1 MONTH OF
FREE
READING

at

www.ForgottenBooks.com

By purchasing this book you are
eligible for one month membership to
ForgottenBooks.com, giving you
unlimited access to our entire
collection of over 700,000 titles via
our web site and mobile apps.

To claim your free month visit:

www.forgottenbooks.com/free199255

ISBN 978-0-483-82154-5
PIBN 10199255

TRACTS

IN

CONTROVERSY WITH DR PRIESTLEY UPON THE HISTORICAL QUESTION

OF THE

BELIEF of the FIRST AGES

IN

OUR LORD'S DIVINITY.

ORIGINALLY PUBLISHED

IN THE YEARS 1783, 1784, AND 1786

AFTERWARDS REVISED AND AUGMENTED

WITH A LARGE ADDITION OF NOTES AND SUPPLE-
MENTAL DISQUISITIONS,

By the Author,

SAMUEL, LATE LORD BISHOP OF ST ASAPH.

THE THIRD EDITION.

TO WHICH IS ADDED

AN APPENDIX

BY

The Rev. HENEAGE HORSLEY, *A. M.*

PREBENDARY OF ST ASAPH, AND LATE STUDENT OF CHRIST

CHURCH, OXON.

Αγνοιας γαρ μεγα τι μοι δοκει και χαλεπον αφωρισμενον οραν ειδος,
πασι τοις αλλοις αυτης αντιςαθμον μερισι—Το, μη κατειδοτα τι,
δοκειν ειδεναι· δι ο κινδυνευει παντα, οσα διανοια σφαλλομεθα,
γιγνεσθαι πασι—............PLATO IN SOPHISTA.

DUNDEE:

Printed by A. Smith & Company,

FOR J. CHALMERS,

AND SOLD BY LONGMAN, HURST, REES, ORME, AND BROWN,
F. C. AND J. RIVINGTON, AND T. HAMILTON, LONDON;
AND A. CONSTABLE & CO. EDINBURGH.

1812.

to

HIS ROYAL HIGHNESS

THE

PRINCE REGENT.

Sir,

THE remembrance of the attention and regard with which Your ROYAL HIGHNESS condescended to honour during the latter years of his life the Author of the following Tracts, first suggested to my mind the wish of introducing under the sanction of YOUR High Patronage the present edition of them to the public.

This wish received additional strength from the reflection that the republication of the Tracts being intended as an antidote to the dissemination of false doctrine, the success of the design would be greatly promoted, were the work to appear under the immediate auspices of HIM to whom the Church of England looks up as her legitimate Protector.

The ready and condescending manner in which Your Royal Highness hath been graciously pleased to accede to the petition expressive of my wish, affords to the Church of England at a crisis when "those who hate her wrongfully are many in number and mighty" the high consolation, that she finds in You what she hath ever found in Your Illustrious Father, not merely a nominal but a real Defender of her Faith——while the personal honour conferred upon myself, and the expressions of regard with which Your Royal Highness has been pleased to speak of the memory of the late Bishop of St Asaph must ever be remembered with a sense of the deepest gratitude, and with feelings of unfeigned loyalty and zealous attachment to YOUR ROYAL PERSON, by

HIS MAJESTY'S

and

YOUR ROYAL HIGHNESS'S

Faithful

Subject and Servant,

Heneage Horsley.

Dundee,
20th March, 1812.

EDITOR'S

PREFACE.

Iɴ the interval between the time of Dr Priestley's emigration to America and the death of Bishop Horsley, the exertions of the Unitarians appear to have lost much of their wonted activity. " The patriarch of the sect *(strange result of victory)* had fled; and the oracles and orators of Birmingham and Essex-Street were dumb; or if they spoke, spoke only to be disregarded."* No sooner however had happened the melancholy event which deprived the church of England of one of her most able champions, and at the same time released the Unitarians from the fears which they had justly entertained of their indefatigable opponent, than the party again ventured forth from their hiding places. The columns of the daily papers were once more filled with their speeches at public meetings, and the press again groaned under their pamphlets. At a meeting of the friends to the Unitarian fund held at the London Tavern immediately after the rejection of Lord Sidmouth's bill in 1811, one orator insisted upon the necessity of diffusing the *advantages* of the

---

* See the Bishop of Rochester's Charge to the Clergy of his Diocese in the year 1800.

Unitarian system among the poor; another suggested the propriety of instituting an academy for students between 18 and 25 years of age; and a third, to raise the spirits of the party to the highest pitch of hope, did not scruple to declare that so far from Socinianism not becoming the religion of the people, he expected to live to see the day, when by means of missions among them, and through the endeavours of the Socinians' friend Mr JOSEPH LANCASTER, Roman Catholics would become good Unitarians.* Glorious æra, when all errors in faith shall be for ever done away and abolished by the joint exertions of Socinian Missionaries, and Mr JOSEPH LANCASTER!

His amor unus erat, pariterque in bella ruebant.

---

* See the Morning Chronicle for the 6th of June 1811.

To give reality to such delightful hopes, the activity and zeal of the writers of the party corresponded with the vaunting language of their orators. A bold endeavour to over-turn the faith of the Christian world was first made by the publication of an *improved* version of the New Testament with a *corrected* text and notes critical and explanatory; in which every text relative to the divinity of our Lord is either expunged as a Trinitarian interpolation, or its genuine sense frittered away by some allegorical or figurative interpretation. This daring attempt was quickly followed up by a work on THE SCRIPTURE DOCTRINE CONCERNING THE PERSON OF CHRIST, the author of which introduces himself to the notice of the public in the *attractive*, but in the present instance, *masquerade* dress of a *calm* inquirer; and to this *calm* inquiry he affixes what he presumes to call a *review* of the controversy between Dr Horsley and Dr Priestley.

Of that controversy, the part of which Bishop Horsley was the author, has long been out of print; and the CALM INQUIRER aware of this fact, has not scrupled to pervert the Bishop's reasoning by partial quotations and prudent omissions; *presuming perhaps on the scarcity of the book, that he might escape detection,* whilst he should *thus* destroy the authority of the greatest modern champion of the Catholic faith!

Under these circumstances the Editor was strongly urged by several of the clergy of the church of England, as well as by many both of the established and of the episcopal church in the country in which he now resides, to reprint the Bishop's Tracts. With such a request he thought it his duty to comply, and he sent an intimation of his intention to carry the work immediately to press to the British Critic for October 1811. At the time when he made that communication he had by him only copies of the Tracts as they were published in separate pamphlets in the years 1783, 1784, and 1786. In each of these pamphlets and in the Editor's copy of Dr Priestley's part of the controversy, he found numerous marginal notes in the Bishop's hand writing; and this led him, somewhat too hastily he confesses, to state that he was in possession of new matter of the Bishop's, and to promise the publication of it. But when he came to compare these marginal notes with the copy of the Tracts published by the Bishop himself in the year 1789, he found that the greater part of them were already embodied in that edition, and that in the substance of what remained he was completely anticipated by Mr Edward Nares, Dr Laurence, and Mr Rennel, in their able remarks on the Unitarian version of the New Testament.

When offering the present edition of the Tracts to the public, the Editor found himself called upon by the most imperious sense of duty to vindicate the character of the author of them from the foul aspersions cast upon it by an unfair and ungenerous adversary. That the task might have fallen into abler hands no one is more ready to admit than the Editor himself: but moderate abilities are sufficient to vindicate truth against error and palpable misrepresentation; and therefore he trusts that the vindication in the Appendix will be fonnd complete.

When the reader shall have become acquainted with the arts of controversy which the *calm* inquirer has employed to make " the worse appear the better argument," and shall have read the contemptuous abuse he has heaped upon the head of Bishop Horsley, when the object of that abuse to use the Bishop's emphatic words was gone " to those unseen abodes where the din of controversy and the din of war are equally unheard," he will perhaps think that he has discovered ANOTHER PERSON to whom the terms of reproach which in the heat of debate fell from the pen of one of the original disputants, may now with greater propriety be applied, A FALSIFIER OF HISTORY and A DEFAMER OF THE CHARACTER OF THE DEAD !

THE
TRACTS.

PREFACE.

A GENERAL view of the controversy between Dr Priestley and the author of the tracts of which the ensuing volume is composed, may not be unacceptable to such of its readers, who for want of leisure or of opportunity, or perhaps of curiosity to peruse the pieces on either side as they were first successively published in separate pamphlets, may be supposed to be as yet unacquainted with the rise and progress and with the present state of the dispute.

In the year 1782 an open and vehement attack was made by Dr Priestley upon the creeds and the established discipline of every church in Christendom, in a work in two volumes octavo, entitled, *A History of the Corruptions of Christianity.* At the head of these the author placed both the Catholic doctrine of our Lord's divinity and the Arian notion of his pre-existence in a nature far superior to the human, representing the Socinian doctrine of his mere humanity as the unanimous faith of the first Christians. It seemed that the most effectual preservative against the intended mischief would be to destroy the writer's credit and the authority of his name, which the fame of certain lucky discoveries in the prosecution of physical experiments had set high in popular esteem, by proof of his incompetency in every branch of literature connected with his present subject, of which the work itself afforded evident specimens in great abundance. For this declared purpose a review of the imperfections of his work in the first part relating to our Lord's divinity, was made the subject of a Charge delivered to the Clergy of the Archdeaconry of St Alban's the spring next following Dr Priestley's publication. The specimens alleged of the imperfections of the work and the incompetency of its author, may be reduced to six general classes.—Instances of reasoning in a circle; instances of quotations misapplied through ignorance of the writer's subject; instances of testimonies perverted by artful and forced constructions; instances of passages in the Greek fathers misinterpreted through ignorance of the Greek language; instances of passages misinterpreted through the same ignorance driven further out of the way by an ignorance of the Platonic philosophy; instances of ignorance of the phraseology of the earliest ecclesiastical writers. This discourse was received by the venerable body to which it was addressed, with marks of favour and

approbation ever to be remembered by its
author with pride and satisfaction. At their
request it was given with considerable en_
largement to the public. It is the first
tract in the present collection. The first
publication of this discourse gave no small
alarm to the well-wishers and admirers of
Dr Priestley's doctrines. Dr Priestley however kept up the spirits of his party by promising an early and satisfactory answer.

> Per damna, per cædes, ab ipso
> Ducit opes animumque ferro——

was his vaunting language. He predicted
that he should rise more illustrious from his
supposed defeat; he promised to strengthen
the evidence of his favourite opinion by the
very objections that had been raised against
it; he seemed to flatter himself that he
should find a new convert in his antagonist
himself; and his new performance had
scarce made its appearance when he had the
ridiculous vanity to boast even in print of

the shame and remorse with which he was confident his adversary must be penetrated. A controversy that was in the meanwhile going on upon the same subject between Dr Priestley and the Rev. Mr Samuel Badcock, the author of a learned critique upon the first part of Dr Priestley's history, inserted in the Monthly Review for the month of June 1783, gave Dr Priestley the occasion of raising these expectations in the public. It was late in the autumn of the same year (1783) when the work which was to effect these wonders appeared in the form of *Letters to Dr Horsley*. These Letters gave occasion to the tract which is the second in this collection, entitled, *Letters from the Archdeacon of St Alban's in Reply to Dr Priestley*, which was first published in the summer of the year 1784. Dr Priestley in his Letters expressed a great desire to draw his adversary into a tedious controversy on the main question,—the article of our Lord's divinity. His adversary knowing that question to have been long since exhausted, and that nothing new was to be said on either side, chose in his *Letters in Reply* to adhere closely to *his own* main question. He defended his former argument, and he collected new specimens from Dr Priestley's new publication, of his utter inability to throw light upon the subject. Thus a useless and endless contention upon the main question was avoided; but many discussions necessarily arose upon secondary points more or less connected with it. The authority of the writings that go under the name of the apostolical fathers—the rise of the two sects of the Nazarenes and the Ebionites—the difference between the two—and the difference of both from the orthodox Hebrew Christians—these the learned reader will probably esteem the most interesting parts of the whole controversy, as on the other hand he will certainly judge the long dispute whether the word *Jews* means Jews, on Dr Priestley's part at least to be the most

frivolous. In these Letters in Reply Dr
Priestley's antagonist declared himself resolved to give no answer to any thing that
Dr Priestley might find to say further upon
the subject. A declaration in which at the
time he was much in earnest.

Dr Priestley mortified to find that his
Letters had failed of the expected success;
that his antagonist touched with no shame,
with no remorse, remained unshaken in his
opinion; and that the authority of his own
opinion was still set at nought, his learning
disallowed, his ingenuity in argument impeached; and what was least to be borne,—
finding that a haughty churchman ventured
incidentally to avow his sentiments of the
Divine commission of the Episcopal ministry, and presumed to question the authority
of those teachers who usurp the preacher's
office without any better warrant than their
own opinion of their own sufficiency,—lost
all temper. A second set of *Letters to the*

Archdeacon of St Alban's appeared in the autumn of the year 1784, in which all profession of personal regard and civility was laid aside. The charge of insufficiency in the subject was warmly retorted, and the incorrigible dignitary was taxed with manifest misrepresentation of his adversary's argument; with injustice to the character of Origen whose veracity he had called in question, and with the grossest falsification of ancient history. He was stigmatized in short, in terms as *a falsifier of history, and a defamer of the character of the dead.*

Under all this reproach he continued silent almost eighteen months: the character of Origen and an intricate question of ancient history upon which the charge of direct falsification had been advanced against him, were indeed the only points on which he felt the least desire to reply. *A Sermon on the Incarnation* preached in his parish church of St Mary Newington, in Surrey, upon the feast of the nativity, in the year 1785, which is the third tract in this collec-tion, was the prelude to a renewal of the contest upon his side, and was followed early in the ensuing spring by his *Remarks on Dr Priestley's Second Letters to the Archdeacon of St Alban's, with Proofs of certain facts as-serted by the Archdeacon.* This tract is the fourth in order in this volume. It consists of two parts: The first is a collection of new specimens of Dr Priestley's temerity in assertion. The second defends the attack upon the character of Origen, and proves the existence of a body of Hebrew Chris-tians at Ælia after the time of Adrian,—the fact upon which the author's good faith had been so loudly arraigned. It also contains confirmation of another fact which had been incidentally mentioned,—the decline of Cal-vinism among our English dissenters, and a chapter on the general spirit of Dr Priest-ley's controversial writings. With this pub-lication he again promised himself that the controversy on his part would be closed. But having at last yielded with reluctance to the solicitations of his friends to republish these four tracts in the present form, he hath taken this occasion to give Dr Priestley's Letters a second perusal; and to many things which he had before passed unnoticed he hath now replied, partly in notes occasionally interspersed in the former tracts, and where the matter arising upon any particular question hath turned out to be more than could be conveniently comprised within the compass of a note, in Supplemental Disquisitions of considerable length. The Remarks upon Dr Priestley's Second Letters produced a *third* set of *Letters from Dr Priestley* upon the two questions of Origen's veracity and the orthodox Hebrews of the church of Ælia. These too are answered, partly in notes interspersed in the Remarks, and partly in the two last of the Supplemental Disquisitions, which in all are six in number. It is conceived that nothing of any consequence in Dr Priestley's three sets of Letters now remains unanswered. The author indeed is well aware that Dr Priestley will charge him with one capital omission.—That he hath taken no notice of any thing that may be contained relating to the various points of this controversy in Dr Priestley's *History of Early Opinions concerning Christ;* that large work in four volumes, the result of a *whole two-years* study of the writers of antiquity, which as it hath been published since Dr Priestley's last Letters, may be supposed to contain better arguments, or at least his old arguments in a better form. The only apology to be made is a simple declaration of the truth. Not conceiving himself obliged to engage in the insipid task of reading so long a book without better hope of information from it than his past experience of the writer's knowledge in the subject gives, Dr Priestley's adversary is as ignorant of the contents of that work as he could have

been had it never been published. It is
reported indeed that the work, whatever
may be its merits, hath a very slow sale.
Of consequence it hath found but few
readers. The antagonist of Dr Priestley
were he better acquainted with its contents,
would still disdain to do the office of the
midwife for this laborious birth. He would
not by an unnecessary and unseasonable opposition to neglected arguments be the instrument of drawing four volumes, fraught
as the very title imports, with pernicious
heretical theology, from the obscurity in
which they may innocently rot in the
Printer's warehouse.

CONTENTS.

CONTENTS

OF THE

Letters in Reply to Dr Priestley.

———

LETTER FIRST.

LETTER SECOND.

LETTER THIRD.

LETTER FOURTH.

LETTER FIFTH.

LETTER SIXTH.

LETTER SEVENTH.

LETTER EIGHTH.

LETTER NINTH.

LETTER TENTH.

LETTER ELEVENTH.

LETTER TWELFTH.

LETTER THIRTEENTH.

LETTER FOURTEENTH.

LETTER FIFTEENTH.

LETTER SIXTEENTH.

LETTER SEVENTEENTH.

CONTENTS

CONTENTS

OF THE

Supplemental Disquisitions.

———

DISQUISITION FOURTH.

DISQUISITION FIFTH.

DISQUISITION SIXTH.

CHARGE

TO THE

CLERGY

OF THE

ARCHDEACONRY OF ST ALBAN'S,

&c.

CHARGE,

&c.

MY REVEREND BRETHREN,

THE business of the Christian priesthood, like
that of every secular occupation, consisting in two
branches, the speculative, and the practical; if any
of us, by a particular blessing of Providence attending our temporal fortunes, are released from
the necessity, to which the greater part submit, of
a severe and constant toil in the practical branch
of the profession, as the labour by which they
have to earn their daily bread; it seems to be our
particular duty to consecrate the leisure we enjoy,
if I may borrow an expression from the profane
sciences, to the theory of religion. And in the
present state of religious learning in this country,
it should seem that the cultivation of that branch

A

of it, which is called sacred criticism, and particu
larly the elucidation of the text of the Old Testament, by a diligent use of the materials which the
unwearied industry of a learned critic, supported
by the munificence of the best of Princes, hath
supplied, is the study in which, of all others, our
talents and our industry might be best employed.
It is, however, to be remembered, that the writings of the Old Testament are only of a secondary importance; for the evidence which they
afford of the truth of our Lord's pretensions, and
for the light which they throw upon the doctrines
of the gospel: which is indeed so great, that an
inattention to these more ancient parts of the code
of revelation, is likely to be one principal cause of
the scepticism which unhappily prevails among our
modern sectaries, concerning the original dignity
of the Redeemer's nature, and the expiatory virtue of his sufferings.   But in whatever degree the
Jewish Scriptures may be useful for the general
confirmation of Christianity; it is from their relation to the gospel, to which, we have been told by
the highest authority, the Mosaic dispensation was
but a prelude or preparative, that they derive the
whole of the importance which they yet retain.
A profound and critical acquaintance with them,
is useful only as means conducive to an end: and
in this, as in other cases, every solid advantage
will be lost, that might be reaped from the improvement of the means, if, in the too assiduous

pursuit of these, we lose sight of the end to which they should be made subservient. The theology of the Christian revelation is the great object, to which every other branch of sacred literature is naturally subordinate. To extract it from the writings of the apostles and evangelists, connected with the earlier revelations; to assert and defend their genuine doctrine; to preserve it entire; and to maintain it in its native purity, unadulterated by the additions of superstition, undebased and undiminished by the refinements of philosophy; this is the great business to which those of us, who feel themselves at ease and in affluence, and masters of the leisure which affluence affords, should consider their talents and their studies to be solemnly devoted.

2. My Reverend Brethren, I would be understood to speak with sentiments of respect, of those whom I shall take the liberty to call the labouring part of the parochial clergy: of those whose lives are spent in a constant attendance on the public ceremonies of external worship, or in the charitable and necessary business of instructing the people of the lower ranks in the first principles of the doctrine of Christ. Of these venerable men, of their godly labours, and honourable occupations, I would be understood to speak with reverence and respect. Of all the departments of the sacred office, the business of that which it is their lot to

fill, is perhaps the most immediately conducive to
general edification: and for the zeal and ability
with which it is discharged by them, they are
justly entitled to the highest degrees of veneration
and esteem. It is matter of concern and grief to
every serious Christian, that their rewards in this
life should but seldom correspond, in any fair proportion, with the worth of their characters, and
the importance of their services. Thanks be to
Him, of whom the whole family is named, their
hope is full of glory. It is felt, I am persuaded,
by themselves, as the heaviest inconvenience of
their present situation, that their employment, useful and honourable as it must ever be confessed to
be, partakes in some degree of the nature of a
worldly business; requiring a labour of the body,
and a distracting intercourse with the world, which
leave little opportunity for private study and solitary meditation. In circumstances so unfriendly
to literary improvement, it redounds highly to their
praise, that they are so eminently well qualified,
as they generally approve themselves to be, to discharge the plain duty of Catechists, with credit to
themselves, and advantage to the church of God.
To deliver the doctrine of the gospel in that plain
and general way, which, if it were to meet with
no opposition from the disputers of the world,
might be sufficient to give it its full effect upon
the heart of the hearer. But occasions will from
time to time arise, when the truth must be not

only taught, but defended. The stubborn infidel
will raise objections against the first principles of
our faith: and objections must be answered. The
restless spirit of scepticism will suggest difficulties
in the system, and create doubts about the particulars of the Christian doctrine: difficulties must
be removed, and doubts must be satisfied. But
above all, the scruples must be composed, which
the refinements of a false philosophy, patronized
as they are in the present age, by men no less amiable for the general purity of their manners, than
distinguished by their scientific attainments, will
be *too* apt to raise in the minds of the weaker brethren. And this is the service to which they,
whom the indulgence of Providence hath released
from the more laborious offices of the priesthood,
stand peculiarly engaged. To them their more occupied brethren have a right to look up, in these
emergencies, for support and succour in the common cause. It is for them to stand forth the
champions of the common faith, and the advocates
of their order. It is for them to wipe off the aspersions injuriously cast upon the sons of the establishment, as uninformed in the true grounds of
the doctrine which they teach, or insincere in the
belief of it. To this duty they are indispensably
obliged, by their providential exemption from work
of a harder kind. It is the proper business of the
station which is allotted them in Christ's household. And deep will be their shame, and insup-

portable their punishment, if, in the great day of reckoning, it should appear, that they have received the wages of a service, which hath never been performed.

3. You will easily conjecture, that what has led me into these reflections, is the extraordinary attempt, which hath been lately made, to unsettle the faith, and to break up the constitution of every ecclesiastical establishment in Christendom. Such is the avowed object of a recent publication, which bears the title of " A History of the Corruptions of Christianity;" among which the Catholic doctrine of the Trinity, in the author's opinion, holds a principal place. With what success he hath attacked this fundamental article, and how far he hath been able to invalidate the argument from early and uniform tradition, this reverend assembly will be competent to judge, from the brief view which shall be laid before them, of the account which he attempts to give of the rise and progress of the doctrine in the three first ages, accompanied with specimens of the proofs by which his pretended history, in this part of it, is supported,

I.

1. The opinion which he maintains, is in general the same which was first, I think, propagated

in the last century, by Daniel Zuicker, a Prussian physician, of the Socinian persuasion; and, upon the authority of that writer, hath been current ever since, among the Unitarians of this country. " That the doctrine of the Trinity, in the form in which it is now maintained, is of no greater antiquity than the Nicene council: that it is the result of a gradual corruption of the doctrine of the gospel, which took its rise in an opinion first advanced in the second century, by certain converts from the Platonic school; who, expounding the beginning of St John's gospel by the Platonic doctrine of the Logos, ascribed a sort of secondary divinity to our Saviour, affirming that he was no other than the second principle of the Platonic Triad, who had assumed a human body to converse with man: that before this innovation, of which Justin Martyr is made the author, the faith of the whole Christian church, but particularly of the church of Jerusalem, was simply and strictly Unitarian. The immediate disciples of the apostles conceived our Saviour to be a man, whose existence commenced in the womb of the Virgin; and they thought him in no respect the object of worship. The next succeeding race worshipped him indeed, but they had however no higher notions of his divinity, than those which were maintained by the followers of Arius in the fourth century." In short, the first race of Christians, in Dr Priestley's opinion, were Unitarians in the

strictest sense of the word; the second, Arians.*
As Dr Priestley follows Zuicker in these extravagant assertions, so the arguments, by which he
would support them, are in all essential points the
same which were alleged to the same purpose,
either by that writer, or by Simon Episcopius.
Episcopius, though himself no Socinian, very in-
discreetly concurred with the Socinians of his
time, in maintaining, that the opinion of the mere
humanity of Christ, had prevailed very generally
in the first ages; and was never deemed heretical
by the fathers of the orthodox persuasion; at least
not in such degree, as to exclude from the communion of the church. The opinion, I believe,
had its rise in no worse principle than the charitable temper of the man, and his just abhorrence
of the spirit of persecution, with which Christians
of every denomination, were in his time much infected: which is indeed itself of all heresies by far
the most malignant, being the most opposite to
that general philanthropy, which is the root of all
social virtue, and the highest ornament of the
Christian profession. Episcopius wished, as every
good man must wish, to see a general toleration
established; which he thought could not be more
effectually recommended, than by the example of

---

* See this brief statement of Dr Priestley's opinion defended
against his objections to it, in the 13th of my Letters in Reply.

the harmony which subsisted among Christians in the earliest ages. The force of his example he would naturally think improved, in proportion as the idea of the harmony was heightened; the idea of the harmony heightened, as the controversies of the first Christians were magnified and multiplied. These sentiments inclined him to credit as historians, the same writers whom, as divines, he held in little estimation. He gave easy credit to Unitarian writers, when they represented the differences of opinion in the early churches, as much greater than ever really obtained; and the tenderness for sectaries, as more than was ever practised; and while he opposed their doctrine, he vouched their story. The purposes of charity had been better served, without injury to the cause of truth, had the talents of this able writer been employed to set the doctrine of universal toleration on its only firm and proper basis: to shew, that although in dubious points of doctrine, the judgment of antiquity, wherever it is clear, must be allowed to be decisive; yet the just severity of the primitive church towards the refractory heretics, whose visionary doctrines, joined with their contempt of apostolic authority, disgraced the rising community, and obstructed the propagation of the truth, constitutes no example for the controul of fair inquiry, or for the punishment of mere speculative heresy in these later times; by any harsher means than the necessary exclusion of dissenters from the honours and emoluments of national establishments. Had the opinion which he chose to adopt been true, Simon Episcopius, with his scanty knowledge of ecclesiastical antiquities, was but ill qualified to maintain it. False and groundless as it was, his natural acuteness enabled him to furnish the Socinians of his time, whose cause in the doctrinal part he little thought to serve, with the best arguments that have ever been produced on the Unitarian side of the question. Our modern historian, in support of his imaginary progress of opinions from the Unitarian doctrine to the Nicene faith, hath produced few, if any, arguments which make directly for his purpose, but what are to be found in the writings either of Zuicker or Episcopius. Nor is a single argument to be found in the writings either of Zuicker or Episcopius, which is not unanswerably confuted by our learned Dr George Bull, afterwards Lord Bishop of St David's, in three celebrated treatises, which deserve the particular attention of every one, who would take upon him to be either a teacher or an historian of the Christian faith. The first, " A Defence of the Nicene faith;" the second, " The Judgment of the Catholic church, in the first ages, concerning the necessity of believing that our Lord Jesus Christ is very God;" the third, " The Primitive and Apostolical Tradition concerning the true Divinity of Jesus Christ."

2. It seems very extraordinary, that any one should presume to revive the defeated arguments of Zuicker and Episcopius, without attempting to make them good against the objections of a writer of Dr Bull's eminence. Nor is it easy to conceive, what apology can be made, for what should seem so gross an insult on the learning and discernment of the age; unless it be, that Dr Priestley imagines, that although he hath abstained from a particular discussion of Dr Bull's arguments, he hath in effect answered them, by the new light which he persuades himself he has thrown upon the subject: that by the evidence which he thinks he hath brought of the truth of his own narrative, in every branch of it, he supposes that he hath virtually replied to all objections: that he hath confirmed the assumptions from which Zuicker and Episcopius reasoned, which Dr Bull pretended to deny: and that, by confirming their assumptions, he hath made good their arguments, although he may have taken no notice of their learned antagonist. What new illustrations the subject hath received from Dr Priestley's labours, will best appear from specimens of the arguments by which he would support his three principal assumptions: namely, that the first Christians were Unitarians in the strictest sense of the word; that the deity of Christ was first taught by a Platonizing sect; and that the doctrine, which they introduced, was the very same, for which, in a later age, Arius was con-

demned. If his proof of these fundamental propositions should be found to rest upon precarious
assumptions, perverted history, misconstrued and
misapplied quotations : if his facts should appear
to be confuted by his own authorities, and his conclusions to be defeated by his own arguments : if
the resemblance between the Christian and the
Platonic Trinity should appear to be no mark of
corruption in the prevailing opinions ; the Catholic
faith, which hath heretofore sustained so many
rude assaults, will hardly find its mortal wound in
the stroke which Dr Priestley imagines he hath
inflicted.

3. The first argument which is produced in
support of the first assertion, " that the faith of
the first Christians was simply Unitarian,". is built
upon an assumption, which, could it be proved to
be true, would indeed render the conclusion obvious and inevitable. " That the doctrine of our
Lord's mere humanity is the clear doctrine of the
Scriptures, and that the apostles never taught any
other."* It will easily be granted, that the apostles never taught the contrary of any doctrine that
is clearly delivered in their writings ; and that the
faith of the first converts was a belief of neither
more nor less, than the apostles taught. So that

---

* History of Corruptions, vol. i. p. 6.

the sense of the Scriptures in any article being once clearly ascertained, the argument from the clear confessed sense of Scripture to the preaching of the apostles, and from the preaching of the apostles to the primitive faith, will be firm and valid. But the professed object of our learned adversary's undertaking, requires an argument, that should go the contrary way:—from the primitive faith to the sense of the Scriptures. It is the professed object of his undertaking, to exhibit a view of the gradual changes of opinions, in order to ascertain the faith of the first ages: and he would ascertain the faith of the first ages, in order to settle the sense of the Scriptures in disputed points. He is therefore not at liberty, to assume any sense of the Scriptures, which, because, it is his own, he may be pleased to call the clear sense, for a proof that the original faith was such, as would confirm the sense he wishes to establish. His sense of the Scriptures being not acknowledged by the majority of the Christian church, whatever may be his own judgment of its clearness, it can only pass for a particular interpretation. When this particular interpretation is alleged, in proof that the original faith of the church of Jerusalem was such as might justify that interpretation; the middle term of the argument is no otherwise confirmed than by an assumption of the principal matter in debate: and so long as the sixth page of the first volume of Dr Priestley's history shall be extant, the masters of the dialectic art will be at no loss for an example of the circulating syllogism. To Dr Priestley it may be very clear, that when St John, speaking of the Logos, of which he had already affirmed, that it was in the beginning, says, " This person" (for that is the natural force of the Greek pronoun ὁυῖος*) " This person was in the beginning with God; all things were made by him, and without him was not any thing made that was made :" it may be very clear to Dr Priestley, that St John, speaking of the Logos, as of a person who had been from the beginning, and had done these great things, means to affirm that the Logos is no person; nor is, otherwise than in a figurative sense, to be called an agent in any business: that he means to contradict those, who held that the Logos was any thing more than an attribute of the Divine mind; to silence them; to extinguish their profane innovation, by his definitive sentence upon the question: and that when he speaks of eternity as belonging to the Logos as a person, it is, that this was the most explicit way, in which he could give the Christian church to understand, that eternity is only accidental to the Logos, the substance to which it properly belongs, being that mind of

___

* See the third of my Letters in Reply, and the Appendix to the Letters, No. 2.

which the Logos itself is only another attribute.*
It may be very clear to Dr Priestley's apprehension, that when St Paul affirms of Christ, that he
is the " image of the invisible God, the first born
of every creature, by whom all things were created," and explains in what extent the words " all
things" are to be understood, by an enumeration
of the constituent parts, and governing powers of
the universe; " things in heaven and things in
earth, visible and invisible, whether they be
thrones, or dominions, or principalities, or powers,
all things were created by him and for him, and
he is before all things, and by him all things consist;"† it may be very clear to Dr Priestley, that
St Paul in these expressions would be understood
to assert, that Christ was nothing more than a
man, and was no otherwise the creator of any
thing, than as he was the founder of the Christian
church.   All this may be very clear to Dr Priestley's apprehension; and equal to the clearness of
the apprehension, which he imagines he enjoys,
that this was the doctrine of the apostles, will be
the confidence of his persuasion, that it was also
the faith of their first converts.   But to others,
who have not the sagacity to discern, that the true
meaning of an inspired writer must be the reverse

---

* Hist. of Corrup. vol. i. p. 10, 12.
† Coloss. i. 15, 17.

of the natural and obvious sense of the expressions which he employs; the force of the conclusion, that the primitive Christians could not believe our Lord to be more than a mere man, because the apostles had told them he was the Creator of the universe, will be little understood.

4. Another argument is built upon a pretended silence of St John, about the error of those who maintained the mere humanity of Christ,* in his first epistle: in which he is supposed to censure those, who believed Christ to be a man only in appearance, in the severest manner; but upon those who believed him to be nothing more than man, the apostle, as he is understood by Dr Priestley, passes no censure. From which it is to be concluded, that the latter opinion is no error, but the very truth of the gospel.

5. But here the question is, whether the opinion of Christ's mere humanity is really passed over by St John, as Dr Priestley supposes, uncensured and unnoticed. This question will be differently resolved, according as different interpretations of the apostle's expressions are adopted. This argument, therefore, is of the same complexion with the former, and labours under the

---

* Hist. of Corrup. vol. i. p. 10, 13; and vol. ii. p. 485.

same defect. A particular sense of the epistle is alleged, in proof of a pretended fact; which fact must itself support the interpretation. " Every spirit," says St John, " which confesses that Jesus Christ is come in the flesh, is of God."* " That is," says Dr Priestley, " every spirit is of God, that confesses that Jesus Christ is truly a man."† But it should seem, that the proposition that he was truly a man, if he was nothing more than man, is very aukwardly and unnaturally expressed by the phrase of his " coming in the flesh :" for in what other way was it possible for a mere man to come? The turn of the expression seems to lead to the notion of a being, who had his choice of different ways of coming; a notion which is implied in other passages of holy writ, and is explicitly expressed in a book little inferior in authority to the canonical writings,—in the first epistle of Clemens Romanus; in a passage of that epistle which Dr Priestley, somewhat unfortunately for his cause, hath chosen for the basis of an argument of that holy father's heterodoxy. " The sceptre of the majesty of God," says Clemens, " our Lord Jesus Christ, came not in the pomp of pride and arrogance, *although he had it in his power.*"‡ Clemens, it seems, conceived, that the manner of coming

---

* 1 John iv. 2.
† Hist. of Corrup. vol. i. p. 10.   ‡ Chap. xvi.

B

was in the power and choice of the person who was to come. St John's expressions evidently lead to the same notion. It should seem, therefore, that St John's assertions, concerning the spirits that maintain or deny that Jesus is come in the flesh; that the one are of God, and the other of antichrist; were levelled not singly at the heresy of the *Docetæ*, as Dr Priestley imagines, but equally at that and at another branch of the Gnostic heresy, which divided Jesus Christ into two persons: Jesus, who was supposed to be a mere man, the son of Mary, by her husband Joseph; and the Christ, a divine being, who was considered as the genius, or tutelary angel, of the man; not however so united with the man, as to constitute one person, or to partake of the man's sufferings. The first epistle of St John asserts the doctrine of a true and proper incarnation, in opposition to the extravagancies of both these sects. The apostle makes the acknowledgment of the incarnation, in which both an antecedent divinity and an assumed humanity are implied,—the criterion by which the true teachers are to be distinguished from the false. And in the positive assertion of the incarnation, and the express censure of the opposite doctrine as antichristian, he reprobates the notion of Christ's mere humanity, in the only sense in which we have any certain evidence that he lived to see it maintained. It appears, therefore, that to confess that " Jesus Christ is

A CHARGE TO THE CLERGY.

come in the flesh,"* and to affirm that Jesus Christ
is truly a man, are propositions not perfectly equivalent. Dr Priestley indeed hath shewn himself
very sensible of the difference. He would not
otherwise have found it necessary, for the improvement of his argument, in reciting the third
verse of the fourth chapter of St John's first epistle, to change the expressions which he found in
the public translation, for others which correspond
far less exactly with the Greek text. For the
words " Jesus Christ is come *in* the flesh," Dr
Priestley substitutes these, " Jesus Christ is come
of the flesh."† That he is come *in* the flesh, and
that he is come *of* the flesh, are two very distinct
propositions. The one affirms an incarnation;
the other a mortal extraction. The first is St
John's assertion ; the second is Dr Priestley's.
Perhaps Dr Priestley hath discovered of St John
as of St Paul, that his reasoning is sometimes inconclusive,‡ and his language inaccurate: and he
might think it no unwarrantable liberty to correct
an expression, which, as not perfectly corresponding with his own system, he could not entirely approve. It would have been but fair to advertise
his readers of so capital an emendation. An

---

* 1 John iv. 2. Ιησυν Χριστον εν σαρκι εληλυθοτα.
† Hist. of Corrup. vol. i. p. 10. line 15.
‡ " ———— I think I have shewn that the apostle Paul often
reasons inconclusively." Dr P.'s Hist. of Corrup. vol. ii. p. 370

emendation for which no support is to be found
in the Greek text, nor even in the varieties of any
manuscripts. We are informed, indeed by Socrates the historian,* (and his testimony is confirmed
by the Latin of the vulgate,) of a very considerable
variety of some of the ancient manuscripts. But
it is such as only serves to prove, that the principal object of this epistle of St John was understood in the primitive church, to be the confutation of the Cerinthian Gnostics; the sect which
divided Christ into two persons, of which they
made Jesus a mere man; differing in this essentially from the *Docetæ*, who made the body of the
man Jesus a mere phantom.

6. And this view of St John's epistle receives a
further confirmation from the genuine epistles of
Ignatius. In these the error of the *Docetæ*, which
Dr Priestley supposes to be the sole object of St
John's epistle, is indeed particularly censured.
But lest, in asserting the truth of our Lord's humanity, he should be understood to support the
opinion of his mere humanity, the holy father
hardly ever mentions Christ, without introducing
some explicit assertion of his divinity, or without
joining with the name of Christ some epithet in
which it is implied.

---

* Lib. vii. c. 32.

7. The mention of Ignatius having occurred, it were unpardonable not to suggest to the recollection of this learned assembly, one passage in particular in the epistle to the Magnesians, in which the eternal existence of the Word, as a distinct person from the Father, is asserted in terms, which, though highly figurative, are perfectly unequivocal: " There is one God who hath manifested himself through Jesus Christ his Son, who is his eternal Word, who came not forth from silence."* The name of the Logos led the early fathers to conceive the generation of the Son as an utterance; or at least to speak of it under that figure: as on the contrary the heretics who denied the eternity of the Son, described the period preceding his generation as a time of silence.† Under that figure Ignatius speaks of the generation of the Son in this passage: and he affirms, that no period of silence had preceded the utterance of the eternal Word. Or if it should seem more reasonable to suppose an allusion, in these expressions of Ignatius, to the *Sige* of the Gnostics, the consort of their *Buthos*, upon whom the Æons were engendered; and to understand the holy father

---

* Εις Θεος ἐςιν ὁ φανερωσας ἑαυτον δια Ιησου Χριςου τυ υιυ αυτυ, ἐς ἐςιν αυτυ λογος ἀιδιϑ, ουκ ἀπο σιγης προελθων. Ign. ad Magn. sec. 8.

† So Marcellus of Ancyra:—Προ γαρ της δημιυργιας ἁπασης, ἡσυχια τις ἠν, ὡς εἰκος, ἐν τῳ Θεῳ τυ Λογυ ὀντος. Euseb. contra Marcell. p. 39.

as maintaining the immediate connexion of the Father and the Son, unbroken by the intervention of any such intermediate intelligences, as the impious theogeny of the Gnostics interposed; still the eternity of the Son is asserted. For the passage, in this view of it, amounts to this disjunctive proposition: " The Son's existence holds not of the Father's by any such remote relation as these fabulous genealogies describe; but he is the eternal Logos of the Paternal Mind." According to either interpretation, the passage contains an evident assertion of the divinity of the Son of God. And this assertion being found in the writings of Ignatius, the familiar friend and companion of the apostles, who suffered martyrdom so early as in the sixteenth year of the second century, and had been appointed to the bishopric of Antioch full thirty years before, it is an unanswerable confutation of our author's confident assertions, that " we find nothing like divinity ascribed to Jesus Christ before Justin Martyr,"* and " that all the early fathers speak of Christ as not having existed always."†

8. We have seen the sort and fashion of the argument which, in proof of his first assertion, Dr

---

* Hist. of Corrup. vol. i. p. 32.
† Ibid. vol. i. p. 42.

Priestley builds on holy writ. Let us take a view of those which he hath drawn from other writers.

9. One principal argument, " that the primitive church of Jerusalem was properly Unitarian," maintaining the simple humanity of Christ, is this:—" Athanasius himself was so far from denying it," says Dr Priestley, " that he endeavours to account for it, by saying,"—" that all the Jews were so firmly persuaded that their Messiah was to be nothing more than a man like themselves, that the apostles were obliged to use great caution in divulging the doctrine of the proper divinity of Christ."* The latter clause of the sentence, which contains what Athanasius is supposed to have said, is marked with inverted commas; which should seem to intimate, that it is an exact translation of some passage in the holy father's writings: and the lower margin of Dr Priestley's book refers to Athanasius's celebrated piece on the orthodoxy of his predecessor Dionysius. Now in this piece upon the orthodoxy of Dionysius, Athanasius no where, I confess, denies that the primitive church of Jerusalem was Unitarian. Nor on the other hand do I recollect, that Dr Priestley hath asserted it, in any part of his " History of Electricity." The truth is, that in either of these

---

* Hist. of Corrup. vol. i. p. 12.

valuable works, the faith of the primitive church
of Jerusalem never comes in question. In the defence of Dionysius, not a single passage is to be
found, which may be fairly understood as a tacit
confession, that the primitive faith of the church
of Jerusalem was Unitarian: much less is there
any attempt to account for its supposed heterodoxy. Athanasius says indeed of the Jews of the
apostolic age, that is, of the unbelieving Jews,
(for Athanasius is a writer who calls things by
their names; and when he speaks of Jews, means
not, as Dr Priestley would persuade us,* Jewish
Christians, except when he sarcastically gives the
Arians the name of Jews, as resembling the Jews,
in his judgment, in an obstinate denial of the Lord
who bought them; but otherwise when he speaks
his usual, plain, unfigured language, the unconverted Jews of the apostolic age are they, of whom
he says,) that they had so little insight into the
true meaning of the prophecies, as to look for nothing more than a MAN in the promised Messiah.
He says, that this error of the Jews had been the
means of spreading the like mistake among the
Gentiles; meaning probably the proselytes of the
Gate; who, acknowledging in some degree the
divinity of the Jewish scriptures, looked for the
completion of the prophecies, and were the first

---

* Hist. of Corrup. vol. ii. p. 486.

Gentiles to whom the preaching of the apostles
was addressed. These Gentiles, with something
of the Jewish faith, it may easily be supposed, had
imbibed many of the Jewish errors; and among
others, as Athanasius imagines, the expectation of
a Messiah of mortal extraction. This general
mistake, he says, made it necessary, that the apostles, in their first public sermons, should insist
largely on the miracles of our Saviour's life on
earth, before they entered into a detail of the particulars of the gospel doctrine, or explained what
sort of person the promised Messiah was to be,
and Jesus was. For their doctrine upon that article was not likely to meet with credit, till their
divine commission to teach it was acknowledged,
and their Master's general claim to the character
of the Messiah, whatever that might be, previously
admitted. The example of the apostles' practice
in this particular is alleged, to shew what prudence requires of every preacher of the gospel;
who must allow himself to be determined in the
arrangement of his matter, the choice of his topics,
and the composition of his language, by the degree
of previous knowledge, and the state of opinions,
which may actually obtain, among those to whom
his instructions are addressed. What the ignorant will most easily apprehend must be first
taught: those points, which are supposed to be
most generally misunderstood, must be most particularly explained: and the truth must be con-

veyed in that language, which may the most evidently shew its disagreement with any false opinions, to which the hearer may be particularly addicted.　Athanasius contends, that upon these
principles Dionysius was to be justified, if he dwelt
more on the topic of our Lord's humiliation, than
on that of his divinity: the Sabellian heresy being
the error with which Dionysius was engaged.
The consideration that the Son became man, afforded the most obvious proof that he was not the
Father: and the Sabellians were to be convinced,
that the Word was made flesh, gross, corruptible
flesh, before they could be brought to acknowledge
that he was God of God.　Athanasius shews, that,
in the controversy with these heretics, Dionysius
was inevitably led to the use of expressions, which
the Arian party interpreted in their own favour;
though Dionysius always disclaimed the sense, to
which his words were wrested.　He contends, that
to tax Dionysius with a propensity to the Arian
party, on account of these expressions, were no
less unreasonable and injurious, than it would be
to entertain the like suspicion of the apostles themselves; because they had found it necessary to persuade the Jews, that Jesus had been approved of
God, by signs and wonders, as a man, before they
could hope to persuade them, that he was so much
more than man; that his being found in fashion as
a man, was really the most extraordinary part of
his history and character.　It is in no other way

than this, that Athanasius speaks of the apostles
as teaching the Jews the humanity of Christ. The
holy father never speaks of any caution which they
used in divulging the doctrine of his full divinity;
unless an historian's distribution of the matter of
his narrative, or a master's accommodation of his
lessons to the previous attainments of his pupils, is
to be called a caution of divulging, what, in the
natural order of tradition, is to be the last disclosed. Was it ever said of Livy, that he relates the
tragedy of Lucretia's death, from a caution of divulging the expulsion of the Tarquins? Of Porphyry, that he treats of the five words, from a
caution of divulging the doctrine of the Categories? The beginning of every story must be first
told. The easiest part of every science must be
first taught. Of the great ability and judgment,
with which the apostles conducted the first preaching of the gospel; of their happy art in the perspicuous arrangement of their lofty argument;
with what readiness they led their Catechumens
on, from the simplest principles to the highest
mysteries; of this consummate ability of the apostles in the capacity of teachers, Athanasius speaks
with due commendation. Their caution he never
mentions. On the contrary, the rapid progress of
their instruction, how they passed at once from
the detail of our Lord's life on earth, to the mystery of his Godhead, is one principal branch of his
encomium. I wish that Dr Priestley had produ-

ced the passage, in which he thinks the apostles are taxed with caution; and of which he certainly imagines (he would not otherwise have led his reader to imagine) he hath given an exact translation.*

10. Nearly allied to this argument from Athanasius's omission to *deny*, is another from Epiphanius's omission to *assert*. " Epiphanius in his account of the Nazarenes—makes no mention of any of them believing the divinity of Christ in any sense of the word."† It is granted. Epiphanius, in his account of these ancient heretics,‡ makes indeed no mention, that they believed the divinity of Christ in any sense of the word. But what is this *no-mention* which Epiphanius makes, and of what importance is it to our author's system? It is only that Epiphanius confesses, that he had no certain information, what the opinion of the Nazarenes might be upon this article. He had described them in general as a sect half Jew and half Christian: not Jews, because they had something of a belief in Christ: not Christians,

---

* See the passage produced and critically examined, in the Fourth of Dr Priestley's First Letters to me, the Eleventh of my Letters in Reply, and the Tenth of Dr Priestley's Second Letters; and in my Remarks upon Dr Priestley's Second Letters,—Part II. chap. i. sec. 11.

† Hist. of Corrup. vol. i. p. 8.

‡ Hæres. 29.

because they lived in bondage to the ritual law. " But concerning Christ," he says, " I cannot say whether they think him a mere man; or affirm, as the truth is, that he was begotten of Mary, by the Holy Ghost."* . It is thus, and thus only, that Epiphanius *makes no mention* of the belief of the Nazarenes in Christ's divinity. But he equally makes no mention of their disbelief. And had it been Dr Priestley's point to prove, that the Nazarenes held the Nicene faith upon the subject of the Trinity, he might have alleged, with equal fairness and propriety, Epiphanius's no-mention of their heterodoxy.

11. Indeed that they were believers in our Lord's divinity were the fairer conclusion from the neutrality of Epiphanius's evidence. It was little the temper of the age in which Epiphanius lived; it was little the temper of Epiphanius, to think or to speak favourably of those who were deemed heretics. It was rather the practice to aggravate and to multiply their errors, and to vilify their characters: to charge them upon the slightest grounds with every enormity both in faith and practice. It is very unlikely that Epi-

•

---

* Περι Χριςυ δε, εκ οιδα ειπειν, ει και αυτοι τη των προειρημενων περι Κηρινθον και Μηρινθον μοχθηρια αχθειλις, ψιλον ανθρωπον νομιζυσιν· η, ταθως η αληθεια εχει, δια πνευματ⊙ αγιυ γεγεννησθαι εκ Μαριας διαδεδαωνεται.

phanius would have been so tender of the reputation of these Nazarenes, as to confess his want of
information about their opinions of the nature of
Christ, had there been the least ground to suspect,
or had there been so much as a suspicion current
in his times, although it had been founded only on
a general bad opinion of the sect, that they were
heretical in this article. A general clamour, or
the bare assertion of an earlier writer, would have
fixed the imputation, without any nice enquiry into the evidence, by which the charge might be
supported. And since Epiphanius confesses, that
he had no ground to say, that these Nazarenes
held Christ to be a mere man; the presumption is,
that he ought to have said, that they affirmed, as
the truth is, that he was begotten of Mary, by the
Holy Ghost. But to affirm, as the truth is, that
he was begotten of Mary, by the Holy Ghost, in
Epiphanius's sense of those words, was a full confession of his divinity. So that if the opinions of
these Nazarenes, be of any importance for ascer-
taining the primitive faith; and conjectures are
to be drawn, concerning their opinions, from Epiphanius's profession of his want of information,
the fair conjecture is the opposite of Dr Priestley's: namely, that the Nazarenes homologated
with the church; with the church, as its opinions
stood in the age of Epiphanius, when I suppose
he will allow it to have been far gone from the
primitive purity of his Unitarian faith; with this

corrupt church, as Dr Priestley deems it, his friends, the Nazarenes, homologated upon the article of Christ's divinity.

12. But after all, of what importance is the opinion of these Nazarenes? Or how may the Catholic tradition be affected by the singularities of a sect? Of a sect which lay under the censure of the church as heretical? Attend, my Reverend Brethren. It is in this that we have been so long, I believe I ought to add, so fatally mistaken. The Nazarenes were never censured! They were no sectaries! They were the very first, and because the first, they were the purest, the very best of Christians! Nazarene was the ancient name of the Jewish Christians!* Of the first members of the primitive church of Jerusalem, that original, parent church, the mother of us all; where James the brother of our Lord was bishop! In the opinions therefore of these Nazarenes, we have the opinions of those first Christians, who received, not only the baptismal ablution, but the illumination of the Spirit, at the hands of the apostles! You seem to ask me, by what evidence this important discovery is confirmed? By no evidence. The thing is not proved. It is asserted. In philoso-

---

* —— the Nazarenes (and the Jewish Christians never went by any other name). Hist. Corrup. vol. i. p. 8.

phical subjects Dr Priestley would be the last to reason from principles assumed without proof. But in divinity and ecclesiastical history, he expects that his own assertion, or that of writers of his own persuasion, however uninformed or prejudiced, should pass with the whole Christian world for proof of the boldest assumptions: The Nazarenes, it is confessed, were the progeny of the first Christians of the church of Jerusalem. But the name of Nazarene, you will bear me witness, was never heard of in the Christian church, as descriptive of the Jewish Christians, before their settlement in the northern parts of Galilee, upon the banishment of the Jews from Jerusalem, in the reign of Adrian.* *The Hebrews*, and *they of the circumcision*, were the earlier names, by which the Jewish converts, who formed the church of Jerusalem, had been distinguished from the Christians of the Gentiles. Their descendants, the Nazarenes, were at first perhaps heretical but in a single article; in maintaining the necessity of the observance of the Mosaic law, for the attainment of salvation under the gospel: whereas their ancestors, had indeed themselves adhered to their old law, but had declared against the absurdity of exacting a submission to the ceremonial part of it from the

---

* See the last paragraph of the sixth of my Letters in Reply, and the seventh of those Lettters, sec. 5.

Gentile converts. By degrees, however, these Nazarenes declined so far from the pure faith of that
first race of Christians, from which they boasted
their descent; that in Jerome's time they were become heretical in that degree, that Jerome considered them as a Jewish sect rather than a Christian. " To this day," says Jerome, " a heresy prevails among the Jews in all the synagogues of the
East, which is called that of the Minæi, who commonly go by the name of Nazarenes: who believe
in Christ, the Son of God, born of the Virgin;
and say that he was the person who suffered under
Pontius Pilate, and rose again; in whom we ourselves believe. But from a desire of being Jews
and Christians both at once, they are neither Jews
nor Christians."*

18. It is rather for the sake of general truth,
than for the attainment of victory in the present
argument, that I am desirous to maintain the distinction which was ever made, till Zuicker attempted to confound it, between the primitive
church of Jerusalem, and the sect of the Nazarenes, its heretical offspring. In the Trinitarian
controversy the distinction is of little importance.
Or rather it would be of advantage to the argu-

---

* Epist. ad Augustinum de dissidio Petri et Pauli. tom. iii.
fol. 155. B. edit. Froben.

ment of the orthodox party, if our faith needed
other support, than that which the plain sense of
the Scriptures, and the whole tenor of ecclesiastical
history supply; it would be of singular advantage
to our argument, that Dr Priestley should be able
to establish Zuicker's extravagant position, that
these Nazarenes were no other than the original
members of the Hebrew church. Whoever they
were, their orthodoxy, in the article of our Lord's
divinity, is notorious. It is attested by most of
the writers of antiquity that mention them. It is
acknowledged by Jerome, at the very same time
that he taxes them with the grossest heresy in
other points. And were no express testimony to
be produced, still it would be the fair and probable
conclusion, from that very passage of Epiphanius,
upon which Dr Priestley would build the contrary
opinion. If therefore it could be proved, that these
Nazarenes really were, what Dr Priestley hath
been taught by Zuicker to believe, the first converts of the circumcision; we who maintain the
full divinity of Christ, should find, in the confession of the Nazarenes, the verdict of those first
Christians in our favour. But since the fact is,
that they were an heretical sect, which arose in
the second century, from the ashes of the church
of Jerusalem;* their opinions upon any article are

* See Letters in Reply, vi. and vii.

totally insignificant, and can in no way affect the
Catholic tradition.   Still, therefore, the modern
Unitarian would serve his own cause but ill, who
should be able to succeed in the attempt to prove,
that the mere humanity of Christ was a tenet of
the Nazarenes.

14. The neutrality of Epiphanius's evidence is
however not the whole of the proof, by which our
modern historian hath taken the pains to support
an assertion so little to his purpose.   It is alleged
only to corroborate a more direct proof, which is
very proper to be produced as another specimen
of the sort of argument upon which our author's
first proposition rests.

15. The Nazarenes, and the Ebionites, he tells
us, were the same people, and held the same tenets.*   By the appellation of Ebionites, it is confessed, a certain sect, which denied the divinity of
our Saviour, was originally distinguished.   But
how is it proved, that these Ebionites were the
same with the Nazarenes? By a pretended acknowledgment of Origen and Epiphanius.†   It
is of great importance, for a just apprehension of

---

* Hist. of Corrup. vol. i. p. 7.
† "—— both Origen and Epiphanius acknowledge, that the
Nazarenes and Ebionites were the same people, and held the
same tenets." Hist. of Corrup. vol. i. p. 7.

the exact force of any writer's arguments, to catch
the idioms of his style: and an attention to this
circumstance, must be particularly recommended
to Dr Priestley's readers. One of the most striking peculiarities of his language, is a very singular
use of the words *acknowledge*, and *acknowledgment*.
Acknowledgment, in the usual acceptation of the
word in controversial writing, signifies a writer's
avowal of a principle or a fact, which, as making
for his adversary's argument, it might have been
for his purpose to conceal or to deny, but that the
evidence of the thing extorted the confession. But
with Dr Priestley, any expressions, which are capable of being drawn, by construction and refinement, to a sense that may seem but indirectly favourable to his own notions, are an explicit *acknowledgment* of the writer who uses them, that
things actually were, as Dr Priestley is inclined
to represent them. If such expressions of one
writer are quoted by another; they amount to an
acknowledgment to the same purpose, on the part
of the writer who makes the quotation. On the
other hand, the acknowledgment of an original
writer may sometimes be inferred from a negligent
citation. Hath Eusebius, complaining of a total
disregard to truth among the sectaries who denied
our Lord's divinity, appealed, in confirmation of
the charge, to a writer of the second century;
who alleges it against the Unitarians of his own
time, as an instance of the most hardened effron-

tery, that they had the audacity to assert, that their tenets had been originally taught 'by the apostles, and were maintained by all the Roman bishops in succession, to the time of Victor?* This heavy accusation, thus supported by the testimony of an earlier writer, is a plain *acknowledgment* † on the part of Eusebius, that the Unitarians constantly claimed this high antiquity of their doctrine. And what may seem more paradoxical, this writer's appeal to " certain psalms and odes, the compositions of faithful brethren in the first age, which celebrate the divinity of the Christ, the Word of God,"‡ is only a proof of Eusebius's inability to confute the claim, which, by his own acknowledgment, was set up.§ Hath the learned Dr Samuel Clarke, in an accurate citation of a passage in Origen, made Origen speak of the Unitarians of his time as pious persons? This is a candid acknowledgment,‖ on the part of Origen,

---

* Euseb. Hist. Eccl. lib. v. c. 28.

† " It is *acknowledged* by Eusebius, and others, " that the ancient Unitarians themselves constantly asserted, that their doctrine was the universal opinion of the Christian church, till the time of Victor." Hist. of Corrup. vol. ii. p. 486. Compare vol. i. p. 18, 19.

‡ Ψαλμοι δι οσοι και ωδαι, αδιλφων απ' αρχης υπο πιςων γραφιισαι, των λογον τυ θιυ τον Χριςον υμνιυσι θιολογυιλις. Euseb. Hist. Eccl. lib. v. c. 28. Compare Ephes. v. 19. Col. iii. 16. James v. 13.

§ " —— in refuting their pretensions to antiquity, he goes no farther back than Irenæus and Justin Martyr." Hist. of Corrup. vol. i. p. 19.

‖ " Origen candidly calls these adherents to the strict unity of God, pious persons." Hist. of Corrup. vol. i. p. 57.

of the piety of those sectaries; whereas Origen says not that they were pious, but that they boasted * that they were pious, or affected piety. Piety, and the affectation of piety, belong to opposite characters.   According to this enlarged use of the word *acknowledgment*, it will indeed be very hazardous to deny but that an acknowledgment to any purpose may be found in any writer, or be drawn from any words.   It is necessary therefore to declare, that it is only in the usual meaning of the word, that I take upon me to aver, that no acknowledgment of the supposed identity of the Nazarenes and the Ebionites, is to be found either in Origen or Epiphanius.† Origen says, indeed, of the Jewish Christians of his own time, that they were Ebionites :‡ not meaning to make any acknowledgment in favour of the proper Ebionites, as no worse heretics than the Nazarenes; but rather to stigmatize the Nazarenes with an opprobrious appellation.   And the only conclusion which is to be drawn from this passage of Origen, is, that the word Ebionite had, in his time, out-grown its original meaning; which it easily might do; inasmuch as, by its derivation, it is not naturally descriptive of any particular set of opinions; but barely expressive of the contempt, in which those who bestowed it, held the

---

* —— πολλὰς φιλοθεὺς ἱιναι ἰυγομένες ——
† See Appendix.   ‡ Contra Cels. lib. 2.

knowledge and understanding of the party on
which it was bestowed. It was therefore likely
to be variously applied at different times, according as one or another folly incurred the contempt
either of any particular writer, or of the age in
which he flourished. Accordingly it appears from
ecclesiastical history, that the use of it was various and indefinite. Sometimes it was the peculiar
name of those sects, which denied both the divinity of our Lord, and his miraculous conception.
Then its meaning was extended to take in another party; which, admitting the miraculous conception of Jesus, still denied his divinity, and
questioned his previous existence. And at last, it
seems the Nazarenes, whose error was rather a
superstitious severity in their practice, than any
deficiency in their faith, were included by Origen
in the infamy of the appellation. It was natural
indeed for Origen, fond as he was of mystic interpretations of the Jewish Scriptures, and possessed
with the imagination that every particular of the
ritual service, and every occurrence in the Jewish
story, was typical of something in the gospel dispensation; it was natural for Origen to think
meanly of a sect, who held the observance of the
letter of the ceremonial law to be an essential
part of a Christian's duty. They certainly had
little apprehension of the free spirit of the religion they professed; and this with Origen would
be the surest mark of a low and beggarly under-

standing. It is in this reproachful appellation, which he alone of all the writers of antiquity hath bestowed upon the Nazarenes, that Dr Priestley hath discovered his acknowledgment in favour of the Ebionites. For Epiphanius, who is joined with Origen in this acknowledgment, he describes the Nazarenes and the Ebionites as different sects, maintaining different opinions; except that they agreed in retaining more or less of the Mosaic service.*

16. Among other specimens of our author's happy art of turning every thing, by a dexterous interpretation, to his own purpose, it were injustice to the injured memory of Eusebius, not to mention the attempt that is made to shake the credit of his history, by representing the unfairness with which that candid writer is supposed to treat the Unitarians; where he says, "that Theodotus, who appeared about the year 190, was the first who held that our Saviour was a mere man; when in refuting their pretensions to antiquity, he goes no farther back than to Irenæus and Justin Martyr, though in his own writings alone he might

---

* See this two-fold question, concerning the faith of the Nazarenes, and the distinction between the Nazarenes and Ebionites, largely discussed in the second of Dr Priestley's Letters to me, the sixth and seventh of my Letters in Reply, the third of Dr Priestley's Second Letters, and my Remarks on his Second Letters,—Part II. chap. ii. and iii.

have found a refutation of his assertion."* It must be confessed, that any one who should assert that Theodotus was the first who taught a doctrine, which sunk our Lord into the rank of mere man, might easily be confuted from the ecclesiastical history of Eusebius; in which the Cerinthians and the Ebionites, who are taxed by all antiquity with that impiety, are referred to an earlier period. The truth however seems to be, that the doctrine of our Lord's humanity, like all corruptions, had its stages; that it was carried by degrees to the height, which it at last attained: and that Theodotus, in this article, so far surpassed the earlier heresiarchs, that the merit of being the inventor of the mere humanity, in the precise and full meaning of the words, is with great propriety and truth ascribed to him. When the Cerinthians and the Ebionites affirmed that Jesus had no existence previous to Mary's conception, and that he was literally and physically the carpenter's son; it might justly be said of them, that they asserted the mere humanity of the Redeemer: especially as it could not be foreseen, that the impiety would ever go a greater length than this, of ascribing to him an origin merely human. These heretics, however, went no farther, as I conceive, than to deny our Lord's original divinity: they admitted

---

* Hist. of Corrup. vol. i. p. 19.

I know not what unintelligible exaltation of his nature,* which took place, as they conceived, upon his ascension, by which he became no less the object of worship, than if his nature had been originally divine. But when a more daring (though, I confess, a far more consistent) sect arose; denying that our Lord in glory is more than a mortal man, raised, as all the just will one day be, to immortality; or that he is more the object of adoration than Enoch or Elijah: these younger heretics eclipsed the glory of their timid ancestors, and might justly claim the honour of being the first assertors of the mere humanity of Christ; for they were indeed the first, who made humanity the whole of his condition. It was un-doubtedly in this exalted sense, that the humanity of Christ was taught by Theodotus. For nothing short of this might serve his purpose: which, as we learn from Epiphanius, was to extenuate the guilt of a renunciation of his faith, which he had made under the terrors of persecution, by setting up a plea, that, in renouncing Christ, he had not renounced his God, but a man. This plea could be of no service to Theodotus's cause, unless Christ were a man, not only in his origin, but at the time when Theodotus renounced him. It was therefore that sublime doctrine, which is at this

---

* See the fourteenth of my Letters in Reply, sec. 5.

day taught in the conventicles* of Dr Priestley and Mr Lindsey, the doctrine of our Lord's mere undeified humanity, which Theodotus, the learned tanner of Byzantium, a deserter of his Lord, and a fugitive from his country, broached at Rome, in the end of the second century. This doctrine Dr Priestley will perhaps find it difficult to trace to any earlier period, or to any more respectable origin. No injury, therefore, is done to the Unitarian cause, when Theodotus is said to be the first author of the Unitarian doctrine in this exalted, finished, form. But after all, this is not, what Dr Priestley imagines it to be, the assertion of Eusebius. It is the assertion of a writer cited by Eusebius without any name. It should seem that he was of the Latin church, and that his expressions are to be understood with particular reference to the state of religion in the western world, especially at Rome. Now it was probably true, that Theodotus was the very first who at Rome, in any sense, taught the mere humanity of Christ. For notwithstanding the corrupt state of

---

* That the assemblies held by Mr Lindsey, in Essex-Street, and by Dr Priestley, at Birmingham, are strictly CONVENTICLES, in the genuine forensic meaning of the word, see proved in the seventeenth of my Letters in Reply, sec. 8; and my Remarks on Dr Priestley's Second Letters,—Part II. chap. iv. sec. 6. And that Dr Priestley is, by his principles, disqualified to be the pastor of any thing better than a Conventicle, see proved by his own confession, in the seventeenth of his Second Letters to me.

the Roman church in later ages, it is notorious
that she was the last of all infected with any gross
heresy. As for the pretensions of the Unitarians,
which it might be incumbent upon Eusebius to refute, they were not simply pretensions to antiquity. The antiquity of the Unitarian doctrine,
in a certain form, is confessed. Its antiquity is
proved by the express censure which is passed
upon it in St John's writings, both in his first
epistle and in his gospel, as a dangerous error
which was in being when he wrote. But the pretensions of the Unitarians, which Eusebius contradicts, were pretentions to a *prior* antiquity :
the pretence that their own doctrine was original ; and the doctrine of the church, in the time
of Zephyrinus, novel. And in refuting these pretensions, the writer quoted by Eusebius, goes back
to the apostolic age : he goes back to those psalms
and odes, which seem to be alluded to in the
apostolic epistles, and to the books of holy writ.*

II.

1. By these specimens, a judgment may be formed of the arguments and of the facts by which our
author's first assumption is supported. By expos-

---

* See this question about Theodotus, pursued in the eighth
of Dr Priestley's First Letters to me, the postscript, sec. 4 ; and
the fourteenth of my Letters in Reply.

ing the weakness of our author's arguments, and
by the proof which hath been produced from the
writings of Ignatius, that the divinity of the Son,
his full divinity, was acknowledged by the immediate disciples of the apostles, (a proof, which had
not the work been long since done by the learned
Bishop Bull, might have been strengthened with
a copious collection of passages to the same purpose from Ignatius, Barnabas, Clemens Romanus,
Hermas, and the authentic acts of the martyrdom
of Polycarp,) by the detection of the fallacy of the
arguments on the one side, and by the positive
proof adduced on the other; our author's notion
of the faith of the first Christians, that it was purely Unitarian, is overturned. And if this notion of
the first Christians be overturned; the assertion,
that the doctrine of our Lord's divinity was an
invention of the second race, falls with it. For
what was believed by the first race, could be no
invention of the second. Nor can any argument
be drawn, from any resemblance that may be imagined between the Trinity of the Christian church,
and the three principles of the Platonists, that the
doctrine of the apostles was not rightly understood by their first converts; unless indeed it could
be proved, (which is the tacit assumption upon
which this objection is founded,) that the discoveries of revelation, and the investigations of philosophy, may never coincide. But why is it supposed that nothing can be a part of an inspired

teacher's doctrine, which had been taught before by wise men, who were not inspired? Were every iota of the gospel doctrine to be found in the writings of the Greek philosophers, this would not be sufficient to set aside the pretensions of the first preachers of Christianity to a divine commission. The just conclusion from so perfect an agreement would only be, that for the great importance of these doctrines to the manners of mankind, it had pleased God to make discoveries to all men by revelation, to which a few only could attain by abstract reasoning. The case indeed is far otherwise. It is ever to be remembered, for the mortification of man's pride, and to the praise of God's mercy, that "when the world by wisdom knew not God," when philosophy had made its utmost efforts, not entirely without success, but with little general advantage, "it pleased God by the foolishness of preaching," by a method of instruction, which in the article of religious information, hath abolished the distinction between the philosopher and the idiot, "to save them that believe." But had our supposed case actually obtained, had revelation discovered nothing more to all, than reason had previously taught a few, still to teach all and to teach a few is so different a business, that the previous attainments of philosophers would have afforded no objection against the pretensions of the first preachers of the gospel, sufficient to overturn the evidence by which their claim to a divine commission is supported. Much less may a resemblance, more or less exact, between faith and philosophy in single articles, create a presumption, that those articles of faith, of which certain philosophical opinions seem to carry a resemblance, made no part of the doctrine which those inspired teachers taught. The resemblance may seem indeed a wonderful fact, which may justly draw the attention of the serious and inquisitive. And if it should be deemed incredible, as well it may, that reason, in her utmost strength, should ever ascend so high, as to attain even to a distant glimpse of truths, which have ever been esteemed the most mysterious discoveries of revelation; it will become a question of the highest curiosity and importance, to determine by what means the Platonic school came by those notions of the Godhead, which, had they been of later date than the commencement of Christianity, might have passed for a very mild corruption of the Christian faith; but being in truth much older, have all the appearance of a near, though very imperfect view, of the doctrine which was afterwards current in the Christian church.

2. The inquiry becomes more important, when it is discovered, that these notions were by no means peculiar to the Platonic school: that the Platonists pretended to be no more than the expositors of a more ancient doctrine; which is traced

from Plato to Parmenides; from Parmenides to his masters of the Pythagorean sect; from the Pythagoreans to Orpheus, the earliest of the Grecian Mystagogues; from Orpheus to the secret lore of the Egyptian priests, in which the foundations of the Orphic theology were laid. Similar notions of a triple principle prevailed in the Persian and Chaldæan theology; and vestiges even of the worship of a Trinity were discernible in the Roman superstition in a very late age. This worship the Romans had received from their Trojan ancestors. For the Trojans brought it with them into Italy from Phrygia. In Phrygia it was introduced by Dardanus so early as in the ninth century after Noah's flood. Dardanus carried it with him from Samothrace; where the personages, that were the objects of it, were worshipped under the Hebrew name of the Cabirim. Who these Cabirim might be, has been matter of unsuccessful inquiry to many learned men. The utmost that is known with certainty is, that they were originally three, and were called by way of eminence, the Great or Mighty Ones: for that is the import of the Hebrew name. And of the like import is their Latin appellation, *Penates*. *Dii per quos penitus spiramus, per quos habemus corpus, per quos rationem animi possidemus.** *Dii qui sunt intrinsecus,*

---

* Macrob. Saturnal. lib. iii. c. 4.

atque in intimis penetralibus cœli.* Thus the joint worship of Jupiter, Juno, and Minerva, the Triad of the Roman Capitol, is traced to that of the THREE MIGHTY ONES in Samothrace;† which was established in that island, at what precise time it is impossible to determine, but earlier, if Eusebius may be credited, than the days of Abraham.

8. The notion therefore of a Trinity, more or less removed from the purity of the Christian faith, is found to have been a leading principle in all the ancient schools of philosophy, and in the religions of almost all nations ; and traces of an early popular belief of it, appear even in the abominable rites of idolatrous worship. If reason was insufficient for this great discovery, what could be the means of information, but what the Platonists themselves assign, Θεοπαραδολος Θεολογια. " A theology delivered from the gods," *i. e.* a revelation. This is the account which Platonists, who were no Christians, have given of the origin of their master's doctrine. But from what revelation could they derive their information, who lived before the Christian, and had no light from the Mosaic ? For whatever some of the early fathers may have imagined,

---

* Varro apud Arnob. lib. iii. p. 123.   Lugd. Bat. 1651.

† —— Tarquinius Demarati Corinthii filius,—*Samothraciis mystici imbutus,* uno templo ac sub eodem tecto, numina memorata conjungit.   Macrob. Saturnal. lib. iii. c. 4.

there is no evidence that Plato or Pythagoras were at all acquainted with the Mosaic writings: not to insist, that the worship of a Trinity is traced to an earlier age than that of Plato or of Pythagoras, or even of Moses. Their information could be only drawn from traditions founded upon earlier revelations; from scattered fragments of the ancient patriarchal creed; that creed, which was universal before the defection of the first idolaters, which the corruptions of idolatry, gross and enormous as they were, could never totally obliterate.* Thus the doctrine of the Trinity is rather confirmed than discredited by the suffrage of the heathen sages; since the resemblance of the Christian faith and the Pagan philosophy in this article, when fairly interpreted, appears to be nothing less than the consent of the latest and the earliest revelations.

III.

1. Our author's assumption, that the doctrine of our Lord's divinity was an innovation of the Platonic Christians of the second century, being overthrown by direct proof, that this pretended

---

* " ——What Socrates said of him, what Plato writ, and the rest of the heathen philosophers of several nations, is all no more than the twilight of revelation, after the sun of it was set in the race of Noah." Dryden's Preface to *Religio Laici*.

innovation was a part of the faith of the first
Christians : all oblique and secondary arguments,
that might otherwise create a presumption in our
author's favour, are rendered wholly insignificant.
To Dr Priestley it seems a circumstance of great
importance, that these early writers " sometimes
drop the personification of the Logos, (which in
his opinion had been their first step towards the
deification of our Saviour,*) and speak of it as the
mere attribute of God."† This he imputes to the
difficulty, with which new opinions lay hold upon
the mind; and to the natural prevalency of good
sense, which is such, that it will in all cases often
get the better of imagination.‡ Facts themselves
should be established, before consequences are deduced from them. Let us therefore consider the
example by which this assertion is supported.

2. Theophilus of Antioch says, " that when
God said, *Let us make man,* he spake to nothing
but his own Logos, or Wisdom."§ It must be
confessed, that the example is happily chosen. It
is clear that in this passage of Theophilus, as it is
expressed in Dr Priestley's translation, the Logos
is described as *nothing but* the Wisdom of God :
nothing but *His own* wisdom. His own Wisdom

---

* Hist. of Corrup. part i. sec. ii.
† Ibid. vol. i. p. 35.
‡ Ibid.   § Ibid.

must be that internal Wisdom, which is a power
of his own Mind, a property of his own Person:
and, to say that God spake to " nothing but his
own Wisdom," is to say, that he spake to no one
but himself. Dr Priestley methinks hath spared
to make the use he might have done of this passage of Theophilus; which seems not only to be
an instance in which Theophilus drops the personification of the Logos in his own writings; but
to prove, that as far as the interpretation of the
Old Testament is of any importance, the authority
of this learned and ancient bishop of Antioch
stands with the Unitarian scheme. This learned
bishop tells us, that the writers of the Old Testament, if ever they seem to allude to a plurality of
persons in the Godhead, speak figuratively, and
are to be understood accordingly. The allusion is
perhaps no where stronger, than in those words of
Moses, in the book of Genesis, " God said, Let us
make." God not only speaks, " God said;" but
God speaks in the plural number, " Let us make;"
as though persons were addressed, who were to
take part with the speaker in the business to be
done. Theophilus, the celebrated bishop of Antioch; Theophilus, so respectable for his antiquity,
his piety, and his learning; Theophilus cautions
us, not to be over-confident of the consequences
which we draw from this rigid exposition of the
sacred writer's words. Theophilus affirms, that
the expression is purely figurative; signifying

only, that before man was made, the purpose of making him arose, and was contemplated, in the Divine intellect. The expression describes an internal deliberation of the Divine Mind concerning the intended work; just as the private thoughts and purposes of a man are sometimes expressed under the figure of a discourse passing within himself. All this Theophilus affirms in Dr Priestley's English. Nothing of this Theophilus affirms speaking for himself, in his own language,* ἐκ ἀλλῳ δὲ τινι εἴρηκι, Ποιησωμιν, ἀλλ' ἢ τῳ ἱαυλ Λογι, καὶ τῃ ἱαυλ Σοφιᾳ. The " nothing but" of Dr Priestley's English, conveys quite another idea than the ἐκ ἀλλῳ τινι ἀλλ' ἢ of Theophilus's Greek. The Logos and the Wisdom, as different names of one thing, are connected by the disjunctive *or*, in Dr Priestley's English; as names of different things they are connected by the copulative *and*, (Καὶ,) in Theophilus's Greek. The exact rendering of Theophilus's words is to this effect: " It was to no other person" (that is the proper force of ἐκ ἀλλῳ τινι, *haud alii cuipiam*) " It was to no other person that he said, *Let us make*, than to his own Word, and to his own Wisdom." τῳ ἱαυλ Λογι καὶ τῃ ἱαυλ Σοφιᾳ. The repetition of the demonstrative article with the pronoun, as well as the connection by the copulative, clearly shews that Λογι and Σοφια, the Word and the Wis-

---

* Ad. Autolyc. p. 114. Oxon. 1684.

dom, are different things. Hath Dr Priestley written a history of the Corruptions of Christianity, and hath he yet to learn, that in the language of Theophilus, and of the best writers of his age, the Word and the Wisdom, (Λογος and Σοφια,) are used as proper names of the second and third persons of the Trinity? If his own reading in those early fathers hath been so confined, that not one of the clear unequivocal instances that occur in Theophilus himself, in Origen, in Tatian, and Irenæus, hath ever fallen under his own proper observation, he might have been informed of this peculiarity of their style, from the notes which accompany the text of Theophilus, in Bishop Fell's edition, printed at Oxford in 1684; which, as it is inserted in his catalogue* of *principal* editions, it is possible he may have seen. Theophilus's assertion, that God spake to no other person than his Word and his Wisdom, is an assertion, that he spake to persons of no less dignity, than the Son and the Holy Ghost. It is an assertion of the Catholic exposition† of the text, and of the consequences deduced from it, in opposition to the Jewish expositors of that age; who contended,

---

* Dr Priestley's Preface, p. xxii.

† That this is the true exposition, that the text describes a consultation which passed between the persons of the Godhead, is shewn with great brevity, but with the highest degree of evidence and perspicuity in Dr Kennicott's dissertation on the Tree of Life, p. 29, 30.—Compare the same dissertation, p. 71.

that this speech of God was addressed to the angels. Theophilus therefore in this passage hath
not dropped the personification of the Logos; that
is, he hath not receded from the assertion of the
personality of the Word. He affirms not, that
the Logos, so often mentioned by himself and
other writers as a person, is no person, but merely
the Divine Attribute of Wisdom; which, in the
usual language of grammarians, were rather to
assert the personification* than to drop it: but by
the names of the Word and the Wisdom, he distinguishes two different persons; saying, these
were the persons to whom God spake.

IV.

1. We have seen by what sort of arguments
our author's two first assertions, " That the faith
of the first age was Unitarian, and that the doctrine of our Lord's divinity was an invention of
the second," are supported. If he hath succeeded
no better in the proof of his third assertion, concerning the Platonic Christians of the second age,
the inventors, as he would have it, of our Lord's
divinity,—that the divinity which they set up was

---

* Of my misapprehension of the word *personification*, as
used by Dr Priestley, and how little it affects my argument,
see the thirteenth of my Letters in Reply, sec. 2—5.

only of that secondary sort, which was admitted
by the Arians, including neither eternity, nor any
proper necessity of existence, having the mere
name of divinity, without any thing of the real
form; if the proof of this third assertion should
be found to be equally infirm with that of the
other two, his notion of the gradual progress of
opinions, from the mere Unitarian doctrine to the
Arian, and from the Arian doctrine to the Athanasian faith, must be deemed a mere dream or
fiction, in every part.

2. It must be acknowledged, that the first converts from the Platonic school, took advantage of
the resemblance between the evangelic and Platonic doctrine, on the subject of the Godhead, to
apply the principles of their old philosophy to the
explication and the confirmation of the articles of
their faith.   They defended it by arguments
drawn from Platonic principles; they even propounded it in Platonic language: which to themselves and their contemporaries was the most familiar and intelligible, that could be employed
upon so abstruse a subject.   Nor was this practice
to be condemned, so long as the Scriptures and the
Catholic traditions were made the test of truth;
so long as revelation was not pressed into the
service of philosophy, by any accommodation of
the pure evangelical doctrine to preconceived opinions: but philosophy was made to exert her

powers in the defence of revelation, and to lend her language to be the vehicle of its sacred truths. These might be deemed the most promising means that could be employed, for bringing over more converts from the Pagan schools. And the writers, who evangelized in this philosophical style, conceived perhaps, that they had the sanction of an apostle's example, " for becoming all things to all men, that they might gain some."

3. But whatever might be the purity of their intentions, they were guilty of an unpardonable deviation from the primitive faith, if it be true that they maintained the doctrine which Dr Priestley ascribes to them; namely, that the Son is the mere contingent creature of the Father's will and power; a production which hath not always existed.* We have seen that this was not the belief of the first age; and if it is to be found in the writings of the second, it could indeed be nothing better than a corruption of religon by philosophy.

4. To judge of the truth of a writer's proposition, and even to divine of what sort the arguments will be, which he will allege in support of it, it is sometimes sufficient that the precise tenor of it be clearly understood. They were converts

---

* Hist. of Corrup. vol. i. p. 42, 44, 62.

from Platonism, they were Christians, who, with their Christianity, are supposed to have retained their Platonism, to whom Dr Priestley ascribes the notion of a Logos which had not always existed, but began to be, like other creatures, by an act of the Father's will. After all that Dr Priestley hath written, about the resemblance between the ecclesiastical and the Platonic Trinity; he hath yet, it seems, to learn that a created Logos, a Logos which had ever not existed, was no less an absurdity in the academy, than it is an impiety in the church. The converts from Platonism must have renounced their philosophy, before they could be the authors of this absurd, this monstrous opinion.* As the notion that this doctrine took its rise with them, betrays a total ignorance of the genuine principles of their school; it is easy to foresee, that the arguments brought in support of it, can only be founded in gross misconstructions of their language. That this is indeed the case, will be abundantly proved by a single instance.

5. Athenagoras is one of the writers to whom Dr Priestley refers for a proof of his assertion. The passage which he cites, as affording a proof that Athenagoras believed not that Christ had al-

---

* See more upon this subject in the eighth of Dr Priestley's First Letters to me, and the thirteenth of my Letters in Reply, sec. 8.

ways existed, or that the Logos had always existed, otherwise than as an attribute of the Divine Mind, happens to be one, in which that philosophic father asserts the eternity of the Logos, as a distinct person, in the most explicit terms; and argues in support of it from a certain relation of the Logos to the paternal intellect, which the name, Logos, implies. " Athenagoras," says Dr Priestley, " calls Christ the first production of the Father; but says, he was not always actually produced; for that from the beginning, God, being an eternal mind, had reason in himself, being from eternity rational."* But let us hear Athenagoras himself.† " If," says he, " endowed as you are with superior understanding," (he addresses the Emperors Marcus Aurelius Antonius, and Lucius Aurelius Commodus,) it should occur to you to enquire, whence it is that he is called a Son, I will explain it in a few words. (It is) that he is to the Father (as) the first offspring. Not as something made" (This is the true sense of the words, in which Dr Priestley imagines that it is said that Christ was not always produced) " Not as something made. For God, being an eternal intelligence, himself from the beginning had the Logos in himself, being eternally rational." The learned

---

* Hist. of Corrup. vol. i. p. 36.
† See the entire Greek passage, p. 62.

father undertakes to explain to the philosophical
emperors, why the second person in the ever-bles-
sed Trinity, is called the Son. He tells them, that
this name is expressive of a certain relation, which
the second person stands in to the first, who is
called the Father; which relation is that of the
eldest born. But lest the relation of primogeni-
ture should lead to the notion of a proper physical generation, which would sink the Son into
the rank of a creature, (for generation is only a
particular way in which certain things are made,)
he says, that the birth or generation of the Son,
is not to be understood as if he were something
that had been ever made; as if his being had
commenced, at any certain time, by the inducement of a form upon a preexisting material. For
that is the general notion of a making; although
in common speech it is usual to say of those
things only, that they are made, to which the
form is given at once by the hand of the artist.
When the form is gradually brought on by the
·plastic powers of nature, the secret process is called generation: which is therefore but a sort of
making, and differs from that which is usually
called a making, in the means only by which the
end is compassed. Athenagoras therefore gives
the emperors a caution, not to understand by the
generation of a Son, a generation in the literal
sense of the word, which comes under the general notion of a making: not to understand by it

any thing like that natural process, by which the bodies of plants and animals, and some other substances, are carried forward from a potential to an actual existence. The generation of the Son cannot be understood, he says, of any such production, because his actual existence is from eternity. This, he says, is the necessary consequence of the confessed eternity of the Father. The Logos hath existed from eternity, in union with the Father; " because God, being eternally rational, ever had the Logos in himself." The sense is, that the personal subsistence of a Divine Logos is implied in the very idea of a God. And the argument rests on a principle which was common to all the Platonic fathers, and seems to be founded in Scripture, that the existence of the Son flows necessarily from the Divine Intellect exerted on itself; from the Father's contemplation of his own perfections. But as the Father ever was, his perfections have ever been, and his intellect hath been ever active. But perfections, which have ever been, the ever-active Intellect, must ever have contemplated; and the contemplation which hath ever been, must ever have been accompanied with its just effect, the personal existence of the Son. Athenagoras having thus proved, that the generation of the Son can be only a figurative generation, proceeds to explain the figure, by assigning the particular transaction to which he conceives it to allude;

which is no commencement of the Son's existence; not even that act of the Paternal Mind, in
which the existence of the Son originates; but
the going forth of the Son to exert his powers in
the business of creation. "He is," says Athenagoras, "to the Father as the first offspring; not
as something that was ever made: but that he
went forth to be idea and energy in material substances, which lay yet in chaos, unqualified and
undistinguished; the dense promiscuously mingled with the rare, waiting the operation of the active spirit to impregnate them with form."* Here,
indeed, the Son of God is called an idea, and

---

* εἰ δὲ, δὲ ὑπερβολην συνεσιως, σκοπειν ὑμιν ἐπεισιν, ὁ παις τι βε-
λεται· ἐρω δια βραχεων, πρῶτον γεννημα εἶναι τῳ πατρι. ἐκ ὡς γενομενον·
ἐξ ἀρχης γαρ ὁ Θεος, νες ἀϊδιος ὤν, εἶχεν αὐτος ἐν ἑαυτῳ τον λογον,
ἀϊδιως λογικος ὤν· ἀλλ᾿ ὡς των ὑλικων συμπαντων ἀποιη φυσεως και γης
ὀχειας ὑποκειμενων δικην, μεμιγμενων των παχυμεριστερων προς τα κυφο-
τερα, ἐπ᾿ αὐτοις ἰδεα και ἐνεργεια εἶναι προελθων. There seems to be
some corruption in the words και γης. A learned clergyman of
the archdeaconry of St Alban's, conjectures, that γης should be
της. Nor can I devise any better emendation. The general
sense of the passage cannot but be very clear, to those to whom
the imagery of the Platonists is in any degree familiar.

A passage of Hermes Trismegistus, preserved by Suidas, and
Cedrenus, and Melela, may somewhat illustrate this passage of
Athenagoras. Ἢν φως νοερον προ φωτος νοερου, και ἀδεν ἱερον ἢν ἢ τελεη
ἐνοης· ἀει ἐν ἑαυτῳ ὤν, ἀει τῳ ἑαυτῳ νοι και φωτι και πνευματι παντα
περιεχει· ἐκτος τελεη ὁ Θεος, ἐκ ἀγγελος, ἐ δαιμων, ἐκ ἐσια τις ἀλλη,
παντων γαρ κυριος, και Θεος, και παντη, και παντα ὑπ᾿ αὐτου και ἐν αὐτῳ
ἐστιν. ὁ γαρ Λογος αὐτου προελθων, παντελειος και γονιμος και δημιουργος
ἐν γονιμῳ ὑδατι πεσων· ἐγκυον ἐποιησε το ὑδωρ.

---

* Malela has ἐν γενιμω Θεου πεσων, for ἐν γονιμω ὑδατι.

an energy. But it is not, that he is understood to be an unsubstantial idea, or energy, of the Paternal Mind; but a living idea, energising on the matter of the universe, to stamp it with the forms of things. And his generation is affirmed to be no commencement of his existence, but the first exertion of his powers in the production of external substances: or to use a more Platonic phrase, the first projection of his energies. προϛολη των ἐπιγγημαlων.

6. If any thing be justly reprehensible in the notions of the Platonic Christians, it is this conceit, which seems to be common to Athenagoras with them all, and is a key to the meaning of many obscure passages in their writings, that the external display of the powers of the Son, in the business of creation, is the thing intended, in the Scripture language, under the figure of his generation.* A conceit which seems to have no certain foundation in holy writ, and no authority in the opinions and the doctrines of the preceding age: and it seems to have betrayed some of those, who were the most wedded to it, into the use of a very improper language; as if a new relation had taken place between the first and the second person, when the creative powers were first exerted.

---

* See the thirteenth of my Letters in Reply, sec. 12, 15.

The indiscretion of presuming to affix a determinate meaning upon a figurative expression, of which no particular exposition can be safely drawn from holy writ, is in some degree atoned by the object, which these writers had in view. It was evidently their intention, to guard the expressions of Scripture from misconstruction. They thought to lead men away from the notion of a literal generation, by assigning to the figure a particular meaning, which it might naturally bear, and which, whether it was the true sense of it or no, seemed not to clash with any explicit part of the revelation. The conversion of an attribute into a person, whatever Dr Priestley may imagine, is a notion to which they were entire strangers. They held indeed, that the existence of the Son necessarily and inseparably attached to the attributes of the Paternal Mind: insomuch that the Father could no more be without the Son, than without his own attributes. But that the Son had been a mere attribute, before he became a person; or that the Paternal attributes were older than the Son's personal existence, is a doctrine which they would have heard with horror and amazement. With horror, as Christians; with amazement, as philosophers!

7. It is but justice to Dr Priestley, to acknowledge, what indeed he ought to have acknowledged for himself, that in this misinterpretation

of the Platonic fathers, he is not original : that he hath upon his side the respectable authority of two very eminent divines of the Roman church,— Petavius and Huetius : which however is no more than a single authority; the pious bishop of Avranches, upon this subject, being but the echo of the very learned Jesuit. It is not the season to revive past quarrels : one is therefore unwilling to recollect the motives, which induced Petavius to belie his better knowledge, and to charge the philosophical fathers of the second century with errors, which he was too learned not to know no Platonist could entertain. But at the time when Petavius wrote, the minds of the most enlightened and liberal of the Romanists, were so ill reconciled to the separation of the reformed churches from their communion, that it was the fashion for the champions of the Papal superstition, in order to weaken the support which they were sensible the Protestant cause received from the writings of the fathers of the three first centuries, to take every method to derogate from their authority. And this it was thought could in no way be more effectually done, than by bringing them under a suspicion of misbelief, in doctrines which the reformed churches, and the Roman, hold in equal reverence. The learned Petavius considered not, that he sacrificed the cause of our common Christianity to the private views of his own church, in

E

thus attempting to corrupt the stream of tradition at the very fountain-head. His arguments, which Dr Priestley hath attempted to revive, are examined and confuted, with great erudition and ability, by the excellent Bishop Bull, in the third section of his " Defence of the Nicene Faith."

8. The last specimen which I shall produce of Dr Priestley's manner of arguing from authorities, shall be taken from his short account of the word TRINITY.* This word, he says, first made its appearance in the writings of Theophilus, bishop of Antioch. But Dr Priestley thinks " it is not clear that by it he meant, a Trinity consisting of the same persons that it was afterwards made to consist of:" and he affirms, that it is certain a Trinity of persons in the Godhead, was not meant by Theophilus. And thus Theophilus, for the second time, is brought to give evidence against his own opinion. But whence arises the certainty, that a Trinity of persons is not meant by Theophilus? From no other circumstance that I can perceive, but that the word Trinity is expressly expounded in the text of Theophilus, by God, his Word, and his Wisdom. " The three days," says Theophilus, " which preceded the creation of the luminaries, were types of the Trinity; of God, and

* Hist. of Corrup. vol. i. p. 99.

of his Word, and of his Wisdom."* It hath already been observed that God, his Word, and his Wisdom, in the praseology of Theophilus's age, were used for Father, Son, and Holy Ghost. It is unnecessary in this assembly to cite the numerous examples that occur in Theophilus, Tatian, Irenæus, and Origen. It may be more useful to explain the grounds upon which, as I conceive, this language was adopted.

9. We have seen that the Platonic fathers, although they held the eternity of the second person no less than of the first, imagined that his generation signified a particular transaction, which took place at a certain time. And it is probable that, although they held the eternity of the Holy Spirit, yet they conceived that the procession expressed some projection of his energies, which took place at the same time with that, which they understood to be the generation of the Son. They imagined that the second person was not properly a Son, before that event, which they understood by his generation: and they would equally imagine, that the third was not properly the Spirit, before the event which they understood by his procession.

---

* ὡσαύτως καὶ ἀι τρεῖς ἡμέραι (πρὸ) τῶν φωστηρων γεγονυιαι, τυποι ἱσιν τῆς τριαδος· τυ Θευ, καὶ τυ Λογυ ἀυτυ, καὶ τῆς Σοφιας ἀυτυ. Theoph. ad Autolyc. lib. ii. p. 106. Oxon. 1684. I have taken the liberty to insert the preposition πρὸ, the want of it being evidently an omission.

But they conceived, that the second person had
ever been the Word; and that the third had ever
been the Wisdom. Of the first they conceived,
that he was not properly a Father, before the second was a Son; although he ever had been God.
I have already given my opinion of these subtle
distinctions; for which the best apology (for an
apology they need) is the evident good intention of
the writers, who first maintained them. But upon
these distinctions, whether just or visionary, their
phraseology seems to have been founded. They
thought the names of God, the Word, and the
Wisdom, which express of each of the three divine persons, what each hath always been, were
appellations to be generally preferred to those of
Father, Son, and Holy Ghost; which express relations only, which, according to their fancy, had
not always been. And this explains the reason,
why they used the word God, as the peculiar appellation of the Father. It was not that they
scrupled to ascribe an equal divinity to all the
Three Persons; but that rejecting the simpler nomenclature founded on relations, they desired to
call each person by the name which they conceived to be most descriptive of his essence : and
of the essence of the Father, they could find no
name at all descriptive, but the general appellation,—God.

10. The three names therefore, God, the Word,

and the Wisdom, in the language of Theophilus's
age, were understood to be equivalent to Father,
Son, and Holy Ghost: and when Theophilus expounds the word TRINITY, by God, his Word, and
his Wisdom, it is just the same thing as if he had
rendered it by Father, Son, and Holy Ghost.
How this exposition may create a.doubt, whether
Theophilus's Trinity consisted of the same persons
with the Trinity of later ages; how it may produce a certainty that Theophilus's was not a Trinity of persons in the Godhead, it is not my business to explain. Dr Priestley should have opened
this mystery; but he hath not condescended to
give his readers any farther light, than his own
naked assertion, that the thing is, as he would
choose that it should be; which in this, as in other
cases, he seems to think may pass for a sufficient
proof of any of the paradoxes of his own party.

11. Perhaps his doubt about the real meaning
of the word, and his confident persuasion that it
was no Trinity of persons in the Godhead, have
arisen from the obscurity of which he complains,
in the subsequent part of the sentence, where the
Word and the Wisdom are mentioned again. It
is indeed but reasonable to suppose, that these
words are used in the same sense in both places.
But in this second place, the Wisdom, Dr Priestley might imagine, could be no divine person.
For in Dr Priestley's English, the latter clause of

the sentence runs thus: " The fourth day is the type of Man, who needs light, that the Word may be God, and the Man Wisdom." This passage, Dr Priestley observes, is " certainly obscure enough." You all, I am persuaded, agree in the truth of his remark; and you will equally agree in mine, if I venture to say much more of the latter clause: that it is certainly unintelligible—in Dr Priestley's translation. But turn to the original—the whole obscurity will vanish; and instead of it, you will find that striking perspicuity of language, which is the characteristic beauty of Theophilus's style. Having said that the three first days of creation were types of the Trinity, Theophilus adds, " That the fourth was a type of Man, who is in need of light. That there might be, or, so that there is, God, the Word, the Wisdom, Man."* This last clause is nothing but an enumeration of all that had been mentioned, as typified in the first four days of creation.. To explain how these days were types of what they are supposed to represent, might indeed be difficult: but in the age of Theophilus, the great art of interpreting the Old Testament, was supposed to consist in making types out of every thing. The

---

* ὡσαύτως καὶ αἱ τρεῖς ἡμέραι (πρὸ) τῶν φωστήρων γεγονυῖαι, τύποι εἰσιν τῆς τριάδος· τῦ Θεῦ, καὶ τῦ Λόγυ ἀὐτ, καὶ τῆς Σοφίας ἀὐτ. τέταρτη δὲ τύπος ἐστὶν ἀνθρώπυ· ὁ προσδεὴς τῦ φωτός· ἵνα ᾖ Θεος, Λόγος, Σοφία, Ανθρωπος. Ad Autolyc. lib. ii. p. 106. Oxon. 1684.

sense, however, of the writer, is expressed with the greatest perspicuity. It is evident from his own exposition of the word, that he speaks of no other Trinity than Father, Son, and Holy Ghost. It appears therefore, from the testimony of Theophilus, that the word was used at first in no other sense, than that which it hath borne in later ages. The word hath not changed its original meaning; but in this, as in most of his assertions, Dr Priestley is confuted by his own authorities.

12. I feel no satisfaction in detecting the weaknesses of this learned writer's argument, but what arises from a consciousness, that it is a discharge of some part of the duty, which I owe to the church of God. It is a mortifying proof of the infirmity of the human mind, in the highest improvement of its faculties in the present life, that such fallacies and reasoning, such misconstructions of authorities, such distorted views of facts and opinions, should be found in the writings of a man, to whom of all men of the present age, some branches of the experimental sciences are the most indebted.

V.

1. May I be permitted to close this long address, with a word of exhortation to the younger members of the priesthood.

2. The actual state of things is such, that, to the greater part of those who engage in it, our holy profession must furnish the means of a subsistence. The consequence is, that we are obliged to enter upon it in an early season of our lives, when it is well if we have previously laid a good foundation in our minds, of the very first principles of the doctrine of Christ: and a due proficiency in theological studies, must be the attainment of future industry. To the novitiates therefore of our order, considered as unfinished theologians, I take the liberty to recommend the diligent study of the works of Bishop Bull; especially of his writings on the subject of the Trinity, with the annotations of Grabe, his learned editor. In these they will find an exact and critical detail of the opinions of the fathers of the three first centuries. They will find the faith of the church of England confirmed, and proved to be the original faith, by a tradition traced with certainty, to the apostolic age. And they will find every argument refuted, which the Unitarian party have yet been able to form upon their own views of the opinions of the earliest ages.

3. The study of Bishop Bull, if leisure is not wanting, may be followed, or accompanied with advantage by that of the ecclesiastical historians: of the original historians, I mean, Eusebius, Socrates, Sozomen, and Theodorit. As for modern

histories, the use of them, without a previous acquaintance with the ancient writers, is rather to be discouraged than recommended. By those who are already learned in the subject, they may be read indeed with emolument; as commentaries on the ancient text of history, as it lies in the original writers, which may occasionally throw light upon dark and doubtful questions. But as books of elementary instruction for beginners, they will generally be pernicious. For it will too often be found to be the case, that the narrative is accommodated, not through premeditated fraud, but in the mere error of prejudice, either to the private opinions of the writer, or to the interests of his sect. Of this Dr Priestley's work is a striking example. No work was perhaps ever sent abroad, under the title of a history, containing less of truth than his, in proportion to its volume.

4. From ecclesiastical history the student learns what the faith of the church hath at all times been; and he is enabled to separate the pure doctrine of the first age from all later innovations: a matter at all times of the highest moment; but of particular importance in the present juncture, when the whole ability and learning of the Unitarian party is exerted, to wrest from us the argument from tradition. The importance of the argument from tradition rests upon the supposed infallibity of the first preachers. The opinion of their infallibility

rests upon the belief of their divine illumination. The consequence of a divine illumination is, that their whole doctrine must have been, not indeed obvious to the human understanding, not within the reach of its unassisted power to discover, but consonant to the highest reason, nor too difficult, when propounded, for the human apprehension; and though not free from paradoxes, certainly not encumbered with contradictions. No tradition therefore, may avail to prove, that any manifest contradiction, that a part, for instance, is equal to the whole, or that the same thing in the same respect, is at the same time one and many, was a part of the apostolic doctrine; if the inspiration of the apostles be admitted. Or, if it should appear, from the evidence of a tradition which cannot reasonably be questioned, that the apostles really required the belief of contradictions under the name of mysteries; their pretence to inspiration will be refuted, and the credit of their doctrine overturned. For as the evidence of intuition is far superior to that of sense; no external evidence may establish the belief of a contradiction; since no testimony that a contradiction is, should be allowed to overpower the intuitive conviction that it cannot be. An inquiry therefore into the reasonableness of our faith, as well as just views of its history, is of great importance.

5. The reasonableness of our faith will be best

understood from the writings of the fathers of the three first centuries. And among these, those wicked Platonists of the second age, who, in Dr Priestley's judgment, sowed the seeds of the anti-christian corruption, deserve particular attention; for the great perspicuity with which in general they expound the faith, and the great ability with which they defend it. And as these corrupters brought with them into the church, the language of their school, (I say the language, for its opi-nions, except so far as they harmonized with the gospel, they had the ingenuity to retract,*) the writings of the Pagan philosophers, particularly the Platonists, will be of considerable use to the Christian student; as they will bring him more acquainted with a phraseology, which is used even by the Christian Platonists: nor for this purpose only, but for some degree of light which they will throw upon the argument. The error of the later Platonists was, that they warped the genuine doc-trine of the original tradition, their Θιοπαραδόλος Θιολογια, to a form in which it might be in friendship with the popular idolatry. Their writings there-fore are a mine, in which the true metal is indeed mingled with a dross of heterogeneous substan-ces; but yet the richness of the ore is such, as

---

* See the beginning of Justin Martyr's Dialogue with Try-pho; and Theoph. ad Autolyc. lib. ii.

may well repay the cost and trouble. of the separation. Or if leisure should be wanting for a minute study of a subject, which may seem but of a secondary importance, it will at least be expedient, I had almost said it will be necessary, to know so much of the opinions of heathen antiquity, as is to be learned from those authentic documents, which the industry of the indefatigable Cudworth, hath collected and arranged, with great judgment, in his Intellectual System.

6. The advantage to be expected from these deep researches, is not any insight into the manner in which the three Divine Persons are united; a knowledge which is indeed too high for man, perhaps for angels; which in our present condition at least is not to be attained, and ought not to be sought. But that just apprehension of the Scripture doctrine, which will shew that it is not one of those things that " no miracles can prove,"* that will be the certain fruit of the studies recommended. They will lead us to see the Scripture doctrine in its true light: that it is an imperfect discovery, not a contradiction. That the Catholic faith is not properly compared with the tale of

---

* " They are things which no miracles can prove," says Dr Priestley, in his Address to Mr Gibbon, speaking of the doctrines of the Trinity, and the Atonement. See Hist. of Corrup. vol. ii. p. 861.

Mahomet's journey to the third heaven; his conferences there, while the pitcher of water fell; or
even with the doctrine of transubstantiation :*
that even the Athanasian creed is something very
different from a set "·of contradictions, the most
direct which any person the most skilled in logic
might draw up."† A censure, which could hardly
have fallen from our learned adversary, Unitarian
as he is, had he but known so common a book as
Dr Waterland's History and Paraphrase. In the
opinions of the Pagan Platonists, we have in some
degree an experimental proof, that this abstruse
doctrine cannot be the absurdity, which it seems to
those who misunderstand it. Would Plato, would
Porphyry, would even Plotinus, have believed the
miracles of Mahomet, or the doctrine of transubstantiation? But they all believed a doctrine,
which so far at least resembles the Nicene, as to
be loaded with the same, or greater objections. By
every one who will thus combine the studies of
divinity and philosophy, the truth of Plato's observation, I am persuaded, will be soon experienced: that to those who apply themselves to these
speculations, with a humble disposition to be
taught, rather than with the unphilosophical and
irreligious habit of deciding hastily upon the first
view of difficulties, what at first appeared the most

---

* Hist. of Corrup. vol. ii. p. 461.
† Ibid. vol. i. p. 87.

incredible, will in the end seem the most evident and certain; and maxims, which seemed at first indisputable, will be discarded.*

7. An extensive erudition in Pagan as well as Christian antiquity, joined with a critical understanding of the sacred text, is that which hath so long enabled the clergy of the church of England, to take the lead among Protestants, as the apologists of the apostolic faith and discipline; and to baffle the united strength of their adversaries of all denominations. God forbid, that through an indolence, which would be unpardonable, we should ever lose the superiority, which we have so long maintained. The acquisition of learning is indeed laborious, but the fruit is sweet. The private satisfaction that it must give to every minister of the church of England, to understand, that his engagements to the establishment are perfectly consistent with his higher obligations to God and Christ, is alone sufficient to repay the labour of the studies, which afford this comfortable conviction, and contribute to its daily growth. But private satisfaction is not the end of our pursuits. The nobler end is public edification. It is a maxim of Dr Priestley's, that every man, who in his conscience dissents from the established

---

* Plato in Epist. ad Dionys.

church, is obliged in conscience to be a declared
dissenter. I honour the generosity of the sentiment.

——————— φιλον ἱιη
Φιλιιν· ποῖι δ' ἰχϑρον, ά-
τ' ἰχϑρος ἰων, λυκοιο δικαν ὑποϑιυσομαι,
Αλλ' ἀλλαῖι παλιων, ὁδοις σκολιαις——

It ought much more to be the sentiment of every
one who stands with the received doctrine,—to
be a declared churchman. If he would reap any
solid advantage from the purity of his faith, he
must be an open and avowed believer; lest if he
confess not Christ, his God and Saviour, before
men, he should not be at last confessed before the
angels of heaven. If this confession be the general duty of every man, who feels conviction; it is
the particular duty of every one, who hath been
called to the evangelist's office. He holds the authority of his commission for no other purpose, but
to be a witness of the truth. A conviction that it
is the truth, founded on a deep investigation of the
subject, will supply him with firmness to persevere
in the glorious attestation, unawed by the abilities
of his antagonists, undaunted by obloquy, unmoved by ridicule: which seem to be the trials which
God hath appointed, instead of persecution, in the
present age, to prove the sincerity and patience
of the faithful. The advocate of that sound form
of words, which was originally delivered to the

saints, hath to expect that his opinions will be the
open jest of the Unitarian party : that his sincerity will be called in question; or if " a bare
possibility of his being in earnest"* be charitably
admitted, the misfortune of his education will be
lamented, and his prejudices deplored. All this
insult will not alarm nor discompose him. He
will rather glory in the recollection, that his adherence to the faith of the first ages hath provoked it. The conviction, which he will all the while
enjoy, that his philosophy is Plato's, and his creed
St John's, will alleviate the mortification he might
otherwise feel in differing from Dr Priestley; nor
suffer him to think the evil insupportable, although the consequence of this dissent, should be,
that he must share with the excellent Bishop of
Worcester, in Dr Priestley's " pity and indignation."† Not indeed that he will hold any good
man's good opinion cheap; or esteem it a light
evil, that a conscientious attachment to the truth
should embroil him with those, whose talents he
will revere, and whose virtues he will love. But
he will esteem it but a temporary evil: an evil
which providence in mercy hath appointed for the

---

* Hist. of Corrup. vol. ii. p. 471.

† " To see such men as Bishop Hurd in this class of writers,
(the defenders of the establishment,) when he is qualified to
class with Tillotson, Hoadley, and Clarke, equally excites one's
pity and indignation." Hist. of Corrup. vol. ii. p. 471.

trial of his faith, and the improvement of his habits of disinterested obedience: an evil therefore which the spirit of a Christian will support; suffering neither the misfortune to detect, nor the injury to irritate. Adoring the wisdom of that mysterious dispensation, which, to heighten human virtue, ordains that it should often miss the reward, which disinterested virtue ever covets most; of that dispensation, which makes even error and rash judgment a useful part of the discipline of the present life: he will not disgrace the cause, which he should support, by any uncharitable conclusions concerning the actual motives, or the future doom, of those whose opinions he may think it his duty to oppose. Nor, in the necessary asperity of debate, will he hastily retaliate their unjust aspersions. He will admit much more than a possibility, that Dr Priestley may be in earnest in all his misinterpretations of the Scriptures and the fathers, and in all his misrepresentations of facts. Appearances to the contrary, however strong, he will refer to the fascinating power of prejudice, and to the delusive practice of *looking through* authors,* which the historian of religious opinions ought to have read. Though truth in these controversies can be only

---

* " I have taken a good deal of pains to read, or at least look carefully through, many of the most capital works of the ancient Christian writers." Dr Priestley's Preface, p. xvii.

F

on one side; he will indulge, and he will avow, the charitable opinion, that sincerity may be on both: And he will enjoy the reflection, that by an equal sincerity, through the power of that blood, which was shed equally for all, both parties may at last find equal mercy. In the transport of this holy hope, he will anticipate that glorious consummation, when faith shall be absorbed in knowledge; and the fire of controversy for ever quenched. When the same generous zeal for God and truth, which too often, in this world of folly and confusion, sets those at widest variance, whom the similitude of virtuous feelings, should the most unite, shall be the cement of an indissoluble friendship; when the innumerable multitude of all nations, kindreds, and people, (why should I not add of all sects and parties,) assembled round the throne, shall, like the first Christians, be of one soul, and one mind, giving praise, with one consent, to Him that sitteth on the throne, and to the Lamb that was slain to redeem them by his blood.

APPENDIX.

WHILE these sheets were in preparation for the press, Dr Priestley was challenged by a writer in the Monthly Review, for June, (who the critic may be, I know not—he appears to be learned in ecclesiastical history: and I am well pleased to find, that his views of Dr Priestley's argument in many particulars agree with mine,) Dr Priestley was challenged by this writer, to point out the particular passages in Origen's writings, in which he had conceived an acknowledgment of the identity of the Nazarenes and the Ebionites to be contained. Dr Priestley's Reply hath already made its appearance; in which he is reduced to the necessity of confessing, that he hath no such passage to produce.* Still, however, he maintains, that the identity of these sectaries, although not ac-

---

* See Dr Priestley's Reply to the Monthly Review, p. 5.

knowledged by Origen, is to be inferred from Origen, Epiphanius, and Eusebius.* But this is still affirmed, without reference to the particular passages, either of Origen or of Eusebius, from which the inference is to be drawn: nor is the reader informed, in which of Origen's works that *description* is to be found, of the opinions of the Ebionites, which represents them as the same opinions which others ascribe to the Nazarenes; and makes it appear, that Origen had no idea of any difference between the two sects.† Dr Priestley makes a reference indeed to the 13th tract of Origen's Commentary upon St Matthew's Gospel;‡ but this is for another purpose: for proof, of what needs indeed no proof at all,—that the Ebionites were of two sorts;. the one admitting, the other denying, the miraculous conception, while both rejected the divinity of the Redeemer. What proof of this secondary proposition is to be found in the 18th of the Exegetics upon St Matthew's Gospel, I know not. I suspect an error of the press; and that the reference should have been to the 16th of the Exegetics, in the 3d section, which treats of the cure of the blind near Jericho. In that transaction, as St Mark relates it, Origen imagines that the two divisions of the

---

* See Corrections and Additions, &c. at the end of the Reply.
† Reply, p. 5.
‡ See the References, p. 4, of the Reply.

primitive church, the Gentile and the Jewish converts, are allegorised. Jericho is the world. The
multitudes which follow our Lord from Jericho,
are the converts from Paganism to the true faith;
who forsake the world, to follow Christ. The
blind beggar is a half-converted Jew, addicted to
the Ebionæan heresy; whose eyes are at last
opened to the truth of the gospel. If this be not
the reference which Dr Priestley meant to make,
let me advise him to adopt it in the emended edition of his work, which he seems to promise. Besides that, the very purport of the exposition,
which places the characteristic distinction between
the Gentile and the Jew convert, in a belief or
disbelief of Christ's divinity, may seem to militate
strongly for his favourite opinion, that the whole
Hebrew church was Unitarian : he will find one
sentence in particular in this discourse, or a part
at least of one sentence, which, I am persuaded,
he will think worthy to be written in characters
of gold. Και ιπαν ιδης των απο Ιυδαιων πιστιοιτων ης τον Ιησυν
την περι τυ σωτηρος πιστιν, ότι μιν ικ Μαριας και Ιωσηφ διομινων αυτον
ιιναι, ότι μην ικ Μαριας μονης και τυ θιιυ πνευματΟ, ὁ μην και μιζα
της περι αυτυ θιολογιας, όψιι κ. τ. λ.—— " ——and when
you consider, what belief they of the Jewish race,
who believe in Jesus, entertain of the Redeemer;
some thinking that he took his being from Mary
and Joseph, some indeed from Mary only, and the
Divine Spirit, but still without any belief of his
divinity: you will understand, &c." These ex-

'pressions taken by themselves, may seem to intimate, that the sect of the Ebionites, in its two
great branches, embraced, in the time of Origen,
the whole body of the Hebrew Christians. But
let the learned reader attentively peruse the whole
discourse; let him consider well the subject and
the style; and he will perceive, that as the subject
is not history, neither is the style of the sedate
historic kind. The object of the discourse is to
spiritualize a plain story. An attempt in which
the imagination of the writer is always busier than
the judgment: and the style, even in allusion to
historical facts, is generally rather warm than exact; and is apt to border on the vehement and
the exaggerated. This is in some degree the case
in this discourse of Origen's. His expressions are
therefore to be interpreted by the known tenor of
ecclesiastical history: ecclesiastical history is not
to be accommodated to his expressions. That the
Jewish converts were remarkably prone to the
Ebionæan heresy, from which the Gentile churches
in general were pure, is the most that can be concluded from this passage, strengthened as it might
be with another, somewhat to the same purpose,
in the Commentaries upon St John's Gospel. But
what if it were proved, that the whole sect of the
Nazarenes was absorbed in the Ebionæan heresy
in the days of Origen? What evidence would
that afford of the identity of the Nazarenes and
the Ebionites, in earlier times? And even that

identity, if it were proved, what evidence would it afford, that the church of Jerusalem had been originally Unitarian, under her first bishops of the circumcision?

2. But however indecisive the pretended testimony of Origen may be, Dr Priestley makes himself very sure that Epiphanius is on his side. " Epiphanius expressly says, that Ebion held the same opinion with the Nazarenes.*" The only inference to be made from this assertion, is this : that Dr Priestley hath never troubled himself to read more of Epiphanius's account of the Ebionites, than the first eleven words of the first sentence. Had he read the first sentence to the end, he would have found that Ebion, although he arose from the school of the Nazarenes, and held similar opinions, preached also other doctrines, of which he was the first inventor. Among these novelties, by the consent of all antiquity, though not with Dr Priestley's leave, we place the mere humanity of Christ, with or without the miraculous conception.

3. Still Dr Priestley triumphs in the silence of Hegesippus, and the concessions of Justin Martyr. It were not difficult, to shew the insufficiency of

---

* Reply, p. 4.

his Reply to the learned reviewer of his work, upon both these articles : but I forbear to put my sickle into another's harvest. But that it may not be thought strange, that these cogent arguments should have been suffered to pass unnoticed in my own animadversions, and that the omission may not be imputed to the wrong cause; it seems proper to declare the true reason of it, which was this : I wished to confine my strictures to those arguments, in which the learned author seemed to me the most original. In these two he is the least so. Both are stale. The one is from Zuicker's mint; the other from Episcopius. Both have been canvassed with great accuracy, and both have been effectually overturned, by that excellent divine, whom I have so often found occasion to mention, and who never must be mentioned without praise, the learned and pious Bishop Bull.

LETTERS

FROM THE

ARCHDEACON OF ST ALBAN'S,

IN

REPLY

TO DR PRIESTLEY.

LETTERS,

&c.

LETTER FIRST.

The Archdeacon of St Alban's declines a regular controversy with Dr Priestley.—Produces new instances of Dr Priestley's inaccuracies and misrepresentations.

DEAR SIR,

WHEN at the request of the clergy of my archdeaconry, I published the discourse, in which I had given them my thoughts of your late attack on the doctrine of the Trinity; it was not at all my intention to open a regular controversy with you upon the subject. I cannot think, that you have read my publication with so little discernment, as not to perceive in it, a design of quite another kind; which yet, I fear, I shall find it difficult to avow in explicit terms, without giving an offence, which, were it possible, I would avoid. But since you challenge me to a contest, in which it is my

resolution never to engage; not from any distrust
of my own cause, nor from any dread of the abilities by which I should be opposed; but from a
persuasion that a controversy, in which so little
new is to be said on either side, could not terminate in the satisfaction of either party; it is necessary that both yourself and the public should
be made to understand, upon what grounds I conceive myself at liberty to decline a discussion to
which you seem to think me pledged: and for
this purpose, I must declare in very plain language, what I would rather have left you to collect: that my original attack upon your history
was such, as to lay me under no obligation to
prosecute the argument. My attack was not so
much upon the opinions, which you maintain,
however I may hold them in abhorrence, as upon
the credit of your narrative: and if I have succeeded in overthrowing that, which the judgment
of the learned must decide, I am not at all obliged to go into new arguments upon the main
question. The objections, which were brought
against you in my Charge, all went to the proof of
this single proposition.—That, on which ever side
the truth may lie in the Trinitarian controversy
—I have no doubt on which it lies; but the footing, upon which I put the dispute with you, leaves
me at liberty to suppose the matter doubtful;
with whatever metaphysical difficulties the Catholic doctrine may be encumbered—those difficul-

ties, when the doctrine is rightly apprehended,
are in my judgment not great, but I will allow
you to say they are insuperable: whatever ambiguity may be pretended in the expressions of
holy writ, in which the Divinity of the Son is
generally supposed to be asserted—in the greater
part of the texts I perceive no ambiguity, but you
may assume, if you please, that not one of them
renders a certain meaning; whatever variety and
disagreement is to be found in the orthodoxy of
different ages—for the three first centuries the
opinion of the church upon this point was uniform, but I give you leave to suppose it as unstable as the world of Heraclitus: whatever may
be the intrinsic difficulty of the doctrine of the
Trinity, however deficient the proof of it from
holy writ, and however discordant the opinions of
different ages, still I affirm, and the proof of this
was the whole object of my Charge, that Dr
Priestley, great as his attainments are confessed
to be in the profane sciences, is altogether unqualified to throw any light upon a question of ecclesiastical antiquity.

2. If the instances, which I have alleged, of
misinformation and inaccuracy, are only secondary
oversights, such as affect not the main argument,
and are incident to the best writers in undertakings of such extent as yours; the attempt to de-
preciate a work of merit, by uncandid censure,

must redound to my own disgrace.　But whoever will take the trouble to compare your work and mine, will find, that with all the illiberal zeal which you ascribe to me, I was not disposed to cavil about trifles.　I fear it will be rather found, that I have erred in the opposite extreme; and, lest I should seem too much inclined to censure, have passed over many inaccuracies, which ought to have been pointed out.

3. Such, for instance, is your inversion of the order of succession of the Roman pontiffs: when you mention Victor as the successor of the bishop who came after him.*

4. Such is your assertion,† that in the age of Tertullian it was not pretended " that the subject of the Trinity was above human comprehension;" when but a few pages back ‡ you had produced a passage from Irenæus, in which the generation of the Son, which is a part only of the subject, is mentioned as so wonderful a thing, as to be understood by none " except the Father, who begat, and the Son, who is begotten."

5. Such is your misrepresentation of the opinion of Valesius, concerning the cause of the loss of

---

* Hist. of Corrup. vol. i. p. 19.
† Ibid. p. 61.　　‡ Ibid. p. 37.

Hegesippus's history. Valesius, you say, "was of opinion, that the history of Hegesippus was ne. glected and lost by the ancients, because it was observed to favour the Unitarian doctrine."* Va. lesius hath indeed expressed an opinion, that the work of Hegesippus was neglected by the an. cients, on account of errors which it contained. But what the errors might be, which might occasion this neglect, is a point, upon which Valesius is silent. And what right have you to suppose, that the Unitarian doctrine was the error which Valesius ascribed to Hegesippus, more than to Clemens Alexandrinus, upon whose lost work of the Hypotyposes he passes the same judgment.†

6. Such another inaccuracy, to use no harsher word, is your appeal to the testimony of Epipha-

---

* Hist. of Corrup. vol. i. p. 9.

† Dr Priestley, in the nineteenth of his Second Letters, to extricate himself from this question, endeavours to prove, that the Unitarian doctrines are the only errors that can with probability be ascribed to Hegesippus, in his lost work; and that Clemens Alexandrinus, though he was himself no Unitarian, might, for aught any one now knows to the contrary, have said things in favour of Unitarians, in his lost work of the Hypotyposes. But whatever proof Dr Priestley may be able to make out, that Hegesippus was an Unitarian, and that Clemens Alexandrinus spoke favourably of Unitarians, still I complain, that he alleges the authority of Valesius for more than Valesius himself affirms: and I maintain, that this inaccuracy, (for I have called it in this instance by no worse name,) in the allegation of authorities, is a circumstance that ought to lessen his credit as an historian.

nius, in favour of Noetus; to prove that he was
wronged by his adversaries, when he was accused
of the Patripassian heresy. Noetus's confession,
according to Epiphanius, was this: " that he acknowledged one God, who was begotten, who
suffered and died." But suppressing, or in your
rapid glances having not observed, the latter part
of this acknowledgment, asserting the sufferings
and death of his one God; you produce Epiphanius as an evidence, that—" Noetus was simply
an Unitarian, declaring upon all occasions with
great boldness, that he neither knew nor worshipped any God but one."* (†) Having thus vindicated the injured character of Noetus, you proceed to inform your readers, how it came to pass,
that the Unitarians of that age fell under the imputation of the Patripassian error.

7. Such another inaccuracy we have in your relation of the judgment, which the Roman Diony-

---

* Hist. of Corrup. vol. i. p. 74.
(†) In the nineteenth of his Second Letters, Dr Priestley acknowledges that he ought not to have exempted Epiphanius
from the impropriety of charging Noetus with the Patripassian
heresy. But he says, " this like the former," the misquotation
of Valesius, " is a circumstance of little consequence to the main
argument." Dr Priestley forgets, that the main argument with
him and with me goes to different points. His point is the antiquity and the truth of the Unitarian doctrine. Mine is Dr
Priestley's incompetency in the subject, which he pretends to
treat.

sius passed upon certain injudicious antagonists
of Sabellius; who, to avoid his error, divided the
Holy Trinity into three persons *unrelated* to each
other, and distinct *in all respects.* Εἰς τρεις ὑπορασεις,
ξενας ἀλληλων, παντατασι κεχωρισμενας, διαιρουλας την ἁγιαν τριαδα.
These are the words, in which Athanasius states
the opinion, which Dionysius censures: and the
censure of Dionysius upon this opinion, Athanasius quotes with approbation: as well indeed he
might; for the opinion of three persons in the
Godhead, *unrelated to each other, and distinct in
all respects,* is rank Tritheism; because what are
unrelated and distinct in all respects, are many in
all respects; and being many in all respects, cannot in any respect be one. But in your translation of the passage, by omitting the very significant adjective ξενας and the very emphatical adverb παντατασι, you leave hardly any difference between the opinion which Dionysius censured, and
the Catholic faith, which Athanasius maintained:
and thus you procure yourself a fine opportunity
of introducing an oblique sarcastic stroke at
Athanasius, for concurring in a censure upon his
own opinions. " Some persons in opposing Sabellius having made three hypostases, which we
render persons, separate from each other, Dionysius, bishop of Rome, quoted with approbation by
Athanasius himself, said, that it was making three

Gods."*   Surely truth, candour, and consistency,
are conspicuous in the writings of our modern
Unitarians; and the Archdeacon of St Alban's is
the only writer of the age, who deals in sarcasms!

8. These, and other inaccuracies, which might
have been remarked without any impeachment of
my candour, and with advantage to my argument,
I suffered to pass unnoticed.   I chose to rest the
strength of my attack rather on the importance,
than the variety, of the matter of complaint.   If
the instances of mistake, which I have alleged, be
few in number, yet if they are singly too considerable in size, to be incident to a well-informed
writer; if they betray a want of that general
comprehension of your subject, which might enable you to draw the true conclusions from the
passages you cite; if they prove you incompetent
in the very language of the writers, from which
your proofs should be drawn; unskilled in the
philosophy, whose doctrines you pretend to compare with the opinions of the church; a few clear
instances of errors of this enormous size may release me from the task, which you would impose
upon me, of canvassing every part of your argument, and of replying to every particular quotation.   A writer, of whom it is once proved that

---

* Hist. of Corrup. vol. i. p. 65.

he is ill-informed upon his subject, hath no right
to demand a further hearing. It is a fair presumption against the truth of his conclusion, be it
what it may, that it cannot be right, but by mere
accident. To be right by accident, will rarely
happen to any man in any subject; because in all
subjects truth is single, and error infinite.

9. Not long since, I was consulted about a new
opinion concerning the actual figure of the earth.
I objected, that while the basis of the author's
argument was an assumption, that the figure of
the meridian is an ellipsis, in his inquiry after the
particular species of the ellipsis, he had assigned
properties to the curve of the earth's meridian,
which the known nature of the ellipsis would not
admit. I was challenged to prove a certain relation, which I asserted, between the rays of curvature in different parts of the curve—to prove the
curvature at the second, less than at the principal
vertex—and at last I was challenged, to prove
the property from which the ellipsis takes its
name. Was I to blame, that I broke off the conference—that I refuse to contemplate another
scheme, or to examine another computation?

10. Pardon me, Sir, if plain dealing compels
me to profess, that I think little less respectfully
of this philosopher's learning in the conics, than
of your attainments in ecclesiastical history. I

make this avowal with the less hesitation, because
I find my opinion in some measure justified by
your own confessions.   You confess, that my late
publication first brought you acquainted with the
very name of Daniel Zuicker: that from me you
have received your first information of the concessions of Episcopius; and the first notice of the
coincidence of your own opinions, concerning the
Platonizing fathers of the second century, with
those of Petavius and Huetius: that you had
never in your life *looked through* the writings of
Bishop Bull, till my frequent references to them
excited your curiosity; as they gave you to understand, what before you had never known, that
the author is in high esteem with the clergy
of the establishment. What is this but to confess,
that you are indeed little read in the principal
writers, either on your own side of the question
or the opposite? But as no man, I presume, is
born with an intuitive knowledge of the opinions
or the facts of past ages, the historian of Religious Corruptions, confessing himself unread in
the polemical divines, confesses ignorance of his
subject. The opinion therefore, which I formed,
upon a diligent perusal of your work, is confirmed
by your own acknowledgments; and my victory
is already so complete, that I might well decline
any further contest.

11. My alarms (if I ever felt alarm) for the

Catholic faith, or for the national establishment,
as in danger from your attacks, must now be laid
asleep; and will be no incentive to any very
vigorous exertions against a prostrate enemy.*
But the truth is, that I never was alarmed, and it
is necessary that I should set you right in that
point. When I spake of your extraordinary attempt to unsettle faith, and to break up establishments,† I spake of the end, to which your wishes
seem to be carried, not of an event which I
thought likely to ensue. The utmost danger, that
I feared, was of an inferior kind: a present
danger, not to the church, but to the more unwary of her members, who might be misled by
the justly celebrated name of Dr Priestley: a
future danger to myself, if I forbore to bear my
witness to the truth. For although we have a
promise, that the gates of hell shall not prevail
against the church, yet the vigilance of the priesthood I conceive to be the ordinary means, which
God hath provided for its security. I therefore
thought it my duty to prevent the mischief, which
might arise to the unlearned and unstable, by demolishing the credit of your narrative, and in these
subjects, the authority of your name.

---

* —" you seem to have taken a particular alarm—I hope
you will exert yourself with proportionable vigour——to save a
falling state." Letters to Dr Horsley, p. 2.
† Charge, sec. 3.

12. The letters, which you have lately addressed to me, give me no reason to alter my opinion or retract my accusation. They only fix me in the persuasion, that to prosecute the dispute with you, would be to little purpose. You will therefore excuse me, if I decline a controversy to be carried on, for such I understand to be the conditions of the challenge, " till you shall have nothing left, which you may think of consequence to allege."* When I have shewn the insufficiency of the defence which you have now set up, and have collected the new specimens of your historical abilities, which this new publication supplies in great abundance, whatever more you may find to say upon the subject, in me you will have no antagonist.

I am, &c.

---

* Preface to Letters, p. iii. and xviii.

LETTER SECOND,

A recapitulation of the Archdeacon's Charge.

DEAR SIR,

IF I could adopt your heroic plan, of writing on till I should have nothing left to say, our correspondence would run to an enormous size: for I should have more than a single remark to make upon almost every sentence of every one of your Ten Letters. But as we both write for the edification of the public, and yet few, I fear, will be disposed to give a long or a close attention to our subject; the ease of our readers, if we mean to be read, must be consulted. You, I am told, in defiance of your bookseller's sage counsels, despise such considerations. But they will have their weight with me. I shall be unwilling either to fatigue by the length, or to perplex by the intricacy or obscurity of my reasoning. To avoid the first miscarriage, I shall be content to give you a sufficient, rather than a full reply; and to avoid the second, I shall endeavour so to frame my argument, that my readers may perceive the force of it, without the trouble and interruption of frequent recourse to our former publications. For this purpose, I shall begin with a recapitulation of the substance of my Charge; that before I enter upon particular discussions, the points to be disputed may be brought at once in view.

2. The general argument of my Charge was a critical review of your History, in that part of it which relates to the doctrine of the Trinity in the three first ages. This review consisted of two parts: a summary of the account, which you pretend to give, of the rise and progress of the Trinitarian doctrine; and a view of the evidence, by which your narrative is supported, consisting of nine select specimens of the particular proofs of which the body of that evidence is composed.

3. Of your account of the rise and progress of the Trinitarian doctrine, I said in general, that it is nothing new; that it is in all its essential parts the same, which was propagated by the Unitarian writers of the last century, and, upon its first appearance, refuted by divines of the church of England. Your answer to this part of my Charge, is, as I have already had occasion to observe, complete. You repel the imputation of plagiarism, by the most disgraceful confession of ignorance, to which foiled polemic ever was reduced. To this part of your defence I have nothing to reply.

4. To your evidence, I made the same general objection, that it is destitute of novelty; consist-

ing of proofs long since set up, and long since confuted: that if you have attempted any thing new,
it is only to confirm the gratuitous assumptions of
former Unitarians, by inconclusive arguments, and
false quotations. The nine specimens of your
proofs, by which this heavy accusation was supported, were nothing less than your principal arguments in support of your three fundamental
assertions: that the primitive church was simply
Unitarian; that our Lord's divinity was an innovation of the second century; and that the innovation was made by the Platonizing fathers. If
your principal arguments were fairly adduced, as
instances of weak, insufficient proof; your whole
notion of the gradual progress of opinions, from
the Unitarian doctrine to the Arian, and from the
Arian to the Nicene faith, is overthrown. Of this
you have shewn yourself not insensible, by the
great pains which you have taken, to what purpose will soon appear, to answer my objections.

5. The nine specimens of insufficient proof were
these.

6. Two instances of the circulating syllogism.
The first, when you allege your own sense of
Scripture as the clear sense, in proof of your pretended fact, that the primitive faith was Unitarian; whereas the fact must be first proved, before
your particular interpretation can be admitted.

The second, when in like manner you allege the
pretended silence of St John about the error of
the Unitarians, in proof that the Unitarian doctrine is no error, but the very truth of the gospel.
The assumption that St John is silent upon this
subject in his first epistle, is gratuitous and disputable.   It rests upon a particular interpretation
of St John's expression, that " Christ is come
in the flesh," which will be admitted by none,
who are not previously convinced that St John's
own faith was Unitarian.   If St John's faith was
Unitarian, the phrase that " Christ is come in the
flesh," signifies only, that Christ was a man : and
thus we shall find no censure of the Unitarian
doctrine in St John's first epistle.   But if St John
was no Unitarian, but a believer in the incarnation and divinity of our Lord ; then the phrase of
Christ's coming in the flesh cannot but be understood to allude to both these articles, as parts of
the true faith ; and alluding to both these articles,
as parts of the true faith, it conveys a censure
upon the Unitarian doctrine in every form.   The
assumption therefore of St John's silence, concerning the Unitarian doctrine, presumes another fact,
that St John was himself an Unitarian.   This is
the primary, though tacit assumption, on which
this argument is built.   This argument therefore,
fairly analysed, is found to circulate like the former.   For the conclusion to be established, is the
pretended fact, that the faith of the primitive

church was Unitarian. The mean of proof is the gratuitous assumption, that the faith of St John was Unitarian. But to assume the faith of an inspired apostle, is the same thing as to assume the faith of the primitive church.

7. My third specimen was an instance, in which you cite a testimony, which no where exists. The pretended testimony is of no less a person than Athanasius. The fact, to which Athanasius is made to depose, is the high antiquity of the Unitarian faith. His testimony to this fact, you find in his piece upon the orthodoxy of the Alexandrine Dionysius; in a certain passage in which he affirms, that the Jews were firmly persuaded that the Messiah was to be a mere man; and alleges, as you understand him, this persuasion of the Jews as an apology for a caution, used by the apostles, in divulging the doctrine of our Lord's divinity. The Jews, of whom Athanasius speaks, you preposterously imagine were Christians, the first converts from Judaism. Whereas he speaks of plain downright Jews; and what you take for his apology for caution in the apostles, is in truth a commendation of the sagacity, which they displayed in a judicious arrangement of the matter of their doctrine.

8. My fourth specimen was your capital argument for the antiquity of the Unitarian faith,

founded on the opinions of the Nazarenes. This
argument I maintain to be lame and impotent in
every part. It is built upon two assumptions, of
which the one is a mere gratuitous assertion, of
which no proof is attempted; the other is accompanied with a pretended proof, which arises however from a forged testimony, and an ill-founded
assertion. The gratuitous assumption is, that the
Nazarenes and the Hebrew Christians, were the
same people: whereas the fact is, that the sect
of the Nazarenes arose after the extinction of
the proper church of Jerusalem. The other assumption is, that the faith of these Nazarenes was
Unitarian. This is proved by the testimony of
Epiphanius, and by an assumption, that the Nazarenes and the Ebionites were the same. This
assertion is unfounded, and the testimony of Epiphanius is in fact forged; since it is drawn by
torture from his words. Indeed it is not preten-
ed to be more than this: that Epiphanius makes
no mention " that the Nazarenes believed in the
divinity of Christ:" and this no-mention is only
his confession, that he was totally uninformed,
whether they believed the divinity of Christ, or
not. Were both these assumptions true, the argument would be complete. Both are false: and
were either singly true; yet the other being false,
the conclusion would be either the reverse of
your's, or altogether precarious.

9. My fifth specimen was your misrepresentation of Eusebius; whom you charge with inconsistency, because another writer, who is quoted by him, speaks of Theodotus, who appeared about the year 190, as the first who held that our Saviour was a mere man; when in refuting the pretensions of the Unitarians to antiquity, he goes no further back than to Irenæus and Justin Martyr; although the writings of Eusebius himself afford a refutation of the assertion. But although the assertion, as you choose to understand it, would be liable to refutation from the writings of Eusebius, it admits an interpretation, by which the seeming inconsistency is entirely removed. The pretensions to antiquity, which it was incumbent upon Eusebius, or the author quoted by him, to refute, were not simply pretensions to antiquity, but to a prior antiquity: and in refuting these, the author quoted by Eusebius, goes back to the apostolic age.

10. Your objection to the doctrine of the church, drawn from the resemblance which you find between the Christian and the Platonic doctrine, furnished my sixth specimen of insufficient proof. I acknowledge the resemblance; but I insist, that it leads to an inquiry into the sentiments of heathen antiquity, which, pursued to its just consequences, rather corroborates, than invalidates, the traditional evidence of the Catholic faith.

11. Your proofs of your second assertion, that the doctrine of our Lord's divinity was an innovation of the second age, are all of an oblique and secondary kind: such as, were they liable to no other objection, would lead to no conclusion, without a distinct previous proof, that the faith of the first age was Unitarian. One of these arguments furnished my seventh specimen of insufficient proof. It is an instance, in which you cite the testimony of a Greek writer, to prove the very reverse of what he says. It is alleged by me as an instance of your competency in the Greek language in general, and of your particular acquaintance with the phraseology of the early fathers.

12. My eighth specimen was taken from your attempt to translate a passage of Athenagoras, at which an abler philologer, than you have shewn yourself to be, unread in the Platonists, might be allowed to stumble. I produced it, to convict you of incompetency in the language of the Platonists; and to confirm a suspicion, which the very tenor of your third assertion might create, that you are ignorant of the genuine doctrines of the Platonic school. Thence it is to be inferred, that you are little to be trusted, when you take upon you to compare the opinions of the first Christians, in which you are not learned, with Platonism, in which you are a child.

13. My ninth specimen was another instance of your skill in the Greek language. A passage of Theophilus, in which he expounds the word Trinity, by Father, Son, and Holy Ghost, is produced by you, to prove that the use of the word Trinity, to denote Father, Son, and Holy Ghost, was unknown to Theophilus. Theophilus's words are so very clear, that the sense was hardly to be missed, at first sight, by a school boy in his second year of Greek.

14. These are the nine specimens, by which I support my general Charge of the inaccuracy of your narrative, and in these subjects, the insufficiency of its author. To all of them, except the seventh and the ninth, you have attempted to reply. With what success is to be considered.

I am, &c.

LETTER THIRD..

*In Reply to Dr Priestley's introductory, and to part of his First
Letter.—His defence of his argument from the clear sense of
Scripture confuted.—Of the argument against our Lord's pre-
existence to be drawn from the materiality of man.—Of the
Greek pronoun ἑτος.*

DEAR SIR,

To remove the imputation of having argued in
a circle, when alleging your own sense of Scripture as the clear sense, you infer, that the faith of
the first ages was exactly conformable to your
own opinions; you tell me, that the clear sense of
Scripture and the historical evidence, are collateral
proofs* of the early prevalence of the Unitarian
faith.   I shall admit this, and shall retract all that
I have written, when once you shall have proved
to the satisfaction of the Christian world, that the
Unitarian doctrine is delivered in the holy Scriptures, taken in their plain and obvious meaning.
But while your sense of Scripture is disallowed by
the majority of Christians, I must still contend,
that you have no right to call it the clear sense;
and that any argument built on a supposition, that

---

* Letters to Dr Horsley, p. 4—6.

the Scriptures speak a sense not generally perceived in them, rests at best upon a gratuitous
assumption. I confess, that an argument drawn
from a gratuitous assumption is not necessarily an
argument running in a circle, unless the only
means of reducing the assumption to a certainty,
be a previous proof of the conclusion to be drawn.
But this I affirm to be the case in the instance
under consideration. When we speak of the clear
sense of any piece of writing, this very expression
admits a twofold interpretation. The clear sense,
may be either that which is clearly conveyed in the
words; or a sense, which though it be not clearly conveyed in the words, may be clearly proved,
from the context, or from other considerations, to
be the sense which was really present to the mind
of the writer. If you allege the clear sense of the
Scriptures, in the first sense of the expression, in
proof that the primitive faith was Unitarian; I
ask, whether it be not the sole end and purpose
of the inquiry into the primitive faith, to settle
the differences of Christians upon points in which
the Scriptures if there be any ground in them for
the disputes which have arisen, are not clear?
You now assume a sense, which you call their
clear sense, upon those very points, in order to
ascertain the primitive faith. This is to reason
in a circle.

2. But in truth the Unitarian doctrine will

never be proved to be the clear sense of Scripture
in the first sense of clearness. On the contrary,
if ever it should be clearly proved to have been
the sense of the sacred writers; the just conclusion will be, that of all writers, these have been
the most unnecessarily and the most wilfully obscure. The Unitarians themselves, pretend not
that their doctrine is to be found in the plain literal sense of holy writ; on the contrary, they
take the greatest pains to explain away the literal
meaning. They pretend that the sacred writers
delight in certain metaphors and images, which,
however unnatural and obscure they may seem
at this day, are supposed to have been of the
genius of the eastern languages, and of consequence familiar to the first Christians; who, in
the greater part, were of Jewish extraction.
By the help of these supposed metaphors, the
Unitarian expositors contrive to purge the Scripture of every thing which they disapprove, and
make it the oracle, not of God's wisdom, but of
their own fancies. When you therefore, as a Unitarian, say, that your doctrine is the clear sense
of Scripture, which, according to the scheme of
interpretation which you follow, hath no clear
sense at all; you can only mean, that this doctrine may be clearly proved to be the sense intended by the inspired writers. Perhaps in my
Charge I was too negligent in the interpretation
of your expressions, when I pretended to expose

the infirmity of your argument. Be it so. This then is your assertion. The Unitarian doctrine is clearly the true sense of Scripture. But where is the proof? You can bring no proof that will be generally convincing, unless you can find it in the faith of the apostolic ages. The faith of the first Christians, once clearly ascertained, must be allowed indeed to be an unerring exposition of the written word. To prove therefore, that the Unitarian doctrine is clearly the true sense of Scripture, which is your assumption, you must first prove that the primitive faith was Unitarian, which should be your conclusion. Still this argument circulates, and was not improperly alleged by me as my first specimen of insufficient proof.

3. But it is of no great importance to dispute, where the particular infirmity of this argument may lie; when you confess that it is of such a sort, " that you could not suppose it would have any weight with Trinitarians."* While you condescend to employ your rare abilities in framing arguments, which will persuade those only who are previously persuaded, you will do little harm. Why should I disturb you in this innocent amusement?

---

* Letters to Dr Horsley, p. 5.

4. To compensate for the confessed inefficacy of this argument, you tell me of another, which you might have urged, to disprove not only the divinity, but the preexistence of our Lord; such an argument it seems might have been drawn " from the doctrine of the materiality of man, which has been sufficiently proved in your disqui- sitions on matter and spirit."* In which, by an analogical proof, you have refuted the vulgar error of the immateriality of the human soul, and have in consequence overthrown the whole system of preexistence. I believe, Sir, the opponents of the Unitarian scheme will not be displeased to understand, that it is at last to stand or fall with Dr Priestley's System of Materialism, and Dr Hartley's Theory of the Mind.

5. As a striking instance of the conformity be- tween the Unitarian doctrine and the clear sense of Scripture, I produced the initial sentences of St John's gospel; in which, you know, you find a clear refutation of the personality of the Logos. In rendering these sentences in English, I took occasion to remark, that the Greek pronoun ἐτος naturally renders a person. You tell me, " it may refer to any thing that is of the same gender in the Greek language, whether it be a person or

---

* Letters to Dr Horsley, p. 5.

not."*   I never meant to insinuate the contrary. Give me leave to refer you to a letter which was published in the Gentleman's Magazine, for November last, under the signature of PERHAPS. You will find it in my Appendix,† and I now declare myself the writer of it.

I am, &c.

* Letters to Dr Horsley, p. 7.
† Appendix, No. 1, and 2.

LETTER FOURTH.

In Reply to Dr Priestley's First Letter.—His defence of his argument from St John's first epistle confuted.—The phrase " come in the flesh," more than equivalent to the word " to come."—St John's assertion that " Christ came in the flesh," not parallel with St Paul's, that " he partook of flesh and blood."

DEAR SIR,

YOUR argument for the antiquity of the Unitarian doctrine from St John's first epistle, the second among my specimens of insufficient proofs, rests on a supposition, that in that epistle the Unitarian doctrine is not censured. I have shewn,* that this supposition will stand or fall, according as one or another interpretation of the phrase of " coming in the flesh," shall be admitted. That single expression, as it is generally understood, reprobates the Unitarian doctrine, and overthrows your supposition. You must therefore establish your own sense of the phrase, before you can be permitted to assume, that St John is silent about the Unitarian doctrine. Now to make good this argument, you tell me that " you think," and that " it is your opinion," that the phrase of " coming

---

* Charge, and Letter ii.

in the flesh," is merely an assertion of our Lord's humanity.* Sir, I understood from the first, that this is *your opinion,* and I doubt not in the least your firmness in it. But I contend, that no such authority belongs to your opinion, that the bare notification of it should command the assent of the whole Christian world, in preference to other opinions, which have more generally prevailed. You must justify that opinion, if you would give any colour of plausibility to your argument. But the opinion cannot be justified, unless it might be previously assumed, that St John himself was an Unitarian. You will hardly say, that any believer in our Lord's divinity and incarnation, could employ the phrase of Christ's " coming in the flesh," without an allusion, in his own mind, to both those articles, as branches of the true faith. But such an allusion implies a censure of the Unitarians. ·Till you shall have proved, therefore, that St John was an· Unitarian, the phrase of " Christ's coming in the flesh," may be thought to contain a censure of the Unitarian tenets; and your opinion, that no censure of them is contained in St John's first epistle, will be disputable.

2. You say, that this phrase of coming in the flesh, " refers naturally to the doctrine of the

---

* Letters to Dr Horsley, p, 8, 10.

Gnostics."* I say the very same thing. But I say, that in the sense in which the church hath ever understood it, this phrase refers to two divisions of the Gnostics: the Docetæ, and the Cerinthians; affirming a doctrine, which is the mean between their opposite errors. The Docetæ affirmed, that Jesus was not a man in reality, but in appearance only; the Cerinthians, that he was a mere man, under the tutelage of the Christ, a superangelic being, which was not so united to the man as to make one person. St John says, " Jesus Christ is come in the flesh;" that is, as the words have been generally understood, Jesus was a man, not in appearance only, as the Docetæ taught, but in reality; not a mere man, as the Cerinthians taught, under the care of a superangelic guardian, but Christ himself come in the flesh; the Word of God incarnate. St John says, that whoever denies this complex proposition, is of antichrist. It surprises me, that you should find an improbability, upon the first face of the thing, in supposing, that the same expression should be equally levelled† at two heresies, which you confess to be opposite. For it is not always the case, that expressions which predicate a truth lying in the middle between two opposite falsehoods, equally impugn both the false extremes?

If I say, that when Fahrenheit's thermometer in the open air stands at 60° in the shade, the weather is mild; do I not equally deny that it is insufferably hot, or insufferably cold? " Gnosticism, you say, is certainly condemned by the apostle, but not the doctrine of the Ebionites, though it is allowed to have existed in his time."[*] The doctrine of the original Ebionites, and that of the Cerinthian Gnostics, upon the point of Christ's divinity, was the same. If the apostle condemns the one, he condemns the other, whether he lived or lived not to see the rise of the Ebionæan sect.[†] I shall hereafter have occasion to shew, that the Ebionæan sect was of a later date than you imagine.

3. It is perhaps from something of a secret misgiving, that your interpretation of the phrase of

---

[*] Letters to Dr Horsley, p. 10.

[†] " You insist upon it," says Dr Priestley, in the fifth of his Second Letters, " that John does censure the Unitarian doctrine: which is curious enough; when, *according to your account*, there were no Ebionites or Nazarenes; that is, none who denied the preexistence of Christ, till long after the time of John." But this is not *according to my account*. My account is, that Cerinthus, who was unquestionably contemporary with St John, denied our Lord's preexistence, and was in this point the precursor of the Ebionites. And what if I had said, that St John had censured a doctrine not taught till after his death? Do not the fathers perpetually refer to proleptic censures of late heresies in the sacred writings? Is no proleptic reprobation of the late errors of the Roman church to be found in St Paul's epistles?

" coming in the flesh," will not be allowed to be its natural and obvious meaning; that you are so desirous to retreat into the strong-hold of Jewish idioms. You think the phrase in question " is similar to other Jewish phrases,"* which you think will be allowed to be merely expressive of humanity. I fear, Sir, it hath been the custom of late, to lay too much stress upon Jewish idioms, in the exposition of the didactic parts of the New Testament. The gospel is a general revelation.† If it is delivered in a style, which is not perspicuous to the illiterate of any nation except the Jewish; it is as much locked up from general apprehension, as if the sacred books had been written in the vernacular gibberish of the Jews of that age. The Holy Spirit, which directed the apostles and the evangelists to the use of the tongue, which in their day was the most generally understood—the Greek, would for the same reason, it may be presumed, suggest to them a style which might be generally perspicuous. It is therefore a principle with me, that the true sense of any phrase in the New Testament is, for the most part, what may be called a standing sense: that which will be the

---

* Letters to Dr Horsley, p. 8.
† " The religion of Christ was an universal religion, and the doctrines of the gospel were calculated for the western as well as the eastern hemisphere." See Mr Shepherd's Preface to his *Free Examination of the Socinian Exposition of the Prefatory Verses of St John's Gospel.*

first to occur to common people of every country, and in every age : and I am apt to think, that the difference between this standing sense and the Jewish sense will, in all cases, be far less than is imagined, or none at all; because, though diffe-rent languages differ widely in their refined and elevated idioms, common speech is in all langua-ges pretty much the same.

4. But what are those Jewish phrases, with which you would compare the Jewish phrase of " coming in the flesh ?"   They are the word " to come," and the phrase " partaker of flesh and blood."

5. The word " to come," is used by metaphor I believe in all languages, to signify either a man's birth, or first entrance into public life. *He came into the world; he came into life; he came into business.*   I have no where affirmed, that such phrases denote any thing more than human, in any person to whom they may be applied.   But is the phrase " to come in the flesh," no more than equi-valent to the word " to come ?" Are the words " in the flesh," mere expletives ?—If they are not expletives, what is their import, but to limit the sense of the word *to come* to some particular man-ner of coming ?—This limitation either presumes a possibility of other ways of coming; or it is nu-gatory.   But was it possible for a mere man to

come otherwise than in the flesh?—Nothing can be more decisive for my purpose, than this comparison which you have suggested, between the word "to come," which is general, and the phrase "to come in the flesh," which is specific.—My thanks are due to you for this illustration of my argument; which may be rendered still more evident by applying the two phrases successively to a familiar instance. If some future historian of these planet-stricken times, should say, "In the latter end of the eighteenth century, came Dr Priestley preaching the Unitarian doctrine," no one will suspect any thing more, than that a man of this name preached this doctrine.—But if the historian should say, "Dr Priestley came *in the flesh* preaching this doctrine;" if the writer, who may use this expression, shall have any credit in his day, a general curiosity will be excited to know, whether Dr Priestley had it in his power to come in any way without his flesh, "unmanacled with membrane, joint, or limb:" and when once it shall be found, that he had not; the style of the writer will be condemned, and his credit perhaps lessened.—I leave you to make the application.

6. But you think, that St John's phrase that "Christ came in the flesh," may be expounded by St Paul's phrase, that "he was partaker of flesh and blood." The passage to which you refer is this.—"Forasmuch then as the children are par-

takers of flesh and blood, he also himself likewise took part of the same."* As you have only hinted, that some argument might be drawn from this text, to confirm your sense of St John's phrase; I am left to divine what your argument might be. Perhaps you would reason thus.—In this passage it is said of men, that they are partakers of flesh and blood: and this expression is evidently descriptive of the condition of humanity. It appears therefore, that to be " a partaker of flesh and blood," is a Jewish phrase, which signifies " to be a man." But in this same passage it is said of Christ, that " he likewise took part of flesh and blood." It is said of Christ therefore that he was a man like other men: consequently nothing more can be meant by his " coming in the flesh."—If this be your intended argument, I reply, that Christ was indeed a man like other men: and this perhaps is all that is implied in St Paul's assertion, that he was " partaker of flesh and blood." But it follows not, that this is all which is implied in St John's expression, that " Jesus Christ came in the flesh;" which asserts indeed his humanity; but with an evident allusion to a prior condition: and the proper conclusion from the comparison of St John's expression with St Paul's, is this: that the two are not, as you suppose, equivalent.

---

* Heb. ii. 14.

7. But I suspect, that you connect St Paul's expression with your own doctrine of materialism; and that you would argue thus.—Since it is said of men, who are flesh and blood, and nothing else, that they partake of flesh and blood; therefore " to *partake* of flesh and blood," in the Jewish language, and " to *be* flesh and blood," in other languages, are equivalent phrases. Therefore Christ, of whom it is also said, that he partook of flesh and blood, was mere flesh and blood; a man like other men, in whom the mental faculties were the result of organization. Thus, you will say, the notion of Christ's preexistence, much more of his divinity, is overturned by the apostle's assertion; and, whatever may have been imagined, no allusion to his preexistence or his divinity, was intended in any expressions of the sacred writers. The assertion therefore of Christ's real manhood, is all that can be obtained in St John's expressions, that " Christ is come in the flesh." But in this argument the conclusion results not from any evident parallelism of the different phrases used by St Paul and by St John; but it is a consequence from a particular interpretation of St Paul's phrase: which interpretation of St Paul rests not upon any thing in his expressions, but upon something quite out of Scripture: upon your notion of the mere materiality of man. To have shewn the true foundation of this argument is to have confuted it.

8. I must remark, that in whatever form this argument may be drawn, it will rest solely on the translation of the sacred text. For in the original, man's connexion with flesh and blood, and Christ's connexion, are expressed by different words: κικοινωνηκε and μετεσχε. A difference, which, however slight it may appear to you, was thought of sufficient importance to be preserved in the Vulgate ;. *communicaverant—participavit.**

9. But not to lay a stress upon any critical refinements upon single expressions, let me ask your opinion, Sir, upon the general sense of the passage, in which this phrase, " to partake of flesh and blood," occurs. I would appeal to yourself, whether the conclusion, which you would build upon that particular expression, is not overthrown by the general sense of the passage. The purport of the passage is to assign a reason why the Redeemer should partake of flesh and blood; that is, why he should be a man. But a reason why a man should be a man, one would not expect to find in a sober man's discourse. For why any thing should be what it is, rather than what it is not, is a question which few, I think, would ask, and none would attempt to answer. The attempt to assign a reason, why the Redeemer should be

---

* That κοινωνειν is more than μετεχειν. See Iamblich. de Myst. sect. 2. cap. v.

a man, implies both that he might have been, without partaking of the human nature, and by consequence, that in his own proper nature he was originally something different from man; and that there might have been an expectation, that he would make his appearance in some form above the human. It particularly implies, that an expectation of his appearance in some higher form, might be expected to prevail among the persons, to whom this reason is assigned; so that the manifest manhood of Christ would be likely to be an objection with them, to his claim to the character of the Messiah. This, Sir, seems to deserve your particular attention. For the persons, to whom the apostle renders these reasons for the manhood of the Redeemer, were the Hebrews; the first Jewish Christians; of whom you say, that before their conversion at least, " they had no idea that their Messiah was to come down from heaven,"* having never been taught by their prophets to expect " any other than a man like themselves, in that illustrious character."†

10. Upon the whole, since the phrase of " coming in the flesh," must be more than equivalent to the word " to come;" since there is no evidence of its supposed parallelism with St Paul's phrase

---

* Letters to Dr Horsley, p. 49.
† Hist. of Corrup. vol. i. p. 2.

of " partaking of flesh and blood;" since in the
discourse of any but an Unitarian, it must involve
an allusion to the incarnation and divinity of our
Lord; your defence of your argument from St
John's first epistle is insufficient: the argument is
still to be considered as running in a circle, and
it was properly adduced as the second among
my specimens of insufficient proof.

I am, &c.

N. B. The argument, which Dr Priestley has
advanced in the fifth of his Second Letters, in favour of his own interpretation of the phrase " coming in the flesh," from a passage in St Polycarp's
epistle, is considered and refuted in the first of
the Supplemental Disquisitions.

LETTER FIFTH.

The Archdeacon's interpretation of Clemens Romanus defended.
—The shorter epistles of Ignatius genuine.

DEAR SIR,

HAVING, to your own entire satisfaction, made good your argument from St John's first epistle, against my exceptions; you proceed to reply to the testimonies which I produced from Clemens Romanus, for the preexistence and divinity of our Lord.

2. When Clemens says, " our Lord Jesus Christ came not in the pomp of pride and arrogance, although he had it in his power," you say, that the coming alluded to was " no coming from heaven to earth; and that the pomp of pride and arrogance, in which our Lord came not, stands for an " ostentatious display" of the miraculous powers which our Lord never made.* To this it is sufficient to reply, that my interpretation rests upon the literal sense of the holy father's words, which you suppose to be figurative; that you have nothing to object to the literal interpreta-

---

* Letters to Dr Horsley, p. 13.

tion, but that it suits not with your own opinions; whereas I have something of great importance to say in its defence; that it is established by the context. " He came not (says Clemens) in the pomp of pride and arrogance, although he had it in his power, but in humility, as the Holy Spirit spake concerning him." The pomp therefore of pride and arrogance, in which our Lord came not, is that pomp, which is the proper opposite of the humility, in which the Holy Spirit had foretold that he should come. For he came not in that, but in this he came. Now to determine what this humility is, Clemens immediately goes on to cite the prophecies, which describe the Messiah's low condition. The humility, therefore, of an ordinary condition, is that in which it is said the Messiah came. The pomp, therefore, of a high condition, is the pomp, in which it is said he came not, although he had it in his power so to come. The expressions therefore clearly imply, that our Lord, ere he came, had the power to choose, in what condition he would be born.

3. In citing this passage of Clemens Romanus, I dealt very liberally with you; as I trust indeed that I have done in every part of the argument. I cited the passage, as it stands in our modern copies. More ancient copies, those which Jerome used, instead of *καιπερ δυναμενος,* " although he had it in his power," had *καιπερ παντα δυναμενος,* although he

had *all things* in his power." This appears from
Jerome's translation of the passage, which is in
these words, " Sceptrum Dei, Dominus Jesus
Christus non venit in jactantia superbiæ, cum
possit omnia."* Now with this emendation of
the last clause, which it seems was an assertion
of our Lord's omnipotence, you are welcome to
make what you can of the preceding clause, by
figurative interpretations.†

4. No figurative interpretations will elude the
force of my citations from Ignatius. But it is the

---

* Hieronym. in Esaiam, cap. lii.
† Dr Priestley, to whom it is a matter of equal ease to bring
the holy Scriptures, or the fathers, upon all occasions to speak
his own sentiments, finds no assertion of our Lord's omnipotence in this clause of Clemens thus rendered by Jerome: nothing more than an allusion " to the great power of which he
became possessed, after the descent of the Spirit of God upon
him at his baptism." (See the second of Dr Priestley's Second
Letters to me). That is, to affirm that a person hath *all* things
in his power, is, in Dr Priestley's apprehension of the terms, to
affirm that at a certain time he had *some* things in his power.
Had any such allusion been intended to the miraculous powers,
the verb *possit* in Jerome's Latin, should have been in one or
the other of the preterite tenses. By the use of the present
tense, Jerome describes a plenitude of power now enjoyed.
This plenitude of power now enjoyed, is alleged as what might
have been exercised by our Lord in time past, with respect to
the manner of his own coming. It is a plenitude of power therefore ever present to our Lord, now and in time past; and being
allowed to be now present, is supposed of necessary consequence
to be capable of effects in time past. But this describes nothing
less than the attribute of omnipotence. But language is no key
to " unlock the mind of a Socinian."

particular happiness of the Unitarian writers, that they are never found at a loss for an expedient. All that I say of the repeated assertion of our Lord's divinity in the epistles of Ignatius, you allow to be true, " according to our present copies of his epistles. But the genuineness of them, (you say,) is not only very much doubted, but generally given up by the learned." And lest this assertion should want that appearance of weight, which an air of confidence gives, you even tax my ingenuity " for concealing a circumstance, which, (you say,) I must have known;" and you challenge me to prove these epistles, " as we now have them, to be the genuine epistles of Ignatius."*

5. Sir, if the genuineness of these epistles be generally given up by the learned, my ignorance, not my ingenuity, is to be blamed, that I cited them as genuine. I indeed knew nothing of this general giving up. But since the testimony of Ignatius is allowed to be express, if the epistles be genuine from which it is produced; permit me to tell you, in few words, what I know of these epistles.

6. I know that ancient writers mention seven epistles of Ignatius, written upon his journey from

---

* Letters to Dr Horsley, p. 13.

Antioch, where he was bishop, through Asia Minor; for that way his journey lay, when he was
carried to Rome, by Trajan's order, to be exposed to wild beasts. Of these epistles six are
said to have been addressed to the churches of six
different cities: Ephesus, Magnesia upon Mæan-
der, Tralles, Rome, Philadelphia, Smyrna; and
the seventh was addressed to Polycarp. I know,
that besides some other epistles, confessedly spurious, two editions, a longer and a shorter, are at
this day current, of seven epistles under the name
of Ignatius, inscribed to those to whom the real
epistles of the blessed martyr, according to the
ecclesiastical historians, were addressed. The
longer epistles first appeared in print, in an old
Latin version, published by Father Stapulensis, in
1498; a corresponding Greek text was published
by Valentine Pacæus, from a manuscript in the
Augustan library, in the year 1557. The shorter
edition likewise made its first appearance in print,
in an old Latin version, published by Usher, from
two manuscripts, in the year 1644. The Greek
was published by Isaac Vossius, in 1646, from a
manuscript in the Medicæan library at Florence.
The Medicæan manuscript being imperfect in the
end, wanted the epistle to the Romans. But a
Greek text of this epistle, perfectly corresponding
with Usher's Latin version, was published at
Paris, from a manuscript of Colbert's, by Mr
Ruinard, in the year 1689.

7. It has been made a question, whether the shorter epistles are from abridged, or the longer from interpolated copies. The phraseology of the longer, seems in some parts accommodated to the Arian notions: that of the shorter, is every where agreeable to the Catholic faith. The shorter edition hath the suffrage of the fathers of the five first centuries; their quotations, which are numerous, every where agreeing with this text. William Whiston, a man whose memory is 'more to be esteemed for his integrity, and the extent and variety of his reading, than for the soundness of his judgment, from pure attachment to the Arian cause, maintained the authority of the longer copies; but his opinion hath found but few abettors, and those of inconsiderable name, even in his own party. The Presbyterian divines, desirous to get rid of so great an authority as that of Ignatius in favour of Episcopacy, the rights of which are set very high in these epistles, were unwilling to allow their authenticity in either form. But with a majority of the learned, these seven epistles are received as authentic; and the shorter edition is supposed to exhibit the genuine text. This at least was the opinion of Isaac Vossius, Usher, Hammond, 'Petavius, Grotius, Pearson, Bull, Cave, Wake, Cotelerius, Grabe, Dupin, Tillemont, Le Clerc. On the other side stand no names to be compared with these, except the three of Salmasius, Blondel, and Dallæus. Perhaps

you will add that of Bochart. But the great
Bochart's doubts went to one only of the seven,[*]
the epistle to the Romans; and they are founded
on a chronology of the word *Leopardus*, which
Pearson hath proved to be erroneous.[†]

8. Mosheim holds a middle opinion. The question of preference between the two editons, he
thinks undecided. Whichever edition be preferred, he thinks the suspicion of interpolation and
corruption cannot be entirely removed. That
these epistles are of great antiquity, he thinks
certain. That they are not altogether forgeries,
so credible, that nothing can be more. But how
far they are sincere, he takes to be a knot which
cannot be untied.[‡] At the same time he allows,
what with me entirely overturns his singular opinion, that the authenticity of them would never
have been called in question, had they not contained, what the advocates of Episcopacy knew
how to turn to the advantage of their cause;
which when the Presbyterians and others, who
were for abolishing the privileges of the clergy,
understood, they attacked them with a warmth,
by which they more harmed their own reputation
than the authenticity of those writings.[§] It is

---

[*] Hierozoic. P. I. lib. iii. cap. 8.
[†] Vindiciæ Ignatianæ, P. II. p. 91—94.
[‡] De Rebus Christianorum ante Constantinum, p. 161.
[§] Ibid. p. 165.

true, he taxes the writers on the other side, but
not so generally, with no less intemperance. But,
in my judgment, the authenticity of ancient writings must be set very high, which could never
have been brought in question, but through prejudice.

9. With this preponderance therefore, of authorities on the side of the epistles, and with this confession of Mosheim against his own opinion, I
shall take the liberty to appeal to them, as they
stand in the shorter edition, as the genuine writings
of the blessed martyr: not free indeed from those
blemishes, which arise from the haste, the carelessness, and the ignorance of transcribers; but upon
the whole, not less sincere, than most other pieces
of the same antiquity. I shall appeal to them with
the less scruple, forasmuch as the same sincerity,
which I ascribe to them, and which is quite sufficient for my purpose, is allowed by the learned
and the candid Lardner; whose judgment must
have been biassed by his opinions in prejudice of
these writings, if any thing could have biassed
his judgment in prejudice of the evidence of truth.
After suggesting in no very confident language,
that " even the smaller epistles may have been
tampered with by the Arians, or the orthodox, or
both;" he adds, " I do not affirm, that there are
in them any considerable corruptions or altera-

tions."* If no considerable corruptions or alterations, certainly none respecting a point of such
importance, as the original nature of Christ. I
will therefore still appeal to these epistles, as
sufficiently sincere to be decisive upon the point in
dispute. Nor shall I think myself obliged to go
into the proof of their authenticity, till you have
given a satisfactory reply to every part of Bishop
Pearson's elaborate defence: a work, which I
suspect you have not yet *looked through.*

I am, &c.

P. S. To the authorities of the epistles of Ignatius, according to the shorter copies, I must add
Fabricius.

---

* These words of Dr Lardner, are cited by Dr Priestley
himself, in his Reply to the Animadversions, in the monthly
Review of June, 1783, p. 36. They make a part of his proof,
that these epistles are so corrupted, as not to be quoted with
safety. See Reply to Animadversions, p. 35.

LETTER SIXTH.

DEAR SIR,

THE citadel of your strength is the argument from the Nazarenes; to which however I have given a place among my specimens of insufficient proof. You find the attack upon this fortress warm on every side; and your resistance is proportionably vigorous. So impatient are you for its defence, that you take it out of its turn, passing by my third specimen—the argument from Athanasius; which you very properly consider as an outwork, which will be indeed of little consequence, if the citadel should surrender—which however, must be the case; neither force nor stratagem can defend it.

2. Two points, you know, must be made out to save this argument: the one, that the faith

of the Nazarenes was Unitarian; the other, that
these Unitarian Nazarenes were the Hebrew
Christians, or the members of the primitive church
of Jerusalem. To prove the first point, you abide
by your original assertion, that the Nazarenes and
the Ebionites, were one and the same people, under
different names. This assertion you attempt to
defend against my objections. We shall see with
what success.

3. You allow " it has been imagined by some,
that there was a difference between the doctrine of the Ebionites and the Nazarenes, concerning the person of Christ."* Something of a
difference, some half-witted critics have, it seems,
imagined. But you take care to insinuate in the
next sentence, that none before me ever dreamed
of so wide a difference, as I would put between
them. It had only been imagined " that the
Ebionites disbelieved, while the Nazarenes maintained, the miraculous conception;"† both concurring in the disbelief of our Lord's divinity.
" For as to any Nazarenes, who believed that
Christ was any thing more than man, you find no
trace of them in history."‡ And you think it extraordinary, " that it should now be made a point
to find some difference between the Nazarenes

---

* Letters to Dr Horsley, p. 14.   † Ibid.   ‡ Ibid.

and the Ebionites, inasmuch as you believe, no
critic of any name in the last age pretended to
find any."* Indeed, you may well be astonished.
For, " the learned Jeremiah Jones"† wrote a
chapter to prove them the same people.

4. Indeed, Sir, I must take shame to myself,
and confess, that this learned Jeremiah Jones is
not of my acquaintance. I find upon inquiry,
that he is very much unknown among my brethren
of the establishment. I am informed, however,
that he was not undeserving of the epithet which
you have coupled with his name. He was, it
seems, the tutor of the venerable Lardner, and
was thought in natural ability to excel his pupil.
Nevertheless, Sir, I conceive I may be pardoned,
if I presume to dissent from the opinion of Jeremiah Jones, notwithstanding the importance that
may have accrued to it from the approbation of
Dr Priestley. That, Sir, which you are pleased
to call an imagination of some, the notion of a
difference between the Nazarenes and the Ebionites, was the decided opinion of a writer better
known than Jeremiah Jones, the illustrious Mosheim. " This little body of Christians," says that
learned historian, " which coupled Moses with
Christ, split again into two sects, distinguished

---

* Letters to Dr Horsley, p. 23.   † Ibid.

from each other by their doctrines concerning Christ, and the permanent obligation of the law, and perhaps by other circumstances."* As a certain proof that they were two distinct sects, he observes that each had its own gospel. He says, that " the Nazarenes had a better and truer notion of Christ than the Ebionites."†

6. It may be Mosheim was the inventor of this distinction, since you have not found it in any critic of any name of the last age. Perhaps, Sir, you and I, when we speak of critics of any name, may not always agree in the persons, to whom we would apply that description. May I then take leave to ask, what you think of Hugo Grotius? Was He a critic of any name? Vossius, Spencer, Huetius, were These critics of any name? If they were, Sir, you must come again to your confessions. For Hugo Grotius, Vossius, Spencer, and Huetius ‡ agree that the Nazarenes and Ebionites, though sometimes confounded, were distinct

---

* Pusillum vero hoc Christianorum agmen, quod Mosen Christo sociabat, in duas iterum dissiliebat sectas; dogmatibus de Christo, legisque necessitate, forte aliis etiam rebus sejunctas. *Mosheim de Rebus Christianorum ante Constantinum.* Sæc. 2. sec. xxxix.

† Nazarei nimirum et de Christo multo rectius et verius sentiebant quam Ebionei. Ibid. n. * * *.

‡ Grotius in Matth. c. i. Vossius de genere Jesu Christi, cap. ii. sec. 1. Spencer in Origen contra Celsum, ad p. 56. Huetius in Origenis commentaria, p. 74.

sects; and they maintain the opinion, which I now maintain, of the high orthodoxy of the proper Nazarenes, in the article of our Lord's divinity.

6. But it may be that the Nazarenes were Unitarian, though they were not Ebionites. For the doctrine concerning our Lord's divinity is not the only point, in which the pretended difference is placed: and " as to any Nazarenes, who believed that Christ was any thing more than man, you find no trace of them in history."* You have then been less successful than Hugo Grotius, Vossius, Spencer, and Huetius: not to mention others of inferior note.

7. You see, Sir, (our readers at least will see,) that you had little ground to represent the opinion, which I maintain, of a difference between the Nazarenes and Ebionites, as singular or novel. Your attempt to set it forth in that light, I cannot but consider as a stratagem, which you are willing to employ for the preservation of your battered citadel—the argument from the Nazarenes. In this stratagem, if I mistake not, you are completely foiled. In your sallies against the batteries which I have raised, I trust you will be little more successful. But as too much of stratagem is apt

---

* Letters to Dr Horsley, p. 14.

to mix itself with all your operations, it will be necessary that I watch very narrowly the manner of your approaches.

8. You reply to my objections against the testimony, which Epiphanius is supposed to bear to the identity of the two sects, is opened with a complaint, that I have said nothing " to the arguments from Origen and Eusebius."* Sir, either here is more stratagem, or you have dealt by me, as you profess to do by the ancients. You have only looked through my Charge. Had you read it through, you could hardly have missed something that I say to the arguments from Origen and Eusebius. I flatly deny any direct testimony of Origen, in favour of the identity which you would prove; and I have shewn that the passages, from which you would draw the inference, are little to your purpose."† The argument from Eusebius, you will be pleased to recollect, made no part of your original proof. It first appeared among certain corrections and additions, which are annexed to your " Reply to the Animadversions" of a learned writer in the Monthly Review. It was impossible therefore, that I should take notice of it in my Charge, which had been sent to the

---

* Letters to Dr Horsley, p. 14.
† Charge I. sec. 15, and Appendix, sec. 2.

press, and was in great part printed, before I had any knowledge of the Reply, or indeed of the Animadversions which occasioned it.   But in the Appendix to my Charge, which was written after I had read your Reply, and in consequence of it, I complained, that you had made no reference to the particular passages of Eusebius, upon which you would found your argument.*

9. However, that I said something very material to the argument from Epiphanius, you deny not.   I said indeed that no man could allege, as you do, the testimony of Epiphanius to the identity of the Ebionites and Nazarenes, who had read to the end so much as the first sentence of Epiphanius's account of the Ebionites.   And I still say the same thing.   For in that first sentence Epiphanius asserts, that Ebion made additions to the doctrine of the Nazarenes.   Among these additions I place, although you will not, the mere humanity of Christ.

10. You tell me in reply, that if I had myself read the second paragraph of this same chapter of Epiphanius, it would have shewn me the error of my own remark; for in that second paragraph, you say it appears, that the difference between the Ebionites and the Nazarenes lay in other par-

---

* Appendix to Charge, sec. 2.

K

ticulars, not in the doctrine of the mere humanity of Christ.* You then produce that paragraph, with a string of . other passages, confirming, as you think,' the assertion, which you pretend to find in it, of the agreement of the two sects upon the point in question. Epiphanius tells us, as you think, in the second paragraph of his first section about the Ebionites, " That Ebion borrowed his abominable rites (so you render βδιλυρον) from the Samaritans; his opinion (γνωμην) from the Naza-renes; his name from the Jews." In the second section, as. you understand him, he .places the whole difference between the Nazarenes and the Ebionites, in a single circumstance, totally uncon-nected with the opinions about Christ. In 'the same section, you say, he speaks of the two sects as inhabiting the said country, and adds, that " agreeing together they communicated of their perverseness to each other."†

11. Now, Sir, in these quotations, I have to complain partly of the want of critical discern-ment; partly of stratagem; partly of unskilful interpretation; and I affirm, that not one of the passages alleged, is to your purpose.

12. For the second paragraph of the first sec-tion, the only clause in it of which you can avail

---

* Letters to Dr Horsley, p. 15—17.   † Ibid. 15.

yourself, is that in which it is asserted, according
to your translation, that " Ebion took——his opinion from the Nazarenes."* But here, Sir, is
stratagem. Why is not the entire clause produced? Because the entire clause would defeat
the conclusion, which it is brought to establish.
Does Epiphanius say, that Ebion took his opinion
simply from the Nazarenes? He says it not; even
if it be admitted, that the word γνωμην is rightly
rendered by *opinion*. If *opinion* be indeed what
is here signified by γνωμην, Epiphanius says that
Ebion took his opinion from the " the Ossæans,
the Nazoræans, and the Nasaræans." The Nazoræans of Epiphanius (Ναζωραιοι) were the Christian Nazarenes. But his Nasaræans were no
Christians. They were a Jewish sect; one of the
seven which were subsisting at the time of our
Lord's appearance; the fifth in Epiphanius's enumeration. The Ossæans were the sixth of those
seven sects of Judaism. So that if any thing is
asserted in this clause concerning the opinions of
Ebion, it is, that they were a mixture of the extravagancies of three sects; two Jewish, and one
Christian. But this general assertion will never
determine, to which of these three sources any
particular opinion, maintained by Ebion, is to be
referred. It will be probable, that his doctrine of
our Lord's humanity was an accommodation of
the old doctrine of the Nazarenes to the preju-

---

* Letters to Dr Horsley, p. 15.

dices of his Jewish friends. For how will you prove, Sir, that Ebion, if he taught the same opinions which you now maintain, was not actuated by the same generous motives: a tender charity for the Jews, whom he might propose, as you do, to reconcile to the evangelic doctrine, by divesting the doctrine of every thing properly evangelic?

13. But I contend further, that the word γνωμη, in this passage of Epiphanius, is not rightly rendered by *opinion*. It often indeed denotes *opinion* in good Greek writers; but it is not used in that sense here. That it is not, appears from the subsequent part of the same sentence; in which γνωμη is mentioned as something distinct from γνωσις and συγκαταθεσις των ευαγζιλιων (perhaps we should read ευαγγελισων) και αποτολων περι πιστεως. "Ebion, says Epiphanius, desired to bear the appellation of a Christian, but not to adopt the practice of Christians, nor their γνωμη, nor their knowledge, nor their assent to the evangelists and apostles concerning the faith."* Now knowledge and assent concerning faith to the evangelists and apostles, include religious opinion; γνωμη, therefore, being mentioned as distinct from these, is not opinion. It seems to be rather used here, for what is expressed in English by the word *sentiment*; a thing

---

* Χριστιανων βελεται εχειν την προσηγοριαν, ε γαρ δηπεθεν τοτε πραξιν, και την γνωμην, και την γνωσιν, και την των ευαγζιλιων και αποτολων περι πιστεως συγκαταθεσιν.

which often modifies opinion, but itself is not opinion.   Of this use of the word, examples are not
wanting.   " Ebion, it is said, possessed the sentiments of Ossæans, Nazarenes, and Nasaræans."
He resembled these Christian and Jewish sectaries, in that illiberality of sentiment, which inclined the Nazarenes to think the observance of
the ritual law necessary to a Christian's salvation,
and disposed the Ossæans and the Nasaræans to
many senseless superstitions.   But this resemblance
is no proof, that he took his opinion of the mere
humanity of Christ from the Christian Nazarenes.

14. But if this passage is not sufficiently explicit, the second section you will tell me is decisive.
Unfortunately the long passage, which you have
produced from this section, wants to be set in order before any use can be made of it : and when
we have made the best of the present text, which
I fear is too corrupt to be perfectly restored without manuscripts, it will little serve your purpose.
Much indeed of the confusion arises from a false
punctuation, which your own translation sets in a
most conspicuous light, as a little remark which
you have thrown in, points out the correction of
it.   " ——— and first, he asserted that Christ was
born of the commerce and seed of a man, namely
Joseph, *as we signified above.*"*   This assertion of

---

* Letters to Dr Horsley, p. 16.

Ebion's, had not been signified above: it is mentioned in this passage for the first time.   You
remark, that these words, " as we signified above,"
refer to the first words of the first section.   But
in the first words of the first section, we have no
signification of Ebion's denial of the miraculous
conception, nor in any words previous to this
clause of the second section: and the reference
cannot be to previous words, for that which no
previous words contain.   The reference therefore,
which is explicitly to something previous, can have
no connexion with the denial of the miraculous
conception, which is now mentioned for the first
time.   It must connect however, with something
in the writer's present narrative, or it hath no
meaning.   Now in the words which immediately
precede the clause, which regards Ebion's heterodoxy upon the article of the conception, that is in
the initial clauses of this section, Epiphanius actually repeats what he had said before.   With
these clauses therefore, this reference to the former part of his narrative is to be connected; and
the intervening clause, regarding the conception,
should be set out as a parenthesis.   I will now
present you with the Greek text properly pointed,
accompanied with two translations; your own on
one side, and mine upon the other; that our
readers, comparing both with the original, may
judge for themselves of the propriety of each.

Dr Priestley.

——be was cotemporary with the former, and had the same origin with them; and first he asserted, that Christ was born of the commerce and seed of a man, namely Joseph, as we signified above, [referring to the first words of his first section,] when we said, that in other respects he agreed with them all, and differed from them only in this, *viz.* in his adherence to the laws of the Jews, with respect to the Sabbath, circumcision, and other things that were enjoined by the Jews and the Samaritans. He moreover adopted many more things than the Jews, in imitation of the Samaritans.

Ουτος γαρ ὁ Εβιων συγχρονος μεν τυτων ὑπαρχει, απ᾽ αυτων δε ουν αυτοις ὁρμαται· τα πρωτα δε εκ παραξησεως και σπερματος ανδρος, τυτεσι τυ Ιωσηφ, τον Χριστον γεγενησθαι ελεγεν· ὡς και ηδη ἡμιν προειρηται. ὁτι τα ισα τους αλλοις εν ἁπασιν φρονων, εν τυτω μονω διαφερω· εν τω τω νομω τυ Ιυδαιωμω προσανεχειν, κατα σαββατισμον, και κατα την περιτομην, και κατα τα αλλα παντα ὁσαπερ παρα Ιυδαιοις και Σαμαρειταις εμπολιτευεται. επι δε πλειω ετος, παρα τας Ιυδαιοις, ὁμοιως τοις Σαμαρειταις διαπραττεται.

Dr Horsley.

For this Ebion was contemporary with these, and he sets out from the same principles with them (but first of all he asserted, that Christ was begotten of the commerce and seed of a man, namely Joseph) as hath been already related by us. For agreeing with other [heretics] in all things [else] he differed in this single point, in that he adhered to the Judaic law, with respect to the observation of the Sabbaths, and to circumcision, and to all other things which are common to the rites of the Jews and the Samaritans. And besides, he is punctual in many things, not regarded by the Jews, in conformity with the Samaritans.

15. The manner in which Ebion's opinion concerning the conception of our Lord is mentioned in parenthesis, seems to exclude it from those principles, which he borrowed from other sectaries. If those other sectaries therefore were the Nazarenes, then this opinion, as it should seem, was no principle with them; and this passage, like most of your quotations, contradicts what you have brought it up to prove.

16. You will perhaps object, that if Epiphanius meant to insinuate, that Ebion and the Nazarenes held different opinions about Christ; he would not have named another thing as the single point in which they differed. Nor hath he done this. Having described Ebion's doctrine as a compilation of the extravagancies of other sects, he says, he differed only in a single point. That is, there was but a single point in his whole system, in which he differed from *all* the sects from which he borrowed: which was this, that his Juadism was of the Samaritan cast. But it follows not from this, that whatever he maintained besides, was to be found in the doctrines of the Nazarenes, or of any other in particular of the various heresies of which the Ebionæan was composed.

17. But, to deal sincerely, I must confess, that it is not at all clear to me, that the Nazarenes are the sect intended, in the beginning of this section,

under the description of Ebion's contemporaries, from whom he borrowed his principles. If they were not, this section will neither afford any proof of your opinion, nor be conclusive on the other side. The persons intended are not named, otherwise than by the pronoun τυλων: and for this pronoun, if you examine the original text, you will be much at a loss to find an antecedent. This pronoun used as it is here, as a relative, is generally to be referred to the persons mentioned last before in the author's discourse. But in all the preceding part of this discourse about the Ebionites, the Nazarenes are no where mentioned, except in that sentence in which they are joined with the Ossæans and the Nasaræans, and at the very beginning of the chapter, where they are intended by this same pronoun as the sect described in the chapter next preceding. The persons last mentioned in the present discourse, are the Jews and the Samaritans: and of these the pronoun τυλων may be redditive. Ebion might be called their contemporary, if he lived before the Jews entirely lost their consideration in the world, as a religious sect; and while the Samaritans were yet subsisting as a distinct set of Judaism. He set out from the same principles with them, because he maintained the permanent obligation of the ritual law. If this be the true exposition of the two first clauses of this section; it is the purport of the parenthesis, which follows them, to re-

mark, that Ebion, even in that part of his doctrine which could not be borrowed either from
Jews or Samaritans, carried his desire of accommodating to Jewish principles, such a length, as to
acknowledge our Lord for nothing more than a
preacher of righteousness. But this leads to no
conclusion about the faith of the Nazarenes.

. 18. I have sometimes thought, that the pro.
noun τουτων might be redditive, not of the Nazarenes singly, but of all. the sects which are mentioned in the preceding part of the narrative, as
furnishing the constituent parts of Ebion's system;
namely, of the Jews, the Samaritans, the Ossæans,
the Nasaræans, the Nazarenes, the Cerinthians,
and the Carpocratians. With all these, according to the confused chronology of this inaccurate
writer, Ebion, as a junior with an elder, was contemporary: and he set out from the same principles with them; inasmuch as all his principles
were borrowed, some from one of these sects, some
from another: the only thing which was peculiar
to himself being this: that the Juadism, which he
practised, was of the Samaritan cast. In this exposition of the pronoun τουτων, the importance of the
parenthesis must be to signify, that the mere humanity of Christ was made a principle by Ebion,
although it was no principle with those from
whom he borrowed. It was indeed a part of the
Cerinthian doctrine, not as a principle, but as a

consequence from principles. The principles of
the Cerinthian doctrine were the principles of the
Oriental philosophy: and the denial of our Lord's
divinity, and of his miraculous conception, in the
system of Cerinthus, was a consequence of that
cardinal principle of the Oriental philosophy,
which put eternal enmity between God and every
thing material. But with Ebion the denial of the
miraculous conception was itself a first principle,
independent of every thing else. In this view of
it again, the parenthesis leads to no conclusion
concerning the Nazarenes.

19. Which exposition of the pronoun τινων is to
be preferred, is a point upon which I can bring
myself to no fixed opinion. I very much suspect,
as I have already observed, some considerable corruption of the text. For, although Epiphanius is
indeed a wretched writer, the obscurity of this
sentence, as it stands, is more than mere bad writing is apt to create. But expound the pronoun as
you please, the passage will be either against you,
or at the best nothing to your purpose.

20. But in a subsequent sentence, Epiphanius
speaks, it seems, " of the Ebionites, as inhabiting
the same country as the Nazarenes;" and adds,
" that *agreeing together, they communicated of their
perverseness to each other.*" It is true, that in the

passage which you have produced, Epiphanius
speaks of the Ebionites as the near neighbours of
certain Nazarenes, and of a resemblance which the
vicinity of situation produced.   But the Nazarenes intended, were they the Christian Nazarenes, or the Nasaræan Jews? They are called
" the lawless Nazarenes" [Ναζαρηνοι οι ανομοι]. The
Christian Nazarenes had nothing in their conduct,
that might render them deserving of this epithet.
Their error was, that they feared to use their
liberty, not that they abused it.   The Nasaræan
Jews, as Jews, were lawless in a very emphatic
sense; inasmuch as they renounced the whole of
the Mosaic law, except that they circumcised,
kept the Sabbath, and paid some regard to the
stated festivals.   It was not, that they denied the
authority of Moses: but, by what may be gathered from Epiphanius's account of them, they
pretended that the real laws of Moses were lost,
and that the Pentateuch of the Jews was, in all
but the historical parts, a spurious work.*   Upon
these principles they held themselves released
from all rites, but those which the history itself

---

* This conjecture, which I formed from Epiphanius's account
of this sect, I have since found confirmed by Damascenus; who
says, that they held the Pentateuch of the Jews to be a spurious
work, and pretended to have the original in their own hands.
Τας δε της πεντατευχη γραφας ουκ ειναι Μωσεως δογματιζουσι, αλλας δε
τας αυτας διαβεβαιουνται. Joan. Damascen. de Hæresibus.

confirmed.   This sect was found chiefly in the
region of Basantis: and in a town called Cochaba,
in the same region, Epiphanius places the original residence of Ebion.   These Nasaræans therefore, were neighbours of the Ebionites, and they
seem to be the people intended in this passage.

21. It may perhaps seem strange, that any resemblance should be pretended, between a Christian sect which adhered to the Mosaic law, and a
Jewish sect which rejected it.   But the first Ebionites, if Epiphanius is to be trusted in his description of them, retained nothing more of genuine Judaism, than the Nasaræans.   Whatever
more they had which looked like Judaism, it was
borrowed from the Samaritan superstition.

22. But whoever these lawless Nazarenes might
be, their agreement with the Ebionites, is an addition of your own, founded on a misinterpretation of the original.   Epiphanius answers for nothing more than some general resemblance.   His
words are to this effect.   " From hence he began
to propagate his pernicious doctrine; namely,
from the same parts which it hath before been
said those lawless Nazarenes inhabited.   For being contiguous, he to them, and they to him, each
imparted to the other of his own particular impiety.   And yet in certain things they differ; but
in evil disposition they were counterparts one to

the other."* . What you took for agreement is contiguity of situation; and the resemblance comes at last to nothing more, than an undefined general resemblance, with specific differences. An entire likeness is not pretended in any circum- stance, but the common depravity of disposition.

23. To these passages from the chapter about the Ebionites, you subjoin another, from the 7th section of the preceding chapter, which treats of the Nazarenes. " He says, that they were Jews in all respects, except that they believed in Christ; *but I do not know, whether they hold the miraculous conception or not.*"† This you say, " amounts to no more than a doubt, which he af- terwards abandoned, by asserting that the Ebio- nites held the same opinion concerning Christ with the Nazarenes; which opinion he expressly states to be their belief, that Jesus was a mere man, and the son of Joseph."‡ I lament, Sir, that, in jus- tice to my own cause, I must here openly com- plain of the perverseness of your translation. When you cite an ancient author, why will you

---

* Ενθεν αρχεται της κακης αυτη διδασκαλιας, οθεν δηθεν και Ναζαρηνοι οι ανομοι προδιδηλωνται. Συναφθεις γαρ, ουτος εκεινοις και εκεινοι τελα, εκατερος απο της εαυτου μοχθηριας τω ετερω μετεδωκε. και διαφεροιλαι μεν ετερος προς τον ετερον κατα τι, εν δε τη κακονοια αλληλους ατιμαζουσι.

† Letters to Dr Horsley, p. 17.   ‡ Ibid.

make him say more or less, than he hath said for himself? Why not translate literally? that your readers might see, how far your account of things is supported by express testimony, how far it is mere inference; and be enabled to estimate the degree of probability, with which each inference is accompanied.. " ——they believed in Christ; but I do not know, whether they held the miraculous conception or not." Is this a translation of the words of Epiphanius? It is not. It is an artful substitution of an inference of your own, from the author's words, for the words of the author. I, Sir, in my Charge had furnished you with a more exact translation.* Why would you not adopt it; unless you could have made a better of your own, or could have shewn its impropriety? " Concerning Christ," says Epiphanius, " I cannot say with certainty (or, I am not informed to say, ὃκ ὃιδα εἰπτιν) whether they too, carried away with the impiety of the aforementioned Cerinthus and Merinthus, think him a mere man; or affirm, as the truth is, that he was begotten of Mary, by the Holy Ghost." To affirm, " as the truth is, that Christ was begotten of Mary, by the Holy Ghost," in Epiphanius's sense of those words, was to affirm much more than the miraculous conception, in any sense in which an Unitarian might affirm it.

---

* Charge I. sec. 10.

It was to affirm our Lord's divinity. Epiphanius's confession, that he had no ground to assert, that the Nazarenes held the contrary opinion, amounts to much more than a doubt. It amounts to an unwilling confession of a base accuser; who had not the liberality to absolve in explicit terms, when he found himself unable to convict. As you have not yet produced the passage, in which Epiphanius asserts, that the Nazarenes and Ebionites held one opinion concerning Christ; your assertion, that he afterwards abandoned this donbt, or this acknowledgment, is destitute of proof; and it is the fair conclusion from this passage of Epiphanius, that the Nazarenes were orthodox in their opinions concerning Christ. This I shewed at large in my Charge.* You now attempt to elude my argument, by setting up an unfair and sophisticated translation of the passage, upon which my reasoning was founded.†

---

* Charge I. sec. 10, 11.

† In the third of his Second Letters to me, Dr Priestley has produced a passage from another part of Epiphanius's work, his chapter against the Arians, which clearly proves that the Ebionites and the Nazarenes, in the judgment of that writer, were different sects; in as much as both are separately mentioned. Dr Priestley perhaps may say, that whatever distinction this passage may prove between the Nazarenes and the Ebionites, upon the whole of their doctrine; it clearly proves that they held one opinion concerning Christ, which is sufficient for his purpose. It must be acknowledged, that, in this passage, the Nazarenes are mentioned together with the Ebionites, as sects in error in their opinions about Christ, and confuted by the beginning of St John's Gospel; still I maintain, that, in that

24. Were the identity of the Nazarenes and Ebionites clearly established, still you could turn it to no advantage, without making good your other assertion, that the Názarenes were originally the very same with the Hebrew Christians, or the members of the primitive church of Jerusalem. But of this I cannot find that you have brought a shadow of a proof, except what you pretend to derive from the testimony of Origen; which I shall consider in my next letter. You talk indeed of the antiquity of the Nazarenes. You bid me observe, " that they were prior to

---

part of his work where he professedly treats of the heresy of the Nazarenes, Epiphanius expresses a doubt of their heterodoxy upon the article of our Lord's divinity, in such terms as ought to leave no doubt upon the mind of his reader, of their orthodoxy in that particular. And what he says of them, when they are only incidentally mentioned, ought to have much less weight than what he says, or shews himself averse to say, in that part of his work where the errors of that sect are the immediate subject.

Dr Priestley, allowing Epiphanius to have been " in some things weak enough," exults however, in the testimony which, in his chapter against the Arians, he bears against the Nazarenes as a sect, which, together with the Ebionites, " held the doctrine of the simple humanity of Christ." And he says, that in this Epiphanius " stands uncontradicted by any authority whatever." Dr Priestley is mistaken; rashly venturing to assert, that where no authority is known to him, none is extant. Epiphanius is in this contradicted, not only by himself, as I have already shewn, but by a writer of far superior credit; by Joannes Damascenus, who, in his book *De Hæresibus*, says expressly, that the Nazarenes confessed Jesus to be the Son of God. Damascenus would not have said of Dr Priestley, or of any one maintaining the simple humanity of Christ, that he confesses Jesus to be the Son of God.

Ebion."* Of whom you say, that "he was himself cotemporary with the apostle John."† And
you tell me, that in allowing that the " Jewish
Christians were distinguished by the name of
Nazarenes————from the time that they were
settled in the country beyond the sea of Galilee,
I carry the opinions of the Ebionites, as universally held by the Jewish Christians, to the very
age of the apostles."‡ When you do me the honour to argue from my concessions, I wish, Sir,
you would report them with more fidelity and exactness. I have allowed no such antiquity to the
Nazarenes, as you would claim for them upon
the ground of my concessions. I said not, that
the Jewish Christians were distinguished by the
name of Nazarenes, from the time when the
first settlements were made beyond the sea of
Galilee. I said, that the sect of the Nazarenes
first arose when those of the Jewish Christians,
who pertinaciously retained their Judaism, made
their final settlement in those parts, in consequence of Adrian's severe edicts, by which the
Jews were banished from the ancient site of Jerusalem and the adjacent region. Thus I carried not the opinions of the Ebionites up to the
apostolic age: but I fixed the rise of a prior sect,
to an epoch little earlier than the middle of the

---

* Letters to Dr Horsley, p. 18.   † Ibid.   ‡ Ibid. p. 21.

second century. I maintained, that the Nazarenes at that time separated from the main body of the Jewish Christians, and appeared as a
distinct sect. It is not. allowed by me, that
from that time, or in any age of the church,
" the whole body of the Jewish Christians were
distinguished by the name of Nazarenes." If any
such concession may seem to be implied in the
expressions, in which I speak of the Nazarenes
in my Charge, (I. sec. 12.) I disavow it. Appealing against your assertions, to the sense of
the learned and reverend assembly, which I had
the honour to address; I rather sought expressions, which might convey the general part of
an opinion common to us all, than such as
might more precisely mark the particulars of
my own. That the name of Nazarene was descriptive of a heresy, I was confident none in
that assembly doubted. I was not equally confident but that some might doubt, whether that
heresy, from the time the name was used, embraced not the main body of the Jewish Christians. Whatever doubts might subsist about the
extent, I was confident there could be but one
opinion, in that assembly, about the chronology
of the name. But Ebion, you say, was contemporary with St John. To that circumstance,
when it is proved, I shall be disposed to give
great attention. I believe the opinion hath no
foundation, but in the foolish story told by Epi-

phanius, of St John and Ebion in the bath. The same is told by other writers, of St John and Cerinthus; and it hath altogether the air of fiction. But suppose I were to allow the highest antiquity to these Nazarenes; suppose that with you I were to place them in the apostolic age; would this oblige me to allow, that they were the true members of the primitive church? Had not the apostolic age its schisms and its heresies? The Simonians, the Nicolaitans, the Cerinthians; were not all these contemporary with the apostles? Were they therefore sound members of the church of Jerusalem? Be pleased, Sir, to consider this question.

I am, &c.

POSTSCRIPT.

1. Eusebius, in his *Ecclesiastical Theology*, speaks as if he thought the name *Ebionites* had been imposed by the apostles themselves, upon those who disowned our Lord's divinity; which necessarily implies, that, in his opinion, the sect and the name were of the apostolic age. " Our Saviour's own heralds," says Eusebius, " named those Ebionites————who acknowledged

not the Godhead of the Son."* Our Saviour's own first heralds must be the preachers, it should seem, of his own appointment; namely, the apostles: and that they are the persons intended, is the more probable, for the distinction seems to be made between these *first heralds* and *ecclesiastical fathers*, who are afterwards mentioned. Strenuously as you assert the antiquity of the Ebionites, you have no where, that I remember, alleged this testimony. You were aware perhaps, that were it good for the antiquity of the sect, it would be equally good for the reason and origin of the name. For my own part, I am not inclined to avail myself of it. I consider it as a hasty assertion of a writer, over zealous to overwhelm his adversary by authorities. I mention it only to protest against any use, which you may hereafter be disposed to make of it, in a dearth of proof of Ebion's antiquity. Should you urge me with any part of this testimony, I shall have a right to insist, that you accept the whole. Should you produce it in proof, that an Unitarian sect existed in the apostolic age; you will be obliged to allow, that it is equally a proof that the Unitarian doctrine was

---

* Καὶ αὐτὶ δὶ τῳ σωτηρος ἡμων πρωτοκηρυκες Εβιωναιυς ὀνομαζοι, ἑβραϊκη φωνη πτωχυς την διανοιαν ἀποκαλυντες τυς ἱνα μεν θεον λεγωντας ἐιδεναι, καὶ τυ σωτηρος το σωμα μη ἀγνωμισυς, την δὲ τυ ἱυν θεοτητα μη ἐιδωτας. Ecc. Theol. lib. i. c. 14.

expressly condemned by the apostles. It will be
no concern of mine to disprove the antiquity of
Ebion, however I may disbelieve it, so long as the
very ground of his claim seals his condemnation ;
so long as his pretensions to an early existence
rest on a presumption, that he had the honour to
be the object of apostolical censure.

2. Upon the story of St John and the hæresiarch, in the public baths at Ephesus, I passed
judgment hastily, when I spake of it as a foolish
story, carrying *altogether* the air of fiction.   I
ought to have recollected, that Irenæus* vouches
strongly for so much of it as he relates.   He even
cites the testimony of Polycarp, in terms which
may be understood to imply, that he was himself
one of many, still living when he wrote, who had
heard the story from the mouth of Polycarp. The
testimony of Irenæus is hardly to be disbelieved ;
the testimony of Polycarp is irresistible.   But the
story, which Irenæus relates after Polycarp, he
relates of St John and Cerinthus.   It makes
nothing therefore for the antiquity of Ebion.   As
related of him, with the addition of many improbable circumstances not mentioned by Irenæus, it
may be deemed a fiction.†

---

* Lib. iii. c. 3.
† Dr Priestley, in the third of his Second Letters to me, to
corroborate the testimony of Epiphanius, alleges that of Jerome ;

LETTER SEVENTH.

Continuation of Reply to Dr Priestley's Second.—Of the argu-
ment from Origen.—That it rests on two passages in the books
against Celsus. The first misinterpreted by Dr Priestley in
a very important point.—No argument to be drawn from the
two passages in connexion.—Origen convicted of two false as-
sertions in the first passage.—The opinions of the first age
not to be concluded from the opinions of Origen.

DEAR SIR,

IN failure of all other proof of your supposed
identity of the Ebionites and Nazarenes, you still
appeal to the testimony of Origen. You have
however, given a new turn to this part of your
argument. Your appeal was originally* to a pretended acknowledgment of Origen's, that the Nazarenes and the Ebionites were the same people.
But being made sensible,† how difficult it must

---

who, he says, " mentions the Ebionites, not only as a sect,
but a flourishing sect, in the time of St John." But Jerome
makes no such mention of the Ebionites. He says, that St John
wrote his Gospel in opposition to Cerinthus, and other heretics,
and principally the doctrine of the Ebionites (not then flourishing, but) *tunc consurgens*, then making its first appearance. This
I readily allow; for what was afterwards the doctrine of the
Ebionites, was first propagated by the Cerinthian Gnostics.

* Hist. of Corrup. vol. i. p. 7.

† See the Monthly Review for June, 1783, and for September, 1783.

be to find an acknowledgment of this identity, in
a writer who never once names the Nazarenes;
you abandon that project, and in the passages
which were at first cited to establish. this supposed identity, you have at last the good fortune
to discover an immediate proof of your main proposition, that the primitive faith of the Hebrew
·church was Unitarian.   Your method is, to trace
from Origen the faith of the Jewish Christians in
his age, and from their faith to infer that of their
ancestors.

2. The strength of this argument lies in two
passages in the books against Celsus; which are
very distant from each other: for the one is in the
second, the other in the fifth book; and yet they
must be taken in connexion, to give any colour to
your reasoning. You set it off indeed to great advantage, when, appealing to the first of these passages, you say, that it appears, and that I deny not
that it appears, " that the unbelieving Jews called
all those of their race, who were Christians, by
the name of Ebionites, in the time of Origen;" and
that " Origen's own words are too express, to admit any doubt of this."*   Truly, Sir, I was not
likely to deny a groundless assertion, before it
was made by my antagonist; and you now make

* Letters to Dr Horsley, p. 18.

it for the first time; at least I remember nothing like it in your former publications. I believe I was myself the first to bring forward this passage from the second book against Celsus. In your history, you have appealed to Origen's acknowledgment of the identity of the Ebionites and Nazarenes, without any reference to particular passages. I produced this passage, as of all that I could recollect the most for your purpose.* I produced it in order to shew, that when it is rightly understood, it is nothing to your purpose: for, although the Christians of the circumcision, in general, are in this passage called Ebionites, it is according to a peculiar definition of the word, which includes not what by other writers always, and by Origen himself in others places, is included in the notion of the Ebionæan doctrine; namely, a denial of our Lord's divinity. The Nazarenes therefore, might be Ebionites, in the sense which is here given to that word, although they doubted not our Lord's divinity, and were quite another set of people than the proper Ebionites. I acknowledge therefore, that in this passage, " Origen says of the Jewish Christians of his own time, that they were Ebionites."† These were my very words. But I said not, that they were the unbelieving Jews,

---

* Charge I. sec. 15.   † Ibid.

who imposed this name upon the converted:
and now that you have been pleased to say it
for me, I deny it; and I maintain, that Origen's words are too express to admit a doubt,
that you have mistaken his meaning. The entire passage of Origen* is to this effect———
" they of the Jews who believe in Christ, have
not abandoned the law of their ancestors; for
they live according to it; bearing a name, which
corresponds with the poor expectations which
the law holds out.† For a beggar is called
among the Jews, (that is, in the Hebrew language,) Ebion. And they of the Jews who have
received Jesus as the Christ, go by the name
of Ebionæans." The converted Jews went, it is
said, by this name. But where have you found
that the unbelieving Jews imposed it? Not in
Origen, Sir; but in the Latin translation of Ge-
lenius. Attend to the reasons assigned by Origen for the name, and you cannot but perceive,
that it could never be imposed by Jews. It
was given in contempt: the objects of the contempt were observers of the Mosaic law; and

---

* ———Οἱ ἀπο Ινδαιων εἰς Ιησνν πιστευοιλις ἡ καταλελοιπασι τον
παλριον νομον, βινσι γαρ κατ᾽ αυτον, επωνυμοι της κατα τον εκδοχην
πτωχειας τν νομν γεγενημενοι. Εβιων τε γαρ ὁ πτωχος παρα Ινδαιοις
καλειλαι, και Εβιωναιοι χρημαλιζνσιν οἱ ἀπο Ινδαιων τον Ιησνν ὡς Χριστα
τπαραδιξαμενοι. Origen in Celsum, p. 56. edit. Spencer.
† Literally, *being named after the poverty of the law in expectation.*

the cause of the contempt was the mean opinion, which was entertained by those who gave
the name, of expectations built on legal righteousness. Could these, Sir, be the sentiments
of unconverted Jews?

3. It would have been a circumstance of much
advantage to your argument, which I doubt not
you well understand, that the unconverted Jews
should have been the coiners of the name: because it would have followed, that the name
was originally common to the whole body of
the Hebrew Christians. Then since Origen, in
the other passage in the fifth book, makes, as
you observe, only two sorts of Ebionites, the
one believing, the other denying the miraculous
conception, the deduction might have seemed
not unfair, that Origen knew of no Hebrew
Christians that were not Unitarians.

4. You will say, perhaps, that since we have
Origen's testimony for the universality of the
name, the argument from the two passages, taken
in connexion, may still proceed. If I could admit the universality of the name upon Origen's
testimony, I should insist, that his description of
the twofold Ebionites, in the fifth book, is not
exactly what you take it to be. I should remark,
that the words, ὁμοίως ἡμῖν, " in like manner as we
do," make an important branch of the character

of the milder sort——————" these," says he, " are
the double Ebionites; who either confess Jesus
born of a virgin, *in like manner as we do*, or
think he was not born in that manner, but like
other men."* I should maintain, that the words
" in like manner as we do," are equivalent to
the words " as the truth is," in Epiphanius's
description of that belief in the miraculous conception, which he says the Nazarenes, for aught
he, knew to the contrary, might hold; and I
should contend, that Origen affirms, but with
less equivocation, of these better Ebionites, what
Epiphanius reluctantly confesses of the Nazarenes, that they held the Catholic doctrine concerning the nature of our Lord. And in this
manner the words of Origen seem to have been
understood both by Grotius and Vossius; when
they allow, that the Nazarenes, though orthodox
in this part of their faith, are included, in this
passage of Origen's fifth book, in the appellation
of Ebionites. I should contend, that if the former passage proves the name general for the whole
body of the Hebrew Christians, the latter equal-

---

* Εγωσαν δι τοις και τον Ιησυ αποδιχομενοι, ως παρα τυτο Χριστια-
νοι ειναι αυχυντες, ιτι δι καια τον Ιυδαιων νομον, ως τα Ιυδαιων πληθυ,
βιων εθιλοντες· υτοι δι εισιν οι διπλοι Εβιωναιοι, ητοι ιχ παρθινυ ομολ-
ογυντες αμοιως ημιν τον Ιησυν, η υχ υτω γιγινοσθαι, αλλ' ως τας λοιπας
ανθρωπυς· τι τυτο φιρι ιγχλαμα τοις απο της ιχχλησιας. Contra
Cels. p. 272.

ly proves, that the notion of an Unitarian was not necessarily included in it. The connexion therefore of these two passages, makes little for your purpose; since the second serves to overthrow the argument, which might be built upon the first. It justifies what I advanced in my Charge, upon a presumption that the first singly would be made the foundation of the argument from Origen; that the word Ebionite, in Origen's time, or at least in his use of it, had outgrown its original meaning.

5. In this manner I should combat your argument from these two passages; were it not that I think too lightly of the testimony of Origen, in what relates to the Hebrew Christians, to be solicitous to turn it to my own advantage. Let his words be taken as you understand them; and so far as the faith of the Hebrew Christians of his own time is in question, let him appear as an evidence on your side.—I shall take what you may think a bold step. I shall tax the veracity of your witness—of this Origen. I shall tell you, that whatever may be the general credit of his character, yet in this business, the particulars of his deposition are to be little regarded, when he sets out with the allegation of a notorious falsehood. He alleges of the Hebrew Christians in general, that they had not renounced the Mosaic law. The assertion served him for

an answer to the invective, which Celsus had
put in the mouth of a Jew, against the converted Jews, as deserters of the laws and customs
of their ancestors. The answer was not the
worse for wanting truth, if his heathen antagonist was not sufficiently informed in the true distinctions of Christian sects, to detect the falsehood. But in all the time which he spent in Palestine, had Origen never conversed with Hebrew
Christians of another sort? Had he met with no
Christians of Hebrew families, of the church of
Jerusalem? Was the Mosaic law observed, was
it tolerated, in Origen's days, in the church of
Jerusalem, when that church was under the government of bishops of the uncircumcision? The
fact is, that after the demolition of Jerusalem by
Adrian, the majority of the Hebrew Christians,
who must have passed for Jews with the Roman
magistrates, had they continued to adhere to the
Mosaic law, which to this time they had observed more from habit than from any principle
of conscience, made no scruple to renounce it;
that they might be qualified to partake in the
valuable privileges of the Ælian colony, from
which Jews were excluded. Having thus divested
themselves of the form of Judaism, which to that
time they had born, they removed from Pella,
and other towns to which they had retired, and
settled in great numbers at Ælia. The few, who
retained a superstitious veneration for their law,

remained' in the north of Galilee, where they
were joined perhaps by new fugitives of the same
weak character, from Palestine. And this was the
beginning of the sect of the Nazarenes. But
from this time, whatever Origen may pretend to
serve a purpose, the majority of the Hebrew
Christians forsook their law, and lived in communion with the Gentile bishops of the new-
modelled church of Jerusalem; for the name was
retained, though Jerusalem was no more, and the
seat of the bishop was at Ælia.* All this I affirm with the less hesitation, being supported by
the authority of Mosheim.† From whom indeed
I first learnt to rate the testimony of Origen, in
this particular question, at its true value.‡

6. It is in defiance thereof of the fact, and I
fear of his own knowledge of the fact, that
Origen affirms of the Hebrew Christians in general, that they lived in the observance of the
Mosaic law: and it must be equally in defiance
of the fact, that he affirms, that they were all in

---

* See Dr Priestley's objections to this representation of facts,
in the fourth of Dr Priestley's Second Letters to me, and my
Defence, in my Remarks on his Second Letters, p. 2. c. ii.

† De rebus Christianorum ante Constantinum. Sæc. II. sec.
38. Note *

‡ See his Dissertation about Ebion, which is the tenth in order in the first volume of a Collection, entitled, *Dissertationes
ad Historiam Ecclesiasticam pertinentes.*

general called Ebionites: for he pretends not, that this name generally belonged to them otherwise than as Judaizers. His expressions in the passage in the fifth book, seem to imply a retractation of both these assertions. For there 'he speaks only of *some*, who, with the profession of Christianity, retained the practice of Judaism. These *some*, he says, were the Ebionites; and, which is more, he describes these Ebionites, not indeed as universally Unitarians, but as despicable wretched heretics, whose extravagancies could bring no disgrace upon the Christian church, of which they were no part. Were the Hebrew Christians, living in communion with the bishop of Jerusalem, in the days of Origen, no part of the true church of Christ? If they were a part of it, in Origen's own judgment they were no Ebionites. " I would not believe this witness upon his oath," says Mosheim, " vending, as he manifestly does, such flimsy lies."*

7. I may now, Sir, without damage to my cause, freely make you a present of the whole testimony of Origen, not only as it is given by

---

* Ego huic testi, etiamsi jurato, qui tam manifesto fumos vendit, me non crediturum esse confirmo. Mosheim de Ebione. sec. x. See the veracity of Origen defended by Dr Priestley, and further impugned by me, in the fourth of Dr Priestley's Second Letters to me, and in my Remarks on the Second Letters, p. 2. c. i.

him, but as it is interpreted by you. As it is given by him, it states, that the Hebrew Christians in his time, were generally Judaizers. As interpreted by you, it states, that in his time, they were generally Unitarian. But if this testimony were more unexceptionable than it is, and this sense of the testimony less doubtful, what evidence would it afford, that the first Hebrew Christians were Unitarians in the time of the apostles?

8. You pretend not, that this would follow by necessary consequence. But you say, " if the Jewish Christians were universally Ebionites in the time of Origen, the probability is, that they were very generally so in the time of the apostles."[*] Whence should this probability arise? From this general maxim, it seems: that " whole bodies of men do not soon change their opinion."[†] You are indeed, Sir, the very last person, who might have been expected to form conclusions upon an historical question from mere theory, in defiance of the experience of mankind: in defiance of the experience of our own country and our own times. How long is it, since the whole body of dissenters in this kingdom, (the single sect of the Quakers excepted,) took their standard of or-

---

[*] Letters to Dr Horsley, p. 21.   [†] Ibid.

thodoxy from the opinions of Calvin? Where shall we now find a dissenter, except perhaps among the dregs of Methodism, who would not think it an affront to be taken for a Calvinist?*

9. I now, Sir, take my leave of your argument from the Nazarenes. I trust I have shewn, that, although it is the chief strength of your cause, it was well entitled to a place among my specimens of insufficient proof, of which it was the fourth in order. Before I proceed to examine other parts of the evidence, by which you think to establish the high antiquity of the Unitarian doctrine; give me leave to remind you, that, although you have overlooked it, a very positive proof is at this day extant in the world: that the divinity of Christ was the belief of the very first Christians. This shall be the subject of my next letter.

I am, &c.

POSTSCRIPT.

A learned correspondent of mine, an eminent

---

* Of the numbers of the Calvinists among the dissenters of the present day, see the fourth of Dr Priestley's Second Letters, and my Remarks, p. 2. c. iv.

divine of the church of Scotland, a Calvinist,* and
by consequence, a serious and devout believer in
the Catholic doctrine of the Trinity, hath remarked to me, that your assertion, that the Nazarenes were the first Hebrew Christians, might
have had some colour given to it, from the history
of the accusation of St Paul before Felix, in the
Acts of the apostles.   St Paul was charged upon
that occcasion, by Tertullus the orator, as he is
called, as a ringleader " *of the sect of the Nazarenes.*"   Whence it might have been argued,
that this was the name, which Christians in general at that time bore. This argument, I think,
is far more specious, than any you have produced
for yourself; but it is only an instance, by which
it may be seen how easy it is, to frame arguments, in that oblique kind in which you so much
delight, which may give a false colouring to
things, and impose upon the ignorant or heedless.
It is for this purpose, I believe, that it is produced
by my learned and much honoured correspondent;
not as a proof which, had it been set up by you,
would have convinced, or even staggered, either
him or me.   It only proves, that in the infancy of
Christianity, Christians, among the unbelieving
Jews, who considered them as an heretical sect in

---

* The person meant, was my maternal uncle, the Rev. Robert Hamilton, D.D. many years professor of divinity in the
college of Edinburgh.

their own religion, went by the name of Nazarenes, as followers of the Nazarene; for that
was the appellation which, in contempt, they
gave our Lord himself, from the obscure village
to which his family belonged. But while the
Christians were called Nazarenes by the unbelieving Jews, they were called among themselves
The Brethren, They of the Faith, and *The Faith;*
till at length, when they became more numerous,
and received a large accession of converts from
the Gentiles, *Christians* became the general name,
and the Hebrew Christians, who still perhaps bore
the name of Nazarenes among the Jews, were distinguished among Christians by the names of
The Hebrews, and *They of the Circumcision.*
I still therefore abide by my assertion, that the
name of Nazarene was never heard of *in the
church*, that is, among Christians themselves,
as descriptive of a sect, (as a general name for the
whole fraternity of believers, it was never heard
of in the church at all,) but as descriptive of a
sect, it was never heard of before the final destruction of Jerusalem by Adrian; when it became
the specific name of the Judaizers, who at that
time separated from the church of Jerusalem,
and settled in the north of Galilee. The name
was taken from the country in which they settled; but it seems to have been given in contempt,
and not without allusion to the earlier application
of it by the Jews to the Christians in general.

The intent of it was, to signify that these Judaizers, who were for imposing the yoke of the
Mosaic law upon the brethren of the uncircumcision, knew so little of the spirit of the gospel,
that they were only to be considered as a sect of
Jews; and were undeserving of any more honourable name, than that by which the unbelieving
Jews, of the apostolic age, had been accustomed
to express their contempt for the then new and
little family of Christ; that they could not be
more properly described than as heretical Jews,
living in the poorest village of the poorest province.

LETTER EIGHTH.

A positive proof still extant, that our Lord's divinity was the belief of the very first Christians.—The Epistle of St Barnabas not the work of an apostle, but a production of the apostolic age.—Cited as such by Dr Priestley.—The author a Christian of the Hebrews.—A believer in our Lord's divinity. —Writes to Christians of the Hebrews concurring in the same belief.

DEAR SIR,

I AM to produce a positive proof, that the divinity of our Lord was the belief of the very first Christians. Give me leave then to ask your opinion of that book, which had been current in the church from the very first ages, under the title of *The Epistle of St Barnabas.* It is quoted, you know, by Clemens Alexandrinus, not to mention later writers, as the composition of Barnabas the apostle. Take no alarm, Sir—I shall not claim a place for it in the canon. I shall not contend, that any apostle was its author. I am well persuaded of the contrary. But the reasons which persuade me, are such as ought to have no weight with you, if you will be true to your own principles. The style is indeed embarrassed and undignified; the reasoning is often unnatural and weak. Texts of the Old Testament are drawn

by violence to allegorical senses, which are inadmissible : as when Moses, encouraging the Israelites to take possession of the promised land, is
supposed to exhort the Jews to embrace the
Christian religion; and in the description of Canaan, as a land flowing with milk and honey, the
land is our Saviour's body, the milk and honey
are the doctrines and promises of the gospel.
The attempt to find evangelical types in the Jewish rites, is injudiciously conducted. The essential part of a rite, which was of divine appointment, is often superficially treated ; and the supposed sense of subordinate ceremonies, and those
very often of human institution, and of no significance, is pursued with a trifling exactness: thus,
in the exposition of the red heifer, and in that
of the scape goat; the stress is principally laid
upon circumstances, about which the divine law
is silent. But what may least of all be reconciled
with the apostolic spirit, is that strange cabalistic
process, by which the name of Jesus, and the cross,
are drawn from the number of Abraham's armed
domestics; and the great credit which the author
gives himself for such discoveries. My notion of
inspiration will not allow me to believe, that an
inspired apostle could be the writer of such a book,
and be vain of having written it. Your principles leave you at liberty to be less scrupulous.
You, who have convicted St Paul of reasoning to

precarious conclusions,* may easily admit that St Barnabas, the companion of St Paul, might reason from false premises. You, who think that one apostle " has strained his imagination very much"† to find analogies between the rites of Judaism and something in Christianity, may easily suppose, that another apostle from the same motive— a desire of reconciling the Jews to Christianity, may have strained much more to make the analogy much more complete. I can therefore see no reason, why you should not receive what is called the Epistle of St Barnabes, extravagant and nonsensical as it is in many parts, for the genuine work of Barnabas the apostle. But this is much more than I desire, and much more than is necessary to my argument.‡ I suppose, however, that you will allow, what all allow, that the book is a production of the apostolic age: in the fifth section of your history of the doctrine of atonement, you quote it among the writings of the apostolic fathers. I think it fair to remind you of this circumstance, lest you should hastily ad-

---

* Hist. of Corrup. vol. ii. p. 370.

† Ibid. vol. i. p. 24.

‡ Modica sunt, quæ in ejus gratiam, nec (ut puto) facile recusanda: ut nimirum, si non ipsis saltem annis ejus honos habeatur: si non apostolum agnoscamus; eum tamen ceu patrem revereamur; et demum, si non in canonem illum recipiendum ducamus, saltem in classicis scriptoribus, pro dignitate quam olim obtinuit apud ecclesiæ scriptores antiquissimos, numeremus. *Præfat. Editoris Oxoniensis.*

vance a contrary opinion, when you find the testimony of this writer turned against you.

2. You allow him a place, then, among the fathers of the apostolic age: and will you not allow, that he was a believer in our Lord's divinity? I will not take upon me, Sir, to answer this question for you; but I will take upon me to say, that whoever denies it, must deny it to his own shame. " The Lord, says Barnabas, submitted to suffer for our soul, although he be THE LORD OF THE WHOLE EARTH, unto whom he said, the day before the world was finished, Let us make man after our image and our likeness."* Again, " —— for if he had not come in the flesh, how could we mortals, seeing him have been preserved; when they who behold the sun, which is to perish, and is the work of his hands, are unable to look directly against its rays."† Compare Deut. xviii. 16. Exod. xxxiii. 20. Judges vi. 23. and xiii. 22. Again " —— if then the Son of God, being Lord, and being to judge the quick and dead, suffered to the end, that his wound

---

* Dominus sustinuit pati pro animâ nostrâ, cum sit orbis terrarum dominus, cui dixit die ante constitutionem sæculi " Faciamus hominem ad imaginem et similitudinem nostram." sec. v.

† —— Ει γαρ μη ηλθεν εν σαρκι, πως αν εσωθημεν ανθρωποι βλεποντες αυτον, οτι τον μελλοντα μη ειναι ηλιον, εργον χειρων αυτε υπαρχοντα, εκ ισχυωσιν εις ακτινας αυτοφθαλμησαι. sec. v.

might make us alive; let us believe that the Son of God had no power to suffer, had it not been for us."* And again, " Mean while thou hast [the whole doctrine] concerning the majesty of Christ; how all things were made for him and through him; to whom be honour, power, and glory, now and for ever."† He who penned these sentences was surely a devout believer in our Lord's divinity. It is needless to observe, that he was a Christian; and almost as needless to observe, that he had been a Jew. For in that age none but a person bred in Judaism could possess that minute knowledge of the Jewish rites, which is displayed in this book. In the writer therefore of the Epistle of St Barnabas, we have one instance of a Hebrew Christian of the apostolic age, who believed in our Lord's divinity.

8. But this is not all. They must have been originally Jews to whom this epistle was addressed. The discourse supposes them well acquainted with the Jewish rites, which are the chief subject of it : and indeed to any not bred in Judaism, the book had been uninteresting and unintelli-

---

* —— Ei ὖν ὁ ὑιος τȣ Θεȣ, ὡν Κυριος, καὶ μελλων κρινειν ζωιλος καὶ νεκρȣς, ἐπαθιν, ἱνα ἡ πληγη ἀυτȣ ζωοπωιηση ἡμας· πιςιυσωμεν, Jh ὁ ἱιοχ τȣ Θεȣ ȣκ ἰδυναλο παθειν, ἰι μη διἁ ἡμας. sec. vii.

† Habes interim de majestate Christi, quo modo omnia in illum et per illum facta sunt: cm sit honor, virtus, gloria nunc et in sæcula sæculorum. sec. xvii. -

gible. They were Hebrew Christians, therefore, to whom a brother of the uncircumcision holds up the doctrine of our Lord's divinity. He upholds it, not barely as his own persuasion, but as an article of their common faith. He brings no arguments to prove it—he employs no rhetoric to recommend it. He mentions it as occasion occurs, without shewing any anxiety to inculcate it, or any apprehension, that it would be denied or doubted. He mentions it in that unhesitating language, which implies that the public opinion stood with his own. So that in this writer we have not only an instance of an Hebrew Christian, of the apostolic age, holding the doctrine of our Lord's divinity; but in the book we have the clearest evidence, that this was the common faith of the Hebrew Christians of that age, or in other words, of the primitive church of Jerusalem.

4. This, Sir, is the proof, which I had to produce, of the consent of that church with the later Gentile churches in this great article. It is so direct and full, though it lies in a narrow compass, that if this be laid in the one scale, and your whole mass of evidence, drawn from incidental and ambiguous allusions, in the other,

" The latter will fly up, and kick the beam."

I am, &c.

LETTER NINTH.

The proof of the orthodoxy of the first age, overturns Dr Priest-
ley's arguments from Hegesippus and Justin Martyr.—Hege-
sippus a voucher for the Trinitarian faith.—Dr Priestley's
own principles set aside his interpretation of Justin Martyr.—
Dr Priestley himself gives it up.—Tertullian makes no ac-
knowledgment of any popularity of the Unitarian tenets in his
own time.

DEAR SIR,

SINCE it is proved of the first Christians of
the circumcision, that they were believers in our
Lord's divinity ; what becomes of your two arguments to the contrary, from Hegesippus and Justin Martyr?

2. The argument from Hegesippus rested on
a presumption, that Hegesippus himself was an
Unitarian. That Hegesippus himself was an Unitarian was presumed, because he was a Christian of the Hebrews, and the Christians of the
Hebrews were supposed to be generally of that
persuasion. But now that the reverse is proved
of the Hebrew Christians, the presumption must
be reversed concerning Hegesippus. Hegesippus
must be deemed no Unitarian, and all consequences deduced from the contrary supposition must
be reversed, or at least they will vanish.

3. You remark indeed that Hegesippus, enu-merating the heresies of his time, makes no men-tion of the Ebionæan."* But this, I suppose, is mentioned only as a circumstance, that might seem to corroborate the inference from the suppo-sed prevalency of the Ebionæan tenets in the an-cient Hebrew church, if that supposition might be allowed to stand. It will hardly be pretended, that this circumstance alone will amount to a proof, that Hegesippus was a dissenter from what hath been shewn to be the prevailing opinion of his church. Of the five books of his Ecclesiastical Commentaries, nothing more survives, than a few sentences, cited by Eusebius in different parts of his history; which all brought together, might per-haps fill two pages and a half, in a folio of a mid-dling size. In these fragments, no mention occurs of the Ebionæan heresy. Is it therefore to be concluded, that the Ebionites were not mentioned, or not mentioned as heretics, in the entire work? Or where is the cogency of this argument? In certain fragments of the work of Hegesippus, the Ebionites are not mentioned as heretics; there-fore the author was himself an Ebionite.

4. Scanty as these fragments are, Providence hath so ordered, that clear evidence is to be found

---

* Hist. of Corrup. vol. i. p. 8. and vol. ii. p. 486. Reply to Monthly Review for June, p. 8. Letters to Dr Horsley, p. 143.

in them, that Hegesippus was no Ebionite; and that his testimony is to be found in them in favour of the Catholic faith. That he was no Ebionite, appears with the highest evidence from a little circumstance incidentally mentioned by Eusebius, which those who only *look through* ancient writers, may be very apt to overlook. Eusebius relates, that Hegesippus cited the Proverbs of Solomon, by a title which implied his acknowledgment of the book :* whereas the Ebionites acknowledged no part of the Old Testament but the Pentateuch, nor the whole of that.† His testimony in favour of the Catholic faith, is contained in his declaration—" that he found in all the churches which he visited, in his journey to Rome, that faith maintained, which was agreeable to the law, the prophets, and the doctrine of our Lord."‡ Hegesippus, in this declaration, bears his testimony to the faith of all the

---

* Euseb. Ecc. Hist. lib. iv. c. 22.

† Dr Priestley, in the third of his Second Letters, questions this fact : that the Ebionites acknowledged no part of the Old Testament but the Pentateuch ; and I must confess that his objections carry some weight. He remarks in particular, that Irenæus says of them, that they were over-curious in the exposition of the prophecies ; and that Grabe mentions fragments, which he had seen, of an exposition of prophets, ascribed to Ebion. Still that Hegesippus was no Ebionite, is evident from the favourable testimony which he bears to the general doctrine of the church in his own time.

‡ Euseb. Ecc. Hist. lib. iv. c. 22.

churches at this time, that it was the faith
which Christ had taught. But what faith the
churches at this time maintained, let Irenæus
and Justin testify: and where is the Unitarian
who will have the forehead to affirm, that the
faith, described as the faith Catholic, by Irenæus
and by Justin, was any other than the Trinitarian?

5. So much for Hegesippus. Now for Justin
Martyr: your argument from his supposed apology
for his own opinions, as contrary to the general
and prevailing, rests on a particular interpretation of certain expressions, which in themselves
perhaps are not free from ambiguity. But this interpretation, Sir, rests on your assumption, that
the first Christians were Unitarian. This being
now disproved, I will reason against your interpretation, from your own principles, and, with
little variation, in your own words; and from the
contrary interpretation, I will deduce the contrary
conclusion.

6. Justin wrote, you know, " about the year
140, *i. e.* about eighty years after the time of the
apostles."* If we consider the state of opinions
in their time " we can hardly doubt, whether Jus-

---

* Reply to Monthly Review for June, p. 17.

tin asserts it or not, that the doctrine of *our Lord's divinity** *must* have been the prevailing one in his time."[†] For we have certain evidence,[‡] that it was the opinion of the church in the age of the apostles; and it is not likely, that so important a doctrine should be generally abandoned " in so short a time as fourscore years.[§] And if we take in another well authenticated circumstance, we shall be obliged to reduce this short space to one still shorter. Hegesippus says——that the church of Jerusalem continued a virgin, or free from heresy, till the death of Simeon, who succeeded James the Just, that is, till the time of Trajan,[||] or about the year 100 or perhaps 110.——Knowing therefore, *(from another evidence, that of Barnabas,)* what this purity of Christian faith was, and what Hegesippus must have known it to be, we have only the space of forty, or perhaps thirty years, for so great a change. So rapid at that particular period must have been that movement, which we find by experience to be naturally one of the very slowest in the whole system of nature, *viz.* the revolution of opinions in great bodies of men. Can it then be thought probable, that the

---

* Dr Priestley's words are *the simple humanity of Christ.*
† Reply to Monthly Review for June, p. 17.
‡ See my last Letter.
§ Reply to Monthly Review for June, p. 17.
|| Euseb. Ecc. Hist. lib. iii. c. 32.

generality either of Jewish or Gentile Christians, or both considered as one body, the οἱ πλεῖστοι, should have abandoned the doctrine of *our Lord's divinity** in the time of Justin Martyr."† Certainly not. The words therefore, *εἰ ἂν ἃ πλεῖστοι ταῦτα μοι δοξασωσιν εἴποιεν* could not be intended to convey the sense, which you and your vindicator would impose upon them. On the contrary, they must be understood as an assertion, or at least as an insinuation, that the opinion of our Lord's mere humanity was generally condemned.

7. I once thought to have entered minutely into every part of the argument, which you and your vindicator have framed from this passage of Justin. But I find myself excused from that task, by your candid acknowledgment, in the sixth article of your postscript, that you are influenced in your construction of this passage, by your own particular opinions; and that another person having a different persuasion concerning the state of opinions in that age, will naturally be inclined to put a different construction upon it."‡ A passage, which may bear one or another construction, according to the previous persuasions of the reader, can be of little avail on either side. You

---

* Dr Priestley's words are, *the simple humanity of Christ.*
† Reply to Monthly Review for June, p. 18, 19.
‡ Letters to Dr Horsley, p. 130.

are welcome to all the proof of that sort, which you will take the trouble to amass. You seem, Sir, not insensible of its insignificance. Perceiving at last, that the expressions of Justin, when you have made the most of them, are but ambiguous, you are inclined to lay but little stress upon the passage. You resume the consideration of it, with a declaration that you are not " solicitous about trifles."* I must remark however, that expressions, which in themselves might be very ambiguous, may receive a definite sense from the known history of the writer's times. This is the case in this passage of Justin. His words, considered by themselves, are ambiguous; but connected with the opinions of the writer and of his age, they afford a decisive testimony against you.

8. But you think, if Justin Martyr and Hegesippus fail, you have still the positive testimony of Tertullian to oppose to my conclusions from the faith of the first Christians. Tertullian, who was little younger than Justin, complains, that in his time the Unitarian doctrine was the general persuasion. " The simple, the ignorant, and the unlearned, who are always a great part of the body of Christians, because the rule of faith transfers their worship of many gods

---

* Letters to Dr Horsley, p. 127.

to the one true God, not understanding that the unity of God is to be maintained, but with the economy, dread this economy."* I must confess, Sir, here seems to be a complaint against the unlearned Christians, as in general unfavourable to the Trinitarian doctrine. But the complaint is of our own raising. Tertullian will vouch but for a very small part of it. " Simple persons,† says Tertullian, (not to call them ignorant, and idiots,) who always make the majority of believers, because the rule of faith itself carries us away from the many gods of the heathen, to the one true God, not understanding that one God is indeed to be believed, but with an economy (or arrangement) of the Godhead, startle at the economy. They take it for granted, that the number and disposition of the Trinity is a division of the unity. They pretend that two, and even three, are preached by us, and imagine that they themselves are the worshippers of one God. We, they say, *hold the monarchy.* Latins have caught up the word *monarchia,* Greeks will not understand *œconomia.*" Let the author's words be thus exactly rendered, and you will find in

---

* Hist. of Corrup. vol. i. p. 55.

† Simplices enim (nec dixerim imprudentes et idiotæ) quæ major semper credentium pars est, quoniam et ipsa regula fidei, a pluribus diis sæculi, &c. non intelligentes unicum quidem, sed cum suâ œconomiâ credendum, expavescunt ad œconomiam.

them neither complaint, nor acknowledgment, of
a general prevalence of the Unitarian doctrine
among Christians of any rank. Tertullian alleges, that what credit it obtained, was only with
the illiterate; nor with all the illiterate, but with
those only, who were ignorant and stupid in the
extreme. To preclude the plea of numbers, he
remarks, that the illiterate will always make the
majority of believers. " Some simple people, he
says, " take alarm at the notion of a plurality
of persons in the unity of the Godhead. Simple
people, said I! I should have said, ignorant and
dull; who have never been made to comprehend
the true sense of the apostle's creed; which speaks
of one God, in opposition only to a plurality of
independent gods, worshipped by the heathen,
without any respect to the metaphysical unity of
the Deity. When it is considered, that persons
of mean endowments must always be the majority of a body, collected, as the church is, from
all ranks of men; it were no wonder, if the followers of the Unitarian preachers were more numerous than they really are." This, Sir, is the
natural exposition of the passage, which you cite
as Tertullian's testimony of the popularity of your
favourite opinions, in his own time. It is no such
testimony. It is a charge of ignorance against
your party; of such ignorance as would invalidate
the plea of numbers, if that plea could be set up.
The argument, which you build upon the rank

and condition of Tertullian's Unitarians, who were common or unlearned people, can be of no force, unless it could be proved, that the Unitarian opinion was general in this rank of Christians. The common people, who will be the last to depart from the opinions of their ancestors, when they are left to themselves, will on the other hand be the first to be staggered with difficulties, and, for that reason, the first to be misled. Whatever therefore, might be the novelty of the Unitarian doctrine, in the age of Tertullian, it is no wonder that it should find admirers among the most ignorant and stupid of the common people.*

9. You must search, Sir, for some clearer testimony, than any that is to be found in Tertullian, Justin Martyr, or the few surviving fragments of Hegesippus, to oppose to my proof from the epistle of St Barnabas.

I am, &c.

---

* See the Second of the Supplemental Disquisitions.

LETTER TENTH.

In Reply to Dr Priestley's third letter, in which he would prove that the primitive Unitarians were not deemed heretics.—His arguments from Tertullian, Justin Martyr, and Irenæus, confuted by the Monthly Reviewer.—The insufficiency of Dr Priestley's reply.—The arguments from Clemens Alexandrinus, and from Jerome, confuted.

DEAR SIR,

IT should seem, that you have some secret mistrust in your own heart, of the proof which you pretend to bring, that the Unitarian doctrine was orthodoxy in the first age; or you would have been less solicitous to shew, that the primitive Unitarians were not deemed heretics. For a proof that confessed orthodoxy was not deemed heresy, or in other words, that the orthodox did never excommunicate themselves, might have been spared. This however, is the subject of your third letter. Your arguments from the apostles' creed, as it is stated by Tertullian;[*] from the little severity with which Irenæus speaks of the Ebionites;[†] and from the respect with which Justin Martyr treats those blasphemers,[‡] for that is the

---

[*] Letters to Dr Horsley, p. 27, 28,
[†] Ibid. p. 32.   [‡] Ibid. p. 31,

appellation by which his regard for them is expressed, have been already so completely answered by my good and able *ally*,* the Monthly Reviewer,† that little is left for me to say upon the subject.

2. I must take this occasion to declare, that you are perfectly right in your conjecture,‡ that I entertain an high opinion of that gentleman's learning in ecclesiastical history. Indeed my opinion of his learning hath been gradually rising, while yours hath been going down :§ and what you predicted is at last come to pass; I think myself happy in the alliance of that able critic. I am informed by your last publication,‖ that my valuable ally is the Rev. Mr Samuel Badcock, a dissenting minister at South Molton, in Devonshire. To what ever denomination of Christians my worthy fellow-labourer may belong, he is learned, and an able advocate of the faith which was at first delivered to the saints, and his alliance will not be disgraceful, though he chooses to fight in a reviewer's armour. Indeed I cannot see for what

---

* " Dr Horsley considers this writer as learned in ecclesiastical history, and may wish to have him for an ally."

† In the Monthly Review for January, 1784.

‡ See note (*).

§ Letters to Dr Horsley, p. 159.

‖ Remarks on the Monthly Review of the Letters to Dr Horsley, &c.

reason the alliance of a Christian divine, although he be a reviewer by profession, should be less creditable than that, which you, Sir, so obsequiously court, with Jew, Turk, heretic, and infidel. You seem to think it unfair, that your antagonist should avail himself of the prodigious advantage, which the review gives him, of a cheap and immense circulation.* This complaint, Sir, really comes with an ill grace from you; who are every day diffusing your dangerous doctrines among the common people, in pamphlets published for their benefit, in an ordinary form, to be purchased at the easy price of sixpence, a groat, and even twopence. Some reserve on our part might be proper, if any were observed on yours. But while you invite the most illiterate of the laity to take a part in the dispute, it is our duty to guard them, what we can, from seduction; to take advantage of every mode of cheap and general circulation, that the antidote may be as widely spread, and as easy to be had, as the medicated phials.—I return to my subject.

3. Justin Martyr's respect for the Unitarians of his time, you collect from certain passages, in which, speaking of heretics with the highest indignation, he makes no allusion, as you conceive,

---

* Preface to the Letters to Dr Horsley, p. xxi.

to the Unitarians. My learned ally replies,* that in one of these passages Justin Martyr expressly alludes to the Unitarians, under the very honourable character of blasphemers of the Christ, whose coming had been announced by the prophets. He remarks, that in this passage Justin couples the name of Christ, with the title " of God of Abraham, Isaac, and Jacob," in a manner which, as it must bring to every learned reader's recollection other passages of the holy martyr's writings, in which Christ and the God of Abraham are described as the very same person, clearly defines the particular blasphemy, which was the subject of the accusation. My learned ally complains, that your translation of this passage is so *managed,* as to conceal this allusion to the Unitarian heresy; and to convey " no idea of distinction between the Maker of the world and the God of Abraham, Isaac, and Jacob." He might have added another complaint: that in your translation you have suppressed another clause in the same period, in which certain persons are treated with great severity, " who instead of worshipping Jesus" [instead of paying him divine worship, for that is the proper force of the verb σέβω] " confessed him only in name." Your re-

---

* Monthly Review for January, 1784, p. 61, 62.

ply* is indeed very extraordinary. It consists of three parts. An apology for the omissions; a defence of your argument; a flat denial † that you have made the omissions, for which however you have condèscended to apologize.

4. Your apology is, that the omissions were made to *shorten a long Greek quotation.*‡ But, Sir, the omissions are in your English translation; and the Greek, which is given at length at the bottom of your page, is nothing shortened by them. If the passage was to be shortened, either in Greek or in English, why was this shortening effected by the omission of those clauses in particular, which might seem at least adverse to your argument? Your defence is, that the omitted passages affect not the argument either way. For the whole of Mr Badcock's remark is answered, you say, at once,§ by observing " that it is to no sort of purpose, who it was that Justin meant by the God of Abraham, Isaac, and Jacob: but who it was, that the heretics he is speaking of meant by the person so described, and whom they meant to blaspheme: and this certainly was not Jesus

---

* Remarks on the Monthly Review of the Letters to Dr Horsley, sect. I.
† Appendix to the Remarks.
‡ Remarks, p. 14.   § Ibid. p. 13.

Christ, but another being, the supposed maker of the world, the author of the Jewish dispensation, and the introducer of much evil, which they said Christ was sent to rectify." Sir, I apprehend, and my learned ally, I believe, will be of the same opinion, that the true, not the supposed, maker of the world, was the person blasphemed, by the introduction of the fabulous *Demiurgus* of the Gnostics. Of the same opinion was Justin. You cannot, Sir, know so little of his language as to imagine, that by the title of ποιητὴς τῶν ὅλων, *the Maker of the Universe*, he describes the Gnostic *Demiurgus*, not the true Creator, the Father of our Lord Jesus Christ. But how is it that you maintain, that Jesus Christ was not blasphemed, by those whom Justin accuses? Justin describes those whom he would accuse, as blasphemers of Jesus Christ. This is in part the matter of his accusation. That you should attempt to deny it, is extraordinary, Sir, when you confess, that you omitted it " to shorten." It appears, however, that your arguments rest entirely upon a supposition, that the blasphemy of Jesus was no part of Justin's accusation. You took therefore, that method of shortening, which might best serve your purpose.

5. But you insist, that " they were Gnostics only, not Unitarian Christians, that Justin was

reflecting upon or alluding to."* Sir, will you take upon you to define on whom Justin would reflect, in contradiction to Justin's own declaration. I think with you, that the phrase ἀλλα γαρ καῖ ἀλλον τροπον is distributive; introducing, not the mention of any new sect, but a specific enumeration of the sects which had been already mentioned, under the general description of " those who taught men to say and to do many impious and blasphemous things." But the force of the objection, which my learned ally hath brought against your argument, depends not on the exact sense of this phrase. It is sufficient for our purpose, that a blasphemy of Christ, by denying his divinity, and refusing to honour him with divine worship, is a part of Justin's description of the heresies to which he alludes. Whence it is manifest, that his reflections allude to other heretics beside the Gnostics; unless indeed you will choose to say, that some of the Gnostics had a principal share in this Unitarian blasphemy: which, if you should affirm, you will in me have no antagonist. It is indeed my opinion, that the Cerinthian Gnostics were the first who denied the divinity of our Lord. Cerinthus was much earlier than Ebion; and Ebion, in his notions of the Redeemer, seems to have been a mere Cerinthian. But if

---

* Remarks, p. 13.

you concur with me in these opinions, it is little
to your purpose to insist, that Justin Martyr's reflections are levelled only at the Gnostics; since
in the Gnostics, according to this view of their
opinions, he censures the Unitarians. If you
deny, that our Lord's mere humanity was a doctrine maintained by any branch of the Gnostics,
still Justin expressly censures the Unitarians. If
the Ebionites are not mentioned by name, are you
sure they are not included among the [ἄλλοι ἄλλῳ
ὀνόματι] " others of various denominations," thus
generally mentioned after an enumeration of the
principal Gnostic sects. The Ebionæan heresy
was at this time in its infancy, and probably too
inconsiderable to deserve particular notice.

6. Such, Sir, is your apology for your omission,
and such is your defence of your argument. After
this apology, and after this defence, comes in your
appendix a flat denial of the omissions, for which
you have apologized. A friend has told you, that
the passage of Justin is entire, and in its proper
place in your letters to me, page 81.* It is true,
Sir, the passage is entire, in the Greek in the
margin of your book. But has your friend told
you, that it is entire in your translation? My
learned ally complains, and indeed, Sir, with too

---

* Appendix to Remarks.

much reason, that you .write for the unlearned.
The entire passage, as long as it appears not in
your translation, lay innocently enough in the
Greek, at the bottom of your page.

7. To your argument from the apostle's creed,
as recited by Tertullian,* it might, Sir, be a
sufficient reply, that Jesus Christ is mentioned in
it as the Son of God ; a title which, in the sense
in which it was constantly expounded and understood, reprobates the Unitarian heresy. But my
learned ally refers you † to another creed, produced by Tertullian in the book, *De Præscrip-
tione, &c.* in which the divinity of Christ is more
explicitly asserted. This you say is not simply a
creed, but an exposition of the creed,‡ and expresses no more than Tertullian's own faith."§
Tertullian himself, Sir, " was of another opinion.
He calls this exposition a rule of faith appointed
by Christ. He says, it expressed the general
faith, which was . disputed by none but heretics."
After this, Sir, will you say, that " Tertullian did
not consider Unitarians as excluded from the
name and assemblies of Christians ?"‖

---

* Letters to Dr Horsley, p. 27, 28.
† Monthly Review for January, 1784, p. 60.
‡ Remarks, &c. p. 18.
§ Ibid. p. 21.
‖ Letters to Dr Horsley, p. 27.

8. Clemens Alexandrinus, who makes frequent mention of heretics, hath been very silent, you think, about the Ebionites. Hence, you seem desirous to infer, that Clemens thought them not heretical. "Almost the whole," these are your words, "Almost the whole of his seventh book of *Stromata,* relate to that subject [heresies]. He mentions fourteen different heresiarchs by name, and ten heresies by character; but none of them bear any relation to the Ebionites, or any species of Unitarians."[*] Indeed, Sir, it was not without reason, that I complained, in my former publication, of the peculiarities of your style. I hope, that the great work which you are preparing upon the subject of our present controversy, will be accompanied with a glossary, to explain the words of the English language, upon which you shall be pleased to impose new senses: and that in particular, you will not omit to inform your readers, how much of a thing may be meant by the WHOLE, in your new phraseology.

9. I find, Sir, by the best computation I can form upon a single example, which I am sensible must be liable to great inaccuracies, I speak therefore under the correction of your authoritative decision—but by the best computation I can

---

[*] Letters to Dr Horsley, p. 118.

form, the WHOLE may be any part of a thing not
less than a forty-eighth. I beg your pardon—I
had written this, when turning back to the errata,
at the beginning of your book, I there find, that
you have been yourself very properly shocked at
the extravagant hyperbolism of your own expressions; and for the words *almost the whole*, you
advise the reader to substitute these, *a great part*.
Sir, a reluctant and imperfect retractation is more
unseemly than the first error, be it ever so enormous. If you would not be thought to impose
upon your reader's ignorance, or to presume upon
his inattention, you must correct again; and for
a great, bid him read *a very little part*. The
seventh book of the *Stromata*, in Sylburgius's edition, which I use as most convenient for my present purpose, because the pages, not incumbered
with notes, all contain equal quantities of text:
in this edition the seventh book, Greek and Latin,
fills 48 pages. The general subject of the book
is the excellence of Christian Knowledge in preference to Philosophy. This argument fills more
than 38 pages of the 48, that is, more than three-
fourths of the whole book, without any mention
of heretics. Then the author answers an objection to the certainty of Christian knowledge,
taken from the differences of opinion that subsisted among the different sects. This introduces a
general invective against heretics, and a dissuasive
of heresy, drawn from general topics, not from

the enormities of particular sects; which fills eight pages more. The dissuasive of heresy, leads to an argument for the authority of the church upon the footing of antiquity: and this introduces the names of some remarkable heresies, which are mentioned for no other purpose, but to shew that the very denominations, which they bore, argued a late origin, singularity of opinion, and separation from a more ancient society. This list, with many interspersed remarks upon the origin of each sect, and assertions of the unity of the true church, fills perhaps three-fourths of one of the two remaining pages of the book: for the last page is taken up with a whimsical explanation of the Levitical marks of clean and unclean beasts; which are supposed to be types of the good and bad qualities of true Christians and of heretics. Thus it appears, that that great part of the seventh book of the *Stromata*, which you had well nigh mistaken for the whole, is somewhat less than one part in forthy-eight.

10. But the Ebionites have no place in that long list of heretics, which occupies almost the whole, or, to speak more accurately, a great part, or, to speak exactly, almost a forty-eighth part of the seventh book of the *Stromata*.* I think in-

---

* Letters to Dr Horsley, p. 118.

deed they have not, unless they be included, which I suspect may be the case, among the Peratic heretics. But I will grant that they are omitted. Is it, Sir, a consequence, that Clemens thought their opinions indifferent? I cannot see the necessity of this conclusion, unless indeed it had been of importance to the argument of Clemens, that he should make an exact enumeration of all the sects, which he deemed heretical: but this was not the case. A few instances sufficed for the illustration of his reasoning; and these, in a discussion with Greek philosophers, he would naturally select from those heresies, which, for something of subtlety and refinement in their doctrine, were the most likely to have attracted the notice of the Gentiles. A sect, which lived in obscurity in the north of Galilee, of no consideration for number, learning, or abilities, was likely to be the last that he would mention.

11. It is another circumstance which you urge, Sir, in favour of the early Unitarians, that it is confessed by Jerome, that the Ebionites were anathematised, not for their Unitarian opinions, but for their rigid adherence to the Mosaic law,* ——*propter hoc solum a patribus anathematizati*

---

* Letters to Dr Horsley, p. 34.

*sunt, quod legis cærimonias Christi evangelio mis-
cuerunt.*

12. I shall frankly confess, Sir, that if nothing
more were known either of the Ebionites or Cerinthians, from ecclesiastical history, than what
might be gathered from this sentence of Jerome,
I should be apt to conclude, that the single error
of either sect was this: that they judaized. The
words however are capable of another meaning;
namely, that the Judaic superstition was a thing
so criminal in the judgment of the primitive Christians, as to constitute, *by itself,* one very sufficient
reason for the excommunication of the sects which
were addicted to it. For it is to be observed, that
the Ebionites are coupled in this passage with the
Cerinthians. It is said of both, that " for this
single thing they were anathematised, that they
mixed the ceremonies of the law, with the gospel
of Christ." This being said of both without distinction, must be said of either in some sense in
which it may be true of both: and if it acquit the
Ebionites of heresy, except in the single article of
their Judaism, it equally acquits the Cerinthians.
If it be to be concluded from these expressions of
Jerome, that to deny our Lord's divinity was no
heresy in the Ebionites; it is equally to be concluded from these same expressions, that to deny
that God was the Creator of the universe, was no
heresy in the Cerinthians. If this passage of Je-

rome be no testimony in favour of the Cerinthian doctrine about the creation, it is no testimony in favour of the Ebionæan doctrine about our Lord. It is lame and defective, like every other testimony which you have produced to the same purpose; and your opinion, that the primitive Unitarians were not considered as heretics, I must still, Sir, in defiance of all your testimonies, take the liberty to place among the extravagant assertions of Daniel Zuicker, of which Simon Episcopius was the charitable but insufficient advocate.

I am, &c.

POSTSCRIPT.

You are pleased, Sir, to say in the conclusion of your third letter, that the Unitarian doctrine, even in its most obnoxious form, existed in the very time of the apostles. I deny that the Unitarian doctrine existed at that time, in the most obnoxious form. Produce your indisputable evidence. Observe that by the most obnoxious form, I understand that form, which excludes the worship of Christ.

N. B. In answer to Dr Priestley's argument from the writings of Irenæus in particular, see the Third of the Supplemental Disquisitions.

LETTER ELEVENTH.

In Reply to Dr Priestley's fourth, in which he defends his argu-
ment from a passage in Athanasius.—The sense of the words
ἀιδια ιυλογος mistaken by Dr Priestley.—The sense of the word
συνεσις mistaken by Dr Priestley.—Prudence and caution not
synonymous.—The matter of fact, as represented by Athana-
sius, mistaken by Dr Priestley.—His grammatical argument
refuted.—That Athanasius speaks of unconverted Jews, proved
from a comparison of the two clauses in which Jews are men-
tioned.—The Gentiles not uninterested in questions about the
Messiah.—Of deference to authorities.

DEAR SIR,

A SUPPOSED testimony of Athanasius made a
principal branch of your original proof, that the
faith of the first Christians was Unitarian; and
this, with other principal branches of your proof,
found a place among my specimens of your evidence, of which it was the third in order. For
this testimony of Athanasius, you refer your reader to Athanasius's defence of the Alexandrine
Dionysius, where you think you find a confession
of two very important circumstances: that the
apostles used great caution in divulging the doctrine of the proper divinity of Christ; and that
the occasion of this caution was the prevalency of
a contrary persuasion among the first Hebrew
Christians.

2. In opposition to this, I took upon me to assure the reverend assembly which I had the honour to address, that no mention of the caution of the apostles, or of the heterodoxy of the first Jewish Christians, is to be found in the defence of Dionysius—I believe I might have added, in any part of the writings of Athanasius.

3. You have now, Sir, in your fourth letter, produced the passage, from the defence of Dionysius, in which you conceive that these important secrets are betrayed. This passage, you say, you " only abridged before."* (I am sorry, Sir, to remind you, that the manner in which your abridgments are managed, has appeared in other instances.) You abridged it before, but now you " give a larger portion of it at full length :" not the whole, by your own confession; " for the whole is much too long to transcribe." Pardon me, Sir, if I add, that the whole, were it transcribed, would justify the summary which I have given of it in my Charge: it would prove, that the example of the apostles is alleged for the purpose which I assign, and in the manner which I mention: it would prove, therefore, that this " larger portion," which you have given " at full length," is nothing to your purpose. But to bring

---

* Letters to Dr Horsley, p. 39.

the matter to a short issue, I will set the general scope of the discourse quite out of the question. I will take the particular portion, which you have produced, by itself, as you desire it should be taken: and I will shew, that even thus taken, it will give no support to your assertions, without a singular construction of certain words and phrases, which cannot be admitted.

4. The apostles, it is said, spake of Christ as a man; a man of Nazareth; a man obnoxious to sufferings. Was it that the apostles were in the sentiments of Arius? No such thing. " But this they did, as wise master-builders and stewards of the mysteries of God; and they had this specious pretence for it ————."* Stop, Sir, a moment. What do I hear? A specious pretence for it! For what? For doing as wise master-builders and stewards of the mysteries of God. Are specious pretences needed then for wise conduct? Or were the apostles men to make pretences? Surely this is the language of Dr Priestley, not of Athanasius. He thought more reverently of the apostles. Let him speak for himself. Καὶ τὴν αἰλίαν ἱχυσιν ἰυλογον. Is *pretence* the sense of αἰλία? The true Greek word for *pretence* is προφασις. And even had this word been used, the adjective ἰυλογος would have carried it

---

* Letters to Dr Horsley, p. 39.

away from that base meaning, which is inseparable from the English words *specious pretence.*
For ιυλογος is not *specious* in the English sense.   It
may be applied to any thing *in quo species cerni-
tur honesti;* but it is not mere seeming.   Had
Athanasius meant to'say, that the apostles had a
specious pretence only for their conduct, the adjective must have been πιθανος. He must have said,
και προφασιν τινα ισχον πιθανην.   Or, και ουκ απιθανον τινα ισχον
προφασιν.

5. The word αιτια hath two principal senses: a
philosophical and a popular.   Either of the two
may suit this place.   Amongst the philosophers it
signifies a cause, in any one of the four kinds of
causes; the material, the efficient, the formal, or
the final.   Hence it comes to signify a motive,
motives being final causes considered in their relation to the mind of a rational agent. Thus
Plato, speaking of the Creator's motive for a particular arrangement of the heavenly bodies, τα δ'
αλλα, οι δη και δι ας 'ΑΙΤΙΑΣ ιδρυσατο, ειτις επιξιοι πασας, &c. *in
Timæo.* Again, δια δη την ΑΙΤΙΑΝ και τον λογισμον τονδε ιν
ολον εξ απαιλων ——ιτεκληρατο. *in Timæo.* A motive may
be either good or bad, but αιτια ιυλογος can be only
good. It must be a wise and honourable motive;
or, in plain English, *a good reason.*

6. Αιτια, in the rhetorical or popular sense, answers to the English word *cause,* in its forensic

meaning. It signifies an action or suit at law, or a criminal indictment. In this sense αἰτία εὔλογος is a cause fairly defensible, upon a just and honourable plea. I am inclined to prefer this sense of the word in this place, because the verb ἔχουσι is in the present time, when the preceding and the following, are in the past. " If the conduct of the apostles should be at any time questioned, they have a fair and substantial plea." This may still be expressed in English by *a good reason*. This therefore is the proper English phrase to convey the holy father's meaning, whether αἰτία be taken in its philosophical, or in its popular sense.

7. Now, Sir, if for *specious pretence* you will be pleased to substitute *good reason*, you will find that this passage, even in your own translation, will afford no ground for the inferences you would build upon it. Athanasius proceeds to shew what this good reason was; and he commends the great sagacity, which was displayed in the conduct of the apostles.

8. The deficiencies of your translation, I must however confess, are abundantly compensated in your comment. " I now have produced the passage, you say, and have pointed out a word, *viz.* συνεσις, which, in the connexion in which it stands, can bear no other sense than caution, and great

caution; μila πολλης συνισιως ———."* Sir, may I ask in what lexicon (you must excuse me if I suspect that you are used to take the senses of Greek words from ordinary lexicons) in what lexicon, good or bad, have you found that συνσις, in any connexion may stand for *caution?* It is literally the meeting or coming together of different things; and applied to the mind, it is properly that faculty, or that act of the mind, by which it brings things together, and compares them, and forms a ready judgment of fitnesses and discongruities. It is expounded by the ancient Greek lexicographers, who best understood their own language, to be the " knowledge of comparables and incomparables; or a ready following of the mind quickly bringing together the notions of things, readily discovering what is proper and beseeming to each."† Plato says more concisely, συνιναι means that the mind *goes along* with things.‡ *Sagacity* is the English word, which most nearly renders the same idea. *Prudence,* the word which you have used in your translation, may be born, but the idea, which it gives, is rather similar, than the same. You have shewn, you say, " from the whole tenor of the discourse, that Athanasius could have intended nothing else than to describe

---

* Letters to Dr Horsley, p. 45.
† See Phavorinus.   ‡ In Cratylo.

their prudence, or extreme caution."* *Prudence,
or extreme caution!* Do you really think, Sir, that
prudence and caution in the English language are
synonymous? If that be your opinion, I must beg
that one or both of these words may go into the
glossary,† and be declared equivalent. *Caution*
is indeed sometimes used abusively for *discretion;*
but in its proper sense it carries with it the notion
of some dishonest art: and caution, in a teacher
or disputant, always denotes an artful provision
by some dishonest reserve, for the success of doctrine or of argument. In the present case, if you
use the word without affixing to it the notion of
concealment, it will not serve your purpose. But
nothing of concealment is implied in the Greek
word. Athanasius extols the sagacity of the
apostles: their caution he never mentions.

9. Still you will insist that he describes the
thing, though he may not have called it by its
proper name. "He evidently, you say, does not
represent them as deferring the communication of
the doctrine of the divinity of Christ, on account
of its being more conveniently taught afterwards,
as part of a system of faith; but only lest it
should have given offence to the Jews."‡ I cannot
read this sentence without astonishment, when I

---

* Letters to Dr Horsley, p. 45.   † See page 207.
‡ Letters to Dr Horsley, p. 45.

turn back to the quotation, and find that you have fairly produced the passage, in which Athanasius, in your own translation as well as in the original, affirms, that what related to our Lord's humanity was taught *first*, for no other reason, but that the doctrine of his divinity might be taught *afterwards* with more effect. The desire of instructing the Jews, not the fear of offending them, was the motive with the apostles for propounding first what was the easiest to be understood, and the most likely to be admitted.

10. But whatever the motive may have been with the apostles, for their conduct, you insist that the fact was, that the doctrine of the Trinity was not divulged by them: and of this you think you find a proof in this passage of Athanasius; in which you think it is confessed, that the apostles in the opening of their ministry, were very reserved upon this article; and you observe, and I think not improperly, that the reasons for that reserve (if they ever subsisted) would operate till within a short time of the dispersion and death of the apostles. Whence you conclude, that if ever they divulged this doctrine, it must have been at so late a period, that the church, in consequence of their former silence upon the subject, must have been fixed in the contrary persuasion.[*]

---

[*] Letters to Dr Horsley, p. 42—44.

11. But what if the foundation of this whole argument should be rotten? What if the whole should be built on a misinterpretation of Athanasius? Athanasius affirms not, that the apostles, in any period of their ministry, kept the doctrine of our Lord's divinity a secret: or that they were reserved upon this or any article of faith, with those who were so far converted as to be catechumens. In their first public sermons, addressed to the unbelieving multitude, they were content to maintain, that Jesus, whom the Jews had crucified, was risen from the dead; without touching his divinity otherwise than in remote allusions. But to suppose that they carried their converts no greater length, is to suppose that their private instruction was not more particular than their public. For this you will find little support in Athanasius; or in Chrysostom; who is called upon to corroborate the argument from the concessions of Athanasius.

12. But whatever the doctrine of the apostles might be, or whatever opinion Athanasius, or Chrysostom might entertain concerning it, Athanasius, it seems, acknowledges that the first Jewish Christians were Unitarians. Οἱ τότε Ἰουδαῖοι, "The Jews of that time," or, "The then Jews," is the name, by which the persons are described, who are said to have holden the erroneous belief of the mere humanity of the Messiah. Now, Sir, if

" The then Jews," Οι τότε Ιουδαιοι, may denote Jewish
Christians, will you be pleased to inform me,
what more precise expressions the holy father
might have found in the whole compass .of the
Greek language, to denote genuine Jewish Jews,
had he had occasion to mention them? But the
verbs, it seems, " in that part of the passage which
mentions *Christ being come of the seed of David,*
and the *word being made flesh,* are. not in the *future tense.*"* In this remark, Sir, I cannot but
admire the singular *caution* of .the expression.
" The verbs——are not in the future tense." It
is true, they are not. But the most important of
these verbs, in that part of the passage which
mentions the Messiah's coming, although it be
not in the future form, carries a future signification. It is in the infinitive mood of the present
tense; which often denotes an instant futurity,
but never denotes time either long since, or just
now, past. This obtains in all the Greek verbs,
but particularly in the verb ἐρχομαι; which, not
only by use, but naturally involves a notion of
futurity even in the present tense. Ενομιζον τον Χριστον
ψιλον ανθρωπον μονον——ιεχεσθαι. " They thought the
Christ was *a-coming* as a mere man only." This
expression refers to the Messiah not as come,
but as coming. Another verb, I confess, which

---

* Letters to Dr Horsley, p. 42.

relates to the incarnation of the Word, is in a preterite tense. *ὐδι ὅτι λογος σαρξ ἐγινιλο ἐπισιυον.* "Neither believed they, that the word *was made* flesh." *ὁ λογος σαρξ ἐγινιλο,* "the word was made flesh," these are the words in which St John mentions the incarnation. The holy father, it is likely, chose to use the very words of the evangelist, in speaking of this mystery; and for that reason, he may have sacrificed somewhat of the accuracy of his syntax to the exactness of his quotation. The passage should be printed thus: *ὐδι* "*ὅτι ὁ λογος σαρξ ἐγινιλο*" *ἐπισιυον.* In this grammatical argument your *prudence* appears, not only in the very guarded expressions, in which you have stated it; but in the declaration, with which it is prefaced, that you desire to lay no great stress upon it. What you have respect to in this passage "is the obvious general tenor and spirit of it."* Indeed, Sir, you would do well to be cautious, upon all occasions, how you handle these briars of criticism. Let us return then to the general tenor of the passage.

13. You know, Sir, that Jews are twice mentioned in it. "The Jews of that age being deceived themselves, and having deceived the Gentiles." And again, "——the blessed apostles ——taught what related to the humanity of our

---

* Letters to Dr Horsley, p. 42.

Saviour to the Jews." Is it your opinion, Sir,
that they are the same or different persons, who
are mentioned under the name of Jews, in these
two different clauses? If they are different persons, I desire to know, what circumstance or note
of difference you find in the author's expressions?
If you find none, on what is your opinion of a difference founded? Or not to entangle you again in
grammatical disquisitions, I will for a moment suppose the persons different, and desire you to shew
me, what will then be the sense or coherence of
the writer's argument. If you allow that the
same persons are designed in both places under
the same name; I must desire you to remark, that
the Jews, mentioned in the second instance, were
persons who were " at any rate to be persuaded
(*at any rate,* that is the force of ὅλως, which you
have erroneously rendered by the word *fully*) at
any rate to be persuaded, from the actual state of
things, and from the evidence of the miracles
which had been wrought, that the Christ was
come."* Could these, Sir, be converted Jews?
Could they be already Christians, in whom this general persuasion, " that the Christ was come," was
yet to be wrought? Wanting this persuasion they
were clearly Jews, whose conversion was not yet
begun: and of the same description, since they

---

* Ἱνα ὅλως πεισαιλες αὐτος ἐκ των φαινομενων και γενομενων σημειων.

were indeed the very same persons, were the
Jews, to whom it is imputed, that they held the
erroneous belief of the Messiah's mere humanity,
and that they spread the like error among the
~~Gentiles.~~

14. But the Gentiles, you say, who were thus
misled, must have been Christian Gentiles; and
by consequence the Jews, who misled them, were
Jewish Christians.* But, Sir, whence is the certainty that Christian Gentiles were intended by
Athanasius? It hangs upon this principle, that to
any other Gentiles the whole doctrine of a Messiah must have been uninteresting.† Have you
forgotten, Sir, have you never known, or would
you deny, what is not denied by candid infidels,
that the expectation of a great deliverer or benefactor of mankind, was universal even in the Gentile
world, about the time of our Lord's appearance?
If you acknowledge this, where is the improbability, that the general opinion concerning this per-
sonage should be modified by the opinions which
prevailed in Judea, which was the centre of the
tradition? especially when it is considered, that
the proselytes of the gate, made an easy channel
of communication between the Jews and the idolatrous Gentiles. But whatever you may be dis-

---

* Letters to Dr Horsley, p. 41.   † Ibid.

posed to grant, or to deny, this argument is easily
inverted, and turned against you. It hath been
shewn, that none but Jew Jews can be intended
by Athanasius, when he speaks of the Jews as
misleaders of the Gentiles. They were Gentile
Gentiles, therefore, who were misled: for, from
unbelieving Jews, Christians of the Gentiles would
hardly take instruction.

15. Your last resource is to flee for shelter to
the authority of Beausobre. "The learned Beausobre, a Trinitarian, and therefore an unexceptionable judge in this case, quoting this very passage, does not hesitate to pronounce, that they
were believing Jews, who were intended by the
writer."* It is for you, Sir, to judge, what deference is due from you to the authority of Beausobre. For my own part—I shall not affect a modesty which I feel not—when the sense of a Greek
sentence is the thing in question, if I have the writer upon my own shelf, or can find him upon my
friend's, it is not much my practice to stand bow-
ing at a distance to authorities; unless indeed it
be the authority of a Casaubon, a Scaliger, or a
Bentley. But these men would laugh, or they
would storm, at your attempts to construe Greek,
with Beausobre at your elbow. To construe

---

* Letters to Dr Horsley, p. 42.

Greek! I fear, Sir, they would think but lightly of your Latin erudition, after the specimen which you have given of it, in your attempt to wrest from my learned ally, his strong argument for the difference, which we assert, in articles of faith, between the Nazarenes and the Ebionites. The feats of criticism, which you have performed for this purpose, upon certain plain words of Jerome,[*] to draw them from the only meaning of which they are capable, had you been a Westminster man, were enough to bring old Busby from his grave. But, alas! Sir, you are not to be persuaded, though one should rise from the dead. I trust our readers are persuaded, that the argument from Athanasius [†] was with great justice and propriety, placed among my specimens of insufficient proof.

I am, &c.

---

[*] Letters to Dr Horsley, p. 152—156.

[†] Of the testimonies of other writers, by which Dr Priestley attempts to confirm his argument from Athanasius, see the tenth of his Second Letters to me, and my Remarks upon his Second Letters, Part II. c. i. sec. 10—14.

LETTER TWELFTH.

*In Reply to Dr Priestley's fifth; in which he moves certain
chronological difficulties.—Himself chiefly concerned to find
the solution.—His question divided.—The divinity of our
Lord preached from the very beginning, by the apostles.—
St Stephen a martyr to this doctrine.—His dying ejaculations
justify the worship of Christ.—Christ deified in the story of
St Paul's conversion.—The divinity of Jesus acknowledged by
the apostles, from the time when they acknowledged him for
the Messiah.—Notions of a Trinity, and of the Deity of the
Messiah, current among the Jews in the days of our Saviour.*

DEAR SIR,

IN your fifth letter, you call upon me to assign
the particular time, when the knowledge of our
Lord's divinity, which, in the persuasion that the
apostles were taxed by the fathers with a reserve
upon the subject, you are pleased to call " the
great secret of Christ being not a mere man, but
the eternal God;"* you call upon me to assign
the time, when this great secret " was communicated first to the apostles, and then by them to
the body of Christians."† You " request my opinion" upon this question, with a certain air of
triumph, which seems to imply, that, in your ap-

---

* Letters to Dr Horsley, p. 55.   † Ibid.

prehension, I must be much at a loss to frame
an opinion upon it, which may be consistent with
my creed. But the truth is, that you are yourself the person most concerned to find the solution. Or, to express myself more accurately, the
question splits into two, of which the one concerns
not me, and the other concerns not either of us.

2. When was the doctrine of our Lord's divinity first published in the church by the apostles?

3. When was the knowledge of the thing first
conveyed to the minds of the apostles themselves?

4. These, Sir, are two distinct questions. Of
the first, it is your concern, not mine, to seek
the solution. For since I have clearly traced the
belief of Christ's proper deity up to the apostolic
age; unless you can assign the particular epocha
of the publication, I have a right to conclude,
that it was a part of the very earliest doctrine.
Nay, if you should even be able to assign some
later time of its commencement, yet since that
time must fall within the compass of the apostolic age, to which you are limited, by virtue of
my proof from the epistle of St Barnabas, a question might indeed arise, which might be of difficult resolution : why was this doctrine, for a certain time, kept back ? But this difficulty would
not shake the credit of the doctrine. For since

there is no reason to suppose, that any of the
apostles, having once received the light of inspiration, was in any future period of his life deprived of it, any doctrine published by them,
claims implicit credit, whatever might be the time
of its first publication.   A discovery that St John
had made, in the last moments of his life, had
been equally to be believed, as any thing that
St Peter preached, in his first sermon, on the day
of Pentecost.   You will therefore choose your
own epocha for the discovery of " the great secret."   Place it, where it best may please you
in the apostolic age ; I will hold no argument with
you upon the subject.   In my own congregations
I shall think it my duty to bear my witness, that
from the very beginning of the gospel, the thing
had been no secret.   For proof from holy writ, I
shall have recourse to those very passages of the
apostolic history, from which you draw the contrary inference.   I shall remind my hearers, that
in St Peter's first public sermon, when it was reasonable to keep to the general assertion, that
Jesus was the Messiah, rather than to enter into
the particulars which that character might involve ;
allusions are nevertheless used, which discover
that the mind of the speaker was strongly impressed with notions, which it was his policy to
conceal.   I shall particularly desire them to remark, that it is said of our Lord Jesus, that " it
was not possible that he should be holden of

death."* The expressions clearly imply a physical impossibility. I shall bid them observe, that the great miracle of that day, is said to be an exertion of the power of Jesus exalted by God's right hand.† And I shall maintain, that the three persons are distinctly mentioned, in a manner which implies the divinity of each, "Jesus—being by the right hand of God exalted, and having received of the Father the promise of the Holy Ghost"‡—of the Father—ταρα τυ ταλψ.—*The Father :* the substantive, with the article prefixed, describes a person, whose character it is to be the Father. Paternity is the property, which individuates the person. But from whom is the first principle thus distinguished? From his creatures? From them he were more significantly distinguished by the name of God. Not generally therefore from his creatures, but particularly from the two other persons mentioned in the same period, Jesus and the Holy Ghost. And since this is his distinction, that he is the Father of that Son, from whom, together with himself, the Holy Ghost proceeds; it follows, that the interval, between him and them, is no more than relation may create; that the whole difference lies in personal distinctions, not in essential qualities. Thus I will ever reason, Sir, for the edification of my

---

* Acts ii. 24.   † Ibid. ii. 32, 33.   ‡ Ibid.

own flock, but with little hope of your conviction from St Peter's first sermon.

5. I shall always insist, Sir, that the blessed Stephen died a martyr to the DEITY of Christ. The accusation against him, you say, was " his speaking blasphemous things against the temple and the law."* You have forgotten to add the charge of blasphemy " against Moses and against God."† The blasphemy against the temple and the law, probably consisted in a prediction, that the temple was to be destroyed, and the ritual law, of course, abolished. The blasphemy against Moses was probably his assertion, that the authority of Moses was inferior to that of Christ. But what could be the blasphemy against God? What was there in the doctrine of the apostles, which could be interpreted as blasphemy against God, except it was this, that they ascribed divinity to one who had suffered publicly as a malefactor. That this was the blessed Stephen's crime, none can doubt, who attends to the conclusion of the story. He " looked up stedfastly into heaven," says the inspired historian, " and saw the glory of God," [that is, he saw the splendour of the Shechinah, for that is what is meant, when the glory of God is mentioned as something to be seen,]

---

* Letters to Dr Horsley, p. 60.   † Acts vi. 11.

" and Jesus standing on the right hand of God."[*]
He saw the man Jesus in the midst of his divine
light. His declaring what he saw,[†] the Jewish
rabble understood as an assertion of the divinity of
Jesus. They stopped their ears; they overpowe-
red his voice with their own clamours; and they
hurried him out of the city, to inflict upon him
the death which the law appointed for blasphemers.[‡] He died, as he had lived, attesting the
deity of our crucified Master. His last breath
was uttered in a prayer to Jesus, first for himself,
and then for his murderers. " They stoned Stephen calling upon *God*, and saying, Lord Jesus
receive my spirit—and he cried with a loud voice,
Lord lay not this sin to their charge."[§] It is to
be noted, that the word *God* is not in the original text, which might be better rendered, thus:
" They stoned Stephen, invocating and saying,
&c." Jesus therefore was the God, whom the dying martyr invocated in his last agonies; when
men are apt to pray, with the utmost seriousness,
to him whom they conceive the mightiest to save.

6. It seems the holy Stephen, full, as we are informed he was, in those trying moments, of the
Holy Ghost, was not in the opinion, which you
are pleased to impute to me; but you will observe,

---

* Acts vii. 55.   † Ibid. 56.   ‡ Ibid. 57, 58.   § Ibid. 59, 60.

that I disclaim it, that " the proper object of prayer is God the Father."* This, you tell me, I cannot but acknowledge. That the Father is *a* proper object of prayer, God forbid that ever I should not acknowledge. That he is *the* proper object, in the sense in which you seem to make the assertion, in prejudice and exclusion of the other persons, God forbid that ever I should concede. I deny not, that there is an honour personally due to him as the Father. There is also an honour personally due to the Son, as the Son; and to the Spirit, as the Spirit. But our knowledge of the personal distinctions is so obscure, in comparison of our apprehension of the general attributes of the Godhead, that it should seem that the Divinity [the το Θειον] is rather to be generally worshipped in the three persons jointly and indifferently, than that any distinct honours are to be offered to each separately. Prayer, however, for succour against external persecution, seems addressed with particular propriety to the Son.

7. When you deny, not only that any precept, but that any proper example is to be found in Scripture, to authorise the practice,† you seem to have forgotten, beside many other passages, the initial salutations of St Paul's epistles. St Ste-

---

* Letters to Dr Horsley, p. 81.   † Ibid.

phen's "short ejaculatory address" you had not
forgotten; but you say, " it is very inconsiderable."* But, Sir, why is it inconsiderable? Is it
because it was only an ejaculation? Ejaculations
are often prayers of the most fervent kind; the
most expressive of self-abasement and adoration.
Is it for its brevity that it is inconsiderable? What
then is the precise length of words, which is requisite to make a prayer an act of worship? Was
this petition preferred on an occasion of distress,
on which a Divinity might be naturally invoked?
Was it a petition for a succour, which none but a
Divinity could grant? If this was the case, it was
surely an act of worship. Is the situation of the
worshipper the circumstance, which in your judgment, Sir, lessens the authority of his example?
You suppose perhaps some consternation of his faculties, arising from distress and fear. The history
justifies no such supposition. It describes the utterance of the final prayer, as a deliberate act of one
who knew his situation, and possessed his understanding. After praying for himself, he kneels
down, to pray for his persecutors: and such was
the composure with which he died, although the
manner of his death was the most tumultuous and
terrifying, that, as if he had expired quietly upon
his bed, the sacred historian says, that " he fell
asleep."† If therefore you would insinuate, that

---

* Letters to Dr Horsley, p. 81.   † Acts vii. 60

St Stephen was not himself, when he sent forth this "short ejaculatory address to Christ," the history refutes you. If he was himself, you cannot justify his prayer to Christ, while you deny that Christ is God, upon any principle that might not equally justify you, or me, in praying to the blessed Stephen. If St Stephen, in the full possession of his faculties, prayed to him who is no God; why do we reproach the pious Romanist, when he chaunts the litany of his saints? If the persuasion of Christ's divinity prompted the holy martyr's dying prayer; then there is no room to doubt, but that the assertion of Christ's divinity was the blasphemy, for which the Jews, hardened in their unbelief, condemned him.

8. Another instance, to which I ever shall appeal, of an early preaching of our Lord's divinity, though it may not conduce to your conviction, is the story of St Paul's conversion: in which, as it is twice related by himself, Jesus is deified in the highest terms. I know not, Sir, in what light this transaction may appear to you. To me, I confess, it appears to have been a repetition of the scene at the bush, heightened in terror and solemnity. Instead of a lambent flame appearing to a solitary shepherd amid the thickets of the wilderness, the full effulgence of the Shechinah, overpowering the splenduor of the mid-day sun, bursts upon the commissioners of the sanhedrim, on the

public road to Damascus, within a small distance of the city. Jesus speaks, and is spoken to, as the Divinity inhabiting that glorious light. Nothing can exceed the tone of authority on the one side, the submission and religious dread upon the other. The recital of this story seems to have been the usual prelude to the apostle's public apologies; but it only proved the means of heightening the resentment of his incredulous countrymen.

9. These instances, Sir, will bear me out in the assertion, that our Lord's divinity was preached from the very beginning, till you can fix the first discovery to some latter epocha. I am therefore, not at all concerned in the solution of your first question.

10. The second, " when was the knowledge of our Lord's divinity first imparted to the minds of the apostles?" is wholly insignificant, and uninteresting to all parties. It concerns not me; because, with my notions of inspiration, I am obliged to believe what the inspired apostles taught, however late the time might be when they themselves received their information. It concerns not you; because with your notions of inspiration, you are at liberty to dispute what the inspired apostles taught, whatever pretensions they may have to the earliest information. If the knowledge was infallible which they received from inspiration, it

matters not how late; if not infallible, it matters not how early they received it. If no positive proof were extant, that the deity of Christ was an article of faith among the first Christians; the difficulty of assigning the precise time, when the apostles were first made acquainted with it, might be something of an objection against the antiquity of the doctrine, and against its truth. But in opposition to direct proof, the objection, were it founded, could have no weight.

11. Upon this question therefore, as the former, you must not take it amiss if I leave you to yourself. Choose any time, within the compass of each apostle's life, for the epocha of his illumination. I will hold no argument upon the subject; although I have an opinion upon the question, as upon the former, which I ever shall inculcate in my own congregation: and this, Sir, happens to be the very reverse of that, which you imagine I must allow. "You must allow," you say to me, "that at first the apostles were wholly ignorant of this."* *At first* indeed, before their acquaintance with our Lord, or at least with the Baptist, they were ignorant, I believe, of every thing. But from their first acknowledgment of our Lord as the Messiah, they equally acknowledged his divinity. Their faith,

* Letters to Dr Horsley, p. 56.

I believe, was but unsettled, as their notions of the Messiah's kingdom were certainly very confused, till the descent of the Holy Ghost. But so far as they believed in Jesus as the Messiah, in the same degree they understood and acknowledged his divinity. The proof, which I have to produce of this from holy writ, consists of too many particulars, to be distinctly enumerated in the course of our present correspondence. I shall mention two, which to any but a decided Unitarian, will be very striking: Nathaniel's first profession, and Peter's consternation at the miraculous draught of fishes. It was in Nathaniel's very first interview with our Lord, that he exclaimed, " Rabbi, thou art the Son of God! thou art the king of Israel!"* And this declaration was drawn from Nathaniel by some particulars in our Lord's discourse, which he seems to have interpreted as indications of Omniscience. When Simon Peter saw the number of fishes taken at a single draught, when the net was cast at our Lord's command, after a night of fruitless toil, " he fell down at the knees of Jesus, saying, depart from me, for I am a sinful man, O Lord."† Peter's consternation was evidently of the same sort, of which we read in the worthies of earlier ages, upon any extraordinary appearance of the light of the Shechinah, which was founded on a

---

* John i, 49.   † Luke v. 8.

notion, that a sinful mortal might not *see God and live.* These, and many other passages of the evangelical history, discover that our Lord's associates, although it was not till after his ascension that the Holy Ghost led them into all truth, had an early apprehension of something more than human in his character. Nor indeed were early intimations of it wanting: in the first annunciation of his birth, by the angelic host; in the Baptist's declarations; and in our Lord's own assertions of a power to forgive sins, and of an authority to dispense with ordinances of divine appointment; and in his claim to be the proper Son of God, which the unbelieving Jews ever understood as an express deification of his own person.

12. But Judas Iscariot, you think, " could not possibly have formed a deliberate purpose of betraying our Lord,"* had the belief of his divinity been general among the apostles before his crucifixion. Or had any such pretension been set up, which had not gained belief, Judas would have taken advantage of the imposition, and would have made a discovery of it, to the prejudice of our Lord. It should seem, Sir, that you think your own cause almost desperate, if you would desire that Judas Iscariot should be admitted as an evi-

---

* Letters to Dr Horsley, p. 58.

dence for you, or as an advocate. But what if your cause should turn out to be, what Judas Iscariot himself would scruple to undertake. I would not willingly be the apologist of that traitor. But I am inclined to think, that, traitor as he was, his intentions went not to the mischief which he effected. It was rather perhaps his meaning, to cheat the chief priests of their money, than actually to sell his Master's life. When he bargained to lead them, for a certain sum, to the place of our Lord's retirement, he thought, perhaps, that he might safely trust to his Master's power, to repel any attack upon his person. This is very consistent with a belief of our Lord's divinity; as the most dishonourable designs are often found to consist with the truest speculative principles. That he meant not the mischief which ensued, may be presumed, from the remorse which followed, and the vengeance which in despair he executed upon himself. But I care little about his testimony. Only, I think, that, with the devils he might believe and tremble, and trembling, might be still a devil.

13. After all, Sir, I might have spared so particular an answer as I have given to your fifth letter. In the conclusion of it, you furnish me with a short reply, of which I might have availed myself. " Had there been any pretence, you say, for imagining that the Jews in our Saviour's time had

any knowledge of the doctrine of the Trinity, and that they expected the second person in it, in the character of their Messiah, the question I propose to you would have been needless."* Then, Sir, the question which you propose to me, is needless. The Jews, in Christ's days, had notions of a Trinity in the Divine nature. They expected the second person, whom they called the Logos, to come as the Messiah. For the proof of these assertions, I refer you to the work of the learned Dr Peter Allix, entitled, *The Judgment of the Ancient Jewish Church against the Unitarians.* A work, which it is to be hoped, Sir, you will carefully *look through*, before you send abroad your intended view of the doctrine of the first ages concerning Christ.† That you will be convinced by Dr Allix's proof, I have indeed little hope. I shall produce, however, another authority, to which you will perhaps be more inclined to pay regard : the authority of a learned Unitarian of the last century, who wrote in vindication of a former Unitarian work, of great fame, called, *The Naked Gospel.* The Naked Gospel, you know, was printed at Oxford, in the year 1690, and was burnt the same year, by order of the convocation. The anonymous author of the *Historical Vindication*, was

---

* Letters to Dr Horsley, p. 64.
† Preface to Letters, p. xviii.

supposed to be Le Clerc. He it is, who says in his preface, that the Platonic enthusiasm crept first into the Jewish, afterwards into the Christian church. Then he tells his readers how the Jews picked up their Platonism. Of which, he says, the principal doctrines were two: the one, that of the preexistence of souls; the other, that of the Divine Trinity. These, he says, were the opinions of the Jews in the days of our Saviour and his apostles: and hence, perhaps, it hath come to pass, that, as the learned have observed, certain Platonic phrases and expressions are to be found in the New Testament, especially in St John's Gospel. You, Sir, and this Unitarian brother, seem to agree but ill in your notions of the doctrine of the first ages. He thought the doctrine of the Trinity one of the ancient corruptions of Judaism; which, in laying the foundations of Christianity, the heaven-taught builders some how or other forget to do away. You have discovered, that every notion of the Trinity, whatever may be fancied with respect to more ancient times, was obliterated from the minds of the Jews, in our Saviour's time."[*] I believe, Sir, I shall never sit down to the task, which you desire me to undertake,—a translation of the works of Bishop Bull.[†] For as his argument is not for the unlearned, the labour would

---

[*] Letters to Dr Horsley, p. 64.   [†] Ibid. p. 113.

be thrown away. A work which might be more generally edifying, and in which I might engage, if it were not that I really grudge every moment which I give to controversy, would be,—a harmony of the Unitarian divines.

14. You will ask me, whence was the offence which the assertion of our Lord's divinity, by my own confession, gave the Jewish people, if divinity made a part of their own notion of the Messiah's character? I answer, the deification of the Messiah was not that which gave offence, but the assertion that a crucified man was that divine person; and before his crucifixion, the meanness of his birth gave an offence, less in degree, but of the same kind.

I am, &c.

LETTER THIRTEENTH.

In Reply to Dr Priestley's sixth.—Dr Priestley's ignorance of the true principles of Platonism, appears in his disquisitions concerning matter and spirit.—The equality and unity of the three principles of the Platonists.—Dr Priestley's peculiar sense of the word PERSONIFICATION, *not perceived either by the archdeacon, or the reviewer.—The outline, however, of Dr Priestley's work not misrepresented by the archdeacon.—The conversion of an attribute into a substance, differs not from a creation out of nothing.—Never taught by the Platonists.— The eternity of the Logos independent of any supposed eternity of the world.—Not discarded therefore by the converted Platonists.—Dr Priestley's arguments from the analogy between the divine Logos and human reason, answered.—The archdeacon abides by his assertion, that Dr Priestley hath misrepresented the Platonic language.—The archdeacon's interpretation of the Platonists rests not on his own conjecture, but on the authority of Athenagoras.—Confirmed by other authorities.—Dr Priestley's quotations from Tertullian, considered.—From Lactantius.*

DEAR SIR,

You must forgive me, if I confess to you, that so long since as when I first read your disquisitions concerning matter and spirit, I formed no very high opinion of your learning in the Platonic philosophy. What gave me my first suspicion, as I well remember, was a surprise which you express, that a certain French writer should speak of the idea of a circle as itself not round,* and of the ideas of extended things as not extended. Your apprehension, that ideas could not be divisible, unless they were extended,† heightened my suspicion; which became something more than suspicion when I found you speaking of the soul's need of *a repository for her ideas‡ especially during sleep;* as if ideas were things to be locked up, with our china, in a cupboard. Dr Priestley, I said to myself, confounds ideas with the impressions of external objects, on the material sensory: which impressions are in truth as much external to the mind, as the objects which make them. What pity, that he hath not been more conversant with the Platonists! These previous indications, of your deficiency in this branch of learning, in some measure prepared me for what I was to find in your *History of the Philosophical Doctrine concerning the soul;* insomuch, that I read your assertion, that " Plato's philosophy was the oriental system, with very little variation,"§ without indignation; because I considered it as the reproach of an enemy, whom better information might make a friend. I was indeed surprised at your want of information in this particular instance; because Mosheim, whose

---

* Disquisitions, p. 39.
‡ Ibid. p. 79, 93.
† Ibid. p. 37, 38.
§ Ibid. p. 274.

authority as an historian, you seem to hold in due
respect, indisposed, as he is in general, to be partial to the Platonists, hath however so far done
them justice, as to point out the total discordance
in principle at least, between the sober philosophy of Plato, and the extravagancies of the Gnostics; whose principles were those of the oriental
system. After this, Sir, it gives me no surprise
at all, that you should now assert, " that it was
never imagined that the three component members of the Platonic Trinity, are either equal to
each other, or, strictly speaking, one."* They are,
Sir, more strictly speaking, one, than any thing
in nature of which unity may be predicated. No
one of them can be supposed without the other
two. The second and third being, the first is necessarily supposed; and the first (Αγαθον) being,
the second and third, (Νας & Ψυχη) must come
forth. Concerning their equality, I will not say
that the Platonists have spoken with the same accuracy which the Christian fathers use; but they
include the three principles in the Divine nature,
in the το Θειον; and this notion implies the same
equality, which we maintain; at the same time I
confess, that the circumstance of their equality
was not always strictly adhered to by the younger
Platonists, for reasons which I have explained.†

---

* Letters to Dr Horsley, p. 99.　　† See Charge V. sec. 5.

2. The want of perspicuity is a fault in writing, of which indeed, Sir, you are little guilty.
It is the more extraordinary, that your *personification* of the Logos should not be distinctly understood, either by myself, or by my learned ally.
For my own part, I confess, I had not the least
apprehension, that you used the word *personification* in any other than its usual sense; till, in your
reply to the animadversions of my learned ally,
you distinguished between the personification of
the Logos, which you impute to Justin, and the
earlier doctrines of the Gnostics.* By personification, I had no suspicion that you meant any
thing more than a grammatical *prosopopeia;*
which you seemed to think had been used both
by Plato and St John, in speaking of the divine
attribute of wisdom. Certainly, Sir, you express
yourself in your history, as if you thought, that a
literal acceptation of such figured language was the
occasion, that a mere attribute was mistaken for a
real person, first in the academy, and afterwards
in the church: and that this error led to another,
still founded on a literal interpretation of figurative expressions: the expressions in which St
John describes, as you conceive, the extraordinary
degree in which wisdom and power were conferred on Christ, being understood as assertions that

---

* Reply to Monthly Review, for June, sec. 5.

Christ was that very person, which was supposed
to have been previously described by the evangelist, as a branch of the Divinity. I thought, Sir,
that you conceived that a mere grammatical *prosopopeia* had been, in this way, the first step towards
the deification of Christ. Upon looking again into the second section of your history, I see no
great reason to be ashamed of my mistake. I
believe, Sir, that, without the assistance of the
comment, which your Reply to the Monthly Reviewer furnishes, no reader of your work would
discover any other meaning in your expressions.
It seems, however, that the word *personification*,
is a new term of theology, invented by you, for a
doctrine which is also of your own invention,
though you are pleased to give the credit of it to
the Platonic fathers: the doctrine of the conversion of an attribute into a person; which was
supposed, you say, by its first advocates, to take
place immediately before the creation of the
world, but being afterwards " carried farther
back, namely to all eternity, it led to the present
doctrine of the Trinity."* The distinction between this personification of the Logos, and the
earlier doctrines of the Gnostics, is, it seems, an
important feature in the great outline of your
work. The outline of your work, as sketched by

---

* Reply to Monthly Review, for June, p. 34, 35.

yourself, is briefly this.—The exaltation of the person of Jesus Christ began with the Gnostics, who maintained the preexistence of human souls. When their errors were exploded, the personification was adopted.—The Arian doctrine was subsequent to this; and it was after all these, that, from improvements upon the doctrine of personification, the present doctrine of the Trinity was brought out.* It is a heavy accusation against my learned ally and me, that we have not sufficiently attended to these distinctions; and the omission shews, that " we have never formed a right conception of what we undertook to exhibit."†

8. Every writer must be allowed to be the best interpreter of his own expressions. But in the sense in which I am now taught to understand the personification of the Logos, I cannot perceive, Sir, with what propriety it is called the first step towards the deification of Christ; since the doctrines of the Gnostics, which you maintain to be more ancient, had, in your judgment, the same tendency. I am sometimes inclined to suspect, that you are apt yourself to fluctuate between your own and the vulgar sense of personification.

---

* Reply to Monthly Review, for June, p. 34, 35.
† Ibid. p. 35; and Letters to Dr Horsley, p. 66.

4. But although I should allow, that I missed the sense of a particular expression; I am not sensible, that I misconceived, or misrepresented, your account of the ancient opinions. You certainly make the Unitarian doctrine the general opinion of the first Christians. In the second age you allow, that something of divinity was ascribed to Christ; but you think it was a divinity of an inferior kind, including neither necessity, nor eternity, of a distinct personal existence. I therefore misrepresented not the great outline of your work, when I said, that the first race of Christians were, in your opinion, Unitarians in the strictest sense of the word; the second, Arians.* This is the sum of your account, stated not in your words, but in my own. You complain however, that I " have misconceived your idea."† You inform me, that " the Platonizing Christians were not Arians. That it is well known that they were not Arians, but the orthodox who Platonized."‡

5. Sir, I am very sensible that the Platonizers of the second century, were the orthodox of that age. I have not denied this. On the contrary, I have endeavoured to shew, that their Platonism brings no imputation upon their orthodoxy. The

---

* Charge I. sec. 1.　　　† Letters to Dr Horsley, p. 66.
‡ Ibid.

advocates of the Catholic faith, in modern times, have been too apt to take alarm at the charge of Platonism. I rejoice and glory in the opprobrium. I not only confess, but I maintain, not a perfect agreement, but such a similitude, as speaks a common origin, and affords an argument in confirmation of the Catholic doctrine, from its conformity to the most ancient and universal traditions. Nor is this the only article, in which heathen antiquity, however you may slight the argument, by the vestiges, which are to be traced even in idolatrous rites, of the patriarchal history and the patriarchal creed, bears its testimony to revelation. But, Sir, I well know that these Platonizers of the second century, were far more ancient than Arius : nor did I mean to charge you with the absurdity of maintaining a contrary opinion. I thought that the notion which you express, of what was orthodoxy in the second century, was conveyed in a single word; when it was said, that you represent the Christians of the second race as Arians; that is, as Arians in belief; because the divinity which you suppose to have been ascribed by them to Christ, was only of that secondary sort, which Arius and his followers, in a later age, allowed. But to convict me of an error in this representation of your opinion, you now set up a distinction, between the opinions which you would ascribe to the early Platonists and the Arian tenets. " The Logos of the Platonizers, you say, was an attribute of the Father, and not any thing that was created out of nothing, as the Arians held Christ to have been."* However, when this distinction hath served the purpose of convicting me of one error, it is cleared away again to convict me of another. This Logos of the Platonists, I am told, " was originally nothing more than a property of the Divine mind, which assumed a separate personal character in time."† This is the same notion which is expressed in your history, in these words. " All the early fathers speak of Christ as not having existed always, except as reason exists in man, *viz.* as an attribute of the Deity."‡ And the assumption of a personal character, seems to be the same thing, which in your history you call " the conversion of a mere attribute into a thinking substance."§ Indeed, it is not easy to conceive, how a personal character may be assumed, otherwise than by being made a person. Now, what the difference may be between a making out of nothing, and the conversion of a mere attribute into a substance; or how a person made out of an attribute, may differ from a person made out of nothing, I would rather, Sir, that you than I, should take the trouble to explain. If this was the diffe-

---

* Letters to Dr Horsley, p. 66.   † Ibid. p. 72.
‡ Hist. of Corrup. p. 42.   § Ibid. p. 40.

rence between the doctrines of the early Platonizers and the Arians, and this is the whole difference which you put between them, they might
pass, I think, for the same: and your account of
the Platonic orthodoxy, was not misrepresented
by me, when I said, that you made it the same
thing, the same in form, not in time, with Arianism.

6. But, Sir, I maintain, that this is an erroneous
and injurious account of the Platonic Christians.
This conversion of an attribute into a substance,
was never taught by them; nor by any except
the Sabellians, and those earlier visionaries described by Justin Martyr, who imagined occasional emissions and absorptions of the Divine Logos.
" Which opinion (you say) was not very remote
from the Unitarian doctrine."* I am happy, Sir,
to be informed by you, that the Unitarian doctrine approaches to opinions so mysterious. I
thought, that to be clear of mysteries, had been
its particular recommendation. I now find, that
were I even to turn Unitarian, I should have mysteries to digest: and mysteries much too hard for
my digestion. I will therefore, adhere to my
creed; in which I know no mystery to be compared with this notion, of a thing which may be
a person, and no person by fits and starts. But

---

* Letters to Dr Horsley, p. 73.

for any production of the Logos, by a conversion, either permanent or occasional, of an attribute into a thinking substance; I still maintain, that, were the thing conceivable, the Platonists were likely to be the last to adopt it: because a crea‑ ted Logos, to use my former expression, had been no less an absurdity in the academy, than it is an impiety in the church: and the notion, that this doctrine took its rise among the Platonists, betrays an entire ignorance of the genuine prin‑ ciples of their school."[*]

7. You tell me, that " I discover in these ani‑ madversions, a total ignorance of what you have asserted.—That you have nowhere said, that either the Platonists, or the Platonizing Chris‑ tians, held, that the Logos was created, or that it had ever not existed."[†] What then have you said? You said in your History, that " All the early fathers speak of Christ as not having ex‑ isted always, except as———an attribute of the deity:"[‡] that they taught " the conversion of this attribute into a substance."[§] And what is it you say now? You say now that the Platoni‑ zing Christians held, that " whereas the Logos was originally nothing more than a property of

---

* Charge IV. sec. 4.　　† Letters to Dr Horsley, p. 72.
‡ Hist. of Corrup. p. 42.　　　　　§ Ibid. p. 40.

the Divine mind, it assumed a separate personal character in time."*   Be pleased, Sir, to explain the difference between this conversion of
attribute into substance, or property into person, and a creation out of nothing.

8. You admit however, that the eternity of
the Logos was a doctrine of Platonism; but
you attempt to assign a reason, why the converted Platonists, when they entered into the
church, must have parted with this opinion.
" The Logos (you say) of the Platonists, had, in
their opinion, always had a personal existence,
because Plato supposed creation to have been
eternal; but this was not the opinion of the
Platonizing Christians, who held, that the world
was not eternal; and therefore, retaining as
much of Platonism as was consistent with that
doctrine, they held, that there was a time when
the Father was *alone,* and without a Son."†   Sir,
if I thought proper to deny your assertion, that
Plato supposed creation to have been eternal; it
would require much more skill in the Platonic
philosophy, than is to be gotten at second hand,
from modern authors, who pretend to give an account of it, to confute the proof which I might
bring to the contrary from Plato's own writings.

---

* Letters to Dr Horsley, p. 72.   † Ibid.

But as the younger Platonists generally held the eternity of creation, and Plato in some parts of his writings seems to favour that opinion, not-withstanding what he says to the contrary in the Timæus, I shall take no advantage of the uncertainty of your assumption. Indeed it would be sufficient for your purpose, were your argument sound in other parts, that the opinion of the world's eternity was current in that school in which the Christian Platonists were trained, and was probably entertained by them all, before their conversion. Still your conclusion will not stand, unless you can prove, that the Platonists, whether Christian or Pagan, held the Logos to be a part of the world, or thought the eternity of the Logos, a consequence only of the world's eternity. Whereas neither the one nor the other of these principles would have been allowed, even by those Platonists who deemed the world eternal. The eternity of the world seemed to them a consequence of that eternal activity, which they ascribed to the Deity; that is, to the three principles of Goodness [Τ'αγαθόν], Intelligence [Νας], and Vitality [Ψυχη]: and chiefly to the two last. For to the first principle they ascribed indeed an activity, but of a very peculiar kind; such as might be consistent with an undisturbed immutability. He acts, μενων ἱ, ἱαυτω ἱθυ, by a simple indivisible unvaried energy; which as it cannot be broken into a multitude of distinct acts, cannot be adapted to the variety of external things; on which therefore the First Good acts not, either to create or to preserve them, otherwise than through the two subordinate principles. The eternal activity therefore of the Deity, and by consequence the existence of Intellect and the vital principle, in which alone the Divine nature is active upon external things, was necessary in this system to the eternity of the world. And this eternal activity was supposed to be the consequence of that goodness of the Deity, which could not suffer that to be delayed, which, because he hath done it, appears to be fit to be done. The world therefore, however the fact may actually be, might or might not have been eternal. If it hath been eternal, it hath been such, not by its own nature, but by the choice of a free agent, who might have willed the contrary. But intellect, and the vital principle, have been eternal by necessity, as branches of the divinity. These therefore must have been eternal, even if the world had never been, although the world could not be without them; and this, upon the principles of those philosophers who deemed the world eternal. The converted Platonists therefore, when upon the authority of revelation they discarded the notion of the world's eternity, would not find themselves obliged to discard with this the eternity of Intellect, or the Logos: for that stands upon another ground, and is indeed eternity of quite another kind.

9. But whatever they might be at liberty to do, you are confident of the fact, that the eternal existence of the Logos, as a person, is a notion which was discarded by the Christian Platonists, when they became Christian. Your proof is drawn from the analogy which some of them imagined between the Divine Logos, and the reason of the human soul, or between the Logos and human speech; and from the doctrine of the conversion of an attribute into a substance, which you persuade yourself they deliver in the most unequivocal language.

10. " That the Logos of the Father, the same that constituted the second person in the Trinity, exactly corresponded to the Logos, or reason, or word of man, was the idea of Athanasius himself."* In proof of this assertion, you bring a passage from Athanasius, in which, to prevent as it should seem a conclusion which the unwary might draw from the agreement of the name, instead of the exact correspondence which you may imagine, he shews the great difference between the Divine Logos and human speech. Tertullian, in a passage cited in your history,† sets up something of an analogy between the Divine Logos

---

* Letters to Dr Horsley, p. 69,
† Hist. of Corrup. p. 38.

and the human reason. This analogy, if I mistake not, hath been pursued by the schoolmen, with their peculiar subtley; and, as far as it obtains, is well explained by the learned Dr Charles Leslie, in his dialogues, entitled, *The Socinian Controversy discussed.* Tertullian, to prevent the very conclusion which you draw from this analogy, that the Logos was at some time or another a mere attribute, remarks, that nothing empty and unsubstantial can proceed from God; for the Divine nature, admitting neither quality nor accident, every thing belonging to it must, be substance. This argument is ably stated in the work just mentioned, the dialogues of the learned Dr Leslie.

11. For the conversion of an attribute into a substance, I abide by my assertion, that it is the offspring of your own imagination; and can only have arisen from a misapprehension of the language of the Platonic fathers, It is true, that they speak of the Son's generation as taking place at a particular time, as commencing indeed with the creation. But by this generation they understood not any beginning of his personal existence, but the projection of his energies ; the display of his powers in the production of external substances.

12. You reply, " that any mere external dis-

play of powers should ever be termed generation, is so improbable, from its manifest want of analogy to any thing that ever was called generation before or since, that such an abuse of words is not to be supposed of these writers, or of any person without very positive proof; and, in this case," you say to me, " you advance nothing but a mere conjecture, destitute of any thing that can give it a colour of probability."* This sentence, Sir, only finishes the proof, if it was before defective, of your incompetency in the subject. It shews that you have so little acquaintance with Platonism, that your mind cannot readily apprehend a Platonic notion, when it is clearly set before you. What you take for my mere conjecture, is the express assertion of Athenagoras, in the very passage which you have quoted: and Athenagoras, I should think, might be a sufficient evidence of his own meaning. He says,—that the Son was called the Son, as being the first offspring of the Father—not because he was ever made, but because he went forth to act upon material substances.† He explains the generation of the Son, by declaring first what it signifies not; then, what it signifies. A making it signifies not: a going forth, according to Athenagoras, it signifies. That the generation of the Son of God is something

---

* Letters to Dr Horsley, p. 70.   † Charge IV. sec. 5.

figuratively called a generation, will hardly be denied. Athenagoras declares what he understood by the figure; and the interpretation which he puts upon it, seems to have been general among the writers who came from the same school. It rests not however upon any conjecture, but upon his authority: the fault, Sir, is not in me, if you cannot perceive his meaning when it is rendered in our own language. You object a want of analogy, between the figure and the thing which it is supposed to represent. This, I think, with an Unitarian, should be but a slight objection; since the whole language of the New Testament, in their view of it, is made up of figures, in which analogy is wanting. But the question is not what may be the natural sense of the word generation, when it is applied to the Son of God, or what may be its true sense when it is so applied in Scripture; but in what sense it was accepted by the Platonizing Christians. I affirm, upon the authority of Athenagoras, that it was understood by them, when they speak of it as taking place at a certain time, not of a beginning of the Son's existence, but of a display of his powers. To confute this assertion, instead of critical reasoning upon the propriety of the language, you must produce some better authority upon your own side, than that of Athenagoras, whose testimony is express and full, on mine.

13. But for the sense which these Platonists put upon the word generation, I am not solicitous to defend it. I have spoken of it in my Charge as a conceit; and I have spoken of the attempt, to put a determinate sense upon a figurative expression, of which no particular exposition can be drawn from holy writ, as highly presumptuous.* Still, Sir, the Platonists are not without a defence, against what you have found to object to the propriety of the expression, in the sense in which they understand it. You say to me, " Since according to your hypothesis, the Logos was always an intelligent person, he must have exerted his intellectual faculties in some way or other from all eternity, as much as the Father himself."† It is true, Sir. But it was not an exertion of his faculties *in some way or other*, but the first exertion of them on external things, that the Platonic fathers understood by generation. This was the exertion in which the Son came forth. Before this he-energized only within himself: he lay, as it were, unissued in the bosom of the Father. You go on ——" was the exertion of the faculties of the Father in the creation of the world, ever called a generation of the Father?——and yet, according to you, this language must have been equally proper with respect to the Father."‡

---

* Charge IV. sec. 6.
† Letters to Dr Horsley, p. 71.   ‡ Ibid.

———Not according to me, Sir. I hold with the Platonists, that the Father's faculties are not exerted on external things, otherwise than through the Son and Holy Ghost: these two persons being, as it were, the two faculties, in which alone the Divine nature is active on created things. Although I approve not the attempt to determine the meaning of a figure, which the holy Scriptures leave undetermined; yet I cannot allow, that the language, in that interpretation of it which I ascribe to the Platonists, is as improper of the Son as it would be of the Father. I perceive indeed no impropriety in it, as applied to the Son; I only complain of the want of authority from holy writ.

14. Still I maintain, that the thing in question is, not the propriety or impropriety of an expression; but the fact, how an expression was used and understood by certain writers. It were endless to accumulate authorities; but if the single testimony of Athenagoras is not sufficient, I will produce two more; to one of which at least I expect that you will pay some regard, because it is given by heretics. The first is that of Constantine the Great. The emperor may be numbered among the Platonizing Christians; because, as you have yourself observed, he alleges the authority of Plato in support of the Catholic doctrine. Now Constantine the Great, in his epistle to the Nico-

medians, written after the Nicene council, uses
these expressions———" he was begotten, or rather
he himself came forth (being even ever in the
Father) for the setting in order of the things
which were made by him."* Here the emperor
expounds generation, by coming forth : he thinks,
" that he came forth," the more significant expression : and he asserts the eternal co-existence
of the Son and Father. The other testimony, on
which I should more rely for your conviction, if I
could hope that any testimony might produce it,
is that of Arius the hæresiarch, and the priests
and deacons of his faction. In their common
letter to Alexander, bishop of Alexandria, (the
seat you know of the Platonic school,) stating what
they believed, and what they disbelieved; among
the articles which they disbelieved is this : " that
the Son, previously existing, was afterwards begotten."† And it is remarkable, that this stands
last in a list of articles of disbelief. In the preceding articles their disbelief is justified, by a reference of the rejected propositions to certain
heretics, as the first authors of them : of one to
Valentinus, of another to Manes, and another to
Sabellius. But this article is not referred to any
heretic ; which argues that they were conscious,

---

* Εγιννϑη, μαλλον δι προηλϑιν αυλος, και ταιϑϑλι ιν τῳ ταλρι ιν,
ιπι την των απ' αυλ πιποιημινων διαχοσμησιν.

† ιδι τον ονλα προτιρον υσιρον γιννϑιιτα.

that this was the opinion of the church. It is
true they immediately subjoin, that " Alexander
himself had often publicly declared against those
who introduced such things;" as if this had been
one of the things, which Alexander condemned.
But the falsehood of this insinuation appears from
another epistle of Arius to Eusebius of Nicome-
diá, to whom as a friend, the heretic may be supposed to write without art or disguise. In this
epistle he mentions the proposition, " that the
Son is coexistent with God, without generation,"*
as one of the articles of Alexander's public doctrine, to which he could not give assent. You
will find both these epistles, in Epiphanius's account of the Arians.

15. From these testimonies it is indisputable,
that the early Platonists, by the generation of
the Son, when they speak of it as taking place at
a particular time, understand not any beginning
of his existence: and it appears that it was the
language of the orthodox, at the time of the
Nicene council, that the existence of the Son was
prior to his generation, and independent of it;
coeval indeed with the eternal Father's. Later
writers distinguish three generations: the incar-

---

* Επειδη ὁ συμφωνημεν ἀιλω δημοσια λιγοιλι——συπαρχιι ὁ ἐιας
ἀγιππιλως τῳ Θιῳ.

nation; the going forth to the business of creation; and an eternal generation; which last is
only a name for the unknown manner in which
the Son's existence is connected with the Father's.
Tertullian, in the passage which you have quoted
in your History,* which you call upon me so particularly to consider,† only speaks the language of
his times, and never dreamed that he should be
understood to assert a beginning of the Son's existence, when he said, " that the nativity of the
word was perfected, when God said, *Let there be
Light.*"

16. You now, Sir, produce another passage of
Tertullian, to·prove " how ready the Platonizing
Christians were to revert to the idea of an attribute of God, in their use of the word Logos."‡
But the passage, instead of proving this readiness
of the Platonizing Christians, proves the readiness of the Pagan philosophers to apply this same
name to a person; even to the Maker of the Universe.

17. You call upon me to consider also a passage cited in your History, from Lactantius, whose

---

* Vol. I. p. 38—40.   † Letters to Dr Horsley, p. 67.
‡ Letters to Dr Horsley, p. 76.

orthodoxy, you tell me, I cannot question.* Sir, you are not more inaccurate in your citations from the ancients, than unfortunate in your divinations about the principles of your contemporaries, and the concessions which they will be willing to make to you. The orthodoxy of Lactantius I shall question, I shall deny. He had not perhaps the dispositions of an heretic. He did not set himself to oppose, what he knew to be the approved doctrine of the church. But his talent was eloquence, which he possessed in a high degree, and his learning was in mythological antiquity. In philosophy his information was small; in divinity he was a child. The common places of morality and natural religion, he touches with elegance; and he inveighs against the Pagan superstition in a masterly strain. But in his attempt to philosophize, or to expound articles of faith, he is contemptible. In the seventh chapter of his first book, he ascribes a beginning to the existence of the eternal Father. No wonder then that he should ascribe a beginning to the Son's existence. You are welcome, Sir, to any advantage you may be able to derive from the authority of such a writer.

16. I persuade myself I have now shewn, that

---

* Letters to Dr Horsley, p. 76.

your objection to the Catholic doctrine, founded on its supposed Platonism, and your argument for what I shall call the Arianism of the Platonizers from Athenagoras, are well entitled to the places which they hold among my specimens of insufficient proof, of which the one is the sixth, and the other the eighth in order.

I am, &c.

LETTER FOURTEENTH.

*In Reply to Dr Priestley's eighth.—The archdeacon's supposi-
tion, that the first Ebionites worshipped Christ, defended.—
His supposition, that Theodotus was the first person who
taught the Unitarian doctrine at Rome, defended.*

DEAR SIR,

OF all my nine specimens of insufficient proof,
selected from the first book of your History, the
fifth is the only one about which any doubt is
likely to remain (except with yourself) that it was
properly alleged.   For the seventh and the ninth
you give up; and the other six have been considered.

2. My fifth specimen was your misrepresentation
of Eusebius, a writer of acknowledged veracity and
candour, whom you very rashly charge with inconsistency, and even with unfairness; because in his
account of Theodotus the hæresiarch, who appeared at Rome about the year 190, he cites another writer, who says, that this Theodotus was the
first who taught the mere humanity of Christ;
whereas it appears from his own history, that the
Ebionites, who held the mere humanity of Christ,
were far more ancient than Theodotus.   Admitting the antiquity of the Ebionites, I maintain,

that Eusebius is so easily reconciled with the author whom he cites, that the difference between
them is no just ground to tax the veracity of either.
It is very certain, that Theodotus maintained the
mere humanity of Christ in the grossest sense: in
that gross and shocking sense, in which it is at
this day taught by yourself and Mr Lindsey.   It
is not certain that the Ebionites, before Theodotus, had gone further than to deny our Lord's ori-
nal divinity.   They probably, like Socinius, admitted some unintelligible exaltation of his nature
after his resurrection, which rendered him the object of worship.   If this was the case, Theodotus
might justly claim the honour of being the first
assertor of our Lord's humanity, being indeed the
first who made humanity the whole of his condition.   By this very natural supposition, that the
Ebionites were Unitarians of a milder sort than
Theodotus, Eusebius might have been reconciled
with himself, had it been his own assertion, that
Theodotus was the first who taught the mere humanity of Christ.*   .

3. But this is not the assertion of Eusebius, but
of another writer cited by Eusebius.   Now, since
Theodotus broached his heresy at Rome, it is very
probable, that the writer cited by Eusebius was a

---

* See Charge I. sec. 16.

Roman, and that he treated of the state of religion in the western church, and especially at
Rome; where Theodotus was probably the first,
who, in any sense, taught the mere humanity of
Christ.*

4. You tell me, in your eighth letter, that the
difference which I put between Theodotus and
Ebion, is advanced upon my own authority.†
Truly, Sir, I think that a supposition, which reconciles a writer of established credit with himself, or which is nearly the same thing, with another writer whom he cites with approbation, should
need no great authority to support it; unless it be
contrary to known fact, in which case indeed no
authority might support it, or in itself improbable.
Now, Sir, can you prove, that Christ was not worshipped by the original Ebionites? Can you prove
this, I would ask, by explicit evidence? For as for
that kind of proof, in which you so much delight,
which is drawn by abstract reasoning from general and precarious maxims; it is of no more significance in history, than testimony would be in mathematics. To think to demonstrate a fact by
syllogism, is not less absurd, than to go about to
establish a geometrical theorem by an *affidavit*.
Excuse me, if I insist upon the difference, in the

---

* See Charge, p. 43.　　† Letters to Dr Horsley, p. 103.

nature of things, between historic certainty and scientific truth. I apprehend an inattention to this distinction hath misled many, and hath been the cause of much fruitless labour in many subjects. Scientific truth can only be established by abstract reasoning. Testimony can in science produce nothing more than probability. In history it is quite the reverse; abstract reasoning can never go beyond a probability: proof must arise from evidence. And the reason of this is plain. The principles of scientific truth are all within the mind itself: the truths of history are the occurrences of the external world. Neglecting this necessary distinction, the great Berkley questioned the existence of the material world, because he found it incapable of demonstration; and I have known many seek a confirmation of geometrical theorems from experiment. Now to return to my subject: have you evidence, for that is the only proof to which, in this case, the judicious will attend; have you evidence, that Christ was not worshipped by the Ebionites? If you have none, my supposition is not contrary to known fact. Is it in itself improbable, since all innovations have a progress, and the divinity of Christ was the belief, and the worship of Christ the practice, of the first ages, that presumptuous men would begin to question the ground, on which his right to worship might be thought to stand, before they abandoned the worship to which they had been long

habituated? Hath not this been the progress of
the corruption (you will call it reformation, but I
must speak'my own language) in later times: Socinius, although he denied the original divinity of
our Lord, was nevertheless a worshipper of Christ,
and a strenuous assertor of his right to worship.
It was left to others to build upon the foundation
which Socinius laid; and to bring the Unitarian
doctrine to the goodly form, in which the present
age beholds it.

5. But, Sir, my supposition is not only free
from improbability; it is highly probable. Ebion
in his notions of the Redeemer, as I have already
had occasion to observe, seems to have been a
mere Cerinthian. Epiphanius and Irenæus say,
that he held the Cerinthian doctrine of a union of
Jesus with a superangelic being. The Cerinthian
doctrine was,—that this union commenced at our
Lord's baptism; was interrupted during the crucifixion, and at the time of our Lord's interment,
but restored again after his resurrection; and being restored, it rendered the man Jesus an object
of divine honours. As Epiphanius says in general of Ebion, that he held the Cerinthian doctrine
concerning Christ, without specifying parts that he
received, and parts that he rejected; the probability is, that he received the whole; and of consequence, that he worshipped Christ as a deified
man, notwithstanding that he denied his original

divinity. This supposition of mine hath, you see, a probability of its own; which is quite distinct from that which accrues to it from its use in re-conciling Eusebius with the historian that he quotes; and is founded on the acknowledged agreement of Ebion with Cerinthus.

6. For my other supposition, that Theodotus might be the first person who taught the Uni-tarian doctrine at Rome, you think it highly im-probable, " because Tertullian says, that in his time the Unitarians were the greater part of be-lievers."* At Rome therefore, " where there was a conflux of all religions, and of all sects," the probability is little, that there should be no Uni-tarians. Sir, I will grant—I am liberal, I am sure, in my concessions—I will grant, that Rome swarmed with Unitarians in the time of Tertul-lian. Not for the reason which you assign; that Tertullian says, the Unitarians were the majority of believers. For this Tertullian hath not said; with whatever confidence you may ascribe to him the dreams of Zuicker and his credulous disciples. I must take the liberty to say, Sir, that a man ought to be accomplished in ancient learning, who thinks he may escape, with impunity, and

---

* Letters to Dr Horsley, p. 103.—See also p. 121; and Se-cond Letters, p. 71.

without detection, in the attempt to brow-beat the world with a peremptory and reiterated allegation of testimonies that exist not. But, Sir, although I deny that Tertullian says, that the Unitarians were in his time the majority of believers; yet I will grant, that they were numerous at Rome in the time of Tertullian. I profess I know not how numerous, or how few they were. But to shew the strength of my cause, since you are pleased to have it so, let them be numerous. How will their numbers affect my supposition, that Theodotus was the first person who at Rome taught the Unitarian doctrine? Might not this be, although the Unitarians swarmed at Rome in the time of Tertullian? Believe me, Sir, it well might be; for the times of Tertullian were the very times of Theodotus. About the year of our Lord 185, Tertullian embraced Christianity. About the year of our Lord 190, came Theodotus the apostate, the tanner of Byzantium, preaching at Rome the doctrine of antichrist.

7. My learned ally has a third conjecture for the reconciling of Eusebius and his author. It is by no means necessary to our argument, that either of my suppositions, or that his, or that any particular conjecture which may be made upon the subject, should be brought to a certainty. You tax Eusebius with want of candour and consistency. The charge rests upon an assumption, that

what Eusebius relates of the antiquity of the
Ebionites, and what his author affirms of the first
assertion of our Lord's mere humanity, by Theodotus, cannot be interpreted but in contradictory
senses. If we have shewn, by a variety of probable conjectures, that the two assertions admit
consistent interpretations, that each may be true
in the sense in which each writer understood
himself, without contradiction of the other,
the whole evidence of your accusation is demolished, and the charge of temerity and presumption lies heavy on yourself for an attack, which
you cannot support with proof, upon the character of a grave and respectable historian.

I am, &c.

LETTER FIFTEENTH.

DEAR SIR,

AFTER the declaration which I have made, that I will not enter into a regular controversy with you, upon the subject of the Trinity, you will not wonder, if you receive only a general reply to some parts of your seventh letter. A particular answer to the several objections which it contains, would lead me into metaphysical disquisitions, which I wish to decline, because in that subject I forsee that we should want common principles and a common language. The questions which you propose in the second and the fourth sections of this letter, are not new, and have been answered. But if they were unanswerable, what would be the inference? The inference would only be, that the doctrine of the Trinity hath its difficulties. And is it possible, that any doctrine concerning the nature of the Deity, should be without its difficulties? When the infinite distance is considered between man and his Maker, it seems reasonable to presume, that there must be mysteries, far above the reach of the human understanding, both in the nature of God, and in the plan of his government; that the fullest discovery that could be made, of God and of his ways, to the human intellect, must be imperfect; because, however perfect in itself, it could be but imperfectly apprehended. No difficulties, therefore, short of a contradiction, can be allowed to constitute an objection to a doctrine claiming divine original. On the contrary, it should rather seem, that to involve difficulties, must be one characteristic of a divine revelation; and its greatest difficulties may reasonably be expected to lie in those parts, which immediately respect the nature of God, and the manner of his existence. If you would suppose the contrary, if you would insist that a divine revelation, being intended for the general information of mankind, must be perspicuous and free from difficulty; I would ask, is Christianity clear of difficulties in any of the Unitarian schemes; hath the Arian hypothesis no

difficulty, when it ascribes both the first formation and the perpetual government of the universe, not to the Deity, but to an inferior being?
Can any power or wisdom, less than the supreme,
be a sufficient ground for the trust we are required to place in Providence? Make the wisdom
and the power of our ruler what you please; still
upon the Arian principle, it is the wisdom and the
power of a creature. Where then will be the
certainty, that the evil, which we find in the
world, hath not crept in through some imperfection in the original contrivance, or in the present
management? since every intellect, below the
first, may be liable to error, and any power, short
of the supreme, may be inadequate to purposes of
a certain magnitude. But if evil may have thus
crept in, what assurance, can we have, that it will
ever be extirpated? In the Socinian scheme, is it
no difficulty, that the capacity of a mere man
should contain that wisdom, by which God made
the universe? Whatever is meant by *the Word* in
St John's gospel, it is the same Word of which
the evangelist says, that all things were made by
it, and that it was itself made flesh. If this Word
be the Divine attribute Wisdom; then that attribute, in the degree which was equal to the formation of the universe, in this view of the Scripture
doctrine, was conveyed entire into the mind of a
mere man, the son of a Jewish carpenter. A much

greater difficulty, in my apprehension, than any that is to be found in the Catholic faith.*

2. In the third section of your seventh letter, you build an argument for the sole deity of the Father, upon an assumption that he is the sole object of worship. To this argument I have replied.† I deny the assumption. I cite the example of St Stephen, whose last act of worship was addressed to Christ. You allege, on the

---

* In reply to this, Dr Priestley says to me, in the thirteenth of his Second Letters, sec. 3. " Pray, Sir, what Socinian ever maintained, that the Divine attribute Wisdom, in the degree which was equal to the formation of the universe, was conveyed entire into the mind of Jesus Christ.". I say, that St John maintains it, if St John was, what Dr Priestley believes him to have been, a Socinian. It is maintained in the beginning of St John's gospel, if the evangelist's words·be expounded in the true sense by the Unitarians. The Word, which was with God from the beginning, according to St John, was made flesh. If the Word, which was made flesh, was not the same Word which was in the beginning with God, by which all things were made, there is no meaning in the evangelist's words, literal or figurative. The Word's being made flesh, according to the Socinians, was only a communication of the word to the mind of Christ. What was communicated to the mind of Christ? That Word which was from the beginning, which made the world. Dr Priestley says, this is more than the Unitarians believe. " What we believe is——that a *portion* only of the same wisdom, which formed the universe, was communicated to Christ." It may be so. Far be it from me to tax Dr Priestley, or his brethren, with a larger faith than they profess. But if they believe no more than Dr Priestley in this passage acknowledges, they believe much less than St John asserts in the most reduced sense of his expressions.

† Letter XI.

other side, the example of our Saviour, who himself prayed to the Father; the authority of Origen; and I know not what early and universal practice. I reply, that our Saviour, as a man, owed worship to the Father. I maintain, that neither the authority of Origen, nor any universal practice of a later age, can outweigh the example of St Stephen, were it single; much less supported as it is by other examples of equal weight. The worship addressed to Christ by St Stephen, and the apostles, either proves the divinity of Christ, or it justifies the worship of the saints and martyrs in the Roman church; and they who live in countries, where the papal superstition is established, may, without scruple, invocate St Michael, St Raphael, St Abel, St Abraham, St Stephen, St Sebastian, and all the saints, angelic, and human, Jewish, and Christian, of the Roman calendar.

3. The text of St Paul (Col. i. 15.) was produced by me,* not as the most explicit assertion that may be found in Scripture, of our Lord's divinity; but as an explicit assertion, that he is at least something much more than man, and that the universe was made by him. If the dignity of his nature were mentioned only in this single pas-

---

* See Charge, p. 15.

sage, or were no where described by higher titles
than those which the apostle uses here, "the
image of the invisible God, and the *first-born* of
every creature," divinity might seem more than is
implied in them.   But when we recollect the
stronger expressions, which occur in other places;
in particular, St Paul's assertion, that he was
originally in the form of God, of which he emptied himself to take the form of a servant, *i. e.*
of a man; and when to all other proofs of the
high dignity of his nature, we add St John's explicit doctrine of his eternity and Godhead; it
must be very evident, that it could not be the intention of St Paul, in this passage, to sink the Son
of God into the rank of a creature, or to separate
him from the Divine nature.   The force of St
Paul's description in both its branches, lies rather
in the adjectives, *invisible* and *first-born*, than in
the substantives, *image* and *creature*.   The first
branch of the description, that " he is the image
of the invisible God," points to a circumstance,
upon which the early fathers dwell, as one of the
principal personal distinctions: that it is in the
person only of the Son, that the glory of the Godhead can be rendered visible.   *For God*, in the
person of the Father, *no man hath seen at any
time.** The Son is therefore an image of the In-

---

* John i. 18; and vi. 46.

visible Deity; not as a likeness formed in a distinct substance, but as he, who in every instance
of an immediate intercourse between God and
man, hath been the appearing person.* The second branch of the description, holds out a distinction between birth and creation, which implies
that the Son's existence is dependent on the
Father's, in some other manner than that in
which any creature's existence is dependent on
its Maker's. You must know, that the words in
the original text, πρωτότοκος πάσης κτίσεως, are equivalent
to these: ὁ τεχθεὶς πρὸ πάσης κτίσεως, *he who was born or
begotten before any creation, or before any thing
was made.* " It is observable, says Dr Clarke,
that St Paul does not here call our Saviour πρωτό-
τιστος πάσης κτίσεως, *the first created of all creatures,* but
πρωτότοκος πάσης κτίσεως, *the first-born of every creature ;
the first begotten before all creatures.*"

4. I allow, that " there is nothing that can be
called an *account* of the divine nature of Christ,
in the gospels of St Matthew, St Mark, or St
Luke."† But every one of the gospels abounds
with passages, in which it is so evidently implied,

---

* ——*image of the invisible God.* " A lively description of
the person of Christ ; whereby we understand, that in him only
God sheweth himself to be seen." Marginal note, in Barker's
quarto Bible, 1599.
† Letters to Dr Horsley, p. 94.

that no room is left to doubt, that the four evangelists had but one opinion upon the subject. I
cannot admit your position, that " each of the
gospels was intended to be a sufficient instruction
in the fundamental principles of the doctrine of
Christianity."* Nothing seems to have been less
the intention of any of the evangelists, than to compose a system of fundamental principles. Instruction in fundamentals, in that age, was orally delivered. The general design of the evangelists,
seems to have been nothing more, than to deliver in
writing a simple, unembellished narrative of our
Lord's principal miracles; to record the occurrences and actions of his life, which went immediately to the completion of the ancient prophecies, or
to the execution of the scheme of man's redemption; and to register the most interesting maxims
of religion and morality, which were contained
in his discourses. The principles of the Christian
religion, are to be collected neither from a single
gospel, nor from all the four gospels; nor from
the four gospels, with the acts and the epistles;
but from the whole code of revelation, consisting
of the canonical books of the Old and New Testament: and for any article of faith, the authority
of a single writer, where it is express and unequivocal, is sufficient. Had St Paul related what

---

* Letters to Dr Horsley, p. 91.

he saw in the third heaven, I hope, Sir, you would have given him implicit credit, although the truth of the narrative must have rested on his single testimony.

5. I cannot however grant, that the general tenor of Scripture, supposes not such a Trinity, as I contend for.* I contend, that your doctrine is what stands upon particular texts; while the Catholic faith, is supported by the general tenor of the sacred writings, and by the consent of those writings, in many parts, with an universal tradition of unexplored antiquity.

6. You ask me, " why the doctrine of the Trinity, if it be a truth, was not taught as explicitly in the New Testament, as the doctrine of the Divine unity both in Old and New?"† And you say, that many passages in Scripture inculcate the doctrine of the Divine unity, in the clearest and strongest manner."‡ Be pleased, Sir, to produce one of the many. I know of no doctrine of the Divine unity, taught either in the Old Testament or in the New, but the doctrine, that Jehovah, the God of Abraham, Isaac, and Jacob, the Creator of heaven and earth, is the one true God, in opposition to the variety of imaginary gods worshipped

---

* Letters to Dr Horsley, p. 87.
† Ibid. p. 92.   ‡ Ibid. p. 93.

by the heathen.* Concerning the metaphysical unity of the Divine nature, the Scriptures are silent; except that by discovering a Trinity of persons, they teach clearly what the unity is not; namely, that it is not personal. If you imagine, that the absolute unity of the Divine substance, is more easy to be explained than the Trinity, let me intreat you, Sir, to read the Parmenides. It is indeed in Plato's school, if any where, that a man's eyes are likely to be opened to his own ignorance. Read the Parmenides—you will then perhaps perceive, that that unity, which must be the foundation of all being, is itself of all things the most mysterious and incomprehensible. I must know more of it than I do, before I can pretend to perceive, what is so clear to you, that you think that I cannot deny it, " that the doctrine of the Trinity looks like an infringement of the unity."†

7. The argument contained in the seventh section of your seventh letter, splits, I think, into three, resting on the three different assumptions. The apostles both in the book of Acts, and in their epistles, usually call Christ a man; therefore

---

* Τὸ μὲν γὰρ θεὸν ὁμολογεῖν ἕνα, πρὸς ἀντιδιαστολὴν τῆς ἑλλήνων πολυ-θεοῦ πλάνης, πρῶτοι παρειλήφασιν Ἰουδαίων παῖδες. Euseb. Ecc. Theol. lib. i. c. 2.

† Letters to Dr Horsley, p. 92.

they knew not that he was God; for the discovery would have changed their language.*

8. They speak of him as a man, in reasoning and argumentation. Therefore he was a man.†

9. They behaved to him as a man, in their ordinary intercourse with him; therefore they had no apprehension that he was God.‡

10. To the two first arguments it is an answer, that according to the faith which I defend, Christ is truly a man as well as God. It is no wonder therefore, that he should be mentioned as a man, when nothing in the narrative, or in the argument, requires that his divinity should be particularly brought to view.

11. To the first argument in particular, it is a further answer, that it was the style of all the sacred writers, and it is the style of all writers, to name things rather after their appearances than their internal forms. The tempter you know, in the Mosaic history of the fall, is called the serpent; and is not once mentioned by any other name. The three angels, who appeared to Abra-

---

* Letters to Dr Horsley, p. 93.   † Ibid. 94.
‡ Ibid. 93, and 94.

ham in the form of men, are called men, throughout the story.

12. To the second argument in particular, it is a further answer, that, as the scheme of man's redemption required the incarnation of the Son of God, the apostles would often find it necessary, in reasoning upon that scheme, and in argumentation in defence of it, to insist on his humanity.

13. The third branch of the argument cannot be allowed to have any force at all, even though the assumption upon which it rests should be admitted, if we have the authority of the apostles, in their writings, for the deity of Christ. The most that could be inferred, were the assumption true, would be something strange in their conduct; and even this might be a hasty inference. The singularity of their conduct might disappear, if the accounts which they have left of our Lord's life on earth, and of their attendance upon him, were more circumstantial. But the truth is, that the foundations of this argument are unsound. It may be gathered from the evangelical history, imperfect as it is, that the behaviour of the apostles to our Lord during his life, possessed as they were with an imperfect wavering belief in him as the Messiah, and with indistinct notions of the Messiah's divinity, was the natural behaviour of men under these impressions. They treat him upon

T

all occasions with a very distant reserve: sometimes they invoke him as a deity; as St Peter, when he was sinking in the sea, and all the disciples in the storm. If the angels Michael or Gabriel should come and live among us, in the manner which you suppose,* I think we should soon lose our habitual recollection of their angelic nature. It would be only occasionally awaked by extraordinary incidents. This at least would be the case, if they mixed with us upon an even footing, without assuming any badges of distinction, wearing a common garb, partaking of our lodging and of our board, suffering in the same degree with ourselves from hunger and fatigue, and seeking the same refreshments. The wonder would be, if angels, in this disguise, met with any other respect, than that which dignity of character commands, with something of occasional homage, when their miraculous help was needed. This was the respect which our Lord met with from his followers. You say, " he could not divest himself of his superior and proper nature :"† but St Paul says quite the contrary,—that he emptied himself, and assumed a form, which set out of sight the transcendent dignity of his nature, and deprived him of the homage due to it. The scheme of man's redemption required this humiliation, which made

---

* Letters to Dr Horsley, p. 94.   † Ibid. p. 24.

a part of the sufferings by which our guilt was to be atoned.

14. In the eighth section of this seventh letter, you argue against our Lord's divinity, from " the manner in which he speaks of the power by which he worked miracles, as not his own, but the Father's;"* and from the manner in which he speaks of himself, saying, *My Father is greater than I.* If from such expressions, you would be content to infer, that the Almighty Father is indeed the fountain and the centre of divinity; and that the equality of Godhead is to be understood, with some mysterious subordination of the Son, to the Father; you would have the concurrence of the ancient fathers, and of many advocates of the true faith, in all ages. If you would infer any other inferiority, than what is necessarily implied in the relation of a Son, some of the very passages to which you allude, will serve to your confutation. Such are those sayings of our Lord, recorded in St John's gospel, that " the Son can do nothing of himself †—the word which you hear, is not mine, but the Father's which sent me‡——the Father which dwelleth in me, he doeth the works."§ Refer the expressions to the context,

---

* Letters to Dr Horsley, p. 95.   † John v. 19.
‡ John xiv. 24.   § Ibid. xiv. 10.

and it will appear, that, with something of a subordination on the part of the Son, they assert the most perfect identity of nature, the most entire unity of will, and consent of intellect, and an incessant co-operation in the exertion of common powers to a common purpose. You are, Sir, very positive in the assertion, that Dr Waterland in particular, and all the strict Athanasians of the last age, maintained, " that the Trinity consists of three persons, all truly independent of each other."* Upon this opinion, which you ascribe to the strict Athanasians, you remark in your History,† that to make three proper distinct persons, independent of each other, is to make three distinct gods. I concur with you in this remark, in which you have been anticipated by the Roman Dionysius; whose judgment you know, upon certain persons of his own time, who, in their zeal against Sabellius, ran into this error, " is quoted with approbation by Athanasius himself."‡ But, Sir, I deny of Dr Waterland in particular, and of the strict Athanasians of the last age in general, that they fall justly under this censure.

15. Bishop Bull, in his defence of the Nicene faith, spends a whole chapter, and a very long

---

* Letters to Dr Horsley, p. 80.   † Vol. i. p. 147.
   ‡ See Dr Priestley's Hist. vol. i. p. 65 ; and the first of these Letters.

chapter it is, upon the subject of the Son's subordination; which he maintains to be as much a
branch of the true faith, as the doctrine of the
Son's eternity or consubstantiality.

16. The same thing is asserted by Bishop Pearson, in his exposition of the apostles' creed. He
observes, that " in the very name of Father there
is something of eminence, which is not in that of
Son; and something of priority we must ascribe
unto the first, in respect of the second person."[*]
" ———We must not therefore so far endeavour to
involve ourselves in the darkness of this mystery,
as to deny that glory which is clearly due unto
the Father—he is God, not of any other, but of
himself;———there is no other person who is God,
but is God of him. It is no diminution of the Son
to say, he is from another—but it were a diminution of the Father to speak so of him; and there
must be some pre-eminence, where there is a place
for derogation.—The first person is a Father indeed, by reason of his Son, but he is not God by
reason of him; whereas the Son is not only Son
in regard of the Father, but also God, by reason
of the same."[†] Upon this pre-eminence of the
Father, the learned bishop founds the congruity
of the Divine mission;[‡] and he maintains, that

---

[*] Pearson on the creed, p. 34.   [†] Ibid.   [‡] Ibid. p. 37.

" the dignity of the Father appears from the order
of persons in the blessed Trinity, of which he is
undoubtedly the first. Although in some passages of the apostolical discourses, the Son may be
first named——and in others the Holy Ghost
precede the Son——yet where the three persons
are barely enumerated, and delivered unto us as
the rule of faith, there that order is observed
which is proper to them——this order hath been
perpetuated in all confessions of faith, and is for
ever to be inviolably observed."* And this order
being so generally acknowledged by the fathers,
the bishop remarks in a note, that " when we read
in the Athanasian creed, that *in this Trinity none
is afore or after other*, we must understand the
negation of the priority of perfection or time."†

17. To the same purpose the learned Mr William Stephens, author of some able discourses on
the Trinity, in his sermon *On the Eternal Generation of the Son of God*, preached before the university of Oxford, August 5th, 1722, affirms, that
" on the communication of the Godhead from the
Father to the Son—is founded and established all
that subordination which we assert among the
persons of the Trinity." He adds, that " unless
some subordination be maintained, we run into

---

* Pearson on the creed, p. 37.   † Ibid.

Tritheism." For he agrees with you and me, that "three *co-ordinate* persons would be manifestly three gods."

18. The same sentiments are acknowledged by Dr Waterland, in his commentary on the Athanasian creed. " When it is said, *none is afore or after other*, we are not to understand it of order; for the Father is first, the Son second, the Holy Ghost third in order. Neither are we to understand it of office; for the Father is supreme in office, while the Son and Holy Ghost condescend to inferior offices. But we are to understand it, as the creed itself explains it, of duration and dignity."*

19. From these passages it appears, that you misrepresent the strict Athanasians of the last age, when you charge them with asserting such a separation and independence of the three persons, as would amount to Tritheism: and you misrepresent me, when you insinuate, that I would set the three persons at a greater distance, than the Athanasians of the last age allowed. I maintain that the Three Persons are one Being; One by mutual relation, indissoluble connexion, and gradual subordination: so strictly One, that any in-

---

* Waterland on the Athanasian creed, p. 144.

dividual thing, in the whole world of matter and
of spirit, presents but a faint shadow of their unity.
I maintain, that each person by himself is God;
because each possesses fully every attribute of the
Divine nature. But I maintain, that these persons
are all included in the very idea of a God; and
that for that reason, as well as for the identity of
the attributes in each, it were impious and absurd
to say, there are three Gods. For to say there
are three Gods, were to say there are three Fathers, three Sons, and three Holy Ghosts. I maintain the equality of the three persons in all the
attributes of the Divine nature. I maintain their
equality in rank and authority, with respect to all
created things, whatever relations or differences
may subsist between themselves. Differences there
must be, lest we confound the persons, which was
the error of Sabellius. But the differences can
only consist in the personal properties, lest we divide the substance, and make a plurality of independent gods. It will not put me out of conceit
with the arguments, which I have brought to support these sacred truths, or with the illustrations
which I have attempted, that you pronounce them
equal in absurdity to any thing in the Jewish ca-
bala,* (of which I suspect you hardly know enough
to judge with certainty of this pretended resem-

---

* Letters to Dr Horsley, p. 80.

blance,) or that you imagine, when you read me, that you are reading Peter Lombard, Thomas Aquinas, or Duns Scotus.* Perhaps, Sir, though a Protestant divine, I may sometimes condescend to look into the *Summa*,† and may be less mortified, than you conceive, with this comparison. It was well meant however, and is one of those general depreciatory insinuations, which are apt to catch the vulgar, and may serve the purpose of a reply, upon any occasion, when a real reply is not to be framed.

I am, &c.

---

* Letters to Dr Horsley, p. 99.

† ⸺ no Protestant, I imagine, will ever think it worth his while to read many sections in that work—the *Summa.* Hist. of Corrup. vol. i. p. 119.

LETTER SIXTEENTH.

The Unitarian doctrine not well calculated for the conversion of Jews, Mahometans, or Infidels, of any description.

DEAR SIR,

You express in your history, and in your letters to me, a very charitable anxiety about Jews, Mahometans, and Infidels. It is one of your great objections to the doctrine of the Trinity, that it is, as you conceive, an obstruction to their conversion; which you think might be speedily effected, by reducing Christianity to the Unitarian creed. My notion is, that it is our duty to adhere to the letter of the gospel; and to leave it to God to open the eyes of Jews, Mahometans, and Infidels, in his own time, and in his own way. Your device of bringing them to believe Christianity, by giving the name of Christianity to what they already believe, in principle exactly resembles the stratagem of a certain missionary of the Jesuits, of whom I have somewhere read; who, in his zeal for the conversion of an Indian chief, on whom the sublimity of the doctrine of the gospel, and the purity of its moral precepts, made little impression, told him,—that Christ had been a valiant and successful warrior, who, in the space of three years, scalped men, women, and children, without

number. The savage was well-disposed to become
a disciple of such a master.—He was baptized,
with his whole tribe, and the Jesuit gloried in his
numerous converts.

2. Pardon me, Sir, if I express a doubt, whether your stratagem promise equal success. For
the Jews, whenever they begin to open their eyes
to the evidences of our Saviour's mission, they will
still be apt to consider the New Testament in
connexion with the Old. They will look for an
agreement, in principle at least, between the
gospel and the law. When they accept the Christian doctrine, it will be as a later and a fuller
discovery. They will reject it, if they conceive it
to be contradictory to the patriarchal and the
Mosaic revelations. Successive discoveries of divine truth may differ, they will say, in fullness
and perspicuity; but in principle they must har-
monize, as parts of one system. They will retain
some veneration for their traditional doctrines;
and in their most ancient Targums, as well as in
allusions in their sacred books, they will find the
notion of one Godhead in a Trinity of persons;
and they will perceive, that it was in contradiction to the Christians, that their later rabbin
abandoned the notions of their forefathers. The
Unitarian scheme of Christianity, is the last therefore, to which the Jews are likely to be converted,

as it is the most at enmity with their ancient faith.

3. With the Mahometans indeed, your prospects may seem more promising; as the whole difference between you and them seems very inconsiderable. The true Mussulman believes as much, or rather more of Christ, than the Unitarian requires to be believed; and though the Unitarians have not yet recognised the divine mission of Mahomet, there is good ground to think, they will not long stand out.* In Unitarian writings of the last century, it is allowed of Mahomet, that he had no other design than to restore the belief of the unity of God—of his religion, that it was not meant for a new religion, but for a restitution of the true intent of the Christian—of the grand prevalence of the Mahometan religion, that it hath been owing, not to force and the sword, but to that one truth contained in the Alcoran,

---

* Dr Priestley, in his Second Letters, p. 163, wittily remarks, " that I might almost as well assert that all the Unitarians in England are already so far Mahometans, that, to my certain knowledge, they are actually circumcised." Upon this occasion I cannot but remind him, of what history records of an elder brother of our modern Unitarians. In the latter end of the sixteenth century, Adam Neuser, pastor of the church of Heidelberg, the first, or among the first propagators of the Socinian heresy in the Palatinate, began in Socinianism, and finished his career with turning Mahometan, and submitting to circumcision, at Constantinople.

the unity of God. With these friendly dispositions towards each other, it should seem that the
Mahometan and the Unitarian might easily be
brought to agree. But the experiment hath been
very seriously tried, without any event answerable to the expectation. You may not know it,
Sir, but so it was,—that in the reign of Charles the
Second, a negociation was regularly opened, on
the part of our English Unitarians, with his excellency Ameth Ben Ameth, ambassador of the
emperor of Morocco at the British court, in order
to form an alliance with the Mahometan prince,
for the more effectual propagation of the Unitarian principles. The two Unitarian divines, who
undertook this singular treaty, address the ambassador and the Mussulmen of his suite, as " votaries and fellow-worshippers of the sole supreme
Deity." They return thanks to God, that he
hath preserved the emperor of Morocco, and his
subjects, in the excellent knowledge of one only
sovereign God, who hath no distinction nor plurality of persons; and in many other wholesome
doctrines. They say, that they, with their pens,
defend the faith of one supreme God, and that
God raised up Mahomet to do the same with the
sword, as a scourge on idolizing Christians. They
therefore style themselves the fellow-champions,
with the Mahometans, for these truths. They
offer their assistance, to purge the Alcoran of certain corruptions and interpolations; which, after

the death of Mahomet, had crept into his papers, of which the Alcoran was composed. For of Mahomet they think too highly, to suppose that he could be guilty of the many repugnancies, which are to be found in the writings that go under his name. This work they declare themselves willing to undertake for the vindication of Mahomet's glory. They intimate, that the corrections, which they would propose, would render the Alcoran more consistent, not with itself only, but with the gospel of Christ; of which they say Mahomet pretended to be but a preacher. They tell the ambassador, that the Unitarian Christians are a great and considerable people. To give weight to the assertion, they enumerate the hæresiarchs of all ages who have opposed the Trinity, from Paulus Samosatensis, down to Faustus Socinus, and the leaders of the Polonian fraternity: they celebrate the modern tribes of Arianizing Christians, as assertors of the proper unity of God: and they close the honourable list, with the Mahometans themselves. " All these (they say) maintain the faith of one—God. And why should we forget to add you Mahometans, who also consent with us in the belief of one only supreme Deity." Such is the substance of a letter, which they presented to the ambassador, with some Latin manuscripts respecting the differences between Christianity and the Mahometan religion, and containing an ample detail of the Unitarian tenets. They apply to the Mussulman as to a peson of " known discernment in spiritual and sublime matters;" and they intreat him to communicate the import of their manuscripts to the consideration of the fittest persons of his countrymen. This singular epistle may be seen entire, in Dr Leslie's *Socinian Controversy Discussed.* An hundred years are almost elapsed, since these overtures were made to the Moor; and as no effect hath yet followed, it should seem, that the conversion of the Mahometans to the Unitarian Christianity, is as unlikely as that of the Jews.

4. For the unbelievers, Sir, Mr Gibbon, as you seem yourself to intimate, hath given you but slender hopes.* Unbelievers indeed are of two descriptions. The sober Deists; who, rejecting revelation, acknowledge however the obligations of morality; believe a Providence; and expect a future retribution: and the Atheists; who have neither hope nor fear beyond the present life; deny the Providence of God; and doubt at least of his existence.

5. Infidels of the first description will hardly become your disciples, because you have nothing

---

* "——— Mr Gibbon has absolutely declined to discuss with me, as I proposed to him, the historical evidences of Christianity." Preface to Reply to Monthly Review, for June, p. 8.

to teach them, but what they think they know. " We think, they will say, no less reverently than you of the moral attributes of God. Upon our notions of his attributes we build an expectation of a future existence; and we look for·a lot of happiness or misery, in our future life, according to our deserts in this. The whole difference be- tween you and us is this: that we believe the same things upon different evidence; you, upon the testimony of a man, who, you say, was raised· up to preach these truths: we, upon the evidence of reason; which we think a higher evidence than any human testimony. We think that a revela- tion is pretended with a very ill grace, when no- thing hath been actually revealed. Revelation is discovery. The doctrines of a God, a Provi- dence, and a future state were known to the Jews before Christ; to the patriarchs before Moses; they have been known to thinking men in all ages: and there can be no place for discovery, where there hath been no concealment." If you would say, that the end of revelation is, to extend to all mankind that useful knowledge, which must otherwise have been enjoyed but by a few; to convey information by testimony to those who are incapable of informing themselves by abstract reasoning; that the gospel is therefore a revela- tion, because to the bulk of mankind it is a dis- covery, and a discovery of sufficient importance to claim a divine original: they will reply, that whatever weight this argument might carry, if it were urged by those who take the Scriptures in their literal meaning, and conceive that the revelation is conveyed in a plain undisguised language; it is a feeble weapon in the hand of an Unitarian. " If your method of interpretation be the true one, the first preachers of Christianity, they will say, differed not from other moralists, otherwise than by the wonderful obscurity of their language, and the air of mystery which they have contrived to throw over the simplest truths. Their enigmatic language is as little adapted to popular apprehension, as the abstruse reasonings of philosophers. The success of their doctrine hath been such, as might have been well foreseen. They were studious of obscurity—they have attained their end. They have been misunderstood by a great majority of their followers, for almost two thousand years. They professed to teach the pure worship of the true God. The language, in which they conveyed their doctrine, hath been the means of introducing the grossest idolatry. We will not trust ourselves to such dangerous guides, who, as you expound their writings, never spake upon the most interesting subjects, without figure and equivocation."

6. For the Atheistic infidels, who are in the first place to be convinced of the existence of a Deity ; your doctrine, that there is no mind in

man, but what results from the organization of the brain, will never lead them to conclude, that mind is older than body, in the universe. " You would persuade me, the Atheist will say, that there is an higher intellect than mine, the cause of all things. But if intellect in me be the result of motion, why not in any other intelligent? You only confirm my incredulity, and multiply my doubts. You make me doubt of my own intellect, while you would account for its production; and you confirm the suspicion, which I have long entertained, that the material world is older than its supposed maker: that mind, if indeed such a thing exist, hath like all other things started spontaneously from a corporeal chaos; and, instead of being the first cause and the governing principle, is the youngest of all nature's productions." Your principle that death is an utter extinction of the man, your Atheistical pupil will easily admit. But it is little likely to awaken him to the hope of a future existence. The hope which you hold out of a resurrection, he will tell you, is no hope at all, even admitting that the evidence of the thing could, upon your principles, be indisputable. " The atoms which compose *me*, your Atheist will say, may indeed have composed a man before, and may again. But *me* they will never more compose, when once the present *me* is dissipated. I have no recollection of a former, and no concern about a future self.

> Et nunc nihil ad nos de nobis attinet, anté
> Qui fuimus; nec jam de illis nos afficit angor,
> Quos de materiâ nostrâ nova proferet ætas.
>
> ....
>
> ....
>
> Inter enim jecta est vitäi pausa, vageque
> Decrârunt passim motus ab sensibus omnes."

7. It should seem, Sir, that your doctrines are ill calculated for the conversion of Jews or Infidels. Upon the Mahometans, their efficacy hath been tried without success. The Unitarians therefore, are not likely to be the instruments of these conversions.

I am, &c.

N. B. The story of the negociation on the part of the English Unitarians, in the reign of Charles the Second, with the ambassador of the emperor of Morocco, Dr Priestley, in the fifteenth of his Second Letters, is pleased to treat with great contempt, as an invention, that is to say, a lie or forgery, of Dr Leslie's. Fortunately the evidence of this extraordinary fact is yet extant in the Archiepiscopal Library at Lambeth. Among the *Codices Manuscripts Tenisoniani*, is a thin folio, marked with the number 678, and entered in the catalogue, under the article *Socinians*, by the title of *Systema Theologiæ Socinianæ.* It contains four tracts. The first is the very letter to Ameth Ben

Ameth, published by Dr Leslie, written in a very fair hand. On the preceding leaf are these remarks. " These are the original papers, which a cabal of Socinians in London offered to present to the Embassadour of the King of Fez and Morocco, when he was taking leave of England. August 1682. The said Embassadour refused to receive them, after having understood that they concerned religion. The agent of the Socinians was Monsieur Verze. Sir Charles Cottrell, Kn. Mr of the Cerem. then præsent, desired he might have them; which was graunted: and he brought them and gave them to me, Thomas Tenison, then Vicar of St Martin's in the Fields, Middl.

The second tract is in Latin, entitled, *Epistola Ameth Benundula Mahometani ad Auriacum Principem Comitum Mauritium, et ad Emmanuelem Portugalliæ Principem.*

The third tract is again in Latin, entitled, *Animadversiones in præcedentem Epistolam.* These two tracts are the Latin letter, and the remarks of the Unitarian divines upon it, which are mentioned in the English letter to Ameth Ben Ameth, and of which Dr Leslie, in his preface, says he had seen a printed copy.

The fourth tract I take to be the preface to the printed edition, or intended edition. This also is in Latin, and is inscribed *Theognis Irenæus Christiano Lectori salutem.*

I do most solemnly aver, that I have this day, Jan. 15, 1789, compared the letter to Ameth Ben Ameth, as published by Dr Leslie, in his *Socinian Controversy Discussed,* with the manuscript in the Archbishop's Library, and find that the printed copy, with the exception of some trivial typographical errors, which in no way affect the sense, and are such as any reader will discover and correct for himself, is exactly conformable to the manuscript, without the omission or addition of a single word. I do moreover aver, that the remarks in the leaf at the beginning of the manuscript, giving an account of its contents, and of the manner in which these papers came into the possession of Dr Tenison, were this same day copied verbatim from the manuscript, by myself upon the spot.

If Dr Priestley should mistrust my veracity in these assertions, (which I think he will not,) I promise him that I will at any time use my endeavours to procure him a sight of the manuscript, that he may satisfy himself.

LETTER SEVENTEENTH.

The archdeacon takes leave of the controversy.

DEAR SIR,

IT might be but consistent with the *pride*, which you impute to me as a churchman, and with the *contemptuous airs*, which I am apt to give myself with respect to dissenters,* were I to close our present correspondence without any notice of your animadversions upon that part of my Charge, which regards the studies of the younger clergy, and what you are pleased to call my terms of communion. It might be a sufficient, and not an unbecoming reply, to remind you that I spoke *ex cathedra*, and hold myself accountable for the advice which I gave, to no human judicature, except the KING, the Metropolitan, and my Diocesan. This would indeed be the only answer, which I should condescend to give to any one for whom I retained not, under all our differences, a very considerable degree of personal esteem. But as Dr Priestley is my adversary, in some points I could

---

* " If your pride as a churchman, and the contemptuous airs you give yourself with respect to dissenters, &c." Letters to Dr Horsley, p. 112.

wish to set him right, and in some I desire to explain.

2. If I have any where expressed myself contemptuously, the contempt is not of you, but of your argument upon a particular subject, upon which I truly think you argue very weakly; and of your information upon a point, in which I truly think you are ill informed. This hinders not, but that I may entertain the respect, which I profess, for your learning in other subjects; for your abilities in all subjects in which you are learned; and a cordial esteem and affection for the virtues of your character, which I believe to be great and amiable. Your attack being made upon those parts of the established faith, which I conceive to be fundamental principles of the Christian religion, I hold it my duty to shew the weakness of your reasoning; to expose your insufficiency in these subjects; and to bear my testimony aloud against your doctrine. Between duty to God and to his church, and respect for man, it were criminal to hesitate. Upon any occasion, wherein complaisance might be allowed to operate, you are the last person, whose feelings I would have wounded.

3. You seem to think that I secretly suspect you of artifices, which are incompatible with that purity of intention, which I would seem willing

to allow.* In your last pamphlet, you complain
that I have charged you with several instances of
gross disingenuity.† I am sensible, that, in these
letters, you will find more and stronger instances
of charges, which you will be apt to interpret as
unfavourably; and this, I fear, will heighten the
suspicion which you express, that even the compliments I sometimes pay you, are ironically
meant.‡

4. Indeed, Sir, in quoting ancient authors,
when you have understood the original, which
in many instances is not the case, you have too
often been guilty of much reserve and management. This appears in some instances, in which
you cannot pretend, that your own inadvertency,
or your printer's, hath given occasion to unmerited imputations. I wish that my complaints upon
this head had been groundless; but in justice to
my own cause, I could not suffer unfair quotations to pass undetected. I am unwilling to
draw any conclusion from this unseemly practice,
against the general probity of your character.
But you must allow me to lament, that men of
integrity, in the service of what they think a good
end, should indulge themselves so freely as they

---

* Letters to Dr Horsley, p. 12.
† Remarks on Monthly Review, p. 12, note.
‡ Letters to Dr Horsley, p. 110.

often do, in the use of unjustifiable means. Time was when the practice was openly avowed; and Origen himself was among its defenders. The art which he recommended, he scrupled not to employ. I have produced an instance, in which to silence an adversary, he had recourse to the wilful and deliberate allegation of a notorious falsehood. You have gone no such length as this, I think you may believe me sincere, when I speak respectfully of your worth and integrity, notwith-standing that I find occasion to charge you with some degree of blame, in a sort in which the great character of Origen was more deeply infected. Would God it had been otherwise. Would God I could with truth have boasted, " To these low arts stooped Origen; but my contemporary, my great antagonist, disdains them." How would it have heightened the pride of victory, could I have found a fair occasion to be thus the herald of my adversary's praise !

5. I am not sensible, that I have spoken con-temptuously of dissenters in general. A fair and consciencious dissent is not the object of con-tempt; neither is a petulant hostility against es-tablishments respectable. The praise which I give the Church of England, that she is the first in consideration of all the Protestant churches, is no more than liberal dissenters have themselves allowed. I have heard, from very good authori-

ty, of a conversation that passed between the late Dr Chandler, and a clergyman of the Church of Scotland, in which Chandler was a warm advocate for the constitution of the Church of England, in preference to any of the reformed churches. You will remember, that I make the learning and the piety of her clergy, of which ample monuments are extant, the basis of her pre-eminence; to which, however, another circumstance hath in some degree contributed; namely, that she had the discretion to observe some decency and moderation, in the business of reforming. I cannot admit, that mere distance from the Church of Rome, is the true standard of purity; and when you recollect, how strongly that maxim savours of Jack's spleen against Lord Peter, I am apt to think you will regret, that such a sentiment should stain your page.*

6. It is still my opinion, that any young clergyman who will diligently apply to the course of studies, which I took the liberty to recommend, may do without Dr Whitby's *Disquisitions,* or Dr Clarke's *Scripture Doctrine.*† The last treatise contains indeed a very full collection of the texts relating to the Trinity. The compilation from the fathers is incomplete; the learned au-

---

* Letters to Dr Horsley, p. 112.   † Ibid. p. 3,

thor having carefully selected those passages, which, taken by themselves in detachment from their contexts, seem favourable to his own opinions. I will not however deny, that to students of a certain description, the book may have its use. I myself perhaps owe something to it; which, as you recommend it to my particular attention, it seems incumbent upon me to declare. I believe, Sir, that few have thought so much upon these subjects, as you and I have done, who have not at first wavered. Perhaps nothing but the uneasiness of doubt, added to a just sense of the importance of the question, could engage any man in the toil of the inquiry. For my own part, I shall not hesitate to confess, that I set out with great scruples. But the progress of my mind hath been the very reverse of yours. It was at first my principle, as it is still yours, that all appearance of difficulty in the doctrine of the gospel must arise from misinterpretation; and I was fond of the expedient of getting rid of mystery, by supposing a figure in the language. The harshness of the figures, which I had sometimes occasion to suppose, and the obvious uncertainty of all figurative interpretations, soon gave me a distrust of this method of expounding : and Butler's Analogy, cured me of the folly of looking for nothing mysterious in the true sense of a divine revelation. By this cure I was prepared to become an easy convert to the doctrine of atonement and satisfaction; which seemed to furnish incentives to piety, that no other doctrine could supply. I soon perceived, how the value of the atonement was heightened, and what a sublimity accrued to the whole doctrine of redemption, by the notion, clearly conveyed in the Scriptures literally taken, of a Redeemer descending from a previous state of glory, to become our teacher, and to make the expiation. Thus I was brought to a full persuasion of our Lord's pre-existent dignity. Having once admitted his pre-existence in an exalted state, I saw the necessity of placing him at the head of the creation. " For a derived pre-existent being, supposed to animate the body of Jesus, who is not also the maker of the world, is, as you well observe, a mere creature of the imagination, whose existence is not to be inferred, with the least colourable pretext from the Scripture:"* since it is not to be found either in the literal, or in the figurative meaning. Not in the literal confessedly. Not in the figurative; because if the texts, which speak of Christ as the maker of the world, admit a figurative construction; much more those which refer only to his pre-existence."† I thank you, Sir, for expressing my own sentiments with so much perspicuity, and

---

* Letters to Dr Horsley, p. 84.
† Hist. of Corrup. vol. i. p. 146.

for proving them with so much evidence. Being thus convinced, that our Lord Jesus Christ is indeed the Maker of all things; I found, that I could not rest satisfied with the notion, of a Maker of the universe *not God.* I saw that all the extravagancies of the Gnostics hung upon that one principle: and I could have little opinion of the truth of a principle, which seemed so big with mischief. I then set myself to consider, whether I knew enough of the divine unity, to pronounce the " Trinity an infringement of it." Upon this point the Platonists, whose acquaintance I now began to cultivate, soon brought me to a right mind. It was in this stage of my inquiries, while I was wavering between the Arian tenets in their original extent, and the true faith, that I first opened Dr Clarke's *Scripture Doctrine of the Trinity.* I sat seriously down to the perusal of the book—I rose a firm and decided Trinitarian. And why not recommend to others, you will say, a book which had so principal a share in your own conversion? I will tell you. It is one of those books, which may either instruct or mislead, according to the previous attainments and habits of the student. I was much at home in the Greek language; I had read the ecclesiastical historians; and I had been many years in the habit of thinking for myself, upon a variety of subjects, before I opened Dr Clarke's book. There is in most men a culpable timidity; you and I perhaps have

overcome that general infirmity; but there is in
most men a culpable timidity, which inclines them
to be easily overawed by the authority of great
names: and, much as we talk of the freedom and
liberality of thinking and inquiry, it is this slavish
principle, not, as is pretended, any. freedom of
original thought, which makes converts to infidelity and heresy. Fools imagine, that the greatest
authorities are always on the side of new and
singular opinions; and that, by adopting them,
they get themselves into better company, than
they have naturally any right to keep: and thus
they are secretly worshippers of authority, in that
very act in which they pretend to fly in the face
of it. They worship private authority, while
they fly in the face of universal. They deride an
old and general tradition, because they have not
sagacity to trace the connexion of its parts, and
to perceive the force of the entire evidence: and
while they thus trample on the accumulated authority of ages, with an idiot simplicity they suffer themselves to be led by the mere name of
the writer of the day,—a Bolingbroke, a Voltaire,
a Gibbon, or a Priestley; as if they thought to
become wise and learned, by taking a share and
an interest in the follies, or the party-views, of
men of abilities and learning. And where a secret consciousness of ignorance is not accompanied with the vain ambition of being thought wise;
still an undue deference to private authority, in

prejudice of established opinion, seems to be the side upon which, even modest men, are liable to err. Insomuch, that every man may be supposed to partake of this infirmity, in subjects in which he feels himself unlearned. To those, therefore, who are qualified to use Dr Clarke's book as a digest, which, though incomplete, may assist them in forming a judgment for themselves; to those who can and will turn it to this use, it may be serviceable. But they, who from a modest sense of their own insufficiency in the learned languages, and in ecclesiastical history, may be disposed to listen to the opinion of the writer, will be more misled by his authority, than they will be informed by the compilation. In a word, it is a book of which a scholar may make his use; but I cannot recommend it to young divines, in the beginning of their studies.

7. In the conclusion of your seventh letter, you speak of a certain defence of Bishop Bull's, of the damnatory clause in the Athanasian creed; of which, inasmuch as I have recommended the writings of Bishop Bull without exception, you " presume, you tell me, that I approve." And to correct these expressions, which state as a presumption only, or an inference, what might be directly proved upon me by my own words, you add in a parenthesis, that I have mentioned this among the most valuable works of that learned

prelate.* Of whatever importance, Sir, I may conceive it to be, that the faith which was first delivered to the saints, should be preserved whole and undefiled; whatever I may think of the folly and the crime of setting up private judgment for the rule of public opinion, in opposition to a tradition traced to the first ages, and by consequence of the same authority with that on which the credit of the canon rests, I am no lover of damnatory clauses. I am an enemy to any application of damnatory clauses to particular persons. I am hopeful, that there is more folly in the world than malignity; more ignorance than positive infidelity; more error than heretical perverseness. How is it then, that I recommend a defence of the damnatory clause, among the most valuable of a learned Bishop's works? Sir, did you write this in your sleep? Or is it in a dream only that I seem to read it; Bishop Bull's defence of the damnatory clause! From you, Sir, I have now my first information that Bishop Bull ever wrote upon the subject. The writings of Bishop Bull, which I have particularly recommended, are these three Latin treatises: *Defensio fidei Nicenæ; Judicium Ecclesiæ Catholicæ de necessitate credendi Jesum Christum esse verum Deum; Primitiva et Apostolica traditio de Jesu Christi divinitate.* To

---

* Letters to Dr Horsley, p. 100.

which I might have added a fourth, of less importance, *Animadversiones in brevem tractatum Gul.
Clerke,* &c. These are all his writings upon the
Trinitarian controversy, which are contained in
the edition of his Latin works, by Grabe. In
these treatises there is no defence of the damnatory clause; nor, that I recollect, any mention of
the Athanasian creed. There is no defence of
the damnatory clause in the sermons and English
tracts published by Mr Nelson. Nor can I find
any such tract mentioned by Mr Nelson among
the Bishop's lost works; for many small pieces,
which it was known that he had written, were
never found after his death. Where have I mentioned, Sir, with such high approbation, a work
which I declare I have never seen; and of which,
you will forgive me, if I still doubt the existence?*

---

* Dr Priestley is reduced to the necessity of confessing, in the
sixteenth of his Second Letters, that he knows no more than I,
in what library any work of Bishop Bull's, upon the damnatory
clause in the Athanasian creed, is to be found. And yet he affects to be indignant, that I should presume to resent a false accusation; a calumny, founded on my pretended admiration of a
work that never existed. It seems, when he spoke of this defence, he had in his mind the *Judicium Ecclesiæ Catholicæ,* but,
" not looking into the title-page of the book," he described it by
a wrong name. But unfortunately, his description is not more
erroneous in the name, than in the subject. The occasion and
manner of his error, may easily be divined. Having no acquaintance with Bishop Bull's writings, but what his controversy
with me hath occasioned, when he wrote his First Letters, he
made a guess about the particular subject of each work, from
the titles enumerated by me. Among these he found the " *Ju-*

' 8. Had I been aware of the offence which I find the word *conventicle* hath given, I would have avoided the use of it. We are engaged in a subject, in which I hold it my duty to display my ar-

---

dicium Ecclesiæ Catholicæ," &c. He guessed that this judgment of the Catholic church, which Bishop Bull defended, was a judgment founded on the damnatory clause in the Athanasian creed. So he guessed, that Bishop Bull, defending that judgment, must have defended the damnatory clause: and he chose to guess further, that I, the professed admirer of Bishop Bull, of all parts of his writings the most admired that defence.

Dr Priestley hath since indeed looked further into this matter. And at the time when he drew up his Second Letters, he had discovered that the judgment of the church, defended by Bishop Bull, is the anathema of the Nicene council against those, who should in any way impugn the article of our Lord's divinity. This Bishop Bull indeed defends; that is, he maintains the historical fact, that the fathers of the Nicene council enforced the belief of that article, under the solemn sanction of a public sentence; which fact Episcopius had denied.

Dr Priestley, being now informed of the real subject of Bishop Bull's treatise, says, " that the damnatory clause in the Athanasian creed, and the anathema annexed to the Nicene, are things exactly of the same nature." Were I to undertake the defence of the damnatory clause in the Athanasian creed, it should indeed be upon this principle,—that it is a thing somewhat of the same nature with the anathema annexed to the Nicene. The anathema is no part of the Nicene creed; it is only a sentence of the church, against the impugners of a particular article. What is called the damnatory clause, is no part of the Athanasian. It is a clause, not of the creed, but of a prefatory sentence, in which the author declares his opinion of the importance of the rule of faith he is about to deliver. But in whatever degree the damnatory clause may be capable or incapable of apology, Dr Priestley is, I believe, the only writer, who ever confounded two things so totally distinct, as an anathema, and an article of faith; which he conceives the damnatory clause to be. An anathema is simply a sentence of excommunication. The church of England anathematizes those, who speak disre-

gument in its utmost force; and even to use pretty freely that high seasoning of controversy, which
may interest the reader's attention; but I would
not wilfully give offence by harsh words, from
which the reasoning may acquire neither force
nor lustre. You say, that the word conventicle
usually signifies, an unlawful assembly. For my
own part I thought it barely equivalent to the old
Greek word συνλυσις, which was the name for certain irregular assemblies, not as illegal; for the
word was brought into use in an age when all assemblies of Christians were, in the civil sense, equally illegal; but it was the name for assemblies,
meeting for the purpose of religious worship, without authority from the bishop. Such assemblies,
in the primitive ages, were thought to be spiritually unauthorised; and in this sense, the word
conventicle is applicable at this day to many religious meetings, which are not liable to any legal

---

spectfully of her Book of Common Prayer, (see the IVth Canon). But that every person, who shall incur the anathema of
the IVth Canon, shall perish everlastingly, is no clause of the
church of England's creed.

Dr Priestley hath lengthened his sixteenth letter, with a recital of several passages from Bishop Bull's works, which, he
thinks, must compel me to acknowledge, that, whatever I may
be, Bishop Bull at least was a friend to damnatory clauses.
The sentiments expressed by Bishop Bull, in the passages produced by Dr Priestley, I would be understood to cherish and
embrace, with the most entire unqualified approbation. If to
cherish such sentiments, and to be a friend to damnatory clauses,
be the same thing, I stand convicted. *Habet confitentem reum.*

penalties. I could have wished, that the use of it
had been considered as one of the mere archaisms
of my style, in which nothing of insult was intended. I must however declare, that it would give
me particular pleasure to receive conviction, that
Mr Lindsey's meeting-house, and your own, are
not more emphatically conventicles, in your sense,
that is, in the worst sense of the word. From
personal respect for you and him, I should be
happy to be assured, that you stand not within
the danger of the 35th of Eliz. c. i; or the 17th
C. ii. c. 2. To the penalties of which, and of other
statutes, I must take the liberty to tell you, you
are obnoxious, notwithstanding the late act of the
19th of His present Majesty, in favour of dissenters, unless at the quarter-sessions of the peace for
the county where you live, you have made a certain declaration,* which is required by that act,
instead of the subscription to articles required by
the former acts of toleration. I am sorry, Sir, to
inform you, that I find no entry of Mr Lindsey's
declaration, in the office of the clerk of the peace,
either for the county of Middlesex, or the city of
Westminster. Could I make the same inquiry
concerning you, (which the distance of your residence prevents,) I fear I should have the mortification to find, that you have, no more than your

---

* Appendix, No. VI.

friend, complied with the laws, from which you claim protection. A report prevails, that you both object to the declaration, from conscientious scruples. A very sufficient excuse for not making it; but no excuse at all for doing what the law allows not to be done, except upon the express condition, that the declaration be previously made. Had you made the declaration, you might indeed be-entitled to the same indulgence, by virtue of the late act, to which you would have been entitled, by a subscription to certain articles under former acts of toleration; but not without the performance of certain other conditions, required by the 1st of William and Mary, c. 18, from which other conditions, dissenters are not released by any subsequent statutes. For the single operation of the 19th of our present gracious Sovereign, c. 44, is to substitute a short and general declaration, instead of a more particular subscription. All other limitations of the indulgences granted by the first of William and Mary, stand as they were. Had you therefore made the declaration, which the law demands, still to entitle your meetings to the benefit of the toleration, it would have been necessary that the places of them should be certified, (according to the last clause of 1st of William and Mary, c. 18,) either to the bishop of the diocese, or to the archdeacon of the archdeaconry, or to the justices of the peace at the general or quarter-sessions of the peace for the county, city, or place

where such meeting may be held.*——I have
searched the registers of the episcopal court of
London, of the archdeacon's court of Middlesex,
and the records of the sessions for the county of
Middlesex, and for the city of Westminster, for
an entry of the house in Essex-street, without
success.† About your meeting-house I am pre-
cluded, as before, from making a regular inquiry.
But I fear you have not taken the proper measures
for your legal security; because the professed
ground of your dissent from the church of England, is not a mere disagreement about particular
articles, but a general denial of the magistrate's
authority, either to prohibit or to tolerate.‡ Still,
Sir, were you ready to comply with the requisi-
tions of the law in these two particulars, the declaration of your own belief in the holy Scriptures,
and the notification of the place of meeting, to the
ecclesiastical or the secular magistrate, Mr Lindsey and you, by the doctrines which you publicly
maintain,§ are excluded from all benefits of the
acts of toleration. Your meeting-house and his,

---

* Appendix, No. V.

† See the seventeenth of Dr Priestley's Second Letters, and
my Remarks upon the Second Letters, Part II. cap. iv. sec. 6.

‡ " Exclusive of every thing contained in the religion of the
church of England, it is chiefly the authority by which it is enjoined, that dissenters object to in it." Hist. of Corrup. vol. ii.
p. 357.

§ Appendix, No. IV.

contrary to your imagination, are *illegal*; UN-
KNOWN to the laws, and UNPROTECTED by them.
If this be the definition of a conventicle, they are
CONVENTICLES by the express letter of the law,
and in your own construction of the word. Still,
Sir, I had no thought to insult over your miserable *unprotected* state. The extravagant outcry
which you have made, and the arrogance with
which you presume to set your conventicles upon
a footing with our own churches,* have provoked
me to salute you with these unwelcome truths.
Respect for individuals in Mr Lindsey's congregation and in yours, as well as for you and him,
would have restrained me from the use of a word,
which I had perceived to be any otherwise reproachful, than as it might contain a strong disapprobation and censure of your doctrine, and a serious disavowal of your authority to exercise the
sacred function. If this is to be deemed reproach,
I am not at liberty to abstain from it. Your doctrine I must disapprove and censure; because I
conceive it to be a gross, I trust not a wilful, corruption of the word of God. If your authority,—
I speak not now of the authority which derives
from human laws; but even in *that* you are deficient; for a mere exemption from civil penalties,

---

* "—— our places of worship are as legal as yours—equally
known to the laws, and protected by them." Letters to Dr
Horsley, p. 112.

which still is more than you enjoy, differs from
authority, just as the king's pardon differs from
his favour: if your spiritual authority, as ministers of the word and sacraments, is wrongfully
called in question, you must bear with the prejudices of a churchman, who, when he reviews the
practice of the primitive ages; when he ponders
our Saviour's parting promise to be always present with the apostles, the delegated preachers
of the gospel, even to the end of the world; when
he connects it with the history of the first ordina-
tions, and with the great stress laid upon the
Bishop's authority, by Clemens, the fellow-labourer of St Paul, by Ignatius, the disciple of St
John, and by the whole church for many ages,
allows himself to be easily persuaded, that the
authority of the commission, under which he acts,
is something more than mere human legislation
can convey; and, while he would abhor to enforce civil penalties, may think it his duty occasionally to protest against a spiritual usurpation.
Indeed, Sir, when I revolve in my thoughts the
various disorders and distractions, which I have
seen in my own country, within the compass of
my own life, arising from the irregular zeal of
self-constituted teachers of religion; when I reflect, how the unity of the church hath been torn,
how tender consciences are every day disturbed
with groundless scruples, and melancholy tempers
driven to insanity; how the simplicity of the vul-

gar hath been first abused, and their principles in
the end' unsettled; when I recollect, how eminently the state hath been lately endangered, and
the Protestant cause disgraced, by a combination
of wild fanatics, pretending to associate for the
preservation of the reformed religion; when I
consider, how by these scandals the true religion
hath itself been brought into discredit; how it
hath been injured by attempts to inflame devotion
on the one hand, and by theories fabricated to reduce the mystery of its doctrines on the other;
when I consider, that the root of all these evils
hath been the prevalency of a principle, of which
you seem disposed to be an advocate, that every
man who hath credit enough to collect a congregation, hath a right, over which the magistrate
cannot without tyranny exercise controul, to celebrate divine worship according to his own form,
and to propagate his own opinions; I am inclined
to be jealous of a principle, which hath proved, I
had almost said, so ruinous; and I lean the more
to the opinion, that the commission of a ministry,
perpetuated by regular succession, is something
more than a dream of cloistered gownmen, or a
tale imposed upon the vulgar, to serve the ends of
avarice and ambition. For whatever confusion
human folly may admit, a divine institution must
have within itself a provision for harmony and
order. And upon these principles, though I wish

that all indulgence should be shewn to tender
consciences, and will ever be an advocate for the
largest toleration that may be consistent with political wisdom, being indeed persuaded, that the
restraints of human laws must be used with the
greatest gentleness and moderation, to be rendered means of strengthening the bands of Christian peace and amity; yet I could wish to plant a
principle of severe restraint in the consciences of
men. I could wish, that the importance of the
ministerial office were considered; that the practice of antiquity were regarded; and that it might
not seem a matter of perfect indifference to the
laity, to what house of worship they resort. I
cannot admit, that every assembly of grave and
virtuous men, in which grave and virtuous men
take upon them to officiate, is to be dignified with
the appellation of a church; and for such irregular assemblies, which are not churches, I could
wish to find a name of distinction void of opprobrium. As such I used the word conventicle,
as expressing great irregularity, (which I must express, wo! is me if I express it not,) but no infamy of the assemblies to which I applied it. If
you are still disposed to be indignant about this
harmless word, recollect I beseech you, with
what respect you have yourself treated the venerable body to which I belong,—the clergy of the
establishment. You divide it into two classes

only: the ignorant, and the insincere.* Have I no share in this opprobrium of my order? Have I no right to be indignant in my turn?

9. Still looking forward to the time, when after all that is past, we shall mutually forgive, and be ourselves forgiven, I remain,

DEAR SIR,

Your very humble Servant, &c.

Fulham Palace,
June 15th, 1784.

---

* Dr Priestley, in his History of Corruptions, vol. i. p. 147, says of the Trinitarians of the present age, under which denomination it is evident he alludes to the clergy of the established church, for he afterwards describes these Trinitarians, as persons " to all of whom the emoluments of the establishment are equally accessible;" he says of these persons, that " they are all reducible to two classes, *viz.* that of those, who, if they were ingenuous, would rank with Socinians, believing that there is no proper divinity in Christ besides that of the Father; or else with Tritheists, holding three equal and distinct Gods." The first class surely must be insincere, as not believing what they profess; the second ignorant, as not perceiving what it is that they believe. In the conclusion of his History, vol. ii. p. 471, he says, that all that is urged in defence of the present system, by men of the greatest eminence in the church, who have appeared as its advocates, " is so palpably weak, that it is barely possible they should be in earnest—in thinking their arguments have that weight in themselves, which they wish them to have with others." And he speaks of this insincerity of the defenders of the establishment, as a thing so notorious, that it may be reckoned " one of the worst symptoms of the present times." After all this, in his appendix to his Second Letters, he denies that he ever intended to make that division of the whole body

APPENDIX.

―――――

No. I.

Gentleman's Magazine, for October, 1783, *p.* 842.

MR URBAN,

I was formerly a pupil of Dr Harwood, and read with my learned and worthy master Thucydides, Sophocles, and the life of Moses, in a magnificent edition of Philo, printed by the learned Mr Bowyer; and wonder that Dr Horsley should assert, as he is represented to do by the learned and ingenious Mr Maty, in his New Review, that ἀτος is spoken of *persons* only; when it is applied to any thing of which the writer is speaking, that happens to be of the masculine gender. For instance, it is predicated of bread *twice* in John vi.

―――――

of the established clergy, which I ascribe to him, into the two classes of the ignorant and the insincere: he treats the charge as a calumny, from which he justifies himself, by producing a long passage from one of his sermons, in which he professes to hold the church of England in no less estimation than the church of Rome.

50, 58, ἔτος ἔτι ὁ ἀρλος, and of a stone, Luke xx. 17, *the same; viz.* stone, ἔτος is *become head of the corner.* Controversialists are apt to overshoot the mark.

GRÆCULUS.

No. II.

Gentleman's Magazine, for November, 1783, *p.* 944.

MR URBAN,

BE pleased, Sir, to inform your correspondent, *Græculus,* that Dr Horsley has not asserted of the Greek pronoun ἔτος, that it is spoken of persons *only.* He renders it indeed, in the second verse of the first chapter of St John's gospel, by the words " This Person," and he says, in a parenthesis, that " this is its natural force." And this, Sir, may be, although by the usage of the Greek writers, it is applicable, as *Græculus* with great truth remarks, to any thing of which the writer is speaking, that happens to be of the masculine gender: for few words, in any language, are confined to their natural and primary meaning. But, since the application of the word is confessedly so general in the best writers, *Græculus* will perhaps be apt to put the question, how should Dr Horsley know, that " This Person," is more the natural sense of ἔτος, than " This Loaf,"

or this any thing? Perhaps Dr Horsley has observed, that it is peculiar to the two pronouns
ἑτος, and αὐτος, to be used to any one of the three
persons. Which is one argument, that their proper sense is personal. Perhaps Dr Horsley has
observed, that the pronoun ἑτος, when it is demonstrative of any thing which has no person, and
which the writer would not personify, is often
put in the *neuter* gender, although the noun,
which it represents, be masculine——ἐπειδαν δε ταυτα
λυσητε——*after you have abrogated these* LAWS——
νομους. Demosth. Olynth. iii.——τουτο ἐστι το σωμα μυ. this
[*i. e.* this bread, αρτος] is my body. Matt. xxvi. 6.
This is another argument, that ἑτος is naturally demonstrative of a person. For there are but three
causes, to which the various anomalies of speech
may be referred. Ignorance, negligence, design.
Those, which are frequent in the best writers,
can be ascribed to neither of the two first causes.
They must have arisen therefore from the third.
But the third, design, implies an end. And what
should be the end of this anomaly of gender, in
the word ἑτος, but that it was the means of avoiding an appearance of a *prosopopœia*, where no *prosopopœia* was intended.

2. Perhaps *Græculus*, though perfectly right in
his remark, that ἑτος may be demonstrative of any
thing of which the Greek name is masculine, has
been unfortunate in his selection of passages in

proof of it. Perhaps of the three, which he has produced, two are nothing to his purpose. Perhaps ὃτος ἐστιν ὁ ἁγίος, &c. in both the texts in St John, should be rendered " This person is the bread, &c." *i. e.* I am the bread, &c. It may be supposed that our Lord pointed to himself, when he said this. As the Baptist points to himself, when he says, Οὗτος γὰρ ἐστιν ὁ ῥηθεὶς, &c. " For this person is the person spoken of, &c." *i. e.* For I am the person spoken of, &c. Matt. iii. 3. For that these are the Baptist's, not the historian's words, is evident from the form, in which the following sentence is begun. Αὐτὸς δὲ ὁ Ἰωάννης. " Now this same John, &c." a form which marks the writer's resumption of his narrative, interrupted by the insertion of John's words.

3. Perhaps Dr Horsley had not erred, had he affirmed, that, in John i. 2. ἐτος must necessarily be rendered by " This Person." The utmost liberty of choice, which the context leaves, is between *two* expositions only : " This Person," or " This Word." If the latter be adopted, the second verse will be only a useless repetition of what had been before affirmed. Whereas in Dr Horsley's view of it, it contains an explicit assertion of the personality of the Logos, which with great propriety and significance, precedes the mention of his agency in the next verse,

4. Perhaps to have read some two or three difficult authors with a master, may have made *Græculus* almost a match for the brightest boys in the upper forms of our public schools. Perhaps something more should be done in the study of the Greek language, before a man begin to play the critic in it. Ἡ γαρ των λογων κρισις πολλης ἰστι πιιρας τιλιυταιον ἰπιγιννημα.

I am, Sir,

Your most obedient,

PERHAPS.

No. III.

Short strictures on Dr Priestley's Letters to Dr Horsley, by an unknown hand.

LETTERS to Dr Horsley, page 9. Jesus Christ is come in the flesh. Dr Priestley should produce an instance, where the whole phrase of *coming in the flesh,* is applied to the birth or appearances of any mere man. The instances alleged by him, prove nothing to his purpose.

Page 18. The epistles of Ignatius. Dr Priestley is certainly in the right to reprobate these epistles, if he can. They subvert all his theology and history.* But who are these learned in general, that have given them up as spurious? There are the names of great critics on the other side, of whose arguments Archbishop Wake has given a judicious summary, in his preliminary discourse: and till they are refuted, Dr Horsley has an undoubted right to appeal to these epistles, as containing the sentiments of an apostolical father.

Page 14. If Dr Priestley could prove, that the Nazarenes held the same doctrines with the Ebionites, what would it avail his cause? Could he prove by this medium, that the Nazarenes *continued* in the doctrine of the apostles, and that the reputed Catholic church fell off from it? Did the Ebionites learn from the apostles, that John the Baptist came preaching in the days of Herod the king of Judea; that Christ descended into Jesus, in the form of a dove, at his baptism; *cum multis aliis?* See Epiphan. Hæres. xxx. sec. 14.

24. Here, and throughout, Dr Priestley supposes the Unitarian doctrine to have had a general prevalence among the Gentile Christians, and universal among the Jewish. Does this well agree, with respect to the Gentiles, with his quotation from Origen, at the bottom of page 20?

---

* The chief of them are mentioned by Cave, under Ignatius.

Y

The much controverted passage of Justin Martyr, in his Dialogue with Trypho,* and the meaning of Ἡμετερου γἰνους, are well illustrated by Mr Bingham, in his Vindication of the doctrine and liturgy of the Church of England, printed at Oxford, 1774, page 23. There were according to Justin, SOME countrymen of his, Jews, and Samaritans, " who confess him to be the Christ, yet affirm him to be a mere man." The same Justin says in another place, First Apol. p. 78, Ed. Thirlby,—that he had observed more and truer Christians, from among the Gentiles, than from among the Jews and Samaritans. This passage, (which helps to confirm Mr Bingham's translation of Ἡμετερου γἰνους,) compared with the other, contains the testimony of Justin, that there were only SOME of the Jews and Samaritans, and still fewer of the Gentiles, professing to believe in Christ, who affirmed him to be a mere man.

Page 39. Dr Priestley, who seems to be very moderately skilled in Greek, may give a faulty translation sometimes, through inadvertency. But what shall we say for his rendering αἰτίας εὐλογω, a specious pretence? Can he really think, that Athanasius meant to speak in this style, of the conduct of the apostles? Ἀιτία εὐλογος occurs in Chrysostom

* See Priestley, page 127.

on Matt. xxiv. 42. (tom. ii, p. 448. Ed. Savil,) where though ἀιλία signifies somewhat differently, ἴυλογος bears the same sense, as here, of wise and reasonable.

In the same passage ἔρχισθαι is mistranslated. As the present infinitives have sometimes a future sense in the best classic authors, it here means a Messiah TO COME, as the next sentence evinces, where Christ already come, is said ἐληλυθέναι.

49. Another inaccurate version of Athanasius.

50. Another of the like kind from Chrysostom. Dr Priestley makes him say,—our Saviour *never* taught his own divinity in express words. Chrysostom, I apprehend, says,—that he did not every where, or, on all occasions, ὀυ παιλαχὸυ, speak plainly of his own divinity. In the judgment of Chrysostom, he sometimes did so. See on John vi. 35, 36. viii. 58, x. 30.

56. Last paragraph. Caiaphas adjures our Saviour, by the living God, to tell them, *Whether thou be the Christ, the Son of God?* Our Lord avows, these characters, and adds, *Nevertheless* (rather, moreover) *I say unto you, Hereafter ye shall see the Son of Man sitting on the right hand of power.* How can Dr Priestley be sure, in what sense Caiaphas understood our Lord's answer,

when he rent his clothes, and accused him of blasphemy? Was the notion of a Son of God superior
to all created beings, then unknown among the
Jews? See, besides Bishop Bull's Defens. Fidei
Nicænæ, cap. i. sect. 1, § 16, p. 13, a remarkable
passage quoted from Philo Jud. by Dr Randolph,
Vindication of the doctrine of the Trinity, part I.
p. 29.

LETTER V.

Dr Priestley makes the fathers *acknowledge,*
that the apostles did not preach the divinity of
Christ *early,* and confidently supposes them *never*
to have taught it.

According to the more general opinion, St Matthew wrote his gospel early, and for the Jews.
In the opening of this gospel, he applies the name
Emmanuel to our Lord, and gives his own interpretation of it, *God with us :* by which, plain people conceive him to mean what St Paul expresses,
God manifest in the flesh ; and the apostolical Ignatius, *God appearing in the form of a man.* Ad.
Eph. xix. If we are led into an error, it is by
taking St Matthew's words in their literal and ob-

vious sense: and was he less solicitous about the truth than even Dr Priestley himself? If Dr Priestley had been to write a gospel, according to his own theology, would he have set out with such an application and interpretation of the name Emmanuel? *Quod tu non feceris, Ego feci?* might St Paul ask; who writes with the greatest simplicity, and never uses any amplification of any subject treated by him: and, as we may justly conclude, would not here have spoken of Christ as he has done, but because he had very different notions of his dignity, from those of Dr Priestley: to declare which notions, he was not afraid of Jewish prejudices and clamour.

In the same gospel, our Lord is introduced declaring, " No one knoweth the Son but the Father; neither knoweth any one the Father, save the Son, and he to whomsoever the Son will reveal him." Here the negative *ουδεις* being universal, we seem to be told, that the Father and Son are incomprehensible to all created intelligences; and that all they can really know of the Father, must be in and through the Son, by his illuminating spirit. Does such a declaration consist with Dr Priestley's plan, with what our Lord says of himself in the next verse but one, " I am meek and lowly in heart?" *Utique parum modeste (sit verbo venia) de seipso locutus est Christus, aut alios loquentes audivit, si nihil interea præter me-*

rum hominem se esse noverit. Burnet de Fide et
Officiis, p. 20.[*]

The same Saviour, in the concluding paragraph
of this gospel, commands his apostles to evange-
lize all nations, baptizing them in the name of
the Father, and of the Son, and of the Holy
Ghost. Dr Priestley considers the Holy Spirit as
an attribute of the Father, not a person. But
does our Lord, if he had only an exalted humanity, thrust himself in between the Most High, and
one of his incommunicable attributes? or does he
join two persons with an attribute, in a most solemn form of words, which leads us almost inevitably to believe, that the third is a person also?
Would such a conduct appear suitable to his care
and tenderness to guide his flock into the whole
truth? The supposition seems impossible; and
nothing can be more certain, than that the very
first evangelist, in full harmony with all the succeeding sacred writers, exhibits to us the divinity
of Christ, in the beginning, middle, and end of
his gospel.

It is objected to this form of baptism, that the
use of it does not appear any where in the Acts

---

[*] This is quoted by Dr Randolph, Vind. Part II, p. 42,
where a similar passage is cited from St Chrysostom.

of. the apostles. This objection is, I think, well answered by Mr Bingham, Vindicat. p. 37—41. particularly from Acts xix.

Page 63. Towards the end of the first paragraph, Dr Priestley seems to betray some suspicions, that St Paul did in truth teach the divinity of Christ.

Page 69. Last paragraph. The reasoning appears rather extraordinary on the passage of Athanasius, who seems made, by Dr Priestley, to consider things in the same light, between which he is studious to point out an eternal difference.

LETTER VII.

PAGE 92. " If the doctrine of the Trinity be true, it is no doubt in the highest degree important and interesting." So Dr Priestley can say, when it serves his purpose. But how does this agree with his previous observations, No. IV. p. 85, &c.?

Page 133. It is somewhat hard to discover, how the remark on Eusebius, and his treatment of the

Unitarians, *at that time very numerous,* agrees with the observation in the preceding paragraph.

Page 135. Was the hymn, which as Pliny tells us in his noted epistle, was sung to Christ *quasi Deo,* novel, in the time of Paul of Samosata?

Page 136. Dr Priestley should, I think, have prefixed that which seems to be his ruling maxim, that the human mind is competent to search all things, even the deep things of God.

Whether he, or Mr Burgh, in the first chapter of his Scriptural Confutation, lays down the province of reason in the better way, let others determine.

No. IV.

1 *W. & M. c.* 18.

PROVIDED always, That neither this act, nor any clause, article, or thing herein contained, shall extend————to give any ease, benefit, or advantage to————any person that shall deny in his preaching or writing, the doctrine of the Blessed Trinity, as it is declared in the aforesaid articles of religion.

No. V.

1 *W. & M. c.* 18.

PROVIDED always, That no congregation or
assembly for religion, shall be permitted or allowed by this act, until the place of such meeting
shall be certified to the bishop of the diocese, or
to the archdeacon of the archdeaconry, or to the
justices of the peace, at the general or quarter-
sessions of the peace for the county, city, or
place in which such meeting shall be held, and registered in the said bishop's or archdeacon's court
respectively, or recorded at the said general or
quarter-sessions.

No. VI.

19 *G. III. c.* 44.

———— be it enacted, ———— That every person dissenting from the church in holy orders, or
pretended holy orders, or pretending to holy
orders, being a preacher or teacher of any congregation of dissenting Protestants, who————shall
take the oaths, and make and subscribe the declaration against popery, required by the said act,
(1 W. & M. c. 18,) and shall also make and subscribe a declaration in the words following, *videlicet:*

" I A. B. do solemnly declare, in the presence of Almighty God, that I am a Christian and a Protestant, and as such, that I believe that the Scriptures of the Old and New Testament, as commonly received among Protestant churches, do contain the revealed will of God; and that I do receive the same as the rule of my doctrine and practice." Shall be——entitled to all the exemptions, benefits, privileges, and advantages granted to Protestant dissenting ministers, by 1 W. & M. c. 18, and by 10 A. c. ——and every such person, qualifying himself as aforesaid, shall be exempted from serving in the militia of this kingdom, and shall also be exempted from any imprisonment or other punishment, by virtue of the act of uniformity, &c.

A

SERMON

ON THE

INCARNATION,

PREACHED IN THE

PARISH CHURCH

OF

S<small>T</small> MARY NEWINGTON,

I<small>N</small> S<small>URREY</small>, Dec. 25, 1785.

SERMON,

&c.

LUKE i. 28.

———Hail thou that art highly favoured, the Lord is with thee: Blessed art thou among women.

THAT she, who in these terms was saluted by an angel, should in after ages become an object of superstitious adoration, is a thing far less to be wondered, than that men, professing to build their whole hopes of immortality on the promises de-livered in the sacred books, and closely inter-woven with the history of our Saviour's life, should question the truth of the message which the angel brought. Some nine years since, the Christian Church, was no less astonished than offended, by an extravagant attempt* to heighten, as it was pretended, the importance of the Christian revelation, by overturning one of those first principles of natural religion, which had for ages been considered as the basis, upon which the whole superstructure of revelation stands. The notion of an immaterial principle in man, which, without an immediate exertion of the Divine power, to the express purpose of its destruction, must necessarily survive the dissolution of the body; the notion of an immortal soul, was condemned and exploded, as an invention of heathen philosophy. Death was represented as an utter extinction of the whole man, and the evangelical doctrine of a resurrection of the body, in an improved state, to receive again its immortal inhabitant, was heightened into the mystery of a reproduction of the annihilated person. How a person once annihilated could be re-produced, so as to be the same person which had formerly existed, when no principle of sameness, nothing necessarily permanent, was supposed to enter the original composition; how the present person could be interested in the future person's fortunes; why *I* should be at all concerned for the happiness or misery of the man, who some ages hence shall be

---

* Disquisitions relating to Matter and Spirit, &c. London 1777.

raised from my ashes; when the future man could be no otherwise the same with me, than as he was arbitrarily to be called the same, because his body was to be composed of the same matter which now composes mine: these difficulties were but ill explained. It was thought a sufficient recommendation of the system, with all its difficulties, that the promise of a resurrection of the body seemed to acquire a new importance from it, (but the truth is, that it would lose its whole importance, if this system could be establised, since it would become a mere prediction concerning a future race of men, and would be no promise to any men now existing,) and the notion of the soul's natural immortality, was deemed an unseemly appendage of a Christian's belief, for this singular reason, that it had been entertained by wise and virtuous heathens, who had received no light from the Christian, nor, as it was supposed, from any earlier revelation.

It might have been expected, that this anxiety to extinguish every ray of hope, which beams not from the glorious promises of the gospel, would have been accompanied with the most entire submission of the understanding to the letter of the written word; the most anxious solicitude for the credit of the sacred writers; the warmest zeal to maintain every circumstance in the history of our Saviour's life, which might add authority to his

precepts, and weight to his promises, by heightening the dignity of his person. But so inconsistent
with itself is human folly, that they who at one
time seemed to think it a preliminary, to be required of every one who would come to a right
belief of the gospel, that he should unlearn and
unbelieve what philosophy had been thought to
have in common with the gospel, as if reason and
revelation could in nothing agree; upon other ac-
casions discover an aversion to the belief of any
thing, which at all puts our reason to a stand:
and in order to wage war with mystery, with the
more advantage, they scruple not to deny, that
that Spirit which enlightened the first preachers
in the delivery of their oral instruction, and rendered them infallible teachers of the age in which
they lived, directed them in the composition of
those writings, which they left for the edification
of succeeding ages.* They pretend to have
made discoveries of inconclusive reasoning in the
epistles;† of doubtful facts in the gospels: and
appealing from the testimony of the apostles to
their own judgments, they have not scrupled to
declare their opinion, that the *miraculous conception of our Lord,* is a subject, " with respect to

---

* " I have frequently declared myself not to be a believer in
the inspiration of the evangelists and apostles as writers." Dr
Priestley's Letters to Dr Horsley, Part I. p. 132.

† Hist. of Corrup. vol. ii. p. 370.

which, any person is at full liberty to think, as the evidence shall appear to him, without any impeachment of his faith or character as a Christian."* And lest a simple avowal of this extraordinary opinion should not be sufficiently offensive, it is accompanied with certain obscure insinuations,† the reserved meaning of which we are little anxious to divine, which seem intended to prepare the world not to be surprised, if something still more extravagant, if more extravagant may be, should in a little time be declared.

We are assembled this day to commemorate our Lord's Nativity. It is not as the birth-day of a prophet that this day is sanctified; but as the anniversary of that great event, which had been announced by the whole succession of prophets, from the beginning of the world; and in which the predictions concerning the manner of the Messiah's advent, received their complete and literal accomplishment. In the predictions, as well as in the corresponding event, the circumstance of the miraculous conception, makes so principal a part, that we shall not easily find subjects of meditation, more suited either to the season, or to the times, than these two points; the importance of this doctrine, as an article of the Christian faith,

---

* Letters to Dr Horsley, Part I. p. 132.   † Ibid. p. 54.

and the sufficiency of the evidence by which the fact is supported.

First, for the importance of the doctrine, as an article of the faith; it is evidently the foundation of the whole distinction between the character of Christ, in the condition of a man, and that of any other prophet. Had the conception of Jesus been in the natural way; had he been the fruit of Mary's marriage with her husband, his intercourse with the Deity could have been of no other kind, than the nature of any other man might have equally admitted: an intercourse of no higher kind than the prophets enjoyed, when their minds were enlightened by the extraordinary influence of the Holy Spirit. The information conveyed to Jesus, might have been clearer and more extensive, than any imparted to any former prophet; but the manner and the means of communication, must have been the same. The holy Scriptures speak a very different language: they tell us, that the " same God who spake in times past to the fathers by the prophets, hath in these latter days spoken unto us by his Son;"* evidently establishing a distinction of Christianity from preceding revelations, upon a distinction between the two characters of a prophet of God,

---

* Hebrews i. 1, 2.

and of God's Son. Moses, the great lawgiver of
the Jews, is described in the book of Deuteronomy, as superior to all succeeding prophets, for
the intimacy of his intercourse with God, for the
variety of his miracles, and for the authority with
which he was invested. " There arose not a prophet in Israel like unto Moses, whom Jehovah
knew face to face: 'in all the signs and wonders
which Jehovah sent him to do in the land of
Egypt, to Pharoah, and all his servants, and to all
his land: and in all that mighty hand, and in all
the great terror, which Moses shewed in the sight
of all Israel."* Yet this great prophet, raised up
to be the leader and the legislator of God's
people; this greatest of the prophets, with whom
Jehovah conversed face to face, as a man talketh
with his friend; bore, as we are told, to Jesus, the
the humble relation of a servant to a son.† And
lest the superiority on the side of the Son, should
be deemed a mere superiority of the office to which
he was appointed, we are told, that the Son is
" higher than the angels," being the effulgence of
God's glory, the express image of his person,"‡
the God " whose throne is forever and ever, the
sceptre of whose kingdom is a sceptre of righteousness :"§ and this high dignity of the Son, is

---

* Deut. xxxiv. 10—12.   † Heb. iii. 5, 6.
‡ Heb. i. 3—6.   § Heb. i. 8.

alleged as a motive for religious obedience to his commands, and for reliance on his promises. It is this indeed which gives such authority to his precepts, and such certainty to his whole doctrine, as render faith in him the first duty of religion. Had Christ been a mere prophet, to believe in Christ had been the same thing as to believe in John the Baptist. The messages indeed, announced on the part of God by Christ, and by John the Baptist, might have been different; and the importance of the different messages unequal; but the principle of belief in either, must have been the same.

Hence it appears, that the intercourse which Christ, as a man, held with God, was different in kind, from that which the greatest of the prophets ever had enjoyed: and yet how it should differ, otherwise than in the degree of frequency and intimacy, it will not be very easy to explain, unless we adhere to the faith transmitted to us from the premitive ages, and believe that the Eternal Word, who was in the beginning with God, and was God, so joined to himself the holy thing which was formed in Mary's womb, that the two natures, from the commencement of the virgin's conception, made one person. Between God and any living being, having a distinct personality of his own, separate from the Godhead, no other communion could obtain, than what should consist in the action of the Divine Spirit upon the faculties of the separate person. This communion with God, the prophets enjoined. But Jesus, according to the primitive doctrine, was so united to the ever-living Word, that the very existence of the man, consisted in this union.* We shall not indeed find this proposition, that the existence of Mary's Son consisted from the first, and ever shall consist, in his union with the Word; we shall not find this proposition, in these terms in Scripture. Would to God the necessity never had arisen, of stating the discoveries of revelation in metaphysical propositions! The inspired writers delivered their sublimest doctrines in popular language, and

---

* So Theodoret, in the fourth of his Seven Dialogues about the Trinity, published under the name of Athanasius. The persons in this dialogue, are an Orthodox Believer, and an Apollinarian. The Apollinarian asks, Ουκ ἐστιν ὁν Ιησυς ἀνθρωπος; the Believer replies, ἀπυ τυ Λογυ ὁτι ἀνθρωπον αυτον ειδα ὑπογαιλα, την γαρ ὑπαρξιν αυτυ ιν τη ἑνωσιι τυ Λογυ γνωριζω. To the same purpose Joannes Damascenus, —— ἡ γαρ προυπογασην καθ᾽ ἑαυτην σαρκι ἡνωθη ὁ θειος Λογος, αλλ᾽ ἐνοικησας τη γαστρι της ἁγιας παρθενυ ἀπεριγραπλως, ἐν τη ἑαυλυ ὑπογασιι ἐκ των ἁγιων της ἀειπαρθενυ αἱματων, σαρκα ἐψυχωμενην ψυχη λογικη τε και νοερα ὑπεστησαλο, ἀπαρχην προσλαβομενο τυ ἀνθρωπινυ φυραμαλο, ΑΥΤΟΣ Ὁ ΛΟΓΟΣ ΓΕΝΟΜΕΝΟΣ ΤΗ ΣΑΡΚΙ ῾ΥΠΟΣΤΑΣΙΣ. De Fide Orthodoxâ, lib. 3. cap. ii; and again, cap. vii. Εσαρκωλαι τοινυν—————ἐγι αὑτην χρημαλισαι τη σαρκι ὑπογασιν ἡ τε Θευ Λογυ ὑπογασις. So also Gregory Nazianzen, ἡ τις διαπεπλασθαι τον ανθρωπον, ειθ᾽ ὑποδιδυκεναι λεγοι θεον, καθαιρετεος.—————Ειτις ὡς ἐν προφηλη λεγοι καλα χαριν ἐνεργηκεναι, ἀλλα μη καθ᾽ ἑσιαν συνηφθαι τε και συναπλισθαι, ἐιη κενος της κρειτλονο ἐνεργειας, μαλλον δι πληρης της ἐναιλιας. Epist. ad Cledon. I.

abstained, as much as it was possible to abstain, from a philosophical phraseology. By the perpetual cavils of gainsayers, and the difficulties which they have raised, later teachers, in the assertion of the same doctrines, have been reduced to the unpleasing necessity of availing themselves of the greater precision of a less familiar language.

But if we find not the same proposition in the same words in Scripture, we find in Scripture what amounts to a clear proof of the proposition. We find the characteristic properties of both natures, the human and the divine, ascribed to the same person. We read of Jesus, that he suffered from hunger and from fatigue; that he wept for grief, and was distressed with fear; that he was obnoxious to all the evils of humanity, except the propensity to sin. We read of the same Jesus, that he had " glory with the Father before the world began;"* that " all things were created by him,† both in heaven and in earth, visible and invisible; whether they be thrones, or dominions, or principalities, or powers; all things were created by him, and for him,"‡ and " he upholdeth all things by the word of his power."§   And that we may in some sort understand, how infirmity and

---

* John xvii. 5.

† Ibid. i. 3.

‡ Coloss. i. 16.

§ Heb. i. 3.

perfection should thus meet in the same person, we are told by St John, that the " Word was made flesh."

It was clearly, therefore, the doctrine of holy writ, and nothing else, which the fathers asserted, in terms borrowed from the schools of philosophy, when they affirmed, that the very principle of personality and individual existence, in Mary's Son, was union with the uncreated Word.* A doctrine in which a miraculous conception would have been implied, had the thing not been recorded; since a man, conceived in the ordinary way, would have derived the principles of his existence from the mere physical powers of generation. Union with the Divine nature, could not have been the principle of an existence physically derived from Adam; and that intimate union of God and man in the Redeemer's person, which the Scriptures so clearly assert, had been a physical impossibility.

---

* Ὁ ἐν Θεος Λογος σαρκωθεις, ωτι την ἐστη ψιλη θεωρια καἰανοϑμι-ηις φυσιν ἀιελαϐιν (ὁ γαρ σαρκωσις τϑιε, ἀλλ᾽ ἀπαῖη και ϖλασμα σαρκωσιως) ἀλλα την ιν αἰομϑ, την αὐτην ϑσαι τῃ ιν τῳ ἰιδιι (ἀπαρχην γαρ ἀιιλαϐι τϑ ἡμιϊιρϑ φυραμαῖ⊕) ἠ καθ᾽ ἱαὐῃι ὑποϛασαι και ἀτομον χϛημαλιϛασαι ϖϛοϊιρον, και ἰτϑς ὑπ᾽ αὐῃ ϖϛοσληφθιισαι, ἀλλ᾽ ἐν τῃ αὐῃ ὑποϛασιι ὑπαϛξασαι· αὐῃ γαρ ἠ ὑποϛασις τϑ Θεϑ Λογϑ ἰγιιῖο τῃ σαϛκι ὑποϛασις. Joann. Damascen. De Fide Orthodoxâ. lib. 3. cap. xi.

But we need not go so high, as to the Divine nature of our Lord, to evince the necessity of his miraculous conception. It was necessary to the scheme of redemption, by the Redeemer's offering of himself as 'an expiatory sacrifice, that the manner of his conception should be such, that he should in no degree partake of the natural pollution of the fallen race, whose guilt he came to atone, nor be included in the general condemnation of Adam's progeny. In what the stain of original sin may consist, and in what manner it may be propagated, it is not to my present purpose to inquire. It is sufficient, that Adam's crime, by the appointment of Providence, involved his whole posterity in punishment. " In Adam," says the apostle, " all die."* And for many lives thus forfeited, a single life, itself a forfeit, had been no ransom. Nor by the Divine sentence only, inflicting death on the progeny, for the offence of the progenitor; but by the proper guilt of his own sins, every one sprung by natural descent from the loins of Adam, is a debtor to Divine Justice, and incapable of becoming a mediator for his brethren. " In many things," says St James, " we offend all."† " If we say that we have no sin, we deceive ourselves," saith St John, " and the truth is not in us. And if any man

---

* 1 Cor. xv. 22.   † James iii. 2.

sin, we have an advocate with the Father, Jesus Christ the righteous, and he is the propitiation for our sins."[*] Even we Christians all offend, without exception even of the first and best Christians, the apostles. But St John clearly separates the righteous advocate from the mass of those offenders. That any Christian is enabled, by the assistance of God's Spirit, to attain to that degree of purity, which may entitle him to the future benefits of the redemption, is itself a present benefit of the propitiation which hath been made for us: and he, who under the assault of every temptation, maintained that unsullied innocence, which gives merit and efficacy to his sacrifice and intercession, could not be of the number of those, whose offences called for an expiation, and whose frailties needed a Divine assistance, to raise them effectually from dead works, to serve the living God. In brief, the condemnation and the iniquity of Adam's progeny, were universal. To reverse the universal sentence, and to purge the universal corruption, a Redeemer was to be found, pure of every stain of inbred and contracted guilt. And since every person produced in the natural way, could not but be of the contaminated race; the purity, requisite to the efficacy of the Redeemer's atonement, made it neces-

---

[*] 1 John i. 8 ; and ii. 1.

sary, that the manner of his conception should
be supernatural.

Thus you see the necessary connexion of the
miraculous conception, with the other articles of
the Christian faith. The incarnation of the
Divine Word, so roundly asserted by St John,
and so clearly implied in innumerable passages
of holy writ, in any other way had been impossible; and the Redeemer's atonement inadequate and ineffectual. Insomuch that, had the
extraordinary manner of our Lord's generation
made no part of the evangelical narrative, the
opinion might have been defended, as a thing
clearly implied in the evangelical doctrine.

On the other hand, it were not difficult to
shew, that the miraculous conception, once admitted, naturally brings up after it, the great doctrines of the atonement and the incarnation.
The miraculous conception of our Lord, evidently implies some higher purpose of his coming,
than the mere business of a teacher. The business of a teacher might have been performed by
a mere man, enlightened by the prophetic spirit.
For whatever instruction men have the capacity
to receive, a man might have been made the instrument to convey. Had teaching, therefore,
been the sole purpose of our Saviour's coming, a
mere man might have done the whole business;

and the supernatural conception had been an unnecessary miracle. He, therefore, who came in
this miraculous way, came upon some higher business, to which a mere man was unequal. He
came to be made a sin-offering for us, " that we
might be made the righteousness of God in him."*

So close, therefore, is the connexion of this extraordinary fact with the cardinal doctrines of the
gospel, that it may be justly deemed a necessary
branch of the scheme of redemption : and in no
other light was it considered by St Paul, who
mentions it among the characteristics of the Redeemer, that he should be " made of a woman."†
In this short sentence, St Paul bears a remarkable
testimony to the truth of the evangelical history,
in this circumstance. And *you*, my brethren,
have not so learned Christ, but that you will prefer the testimony of St Paul to the rash judgment
of those, who have dared to tax this " chosen
vessel" of the Lord, with error and inaccuracy.

The opinion of these men is indeed the less to
be regarded, for the want of insight, which they
discover, into the real interests and proper con-

---

* 2 Cor. v. 21.
† Gal. iv. 4. " There is no reference to the miraculous con-
ception, either in the book of Acts, or *in any of the Epistles.*"
Dr Priestley's Letters to Dr Horsley, p. 53.

nexions of their own sytem. It is by no means
sufficient for their purpose, that they insist not on
the belief of the miraculous conception. They
must insist upon the disbelief of it, if they expect
to make discerning men proselytes to their Socinian doctrine. They must disprove it, before
they can reduce the gospel to what their scheme
of interpretation makes it,—a mere religion of nature, a system of the best practical Deism, enforced by the sanction of high rewards, and formidable punishments, in a future life; which are
yet no rewards and no punishments, but simply
the enjoyments and the sufferings of a new race
of men, to be made out of old materials; and therefore constitute no sanction, when the principles of
the materialist are incorporated with those of the
Socinian, in the finished creed of the modern Unitarian.

Having seen the importance of the doctrine of
the miraculous conception, as an article of our
faith; let us in the next place consider the sufficiency of the evidence, by which the fact is supported.

We have for it the express testimony of two
out of the four evangelists: of St Matthew,
whose gospel was published in Judea, within a
few years after our Lord's ascension; and of St
Luke, whose narrative was composed, as may be

collected from the author's short preface, to prevent the mischief that was to be apprehended
from some pretended histories of our Saviour's
life, in which the truth was probably blended
with many legendary tales. It is very remarkable, that the fact of the miraculous conception,
should be found in the first of the four gospels;
written at a time when many of the near relations
of the Holy Family must have been living, by
whom the story, had it been false, had been easily
confuted: that it should be found again in St
Luke's gospel; written for the peculiar use of
the converted Gentiles, and for the express purpose of furnishing a summary of authentic facts,
and of suppressing spurious narrations. Was it
not ordered by some peculiar providence of God,
that the two great branches of the primitive
church, the Hebrew congregations, for which St
Matthew wrote, and the Greek congregations, for
which St Luke wrote, should find an express
record of the miraculous conception, each in its
proper gospel? Or if we consider the testimony
of the writers, simply as historians of the times in
which they lived, without regard to their inspiration, which is not admitted by the adversary:
were not Matthew and Luke, Matthew, one of
the twelve apostles of our Lord, and Luke, the
companion of St Paul, competent to examine the
evidence of the facts which they have recorded?
Is it likely that they have recorded facts, upon

the credit of a vague report, without examination? And was it reserved for the Unitarians of the eighteenth century, to detect their errors ? St Luke thought himself particularly well qualified for the work, in which he engaged, by his exact knowledge of the story, which he undertook to write, in all its circumstances, from the very beginning. It is said indeed by a writer of the very first antiquity, and high in credit, that his gospel was composed from St Paul's sermons. " Luke, the attendant of St Paul," says Irenæus, " put into his book the gospel preached by that apostle." This being premised, attend I beseech you, to the account which St Luke gives of his own undertaking. " It seemed good to me also, having had perfect understanding of all things from the very first, to write unto thee in order, most excellent Theophilus, that thou mightest know the certainty of those things wherein thou hast been instructed." The last verse might be more literally rendered " that thou might know the exact truth of those doctrines, wherein thou hast been CATECHISED." St Luke's gospel therefore, if the writer's own word may be taken about his own work, is an historical exposition of the *Catechism*, which Theophilus had learned, when he was first made a Christian. The two first articles, in this historical exposition, are the history of the Baptist's birth, and that of Mary's miraculous impregnation. We have much more therefore, than the

testimony of St Luke, in addition to that of St
Matthew, to the truth of the fact of the miraculou,
conception; we have the testimony of St Luke
that this fact was a part of the earliest catechetica.
instruction: a part of the catechism, no doubt,
which St Paul's converts learnt of the apostle.
Let this then be your answer, if any man shall
ask you a reason of this part of your faith; tell
him, that you have been learning St Paul's cate.
chism.

From what hath been said, you will easily per.
ceive, that the evidence of the fact of our Lord's
miraculous conception, is answerable to the great
importance of the doctrine; and you will esteem
it an objection of little weight, that the modern
advocates of the Unitarian tenets, cannot other.
wise give a colour to their wretched cause, than
by denying the inspiration of the sacred historians, that they may seem to themselves at liberty
to reject their testimony. You will remember,
that the doctrines of the Christian revelation, were
not originally delivered in a system; but inter.
woven in the history of our Saviour's life. To
say therefore, that the first preachers were not
inspired in the composition of the narratives in
which their doctrine is conveyed, is nearly the
same thing, as to deny their inspiration in the
general. You will perhaps think it incredible,
that they, who were assisted by the Divine Spirit,

when they preached, should be deserted by that
Spirit, when they committed what they had
preached to writing. You will think it improbable that they, who were endowed with the gift
of discerning spirits, should be endowed with no
gift of discerning the truth of facts. You will
recollect one instance upon record, in which St
Peter detected a falsehood by the light of inspiration: and you will perhaps be inclined to think,
that it could be of no less importance to the
church, that the apostles and evangelists should
be enabled to detect falsehoods in the history of
our Saviour's life; than that St Peter should be
enabled to detect Ananias's lie about the sale of
his estate. You will think it unlikely, that they
who were led by the Spirit into all truth, should
be permitted to lead the whole church for many
ages into error: that they should be permitted to
leave behind them, as authentic memoirs of their
master's life, narratives compiled with little judgment or selection, from the stories of the day,
from facts and fictions in promiscuous circulation.
The credulity, which swallows these contradictions, while it strains at mysteries, is not the faith
which will remove mountains. The Ebionites of
antiquity, little as they were famed for penetration and discernment, managed however the affairs of the sect with more discretion than our
modern Unitarians. They questioned not the
inspiration of the books which they received; but

they received only one book, a spurious copy of St Matthew's gospel, curtailed of the two first chapters. You will think it no inconsiderable confirmation of the doctrine in question, that the sect, which first denied it, to palliate their infidelity, found it necessary to reject three of the gospels, and to mutilate the fourth.

Not in words therefore and in form, but with hearts full of faith and gratitude, you will join in the solemn service of the day, and return thanks to God, " who gave his only begotten Son to take our nature upon him, and, as at this time, to be born of a pure Virgin." You will always remember, that it is the great use of a sound faith, that it furnishes the most effectual motives to a good life. You will therefore not rest in the merit of a speculative faith. You will make it your constant endeavour, that your lives may adorn your profession——that " your light may shine before men, that they, seeing your good works, may glorify your Father which is in heaven,"

REMARKS

UPON

DR PRIESTLEY'S

SECOND LETTERS

TO THE

ARCHDEACON OF ST ALBAN'S,

WITH

PROOFS OF CERTAIN FACTS ASSERTED BY THE ARCHDEACON.

PART FIRST.

REMARKS.

W HEN first I had the pleasure to peruse the Second Letters addressed to me by Doctor Priestley, upon the subject of our Lord's divinity; I was not ill satisfied to find the performance such, both in matter and style, as might have released me from all obligation to a formal reply; although I had made no previous declaration of the resolution, in which I am fixed, never to enter into a useless disquisition upon the main question—an exhausted subject, in which nothing new is to be said on either side;—nor to pursue an interminable controversy, with one, whom, with high respect for his natural abilities, and for his attainments in some parts of learning, I must still call an insufficient antagonist. The dislike of trouble in my natural disposition is so strong, as too often, I fear, to strive for the mastery with better principles. I was well satisfied to find, that in the contest with Dr Priestley, I was at liberty to indulge my indolence, without seeming to desert my cause: that his book, abounding in new specimens of that confident ignorance, which in these subjects is the most prominent feature in his writings, and in expressions of fiery resentment and virulent invective, carried with it, as I thought, its own confutation to unprejudiced readers of all descriptions: to the learned reader, by the proof which it furnishes of the author's incompetency in the subject; to the unlearned, by the consciousness which the fierceness of his wrath betrays of a defect of argument.

2. To mention a few instances: it gave me great satisfaction to perceive, that the whole confutation of the proof, which I had built upon the epistle of St Barnabas, of the orthodoxy of the first Hebrew Christians,[*] was to consist in an insinuation, that " doubts had been entertained by many learned men concerning the genuineness of that epistle;"[†] and in an assertion of my antagonist's, that it is most evidently interpolated; and that the interpolations respect the very subject of which we treat."[‡] The genuineness of the epistle,

---

[*] See Letter eighth in Reply to Dr Priestley.
[†] Second Letters to the Archdeacon of St Alban's, p. 7.
[‡] Ibid.

as a work of St Barnabas the apostle, had been expressly given up by me; its age being the only circumstance of importance to my argument. For the notion that it is evidently interpolated, particularly in what respects the subject of which we treat; the evidence by which the assertion is supported, is of that sort, which every one, who engages in controversy, must rejoice that his adversary should condescend to employ. Some passages in the Greek text, which allude to our Lord's divinity, are not found, it seems, in the old Latin version; others relating to the same subject, appear in the old Latin version only, and are not found in the Greek text.[*] That both the Greek text and Latin version, carry evident marks of the injuries of time; that defects, sometimes of a single word, sometimes of many words, sometimes of whole periods, abound in both, is known to every one who hath ever looked into the work. It is doubtless therefore, a very rational conclusion, that whatever is not found both in the original, and in the version, is in either an interpolation. That the hand of time must always have fallen upon the corresponding passages in the two copies, may be taken as a self-evident proposition! If any assertion therefore, of our Lord's divinity, occur in

---

[*] Second Letters, p. 7.

either copy, which is ·not found·in both, the suspicion must be but too well founded, that some wicked Athanasian hath been tampering!

8. I was well pleased to find, that the two passages which my antagonist hath produced from the Greek text, as · evident instances of interpolation, are not among those which I have cited. In these two passages, the divinity of our Lord is briefly alluded to. In every one of the four, cited by me, it is distinctly asserted, or strongly implied : of these four two are found, with inconsiderable varieties, both in the Greek and in the Latin; the other two in the Latin only. But that I lay the chief stress * upon either of the two, which are in the Latin version only, is a mere imagination of my adversary.

4. The satisfaction, which this confutation of my argument from Barnabas afforded me, was not a little heightened, by the manner in which I am convicted of an error, in the appeal, which, in my sixth letter to Dr Priestly, I made to the authority of Grotius, among others, in support of the opinion, which I maintain, of the orthodoxy of the Nazarenes, in the article of our Lord's divinity. Dr Priestley, in his First Letters to me, said, that

---

* Second Letters, p. 8.

I was singular in asserting this. To shew that I was not singular in the assertion, (not to prove the thing asserted ; for the proof of that I build entirely upon what is to be found in ancient writers; but to disprove the pretended novelty of the assertion,) I alleged the authorities of Grotius, Vossius, Spencer, and Huetius. " Having examined, says my antagonist, in the third of his Second Letters, the most respectable of these authorities, *viz.* Grotius, I find him entirely failing you, and saying no such thing as you ascribe to him ."[*] Then, to prove that Grotius fails me, and says no such thing as I ascribe to him, Dr Priestley produces a passage from Grotius, to which I never meant to allude, and which is indeed nothing to the purpose. But he takes no notice of the passage upon which my assertion was built, and to which the margin of my publication referred him.

5. The satisfaction, which it gave me to find myself thus confuted, was still increased, by the retractation of this confutation in my adversary's Appendix, No. III. A retractation, which in effect is little less than a confession of the fraudulent trick, which, had not the advice of friends seasonably interposed, it is too evident, he meant to put upon the public. I say upon the public ; for upon

---

[*] Second Letters, p. 30.

me he could not think that it would pass. Whatever may be his opinion of my learning; he has,
I believe, had some experience of my vigilance, in
watching the movements of an enemy; and he
could not imagine, that the passage, which he produces, would pass with myself, for that which I
cited. But he has heard perhaps from those who
know me, of the constitutional indolence which
domineers in my disposition; and under this circumstance, and the declaration which I had made
of my intention to give him no reply, he thought
himself secure against detection.

6. I must acknowledge another gratification,
which I received from this same No. III. of Dr
Priestley's Appendix. I learnt from it, that Grotius, " when he speaks of the Nazarenes as holding the common faith of other Christians, with respect to Christ;" meant only that they held something, which was *not* the common faith of other
Christians.* And that Sulpitius Severus, when
he says that " all the Jewish Christians till the
time of Adrian, held that Christ was God, though
they observed the law of Moses, *(Christum Deum
sub legis observatione credebant,)* is to be considered as having said nothing more, than that almost

---

* " By the common faith of Christians in that early age, Grotius no doubt meant his *own opinion*, &c." Second Letters, p.
217.

all the Jews of Jerusalem were Christians, though
they observed the law of Moses."*   Certainly the
learned commentator and the historian, are to be
so understood. For were they to be understood in
the plain meaning of their words, they would flatly contradict Dr Priestley; which however if they
had done, it would have been no great matter : for
any writer, who may contradict Dr Priestley, is
little to be regarded.

7. Dr Priestley has been reading the Parmenides !†   Having taught the Greek language several years at Warrington, he conceived himself
well qualified to encounter that profound book.
The benefit, which he has received from the performance of this knotty task, exactly corresponds
with my notion of his abilities for the undertaking.   He has found the whole treatise unintelligible !‡   Perhaps he has, 'ere this, *looked through* the
Enneads of Plotinus, with the like emolument.
He must therefore be well qualified to illustrate
the history of the Platonic doctrines, in the most
mysterious parts : and in the GREAT WORK, with
which the press now labours, his promise will, I
dare say, be fulfilled, of teaching the world many
things respecting them, of which his antagonist is
ignorant.   He can produce hundreds of passages

---

* Second Letters, p. 218.   † Ibid. p. 145.   ‡ Ibid.

to prove, that the " divinity which the orthodox Christians ascribed to Christ, was the very same principle which constituted the wisdom and other powers of God the Father;" and he can prove, that " this was agreeable to the principles of those Platonists, from whom Philo and the Christian fathers derived their opinion."* That the second person in the Platonic triad was, according to the theology of that school, the *principle of intelligence* in the Godhead, he will find indeed not difficult to prove. But unless he can shew, that this principle of Divine intelligence was not supposed, by the Platonists, to have had from all eternity a personality of its own, distinct from the personality of either of the two other principles, he will prove nothing, but what is already known to every child in Platonism.

8. The GREAT WORK will probably abound in new specimens of the proficiency which he has made in logic, under the tuition of the great Locke. It was not unpleasant to me to find this great logician confounding *being, substance,* and *substratum;*† that is, ignorant of the distinctions of ὑπόστασις (which seems to be Being in his language) οὐσία and ὑποκείμενον: to find him unapprized of that great principle, without which a logician will handle

---

* Second Letters, p. 124.   † Second Letters, p. 138.

his tools but aukwardly, that the genus cannot be predicated of the specific differences * (a); and, from an ignorance of this principle, falling into an error, into which indeed greater men than he have fallen, that Being is the universal *genus,* under which all other *genera* rank as *species.*

9. These, and many other glaring instances of unfinished erudition, shallow criticism, weak argu_ment, and unjustifiable art to cover the weakness, and to supply the want of argument, which must strike every one who takes the trouble to *look through* these Second Letters, put me quite at ease with respect to the judgment, which the public would be apt to form between my antagonist and me; and confirmed me in the resolution of mak_ing no reply to him, and of troubling the public no more upon the subject, except so far as might

---

* "——The former [being] is the genus, and the latter [person] the species," &c. p. 140.

(a) In the sixth of his Third Letters, sec. 3. Dr Priestley courageously encounters this principle. To prove the fallacy of it, he says, " According to it, since *men* are divided into *Whites* and *Blacks,* &c. &c. it would follow, that it cannot with proprie- ty be said of any Whites or Blacks, that they are *men."* A more curious instance of logical accuracy will not easily be found, than this deduction. The common *genus* of White men and Black men, I take to be *Man.* The specific difference between them lies in colour. Of this I apprehend manhood cannot be predi- cated. But how does this lead to Dr Priestley's inference, that manhood is not predicable of any subject in which colour is found.

be necessary, to establish some facts, which he hath somewhat too peremptorily denied; and to vindicate my character from aspersions, which he hath too inconsiderately thrown out.

10. The matters of fact which I mean to prove are these.

I. Origen's want of veracity in disputation.

II. The existence of orthodox Hebrew Christians at Jerusalem, after the time of Adrian.

III. The decline of Calvinism, amounting almost to a total extinction of it, among the English dissenters.

11. The slander, which I mean to repel, is contained in my adversary's insinuation, that I have spoken with contempt of the doctrines of Calvin.

12. As for the outcry which he makes about my intolerance, and my bigotry to what he calls high-church principles, it gives me rather pleasure than uneasiness. I consider it, as the vain indignant struggle of a strong animal which feels itself overcome; the mere growling of the tiger in the toils; and I disdain to answer. I glory in my principles; I am proud of the abuse, which they may draw upon me. Nor shall I pretend to

apologize for the severity and warmth of my present language, or of any which I may think proper to employ in the ensuing pages. After the
avowal·which Dr Priestley has made, in his last
publication,* of the spirit in which he has drawn
his polemical sword; it is time, that on our part
also the *scabbard should be thrown away.*   ›

13. Dr Priestley's Second Letters to the Archdeacon of St Alban's are, at this instant, lying
open before me, at the 53d page. My eye is attracted to a passage near the bottom, distinguished by a mark, which in the first perusal of the
work, I had set against it in the margin; which
reminds me, that it is one of those, in which I
was the most captivated with the justness of the
reasoning, and the frankness of the writer's declarations.   Although I have already spent more
time, than when I first took up my pen I thought
to do, in culling the flowers of my adversary's
composition, I cannot resist the temptation of
stopping (although it delay for a few moments
the business to which I hasten) to pluck this delicious blossom, which I had well nigh overlooked,
sensible how much it will add to the brilliancy
and fragrance of my posey.

---

* See the Animadversions on Dr White's Sermons, annexed
to Dr Priestley's discourse upon the Importance of Free Inquiry,
p. 78.

14. Bishop Pearson alleges, that Ignatius in his epistles to Polycarp, to the Ephesians, Magnesians, and Philadelphians, refers to the doctrine of the Ebionites as an heretical doctrine. These references would demolish Dr Priestley's notion, that the Ebionites were not considered as heretics, so early as in the times of Ignatius. Dr Priestley " therefore finds no such references," in these epistles, " except perhaps two passages." Two clear references are just as good as two thousand. How then shall we dispose of these two passages? Very easily. " They may easily be *supposed* to have been altered." Yes. Suppositions are easily made; and for that very reason, they are not easily admitted by wary men, without some other recommendation than the bare ease of making them, joined to the consideration of the service, which a particular supposition may render to a party-writer, as a crutch for a lame argument. Upon what ground then may we build this supposition, which is so easily made, of an alteration in two passages in the epistles of Ignatius? which, as they now stand, contradict Dr Priestley? Upon the firmest ground imaginable. " When CORRECTED by an UNITARIAN, nothing is wanting to the evident purpose of the writer." *Corrected by an Unitarian!* The Unitarians, if they are not shamefully belied by the ecclesiastical historians, have ever indeed been ready at this business of *correction.* The Arians took the trouble to cor-

rect a treatise of Hilary of Poictou, in which the heretical confession of the council of Ariminum was the subject: they córrected, and corrected, till the work became a novelty to its author. They, or the Macedonians, did the same good office for St Cyprian's epistles; and to circulate their amended copies more widely, they sold them at Constantinople, at a low price. Similar liberties were taken with the works óf the two Alexandrians, Clemens and Dionysius. They, who thus corrected, were not deficient in the kindred art of forging whole treatises, under the names of the brightest luminaries of the church, in which the holy fathers were made to support heretical doctrines. The holy Scriptures were not unattempted, as appears by the testimony of those * who lived at the time when the *amended* copies were extant in the world; who, in proof of the heavy accusation, appeal to the notorious disagreement of different copies, which had undergone the revision of different heresiarchs. This is indeed the confutation of the Unitarian doctrine, that both the primitive fathers, and the holy Scriptures, must be corrected in every page, before they can be brought to give evidence in its favour. It is because the Unitarians themselves have always understood this, that they have ever

---

* See Euseb. Ecc. Hist. lib. v.

been ready to apply the needful *corrections*, when they thought the thing might be done without danger of detection. But the modern *Coryphæus* of the company is, I believe, the first who ever had the indiscretion to avow the practice, and confess that he could not otherwise stand his ground, than by an appeal to the testimony of CORRECTED FATHERS! He is himself indeed a master of the art of correction. His attempt upon a passage in St John's first epistle, will never be forgotten.*

15. Will he dare to recriminate? He will.— " The orthodox, he says, as they are commonly called, have tampered with the New Testament itself, having made interpolations favourable to the doctrine of the Trinity, especially the famous passage concerning *the three that bear record in heaven.*"† The great name of NEWTON is brought up, to give weight to the accusation. " Newton among others has clearly proved, &c." And this he imagines, I myself will acknowledge. Dr Priestley, even before the inditing of these Second Letters, must have found himself deceived in so many instances, in his imaginations about me; how I would acknowledge, and how I would re-

---

* See the charge to the clergy of the archdeaconry of St Alban's, I. sec. 5.

† Second Letters, p. 13.

cant; how my eyes would be opened by the information which he had to give me; that I wonder he should venture to imagine any more, in a
subject in which he hath found himself so liable
to error. He imagines, that I must acknowledge,
that Newton hath clearly proved, that the record
of the three in heaven in St John's first epistle, is
an interpolation made by some of those, whom I
call the orthodox.—No: I acknowledge no such
thing. Suppose I were to make the first part of
the acknowledgment, that the passage is an interpolation, what consequence would bind me to
the second, that the orthodox have been the wilful falsifiers? Is it because their purpose might
have been served by the pretended falsification?
Truly their purpose had been poorly served by it.
It is not agreed, among the orthodox themselves,
that this text relates to the consubstantiality of
the three persons in the Godhead. It is my own
opinion, that it does not: and this I take to be
the reason,—that it is so seldom alleged by the
ancient writers in proof of the Trinity. But why
must I acknowledge, that the passage is at all an
interpolation? Because Newton and others have
clearly proved it. To me the proof is not clear.
Were the defect of positive proof in favour of the
passage much greater, than Newton and others
have been able to make out, it would still be
with me an argument of its authenticity, that the
omission of it breaks the connexion, and wonder-

fully heightens the obscurity, of the apostle's discourse. Dr Priestley perhaps imagines, that I hold myself bound to acknowledge whatever Newton hath attempted to prove. In his letters to me, and in his animadversions upon Dr White's celebrated discourses, he is often pleased to boast of the probability * of what he knows, more than his antagonists; and that too in subjects, in which he hath been convicted of the greatest want of knowledge. I hope I may say, without arrogance, that it is probable that Sir Isaac Newton's talents in demonstration, are as well known to me, as to Dr Priestley. It is probable too, that, after the pains which I have taken to examine the principles and the authorities on which his ancient chronology is founded, I am as well qualified, as Dr Priestley, to judge of his talents in other subjects, which are not capable of demonstration. Now in these, I scruple not to say with a writer of our own times, that the great Newton went out like a common man. For the exposition, which to complete his argument against the record of the three in heaven, he gives of the context of the apostle's discourse, I hold it to be a model of that sort of paraphrase, by which any given sense may be affixed to any given words.

---

* Second Letters, p. 135, 146, 200, 202. Animadversions on Dr White, p. 66, 72.

But that even the external evidence of the authenticity of the passage is so far less defective, than
Newton and others have imagined, will be denied, I believe, by few, who have impartially considered the very able vindication of this celebrated text, which hath lately been given by Mr
Travis, in his Letters to Mr Gibbon.   Dr Priestley perhaps hath not found leisure to *look through*
that performance.   Or, if he have, he hath formed,
I suppose, " no very high opinion of the author's
acquaintance with Christian antiquity."*   For in
this, all who oppose the Socinian tenets, are miserably deficient.

16. Here I close my remarks upon my adversary's reasoning ; and I now proceed to the proof
of my own facts, and the vindication of my own
character.

---

* See Remarks on Mr Howes's discourse.

PART SECOND.

PROOFS.

CHAPTER FIRST.

Of Origen's want of veracity.—Of the fathers in general.—Of the passages in which St Chrysostom is supposed to assert that the apostles temporized.—A specimen of CORRECTION *by an Unitarian.*

THE first fact that comes in question, is the want of veracity in disputation, which I impute to Origen.

2. In the second book against Celsus, near the beginning of the book, Origen asserts of the Hebrew Christians of his own times, without exception, that they had not abandoned the laws and customs of their ancestors; and that, for that rea-

son, they were called Ebionites. Dr Priestley sets
a high value upon this testimony of Origen, as
clearly establishing his great point, that the
Ebionites were nothing worse than the Christians
of the circumcision. I maintain, that if the truth
of Origen's assertion were admitted, still his testimony would be less to Dr Priestley's purpose,
than he imagines. It would prove, indeed, the
Hebrew Christian, and the Ebionite, to be the
same; but it would equally prove, that the disbelief of our Lord's divinity was no necessary part
of the Ebionæan doctrine. But I go further. I
deny the truth of Origen's assertion in both its
branches. I deny, that it is universally true of
the Hebrew Christians, in his time, that they had
not abandoned the. Mosaic law; and I deny that
it is true, that they were all called Ebionites. I
say, that Origen himself knew better, than to believe his own assertion. And I say that it was a
part of Origen's character, not to be incapable of
asserting, in argument, what he believed not.

3. Dr Priestley ill brooks this open attack upon
the credibility of one, whom he considers as a
principal witness. He defends Origen, by retort-
ing a similar accusation upon me; and, with the
utmost vehemence of indignant oratory, he arraigns me at the tribunal of the public, as a falsifier of history, and a defamer of the character of

the dead.* From assertions which I have not rashly made, it must be something more terrible to my feelings, than the reproaches of Dr Priestley, loudly re-echoed by his whole party, that shall compel me to recede.

4. I say, then, that in the particular matter in question, Origen asserted a known falsehood. I say, in general, that a strict regard to truth, in disputation, was not the virtue of his character.

5. With respect to the particular matter in question; if I prove, that Origen knew the falsehood of his own assertion in the first branch of it, in which he avers, " that the Hebrew Christians in his time had not abandoned their ancient laws and customs," no great stress, I presume, will be laid upon the second, " that they were all called Ebionites." For, according to Origen's account of the reason of the name, (which yet I believe not to be the true one,) the two branches of his assertion must stand or fall together.

9. It is an inconvenience which attends controversy, that it obliges both the writer and the reader to go frequently over the same ground. I must here repeat, what I observed in the seventh of my letters to Dr Priestley, that it is in

---

* Second Letters, &c. Preface, p. xviii. p. 47, 192.

answer to a reproach upon the converted Jews,
which Celsus had put in the mouth of an unbelieving Jew, that, by embracing Christianity, they
were deserters of their ancient law, that Origen
asserts, that the Jews believing in Christ had not
renounced their Judaism. This assertion is made
at the beginning of Origen's second book. Now,
at no greater distance than in the third section of
the same book, the good father takes quite another ground to confute his adversary. He insults,
over his adversary's ignorance, for not making the
distinctions, which he himself, in the allegation in
question, had confounded. "It is my present
point," says Origen, "to evince Celsus's ignorance, who has made a Jew say to his countrymen, to Israelites believing in Christ, *Upon what
motive have you deserted the law of your ancestors?* But how have they deserted the law of
their ancestors, who reprove those that are inattentive to it, and say, *Tell me ye &c.?*"[*] Then,
after a citation of certain texts from St. Paul's
epistles, in which the apostle avails himself of the
authority of the law, to enforce particular duties;
which texts make nothing either for or against the
Jew's assertion, that the Christians of the circum-

---

[*] Νυν δε προκειται ελεγξαι την τε Κελσου αμαθιαν, παρ᾽ ᾧ ὁ Ιουδαιος
λεγει τοις παλιλαις, και τοις Ισραηλιταις πιστευσασιν επι τον Ιησουν, τε.
Τι παθοντες καταλιπητε τον πατριον νομον; και τα εξης. Πως δε καταλι-
λοιπασι τον πατριον νομον οι επιτιμωντες τοις μη ακουουσιν αυτα, και λεγοντες·
λεγετε μοι οι τον νομον, &c.

cision had abandoned their ancient law; but prove only, that the disuse of the law, if it was actually gone into disuse, could not be deemed a desertion; because it proceeded not from any disregard to the authority of the Lawgiver: after a citation of texts to this purpose, Origen proceeds in this remarkable strain. " And how confusedly does Celsus's Jew speak upon this subject? when he might have said more plausibly, SOME of you *have relinquished the old customs* upon pretence of expositions and allegories. SOME again, expounding, as you call it, spiritually, nevertheless observe the institutions of our ancestors. But SOME, not admitting these expositions, are willing to receive Jesus as the person foretold by the prophets, and to observe the law of Moses according to the ancient customs, as having in the letter the whole meaning of the Spirit."* In these words Origen confesses all that I have alleged of him. He confesses, in contradiction to his former assertion, that he knew of three sorts of Jews professing Christianity. One sort adhered to the letter of the Mosaic law, rejecting all figurative interpretations; another sort admitted a figura-

---

* —— Και ὡς συγκεχυμένως γε ταυ{ ὁ παρα τῳ Κελσῳ Ιουδαιος λεγει, δυναμενος πιθανωτερον ειπειν, ὁτι ΤΙΝΕΣ μεν ὑμων καταλελοιπασι τα ἰδ., προφασει διηγησεων και ἀλληγοριων· ΤΙΝΕΣ δε και διηγουμενοι, ὡς ἐπαγγελλεσθε, πνευματικως, ὑδεν ἡτλον τα πατρια τηρειτε· ΤΙΝΕΣ δε, ὑδε διηγουμενοι, βελεσθε και τον Ιησουν παραδεξασθαι ὡς προφητευθεντα, και τον Μωυσεως νομον τηρησαι κατα τα πατρια, ὡς εν τῳ λεξει εχοντες τον παντα τε πνευματ[ος] νεν.

tive interpretation, conforming, however, to the letter of the precept; but a third sort (the first in Origen's enumeration) had relinquished the observance of the literal precept, conceiving it to be of no importance, in comparison of the latent figurative meaning.

7. But this is not all. In the next sentence, he gives us to understand, though I confess more indirectly, but he gives us to understand, that of these three sorts of Hebrews professing Christianity, they only, who had laid aside the use of the Mosaic law, were in his time considered as true Christians. For he mentions it as a further proof of the ignorance of Celsus, pretending, as it appears he did, to deep erudition upon all subjects, that in his account of the heresies of the Christian church, he had omitted *the Israelites believing in Jesus, and not laying aside the law of their ancestors.* " But how should Celsus, he says, make clear distinctions upon this point; who, in the sequel of his work, mentions impious heresies altogether alienated from Christ, and others, which have renounced the Creator, and hath not noticed [or knew not of] Israelites believing in Jesus and not relinquishing the law of their fathers?"* What opinion is to be entertain-

---

* Αλλα γαρ ωθεν Κιλσος τα καλα του τοπου τραινωσαι, ὡς και ἀφισ-
των μεν ἐθεων, και τα Ιησου σαιλη ἀλλοιων ἐν τοις ἰξης ἐριμμονιωσι,

ed of a writer's veracity, who, in one page, asserts that the Hebrews professing Christianity had not renounced the Jewish law; and, in the next af firms that a part of them had renounced it, not without an insinuation, that they, who had not, were heretics, not true Christians? EGO HUIC TESTI, ETIAMSI JURATO, QUI TAM, MANIFESTO FU. MOS VENDIT, ME NON CREDITURUM ESSE CONFIRMO.

8. I flatter myself, that I have established my charge against Origen, with respect to the par. ticular fact in question. That a strict regard to truth in disputation, was not the virtue of his character, I shall now shew by another strange instance of prevarication, which occurs in these same books against Celsus. Celsus, to deprive the Christian cause of all benefit from Isaiah's prophecy of the Virgin's conception, makes his Jew say, what hath since been said by many Jewish critics without the least foundation, that the Hebrew word in Isaiah vii. 14, which is rende- red by the LXX, *a virgin*, denotes only *a young woman*. Origen, in justification of the sense in which Christian interpreters understand the pas- sage, cites * the law against the incontinence of betrothed virgins, in Deut. xxii. 23, 24, the word

---

ται άλλων καλαλιπωσιν τον δημιεργον· εκ ειδε δε και Ισεανλιλας εις Ιησεν πισευοιλας και ό καλαλιπονλας τον παλειον νομον.

. * Contra Cels. lib. i. sec. 34.

עלמה, which Christians understand of a virgin in Isaiah, being allowed, as Origen will have it, to denote a virgin in this passage of the law. But in this passage, according to our modern Hebrew text, the word is not עלמה, but בתולה. Were it certain that עלמה had been the reading in the copies of the age of Origen, a suspicion might arise, that the text had been corrupted by the Jews, for the purpose of depriving the Christians of one argument in vindication of their interpretation of Isaiah. But there is something so suspicious in the manner of Origen's appeal to this text, that he is rather to be suspected of prevarication, than the synagogue of fraud.——ἡ μὲν λέξις ἡ Αλμα, ἣν οἱ μὲν ἑξδομήκοντα μεθερμηνεύσαντι πρὸς τὴν παρθένον, ἄλλοι δὲ εἰς τὴν νεάνιν, κεῖλαι, ΩΣ ΦΑΣΙ, καὶ ἐν τῷ Δευτερονομίῳ ἐπὶ παρθένου, &c. "The word עלמה which the LXX have translated into the word παρθένος [a virgin], but other interpreters, into the word νεάνις [a young woman], is put too, AS THEY SAY, in Deuteronomy, for a virgin." What is this, *As they say?* Was it unknown to the compiler of the Hexapla, what the reading of the Hebrew text, in his own time was? If he knew that it was, what he would have thought it to be; why does he seem to assert upon hearsay only? If he knew not; why did he not inform himself? that he might either assert, with confidence, what he had found upon inquiry to be true; or not assert what could not be maintained. EGO HUIC TESTI, ETIAMSI

JURATO, QUI TAM MANIFESTO FUMOS VENDIT, ME
NON CREDITURUM ESSE CONFIRMO.

9. So much for Origen's veracity in argument,
so unjustly aspersed by me, so completely vindicated by Dr Priestley.*

10. I will here take the liberty to remark upon
the early fathers in general, whose memories are
nevertheless to be revered, for their learning and
the general sanctity of their characters; that in
their popular discourses, and in argument, they
were too apt to sacrifice somewhat of the accuracy of fact to the plausibility of their rhetoric; or,
which is much the same thing, they were too
ready to adopt any notion, which might serve a
present purpose, without nicely examining its solidity or its remote consequences. For this reason
the great profit, which may arise from the study
of their works, is rather that we may gather from
them, what were the opinions and the practice
of the whole body of the church, in the times
wherein they lived; than that any one of these
writers is safely to be followed in all his asser-

---

* " I have completely vindicated the character of Origen,
which you have endeavoured to blot."   Second Letters, &c. p.
189.   See a further defence of Origen's veracity, in the first
of Dr Priestley's Third Letters, and my Reply to that further
defence, in the fifth of the Supplemental Disquisitions.

tions. Instances of precipitation, in advancing what occurred at the moment, and served a present purpose, may be found, I believe, in the writings of no less a man than St Chrysostom. I shall mention one instance which occurs to me, which is very remarkable, though perhaps of little consequence. In his homilies upon the second epistle to the Corinthians, Chrysostom relates that it was not agreed, in his time, who the person might be, who is described by St Paul as the " brother whose praise is in the gospel in all the churches:" that some thought St Luke was meant under this description; others St Barnabas: and, for a reason which he mentions, he gives it as his own opinion, that St Barnabas was probably the person intended. But, in his first homily upon the Acts of the Apostles, he no less than three times brings up this text as an attestation of St Paul to St Luke's merit: for no other reason, but that this application of it served the purpose of a rhetorical amplification of St Luke's praise.

11. Upon this circumstance, the notorious carelessness of the fathers in their rhetorical assertions, I should build my reply to the several passages which Dr Priestley hath produced from St Chrysostom, to prove that it was allowed by St Chrysostom, that the doctrine of the Trinity had never been openly taught by the apostles; if those passages appeared to me, in the same light in which

they appear to my antagonist. As for the particular passage in Athanasius, if any Unitarian, who reads the entire passage, thinks that the Jews there mentioned were converted, not unbelieving Jews, I must apply to him, what Dr Priestley remarks of those whom I esteem as orthodox, that "the minds of a few individuals may be so locked up, that no keys we can apply will be able to open them."* For St Chrysostom, I cannot find that he says any thing, but what I myself would say; that the apostles taught first what was easiest to be learned, and went on to higher points, as the minds of their catechumens became able to bear them. If I could allow that he hath any where said, what Dr Priestley thinks he finds in his expressions, that the apostles had been reserved and concealed upon an article of faith; I should say, that it was a thought that had hastily occurred to him, as a plausible solution of a difficulty, which deserved, perhaps, no very diligent discussion in a popular assembly; and that he had hastily let it escape him. I am well persuaded, that any priest in Chyrsostom's jurisdiction, who should have maintained this extraordinary proposition, that "the apostles had temporized, in delivering the fundamentals of the Christian faith," would have met with no very

---

* Importance of Free Inquiry, p. 59.

gentle treatment from the pious Archbishop of
Constantinople. Had the priest, in his own vindication, presumed to say: " Holy father, if I
am in error, you yourself must answer for it.
Upon your authority I adopted the opinion, which
you now condemn; you have repeatedly said in
your commentaries upon the sacred books, that
the apostles and the evangelists stood in awe of
the prejudices of their hearers." St Chrysostom
would have replied: " Faithless monster! is it
thy stupidity, or thy baseness, that interprets, as
an impeachment of the sincerity of the first inspired preachers, my encomium of their wisdom ?
But why should I wonder, that he should not
scruple to slander his bishop, who spares not the
apostles and evangelists." Had the priest been
able to prove against St Chrysostom, that he had
indeed given countenance in his writings to such
an error, the good father would have repented
in sackcloth and ashes.

12. As the mention of Dr Priestley's quotations
from St Chrysostom hath occurred, I must not
omit to do justice to a passage, which hath suffered a little in the hands of this *emeritus* professor
of Greek * in the late academy at Warrington. I

---

* " I —— taught it nine years, the last six of them at
Warrington." Second Letters, p. 202.
  Ad summum, non Maurus erat, nec Sarmata, nec Thrax,
  Qui sumpsit pennas, *mediis sed natus Athenis.*

speak of the passage cited by Dr Priestley, in his Second Letters, page 94, from the first homily on the epistle to the Hebrews. In the Greek, as Dr Priestley gives it, it is rank nonsense; and not very intelligible, in Dr Priestley's English. Dr Priestley, to get it into English at all, has had recourse to an emendation. An " *ὁ* must be turned into *και, or something else.*" Suppose *ὁ* turned into *και,* what will be the antecedent of the pronoun *αὐλος* in the Greek, or of *himself* in Dr Priestley's English? Had Dr Priestley consulted any good edition of St Chrysostom, either the Paris edition of 1735, or the old Paris edition of Fronto Ducæus, or the Eton edition, he would have found that *ὁ γαρ ἡμιν ὁ Θεος* should be *ὁ γαρ ἡμιν ὁ Χριστος* and that *ὁ* should keep its place. " Observe," says St Chrysostom, " the apostle's prudence in the choice of his expressions. For he hath not said, *Christ spake,* although he [*i. e.* Christ] was the person who spake; but because their minds were weak, and they were not yet able to bear the things concerning Christ, he says, *God spake by him.*"

13. The particular notion that Christ was the Jehovah of the Old Testament, the person who

---

But " the elements of the language, it seems, were not taught there." [Ibid.] The professor indeed, had the elements been to be taught, had been ill qualified for his chair.

conversed with the patriarchs, talked with Moses
in the bush, displayed his tremendous · glory at
Sinai, and . spake by the prophets, is what St
Chrysostom thought the Hebrews not far enough
advanced in the theory of revelation to bear. If
he thought them too weak, to bear the general
doctrine of our Lord's DEITY, his judgment
would be of little weight, since St Paul thought
otherwise. For, in the second verse of the first
chapter of this epistle, the apostle enters upon
that abstruse subject, which, in the first verse, according to Dr Priestley's interpretation of St
Chrysostom, he is supposed to shun; in the third
verse, he goes deep into the mystery; and, in the
eighth, he applies to Christ what the Psalmist
says of God, that " his throne is for ever and ever,
the sceptre of his kingdom a sceptre of righteousness:" and the manner, in which the words of the
Psalmist are introduced, shews that the apostle
thought, that they, to whom he wrote, could not
but join with him in this application. Dr Priestley, I suppose, thought it as well to keep it out of
the reader's sight, that St Chrysostom, in this
very passage, speaks of Christ as the Jehovah of
the Old Testament. He thought it best to keep
the true meaning of the passage out of sight; and
for this reason he chose to take up the corrupt
and senseless reading of the Heidelberg edition,
(a bad copy of the Veronese text, in a very small

part only collated with the Palatin and Augustan manuscripts,) and rejecting an emendation, unanimously received by later editors, who took the pains to rectify the text by a laborious collation of many manuscripts, to make the best of the passage for himself, by *correcting* in the wrong place. Thus indeed we have a beautiful specimen of an ancient father *corrected by an Unitarian!*

14. I must not quit the subject of these quotations, without observing, that the learned reader, in his first homily of St Chrysostom upon the epistle to the Hebrews, will find St Chyrsostom's own confutation of the proof, which Dr Priestley' attempts to bring from his works; that it was a thing known and admitted in his time, that the apostles had been silent upon the subject of our Lord's divinity; and that the orthodox, to account for this acknowledged fact, were reduced to the necessity of supposing, that they temporized. What the silence of the apostles, upon this subject was, may be learned from the epistle to the Hebrews. What St Chrysostom's opinion of their temporizing caution was, may be learned from his first homily upon that epistle. Whoever reads only the two first sections of that homily, will perceive, that the prudence, which St Chrysostom ascribes to the apostles, was a prudence in

the manner of preaching mysterious doctrines, not
a dishonest caution in dissembling difficulties.
Had he ascribed to them any such base art, the
epistle to the Hebrews had been his confutation.
His first homily on that epistle is the confutation
of those, who, in ignorance, or in art, would ascribe to him so unworthy a notion of the founders
of our faith.

CHAPTER SECOND.

Of the church of Ælia, or Jerusalem, after Adrian.—Mosheim's
narration confirmed.—Christians not included in Adrian's
edicts against the Jews.—The return from Pella, a fact af-
firmed by Epiphanius.—Orthodox Hebrew Christians existing
in the world long after the times of Adrian.

THE next fact that comes in question, is the
existence of a body of orthodox Hebrew Christians at Jerusalem, after the final dispersion of the
Jews by Adrian,

2. In the seventh of my letters to Dr Priestley,
I stated briefly, what I take to be the true account
of the changes, which took place in the ecclesiastical state of Palestine, upon the banishment of
the Jews by Adrian. The ecclesiastical history of
those times is so very general and imperfect, that
whoever attempts to make out a consistent story
from the ancient writers, which are come down to
us, will find himself under a necessity of helping
out their broken accounts by his own conjectures.
In the general view of the transactions of that
time, I agree almost entirely with Mosheim; who,
in my judgment, hath, with great penetration,
drawn forth the whole truth; or what must seem
to us the truth, because it carries the highest air

of probability, from the obscure hints, which the
historian Sulpitius furnishes, connected with other
hints, which, though unobserved by Dr Priestley,
are to be found in other writers of antiquity.   Dr
Priestley speaks of a series of facts,* and of many
circumstances, which, he says, I have added to
Mosheim's account, and " must know that I added."   If Dr Priestley consulted that part of Mosheim's work, *De Rebus Christianorum ante Constantinum*, to which the margin of my letters referred him (but in Mosheim, as in Grotius, it is
likely that he turned to the wrong place), if he
opened Mosheim in the place to which I referred,
he must know that I have added no circumstance,
to Mosheim's account; but such as every one must
add, in his own imagination, who admits Mosheim's representation of the fact in its principal
parts.   He must know, that three circumstances
in particular, which he is pleased to mention
among my additions, are affirmed by Mosheim:
the conflux of Hebrew Christians to Ælia; the
motive, which induced the majority to give up
their ancient customs; namely, the desire of sharing in the privileges of the Ælian colony; and
the retreat of those, who could not bring themselves to give their ancient customs up, to remote

---

* Second Letters, p. 192.

corners of the country.* These were Mosheim's assertions before they were mine: and Dr Priestley either knows this, or, pretending to separate Mosheim's own account from my additions, he hath not taken the trouble to examine what is mine, and what is Mosheim's.

3. It may seem, however, that to convict my adversary of the crime of shameful precipitance, in asserting what he hath not taken the pains to know; or of the worse crime, of asserting the contrary of what he knows, absolves not me of the imputation, that I have related upon the authority of Mosheim, what Mosheim related upon none.† I will therefore briefly state the principles, which determine me to abide by Mosheim's account of the transactions in question. I take for granted, then, these things.

I. A church of Hebrew Christians, adhering to the observance of the Mosaic law, subsisted for a time at Jerusalem, and for some time at Pella, from the beginning of Christianity until the final dispersion of the Jews by Adrian.

II. Upon this event a Christian church arose at Ælia.

---

* Second Letters, p. 39.   † Ibid. p. 192.

III. The church of Ælia, often, but improperly, called the church of Jerusalem, for Jerusalem was no more; the church of Ælia in its external form, that is, in its doctrines and its discipline, was a Greek church; and it was governed by bishops of the uncircumcision. In this my adversary and I are agreed. The point in dispute between us is, of what members the church of Ælia was composed. He says, of converts of Gentile extraction. I say, of Hebrews; of the very same persons, in the greater part, who were members of the ancient Hebrew church, at the time when the Jews were subdued by Adrian. For again, I take for granted,

IV. That the observation of the Mosaic law, in the primitive church of Jerusalem, was a matter of mere habit and national prejudice, not of conscience. A matter of conscience it could not be; because the decree of the apostolical college, and the writings of St Paul, must have put every true believer's conscience at ease upon the subject. St Paul, in all his epistles, maintains the total insignificance of the Mosaic law, either for Jew or Gentile, after Christ had made the great atonement; and the notion that St Paul could be mistaken, in a point which is the principal subject of a great part of his writings, is an impiety, which I cannot impute to our holy brethren, the saints of the primitive church of Jerusalem.*   Again, I take for granted,

V. That with good Christians, such as I believe the Christians of the primitive church of Jerusalem to have been; motives of worldly interest, which would not overcome conscience, would, nevertheless, overcome mere habit.

VI. That the desire of partaking in the privileges of the Ælian colony, from which Jews were excluded, would accordingly be a motive, that would prevail with the Hebrew Christians of Jerusalem, and other parts of Palestine, to divest themselves of the form of Judaism, by laying aside their ancient customs.

4. Dr Priestley asks me, " Where, Sir, do you find in this passage (a passage of Sulpitius Severus which he cites) any promise of immunities to the Jewish Christians, if they would forsake the law of their fathers."† Nowhere, I confess, in this passage; nor in any other passage of Sulpitius; in any passage of any ancient, I may add, nor of

---

* By the primitive church of Jerusalem, I mean the Hebrew church, before Adrian.   The retreat to Pella was temporary; and, I am inclined to think, of short duration ; and the bishop, while he sat there, was still called the Bishop of Jerusalem.

† Second Letters, p. 42.

any modern writer. But the question implies a false and fraudulent representation of my argument. I never spake, I never dreamed, of any promise of *particular* immunities to Jewish Christians, upon condition that they renounced the Mosaic law. I spake only of the general immunities of the Ælian colony, of which Christians might, and Jews might not partake.*

5. Dr Priestley alleges, that " the historian (Sulpitius) says, that the object of Adrian was to overturn Christianity."† But whatever the emperor's dislike to Christianity might be, there is little probability that, upon this occasion, he would be disposed to treat Christians with severity. The

---

* Notwithstanding the explanation, which I have here given, of what I said, in the seventh of my Letters in Reply, of the exclusion of Jews, and of Jews only, from the privileges of the Ælian colony; Dr Priestley in his Third Letters, has the assurance to tell me, " You say that the Jews were allowed to remain in the place, and enjoy the privileges of the Ælian colony, on condition of their becoming Christians." As if I had mentioned this as an article of capitulation between the emperor and the Jews. I conceive, that I have expressed my meaning too plainly to be misapprehended, by those who choose to understand. I never conceived, I have nowhere said, " that Adrian was so well disposed to Christianity, as to permit the rebellious Jews to remain in Jerusalem, on condition of their embracing it." But I suppose that the emperor might distinguish between rebels and those who had been good subjects. The Hebrew Christians had taken no part in the rebellion. And yet, had they not discarded the Jewish rites, they might have been mistaken for Jews.

† Second Letters, p. 42.

historian Sulpitius nowhere says, that the emperor's edicts against the Jews extended to Christians; and the historian Orosius says expressly,
that to Christians they extended not.* Was Orosius too late a writer to give evidence about these
transactions? The historian of Corruptions is, I
believe, some centuries later. His means of information therefore, are fewer; and, were he well informed, his precipitance in assertion, and his talent of accommodating his story to his opinions,
should annihilate the credit of his evidence. The
testimony of Orosius, however inconsiderable,
might of itself therefore outweigh the opinion of
Dr Priestley; if a feather only, in the one scale,
be more than a counterpoise for a nothing in the
other.

6. The testimony however, of Orosius, is not
without some indirect confirmation from other
writers; and, what is more, from its consistency
with other circumstances in the history of those
times, with which the assertion of Sulpitius, that
Adrian meant to wound Christianity through the
sides of Judaism, will not easily accord. It is a
notorious fact, that Adrian was not unfavourable
to the Christians. The church, in his reign, ob-

---

* ——præcepitque ne cui Judæo introeundi Hierosolymam
esset licentia, Christianis tantum civitate permissâ. Oros. Hist.
lib. 7. cap. xiii.

tained a respite from persecution. The fury of
its persecutors was restrained by the imperial rescripts to the provincial governors; who were directed not to proceed against the Christians, except by way of regular trial, upon the allegation of
some certain crime : and when nothing more was
alleged than the bare name of Christianity, to
punish the informer as a sycophant. A rescript
to this effect, addressed to Minucius Fundanus,
proconsul of Asia, is preserved by Justin Martyr
in his first apology; and, after Justin, by Eusebius in his history.*(a) This equitable disposition of the emperor towards the Christians, is ascribed by Eusebius to the eloquent apologies of
Quadratus and Aristides, and to the remonstrances of Serenius Granianus, the predecessor of Fundanus in the Asiatic proconsulate.† When the
Jewish war broke out, reasons of state immediately took place, which would greatly heighten
the effect of any impressions, previously made
upon the emperor's mind by the pleadings of
the Christian apologists, and the intercessions of

---

* Hist. Eccl. lib. iv. c. 8, 9.

(a) Dr Priestley in the second of his Third Letters, contends that these rescripts meant nothing more, than that no one
should be punished as a Christian, until he was proved to be
such. But this had been no indulgence; for every Christian
might have been proved to be a Christian by his own confession. The writers of the times boast of these rescripts as indulgences.

† Hist. Eccl. lib. iv. c. 3; and in Chron. ad ann. MMCXLII.

what friends they might have among his courtiers. The Christians of Palestine refused to take any part in the Jewish rebellion; and they smarted under the resentment of Barchochebas, the leader of the insurgents. The earliest testimony now extant of this fact is, I believe, that of Eusebius in his chronicle.* But the known impiety of Bar-chochebas, which renders it incredible that the Christians should inlist under his banners, sufficiently avouches the truth of the chronologer's assertion. The thing therefore in itself is highly probable, that the emperor should make the distinction which, Orosius says, he made between the seditious Jews and the harmless Christians; who had, indeed, been sufferers by their loyalty. The probability is still increased by certain circumstances mentioned by historians, which indicate a particular antipathy in the imperial court, at this time, to the rites of Judaism; which the refractory manners of the Jews might naturally excite. Spartian says, that a prohibition of circumcision was one of the pretences of the Jewish rebellion.† Modestinus the lawyer, as he is cited by Casaubon, alleges a rescript of Antoninus, granting a permission to the Jews, to circumcise their own children. This rescript of permission, as it

---

* Ad annum MMCXLIX.

† Movebant eâ tempestate et Judæi bellum, quòd vetabantur mutilare genitalia. *Spartian in Adriano.*

plainly implies, that the practice had been forbidden by some preceding emperor, in some measure confirms Spartian's relation. All these circumstances put together, create, as the thing appears to me, the highest probability of the truth of Orosius's assertion: that Christians were not included in the edicts of Adrian, by which the Jews were banished from Jerusalem. And although no author that I know of, beside Orosius, expressly mentions the distinction; the contrary, that the Christians were included, is affirmed by no ancient writer. The distinction indeed, though not mentioned, is clearly implied in Epiphanius's assertion; that the Hebrew Christians, after Adrian's settlement of the Ælian colony, returned from Pella, whither they had retired from the distresses of the war, to Ælia. For it happens, that this fact, of which Dr Priestley does me the honour to make me the inventor, is asserted by Epiphanius. Epiphanius, having related that Aquila, the same person who afterwards made a translation of the scriptures of the Old Testament into Greek, was employed by Adrian, as overseer of the works at Ælia, proceeds in these words: ὁ τωτων Ακυλας, διαγων ἐν τῃ Ἱερυσαλημ, και ὁρων τας μαθηίας των μαθηίων των ἀποςολων ἀνθεύίας τῃ πιςίι, και σημεια μεγαλα ἐργαζομιυς ἰαςιων και ἄλλων θαυμαίων· ἡσαν γαρ 'ΥΠΟΣΤΡΕΨΑΝΤΕΣ' ΑΠΟ ΠΕΛΛΗΣ της δικαιπολιως εἰς Ἱερυσαλημ, και διδασκοήις· ἡνικα γαρ ἑμελλεν ἡ πολις ἁλισκισθαι ὑπο των Ρωμαιων, προιχρημαίισθησαν ἱπο ἀγγελω παιδις ὁι μαθηίαι μίαςηναι ἀπο της πολιως, μελλυσης ἀρδην ἀπολλισθαι· ὁιτινις και μίανασαι γινομινοι ὤκησαν ἐν Πελλη τη προγιγραμμμεση συλλι στρας τυ Ιεδασυ, ητις δκ δικασπολιας λογίλαι είναι· μίλα δί τω ίρημωσιν Ιερμσαλημ 'ΕΠΑΝΑΣΤΡΕΨΑΝΤΕΣ, ἱς ἱφχι, σημιτα μιγαλα ἱπιτιλιν· ὁ τοισυι Αχυλας, κ. τ. λ. Epiph. *De Pond et Mens.* Whether this return of the Christians of Jerusalem from Pella took place in the interval between the end of Titus's war and the commencement of Adrian's, or after the end of Adrian's, is a matter of no importance. It is sufficient for my purpose, that these returned Christians were residing at Jerusalem, or more properly at Ælia, at the same time that Aquila was residing there as overseer of the emperor's works. Let not the public therefore be abused by any cavils, which ignorance or fraud may raise, about the chronology of the return.* To this assertion

---

* Dr Priestley in the third of his Third Letters, has treated this testimony of Epiphanius just as I expected and indeed predicted. He first endeavours to embarrass the argument with some chronological difficulties; and then gets rid of it in his own peculiar manner, by making positive testimony submit to his own theory. "What can be more evident," he says, "than that the return of the Jewish Christians from Pella, mentioned in this passage by Epiphanius, is that return which followed the destruction of Jerusalem by Titus?" Be it so. It is granted then that some of the Jewish Christians, who fled to Pella during Titus's war, returned to Jerusalem afterwards. But the question is, not at what time the Jewish Christians, whom Aquila found at Ælia, had returned thither, but at what time he conversed with them. Epiphanius says he conversed with them at the time that he was superintendent of Adrian's works at Ælia. At that time therefore there were Hebrew Christians settled at Ælia, or they could not then have conversed with Aquila. I maintain, that there is no reason to believe that the Hebrew Christians quietly set-

of Epiphanius, Mosheim, relating the fact, refers.
Relating the same fact to Mosheim, I referred *
to the very passage,† where Dr Priestley, had he
known what it is to examine authorities before he

---

tied at Ælia, before the Jewish rebellion, were included in
Adrian's edict for the banishment of the Jews.

But Dr Priestley remarks further, upon the authority of Cave,
that Aquila's translation of the Old Testament was made in the
11th or 12th year of Adrian.   Then, since that translation was
undertaken in consequence of his apostacy, and his apostacy was
some considerable time after his conversion, Dr Priestley infers,
that his conversion " was probably prior to the reign of Adrian,"
and so the whole story of his intercourse with the Jewish Christians at Ælia, while he was residing there in the time of Adrian,
is discredited.

Perhaps to assign the exact year of Aquila's translation, would
prove a task of no less difficulty to any who should attempt it,
than to determine the day of the week, and the hour of the day,
when the last word of that work was written.   The learned Cave
had, as far as I know, no reason for fixing Aquila's translation
to the 11th or 12th of Adrian ; but that Epiphanius says, that
in the 12th year of Adrian, " Aquila first became known." But
if Epiphanius is to be believed, Aquila first became known by
Adrian's appointment of him to so considerable an office, as that
of overseer of the public works at Ælia.   This was in the 12th
year of Adrian.   His conversion to Christianity was some time
subsequent to that appointment ; his apostacy, at some considerable distance of time, subsequent to his conversion ; and his
translation of the Old Testament subsequent to his apostacy.
So that the time of that translation, can be no otherwise defined
than thus: that it certainly was not earlier than the 12th of
Adrian, and probably was later by an interval of many years.

My argument therefore from Epiphanius stands its ground,
and the caution which I gave the public not to be abused by cavils which might be raised about the chronology of the return
from Pella, is but too much justified by the event.

* Letters to Dr Priestley, p. 61.

 + De Rebus Christianorum ante Constantinum.   Sæc. II. sec.
38. note *.

pronounces upon them, might have found the reference to the original author. The confidence
with which he mentions this, as a fact forged by
me, is only one instance, out of a great number, of
his own shameless intrepidity in assertion.

7. But to return from the detection of Dr
Priestley's fictions, to the historical discussion. It
may seem, that my six positions go no further,
than to account for the disuse of the Mosaic law,
among the Christians of Palestine, upon the supposition that the thing took place; and that they
amount not to a proof, that a church of Hebrew
Christians, not adhering to the rites of Judaism,
actually existed at Ælia. To complete the proof
therefore, I might appeal to Epiphanius's assertion
of the return of the Christians of Jerusalem from
Pella. But I will rather derive the proof, from a
fact which I think more convincing than the testimony of Epiphanius; a fact, by which that testimony is itself indeed confirmed. I affirm then,

VII. That a body of orthodox Christians of
the Hebrews, were actually existing in the world,
much later than in the time of Adrian.

8. The testimony of Origen I hold too cheap,
to avail myself of his triple division of the Hebrew
Christians, to prove the existence of the orthodox
set, in his time. It must be observed, however,

that, were his evidence at all admissible, his distinction would be somewhat a stronger proof for
me, than his general assertion, of which the generality is discredited by the distinction afterwards
alleged, can be allowed to be for my antagonist.
But I give him Origen. I will rest the credit of
my seventh position, upon the mention which occurs in St Jerome's commentary upon Isaiah, of
Hebrews believing in Christ as distinct from the
Nazarenes. St Jerome relates two different expositions of the prophecy concerning Zabulon and
Naphtali, delivered in the beginning of the ninth
chapter of Isaiah ; of which expositions he ascribes
the one to the *Hebrews believing in Christ;* the
other, to the *Nazarenes.* The character given of
these Hebrews, that " they believed in Christ,"
without any thing to distinguish their belief from
the common belief of the church, without any
note of its error or imperfection, is a plain character of complete orthodoxy. For it was neither
the disposition of St Jerome, nor the fashion of
his age, to miss any opportunity of proclaiming
the vices of those, who were deemed heretics;
unless upon occasions when some rhetorical purpose might be answered by concealing them.
But no rhetorical purpose was to be answered,
in these notes upon Isaiah, by a concealment of
any error, that had been justly to be imputed
to these Hebrews; nor was St Jerome at all
concerned to maintain the particular exposition,

which he ascribes to them. He had therefore
no inducement to conceal their errors. But he
taxes them with none. He had therefore no
harm to say of them. They were orthodox believers: and the distinction of them from the Nazarenes, made by St Jerome, is a plain proof that
they were not observers of the Mosaic law. For
although the Mosaic law was observed in the orthodox church of Jerusalem, until the time of the
suppression of the Jewish rebellion by Adrian, it
was after his time, by my adversary's own confession, confined to the Nazarenes and the Ebionites.
If then the Hebrews believing in Christ observed
not the Mosaic law in the time of St Jerome, since
the Mosaic law had been observed by the first
race of believing Hebrews; it follows, that the
practice of the Hebrew congregations had undergone a change, at some time before the age of St
Jerome. Dr Priestley says, that great bodies of
men change not their opinions soon. I say, they
never change their old customs and inveterate habits, but from some powerful motive. Now, in
what period of the history of the church shall we
find a posture of affairs, so likely to induce the
Hebrew Christians to forsake the Mosaic law, as
that which obtained in Palestine, upon the final
dispersion of the Jews by Adrian? If the orthodox Christians of the Hebrews, actually existing
somewhere in the world from the reign of Adrian
to the days of St Jerome, were not members of the

church of Ælia, dwelling at Ælia, and in the adjacent parts of Palestine, Dr Priestley, if he be so
pleased, may seek their settlement.　It is no small
difficulty upon my adversary's side, that he can neither tell " what became of the Christian Jews,"
upon his supposition, that with the unbelieving
Jews they " were driven out of Jerusalem by A-
drian;"* nor from what quarter the Greek church
of Ælia was furnished with its members.

9. Upon these foundations, which a stronger
arm than Dr Priestley's shall not be able to tear
up, stands " the church of orthodox Jewish Christians at Jerusalem:"† to which the assertors of
the Catholic faith will not scruple to appeal, in
proof of the antiquity of their doctrine, whatever
offence the very mention of the orthodox church
of Jerusalem, may give to the enraged hæresiarch.‡

10. He asks me, what evidence I can bring
that this church, even before the time of Adrian,

---

* " What became of the Christian Jews who were driven out
of Jerusalem by Adrian, does not appear."　Second Letters, &c.
p. 45.

† " Thus ends this church of orthodox Jewish Christians at
Jerusalem, &c."　Second Letters, p. 44.

‡ " — I hope, *(id populus curat scilicet)* I hope, however,
we shall hear no more of them as an evidence of the antiquity
of the Trinitarian doctrine."　Second Letters, p. 45.

was Trinitarian. I brought evidence in my letters,* which he hath not been able to refute. Upon his own principles, the acknowledgment of their orthodoxy in later times, by writers who would have acknowledged no orthodoxy of any Unitarian sect, might be a sufficient evidence of their earliest orthodoxy. The evidence which I have brought, is nothing less than an attestation of a member of this earliest Hebrew church to the belief of himself, and his Hebrew brethren, in our Lord's divinity. But " *If* they were Nazarenes, (says Dr Priestley,) Epiphanius represents them as Unitarian, when John wrote."† I have said, and I will never cease to say, that Epiphanius's representation justifies no such opinion. But what is Epiphanius's account of the Nazarenes, or what is any account of the Nazarenes, to the purpose, *if* the Hebrews of the church of Jerusalem were no Nazarenes? With St Jerome, the Hebrews believing in Christ, and the Nazarenes, are different people.

N. B. Dr Priestley's objections to the evidence brought from St Jerome, in proof of my seventh position, which he hath advanced in the fourth of his Third Letters, are answered in the sixth of the Supplemental Disquisitions.

---

* See particularly Letter VIII.
† Second Letters, p. 45.

CHAPTER THIRD.

Of the Hebrew church, and its sects.

IT must strike the learned reader, that the Nazarenes mentioned by St Jerome, in the passage to which I now refer of his annotations on Isaiah, must have been a different people from those mentioned by him with such contempt in his epistle to St Austin, and described by Epiphanius. The Nazarenes, here mentioned by St Jerome, held the scribes and pharisees in detestation; their traditions in contempt; and the apostle St Paul in high veneration.* And yet these Nazarenes, of the best sort, were still a distinct set of people from the Hebrews believing in Christ; that is, from the orthodox church of Jerusalem, divested, in consequence of Adrian's edicts against the Jews, of what, until the time of those edicts, it had retained of the exterior form of Judaism. These remarks lead, I think, to a more distinct notion of the different sects of Hebrews professing the Christian religion, than I have met with in writers of ecclesiastical antiquity; a much more distinct one, I confess, than I had myself formed,

---

* See St Jerome in Is. ix. 1, 2, 3, et viii. 14, 19—22,

when I delivered the Charge to the clergy of my archdeaconry, which gave the beginning to this controversy; a notion however perfectly consistent with every thing which I then maintained; and tending to establish the points, in which I differ from Dr Priestley. As the question about the Hebrew sects is of great importance, I shall here briefly state the sum of what I have found concerning them in ancient writers, and then propound my own conclusions.

2. The Nazarenes are not mentioned by Irenæus. Irenæus says of the Ebionites,* that they acknowledged God for the maker of the world;— that they resembled not Cerinthus or Carpocrates in their opinions about Christ;—that they used only the Gospel by St Matthew;—were over curious in the exposition of the prophets;—disowned the apostle Paul, calling him an apostate from the law;—circumcised, and retained the Jewish law and Jewish customs. This description of the Ebionites occurs in that part of the great work of Irenæus, which is extant only in a barbarous Latin translation. In the passage which relates to their opinions about Christ, Cotelerius suspects a corruption; and for *non similiter*, he would read *consimiliter*; supposing that Irenæus

---

* Irenæus, lib. i. c. 26.

must have affirmed, and that he could not deny, their resemblance of Cerinthus and Carpocrates in that article; and this indeed is agreeable, as will appear, to the descriptions given of the Ebionites by other writers.

3. Irenæus in another place insinuates, that for wine, in the Eucharist, the Ebionites substituted pure water.[*]

4. Tertullian says, that Ebion made Jesus a mere man, of the seed of David only, that is, not also the Son of God; in some respect higher in glory than the prophets.[†] In another place [‡] he says, that Ebion was the successor of Cerinthus; not agreeing with him in every particular, inasmuch as he allowed that the world was made by God, not by angels: that as a consequence of Christ's mere humanity, he maintained the lasting obligation of the Mosaic law; because it is written, that the disciple is not above the master, nor the servant above his lord. Tertullian says nothing expressly about the agreement, or disagreement of Ebion and Cerinthus, in their notions of Christ; but the impiety of maintaining that he was a mere man, the son of Joseph, he ascribes to Carpocrates and Cerinthus as well as Ebion;

---

[*] Irenæus, lib. v. c. 2.   [†] De carne Christi, c. 14.
[‡] De Præscript. Hæret. c. 48.

which renders the emendation, proposed by Cotelerius, in the Latin version of Irenæus, *consimiliter* for *non·similiter*, very probable : especially, as
a further agreement of the Ebionites and Gnostics, in their notions about Christ, is maintained
by other writers. Tertullian again in another
place, having mentioned " that St Paul, writing
to the Galatians, inveighs against the observers
and defenders of circumcision and the law," adds,
" this was Ebion's heresy."* This however is no
argument, that Ebion lived when that epistle was
written. Tertullian means only to remark, that
Ebion's tenets, in this article, were clearly confuted by St Paul's writings. In the same place
he mentions the denial of the resurrection of the
body, by Marcion, Apelles, and Valentinus, as an
error reproved in St Paul's first epistle to the
Corinthians. But no one, I imagine, would
thence conclude that Marcion, Apelles, and Valentinus, were contemporaries of the apostle.

5. Origen, in the second book against Celsus,
seems to comprehend the whole body of the Hebrew Christians under the name of Ebionites;
and affirms, that they adhered to the law of their
fathers.† But in another place, where he profes-

---

* De Præscript. Hæret. c. 33.
† Contra Cels. lib. ii. sec. 1.

ses to describe the Christianity of the Hebrews
with the greatest accuracy, he divides the whole
body into three sects. The first, like other Christians, entirely discarded the Mosaic law; the second retained the observation of the law in the
letter of the precept, admitting however the same
spiritual expositions of it, which were set up by
those who discarded it; the third sort not only
observed the law according to the letter, but rejected all spiritual expositions of it.*

6. Eusebius divides the Ebionites into two
sorts, both denying our Lord's divinity; but the
better sort believing the miraculous conception.†
Both rejected the epistles of St Paul, whom they
called an apostate from the law. They used the
Gospel according to the Hebrews, and held the
canonical gospels in little esteem. They kept
both the Jewish Sabbath and the Christian Sunday. Origen and Eusebius, like Irenæus, mention not the Nazarenes by name.

7. St Jerome, in his commentary upon Isaiah,
mentions Hebrews believing in Christ;‡ and, as a
distinct set of people from these believing Hebrews, he mentions Nazarenes who observed the
law,§ but despised the traditions of the pharisees,

---

* Contra Cels. lib. ii. sec. 3.   † Hist. Ecc. lib. iii. c. 27.
‡ In Is. ix. 1, 2, 3.   § Ibid. and viii. 14, 19—21.

thought highly of St Paul,* and held the doctrine of our Lord's divinity. For, by an exposition of Isaiah viii. 13, 14, which St Jerome ascribes
to them, it appears that they acknowledged in
Christ the נחוה צבאות [the Lord God of hosts] of
the Old Testament. In his epistle to St Au-
gustin,† St Jerome describes Nazarenes of another sort, " who believed in Christ the Son of
God, born of the Virgin Mary, in whom the orthodox believe;" but were, nevertheless, so bigotted to the Mosaic law, that they were rather
to be considered as a Jewish sect than a Christian. In the same place, he speaks of the
Ebionites as a sect anathematized for their Judaism, and falsely pretending to be Christians ;
and in his commentary upon St Matthew xii. he
says they acknowledged not St Paul's apostolical
commission.

8. Epiphanius describes the sect of the Nazarenes as a set of people hardly to be distinguished from Jews. He expresses a doubt, whether
they acknowledged our Lord's divinity: but the
terms, in which his doubt is expressed, argue
that it was groundless.‡ He describes the Ebio-

---

* In Is. ix. 1, 2, 3 ; and viii. 14, 19—21.
† Hieron. Op. tom. ii. f. 341. A. edit. Froben.
‡ Charge to the Clergy of the Archdeaconry of St Alban's.
I. sec. 10, 11.

nites as resembling the Samaritans, rather than the Jews;—as maintaining that Jesus was the son of Mary, by her husband;—that the Christ, descending from heaven in the figure of a dove, entered into Jesus at his baptism. He says, that the Nazarenes and the Ebionites had each a Hebrew gospel, (the only one which they received,) which they called the gospel by St Matthew;—that the copies received by the two sects were different: compared with the true gospel by St Matthew, which the church receives, the Ebionæan copy was the least entire, and the most corrupt. He speaks of the Ebionites as a sect, which branched off from the Nazarenes, and appeared not till after the destruction of Jerusalem.*

9. From the testimony of an ancient writer, cited by Eusebius, it appears, that one Theodotus, a native of Byzantium, a tanner by trade, at the very end of the second century, was the first who taught the mere humanity of Christ.† He preached at Rome. His doctrine was an extension of the impiety of the first Ebionites: for, with them, the humanity of Christ was over at his baptism.‡ He was then deified; or, at least

---

* Epiph. Hær. 30.
† Hist. Ecc. lib. v. c. 28.
‡ See more upon this point, in Mr Howes's sermon.

exalted above humanity, by the illapse of the Christ.

10. Now, from all this, I seem to gather, that, after the destruction of Jerusalem, the Hebrew church, if under that name we may comprehend the sects which separated from it, were divided into five different sets of people.

I. St Jerome's Hebrews believing in Christ: these were orthodox Christians of Hebrew extraction, who had laid aside the use of the Mosaic law. They are the same with the first set in Origen's threefold division of the Hebrew Christians.

II. Nazarenes of the better sort, orthodox in their creed, though retaining the use of the Mosaic law. As they were admirers of St Paul, they could not esteem the law generally necessary to salvation. If these people were at all heretical, I should guess that it was in this single point, that they received the gospel of the Nazarenes, instead of the canonical gospels.

III. Nazarenes of a worse sort, bigotted to the Jewish law, but still orthodox, for any thing that appears to the contrary in their creed. These were the proper Nazarenes, described under that name by Epiphanius, and by St Jerome in his epistle to St Austin. These two sects, the better and the worse sort of Nazarenes, make the middle set in Origen's threefold division.

IV. Ebionites denying our Lord's divinity, but admitting the fact of the miraculous conception.

V. Ebionites of a worse sort, denying the miraculous conception, but still maintaining an union of Jesus with a divine being, which commenced upon his baptism. These two sects, the better and the worse sort of Ebionites, make the last set in Origen's threefold division.

11. Thus we find a regular, and no unnatural gradation, from the orthodox Hebrew Christian to the blaspheming Ebionite. It appears, however, that the impious degradation of the Redeemer's nature, though it took its rise among the Hebrew sects, was not carried to its height among them. A sect of proper Unitarians, holding the perpetual undeified humanity of the Saviour, made its first appearance at Rome, and boasted for its founder Theodotus, the apostate tanner of Byzantium, if, indeed, it was not the growth of still later times, which seems to be the opinion of the learned Mr Howes, to whose judgment I am inclined to pay great regard. These two points, however, seem certain: that the Nazarenes, even of the best sort, were a different people from the Hebrew brethren of the orthodox church of Je-

rusalem; and that the Nazarenes, even of the worst sort, were believers in the divinity of our Lord. In what extent they believed it, may, perhaps, seem to some a question in some degree still open to discussion. At present, I see no reason to recede from the opinion, which, with great authorities upon my side, I have hitherto, maintained, of their entire orthodoxy upon that article. If, upon that particular point, I should, at any time hereafter, see cause to think myself mistaken, my conviction is not likely to come from Dr Priestley, but from a very different quarter. Mr Howes's 9th number is just fallen into my hands. That learned writer, I perceive, thinks that it was but a subordinate divinity, which the Nazarenes acknowledged in our Lord. For his opinion I feel all the deference, which one scholar owes to the sentiments of another; but not without the strongest prepossessions, I confess, at present, in favour of my own.

2 c

CHAPTER FOURTH.

Of the decline of Calvinism.—Of Conventicles.

I now pass to the third fact, which I have taken upon me to establish: the decline of Calvinism, amounting almost to a total extinction of it, among our English dissenters, who, no long time since, were generally Calvinists.

2. This fact is of no great importance in our controversy; as it is but very remotely connected with the question about the opinions of the first ages. The rapid decline of Calvinism, here in England, was alleged by me as an instance, in which Dr Priestley's *theorem* about the rate of velocity, with which the opinions of great bodies of men change, would lead, in the practical application of it, to very erroneous conclusions. If my instance was ill-chosen, it will not immediately be a consequence, that Dr Priestley's theorem is a false principle for the reformation of the history of the primitive church, in defiance of the testimony of the earliest writers extant. It would give me great pleasure to find myself in an error with respect to this fact; and to see reason to believe Dr Priestley, in his assertion, that the body of our dissenters at this day are Calvinists. So

many Calvinists as are among them, so many friends there are to the Catholic faith in all its essential branches; for the peculiarities of Calvinism affect not the essentials of Christianity. But I am sorry to say, that I must still believe, that the genuine Calvinists among our modern dissenters, are very few; unless, in a matter, which hath so lately fallen under the cognisance of the British legislature, I could allow Dr Priestley's assertion, to outweigh the plain testimony of facts of public notoriety.

8. If the great body of the dissenters are, at this day, Calvinists; upon what pretence was it, that the dissenting ministers, who, in the years 1772 and 1773, petitioned Parliament to be released from the subscriptions to which they were held by the 1st of William any Mary, arrogated to themselves the title of the GENERAL BODY of dissenting ministers of the three denominations in and about London? No true Calvinist could concur in that petition. For although I cannot admit, that the articles of our church, in the doctrinal part, affirm the strict tenets of Calvinism; yet they are in this part, what, as I conceive, no true Calvinist would scruple to subscribe; and, with respect to the great doctrines of the Trinity, the Incarnation, Justification, and Grace, every genuine Calvinist would start at the very thought of being supposed, even tacitly to concur in a re-

quest to be released from a confession of his faith: for none better understands, than the genuine Calvinist, the force of that sacred maxim, " with the heart man believeth unto righteousness, and with the mouth confession is made unto salvation." Would Dr Priestley insinuate, that his brethren of the Rational dissent approached the august assembly of the British Parliament, with a petition founded upon false pretensions? Will he say, that they were, in fact, the minority of the body, of which they called themselves the generality? Will he say, that the Thirteen,* who in the meeting of the General Body at the Library, in Red-cross Street, on Wednesday, December the 23d, 1772, divided against the vote for an application to Parliament to remove the restraints, which the wisdom of our forefathers, by the Act of Toleration, had imposed, were the representatives of a more numerous body, than the Fifty-five who gave their suffrages for the motion:† who, at a subsequent meeting, suffered not the protest of the thirteen orthodox ministers, to be recorded in the minutes of the business of the day; and with difficulty permitted their reasons to be read.‡ A proceed-

---

* See a pamphlet entitled, " A Collection of the several Papers relating to the Application made to Parliament, in 1772 and 1773, by some of the Protestant Dissenters, for Relief in the matter of Subscription, &c." London, printed for J. Wilkie, No. 71, St Paul's Church-yard. MDCCLXXIII.

† See Wilkie's Collection, No. III.   ‡ Ibid. No. II.

ing, by the way, which clearly shews, how cordially these pretended friends of general toleration would delight, were they in power, to tolerate opinions which might differ from their own; and evinces the propriety of the prayer, which a sense of such wrongs, drew from a member of the orthodox minority, " From the power of such pretenders to superior reason, may GOD and THE BRITISH GOVERNMENT ever defend the orthodox dissenters."* These thirteen spake only the sentiments of every Calvinist, when they said, " We believe the doctrines of the articles to be both true and important. We dare not therefore consent, to be held up to view as those, who indulge any doubts respecting their truth, or at all hesitate about their importance. We consider them as the basis of our hope, the source of our comfort, and the most powerful incentive to a course of sincere, stedfast, cheerful obedience."† It were injustice to these worthy men, to let any occasion pass of mentioning their names with the reverence which is due to them. David Muire, John Rogers, Thomas Towle, Samuel Brewer, Edward Hitchin, Thomas Oswald, John Potts, John Trot-

---

* See " Candid Thoughts on the late Application of some Protestant dissenting ministers, &c. By an Orthodox Dissenter." London, printed for W. Goldsmith, No. 20, Paternoster-Row, 1772.
† See Wilkie's Collection, No. II. sec. 3.

ter, John Macgowan, George Stephens, Joseph
Popplewell, Henry Hunter, John Kello; these
were the venerable confessors, who, on the 23d
of December, 1772, and on the 27th of January
in the following year, in meetings of the General Body of the three denominations, stood *for
the faith once delivered to the saints.* " They
thought themselves bound, they said, to contend
earnestly for it against all who' should oppose it."
For this purpose they formed, as I gather from
the documents of the times, * into a distinct association.   When the petition of the Rationalists
was laid before the Parliament, they were firm
and active in their opposition to it; considering
the request as little less than a blow craftily aimed at the very vitals of the reformed religion,
and of Christianity, indeed, itself. They presented a cross petition, † signed, as they themselves
said, by the ministers, as well as the laity of the
most respectable congregations of real Protestant
dissenters in town and country. But, when they
wished to give credit and authority to their opposition, by boasting of their numbers, the most
that they could say of the number of ministers,
who had signed the cross petition was this: that
they were " upwards of Fifty." The number of
dissenting ministers in the whole kingdom, was

---

* See Wilkie's Collection, No. III. and IV.   † Ibid. No. V.

reckoned at that time to be about 2000. Of which
50 is just the fortieth part. When Dr Priestley
therefore affirms, that the " majority of the dissenting ministers are still Calvinists," he must be
understood to use the same rhetorical figure, by
which, in the Postscript of his First Letters to me,
he swelled a few periods of Clemens Alexandrinus
to the size of a whole book. By a computation
formed upon that instance, I concluded the proportion of the Priestleian to the vulgar *whole*, to
be that of 1 to 48; from this new instance it turns
out somewhat larger.

4. Thus, from the evidence of public facts, I
have the mortification to find Dr Priestley's sentiments confuted, and my own confirmed, concerning the present state of Calvinism among the
English dissenters. And however it may now
serve Dr Priestley's purpose, to magnify the numbers of the Calvinists; his Rational brethren, in
the year 1772, spoke of their own majority in
terms which implied, that the Calvinists were, in
their judgment, a very inconsiderable part of the
whole body of the dissenters. " It is admitted,"
says the Rationalists, in the *Case of the Protestant dissenting Ministers and Schoolmasters*, "that
the greater part of the dissenting ministers have
not complied, and cannot in conscience comply
with the subscription required by the Act of Toleration. The dissenting ministers in general are

consequently liable to the penalties abovemen-
tioned." After stating the relief which they desired to obtain, they allege that the " generality
of Protestant dissenting ministers, together with
their people, are happily united in the object of
the present application."* The petitioning dissenters, it seems, in the year 1772, thought the
Calvinists so few and inconsiderable, that the
ministers, who could not in conscience comply
with the 1st of William and Mary, and were happily united in-the object of the application at that
time made to Parliament, seemed to them the
generality of Protestant dissenting ministers.
These gentlemen knew, it is to be presumed, the
state of the dissent. They meant not to impose
a lie upon the three estates of the British legislature. For *they were all, all honourable men!* If
then my notion of the decline of Calvinism is erroneous, Dr Priestley will at least confess, that I
am countenanced and supported, in my error, by
a very respectable authority.

5. I am not ignorant indeed, that this authority was treated with little respect by the protesting Calvinists; who allowed no superiority of
numbers on the side of the Rationalists.† It was
pretended that many Calvinists concurred in the

---

* See Wilkie's Collection, No. I.

† See " Candid Thoughts, &c. by an Orthodox Dissenter,"
sec. II.

petition: some in mere tenderness for scrupulous
consciences; many more upon that goodly principle, the source of all that orderly submission to
the higher powers, which hath ever been so conspicuous in the Puritans of this country, that even
a true faith is not to be confessed at the requisition of the magistrate. I bear that good will to
Calvinism, that it gives me real concern to remember, that it hath ever been disgraced by a
connexion with such a principle. I am inclined
however to believe, that the Calvinists, who, upon
puritanical principles, concurred in the petition of
the Rationalists, in the year 1772, were very few;
and that the orthodox dissenters were deceived,
in the idea, which they had formed, of the numbers of their own party. The requisition of the
magistrate is now removed; and no pretence exists for a puritanical reserve. I would ask then,
what is now the state of the dissenting ministry?
Are they at this time a majority, are they any
considerable part, of the dissenting ministers, who
have qualified under the 1st of William and
Mary? Every dissenting minister hath now the
alternative of qualifying, either by subscribing the
doctrinal articles; or by a declaration, which, by
the 19th of his present Majesty, is accepted instead of subscription. But the Calvinist, even of
the puritanical cast, holds himself bound to an
open declaration of his faith; except in that extraordinary case, when the interference of the ma-

gistrate makes it a duty, to disown his usurped authority, by refusing to confess with the mouth, what the heart believes. Every true Calvinist therefore will now qualify under the old Act of Toleration. And if they are but an inconsiderable part of the dissenting ministry, who have qualified in this manner, it is but too plain that Calvinism among the dissenters is almost extinguished. Inconsiderable, however, as I fear their numbers are, the Calvinists, for the soundness of their faith, are the most respectable part of our modern dissenters: and though few, in comparison with the general mixed body of the Rationalists, I hope they are more numerous than the proper Unitarians.

6. So much for the principal facts which I engaged to establish. It may, perhaps, be expected, that I should take some notice of another, in which I have been charged with 'misrepresentation. Dr Priestley, in his First Letters to me, expressed high resentment, at the use which I had made in my Charge of the word *conventicle;* as descriptive of meetings in which he, and friends of his, preside. To inform myself how far this resentment might be well founded, and for no other purpose, I searched the registers of certain courts, for such an entry of the house in Essex-Street, and for a record of such declarations on the part of the minister, as, by the 19th of his

present Majesty, are requisite to make a meeting, upon the pretence of divine worship, not a conventicle in the strict sense of the word. I told Dr Priestley, that I had found neither entry of the house, nor record of the minister's declaration. Dr Priestley replies, that I could, indeed, find no record of declaration; for none was ever made: but that I ought to have found an entry of the house; for the entry was duly made. Now the truth is, that I employed the clerks at the different offices to make the search, for which I paid the accustomed fee. I trusted to their report, which I find was not accurate. I believe the fact to be, as Dr Priestley states it. The house is entered; but the minister hath never declared his principles, as the law requires. The defence of a strong word, which hath been taken personally, would be to me the most unpleasant part of the controversy, were it not that the style of Dr Priestley's Second Letters, and of some other publications upon that side, hath put an end to all ceremony between me and the leaders of the Unitarian party. I therefore still insist, that all meetings under ministers who have not declared, whether the place of meeting be entered or be not entered, are illegal; and that the word *conventicle*, as it was used by me in my Charge, was not misapplied.*

---

* Dr Priestley in his Third Letters, insists that his own

N. B. The preceding chapter gave occasion to a pamphlet, entitled, *The Calvinism of the Protestant Dissenters asserted: in a Letter to the Archdeacon of St Alban's.* By Samuel Palmer, *Pastor of the Independent Congregation at Hackney.* London, Printed for J. Buckland, &c. 1786.

The sum of Mr Palmer's argument, is contained, I think, in these three propositions. That of the thirteen ministers who signed the protest against the resolution for the application to Parliament, six were Scotsmen, true members of the Kirk, and therefore not properly among our English disenters. That the cross petition was not presented by the thirteen; that the fifty who signed it were chiefly lay-preachers, not belonging to the body of the London ministers; Methodists; unacquainted with the fundamental principles of the Protestant dissenters. That a great

---

meeting-house, and Mr Lindsey's, cannot be brought under the denomination of *conventicles* merely because they, who preach in them, are not authorised by law. He thinks, "that if, by any accident, an unauthorised dissenting minister, like himself, should preach in *a parish church,* it would not on that account become a *conventicle.*" But whatever he may think, an assembly in a parish church to hear Dr Priestley preach, or even to assist at divine worship performed by a priest of the church of England, otherwise than according to the form prescribed by the Book of Common Prayer, would be a *conventicle;* and all persons resorting to it would be liable to the penalties, which the laws denounce against persons frequenting conventicles.

body of Calvinists concurred in the application to
Parliament upon a general principle of Liberty,
disliking any interference of the magistrate in religious matters.

Of these three propositions, the two first seem
to militate strongly on my side, heightening the
appearance at least of a paucity of Calvinists
among our dissenters, since six of the thirteen who
protested, and all the fifty who petitioned, according to Mr Palmer, were not English dissenters.
As for the third, if the fact be as Mr Palmer
states it, I can only lament that a republican principle should so strongly have infected so respectable a branch of the Christian church, as the Calvinists are in my estimation. I believe however,
that the truth is, and is pretty notorious, that
Calvinism is gone among the dissenters of the
present times; though, for what reason I presume
not to say, the dissenting teachers dislike to be
told of its extinction.

CHAPTER FIFTH.

Of the doctrines of Calvin.—Of Methodists.

I now proceed to reply to Dr Priestley's insinuation, that I have spoken with contempt of the doctrines of Calvin, which at the same time he presumes, I really believe.* He was in good humour with me, when he drew up this concluding paragraph of his third letter; for his reason for presuming that I believe what, he imagines, I speak of with contempt, is, that he is unwilling " to tax me with insincerity."†

2. If any where I seem to speak with contempt of the doctrines of Calvin, I have certainly been unfortunate in the choice of my expressions. It is one thing not to assent to doctrines in their full extent; quite another to despise them. I am very sensible that our articles affirm certain things, which we hold in common with the Calvinists: so they affirm many things which we hold in common with the Lutherans; and some things which we hold in common with the Romanists. It cannot well be otherwise; for as there

---

* Second Letters, p. 35. † Ibid.

are certain principles which are common to all Protestants, so the essential articles of faith are common to all Christians. Perhaps, in points of mere doctrine, the language of our articles agrees more nearly with the Calvinistic, than with any other Protestant confession, except the Lutheran. But I never was aware, till Dr Priestley informed me of it, that I am obliged, by my subscription to the thirty-nine articles, to believe *every* tenet that is generally known by the name of Calvinistic :* and, till the obligation is enforced upon me by some higher authority than his, I shall, in these matters, " stand fast in my liberty." Nevertheless, I hold the memory of Calvin in high veneration; his works have a place in my library; and in the study of the holy Scriptures, he is one of the commentators whom I frequently consult. I may appeal to my own congregation at Newington, and to other congregations to which, by my situation, I am occasionally called to preach, to witness for me, that I never mention the Calvinistic divines without respect; even when I express, what I often express, a dissent, upon particular points, to their opinions. The respect with which they are mentioned in my Good-Friday sermon, in which I asserted the doctrines of Providence on the one hand, and of Free-agency on the other, is, per-

---

* Second Letters, p. 35.

haps in Dr Priestley's own recollection. In the passage to which he alludes, in my seventh letter to himself, he will find no contempt expressed of Calvinists, or of their opinions. The severity of the reflection falls on those, who have so speedily deserted a doctrine to which, for a long time, they were not without bigotry attached; while they not only maintained Calvin's tenets without exception, but seemed to think there could be no orthodoxy out of Calvinism. I consider it as the reproach of the dissenters of the present day, that a genuine Calvinist is hardly to be found; except in a sect, conspicuous only for the encouragement, which the leaders of it seem to give to a disorderly fanaticism. The rational dissenter hath nothing in common with the Calvinist, except it be an enmity to the episcopal establishment of this country; and this he hath not so much in common with the Calvinistic churches, as with his own ancestors the factious Puritans.

3. It was, perhaps, an omission, that when the scarcity of Calvinists among the English dissenters was mentioned, a distinct exception was not made in favour of natives of Scotland, formed into Calvinistic congregations, under respectable pastors of their own country, and of the true Calvinistic persuasion, here in London, and perhaps in other parts of England. But I consider these as no part of our English dissenters. They are

members of another national establishment; who,' residing here, may think that a conformity with the church of England might be interpreted as a desertion of their own communion. The rational dissenter may take no credit to himself for their adherence to their old principles; nor are they involved in the reproach of his degeneracy.

4. While I thus repel my adversary's slanderous insinuation of contempt expressed by me of Calvin's doctrines, the reflection, I doubt not, is arising in his breast, and with much secret satisfaction he says within himself, " He is making his peace, I see, with the Calvinists; but how will he get over my remark upon the disrespectful language in which he has spoken of the Methodists, his brother churchmen ?"* To the burden of that crime, my shoulders, I trust, are not unequal. What if I frame my reply in terms which Dr Priestley's late publication furnishes? that whenever occasions shall arise, which may make it my duty, as a minister of the gospel, to declare my sentiments, I shall not wait for Dr Priestley's leave to " express my contempt of what I think to be despicable, and my abhorrence of what I think to be shocking."† The Methodist, I am sensible, pro-

---

* Second Letters, p. 35.
† Importance of Free Inquiry, p. 29.

fesses much zeal for our common faith.   Many of
his follies, I am willing to believe, proceed more
from an unhappy peculiarity of temperament than
from any thing amiss in the moral dispositions of
his heart.   Let him then renounce his fanatical
attachment to self-constituted uncommissioned
teachers: let him shew his faith by his works;
not the formal works of superstition and hypocrisy, but the true works of everlasting righteousness; the works of fair-dealing, charity, and con-
tinence: let him do this, and churchmen will turn
to him, and call him brother.

CHAPTER SIXTH.

Of the general spirit of Dr Priestley's Controversial Writings.—
Conclusion.

I HAVE replied more largely than I thought to do, to more than is deserving of reply in Dr Priestley's Second Letters. But, as the controversy between him and the advocates of the Catholic faith is now brought, by his own declarations, to a state resembling that of a war in which no quarter is to be given or accepted, I think myself at liberty to strike at my enemy, without remorse, in whatever quarter I may perceive an opening; and I think myself called upon, by the present situation of the controversy, not to suppress the remarks which have spontaneously arisen in my own mind upon the perusal of his late writings. I fear he is too little read but by his own party; and it is fit that it should be generally known what spirit he is of.

2. He avows, indeed, with the greatest frankness, that the great object of his essays upon theological subjects, is to spread opinions among his countrymen, from the press and from his pulpit, which he flatters himself must end in the total demolition of the polity of his country in the ecclesiastical branch, the only branch against

which he thinks it prudent, as yet, to declare his antipathy. In his *View of the Principles and Conduct of the Protestant Dissenters, with respect to the Civil and Ecclesiastical Constitution of England*, a pamphlet first published in the year 1769, after a picture, highly exaggerated I hope, of certain abuses among the clergy, which he refers to the principles of our hierarchy, but which, so far as they are real, are easily traced to very different causes; he, in the true spirit of patriotism, points out the remedy. His salutary advice is conveyed in the form of a prediction. He foretells, that in " some general convulsion of the state," such as he might hope our disputes with the American colonies, which were then visibly tending to an open rupture, might in no long time produce, " some bold hand, secretly impelled by a vengeful providence, shall sweep down the whole together."* In later publications he discovers no aversion to be himself the hand employed in that vindictive business; although his indiscretion, which he avows, and which seems indeed to be very great, when the glorious prospect of state convulsions warms and elevates his patriotic mind, should render him, it may be thought, unfit to have a part in the execution of any project, in which the success

---

* View of the Principles, &c. p. 12.

may at all depend on secresy. In the dedication of his late *History of Corruptions* to Mr Lindsey, he tells his friend (what might be fitting for an associate's ear, but it is a strange thing to be mentioned in public) " that while the attention of men in power is engrossed by the difficulties, which more immediately press upon them; the endeavours of the friends of reformation [that is, of those concealed instruments of vengeance on their devoted country], their endeavours in points of doctrine pass with *less notice,* and operate *without obstruction.*"* In his last publication he has thrown out many acute remarks upon the efficacy of " small changes in the political state of things, to overturn the best compacted establishments;"† upon the certainty with which the exertions of himself and his associates operate to the ruin of the ecclesiastical constitution; upon the violence with which causes that lie dormant for a time at last act. " We," he says, " are, as it were, laying *gunpowder* grain by grain under the old building of error and superstition, which a single spark may hereafter inflame, so as to produce an instantaneous explosion."‡ He shews, with great ability, that all measures of government, to support the ecclesiastical constitution, will be of no avail, if

---

* Dedication of History of Corruptions, p. vii.
† Importance of Free Inquiry, p. 39.　　‡ Ibid. p. 40.

once a great majority of the people can be made
its enemies.* And, for this good purpose, he de-
claims in his *conventicle* to " enlighten the minds
and excite the zeal"† of the mechanics of the populous town of Birmingham, with respect to the
doctrines in dispute between himself and the assertors of that faith which the church of England holds in common with the first Christians.
The avowal of these sentiments in himself, of
hostility to the political constitution of his country; the attempt, to excite similar sentiments in
the breasts of the " commonest people," in whose
breasts they cannot be expected to lie inactive,
quietly expecting the event of literary discussion;
such avowal, and such attempts are more, I should
think, than can be justified by the right of private
judgment upon speculative questions. Not that
I would insinuate that they, in any degree, deserve
the attention of our governors; for I am well persuaded, that neither his doctrine nor his principles are gaining that ground among the people
which he seems to imagine. I am inclined indeed
to think, that the advancement even of his Unitarian doctrine is but slow, except in his own head;
in which it seems to be making hasty strides. In
his good wishes to the constitution, I think better
of many of his Unitarian friends than to believe

---

* Importance of Free Inquiry, p. 41—44.   † Ibid. p. 29.

that they concur with him. And while trade and manufactures flourish at Birmingham, we may safely trust to the inducements which every man there will find to mind his own business to defeat the success of Dr Priestley's endeavours to " enlighten and excite." It seems therefore unnecessary at present to think of " raising the dam or of making it stronger." It will be the better policy of government to let the brawling torrent pass. The attempt to provoke severities by audacious language, in order to raise a cry of persecution, if sedition, making religion its pretence, should meet with a premature check from the secular power, is a stale trick, by which the world is grown too wise to be taken in. If Dr Priestley ever should attempt to execute the smallest part of what he would now be understood to threaten, it may then indeed be expedient that the magistrate should shew that he beareth not the sword in vain. But whatever Dr Priestley may affect to think of the intolerance of churchmen in general, and of the Archdeacon of St Alban's in particular, a churchman lives not in the present age so weak, who would not in policy, if not in love, discourage, rather than promote, any thing that might be called a persecution of the Unitarian blasphemy, in the person of Dr Priestley, or of any of his admirers. A churchman lives not so weak as not to know, that persecution is the hot-bed, in which nonsense and impiety have ever thrived. It is so friendly to the growth of religion, that it nourishes even the noxious weeds, which carry but a resemblance of the true plant in the external form. Let us trust, therefore, for the present, as we securely may, to the trade of the good town of Birmingham, and to the wise connivance of the magistrate, (who watches, no doubt, while he deems it politic to wink,) to nip Dr Priestley's goodly projects in the bud; which nothing would be so likely to ripen to a dangerous effect, as constraint excessively or unseasonably used. Thanks, however, are due to him, from all lovers of their country, for the mischief which he wants not the inclination to do, if he could find the means of doing it. In gratitude's estimation, the will is ever to be taken for the deed.

3. In his First Letters to me, and in former publications, Dr Priestley professed to disbelieve an inspiration of the apostles and evangelists, in any greater extent than might be consistent with the liberty which he uses of criticising their reasonings and their narrations. I had a hope that denying, as he does, our Lord's divinity, he still admitted, in some figurative sense, that " all the fulness of the Godhead dwells in him bodily." I had a hope, that he believed, at least, an unlimited inspiration (since he disbelieves any nearer communion with the Godhead) of him to whom " the Spirit was not given by measure." I per-

ceived, with concern, by his late publication, that
" the plenary inspiration of Christ"* is to be disbelieved, no less than that of the apostles. The
assertion, indeed, is qualified, by confining it to
cases " with respect to which the object of their
mission did not require inspiration." The object
of their mission required, that the first preachers
of Christianity should be infallible, in whatever
opinions they maintained, either about the nature
of God or the principles of his moral government;
in whatever they taught concerning the terms or
the means of man's acceptance and salvation; and
in the facts which they have related of the Redeemer's life. If in these things they were not
infallible; if an appeal lies from their assertions,
to any man's private opinions; who shall draw
the line, where the truth of their preaching ends,
and their error commences? If their inspiration
was complete upon these subjects, it was to all
intents and purposes *plenary*. If it gave them no
light about the true system of the world, the circulation of the blood, or the properties of the Leyden
Phial, it was not upon that account defective as
a religious inspiration. The distinction, therefore,
between a plenary inspiration, and an inspiration
extending only to cases in which the object of
their mission required it, is vain and imaginary:

---

* Importance of Free Inquiry, p. 35.

and it is a mere pretence to profess a belief in the one when the other is openly denied.

4. In his First Letters to me, Dr Priestley disavowed his belief of the inspiration of the apostles as *writers* only.* Our blessed Lord left no writings. When, therefore, the fulness of his inspiration is denied, the denial must be understood of his inspiration as an oral teacher. Dr Priestley, therefore, must extend his disbelief of the inspiration of the apostles to their oral doctrine; unless he would be guilty of the folly of setting the disciple above his Lord.

5. It is some time since it was told me, that an admirer of Dr Priestley's tenets, in conversation with a divine of the church of England, high in station and in learning, had maintained, that our dying Lord's promise to the thief, that he should be with our Lord that day in Paradise, was founded on a mistaken notion of him who gave it about the state of the dead. Dr Priestley's disciples well know, that the thief at this time is nowhere, and will not be in Paradise before the resurrection. The leader of a party is not answerable for the absurdities of all his followers: I was unwilling, therefore, to make the conclusion, that Dr Priest-

* First Letters, p. 132.

ley himself ever would maintain, what he now maintains, the fallibility of Christ! I shudder while I relate these extravagancies, though it be only to expose them.

6· Dr Priestley hath given free scope to the powers of his eloquence, upon the subject of my pretended injustice to illustrious characters, living and dead. If injustice may be committed by praise bestowed where it is unmerited, no less than by censure injuriously applied, Dr Priestley may find it more difficult, than I have done to refute the accusation. A character now lives, not without its eminence, nor, I hope, without its moral worth, which Dr Priestley seems to hold in excessive admiration, and upon which he is too apt to be lavish of his praise. Few, who are acquainted with his writings, will be at a loss to guess that the character I speak of is—HIMSELF. As the analyzer of elastic fluids, he will be long remembered : but he sometimes seems to claim respect as a GOOD CHRISTIAN, and a GOOD SUBJECT. If upon any branch of Christian duty my conscience be at perfect ease, the precept " Judge not," is that which, I trust, I have not transgressed. The motives by which one man is impelled, are, for the most part so imperfectly known to any other, that it seems to me cruel to suppose, that the evil which appears in men's actions is always answered by an equal malignity in their minds. I have

ever, therefore, held it dangerous and uncharitable, to reason from the actions of men to their
principles; and, from my youth up, have been
averse to censorious judgment. But when men
declare their motives and their principles, it were
folly to affect to judge them more favourably
than they judge themselves. I shall, therefore,
not hesitate to say, that after a denial of our
Lord's divinity, his pre-existence, and the virtue
of his atonement; after a denial, at last, of our
Lord's plenary inspiration; after a declaration of
implacable enmity to the constitution under which
he lives, under which he enjoys the license of
saying what he lists, in a degree in which it never
was enjoyed by the first citizens of the freest democracies; the goodness of his Christianity, and
his merit as a subject, are topics upon which it
may be indiscreet for the encomiast of Dr Priestley to enlarge.

7. For eighteen months or more, it hath been
the boast of the Unitarian party, that the Archdeacon of St Alban's hath been challenged to
establish facts which he had averred; that he
hath been insulted in his character, as a scholar
and a man; charged with ignorance, misrepresentation, defamation, and calumny;* and that un-

---

* Second Letters, &c. Preface, p. xviii. p. 1, 39, 47, 160, 161,
163, 208, *et alibi passim.*

der all this he hath continued speechless.* He
hath at last spoken, in a tone, which, perhaps,
will little endear him to the Unitarian zealots.
It matters not. The time seems yet so distant
when the train which they are laying may be expected to explode, that the danger is exceedingly
small that he will ever be reduced to the alternative of renouncing his faith or relinquishing his
preferments, or to the harder alternative which
Dr Priestley seems to threaten,† " of a prison,
with a good conscience, or his present emoluments without one." If those happy times of
which Dr Priestley prophesies should overtake
him ere his course is finished when an Arian or
Socinian parliament‡ shall undertake the blessed
business of a second reformation, and depose archbishops from their thrones and archdeacons from
their couches of preferment, he humbly hopes,
that he may be supplied with fortitude to act the
part which may not disgrace his present professions. The probability, however, seems to be,
that ere those times arrive, (if they arrive at all,
which we trust they will not,) my antagonist and
I shall both be gone to those unseen abodes,
where the din of controversy and the din of war
are equally unheard. There we shall rest to-

---

* See Animadversions on Mr White, p. 84.
† Second Letters, p. 88.   ‡ Ibid. p. 87.

gether till the last trumpet summon us to stand
before our God and King.   That whatever of intemperate wrath and carnal anger hath mixed
itself, on either side, with the zeal with which we
have pursued our fierce contention, may then be
forgiven to us both, is a prayer which I breathe
from the bottom of my soul; and to which my antagonist, if he hath any part in the spirit of a
Christian, upon his bended knees will say, AMEN.

SUPPLEMENTAL

DISQUISITIONS

UPON

CERTAIN POINTS

IN

DR PRIESTLEY'S

SECOND AND THIRD LETTERS

TO THE

ARCHDEACON OF ST ALBAN'S,

BY

SAMUEL,

LORD BISHOP OF ST DAVID'S.

DISQUISITIONS.

DISQUISITION FIRST.

Of the phrase of " coming in the flesh," as used by St Polycarp in his epistle to the Philippians.

Dr Priestley, in the fifth of his Second Letters to me, to prove that the phrase of " coming in the flesh" asserts nothing more than our Lord's manhood, without any reference to a prior state of existence, alleges that the phrase is so used by St Polycarp, the disciple of St John, in his epistle to the Philippians. The passage in which Dr Priestley imagines that he hath found this use of the phrase stands thus in Archbishop Wake's translation, from which Dr Priestley makes his quotation:

" Whosoever does not confess that Jesus Christ is come in the flesh, he is antichrist; and whosoever does not confess his suffering upon the cross, is from the Devil; and whosoever perverts the oracles of the Lord to his own lusts, and says that there shall be neither any resurrection nor judgment, he is the first-born of Satan."

By an argument, the force of which will, I believe, be perceived by few but his Unitarian brethren, Dr Priestley persuades himself, that the blessed martyr, in this passage, is not describing three different sects, but that "he alludes to no more than one and the same kind of persons by all the three characters," i. e. by the denial of our Lord's coming in the flesh, the denial of his sufferings, and the denial of the general resurrection and the future judgment.

Hence he would infer, that the phrase of "coming in the flesh" predicates the manhood of our Lord, and nothing more; as I conceive for this reason: (for he hath not stated his argument very clearly.) The denial of our Lord's coming in the flesh must be something that might consist with the denial of his sufferings; since the two errors (by Dr Priestley's hypothesis) were found in the same persons. They who denied the reality of our Lord's sufferings, denied his manhood; and in that sense they might, and they did, deny his coming in the flesh. But his divinity they denied not; on the contrary, they strenuously asserted a nature in him superior at least to the human. Any allusion, therefore, which may be supposed in the phrase of his "coming in the flesh," to an original nature in him more than human, they denied not. His manhood therefore, which is all that they who are charged with a denial of his " coming in the flesh" denied, is all that the phrase imports.

This is the very most that I can make of my adversary's argument. And in this state of it (if I have misrepresented it, I most seriously declare it is without design) I confess myself too dull to perceive the connexion of the premises and the conclusion. We of the orthodox persuasion conceive that the phrase of " coming in the flesh" expresses the INCARNATION; that is to say, it contains this complex proposition, that a Being originally divine assumed the human nature. This complex proposition, they who denied the reality of our Lord's sufferings denied; not in that part which affirms his divinity, but in that part which affirms his assumption of the manhood; and the denial of this was the foundation of their error about the sufferings on the cross. These three characters of error, therefore, mentioned by St Polycarp, might belong to one and the same sort of persons, as Dr Priestley supposes that they did, and yet the phrase of " coming in the flesh" in its natural sense may, for any thing that appears from St Polycarp's own words, allude not to the manhood simply; but to the Catholic doctrine of the incarnation.

It must be observed however, and the fact is too well known to the learned in ecclesiastical history to require proof, that a great variety of sects, differing from each other in the wild and impious opinions which they severally maintained, were comprised under the general name of GNOS-TICS. To say, therefore, that the one and same kind of persons, alluded to by St Polycarp under all these three different characters, was the Gnostics, is to say that this one and same kind of persons was many different kinds. Of the various sects that went under this common name, the Docetæ, who denied our Lord's genuine manhood, were one general branch,—itself subdivided, if I mistake not, into many distinct denominations; the Cerinthians, who denied his original divinity, were another. Both these equally, though in different ways, denied the proposition that " Jesus Christ was come in the flesh," in the sense in which the orthodox understand it. And I confess I am not sure, though Dr Priestley says we are sure of it, that the denial of the resurrection was not to be found in a third class, distinct from either of these two, and from every branch of the Gnostics. The two ancient heretics mentioned by St Paul, (2 Tim. ii. 17, 18,) who said that the resurrection was past, and in that assertion, as St Chrysostom observes, denied a resurrection to come and the general judgment, are not num-bered, by the writers of antiquity, among the

Gnostic teachers. (See Dr Whitby's note upon 2 Tim. ii. 17, 18.) The future judgment was more explicitly denied by these than by the Gnostics, who only denied the resuscitation of the body. And I think it not unlikely, that they might be the persons to whom St Polycarp, in his third character of damnable heresy, alludes. Be that as it may, it seems clear to me, that St Polycarp, in the passage alleged by Dr Priestley, describes three different sets of people; and I should paraphrase the whole passage thus:

" Whoever confesses not that Jesus Christ, the ever blessed and only begotten Son of God, the brightness of his glory and the express image of his person, the eternal Word by whom he made the worlds, is come in the flesh, he is antichrist. And if any one pretending to confess this, shall yet deny the reality of his sufferings, in his own proper and entire person, on the cross, he also, notwithstanding he confess the truth in the former article, is of the Devil. Again, if any one confessing both our Lord's coming in the flesh and his sufferings and death, shall however pervert the oracles of God, accommodating the divine doctrine to his own prejudices and conceits, and say that there shall be neither resurrection nor judgment, this man, notwithstanding his confession of our Lord's incarnation and passion, is the first-born of Satan."

But whether St Polycarp in this passage describe three different sort of heretics, or one sort
by three characters, it is not very material to dispute. The blessed martyr is not enumerating
sects, as an ecclesiastical historian; but as a
preacher of the truth, he is warning the faithful
against errors. He mentions three; any one of
which would avail, in his judgment, to the perdi-
tion of him who should maintain it. For I contend, that nothing in the words of St Polycarp
himself, nor any known and admitted fact in the
history of the heresies of his times, makes it necessary to apply the description in the whole to
one sect, rather than in the parts of it to three.
I contend, that the coming of our Lord in the
flesh, his passion, and the general resurrection,
are three distinct things: the two first, for any
thing that appears from St Polycarp's words, as
distinct from each other as either is from the
third; so distinct therefore from each other, that
a person admitting the one might possibly not
confess the other. I contend therefore, that for
any thing that appears from the words of St Polycarp, a person confessing that our Lord came in
the flesh might still deny his sufferings. The
phrase, therefore, of " coming in the flesh," for
any thing that appears from St Polycarp's own
words, may denote something more than our Lord's
mere manhood. And I contend yet further, that
although it could be proved that St Polycarp al-

ludes to one sect, so that the coming in the flesh must necessarily be so understood that the denial of that coming and the denial of the sufferings should be consistent errors, still it will not follow that the coming in the flesh must be understood as descriptive simply of the manhood. If any one sect indeed singly be described, the Docetæ must be that one, since their characteristic error makes an explicit part of the description. But with their error the denial of the incarnation was perfectly consistent. Dr Priestley thinks, that St Polycarp condemns the Docetæ, because they admitted not that Christ was a mere man. But if I say that St Polycarp condemns them, not for maintaining that he was more than man, but for denying that being more than man, being indeed God, he was made man; and that for this reason he made choice of the phrase of " coming in the flesh," that he might not seem to condemn more of their doctrine than he really disapproved. What is there in St Polycarp's words to prove that I, rather than Dr Priestley, misinterpret?

It may seem, that if, for any thing that appears from the writer's words, the phrase may be interpreted in either sense, the true inference is, that it is ambiguous. This conclusion indeed follows, with respect to the use of the phrase in this particular passage; and it is upon this very ground that I maintain the total insignificance of the passage to decide the matter in dispute. In the fourth of my letters in reply to Dr Priestley, I have considered the natural and internal force of this phrase of " coming in the flesh." I have shewn, that it contains such evident allusion to a prior condition of the person who so came, and to the power that he had of coming in various other ways, had it pleased him otherwise to come, that if the sacred writers really meant to affirm that our Lord was a mere man, and nothing more, no reason can be devised why they should make choice of such uncouth mysterious words for the enunciation of so simple a proposition, which they might easily have stated in plain terms incapable of misconstruction. Dr Priestley appeals from this reasoning of mine upon the natural sense of the words, to the usage of writers; which indeed, when it is clear and constant, must be allowed to outweigh all reasoning from general principles, because the particular sense of a phrase is a question about a fact; and in all such questions external evidence, when it can be had, must overpower theory. To prove that the usage of the writers of antiquity settles the sense of the phrase in his favour, he alleges this passage of St Polycarp's epistle, as an instance " that might satisfy me." But I say, that no one who thinks the meaning of the phrase dubious will be satisfied by this instance. For, not to insist that the usage of writers is very insufficiently proved by a single instance, I maintain, that if the phrase in question were in itself equally capable of the two senses, the low sense to which the Unitarians would confine it, and the sublimer sense in which it is generally understood, it certainly might be taken in either in this passage of St Polycarp; and that, in whatever light the passage be consi. dered, whether as descriptive of three sects, as I believe it to be, or of one only, as Dr Priestley understands it. This passage, therefore, is of no significance in the argument; since no passage can be alleged, as an instance of any particular use of any phrase, in which various senses of the phrase may equally suit the purpose of the writer.

To this neutral passage of St Polycarp, I have on my side to oppose a very decisive passage of St Barnabas; in which the allusion to a prior con. dition of our Lord, which I contend to be the natural import of the phrase, is manifest; and is so necessary to the writer's purpose, that if the phrase be understood without such allusion, the whole sentence is nonsense. " For if he had not come in *the flesh*, how should we mortals, seeing him, have been preserved? when they who behold the sun, which is to perish and is the work of his hands, are unable to look directly against its rays." Let Dr Priestley find a passage in which the allusion to our Lord's original glory is as necessarily excluded from the import of the

phrase as it is included in it in this passage of St
Barnabas.   And even then the only just inference
will be, that the phrase is used variously, in a
more restrained or larger signification, as may
suit the particular occasion on which it is introduced; but that in its full and natural import it
affirms the incarnation.

But in truth Dr Priestley seems to deal by St
Polycarp as by St John; by the disciple as by the
master.   Devoted himself to the Unitarian doctrine, he takes it with him as a principle in the
study of St Polycarp, as of the New Testament,
that the creed of St Polycarp, as of all the primitive Christians, was Unitarian.   Then, whatever
expressions occur alluding to opinions of a different cast, he interprets in the sense in which he
and his Unitarian brethren would use them. From
these expressions, so interpreted, he goes back to
his original prejudice, that St Polycarp held and
taught an Unitarian creed, as to a conclusion
which he hath drawn, and can teach others to
draw, from St Polycarp's own writings.   Alas!
the sum of all such reasonings is no more than
this: I JOSEPH PRIESTLEY am an Unitarian;
therefore such was Polycarp.   And the basis of
this argument is the supposed infallibility of Jo-
SEPH PRIESTLEY.

DISQUISITION SECOND.

*Of Tertullian's testimony against the Unitarians, and his use of the word I*DIOTA.

D<small>R</small> P<small>RIESTLEY</small> has made it an occasion of great triumph to himself and to his party, that he has caught me tripping, as he thinks, in my Greek and Latin, in the translation which I have given, in the ninth of my Letters in Reply, of a certain passage in Tertullian's book against Praxeas, which is produced by him as an acknowledgment of Tertullian that the Unitarians were in his time the majority of Christians, and is represented by me as an assertion of the contrary. None but an idiot, as Dr Priestley conceives, in the learned languages, would imagine that the English word " idiot," which I have used in my translation of that passage, might in any sense render the ιδιώτης of the Greek or the *Idiota* of the Latins, which is the name by which, with other adjuncts, Tertullian describes the Unitarians of his time. Dr Priestley says in the nineteenth of his Second Letters, sec. 3. " What will be said of the man who can translate *Idiota*, idiot ?" He hath now for some considerable time been receiving the incense of his own applause, and the triumphant acclamations of his party, on the occasion of this victory gained over his daring adversary, on the very ground on which the enemy had taken his stand with particular security. But it will be time enough to bind the laurel on their chieftain's spear, when they are sure he is in possession of the field.

In the seventh of his Second Letters, Dr Priestley says to me, " I will venture to say that it properly signifies [the word *Idiota* in Latin, or ιδιω in Greek properly signifies] an unlearned man, or a person who has not had a liberal education." This Dr Priestley ventures to affirm, and this I venture to deny. The word ιδιωτης hath ten distinct senses; which I shall recite in order.

I. *A private person; i. e.* a person in private life, in opposition to a person in public office or employment, civil or military. In this sense the word is chiefly used by the orators and historians, and by all writers who treat of popular subjects; and this is its first and proper sense, as it is of all its senses the most immediately connected with the sense of the adjective ιδιος, from which the substantive ιδιωτης is immediately derived.

II. *A person in low life, one of the common people,* in opposition to persons of condition. This is nothing more than an intension of the former scure and low.

III. *A laic*, as distinguished from a clerk. This sense the Greek fathers easily grafted upon the first; the church being considered as a polity of its own kind, in which the clergy bear the public offices, the laity are citizens in private life. In a sense nearly allied to this, the word seems to be used by St Paul, 1 Cor. xiv. 16, to denote a private member of a congregation as distinguished from the minister.

IV. *A person unskilled in any particular science or art*, in opposition to the professors of it. The word, thus used, rather expresses the want of professional skill than of ordinary knowledge. In this sense the word is sometimes constructed by the Attic writers with a genitive of the thing, and by ordinary writers with an accusative, either with or without a preposition. ἰδιωτος ἰδιωτην τινα. Plat. in Tim. ἰδιωτης τινα, κατα τινα, or ὡς προς τινα.

V. *A person deficient in any particular talent, habit, or accomplishment*. In this sense the word is sometimes constructed with a dative of the thing. ἰδιωτης τῳ λογῳ, 2 Cor. xi. 16. In this sense the word is used by St Paul, 1 Cor. xiv. 23, 24, to denote a common Christian, not endowed with any of the extraordinary gifts of the Holy Spirit, as distinguished from persons so gifted.

VI. *A person generally unlearned;* one who has not had a learned and liberal education. In this sense, in conjunction with the epithet ἀγραμμαλοι, the word is applied to the apostles by the rulers of the Jews. Acts iv. 13.

VII. The plural ιδιωλαι, signifies *individuals;* citizens, individually considered, as distinguished from the collective body, the state.

VIII. The plural ιδιωλαι, is a collective name for the illiterate vulgar, in particular reference to their general want of accomplishment in literature, the sciences and the arts. ο πολυς. ὁμιλος, ὡς ιδιωλας ἐκ σοφοι καλυσι. Lucian.

IX. Hence among philosophers and sophists, and pretenders to that sort of taste which is now called *virtù,* it became a name of reproach which they gave to those whom they thought disgracefully deficient in those accomplishments which they valued and admired in themselves. Thus the great Roman peculator, seeking to hide his avarice under a mask of affected taste for the works of the Greek masters, reproached his accusers with idiotcy in this sense of the word. *Erat apud Heium sacrarium——perantiquum, in quo signa pulcherrima quatuor——quæ non modo istum, hominem ingeniosum et intelligentem, verum etiam quemvis nostrum, quos iste idiotas appellat, delectare possent.*   Cic. in Verrem. Act 2. Lib. iv. c. 2.

X. And because the faculties are apt to be dull, when they have not been sharpened by exercise upon any subject whatsoever, ιδιωται, from its use in the sense of illiterate and uncultivated, comes to be an opprobrious name for the *dull* and *stupid*, without any reference to the want of education as the cause of the stupidity.   It never indeed, as far as I know, refers to that constitutional defect of the faculty of reason which is the peculiar sense of the corresponding word of our language in our statutes and law books.   But it denotes the goodly qualities of stupidity and ignorance in the gross, like our vernacular words *dunce, booby,* and their synonymes.

That this last is the sense in which it is used by Tertullian, in the passage in question, is sufficiently evident from the very structure of the sentence.   Whoever knows the force of the phrase *pœne dixerim,* which is probably as little understood by Dr Priestley as St Jerome's *quid dicam;* but whoever knows the true force of this phrase, will allow that the epithets *imprudentes* and *idiotæ,* which are introduced by it, must contain some high intension and aggravation of the qualities, whatever they may be, which are contained in the notion of the preceding adjective, *simplices*; an aggravation in such degree, that the writer thinks it necessary to apologize for the strength and severity of the terms which he finds himself obliged to employ. This is the force of the phrase *pœne dixerim*: to take away what may seem too much in the terms which a writer is about to employ, when he fears they may seem excessive, notwithstanding that they are the lowest which will convey his full meaning, and do justice to his argument. The *imprudentes* therefore of Tertullian, are a sort of people in discernment and information many degrees below his *simplices*; and his *idiotæ* are still below his *imprudentes*. All this is evident, to those who have any real knowledge of the Latin language, from the bare structure of the sentence, whatever the proper use of each of the three words may be among the polite writers of the Augustan age. As equivalent to the Latin *idiotæ*, as it is used by Tertullian in this passage, I employed our English word *idiots*. I employed the English word, to express that extreme degree of ignorance and stupidity, for which our language furnishes no other word sufficiently contemptuous, of which Tertullian affirms the Unitarians of his day, like their younger brethren in our own, exhibited a notable example. It was little to be apprehended, that even Unitarian prejudice would render any one so much an idiot in style and phraseology, as not to perceive that I used not the word in what in English is its forensic sense, especially when in an exposition of the passage, which at the distance of a few lines follows my translation, I explain it by the words " dull," and " persons of mean attainments."

Dr Priestley asks me, in the seventh of his Second Letters, " Pray, Sir, in what lexicon or dictionary, ordinary or extraordinary, did you find this sense of the term *idiota* in Latin, or ἰδιώτης in Greek ?" Dr Priestley is venturesome in propounding questions like this, and seems to be one of those, whom repeated miscarriages cannot render wary and discreet. I certainly consulted no lexicon, for the purpose of making my translation of that plain passage of Tertullian ; and it is within these very few days that I have taken the trouble to consult lexicons, in order to discover what ground my adversary may have found in their defects, for the confidence which the question bespeaks. I will now refer him to certain lexicons, never known perhaps in the academy at Warrington, but such as a late Greek professor there might occasionally have condescended to consult, with advantage to himself and to his pupils. The first is that old glossary, which was found annexed to some copies of St Cyril, and is published by Henry Stephens, in the appendix to his Greek

Thesaurus. In this glossary the word ܐܝܕܝܘܛܐ is expounded by *ὁ μὴ νοημων*, words which express not the want of education, but dulness of the natural faculties. The second is Robert Stephens's *Dictionarium Latino-Gallicum,* in which the word *idiota* is rendered *Ung lourdault, qui n'est pas des plus fins du monde, qui n'ha pas grand esprit, Idiot.* The third is the learned Calepini's *Dictionarium Octolingue,* in which the author gives the French words *lourdaut, sot, ignorant,* and the English words, *an idiot, a fool,* as rendering the Latin *idiota.* The fourth is the Thesaurus of our learned countryman Cooper, in which *idiota* is thus expounded: *One that is not very fine-witted; an idiot.* If my adversary demand the authority of an ordinary dictionary, I will refer him to a very ordinary dictionary indeed; to a dictionary in every school-boy's hand. Let him turn to the word *idiota* in Ainsworth; he will find among its first senses, *an idiot.*

I abide therefore by my assertion, that this passage of Tertullian, which Dr Priestley mistakes for a testimony of the popularity of his favourite opinions in Tertullian's time, is no such testimony, but a charge of ignorance against his party; of such ignorance, as would invalidate the plea of numbers, if that plea could be set up.

And that this is the true representation of

Tertullian's meaning, may be proved, without insisting upon any particular force of the word
idiotæ, from the necessary indisputable sense of
the adverb *semper*, which extends Tertullian's
proposition, concerning the majority of believers,
from his own time in particular to all time.   He
says not what were, or what were not, the prevailing opinions of his own times; but he says,
that those persons who come under the characters of *simplices, imprudentes,* and *idiotæ* (that is,
according to Dr Priestley's own translation, which
yet I admit not otherwise than *disputandi gratia,*
for I have still " the assurance" to call my own
an exact translation) but according to Dr Priestley's own translation, Tertullian says, that persons who come under the character of " the
simple, the ignorant, and the unlearned," whatever their opinions at one time or another may
be, are, in all times, the greater part of believers:
as indeed they must be of every society collected
indiscriminately, as the church is, from all ranks
of men.   Tertullian alleges that persons of that
description, in his time, meaning to assert what
they little understood, the Divine Monarchy,
were startled at the doctrine of the Trinity,
which they as little understood.   This is the only
sense in which Tertullian's words can be taken,
unless some Unitarian adventurer in criticism
shall be able to prove, that the adverb *semper*

is equivalent to *nunc*, expressive of present time exclusively.

Dr Priestley " wonders at my assurance" in another circumstance; namely, that I should limit, as he says, what Tertullian affirms, as he would have him understood, of the whole body of the *simplices* and *idiotæ* to some of them. In this limitation, he says, I am altogether unwarranted. But when Tertullian says, that simple persons and *idiotæ* are startled at the economy, the natural sense of the words is, that this scruple was incident chiefly to persons of that description; not that it was to be found in the whole body of the common people. He insinuates, that persons of that weak character *only* were liable to that alarm. Had he meant to speak of the whole body of the common people, he must have used phrases of another cast, as *vulgus indoctum*, or *genus hominum simplex*. Dr Priestley's complaint against me might have seemed to have some foundation, had the word " some" been prefixed to " simple persons" in my translation. But it only appears in an exposition of the passage, which follows the translation. And surely having translated the passage exactly, I took no unwarrantable liberty in adding an explanation of the author's sense (or of what I take to be his sense) in my own words. Had Dr Priestley's loose expositions of the passages in ancient writers, which he cites, been always accompanied with exact translations, the world would have had less reason to stand aghast at his assurance and ill-dissembled management. But to what purpose can it be to hold an argument with a man, who is too hasty to distinguish between what professes to be paraphrase, and what pretends to be exact translation; who has the vanity to play the critic in languages, to the idioms of which he is a stranger; and the audacity to challenge the production of authorities, without taking the pains to inform himself, in which scale the weight of authority may preponderate? " Pray, Sir, in what lexicon or dictionary, ordinary or extraordinary, do you find *idiota* in Latin, or ιδιωτης in Greek rendered *idiot?*" Vide Glossarium Vetus, R. Steph. Calepin. Cooper, Ainsworth.

DISQUISITION THIRD.

*On what is found relating to the Ebionites in the writings of
IRENÆUS, in confutation of an argument advanced by Dr
Priestley in favour of the Ebionites, in the third of his First,
and the fourth of his Second Letters, from the writings of
Irenæus in particular.*

THE particular argument in favour of the Ebionites, which Dr Priestley, in the third of his First
Letters to me, attempted to draw from the writings of Irenæus, was so ably, though concisely
answered in the Monthly Review for January
1784, by Mr Badcock, who, taking facts as Dr
Priestley chose to state them, shewed, even upon
his own statement of the facts, the utter futility of his conclusion, inasmuch as the contrary
conclusion might be drawn with equal probability from the same assumptions, that when I
wrote my Letters in Reply, I thought I might
be excused if I passed by this argument without any other notice, than a slight reference to
Mr Badcock's confutation.   But in the sixth
of his Second Letters, Dr Priestley hath attempted to refit this shattered piece of his artillery, and to bring it again into action.

He says to me, " It is truly remarkable, and
may not have been observed by you, as indeed

it was not by myself till very lately,"—It had indeed been strange, if any sagacity of remark in me had outrun Dr Priestley's !—" that Irenæus, who has written so large a work on the subject of heresy, after the time of Justin, in a country where it is probable there were fewer Unitarians, again and again characterises them in such a manner as makes it evident, that even he did not consider any other persons as heretics besides the Gnostics. He expresses a great dislike of the Ebionites, but he never calls them heretics."*

. Freely I resign to Dr Priestley the honour of having been the first to make this remark. At least I shall put in no claim for myself, or for my friends. If any plagiarism hath been committed, which I pretend not in this particular instance to assert, the depredation must have been made upon some of his own party. For I will venture to affirm, that the remark, so far as it extends to Irenæus's acquittal of the Ebionites from the imputation of heresy, could have occured to none, that had not been in some good degree an IDIOT in the writings of Irenæus. It could have occurred to none, that had known more of the work of Irenæus, than is to be learned from an occasional re-

---

* Second Letters, p. 56.

ference to particular passages, by the help of an
index.

The great object of Irenæus, in his work
against heresies, is to assert the Scripture doctrines of the unity of God, and the incarnation of
the Divine Word, in their original simplicity,
against the numerous sectaries of his times, who,
from various views and motives, had variously disfigured and disguised them. Some thought, that
they gave a clear solution of the dark question
about the origin of evil, when they maintained
that the world is the work of one or more intelligences, far inferior to the First Mind. Some, to
account for some circumstances of contrariety
that may appear upon a superficial view of the
Old and the New Testament, taught that the God
of the Jews was a distinct being from the Father
of our Lord Jesus Christ. Some, to solve the
difficulties in the great doctrine of the incarnation, indulged in a most criminal wantonness of
speculation concerning the person of Christ.
Some, affecting a deep mysterious wisdom, endeavoured to explain, in obscure and ill-imagined
allegories, the procession of the different orders
of intellect and life from the Divine Mind, and
the production of the visible world. Some, the
most profane and hardened, artfully availed themselves of certain mysterious points of the Christian doctrine, to give personal consequence to

themselves, and to gain credit among the vulgar to the most impious pretensions. To guard the faithful against these various seductions, and to establish them in the belief of the true Scripture doctrine of ONE-GOD, absolute in power and in all perfection, who, by his Eternal Word, created all things in heaven and in earth, visible and in. visible; and, having in time past spoken to the fathers by the prophets, hath spoken in the last days by his Son, the same Divine Word incarnate, and hath reconciled mankind to himself, through him, who, to effect this reconciliation, united the manhood to the Godhead in his own person,—to establish the faithful in this doctrine, Irenæus undertakes the confutation of those extravagant conceits, by which it is either contradicted, or perverted and disgraced, never losing sight of his two cardinal points, the unity of God, and the incarnation of the Word.

His whole work consists of five books. Of these, the first is historical, exhibiting a general view of heretical opinions, in those points in which they differed most essentially from genuine Christianity; reciting the names of the principal hæresiarchs, describing their characters, and relating the varieties of opinion by which the different sects were distinguished.

In the second book, the author professes to re-

fute the extravagant opinions recited in the first,
by general arguments, exposing the incoherence
and intrinsic absurdity of each. In the third, he
engages to bring a confutation of the same opinions from Scripture in general; in the fourth,
from our Lord's own discourses in particular; in
the fifth, from our Lord's own words, and the
writings of St Paul.

In the first book, after a general recital of the
principal extravagancies of the Valentinians, the
author undertakes to shew, that Simon Magus
was the parent of all heresy, and that the distinguishing conceits of every sect attached to one
point or another of his doctrine. For this purpose he gives a list of hæresiarchs and sects from
Simon Magus in succession to his own time, specifying the particular doctrines of each. In this
list, the Ebionites have the honour to have the
name of their sect enrolled * between the Cerinthians and Nicolaitans. If Irenæus deemed them
not heretics, he has surely put them in bad company. At no great distance from the Ebionites,
he introduces Marcion.† This Marcion was a
most distinguished heretic, not only for the extravagance and impiety of his doctrine, but for the
liberty which he took with the books of the New

---

* Lib. I. cap. xxvi.   † Ibid. xxix.

Testament, altering or expunging whatever he disliked, till he made the holy Scriptures, as he thought, speak his own sentiments. Irenæus pro. mises a particular confutation of the opinions of Marcion, from the Scriptures as Marcion himself received them. But notwithstanding this design, he found it necessary, he says, to mention him in this place, in order to make out his assertion, " that all who adulterated the truth, and im. pugned the public doctrine of the church, were disciples of Simon the Samaritan sorcerer;"* inti. mating, that having in his contemplation a parti. cular work upon the heresy of Marcion, he would have omitted the mention of him in this place, but that the omission would have rendered the list of hæresiarchs, descending from Simon Magus, de. fective. Here then we see both the author's at. tention to the accuracy of his list, and his own notion of what sort of persons they were who had a right to a place in it. The accuracy of his list had certainly been as much vitiated by an impro. per insertion as by an omission. Where then is

---

* Sed huic quidem———seorsum contradicemus; ex ejus scriptis árguentes eum, et ex iis sermonibus, qui apud eum ob. servati sunt, Domini et Apostoli, quibus ipse utitur, eversionem ejus facientes præstante Deo. Nunc autem necessario memini. mus ejus, ut scires quoniam omnes, qui quoquo modo adulte. rant veritatem, et præconium Ecclesiæ lædunt, Simonis Sama. ritani Magi discipuli et successores sunt. Lib. I. cap. xxix. et XXX.

the probability, that an author, who declares he
would have omittèd Marcion, but from a scrupulous attention to the accuracy of his catalogue of
hæresiàrchs, in defiance of any such scruple, would
have inserted the Ebionites, had not their notorious heresy, and their affinity with Simon Magus,
given them an equal claim with Marcion, and
with their next neighbours the Cerinthians and
Nicolaitans, to admission? Again, the author's
notion of the sort of persons that were to be included in his list, namely, " adulterators of the
truth, impugners of the public doctrine of the
church, and disciples of Simon the Samaritan sorcerer," clearly proves what the public character of
the Ebionites was, whom he hath enrolled among
these worthies. To have registered among the
sects allied to Simon Magus, persons who lay
under no public imputation of heresy, however in
his own private judgment he might see reason to
reprobate their tenets, had been a very awkward
proof of the general affinity between heresy and
Simon Magus. To the proof of this, a consent or
resemblance of opinion between Simon Magus
and those who were no heretics, or not generally
deemed such, could little contribute. It would
rather indeed conduce to the acquittal of Simon
than the condemnation of an innocent sect said to
resemble him. The Ebionites, therefore, having
a place in this list, by which Simon is to be proved
the common parent and founder of all heresies,

unquestionably partook of that character which Irenæus makes the peculiar mark of that family. They were adulterators of the truth, not barely of what was truth in the private judgment of Irenæus, but they were impugners of the public doctrine of the church. If such persons were not heretics, I have yet to learn the meaning of the name.

I am well aware, that a laudable concern for the reputation of his ancestors will incline Dr. Priestley to put the question, in what circumstance the Ebionites resembled Simon Magus? Some resemblance, he will say, according to Irenæus's notions, was necessary to constitute a heresy. For if all heretics resembled Simon Magus in some circumstance or another, they who resembled him in none were no heretics.

To this it may be answered, that Epiphanius, when he tells us that Ebion's Judaism was of the *Samaritan* cast, says what may be thought to imply a resemblance, in many circumstances, between this sect and the Samaritan sorcerer. But the principle in which Irenæus, I doubt not, placed the resemblance, was no other than the cardinal doctrine of the Ebionites of the mere humanity of our Lord. This, as it was taught by the Cerinthians and the first Ebionites, was indeed nothing more than a refinement upon the older error of the Docetæ, of which Simon was the first teacher. The Docetæ, thinking it beneath the dignity of a celestial being to undergo the life of a man, and to submit to a violent and painful death, maintained that the body of Jesus was a mere illusion, and the whole scene of his sufferings phantastic. Or if any of them admitted the reality of the sufferings, they denied, however, that Jesus was the sufferer. The Cerinthians, whose doctrines the first Ebionites followed in what related to the person of our Lord, thought it more reasonable to admit that Jesus was a real man, the subject of real sufferings. They maintained that he was a mere man, and they supposed a superangelic being, which they called the Christ, to have been through life the guide and guardian of the man; something more perhaps than a Socratic dæmon, but yet distinct from the man, and exempt from all participation of his sufferings. This is evidently a refinement upon the doctrine of the Docetæ. Both doctrines had a common object,— to give the doctrine of the incarnation such a turn, that a divine or superangelic nature might not be involved in the miseries of mortality. For this purpose the Docetæ denied the reality of the manhood; and the Ebionites, with the Cerinthians, maintained a separate personality and distinct conditions of the man and the superior being. Thus the affinity between the Ebionites and the Simonians is manifest; and the derivation of the

one from the other easy and natural: and I cannot but remark, that as the ancient Ebionæan
doctrine passes by a single step, the dismission of
the superangélic being, into the modern Unitarian,
that too is traced to its source in the chimeras of
the Samaritan. sorcerer. And thus both the Ebionites of antiquity, and the Unitarians of our own
time, are in truth branches, or the offspring at
least of Gnosticism. And in this extended meaning of the word, I am ready to allow that Irenæus
knew of no heretics but what are included under
the general name of Gnostics. Be that as it may,
I maintain, that the first book of Irenæus, by the
enrolment therein made of the Ebionites, in a
list, in which the author had done disservice to
his own argument had he inserted any but known
heretics, affords a clear argument that the Ebionites were heretics in the judgment of the church,
in the time of Irenæus.

In the second book of Irenæus, no mention of
the Ebionites occurs either by name or by description. Nor is this, indeed, the place where
any mention of that sect might be expected. The
argument of the second book is a confutation of
heretical opinions from principles of mere reason;
from general views of their intrinsic absurdity and
incoherence. But the error of the Ebionites is
not of the number of those that may be so confuted. The great mystery of godliness, the incarna-

tion of the Divine Word, was no discovery of natural reason. Reason, therefore, whose natural powers, upon this subject, gave no knowledge of the truth, is insufficient, without the aid of revelation, to the refutation of the contrary falsehood. The conviction of the Ebionites must rest entirely upon holy writ.

Accordingly, in the third book, in which the confutation is drawn from Scripture, the Ebionites are thus mentioned : " They again who say, that he was merely a man engendered of Joseph, die; continuing in the bondage of the former disobedience, having to the last no conjunction with the word of God the Father, nor receiving freedom through the Son, according to that saying of his own, *If the Son give you manumission, ye shall be free indeed.* But not knowing him, who is the Emmanuel of the Virgin, they are deprived of his gift, which is eternal life. And not receiving the incorruptible word, they continue in the mortal flesh, and are liable to the natural debt of death, not accepting the antidote of life."*

---

* Rursus autem qui nudè tantum hominem eum dicunt ex Joseph generatum, perseverantes in servitute pristinæ inobedientæ moriuntur, nondum commixti verbo Dei Patris, neque per Filium percipientes libertatem, quemadmodum ipse ait; *si Filius vos manumiserit, vere liberi eritis.* Ignorantes autem eum qui ex Virgine est Emmanuel, privantur munere ejus,

That the Ebionites are the persons intended in this passage we need not be solicitous to prove, since a part of the passage is cited by Dr Priestley himself in the appendix of his First Letters as unquestionably relating to that sect. In this passage their error, and their crime, is placed in their assertion, that our Lord was a mere man the son of Joseph. This error is called a rejection of the incorruptible word, a refusal of the antidote of life. These are phrases evidently descriptive of a hardened infidelity, which listens not with a due submission of 'the understanding to the evangelical doctrine. The Ebionites therefore, by their wicked doctrine of our Lord's mere humanity, seemed to Irenæus to be mere infidels; and in consequence of this infidelity " to die in the bondage of the former disobedience, having to the last no connexion with the word of God the Father, continuing in the mortal flesh, and liable to the natural debt of death." These expressions describe the miserable condition of the unconverted and impenitent; who, notwithstanding what the Son of God hath done and suffered for those who will believe in him remain obnoxious to the guilt and punishment of their own sins, as

---

quod est vita æterna: non recipientes autem verbum incorruptionis perseverant in carne mortali, et sunt debitores mortis, antidotum vitæ non accipientes. Lib. 3. cap. xxi.

2 H

well as to all the dreadful consequences of the
first transgression. Such Irenæus deemed the
dangerous situation of these infidel Ebionites. He
says further, that for their ignorance of him who
is the Emmanuel of the Virgin, and in consequence of the infidelity and impenitence of which
that ignorance was in his judgment a sure symptom, " they are deprived of the gift of that Emmanuel, which gift is eternal 'life." To be deprived of that life eternal, which is the gift of the
Emmanuel is the same thing in the phraseology
of the ancient writers, as to be under a sentence
of eternal damnation. These Ebionites therefore,
who said that our Lord was a mere man, convicted by that wicked assertion of an *evil heart* of
impenitence and unbelief, in the opinion of Irenæus lay under a sentence of eternal punishment,
which nothing but a renunciation of their error
and a sincere repentance might avert. Nothing
can be clearer, than that in this passage they are
taxed with infidelity and impenitence, and threatened with the doom which awaits such crimes.
But Dr Priestley can find no such sentence of
damnation in this passage passed upon the
Ebionites. " Irenæus *must* have meant not that
the Ebionites in particular, but that mankind in
general, could have had no resurrection, if the
Ebionæan doctrine had been true."* That is,

---

* First Letters, p. 118.

Irenæus expressly speaking of the Ebionites in particular, *must* be understood of mankind in general. Speaking of their particular punishment, he *must* be understood to speak of a general calamity. The ground of the necessity is obvious. In no other way of interpretation can what Irenæus hath actually said of the Ebionites be brought to agree with what Dr Priestley, for the interest of his cause *must* wish he had said about them. The learned Feuardentius, who lived not to be enlightened by the new revelations of our modern Unitarians, and above all by Dr Priestley's ingenious expositions of the Scriptures and the fathers, was blind to this necessity. " Irenæus contends in this chapter," says Feuardentius, " that they who make Christ the son of Joseph, attain neither remission of sins nor the adoption of the sons of God, nor so much as the right of a blessed resurrection."*

In the fourth book after a confutation of many heretical opinions, Irenæus lays down this maxim :† that the believer, who steadily adheres to the great principle of one God who created

---

* Contendit autem hoc capite Irenæus, illos nec peccatorum remissionem, nec adoptionem filiorum Dei; imo nec jus beatæ resurrectionis assequi, qui Christum filium Joseph constituunt. *Feuardentius ad laudatum locum Irenæi.*

† Lib. 4. cap. lii.

all things by his word, and studies the Scriptures with the assistance of the presbyters of
the church, who were in possession, as Irenæus
says, of the doctrine of the apostles, will extricate himself from the difficulties which were
the stumbling-blocks of heretics. In particular,
he will perceive the connexion and affinity between the Old Testament and the New, and
will understand that the same God was the
author of both. " Such a disciple,". he says,
" being truly spiritual, inasmuch as he receiveth
the Spirit of God, who under all the dispensations of God was present with men, and announced the future, and sheweth the present,
and relateth the past; [such a spiritual disciple]
judgeth all, but is judged himself of none."*
He judgeth all; that is, he discerns in what
point the error of any erroneous doctrine lies,
and he can evince its inconsistence with the
truth. But he himself having the written word
and the doctrine of the apostles for his guide, and
enjoying the secret illumination of the Spirit, is
inconfutable. Irenæus illustrates and amplifies
this aphorism by an application of it to different

---

* Talis discipulus verè spiritalis, recipiens Spiritum Dei, qui
ab initio, in universis dispositionibus Dei, affuit hominibus, et
futura annuntiavit, et præsentia ostendit, et præterita enarrat,
judicat quidem omnes, ipse autem à nemine judicatur. Lib. 4.
cap. liii.

sects; shewing how and upon what principles the spiritual disciple will *judge them; i. e.* expose and refute their errors. This amplification of the general sentiment makes a very long period, which some of the early editors (Grynæus I believe) hath broken into no less than nine chapters, prefixing to each a proper title. This spiritual disciple, Irenæus says, will judge the Gentiles,*—will judge the Jews,†—will judge the Marcionites,‡—will judge the Valentinians.§—" He will also judge the vain babblings of wicked Gnostics, shewing them to be the disciples of Simon Magus.‖—He will also judge the Ebionites. How can they be saved, unless he, who wrought their salvation upon earth, be God."¶ Dr Priestley imagines that Irenæus says of the Ebionites, that " God will judge them."** This mistake, of putting God's judgment for the sound believer's judgment is indeed of no importance in the argument. I mention it only as one instance of that practice of which I accuse Dr Priestley, of taking short detached passages in the sense which may first occur to him without knowing, and

---

* Lib. 4. cap. liv.   † Cap. lv.   ‡ Cap. lvii.   § Cap. lviii.
‖ Judicabit autem et vaniloquia pravorum Gnosticorum, Simonis eos Magi discipulos ostendens.   Cap. lviii.
¶ Judicabit autem et Ebionitas; quomodo possunt salvari, nisi Deus est qui salutem eorum super terram operatus est? Cap. lix.
** First Letters, p. 33.

without examining with what they may be connected in the context of the author's discourse.
Talis discipulus vere spiritalis is the subject of
the verb *Judicabit* from the LIIId. chapter to the
end of the LXIId. Irenæus says then, that the
spiritual disciple " will judge the Ebionites."
And this is the principle upon which he will
judge them, " that they could not be saved, unless he, who wrought their salvation upon earth,
be God." But this, Dr Priestley says, " is no
sentence of damnation passed upon them in particular for holding their doctrine, but an argument used by him to refute them; and is the
same as if he had said, mankind in general could
not be saved, if Christ had not been God as well
as man."* This shall be granted. What Irenæus says in the passage now under consideration is nothing more than an argument for the
refutation of the Ebionites; and the principle of
this argument is rightly stated by Dr Priestley.
But by whom is this argument used? By Irenæus. Not simply by Irenæus in his own person:
it is the argument which Irenæus puts in the
mouth of the spiritual disciple. The spiritual
disciple, that is, every spiritual disciple, every
sound believer is the person, who upon these
principles will confute the Ebionites. Irenæus,

---

* First Letters, p. 33,

therefore distinguishing the Ebionites who are confuted from every spiritual disciple who confutes, sets the former out of the society of spiritual disciples, of sound believers, and puts them in the class of those who are not spiritual; that is, of those who have not the spirit. For were they spiritual, they could not be the objects of the spiritual disciple's opposition and confutation. But the class of those, who are not spiritual, is the choice society of heretics and infidels. For *he, who hath not the spirit of Christ, is none of his.* In this passage therefore the Ebionites are clearly ranked with heretics.

It deserves particular notice, that one circumstance in Irenæus's description of the spiritual disciple who judges these Ebionites, is, that " he is a follower of the public doctrine of the church."* Whence it might seem no unnatural conclusion, if other proof of the thing were wanting, that the public judgment of the church, no less than the sentiments of Irenæus, was against the Ebionites; that they were opposers of the public doctrine, and of course in the public estimation heretics. But the same thing indeed is sufficiently implied in the representation given

---

* Si et scripturam diligenter legerit, apud eos qui in ecclesiâ sunt presbyteri, apud quos est apostolica doctrina. Cap. lii.

them, as maintainers of an opinion which struck at the very root of the doctrine of redemption, and lay open to every sound believer's confutation.

In the fifth book the Ebionites are mentioned among heretics whose doctrines fall all together, when the great scheme of man's redemption is rightly understood. " Our Lord redeeming us by his own blood, and giving his own soul for our soul, and his body for our bodies, and pouring out the spirit of the Father for the adunion and communion of God with men, bringing God down to men by the spirit, and again, by his incarnation, raising man to God, and in his advent actually and assuredly conferring on us incorruptibility by communion with God, the doctrines of heretics fall all together. For they are vain, who say that his appearance was phantastic.—The Valentinians therefore are vain, who hold this doctrine. —The Ebionites also are vain, not receiving the union of God and man by faith, &c."[*]

---

[*] Suo igitur sanguine redimente nos Domino, et dante animam suam pro nostrâ animâ, et carnem suam pro nostris carnibus, et effundente Spiritum Patris in adunitionem et communionem Dei et hominum, ad homines quidem deponente Deum per Spiritum, ad Deum autem rursus imponente hominem per suam incarnationem, et firmé et veré in suo adventu donante nobis incorruptelam, per communionem quæ est ad Deum; perierunt omnes hæreticorum doctrinæ. Vani autem sunt qui putativè

The only use which Dr Priestley makes of this passage is to take the clause relating to the Ebionites by itself, and to remark that " the harshest epithet which Irenæus here applies to that sect is that of *Vani;* which, considering the manner of the ancients, he says, is certainly very moderate."[*] But however moderate he may think this epithet, had he attended to the context he would have seen that it is the very same epithet which Irenæus in this same place applies to the Docetæ, the Valentinians, and the most impious of the Gnostics. It should seem therefore, that it is a term of more severe reproach than Dr Priestley apprehends. It imports indeed that they to whom it is applied, were persons *become vain in their imaginations,* cherishing opinions void of foundation in Scripture and in truth, such as arose out of a misapprehension of the whole scheme of revealed religion. And whatever the particular sense of this epithet may be, the manner in which the mention of the Ebionites is introduced, shews that they are mentioned as affording one instance of heretics of that description.

---

* dicunt eum apparuisse——Vani igitur qui á Valentino sunt, hoc dogmatizantes——Vani autem et Ebionæi, unitionem Dei et Hominis per fidem non recipientes in suam *animam.* Lib. 5. cap. i.

† First Letters, p. 33.

In another passage of this fifth book Irenæus says of heretics in general, that "they are unlearned, ignorant of the divine dispensations, particularly of the scheme respecting man, blind to the truth, and that they contradict their own salvation." This general charge he illustrates and confirms by specifying the particular absurdities of different sects. " Some," he says, " introducing another Father beside the Demiurgus. Some again saying that the world, and the substance of it were made by certain angels. Some, that the substance of the world sprang up from itself, and is self-produced, far separate from him, who according to them is the Father. Some, that it took its substance from corruption and ignorance, being among the things within the Father. Some treat the doctrine of our Lord's visible advent with contempt, not admitting the incarnation. Some ignorant of the dispensation of the Virgin, say, that he was begotten by Joseph, Some, &c."*

* Indocti omnes hæretici, et ignorantes dispositiones Dei, et inscii ejus quæ est secundum hominem dispensationis, quippe cæcutientes circa veritatem, ipsi suæ contradicunt saluti, alii quidem alterum introducentes, præter Demiurgum, patrem. Alii autem ab angelis quibusdam dicentes factum esse mundum, et substantiam ejus. Alii quidem porro et longe separatum ab eo, qui est secundum ipsos, patre, a semetipsá floruisse, et esse ex se natam. Alii autem in his quæ continentur a patre, de labe et 'ignorantiâ substantiam habuisse. Alii autem manifestum adventum domini contemnunt, incarnationem eius non recipientes. Alii autem rursus ignorantes virginis dispensationem, ex Joseph dicunt eum generatum. Lib. 5. cap. xix.

Dr Priestley " once thought"[*] that in this passage the Ebionites were included in the appellation of heretics; as indeed any one would think, who could explain the grammatical construction of the sentence ,in every clause of which *heretici* [heretics] is understood as the substantive to be joined with *Alii* [Some]. They therefore, who maintained that our Lord was literally and naturally Joseph's son are here expressly called " Some heretics." But Dr Priestley has reconsidered the passage; and perceiving how strongly the natural sense of it makes against him, he has found himself mistaken in that construction of it. He says, " as Cerinthus and Carpocrates, and other Gnostics denied the miraculous conception as well as the Ebionites, and all the rest of this description, both before and after this circumstance, evidently belongs to the Gnostics only, and as in no other place whatever does he comprehend them in his definition of heresy, it is natural to conclude that he had no view to the Ebionites even here, but only to those Gnostics who in common with them denied the miraculous conception."[†] This conclusion might indeed be somewhat more natural than it is, if the passage really were, what Dr Priestley when he calls it " this description," would represent it to be,—

---

[*] Second Letters, p. 57.   [†] Ibid. p. 58.

a description of one sect by various characters.
For in that case it might be said, that all the
parts of the description must be united to make
up the complete character of an heretic. But the
passage is plainly an enumeration of different
sects, to which the name of heretics, and the
charge of ignorance and blindness belong in common; an enumeration describing each by its particular error. This appears, not only from the
grammatical structure of the period, in which the
repetition of *Alii, Alii, Alii,* &c. *Some, Some,
Some,* distinguishes and enumerates, and hath
no other force; but still more evidently from
this circumstance: that the opinions mentioned
in the different clauses are, in some *instances,*
manifestly repugnant; insomuch that they could
not all be maintained by the same persons.
Thus the second, third, and fourth clauses, mention contradictory opinions about the origin of
the visible world; and the " some heretics" who
held any one of these opinions must have been a
different set from the " some heretics" who held
another. And indeed that they were different,
is clearly expressed in the Latin words. For I
have been favourable to Dr Priestley in rendering the repeated *Alii, Some,* and *Some* and *Some.*
The proper rendering would be, *Some, Others,
Others,* &c. In this enumeration of heresies the
error ascribed to each is alleged as an instance
of the ignorance of that sect, of their blindness to

the truth, and their opposition to their own salvation. The enumeration being made in proof of that general charge, it is natural to suppose, that each sect is described by that error, which, of all their absurd opinions was the fittest for the purpose of that proof, the clearest instance of their ignorance and blindness, and their contradicting of their own salvation. The particular error therefore mentioned in each 'clause is not indeed by itself a definition of heresy, but it is by itself a sure mark of a heretic; by which, every one maintaining that opinion might be known to come under that general character. One of these marks of a heretic is the opinion, that our Lord was literally and naturally the son of Joseph. All therefore were heretics in the judgment of Irenæus, upon whom that mark was to be found, whether they were Cerinthians, Carpocratians, or Ebionites. If this was a mark that might in the judgment of Irenæus convict a Carpocratian or Cerinthian, why should it not equally in his judgment, convict the Ebionites? because in the Cerinthians and Carpocratians, Dr Priestley will say, this opinion was blended with impieties which were indeed heretical. But this is to place the mark of the heresy in the judgment of Irenæus, not in the circumstance which he expressly mentions as the mark, but in others which he suppresses. A mode of interpretation by which every writer may be brought to say whatever his expositor shall be pleased to say for him.

" If there be any other passage in Irenæus in which he calls or seems to call the Ebionites heretics,"* Dr Priestley declares he hath overlooked it. He hath then overlooked a very remarkable passage in the third book, the mention of which I have reserved for this place. Irenæus speaking of the universal credit and authority of the gospels, says, that " even heretics bear witness to it, since each of them endeavours to confirm his own doctrines by proofs from those writings. For the Ebionites using only the gospel according to St Matthew, are by that convicted of error in their notions of our Lord. Marcion, cutting off much of the gospel according to St Luke, may be proved a blasphemer against the only God from the parts which he retains, &c."†

As Dr Priestley mentions a definition of heresy given by Irenæus, in terms which exclude, or at

---

* Second Letters, p. 58.

† Tanta est autem circa evangelia hæc firmitas, ut et ipsi hæretici testimonium reddant eis, et ex ipsis egrediens unus quisque eorum conetur suam confirmare doctrinam. Ebionæi ctenim, eo evangelio quod est secundum Matthæum solo utentes, ex illo ipso convincuntur non recte præsumentes de Domino. Marcion autem id quod est secundum Lucam circumcidens, ex his quæ adhuc servantur penes eum, blasphemus in solum existentem Deum ostenditur. Lib. 3. cap. xi.

least comprehend not the Ebionites,* I shall just
take the liberty to suggest, that he might confer
an obligation upon the learned world, if he would
be pleased to give information, in what part of
the whole work of Irenæus that definition may
be found.

Meanwhile it appears, that the Ebionites are
repeatedly mentioned by Irenæus, and never
mentioned but as heretics. When any heavy
charge against heretics is to be confirmed by particular instances, the Ebionites seldom are forgotten. In the first book they appear in a list
of heretical sects as one instance among many
confirming the author's general assertion, that all
the heretical sects of his own and the preceding
age had their root and origin in the doctrines of
Simon Magus. In the third book they are mentioned as one instance of heretics, who rejecting
the greater part of the four gospels contribute
to the general evidence of the authenticity and
credit of those writings by their solicitude to
build their particular opinions upon the parts
which they receive, and yet are convicted of error
in those opinions by those very parts to which
they appeal. In another passage of the third
book they are described as persons in a state of

---

* Second Letters, p. 53.

impenitence and hardened infidelity, lying under
the dreadful sentence of eternal damnation. In
the fourth book their sect is mentioned among
those, whom the spiritual disciple, *i. e.* the sound
believer will judge. In the fifth book they are
mentioned among heretics whose doctrines are
demolished all in the lump, and at one blow, by
being contrasted with the scheme of man's redemption truly stated. And in another passage
of the same book their distinguishing tenet of
the mere humanity of our Lord is alleged as an
instance of the ignorance and blindness of heretics, and of the forwardness of such persons to
oppose their own salvation.

Of the truth of that remark of Dr Priestley's
which provoked this long disquisition, that the
Ebionites in Irenæus's large work " are again and
again characterised by him in such a manner as
makes it evident that even he did not consider
them. as heretics, and that he never calls them by
that name;" of the truth of this remark, and of
the qualifications of the man who could make it,
and take credit to himself that he had been the
first to make it, to enlighten the age upon points
of ecclesiastical antiquity, let the intelligent reader
now form his own judgment.

DISQUISITION FOURTH.

Of the sentiments of the fathers and others, concerning the eternal origination of the Son in the necessary energies of the paternal intellect.

In a subject so far above the comprehension of the human mind, as the doctrine of the Trinity must be confessed to be in all its branches, extreme caution should be used to keep the doctrine itself, as it is delivered in God's word, distinct from every thing that hath been devised by man, or that may even occur to a man's own thoughts to illustrate it, or explain its difficulties. Every one who hath ever thought for any length of time upon the subject, cannot but fall insensibly and involuntarily upon some way or other of representing the thing to his own mind. And if a man be ever so much upon his guard to check the licentiousness of imagination, and bridle an irreverent curiosity upon this holy subject, yet if he read what others have written, orthodox or heretics, he will find opinions proposed with too much freedom upon the difficulties of the subject; and among different opinions he cannot but form some judgment of the different degrees of probability with which they are severally accompanied; nor can he so far command himself, as not in some measure to embrace the opinion which seems the most probable. In this manner, every one who meddles at all with the subject, will be apt to form a solution for himself of what seem to him the principal difficulties. But since it must be confessed, that the human mind in these inquiries is groping in the dark every step that she ventures to advance beyond the point to which the clear light of revelation reaches, the probability is, that all these private solutions are in different ways and in different degrees, but all in some way and in some degree erroneous; and it will rarely happen, that the solution invented by one man will suit the conceptions of another. It were therefore to be wished, that in treating this mysterious subject, men would not, in their zeal to illustrate what after their utmost efforts must remain in some parts incomprehensible, be too forward to mix their private opinions with the public doctrine. Many curious questions were moved by the heretics of antiquity, and are now revived by Dr Priestley, about the nature and the limit of the Divine generation. Why the Father generates but one Son? Why that Son generates not another? Why the generation is not infinite? Instead of answering such questions, it seems to me that except when the necessity may arise, as indeed it too often will, of " answering a fool according to his folly," it should be a point of conscience with every writer to keep any particular opinions he may have formed, as much as possible out of sight, that divine truth may not be debased with a mixture of the alloy of human error, and that controversies may not be raised upon points in which no man or set of men can be authorised or qualified to prescribe to the belief of others. Upon these principles I should wish to decline all dispute upon the metaphysical difficulties of the subject, even with an adversary better qualified than I take Dr Priestley to be for such discussions. I should think indeed that I had already been guilty of an indiscretion, in the avowal that I have made in my Charge* of my own opinion about the manner in which the Son's eternal existence, without any diminution of its own necessity, may be connected with the Father's, were it not that what I am there attempting to illustrate, is not so much the Scripture doctrine itself, as the manner in which that doctrine was understood by the Platonizing fathers.

I said, and I still say, that it was their common principle " that the existence of the Son flows, necessarily from the Divine Intellect exerted on itself."† I shewed how the Son's eternity will follow from this principle. And I discovered what indeed I might have concealed, that I myself con-

---

* Charge IV. sec. 5. † Ibid.

cur in this principle with the Platonists; for I
said, that " it seems to me to be founded in
Scripture."[*]   By which I meant not to assert
that it is so expressly declared in Scripture
that I would undertake to prove it by the Scriptures to others, in the same manner that I
would undertake to prove that the world was
created by Jesus Christ; or that the one like
the other ought to be made a branch of the public confession of the church; or that the belief or
disbelief of this particular principle is a circumstance that may in the least affect the integrity
of any Christian's faith.   It was not alleged as a
principle on which I meant at all to rest the credit of the Scripture doctrine; it was mentioned
only as a principle which, true or false, was embraced by a certain set of writers, and serves to
explain certain things said by them, which without it are unintelligible, or at least liable to misinterpretation.   At the same time, I discovered
my own opinion about this principle, that I think
it true, or likely to be true; for it *seems* (that is
the word I used) to be founded in Scripture.
Many phrases of holy writ seem to me to allude
to it; and to those who first thought of it, I
doubt not but that the same allusions seemed
couched in the same phrases.   Yet I will not un-

---

[*] Charge IV. sec. 5.

dertake to teach every one to read the same sense
in the same expressions. When I shewed, that
from this principle once admitted, a strict demonstration might be drawn of the eternity of the second person, it was not that I set any value upon
that demonstration as adding in the least degree
to the certainty of the Scripture doctrine. Upon
such points the evidence of Holy Scripture is indeed, the only thing that amounts to proof. The
utmost that reasoning can do, is to lead to the
discovery, and by God's grace to the humble
acknowledgment of the weakness and insufficiency of reason; to resist her encroachments upon
the province of faith; to silence her objections
and cast down imaginations, and prevent the innovations and refinements of philosophy and vain
deceit. Had philosophical reasoning upon points
of express revelation been held as cheap by Dr
Priestley as it is by me, the present controversy
never had arisen. But this demonstration of the
Son's eternity, was produced for no other purpose but to shew the disagreement between the
immediate consequences of the principle from
which it was deduced, and certain notions which
Dr Priestley would ascribe to those who held that
principle. But Dr Priestley mistaking for an illustration of Scripture what is only an illustration of writers whose meaning had been perverted by him, conceiving that the whole Catholic doctrine of the Trinity would be confuted, if a

certain principle, which being admitted might furnish a demonstrative proof of a particular part of it, might be shewn to be without foundation, calls upon me in the seventh of his First Letters,* to " shew what it is in the Scriptures, or indeed in the fathers, that gives any countenance to that curious piece of reasoning." In another part of the same letter he tells me, that " in reading my attempt to explain the doctrine of the Trinity [so he calls it], he fancies himself got back to the darkest of the dark ages, or at least that he is reading Peter Lombard, Thomas Aquinas, or Duns Scotus."† In his Second Letters, waxing confident by my neglect, which he interpreted as a cowardly desertion of my argument, he is louder in his challenge, and more stout in his defiance. Upon every occasion of these *challenges* and *calls*, of which sometimes the Dean of Canterbury, sometimes Dr White, sometimes Bishop Prettyman, sometimes I myself have the honour to be the object,—upon every such occasion, but particularly on this, his tone reminds me of the strutting actor on the stage :

> Clifford of Cumberland, 'tis Warwick calls.
> And if thou dost not hide thee from the bear,
> Now, when the angry trumpet sounds alarum,
> Clifford, I say, come forth and fight with me.

---

* First Letters, p. 78.   † Ibid. p. 99.

Proud Northern Lord————————
Warwick is hoarse with calling thee to arms.

" I challenge him," he says, " to produce any
authority whatever, ancient or modern, for that
opinion of the origin of the Son from the Father's
contemplation of his own perfections."*　In another place he speaks of it as " my own peculiar
notion."　He expresses " great mortification,"
that in my Letters in Reply to his First Letters,
" he found not one gleam of more light on this
curious subject".†　He reminds me of his most
magnanimous " CHALLENGE to produce any authority for it, except what may exist in my own
imagination."‡　He makes no doubt but that, had
it been possible for me to give an answer, I should
have answered.§

As for the question about the opinion itself,
how far it may be reasonable or unreasonable,
how far the allusion to it may be real or imaginary, which I think I perceive in some scriptural
phrases, no challenge of Dr Priestley's, no call,
taunt, defiance, insult, will move me from my
vow of silence.　But upon the question of fact,
concerning my own exclusive property in whatever there may be of truth or falsehood in the no-

---

* Second Letters, p. xxxiv.　　† Ibid. p. 135.
‡ Ibid.　　　　　　　　　　§ Ibid. p. 134.

tion, I think myself more at liberty, and feel more stomach for the contest. I cannot indeed resist the temptation which Dr Priestley's challenge " to produce any authority whatever, ancient or modern," presents, to seize the occasion of strengthening the proof of my *main point*, by exhibiting in its true light an instance, which, more perhaps, than any other singly taken, evinces Dr Priestley's ignorance of the religious opinions of every age, and shews how much the oldest things to him are novelties.

The fathers, it must be confessed, were in general very properly reserved and shy, when they were directly pressed with questions about the manner in which the existence of the three Divine Persons is connected. At the same time the analogy, which the Platonizing fathers in particular suppose between the relation of the Father to his Word, and the relation of every man's mind to its own thoughts, so necessarily implies this principle concerning the Son's origination, that with this principle as a key what they say upon the subject is very intelligible; and without this key impenetrably obscure. Insomuch that to me it is matter of astonishment, that any one can read some of the passages which Dr Priestley himself hath produced from Athenagoras, Tatian, Tertullian, and others, and not perceive that this notion was common to all those writers, and is the principle upon which all they have said upon the subject rests. But if the sentiments of the fathers upon this abstruse point were not to be collected with certainty from the tenor of their reasoning, and from their language, St Basil and St Cyril are sufficiently explicit: St Basil, when he says that the son of God is called the Λογος, " to shew that he came forth from intellect."[*] Which he endeavours to illustrate by the example so generally in use among the writers of antiquity, of the human mind producing an image of itself in its own thoughts: St Cyril, when he says, that " if any one would investigate the manner of that generation, he ought to consider the fructifications of intellect, and to endeavour rather to compare with them [than with physical propagations] the generation of the Word; and not to say that God is less capable of generating than body, because he generates not in a corporeal way. That the human intellect generates good thoughts, must necessarily be confessed. If it be impious to suppose that the human intellect is unfruitful, how much more absurd to think, that the Supreme Intellect should be unproductive, and to deprive it of its proper fructification."[†] In

---

[*] Διατι Λογος ; ινα διιχθη, ὅτι ἐκ τȣ Νȣ προηλθι. Homil. in verba illa " In Principio erat verbum." Tom. i. p. 506.

[†] Δια ταυτην οιμαι την αἰτιαν χρηναι διιν τȣς ὁσοι την ἐπ αὐτȣ γιννησιν ἐξιλαζιιν βȣλονται, τας ἐκ τȣ καρποφοριας ζητιιν, και ταυταις μαλ-

these words, St Cyril evidently places the generative faculty (if the expression may be allowed) of the Divine nature in the necessary fecundity of intelligence. In another part of the same discourse he says, that it is to be conceived, that " the Son is in such sort begotten of the Father, as wisdom of intellect."[*] And again, in another place he illustrates the intimate union of the Father and the Son, by its analogy to the union between the human intellect and its internal operations.[†]

From the fathers if we pass to the schoolmen, we shall find among them in this, as in most subjects, more philosophical subtlety and much less of a laudable reserve. With them the question was expressly agitated, whether the Divine generation was effected by intellect or by will. If by intellect, there arose a second question, from which they had not the modesty to abstain; what the object of the intellect might be; whether the

---

λον ἐξομοιως ἐπιγιγῦαι τε λογε την γεννησιν· και μη λεγειν σωμαλον ἀγονωλεροι εἰναι τον Θεον, ἐπει μη ὡς σωμα γεννα. Γεννὰν μεν γαρ και τιν ἀνδρωπινον νεν παιλως ἀν ὁμολογησαιμεν διαλογισμους· ἀγαθεκ.—: τοινυν ἀσιθεις εἰπειν τον ἀνθρωπινον νεν καρπον εν. ἐχειν——πως εκ ἀλ- πον τον ὑπερ παιλα νεν ἀναρπον εἰναι λεγειν, και της πρεπεσης αιλε εκπτοφοριας ἀποσιρειν. Cyril in Thesauro. tom. v. p. 45. edit. Auberti.

[*] ——Νοηῖιον ἐῖν γιγεννησθαι τον υἱον ἐκ τε παῖρα, ὡς σοφιαν ἐν νεν. p. 48.

[†] Ἐι ὁ ἀνθρωπινος νες, &c. p. 31.

Divine essence simply, as Scotus maintained, or the totality of the Divine nature, in the essence, the persons, and the works of creation, which was the notion of Thomas and his followers. And for this unbounded curiosity of speculation, they are justly censured by Simon Episcopius;* whose censure is a testimony which Dr Priestley perhaps will regard, that such opinions were maintained, and such questions agitated.

After the council of Trent, this peculiar no-tion of mine, this singular conceit, for which no authority whatever can be produced, ancient or modern, became the public doctrine of the church of Rome, being expressly asserted in the rule of public teaching set forth by the authority of that council, for the assistance and direction of the parochial clergy, under the title of *Catechismus ad Parochos.* The first part of that work is an exposition of the apostles' creed. In the explanation of the first article, the comment upon the word " *patern,*" is closed with an exhortation to the true believer to pray without intermission, " that being at some time or other admitted into the eternal tabernacles, he may be thought worthy to be allowed to see what that wonderful fecundity of God the Father is, that *contemplating and ex-*

---

* Episcop. Inst. lib. iv. sec. 11. c. 33.

erting his intelligence upon himself, he should beget a Son the exact counterpart and equal of himself."[*]　In the exposition of the second article, upon the words " *Filium ejus unicum,*" it is said, " That of all similitudes that are usually brought to explain the manner and way of the eternal generation, that seems to come the nearest to the thing which is taken from the reflection of our own mind ; upon which account St John calls the Son the Word.　For as our mind, exercising its intelligence upon itself, forms as it were an image of itself, which divines have called its word ; so God, so far as human things may be put in comparison with divine, exercising intelligence upon himself, generates the eternal Word."[†]

This however, was not so peculiarly the doctrine of the Roman church, but that it had its advocates among the most eminent of the Protestant divines.　Philip Melancthon, that great luminary

---

[*] Oret sine intermissione—ut aliquando in æterna tabernacula receptus dignus sit qui videat, quæ tanta sit Dei Patris fœcunditas, ut *seipsum intuens atque intelligens* parem et æqualem sibi Filium gignat.　Artic. Prim. sec. xiv.

[†] Ex omnibus autem, quæ ad indicandum modum rationemque æternæ generationis similitudines afferuntur, illa propius ad rem videtur accedere, quæ ab animi nostri cogitatione sumitur ; quamobrem sanctus Joannes Filium ejus verbum appellat.　Ut enim mens nostra, se ipsum quodam modo intelligens sui effingit imaginem, quam verbum Theologi discerunt ; ita Deus, quantum tamen divinis humana conferre possunt, *seipsum intelligens,* verbum æternum generat.　Artic. Secund. sec. xv.

of the reformation, was its constant and strenuous assertor; and he repeatedly resorts to it as a principle for the explanation of the phraseology of Scripture. Philip Melancthon, a man with whom it were more honourable to err, than to be in the right with Socinus or Dr Priestley, thought as I think, that the notion was founded in holy writ. He thought it indeed so clearly implied in the Scripture phrases, that he was less scrupulous than I would be in asserting it as a part of the Scripture doctrine.

In his Loci Theologici, he says, " the Son therefore is an image generated by the Father's *Thought.*———The eternal Father, *contemplating himself*, begets a thought of himself [or a conception of himself in his own thoughts] which is an image of himself never vanishing away, but subsisting, the essence being communicated to the image.———He is called the Word, because he is generated by thought. He is called the Image, because thought is an image of the thing thought upon."[*]

---

[*] Est igitur imago cogitatione Patris genita.———Pater æternus *sese intuens* gignit cogitationem sui, quæ est imago ipsius non evanescens, sed subsistens, communicatâ ipsi essentiâ. ———Dicitur Λογος, quia cogitatione generatur. Dicitur imago, quia cogitatio est imago rei cogitatæ. Op. Melanct. tom. i. p. 152.

Let me by the way entreat the learned reader to compare these sentences of Melancthon with Tertullian's fifth chapter against Praxeas, and judge for himself whether Tertullian and Melancthon had not the same view of the subject.

Again, in the form of examination of candidates for holy orders, Melancthon says, " The eternal Son is the second person of the Divinity, which person is the substantial and entire image of the eternal Father, which the Father *contemplating and considering himself*, generates from eternity."* The same thing is repeated nearly in the same words in his definitions of appellations,† and again in his second exposition of the Nicene creed.‡

In his first exposition of the Nicene creed, he says, " The eternal Father is a divine person, eternal, not sprung of any other, but *by thought upon himself* generating from eternity the coeternal Son, his own image.——The Son is a divine person begotten by the Father *thinking upon and contemplating himself*."§

---

* Filius æternus est secunda persona divinitatis, quæ est substantialis et integra imago cæterni Patris, quam Pater *sese intuens et considerans* ab æterno gignit. Opera Melanct. tom. i. p. 307.
† Tom. i. p. 350.   ‡ Tom. ii. p. 213, and p. 315.
§ Pater æternus est persona divina, æterna, non nata ali-

In the second exposition, he says, " To be born, is of the intelligent power; because the Son is born by thought."*

In his annotations upon the gospel for the feast of the nativity he says, " Basil and others say, that the Son is called the Word, because he is the image of the Father, generated by the Father *thinking upon himself.* For the Father *contemplating himself,* generates a thought, which is called the Word; which thought is the image of the Father; into which image the Father, if we may so speak, transfuses his own essence."†

So possessed was Melancthon with this notion, which Dr Priestley learned only in his own imaginations conceives to have been first hatched in my brain, ages since the good Melancthon fell asleep, that upon every occasion, when he mentions the generation of the Son, he introduces this

---

unde, sed *cogitatione sui* gignens ab æterno Filium coæternum, imaginem suam.——Filius est persona divina genita à Patre cogitante ac intuente seipsum. Symb. Nicen. De Tribus personis.

* Nasci est à potentiâ intelligente; quia Filius cogitatione nascitur. Tom. ii. p. 228.

† Basilius et alii dicunt, Filium dici Λογον quia sit imago Patris, genita à Patre *sese cogitante.* Pater enim *intuens se,* gignit cogitationem, quæ vocatur verbum; quæ cogitatio est imago Patris, in quam imaginem Pater, ut ita dicamus, transfundit suam essentiam. Tom. iii. p. 12.

notion of the manner of it. And Melancthon, the learned reader will observe, never dreamed that in this he was setting up a notion of his own. He thought, as I do, that the fathers entertained the same view of the subject; and that this view of the subject was countenanced by the phraseology of holy writ.

Zanchius indeed, an orthodox writer of great piety and learning, speaks of this same notion in terms, as it may seem, of strong disapprobation. " What some, he says, as the schoolmen write, that God the Father, by seeing and considering himself begot the Word, and that the emanation of the Son from the Father, is after the manner of an emanation of intellect and other things of that kind, which have no proof from the word of God, we must reject them as rash and vain ; that is to say, if the thing be positively asserted so to be."* Zanchius therefore, were he now living to be a witness of this controversy between Dr Priestley and me, would have taxed me, it seems, with rashness and presumption, had he found me

---

* Cæterum quod quidam, ut scholastici, scribunt, Deum patrem se videndo et considerando genuisse Λογοι, et quòd emanatio Filii a Patre est secundum emanationem intellectûs, et alia id genus, quæ nullum habent ex verbo Dei testimonium, rejicienda nobis sunt tanquam temeraria et vana ; nempe si res ita sese habere asseveretur. Zanchius De Tribus Elohim. Lib. v. c. 8.

propounding this notion of the Divine generation, *as the way in which the thing must certainly be.* But he would have little admired my adversary's learning or commended his modesty, when he upbraids me as a setter forth of new doctrines of my own coinage, and challenges me to produce any authority ancient or modern, in support of this opinion. Zanchius well knew, though the thing is unknown to Dr Priestley, that the authority of the schoolmen, and of others, is on the side of the opinion. And in the very censure which he passes upon the doctrine he acquits all of his own, or later times, of the invéntion.

But in truth, this learned Calvinist seems to have thóught no worse of this opinion than I myself think of it,—that it is not a thing to be too positively asserted so to be. In itself he seems to have thought it not improbable. For in another part of his works he mentions it as a notion furnishing the best answer to those who would deny the Son's eternity, upon the principles so frequently alleged by the Arians and other Antitrinitarians, that that which is begotten must always have a later beginning of its existence than that which begets; and that all generation is effected by motion and change. Such objections he says, may be answered by analogies taken from the material world. The sun at all times generates rays from his own body. These rays are emitted without any change in the sun himself. " But a clearer refutation," he says, " may be drawn from the example of our own incorporeal intellect.———Intellect in the energy of intelligence generates another *quasi-intellect,* as the philosophers call it, like unto itself; which for this reason is called by us a conception of the mind; by the Platonists, mind generated of mind; and by the fathers, the word and Λογος of the mind. And this it begetteth within itself. And there is no such thing as intellect actually intelligent, that is, which is truly intellect, without this other generated intellect; and the parent intellect generates without suffering in itself any change."[*] Zanchius suggests these philosophical topics of reply to philosophical arguments against the eternity of God the Son. This analogy therefore, between the Father's generation of the Son, and the mind's generation of a conception of itself in thought, he esteemed an hypothesis philosophically probable; which might be very properly em-

---

[*] Clarius etiam hæc refutari possunt exemplo intellectûs nostri incorporei.———Intellectus, dum intelligit, gignit (ut philosophi vocant) alium quasi intellectum, sibi similem, quem hanc ob causam nos conceptum mentis, Platonici mentem genitam a mente, Patres verbum et Λογον mentis appellarunt. Et illum gignit intra se; et nunquam intellectus est actu intelligens, et ideo verè intellectus, sine hoc genito altero intellectu: et quidem sine ullâ sui mutatione gignit. Zanchius De Naturâ Dei. Lib. ii. c. 7.

ployed to convince those who upon philosophical grounds made a difficulty of the only begotten Son's eternity, that what they called in question might easily be, though he thought it presumptuous in any one to assert too positively that this analogy represents the way in which the thing actually is.

If the Calvinists have been shy of resorting in their disputes with Antitrinitarians to the arguments which Zanchius suggests and recommends, I take the reason of this to be, that the analogy on which those arguments were founded seemed repugnant to an opinion which Calvin himself was thought to hold. Calvin, in the heat of his disputes with Valentinus Gentilis and Blandratta, was carried to the use of some unguarded expressions which seemed to imply that the existence of the Son was entirely independent of the Father's. He went indeed so far as to question the propriety of the expression in the Nicene creed, " God of God." This notion was considered as a dangerous novelty, and gave much alarm to some of the most eminent divines of those times, as necessarily terminating in one or the other of two horrible extremes: Sabellianism on the one hand, or Tritheism on the other. It was treated with great severity by writers of the Roman church, and was strenuously opposed, though with much moderation and

candour, by my illustrious predecessor Bishop
Bull among ourselves, and in Holland by Armi-
nius. Beza, in his preface to Athanasius's dialogues, makes the apology of Calvin; confessing
that he had not been sufficiently circumspect in
the choice of expressions, and alleging that his
expressions had been misunderstood; which I
take indeed to be the truth. It seems to me
that Calvin meant only to deny that the Son was
a contingent being, the creature of the Father's
will; to assert that he is, strictly speaking, God;
and that the existence of the three persons, of
the second and third no less than of the first,
is contained in the very notion of a God, when
that notion is accurately developed. However,
his words were otherwise understood by many
of his followers; his authority gave credit and
currency to an error which was supposed to be
his doctrine, and the notion of the Son's origination in the necessary energies of the paternal intellect is rejected by many of the Calvinists,
more peremptorily than by Zanchius.

The church of England, with her usual caution, hath abstained from giving her sanction to
any particular opinion concerning the manner of
the Divine generation. Of her divines, some
have embraced the opinion which I have acknowledged for my own, (particularly Dr Leslie, in
his *Socinian Controversy Discussed,*) and a great

majority acknowledge a dependence of the Son's existence on the Father, strenuously asserting in the language of the Nicene creed, that the Son is " God of God." But some of no inconsiderable name have adopted what was thought to be Calvin's doctrine, in an extent to which I think with Beza, Calvin himself never meant it should be carried.

Upon the whole, I trust it appears that this singular conceit of mine, this invention for which I am challenged to produce any authority ancient or modern, is a principle that was tacitly assumed by many of the fathers; openly maintained by some ; disputed about by the schoolmen; approved by the church of Rome; maintained by the greatest of the Lutheran divines; objected to by the Calvinists as a point of doctrine, but received by some of the most learned of that persuasion as at least a probable surmise. About the truth of the opinion, I have declared that I will not dispute; and I shall keep my word. But Dr Priestley's rash defiance I may place among the specimens with which his history and his letters to me abound, of his incompetency in this subject, and of the effrontery of that incurable ignorance which is ignorant even of its own want of knowledge.

DISQUISITION FIFTH.

Of Origen's want of veracity.

THE defence of Origen's veracity, which Dr Priestley hath attempted to set up in the second of his Third Letters, is in some parts so weak, and in others so disingenuous, that it would deserve no serious reply if the reader might be considered as a judge before whom Origen was arraigned, who would be obliged by his office to canvass the arguments and weigh the evidence on both sides with a scrupulous attention, in order to a solemn condemnation or acquittal of the accused party. But it may be expected of a controversial writer to save trouble to the reader, who is bound to no such official duty, to assist him in forming a final judgment upon the evidence produced on either side, and to expose the futility of arguments and the fallacy of assertions, which in a criminal process before any of his Majesty's judges of assize, might safely be trusted to expose themselves.

The work of Celsus against Christianity being lost, neither the plan nor the matter of it is otherwise to be known, than by what may be gathered from Origen's answer. It appears from Origen, that it was a composition of much art, and highly laboured. Many of Celsus's objections were delivered in the person of a Jew, who is supposed to address his discourse first to Jesus and afterwards to the Hebrew Christians. In the discourse addressed to the Hebrew Christians, Celsus makes his Jew upbraid them with a desertion of the Mosaic law. To this reproach Origen in vindication of the Hebrew brethren, gives a double answer, which I have shewn to be inconsistent with itself in the two different branches.[*] First, he asserts that the Jews believing in Christ had not renounced their Judaism. Upon occasion of this assertion he goes into a discourse of some length about St Peter's adherence to the Mosaic law, and the information which was conveyed to that apostle in a vision concerning the extinction of its authority. From this discourse he runs into a second, upon a saying of our Lord's, which he expounds as an ænigmatical allusion to the intended abrogation of the law. And when in this digressive way he hath written " about it and about it," till he had himself forgotten, or might reasonably trust that his reader would have forgotten, the position with which this prolix discourse began, he enters upon the second branch

---

[*] Remarks on Dr Priestley's Second Letters, P. II. chap. i. sec. 6.

of his defence of the Hebrew brethren, in which
he flatly contradicts his first assertion, insulting
over Celsus's ignorance, who had not made his
Jew distinguish the different sects of the converted Hebrews,—two of which observed the law, and
one of which had to all intents and purposes abandoned it.   I have given this passage at length in
my Remarks on Dr Priestley's Second Letters,*
and shall not tire my readers' patience with a
needless repetition of it.

Dr Priestley to vindicate Origen from the
charge of self-contradiction in this instance, hath
recourse to a very curious piece of criticism. He
bids me observe, that Origen contends *not* that
Celsus's Jew, had he said what Origen says he
should have said, would have said what was *true*,
but what was *plausible*.† The same critical sagacity that struck out this distinction, might
have perceived that the want of plausibility with
which Celsus's Jew is taxed, consisted in the confounding of distinctions which actually existed;
and that the existing distinctions which Celsus's
Jew confounded, were the distinctions between
the Hebrew sects, two observing the law, and one
disusing it. For this is the language of Origen's

---

* Remarks on Dr Priestley's Second Letters, P. II. chap. i.
sec. 6.
† Third Letters, p. 10.

reproach. " How *confusedly* does Celsus's Jew speak, when he might have said, &c." and by saying so have avoided the imputation of confusion.

The plausibility, of the want of which Origen complains in the discourse of Celsus's Jew, is what may be called poetical plausibility. It is that general air of truth which a writer of judgment and good taste contrives to give to the fable of a drama, by an attention to the peculiarities of times, places, manners, and characters; a neglect of which stamps a manifest character of clumsy fiction on what ought to seem reality; as would be the case in any serious play in which the Maid of Orleans should be seated on the Delphic tripod, or Hugh Peters introduced maintaining the divine rights of kings and bishops. This is the want of plausibility, with which Origen taxes Celsus. He says that Celsus with all his great pretensions to learning and taste knew not the common rules of art about maintaining character in the fiction of persons. Το ἀκολυθον ἐπ' οὐδὲ καλυτον του σω τας προυτοντας. He made his Jew say what no real Jew would have said,—that the Hebrew Christians in general had deserted the law of their ancestors. This no Jew would have said, because it was a downright falsehood, which every Jew must have known to be such. Had Origen stopt short here he would not have himself betrayed the want of truth in his first assertion that the whole body of the Hebrew Christians retained the observation of the law. · For the two propositions concerning the Hebrew Christians, that they had all forsaken their law, which was Celsus's Jew's assertion, and that none of them had forsaken it, which was Origen's, are so completely opposite, that the entire falsehood of the one were perfectly consistent with the entire truth of the other. But Origen unfortunately for his own credit, goes on to tell his reader what Celsus's Jew might have said with more plausibility, *i. e.* with more propriety of character —more consistently with a Jew's knowledge of the truth—that is, more truly : so that plausibility and truth, in this use of the word plausibility, are the very same thing. Had Celsus made his Jew reproach the Hebrew converts, not as he did, with a general desertion of their law, but with great disagreements among themselves about the extent and duration of its authority, and the respect due to it under the Christian dispensation, he would have made his Jew speak more in character; because he would have spoken more consistently with what every Jew must have known to be the real state of opinions among the Christians of the circumcision. Had Celsus's Jew talked like a Jew upon this subject, he would not have said that all the Hebrew brethren were deserters of their law; but he might it seems with great propriety have said, that some of them had forsaken it. This had been very consistent with that accurate information which a Jew might be expected to possess. Consequently, it appears that Origen should not have said that they all adhered to it. And his own representation of the fact when he comes to state it accurately, betrays the falsehood of that first assertion.

That the distinctions which Origen says Cel. sus's Jew might have put between the Hebrew Christians, were differences really subsisting in that body at the time, is strongly implied in the form of the expression, δυαμενος ἱστιν; the force of which is very imperfectly rendered in my translation of the passage by the words " when he might have said." It had been better rendered, " when he had it to say." The Greek words δυαμενος ἱστιν, like the English " he had it to say," are applicable only to substantial facts, which might safely be averred without danger of refutation.

Dr Priestley indeed seems willing to concede, that Origen in this second branch of his reply to Celsus's Jew's reproach, " may allude to a few" of the Hebrew Christians, " who had abandoned their ancient customs."* So that the question at

---

* Third Letters, p. 10.

last comes to this; how many of the Hebrew Christians had abandoned those customs? for that some had abandoned them is at last confessed. These *some* were by Origen's account enow to be reckoned a sect. But Dr Priestley hath taken care to settle the proportion to the advantage of his own argument. " There might be," he says, " a few Jewish Christians who had deserted their former customs, which would have given Celsus a *plausible pretence* for making such a division of them as to make these one of the classes, yet the great body of them had not."[*] But there is nothing in Origen's expressions which should imply that either of the two sects of the Hebrew Christians which retained the law, was a greater body than the sect which had abandoned it. *Some* and *Some* and *Some* is the word by which the mention of each class is introduced. In what proportion the first " Some" might fall short of, or exceed the second or the third, it exceeds my skill in computation to investigate. Dr Priestley perhaps solved the problem in that early period of his life when he was addicted to mathematical pursuits.[†]

But I have maintained, that Origen in the sentence which follows this division of the Hebrews

---

* Second Letters, p. 191.   † Ibid,

professing Christianity into three classes, gives us
to understand, that of these three sorts they only
who had laid aside the observation of the Mosaic
law were in his time considered as true Christians. For he mentions it as a further proof of
Celsus's ignorance, that in his account of the heresies of the Christian church he had omitted *the
Israelites believing in Jesus and not laying aside
the law of their ancestors.* I refer the reader to an
exact translation of Origen's words in my Remarks
upon Dr Priestley's Second Letters.*

Upon this Dr Priestley says to me in the first
of his Third Letters, " From this construction of
the passage a person might be led to think that
Origen represented Celsus as having undertaken
to give an account of the heresies in the Christian
church, and as having in that account omitted the
Israelites believing in Christ, and not laying aside
the rites of their ancestors; and upon no other
ground can your insinuation stand."† On no
other ground I declare, does my insinuation stand.
But I am confident, that with the exception of
Dr Priestley and his associates and admirers,
every person who will take the trouble to consider the passage as it stands in Origen's discourse,
will perceive that mine is the plain and natural

---

* P. II. chap. i. sec. 7.   † Third Letters, p. 13.

construction of it. Every unprejudiced person
who can construct the passage for himself, will
perceive that Origen hath indeed thus represented
Celsus as pretending to give an account of the heresies among Christians, and in that account in-
serting some who had not a right to be inserted,
and omitting others who had. Of Celsus's work,
as hath been before remarked, we know not the
contents but so far as they may be gathered from
Origen's reply. It should seem from this passage
in Origen, that Celsus in some part of his work
had found it to his purpose to enumerate the principal sects of which he would have it believed the
general body of the Christians was composed. It
is not difficult to conceive how it might be to his
purpose to enumerate sects, and make as many
of them as he could. He might intend by this
to throw discredit on Christians in general as dis-
agreeing among themselves, and broken into parties about the particulars of the revelations which
they professed in common to believe. Origen
says, that in the execution of this design he numbered among the heresies of the church impious
sects, which were not to be deemed in any degree
Christian, and passed unnoticed or knew not of
the real heresy of the Judaizing Hebrews. This
is in itself a very just and pertinent objection to
Celsus's enumeration. But then it is a confession
that the Judaizing Hebrews were an heretical
sect, and of consequence that Origen asserted

what was false when he said of the Hebrew Christians in general that they Judaized. For that the great body of the Hebrew Christians was deemed heretical, is what I believe no adventurer in ecclesiastical history hath ever yet affirmed.

Another instance which I produced* of Origen's disposition to prevaricate, is his answer to Celsus's Jew's objection to the famous prophecy of the miraculous conception, contained in Isaiah vii. 14. Celsus's Jew maintains, that the Hebrew word in that text which the Christians with the old Greek translators, understand to signify a virgin, properly renders not the condition of virginity, but the season of youth; not a virgin but a young woman. Origen to prove on the contrary that this word properly renders a woman in the state of virginity, cites a text in Deuteronomy, where he would have it believed that the word in question is clearly used in that sense. But according to our modern copies of the Hebrew text, the words which correspond to the Greek παρθως in the two passages in Isaiah and Deuteronomy, are two different words. And there is much reason to believe, as I have shewn in my Remarks on Dr Priestley's Second Letters,†

---

* Remarks on Dr Priestley's Second Letters, P. II. chap. i. sec. 8.   † Ibid.

that the same two different words occurred in the
two passages in the copies of Origen's time, and
that Origen himself was apprised of the difference.
The text in Deuteronomy therefore, as it stands
in the modern Hebrew text, and as it probably
stood in the more ancient copies, affords no illustration of Isaiah's words; and Origen's expressions give the greatest cause to suspect that he
well knew the infirmity of his own argument;
and by consequence that in the use of such an
argument he was guilty of prevarication.

Dr Priestley says to me in the first of his Third
Letters, " The question between Origen and the
Jews was not what was the word in the Hebrew,
but what was the meaning of it in a particular
place."* It is true. The main question between
Origen and Celsus's Jew, was about the meaning
of a word in a text. But then the question was
not indefinite about one or another of different
words in different places. It was about a particular word in a particular place. About the meaning of the word עלמה in Isaiah vii. 14. This was
indeed the question between Origen and Celsus's
Jew. But the question between Dr Priestley and
me is by what sort of argument Origen attempted
to sustain his own opinion upon the matter in de-

---

* Third Letters, p. 14.

bate between him and the Jew? Whether by such
an argument as might have been employed by an
honest disputant who had preferred general truth
to victory in a particular question. Origen to
justify the sense in which he understood the word,
resorts to a critical argument. He appeals to a
passage in Deuteronomy, in which he would have
it believed that the word was indisputably used
in the same sense in which he understood it to be
used in the text in question in Isaiah. Now it is
evident, that this critical argument rests entirely
upon the identity of the word in the two different
texts; and Origen's good faith in the use of that
argument rests on his knowledge or belief of the
identity. I remark that Origen takes not upon
him to affirm positively this identity of the word
upon which his whole argument depends, but
speaks of it as from hearsay only. I remark that
from the present state of the Hebrew text there
is great reason to think that this hearsay was a
false report. For in the text in Deuteronomy we
find not עלמה but בתולה. Nor did Dr Kennicott
find עלמה in the text cited by Origen from Deuteronomy, in any one of the innumerable copies
which he collated. Now I say, that the confessed sense of the word בתולה in Deuteronomy can
never settle the disputed sense of the word עלמה
in Isaiah. And I say, that the doubtful manner
in which Origen speaks of the identity of the two

words in Isaiah and Deuteronomy, creates a vehement suspicion that the words were different
in the copies of his time, as they are in those of
the present day; and that Origen well knew that
his argument was founded on a misrepresentation
of the text in Deuteronomy.*

Dr Priestley adds, " admitting that the dispute
was about the true reading in the original, what
great matter was there in Origen's saying *the
Jews said so*, when he knew that what they said
was true?"† Here again we have a beautiful
specimen of our Greek professor's readiness in the
Greek language. *The Jews said so!* Origen says
nothing of what the Jews said. There is no mention of Jews more than of Cherokees, except of
Celsus's fictitious Jew, in this part of Origen's
discourse. The nominative of the verb φασι is not
the Jews, but the indefinite plural understood;
which is usually expressed in the English language by the pronoun *they* used indefinitely, and
in the French by *on*; but in the Greek and the
Latin languages is always understood, never is
expressed: ὡς φασι, *ut aiunt*. " As they say," i. e.
" As is generally said." Origen affirms not that

* Remarks on Dr Priestley's Second Letters, P. II. chap. i.
sec. 8.
† Third Letters, p. 14.

what was thus generally said was true. That he should shelter himself under the authority of a vague report in a point so essential to his argument, in which he was so competent to judge how the case really stood, is a strong presumption that he knew, not that this report was true, but that it was the reverse of truth. That it was the reverse of truth is in the highest degree probable from the present state of the Hebrew text. That Origen knew it to be the reverse is highly probable from the suspicious manner in which he appeals to it. And upon the ground of this strong presumptive evidence my impeachment of his veracity in this instance stands.

Dr Priestley in relating my remark upon Origen's critical argument, hath taken care to omit that very material part of it, that in our modern copies of the Hebrew Bible, the word which by the consent of all interpreters denotes a virgin in the text cited from Deuteronomy, is a different word from that which the LXX with great propriety render a virgin in Isaiah. This art which Dr Priestley is so apt to employ, of reducing an argument which he would refute, by well-managed abridgements, to a form in which it may be capable of refutation, indicates so near a resemblance between the characters of Origen and his *Hyperaspistes*

in the worst part of Origen's, that perhaps I
might not be altogether unjustifiable were I to
apply to the Squire the words which Mosheim
so freely uses of the Knight, EGO HUIC TESTI,
ETIAMSI JURATO, QUI TAM MANIFESTO FUMOS
VENDIT, ME NON CREDITURUM ESSE CONFIRMO.

DISQUISITION SIXTH.

Of St Jerome's orthodox Hebrew Christians.

In the fourth of his Third Letters, Dr Priestley professes to consider *the evidence from Jerome in favour of the existence of a church of orthodox Jewish Christians at Jerusalem after the time of Adrian.*[*] The learned reader will be pleased to recollect that my proof of the existence of such a church rests in part only upon St Jerome's evidence. The entire proof rests upon seven positions laid down by me in my Remarks upon Dr Priestley's Second Letters, P. II. chap. ii; and St Jerome's evidence goes barely to the proof of the last of those positions, the seventh: namely, " that a body of orthodox Christians of the Hebrews was actually existing in the world much later than in the time of Adrian."[†] St Jerome's evidence is brought for the proof of this position singly; and this proved by St Jerome's evidence, in conjunction with six other principles previously laid down, in the proof of which St Jerome is not at all concerned, makes the whole evidence of the main fact which I affirm, that a church of or-

---

[*] See the title of the fourth Letter. Third Letters, p. 25.
[†] Remarks on Dr Priestley's Second Letters, P. II. c. ii. sec. 7.

thodox Christians of the Hebrews existed at Ælia
from the final dispersion of the Jews by Adrian
to a much later period.[*]

Dr Priestley tells me that " before I can shew
that the passage in Jerome on which I lay so
great a stress is at all to my purpose, I must
prove the three following things : first, that the
Hebrews believing in Christ were different from
the Nazarenes; secondly, that the former were
completely orthodox; and thirdly, that those orthodox Jewish Christians resided at Jerusalem."[†]

Certainly it must be an argument of little significance that cannot be applied to the matter in
question till the thing to be proved by it hath
been previously proved from other principles.   Dr
Priestley hath confessed, that he sometimes con-
descends to amuse himself with the fabrication of
such arguments.[‡]   But I would not willingly be
detected in the use of them.   I contend that the
passage in St Jerome's commentary on Isaiah, to
which I refer in my Remarks on Dr Priestley's
Second Letters, (Part II. chap. ii. sec. 8.) which
Dr Priestley hath given at length in the fourth

---

[*] Remarks on Dr Priestley's Second Letters, P. II. chap. ii.
[†] Third Letters, p. 28·
[‡] First Letters, p. 130 ; and see my Letters in Reply, Let-
ter ninth.

of his Third Letters ;*' I contend that this passage itself contains a clear proof that the persons
there mentioned under the description of " Hebrews believing in Christ," and under the name
of " Nazarenes," were different persons. I contend that this same passage affords a strong presumptive argument that the former were completely orthodox. The existence of these orthodox Hebrew believers in the time of St Jerome
being thus proved by St Jerome's evidence, the
probability of the fact that they resided at Ælia,
and that such a body had been settled at Ælia
from the time of Adrian downwards, rests upon
my six former positions.

St Jerome relates, as I have observed, (Remarks, Part II. chap. ii. sec. 8.) two different expositions of the prophecy delivered by Isaiah in
the beginning of the ninth chapter, concerning
Zabulon and Naphtali. The first of these expositions he ascribes to " the Hebrews believing in
Christ," the other to " the Nazarenes, *whose opinion he had given above.*" Dr Priestley thinks
that by these Nazarenes St Jerome " did not
intend any other than the Hebrews believing in
Christ, but only meant to vary his mode of expression."† This might seem probable, if the·

---

* Third Letters, p. 28.   † Ibid. p. 29.

difference of name were the only note of difference between the people; and if the Nazarenes had not been mentioned before by their proper name, and a particular opinion mentioned as peculiar to the persons so named. But to suppose that under all these circumstances St Jerome hath described the same people under different names, merely for the sake of varying his mode of expression, is to suppose that he hath varied his expression when it ought least of all to have been varied, and when a variation could serve no purpose but to create confusion. An imputation to which St Jerome is too good a writer to be liable. The Nazarenes are twice mentioned by St Jerome under their proper name, *in his* commentary on the next preceding chapter of Isaiah's prophecies: the eighth. Upon the passage—*in lapidem autem offensionis et petram scandali duabus domibus Israel.*—St Jerome remarks that " the Nazarenes who so receive Christ that they discard not the rites of the ancient law, interpret these two houses of the two schools of Sammai and Hillel, from which sprang the Scribes and Pharisees,—and that these are the two houses that received not the Saviour," &c. Again upon the passage at the conclusion of the same chapter,—*cum dixerint ad vos quærite a Pythonibus,*—he remarks, that the Nazarenes expound this passage also to the disadvantage of the Scribes and Pharisees. The persons

whom he mentions under the same name in his
commentary upon the ninth chapter, put as he
affirms, a similiar sense upon the first verses of
that: expounding the darkness and shadow of
death which overspread the land of Zabulon and
Naphtali, of the load of Pharisaical ceremonies
from which they were delivered by the gospel.
Certainly these persons mentioned by the same
name, as expounding passages so near to each
other in the 8th and 9th chapters of Isaiah so
much to the same purpose, were the same persons; and when St Jerome in his commentary
on the ninth chapter mentions " the Nazarenes,
whose opinion he had given above," he refers to
that opinion of the Nazarenes which he had actually related just above in his commentary on
the eighth chapter. But " the Hebrews believing in Christ," gave, according to St Jerome, an
exposition of this prophecy concerning the land
of Zabulon and Naphtali, very different from
that which is ascribed by him to the Nazarenes.
They imagined that the prophet in the miseries
which he describes of those northern provinces,
alluded to the miseries of the captivity which
they were the first to undergo; as in compensation they were the first who enjoyed the light of
our Lord's own preaching. What similitude can
Dr Priestley find between these two expositions?
What connexion between the miseries of the captivity and the load of Pharisaical ceremonies?

To say as Dr Priestley says, that the Nazaræan exposition was only " a farther illustration"* of this of the Hebrew Christians, is as if any one should say that Dr Priestley's exposition of the beginning of St John's gospel is only an illustration of mine.

Here then two different expositions of one and the same prophetic text are ascribed to expositors described under two different names. The necessary inference is, that these expositors differing in their names and in their sentiments, were different persons; or to speak more accurately, since they are names of bodies by which they are severally described, two different sects. This is St Jerome's evidence, that the Hebrews believing in Christ were different people from the Nazarenes.

Dr Priestley thinks it a presumptive argument that these Hebrew Christians were the same with the Nazarenes, and indeed with the Ebionites; that St Jerome introduces their interpretation of the prophecy, " after giving a translation of the passage by Aquila and Symmachus, both Ebionites."† Due regard being paid to this circumstance, Dr Priestley thinks this passage of St Je-

---

* Third Letters, p. 29.   † Ibid.

rome " furnishes an argument that in the idea of
Jerome" these Hebrews " were the very same
people" with the Nazarenes; " if it does not also
prove that their opinions were the same with
those of Aquila and Symmachus, or of the Ebionites."*

The fact however is, that these Hebrew
Christians, as it should seem from their exposition of the prophecy in this passage at least,
followed not the translation either of Aquila or
Symmachus, so far as we know what their translations of this passage were from the information which St Jerome hath given. The Hebrew
Christians took the word גליל to be the proper
name of the region of Galilee; whereas both
Aquila and Symmachus, as St Jerome tells us,
took it for an appellative. And this circumstance, their different interpretations of that
single word with Symmachus's interpretation of
another single word in the first verse, is all that
St Jerome hath " given" us of the translations of
this passage by Aquila and Symmachus; though
Dr Priestley hath thought proper to speak as if St
Jerome in his commentary had given their entire
translations of the prophecy, and would lead his
readers to believe that the exposition of the Hebrew Christians was founded on those translations.

---

* Third Letters, p. 29.

The probable argument that the Hebrew Christians were orthodox is this: that the character given of them by an orthodox writer is simply this, " that they believed in Christ," without any thing to distinguish their belief from the common belief of the church, without any note of its error or imperfection. This argument acquires great weight from the well known temper of St Jerome and his times.[*]

Dr Priestley thinks it " remarkable, that having before maintained that those whom Jerome called Christians in his epistle to Austin were orthodox, I should now allow that by the same term he here means heretics; and that the phrase *believing in Christ* should now be a character of complete orthodoxy, when in that epistle it is predicated of the heretical Ebionites."[†] I never maintained that the Nazarenes mentioned by St Jerome in his epistle to St Austin were orthodox Christians. I maintained the contrary.[‡] I only maintain, that upon the particular article of our Lord's divinity they were certainly orthodox; and so far as we know, in most other articles of their creed. But by their bigotted attachment to the law they were heretics. I have

---

[*] Remarks on Dr Priestley's Second Letters, P. II. chap. ii. see. 8.

[†] Third Letters, p. 26.   [‡] Charge I. sec. 12.

given my reasons* why I think the Nazarenes mentioned here a different set of people from the Nazarenes mentioned in the epistle to St Austin; and still less if at all heretical. Of the Ebio-nites, the belief in Christ is not predicated in that epistle simply, as here of the Hebrews, without any thing to distinguish their belief from the common belief of the church, without any note of its error or imperfection. St Jerome when he speaks of the belief of the Ebionites marks and reprobates their misbelief in the distinctest and severest terms. At this day the word *believer* in its common acceptation, signifies a sound Chris-tian. But with certain additions to qualify and restrain its meaning, I uncharitable and intole-rant as I am, might apply it even to Dr Priest-ley. But it would hardly be understood that by such an application of it I could mean to allow that Dr Priestley is a believer in the full sense of the word. It would certainly be in very differ-ent senses that I should apply this same word to Dr Priestley, and to the Dean of Canterbury, Professor White, or Mr Parkhurst.

If there be any thing in Dr Priestley's Let-ters which I receive with particular compla-

* Remarks on Dr Priestley's Second Letters, P. II. chap. iii. sec. 1.

cency, it is the kind concern which he sometimes discovers, lest in my heedless zeal to oppose his opinions I should suffer my own foot to
slip from the strait line of orthodoxy. In reply
to my reasoning for the orthodoxy of one branch
at least of the Nazarenes, from the exposition
ascribed to them by St Jerome of Isaiah viii. 13,
14,* by which it clearly appears that they
thought the Saviour of the world designed in
that passage by the title of יהוה צבאות, he tells
me that " he wonders that this mode of interpreting Scripture should not stagger even myself. *He* thought that the most orthodox of the
present day had believed that the person characterised by the title of the Lord of hosts had
been not the Son, but the Father."† So he
may have thought. That he hath so thought,
only proves that he is as little acquainted with
the orthodoxy of the present as of past days.
The orthodox of the present day well know
that the Son no less than the Father, is often
characterised in the Old Testament by the word
Jehovah put absolutely. They hold it one ir-
refragable argument of the Son's divinity, that
the writers of the New Testament usually mention Christ by the title of Κυριος, " the Lord ;"

---

* Remarks on Dr Priestley's Second Letters, P. II. chap. iii.
sec. 7.

† Third Letters, p. 34.

which is the word that throughout the Old Testament, in the Greek version of the LXX, is used as equivalent to the Hebrew Jehovah. Him whom the apostles and evangelists called Κυριος writing in the Greek, they must have called יהוה (Jehovah) had they written in the Hebrew language. The orthodox of the present day believe, because they know St John believed it, that Christ Jesus is the JEHOVAH whom the prophet Isaiah saw upon his throne the year that King Uzziah died, whose praises were the theme of the Seraphic Song, whose glory filled the temple.

The disturbed foundations of the church of Ælia are again settled. I could wish to trust them to their own solidity to withstand any future attacks. I could wish to take my final leave of this unpleasing task of hunting an uninformed uncandid adversary through the mazes of his blunders and the subterfuges of his sophistry. But I have found by the experience of this conflict, that a person once engaging in controversy is not entirely at liberty to choose for himself to what length he will carry the dispute, and when he will desist. I perceive that I was guilty of an indiscretion in discovering an early aversion to the continuance of the contest. My adversary perhaps would have been less hardy in assertion and more circumspect in

argument, had I not given him reason to expect that every assertion would pass uncontradicted, and every argument uncanvassed. Un-
ambitious therefore as I still remain of the honour of the last word, be it however understood,
that if Dr Priestley should think proper to make
any further defence or any new attack, I am not
pledged either to reply or to be silent.

APPENDIX.

Bishop Horsley has declared, that in publishing the preceding Tracts, his object was not to bring forward any new argument in support of the divinity of our Blessed Lord, or of the Catholic doctrine of the Trinity; but to destroy the credit of an author by whom these doctrines had been attacked, by showing that as an ecclesiastical historian and Greek scholar he had no claim to such deference as had been generally paid to him in the character of a chemical philosopher. That the Bishop has incidentally added strength to the arguments by which others had defended the Catholic doctrine against the insults of infidelity and the sophistry of Unitarianism, has been gratefully acknowledged indeed by every lover of the truth as it is in Jesus; but his *main object* was to show, that a man may have made valuable discoveries in physical science, without being entitled to implicit belief when professing to have made discoveries likewise in Christian theology.

To a superficial thinker this may appear an object unworthy of the talents and erudition which the Bishop is universally allowed to have possessed; but he who reflects how large a proportion of mankind are *implicit* believers, whether in the truth or in error, will view it in a different light. We talk much of the right of private judgment,—and we talk well; for every man has an unquestionable right to judge for himself of the truth or falsehood of what is proposed to his belief: But with respect to the questions discussed in this volume, the only judgment which the illiterate multitude can form, is, whose *report* is best entitled to be implicitly adopted by them as the truth. Their education does not enable them by consulting the records of Christian antiquity to discover for themselves what was the faith of the primitive church. They *must* rely therefore with unbounded confidence on the testimony of such as having consulted those records make their report of that faith; and they will always place, as they ought to place, the greatest confidence in those who appear to them best entitled to it, by their reputation for learning, integrity, and the love of truth.

Dr Priestley's natural talents were unquestionable; his successful experiments had raised him high in the republic of letters, or rather of philosophy; by those who were attached to him he was extolled for his kindness and benevolence; and he took care on all occasions to boast, that as his theological opinions led neither to honour nor to emolument, he was induced to publish them solely by his love of truth. That the mere name of such a man must have decided the faith of many cannot be doubted. The vulgar know not that the love of novelty, and the ambition of becoming the founder of a sect, which sometimes steals insensibly even into the most vigorous and upright minds, are as apt to pervert the judgment as the love of money or the ambition of rank. Nor is it among the vulgar only that the authority of names supplies too often the place of argument: Philosophers themselves are all more or less partial to their own pursuits and their own theories; and the chemist who is desirous to know what was the faith of the earliest Christians, and who has not leisure to read the voluminous writings of the fathers of the church, having found that Dr Priestley's reports of his own experiments on air are entitled to the fullest credit, even when his inferences from those experiments have been untenable and absurd, not unnaturally concludes that the same confidence may be placed in his reports of the doctrine of the early church.

Such being the case, it is of the utmost importance to the diffusion of truth that the authority of celebrated names be duly appreciated; and Bishop Horsley could not have employed his time or his talents to better purpose than in bringing down the name of Dr Priestley to its proper level. Since the first publication of the Tracts which are now offered a third time to the church of Christ, no man until very lately has presumed to boast of the weight of *Dr Priestley's name* in theological controversy; and thus has one bias been removed from the youthful mind when entering on the investigation of Catholic truth.

Of all this Mr Belsham appears to be fully aware; and therefore, in the appendix to the twelfth section of his late work entitled *A Calm Inquiry into the Scripture Doctrine concerning the Person of Christ*, he sets himself in good earnest to destroy the authority of Bishop Horsley's name, as his Lordship had destroyed the authority of Dr Priestley's. He probably thinks, that as one of those names sinks the other will rise, and that when the equipoise between the two shall be restored the *weight of his own name* thrown into the scale of Dr

Priestley's will instantly make the Bishop's kick the beam. With this view he lays hold of one or two passages, certainly not of the greatest importance to the question at issue between the Catholics and the Unitarians, but where he may most easily employ all the arts of modern controversy; and when by partial quotations and contemptuous language he imagines that he has thrown a sufficient quantity of dust into the eyes of his readers, he claims to himself what he will not allow to his Redeemer, the divine attribute of searching the heart; and declares, " that both the contending parties retired from the field *well satisfied* with the result of the conflict,—Dr Priestley with his VICTORY, and Dr Horsley with his MITRE."

Affecting after his master in theology a great reverence for the character of Origen, he begins his attack of Bishop Horsley with accusing him of defaming either ignorantly or wilfully that learned presbyter of the ancient church, for the purpose of falsifying history respecting the faith of the Hebrew Christians.

" Dr Priestley," he says, " having asserted upon the authority of Origen that the Jews who believed in Jesus were called Ebionites; that these Ebionites were of two sorts, one of them believing the miraculous conception, the other not, but all of them considering Christ as a mere man;[*] Dr Horsley in reply, after endeavouring to show that Origen's words might be interpreted differently, proceeds in a very triumphant tone to remark, " Let his words be taken as you understand them; *and so far as the faith of the Hebrew Christians of his own time is in question, let him appear as an evidence on your side.* I shall take what you may think a bold step; I shall tax the veracity of your witness—of this Origen."

This is part of a quotation from the seventh of Dr Horsley's Letters to Dr Priestley; but the clause which is here printed in the Italic character Mr Belsham has *prudently* omitted. The quotation proceeds to the end of the fifth section of that letter; to the whole of which the reader is requested to pay particular attention. If he comply with this request, he will find that in the four first sections, Dr Horsley has not only *endeavoured to show* that Origen's words might be differently interpreted, but *actually proved* that they will *not admit* of the sense in which Dr Priestley has chosen to interpret them. Convinced however of the goodness of his own cause, and knowing how little

---

[*] Belsham, p. 422.

Origen is to be relied on when writing controversy,. Dr Horsley made a concession to which
he could not have been driven, and which he
probably would not have made, could he have
foreseen the unfair advantage of it that was to
be taken by his adversaries. To deprive Mr
Belsham of that advantage in which he vain-
gloriously affects to triumph, it is proper to inform the reader, that in the quotation which
he has made from the Bishop's letter there is
another *prudent omission* of no fewer than *three
sentences* which all affect the question at issue
of Origen's veracity.

The object of the Bishop was to tax the veracity of Origen in what he says *only of the
faith of the Hebrew Christians of his own time;*
but the object of Mr Belsham seems to be to
charge the Bishop with taxing the veracity of
Origen *on every question.* He is probably aware
that Origen being strongly attached to the philosophy of his age, which led her votaries to
contend in controversy for victory rather than
for truth, might readily be believed to have asserted a falsehood in answer to the invective
which his antagonist had put into the mouth
of a Jew; but he is aware at the same time,
that the character of Origen stands so high in
the learned world, that he who should charge
him with disregard to *truth in general* would

excite against himself the indignation of every
man of letters. Whether all this occurred to
Mr Belsham's mind, and induced him to omit
the sentences to which I allude, is unknown to
me, who possess not the faculty of discerning
the secrets of other men's hearts; but he could
not have acted otherwise than he has done, if
it *had* occurred to him *and influenced his conduct.*

If the reader has turned to the fifth section
of the Bishop's seventh Letter to Dr Priestley,
he has found him modestly saying, " All this I
affirm with the less hesitation, being *supported*
by the authority of Mosheim; from *whom* indeed *I first learned* to rate the testimony of
Origen *in this particular question* at its true
value."

This sentence Mr Belsham has *not* omitted;
but he draws from it an inference which by all
the arts of controversy it cannot be made to
support. " One would conclude," says he,
" from the manner in which Dr Horsley appeals
to the testimony of Mosheim, that having first
from his own extensive researches into ecclesiastical history made this notable discovery of a
church at Ælia, he was confirmed in his judgment by finding that Mosheim had also made
the same discovery. *But the truth is, that the*

learned dignitary, *placing implicit confidence* in Mosheim's testimony, having borrowed all the circumstances related by that celebrated historian, and mixed up a little of his own, has stated with great parade and as an incontrovertible fact a narrative most improbable in itself, and utterly destitute of foundation in ecclesiastical antiquity."*

I have been told by a learned friend of mine much conversant in works on the laws of reasoning, that Mr Belsham published some years ago a *Compendium of Logic*, remarkable for such definitions as the world had never before seen. It must be by the aid of such definitions that one would *artificially* conclude from the manner in which Bishop Horsley appeals to the testimony of Mosheim, that he had first by his own researches discovered a church of Jewish Christians at Ælia, and was afterwards confirmed in his judgment by finding that Mosheim had made the same discovery before him; for by the laws of such logic as is known in the schools, a conclusion directly contrary to this must *naturally* be made from the Bishop's words. He says expressly, " that it was from Mosheim *that he first learned* to rate the testi-

---

* Belsham, p. 423.

mony of Origen *in this particular question* at its true value;" and though he was a greater master than most men both of the Aristotelian and of the Baconian logic, I am persuaded that he could not have conceived it possible to draw from his own words such a conclusion as Mr Belsham has drawn from them.

With respect to what the same original logician here calls *the truth,* I can only say that it was not Bishop Horsley's practice to put *implicit confidence* in any uninspired testimony; but I cannot affirm as an *unquestionable truth* that on this occasion he did not deviate from his usual practice. What that practice was, no man not possessing the faculty of discerning the secrets of his neighbour's heart could have better opportunities of knowing than I enjoyed; and although I may not have derived from them all the advantages which I might and ought to have done, yet I was sufficiently attentive to the Bishop's mode of investigating the truth, to be able to say that it was exactly what to ordinary readers his words declare it to have been on this particular occasion. When he found any thing of importance asserted by a modern writer on ancient authority, far from placing implicit confidence in the modern *testimony,* he did not rely even on modern *criticism;* nor had he ever recourse to an English

or French translation of a Greek or Latin author of antiquity, as is the common practice of
the most arrogant polemics of the Unitarian
school: It was Bishop Horsley's practice to
consult the authorities referred to with his own
eyes, and to draw from them whatever conclusion his own reason and critical sagacity enabled him to draw; though, not deeming himself infallible, he was happy, as every man not
lost to all sense of modesty would be, to have
his own judgment *supported* by the concurrence
of a scholar so eminent as Mosheim.

But says Mr Belsham, " the learned dignitary,
placing implicit confidence in Mosheim, borrowed all the circumstances related by that celebrated historian, and *mixed up* (with them) *a little of his own*." At the distance of two pages
indeed, the same Mr Belsham, after representing a *very common book* as not easily to be met
with in England, affirms that the Bishop had
in fact advanced *nothing* but what he had borrowed from Mosheim. Both these assertions
cannot be true. Whether either of them be
entitled to the fullest credit, the reader will
judge for himself when he has read with attention the first and second chapters of the second
part of the Bishop's Remarks on Dr Priestley's
Second Letters to the Archdeacon of St Alban's,

and compared them with the following extract from Mosheim's work.

"Quum HADRIANUS Hierosolymam ex cineribus suis paullatim renascentem denuo funditus evertisset, severasque in Judaicam gentem leges tulisset, maxima Christianorum in Palæstina degentium pars a lege Mosis, cui antea paruerat, desciscebat, atque antistitem sibi MARCUM creabat, non Judæum, sed alienigenam, quo nihil sibi cum Judæis commune esse doceret. Quod factum indigne ferentes illi, qui Mosaicæ legis immoderato studio ducebantur, secedebant a fratribus, atque in illa Palæstinæ parte quæ Peræa dicebatur, vicinisque locis peculiarem cœtum condebant, in quo cærimoniis a MOSE præscriptis vetus sua dignitas incolumis manebat. Familia hæc, exigua sine dubio, claritatem nusquam adepta est, quumque per aliquot sæcula in Palæstina vixisset, post CONSTANTINUM M. paullatim esse desiit."

To this passage, which is part of the text of his work entitled *De Rebus Christianorum ante Constantinum Magnum Commentarii*, Mosheim subjoins the following important note.

" Eximius est hac de re SULPITII SEVERI locus Histor sacr. Lib. II. cap. xxxi. p. 245. *Et quia Christiani* (in Palæstina viventes) *ex Judæis potissimum putabantur (namque tum Hierosolymæ non*

*nisi ex circumcisione habebat ecclesia sacerdotem)
militum cohortem custodias in perpetuum agitare jus-
sit, quæ Judæos omnes Hierosolymæ aditu arceret.
Quod quidem Christianæ fidei proficiebat ; quia tum
pæne omnes Christum Deum sub legis observatione
credebant. Nimirum id Domino ordinante disposi-
tum, ut legis servitus a libertate fidei atque ecclesiæ
tolleretur. Ita tum primum Marcus ex gentibus
apud Hierosolymam episcopus fuit."*

This is the passage which furnishes the basis of
Bishop Horsley's reasoning in that part of the preceding Tracts to which we have immediately referred ; and it is on the same passage that Mosheim makes the following observations.

" Etsi nec lucis, nec ordinis satis habet hic
Sulpitii locus, clare tamen origines ostendit illius
inter Christianos ecclesiæ, quæ Christum ita sibi
colendum esse censuit, ut Mosis tamen legibus
simul obtemperaret. Constat enim (I) ex eo
Christianos in Palæstina viventes Judaici generis,
quamdiu spes erat, fore, ut Hierosolyma post primum excidium instauraretur, ritus a Mose impe-
ratos cum Christi cultu conjunxisse. (II) Repu-
diasse maximam partem horum Christianorum legem Mosaicam sub Hadriano quum spes omnis,
fore, ut Hierosolyma resurgeret, occidisset, atque
Marcum, alienigenam, episcopum elegisse. Hoc
ideo sine dubio fiebat, ne forte episcopus gente

Hebræus, innato patriæ leges amore ductus, abro-
gatas cærimonias paullatim reduceret. (III). Causam sublatæ hos inter Christianos legis Mosaicæ
fuisse HADRIANI, Imperatoris, severitatem, qui mi-
lite cingebat spatium, quod urbs Hierosolyma
quondam occupaverat, omnesque Judæos ab ejus
aditu cohiberi jubebat. In hac re explicanda minus est, quam decebat, perspicuus et luculentus
SULPITIUS, multaque retinet animo, quæ rectius
enuntiasset. At liquet tamen in universum, quid
sibi velit, nec difficile est addere, quæ omissa sunt
ab eo. Christiani Palæstinæ quamdiu legi Mosaicæ serviebant, a Romanis pro Judæis habeban-
tur: nec temere prorsus. HADRIANUS igitur quum
Judæis aditum ad loca, quæ Hieorosolyma quondam occupaverat, occlusisset, Christianis pariter
non licebat ad illud spatium accedere. Atqui
Christiani hi facultatem sibi dari cum maxime cupiebant Hierosolymam proficiscendi, quum vellent.
Ea ergo ut potirentur, cærimonias legis Mosaicæ
dimittebant, atque, ne Romani dubitarent, seriose
hoc fecissent, an simulatæ, gubernationem cœtus
sui non Judæo, sed alienigenæ, committebant.
Post hoc apertum cum lege Judæorum divortium,
patiebantur eos Romani regionem illam ingredi, a
cujus aditu milites Judæos arcere jussi erant.
Hæc omnia ex SULPITIO, valde licet negligenter
scribat, mediocri attentione adhibita eliciuntur."

Mosheim then inquires into what was probably

the motive which induced the greater part of the
Jewish Christians to cherish so strong a desire to
return to Jerusalem, as, for the attainment of that
object, to abandon the laws and rites of their fathers. After stating several possible motives, and
rejecting them all as in the highest degree improbable, he says,

" Alia ergo sine dubio his Christianis ratio fuit,
cur facultatem Hierosolymam adeundi majorem
patriis suis cærimoniis et institutis esse, putarent,
atque illam legis Mosaicæ contentione redimere
non dubitarent. Neque magno, ut opinor, labore
opus erat ad eam investigandam. Construxerat
HADRIANUS non longe ab illo loco, quo steterat
Hierosolyma, novam urbem, cui *Æliæ Capitolinæ*
nomen dederat, quamque magnis juribus donaverat.
Huic novæ coloniæ adscribi valde cupiebant Christiani, qui partim Pellæ, exiguo oppido, partim in
agris, parum commode et liberaliter vivebant.
Excluserat vero Imperator a nova urbe sua gentem Judaicam ; cujus portio quum Christiani esse
viderentur, qui legi Mosaicæ obediebant, ad eos
quoque lex HADRIANI de Judæis non in civitatem
recipiendis pertinebat. Quocirca maxima eorum
pars, quo jus civitatis Æliæ consequi, domicilium-
que suum Pella Æliam transferre libere posset,
cærimoniarum legem a MOSE præscriptam abro-
gabat. Auctor hujus consilii, quod in primis ve-
risimile est, is ipse MARCUS erat, quem episcopum

sibi præficiebant, homo, quod nomen docet, Romanus et sine dubio Romanis in Palæstina do-
minantibus non ignotus, forte principem quem-
dam inter Romanos virum cognatione attingens.
Suæ igitur gentis hominem quum caput Christianorum præfecti Romanorum viderent, timeri
desinebant, ne quid novæ civitati periculi ex
Christianis oriretur, neque amplius Judæorum eos
numen habebant : ex quo consequebatur, ut fa-
cultas illis concederetur, in novam Imperatoris
urbem migrandi et civium ejus juribus, quæ exi-
mia erant, fruendi.   Nihil est in his difficile cre-
ditu : omnia vero egregie ex eo, quod diserte
scriptum legitur apud EPIPHANIUM *de ponderi-*
bus et mensuris § XV. p. 171. confirmantur, Christianos, lege Judaica dimissa, Pella Hierosolymam migrasse.   Hierosolymæ vero nomine nova
HADRIANI urbs intelligi debet, quæ post CON-
STANTINI M. ætatem verum nomen suum amitte-
bat et Hierosolyma vocabatur. Vid. HENR. VALE-
SIUS *Adnot. ad Eusebium,* p. 61.   Quamquam si
vel hoc memoriæ non esset proditum, omni tamen
vacaret controversia. Certissimum enim est, Æ-
liæ Christianorum ab HADRIANI jam ætate cele-
brem extitisse ecclesiam, atque episcopos, qui vul-
go Hierosolymitani nominantur, Ælienses revera
fuisse."

" Non addit SULPITIUS, cujus locum illustra-
mus, non omnes Christianos in Judæa viventes

insignem hanc mutationem, probasse, verum partem eorum legis Mosaicæ studium retinuisse, atque a societate eorum, qui legi nuntium miserant, recessisse. Sed nec opus erat, ut hoc adderet, quum in vulgus notum esset. Extitisse in Palæstina cœtum Christianorum legis cultum cum Christiana religione conjungentium, alium item cœtum Mosaicis cærimoniis nihil loci et honoris tribuentem, testatissimum est. Divisio hæc Christianorum ex Judæis ortorum non contigit ante tempora HADRIANI; scimus enim, ante hunc omnes Christianos in Palæstina commorantes in servandis majorum cærimoniis concordes fuisse. Quocirca sine dubio discidium hoc tum extitit, quum, duce MARCO, sub HADRIANO plerique eorum jugum rituum abjicerent, quo securius vivere, atque inter cives novæ urbis, Æliæ Capitolinæ, recipi possent."

The reader who attentively compares this long extract with those parts of the preceding Tracts to which I have already referred as relating to the same subject, will perceive with what *justice* Mr Belsham charges Bishop Horsley with the intention of passing off Mosheim's discoveries for his own, presuming upon security from detection by the scarcity of Mosheim's book. He will likewise perceive the *modesty* of Mr Belsham, when he affirms that the Bishop was " nothing more than the humble, and we may charitably hope the *ignorant* plagiary of the falsehood and defamation of another."* Bishop Horsley ignorant, and Mr Belsham learned!

The Bishop must have been ignorant indeed if he presumed on the *scarcity* of Mosheim's book entitled *De Rebus Christianorum ante Constantinum Magnum Commentarii*; for though I brought it not with me into Scotland, I found it in the libraries of the two first clergymen to whom I applied for the loan of it. But what detection had the Bishop to dread? He expressly declared that Mosheim first pointed out to him the ground over which he afterwards travelled, and taught him to rate the veracity of Origen on a particular question at its true value. He boasts of no discoveries of his own, nor attempts to defraud Mosheim of his. He consulted the same ancient authors which had been consulted by Mosheim before him, and by Cave before Mosheim; and as a lover of truth he could not pass them by without examination. But though from the facts recorded by Sulpitius and Epiphanius he draws most of the conclusions which had been drawn by his learned predecessors in this investigation, he does not infer from these facts every thing which Mosheim had inferred from them. In a passage of that

* Belsham, p. 427.

historian's long note which I thought it not worth while to transcribe, he says that "without doubt Marc the Roman bishop of the church of Hebrew Christians at Ælia demonstrated to those Christians, before they left Pella, that the ritual law of Moses was abolished by Christ." This seems to have been said, I know not on what authority, with the view of vindicating the Hebrew Christians from the charge that might otherwise be brought against them of having abandoned the customs of their ancestors from mere worldly motives. Mosheim has not the smallest doubt but that the arguments of Marc amounted to demonstration. "Minus vero (he adds) argumenta ejus valuissent apud homines a teneris legi Mosaicæ adsuetos, nisi desiderium accessisset ad ea Æliæ habitandi, civiumque ejus commoditatibus et juribus fruendi," &c. *

Bishop Horsley, though he professedly goes over the same ground with the justly celebrated Chancellor of the university of Gottingen, does not with him attribute the merit of weaning the affections of the Hebrew Christians from the ritual law of Moses to this Bishop Marc; but to the writings of St Paul, and the decree of the apos-

---

* Mosh. De Reb. Chris. Ant. Con. Mag. Com. § XXXVIII. p. 327.

tolical college, which, as he justly observes, must have put every believer's conscience at ease on the subject. He admits however that the desire of enjoying the benefits of the Ælian colony would have its effect. " I take it for granted (says he) that with good Christians motives of worldly interest which would not overcome conscience would nevertheless overcome mere habit;"* and this he might surely take for granted in the present case, since the most important parts of the ritual law to which the Christians at Pella were *habitually* attached, the severity and vigilance of Adrian had rendered it impossible for them to observe. Sacrifices could be offered only on the site of the temple, of which Titus had ploughed up the very foundations; but the site of the temple was by Adrian's command surrounded by a cohort of soldiers, stationed there for the very purpose of driving away every person who should approach it with the view of offering sacrifice.

In confirmation of the inferences drawn from the narrative of Sulpitius Severus, Bishop Horsley appeals to the same passage in the writings of Epiphanius to which Mosheim had appealed before him; but he does what Mosheim did not

---

* See Remarks upon Dr Priestley's Second Letters, Part II. chap. ii.

do: He analyses that passage; · vindicates it against the cavils of Dr Priestley; shows the full force of the evidence which Epiphanius in conjunction with Sulpitius affords for the existence of a church of Hebrew Christians at Ælia; and the testimony of these two ancient authors he confirms by the testimony of Orosius and of Jerome, to neither of whom Mosheim had made any appeal. He was not therefore a mere humble and ignorant plagiary of the German historian; but surely his inferences from the united testimony of three or four ancient authors cannot be entitled to the less regard for their being nearly the same which other men of such learning as Mosheim and Cave had drawn before him.

The perversion of the sense of the Bishop's words in some parts of his disquisitions on this subject, by Mr Belsham, who represents him as TAKING EVERY THING FOR GRANTED, because he occasionally makes use of that phrase where there is no room for difference of opinion, is scandalous, because it must have been wilful. It can deceive no man however who will take the trouble to have recourse to the Bishop's Tracts in order to discover what he *really* took for granted; though the humble Unitarians, who place implicit confidence in Mr Belsham, may take it for granted, on his report, that the editor of the works of

Newton knew nothing of the laws of reasoning or of demonstration.

But, according to Mr Belsham, the reasonings and criticisms of Bishop Horsley can derive little support from their coincidence with those of Mosheim. " This migration of the Hebrew Christians from Pella to Ælia is stated, says he, by Mosheim in his Ante-Constantine History; but upon *more mature reflection and better information*, it had been omitted in the General Ecclesiastical History, which alone Dr Priestley had consulted.[*]

This is an assertion at least as precipitate as any that Dr Priestley himself ever hazarded. As I have not in this remote corner access to the *first edition* of what Mr Belsham calls the *General Ecclesiastical History*, I cannot say with confidence in what year it was first published; but I know from the testimony of Mosheim himself now lying before me, that the work entitled *De Rebus Christianorum ante Constantinum Magnum Commentarii*, which suggested to Bishop Horsley what he has said of the church at Ælia, was *first* published in the end of the year 1753; the preface and the dedication being both dated at Gottingen, on the 6th day of September in that year.

---

[*] Belsham, p. 435.

I knew from the same testimony that Mosheim employed *two years* on his *General Ecclesiastical History;*[*] and Dr Maclaine, the learned translator of that history, informs us[†] that the author died at Gottingen in the year 1755. The General History therefore must have been *begun* the instant that the other work was published; so that there could not have been time for much *mature reflection* or the acquisition of *better information* between the publication of the one work and the commencement of the other; even on the supposition that the General History was first published *after* the other,—a fact of which I am very far from being certain.

It was indeed published many years after the *Institutiones Historiæ Christianæ Majores;* and as that work is bound up in the same volume with the edition of the *De Rebus Christianorum ante Constantinum Magnum Commentarii* now lying before me, I think it not improbable that Mr Belsham, with the usual heedlessness of his master, has looked at the date affixed to the first work in the volume, when he should have looked at the date of the second; and finding the former dated IV. Kalend. Octobr. 1739, hazarded the assertion

---

[*] See his Preface to that History.
[†] See his Preface.

that Mosheim after *mature reflection* and *better information* had omitted in his *General History* a detail which he had published in his Commentaries.

But has he omitted this detail in his larger history? No; he has given the detail as fully as was possible in such a work,[*] and refers, as he had done in his Commentaries, to Sulpitius and Epiphanius as his authors; but he has omitted the critical disquisition on the words of Sulpitius which in the Commentaries was published in a long note, too long to be inserted in a compendium of general history. He probably thought indeed that there was no occasion for such a disquisition; for Dr Priestley had not then appeared; and before him I am not aware that any writer of name had called in question the existence of a church of orthodox Hebrew Christians at Jerusalem, though many were ignorant that what was called Jerusalem was in fact Ælia.

I have already observed that the Bishop vindicated the united testimony of Sulpitius and Epiphanius against the cavils of Dr Priestley. The cavils to which I more particularly alluded refer chiefly to Epiphanius, and were founded in chro-

---

[*] See Maclaine's translation of Mosheim's Eccles. Histor. Cent. II. Part I. chap. I. § XI; and Part II. chap. V. § I. &c.

nological difficulties; but they are revived by Mr
Belsham, and brought into view in the following
triumphant manner.

" The FACT is, and the Archdeacon does not
deny it, that the desolation of Jerusalem of which
Epiphanius speaks, was that by Titus, A. D. 70,
MORE THAN SIXTY YEARS BEFORE THE COLONY OF
ÆLIA EXISTED. ' But this, says the learned dignitary, is a matter of no importance: It is sufficient for my purpose that these returned Christians were residing at Jerusalem, or more properly at Ælia, at the same time that Aquila resided
there as overseer of the Emperor's works.' So
then, we are now to believe that these Hebrew
Christians, who returned in great numbers to
Ælia after Adrian's settlement of the Ælian colony, who abandoned the rites of Moses, and
placed themselves under a Greek bishop (a Roman bishop), and worshipped in an unknown
tongue,* that they might be qualified to par-

---

* Why in an unknown tongue? Has Mr Belsham forgotten
that Greek, Latin, and the dialect of Hebrew which was then
vernacular, were all spoken by every man of learning, whether
Jew or Roman, who had been for any time resident in Judea?
During the trial (if trial it may be called) of our Saviour before Pilate, we never hear of the governor making use of an interpreter; and may not Marc the bishop have been as much
master of Hebrew as Pilate the governor? Nay, may not the
Hebrew Christians from their long residence among the Gen-

take of the valuable privileges of the Ælian colony, *were the very same persons who had quit-*
ted Jerusalem to avoid the calamities of the
siege by Titus SIXTY YEARS before! Now if we
allow that at the time of their retreat they were
upon an average twenty years of age, they must
have been fourscore at the time of their return.
And it is really quite edifying to figure to one's
self these illustrious Octogenaries, ' *our holy
brethren the saints of the primitive church of
Jerusalem,*' upon the first intelligence of the
good news, hasting away from Pella and the
North of Galilee, where they had been passing threescore years in obscurity and tranquillity, and in heroic defiance of the most inveterate attachments, and of the habits and prejudices of fourscore, abandoning at once the rites
of their forefathers, and the *forms* and even
the *language* of the devotions to which they

---

tiles at Pella have acquired such a knowledge of the Greek
tongue as enabled them to read the whole New Testament in
that language, in which by far the greater part of it was written, as well as to bear their part in the same language in the
public devotions of the church? I am unwilling to charge a
man probably much older than myself with ignorance; but
what Mr Belsham says of abandoning *the forms of public worship* to which the Hebrew Christians had been accustomed,
would lead one to imagine that he is not aware that in the primitive church every diocese had its own liturgy, the mere *forms*
of which were liable to be altered by every bishop in succession
according to his own taste and judgment.

had been ever accustomed,—in order to obtain
what?—the valuable privileges and immunities
of the Ælian colony! And how gratifying must
it be to every pious mind to learn, upon the
high authority of Epiphanius, that after all the
fatigues and hazards of their journey, they
were still in a flourishing state, teaching and
working miracles with great effect, at the time
when Aquila, who was converted by them, was
superintendant of Adrian's works!"*

Whether Mr Belsham was restrained by any
prudential motive from making these observations on the reasoning of Bishop Horsley during that prelate's life is probably known to
Mr Belsham himself; but I will venture to assure him that the Bishop, were he now alive
and possessed of all his youthful ardour, would
not deign to take the smallest notice of them.
Even I, however inferior to him, will not condescend to make a *serious* reply to such a tis-
sue of petulance and absurdity. I think it but
fair however to observe, that Mr Belsham has
not employed this mode of *reasoning* so successfully as he might have employed it in confirmation of his favourite doctrine of Unitarianism; and to convince him that I have a great-

---

* Belsham, p. 435.

er regard for the truth than even for the memory of my ever-honoured father, I will here supply what he has so strangely omitted.

In the year 1682 the English Unitarians expressed a strong desire to convert the Mahometans to their creed of Christianity; and with that view presented an address on the subject to the Ambassador of the Emperor of Morocco, who refused to receive it.* About the same period, the English Unitarians distributed *gratis* among the people an immense number of pamphlets, printed on a public stook, of which one object was to prove that the Scriptures of the New Testament had been interpolated by the Trinitarians to support their own doctrines.† When they were performing these notable exploits, the English Unitarians cannot on an average have been less than twenty years of age; and yet we find the *very same persons*, the English Unitarians, a full century afterwards doing the very same things,—publishing Unitarian pamphlets by subscription,‡ expressing the same earnest desire for the conversion of Mahomet,§ and accusing the Catholics of

---

* See Bishop Horsley's sixteenth letter to Dr Priestley.
† See Pref. to Leslie's Sos. Cont. Discussed.
‡ See Dr Priestley's Memoirs of himself.
§ See Dr Priestley's History of the Corruptions of Christianity, and the first series of his Letters to Dr Horsley.

having wilfully interpolated the Greek Scriptures.* True indeed it is that they had so completely forgotten their address to " His Illustrious Excellency AMETH BEN AMETH, Ambassador of the Mighty Emperor of *Fez* and *Morocco*, to Charles the Second, King of Great Britain," that in the year 1784 they denied that such an address had ever existed.† This however was not wonderful in men a *hundred and twenty-two years old;* for the memory is the faculty which generally decays first through age. But it is really quite edifying to see with what condescension these aged Unitarians have adapted their style to the varying tastes of the several generations that have passed away since they addressed AMETH BEN AMETH; and how gratifying must it be to every lover of the *truth* to learn, on the high authority of the *New Testament in an improved version, with a corrected text, and notes critical and explanatory,* that these Unitarians have retained all their other faculties in such perfection as to be able, when no less than one hundred and thirty-eight years old, to perform what they ventured not to promise in their youth: They have now expunged from the Chris-

---

* See the writings of the Unitarians in general, and of Mr Belsham in particular, since the commencement of the nineteenth century.

† See the fifteenth of Dr Priestley's second series of Letters to Dr Horsley.

tian Scriptures the Trinitarian interpolations, and brought those Scriptures to teach that faith which in their address to the Morocco Ambassador they say God had raised up Mahomet to defend with the sword. If the Trinitarians be of opinion that the preservation of their *holy brethren the saints of the primitive church of Jerusalem* in so flourishing a state as at the age of eighty to be able to teach with great effect, be any proof of the Catholic doctrine (and if this be not the opinion of the Trinitarians, it is not easy to conceive for what purpose a calculation was made by Mr Belsham of the age of their holy brethren), how much stronger is the proof of the Unitarian doctrine from the preservation of the fellow-worshippers with the Ambassador of Morocco, in a state so flourishing as at the more advanced age of ONE HUNDRED AND THIRTY-EIGHT to be able to correct the ORACLES of GOD with great effect!

If the extract which I have made from Mr Belsham's *confutation* of Bishop Horsley be of any importance in the Unitarian controversy, this addition which I have proposed to it is of so much greater importance, that I really expect Mr Belsham's thanks for having suggested it. If its effect go to prove that there could be no English Unitarians in the reign both of Charles the Second and of George the Third, then has Mr Belsham succeeded in proving

that there could be no church of Hebrew
Christians at Pella in the reign of Titus, and
afterwards at Ælia in the reign of Adrian! Or
should it be impossible, as I think it is, to
deny that there were English Unitarians in the
reign of Charles the Second, then, though it
must be granted that there were likewise Hebrew Christians at Ælia under a Roman bishop in the reign of Adrian, I have at least
deprived the Trinitarians of the argument which
they might draw for the truth of their doctrine
from the miraculous preservation of their orthodox Octogenaries, and have transferred that argument in all its force to the English Unitarians of the nineteenth century.

Of the remainder of Mr Belsham's arguments
against Mosheim and the Bishop, I confess that
I can make nothing. He goes over the same
ground with Dr Priestley, from whom he occasionally differs; but these differences certainly
add nothing to the force of the Doctor's original reasoning. He contrives however to weak-
en the Bishop's by making him occasionally say
what he has *not* said, and quoting *partially*
what he *has* said; and upon those implicit believers the Unitarians, this will have as good
an effect as if he had raised the conjectures
and arguments of Dr Priestley to the height

of demonstration. To such however, whether Trinitarians or Unitarians, as do not repose im-plicit confidence in Mr Belsham, I have only to recommend the old adage *audi alteram partem ;* and if they pay attention to it, I am under no apprehension of injury to my father's fair fame from this rude attack, even in the judgment of candid Unitarians.

The man who can burlesque the Scriptures for the purpose of turning into ridicule argu-ments which he does not fairly state, and can-not answer, is not I hope likely *long* to *retain* implicit credit with serious Christians of any denomination.

" Whether the easy simplicity," he says, " of the Roman magistrates was really imposed upon by the specious artifices of our ' holy brethren,'— or whether their good-nature, at the hazard of incurring the Emperor's displeasure, winked at the pious frauds,—or finally, since by the testi-mony of the Bishop's great authority, St Epi-phanius, miracles had not yet ceased in the Je-rusalem church, whether *their eyes might not be holden so that they did not know them,*—does not appear."*

---

* Belsham, p. 437.

To the admirers of the *improved version of the New Testament* this may for aught that I know to the contrary, appear genuine wit and sound reasoning against the *possibility* of such a church of Hebrew Christians as the Bishop contends for, enjoying the privileges of the Ælian colony; but those who do not admire that version will probably consider such a ludicrous application of one of the proofs of Christ's resurrection as a mere subterfuge,— nay, as a profane artifice for withholding the reader's attention from arguments which Mr Belsham is conscious that he could not have answered.

But says Mr Belsham in the words of his master, " My Lord——the foundations of your church of Trinitarian Jews at Jerusalem (Ælia) after the time of Adrian, were attempted to be laid on the grossest calumny, and on the ruins of the fairest character that Christian history has to exhibit; and therefore they could expect no better fate, than to be overturned for ever."*

Foundations laid in this manner certainly *deserve* no better fate than to be " overturned for ever;" but how comes Origen to be such a

* Belsham, p. 439.

favourite with the present race of Unitarians
that his character should be deemed fairer than
the character even of Christ Jesus? According
to the creed of Dr Priestley and Mr Belsham
Jesus and Origen were both men, and nothing
more than men; the characters of both are exhibited in Christian history; and here we are
solemnly told that the character of Origen is the
fairest which that history has to exhibit! That
Origen was a man of great talents and of most
extensive erudition is universally admitted; but
that he asserted at one time the very reverse of
what he had taught at another, and was in controversy more earnest to vanquish his antagonist
than to maintain the truth, without being very
scrupulous about the means by which the victory was to be gained, is known to all who
know any thing of his writings. Of all this
Bishop Horsley has given specimens from his
works, and I shall add another from Dr Cave,
because Cave was one of his most learned and
ardent admirers, and has made perhaps the
best apology possible for his tergiversation in
controversy.

" Whilst Origen continued at Athens (which
was not long) he returned an answer to a letter which he had received from *Julius Africanus* concerning the history of Susanna, which
Africanus, by short but very forcible argu-

ments* maintained to be a fictitious and spurious relation. Origen undertook the case, and justified the story to be sincere and genuine, but by arguments which rather manifest the acuteness of his parts than *the goodness of his cause;* and clearly show how much men of the greatest learning and abilities are put to it when engaged to uphold a weak side, *which has no truth of its own to support it.*"†

The learned biographer attributes this disregard of truth in controversy to Origen's delight in argument, which led him according to his apologist in Photius to write and say many things γυμνασίας χαίρειν which in his cooler and more considering moments he would not have advanced; and this again he attributes to the natural ardour of his mind impelling him to write on a variety of subjects *which he had not thoroughly studied,* ‡ and to his attachment to the philosophy of his age, of which the very essence was the spirit of disputation. Of any thing more than this Bishop Horsley has not accused Ori-

---

* The substance of these arguments which are indeed unanswerable, may be seen in Cave's *Historia Literaria*, in the short biographical account of Julius Africanus.

† Cave's Lives of the Fathers, fourth edition, folio, p. 159.

‡ Was it for this conduct that Dr Priestley considered the character of Origen as the fairest that Christian history has to exhibit? It is conduct in which he himself certainly imitated the learned and ingenious presbyter of Alexandria.

gen.—He has not insinuated that he would not have been entitled to at least as much credit as either Sulpitius, Epiphanius, or Jerome, had he like them been coolly writing history or criticisms on the Old Testament; but the Bishop has accused him of misrepresenting facts through design or inattention when writing controversy; and I am afraid that such an accusation might be brought against zealous controvertists in every age.

Thus Dr Buchanan in his zeal, a laudable zeal certainly, to have Christian missionaries sent into our dominions in the East, has said in some of his late writings that missionaries of all denominations live in perfect harmony with each other in India, and know not those distinctions which are the sources of dissension among Christians in Europe. Nay, he says that even the distinctions between Papists and Protestants are in the East considered as sectarian; the only controversy there being between the true God and an idol. Others again who have come from India as well as he, who have had the same opportunities of making observations, and of whose zeal for religion there appears to be no room for doubt, give a very different account of the light in which the various missionaries view one another in the East; and represent the preaching

of unsent enthusiasts as in the highest degree prejudicial to the propagation of genuine
Christianity. Which of these accounts are we
to believe? Probably neither of them to its full
extent; for the authors of both have each a
favourite object in view, as Origen had in his
controversy with Celsus; and these objects have
got such complete possession of their respective·
minds as to make them view through different
mediums the very same matters of fact, or overlook those facts entirely. That ·the distinction
between Papists and Protestants is well known
in the East, and deemed of great importance,·
Dr Buchanan himself has furnished complete
proof in the account which he gives of the
Syrian Christians ;* though, like Origen in his
book against Celsus, he has expressed himself
so very differently within the compass of one
small volume.

Even Mr Belsham himself is not free from this
weakness to which controvertists of every description are indeed very liable. Though I am as
far from suspecting him of a disregard to truth in
general, as my father was of suspecting Origen
of such a disregard, it is impossible to doubt but
that in the heat of controversy he has, through
inattention no doubt, asserted at least one false-

---

* See his Christian Researches in Asia.

hood as notorious as that of which the Bishop accused Origen. In his zeal to degrade the Son of God from the dignity of the Creator to the rank of a mere man in the creation, he finds the epithet μονογενης, which is applied to him by St John so much in his way, that to get rid of it, he supposes it to be employed by that apostle in no other sense than as equivalent to αγαπητος, which he boldly affirms does *not occur in St John.* As he is one of the authors of the improved version we cannot suspect him of having never read the original, or of having read it with so little attention as to have totally overlooked any thing of importance which it contains. We can only suppose that his mind was so completely occupied by the object of the controversy in which he was engaged with the celebrated Dr Clarke, as to make him lose sight at the instant of at least six different sentences in which St John employs the word αγαπητος in the sense in which it is commonly employed by other Greek writers.*

---

* See the British Critic for January 1812, to which I am indebted for pointing out to me this blunder, as Mosheim pointed out to my father the passages in Sulpitius and Epiphanius. I hope however that even Mr Belsham will give me credit for having consulted my Greek Testament myself, though I admit that it is at least as probable that I should have relied with implicit confidence on the British Critic as that Bishop Horsley relied with implicit confidence on the Chancellor of the University of Gottingen.

Having discussed the questions agitated by Mr Belsham concerning the veracity of Origen and the existence of a church of Jewish Christians at Ælia, the question respecting the æra of the epistle of Barnabas, the only thing remaining on which he has chosen to enter the lists with Bishop Horsley, will be easily disposed of.

Whoever has paid to the Bishop's Tracts that attention, to which the questions discussed in them have so powerful a claim from every Christian, must be aware that the epistle of Barnabas was quoted merely as evidence of the faith of the first Hebrew Christians; and until I met with Mr Belsham's book I did not think it possible that any man could have insinuated that the Bishop had attributed to that epistle any authority to which even an apocryphal book written with no obviously wicked intention may not be justly entitled. Mr Belsham does not *directly* charge him with having attributed to it any undue authority; but the manner in which he labours to set aside its evidence, must lead the unthinking multitude who have never looked into the Bishop's Tracts, to imagine that he considers it as the work of an inspired apostle.

" The venerable Archdeacon (says Mr Bel-

sham) having pledged himself to prove that
the divinity of our Lord was the belief of the
very first Christians, appeals in his eighth letter to a work of great antiquity, under the
title of ' The Epistle of Barnabas,' which
though it is admitted not to have been written
by the companion of St Paul, the learned
writer contends to have been a production of
the apostolic age, and addressed by a Hebrew
Christian to his Jewish brethren. From this
epistle he cites the following passage: ' The
Lord submitted to suffer for our souls although he be the Lord of the whole earth,
unto whom he said the day before the world
was finished, Let us make man after our
image and our likeness.' He adds two or
three other passages of the same import. He
then remarks that the writer mentions this
doctrine as an article of their common faith;
he brings no arguments to prove it; he mentions it as occasion occurs, without showing any
anxiety to inculcate it, or any apprehension that
it would be denied or doubted, and he triumphantly concludes, ' This, Sir, is the proof
which I had to produce.' It is so direct and
full that if this be laid in one scale, and your
whole mass of evidence drawn from incidental
and ambiguous allusions in the other, the latter will fly up and kick the beam. To this
argument Dr Priestley replies in the second of

his second series of Letters to Dr Horsley, by reminding his antagonist of the doubts entertained by many learned men (and by his antagonist among them) of the genuineness of this epistle and of the certainty of numerous interpolations, and those such as respect the very subject in question. Adding, I must see other evidence than this' from Barnabas before I can admit that the divinity or pre-existence of Christ was the belief of the apostolic age."* This reply sufficiently impeaches the testimony of the pseudo-Barnabas.

It does so, if by the word *impeaches* Mr Belsham mean *challenges*.† Dr Priestley might in this sense impeach any testimony whatever—even the testimony of the apostles, that they " had eaten and drunk with Jesus of Nazareth after he rose from the dead." And Mr Belsham if it seemed good to him, might have joined in that impeachment; but he would claim.to himself and his master a degree of deference which surely is not due to them, were he to expect even Unitarians to admit on their bare *impeachment* unsupported by proof, that the apostles were false witnesses! Just so it is in the present case with re-

---

* See Belsham, p. 440.
† See Johnson's Dictionary under the word IMPEACH.

spect to the testimony of Barnabas. He may, or may not be a false witness; but as the Bishop did not expect the public to believe on his αὐτος ἰφη that Barnabas bears testimony to the faith of the very first Christians in the divinity of our Lord, so neither will the public believe Barnabas to be a false witness on the impeachment of his veracity by Dr Priestley and Mr Belsham! It would be very unjust however to the memory of Dr Priestley not to apprise my readers that he expects from the public no such implicit confidence in what Mr Belsham calls his *impeachment* of the testimony of Barnabas. He assigns his reasons not for *impeaching* that testimony (which he does not) but for contending that it will by no means bear the *stress that his antagonist had laid upon it*; and to be satisfied whether those reasons have any validity the reader has only to compare them with Dr Horsley's reply in this volume.*

Mr Belsham himself seems to have instantly discovered that his mode of *impeaching* ancient testimonies is not alone sufficient to *destroy them*. He proceeds therefore to give an answer " *still more satisfactory*" he says, from the learned Jeremiah

---

* See the eighth of Dr Horsley's Letters to Dr Priestley, the first of Dr Priestley's second series of Letters to Dr Horsley, and Part 1. sec. 2, 3, of Dr Horsley's Remarks on Dr Priestley's Second Letters to the Archdeacon of St Alban's.

Jones, and begins with correcting some mistakes
into which Dr Horsley had fallen with respect
to that gentleman's pedigree and private history.
What this has to do with the question at issue
about the deference due to the testimony of St
Barnabas or of the author assuming that name I
confess myself unable to imagine. We are next
informed that Mr Jones was the relation and
pupil of the very learned Samuel Jones, who
was also tutor to Dr Lardner, Maddox bishop
of Worcester, Butler bishop of Durham, Secker
archbishop of Canterbury, and Dr Samuel Chandler " many years the able and admired pastor of
the highly respectable Presbyterian congregation
of the Old Jewry."*

This is somewhat more to the purpose, as it
shews that Jeremiah Jones had the best opportunity of being well educated: and I have not a
doubt but that he derived every advantage which
could be derived from the tutor of so many eminent men. Still the circumstance of Mr Jones
having been well educated does not tend in the
smallest degree to destroy the evidence given in
the epistle of Barnabas that the divinity of our
Lord was the belief of the first Christians. Secker
and Butler, and Maddox and Chandler, were all

* Belsham, p. 441.

convinced that the " divinity of our Lord was the belief of the very first Christians; and since they were all educated by the same tutor, and all possessed of eminent abilities, why should not we pay as much deference to their judgment as to the judgment of Jeremiah Jones? The evidence possessed by us of what was the belief of the first Christians will lose *something*, I do not think *much*, but it will lose *something* of its weight, if the testimony of Barnabas be set aside; and no orthodox Christian will allow it to be set aside without proof by the *ipse dixit* of Mr Jones, merely because he was a man of learning and the fellow pupil of three eminent English bishops, of one very learned Socinian, and of one eminent Presbyterian divine!

Mr Belsham seems to be aware of this, and therefore gives in the following words the answer supplied by the learned Jeremiah Jones, which he says is still more satisfactory than the impeachment of the testimony of Barnabas by himself and Dr Priestley.

" In the second volume of his admirable treatise on the canon of Scripture, republished a few years ago by the University of Oxford, Part III. ch. 37, after a very full and impartial inquiry into the subject, Mr Jones states it as his *opinion* which he substantiates by abundant evidence, that the epistle was written not by Barnabas nor by any other Jew, but by some person who was originally a pagan idolater, that it is an apocryphal book, and was never read in the churches till the time of Jerome; that it contains many assertions which are absolutely false, and a great number of trifling, silly, and idle things. And upon the whole he concludes from its having been cited only by *Clemens Alexandrinus and Origen,*° that it was forged at Alexandria; and because there are so many pious frauds in it; that it was the forgery of some such person as corrupted the books of the Sybils, and that it was written about the middle of the second century."†

But all this is only the *opinion* of Mr Jones, and learned as I doubt not he was, I am not bound, nor is the public bound to adopt his opinions without proof in preference to the opinions of those who think differently of the epistle of Barnabas. That the epistle contains

---

° That it is cited by other ancient writers besides Clemens and Origen, the reader may easily satisfy himself by perusing the *Veterum Testimoniæ de Epistola Sd Barnabæ*, prefixed to Cotelerius's edition of the apostolical fathers.

† Belsham, p. 441.

several trivial, silly, and idle things, and was
not written by Barnabas the apostle was the
opinion of Bishop Horsley as well as of Mr
Jones; and the Bishop assigns the reasons on
which his opinion was founded: but that the
epistle is the work of some apostolical writer,
and no forgery of a converted heathen about
the middle of the second century is the joint
opinion of Bishop Horsley and Dr Priestley.*
Now throwing the Bishop's opinion out of the
scale, whether is the opinion of the learned
Jeremiah Jones, or of the learned Dr Joseph
Priestley to preponderate on this occasion? If
Mr Belsham think that two such names must
keep the balance in equipoise, what is to happen when we throw into the Doctor's scale
the opinions of Archbishop Wake, Dr Cave,
Cotelerius, and Bishop Pearson,† whose opinion
alone is on questions of this sort of greater
weight than the opinions of twenty Joneses and
of as many Belshams, of greater weight indeed
than the opinion of any other modern, with

---

* See the fifth section of Dr Priestley's *History of the Doctrine of Atonement*, in his *Appeal to the serious professors of
Christianity*, and the eighth of Dr Horsley's Letters in the preceding Tracts.

† This prodigy of learning says (Lect. II. in act. App. § 10.)
Nemo certe fuit (veterum) qui hanc epistolam Barnabæ non
tribuerit, neque in ea quidquam apparet, quod eam ætatem non
ferat.

whose writings I am at all acquainted. But they are not *modern* opinions only that must be thrown into the scale of Bishop Horsley and Dr Priestley.

Origen himself, " the fairest character which Christian history has to exhibit," quotes this epistle not barely as the writing of some apostolical men, but as the genuine writing of the apostle whose name it bears. In answer to an objection which Celsus puts into the mouth of his Jew, to the characters of those whom our Lord called to the apostleship, that they were *infamous wretches, publicans* and *fishermen*, Origen after observing that Celsus seems willing enough to believe the writings of the evangelists when they furnish matter for detraction, but not in matters of importance, least he should be obliged to confess the Divinity openly preached in their writings, adds—Γέγραπται δὴ ἐν τῇ Βαρνάβα Καθολικῇ Ἐπιστολῇ (ἔνθεν ὁ Κέλσος λαβὼν τάχα εἶπεν, εἶναι ἐπιρρήτους καὶ πονηροτάτους τοὺς ἀποστόλους) ὅτι ἐξελέξατο τοὺς ἰδίους ἀποστόλους Ἰησοῦς, ὄντας ὑπὲρ πᾶσαν ἀνομίαν ἀνομωτέρους. Καὶ ἐν τῷ εὐαγγελίῳ δὲ τῷ κατὰ Λουκᾶν φησι πρὸς τὸν Ἰησοῦν ὁ Πέτρος, Ἔξελθε ἀπ᾿, ἐμοῦ, ὅτι ἀνὴρ ἁμαρτωλός εἰμι κύριε.*

That the epistle of Barnabas which is here

---

* Vid. Orig. contra Celsum, lib. I. p. 49. ed. Cantab. 1658.

cited by Origen is the epistle which Messrs
Jones and Belsham think unworthy of all credit is unquestionable; for the very words quoted
are in the fifth chapter of that epistle published
by Cotelerius. It is true Barnabas adds that our
Lord chose for his apostles the greatest of sin-
ners, ἵνα δείξη, ὅτι οὐκ ἦλθε καλέσαι δικαίους, ἀλλὰ ἁμαρτωλοὺς εἰς μετ-
άνοιαν; and Origen after citing several passages
from St Luke and St Paul acknowledging the
apostles to have been great sinners, assigns a similar reason for our Lord having made choice of
such men to be the first preachers of his gospel.

Here then we have Origen bearing testimony
not barely to the antiquity of the epistle ascribed
to Barnabas, but even to its genuineness as the
work of that apostle himself; and quoting it as of
equal authority when relating a matter of fact
with the gospel of St Luke. In ascribing it to
the apostle I think indeed for the reasons assigned
by Bishop Horsley that Origen was mistaken;
but into such a mistake an inquirer into the records of the church so indefatigable as Origen
could not possibly have fallen, had the epistle
been forged by a converted heathen in the very
city in which he was born, and within thirty or
forty years of his birth. At any rate Mr Belsham must admit that if Origen was liable to fall
into such a mistake as this, he is no competent

witness respecting the church of orthodox Jewish
Christians at Ælia during the reign of Adrian;
for though he was more than once at Ælia or Jerusalem, he was not so long there as he was at
Alexandria; nor had he equal opportunities of
making himself acquainted with the original state
of the Ælian church. Indeed the epistle itself
bears internal evidence little short of demonstration that it could not have been composed by a
converted pagan as Mr Jones alleges; for as Bishop Horsley observes, " none but a person bred
in Judaism could in that age possess such a minute knowledge of the Jewish rites as is displayed
in that book."

Here then we have a number of eminent men,
Bishop Horsley, Dr Priestley, Archbishop Wake,
Dr Cave, Cotelerius, and Bishop Pearson himself
a host, besides Origen " the fairest character that
Christian history has to exhibit,"—all opposed to
the learned Jeremiah Jones and the learned Thomas Belsham; and if the question is to be decided by *authority* or by *votes*, the Catholic epistle
of Barnabas must be deemed a writing of the
apostolical age.

" No," says Mr Belsham, it is not of the apostolical age, for Jeremiah Jones substantiates his
opinion by abundant evidence;" but where is that

2 P

evidence?—Mr Jones has indeed cited a great variety of testimonies—all, it is to be supposed that he thought of any weight in deciding the authenticity of the epistle, and among these not one is found to favour Mr Jones's own opinion. Three out of the four ancient authorities produced by him, Clemens Alexandrinus, Origen, and Jerome, contend that the epistle is genuine, the work of the apostle whose name it bears, and the fourth—Eusebius—though he ranks it among the books which are spurious believes it to have been written in the apostolic age. Of the eighteen modern writers whose sentiments upon the subject Mr Jones has detailed, *eight** agree in the opinions of Clemens Alexandrinus, Origen, and Jerome, and the remaining *ten*† in that of Eusebius. In the *conjecture* therefore that the epistle of Barnabas was written " originally by a pagan about the middle of the second century, and was the forgery of some such person as corrupted the books of the Sybils" Mr Jones stands *single* ;‡—or at

---

* J. Vosius. Dr Bernard. Du Pin. Dr Cave. Archbishop Wake. Dr S. Clarke. Mr Le Clerc. Dr Jenkin.

† Archbishop Usher. Hugo Menardus. Archbishop Land. Cotelerius. Bishop Fell. Mr Dodwell. Mr Toland. Dr Mill. Mr Eachard. Mr Whiston.

‡ It must be confessed by every candid man who consults Mr Jones's work on the Canon of Scripture, that the author has displayed great ingenuity and considerable powers of reasoning

least stood single till the appearance of Mr Belsham; and how unreasonable it would be to suffer the opinion of a *single* writer to decide the
authority of any book in opposition to the general sense of the learned world cannot be more
forcibly illustrated than by applying with a slight
verbal alteration to Mr Jones's conjecture the observations which he himself makes on the opinions of Clemens Alexandrinus.

*" Suppose then that one writer (Jeremiah Jones)
had too low an opinion of a book, are we to be governed in determining its authenticity by the private opinion of one single writer, contrary to the
known sentiments of every other writer? Must one
man judge for the whole Christian world? and
must his rejection of a book prove its insufficiency
when it appears to have been received by every
Christian writer besides, and admitted on its own
internal evidence to have been the work of the
apostolic age by every one who has mentioned it.
I shall add no more here, but repeat what I observed* Vol. I. Prop. v. *that we are not to deter-*

---

in support of his conjecture; *(" for Mr Jones was really a
learned man, and dealt not in contemptuous but argumentative
language.)* But if the reader will take the trouble to compare
the arguments of Dr S. Clarke, Bishop Pearson, and Bishop
Horsley upon the point at issue, with the reasoning of Mr
Jones, he will find the latter completely refuted.

mine the authority of any book or books upon the credit of any one or two particular writers but the **WHOLE BODY OF THE WRITERS OF THE CHURCH.**"[*]

The reader is by this time satisfied I trust with what propriety Mr Belsham has applied to Bishop Horsley such epithets as *ignorant* and *pitiful!* Of this modern champion of Unitarianism I know nothing but from his inquiry into the person of Christ, and his share whatever it may be in the merits of the improved version of the New Testament: but from these specimens of his literature and powers of reasoning it seems not too much to say that he is at least as inferior to Dr Priestley, as I readily acknowledge myself *to be* to Bishop Horsley. Dr Priestley, as the Bishop always declared, was in the departments of physical science, to which he had devoted his attention, a great man, though he had no pretensions to superiority as a Greek scholar, or a Scripture critic. There may be departments in science in which Mr Belsham too is great; but what they are I have not heard. I have therefore treated him without ceremony; though I trust that I have never expressed myself in language unworthy of a gentleman or a Christian.—If I acknowledge

---

[*] Jones' Can. of Scrip. Vol. II. Part III. cap. XL.

that I have sometimes felt it difficult to repress my indignation, and that I have treated with ridicule what being unsupported by argument admits not of an argumentative reply, I am persuaded that by the candid part of the public I shall be forgiven; and the sentiments of Mr Belsham himself will give me no concern. Τίς πονηρὸς καὶ τίνι τῶλων τί πόλι πίπρηκται, μη μιλοιμι; ιιδιίηι δι τὺς ἀγαθὺς και τύτοις μιλαδιώκοιμι. Οφιιλοιμι μηδινὶ μηδιν' ειδί πόλι ιπ' ἀνάγκης μιγάλης ις τηλο καλασλαίηι, γίνοιλό μοι τάχισλα ιλιυθίρω γινίσθαι δυνηθῆναι. Αιντοιμι τὺς αγαθὺς ἀφθόιως. Φιλοψογον δι γλῶσσαν παιλὸς ἀποσλυγίιηι.

FINIS.

DUNDEE.
Printed by A. Smith & Co.

ERRATA.

Page 22, line 4, *for* theogeny *read* theogony
...... 37, line 16, *for* accurate *read* inaccurate
...... 59, line 16, *for* Antonius *read* Antoninus
...... 60, line 3d from the bottom, *for* a Son *read* the Son.
...... 71, line 18, *for* fallacies and reasoning *read* fallacies in reasoning
...... 72, bottom line, *for* Theodorit *read* Theodoret
...... 76, line 5 from the bottom, *dele* that
...... 81, line 4, *for* detect *read* deject
...... 110, line 5 from the bottom, *for* Thence *read* Whence
...... 122, line last of the text, *for* a standing sense *read* its standing sense
...... 126, line 19, *for* obtained *read* contained
...... 138, Postscript, *for* authorities of *read* authorities for
...... 144, 2d foot note, *for* appendix, sect. 2. *read* sect. 1.
...... 146, line 17, *for* said country *read* same country
...... 148, line 8, *for* γνωμιν *read* γνωμην
...... 164, line 2d from the bottom, *for* heralds *read* first heralds
...... 165, line 6, *for* seems *read* which seems
...... 173, line 4, *for* serves to *read* serves but to
...... 176, line 9, *for* which is more *read* what is more
...... 182, line 4, *for* had *read* hath
...... 187, line 2, *for* uncircumcision *read* circumcision
...... 195, line 7, *for* our own *read* your own
...... 199, line 18, *for* learned *read* a learned
...... 233, line 2, *for* his *read* this
...... 271, line 10, and several other places, *for* Socinius *read* Socinus
...... 307, line 5, *for* decrârunt *read* deërârunt
...... 307, line 5th from the bottom, *for* Manuscripts *read* Manuscripti
...... 334, line 3, *for* used to any *read* used of any
...... 357, line 3, *for* enjoined *read* enjoyed
...... 359, note, line 1, *for* ἱιλη *read* ἰν τη
...... 369, line 3d from the bottom, *for* may shine *read* may so shine
...... 405, line 12, *for* his first *read* this first
...... 411, line last of the text, *for* in any passage *read* nor in any passage
...... 431, line 6, *for* were divided *read* was divided
...... 434, line 7th from the bottom, *for* false principle *read* safe principle
...... 434, line 2d from the bottom, *for* body *read* great body
...... 439, line 6th from the bottom, *for* says *read* say
...... 568, line 3d from the bottom, *for* church at Ælia *read* Jewish church at Ælia

Lightning Source UK Ltd.
Milton Keynes UK
UKHW02n1213120218
317657UK00006B/1102/P

Chambers
Book of Great Speeches

Editor
Andrew Burnet

Chambers

CHAMBERS
An imprint of Chambers Harrap Publishers Ltd
338 Euston Road, NW1 3BH
Chambers Harrap Publishers is an Hachette UK company

This edition published 2013
First published 2006

Database right Chambers Harrap Publishers Ltd (makers)

A CIP catalogue record for this book is available from the British Library.

ISBN 9781471801747

10 9 8 7 6 5 4 3 2 1

Typeset by Cenveo® Publisher Services.

www.chambers.co.uk

Printed and bound in India.

All dates and information are correct at the time of going to press.

Contributors

Editor
Andrew Burnet

Contributors
Nancy E M Bailey
Allan Burnett
Andrew Campbell
Steve Cramer
Catherine Gaunt
Professor John Richardson

Editorial assistant
Vicky Aldus

Proofreader
Hilary Marsden

Index
Meg Davies

Managing editor
Camilla Rockwood

Publishing manager
Patrick White

Prepress
David Reid
Sharon McTeir

Contents

Introduction

The art of oratory has been developing since the very moment of humankind's first utterance. How could it be otherwise? Could speech have emerged, a talent so potent and ripe with possibilities, and been allowed to languish? Surely not: the instinctive human response to a new skill is to hone it, develop it, give rein to it. We know that the roots of human culture are embedded in myth and legend, and that skilful, charismatic storytellers were the channels by which they were preserved and passed on.

Certainly, oratory thrived in the two great civilizations we regard as forerunners to our own. Both the Greeks and the Romans held their most gifted speakers in high esteem, an accolade they were not reluctant to accept. One of the earliest speeches in this book, given by the Athenian orator Isocrates, begins by dwelling on the importance of oratory; while the great Roman speaker Cicero wrote several books on the subject, arguing that rhetoric was a discipline to be prized above law and philosophy.

The short attention span that shapes our culture today has banished verbosity from many areas of public life, but public speaking is still vigorously alive – at political party conferences, in presidential addresses, and on the thriving after-dinner speaking circuit.

Opinions vary over what constitutes great oratory. 'True eloquence ... does not consist in speech,' declared the US senator Daniel Webster during a eulogy on the former presidents John Adams and Thomas Jefferson. 'Words and phrases may be marshalled in every way, but they cannot compass it. It must exist in the man, in the subject, and in the occasion.'

'Eloquent speech,' offered the American lawyer and politician W J Bryan, 'is not from lip to ear, but rather from heart to heart.'

The journalist, novelist and former presidential speechwriter William Safire has attributed the success of a speech to a 'tripod' of factors: an 'occasion of emotional turmoil', a setting which provides the speaker with a momentous 'forum', and – relegated to third place – the speech's content and phrasing.

This is a telling analysis. Both Bryan and Safire had compiled their own anthologies of speeches, and knew that such a book can at best tell half the story. The point was tartly made by the 19th-century English politician John Bright, one of the most brilliant orators of his day: 'If a speech reads well it must be a damned bad speech.'

It would be wrong to downplay the importance of delivery – of Martin Luther King's evangelical rhapsody, Adolf Hitler's puppet-master demagoguery, Winston Churchill's slurring bulldog snarl – and you don't have to be Harold Pinter to value the judicious use of pause. But my own view is that Bright protested too much. A novel with real pulse and sinew – *Crime and Punishment*, say, or *Madame Bovary* – can survive translation with barely a scratch. By the same token, a really good speech, when written down, is not confined to the page but strides forth and grasps the lectern squarely, clearing its throat. Many of the speeches included here can be obtained in audio or video format; but there is nothing to prevent you, dear reader, from clearing your own throat and trying out these words on your family, your dog, or your bedroom wall.

With regard to the front two feet of Safire's tripod, my fellow contributors and I have done some of the work for you. Each speaker represented in this book is introduced by a brief biography, and each speech has its own scene-setting preamble. As well as describing the historical circumstances surrounding the speeches, we have tried to suggest something of the atmosphere in which they were delivered and the results they produced. We have also provided marginal notes, which will enable you to understand quickly the people and references mentioned by the speakers.

In choosing the speeches, I have been guided by various criteria. Relatively few speeches seemed so iconic that they simply could not be omitted. Friends, colleagues and relatives all put forward candidates; I also consulted a number of experts in a range of academic fields, some of whom suggested speeches from other fields entirely. I spent many hours in libraries, surfed the untameable seas of the Internet, pored laboriously over weathered old editions of Hansard and scoured my own memory for examples of great oratory.

When quizzed about my quest, I would mutter phrases such as 'inspirational rhetoric', 'moments of historical significance' and 'ideally both'. But then I came across a speech which was neither – Stanley Baldwin's rigorous debunking of rhetoric at the Cambridge Union – and took relish in including it too.

I was allowed a free hand in making my selection, and there can be little doubt that it reflects my own passions and obsessions. But I have tried to assemble a varied anthology that reflects and celebrates the diversity of human thought over distances of geography and chronology, culture and ideology. I cannot deny that the contemporary era and the western mindset loom larger than voices more remote in space and time; but I also hope that even the most foreign, most ancient, most contentious voices are recognizable as germane to our own.

Tempting as it was to include Henry V urging his followers once more unto the breach, or Richard II telling sad stories of the death of kings, I have refrained from embracing the inventions of dramatists or novelists. Admit Shakespeare's kings and where do you stop? Peter Shaffer's Mozart? John Osborne's Luther? Charlton Heston's Michelangelo? (Instead, we have Heston in his own voice, railing against the dangers of political correctness.)

Speeches are rarely written with publication in mind (and when they are, they are often carefully rewritten). Therefore, it is often far from easy to determine the authenticity of any given 'version'. In each case, I have done my best to locate the most authentic transcript, or – for speeches given in foreign languages – the most faithful translation. I have also, where possible, recorded the reactions of the audience who first heard it.

However, I must confess to some deliberate rule-bending. Certain speeches in this book are attributed to people who never delivered them, though they may have said something similar. The 1st-century Scottish warrior Calgacus is remembered for his scornful diatribe against Roman 'civilizers', but the words generally attributed to him were in fact composed two decades later by the Roman historian Tacitus. Another unruly Scot, William Wallace, is here credited with a defiant scaffold speech, which was probably written some six centuries after his grisly execution.

Similarly, the speech allegedly given by the Carthaginian general Hannibal to his expeditionary force around 218 BC was in fact 'recorded' by the Roman historian Livy about 200 years after the event; and the famous funeral oration given by Pericles in 431 BC has come down to us in an account written by his near-contemporary Thucydides. Although the authenticity of these speeches is at best highly dubious, I commend them to you as capable of standing up for themselves, and – to varying degrees – true to the spirit of the figures they represent.

Then there are the speeches whose authors failed to deliver them. Cicero's bitter denunciation of Marc Antony, written in 44 BC, was clearly his own work, but he wisely decided not to declaim it before the Senate. (Antony had him killed the following year anyway.) Other speeches were delivered by proxy: in 1787, an aging Benjamin Franklin was too ill to bestow his qualified blessing on the US Constitution, so his speech was read out by a colleague. And in 1953, Nelson Mandela was bound by a government gagging order, so his famous 'no easy walk to freedom' speech was read on his behalf. These seemed to me exceptions worth tolerating.

This is not the place for a discussion on the reliability of the Gospel-writers in recording the words of Jesus: they are included here in the King James Version, perhaps the least accurate translation, but certainly the most resonant. I should, however, declare one sermon which, though delivered by a preacher of no great renown, was written by a towering literary figure. Dr Samuel Johnson's treatment of Ecclesiastes 1:14 – 'all is vanity' – has a spirit and vitality that belie its gloomy theme.

This brings us to the dark art of the political speechwriter. It would be both pedantic and confusing to attribute speeches by John F Kennedy and Ronald Reagan to their speechwriters Theodore Sorensen and Peggy Noonan – however, in many cases it is these backroom script editors who have devised the most memorable phrases delivered by their employers. Even the literary lion Rudyard Kipling (who appears here in his own right, bemoaning the curse of linguistic talent) is rarely credited as the author of the first Christmas Day broadcasts delivered by King George V.

Speechwriting is by its nature an anonymous trade, and often a thankless one. As Peter Hyman, former speechwriter to Tony Blair, writes in his book *1 Out of 10*, 'It is very hard to write in someone else's voice, particularly if they increasingly know what they want to say and would rather write it themselves.' And of course, a speaker is at liberty to depart from the script, as Reagan famously did when he urged Berliners to 'tear down this wall'.

Some of history's most celebrated speeches have been based on the most minimal of scripts, or not scripted at all. Richard M Nixon's television speech about his daughter's dog Checkers – the first of his many high-profile attempts to deny corruption – was delivered live to the nation, without reference to notes, and probably without an autocue. And although the former Labour leader Neil Kinnock tells stories of sitting up all night to hone his conference speeches, his most inspired and affecting piece of oratory – 'Why am I the first Kinnock in a thousand generations to be able to get to university?' – was reputedly scrawled on an envelope during his journey to the conference hall.

Military men, one might suppose, have little use for scripts: both General George Patton and Colonel Tim Collins are said to have extemporized their battlefield resolve-stiffeners. However, General Douglas MacArthur's astonishing farewell addresses – of which one is included here – were clearly prepared in detail.

Speeches have themselves often provided inspiration for future speakers. Readers familiar with Jesus's words will find them echoed repeatedly throughout this book, and not only in a Christian context. One phrase in particular –

the 'city upon a hill' – can be traced from the Sermon on the Mount, via the early American settler John Winthrop to Presidents Kennedy and Reagan, and thence to Mario Cuomo, former governor of New York, who took Reagan to task over it. That did not, however, deter the Austrian-born film star Arnold Schwarzenegger from citing the phrase on taking office as governor of California.

Abraham Lincoln's truly iconic Gettysburg Address has been a frequent point of reference: the untarnishable phrase 'government of the people, by the people and for the people' was even quoted by Patrice Lumumba during his tragically brief premiership of the Democratic Republic of the Congo. Similarly, Winston Churchill's wartime stoicism has inspired many a speaker seeking to bolster morale: one example is Rudolph Giuliani, former mayor of New York, who led the city through the trauma of 11 September 2001.

Imitation may be sincere flattery, but plagiarism can lead to trouble. In 1988, Senator Joe Biden was a promising candidate for the Democratic presidential nomination until he failed to credit Neil Kinnock for that famous speech, whose 'thousand generations' refrain he had borrowed.

I too am dependent on the words of others, and I have attempted to treat them with due respect. However, many of the speeches included here were simply too long to reproduce in full. I could easily have filled these pages with a handful of complete speeches by such verbose figures as Edmund Burke, Adolf Hitler, Oliver Cromwell, William Gladstone and Fidel Castro, but it seemed more interesting and more valuable to represent a wider variety of speakers. I have therefore, with great care, abridged or excerpted those speeches which could not be given in full. Although in some cases this has meant omitting fascinating material or marring the overall structure, I have made every possible effort to preserve the essence of each original speech. I have also modernized and anglicized spellings, and amended punctuation where I believe it will improve clarity.

In all this, my goal has been to allow the voices of these speakers to be heard clearly, without compromising their spirit, their beliefs or their rhetorical style; without passing judgement on their opinions; above all without distorting their meaning.

Like the text of a play, this book sits at the meeting point between two distinct forms of language: speech and writing. And like every good script, it requires only the spark of imagination to bring it to life.

Andrew Burnet

Acknowledgements

I am indebted to the following people, whose time, knowledge and expertise were crucial to the development and completion of this book: Liz and Eve Abzug; Lord Baldwin; Libby Bassett,Women's Environment & Development Organization; Tony Benn; Lucy Bright, Warner Classics; Simon Bourn, Taylor Wessing; Stephanie Brinkman, University of Edinburgh; Mark Brown; Stéphane Bruchweld, University of Uppsala; Dr Douglas Cairns; Angus Calder; Sara Chenoweth, People for the Ethical Treatment of Animals; Julie Christensen, Mary Fisher CARE Fund; Louise Clarke, Cambridge University Library; Dr Frank Cogliano, University of Edinburgh; Chris Collins, Margaret Thatcher Foundation; Dr Markus Daechsel, University of Edinburgh; Dr John Doyle, Dublin City University; Barry Eaden, Cambridge University Library; Owen Dudley Edwards, University of Edinburgh; Bashabi Fraser, University of Edinburgh/Open University; Sir Edward Ford; Rob Fraser; Milton Friedman; Diane S Gianelli, the President's Council on Bioethics; Professor Robert F Goheen, Princeton University; Simon Gray; Grizelda Grimond; Lord Healey; Aura Herzog; John R Hodgson, John Rylands Library, Manchester; Ieuan Hopkins, Churchill Archives Centre, Cambridge; Lord Howard; Ami Isseroff, mideastweb.org; Prof Rhodri Jeffreys-Jones, University of Edinburgh; Lord Kinnock; Sergei Khrushchev; Maude Laflamme, David Wilkinson Associates; Helen Langley, Bodleian Library, Oxford; Janet Lorenz, oscars.org; Jen McClure, People for the Ethical Treatment of Animals; Leon McDermott; Lizzie MacGregor, Scottish Poetry Library; Eric MacLeod, The Scottish Parliament; Michael McManus; Joyce McMillan; Aurelie Martot; Dr Jolyon Mitchell, University of Edinburgh; Alan Morrison; Brian Morton; Dr Graeme Morton, University of Edinburgh; Judy Nokes, the Office of Public Sector Information; Barry Pateman, University of California, Berkeley; Patrick Price, The Northern Ireland Assembly; Sister M Ozana, the Missionaries of Charity Calcutta Centre, San Diego; Joan Ross-Frankson,Women's Environment & Development Organization; Trevor Royle; Aaron Rule, Office of Gough Whitlam; Andrew Sergeant, National Library of Australia; Lord Steel; Elaine Steel, literary agent; Emily Tarrant, Bodleian Library, Oxford; Alan Taylor; Martin Tod, MP; Darren Treadwell, the People's History Museum, Manchester; Sue Vale, BAFTA; Barbara Walker; Colin Webb, Palazzo Editions; John Wells, Cambridge University Library; Louise Weston, BBC Written Archives Office; Prof Philip Williamson, University of Durham; Clive Wolfe, National Student Drama Festival; the staff of the National Library of Scotland, Edinburgh City Libraries and Edinburgh University Library.

Above all my thanks are due to my wife Susie, for her support, advice, patience and unshakeable good nature.

AB

Sources

Thanks are due to the following for their kind permission to reproduce copyright material:

Bella Abzug: to Liz and Eve Abzug; Lady Astor: to the Rt Hon Viscount Astor and the BBC; Clement Attlee: to the People's History Museum, Manchester, Archive and the Labour Party; Stanley Baldwin: to Rt Hon the Earl Baldwin of Bewdley; Daniel Barenboim: to Daniel Barenboim; David Ben-Gurion: to Philosophical Library, New York (reprinted from *Rebirth and Destiny of Israel*, copyright © 1954 by Philosophical Library); Tony Benn: to Tony Benn; Aneurin Bevan: to the People's History Museum, Manchester, Archive and the Labour Party; Benazir Bhutto: to The Wylie Agency (UK) Ltd, copyright © 1995 Benazir Bhutto; Tony Blair: to the Controller of Her Majesty's Stationery Office and the Queen's Printer for Scotland, reproduced with permission from www.number10.gov.uk; Simón Bolívar: to Oxford University Press USA (reprinted from *El Libertador: Writings of Simón Bolívar*, ed. David Bushnell, trans. Frederick H Fornoff, copyright © 2003 by Oxford University Press, Inc.); Calgacus: to Penguin Books Ltd (reprinted from *On Britain and Germany: Tacitus*, trans. H Mattingly, Penguin Classics 1948, copyright © the Estate of H Mattingly, 1948); Charles, Prince of Wales: to Clarence House, copyright © Clarence House; St John Chrysostom: to The Lutterworth Press (reprinted from *Chrysostom and His Message*, selected and translated by Stephen Neill, United Society for Christian Literature/Lutterworth Press, 1962); Sir Winston Churchill: to Curtis Brown Ltd,

Bella Abzug
American feminist, lawyer and politician

Bella Abzug *née Savitzky* (1920–98) was born in the Bronx, New York. She was educated at Hunter College, New York and Columbia University and practised as a lawyer in New York (1944–70). She became noted for defending those accused of un-American activities during the anti-communist campaign of the 1950s and was a prominent peace campaigner, founding Women Strike for Peace (1961) and the National Women's Political Caucus. After winning a seat in Congress (1971), she vigorously championed welfare issues, and became known as 'Battling Bella'. She ran unsuccessfully for a Senate seat (1976) and for appointment as Mayor of New York (1977). She returned to legal practice in 1980, but continued as a political campaigner. Her publications include *Gender Gap: Bella Abzug's Guide to Political Power for American Women* (1984).

'The end of the human race'
25 May 1982, New York City, USA

During the Cold War, the USA and USSR became rivals in a nuclear arms race. By the end of the 1970s, both sides had developed sufficient warheads to destroy the world several times over. Treaties were negotiated which aimed to limit each side's arsenal; but both 'superpowers' continued to pursue research into new forms of weapon, while politicians on each side stressed the threat posed by the other.

In the early 1980s, western activists proposed a 'nuclear freeze': a halt to the production of new warheads. President RONALD REAGAN opposed the nuclear freeze, and in 1981 began a major increase in defence development, while claiming to support bilateral arms reductions.

At a meeting in New York's Town Hall, Abzug gave this passionate but carefully argued speech in support of the Kennedy–Hatfield freeze resolution, which had been introduced to the US Senate. After a chilling survey of the potential consequences of the arms race, she ridicules Nuclear Use Theorists as 'NUTS' and urges restraint.

Three weeks later, on 12 June, one million people took part in a pro-nuclear freeze march from the United Nations building to Central Park in New York City – the biggest demonstration in history to that date. US–Soviet talks aimed at reducing numbers of nuclear weapons began later that month, but only bore fruit later in Reagan's presidency, after Mikhail Gorbachev became Soviet leader in 1985.

A nuclear freeze.

The idea is simple. It is practical. It is urgent.

It is a logical response to the terrible threat that faces us and all the people of the world. The end of the human race. The death of our planet. As Jonathan Schell points out in his profoundly moving book, *The Fate of the Earth*, if we allow ourselves and our earth to be destroyed by a nuclear holocaust, all human meaning, all human history, all human achievements, all human memory will be lost forever. The past will disappear. The future will be a void. Death itself will die.

The way to stop an arms race leading us madly toward this awesome, almost unimaginable fate is to stop. Just stop. Freeze in position. Stop testing new nuclear weapons. Stop producing more nuclear weapons. Stop deploying more nuclear weapons on land and in the sea and air, and for heaven's sake – and I mean that literally – stop trying to pollute space with nuclear weapons, the new plan being worked on by the soulless technologists in the Pentagon who play with our fate as though we were little blips in an electronic war game on a video screen.

And while we take a breather in a nuclear freeze, let us use that time to analyse what goal it is we have been racing toward since 1945 – the year we ended the second world war and began preparing for the third. And what kind of arms race is it anyway, if the rules keep changing and the goal-line keeps moving out of reach? Does anyone here expect that a time will ever come when the Pentagon planners and the industrial complex that profits from planning and producing weapons of death will say, 'Yes, we have enough? We have enough to protect our nation from any enemy. Yes, it is time to stop.'

You can depend on this if we leave these decisions to the military-industrial complex[1] and their political spokesmen: The arms race will end only when the superpowers go bankrupt or destroy us all. But, we are told repeatedly, we are only in the nuclear arms race because of the Soviet threat. We are peaceful. They are warlike. For more than 30 years, the relentless build-up of American military power has been structured on the hypothesis that the leaders of the Soviet Union want to destroy our country and our people with a surprise nuclear attack.

What does that mean? Try to envision it. If the Russians did succeed in obliterating us in a first strike without our having a chance to respond – and there is no responsible military official who has said they can do that – what would happen next? Would those Russian madmen then just happily rule the rest of the world, supreme, contented, unopposed? Would they and their people be unaffected by nuclear fallout? Would they be untouched by the disease and epidemics that would result from several hundred million American bodies lying amidst the burning rubble of our land? Would they be untouched by the economic, political and social chaos that would follow such a catastrophe? How would they feed and protect their own population? Could they survive, in any rational meaning of that word?

When we begin to think about the real problems behind the scenarios of nuclear destruction that the experts keep producing, we realize the total absurdity of what passes for military planning and what is done in the name of national security.

It is not necessary to like the Soviet system – and I know that if I had to live there, I'd probably be in jail or a work camp or be trying desperately, along with my fellow and sister Jews, to get an exit visa – it is not necessary to admire the Soviet Union to challenge the widely held belief that the Russians want to destroy us in a nuclear attack.

One of the most thoughtful challenges I have read was in an article by George Kennan, our former ambassador to the Soviet Union. He wrote: 'The view of the Soviet Union that prevails today in large portions of our governmental and journalistic establishments [is] so extreme, so subjective, so far removed from what any sober scrutiny of external reality would reveal, that it is not only ineffective but dangerous as a guide to political action.'[2]

And he went on to say that these views 'are not the marks of the maturity and discrimination one expects of the diplomacy of a great power; they are the marks of an intellectual primitivism and naïveté unpardonable in a great power. I use the word naïveté,' he said, 'because there is a naïveté of cynicism and suspicion just as there is a naïveté of innocence.'

As a great world power, we can no longer pretend to be innocents abroad. As George Kennan reminds us, 'It was we who first produced and tested a nuclear device; we who were the first to raise its destructiveness to a new level with the hydrogen bomb; we who introduced the multiple warhead; we who have declined every proposal for the renunciation of the principle of 'first use',[3] and we alone, so help us God, who have used the weapon in anger against others, and against tens of thousands of helpless non-combatants at that.'

And it is the United States, I might add, that by the early 1970s had

[1] This term was first coined by US President DWIGHT D EISENHOWER in 1961, in a speech expressing concern about a network of the military and its suppliers, with the potential to influence government policy. The speech is included in this book.

[2] Kennan's article appeared in *The New York Review of Books* on 21 January 1982.

[3] A pre-emptive use of nuclear weapons, designed to disable enemies before they can launch a retaliation.

initiated 23 out of the 25 existing major nuclear weapons systems. The nature of the arms race is that it is a contest. Whatever nuclear weapon system we introduce, we can be sure that the Russians will try, and probably succeed, in catching up with us.

Where do we stand now? According to Senator Mark Hatfield, the Oregon Republican who is co-author of the Kennedy[4]–Hatfield nuclear freeze resolution, in 1960 both sides together had about 6,500 strategic nuclear weapons. Today they have about 16,000. The Union of Concerned Scientists tells us that the US and the Soviet Union share 'rough equality' in nuclear weaponry – 9,500 strategic nuclear warheads on the American side, 7,000 on the Soviet side – with neither having the capacity to disarm the other in an effective first strike.

[4] The Democrat Senator from Massachusetts Edward 'Ted' Kennedy (1932–2009), younger brother of US President JOHN F KENNEDY.

Senator Hatfield tells us: 'The United States and Soviet Union have never been as strategically equal as they are today. A new arms race will make mincemeat of the present strategic balance. This then is a moment of historic opportunity.' And Senator Ted Kennedy tells us: 'The prevention of nuclear war is not only the great issue of our time, but perhaps the greatest issue of all time. Today the two superpowers possess the equivalent of one million Hiroshima bombs – an amount equal to four tons of TNT for every man, woman and child presently living on this planet.'

A million Hiroshimas! Can you conceive of it? And do you know that just one of the thousands of so-called tactical nuclear weapons the US has stored in western Europe far exceeds the destructive power of the atom bomb our Air Force dropped on Hiroshima? And, remember, it was one of these tactical weapons Secretary of State Alexander Haig[5] was probably referring to when he told a Senate committee last November that NATO has contingency plans to fire a nuclear weapon (quote) 'for demonstrative purposes' if there should be a conventional war in Europe involving the Soviet Union.

[5] The US soldier and politician Alexander M Haig, Jr (1924–2010) served as Secretary of State under President Reagan, 1981–2. He resigned his post, allegedly over Reagan's insistence that he negotiate with Soviet officials over nuclear weapons.

That was when the administration and the Pentagon were trying to get us used to the idea of what they called a 'limited' nuclear war, when we were being told that a nuclear war was winnable, that we in the US could survive a nuclear attack if we just spent a couple of billion dollars on a civil defence programme. The concept of a winnable so-called limited nuclear war is still prevalent among American military strategists. The Nuclear Use Theorists, known for short as the NUTS, those who believe the US must seek a first-strike capability, are still prevalent in our strategic planning. And the assistant NUTS, the bureaucrats in the Federal Emergency Management Agency,[6] are still pushing their civilian defence plans.

[6] The body established in 1979 to co-ordinate responses to national disasters.

They contend they can save up to 80 per cent of the American people in a nuclear war. Notice that qualifying 'up to'. But let's say only 20 per cent of Americans lose their lives. That's only 46 million dead children, women and men. Surely a horrifying, unacceptable prospect. But the FEMA bureaucrats are very cool about it. They're thinking of the 80 per cent who might be saved.

And how do they propose to save them? Well, first they admit that they would need three days' warning that we were going to be attacked. Then mass evacuations would start. People would be told to get into their cars and leave town. Wherever they are they should go some place else – maybe out into the country, but the country is where most of our nuclear weapons are stocked. A minor problem. People who don't have cars will be picked up by buses, which presumably will be in perfect working order. In New York State we might have some difficulty figuring out where to go –

because there are four locations spread out in New York State where nuclear weapons are stocked. New Jersey, Connecticut and indeed, almost every state in the nation has supplies of nuclear weapons or nuclear material.

In New York, if the buses don't come, we could always use the subways and maybe our Guardian Angels[7] would save us, because you can be sure that FEMA's plan will not. In fact, the administration's revived civil defence programme is so fraudulent in its assurance of safety that many communities in our nation are refusing to co-operate with it. They say the only defence against nuclear war is no nuclear war.

That is a common-sense response, and we owe it to the common sense of millions of ordinary people in western Europe, Japan, in other countries, and increasingly here in the US, that we are now seeing a mini-competition between the American and Soviet governments on proposals for reducing nuclear armaments. A peace race? Isn't it about time? Thanks to the growing anti-nuke movement and the gratifying emergence of the rapidly spreading nuclear freeze campaign here in the US, the harsh rhetoric and talk of limited nuclear war that had been coming out of Washington has been cooled, and President Reagan is now talking about the need to restrain nuclear weapons. We certainly welcome that, and we can take comfort in the belief that because of our efforts, the common sense of the people, there will probably be serious arms control talks between the two superpowers.

We must encourage the administration and Congress to go in that direction. But let us not be fooled. The Senate has just voted against a reduction in the administration's huge military spending and the President remains opposed to a nuclear freeze. Administration spokesmen say we must have more new weapons so that we can have more bargaining chips in future negotiations. We must have more now so that we can have less later! The Senate has just voted against a reduction in the administration's huge spending programme. In fact, the President tells us that peace depends on public support for a continuing military build-up.

If the arms control or actual arms reduction talks take place with the Soviet Union, the likelihood is that they will require several years to produce an agreement – if they do agree. And, meanwhile, the arms race will escalate. President Reagan's START[8] proposal permits the continued testing, production, and deployment of the MX missile, the Trident II missile, the cruise missile, the BI bomber, the stealth bomber and other advanced nuclear weapons. Indeed, the Reagan proposal does not cover bombers of cruise missiles at all ...

And while the US builds more weapons, the Soviet Union will also be building more. They have their own new weapons on their drawing boards, including the Typhoon submarine and a new generation of missiles beyond their current SS-18s and SS-19s.

The history of past arms control negotiations between the US and Soviet Union shows that the arms race has rushed ahead while the talks drag on ... That is why a mutual freeze now is the only practical idea that can put a stop to this runaway race toward catastrophe. Once armaments and technological advances are frozen at present levels, the two superpowers can get on with the real job of negotiating phased and balanced reductions of existing nuclear weapons and banning the development and production of new arms systems. Our ultimate goal should be an international agreement for a nuclear-free world.

[7] An organization of volunteers, formed by Curtis Sliwa in 1979, who patrolled the streets and subways to protect New York citizens from crime, under the motto 'Dare to Care'.

[8] Strategic Arms Reduction Talks, which eventually led to a treaty signed in 1991.

4

The question before the leaders of these two governments now is whether they will have the vision, determination and responsibility to move past the nitpicking, name-calling, competitive stage and give the people of the world what we so desperately need and want – a peace race so that the human race can survive and flourish. One thing is clear. We cannot afford to continue in the old way – a way that wastes lives, resources and the creative talents of humanity and ignores human needs.

Samuel Adams
American politician

Samuel Adams (1722–1803) was born in Boston, the second cousin of John Adams (1735–1826), the first vice president and second president of the USA. After attending Harvard, he became a tax-collector and then a member of the Massachusetts legislature (1765–74). He organized opposition to the Stamp Act (1765), as well as the Non-Importation Association (1798) and the Boston Committee of Correspondence (1772). He was chief instigator of the so-called Boston Tea Party (1773), during which crates of tea were thrown from British cargo ships into the sea, to protect a boycott on imports. After this, he became a delegate to the First and Second Continental Congresses (1774–5), and signed the Declaration of Independence (4 July 1776). He was lieutenant-governor (1789–94) and later governor (1794–7) of Massachusetts.

'The spirit of liberty which now animates our hearts'
1 August 1776, Philadelphia, Pennsylvania, USA

Samuel Adams came from a respected Puritan family in Massachusetts, which was then ruled by a governor appointed by the British king. At Harvard, he was influenced by theories of the Enlightenment movement, which questioned existing ideas and social institutions and stressed the importance of reason. Adams was also greatly influenced by the Great Awakening, the Protestant Christian revival which swept through the American colonies during the late 18th century, and he devoted much time to prayer and Bible study.

These influences gave him a dislike not only for the existing government, but for any central government. He came to believe that individuals should be free to direct their own lives, under the influence of God, their only true king. He began to campaign for reform, writing and speaking against the government.

In this speech, given at the State House in Philadelphia shortly after the Declaration of Independence, he supports American independence and opposes government by monarchy and the hereditary principle. He describes the British as a 'nation of shopkeepers', a phrase used by Adam Smith in his *Wealth of Nations* (published the same year), implying that the British government's concern for the American colonies was merely that of a shopkeeper's for his customers. He also rails against those fellow citizens who preferred the security of remaining subjects of a British king to 'the animating contest of freedom'.

Countrymen and brethren: I would gladly have declined an honour to which I find myself unequal. I have not the calmness and impartiality which the infinite importance of this occasion demands. I will not deny the charge of my enemies, that resentment for the accumulated injuries of our country, and an ardour for her glory, may deprive me of that accuracy of judgement and expression which men of cooler passions may possess. Let me beseech you, then, to hear me with caution, and to correct the mistakes into which I may be hurried by my zeal.

Truth loves an appeal to the common sense of mankind ... He who made all men hath made the truths necessary to human happiness obvious to all.

Our forefathers threw off the yoke of Popery in religion; for you is reserved the honour of levelling the popery of politics. They opened the Bible to all, and maintained the capacity of every man to judge for himself in religion. Are we sufficient for the comprehension of the sublimest spiritual truths, and unequal to material and temporal ones?

... This day, I trust, the reign of political protestantism will commence. We have explored the temple of royalty, and found that the idol we have bowed down to has eyes which see not, ears that hear not our prayers, and a heart like the nether millstone. We have this day restored the Sovereign to whom alone men ought to be obedient. He reigns in Heaven, and with a propitious eye beholds his subjects assuming that freedom of thought and dignity of self-direction which he bestowed on them. From the rising to the setting sun, may his kingdom come!

… To the eye of reason what can be more clear than that all men have an equal right to happiness? Nature made no other distinction than that of higher and lower degrees of power of mind and body. But what mysterious distribution of character has the craft of statesmen, more fatal than priestcraft, introduced?

According to their doctrine, the offspring of the lewd embraces of a successful invader shall, from generation to generation, arrogate the right of lavishing on their pleasures a proportion of the fruits of the earth, more than sufficient to supply the wants of thousands of their fellow-creatures; claim authority to manage them like beasts of burden, and, without superior industry, capacity, or virtue – nay, though disgraceful to humanity, by their ignorance, intemperance and brutality – shall be deemed best calculated to frame laws and to consult for the welfare of society.

Were the talents and virtues which Heaven has bestowed on men given merely to make them more obedient drudges, to be sacrificed to the follies and ambition of a few? Or, were not the noble gifts so equally dispensed with a divine purpose and law, that they should as nearly as possible be equally exerted, and the blessings of Providence be equally enjoyed by all?

Away, then, with those absurd systems which to gratify the pride of a few debase the greater part of our species below the order of men. What an affront to the King of the universe, to maintain that the happiness of a monster, sunk in debauchery and spreading desolation and murder among men – of a Caligula,[1] a Nero,[2] or a **CHARLES**[3] – is more precious in his sight than that of millions of his suppliant creatures, who do justice, love mercy, and walk humbly with their God!

No, in the judgement of Heaven there is no other superiority among men than a superiority in wisdom and virtue. The Deity, then, has not given any order or family of men authority over others; and if any men have given it, they only could give it for themselves.

Our forefathers, 'tis said, consented to be subject to the laws of Great Britain. I will not, at present, dispute it, nor mark out the limits and conditions of their submission; but will it be denied that they contracted to pay obedience and to be under the control of Great Britain because it appeared to them most beneficial in their then present circumstances and situations? We, my countrymen, have the same right to consult and provide for our happiness which they had to promote theirs …

Ye darkeners of counsel, who would make the property, lives, and religion of millions depend on the evasive interpretations of musty parchments; who would send us to antiquated charters of uncertain and contradictory meaning: prove that the present generation are not bound to be victims to cruel and unforgiving despotism, tell us whether our pious and generous ancestors bequeathed to us the miserable privilege of having the rewards of our honesty, industry, the fruits of those fields which they purchased and bled for, wrested from us at the will of men over whom we have no check …

No man had once a greater veneration for Englishmen than I entertained. They were dear to me as branches of the same parental trunk, and partakers of the same religion and laws; I still view with respect the remains of the constitution as I would a lifeless body, which had once been animated by a great and heroic soul.

But when I am aroused by the din of arms; when I behold legions of foreign assassins, paid by Englishmen to imbrue their hands in our blood;

[1] The despotic Roman Emperor Gaius Julius Caesar Germanicus (AD 12–41).
[2] The despotic Roman Emperor Nero Claudius Caesar Augustus Germanicus (AD 37–68).
[3] The King of England, Scotland and Ireland, Charles I (1600–49) was executed after a long power struggle with Parliament, culminating in the English Civil War.

when I tread over the uncoffined bodies of my countrymen, neighbours and friends; when I see the locks of a venerable father torn by savage hands, and a feeble mother, clasping her infants to her bosom, and on her knees imploring their lives from her own slaves, whom Englishmen have allured to treachery and murder; when I behold my country, once the seat of industry, peace, and plenty, changed by Englishmen to a theatre of blood and misery, Heaven forgive me if I cannot root out those passions which it has implanted in my bosom, and detest submission to a people who have either ceased to be human, or have not virtue enough to feel their own wretchedness and servitude!

Men who content themselves with the semblance of truth talk much of our obligations to Great Britain for protection. Had she a single eye to our advantage? A nation of shopkeepers are very seldom so disinterested. Let us not be so amused with words; the extension of her commerce was her object. When she defended our coasts, she fought for her customers, and convoyed our ships loaded with wealth, which we had acquired for her by our industry. She has treated us as beasts of burden, whom the lordly masters cherish that they may carry a greater load.

Let us inquire also against whom she has protected us? Against her own enemies, with whom we had no quarrel, or only on her account … Did the protection we received annul our rights as men, and lay us under an obligation of being miserable? Who among you, my countrymen, that is a father, would claim authority to make your child a slave because you had nourished him in infancy?

'Tis a strange species of generosity which requires a return infinitely more valuable than anything it could have bestowed; that demands as a reward for a defence of our property a surrender of those inestimable privileges, to the arbitrary will of vindictive tyrants, which alone give value to that very property …

The Author of nature directs all his operations to the production of the greatest good, and has made human virtue to consist in a disposition and conduct which tends to the common felicity of his creatures. An abridgement of the natural freedom of men, by the institutions of political societies, is vindicable only on this foot. How absurd, then, is it to draw arguments from the nature of civil society for the annihilation of those very ends which society was intended to procure! … Dismissing, therefore, the justice of our cause as incontestable, the only question is, what is best for us to pursue in our present circumstances?

The doctrine of dependence on Great Britain is, I believe, generally exploded; but as I would attend to the honest weakness of the simplest of men, you will pardon me if I offer a few words on that subject. We are now on this continent, to the astonishment of the world, three millions of souls united in one cause. We have large armies, well disciplined and appointed, with commanders inferior to none in military skill, and superior in activity and zeal. We are furnished with arsenals and stores beyond our most sanguine expectations, and foreign nations are waiting to crown our success by their alliances … Our success has staggered our enemies.

The hand of Heaven appears to have led us on to be, perhaps, humble instruments and means in the great providential dispensation which is completing. We have fled from the political Sodom;[4] let us not look back,[5] lest we perish and become a monument of infamy and derision to the world. For can we ever expect more unanimity and a better preparation for defence; more infatuation of counsel among our enemies, and more valour

[4] According to Genesis 19, Sodom was destroyed by God as a punishment for the depravity of its citizens.
[5] Lot's wife was turned into a pillar of salt because she turned to look back at Sodom as she fled from the city. See Genesis 19:26.

and zeal among ourselves? The same force and resistance which are sufficient to procure us our liberties will secure us a glorious independence and support us in the dignity of free, imperial states. We cannot suppose that our opposition has made a corrupt and dissipated nation more friendly to America, or created in them a greater respect for the rights of mankind …

From the day on which an accommodation takes place between England and America, on any other terms than as independent States, I shall date the ruin of this country. A politic minister will study to lull us into security, by granting us the full extent of our petitions … Every art of corruption would be employed to loosen the bond of union which renders our resistance formidable. When the spirit of liberty which now animates our hearts and gives success to our arms is extinct, our numbers will accelerate our ruin and render us easier victims to tyranny …

Contemplate the mangled bodies of your countrymen, and then say, 'What should be the reward of such sacrifices? Bid us and our posterity bow the knee, supplicate the friendship, and plough and sow and reap to glut the avarice of the men who have let loose on us the dogs of war to riot in our blood and hunt us from the face of the earth?'

If ye love wealth better than liberty, the tranquillity of servitude than the animating contest of freedom – go from us in peace. We ask not your counsels or arms. Crouch down and lick the hands which feed you. May your chains sit lightly upon you, and may posterity forget that ye were our countrymen!

Jane Addams
American reformer

Jane Addams (1860–1935) was born in Cedarville, Illinois, and attended Rockford College, Illinois. In 1899 she founded the first US settlement house, Hull House in Chicago, dedicated to work among the immigrant poor, where she made her home. Addams worked to secure social justice by sponsoring legislation relating to housing, factory inspection, female suffrage and pacifism. She also campaigned for the abolition of child labour and the recognition of labour unions. Many of these reforms were adopted by the Progressive Party as part of its platform at the presidential election of 1912; Addams seconded THEODORE ROOSEVELT's nomination for president and was an active campaigner on his behalf. She was the first woman president of the National Conference of Social Work (1910), the founder and president of the national Federation of Settlements (1911–35) and the vice president of the National American Woman Suffrage Association (1911–14). She also helped to found the American Civil Liberties Union in 1920. As president of the Women's International League for Peace and Freedom (1919–35), she shared the 1931 Nobel Peace Prize, awarded in recognition of her efforts to end hostilities in World War I. Her many publications include *Democracy and Social Ethics* (1902) and *Peace and Bread in Time of War* (1922).

'The dependence of classes on each other is reciprocal'
Summer 1892, Plymouth, Massachusetts, USA

This speech, given at the Ethical Culture Societies summer school, illustrates Addams's idealistic energy and determination, despite chronic ill-health, to apply her solution of education and social inclusion to the problems of the urban poor. Along with the temperance movement, new child labour laws, women's suffrage and anti-trust legislation, the settlement movement was a reaction against the excesses of the rapid industrialization of 1865–1914. (This period is known as 'The Gilded Age', after a book of that title, published in 1873, by MARK TWAIN and Charles Dudley Warner.)

Founded by Addams and her friend Ellen Gates Starr in 1899, Hull House's success was inspirational in an era before centralized welfare provision. Social settlements provided wide-ranging support for their residents, and the facilities at Hull House included a day nursery, a gymnasium, social clubs, shops and university-level educational courses, as well as boarding facilities for young women. It became a centre for social and civic life among Chicago's immigrant population.

Addams's style of oratory is dense by modern standards, but was not unusual in a time when speeches and lectures often lasted several hours. She used this platform to reinforce the major themes which galvanized her career: social democracy, the role of a newly-educated class (particularly women) and Christianity. In the speech, she observes that political equality does not naturally result in social equality, and argues that a more equitable society can develop if those with wealth, education and social advantages willingly pass on their 'high' culture to the aspiring masses.

Hull House, which was Chicago's first Settlement, was established in September, 1889. It represented no association, but was opened by two women, backed by many friends, in the belief that the mere foothold of a house, easily accessible, ample in space, hospitable and tolerant in spirit, situated in the midst of the large foreign colonies which so easily isolate themselves in American cities, would be in itself a serviceable thing for Chicago.

Hull House endeavours to make social intercourse express the growing sense of the economic unity of society. It is an effort to add the social function to democracy. It was opened on the theory that the dependence of classes on each other is reciprocal …

This paper is an attempt to treat of the subjective necessity for Social Settlements, to analyse the motives which underlie a movement based not only upon conviction, but genuine emotion. Hull House of Chicago is used as an illustration, but so far as the analysis is faithful, it obtains wherever educated young people are seeking an outlet for that sentiment of universal brotherhood, which the best spirit of our times is forcing from an emotion into a motive.

I have divided the motives which constitute the subjective pressure toward Social Settlements into three great lines: the first contains the desire to make the entire social organism democratic, to extend democracy beyond its political expression; the second is the impulse to share the race life, and to bring the accumulation of civilization to those portions of the race which have little; the third springs from a certain renaissance of Christianity, a movement toward its early humanitarian aspects.

It is not difficult to see that although America is pledged to the democratic ideal … democracy has made little attempt to assert itself in social affairs. We have refused to move beyond the position of its 18th-century leaders, who believed that political equality alone would secure all good to all men. We conscientiously followed the gift of the ballot hard upon the gift of freedom to the negro, but we are quite unmoved by the fact that he lives among us in a practical social ostracism. We hasten to give the franchise to the immigrant from a sense of justice, from a tradition that he ought to have it, while we dub him with epithets deriding his past life or present occupation, and feel no duty to invite him to our houses …

The social organism has broken down through large districts of our great cities. Many of the people living there are very poor, the majority of them without leisure or energy for anything but the gain of subsistence. They move often from one wretched lodging to another. They live for the moment side by side, many of them without knowledge of each other, without fellowship, without local tradition or public spirit, without social organization of any kind. Practically nothing is done to remedy this.

The people who might do it, who have the social tact and training, the large houses, and the traditions and custom of hospitality, live in other parts of the city. The clubhouses, libraries, galleries and semi-public conveniences for social life are also blocks away. We find working men organized into armies of producers because men of executive ability and business sagacity have found it to their interests thus to organize them. But these working men are not organized socially.

Although living in crowded tenement-houses, they are living without a corresponding social contact … They have no share in the traditions and social energy which make for progress. Too often their only place of meeting is a saloon, their only host a bartender; a local demagogue forms their public opinion. Men of ability and refinement, of social power and university cultivation, stay away from them …

It is constantly said that because the masses have never had social advantages they do not want them, that they are heavy and dull, and that it will take political or philanthropic machinery to change them. This divides a city into rich and poor; into the favoured, who express their sense of the social obligation by gifts of money, and into the unfavoured, who express it by clamouring for a 'share' — both of them actuated by a vague sense of justice.

This division of the city would be more justifiable if the people who thus isolate themselves on certain streets and use their social ability for each other gained enough thereby to justify the withholding of the pleasures and results of progress from so many people who ought to have them. But they cannot accomplish this … They have been shut off from the common labour by which they live. They feel a fatal want of harmony between their theory and their lives, a lack of co-ordination between thought and action. I think it is hard for us to realize how seriously many of them are taking to the notion of human brotherhood, how eagerly they long to give tangible expression to the democratic ideal. These young men and women, longing to socialize their democracy, are animated by certain hopes.

These hopes may be loosely formulated thus: that if in a democratic country nothing can be permanently achieved save through the masses of the people, it will be impossible to establish a higher political life than the people themselves crave; that it is difficult to see how the notion of a higher civic life can be fostered save through common intercourse; that the blessings which we associate with a life of refinement and cultivation must be made universal if they are to be permanent; that the good we secure for ourselves is precarious and uncertain, is floating in mid-air, until it is secured for all of us and incorporated into our common life.

These hopes are responsible for results in various directions, pre-eminently in the extension of educational advantages. The public schools in the poorest and most crowded wards of the city are inadequate to the number of children, and many of the teachers are ill-prepared and overworked; but in each ward there is an effort to secure public education. The schoolhouse itself stands as a pledge that the city recognizes and endeavours to fulfil the duty of educating its children.

But what becomes of these children when they are no longer in public schools? Many of them never come under the influence of a professional teacher nor a cultivated friend after they are twelve. Society at large does little for their intellectual development ...

The University Extension movement[1] – certainly when it is closely identified with Settlements – would not confine learning to those who already want it, or to those who, by making an effort, can gain it, or to those among whom professional educators are already at work, but would take it to the tailors of East London and the dock-labourers of the Thames. It requires tact and training, love of learning, and the conviction of the justice of its diffusion to give it to people whose intellectual faculties are untrained and disused. But men in England are found who do it successfully, and it is believed there are men and women in America who can do it.

I also believe that the best work in University Extension can be done in Settlements, where the teaching will be further socialized, where the teacher will grapple his students, not only by formal lectures, but by every hook possible to the fuller intellectual life ... The social and educational activities of a Settlement are but differing manifestations of the attempt to socialize democracy, as is the existence of the Settlement itself.

I find it somewhat difficult to formulate the second line of motives which I believe to constitute the trend of the subjective pressure toward the Settlement. There is something primordial about these motives, but I am perhaps over-bold in designating them as a great desire to share the race life. We all bear traces of the starvation struggle which for so long made up the life of the race. Our very organism holds memories and glimpses of that long life of our ancestors which still goes on among our contemporaries ...

You may remember the forlorn feeling which occasionally seizes you when you arrive, early in the morning, a stranger in a great city. The stream of labouring people goes past you. You see hard-working men lifting great burdens; you hear the driving and jostling of huge carts. Your heart sinks with a sudden sense of futility. The door opens behind you and you turn to the man who brings you your breakfast with a quick sense of human fellowship ... You find yourself praying that you may never lose your hold

[1] The University Extension movement emerged in the UK during the 19th century and aimed – in the words of the Cambridge University academic Samuel Earnshaw (1805–88) – to 'place its resources at the disposal of the towns of the country, bringing the advantages of University education to the very doors of the people'.

on it at all. You turn helplessly to the waiter. You feel that it would be almost grotesque to claim from him the sympathy you crave. Civilization has placed you far apart, but you resent your position with a sudden sense of snobbery ...

We have in America a fast-growing number of cultivated young people who have no recognized outlet for their active faculties. They hear constantly of the great social maladjustment, but no way is provided for them to change it, and their uselessness bangs about them heavily. Huxley[2] declares that 'the sense of uselessness is the severest shock which the human system can sustain', and that, if persistently sustained, it results in atrophy of function. These young people have had advantages of college, of European travel and economic study, but they are sustaining this shock of inaction.

[2] The English biologist Thomas Huxley (1825–95).

They have pet phrases, and they tell you that the things that make us all alike are stronger than the things that make us different. They say that all men are united by needs and sympathies far more permanent and radical than anything that temporarily divides them. If they affect art, they say that the decay in artistic expression is due to the decay in ethics, that art when shut away from the great mass of humanity is self-destructive. They tell their elders with all the bitterness of youth that if they expect success from them in business or politics, they must let them consult all of humanity ...

It is not philanthropy, nor benevolence. It is a thing fuller and wider than either of these. This young life, so sincere in its emotion and yet so undirected, seems to me as pitiful as the other great mass of destitute lives. Mr Barnett,[3] who urged the first Settlement – Toynbee Hall, in East London – recognized this need of outlet for the young men of Oxford and Cambridge, and hoped that the Settlement would supply the communication.

[3] The English missionary Canon Samuel Barnett (1844–1913). With his wife Henrietta *later Dame Henrietta Barnett* (1851–1936) he established the first university settlement in Whitechapel, East London, in 1884.

It is easy to see why the Settlement movement originated in England, where the years of education are more constrained and definite than they are here, where class distinctions are more rigid. The necessity of it was greater there, but we are fast feeling the pressure of the need and meeting the necessity for Settlements in America. Our young people feel nervously the need of putting theory into action, and respond quickly to the Settlement form of activity.

The third division of motives which I believe make toward the Settlements is the result of a certain renaissance in Christianity. The impulse to share the lives of the poor, the desire to make social service, irrespective of propaganda, express the spirit of Christ, is as old as Christianity itself ...

The early Christians were pre-eminently non-resistant. They believed in love as a cosmic force. There was no iconoclasm during the minor peace of the Church. They did not yet denounce, nor tear down temples, nor preach the end of the world. They grew to a mighty number, but it never occurred to them to regard other men as their foes or as aliens. The spectacle of the Christians loving all men was the most astounding Rome had ever seen. They were eager to sacrifice themselves for the weak, for children and the aged ... A happiness ranging from the heroic to the pastoral enveloped them. They were to possess a revelation as long as life had new meaning to unfold, new action to propose.

I believe that there is a distinct turning among many young men and women toward this simple acceptance of Christ's message ... The Settlement movement is only one manifestation of that wider humanitarian movement which throughout Christendom, but pre-eminently in England, is endeavouring to embody itself, not in a sect, but in society itself …

It would, I think, be unfair to Hull House not to emphasize the conviction with which the first residents went there, that it would be a foolish and an unwarrantable expenditure of force to oppose or to antagonize any individual or set of people in the neighbourhood; that whatever of good the House had to offer should be put into positive terms; that its residents should live with opposition to no man, with recognition of the good in every man, even the meanest. I believe that this turning, this renaissance of the early Christian humanitarianism, is going on in America – in Chicago, if you please – without leaders who write or philosophize, but with a bent to express in social service, in terms of action, the spirit of Christ. Certain it is that spiritual force is found in the Settlements movement, and it is also true that this force must be evoked and must be called into play before the success of any Settlements is assured …

It is quite impossible for me to say in what proportion or degree the subjective necessity, which led to the opening of Hull House, combined the three trends: first the desire to interpret democracy in social terms; secondly, the impulse beating at the very source of our lives, urging us to aid in the race progress; and, thirdly, the Christian movement toward Humanitarianism. It is difficult to analyse a living thing; the analysis is at best imperfect.

Many more motives may blend with the three trends. Possibly the desire for a new form of social success, due to the nicety of imagination, which refuses worldly pleasures unmixed with the joys of self-sacrifice; possibly a love of approbation, so vast that is it not content with the treble clapping of delicate hands, but wishes also to hear the bass notes from toughened palms, may mingle with these.

Salvador Allende
Chilean politician

Salvador Allende (Gossens) (1908–73) was born in Valparaíso. He studied medicine at the University of Chile in Santiago, where he took an active interest in politics and was arrested several times for radical activities. He helped found the Chilean Socialist Party (1933), a Marxist organization distinct from the Soviet-orientated Communist Party. He was elected to the Chamber of Deputies (1937–41), and later became Minister of Health (1939–42) and a senator (1945–70). He sought, and failed to win, the presidency in 1952, 1958 and 1964 but was narrowly successful in 1970, when he represented *Unidad Popular* 'Popular Unity', a coalition of socialists, communists, radicals and dissident Christian Democrats. He tried to build a socialist society within the framework of a parliamentary democracy but met widespread opposition from business interests, which was supported by the US Central Intelligence Agency (CIA). He was overthrown and killed in September 1973 during a military coup, led by General Augusto Pinochet.

'I will offer my life to defend the principles of this nation'
11 September 1973, radio broadcast from Santiago, Chile

This desperate speech, broadcast from Santiago's besieged presidential palace, marks the end of Allende's three-year effort to establish a socialist democracy in Chile.

Well-intentioned but politically clumsy, Allende had launched education and health programmes, nationalized banks and industries – including some US-owned copper companies – and redistributed wealth through land reform and wage increases. But his economic policies – which included price freezes, printing unsupported currency and defaulting on foreign debts – brought short-lived success. By 1972, the country was in economic turmoil, with rocketing inflation, food shortages and a flourishing black market.

Allende also established diplomatic links with Communist China and Cuba, and the Cuban leader FIDEL CASTRO spent a month in Chile in an advisory role. None of this endeared Allende to RICHARD M NIXON's US government; and a series of crippling strikes – some financed by the CIA – began in 1972.

Unidad Popular retained enough support to win the congressional election of March 1973, but a storm was gathering. A failed coup in June was followed in August by Pinochet's appointment as military commander-in-chief. He soon launched his successful coup and established a brutal dictatorship, which endured for 17 years.

Allende died soon after making this speech. The authorities claimed he had committed suicide, but many believed he had been murdered. The episode is vividly described in the novel *The House of the Spirits* by Isabel Allende, Salvador's niece.

In 1974, Pinochet declared 11 September a national holiday in Chile. In 1999, it was replaced with a Day of National Unity, held in the first week of September.

I will offer my life to defend the principles of this nation. A deluge will fall on those who have broken their word and torn to pieces the honour of the armed forces. The nation must be alert and vigilant. The people must not be provoked and allow themselves to be massacred, but must also defend their conquests. The people must defend their right to live with dignity and to lead a better life.

I call on you to have faith in the name of the most sacred interests of the people and in the name of our beloved nation. The march of history does not stop with crime or repression. We will overcome this most difficult chapter. It is possible they will crush us, but the future will belong to the people; it will belong to the workers. Humanity marches on towards better living conditions.

Fellow countrymen: it is possible they will silence the radios and so I bid you farewell. At this moment, jet planes are passing overhead. It is possible a rain of bullets will fall upon us. But let me tell you that we remain here to show that there are still men in this country who know how to carry out their duties and obligations. I will do my duty, as mandated by the people and with the conscious will of a president who is equal to the dignity of the title …

This might be the last time I will be able speak to you. The Air Force has bombarded the towers of Radio Portales and Radio Corporación.[1] My words do not taste of bitterness but of deception, and those same words will be the moral punishment for those who have betrayed their sworn duties.

Workers of the nation: I want to thank you for your loyalty and the confidence you always had in a man who was only the interpreter of your great yearnings for justice, and who gave his word that he would respect the constitution and the law, and did so. This is the definitive moment, the last time I will be able to address you. I hope you make the most of the lesson.

Foreign capital, imperialism and reactionary forces created the conditions by which the armed forces broke with the tradition – a tradition taught by Schneider[2] and reaffirmed by Commodore Araya,[3] victims of the same tendency that today will be in their houses, waiting for the chance to win back power with somebody else's hand and keep hold of their profits and privileges.

Most of all, I want to direct my words to the modest women of our country: the farm woman who believed in us; the labourer who worked a little more; the mother who knew how to take care of her children. I want to speak to the country's professionals, professional patriots, who battle the sedition sponsored by their colleges – institutions which are working to protect their capitalist privileges.

I want to direct my words to the youth of this nation, to those who sang and who shared their happiness and fighting spirit. I want to speak to the men of Chile – the worker, the farm labourer, the intellectual – and to those who will be persecuted by forces of fascism, forces which were present in terrorist attempts, blown bridges, cut-off railways, the destruction of oil and gas pipelines, in the face of the silence of those who had the obligation to stop them. History will judge them.

Surely Radio Magallanes[4] will soon be silent and my quiet, metallic voice will no longer reach you. It does not matter, because you will continue to hear me. I will always be with you. At least I will be remembered as a man of dignity who was loyal to his nation. The people must not allow themselves to be crushed or shot down, but nor must they allow themselves to be humiliated.

Workers of my country: I have faith in Chile and its destiny. Other patriots will overcome this bitter and grey moment. Always keep in mind that sooner rather than later, the grand avenues through which the free man passes will open up, to build a better society.

Long live Chile! Long live the people! Long live the workers!

These are my last words and I am certain my sacrifice will not be in vain.

[1] Socialist radio stations based in Santiago.

[2] The former commander of the Chilean army General René Schneider (1913–70), a close ally of Allende. He was fatally wounded while resisting a kidnap attempt in October 1970. In 2001, a lawsuit was filed against Henry Kissinger (1923–), former national security adviser to President Nixon, alleging CIA involvement in the plot.
[3] Allende's naval aide Commodore Arturo Araya Peter was murdered at his home in July 1973. A rebel group of military police was blamed.

[4] The Socialist radio station on which this speech was broadcast.

Yasser Arafat

Palestinian resistance leader and politician

Yasser Arafat *real name Mohammed Abed Ar'ouf* (1929–2004) was born in Jerusalem and educated at Cairo University (1952–6). He co-founded the Al Fatah resistance group in 1956. In 1959 he began contributing to a new Beirut magazine, *Filastinuna* ('Our Palestine'). In 1964 the Arab states founded the Palestine Liberation Organization (PLO). By 1969, Arafat's Al Fatah group had gained control of the organization, and he became its acknowledged (though not universally popular) leader. The organization was formally recognized by the United Nations in 1974. Under Arafat's leadership, the PLO's original aim – to create a secular state over the whole of former Palestine – was modified to one of establishing an independent state within the territory. In the 1980s, growing factionalism reduced his power and in 1983, he was forced to leave Lebanon. In 1985, he agreed with King Hussein of Jordan to recognize the state of Israel, provided that occupied territory was restored. This initiative failed but Hussein later renounced Jordan's claim to the West Bank, indicating that the PLO might take over. Arafat persuaded many colleagues to acknowledge the right of Israel to co-exist with an independent Palestine. In 1993 Arafat and the Israeli prime minister YITZHAK RABIN negotiated a peace agreement in the USA (signed in Cairo in 1994), under which Israel withdrew from Jericho and the Gaza Strip. Arafat and Rabin, together with Israel's Foreign Minister Shimon Peres, were awarded the Nobel Prize for peace in 1994. Arafat returned as head of a Palestinian state (1994). In 1995, he negotiated Israeli withdrawal from the West Bank. Peace was jeopardized later that year by Israeli encroachment into the West Bank, suicide attacks by Hamas terrorists, and above all the assassination of Rabin. In January 1996, Arafat was comfortably elected president of the Palestinian Authority. In 2000, he attended the Camp David Summit convened by American president BILL CLINTON with the new Israeli prime minister Ehud Barak, but rejected their proposals. In 2002, Israel occupied Arafat's headquarters at Ramallah, confining him there and alleging documentary evidence of his links with terrorism. Later that year, the Arab League made an offer to recognize Israel in exchange for territory and recognition of the Palestinian Authority. However, this was followed by terrorist strikes against Israeli civilians and Israeli military retaliation. By 2003, Arafat was widely considered unable to control Arab militancy. He died in November 2004 of an illness whose nature was disputed.

'I have come bearing an olive branch and a freedom fighter's gun'

13 November 1974, New York City, USA

Yasser Arafat was the first representative of a non-governmental organization to be invited to address the General Assembly of the United Nations. He appeared at their New York headquarters wearing a *kaffiyeh* headscarf, with his gun-belt strapped around his waist. Although it is unlikely that there was a weapon in the holster, the timing was remarkable. In 1972 the Black September Organization – believed to be linked to the PLO – had murdered eleven Israeli athletes at the Munich Summer Olympics. The following year, Egypt and Syria had attacked Israeli positions on the Suez Canal and the Golan Heights, supported by other Arab states and probably the Soviet Union. Cold War politics influenced both Arafat's invitation to speak and its outcome.

In this speech, translated from Arabic, Arafat blames the troubles of the Middle East on imperialism and Zionism. These, he says, conspired in the partition of Palestinian land following the Balfour Declaration (1917), by which the British Foreign Secretary ARTHUR BALFOUR expressed British support for the establishment of a Jewish homeland in Palestine. Arafat seeks to legitimize the PLO as freedom fighters by reiterating the themes of just cause and legitimate struggle, and reminds his listeners that many of them achieved independence through similar colonial wars. His repetition of the word 'exile' also has echoes in the Jewish history of exile and diaspora. Arafat ends his speech with a veiled threat of further violence.

Despite this, he received a standing ovation from most of the audience. A year later, Resolution 3237 granted the PLO observer status at the UN. It was the first non-governmental body to be recognized in this way.

Mr President: I thank you for having invited the Palestinian Liberation Organization to participate in this plenary session of the United Nations General Assembly. This is a very important occasion. The question of Palestine is being re-examined by the United Nations, and we consider that step to be a victory for the world organization as much as a victory for the cause of our people ...

Our world aspires to peace, justice, equality and freedom. It wishes that oppressed nations, at present bent under the weight of imperialism, might gain their freedom and their right to self-determination. It hopes to place the relations between nations on a basis of equality, peaceful coexistence, mutual respect for each other's internal affairs, secure national sovereignty, independence and territorial unity on the basis of justice and mutual benefit. This world resolves that the economic ties binding it together should be grounded in justice, parity and mutual interest. It aspires finally to direct its human resources against the scourge of poverty, famine, disease and natural calamity, toward the development of productive scientific and technical capabilities to enhance human wealth – all this in the hope of reducing the disparity between the developing and the developed countries …

Great numbers of peoples, including those of Zimbabwe, Namibia, South Africa and Palestine, among many others, are still victims of oppression and violence … It is imperative that the international community should support these peoples in their struggles, in the furtherance of their rightful causes, in the attainment of their right to self-determination …

[But] despite abiding world crises, despite even the gloomy powers of backwardness and disastrous wrong, we live in a time of glorious change. An old world order is crumbling before our eyes, as imperialism, colonialism, neo-colonialism and racism, the chief form of which is Zionism, ineluctably perish. We are privileged to be able to witness a great wave of history bearing peoples forward into a new world which they have created. In that world just causes will triumph. Of that we are confident.

The question of Palestine belongs to this perspective of emergence and struggle … Present at this very moment in our midst are those who, while they occupy our homes, as their cattle graze in our pastures, and as their hands pluck the fruit of our trees, claim at the same time that we are disembodied spirits, fictions without presence, without traditions or future …

Until recently some people have regarded – and continued to regard – our problem as merely a problem of refugees. They have portrayed the Middle East question as little more than a border dispute between the Arab states and the Zionist entity. They have imagined that our people claims rights not rightfully its own and fights with neither logic nor valid motive, with a simple wish only to disturb the peace and to terrorize wantonly.

For there are amongst you – and here I refer to the United States of America and others like it – those who supply our enemy freely with planes and bombs and with every variety of murderous weapon. They take hostile positions against us, deliberately distorting the true essence of the problem. All this is done not only at our expense, but at the expense of the American people, and of the friendship we continue to hope can be cemented between us and this great people, whose history of struggle for the sake of freedom we honour and salute.

I cannot now forgo this opportunity to appeal from this rostrum directly to the American people, asking it to give its support to our heroic and fighting people. I ask it whole-heartedly to endorse right and justice, to recall GEORGE WASHINGTON to mind, heroic Washington whose purpose was his nation's freedom and independence; ABRAHAM LINCOLN, champion of the destitute and the wretched; also WOODROW WILSON, whose doctrine of Fourteen Points[1] remains subscribed to and venerated by our people …

[1] President Wilson set out a programme for world peace in his 'Fourteen Points' speech of January 1918, which is included in this book.

18

As our discussion of the question of Palestine focuses upon historical roots, we do so because we believe that any question now exercising the world's concern must be viewed radically, in the true root sense of that word, if a real solution is ever to be grasped … The roots of the Palestinian question reach back into the closing years of the 19th century, in other words, to that period which we call the era of colonialism and settlement, as we know it today. This is precisely the period during which Zionism as a scheme was born; its aim was the conquest of Palestine by European immigrants, just as settlers colonized, and indeed raided, most of Africa …

Just as colonialism and its demagogues dignified their conquests, their plunder and limitless attacks upon the natives of Africa with appeals to a 'civilizing and modernizing' mission, so too did waves of Zionist immigrants disguise their purposes as they conquered Palestine … Just as colonialism heedlessly used the wretched, the poor, the exploited as mere inert matter with which to build and to carry out settler colonialism, so too were destitute, oppressed European Jews employed on behalf of world imperialism and of the Zionist leadership. European Jews were transformed into the instruments of aggression; they became the elements of settler colonialism intimately allied to racial discrimination.

Zionist theology was utilized against our Palestinian people: the purpose was not only the establishment of western-style settler colonialism but also the severing of Jews from their various homelands and subsequently their estrangement from their nations. Zionism is an ideology that is imperialist, colonialist, racist; it is profoundly reactionary and discriminatory; it is united with anti-Semitism in its retrograde tenets and is, when all is said and done, another side of the same base coin. For when what is proposed is that adherents of the Jewish faith, regardless of their national residence, should neither owe allegiance to their national residence nor live on equal footing with its other, non-Jewish citizens – when that is proposed we hear anti-Semitism being proposed.

So the Zionist movement allied itself directly with world colonialism in a common raid on our land. Allow me now to present a selection of historical truths about this alliance.

The Jewish invasion of Palestine began in 1881. Before the first large wave of immigrants started arriving, Palestine had a population of half a million; most of the population was either Muslim or Christian, and only 20,000 were Jewish. Every segment of the population enjoyed the religious tolerance characteristic of our civilization. Palestine was then a verdant land, inhabited mainly by an Arab people in the course of building its life and dynamically enriching its indigenous culture.

Between 1882 and 1917 the Zionist movement settled approximately 50,000 European Jews in our homeland. To do that it resorted to trickery and deceit in order to implant them in our midst. Its success in getting Britain to issue the Balfour Declaration[2] once again demonstrated the alliance between Zionism and imperialism. Furthermore, by promising to the Zionist movement what was not hers to give, Britain showed how oppressive was the rule of imperialism.

As it was constituted then, the League of Nations abandoned our Arab people, and Wilson's pledges and promises came to nought. In the guise of a mandate, British imperialism was cruelly and directly imposed upon us, to enable the Zionist invaders to consolidate their gains in our homeland.

In the wake of the Balfour Declaration and over a period of 30 years, the Zionist movement succeeded, in collaboration with its imperialist ally, in

[2] Arthur Balfour defended the provisions of the Balfour Declaration in a speech of 1922, which is included in this book.

19

settling more European Jews on the land, thus usurping the properties of Palestinian Arabs.

By 1947 the number of Jews had reached 600,000; they owned about six per cent of Palestinian arable land. The figure should be compared with the population of Palestine, which at that time was 1,250,000.

As a result of the collusion between the mandatory power and the Zionist movement and with the support of some countries, this General Assembly early in its history approved a recommendation to partition our Palestinian homeland ... When we rejected that decision, our position corresponded to that of the natural mother who refused to permit King Solomon to cut her son in two when the unnatural mother claimed the child for herself and agreed to his dismemberment.

Furthermore, even though the partition resolution granted the colonialist settlers 54 per cent of the land of Palestine, their dissatisfaction with the decision prompted them to wage a war of terror against the civilian Arab population. They occupied 81 per cent of the total area of Palestine, uprooting a million Arabs. Thus, they occupied 524 Arab towns and villages, of which they destroyed 385, completely obliterating them in the process. Having done so, they built their own settlements and colonies on the ruins of our farms and our groves.

The roots of the Palestine question lie here. Its causes do not stem from any conflict between two religions or two nationalisms. Neither is it a border conflict between neighbouring states. It is the cause of a people deprived of its homeland, dispersed and uprooted, and living mostly in exile and in refugee camps.

With support from imperialist and colonialist Powers, [Israel] managed to get itself accepted as a United Nations member. It further succeeded in getting the Palestine question deleted from the agenda of the United Nations and in deceiving world public opinion by presenting our cause as a problem of refugees in need either of charity from do-gooders, or settlement in a land not theirs.

Not satisfied with all this, the racist entity, founded on the imperialist-colonialist concept, turned itself into a base of imperialism and into an arsenal of weapons. This enabled it to assume its role of subjugating the Arab people and of committing aggression against them, in order to satisfy its ambitions for further expansion on Palestinian and other Arab lands. In addition to the many instances of aggression committed by this entity against the Arab States, it has launched two large-scale wars, in 1956 and 1967, thus endangering world peace and security.

As a result of Zionist aggression in June 1967, the enemy occupied Egyptian Sinai as far as the Suez Canal. The enemy occupied Syria's Golan Heights, in addition to all Palestinian land west of the Jordan. All these developments have led to the creation in our area of what has come to be known as the 'Middle East problem'. The situation has been rendered more serious by the enemy's persistence in maintaining its unlawful occupation and in further consolidating it, thus establishing a beachhead for world imperialism's thrust against our Arab nation.

All Security Council decisions and appeals to world public opinion for withdrawal from the lands occupied in June 1967 have been ignored. Despite all the peaceful efforts on the international level, the enemy has not been deterred from its expansionist policy ...

The fourth war broke out in October 1973, bringing home to the Zionist enemy the bankruptcy of its policy of occupation, expansion and its reliance on the concept of military might. Despite all this, the leaders of the Zionist entity are far from having learned any lesson from their experience. They are making preparations for the fifth war, resorting once more to the language of military superiority, aggression, terrorism, subjugation and, finally, always to war in their dealings with the Arabs.

It pains our people greatly to witness the propagation of the myth that its homeland was a desert until it was made to bloom by the toil of foreign settlers, that it was a land without a people, and that the colonialist entity caused no harm to any human being. No: such lies must be exposed from this rostrum, for the world must know that Palestine was the cradle of the most ancient cultures and civilizations. Its Arab people were engaged in farming and building, spreading culture throughout the land for thousands of years, setting an example in the practice of freedom of worship, acting as faithful guardians of the holy places of all religions.

As a son of Jerusalem, I treasure for myself and my people beautiful memories and vivid images of the religious brotherhood that was the hallmark of our holy city before it succumbed to catastrophe … Our revolution has not been motivated by racial or religious factors. Its target has never been the Jew as a person, but racist Zionism and undisguised aggression. In this sense, ours is also a revolution for the Jew as a human being as well. We are struggling so that Jews, Christians and Muslims may live in equality, enjoying the same rights and assuming the same duties, free from racial or religious discrimination.

We do distinguish between Judaism and Zionism. While we maintain our opposition to the colonialist Zionist movement, we respect the Jewish faith. Today, almost one century after the rise of the Zionist movement, we wish to warn of its increasing danger to the Jews of the world, to our Arab people and to world peace and security …

Those who call us terrorists wish to prevent world public opinion from discovering the truth about us and from seeing the justice on our faces. They seek to hide the terrorism and tyranny of their acts, and our own posture of self-defence.

The difference between the revolutionary and the terrorist lies in the reason for which each fights. For whoever stands by a just cause and fights for the freedom and liberation of his land from the invaders, the settlers and the colonialists cannot possibly be called terrorist, otherwise the American people in their struggle for liberation from the British colonialists would have been terrorists; the European resistance against the Nazis would be terrorism; the struggle of the Asian, African and Latin American peoples would also be terrorism – and many of you who are in this assembly hall were considered terrorists.

This is actually a just and proper struggle, consecrated by the United Nations Charter and by the Universal Declaration of Human Rights. As to those who fight against the just causes, those who wage war to occupy, colonize and oppress other people, those are the terrorists … Thousands of our people were assassinated in their villages and towns; tens of thousands of others were forced at gunpoint to leave their homes and the lands of their fathers. Time and time again our children, women and aged were evicted and had to wander in the deserts and climb mountains without any food or water …

Their terrorism fed on hatred and this hatred was even directed against the olive tree in my country, which has been a proud symbol and which reminded them of the indigenous inhabitants of the land, a living reminder that the land is Palestinian – thus they sought to destroy it … Their terrorism even reached our sacred places in our beloved and peaceful Jerusalem. They have endeavoured to de-Arabize it and make it lose its Muslim and Christian character by evicting its inhabitants and annexing it …

Need one remind this assembly of the numerous resolutions adopted by it condemning Israeli aggressions committed against Arab countries, Israeli violations of human rights and the articles of the Geneva Conventions, as well as the resolutions pertaining to the annexation of the city of Jerusalem and its restoration to its former status? The only description for these acts is that they are acts of barbarism and terrorism. And yet, the Zionist racists and colonialists have the temerity to describe the just struggle of our people as terror. Could there be a more flagrant distortion of truth than this?

… I am a rebel and freedom is my cause. I know well that many of you present here today once stood in exactly the same resistance position as I now occupy and from which I must fight. You once had to convert dreams into reality by your struggle … Why therefore should I not dream and hope? For is not revolution the making real of dreams and hopes? So let us work together that my dream may be fulfilled, that I may return with my people out of exile, there in Palestine to live with this Jewish freedom-fighter and his partners, with this Arab priest and his brothers, in one democratic state where Christian, Jew and Muslim live in justice, equality, fraternity and progress. Is this not a noble dream? … In my formal capacity as Chairman of the Palestine Liberation Organization and leader of the Palestinian revolution, I appeal to you to accompany our people in its struggle to attain its right to self-determination …

Today I have come bearing an olive branch and a freedom fighter's gun. Do not let the olive branch fall from my hand. I repeat: do not let the olive branch fall from my hand.

Nancy Astor
Anglo-American politician and socialite

Nancy Witcher Astor, *née Langhorne; later Viscountess Astor* (1879–1964) was born in Danville, Virginia, USA, the daughter of a wealthy tobacco auctioneer. In 1906 she married her second husband Waldorf Astor, *later 2nd Viscount Astor*, whom she succeeded as Conservative MP for Plymouth Sutton in 1919, becoming the first woman MP to sit in the House of Commons. She held the seat until 1945, when she retired under pressure from her husband. She was known for her interest in social problems, especially women's rights and temperance.

'The best club in Europe'
November 1937, broadcast on the BBC Empire Service from London, England

Nancy Astor was the second woman to be elected to the British Parliament, but the first to take her seat. She had retained her husband's constituency in a by-election when he moved to the House of Lords following the death of his father. The Representation of the People Act (1918) not only gave the vote to women over 30, but also allowed them to stand for Parliament and, although she had never been a suffragette, she benefited from the new legislation.

At this time it was not unusual for parliamentarians to continue in their primary employment; and the hours and social life of government reflected this. Lady Astor campaigned against the sale of alcohol to minors (her maiden speech was in support of the Temperance Society) and disliked smoking, so the Commons' *modus operandi* was bound to be irritating. She was also known for her irreverent attitude towards the more arcane procedures of the House, and for her tendency to interrupt debates.

She brought to the Commons not only her progressive views on the role of women – including equal opportunity in the Civil Service, and support for nursery schools – but also her wit and social contacts. Her 'Clevenden set' included many influential people, among them WINSTON CHURCHILL, her sparring partner in the Commons.

In retort to the anecdote given here, Lady Astor seems to have had the last word. She reportedly told Churchill, 'You're not handsome enough to have such fears.'

It's often been called, you know, the House of Commons, 'The Best Club in Europe' – well it certainly did not seem the best club to me. In fact, I can't think of anything worse, in the way of havin' a good time, than being among 600 men, none of whom really wanted you there. Of course, they believed in equality – I mean, theoretically. But a woman in their club? Oh no, that was too much.

Well I don't blame them. No doubt we as women would have felt the same way, and probably behaved far worse, if we'd had it for all those years to ourselves.

Winston Churchill, you know, who I knew quite well, like many other Members of the House, who I knew intimately, simply could not bring themselves to speak to me, once I was in the House. But after about two years I met Winston at dinner and he congratulated me on my performance. I asked him why he'd not spoken to me before, and he replied: 'We thought that if we could freeze you out we could get rid of the lot.'

'Why,' asked I, 'why did you want to get rid of the lot?'

'Well,' replied Winston, 'when you entered the House of Commons, I felt as though some woman had entered my bath, and I'd nothin' to protect myself with except my sponge.'

Clement Attlee
English politician

Clement Richard Attlee *later 1st Earl Attlee* (1883–1967) was born in Putney, London. He was educated at University College, Oxford, and was called to the Bar in 1905. Through Haileybury House, a boys' club in the Stepney slums, he developed a practical interest in social problems which, alongside the works of John Ruskin and William Morris, converted him to socialism, and in 1910 he became secretary of Toynbee Hall in London. A lectureship at the newly-founded London School of Economics (1913–23) was interrupted by service in World War I, in which he attained the rank of major and was wounded. In 1919 he became the first Labour Mayor of Stepney, and in 1922 he entered Parliament and became RAMSAY MACDONALD's parliamentary secretary (1922–4), then Under-Secretary of State for War (1924). He served on the Simon Commission on India (1927–30) and was Postmaster-General (1931). One of the few Labour MPs to retain his parliamentary seat in the following election, he became deputy leader of the opposition (1931–5) under George Lansbury, whom he succeeded as Labour leader in 1935. He paved the way for WINSTON CHURCHILL's wartime premiership by refusing to join a coalition under NEVILLE CHAMBERLAIN. He was Dominions Secretary (1942–3) and Deputy Prime Minister (1942–5) in Churchill's War Cabinet. As leader of the opposition he accompanied Sir ANTHONY EDEN to the San Francisco and Potsdam Conferences (1945), and returned to the latter as prime minister after the 1945 Labour victory. Despite severe economic problems during his six years in office, he carried through a vigorous programme of nationalization and reform – the National Health Service was introduced and independence was granted to India (1947) and Burma (1948). Labour's foreign policy of support for NATO in the face of Russian intransigence, particularly the necessity for re-arming the Germans and the manufacture of British atom bombs, precipitated continuing party strife which at times taxed Attlee's competent chairmanship. He earned affection and respect through his sheer lack of dogma, oratorical gifts or showmanship; by his balanced judgement; and by the quiet authority which belied the public image of 'Little Clem'. He was leader of the opposition 1951–5, then resigned and accepted an earldom. His many books include *The Labour Party in Perspective* (1937), with the supplement *Twelve Years Later* (1949), and an autobiography, *As It Happened* (1954).

'We are determined not only to win the war but to win the peace'
29 October 1941, New York City, USA

Clement Attlee's call to 'win the peace' was one of the great rousing slogans of World War II; he repeated it in 1945 to lead Labour to a post-war victory. The occasion for the words' first airing, however, was an address to the International Labour Organization in New York in October 1941.

Attlee's main aim in the speech was to promote the joint declaration known as the Atlantic Charter, made in August that year by Winston Churchill and US president FRANKLIN D ROOSEVELT. This was a set of broad principles that promised a collaborative approach to international relations after the war. Attlee's support for the charter was twofold: as the senior Labour figure in the wartime coalition government, he had long pressed for post-war planning to ensure a fairer world; in addition, like Churchill, he knew the importance of the declaration in bringing the USA closer to entering the war. Two months later, the Japanese attack on Pearl Harbor would achieve precisely that.

Attlee is a towering figure in British politics of the 20th century, but is not remembered as a great public speaker: his style of oratory – as demonstrated by this example – is dry and precise. Comparing his delivery to Churchill's, he once wrote, 'I eschew embroidery and stick to a plain statement.' Like its speaker, this speech – which draws on the wording of the Atlantic Charter itself – is a study in quiet determination.

We do not envisage an end to this war save victory. We are determined not only to win the war but to win the peace. Plans must be prepared in advance. Action must be taken now if the end of the war is not to find us unprepared. But the problems of the peace cannot be solved by one nation in isolation. The plans of a post-war Britain must be fitted into the plans of a post-war world, for this fight is not just a fight between nations. It is a fight for the future of civilization. Its result will affect the lives of all men and women – not only those now engaged in the struggle.

It is certain that until the crushing burden of armaments[1] throughout the world is lifted from the backs of the people, they cannot enjoy the

[1] This phrase is one of several taken directly from the Atlantic Charter. The charter also urged 'for realistic as well as spiritual reasons ... the abandonment of the use of force'.

maximum social well-being which is possible. We cannot build the city of our desire under the constant menace of aggression. Freedom from fear and freedom from want must be sought together.

The joint expression of aims – common to the United States and the British Commonwealth of Nations – known as the Atlantic Charter includes not only purposes covering war but outlines of more distant objectives.

It binds us to endeavour, with due respect to our existing obligations, to further the enjoyment by all states – great and small, victors and vanquished – of access on equal terms to trade and raw materials which are needed for their economic prosperity. In addition, it records our desire to bring about the fullest collaboration between all nations in the economic field with the object of securing for all labour standards, economic advancement and social security.[2]

But it is not enough to applaud these objectives. They must be attained. And if mistakes are to be avoided, there must be the closest international collaboration in which we in the United Kingdom will gladly play our part.

We are determined that economic questions and questions of the universal improvement of standards of living and nutrition shall not be neglected, as they were after the last war, owing to the preoccupation with political problems.[3] The fact is that wars do not enrich but impoverish the world; and bold statesmanship will be needed if we are to repair the ravages of war and to insure to all the highest possible measure of labour standards, economic advancement and social security to which the Atlantic Charter looks forward.

[3] A series of events at the end of World War I, including the Bolshevik revolution in Russia and the collapse of imperial dynasties across central and eastern Europe, served to increase the instability caused by the war itself.

[2] The call for 'improved labour standards, economic advancement and social security', also echoing the Atlantic Charter, was first made by the English trade union leader Ernest Bevin (1881–1951), who served as Minister of Labour in the wartime coalition government and as Foreign Minister in Atlee's post-war government.

Aung San Suu Kyi
Burmese political leader

Aung San Suu Kyi (1945–) was born in Rangoon, the daughter of the nationalist hero General Aung San (1915–47), who founded the Anti-Fascist People's Freedom League and led Burma's fight for independence until his assassination a few months before it was achieved. Her mother was Khin Kyi (1914–88) who became Burma's ambassador to India in 1961. Suu Kyi went with her to India, and later attended Oxford University, where she read Politics, Philosophy and Economics. In 1969, she worked for the United Nations in New York. After a period in Bhutan, she went to Kyoto University in Japan, and later returned to Oxford where she and her husband Michael Aris (1946–99), whom she married in 1972, pursued their academic careers and raised their two sons. In 1988 she returned to Burma, which was in a state of extreme political unrest under a new military junta. After appeals to the government for more open consultation, she helped found the National League for Democracy (NLD) and became its general secretary. The government had established its State Law and Order Restoration Council, introduced martial law and imprisonment without trial, and banned public meetings, forbidding Suu Kyi to hold her office. Nonetheless, she toured the country addressing supporters and as a result was held under house arrest by the military junta (1989–95), allowed only two visits from her husband and one from her sons. Despite this, the NLD won 80 per cent of the popular vote in the elections of 1990, although the result was ignored and many newly elected MPs were jailed. Her release in July 1995 did not change her long-standing conviction that the military had no place in politics, but she emphasized the need for dialogue and reconciliation, appealing to exiled Burmese opposition groups to practise patience. She was reappointed general secretary of the NLD in October 1995, but was continually vilified by the pro-government newspapers. She continued to address supporters and work towards the framing of a new constitution but experienced constant persecution by the government, including restrictions on her movements (1998), further periods of house arrest (2000–2, 2003–10) and imprisonment (May 2003). She was finally released on 13 November 2010, in the wake of a much criticized general election, and in 2012 the NLD successfully contested that year's by-elections, with Suu Kyi assuming a seat in the lower house of the Burmese Parliament and the position of Leader of the Opposition. She has been awarded the Sakharov Prize for Freedom of Thought (1990), the Nobel Peace Prize (1991), the Simón Bolívar Prize (1992), the Presidential Medal of Freedom (2000) and the Congressional Gold Medal (2012).

'No war was ever started by women'
31 August 1995, delivered via videotape in Huairou, China

The 1995 NGO Forum on Women 'Looking at the World through Women's Eyes' was held between 30 August and 8 September. Originally scheduled to take place alongside the Fourth United Nations Conference on Women in Beijing, it was relocated by the Chinese government to Huairou, 45 miles away. At the time of the forum, many of the facilities at the Huairou site were unfinished, transport into Beijing was sporadic and interpretation facilities were lacking.

Forum convenor Supatra Masdit had invited Aung San Suu Kyi to address the forum but, recently freed following six years of house arrest, Suu Kyi declined the invitation, fearing that she would not be allowed to return to Burma if she left. Masdit visited Suu Kyi in August, asking her to prepare a speech which she would record on a subsequent visit. When Masdit was refused a visa to return, Suu Kyi recorded a videotape of her speech and had it smuggled out of the country.

Suu Kyi's video began the first working session of the Forum. It was played to an appreciative audience of around 4,000, packed into a converted cinema which notionally held 1,500. The Chinese authorities (key supporters of the Burmese military leaders) had attempted to divert potential attendees by making misleading announcements about the venue.

In this, her first international speech following her release from detention, Suu Kyi spoke calmly and clearly in English about the need for peace, security, human rights and democracy.

It is a wonderful but daunting task that has fallen on me to say a few words by way of opening this forum, the greatest concourse of women – joined by a few brave men – that has ever gathered on our planet. I want to try and voice some of the common hopes which firmly unite us in our splendid diversity.

But first I would like to explain why I cannot be with you in person today.

Last month I was released from almost six years of house arrest. The regaining of my freedom has in turn imposed a duty on me to work for the freedom of women and men in my country who have suffered far more – and who continue to suffer far more – than I have. It is this duty which prevents me from joining you today.

Even sending this message to you has not been without difficulties. But the help of those who believe in international co-operation and freedom of expression has enabled me to overcome the obstacles. They have made it possible for me to make a small contribution to this great celebration of the struggle of women to mould their own destiny and to influence the fate of our global village.

The opening plenary of this forum will be presenting an overview of the global forces affecting the quality of life of the human community and the challenges they pose for the global community as a whole and for women in particular as we approach the 21st century. However, with true womanly understanding, the convener of this forum suggested that among these global forces and challenges, I might wish to concentrate on those matters which occupy all my waking thoughts these days: peace, security, human rights and democracy. I would like to discuss these issues particularly in the context of the participation of women in politics and governance.

For millennia, women have dedicated themselves almost exclusively to the task of nurturing, protecting and caring for the young and the old, striving for conditions of peace that favour life as a whole. To this can be added the fact that, to the best of my knowledge, no war was ever started by women. But it is women and children who have always suffered most in situations of conflict. Now that we are gaining control of the primary historical role imposed on us of sustaining life in the context of the home and family, it is time to apply in the arena of the world the wisdom and experience thus gained in activities of peace over so many thousands of years. The education and empowerment of women throughout the world cannot fail to result in a more caring, tolerant, just and peaceful life for all.

If to these universal benefits of the growing emancipation of women can be added the 'peace dividend' for human development offered by the end of the Cold War, spending less on the war toys of grown men and much more on the urgent needs of humanity as a whole, then truly the next millennium will be an age the like of which has never been seen in human history. But there still remain many obstacles to be overcome before we can achieve this goal. And not least among those obstacles are intolerance and insecurity.

This year is the International Year for Tolerance. The United Nations has recognized that 'tolerance, human rights, democracy and peace are closely related. Without tolerance, the foundations that form democracy and respect for human rights cannot be strengthened, and the achievement of peace will remain elusive.'

My own experience during the years I have been engaged in the democracy movement of Burma has convinced me of the need to emphasize the positive aspect of tolerance. It is not enough simply to 'live and let live': genuine tolerance requires an active effort to try to understand the point of view of others; it implies broad-mindedness and vision, as well as confidence in one's own ability to meet new challenges without resorting to intransigence or violence. In societies where men are truly confident, women are not merely tolerated, they are valued. Their opinions are listened to with respect; they are given their rightful place in shaping the society in which they live.

There is an outmoded Burmese proverb still recited by men who wish to deny that women too can play a part in bringing necessary change and progress to their society: 'The dawn rises only when the rooster crows'. But Burmese people today are well aware of the scientific reasons behind the rising of dawn and the falling of dusk. And the intelligent rooster surely realizes that it is because dawn comes that it crows and not the other way round. It crows to welcome the light that has come to relieve the darkness of night. It is not the prerogative of men alone to bring light to this world: women, with their capacity for compassion and self-sacrifice, their courage and perseverance, have done much to dissipate the darkness of intolerance and hate, suffering and despair.

Often the other side of the coin of intolerance is insecurity. Insecure people tend to be intolerant, and their intolerance unleashes forces that threaten the security of others. And where there is no security there can be no lasting peace. In its Human Development Report for this year, the UNDP[1] noted that human security 'is not a concern with weapons – it is a concern with human life and dignity'. The struggle for democracy and human rights in Burma is a struggle for life and dignity. It is a struggle that encompasses our political, social and economic aspirations. The people of my country want the two freedoms that spell security: freedom from want and freedom from fear. It is want that has driven so many of our young girls across our borders to a life of sexual slavery where they are subject to constant humiliation and ill-treatment. It is fear of persecution for their political beliefs that has made so many of our people feel that even in their own homes they cannot live in dignity and security.

Traditionally the home is the domain of the woman. But there has never been a guarantee that she can live out her life there safe and unmolested. There are countless women who are subjected to severe cruelty within the heart of the family which should be their haven. And in times of crisis when their menfolk are unable to give them protection, women have to face the harsh challenges of the world outside while continuing to discharge their duties within the home.

Many of my male colleagues who have suffered imprisonment for their part in the democracy movement have spoken of the great debt of gratitude they owe to their womenfolk, particularly to their wives who stood by them firmly, tender as mothers nursing their newly born, brave as lionesses defending their young. These magnificent human beings who have done so much to aid their men in the struggle for peace and justice – how much more could they not achieve if given the opportunity to work in their own right for the good of their country and of the world?

Our endeavours have also been sustained by the activities of strong and principled women all over the world who have campaigned not only for my release but, more importantly, for our cause. I cannot let this opportunity pass without speaking of the gratitude we feel towards our sisters everywhere, from heads of government to busy housewives. Their efforts have been a triumphant demonstration of female solidarity and of the power of an ideal to cross all frontiers ...

The adversities that we have had to face together have taught all of us involved in the struggle to build a truly democratic political system in Burma that there are no gender barriers that cannot be overcome. The relationship between men and women should, and can be, characterized not by patronizing behaviour or exploitation, but by *metta* (that is to say loving kindness), partnership and trust. We need mutual respect and understanding between men and women, instead of patriarchal domination and degradation, which are expressions of violence and engender counter-violence. We can learn from each other and help one another to moderate the 'gender weaknesses' imposed on us by traditional or biological factors.

There is an age-old prejudice the world over to the effect that women talk too much. But is this really a weakness? Could it not in fact be a strength? Recent scientific research on the human brain has revealed that women are better at verbal skills while men tend towards physical action. Psychological research has shown on the other hand that disinformation engendered by men has a far more damaging effect on its victims than feminine gossip. Surely these discoveries indicate that women have a most valuable contribution to make in situations of conflict, by leading the way to solutions based on dialogue rather than on viciousness and violence. ... All the world's great religions are dedicated to the generation of happiness and harmony. This demonstrates the fact that together with the combative instincts of man there exists a spiritual aspiration for mutual understanding and peace ...

The last six years afforded me much time and food for thought. I came to the conclusion that the human race is not divided into two opposing camps of good and evil. It is made up of those who are capable of learning and those who are incapable of doing so. Here I am not talking of learning in the narrow sense of acquiring an academic education, but of learning as the process of absorbing those lessons of life that enable us to increase peace and happiness in our world. Women in their role as mothers have traditionally assumed the responsibility of teaching children values that will guide them throughout their lives. It is time we were given the full opportunity to use our natural teaching skills to contribute towards building a modern world ...

As we strive to teach others, we must have the humility to acknowledge that we too still have much to learn. And we must have the flexibility to adapt to the changing needs of the world around us. Women who have been taught that modesty and pliancy are among the prized virtues of our gender are marvellously equipped for the learning process. But they must be given the opportunity to turn these often merely passive virtues into positive assets for the society in which they live.

These, then, are our common hopes that unite us – that as the shackles of prejudice and intolerance fall from our own limbs we can together strive to identify and remove the impediments to human development everywhere. The mechanisms by which this great task is to be achieved provide the proper focus of this forum. I feel sure that women throughout the world who, like me, cannot be with you join me now in sending you all our prayers and good wishes for a joyful and productive meeting.

I thank you.

❧

'The time of our greatest need'

21 June 2012, Westminster Hall, London

❧

In June 2012 the newly elected MP and National League for Democracy leader Aung San Suu Kyi visited the UK. On the 21 June she addressed the joint Houses of Commons and Lords in Westminster Hall, giving an impassioned plea for Britain to assist her country as it struggled to recreate itself as a parliamentary democracy.

Lord Speaker, Mr Speaker, Mr Prime Minister, My Lords, and Members of the House of Commons. Thank you for inviting me to speak to you here in this magnificent hall. I am very conscious of the extraordinary nature of this honour. I understand that there was some debate as to whether I would speak here in this splendid setting or elsewhere in the Palace of Westminster.[1] I welcome that debate and discussion. It is what Parliament is all about.

I have just come from Downing Street. It is my first visit there, and yet for me it is a familiar scene. Not just from television broadcasts, but from my own family history. As some of you may be aware, the best-known photograph of my father, Aung San, taken shortly before his assassination in 1947 was of him standing in Downing Street with CLEMENT ATLEE[2] and others with whom he had been discussing Burma's transition to independence.

He was pictured wearing a large British military-issue greatcoat. This had been given to him by JAWAHARLAL NEHRU[3] en route to the UK to protect him against the unaccustomed cold. And I must say that not having left my tropical country for 24 years, there have been the odd moments this week when I have thought of that coat myself.

A couple of hours ago I was photographed in the same place where my father was photographed, together with Prime Minister David Cameron,[4] and it was raining. Very British!

My father was a founding member of the Burmese Independence Army[5] in World War II. He took on this responsibility out of a desire to see democracy established in his homeland. It was his view that democracy was the only political system worthy of an independent nation. It is a view of course that I have long shared.

General Slim,[6] commander of the 14th Army, who led the Allied Burmese campaign, wrote about his first encounter with my father in his memoir *Defeat until Victory*. The meeting came towards the end of the war, shortly after my father had decided that the Burmese Independence Army should join forces with the Allies. General Slim said to my father: 'You've only come to us because we are winning.' To which my father replied, 'It wouldn't be much good coming to you if you weren't!' Slim saw in my father a practical man with whom he could do business. Six decades later, I strive to be as practical as my father was.

And so I am here, in part, to ask for practical help. Help as a friend and as an equal. In support of the reforms which can bring better lives and greater opportunities to the people of Burma who have been for so long deprived of their rights and place in the world.

As I said yesterday in Oxford,[7] my country today stands at the start of a journey toward I hope a better future. So many hills remain to be climbed, chasms to be bridged, obstacles to be breached. Our own determination can get us so far. The support of the people of Britain and of peoples around the world can get us so much further.

[1] The largely 19th-century building that is the meeting place of the two houses of Parliament of the UK. Westminster Hall is the oldest existing part of the Palace, dating back to the 11th century, and it is considered a high honour for a foreign leader to address both houses there.

[2] Clement Attlee later 1st Earl Attlee (1883–1967), British Prime Minister, 1945–51.
[3] Jawaharlal Nehru (1889–1964), Indian statesman.

[4] David Cameron (1966–), British Prime Minister, 2010–.
[5] The Burmese Independence Army was the army set up by Burmese independence leaders in 1941. Initially, the army fought in collaboration with the Japanese as they sought to end British colonial rule in Burma, but later switched sides.

[6] William Slim later 1st Viscount Slim (1891–1970), commander of the 14th Army, 1943–5, which comprised multinational forces drawn from Commonwealth countries.

[7] On the previous day Suu Kyi had given a speech at her former university when receiving an honorary doctorate.

In a speech about change and reform, it is very appropriate to be in Westminster Hall, because at the heart of this process must be the establishment of a strong, parliamentary institution in my own country. The British Parliament is perhaps the pre-eminent symbol to oppressed peoples around the world of freedom of speech. I would imagine that some people here, to some extent, take this freedom for granted.

For us in Burma, what you take for granted, we have had to struggle for long and hard. So many people in Burma gave up so much, gave up everything in Burma's ongoing struggle for democracy, and we are only now just beginning to see the fruits of our struggle.

Westminster has long set a shining example of realizing the people's desire to be part of their own legislative process. In Burma our parliament is in its infancy, having been established only in March 2011. As with any new institution, especially an institution which goes against the cultural grain of 49 years of direct military rule, it will take time to find its feet and time to find its voice.

Our new legislative processes, which undoubtedly are an improvement on what has gone before, are not as transparent as they might be. I would like to see us learn from established examples of parliamentary democracies elsewhere, so that we might deepen our own democratic standards over time.

Perhaps the most critical moment in establishing the credibility of the parliamentary process happens before parliament even opens, namely the people's participation in a free fair inclusive electoral process. Earlier this year I myself participated in my first election as a candidate. To this day, however, I have not yet had the chance to vote freely in any election. In 1990 I was allowed to cast an advanced vote while under house arrest.

But I was prevented from contesting as a candidate for my party, the National League for Democracy. I was disqualified on the grounds that I had received help from foreign quarters. This amounted to BBC broadcasts that the authorities considered to be biased in my favour. What struck me most ahead of this year's by-elections, was how quickly people in the constituencies around Burma grasped the importance of participating in the political process. They understood first hand that the right to vote was not something given to all. They understood that they must take advantage when the opportunity arose, because they understood what it meant to have that opportunity taken away from them.

During the years that I lived in the United Kingdom, I never had the right to vote myself. But I can remember, even during my university days, that I was always trying to encourage my friends to exercise their right to vote. It was never clear to me if they followed these instructions. But it was very clear to me even then that if we do not regard the rights we have, we run the risk of seeing those rights erode away.

To those who feel themselves to be somehow above politics I want to say that politics should be seen neither as something that exists above us, nor as something that happens beneath us, but something that is integral to our everyday existence.

After my marriage, I constantly preached my gospel of political participation to my late husband, Michael. I still distinctly recall the occasion when a canvasser knocked on the door of our Oxford home during an election campaign. Michael opened the door and when he saw the gentleman poised to deliver his campaign pitch, said, 'It's no use trying to win me over. It's my wife who decides how I should vote. She's out now. Why don't you come back later?'

The canvasser did come back later mainly I think to see what a wife who decided how her husband should vote looked like.

It has been less than 100 days, since I together with my fellow National League for Democracy candidates was out on the campaign trail across Burma. Our by-elections were held on April 1st, and I was conscious there was a certain scepticism that this would turn out to be an elaborate April Fool's joke. In fact, it turned out to be an April of new hope.

The voting process was largely free and fair, and I would like to pay tribute to President Thein[8] for this and for his commitment and his sincerity in the reform process.

[8] Thein Sein (1945–), Burmese politician and former military commander, Prime Minister, 2007–11, President, 2011– ; considered by many as a moderate who has led the way in the post-junta reforms.

As I have long said, it is through dialogue and through cooperation that political differences can best be resolved, and my own commitment to this path remains as strong as ever.

Elections in Burma are very different to those in many more established democracies such as yours. Apathy, especially amongst the young, is certainly not an issue. For me, the most encouraging and rewarding aspect of our own elections was the participation in such vast numbers and with such enthusiasm of our young people. Often our biggest challenge was in restraining the crowds of university students, schoolchildren and flag-waving toddlers who greeted us on the campaign, blocking the roads throughout the length of towns.

The day before the elections, on the way to my constituency, I passed a hillock which had been occupied by a group of children, the oldest about 10 or 11, their leader standing at the summit holding the NLD flag.

The passion of the electorate was a passion born of hunger for something long denied.

Following Burma's independence in 1948, our parliamentary system was of course based on that of the United Kingdom. The era became known in Burmese as the Parliamentary Era, a name which, by the mere necessity of its application, speaks of the unfortunate changes which followed.

Our parliamentary era, which lasted more or less until 1962, could not be said to have been perfect. But it was certainly the most progressive and promising period until now in the short history of independent Burma. It was at this time that Burma was considered the nation most likely to succeed in South East Asia. Things did not, however, go entirely to plan. They often don't in Burma and indeed in the rest of the world.

Now once again we have an opportunity to re-establish true democracy in Burma. It is an opportunity for which we have waited many decades. If we do not use this opportunity, if we do not get things right this time around, it may be several decades more before a similar opportunity arises again.

And so it is for this reason that I would ask Britain as one of the oldest parliamentary democracies to consider what it can do to build the sound institutions needed to support our nascent parliamentary democracy.

The reforms taking place led by President Thein Sein are to be welcomed. But this cannot be a personality-based process. Without strong institutions this process will not be sustainable. Our legislature has much to learn about the democratization process, and I hope that Britain and other democracies can help by sharing your own experiences with us.

Thus far I have only spent a matter of minutes inside the Burmese Parliament when I took the oath as a new MP last month. I must say that I found the atmosphere rather formal. Men have to wear formal headgear. There is certainly no heckling. I would wish that over time perhaps we would reflect the liveliness and relative informality of Westminster. I am not unaware of the saying that more tears have been shed over wishes granted than over wishes denied.

Nevertheless, it is when Burma has its own satisfactory equivalent of Prime Minister's Questions that we will be able to say that parliamentary democracy has truly come of age.

I would also like to emphasize the importance of establishing requisite parliamentary control over the budget.

In all this, what is most important is to empower the people, the essential ingredient of democracy. Britain is living proof that a constitution does not need to be written down to be effective. It is more important that a constitution should be accepted by the people, that the people feel it belongs to them, that it is not an external document imposed on them.

One of the clearly stated aims of my party, the National League for Democracy, is constitutional reform. [Burma's] original constitution was drawn up following the meeting between my father Aung San and Clement Attlee here in London in 1947. This constitution may not have been perfect, but at its core was a profound understanding of and respect for the aspirations of the people.

The current constitution, drawn up by the military government in 2008, must be amended to incorporate the basic rights and aspiration of Burma's ethnic nationalities. In over 60 years of independence Burma has not yet known a time when we could say that there is peace throughout the land.

At this very moment, hostilities continue between the Kachin[9] forces and the state armed forces in the north. In the west, communal strife has led to the loss of innocent lives and the displacement of tens of thousands of hapless citizens. Since this speech was drafted, I've also heard that hostilities have resumed in the east of the country between Shan troops and the troops of the government.

We need to address the problems that lie at the root of conflict. We need to develop a culture of political settlement through negotiation and to promote the rule of law, that all who live in Burma may enjoy the benefits of both freedom and security.

In the immediate term, we also need humanitarian support for the many peoples in the north and west, largely women and children, who have been forced to flee their homes.

As the long history of the United Kingdom shows clearly, people never lose their need to preserve their national or ethnic identity. This is something which goes beyond, which supersedes economic development. And that is why I hope that in working for Burma's national reconciliation, the international community will recognize that it is political dialogue and political settlement which must be given precedence over short-term economic development.

If differences remain unresolved, if basic aspirations remain unfulfilled, there cannot be an adequate foundation for sustainable development of any kind – economic, social or political.

Britain has for so long, under successive governments, including the present Conservative / Liberal Democratic coalition, and the previous

[9] Kachin is the most northerly constituent state of Burma and home to the Kachin peoples. For much of the late 20th century, the Kachin Independence Army was engaged in a bloody civil war with the Burmese government. Fighting restarted in 2011, though intermittent peace talks began early in 2013. Shan State, in eastern Burma, has also long been embroiled in intermittent civil war.

Labour government, been a staunch and unshakeable supporter of aid efforts in Burma. I hope that you can continue to help our country through targeted and coordinated development assistance. Britain has been until now the largest bilateral donor to Burma. It is in education in particular that I hope the British can play a major role. We need short-term results so that our people may see that democratization has a tangible positive impact on their lives.

Vocational training and creation of employment opportunities to help address Burma's chronic youth unemployment are particularly important. Longer term, Burma's education system is desperately weak. Reform is needed, not just of schools and the curriculum, and the training of teachers, but also of our attitude to education, which is too narrow and rigid.

I hope also that British businesses can play a role in supporting the democratic reform process, through what I have termed democracy-friendly investment. By this I mean investment that prioritizes transparency, accountability, workers' rights, and environmental sustainability. Investment particularly in labour-intensive sectors when carried out responsibly and with positive intent, can offer real benefits to our people.

One test will be whether new players will benefit from the investment coming in. Britain has played an important role in facilitating the forthcoming visit next month of the Extractive Industries Transparency Initiative Secretariat.[10] I hope this will be the start of many similar initiatives in the month ahead.

It is through learning, while at Oxford, about two great British leaders, GLADSTONE[11] and DISRAELI,[12] that I first developed my understanding of parliamentary democracy: that one accepts the decision of the voters; that the governing power is gained and relinquished in accordance with the desires of the electorate, and that ultimately everyone gets another chance.

These are things taken for granted here in Britain, but in 1990 the winner of the elections was never allowed even to convene parliament. I hope that we can leave such days behind us, and that as we look forward to the future, it will be the will of the people that is reflected faithfully in Burma's changing political landscape.

This journey out of Burma has not been a sentimental pilgrimage to the past, but an exploration of the new opportunities at hand for the people of Burma. I have been struck throughout my trip by how extraordinarily warm-hearted and open the world has been to us.

To experience this first hand after so long physically separated from the world has been very moving. Countries that geographically are distant have shown that they are close to Burma in what really matters: they are close to the aspirations of the people of Burma. We are brought into proximity through our shared values, and no geographical distance, no human-made barriers can stand in our way.

During the years of my house arrest, it was not just the BBC and other broadcasting stations that kept me in touch with the world outside. It was the music of Mozart and Ravi Shankar and the biographies of men and women of different races and religions that convinced me I would never be alone in my struggle. The prizes and honours I received were not so much a personal tribute as a recognition of the basic humanity that unites one isolated person to the rest of the world.

[10] The Extractive Industries Transparency Initiative (EITI), whose secretariat is based in Oslo, Norway, works to promote transparency in the exploitation of countries' oil, gas and mineral resources. Burma has rich gas and oil resources and is the world's biggest producer of rubies.

[11] William Ewart Gladstone (1809–98), British Prime Minister 1853–5, 1859–66, 1873–4 and 1880–2. [12] Benjamin Disraeli *1st Earl of Beaconsfield* (1804–81), British Prime Minister 1874–80.

During our dark days in the 1990s a friend sent me a poem by Arthur Hugh Clough.[13] It begins – I think many of you will know it—'Say Not the Struggle Naught Availeth'. I understand that WINSTON CHURCHILL, one of the greatest parliamentarians this world has known, used this poem as a plea to the United States to step in against Nazi Germany.

Today I want to make a rather different point that we can work together, combining political wisdom from East and West to bring the light of democratic values to all peoples in Burma and beyond.

I will just read the final verse (I was advised that the whole poem was far too long):

> And not by eastern windows only,
>   When daylight comes, comes in the light;
> In front the sun climbs slow, how slowly,
>   But westward, look, the land is bright.

I would like to emphasize in conclusion that this is the most important time in Burma. That this is the time of our greatest need. And so I would ask that our friends both here in Britain and beyond participate in and support Burma's efforts towards the establishment of a truly just and democratic society.

Thank you for giving me this opportunity to address the members of one of the oldest democratic institutions in the world. Thank you for letting me into your midst. My country has not entered the ranks of truly democratic societies but I am confident that we will get there before too long.

With your help.

[13] Arthur Hugh Clough (1819–61), Victorian poet. Suu Kyi quotes the fourth stanza of 'Say Not the Struggle Naught Availeth' – a rousing call to weary soldiers to keep up their struggle.

Stanley Baldwin
English politician

Stanley Baldwin *later 1st Earl Baldwin of Bewdley* (1867–1947) was born in Bewdley, Worcestershire and educated at Harrow and Trinity College, Cambridge. He succeeded his father as Conservative MP for West Worcestershire in 1908. He became joint financial secretary of the Treasury (1917) and president of the Board of Trade (1921). In October 1922 he was instrumental in bringing down the coalition government with a speech that revealed Conservative distrust of its leader, DAVID LLOYD GEORGE. He served as Chancellor of the Exchequer in Andrew Bonar Law's brief administration (1922–3) and in January 1923 visited the USA to settle the British debt incurred during World War I. This was accomplished at terms less favourable than had been hoped, and Baldwin faced criticism. Nonetheless he became prime minister in May 1923, after illness forced Bonar Law to retire. Baldwin served three periods as prime minister (1923–4; 1924–9; 1935–7), interrupted by RAMSAY MACDONALD'S two Labour administrations (1924; 1929–31) and National coalition government (1931–5). He lost the election of 1929, but from 1931, he served as Lord President of the Council in MacDonald's coalition. After ADOLF HITLER became German Chancellor in 1933, Baldwin sought to remedy deficiencies in defence, steadily stepping up the pace of rearmament. He placed the issue at the centre of his 1935 election campaign, while also seeking to preserve peace (eg with the Anglo-German naval agreement of 1935, which limited the size of Hitler's fleet). Baldwin was widely criticized for Anglo-French negotiations of December 1935, which proposed to cede Ethiopian territory to Italy, and declined to intervene in the Spanish Civil War of 1936. He was noted for his tact and resolution during the constitutional crisis culminating in EDWARD VIII's abdication (1936). Having resolved to step down at 70, he took the opportunity to do so following the coronation of George VI. On retiring, he received his peerage. His political career was marked by liberal conservatism, commitment to parliamentary democracy and high standards in public life. Although an enduring myth sprang up after Dunkirk that he had neglected rearmament, at the time of his retirement he was held in high esteem among colleagues, opponents and much of the public. WINSTON CHURCHILL wrote in 1948 that Baldwin left office 'loaded with honours and enshrined in public esteem'.

'To tell the truth needs no art at all'
11 March 1924, Cambridge, England

The entry given for 'rhetoric' in *The Chambers Dictionary* includes the definition, 'the whole art of using language so as to persuade others'. Given the role of such an art in politics, it is perhaps surprising to find a politician describing it as 'one of the greatest dangers of modern civilization'.

In spring 1924, Baldwin was both a past and a future prime minister. He was invited to take part in a debate on rhetoric at Cambridge Union, the university's prestigious debating society, where many an aspiring statesman has honed his rhetorical skills. Indeed, the future Cabinet minister 'Rab' Butler was its president at this time.

Baldwin opposed the motion, 'That this House has the highest regard for rhetoric', supporting his argument with a range of references both literary and political. These included allegations of deceit levelled at his parliamentary foe Lloyd George.

Butler later wrote: 'The Union, having a high regard for rhetoric, were puzzled as to why [Baldwin] should avoid the very art which justified our Union's existence.' In fact, Baldwin's speech is consistent with his political goals of the time: exposing the extravagant rhetoric employed by Labour and Liberal leaders as misleading; and presenting the Conservatives as a sober and reliable alternative.

The outcome was a tied vote. Butler, in keeping with tradition, used his casting vote to uphold the motion. The following morning, as he accompanied the distinguished guest to the railway station, Baldwin told him, 'that intellectualism was a sin, and would lead a young man to a fate worse than death'.

I sometimes think that possibly a man's views of rhetoric may be coloured according to whether he possesses it or is without it; this may be the reason why Mr Mitchell Banks,[1] who has made such an eloquent plea, finds himself in opposition to me. I have never been a rhetorician or an orator. I attribute this largely to the fact that, much as I used to enjoy reading speeches, I was greatly struck when I was about 18, at coming across a phrase in Froude,[2] 'Oratory is the harlot of the arts,' illustrated, as Froude

[1] The Unionist MP Reginald Mitchell Banks (1880–1940).

[2] The English historian James Anthony Froude (1818–94).

could illustrate it, with a wealth of eloquence! There is nothing odd about that, because you will remember that there was no-one who fulminated more against rhetoric than Carlyle,[3] probably the greatest rhetorician who ever put pen to paper. I was reading in him only the other day that the best thing man could do was to doom himself to eternal silence, which Carlyle never could do, except when he was smoking a pipe with Tennyson.[4]

MrTheobald [the mover of the resolution] made a most characteristic remark in his definition of rhetoric, a definition on which a good deal depends. He defined it as a marshalling of facts which were likely to persuade people. I entirely agree with him, except that he has left out the other half of the sentence, which is the essence of my case: 'concealing the facts which are likely to dissuade people'. There is a good deal more in rhetoric than the marshalling of facts, otherwise *The Origin of Species*[5] would have been the greatest work of rhetoric the world has produced.

To tell the truth needs no art at all, and that is why I always believe in it. We have each attempted our own definition of rhetoric. I would rather define it by illustrations of what I mean by rhetoric, which I regard as one of the greatest dangers of modern civilization. I am going to give you two or three phrases which I call rhetorical phrases, and each of them, to my mind, is pregnant with darkness and confusion. Consider this one of three words from one of the greatest rhetoricians of the ages: 'Bulging corn bins'.[6] 'The democratic control of the means of production'[7] is another. I tried in the House of Commons to get that last phrase translated from rhetorical English into English that I could understand, and the only answer I got was that it was impossible to produce rabbits from a top hat. 'Self-determination' is another rhetorical term that may some day lead the nations into a bloody war. That is what rhetoric does. 'Homes fit for heroes to live in'[8] and 'A world safe for democracy!'[9] These, to my mind, are the quintessence of rhetoric, and it is against rhetoric in this sense that I am going to vote tonight.

I suppose everyone will admit that a great rhetorician was CHARLES FOX, who said something which illustrates my point very clearly: 'If a speech reads well it must be a damned bad speech.' I mean by this that Mr Mitchell Banks will read his speech tomorrow morning with less pleasure than that with which he heard the cheers for it tonight. Rhetoric is meant to get the vote of a division or at an election, but God help the man who tries to think on it!

Such speeches as have been quoted in support of rhetoric could not be delivered nowadays. The character and temper of the audience and the people have so changed that what may have been possible for Macaulay[10] is impossible today. The rhetoric of today, the rhetoric we have to consider, is the rhetoric of the 'bulging corn bins'. I suppose that this gift has been responsible for more bloodshed on this earth than all the guns and explosives that have ever been invented. If we look back only over the last century, was there anything more responsible for the French Revolution than the literary rhetoric of Rousseau,[11] fanned by the verbal rhetoric of Robespierre[12] and others, just as the Russian Revolution was due to the rhetoric of Kerensky[13] – flatulent rhetoric which filled the bellies of his people with the east wind?

That appalling twopenny-ha'penny gift of fluency, with the addition of a certain amount of training and of imagination in word-spinning, is the kind of rhetoric which stirs the emotions of the ignorant mob and sets it moving. It is because such forces can be set in motion by rhetoric that I have

[3] The Scottish essayist and historian Thomas Carlyle (1795–1881).

[4] The English poet and poet laureate Alfred Tennyson, 1st Baron Tennyson (1809–92).

[5] The book (correctly titled *On the Origin of Species*) published in 1859 by the English naturalist Charles Darwin (1809–82), in which he put forward his revolutionary theory of evolution.

[6] In March 1920, Lloyd George raised hopes of resolving a food shortage with reference to Russian corn bins 'bulging with grain'.
[7] A phrase associated with the core principles of democratic Socialism.

[8] Another dictum of Lloyd George, associated with the Housing Act of 1919, which addressed a housing shortage by compelling councils to build accommodation.
[9] A phrase used by US President WOODROW WILSON in his speech of April 1917, calling for a declaration of war on Germany. The speech is included in this book.

[10] The English historian and politician THOMAS MACAULAY.

[11] The French philosopher and writer Jean-Jacques Rousseau (1712–78) was a key influence on French revolutionary thinking. His book *The Social Contract* (1762) contains the famous phrase 'Liberté, égalité, fraternité', an inspirational slogan during the French Revolution of 1789.

[12] The French Revolutionary leader MAXIMILIEN ROBESPIERRE was much influenced by Rousseau.
[13] Alexander Fyodorovich Kerensky (1881–1970) was a Russian revolutionary leader who served as Prime Minister of the provisional government from July 1917 until Lenin seized power in the October Revolution of the same year.

no regard for it, but a positive horror. Very rarely do we find the gift given to men who have wisdom and constructive power, and for the time being it would seem that it was in this world a force far beyond its merits, although in the more advanced countries I sometimes hope that it is past its prime. At least I believe that in England and Scotland at any rate rhetoric of the kind I have tried to describe no longer makes that appeal to the people.

I think that it may be that the people of this country are getting just the least bit suspicious of the literary rhetoric of our Sunday press, and of our daily press, and that this very wholesome dread, this wholesome nervousness, is being transferred from the press to the platform. I think that throughout this country there is today a far greater desire than there has ever been before to hear plain, unadorned statements of cases. I believe that anyone who has taken part in recent elections – a few constituencies excepted – will agree with me that one of the most remarkable features is the way in which large audiences all over the country will listen to a statement of a case, whether they agree with it or not, provided they feel that the statement is made honestly and fairly, and with due consideration for the opposite view.

Let us always remember this: when we come to big things we do not need rhetoric. Truth, we have always been told, is naked. She requires very little clothing. After all, St Paul[14] was no orator, and yet his speeches and his teaching seem to have spread and to have lasted a long time. I cannot help feeling that if we were to go back 2,000 years I would back St Paul and the results of his teaching against all the rhetoric of a Sunday paper or of the leading orators of the age.

If there is one thing which those who have been in any other profession than the Bar distrust more than another it is the eloquent man. In the business world, other things being equal, the man who has the power of talking is not the man who gets promotion. To be able to express oneself in business is always to be written down as being not quite first-class, and it is a joyous fact that in most of the towns of the kingdom we find that the men of business who talk most in such places as Chambers of Commerce are not the men who are making a success of the big businesses in the country. From this I argue that it is not necessarily the man most fluent of speech to whom we should entrust the destinies of the country.

[14] Paul of Tarsus (AD 3–67) was a leading evangelist of the early Christian Church. A number of his 'epistles' offering guidance to followers of JESUS around the Mediterranean are recorded as books of the New Testament.

'It is necessary for this country to put its defensive house in order'
30 July 1934, London, England

The deliberate steps by which Britain moved towards rearmament during the 1930s are at the heart of Baldwin's legacy. Though his reputation suffered during the 1940s and afterwards from the allegation that he had resisted rearmament, he was in fact instrumental in building up British military strength.

In 1932, recognizing the threat from advances in aircraft technology, he had supported rearmament, warning Parliament that 'the bomber will always get through'. In 1934 – two weeks after announcing a major expansion of the Royal Air Force – he reiterated the same phrase in this speech. By now, however, he was defending a policy of armed deterrence.

At this time, Baldwin was Lord President of the Privy Council, effectively second-in-command in RAMSAY MACDO-NALD's coalition government. In the aftermath of World War I, disarmament negotiations had been under way since the mid-1920s; and a disarmament conference held in Geneva, Switzerland had been in progress for over two years. But with ADOLF HITLER installed as Chancellor, Germany and other countries were rearming rapidly, and Baldwin was convinced of the need to rearm Britain.

The occasion of this speech was a censure motion brought by the Labour MP Charles Edwards, attacking the government's rearmament policy as 'certain to jeopardize the prospects of international disarmament and to encourage a revival of dangerous and wasteful competition in preparation for war'. Baldwin was called upon to defend a policy that was both politically under attack and unpopular with the public.

The Labour opposition motion was defeated and Baldwin persevered with rearmament. This became central to his mandate when he won the election of 1935.

❧

The main obstacle, as the whole House knows, to the conclusion of the Disarmament Convention today is the insistence of Germany on an immediate measure of rearmament and France's refusal to agree to it. This gulf is not easy to bridge, but it is not likely to be made any wider by our remedying the deficiencies in our own national defences. It is even possible that, had our own scale of armaments been higher, we should have been better able to influence the course of the Disarmament Conference.

Our representatives at Geneva have not always had an easy task in making proposals which involved much greater concessions from the more heavily armed nations, and they have got tired of hearing us descanting on our own virtue in not having increased our armaments. On the other hand, if the other nations find that we are no longer content to remain comparatively disarmed in this respect when they are all armed, and that increasing expenditure on their part may be met in like manner by ourselves, that in itself will be no mean weapon to use in inclining them to discuss more seriously than some of them have yet done the question of aerial disarmament.

The figures which we have announced do not achieve that parity which is our ultimate aim within the next five years.[1] We would much rather, if it were possible, attain that parity by agreement at the lower figure for which we have worked so hard at Geneva.[2] But remember this: if we were to wait until danger was imminent … which is what many people would do, we should run the risk of precipitating that very danger which we seek to avoid. No expectant intending aggressor would give us time, and as I said a few minutes ago, air defences cannot be improvised, nor can they be brought about in a moment. It takes time, and there must come a moment when it is necessary for this country to put its defensive house in order, unless we can achieve the disarmament for which we have been trying.

No government dare take the responsibility of reducing this country, in the world as it is today, to a state of defencelessness, and from a careful review of the whole situation and from a study of the information of every kind at our disposal, we are convinced that we shall be neglecting our duty to the people of this country if we delay any longer in bringing these proposals forward …

We have to provide for the safety not only of these islands, but of a widespread empire with trade routes that run from country to country. A glance at the map of the world will show that on these trade routes the power of air, unless it be used from shipboard, is very limited and that the bulk of the trade routes are on the open sea, where they can be attacked only by ships and defended only by ships. In the long years of financial depression – and do not let us think we are through those years yet; I throw out that caveat – we have regretfully allowed, and every government has regretfully allowed, deficiencies to accumulate. Those deficiencies, so far as it may be possible, will have to be rectified in the next few years …

The truth is that a bomber will always get through. That is perfectly true, but it is not true to say that because of that it is a waste of money to increase your air force. The stronger your force to attack the enemy when

[1] A manufacturing programme was under way which aimed to increase the number of British military aircraft from 844 to 1,304 within five years, bringing the RAF roughly in line with the air forces of other European countries, particularly Germany.

[2] At Geneva, the British Draft Convention had proposed complete abolition of military aircraft, with a ceiling of 500 per country by the end of the convention.

he tries to bomb you, the more difficult you make it for him. Some will always get through; but there comes a point when he has to think very seriously whether the game is worth the candle. The last German air raid on London[3] was a very severe one, but it was the last, and I may remind the House that a large number of those raiders were turned back at the coast. Of those getting across the coast, a quarter were brought down and killed. That kind of proportion is true of later raids over Paris. Sixty per cent of the raiders were turned back that night at the coast and more than a quarter of those crossing the coast were destroyed.

Have honourable Members ever asked themselves this question? No naval authority would guarantee to us that in the event of war a submarine of the enemy will not sink one of our ships or will not sink one of our food ships. No naval authority will assure us immunity for all our food ships, however many cruisers we have got. Do we therefore say, 'We will do without cruisers altogether, because there is no defence?' Do we say, 'We will do without attempting to destroy the submarine, because the submarine will always get through?' Of course we do not; and that is true of the air. There is no deterrent to any country which is contemplating the use of the air like knowing that the other country which it may be thinking of invading is not going to sit, shivering, waiting for the invasion, but is, while realizing perfectly well that it will suffer, prepared to defend itself and to make it as difficult for the aggressor as possible. That is our position.

In exactly the same way, let us just remember this. The president of the Board of Trade,[4] at the end of last week, was speaking about his trade agreements. We all remember, in the lifetime of the last government, our late friend Mr William Graham[5] going to Geneva full of hope, but weaponless, unarmed, to make trade agreements on the Continent. We know that that visit was a complete failure, in spite of his being – so far as arguments went, and qualifications – as well-equipped for that purpose and that task as any man in this country. My right honourable friend was successful, not because he is a better man than the late president of the Board of Trade, but because he was armed.

That lesson shows that there is a certain truth in what I hinted at in the earlier part of my speech, that we may well have suffered in the past at Geneva in having so little to give away and nothing with which to bargain. Honourable Members opposite will, of course, think that a ridiculous statement. Honourable Members opposite, even my right honourable friend the leader[6] has not, I think, been in a Cabinet that has had to consider these matters, and to take the responsibility of decisions on their shoulders and justify them to the country. Let me remind him, and I shall be glad to hear his criticism of it, of these words: 'We wish to reduce armaments and expenditure, but we cannot get anything accomplished with a diplomacy that is impotent for want of power behind it.'

Those words were not written by me; they were written by Lord Haldane[7] to the present prime minister after the defeat of the Labour Party in the winter of 1924. Lord Haldane was a man who, on questions of defence and armaments, knew as much as if not more than any man in that government or in any government since the war. That was his deliberate opinion, written privately and published in his autobiography, and I think those words are well to be considered …

There is one other thing. The greatest crime to our own people is to be afraid to tell the truth.[8] I notice with great regret that in a good deal of the propaganda that goes about in this country the truth is not being told. We

[3] Between November 1916 and the end of the war two years later, German raids dropped more than 250 tonnes of bombs over England. There were around 9,000 casualties.

[4] The English Liberal politician Walter Runciman *later 1st Viscount Runciman of Doxford* (1870–1949) served as President of the Board of Trade, 1931–7, under both MacDonald and Baldwin.
[5] The Scottish Labour politican William Graham (1887–1932) served as President of the Board of Trade, 1929–31, and had attended the Geneva Disarmament Conference in that capacity.

[6] The Socialist and pacifist politician George Lansbury (1859–1940) was leader of the opposition at this time.

[7] The English Liberal politician and philosopher Richard Burdon Sanderson Haldane, 1st Viscount Haldane (1856–1928), who had served as Lord Chancellor in the UK's first Labour government under MacDonald.

[8] Baldwin here accuses Liberal and Labour politicians of failing to acknowledge Germany and Italy as aggressive dictatorships. The phrase was later used against him in claims that he was responsible for delays in rearmament, having failed to 'tell the truth' during the 1935 election campaign.

are too apt in this country to believe that all the peoples of the world are animated by the ideals which animate us. That is not true at this moment. There are in this world signs of a form of force being used which shows a spirit which, if it became powerful enough, might mean the end of all that we in this country value and which we believe makes our life worth living.

Let us never forget this: since the day of the air, the old frontiers are gone. When you think of the defence of England you no longer think of the chalk cliffs of Dover; you think of the Rhine.

[*Honourable Members: 'Hear, hear.'*]

That is where our frontier lies. To show that I am no alarmist in what I have said of the air, I would remind the Liberals in this House … that on the occasion of the Labour party's budget ten years ago, Mr Asquith,[9] while critical of the amount of the figures of the defence services in that budget, said that he had no disposition to pare down defensive expenditure to danger point, and this is what he added, and it is a remark to which I would call the attention of the House: 'In regard to the Air Service, I have more than once expressed the view that we were spending not too much but too little.'[10]

Having regard to the circumstances existing in the world today, circumstances which I have endeavoured to make clear to the House and which are connected both with our own position and with the position of other countries; having regard to political tendencies in Europe today and having regard to what our own people stand for, I am confident that I am asking the House today to approve not only what is absolutely necessary but what is the least that I think we ought to ask the House to give its assent to, and I ask for that confidence in the certainty that the vast majority will agree with the proposals.

[9] The English Liberal statesman Herbert Henry Asquith, 1st Earl of Oxford and Asquith (1852–1928), had served as Liberal Prime Minister, 1908–16, and continued as leader of the Liberal Party, supporting MacDonald in his successful bid to become the UK's first Labour Prime Minister in January 1924.

[10] Baldwin quotes from Hansard, 27 May 1924.

Arthur Balfour
Scottish statesman and philosopher

Arthur James Balfour, *later 1st Earl of Balfour* (1848–1930) was born into an ancient Scottish family, and succeeded to the family estate in East Lothian in 1856. Educated at Eton and Trinity College, Cambridge, he entered Parliament in 1874, becoming Secretary for Scotland (1886) and Chief Secretary for Ireland (1887–91), where his policy of suppression earned him the name of 'Bloody Balfour'. A Conservative, he succeeded his uncle Robert Cecil, 3rd Marquess of Salisbury, as prime minister (1902–5), and later served as First Lord of the Admiralty (1915–16). As Foreign Secretary (1916–19), he was responsible for the Balfour Declaration (1917), which expressed British support for a Jewish homeland in Palestine. He resigned in 1922 and was ennobled, but served again as Lord President of the Privy Council (1925–9).

'Is there anyone here who feels content with the position of the Jews?'
21 June 1922, London, England

Balfour's qualities as a philosopher and debater are brilliantly displayed in this speech, his defence of the British promise of support for a Jewish homeland in Palestine. The promise, made in his famous Balfour Declaration of 1917, had taken on greater meaning when Britain drove the Ottoman Turks from Palestine at the end of World War I. The British set up a colonial government in the region, receiving a mandate from the League of Nations to facilitate the establishment of a Jewish national home.

But many people were concerned that this policy would give rise to Jewish dominance over the Arab population in Palestine, leading to bloodshed. Arab anti-Zionist riots, which erupted in 1920 and 1921, gave credence to these fears. Balfour, however, strongly believed that a Jewish homeland was in the interests of the Middle East and the wider world. Moreover, he felt that the Christian West had an obligation to support the Jews, whose achievements it had overlooked and whose culture it had persecuted for centuries.

His speech to the House of Lords, responding to an attack by Lord Islington on Britain's acceptance of the Palestine mandate, contains all the oratorical mastery for which he had won renown in the House of Commons. It appeals directly to his audience, in particular his fellow peers' sense of religious duty and idealism, and builds to a heartfelt conclusion.

[1] The English Conservative politician John Poynder Dickson-Poynder, 1st Baron Islington (1866–1936).

My noble friend[1] tries to maintain the paradox that the powers who adopted the mandatory system[2] – the powers who laid down the lines on which that system was to be carried out and have embodied it in the League of Nations[3] – are so ignorant that they do not know their own child, and are violating all their principles when they establish the policy of a Jewish home in Palestine. I think my noble friend is asking us to accept a proposition which, as men of common sense, we should certainly repudiate. I will therefore leave what I may call the legal aspect of the criticism of my noble friend, which I think he will admit is essentially paradoxical, and will come to his more particular charges.

Those particular charges were, as I understood him, that it was impossible to establish a Jewish home in Palestine without giving to the Jewish organisations political powers over the Arab race with which they should not be entrusted and which – even if they exercised them well – were not powers that should be given under a British mandate to one race over another. But I think my noble friend gave no evidence of the truth of these charges. He told us that it was quite obvious that some kind of Jewish domination over the Arabs was an essential consequence of the attempt to establish a Jewish home. It is no necessary consequence, and it is surely a very poor compliment to the British government, to the Mandates Commission, whose business it will be to see that the spirit of the mandate as well as the letter is carried out, and beyond them to the council of the League of Nations, to suppose that all these bodies will so violate every

[2] Balfour refers to the victorious Allied Powers of World War I.
[3] The League of Nations was established in 1920 to promote international co-operation and prevent wars. It ceased to operate during World War II, and officially dissolved itself in 1946, at a meeting of its successor organization, the United Nations.

pledge that they have ever given and every principle to which they have ever subscribed, as to use the power given to them to enable one section of the community in Palestine to oppress and dominate any other.

My noble friend told us in his speech, and I believe him absolutely, that he has no prejudice against the Jews. I think I may say that I have no prejudice in their favour. But their position and their history, their connection with world religion and with world politics is absolutely unique. There is no parallel to it, there is nothing approaching to a parallel to it, in any other branch of human history.

Here you have a small race, originally inhabiting a small country, I think of about the size of Wales or Belgium, at any rate of comparable size to those two, at no time in its history wielding anything that can be described as material power, sometimes crushed in between great Oriental monarchies, its inhabitants deported, then scattered, then driven out of the country altogether into every part of the world, and yet maintaining a continuity of religious and racial tradition of which we have no parallel elsewhere.

That itself is sufficiently remarkable, but consider – it is not a pleasant consideration, but it is one that we cannot forget – how they have been treated during long centuries, during centuries which in some parts of the world extend to the minute and the hour in which I am speaking; consider how they have been subjected to tyranny and persecution; consider whether the whole culture of Europe, the whole religious organization of Europe, has not from time to time proved itself guilty of great crimes against this race.

I quite understand that some members of this race may have given, doubtless did give, occasion for much ill-will, and I do not know how it could be otherwise, treated as they were; but, if you are going to lay stress on that, do not forget what part they have played in the intellectual, the artistic, the philosophic and scientific development of the world. I say nothing of the economic side of their energies, for on that Christian attention has always been concentrated.

I ask your Lordships to consider the other side of their activities. Nobody who knows what he is talking about will deny that they have at least – and I am putting it more moderately than I could do – rowed all their weight in the boat of scientific, intellectual and artistic progress, and they are doing so to this day. You will find them in every university, in every centre of learning; and at the very moment when they were being persecuted, when some of them, at all events, were being persecuted by the church, their philosophers were developing thoughts which the great doctors of the church embodied in their religious system.

As it was in the Middle Ages, as it was in earlier times, so it is now. And yet, is there anyone here who feels content with the position of the Jews? They have been able, by this extraordinary tenacity of their race, to maintain this continuity, and they have maintained it without having any Jewish home.

What has been the result? The result has been that they have been described as parasites on every civilization in whose affairs they have mixed themselves – very useful parasites at times, I venture to say. But however that may be, do not your Lordships think that if Christendom – not oblivious of all the wrong it has done – can give a chance, without injury to others, to this race of showing whether it can organize a culture in a home where it will be secured from oppression, that it is not well to say, if we can do it, that we will do it? And, if we can do it, should we not be doing something material to wash out an ancient stain upon our own civilization if we absorb the Jewish race in friendly and effective fashion in these countries in which they are the citizens? We should then have given them what every other nation has: some place, some local habitation, where they can develop the culture and the traditions which are peculiarly their own.

I could defend – I have endeavoured, and I hope not unsuccessfully, to defend – this scheme of the Palestine Mandate from the most material economic view, and from that point of view it is capable of defence. I have endeavoured to defend it from the point of view of the existing population, and I have shown, I hope with some effect, that their prosperity also is intimately bound up with the success of Zionism. But having endeavoured to the best of my ability to maintain those two propositions, I should, indeed, give an inadequate view to your Lordships of my opinions if I sat down without insisting to the utmost of my ability that, beyond and above all this, there is this great ideal at which those who think with me are aiming, and which, I believe, it is within their power to reach.

It may fail. I do not deny that this is an adventure. Are we never to have adventures? Are we never to try new experiments? I hope your Lordships will never sink to that unimaginative depth, and that experiment and adventure will be justified if there is any case or cause for their justification.

Surely, it is in order that we may send a message to every land where the Jewish race has been scattered, a message which will tell them that Christendom is not oblivious of their faith, is not unmindful of the service they have rendered to the great religions of the world – and most of all, to the religion that the majority of your Lordships' House profess – and that we desire to the best of our ability to give them that opportunity of developing, in peace and quietness under British rule, those great gifts which hitherto they have been compelled from the very nature of the case only to bring to fruition in countries which know not their language, and belong not to their race.

That is the ideal which I desire to see accomplished; that is the aim which lay at the root of the policy I am trying to defend; and, though it be defensible indeed on every ground, that is the ground which chiefly moves me.

Daniel Barenboim
Argentinian-Israeli musician

Daniel Barenboim (1942–) was born to Russian Jewish parents in Buenos Aires, Argentina, and made his debut there at the age of seven. His family moved to Austria and then to Israel in 1952. He studied with Igor Markevich (1912–83) and Nadia Boulanger, and has performed regularly in Europe since 1954. He became an Israeli citizen in 1967, and married the English cellist Jacqueline du Pré (1945–87) the same year. A noted exponent of Mozart and Beethoven, he gained his reputation as pianist/conductor with the English Chamber Orchestra, then became musical director of the Orchestre de Paris (1975–89) and of the Chicago Symphony Orchestra (1991–), and musical and artistic director of the Deutsche Staatsoper, Berlin (1992–). In the early 1990s, he formed a close friendship with the Palestinian academic Edward Said (1935–2003), which led to the formation of the West–Eastern Divan, a youth orchestra made up of Arab, Israeli and European musicians. In 2000, he was appointed Chief Conductor for Life of the Staatskapelle Berlin and in 2011 the music director of La Scala, Milan. He has received numerous awards, including the Prince of Asturias Concord Prize in Spain (2002), the Grosses Bundesverdienstkreuz in Germany (2002) and the Wolf Prize for the Arts in Israel (2004).

'There is no military solution to the Jewish–Arab conflict'
9 May 2004, Jerusalem, Israel

In an interview published in 2005, Daniel Barenboim declared: 'With notoriety, you can do what you think is right.' Having achieved global fame as a pianist and conductor, he has become increasingly outspoken about Jewish identity and Arab–Israeli relations. In 2001, as conductor of the Staatskapelle Berlin, he caused a furore at a concert in Jerusalem by performing an encore from *Tristan and Isolde* by the German composer Richard Wagner (1813–83). Wagner was notable for his anti-Semitism and much admired by ADOLF HITLER, and his work had long been considered taboo in Israel.

Barenboim's work with the late Edward Said through the Barenboim–Said Cultural Foundation and the West–Eastern Divan orchestra has been a practical expression of his views.

In 2004, he received the Wolf Prize for the Arts, an Israeli award established in 1978 to honour 'achievements in the interest of mankind and friendly relations among peoples'. At the award ceremony, held in the Israeli parliament, the Knesset, Barenboim gave this provocative but heartfelt speech. In it, he quotes from the country's Declaration of Independence of 1948, hoping to shame the Israeli state for according unequal status to Palestinian citizens and failing to maintain friendly relations with neighbouring Arab nations. Rejecting intransigent ideology, Barenboim makes a reasoned case for pragmatism and humanitarianism.

The speech drew criticism from many Israelis, including President Moshe Katsav, but was reported around the world as an articulate plea for peace and justice.

> I would like to express my deep gratitude to the Wolf Foundation for the great honour that is being bestowed upon me today. This recognition is for me not only an honour, but also a source of inspiration for additional creative activity.
>
> It was in 1952, four years after the Declaration of Israel's Independence, that I, as a ten-year-old boy, came to Israel with my parents from Argentina. The Declaration of Independence was a source of inspiration to believe in ideals that transformed us from Jews to Israelis.
>
> This remarkable document expressed the commitment: 'The state of Israel will devote itself to the development of this country for the benefit of all its people; It will be founded on the principles of freedom, justice and peace, guided by the visions of the prophets of Israel; It will grant full equal, social and political rights to all its citizens, regardless of differences of religious faith, race or sex; It will ensure freedom of religion, conscience, language, education and culture.'
>
> The founding fathers of the state of Israel who signed the Declaration also committed themselves and us: 'To pursue peace and good relations

with all neighbouring states and people'.

I am asking today with deep sorrow: can we, despite all our achievements, ignore the intolerable gap between what the Declaration of Independence promised and what was fulfilled, the gap between the idea and the realities of Israel? Does the condition of occupation and domination over another people fit the Declaration of Independence? Is there any sense in the independence of one at the expense of the fundamental rights of the other?

Can the Jewish people, whose history is a record of continued suffering and relentless persecution, allow themselves to be indifferent to the rights and suffering of a neighbouring people? Can the State of Israel allow itself an unrealistic dream of an ideological end to the conflict, instead of pursuing a pragmatic, humanitarian one, based on social justice?

I believe that despite all the objective and subjective difficulties, the future of Israel and its position in the family of enlightened nations will depend on our ability to realize the promise of the founding fathers as they canonized it in the Declaration of Independence.

I have always believed that there is no military solution to the Jewish–Arab conflict, neither a moral nor a strategic one and since a solution is therefore inevitable I ask myself, why wait? It is for this very reason that I founded, with my late friend Edward Said, a workshop for young musicians from all the countries of the Middle East, Jews and Arabs.[1]

[1] Barenboim refers to his West–Eastern Divan orchestra, which takes its name from a cycle of poems in a Persian style by the German writer Johann von Goethe (1749–1832).

Despite the fact that as an art, music cannot compromise its principles – and politics, on the other hand, is the art of compromise – when politics transcends the limits of the present existence and ascends to the higher sphere of the possible, it can be joined there by music. Music is the art of the imaginary par excellence, an art free of all limits imposed by words, an art that touches the depth of human existence, an art of sounds that crosses all borders. As such, music can take the feelings and imagination of Israelis and Palestinians to new, unimaginable spheres.

I therefore decided to donate the monies of the prize to music education projects in Israel and in Ramallah.[2]

[2] A prosperous city, nine miles north-west of Jerusalem, which was handed over to Palestinian control in 1995 under the terms of the Oslo Accords.

Thank you.

J M Barrie
Scottish writer

Sir James Matthew Barrie (1860–1937) was born in Kirriemuir, Angus. The son of a weaver, he graduated from Edinburgh University in 1882, then settled in London and became a regular contributor (under the name 'Gavin Ogilvy') to the *St James's Gazette* and *British Weekly*. He wrote a series of autobiographical prose works, including *The Little Minister* (1891, dramatized 1897), set in his native village disguised as 'Thrums'. From 1890 he wrote for the theatre. He established a reputation with works such as the successful *Walker, London* (1892) and *The Admirable Crichton* (1902), a good-humoured social satire. But it is as the creator of *Peter Pan* (1904) that he will be chiefly remembered. Aware of the popular demand for sentimentality on the London stage, Barrie provided surface romance within dramatic structures which indirectly suggested a bleaker vision of life. He continued his excursions into fairyland in later plays such as *Dear Brutus* (1917) and *Mary Rose* (1920). His last play, *The Boy David* (1936), tried a biblical theme, but despite containing some of his finest writing won no laurels in the theatre.

'After the lapse of centuries, our greatest Scottish case is closed'
11 October 1928, Jedburgh, Scotland

This boyish yet masterful oratory was delivered by J M Barrie at the opening of a fundraising bazaar. Its purpose was to encourage generosity at the event, which was intended to raise funds for the upkeep of a house briefly occupied by Mary, Queen of Scots in 1566. Barrie had been preparing the speech for some months, and it turned out to be one of his very best.

It is not a speech by one man, but two, since it is a product of Barrie's famously divided self. The unruly, writerly and romantic half he called M'Connachie; the dour, practical and canny half he referred to as his real self, J M Barrie. During the address, Barrie transforms into M'Connachie when he dazzles his audience with news of a magical tryst he has had with the ghost of Mary, Queen of Scots on the previous night.

M'Connachie-Barrie reveals how the meeting allowed him to 'solve' the case of the infamous Casket Letters, which implicated Mary in the murder of her first husband, the Englishman Lord Darnley. Exonerating the queen of any wrongdoing, Barrie paves the way for those 'Southerners' present to show unbridled generosity at the bazaar.

A fascinating blend of romantic Scottish nationalism and understated British patriotism, the speech is both typical of the ambivalent sense of identity ascribed to middle-class Scots of the period, and unique in terms of the infectiousness of Barrie's historical imagination. Needless to report, the bazaar was a triumph.

Before I begin, may I ask you to make sure that all the doors are locked? We want no government spies in here. However innocent our intention, there is no denying that this meeting for the preservation of the house of Mary, Queen of Scots has many of the marks of a Stuart rising.[1] Though great efforts have been made to keep this assemblage secret, we cannot be certain that something has not leaked out. Quite possibly tomorrow's news-sheets may bear startling headlines: 'Extraordinary Jacobite Gathering at Jedburgh – The Town Council Involved – J M Barrie escaped to France – F S Oliver[2] arrested at Edgerston.'

How strange if Mr Oliver, who has done such manful deeds for Queen Mary's House – Ah, don't cheer him, it may be remembered against you at the trials – how strange if, as a result of this meeting, he were to end his days confined in a dungeon in that very house. Nevertheless, we must remember in this connection that the inventor of the guillotine himself perished by it.[3]

I think in any further references I may feel constrained to make about Mr Oliver I shall be giving him a better chance if I simply call him X. No doubt you are planning, if the worst comes to the worst, to succour him at his little window, with provender thrust between the bars. Disabuse yourselves of that idea. If X is under lock and key, you will be in full flight. Winter is coming

[1] Barrie refers to the Jacobite rebellions of the 18th century, which attempted to restore Scotland's Stuart monarchs, descendants of Mary, to the British throne.

[2] Mr and Mrs F S Oliver of Edgerston were well-known local figures who had donated the house to the town of Jedburgh, and invited their old friend Barrie to open the bazaar. The reference to France is deliberate, since it was the place of exile for Jacobite kings, and is designed to elevate Barrie subtly in the mind of his audience.

[3] The French revolutionary politician Dr Joseph-Ignace Guillotin (1738–1814) did not, in fact, invent the guillotine, though he did propose such a device. Nor did he perish by it, though this myth persists.

on, and I hope you have brought warm clothing with you. In dank caves on Western Isles you will lay your heads – such of them as have not been laid elsewhere.

Is there no bright side to this gloomy picture? Yes. Bank-notes will be of no use to you among the bracken; indeed, to be tracked down with them on you will be a suspicious circumstance. Be thankful that a number of courageous ladies are here today to relieve you of them. Before you start for the misty Hebrides, don't miss this opportunity of getting rid of those incriminating documents.

And now, ladies and gentlemen, leaving you in the wind-driven haunts where the whaup and the seagull build their lonely nests, I return to Queen Mary's picturesque house at Jedburgh. It is chiefly historical, if I remember aright, because she rushed to it, womanlike, to visit a sick friend. Somehow that has always troubled the Southerner; What is the vital difference between the Scot and his friendly brother? Of course it has to do with Mary, Queen of Scots. A Scot, wherever he may be, has always at least one moment of the day when he leans against the nearest object and thinks about her. That is our romantic secret, at last divulged.

In England they had a contemporary queen, a far greater than Mary, though I am not going to advertise her here by mentioning her name. But do they think of her every day? You Scotsmen in the hall are leaning and thinking of Mary now; I can even tell you what you are thinking of her; you are wondering whether if you had lived in her day – whether she would have liked you.

Of course, I would not have dared to speak in Jedburgh unless I could answer that question. It seems only fair to tell you how I found the answer. By the way, I hope I didn't wake up any of you last night? I mean by the galloping of my horse? I couldn't sleep, and after X had gone to bed – the last downy couch he may stretch himself upon for many a day – I saddled my steed and galloped into Jedburgh. A call irresistible was drawing me to Queen Mary's House. I stood beneath the glamorous pile and not one of its many windows showed a gleam.

[4] The Scottish novelist, poet and antiquarian Sir Walter Scott (1771–1832). His non-fiction works include *From Gileskirk to Greyfriars: Mary Queen of Scots, John Knox and the Heroes of Scotland's Reformation.*

And yet – I remembered from our beloved Sir Walter's pages,[4] how at Loch Leven there was at all hours someone ready to place a lamp in a darkened eye of the castle in response to a light across the loch, a signal that friends were near … I dared to flash my lantern, and almost immediately a lamp shone for a moment in a turret window. Without a sound, the celebrated key turned in the lock, the door opened softly, and I found myself in the presence of Mary of Scots. She was but a moving part of the night; but a mother will forget her child and rivers flow uphill before a Scotsman is unable to recognize that face and form.

Inside, I went on one knee to her and she extended her pretty hand. I called her 'My Liege'. It may mean caves for me, but it was worth it. I said there was one question I craved to ask of her:– Were the Casket Letters[5] genuine? You will be glad to know that the answer was in the negative.

[5] The Casket Letters were poems and correspondence allegedly written by Mary that proved her complicity in the murder of her first husband, Lord Darnley.

So, after the lapse of centuries, our greatest Scottish case is closed. There was much else I wanted to learn about the past, but strangely enough she was more interested in the present. She made many inquiries about Jedburgh itself, as, for instance, did 'Jeddart Justice' still hold,[6] and who was provost now. She had been puzzling why there was of late so much stir around this hall, and when I hazarded the guess that it was probably preparation for the bazaar, I was touched to find that she did not know what bazaars were.

[6] During the 'Border Wars' of the 13th to 16th centuries, English raiders captured in Scottish territory were often hanged first, then tried posthumously. This practice came to be known as 'Jeddart Justice'.

But when I explained, and told her the object of this one, she wept tears of joy because her Jedburgh still remembered her kindly. She said she must see the bazaar – you know how … how hasty she was – and putting her hands in mine in that confiding way which is either the best or the worst thing in woman – she was dressed in black velvet with a white ruff about her neck and a white veil flying – and so we came here – by the longest route. When she saw the lovely stalls, she fingered the display, calling them by old lavender names, and some of them she tried on, and she clapped her hands, and exclaimed, 'Whoever buys at my bazaar, I will always have a leaning to him.'

'Him,' she said, though I had told her that most of the work was done by ladies. I told her there would be Southerners here today, and asked her whether she would be vexed if they were purchasers, and she said 'No,' that she wanted them to have the same rights as the others, for old wounds were healed, and she touched her neck and smiled.

Then I did a foolish thing. I asked her whether she would like to buy some little article herself, and at that she began to fade away – a sure proof that she was no Frenchwoman, but Scotch to the core.[7] Before she was quite obliterated – when there was no more of her than the veil, she placed in my hand a sprig of white heather.[8] [*Here the speaker drew attention to white heather in his button-hole.*] Seeing is believing! I have an uneasy feeling that this was not meant for me, but for a better man, whom she had been mistaking me for all the time – our friend, X. However – [*Here he resumed the button-hole.*]

Ah! Great Queen Bess, that famous chop at Fotheringhay – the third hack – has not silenced Mary Stuart.[9] Rather has it decreed that she live on alluringly and find new servants. We see the charming, dangerous creature even now, after more than 300 years, sailing away from us, not into the past, but into the future, in the barque of her royal sister's contrivance – her white ruff concealing the rim of red – her hazel eyes sparkling, her form disdainfully melting – mocking all our attempts to solve her – Scotia's proud-fated, starry mistress. And now, ladies and gentlemen, if you want her to have a leaning to you, fall to. Her bazaar is open.

[7] Mary was born in Linlithgow, Scotland, in 1542 but at six she was taken to France, where she was raised until her return in 1561.

[8] White heather is a traditional Scottish token of good luck, said to be exchanged by lovers. It was popularized by the Victorians.

[9] Mary was beheaded at Fotheringhay, Northamptonshire, in 1587 on the orders of her cousin ELIZABETH I. It is said that the first two blows of the executioner's axe failed to sever her head completely.

David Ben-Gurion

Israeli statesman

David Ben-Gurion *originally David Gruen* (1886–1973) was born in Plonsk, Poland, and emigrated to Palestine in 1906. Expelled by the Turks during World War I, he recruited Jews to the British Army in North America. In Palestine in 1919 he founded a socialist party and became Secretary to the Histadrut – the Israeli trade union congress – in 1921. A keen Zionist, he led the Mapai (Labour) Party from its formation in 1930 and in 1935 headed the Sochnut or Jewish Agency, which represented the interests of the Yishuv, the Israeli community in Palestine. Ben-Gurion moulded Mapai into the main party of the Yishuv during British rule and after independence became prime minister of Israel (1948–53). During this period, he was responsible for the country's absorption of large numbers of refugees from Europe and Arab countries. He served as prime minister again from 1955 to 1963. He retired from politics in 1970, and spent the remainder of his life on a kibbutz. In 1998, *Time* magazine named him one of the 100 most influential figures of the century.

'We dedicate today this Road of Valour'

12 December 1948, Ayalon, Israel

The roots of this speech can be traced back many centuries. The Jewish people believe that God promised them Canaan (or Palestine, the land between the Jordan and the Mediterranean) following their escape from Egypt. Despite a period of exile, they dominated the area until Roman times, when they were dispersed, and Palestine became home to Arabs. Following World War I, Britain administered Palestine under a League of Nations mandate (1922–47), during which time many Jews escaped from Nazi persecution to Palestine. Jews and Arabs lived together, but calls for a Jewish homeland provoked conflict with the majority Arab population.

In November 1947, the United Nations adopted a plan to partition Palestine into Jewish and Arab states, each comprising sections linked by extraterritorial roads. The Arabs rejected this scheme and war broke out. Roads linking Jewish settlements ran through Arab-controlled areas, enabling them to control access.

Operation Nachshon began in April 1948, with the aim of clearing a road to Jerusalem. After initial success, Jerusalem was again besieged. On 14 May, David Ben-Gurion announced Israel's independence; the following day the British mandate ended and Israel was invaded by her Arab neighbours. A route through the mountains to Jerusalem was forged on 9 June, and following further Israeli military successes, the country's borders were largely secured by the end of October.

On 11 December, UN Resolution 194 proposed a Conciliation Commission for the area and the following day Ben-Gurion gave this rousing speech, dedicating the road to Jerusalem and celebrating the city's deliverance by Israeli troops.

On the road we open today is set the crown of our fight for the homeland and freedom. Into its making went the most tragic heroism and the greatest grandeur of that fight, since the day we were called to face our many enemies and save Jerusalem.

This was the heart and soul of the War of Independence that has raged over the country now for more than a year. It was, it still is, a struggle in the eternal city[1] and round about it, and even more a struggle for the road to it. On mastery of the road hangs the city's fate.

Our Third Return[2] to Israel took a course opposite to the First and the Second. We have come now not westering from the East, but from the Occident moving eastward; not from desert to sea, but from sea to desert. Of the three regions of the land – mountains, lowland and valley – we possessed the valley first. We took only little of the lowlands, and late. Of the mountains, we held almost nothing except for Jerusalem, which in every generation from every quarter drew Jews to it.

Within the last century, this magnetism has turned Jerusalem into a Jewish metropolis, with a great and growing Jewish majority. But it also meant that Jewish Jerusalem stood severed from the main centres of rural

[1] Jerusalem.

[2] In Jewish tradition, the First Return followed the Jews' period of captivity in Egypt in 1300 BC; the Second Return followed their period of exile in Babylon in 538 BC. The Third Return followed their period of dispersal by the Romans in AD 135.

and urban settlement, for it was the coastal belt we held for the most part, and the valleys of Jezreel and Jordan, north of Lake Tiberias and south of it. In normal times, the threat to Jerusalem did not strike the eye. An hour's journey to Tel Aviv seemed of little concern, so long as it was safe.

How deadly was the danger soon appeared when the Arab states sought to encompass us. Many and bitter were the hurts our settlements endured in this War of Independence: the suffering of Jerusalem alone was sevenfold. Our enemy knew the mortal stroke he might with ease deliver was to seize and destroy this city of ours, distant from all concentrations of Jewish force and surrounded on all sides by a numerous, compact and daring Arab population in towns and villages whence every road led to Jerusalem.

The Jews had only one and almost its entire length traversed Arab areas, up hill and down dale, from Abu Kebir near Tel Aviv to Lifta at the gates of Jerusalem. With strategic astuteness, the enemy deployed his strength from the start in the effort to sunder Jerusalem from Tel Aviv and the lowland, to halt all Jewish traffic to the city; and this while the Mandate was still in being, as long ago as December 1947.

The Mandate undertook to maintain freedom of movement on the road: its promises were not kept, and while yet British troops garrisoned Palestine, hunger and the sword were menacing the Jewish capital. The state was still far off when we realized that, unless unaided we could blast a way through to Jerusalem and occupy a sufficient space on either side of this corridor, the city was doomed and our whole campaign might be lost.

With the incursion of Arab regulars right upon the Proclamation of the State,[3] the concentrated wrath of the enemy was vented upon Jerusalem, as it was in the days of the Prophet Ezekiel: 'For the king of Babylon standeth at the parting of the way, at the head of the two ways, to use divination; he shaketh the arrows to and fro, he inquireth of teraphim, he looketh in the liver. In his right hand is the lot Jerusalem, to set battering rams, to open the mouth for the slaughter, to lift up the voice with shouting, to set battering-rams against the gates, to cast up mounds, and to build forts.'[4]

In our days the king of Babylon[5] was joined by the king of the sons of Ammon,[6] but the army and champions of Israel, its builders and engineers, its warriors and workers, set the schemes of Babylon and Ammon at naught; they broke through to right and left, they thrust back the invaders and scattered them. Jerusalem was liberated and a broad, untroubled approach secured.

Thus, as April began, our War of Independence swung decisively from defence to attack. Operation Nachshon, to free the road, was launched with the capture of Arab Hulda, near where we stand today, and of Dir Muhsin, and culminated in the storming of Kastel, the great hill-fortress near Jerusalem, where Abdul Qader el Husseini,[7] perhaps the only real commander among the Arabs of Palestine, fell in action.

Jerusalem drew breath freely again, but not for long: reinforcements arrived from other Arab states, and it was beleaguered a second time. Upon it the enemy rained his fiercest blows indiscriminately, viciously, night and day without surcease. British guns, primed by British gunners, bombarded it. Our relief column was led by a gallant and honoured American Jew, Colonel David Michael Marcus.[8] He was not fated, alas!, to enter the Jerusalem he came to free, and on the very eve of the first truce, he died in the Judean hills.

[3] The proclamation of Israeli independence, made by Ben-Gurion on 14 May 1948.

[4] Ezekiel 21:21–2.

[5] An ancient city in Mesopotamia, south of modern Baghdad.
[6] Closely related to the Jews, but their traditional enemy.

[7] The Palestinian guerrilla Abdul Qader el-Husseini was mortally wounded fighting Israeli forces in Jerusalem, in April 1948. Following his death the Arab forces retreated.

[8] The Jewish-American soldier Brigadier General David Michael Marcus was a US Army officer who fought for Israel and led construction of the path (known as the Burma Road) through the mountains to Jerusalem. He was accidentally killed by an Israeli sentry near Jerusalem, just hours before the ceasefire of 11 June 1948.

[9] A strategically important area of Israel (the scene of David's fight against Goliath, among many other battles) between Bet Guvrin and Latrun.
[10] The British authorities controlling Palestine had transported some illegal Jewish immigrants to detention camps in Cyprus.

Here, in the Valley of Ayalon,[9] the Defence Army of Israel, only just taking form, made its first assault on the Arab lines at Latrun. In the van was the Seventh Brigade, newly mobilized, in the main of men landed a few days earlier from the detention camps of Cyprus.[10] Its units in a brave engagement penetrated the village and burned it down, but were forced back by massed artillery. A Palmach brigade,[11] with typical courage, renewed the assault, but it too had to withdraw, not unscathed. So the Arab Legion held the key still to Sha'ar Hagai,[12] the portal of the valley-way, and Jerusalem was in the toils.

[11] The first mobilized regiment of the Haganah – the Jewish underground militia.
[12] The Valley Gate, leading to Jerusalem.

It seemed as though we had been worsted at Latrun, yet the fighting there in actuality saved Jerusalem, even before the first truce gave it a brief respite, for we had compelled the enemy to shift a large part of his strength from the city to the valley. The shelling was more fitful and the citizens were heartened to hold out until the end. And more: the fighting gave us a new and open access from the coast through the foothills to Jerusalem.

[13] An Arab village.
[14] An Arab hamlet.
[15] A town west of Jerusalem, also known as Zora.

At the end of May, the Eleventh Brigade took Beit Jiz[13] and Beit Susin[14] and the Palmach entered Zar'a,[15] birthplace of Samson.[16] These actions hewed out the line of shock and valour we call Burma Road,[17] on to deliverance and the salvation of Jerusalem. Afterwards, it was retraced along an easier and apter line, no longer to be makeshift in emergency but an established and enduring link, flanked by multiplying settlements that will unite to form a living bridge of men and husbandry from the principal zones of Jewish occupancy and power in the state to imperishable Jerusalem.

[16] Samson was a Hebrew judge and warrior who was betrayed to the Philistines by his lover Delilah. See Judges 16.
[17] The route built through the mountains which relieved the besieged city of Jerusalem on 9 June 1948 was called the Burma Road after the road built by the slave labour of Allied prisoners-of-war during World War II.

As we dedicate today this Road of Valour, this path of deliverance, let us remember in deepest thankfulness the soldiers and workers in their thousands who helped in its making, the battalions of infantry and the armoured cars, the artillery and the engineers who contrived it, the men who laid the pipeline, the men of Solel-Boneh,[18] from Jerusalem and Tel Aviv, the stout-hearted drivers.

[18] A Histadrut public works and construction operation.

They had a proud share in this feat of combat and development, one that will be immortalized in the ageless annals of Zion set free, that will be a monument to Jewish prowess in arms and in labour, the passport, now and always, to victory.

Tony Benn

English politician

Anthony Neil Wedgwood Benn *briefly 2nd Viscount Stansgate* (1925–) was born in London, the son of William Wedgwood Benn, 1st Viscount Stansgate (1877–1960), a Liberal MP who later joined the Labour Party. He was educated at Westminster School and New College, Oxford. He became a Labour MP in 1950, but was debarred from the House of Commons on succeeding to his father's title in 1960. He was able to renounce it in 1963 and was re-elected to Parliament the same year. He was Postmaster-General (1964–6), Minister of Technology (1966–70), and assumed responsibility for the Ministry of Aviation in 1967 and Ministry of Power in 1969. He was opposition spokesman on trade and industry (1970–4) and on Labour's return to government in March 1974 he was made Secretary of State for Industry, and Minister for Posts and Telecommunications. The following year he became Secretary of State for Energy, a position he held until the Conservative victory in the 1979 general election. Representing the left wing of Labour opinion, he unsuccessfully stood for the deputy leadership of the party in 1981. He lost his seat in the general election of 1983, but returned to represent Chesterfield from 1984 until his retirement at the 2001 general election, 'to devote more time to politics'. He was taken ill at the Labour Party conference in September 2005, and subsequently fitted with a pacemaker. He remains an outspoken political critic and active defender of his socialist and democratic ideals. Among his publications are *Arguments for Socialism* (1979), *Arguments for Democracy* (1981) and *Years of Hope* (1994).

'The New Women's Movement draws much of its energy from a history of clear injustice'

5 June 1971, Rotherham, England

This address was given at a Yorkshire Labour Women's rally at Clifton Hall in Rotherham, South Yorkshire – one of the heartlands of British radicalism. It was a critical moment for both socialism and feminism. Having alienated its supporters by drifting to the right, the Labour government had been defeated the previous year by the Conservative Party and the political left was in disarray. This had provoked political struggle of an intensity not seen since the 1920s. One major force threatening the unity of radical politics was the post-war New Women's Movement, which grew up under the influence of Marxism, but had since become disillusioned by the patriarchal character of organized labour.

Placing women's rights at the heart of an epic struggle that takes in Chartism and colonial liberation, Benn presents the causes of women and organized labour as comrades in the same political battle. Calling for a reversal of a culture that had seen women marginalized by British socialism, particularly the trade unions, Benn warns against allowing the women's and trade-union movements to come into conflict with each other, to their mutual detriment.

He demonstrates a keen grasp of contemporary feminism by emphasizing the importance of changing attitudes, rather than merely writing new laws, in creating gender equality. His sensitive delivery can be attributed not only to his native gifts as speaker, which made him a figurehead of the left-wing challenge to the Labour leadership throughout the 1970s and early 1980s, but also the formative influence of his mother, Margaret Benn (née Eadie), a radical Christian feminist.

I want to speak today about the role of women in society. It is a very risky thing for a man to presume to talk to women, about women, and so I hope you'll be patient with me …

Incredible as it now seems, women were altogether denied even the vote until 53 years ago, and only won the franchise at 21 ten years after that. If we are considering what is still called 'the women's question' we have got to see it against a background of centuries when women were specifically and categorically discriminated against by men, as indeed they still are. Even after some of them escaped from male domination, they were denied political representation.

Today, even in Britain, they still suffer from laws passed by Parliament before women had the right to vote, which are enforced by the courts in such a way as to keep them as second-class citizens. But the problem goes far deeper than that. Public attitudes, adopted by many men, and accepted by many women, are now a hundred years out of date.

It is appropriate that the New Women's Movement[1] … should have demanded liberation, for that is what the battle is about. In part inspired by the colonial liberation movements, and in part by the powerful pressure groups for racial equality established by those who had suffered discrimination, the New Women's Movement draws much of its energy from a history of clear injustice. And it is no good ignoring it in the hope that it will go away – because it won't. Moreover it has tremendous and untapped political potential.

Many people mock the women's movement today by picking on some of its tactics, just as the feminist movement was mocked at the time the suffragettes began their campaigns. But every struggle for rights by an oppressed group is exposed to ridicule by those who are frightened of the power it generates. Those who are privileged know that if a progressive movement succeeds in its objectives the privileges which they have enjoyed will be threatened. No wonder some men are uneasy …

It is also true that the leaders of a new movement for social change are always liable to be accused of being unrepresentative. How easy to dismiss them as a lunatic fringe, commanding no real support amongst their own constituency of women. But just the same was said of the trade union and socialist pioneers or the Chartists in the 19th century, who were written off as wild men and agitators, in a deliberate effort to separate them from a supposedly sensible body of people who, the public was told, were quite content with their lot.

I have mentioned this because if we are to see this new movement in its proper historical perspective we must see it as part of a much wider movement for human rights and human equality which is being fought for against all sorts of privileges all over the world. It is, in fact, a natural part of our fight for a socialist society. Our campaign for women's rights must include women's right to be fully equal with men as workers and individuals.

One of the most interesting things about the New Women's Movement is the extent to which it has struck a responsive chord in women of all ages and cuts across class barriers. It is perhaps not surprising that many young women should be profoundly discontented when they come across examples of the discrimination in education and jobs and opportunity that are still tolerated in modern society.

But it is equally true that many older women whose first political experience was the fight for the vote should now, sometimes as pensioners, be waking up to the fact that the winning of the vote did not achieve what they expected it would. It was only the first step, giving women the outward form of political freedom with some marginal liberalisation, but leaving the inner substance of human equality beyond their grasp. They find they are excited by the new wave of feeling among their children and grandchildren. They want to see them succeed where they failed …

The generalized discontent among women has now assumed the proportions of a real national – indeed international – movement. Whether we support it or not – and I am arguing strongly that we should do – it is a political force to be reckoned with.

The movement towards greater women's rights has remained for too long on the edge of our policy-making. We have not been concerned as we ought to have been with it. We must now integrate it more clearly into our

[1] The New Women's Movement had its origins in the entry of women into the industrial labour force during World War II, and was given ideological expression in the 1950s and 1960s by such writers as Simone de Beauvoir and BETTY FRIEDAN, who criticized the dehumanizing position of women in society.

own political philosophy as a movement based upon human equality, and human development …

An extraordinary gap still exists between the accepted national view – about the way that people are supposed to behave and the way in which society has actually been moving … Take a simple example. Though most women marry; and nowadays marry younger, some women don't marry; they want to be educated for a job and to get a job appropriate to their qualifications. And many find it hard because some people treat them as if they were kicking over the traces instead of settling down with a 'nice man', washing his shirts and raising his children and having his slippers ready when he comes back at night.

Some do get married, but things don't work out and they part, and they marry again; and perhaps have children or perhaps not.

Some women have children without marrying, and some want to marry and not have children, and some don't like men at all.

All this … means that a lot of women want to do things, or are doing things, that in a way aren't accepted by society and they find themselves discriminated against because of it. The traditional role of the family as a united partnership for life, which it is for the majority, is not threatened by accepting other lifestyles for the minority, though some try to argue that it is.

Remember one thing. This freedom has been accepted for centuries, but for men only. Men have always been generous to themselves, in approving their own lifestyles. But the old double standards are no longer acceptable. Now new options are beginning to open up for women. This is the stuff of which revolutions are made, because it involves a change of values which threatens the existing pattern of male domination …

It is very difficult to run a modern community successfully and it is particularly difficult to see things changing so rapidly without getting frightened. Yet you and I know that we are aiming for unity in diversity; for letting people lead their own lives so long as they do not make life hell for everyone else. And if women are to be allowed to lead fuller lives there will have to be a lot of changes made, and most of them will require a complete re-education of men.

To start with we have got to change the whole educational system and completely abandon the conditioning of girls in our schools, designed to brainwash them into accepting a subordinate role in life. We have got to break the monopoly of good jobs enjoyed by men. We have also got to open up job opportunities and provide far more day nurseries and other facilities women need to free them for work. We must make provision for women of any age who want to upgrade their level of skill or re-enter the working population if they can't have children or have had their children or for any other reason they want or need to work. Here the second chance of adult education, or the Open University,[2] could be so important for women.

[2] Founded in 1969 by the Labour government, the Open University was established to offer further education on the basis of part-time study and/or distance learning. It is particularly geared to improving access to degree studies for mature students without educational qualifications.

We have got to sweep away all the discrimination against women that clutters up our statute-book and tax laws, and that disfigures our working practices in industry, especially the continued denial of equal pay. We must make it clear that a person is a person, whether male or female, black or white, rich or poor. That's what socialism is all about. And in doing so we are no more attacking femininity than we would be attacking masculinity if men were the victims of discrimination. The issue is one of freedom, and where femininity is used as an excuse to deny that freedom it must be exposed as an unfair practice.

But it would be wrong to suggest that the only thing we need is changes in the law. The Labour Party, which itself has a long way to go, has sometimes been too ready to believe that if you passed a bill you solved the problem. We will have to change the law and we will have to make resources available to advance women's rights. But above all we will have to change attitudes. And there are real conflicts of interest at the heart of this issue that have to be faced and resolved.

In the end the whole character of any society is dictated by its values. You can have any number of laws, but if they don't reflect the spirit of the people they are just dead letters. It is how people regard their fellow creatures and how much responsibility they feel for them that makes a healthy society, or a happy family, or a happy person.

Looked at like this, the women's movement can be clearly seen as a powerful ally in the struggle for human rights which, if it wins, will help to liberate men too. We are all fighting the same battle. The things that women are fighting against – bad housing, inadequate social services, bad education, discrimination, lack of opportunity and outdated ideas – are the very same enemies that men are fighting. A victory for the one is a victory for us all …

And what better time to start than now, when so many women are utterly disillusioned with the total failure and cynicism of the government they helped to elect last year[3] … It would be a good start to give women their proper role in the Labour and Trade Union Movement, where they still do not enjoy full equality … Above all, let us listen to what the Women's Movement is saying to us, because their message is a very important one.

[3] The Conservative government of EDWARD HEATH, who had defeated HAROLD WILSON at the general election of July 1970.

Theobald von Bethmann-Hollweg
German politician

Theobald von Bethmann-Hollweg (1856–1921) was born in Hohenfinow, Brandenburg. He qualified in law, then rose in the service of Prussia and the German Empire, becoming Imperial Chancellor in 1909. Although not identified with the German élite's most bellicose elements, and fearing the effects of war upon German society, he nevertheless played an important part in the events which led to World War I in 1914. Anxious for a negotiated peace in 1917, he was forced from office. He wrote *Reflections on the World War* (1920).

'England is answerable for this catastrophe'
2 December 1914, Berlin, Germany

❧

This speech illustrates the web of treaties and alliances underlying the rapid escalation of World War I.

Following the assassination of the Austrian Archduke Franz Ferdinand by the Serb nationalist Gavrilo Princip on 28 June 1914, Austria–Hungary threatened war on Serbia, partly seeking to pre-empt a Slav attack on its own territory. As Chancellor of Germany, Bethmann-Hollweg feared Russian intervention on Serbia's behalf and, hoping to discourage this, pledged support to Austria–Hungary. However, Serbia appealed for Russian help; and when Austria–Hungary finally declared war on Serbia, Russia mobilized its army. Germany then mobilized, as did France, Russia's ally. This led Britain – fearing a German invasion of Belgium en route for France, and committed to guarding Belgian neutrality – to demand that Germany respect Belgium's neutral status. Bethmann-Hollweg initially doubted Britain's intention to become involved and, fearing a French attack, sent an ultimatum to Belgium, requiring passage for German troops, but this was rejected. On 4 August, Germany declared war on France, which it invaded via Belgium.

Addressing the Reichstag that day, Bethmann-Hollweg spoke of the necessity of attacking France, but expressed regret for violating Belgian neutrality. Citing this violation, Britain then declared war on Germany. Later that day, Bethmann-Hollweg said he was surprised at such a response over a 'scrap of paper': this was interpreted as a lack of respect for international treaties.

Four months later, with Europe engulfed in conflict, Bethmann-Hollweg gave this speech at the Reichstag, giving rein to his fury with Britain and querying its reasons for declaring war. In it, he refutes British claims of concern for Belgian neutrality, claiming Britain had secretly promised support to France and Russia long before the invasion of Belgium.

❧

Where the responsibility in this greatest of all wars lies is quite evident to us. Outwardly responsible are the men in Russia who planned and carried into effect the general mobilization of the Russian army. But in reality and truth, the British government is responsible.

The London Cabinet could have made war impossible if they had unequivocally told St Petersburg that England was not willing to let a continental war of the Great Powers result from the Austro-Hungarian conflict with Serbia. Such words would have compelled France to use all her energy to keep Russia away from every warlike measure. Then our good offices and mediation between Vienna and Petersburg would have been successful, and there would have been no war.

But England has chosen to act otherwise. She knew that the clique of powerful and irresponsible men surrounding the Czar were spoiling for war and intriguing to bring it about. England saw that the wheel was set rolling, but she did not think of stopping it. While openly professing sentiments of peace, London secretly gave St Petersburg to understand that England stood by France and therefore by Russia too ...

Up to this summer, English statesmen have assured their parliament that no treaty or agreement existed influencing England's independence of action. Should a war break out, England was free to decide whether she would participate in a European war or not.

Hence, there was no treaty obligation, no compulsion, no menace of the homeland which induced the English statesmen to originate the war and then at once to take part in it.

The only conclusion left is that the London Cabinet allowed this European war, this monstrous world war, because they thought it was an opportune moment to destroy the nerve of her greatest European competitors in the markets of the world. Therefore, England, together with Russia … is answerable before God and man for this catastrophe which has come over Europe and over mankind.

The Belgian neutrality, which England pretended she was bound to shield, is but a mask. On 2 August, 7pm, we informed Brussels that France's plan of campaign was known to us and that it compelled us, for reasons of self-preservation, to march through Belgium. But as early as the afternoon of the same day, before anything was known of this step, the British government promised unconditional aid to France in case the German navy attacked the French coastline.

Not a word was said of Belgian neutrality. This fact is established by the declaration made by Sir Edward Grey[1] in the House of Commons on 3 August … How, then, can England allege that she drew the sword because we violated Belgian neutrality? How could British statesmen, who accurately knew the past, talk at all of Belgian neutrality?

… The whole world is now acquainted with two outstanding facts. One: on the night of 3 August, when our troops entered Belgian territory, they were not on neutral soil, but on the soil of a state that had long abandoned its neutrality.

Two: England has declared war on us, not for the sake of Belgian neutrality, which she herself had helped to undermine, but because she believed that she could overcome and master us with the help of two great military powers on the Continent.

Ever since 2 August, when England promised to back up the French in this war, she was no longer neutral, but actually in a state of war with us. On 4 August she declared war, the alleged reason being our violation of Belgian neutrality. But that was only a sham motive and a spectacular scene intended to conceal the true war motive and thus to mislead both the English people and foreign neutral countries.

The military plans which England and Belgium had worked out to the minutest details now being unveiled, the policy of English statesmen is branded for all times of history to come. But English diplomacy still added to this. At its call, Japan snatched from us Kiautschau, so bravely defended, and thus violated Chinese neutrality. Has England interfered with that breach of neutrality? Has she shown in this instance her scrupulous anxiety about the neutral states?

When, in 1910, I became Chancellor, the Triple Alliance[2] had to reckon with a solid counter-combination of powers. England had created the Triple Entente[3] and knitted it firmly for the purpose of maintaining the 'balance of power'.

For centuries it had been a fundamental tenet of British policy to turn against that continental power which was strongest, and this principle was to find its most efficient instrument in the Triple Entente. Thus, whilst the Triple Alliance was of a strictly defensive character, the nature of the Triple Entente was offensive from the beginning. In this lay all the elements of a terrific explosion.

A nation as great and efficient as Germany does not allow its free and

[1] The English politician Sir Edward Grey *later 1st Viscount Grey of Fallodon* (1862–1933) was the British Foreign Secretary, 1905–16.

[2] A non-aggression treaty between Germany, Austria–Hungary and Italy, signed in 1882.

[3] An alliance between the UK, France and Russia, formed when the Anglo-Russian Entente was signed in 1907.

pacific development to be thwarted. In the face of this aggressive combination the course of German policy was clear. We had to try to come to a separate understanding with each member of the Triple Entente in order to dispel the clouds of war, and at the same time we had to increase our armaments so as to be ready if war actually broke out.

Gentlemen, you know that we have done both. In France we encountered, again and again, sentiments of revenge.[4] Fed and fostered by ambitious politicians, these sentiments proved stronger than the wish, undoubtedly cherished by some of the French people, to live with us, as neighbours should, on friendly terms.

We made, indeed, some specific agreements with Russia, but her close alliance with France, her opposition to our Austro-Hungarian ally and an anti-German feeling, born and bred of the Pan-slavistic craving for power, made agreements impossible which would have averted all dangers of war in the case of a political crisis.

Freer than France and Russia was England. I have already reminded you how British statesmen in Parliament, again and again, proudly affirmed Great Britain's absolutely unrestricted right to steer her own course. The attempt to come to an understanding, which would have safeguarded the peace of the world, was easiest to make with England.

On these lines I had to act and I did act. I well knew that it was a narrow road, not easy to tread. In the course of centuries, the English insular way of thinking had evolved the political maxim that England had a right to an *arbitrium mundi*,[5] which she could only uphold by an unrivalled supremacy on sea and by the maintenance of the balance of power on the Continent. I never had any hopes that my persuasion could break that old English maxim.

What I did hope and thought possible was that the growth of German power and the increase of the risks of a war might open England's eyes to the fact that her old-fashioned maxim had become untenable and impracticable, and that an amicable settlement with Germany was preferable. But that old doctrine of hers more than once stood in the way of a peaceful understanding …

Popular sentiment forced the British government to a rapprochement with Germany. After long and arduous negotiations, we finally arrived at an understanding on various disputed questions of an economic character, regarding Africa and Asia Minor. This understanding was to lessen every possible political friction. The world is wide. There is room enough for both nations to measure their strength in peaceful rivalry, as long as our national strength is allowed free scope for development.

German policy always stood up for that principle. But during the negotiations, England was indefatigable in her endeavours to enter into closer relations with France and Russia. The decisive point was that beyond the political sphere of action, one military agreement after the other was made in view of a possible continental war.

England kept these negotiations as secret as possible … But things could not be concealed, as you know from the official papers that were published by me. The general situation was this: England was indeed ready to come to an understanding, but the first and foremost principle of her policy was the 'balance of power' as a means of checking German strength in its free development.

This forms the borderline of England's amicable relations with Germany; and the purpose was the utmost strengthening of the Triple Entente. When

[4] Feelings of resentment towards Germany and its allies had beeen harboured by many in France since its defeat in the Franco-Prussian War of 1870–1.

[5] Latin: 'Power of judgement over the world'.

the Allies demanded military assurances in return, England was at once ready to give them. The circle was closed. The English were sure of the following of France and hence of Russia. But they, too, had to abandon their free will … England, as soon as either of the two Allies began the war, was morally bound to support them.

And all this was done to what purpose? Because Germany was to be kept down. We have not been remiss in warning the British government. As late as the beginning of last July I gave them to understand that their secret negotiations with Russia about a naval agreement were well known to me. I called their attention to the grave danger which such policy implied for the peace of the world. A fortnight afterward my predictions came true.

We have taken the consequences of the general situation. In quick succession I have laid before you the hugest war bill which history ever recorded, and you, gentlemen, fully recognizing the country's danger, have gladly made the sacrifice and have granted what was necessary for our national self-defence.

And when war broke out, England dropped the mask of hypocrisy. Loudly and openly she declares her determination to fight until Germany is laid prostrate both in an economic and military sense. Anti-German Pan-slavism joins its jubilant notes, France with the full strength of an old warlike nation hopes to redeem the humiliation inflicted on her in 1870.

Our only answer to our enemies is Germany does not allow herself to be crushed!

Aneurin Bevan
Welsh politician

Aneurin Bevan *known as Nye Bevan* (1897–1960) was born in Tredegar, Monmouthshire, one of 13 children of a miner. He began work in the pits at the age of 13. Six years later he became chairman of a Miners' Lodge of more than 4,000 members. Active in trade unionism in the South Wales coalfield, he led the Welsh miners in the 1926 General Strike. Elected as the Independent Labour Party (ILP) MP for Ebbw Vale (1929), he joined the more moderate Labour Party in 1931, establishing a reputation as a brilliant, irreverent and often tempestuous orator. In 1934 he married Jennie Lee. During World War II he was frequently a 'one-man opposition' against Prime Minister WINSTON CHURCHILL. Appointed Minister of Health in the 1945 Labour government led by CLEMENT ATTLEE, he introduced the revolutionary National Health Service in 1948. He became Minister of Labour in 1951, but resigned the same year over the National Health Service charges proposed in the Budget. From this period dated 'Bevanism', the left-wing movement aimed at making the Labour Party more socialist and less 'reformist'. It made Bevan the centre of prolonged and often bitter disputes with his party leaders, but the movement began to wither towards the end of 1956 when he became shadow spokesman on foreign affairs. He ceased to be a 'Bevanite' at the 1957 Brighton party conference, when he opposed a one-sided renunciation of the hydrogen bomb by Great Britain. The most publicized Labour politician of his time, he brought to the Commons radical fervour, iconoclastic restlessness and an acute intellect. He published a collection of essays, *In Place of Fear*, in 1952.

'What control had I over that destiny?'
4 December 1933, London, England

During a debate on the 1933 Unemployment Bill in the House of Commons, Nye Bevan made this highly personal plea for the plight of the jobless. His argument was that technological developments and international economics left ordinary men and women with little control over their working lives. The Great Depression of the early 1930s partly proved his point: the collapse of the American economy caused British unemployment to double between 1928 and 1931. In the north of England, too, steel manufacturing, shipbuilding and mining were all in decline, while automobile and service industries had begun to spring up in the south and the Midlands.

As Bevan mentions in his speech, he knew what it was like to be without a job: between 1921 and 1924 he had failed to find work as a miner. One of the greatest orators of his time, he used his fierce wit to attack the bill for failing to provide adequate support for the unemployed, and for its implicit assumption that unemployment was the fault of the individual. The Conservative-dominated coalition government had no such qualms, Bevan argued, in helping wealthy investors when they ran into difficulties: 'Christ drove the money-changers out of the temple, but you inscribe their title deeds on the altar cloth.'

The House will perhaps pardon me if, in resuming this debate, I offer a few general observations. I have listened, as have many other honourable Members, from time to time, to many debates on unemployment insurance – and indeed upon unemployment generally – and it seems to me that the House is divided in this matter upon grounds of general principle ... The party to which I belong hold the view that the ideas which have inspired the Minister of Labour[1] and the government in drafting this bill are entirely out of accord with the realities of society today and that they are founded upon assumptions which belong, not so much even to pre-war days as to the early 19th century. The Minister of Labour, indeed, has failed to keep pace not only with the change in society, but with the change in the views held by people in the course particularly of the last two years.

The assumption upon which the government have proceeded in this bill is that unemployment is primarily the responsibility of the individual citizen. The assumption upon which we proceed is that unemployment is not an individual but a social act, and that over that circumstance the individual has comparatively little control.

[1] The Unionist politician Sir Henry Betterton *later 1st Baron Rushcliffe* (1872–1949).

Almost all the assumptions underlying public assistance were to the effect that if a man became idle, he was committing a crime against society and the longer that crime continued, the heavier his punishment should be. Indeed, the principle which has governed the administration of the Poor Law[2] in this country has been that an idle person was a shiftless person and that as long as he was idle it should be impressed upon him that he was an undesirable member of the community. That principle is contained in this Bill. The Minister of Labour has impressed upon the unemployed person that somehow or other he must, by the use of his own resources, attempt to secure employment.

I was brought up in a mining community in South Wales, and I mention this not because I want to influence the House by personal considerations, but simply because my circumstances are typical of those of millions of my fellow creatures in this country. I was born the son of a miner, and I went underground when I was 13 years of age, inevitably.

Down the pit was the only place to go. I was as inevitably made into a collier as I would have been made into a shooter of big game if I had been born in Mayfair. I went down the colliery then because of the fact that I lived in a mining community and that there was no other way in which I could earn my livelihood. There were very few choices. I might have become a railwayman or a shop assistant, but I had to become a collier, because most of the people in my district were colliers.

I worked underground until I was about 21 years of age, and then I became unemployed, because society discovered that it no longer wanted the product of my labour. The eight years which I had spent serving an apprenticeship became entirely valueless and for three years I was out of employment.

I ask the Minister of Labour, what control had I over that destiny? Was there any other course available to me? For practically three years – indeed for ten years – in my district, steel workers and miners, living in hamlets and villages, largely cut off from the rest of the community, have been living in helplessness and despair and have no way of escape at all … Those men are completely helpless, and the longer they are idle the more helpless they become.

[*An honourable Member: 'Unless they go in for politics!'*]

That is the kind of observation one would expect from the product of the Oxford Union.[3] The circumstances I have attempted to describe are the circumstances of millions of our fellow countrymen.

This House has indeed recognized in the course of the last two years that the individual has comparatively little control over the destiny of his economic enterprises. If the House has abandoned anything, it has abandoned the principles of 19th-century Liberalism. It has declared that modern society has called up forces which are overwhelmingly against us. The individual can make little headway, and it is declared that so little control has the individual that the state must come to his assistance when those economic enterprises fail …

The House has recognized that society has fundamentally changed, and that there is an obligation upon the state to come to the assistance of the individual when the individual is brought face to face with social circumstances over which he has no control. Why should that apply to the Lancashire cotton owner and coal owner and not to the textile worker and the miner?

… I submit that if this reasoning holds good for the owner of property, it

[2] Britain's Poor Laws, the first of which date from the late 16th century, provided relief for the very young, the sick and the old. Those who were capable of it were employed in workhouses. Legislation between the 1910s and 1940s replaced the Poor Laws with a welfare system.

[3] The debating society at Oxford University.

holds good with respect to the owner of labour. We therefore ask the House in face of this problem of unemployment to start off on the fundamental principle that the individual worker is caught up in circumstances over which he has no control and that consequently the state should comport itself towards him as it does towards the owner of property.

Our first principle, therefore, is that the individual worker when he is unemployed is helpless, and consequently ought not to be punished for a circumstance over which he has no control. But compare the treatment in this bill of the unemployed worker, the miner, the textile worker and the agricultural labourer with the treatment which the government propose to mete out next Thursday to the owner of Newfoundland bonds. Compare it with the treatment that they mete out to the owners of American stock, or to the treatment meted out to the Rothschilds[4] in connection with the Austrian loan, or to the owners of German stock.

> [4] The Rothschilds are a banking dynasty which began to exert an influence on European economies and politics from the late 18th century.

These people have invested their money in Austria or Newfoundland or Germany or America and the government say, 'These poor creatures cannot be blamed for what has overtaken their investments', and a generous state rushes to their assistance. That is characteristic of the Tory party, which never shares the point of view of the Liberals.

The Liberals say that the state should hold itself aloof from economic enterprises. The Tories were never of that view. They always held the view that the state is an apparatus for the protection of the swag of the property owners. They are true to it in this House, and they instruct the Minister of Labour to punish the unemployed person, to depress his standard of livelihood, to pursue him and to whip him whenever possible by the most malignly conceived regulations, but they put the whole resources of the state behind the bondholders and the rich when they get into difficulties.

Christ drove the money-changers out of the temple, but you inscribe their title deeds on the altar-cloth. The individual worker, if he wanted to have economic security, should not have invested his labour in the valleys of Wales or the looms of Lancashire; he should have invested his resources in Germany or Austria and a grateful country would have come to his rescue. The only investment which the worker made in foreign lands was his blood; and those who fought came back and dragged their tortured limbs through the streets of our towns, and they were told by a grateful country that they are still allowed to retain half the miserable compensation which they received …

The Minister of Labour takes the view that the longer a man has been idle, the more undesirable he becomes. If you are going to be equitable, you should take the opposite view, namely that the longer a man is idle, the heavier crime society has committed against him. Indeed if you are going to measure the treatment of him according to his need, the longer he is idle the more he wants. The Minister of Labour, despite his urbanity and his kindliness of demeanour, proceeds upon a principle which is fundamentally bad, and the heavier a man's need, the heavier the burden he is putting upon his shoulders …

This is a bill to make the poor dumb. Indeed, that very point is emphasized in the language of the bill. I believe that it is in Clause 38 that the Minister of Labour protects himself against appeal … [He] not only refuses to accept responsibility in this chamber, and abolishes the natural representatives of the unemployed man – the local council – but he is also suffocating and stifling that man by saying that he has to be satisfied with a paid lawyer – because lawyers are usually the persons appointed, before whom one has to make a grievance articulate.

The only recourse that an unemployed man will have, in order to attract public attention to his grievances, will be to throw a stone through a shop window. Unless he does that, no-one will know that he has a grievance. At the moment, the Public Assistance Committee can be approached, or individual councillors can be spoken to. An unemployed man can knock upon the door of his alderman, or he can hold his meeting and pass his resolution for submission to the local council. He can make his grievance articulate; but he will not be able to do so from now on.

If this bill is passed, it will be an attempt to suffocate the cries of the unemployed man in the mazes of bureaucratic machinery. This bill is going to do for this Conservative majority what the not-genuinely-seeking-work clause did for the Conservative majority in 1929 – abolish it.[5]

[5] The Conservatives lost the 1929 general election to RAMSAY MACDONALD'S Labour Party. In 1931, however, a split over reducing welfare payments caused the cabinet to resign. A coalition government was formed, headed by MacDonald but dominated by Conservatives, who won 473 seats to Labour's 52 in the election of that year.

'The advent of the hydrogen bomb has stalemated power'
1 November 1956, London, England

At the time of the Suez crisis, Bevan was shadow foreign secretary and one of the fiercest critics of the government's policy towards Egypt. The Egyptian president Gamal Abdel Nasser had nationalized the Suez Canal, which was almost half-owned by British banks and businesses. The British prime minister Sir ANTHONY EDEN urged the need for war, and had formed a coalition with Israel and France. On 31 October, British and French air strikes had lent support to an Israeli land invasion. Bevan gave this speech during a House of Commons debate the following day.

Attacking and ridiculing Eden's response to the crisis, he also draws out the wider implications of the 'attempt to impose our will by force upon any nation'. In the nuclear age, he argues, the threat of war is no longer a viable bargaining tool – the consequences are simply too terrifying.

Bevan's plea for restraint was unsuccessful: British troops landed in Egypt a few days later. However, the speech is entirely consistent with arguments he had made since the early 1950s, criticizing Britain's high defence expenditure and, in particular, its nuclear weapons programme, which resulted in the first British hydrogen bomb tests in 1957.

By the time of those tests, though, Bevan had changed his mind. At that year's Labour Party Conference in Brighton he dismayed his followers by famously announcing that, if Britain pursued a policy of unilateral nuclear disarmament, it would 'send a British Foreign Secretary, whoever he may be, naked into the conference chamber'.

Mankind is faced with an entirely novel situation. There has never been anything like it in the history of nations. Two major events have completely cancelled – if I may be allowed to use the term – all the finesse and the sophistication of conventional diplomacy. There is nothing in the White House, in London, in the Quai d'Orsay[1] or in the Kremlin that furnishes statesmen with lessons from history to enable them to judge what to do in the existing circumstances.

[1] The location of the French ministry of foreign affairs in Paris.

The advent of the hydrogen bomb has stalemated power among the Great Powers. The use of the threat of war, which formerly helped to save many international difficulties – and when the threat could not do it, war tried to do it – is no longer available to statesmen. The great powers are stalemated by their own power. This fact has created a vacuum in diplomatic thinking. In the last four or five years, the tragedy of the world has been that the statesmen of the world have not adjusted themselves to that reality. I know it is an obvious thing to say, but we do not leave a thing behind merely because it is obvious. There is an old German saying that to understand is not necessarily to leave behind.

To state that the hydrogen bomb has introduced an entirely novel relationship between nations does not mean that we should then forget it and mean that we can go on as we were before. The fact is that, there being no way of settling disputes between major nations by the resort to major war, the statesmen of the world have not got together to attempt to solve those problems which formerly were attempted to be solved by war. The Middle East is a characteristic example.

There is another novel situation. I have ventured to mention it on several occasions before. It is an extremely novel situation, and it has stolen upon us in so stealthy a fashion that we have scarcely recognized its arrival. It is that not only does the use of force become utterly inadmissible in determining quarrels between nations without running the risk of universal destruction, but the use of force in domestic affairs is now demonstrably failing. The most extraordinary and the most optimistic of all the news that we have had in the last few months is the fact that the Soviet Union itself is recognizing that it cannot hold down whole populations merely by terror and by police action. For myself, I find that an infinitely encouraging fact.

I would venture to point out – if I may be allowed to do so without immodesty – that in 1951, in speaking from the other side of the House on the defence programme of the Labour government, I pointed out that one of the most encouraging things that we could expect was that with the increasing industrialization of the Soviet Union, and with the increasing use of industrial techniques in the satellite countries and in Russia, we could look forward before very long to an increased democratization of the regime. Because I profoundly believe – and this is an article of faith with me, as I think it should be with almost every Member of the House – that there is only one form of government which is consistent with the modern industrial community, and that is political democracy.

Those are two very important events that lie at the background of what we are discussing this evening. The tragedy has been that in the meantime, although those facts have been there, they have not inspired statesmen to intelligent action. Indeed, there are commentators in the United States, like Mr Lippmann,[2] who – speaking of President EISENHOWER[3] the other day – said that the difficulty about the President was that he did not act for peace but merely reacted against trouble.

I am not one, therefore, who is going to say that the British government are themselves reacting with complete guilt towards this situation, because I think it is one which is shared by everybody, and every public man ought to have a sense of humility in face of these intractable problems. I therefore think that it would be a profound blunder if any party in this state tried to mislead the people of the country into imagining that there is any simple or quick solution to these problems before us.

But, having said that, I am bound to say that I have not seen from the Prime Minister, in the course of the last four or five months, any evidence of that sagacity and skill that he should have acquired in so many years in the Foreign Office.[4] Indeed, I have been astonished at the amateurishness of his performance. There is something the matter with him. I have often listened to bad cases in this House, but rarely have I listened to them so badly put as I have heard them in the last few days. The Prime Minister has made several speeches in which he has repeated himself over and over again, but each speech becomes more tawdry and barren than the last …

Our view is this. It has been stated, and I repeat it, that we believe it is highly consistent with the welfare and security of Great Britain that we should not ourselves attempt to impose our will by force upon any nation,

[2] The US political journalist and author Walter Lippmann (1889–1974).
[3] Eisenhower ultimately pressured Britain and France to withdraw from Egypt.

[4] Eden served as Foreign Secretary, 1935–8, 1940–45 and 1951–5.

and that only by the maintenance of that position can we ever give to the people of Great Britain the hope that they will not be exterminated by war.

Right honourable and honourable Members have said that the United Nations is too weak and it cannot be relied upon. Every gang that wanted to lynch some poor prisoner always pleaded that the court might not be effective. It is the way in which lynchers have always justified themselves.

We are perfectly prepared to admit that the institutions of the United Nations are not by any means as effective as we should like them to be. But what we say is that it is our duty to build them up to a strength at which they can be relied upon. It is not enough to say they are weak, and therefore we destroy them. If we destroy them, where does the hope lie? Is the appeal to be to anarchy? For it is anarchy we are being asked to support. It is the action of the bully.

Benazir Bhutto
Pakistani politician

Benazir Bhutto (1953–2007) was born in Karachi, the daughter of the former prime minister Zulfikar Ali Bhutto, and of Begum Nusrat Bhutto, also a politician. She was educated at Oxford University, where she became the first Asian woman president of the Oxford Union debating society. She returned to Pakistan in 1977. After the military coup led by General Mohammed Zia ul-Haq – in which her father was executed (1979) – she was placed under house arrest at frequent intervals until 1984. Between 1984 and 1986, she and her mother lived in England, and she became the joint leader-in-exile of the opposition Pakistan People's Party (PPP). Martial law was lifted in Pakistan in December 1985, and she returned the following April to launch a nationwide campaign for open elections. In 1987 she married Asif Ali Zardari, a wealthy landowner, and the following year she gave birth to her first child. Just three months later she was elected prime minister after the death of Zia in mysterious circumstances, becoming the first modern-day woman leader of a Muslim nation. In her first term, she achieved an uneasy compromise with the army and improved relations with India. She led Pakistan back into the Commonwealth in 1989. She also became, in 1990, the first head of government to bear a child while in office. That year her government was removed from office by presidential decree, and she was accused of corruption. She was later defeated in the elections, but was returned to power in the election of 1993. In September 1995 the armed forces were discovered to have hatched a plot to remove her; and a year later her brother Murtaza was killed during a gun battle with police. In 1996, she appointed her husband Minister of Investments. Defeated in the 1997 election, she was later sentenced to five years' imprisonment for corruption, disqualified from politics and sent into exile. Her appeal against the conviction was upheld in 2001, but further charges followed and she faced jail if she returned to Pakistan. Asif Ali Zardari spent seven years in jail without being convicted, and was released in November 2004, to be reunited with his wife and children. Having reached an agreement with President Pervez Musharraf, she finally returned to Pakistan in October 2007 and prepared to fight the 2008 general elections as the leading opposition candidate. She was assassinated just two months later, on 27 December, while returning from an election rally at Rawalpindi.

'The ethos of Islam is equality, equality between the sexes'
4 September 1995, Beijing, China

'Action for Equality, Development and Peace' was the mandate of the Fourth United Nations World Conference on Women, held in Beijing between 4 and 15 September 1995. However, disagreement on the role of the family and female sexuality arose between groups of largely western feminists and a coalition of fundamentalist Christians, Islamists and traditional Catholics, which marred meetings convened to prepare the 'Platform of Action', the paper to be discussed at the conference.

The conference's opening ceremony was held at the Great Hall of the People in Tiananmen Square, and representatives from 189 countries sat through a display of dancing, music, fashion and gymnastics felt by many to have been more suited to an Olympic opening ceremony than a conference discussing the role of women. Following this extravaganza and the formal opening of the conference, Benazir Bhutto addressed the first plenary meeting, speaking in a dazzling style honed at Oxford Union. In her speech she defended Islam while condemning fundamentalism, and although she conformed with the Islamic requirement to cover her head in public, her headscarf continually slipped from her head as she spoke.

As the female leader of an Islamic nation educated in the West, Bhutto exemplified the tension between the opposite sides at the conference, and her speech trod a careful line between these extremes.

> As the first woman ever elected to head an Islamic nation, I feel a special responsibility about issues that relate to women.
>
> In addressing the new exigencies of the new century, we must translate dynamic religion into a living reality. We must live by the true spirit of Islam, not only by its rituals. And for those of you who may be ignorant of Islam, cast aside your preconceptions about the role of women in our religion. Contrary to what many of you may have come to believe, Islam embraces a rich variety of political, social, and cultural traditions. The fundamental ethos of Islam is tolerance, dialogue, and democracy.
>
> Just as in Christianity and Judaism, we must always be on guard for those who will exploit and manipulate the Holy Book[1] for their own narrow

[1] The Koran.

political ends, who will distort the essence of pluralism and tolerance for their own extremist agendas.

To those who claim to speak for Islam but who would deny to women our place in society, I say:

The ethos of Islam is equality, equality between the sexes. There is no religion on earth that, in its writing and teachings, is more respectful of the role of women in society than Islam.

My presence here, as the elected woman prime minister of a great Muslim country, is testament to the commitment of Islam to the role of women in society.

It is this tradition of Islam that has empowered me, has strengthened me, has emboldened me. It was this heritage that sustained me during the most difficult points in my life, for Islam forbids injustice; injustice against people, against nations, against women. It denounces inequality as the gravest form of injustice. It enjoins its followers to combat oppression and tyranny. It enshrines piety as the sole criterion for judging humankind. It shuns race, colour, and gender as a basis of distinction amongst fellow men.

When the human spirit was immersed in the darkness of the Middle Ages, Islam proclaimed equality between men and women. When women were viewed as inferior members of the human family, Islam gave them respect and dignity. When women were treated as chattels, the Prophet of Islam (peace be upon him) accepted them as equal partners.

Islam codified the rights of women. The Koran elevated their status to that of men. It guaranteed their civic, economic, and political rights. It recognized their participative role in nation building.

Sadly, the Islamic tenets regarding women were soon discarded. In Islamic society, as in other parts of the world, their rights were denied. Women were maltreated, discriminated against, and subjected to violence and oppression, their dignity injured and their role denied.

Women became the victims of a culture of exclusion and male dominance. Today more women than men suffer from poverty, deprivation, and discrimination. Half a billion women are illiterate. Seventy per cent of the children who are denied elementary education are girls.

The plight of women in the developing countries is unspeakable. Hunger, disease, and unremitting toil is their fate. Weak economic growth and inadequate social support systems affect them most seriously and directly. They are the primary victims of structural adjustment processes, which necessitate reduced state funding for health, education, medical care and nutrition. Curtailed resource-flows to these vital areas impact most severely on the vulnerable groups, particularly women and children.

This, Madam Chairperson, is not acceptable. It offends my religion. It offends my sense of justice and equity. Above all, it offends common sense.

That is why Pakistan, the women of Pakistan, and I personally have been fully engaged in recent international efforts to uphold women's rights. The Universal Declaration of Human Rights enjoins the elimination of discrimination against women.

The Nairobi Forward-looking Strategies[2] provide a solid framework for advancing women's rights around the world. But the goal of equality, development and peace still eludes us.

Sporadic efforts in this direction have failed. We are satisfied that the Beijing Platform of Action[3] encompasses a comprehensive approach toward the empowerment of women. This is the right approach and should

[2] 'The Nairobi Forward-looking Strategies for the Advancement of Women' was a document produced by the United Nations as the outcome of a conference held in Nairobi in July 1985.
[3] A document signed by 189 governments in 1995, which analysed and prioritized issues and strategies relating to women's rights.

be fully supported.

Women cannot be expected to struggle alone against the forces of discrimination and exploitation. I recall the words of Dante, who reminded us that, 'The hottest place in Hell is reserved for those who remain neutral in times of moral crisis.'[4]

Today in this world, in the fight for the liberation of women, there can be no neutrality. My spirit carries many a scar of a long and lonely battle against dictatorship and tyranny. I witnessed, at a young age, the overthrow of democracy, the assassination of an elected prime minister,[5] and a systematic assault against the very foundations of a free society.

But our faith in democracy was not broken. The great Pakistani poet and philosopher Dr Allam Iqbal[6] says, 'Tyranny cannot endure forever'. It did not. The will of our people prevailed against the forces of dictatorship.

But, my dear sisters, we have learned that democracy alone is not enough. Freedom of choice alone does not guarantee justice. Equal rights are not defined only by political values. Social justice is a triad of freedom, an equation of liberty.

Justice is political liberty. Justice is economic independence. Justice is social equality.

Delegates, sisters, the child who is starving has no human rights. The girl who is illiterate has no future. The woman who cannot plan her life, plan her family, plan a career, is fundamentally not free.

I am determined to change the plight of women in my country. More than 60 million of our women are largely sidelined. It is a personal tragedy for them. It is a national catastrophe for my nation. I am determined to harness their potential to the gigantic task of nation-building.

I dream of a Pakistan in which women contribute to their full potential. I am conscious of the struggle that lies ahead. But, with your help, we shall persevere. Allah willing, we shall succeed.

[4] The Florentine poet Durante degli Alighieri, or Dante (1265–1321), is best known for his *Divine Comedy* trilogy. Bhutto quotes from the *Inferno* section, which deals with damnation.

[5] Bhutto refers to her father.

[6] The Punjab-born poet and philosopher Allam Iqbal (1877–1938) was one of Muslim India's cultural figureheads. Although he died before the creation of Pakistan as a state, he was one of the first Indians to call for partition.

Osama bin Laden
Saudi Arabian terrorist

Osama bin Mohammad bin Laden (1957–2011) was born in Riyadh, the son of a Yemeni-born construction billionaire. He was educated at the King Abdul Aziz University in Jiddah. During the 1980s he used his wealth to support rebels resisting the Soviet occupation of Afghanistan, establishing centres to recruit and train fighters. In 1988 he founded the al-Qaeda organization to support Islamic opposition movements across the world. By 1991 he had identified the USA as his chief enemy. He was expelled from Saudi Arabia in 1991 and had to leave Sudan in 1996 after pressure from the USA and the United Nations. In 1998 he called upon Muslims everywhere to attack Americans and US interests and was strongly suspected of being involved in various terrorist attacks against the West. He was linked with terrorist bombings of the US embassies in Dar es Salaam, Tanzania and Nairobi, Kenya on 7 August 1998, but his global notoriety came three years later. On 11 September 2001, four commercial air-liners were hijacked by terrorists: two were used to destroy the World Trade Center in New York, a third to destroy part of the Pentagon in Washington, DC; the fourth, also believed to be bound for Washington, crashed in rural Pennsylvania, following an attempt by passengers to overwhelm the hijackers. In total, almost 3,000 people were killed. Soon afterwards, bin Laden was identified as the chief culprit. US president GEORGE W BUSH responded by declaring an international 'war on terrorism', organizing assaults against Bin Laden's bases in Afghanistan and against the Taliban regime, which was accused of sheltering him. Considered the world's most wanted criminal, he made sporadic broadcasts, recorded in unidentified locations, but for a decade consistently eluded capture. On 2 May 2011, he was assassinated during a controversial covert operation ordered by President BARACK OBAMA at what seems to have been his long-standing home in a private residential compound in Abbottabad, Pakistan.

'Our acts are reaction to your own acts'
15 April 2004, sound recording made in an undeclared location

Since the catastrophe of 2001, Osama bin Laden has continued to taunt his enemies with a series of taped audio and video messages, delivered to broadcasting organizations. In April 2004, one such audio tape, believed to be a recording of his voice, was broadcast by the pan-Arab satellite channels al-Arabiya and al-Jazeera.

On the tape, bin Laden outlines his view of the global security situation. He argues that his followers are targeting the West because western nations have harmed Muslim interests, denying them power and security. This, he suggests, is morally equivalent to the acts of terrorism pursued by al-Qaeda – 'your commodity that was returned to you'.

He points specifically to the plight of the Palestinians displaced and dispossessed by Israel, with the support of the USA. Westerners who desire peace, he says, should promote the cause of Palestinians and other oppressed Muslim people. He emphasizes this message with a blunt threat: 'stop shedding our blood so as to preserve your blood'.

This 'peace offer' was interpreted by most western commentators as propaganda designed to appeal to western intellectuals, who might influence their governments to reduce support for Israel and withdraw troops from Iraq. However, sympathy for bin Laden's position is still very limited in the West.

Praise be to Almighty God; peace and prayers be upon our Prophet Muhammad, his family, and companions. This is a message to our neighbours north of the Mediterranean, containing a reconciliation initiative as a response to their positive reactions.

Praise be to God; praise be to God; praise be to God who created Heaven and earth with justice and who allowed the oppressed to punish the oppressor in the same way.

Peace upon those who followed the right path. In my hands there is a message to remind you that justice is a duty towards those whom you love and those whom you do not. And people's rights will not be harmed if the opponent speaks out about them.

The greatest rule of safety is justice, and stopping injustice and aggression. It was said: Oppression kills the oppressors and the hotbed of injustice is evil. The situation in occupied Palestine is an example. What happened on 11 September and 11 March[1] is your commodity that was

[1] On 11 March 2004, ten bombs were detonated on commuter trains in Madrid, Spain, killing 191 people and wounding over 1,800. Spain had been a member of the US-led coalition that invaded Iraq in 2003, and had been cited as a target in a bin Laden broadcast of October 2003.

returned to you.

It is known that security is a pressing necessity for all mankind. We do not agree that you should monopolize it only for yourselves. Also, vigilant people do not allow their politicians to tamper with their security.

Having said this, we would like to inform you that labelling us and our acts as terrorism is also a description of you and of your acts. Reaction comes at the same level as the original action. Our acts are reaction to your own acts, which are represented by the destruction and killing of our kinfolk in Afghanistan, Iraq and Palestine. The act that horrified the world – that is, the killing of the old, handicapped Sheikh Ahmed Yassin,[2] may God have mercy on him – is sufficient evidence.

We pledge to God that we will punish America for him, God willing.

Which religion considers your killed ones innocent and our killed ones worthless? And which principle considers your blood real blood and our blood water? Reciprocal treatment is fair and the one who starts injustice bears greater blame.

As for your politicians and those who have followed their path, who insist on ignoring the real problem of occupying the entirety of Palestine and exaggerate lies and falsification regarding our right in defence and resistance: they do not respect themselves. They also disdain the blood and minds of peoples. This is because their falsification increases the shedding of your blood instead of sparing it.

Moreover, the examining of the developments that have been taking place – in terms of killings in our countries and your countries – will make clear an important fact; namely, that injustice is inflicted on us and on you by your politicians, who send your sons – although you are opposed to this – to our countries to kill and be killed.

Therefore, it is in both sides' interest to curb the plans of those who shed the blood of peoples for their narrow personal interest and subservience to the White House gang.

The Zionist lobby is one of the most dangerous and most difficult figures of this group. God willing, we are determined to fight them. We must take into consideration that this war brings billions of dollars in profit to the major companies, whether it be those that produce weapons or those that contribute to reconstruction, such as the Halliburton Company,[3] its sisters and daughters.

Based on this, it is very clear who is the one benefiting from igniting this war and from the shedding of blood. It is the warlords, the bloodsuckers, who are steering the world policy from behind a curtain.

As for President Bush: the leaders who are revolving in his orbit, the leading media companies and the United Nations, which makes laws for relations between the masters of veto[4] and the slaves of the General Assembly – these are only some of the tools used to deceive and exploit peoples. All these pose a fatal threat to the whole world.

Based on the above, and in order to deny war merchants a chance – and in response to the positive interaction shown by recent events and opinion polls, which indicate that most European peoples want peace – I ask honest people … to form a permanent committee to enlighten European peoples of the justice of our causes, above all Palestine. They can make use of the huge potential of the media.

The door of reconciliation is open for three months from the date of announcing this statement. I also offer a reconciliation initiative to them, whose essence is our commitment to stopping operations against every

[2] The Palestinian activist Ahmed Yassin (c.1937–2004) was the founder and spiritual leader of Hamas, the Palestinian Islamic Resistance Movement. He was assassinated by Israeli security forces on 22 March 2004.

[3] The Halliburton Company, whose chief executive 1995–2000 was Dick Cheney (US Vice President, 2001–9) was awarded reconstruction contracts in Iraq after the 2003 invasion without a competitive tender process taking place. A US government inquiry into the contracts was established in 2004.

[4] The voting procedures of the 15-member UN Security Council give the five permanent members (China, France, Russia, the UK, the USA) the power of veto over Security Council resolutions. Although the General Assembly can adopt resolutions, authorization of external action must come from the Security Council, except in exceptional circumstances.

country that commits itself to not attacking Muslims or interfering in their affairs – including the US conspiracy on the greater Muslim world ... The reconciliation will start with the departure of its last soldier from our country.

The door of reconciliation is open for three months from the date of announcing this statement. For those who reject reconciliation and want war, we are ready ...

Stop shedding our blood so as to preserve your blood. It is in your hands to apply this easy, yet difficult, formula. You know that the situation will expand and increase if you delay things. If this happens, do not blame us – blame yourselves. A rational person does not relinquish his security, money and children to please the liar of the White House ...

It is said that prevention is better than cure. A happy person is he who learns a lesson from the experience of others. Heeding right is better than persisting in falsehood.

Peace be upon those who follow guidance.

Tony Blair
British politician

Anthony Charles Lynton Blair (1953–) was born in Edinburgh and raised in Adelaide, Australia, then Durham, England. He was educated at Fettes College, Edinburgh and St John's College, Oxford. He became a barrister specializing in employment law and was elected as Labour MP for Sedgefield in 1983. He achieved success as opposition home affairs spokesman in 1992, and in July 1994 he became leader of the Labour Party. He swiftly reinvented it as a centrist party. After a landslide election victory in 1997, he became prime minister. During his first term, Blair invested in education and health, signed the Good Friday Agreement in a bid to settle conflicts in Northern Ireland, introduced the Human Rights Act and a minimum wage, urged NATO intervention in the ethnic conflict in Kosovo, oversaw the establishment of the Scottish Parliament and the Welsh Assembly, and reformed the House of Lords. The Freedom of Information Act (2000) granted citizens access to data held by public bodies. After winning the election of 2001, he became the first Labour prime minister to serve a full second term. He developed a close relationship with American president GEORGE W BUSH, receiving, in 2003, a Congressional Gold Medal. However, he faced harsh criticism for British involvement in the invasion of Iraq (March 2003). This controversy persists, and led to calls for Blair's impeachment and indictment for war crimes. He also met sustained protest over university tuition fees, though the Higher Education Act was narrowly passed in January 2004. In 2004, he revealed his intention to serve a third term; and in May 2005, he was re-elected, with a substantially reduced majority. In July 2005 he announced the success of London's bid to host the 2012 Olympic Games; this was swiftly followed by terrorist strikes in the city. In November 2005, he was defeated in the Commons over a provision in the terrorism bill to hold suspects for 90 days without charge. This was considered a serious blow to his authority. Blair was criticized for media manipulation, for authoritarian leadership and for uncritical compliance with Bush and in 2006 his reputation was further damaged by allegations that he had conferred peerages in return for loans to Labour Party funds. In June 2007 he resigned as Prime Minister and was replaced by Gordon Brown, and that same day took up his appointment as Envoy of the Quartet of the Middle East. His publications include *Socialism* (1994), *The Third Way: New Politics for the New Century* (1998), and a volume of memoirs, *A Journey* (2010).

'Removing Saddam will be a blessing to the Iraqi people'
20 March 2003, television broadcast from London, England

In this live televised statement to the British people, Blair announced the start of the offensive against Iraq. Acknowledging the thousands of anti-war protestors who had taken to the streets in cities across Britain, his speech was both an appeal for unity and a last-minute attempt to argue the case for war. In it, he argues that dictators such as SADDAM HUSSEIN pose as much of a threat to global stability as terrorist groups such as al-Qaeda, and must be dealt with resolutely.

Blair appeared tired and drawn as he delivered his message, the result of a gruelling schedule that involved travelling across the world in an attempt – often unsuccessful – to persuade other nations of his case. While the US-led coalition would depose Saddam's regime by mid-April, two phrases from Blair's speech – 'weapons of mass destruction' and 'intelligence' – would haunt him and his government in the months to come. Investigations after the war found no evidence for such weapons, while intelligence claims that Iraq could launch chemical or biological strikes against Britain in 45 minutes were found to be false.

On Tuesday night I gave the order for British forces to take part in military action in Iraq.

Tonight, British servicemen and women are engaged from air, land and sea. Their mission: to remove Saddam Hussein from power, and disarm Iraq of its weapons of mass destruction.

I know this course of action has produced deep divisions of opinion in our country. But I know also the British people will now be united in sending our armed forces our thoughts and prayers. They are the finest in the world and their families and all of Britain can have great pride in them.

The threat to Britain today is not that of my father's generation. War between the big powers is unlikely. Europe is at peace. The Cold War already a memory. But this new world faces a new threat: of disorder and chaos born either of brutal states like Iraq, armed with weapons of mass destruction; or of extreme terrorist groups. Both hate our way of life, our freedom, our democracy.

My fear, deeply held, based in part on the intelligence that I see, is that these threats come together and deliver catastrophe to our country and world. These tyrannical states do not care for the sanctity of human life. The terrorists delight in destroying it.

Some say if we act, we become a target. The truth is, all nations are targets. Bali was never in the front line of action against terrorism.[1] America didn't attack al-Qaeda. They attacked America.

[1] On 12 October 2002, 202 people – mostly Australian tourists – were killed by a car bomb detonated on the Indonesian island of Bali. The Islamic terrorist group Jemaah Islamiyah is believed to have been responsible.

Britain has never been a nation to hide at the back. But even if we were, it wouldn't avail us. Should terrorists obtain these weapons now being manufactured and traded round the world, the carnage they could inflict to our economies, our security, to world peace, would be beyond our most vivid imagination.

My judgement, as prime minister, is that this threat is real, growing and of an entirely different nature to any conventional threat to our security that Britain has faced before.

For twelve years, the world tried to disarm Saddam; after his wars in which hundreds of thousands died.[2] UN weapons inspectors say vast amounts of chemical and biological poisons, such as anthrax, VX nerve agent, and mustard gas remain unaccounted for in Iraq.

[2] Around 500,000 Iraqis are thought to have died in the Iran–Iraq War (1980–8); in the final months of the conflict Iraqi forces massacred approximately 100,000 Kurds.

So our choice is clear: back down and leave Saddam hugely strengthened; or proceed to disarm him by force. Retreat might give us a moment of respite, but years of repentance at our weakness would, I believe, follow.

It is true Saddam is not the only threat. But it is true also – as we British know – that the best way to deal with future threats peacefully is to deal with present threats with resolve.

Removing Saddam will be a blessing to the Iraqi people. Four million Iraqis are in exile. Sixty per cent of the population dependent on food aid. Thousands of children die every year through malnutrition and disease. Hundreds of thousands have been driven from their homes or murdered.

I hope the Iraqi people hear this message. We are with you. Our enemy is not you, but your barbarous rulers.

Our commitment to the post-Saddam humanitarian effort will be total. We shall help Iraq move towards democracy, and put the money from Iraqi oil in a UN trust fund so that it benefits Iraq and no-one else.

Neither should Iraq be our only concern. President Bush and I have committed ourselves to peace in the Middle East based on a secure state of Israel and a viable Palestinian state. We will strive to see it done.

But these challenges and others that confront us – poverty, the environment, the ravages of disease – require a world of order and stability. Dictators like Saddam, terrorist groups like al-Qaeda threaten the very existence of such a world.

That is why I have asked our troops to go into action tonight. As so often before, on the courage and determination of British men and women, serving our country, the fate of many nations rests.

Thank you.

'It is now that timely action can avert disaster'
14 September 2004, London, England

Speaking at an anniversary lecture for the PRINCE OF WALES's Business and Environment programme, Blair made an impassioned case for dealing with climate change. In it, he summarizes the scientific evidence for global warming and its effect on weather patterns and sea levels, and demands urgent action on an international, national and individual scale. He also gives details of government policies to tackle climate change.

The speech emphasizes Britain's leading role in reducing greenhouse gas emissions, but campaigners were quick to point out that Blair's government was then pursuing a major expansion of road and air transport, which threatened to undermine any environmental gains, and that the key sticking point for international action remained the USA's refusal to ratify the Kyoto Protocol on climate change.

Tonight I want to concentrate on what I believe to be the world's greatest environmental challenge: climate change. Our effect on the environment, and in particular on climate change, is large and growing.

To summarize my argument at the outset: from the start of the industrial revolution more than 200 years ago, developed nations have achieved ever greater prosperity and higher living standards. But through this period our activities have come to affect our atmosphere, oceans, geology, chemistry and biodiversity.

What is now plain is that the emission of greenhouse gases, associated with industrialization and strong economic growth, is causing global warming at a rate that began as significant, has become alarming and is simply unsustainable in the long term.

And by long term I do not mean centuries ahead. I mean within the lifetime of my children certainly; and possibly within my own. And by unsustainable, I do not mean a phenomenon causing problems of adjustment. I mean a challenge so far-reaching in its impact and irreversible in its destructive power, that it alters radically human existence …

The challenge is complicated politically by two factors. First, its likely effect will not be felt to its full extent until after the time for the political decisions that need to be taken has passed. In other words, there is a mismatch in timing between the environmental and electoral impact. Secondly, no one nation alone can resolve it. It has no definable boundaries. Short of international action, commonly agreed and commonly followed through, it is hard even for a large country to make a difference on its own.

But there is no doubt that the time to act is now. It is now that timely action can avert disaster. It is now that with foresight and will such action can be taken without disturbing the essence of our way of life, by adjusting behaviour, not altering it entirely.

There is one further preliminary point. Just as science and technology has given us the evidence to measure the danger of climate change, so it can help us find safety from it. The potential for innovation, for scientific discovery – and hence of course for business investment and growth – is enormous. With the right framework for action, the very act of solving it can unleash a new and benign commercial force to take the action forward, providing jobs, technology spin-offs and new business opportunities, as well as protecting the world we live in.

But the issue is urgent. If there is one message I would leave with you and with the British people today it is one of urgency.

Let me turn now to the evidence itself. Apart from a diminishing handful of sceptics, there is a virtual worldwide scientific consensus on the scope of the problem. As long ago as 1988, concerned scientists set up an unprecedented Intergovernmental Panel to ensure that advice to the world's decision-makers was sound and reliable.

Literally thousands of scientists are now engaged in this work. They have scrutinized the data and developed some of the world's most powerful computer models to describe and predict our climate … And from Arnold Schwarzenegger's California[1] to Ningxia Province in China, the problem is being recognized.

[1] The Austrian-born film star Arnold Schwarzenegger (1947–) was elected governor of California in 2003.

Let me summarize the evidence. The ten warmest years on record have all been since 1990. Over the last century average global temperatures have risen by 0.6 degrees Celsius: the most drastic temperature rise for over a thousand years in the northern hemisphere. Extreme events are becoming more frequent. Glaciers are melting. Sea-ice and snow cover is declining. Animals and plants are responding to an earlier spring. Sea levels are rising and are forecast to rise another 88 cm by 2100, threatening 100 million people globally, who currently live below this level.

The number of people affected by floods worldwide has already risen from seven million in the 1960s to 150 million today. In Europe alone, the severe floods in 2002 had an estimated cost of $16 billion. This summer we have seen violent weather extremes in parts of the UK[2] …

[2] The most extreme British weather event of 2004 was the flooding of the village of Boscastle in Cornwall, during which an estimated 440 million gallons of water destroyed historic buildings and swept away cars and other large objects.

There is good evidence that last year's European heatwave was influenced by global warming. It resulted in 26,000 premature deaths and cost $13.5 billion. It is calculated that such a summer is a one-in-about-800-year event. On the latest modelling, climate change means that as soon as the 2040s, at least one year in two is likely to be even warmer than 2003.

That is the evidence. There is one overriding positive: through the science we are aware of the problem and, with the necessary political and collective will, have the ability to address it effectively.

The public, in my view, do understand this. The news of severe weather abroad is an almost weekly occurrence. A recent opinion survey by Greenpeace[3] showed that 78 per cent of people are concerned about climate change. But people are confused about what they can do. It is individuals as well as governments and corporations who can make a real difference. The environmental impacts from business are themselves driven by the choices we make each day.

[3] The international environmental organization Greenpeace was founded in Canada in 1971.

To make serious headway towards smarter lifestyles, we need to start with clear and consistent policy and messages, championed both by government and by those outside government.

I said earlier it needed global leadership to tackle the issue. But we cannot aspire to such leadership unless we are seen to be following our own advice. So, what is the UK government doing? We have led the world in setting a bold plan and targets for reducing greenhouse gas emissions … We need both to invest on a large scale in existing technologies and to stimulate innovation into new low-carbon technologies for deployment in the longer term …

In short, we need to develop the new green industrial revolution that develops the new technologies that can confront and overcome the challenge of climate change; and that above all can show us not that we can avoid changing our behaviour but we can change it in a way that is environmentally sustainable …

None of this is easy to do. But its logic is hard to fault. Even if there are those who still doubt the science in its entirety, surely the balance of risk for action or inaction has changed. If there were even a 50 per cent chance that the scientific evidence I receive is right, the bias in favour of action would be clear. But of course it is far more than 50 per cent.

And in this case, the science is backed up by intuition. It is not axiomatic that pollution causes damage. But it is likely. I am a strong supporter of proceeding through scientific analysis in such issues. But I also, as I think most people do, have a healthy instinct that if we upset the balance of nature, we are in all probability going to suffer a reaction. With world growth and population as it is, this reaction must increase.

We have been warned. On most issues we ask children to listen to their parents. On climate change, it is parents who should listen to their children.

Now is the time to start.

Simón Bolívar
Venezuelan-born revolutionary leader

Simón Bolívar *known as El Libertador ('The Liberator')* (1783–1830) was born in Caracas, of an aristocratic creole family. He studied law in Madrid and travelled extensively in Europe. In 1802, he married a Spanish noblewoman, María Teresa Rodríguez del Toro y Alaysa; she died of yellow fever the following year, after he brought her to the Caribbean. He renounced Spain altogether when he resolved, around 1807, to liberate his country. He was active in the resistance junta that declared Venezuela's independence from Spain in 1810. In 1811, he was placed in command of the strategically important port of Puerto Cabello. However, one of his lieutenants colluded with the Spanish, bringing about defeat and the surrender of the junta's leader, Francisco de Miranda, in July 1812. Bolívar fled to Cartagena in New Granada, where he was given command of an army. In August 1813, he entered Caracas as conqueror and proclaimed himself dictator of western Venezuela. Driven out in 1814, he repeatedly led raids on Venezuela from the West Indies. In 1817 he began to make headway against the Spaniards, but it was only in 1821 that the victory of Carabobo virtually ended the war; and it was not until 1824 that the royalist troops were finally driven out. In 1819 Bolívar became president of the new republic of Colombia (comprising modern Venezuela, Colombia and, from 1822, Ecuador). In 1824 he joined with other rebel leaders including Antonio de Sucre and José de San Martin to drive the Spaniards out of Peru, and made himself dictator there for a time. Upper Peru was made a separate state, and called Bolivia in his honour, while he was named perpetual protector, but his Bolivian constitution provoked political dissent, and led to the expulsion of the Colombian troops. His assumption of supreme power, after his return to Colombia in 1828, roused the apprehension of the republicans there, and in 1829 Venezuela separated itself from Colombia. Bolívar resigned in 1830. Although his life ended in dictatorship, his ideal of a federation of all Spanish-speaking South American states exerted a lasting influence.

'Our sole mission is to break the chains of servitude'
15 June 1813, Trujillo, Venezuela

Bolívar launched his *campaña admirable* ('admirable campaign') to reconquer Venezuela on 14 May 1813. By the end of the month, he had taken the city and state of Mérida. On 9 June, he captured Trujillo where, six days later, he read out this famous call to arms, known as the *Decreto de Guerra a Muerte* ('Decree of War to the Death').

Translated here by Frederick H Fornoff, Bolívar's triumphal declaration presents a stirring appeal to solidarity and national pride, offering immunity to Spaniards and even turncoats, provided they join his cause. But mindful of his disastrous betrayal at Puerto Cabello the previous year, he makes an unambiguous demand for loyalty, enforced by the threat of summary execution.

Within two months, Bolívar had recaptured Caracas and established the Second Venezuelan Republic. Thereafter – despite his autocratic tendencies – he was hailed as *El Libertador*, the name by which he is still revered. His statue stands in countless Latin American plazas to this day. Hugo Chávez, left-wing president of Venezuela since 1999, has expressed great admiration for Bolívar, frequently citing the Decree of War.

[1] A union of Spanish colonies in the northern part of South America, created in 1717, and roughly corresponding to modern Colombia.

Venezuelans: an army of brothers, sent by the Supreme Congress of New Granada,[1] has come to liberate you, and it now stands among you, after having expelled the oppressors from the provinces of Mérida and Trujillo.

We are sent to destroy the Spaniards, to protect Americans,[2] and to re-establish the republican governments that formed the Federation of Venezuela. The states protected by our arms are once again ruled by their former constitutions and leaders, in the full enjoyment of their freedom and independence, because our sole mission is to break the chains of servitude that still oppress some of our people, not to make laws or seize power, as the rules of war might authorize us to do.

Moved by your misfortunes, we could not witness with indifference the afflictions visited upon you by the savage Spaniards, who have annihilated and destroyed you with pillage and death, who have violated the sanctity of human rights, rendered null the most solemn articles of surrender and

[2] Bolívar refers to Latin Americans. The American continents are named after the Florentine adventurer Amerigo Vespucci (1454–1512), whose first landing in the 'new world' around 1499 was probably on the north coast of South America, in what is now Guyana.

treaty, and committed every imaginable crime, reducing Venezuela to the most horrific desolation. Thus, justice demands retribution, and necessity obliges us to take it.

Let the monsters who have infested Colombian soil, covering it with blood, vanish forever; let their punishment be equal to the enormity of their perfidy, thus washing away the stain of our ignominy and demonstrating to the nations of the world that one cannot offend the sons of America with impunity.

Despite our just resentment against the foul Spaniards, our generous hearts still see fit one last time to pen the way to reconciliation and friendship; we invite them once again to live peacefully among us under the condition that, renouncing their crimes and acting henceforth in good faith, they co-operate with us in the destruction of the Spanish government of occupation and in the re-establishment of the Venezuelan Republic.

Any Spaniard who does not join our fight against tyranny to further this just cause, actively and effectively, will be regarded as an enemy and punished as a traitor to the country and consequently put to death without appeal. On the other hand, a general and absolute pardon is hereby granted to those who come over to our armies, with or without their weapons, and who lend their support to the good citizens who are struggling to shake off the yoke of tyranny.

Military officers and civil leaders who join us in proclaiming the government of Venezuela will keep their rank and offices; in a word, Spaniards who render distinguished service to the state will be regarded and treated as Americans.

And you Americans who have been led from the path of justice by error or perfidy, be sure that your brothers forgive you and sincerely lament your offences, convinced in our hearts that you cannot be to blame, and that only the blindness and ignorance in which you have been held hitherto by the instigators of your crimes could have led you to commit them. Do not fear the sword that comes to avenge you and to sever the ignominious bonds that bind you to the fate of your executioners. You may count on absolute immunity regarding your honour, your lives, and your property: the mere title of Americans will be your guarantee and your safeguard. Our weapons are here to protect you and will never be turned against a single one of our brothers.

This amnesty extends even to the traitors who have most recently committed acts of felony, and it will be so religiously fulfilled that no reason, cause, or pretext will be sufficient to cause us to break our promise, no matter how grievous and extraordinary the motives you give us to arouse our loathing.

Spaniards and Canarians, even if you profess neutrality, know that you will die unless you work actively to bring about the freedom of America. Americans, know that you will live, even if you are guilty.

Napoleon Bonaparte
French military leader and emperor

Napoleon Bonaparte *later Napoleon I* (1769–1821) was born in Corsica, the son of a lawyer. In 1785 he was commissioned as an artillery officer. He organized a revolution in Corsica (1792), but was given command of the artillery at the Siege of Toulon (1793) and promoted to brigadier general. In 1796 he became commander of the army of Italy (1796), where he occupied Milan and took Verona and Legnago from neutral Venice. He then advanced on Vienna. Austria signed the Treaty of Campo Formio (1797), by which France obtained Belgium and Lombardy. The Directory, fearing Napoleon's ambition, gave him command of the army of England. Instead, he launched an expedition to Egypt, hoping to damage Britain's trade with India. He entered Cairo in 1798, but his fleet was destroyed by Nelson at the Battle of the Nile. Napoleon returned to Paris, taking part in the revolution of 1799. He helped draft a new constitution, and was nominated First Consul. He proposed a Bank of France and reformed local government and the judiciary. In 1800, he returned to Italy, occupying Milan. Further victories at Marengo and Hohenlinden led to the Treaty of Luneville (1801). France's power was strengthened by a concordat with Rome and peace with England. Napoleon continued domestic reforms, becoming emperor in 1804. In 1805 he faced both England and an Austro-Russian coalition. He surprised the Austrians at Ulm and took Vienna, but meanwhile the French fleet was destroyed at the Battle of Trafalgar. He defeated an Austro-Russian army at Austerlitz, then began peace negotiations. Defeating Prussia in 1806, he gained control of a huge European empire. He tried to cripple the UK with a trade boycott. To enforce the blockade, he sent armies to occupy Spain and Portugal, precipitating the Peninsular War. British forces drove French troops from Portugal (1808) and Spain (1813). In 1812, Napoleon invaded Russia, occupying Moscow, but was forced to retreat in the winter, losing much of his army. He returned to Paris but was defeated at the Battle of the Nations near Leipzig. The allies invaded France and took Paris (1814). Forced to abdicate, Napoleon retained sovereignty of Elba and the title of emperor. Louis XVIII was restored to the throne but proved unpopular. Napoleon returned to France in 1815, occupying Paris. Europe declared war. After initial victory against the Prussians, Napoleon was defeated at Waterloo. Banished to St Helena, he died there of a stomach illness.

'With men such as you our cause could not be lost'
Speeches to the French troops, 1796–1814

Napoleon's outstanding military career was well under way when he became commander of the French army of Italy in 1796. He found this army demoralized, poorly equipped and badly organized, but he inspired his men, gaining their respect and loyalty. He promised them victories and great rewards and encouraged them to begin campaigning in a speech which demonstrates his understanding of their condition and inspired confidence.

He was a brilliant military strategist, and the campaign's success was largely due to his excellent planning. He was aware of the importance of supplies (hence his famous dictum 'an army marches on its stomach'), but directed his troops to live off the land rather than relying on army headquarters. By the time they reached Milan, the army had enjoyed considerable success, for which Napoleon gave them credit in a speech before entering the city.

Following Russia's defeat at Friedland, France's relations with Russia were strengthened by the treaty of Tilsit, but soon deteriorated. In 1812 Napoleon acted to counter a threatened Russian attack, assembling a huge army on the Russian border. He invaded Russia, hoping for a quick victory, encouraging his men in a speech reminding them of their previous success and of Russian bad faith.

The failure of the Russian invasion and the disastrous retreat from Moscow marked the beginning of Napoleon's decline. Before leaving for exile in Elba, he paraded a group of faithful followers in the courtyard at Fontainebleau, called for his eagle standard and cradled it in his arms, causing cries of despair from the men, to whom he then said farewell.

On launching the Italian campaign, March 1796:
Soldiers: You are naked and ill-fed! Government owes you much and can give you nothing. The patience and courage you have shown in the midst of this rocky wilderness are admirable; but they gain you no renown; no glory results to you from your endurance.

It is my design to lead you into the most fertile plains of the world. Rich provinces and great cities will be in your power; there you will find honour, glory, and wealth. Soldiers of Italy, will you be wanting in courage or perseverance?

On entering Milan, 15 May 1796:
Soldiers: You have rushed like a torrent from the top of the Apennines; you have overthrown and scattered all that opposed your march. Piedmont, delivered from Austrian tyranny, indulges her natural sentiments of peace and friendship toward France. Milan is yours, and the republican flag waves throughout Lombardy. The dukes of Parma and Modena owe their political existence to your generosity alone.

The army which so proudly threatened you can find no barrier to protect it against your courage; neither the Po, the Ticino, nor the Adda could stop you for a single day. These vaunted bulwarks of Italy opposed you in vain; you passed them as rapidly as the Apennines.

These great successes have filled the heart of your country with joy. Your representatives have ordered a festival to commemorate your victories, which has been held in every district of the republic. There your fathers, your mothers, your wives, sisters and mistresses rejoiced in your good fortune and proudly boasted of belonging to you.

Yes, soldiers, you have done much − but remains there nothing more to do? Shall it be said of us that we knew how to conquer, but not how to make use of victory? Shall posterity reproach us with having found Capua[1] in Lombardy?

But I see you already hasten to arms. An effeminate repose is tedious to you; the days which are lost to glory are lost to your happiness. Well, then, let us set forth!

[1] In ancient Italy, Capua was a city whose size and importance rivalled that of Rome.

On war with Russia, June 1812:
Soldiers: The Second War of Poland[2] has begun. The first war terminated at Friedland and Tilsit. At Tilsit, Russia swore eternal alliance with France and war with England. She has openly violated her oath, and refuses to offer any explanation of her strange conduct till the French eagle[3] shall have passed the Rhine, and consequently shall have left her allies at her discretion. Russia is impelled onward by fatality. Her destiny is about to be accomplished. Does she believe that we have degenerated − that we are no longer the soldiers of Austerlitz? She has placed us between dishonour and war. The choice cannot for an instant be doubtful.

Let us march forward, then, and, crossing the Niemen, carry the war into her territories. The second war of Poland will be to the French army as glorious as the first. But our next peace must carry with it its own guarantee and put an end to that arrogant influence which for the last 50 years Russia has exercised over the affairs of Europe.

[2] Napoleon refers to this war as the 'Second Polish War' to increase support from Polish allies. The First Polish War had been the liberation of Poland from Russia, Prussia and Austria in 1809.
[3] The symbol of ancient Rome, associated with military victory, which was adopted by Napoleon in his coat of arms and used by his army on regimental standards.

On his abdication, April 1814:
Soldiers of my Old Guard: I bid you farewell. For 20 years I have constantly accompanied you on the road to honour and glory. In these latter times, as in the days of our prosperity, you have invariably been models of courage and fidelity. With men such as you our cause could not be lost; but the war would have been interminable; it would have been civil war, and that would have entailed deeper misfortunes on France.

I have sacrificed all my interests to those of the country. I go, but you, my friends, will continue to serve France. Her happiness was my only thought. It will still be the object of my wishes. Do not regret my fate; if I have consented to survive, it is to serve your glory. I intend to write the history of the great achievements we have performed together. Adieu, my friends. Would I could press you all to my heart.

John Bright
English orator and politician

John Bright (1811–89) was born in Rochdale, Lancashire, the eldest surviving son of a Quaker cotton-spinner. Educated in Ackworth, York, Newton and Clitheroe, he joined his father's firm, eventually becoming a partner. In 1839, he became, with Richard Cobden and others, a founding member of the Anti-Corn Law League, which was formed to challenge tariffs that protected the interests of wealthy landowners and to agitate for free trade. He became MP for Durham (1843) and continued to oppose the Corn Laws until they were repealed in 1846. He was elected MP for Manchester in 1847. Like Cobden, he was a member of the Peace Society and energetically denounced the Crimean War (1854–6). Elected as MP for Birmingham in 1857, he seconded the motion against the conspiracy bill which led to the overthrow of Lord Palmerston's government. He was closely involved with the Reform Act of 1867, which greatly increased male suffrage. In 1868 he accepted office as president of the Board of Trade but he retired through illness in 1870. He returned to politics in 1881 as chancellor of the Duchy of Lancaster. He retired from WILLIAM GLADSTONE's ministry in 1882 over the British bombardment and occupation of Egypt, and later opposed Gladstone's Home Rule policy in Ireland (1886–8).

'The Angel of Death has been abroad'
23 February 1855, London, England

Often a fiery and pugnacious debater, John Bright was never more passionate than when opposing war. This, the most famous speech of his distinguished parliamentary career, was given during the Crimean War, four months after the disastrous charge of the Light Brigade. Lord John Russell, Secretary of State for the Colonies, had been instructed to represent Britain at a peace conference in Vienna, and Bright saw in this the possibility of an armistice. In his speech, he urges the government to negotiate for peace.

Its chilling core is the biblical vision of the Angel of Death, visiting its message of bereavement on the families of those killed in combat. But devout as he was, Bright does not rest his argument on purely religious foundations. Considered a champion of the working class, he touches briefly on the growth of civil unrest, but addresses his appeal to members of all classes. All strata of British society were involved in the war, he argues, and whatever the outcome, some casualties were inevitable.

He also appeals to the prime minister Lord Palmerston – advanced in years but not, as it turned out, nearing the end of his career – to 'return the sword to the scabbard' as an act of statesmanship to be remembered with pride.

Bright's opposition to the war received a hostile response, which contributed to his nervous breakdown of 1856 and his defeat at the election of 1857. He withdrew briefly from politics but returned to Parliament months later as MP for Birmingham, a seat he held for 30 years.

There is one subject upon which I should like to put a question to the noble Lord at the head of the government.[1] I shall not say one word here about the state of the army in the Crimea, or one word about its numbers or its condition. Every Member of this House, every inhabitant of this country, has been sufficiently harrowed with details regarding it. To my solemn belief, thousands – nay, scores of thousands of persons – have retired to rest, night after night, whose slumbers have been disturbed or whose dreams have been based upon the sufferings and agonies of our soldiers in the Crimea.

I should like to ask the noble Lord at the head of the government – although I am not sure if he will feel that he can or ought to answer the question – whether the noble Lord the Member for London[2] has power, after discussions have commenced (and as soon as there shall be established good grounds for believing that the negotiations for peace will prove successful) to enter into any armistice?

[*An honourable Member: 'No, no!'*]

I know not, Sir, who it is that says 'No, no,' but I should like to see any man get up and say that the destruction of 200,000 human lives lost on all sides

[1] The English statesman Henry John Temple, 3rd Viscount Palmerston (1784–1865) served as Foreign Secretary 1830–4, 1835–41 and 1846–51, and as Prime Minister, 1855–8 and 1859–65.

[2] The English politician Lord John Russell *later 1st Earl Russell* (1792–1878) served as Prime Minister 1846–52 and 1865–6. In March–April 1855, he represented Britain at the Vienna peace talks, which failed to bring an end to the Crimean War.

during the course of this unhappy conflict is not a sufficient sacrifice. You are not pretending to conquer territory; you are not pretending to hold fortified or unfortified towns; you have offered terms of peace which, as I understand them, I do not say are not moderate. And breathes there a man in this House or in this country whose appetite for blood is so insatiable that, even when terms of peace have been offered and accepted, he pines for that assault in which of Russian, Turk, French and English as sure as one man dies, 20,000 corpses will strew the streets of Sebastopol?

I say I should like to ask the noble Lord – and I am sure that he will feel, and that this House will feel, that I am speaking in no unfriendly manner towards the government of which he is at the head – I should like to know, and I venture to hope that it is so, if the noble Lord the Member for London has power, at the earliest stage of these proceedings at Vienna, at which it can properly be done (and I should think that it might properly be done at a very early stage) to adopt a course by which all further waste of human life may be put an end to, and further animosity between three great nations be, as far as possible, prevented?

I appeal to the noble Lord at the head of the government and to this House; I am not now complaining of the war – I am not now complaining of the terms of peace, nor, indeed, of anything that has been done – but I wish to suggest to this House what, I believe, thousands and tens of thousands of the most educated and of the most Christian portion of the people of this country are feeling upon this subject – although, indeed, in the midst of a certain clamour in the country, they do not give public expression to their feelings.

Your country is not in an advantageous state at this moment; from one end of the kingdom to the other there is a general collapse of industry. Those Members of this House not intimately acquainted with the trade and commerce of the country do not fully comprehend our position as to the diminution of employment and the lessening of wages. An increase in the cost of living is finding its way to the homes and hearts of a vast number of the labouring population.

At the same time there is growing up – and, notwithstanding what some honourable Members of this House may think of me, no man regrets it more than I do – a bitter and angry feeling against that class which has for a long period conducted the public affairs of this country. I like political changes when such changes are made as the result not of passion, but of deliberation and reason. Changes so made are safe, but changes made under the influence of violent exaggeration, or of the violent passions of public meetings, are not changes usually approved by this House or advantageous to the country. I cannot but notice – in speaking to gentlemen who sit on either side of this House; or in speaking to anyone I meet between this House and any of those localities we frequent when this House is up – I cannot, I say, but notice that an uneasy feeling exists as to the news which may arrive by the very next mail from the east. I do not suppose that your troops are to be beaten in actual conflict with the foe, or that they will be driven into the sea; but I am certain that many homes in England in which there now exists a fond hope that the distant one may return – many such homes may be rendered desolate when the next mail shall arrive.

The Angel of Death has been abroad throughout the land; you may almost hear the beating of his wings. There is no-one, as when the first-born were slain of old, to sprinkle with blood the lintel and the two side-

[3] Bright alludes to Exodus 12:1–30, which describes how the Israelites were spared the final plague of Egypt – the death of the first-born – after marking their door-frames with the blood of a sacrificial lamb. This is the origin of the Jewish festival of Passover.

posts of our doors, that he may spare and pass on;[3] he takes his victims from the castle of the noble, the mansion of the wealthy, and the cottage of the poor and the lowly, and it is on behalf of all these classes that I make this solemn appeal.

I tell the noble Lord that if he be ready honestly and frankly to endeavour, by the negotiations about to be opened at Vienna, to put an end to this war, no word of mine, no vote of mine, will be given to shake his power for one single moment, or to change his position in this House. I am sure that the noble Lord is not inaccessible to appeals made to him from honest motives and with no unfriendly feeling.

The noble Lord has been for more than 40 years a member of this House. Before I was born, he sat upon the treasury bench, and he has spent his life in the service of his country. He is no longer young, and his life has extended almost to the term allotted to man.[4] I would ask, I would entreat the noble Lord to take a course which, when he looks back upon his whole political career – whatever he may therein find to be pleased with, whatever to regret – cannot but be a source of gratification to him. By adopting that course he would have the satisfaction of reflecting that, having obtained the object of his laudable ambition – having become the foremost subject of the Crown, the director of, it may be, the destinies of his country, and the presiding genius in her councils – he had achieved a still higher and nobler ambition: that he had returned the sword to the scabbard. That at his word, torrents of blood had ceased to flow. That he had restored tranquillity to Europe, and saved this country from the indescribable calamities of war.

[4] According to Psalm 90:10, 'the days of our years are threescore years and ten' – ie human life expectancy is 70 years. At this time, Lord Palmerston was 68.

'The huge, foul blot upon the fame of the American republic'
18 December 1862, Birmingham, England

During his long career in politics, Bright consistently opposed war and upheld the cause of human rights and liberties. During the American Civil War of 1861–5, his principles were put to the test. War had broken out when the slave-owning southern states seceded from the Union, largely because they feared President ABRAHAM LINCOLN would abolish slavery. (Their fears were well founded: the Emancipation Proclamation was announced in September 1862, and came into effect at the start of 1863, two weeks after this speech was made).

Deeply disgusted by slavery, Bright naturally supported the US government and considered the breakaway Confederate States of America a blasphemous entity: 'a new state intending to set itself up on the sole basis of slavery'. At the same time, he was appalled by the brutalities of the war, whose death toll rose to above half a million. He tackled these issues in this address to his Birmingham constituents.

There is both compromise and contradiction in his speech. At one point – probably prompted by political pragmatism – he concedes that trade and good relations might be maintained with nations practising slavery by 'accident' of history. Later, he declares the war the only imaginable means of bringing US slavery to an end, yet still condemns it as 'a measureless calamity'.

The outcomes Bright sought – abolition of slavery, survival and harmonization of the Union – were ultimately achieved, but not without bloodshed on a grand scale.

Is there a man here that doubts for a moment that the object of the war on the part of the South – they began the war – that the object of the war on the part of the South is to maintain in bondage four millions of human beings? That is only a small part of it. The further object is to perpetuate for ever the bondage of all the posterity of those four millions of slaves.

[*A few cries of 'No! No!'*]

You will hear that I am not in a condition to contest vigorously anything that may be opposed, for I am suffering, as nearly everybody is, from the state of the weather, and a hoarseness that almost hinders me from speaking. I could quote their own documents till midnight in proof of what I say; and if I found a man who denied it, upon the evidence that had been offered, I would not offend him, or trouble myself, by trying further to convince him.

The object is that a handful of white men on that continent shall lord it over many millions of blacks, made black by the very hand that made us white. The object is that they should have the power to breed negroes, to work negroes, to lash negroes, to chain negroes, to buy and sell negroes, to deny them the commonest ties of family, or to break their hearts by rending them at their pleasure, to close their mental eye to but a glimpse even of that knowledge which separates us from the brute – for in their laws it is criminal and penal to teach the negro to read – to seal from their hearts the book of our religion, and to make chattels and things of men and women and children.

Now, I want to ask whether this is to be the foundation, as it is proposed, of a new slave empire, and whether it is intended that on this audacious and infernal basis England's new ally is to be built up …

I should have no kind of objection to recognize a country because it was a country that held slaves – to recognize the United States, or to be in amity with it. The question of slavery there, and in Cuba and in Brazil, is – as far as respects the present generation – an accident, and it would be unreasonable that we should object to trade with and have political relations with a country, merely because it happened to have within its borders the institution of slavery, hateful as that institution is. But in this case it is a new state intending to set itself up on the sole basis of slavery. Slavery is blasphemously declared to be its chief cornerstone.

I have heard that there are, in this country, ministers of state who are in favour of the South; that there are members of the aristocracy who are terrified at the shadow of the great republic; that there are rich men on our commercial exchanges, depraved, it may be, by their riches, and thriving unwholesomely within the atmosphere of a privileged class; that there are conductors of the public press who would barter the rights of millions of their fellow-creatures that they might bask in the smiles of the great.

But I know that there are ministers of state who do not wish that this insurrection should break up the American nation; that there are members of our aristocracy who are not afraid of the shadow of the republic; that there are rich men, many, who are not depraved by their riches; and that there are public writers of eminence and honour who will not barter human rights for the patronage of the great. But most of all, and before all, I believe – I am sure it is true in Lancashire, where the working men have seen themselves coming down from prosperity to ruin – I say that I believe that the unenfranchised but not hopeless millions of this country will never sympathize with a revolt which is intended to destroy the liberty of a continent, and to build on its ruins a mighty fabric of human bondage.

When I speak to gentlemen in private upon this matter, and hear their own candid opinion – I mean those who differ from me on this question – they generally end by saying that the republic is too great and too powerful, and that it is better for us – not by 'us' meaning you, but the governing classes and the governing policy of England – that it should be broken up. But we will suppose that we are in New York or in Boston, discussing the policy and power of England. If any one there were to point to England – not to the 31 millions of population in these islands, but to her 150 millions in India, and nobody knows how many millions more in every other part of the globe – might he not, whilst boasting that America has not covered the ocean with fleets of force, or left the bones of her citizens to blanch on a hundred European battlefields – might he not fairly say, that England is great and powerful, and that it is perilous for the world that she is so great?

But bear in mind that every declaration of this kind, whether from an Englishman who professes to be strictly English, or from an American strictly American, or from a Frenchman strictly French – whether it asserts in arrogant strains that Britannia rules the waves,[1] or speaks of 'manifest destiny'[2] and the supremacy of the 'Stars and Stripes',[3] or boasts that the Eagles of one nation,[4] having once overrun Europe, may possibly repeat the experiment – I say all this is to be condemned. It is not truly patriotic; it is not rational; it is not moral. Then, I say, if any man wishes the great republic to be severed on that ground: in my opinion, he is doing that which tends to keep alive jealousies which, as far as he can prevent it, will never die; though if they do not die, wars must be eternal …

My countrymen who work for your living, remember this: there will be one wild shriek of freedom to startle all mankind if that American republic should be overthrown.

Now for one moment let us lift ourselves, if we can, above the narrow circle in which we are all too apt to live and think; let us put ourselves on an historical eminence, and judge this matter fairly. Slavery has been, as we all know, the huge, foul blot upon the fame of the American republic; it is a hideous outrage against human right and against divine law; but the pride, the passion of man, will not permit its peaceable extinction. The slave-owners of our colonies, if they had been strong enough, would have revolted too.[5] I believe there was no mode – short of a miracle more stupendous than any recorded in holy writ – that could in our time, or in a century, or in any time, have brought about the abolition of slavery in America, but the suicide which the South has committed and the war which it has begun.

Sir, it is a measureless calamity, this war. I said the Russian war[6] was a measureless calamity, and yet many of your leaders and friends told you that it was a just war to maintain the integrity of Turkey, some thousands of miles off. Surely the integrity of your own country at your own doors must be worth as much as the integrity of Turkey? Is not this war the penalty which inexorable justice exacts from America, North and South,[7] for the enormous guilt of cherishing that frightful iniquity of slavery for the last 80 years? I do not blame any man here who thinks the cause of the North hopeless and the restoration of the Union impossible. It may be hopeless; the restoration may be impossible. You have the authority of the Chancellor of the Exchequer[8] on that point. The Chancellor of the Exchequer, as a speaker, is not surpassed by any man in England, and he is a great statesman; he believes the cause of the North to be hopeless; that their enterprise cannot succeed.

Well, he is quite welcome to that opinion, and so is anybody else. I do not hold the opinion; but the facts are before us all, and – as far as we can discard passion and sympathy – we are all equally at liberty to form our own opinion. But what I do blame is this. I blame men who are eager to admit into the family of nations a state which offers itself to us, based upon a principle, I will undertake to say, more odious and more blasphemous than was ever heretofore dreamed of in Christian or pagan, in civilized or in savage times. The leaders of this revolt propose this monstrous thing – that over a territory 40 times as large as England, the blight and curse of slavery

[1] A line from the patriotic British anthem 'Rule Britannia' written in 1740 by James Thomson and Thomas Arne.
[2] A phrase originally coined in 1844 by the US journalist John L O'Sullivan, who referred to 'our manifest destiny to overspread the continent allotted by Providence for the free development of our yearly multiplying millions'. It became widely used in 19th-century America as a byword for the nation's expansion towards the west coast.
[3] A nickname for the US flag.
[4] The eagle, previously used as a symbol of Roman imperial power, was adopted by the French emperor NAPOLEON BONAPARTE and cast in bronze on the flagpoles of his armies.

[5] The Abolition of Slavery Act of 1833 had a severe economic impact on the sugar trade in the British-owned West Indies, which relied on slave labour.
[6] Bright refers to the Crimean War (1854–6). See his previous speech.

[7] Bright means the northern and southern states of the USA.

[8] The Chancellor of the Exchequer, WILLIAM GLADSTONE, had made a contentious speech in October 1862 – which he later regretted – apparently in support of the South.

shall be forever perpetuated.

I cannot believe, for my part, that such a fate will befall that fair land, stricken though it now is with the ravages of war. I cannot believe that civilization, in its journey with the sun, will sink into endless night in order to gratify the ambition of the leaders of this revolt, who seek to 'wade through slaughter to a throne, And shut the gates of mercy on mankind.'[9]

I have another and a far brighter vision before my gaze. It may be but a vision, but I will cherish it. I see one vast confederation stretching from the frozen North in unbroken line to the glowing South, and from the wild billows of the Atlantic, westward to the calmer waters of the Pacific main. And I see one people, and one language, and one law, and one faith and – over all that wide continent – the home of freedom and a refuge for the oppressed of every race and of every clime.

[9] From *Elegy Written in a Country Churchyard* (1751) by Thomas Gray.

John Brown

American abolitionist

John Brown (1800–59) was born in Torrington, Connecticut, of Pilgrim descent. He was successively a tanner, a land surveyor, a shepherd and a farmer. A committed abolitionist, he travelled throughout the USA on anti-slavery enterprises. He was twice married and had 20 children. In 1854, five of his sons moved to Kansas. When border skirmishes broke out with Missouri over the right to own slaves, he moved to Kansas and became a leader in the struggle. In 1856, his home was burned and one of his sons was killed. When the fighting in Kansas ended, Brown began to drill men in Iowa. His next scheme was to establish a stronghold in the mountains of Virginia as a refuge for runaway slaves, and in 1859 he seized the Federal arsenal at Harpers Ferry in Virginia, apparently intending to launch a slave insurrection. The arsenal was stormed by a company of marines, leading to losses on both sides, and Brown was wounded. Tried by a Virginia court for insurrection, treason and murder, he was convicted and hanged at Charlestown, Virginia. A song commemorating the Harpers Ferry raid – 'John Brown's Body Lies a-Mouldering in the Grave', attributed to Thomas B Bishop – became highly popular as a marching song for Unionist soldiers during the American Civil War. Provided with alternative lyrics by Julia Ward Howe, it later became 'The Battle Hymn of the Republic'.

'I feel no consciousness of guilt'

2 November 1859, Charlestown, Virginia, USA

John Brown's legacy divides opinion. Some see him as a martyr to the cause of abolitionism; others as a dangerous extremist and terrorist. His execution certainly stirred controversy and helped nudge the USA towards civil war.

The political roots of Brown's activities lie in the Kansas–Nebraska Act of 1854, which allowed citizens of the two newly established states to determine their own slavery laws. This appeased the pro-slavery South, and neighbouring Missouri (politically aligned to the South) sought to expand slavery into Kansas, provoking a series of violent cross-border confrontations.

In May 1856, the abolitionist senator CHARLES SUMNER gave a speech on Kansas in the Senate and was afterwards savagely beaten. Brown was outraged and probably led a retaliation at Pottawatomie, Kansas, in which five pro-slavery settlers were brutally murdered, though he denied involvement. In further skirmishes, including one at Osawatomie, Kansas, he led brave actions against superior numbers of Missourian troops, gaining the nickname 'Osawatomie Brown'. In December 1858, he led a mission into Missouri to liberate eleven slaves, whom he conducted to Canada.

But his most audacious raid was at Harpers Ferry in the southern state of Virginia, in October 1859. With 21 heavily armed supporters, he seized the federal armoury, murdering a railwayman and taking hostages, apparently intending to initiate a slaves' rebellion. When US Marines under Robert E Lee stormed the building, Brown and six men, barricading themselves in an engine house, continued to fight until two of Brown's sons were killed and Brown was severely wounded.

His trial lasted two weeks, but its outcome can have surprised no-one. After being sentenced to hang, Brown gave this plaintive but dignified speech.

I have, may it please the court, a few words to say. In the first place, I deny everything but what I have all along admitted: of a design on my part to free slaves. I intended certainly to have made a clean thing of that matter, as I did last winter, when I went into Missouri and there took slaves without the snapping of a gun on either side, moving them through the country, and finally leaving them in Canada. I designed to have done the same thing again on a larger scale. That was all I intended. I never did intend murder, or treason, or the destruction of property, or to excite or incite slaves to rebellion, or to make insurrection.

I have another objection, and that is that it is unjust that I should suffer such a penalty. Had I interfered in the manner which I admit, and which I admit has been fairly proved – for I admire the truthfulness and candour of the greater portion of the witnesses who have testified in this case – had I so interfered in behalf of the rich, the powerful, the intelligent, the so-called great, or in behalf of any of their friends, either father, mother, brother, sister, wife or children, or any of that class, and suffered and sacrificed what I have in this interference, it would have been all right. Every man in this court would have deemed it an act worthy of reward rather than punishment.

This court acknowledges, too, as I suppose, the validity of the law of God. I see a book kissed, which I suppose to be the Bible, or at least the New Testament, which teaches me that all things whatsoever I would that men should do to me, I should do even so to them.[1] It teaches me, further, to remember them that are in bonds as bound with them. I endeavoured to act up to the instruction.

[1] See Luke 6:31.

I say I am yet too young to understand that God is any respecter of persons. I believe that to have interfered as I have done, as I have always freely admitted I have done, in behalf of his despised poor, I did not wrong but right. Now, if it is deemed necessary that I should forfeit my life for the furtherance of the ends of justice, and mingle my blood further with the blood of my children and with the blood of millions in this slave country whose rights are disregarded by wicked, cruel, and unjust enactments – I say, let it be done.

Let me say one word further. I feel entirely satisfied with the treatment I have received on my trial. Considering all the circumstances, it has been more generous than I expected. But I feel no consciousness of guilt. I have stated from the first what was my intention, and what was not. I never had any design against the liberty of any person, nor any disposition to commit treason, or incite slaves to rebel, or make any general insurrection. I never encouraged any man to do so, but always discouraged any idea of that kind.

Let me say, also, in regard to the statements made by some of those who were connected with me, I hear it has been stated by some of them that I have induced them to join me. But the contrary is true. I do not say this to injure them, but as regretting their weakness. Not one but joined me of his own accord, and the greater part at his own expense. A number of them I never saw, and never had a word of conversation with, till the day they came to me, and that was for the purpose I have stated.

Now, I have done.

W J Bryan
American lawyer and politician

William Jennings Bryan (1860–1925) was born in Salem, Illinois. He graduated from Illinois College in 1881 and studied law at Chicago. He served in the US House of Representatives as a Democrat from Nebraska (1891–5). He was a delegate to the 1896 Democratic National Convention where, with the backing of the short-lived Populist Party, he received the presidential nomination. He lost to William McKinley in that year and again in 1900; in 1908 he gained the nomination for the third time but lost to William Howard Taft. In the course of his campaigns he became known as a great populist stump-orator, styling himself as an advocate of the common people and denouncing expansionism and monopolies. He also promoted his views through a political weekly, *The Commoner*, which he founded and edited from 1901. In 1913, he was appointed Secretary of State by President WOODROW WILSON, but as an ardent pacifist he resigned in June 1915 over the aggressive American response to the German submarine attack on the British passenger ship *Lusitania*, in which 124 American citizens were killed. His last public act was assisting the anti-evolutionist prosecutor in the 'Scopes Monkey Trial'. He was the father of the prominent feminist Ruth Rohde (1885–1954).

'You shall not crucify mankind upon a cross of gold'
9 July 1896, Chicago, Illinois, USA

This famous speech, which won W J Bryan the first of his three nominations for the presidency, hinges on a question of monetary policy, but appeals to the listener's moral and social conscience. Given at the Democratic National Convention, it concerns an economic issue which occupied politicians in the USA and elsewhere for much of the 19th and early 20th centuries.

The gold standard – a monetary system which links the unit of currency to a precise value in gold – was by now unofficially operating in the USA. The Democrats from the financial centres of the east coast favoured this as a means of securing the economy against inflation. Bryan, however, sided with the 'silver Democrats': he favoured bimetallism, which allows money to be expressed in either silver or gold.

Because the relative value of silver and gold fluctuates, this system is less stable, but Bryan believed 'free silver' was in the interests of the country as a whole, and in particular of the impoverished rural west.

In his speech, Bryan displays his Populist credentials, portraying these 'hardy pioneers' in stirring, romantic terms, and memorably redefining the word 'businessman'. But Bryan was also a devout Christian, and the most striking feature of his rhetoric is its use of biblical references – notably in the steely final passage.

Having won the nomination, Bryan used the 'cross of gold' motif in some 600 campaign speeches. But in November, the election was won by the Republican candidate William McKinley, who believed bimetallism should only be introduced by international agreement. He passed the Gold Standard Act in 1900.

Mr Chairman and gentlemen of the convention … this is not a contest between persons. The humblest citizen in all the land, when clad in the armour of a righteous cause, is stronger than all the hosts of error. I come to speak to you in defence of a cause as holy as the cause of liberty – the cause of humanity.

When this debate is concluded, a motion will be made to lay upon the table the resolution offered in commendation of the administration, and also the resolution offered in condemnation of the administration. We object to bringing this question down to the level of persons. The individual is but an atom; he is born, he acts, he dies; but principles are eternal; and this has been a contest over a principle.

Never before in the history of this country has there been witnessed such a contest as that through which we have just passed. Never before in the history of American politics has a great issue been fought out as this issue has been, by the voters of a great party. On 4 March 1895, a few Democrats, most of them members of Congress, issued an address to the Democrats of the nation, asserting that the money question was the paramount issue of the hour; declaring that a majority of the Democratic Party had the right to control the action of the party on this paramount issue; and concluding with the request that the believers in the free coinage of silver should organize, take charge of, and control the policy of the Democratic Party.

Three months later, at Memphis, an organization was perfected, and the silver Democrats went forth openly and courageously proclaiming their belief, and declaring that, if successful, they would crystallize into a platform the declaration which they had made. Then began the conflict.

With a zeal approaching the zeal which inspired the Crusaders who followed Peter the Hermit,[1] our silver Democrats went forth from victory unto victory until they are now assembled, not to discuss, not to debate, but to enter up the judgement already rendered by the plain people of this country. In this contest, brother has been arrayed against brother, father against son.[2] The warmest ties of love, acquaintance, and association have been disregarded … Thus has the contest been waged, and we have assembled here under as binding and solemn instructions as were ever imposed upon representatives of the people …

When you [*turning to the gold delegates*] come before us and tell us that we are about to disturb your business interests, we reply that you have disturbed our business interests by your course.

We say to you that you have made the definition of a businessman too limited in its application. The man who is employed for wages is as much a businessman as his employer; the attorney in a country town is as much a businessman as the corporation counsel in a great metropolis; the merchant at the crossroads store is as much a businessman as the merchant of New York; the farmer who goes forth in the morning and toils all day, who begins in spring and toils all summer, and who by the application of brain and muscle to the natural resources of the country creates wealth, is as much a businessman as the man who goes upon the Board of Trade and bets upon the price of grain; the miners who go down 1,000 feet into the earth, or climb 2,000 feet upon the cliffs, and bring forth from their hiding places the precious metals to be poured into the channels of trade are as much businessmen as the few financial magnates who, in a back room, corner the money of the world. We come to speak of this broader class of businessmen.

Ah, my friends, we say not one word against those who live upon the Atlantic coast, but the hardy pioneers who have braved all the dangers of the wilderness, who have made the desert to blossom as the rose – the pioneers away out there, who rear their children near to nature's heart, where they can mingle their voices with the voices of the birds – out there where they have erected schoolhouses for the education of their young, churches where they praise their Creator, and cemeteries where rest the ashes of their dead – these people, we say, are as deserving of the consideration of our party as any people in this country. It is for these that we speak.

We do not come as aggressors. Our war is not a war of conquest; we are fighting in the defence of our homes, our families, and posterity. We have petitioned, and our petitions have been scorned; we have entreated, and our entreaties have been disregarded; we have begged, and they have mocked when our calamity came. We beg no longer; we entreat no more; we petition no more. We defy them!

They tell us that this platform was made to catch votes. We reply to them

[1] The French monk Peter the Hermit (c.1050–c.1115) was a fervent preacher who claimed appointment by Christ himself. He led the People's Crusade of 1096, which became part of the First Crusade.

[2] See Matthew 10:21.

that changing conditions make new issues; that the principles upon which democracy rests are as everlasting as the hills, but that they must be applied to new conditions as they arise. Conditions have arisen, and we are here to meet those conditions …

They say that we are opposing national bank currency; it is true. If you will read what Thomas Benton[3] said, you will find he said that, in searching history, he could find but one parallel to **ANDREW JACKSON**;[4] that was **CICERO**,[5] who destroyed the conspiracy of Catilina and saved Rome. Benton said that Cicero only did for Rome what Jackson did for us when he destroyed the bank conspiracy and saved America.

We say in our platform that we believe that the right to coin and issue money is a function of government. We believe it. We believe that it is a part of sovereignty, and can no more with safety be delegated to private individuals than we could afford to delegate to private individuals the power to make penal statutes or levy taxes … Those who are opposed to this proposition tell us that the issue of paper money is a function of the bank, and that the government ought to go out of the banking business … I tell them that the issue of money is a function of government, and that the banks ought to go out of the governing business …

Why is it that within three months such a change has come over the country? Three months ago – when it was confidently asserted that those who believe in the gold standard would frame our platform and nominate our candidates – even the advocates of the gold standard did not think that we could elect a president. And they had good reason for their doubt, because there is scarcely a state here today asking for the gold standard which is not in the absolute control of the Republican Party.

But note the change. Mr McKinley[6] was nominated at St Louis upon a platform which declared for the maintenance of the gold standard until it can be changed into bimetallism by international agreement. Mr McKinley was the most popular man among the Republicans, and three months ago everybody in the Republican Party prophesied his election. How is it today? Why, the man who was once pleased to think that he looked like **NAPOLEON** – that man shudders today when he remembers that he was nominated on the anniversary of the battle of Waterloo …

Why this change? Ah, my friends, is not the reason for the change evident to anyone who will look at the matter? No private character, however pure; no personal popularity, however great, can protect from the avenging wrath of an indignant people a man who will declare that he is in favour of fastening the gold standard upon this country, or who is willing to surrender the right of self-government and place the legislative control of our affairs in the hands of foreign potentates and powers.

We go forth confident that we shall win. Why? Because upon the paramount issue of this campaign there is not a spot of ground upon which the enemy will dare to challenge battle. If they tell us that the gold standard is a good thing, we shall point to their platform and tell them that their platform pledges the party to get rid of the gold standard and substitute bimetallism. If the gold standard is a good thing, why try to get rid of it?

… If they come to meet us on that issue we can present the history of our nation. More than that; we can tell them that they will search the pages of history in vain to find a single instance where the common people of any land have ever declared themselves in favour of the gold standard …

My friends, we declare that this nation is able to legislate for its own people on every question, without waiting for the aid or consent of any

[3] The US politician Thomas Benton (1782–1858) was known as 'Old Bullion' for his opposition to the use of paper currency.
[4] As US President (1828–37), Jackson vehemently opposed the rechartering of the Bank of the United States, which he considered was unconstitutional and favoured the interests of the north-eastern states.
[5] Cicero's first speech exposing Catilina's conspiracy is included in this book.

[6] William McKinley (1843–1901), the Republican candidate, who won the election and served as President from 1897 until his assassination in 1901.

other nation on earth … Our ancestors, when but three millions in number, had the courage to declare their political independence of every other nation. Shall we, their descendants, when we have grown to 70 millions, declare that we are less independent than our forefathers?

No, my friends, that will never be the verdict of our people. Therefore, we care not upon what lines the battle is fought. If they say bimetallism is good, but that we cannot have it until other nations help us, we reply that, instead of having a gold standard because England has, we will restore bimetallism, and then let England have bimetallism because the United States has it.

If they dare to come out in the open field and defend the gold standard as a good thing, we will fight them to the uttermost. Having behind us the producing masses of this nation, supported by the commercial interests, the labouring interests and the toilers everywhere, we will answer their demand for a gold standard by saying to them: you shall not press down upon the brow of labour this crown of thorns,[7] you shall not crucify mankind upon a cross of gold.

[7] Bryan alludes to the crown of thorns JESUS was forced to wear prior to his crucifixion, intended to mock his status as 'King of the Jews'. See Mark 15:17–18.

'They shut God out of the world'
16 July 1925, Dayton, Tennessee, USA

Bryan's final public act was an attempt to defend a biblical principle close to his heart. In February 1922, he had published 'God and Evolution', an essay defending Creationism, in the *New York Times*. Three years later, the Butler Act was introduced in Tennessee, banning the teaching of evolution in schools. It was put to the test at the celebrated 'Scopes Monkey Trial' of July 1925.

John T Scopes was a schoolteacher in the small town of Dayton, Tennessee, who had been using George William Hunter's book *A Civic Biology* (1914) to explain the theory of evolution. He was charged under the new legislation and his case attracted two of the finest legal minds of the day: Bryan, and the famous defence attorney CLARENCE DARROW.

Introduced as visiting council, Bryan saw the trial as a showcase, and used his one major speech – of which this is an edited version – to ridicule Hunter's book and the theory of evolution itself. His speech displays a palpable sense of outrage over children being robbed, as he saw it, of their faith in God as creator.

Although Scopes was ultimately found guilty, Bryan was exhausted by the trial. A few days after it finished, he fell ill and died. The debate lived on, however. In 2004, the Dover Area School District in Pennsylvania instructed its science staff to teach the theory of 'intelligent design' as an alternative to Darwin's theory of evolution. Following a court case brought by parents, a judge in Harrisburg, Pennsylvania ruled against the school board in December 2005.

Your Honour: I want to show you that we have evidence enough here. We do not need any experts to come in here and tell us about this thing. Here we have Mr Hunter. Mr Hunter is the author of this biology and this is the man who wrote the book Mr Scopes was teaching. And here we have a diagram …

[*Bryan shows* A Civic Biology *to the court.*]

On page 194 we have a diagram, and this diagram purports to give someone's family tree. Not only his ancestors but his collateral relatives. We are told just how many animal species there are: 518,900. And in this diagram, beginning with protozoa, we have the animals classified. We have circles differing in size according to the number of species in them … Of course, it is only a guess. I see they are round numbers, and I don't think all of these animals breed in round numbers, so I think it must be a generalization of them.

[*Laughter in the courtroom. The Court: 'Let us have order!'*]

Eight thousand protozoa; 3,500 sponges. I am satisfied from some I have seen there must be more than 35,000 sponges.

[*Laughter in the courtroom.*]

And then we run down to the insects: 360,000 insects. Two-thirds of all the species of all the animal world are insects – and sometimes, in the summer time, we feel that we become intimately acquainted with them. A large percentage of the species are molluscs and fishes. Now, we are getting up near our kinfolks: 13,000 fishes. Then there are the amphibia … and then we have the reptiles: 3,500. And then we have 13,000 birds. Strange that this should be exactly the same as the number of fishes; round numbers. And then we have mammals: 3,500.

And there is a little circle and man is in the circle. Find him, find man.

There is that book. There is the book they were teaching your children: that man was so indistinguishable among the mammals that they leave him there with 3,499 other mammals.

[*Laughter and applause.*]

Including elephants? Talk about putting Daniel in the lions' den! [1] How dared those scientists put man in a little ring like that, with lions and tigers … and all these animals that have an odour that extends beyond the circumference of this circle, my friends.

[*Extended laughter.*]

He tells the children to copy this diagram and take it home in their notebooks, to show their parents that you cannot find man. That is the great game in the public schools – to find man among animals, if you can.

Tell me that the parents of this day have not any right to declare that children are not to be taught this doctrine … If they believe it, they go back to scoff at the religion of their parents! And the parents have a right to say that no teacher paid by their money shall rob their children of faith in God and send them back to their homes, sceptical, infidels, agnostics or atheists.

This doctrine that they want taught, this doctrine that they would force upon the schools, where they will not let the Bible be read! Why, up in the state of New York they are now trying to keep the schools from adjourning for one hour in the afternoon, not that any teacher shall teach them the Bible, but that the children may go to the churches to which they belong and there have instruction in the work. And they are refusing to let the schools do that. These lawyers, who are trying to force Darwinism [2] and evolution on your children, do not go back to protect the children of New York in their right to even have religion taught to them outside of the schoolroom – and they want to bring their experts in here!

As we have one family tree this morning given to us, I think you are entitled to have a more authentic one. My esteemed friend from New York [3] gave you the family tree according to Linnaeus [4] … I will give you the family tree according to Darwin. If we are going to have family trees here, let us have something that is reliable. I will give you the only family tree that any believer in evolution has ever dared to outline – no other family tree that any evolutionist has ever proposed has as many believers as Darwin has in his family tree.

Some of them have discarded his explanations … They did not use to complain. It was not until Darwin was brought out into the open – it was not until the absurdities of Darwin had made his explanations the laughing stock – that they began to try to distinguish between Darwinism and evolution … But my friends, when they discard his explanations, they still

[1] In the Old Testament, the scholar Daniel was pressed into service as a tutor in the Babylonian court, and persecuted for his observance of Mosaic law. He was thrown into a den of lions, but survived unharmed. See Daniel 6.

[2] The English naturalist Charles Darwin (1809–82) developed the theory of evolution with Alfred Wallace (1823–1913). His books include *On the Origin of Species* (1859) and *The Descent of Man* (1871), which proposed that humankind and apes evolved from the same ancestors.

[3] The US lawyer Arthur Garfield Hays (1881–1954), who managed the defence team, and had worked extensively with the American Civil Liberties Union.
[4] The Swedish naturalist Carolus Linnaeus (1707–78) created a system of classification and nomenclature for plants and later for animals.

teach his doctrines. Not one of these evolutionists have discarded Darwin's doctrine that makes life begin with one cell in the sea and continue in one unbroken line to man. Not one of them has discarded that.

Let me read you what Darwin says, if you will pardon me ... Here is the family tree of Darwin – and remember that it is Darwin that is spoken of in Hunter's biology, that it is Darwin he has praised ...

[*Bryan reads at some length from Darwin's* The Descent of Man.]

'... The Simiadae then branched off into two great stems, the new world and the old world monkeys, and from the latter, at a remote period, man, the wonder and glory of the universe, proceeded.'

Not even from American monkeys, but from old world monkeys!

[*Laughter.*]

Now, here we have our glorious pedigree, and each child is expected to copy the family tree and take it home to his family ...

[*The Court: 'Let me ask you a question. Do you understand the evolution theory to involve the divine birth of divinity, or Christ's virgin birth, in any way or not?'*]

I am perfectly willing to answer the question. My contention is that the evolutionary hypothesis is not a theory, Your Honour.

[*The Court: 'Well, hypothesis.'*]

The legislature paid evolution a higher honour than it deserves. Evolution is not a theory, but a hypothesis. Huxley[5] said it could not raise to the dignity of a theory until they found some species that had developed according to the hypothesis. At that time there had never been found a single species, the origin of which could be traced to another species.

Darwin himself said he thought it was strange that with two or three million species they had not been able to find one that they could trace to another.

About three years ago, Bateson of London[6] came all the way to Toronto at the invitation of the American Academy for the Advancement of Sciences – [of] which, if the gentlemen will brace themselves for a moment, I will say I am a member. They invited Mr Bateson to come over and speak to them on evolution ... And Bateson told those people – after having taken up every effort that had been made to show the origin of species and find it – declared that every one had failed. Every one. Every one.

And it is true today: never have they traced one single species to any other ... There is not a scientist in all the world who can trace one single species to any other. And yet they call us ignoramuses and bigots because we do not throw away our Bible and accept it as proved that out of two or three million species, not a one is traceable to another ... and yet they demand that we allow them to teach this stuff to our children, that they may come home with their imaginary family tree and scoff at their mother's and father's Bible.

Now, my friends, I want you to know that they not only have no proof, but they cannot find the beginning. I suppose this distinguished scholar who came here[7] shamed them all by his number of degrees. He did not shame me, for I have more than he has, but I can understand how my friends felt when he unrolled degree after degree.

Did he tell you where life began? Did he tell you that ... there was a God? Not a word about it. Did he tell you how life began? Not a word; and not one of them can tell you how life began.

The atheists say it came some way without a God; the agnostics say it came in some way, they know not whether with a God or not. And the

[5] The English scientist Thomas Henry Huxley (1825–95) championed Darwin's theories.

[6] The English geneticist William Bateson (1861–1926).

[7] The US zoologist Maynard M Metcalf (1868–1940), then based at Johns Hopkins University in Baltimore.

Christian evolutionists say it came away back there somewhere, but they do not know how far back – they do not give you the beginning. That gentleman that tried to qualify as an expert; he did not tell you how life began. He did not tell you whether it began with God – or how.

No, they take up life as a mystery that nobody can explain, and they want you to let them commence there and ask no questions. They want to come in with their little padded-up evolution that commences with nothing and ends nowhere … They tell you that everybody believes in [it], but they do not explain the great riddle of the universe. They do not deal with the problems of life. They do not teach the great science of how to live.

And yet they would undermine the faith of these little children in that God who stands back of everything and whose promise we have that we shall live with Him forever by and by. They shut God out of the world. They do not talk about God … They did not tell us where immortality began. They did not tell us where in this long period of time, between the cell at the bottom of the sea and man, where man became endowed with the hope of immortality.

They did not, if you please, and most of them do not go to the place to hunt for it, because more than half of the scientists of this country … do not believe there is a God, or personal immortality, and they want to teach that to these children, and take that from them, to take from them their belief in a God who stands ready to welcome his children.

And Your Honour asked me whether it has anything to do with the principle of the virgin birth. Yes, because this principle of evolution disputes the miracle; there is no place for the miracle in this train of evolution … If this doctrine is true, this logic eliminates every mystery in the Old Testament and the New, and eliminates everything supernatural, and that means they eliminate the virgin birth. That means that they eliminate the resurrection of the body.

That means they eliminate the doctrine of atonement and they believe man has been rising all the time; that man never fell; that when the Saviour came, there was not any reason for His coming … and that He lies in his grave.

And when the Christians of this state have tied their hands and said, 'We will not take advantage of our power to teach religion to our children, by teachers paid by us', these people come in from the outside of the state and force upon … the children of the taxpayers of this state a doctrine that refutes not only their belief in God, but their belief in a Saviour and belief in Heaven, and takes from them every moral standard that the Bible gives us.

Edmund Burke
Irish philosopher and statesman

Edmund Burke (1729–97) was born in Dublin and educated at Trinity College, Dublin. He entered the Middle Temple, London in 1750, but abandoned law for literary work. His early works include *Vindication of Natural Society* (1756) and *Philosophical Inquiry into the Origin of our Ideas of the Sublime and Beautiful* (1757). He was appointed Secretary for Ireland, and in 1765 became MP for Wendover. Burke's eloquence soon earned him a high position in the Whig Party. The best of his writings and speeches belong to the turbulent and corrupt period of Lord North's long administration (1770–82), and were a defence of sound constitutional statesmanship against prevailing abuse and misgovernment. *Observations on the Present State of the Nation* (1769) was a reply to the former prime minister George Grenville; *On the Causes of the Present Discontents* (1770) deals with the Wilkes controversy, whereby the MP John Wilkes was expelled from Parliament and arrested for seditious libel after publishing a critique of Grenville in 1763. Perhaps the finest of Burke's many efforts are his speeches on American taxation (1774) and on conciliation with America (1775) and the 'Letter to the Sheriffs of Bristol' (1777), all of which advocate wise and liberal measures, though Burke never systematized his inconsistent political philosophy. Opposed to the doctrine of 'natural rights', he took over the concept of 'social contract', and attached to it a divine sanction. After the fall of the Whig ministry in 1783, Burke was never again in office. He opposed William Pitt, the Younger's measure for free trade with Ireland and the Commercial Treaty with France. In 1788 he opened the trial of Warren Hastings, former governor-general of British India, with a famous speech. His *Reflections on the Revolution in France* (1790) was read all over Europe, and he ranks as one of the foremost political thinkers of the British Isles. He had a vast knowledge, a glowing imagination, passionate sympathies and an inexhaustible wealth of powerful and cultured expression; however, he suffered prolonged financial difficulties, despite two pensions granted him in 1794. He was buried at Beaconsfield, where in 1768 he had purchased the estate of Gregories.

'This fierce spirit of liberty'
22 March 1775, London, England

This is one of Burke's most famous and brilliant speeches, given in the House of Commons during the crisis of American independence. Its keynote is the phrase, 'let us seriously and coolly ponder'. Burke's appeal is not moral or ideological, but rational and pragmatic; his rhetoric is lucid, carefully weighted and logically ordered.

With war looming, Burke persuasively counsels conciliation rather than force of arms. This excerpt begins with his reply to those MPs who had called for a military response to growing unrest in the American colonies: this he firmly but courteously dismisses as unwise on several counts.

He then moves on to analyse the American character. Here again this cunning Irishman deploys tact, flattering his English listeners that Americans owe their noble spirit of liberty to their roots in England. He specifies unfair taxation as a cause of civil unrest in both countries.

Maintaining this non-judgemental position, Burke is careful throughout the speech to attribute Americans' rebellious spirit to positive or neutral qualities – their devotion to religion, 'always a principle of energy'; their study of law. And he soothes British pride by presenting America as too distant to be successfully governed by any colonial power: 'No contrivance can prevent the effect of this distance in weakening government'.

Burke's argument is very hard to refute, but the concessions he urged were not energetically pursued. War broke out less than a month later – and when, on 14 August, the Olive Branch Petition arrived from America, King George III refused to receive it.

America, gentlemen say, is a noble object. It is an object well worth fighting for. Certainly it is, if fighting a people be the best way of gaining them. Gentlemen in this respect will be led to their choice of means by their complexions and their habits. Those who understand the military art will, of course, have some predilection for it. Those who wield the thunder of the state may have more confidence in the efficacy of arms. But I confess, possibly for want of this knowledge, my opinion is much more in favour of prudent management than of force; considering force not as an odious, but a feeble instrument for preserving a people so numerous, so active, so growing, so spirited as this, in a profitable and subordinate connection with us.

First, Sir, permit me to observe that the use of force alone is but *temporary*. It may subdue for a moment, but it does not remove the necessity of subduing again; and a nation is not governed which is perpetually to be conquered. My next objection is its *uncertainty*. Terror is not always the effect of force; and an armament is not a victory. If you do not succeed, you are without resource; for, conciliation failing, force remains; but, force failing, no further hope of reconciliation is left. Power and authority are sometimes bought by kindness, but they can never be begged as alms by an impoverished and defeated violence.

A further objection to force is that you *impair the object* by your very endeavours to preserve it. The thing you fought for is not the thing which you recover; but depreciated, sunk, wasted and consumed in the contest … Lastly, we have no sort of *experience* in favour of force as an instrument in the rule of our colonies. Their growth and their utility have been owing to methods altogether different. Our ancient indulgence has been said to be pursued to a fault. It may be so; but we know, if feeling is evidence, that our fault was more tolerable than our attempt to mend it; and our sin far more salutary than our penitence.

These, Sir, are my reasons for not entertaining that high opinion of untried force by which many gentlemen – for whose sentiments in other particulars I have great respect – seem to be so greatly captivated.

But there is still, behind, a third consideration concerning this object, which serves to determine my opinion on the sort of policy which ought to be pursued in the management of America, even more than its population and its commerce – I mean its *temper and character*. In this character of the Americans, a love of freedom is the predominating feature which marks and distinguishes the whole; and, as an ardent is always a jealous affection, your colonies become suspicious, restive and untractable whenever they see the least attempt to wrest from them by force, or shuffle from them by chicane, what they think the only advantage worth living for.

This fierce spirit of liberty is stronger in the English colonies, probably, than in any other people of the earth, and this from a variety of powerful causes, which – to understand the true temper of their minds and the direction which this spirit takes – it will not be amiss to lay open somewhat more largely.

First, the people of the colonies are descendants of Englishmen. England, Sir, is a nation which still, I hope, respects – and formerly adored – her freedom. The colonists emigrated from you when this part of your character was most predominant; and they took this bias and direction the moment they parted from your hands. They are, therefore, not only devoted to liberty, but to liberty according to English ideas and on English principles.

Abstract liberty, like other mere abstractions, is not to be found. Liberty inheres in some sensible object; and every nation has formed to itself some favourite point which, by way of eminence, becomes the criterion of their happiness. It happened, you know, Sir, that the great contests for freedom in this country were, from the earliest times, chiefly upon the question of taxing. Most of the contests in the ancient commonwealths turned primarily on the right of election of magistrates, or on the balance among the several orders of the state. The question of money was not with them so immediate. But in England it was otherwise. On this point of taxes the ablest pens and most eloquent tongues have been exercised; the greatest spirits have acted and suffered ...

The colonies draw from you, as with their life-blood, these ideas and principles. Their love of liberty, as with you, fixed and attached on this specific point of taxing. Liberty might be safe – or might be endangered – in 20 other particulars without their being much pleased or alarmed. Here, they felt its pulse; and as they found that beat, they thought themselves sick or sound.

I do not say whether they were right or wrong in applying your general arguments to their own case. It is not easy indeed to make a monopoly of theorems and corollaries. The fact is that they did thus apply those general arguments; and your mode of governing them, whether through lenity or indolence, through wisdom or mistake, confirmed them in the imagination that they, as well as you, had an interest in these common principles.

They were further confirmed in this pleasing error by the form of their provincial legislative assemblies. Their governments are popular in a high degree; some are merely popular; in all, the popular representative is the most weighty; and this share of the people in their ordinary government never fails to inspire them with lofty sentiments, and with a strong aversion from whatever tends to deprive them of their chief importance.

If anything were wanting to this necessary operation of the form of government, religion would have given it a complete effect. Religion, always a principle of energy, in this new people is no way worn out or impaired; and their mode of professing it is also one main cause of this free spirit. The people are Protestants; and of that kind which is the most adverse to all implicit submission of mind and opinion. This is a persuasion not only favourable to liberty, but built upon it ...

All Protestantism, even the most cold and passive, is a sort of dissent. But the religion most prevalent in our northern colonies is a refinement on the principle of resistance; it is the dissidence of dissent, and the Protestantism of the Protestant religion. This religion, under a variety of denominations agreeing in nothing but in the communion of the spirit of liberty, is predominant in most of the northern provinces; where the Church of England, notwithstanding its legal rights, is in reality no more than a sort of private sect, not composing most probably the tenth of the people.

The colonists left England when this spirit was high, and in the emigrants was the highest of all; and even that stream of foreigners which has been constantly flowing into these colonies has, for the greatest part, been composed of dissenters from the establishments of their several countries, and have brought with them a temper and character far from alien to that of the people with whom they mixed ...

Permit me, Sir, to add another circumstance in our colonies, which contributes no mean part toward the growth and effect of this untractable spirit – I mean their education. In no country perhaps in the world is the law so general a study. The profession itself is numerous and powerful, and in most provinces it takes the lead. The greater number of the deputies sent to Congress were lawyers. But all who read – and most do read – endeavour to obtain some smattering in that science. I have been told by an eminent bookseller that in no branch of his business, after tracts of popular devotion, were so many books as those on the law exported to the plantations ... This study renders men acute, inquisitive, dexterous, prompt in attack, ready in defence, full of resources.

In other countries, the people, more simple, and of a less mercurial cast, judge of an ill principle in government only by an actual grievance; here they anticipate the evil, and judge of the pressure of the grievance by the badness of the principle. They augur misgovernment at a distance; and snuff the approach of tyranny in every tainted breeze.

The last cause of this disobedient spirit in the colonies is hardly less powerful than the rest, as it is not merely moral, but laid deep in the natural constitution of things. Three thousand miles of ocean lie between you and them. No contrivance can prevent the effect of this distance in weakening government. Seas roll and months pass between the order and the execution; and the want of a speedy explanation of a single point is enough to defeat the whole system. You have, indeed, winged ministers of vengeance, who carry your bolts in their pouches to the remotest verge of the sea. But there a power steps in that limits the arrogance of raging passion and furious elements, and says: 'So far shalt thou go, and no farther.'[1]

Who are you that should fret and rage, and bite the chains of nature? Nothing worse happens to you than does to all nations who have extensive empire; and it happens in all the forms into which empire can be thrown. In large bodies, the circulation of power must be less vigorous at the extremities. Nature has said it …

I do not mean to commend either the spirit in this excess, or the moral causes which produce it. Perhaps a more smooth and accommodating spirit of freedom in them would be more acceptable to us. Perhaps ideas of liberty might be desired, more reconcilable with an arbitrary and boundless authority. Perhaps we might wish the colonists to be persuaded that their liberty is more secure when held in trust for them by us – as their guardians during a perpetual minority – than with any part of it in their own hands.

But the question is not whether their spirit deserves praise or blame. What, in the name of God, shall we do with it? You have before you the object, such as it is, with all its glories, with all its imperfections on its head.[2] You see the magnitude, the importance, the temper, the habits, the disorders. By all these considerations we are strongly urged to determine something concerning it. We are called upon to fix some rule and line for our future conduct, which may give a little stability to our politics and prevent the return of such unhappy deliberations as the present. Every such return will bring the matter before us in a still more untractable form.

For what astonishing and incredible things have we not seen already? What monsters have not been generated from this unnatural contention?[3] Whilst every principle of authority and resistance has been pushed, upon both sides, as far as it would go, there is nothing so solid and certain, either in reasoning or in practice, that has not been shaken.

Until very lately, all authority in America seemed to be nothing but an emanation from yours. Even the popular part of the colony constitution derived all its activity, and its first vital movement, from the pleasure of the Crown. We thought, Sir, that the utmost which the discontented colonists could do was to disturb authority; we never dreamed they could of themselves supply it; knowing in general what an operose[4] business it is to establish a government absolutely new.

But having, for our purposes in this contention, resolved that none but an obedient assembly should sit;[5] the humours of the people there, finding all passage through the legal channel stopped, with great violence broke out another way. Some provinces have tried their experiment, as we have

[1] Burke refers to David Hume's account of Canute in *The History of England*, vol 1 (1754), which in turn refers to Job 28:11.

[2] Burke refers to Shakespeare's *Hamlet*, I.5, in which the ghost of Hamlet's father describes being murdered while in a state of sin.

[3] Burke refers to events such as the Boston Massacre (1770), in which British troops fired into a mob, killing five civilians; and the Boston Tea Party (1773), when around 60 Bostonian rebels boarded three British ships loaded with tea and threw their cargo overboard.

[4] Laborious.
[5] Burke refers to the Massachusetts Government Act, Administration of Justice Act, Boston Port Act and the second Quartering Act (all 1774), which reinforced British rule in America and came to be known as the Intolerable Acts.

[7] The Scottish nobleman John Murray, 4th Earl of Dunmore served as Governor of New York (1770–1) and of Virginia (1771–5). He fled to Britain when war broke out in 1775.

tried ours; and theirs has succeeded.[6] They have formed a government sufficient for its purposes, without the bustle of a revolution, or the troublesome formality of an election. Evident necessity and tacit consent have done the business in an instant.

So well they have done it, that Lord Dunmore[7] (the account is among the fragments on your table) tells you that the new institution is infinitely better obeyed than the ancient government ever was in its most fortunate periods. Obedience is what makes government, and not the names by which it is called; not the name of governor, as formerly, or committee, as at present. This new government has originated directly from the people; and was not transmitted through any of the ordinary, artificial media of a positive constitution. It was not a manufacture ready-formed, and transmitted to them in that condition from England.

The evil arising from hence is this: that the colonists having once found the possibility of enjoying the advantages of order in the midst of a struggle for liberty, such struggles will not henceforward seem so terrible to the settled and sober part of mankind as they had appeared before the trial …

In this situation, let us seriously and coolly ponder what is it we have got by all our menaces, which have been many and ferocious. What advantage have we derived from the penal laws we have passed, and which, for the time, have been severe and numerous? What advances have we made toward our object by the sending of a force which, by land and sea, is no contemptible strength? Has the disorder abated? Nothing less. When I see things in this situation, after such confident hopes, bold promises, and active exertions, I cannot, for my life, avoid a suspicion that the plan itself is not correctly right.

If, then, the removal of the causes of this spirit of American liberty be, for the greater part, or rather entirely impracticable; if the ideas of criminal process be inapplicable – or, if applicable, are in the highest degree inexpedient – what way yet remains? No way is open but the third and last – to comply with the American spirit as necessary; or, if you please, to submit to it as a necessary evil.

[6] American experiments in collective self-government began in September–October 1774 with the short-lived Continental Congress, which drafted an association of twelve colonies and a boycott on trade with Britain. The Second Continental Congress was formed in May 1775 and immediately raised an army.

'Every rupee of profit made by an Englishman is lost forever to India'

1 December 1783, London, England

Burke's capacity for cool analysis is revealed in the previous speech. Here, Burke the moralist emerges, determined to shame Parliament into action on a situation which, he declares, 'cannot be indifferent to our fame'.

He was speaking in support of CHARLES JAMES FOX's East India Bill, which he himself had drafted. The bill exposed severe abuses committed by the British East India Company, and proposed transferring its powers to a commission based in London.

In the 1760s and 1770s, Burke had opposed government intervention in the affairs of the company, upholding the rights bestowed by its charter. But in 1781, he was appointed to a select committee charged with investigating the company's administration, and became appalled by its laxity and corruption.

The central thrust of his long speech – given here in abridged form – is that colonial power should be exercised for the benefit of the colonized people. Evoking India's past as an advanced and affluent society, he draws a contrast between conquerors past and present. Earlier invaders, he argues, occupied and integrated, feeding Indian culture and infrastructure. By contrast, he paints British traders as rapacious dilettantes, ruthlessly stripping India of its assets.

Burke's appeal for the rights of 30 million people won more than two-thirds of votes in the Commons. The bill was, however, overthrown by the House of Lords – though it led, the following year, to the India Act, which curbed the East India Company's powers.

[1] Decisions about the future of the East India Company had been deferred during the war with America. But in 1781 a select committee was established to investigate the company's affairs. Burke played an active role on it.

It is now to be determined whether the three years of laborious parliamentary research,[1] whether the 20 years of patient Indian suffering,[2] are to produce a substantial reform in our Eastern administration; or whether our knowledge of the grievances has abated our zeal for the correction of them, and whether our very enquiry into the evil was only a pretext to elude the remedy which is demanded from us by humanity, by justice and by every principle of true policy. Depend upon it: this business cannot be indifferent to our fame. It will turn out a matter of great disgrace or great glory to the whole British nation …

[2] At the Battle of Buxar in October 1764, the East India Company's forces had defeated those of Mughal emperor Shah Alam II (1728–1806), the Mughal governor of Oudh, Shuja 'ud-Dawlah (1731–75), and Mir Qasim Ali Khan (c. 1730–77) dispossessed governor of Bengal. The battle secured the company's rule of eastern India.

I must observe that the phrase, 'the chartered rights of men' is full of affectation; and very unusual in the discussion of privileges conferred by charters of the present description. But it is not difficult to discover what end that ambiguous mode of expression, so often reiterated, is meant to answer.

The rights of men, that is to say, the natural rights of mankind, are indeed sacred things; and if any public measure is proved mischievously to affect them, the objection ought to be fatal to that measure, even if no charter at all could be set up against it. If these natural rights are further affirmed and declared by express covenants, if they are clearly defined and secured against chicane, against power and authority, by written instruments and positive engagements, they are in a still better condition: they partake not only of the sanctity of the object so secured, but of that solemn public faith itself which secures an object of such importance.

Indeed, this formal recognition, by the sovereign power, of an original right in the subject can never be subverted but by rooting up the holding radical principles of government, and even of society itself. The charters which we call by distinction *great* are public instruments of this nature; I mean the charters of King John[3] and Henry III.[4] The things secured by these instruments may, without deceitful ambiguity, be very fitly called the 'chartered rights of men'.

[3] The English monarch King John (1166–1216) reigned 1199–1216. He is chiefly remembered for signing Magna Carta (1215) which limited his absolute rule and is regarded as an early precursor of constitutional law.

These charters have made the very name of a charter dear to the heart of every Englishman. But, Sir, there may be, and there are, charters not only different in nature, but formed on principles the very reverse of those of the great charter. Of this kind is the charter of the East India Company. Magna Carta is a charter to restrain power, and to destroy monopoly. The East India Charter is a charter to establish monopoly, and to create power. Political power and commercial monopoly are not the rights of men; and the rights to them derived from charters it is fallacious and sophistical to call 'the chartered rights of men'. These chartered rights (to speak of such charters and of their effects in terms of the greatest possible moderation) do at least suspend the natural rights of mankind at large; and in their very frame and constitution are liable to fall into a direct violation of them.

[4] The English monarch Henry III (1207–72) was King John's son and successor, reigning 1216–72. In 1217, aged ten, he reissued the Magna Carta. In 1258 he was coerced into accepting the Provisions of Oxford, which devolved power to a 15-strong council of barons.

It is a charter of this latter description (that is to say, a charter of power and monopoly) which is affected by the bill before you. The bill, Sir, does without question affect it; it does affect it essentially and substantially. But, having stated to you of what description the chartered rights are which this bill touches, I feel no difficulty at all in acknowledging the existence of those chartered rights in their fullest extent. They belong to the Company in the surest manner; and they are secured to that body by every sort of public sanction. They are stamped by the faith of the King;[5] they are stamped by the faith of Parliament; they have been bought for the money, for money honestly and fairly paid; they have been bought for valuable consideration, over and over again.

[5] The English monarch George III (1738–1820) reigned from 1760, but from 1810 succumbed to mental illness and his eldest son the Prince of Wales (later George IV) became Prince Regent, exercising all his father's powers.

I therefore freely admit to the East India Company their claim to exclude their fellow-subjects from the commerce of half the globe. I admit their claim to administer an annual territorial revenue of seven millions sterling; to command an army of 60,000 men; and to dispose (under the control of a sovereign imperial discretion, and with the due observance of the natural and local law) of the lives and fortunes of 30 millions of their fellow creatures. All this they possess by charter and acts of Parliament, in my opinion without a shadow of controversy.

Those who carry the rights and claims of the company the furthest do not contend for more than this; and all this I freely grant. But granting all this, they must grant to me in my turn that all political power which is set over men, and that all privilege claimed or exercised in exclusion of them, being wholly artificial, and for so much a derogation from the natural equality of mankind at large, ought to be some way or other exercised ultimately for their benefit …

This multitude of men does not consist of an abject and barbarous populace; much less of gangs of savages, like the Guaranies[6] and Chiquitos,[7] who wander on the waste borders of the river of Amazons, or the Plate; but a people for ages civilized and cultivated; cultivated by all the arts of polished life, whilst we were yet in the woods. There have been (and still the skeletons remain) princes once of great dignity, authority and opulence. There are to be found the chiefs of tribes and nations. There is to be found an ancient and venerable priesthood, the depository of their laws, learning and history, the guides of the people whilst living and their consolation in death; a nobility of great antiquity and renown; a multitude of cities, not exceeded in population and trade by those of the first class in Europe; merchants and bankers, individual houses of whom have once vied in capital with the Bank of England; whose credit had often supported a tottering state, and preserved their government in the midst of war and desolation; millions of ingenious manufacturers and mechanics; millions of the most diligent, and not the least intelligent, tillers of the earth …

All this vast mass, composed of so many orders and classes of men, is again infinitely diversified by manners, by religion, by hereditary employment, through all their possible combinations. This renders the handling of India a matter in a high degree critical and delicate. But oh, it has been handled rudely indeed! Even some of the reformers seem to have forgot that they had anything to do but to regulate the tenants of a manor, or the shopkeepers of the next county town …

The several irruptions of Arabs, Tartars and Persians into India were, for the greater part, ferocious, bloody and wasteful in the extreme. Our entrance into the dominion of that country was, as generally, with small comparative effusion of blood; being introduced by various frauds and delusions, and by taking advantage of the incurable, blind and senseless animosity which the several country powers bear towards each other, rather than by open force. But the difference in favour of the first conquerors is this: the Asiatic conquerors very soon abated of their ferocity, because they made the conquered country their own. They rose or fell with the rise or fall of the territory they lived in. Fathers there deposited the hopes of their posterity; and children there beheld the monuments of their fathers. Here their lot was finally cast; and it is the natural wish of all that their lot should not be cast in a bad land …

But under the English government, all this order is reversed. The Tartar invasion was mischievous, but it is our protection that destroys India. It was

[6] A tribal group occupying territory between the Uruguay and Paraguay rivers, which now falls into Paraguay and Argentina.
[7] A tribal group occupying territory in the rain savannas of what is now eastern Bolivia.

their enmity, but it is our friendship. Our conquest there, after 20 years, is as crude as it was the first day. The natives scarcely know what it is to see the grey head of an Englishman. Young men (boys almost) govern there, without society, and without sympathy with the natives. They have no more social habits with the people than if they still resided in England; nor, indeed, any species of intercourse but that which is necessary to making a sudden fortune, with a view to a remote settlement. Animated with all the avarice of age and all the impetuosity of youth, they roll in, one after another, wave after wave; and there is nothing before the eyes of the natives but an endless, hopeless prospect of new flights of birds of prey and passage, with appetites continually renewing for food that is continually wasting.

Every rupee of profit made by an Englishman is lost forever to India. With us are no retributory superstitions by which a foundation of charity compensates, through ages, to the poor, for the rapine and injustice of a day. With us no pride erects stately monuments which repair the mischiefs which pride had produced and which adorn a country out of its own spoils. England has erected no churches, no hospitals, no palaces, no schools; England has built no bridges, made no high-roads, cut no navigations, dug out no reservoirs. Every other conqueror of every other description has left some monument, either of state or beneficence, behind him. Were we to be driven out of India this day, nothing would remain to tell that it had been possessed, during the inglorious period of our dominion, by anything better than the orang-utan or the tiger.

There is nothing in the boys we send to India worse than the boys whom we are whipping at school, or that we see trailing a pike or bending over a desk at home. But as English youth in India drink the intoxicating draught of authority and dominion before their heads are able to bear it – and as they are full-grown in fortune long before they are ripe in principle – neither nature nor reason have any opportunity to exert themselves for remedy of the excesses of their premature power.

The consequences of their conduct, which in good minds (and many of theirs are probably such) might produce penitence or amendment, are unable to pursue the rapidity of their flight. Their prey is lodged in England, and the cries of India are given to seas and winds, to be blown about in every breaking up of the monsoon, over a remote and unhearing ocean. In India, all the vices operate by which sudden fortune is acquired; in England are often displayed by the same persons the virtues which dispense hereditary wealth.

Arrived in England, the destroyers of the nobility and gentry of a whole kingdom will find the best company in this nation at a board of elegance and hospitality. Here the manufacturer and husbandman will bless the just and punctual hand that in India has torn the cloth from the loom, or wrested the scanty portion of rice and salt from the peasant of Bengal, or wrung from him the very opium in which he forgot his oppressions and his oppressor. They marry into your families, they enter into your senate, they ease your estates by loans, they raise their value by demand, they cherish and protect your relations which lie heavy on your patronage; and there is scarcely a house in the kingdom that does not feel some concern and interest that makes all reform of our eastern government appear officious and disgusting; and, on the whole, a most discouraging attempt.

In such an attempt you hurt those who are able to return kindness or to resent injury. If you succeed, you save those who cannot so much as give you thanks. All these things show the difficulty of the work we have on hand: but they show its necessity too. Our Indian government is in its best state a grievance. It is necessary that the correctives should be uncommonly vigorous; and the work of men sanguine, warm and even impassioned in the cause.

George W Bush
American politician

George Walker Bush (1946–) was born in New Haven, Connecticut, the son of the American politician George Bush, who became the 41st US president. He studied at Yale University and Harvard Business School. His early career was in the oil industry. In 1977 he founded Arbusto Oil, which became Bush Exploration in 1982 and merged with the Spectrum 7 Energy Corporation in 1984, with Bush as chief executive. In 1989 he was manager of a consortium that bought the Texas Rangers baseball team. He was elected governor of Texas in 1994 and proved popular, winning re-election four years later. In 2000 he stood as the Republican presidential candidate against Al Gore, winning by the tightest margin for more than a century, and engendering legal disputes over the ballot count in Florida that lasted for months. In contrast to the left-leaning presidency of BILL CLINTON, Bush has led a swing to the right. He is closely associated with the Neoconservative movement and the Christian right: his policies include tax cuts, support for a National Missile Defence system and an illiberal approach to issues of personal morality. On becoming president, he had little experience in foreign affairs, and most commentators expected a withdrawal of the USA from the world stage. However, in September 2001, following the terrorist strikes on New York and Washington, Bush was plunged into the international arena and became committed to military action against perceived enemies in the Middle East. In 2003, with the support of a number of allies – notably British prime minister TONY BLAIR – but without the approval of the United Nations, he launched a war on Iraq which resulted in the overthrow and eventual arrest of President SADDAM HUSSEIN. Following Saddam's capture, Bush made it known that God had advised him to launch the war. In 2004 Bush was re-elected president but faced a rising tide of popular criticism, especially for his handling of the ongoing Iraq War, Hurricane Katrina (2005) and the so-called 'Great Recession' that began in 2007. He left office in 2009, succeeded by the Democrat BARACK OBAMA and retired to Dallas, Texas.

'America, at its best'
20 January 2001, Washington, DC, USA

The inauguration of President George W Bush on a wet winter's day in 2001 ushered in a new era in American politics. His defeat of outgoing vice president Al Gore in the November election had been extremely narrow, bitterly contested and ultimately decided in court. Bush was the first president in more than a century who had not won a majority of the popular vote – while his predecessor, Bill Clinton, was leaving office with very high approval ratings.

Bush – and his speech-writers – were mindful of this as he spoke for the first time as president, after taking a tearful oath of office. The Washington crowd numbered several hundred thousand, among them members of the Supreme Court in rainproof ponchos, and protestors with banners carrying slogans such as 'Fraud' and 'Hail to the thief!' – a corruption of the presidential anthem 'Hail to the Chief'.

'[Some citizens] doubt the promise, even the justice, of our own country,' Bush concedes, but he urges national unity by appealing to Americans' patriotic, democratic and egalitarian instincts. Bush's Christian faith is also to the fore – as it would be in his re-election campaign of 2004.

The speech's overall tone is sombre and purposeful, encouraging aspiration and optimism with the refrain 'America, at its best'. In promoting participation and volunteerism, Bush knowingly recalls the inauguration speeches of his father George Bush in 1989 and JOHN F KENNEDY in 1961. He wisely resists attacking Clinton's presidency, but signals a change of direction on key issues such as tax, social security and health care, pleasing his neoconservative allies.

President Clinton, distinguished guests and my fellow-citizens: the peaceful transfer of authority is rare in history, yet common in our country. With a simple oath, we affirm old traditions and make new beginnings.

As I begin, I thank President Clinton for his service to our nation. And I thank Vice President Gore for a contest conducted with spirit and ended with grace.

I am honoured and humbled to stand here, where so many of America's leaders have come before me, and so many will follow.

We have a place, all of us, in a long story – a story we continue, but whose end we will not see. It is the story of a new world that became a friend and liberator of the old, a story of a slave-holding society that became a servant of freedom, the story of a power that went into the world to protect but not possess, to defend but not to conquer.

It is the American story — a story of flawed and fallible people, united across the generations by grand and enduring ideals. The grandest of these ideals is an unfolding American promise that everyone belongs, that everyone deserves a chance, that no insignificant person was ever born.

Americans are called to enact this promise in our lives and in our laws. And though our nation has sometimes halted, and sometimes delayed, we must follow no other course.

Through much of the last century, America's faith in freedom and democracy was a rock in a raging sea. Now it is a seed upon the wind, taking root in many nations. Our democratic faith is more than the creed of our country, it is the inborn hope of our humanity, an ideal we carry but do not own, a trust we bear and pass along. And even after nearly 225 years, we have a long way yet to travel.

While many of our citizens prosper, others doubt the promise, even the justice, of our own country. The ambitions of some Americans are limited by failing schools and hidden prejudice and the circumstances of their birth. And sometimes our differences run so deep, it seems we share a continent, but not a country.

We do not accept this, and we will not allow it. Our unity, our union, is the serious work of leaders and citizens in every generation. And this is my solemn pledge: I will work to build a single nation of justice and opportunity. I know this is in our reach because we are guided by a power larger than ourselves who creates us equal in His image. And we are confident in principles that unite and lead us onward.

America has never been united by blood or birth or soil. We are bound by ideals that move us beyond our backgrounds, lift us above our interests and teach us what it means to be citizens. Every child must be taught these principles. Every citizen must uphold them. And every immigrant, by embracing these ideals, makes our country more, not less, American.

Today, we affirm a new commitment to live out our nation's promise through civility, courage, compassion and character. America, at its best, matches a commitment to principle with a concern for civility. A civil society demands from each of us good will and respect, fair dealing and forgiveness.

Some seem to believe that our politics can afford to be petty because, in a time of peace, the stakes of our debates appear small. But the stakes for America are never small. If our country does not lead the cause of freedom, it will not be led. If we do not turn the hearts of children toward knowledge and character, we will lose their gifts and undermine their idealism. If we permit our economy to drift and decline, the vulnerable will suffer most. We must live up to the calling we share.

Civility is not a tactic or a sentiment. It is the determined choice of trust over cynicism, of community over chaos. And this commitment, if we keep it, is a way to shared accomplishment.

America, at its best, is also courageous. Our national courage has been clear in times of depression and war, when defending common dangers defined our common good. Now we must choose if the example of our fathers and mothers will inspire us or condemn us. We must show courage in a time of blessing by confronting problems instead of passing them on to future generations.

Together, we will reclaim America's schools, before ignorance and apathy claim more young lives. We will reform Social Security and Medicare, sparing our children from struggles we have the power to prevent. And we will reduce taxes, to recover the momentum of our economy and reward the effort and enterprise of working Americans.

We will build our defences beyond challenge, lest weakness invite challenge. We will confront weapons of mass destruction, so that a new century is spared new horrors. The enemies of liberty and our country should make no mistake: America remains engaged in the world by history and by choice, shaping a balance of power that favours freedom. We will defend our allies and our interests. We will show purpose without arrogance. We will meet aggression and bad faith with resolve and strength. And to all nations, we will speak for the values that gave our nation birth.

America, at its best, is compassionate. In the quiet of American conscience, we know that deep, persistent poverty is unworthy of our nation's promise. And whatever our views of its cause, we can agree that children at risk are not at fault. Abandonment and abuse are not acts of God, they are failures of love. And the proliferation of prisons, however necessary, is no substitute for hope and order in our souls.

Where there is suffering, there is duty. Americans in need are not strangers, they are citizens; not problems, but priorities. And all of us are diminished when any are hopeless. Government has great responsibilities for public safety and public health, for civil rights and common schools. Yet compassion is the work of a nation, not just a government.

And some needs and hurts are so deep they will only respond to a mentor's touch or a pastor's prayer. Church and charity, synagogue and mosque lend our communities their humanity, and they will have an honoured place in our plans and in our laws.

Many in our country do not know the pain of poverty, but we can listen to those who do. And I can pledge our nation to a goal: when we see that wounded traveller on the road to Jericho, we will not pass to the other side.[1]

America, at its best, is a place where personal responsibility is valued and expected. Encouraging responsibility is not a search for scapegoats, it is a call to conscience. And though it requires sacrifice, it brings a deeper fulfilment. We find the fullness of life not only in options, but in commitments. And we find that children and community are the commitments that set us free.

Our public interest depends on private character, on civic duty and family bonds and basic fairness, on uncounted, unhonoured acts of decency which give direction to our freedom. Sometimes in life we are called to do great things. But as a saint of our times has said, every day we are called to do small things with great love.[2] The most important tasks of a democracy are done by everyone.

I will live and lead by these principles: to advance my convictions with civility, to pursue the public interest with courage, to speak for greater justice and compassion, to call for responsibility and try to live it as well. In all these ways, I will bring the values of our history to the care of our times.

What you do is as important as anything government does. I ask you to seek a common good beyond your comfort; to defend needed reforms against easy attacks; to serve your nation, beginning with your neighbour. I ask you to be citizens: citizens, not spectators; citizens, not subjects; responsible citizens, building communities of service and a nation of character.

[1] Bush refers to the parable of the Good Samaritan, used by JESUS to instruct his followers in the meaning of loving one's neighbour. See Luke 10:25–37.

[2] A famous dictum of MOTHER TERESA.

Americans are generous and strong and decent, not because we believe in ourselves, but because we hold beliefs beyond ourselves. When this spirit of citizenship is missing, no government programme can replace it. When this spirit is present, no wrong can stand against it.

After the Declaration of Independence was signed, Virginia statesman John Page[3] wrote to THOMAS JEFFERSON: 'We know the race is not to the swift nor the battle to the strong. Do you not think an angel rides in the whirlwind and directs this storm?'

Much time has passed since Jefferson arrived for his inauguration. The years and changes accumulate. But the themes of this day he would know: our nation's grand story of courage and its simple dream of dignity. We are not this story's author, who fills time and eternity with his purpose. Yet his purpose is achieved in our duty, and our duty is fulfilled in service to one another.

Never tiring, never yielding, never finishing, we renew that purpose today, to make our country more just and generous, to affirm the dignity of our lives and every life. This work continues. This story goes on. And an angel still rides in the whirlwind and directs this storm.

God bless you all, and God bless America.

[3] The US soldier and politician John Page (1743–1808) was a colonel in the Revolutionary Army and served as Lieutenant Governor of Virginia, 1776–9, Congressman from Virginia, 1789–97, and Governor of Virginia, 1802–5.

'Today, our nation saw evil'

11 September 2001, Washington, DC, USA

The terrorist strikes of 11 September 2001 were unquestionably a turning point in history, though their significance may not be fully understood for some years. They led to war in Afghanistan and a raft of security measures and legislation under the umbrella title the 'War on Terror'. They were also used to justify the 2003 invasion of Iraq.

Bush was in a classroom at Emma Booker Elementary School in Florida when he was told about the attacks in New York. Photographs and film footage show anguish settling over his features as he clutches the children's book *My Pet Goat*. 'I was very aware of the cameras,' he later revealed. 'America is under attack. I'm trying to absorb that knowledge.'

He made a brief media announcement from the school, then travelled to Louisiana, where he made a further announcement. By now, the World Trade Center had collapsed, and two further hijacked planes had crashed, one destroying part of the Pentagon in Washington.

Bush spent most of the afternoon flying cross-country to Nebraska, then Maryland, before finally arriving at the White House just before 7pm. His 'disappearance' during the crisis – a security measure urged by Vice President Dick Cheney – was criticized in some quarters as a dereliction of duty.

By 8.30pm, though, he was ready to address the nation, which he did in this televised address from the Oval Office. Visibly rattled, and stumbling on a few words, he gave a competent performance nonetheless. This disaster was, in a sense, a gift for Bush: his hawkish response propelled a president formerly considered inward-looking into the international arena.

Good evening. Today, our fellow citizens, our way of life, our very freedom came under attack in a series of deliberate and deadly terrorist acts. The victims were in airplanes, or in their offices; secretaries, businessmen and women, military and federal workers; moms and dads, friends and neighbours. Thousands of lives were suddenly ended by evil, despicable acts of terror.

The pictures of airplanes flying into buildings, fires burning, huge structures collapsing, have filled us with disbelief, terrible sadness and a quiet, unyielding anger. These acts of mass murder were intended to frighten our nation into chaos and retreat. But they have failed; our country is strong.

A great people has been moved to defend a great nation. Terrorist attacks can shake the foundations of our biggest buildings, but they cannot touch the foundation of America. These acts shattered steel, but they cannot dent the steel of American resolve.

America was targeted for attack because we're the brightest beacon for freedom and opportunity in the world. And no-one will keep that light from shining.

Today, our nation saw evil, the very worst of human nature. And we responded with the best of America – with the daring of our rescue-workers, with the caring of – for strangers and neighbours who came to give blood and help in any way they could.

Immediately following the first attack, I implemented our government's emergency response plans. Our military is powerful, and it's prepared. Our emergency teams are working in New York City and Washington, DC to help with local rescue efforts. Our first priority is to get help to those who have been injured, and to take every precaution to protect our citizens at home and around the world from further attacks.

The functions of our government continue without interruption. Federal agencies in Washington which had to be evacuated today are reopening for essential personnel tonight, and will be open for business tomorrow. Our financial institutions remain strong, and the American economy will be open for business, as well.

The search is under way for those who are behind these evil acts. I've directed the full resources of our intelligence and law-enforcement communities to find those responsible and to bring them to justice. We will make no distinction between the terrorists who committed these acts and those who harbour them.

I appreciate so very much the members of Congress who have joined me in strongly condemning these attacks. And on behalf of the American people, I thank the many world leaders who have called to offer their condolences and assistance.

America and our friends and allies join with all those who want peace and security in the world, and we stand together to win the war against terrorism. Tonight, I ask for your prayers for all those who grieve, for the children whose worlds have been shattered, for all whose sense of safety and security has been threatened. And I pray they will be comforted by a power greater than any of us, spoken through the ages in Psalm 23: 'Even though I walk through the valley of the shadow of death, I fear no evil, for you are with me.'

This is a day when all Americans from every walk of life unite in our resolve for justice and peace. America has stood down enemies before, and we will do so this time. None of us will ever forget this day. Yet we go forward to defend freedom and all that is good and just in our world.

Thank you. Good night, and God bless America.

❧

'The tyrant has fallen and Iraq is free'
1 May 2003, at sea near San Diego, California, USA

❧

When Iraq was invaded by a US-led coalition in March 2003, the outcome was never in doubt, despite the blood-curdling threats of SADDAM HUSSEIN.

In October 2002, the title of commander-in-chief had been reserved for the president alone. With Iraqi forces largely subdued, Bush seized the opportunity to play up his military role.

He arrived on board the aircraft carrier USS *Abraham Lincoln*, which had played an active role in the conflict, as co-pilot of a US Navy fighter jet. In 1968, he had flown fighters in the Texas Air National Guard. Now, when he emerged beaming from the cockpit, he confirmed that he had taken a turn flying the plane. He then saluted, shook hands and posed for photographs with members of the crew.

Later, under a banner reading 'Mission Accomplished', Bush addressed the crew and the cameras. It was an archetypal triumphal speech, but there are subtleties worth noting. Bush does not refer to victory, which would have created legal barriers to further pursuit of Saddam and his followers. He does, however, link the Iraqi regime – spuriously, many believed – to al-Qaeda. He also refers to weapons of mass destruction, though no stockpiles were ever discovered in Iraq. Finally, he uses the contentious term 'Palestine' to refer to a disputed geographical region.

The staging of the speech was highly effective, but not everyone was impressed. Senator John Kerry, who would stand against Bush in the 2004 presidential election, remarked: 'The President's going out to an aircraft carrier to give a speech far out at sea ... while countless numbers of Americans are frightened stiff about the economy at home.'

❧

[1] The US naval officer Rear Admiral John M Kelly commanded strike forces for four carrier battle groups during Operation Iraqi Freedom.

Admiral Kelly,[1] Captain Card,[2] officers and sailors of the USS *Abraham Lincoln*, my fellow Americans: major combat operations in Iraq have ended. In the battle of Iraq, the United States and our allies have prevailed.

[*Applause.*]

And now our coalition is engaged in securing and reconstructing that country.

In this battle, we have fought for the cause of liberty, and for the peace of the world. Our nation and our coalition are proud of this accomplishment – yet it is you, the members of the United States military, who achieved it. Your courage, your willingness to face danger for your country and for each other, made this day possible. Because of you, our nation is more secure. Because of you, the tyrant has fallen and Iraq is free.

[*Applause.*]

Operation Iraqi Freedom was carried out with a combination of precision and speed and boldness the enemy did not expect, and the world had not seen before. From distant bases or ships at sea, we sent planes and missiles that could destroy an enemy division or strike a single bunker. Marines and soldiers charged to Baghdad across 350 miles of hostile ground, in one of the swiftest advances of heavy arms in history. You have shown the world the skill and the might of the American armed forces.

This nation thanks all the members of our coalition, who joined in a noble cause. We thank the armed forces of the United Kingdom, Australia and Poland, who shared in the hardships of war. We thank all the citizens of Iraq who welcomed our troops and joined in the liberation of their own country. And tonight, I have a special word for Secretary Rumsfeld,[3] for General Franks,[4] and for all the men and women who wear the uniform of the United States: America is grateful for a job well done.

[*Applause.*]

The character of our military through history – the daring of Normandy,[5] the fierce courage of Iwo Jima,[6] the decency and idealism that turned enemies into allies – is fully present in this generation. When Iraqi civilians looked into the faces of our servicemen and women, they saw strength and kindness and goodwill. When I look at the members of the United States military, I see the best of our country, and I'm honoured to be your commander-in-chief.

[*Applause.*]

In the images of falling statues,[7] we have witnessed the arrival of a new era. For a hundred years of war, culminating in the nuclear age, military technology was designed and deployed to inflict casualties on an ever-growing scale. In defeating Nazi Germany and imperial Japan, Allied forces destroyed entire cities, while enemy leaders who started the conflict were

[2] The US naval officer Captain Kendall L Card had been commanding officer of the USS *Abraham Lincoln* since November 2002.

[3] The US businessman and politician Donald H Rumsfeld (1932–) had been US Secretary of Defence since January 2001.

[4] The US army officer General Tommy R Franks (1945–) served as Commander-in-Chief of US Central Command from June 2000 until his retirement in July 2003.

[5] The D-Day landings of 6 June 1944, when Allied troops invaded German-occupied northern France in the greatest amphibious operation in history.

[6] A Japanese island in the Pacific Ocean that was the scene of a major battle of World War II in 1944–5 and was taken by US troops after a three-month campaign.

[7] The overthrow of the Iraqi regime was memorably symbolized on 9 April 2003, when a statue of Saddam Hussein in central Baghdad, erected a year previously to mark the dictator's 65th birthday, was toppled by Iraqi civilians with assistance from US Marines.

safe until the final days. Military power was used to end a regime by breaking a nation.

Today, we have the greater power to free a nation by breaking a dangerous and aggressive regime. With new tactics and precision weapons, we can achieve military objectives without directing violence against civilians. No device of man can remove the tragedy from war; yet it is a great moral advance when the guilty have far more to fear from war than the innocent.

[*Applause.*]

In the images of celebrating Iraqis, we have also seen the ageless appeal of human freedom. Decades of lies and intimidation could not make the Iraqi people love their oppressors, or desire their own enslavement. Men and women in every culture need liberty like they need food and water and air. Everywhere that freedom arrives, humanity rejoices; and everywhere that freedom stirs, let tyrants fear.[8]

[*Applause.*]

We have difficult work to do in Iraq. We're bringing order to parts of that country that remain dangerous. We're pursuing and finding leaders of the old regime, who will be held to account for their crimes. We've begun the search for hidden chemical and biological weapons and already know of hundreds of sites that will be investigated. We're helping to rebuild Iraq, where the dictator built palaces for himself, instead of hospitals and schools. And we will stand with the new leaders of Iraq as they establish a government of, by and for the Iraqi people.

[*Applause.*]

The transition from dictatorship to democracy will take time, but it is worth every effort. Our coalition will stay until our work is done. Then we will leave, and we will leave behind a free Iraq.

[*Applause.*]

The battle of Iraq is one victory in a war on terror that began on September 11, 2001 – and still goes on. That terrible morning, 19 evil men – the shock-troops of a hateful ideology – gave America and the civilized world a glimpse of their ambitions. They imagined, in the words of one terrorist, that September 11 would be 'the beginning of the end of America'.[9] By seeking to turn our cities into killing fields, terrorists and their allies believed that they could destroy this nation's resolve, and force our retreat from the world. They have failed.

[*Applause.*]

In the battle of Afghanistan, we destroyed the Taliban, many terrorists and the camps where they trained. We continue to help the Afghan people lay roads, restore hospitals, and educate all of their children. Yet we also have dangerous work to complete. As I speak, a Special Operations task force, led by the 82nd Airborne, is on the trail of the terrorists and those who seek to undermine the free government of Afghanistan. America and our coalition will finish what we have begun.

[*Applause.*]

From Pakistan to the Philippines to the Horn of Africa, we are hunting down al-Qaeda killers. Nineteen months ago, I pledged that the terrorists would not escape the patient justice of the United States. And as of tonight, nearly one half of al-Qaeda's senior operatives have been captured or killed.

[*Applause.*]

The liberation of Iraq is a crucial advance in the campaign against terror.

[8] A phrase drawn from the speech of ELIZABETH I at Tilbury on 9 August 1588, which is included in this book.

[9] Words attributed to Ramzi Binalshibh, a member of al-Qaeda who allegedly planned to take part in the terrorist strikes of September 2001, but was refused entry to the USA.

We've removed an ally of al-Qaeda, and cut off a source of terrorist funding. And this much is certain: no terrorist network will gain weapons of mass destruction from the Iraqi regime, because the regime is no more.

[*Applause.*]

In these 19 months that changed the world, our actions have been focused and deliberate and proportionate to the offence. We have not forgotten the victims of September 11 – the last phone calls, the cold murder of children, the searches in the rubble. With those attacks, the terrorists and their supporters declared war on the United States. And war is what they got.

[*Applause.*]

Our war against terror is proceeding according to principles that I have made clear to all: any person involved in committing or planning terrorist attacks against the American people becomes an enemy of this country, and a target of American justice.

[*Applause.*]

Any person, organization, or government that supports, protects, or harbours terrorists is complicit in the murder of the innocent, and equally guilty of terrorist crimes.

Any outlaw regime that has ties to terrorist groups and seeks or possesses weapons of mass destruction is a grave danger to the civilized world – and will be confronted.

[*Applause.*]

And anyone in the world, including the Arab world, who works and sacrifices for freedom has a loyal friend in the United States of America.

[*Applause.*]

Our commitment to liberty is America's tradition – declared at our founding; affirmed in FRANKLIN ROOSEVELT's Four Freedoms;[10] asserted in the TRUMAN Doctrine[11] and in RONALD REAGAN's challenge to an evil empire.[12] We are committed to freedom in Afghanistan, in Iraq and in a peaceful Palestine.

The advance of freedom is the surest strategy to undermine the appeal of terror in the world. Where freedom takes hold, hatred gives way to hope. When freedom takes hold, men and women turn to the peaceful pursuit of a better life. American values and American interests lead in the same direction: we stand for human liberty.

[*Applause.*]

The United States upholds these principles of security and freedom in many ways – with all the tools of diplomacy, law enforcement, intelligence, and finance. We're working with a broad coalition of nations that understand the threat and our shared responsibility to meet it. The use of force has been – and remains – our last resort. Yet all can know, friend and foe alike, that our nation has a mission: we will answer threats to our security, and we will defend the peace.

[*Applause.*]

Our mission continues. Al-Qaeda is wounded, not destroyed. The scattered cells of the terrorist network still operate in many nations, and we know from daily intelligence that they continue to plot against free people. The proliferation of deadly weapons remains a serious danger. The enemies of freedom are not idle, and neither are we. Our government has taken unprecedented measures to defend the homeland. And we will continue to hunt down the enemy before he can strike.

[*Applause.*]

[10] President Roosevelt's 'Four essential human freedoms' speech of 6 January 1941 is included in this book.
[11] President Truman's 'Truman Doctrine' speech of 12 March 1947 is included in this book.
[12] President Reagan's 'evil empire' speech of 8 March 1983 is included in this book.

The war on terror is not over; yet it is not endless. We do not know the day of final victory, but we have seen the turning of the tide. No act of the terrorists will change our purpose, or weaken our resolve, or alter their fate. Their cause is lost. Free nations will press on to victory.

[*Applause.*]

Other nations in history have fought in foreign lands and remained to occupy and exploit. Americans, following a battle, want nothing more than to return home. And that is your direction tonight. [*Applause.*] After service in the Afghan and Iraqi theatres of war; after 100,000 miles, on the longest carrier deployment in recent history, you are homeward bound.

[*Applause.*]

Some of you will see new family members for the first time – 150 babies were born while their fathers were on the *Lincoln*. Your families are proud of you, and your nation will welcome you.

[*Applause.*]

We are mindful, as well, that some good men and women are not making the journey home. One of those who fell, Corporal Jason Mileo, spoke to his parents five days before his death. Jason's father said, 'He called us from the centre of Baghdad, not to brag, but to tell us he loved us. Our son was a soldier.'

Every name, every life is a loss to our military, to our nation, and to the loved ones who grieve. There's no homecoming for these families. Yet we pray, in God's time, their reunion will come.

Those we lost were last seen on duty. Their final act on this earth was to fight a great evil and bring liberty to others. All of you – all in this generation of our military – have taken up the highest calling of history. You're defending your country, and protecting the innocent from harm. And wherever you go, you carry a message of hope – a message that is ancient and ever new. In the words of the prophet Isaiah, 'To the captives, "Come out"; and to those in darkness, "Be free".'[13]

Thank you for serving our country and our cause. May God bless you all, and may God continue to bless America.

[*Applause.*]

[13] Isaiah 49:9.

Calgacus
Caledonian chieftain

Calgacus *also called Galgacus* (1st century AD) was leader of the tribes defeated by Gnaeus Julius Agricola (AD 40–93) at the Battle of Mons Graupius (AD 83). Agricola's biographer, the Roman historian Tacitus (c. 56–11 AD) attributes to Calgacus a heroic speech on the eve of a battle, with a ringing denunciation of Roman imperialism.

'They create a desolation and call it peace'
AD 83, Northern Britain

The speech attributed here to Calgacus was not given by him, but was written by Tacitus at the very end of the 1st century AD in his biography of Agricola, the commander of the Roman army in Britain, who was Tacitus's father-in-law. The translation is by Hugh Mattingly (1948).

In the tradition of all writers of history in the ancient world, Tacitus places speeches by the leaders of each side to their soldiers immediately before his account of the battle, which Tacitus places at Mons Graupius (the Graupian Mountain), which is probably Bennachie in the Grampians, some 20 miles north-west of Aberdeen; and, again in the tradition of ancient historiography, these speeches are the product of the historian rather than of the speakers.

Consequently the fierce and eloquent critique of Roman imperialism that the speech contains comes from a Roman writer, however accurately it may reflect the feelings of Calgacus and his followers. Tacitus elsewhere in the *Agricola* – and in his other early work, *Germania*, on the peoples with whom the Romans came in contact east of the Rhine – writes glowingly of the superiority of the way of life of these 'noble savages', compared with the decadence (as he saw it) of contemporary Rome. Nonetheless, this speech has justifiably been seen throughout the ages as an attack on the arrogance of military imperialism, however benign the intentions of the imperialists (such indeed as Agricola) are alleged to be.

Nothing is known of Calgacus apart from his appearance here, though the name seems to be connected to the Irish *calgach*, meaning a swordsman. His is the first name from the area of modern Scotland to be mentioned in any ancient source.

Whenever I consider why we are fighting and how we have reached this crisis, I have a strong sense that this day of your splendid rally may mean the dawn of liberty for the whole of Britain. You have mustered to a man, and to a man you are free. There are no lands behind us, and even the sea is menaced by the Roman fleet. The clash of battle – the hero's glory – has become the safest refuge for the coward. Battles against Rome have been lost and won before – but never without hope; we were always there in reserve. We, the choice flower of Britain, were treasured in her most secret places. Out of sight of subject shores, we kept even our eyes free from the defilement of tyranny. We, the last men on earth, the last of the free, have been shielded till today by the very remoteness and the seclusion for which we are famed.

But today the boundary of Britain is exposed; beyond us lies no nation, nothing but waves and rocks and the Romans, more deadly still than they, for you find in them an arrogance which no reasonable submission can elude. Brigands of the world, they have exhausted the land by their indiscriminate plunder, and now they ransack the sea. The wealth of an enemy excites their cupidity, his poverty their lust of power. East and West have failed to glut their maw. They are unique in being as violently tempted to attack the poor as the wealthy. Robbery, butchery, rapine, the liars call Empire; they create a desolation and call it peace.[1]

We instinctively love our children and our kinsmen above all else. These are torn from us by conscription to slave in other lands. Our wives and

[1] The blessings of peace as an accompaniment to empire appeared frequently in Roman imperial propaganda.

sisters, even if they are not raped by Roman enemies, are seduced by them in the guise of guests and friends. Our goods and fortunes are ground down to pay tribute, our land and its harvest to supply corn, our bodies and hands to build roads through woods and swamps – all under blows and insults. Slaves born into slavery, once sold, get their keep from their masters. But as for Britain, never a day passes but she pays and feeds her enslavers.

In a private household it is the latest arrival who is always the butt of his fellow-slaves; so, in this establishment, where all the world have long been slaves, it is we, the cheap new acquisitions, who are picked out for extirpation. You see, we have no fertile lands, no mines, no harbours, which we might be spared to work. Courage and martial spirit we have, but the master does not relish them in the subject. Even our remoteness and seclusion, while they protect, expose us to suspicion.

Abandon, then, all hope of mercy and at last take courage, whether it is life or honour that you hold most dear. The Brigantes, with only a woman to lead them, burned the colony, stormed the camp and, if success had not made them grossly careless, might have cast off the yoke.[2] Let us, then, uncorrupted, unconquered as we are, ready to fight for freedom but never to repent failure, prove at the first clash of arms what heroes Caledonia[3] has been holding in reserve.

Can you really imagine that the Romans' bravery in war comes up to their wantonness in peace? No! It is our quarrels and disunion that have given them fame. The reputation of the Roman army is built up on the faults of its enemies. Look at it: a motley agglomeration of nations that will be shattered by defeat as surely as it is now held together by success!

Or can you seriously think that those Gauls or Germans – and, to our bitter shame, many Britons too! – are bound to Rome by genuine loyalty or love? They may be lending their life-blood to foreign tyrants, but they were enemies of Rome much longer than they have been her slaves. Apprehension and terror are weak bonds of affection; once break them, and, where fear ends, hatred will begin.

All that can goad men to victory is on our side. The enemy have no wives to fire their courage, no parents ready to taunt them if they run away. Most of them have no country, or, if they have one, it is not Rome.

See them, a scanty band, scared and bewildered, staring blankly at the unfamiliar sky, sea and forests around! The gods have given them, spellbound prisoners, into our hands. Never fear the outward show that means nothing, the glitter of gold and silver that can neither avert nor inflict a wound. In the ranks of our very enemies we shall find hands to help us.

The Britons will recognize our cause as their own, the Gauls will remember their lost liberty, the rest of the Germans will desert them as surely as the Usipi have just done. They have nothing in reserve that need alarm us – only forts without garrisons, colonies of greybeards, towns sick and distracted between rebel subjects and tyrant masters.

Here before us is their general, here his army; behind are the tribute, the mines and all the other whips to scourge slaves. Whether you are to endure these for ever or take summary vengeance, this field must decide. On, then, into action and, as you go, think of those that went before you and of those that shall come after.

[2] This seems to be an error by Tacitus. The Brigantes, a populous tribe in northern England, were indeed led by a queen, Cartimandua, for some decades until AD 69; but the revolt here described is that of Boudicca (Boadicea), queen of the Iceni in East Anglia, in AD 61, in which Colchester (a Roman *colonia*), London and St Albans were sacked.

[3] Caledonia is used by Tacitus to describe the Highland region. The Caledonii were a tribe who occupied the area between the Great Glen and the upper Tay valley.

John C Calhoun
American politician

John Caldwell Calhoun (1782–1850) was born in Abbeville County, South Carolina, of Scottish–Irish Presbyterian descent, and became a successful lawyer. In Congress, he supported the measures which led to the war of 1812–15 with Great Britain, and promoted the protective tariff. In 1817 he joined President James Monroe's Cabinet as Secretary of War, and reorganized the war department. He was vice president under both John Q Adams, 1825–9, and ANDREW JACKSON, 1829–32. His 'Address to the People of South Carolina' (1831) set forth his theory of States' Rights, by which, he maintained, individual states were sovereign and could nullify federal legislation. In 1832, South Carolina passed the Ordinance of Nullification, rejecting the import tariffs imposed by Congress in 1828 and 1832. As a result, Calhoun found himself in bitter dispute with Jackson. He resigned the vice-presidency and entered the Senate, becoming a leader of the States' Rights movement, and throughout the 1830s and 1840s he was a champion of the interests of the slave-holding southern states. In 1844, as Secretary of State, he signed a treaty annexing Texas, but after returning to the Senate in 1845, he strenuously opposed the war of 1846–7 with Mexico. He, Henry Clay, and Daniel Webster were the 'great triumvirate' of American political orators. The US Senate honoured him in 1957 as 'one of the five greatest senators of all time' and, in a similar resolution of 2000, as one of the seven greatest.

'Abolition and the Union cannot co-exist'
6 February 1837, Washington, DC, USA

It was said of Calhoun that he took an unusual approach to logical thinking: he would start from a desired conclusion, then work backwards. This may help account for the extraordinary assertion he puts forward in this speech, that slavery provided a 'positive good' for slaves. He supports this theory with a discourse on the unequal division of wealth in other societies; and with a homely vision of the American slave growing old 'under the kind, superintending care of his master and mistress'.

But Calhoun was far from alone in upholding the right to keep slaves. Regarded as a bulwark of the Old South, he was trying to defend an economy dependent on slave labour, which was threatened by the growing strength of the abolitionist movement.

This speech was delivered in the Senate, and is in part a response to William Rives, senator from Virginia, who had argued that slavery was an evil, but could sometimes be considered a 'lesser evil'. To Calhoun, this smelled of compromise.

Known as the 'cast-iron man', Calhoun was a belligerent debater. His colleague James H Hammond (who later became governor of South Carolina) remarked: 'He was so wanting in judgement in the managing of men, was so unyielding and unpersuasive, that he never could consolidate sufficient power to accomplish anything great'. Yet Calhoun's forceful oratory was widely admired – and his prediction that slavery would divide the Union proved accurate, though he died long before the outbreak of war.

The peculiar institution of the South – that on the maintenance of which the very existence of the slaveholding States depends – is pronounced to be sinful and odious, in the sight of God and man; and this with a systematic design of rendering us hateful in the eyes of the world, with a view to a general crusade against us and our institutions. This, too, in the legislative halls of the Union; created by these confederated states for the better protection of their peace, their safety, and their respective institutions.

And yet, we, the representatives of twelve of these sovereign[1] states against whom this deadly war is waged, are expected to sit here in silence, hearing ourselves and our constituents day after day denounced, without uttering a word; for if we but open our lips, the charge of agitation is resounded on all sides, and we are held up as seeking to aggravate the evil which we resist. Every reflecting mind must see in all this a state of things deeply and dangerously diseased.

I do not belong to the school which holds that aggression is to be met by

[1] The slave-owning states of the South; Calhoun's description of them as 'sovereign' states was central to his States' Rights scheme.

concession. Mine is the opposite creed, which teaches that encroachments must be met at the beginning, and that those who act on the opposite principle are prepared to become slaves. In this case, in particular.

I hold concession or compromise to be fatal. If we concede an inch, concession would follow concession – compromise would follow compromise, until our ranks would be so broken that effectual resistance would be impossible. We must meet the enemy on the frontier, with a fixed determination of maintaining our position at every hazard. Consent to receive these insulting petitions, and the next demand will be that they be referred to a committee in order that they may be deliberated and acted upon … I already see indications that such is now the intention. If we yield, that will be followed by another, and we will thus proceed, step by step, to the final consummation of the object of these petitions.

We are now told that the most effectual mode of arresting the progress of abolition is to reason it down; and with this view it is urged that the petitions ought to be referred to a committee … The most unquestionable right may be rendered doubtful, if once admitted to be a subject of controversy, and that would be the case in the present instance. The subject is beyond the jurisdiction of Congress – they have no right to touch it in any shape or form, or to make it the subject of deliberation or discussion …

As widely as this incendiary spirit has spread, it has not yet infected this body, or the great mass of the intelligent and business portion of the North; but unless it be speedily stopped, it will spread and work upwards till it brings the two great sections of the Union into deadly conflict.

This is not a new impression with me. Several years since, in a discussion with one of the senators from Massachusetts,[2] before this fell spirit had showed itself, I predicted that the doctrine of the proclamation[3] and the Force Bill[4] – that this government had a right, in the last resort, to enforce its decision at the point of the bayonet, which was so warmly maintained by that senator – would at no distant day arouse the dormant spirit of abolitionism. I told him that the doctrine was tantamount to the assumption of unlimited power on the part of the government, and that such would be the impression on the public mind in a large portion of the Union.

The consequence would be inevitable. A large portion of the northern States believed slavery to be a sin, and would consider it as an obligation of conscience to abolish it if they should feel themselves in any degree responsible for its continuance, and that this doctrine would necessarily lead to the belief of such responsibility. I then predicted that it would commence as it has with this fanatical portion of society, and that they would begin their operations on the ignorant, the weak, the young, and the thoughtless – and gradually extend upwards till they would become strong enough to obtain political control, when he and others holding the highest stations in society, would, however reluctant, be compelled to yield to their doctrines, or be driven into obscurity. But four years have since elapsed, and all this is already in a course of regular fulfilment.

Standing at the point of time at which we have now arrived, it will not be more difficult to trace the course of future events now than it was then. They who imagine that the spirit now abroad in the North will die away of itself, without a shock or convulsion, have formed a very inadequate conception of its real character. It will continue to rise and spread, unless prompt and efficient measures to stay its progress be adopted. Already it

[2] The US politician Daniel Webster (1782–1852) served as a senator for the Adams, Anti-Jacksonian and Whig Parties, 1827–41 and 1845–50.

[4] The Force Bill of 1833 authorized the government to use force to impose federal laws, and was introduced after South Carolina declared itself exempt from tariffs. Calhoun responded by nullifying it, but was placated by a Compromise Tariff, passed the same day.

[3] President Jackson issued a proclamation in December 1829, which declared 'the power to annul a law of the United States, assumed by one state, incompatible with the existence of the Union'.

has taken possession of the pulpit, of the schools and – to a considerable extent – of the press; those great instruments by which the mind of the rising generation will be formed.

However sound the great body of the non-slaveholding States are at present, in the course of a few years they will be succeeded by those who will have been taught to hate the people and institutions of nearly one-half of this Union, with a hatred more deadly than one hostile nation ever entertained towards another. It is easy to see the end. By the necessary course of events, if left to themselves, we must become, finally, two people. It is impossible – under the deadly hatred which must spring up between the two great nations, if the present causes are permitted to operate unchecked – that we should continue under the same political system. The conflicting elements would burst the Union asunder, powerful as are the links which hold it together.

Abolition and the Union cannot co-exist. As the friend of the Union I openly proclaim it – and the sooner it is known the better. The former may now be controlled, but in a short time it will be beyond the power of man to arrest the course of events. We of the South will not, cannot, surrender our institutions. To maintain the existing relations between the two races, inhabiting that section of the Union, is indispensable to the peace and happiness of both. It cannot be subverted without drenching the country in blood, and extirpating one or the other of the races. Be it good or bad, it has grown up with our society and institutions, and is so interwoven with them, that to destroy it would be to destroy us as a people.

But let me not be understood as admitting, even by implication, that the existing relations between the two races in the slaveholding States is an evil. Far otherwise. I hold it to be a good, as it has thus far proved itself to be to both, and will continue to prove so if not disturbed by the fell spirit of abolition. I appeal to facts. Never before has the black race of Central Africa, from the dawn of history to the present day, attained a condition so civilized and so improved, not only physically, but morally and intellectually.

In the meantime, the white or European race has not degenerated. It has kept pace with its brethren in other sections of the Union where slavery does not exist. It is odious to make comparison; but I appeal to all sides whether the South is not equal in virtue, intelligence, patriotism, courage, disinterestedness and all the high qualities which adorn our nature.

But I take higher ground. I hold that in the present state of civilization, where two races of different origin – and distinguished by colour and other physical differences, as well as intellectual – are brought together, the relation now existing in the slaveholding states between the two is, instead of an evil, a good, a positive good. I feel myself called upon to speak freely upon the subject where the honour and interests of those I represent are involved. I hold then, that there never has yet existed a wealthy and civilized society in which one portion of the community did not, in point of fact, live on the labour of the other. Broad and general as is this assertion, it is fully borne out by history.

This is not the proper occasion, but, if it were, it would not be difficult to trace the various devices by which the wealth of all civilized communities has been so unequally divided, and to show by what means so small a share has been allotted to those by whose labour it was produced, and so large a share given to the non-producing classes. The devices are almost innumerable, from the brute force and gross superstition of ancient times, to the subtle and artful fiscal contrivances of modern.

I might well challenge a comparison between them and the more direct, simple and patriarchal mode by which the labour of the African race is, among us, commanded by the European. I may say with truth that in few countries so much is left to the share of the labourer, and so little exacted from him; or where there is more kind attention paid to him in sickness or infirmities of age. Compare his condition with the tenants of the poor houses in the more civilized portions of Europe – look at the sick, and the old and infirm slave, on one hand, in the midst of his family and friends, under the kind, superintending care of his master and mistress and compare it with the forlorn and wretched condition of the pauper in the poorhouse.

But I will not dwell on this aspect of the question. I turn to the political; and here I fearlessly assert that the existing relation between the two races in the South – against which these blind fanatics are waging war – forms the most solid and durable foundation on which to rear free and stable political institutions. It is useless to disguise the fact. There is and always has been, in an advanced stage of wealth and civilization, a conflict between labour and capital. The condition of society in the South exempts us from the disorders and dangers resulting from this conflict; and explains why it is that the political condition of the slaveholding states has been so much more stable and quiet than that of the North ...

Be assured that emancipation itself would not satisfy these fanatics. That gained, the next step would be to raise the negroes to a social and political equality with the whites; and that being effected, we would soon find the present condition of the two races reversed. They and their northern allies would be the masters, and we the slaves; the condition of the white race in the British West India Islands, bad as it is, would be happiness to ours.[5] There the mother country is interested in sustaining the supremacy of the European race. It is true that the authority of the former master is destroyed, but the African will there still be a slave, not to individuals but to the community – forced to labour, not by the authority of the overseer, but by the bayonet of the soldiery and the rod of the civil magistrate.

Surrounded as the slaveholding states are with such imminent perils, I rejoice to think that our means of defence are ample, if we shall prove to have the intelligence and spirit to see and apply them before it is too late. All we want is concert, to lay aside all party differences and unite with zeal and energy in repelling approaching dangers. Let there be concert of action, and we shall find ample means of security without resorting to secession or disunion.

I speak with full knowledge and a thorough examination of the subject, and for one see my way clearly ... I dare not hope that anything I can say will arouse the South to a due sense of danger; I fear it is beyond the power of mortal voice to awaken it in time from the fatal security into which it has fallen.

[5] Calhoun refers to the severe economic impact of the Abolition of Slavery Act (1833) on landowners in the British West Indies.

George Canning
English statesman

George Canning (1770–1827) was born in London, and raised and educated by his uncle after his father died when he was only one year old. He attended Eton and Christ Church, Oxford, and was admitted to the Bar before entering Parliament in 1794. He became Under-Secretary of State under William Pitt, the Younger (1796), and was appointed Navy Treasurer in 1801. As Foreign Affairs Minister in Lord Portland's Cabinet (1807–9), he planned the seizure of the Danish fleet that prevented NAPOLEON BONAPARTE's planned invasion. In 1809, he was wounded in the thigh during a duel with his former Cabinet colleague Lord Castlereagh. They had argued over the Walcheren Expedition of 1809, in which 39,000 British troops Canning planned to send to Portugal were sent instead to Flanders to assist Austria against Napoleon, at a cost of over 4,000 lives. As MP for Liverpool from 1812, he was a strong advocate of Catholic emancipation. He supported Lord Liverpool until the succession of George IV in 1820. Canning resigned in protest at the government's attempt to dissolve George's marriage to Queen Caroline, with whom he is alleged to have had an affair. After Castlereagh's suicide in 1822, Canning became Foreign Minister again, and on the death of Liverpool in 1827 he became prime minister in a coalition with the Whigs, but he died later the same year. A notable orator, he was buried in Westminster Abbey.

'The resources created by peace are means of war'
October 1823, Plymouth, England

On receiving the freedom of the town of Plymouth, George Canning displayed the flair for oratory for which he was rightly renowned. But his speech required a careful, diplomatic approach. Plymouth was a town associated with naval warfare, and Britain, for the first time in over 20 years, was not at war.

By this time, Canning had become Foreign Secretary and Leader of the House of Commons, a dual role vacated by the suicide of his old rival Lord Castlereagh. Mistrusted by the aristocracy as an upstart from the lower orders, and by George IV as a supporter of Catholic emancipation, he nonetheless enjoyed great support from the middle classes. From his powerful new position, he was able to resist British involvement in the affairs of continental Europe, distancing Britain from the unpopular monarchs Ferdinand VII of Spain and Louis XVIII of France, and from the 'Holy Alliance' formed by Alexander I of Russia after the defeat of Napoleon in 1815.

In his speech, Canning set out to convince his audience that the Royal Navy was still a force of awesome power; and that Britain could reap great benefits from peace. He describes the dormant warships in glowing, romantic terms: 'those stupendous masses now reposing on their shadows in perfect stillness'. And perhaps mindful of the New World – which he helped protect from Spanish and French domination – he concludes with a vision of the port as a gateway to trade and 'commercial prosperity'.

Gentlemen: the end which I confess I have always had in view, and which appears to be the legitimate object of pursuit to a British statesman, I can describe in one word. The language of modern philosophy is wisely and diffusely benevolent; it professes the perfection of our species and the amelioration of the lot of all mankind. Gentlemen: I hope that my heart beats as high for the general interest of humanity – I hope that I have as friendly a disposition towards other nations of the earth as anyone who vaunts his philanthropy most highly; but I am contented to confess that in the conduct of political affairs, the grand object of my contemplation is the interest of England.

Not, gentlemen, that the interest of England is an interest which stands isolated and alone. The situation which she holds forbids an exclusive selfishness; her prosperity must contribute to the prosperity of other nations, and her stability to the safety of the world. But intimately connected as we are with the system of Europe, it does not follow that we are therefore called upon to mix ourselves, on every occasion, with a restless and meddling activity, in the concerns of the nations which surround us. It is upon a just balance of conflicting duties, and of rival but sometimes incompatible advantages, that a government must judge when to put forth its strength, and when to husband it for occasions yet to come.

Our ultimate object must be the peace of the world. That object may sometimes be best attained by prompt exertions; sometimes by abstinence from interposition in contests which we cannot prevent. It is upon these principles that … it did not appear to the government of this country to be necessary that Great Britain should mingle in the recent contest between France and Spain.[1]

Your worthy recorder has accurately classed the persons who would have driven us into that contest. There were undoubtedly among them those who desired to plunge this country into the difficulties of war, partly from the hope that those difficulties would overwhelm the administration; but it would be most unjust not to admit that there were others who were actuated by nobler principles and more generous feelings, who would have rushed forward at once from the sense of indignation at aggression, and who deemed that no act of injustice could be perpetrated from one end of the universe to the other, but that the sword of Great Britain should leap from its scabbard to avenge it. But as it is the province of law to control the excess even of laudable passions and propensities in individuals, so it is the duty of government to restrain within due bounds the ebullition of national sentiment, and to regulate the course and direction of impulses which it cannot blame.

Is there anyone among the latter class of persons … (for to the former I have nothing to say), who continues to doubt whether the government did wisely in declining to obey the precipitate enthusiasm which prevailed at the commencement of the contest in Spain? Is there anybody who does not now think that it was the office of government to examine more closely all the various bearings of so complicated a question, to consider whether they were called upon to assist a united nation, or to plunge themselves into the internal feuds by which that nation was divided – to aid in repelling a foreign invader, or to take part in a civil war? Is there any man that does not now see what would have been the extent of burdens that would have been cast upon this country? Is there anyone who does not acknowledge that, under such circumstances, the enterprise would have been one to be characterized only by a term borrowed from that part of the Spanish literature with which we are most familiar: quixotic[2] – an enterprise romantic in its origin and thankless in the end?

But while we thus control even our feelings by our duty, let it not be said that we cultivate peace either because we fear or because we are unprepared for war. On the contrary: if eight months ago the government did not hesitate to proclaim that the country was prepared for war (if war should be unfortunately necessary) every month of peace that has since passed has but made us so much the more capable of exertion.

The resources created by peace are means of war; in cherishing those resources, we but accumulate those means. Our present repose is no more a proof of our inability to act, than the state of inertness and inactivity in which I have seen those mighty masses that float in the waters above your town is a proof they are devoid of strength, and incapable of being fitted for action. You well know, gentlemen, how soon one of those stupendous masses now reposing on their shadows in perfect stillness, how soon, upon any call of patriotism or necessity, it would assume the likeness of an animated thing, instinct with life and motion; how soon it would ruffle, as it were, its swelling plumage; how quickly it would put forth all its beauty and

[1] At the request of Ferdinand VII of Spain (1784–1833), Louis XVIII of France (1755–1824) sent French troops to intervene in the Spanish Civil War of 1820–3, helping to crush a rebellion and restore Ferdinand to absolute monarchy. Canning later took action to prevent Louis intervening in revolts against Spanish rule in Latin America.

[2] Canning refers to Don Quixote, the central character of the novel of the same name (1605–15) by Spanish writer Miguel de Cervantes (1547–1616). Quixote is an impetuous fantasist driven by an idealistic obsession with medieval chivalry.

its bravery, collect its scattered elements of strength, and awaken its dormant thunder.

Such as is one of these magnificent machines when springing from inaction into a display of its might, such is England herself, while, apparently passive and motionless, she silently concentrates the power to be put forth on an adequate occasion. But God forbid that that occasion should arise!

After a war sustained for nearly a quarter of a century, sometimes single-handed, and with all Europe arranged at times against her, or at her side, England needs a period of tranquillity, and may enjoy it without fear of misconstruction. Long may we be enabled, gentlemen, to improve the blessings of our present situation; to cultivate the arts of peace; to give to commerce, now reviving, greater extension and new spheres of employment; and to confirm the prosperity now generally diffused throughout this island.

Of the blessings of peace, gentlemen, I trust that this borough, with which I have now the honour and happiness of being associated, will receive an ample share. I trust the time is not far distant when that noble structure,[3] of which, as I learn from your recorder, the box with which you have honoured me through his hands formed a part, that gigantic barrier against the fury of the waves that roll into your harbour, will protect a commercial marine, not less considerable in its kind than the warlike marine of which your port has been long so distinguished an asylum; when the town of Plymouth will participate in the commercial prosperity as largely as it has hitherto done in the naval glories of England.

[3] The limestone and granite breakwater at Plymouth was constructed 1811–41, protecting Plymouth Sound from severe south-westerly gales.

Roger Casement
Irish nationalist

Roger David Casement (1864–1916) was born in Sandycove, County Dublin. He joined the British consular service and went to Africa, where he condemned the treatment of native workers (1904). As Consul-General at Rio de Janeiro he exposed the exploitation of rubber workers in the Congo and Peru, for which he was knighted in 1911. He joined the Irish Volunteers in 1913, and at the outbreak of World War I the following year, he visited Berlin to try to obtain German support for Irish independence, attempting to form an Irish Brigade of prisoners of war, with which he intended to invade Ireland and end British rule. In 1916 he was arrested on landing in Ireland from a German submarine to participate in the Sinn Féin rebellion. He was tried in England for high treason, and hanged. Extracts from his controversial 'Black Diaries', revealing, among other things, homosexual practices, were circulated in 1916 by the government to turn opinion against him and discourage appeals for clemency; the diaries were not published until 1959. In 1965, the British government allowed his remains to be reinterred in Ireland.

'This court is to me, an Irishman, a foreign court'
29 June 1916, London, England

In May 1914, Irish Home Rule legislation was passed by Parliament, despite persistent opposition in the House of Lords. But that August, the legislation was suspended when Britain declared war on Germany. Meanwhile, the Ulster Volunteer Force had been assembled and armed to resist the anticipated introduction of home rule.

Determined to advance the Republican project, Casement travelled to the USA, then Germany, to acquire arms. In April 1916, he arrived back in Ireland, but was quickly arrested and linked to a planned shipment of 20,000 German guns.

Days later, the Republican Easter Rising occurred in Dublin. It was quickly crushed and its leaders were executed. Casement, however, was charged with high treason under the Statute of Treasons of 1351 and held in the Tower of London. At his trial, he argued that as an Irishman he did not owe loyalty to the English Crown and should be tried by his Irish peers.

Casement was prosecuted by the Attorney-General F E Smith, a staunch opponent of Home Rule. Ironically, Smith had himself helped arm the Ulster Volunteers with German weapons (though prior to the outbreak of war). Smith was ruthless, declaring, 'The prisoner, blinded by a hatred for this country, as malignant in quality as it was sudden in origin, has played a desperate hazard … Today the forfeit is claimed.'

As Casement spoke from the dock, anticipating his execution, Smith strode from the court. Casement's conviction was widely criticized in legal circles, but no appeal could be made other than via Smith. Casement was hanged on 3 August.

As I wish my words to reach a much wider audience than I see before me here, I intend to read all that I propose to say. What I shall read now is something I wrote more than 20 days ago. There is an objection – possibly not good in law but surely good on moral grounds – against the application to me here of this English statute, 565 years old, that seeks to deprive an Irishman today of life and honour, not for 'adhering to the King's enemies' but for adhering to his own people.

When this statute was passed, in 1351, what was the state of men's minds on the question of a far higher allegiance – that of man to God and his kingdom? The law of that day did not permit a man to forsake his church or deny his God, save with his life. The heretic then had the same doom as the traitor.

Today, a man may forswear God and his heavenly realm without fear or penalty, all earlier statutes having gone the way of Nero's edicts against the Christians.[1] But that constitutional phantom the King can still dig up from the dungeons and torture chambers of the Dark Ages a law that takes a man's life for an exercise of conscience.

[1] In the wake of the great fire of Rome in AD 64, Emperor Nero (AD 37–68) diverted criticism for his handling of reconstruction by scapegoating Christians. Many were thrown to the lions or crucified.

Loyalty is a sentiment, not a law. It rests on love, not on restraint. The government of Ireland by England rests on restraint and not on law; and, since it demands no love, it can evoke no loyalty. Judicial assassination today is reserved only for one race of the King's subjects, for Irishmen; for those who cannot forget their allegiance to the realm of Ireland.

What is the fundamental charter of an Englishman's liberty? That he shall be tried by his peers. With all respect I assert that this court is to me, an Irishman, a foreign court – this jury is for me, an Irishman, not a jury of my peers.

It is patent to every man of conscience that I have an indefeasible[2] right, if tried at all under this statute of high treason, to be tried in Ireland, before an Irish court, and by an Irish jury.

> [2] Not to be annulled, forfeited or made void.

This court, this jury, the public opinion of this country, England, cannot but be prejudiced in varying degree against me, most of all in time of war. From this court and its jurisdiction I appeal to those I am alleged to have wronged, and to those I am alleged to have injured by my 'evil example', and claim that they alone are competent to decide my guilt or my innocence.

This is so fundamental a right, so natural a right, so obvious a right, that it is clear the Crown were aware of it when they brought me by force and by stealth from Ireland to this country. It was not I who landed in England, but the Crown who dragged me here, away from my own country, to which I had returned with a price upon my head, away from my own countrymen, whose loyalty is not in doubt, and safe from the judgement of my peers, whose judgement I do not shrink from.

I admit no other judgement but theirs. I accept no verdict save at their hands.

I assert from this dock that I am being tried here not because it is just, but because it is unjust. My counsel has referred to the Ulster Volunteer movement,[3] and I will not touch at length upon that ground, save only to say that neither I nor any of the leaders of the Irish Volunteers[4] – who were founded in Dublin in November 1913 – had quarrel with the Ulster Volunteers as such, who were born a year earlier.

> [3] The Ulster Volunteer Force was formed in 1912 by Edward Carson (1854–1935) and James Craig (1871–1940) to resist, by force if necessary, the establishment of home rule in Ireland.
>
> [4] The Irish Volunteers (*Óglaigh na hÉireann*) were formed in 1913 by the Irish nationalists PÁDRAIG PEARSE (1879–1916), Eamonn Ceannt (1881–1916) and Sean MacDermott (1883–1916) to help enforce Home Rule and 'to secure and maintain the rights and liberties common to the whole people of Ireland'.

Our movement was not directed against them, but against the men who misused and misdirected the courage, the sincerity, and the local patriotism of the men of the North of Ireland. On the contrary, we welcomed the coming of the Ulster Volunteers, even while we deprecated the aims and intentions of those Englishmen who sought to pervert to an English party use – to the mean purposes of their own bid for place and power in England – the armed activities of simple Irishmen.

We aimed at winning the Ulster Volunteers to the cause of a united Ireland – we aimed at uniting all Irishmen in a natural and national bond of cohesion, based on mutual self-respect. Our hope was a natural one, and, if left to ourselves, not hard to accomplish.

If external influences of disintegration would but leave us alone, we were sure that nature itself must bring us together. It was not the Irish Volunteers who broke the law, but a British party.

The government had permitted the Ulster Volunteers to be armed by Englishmen, to threaten not merely an English party in its hold on office, but to threaten that party through the lives and blood of Irishmen. Our choice lay between submitting to foreign lawlessness and resisting it, and we did not hesitate. I for one was determined that Ireland was much more to me than empire, and that if charity begins at home so must loyalty.

Since arms were so necessary to make our organization a reality and to give to the minds of Irishmen menaced with the most outrageous threats a sense of security, it was our bounden duty to get arms before all else. I decided, with this end in view, to go to America. If − as the right honourable gentleman, the present Attorney-General, asserted in a speech at Manchester, Nationalists would neither fight for home rule nor pay for it − it was our duty to show him that we knew how to do both.

Then came the war. As Mr Birrell[5] said, in his evidence recently laid before the commission of inquiry into the causes of the late rebellion in Ireland, 'The war upset all our calculations'. It upset mine no less than Mr Birrell's, and put an end to my mission of peaceful effort in America. War between Great Britain and Germany meant, as I believed, ruin for all the hopes we had founded on the enrolment of the Irish Volunteers.

I felt, over there in America, that my first duty was to keep Irishmen at home in the only army that could safeguard our national existence. If small nationalities were to be the pawns in this game of embattled giants, I saw no reason why Ireland should shed her blood in any cause but her own − and if that be treason beyond the seas, I am not ashamed to avow it or to answer for it here with my life.

And when we had the doctrine of Unionist loyalty at last − 'Mausers and Kaisers and any king you like'[6] − I felt I needed no other warrant than that these words conveyed: to go forth and do likewise. The difference between us was that the Unionist champions chose a path which they felt would lead to the Woolsack,[7] while I went a road that I knew must lead to the dock.

And the event proves that we were both right. But let me say that I am prouder to stand here today in the traitor's dock to answer this impeachment than to fill the place of my accusers. If there be no right of rebellion against a state of things that no savage tribe would endure without resistance, then am I sure that it is better for men to fight and die without right than to live in such a state of right as this.

Where all your rights become only an accumulated wrong; where men must beg with bated breath for leave to subsist in their own land, to think their own thoughts, to sing their own songs, to garner the fruit of their own labours − and even while they beg to see these things inexorably withdrawn from them − then surely it is a braver, a saner, and a truer thing to be a rebel in act and deed against such circumstances as this than tamely to accept it as the natural lot of men.

My Lord, I have done. Gentlemen of the jury, I wish to thank you for your verdict. I hope you will not think that I made any imputation upon your truthfulness or your integrity when I said that this was not a trial by my peers.

[5] The English writer and politician Augustine Birrell (1850–1933) served as Chief Secretary for Ireland, 1907–16.

[6] German-made Mauser guns were issued to German forces during the 19th and 20th centuries; Kaiser is the German word for emperor. Casement refers to the purchase of German weapons for the Ulster Volunteers by F E Smith and Carson, who had declared a willingness to 'resist the King and Commons'.

[7] The seat of the Lord Chancellor in the House of Lords, which office was occupied by F E Smith, as Lord Birkenhead, from 1919 until 1922.

Fidel Castro
Cuban revolutionary and politician

Fidel Castro Ruz (1926–) was born near Birán, the son of a Spanish sugar planter. He studied law and practised in Havana, fighting cases on behalf of the poor and against corruption, which was rife under President Fulgencio Batista. In 1953, with his brother Raúl, Castro led an unsuccessful rising in Santiago de Cuba and was jailed for 15 years. Released under an amnesty after two years, the Castro brothers went to the USA, then Mexico, where they continued to plot revolution and met the Argentinian doctor ERNESTO 'CHE' GUEVARA, who joined their movement. In December 1956, Castro led an invasion force of around 80 insurgents, who sailed from Mexico to Cuba. They were betrayed and ambushed, and only a dozen men survived, escaping into the Sierra Maestra mountains, where they established a stronghold and began to recruit a peasants' army. For two years they waged a guerrilla campaign against Batista's regime. In 1958 Castro mounted a full-scale attack and by the end of the year Batista had fled. As prime minister from February 1959, Castro introduced radical reforms in agriculture, industry and education. Not all were immediately successful, but his regime gathered strength. He nationalized Cuban industries, expropriating American interests, which led to a trade embargo; and routed the American-backed émigré invasion at the Bay of Pigs (1961). He also proclaimed a 'Marxist–Leninist programme', which enabled him to form strong trade links with the USSR but this led to dependence and the near-disaster of October 1962, when a Soviet plan to site nuclear warheads in Cuba met with a bullish response from US president JOHN F KENNEDY. Despite problems in sugar and tobacco production and two mass exoduses, Castro's popularity remained high. In 1979 he became president of the Non-Aligned Countries Movement, despite Cuba's continuing substantial economic and political involvement with the Kremlin, but by the late 1980s, Cuba's status as the world's largest supplier of sugar was beginning to suffer from outdated and poorly maintained equipment. Communist Cuba suffered its worst economic crisis in the early 1990s, caused largely by the collapse of the USSR, which had become Cuba's main trading partner. The economic crisis accelerated moves to open up the country to the West, especially to tourism. In 1993–4 Castro suffered embarrassment when his daughter Alina Fernandez-Revuelta fled Cuba and sought asylum in the USA, where she publicly criticized the way her homeland was being run. From 2006, with his health failing, he increasingly passed his powers to his brother, Vice-President Raúl Castro, who assumed the presidency in 2008.

'History will absolve me'
16 October 1953, Santiago, Cuba

Castro's initial foray into politics had been as a democratic activist for the Cuban People's Party. He was a candidate for the elections of 1952, but Batista had intervened with a military coup, unseating President Carlos Prío. After this, Castro took to armed struggle. On 26 July 1953, he led his disastrous attack upon the Moncada Barracks in Santiago. Eight of the 123 participants died in the attack; a further 80 were murdered in custody.

Castro was denied representation at his trial, which was conducted in secret at the nurses' lodge of the Saturnino Lora hospital. A skilled lawyer, he conducted his own defence, drawing attention to these legal improprieties. His famous speech took several hours to deliver, and is presented here in much abridged form. Its culmination is a long parade of heroic figures from world history who – in one way or another – took a stance against tyranny. The speech was published as a book, and is still widely sold in Cuba and elsewhere.

Castro was sentenced to 15 years in jail. At the outset of his sentence, a prison officer, Captain Jesus Pelletier, was ordered to poison his food. He refused and, at his court martial, drew attention to Castro's cause. Such was the local and international outcry at Castro's treatment that no further attempts were made on his life. His popularity grew, and after two years Batista was forced to release him.

The date of the uprising gave its name to the revolutionary Movimiento de 26–7 (which overthrew Batista in the revolution of 1956–9) and remains a public holiday in Cuba.

Honourable Judges: never has a lawyer had to practise his profession under such difficult conditions; never has such a number of overwhelming irregularities been committed against an accused man. In this case, counsel and defendant are one and the same. As attorney he has not even been able to take a look at the indictment. As accused, for the past 76 days he has been locked away in solitary confinement, held totally and absolutely incommunicado, in violation of every human and legal right …

If I have had to assume my own defence before this court it is for two reasons. First: because I have been denied legal aid almost entirely, and second: only one who has been so deeply wounded, who has seen his country so forsaken and its justice trampled so, can speak at a moment like this with words that spring from the blood of his heart and the truth of his very gut ...

The accused, who is now exercising this right to plead his own case, will under no circumstances refrain from saying what he must say ... You have publicly called this case the most significant in the history of the republic. If you sincerely believed this, you should not have allowed your authority to be stained and degraded.

The first court session was on 21 September. Among 100 machine guns and bayonets, scandalously invading the hall of justice, more than 100 people were seated in the prisoner's dock. The great majority had nothing to do with what had happened. They had been under preventive arrest for many days, suffering all kinds of insults and abuses ... But with the cause of justice on our side, we would wage the terrible battle of truth against infamy! Surely the regime was not prepared for the moral catastrophe in store for it!

How to maintain all its false accusations? How to keep secret what had really happened, when so many young men were willing to risk everything – prison, torture and death, if necessary – in order that the truth be told before this court?

I was called as a witness at that first session ... I spoke of the goals that inspired us in our struggle and of the humane and generous treatment that we had at all times accorded our adversaries ... The structure of lies the regime had erected about the events at Moncada Barracks began to collapse like a house of cards ...

At that point what I consider my most important mission in this trial began: to totally discredit the cowardly, miserable and treacherous lies which the regime had hurled against our fighters; to reveal with irrefutable evidence the horrible, repulsive crimes they had practised on the prisoners; and to show the nation and the world the infinite misfortune of the Cuban people who are suffering the most inhuman oppression of their history ...

As the trial went on, the roles were reversed: those who came to accuse found themselves accused, and the accused became the accusers! It was not the revolutionaries who were judged there; judged once and forever was a man named Batista ...

If there is in your hearts a vestige of love for your country, love for humanity, love for justice, listen carefully. I know that I will be silenced for many years; I know that the regime will try to suppress the truth by all possible means; I know that there will be a conspiracy to bury me in oblivion. But my voice will not be stifled – it will rise from my breast even when I feel most alone, and my heart will give it all the fire that callous cowards deny it.

From a shack in the mountains on Monday 27 July, I listened to the dictator's voice on the air, while there were still 18 of our men in arms against the government. Those who have never experienced similar moments will never know that kind of bitterness and indignation. While the long-cherished hopes of freeing our people lay in ruins about us, we heard those crushed hopes gloated over by a tyrant more vicious, more arrogant than ever. The endless stream of lies and slanders, poured forth in his crude, odious, repulsive language, may only be compared to the endless stream of clean young blood ... spilled by the most inhuman gang of assassins it is possible to imagine.

To have believed him for a single moment would have sufficed to fill a man of conscience with remorse and shame for the rest of his life … Already a circle of more than 1,000 men – armed with weapons more powerful than ours and with peremptory orders to bring in our bodies – was closing in around us. Now that the truth is coming out, now that speaking before you I am carrying out the mission I set for myself, I may die peacefully and content. So I shall not mince my words about those savage murderers …

It is common knowledge that in 1933, after the battle at the National Hotel,[1] some officers were murdered after they surrendered … It is also known that after the surrender of Fort Atarés[2] the besiegers' machine-guns cut down a row of prisoners … It is well known in Cuban history that assassination of prisoners was fatally linked with Batista's name. How naïve we were not to foresee this! However, unjustifiable as those killings of 1933 were, they took place in a matter of minutes, in no more time than it took for a round of machine-gun fire. What is more, they took place while tempers were still on edge.

This was not the case in Santiago de Cuba. Here, all forms of ferocious outrages and cruelty were deliberately overdone. Our men were killed not in the course of a minute, an hour or a day. Throughout an entire week the blows and tortures continued. Men were thrown from rooftops and shot. All methods of extermination were incessantly practised by skilled artisans of crime.

Moncada Barracks were turned into a workshop of torture and death. Some shameful individuals turned their uniforms into butchers' aprons. The walls were splattered with blood. The bullets embedded in the walls were encrusted with singed bits of skin, brains and human hair, the grisly reminders of rifle shots fired full in the face. The grass around the barracks was dark and sticky with human blood. The criminal hands that are guiding the destiny of Cuba had written for the prisoners at the entrance to that den of death the very inscription of Hell: 'Forsake all hope'.

They did not even attempt to cover appearances. They did not bother in the least to conceal what they were doing. They thought they had deceived the people with their lies and they ended up deceiving themselves. They felt themselves lords and masters of the universe, with power over life and death. So the fear they had experienced upon our attack at daybreak was dissipated in a feast of corpses, in a drunken orgy of blood … Never has such a sad and bloody page been written in numbers of victims and in the viciousness of the victimizers, as in Santiago de Cuba …

Even greater is his crime, and even more condemnable, because the man who perpetrated it had already, for eleven long years, lorded over his people … This man has furthermore never been sincere, loyal, honest or chivalrous for a single minute of his public life … I know many details of the way in which these crimes were carried out, from the lips of some of the soldiers who, filled with shame, told me of the scenes they had witnessed.

When the fighting was over, the soldiers descended like savage beasts on Santiago de Cuba and they took the fury of their frustrations out against the defenceless population …

In every society there are men of base instincts. The sadists, brutes, conveyors of all the ancestral atavisms go about in the guise of human beings, but they are monsters, only more or less restrained by discipline and social habit. If they are offered a drink from a river of blood, they will not be

[1] Batista effectively seized control of Cuba during the 'Sergeants' Revolt' of September 1933. The following month, his men attacked the National Hotel in Havana. Fourteen officers were killed and 17 injured; the remainder were taken prisoner.

[2] One of the fortifications defending Havana's harbour, where Batista crushed a rising led by the peasant guerrilla Juan Blas Hernández in November 1933. Hernández was summarily executed after surrendering.

satisfied until they drink the river dry. All these men needed was the order. At their hands the best and noblest Cubans perished: the most valiant, the most honest, the most idealistic. The tyrant called them mercenaries. There they were, dying as heroes at the hands of men who collect a salary from the republic and who, with the arms the republic gave them to defend her, serve the interests of a clique and murder her best citizens.

Throughout their torturing of our comrades, the army offered them the chance to save their lives by betraying their ideology and falsely declaring that Prío[3] had given them money. When they indignantly rejected that proposition, the army continued with its horrible tortures. They crushed their testicles and they tore out their eyes. But no-one yielded. No complaint was heard nor a favour asked. Even when they had been deprived of their virile organs, our men were still a thousand times more men than all their tormentors together. Photographs, which do not lie, show the bodies torn to pieces …

In the early morning hours, groups of our men were removed from the barracks and taken in automobiles to Siboney, La Maya, Songo and elsewhere. Then they were led out – tied, gagged, already disfigured by the torture – and were murdered in isolated spots. They are recorded as having died in combat against the army. This went on for several days, and few of the captured prisoners survived. Many were compelled to dig their own graves … Others were even buried alive, their hands tied behind their backs …

Honourable Judges: a great deal of what I have just related you already know, from the testimony of many of my comrades. But please note that many key witnesses have been barred from this trial … For my dead comrades, I claim no vengeance. Since their lives were priceless, the murderers could not pay for them, even with their own lives. It is not by blood that we may redeem the lives of those who died for their country. The happiness of their people is the only tribute worthy of them. What is more, my comrades are neither dead nor forgotten; they live today, more than ever, and their murderers will view with dismay the victorious spirit of their ideas rise from their corpses …

Since this trial may, as you said, be the most important trial since we achieved our national sovereignty, what I say here will perhaps be lost in the silence which the dictatorship has tried to impose on me, but posterity will often turn its eyes to what you do here. Remember that today you are judging an accused man, but that you yourselves will be judged not once, but many times, as often as these days are submitted to scrutiny in the future. What I say here will be then repeated many times, not because it comes from my lips, but because the problem of justice is eternal …

Honourable Judges: I am a humble citizen who one day demanded in vain that the Courts punish the power-hungry men who had violated the law and torn our institutions to shreds. Now that it is I who am accused for attempting to overthrow this illegal regime and to restore the legitimate constitution of the republic, I am held incommunicado for 76 days and denied the right to speak to anyone … I am transferred to this hospital to be tried secretly with the greatest severity; and the prosecutor with the Code in his hand solemnly demands that I be sentenced to 26 years in prison …

The right of rebellion against tyranny, Honourable Judges, has been recognized from the most ancient times to the present day by men of all creeds, ideas and doctrines.

[3] Carlos Prío (1903–77) was President of Cuba 1948–52, ousted by Batista. He subsequently lived in exile in Florida, where he died of gunshot wounds when about to give evidence to the US House Committee on Assassinations.

It was so in the theocratic monarchies of remote antiquity. In China it was almost a constitutional principle that when a king governed rudely and despotically he should be deposed and replaced by a virtuous prince. The philosophers of ancient India upheld the principle of active resistance to arbitrary authority. They justified revolution and very often put their theories into practice … The city states of Greece and Rome not only admitted, but defended the meting out of violent death to tyrants.

In the Middle Ages, John Salisbury[4] in his *Book of the Statesman* says that when a prince does not govern according to law and degenerates into a tyrant, violent overthrow is legitimate and justifiable. St Thomas Aquinas,[5] in the *Summa Theologica*, rejects the doctrine of tyrannicide, and yet upholds the thesis that tyrants should be overthrown by the people. MARTIN LUTHER proclaimed that when a government degenerates into a tyranny that violates the laws, its subjects are released from their obligations to obey … Calvin,[6] the outstanding thinker of the Reformation, postulates that people are entitled to take up arms to oppose any usurpation.

No less a man that Juan Mariana,[7] a Spanish Jesuit during the reign of Philip II, asserts in his book, *De Rege et Regis Institutione*, that when a governor usurps power or governs in a tyrannical manner, it is licit for a private citizen to exercise tyrannicide … The French writer, François Hotman,[8] maintained that between the government and its subjects there is a bond or contract, and that the people may rise in rebellion against the tyranny of government when the latter violates that pact …

The Scottish reformers John Knox[9] and John Poynet[10] upheld the same points of view. And, in the most important book of that movement, George Buchanan[11] stated that if a government achieved power without taking into account the consent of the people, or if a government rules their destiny in an unjust or arbitrary fashion, then that government becomes a tyranny and can be divested of power; or, in a final recourse, its leaders can be put to death.

John Althus,[12] a German jurist of the early 17th century, stated in his *Treatise on Politics* that sovereignty as the supreme authority of the state is born from the voluntary concourse of all its members; that governmental authority stems from the people and that its unjust, illegal or tyrannical function exempts them from the duty of obedience and justifies rebellion …

It is well known that in England during the 17th century two kings, CHARLES I and James II,[13] were dethroned for despotism. These actions coincided with the birth of liberal political philosophy and provided the ideological base for a new social class, which was then struggling to break the bonds of feudalism.

Against divine-right autocracies, this new philosophy upheld the principle of the social contract and of the consent of the governed, and constituted the foundation of the English Revolution of 1688,[14] the American Revolution of 1775 and the French Revolution of 1789. These great revolutionary events ushered in the liberation of the Spanish colonies in the New World – the final link in that chain being broken by Cuba.

The new philosophy nurtured our own political ideas and helped us to evolve our constitutions … The right of insurrection against tyranny then underwent its final consecration and became a fundamental tenet of political liberty.

As far back as 1649, John Milton[15] wrote that political power lies with the

---

[4] The English churchman, diplomat and philosopher John of Salisbury (c. 1115–80) is best known for his seminal political treatise *Policraticus* or *Book of the Statesman*, published in 1159.

[5] The Italian philosopher and theologian St Thomas Aquinas (c. 1225–74) was the leading religious writer of his time. The *Summa Theologica* (1265–72), his most important work, mainly concerns the theory and practice of Christian faith, but touches on issues of politics and governance.

[6] The French theologian John Calvin (1509–64).

[7] The Spanish Jesuit writer Juan Mariana (1536–1624) is best known for his incendiary work *De Rege et Regis Institutione* (1599), which called for the execution of despots.

[8] The French jurist François Hotman (1524–90) wrote several controversial works on political and religious themes, including *Franco-gallia* (1573), in which he denounced the absolute power of the French monarchy.

[9] The Scottish churchman John Knox (c. 1513–72) led the Presbyterian reform of the Church of Scotland and maintained a bullish stance towards the Catholic Mary Queen of Scots.

[10] The English churchman John Poynet (c. 1514–56) became Bishop of Winchester. In 1556, he published *A Short Treatise of Political Power*, which affirmed the right of citizens to oppose unjust secular power.

[11] The Scottish historian and poet George Buchanan (1506–82) was a leading member of the early Protestant movement but also tutor to the Catholic Mary Queen of Scots. His book *De Jure Regni apud Scotos* ('The Powers of the Crown of Scotland', 1579) asserts that political power resides with the people rather than the ruler, and that tyrants can be lawfully overthrown.

[12] The German legal philosopher John Althus (1557–1638) was a specialist in Roman law.

[13] The British monarch James II of England and VII of Scotland (1633–1701) was deposed in 1688 because his pursuit of pro-Catholic policies alienated his staunchly Protestant kingdoms.

[14] The 'Glorious Revolution', in which William of Orange deposed James II and VII to become joint monarch of England, Scotland and Ireland with his wife Mary, James's elder daughter.

[15] The English poet John Milton (1608–74) is best known for his epic poem *Paradise Lost* (1667), which contains a strong theme of tyranny and liberty. He also wrote on political philosophy, including *A Treatise of Civil Power* (1659). His works were consulted during the drafting of the US Constitution.

[16] The English philosopher John Locke (1632–1704) developed a theory of social contract between citizen and state, including the principle of 'government with the consent of the governed', and became a major influence on modern democracy. He wrote two *Treatises on Government* around 1679–82 and published them in 1690.
[17] The French philosopher and writer Jean-Jacques Rousseau (1712–78) is best known for *The Social Contract* (1762), advocating a collectivist society. A key influence on French revolutionary thinking, it contains the famous phrase '*Liberté, égalité, fraternité*', adopted as a slogan during the Revolution of 1789.

people, who can enthrone and dethrone kings and have the duty of overthrowing tyrants. John Locke,[16] in his essay on government, maintained that when the natural rights of man are violated, the people have the right and the duty to alter or abolish the government. 'The only remedy against unauthorized force is opposition to it by force.'

Jean-Jacques Rousseau[17] said with great eloquence in his *Social Contract*: 'While a people sees itself forced to obey and obeys, it does well; but as soon as it can shake off the yoke and shakes it off, it does better, recovering its liberty through the use of the very right that has been taken away from it.' …

Thomas Paine[18] said that 'one just man deserves more respect than a rogue with a crown' … The famous French *Declaration of the Rights of Man*[19] willed this principle to the coming generations: 'When the government violates the rights of the people, insurrection is for them the most sacred of rights and the most imperative of duties.' 'When a person seizes sovereignty, he should be condemned to death by free men.'

I believe I have sufficiently justified my point of view … All these reasons support men who struggle for the freedom and happiness of the people. None support those who oppress the people, revile them, and rob them heartlessly …

Still there is one argument more powerful than all the others. We are Cubans and to be Cuban implies a duty; not to fulfil that duty is a crime, is treason. We are proud of the history of our country; we learned it in school and have grown up hearing of freedom, justice and human rights … We were taught that the Titan[20] once said that liberty is not begged for but won with the blade of a machete. We were taught that for the guidance of Cuba's free citizens, the Apostle[21] wrote in his book *The Golden Age*: 'The man who abides by unjust laws and permits any man to trample and mistreat the country in which he was born is not an honourable man …'

… … We were taught that 10 October[22] and 24 February[23] are glorious anniversaries of national rejoicing, because they mark days on which Cubans rebelled against the yoke of infamous tyranny. We were taught to cherish and defend the beloved flag of the lone star, and to sing every afternoon the verses of our National Anthem: 'To live in chains is to live in disgrace and in opprobrium,' and 'To die for one's homeland is to live forever!'.

All this we learned and will never forget, even though today in our land there is murder and prison for the men who practise the ideas taught to them since the cradle. We were born in a free country that our parents bequeathed to us, and the island will first sink into the sea before we consent to be the slaves of anyone.

It seemed that the Apostle would die during his centennial.[24] It seemed that his memory would be extinguished forever. So great was the affront! But he is alive; he has not died. His people are rebellious. His people are worthy. His people are faithful to his memory …

I come to the close of my defence plea but I will not end it as lawyers usually do, asking that the accused be freed. I cannot ask freedom for myself while my comrades are already suffering in the ignominious prison of the Isle of Pines. Send me there to join them and to share their fate. It is understandable that honest men should be dead or in prison in a republic where the President is a criminal and a thief.

To you, Honourable Judges, my sincere gratitude for having allowed me to express myself, free from contemptible restrictions. I hold no bitterness

[21] The revolutionary journalist and poet José Martí (1853–95) was a figurehead of the Cuban independence movement. He was one of the leaders of the Second War of Independence which ended centuries of Spanish rule, but was killed during his first battle. He is often called the Apostle of Cuban Independence, and is ubiquitous in statuary and portraiture.
[22] The First War of Independence began on 10 October 1868.
[23] The Second War of Independence began on 24 February 1895.
[24] In 1953, Cuba held no major celebrations of the centenary of Martí's birth.

[18] The English philosopher Thomas Paine (1737–1809) wrote the pamphlet 'Common Sense' (1776), advocating American independence, and the book *The Rights of Man* (1791), which supported the French Revolution and proposed abolition of the British monarchy.
[19] On 26 August 1789, the National Assembly of France ratified a 17-article *Declaration of the Rights of Man and the Citizen*, asserting democratic and republican principles. Based on the constitutions of the US states of New Hampshire and Virginia, it was also influenced by Locke, Rousseau and the French author Voltaire (1694–1778).
[20] The guerilla leader Antonio Maceo (1848–96) was a key figure in Cuba's struggle for independence, known as the 'Titan of Bronze'.

towards you; I recognize that in certain aspects you have been humane ... Still, a more serious problem remains for the court of appeals: the indictments arising from the murders of 70 men – that is to say, the greatest massacre we have ever known. The guilty continue at liberty and with weapons in their hands – weapons which continually threaten the lives of all citizens. If all the weight of the law does not fall upon the guilty because of cowardice, or because of domination of the courts, and if then all the judges do not resign, I pity your honour. And I regret the unprecedented shame that will fall upon the judicial power.

I know that imprisonment will be harder for me than it has ever been for anyone, filled with cowardly threats and hideous cruelty. But I do not fear prison, as I do not fear the fury of the miserable tyrant who took the lives of 70 of my comrades. Condemn me. It does not matter. History will absolve me.

'Never has a people had such sacred things to defend'

1 May 2003, Havana, Cuba

Plaza de la Revolución is a large, rather shabby civic square in the Cuban capital, dominated by monuments to two of the country's national figureheads. In one corner, a vast likeness of CHE GUEVARA in wrought steel glowers down from the side of a building; but the plaza's focal point is a star-shaped white tower dedicated to José Martí, who died liberating his country from Spanish rule in 1895. At the foot of the Martí Memorial is a dais, from which Castro addresses the annual May Day parade.

By 2003, Castro had controlled Cuba as a one-party state for well over four decades, and had developed an oratorical style chiefly notable for its verbosity. Spirited as they are, his addresses can resemble the kind of rosy inventory of grain yields and iron production favoured by long-serving Communist leaders such as JOSEPH STALIN and Mao Zedong.

Most Cubans are highly patriotic, and support for the government remains strong, but the economy has rarely flourished since the US trade embargo imposed following Castro's coup. Cuba is still recovering from the crisis of the early 1990s, caused by the collapse of its main trading partner the Soviet Union. Illiteracy is rare thanks to the much-vaunted education system, and free health care is available to all; but medicines are scarce, prices are high, and infrastructure is crumbling.

Self-congratulatory as it is, this speech is leavened by Castro's lively defiance towards US president GEORGE W BUSH. Never an ally of Communism, Bush was at the time wooing the large (anti-Castro) Cuban community of Florida, ahead of the 2004 elections. Shortly after this speech, Bush spoke of 'driving Cuba into democracy'. Castro did not attempt reconciliation. 'Bush couldn't debate a Cuban ninth-grader,' he retorted.

Distinguished guests, dear fellow Cubans: our heroic people have struggled for 44 years from this small Caribbean island just a few miles away from the most formidable imperial power ever known by mankind. In so doing, they have written an unprecedented chapter in history. Never has the world witnessed such an unequal fight.

Some may have believed that the rise of the empire to the status of the sole superpower, with a military and technological might with no balancing pole anywhere in the world, would frighten or dishearten the Cuban people. Yet today they have no choice but to watch in amazement the enhanced courage of this valiant people. On a day like today, this glorious international workers' day ... I declare, on behalf of the one million Cubans gathered here, that we will face up to any threats, we will not yield to any pressures, and that we are prepared to defend our homeland and our Revolution with ideas and with weapons to our last drop of blood.

What is Cuba's sin? What honest person has any reason to attack her? With their own blood and the weapons seized from the enemy, the

Cuban people overthrew a cruel tyranny with 80,000 men under arms, imposed by the US government.

Cuba was the first territory free from imperialist domination in Latin America and the Caribbean, and the only country in the hemisphere, throughout post-colonial history, where the torturers, murderers and war criminals that took the lives of tens of thousands of people were exemplarily punished.

All of the country's land was recovered and turned over to the peasants and agricultural workers. The natural resources, industries and basic services were placed in the hands of their only true owner: the Cuban nation.

In less than 72 hours, fighting ceaselessly, day and night, Cuba crushed the Bay of Pigs mercenary invasion organized by a US administration, thereby preventing a war of incalculable consequences[1] … In 1962, Cuba confronted with honour, and without a single concession, the risk of being attacked with dozens of nuclear weapons.[2]

It defeated the dirty war that spread throughout the entire country, at a cost in human lives even greater than that of the war of liberation. It stoically endured thousands of acts of sabotage and terrorist attacks organized by the US government. It thwarted hundreds of assassination plots against the leaders of the Revolution.[3]

While under a rigorous blockade and economic warfare that have lasted for almost half a century,[4] Cuba was able to eradicate in just one year the illiteracy that has still not been overcome in the course of more than four decades by the rest of the countries of Latin America, or the United States itself. It has brought free education to 100 per cent of the country's children … Its elementary school students rank first worldwide in the knowledge of their mother language and mathematics. The country also ranks first worldwide with the highest number of teachers per capita and the lowest number of students per classroom …

Today, the country has 30 university graduates, intellectuals and professional artists for every one there was before the Revolution. The average Cuban citizen today has at the very least a ninth-grade level of education. Not even functional illiteracy exists in Cuba …

University campuses are progressively spreading to all of the country's municipalities. Never in any other part of the world has such a colossal educational and cultural revolution taken place as this that will turn Cuba, by far, into the country with the highest degree of knowledge and culture in the world, faithful to Martí's profound conviction that 'no freedom is possible without culture'.

Infant mortality has been reduced from 60 per 1,000 live births to a rate that fluctuates between 6 and 6.5, which is the lowest in the hemisphere, from the United States to Patagonia. Life expectancy has increased by 15 years …

Today, in our country, people die of the same causes as in the most highly developed countries: cardiovascular diseases, cancer, accidents, and others, but with a much lower incidence …

Cuba is today the country with the highest number of doctors per capita in the world, with almost twice as many as those that follow closer. Our scientific centres are working relentlessly to find preventive or therapeutic solutions for the most serious diseases. Cubans will have the best healthcare system in the world, and will continue to receive all services absolutely free of charge.

[1] In April 1961, a group of Cuban expatriates – funded by the CIA with the approval of US President JOHN F KENNEDY – attempted to invade Cuba and topple Castro. The operation ended in fiasco and rapid defeat at the Bay of Pigs.

[2] The Cuban Missile Crisis was a diplomatic confrontation between the USA and the USSR, widely seen as the Cold War's closest brush with nuclear conflict. Soviet plans to site nuclear missiles in Cuba, within range of the USA, were eventually abandoned in return for the removal of US missiles from Turkish soil close to the borders of the USSR.

[3] The CIA sponsored repeated attempts on Castro's life, most farcically with an exploding cigar.

[4] US trade sanctions were first imposed in August 1960 and remain in place, constituting the most enduring trade embargo in modern history.

Social security covers 100 per cent of the country's citizens. In Cuba, 85 per cent of the people own their homes and they pay no property taxes on them whatsoever. The remaining 15 per cent pay a wholly symbolic rent, which is only 10 per cent of their salary.

Illegal drug use involves a negligible percentage of the population, and is being resolutely combated. Lottery and other forms of gambling have been banned since the first years of the Revolution to ensure that no-one pins their hopes of progress on luck.

There is no commercial advertising on Cuban television and radio or in our printed publications. Instead, these feature public service announcements … Our media educate, they do not poison or alienate. They do not worship or exalt the values of decadent consumer societies.

Discrimination against women was eradicated, and today women make up 64 per cent of the country's technical and scientific workforce.

From the earliest months of the Revolution, not a single one of the forms of racial discrimination copied from the south of the United States was left intact. In recent years, the Revolution has been particularly striving to eliminate any lingering traces of the poverty and lack of access to education that afflicted the descendants of those who were enslaved for centuries … Soon, not even a shadow of the consequences of that terrible injustice will remain.

There is no cult of personality around any living revolutionary, in the form of statues, official photographs, or the names of streets or institutions. The leaders of this country are human beings, not gods.

In our country there are no paramilitary forces or death squads, nor has violence ever been used against the people. There are no executions without due process and no torture. The people have always supported the activities of the Revolution. This rally today is proof of that …

We cultivate brotherhood and solidarity among individuals and peoples both in the country and abroad. The new generations and the entire people are being educated about the need to protect the environment. The media are used to build environmental awareness.

Our country steadfastly defends its cultural identity, assimilating the best of other cultures while resolutely combating everything that distorts, alienates and degrades. The development of wholesome, non-professional sports has raised our people to the highest ranks worldwide in medals and honours.

Scientific research, at the service of our people and all humanity, has increased several-hundredfold. As a result of these efforts, important medications are saving lives in Cuba and other countries. Cuba has never undertaken research or development of a single biological weapon, because this would be in total contradiction with the principles and philosophy underlying the education of our scientific personnel, past and present.

In no other people has the spirit of international solidarity become so deeply rooted … Over 2,000 heroic Cuban internationalist combatants gave their lives fulfilling the sacred duty of supporting the liberation struggles for the independence of other sister nations. However, there is not one single Cuban property in any of those countries. No other country in our era has exhibited such sincere and selfless solidarity.

Cuba has always preached by example … It has never betrayed its principles. There must be some reason why, just 48 hours ago, it was re-elected by acclamation in the United Nations Economic and Social Council to another three years on the Commission on Human Rights, of which it has now been a member for 15 years.

More than half a million Cubans have carried out internationalist missions as combatants, as teachers, as technicians or as doctors and healthcare workers. Tens of thousands of the latter have provided their services and saved millions of lives over the course of more than 40 years … Through preventive and therapeutic methods they save hundreds of thousands of lives every year, and maintain or restore the health of millions of people, without charging a penny for their services …

After the demise of the USSR and the socialist bloc, nobody would have bet a dime on the survival of the Cuban Revolution. The United States tightened the blockade … We abruptly lost our main markets and supplies sources. The population's average calorie and protein consumption was reduced by almost half. But our country withstood the pressures and even advanced considerably in the social field.

Today, it has largely recovered with regard to nutritional requirements and is rapidly progressing in other fields … Why have we endured? Because the Revolution has always had, as it still does and always will to an ever-greater degree, the support of the people, an intelligent people,   - increasingly united, educated and combative.

Cuba was the first country to extend its solidarity to the people of the United States on September 11, 2001. It was also the first to warn of the neo-fascist nature of the policy that the extreme right in the United States, which fraudulently came to power in November of 2000, was planning to impose on the rest of the world. This policy did not emerge as a response to the atrocious terrorist attack perpetrated against the people of the United States … It was coldly and carefully conceived and developed, which explains the country's military build-up and enormous spending on weapons at a time when the Cold War was already over, and long before September 11, 2001. The fateful events of that day served as an ideal pretext for the implementation of such policy …

In Miami and Washington they are now discussing where, how and when Cuba will be attacked or the problem of the Revolution will be solved.

For the moment, there is talk of economic measures that will further intensify the brutal blockade, but they still do not know which to choose, who they will resign themselves to alienating, and how effective these measures may be. There are very few left for them to choose from. They have already used up almost all of them …

What methods are they considering? Physically eliminating me with the sophisticated modern means they have developed, as Mr Bush promised them in Texas before the elections? Or attacking Cuba the way they attacked Iraq? If it were the former, it does not worry me in the least. The ideas for which I have fought all my life will not die, and they will live on for a long time.

If the [US's] solution were to attack Cuba like Iraq, I would suffer greatly because of the cost in lives and the enormous destruction it would bring on Cuba. But it might turn out to be the last of this administration's fascist attacks, because the struggle would last a very long time.

The aggressors would not merely be facing an army, but rather thousands of armies that would constantly reproduce themselves – and make the enemy pay such a high cost in casualties that it would far exceed the cost in lives of its sons and daughters that the American people would be willing to pay for the adventures and ideas of President Bush. Today, he enjoys majority support, but it is dropping, and tomorrow it could be reduced to zero.

The American people, the millions of highly cultivated individuals who reason and think, their basic ethical principles, the tens of millions of computers with which to communicate … will show that you cannot fool all of the people, and perhaps not even part of the people, all of the time. One day they will put a straitjacket on those who need it before they manage to annihilate life on the planet.

On behalf of the one million people gathered here this May Day, I want to convey a message to the world and the American people. We do not want the blood of Cubans and Americans to be shed in a war. We do not want a countless number of lives of people who could be friends to be lost in an armed conflict. But never has a people had such sacred things to defend, or such profound convictions to fight for, to such a degree that they would rather be obliterated from the face of the earth than abandon the noble and generous work for which so many generations of Cubans have paid the high cost of the lives of many of their finest sons and daughters.

We are sustained by the deepest conviction that ideas are worth more than weapons, no matter how sophisticated and powerful those weapons may be.

Let us say, like CHÉ GUEVARA when he bade us farewell:[5] ever onward to victory!

[5] Differences emerged between Castro and his idealistic lieutenant in the mid-1960s. On deciding to leave Cuba in 1965, Guevara wrote a frank private letter to Castro, which Castro made public, further alienating his old ally.

Neville Chamberlain
English statesman

Arthur Neville Chamberlain (1869–1940) was born in Birmingham, the son of the English statesman Joseph Chamberlain by his second marriage. He was educated at Rugby and Birmingham University. He was Lord Mayor of Birmingham (1915–16) and a Conservative MP from 1918. He was Chancellor of the Exchequer (1923–4 and 1931–7), Minister for Health (1924–9) and became prime minister in 1937. For the sake of peace, and with the country unprepared for war, he chose initially to follow a policy of appeasing Italy and Germany. In September 1938, he signed the Munich Agreement with German Chancellor ADOLF HITLER, Italian prime minister BENITO MUSSOLINI and French prime minister Edouard Daladier, afterwards claiming to have found 'peace in our time'. Having meanwhile pressed on with rearmament, he declared war in 1939. Criticism of his war leadership accompanied initial military reverses, and in 1940 he yielded the premiership to WINSTON CHURCHILL. He died six months later. Subsequent re-evaluations of Chamberlain's career have shown his policy of appeasement in a more favourable light.

'We have no quarrel with the German people'
1 September 1939, London, England

The slaughter of a generation of young men in World War I had made a profound impression on British public opinion. In early 1933, just after Hitler became Germany's Chancellor, the Oxford Union supported the motion 'this House will in no circumstances fight for its king and its country', and the people's mood of antipathy toward war underlay Chamberlain's policy of appeasement.

No action was taken by Britain when, in March 1938, German troops entered Austria and claimed it for Germany. The Munich Agreement allowed for Germany's military occupation of the Sudetenland (part of Czechoslovakia) and a guarantee of Czechoslovakia's remaining frontiers. But although Chamberlain's claim that the Agreement had brought 'peace with honour', Czechoslovakia was dismembered over the following months, and Hitler made a triumphal entry into Prague on 15 March 1939.

Following increasing German pressure, Chamberlain warned Hitler that Britain would stand by Poland, but by now Hitler showed little interest in peace negotiations. On the night of 31 August, the Nazis staged a fake attack on a German radio outpost along the German–Polish border – forcing concentration camp prisoners to masquerade as Polish soldiers – and used it as a pretext for invasion.

In this speech to the House of Commons, given a few hours later, Chamberlain explains to the British public that while every possible measure had been taken to avert war, it was now probably inevitable. This was of course the case.

[1] Chamberlain refers to his response to the German annexation of Austria.

I do not propose to say many words tonight. The time has come when action rather than speech is required. Eighteen months ago, in this House, I prayed that the responsibility might not fall upon me to ask this country to accept the awful arbitrament of war.[1] I fear that I may not be able to avoid that responsibility. But, at any rate, I cannot wish for conditions in which such a burden should fall upon me in which I should feel clearer than I do today as to where my duty lies. No man can say that the government could have done more to try to keep open the way for an honourable and equitable settlement of the dispute between Germany and Poland.

Nor have we neglected any means of making it crystal clear to the German government that if they insisted on using force again in the manner in which they had used it in the past, we were resolved to oppose them by force. Now that all the relevant documents are being made public, we shall stand at the bar of history knowing that the responsibility for this terrible catastrophe lies on the shoulders of one man – the German Chancellor, who has not hesitated to plunge the world into misery in order to serve his own senseless ambitions.

I would like to thank the House for the forbearance which they have shown on two recent occasions, for not demanding from me information which they recognized I could not give while these negotiations were still in progress. I have now had all the correspondence with the German government put into the form of a White Paper[2] ...

I do not think it necessary for me to refer in detail now to these documents, which are already past history. They make it perfectly clear that our object has been to try and bring about discussions of the Polish – German dispute between the two countries themselves on terms of equality, the settlement to be one which safeguards the independence of Poland and of which the due observance would be secured by international guarantees. There is just one passage from a recent communication, which is dated 30 August, which I should like to quote, because it shows how easily the final clash might have been avoided had there been the least desire on the part of the German government to arrive at a peaceful settlement. In this document we said:

> 'His Majesty's government fully recognize the need for speed in the initiation of discussions and they share the apprehensions of the Chancellor arising from the proximity of two mobilized armies standing face to face. They would accordingly most strongly urge that both parties should undertake that during the negotiations no aggressive military movements should take place. His Majesty's government feel confident that they could obtain such an undertaking from the Polish government if the German government would give similar assurances.'

That telegram, which was repeated in Poland, brought an instantaneous reply from the Polish Government, dated 31 August, in which they said:

> 'The Polish government are also prepared on a reciprocal basis to give a formal guarantee in the event of negotiations taking place that Polish troops will not violate the frontiers of the German Reich, provided a corresponding guarantee is given regarding the non-violation of the frontiers of Poland by troops of the German Reich.'

We never had a reply from the German government to that suggestion, one which, if it had been followed, might have saved the catastrophe which took place this morning. In the German broadcast last night, which recited the 16 points of the proposals which they have put forward, there occurred this sentence: 'In these circumstances the Reich government considers its proposals rejected.'

I must examine that statement. I must tell the House what are the circumstances. To begin with, let me say that the text of these proposals has never been communicated by Germany to Poland at all. The history of the matter is this. On Tuesday 29 August, in replying to a note which we had sent to them, the German government said, among other things, that they would immediately draw up proposals for a solution acceptable to themselves and '... will, if possible, place these at the disposal of the British government before the arrival of the Polish negotiator.'

It will be seen by examination of the White Paper that the German government had stated that they counted upon the arrival of a plenipotentiary from Poland in Berlin ... on the following day. In the meantime, of course, we were awaiting these proposals. The next evening, when our ambassador saw Herr von Ribbentrop, the German Foreign

[2] A policy statement issued by a British government for discussion in Parliament, which signifies its intention to take legislative action.

140

Secretary, he urged … that when these proposals were ready – for we had heard no more about them – he should invite the Polish ambassador to call and should hand him the proposals for transmission to his government. Thereupon, reports our ambassador, in the most violent terms Herr von Ribbentrop said he would never ask the ambassador to visit him. He hinted that if the Polish ambassador asked him for an interview it might be different.

The House will see that this was on Wednesday night, which according to the German statement of last night, is now claimed to be the final date after which no negotiation with Poland was acceptable. It is plain, therefore, that Germany claims to treat Poland as in the wrong because she had not by Wednesday night entered upon discussions with Germany about a set of proposals of which she had never heard.

Now what of ourselves? On that Wednesday night, at the interview to which I have just referred, Herr von Ribbentrop produced a lengthy document which he read out in German, at top speed. Naturally, after this reading our ambassador asked for a copy of the document, but the reply was that it was now too late, as the Polish representative had not arrived in Berlin by midnight. And so, Sir, we never got a copy of those proposals, and the first time we heard them – *we* heard them – was on the broadcast last night.

Well, Sir, those are the circumstances in which the German government said that they would consider that their negotiations were rejected. Is it not clear that their conception of a negotiation was that on almost instantaneous demand a Polish plenipotentiary should go to Berlin – where others had been before him – and should there receive a statement of demands to be accepted in their entirety or refused?

I am not pronouncing any opinion upon the terms themselves, for I do not feel called upon to do so. The proper course, in our view – in the view of all of us – was that these proposals should have been put before the Poles, who should have been given time to consider them and to say whether, in their opinion, they did or did not infringe those vital interests of Poland which Germany had assured us on a previous occasion she intended to respect.

Only last night the Polish ambassador did see the German Foreign Secretary, Herr von Ribbentrop. Once again he expressed to him what, indeed, the Polish government had already said publicly, that they were willing to negotiate with Germany about their disputes on an equal basis. What was the reply of the German government? The reply was that without another word the German troops crossed the Polish frontier this morning at dawn and are since reported to be bombing open towns.

In these circumstances there is only one course open to us. His Majesty's ambassador in Berlin and the French ambassador have been instructed to hand to the German government the following document:

'… It appears to the governments of the United Kingdom and France that by their action the German government have created conditions, namely, an aggressive act of force against Poland threatening the independence of Poland, which call for the implementation by the governments of the United Kingdom and France of the undertaking to Poland to come to her assistance. I am accordingly to inform your Excellency that unless the German government are prepared to give His Majesty's government satisfactory assurances that the German government have suspended all aggressive action against Poland and are prepared promptly to withdraw their forces from Polish territory, His Majesty's government in the United Kingdom will without hesitation fulfil their obligations to Poland.'

If a reply to this last warning is unfavourable – and I do not suggest that it is likely to be otherwise – His Majesty's ambassador is instructed to ask for his passports.

In that case we are ready. Yesterday, we took further steps towards the completion of our defensive preparation. This morning we ordered complete mobilization of the whole of the Royal Navy, Army and Royal Air Force. We have also taken a number of other measures, both at home and abroad, which the House will not perhaps expect me to specify in detail. Briefly, they represent the final steps in accordance with pre-arranged plans. These last can be put into force rapidly, and are of such a nature that they can be deferred until war seems inevitable …

The thoughts of many of us must at this moment inevitably be turning back to 1914, and to a comparison of our position now with that which existed then. How do we stand this time? The answer is that all three Services are ready, and that the situation in all directions is far more favourable and reassuring than in 1914, while behind the fighting Services we have built up a vast organization of Civil Defence under our scheme of Air Raid Precautions.

As regards the immediate manpower requirements, the Royal Navy, the Army and the Air Force are in the fortunate position of having almost as many men as they can conveniently handle at this moment. There are, however, certain categories of service in which men are immediately required, both for military and civil defence. These will be announced in detail through the press and the BBC. The main and most satisfactory point to observe is that there is today no need to make an appeal in a general way for recruits such as was issued by Lord Kitchener 25 years ago.[3] That appeal has been anticipated by many months, and the men are already available.

So much for the immediate present. Now we must look to the future. It is essential in the face of the tremendous task which confronts us, more especially in view of our past experiences in this matter, to organize our manpower this time upon as methodical, equitable and economical a basis as possible. We therefore propose immediately to introduce legislation directed to that end.

A bill will be laid before you which for all practical purposes will amount to an expansion of the Military Training Act. Under its operation, all fit men between the ages of 18 and 41 will be rendered liable to military service if and when called upon. It is not intended at the outset that any considerable number of men other than those already liable shall be called up, and steps will be taken to ensure that the manpower essentially required by industry shall not be taken away.

There is one other allusion which I should like to make before I end my speech, and that is to record the satisfaction of His Majesty's government, that throughout these last days of crisis Signor Mussolini also has been doing his best to reach a solution.

It now only remains for us to set our teeth and to enter upon this struggle, which we ourselves earnestly endeavoured to avoid, with determination to see it through to the end. We shall enter it with a clear

[3] The English soldier and politician Horatio Herbert Kitchener, 1st Earl Kitchener (1850–1916), launched a military recruitment drive at the start of World War I in 1914, his image appearing on posters alongside the famous slogan 'Your Country Needs You'.

conscience … and the moral approval of the greater part of the world. We have no quarrel with the German people, except that they allow themselves to be governed by a Nazi government. As long as that government exists and pursues the methods it has so persistently followed during the last two years, there will be no peace in Europe. We shall merely pass from one crisis to another, and see one country after another attacked by methods which have now become familiar to us in their sickening technique. We are resolved that these methods must come to an end. If out of the struggle we again re-establish in the world the rules of good faith and the renunciation of force, why then even the sacrifices that will be entailed upon us will find their fullest justification.

❧

'This country is now at war with Germany'
3 September 1939, radio broadcast from London, England
❧

ADOLF HITLER had agreed a ten-year non-aggression pact with Poland in 1934, but early in 1939 he began laying claim to the 'Polish Corridor', which divided Germany from the Baltic and included the port of Gdánsk (known as Danzig to the Germans). Poland rejected this territorial claim and received guarantees of support from France and Britain. By early April, Hitler had formulated a plan for the invasion of Poland, and at the end of the month he renounced the Polish–German non-aggression pact. Meanwhile, diplomacy continued between Poland, Britain and France, which eventually led to military alliances being expanded and formalized. Chamberlain warned Hitler that Britain would stand by Poland on 23 August, though the treaty was not signed until 25 August. Meanwhile, the Nazis were signing their own alliance with Russia, the Molotov–Ribbentrop Pact, which they would also violate in due course.

When Germany finally invaded Poland on 1 September, the British people had little wish to go to war, but Chamberlain saw there was no alternative. Hitler's expansionist aspirations were now unmistakable, and the policies espoused by his Nazi Party had made Europe increasingly dangerous.

Britain, together with France, was obliged to declare war on Germany. In this famous radio broadcast to the British people, the Prime Minister outlines the events that had made this declaration unavoidable.

❧

This morning, the British ambassador in Berlin handed the German government a final note, stating that unless we heard from them by eleven o'clock that they were prepared at once to withdraw their troops from Poland, a state of war would exist between us. I have to tell you now that no such undertaking has been received and that consequently this country is at war with Germany.

You can imagine what a bitter blow it is to me that all my long struggle to win peace has failed, yet I cannot believe that there is anything more, or anything different, that I could have done and that would have been more successful. Up to the very last, it would have been quite possible to arrange a peaceful and honourable settlement between Germany and Poland, but Hitler would not have it. He had evidently made up his mind to attack Poland whatever happened; and although he now says he put forward reasonable proposals which were rejected by the Poles, that is not a true statement. The proposals were never shown to the Poles, nor to us. And though they were announced in the German broadcast on Thursday night, Hitler did not wait to hear comments on them, but ordered his troops to cross the Polish frontier the next morning.

His action shows convincingly that there is no chance of expecting that this man will ever give up his practice of using force to gain his will. He can only be stopped by force.

We and France are today, in fulfilment of our obligations, going to the aid of Poland, who is so bravely resisting this wicked and unprovoked attack on her people. We have a clear conscience. We have done all that any country could do to establish peace. The situation in which no word given by Germany's ruler could be trusted and no people or country could feel themselves safe has become intolerable. And now that we have resolved to finish it, I know that you will all play your part with calmness and courage.

When I have finished speaking, certain detailed announcements will be made on behalf of the government. Give these your closest attention. The government have made plans under which it will be possible to carry on the work of the nation in the days of stress and strain that may be ahead. But these plans need your help. You may be taking your part in the fighting services, or as a volunteer in one of the branches of civil defence. If so, you will report for duty in accordance with the instructions you have received. You may be engaged in work essential to the prosecution of war or for the maintenance of the life of the people – in factories, in transport, in public utility concerns, or in the supply of other necessaries of life. If so, it is of vital importance that you should carry on with your jobs.

Now may God bless you all. May he defend the right. It is the evil things that we shall be fighting against – brute force, bad faith, injustice, oppression and persecution – and against them I am certain that the right will prevail.

Charles I
King of Great Britain and Ireland

Charles I (1600–49) was born in Dunfermline, the son of JAMES VI AND I. He suffered from childhood frailty, but became a skilled marksman, and a gifted student of theology. He became Prince of Wales in 1616, four years after his brother's death left him heir to the throne. He was betrothed in 1625 to Princess Henrietta Maria of France, with the promise that she would be allowed to practise her religion freely, an arrangement which received a hostile reception from the Puritans. After succeeding his father in 1625, he welcomed his new bride at Dover. Henrietta Maria exercised growing influence, and it was largely at her behest that Charles dissolved three parliaments within the first four years of his reign and then ruled without one for 12 years. With England now at peace with France and Spain, Charles attempted to refresh his dwindling treasury by increasing taxation, and to pull Presbyterian Scotland into line, imposing a common prayer book. Both issues provoked hostility, forcing Charles to recall Parliament in 1640, but it frustrated almost his every action. To divert hostility from Henrietta Maria, he was compelled to approve the Act of Attainment (1641), by which Parliament could not be dissolved without its consent, and to allow the execution of the Earl of Strafford, his loyal Lord Deputy for Ireland, after a secret plan to suppress the King's opponents was exposed. Resentful of the power that Parliament now held, Charles went to Edinburgh in an unsuccessful bid to win over the Scottish lords. In 1642, his arrival in the House of Commons to supervise the arrest of John Pym and four other MPs – prompted by the Queen's fear of impeachment – made the Civil War inevitable. In August 1642 the royal standard was raised at Nottingham and three years of bitter fighting followed. The war was effectively ended by the defeat of Royalist forces at Naseby (June 1645), but Charles spent another year trying to rally support, before finally surrendering to the Scots at Newark in May 1646. He was handed over to Parliament and held near Northampton, where he negotiated a treaty with the Scots and fomented a brief resurgence of civil war. In November 1647 he escaped to the Isle of Wight, but was soon recaptured. He stood trial at Westminster, where his three refusals to plead were interpreted as a silent confession, and he was beheaded at Whitehall in January 1649.

'I go from a corruptible, to an incorruptible crown'
30 January 1649, London, England

Convicted of high treason and 'other high crimes against the realm of England', Charles cannot have hoped for mercy, but during the few days left to him after his death sentence was pronounced, he conducted himself with dignity. When the day of his execution came, he walked calmly from St James's Palace, where he had been held, to the scaffold erected outside the Banqueting Hall in Whitehall.

According to a contemporary account, he 'look'd very earnestly on the Block, and asked Col Hacker if there were no higher'. (Colonel Francis Hacker was the commander of the Ironsides, the parliamentary troops loyal to Cromwell. He had guarded the King during his imprisonment, and was among the first to be arrested and executed when the monarchy was restored in 1660. The executioner himself wore a mask and his identity is still debated.)

Though it was audible to very few members of the large crowd, Charles's final speech did much to gild his reputation after a reign marked by tyranny, including religious persecution and illegally levied taxes. Calm, noble and deferential, Charles declares his innocence, but admits to being subject to judgement by God; he professes his faith and bestows forgiveness on his prosecutors.

But the speech's most notable feature is Charles's description of himself as 'the martyr of the people', a title embraced by those witnesses who leant forward to dip their handkerchiefs in the blood of the freshly decapitated King.

> I shall be very little heard of anybody here. I shall therefore speak a word unto you here; indeed I could hold my peace very well, if I did not think that holding my peace would make some men think that I did submit to the guilt, as well as to the punishment. But I think it is my duty to God first, and then to my country, for to clear myself both as an honest man, and a good king and a good Christian.
>
> I shall begin first with my innocency. In truth I think it not very needful for me to insist long upon this, for all the world knows that I never did begin a war with the two Houses of Parliament, and I call God to witness, to whom I must shortly make my account, that I never did intend for to encroach

upon their privileges. They began upon me; it is the militia they began upon. They contest that the militia was mine, but they thought it fit for to have it from me; and to be short, if anybody will look to the dates of the commissions – of their commissions and mine, and likewise to the declarations – [they] will see clearly that they began these unhappy troubles, not I.

So that as the guilt of these enormous crimes that are laid against me, I hope in God that God will clear me of it, I will not I am in charity; God forbid that I should lay it upon the two Houses of Parliament: there is no necessity of either. I hope they are free of this guilt, for I do believe that ill instruments between them and me has been the chief cause of all this bloodshed; so that by way of speaking, as I find myself clear of this, I hope (and pray God) that they may too.

Yet for all this, God forbid that I should be so ill a Christian, as not to say that God's judgements are just upon me. Many times he does pay justice by an unjust sentence, that is ordinary. I will only say this: that an unjust sentence – that I suffered for to take effect[1] – is punished now, by an unjust sentence upon me. That is, so far I have said, to show you that I am an innocent man.

[1] Charles probably refers to Thomas Wentworth, 1st Earl of Strafford (1593–1641) whose execution he had been compelled to allow.

Now for to show you that I am a good Christian. I hope there is a good man that will bear me witness, that I have forgiven all the world; even those in particular that have been the chief causes of my death. Who they are, God knows, I do not desire to know. I pray God forgive them. But this is not all; my charity must go farther. I wish that they may repent, for indeed they have committed a great sin in that particular. I pray God with St Stephen, that they may take the right way to the peace of the kingdom, for my charity commands me not only to forgive particular men, but my charity commands me to endeavour to the last gasp the peace of the kingdom. So, sirs, I do with all my soul, and I do hope there is some here will carry it further, that they may endeavour the peace of the kingdom.

Now, sirs, I must show you both how you are out of the way, and will put you in a way. First, you are out of the way, for certainly all the way you ever had yet as I could find by any thing, is in the way of conquest. Certainly this is an ill way, for conquest, sir, in my opinion, is never just, except there be a good just cause, either for the matter of wrong or just title; and then if you go beyond it, the first quarrel that you have to it, that makes it unjust at the end, that was just at first …

Now sir, for to put you in the way, believe it you will never do right, nor God will never prosper you, until you give God his due, the King his due (that is, my successor) and the people their due. I am as much for them as any of you. You must give God his due by regulating rightly his church according to his scripture which is now out of order. For to set you in a way particularly now, I cannot, but only this, a national synod freely called, freely debating among themselves, must settle this; when that every opinion is freely and clearly heard.

For the King, indeed I will not …

[*At this point a gentleman touched the axe.*]

Hurt not the axe that may hurt me. For the King: the laws of the land will clearly instruct you for that; therefore, because it concerns my own particular, I only give you a touch of it.

For the people – and truly I desire their liberty and freedom, as much as anybody whomsoever – but I must tell you that their liberty and their freedom consists in having of government, those laws by which their life

146

and their goods may be most their own. It is not for having share in government, sir. That is nothing pertaining to them. A subject and a sovereign are clean different things; and therefore, until they do that – I mean, that you do put the people in that liberty, as I say – certainly they will never enjoy themselves.

Sirs, it was for this that now I am come here. If I would have given way to an arbitrary way, for to have all laws changed according to the power of the sword, I needed not to have come here. And therefore, I tell you, (and I pray God it be not laid to your charge) that I am the martyr of the people.

In truth, sirs, I shall not hold you much longer, for I will only say this to you: that in truth, I could have desired some little time longer, because that I would have put this I have said in a little more order, and a little better digested, than I have done; and therefore I hope you will excuse me.

I have delivered my conscience. I pray God that you do take those courses that are best for the kingdom, and your own salvation.

[*Dr Juxon:*[2] *'Will Your Majesty – though it may be very well known Your Majesty's affections to religion, yet it may be expected that you should – say somewhat to the world's satisfaction?'*]

I thank you very heartily, my lord, for that. I had almost forgotten it. In truth, sirs, my conscience in religion, I think, is very well known to the world; and therefore I declare before you all, that I die a Christian according to the profession of the Church of England, as I found it left me by my father. And this honest man [*pointing to Dr Juxon*] will witness it.

Sirs, excuse me for this same. I have a good cause, and I have a gracious God; I will say no more. I go from a corruptible, to an incorruptible crown; where no disturbance can be, no disturbance in the world.

[2] The English clergyman William Juxon (1582–1663) was Bishop of London, 1633–49. Charles had also appointed him to secular posts, including Lord High Treasurer and First Lord of the Admiralty. He was removed from power after Charles's death, but became Archbishop of Canterbury after the Restoration in 1660.

Charles, Prince of Wales
Heir to the British throne

The Prince of Wales *full name Charles Philip Arthur George Mountbatten-Windsor* (1948–) is the eldest son of Queen ELIZABETH II and Prince Philip, Duke of Edinburgh and heir apparent to the British throne. He was given the title of Prince of Wales in 1958 and invested at Caernarvon in 1969. Educated at Cheam School, Berkshire and Gordonstoun School in Scotland, he spent a term at Geelong Grammar School, Australia (1966), and studied at Trinity College, Cambridge (1967–70). He served in the RAF and Royal Navy (1971–6), and in 1981 married Lady Diana Frances Spencer (1961–97), younger daughter of the 8th Earl Spencer. They announced their separation in 1992 and were divorced in 1996. They had two children: Prince William (1982–), and Prince Harry (1984–). In April 2005, he married Camilla Rosemary Parker Bowles (née Shand). Since leaving the Navy, the Prince has established a unique role for himself. He has founded 14 charities and is president of two others. They are concerned with inner city deprivation, the rural community, disadvantaged young people, education, the arts, health and the environment. He has a farm in Gloucestershire, with which he is directly involved, and is a skilled fisherman, skier, rider and painter. His publications include the children's book *The Old Man of Lochnagar* (1980) and *A Vision of Britain: A Personal View of Architecture* (1989).

'A monstrous carbuncle on the face of a much-loved friend'
30 May 1984, London, England

On the 150th anniversary of the Royal Institute of British Architects (RIBA), a reception was held at Hampton Court Palace. The guest of honour was the Prince of Wales, who had been invited to present the RIBA's annual gold medal. He was required to utter a few congratulatory platitudes. Instead, quite unexpectedly, he launched what became a long-running and heated debate over current trends in British architecture.

The architectural profession and its pundits were outraged, but the Prince's opinions were widely discussed, and architecture gained a higher profile among the British public than it had ever enjoyed before.

There were immediate effects. Peter Ahrends' proposed extension to the National Gallery – the 'monstrous carbuncle' itself – was abandoned. So too was a planned tower at Mansion House Square, alluded to in the speech as 'yet another giant glass stump'.

But if the Prince's aesthetic judgement is controversial, he has been widely praised for demanding greater consultation with tenants and the integration of social and private housing in place of ghettoized estates and tower blocks. His views on urban planning have been cited in government planning guidance.

He continued to campaign, famously remarking in 1987 that when the Luftwaffe bombed British buildings 'it didn't replace them with anything more offensive than rubble'. Results soon became perceptible: for some years, British developers tended to favour more 'traditional' designs; though more recently British architecture has entered a phase of renewed audacity and vigour.

The Prince's interest in architecture has not waned. In 1992, he founded an Institute of Architecture, now The Prince's Foundation for the Built Environment. The following year, construction work began on the urban extension to Dorchester named Poundbury, a pedestrian-orientated community that reflects local character and local tradition. He summarized his credo in February 1999: 'We should build legacies, not blots, on our landscape.'

Ladies and gentlemen: it seems entirely appropriate in this anniversary year that the Royal Institute of British Architects should nominate Mr Charles Correa[1] to the Queen to receive the Royal Gold Medal for Architecture. I have heard that he is a brilliant modern architect who has been responsible for splendidly brilliant and sensitive modern architecture, invariably of low cost. But it is for his imaginative concern for those who suffer the disability of poverty in Bombay and the third world generally that he is justly famous. It is for this as well as his supreme skill as an architect that he is being honoured this evening.

It would seem that sesquicentenaries are coming thick and fast nowadays. Last year I was invited to become president of the British Medical Association for its 150th anniversary and greatly enjoyed holding that particular office. I am enormously relieved, I must say, that you have

[1] The Indian architect Charles Correa (1930–) trained in the USA, and established a practice in Bombay in 1958.

not asked me to be president of the RIBA this year because – while it is comparatively easy to be a practising hypochondriac – it is probably much more difficult to become the architectural equivalent. On the other hand, my great, great, great grandfather, the Prince Consort,[2] indulged himself wholeheartedly in a kind of architectural hypochondria as often as he could.

Osborne[3] and Balmoral[4] are, of course, the most obvious examples of his personal involvement with the design of buildings, but he also busied himself with the design of farm buildings and the interiors of houses. No detail seemed to be too small to escape his attention and, as a result, we have been left with a series of buildings which never fail to fascinate and which display great individuality. (Although always inspired originally by some earlier style of architecture.) Embellishment appears to have been a vital ingredient, as far as Prince Albert was concerned, to any building and the more symbolic it was the better.

I sometimes can't help wondering whether planning permission would be forthcoming nowadays for some of his designs. But with the present, welcome reaction to the modern movement, which seems to be taking place in our society, it would be forthcoming. For at last people are beginning to see that it is possible, and important in human terms, to respect old buildings, street plans and traditional scales and at the same time not to feel guilty about a preference for façades, ornaments and soft materials. At last, after witnessing the wholesale destruction of Georgian and Victorian housing in most of our cities, people have begun to realize that it is possible to restore old buildings and, what is more, that there are architects willing to undertake such projects.

For far too long, it seems to me, some planners and architects have consistently ignored the feelings and wishes of the mass of ordinary people in this country. Perhaps, when you think about it, it is hardly surprising as architects tend to have been trained to design buildings from scratch – to tear down and rebuild. Except in interior design courses, students are not taught to rehabilitate, nor do they ever meet the ultimate users of buildings in their training – indeed, they can often go through their whole career without doing so.

Consequently a large number of us have developed a feeling that architects tend to design houses for the approval of fellow architects and critics, not for the tenants. The same feelings, by the way, have been shared by disabled people who consider that with a little extra thought, consultation and planning, their already difficult lives could be made that much less complicated. Having said that, I am told that the Department of the Environment is preparing an amendment to the building regulations which will mean that in future buildings will have to be designed so that they are accessible, which in turn will make it easier for architects who are working for clients. This is excellent news and could ultimately transform the lives of over two million people throughout the country.

I want to take this opportunity too, to express my gratitude to the president of the RIBA[5] for his willingness to join with a group of architects, planners, government officials, journalists and disabled people who came to lunch with me in March to discuss this very problem. I would also like to say how impressed I am to see how the RIBA has overcome the difficulty of access to their HQ in London by means of an ingenious combination of steps and ramps. I know that many architects are now fully aware of the needs of disabled people and of their understandable desire to live as near 'normal' a life as possible. Because of this increasing awareness on the part

[2] The German-born nobleman Prince Albert of Saxe-Coburg-Gotha (1819–61) married Queen Victoria in 1840 and was given the official title Prince Consort in 1857. He remains the only person ever to have held it.

[3] A former royal residence on the Isle of Wight, built for Victoria and Albert 1845–51.
[4] A royal residence in Aberdeenshire, also commissioned by Victoria, built 1853–6.

[5] The English architect Michael Manser (1929–) served as president of the RIBA, 1983–5.

149

of architects and planners, I am sure that there will be considerable progress in the field.

But there is a particular problem to overcome and that is the fire regulations which apply to all public buildings. Selwyn Goldsmith[6] wrote about this in his *Designing for the Disabled*, which the RIBA helped initiate in 1961. Referring to building hazards to disabled people and the demands that exist for strict controls, he says: 'For those who administer fire regulations the easy way out is always to say, "yes, we must impose more controls because we are bothered about people dying". The more difficult alternative is to say, "no, we shall not, because we are concerned about people living".'

To be concerned about the way people live; about the environment they inhabit and the kind of community that is created by that environment should surely be one of the prime requirements of a really good architect. It has been most encouraging to see the development of community architecture as a natural reaction to the policy of decamping people to new towns and overspill estates, where the extended family patterns of support were destroyed and the community life was lost.

Now, moreover, we are seeing the gradual expansion of housing co-operatives, particularly in the inner-city areas of Liverpool, where the tenants are able to work with an architect of their own who listens to their comments and their ideas and tries to design the kind of environment they want, rather than the kind which tends to be imposed upon them without any degree of choice.

This sort of development, spearheaded as it is by such individuals as a vice president of the RIBA, Rod Hackney and Ted Cullinan[7] – a man after my own heart, as he believes strongly that the architect must produce something that is visually beautiful as well as socially useful – offers something very promising in terms of inner-city renewal and urban housing, not to mention community garden design. Enabling the client community to be involved in the detailed process of design, rather than exclusively the local authority, is, I am sure, the kind of development we should be examining more closely. Apart from anything else, there is an assumption that if people have played a part in creating something they might conceivably treat it as their own possession and look after it, thus making an attempt at reducing the problem of vandalism.

What I believe is important about community architecture is that it has shown 'ordinary' people that their views are worth having; that architects and planners do not necessarily have the monopoly of knowing best about taste, style and planning; that they need not be made to feel guilty or ignorant if their natural preference is for the more 'traditional' designs – for a small garden, for courtyards, arches and porches; and that there is a growing number of architects prepared to listen and to offer imaginative ideas.

On that note, I can't help thinking how much more worthwhile it would be if a community approach could have been used in the Mansion House Square project.[8] It would be a tragedy if the character and skyline of our capital city were to be further ruined and St Paul's dwarfed by yet another giant glass stump, better suited to downtown Chicago than the City of London.

It is hard to imagine that London before the last war must have had one of the most beautiful skylines of any great city, if those who recall it are to be believed. Those who do say that the affinity between buildings and the

[6] The English architect and writer Selwyn Goldsmith published the influential work *Designing for the Disabled* through the RIBA in 1963.

[7] The English architect Edward Cullinan (1931–) established his own practice in 1959 and received a CBE in 1987.

[8] The property developer Peter Palumbo *later Baron Palumbo* (1935–), present at the speech, was at this time redeveloping a square at Mansion House in London. His plans included a glass tower designed by Mies van der Rohe.

earth, in spite of the city's immense size, was so close and organic that the houses looked almost as though they had grown out of the earth and had not been imposed upon it – grown moreover, in such a way that as few trees as possible were thrust out of the way.

Those who knew it then and loved it – as so many British love Venice without concrete stumps and glass towers, and those who can imagine what it was like – must associate with the sentiments in one of Aldous Huxley's earliest and most successful novels, *Antic Hay*,[9] where the main character, an unsuccessful architect, reveals a model of London as Christopher Wren[10] wanted to rebuild it after the Great Fire, and describes how Wren was so obsessed with the opportunity the fire gave the city to rebuild itself into a greater and more glorious vision.

What, then, are we doing to our capital city now? What have we done to it since the bombing during the war? What are we shortly to do to one of its most famous areas – Trafalgar Square? Instead of designing an extension to the elegant façade of the National Gallery which complements it and continues the concept of columns and domes, it looks as if we may be presented with a kind of municipal fire station, complete with the sort of tower that contains the siren. I would understand better this type of high-tech approach if you demolished the whole of Trafalgar Square and started again, with a single architect responsible for the entire layout, but what is proposed is like a monstrous carbuncle on the face of a much-loved and elegant friend.

Apart from anything else, it defeats me why anyone wishing to display the early Renaissance pictures belonging to the gallery should do so in a new gallery so manifestly at odds with the whole spirit of that age of astonishing proportion. Why can't we have those curves and arches that express feeling in design? What is wrong with them? Why has everything got to be vertical, straight, unbending, only at right angles – and functional?

As if the National Gallery extension wasn't enough, they are now apparently planning to redevelop the large, oval-bellied 19th-century building known as the Grand Hotel, which stands on the south-west corner of Trafalgar Square and which was saved from demolition in 1974 after a campaign to rescue it. As with the National Gallery, I believe the plan is to put this redevelopment out to competition, in which case we can only criticize the judges and not the architects, for I suspect there will be some entries representative of the present-day school of romantic pragmatism, which could at least provide an alternative.

Goethe[11] once said, 'There is nothing more dreadful than imagination without taste'. In this 150th anniversary year, which provides an opportunity for a fresh look at the path ahead – and in which by now you are probably regretting having asked me to take part – may I express the earnest hope that the next 150 years will see a new harmony between imagination and taste and in the relationship between the architects and the people of this country.

[9] The English novelist and essayist Aldous Huxley (1864–1963), best known for his dystopian novel *Brave New World* (1932). He published *Antic Hay* in 1923.

[10] The English architect Sir Christopher Wren (1632–1723) planned the rebuilding of London after the devastating fire of 1666. His buildings include St Paul's Cathedral (completed 1710), 50 other churches and Greenwich Observatory.

[11] The German poet, dramatist and scientist Johann Wolfgang von Goethe (1749–1832).

St John Chrysostom

Syrian preacher and one of the Doctors of the Church

St John Chrysostom (c.347–407 AD) was born in Antioch, and was named from the Greek meaning 'golden-mouthed', due to his eloquence. He spent six years as a monk in the mountains, but illness forced his return in AD 381 to Antioch, where he was ordained and gained his reputation as a great religious orator. In AD 398 he became Archbishop of Constantinople, where he carried out many reforms, but his reproof of vices caused the Empress Eudocia (wife of Arcadius) to have him deposed and banished (AD 404), after which he moved from one place of exile to another. His works include commentaries on the whole Bible, parts of which have perished, as well as homilies, epistles, treatises and liturgies. His feast day is 27 January.

'The courage of the hermits'
March/April AD 387, Antioch, Syria (now in Turkey)

The patron saint of orators, Chrysostom is best known for his biblical commentaries but his series of 21 homilies delivered in AD 387 shows his ability to engage, calm and inspire audiences. The homilies were a response to riots which had broken out in Antioch after the imposition of new taxes by the Roman emperor Theodosius I (AD 347–95). During the uprising, rioters attacked bronze statues of the Emperor, his father and his wife – a treasonable offence. The riot was quickly suppressed, leaving the people of Antioch to wait in dread while an imperial commission decided what punishment to mete out.

Translated here by Stephen Neill, this extract from Homily 17 demonstrates the role of priest as news-giver – a role that continued until modern times. Chrysostom tells his congregation what has happened so far in the city; how monks and hermits successfully appealed to the commissioners to show mercy to the people of Antioch.

But Chrysostom's role involved much more than passing on information. By describing the holy men, who 'manifested the strength of lions', he invokes the Christian values of virtue, courage and sacrifice. According to some accounts, the homilies encouraged many pagans to convert. They also helped soothe a fearful city which, as Chrysostom here predicts, was duly pardoned by the Emperor.

We were expecting countless evils. We thought that we should be dispossessed of all our possessions, that the houses of the city would be burned with all their inhabitants, that the city would be erased from existence in the world, that its very ruins would be destroyed, and that the site on which it stood would be ploughed up. But all this remained a matter of mere expectation; none of it actually came to pass. And this is the most wonderful thing of all – God did not merely deliver us from this terrible danger; he poured great benefits upon us; he added glory to our city; through this time of trial and disaster he raised our credit higher than it had ever stood before. I will now record how all this came about.

When the commissioners sent by the Emperor to hold an enquiry into these events had set up that terrible tribunal, and had summoned to trial all those who had in any way been involved in the crimes, and we were in expectation of various kinds of death, the hermits who dwell on the high ridges of the mountains revealed the true quality of their manner of life. For many years they had lived apart in their seclusion; but now, though no-one had called them and no-one had so advised them, seeing this great cloud of disaster hanging over the city they left their caves and their huts, and ran together from every quarter, as it were a host of angels descending from the heavens.

And indeed the appearance of the city at that time was like Heaven, with so many holy men appearing everywhere in it, and by their very appearance giving confidence to those who were in distress, and helping them to bear with equanimity the disaster that had befallen them. For who, seeing these men, would not learn to laugh at death? Who would not learn to think lightly of life?

This was only the first of the marvels. The next was that these men entered the presence of the judges, and boldly appealed to them on behalf of the accused. They said that they were all ready to shed their own blood, and to lose their own heads, if only they might be allowed to deliver the captives from the calamity that seemed ready to fall upon them. And they affirmed that they would not desist from their appeal, until the judges either agreed to spare the people, or consented to send them, together with the accused, as a delegation to the Emperor.

'Theodosius,' they said, 'the Emperor of all the world is a believer, a man who leads a godly life. We shall certainly be able to persuade him to be merciful. We do not authorize or permit you to stain the sword with blood or to sever a single head. If you do not agree to postpone sentence, we will certainly all die with them. The crimes committed were terrible; that we frankly admit; but great as was this lawlessness, the human kindness of the Emperor is even greater'.

We hear that another of them spoke a word full of shrewd wisdom: 'The statues which had been thrown down have been put back in their places and have resumed their accustomed appearance; in a very short time what was wrong has been put right. But, if you destroy the image of God,[1] how will you ever be able to put right the wrong that you have done? Will you be able to bring dead men back to life? Will you be able to bring back the souls to the bodies?' They also spoke to them at great length about the judgement of God.

Who could fail to be astonished, to be lost in admiration for the character of these men? When the mother of one of the accused, baring her head and exposing her grey hairs, caught hold of the horse of one of the judges by the bridle, and ran with him through the open street, and so entered into the judgement hall, we were all amazed, we were lost in admiration of her love and her courage.

Ought we not to be far more amazed at the actions of these men? For there would be no such great cause for astonishment, if such a mother had given her life for her son. The force of nature is very great, and the love of a mother for the son that she herself has borne is irresistible. But these men showed such love for those whom they had not begotten or brought up, whom they had never seen or heard of or encountered, that, even if they had had ten thousand lives, they would have been willing to surrender them all in order to deliver the accused from death.

Now, do not reply that they were not actually put to death, and did not in actual reality shed their blood; or that the boldness with which they spoke before the tribunal was only such as was natural to men who had already renounced their own lives, and that it was with this understanding that they came down from the mountains to the judgement hall. For, unless they had resolutely prepared themselves in advance for every kind of death, they would not have been able to use such freedom of speech to the judges and to manifest so notable a degree of courage. They remained sitting before the doors of the judgement hall all day long, ready to snatch from the very hands of the executioners those who might be led out to die.

Where now are those who ostentatiously wore the philosopher's cloak, and grew their beards long, and carried a staff in their right hand, those worthless Cynics,[2] those philosophers in outward show, whose behaviour was worse than that of the dogs under the table, who were prepared to do

[1] Chrysostom means a human being, created by God 'in his own image'. See Genesis 1:27.

[2] The Cynics were a philosophical sect established in the 4th century BC who strove to challenge social convention. Chrysostom's comparison of them to dogs is pointed: Cynics urged people to express their animalistic nature; and their name is derived from the Greek word for dog.

anything for the sake of their bellies? All at that time had left the city; they had sped away, and hidden themselves in caves. And only those who by their works showed what philosophy truly is walked without fear through the open streets, as though no cloud of danger hung over the city.

So those who dwelt in the city fled away to the mountains and the deserts, and the dwellers in the desert came into the city, thus showing by their deeds what they had previously affirmed constantly in word, that not even a furnace of fire can harm the man who lives virtuously. So great is this philosophy, which is far superior to all other things, and rises above the chances of good and evil fortune; for it is not puffed up by prosperity, and is not cast down or discouraged by adversity, but keeps an even balance at all times, thus manifesting its own intrinsic strength and power.

Who was there who was not convicted of weakness by the painful circumstances of that time? Those who held the first positions in the city, men of rank and power, those who had boundless wealth and ready access to the Emperor, all left their houses and fled away to the wilderness, taking counsel only for their own safety. All friendship and kinship was then tested and found wanting.

In this time of disaster, men refused to recognize those whom previously they had known quite well, and preferred not to be recognized by them. But these hermits, poor men who possessed nothing more than a single cheap garment, who had lived in rustic surroundings, men who previously had been little regarded, dwelling in mountains and ravines, now manifested the strength of lions. With high and lofty courage they stood forth in the midst. At a time when all were trembling and cowering from fear, they dispelled the cloud of disaster. And this they achieved not by long and painful effort, but as it were in the twinkling of an eye.

The greatest and most mighty warriors do not need to enter into close conflict with their adversaries; if they appear in armed array and shout their warcry, that is enough to put their enemies to flight. So in one single day these men came down, conferred, relieved disaster, and went back to their own dwelling place. So wonderful is the way of life, the philosophy, that has been taught by Christ to men.

And what shall I say of the eminent men, those who were in a position to exercise authority? When the commissioners, who had received from the Emperor the highest authority to enquire into this affair, were appealed to by the hermits to exercise clemency and to let their judgement be tempered by mercy, they replied that their authority did not go so far as this; when the Emperor had been insulted, to release without punishment those who had insulted him might be regarded as compounding the insult, and this would be fraught with grave danger for themselves.

But the monks were simply unwilling to take 'no' for an answer. With their high-minded importunity, they besieged the judges, and in the end so put them to shame that they were willing to take the risk of going beyond the authority which they had received from the Emperor. They were able to persuade the judges, even though the guilt of the guilty had been proved, not to proceed to pronounce sentence upon them, but to refer the matter to the Emperor for his final decision.

They undertook with absolute confidence to persuade the Emperor to pardon those who had offended him, and they themselves were ready at once to set off for the capital city. In admiration for the courage of the hermits, the judges manifested the highest respect for them …

This will be an adornment to our city richer than any crown. For the

Emperor will hear what has happened here. The capital will hear, the whole inhabited world will hear, that the hermits of Antioch are men of apostolic courage. And when these letters are read at court, everyone will be amazed at their nobility; everyone will congratulate our city, and thus we shall be able to wipe away the evil repute into which we have come.

And everyone will come to understand that these crimes were the work not of citizens of the city, but of strangers of depraved character. And the evidence of the hermits will be quite sufficient testimony to vindicate the character of our city.

Winston Churchill
English statesman and historian

Winston Leonard Spencer Churchill (1874–1965) was born at Woodstock, the eldest son of Lord Randolph Churchill. Educated at Harrow and Sandhurst, he was commissioned in 1895. He served in the Malakand and Nile campaigns (1897–8) and, as a London newspaper correspondent in the Boer War, was captured but escaped. In 1900 he entered Parliament as a Conservative MP, crossing the floor in 1906 to join the Liberal majority. He was appointed Colonial Under-Secretary and, as president of the Board of Trade (1908–10), he introduced labour exchanges. In 1910, he became Home Secretary, then First Lord of the Admiralty (1911–15), strengthening the army and navy in preparation for the war he foresaw. He rebuilt his reputation after the disastrous Dardanelles expedition of 1915, and Prime Minister DAVID LLOYD GEORGE appointed him Minister of Munitions in 1917. He was Secretary of State for War and Air, 1919–21, but was excluded from the Cabinet. He warned of the rising Nazi threat in the mid-1930s and in 1940, NEVILLE CHAMBERLAIN stepped down and Churchill became prime minister, seeing Britain through World War II, one of the most momentous periods in its history. Churchill quickly gained the loyalty of the British people and the confidence of the Allies; and was the first premier since THE DUKE OF WELLINGTON with first-hand experience of battle. He was an accomplished orator, able to convince audiences that Britain would eventually prevail, even in the blackest moments. During the war, he travelled thousands of miles, shaped the Atlantic Charter of 1941 with US president FRANKLIN D ROOSEVELT, drew an initially reluctant American people into the war, and masterminded the strategies adopted for the Battle of Britain (1940) and the North Africa campaign (1942). After ADOLF HITLER had been defeated, he contrived with US President HARRY S TRUMAN and Soviet leader JOSEPH STALIN the post-war settlement in Europe. Churchill was defeated in the general election of July 1945; but in 1951, at the age of 77, he became prime minister again. In 1951–2 he vigorously promoted the development of Britain's first nuclear weapons. Meanwhile, he set about reconstructing a country ravaged by war, and when he finally relinquished the premiership at the age of 81, its recovery was nearly complete. After his death, the public queued for hours to pay homage as he lay in state in Westminster Hall, and tens of thousands lined the route of his funeral procession.

'I have nothing to offer but blood, toil, tears and sweat'
13 May 1940, London, England

This was Churchill's debut speech to the House of Commons as prime minister, a position he had occupied for just three days. His rousing oratory was designed to unite the House behind his new coalition government. He had already secured the support of the Labour Party, but many Conservatives were less enthusiastic, preferring the ailing Neville Chamberlain, who had relinquished power the previous week.

Churchill's speech was also designed to bolster the British people, who were acutely aware that since the Germans had occupied Poland, Denmark, Norway, Belgium, the Netherlands and Luxembourg already and had invaded France three days earlier, an attempt to invade Britain was almost certain.

As the speech acknowledges, Britain's prospects were enormously daunting – indeed, the months that followed were among the most desperate in the country's history. Italy was about to join the war; France would soon fall; Dunkirk was three weeks away; the Channel Islands were occupied less than two weeks later. Then came the Battle of Britain.

As Churchill admitted privately around this time, 'Poor people, poor people. They trust me, and I can give them nothing but disaster for quite a long time.' His implication that Britain would ultimately prevail was, however, justified; and his own famous 'bulldog' spirit made an immeasurable contribution. It was made evident in this speech, after which Churchill is said to have muttered, 'That got the sods, didn't it?'

[1] The British monarch George VI (1895–1952) who reigned 1936–52.

[2] Churchill refers to Neville Chamberlain's administration of 1937–40.

On Friday evening last I received His Majesty's[1] commission to form a new administration. It was the evident wish and will of Parliament and the nation that this should be conceived on the broadest possible basis and that it should include all parties, both those who supported the late government[2] and also the parties of the opposition.[3] I have completed the most important part of this task. A War Cabinet has been formed of five members, representing, with the opposition Liberals, the unity of the nation.

[3] The opposition was then divided between the Labour Party, led by CLEMENT ATTLEE; and the Liberal Party led by David Lloyd George.

[4] The Royal Navy, British Army and Royal Air Force. Churchill refers to a period of rearmament from 1933 onwards, instigated by STANLEY BALDWIN, among others.

The three party leaders have agreed to serve, either in the War Cabinet or in high executive office. The three fighting services[4] have been filled. It was necessary that this should be done in one single day, on account of the extreme urgency and rigour of events. A number of other key positions were filled yesterday, and I am submitting a further list to His Majesty tonight. I hope to complete the appointment of the principal ministers during tomorrow. The appointment of the other ministers usually takes a little longer, but I trust that when Parliament meets again, this part of my task will be completed, and that the administration will be complete in all respects …

To form an administration of this scale and complexity is a serious undertaking in itself, but it must be remembered that we are in the preliminary stage of one of the greatest battles in history; that we are in action at many points in Norway and in Holland, that we have to be prepared in the Mediterranean; that the air battle is continuous and that many preparations have to be made here at home.

In this crisis I hope I may be pardoned if I do not address the House at any length today. I hope that any of my friends and colleagues, or former colleagues, who are affected by the political reconstruction, will make all allowance for any lack of ceremony with which it has been necessary to act. I would say to the House, as I said to those who have joined the government: 'I have nothing to offer but blood, toil, tears and sweat.'

We have before us an ordeal of the most grievous kind. We have before us many, many long months of struggle and of suffering. You ask, what is our policy? I will say: it is to wage war, by sea, land and air, with all our might and with all the strength that God can give us; to wage war against a monstrous tyranny, never surpassed in the dark, lamentable catalogue of human crime. That is our policy.

You ask, what is our aim? I can answer in one word: victory – victory at all costs, victory in spite of all terror, victory, however long and hard the road may be; for without victory, there is no survival. Let that be realized; no survival for the British Empire;[5] no survival for all that the British Empire has stood for; no survival for the urge and impulse of the ages, that mankind will move forward towards its goal.

[5] By 1940, the British Empire was in decline and had been officially known, since the Statute of Westminster (1931), as the British Commonwealth of Nations.

But I take up my task with buoyancy and hope. I feel sure that our cause will not be suffered to fail among men. At this time I feel entitled to claim the aid of all, and I say, 'Come, then, let us go forward together with our united strength.'

'We shall fight on the beaches'
4 June 1940, London, England

The German attack on northern Europe began on 10 May 1940. It had been expected since the declaration of war by Britain and France on 3 September 1939, and during the intervening months Allied commanders had drawn up plans both defensive and offensive. When the attack began, German Panzer columns raced through Luxembourg, eastern Belgium and the Netherlands into northern France. Overwhelmed, Allied forces were forced to retreat, impeded by the surrender of the Belgian army. British and French forces fought to reach Dunkirk, where they were confined to a small area but faced annihilation after only two weeks' fighting. Churchill prepared to make a speech to the House explaining the prospect of defeat.

However, between 26 May and 2 June over 330,000 Allied troops were successfully evacuated from the beaches in what was called the 'Miracle of Dunkirk'. Although the troops had to abandon most of their equipment, their safe return to Britain averted a great catastrophe and there was national rejoicing.

Churchill's speech describes the heroic efforts of the Royal Navy and hundreds of merchant seamen in evacuating the Allied army, and the Royal Air Force for its success in defending the evacuation. But it also seeks to prepare listeners for difficult times ahead for Britain, warning that the struggle to overcome German aggression would not be easy, but assuring British people of their ability to win through. The speech's eloquence moved many to tears – a response shared by the speaker himself.

When a week ago today I asked the House to fix this afternoon as the occasion for a statement, I feared it would be my hard lot to announce the greatest military disaster in our long history … The whole root and core and brain of the British army – on which and around which we were to build and are to build the great British armies in the later years of the war – seemed about to perish upon the field or to be led into an ignominious and starving captivity.

That was the prospect a week ago. But another blow which might well have proved final was yet to fall upon us … The surrender of the Belgian army compelled the British at the shortest notice to cover a flank to the sea more than 30 miles in length … It seemed impossible that any large number of Allied troops could reach the coast.

The enemy attacked on all sides with great strength and fierceness, and their main power, the power of their far more numerous air force, was thrown into the battle or else concentrated upon Dunkirk and the beaches. Pressing in upon the narrow exit, both from the east and from the west, the enemy began to fire with cannon upon the beaches by which alone the shipping could approach or depart. They sowed magnetic mines in the channels and seas; they sent repeated waves of hostile aircraft, sometimes more than 100-strong in one formation, to cast their bombs upon the single pier that remained, and upon the sand dunes upon which the troops had their eyes for shelter.

Their U-boats, one of which was sunk, and their motor launches took their toll of the vast traffic which now began. For four or five days, an intense struggle reigned. All their armoured divisions – or what was left of them – together with great masses of infantry and artillery, hurled themselves in vain upon the ever-narrowing, ever-contracting appendix within which the British and French armies fought.

Meanwhile, the Royal Navy, with the willing help of countless merchant seamen, strained every nerve to embark the British and Allied troops; 220 light warships and 650 other vessels were engaged. They had to operate upon the difficult coast, often in adverse weather, under an almost ceaseless hail of bombs and an increasing concentration of artillery fire. Nor were the seas, as I have said, themselves free from mines and torpedoes. It was in conditions such as these that our men carried on, with little or no rest, for days and nights on end, making trip after trip across the dangerous waters, bringing with them always men whom they had rescued. The numbers they have brought back are the measure of their devotion and their courage. The hospital ships, which brought off many thousands of British and French wounded, being so plainly marked, were a special target for Nazi bombs; but the men and women on board them never faltered in their duty.

Meanwhile, the Royal Air Force, which had already been intervening in the battle, so far as its range would allow from home bases, now used part of its main metropolitan fighter strength and struck at the German bombers, and at the fighters which in large numbers protected them. This struggle was protracted and fierce.

Suddenly the scene has cleared, the crash and thunder has for the moment – but only for the moment – died away. A miracle of deliverance, achieved by valour, by perseverance, by perfect discipline, by faultless service, by resource, by skill, by unconquerable fidelity, is manifest to us all … We must be very careful not to assign to this deliverance the attributes of a victory. Wars are not won by evacuations. But there was a victory inside this deliverance, which should be noted …

This was a great trial of strength between the British and German air forces. Can you conceive a greater objective for the Germans in the air than to make evacuation from these beaches impossible, and to sink all these ships which were displayed, almost to the extent of thousands? Could there have been an objective of greater military importance and significance for the whole purpose of the war than this? They tried hard, and they were beaten back; they were frustrated in their task.

We got the army away; and they have paid fourfold for any losses which they have inflicted. Very large formations of German aeroplanes – and we know that they are a very brave race – have turned on several occasions from the attack of one-quarter of their number of the Royal Air Force, and have dispersed in different directions. Twelve aeroplanes have been hunted by two. One aeroplane was driven into the water and cast away, by the mere charge of a British aeroplane which had no more ammunition. All of our types – Hurricane, the Spitfire and the new Defiant – and all our pilots have been vindicated as superior to what they have at present to face …

There never had been, I suppose, in all the world, in all the history of war, such an opportunity for youth. The Knights of the Round Table, the Crusaders, all fall back into the past: not only distant but prosaic; these young men, going forth every morn to guard their native land and all that we stand for, holding in their hands these instruments of colossal and shattering power … deserve our gratitude, as do all of the brave men who, in so many ways and on so many occasions, are ready, and continue ready, to give life and all for their native land …

I return to the army. In the long series of very fierce battles, now on this front, now on that, fighting on three fronts at once … our losses in men have exceeded 30,000 killed, wounded and missing. I take occasion to express the sympathy of the House to all who have suffered bereavement or who are still anxious … But I will say this about the missing. We have had a large number of wounded come home safely to this country, but I would say about the missing that there may be very many reported missing who will come back home, some day, in one way or another …

Against this loss of over 30,000 men, we can set a far heavier loss certainly inflicted upon the enemy. But our losses in material are enormous … The best of all we had to give had gone to the British Expeditionary Force, and although they had not the numbers of tanks and some articles of equipment which were desirable, they were a very well and finely equipped army. They had the first fruits of all that our industry had to give, and that is gone. And now here is this further delay. How long it will be, how long it will last, depends upon the exertions which we make in this island.

An effort the like of which has never been seen in our records is now being made. Work is proceeding everywhere, night and day, Sundays and weekdays. Capital and labour have cast aside their interests, rights and customs and put them into the common stock. Already the flow of munitions has leapt forward. There is no reason why we should not in a few months overtake the sudden and serious loss that has come upon us, without retarding the development of our general programme.

Nevertheless … the French army has been weakened, the Belgian army has been lost, a large part of those fortified lines upon which so much faith had been reposed is gone, many valuable mining districts and factories have passed into the enemy's possession, the whole of the Channel ports are in his hands, with all the tragic consequences that follow from that, and we must expect another blow to be struck almost immediately at us or at France. We are told that Herr Hitler has a plan for invading the British Isles …

We have, for the time being in this island, incomparably more powerful military forces than we have ever had at any moment in this war or the last. But this will not continue. We shall not be content with a defensive war. We have our duty to our Ally.[1] We have to reconstitute and build up the British Expeditionary Force once again, under its gallant commander-in-chief, Lord Gort. All this is in train; but in the interval we must put our defences in this island into such a high state of organization that the fewest possible numbers will be required to give effective security and that the largest possible potential of offensive effort may be realized. On this we are now engaged …

Turning once again, and this time more generally, to the question of invasion, I would observe that there has never been a period in all these long centuries of which we boast when an absolute guarantee against invasion, still less against serious raids, could have been given to our people … There was always the chance, and it is that chance which has excited and befooled the imaginations of many Continental tyrants.

Many are the tales that are told. We are assured that novel methods will be adopted, and when we see the originality of malice, the ingenuity of aggression which our enemy displays, we may certainly prepare ourselves for every kind of novel stratagem and every kind of brutal and treacherous manoeuvre. I think that no idea is so outlandish that it should not be considered and viewed with a searching – but at the same time, I hope, with a steady – eye. We must never forget the solid assurances of sea-power and those which belong to air power if it can be locally exercised.

I have, myself, full confidence that if all do their duty … we shall prove ourselves once again able to defend our island home, to ride out the storm of war and to outlive the menace of tyranny, if necessary for years, if necessary alone. At any rate, that is what we are going to try to do. That is the resolve of His Majesty's Government – every man of them. That is the will of Parliament and the nation …

Even though large tracts of Europe and many old and famous states have fallen or may fall into the grip of the Gestapo[2] and all the odious apparatus of Nazi rule, we shall not flag or fail.

We shall go on to the end, we shall fight in France, we shall fight on the seas and oceans, we shall fight with growing confidence and growing strength in the air, we shall defend our island, whatever the cost may be, we shall fight on the beaches, we shall fight on the landing grounds, we shall fight in the fields and in the streets, we shall fight in the hills; we shall never surrender, and even if – which I do not for a moment believe – this island or a large part of it were subjugated and starving, then our empire beyond the seas, armed and guarded by the British fleet, would carry on the struggle, until in God's good time, the new world, with all its power and might, steps forth to the rescue and the liberation of the old.

[1] Churchill refers to France, which was still attempting to repel the German invasion, though it would surrender three weeks later.

[2] Germany's *Geheime Staatspolizei* ('Secret State Police'), shortened to *Gestapo*, was known for its brutality.

'So much owed by so many to so few'
20 August 1940, London, England

Following the fall of France in June 1940, Britain stood alone against Germany and an invasion attempt was anticipated. Sure enough, *Unternehmen Seelöwe* ('Operation Sealion') began in July 1940, when Adolf Hitler called for the destruction of Royal Air Force (RAF) fighters, bombers and bases. For the following two months, RAF fighter planes desperately fought waves of incoming German bombers and fighters in what became known as the Battle of Britain.

At the height of this struggle, during which the RAF gradually gained supremacy over Germany's mighty *Luftwaffe*, Churchill addressed the House of Commons in a speech that famously emphasizes the debt owed by the people of Britain (the 'many') to the RAF personnel (the 'few') who were engaged in the airborne combat. The speech also refers to the recent promise of American assistance to Britain, the result of Churchill's persistent approaches to US president Franklin D Roosevelt. Many American citizens were reluctant to take part in what they saw as a European war, although most were sympathetic to Britain's plight.

By late September, attacks by the *Luftwaffe* dwindled owing to the RAF's effectiveness and the invasion threat receded, and Britain had acquired 50 American destroyers in exchange for naval bases in the Caribbean. In 1941, under the Lend–Lease scheme, the USA began supplying war materials to Britain.

Almost a year has passed since the war began, and it is natural for us, I think, to pause on our journey at this milestone and survey the dark, wide field. It is also useful to compare the first year of this second war against German aggression with its forerunner a quarter of a century ago. Although this war is in fact only a continuation of the last, very great differences in its character are apparent. In the last war, millions of men fought by hurling enormous masses of steel at one another. 'Men and shells' was the cry, and prodigious slaughter was the consequence.

In this war nothing of this kind has yet appeared. It is a conflict of strategy, of organization, of technical apparatus, of science, mechanics and morale. The British casualties in the first twelve months of the Great War amounted to 365,000. In this war, I am thankful to say, British killed, wounded, prisoners and missing, including civilians, do not exceed 92,000, and of these a large proportion are alive as prisoners of war. Looking more widely around, one may say that, throughout all Europe, for one man killed or wounded in the first year perhaps five were killed or wounded in 1914–15.

The slaughter is only a small fraction, but the consequences to the belligerents have been even more deadly. We have seen great countries with powerful armies dashed out of coherent existence in a few weeks … Although up to the present the loss of life has been mercifully diminished, the decisions reached in the course of the struggle are even more profound upon the fate of nations than anything that has ever happened since barbaric times. Moves are made upon the scientific and strategic boards, advantages are gained by mechanical means, as a result of which scores of millions of men become incapable of further resistance …

There is another, more obvious, difference from 1914. The whole of the warring nations are engaged, not only soldiers, but the entire population – men, women and children. The fronts are everywhere. The trenches are dug in the towns and streets. Every village is fortified. Every road is barred. The front line runs through the factories. The workmen are soldiers with different weapons but the same courage …

If it is a case of the whole nation fighting and suffering together, that ought to suit us, because we are the most united of all the nations, because we entered the war upon the national will and with our eyes open, and because we have been nurtured in freedom and individual responsibility and are the products, not of totalitarian uniformity but of tolerance and variety … Our geographical position, the command of the sea and the friendship of the United States enable us to draw resources from the whole world and to manufacture weapons of war of every kind, but especially of the superfine kind, on a scale hitherto practised only by Nazi Germany. The road to victory may not be so long as we expect, but we have no right to count upon this. Be it long or short, rough or smooth, we mean to reach our journey's end …

Rather more than a quarter of a year has passed since the new government came into power in this country.[1] What a cataract of disaster has poured out upon us since then … The whole western seaboard of Europe, from the North Cape to the Spanish frontier, in German hands; all the ports, all the airfields on this immense front employed against us as potential springboards of invasion. Moreover, the German air power, numerically so far outstripping ours, has been brought so close to our island that what we used to dread greatly has come to pass and the hostile bombers not only reach our shores in a few minutes and from many directions, but can be escorted by their fighting aircraft.

Why, Sir, if we had been confronted at the beginning of May with such a prospect, it would have seemed incredible that at the end of a period of horror and disaster – or at this point in a period of horror or disaster – we should stand erect, sure of ourselves, masters of our fate and with the conviction of final victory burning unquenchable in our hearts. Few would have believed we could survive; none would have believed that we should today not only feel stronger but should actually be stronger than we have ever been before.

Let us see what has happened on the other side of the scales. The British nation and the British Empire, finding themselves alone, stood undismayed against disaster. No-one flinched or wavered; nay, some who formerly thought of peace now think only of war. Our people are united and resolved as they have never been before. Death and ruin have become small things compared with the shame of defeat or failure in duty. We cannot tell what lies ahead. It may be that even greater ordeals lie before us. We shall face whatever is coming to us. We are sure of ourselves and of our cause and that is the supreme fact which has emerged in these months of trial.

Meanwhile, we have not only fortified our hearts but our island … Our navy is far stronger than it was at the beginning of the war … The seas and oceans are open. The U-boats are contained. The magnetic mine is, up to the present time, effectively mastered … Our stocks of food of all kinds are far more abundant than in the days of peace and a large and growing programme of food production is on foot.

Why do I say all this? Not assuredly to boast; not assuredly to give the slightest countenance to complacency. The dangers we face are still enormous, but so are our advantages and resources. I recount them because the people have a right to know that there are solid grounds for the confidence which we feel; and that we have good reason to believe ourselves capable – as I said in a very dark hour two months ago – of continuing the war 'if necessary alone, if necessary for years'.[2]

I say it also because the fact that the British Empire stands invincible, and that Nazidom is still being resisted, will kindle again the spark of hope in the breasts of hundreds of millions of downtrodden or despairing men and women throughout Europe, and far beyond its bounds, and that from these sparks there will presently come cleansing and devouring flame.

[1] On 10 May 1940, Churchill had become prime minister of a coalition government, comprising Conservative, Liberal and Labour members.

[2] See previous speech.

The great air battle which has been in progress over this island for the last few weeks has recently attained a high intensity. It is too soon to attempt to assign limits either to its scale or to its duration. We must certainly expect that greater efforts will be made by the enemy than any he has so far put forth. Hostile airfields are still being developed in France and the Low Countries, and the movement of squadrons and material for attacking us is still proceeding.

It is quite plain that Herr Hitler could not admit defeat in his air attack on Great Britain without sustaining most serious injury. If, after all his boastings and blood-curdling threats and lurid accounts, trumpeted round the world, of the damage he has inflicted, of the vast numbers of our air force he has shot down, so he says, with so little loss to himself; if after tales of the panic-stricken British, crushed in their holes, cursing the plutocratic Parliament which has led them to such a plight; if, after all, this his whole air onslaught were forced after a while tamely to peter out, the Führer's reputation for veracity of statement might be seriously impugned. We may be sure, therefore, that he will continue as long as he has the strength to do so, and as long as any preoccupations he may have in respect of the Russian air force allow him to do so.

On the other hand, the conditions and course of the fighting have so far been favourable to us. I told the House two months ago that whereas in France our fighter aircraft were wont to inflict a loss of two or three to one upon the Germans, and in the fighting at Dunkirk, which was a kind of no-man's-land, a loss of about three or four to one, we expected that in an attack on this island we should achieve a larger ratio. This has certainly come true …

The enemy is, of course, far more numerous than we are. But our new production already, as I am advised, largely exceeds his, and the American production is only just beginning to flow in. It is a fact – as I see from my daily returns – that our bomber and fighter strength now, after all this fighting, are larger than they have ever been. We believe that we shall be able to continue the air struggle indefinitely and as long as the enemy pleases, and the longer it continues, the more rapid will be our approach, first towards that parity, and then into that superiority in the air upon which in a large measure the decision of the war depends.

The gratitude of every home in our island, in our empire, and indeed throughout the world (except in the abodes of the guilty) goes out to the British airmen who, undaunted by odds, unwearied in their constant challenge and mortal danger, are turning the tide of the world war by their prowess and by their devotion. Never in the field of human conflict was so much owed by so many to so few. All hearts go out to the fighter pilots, whose brilliant actions we see with our own eyes, day after day; but we must never forget that all the time, night after night, month after month, our bomber squadrons travel far into Germany, find their targets in the darkness by the highest navigational skill, aim their attacks, often under the heaviest fire, often with serious loss, with deliberate careful discrimination, and inflict shattering blows upon the whole of the technical and war-making structure of the Nazi power.

On no part of the Royal Air Force does the weight of the war fall more heavily than on the daylight bombers, who will play an invaluable part in the case of invasion and whose unflinching zeal it has been necessary in the meanwhile on numerous occasions to restrain.

We are able to verify the results of bombing military targets in Germany, not only by reports which reach us through many sources, but also, of course, by photography. I have no hesitation in saying that this process of bombing the military industries and communications of Germany and the air bases and storage depots from which we are attacked – which process will continue upon an ever-increasing scale until the end of the war, and may in another year attain dimensions hitherto undreamed of – affords one at least of the most certain, if not the shortest of all the roads to victory.

'Little does he know the spirit of the British nation'
11 September 1940, radio broadcast from London, England

By now, the Battle of Britain was drawing to an end. The Royal Air Force had effectively thwarted the German effort to neutralize British air defences to make way for a planned land invasion from the English Channel, for which large numbers of ships and men were standing by. The south coast was fortified and the British people were prepared – through mobilization of the army and the creation of the Home Guard – to defend their country.

But on 5 September, Adolf Hitler had launched a new strategy: German bombers began attacking the civilian populations of London and other major cities. Churchill was outraged by this and broadcast to the nation, reavowing his determination to secure victory and praising those who were enduring the air raids.

Throughout the winter of 1940–1 German bombers pounded British cities by night in what became known as 'the Blitz' (from the German *Blitzkrieg*, literally 'lightning war'). Although many civilians died and cities were devastated, stoic determination was embraced as a characteristic of the British public, and 'the spirit of the Blitz' became a rallying cry whenever the country needed to pull together against a common enemy. This speech was referred to by Rudolph Giuliani, Mayor of New York City, after the terrorist attacks of 11 September 2001.

When I said in the House of Commons the other day that I thought it improbable that the enemy's air attack in September could be more than three times as great as it was in August, I was not, of course, referring to barbarous attacks upon the civil population, but to the great air battle which is being fought out between our fighters and the German air force.

You will understand that whenever the weather is favourable, waves of German bombers, protected by fighters, often 300 or 400 at a time, surge over this island, especially the promontory of Kent, in the hope of attacking military and other objectives by daylight. However, they are met by our fighter squadrons and nearly always broken up; and their losses average three to one in machines and six to one in pilots.

The effort of the Germans to secure daylight mastery of the air over England is, of course, the crux of the whole war. So far it has failed conspicuously. It has cost them very dear, and we have felt stronger, and actually are relatively a good deal stronger, than when the hard fighting began in July. There is no doubt that Herr Hitler is using up his fighter force at a very high rate, and that if he goes on for many more weeks he will wear down and ruin this vital part of his air force. That will give us a very great advantage.

On the other hand, for him to try to invade this country without having secured mastery in the air would be a very hazardous undertaking. Nevertheless, all his preparations for invasion on a great scale are steadily going forward. Several hundreds of self-propelled barges are moving down the coasts of Europe, from the German and Dutch harbours to the ports of northern France; from Dunkirk to Brest; and beyond Brest to the French harbours in the Bay of Biscay.

Besides this, convoys of merchant ships in tens of dozens are being moved through the Straits of Dover into the Channel, dodging along from port to port under the protection of the new batteries which the Germans have built on the French shore. There are now considerable gatherings of shipping in the German, Dutch, Belgian and French harbours — all the way from Hamburg to Brest. Finally, there are some preparations made of ships to carry an invading force from the Norwegian harbours.

Behind these clusters of ships or barges, there stand very large numbers of German troops, awaiting the order to go on board and set out on their very dangerous and uncertain voyage across the seas. We cannot tell when they will try to come; we cannot be sure that in fact they will try at all; but no-one should blind himself to the fact that a heavy, full-scale invasion of this island is being prepared with all the usual German thoroughness and method, and that it may be launched now — upon England, upon Scotland, or upon Ireland, or upon all three.

If this invasion is going to be tried at all, it does not seem that it can be long delayed. The weather may break at any time. Besides this, it is difficult for the enemy to keep these gatherings of ships waiting about indefinitely, while they are bombed every night by our bombers, and very often shelled by our warships which are waiting for them outside.

Therefore, we must regard the next week or so as a very important period in our history. It ranks with the days when the Spanish Armada was approaching the Channel, and Drake was finishing his game of bowls;[1] or when Nelson stood between us and NAPOLEON's Grand Army at Boulogne.[2] We have read all about this in the history books; but what is happening now is on a far greater scale and of far more consequence to the life and future of the world and its civilization than these brave old days of the past.

Every man and woman will therefore prepare himself to do his duty, whatever it may be, with special pride and care. Our fleets and flotillas are very powerful and numerous; our Air Force is at the highest strength it has ever reached, and it is conscious of its proved superiority, not indeed in numbers, but in men and machines. Our shores are well fortified and strongly manned, and behind them, ready to attack the invaders, we have a far larger and better equipped mobile Army than we have ever had before.

Besides this, we have more than a million and a half men of the Home Guard, who are just as much soldiers of the regular army as the Grenadier Guards, and who are determined to fight for every inch of the ground in every village and in every street.

It is with devout but sure confidence that I say: let God defend the right.

These cruel, wanton, indiscriminate bombings of London are, of course, a part of Hitler's invasion plans. He hopes, by killing large numbers of civilians, and women and children, that he will terrorize and cow the people of this mighty imperial city, and make them a burden and an anxiety to the government and thus distract our attention unduly from the ferocious onslaught he is preparing.

Little does he know the spirit of the British nation, or the tough fibre of the Londoners, whose forebears played a leading part in the establishment of parliamentary institutions and who have been bred to value freedom far above their lives.

This wicked man, the repository and embodiment of many forms of soul-destroying hatred, this monstrous product of former wrongs and shame, has now resolved to try to break our famous island race by a process of indiscriminate slaughter and destruction.

[1] According to legend, the English sailor Sir Francis Drake (c.1540–96) was playing bowls in Plymouth when he learned of the Spanish Armada's approach via the English channel in July 1588. He declared that he had time enough to finish his game and defeat the Spanish – and in fact did so.

[2] In 1805, Napoleon planned an invasion of Britain and assembled his forces at Boulogne. But his plans were wrecked by the decisive defeat of the French navy at Trafalgar, off south-west Spain, by the British Admiral Horatio Nelson (1758–1805), who was mortally wounded during the battle.

What he has done is to kindle a fire in British hearts, here and all over the world, which will glow long after all traces of the conflagration he has caused in London have been removed. He has lighted a fire which will burn with a steady and consuming flame until the last vestiges of Nazi tyranny have been burnt out of Europe, and until the Old World – and the New – can join hands to rebuild the temples of man's freedom and man's honour, upon foundations which will not soon or easily be overthrown.

This is a time for everyone to stand together, and hold firm, as they are doing. I express my admiration for the exemplary manner in which all the Air Raid Precautions services of London are being discharged, especially the fire brigade, whose work has been so heavy and also dangerous. All the world that is still free marvels at the composure and fortitude with which the citizens of London are facing and surmounting the great ordeal to which they are subjected, the end of which or the severity of which cannot yet be foreseen.

It is a message of good cheer to our fighting forces on the seas, in the air, and in our waiting armies in all their posts and stations, that we send them from this capital city. They know that they have behind them a people who will not flinch or weary of the struggle – hard and protracted though it will be; but that we shall rather draw from the heart of suffering itself the means of inspiration and survival, and of a victory won not only for ourselves but for all – a victory won not only for our own time, but for the long and better days that are to come.

❧

'An iron curtain has descended'
5 March 1946, Fulton, Missouri, USA
❧

In the general election of July 1945, Churchill was decisively defeated by the Labour Party under CLEMENT ATTLEE. He would return as prime minister in 1951, but spent the intervening years working on his vast, Nobel Prize-winning chronicle *The Second World War* (published 1948–53) and participating in global diplomacy. He was a keen advocate of European union, and had established a solid working relationship with the US government.

During the Potsdam Conference of July–August 1945, Attlee had replaced Churchill at talks with Soviet leader JOSEPH STALIN and US president HARRY S TRUMAN to agree political arrangements which would restore order to Europe. Stalin had agreed to allow eastern European countries to decide their own form of post-war government, but the domination of these countries by their powerful neighbour was conspicuous. The resulting map of Europe was starkly divided between Soviet and Allied spheres of influence.

The following year, Churchill accepted an invitation to speak at Westminster College, a liberal arts institution in Missouri. By now convinced of the dangers posed by the emerging Eastern bloc, he gave perhaps the most influential speech of his post-war career.

In it, he describes the political and cultural fraternity between Britain and the USA as a 'special relationship', in what appears to be the first use of this enduring phrase. His speech also introduced the term 'Iron Curtain' to the English language, and it is sometimes attributed to Churchill. In fact, it was originally coined by the Nazi propagandist JOSEPH GOEBBELS in an anti-communist newspaper article of February 1945.

❧

The United States stands at this time at the pinnacle of world power. It is a solemn moment for the American democracy. For with primacy in power is also joined an awe-inspiring accountability to the future … Opportunity is here now, clear and shining for both our countries. To reject it or ignore it, or fritter it away, will bring upon us all the long reproaches of the after-time. It is necessary that constancy of mind, persistency of purpose and the grand simplicity of decision shall guide and rule the conduct of the English-speaking peoples in peace as they did in war. We must, and I believe we shall, prove ourselves equal to this severe requirement.

When American military men approach some serious situation they are wont to write at the head of their directive the words 'overall strategic concept'. There is wisdom in this, as it leads to clarity of thought. What then is the overall strategic concept which we should inscribe today? It is nothing less than the safety and welfare, the freedom and progress, of all the homes and families of all the men and women in all the lands. And here I speak particularly of the myriad cottage or apartment homes where the wage-earner strives, amid the accidents and difficulties of life, to guard his wife and children from privation and bring the family up in the fear of the Lord, or upon ethical conceptions which often play their potent part.

To give security to these countless homes, they must be shielded from the two giant marauders, war and tyranny. We all know the frightful disturbances in which the ordinary family is plunged when the curse of war swoops down upon the breadwinner and those for whom he works and contrives. The awful ruin of Europe, with all its vanished glories, and of large parts of Asia glares us in the eyes. When the designs of wicked men or the aggressive urge of mighty states dissolve over large areas the frame of civilized society, humble folk are confronted with difficulties with which they cannot cope. For them, all is distorted, all is broken, even ground to pulp.

When I stand here this quiet afternoon, I shudder to visualize what is actually happening to millions now and what is going to happen in this period when famine stalks the earth … Our supreme task and duty is to guard the homes of the common people from the horrors and miseries of another war. We are all agreed on that.

Our American military colleagues, after having proclaimed their 'overall strategic concept' and computed available resources, always proceed to the next step – namely, the method. Here again there is widespread agreement. A world organization has already been erected for the prime purpose of preventing war. UNO,[1] the successor of the League of Nations[2] – with the decisive addition of the United States and all that that means – is already at work. We must make sure that its work is fruitful, that it is a reality and not a sham; that it is a force of action and not merely a frothing of words; that it is a true temple of peace, in which the shields of many nations can some day be hung up, and not merely a cockpit in a Tower of Babel[3] …

Anyone can see with his eyes open that our path will be difficult and also long, but if we persevere together as we did in the two world wars – though not, alas, in the interval between them – I cannot doubt that we shall achieve our common purpose in the end.

I have, however, a definite and practical purpose to make for action. Courts and magistrates may be set up, but they cannot function without sheriffs and constables. The United Nations Organization must immediately begin to be equipped with an international armed force … This might be started on a modest scale and would grow as confidence grew. I wished to see this done after the First World War, and I devoutly trust it may be done forthwith …

Now I come to the second danger of these two marauders which threatens the cottage, the home and the ordinary people – namely, tyranny. We cannot be blind to the fact that the liberties enjoyed by individual citizens throughout the British Empire are not valid in a considerable number of countries, some of which are very powerful. In these states, control is enforced upon the common people by various kinds

[1] The United Nations Organization was established on 24 October 1945.

[2] The League of Nations was established in 1920 to promote international co-operation and prevent wars. It ceased to operate during World War II, and formally dissolved itself at a meeting of the United Nations in 1946.

[3] According to the Old Testament, humankind, possessed by pride, attempted to build the Tower of Babel, a structure reaching up to the heavens. In order to prevent this, God caused them to speak in different languages. Unable to communicate, they were forced to abandon the project. See Genesis 11:1–9.

of all-embracing police governments. The power of the state is exercised without restraint, either by dictators or by compact oligarchies operating through a privileged party and a political police ...

People of any country have the right – and should have the power by constitutional action, by free unfettered elections, with secret ballot – to choose or change the character or form of government under which they dwell; that freedom of speech and thought should reign; that courts of justice, independent of the executive, unbiased by any party, should administer laws which have received the broad assent of large majorities or are consecrated by time and custom.

Here are the title deeds of freedom which should lie in every cottage home. Here is the message of the British and American peoples to mankind. Let us preach what we practise – let us practise what we preach ...

Now, while still pursuing the method of realizing our overall strategic concept, I come to the crux of what I have travelled here to say. Neither the sure prevention of war, nor the continuous rise of world organization will be gained without what I have called the fraternal association of the English-speaking peoples. This means a special relationship between the British Commonwealth and Empire and the United States.

This is no time for generalities, and I will venture to be precise. Fraternal association requires not only the growing friendship and mutual understanding between our two vast but kindred systems of society, but the continuance of the intimate relationship between our military advisers, leading to common study of potential dangers, the similarity of weapons and manuals of instructions, and to the interchange of officers and cadets at technical colleges ... Eventually there may come – I feel eventually there will come – the principle of common citizenship, but that we may be content to leave to destiny, whose outstretched arm many of us can already clearly see ...

I spoke earlier of the temple of peace. Workmen from all countries must build that temple. If two of the workmen know each other particularly well and are old friends, if their families are intermingled ... why cannot they work together at the common task as friends and partners? Why cannot they share their tools and thus increase each other's working powers? Indeed they must do so, or else the temple may not be built – or, being built, it may collapse, and we shall all be proved again unteachable and have to go and try to learn again for a third time in a school of war incomparably more rigorous than that from which we have just been released.

The Dark Ages may return; the Stone Age may return on the gleaming wings of science, and what might now shower immeasurable material blessings upon mankind may even bring about its total destruction. Beware, I say; time may be short. Do not let us take the course of allowing events to drift along until it is too late. If there is to be a fraternal association of the kind I have described – with all the extra strength and security which both our countries can derive from it – let us make sure that that great fact is known to the world, and that it plays its part in steadying and stabilizing the foundations of peace. There is the path of wisdom. Prevention is better than cure.

A shadow has fallen upon the scenes so lately lighted by the Allied victory. Nobody knows what Soviet Russia and its Communist international organization intends to do in the immediate future, or what are the limits, if any, to their expansive and proselytizing tendencies. I have a strong admiration and regard for the valiant Russian people and for my wartime comrade, Marshal Stalin. There is deep sympathy and goodwill in Britain – and I doubt not here also – towards the peoples of all the Russias and a resolve to persevere, through many differences and rebuffs, in establishing lasting friendships.

We understand the Russian need to be secure on her western frontiers by the removal of all possibility of German aggression. We welcome Russia to her rightful place among the leading nations of the world. We welcome her flag upon the seas. Above all, we welcome constant, frequent and growing contacts between the Russian people and our own people on both sides of the Atlantic. It is my duty, however – for I am sure you would wish me to state the facts as I see them to you – to place before you certain facts about the present position in Europe.

From Stettin in the Baltic to Trieste in the Adriatic, an iron curtain has descended across the Continent. Behind that line lie all the capitals of the ancient states of central and eastern Europe. Warsaw, Berlin, Prague, Vienna, Budapest, Belgrade, Bucharest and Sofia: all these famous cities and the populations around them lie in what I must call the Soviet sphere, and all are subject, in one form or another, not only to Soviet influence but to a very high and, in many cases, increasing measure of control from Moscow …

Whatever conclusions may be drawn from these facts – and facts they are – this is certainly not the liberated Europe we fought to build up. Nor is it one which contains the essentials of a permanent peace.

The safety of the world requires a new unity in Europe, from which no nation should be permanently outcast. It is from the quarrels of the strong parent races in Europe that the world wars we have witnessed – or which occurred in former times – have sprung. Twice in our own lifetime we have seen the United States – against their wishes and their traditions, against arguments the force of which it is impossible not to comprehend – drawn by irresistible forces into these wars, in time to secure the victory of the good cause, but only after frightful slaughter and devastation had occurred. Twice the United States has had to send several millions of its young men across the Atlantic to find the war; but now war can find any nation, wherever it may dwell between dusk and dawn …

On the other hand I repulse the idea that a new war is inevitable; still more that it is imminent. It is because I am sure that our fortunes are still in our own hands, and that we hold the power to save the future, that I feel the duty to speak out, now that I have the occasion and the opportunity to do so.

I do not believe that Soviet Russia desires war. What they desire is the fruits of war and the indefinite expansion of their power and doctrines. But what we have to consider here today, while time remains, is the permanent prevention of war and the establishment of conditions of freedom and democracy as rapidly as possible in all countries. Our difficulties and dangers will not be removed by closing our eyes to them. They will not be removed by mere waiting to see what happens; nor will they be removed by a policy of appeasement. What is needed is a settlement – and the longer this is delayed, the more difficult it will be and the greater our dangers will become.

From what I have seen of our Russian friends and allies during the war, I am convinced that there is nothing they admire so much as strength, and there is nothing for which they have less respect than for weakness, especially military weakness. For that reason, the old doctrine of a balance of power is unsound. We cannot afford, if we can help it, to work on narrow margins, offering temptations to a trial of strength. If the western democracies stand together in strict adherence to the principles of the United Nations Charter, their influence for furthering those principles will be immense and no-one is likely to molest them. If, however, they become divided or falter in their duty; and if these all-important years are allowed to slip away, then indeed catastrophe may overwhelm us all …

[But] if we adhere faithfully to the Charter of the United Nations and walk forward in sedate and sober strength, seeking no-one's land or treasure, seeking to lay no arbitrary control upon the thoughts of men; if all British moral and material forces and convictions are joined with your own in fraternal association, the high roads of the future will be clear, not only for us but for all; not only for our time, but for a century to come.

Cicero
Roman orator and politician

Marcus Tullius Cicero (106–43 BC) was born at Arpinum into a wealthy family. At Rome he studied law and oratory. He saw military service in the Social War (90–88 BC). He was elected Quaestor in 76 BC, thereby qualifying for membership of the Senate, and obtained an appointment in Sicily. At the request of the Sicilians, he brilliantly impeached the corrupt governor Gaius Verres in 70 BC. Cicero made clear his support for Gnaeus Pompeius Magnus (Pompey) and the supremacy of the Senate, and in 66 BC he became praetor, supporting the appointment of Pompey to conduct the war with Mithridates. In 63 BC he held the consulship, and foiled the plot of Catilina; the Senate voted on the death penalty for the conspirators, and Cicero had the sentence carried out immediately. He was for a brief time the great man of the day. Then the tide turned against him. In 59 BC he had declined an invitation to join the triumvirate of Pompey, Caesar and Crassus. He was now without real support, and his enemies accused him of having violated the constitution by putting a citizen to death without trial. Cicero was condemned to exile, and his houses were plundered. But in 57 BC the people, with Pompey's support, almost unanimously voted his recall. He subsequently tried to secure compensation. However, he was no longer a power in politics; and, sensitive to the fluctuations of public opinion, swithered between Pompey and the aristocracy, and Caesar and the new democracy. He ultimately inclined toward Caesar, but lost the esteem of both parties. In 52 BC he composed his speech in defence of Milo, who had killed Clodius in a riot; but Clodius's supporters filled the court and Cicero lost his nerve; Milo was exiled. Cicero served with Pompey's army in Greece (49–48 BC) but after the defeat at Pharsalia (48 BC) he threw himself on Caesar's mercy. A series of personal catastrophes, combined with his loss of faith in Caesar, forced him to withdraw from public life. Living in brooding retirement, he took refuge in writing. In 46–44 BC he wrote most of his chief works on rhetoric and philosophy. He delivered his most famous speeches – against Mark Antony – in 43 BC after Caesar's death, and they cost him his life. As an orator, Cicero stands in the first rank; as a politician, he was an outstanding figure of the late Republic, but he was ultimately defeated.

'Catilina, your hopes must obviously be at an end'
7 November 62 BC, Rome, Italy

In 63 BC Cicero was consul, one of the two chief magistrates of the city of Rome, a remarkable achievement for a man who was not a member of one of the noble families which dominated the magistracies. He had been elected in the previous year, when one of his two chief competitors had been Lucius Sergius Catilina, from an ancient but recently insignificant noble family, who (if we are to believe Cicero) had run up sizeable debts through an extravagant lifestyle. In the following year, Catilina was determined to try again. His policy statements became increasingly popularist, with promises of debt cancellation and land redistribution, which seems to have frightened off some of the influential men who had backed him in 64 BC. At the elections in 63 BC which were presided over by Cicero, Catilina again failed to be elected.

Catilina now moved to more openly revolutionary methods: he sent Gaius Manlius to Etruria, just north and east of Rome, to stir up disaffected farmers, gather an armed force and attack the city of Praeneste (modern Palestrina), while in Rome plans were laid to assassinate the leaders of the state and seize power.

Cicero, who had an excellent network of informers, announced all this to a startled and not altogether convinced Senate on 21 October, and managed to extract from them the emergency decree that gave the consuls *carte blanche* to take military action. However nothing was done until Manlius took to the field on 1 November, just as Cicero had predicted. On 7 November, he summoned an emergency meeting of the Senate. Catilina, against whom at that stage there had been no formal allegations, attended, and in this speech Cicero at last convinced the Senate of the reality of the threat posed by Catilina, who left Rome immediately to join Manlius. This is the first third of Cicero's speech to the Senate. The translator is Michael Grant (1969).

In the name of Heaven, Catilina, how long do you propose to exploit our patience? Do you really suppose that your lunatic activities are going to escape our retaliation for ever more? Are there to be no limits to this audacious, uncontrollable swaggering? Look at the garrison of our Roman nation which guards the Palatine[1] by night, look at the patrols ranging the city, the whole population gripped by terror, the entire body of loyal

[1] One of the seven hills of Rome, which overlooks the area of the Forum.

citizens massing at one single spot!

Look at this meeting of our Senate behind strongly fortified defences;[2] see the expressions on the countenances of every one of these men who are here! Have none of these sights made the smallest impact on your heart? You must be well aware that your plot has been detected. Now that every single person in this place knows all about your conspiracy, you cannot fail to realize it is doomed. Do you suppose there is a single individual here who has not got the very fullest information about what you were doing last night and the night before: where you went, the men you summoned, the plans you concocted?

What a scandalous commentary on our age and its standards! For the Senate knows about all these things. The consul sees them being done. And yet this man still lives! Lives? He walks right into the Senate. He joins in our national debates – watches and notes and marks down with his gaze each one of us he plots to assassinate. And we, how brave we are! Just by getting out of the way of his frenzied onslaught, we feel we are doing patriotic duty enough.

But yours was the death which the consul should have ordered long ago. The calamity which you have long been planning for each one of us ought to have rebounded onto yourself alone. The noble Publius Scipio Nasica, who was chief priest but held no administrative office, killed Tiberius Gracchus, although his threat to the national security was only on a limited scale.[3] Shall we, then, who hold the office of consuls, tolerate Catilina when he is determined to plunge the entire world into fire and slaughter?

Upon precedents that go too far back into antiquity, such as the act of Gaius Servilius Ahala, who with his own hand slew Spurius Maelius for plotting a revolution,[4] I shall not dwell: except to say that at former epochs, in this country of ours, brave men did not lack the courage to strike down a dangerous Roman citizen more fiercely even than they struck down the bitterest of foreign foes. Moreover, we have in our hands, Catilina, a decree of the Senate that is specifically aimed against yourself; and a formidable and stern decree it is.[5] From this body, then, the state has no lack of counsel and authority. I tell you frankly, it is we, the consuls, who are not doing our duty.

The Senate once ordained that Lucius Opimius, who was at that time consul, should take measures to protect the state from harm.[6] Thereafter, not one single night was allowed to elapse. Because of a mere suspicion of treason, Gaius Gracchus, the son, grandson and descendant of highly distinguished men, was put to death. A man of consular rank, Marcus Fulvius, was also killed, and so were his children. A similar resolution of the Senate entrusted the national safety to the consuls Gaius Marius and Lucius Valerius; and thereafter not one day went by before the vengeance of the state brought a violent end to the tribune of the people Lucius Saturninus and the praetor Gaius Servilius.[7]

But look at us, on the other hand. For the past 20 days we have allowed the powers which the Senate has given into our grasp to become blunt at the edges. We have an entirely appropriate decree – but it is left buried in the archives like a sword hidden in its sheath. According to this decree, Catilina, it is evident to all that you should have been instantly executed. And yet you are still alive – and living with an effrontery which bears not the smallest sign of subsiding and is indeed more outrageous than ever.

Members of the Senate, my desire is to be merciful. Yet in this grave

[2] Cicero had summoned the Senate to meet in the Temple of Jupiter Stator, at the foot of the Palatine hill.

[3] Scipio Nasica initiated the killing of the popularist reforming tribune Tiberius Sempronius Gracchus in 133 BC when the Senate hesitated.
[4] Ahala killed Maelius, who was alleged to have been aiming at tyranny by selling corn at low prices, in 439 BC.

[5] Cicero refers to the emergency decree, voted by the Senate on 21 October, though the form of the decree did not mention any individual by name.
[6] This is the emergency decree, first used in 121 BC against the reforming tribune Gaius Gracchus and his followers.

[7] Saturninus was another popularist tribune, who was killed in 100 BC when his support for the candidacy of Gaius Servilius Glaucia led to rioting.

national emergency I also do not want to seem negligent; and as things are I blame myself for culpable inaction. Inside Italy, within the passes of Etruria, there is a camp occupied by men who plan the destruction of the Roman people. The number of these enemies increases every day. But as for the real commander of that camp, the leader of the hostile force, he is to be seen within our own walls and even inside the Senate itself, plotting every day, from this interior vantage point, some form of ruin for our country. If, therefore, Catilina, I order your arrest and execution, surely all honest men will complain, not that I am acting with undue brutality, but that I have delayed too long.

Yet there is a particular reason why I still cannot bring myself to do what I ought to have done long ago. For I intend that your execution shall be timed to coincide with that day when even the most abandoned rascals, the people most resembling yourself, will be admitting one and all that this is your just fate. As long as one man exists who can dare to defend you, you will continue to live – and live as you are living now, surrounded by large numbers of my trusty guards whose duty it is to ensure that you make no move against the government. Although you may not know it, many eyes and ears will be paying you their alert attention. They have been doing so already.

For now, Catilina, your hopes must obviously be at an end. The darkness of night no longer avails to conceal your traitorous consultations. A private house does not suffice to keep the voices of your conspiracy secret. Everything is patently apparent. It all bursts out into the open; you are forced to give up the whole outrageous design. So do as I say: dismiss all those projects of carnage and conflagration from your mind. You are hemmed in on every side. All your schemes are more glaringly evident to us than the light of day.

Let us just go over them together. Do you remember how I said in the Senate on 21 October that Gaius Manlius, your henchman and satellite in this frightful project, would take up arms on a particular date, and that the date in question would be 27 October? Was I mistaken, Catilina, in prophesying this significant, deplorable and unbelievable event? And, more remarkable still, was I wrong about the day?

I also informed the Senate that you had put off the massacre of our national leaders until 28 October, although by that time many of the chief men in the state had fled from Rome, less from a desire for self-preservation than in order to thwart your plans. But you went around saying that, in spite of their departure, you would still be content with the slaughter of the rest of us who remained.

After that admission of failure, you cannot very well deny that my guards and my vigilant attentions encompassed you so completely that you were quite unable to take any effective revolutionary action. When you were confident you would be able to seize Praeneste on 1 November by a night attack, you had no idea that the town was defended, on my orders, by my police and garrisons and protective forces. No single thing you do, nothing you attempt or even contemplate, escapes my notice. I hear and see and plainly understand your every move.

Review with me what happened on the night before last, and you will appreciate that I watch for the safety of our country far more keenly even than you watch for its destruction. I am able to report how on that night you came into Scythe-makers' Street (I will be perfectly specific) and entered the home of Marcus Laeca; and many of your accomplices in this lunatic, criminal enterprise joined you there.

Do you dare to deny it? What can be the reason for your silence? But indeed, if you attempt a denial, I will prove that it is true. For here in the Senate today I can see with my own eyes some of the men who were with you in that house.

By heaven, Senators, it is difficult to imagine where on earth we can be, or what sort of a system of government is ours, or what kind of a city we inhabit, when there are men sitting here among ourselves, in this most solemn and dignified of all the world's assemblies, who are actually plotting the destruction of every single one of us, and of all Rome, and of everything upon the face of the earth! I, the consul, am gazing upon them now; they are taking part in this national debate. They ought to have been put to death by the sword. And yet, so far, I have not even succeeded in marking them with a verbal wound.

So you were at Laeca's house that night, Catilina. You parcelled out the regions of Italy. You decided where you wanted each of your agents to go. You chose the men to leave at Rome and the men you would take with you. You divided up the city into sections for the benefit of the incendiaries. You confirmed that you yourself would be leaving, and added that the only thing which still held you back for a bit was the fact that I was still alive. But two Roman knights were found to relieve you of this worry. They promised they would kill me in my bed during that same night, a little before dawn.

However, almost before your meeting dispersed, I knew about all these projects. Thereupon I proceeded to strengthen and fortify my home with an increased number of bodyguards; and the individuals you had sent me, to convey the morning's greetings, were refused admission. I had foretold the arrival of these visitors to many leading personages. And the men made their appearance at the very hour I had indicated.

Since that is the position, Catilina, I call upon you to leave for the destination you already have in mind. Depart, at last, from our city! The gates are open; be on your way. Your camp run by Manlius has been waiting all too long for you to take over its command. And take all your friends with you, or as many as you can – clean the city up. Once there is a wall between you and ourselves, you will have delivered me from grave anxiety. With us, you can remain no longer. I find it unendurable that you should still be here: unendurable, intolerable, impermissible.

'The only proper verdict is Milo's acquittal'
52 BC, Rome, Italy

The political scene in Rome in the mid-50s BC was chaotic and violent, with the streets frequently occupied by rival gangs. Two of these were led respectively by Publius Clodius, a long-term enemy of Cicero, who came from an ancient noble family but had adopted extreme popularist tactics, and Titus Annius Milo, supported by the more conservative elements in the city. Elections were regularly disrupted and postponed, so that at the beginning of the year 52 BC there were no magistrates in post. This was in part because both Clodius and Milo were running for office, respectively as praetor and consul.

On 18 January the two men and their followers met on the Appian Way, south of Rome. Clodius was killed, and his followers brought the corpse back to Rome, where it was burned in the Senate House, causing severe damage.

The Roman general Pompey was summoned back to Rome to restore order. Among other measures, he introduced a court to deal with cases of violence, before which Milo was tried, with Cicero appearing for the defence. The court Cicero addressed was surrounded by soldiers to prevent disruption, and Cicero uncharacteristically lost his nerve, and consequently the case.

Milo was banished shortly afterwards to Marseilles. Cicero later revised and published the speech, which is widely regarded as one of his finest forensic orations. Milo, on reading it, is said to have been grateful that Cicero never gave it in this form, since otherwise he would not have had the opportunity of enjoying the excellent red mullet of Marseilles.

This extract is taken from the middle of the speech, in which Cicero gives an account of the encounter between the two sides. The translation is by Michael Grant (1969).

Now, gentlemen: we must come to the charge which is the reason for this trial. I have shown that confession of such a deed is not wholly without precedent. I have suggested that the only pronouncements the Senate has offered about our case were in complete conformity with what we ourselves should have wished. I have pointed out that the proposer of the law himself,[1] even though there is no argument about the facts, desired the investigation to go further and look into the rights of the matter. And I have stressed that the judges and president chosen to conduct the action are personages whose deliberations will be both just and wise. It only remains then, gentlemen, for you to decide which of the two men involved laid the plot against the other. So as to help you to obtain a clearer view of the true circumstances, I will now give a brief account of what happened; and I ask for your close attention.

[1] The Roman soldier and politician Gnaeus Pompeius Magnus *known as Pompey* (106–48 BC) had been appointed as sole consul for the year, after his return to Rome.

Publius Clodius was determined to use the post of praetor to convulse the government by every sort of evil-doing. But the elections of the previous year had dragged on so protractedly that he saw his own praetorship would be restricted to a period of no longer than a few months. Advancement in rank, which appeals to other men, was not his object at all. One of the purposes that carried more weight in his mind was a strong desire to avoid having an excellent man like Lucius Paullus[2] as his colleague.

[2] The Roman soldier and politician Lucius Aemilius Lepidus Paullus (d. 13 BC) was elected praetor for 53 BC and became consul in 50 BC. He was a friend and supporter of Cicero.

But Clodius's main ambition was to have an entire year to devote to the disruption of our state. And so he suddenly abandoned the idea of being praetor in the earliest year to which he was entitled, and transferred his candidature to the following year instead. His motive in so doing was very far from involving the religious scruples which sometimes cause people to take such a step. On the contrary – as he himself admitted – what he wanted was to have a full and continuous year for the exercise of his praetorship: that is to say, for the subversion of the republic.

All the same, in regard to the latter year as well, a worrying thought continued to nag him. This was the consideration that if Milo was elected to the consulate for that year, his own praetorship would once again be hampered and paralysed. Indeed, as Clodius clearly appreciated, there was every likelihood of Milo becoming consul, and by the unanimous vote of the Roman people at that. In this situation, he attached himself to Milo's competitors, and did so in such a way that he himself should have complete control of their electoral campaigns – whether they liked it or not. That is to say, as he himself frequently expressed it, his intention was to carry the entire election upon his own shoulders. And so he proceeded to marshal the tribes, acting as a go-between in every negotiation and mobilizing disreputable toughs who virtually amounted to a new Colline tribe[3] in themselves.

[3] The Colline tribe was one of the four urban tribes (geographically based voting units) in the Roman political assemblies, out of a total of 35 tribes.

And yet the more flagrantly Clodius's disturbances raged, the stronger waxed Milo's position every day, until finally it became evident to Clodius, through the unmistakable voice of public opinion expressing itself in a series of popular votes, that this courageous man, his inveterate enemy, was certain to become consul. And so Clodius, who was ready to stop at nothing, now began to operate openly, and he declared straight out that Milo must be killed.

Clodius had a gang of rustic and barbarous slaves whom he had recruited to ravage the national forests and harass the Etrurian countryside. These he now brought down from the Apennines — and you have seen the creatures yourselves. There was not the slightest concealment, for he himself asserted repeatedly and publicly that even if the consulate could not be taken away from Milo, the same could not be said about his life. Clodius frequently gave indications to this effect in the Senate, and he said it at mass meetings too. Moreover, when the gallant Marcus Favonius asked him what purpose all this violence could possibly serve while Milo was alive to resist it, Clodius replied that within three or, at most, four days Milo would be dead. And Favonius promptly reported this remark to Marcus Cato here.[4]

Meanwhile Clodius became aware (and it was an easy enough fact to discover) that on 18 January Milo was under an obligation, prescribed by ritual and law, to proceed to Lanuvium. He held the local office of Dictator,[5] and it was his duty to make a nomination to the priesthood of the town. Equipped with this knowledge, Clodius left Rome without notice on the previous day. As subsequent events demonstrated, his plan was to take up a position in front of his own country manor, and set an ambush for Milo on that spot.

Clodius's departure from Rome meant that he had to absent himself from a turbulent public gathering on that same day. His usual violent contributions were greatly missed at the meeting, and he would certainly never have failed to play his part had he not formed the deliberate intention to be punctually in the locality set for the ambush at the appropriate time.

Meanwhile Milo, on the other hand, attended the Senate on that day, until the meeting was concluded. Then he proceeded to his home, changed his shoes and his clothes, waited for the usual period while his wife got ready, and then started off at just about the time when Clodius could have got back to Rome if it had been his intention to return at all on the day in question. But instead, he encountered Clodius in the country.

The man was lightly equipped, not seated in a coach but riding on horseback, unimpeded by any baggage, with none of his usual Greek companions and even without his wife, who nearly always travelled with him. Milo, on the other hand, was sitting in a coach with his wife, wearing a heavy travelling cloak and accompanied by a substantial, heavily laden, feminine, unwarlike retinue of maids and pages. And this was our so-called waylayer, the man who had allegedly planned the expedition with the explicit purpose of committing a murder!

And so at about five in the afternoon, or thereabouts, he found himself confronted by Clodius before the gates of the latter's house. Milo was instantly set upon by a crowd of armed men, who charged down from higher ground; while, simultaneously, others rushed up from in front and killed the driver of the coach. Milo flung back his cloak, leapt out of the vehicle, and defended himself with energy. But meanwhile the people with Clodius were brandishing their drawn swords, and while some of them ran towards the coach in order to fall upon Milo from the rear, others believed he was already slain and began to attack his slaves who had been following behind him.

A number of these slaves of Milo's lost their lives defending their master with loyal determination. Others, however, who could see the fight round

[4] Marcus Porcius Cato Uticencis *known as Cato the Younger* (95–46 BC) and Marcus Favonius were both staunch members of the conservative section of the Senate. Cato was later to commit suicide at Utica in north Africa, after Caesar's victory over Pompey in the civil war.

[5] 'Dictator' was the name of an ancient magistracy in Lanuvium, in the Alban hills, south of Rome, where Milo was born.

the coach but were unable to get to their master's help, heard from Clodius's own lips that Milo was slain, and believed the report. And so these slaves, without the orders or knowledge or presence of their master – and I am going to speak quite frankly, not with any aim of denying the charge, but just exactly as the situation developed – did what every man would have wished his own slaves to do in similar circumstances.

The incident, gentlemen, took place precisely as I have described it. The attacker was defeated. Force was frustrated by force; or, to put the matter more accurately, evil was overcome by good. Of the gain to our country and yourselves and all loyal citizens, I say nothing. It is not my intention to urge that the deed be counted in favour of Milo – the man whose self-preservation was destined to mean the preservation of the republic and yourselves. No, my defence is that he was justified in acting to save his life.

Civilized people are taught this by logic, barbarians by necessity, communities by tradition; and the lesson is inculcated even in wild beasts by nature itself. They learn that they have to defend their own bodies and persons and lives from violence of any and every kind by all the means within their power. That being so, if you come to the conclusion that this particular action was criminal, you are in the same breath deciding that every other man in the history of the world who has ever fought back against a robber deserves nothing better than death – and that if the robber's weapons did not manage to produce this result, then you yourself would be quite prepared to bring it about! If Milo had been of the same mind, he would have done better to offer his throat to Clodius, who had already attacked him repeatedly, than to refuse the death-blow from Clodius merely so that it could be dealt him subsequently by yourselves.

If, then, you are all agreed that self-defence is not necessarily wrong, you need not trouble about the question *whether* Clodius was killed. For we fully admit that he was. What you have to consider instead is that issue which has so frequently been raised in a variety of different cases – namely, whether the act was justifiable or not. That a plot existed is generally agreed – and indeed the plot is what the Senate has denounced as having been contrary to the national interests.

But the point that needs to be settled is which of the two men was the conspirator, and this is the problem you were appointed to investigate. What the Senate censured was the deed itself, and not any particular individual; and the inquiry set up by Pompeius was intended to determine not the facts, but the question of justification. So quite clearly the only matter before the court is this: which man plotted against the other? If Milo plotted against Clodius, let him be punished; if Clodius plotted against Milo, then the only proper verdict is Milo's acquittal.

❧

'Antony's action proves he is totally uncivilized'

October 44 BC, Rome, Italy

❧

After the assassination of Julius Caesar on 15 March 44 BC, the assassins (or 'Liberators' as they were called by their friends) hoped for the restoration of the oligarchic government, based on the Senate and its members. At first Mark Antony – who, as one of Caesar's closest associates, was one of the two consuls for the year – seemed to accommodate the 'Liberators'; but once in control of Rome (despite the arrival on the scene of Octavian, Caesar's heir and the future emperor Augustus), he began to act more autocratically, and when Cicero returned to the Senate on 1 September, having laid low for some months, Antony attacked him violently for having absented himself.

Cicero responded on 2 September in fairly moderate terms in a speech, which was the first of what he later called jokingly called his Philippics, a reference to the speeches which the Athenian orator DEMOSTHENES had made against Philip II of Macedon in the 4th century BC. After a furious rejoinder from Antony, Cicero retired to the country once again, where he wrote the Second Philippic, from which the extracts given here are taken. The translation is by Michael Grant (1960).

Although written as though a speech to the Senate, this was never delivered, but remains one of the great pieces of political invective. Cicero compares Antony to the enemies of Rome whom he has overcome in his career, and to Caesar, showing him as both worse and more dangerous than any of them. It was followed by twelve more Philippics, and undoubtedly led to Antony's brutal murder of Cicero on 7 December 43 BC once Antony had come to power along with Octavian and Marcus Lepidus, after a year of tumultuous fighting and politicking.

Members of the Senate: why is this my fate? I am obliged to record that, for 20 years past, our country has never had an enemy who has not, simultaneously, made himself an enemy of mine as well. I need mention no names. You remember the men for yourselves. They have paid me graver penalties than I could have wished.

Antony, you are modelling your actions on theirs. So what happened to them ought to frighten you; I am amazed that it does not. When those others were against me as well as against Rome I was less surprised. For they did not seek me out as an enemy. No, it was I who, for patriotic reasons, took the initiative against every one of them. But you I have never injured, even in words. And yet, without provocation, you have assailed me with gross insults. Catilina[1] himself could not have been so outrageous, nor Publius Clodius[2] so hysterical. Evidently you felt that the way to make friends, in disreputable circles, was by breaking off relations with me.

Did you take this step in a spirit of contempt? I should not have thought that my life, and my reputation, and my qualities – such as they are – provide suitable material for Antony's contempt. Nor can he have believed, surely, that he could successfully disparage me before the Senate. Accustomed though it is to complimenting distinguished Romans for good service to the state, the Senate has praised only one man for actually rescuing it from annihilation: and that is myself. But perhaps Antony's ambition was to compete with me as a speaker? If so, how extremely generous of him to present me with such a subject – justification of myself, criticism of him: the richest and most promising theme imaginable! No, the truth is clearly this. He saw no chance of proving to people like himself that he was Rome's enemy, unless he became mine too ...

Before I reply to his other accusations, I should like to say a few words in answer to one particular complaint, namely that it was I who broke our friendship. Because I regard this as a very serious charge. He has protested that I once spoke against him in a lawsuit ... I admit that there was no lack of grief and misery in my complaints. But a man in my position, the position conferred on me by the Senate and people of Rome, could not help that. And my words were restrained and friendly, never insulting. Surely that is real moderation – to protest about Antony and yet refrain from abuse!

For what was left of Rome, Antony, owed its final annihilation to yourself. In your home everything had a price: and a truly sordid series of deals it was. Laws you passed, laws you caused to be put through in your interests, had never even been formally proposed. You admitted this yourself. You were an augur, yet you never took the auspices. You were a consul, yet you blocked the legal right of other officials to exercise the veto. Your armed escort was shocking. You are a drink-sodden, sex-ridden wreck. Never a day passes in that ill-reputed house of yours without orgies of the most repulsive kind.

In spite of all that, I restricted myself in my speech to solemn complaints

[1] Cicero's speech against Catilina is included in this book.

[2] Cicero's attack on Clodius, as part of his defence of Milo, is included in this book.

concerning the state of our nation. I said nothing personal about the man. I might have been conducting a case against Marcus Licinius Crassus[3] (as I often have, on grave issues) instead of against this utterly loathsome gladiator.

Today, therefore, I am going to ensure that he understands what a favour I, on that occasion, conferred upon himself. He read out a letter, this creature, which he said I had sent him. But he has absolutely no idea how to behave – how other people behave. Who, with the slightest knowledge of decent people's habits, could conceivably produce letters sent him by a friend, and read them in public, merely because some quarrel has arisen between him and the other? Such conduct strikes at the roots of human relations; it means that absent friends are excluded from communicating with each other. For men fill their letters with flippancies which appear tasteless if they are published – and with serious matters which are quite unsuitable for wide circulation. Antony's action proves he is totally uncivilized …

Your behaviour today, at the present day and moment at which I am speaking – defend that if you can! Explain why the Senate is surrounded by a ring of men with arms; why my listeners include gangsters of yours, sword in hand; why the doors of the temple of Concord are closed; why you bring into the forum the world's most savage people, Ituraeans,[4] with their bows and arrows. 'I do these things in self-defence,' says Antony. But surely a thousand deaths are better than the inability to live in one's own community without an armed guard.

A guard is no protection, I can tell you! The protection you need is not weapons, but the affection and goodwill of your fellow-citizens. The people of Rome will seize your weapons and wrench them from you. I pray that we shall not perish before that is done! But however you behave towards ourselves, believe me, these are methods which cannot preserve you for long …

Here, for the first time, are men raising their swords to kill one who was not merely aiming at monarchy, but actually reigning as monarch.[5] Their action was superhumanly noble in itself, and it is set before us for our imitation: all the more conspicuously, because Heaven itself is scarcely immense enough to hold the glory which this deeds has made theirs. The consciousness of a noble achievement was reward enough; yet no-one, I believe, should spurn that further reward which they have also won – immortality.

The day you ought to remember, Antony, is that day on which you abolished the dictatorship for ever.[6] Let your memory dwell on the rejoicing of the Senate and people of Rome on that occasion. Contrast it with the haggling with which you and your friends busy yourselves now. Then you will realize that gain is a different thing from glory. Just as there are diseases, or dullnesses of the senses, which prevent certain people from being able to taste food: so, by the same token, debauchees, misers and criminals are unattracted by glory.

However, if the hope of being praised cannot entice you to behave decently, is fear equally incapable of scaring you out of your repulsive behaviour? I know the law courts cause you no alarm. If that is due to innocence, you are to be commended. But if the reason is your reliance upon force, do you not understand this: that the man whose imperviousness to judicial processes is due to such a cause has pressing reason to feel terrors of quite another kind? For if you are not afraid of

---

[3] The Roman soldier and statesman Marcus Licinius Crassus Dives (c. 115–53 BC) was an associate of Julius Caesar and Pompey in the 50s BC who was killed on campaign against the Parthians in 53 BC. Though often an opponent of Cicero, and renowned for his wealth, he is here mentioned as a distinguished politician of the old school.

[4] From the Beqa'a valley in Lebanon, and famed for their skill at archery.

[5] The 'Liberators', who had assassinated Caesar.

[6] The dictatorship was an old Roman office for use in times of emergency, and normally for a maximum of six months. Caesar had turned it into the basis of a monarchy by being declared 'perpetual dictator'.

brave men and good Romans — seeing that armed satellites keep them away from your person — believe me, your own supporters will not stand you for very much longer. To be afraid of danger from one's own people night and day is no sort of a life; and you can hardly have men who owe you more, in terms of benefactions, than some of Caesar's killers owed to him.

However, you and he are not in any way comparable! His character was an amalgamation of genius, method, memory, culture, thoroughness, intellect, and industry. His achievements in war, though disastrous for our country, were none the less mighty. After working for many years to become king and autocrat, he surmounted tremendous efforts and perils and achieved his purpose. By entertainments, public works, food-distributions, and banquets, he seduced the ignorant populace; his friends he bound to his allegiance by rewarding them, his enemies by what looked like mercy. By a mixture of intimidation and indulgence, he inculcated in a free community the habit of servitude.

Your ambition to reign, Antony, certainly deserves to be compared with Caesar's. But in not a single other respect are you entitled to the same comparison. For the many evils which Caesar inflicted upon our country have at least yielded certain benefits. To take a single example, the people of Rome have now discovered what degrees of confidence they can repose in this or that person. They have discovered who are fit to be entrusted with their fortunes, and who, on the other hand, need to be shunned. Do these facts never occur to you? Do you never understand the significance of this: that brave men have now learnt to appreciate the noble achievement, the wonderful benefaction, the glorious renown, of killing a tyrant? When men could not endure Caesar, will they endure you? Mark my words, this time there will be crowds competing to do the deed. They will not wait for a suitable opportunity — they will be too impatient.

Antony: some time, at long last, think of your country. Think of the people from whom you come — not the people with whom you associate. Let your relationship with myself be as you please: but your country I pray you to make your friend once again. However, your behaviour is a matter for yourself to decide. As for mine, I will declare how I shall conduct myself. When I was a young man I defended our state: in my old age I shall not abandon it. Having scorned the swords of Catilina, I shall not be intimidated by yours. On the contrary, I would gladly offer my own body, if my death could redeem the freedom of our nation — if it could cause the long-suffering people of Rome to find final relief from its labours.

For if, nearly 20 years ago, I declared in this very temple that death could not come prematurely to a man who had been consul, how much greater will be my reason to say this again now that I am old. After the honours that I have been awarded, Senators, after the deeds that I have done, death actually seems to me desirable. Two things only I pray for. One, that in dying I may leave the Roman people free — the immortal gods could grant me no greater gift. My other prayer is this: that no man's fortunes may fail to correspond with his services to our country!

John Cleese
English comic actor and writer

John Marwood Cleese (1939–) was born in Weston-super-Mare. He studied at Cambridge University, where he joined the Footlights (1963), subsequently performing with them in London, New Zealand and the USA. He appeared in the Broadway production of *Half a Sixpence* (1965) and returned to the UK to write and perform in such television series as *The Frost Report* (1966) and *At Last the 1948 Show* (1967). With Graham Chapman (1941–89) he wrote scripts for television (*Doctor in the House*, 1968) and film (*The Rise and Rise of Michael Rimmer*, 1970). He then joined *Monty Python's Flying Circus* (1969–74), an anarchic series that changed the face of British television humour with its surreal comedy and animated graphics. The Monty Python team subsequently collaborated on such films as *Monty Python's Life of Brian* (1979) and *Monty Python's Meaning of Life* (1983). He had further success as the writer and star of the series *Fawlty Towers* (1975, 1979) and the films *A Fish Called Wanda* (1988) and *Fierce Creatures* (1996). His other film appearances include *Privates on Parade* (1982), *Clockwise* (1985), *Bullseye!* (1990) and two Harry Potter films (2001, 2002); subsequent film roles have largely been voice-overs such as the last three *Shrek* films (2004, 2007, 2010). On television, he played a straight role in *The Taming of the Shrew* (1980) and presented the documentary *The Human Face* (2001).

'I'd obviously like to thank some people'
19 March 1989, satellite link to London, England, from Los Angeles, California, USA

🐦

By the mid-1980s, John Cleese had become one of Britain's most successful and admired comic writer/performers. His next project was a collaboration with the veteran British film director Charles Crichton (1910–99), known for Ealing comedies such as *The Lavender Hill Mob* (1951) and *The Titfield Thunderbolt* (1953). Co-written and co-directed by Cleese and Crichton, *A Fish Called Wanda* stars Cleese as starchy London lawyer Archie Leach (the real name of British-born Hollywood star Cary Grant). When Leach becomes embroiled with an Anglo-American gang of criminals, his principles are swayed by romantic feelings for Wanda (played by American actress Jamie Lee Curtis).

Co-starring Michael Palin (a fellow member of the Monty Python group) and American actor Kevin Kline, the film was a hit on both sides of the Atlantic, winning BAFTA awards for Cleese (best actor) and Palin (best supporting actor) and a best supporting actor Academy Award for Kline. At the BAFTA ceremony, Cleese – appearing by satellite link-up with fellow British comic Dudley Moore, who presented the award to him – gave this extraordinary acceptance speech.

He begins along conventional lines, thanking members of the cast (including his daughter Cynthia Caylor, who played Archie's daughter) and crew. There is perhaps a hint of satire in Cleese's opening remarks – a pastiche of the faux modesty often apparent in actors receiving awards. But before long, Cleese's anarchic sense of bathos manifests itself in a string of tributes of escalating irrelevance and absurdity.

Cleese's final acknowledgement may not be altogether facetious. Following the release of *Monty Python's Life of Brian*, the Pythons had been widely accused of blasphemy.

🐦

[*Dudley Moore (handing over the BAFTA award):* 'John … and this is yours I believe.']

Isn't it nice?

[*Moore:* 'May I hand it to you?']

I wish they'd given it to Kevin, because I thought his performance was better than mine, but I'm very happy to accept it on his behalf.

And erm … I'd obviously like to thank some people. I'll keep it short. I want to thank Charlie Crichton for doing the plot with me and Jamie and Kevin for writing their parts. I would like to thank Michael Palin[1] for checking the scene numbers. I'd also like to thank John Comfort,[2] Jonathan Benson,[3] Roger Murray-Leach,[4] Hazel Pethig,[5] Glenn Palmer-Smith,[6] Cynthia Caylor, Maria Aitken,[7] Jonathan Aitken,[8] Lord Beaverbrook,[9] Eleanor Roosevelt,[10] Jacques Cousteau and his wife Mimi,[11] Søren Kierkegaard,[12] Gisela Werbisek-Piffle,[13] Sonny Liston,[14] Anne Haydon-Jones and her husband Pip,[15] Gregor Mendel, the founder of the science of genetics, my tailor, Harriet Beecher-Stowe, author of *Uncle Tom's Cabin*,

[1] Incorrectly pronounced 'Pallin'.
[2] Associate producer.
[3] Assistant director.
[4] Production designer.
[5] Costume designer.
[6] The US photographer Glenn Palmer-Smith is a friend of Cleese.
[7] The English actress Maria Aitken (1945–) played Archie Leach's wife Wendy.
[8] The English politician Jonathan Aitken (1942–), the elder brother of Maria Aitken, was then a Conservative MP.
[9] The Canadian-born British press baron William Maxwell Aitken, 1st Baron Beaverbrook (1879–1964).
[10] The US humanitarian Eleanor Roosevelt (1884–1962) was the niece of President THEODORE ROOSEVELT and wife of President FRANKLIN D ROOSEVELT.
[11] The French marine biologist Jacques Cousteau (1910–97) married Simone Melchior in 1937.

[12] The Danish philosopher Søren Kierkegaard (1813–55) was one of the founders of Existentialism.

[13] The Austro-Hungarian actress Gisela Werbisek (1875–1956) married the Austro-Hungarian actor John Piffle (1886–1951).

[14] The US boxer Charles 'Sonny' Liston (1932–70) was world heavyweight champion, 1962–4.

[15] The British tennis player Ann Haydon-Jones *née Adrianne Haydon* (1938–) was a British tennis star who won at Wimbledon in 1969. She married the tennis player Pip Jones in 1962. Cleese had mentioned them in a Monty Python sketch.

[16] An east London football team.

[17] The Prusso-German statesman Otto von Bismarck (1815–98). Kline's character in the film was named Otto.

[18] The organization does not exist; there is a Royal Society for the Protection of Birds, founded in 1889.

[19] The English businessman Basil Smallpiece (1907–92) was best known as chairman of the Cunard shipping line, 1965–71.

the London Symphony Orchestra Brass Section, the Leyton Orient[16] strikers, Mother, Bismarck,[17] The Royal Society for the Prevention of Birds,[18] Sir Basil Smallpiece[19] …

[*Long pause and the sound of Moore's laughter.*]

… **ST FRANCIS OF ASSISI,** Diana Ross and the Supremes,[20] Earl Haig,[21] Wile E Coyote,[22] Herb Alpert and his Tijuana Brass,[23] Herman Goering,[24] Dame Agatha Christie,[25] the Planet Saturn and of course all of its rings, Joan Collins,[26] the publicity department of Turkish Airways, the Unknown Soldier, Tammy Wynette,[27] and last … but of course not least … God.

[20] The US singer Diana Ross (1944–) was the central member of this seminal Motown trio, formed in 1961.

[21] The Scottish general Douglas Haig, 1st Earl Haig (1861–1928) who was Commander-in-Chief of British forces in 1915–18.

[22] The hungry canine predator Wile E Coyote is a Warner Bros cartoon character in perpetual, inept pursuit of the fast-moving bird Road Runner.

[23] The US trumpeter and music business executive Herb Alpert (1935–) and his 'middle-of-the-road' band enjoyed success in the 1960s and early 1970s.

[25] The German politician Hermann Goering (1893–1946).

[26] The English writer Dame Agatha Christie (1890–1976) wrote popular crime fiction and drama.

[27] The English actress Joan Collins (1933–) is known for her racy roles.

[28] The US country singer Tammy Wynette (1942–98) was known for her troubled life and tearjerking lyrics.

Bill Clinton

American politician

William Jefferson Clinton (1946–) was born William Jefferson Blythe in Hope, Arkansas. His father was killed in a road accident before he was born; he later adopted the surname of his stepfather, Roger Clinton. He was educated at Georgetown University and Yale Law School, and at Oxford, where he was a Rhodes scholar. He taught law at the University of Arkansas (1973–6), marrying HILLARY CLINTON (*née* Rodham) in 1975. He was elected Attorney General (1976), then governor (1978) of Arkansas. He was the youngest person ever to hold that office, and served for five terms (1979–81, 1983–92). In 1992, on a platform based on tackling economic recession and voter disillusionment, he defeated President George H W Bush and was elected president, thus ending a twelve-year Republican hold on the office. A popular and charismatic figure, he became, in 1996, the first Democrat president to gain re-election since FRANKLIN D ROOSEVELT in 1936. His presidency saw economic prosperity, with low inflation and unemployment, and a focus on promoting peace on the international stage in Northern Ireland and the Middle East. However, it was also marked by scandal, most notably in 1998 when his affair with White House intern Monica Lewinsky, initially denied, was followed by impeachment on charges of perjury and obstruction of justice; he was subsequently acquitted by the Senate. By the time he stepped down in January 2001, he had the highest approval rating of any outgoing president since records began. He endorsed the presidential bid of Democrat Senator John Kerry in 2004 and those of BARACK OBAMA in 2008 and 2012. In 2012 he became the United Nations Special Envoy to Haiti.

'We will take away their guns and give them books'
13 November 1993, Memphis, Tennessee, USA

This speech was given at the Church of God in Christ, Memphis, the venue where MARTIN LUTHER KING, on the night before his assassination in 1968, had delivered his final speech, 'I have seen the promised land'. Playing to a predominantly African–American audience, Clinton was not slow to embrace King's legacy and align himself with it. He not only quotes a passage from King's famous address; he goes so far as to invent a dialogue between himself and the assassinated folk hero of black America.

Clinton's purpose was to address a raft of problems afflicting the African–American community – social exclusion, broken families, unemployment, underage parenthood, drugs, guns and violent crime, much of it committed by children – and to demonstrate that his administration was tackling them.

Early in the speech he refers to government appointments and legislation designed to include African–Americans in American public life. Later, he lists practical measures he is taking to tackle violent crime and to provide employment. But he underpins his argument with a strong endorsement of family and Christianity: an appeal to values dear to his audience.

For the most part, Clinton's tone is anecdotal, homely and personal – as a counterbalance to shocking stories of violence and deprivation, he refers to 'little bitty kids', to the black Mayor of Baltimore as 'a dear friend', to a 'handsome young [implicitly black] man'. But the speech culminates in a rousing message of intent, laced with religious fervour, one which echoes the oratorical style of King himself.

[1] King's speech of 3 April 1968 is included in this book.

Last year I was elected president of this great country. I never dreamed that I would ever have a chance to come to this hallowed place where Martin Luther King gave his last sermon.[1] I ask you to think today about the purpose for which I ran and the purpose for which so many of you worked to put me in this great office.

I have worked hard to keep faith with our common efforts – to restore the economy; to reverse the politics of helping only those at the top of our totem pole and not the hard-working middle class or the poor; to bring our people together across racial and regional and political lines; to make a strength out of our diversity instead of letting it tear us apart; to reward work and family and community and try to move us forward into the 21st century. I have tried to keep faith.

Thirteen per cent of all my presidential appointments are African–Americans, and there are five African–Americans in the Cabinet of the

United States – two-and-a-half times as many as have ever served in the history of this great land.

[*Applause.*]

I have sought to advance the right to vote with the Motor Voter Bill,[2] supported so strongly by all the churches in our country. And next week it will be my great honour to sign the Restoration of Religious Freedoms Act,[3] a bill supported widely by people across all religions and political philosophies to put back the real meaning of the Constitution – to give you and every other American the freedom to do what is most important in your life, to worship God as your spirit leads you.

[*Applause.*]

… If Martin Luther King – who said, 'Like Moses, I am on the mountaintop and I can see the promised land, but I'm not going to be able to get there with you, but we will get there,' – if he were to reappear by my side today and give us a report card on the last 25 years, what would he say? 'You did a good job,' he would say, 'voting and electing people who formerly were not electable because of the colour of their skin.' You have more political power, and that is good.

'You did a good job,' he would say, 'letting people who have the ability to do so live wherever they want to live, go wherever they want to go in this great country. You did a good job,' he would say, 'elevating people of colour into the ranks of the United States armed forces to the very top, or into the very top of our government.

'You did a very good job,' he would say. He would say, 'You did a good job creating a black middle class of people who really are doing well; and the middle class is growing more among African–Americans than among non-African–Americans. You did a good job. You did a good job in opening opportunity.

'But,' he would say, 'I did not live and die to see the American family destroyed.'

[*Applause.*]

'I did not live and die to see 13-year-old boys get automatic weapons and gun down nine-year-olds just for the kick of it. I did not live and die to see young people destroy their own lives with drugs and then build fortunes destroying the lives of others. That is not what I came here to do.'

[*Applause.*]

'I fought for freedom,' he would say, 'but not for the freedom of people to kill each other with reckless abandon; not for the freedom of children to have children and the fathers of the children walk away from them and abandon them as if they don't amount to anything. I fought for people to have the right to work, but not to have whole communities and people abandoned. This is not what I lived and died for.

'My fellow Americans,' he would say, 'I fought to stop white people from being so filled with hate that they would wreak violence on black people. I did not fight for the right of black people to murder other black people with reckless abandon.'

[*Applause.*]

The other day, the Mayor of Baltimore,[4] a dear friend of mine, told me a story of visiting the family of a young man who had been killed – 18 years old – on Hallowe'en. He always went out with little bitty kids so they could trick-or-treat safely. And across the street from where they were walking on Hallowe'en, a 14-year-old boy gave a 13-year-old boy a gun and dared him to shoot the 18-year-old boy; and he shot him dead. And the Mayor

[2] The National Voter Registration Act of 1993 was designed to encourage American citizens to register as voters. Among other measures, it provided the opportunity to register when applying for a driving licence – hence the nickname 'Motor Voter Act'.

[3] A bill harking back to the First Amendment to the US Constitution, ratified in 1791, which secured the right to free exercise of religion. The bill proposed overturning any law if 'religious exercise is substantially burdened' by it, unless it served a 'compelling governmental interest'. It was passed in 1993.

[4] The African–American Democrat Kurt L Schmoke (1949–) served as Mayor of Baltimore, 1987–99.

had to visit the family.

In Washington, DC, where I live – your nation's capital, the symbol of freedom throughout the world – look how that freedom is being exercised. The other night a man came along the street and grabbed a one-year-old child and put the child in his car. The child may have been the child of the man. And two people were after him and they chased him in the car, and they just kept shooting with reckless abandon, knowing that baby was in the car. And they shot the man dead, and a bullet went through his body into the baby's body and blew the little bootee off the child's foot.

The other day, on the front page of our paper, the nation's capital, are we talking about world peace or world conflict? No – big article on the front page of *The Washington Post* about an eleven-year-old child planning her funeral – 'These are the hymns I want sung; this is the dress I want to wear; I know I'm not going to live very long.' That is not the freedom – the freedom to die before you're a teenager – is not what Martin Luther King lived and died for.

[*Applause.*]

More than 37,000 people die from gunshot wounds in this country every year. Gunfire is the leading cause of death in young men. And now that we've all gotten so cool that everybody can get a semi-automatic weapon, a person shot now is three times more likely to die than 15 years ago, because they're likely to have three bullets in them. A hundred and sixty thousand children stay home from school every day because they are scared they will be hurt in their schools.

The other day I was in California at a town meeting, and a handsome young man stood up and said, 'Mr President, my brother and I, we don't belong to gangs. We don't have guns. We don't do drugs. We want to go to school. We want to be professionals. We want to work hard. We want to do well. We want to have families. And we changed our school because the school we were in was so dangerous. So when we showed up to the new school to register, my brother and I were standing in line and somebody ran into the school and started shooting a gun. My brother was shot down standing right in front of me at the safer school.'

The freedom to do that kind of thing is not what Martin Luther King lived and died for; not what people gathered in this hallowed church for the night before he was assassinated in April of 1968. If you had told anybody who was here in that church on that night that we would abuse our freedom in that way, they would have found it hard to believe. And I tell you, it is our moral duty to turn it around …

So we are beginning. We are trying to pass a bill[5] to make our people safer, to put another 100,000 police officers on the street, to provide boot camps instead of prisons for young people who can still be rescued, to provide more safety in our schools, to restrict the availability of these awful assault weapons, to … require people to have their criminal background checked before they get a gun, and to say, if you're not old enough to vote and you're not old enough to go to war, you ought not to own a handgun, and you ought not to use one unless you're on a target range …

We need this crime bill now. We ought to give it to the American people for Christmas. And we need to move forward on all these other fronts. But I say to you, my fellow Americans, we need some other things as well. I do not believe we can repair the basic fabric of society until people who are willing to work have work. Work organizes life. It gives structure and discipline to life. It gives meaning and self-esteem to people who are parents. It gives a role

[5] The Violent Crime Control and Law Enforcement Act was eventually passed in September 1994. It included a ban on assault weapons, an expansion of the death penalty, increased police recruitment, boot camps for young offenders and measures against hate crimes, crimes against women and gang membership.

model to children. The famous African–American sociologist William Julius Wilson has written a stunning book called *The Truly Disadvantaged*,[6] in which he chronicles in breathtaking terms how the inner cities of our country have crumbled as work has disappeared. And we must find a way, through public and private sources, to enhance the attractiveness of the American people who live there to get investment there. We cannot, I submit to you, repair the American community and restore the American family until we provide the structure, the value, the discipline and the reward that work gives.

[*Applause.*]

… And I say to you, we have to make our people whole again. This church has stood for that. Why do you think you have five million members in this country? Because people know you are filled with the spirit of God to do the right thing in this life by them.

[*Applause.*]

So I say to you, we have to make a partnership – all the government agencies, all business folks – but where there are no families, where there is no order, where there is no hope, where we are reducing the size of our armed services because we have won the Cold War – who will be there to give structure, discipline and love to these children? You must do that. And we must help you.

Scripture says, 'You are the salt of the earth and the light of the world.'[7] That 'if your light shines before men they will give glory to the Father in Heaven'.[8] That is what we must do. That is what we must do. How would we explain it to Martin Luther King if he showed up today and said: 'Yes, we won the Cold War. Yes, the biggest threat that all of us grew up under, communism and nuclear war: communism gone; nuclear war receding. Yes, we developed all these miraculous technologies. Yes, we all have got a VCR in our home. It's interesting. Yes, we get 50 channels on the cable. Yes, without regard to race, if you work hard and play by the rules, you can get into a service academy or a good college, you'll do just great.'

How would we explain to him all these kids getting killed and killing each other? How would we justify the things that we permit that no other country in the world would permit? How could we explain that we gave people the freedom to succeed and we created conditions in which millions abuse that freedom to destroy the things that make life worth living and life itself? We cannot.

And so I say to you today, my fellow Americans, you gave me this job. And we're making progress on the things you hired me to do. But unless we deal with the ravages of crime and drugs and violence; and unless we recognize that it's due to the breakdown of the family, the community and the disappearance of jobs; and unless we say, some of this cannot be done by government because we have to reach deep inside to the values, the spirit, the soul and the truth of human nature, none of the other things we seek to do will ever take us where we need to go.

So in this pulpit, on this day, let me ask all of you in your heart to say: we will honour the life and the work of Martin Luther King; we will honour the meaning of our church; we will somehow, by God's grace, we will turn this around. We will give these children a future. We will take away their guns and give them books. We will take away their despair and give them hope. We will rebuild the families and the neighbourhoods and the communities.

We won't make all the work that has gone on here benefit just a few. We will do it together by the grace of God.

Thank you.

[6] Published in 1987.

[7] Matthew 5:13–14.

[8] Matthew 5:16.

'I have sinned'
11 September 1998, Washington, DC, USA

In January 1998, it was reported in the *Washington Post* that President Bill Clinton had been involved in a sexual relationship with the former White House intern Monica Lewinsky. Months of denials and smokescreens followed, including First Lady Hillary Clinton's assertion, in a television interview, that there had been a 'vast right-wing conspiracy' against her husband.

Finally, on 17 August, Clinton admitted to an 'improper physical relationship' with Lewinsky, in taped testimony to the Office of Independent Counsel and the grand jury. That evening, he made a brief televised address to the nation, in which he offered a rather bullish apology, adding: 'I intend to reclaim my family life for my family. It's nobody's business but ours.'

It soon became apparent that Clinton's approval ratings had not been impaired, but many commentators were not satisfied with his limited contrition. The public apologies continued, but it was not until the annual Religious Leaders' Breakfast at the White House on 11 September that Clinton finally hit the right tone.

The *Time* magazine columnist Lance Morrow wrote that Clinton had 'performed miserably' on 17 August, but reported watching the Dow Jones index steadily rise during the 11 September speech. Clinton had been nicknamed 'Slick Willy' for his polished handling of potential embarrassments – including the much-publicized investigation of the Clintons' failed Whitewater Development Corporation. Yet here his delivery is notably awkward and clumsy. Was this brought on by the shame of a 'broken spirit', or merely – as cynics suspected – a disingenuous show of penitence?

Thank you very much, ladies and gentlemen. Welcome to the White House, and to this day, to which Hillary and the Vice President and I look forward so much every year.

This is always an important day for our country … It is an unusual and, I think, unusually important day today. I may not be quite as easy with my words today as I have been in years past, and I was up rather late last night thinking about and praying about what I ought to say today. And rather unusual for me, I actually tried to write it down. So if you will forgive me, I will do my best to say what it is I want to say to you – and I may have to take my glasses out to read my own writing.

First, I want to say to all of you that, as you might imagine, I have been on quite a journey these last few weeks to get to the end of this, to the rock bottom truth of where I am and where we all are. I agree with those who have said that in my first statement after I testified I was not contrite enough. I don't think there is a fancy way to say that I have sinned.

It is important to me that everybody who has been hurt know that the sorrow I feel is genuine: first and most important, my family; also my friends, my staff, my Cabinet, Monica Lewinsky and her family, and the American people. I have asked all for their forgiveness.

But I believe that to be forgiven, more than sorrow is required – at least two more things. First, genuine repentance – a determination to change and to repair breaches of my own making. I have repented. Second, what my Bible calls a 'broken spirit'; an understanding that I must have God's help to be the person that I want to be; a willingness to give the very forgiveness I seek; a renunciation of the pride and the anger which cloud judgement, lead people to excuse and compare and to blame and complain.

Now, what does all this mean for me and for us? First, I will instruct my lawyers to mount a vigorous defence, using all available appropriate arguments. But legal language must not obscure the fact that I have done wrong. Second, I will continue on the path of repentance, seeking pastoral support and that of other caring people so that they can hold me accountable for my own commitment.

Third, I will intensify my efforts to lead our country and the world toward peace and freedom, prosperity and harmony, in the hope that with a broken spirit and a still strong heart I can be used for greater good, for we have many blessings and many challenges and so much work to do.

In this, I ask for your prayers and for your help in healing our nation. And though I cannot move beyond or forget this – indeed, I must always keep it as a caution light in my life – it is very important that our nation move forward.

I am very grateful for the many, many people – clergy and ordinary citizens alike – who have written me with wise counsel. I am profoundly grateful for the support of so many Americans, who somehow through it all seem to still know that I care about them a great deal, that I care about their problems and their dreams. I am grateful for those who have stood by me and who say that in this case and many others, the bounds of presidency have been excessively and unwisely invaded. That may be.

Nevertheless, in this case, it may be a blessing, because I still sinned. And if my repentance is genuine and sustained, and if I can maintain both a broken spirit and a strong heart, then good can come of this for our country as well as for me and my family.

[*Applause.*]

The children of this country can learn in a profound way that integrity is important and selfishness is wrong, but God can change us and make us strong at the broken places. I want to embody those lessons for the children of this country – for that little boy in Florida who came up to me and said that he wanted to grow up and be president and to be just like me.[1] I want the parents of all the children in America to be able to say that to their children.

A couple of days ago, when I was in Florida, a Jewish friend of mine gave me this liturgy book called *Gates of Repentance*.[2] And there was this incredible passage from the Yom Kippur[3] liturgy. I would like to read it to you: 'Now is the time for turning. The leaves are beginning to turn from green to red to orange. The birds are beginning to turn and are heading once more toward the south. The animals are beginning to turn to storing their food for the winter. For leaves, birds and animals, turning comes instinctively. But for us, turning does not come so easily. It takes an act of will for us to make a turn. It means breaking old habits. It means admitting that we have been wrong, and this is never easy. It means losing face. It means starting all over again. And this is always painful. It means saying I am sorry. It means recognizing that we have the ability to change. These things are terribly hard to do.

'But unless we turn, we will be trapped forever in yesterday's ways. Lord help us to turn, from callousness to sensitivity, from hostility to love, from pettiness to purpose, from envy to contentment, from carelessness to discipline, from fear to faith. Turn us around, O Lord, and bring us back toward you. Revive our lives as at the beginning, and turn us toward each other, Lord, for in isolation there is no life.'

I thank my friend for that. I thank you for being here. I ask you to share my prayer, that God will search me and know my heart, try me and know my anxious thoughts, see if there is any hurtfulness in me, and lead me toward the life everlasting. I ask that God give me a clean heart, let me walk by faith and not sight.

I ask once again to be able to love my neighbour – all my neighbours – as

[3] In Judaism, Yom Kippur is the annual Day of Atonement festival, which falls on the tenth day of the month of Tishri, ie sometime between mid-September and mid-October.

[1] Two days before he gave this speech, Clinton had spoken at Hillcrest School in Orlando, Florida. Later that day, he reported a young boy telling him, 'Mr President, I want to grow up to be president. I want to be a president like you.'
[2] A classic text by Rabbi Yonah of Gerona (1180–1263).

myself, to be an instrument of God's peace; to let the words of my mouth and the meditations of my heart and, in the end, the work of my hands, be pleasing.[4] This is what I wanted to say to you today.

Thank you. God bless you.

[4] See Psalms 19:14.

Robert Clive
English general and colonial administrator

Robert Clive, *later 1st Baron Clive of Plassey, also called Clive of India* (1725–74), was born near Market Drayton, Shropshire. In 1743 he joined the East India Company in Madras, where his moody and quarrelsome behaviour culminated in a suicide attempt. In 1751 he held Arcot with a small force against a Franco-Indian army for 53 days before being relieved. In 1753 he married Margaret Maskelyne, sister of the astronomer Nevil Maskelyne, and returned to England in triumph. In 1755, however, he returned to India, where he was soon called on to avenge the so-called Black Hole of Calcutta (1756) in which British and European prisoners perished in inhumane captivity after the city fell to Siraj-ud-Dawlah, the Nawab of Bengal. Calcutta was soon retaken, and Chandernagore, the French settlement, captured. At Plassey (1757) he defeated Siraj-ud-Dawlah. For three years he was sole ruler in all but name of Bengal on behalf of the East India Company. In 1760 he returned to England, to be hailed by WILLIAM PITT, the Elder as 'a heaven-born general'. In 1761 he entered Parliament, and in 1762 he was elevated to the peerage. Clive was sent to India again in 1764 as governor and commander-in-chief of Bengal. He established British supremacy throughout India, but on his return to England in 1767 he was faced with a parliamentary storm about his handling of the East India Company's affairs. Although ultimately vindicated in 1773, he committed suicide soon afterwards.

'Indostan was always an absolute despotic government'
30 March 1772, London, England

Robert Clive had retired from India in 1767, having vanquished, united and stabilized much of the country under the auspices of the East India Company. Although he had worked to build an administrative structure and tackle endemic bribery, persistent questions were raised at home about the corruption and cruelty rife within the company – and Clive's own conduct in this regard (which had not been unimpeachable). His former ally Pitt the Elder, now ennobled as the Earl of Chatham, was among those who feared British public life might be contaminated by wealth and unscrupulous practices imported from India.

Here, Clive addresses the House of Commons on a 'Motion made for Leave to bring in a Bill, for the Better Regulation of the Affairs of the East India Company and of their Servants in India, and for the due Administration of Justice in Bengal'. Reluctantly sucked back into Anglo-Indian politics, Clive casts himself as a victim to duty, powerless to overhaul a degenerate system.

In his eloquent speech, he vividly dissects the process of corruption, using a prolonged metaphor of sexual adultery. Admitting his own receipt of gifts, he describes the process by which young British men arrived in India, already imbued with avarice at home, and became immersed in a corrupting environment. He acknowledges misdeeds, but attributes them to understandable human frailty.

He was vindicated by Parliament the following year, but his enduring sense of injustice helped drive him to suicide, aged 49.

It is with great diffidence that I attempt to speak to this House, but I find myself so particularly called upon that I must make the attempt, though I should expose myself in so doing. With what confidence can I venture to give my sentiments upon a subject of such national consequence, who myself stand charged with having been the cause of the present melancholy situation of the Company's affairs in Bengal?

This House can have no reliance on my opinion whilst such an impression remains unremoved. The House will therefore give me leave to remove this impression; and to endeavour to restore myself to that favourable opinion which, I flatter myself, they entertained of my conduct before these charges were exhibited against me. Nor do I wish to lay my conduct before the Members of this House only. I speak likewise to my country in general, upon whom I put myself, not only without reluctance, but with alacrity.

It is well known that I was called upon, in the year 1764, to undertake the management of the Company's affairs in Bengal, when they were in a very critical and dangerous situation. It is as well known that my circumstances were independent and affluent. Happy in the sense of my past conduct and services, happy in my family, happy in my connections, happy in everything but my health, which I lost in the Company's service, never to be regained – this situation, this happiness, I relinquished at the call of the Company, to go to a far distant, unhealthy climate, to undertake the envious task of reformation.

My enemies will suppose that I was actuated by mercenary motives. But this House, and my country at large, will I hope think more liberally. They will conceive that I undertook this expedition from a principle of gratitude, from a point of honour and from a desire of doing essential service to that Company, under whose auspices I had acquired my fortune and my fame.

My prospects on going abroad were by no means pleasing or encouraging; for after a violent contest, 13 directors only were chosen who thought favourably of my endeavours to serve the Company; the other eleven were not willing that their good purposes should be accomplished by me. They first gave all possible obstruction to my acceptance of the government, and afterwards declined investing me with those powers without which I could not have acted effectually, for the benefit of the Company.

Upon my arrival in Bengal, I found the powers given were so loosely worded that they were immediately contested by the council.[1] I was determined, however, to put the most extensive construction upon them, because I was determined to do my duty to my country …

[1] The cabinet council of the East India Company, whose power Clive theoretically had the right to overrule.

Dangers and difficulties were on every side, but I resolved to pursue it. In short, I was determined do my duty to the public, although I should incur the odium of the whole settlement. The welfare of the Company required a vigorous exertion, and I took the resolution of cleansing the Augean stable.[2]

It was that conduct which has occasioned the public papers to teem with scurrility and abuse against me, ever since my return to England. It was that conduct which occasioned these charges. But it was that conduct which enables me now, when the day of judgement is come, to look my judges in the face. It was that conduct which enables me now to lay my hand upon my heart and most solemnly to declare to this House, to the gallery and to the whole world at large that I never, in a single instance, lost sight of what I thought the honour and true interest of my country and the Company; that I was never guilty of any acts of violence or oppression, unless the bringing offenders to justice can be deemed so; that as to extortion, such an idea never entered into my mind; that I did not suffer those under me to commit acts of violence, oppression or extortion; that my influence was never employed for the advantage of any man, contrary to the strictest principles of honour and justice; and that so far from reaping any benefit myself from the expedition, I returned to England many thousands of pounds out of pocket …

[2] In Greek mythology, one of the twelve labours allotted to Hercules was cleaning the stables belonging to Augeas, King of Elis, which were inhabited by a large number of cattle. As Clive implies, the task involved tackling a huge quantity of filth.

Indostan[3] was always an absolute despotic government. The inhabitants, especially of Bengal, in inferior stations, are servile, mean, submissive and humble. In superior stations, they are luxurious, effeminate, tyrannical, treacherous, venal, cruel.

The country of Bengal is called, by way of distinction, the paradise of the earth. It not only abounds with the necessaries of life to such a degree as to furnish a great part of India with its superfluity, but it abounds in very curious and valuable manufactures, sufficient not only for its own use, but

[3] Indostan or Hindustan is usually taken to mean the northern part of the Indian subcontinent, roughly equivalent to the extent of the Mughal Empire.

for the use of the whole globe. The silver of the west and the gold of the east have for many years been pouring into that country, and goods only have been sent out in return. This has added to the luxury and extravagance of Bengal.

From time immemorial it has been the custom of that country, for an inferior never to come into the presence of a superior without a present. It begins at the nabob,[4] and ends at the lowest man that has an inferior. The nabob has told me that the small presents he received amounted to £300,000 a year; and I can believe him; because I know that I might have received as much during my last government.

The Company's servants have ever been accustomed to receive presents. Even before we took part in the country's troubles, when our possessions were very confined and limited, the Governor and others used to receive presents; and I will take upon me to assert that there has not been an officer commanding His Majesty's fleet, nor an officer commanding His Majesty's army; not a governor, not a member of council, not any other person, civil or military, in such a station as to have connection with the country government, who has not received presents.

With regard to Bengal, there they flow in abundance indeed. Let the House figure to itself a country consisting of 15 millions of inhabitants, a revenue of four millions sterling, and a trade in proportion. By progressive steps the Company have become sovereigns of that empire. Can it be supposed that their servants will refrain from advantages so obviously resulting from their situation?

The Company's servants, however, have not been the authors of those acts of violence and oppression of which it is the fashion to accuse them. Such crimes are committed by the natives of the country acting as their agents and for the most part without their knowledge. Those agents, and the banyans,[5] never desist, till, according to the ministerial phrase, they have dragged their masters into the kennel; and then the acts of violence begin. The passion for gain is as strong as the passion of love.

I will suppose, that two intimate friends have lived long together; that one of them has married a beautiful woman; that the friend still continues to live in the house, and that this beautiful woman, forgetting her duty to her husband, attempts to seduce the friend; who, though in the vigour of youth, may from high principles of honour, at first, resist the temptation, and even rebuke the lady. But if he still continues to live under the same roof, and she still continues to throw out her allurements, he must be seduced at last or fly.

Now the banyan is the fair lady to the Company's servant. He lays his bags of silver before him today; gold tomorrow; jewels the next day; and if these fail, he then tempts him in the way of his profession, which is trade. He assures him that goods may be had cheap, and sold to great advantage up the country. In this manner is the attack carried on; and the Company's servant has no resource, for he cannot fly. In short, flesh and blood cannot bear it.

Let us for a moment consider the nature of the education of a young man who goes to India. The advantages arising from the Company's service are now very generally known; and the great object of every man is to get his son appointed a writer to Bengal; which is usually at the age of 16. His parents and relations represent to him how certain he is of making a fortune; that my Lord Such-a-one and my Lord Such-a-one acquired so much money in such a time; and Mr Such-a-one and Mr Such-a-one so

[4] A prosperous European merchant in India (from the Hindi word *nawab*).

[5] A Hindu trader or broker.

much in such a time. Thus are their principles corrupted at their very setting out, and as they generally go a good many together, they inflame one another's expectations to such a degree, in the course of the voyage, that they fix upon a period for their return before their arrival.

Let us now take a view of one of these writers arrived in Bengal, and not worth a groat. As soon as he lands, a banyan, worth perhaps £100,000, desires he may have the honour of serving this young gentleman, at four shillings and sixpence per month. The Company has provided chambers for him, but they are not good enough; the banyan finds better. The young man takes a walk about the town, he observes that other writers, arrived only a year before him, live in splendid apartments or have houses of their own, ride upon fine prancing Arabian horses, and in palanquins and chaises; that they keep seraglios,[6] make entertainments, and treat with champagne and claret.

[6] Harems.

When he returns, he tells the banyan what he has observed. The banyan assures him he may soon arrive at the same good fortune; he furnishes him with money; he is then at his mercy. The advantages of the banyan advance with the rank of his master, who in acquiring one fortune generally spends three. But this is not the worst of it: he is in a state of dependence under the banyan, who commits acts of violence and oppression, as his interest prompts him to, under the pretended sanction and authority of the Company's servant.

Hence, Sir, arises the clamour against the English gentlemen in India. But look at them in a retired situation, when returned to England, when they are no longer nabobs and sovereigns of the East. See if there be any thing tyrannical in their disposition towards their inferiors: see if they are not good and humane masters: are they not charitable? Are they not benevolent? Are they not generous? Are they not hospitable? If they are, thus far, not contemptible members of society, and if in all their dealings between man and man, their conduct is strictly honourable: if, in short, there has not yet been one character found amongst them sufficiently flagitious[7] for Mr Foote[8] to exhibit on the theatre in the Haymarket, may we not conclude, that if they have erred, it has been because they were men, placed in situations subject to little or no control?

[7] Guilty of terrible crimes.

[8] The English actor-manager and playwright Samuel Foote (1721–77) was known for his scurrilous plays, staged at the Haymarket Theatre, London. These included *The Nabob* (1772), a satire on the East India Company.

But if the servants of the Company are to be loaded with the demerit of every misfortune in India, let them also have the merit they are entitled to. The court of directors surely will not claim to themselves the merit of those advantages which the nation and the Company are at present in possession of. The officers of the navy and army have had great share in the execution; but the Company's servants were the Cabinet council, who planned everything; and to them also may be ascribed some part of the merit of our great acquisitions.

Sebastian Coe
Athlete and politician

Sebastian Coe *Lord Coe* (1956–) is a former British middle-distance runner who won gold medals for the men's 1500 metres events at the 1980 and 1984 Olympic Games. He served as a Conservative Member of Parliament from 1993 to 1997 and was made a life peer in 2000, taking a seat in the House of Lords. He headed the successful London bid for the Games in 2005 and became chairman of the London Organizing Committee.

'A Games by everyone'
12 August 2012, Olympic Stadium, London

Sebastian Coe's speech delivered at the closing ceremony of the London 2012 Olympic Games was a concise but powerful exercise in crowd-pleasing rhetoric, shot through with just the right note of patriotism. The stadium audience, who had spent an evening being entertained by a spectacular and nostalgic trip through British pop music, received Lord Coe's speech with unmitigated enthusism.

[1] The British queen Elizabeth II was not present at the closing ceremony but was represented by Prince Henry of Wales in the company of the Duchess of Cambridge.

Your Majesty, Your Royal Highnesses,[1] President of the International Olympic Committee,[2] distinguished guests, ladies and gentlemen.

Today sees the closing of a wonderful Games in a wonderful city. We lit the flame and we lit up the world. For the third time in its history, London was granted the trust of the Olympic Movement and once again we have shown ourselves worthy of that trust.

And for that I want to say thank you. Thank you to the people who built the stadiums, the people who created a new neighbourhood in an old city, the people who stood guard to keep us safe.

Thank you to the London organizing team, to every one of you who has worked so hard and who has turned the buildings into a theatre of sport and drama and choreographed these Games, and to the International Olympic Committee, which has been with us every step of the way.

Thank you to the tens of thousands of volunteers, volunteers who gave their time, their boundless enthusiasm and their goodwill and who have the right to say tonight 'I made London 2012'.[3]

And thank you to the people of this country. The British people got behind London's bid and they got behind London's Games. Our opening ceremony proclaimed that these would be a Games for everyone. At our closing ceremony, we can say that these were a Games by everyone.

London 2012 has played host to some incredible sport. To awe-inspiring feats that are the synthesis of incredible dedication and skill by the world's great sportsmen and women. To all the Olympians who came to London to compete – thank you. Those of us who came to watch witnessed moments of heroism and heartbreak that will live long in the memory. You have our admiration and our congratulations.

This may the end of these two weeks of glorious the spirit of thess Games will inspire a generation.

We have seen in these days what tenacity can do, what ambition can, what imagination can do. We know more now both as individuals and as a nation just what we are capable of, and that knowledge will drive us on.

On the first day of these Games I said we were determined to do it right, I said that these Games would see the best of us. On the last day I can finish with these words: 'When our time came, Britain, we did it right.' Thank you.

[2] The Belgian Jacques Rogge (1942–) is the eighth President of the International Olympic Committee (IOC), elected in 2001. He was standing beside Coe as he gave his speech and would go on to officially close the Games, having declared the Games as 'happy and glorious'.

[3] This thank you drew one of the most enthusiastic and sustained cheers from the crowd. The 'Games Makers' were widely seen as one of the most successful features of the London 2012 Games.

Tim Collins
British soldier

Tim Collins (1960–) was born and raised in Belfast, Northern Ireland, and as a schoolboy witnessed sectarian violence. He studied economics at Queen's University, Belfast, then trained as a British Army officer at the Royal Military Academy, Sandhurst. From 1981, he served with the 2nd Battalion, Royal Irish Rangers in Germany, Cyprus, the Falkland Islands, Gibraltar and Northern Ireland. He became a lieutenant colonel and commanding officer of the 1st Battalion, Royal Irish Regiment in 2001. He led the regiment into action during the invasion of Iraq in 2003. His speech to his troops before battle was reported all over the world. He was later accused of having mistreated Iraqi civilians and prisoners of war, but was cleared following an investigation. At this time he also won two libel cases against British newspapers. He was promoted to full colonel, but resigned from the army in January 2004. He was awarded an OBE in 2003. In 2005, he published a memoir, *Rules of Engagement: A Life in Conflict*, and became a frequent media commentator on military affairs. He has publicly criticized American and British policy towards Iraq and has described his own attitude during the war as 'naïve'.

'We go to liberate, not to conquer'
19 March 2003, Fort Blair Mayne, Kuwait

This speech, delivered hours before the invasion of Iraq, made its speaker the most famous soldier of the war. It was addressed to about 800 soldiers of the 1st Battalion of the Royal Irish Regiment at a military base in Kuwait, some 20 miles south of the Iraqi border. A sandstorm had just died down, and the men gathered in a dusty courtyard to listen to their commanding officer.

A hardened soldier – known among colleagues as 'Nails' – Lieutenant-Colonel Collins had not scripted the speech. His intention was to bolster morale; in the UK, Prime Minister TONY BLAIR's decision to commit to the conflict had been hotly debated on legal and ethical grounds. It was also suspected that Iraqi forces loyal to President SADDAM HUSSEIN would use chemical and/or biological weapons.

The speech is remarkable for its lyrical quality – described in at least one newspaper as 'Rimbaud meets Rambo' (Rimbaud was a French poet; Rambo a fictional Vietnam war hero). Collins rouses his troops' fury and courage, urging them to 'show them no pity'. But he also appeals to their nobler instincts, encouraging them to respect Iraq's ancient culture, and to conduct themselves with decency. He also refers repeatedly to the region's biblical legacy. CHARLES, PRINCE OF WALES later wrote to Collins: 'It made me so proud to read what you said. It was in the highest traditions of military leadership.'

The Iraqis did not deploy chemical or biological weapons, and the Iraqi capital, Baghdad, fell within three weeks.

We go to liberate, not to conquer. We will not fly our flags in their country. We are entering Iraq to free a people[1] and the only flag which will be flown in that ancient land is their own. Show respect for them.

There are some who are alive at this moment who will not be alive shortly. Those who do not wish to go on that journey, we will not send. As for the others, I expect you to rock their world. Wipe them out if that is what they choose. But if you are ferocious in battle remember to be magnanimous in victory.

Iraq is steeped in history. It is the site of the Garden of Eden,[2] of the Great Flood[3] and the birthplace of Abraham.[4] Tread lightly there.

You will see things that no man could pay to see – and you will have to go a long way to find a more decent, generous and upright people than the Iraqis. You will be embarrassed by their hospitality even though they have nothing.

Don't treat them as refugees for they are in their own country. Their children will be poor. In years to come they will know that the light of liberation in their lives was brought by you.

If there are casualties of war then remember that when they woke up and got dressed in the morning they did not plan to die this day. Allow them

[1] Iraq had been a repressive dictatorship under Saddam Hussein since 1979.

[2] The original paradise on Earth, from which God expelled Adam and Eve. See Genesis 1–3.

[3] See Genesis 6–8.

[4] In Judaism and Christianity, Abraham is regarded as the founder of the Hebrew people. See Genesis 12. In Islam, he is regarded as a prophet. See, for example, the Koran 2:125.

dignity in death. Bury them properly and mark their graves.

It is my foremost intention to bring every single one of you out alive. But there may be people among us who will not see the end of this campaign. We will put them in their sleeping bags and send them back. There will be no time for sorrow.

The enemy should be in no doubt that we are his nemesis and that we are bringing about his rightful destruction. There are many regional commanders who have stains on their souls and they are stoking the fires of Hell for Saddam.

He and his forces will be destroyed by this coalition[5] for what they have done. As they die they will know their deeds have brought them to this place. Show them no pity.

It is a big step to take another human life. It is not to be done lightly. I know of men who have taken life needlessly in other conflicts. I can assure you they live with the mark of Cain[6] upon them.

If someone surrenders to you then remember they have that right in international law and ensure that one day they go home to their family. The ones who wish to fight, well, we aim to please.

If you harm the regiment or its history by over-enthusiasm in killing or in cowardice, know it is your family who will suffer. You will be shunned unless your conduct is of the highest — for your deeds will follow you down through history. We will bring shame on neither our uniform or our nation.

[*Regarding Iraqi use of chemical or biological weapons*] It is not a question of if, it's a question of when. We know he has already devolved the decision to lower commanders, and that means he has already taken the decision himself. If we survive the first strike we will survive the attack.

As for ourselves, let's bring everyone home and leave Iraq a better place for us having been there. Our business now is north.

[5] The assault on Iraq was led by the USA and the UK, with support from 35 other countries, notably South Korea, Italy and Poland.

[6] The son of Adam and Eve, who murdered his younger brother Abel. God cursed him but also protected him, putting a mark on him to deter anyone from killing him. See Genesis 4.

Robin Cook
Scottish Labour politician

Robin Cook *originally Robert Finlayson Cook* (1946–2005) was born in Bellshill, Lanarkshire and educated at Edinburgh University. He was a teacher and an adult education organizer before embarking on a political career with the Labour Party. An Edinburgh town councillor (1971–4), MP for Edinburgh Central (1974–83) and then for Livingston (1983–2005), he became an opposition spokesman on health and social security in 1987 and was promoted to chief opposition health spokesman two years later. He became trade and industry spokesman in 1992, and in the same year organized John Smith's successful campaign to become leader of the Labour Party. In 1994, he became foreign and Commonwealth affairs spokesman. After Labour won the general election of 1997, Cook entered TONY BLAIR's Cabinet as Foreign Secretary. Widely recognized as one of the most intellectually formidable parliamentarians of recent years, he became Leader of the House of Commons in 2001. He resigned from the government over the invasion of Iraq in 2003. He died aged 59 while hillwalking in Scotland.

'The threshold for war should always be high'
17 March 2003, London, England

Three days before the start of air attacks on Iraq by American and British forces, Robin Cook marked his departure from the British government with one of the most powerful resignation speeches in living memory. In doing so he won a standing ovation and loud applause from many Labour backbenchers, instantly becoming a rallying figure for the anti-war movement.

Cook's address to the House of Commons was a clearly argued attempt to dismantle the government's case for war against Iraq. Britain should not undertake military action without the support of NATO, the European Union and the United Nations, he urged. He dismissed claims that SADDAM HUSSEIN possessed weapons of mass destruction as in all probability untrue (an opinion that later proved correct) and insisted that the presence of UN weapons inspectors was a block to their development, one which war would overturn. Finally, Cook warned, Britain was being pushed into a conflict by an American administration 'with an agenda of its own'.

This is the first time for 20 years that I have addressed the House from the back benches. I must confess that I had forgotten how much better the view is from here.

None of those 20 years were more enjoyable or more rewarding than the past two, in which I have had the immense privilege of serving this House as Leader of the House – which were made all the more enjoyable, Mr Speaker, by the opportunity of working closely with you.

It was frequently the necessity for me as Leader of the House to talk my way out of accusations that a statement had been preceded by a press interview. On this occasion I can say with complete confidence that no press interview has been given before this statement.

I have chosen to address the House first on why I cannot support a war without international agreement or domestic support. The present Prime minister is the most successful leader of the Labour Party in my lifetime. I hope that he will continue to be the leader of our party, and I hope that he will continue to be successful. I have no sympathy with, and I will give no comfort to, those who want to use this crisis to displace him.

I applaud the heroic efforts that the Prime Minister has made in trying to secure a second resolution.[1] I do not think that anybody could have done better than the Foreign Secretary[2] in working to get support for a second resolution within the Security Council.

But the very intensity of those attempts underlines how important it was to succeed. Now that those attempts have failed, we cannot pretend that getting a second resolution was of no importance.

[1] The second UN Security Council resolution – which never materialized – would have been a follow-up to Resolution 1441, issued on 8 November 2002, which demanded that Iraq readmit weapons inspectors and comply with all earlier resolutions. Iraq agreed to these demands, although the USA and UK argued it had failed to co-operate fully.

[2] The English politician Jack Straw (1946–) succeeded Cook as Foreign Secretary in 2001.

France has been at the receiving end of bucketloads of commentary in recent days. It is not France alone that wants more time for inspections. Germany wants more time for inspections; Russia wants more time for inspections; indeed, at no time have we signed up even the minimum necessary to carry a second resolution.

The reality is that Britain is being asked to embark on a war without agreement in any of the international bodies of which we are a leading partner – not NATO, not the European Union and, now, not the Security Council. To end up in such diplomatic weakness is a serious reverse.

Only a year ago, we and the United States were part of a coalition against terrorism that was wider and more diverse than I would ever have imagined possible. History will be astonished at the diplomatic miscalculations that led so quickly to the disintegration of that powerful coalition. The US can afford to go it alone, but Britain is not a superpower. Our interests are best protected not by unilateral action but by multilateral agreement and a world order governed by rules.

Yet tonight the international partnerships most important to us are weakened: the European Union is divided; the Security Council is in stalemate. Those are heavy casualties of a war in which a shot has yet to be fired.

I have heard some parallels between military action in these circumstances and the military action that we took in Kosovo.[3] There was no doubt about the multilateral support that we had for the action that we took in Kosovo. It was supported by NATO; it was supported by the European Union; it was supported by every single one of the seven neighbours in the region. France and Germany were our active allies.

[3] In March 1999, NATO launched air strikes against Serbia after it failed to end violent persecution of ethnic Albanians in the province of Kosovo.

It is precisely because we have none of that support in this case that it was all the more important to get agreement in the Security Council as the last hope of demonstrating international agreement. The legal basis for our action in Kosovo was the need to respond to an urgent and compelling humanitarian crisis. Our difficulty in getting support this time is that neither the international community nor the British public is persuaded that there is an urgent and compelling reason for this military action in Iraq.

The threshold for war should always be high.

None of us can predict the death toll of civilians from the forthcoming bombardment of Iraq, but the US warning of a bombing campaign that will 'shock and awe' makes it likely that casualties will be numbered at least in the thousands.

I am confident that British servicemen and women will acquit themselves with professionalism and with courage. I hope that they all come back. I hope that Saddam, even now, will quit Baghdad and avert war, but it is false to argue that only those who support war support our troops. It is entirely legitimate to support our troops, while seeking an alternative to the conflict that will put those troops at risk.

Nor is it fair to accuse those of us who want longer for inspections of not having an alternative strategy. For four years as Foreign Secretary, I was partly responsible for the western strategy of containment. Over the past decade that strategy destroyed more weapons than in the Gulf War,[4] dismantled Iraq's nuclear weapons programme and halted Saddam's medium and long-range missiles programmes. Iraq's military strength is now less than half its size at the time of the last Gulf War.

[4] The Gulf War began on 16 January 1991. US President George H W Bush declared a ceasefire on 28 February that year.

Ironically, it is only because Iraq's military forces are so weak that we can even contemplate its invasion. Some advocates of conflict claim that

Saddam's forces are so weak, so demoralized and so badly equipped that the war will be over in a few days. We cannot base our military strategy on the assumption that Saddam is weak and at the same time justify pre-emptive action on the claim that he is a threat. Iraq probably has no weapons of mass destruction in the commonly understood sense of the term – namely a credible device, capable of being delivered against a strategic city target. It probably still has biological toxins and battlefield chemical munitions, but it has had them since the 1980s, when US companies sold Saddam anthrax agents and the then British government approved chemical and munitions factories.

Why is it now so urgent that we should take military action to disarm a military capacity that has been there for 20 years, and which we helped to create? Why is it necessary to resort to war this week, while Saddam's ambition to complete his weapons programme is blocked by the presence of UN inspectors?

Only a couple of weeks ago, Hans Blix[5] told the Security Council that the key remaining disarmament tasks could be completed within months. I have heard it said that Iraq has had not months but twelve years in which to complete disarmament, and that our patience is exhausted. Yet it is more than 30 years since Resolution 242 called on Israel to withdraw from the Occupied Territories. We do not express the same impatience with the persistent refusal of Israel to comply.

I welcome the strong personal commitment that the Prime Minister has given to Middle East peace, but Britain's positive role in the Middle East does not redress the strong sense of injustice throughout the Muslim world at what it sees as one rule for the allies of the US and another rule for the rest.

Nor is our credibility helped by the appearance that our partners in Washington are less interested in disarmament than they are in regime change in Iraq. That explains why any evidence that inspections may be showing progress is greeted in Washington not with satisfaction but with consternation: it reduces the case for war. What has come to trouble me most over past weeks is the suspicion that if the hanging chads in Florida

had gone the other way and Al Gore had been elected,[6] we would not now be about to commit British troops.

The longer that I have served in this place, the greater the respect I have for the good sense and collective wisdom of the British people. On Iraq, I believe that the prevailing mood of the British people is sound. They do not doubt that Saddam is a brutal dictator, but they are not persuaded that he is a clear and present danger to Britain. They want inspections to be given a chance, and they suspect that they are being pushed too quickly into conflict by a US administration with an agenda of its own. Above all, they are uneasy at Britain going out on a limb on a military adventure without a broader international coalition and against the hostility of many of our traditional allies.

From the start of the present crisis, I have insisted, as Leader of the House, on the right of this place to vote on whether Britain should go to war. It has been a favourite theme of commentators that this House no longer occupies a central role in British politics. Nothing could better demonstrate that they are wrong than for this House to stop the commitment of troops in a war that has neither international agreement nor domestic support.

I intend to join those tomorrow night who will vote against military action now. It is for that reason, and for that reason alone, and with a heavy heart, that I resign from the government.

Alistair Cooke

Anglo-American broadcaster

Alistair Alfred Cooke *originally Alfred Cooke* (1908–2004) was born in Salford, England and educated at Cambridge, Yale and Harvard universities. He joined the BBC in 1934 as a film critic, then became London correspondent for America's National Broadcasting Corporation. He returned to the USA in 1937 as a commentator on American affairs for the BBC, settled there and became a US citizen in 1941. He also wrote for the *Manchester Guardian* (later *The Guardian*) from 1945 to 1972. In 1946, he began a series of BBC radio broadcasts called *American Letter*; the series was renamed *Letter from America* in 1949 and continued until a month before his death in March 2004. It was broadcast both in the UK and on the World Service. He wrote numerous books, including *A Generation on Trial* (1950), *One Man's America* (1952), and *America Observed* (1988), and wrote and narrated the award-winning television series *America: A Personal History of the United States* (1971–2). He was made an honorary KBE in 1973, and was invited to address the US Congress on its 200th anniversary in 1974.

'I don't have to believe it if I don't want to'

31 May 1974, radio broadcast from New York City, USA

Urbane, perceptive and drily witty, Alistair Cooke was a long-serving observer of American politics and society. His enormously popular *Letter from America* series ran to almost 3,000 broadcasts, covering a broad range of subject matter for his listeners in Britain and around the world. This *Letter*, inspired by the funeral of Duke Ellington, pays tribute to the jazz icon's memory, but does so without undue solemnity. With characteristic lightness of touch, Cooke accords respect to Ellington's musicianship and importance as a cultural figure; but at the heart of this broadcast is an entertaining anecdote about Cooke's own encounter with Ellington, beginning with a visit to the Duke's apartment in New York City.

The story sparkles with astute and amusing detail, affectionately characterizing Ellington as a redoubtable, energetic and gifted figure. While typically downplaying his own role, Cooke allows us to glimpse, through his own eyes, a snapshot of the man at work with his band. The result is an obituary of rare warmth and elegance.

'When it is finished,' says the guidebook, 'it may well be the largest cathedral in the world.' I am always leery of sentences that contain the phrase 'may well be'. But it is certainly a very large cathedral: namely the Episcopal Cathedral Church of St John the Divine on the Upper West Side in New York City. Its foundations were laid in 1892. They've been building it ever since, and the end is not yet.

On Monday, 27 May 1974, St John the Divine housed a ceremony that would have flabbergasted its architect and its early worshippers. Every pew was filled and the aisles were choked and there were several thousands listening to loudspeakers out on the street. And when the 10,000 people inside were asked to stand and pray, there was a vast rustling sound as awesome, it struck me, as that of the several million bats whooshing out of the Carlsbad Caverns in New Mexico at the first blush of dawn.

It is not the size of the crowd that would have shocked the cathedral's founders (they might have taken it jubilantly as a sign of a great religious revival). It was what the crowd was there for. A crowd that ranged through the whole human colour scale, from the most purple black to the most pallid white, came there to honour the life and mourn the death of a man who had become supreme in an art that began in the brothels of New Orleans. The art is that of jazz, and the practitioner of it they mourned was Edward Kennedy Ellington, identified around the world more immediately than any member of any royal family as – the Duke.

The Duke's career was so much his life that there's very little to say about his private ups and downs, if any. He was born in Washington, DC in 1899, the son of a White House butler, and perhaps the knowledge that Father had a special, protected status inside the white establishment had much to do with the Duke's seeming to be untouched, or untroubled, by the privations and public humiliations we should expect of a black born in the nation's capital. Certainly, he must have thought of himself as belonging to one of the upper tiers of black society. But his upbringing could be called normal for any of the black boys who were to turn into great jazzmen. I'm thinking of men like Earl Hines[1] and Fats Waller,[2] the sons of coloured parsons or church organists who, almost automatically as little boys, were hoisted onto a piano stool. The Duke took piano lessons, but also took to sketching and thought of a career as an artist. This dilemma was solved by his becoming a sign painter by day and running small bands by night.

What got him going was the nightly grind and the daily practice. It is something that nightclub habitués seldom credit, it being assumed that while classical pianists must follow a daily regimen, people like Ellington, Hines, Waller, Tatum[3] simply have a 'natural gift' and just rattle the stuff off on request. Nothing could be more false. I remember ten, 15 years ago running into an old and engaging jazzman, a white who was employed in a poky little jazz joint in San Francisco. Muggsy Spanier, a sweet and talented man who had had a long experience of the roller-coaster fortunes of a jazzman: one year you are playing before delirious crowds in a movie theatre or grand hotel, three years later blowing your brains out before a few listless drunks in a crummy roadhouse off the main highway in some place called Four Forks, Arkansas, or New Iberia, Louisiana. Just then, Muggsy was in a lean year playing in a small band with Earl Hines, who was also at a low ebb (this was before Hines, the father of jazz piano, had been discovered by the State Department and the Soviet government,[4] or been re-discovered by a new generation). Well, Muggsy had left his trumpet in this dreadful nightclub and found he needed it, on his night off, for some impromptu gig or other. So he had to go into the nightclub next morning, always a depressing experience, what with the reek of sour air and spilled alcohol and the lights turned down to a maintenance bulb or two. He told me that one of the unforgettable shocks of his stint in San Francisco was coming from the bone-white sunlight into the smelly cave and squinting through the dark and seeing Hines sitting there, as he did for two or three hours every morning, practising not the blues or 'Rosetta' or 'Honeysuckle Rose' but the piano concertos of Mozart and Beethoven.

To the gaping Muggsy, Hines looked up and said, 'Just keeping the fingers loose.' To be the best, it's a sad truth most of us amateurs shrink from admitting, you have to run, fight, golf, write, play the piano every day. I think it was Paganini[5] – it may have been Rubinstein[6] – who said, 'If I go a week without practice, the audience notices it. If I go a day without practice, I notice it.'

This digression is very relevant to the character and the mastery of Duke Ellington. He was at a piano, but he was there as a composer, day in and night out. For a man of such early and sustained success, it is amazing that he not only tolerated the grind, after one-night stands, of the long bus-rides through the day and the pick-up meals, but actually cherished them as the opportunity to sit back and scribble and hum and compose. He did this to the end.

I knew all the records of his first period when I was in college, from 1927 through 1932. And when I first arrived in New York I wasted no time in

[1] The US jazz pianist and bandleader Earl Kenneth Hines (1903–83) was the son of a jazz cornettist father and a church organist mother.

[2] The US jazz pianist, composer and entertainer Thomas Wright Waller *known as Fats Waller* (1904–43) was the son of a Baptist minister father.

[3] The US jazz pianist Arthur Tatum, Jr *known as Art Tatum* (1909–56).

[4] During the Cold War, the US State Department tried to foster diplomatic relations by sponsoring jazz tours in the Soviet Union. In 1966, Earl Hines became one of the first artists to tour under this scheme.

[5] The Italian violinist and composer Niccolò Paganini (1782–1840) was considered a musician of supreme virtuosity.

[6] The Polish-born US classical pianist Arthur Rubinstein (1887–1982).

[7] A legendary nightclub established in Harlem, New York in 1923 by the gangster and bootlegger Owney Madden (1892–1965). It was famous for performances by the black stars of the jazz age, although black people were not usually admitted to the audience. Duke Ellington's orchestra was the house band, 1927–31.

beating it up to the Cotton Club[7] to see the great man in the flesh. But I didn't meet Ellington alone, by appointment so to speak, until the very end of the Second World War. I went up to his apartment on the swagger side of Harlem. The date had been for two in the afternoon. In my mind's eye I had the picture complete: the dapper figure of the Duke seated in a Noel Coward bathrobe[8] deep in composition at a concert grand. For those were the days long before bandleaders got themselves up in gold lamé and sequins. The big band leaders wore dinner jackets. The Duke wore white tie and tails, and was as sleek as a seal.

[8] The English playwright, actor and songwriter Noel Coward (1899–1973) was famous for his elegance.

Well, I was shown into a large and rambling apartment with a living-room that had evidently seen a little strenuous drinking the night before. Off from the living-room, behind curtained French doors, was a bedroom. The doors were open and there in full view was a large bed rumpled and unmade. Beyond that was a bathroom, and out of it emerged what I first took to be some swami in the wrong country. It was the Duke, naked except for a pair of under-drawers and a towel woven around his head. He came in groaning slightly and saying to himself, 'Man!' Then *his* man came in, a coloured butler, and they went into the knotty question of what sort of breakfast would be at once tasty and medicinal. It was agreed on, and the Duke turned and said, 'Now.' Meaning, what's your business at this unholy hour of two in the afternoon?

The breakfast arrived and he went at it like a marooned mountaineer. To my attempts to excite him with the proposal I had come to make, he grunted, 'Uh-huh' and, 'Uh-un' between, or during, mouthfuls.

At last, he pushed the plate away, picked up his coffee cup and sat down and slurped it rapidly and nodded for me to begin again. I had come to suggest that he might like to record a long session with his band for the BBC. This was, remember, the peak period of his big band, and I suggested that we record him not, as we now say, 'in concert', but in rehearsal.

He shot a suspicious glare at me, as if I'd suggested recording him doing five-finger exercises. But slowly and warily he began to see my problem and to respect it. Simply, how to convey to a listener (this was before television) the peculiar genius of the Duke, since it was unique in the practice of jazz music. Which was somehow to be, and feel, present at the act of creation when it was happening to the Duke standing in front of the band in rehearsal. Everybody knows that the best jazz is impossible to write down in the usual musical notation. You can no more make a transcription of Hines playing 'I Can't Give You Anything but Love', or, worse, Art Tatum playing any of his cascading variations on 'Tea for Two', than you can write down three rules for the average swimmer to follow in doing the 200 metres like Mark Spitz.[9] Jazz is always improvisation done best by a group of players who know each other's whimsical ways with such mysteries as harmonics, counterpoint, scooped pitch, jamming in unison. Alone among jazz composers, the Duke's raw material was the tune, scribbled bridge passages, a sketch in his head of the progression of solos and ensembles he wanted to hear, and an instinctive knowledge of the rich and original talents, and strengths and perversities, of his players. They were not just trumpet, trombone, clarinet, E-flat alto sax and so on. They were individual performers who had stayed with him for years, for decades. One of them, Harry Carney, played with the Duke on his first recording date in 1927, and he was with him on the last date, in Kalamazoo, Michigan, last March. In 1927, Ellington had created a weird, compact, entirely personal sound with his band. It was weirder still and richer, but it was just as personal at the

[9] The US swimmer Mark Spitz (1950–) won seven gold medals at the 1972 Olympic Games in Munich, and holds the record for the most medals won at a single games.

end.

Eventually, the Duke appreciated that what we wanted was not just another performance. He agreed, and we had a long and unforgettable session, in a hired studio on Fifth Avenue, where we recorded the whole process of the number dictated, the roughest run-through, with many pauses, trying this fusion of instruments and that, stopping and starting and transferring the obligato from one man to another, the Duke talking and shouting, 'Now, Tricky, four bars!' and, 'Barney, in there eight.' And in the last hour, what had been a taste in the Duke's head came out as a harmonious, rich meal.

The Duke was nicknamed as a boy by a friend who kidded him about his sharp dressing. He was an elegant and articulate man and, as I've hinted, strangely apart from the recent turmoil of his race. Not, I think, because he was ever indifferent or afraid. He was a supremely natural man, and in his later years devout, and he seemed to assume that men of all colours are brothers. And most of the immediate problems of prejudice, and condescension, and tension between black and white dissolved in the presence of a man whom even an incurable bigot must have recognized as a man of unassailable natural dignity. He had a childlike side, which – we ought to remember – is recommended in the New Testament for entry into the kingdom of Heaven.[10]

[10] Cooke refers to Matthew 18:2–3: 'And Jesus called a little child unto him, and set him in the midst of them/ And said, "Verily I say unto you, Except ye be converted, and become as little children, ye shall not enter into the kingdom of Heaven."'

He was very sick indeed in the last few months. He knew, but kept it to himself, that he had cancer in both lungs. A week or two before the end he sent out to hundreds of friends and acquaintances what looked at first like a Christmas card. It was a greeting. On a field of blue was a cross, made of four vertical letters and three horizontal. They were joined by the letter 'O'. The vertical word spelled 'Love' and the horizontal 'God'.

He has left us, in the blessed library of recorded sound, a huge anthology of his music from his 28th birthday to his 75th. He began as a minority cult, too rude for the collectors of dance music. For much, maybe most, of his time he was never a bestseller. He never stuck in the current groove, or in his own groove. He moved with all the influences of the time from blues to bebop and the moderns and transmuted them into his own, and at the end his difficult antiphonies and plotted discords, the newer harmonic structure he was always reaching for, were no more saleable to the ordinary popular music fan than they had ever been. Most people simply bowed to him as an institution.

In 1931, a college room-mate of mine who was something of a pioneer as a jazz critic, on the university weekly, was graduating, and he wrote a farewell piece. He ended with the phrase: 'Bands may come and bands may go, but the Duke goes on for ever.' Ah, how true! We thought it a marvel that the Duke had ridden out all fashions for four long years. In fact, his good and always developing music lasted for 47 years. And we have it all.

[11] The US short-story writer and novelist John Henry O'Hara (1905–70).

So, I am inclined to paraphrase what John O'Hara[11] said on the death of George Gershwin:[12] 'Duke Ellington is dead. I don't have to believe it if I don't want to.'

[12] The US jazz composer George Gershwin (1898–1937).

'The White House is a temporary Versailles'

6 November 1992, radio broadcast from New York City, USA

This *Letter from America*, delivered in the wake of a presidential election, finds Cooke in gently satirical mode as he surveys the approach to interior design adopted by earlier presidents and their First Ladies.

Without a trace of ostentation, Cooke reveals that he has visited the White House on numerous occasions, a privilege which enables him to pass wry judgement on the '18th-century French mansion' created by Jackie, wife of JOHN F KENNEDY and the 'folderols' and ersatz pageantry added by RICHARD M NIXON and his wife Pat.

As always with Cooke, the underlying message is serious and meditative. Here, his point is that a president who sequesters himself in the opulence of the White House does so at his peril. He castigates President George H W Bush, who had just been voted out of office, for failing to pay serious attention to those sectors of the nation beyond his own sphere of influence.

Cooke does not, however, spare himself from gentle mockery. In the final passage, he confesses his own patrician response to the casual dress adopted by President-elect BILL CLINTON.

[1] A(lfred) P(owell) Wadsworth was editor of the *Manchester Guardian*, 1944–56.

When I became the chief American correspondent of a paper whose mission, way back then, was to prompt and protect the thinking of one city, Manchester, I was disturbed at the thought that I was going to have to move myself and my family from New York to Washington. Washington, of course was where all the chief foreign correspondents were based. To my great relief, I soon had a letter from my editor – a small, canny, spiky-haired, bespectacled imp of a Lancastrian.[1] He wrote quite simply: 'No, I don't want you to move to Washington. I don't want you to report Washington, except from time to time. I want you, *all* the time, to report America. New York is the best news base, and the best home base for travel.'

That wise and wily sentence is one that might not only be passed on to editors of papers around the world. It would serve a useful purpose if it could be engraved or done up in needlework, framed and hung in the Oval Office of the White House. It would remind every president of a truth which every president, especially in his second term, is in danger of forgetting: that the White House is not home or anything remotely like the homes of the 200 million people he is there to represent. The White House is a temporary Versailles and not the best place in which to maintain what TEDDY ROOSEVELT called 'a sense of the continent'.

You have to have been in the White House as a guest to appreciate its elegance and patrician comfort, and to have been treated like some venerated old monarch in luxurious exile, in order to feel the benign truth behind the phrase coined by the historian Arthur Schlesinger, 'the Imperial Presidency'. He was referring to the White House – I almost said the court – of Richard M Nixon. And certainly there's been no presidency in our time, or perhaps in any time, when the White House more resembled a royal palace. Mrs Kennedy had done the place over into an 18th-century French mansion more exquisite than most royal palaces. Mr Nixon added some folderols of a monarch's office as imagined by Hollywood. He summoned for ceremonial occasions a row of trumpeters in uniform with tight white pumps and knee breeches, looking for all the world like the wedding guard of honour designed for King Rudolf of Ruritania (Ronald Colman) and Princess Flavia (Madeleine Carroll).[2]

[2] Cooke refers to the stars of the film *The Prisoner of Zenda* (1937) based on Anthony Hope's adventure story set in the fictional European kingdom of Ruritania.

The television pictures of this absurdity evoked such hilarity and mirth (not least in the British Royal Family) that these yeoman of the guard were soon disbanded. But what Mr Nixon had revealed, in exaggeration, was a perception of himself to which a president, after a year or two, is in danger of succumbing: that he is in charge of – that he rules – a nation and that the word is handed down from the White House, not up from the people. It may be said that every prime minister probably feels the same in his official residence. I doubt it. Once, at a White House dinner, I sat next to the son of the British prime minister, who was at that moment the President's guest of honour. The son had been received, as everyone is, by a young Marine officer in a spanking dress uniform. His lady companion took the Marine's proffered arm. They were led through a small suite with a small orchestra playing waltzes by Strauss. Other beautiful rooms or galleries they passed through were ablaze with gilt and glass. On into the main reception room; more Marines, more impeccable manners – the reception line – the shaking hands with the king – I mean the President – and the First Lady. Cocktails and smiling chatter. And on into two linked dining rooms, and a splendid banquet sparkling with a hundred candles. A soothing fountain of music showered from another room. 'Home,' said the Prime Minister's son, 'was never like this.' And in truth, by comparison, Number Ten Downing Street is a modest, upper-middle-class town house.

Apart from this beautiful protective shell in which the president lives, there is the constant human situation, in which he is surrounded by people who defer to him and who pass on to him every day their own view (which might be as blinkered as his) of what is happening. What is being felt and thought, on the Great Outside. The outside is the United States and its people. Only in the past month or so did Mr Bush attempt to listen to their troubles, to emerge from his cocoon of complacency ('Yes, there are people having a bad time, but the economy's growing, 93 million at work – things are getting better all the time').[3] This reminded me of the fatal 1932 assurance Herbert Hoover[4] issued from the White House to millions shivering in tar-paper shacks down by the rivers, and to the quarter of the working people of America who had no work: 'Prosperity is just around the corner.'

Some of you may have expected me to talk about the failures of the Bush campaign, for, only two days after the election, the papers are full of reasons and excuses and explanations by Republicans about failures of technique: he should have had sharper figures, he should have been more insulting earlier, he should have used more women, he should have hired as mean a man as the one who invented the infamous Willie Horton television commercial last time. (He was the Massachusetts black man who, given parole by Governor Dukakis, promptly raped a woman).[5]

One bitter intimate who could enjoy the frankness of having left the administration came a little closer to the central truth when he moaned: 'He surrounded himself with second-rate talent and clones. He was only comfortable with a white-bread crowd, a bunch of white male Protestants and number-crunchers.' I can sympathize with that man's view. I and my generation are probably more comfortable with WASPs[6] (and a Catholic friend or two) than with the polyglot, white – black – Latino – brown – Asian, multi-cultural society that America has increasingly become. But Clinton has reached out to it, and listened to it, is at home with it. His generation is a link with it.

This was never clearer than on Thursday morning, when the *New York Times* carried a front-page photograph of the President-elect with his mother and pals at a friend's house. Clinton in threadbare jeans, a check wool shirt, unzipped windbreaker, bulging Reeboks. Mostly young pals in laughing bunches similarly dressed, or undressed. Not a suit, not a necktie, not a button-down shirt in sight. 'Well,' I said to my wife, 'can you believe this? There is the next president of the United States and his buddies.' I wasn't suggesting that Mr Clinton was putting on an act, as poor Mr Bush had to when he wolfed a hamburger at the local lunch counter and said, 'Gee whillikins, this is great.'

'Clinton,' said my wife sternly, 'is the president of those people and he dresses like them.' Quite right. Unbuttoned, one way or another, is his

[3] Cooke appears to be paraphrasing Bush rather than quoting him directly.

[4] The US engineer and politician Herbert C Hoover (1874–1964) served as President, 1929–33. His remark was not well received during the Great Depression of 1929–33, and contributed to his overwhelming defeat at the election of 1932.

[5] This notorious case was ruthlessly publicized by the 'negative' Bush campaign during the presidential election of 1988. Democratic candidate Michael S Dukakis (1933–) opposed the death penalty and, as Governor of Massachusetts, had backed the 'prison furlough' programme under which Horton was released.

[6] White Anglo-Saxon Protestants – usually considered the dominant racial caste in US public life.

natural style. Along with the passing of George Bush, we shall see, I fear, the passing of the blue blazer.

Oliver Cromwell
English soldier and statesman

Oliver Cromwell (1599–1658) was born in Huntingdon and educated at Sidney Sussex College, Cambridge. He studied law in London, and developed a dislike for CHARLES I after sitting in the House of Commons in 1628. When the King dissolved Parliament the following year, Cromwell took up farming. He was a member of the Short Parliament of 1640, which refused the King funds for war, and of the subsequent Long Parliament. At the start of the English Civil War in 1642, he raised a troop of cavalry for the battles of Edgehill and Gainsborough, and at Marston Moor (1644) mounted a cavalry charge which helped defeat the Royalists. Back in Parliament, he led the faction that rejected reconciliation with the King. He then commanded the army that won a decisive victory at Naseby in June 1645. Cromwell professed willingness to negotiate terms on which the throne might be saved, but Charles's success in rallying the Scots brought further conflict in 1648 and Cromwell resolved to rid himself of the King. His signature was among those on the death warrant that brought Charles's execution in January 1649. The monarchy was abolished and Cromwell declared the establishment of a commonwealth, with himself as chairman of its Council of State. He brutally crushed the last vestiges of Irish resistance at Drogheda and Wexford, and in 1650–1 defeated the supporters of Charles's son Charles II (1630–85), who had declared him king of Scotland, at Dunbar and Worcester. Obstructed by the substantial body of Royalists who remained in the Commons, Cromwell dissolved the Long Parliament in 1653 and ruled briefly as head of the Puritan Convention and then, on the implementation of a new constitution, as Lord Protector. He reorganized the Church of England and established Puritanism, brought prosperity to Scotland and granted Irish representation in Parliament. He dissolved Parliament again in 1655, with a view to imposing regional rule, but the experiment failed, and after recalling the Commons in 1656 he was offered the crown. He declined it, but instead won the right to name his son Richard as Lord Protector. However, his relations with Parliament worsened, bringing another dissolution in 1658, and he continued to rule absolutely until his death later that year. Richard Cromwell failed to emulate his father's iron grip and surrendered the office a year later. On the Restoration in 1660, Oliver Cromwell's body was disinterred from Westminster Abbey; it was later hung from Tyburn gallows and afterwards buried there.

'Truly God hath called you to this work'
4 July 1653, London, England

Cromwell's faith in democracy was a troubled one. He was ideologically committed to the existence of Parliament, but refused to tolerate an ineffectual or self-interested assembly. He had violently dissolved the 'Rump' Parliament on 20 April 1653, following its failure to achieve various goals, including an effective new constitution.

After ten weeks' dictatorship, he convened the Nominated or 'Raw-Bones' Parliament – also known as the Assembly of Saints – through which he hoped to establish a Christian republic. The 'Raw-Bones' would last less than six months, and Cromwell later deemed its appointment an act of 'weakness and folly'. But when the new governing body assembled on a sweltering summer day in 1653, he was filled with optimistic zeal. He addressed the assembly at length, describing the circumstances which led him to dissolve its predecessor, and encouraging his new colleagues to embrace Christian principles.

Cromwell was a coarse and convoluted speaker, who supported his extemporaneous rhetoric with biblical references as they occurred to him. But despite his hardened Puritanism, he favoured religious tolerance. The Royalist Sir Philip Warwick, who had encountered him in the Long Parliament in 1640, described him as follows: 'His countenance swollen and reddish, his voice sharp and untuneable and his eloquence full of fervour ... His temper exceeding fiery, as I have known, but the flame of it kept down, for the most part ... He was naturally compassionate towards objects in distress, even to an effeminate measure ... A larger soul, I think, hath seldom dwelt in a house of clay than his was.'

> Gentlemen: I suppose the summons that hath been instrumental to bring you hither gives you well to understand the occasion of your being here. Howbeit, I have something farther to impart to you, which is an instrument drawn up by the consent and advice of the principal officers of the army; which is a little (as we conceive) more significant than the letter of summons. We have that here to tender you; and somewhat likewise to say farther for our own exoneration; which we hope may be somewhat farther

to your satisfaction. And therefore, seeing you sit here somewhat uneasily, by reason of the scantness of the room and heat of the weather, I shall contract myself with respect thereunto …

You very well know, after divers turnings of affairs, it pleased God, much about the midst of this war, to winnow (if I may so say) the forces of this nation; and to put them into the hands of other men of other principles than those that did engage at the first … The King removed, and brought to justice; and many great ones with him. The House of Peers laid aside. The House of Commons itself, the representative of the people of England, sifted, winnowed and brought to a handful; as you very well remember …

I shall now begin a little to remember to you the passages that have been transacted since Worcester[1] … We may say that, ever since the coming-up of myself and those gentlemen who have been engaged in the military part, it hath been full in our hearts and thoughts to desire and use all the fair and lawful means we could to have had the nation reap the fruit of all the blood and treasure that had been spent in this cause: and we have had many desires, and thirstings in our spirits, to find out ways and means wherein we might be anywise instrumental to help it forward.

We were very tender, for a long time, so much as to petition. For some of the officers being members, and others having very good acquaintance with, and some relations to, divers members of Parliament, we did, from time to time, solicit them; thinking if there should be nobody else to prompt them nor call upon them, these solicitations would have been listened to, out of ingenuity and integrity in them that had opportunity to have answered our expectations.

Truly, when we saw nothing would be done, we did, as we thought according to our duty, a little to remind them by a petition; which I suppose you have seen: it was delivered, as I remember, in August last. What effect that had is likewise very well known. The truth is, we had no return at all for our satisfaction …

Finding the people dissatisfied in every corner of the nation, and all men laying at our doors the non-performance of these things which had been promised and were of duty to be performed, truly we did then think ourselves concerned … And therefore we, divers times, endeavoured to obtain meetings with divers members of Parliament … And in these meetings we did, with all faithfulness and sincerity, beseech them that they would be mindful of their duty to God and men, in the discharge of the trust reposed in them …

At last, when indeed we saw that things would not be laid to heart, we had a very serious consideration among ourselves what other ways to have recourse unto; and when we grew to more closer considerations then they, the Parliament men, began to take the Act for a Representative to heart, and seemed exceeding willing to put it on. And had it been done with integrity, there could nothing have happened more welcome to our judgements than that.

But plainly the intention was not to give the people right of choice (it would have been but a seeming right). The semblance of giving them a choice was only to recruit the House the better to perpetuate themselves …

When we saw all this, having power in our hands, we could not resolve to let such monstrous proceedings to go on, and so to throw away all our liberties into the hands of those against whom we had fought. We came, first, to this conclusion among ourselves: that if we had been fought out of

[1] The final battle of the English Civil War, fought on 3 September 1651, at which Cromwell's forces defeated Charles II's Scottish army.

our liberties and rights, necessity would have taught us patience; but that to deliver them sluggishly up would render us the basest people in the world, and worthy to be accounted haters of God and of his people.

When it pleased God to lay this close to our hearts; and indeed to show us that the interest of his people was grown cheap … this did add more considerations to us, that there was a duty incumbent upon us, even upon us. And – I speak here in the presence of some that was at the closure of our consultations, and as before the Lord – the thinking of an act of violence was to us worse than any engagement that ever we were in, or that could be, to the utmost hazard to our lives: so willing were we, even very tender and desirous, if possible, that these men might quit their places with honour …

But affairs being at this posture that we saw plainly, even in some critical cases, that the cause of the people of God was a despised thing, truly we did believe then that the hands of other men than these must be the hands to be used for the work. And we thought then, it was very high time to look about us, and to be sensible of *our* duty … When we saw, I say, that all tenderness was forgotten to the good people – though it was by their hands and their means, by the blessing of God, that those sat where they did – we thought this very bad requital …

And it pleased these gentlemen who are here, the officers of the army, to desire me to offer their sense to them, which I did, and it was shortly carried thus: we told them, the reason of our desire to wait upon them now was that we might know from them what security lay in the way of their proceeding … and how the whole business should, in actual practice, be executed, of which we had as yet no account of; and having our interest, our lives, estates and families therein concerned … how all this was to be …

Indeed, when this desire was made, the answer was that 'nothing would do good for this nation but the continuance of this Parliament'. We wondered we should have such a return … This being so, we humbly proposed – when neither our counsels, our objections to their way of proceedings, nor their answers to justify them, did give us satisfaction; nor did we think they ever intended to give us any, as indeed some of them have since declared to be the fact – when, I say, we saw this, we proposed to them *our* expedient, which was indeed this: that the government of the nation being in that condition it was, and things being under so much ill sense abroad, and likely to end in confusion if we so proceed – we desired they would devolve the power and trust over to some well-affected men, such as had an interest in the nation, and were known to be of good affection to the commonwealth.

Which, we told them, was no new thing when this land was under the like hurlyburlies and distractions; and it was confessed by them it had been no new thing … They told us, they would take time for the consideration of these things till tomorrow; that they would sleep upon them and consult with some friends … And at parting, two or three of the chief of them, one of the chief and two or three more, did tell us that they would endeavour to suspend farther proceedings about the bill for a new representative until they had a further conference together with us. And upon this we had great satisfaction …

The next morning … word was brought us that the House was proceeding with all speed upon the new representative! We could not believe it, that such persons would be so unworthy; staying till a second and third messenger came, and informed us that the House was really upon that business, and had brought it near to the issue ... Thus, as we apprehended, would have been thrown away the liberties of the nation into the hands of those who had never fought for it. And upon this we thought it our duty not to suffer it. And upon this the House was dissolved ...

I have too much troubled you with this, but we have made this relation, that you might know that that which hath been done in the dissolution of the Parliament was as necessary to be done as the preservation of this cause. And that necessity which led us to do that hath brought us to this issue, of exercising an extraordinary way and course to draw together yourselves here; upon this account, that you are men who know the Lord and have made observations of his marvellous dispensations; and may be trusted as far as men may be trusted with this cause.

It remains now for me to acquaint you a little farther with that which relates to your taking upon you this great business ... It hath been the practice of others who have, voluntarily and out of a sense of duty, divested themselves of power and devolved the government into the hands of others; I say; it hath been the practice of those that have done so ... to lay a charge how to employ it (in such a way as I hope we do), and to press to the duty of employing it well, concerning which we have a word or two to offer you.

Truly God hath called you to this work by, I think, as wonderful providences as ever passed upon the sons of men in so short a time. And truly I think, taking the argument of necessity – for the government must not fall – taking the appearance of the hand of God in this thing, I am sure you would have been loath it should have been resigned into the hands of wicked men and enemies! I am sure God would not have it so.

It's come, therefore, to you by the way of necessity, by the way of the wise providence of God – though through weak hands. And therefore, I think, coming through our hands, though such as we are, it may not be ill taken if we do offer somewhat (as I said before) as to the discharge of the trust which is now incumbent upon you. And although I seem to speak of that which may have the face and interpretation of a charge, it's a very humble one: and if he that means to be a servant to you, who hath now called you to the exercise of the supreme authority, discharge that which he conceives to be a duty to you, we hope you will take it in good part ...

And truly it's better for us to *pray* for you than to *counsel* you in that matter, that you may exercise the judgement of mercy and truth! It's better, I say, to pray for you than counsel you; to ask wisdom from Heaven for you; which I am confident many thousands of saints do this day, and have done, and will do, through the permission of God and His assistance ... And then if God give you hearts to be easy to be entreated, to be peaceably spirited, to be full of good fruits, bearing good fruits to the nation, to men as men, to the people of God, to all in their several stations – this will teach you to execute the judgement of mercy and truth.

And I have little more to say to this. I shall rather bend my prayers for you in that behalf, as I said; and many others will. Truly the judgement of truth, it will teach you to be as just towards an unbeliever as towards a believer; and it's our duty to do so. I confess I have said sometimes, foolishly it may be, I had rather miscarry to a believer than an unbeliever. This may seem a paradox – but let's take heed of doing that which is evil to either! Oh, if God fill your hearts with such a spirit as Moses had, and as Paul had, which was not a spirit for believers only, but for the whole people …

A second thing is to desire you would be faithful with the Saints; to be touched with them. And I hope, whatever others may think, it may be a matter to us all of rejoicing to have our hearts touched (to speak with reverence) as Christ, being full of the spirit, was 'touched with our infirmities', that He might be merciful. So should we be; we should be pitiful. Truly, this calls us to be very much touched with the infirmities of the Saints; that we may have a respect unto all, and be pitiful and tender towards all …

I think I need not advise, much less press you, to endeavour the promoting of the Gospel; to encourage the ministry; such a ministry and such ministers as be faithful in the land; upon whom the true character is. Men that have received the spirit, which Christians will be able to discover and do the will of; men that have received gifts from Him that is ascended up on high …

I have but one word more to say to you; though in that perhaps I shall show my weakness: it's by way of encouragement to go on in this work. And give me leave to begin thus. I confess I never looked to see such a day as this – it may be nor you neither – when Jesus Christ should be so owned as he is, at this day, and in this work … I know you well remember that scripture, in Psalm 110:3: 'He makes His people willing in the day of His power'. God manifests it to be the day of the power of Christ; having, through so much blood, and so much trial as hath been upon this nation, made this to be one of the great issues thereof. He makes this one of the greatest mercies next to his own Son to have his people called to the supreme authority …

Consider the circumstances by which you are called hither; through what strivings, through what blood you are come hither – where neither you nor I, nor no man living, three months ago, had a thought to have seen such a company taking upon them, or rather being called to take the supreme authority of this nation! Therefore, own your call!

Indeed, I think it may be truly said that never was there a supreme authority consisting of so numerous a body as you are – above 140, I believe – never such a body who were ever in the supreme authority before, under such a notion as this in such a way of owning God, and being owned by Him. And therefore I may say also, never such a people so formed, for such a purpose, were so called before …

I say, own your call; for indeed it is marvellous, and it is of God and it hath been unprojected, unthought of by you and us. And indeed it hath been the way God hath dealt with us all along – to keep things from our eyes, so that we have seen nothing in all His dispensations, long beforehand: which is also a witness, in some measure, to our integrity. I say, you are called with an high calling …

I am sorry I have troubled you in such a place of heat as this is so long.[2] All I have to say – in my own name, and that of my fellow officers who have joined with me in this work – is that we shall commend you to the grace of God, to the guidance of His Spirit; that having thus far served you (or rather our Lord Jesus Christ in regard to you) we shall be ready in our stations, according as the providence of God shall lead us, to be subservient to the farther work of God, and to that authority which we shall reckon God hath set over us …

Having said this, we shall trouble you no more. But if you will be pleased that this instrument may be read to you, which I have signed by the advice

[2] This abridged version is around one-third the length of the original speech.

of the Council of Officers, we shall then leave you to your own thoughts
and the guidance of God.

Mario Cuomo
American politician

Mario Matthew Cuomo (1932–) was born in Queens, New York City to poor immigrants from Salerno, Italy. His father had initially found work digging and cleaning sewers, but later opened a small grocery store in South Jamaica, Queens. Cuomo studied at St John's University, graduating in law in 1956 and then became a baseball player until an injury forced him to quit. He became a community activist in Queens and ran unsuccessfully for lieutenant governor in 1974. He was appointed New York Secretary of State in 1975 and was nominated by the Liberal Party for the 1977 mayoral election, but narrowly lost, becoming lieutenant governor in 1978. He won election as governor in 1983 and served for three terms, but was defeated in the Republican landslide of 1994, fought largely on the issue of the death penalty, which he has consistently opposed. He gave the keynote address at the Democratic National Convention of 1984, and was long considered a likely Democratic presidential candidate, though he never sought nomination. His publications include *Reason to Believe* (1995) and *Why Lincoln Matters: Today More than Ever* (2004). He is the father of Andrew Cuomo, elected governor of New York in 2011.

'There's another part to the shining city'
16 July 1984, San Francisco, California, USA

The famous 'City on a Hill' sermon – preached by JOHN WINTHROP to pilgrims crossing the Atlantic in 1630 – has resonated through American oratory for almost four centuries. Derived from Matthew 5:14, it portrays the new country as a paragon of Christian freedom and justice. RONALD REAGAN was fond of quoting from it; but when, as president, he stood for re-election in 1984, he found it turned against him.

As governor of New York, Mario Cuomo was invited to give the keynote address at the Democratic National Convention. He used the platform to take Reagan to task over the millions of Americans who could not share in the President's vision of universal prosperity.

Criticizing Reagan's divisive economic policies and his aggressive approach to defence, Cuomo identifies the Democrats' province as the middle class in its broadest sense: 'the people not rich enough to be worry-free, but not poor enough to be on welfare'. His central appeal is for unity across differences of political opinion, ethnicity and income. He repeatedly champions the excluded and the marginalized – referring vividly to his own impoverished upbringing – before commending the Democratic presidential candidate Walter Mondale and his running mate Geraldine Ferraro, both of immigrant stock.

His forceful, passionate speech was rapturously received and widely admired. Reagan declined to comment on it, though his vice president George H W Bush conceded, 'It was a good speech'. However, it failed to unseat Reagan, who won the election of November 1984 by a landslide.

On behalf of the Empire State and the family of New York, I thank you for the great privilege of being able to address this convention. Please allow me to skip the stories and the poetry and the temptation to deal in nice but vague rhetoric. Let me instead use this valuable opportunity to deal immediately with questions that should determine this election and that we all know are vital to the American people.

Ten days ago, President Reagan admitted that although some people in this country seemed to be doing well nowadays, others were unhappy, even worried, about themselves, their families and their futures. The President said that he didn't understand that fear. He said, 'Why, this country is a shining city on a hill.' And the President is right. In many ways we are a shining city on a hill.

But the hard truth is that not everyone is sharing in this city's splendour and glory. A shining city is perhaps all the President sees from the portico of the White House and the veranda of his ranch, where everyone seems to be doing well. But there's another city; there's another part to the shining city; the part where some people can't pay their mortgages, and most young people can't afford one, where students can't afford the education they need, and middle-class parents watch the dreams they hold for their children evaporate.

In this part of the city, there are more poor than ever, more families in trouble, more and more people who need help but can't find it. Even worse: there are elderly people who tremble in the basements of the houses there. And there are people who sleep in the city streets, in the gutter, where the glitter doesn't show. There are ghettos where thousands of young people, without a job or an education, give their lives away to drug-dealers every day. There is despair, Mr President, in the faces that you don't see, in the places that you don't visit in your shining city. In fact, Mr President, this is a nation …

[*Applause.*]

Mr President, you ought to know that this nation is more a tale of two cities than it is just a shining city on a hill. Maybe, maybe, Mr President, if you visited some more places. Maybe if you went to Appalachia where some people still live in sheds; maybe if you went to Lackawanna,[1] where thousands of unemployed steel workers wonder why we subsidize foreign steel.

[*Applause.*]

Maybe, maybe, Mr President, if you stopped in at a shelter in Chicago and spoke to the homeless there; maybe, Mr President, if you asked a woman who had been denied the help she needed to feed her children because you said you needed the money for a tax break for a millionaire or for a missile we couldn't afford to use.

[*Cheers and applause.*]

Maybe, maybe, Mr President. But I'm afraid not. Because, the truth is, ladies and gentlemen, that this is how we were warned it would be. President Reagan told us from the very beginning that he believed in a kind of social Darwinism.[2] Survival of the fittest. 'Government can't do everything,' we were told, 'so it should settle for taking care of the strong and hope that economic ambition and charity will do the rest. Make the rich richer – and what falls from their table will be enough for the middle class and those who are trying desperately to work their way into the middle class.'

[*Cheers and applause.*]

You know, the Republicans called it 'trickle-down'[3] when Hoover tried it.[4] Now they call it 'supply-side'.[5] But it's the same shining city for those relative few who are lucky enough to live in its good neighbourhoods. But for the people who are excluded – for the people who are locked out – all they can do is to stare from a distance at that city's glimmering towers.

It's an old story. It's as old as our history. The difference between Democrats and Republicans has always been measured in courage and confidence. [*Applause.*] The Republicans believe that the wagon train will not make it to the frontier unless some of the old, some of the young, some of the weak are left behind by the side of the trail. [*Applause.*] The strong, the strong, they tell us, will inherit the land. We Democrats believe in something else. We Democrats believe that we can make it all the way with the whole family intact. And we have, more than once.

[*Cheers and applause.*]

Ever since Franklin Roosevelt lifted himself from his wheelchair to lift this nation from its knees[6] – wagon train after wagon train – to new frontiers of education, housing, peace; the whole family aboard, constantly reaching out to extend and enlarge that family; lifting them up into the

[1] A town near Buffalo in western New York State, whose iron and steel industry declined disastrously in the late 20th century.

[2] A school of thought propagated by the English philosopher Herbert Spencer (1820–1903), which proposed that human society should be governed by 'the survival of the fittest'. The phrase is derived from the theories of the English naturalist Charles Darwin (1809–92) but widely considered to be misapplied.

[3] The 'trickle down' theory proposes that when a wealthy section of society becomes wealthier, the poor benefit indirectly from increased commercial activity.

[4] The US engineer and politician Herbert C Hoover (1874–1964) served as President, 1929–33. His critics believe his anti-interventionist policies did too little to tackle the hardship caused by the Great Depression, which began in 1929.

[5] A term coined in 1975 by the US economist and journalist Jude Wanniski (1936–2005). The 'supply-side' theory proposes that tax cuts and business incentives stimulate growth by encouraging the creation and expansion of businesses.

[6] President FRANKLIN D ROOSEVELT contracted polio in 1921 and was permanently paralysed. He reversed the 'laissez-faire' economic policy of Hoover, ushering in a raft of major economic and social reforms.

wagon on the way; blacks and Hispanics, and people of every ethnic group, and native Americans − all those struggling to build their families and claim some small share of America.

For nearly 50 years, we carried them all to new levels of comfort and security and dignity, even affluence. And remember this: some of us in this room today are here only because this nation had that kind of confidence. And it would be wrong to forget that.

[*Cheers and applause.*]

So, here we are at this convention to remind ourselves where we come from and to claim the future for ourselves and for our children. Today our great Democratic Party, which has saved this nation from depression, from fascism, from racism, from corruption, is called upon to do it again − this time to save the nation from confusion and division, from the threat of eventual fiscal disaster, and most of all from the fear of a nuclear holocaust.

[*Applause.*]

That's not going to be easy … We must win this case on the merits. We must get the American public to look past the glitter, beyond the showmanship − to the reality, the hard substance of things. And we'll do that not so much with speeches that sound good as with speeches that are good and sound. Not so much with speeches that will bring people to their feet as with speeches that bring people to their senses. We must make the American people hear our tale of two cities. We must convince them that we don't have to settle for two cities, that we can have one city, indivisible, shining for all of its people.

[*Applause.*]

Now, we will have no chance to do that if what comes out of this convention is a babble of arguing voices. If that's what's heard throughout the campaign − dissonant sounds from all sides − we will have no chance to tell our message. To succeed, we will have to surrender some small parts of our individual interests to build a platform that we can all stand on at once and comfortably, proudly singing out …

[*Cheers and applause.*]

We need a platform we can all agree to, so that we can sing out the truth for the nation to hear in chorus, its logic so clear and commanding that no slick Madison Avenue commercial,[7] no amount of geniality, no martial music will be able to muffle the sound of the truth. We Democrats must unite. We Democrats must unite so that the entire nation can unite because surely the Republicans won't bring this country together: their policies divide the nation into the lucky and the left-out; into the royalty and the rabble. The Republicans are willing to treat that division as victory. They would cut this nation in half; into those temporarily better off and those worse off than before − and they would call that division 'recovery'.

[*Cheers and applause.*]

Now, we should not − we should not be embarrassed or dismayed or chagrined if the process of unifying is difficult, even wrenching at times. Remember that, unlike any other party, we embrace men and women of every colour, every creed, every orientation, every economic class. In our family are gathered everyone from the abject poor of Essex County in New York, to the enlightened affluent of the gold coasts at both ends of the nation. And in between is the heart of our constituency − the middle class, the people not rich enough to be worry-free, but not poor enough to be on welfare; the middle class − those people who work for a living because they have to, not because some psychiatrist told them it was a convenient

[7] Madison Avenue in Manhattan, New York City became the centre of US advertising in the 1920s and is still associated with the industry.

216

way to fill the interval between birth and eternity. White collar and blue collar. Young professionals. Men and women in small business desperate for the capital and contracts that they need to prove their worth.

We speak for the minorities who have not yet entered the mainstream. We speak for ethnics who want to add their culture to the magnificent mosaic that is America. We speak – we speak for women who are indignant that this nation refuses to etch into its governmental commandments the simple rule 'Thou shalt not sin against equality', a rule so simple –

[*Prolonged cheers and applause.*]

I was going to say – and I perhaps dare not but I will – it's a commandment so simple it can be spelled in three letters: E-R-A.[8]

[*Cheers, applause and chants of 'E-R-A'.*]

We speak, we speak for young people demanding an education and a future. We speak for senior citizens, we speak for senior citizens who are terrorized by the idea that their only security, their social security, is being threatened. We speak for millions of reasoning people fighting to preserve our environment from greed and from stupidity.

[*Cheers and applause.*]

And we speak for reasonable people who are fighting to preserve our very existence from a macho intransigence that refuses to make intelligent attempts to discuss the possibility of nuclear holocaust with our enemy.

[*Cheers and applause.*]

They refuse. They refuse, because they believe we can pile missiles so high that they will pierce the clouds and the sight of them will frighten our enemies into submission …

We Democrats still have a dream. We still believe in this nation's future. And this is our answer to the question, this is our credo: we believe in only the government we need, but we insist on all the government we need.

[*Applause.*]

We believe in a government that is characterized by fairness and reasonableness, a reasonableness that goes beyond labels, that doesn't distort or promise to do things that we know we can't do. We believe in a government strong enough to use the words 'love' and 'compassion' and smart enough to convert our noblest aspirations into practical realities. We believe in encouraging the talented, but we believe that while survival of the fittest may be a good working description of the process of evolution, a government of humans should elevate itself to a higher order.

[*Applause.*]

…We believe as Democrats that a society as blessed as ours, the most affluent democracy in the world's history, one that can spend trillions on instruments of destruction, ought to be able to help the middle class in its struggle, ought to be able to find work for all who can do it, room at the table, shelter for the homeless, care for the elderly and infirm, and hope for the destitute. And we proclaim as loudly as we can the utter insanity of nuclear proliferation and the need for a nuclear freeze, if only to affirm the simple truth that peace is better than war because life is better than death.

[*Cheers and applause.*]

We believe in firm but fair law and order. We believe proudly in the union movement.

[*Cheers and applause.*]

We believe in privacy for people, openness by government, we believe in civil rights, and we believe in human rights. We believe in a single,

[8] The Equal Rights Amendment, drafted in 1921 by the suffragist Alice Paul (1885–1977), demands equality under the law for women and men. Despite persistent efforts, it has never been ratified by the requisite number of states.

217

fundamental idea that describes better than most textbooks and any speech that I could write what a proper government should be. The idea of family. Mutuality. The sharing of benefits and burdens for the good of all. Feeling one another's pain. Sharing one another's blessings, reasonably, honestly, fairly – without respect to race, or sex, or geography or political affiliation. We believe we must be the family of America, recognizing that at the heart of the matter we are bound one to another, that the problems of a retired school teacher in Duluth are our problems. That the future of the child in Buffalo is our future. That the struggle of a disabled man in Boston to survive and live decently is our struggle. That the hunger of a woman in Little Rock is our hunger. That the failure anywhere to provide what reasonably we might to avoid pain is our failure.

Now for 50 years, for 50 years we Democrats created a better future for our children, using traditional Democratic principles as a fixed beacon, giving us direction and purpose, but constantly innovating, adapting to new realities: Roosevelt's alphabet programmes;[9] TRUMAN's NATO[10] and the GI Bill of Rights;[11] KENNEDY's intelligent tax incentives[12] and the Alliance for Progress;[13] JOHNSON's civil rights;[14] Carter's human rights[15] and the nearly miraculous Camp David Peace Accord.[16] Democrats did it –

[*Applause.*]

Democrats did it – and Democrats can do it again … That struggle to live with dignity is the real story of the shining city. And it's a story, ladies and gentlemen, that I didn't read in a book, or learn in a classroom. I saw it, and lived it, like many of you.

I watched a small man with thick calluses on both hands work 15 and 16 hours a day. I saw him once literally bleed from the bottoms of his feet, a man who came here uneducated, alone, unable to speak the language, who taught me all I needed to know about faith and hard work by the simple eloquence of his example. I learned about our kind of democracy from my father. And I learned about our obligation to each other from him and from my mother. They asked only for a chance to work and to make the world better for their children.

[*Cheers and applause.*]

And they, they asked to be protected in those moments when they would not be able to protect themselves. This nation and this nation's government did that for them.

And that they were able to build a family and live in dignity and see one of their children go from behind their little grocery store in South Jamaica[17] on the other side of the tracks where he was born, to occupy the highest seat in the greatest state in the greatest nation in the only world we will know, is an ineffably beautiful tribute to the democratic process.

And, ladies and gentlemen, on January 20, 1985, it will happen again. Only on a much, much grander scale. We will have a new president of the United States, a Democrat born not to the blood of kings but to the blood of pioneers and immigrants.[18] And we will have America's first woman vice president, the child of immigrants.[19] [*Cheers and applause.*]

And she, she, she will open with one magnificent stroke, a whole new frontier for the United States. Now, it will happen. It will happen – if we make it happen; if you and I can make it happen. And I ask you now, ladies and gentlemen, brothers and sisters: for the good of all of us, for the love of this great nation, for the family of America, for the love of God. Please, make this nation remember how futures are built.

Thank you and God bless you.

[9] On being elected president in 1933, Roosevelt quickly established a number of agencies to assist recovery after the Depression, including the Civilian Conservation Corps (CCC) and the Federal Emergency Relief Administration (FERA). Abbreviated to their initials, they became known as 'FDR's alphabet soup'.

[10] Under President Truman, the USA became one of the twelve founder members of the North Atlantic Treaty Organization (NATO) in April 1949.

[11] The GI Bill of Rights was in fact passed under Roosevelt in June 1944, providing for education and unemployment benefit for the armed forces returning from World War II. It was subsequently expanded by Truman.

[12] In 1963, President Kennedy proposed major tax reform, which was passed by Congress after his assassination. Ironically, Kennedy's tax cuts were even greater than Reagan's.

[13] Introduced in 1961, the Alliance for Progress was a programme of economic co-operation between the USA and Latin America, which offered aid as an incentive to land reform and democratization.

[14] President Johnson signed the Civil Rights Act, which was designed to protect ethnic minorities and women from various forms of discrimination.

[15] The US politician Jimmy Carter (1924–) served as President 1977–81, and was highly active in peace negotiations. He agreed arms limitations with the USSR at the Strategic Arms Limitation Talks (SALT II) in 1979; since leaving office in 1980 he has been active in human rights campaigns world-wide.

[16] Carter's great peacemaking achievement was the Camp David Accords of 1978, which he brokered between Egypt and Israel.

[17] An area of Queens, New York City where Cuomo grew up.

[18] The US politician Walter F Mondale (1928–) is descended from Norwegian immigrants.

[19] The US politician Geraldine Ferraro (1935–2011) was the daughter of an Italian immigrant.

The Dalai Lama

Tibetan spiritual and temporal leader in exile

The Dalai Lama *originally Tenzin Gyatso* (1935–) was born into a peasant family in Taktser, Amdo province, and was designated the 14th incarnation of the Dalai Lama by the monks of Lhasa in 1937. He was enthroned in 1940, but his rights were exercised by a regency until 1950. He fled to Chumbi in southern Tibet after an abortive anti-Chinese uprising in 1950, but negotiated an autonomy agreement with China the following year and for the next eight years served as nominal ruler of Tibet. After China's suppression of the Tibetan national uprising in 1959 he was forced into permanent exile, and settled with other Tibetan refugees at Dharamsala in Punjab, India, where he established a democratically-based alternative government and sought to preserve Tibetan culture. A revered figure in his homeland and highly respected internationally, the Dalai Lama has continually rejected Chinese overtures to return home as a figurehead, seeking instead full independence. In 1988 he modified this position, proposing the creation of a self-governing Tibet in association with China. In 1989 he was awarded both the Congressional Human Rights award and the Nobel Prize for peace in recognition of his commitment to the non-violent liberation of his homeland. In 2011 he formally resigned as the political leader of the Tibetan parliament-in-exile.

'Happiness is the purpose of life'

10 December 1989, Oslo, Norway

'No matter what part of the world we come from, we are all basically the same human beings,' remarked the Dalai Lama during his Nobel Peace Prize acceptance speech in December 1989. 'We all seek happiness and try to avoid suffering. We have the same basic human needs and concerns.'

The following day, he delivered his Nobel lecture. A detailed exploration of his principles in relation to the political plight of Tibet, it described his five-point peace plan and his vision of a non-violent 'zone of Ahimsa' in the Tibetan plains (originally proposed in 1987, at the Congressional Human Rights Caucus in Washington, DC).

Between these two major public addresses, he gave an informal evening audience to discuss the spiritual and personal implications of happiness. Few people, it might be said, are better qualified on this subject than the world's most prominent Buddhist. Meditative, gentle and deceptively logical, he focuses on his unshakeable belief in the power of compassion – a virtue to which he accords even greater importance than religion.

Proceeding from this, he uses examples from nature to make a persuasive case for co-operation, constructiveness and non-violence.

What is the purpose of life for a human being? I believe that happiness is the purpose of life. Whether or not there is a purpose to the existence of the universe or galaxies, I don't know. In any case, the fact is that we are here on this planet with other human beings. Then, since every human being wants happiness and does not want suffering, it is clear that this desire does not come from training, or from some ideology. It is something natural. Therefore, I consider that the attainment of happiness, peace and joy is the purpose of life. Therefore, it is very important to investigate what are happiness and satisfaction and what are their causes.

I think that there is a mental factor as well as a physical factor … The mental factor is more important, superior to the physical factor. This we can know through our daily life. Since the mental factor is more important, we have to give serious thought to inner qualities.

Then, I believe compassion and love are necessary, in order for us to obtain happiness or tranquillity. These mental factors are key. I think they are the basic source. What is compassion? From the Buddhist viewpoint, there are different varieties of compassion. The basic meaning of compassion is not just a feeling of closeness, or just a feeling of pity. Rather, I think that with genuine compassion we not only feel the pains and suffering of others but we also have a feeling of determination to overcome that suffering. One aspect of compassion is some kind of determination and responsibility. Therefore, compassion brings us tranquillity and also inner strength. Inner strength is the ultimate source of success.

When we face some problem, a lot depends on the personal attitude toward that problem or tragedy. In some cases, when one faces the difficulty, one loses one's hope and becomes discouraged and then ends up depressed. On the other hand, if one has a certain mental attitude, then tragedy and suffering bring one more energy, more determination.

Usually, I tell our generation we are born during the darkest period in our long history. There is a big challenge. It is very unfortunate. But if there is a challenge then there is an opportunity to face it, an opportunity to demonstrate our will and our determination. So from that viewpoint I think that our generation is fortunate. These things depend on inner qualities, inner strength. Compassion is very gentle, very peaceful and soft in nature, not harsh. You cannot destroy it easily as it is very powerful. Therefore, compassion is very important and useful.

Then, again, if we look at human nature, love and compassion are the foundation of human existence. According to some scientists, the foetus has feeling in the mother's womb and is affected by the mother's mental state. Then the few weeks after birth are crucial for the enlarging of the brain of the child. During that period, the mother's physical touch is the greatest factor for the healthy development of the brain. This shows that the physical needs some affection to develop properly.

When we are born, our first action is sucking milk from the mother. Of course, the child may not know about compassion and love, but the natural feeling is one of closeness toward the object that gives the milk. If the mother is angry or has ill feeling, the milk may not come fully. This shows that from our first day as human beings the effect of compassion is crucial …

Compassion or love has different levels; some are more mixed than others with desire or attachment. For example, parents' attitudes toward their children contain a mixture of desire and attachment with compassion. The love and compassion between husband and wife – especially at the beginning of marriage when they don't know the deep nature of each other – are on a superficial level.

As soon as the attitude of one partner changes, the attitude of the other becomes opposite to what it was. That kind of love and compassion is more of the nature of attachment. Attachment means some kind of feeling of closeness projected by oneself. In reality, the other side may be very negative, but due to one's own mental attachment and projection, it appears as something nice. Furthermore, attachment causes one to exaggerate a small good quality and make it appear 100 per cent beautiful or 100 per cent positive. As soon as the mental attitudes change, that picture completely changes. Therefore, that kind of love and compassion is, rather, attachment.

Another kind of love and compassion is not based on something appearing beautiful or nice, but based on the fact that the other person, just like oneself, wants happiness and does not want suffering and indeed has every right to be happy and to overcome suffering. On such a basis, we feel a sense of responsibility, a sense of closeness toward that being. That is true compassion. This is because the compassion is based on reason, not just on emotional feeling. As a consequence, it does not matter what the other's attitude is, whether negative or positive. What matters is that it is a human being, a sentient being that has the experience of pain and pleasure.

There is no reason not to feel compassion so long as it is a sentient being.

The kinds of compassion at the first level are mixed, interrelated. Some people have the view that some individuals have a very negative, cruel attitude toward others. These kinds of individuals appear to have not compassion in their minds. But I feel that these people do have the seed of compassion. The reason for this is that even these people very much appreciate it when someone else shows them affection. A capacity to appreciate other people's affection means that in their deep mind there is the seed of compassion …

What is my purpose in life, what is my responsibility? Whether I like it or not, I am on this planet, and it is far better to do something for humanity. So you see that compassion is the seed or basis. If we take care to foster compassion, we will see that it brings the other good human qualities. The topic of compassion is not all religious business; it is very important to know that it is human business, that it is a question of human survival, that it is not a question of human luxury. I might say that religion is a kind of luxury. If you have religion, that is good. But it is clear that even without religion we can manage. However, without these basic human qualities we cannot survive. It is a question of our own peace and mental stability.

Next, let us talk about the human being as a social animal. Even if we do not like other people, we have to live together. Natural law is such that even bees and other animals have to live together in co-operation. I am attracted to bees because I like honey – it is really delicious. Their product is something that we cannot produce: very beautiful, isn't it? I exploit them too much, I think.

Even these insects have certain responsibilities: they work together very nicely. They have no constitution, they have no law, no police, nothing, but they work together effectively. This is because of nature. Similarly, each part of a flower is not arranged by humans but by nature. The force of nature is something remarkable. We human beings, we have constitutions, we have law, we have a police force, we have religion, we have many things. But in actual practice, I think that we are behind those small insects …

I will tell you something. I love friends, I want more friends. I love smiles. How to develop smiles? There are a variety of smiles. Some smiles are sarcastic. Some smiles are artificial – diplomatic smiles. These smiles do not produce satisfaction, but rather fear or suspicion. But a genuine smile gives us hope, freshness. If we want a genuine smile, then first we must produce the basis for a smile to come. On every level of human life, compassion is the key thing.

Now, on the question of violence and non-violence. There are many different levels of violence and non-violence. On the basis of external action, it is difficult to distinguish whether an action is violent or non-violent. Basically, it depends on the motivation behind the action. If the motivation is negative, even though the external appearance may be very smooth and gentle, in a deeper sense the action is very violent. On the contrary, harsh actions and words done with a sincere, positive motivation are essentially non-violent. In other words, violence is a destructive power. Non-violence is constructive.

When the days become longer and there is more sunshine, the grass becomes fresh and, consequently, we feel very happy. On the other hand, in autumn, one leaf falls down and another leaf falls down. These beautiful plants become as if dead and we do not feel very happy. Why? I think it is because deep down our human nature likes construction, and does not like destruction. Naturally, every action which is destructive is against human nature. Constructiveness is the human way. Therefore, I think that in terms of basic human feeling, violence is not good. Non-violence is the only way.

Practically speaking, through violence we may achieve something, but at the expense of someone else's welfare. That way, although we may solve one problem, we simultaneously seed a new problem. The best way to solve problems is through human understanding, mutual respect. On one side make some concessions; on the other side take serious consideration about the problem. There may not be complete satisfaction, but something happens. At least future danger is avoided. Non-violence is very safe.

Before my first visit to Europe in 1973,[1] I had felt the importance of compassion, altruism. On many occasions I expressed the importance of the sense of universal responsibility. Sometimes during this period, some people felt that the Dalai Lama's idea was a bit unrealistic. Unfortunately, in the Western world Gandhian non-violence[2] is seen as passive resistance more suitable to the East. The Westerners are very active, demanding immediate results, even in the course of daily life.

But today the actual situation teaches non-violence to people. The movement for freedom is non-violent. These recent events reconfirm to me that non-violence is much closer to human nature.

Again, if there are sound reasons or bases for the points you demand, then there is no need to use violence. On the other hand, when there is no sound reason that concessions should be made to you, but mainly your own desire, then reason cannot work and you have to rely on force. Thus, using force is not a sign of strength but rather a sign of weakness. Even in daily human contact, if we talk seriously, using reasons, there is no need to feel anger. We can argue the points. When we fail to prove with reason, then anger comes. When reason ends, then anger begins. Therefore, anger is a sign of weakness …

We are passing through a most difficult period. I am very encouraged by your warm expression and by the Nobel Peace Prize. I thank you from the depth of my heart.

[1] This included his meeting with Pope Paul VI at the Vatican. The Dalai Lama also visited the UK, Switzerland, Belgium, Ireland, Norway, Sweden, Denmark, the Netherlands, West Germany and Austria.

[2] The Dalai Lama refers to the philosophy of non-violence propounded by the Indian spiritual leader MAHATMA GANDHI.

Clarence Darrow
American lawyer

Clarence Seward Darrow (1857–1938) was born in Kinsman, Ohio, and was admitted to the Bar in 1878. He unsuccessfully defended EUGENE V DEBS, leader of the American Railway Union, for his part in the Pullman strike of 1894. In 1907 he successfully defended 'Big Bill' Haywood and Charles Moyer of the Western Federation of Miners, who had been implicated in the murder of Frank Steunenberg, ex-governor of Idaho. In 1924, he defended Richard Loeb and Nathan Leopold in a highly publicized murder trial; and in the 'Scopes Monkey Trial' of 1925 he defended the biology teacher John Scopes against a prosecution team that included the creationist W J BRYAN. In 1934 he was appointed to investigate Senator Gerald Nye's charge that the codes introduced by the National Recovery Board were favouring monopolies. His report led eventually to the abolition of price control. Darrow was an advocate of progressive reforms and a persistent opponent of the death penalty. He saved over 100 clients from execution, and often used the courtroom as a platform for wry and eloquent arguments which swayed the American public as well as the jury at hand.

'I am pleading that we overcome cruelty with kindness'
22 August 1924, Chicago, Illinois, USA

❧

The Leopold and Loeb case was the most celebrated of Darrow's long and distinguished career as a defence attorney. In May 1924, two privileged and gifted university students, Richard (Dickie) Loeb and Nathan Leopold, Jr, abducted and murdered 14-year-old Bobby Franks, the son of a wealthy Chicago businessman – apparently in an attempt to commit the perfect crime.

Public opinion overwhelmingly favoured hanging the youths, but Darrow agreed to defend them, despite accusations that he was merely pursuing a handsome fee. He began by tendering a guilty plea, resting his defence on evidence of insanity.

The case was held over one hot summer month, provoking intense media attention and riots outside the courtroom. It culminated in Darrow's gruelling, twelve-hour summation. 'The stuffed courtroom was like a black hole,' wrote one reporter. 'Hardly a breath of air moved in it. Yet the crowd ... sat motionless in attention as the weary old man gathered up all the threads of his argument for the final restatement.'

In this, the last part of his speech, Darrow cites the recent war as the root cause of a violent society. He also argues that the youths' reputations might be spared if the sentence were commuted.

It had the desired effect. Judge John R Caverly, reportedly reduced to tears, sentenced the youths to 99 years' imprisonment, 'in accordance with ... the dictates of enlightened humanity'.

Loeb was fatally stabbed in a prison brawl in 1936. Leopold was paroled in 1958, and emigrated to Puerto Rico.

❧

[1] Darrow refers to World War I.

Your Honour: I have spoken about the war.[1] I believed in it. I don't know whether I was crazy or not. Sometimes I think perhaps I was. I approved of it; I joined in the general cry of madness and despair. I urged men to fight. I was safe because I was too old to go. I was like the rest. What did they do? Right or wrong, justifiable or unjustifiable – which I need not discuss today – it changed the world.

For four long years the civilized world was engaged in killing men. Christian against Christian, barbarian uniting with Christians to kill Christians; anything to kill. It was taught in every school, aye in the Sunday schools. The little children played at war. The toddling children on the street. Do you suppose this world has ever been the same since? How long, your Honour, will it take for the world to get back the humane emotions that were slowly growing before the war? How long will it take the calloused hearts of men before the scars of hatred and cruelty shall be removed?

We read of killing 100,000 men in a day. We read about it and we rejoiced in it – if it was the other fellows who were killed. We were fed on flesh and drank blood, even down to the prattling babe. I need not tell you how many upright, honourable young boys have come into this court charged with murder, some saved and some sent to their death, boys who fought in this war and learned to place a cheap value on human life. You know it and I know it. These boys were brought up in it. The tales of death were in their homes, their playgrounds, their schools; they were in the newspapers that they read; it was a part of the common frenzy. What was a life? It was nothing. It was the least sacred thing in existence; and these boys were trained to this cruelty.

It will take 50 years to wipe it out of the human heart, if ever. I know this: that after the Civil War in 1865, crimes of this sort increased marvellously. No-one needs to tell me that crime has no cause. It has as definite a cause as any other disease, and I know that out of the hatred and bitterness of the Civil War, crime increased as America had never seen before. I know that growing out of the Napoleonic Wars there was a an era of crime such as Europe had never seen before. I know that Europe is going through the same experience today; I know it has followed every war; and I know it has influenced these boys so that life was not the same to them as it would have been if the world had not been made red with blood.

I protest against the crimes and mistakes of society being visited upon them. All of us have a share in it. I have mine. I cannot tell and I shall never know how many words of mine might have given birth to cruelty in place of love and kindness and charity.

Your Honour knows that, in this very court, crimes of violence have increased growing out of the war. Not necessarily by those who fought, but by those that learned that blood was cheap, and human life was cheap, and if the state could take it lightly, why not the boy? There are causes for this terrible crime. There are causes, as I have said, for everything that happens in the world. War is a part of it; education is a part of it; birth is a part of it; money is a part of it – all these conspired to compass the destruction of these two poor boys.

Has the court any right to consider anything but these two boys? The state says that your Honour has a right to consider the welfare of the community, as you have. If the welfare of the community would be benefited by taking these lives, well and good. I think it would work evil that no-one could measure. Has your Honour a right to consider the families of these defendants? I have been sorry, and I am sorry for the bereavement of Mr and Mrs Frank, for those broken ties that cannot be healed. All I can hope and wish is that some good may come from it all. But as compared with the families of Leopold and Loeb, the Franks are to be envied – and everyone knows it.

I do not know how much salvage there is in these two boys. I hate to say it in their presence, but what is there to look forward to? I do not know but what your Honour would be merciful if you tied a rope around their necks and let them die; merciful to them, but not merciful to civilization, and not merciful to those who would be left behind. To spend the balance of their days in prison is mighty little to look forward to, if anything. Is it anything?

They may have the hope that as the years roll around they might be released. I do not know. I do not know. I will be honest with this court as I have tried to be from the beginning. I know that these boys are not fit to be at large. I believe they will not be until they pass through the next stage of life, at 45 or 50. Whether they will then, I cannot tell. I am sure of this; that I will not be here to help them. So far as I am concerned, it is over.

I would not tell this court that I do not hope that some time, when life and age have changed their bodies, as they do, and have changed their emotions, as they do – that they may once more return to life. I would be the last person on earth to close the door of hope to any human being that lives, and least of all to my clients. But what have they to look forward to? Nothing. And I think here of the stanza of Housman:[2]

[2] Darrow quotes in full poem LX from the collection *A Shropshire Lad* (1896) by the English poet A E Housman (1859–1936).

'Now hollow fires burn out to black,
And lights are guttering low:
Square your shoulders, lift your pack,
And leave your friends and go.

Oh, never fear, man, nought's to dread,
Look not to left nor right:
In all the endless road you tread
There's nothing but the night.'

I care not, Your Honour, whether the march begins at the gallows or when the gates of Joliet[3] close upon them, there is nothing but the night, and that is little for any human being to expect.

[3] Joliet State Penitentiary, Stateville, Illinois, where Leopold and Loeb would serve their sentences.

But there are others to consider. Here are these two families, who have led honest lives, who will bear the name that they bear, and future generations must carry it on.

Here is Leopold's father – and this boy was the pride of his life. He watched him, he cared for him, he worked for him; the boy was brilliant and accomplished, he educated him, and he thought that fame and position awaited him, as it should have awaited. It is a hard thing for a father to see his life's hopes crumble into dust.

Should he be considered? Should his brothers be considered? Will it do society any good or make your life safer, or any human being's life safer, if it should be handed down from generation to generation, that this boy, their kin, died upon the scaffold?

And Loeb's the same. Here are the faithful uncle and brother, who have watched here day by day, while Dickie's father and his mother are too ill to stand this terrific strain, and shall be waiting for a message which means more to them than it can mean to you or me. Shall these be taken into account in this general bereavement?

Have they any rights? Is there any reason, Your Honour, why their proud names and all the future generations that bear them shall have this bar sinister written across them? How many boys and girls, how many unborn children will feel it? It is bad enough as it is, God knows. It is bad enough, however it is. But it's not yet death on the scaffold. It's not that. And I ask your Honour, in addition to all that I have said, to save two honourable families from a disgrace that never ends, and which could be of no avail to help any human being that lives.

Now, I must say a word more and then I will leave this with you where I should have left it long ago. None of us are unmindful of the public; courts are not and juries are not. We placed our fate in the hands of a trained court, thinking that he would be more mindful and considerate than a jury.[4] I cannot say how people feel. I have stood here for three months as one might stand at the ocean, trying to sweep back the tide. I hope the seas are subsiding and the wind is falling, and I believe they are, but I wish to make no false pretence to this court.

[4] By entering a guilty plea, Darrow had shrewdly ensured that the sentence would be determined by Judge Caverly (whom he considered 'kindly and discerning') and not by a jury.

The easy thing and the popular thing to do is to hang my clients. I know it. Men and women who do not think will applaud. The cruel and thoughtless will approve. It will be easy today; but in Chicago, and reaching out over the length and breadth of the land, more and more fathers and mothers, the humane, the kind and the hopeful, who are gaining an understanding and asking questions, not only about these poor boys, but about their own – these will join in no acclaim at the death of my clients.

These would ask that the shedding of blood be stopped, and that the normal feelings of man resume their sway. And as the days and the months and the years go on, they will ask it more and more.

But Your Honour: what they shall ask may not count. I know the easy way. I know Your Honour stands between the future and the past. I know the future is with me, and what I stand for here; not merely for the lives of these two unfortunate lads, but for all boys and all girls; for all of the young, and as far as possible, for all of the old. I am pleading for life, understanding, charity, kindness, and the infinite mercy that considers all. I am pleading that we overcome cruelty with kindness and hatred with love. I know the future is on my side.

Your Honour stands between the past and the future. You may hang these boys; you may hang them by the neck until they are dead. But in doing it you will turn your face toward the past. In doing it you are making it harder for every other boy who in ignorance and darkness must grope his way through the mazes which only childhood knows. In doing it you will make it harder for unborn children. You may save them and make it easier for every child that sometime may stand where these boys stand. You will make it easier for every human being with an aspiration and a vision and a hope and a fate.

I am pleading for the future; I am pleading for a time when hatred and cruelty will not control the hearts of men. When we can learn by reason and judgement and understanding and faith that all life is worth saving, and that mercy is the highest attribute of man.

I feel that I should apologize for the length of time I have taken. This case may not be as important as I think it is, and I am sure I do not need to tell this court or to tell my friends that I would fight just as hard for the poor as for the rich. If I should succeed in saving these boys' lives and do nothing for the progress of the law, I should feel sad indeed. If I can succeed, my greatest reward and my greatest hope will be that for the countless unfortunates who must tread the same road in blind childhood that these poor boys have trod – that I have done something to help human understanding, to temper justice with mercy, to overcome hate with love.

I was reading last night of the aspiration of the old Persian poet, Omar Khayyám.[5] It appealed to me as the highest that I can vision. I wish it was in my heart, and I wish it was in the hearts of all.

'So I be written in the Book of Love,
I do not care about that Book above.
Erase my name or write it as you will,
So I be written in the Book of Love.'

[5] The Persian poet, mathematician and astronomer Omar Khayyám (1048–1131) is thought to have written at least 250 of the *rubáiyát*, or quatrains, attributed to him, some of which were published in an English translation by Edward Fitzgerald in 1859.

'Everybody loves killing'

27 October 1924, New York City, USA

When Darrow saved Leopold and Loeb from the gallows (see previous speech), the case divided opinion. One withering comment came from the New York City judge Alfred J Talley, who told a newspaper: 'It is not the criminals, actual or potential, that need a neuropathic hospital. It is the people who slobber over them in an effort to find excuses for their crimes.'

A few months later, Darrow rose to Talley's challenge at an event staged by the League for Public Discussion in New York. In front of an audience of 3,000 at the Metropolitan Opera House, the two lawmen debated the motion 'That Capital Punishment is a Wise Public Policy'. Darrow seized the opportunity to air his views.

By turns scathing and eloquent, he proceeds from a series of bold statements ('Everybody loves killing') to a sarcastic endorsement of widespread capital punishment and torture ('Why not boil them in oil, as they used to do?') before closing on a note of sombre sincerity ('I am against it because I believe it is inhuman'). His rhetoric was rarely more persuasive.

❧

I deny [Judge Talley's] statement that every man's heart tells him it is wrong to kill. I think every man's heart desires killing. Personally, I never killed anybody that I know of, but I have had a great deal of satisfaction now and then reading obituary notices; and I used to delight, with the rest of my 100 per cent patriotic friends, when I saw 10,000 or 15,000 Germans being killed in a day.

Everybody loves killing. Some of them think it is too messy for them. Every human being that believes in capital punishment loves killing, and the only reason they believe in capital punishment is because they get a kick out of it. Nobody kills anyone for love, unless they get over it, temporarily or otherwise. But they kill the one they hate. And before you can get a trial to hang somebody or electrocute him, you must first hate him and then get a satisfaction over his death.

There is no emotion in any human being that is not in every single human being. The degree is different, that is all. And the degree is not always different in different people. It depends likewise on circumstances, on time, and on place.

I shall not follow my friend into the labyrinth of statistics. Statistics are a pleasant indoor sport – not so good as crossword puzzles – and they prove nothing to any sensible person who is familiar with statistics. I might just observe, in passing, that in all of these states where the mortality by homicide is great, they have capital punishment and always have had it. A logical man, when he found out that the death rate increased under capital punishment, would suggest some other way of dealing with it …

I will guarantee to take any set of statistics and take a little time to it and prove they mean directly the opposite for what is claimed. But I think I will undertake to say that you can show by statistics that the states in which there was no capital punishment have a very much smaller percentage of homicides.

I know it is true. That doesn't prove anything, because, as a rule, they are states with a less diverse population, without as many large cities, without as much mixtures of all sorts of elements, which go to add to the general gaiety – and homicide is a product of that. There is no sort of question but that those states in the United States where there is no capital punishment have a lower percentage than the others. But that doesn't prove the question. It is a question that cannot be proven one way or the other by statistics. It rests upon things, upon feelings and emotions and arguments much deeper than statistics.

The death rate recently in the United States and all over the world has increased. Why? The same thing has happened that has happened in every country in the world since time began. A great war always increases death rates.

We teach people to kill, and the state is the one that teaches them. If a state wishes that its citizens respect human life, then the state should stop killing. It can be done in no other way, and it will perhaps not be fully done that way. There are infinite reasons for killing. There are infinite circumstances under which there are more or less deaths. It never did depend and never can depend upon the severity of the punishment.

[Judge Talley] talks about the United States being a lawless country. Well, the people somehow prefer it … In any new country, homicide is more frequent than in an old country, because there is a higher degree of equality. It is always true wherever you go. And in the older countries, as a general rule, there are fewer homicides because nobody ever thinks of getting out of his class; nobody ever dreams of such a thing.

But let's see what there is in this argument. He says, 'Everybody who kills dreads hanging.' Well, he has had experiences as a lawyer on both sides. I have had experience on one side. I know that everybody who is taken into court on a murder charge desires to live, and they do not want to be hanged or electrocuted. Even a thing as alluring as being cooked with electricity doesn't appeal to them.

But that hasn't anything to do with it. What was the state of mind when the homicide was committed? The state of mind is one thing when a homicide is committed and another thing weeks or months afterward, when every reason for committing it is gone. There is no comparison …

I don't want to dispute with him about the right of the state to kill people. Of course, they have got a right … That is, they have got the power. And you have got a right to do what you get away with. The words 'power' and 'right', so far as this is concerned, mean exactly the same thing. So nobody who has any knowledge of philosophy would pretend to say that the state had not the right to kill.

But why not do a good job of it? If you want to get rid of killings by hanging people or electrocuting them because these are so terrible, why not make a punishment that is terrible? This isn't so much. It lasts but a short time. There is no physical torture in it. Why not boil them in oil, as they used to do? Why not burn them at the stake? Why not sew them into a bag with serpents and throw them out to sea? Why not take them out on the sand and let them be eaten by ants? Why not break every bone in their body on the rack, as has been done for such serious offences as heresy and witchcraft?

Those were the good old days, in which the judge should have held court. Glorious days, when you could kill them by the million because they worshipped God in a different way from that which the state provided, or when you could kill old women for witchcraft! Those were the glorious days of capital punishment. And there wasn't a judge or a preacher who didn't think that the life of the state depended upon their right to hang old women for witchcraft and to persecute others for worshipping God in the wrong way.

Why, our capital punishment isn't worth talking about, so far as its being a preventive is concerned. It isn't worth discussing. Why not call back from the dead and barbarous past the 160-odd crimes that were punishable by death in England? Why not once more re-enact the blue laws[1] of our own country and kill people right? Why not resort to all the tortures that the world has always resorted to, to keep men in the straight and narrow path? Why reduce it to a paltry question of murder?

Everybody in this world has some pet aversion to something, and on account of that pet aversion they would like to hang somebody. If the prohibitionists made the law, they would be in favour of hanging you for

[1] The 'blue laws', introduced in US and Canadian colonies from around 1780, prohibited commerce on Sundays. A few still operate in certain US states.

taking a drink, or certainly for bootlegging, because to them that is the most heinous crime there is …

Is there anybody who knows what justice is? No-one on earth can measure out justice. Can you look at any man and say what he deserves – whether he deserves hanging by the neck until dead or life in prison or 30 days in prison or a medal? The human mind is blind to all who seek to look in at it and to most of us that look out from it. Justice is something that man knows little about. He may know something about charity and understanding and mercy, and he should cling to these as far as he can …

There is just one thing in all this question. It is a question of how you feel, that is all. It is all inside of you. If you love the thought of somebody being killed, why, you are for it. If you hate the thought of somebody being killed, you are against it.

Let me just take a little brief review of what has happened in this world. They used to hang people on the crossways and on a high hill, so that everybody would be awed into goodness by the sight. They have tortured them in every way that the brain of man could conceive. They have provided every torture known or that could be imagined for one who believed differently from his fellow man – and still the belief persisted. They have maimed and scarred and starved and killed human beings since man began penning his fellow man. Why? Because we hate him. And what has added to it is that they have done it under the false ideal of self-righteousness.

I have heard parents punish their children and tell their children it hurt the parent more than it did the child. I don't believe it. I have tried it both ways, and I don't believe it. I know better.

Gradually, the world has been lopping off these punishments. Why? Because we have grown a little more sensitive, a little more imaginative, a little kindlier, that is all … The only way we got rid of those laws was because juries were too humane to obey the courts. That is the only way we got rid of punishing old women, of hanging old women in New England – because, in spite of all the courts, the juries would no longer convict them for a crime that never existed. And in that way they have cut down the crimes in New England for punishment by death from 170 to two.

What is going to happen if we get rid of them? Is the world coming to an end? The earth has been here ages and ages before man came. It will be here ages and ages after he disappears, and the amount of people you hang won't make the slightest difference with it.

Now, why am I opposed to capital punishment? It is too horrible a thing for a state to undertake. We are told by my friend, 'Oh, the killer does it; why shouldn't the state?' I would hate to live in a state that I didn't think was better than a murderer.

But I told you the real reason. The people of the state kill a man because he killed someone else – that is all – without the slightest logic, without the slightest application to life; simply from anger, nothing else!

I am against it because I believe it is inhuman, because I believe that as the hearts of men have softened they have gradually gotten rid of brutal punishment, because I believe that it will only be a few years until it will be banished forever from every civilized country – even New York – because I believe that it has no effect whatever to stop murder …

There isn't, I submit, a single admissible argument in favour of capital punishment. Nature loves life. We believe that life should be protected and preserved. The greater the sanctity that the state pays to life, the greater the feeling of sanctity the individual has for life.

Eugene V Debs
American socialist and union leader

Eugene Victor Debs (1855–1926) was born in Terre Haute, Indiana, the son of Alsatian immigrants. He became a railroad worker and served as the national secretary of the Brotherhood of Locomotive Firemen until 1893, when he resigned to organize an industrial union of railroad workers, the American Railway Union (ARU). He pledged the ARU's participation in the Pullman strike of 1894, which was broken by féderal authorities and brought Debs a six-month prison sentence. He helped to found the Socialist Party of America, standing unsuccessfully as its candidate in all the presidential elections between 1900 and 1920, except that of 1916. His pacifism during World War I led to his imprisonment (1918–21); he conducted his final presidential campaign from an Atlanta penitentiary, receiving nearly a million votes.

'While there is a soul in prison, I am not free'
18 September 1918, Cleveland, Ohio, USA

On 2 April 1917, President WOODROW WILSON addressed Congress, calling for the USA to intervene in World War I (his speech is included in this book). The declaration of war on Germany came four days later.

Opposition to American involvement in the war was widespread, and led to the introduction of the Espionage Act (1917), which criminalized such activities as disclosing military secrets, refusing military service and disrupting recruitment procedures. Some 900 people were jailed under this legislation. It was extended, in May 1918, by the draconian Sedition Act, which forbade any 'disloyal, profane, scurrilous, or abusive language' against the government, flag and armed forces of the USA.

In June 1918, Eugene Debs, a pacifist, made a speech at the Socialist Party convention in Canton, Ohio, criticizing the imprisonment of colleagues such as Kate Richards O'Hare under the Espionage Act. 'The United States, under plutocratic rule, is the only country that would send a woman to prison for five years for exercising the right of free speech,' he said. 'If this be treason, let them make the most of it.'

He was duly prosecuted for sedition in September 1918. On being convicted, he gave this eloquent, almost poetic speech, laying down his creed and accepting the court's judgement.

Debs nonetheless appealed to the US Supreme Court, though this was unsuccessful. He was sentenced to ten years in jail; however, when the Espionage and Sedition Acts were repealed in 1921, he was pardoned and released.

Your Honour: years ago I recognized my kinship with all living beings, and I made up my mind that I was not one bit better than the meanest on earth. I said then, and I say now, that while there is a lower class, I am in it, and while there is a criminal element, I am of it, and while there is a soul in prison, I am not free.

If the law under which I have been convicted is a good law, then there is no reason why sentence should not be pronounced upon me. I listened to all that was said in this court in support and justification of this prosecution, but my mind remains unchanged. I look upon the Espionage Law as a despotic enactment, in flagrant conflict with democratic principles and with the spirit of free institutions.

Your Honour, I have stated in this court that I am opposed to the form of our present government; that I am opposed to the social system in which we live; that I believe in a fundamental change to both – but if possible by peaceable and orderly means.

Standing here this morning, I recall my boyhood. At 14, I went to work in a railroad shop; at 16, I was firing a freight engine on a railroad. I remember all the hardships and privations of that earlier day, and from that time until now my heart has been with the working class. I could have been in Congress long ago. I have preferred to go to prison.

I am thinking this morning of the men in the mills and the factories; of the men in the mines and on the railroads. I am thinking of the women who for a paltry wage are compelled to work out their barren lives; of the little children who in this system are robbed of their childhood and in their tender years are seized in the remorseless grasp of Mammon and forced into the industrial dungeons, there to feed the monster machines while they themselves are being starved and stunted, body and soul.

I see them dwarfed and diseased and their little lives broken and blasted because in this high noon of our 20th-century Christian civilization, money is still so much more important than the flesh and blood of childhood. In very truth gold is god today and rules with pitiless sway in the affairs of men.

In this country — the most favoured beneath the bending skies — we have vast areas of the richest and most fertile soil, material resources in inexhaustible abundance, the most marvellous productive machinery on earth, and millions of eager workers, ready to apply their labour to that machinery to produce in abundance for every man, woman, and child. And if there are still vast numbers of our people who are the victims of poverty and whose lives are an unceasing struggle — all the way from youth to old age, until at last death comes to their rescue and lulls these hapless victims to dreamless sleep — it is not the fault of the Almighty: it cannot be charged to nature, but it is due entirely to the outgrown social system in which we live, that ought to be abolished, not only in the interest of the toiling masses but in the higher interest of all humanity.

I believe, Your Honour, in common with all socialists, that this nation ought to own and control its own industries. I believe, as all socialists do, that all things that are jointly needed and used ought to be jointly owned — that industry, the basis of our social life, instead of being the private property of a few and operated for their enrichment, ought to be the common property of all, democratically administered in the interest of all.

I have been accused, Your Honour, of being an enemy of the soldier. I hope I am laying no flattering unction to my soul when I say that I don't believe the soldier has a more sympathetic friend than I am. If I had my way, there would be no soldiers, but I realize the sacrifice they are making. I can think of them. I can feel for them. I can sympathize with them. That is one of the reasons why I have been doing what little has been in my power to bring about a condition of affairs in this country worthy of the sacrifices they are making in its behalf.

I am opposing a social order in which it is possible for one man who does absolutely nothing that is useful to amass a fortune of hundreds of millions of dollars, while millions of men and women, who work all the days of their lives, secure barely enough for a wretched existence.

This order of things cannot always endure. I have registered my protest against it. I recognize the feebleness of my effort, but, fortunately, I am not alone. There are multiplied thousands of others who, like myself, have come to realize that before we may truly enjoy the blessings of civilized life, we must reorganize society upon a mutual and co-operative basis; and to this end we have organized a great economic and political movement that spreads over the face of all the earth.

There are today upwards of 60 millions of socialists — loyal, devoted adherents to this cause, regardless of nationality, race, creed, colour or sex. They are all making common cause. They are spreading with tireless energy the propaganda of the new social order. They are waiting, watching, and working hopefully through all the hours of the day and the night.

They are still in a minority. But they have learned how to be patient and to bide their time. They feel – they know, indeed – that the time is coming, in spite of all opposition, all persecution, when this emancipating gospel will spread among all the peoples, and when this minority will become the triumphant majority and, sweeping into power, inaugurate the greatest social and economic change in history. In that day, we shall have the universal commonwealth – the harmonious co-operation of every nation with every other nation on earth.

Your Honour, I ask no mercy and I plead for no immunity. I realize that finally the right must prevail. I never so clearly comprehended as now the great struggle between the powers of greed and exploitation on the one hand and upon the other the rising hosts of industrial freedom and social justice.

I can see the dawn of the better day for humanity. The people are awakening. In due time they will and must come to their own. When the mariner, sailing over tropic seas, looks for relief from his weary watch, he turns his eyes toward the southern cross, burning luridly above the tempest-vexed ocean. As the midnight approaches, the southern cross begins to bend, the whirling worlds change their places, and with starry finger-points the Almighty marks the passage of time upon the dial of the universe. And though no bell may beat the glad tidings, the lookout knows that the midnight is passing – that relief and rest are close at hand.

Let the people everywhere take heart of hope, for the cross is bending, the midnight is passing, and joy cometh with the morning.

Your Honour, I thank you, and I thank all of this court for their courtesy, for their kindness, which I shall remember always.

I am now prepared to receive your sentence.

Charles de Gaulle
French military and political leader

Charles André Joseph Marie de Gaulle (1890–1970) was born in Lille. He served as an army officer in World War I, and drew on this experience to develop a new theory of mechanized strategy. This was expounded in *The Army of the Future*, published in 1932; although largely ignored by the French military, it inspired the German *Blitzkrieg* of 1940. De Gaulle's prescience was rewarded with promotion to general and Under-Secretary of War the same year, but days before France signed an armistice with the German invaders he sought refuge in England to found the Free French Army. Though largely ignored by both WINSTON CHURCHILL and FRANKLIN D ROOSEVELT, he served as a focus for the resistance movement, in which he played an active role during the rest of the war. He returned to Paris in 1944 with the first liberation forces and became the country's first post-war leader. Failing to form an all-party coalition, he resigned in 1946 to found a new party, *Rassemblement du Peuple Français* ('Rally of the French People'), which took 40 per cent of the votes in the 1947 election. He relinquished its leadership in 1953, and, in the wake of the failure by successive administrations to resolve the question of Algerian independence, accepted office as first president of the Fifth Republic in 1958. In 1959–60 he granted self-government to all French African colonies (including Algeria, which finally achieved independence in 1962). At home, he consolidated France's growing international importance by establishing a nuclear deterrent, fostering better relations with West Germany, blocking Britain's attempts in 1962 and 1967 to enter the Common Market, and recognizing the Chinese government in 1964. Despite his extensive use of referenda, his autocratic presidential style and the growing popularity of the Left among younger voters, he won re-election in 1965 after a second ballot, and recovered with an overwhelming victory in 1968, after seeking a mandate in the wake of violent student riots. However, in 1969 a referendum rejected his proposals for Senate and regional reforms. This brought his resignation, and he died a year later. To many British and American politicians, de Gaulle epitomized Gallic obstinacy and self-interest; but while he could not match Churchill's brilliance in wartime, he may be regarded as a more influential and effective national leader in peacetime.

'Is defeat absolute? No!'
18 June 1940, radio broadcast from London, England

Soon after the Nazi occupation of Paris, Charles de Gaulle emerged as France's most defiant voice of resistance. He had campaigned persistently, during the 1920s and 1930s, for a modern mechanized army. However, his advice went unheeded: Marshal Philippe Pétain (who became War Minister in 1934) preferred to rely on the defensive fortifications of the Maginot Line. Following the declaration of war in 1939, French forces prepared for the expected German attack, but when this came in May–June 1940, it outflanked the Maginot Line, quickly overwhelming Belgium, the Netherlands and Luxembourg, and driving back over 300,000 Allied troops to the beaches of Dunkirk.

The French government abandoned Paris on 10 June, retreating to Bordeaux in south-west France. Prime Minister PAUL REYNAUD faced growing pressure to reach an armistice with the Germans, but instead resigned. He was replaced by Pétain, who immediately began negotiations with Germany. As Under-Secretary of War, de Gaulle opposed surrender, and fled to Britain to organize French resistance.

A few days later, despite opposition from his Cabinet, Winston Churchill allowed de Gaulle to broadcast to the French people via BBC radio. In his speech, de Gaulle encourages the French people to resist the German occupation, reminding them that the British Empire and the USA would support them. Although few in France heard the broadcast, word spread that he was in London calling for support.

On 22 June, Pétain surrendered northern France to Germany, and assumed the government of southern France from Vichy. On 28 June, Britain recognized de Gaulle as the leader of the Free French Forces.

> Those military chiefs who for many years led the French armies have formed a government. This government, alleging the defeat of our armies, has negotiated a truce with the enemy.
>
> It's true that we were overwhelmed by the enemy's mechanical force, on the land and in the air. Infinitely more than their numbers, it was the tanks, the aeroplanes, the tactics of the Germans that forced us to retreat. It was the tanks, the aeroplanes, the tactics of the Germans that surprised our generals and brought them to the position they are in today.

But has the final word been spoken? Must hope vanish? Is defeat absolute? No! Believe me: I who speak to you in full possession of the facts, I tell you that France has lost nothing. Those very means that defeated us can one day bring us victory.

For France is not alone! She is not alone! She is not alone! She has a vast empire behind her! She can form an alliance with the British Empire, which holds the sea and perseveres in the struggle. Like England, she can make unlimited demands on the vast industry of the United States.

This war is not limited to the blighted territory of our country. This war is not confined to the battle for France. This war is a world war. All the failures, all the delays, all the miseries do not negate the fact that the means exist within the universe to crush our enemies one day. Stricken today by mechanical force, in the future we shall conquer with a superior mechanical force. That is the destiny of the world.

I, General de Gaulle, currently in London, I invite French officers and soldiers who find themselves on British territory, or who may find themselves here, with or without weapons; I invite engineers and specialists of the armaments industry who find themselves on British territory or who may find themselves here, to contact me.

Whatever happens, the flame of French resistance must not be extinguished and it will not be extinguished.

Tomorrow, I shall speak on London radio again.

'Paris outraged! Paris broken! Paris martyred! But Paris liberated!'
25 August 1944, Paris, France

When de Gaulle made his triumphal return to Paris, France had been under German control for more than four years.

Following his escape to London in 1940, he had been sentenced to death for treason by the Vichy government, which was little more than a puppet regime of the Nazis; but he soon established himself as leader of the Free French Forces. In 1943, he moved his headquarters to the liberated French territory of Algeria.

In summer 1944, Allied forces landed in France (from the north in June; from the south in August), pushing back the German occupiers. As US troops closed in on Paris, the citizens went on strike and launched skirmishes against the occupying Germans. US forces under General DWIGHT D EISENHOWER hesitated, aware that ADOLF HITLER had ordered his troops to destroy the city rather than surrender it. Fearful of a massacre – and eager to pre-empt American military control of Paris – de Gaulle ordered the Free French Forces into Paris, and it was to them that the Germans surrendered on 24 August. This was a triumph for de Gaulle – who had flown in from Algiers that day – not least because US president Franklin D Roosevelt mistrusted him and had initially recognized the Vichy government.

The following day, de Gaulle addressed the expectant crowds from the Hôtel de Ville, announcing the liberation of the city and the restoration of French pride. In his speech, he plays successfully to the crowd's patriotism, personifying Paris as a heroic survivor, 'bleeding but resolute'.

On 28 August, he brought the provisional government home to Paris.

Why try to resist the emotion which now seizes all of us, men and women alike, who are here at home, in a Paris standing tall, liberating herself, and able to do so with her own hands?

No! We shall not hide this profound and sacred emotion. These are overwhelming events in every one of our poor lives.

Paris! Paris outraged! Paris broken! Paris martyred! But Paris liberated! Liberated by herself, liberated by her people, supported by the armies of France, with the support and empowerment of all France, the France who fights back, the only France, the true France, the eternal France.

De Gaulle – 'Paris outraged! Paris broken! Paris martyred! But Paris liberated!'

Well now! Since the enemy who held Paris has surrendered into our hands, France herself may return home to Paris. She returns here, bleeding but resolute. She returns here enlightened by a great lesson, but more certain than ever of her obligations and her rights.

I shall speak first of her obligations, and I summarize them in full when I say that, for the moment, we must concern ourselves with obligations of war. The enemy is flagging but he is not yet beaten. He remains on our soil. We must not consider ourselves satisfied simply because, with the support of our beloved and esteemed allies, we have driven him from our home. We must invade his territory, for that is the victor's duty.

That is why the French advance party entered Paris with cannon fire. That is why the great French army of Italy has disembarked in the Midi,[1] and is making its way swiftly up the Rhône valley. That is why our brave, beloved forces of the interior will equip themselves with modern weapons. We must have revenge, retaliation, justice: that is why we shall continue to fight until the final day, until the day of complete and total victory.

All men here, and all who hear us throughout France, know that this duty of war demands national unity. Those others of us — we who shall have witnessed the greatest hours of our history — need desire nothing but to prove ourselves worthy of France right until the end.

Long live France!

[1] A general term for the south of France.

Demosthenes
Athenian orator and politician

Demosthenes (384–322 BC) was born in Athens, the son of a wealthy sword manufacturer who died when Demosthenes was seven. Most of his inheritance was lost by the neglect or fraud of his guardians, and although he later prosecuted them, the money had gone. This litigation led him to take up law as a profession. Up to the age of 30 he confined himself to speech-writing for others, and gained a reputation as a constitutional lawyer. He did not embark on his political career until 351 BC, around which time the Greek cities were under threat from Philip II of Macedon; Demosthenes from the outset advocated a policy of total resistance. Philip's attack on the northern state of Olynthus gave occasion to the *Olynthiacs* (349 BC), which, with the orations against Philip called the *Philippics* (351 BC, 344 BC and 341 BC), are Demosthenes' greatest speeches. Athens made war with Philip on behalf of Olynthus, but failed to save the city and settled for peace. From 346 BC to 340 BC Demosthenes was engaged in forming an anti-Macedonian movement and in indicting Aeschines, his political opponent, for betraying Athens. War broke out again in 340 BC and ended in the fatal Battle of Chaeronea (338 BC), in which Athens and her allies were totally defeated. At the trial of his supporter Ctesiphon, Demosthenes gave his famous speech *On the Crown*, gloriously vindicating himself against Aeschines. Meanwhile in 336 BC Alexander the Great had succeeded his father Philip to the Macedonian throne. In 324 BC Harpalus, Alexander's treasurer, absconded to Athens with an enormous sum of money. It was placed in the state treasury under the care of Demosthenes and others, and when Alexander demanded it, half was missing. Demosthenes was accused and condemned, but escaped from prison into exile. In 323 BC Alexander died, and Demosthenes was recalled to head a fruitless attempt to throw off Macedonian rule. The Battle of Crannon ended the revolt; sentenced to death, Demosthenes fled to the island of Calauria, where he took poison.

'I was the man who came forth on that day'
330 BC Athens, Greece

Demosthenes was at the height of his political power in the period between the outbreak of war between Athens and Philip II, king of Macedon (349 BC) and the Macedonian victory over Athens, Thebes and their allies at the Battle of Chaeronea. As leader of the anti-Macedonian tendency, opposed by his arch-rival Aeschines, Demosthenes persuaded the Athenian democracy to intervene in the northern Aegean to stop Philip's expansion. When, in late 339 BC, Philip marched south on a pretext and occupied Elateia in Phocis, in striking distance of both Athens and Thebes, it was Demosthenes who spoke to urge defensive measures and an alliance with Thebes, which was in alliance with Macedon but had been disturbed by Philip's evident desire to build his power in central Greece.

Though Demosthenes' advice (and his influence with the Thebans) brought about the alliance, which prevented Philip from dealing severally with Athens and Thebes, the crushing defeat of the allies at Chaeronea led to the success of Philip's designs to dominate Greece and the decline of Demosthenes' influence. However, one of his supporters in Athens, Ctesiphon, proposed that he should be crowned with a golden crown at the festival of the Great Dionysia in 336 BC for his services to the city. Aeschines prosecuted Ctesiphon on the grounds that he had acted illegally, but the trial did not take place until 330 BC. In this speech Demosthenes vindicated his career, and Aeschines was fined for a malicious prosecution and left Athens for good.

In the famous passage from the speech *On the Crown* which follows, Demosthenes describes the panic which struck Athens when the news arrived that Philip had reached Elateia, and his own part in what followed. The translation is by Stephen Usher (1993).

[1] The Presidents of the Council of Five Hundred consisted of the councillors from one of the ten Athenian tribes. One councillor, chosen each day by lot, was the *epistates* (leader) for that day, and was on duty, with some 15 colleagues, for the whole 24 hours. They received meals at public expense.

It was evening. Someone brought a message to the Presidents[1] that Elateia had been taken. They were in the middle of their evening meal but rose from it immediately at the news. Some of them drove the stallholders in the market-place from their booths and set fire to the wicker-frames,[2] while others sent for the generals and summoned the trumpeter; and the city was full of commotion.

At dawn on the next day, the Presidents called the Council[3] to their chamber, and you made your way to the assembly, and before the Council had deliberated and formulated its proposal, all the people were in their seats on the hill.[4] After this, when the councillors had entered and the

[2] Emergencies were signalled by the lighting of bonfires.
[3] The Council of Five Hundred, chosen by lot from among the richer classes, was responsible for preparing the agenda for the meetings of the Assembly.

Presidents had announced the news that had been brought to them and introduced the messenger, and he had spoken himself, the herald asked: 'Who wishes to speak?' And no-one came forward.

The herald asked the question many times, but still not a man got up, though all the generals and all the regular speakers were present, and their country was crying out in her collective voice for a man who would speak to save her: for it is right to regard the voice which the herald gives forth according to the laws as that of the country as a whole.

And yet if men wishing for the city to be saved were required to come forward, all of you and all other Athenians would have risen up and gone to the rostrum; for I know every one of you wanted her to be saved. If it were to have been the richest, then it would have been the Three Hundred;[5] if those who were both patriotic and wealthy, those who subsequently made great contributions, since they made these out of both patriotism and wealth.

But it seems that day and that crisis called not only for the patriot and the rich man, but for the man who had followed the course of events from the beginning, and had calculated correctly the reason and purpose of Philip's actions. For a man who was ignorant of these, and had not been studying them carefully for a long time, was no more likely because of patriotism or wealth to know what should be done or to advise you.

Well, I was the man who came forth on that day and addressed you; and I ask you to listen attentively to what I said for two reasons: firstly, that you may know that I, alone of the speakers and statesmen, did not desert my patriot's post in the hour of peril, but I was to be found there advocating and proposing the measures that your predicament required; and secondly, that by spending a little time you will gain much experience for the future conduct of all affairs of state.

Now I said: 'I consider those who are over-alarmed because the Thebans are already on Philip's side to be ignorant of the actual situation. I am quite sure that if this were really the case, we should be hearing that he was not in Elateia, but at our very border. But I know for a fact that he has come merely to prepare his ground at Thebes.

'Let me tell you how these preparations stand. The man has won over as many Thebans as he could induce by bribery or trickery; but he can by no means persuade those who opposed him from the start and will stand against him. So what does he want and why has he taken Elateia? His object is to display his forces near their borders and station them there, and to encourage and embolden his friends and intimidate his opponents, so that they may concede through fear what they now refuse, or be forced to do so.

'Now if we choose, in the present emergency, to remember anything disagreeable that the Thebans have done to us and to mistrust them, regarding them as our enemies,[6] firstly we shall be doing what Philip would desire; and secondly, I am afraid those who are now resisting him may accept him, and all will unanimously embrace Philip's cause and together march into Attica. If, however, you follow my advice – and apply yourselves to considering what I suggest instead of cavilling at it – I think you will decide I am speaking to the point, and I shall remove the danger that threatens the city.

'What, then, do I recommend? First, relax your present anxiety, then redirect your whole attention to the Thebans and fear for them: for they are much closer to the dangers than we are, and the peril threatens them

[4] The Assembly of all adult male Athenian citizens met on the hill called Pnyx, adjoining the Acropolis.

[5] The Three Hundred were the richest citizens of Athens, who were chiefly responsible for providing the navy with warships at their own expense.

[6] There was a long history of enmity between Athens and Thebes (as often between neighbouring cities in Greece), especially over the previous half-century, when Thebes had grown powerful at the expense of Athens.

7 On the coast east of
Athens, towards the
Boeotian border.

before us. Next, those of military age and the cavalry should march out to
Eleusis,[7] and you should be seen by all to be under arms yourselves. This will
enable your supporters in Thebes to enjoy equal freedom to speak for the
just cause, as they will see that, just as the forces in Elateia are there to
assist those who are selling their country to Philip, so you are ready to
support those wishing to fight for freedom, and you will come to their aid if
anyone attacks them.

'Further I advise you to elect ten ambassadors, and empower them
jointly with the generals to decide the time to go there and the details of
the march itself. And how do I propose we should handle the matter when
the ambassadors reach Thebes? I want your close attention in this. Ask
nothing of the Thebans (for it is a bad time for that), but offer to help if
they so require, on the grounds that they are in the extreme danger,
whereas our perspective is better than theirs. If they accept this and follow
our advice, we shall have managed matters as we desired, and the motive
behind our action will be seen as worthy of our city. But if, after all, we
should not succeed, they will only have themselves to blame for any
mistakes they make now, and we shall have done nothing shameful or
base.'

With these and similar sentiments, I stepped down. After all had joined in
approval and nobody had said anything in opposition, I did not speak
without proposing the motion, nor propose the motion without serving as
ambassador, nor serve as ambassador without persuading the Thebans;
but I followed the process through from beginning to end, and devoted
myself entirely to meeting the dangers that beset the city …

This was the beginning and the first settlement reached in our
negotiations with Thebes. Before this, our cities had been drawn into
enmity, hatred and mistrust by these men. This decree caused the danger
that then beset the city to pass like a cloud.

Camille Desmoulins

French revolutionary leader

Camille Desmoulins (1760–94) was born in Guise. He studied law alongside MAXIMILIEN ROBESPIERRE at the Collège Louis le Grand in Paris. He wrote on classical Republicanism in his pamphlets, *La Philosophie du peuple français* (1788, 'The Philosophy of the French People') and *La France libre* (1789, 'Free France'). In July 1789 he took part in the destruction of the Bastille. His *Discours de la Lanterne aux Parisiens* (1789, 'The Streetlamp's Address to the Parisians') earned him the title of '*Procureur-général de la Lanterne*' ('Prosecutor of the Streetlamp'). In November 1789 he began the witty, sarcastic *Révolutions de France et de Brabant* ('Revolutions of France and Brabant') which appeared weekly until July 1792. In 1790, Desmoulins was a founder member of the Cordeliers' Club, established – in the Franciscan monastery from which it took its name – to scrutinize the National Assembly's approach to human and civil rights. Along with Georges Danton (1759–94) and other moderate members, he sought to end the Terror, and became alienated from the Cordelier movement. In 1793 he was elected by Paris to the National Convention, and voted for the death of the King. He supported Danton in his struggle with the Girondins, but in late 1793 he brought out *Le vieux cordelier* ('The Old Cordelier'), an eloquent expression of his and Danton's longing for clemency. Robespierre took fright at its reception, and soon became actively hostile. On 30 March 1794, Desmoulins and Danton were arrested; on 5 April they were guillotined. A fortnight later his wife Lucile Duplessis (1770–94) was also executed.

'It is a crime to be a king'

January 1793, Paris, France

French kings of the 17th and 18th centuries had, in theory, unlimited authority. In addition, both nobles and clergy enjoyed privileges that were denied to peasants and to the increasingly prosperous middle classes, who were subject to disproportionate levels of taxation. This caused the popular discontent which led to the French Revolution. The revolutionaries formed a government and, in August 1789, pronounced the Declaration of the Rights of Man and Citizen, which proclaimed liberty of conscience, property and the press, using Jean-Jacques Rousseau's slogan *'Liberté, Egalité, Fraternité'* ('Liberty, Equality, Fraternity').

The royal family were taken hostage by the revolutionaries and, following their attempted escape in June 1791, were treated as traitors. In September 1791, King Louis XVI reluctantly signed the Constitution, creating an elected assembly.

Following an insurrection in the summer of 1792, the monarchy was abolished and the royal family was moved to the Temple prison in Paris. The Assembly was replaced by the National Convention, which called for democratic elections, proclaimed France a republic and, on 5 December 1792, began the trial of Louis XVI.

In this speech to the National Convention during Louis's trial, Desmoulins, hindered by a bad stutter, dismisses concerns that the Convention was using powers normally exercised by the judiciary. He argues that since Louis had committed crimes against the French nation he should be tried by the entire nation; and since the Convention members were elected by the nation it was right that they should try him. Louis was executed on 21 January 1793.

It is by the law of nations that this trial ought to be regulated. The slavery of nations during 10,000 years has not been able to rescind their indefensible rights. It was these rights that were a standing protest against the reigning of the Charleses, the Henrys, the Fredericks, the Edwards,[1] as they were against the despotism of Julius Caesar.

It is a crime to be a king. It was even a crime to be a constitutional king, for the nation had never accepted the constitution. There is only one condition on which it could be legitimate to reign; it is when the whole people formally strips itself of its rights and cedes them to a single man ...

It is the prerogative of those who exist, and who are in possession of this Earth, to make the laws for it in their turn. Otherwise, let the dead leave their graves and come to uphold their laws against the living who have repealed them. All other kinds of royalty are imposed upon the people at the risk of their insurrection, just as robbers reign in the forests at the risk of

[1] Desmoulins refers to royal dynasties of Europe.

the provost's punishment befalling them …

Our constituents have not sent us here to follow those feudal laws and that pretended constitution, but to abolish it – or rather, to declare that it never existed, and to reinvest the nation with that sovereignty which another had usurped. Either we are truly republicans, giants who rise to the heights of these republican ideas, or we are not giants, but mere pygmies. By the law of nations, Louis XVI, as king – even a constitutional king – was a tyrant in a state of revolt against the nation, and a criminal worthy of death. And Frenchmen have no more need to try him than had Hercules to try the boar of Erymanthus,[2] or the Romans to try Caesar, who also thought himself a constitutional dictator.

But it is not only a king, it is a criminal accused of crimes that in his person we have to punish.

You must not expect me to indulge in undue exaggeration, and to call him a Nero,[3] as I heard those do who have spoken the most favourably for him. I know that Louis XVI had the inclinations of a tiger, and if we established courts like that of the Areopagus[4] at Athens – which condemned a child to death for putting out his bird's eyes – if we had an Areopagus, it would have a hundred times condemned this man as dishonouring the human race by the caprices of his wanton cruelties.

But as it is not the deeds of his private life but the crimes of his reign that we are judging, it must be confessed that this long list of accusations against Louis, which our committee and our orators have presented to us, while rendering him a thousand times worthy of death, will nevertheless not suggest to posterity the horrors of the reign of Nero but the crimes of constituents, the crimes of Louis the king rather than the crimes of Louis Capet.[5]

That which makes the former king justly odious to the people is the four years of perjuries and oaths, incessantly repeated into the nation's ear before the face of Heaven, while all the time he was conspiring against the nation. Treason was always with every nation the most abominable of crimes. It has always inspired that horror which is inspired by poison and vipers, because it is impossible to guard against it …

The crimes of Louis XVI are the crimes of the constituents who supported him in his position of king rather than his crimes – that is to say, of those who gave him the right by letters patent to be the 'enemy of the nation' and a traitor. But all these considerations, calculated as they may be to soften the horror of his crimes in the eyes of posterity, are useless before the law, in mitigating their punishment.

What? Shall the judges forbear to punish a brigand because in his cave he has been brought up to believe that all the possessions of those who pass his cave belong to him? Because his education has so depraved his natural disposition that he could not be anything but a robber? Shall it be alleged as a reason for letting the treason of a king go unpunished, that he could not be anything but a traitor, and as a reason for not giving the nations the example of cutting down this tree, that it can only bear poisons?

By the declaration of rights, by that code eternal … the articles of which, effaced by the rust of centuries, the French people adopted with joy and – by the enactment (consecrated as the basis of its constitution) that the law is the same toward all, either for punishment or for protection – re-established in all their purity, Louis XVI was divested of his chimerical inviolability.

[2] In Greek mythology, Heracles (Hercules) atoned for killing his own children by carrying out twelve daunting labours. The fourth was to capture a huge wild boar at Mount Erymanthus in Arcadia, which he achieved by trapping the beast in a snowdrift.

[3] The despotic Roman Emperor Nero (AD 37–68).
[4] In ancient Athens, the Areopagus was a council drawn from the richest class who met on the hill of the same name.

[5] Louis XVI was a member of the Bourbon dynasty, which claimed descent from Hugh Capet (938–996), founder of the Capetian dynasty after being elected King in 987. French revolutionaries, refusing to recognize his title, referred to him as Louis Capet.

He can henceforth be regarded only as a conspirator. Followed by the people, he … came to seek an asylum among us, at the foot of the throne of national sovereignty, in the house which was found full of evidences of his plottings and of his crimes. We placed him under arrest and imprisoned him in the Temple, and now it only remains for us to pass sentence upon him.

But who shall judge this conspirator? It is astonishing and inconceivable what trouble this question has given to the best heads of the Convention. Removed as we are from nature and the primitive laws of all society, most of us have not thought that we could judge a conspirator without a jury of accusation, a jury of judgement, and judges who would apply the law …

Who shall judge Louis XVI? The whole people, if it can … But as we cannot hear the pleas of 25 millions of men, we must recur to the maxim of Montesquieu:[6] 'Let a free people do all that it can by itself and the rest by representatives and commissioners!' And what is the National Convention but the commission selected by the French people to try the last king and to form the constitution of the new republic?

Some claim that such a course would be to unite all the powers – legislative functions and judicial functions. Those who have most wearied our ears by reciting the dangers of this cumulation of powers must either deride our simplicity in believing that they respect those limits – or else they do not well understand themselves. For have not constitutional and legislative assemblies assumed a hundred times the functions of judges … ?

To acquit **MIRABEAU**[7] and 'P Equality';[8] or to send Lessart[9] to Orléans – was not that to assume the functions of judges? I conclude from this that those 'Balancers', as Mirabeau called them – who continually talk of 'equilibrium' and the balance of power – do not themselves believe in what they say. Can it be contested, for example, that the nation which exercises the power of sovereignty does not 'cumulate' all the powers? Can it be claimed that the nation cannot delegate, at its will, this or that portion of its powers to whom it pleases?

Can anyone deny that the nation has cumulatively clothed us here with its powers, both to try Louis XVI and to construct the constitution? One may well speak of the balance of power and the necessity of maintaining it when the people, as in England, exercises its sovereignty only at the time of elections. But when the nation, the sovereign, is in permanent activity – as formerly at Athens and Rome, and as now in France … the great necessity cannot be seen of maintaining the equilibrium of powers; since it is the people who, with its arm of iron, itself holds the scales ready to drive out the ambitious and the traitorous, who wish to make it incline to the side opposite the general interest.

It is evident that the people sent us here to judge the king and to give them a constitution. Is the first of these two functions so difficult to fulfil? And have we anything else to do than what Brutus[10] did when the people caused him to judge his two sons himself, and tested him by this, just as the convention is tested now? He made them come to his tribunal, as you must bring Louis XVI before you. It produced for him the proofs of their conspiracy, as you must present to Louis XVI that multitude of overwhelming proofs of his plots.

And it only remains for you to prove, as Brutus proved to the Roman people, that you are worthy to begin the republic and its constitution, and

[6] The French philosopher Charles-Louis de Secondat, Baron de La Brède et de Montesquieu (1689–1755) propounded the theory of separation of powers, advocating the elimination of feudalism and the exclusion of clergy from political power. His theories are enshrined in many modern constitutions.

[9] The French politician Claude Antoine Valdec de Lessart (1741–92) became Foreign Minister in 1791. In 1792 he was imprisoned at Orléans, and later executed.

[7] Mirabeau was a moderate who had argued for retaining a constitutional monarchy and had undertaken secret negotiations with the King.

[8] Louis Philippe Joseph, Duke of Orléans *known as Philippe Égalité* (1747–93) was a member of the royal family who supported the Revolution but was nonetheless guillotined in November 1793.

[10] The Roman hero Lucius Junius Brutus (fl. 500 BC), who drove the royal family from Rome and established republican government. He sentenced his own two sons to death for conspiring to restore the monarchy.

[11] A Roman magistrate's attendant, or lictor, could be called on to punish a wrongdoer by tying him to a stake and beheading him.

to appease the shades of 100,000 citizens whom he caused to perish, in pronouncing the same sentence: 'Go, lictor, bind him to the stake.' [11]

Éamon de Valera
Irish rebel leader and statesman

Éamon de Valera (1882–1975) was born in Brooklyn, New York City, of Spanish–Irish parentage. He was raised in Bruree, County Limerick by a labourer uncle, and became a mathematics teacher. Taking up Irish, he joined the Gaelic League and married his teacher Sinéad Ni Flannagáin (who subsequently became the author of a charming series of Gaelic fairy stories). Under the influence of Thomas MacDonagh he rose in the Irish Volunteers, leading his men into action in the Easter Rising of 1916. The sentence of execution imposed on him after court-martial was commuted through the intervention of the US Consul. After his release from jail (1917) he was elected MP for East Clare, and became the focus of nationalist opposition to conscription (1918). He was again arrested, an event which helped his Sinn Féin Party to massive electoral victory (1918). After a sensational escape, he toured the USA in 1919–20 as president of the Irish Republic (actually of Dáil Éireann, the secret assembly of Irish MPs refusing to participate at Westminster). He drew in massive funds and moral support. Guerrilla warfare had exploded in Ireland without him and on his return he was believed a more moderate influence than Michael Collins, but ultimately Collins signed the Anglo-Irish Treaty of 1921 and incurred de Valera's anger. Narrow victory for the treaty in the Dáil led de Valera to resign as president. He played only a symbolic part in the anti-treaty forces during the Irish Civil War (1922–3), but was ultimately imprisoned (1923–4). In 1926 he formed a Republican opposition party which entered the Irish Free State Dáil (1927), and which brought him to power there in 1932. He severed most of the remaining constitutional links with Britain, and introduced a new constitution (1937) under which his title was altered to *Taoiseach* (a post to which he was re-elected until 1948, and then again in 1951 and 1957). In international affairs he pursued neutrality, partly in response to anti-democratic threats from right and left. In 1959, he resigned his position as Taoiseach and was elected president, being re-elected in 1966 and remaining as head of state until he retired in 1973.

'The Irish genius'
6 February 1933, radio broadcast from Athlone, Ireland

Éamon de Valera had every reason to appreciate the importance of international links for the newly established Irish Free State. His own US citizenship had preserved him from execution alongside the other leaders of the Easter Rising of 1916. His new Fianna Fáil government had survived as a minority administration for most of 1932, and having increased his majority with an election a few weeks before this broadcast, de Valera was ready to dismantle the last vestiges of British influence that had formed part of the 1922 treaty, but hoped to avoid confrontation with the British government.

In doing so, he was keen to ensure support from other governments. He saw that the new high-powered broadcasting system, based in Athlone, County Westmeath, would be of some assistance, promoting Irish interests in places as far away as the USA and Australia – where substantial expatriate Irish populations existed – and supporting the new state. Meanwhile, it was de Valera's chance to play the statesman, distancing himself from his active part in the Civil War.

He spoke to a homeland with threats from within, too. Perhaps the most potent of these was a new fascist movement, led by the former police chief Eoin O'Duffy, whose conflict with the Irish Republican Army subsequently caused instability and the spilling of blood. This was de Valera's moment to rise above the fray.

[1] De Valera's emphasis on Christianity perhaps grew out of his need to reassure the Roman Catholic Church, which had excommunicated him as a result of his actions in the Civil War and remained suspicious of his government. He was a devout Catholic.

The Athlone Broadcasting Station which we are now opening is Ireland's first high-power station. It will enable the world to hear the voice of one of the oldest and, in many respects, one of the greatest of the nations.

Ireland has much to seek from the rest of the world, and much to give back in return, much that she alone can give. Her gifts are the fruit of special qualities of mind and heart, developed by centuries of eventful history. Alone among the countries of western Europe, she never came under the sway of Imperial Rome. When all her neighbours were in tutelage, she was independent, building up her own civilization undisturbed. When Christianity was brought to her shores it was received with a joy and eagerness, and held with a tenacity of which there is hardly such another example.[1]

Because she was independent of the Empire, Ireland escaped the anarchy that followed its fall. Because she was Christian, she was able to take the lead in Christianizing and civilizing the barbarian hordes that had overrun Britain and the west of Europe. This lead she retained until the task was accomplished and Europe had entered into the glory of the Middle Ages. The memories of Irish saints of that time … are still venerated in the lands where they toiled … During most of this early missionary period, Ireland was harassed by Norse invaders … That Ireland in such circumstances continued the work of the apostolate in Europe is an eloquent proof of the zeal of her people, a zeal gloriously manifested once more in modern times in North America and Australia and in the mission fields of Africa and China.

Since the period of her missionary greatness, Ireland has suffered a persecution to which for cruelty, ingenuity and persistence there is no parallel. It did not break — it strengthened — the spirit and devotion of her people and prepared them for the renewal of their mission at a time when it is of no less vital importance to the world than was the mission of the Irish saints of the seventh and eighth centuries to the world of their day.

Next to her services to religion, Ireland's greatest contribution to the welfare of humanity has been the example of devotion to freedom, which she has given throughout 700 years. The invaders who came to Ireland in the twelfth century belonged to a race that had already subjugated England and a great part of western Europe. Like the Norsemen before them, it was in Ireland that they met the most serious resistance — a resistance which was continued generation after generation against the successors of the first invaders until our own time, a resistance which will inevitably continue until the last sod of Irish soil is finally freed.

During the first five centuries of struggle, everything was taken from the Irish people, until in the 17th century an Irish Catholic in the eyes of the law possessed no rights of property, no rights of citizenship, no rights of education, no right to life in the land of his fathers. Little by little, almost all that was taken away has been won back, and today the greater part of the country is once more in the ownership and subject to the rule of the Irish people. Ireland has taught the world that a brave and resolute nation can never be conquered.

The Irish language is one of the oldest, and, from the point of view of the philologist, one of the most interesting in Europe. It is a member of the Indo-European family, principal of the Celtic group … Irish is closely related to Greek and Sanskrit, and still more closely to Latin.

The tradition of Irish learning — the creation of the monastic and bardic schools — was not wholly lost even during the darkest period of the English occupation. So far as the law could do it, education was made impossible for the Catholic population at home, but Irish scholarship was kept alive in the colleges for Irish ecclesiastics in Louvain, Rome, Salamanca, Paris and elsewhere on the Continent. In Ireland itself, the schools of poetry survived in some places until the beginning of the 18th century, maintaining to the end their rigorous discipline. The 'hedge schools', taught by wandering scholars, frustrated in a measure the design to reduce the people to illiteracy, and kept the flame of knowledge alight, however feebly, throughout the island.

In the 18th century — the most terrible period that Ireland has known, when the people were ground down by the Penal Laws[2] — there was a remarkable revival of Irish poetry. Some of the finest poems in the language

[2] The collective name given to statutes enacted in Britain and Ireland, 1695–1728, against the practice of Roman Catholicism. Participation in services attracted various punishments, including execution for officiating priests. The Penal Laws also prevented Catholics from voting or holding public office.

were written during those years by men who spent their lives in poverty, dependent on the hospitality of an impoverished and outcast peasantry. But they were welcome everywhere, and their songs, whether they were inspired by anger at the oppression of their country, by some false hope of foreign aid, by love, by the incidents of their daily lives or by the irrepressible gaiety of their race, were a source of consolation and joy to the people.

Anglo-Irish literature, though far less characteristic of the nation than that produced in the Irish language, includes much that is of lasting worth. Ireland has produced in Dean SWIFT, perhaps the greatest satirist in the English language; in EDMUND BURKE, probably the greatest writer on politics; in William Carleton,[3] a novelist of the first rank; in Oliver Goldsmith,[4] a poet of rare merit. HENRY GRATTAN was one of the most eloquent orators of his time – the golden age of oratory in the English language. Theobald Wolfe Tone[5] has left us one of the most delightful autobiographies in literature. Several recent or still-living Irish novelists and poets have produced work which is likely to stand the test of time. The Irish theatre movement has given us the finest school of acting of the present day, and some plays of high quality.

Ireland's music is of a singular beauty. Based on pentatonic scale, its melodies reach back to a period anterior to the dawn of musical history. It stands pre-eminent amongst the music of the Celtic nations. It is characterized by perfection of form and variety of melodic content. It is particularly rich in tunes that imply exquisite sensitiveness. The strange fitfulness of the lamentations and love songs, the transition from gladness to pathos, have thrilled the experts, and made them proclaim our music the most varied and the most poetical in the world. Equal in rhythmic variety are our dance tunes – spirited and energetic, in keeping with the temperament of our people.

I have spoken at some length of Ireland's history and her contributions to European culture, because I wish to emphasize that what Ireland has done in the past she can do in the future. The Irish genius has always stressed spiritual and intellectual rather than material values. That is the characteristic that fits the Irish people in a special manner for the task, now a vital one, of helping to save western civilization.

The great material progress of recent times, coming in a world where false philosophies already reigned, has distorted men's sense of proportion; the material has usurped the sovereignty that is the right of the spiritual. Everywhere today the consequences of this perversion of the natural order are to be seen. Spirit and mind have ceased to rule. The riches which the world sought, and to which it sacrificed all else, have become a curse by their very abundance. In this day, if Ireland is faithful to her mission – and, please God, she will be – if as of old she recalls men to forgotten truths, if she places before them the ideals of justice, of order, of freedom rightly used, of Christian brotherhood – then, indeed, she can do the world a service as great as that which she rendered in the time of Columcille[6] and Columbanus,[7] because the need of our time is in no wise less.

You sometimes hear Ireland charged with a narrow and intolerant nationalism, but Ireland today has no dearer hope than this: that, true to her own holiest traditions, she may humbly serve the truth and help by truth to save the world. It is in that hope that – calling modern science to the aid of Ireland's age-long mission – we initiate the Athlone Broadcasting Station. *Go gcuire Dia rath ar an obair!*[8]

[3] The Irish novelist William Carleton (1794–1869) is best known for *The Black Prophet* (1847), *The Tithe Proctor* (1849) and *The Squanders of Castle Squander* (1852).

[5] The Irish nationalist leader and pamphleteer Theobald Wolfe Tone (1763–98).

[4] The Irish poet, dramatist, novelist and historian Oliver Goldsmith (1728–74) is best known for the novel *The Vicar of Wakefield* (1766), the poem *The Deserted Village* (1770) and the play *She Stoops to Conquer* (1773).

[6] The Irish missionary Colmcille *also known as St Columba* (521–97) is credited with bringing Christianity to Scotland from 563.

[7] The Irish missionary St Columbanus (543–615) established monasteries in Gaul and the Appenines.

[8] Irish Gaelic: 'May God prosper the work'.

Donald Dewar
Scottish politician

Donald Campbell Dewar (1937–2000) was born in Glasgow and educated at Glasgow University. He qualified as a solicitor, but then moved into politics. He won Aberdeen South for the Labour Party in 1966, but lost his seat in 1970, and spent eight years out of Parliament before winning the Glasgow Garscadden by-election of 1978. He retained the seat with ease in the general elections of 1979, 1983, 1987, 1992 and 1997. Chief opposition spokesman on Scottish affairs from 1983, he moved to social security (1992–5) and was opposition chief whip (1995–7). Following Labour's landslide victory in 1997, he entered TONY BLAIR's Cabinet as Secretary of State for Scotland (1997–9). He was a key figure in establishing the Scottish Parliament and in 1999 became the first person to serve as its First Minister. He was instrumental in the controversial decision to site a new Parliament building at Holyrood, Edinburgh, but did not live to see its completion.

'Wisdom. Justice. Compassion. Integrity'
1 July 1999, Edinburgh, Scotland

Among the first to recognize the threat of Scottish nationalism to the United Kingdom, Donald Dewar made the creation of a devolved Scottish Parliament within the UK his political mission. His speech at its opening session on 12 May 1999 (in a temporary home at The Mound in Edinburgh) was not an acknowledgement of a mission accomplished so much as a recognition that with the securing of a devolution settlement the real struggle to satisfy the demands of the Scottish people had only just begun.

Against a hostile party leadership, Dewar had begun arguing in the 1970s that devolution would satiate the Scottish public's desire for greater autonomy and prevent the break-up of the UK. When Labour regained power at the general election in 1997, Dewar made plain this belief with his acerbic advocate's wit – introducing a devolution White Paper at Westminster with the observation that it would make the task of the Scottish National Party 'a bit more difficult'.

He was elected First Minister in May 1999. This speech at the Parliament's official opening, attended by Queen ELIZABETH II, reveals that behind his frosty attitude towards 'separatism', Dewar maintained a warm sense of patriotic pride in the Scottish symbols that nourished his political vocation. He praises equally the high-flying philosophers and poets of the Scottish Enlightenment and the panel-beating revolutionary socialists of the Clyde shipyards. By the standards of his legendarily ascetic public persona, the speech is positively florid, expressing a nobility of purpose that earned him the soubriquet 'father of the nation'.

Your Majesty: on behalf of the people of Scotland, I thank you for the gift of this mace. It is a symbol of the great democratic traditions from which we draw our inspiration and our strength. At its head are inscribed the opening words of our founding statute:

'There shall be a Scottish Parliament.'

Through long years, those words were first a hope, then a belief, then a promise. Now, they are a reality. This is a moment anchored in our history. Today, we reach back through the long haul to win this parliament, through the struggles of those who brought democracy to Scotland, to that other parliament dissolved in controversy nearly three centuries ago.

Today, we look forward to the time when this moment will be seen as a turning point: the day when democracy was renewed in Scotland, when we revitalized our place in this our United Kingdom.

This is about more than our politics and our laws. This is about who we are, how we carry ourselves. There is a new voice in the land, the voice of a democratic parliament. A voice to shape Scotland as surely as the echoes from our past: the shout of the welder in the din of the great Clyde shipyards;[1] the speak of the Mearns,[2] with its soul in the land; the discourse of the Enlightenment,[3] when Edinburgh and Glasgow were a light held to the intellectual life of Europe; the wild cry of the Great Pipes;[4] and back to

[1] The River Clyde, which links Glasgow to the west coast of Scotland, was a thriving centre for shipbuilding until the decline of heavy industry in the latter half of the 20th century.
[2] A rural area in northeast Scotland, known for its fertile farmland.
[3] An intellectual movement embracing rational approaches to philosophy, economics and political thought. Some of its most influential figures were Scots, including David Hume (1711–76), Adam Smith (1723–90) and James Boswell (1740–95).
[4] A respectful name for the ancient bagpipes of Scotland.

[5] The Scottish nobleman Robert the Bruce (1274–1329) reigned as King Robert I of Scotland, 1306–29. He was among the leaders of the First War of Independence against England (1296–1328) and is considered a national hero.

[7] The Scottish poet Robert Burns (1759–96) is widely considered the greatest Scotland has produced, and is also celebrated for his egalitarianism.

[9] To inaugurate.

the distant cries of the battles of Bruce[5] and WALLACE.

Walter Scott[6] wrote that only a man with soul so dead could have no sense, no feel of his native land. For me, for any Scot, today is a proud moment: a new stage on a journey begun long ago and which has no end. This is a proud day for all of us.

A Scottish Parliament. Not an end: a means to greater ends. And those too are part of our mace. Woven into its symbolic thistles are these four words:

'Wisdom. Justice. Compassion. Integrity.'

Burns[7] would have understood that. We have just heard – beautifully sung – one of his most enduring works.[8] At the heart of that song is a very Scottish conviction: that honesty and simple dignity are priceless virtues, not imparted by rank or birth or privilege, but part of the soul. Burns believed that sense and worth ultimately prevail. He believed that was the core of politics; that without it, ours would be an impoverished profession.

'Wisdom. Justice. Compassion. Integrity.' Timeless values. Honourable aspirations for this new forum of democracy, born on the cusp of a new century.

We are fallible. We will make mistakes. But we will never lose sight of what brought us here: the striving to do right by the people of Scotland; to respect their priorities; to better their lot; and to contribute to the commonweal.

I look forward to the days ahead when this chamber will sound with debate, argument and passion. When men and women from all over Scotland will meet to work together for a future built from the first principles of social justice. But today, we pause and reflect. It is a rare privilege in an old nation to open a new parliament. Today is a celebration of the principles, the traditions, the democratic imperatives which have brought us to this point and will sustain us into the future.

Your Majesty, we are all proud that you are here to handsel[9] this Parliament and with us as we dedicate ourselves to the work ahead.

Your Majesty, our thanks.

[6] The Scottish poet and author Sir Walter Scott (1771–1832), whose novels – many with historical settings – and poetry were extremely popular during his lifetime and for over a century after his death.

[8] The Scottish folk singer Sheena Wellington (1944–) had just performed Burns's famous song 'A Man's a Man for A' That'.

Charles Dickens
English novelist and journalist

Charles John Huffam Dickens (1812–70) was born in Landport, near Portsmouth, the son of John Dickens, a navy pay clerk. In 1817 the family moved to Chatham where Charles received some schooling. In 1821, John Dickens was made redundant and moved the family to London, where he was arrested for debt in 1824 and jailed with his entire family – apart from Charles, who was sent to work in a shoe-blacking factory. On his father's release, Charles returned to school, then worked as an office boy. He decided to pursue journalism, taught himself shorthand, and visited the British Museum to supplement his reading. In 1828 he became a parliamentary reporter for the *Morning Chronicle*; and in 1835 he joined the staff of a London paper. Meanwhile in December 1833, the *Monthly Magazine* published his first sketch, 'Dinner at Poplar Walk', under the pen-name 'Boz'. The *Sketches by Boz* were collected and published early in 1836. In March 1836 the first number of his serialized novel *Pickwick Papers* appeared; the same month Dickens married the daughter of his editor. She bore him ten children, but they separated in 1858. Once established, Dickens allowed himself little respite. Working to publishers' deadlines, he produced *Oliver Twist* (1837–9); *Nicholas Nickleby* (1838–9); *The Old Curiosity Shop* (1840–1) and *Barnaby Rudge* (1841). He travelled widely, visiting the USA (1842 and 1867–8), Genoa (1844–5), Lausanne (1846) and Boulogne (1853, 1854 and 1856). His reception in the USA was somewhat chilled by his criticism of American publishers for pirating English books, and by the unfavourable picture of the country given in *Martin Chuzzlewit*. Dickens died suddenly at Gadshill, near Rochester (the property he had coveted as a boy, and purchased in 1856), and was buried in Westminster Abbey. He is the most widely known British writer after Shakespeare, and no other novelist has managed to find both popular success and critical respect on such a lavish scale. His novels offer a vivid portrayal of life in Victorian England, much of it derived from his own experience. His enduring popularity has been ensured by the breadth and perceptiveness of his writing, his abiding concern with social deprivation and injustice, his gift for memorable characterization, and the comic genius that permeates even his most serious work.

'The two grim nurses, Poverty and Sickness'
9 February 1858, London, England

In the mid-19th century, more than 40 per cent of people dying annually in London were children under ten years old. The Great Ormond Street Hospital opened in 1852, the first children's hospital in Britain, but struggled to enlist support from the moneyed classes. By 1858, it still had only 31 beds.

Dickens, much in demand as a public speaker, resolved to tackle the problem at a fundraising dinner at the nearby Freemasons' Hall. Despite sparse attendance, the event immediately prompted subscriptions amounting to more than £3,000, from which an endowment fund and a building fund were established.

The speech was one of the most brilliant of Dickens's career; a masterpiece of audience manipulation. He begins by engaging his listeners with a string of humorous observations about 'spoilt' children in privileged households, then switches tempo to address the fate of children 'spoilt' by hunger and disease. His central motif is a vividly drawn image of a hopelessly ill child he encountered in the slums of Edinburgh: 'a little decrepit old man, pining to death'. Having conveyed his own lasting horror – 'I can see him now, as I have seen him for several years' – he brightens the mood to paint an idealized picture of the hospital, before concluding with an elegantly worded appeal for contributions. In his report on the event, the journalist T A Reed remarked, 'His speech was magnificent, thoroughly characteristic and extremely telling.'

Great Ormond Street Hospital continues to thrive, treating more than 90,000 patients a year, often children suffering from rare, complex or life-threatening conditions. Its associated charity aims to raise over £20 million a year to supplement its National Health Service funding.

> Ladies and gentlemen: it is one of my rules in life not to believe a man who may happen to tell me that he feels no interest in children … I know, as we all must, that any heart which could really toughen its affections and sympathies against those dear little people must be wanting in so many humanizing experiences of innocence and tenderness, as to be quite an unsafe monstrosity among men.
> [*'Hear, hear.'*]

Therefore I set the assertion down, whenever I happen to meet with it – which is sometimes, though not often – as an idle word, originating possibly in the genteel languor of the hour, and meaning about as much as that knowing social lassitude, which has used up the cardinal virtues and quite found out things in general, usually does mean.

[*Cheers.*]

I suppose it may be taken for granted that we, who come together in the name of children, and for the sake of children, acknowledge that we have an interest in them; indeed, I have observed since we sat down here that we are quite in a childlike state altogether, representing an infant institution, and not even yet a grown-up company.

[*Laughter.*]

A few years are necessary to the increase of our strength and the expansion of our figure; and then these tables, which now have a few tucks in them, will be let out, and then this hall, which now sits so easily upon us, will be too tight and small for us.

[*Cheers and laughter.*]

Nevertheless, it is likely that even we are not without our experience, now and then, of spoilt children. I do not mean of our own spoilt children, because nobody's own children ever were spoilt [*laughter*], but I mean the disagreeable children of our particular friends.

[*Laughter.*]

We know by experience what it is to have them down after dinner, and across the rich perspective of a miscellaneous dessert, to see, as in a black dose darkly, the family doctor looming in the distance.

[*Continued laughter.*]

We know – I have no doubt we all know – what it is to assist at those little maternal anecdotes and table entertainments illustrated with imitations and descriptive dialogue which might not be inaptly called, after the manner of my friend Mr Albert Smith,[1] the toilsome ascent of Miss Mary and the eruption (cutaneous) of Master Alexander.

[*Great laughter.*]

We know what it is when those children won't go to bed; we know how they prop their eyelids open with their forefingers when they will sit up; how, when they become fractious, they say aloud that they don't like us, and our nose is too long, and why don't we go? And we are perfectly acquainted with those kicking bundles which are carried off at last protesting.

[*Cheers and laughter.*]

An eminent eye-witness told me that he was one of a company of learned pundits who assembled at the house of a very distinguished philosopher of the last generation, to hear him expound his stringent views concerning infant education and early mental development, and he told me that, while the philosopher did this in very beautiful and lucid language, the philosopher's little boy, for his part, edified the assembled sages by dabbling up to the elbows in an apple pie which had been provided for their entertainment, having previously anointed his hair with syrup, combed it with his fork, and brushed it with his spoon.

[*Renewed laughter.*]

It is probable that we also have our similar experiences, sometimes, of principles that are not quite practice, and we know people claiming to be very wise and profound about nations of men who show themselves to be rather weak and shallow about units of babies.

[1] The author, entertainer and adventurer Albert Richard Smith (1816–60) was a friend of Dickens and the author of the book *Ascent of Mont Blanc*.

But, ladies and gentlemen, the spoilt children whom I have to present to you after this dinner of today are not of this class. I have glanced at these for the easier and lighter introduction of another, a very different, a far more numerous, and a far more serious class. The spoilt children whom I must show you are spoilt children of the poor in this great city – the children who are, every year, for ever and ever, irrevocably spoilt out of this breathing life of ours by tens of thousands; but who may in vast numbers be preserved, if you, assisting and not contravening the ways of Providence, will help to save them.

[*Cheers.*]

The two grim nurses, Poverty and Sickness, who bring these children before you, preside over their births, rock their wretched cradles, nail down their little coffins, pile up the earth above their graves. Of the annual deaths in this great town, their unnatural deaths form more than one-third.

[*'Hear, hear.'*]

I shall not ask you, according to the custom as to the other class – I shall not ask you on behalf of these children, to observe how good they are, how pretty they are, how clever they are, how promising they are, whose beauty they most resemble – I shall only ask you to observe how weak they are and how like death they are! And I shall ask you … to turn your thoughts to *these* spoilt children, in the sacred names of Pity and Compassion.

[*'Hear, hear.'*]

Some years ago, being in Scotland, I went with one of the most humane members of the humane medical profession, on a morning tour among some of the worst-lodged inhabitants of the Old Town of Edinburgh. In the closes and wynds of that picturesque place – I am sorry to remind you what fast friends picturesqueness and typhus often are – we saw more poverty and sickness in an hour than many people would believe in a life. Our way lay from one to another of the most wretched dwellings – reeking with horrible odours; shut out from the sky; shut out from the air; mere pits and dens.

In a room in one of these places, where there was an empty porridge-pot on the cold hearth, with a ragged woman and some ragged children crouching on the bare ground near it – where, I remember as I speak, that very light, reflected from a high, damp-stained and time-stained house wall, came trembling in, as if the fever which had shaken everything else there had shaken even it – there lay, in an old egg-box which the mother had begged from a shop, a little feeble, wasted, wan, sick child. With his little wasted face, and his little hot worn hands folded over his breast, and his little bright attentive eyes, I can see him now, as I have seen him for several years, looking steadily at us.

There he lay in his little frail box, which was not at all a bad emblem of the little body from which he was slowly parting – there he lay, quite quiet, quite patient, saying never a word. He seldom cried, the mother said; he seldom complained; 'he lay there, seeming to wonder what it was a'aboot'. God knows, I thought, as I stood looking at him, he had his reasons for wondering – reasons for wondering how it could possibly come to be that he lay there, left alone, feeble and full of pain, when he ought to have been as bright and as brisk as the birds that never got near him – reasons for wondering how he came to be left there, a little decrepit old man, pining to death, quite a thing of course, as if there were no crowds of healthy and happy children playing on the grass under the summer's sun within a stone's throw of him, as if there were no bright moving sea on the other side of the great hill overhanging the city; as if there were no great clouds rushing over it; as if there were no life, and movement, and vigour anywhere in the world – nothing but stoppage and decay.

There he lay, looking at us, saying in his silence, more pathetically than I have ever heard anything said by any orator in my life, 'Will you please to tell us what this means, strange man? And if you can give me any good reason why I should be so soon, so far advanced on my way to him who said that children were to come into his presence, and were not to be forbidden,[2] but who scarcely meant, that they should come by this hard road by which I am travelling – pray give that reason to me, for I seek it very earnestly and wonder about it very much.' And to my mind he has been wondering about it ever since.

Many a poor child, sick and neglected, I have seen since that time in this London; many a poor sick child have I seen most affectionately and kindly tended by poor people, in an unwholesome house and under untoward circumstances, wherein its recovery was quite impossible. But at all such times I have seen my poor little drooping friend in his egg-box, and he has always addressed his dumb speech to me, and I have always found him wondering what it meant, and why, in the name of a gracious God, such things should be!

Now, ladies and gentlemen: such things need not be, and will not be, if this company, which is a drop of the life-blood of the great compassionate public heart, will only accept the means of rescue and prevention which is mine to offer. Within a quarter of a mile of this place where I speak stands a courtly old house … In the airy wards, into which the old state drawing-rooms and family bed-chambers of that house are now converted, are such little patients that the attendant nurses look like reclaimed giantesses, and the kind medical practitioner like an amiable Christian ogre.

Grouped about the little low tables in the centre of the rooms are such tiny convalescents that they seem to be playing at having been ill. On the dolls' beds are such diminutive creatures that each poor sufferer is supplied with its tray of toys; and, looking around, you may see how the little tired, flushed cheek has toppled over half the brute creation on its way into the ark;[3] or how one little dimpled arm has mowed down (as I saw myself) the whole tin soldiery of Europe. On the walls of these rooms are graceful, pleasant, bright, childish pictures. At the beds' heads are pictures of the figure which is the universal embodiment of all mercy and compassion, the figure of him who was once a child himself, and a poor one.[4]

Besides these little creatures on the beds, you may learn in that place that the number of small out-patients brought to that house for relief is no fewer than 10,000 in the compass of a single year … In the printed papers of this same hospital, you may read with what a generous earnestness the highest and wisest members of the medical profession testify to the great need of it; to the immense difficulty of treating children in the same hospitals with grown-up people, by reason of their different ailments and requirements; to the vast amount of pain that will be assuaged, and of the life that will be saved, through this hospital – not only among the poor, observe, but among the prosperous too, by reason of the increased knowledge of children's illnesses, which cannot fail to arise from a more systematic mode of studying them.

Lastly, gentlemen, and I am sorry to say, worst of all (for I must present no rose-coloured picture of this place to you – I must not deceive you);

[2] Dickens refers to the injunction of JESUS, 'Suffer the little children to come unto me, and forbid them not: for of such is the kingdom of God.' Mark 10:14. See also Matthew 19:14; Luke 18:16.

[3] Dickens refers to the animals of a toy Noah's Ark.

[4] Dickens refers to the lowly birth of Jesus.

lastly – the visitor to this children's hospital, reckoning up the number of its beds, will find himself perforce obliged to stop at very little over 30; and will learn, with sorrow and surprise, that even that small number, so forlornly, so miserably diminutive, compared with this vast London, cannot possibly be maintained unless the hospital be made better known. I limit myself to saying better known, because I will not believe that in a Christian community of fathers and mothers, and brothers and sisters, it can fail, being better known, to be well and richly endowed.

[*Cheers.*]

Now, ladies and gentlemen: this, without a word of adornment – which I resolved, when I got up, not to allow myself – this is the simple case. This is the pathetic case which I have to put to you; not only on behalf of the thousands who annually die in this great city, but also on behalf of the thousands of children who live half-developed, racked with preventable pain, shorn of their natural capacity for health and enjoyment. If these innocent creatures cannot move you for themselves, how can I possibly hope to move you in their name?

'The acute sagacity of newspaper editors'
20 May 1865, London, England

'Thou ever-bubbling spring of endless lies,' wrote Thomas Cowper in 1782 of that 'god of idolatry', the press. 'You cannot hope/to bribe or twist/thank God! the/British journalist./But, seeing what/the man will do/unbribed, there's/no occasion to,' added Humbert Wolfe in 1930. Few modern commentators would disagree.

But Dickens, himself a distinguished journalist, took a very different view. He expressed it vividly when he chaired the second anniversary dinner of the Newspaper Press Fund, of which he was then vice president. The organization, which still exists, had been formed by members of the press to provide assistance for fellow journalists and their families in cases of hardship.

Mindful, as ever, of his audience, Dickens portrays the profession as upstanding, incorruptible 'artists' making a noble contribution to society; and reserves special praise for editors. He also explores the question, then the subject of public debate, of whether reporters should be allowed to abridge the words of politicians rather than publishing them in full.

But the speech's most intriguing passage comes towards the end, where Dickens recalls, with characteristic vividness, his own exploits as a parliamentary reporter, a fascinating glimpse of the author as an ambitious young cub.

Ladies and gentlemen: when a young child is produced after dinner to be shown to a circle of admiring relations and friends, it may generally be observed that their conversation – I suppose in an instinctive remembrance of the uncertainty of infant life – takes a retrospective turn. As how much the child has grown since the last dinner; what a remarkably fine child it is, to have been born only two or three years ago, how much stronger it looks now than before it had the measles, and so forth.

When a young institution is produced after dinner, there is not the same uncertainty or delicacy as in the case of the child, and it may be confidently predicted of it that if it deserve to live it will surely live, and that if it deserve to die it will surely die.[1] The proof of desert in such a case as this must be mainly sought, I suppose, firstly, in what the society means to do with its money; secondly, in the extent to which it is supported by the class with whom it originated, and for whose benefit it is designed; and lastly, in the power of its hold upon the public.

[*'Hear, hear.'*]

I add this, lastly, because no such institution that I ever heard of ever yet dreamed of existing apart from the public, or ever yet considered it a

[1] The Newspaper Press Fund had not, in fact, survived its original birth in 1858, though it had been revived in 1864.

degradation to accept the public support.

[*'Hear, hear' and cheers.*]

Now, what the Newspaper Press Fund proposes to do with its money is to grant relief to members in want or distress, and to the widows, families, parents, or other near relatives of deceased members, in right of a certain moderate annual subscription ... and its members comprise the whole paid class of literary contributors to the press of the United Kingdom ...

The number of its members at this time last year was something below 100. At the present time it is somewhat above 170 ... This number is steadily on the increase, not only as regards the metropolitan press, but also as regards the provincial throughout the country ... It only remains to add, on this head of desert, the agreeable circumstance that out of all the money collected in aid of the society during the last year more than one third came exclusively from the Press.

[*'Hear, hear' and cheers.*]

Now, ladies and gentlemen, in regard to the last claim – the last point of desert, the hold upon the public – I think I may say that probably not one single individual in this great company has failed today to see a newspaper, or has failed today to hear something derived from a newspaper which was quite unknown to him or her yesterday.

[*'Hear, hear.'*]

Of all those restless crowds that have this day thronged through the streets of this enormous city, the same may be said as the general gigantic rule.

[*'Hear, hear.'*]

It may be said almost equally of the brightest and the dullest, the largest and the least provincial town in the Empire; and this, observe, not only as to the active, the industrious, and the healthy among the population, but also to the bedridden, the idle, the blind and the deaf and dumb.

[*'Hear, hear.'*]

Now, if the men who provide this all-pervading presence, this wonderful ubiquitous newspaper, with every description of intelligence on every subject of human interest, collected with immense pains and immense patience, often by the exercise of a laboriously acquired faculty united to a natural aptitude, much of the work done in the night at the sacrifice of rest and sleep, and (quite apart from the mental strain) by the constant overtasking of the two most delicate of the senses, sight and hearing – I say, if the men who, through the newspapers ... furnish the public with so much to remember, have not a righteous claim to be remembered by the public in return, then I declare before God I know no working class of the community who have.

[*Loud cheers.*]

It would be absurd – it would be actually impertinent in such an assembly as this – if I were to attempt to expatiate upon the extraordinary combination of remarkable qualities involved in the production of any newspaper. But assuming the majority of this associated body to be composed of reporters, because reporters, of one kind or another, compose the majority of the literary staff of almost every newspaper that is not a compilation, I would venture to remind you, if I delicately may, in the august presence of members of parliament, how much we, the public, owe to the reporters, if it were only for their skill in the two great successes of condensation and rejection.[2]

[*Laughter and loud cheering.*]

[2] Dickens refers to abridgement in parliamentary reporting.

Conceive what our sufferings, under an imperial parliament however popularly constituted, under however glorious a constitution, would be if the reporters could not skip.

[*Much laughter.*]

Dr Johnson,[3] in one of his violent assertions, declared that 'the man who was afraid of anything must be a scoundrel, sir'. By no means binding myself to this opinion – though admitting that the man who is afraid of a newspaper will generally be found to be something like it – I still must freely own that I should approach my parliamentary debate with infinite fear and trembling if it were so unskilfully served up for my breakfast.

[*Laughter.*]

Ever since the time when the old man and his son took their donkey home – which were the old Greek days, I believe – and probably ever since the time when the donkey went into the ark (perhaps he did not like the accommodation there), but certainly from that time downwards, he has objected to go in any direction required of him [*laughter*] – from the remotest periods it has been found impossible to please everybody.

[*'Hear, hear.'*]

I do not for a moment seek to conceal that I know this institution has been objected to.[4] As an open fact, challenging the freest discussion and inquiry, and seeking no sort of shelter or favour but what it can win, it has nothing, I apprehend, but itself to urge against objection. No institution conceived in perfect honesty and good faith has a right to object to being questioned to any extent, and any institution so based must in the end be the better for it. [*'Hear, hear.'*] Moreover, that this society has been questioned in quarters deserving of the most respectful attention, I take to be an indisputable fact.

Now I, for one, have given that respectful attention, and I have come out of the discussion to where you see me. [*Cheers.*] The whole circle of arts is pervaded by institutions between which and this I can descry no difference. The painter's art has four or five such institutions. The musician's art, so generously and so charmingly represented here, has likewise several such institutions. In my own art there is one, concerning the details of which my noble friend the president of the society[5] and myself have torn each other's hair to a considerable extent, and which I would, if I could, assimilate more nearly to this.

[*Laughter.*]

In the dramatic art there are four, and I never heard of any objection to their principle, except, indeed, in the cases of some famous actors of large gains, who having through the whole period of their successes positively refused to establish a right in them, became, in their old age and decline, repentant suppliants for their bounty.

[*'Hear, hear.'*]

Is it urged against this particular institution that it is objectionable because a parliamentary reporter, for instance, might report a subscribing MP in large, and a non-subscribing MP in little?

[*Laughter.*]

Apart from the sweeping nature of this charge – which it is to be observed lays the unfortunate Member and the unfortunate reporter under pretty much the same suspicion – apart from this consideration, I reply that it is notorious in all newspaper offices that every such man is reported according to the position he can gain in the public eye, and according to the force and weight of what he has to say.

[3] The English writer, lexicographer and wit Samuel Johnson (1709–84) was much given to pungent social commentary.

[4] *The Times* newspaper had consistently opposed the Newspaper Press Fund, on the grounds that it might encourage bias in parliamentary reporting.

[5] The English politician and writer Richard Monckton Milnes, 1st Baron Houghton (1809–85) was then president of the Newspaper Press Fund.

[*Cheers.*]

And if there were ever to be among the members of this society one so very foolish to his brethren, and so very dishonourable to himself, as venally to abuse his trust, I confidently ask those here, the best acquainted with journalism, whether they believe it possible that any newspaper so ill conducted as to fail instantly to detect him could possibly exist as a thriving enterprise for one single twelvemonth?

[*Loud cheers.*]

No, ladies and gentlemen: the blundering stupidity of such an offence would have no chance against the acute sagacity of newspaper editors. But I will go further, and submit to you that its commission, if it be to be dreaded at all, is far more likely on the part of some recreant camp-follower of a scattered, disunited, and half-recognized profession, than where there is a public opinion established in it, by the union of all classes of its members for the common good: the tendency of which union must in the nature of things be to raise the lower members of the press towards the higher, and never to bring the higher members to the lower level.

[*Cheers.*]

I hope I may be allowed – in the very few closing words that I feel a desire to say in remembrance of some circumstances rather special attending my present occupation of this chair – to give these words something of a personal tone. I am not here advocating the case of a mere ordinary client of whom I have little or no knowledge. I hold a brief tonight for my brothers.

[*Loud and continued cheering.*]

I went into the gallery of the House of Commons as a parliamentary reporter when I was a boy not 18, and I left it – I can hardly believe the inexorable truth – nigh 30 years ago. I have pursued the calling of a reporter under circumstances of which many of my brethren at home in England here, many of my modern successors, can form no adequate conception. I have often transcribed for the printer, from my shorthand notes, important public speeches in which the strictest accuracy was required, and a mistake in which would have been to a young man severely compromising, writing on the palm of my hand, by the light of a dark lantern, in a post chaise and four, galloping through a wild country, all through the dead of night, at the then surprising rate of 15 miles an hour.

The very last time I was at Exeter, I strolled into the Castle Yard, there to identify, for the amusement of a friend, the spot on which I once 'took', as we used to call it, an election speech of my noble friend Lord Russell,[6] in the midst of a lively fight maintained by all the vagabonds in that division of the country, and under such a pelting rain, that I remember two good-natured colleagues, who chanced to be at leisure, held a pocket handkerchief over my notebook after the manner of a state canopy in an ecclesiastical procession.

[*Laughter.*]

I have worn my knees by writing on them on the old back row of the old gallery of the old House of Commons; and I have worn my feet by standing to write in a preposterous pen in the old House of Lords, where we used to be huddled together like so many sheep [*laughter*] kept in waiting, say, until the Woolsack[7] might want re-stuffing.

[*A laugh.*]

I have been, in my time, belated on miry by-roads, towards the small hours, in a wheelless carriage, with exhausted horses and drunken

[6] The English statesman Lord John Russell, 1st Earl Russell (1792–1878), who served as Prime Minister 1846–52 and 1865–6.

[7] The seat of the Lord Chancellor in the House of Lords.

postboys, and have got back in time for publication, to be received with never-forgotten compliments by the late Mr Black,[8] coming in the broadest of Scotch from the broadest of hearts I ever knew.

[*'Hear, hear.'*]

Ladies and gentlemen, I mention these trivial things as an assurance to you that I have never forgotten the fascination of that old pursuit. [*Cheers.*] The pleasure that I used to feel in the rapidity and dexterity of its exercise has never faded out of my breast. Whatever little cunning of hand or head I took to it, or acquired in it, I have so retained as that I fully believe I could resume it tomorrow, very little the worse from long disuse.

[*Cheers.*]

To this present year of my life, when I sit in this hall, or where not, hearing a dull speech – the phenomenon does occur – I sometimes beguile the tedium of the moment by mentally following the speaker in the old way; and sometimes, if you can believe me, I even find my hand going on the table cloth, taking an imaginary note of it all.

[*Laughter.*]

Accept these little truths as a confirmation of what I know; as a confirmation of my undying interest in this old calling. Accept them as a proof that my feeling for the vocation of my youth is not a sentiment taken up tonight to be thrown away tomorrow [*'Hear, hear,'*] but is a faithful sympathy which is a part of myself.

[*Cheers.*]

I verily believe – I am sure – that if I had never quitted my old calling I should have been foremost and zealous in the interests of this institution, believing it to be a sound, a wholesome, and a good one.

Ladies and gentlemen: I am to propose to you to drink 'Prosperity to the Newspaper Press Fund', with which toast I will connect, as to its acknowledgement, a name that has shed new brilliancy on even the foremost newspaper in the world – the illustrious name of Mr Russell.[9]

[*Loud cheers.*]

[8] The Scottish journalist John Black (1783–1855) was Dickens' editor at the *Morning Chronicle*, 1817–40, and had encouraged his literary aspirations.

[9] Dickens perhaps refers to the Irish war correspondent William Howard Russell (1821–1907), who had reported for *The Times* from the Crimean, India and, most recently, the American Civil War.

Benjamin Disraeli

English statesman and novelist

Benjamin Disraeli *later 1st Earl of Beaconsfield* (1804–81) was born in London, the eldest son of Isaac D'Israeli, who, although Jewish, had him baptized in 1817. He was educated in Walthamstow by a Unitarian minister, was articled to a solicitor and kept nine terms at Lincoln's Inn. His first novel, *Vivian Grey* (1826), established his name as an author. After four unsuccessful attempts, he was elected as MP for Maidstone in 1837. His over-ornate maiden speech was drowned in shouts of laughter, but he presciently concluded: 'The time will come when you will hear me'. By 1842 he was leading the 'Young England' group of Tories. He was not appointed to Robert Peel's Cabinet, and fiercely attacked him over the repeal of the Corn Laws (1846); this helped bring about Peel's downfall. In Disraeli's political novels, *Coningsby* (1844) and *Sybil* (1845), his respect for tradition is blended with 'Young England' radicalism. As Chancellor of the Exchequer and Leader of the House of Commons in 1852, he coolly discarded protectionism in favour of free trade; but his budget was rejected, and WILLIAM GLADSTONE succeeded him in Lord Aberdeen's coalition ministry. In opposition, Disraeli displayed talent as a debater, and his spirit and persistence won respect. In 1866, he again became Chancellor of the Exchequer, and introduced and carried a Reform Act (1867) which extended the franchise to the working classes for the first time. In February 1868 he became prime minister; but, in the face of a hostile majority, he resigned in December. He returned to power in 1874 and from this time his curious relationship with Queen Victoria began. In 1875, Britain purchased from Egypt half-ownership of the Suez Canal; and in 1876 Disraeli conferred on the Queen the new title Empress of India. The same year he was ennobled as the Earl of Beaconsfield and continued to lead the government from the House of Lords. The Bulgarian insurrection of 1876, brutally crushed by the Turks, did not move Disraeli as it did Gladstone, but when Russia threatened Constantinople a British fleet was dispatched to the Dardanelles. War was averted by Disraeli's diplomacy at the Congress of Berlin (1878) whose host, Otto von Bismarck, was full of admiration for Disraeli: *'Der alte Jude, das ist ein Mann'* ('The old Jew, now that's what I call a man'). But increased taxation and loss of trade brought about a catastrophic defeat for the Tories in the election of 1880, and Disraeli retired to writing. He was buried at Hughenden, near High Wycombe.

'The wealth of England is not merely material wealth'

2 July 1849, London, England

The roots of this speech lie in the bitter political battle over the Corn Laws, which imposed duties on imported cereal crops, protecting the profits and power of domestic landlords. This system of tariffs, introduced in 1815, had been challenged by the formation of the Anti-Corn Law League in 1838. Supported by Whigs, Radicals and many Conservatives, the League sought repeal of the tariffs as a means of lowering the cost of grain.

When Ireland was struck with potato blight in 1845, the Conservative prime minister Sir Robert Peel tried to provide cheaper bread in Ireland by buying American grain and proposing repeal of the Corn Laws. Disraeli opposed these measures, and articulately led the protectionist wing of the Conservatives against Peel.

When the Corn Laws were largely repealed in June 1846, Disraeli formed an alliance with Whigs and Irish members to defeat Peel's Irish coercion bill. Peel resigned, leaving the Conservatives chaotically and permanently divided. The Whigs under Lord John Russell came to power and full repeal of the Corn Laws followed in 1849.

As effective leader of the new Conservative opposition, Disraeli gave this speech proposing a select committee to examine the state of the nation. Not only had Britain's prosperity been damaged by the reforms, he believed, but also its international standing and the fabric of its society. Meanwhile Ireland was suffering failed crops and a cholera epidemic was claiming thousands of English lives. Disraeli's motion was easily defeated; he was caricatured a few days later in *Punch* magazine, as a tailor measuring up a shabby British lion.

Sir, I have now attempted – but more imperfectly than I could desire – to draw the attention of this House to the state of the country in all its principal relations. The canvas is so wide that it has been to me almost impossible to do more than merely sketch the chief features. But I have endeavoured, without exaggeration, and relying upon documents the accuracy of which cannot and will not be impugned, to lay before the House a fair and impartial statement of our position.

I will not for one moment pretend that what I deem to be our calamitous condition is to be ascribed to any one particular cause. I am ready to admit that in the complicated transactions of a great country like this and in a period of time which in this rapid age of events cannot be considered a brief one, many conjunctures and casualties must occur which the prescience of no statesman could have foreseen, and some of which the power of no minister could remedy.

I am not one of those who look upon the Irish famine as a Cabinet measure.[1] But I am bound to say – taking a general, but I believe not incomplete, view of the government and of the events which have happened within the last three years – that I do recognize one predominant cause to which I attribute the greater part of our calamities – and that is our legislation. Some three years or more ago, as it appears to me, we thought fit to change the principle upon which the economic system of this country had been previously based.[2] Hitherto this country had been, as it were, divided into a hierarchy of industrial classes, each one of which was open to all, but in each of which every Englishman was taught to believe that he occupied a position better than the analogous position of individuals of his order in any other country in the world.

For example, the British merchant was looked on as the most creditable, the wealthiest and the most trustworthy merchant in the world; the English farmer ranked as the most skilful agriculturist – a fact proved by his obtaining a greater amount of produce from the soil than any farmer in Europe or America; while the English manufacturer was acknowledged as the most skilful and successful, without a rival in ingenuity and enterprise. So with the British sailor – the name was a proverb, and chivalry was confessed to have found a last resort in the breast of a British officer.

It was the same in our learned professions. Our physicians and lawyers held higher positions than those in other countries. I have heard it stated that the superiority of these classes was obtained at the cost of the last class of the hierarchy – at the cost of the labouring population of the country. But although I have heard in this House something of the periodical sufferings of that class (as if every class had not its period of suffering); although I have heard in this House epochs referred to of great distress (as if the instances were not exceptional); I know of no great community existing since, I will say, the fall of the Roman Empire, where the working population have been, upon the whole, placed in so advantageous a position as the working classes of England.

I speak not of their civil rights, which are superior to those which princes enjoy in other countries – I speak simply of their material position – I say they have had a greater command over the necessaries of life than any population of equal size in any community of Europe … In this manner, in England society was based upon the aristocratic principles in its complete and most magnificent development.

You set to work to change the basis upon which this society was established, you disdain to attempt the accomplishment of the best, and what you want to achieve is the cheapest. But I have shown you that, considered only as an economical principle, the principle is fallacious – that its infallible consequence is to cause the impoverishment and embarrassment of the people …

But the impoverishment of the people is not the only ill consequence which the new system may produce. The wealth of England is not merely material wealth – it does not merely consist in the number of acres we have tilled and cultivated, nor in our havens filled with shipping, nor in our

[1] The severe Irish famine of 1845–9, believed to have cost up to a million lives, was generally blamed on disastrous mismanagement by Russell's Whig administration of 1846–52. Many commentators have gone further, suggesting a policy of deliberate genocide.

[2] Disraeli refers to the repeal of the Corn Laws in June 1846.

unrivalled factories, nor in the intrepid industry of our mines. Not these merely form the principal wealth of our country. We have a more precious treasure and that is the character of the people. That is what you have injured. In destroying what you call class legislation, you have destroyed that noble and indefatigable ambition which has been the best source of all our greatness, of all our prosperity, and all our power.

I know of nothing more remarkable in the present day than the great discontent which prevails, accompanied as it is on all sides by an avowed inability to suggest any remedy. The feature of the present day is depression and perplexity. That English spirit, which was called out and supported by your old system, seems to have departed from us.

It was a system which taught men to aspire, and not to grovel. It was a system that gave strength to the subject, and stability to the state – that made the people of this country undergo adversity, and confront it with a higher courage than any other people, and that animated them, in the enjoyment of a prosperous fortune, with a higher degree of enterprise. I put it to any gentleman – I care not to what party he belongs, what are his political opinions, or what his pursuits in life – if there be not now only one universal murmur – a murmur of suffering without hope …

As far as I can judge, men in every place – in the golden saloon, and in the busy mart of industry; in the port, and in the Exchange, by the loom, or by the plough, every man says, 'I suffer, and I see no hope'. …

It is because I wish to offer a remedy that I have presumed to call upon the House of Commons today to exercise the highest privilege with which the constitution has invested it. It is because I wish to offer a remedy that I place in your hands, Sir, the resolution I now propose; because I believe in my conscience that it is the best and surest means to save a suffering people, and to sustain a falling country.

Motion made, and question proposed –

'That this House do resolve itself into a committee of the whole House, to take into consideration the state of the nation.'

❧

'The master whose yoke was gentleness'
23 April 1863, London, England

❧

Disraeli was yet to secure his position as friend and confidant of Queen Victoria, but his admiration for her husband Prince Albert seems to have been genuine. Albert had been an important ally to the Conservatives, brokering reconciliation after the 'bedchamber crisis' of 1839, when Victoria's favouritism towards the Whigs prevented Sir Robert Peel from forming a Tory government. Albert had initially regarded Disraeli with contempt, but had warmed to him by the time of his death, aged 42, from typhoid fever.

After Prince Albert's death in December 1861, Disraeli – then in opposition – delivered a string of eulogies to him. This did not go unnoticed by the bereaved queen, who sent him a copy of Albert's speeches with a letter expressing her 'deep gratification at the tribute he had paid to her adored, beloved and great husband'. This extract is from a speech given in Parliament, in which Disraeli urges the construction of a memorial in central London, which would eventually be the Royal Albert Hall.

In praising Prince Albert's mission 'to extend the knowledge, refine the tastes and enlarge the sympathies of a proud and ancient people', Disraeli calls to mind the Great Exhibition of 1851. Albert had instigated and fought hard for the event, which proved highly successful. Profits were ploughed into cultural institutions, including the Victoria and Albert Museum. A permanent building was also proposed for Hyde Park, but progress had been slow.

Partly thanks to Disraeli's campaigning, further funds were raised and in 1867 Queen Victoria laid the foundation stone. The Royal Albert Hall was opened in March 1871 by the Prince of Wales. The queen was too overwhelmed to speak.

❧

The loss was so sudden, so unexpected, that the natural emotions of the community were all directed to the personal character of him who had passed away. The peerless husband, perfect father, the master whose yoke was gentleness, the wise and faithful counsellor of the Sovereign who was his consort – these were the traits in the character of the Prince that attached and appealed to all hearts; and whilst there was a general desire, by public contributions, to show a sense of these qualities, every community felt that it was equally a judge of those virtues with the metropolis; and there was an immense amount of local subscriptions dedicated to the ornament or utility of the district in which the subscriptions were raised. This is the reason why the public contributions were not directed to one centre.

But as time drew on, something of the influence of posterity was exercised upon the opinion of the country, and it became conscious that it had lost not merely a man of virtuous and benignant character, who had exercised the fine qualities he possessed for the advantage of the community of which he was a prominent member, but it felt that it had lost a man of very original and peculiar character, who had exercised a great influence upon the age, and which it felt, as time advanced, would have been still more sensibly experienced.

The character of Prince Albert was peculiar in this respect: that he combined two great qualities which are generally considered to be incompatible, and combined those qualities in a high degree. He united the faculty of contemplation with the talent of action, and was equally remarkable for profundity of thought and promptitude of organization. Add to these qualities all the virtues of the heart, and the House will see that the character thus composed was a very remarkable one. He brought this peculiar temperament to act upon the public mind for purposes of great moment, but of great difficulty.

The task which the Prince proposed to himself was to extend the knowledge, refine the tastes and enlarge the sympathies of a proud and ancient people. Had he not been gifted with deep thought and a singular facility and happiness of applying and mastering details, he could not have succeeded so fully as he did in those efforts, the results of which we shall find so much the greater as time goes on. Such being now the impression of the country – that we have lost not simply an accomplished and benignant Prince, but one of those minds which influence their age and mould the character of a people – a strong feeling prevails that a memorial should be raised in the metropolis of the Empire.

A public memorial such as the country requires should be of a universal and complete description. It should apply to the general sentiments of the country, and should represent, as far as art can represent, the full career of the man, so that future generations may behold a monument which may serve for their instruction and encouragement.

It should, as it were, represent the character of the Prince himself: in the harmony of its proportions, in the beauty of its ornament, and in its enduring nature. It should be something direct, significant, and choice: so that those who come after us may say: 'This is the type and testimony of a sublime life and a transcendent career, and thus they were recognized by a grateful and admiring people!'

❧

'No Caesar or Charlemagne ever presided over a dominion so peculiar'

8 April 1878, London, England

In January 1876, fatigued by the House of Commons, Disraeli became ill. Eager that he continue his work in a less pressured environment, Queen Victoria offered him a peerage. Following a tearful retirement from the Commons in August 1876, he was ennobled as the Earl of Beaconsfield, and thereafter led the government from the House of Lords. It was there that, still ailing, he delivered this speech.

The crisis under discussion was the Russo-Turkish war, which began in 1877 following uprisings against Ottoman rule in Bulgaria and Romania. The Bulgarian revolution had been savagely put down, prompting Russian intervention. Having ousted the Turks from the Balkans, the Russians advanced towards Constantinople (modern Istanbul). Initially reluctant to acknowledge a threat to British interests, Disraeli responded in January 1878, sending the British fleet to the Dardanelles, but was embarrassingly forced to recall it owing to a legal muddle. Turkey signed an uneasy truce with Russia, but towards the end of March, British intervention seemed inevitable.

By now, Disraeli was facing widespread opposition to military action – often couched in terms of flagrant anti-Semitism. The crisis was partly resolved in March when the Cabinet voted to call up reservists and send (non-British) troops from India to Cyprus. Disraeli now sought permanent mobilization of the reservists, building his appeal on patriotism, and depicting the British Empire as a thing of magnificence in peril.

War proved unnecessary. At the Congress of Berlin in June 1878, Disraeli would successfully curb Russian power, restoring part of the Balkans to Turkey.

My Lords: if it was necessary in this state of Europe that Her Majesty should have a sufficient naval and military force, we could take no step but that which we advised the Crown to adopt. And what are the consequences of this step? Her Majesty will be able, in a very brief space of time, to possess an army of 70,000 men, fairly and even completely disciplined. It is double the force of Englishmen that Marlborough or Wellington ever commanded; but it is not a force sufficient to carry on a great war. If England is involved in a great war, our military resources are much more considerable than those you may put into motion by this statute; but this is the only way in which you can place at the disposal of the Crown a considerable and adequate force when the circumstances of the country indicate an emergency. The noble Earl the leader of the opposition,[1] the other night, in his lively and satisfactory answer to one of his own supporters, defended the government, and admitted and approved the satisfactory state in which the country was with regard to defence. He said: 'We happen to know from the Secretary of State that he has a *corps d'armée* ready, and that in a short time he can have another.'

These make up the 70,000 men of whom I speak; and therefore, the noble Earl admitted it was not an unreasonable amount of force we were calling upon Parliament to grant. The question, therefore, between us and the noble Earl is this – I should not say between the noble Earl and us, but between us and any who differ from the policy of the government in this respect. The question is, are the circumstances which exist in the east of Europe at this moment – do the circumstances that prevail in the Mediterranean – constitute an emergency which justifies and demands that Her Majesty shall not only have a powerful navy in these waters, but shall command, if necessary, not a very considerable, but an adequate and an efficient army?

Now, my Lords: I would say that this is a question which comes home to every man's bosom. I cannot understand – I cannot conceive myself – that in the position in which this country now finds itself, when an immense revolution has occurred in the Mediterranean region, a revolution which involves some of the most important interests of this country – I may say,

[1] The Liberal politician Granville George Leveson-Gower, 2nd Earl Granville (1815–91) was then shadow Foreign Secretary and led the opposition in the House of Lords.

even the freedom of Europe – I say, I cannot conceive that any person with a sense of responsibility in the conduct of affairs could for a moment pretend that, when all are armed, England alone should be unarmed ...

I have ever considered that Her Majesty's government, of whatever party formed, are the trustees of the British Empire! That empire was formed by the enterprise and energy of your ancestors, my Lords; and it is one of a very remarkable character. I know no example of it, either in ancient or modern history. No Caesar[2] or Charlemagne[3] ever presided over a dominion so peculiar. Its flag floats on many waters; it has provinces in every zone; they are inhabited by persons of different races, with different religions, different laws, manners, customs.

Some of these are bound to us by the tie of liberty, fully conscious that without their connection with the metropolis, they would have no security for public freedom and self-government. Others, united to us by faith and blood, are influenced by material as well as moral considerations. There are millions who are bound to us by military sway, and they bow to that sway because they know that they are indebted to it for order and justice. But, my Lords, all these communities agree in recognizing the commanding spirit of these islands that has formed and fashioned in such a manner so great a portion of the globe.

My Lords, that empire is no mean heritage; but it is not a heritage that can only be enjoyed. It must be maintained; and it can only be maintained by the same qualities that created it: by courage, by discipline, by patience, by determination, and by a reverence for public law and respect for national rights. My Lords, in the east of Europe at this moment some securities of that empire are perilled. I never can believe that at such a moment it is the peers of England who will be wanting to uphold the cause of their country. I will not believe for a moment but that your Lordships will unanimously vote the address in answer to the message which I now move.

Moved: that an humble address be presented to Her Majesty thanking Her Majesty for her most gracious message communicating to this House Her Majesty's intention to cause the Reserve Force and the Militia Reserve Force, or such part thereof as Her Majesty should think necessary, to be forthwith called out for permanent service.

[2] Julius Caesar (c.100–44 BC) is credited with transforming the Roman republic into an empire. Sometimes considered the first Roman emperor, he was the first to use the name Caesar – though in the context, Disraeli may refer to any or all of his successors.

[3] Charlemagne *literally 'Charles the Great'* (c.745–814) was Holy Roman Emperor from around 800, ruling an empire that included most of modern France and Germany.

Frederick Douglass
American freedman, orator and abolitionist

Frederick Douglass *originally Frederick Augustus Washington Bailey* (1817–95) was born a slave in Tuckahoe, Maryland. He learned to read and write during his childhood as a household servant, but was then returned to a plantation where he laboured as a field hand. He escaped from a Baltimore shipyard in 1838, made his way to New York and, in order to avoid recapture, renamed himself after a character in Sir Walter Scott's *The Lady of the Lake*. He settled in New Bedford, Massachusetts, became an agent of the Massachusetts Anti-Slavery Society and wrote *Narrative of the Life of Frederick Douglass* (1845). He lectured on slavery in Great Britain (1845–7), where his supporters raised the money to buy his freedom. He then travelled in Ireland, but returned to the USA to buy his freedom, thus banishing his fear of recapture. In 1847 he established an abolitionist journal, *The North Star*, in Rochester, New York, which he edited for 16 years. He held various public offices and was US Minister to Haiti (1889–91). He wrote two more autobiographical books, *My Bondage and My Freedom* (1855) and *Life and Times* (1881).

'Allow me to speak of the nature of slavery'
1 December 1850, Rochester, New York, USA

Frederick Douglass was totally self-educated, but was recognized as a first-rate public speaker, a skill perhaps learned from his study of the Roman orator CICERO.

This speech was the first of a series of lectures on slavery. Douglass was uniquely placed to detail the barbarity of the slave system in the southern states of the USA. As a child, he had been separated from his mother and seen family members 'sold south' – ie treated like the chattels they were in law. He himself later fell into the hands of a 'slave breaker'.

In his lectures, Douglass vehemently criticized the laws which continued to make slavery viable in the USA. For example, the Fugitive Slave Law (1793) meant that Douglass himself – until his manumission papers were filed in 1846 – could have been seized and returned to his erstwhile owner in Maryland.

His speeches were widely printed, and his newspaper *The North Star* was made possible through contributions, subscriptions and a printing press provided by British philanthropists. He was a protégé of the American abolitionist and journalist William Lloyd Garrison (1805–79) although he later broke with Garrison, favouring political methods to bring about the end of slavery. Douglass also used his lecture fees to aid fugitive slaves. He was a key figure in the 'Underground Railway' movement which smuggled slaves to freedom, and worked as its 'conductor' in Rochester.

There are times in the experience of almost every community, when even the humblest member thereof may properly presume to teach. When the wise and great ones, the appointed leaders of the people, exert their powers of mind to complicate, mystify, entangle and obscure the simple truth, when they exert the noblest gifts which Heaven has vouchsafed to man to mislead the popular mind, and to corrupt the public heart – then the humblest may stand forth and be excused for opposing even his weakness to the torrent of evil.

That such a state of things exists in this community, I have abundant evidence … Not a day passes over me that I do not meet with apparently good men, who utter sentiments in respect to this subject which would do discredit to savages. They speak of the enslavement of their fellow-men with an indifference and coldness which might be looked for only in men hardened by the most atrocious and villainous crimes …

A very slight acquaintance with the history of American slavery is sufficient to show that it is an evil of which it will be difficult to rid this country. It is not the creature of a moment, which today is, and tomorrow is not; it is not a pygmy, which a slight blow may demolish; it is no youthful upstart, whose impertinent pratings may be silenced by a dignified contempt. No: it is an evil of gigantic proportions, and of long standing.

Its origins in this country date back to the landing of the pilgrims on Plymouth Rock.[1] It was here more than two centuries ago. The first spot poisoned by its leprous presence was a small plantation in Virginia. The slaves, at that time, numbered only 20. They have now increased to the frightful number of three millions; and from that narrow plantation, they are now spread over by far the largest half of the American Union. Indeed, slavery forms an important part of the entire history of the American people. Its presence may be seen in all American affairs. It has become interwoven with all American institutions, and has anchored itself in the very soil of the American Constitution. It … even threatens to bring down that grand political edifice, the American Union, unless every member of this republic shall so far disregard his conscience and his God as to yield to its infernal behests …[2]

Having said thus much upon the power and prevalence of slavery, allow me to speak of the nature of slavery itself; and here I can speak, in part, from experience – I can speak with the authority of positive knowledge. More than 20 years of my life were consumed in a state of slavery. My childhood was environed by the baneful peculiarities of the slave system. I grew up to manhood in the presence of this hydra-headed monster – not as a master – not as an idle spectator – not as the guest of the slaveholder; but as a *slave*, eating the bread and drinking the cup of slavery with the most degraded of my brother bondmen, and sharing with them all the painful conditions of their wretched lot. In consideration of these facts, I feel that I have a right to speak, and to speak strongly …

A master is one (to speak in the vocabulary of the southern states) who claims and exercises a right of property in the person of a fellow man … The law gives the master absolute power over the slave. He may work him, flog him, hire him out, sell him, and in certain contingencies, kill him, with perfect impunity. The slave is a human being, divested of all rights, reduced to the level of a brute – a mere 'chattel' in the eye of the law, placed beyond the circle of human brotherhood, cut off from his kind, his name, which the 'recording angel' may have enrolled in Heaven, among the blessed, is impiously inserted in a master's ledger, with horses, sheep and swine.

In law, the slave has no wife, no children, no country, and no home. He can own nothing, possess nothing, acquire nothing, but what must belong to another. To eat the fruit of his own toil, to clothe his person with the work of his own hands, is considered stealing. He toils that another may reap the fruit; he is industrious that another may live in idleness; he eats unbolted meal, that another may eat the bread of fine flour; he labours in chains at home, under a burning sun and biting lash, that another may ride in ease and splendour abroad; he lives in ignorance, that another may be educated; he is abused, that another may be exalted; he rests his toil-worn limbs on the cold, damp ground, that another may repose on the softest pillow; he is clad in coarse and tattered raiment, that another may be arrayed in purple and fine linen; he is sheltered only by the wretched hovel, that a master may dwell in a magnificent mansion; and to this condition he is bound down as by an arm of iron.

From this monstrous relation, there springs an unceasing stream of most revolting cruelties. The very accompaniments of the slave system, stamp it as the offspring of Hell itself. To ensure good behaviour, the slaveholder relies on the whip; to induce proper humility, he relies on the whip; to rebuke what he is pleased to term insolence, he relies on the whip; to

[1] Plymouth Rock in Cape Cod, Massachusetts is traditionally considered the landing place where the founding fathers of America disembarked from the *Mayflower* on 11 November 1620.

[2] Douglass refers to the threat of southern, slave-holding states to secede from the Union, which would eventually trigger the Civil War of 1861–5.

supply the place of wages as an incentive to toil, he relies on the whip; to bind down the spirit of the slave, to imbrute and destroy his manhood, he relies on the whip, the chain, the gag, the thumb-screw, the pillory, the Bowie knife, the pistol and the bloodhound. These are the necessary and unvarying accompaniments of the system. Wherever slavery is found, these horrid instruments are also found.

Whether on the coast of Africa, among the savage tribes, or in South Carolina, among the refined and civilized, slavery is the same, and its accompaniments one and the same. It makes no difference whether the slaveholder worships the God of the Christians or is a follower of Mahomet, he is the minister of the same cruelty, and the author of the same misery. Slavery is always slavery; always the same foul, haggard, and damning scourge, whether found in the Eastern or in the Western hemisphere.

There is a still deeper shade to be given to this picture. The physical cruelties are indeed sufficiently harassing and revolting; but they are as a few grains of sand on the seashore, or a few drops of water in the great ocean, compared with the stupendous wrongs which it inflicts upon the mental, moral and religious nature of its hapless victims. It is only when we contemplate the slave as a moral and intellectual being, that we can adequately comprehend the unparallelled enormity of slavery, and the intense criminality of the slaveholder. I have said that the slave was a man. 'What a piece of work is man? How noble in reason! How infinite in faculties! In form and moving, how express and admirable! In action, how like an angel! In apprehension how like a God! the beauty of the world! The paragon of animals!'[3]

The slave is a man, 'the image of God', but 'a little lower than the angels'; possessing a soul, eternal and indestructible; capable of endless happiness, or immeasurable woe; a creature of hopes and fears, of affections and passions, of joys and sorrows; and he is endowed with those mysterious powers by which man soars above the things of time and sense, and grasps with undying tenacity the elevating and sublimely glorious idea of a God. It is such a being that is smitten and blasted. The first work of slavery is to mar and deface those characteristics of its victims which distinguish men from things, and persons from property. Its first aim is to destroy all sense of high moral and religious responsibility. It reduces man to a mere machine. It cuts him off from his maker, it hides from him the laws of God, and leaves him to grope his way from time to eternity in the dark, under the arbitrary and despotic control of a frail, depraved and sinful fellow-man.

As the serpent-charmer of India is compelled to extract the deadly teeth of his venomous prey before he is able to handle him with impunity, so the slaveholder must strike down the conscience of the slave, before he can obtain the entire mastery over his victim. It is, then, the first business of the enslaver of men to blunt, deaden and destroy the central principle of human responsibility. Conscience is to the individual soul and to society, what the law of gravitation is to the universe …

Nor is slavery more adverse to the conscience than it is to the mind. This is shown by the fact that in every state of the American Union where slavery exists (except the state of Kentucky) there are laws, absolutely prohibitory of education among the slaves. The crime of teaching a slave to read is punishable with severe fines and imprisonment, and in some instances, with death itself …

I well remember when my mistress first announced to my master that

[3] Douglass quotes from Shakespeare's *Hamlet*, II. 2, in which Hamlet meditates on the nobility of humankind.

she had discovered that I could read. His face coloured at once, with surprise and chagrin. He said that I was ruined, and my value as a slave destroyed; that a slave should know nothing but to obey his master; that to give a Negro an inch would lead him to take an ell; that having learned how to read, I would soon want to know how to write; and that, by and by, I would be running away. I think my audience will bear witness to the correctness of this philosophy, and to the literal fulfilment of this prophecy.

It is perfectly well understood at the South that to educate a slave is to make him discontented with slavery, and to invest him with a power which shall open to him the treasures of freedom; and since the object of the slaveholder is to maintain complete authority over his slave, his constant vigilance is exercised to prevent everything which militates against, or endangers the stability of his authority. Education being among the menacing influences, and perhaps the most dangerous, is therefore the most cautiously guarded against …

We are sometimes told of the contentment of the slaves, and are entertained with vivid pictures of their happiness. We are told that they often dance and sing; that their masters frequently give them wherewith to make merry; in fine, that they have little of which to complain. I admit that the slave does sometimes sing, dance, and appear to be merry. But what does this prove? It only proves to my mind, that though slavery is armed with a thousand stings, it is not able entirely to kill the elastic spirit of the bondsman. That spirit will rise and walk abroad, despite of whips and chains, and extract from the cup of nature occasional drops of joy and gladness. No thanks to the slave-holder, nor to slavery, that the vivacious captive may sometimes dance in his chains, his very mirth in such circumstances, stands before God, as an accusing angel against his enslaver …

But ask the slave: what is his condition? What his state of mind? What he thinks of enslavement? – and you had as well address your inquiries to the silent dead. There comes no voice from the enslaved. We are left to gather his feelings by imagining what ours would be, were our souls in his soul's stead. If there were no other fact descriptive of slavery than that the slave is dumb, this alone would be sufficient to mark the slave system as a grand aggregation of human horrors …

There can be no peace to the wicked while slavery continues in the land. It will be condemned; and while it is condemned there will be agitation; nature must cease to be nature; men must become monsters; humanity must be transformed; Christianity must be exterminated; all ideas of justice, and the laws of eternal goodness, must be utterly blotted out from the human soul, ere a system so foul and infernal can escape condemnation, or this guilty republic can have a sound and enduring peace.

❧

'What to the slave is the Fourth of July?'

4 July 1852, Rochester, New York, USA

❧

In 1845, Douglass had published his autobiography in response to critics who did not believe that an escaped slave could be both self-educated and eloquent. Unfortunately, this also brought him to the attention of the 'slave hunters', who could have seized him under the Fugitive Slave Law and returned him to his owner in Maryland, despite personal liberty laws in northern states designed to protect both free blacks and escaped slaves.

As a result, he spent the next 18 months on a successful lecture tour in Britain, while his British supporters raised the £150 required to buy his freedom. The manumission papers were filed in December 1846, and Douglass returned to Boston the following April.

Ironically, when he delivered this Independence Day address, Douglass had been a truly free man for only five years. His eloquent speech highlights the hypocrisy of the situation, baldly contrasting the pious celebration of 'independence' by free men with the continuing bondage of slaves.

Taking the Declaration of Independence as his basic text, he employs a dogged rhetorical technique, repeatedly posing questions then providing the answers, refusing to spare the feelings of his audience. He hammers home his message, using sarcasm, irony and weight of example to prove that injustice for roughly three million people was no longer a point of debate.

Fellow-citizens, I shall not presume to dwell at length on the associations that cluster about this day. The simple story of it is that, 76 years ago, the people of this country were British subjects. The style and title of your 'sovereign people' (in which you now glory) was not then born. You were under the British Crown … But your fathers, who had not adopted the fashionable idea of this day, of the infallibility of government, and the absolute character of its acts, presumed to differ from the home government in respect to the wisdom and the justice of some of those burdens and restraints. They went so far in their excitement as to pronounce the measures of government unjust, unreasonable, and oppressive, and altogether such as ought not to be quietly submitted to …

Feeling themselves harshly and unjustly treated by the home government, your fathers, like men of honesty, and men of spirit, earnestly sought redress. They petitioned and remonstrated; they did so in a decorous, respectful, and loyal manner. Their conduct was wholly unexceptionable. This, however, did not answer the purpose. They saw themselves treated with sovereign indifference, coldness and scorn. Yet they persevered. They were not the men to look back.

As the sheet anchor takes a firmer hold, when the ship is tossed by the storm, so did the cause of your fathers grow stronger, as it breasted the chilling blasts of kingly displeasure. The greatest and best of British statesmen admitted its justice, and the loftiest eloquence of the British Senate came to its support. But, with that blindness which seems to be the unvarying characteristic of tyrants, since Pharaoh and his hosts were drowned in the Red Sea,[1] the British government persisted in the exactions complained of.

The madness of this course, we believe, is admitted now, even by England; but we fear the lesson is wholly lost on our present rulers. Oppression makes a wise man mad. Your fathers were wise men, and if they did not go mad, they became restive under this treatment. They felt themselves the victims of grievous wrongs, wholly incurable in their colonial capacity. With brave men there is always a remedy for oppression. Just here, the idea of a total separation of the colonies from the Crown was born! It was a startling idea, much more so, than we, at this distance of time, regard it …

On the second of July, 1776, the old Continental Congress, to the dismay of the lovers of ease and the worshippers of property, clothed that dreadful idea with all the authority of national sanction. They did so in the form of a resolution; and as we seldom hit upon resolutions, drawn up in our day, whose transparency is at all equal to this, it may refresh your minds and help my story if I read it.

'Resolved, That these united colonies are, and of right ought to be free and Independent States; that they are absolved from all allegiance to the British Crown; and that all political connection between them and the

[1] When Moses led the Israelites out of slavery in Egypt, God enabled him to part the Red Sea, allowing them to cross the seabed on foot, then to make the water flow back again, drowning their Egyptian pursuers. See Exodus 13:17–14:31.

State of Great Britain is, and ought to be, dissolved.'

Citizens, your fathers made good that resolution. They succeeded; and today you reap the fruits of their success. The freedom gained is yours; and you, therefore, may properly celebrate this anniversary. The Fourth of July is the first great fact in your nation's history – the very ring-bolt in the chain of your yet undeveloped destiny ...

I am not wanting in respect for the fathers of this republic. The signers of the Declaration of Independence were brave men. They were great men too – great enough to give fame to a great age. It does not often happen to a nation to raise, at one time, such a number of truly great men ...

Fellow-citizens, pardon me, allow me to ask, why am I called upon to speak here today? What have I, or those I represent, to do with your national independence? Are the great principles of political freedom and of natural justice, embodied in that Declaration of Independence, extended to us? And am I, therefore, called upon to bring our humble offering to the national altar, and to confess the benefits and express devout gratitude for the blessings resulting from your independence to us?

Would to God, both for your sakes and ours, that an affirmative answer could be truthfully returned to these questions! Then would my task be light, and my burden easy and delightful ... But such is not the state of the case. I say it with a sad sense of the disparity between us. I am not included within the pale of this glorious anniversary! Your high independence only reveals the immeasurable distance between us. The blessings in which you this day rejoice are not enjoyed in common. The rich inheritance of justice, liberty, prosperity and independence, bequeathed by your fathers, is shared by you, not by me.

The sunlight that brought life and healing to you, has brought stripes and death to me. This Fourth [of] July is yours, not mine. You may rejoice, I must mourn. To drag a man in fetters into the grand illuminated temple of liberty, and call upon him to join you in joyous anthems, were inhuman mockery and sacrilegious irony. Do you mean, citizens, to mock me, by asking me to speak today? If so, there is a parallel to your conduct. And let me warn you that it is dangerous to copy the example of a nation whose crimes, lowering up to Heaven, were thrown down by the breath of the Almighty, burying that nation in irrecoverable ruin! I can today take up the plaintive lament of a peeled and woe-smitten people!

'By the rivers of Babylon, there we sat down. Yea! we wept when we remembered Zion. We hanged our harps upon the willows in the midst thereof. For there, they that carried us away captive required of us a song; and they who wasted us required of us mirth, saying, "Sing us one of the songs of Zion". How can we sing the Lord's song in a strange land? If I forget thee, O Jerusalem, let my right hand forget her cunning. If I do not remember thee, let my tongue cleave to the roof of my mouth.'[2]

[2] Psalm 137:1–6.

Fellow-citizens; above your national, tumultuous joy, I hear the mournful wail of millions whose chains, heavy and grievous yesterday, are, today, rendered more intolerable by the jubilee shouts that reach them. If I do forget, if I do not faithfully remember those bleeding children of sorrow this day, 'May my right hand forget her cunning, and may my tongue cleave to the roof of my mouth!'

To forget them, to pass lightly over their wrongs, and to chime in with the popular theme, would be treason most scandalous and shocking, and would make me a reproach before God and the world. My subject, then fellow-citizens, is American slavery. I shall see this day and its popular characteristics from the slave's point of view. Standing there, identified with the American bondman, making his wrongs mine, I do not hesitate to declare, with all my soul, that the character and conduct of this nation never looked blacker to me than on this Fourth of July!

Whether we turn to the declarations of the past, or to the professions of the present, the conduct of the nation seems equally hideous and revolting. America is false to the past, false to the present, and solemnly binds herself to be false to the future. Standing with God and the crushed and bleeding slave on this occasion, I will, in the name of humanity which is outraged, in the name of liberty which is fettered, in the name of the constitution and the Bible, which are disregarded and trampled upon, dare to call in question and to denounce, with all the emphasis I can command, everything that serves to perpetuate slavery – the great sin and shame of America …

What point in the anti-slavery creed would you have me argue? On what branch of the subject do the people of this country need light? Must I undertake to prove that the slave is a man? That point is conceded already. Nobody doubts it. The slaveholders themselves acknowledge it in the enactment of laws for their government. They acknowledge it when they punish disobedience on the part of the slave. There are 72 crimes in the State of Virginia, which, if committed by a black man, (no matter how ignorant he be), subject him to the punishment of death; while only two of the same crimes will subject a white man to the like punishment. What is this but the acknowledgement that the slave is a moral, intellectual and responsible being?

The manhood of the slave is conceded … Is it not astonishing that, while we are ploughing, planting and reaping, using all kinds of mechanical tools, erecting houses, constructing bridges, building ships, working in metals of brass, iron, copper, silver and gold; that, while we are reading, writing and cyphering, acting as clerks, merchants and secretaries, having among us lawyers, doctors, ministers, poets, authors, editors, orators and teachers; that, while we are engaged in all manner of enterprises common to other men, digging gold in California, capturing the whale in the Pacific, feeding sheep and cattle on the hillside, living, moving, acting, thinking, planning, living in families as husbands, wives and children, and above all confessing and worshipping the Christian's God, and looking hopefully for life and immortality beyond the grave, we are called upon to prove that we are men!

Would you have me argue that man is entitled to liberty? That he is the rightful owner of his own body? You have already declared it. Must I argue the wrongfulness of slavery? … There is not a man beneath the canopy of Heaven that does not know that slavery is wrong for him.

What, am I to argue that it is wrong to make men brutes, to rob them of their liberty, to work them without wages, to keep them ignorant of their relations to their fellow men, to beat them with sticks, to flay their flesh with the lash, to load their limbs with irons, to hunt them with dogs, to sell them at auction, to sunder their families, to knock out their teeth, to burn their flesh, to starve them into obedience and submission to their masters? Must I argue that a system thus marked with blood, and stained with pollution, is wrong? No! I will not. I have better employments for my time and strength than such arguments would imply …

At a time like this, scorching irony, not convincing argument, is needed. Oh, had I the ability, and could I reach the nation's ear, I would, today, pour out a fiery stream of biting ridicule, blasting reproach, withering sarcasm, and stern rebuke. For it is not light that is needed, but fire; it is not the gentle shower, but thunder. We need the storm, the whirlwind, and the earthquake …

What, to the American slave, is your Fourth of July? I answer: a day that reveals to him, more than all other days in the year, the gross injustice and cruelty to which he is the constant victim. To him, your celebration is a sham; your boasted liberty, an unholy licence; your national greatness, swelling vanity; your sounds of rejoicing are empty and heartless; your denunciations of tyrants, brass-fronted impudence; your shouts of liberty and equality, hollow mockery; your prayers and hymns, your sermons and thanksgivings, with all your religious parade and solemnity are, to him, mere bombast, fraud, deception, impiety, and hypocrisy – a thin veil to cover up crimes which would disgrace a nation of savages. There is not a nation on the Earth guilty of practices more shocking and bloody than are the people of these United States, at this very hour.

Go where you may, search where you will, roam through all the monarchies and despotisms of the old world, travel through South America, search out every abuse, and when you have found the last, lay your facts by the side of the everyday practices of this nation, and you will say with me that, for revolting barbarity and shameless hypocrisy, America reigns without a rival.

Andrea Dworkin
American feminist

Andrea Rita Dworkin (1946–2005) was born into a Jewish socialist family in Camden, New Jersey, and educated at Bennington College in Vermont. She worked as a waitress, a receptionist and a factory employee before joining the contemporary women's movement. Her early publications include *Woman Hating* (1974), *Out Blood: Prophecies and Discourses on Sexual Politics* (1976) and *The New Women's Broken Heart* (1980). Her crusade against pornography is detailed in *Take Back the Night: Women on Pornography* (1980) and *Pornography: Men Possessing Women* (1981), where she identified pornography as a cause rather than a symptom of a sexist culture. She portrayed contemporary society as one that promotes the hatred of women via debased images of them, and saw this as creating an atmosphere conducive to rape and violence against women. This view was shared by fellow polemicist Catharine MacKinnon (1946–) with whom Dworkin battled to have pornography legally condemned as an infringement of equal rights. Her later works include *Letters from a War-Zone 1976–1987* (1989) and *Mercy* (1990).

'The first principle of all pornography'
20 October 1979, New York City, USA

This address, known as 'The Lie', was given at the conclusion of a march and rally in Bryant Park, near Times Square, an area notorious for drugs, pornography and prostitution. Attended by 5,000 people, mainly women, the event was intended to 'reclaim' the area from an exploitative and violent sex industry. Prominent feminists taking part included Gloria Steinem and BELLA ABZUG.

The event had been organized by Women Against Pornography, a feminist action group formed by Dworkin and others in 1978, a time when many members of the women's movement were more concerned about censorship than about pornography.

Deceptively simple in construction, Dworkin's speech uses reiterated phrases to build and then reinforce her thesis that pornography in all its forms is an abuse of women's civil liberties. Her intent was to dismantle a view, widely held at the time, that women were 'sex objects' who colluded in their own sexual abuse, whether rape, incest or general sexualization, regardless of context. Like many of her later statements, the speech aroused strong feelings in supporters and detractors alike.

Four years later, Dworkin and her collaborator Catharine MacKinnon jointly drafted a civil rights bill which would have recognized pornography as a form of sex discrimination, actionable in US civil courts. The bill was, however, unsuccessful.

There is one message basic to all kinds of pornography, from the sludge that we see all around us, to the artsy-fartsy pornography that the intellectuals call erotica, to the under-the-counter kiddie porn, to the slick, glossy men's 'entertainment' magazines. The one message that is carried in all pornography all the time is this: she wants it; she wants to be beaten; she wants to be forced; she wants to be raped; she wants to be brutalized; she wants to be hurt. This is the premise, the first principle, of all pornography. She wants these despicable things done to her. She likes it. She likes to be hit and she likes to be hurt and she likes to be forced.

Meanwhile, all across this country, women and young girls are being raped and beaten and forced and brutalized and hurt. The police believe they wanted it. Most of the people around them believe they wanted it. 'And what did you do to provoke him?' the battered wife is asked, over and over again, when finally she dares to ask for help or for protection. 'Did you like it?' the police ask the rape victim. 'Admit that something in you wanted it,' the psychiatrist urges. 'It was the energy you gave out,' says the guru. Adult men claim that their own daughters who are eight years old or ten years old or 13 years old led them on.

The belief is that the female wants to be hurt. The belief is that the female likes to be forced. The proof that she wants it is everywhere: the way she dresses; the way she walks; the way she talks; the way she sits; the way she stands; she was out after dark; she invited a male friend into her house; she said hello to a male neighbour; she opened the door; she looked at a man; a man asked her what time it was and she told him; she sat on her father's lap; she asked her father a question about sex; she got into a car with a man; she got into a car with her best friend's father or her uncle or her teacher; she flirted; she got married; she had sex once with a man and said no the next time; she is not a virgin; she talks with men; she talks with her father; she went to a movie alone; she took a walk alone; she went shopping alone; she smiled; she is home alone, asleep, the man breaks in, and still, the question is asked, 'Did you like it? Did you leave the window open just hoping that someone would pop on through? Do you always sleep without any clothes on? Did you have an orgasm?'

Her body is bruised, she is torn and hurt, and still the question persists. Did you provoke it? Did you like it? Is this what you really wanted all along? Is this what you were waiting for and hoping for and dreaming of? You keep saying no. Try proving no. Those bruises? Women like to be roughed up a bit. What did you do to lead him on? How did you provoke him? Did you like it?

A boyfriend or a husband or one's parents or even sometimes a female lover will believe that she could have fought him off – if she had really wanted to. She must have really wanted it – if it happened. What was it she wanted? She wanted the force, the hurt, the harm, the pain, the humiliation. Why did she want it? Because she is female and females always provoke it, always want it, always like it.

And how does everyone whose opinion matters know that women want to be forced and hurt and brutalized? Pornography says so. For centuries men have consumed pornography in secret – yes, the lawyers and the legislators and the doctors and the artists and the writers and the scientists and the theologians and the philosophers. And for these same centuries, women have not consumed pornography and women have not been lawyers and legislators and doctors and artists and writers and scientists and theologians and philosophers.

Men believe the pornography, in which the women always want it. Men believe the pornography, in which women resist and say no only so that men will force them and use more and more force and more and more brutality. To this day, men believe the pornography and men do not believe the women who say no.

Some people say that pornography is only fantasy. What part of it is fantasy? Women are beaten and raped and forced and whipped and held captive. The violence depicted is true. The acts of violence depicted in pornography are real acts committed against real women and real female children. The fantasy is that women want to be abused.

And so we are here today to explain calmly – to shout, to scream, to bellow, to holler – that we women do not want it, not today, not tomorrow, not yesterday. We never will want it and we never have wanted it. The prostitute does not want to be forced and hurt. The homemaker does not want to be forced and hurt. The lesbian does not want to be forced and hurt. The young girl does not want to be forced and hurt.

And because everywhere in this country, daily, thousands of women and young girls are being brutalized – and this is not fantasy – every day women and young girls are being raped and beaten and forced – we will never again accept any depiction of us that has as its first principle, its first premise, that we want to be abused, that we enjoy being hurt, that we like being forced.

That is why we will fight pornography wherever we find it; and we will fight those who justify it and those who make it and those who buy and use it. And make no mistake: this movement against pornography is a movement against silence – the silence of the real victims. And this movement against pornography is a movement for speech – the speech of those who have been silenced by sexual force, the speech of women and young girls. And we will never, never be silenced again.

Anthony Eden
English statesman

> Robert Anthony Eden *later 1st Earl of Avon* (1897–1977) was born at Windlestone Hall, Bishop Auckland, County Durham, and educated at Eton and Christ Church, Oxford. He won the Military Cross in 1917, and became the Conservative MP for Warwick and Leamington (1923–57). In 1931 he became Foreign Under-Secretary, in 1934 Lord Privy Seal and in 1935 Foreign Secretary. He resigned in 1938 following differences with Prime Minister NEVILLE CHAMBERLAIN, principally on the issue of the policy towards fascist Italy. In 1940 he was WINSTON CHURCHILL'S Secretary of State for War, issuing the historic appeal that brought the Home Guard into being. In 1940 he was Foreign Secretary again. Strenuous wartime work culminated in his leadership of the British delegation to the 1945 San Francisco Conference which established the United Nations (UN). With Labour in power from 1945 to 1951, he was deputy leader of the opposition, returning to the Foreign Office once more when Churchill returned to power in 1951. He succeeded Churchill as prime minister in 1955, a year marked by the summit conference at Geneva with the heads of government of the USA, France and the USSR. In 1956 he ordered British and French forces to occupy the Suez Canal Zone ahead of the invading Israeli army. His action was condemned by the UN and caused a bitter and prolonged controversy in Britain which did not subside when he ordered a withdrawal. In failing health, he abruptly resigned the premiership in 1957. He was knighted in 1954 and created an earl in 1961. Regarded as one of the western world's most experienced statesmen, he aimed principally for world peace based on respect for law. His publications included *Days for Decision* (1949), his World War II memoirs – *Full Circle* (1960), *Facing the Dictators* (1962) and *The Reckoning* (1965) – and an account of his pre-political life, *Another World* (1976).

'For us now there will be no turning back'
11 September 1939, radio broadcast from London, England

This stirring broadcast came eight days after Britain and France had declared war on Germany. Hours before Eden spoke, the public had heard of the British Expeditionary Force's arrival in France. Eden had only rejoined the government – to serve as Secretary of State for the Dominions – on the outbreak of war, following his resignation 18 months earlier over Chamberlain's policy of appeasement towards Italy.

Eden was a natural choice to make this morale-boosting address, given his popularity with the British public. He both reflects on and calls for unity and resolve in the face of German duplicity and aggression, at times using poetic imagery to inspire his audience: 'we must fashion a new world that is something better than a stale reflection of the old, bled white'. The speech builds to a rousing conclusion; a series of questions that Britain and its allies must ask themselves after the war, and must remember during the months ahead as a source of hope.

A week has passed since this country found itself at war with Nazi rule in Germany, and today we are a united people, more closely knit one to another in our common resolve than at any time in our history. More united, if that were possible, and certainly no less determined than when, some 25 years ago, we pledged ourselves to fight in a good cause. For such a cause we are fighting with one heart and mind today.

How has this come about? What is it that has levelled the internal barriers – the party and political barriers – and brought our people to be of one mind?

First, we have a good conscience. The White Paper which the government recently made public and which disclosed the story of the ten days that preceded the outbreak of war has made it clear beyond a doubt that the government not only strove to keep the peace, but took great risks for peace.

And yet there was this difference between the days which preceded the outbreak of war in 1914 and the period through which we have just passed. It has sometimes been said that if, before the last great war, we had made our position more plain and clear, peace would have been saved. I am not concerned this evening to argue whether that was a right or a wrong view.

Today one fact stands out and it is this, that before war broke out we did all that words could do to make our attitude unequivocally clear to Germany's rulers so that – and here I use the Prime Minister's own words – there should be no 'tragic ambiguity'. Neither this German government nor any German government in the future will ever have justification for saying that there was doubt as to the action which we must take. Our position was put before the world for all to see, long before the German government decided to submit its fate to the dread arbitrament of war.

You may remember the famous story of the Roman envoys who went to Carthage before the first Punic War.[1] Confronted by the Carthaginian senate, their spokesman said: 'I have here two gifts: peace and war. Take which you choose.'

No such grim alternative was given to Herr Hitler. Every inducement was offered him to enter the way of peaceful negotiation. The Polish government had accepted this principle of negotiation. Herr Hitler deliberately and with set purpose made negotiation impossible. Instead he chose to embark upon a war of naked aggression, and this country and France have in consequence fulfilled their undertaking to Poland, an undertaking with which you are all familiar, an undertaking into which we had entered with full publicity before the world as long ago as last April.[2]

The German Chancellor carried cynical dissimulation so far as finally to invade Poland because Poland had failed to accept peace proposals which she had never even received from the German government. There has never been a more flagrant mockery of international good faith.

We have always desired to live and let live. We considered that there was no dispute that could not be resolved by peaceful means if once the threat of force were removed, and other nations have shared our point of view. Poland was always ready to negotiate, as Czechoslovakia was ready to negotiate a year ago.

Herr Hitler has preferred force. He has made the choice; he must suffer the decision. For us now there will be no turning back. We have no quarrel with the German people, but there can be no lasting peace until Nazism and all it stands for, in oppression, cruelty and broken faith, is banished from the earth. This is an issue that admits of no compromise.

First, then, our conscience is clear.

But secondly, our memory is long. Herr Hitler has claimed that his sole aim was to remedy the injustices of the Treaty of Versailles,[3] which he contended was the root of all evil. This it was, we are told, which had forced him to build his colossal armaments, to march his legions into Austria, to imprison its Chancellor, to absorb Austria into the German Reich. This it was that compelled him to break faith with the British and French governments, and despite his pledge, so recently and so solemnly reaffirmed, to invade and subdue Czechoslovakia and to attempt to reduce her people to the status of hewers of wood and drawers of water.

This it was that left Herr Hitler – we are assured – with no alternative but to turn against Poland, with whom some five years ago he had solemnly signed a pact which was to run for ten years. And a pact, you will recall, which laid down that the status of Danzig and the Polish Corridor[4] would, by consent of both Poland and Germany, remain unchanged until 1944[5].

Faced with such a catalogue of broken vows and discarded pledges, how is it possible to escape the conclusion that the Treaty of Versailles was not a grievance to redress, but a pretext for the use of force?

[1] The First Punic War (264–241BC) was fought between the Roman republic and the Carthaginian empire.

[2] After ADOLF HITLER seized Czechoslovakia in March 1939, Chamberlain arranged an Anglo-French guarantee of support for Poland – as well as Romania and Greece – if it too was invaded.

[3] The Treaty of Versailles, signed in June 1919, demanded Germany pay massive compensation for war damages, and placed severe restrictions on German military development.

[4] The 'Polish Corridor' was a narrow strip of land transferred to Poland at the Treaty of Versailles to provide the country with access to the Baltic Sea. Its ownership was contested by Germany from early 1939; and was a key reason for the German invasion of September 1939.

[5] Germany and Poland signed a ten-year non-aggression pact in January 1934.

Five times in the last 80 years, the rulers of Germany have embarked with only the slightest pretext upon a war of aggression. Against peaceful Denmark in 1864, against Austria in 1866, against France in 1870, against the whole world in 1914 to 1918, and now against France, Poland and Great Britain in 1939.

With such a record, her present rulers, had they been honest and sincere, might well have thought that they should accept to negotiate with nations who wanted nothing more than to live at peace with Germany, and who, as the documents which have been published show, excluded no subjects from peaceful discussion.

Herr Hitler and his Nazi associates would have none of it. Flouting all the lessons of history, ignoring or deriding even their own country's experience of British character, they preferred yet once more the path of lawlessness, the path of misery and of bloodshed, the path of anarchy and want. Let the Nazi leaders ask themselves now to what destiny they are leading the Germany people.

Our conscience then is clear. Our memory is long, and thirdly, our determination is unshaken.

This war has broken out in circumstances which have no parallel. Herr Hitler is invading Poland with the help of overwhelming numbers and the merciless use of the air arm, while he acts on the defensive in the west. These methods are leading to strange illusions among the Nazi leaders, which had best be dispelled at once.

Let there be no mistake about this. Our determination to see this war through to the end is unshaken. We must make it clear to the Nazi leaders and if we can to the German people that this country – as the Prime Minister said – has not gone to war about the fate of a faraway city in a foreign land. We have decided to fight to show that aggression does not pay, and the German people must realize that this country means to go on fighting until that goal is reached.

It is already evident that the Nazi government seeks to delude its people into thinking that a quick victory won in Poland will be followed by the indifference or the capitulation of the western democracies. That is not the truth. The people of this country are ready to fight a very long war to the bitter end if that must be to rid the world of Hitlerism and all that Hitlerism implies.

In the meanwhile, let the Nazi leaders take heed and let us all take encouragement from what has been happening in the British Commonwealth of Nations during the last few days.

One by one the free peoples of that great association have been accepting the risks and responsibilities which the United Kingdom has taken upon itself. Canada, Australia, New Zealand, South Africa, each in turn has given the answer to the challenge, each in turn has made the cause its own.

And not only these great dominions, but India also. The Colonies, too, have offered their aid. From all quarters of the globe have come messages of loyalty to the sovereign[6] and offers of help. Once more, Britain stands armed and resolved with her sister nations at her side.

For some of us, the challenge has come a second time in our generation. There must be no second mistake. Out of the welter of suffering to be endured, we must fashion a new world that is something better than a stale reflection of the old, bled white.

It had been better could we have set ourselves to the task in a world of

[6] The British monarch King George VI (1895–1952) reigned 1936–52.

peace. Herr Hitler has decided otherwise. Nazism, however, is but a passing phase. Like all systems built upon force, it cannot endure. In the long roll of history it will count but as a spasm of acute pain. The suffering will be bitter, the devastation wide. But what really matters is what follows after.

Can we do better this time? Can we finally rid Europe of barriers of castes and creed and prejudice? Can frontiers and faiths, language and commerce serve to unite nations and not divide them? Can we create a true unity in Europe? Can we set before it a common aim of service? Can we inspire it with common ideals of freedom, toleration and mercy? This is what must be. While the Nazi system exists it cannot be, and so the Nazi system and all that it implies must be swept away.

By Herr Hitler's own decision our new civilization must be built through a world at war. We would have wished it otherwise. But our new civilization will be built just the same, for some forces are bigger than men, and in that new civilization will be found liberty and opportunity and hope for all.

🕊

'This is a time for action'
2 November 1956, television and radio broadcast from London, England
🕊

This address to the British public was an attempt by Eden – by now prime minister – to justify military intervention in Egypt during the Suez crisis. What makes the speech remarkable, however, is what he chose not to say. The crisis began when the Egyptian president, Gamal Abdel Nasser, nationalized the Suez Canal, previously controlled by British and French companies. Britain and France, fearful that Nasser might prevent oil shipments reaching Europe, made a secret agreement with Israel. Four days before Eden's address, Israeli troops invaded Egypt and took control of the Canal Zone.

Claiming no prior knowledge of the invasion, Eden announces plans to send British forces to police a ceasefire between the Israeli and Egyptian sides. In the process, of course, Britain would retake the Suez Canal. In conciliatory tones – designed to appease a country divided over the affair – he argues that intervention was necessary to prevent a 'forest fire' in the Middle East from spreading. He also reiterates the Labour leader Hugh Gaitskell's comparison of Nasser to ADOLF HITLER and BENITO MUSSOLINI, an appeal to the patriotism of a Britain that had fought and won World War II in the previous decade. On 5 and 6 November, British and French forces began their occupation of the Canal Zone, but – in response to US diplomacy over the threat of Soviet intervention – they withdrew in December to let a United Nations peacekeeping force take over.

🕊

Good evening. I know that you would wish me, as prime minister, to talk to you tonight on the problem which is in everybody's mind; and to tell you what has happened, what the government has done, and why it has done it.

To look at the matter quietly and thoughtfully together is not to deny our emotions and our differences. But for the moment, let's forget our passions and our parties. Let's look at our problem in the light of our country's needs and dangers. Let's look at it together, as fellow countrymen.

First – the background. For ten years there has been fighting and trouble and turmoil in the Middle East. Again and again passions have come to the boil. There have been raids and counter raids, and shooting and more shooting. Ever since the uneasy armistice of 1949 – Israel and the Arab states – Egypt has been insisting ever since then that she is still at war with Israel. Again and again the United Nations has tried to bring settlement and peace, but with the best will in the world it's failed. And all the time, Heaven knows, this country has worked tirelessly for agreement.

We've tried, for example, to prove our desire for friendship with Egypt.

We made an agreement and withdrew from the Canal Zone. We made another agreement with Egypt about the Sudan. We hoped that these would lead to a new spirit in our relations with Egypt. Some people say we've gone much too far in conciliation; that we gave up too much; that we've been weak where we should have been strong.

Well, be that as it may, we've certainly gone to the limit in our efforts for friendship. All those friendly approaches have failed. It's no use blinking that fact. You've only to read the Egyptian government's own statement – what it intends to do. Its words – not mine. Let me give you two examples. The first refers to Israel. 'There will be no stability until this small but vile state is stifled.' A second example comes nearer home. 'We must not in any circumstances lose sight of our goal: to fight the British serpent and to expel it utterly from our lands' – and 'lands', of course, means the whole of the Middle East. That's been the Egyptian mood. The Egyptian threat – openly and publicly proclaimed.

But deeds speak even louder than words. We've seen the purchase of arms from behind the Iron Curtain;[1] and in early August – when Colonel Nasser seized the canal – Mr Gaitskell[2] called the threats to Israel 'clear notice of aggression to come'. He went on to say: 'It's all very familiar – it's exactly the same as we encountered from Mussolini and Hitler in those years before the war.' Strong words – but justified. No wonder Israel was worried.

Then, a few days ago, came the entry of Israeli troops into Egypt. Was that a dangerous situation? Was it likely to lead to a widespread flare-up in the Middle East? In the judgement of the government, it was. Was it likely to endanger widespread British and international interests? It was.

Well, it's possible to go on arguing who was the aggressor. Was it Israel because she crossed the frontier? Or was it Egypt for what she'd done before? But that's not the real issue for us. If you see afar, the first question isn't how it started, but how to put it out. The hard and inescapable fact was that here was a situation likely to inflame the whole Middle East, with all that this would mean. That, in the government's view, was the fact of the situation – a grim, hard fact. A reality which no words could alter.

As a government we've had to wrestle with the problem of what action we should take, so have our French friends. The burden of that decision was tremendous, but inescapable. In the depths of our conviction we decided that here was the beginning of a forest fire, of immense danger to peace. We decided that we must act and act quickly.

What should we do? We put the matter to the Security Council. Should we have left it to them? Should we have been content to wait to see whether they would act? How long would this have taken? And where would the forest fire have spread in the meantime? Would words have been enough? What we did do was to take police action at once. Action to end the fighting and to separate the armies.

We acted swiftly, and reported to the Security Council, and I believe that before long it will become apparent to everybody that we acted rightly and wisely.

Our friends inside the Commonwealth and outside couldn't, in the very nature of things, be consulted in time. You just cannot have immediate action and extensive consultation as well. But our friends are coming … to see that we acted with courage and speed, to deal with a situation which just could not wait.

There are two things I would ask you not to forget. Never to forget. We

[1] The popularity of the phrase 'Iron Curtain' dates from 1946, when WINSTON CHURCHILL used it in a speech in the USA (included in this book) to describe the parts of Europe under Soviet influence. However, its originator was the Nazi propagandist JOSEPH GOEBBELS, who used the phrase *eiserner Vorhang* ('iron curtain') in a newspaper article in 1945.

[2] The English politician Hugh Gaitskell (1906–63) was leader of the Labour Party from 1955 until his death.

cannot allow – we could not allow – a conflict in the Middle East to spread; our survival as a nation depends on oil and nearly three-quarters of our oil comes from that part of the world. As a Labour Member of Parliament, speaking in support of the government, put it, 'to be without oil' – I quote him – 'to be without oil, is to see our industries grind to a standstill, and starvation overtake the people.'

Yes – chaos in the Middle East could permanently lower the standard of life in this country – in Europe, as well as in many poorer countries of the world.

The other reflection is this. It's a personal one. All my life I've been a man of peace, working for peace, striving for peace, negotiating for peace. I've been a League of Nations man and a United Nations man, and I'm still the same man, with the same conviction, the same devotion to peace. I couldn't be other – even if I wished, but I'm utterly convinced that the action we have taken is right. ...

There are times for courage, times for action. And this is one of them. In the interests of peace, I do hope we've learnt our lesson. Our passionate love of peace, our intense loathing of war have often held us back from using force, even at times when we knew in our heads, if not in our hearts, that its use was in the interests of peace. And I believe with all my heart, and head – for both are needed – that this is a time for action, effective and swift. Yes, even by the use of some force in order to prevent the forest fire from spreading; to prevent the horror and devastation of a larger war.

The government knew – and they regretted it – that this action would shock and hurt some people. The bombing of military targets – and military targets only – it's better to destroy machines on the ground, than let them destroy people from the air. We had to think of our troops, and of the inhabitants of the towns and villages. Above all it was our duty to act and act swiftly – for only by such action could we secure peace.

We learn that the Israeli forces have captured the Egyptian army in Sinai. We learn too, that [the] United Nations truce organization is trying to arrange contact between the two sides to establish terms of surrender. We hope that this organization will be able to arrange for all the captured Egyptians to return to Egypt. We shall certainly give them all the help we can in this.

It seems that Israel has succeeded in destroying the bases in Sinai and Gaza, in which Egyptian commando raiders were trained for attacks on Israel. Once British and French forces have occupied the key points on the canal, Her Majesty's government will ensure that the Israeli forces withdraw from Egyptian territory.

I've no doubt that is their intention, but they will not do so unless we are there to keep the peace, to give the necessary guarantees and prevent a repetition of these events.

So finally, my friends, what are we seeking to do? First and foremost, to stop the fighting, to separate the armies, and to make sure that there's no more fighting. We've stepped in because United Nations couldn't do so in time. If the United Nations will take over this police action we shall welcome it. Indeed we proposed that course to them. And police action means not only to end the fighting now, but also to bring a lasting peace to an area which for ten years has lived, or tried to live, under the constant threat of war.

Until there are United Nations forces there, ready to take over, we and the French must go on with the job, until the job is done. All this could mean

– let's hope and pray it does – that the outcome will be not only peace in the Middle East, but a strengthened United Nations, one with power to act as well as to talk – a real force for peace in the world.

Good night to you all.

Edward VIII
British monarch

Edward VIII *born Edward Albert Christian George Andrew Patrick David Windsor; later HRH The Duke of Windsor* (1894–1972) was the eldest son of GEORGE V (1865–1936). He was born at White Lodge in Richmond, Surrey, and educated at Osborne, Dartmouth, and Magdalen College, Oxford. Invested as Prince of Wales (1911), he served in the Royal Navy and (during World War I) the British Army, travelled much, and achieved considerable popularity. He was forthright in his comments on poverty, especially in South Wales. He succeeded his father in 1936, but abdicated less than eleven months later, prompted by general disapprobation and constitutional difficulties over his proposed marriage to the divorcee Mrs Wallis Simpson. He was thereupon given the title of Duke of Windsor, and the marriage took place in June 1937. He served as governor of the Bahamas (1940–5), as described in his book *A King's Story* (1951). After 1945 he lived in Paris and was not invited back to England with his wife to an official public ceremony until 1967.

'*I lay down my burden*'
11 December 1936, Windsor, England

Edward was a very popular Prince of Wales in the 1920s and 1930s. His manner was charming and informal: impatient of tradition and ceremony, he hoped to modernize the British monarchy. He told his grandmother Queen Alexandra in 1914 that he would only marry someone he loved, and in the years following World War I he was attracted to many women, but none was thought suitable to marry the heir to the throne. In 1930 he met the American divorcee Wallis Simpson – who had already remarried – and became increasingly attached to her. The American newspapers publicized the relationship, but British papers did not.

When Edward succeeded to the throne on 20 January 1936, he was required to behave more formally. However, believing that the British people were beginning to accept the idea of remarriage after divorce, he planned to marry Mrs Simpson following her second divorce in October 1936. Prime Minister STANLEY BALDWIN and church leaders felt strongly that a divorced woman was ineligible to be the wife and queen consort of the monarch because of his role as head of the Church of England. Edward then faced his famous romantic dilemma: he could remain king without marrying Mrs Simpson, or abdicate and marry her. He chose the latter course and broadcast to a stunned nation, which had been largely unaware of the situation.

WINSTON CHURCHILL supported Edward at the time, but later said that it had turned out for the best, since Edward's younger brother George VI was an ideal monarch and his wife, Queen Elizabeth, an ideal consort.

At long last I am able to say a few words of my own. I have never wanted to withhold anything, but until now it has not been constitutionally possible for me to speak.

A few hours ago, I discharged my last duty as king and emperor, and now that I have been succeeded by my brother, the Duke of York,[1] my first words must be to declare my allegiance to him. This I do with all my heart.

You all know the reasons which have impelled me to renounce the Throne. But I want you to understand that in making up my mind I did not forget the country or the empire which, as Prince of Wales, and lately as king, I have for 25 years tried to serve. But you must believe me when I tell you that I have found it impossible to carry the heavy burden of responsibility and to discharge my duties as king as I would wish to do without the help and support of the woman I love.

And I want you to know that the decision I have made has been mine and mine alone. This was a thing I had to judge entirely for myself. The other person most nearly concerned has tried up to the last to persuade me to take a different course. I have made this, the most serious decision of my life, only upon the single thought of what would in the end be best for all.

This decision has been made less difficult to me by the sure knowledge that my brother, with his long training in the public affairs of this country

[1] The British monarch George VI (1895–1952), younger brother of Edward, who reigned 1936–52.

and with his fine qualities, will be able to take my place forthwith, without interruption or injury to the life and progress of the Empire. And he has one matchless blessing, enjoyed by so many of you and not bestowed on me – a happy home with his wife and children.

During these hard days, I have been comforted by Her Majesty my mother and by my family. The ministers of the crown, and in particular Mr Baldwin, the prime minister, have always treated me with full consideration. There has never been any constitutional difference between me and them and between me and Parliament. Bred in the constitutional tradition by my father, I should never have allowed any such issue to arise.

Ever since I was Prince of Wales, and later on when I occupied the Throne, I have been treated with the greatest kindness by all classes of the people, wherever I have lived or journeyed throughout the Empire. For that I am very grateful.

I now quit altogether public affairs, and I lay down my burden. It may be some time before I return to my native land, but I shall always follow the fortunes of the British race and Empire with profound interest, and if at any time in the future I can be found of service to His Majesty in a private station I shall not fail.

And now we all have a new king. I wish him, and you, his people, happiness and prosperity with all my heart. God bless you all. God Save the King.

Jonathan Edwards
American philosopher and theologian

Jonathan Edwards (1703–58) was born in East Windsor, Connecticut. He was educated at Yale University and succeeded his grandfather, Solomon Stoddard, as minister of the Congregationalist Church at Northampton, Massachusetts, in 1729. Renowned for his powerful preaching and hard-line Calvinism, expressed in his sermons, he helped inspire the revivalist movement in the American colonies known as the 'Great Awakening'. He was dismissed in 1750 for his zealous orthodoxy and became a missionary to the Housatonnuck people at Stockbridge, Massachusetts. In 1758, he became president of the College of New Jersey (now Princeton University). He is regarded as the greatest theologian of American Puritanism, his main doctrinal work being the *Careful and Strict Enquiry into the Modern Prevailing Notions of that Freedom of the Will* (1754).

'There will be no end to this exquisite, horrible misery'
8 July 1741, Enfield, Connecticut, America

Jonathan Edward's Enfield sermon – given here in abridged form – is one of the most famous hellfire and brimstone oratories of all time. Its power derives from its stark imagery, in particular that of the sinner prevented from falling into Hell by God's hand – a perfect encapsulation of Calvinist theology. The sermon was made at the peak of the Great Awakening movement, which was inspired by religious ferment in Europe, as well as hostility towards ideas then current in the Anglican church, placing less emphasis on original sin and more on free will.

Though appalled at these ideas, Edwards had an uneasy relationship with some of the movement's more emotional preachers, such as George Whitefield and Gilbert Tennent. His stress on God's wrath, however, was entirely of a piece with the Awakening: like Whitefield and Tennent, he understood that fear was a spur to conversion. The English Nonconformist Isaac Watts described Edwards's address as 'a most terrible sermon, in need of gospel sweetening'. He added, however, 'I think 'tis all true.'

The wrath of God is like great waters that are dammed for the present; they increase more and more, and rise higher and higher, till an outlet is given; and the longer the stream is stopped, the more rapid and mighty is its course, when once it is let loose. It is true that judgement against your evil works has not been executed hitherto; the floods of God's vengeance have been withheld; but your guilt in the meantime is constantly increasing, and you are every day treasuring up more wrath; the waters are constantly rising, and waxing more and more mighty; and there is nothing but the mere pleasure of God that holds the waters back, that are unwilling to be stopped, and press hard to go forward.

If God should only withdraw his hand from the flood-gate, it would immediately fly open, and the fiery floods of the fierceness and wrath of God would rush forth with inconceivable fury, and would come upon you with omnipotent power; and if your strength were ten thousand times greater than it is, yea, ten thousand times greater than the strength of the stoutest, sturdiest devil in Hell, it would be nothing to withstand or endure it.

The bow of God's wrath is bent, and the arrow made ready on the string, and justice bends the arrow at your heart, and strains the bow, and it is nothing but the mere pleasure of God – and that of an angry God, without any promise or obligation at all – that keeps the arrow one moment from being made drunk with your blood. Thus all you that never passed under a great change of heart, by the mighty power of the Spirit of God upon your souls; all you that were never born again, and made new creatures, and raised from being dead in sin, to a state of new, and before altogether unexperienced light and life, are in the hands of an angry God.

However you may have reformed your life in many things, and may have had religious affections, and may keep up a form of religion in your families and closets, and in the house of God, it is nothing but his mere pleasure that keeps you from being this moment swallowed up in everlasting destruction. However unconvinced you may now be of the truth of what you hear, by and by you will be fully convinced of it. Those that are gone from being in the like circumstances with you see that it was so with them; for destruction came suddenly upon most of them; when they expected nothing of it, and while they were saying, 'Peace and safety', now they see that those things on which they depended for peace and safety were nothing but thin air and empty shadows.

The God that holds you over the pit of Hell, much as one holds a spider or some loathsome insect over the fire, abhors you, and is dreadfully provoked; his wrath towards you burns like fire. He looks upon you as worthy of nothing else but to be cast into the fire. He is of purer eyes than to bear you in his sight; you are ten thousand times as abominable in his eyes as the most hateful and venomous serpent is in ours. You have offended him infinitely more than ever a stubborn rebel did his prince, and yet it is nothing but his hand that holds you from falling into the fire every moment. It is ascribed to nothing else that you did not go to Hell the last night that you were suffered to awake again in this world, after you closed your eyes to sleep; and there is no other reason to be given why you have not dropped into Hell since you arose in the morning, but that God's hand has held you up; there is no other reason to be given why you have not gone to Hell, since you have sat here in the house of God provoking his pure eye by your sinful, wicked manner of attending his solemn worship; yea, there is nothing else that is to be given as a reason why you do not this very moment drop down into Hell.

O sinner, consider the fearful danger you are in. It is a great furnace of wrath, a wide and bottomless pit, full of the fire of wrath that you are held over in the hands of that God, whose wrath is provoked and incensed as much against you as against many of the damned in Hell. You hang by a slender thread, with the flames of divine wrath flashing about it, and ready every moment to singe it and burn it asunder, and you have no interest in any mediator, and nothing to lay hold of to save yourself, nothing to keep off the flames of wrath, nothing of your own, nothing that you have ever done, nothing that you can do to induce God to spare you one moment …

It would be dreadful to suffer this fierceness and wrath of Almighty God one moment; but you must suffer it to all eternity. There will be no end to this exquisite, horrible misery. When you look forward, you shall see along forever a boundless duration before you, which will swallow up your thoughts, and amaze your soul; and you will absolutely despair of ever having any deliverance, any end, any mitigation, any rest at all. You will know certainly that you must wear out long ages, millions of millions of ages in wrestling and conflicting with this almighty, merciless vengeance; and then when you have so done, when so many ages have actually been spent by you in this manner, you will know that all is but a point to what remains, so that your punishment will indeed be infinite.

Oh, who can express what the state of a soul in such circumstances is! All that we can possibly say about it gives but a very feeble, faint representation of it; it is inexpressible and inconceivable: for 'who knows the power of God's anger?' How dreadful is the state of those that are daily and hourly in danger of this great wrath and infinite misery! But this is the dismal case of every soul in this congregation that has not been born again, however moral and strict, sober and religious, they may otherwise be. Oh, that you would consider it, whether you be young or old!

There is reason to think that there are many in this congregation now hearing this discourse that will actually be the subjects of this very misery to all eternity.[1] We know not who they are, or in what seats they sit, or what thoughts they now have – it may be they are now at ease, and hear all these things without much disturbance, and are now flattering themselves that they are not the persons, promising themselves that they shall escape.

If we knew that there was one person, and but one, in the whole congregation, that was to be the subject of this misery, what an awful thing it would be to think of! If we knew who it was, what an awful sight it would be to see such a person! How might all the rest of the congregation lift up a lamentable and bitter cry over him! But, alas, instead of one, how many is it likely will remember this discourse in Hell!

And it would be a wonder, if some that are now present should not be in Hell in a very short time, before this year is out. And it would be no wonder if some persons that now sit here in some seats of this meeting-house, in health, and quiet and secure, should be there before tomorrow morning! …

And let every one that is yet out of Christ, and hanging over the pit of Hell, whether they be old men and women, or middle-aged, or young people, or little children, now harken to the loud calls of God's word and providence. This acceptable year of the Lord, a day of such great favour to some, will doubtless be a day of as remarkable vengeance to others. Men's hearts harden, and their guilt increases apace at such a day as this, if they neglect their souls; and never was there so great danger of such persons being given up to hardness of heart and blindness of mind.

God seems now to be hastily gathering in his elect, in all parts of the land; and probably the greater part of adult persons that ever shall be saved will be brought in now in a little time, and that it will be as it was on the great outpouring of the Spirit upon the Jews in the apostles' days; the election will obtain, and the rest will be blinded. If this should be the case with you, you will eternally curse this day, and will curse the day that ever you [were] born, to see such a season of the pouring out of God's spirit, and will wish that you had died and gone to Hell before you had seen it. Now undoubtedly it is, as it was in the days of John the Baptist,[2] the axe is in an extraordinary manner laid at the root of the trees, that every tree which brings not forth good fruit, may be hewn down and cast into the fire.

Therefore, let everyone that is out of Christ now awake and fly from the wrath to come. The wrath of Almighty God is now undoubtedly hanging over a great part of this congregation. Let everyone fly out of Sodom. 'Haste and escape for your lives. Look not behind you. Escape to the mountain, lest ye be consumed.'[3]

[1] The townsfolk of Enfield were late developers as far as the Great Awakening was concerned. One contemporary account tells how the congregation 'hardly conducted themselves with common decency' when Edwards entered the meetinghouse. Before he had finished speaking, however, so many people were crying and moaning that he had to ask them to be quiet so that he could continue.

[2] The Jewish prophet John the Baptist (d. c. 3 AD) was the cousin and harbinger of JESUS, whom he baptized, and was later beheaded by Herod. He is known to Muslims as the prophet Yahya.

[3] Genesis 19:17.

Albert Einstein
German–Swiss–American scientist

Albert Einstein (1879–1955) was born in Ulm, Bavaria, of Jewish parents, and educated in Munich, Aarau and Zurich. He took Swiss nationality in 1901, was appointed examiner at the Swiss Patent Office (1902–5), and began to publish original papers on the theoretical aspects of problems in physics. He achieved world fame through his special and general theories of relativity (1905 and 1916), and won the 1921 Nobel Prize for physics. The special theory provided a new system of mechanics which accommodated James Clerk Maxwell's electromagnetic field theory, as well as the hitherto inexplicable results of the Michelson–Morley experiments on the speed of light. He showed that in the case of rapid relative motion involving velocities approaching the speed of light, puzzling phenomena such as decreased size and mass are to be expected. His general theory accounted for the slow rotation of the elliptical path of the planet Mercury, which Newtonian gravitational theory had failed to do. In 1909 a special professorship was created for Einstein at Zurich; and in 1911 he became professor at Prague. In 1912 he returned to Zurich and from 1914 to 1933 was director of the Kaiser Wilhelm Physical Institute in Berlin. He ranks with Galileo Galilei and Sir Isaac Newton as one of the great contributors to the understanding of the universe, but by 1930 his best work was complete. After ADOLF HITLER's rise to power he left Germany and lectured at Princeton University, New Jersey, from 1934, becoming an American citizen and professor at Princeton in 1940. In 1939 he wrote to President FRANKLIN D ROOSEVELT alerting him to the possibility of constructing an atomic bomb, thus helping to initiate the American effort to produce one. After World War II, Einstein urged international control of atomic weapons and protested against the proceedings of the House Un-American Activities Committee, which had arraigned many scientists. He spent the rest of his life trying, by means of his unified field theory (1950), to establish a merger between quantum theory and his general theory of relativity, thus bringing subatomic phenomena and large-scale physical phenomena under one set of determinate laws. His attempt was not successful.

'Security through national armament is ... a disastrous illusion'
19 February 1950, television broadcast from Princeton, New Jersey, USA

Between 1941 and 1962, Eleanor Roosevelt hosted various radio and television shows. These included a programme during which Einstein, then 71, discussed the issue of nuclear security.

Einstein had written his famous letter to her late husband, President Roosevelt, in August 1939. Recent research in France and America, it explained, meant 'it may become possible to set up a nuclear chain reaction in a large mass of uranium, by which vast amounts of power ... would be generated'. The letter continued: 'This new phenomenon would also lead to the construction of bombs'. Einstein had recommended that the US government maintain permanent contact with the physicists working in that field, urged funding to facilitate progress and warned of evidence that German scientists were exploring the same area of research.

Einstein's letter had prompted Roosevelt to support American nuclear scientists. Their work, which became known as the Manhattan Project, led to development of the bombs that were dropped on Japan in August 1945. Einstein was appalled, and later remarked, 'I could burn my fingers that I wrote that first letter to Roosevelt'. He spent much of his remaining ten years campaigning for international control of nuclear arms.

Though Einstein was a popular figure with a playful public profile, his pacifism and socialism – the latter expressed in a famous essay of 1949 – led to his investigation by the Federal Bureau of Investigation. This did not discourage the liberal-minded Mrs Roosevelt from allowing him a platform for his views.

I am grateful to you for the opportunity to express my conviction in this most important political question.

The idea of achieving security through national armament is, at the present state of military technique, a disastrous illusion. On the part of the United States, this illusion has been particularly fostered by the fact that this country succeeded first in producing an atomic bomb. The belief seemed to prevail that in the end it were possible to achieve decisive military superiority.

In this way, any potential opponent would be intimidated, and security, so ardently desired by all of us, brought to us and all of humanity. The maxim which we have been following during these last five years has been, in short: security through superior military power, whatever the cost.

This mechanistic, technical-military psychological attitude had inevitable consequences. Every single act in foreign policy is governed exclusively by one viewpoint: how do we have to act in order to achieve utmost superiority over the opponent in case of war? Establishing military bases at all possible strategically important points on the globe. Arming and economic strengthening of potential allies.

Within the country: concentration of tremendous financial power in the hands of the military, militarization of the youth, close supervision of the loyalty of the citizens – in particular, of the civil servants – by a police force growing more conspicuous every day. Intimidation of people of independent political thinking.[1] Indoctrination of the public by radio, press, school. Growing restriction of the range of public information under the pressure of military secrecy.

The armament race between the USA and the USSR, originally supposed to be a preventive measure, assumes a hysterical character. On both sides, the means to mass destruction are perfected with feverish haste, behind the respective walls of secrecy. The H-bomb[2] appears on the public horizon as a probably attainable goal. Its accelerated development has been solemnly proclaimed by the President.[3]

If successful, radioactive poisoning of the atmosphere and hence annihilation of any life on Earth has been brought within the range of technical possibilities. The ghost-like character of this development lies in its apparently compulsory trend. Every step appears as the unavoidable consequence of the preceding one. In the end, there beckons more and more clearly general annihilation.

Is there any way out of this impasse created by man himself? All of us, and particularly those who are responsible for the attitude of the US and the USSR, should realize that we may have vanquished an external enemy,[4] but have been incapable of getting rid of the mentality created by the war.

It is impossible to achieve peace as long as every single action is taken with a possible future conflict in view. The leading point of view of all political action should therefore be: What can we do to bring about a peaceful co-existence and even loyal co-operation of the nations?

The first problem is to do away with mutual fear and distrust. Solemn renunciation of violence (not only with respect to means of mass destruction) is undoubtedly necessary.

Such renunciation, however, can only be effective if at the same time a supra-national judicial and executive body is set up, empowered to decide questions of immediate concern to the security of the nations. Even a declaration of the nations to collaborate loyally in the realization of such a 'restricted world government' would considerably reduce the imminent danger of war.

In the last analysis, every kind of peaceful co-operation among men is primarily based on mutual trust and only secondly on institutions such as courts of justice and police. This holds for nations as well as for individuals. And the basis of trust is loyal give and take.

[1] Einstein refers to the purge of alleged Communists from American public life and insitutions in the early 1950s, led by Senator Joseph McCarthy (1908–57).

[2] The hydrogen bomb, developed in the early 1950s, was a more sophisticated and devastating form of nuclear weapon, deriving its power from nuclear fusion.

[3] HARRY S TRUMAN.

[4] Einstein refers to the Axis powers of World War II, principally Germany, Japan and Italy.

Dwight D Eisenhower
American soldier and statesman

Dwight David Eisenhower *nicknamed Ike* (1890–1969) was born in Denison, Texas. He graduated from West Point Military Academy in 1915, took the war college course in 1928 and gained experience under the Secretary for War. By 1939 he had become chief military assistant to General DOUGLAS MACARTHUR in the Philippines. On the outbreak of World War II he returned to the USA. Carefully groomed for the responsibility by General GEORGE C MARSHALL, in 1942 he assumed command of Allied forces mustered for the amphibious assault on North Africa. Perceptive and intelligent, he rapidly learned to translate strategic theory into action. He also exhibited a rare genius for smoothly co-ordinating the activities of diverse forces, perhaps his most valuable contribution to the war effort. His successful conduct of the North African operations led to his selection as supreme commander for the cross-Channel invasion of Normandy in June 1944, which he resolutely launched despite capricious weather conditions. His strategy for the drive to cross the Rhine was a shoulder-to-shoulder advance – a manoeuvre that found some justification in the failure of the 'left-hook' stroke at Arnhem. But his reluctance to push on beyond the Elbe and occupy Berlin, and his compliance in the rather hasty dismantling of the Anglo-American armies, resulted in Russia's emergence as the leading military power in Europe. Among many honours, he received an honorary Order of Merit in 1945, and in 1948 became for a while president of Columbia University. With the establishment of NATO in 1950 he was made Supreme Commander of the combined land forces, but in 1952 the popularity he had gained during World War II swept him to the Republican nomination in the presidential elections. He won by a large majority, and he was re-elected in 1956. During his presidency, the US government was preoccupied with foreign policy and the campaign against communism; and undercurrents of extremism and excess of zeal often placed Eisenhower in an invidious position, but his political inexperience was balanced by sincerity, integrity and a flair for conciliation, maintaining stability during a difficult period.

'The military-industrial complex'
17 January 1961, radio and television broadcast from Washington, DC, USA

One of the most memorable speeches of Eisenhower's presidency occurred right at the end, when, in his nationally televised farewell address from the Oval Office, he warned of the danger of an emerging military-industrial complex coming to exert undue influence on government. From World War II onwards, federal spending on military research had rocketed, while arms manufacturing had become a cornerstone of the American economy – developments, Eisenhower feared, that risked handing too much power to unelected scientists, businessmen and army generals.

Eisenhower's coining of the term 'military-industrial complex', later to become a watchword for anti-Vietnam War activists, at first sight seems surprising given his own background as a four-star general, hero of the Allied vicory against Hitler and pro-business Republican. Yet Eisenhower's conservative political outlook is the key to understanding this speech, which also voices concern about large-scale scientific and agricultural research programmes. It was the expansion of government activity that most troubled him. The keyword in his address is 'balance'; balance between the public and the private sectors of the economy, and between the needs of the moment and the safeguarding of American ideals.

My fellow Americans: three days from now, after half a century in the service of our country, I shall lay down the responsibilities of office as, in traditional and solemn ceremony, the authority of the presidency is vested in my successor.

This evening I come to you with a message of leave-taking and farewell, and to share a few final thoughts with you, my countrymen. Like every other citizen, I wish the new President,[1] and all who will labour with him, Godspeed. I pray that the coming years will be blessed with peace and prosperity for all …

We now stand ten years past the midpoint of a century that has witnessed four major wars among great nations. Three of these involved our own country. Despite these holocausts, America is today the strongest, the most influential and most productive nation in the world.

[1] JOHN F KENNEDY.

Understandably proud of this pre-eminence, we yet realize that America's leadership and prestige depend, not merely upon our unmatched material progress, riches and military strength, but on how we use our power in the interests of world peace and human betterment.

Throughout America's adventure in free government, our basic purposes have been to keep the peace; to foster progress in human achievement, and to enhance liberty, dignity and integrity among people and among nations. To strive for less would be unworthy of a free and religious people. Any failure traceable to arrogance, or our lack of comprehension or readiness to sacrifice would inflict upon us grievous hurt, both at home and abroad.

Progress toward these noble goals is persistently threatened by the conflict now engulfing the world.[2] It commands our whole attention, absorbs our very beings. We face a hostile ideology – global in scope, atheistic in character, ruthless in purpose, and insidious in method. Unhappily the danger it poses promises to be of indefinite duration. To meet it successfully, there is called for, not so much the emotional and transitory sacrifices of crisis, but rather those which enable us to carry forward steadily, surely and without complaint the burdens of a prolonged and complex struggle – with liberty the stake. Only thus shall we remain, despite every provocation, on our charted course toward permanent peace and human betterment.

Crises there will continue to be. In meeting them, whether foreign or domestic, great or small, there is a recurring temptation to feel that some spectacular and costly action could become the miraculous solution to all current difficulties. A huge increase in newer elements of our defence; development of unrealistic programmes to cure every ill in agriculture; a dramatic expansion in basic and applied research – these and many other possibilities, each possibly promising in itself, may be suggested as the only way to the road we wish to travel.

But each proposal must be weighed in the light of a broader consideration: the need to maintain balance in and among national programmes – balance between the private and the public economy, balance between cost and hoped-for advantage – balance between the clearly necessary and the comfortably desirable; balance between our essential requirements as a nation and the duties imposed by the nation upon the individual; balance between actions of the moment and the national welfare of the future. Good judgement seeks balance and progress; lack of it eventually finds imbalance and frustration.

The record of many decades stands as proof that our people and their government have, in the main, understood these truths and have responded to them well, in the face of stress and threat. But threats, new in kind or degree, constantly arise. I mention two only.

A vital element in keeping the peace is our military establishment. Our arms must be mighty, ready for instant action, so that no potential aggressor may be tempted to risk his own destruction. Our military organization today bears little relation to that known by any of my predecessors in peacetime, or indeed by the fighting men of World War II or Korea.

Until the latest of our world conflicts, the United States had no armaments industry. American makers of ploughshares could, with time and as required, make swords as well. But now we can no longer risk emergency improvisation of national defence; we have been compelled to

[2] Eisenhower refers to the Cold War.

create a permanent armaments industry of vast proportions. Added to this, three and a half million men and women are directly engaged in the defence establishment. We annually spend on military security more than the net income of all United States corporations.[3]

This conjunction of an immense military establishment and a large arms industry is new in the American experience. The total influence – economic, political, even spiritual – is felt in every city, every state house, every office of the federal government. We recognize the imperative need for this development. Yet we must not fail to comprehend its grave implications. Our toil, resources and livelihood are all involved; so is the very structure of our society.

In the councils of government, we must guard against the acquisition of unwarranted influence, whether sought or unsought, by the military-industrial complex.[4] The potential for the disastrous rise of misplaced power exists and will persist. We must never let the weight of this combination endanger our liberties or democratic processes. We should take nothing for granted. Only an alert and knowledgeable citizenry can compel the proper meshing of the huge industrial and military machinery of defence with our peaceful methods and goals, so that security and liberty may prosper together.

Akin to, and largely responsible for the sweeping changes in our industrial-military posture, has been the technological revolution during recent decades. In this revolution, research has become central; it also becomes more formalized, complex, and costly. A steadily increasing share is conducted for, by, or at the direction of, the federal government.

Today, the solitary inventor, tinkering in his shop, has been overshadowed by task-forces of scientists in laboratories and testing fields. In the same fashion, the free university, historically the fountainhead of free ideas and scientific discovery, has experienced a revolution in the conduct of research. Partly because of the huge costs involved, a government contract becomes virtually a substitute for intellectual curiosity. For every old blackboard there are now hundreds of new electronic computers.

The prospect of domination of the nation's scholars by federal employment, project allocations, and the power of money is ever-present – and is gravely to be regarded. Yet, in holding scientific research and discovery in respect, as we should, we must also be alert to the equal and opposite danger that public policy could itself become the captive of a scientific-technological elite.

It is the task of statesmanship to mould, to balance, and to integrate these and other forces, new and old, within the principles of our democratic system – ever aiming toward the supreme goals of our free society.

Another factor in maintaining balance involves the element of time. As we peer into society's future, we – you and I and our government – must avoid the impulse to live only for today, plundering, for our own ease and convenience, the precious resources of tomorrow. We cannot mortgage the material assets of our grandchildren without risking the loss also of their political and spiritual heritage. We want democracy to survive for all generations to come, not to become the insolvent phantom of tomorrow.

Down the long lane of the history yet to be written, America knows that this world of ours, ever growing smaller, must avoid becoming a community of dreadful fear and hate, and be instead a proud confederation

[3] During Eisenhower's administration (1952–61), annual defence spending ranged from $42 billion to $49 billion.

[4] Previous drafts of the address had referred to the 'military-industrial-congressional complex', but Eisenhower decided to omit the word 'congressional' because he thought it inappropriate for a President to criticize Congress.

of mutual trust and respect.

Such a confederation must be one of equals. The weakest must come to the conference table with the same confidence as do we, protected as we are by our moral, economic, and military strength. That table, though scarred by many past frustrations, cannot be abandoned for the certain agony of the battlefield.

Disarmament, with mutual honour and confidence, is a continuing imperative. Together we must learn how to compose differences, not with arms, but with intellect and decent purpose. Because this need is so sharp and apparent, I confess that I lay down my official responsibilities in this field with a definite sense of disappointment. As one who has witnessed the horror and the lingering sadness of war – as one who knows that another war could utterly destroy this civilization which has been so slowly and painfully built over thousands of years – I wish I could say tonight that a lasting peace is in sight.

Happily, I can say that war has been avoided. Steady progress toward our ultimate goal has been made. But so much remains to be done. As a private citizen, I shall never cease to do what little I can to help the world advance along that road.

So – in this my last good night to you as your president – I thank you for the many opportunities you have given me for public service in war and peace. I trust that in that service you find some things worthy; as for the rest of it, I know you will find ways to improve performance in the future.

You and I – my fellow citizens – need to be strong in our faith that all nations, under God, will reach the goal of peace with justice. May we be ever unswerving in devotion to principle, confident but humble with power, diligent in pursuit of the nation's great goals.

To all the peoples of the world, I once more give expression to America's prayerful and continuing aspiration:

We pray that peoples of all faiths, all races, all nations, may have their great human needs satisfied; that those now denied opportunity shall come to enjoy it to the full; that all who yearn for freedom may experience its spiritual blessings; that those who have freedom will understand, also, its heavy responsibilities; that all who are insensitive to the needs of others will learn charity; that the scourges of poverty, disease and ignorance will be made to disappear from the earth, and that, in the goodness of time, all peoples will come to live together in a peace guaranteed by the binding force of mutual respect and love.

Elizabeth I
English monarch

Elizabeth I (1533–1603) was the daughter of Henry VIII and his second wife, Anne Boleyn. When Henry married Jane Seymour (1536) Elizabeth and her half-sister Mary Tudor (later Mary I) were declared illegitimate in favour of Jane Seymour's son, the future Edward VI. Her childhood was precarious but well educated, and she was raised a Protestant. In 1549, she rejected the advances of Thomas Seymour, Lord High Admiral, who was subsequently executed for treason. On Edward's death she sided with her Catholic half-sister Mary against Lady Jane Grey and the Earl of Warwick, but her Protestantism aroused Mary's suspicions, and she was imprisoned. Her accession on Mary's death (1558) was greeted with approval. Ably assisted by Sir William Cecil as Secretary of State, she fully established the Church of England (1559–63). Cecil also supported the Reformation in Scotland, where Mary, Queen of Scots had returned in 1561 to face conflict with John Knox's Calvinists. Mary abdicated in 1567, and in 1568 escaped to England, where she was confined and became a focus for Catholic resistance; the northern rebellion (1569) was followed by the Ridolfo plot (1570). The papal bull *Regnans in Excelsis* (1570) excommunicated Elizabeth and absolved Catholics from allegiance to her. Persecution of Catholics became more repressive in the 1580s. Several plots against Elizabeth failed, and the connivance of Mary in another plot in 1586 led to her execution (1587). Support for the Dutch rebellion against Spain, and the licensed piracy of men like Sir Francis Drake against Spanish possessions in the New World provoked an attempted invasion in 1588; the Spanish Armada reached the English Channel, but was dispersed by storms and English harassment, suffering considerable losses. Elizabeth entertained various foreign suitors but never married, preferring to indulge in romances with court favourites. Resentment grew as taxes escalated to meet the costs of foreign expeditions. Drake circumnavigated the known world in 1577 and Sir Walter Raleigh mounted several expeditions to America in the 1580s, but Elizabethan England's only real colony was Ireland, which was now exploited more ruthlessly than ever, provoking a serious rebellion in 1597. Famine in the 1590s brought severe social unrest, only partly alleviated by the Poor Law of 1597. With Elizabeth's death, the Tudor dynasty came to an end. The throne passed to JAMES VI of Scotland, who became James I of England.

'I have the heart and stomach of a king'
9 August 1588, Tilbury, England

At the time of Elizabeth's accession, England was a far weaker nation than Spain, whose interests in the Netherlands and the New World had brought it wealth and power.

Philip II of Spain, widower of Elizabeth's half-sister Mary, was a champion of the Counter-Reformation, eager to crush Protestantism in England and the Netherlands. Elizabeth, however, was a determined defender of the Reformation. She had sent an expedition to support Dutch Protestants in 1585, and authorized Drake and others to attack Spanish treasure fleets.

In 1588 Philip retaliated, assembling a mighty Armada of 130 ships and 30,000 men to overpower Elizabeth's navy and invade England. As the Armada reached the English Channel, the English army assembled at Tilbury on the north bank of the Thames, downstream of London. Elizabeth appeared before her troops clad in armour and mounted on a white horse. In the famous speech she delivered to them, she disparages her 'weak and feeble' sex, but stirringly declares her masculine resolve.

Tilbury was an unwise position for the English army, the wrong side of the river to repel an attack from the south, but England's luck held. The Spanish fleet, unable to rendezvous with the Duke of Parma's forces from the Netherlands, was defeated at the Battle of Gravelines. Forced to circumnavigate the British Isles to escape, only 86 Spanish ships survived. The defeat of the Armada made Elizabeth a legend in Europe and marked the beginning of Spain's decline. Elizabeth's injunction 'let tyrants fear' was later used in a speech by US president GEORGE W BUSH.

My loving people: we have been persuaded by some that are careful of our
safety to take heed how we commit ourselves to armed multitudes, for
fear of treachery; but I assure you, I do not desire to live to distrust my
faithful and loving people.

Let tyrants fear; I have always so behaved myself that, under God, I have
placed my chiefest strength and safeguard in the loyal hearts and goodwill
of my subjects. And therefore I am come amongst you at this time, not as

for my recreation or sport, but being resolved, in the midst and heat of the battle, to live or die amongst you all; to lay down, for my God, and for my kingdom, and for my people, my honour and my blood, even in the dust.

I know I have but the body of a weak and feeble woman; but I have the heart and stomach of a king, and of a king of England, too; and think foul scorn that Parma[1] or Spain, or any prince of Europe, should dare to invade the borders of my realms: to which, rather than any dishonour should grow by me, I myself will take up arms; I myself will be your general, judge, and rewarder of every one of your virtues in the field.

I know already, by your forwardness, that you have deserved rewards and crowns; and we do assure you, on the word of a prince, they shall be duly paid you. In the mean my lieutenant general[2] shall be in my stead, than whom never prince commanded a more noble and worthy subject. Not doubting by your obedience to my general, by your concord in the camp, and by your valour in the field, we shall shortly have a famous victory over the enemies of my God, of my kingdom, and of my people.

[1] The Spanish soldier and diplomat Alessandro Farnese, 3rd Duke of Parma (1546–92), was Governor-General of the Netherlands and Commander-in-Chief of Spanish forces.

[2] The English nobleman Robert Dudley, 1st Earl of Leicester (1532–88) had long been Elizabeth's favourite, and was appointed commander of the land forces at Tilbury.

❧

'The cares and trouble of a crown'

30 November 1601, London, England

❧

During Elizabeth's long reign, England was largely well governed and increased in international status. Elizabeth rewarded those who served her well with trade monopolies. These cost her nothing, but were valuable, as the recipient acquired sole distribution rights for certain common household goods. When the Earl of Essex returned from a mission to Ireland without her permission, she punished him by removing the trade monopolies which had provided his principal income.

At the opening of the 1601 session of Parliament, many Members made it clear to the Queen that the trade monopoly system had become oppressive, increasing the cost of too many commodities. Unaccustomed to dissent, she dismissed them. She then summoned the Speaker, who expected a reprimand, but received promises of reform: Elizabeth now recognized that the Commons were merely reflecting the country's feelings.

The Commons sent a 140-strong deputation to express their gratitude and she received them sitting under a canopy of state. They knelt to hear the first part of her speech; then she allowed them to stand to hear the remainder. Accepting their thanks, she emphasized that she had never benefited from her position as queen, but rejoiced in her ability to protect the country from all threats that had presented themselves.

The speech became known as the 'Golden Speech' after it appeared in a pamphlet under the heading: 'This speech ought to be set in letters of gold'.

❧

Mr Speaker: we perceive your coming is to present thanks unto us. Know I accept them with no less joy than your loves can have desire to offer such a present, and do more esteem it than any treasure or riches – for those we know how to prize; but loyalty, love and thanks: I account them invaluable. And though God hath raised me high, yet this I account the glory of my crown, that I have reigned with your loves.

This makes that I do not so much rejoice that God hath made me to be a queen, as to be a queen over so thankful a people, and to be the means under God to conserve you in safety, and preserve you from danger – yea, to be the instrument to deliver you from dishonour, from shame, and from infamy; to keep you from out of servitude, and from slavery under our enemies, and cruel tyranny, and vile oppression intended against us. For the better withstanding whereof, we take very acceptably your intended helps, and chiefly in that it manifesteth your loves and largeness of heart to your sovereign.

Of myself I must say this: I never was any greedy, scraping grasper, nor a strict fast-holding prince, nor yet a waster. My heart was never set upon any worldly goods, but only for my subjects' good. What you do bestow on me, I will not hoard up, but receive it to bestow on you again. Yea, mine own properties I account yours to be expended for your good, and your eyes shall see the bestowing of it for your welfare.

Mr Speaker: I would wish you and the rest to stand up, for I fear I shall yet trouble you with longer speech.

Mr Speaker: you give me thanks, but I am to thank you, and I charge you, thank them of the Lower-House from me, for had I not received knowledge from you, I might a fallen into lapse of an error, only for want of true information.

Since I was queen, yet did I never put my pen to any grant but upon pretext and semblance made me, that it was for the good and avail of my subjects generally, though a private profit to some of my ancient servants who have deserved well. But that my grants shall be made grievances to my people, and oppressions, to be privileged under colour of our patents – our princely dignity shall not suffer it.

When I heard it, I could give no rest unto my thoughts until I had reformed it, and those varlets, lewd persons, abusers of my bounty, shall know I will not suffer it. And Mr Speaker: tell the House from me, I take it exceeding grateful that the knowledge of these things are come unto me from them. And though amongst them the principal members are such as are not touched in private, and therefore need not speak from any feeling of the grief, yet we have heard that other gentlemen also of the House, who stand as free, have spoken as freely in it; which gives us to know that no respects or interests have moved them, other than the minds they bear to suffer no diminution of our honour, and our subjects' love unto us – the zeal of which affection tending to ease my people and knit their hearts unto us, I embrace with a princely care far above all earthly treasures. I esteem my people's love more than which I desire not to merit.

And God that gave me here to sit, and placed me over you, knows that I never respected myself, but as your good was conserved in me; yet what dangers, what practices, and what perils I have passed, some, if not all of you know: but none of these things do move me, or ever made me fear, but it is God that hath delivered me.

And in my governing this land, I have ever set the last Judgement Day before mine eyes – and so to rule, as I shall be judged and answer before a higher Judge, to whose judgement seat I do appeal, in that never thought was cherished in my heart that tended not to my people's good.

And if my princely bounty have been abused, and my grants turned to the hurt of my people, contrary to my will and meaning; or if any in authority under me have neglected, or converted what I have committed unto them, I hope God will not lay their culps[1] to my charge.

[1] Sins.

To be a king, and wear a crown, is a thing more glorious to them that see it, than it is pleasant to them that bear it. For myself, I never was so much enticed with the glorious name of a king, or the royal authority of a queen, as delighted that God hath made me his instrument to maintain his truth and glory, and to defend this kingdom from dishonour, damage, tyranny and oppression. But should I ascribe any of these things unto myself, or my sexly weakness, I were not worthy to live, and of all most unworthy of the mercies I have received at God's hands. But to God only and wholly, all is given and ascribed.

The cares and trouble of a crown I cannot more fitly resemble than to the drugs of a learned physician, perfumed with some aromatical savour, or to bitter pills gilded over, by which they are made more acceptable or less offensive, which indeed are bitter and unpleasant to take. For my own part, were it not for conscience's sake to discharge the duty that God hath laid upon me, and to maintain his glory, and keep you in safety, in mine own disposition I should be willing to resign the place I hold to any other, and glad to be freed of the glory with the labours, for it is not my desire to live nor to reign longer than my life and reign shall be for your good. And though you have had and may have many mightier and wiser princes sitting in this seat, yet you never had nor shall have any that will love you better.

Thus Mr Speaker, I commend me to your loyal loves, and yours to my best care and your further counsels. And I pray you, Mr Controller and Mr Secretary, and you of my council, that before these gentlemen depart into their countries, you bring them all to kiss my hand.

Elizabeth II

British monarch

Elizabeth II *originally Princess Elizabeth Alexandra Mary of York* (1926–) was born in London. She was proclaimed Queen Elizabeth II on the death of her father, George VI in 1952. Her coronation in June 1953 was the first major royal event to be televised. She is Queen of Great Britain and Northern Ireland, Canada, Australia, New Zealand and of several smaller independent countries, and also head of the Commonwealth. Her husband was created Duke of Edinburgh on the eve of their wedding (1947), and styled Prince Philip (1957). They have three sons – CHARLES, PRINCE OF WALES; Prince Andrew, the Duke of York; and Prince Edward, the Earl of Wessex – and a daughter, Princess Anne, styled the Princess Royal. The Queen has aimed to modernize the monarchy and make it more informal, instituting luncheon parties for distinguished individuals and pioneering royal walkabouts. She shows a strong personal commitment to the Commonwealth as a voluntary association of equal partners.

'It has turned out to be an annus horribilis'

24 November 1992, London, England

The year 1992 should have been an *annus mirabilis* for Queen Elizabeth. It was the 40th anniversary of her accession, and the previous 40 years had seen peace and increasing prosperity in Britain and throughout the Commonwealth. However, during the months preceding this luncheon at the Guildhall to celebrate the anniversary, she had suffered many harrowing moments. One of these – the fire which had devastated Windsor Castle – had occurred only a few days earlier, on 20 November, her 45th wedding anniversary.

The Queen was troubled by public disquiet over statements that the government would pay for repairs to the castle, as many people considered that the Queen, as a wealthy non-tax-payer, should take responsibility. There had also been well-publicized marital problems in her immediate family during the previous year. The City of London had itself experienced a difficult year. An IRA bombing in April 1992 had killed three people, destroyed the Baltic exchange and caused widespread damage to buildings, and the Lloyd's syndicates had suffered their worst-ever trading results. Abroad, there had been tension in the Gulf, ethnic conflict in an unravelling Yugoslavia, anti-apartheid riots in South Africa, and famine in Africa.It was not a pleasant period, but the Queen managed to make a wryly humorous speech in which she reflected on cherished moments of the preceding 40 years.

The coming months were also to be troubled. Two days after giving the speech, the Queen bowed to the inevitable and agreed to pay tax and to fund most of the Royal Family herself, removing them from the Civil List. She celebrated the remarriage of the Princess Royal in December, but was saddened a few days later by a breach of trust which saw the text of her annual Christmas speech leaked to the press.

My Lord Mayor:[1] could I say, first, how delighted I am that the Lady Mayoress is here today.

This great hall has provided me with some of the most memorable events of my life. The hospitality of the City of London is famous around the world, but nowhere is it more appreciated than among the members of my family. I am deeply grateful that you, my Lord Mayor, and the Corporation, have seen fit to mark the 40th anniversary of my accession with this splendid lunch, and by giving me a picture which I will greatly cherish.

Thank you also for inviting representatives of so many organizations with which I and my family have special connections, in some cases stretching back over several generations. To use an expression more common north of the Border, this is a real 'gathering of the clans'.

Nineteen-ninety-two is not a year on which I shall look back with undiluted pleasure. In the words of one of my more sympathetic correspondents, it has turned out to be an *annus horribilis*. I suspect that I am not alone in thinking it so. Indeed, I suspect that there are very few people or institutions unaffected by these last months of worldwide turmoil and uncertainty. This generosity and whole-hearted kindness of the Corporation of the City to Prince Philip and me would be welcome at any

[1] Sir Francis McWilliams (1926–).

time, but at this particular moment, in the aftermath of Friday's tragic fire at Windsor, it is especially so.

And, after this last weekend, we appreciate all the more what has been set before us today. Years of experience, however, have made us a bit more canny than the lady, less well versed than us in the splendours of city hospitality, who, when she was offered a balloon glass for her brandy, asked for 'only half a glass, please'.

It is possible to have too much of a good thing. A well-meaning bishop was obviously doing his best when he told Queen Victoria, 'Ma'am, we cannot pray too often, nor too fervently, for the Royal Family'. The Queen's reply was: 'Too fervently, no; too often, yes'. I, like Queen Victoria, have always been a believer in that old maxim 'moderation in all things'.

I sometimes wonder how future generations will judge the events of this tumultuous year. I dare say that history will take a slightly more moderate view than that of some contemporary commentators. Distance is well-known to lend enchantment, even to the less attractive views. After all, it has the inestimable advantage of hindsight.

But it can also lend an extra dimension to judgement, giving it a leavening of moderation and compassion – even of wisdom – that is sometimes lacking in the reactions of those whose task it is in life to offer instant opinions on all things great and small.

No section of the community has all the virtues, neither does any have all the vices. I am quite sure that most people try to do their jobs as best they can, even if the result is not always entirely successful. He who has never failed to reach perfection has a right to be the harshest critic.

There can be no doubt, of course, that criticism is good for people and institutions that are part of public life. No institution – City, monarchy, whatever – should expect to be free from the scrutiny of those who give it their loyalty and support, not to mention those who don't.

But we are all part of the same fabric of our national society and that scrutiny, by one part of another, can be just as effective if it is made with a touch of gentleness, good humour and understanding.

This sort of questioning can also act, and it should do so, as an effective engine for change. The City is a good example of the way the process of change can be incorporated into the stability and continuity of a great institution. I particularly admire, my Lord Mayor, the way in which the City has adapted so nimbly to what the Prayer Book[2] calls 'The changes and chances of this mortal life'.

You have set an example of how it is possible to remain effective and dynamic without losing those indefinable qualities, style and character. We only have to look around this great hall to see the truth of that.

Forty years is quite a long time. I am glad to have had the chance to witness, and to take part in, many dramatic changes in life in this country. But I am glad to say that the magnificent standard of hospitality given on so many occasions to the sovereign by the Lord Mayor of London has not changed at all. It is an outward symbol of one other unchanging factor which I value above all – the loyalty given to me and to my family by so many people in this country, and the Commonwealth, throughout my reign.

You, my Lord Mayor, and all those whose prayers – fervent, I hope, but not too frequent – have sustained me through all these years, are friends indeed. Prince Philip and I give you all, wherever you may be, our most humble thanks.

[2] The Book of Common Prayer, the authorized prayer book of the Church of England since 1544; it has been repeatedly amended since that first version, and the phrase quoted by the Queen dates back to at least the 18th century.

And now I ask you to rise and drink the health of the Lord Mayor and Corporation of London.

Ralph Waldo Emerson
American essayist and philosopher

Ralph Waldo Emerson (1803–82) was born in Boston, of a long line of ministers. He graduated from Harvard in 1821 and became pastor of the Second Church (Unitarian) in Boston (1829), but his controversial views resulted in his resignation (1832). In 1833 he went to Europe and visited the Scottish historian and essayist Thomas Carlyle, beginning their 38-year correspondence the next year. He moved to Concord, Massachusetts (1834), and in 1836 published a prose rhapsody entitled *Nature*, which expressed his philosophy of transcendentalism – the importance of intuitive understanding as a preparation for experience of the world. This was followed by two major orations given at Harvard: 'The American Scholar' (1837) and the 'Address before the Divinity Class' (1838), which produced a great sensation. In 1849 he revisited England to lecture on *Representative Men* (published in 1850). He also published *English Traits* (1856), *The Conduct of Life* (1860), *Society and Solitude* (1870) and *Letters and Social Aims* (1876). He was an idealist or transcendentalist in philosophy, a rationalist in religion, and a firm advocate of individualism and spiritual independence.

'I draw from nature the lesson of an intimate divinity'
11 August 1841, Waterville, Maine, USA

Emerson's travels in Europe brought him into contact with many of the foremost writers and thinkers of his day. He was particularly influenced by Carlyle and by members of the Romantic movement, including the English poets Samuel Taylor Coleridge and William Wordsworth. These men took a personal and passionate view of the natural world and man's place in it, and expressed it in forms less structured and rigid than those used by their predecessors.

On his return to America, Emerson turned to lecturing and preaching. His lectures and writings attracted much attention: 'The American Scholar' was described by the American writer Oliver Wendell Holmes as 'our Intellectual Declaration of Independence'. However, his controversial address to the Harvard Divinity Class angered the Unitarian establishment. He was banned from speaking there for over 30 years, and abandoned preaching to speak more freely of his transcendentalist ideas.

This powerful oration to the Society of the Adelphi at Waterville College dwells on the superiority of the transcendentalist virtues of experience of the world over the analysis of nature. Emerson contrasts the mystical nature of man's relationship with the glories of the natural world to the narrow Puritan outlook.

He continued developing his ideas for the rest of his life, and exerted a tremendous influence on American literature.

The method of nature: who could ever analyse it? That rushing stream will not stop to be observed. We can never surprise nature in a corner; never find the end of a thread; never tell where to set the first stone. The bird hastens to lay her egg: the egg hastens to be a bird. The wholeness we admire in the order of the world is the result of infinite distribution. Its smoothness is the smoothness of the pitch of the cataract. Every natural fact is an emanation, and that from which it emanates is an emanation also, and from every emanation is a new emanation. If anything could stand still, it would be crushed and dissipated by the torrent it resisted, and if it were a mind, would be crazed; as insane persons are those who hold fast to one thought, and do not flow with the course of nature.

Not the cause, but an ever-novel effect, nature descends always from above. It is unbroken obedience. The beauty of these fair objects is imported into them from a metaphysical and eternal spring. In all animal and vegetable forms, the physiologist concedes that no chemistry, no mechanics can account for the facts, but a mysterious principle of life must be assumed which not only inhabits the organ, but makes the organ.

How silent, how spacious, what room for all; yet without place to insert an atom – in graceful succession, in equal fullness, in balanced beauty, the dance of the hours goes forward still. Like an odour of incense, like a strain of music, like a sleep, it is inexact and boundless. It will not be dissected, nor unravelled, nor shown.

Away profane philosopher! Seekest thou in nature the cause? This refers to that, and that refers to the next, and the next to the third, and everything refers. Thou must ask in another mood. Thou must feel it and love it. Thou must behold it in a spirit as grand as that by which it exists, ere thou canst know the law. Known it will not be, but gladly beloved and enjoyed.

The simultaneous life throughout the whole body, the equal serving of innumerable ends without the least emphasis or preference to any but the steady degradation of each to the success of all, allows the understanding no place to work.

Nature can only be conceived as existing to a universal and not to a particular end, to a universe of ends, and not to one – a work of ecstasy, to be represented by a circular movement, as intention might be signified by a straight line of definite length. Each effect strengthens every other. There is no revolt in all the kingdoms from the commonweal, no detachment of an individual. Hence the catholic character which makes every leaf an exponent of the world. When we behold the landscape in a poetic spirit, we do not reckon individuals. Nature knows neither palm nor oak, but only vegetable life, which sprouts into forests and festoons the globe with a garland of grass and vines …

In short, the spirit and peculiarity of that impression nature makes on us is this: that it does not exist to any one or to any number of particular ends, but to numberless and endless benefit, that there is in it no private will, no rebel leaf or limb, but the whole is oppressed by one superincumbent tendency, obeys that redundancy or excess of life which in conscious beings we call *ecstasy*.

With this conception of the genius or method of nature, let us go back to man … Are there not moments in the history of Heaven when the human race was not counted by individuals, but was only the Influenced, was God in distribution, God rushing into multiform benefit? … This ecstatical state seems to cause a regard to the whole and not to the parts; to the cause and not to the ends; to the tendency and not to the act. It respects genius and not talent; hope and not possession; the anticipation of all things by the intellect, and not the history itself; art and not works of art; poetry and not experiment; virtue and not duties. There is no office or function of man but is rightly discharged by this divine method, and nothing that is not noxious to him if detached from its universal relations …

Here about us coils forever the ancient enigma, so old and unutterable. Behold! There is the sun and the rain and the rocks: the old sun, the old stones. How easy were it to describe all this fitly: yet not word can pass. Nature is a mute, and man, her articulate speaking brother – lo: he also is a mute. Yet when Genius arrives, its speech is like a river, it has no straining to describe, more than there is straining in nature to exist. When thought is best, there is most of it. Genius sheds wisdom like perfume, and advertises us that it flows out of a deeper source than the foregoing silence, that it knows so deeply and speaks so musically because it is itself a mutation of the thing it describes. It is sun and moon and wave and fire in music, as astronomy is thought and harmony in masses of matter.

What is all history but the work of ideas, a record of the incomputable energy which his infinite aspirations infuse into man? Has any thing grand

and lasting been done? Who did it? Plainly not any man, but all men: it was the prevalence and inundation of an idea. What brought the Pilgrims here? One man says, civil liberty; and another, the desire of founding a church; and a third discovers that the motive force was plantation and trade. But if the Puritans could rise from the dust, they could not answer. It is to be seen in what they were, and not in what they designed: it was the growth, the budding and expansion of the human race, and resembled herein the sequent Revolution, which was not begun in Concord or Lexington or Virginia, but was the overflowing of the sense of natural right in every clear and active spirit of the period.

Is a man boastful and knowing, and his own master? We turn from him without hope. But let him be filled with awe and dread before the Vast and the Divine which uses him glad to be used, and our eye is riveted to the chain of events. What a debt is ours to that old religion which, in the childhood of most of us, still dwelt like a sabbath morning in the country of New England, teaching privation, self-denial and sorrow!

A man was born, not for prosperity, but to suffer for the benefit of others, like the noble rock-maple[1] which all around our villages bleeds for the service of man. Not praise, nor men's acceptance of our doing, but the spirit's holy errand through us absorbed the thought. How dignified was this! How all that is called talents and success in our noisy capitals becomes buzz and din before this man-worthiness! How our friendships and the complaisances we use shame us now! Shall we not quit our companions, as if they were thieves and pot-companions, and betake ourselves to some desert cliff of Mount Katahdin,[2] some unvisited recess in Moosehead Lake,[3] to bewail our innocency and to recover it, and with it the power to communicate again with these sharers of a more sacred idea?

And what is to replace for us the piety of that race? We cannot have theirs: it glides away from us day by day, but we also can bask in the great morning which rises for ever out of the eastern seas, and be ourselves the children of the light.

I stand here to say: let us worship the mighty and transcendent soul. It is the office, I doubt not, of this age to annul that adulterous divorce which the superstition of many ages has effected between the intellect and holiness. The lovers of goodness have been one class, the students of wisdom another, as if either could exist in any purity without the other. Truth is always holy, holiness always wise. I will that we keep terms with sin and a sinful literature and society no longer, but live a life of discovery and performance. Accept the intellect and it will accept us. Be the lowly ministers of that pure omniscience, and deny it not before men. It will burn up all profane literature, all base current opinions, all the false powers of the world, as in a moment of time.

I draw from nature the lesson of an intimate divinity. Our health and reason as men needs our respect to this fact against the heedlessness and against the contradiction of society. The sanity of man needs the poise of this immanent force. His nobility needs the assurance of this inexhaustible reserved power. How great soever have been its bounties, they are a drop to the sea whence they flow …

The only way into nature is to enact our best insight. Instantly, we are higher poets and can speak a deeper law. Do what you know, and perception is converted into character, as islands and continents were built by invisible infusories, or as these forest leaves absorb light, electricity and volatile gases, and the gnarled oak to live a thousand years is the arrest and

[1] The sap of the maple tree is collected and used to make maple sugar.

[2] Maine's highest mountain.

[3] A large lake in Maine.

fixation of the most volatile and ethereal currents.

The doctrine of this Supreme Presence is a cry of joy and exultation. Who shall dare think he has come late into nature, or has missed anything excellent in the past, who seeth the admirable stars of possibility, and the yet untouched continent of hope glittering with all its mountains in the vast West? I praise with wonder this great reality which seems to drown all things in the deluge of its light. What man, seeing this, can lose it from his thoughts, or entertain a meaner subject? The entrance of this into his mind seems to be the birth of man.

We cannot describe the natural history of the soul, but we know that it is divine. I cannot tell if these wonderful qualities which house today in this mortal frame shall ever re-assemble in equal activity in a similar frame, or whether they have before had a natural history like that of this body you see before you; but this one thing I know, that these qualities did not now begin to exist, cannot be sick with my sickness, nor buried in any grave; but that they circulate through the Universe: before the world was, they were. Nothing can bar them out or shut them in, but they penetrate the ocean and land, space and time, form and essence, and hold the key to universal nature.

I draw from this faith, courage and hope. All things are known to the soul. It is not to be surprised by any communication. Nothing can be greater than it. Let those fear and those fawn who will. The soul is in her native realm, and it is wider than space, older than time, wide as hope, rich as love. Pusillanimity and fear she refuses with a beautiful scorn: they are not for her who putteth on her coronation robes and goes out through universal love to universal power.

Robert Emmet
Irish revolutionary

Robert Emmet (1778–1803) was born in Dublin, the son of the State Physician of Ireland. He joined the Society of the United Irishmen, formed in 1791 to promote republican reform in Ireland; and took part in the failed Irish rebellion of 1798. He later travelled with its surviving leaders to the Continent, where he interviewed NAPOLEON BONAPARTE and Talleyrand in 1802. Having enlisted French support, he returned home in 1803 and spent his fortune of £3,000 on muskets and pikes. He plotted to seize Dublin Castle and, with putative French assistance, gain Irish independence, but lacked organizational skill. Following an explosion at a cache of his weapons he was forced to begin his insurrection prematurely. A week later, unable to muster all the contingents who had pledged support, he led a chaotic attack on the castle. In the skirmishes which followed, his forces succeeded in killing the Lord Chief Justice, Lord Kilwarden, but were quickly dispersed. Emmet escaped to the Wicklow Mountains, but when he returned to meet his sweetheart, Sarah, daughter of the orator John Curran, he was arrested. He was hanged for treason a month later.

'The man dies, but his memory lives'
19 September 1803, Dublin, Eire

Robert Emmet's status as the doomed romantic hero of Irish patriotism was assured when he delayed his escape to America, hoping to persuade his sweetheart Sarah Curran to accompany him. But it was cemented by his speech from the dock, given at Green Street courthouse at the end of his one-day trial.

Resigned to the death penalty, Emmet spoke eloquently in defence of the reputation that would outlive him, convinced that the authorities would 'consign my character to obloquy' to preserve the impression that justice had been done.

He was repeatedly interrupted by the judge, John Toler *later 1st Earl Norbury* (1745–1831), Chief Justice of the Irish Common Pleas, who was known to be harsh, corrupt and inept, sometimes even falling asleep in court. Gradually, Emmet became rattled by the heckles and retaliated with mounting fury. Finally, he reiterated his famous desire that no epitaph should adorn his grave, for fear that it would mar his good name.

He need hardly have worried on that score: he was soon mythologized as a martyr. His friend, the Irish poet and patriot Thomas Moore (1779–1852) produced two ballads in his honour: 'Oh Breathe Not Her Name' and 'She is Far from the Land', which includes the lines:

> 'He had lived for his love, for his country he died,
> They were all that to life had entwined him,
> Nor soon shall the tears of his country be dried,
> Nor long will his love stay behind him.'

My Lords: what have I to say, why sentence of death should not be pronounced on me according to law? I have nothing to say that can alter your predetermination, nor that will become me to say with any view to the mitigation of that sentence which you are here to pronounce, and I must abide by. But I have ... much to say, why my reputation should be rescued from the load of false accusation and calumny which has been heaped upon it.

I do not imagine that, seated where you are, your minds can be so free from impurity, as to receive the least impression from what I am going to utter. I have no hopes that I can anchor my character in the breast of a court constituted and trammelled as this is. I only wish – and it is the utmost I expect – that your Lordships may suffer it to float down your memories, untainted by the foul breath of prejudice, until it finds some more hospitable harbour to shelter it from the storms by which it is at present buffeted.

Were I only to suffer death, after being adjudged guilty by your tribunal, I should bow in silence, and meet the fate that awaits me without a murmur. But the sentence of the law, which delivers my body to the executioner, will, through the ministry of that law, labour, in its own vindication, to consign my character to obloquy. For there must be guilt somewhere – whether in the sentence of the court, or in the catastrophe, posterity must determine.

A man in my situation has not only to encounter the difficulties of fortune, and the force of power over minds which it has corrupted or subjugated, but also the difficulties of established prejudice. The man dies, but his memory lives. That mine may not perish, that it may live in the respect of my countrymen, I seize upon this opportunity to vindicate myself from some of the charges alleged against me.

When my spirits shall be wafted to a more friendly port; when my shade shall have joined the bands of those martyred heroes who have shed their blood on the scaffold and in the field in defence of their country and of virtue, this is my hope: I wish that my memory and name may animate those who survive me; while I look down with complacency on the destruction of that perfidious government, which upholds its domination by blasphemy of the Most High, which displays its power over men as over the beasts of the forest, which sets man upon his brother, and lifts his hand in the name of God against the throat of his fellow who believes or doubts a little more, or a little less than the government standard, a government which is steeled to barbarity by the cries of the orphans and the tears of the widows which it has made.

[*Here the Judge interrupted Emmet, saying that the mean and wicked enthusiasts who felt as he did were not equal to the accomplishment of their wild designs.*]

I appeal to the immaculate God. I swear by the throne of Heaven, before which I must shortly appear, by the blood of the murdered patriots who have gone before me, that my conduct has been through all this peril, and through all my purposes, governed only by the convictions which I have uttered, and by no other view than that of their cure, and the emancipation of my country from the super-inhuman oppression under which she has so long too patiently travailed; and that I confidently hope, that, wild and chimerical as it may appear, there is still union and strength in Ireland sufficient to accomplish this noblest enterprise …

Think not, my Lord, I say this for the petty gratification of giving you a transitory uneasiness. A man who never yet raised his voice to assert a lie will not hazard his character with posterity by asserting a falsehood on a subject so important to his country, and on an occasion like this. Yes, my Lord, a man who does not wish to have his epitaph written until his country is liberated will not leave a weapon in the power of envy, nor a pretence to impeach the probity which he means to preserve even in the grave to which tyranny consigns him.

[*Here Emmet was again interrupted by the Judge.*]

Again I say that what I have spoken was not intended for your Lordship, whose situation I commiserate, rather than envy. My expressions were for my countrymen. If there is a true Irishman present, let my last words cheer him in the hour of his affliction.

[*Another interruption from the Court.*]

I have always understood it to be the duty of a judge, when a prisoner has been convicted, to pronounce the sentence of the law. I have also understood that judges sometimes think it their duty to hear with patience, and to speak with humanity; to exhort the victim of the laws, and to offer, with tender benignity, his opinions of the motives by which he was actuated in the crime of which he had been adjudged guilty. That a judge has thought it his duty so to have done, I have no doubt; but where is the boasted freedom of your institutions? Where is the vaunted impartiality and clemency of your courts of justice, if an unfortunate prisoner, whom your policy, not pure justice, is about to deliver into the hands of the executioner, is not suffered to explain his motives sincerely and truly, to vindicate the principles by which he was actuated?

… If I stand at the bar of this court, and dare not vindicate my character, what a farce is your justice! If I stand at this bar, and dare not vindicate my character, how dare you calumniate it? Does the sentence of death which your unhallowed policy inflicts on my body, also condemn my tongue to silence, and my reputation to reproach?

Your executioner may abridge the period of my existence; but, while I exist, I shall not forbear to vindicate my character and motives from your aspersions …

I am charged with being an emissary of France. An emissary of France! And for what end? It is alleged that I wished to sell the independence of my country! And for what end? Was this the object of my ambition? And is this the mode by which a tribunal of justice reconciles contradictions? No; I am no emissary. My ambition was to hold a place among the deliverers of my country; not in power; not in profit; but in the glory of the achievement! Sell my country's independence to France? And for what? A change of masters! No; but for ambition! Oh, my country!

Was it personal ambition that influenced me, had it been the soul of my actions, could I not, by my education and fortune, by the rank and consideration of my family, have placed myself amongst the proudest of your oppressors? My country was my idol. To it, I sacrificed every selfish, every endearing sentiment, and to it I now offer up my life. Oh God …

It was the wish of my heart to extricate my country from this doubly-riveted despotism. I wished to place her independence beyond the reach of any power on earth. I wished to exalt her to that proud station in the world which Providence had destined her to fill.

Connection with France was, indeed, intended – but only so far as mutual interest would sanction or require. Were they to assume any authority inconsistent with the purest independence, it would be the signal for their destruction. We sought aid, and we sought it as we had assurances we should obtain it – as auxiliaries in war, and allies in peace. Were the French to come as invaders or enemies, uninvited by the wishes of the people, I should oppose them to the utmost of my strength …

I looked, indeed, for the assistance of France. I wished to prove to France and to the world that Irishmen deserved to be assisted; that they were indignant of slavery, and were ready to assert the independence and liberty of their country. I wished to procure for my country the guarantee which Washington[1] procured for America; to procure an aid which would, by its example, be as important as its valour: disciplined, gallant, pregnant with science and with experience … They would come to us as strangers and leave us as friends, after sharing in our perils, and elevating our destiny. My objects were not to receive new task-masters, but to expel old tyrants. These were my views, and these only became Irishmen. It was for these ends I sought aid from France – because France, even as an enemy, could not be more implacable than the enemy already in the

[1] GEORGE WASHINGTON was Commander-in-Chief of the colonial forces when France entered the War of Independence on the American side in 1778. An alliance had been signed by the United States and France in Feb 1778.

bosom of my country –

[*Another interruption from the Court.*]

I have been charged with that importance, in the efforts to emancipate my country, as to be considered the keystone of the combination of Irishmen, or as your Lordship expressed it, 'the life and blood of the conspiracy'. You do me honour over-much. You have given to the subaltern all the credit of a superior; there are men engaged in this conspiracy who are not only superior to me, but even to your own conceptions of yourself, my Lord. Men before the splendour of whose genius and virtues I should bow with respectful deference, and who would think themselves dishonoured to be called your friend; who would not disgrace themselves by shaking your bloodstained hand –

[*Another interruption.*]

What, my Lord, shall you tell me, on the passage to that scaffold – which that tyranny, of which you are only the intermediary executioner, has erected for my murder – that I am accountable for all the blood that has and will be shed in this struggle of the oppressed against the oppressor? Shall you tell me this, and must I be so very a slave as not to repel it?

I – who fear not to approach the Omnipotent Judge, to answer for the conduct of my whole life – am I to be appalled and falsified by a mere remnant of mortality here? By you too, who, if it were possible to collect all the innocent blood that you have shed, your unhallowed ministry, in one great reservoir, your Lordship might swim in it!

[*Another interruption.*]

Let no man dare, when I am dead, to charge me with dishonour. Let no man attaint my memory, by believing that I could engage in any cause but that of my country's liberty and independence; or that I could become the pliant minion of power in the oppression or the miseries of my countrymen. The Proclamation of the Provisional Government[2] speaks for my views; no inference can be tortured from it to countenance barbarity or debasement at home, or subjection, or humiliation, or treachery, from abroad …

My Lords, you seem impatient for the sacrifice. The blood for which you thirst is not congealed by the artificial terrors which surround your victim; it circulates warmly and unruffled through the channels which God created for noble purposes, but which you are bent to destroy for purposes so grievous, that they cry to Heaven.

Be yet patient! I have but a few words more to say. I am going to my cold and silent grave. My lamp of life is nearly extinguished; my race is run. The grave opens to receive me, and I sink into its bosom. I have but one request to ask at my departure from this world; it is the charity of its silence. Let no man write my epitaph, for as no man who knows my motives dare now vindicate them, let not prejudice or ignorance asperse them. Let them and me repose in obscurity, and my tomb remain uninscribed, until other times and other men can do justice to my character.

When my country takes her place among the nations of the earth, then, and not till then, let my epitaph be written.

I have done.

[2] A declaration of independence, drawn up by Emmet and his colleagues in 1803, which was read by Emmet on the day of the uprising.

William Faulkner
American novelist

William Cuthbert Falkner *later Faulkner* (1897–1962) was born near Oxford, Mississippi, into a long-established Southern family. He amended the spelling of his surname for reasons that remain uncertain. He trained as a pilot in the British Royal Air Force in Canada during World War I, but the war ended before his training finished, and he later attended Mississippi University. He took various jobs, and while working in New Orleans met the short-story writer Sherwood Anderson, who offered to recommend his first novel, *Soldier's Pay* (1926), to a publisher, on condition that he did not have to read it. In 1929 Faulkner took a job as a coal-heaver and while on night-shift at a local power station apparently wrote *As I Lay Dying* (1930) in just six weeks, working between midnight and 4am. *Sanctuary* (1931) was intended as a pot-boiler and was more successful commercially, but had a profound impact on the French authors Jean-Paul Sartre and Albert Camus. However, it is the lyrical style of novels like *The Sound and the Fury* (1929), *Light in August* (1932), *Absalom, Absalom!* (1936), *The Hamlet* (1940) and *Intruder in the Dust* (1948) that account for his reputation as one of the modern masters of the novel. Other titles include *Sartoris* (1929), *The Town* (1957) and *The Mansion* (1959), set, like most of the earlier books, in the imaginary Yoknapatawpha County, and *A Fable* (1954), an ambitious but unsuccessful reworking of Christ's Passion, set on the Western Front. He wrote numerous short stories and from 1932 worked also as a Hollywood screenwriter. He received the 1949 Nobel Prize for literature.

'I decline to accept the end of man'
10 December 1950, Stockholm, Sweden

When William Faulkner was nominated for the Nobel Prize in 1949, the vote in his favour was almost unanimous: the committee cited 'his powerful and artistically unique contribution to the modern American novel'. Speaking hesitantly in his Mississippi drawl, he accepted the award at a banquet at Stockholm City Hall in a brief speech which was somewhat amended for publication.

The speech focuses on Faulkner's concern that the pervasive fear of imminent nuclear holocaust – then widely discussed – was affecting the content of modern literature. Faulkner believed that this fear had affected modern writers so deeply that they were creating works which merely concentrated on the immediate and the ephemeral, showing scant understanding of the human spirit.

He frames his argument as a plea for writers to return to 'the old verities and truths of the heart, the old universal truths', insisting that literature could empower humankind to flourish rather than fall victim to extinction.

I feel that this award was not made to me as a man, but to my work – a life's work in the agony and sweat of the human spirit, not for glory and least of all for profit, but to create out of the materials of the human spirit something which did not exist before. So this award is only mine in trust. It will not be difficult to find a dedication for the money part of it, commensurate with the purpose and significance of its origin. But I would like to do the same with the acclaim too, by using this moment as a pinnacle from which I might be listened to by the young men and women already dedicated to the same anguish and travail, among whom is already that one who will some day stand here where I am standing.

Our tragedy today is a general and universal physical fear so long sustained by now that we can even bear it. There are no longer problems of the spirit. There is only the question: when will I be blown up? Because of this, the young man or woman writing today has forgotten the problems of the human heart in conflict with itself which alone can make good writing because only that is worth writing about, worth the agony and the sweat.

He must learn them again. He must teach himself that the basest of all things is to be afraid; and, teaching himself that, forget it forever, leaving no room in his workshop for anything but the old verities and truths of the heart, the old universal truths, lacking which any story is ephemeral and doomed — love and honour and pity and pride and compassion and sacrifice.

Until he does so, he labours under a curse. He writes not of love but of lust, of defeats in which nobody loses anything of value, of victories without hope and, worst of all, without pity or compassion. His griefs grieve on no universal bones, leaving no scars. He writes not of the heart but of the glands.

Until he relearns these things, he will write as though he stood among and watched the end of man. I decline to accept the end of man. It is easy enough to say that man is immortal simply because he will endure: that when the last dingdong of doom has clanged and faded from the last worthless rock hanging tideless in the last red and dying evening, that even then there will still be one more sound: that of his puny inexhaustible voice, still talking.

I refuse to accept this. I believe that man will not merely endure: he will prevail. He is immortal, not because he alone among creatures has an inexhaustible voice, but because he has a soul, a spirit capable of compassion and sacrifice and endurance. The poet's, the writer's duty is to write about these things. It is his privilege to help man endure by lifting his heart, by reminding him of the courage and honour and hope and pride and compassion and pity and sacrifice which have been the glory of his past. The poet's voice need not merely be the record of man, it can be one of the props, the pillars to help him endure and prevail.

Mary Fisher
American artist, writer and AIDS activist

Mary Fisher (1948–) was born in Louisville, Kentucky, to the philanthropists Max and Marjorie Fisher, and was raised near Detroit, Michigan. She was educated at the Cranbrook Academies, Wayne State University and the University of Michigan. Her career included stints in television production and as assistant to the President in the Gerald R Ford administration (1974–7). She and her husband, Brian Campbell, were parents to two sons, Max (born 1987) and Zachary (born 1989); Brian died of AIDS-related causes in 1993. Since 1992, she has campaigned extensively on HIV/AIDS in America, Europe and Africa. She founded the Family AIDS Network (1992) which in 2000 became the Mary Fisher Center for AIDS Research and Education (CARE) Fund at the University of Alabama, Birmingham. She has frequently given testimony to the US Congress and has twice been named to special presidential councils. She serves as board member and adviser to various international, national and regional charities including the UNAIDS Global Coalition for Women and AIDS, and the Center for Strategic and International Studies (CSIS) Task Force on HIV/AIDS. She is a recognized artist whose work in sculpture, printing and fabrics can be found in distinguished public and private collections. Her publications include *Sleep with the Angels* (1994), *I'll Not Go Quietly* (1995), *My Name Is Mary: A Memoir* (1995), *Angels in Our Midst* (1997), *ABATAKA* (2004) and *Messenger: A Self-Portrait* (2012). In 2006 she became a global emissary for the Joint United Nations Programme on HIV/AIDS.

'AIDS virus is not a political creature'
19 August 1992, Houston, Texas, USA

In the summer of 1991, television producer Mary Fisher was diagnosed with HIV, the virus that causes AIDS. After seven months of deliberation – during which she struggled with despair and alcohol – she decided to make her condition public, and to devote her life to campaigning for research, treatment and an end to the stigmatization of AIDS and HIV sufferers.

Soon afterwards, she found a prominent platform at the annual Republican National Convention. She had close links with the party: her father was a leading Republican adviser and she herself had worked for President Ford.

Her address was delivered with remarkable dignity and composure, and without reference to notes. In this accessible, restrained speech, she calls for awareness, compassion and action, identifying herself – a white, well-to-do, heterosexual mother – with the socially excluded groups often associated with the disease. She also warns against complacency, referring to Pastor Martin Niemöller's famous dictum, 'I was not a Jew, so, I did not protest'.

Fisher's straight-talking appeal won warm support from the convention and the speech quickly became famous under the title 'A Whisper of AIDS'. It was an early landmark in Fisher's long and continuing career as an AIDS campaigner.

[1] The Republican Party, led by President George H W Bush, was then in power.

Thank you. Thank you. Less than three months ago, at platform hearings in Salt Lake City, I asked the Republican Party[1] to lift the shroud of silence which has been draped over the issue of HIV and AIDS. I have come tonight to bring our silence to an end. I bear a message of challenge, not self-congratulation. I want your attention, not your applause.

I would never have asked to be HIV positive, but I believe that in all things there is a purpose; and I stand before you and before the nation gladly. The reality of AIDS is brutally clear. Two hundred thousand Americans are dead or dying. A million more are infected. Worldwide, 40 million, 60 million, or 100 million infections will be counted in the coming few years. But despite science and research, White House meetings and congressional hearings; despite good intentions and bold initiatives, campaign slogans and hopeful promises, it is – despite it all – the epidemic which is winning tonight.

In the context of an election year, I ask you, here in this great hall, or listening in the quiet of your home, to recognize that AIDS virus is not a political creature. It does not care whether you are Democrat or Republican; it does not ask whether you are black or white, male or female, gay or straight, young or old. Tonight I represent an AIDS community whose members have been reluctantly drafted from every segment of American society.

Though I am white and a mother, I am one with a black infant struggling with tubes in a Philadelphia hospital. Though I am female and contracted this disease in marriage[2] and enjoy the warm support of my family, I am one with the lonely gay man sheltering a flickering candle from the cold wind of his family's rejection.

[*Applause.*]

This is not a distant threat. It is a present danger. The rate of infection is increasing fastest among women and children. Largely unknown a decade ago, AIDS is the third leading killer of young adult Americans today. But it won't be third for long, because unlike other diseases, this one travels. Adolescents don't give each other cancer or heart disease because they believe they are in love, but HIV is different; and we have helped it along. We have killed each other with our ignorance, our prejudice and our silence.

We may take refuge in our stereotypes, but we cannot hide there long, because HIV asks only one thing of those it attacks. 'Are you human?' And this is the right question. 'Are you human?' Because people with HIV have not entered some alien state of being. They are human. They have not earned cruelty, and they do not deserve meanness. They don't benefit from being isolated or treated as outcasts. Each of them is exactly what God made – a person, not evil, deserving of our judgement; not victims, longing for our pity. People, ready for support and worthy of compassion.

[*Applause.*]

My call to you, my party, is to take a public stand, no less compassionate than that of the President and Mrs Bush.[3] They have embraced me and my family in memorable ways. In the place of judgement, they have shown affection. In difficult moments, they have raised our spirits. In the darkest hours, I have seen them reaching not only to me, but also to my parents, armed with that stunning grief and special grace that comes only to parents who have themselves leaned too long over the bedside of a dying child.

With the President's leadership, much good has been done. Much of the good has gone unheralded, and as the President has insisted, much remains to be done. But we do the President's cause no good if we praise the American family but ignore a virus that destroys it.

We must be consistent if we are to be believed. We cannot love justice and ignore prejudice, love our children and fear to teach them. Whatever our role as parent or policymaker, we must act as eloquently as we speak – else we have no integrity. My call to the nation is a plea for awareness. If you believe you are safe, you are in danger. Because I was not haemophiliac, I was not at risk. Because I was not gay, I was not at risk. Because I did not inject drugs, I was not at risk.

My father has devoted much of his lifetime guarding against another holocaust. He is part of the generation who heard Pastor Niemöller come out of the Nazi death camps to say, 'They came after the Jews, and I was not a Jew, so I did not protest. They came after the trade unionists, and I was not a trade unionist, so I did not protest. Then they came after the Roman Catholics, and I was not a Roman Catholic, so I did not protest. Then they came after me, and there was no-one left to protest.'[4]

[*Applause.*]

The lesson history teaches is this: if you believe you are safe, you are at risk. If you do not see this killer stalking your children, look again. There is no family or community, no race or religion, no place left in America that is

[2] Fisher and her husband were already divorced when she learned that he had AIDS, and that the infection had been transmitted to her.

[3] The First Lady Barbara Bush (1925–) was then engaged in social programmes relating to AIDS.

[4] Recorded in the US *Congressional Record*, 14 October 1968.

safe. Until we genuinely embrace this message, we are a nation at risk. Tonight, HIV marches resolutely toward AIDS in more than a million American homes, littering its pathway with the bodies of the young: young men, young women, young parents and young children.

One of those families is mine. If it is true that HIV inevitably turns to AIDS, then my children will inevitably turn to orphans. My family has been a rock of support. My 84-year-old father, who has pursued the healing of the nations, will not accept the premise that he cannot heal his daughter. My mother refuses to be broken. She still calls at midnight to tell wonderful jokes that make me laugh. Sisters and friends, and my brother Phillip, whose birthday is today, all have helped carry me over the hardest places. I am blessed, richly and deeply blessed, to have such a family.

[*Applause and cheers.*]

But not all of you have been so blessed. You are HIV positive, but dare not say it. You have lost loved ones, but you dared not whisper the word AIDS. You weep silently; you grieve alone. I have a message for you. It is not you who should feel shame; it is we. We who tolerate ignorance and practise prejudice; we who have taught you to fear. We must lift our shroud of silence, making it safe for you to reach out for compassion. It is our task to seek safety for our children, not in quiet denial, but in effective action.

Someday our children will be grown. My son Max, now four, will take the measure of his mother. My son Zachary, now two, will sort through his memories. I may not be here to hear their judgements, but I know already what I hope they are. I want my children to know that their mother was not a victim. She was a messenger. I do not want them to think, as I once did, that courage is the absence of fear. I want them to know that courage is the strength to act wisely when most we are afraid.

I want them to have the courage to step forward when called by their nation or their party and give leadership, no matter what the personal cost. I ask no more of you than I ask of myself or of my children. To the millions of you who are grieving, who are frightened, who have suffered the ravages of AIDS first-hand – have courage, and you will find support. To the millions who are strong, I issue the plea – set aside prejudice and politics to make room for compassion and sound policy.

[*Applause.*]

To my children, I make this pledge: I will not give in, Zachary, because I draw my courage from you. Your silly giggle gives me hope; your gentle prayers give me strength; and you, my child, give me the reason to say to America, 'You are at risk.' And I will not rest, Max, until I have done all I can to make your world safe. I will seek a place where intimacy is not the prelude to suffering. I will not hurry to leave you, my children, but when I go, I pray that you will not suffer shame on my account.

To all within the sound of my voice, I appeal. Learn with me the lessons of history and of grace, so my children will not be afraid to say the word 'AIDS' when I am gone. Then, their children and yours may not need to whisper it at all. God bless the children, and God bless us all.

Good night.

[*Standing ovation.*]

Michael Foot
English politician and journalist

Michael Mackintosh Foot (1913–2010) was born in Plymouth, Devon, the son of Isaac Foot. He was educated at Oxford, where he became president of the Union in 1933. He became assistant editor of the newly founded left-wing newspaper *Tribune* in 1937; and was later its joint editor (1948–52) and editor (1955–60). He was also acting editor of the *Evening Standard* (1942–4) and a political columnist on the *Daily Herald* (1944–64). He served as Labour MP for Ebbw Vale (1960–83) and Blaenau Gwent (1983–92), and was Secretary of State for Employment (1974–76), Lord President of the Privy Council and Leader of the House of Commons (1976–79) and deputy leader of the Labour Party (1976–80). In 1980 he replaced James Callaghan as Labour Party leader. A man of undoubted political integrity, he was known as a master of rhetoric in parliamentary debates, but proved no match for MARGARET THATCHER in the media-dominated election of 1983, at which Labour was heavily defeated. He was replaced that year by NEIL KINNOCK. A prominent figure on the left of the Labour Party and a pacifist, he was long a supporter of the Campaign for Nuclear Disarmament. His books include the influential *Guilty Men*, written with colleagues and published in 1940, a two-volume biography of ANEURIN BEVAN (1962, 1973) and a biography of the English author H G Wells (whom he had known), entitled *HG: The History of Mr Wells* (1995).

'Those about to die'
28 March 1979, London, England

This speech was delivered on a momentous day in British politics. The leader of the opposition, Conservative leader Margaret Thatcher, had introduced a motion of no confidence in the Labour government, citing 'inept handling' of the devolution referendums held in Scotland and Wales four weeks earlier. 'The essence of the motion,' she said, 'is that the government have failed the nation, that they have lost credibility, and that it is time for them to go.'

As deputy Labour leader, Michael Foot was fighting for his government's survival, yet there is little obvious sense of urgency in his speech. Typically, it is erudite, playful and relaxed.

He begins with a jibe at Donald Stewart, then leader of the Scottish National Party, who had also expressed a lack of confidence in the government. The majority of those who had voted in the referendum favoured devolution, but they had been defeated by a controversial clause that demanded 40 per cent of the *total electorate* must support the motion. This had provoked much bitterness in Scotland.

Foot then attacks another Scot, the relatively youthful Liberal leader DAVID STEEL. The 'Lib–Lab' pact of 1977–8, between the Liberals and a minority Labour government, had not lasted, and Steel had declared his party's intention to vote with the Conservatives to precipitate an election. Foot alludes mockingly to secret negotiations between Steel and Thatcher.

Finally, he turns on his principal foe Mrs Thatcher, whose opposition to devolution was well known, insisting that her party is unfit for power.

Immediately after Foot's speech, the government was defeated by a single vote. This led to the election of 3 May. The Conservatives swept to power, and remained in government for 18 years.

I believe that the right honourable Member for Western Isles[1] and his party have made an error in the way that they propose to vote. However misguided the right honourable gentleman may be if he adheres to his apparent resolution to vote in the Lobby with those who are most bitterly opposed to the establishment of a Scottish Assembly, honourable members who heard his speech must acknowledge the remarkable allegiance that the right honourable gentleman commands from his followers. It is one of the wonders of the world. There has been nothing quite like it since the armies of ancient Rome used to march into battle. It is only now that we see the right honourable gentleman in his full imperial guise.

'Hail Emperor – those about to die salute you.'

Which brings me to the leader of the Liberal Party.[2] He knows that I would not like to miss him out. I am sure that I shall elicit the support and

[1] The Scottish politician Donald Stewart (1920–92) served as Scottish National Party MP for the Western Isles, 1970–87, and as president of the party, 1982–7.

[2] When he was elected in 1965, David Steel was Britain's youngest MP. He became Liberal leader aged 38 in 1976, and led the party into a pact with the Labour Party, 1977–8.

sympathy of the right honourable lady when I say that she and I have always shared a common interest in the development of this young man. If the right honourable lady has anything to say about the matter, I shall be happy to give way to her.

I should very much like to know, as I am sure would everybody else, what exactly happened last Thursday night. I do not want to misconstrue anything, but did she send for him or did he send for her – or did they just do it by *billet-doux*? Cupid has already been unmasked. This is the first time I have ever seen a Chief Whip who could blush. He has every right to blush. Anybody who was responsible for arranging this most grisly of assignations has a lot to answer for.

That brings me to the right honourable lady. I have never in this House – or elsewhere, so far as I know – said anything discourteous to her, and I do not intend to do so. I do not believe that is the way in which politics should be conducted. That does not mean that we cannot exchange occasional pleasantries. What the right honourable lady has done today is to lead her troops into battle snugly concealed behind a Scottish Nationalist shield, with the boy David holding her hand.

I must say to the right honourable lady – and I should like to see her smile – that I am even more concerned about the fate of the right honourable gentleman than I am about her. She can look after herself. But the leader of the Liberal Party – and I say this with the utmost affection – has passed from rising hope to elder statesman without any intervening period whatsoever.

I hope that the House will excuse me if I refer to some of the speeches made by representatives of the smaller parties. Although there have been occasional mischievous attacks made on politicians in this House, and sometimes occasionally on myself, I believe that, especially in a parliament where there is no absolute majority, it is the duty of the Leader of the House[3] to be prepared to enter into conversation with representatives of all parties.

What is more, there is not one spokesman or representative of any smaller party in this House who can say that I have misled him on any occasion in any conversation I have had with him. I believe that that process assists the House in transacting its business, and I believe that the House of Commons will come to learn that ...

The leader of the opposition has not been able to explain very successfully to the House her special policy for dealing with devolution ... She proposed – and I think that this is a fair summary of what she said – talks about talks about talks. That is her proposal for devolution. In fact, I think that my summary of her reply is rather complimentary because what she really proposes is to do nothing at all.

[*Honourable Members: 'Good!'*]

Conservative backbenchers shout 'Good!' – and the honourable member for Stourbridge[4] shouts louder than anyone – but the leader of the opposition has, on the devolution question, torn up all the original policies of her party – the ones on which they fought the last general election – and she now proposes to do nothing. She has no proposals for a Scottish Assembly or any form of devolution or progress in that direction ...

In her speech today, the right honourable lady sought to make us forget what happened in the years of previous Conservative government. She also sought to give a very peculiar impression of the kind of legacy the Conservatives left behind for the Labour government who came into

[3] Foot refers to himself.

[4] The English politician John Stokes *later Sir John Stokes* (1917–2003) was a Conservative MP known for his staunch right-wing views.

power in 1974. It is interesting to note the things that she did not mention at all. She did not say a word about the balance of payments. I do not know whether she regards that as a matter of any significance. The fact is that the deficit in our balance of payments in the year that she and her right honourable friends left office was the biggest in our history – even bigger than the deficit that the Tory Party left us in 1964. But of course she wants all that to be wiped away from the public memory …

So what will happen? What will once again be the choice at the next election? It will not be so dissimilar from the choice that the country had to make in 1945,[5] or even in 1940 when the Labour Party had to come to the rescue of the country –

[*Honourable members: 'Oh!'*]

It was on a motion of the Labour Party that the House of Commons threw out the Chamberlain government in 1940. It was thanks to the Labour Party that Churchill had the chance to serve the country in the war years. Two-thirds of the Conservative Party at that time voted for the same reactionary policies as they will vote for tonight. It is sometimes in the most difficult and painful moments of our history that the country has turned to the Labour Party for salvation, and it has never turned in vain. We saved the country in 1940, and we did it again in 1945. We set out to rescue the country – or what was left of it – in 1974. Here again in 1979 we shall do it again …

We are quite prepared to have an election, but the Conservative Party has always had the idea that it was born to rule, although I should have thought that the country had been cured of that impression long since. It has always thought that everything must be decided according to the desires and whims of Conservative Central Office; that everything else is unpatriotic. Well, we say that this House of Commons should decide when an election takes place, and that the people will decide which government they will have to follow this one.

We believe that once the record is fully put to the country we shall come back here with the real majority that the Labour government require to govern for the next five years.

[5] At the election of July 1945, the wartime prime minister WINSTON CHURCHILL was unexpectedly defeated in a landslide victory for CLEMENT ATTLEE, whose Labour Party was considered better equipped to rebuild the country after World War II.

❧

'They have forgotten the rest of the trick'
29 October 1980, London, England

❧

When this speech was made, the Conservative Party led by MARGARET THATCHER had been in government for 18 months, and rapidly escalating unemployment was a key political issue. Thatcher had won election with the help of the famous campaign slogan, 'Labour isn't working', which referred to high unemployment figures.

Foot was still deputy leader of the Labour Party (he became its leader the following month). In an unemployment debate in the House of Commons, he tackled the government vigorously, declaring that the country was 'slithering into' its worst industrial and economic crisis since World War II. He conceded that unemployment had risen under the previous Labour administration, but insisted it had begun to fall before the election.

Foot's speech is characteristically satirical – and his childhood reminiscence about a conjuror certainly displays a gift for humorous anecdote. But singling out individual members of the Cabinet for gentle mockery may have been unwise, since his intention was to offer encouragement to dissenters, enlisting them to his cause. Yet he acknowledges that Cabinet dissent 'will not solve everything', hinting at Thatcher's notorious tenacity and single-mindedness, as well as the depth of the recession.

Foot's underlying seriousness of purpose is most apparent towards the end of the speech, where he introduces a rousing theme of defiance, threatening to mobilize a major protest campaign. The decade ahead was indeed one of protests – the miners' strike of 1984–5 being the most significant – but it was to be fully ten years before Thatcher was ousted.

❧

The situation is deteriorating much faster than anyone had previously assumed. Also, the prospects are grim. This coming winter will be a winter of fear and desolation for our people. Those are not just my views. They are the views of the CBI.[1] It says:

'We are now in a much more serious recession than that experienced in 1974–75. We would have to go back to before the war to find industry in comparable difficulties … Have we got to go through the next three or four years destroying great tracts of British industry to convince the world that sterling is overvalued?'

These are the sorts of statements that come from the CBI. When the latest report from the CBI reads rather like the front page of the *Tribune*,[2] perhaps we are moving very fast …

I gather that the Prime Minister is not so much impressed by these events because she insists that the policy will not be changed. 'The lady is not for turning.'[3]

[*Honourable members:* 'Burning.']

No, let us not have any misquotation. The lady is not for turning. I suppose that we have to change the old adage – if mother does not turn, none of us will turn. Is that the message that we are sending out from this House today? I do not believe that that is the case. I think that the Cabinet is in a slightly different mood from that.

We read in the newspapers that the Cabinet is to discuss these matters and possibly some aspects of public expenditure cuts tomorrow. I should like to intrude into that meeting, if I may, and offer my assistance to those sections of the Cabinet that deserve it.

The Secretary of State for Employment[4] is sometimes represented as a good man who fell among monetarists. I would not go as far as that. I shall come back to him in a moment. At any rate, I am chalking him up on my slate as one of the good ones.

Now let us look at the others. The situation has changed in the last few weeks. The Secretary of State for Defence[5] – I do not know whether he is here – is a formidable member of the Cabinet. He gets almost as big ovations at Tory conferences as the Prime Minister – and we know that is no accident. The right honourable gentleman has a powerful voice in the Cabinet. If he were to turn himself into the field marshal for the wets,[6] that would cause quite an event, because some of the others might pluck up their courage, too. That is two of them.

Where is the Lord Privy Seal,[7] the philosopher Tory – as H G Wells said, like military intelligence, a contradiction in terms?[8] His contempt for Tory policy is so determined that they all know it. That is three.

Now there is the Leader of the House.[9] We are told that at a fringe meeting at Brighton the Leader of the House came out in his true colours. We can imagine what a gaudy performance that would have been.

Now let us look at some of the others. Where is the Secretary of State for Scotland?[10] He must know what is going on, so we count him on that side.

What about the Secretary of State for Wales?[11] Which side is he on? Maybe they do not count him.

Where is the Minister for Agriculture, Fisheries and Food?[12] We have always counted on him … I bet the right honourable gentleman is upstairs saying that he does not believe in this monetarist malarky any more than we do. So we count him on our side; he is one of us …

[1] The Confederation of British Industry, founded in 1965 to lobby government on behalf of British businesses.

[2] The weekly newspaper produced by left-wing members of the Labour Party. Foot had been its editor, 1955–60.

[3] A famous declaration of intransigence made by Margaret Thatcher in a speech of 10 October 1980, which is included in this book. The phrase alludes to *The Lady's Not for Burning* (1949), a play about Joan of Arc by the English playwright Christopher Fry (1907–2005).

[4] The English politician James Prior *later Baron Prior* (1927–) served as Secretary of State for Employment, 1979–81.

[5] The English politician Francis Pym *later Baron Pym* (1922–2008) served as Secretary of State for Defence, 1979–81.

[6] A usually derogatory term for moderate Conservatives.

[7] The Scottish politician Sir Ian Gilmour, 3rd Baronet *later Baron Gilmour of Craigmillar* (1926–2007) served as Lord Privy Seal, 1979–81.

[8] This may be a mistake on Foot's part. In his satirical novel *Tono-Bungay* (1909), Wells has his protagonist describe the phrase 'trained in research' as a 'ridiculous contradiction in terms'. The phrase 'Military intelligence is a contradiction in terms' is usually attributed to the US comedian Groucho Marx (1890–1977).

[9] The English politician Norman St John-Stevas *later Baron St John of Fawsley* (1929–2012) served as Leader of the House of Commons, 1979–81, following Foot in the post.

[10] The Scottish politician George Younger *later Baron Younger of Leckie* and *4th Viscount Younger of Leckie* (1931–2003) served as Secretary of State for Scotland, 1979–86.

[11] The Welsh politician Nicholas Edwards *later Baron Crickhowell* (1934–) served as Secretary of State for Wales, 1979–87.

[12] The English politician Peter Walker *later Baron Walker of Worcester* (1932–2010) served as Minister of Agriculture, Fisheries and Food, 1979–83.

The Foreign Secretary[13] is an influential chap. I dare say that he is a bit persuaded by the Lord Privy Seal ... I believe that the Foreign Secretary can be persuaded on to the side of enlightenment in the discussions tomorrow.

Whom does that leave? Where is the Home Secretary,[14] the long-playing vice captain? I suppose that we can add him to the list ...

The seriousness of the situation is that the government, I believe, want to apply their minds to the problem. The Cabinet tomorrow will be quite a serious affair. I hope that I have contributed a little to its understanding. I hope that there will be people there to speak for Wales, Scotland, Northern Ireland, Merseyside, the North-East, the Midlands, London and Lancashire – to speak for Britain, for all the places that need a voice to speak for them.

The only people who seriously believe in the policy that the government are pursuing is the diminishing little band headed by the right honourable lady. I sometimes feel that, when the right honourable lady stands on the burning deck all alone at the end, the only person who will be supporting her will be the Minister for Social Security.[15] I have warned the right honourable lady before. Does she not realize that we have put him here as an *agent provocateur* in order to test what damn fool statements can be made in Tory governments? I warn the right honourable lady that she needs a few better companions around her if she wants to deal with unemployment.

I realize that I have discriminated in favour of the wets. I have revealed to the House quite openly, as I would normally do, who are my favourites, but I should not like to miss out the Secretary of State for Industry,[16] who has had a tremendous effect on the Government and our politics generally. As I see the right honourable gentleman walking around the country, looking puzzled, forlorn and wondering what has happened, I try to remember what he reminds me of. The other day I hit on it.

In my youth, quite a time ago, when I lived in Plymouth, every Saturday night I used to go to the Palace Theatre. My favourite act was a magician-conjuror who used to have sitting at the back of the audience a man dressed as a prominent alderman. The magician-conjuror used to say that he wanted a beautiful watch from a member of the audience. He would go up to the alderman and eventually take from him a marvellous gold watch. He would bring it back to the stage, enfold it in a beautiful red handkerchief, place it on the table in front of us, take out his mallet, hit the watch and smash it to smithereens.

Then on his countenance would come exactly the puzzled look of the Secretary of State for Industry. He would step to the front of the stage and say, 'I am very sorry. I have forgotten the rest of the trick.' That is the situation of the government. They have forgotten the rest of the trick. It does not work. Lest any objector should suggest that the act at the Palace Theatre was only a trick, I should assure the House that the magician-conjuror used to come along at the end and say, 'I am sorry. I have still forgotten the trick.'

... The troubled mind in the Conservative Party is widespread. Everyone who has listened to the speeches of Conservative members can see that it is becoming very widespread. I am so generous that I will not even ask those Conservative Members who agree with the government's policies to put up their hands. I do not believe that we would get even the few who enthusiastically obeyed on the previous occasion ...

What will happen if the Cabinet manage to say that the lady must turn?

[13] The English politician Peter Carington, 6th Baron Carrington (1919–) served as Foreign Secretary, 1979–82.

[14] The Scottish politician William Whitelaw *later 1st Viscount Whitelaw* (1918–99) served as Home Secretary, 1979–83, and as Deputy Prime Minister, 1979–88.

[15] The English politician Patrick Jenkin *later Baron Jenkin of Roding* (1926–) served in the post, technically known as Secretary of State for Social Services, 1979–81.

[16] The English lawyer and politician Sir Keith Joseph, 2nd Baronet *later Baron Joseph* (1918–94) served as Secretary of State for Industry, 1979–81.

That will not solve everything. I agree with my right honourable friend the Member for Leeds East,[17] who said that earlier in the debate. However, it will assist, and the sooner we can get it, the better. If they do not succeed in that, they will all go down, because in the meantime we shall organize the biggest protest campaign that this country has seen since the 1930s. We shall have a campaign from one end of the country to the other ...

I believe that in the course of the campaign we shall be able to restore hope to our people, because there is no future for our country in the gospels of despair, in the doctrines of mass unemployment, in the idea that the way in which people can be made to work is by being whipped to work, whether by whips or scorpions.

What we must restore to the country is the proper sense of community in dealing with this great crisis. Just as in the greatest crises of our country in this century it was the Labour movement that came to the rescue, so it will be on this occasion too. We give due notice to the Conservative Party that we intend from this moment on to rouse the country from one end to the other and to ensure that as soon as the opportunity comes we get not merely what we had for five years — a tender, difficult situation with a majority one day and no majority the next — but the full majority to carry through the democratic, socialist reforms that this country requires.

Charles James Fox
English politician

Charles James Fox (1749–1806) was born in London, third son of the English politician Henry Fox *later 1st Baron Holland* (1705–74). Educated at Eton and Hertford College, Oxford, he became the MP for Midhurst at the age of 19. He later became a supporter of Lord North (prime minister 1770–82), and a Lord of the Admiralty. In 1772 he resigned, but the next year was named a commissioner of the Treasury. North dismissed him in 1775 after a quarrel. During the American War of Independence, Fox was the most formidable opponent of the coercive measures of government. After the downfall of North (1782), he was a Secretary of State. In 1783 the short-lived North–Fox coalition was formed, and Fox resumed his former office, but the rejection of his East India Bill by the Lords led to the resignation of his government at the end of the year. When William Pitt, the Younger, came to power, the long contest between him and Fox began. The regency, the trial of Warren Hastings, former governor-general of India, and the French Revolution afforded scope to his talents, and he employed his influence to modify and counteract the policy of his rival. He was a strenuous opponent of the war with France, and an advocate of non-intervention. After Pitt's death in 1806, Fox, recalled to office as Leader of the House of Commons, set into motion negotiations for a peace with France. He was on the point of introducing a bill for the abolition of the slave trade when he died. Although Fox was addicted to gambling and drinking, EDMUND BURKE called him 'the greatest debater the world ever saw'. He was buried, near Pitt, in Westminster Abbey, London.

'What is the most odious species of tyranny?'
1 December 1783, London, England

The occasion of this classic statement of Whig principles was a parliamentary debate on Fox's East India Bill, which sought to bring the British East India Company's growing empire under the control of Parliament. In his speech, Fox criticizes the company's management and accuses its employees of corruption and tyranny. He proposed that, for five years, Parliament appoint seven commissioners to rule company affairs. This would strip the company of the royal charter it had held since 1601, a measure that provoked great hostility.

Fox's speech is a response to that opposition, in advance of a vote on the bill. Besides influential people within the company, Fox had to contend with opposition from King George III, who wanted to maintain his royal prerogative and besides, disliked Fox intensely. Fox pointedly compares those who criticize his bill for violating the company's chartered rights with those who argued that England's constitutional revolution of 1688 – the cornerstone of the 18th-century British state – was a violation of the chartered rights of the deposed James II.

Although Fox pays reverence to the Crown, he skilfully evokes the spirit of 1688 by stating that if trust is abused, a response is justified. The bill went on to be passed comfortably in the Commons, but was defeated by the Lords. Knowing the King would pressure the Lords to reject the bill as a challenge to hereditary authority, Fox boldly suggests that Britain is again faced with the problem of a king intent on abusing his position.

Sir, the necessity of my saying something upon the present occasion, is so obvious to the House, that no apology will, I hope, be expected from me for troubling them even at so late an hour.[1] I shall not enter much into a detailed or minute defence of the particulars of the bill before you, because few particular objects have been made; the opposition to it consisting only in general reasonings, of little application some, and some totally distinct from the point in question.

This bill has been combated through its past stages upon various principles; but to this moment the House has not heard it canvassed upon its own intrinsic merits. The debate this night has turned chiefly upon two points – violation of charter, and increase of influence; and upon both these points I shall say a few words.

The honourable gentleman who opened the debate[2] ... charges me with abandoning that cause, which, he says, in terms of flattery, I had once so successfully asserted. I tell him, in reply, that if he were to search the history of my life, he would find that the period of it, in which I struggled

[1] This speech was given at two o'clock in the morning.

[2] The English politician Thomas Powys *later 1st Baron Lilford* (1743–1800).

most for the real, substantial cause of liberty, is this very moment that I am addressing you. Freedom, according to my conception of it, consists in the safe and sacred possession of a man's property, governed by laws defined and certain; with many personal privileges – natural, civil, and religious – which he cannot surrender without ruin to himself; and of which to be deprived by any other power is despotism. This bill, instead of subverting, is destined to give stability to these principles; instead of narrowing the basis of freedom, it tends to enlarge it; instead of suppressing, its object is to infuse and circulate the spirit of liberty.

What is the most odious species of tyranny? Precisely that which this bill is meant to annihilate. That a handful of men, free themselves, should execute the most base and abominable despotism over millions of their fellow creatures;[3] that innocence should be the victim of oppression; that industry should toil for rapine; that the harmless labourer should sweat, not for his own benefit, but for the luxury and rapacity of tyrannic depredation; in a word, that 30 million of men gifted by Providence with the ordinary endowments of humanity, should groan under a system of despotism, unmatched in all the histories of the world.

What is the end of all government? Certainly the happiness of the governed. Others may hold other opinions; but this is mine, and I proclaim it. What are we to think of a government, whose good fortune is supposed to spring from the calamities of its subjects, whose aggrandizement grows out of the miseries of mankind? This is the kind of government exercised under the East India Company upon the natives of Indostan; and the subversion of that infamous government is the main object of the bill in question. But in the progress of accomplishing this end, it is objected that the charter of the company should not be violated; and upon this point, Sir, I shall deliver my opinion without disguise.

A charter is a trust to one or more persons for some given benefit. If this trust be abused, if the benefit be not obtained, and its failure arises from palpable guilt, or (what in this case is full as bad) from palpable ignorance or mismanagement, will any man gravely say that trust should not be resumed, and delivered to other hands, more especially in the case of the East India Company, whose manner of executing this trust, whose laxity and languor produced – and tend to produce – consequences diametrically opposite to the ends of confiding that trust, and of the institution for which it was granted?

I beg of gentlemen to be aware of the lengths to which their arguments upon the intangibility of this charter may be carried. Every syllable virtually impeaches the establishment by which we sit in this House, in the enjoyment of this freedom, and of every other blessing of our government. These kinds of arguments are batteries against the main pillar of the British constitution.

Some men are consistent with their own private opinions – and discover the inheritance of family maxims – when they question the principles of the revolution; but I have no scruple in subscribing to the articles of that creed which produced it. Sovereigns are sacred, and reverence is due to every king: yet … had I lived in the reign of James II, I should most certainly have contributed my efforts, and borne part in those illustrious struggles which vindicated an empire from hereditary servitude, and recorded this valuable doctrine, 'that trust abused is revocable'.[4]

No man, sir, will tell me that a trust to a company of merchants stands upon the solemn and sanctified ground by which a trust is committed to a

[3] The population of India, which then stood at around 30 million.

[4] The British monarch King James II of England and VII of Scotland (1633–1701) was forced to abdicate by the Whig revolutions of 1688–9, which asserted the respective constitutional rights of the English and Scottish parliaments of the time to remove a tyrannical monarch.

monarch; and I am at a loss to reconcile the conduct of men who approve that resumption of violated trust – which rescued and re-established our unparallelled and admirable constitution with a thousand valuable improvements and advantages at the revolution – and who, at this moment, rise up the champions of the East India Company's charter; although the incapacity and incompetence of that company to a due and adequate discharge of the trust deposited in them by that charter are themes of ridicule and contempt to all the world; and although – in consequence of their mismanagement, connivance, and imbecility, combined with the wickedness of their servants – the very name of an Englishman is detested, even to a proverb, through all Asia, and the national character is become degraded and dishonoured.

To rescue that name from odium, and redeem this character from disgrace, are some of the objects of the present bill; and gentlemen should, indeed, gravely weigh their opposition to a measure which, with a thousand other points not less valuable, aims at the attainment of these objects.

Those who condemn the present bill as a violation of the chartered rights of the East India Company, condemn, on the same ground, I say again, the revolution as a violation of the chartered rights of King James II. He, with as much reason, might have claimed the property of dominion; but what was the language of the people? 'No, you have no property in dominion; dominion was vested in you, as it is in every chief magistrate, for the benefit of the community to be governed; it was a sacred trust delegated by compact; you have abused that trust; you have exercised dominion for the purposes of vexation and tyranny – not of comfort, protection, and good order – and we therefore resume the power which was originally ours. We recur to the first principles of all government, the will of the many; and it is our will that you shall no longer abuse your dominion.'

The case is the same with the East India Company's government over a territory – as it has been said by my honourable friend[5] – of 280,000 square miles in extent, nearly equal to all Christian Europe, and containing 30 million of the human race. It matters not whether dominion arises from conquest, or from compact. Conquest gives no right to the conqueror to be a tyrant; and it is no violation of right to abolish the authority which is misused.

[5] Fox's ally Edmund Burke, who had drafted the East India Bill.

'Your fall is certain and your destruction inevitable'
25 November 1795, London, England

Freedom of speech has called for robust defence at certain points in British history, and this is one such moment. In 1795, Parliament was faced with William Pitt, the Younger's sedition and treason bills, which intended to make subversive words, spoken or written, a treasonable offence, even if they did not lead to direct action. Fox's response was fierce.

The bills had been drafted by Pitt after a stone was thrown that shattered the window of the King's coach on its way to the opening of the Commons. Pitt believed the attack was evidence of a revolution brewing in Britain, and his legislation also proposed banning any public gathering not approved by a magistrate. The latest episode in a trend of state repression following the French Revolution and the declaration of war against France in 1793, Pitt's bills were an attempt to block 'French' ideas.

Whereas Pitt had become increasingly powerful among the elite by defending the status quo, Fox – who had celebrated the fall of the Bastille in 1789, which marked the beginning of the French Revolution – represented radical sympathies among the people. Fox argued that English notions of liberty, which had created the wealth and success of the English nation, were being undermined by Pitt.

In a powerful comparison with the seeds that planted the decline of ancient Rome, Fox argues that Pitt's bills, if passed, would destroy the foundation of England and that – like Rome – its greatness would crumble. Despite popular protests and petitions, during which Fox spoke before large audiences, the bills were passed the following month.

❧

The honourable and learned gentleman, in one part of his speech, and only in one, seems to have a reference to the bill before the House. The honourable and learned gentleman admits that the House is going to make a sacrifice by the measure before them; but contends that what is retained of the rights of the people is still of higher value …

I do not, however, agree with him, that what we are to retain is superior to what we have to lose, if the bill is passed into a law. That which is to be taken away is the foundation of the building. It might, indeed, be said, that there are beautiful parts of the building still left. The same might be said of another building that was undermined: 'Here is a beautiful saloon, there is a fine drawing-room; here are elegant paintings, there elegant and superb furniture; here an extensive and well chosen library.' But if the foundation is undermined, there can be nothing to rest upon, and the whole edifice must soon fall to the ground. Such would be the case with our constitution, if the bill should pass into a law.

Our government is valuable, because it is free. What, I beg gentlemen to ask themselves, are the fundamental parts of a free government? I know there is a difference of opinion upon that subject. My own opinion is that freedom does not depend upon the executive government, nor upon the administration of justice, nor upon any one particular or distinct part, nor even upon forms, so much as it does on the general freedom of speech and of writing. With regard to freedom of speech, the bill before the House is a direct attack upon that freedom.

No man dreads the use of a universal proposition more than I do myself. I must nevertheless say that speech ought to be completely free, without any restraint whatever, in any government pretending to be free. By being completely free, I do not mean that a person should not be liable to punishment for abusing that freedom, but I mean freedom in the first instance.

The press is so at present, and I rejoice it is so. What I mean is that any man may write and print what he pleases, although he is liable to be punished if he abuses that freedom; this I call perfect freedom in the first instance. If this is necessary with regard to the press, it is still more so with regard to speech. An *imprimatur* has been talked of, and it would be dreadful enough; but a *dicatur* would be still more horrible. No man has been daring enough to say that the press should not be free: but the bill before them does not, indeed, punish a man for speaking, it prevents him from speaking.

For my own part, I have never heard of any danger arising to a free state from the freedom of the press, or freedom of speech. So far from it, I am perfectly clear that a free state could not exist without both. The honourable and learned gentleman has said, would we not preserve the remainder by giving up this liberty? I admit that, by passing of the bill, the people would have lost a great deal. A great deal! Aye, all that is worth preserving.

For you will have lost the spirit, the fire, the freedom, the boldness, the energy of the British character, and with them its best virtue. I say, it is not the written law of the constitution of England; it is not the law that is to be found in books, that has constituted the true principle of freedom in any country, at any time. No! it is the energy, the boldness of a man's mind, which prompts him to speak, not in private, but in large and popular assemblies, that constitutes, that creates, in a state, the spirit of freedom.

This is the principle which gives life to liberty; without it the human character is a stranger to freedom. If you suffer the liberty of speech to be wrested from you, you will then have lost the freedom, the energy, the boldness of the British character.

It has been said that the right honourable gentleman rose to his present eminence by the influence of popular favour, and that he is now kicking away the ladder by which he mounted to power. Whether such was the mode by which the right honourable gentleman attained his present situation I am a little inclined to question; but I can have no doubt that if this bill shall pass, England herself will have thrown away that ladder, by which she has risen to wealth (but that is the last consideration), to honour, to happiness and to fame.

Along with energy of thinking and liberty of speech, she will forfeit the comforts of her situation, and the dignity of her character, those blessings which they have secured to her at home, and the rank by which she has been distinguished among the nations. These were the sources of her splendour, and the foundation of her greatness –

'*Sic fortis Etruria crevit, Scilicet et rerum facta est pulcherrima Roma.*'[1]

We need only appeal to the example of that great city, whose prosperity the poet has thus recorded. In Rome, when the liberty of speech was gone, along with it vanished all that had constituted her the mistress of the world. I doubt not but in the days of Augustus[2] there were persons who perceived no symptoms of decay, who exulted even in their fancied prosperity, when they contemplated the increasing opulence and splendid edifices of that grand metropolis, and who even deemed that they possessed their ancient liberty, because they still retained those titles of offices which had existed under the republic.

What fine panegyrics were then pronounced on the prosperity of the Empire! '*Tum tutus bos prata perambulat.*'[3] This was flattery to Augustus: to that great destroyer of the liberties of mankind, as much an enemy to freedom as any of the detestable tyrants who succeeded him. So with us, we are to be flattered with an account of the form of our government, by king, Lords and Commons – '*Eadem magistratuum vocabula.*'[4]

There were some then, as there are now, who said that the energy of Rome was not gone; while they felt their vanity gratified in viewing their city, which had been converted from brick into marble, they did not reflect that they had lost that spirit of manly independence which animated the Romans of better times, and that the beauty and splendour of their city served only to conceal the symptoms of rottenness and decay.

So if this bill passes you may, for a time, retain your institution of juries and the forms of your free constitution. But the substance is gone, the foundation is undermined, your fall is certain and your destruction inevitable. As a tree that is injured at the root and the bark taken off, the branches may live for a while, some sort of blossom may still remain; but it will soon wither, decay, and perish: so take away the freedom of speech or of writing, and the foundation of all your freedom is gone.

You will then fall, and be degraded and despised by all the world for your

[1] Latin: 'Thus Etruria grew to greatness,/And Rome became the loveliest of all things.' Virgil, *Georgics*, II.

[2] Caesar Augustus (63BC–AD14) is usually regarded as the first ruler of the Roman Empire, which Whigs saw as representing moral decay and corrupt government, Augustus's era marks the end of the republican 'golden age'.

[3] Latin: 'The cattle range safely in the meadow.' Horace, *Odes*, IV. 5.

[4] Latin: 'The magistrates held onto their titles.' Tacitus, *Annals*, I.

weakness and your folly, in not taking care of that which conducted you to all your fame, your greatness, your opulence, and prosperity. But before this happens, let the people once more be tried. I am a friend to taking the sense of the people, and therefore a friend to this motion. I wish for every delay that is possible in this important and alarming business. I wish for this adjournment – '*Spatium requiemque furori.*'[5]

Let us put a stop to the madness of this bill; for if you pass it, you will take away the foundation of the liberty of the people of England, and then farewell to any happiness in this country!

[5] Latin: 'To give space and rest to madness.' Virgil, *Aeneid*, IV.

St Francis of Assisi
Italian missionary

St Francis of Assisi *baptized Giovanni; originally Francesco di Pietro di Bernardone* (c.1181–1226) was born in Assisi, the son of a wealthy merchant. He was highly sociable and fond of good living. Around 1205, however, he joined a military expedition, then – following a prophetic dream – returned to live as a hermit and devoted himself to the care of the poor and the sick. By 1210 he had a brotherhood of eleven, for which he drew up a rule repudiating all property, which was originally approved by Pope Innocent III. In 1212 he also founded the 'Poor Clares', a Franciscan order for women. The first General Assembly in 1219 was attended by 5,000 members, and 500 more were claimants for admission. Francis went to Egypt (1223) and preached in the presence of the Sultan, who promised better treatment for his Christian prisoners. On his return to Italy, he is said to have received, while praying, the stigmata of the wounds of JESUS (1224). His works consist of letters, sermons, ascetic treatises, proverbs and hymns, including the well-known 'Canticle of the Sun'. He was canonized by Pope Gregory IX in 1228, and in 1980 was designated patron saint of ecology. His feast day is 4 October.

'My little sisters the birds'
c.1220, Italy

This homily attributed to St Francis emphasizes his special regard for animals – of which he is patron saint – and in particular birds. According to legend, creatures had no fear of him and could understand his words. One story tells how he persuaded a wolf to stop attacking the people and livestock of the town of Gubbio, near Assisi.

Francis regarded nature as a mirror, reflecting God's beauty and bounteousness (which led to his designation as patron saint of the environment). This sermon illustrates his unorthodox belief that all creatures had the ability and duty to worship God. However, his words can also be understood metaphorically, as an exhortation to humans, as much as to birds, to beware of 'the sin of ingratitude'.

My little sisters the birds: much bounden are ye unto God, your creator, and always in every place ought ye to praise Him, for that He hath given you liberty to fly about everywhere, and hath also given you double and triple raiment.

Moreover he preserved your seed in the ark of Noah, that your race might not perish out of the world.[1] Still more are ye beholden to Him for the element of the air which He hath appointed for you. Beyond all this, ye sow not, neither do you reap; and God feedeth you, and giveth you the streams and fountains for your drink; the mountains and valleys for your refuge and the high trees whereon to make your nests; and because ye know not how to spin or sow, God clotheth you, you and your children; wherefore your creator loveth you much, seeing that He hath bestowed on you so many benefits.

And therefore, my little sisters, beware of the sin of ingratitude, and study always to give praises unto God.

[1] See Genesis 6–9.

Benjamin Franklin
American statesman, diplomat and scientist

Benjamin Franklin *also known as Richard Saunders* (1706–90) was born in Boston, the 15th of 17 children. He was apprenticed at the age of twelve to his brother James, a printer, who started a newspaper in 1721. The two later fell out and Benjamin drifted to Philadelphia, where he became a printer. He worked in London (1724–6) before returning to Philadelphia to establish his own printing house, and in 1729 he purchased the *Pennsylvania Gazette*. In 1732 he began publishing *Poor Richard's Almanac*, which became popular for its witty aphorisms. He helped found Philadelphia's first subscription library, paid police force and hospital, volunteer fire department and academy (later the University of Pennsylvania). He was appointed Clerk of the Assembly (1736), Postmaster of Philadelphia (1737), and then Deputy Postmaster-General for the colonies (1753), and was a member of the Assembly almost uninterruptedly until his first mission to England. He invented the Franklin stove and its commercial success encouraged him to abandon printing. In 1746 he commenced his famous researches in electricity. He also researched storms and the Gulf Stream. A staunch advocate of colonial rights, he proposed a Plan of Union in 1754. In 1757 he was sent to England, where he lobbied successfully for the province's right to tax landowners for the cost of defending their territory from the French and the Native Americans. In 1764 he returned to England to contest, unsuccessfully, the taxation of the colonies without representation. He returned to the USA in 1775, and helped draft the Declaration of Independence. He was sent to Paris in 1776 to seek assistance for the war and in February 1778 a treaty of alliance was signed. Munitions and money from France facilitated American victory in the War of Independence. Franklin helped negotiate the Treaty of Paris (1783), ending the war with Great Britain, and remained US Minister in Paris till 1785, when he returned to Philadelphia. In 1787 he was a delegate to the convention which framed the US Constitution. He retired from public life in 1788, but remained active. At 83 he invented bifocal eyeglasses. He suffered from bladder stones and died dependent on opium to relieve the pain. His classic *Autobiography*, not published in full until 1868, reflects his wide-ranging interests and passion for self-improvement, although it reveals little of the irreverent temperament that made him one of the most appealing of the founding fathers.

'I agree to this Constitution with all its faults'
17 September 1787, Philadelphia, Pennsylvania, USA

At the Constitutional Convention held at Philadelphia in May–September 1787, 55 delegates were charged with the task of rewriting the Articles of Confederation, under which the USA had been governed since 1781. The Articles had proved to be unworkable and a new scheme of government was needed. Political compromises were negotiated, particularly over crucial issues such as states' rights, slavery and, especially, representation in Congress. Eventually, the 'Great Compromise' was accepted – creating a bicameral legislature – and other important questions were settled, chief among them the inclusion of ten Amendments, which formed a written Bill of Rights. The Constitution was finally ratified in 1791.

Although Franklin was not universally liked, he was respected as one of the few delegates with an international reputation. His droll sense of humour, which he used to great effect in serious matters, is much in evidence in this speech. His personal reservations concerning the Constitution stemmed from his preference for a unicameral legislature and an executive committee (instead of a presidential executive). However, in the interests of unity he recommended ratification to the delegates and his motion was carried.

Franklin was too ill to give his own speech on the final day of the convention. Although he rose to speak and had, unusually, written his address out on paper, it was delivered instead by James Wilson, his fellow delegate from Pennsylvania. The most common transcriptions come from contemporaneous notes on the debate by the future president James Madison, chief drafter of the Constitution.

> Mr President: I confess that there are several parts of this Constitution which I do not at present approve, but I am not sure I shall never approve them, for having lived long, I have experienced many instances of being obliged by better information, or fuller consideration, to change opinions even on important subjects, which I once thought right, but found to be otherwise.
>
> It is, therefore, that the older I grow, the more apt I am to doubt my own

judgement, and to pay more respect to the judgement of others. Most men indeed, as well as most sects in religion, think themselves in possession of all truth, and that wherever others differ from them it is so far error. Steele[1] (a Protestant) in a dedication tells the Pope that the only difference between our churches in their opinions of the certainty of their doctrines is: the Church of Rome is infallible and the Church of England is never in the wrong.

But though many private persons think almost as highly of their own infallibility as of that of their sect, few express it so naturally as a certain French lady, who in a dispute with her sister, said, 'I don't know how it happens, sister, but I meet with nobody but myself, that's always in the right – *Il n'y a que moi qui a toujours raison.*'

In these sentiments, sir, I agree to this Constitution with all its faults, if they are such; because I think a general government necessary for us, and there is no form of government but what may be a blessing to the people if well administered; and believe farther that this is likely to be well administered for a course of years, and can only end in despotism – as other forms have done before it – when the people shall become so corrupted as to need despotic government, being incapable of any other.

I doubt too whether any other convention we can obtain may be able to make a better constitution. For when you assemble a number of men to have the advantage of their joint wisdom, you inevitably assemble with those men, all their prejudices, their passions, their errors of opinion, their local interests, and their selfish views.

From such an assembly can a perfect production be expected? It therefore astonishes me, sir, to find this system approaching so near to perfection as it does; and I think it will astonish our enemies, who are waiting with confidence to hear that our councils are confounded like those of the builders of Babel;[2] and that our States are on the point of separation, only to meet hereafter for the purpose of cutting one another's throats.

Thus I consent, sir, to this Constitution because I expect no better, and because I am not sure that it is not the best. The opinions I have had of its errors, I sacrifice to the public good. I have never whispered a syllable of them abroad. Within these walls they were born, and here they shall die. If every one of us, in returning to our constituents, were to report the objections he has had to it, and endeavour to gain partisans in support of them, we might prevent its being generally received, and thereby lose all the salutary effects and great advantages resulting naturally in our favour among foreign nations, as well as among ourselves, from our real or apparent unanimity.

Much of the strength and efficiency of any government, in procuring and securing happiness to the people, depends on opinion – on the general opinion of the goodness of the government, as well as of the wisdom and integrity of its governors. I hope, therefore, that for our own sakes as a part of the people, and for the sake of posterity, we shall act heartily and unanimously in recommending this Constitution (if approved by congress and confirmed by the conventions), wherever our influence may extend, and turn our future thoughts and endeavours to the means of having it well administered.

On the whole, sir, I can not help expressing a wish that every member of the convention who may still have objections to it would, with me, on this occasion, doubt a little of his own infallibility, and to make manifest our unanimity, put his name to this instrument.

[1] The Anglo-Irish essayist, dramatist and politician Sir Richard Steele (1672–1729), co-founder of *The Spectator* magazine.

[2] Possessed by pride, humankind attempted to build the Tower of Babel, a structure reaching up to the heavens. In order to prevent this, God caused them to speak in different languages. Unable to communicate, they were forced to abandon the project. See Genesis 11:1–9.

Betty Friedan
American feminist and writer

Elizabeth Naomi Friedan *née Goldstein* (1921–2006) was born in Peoria, Illinois, and educated at Smith College in Northampton, Massachusetts. Her bestselling book *The Feminine Mystique* (1963) analysed the role of women in American society and articulated their frustrations. She was founder and first president of the National Association for Women (1966), and headed the National Women's Strike for Equality (1970). In *The Second Stage* (1981), she emphasized the importance of both the new and the traditional female roles. She also wrote *It Changed My Life* (1977) and *The Fountain of Age* (1993), which explores the virtues and possibilities of old age. Her autobiography *Life So Far* was published in 2000.

'Hostility between the sexes has never been worse'
January 1969, Chicago, Illinois, USA

The socio-political ferment spreading throughout the USA during the 1960s saw an explosion of feminist activity. In *The Feminine Mystique*, Friedan had described 'the problem that has no name': the discontent of an articulate group of university-educated women sublimating their own intellectual, economic and emotional lives to live vicariously through their husbands and children. Towards the end of the decade, the ground-breaking self-help manual *Our Bodies, Ourselves* (1969) was published by the Boston Women's Health Book Collective.

This was also a time of post-war conservatism, when abortion was illegal and reliable contraception was not readily available, even to married women. At the first national conference on abortion law, which laid the foundation for the National Association for the Repeal of Abortion Laws, Friedan gave this address, which she entitled, 'A Woman's Civil Right'.

Her closely argued speech is forceful but not hectoring, advancing the hypothesis that a sexual revolution, leading to absolute equality between men and women, was impossible unless women were able to control their own reproductive lives. Integral to this was a 'woman's right to choose' – a phrase she may have coined.

Friedan later attempted to enshrine women's right to control their own fertility in the Constitution. Proposed in 1971, the Equal Rights Amendment would have ended discrimination based on gender. It was approved by both houses of Congress, but failed to be ratified by three-quarters of the states and was thus narrowly defeated.

This is the first decent conference that's ever been held on abortion, because this is the first conference in which *women's* voices are being heard and heard strongly.

We are in a new stage in the sexual revolution in America. We are moving forward again, after many decades of standing still – which has been in effect to move backward. Belatedly, we have come to recognize that there is no freedom, no equality, no full human dignity and personhood possible for women until we demand control over our own bodies.

Only one voice needs to be heard on the question of whether a woman will or will not bear a child, and that is the voice of the woman herself: her own conscience, her own conscious choice. Then, and only then, will women move out of their definition as sex objects to personhood and self-determination …

Yesterday, an obscene thing happened in the city of New York. A Committee of the State Legislature held hearings on the question of abortion. Women like me asked to testify. We were told that testimony was by invitation only. Only *one* woman was invited to testify on the question of abortion in the state of New York – a Catholic nun. The only other voices were those of men. It is obscene that men, whether they be legislators or priests or even benevolent abortion reformers, should be the only ones heard on the question of women's bodies and the reproductive process, on what happens to the people that actually bear the children in this society.

The right of woman to control her reproductive process must be established as a basic, inalienable, civil right, not to be denied or abridged by the state – just as the right of individual and religious conscience is considered an inalienable private right in both American tradition and in the American constitution.

This is how we must address all questions governing abortion, access to birth control, and contraceptive devices. Don't talk to me about abortion reform. Abortion reform is something dreamed up by men, maybe good-hearted men, but they can only think from their male point of view ... What right have they to say? What right has any man to say to any woman – you must bear this child? What right has any state to say? This is a woman's right, not a technical question needing the sanction of the state, or to be debated in terms of technicalities – they are all irrelevant.

This question can only be confronted in terms of the basic personhood and dignity of woman, which is violated forever if she does not have the right to control her own reproductive process.

It is quite remarkable what has happened in the little more than a year during which some of us have begun to talk about abortion in these terms ... New York State was having a constitutional convention and Larry Lader[1] invited me to the meeting of all the different groups – church groups, medical groups, Planned Parenthood, and the rest – who were working on abortion reform.

I said, we're going into the New York State constitutional convention demanding a Bill of Rights for women, and we are going to demand that it be written into the Constitution that the right of a woman to control her reproductive process must be established as a civil right, a right not to be denied or abridged by the state. Most of the people at that table, people working on abortion reform, were men. They looked at me in absolute horror, as if I was out of my mind. They said, you don't know what you are talking about, you're not an expert on this, you women have never done anything like this ...

If I were easily intimidated, I would have slunk out. But I said, well, you may be right but as far as we are concerned, this is the only way that abortion is worth talking about; we're going to demand it and let's see what happens. As I left, a couple of the women who were sitting quietly at the table came up and said, 'We'd like to help.' Then, lo and behold, I began to hear ministers and ADA[2] and ACLU[3] and others begin to voice the same position, in terms of woman's basic right ...

Women, even though they're almost too visible as sex objects in this country, are invisible people. As the negro was the invisible man, so women are the invisible people who have a share in the decisions of the mainstream of government, of politics, of the church – who don't just cook the church supper, but preach the sermon; who don't just look up the ZIP codes[4] and address the envelopes, but make the political decisions; who don't just do the housework of industry, but make some of the executive decisions. Women, above all, who say what their own lives and personalities are going to be, and no longer listen to or even permit male experts to define what 'feminine' is or isn't.

The essence of the denigration of women is our definition as sex object ... Am I saying that women must be liberated from sex? No. I am saying that sex will only be liberated to be a human dialogue, sex will only cease to be a sniggering, dirty joke and an obsession in this society, when women become active self-determining people, liberated to a creativity beyond motherhood, to a full human creativity.

[1] The US campaigner Lawrence 'Larry' Lader (1920–) wrote the book *Abortion* (1966) and co-founded the National Association for the Repeal of Abortion Laws in 1969.

[2] Americans for Democratic Action, founded in 1947 to promote a liberal political agenda.

[3] The American Civil Liberties Union, founded in 1920 to campaign for civil rights.

[4] The Zone Improvement Plan introduced ZIP codes throughout the USA in 1963 to improve the efficiency of the postal service.

Am I saying that women must be liberated from motherhood? No. I am saying that motherhood will only be a joyous and responsible human act when women are free to make, with full conscious choice and full human responsibility, the decisions to become mothers. Then, and only then, will they be able to embrace motherhood without conflict, when they will be able to define themselves not just as somebody's mother, not just as servants of children, not just as breeding receptacles, but as people for whom motherhood is a freely chosen part of life …

Then, and only then, will motherhood cease to be a curse and a chain for men and for children. For despite all the lip service paid to motherhood today, all the roses sent on Mother's Day, all the commercials and the hypocritical ladies' magazines' celebration of women in their roles as housewives and mothers, the fact is that all television or night-club comics have to do is go before a microphone and say the words 'my wife' and the whole audience erupts into gales of guilty, vicious and obscene laughter.

The hostility between the sexes has never been worse. The image of women in avant-garde plays, novels and movies, and behind the family situation comedies on television is that mothers are man-devouring, cannibalistic monsters, or else Lolitas,[5] sex objects – and objects not even of heterosexual impulse, but of sado-masochism. That impulse – the punishment of women – is much more of a factor in the abortion question than anybody ever admits.

Motherhood is a bane almost by definition, or at least partly so, as long as women are forced to be mothers – and only mothers – against their will. Like a cancer cell living its life through another cell, women today are forced to live too much through their children and husbands …

Perhaps it is the least understood fact of American political life: the enormous buried violence of women in this country today. Like all oppressed people, women have been taking their violence out on their own bodies, in all the maladies with which they plague the MDs and the psychoanalysts. Inadvertently, and in subtle and insidious ways, they have been taking their violence out, too, on their children and on their husbands, and sometimes they're not so subtle.

The battered child syndrome that we are hearing more and more about from our hospitals is almost always to be found in the instance of unwanted children, and women are doing the battering, as much or more than men. In the case histories of psychologically and physically maimed children, the woman is always the villain …

Am I saying that women have to be liberated from men? That men are the enemy? No. I am saying the *men* will only be truly liberated to love women and to be fully themselves when women are liberated to have a full say in the decisions of their lives and their society.

Until that happens, men are going to bear the guilty burden of the passive destiny they have forced upon women, the suppressed resentment, the sterility of love when it is not between two fully active, joyous people, but has in it the element of exploitation. And men will not be free to be all they can be as long as they must live up to an image of masculinity that disallows all the tenderness and sensitivity in a man, all that might be considered feminine.

Men have enormous capacities in them that they have to repress and fear in order to live up to the obsolete, brutal, bear-killing, Ernest Hemingway,[6] crew-cut Prussian, napalm-all-the-children-in-Vietnam, bang-bang-you're-dead image of masculinity. Men are not allowed to

[5] The original Lolita appears in a novel of that name (1955) by the Russian-born US novelist Vladimir Nabokov (1899–1977). A twelve-year-old girl who elopes with her middle-aged stepfather, the character has become a byword for male fantasies about the sexual availability of pubescent girls.

[6] The US novelist Ernest Hemingway (1899–1961) was famous for his machismo and enthusiasm for hunting.

admit that they sometimes are afraid. They are not allowed to express their own sensitivity, their own need to be passive sometimes and not always active. Men are not allowed to cry. So they are only half-human, as women are only half-human, until we can go this next step forward. All the burdens and responsibilities that men are supposed to shoulder alone makes them, I think, resent women's pedestal, much as that pedestal may be a burden for women.

This is the real sexual revolution. Not the cheap headlines in the papers about at what age boys and girls go to bed with each other and whether they do it with or without the benefit of marriage. That's the least of it. The real sexual revolution is the emergence of women from passivity, from the point where they are the easiest victims for all the seductions, the waste, the worshipping of false gods in our affluent society, to full self-determination and full dignity. And it is the emergence of men from the stage where they are inadvertent brutes and masters to sensitive, complete humanity.

This revolution cannot happen without radical changes in the family as we know it today; in our concepts of marriage and love, in our architecture, our cities, our theology, our politics, our art ...

If we are finally allowed to become full people, not only will children be born and brought up with more love and responsibility than today, but we will break out of the confines of that sterile little suburban family to relate to each other in terms of all the possible dimensions of our personalities – male and female, as comrades, as colleagues, as friends, as lovers ...

It's crucial, therefore, that we see this question of abortion as more than a quantitative move, more than a politically expedient move. Abortion repeal is not a question of political expediency. It is part of something greater. It is historic that we are addressing ourselves this weekend to perhaps its first national confrontation by women and men. Women's voices are finally being heard aloud, saying it the way it is about the question of abortion, both in its most basic sense of morality and in its new political sense as part of the unfinished revolution of sexual equality.

In this confrontation, we are making an important milestone in this marvellous revolution that began long before any of us here were born and which still has a long way to go. As the pioneers from Mary Wollstonecraft[7] to Margaret Sanger[8] gave us the consciousness that brought us from our several directions here, so we here – in changing the very terms of the debate on abortion to assert woman's right to choose and to define the terms of our lives ourselves – move women further to full human dignity. Today, we moved history forward ...

[7] The English writer Mary Wollstonecraft (1759–97) was a pioneer of women's rights and her work, which includes *Thoughts on the Education of Daughters* (1787) and *A Vindication of the Rights of Woman* (1792), is now considered a precursor of feminism.

[8] The US birth-control activist Margaret Sanger *née Higgins* (1879–1966) founded the American Birth Control League in 1921.

Milton Friedman

American economist

Milton Friedman (1912–2006) was born in New York City and educated there and in Chicago. After eight years at the National Bureau of Economic Research (1937–45), he became Professor of Economics at Chicago University (1946–83), now emeritus, where he became the foremost exponent of monetarism. In such works as *A Monetary History of the United States, 1867–1960* (1963) and *Inflation: Causes and Consequences* (1963), he argued that a country's economy can be controlled through its money supply. He was awarded the 1976 Nobel Prize for economics, and was a policy adviser to the RONALD REAGAN administration (1981–8). His ideas were also applied in Great Britain by the Conservative government of MARGARET THATCHER. Among his later publications is *Money Mischief* (1992).

'Economic freedom, human freedom, and political freedom'

1 November 1991, Hayward, California, USA

❧

By the early 1960s, Milton Friedman had developed a school of economic thought – later known as monetarism – broadly based on the theories of the English economist John Maynard Keynes (1883–1946). Friedman advocated allowing the free market to match the supply of goods to demand, and enabling governments to control inflation by manipulating money supply and interest rates.

For much of the 20th century, communist countries operated a command economy, the direct opposite of a free market system. In a command economy, economic activity is directed by the state; there is no matching of supply of goods to demand, and citizens lack economic freedom. In *Capitalism and Freedom* (1962), Friedman had argued that economic freedom was a prerequisite of political freedom, but not in itself sufficient.

Almost 30 years later, Friedman gave the inaugural lecture at the Smith Center for Private Enterprise Studies at Hayward. In his speech – given here in abridged form – he reviews the intervening decades, drawing on examples from around the world to illustrate the varying freedoms found in different societies. He exposes the irony that political freedom tends to undermine economic freedom, and criticizes the effect of foreign aid on developing economies. He also examines a third freedom – human freedom – which he considers essential to an ideal society. The speech is remarkable for its lucid and persuasive analysis of complex economic ideas.

The lecture was given two years after the collapse of communist governments in eastern Europe and three months after the failure of a coup in Russia by communist hardliners. During the 1990s, free-market economies were introduced in these countries, though the transition was an economically painful and politically fraught process. It also had a knock-on effect on the economies, though not the political systems, of Soviet satellites such as Cuba.

❧

What I want to talk about tonight is the relationship among economic freedom, human freedom, and political freedom. In *Capitalism and Freedom*, I wrote: 'Historical evidence speaks with a single voice on the relation between political freedom and a free market. I know of no example in time or place of a society that has been marked by a large measure of political freedom that has not also used something comparable to a free market to organize the bulk of economic activity'.[1] I went on to point out that 'History suggests only that capitalism is a necessary condition for political freedom. Clearly it is not a sufficient condition'.[2]

Both of those statements remain valid today, 30 years later. Over the centuries many non-free societies have relied on capitalism and yet have enjoyed neither human nor political freedom. Ancient Greece was fundamentally a capitalist society, but it had slaves. The US South before the Civil War is another example of a society with slaves that relied predominantly on private property. Currently, South Africa has relied predominantly on private markets and private enterprise, yet it has not been a free society. Many Latin American countries are in the same position … So it is clear that capitalism is not a sufficient condition for human or

[1] *Capitalism and Freedom*, page 9.

[2] *Capitalism and Freedom*, page 10.

political freedom, though it is a necessary condition.

While experience has not contradicted the statements I made, it has persuaded me that the dichotomy I stressed between economic freedom and political freedom is too simple. Even at this broad level, I am persuaded that it is important to consider a trichotomy: economic freedom, human freedom, and political freedom.

The example that persuaded me that the relationship was less simple than the one I had sketched in *Capitalism and Freedom* is Hong Kong as it developed in the 1950s and especially as it has developed in the period since *Capitalism and Freedom* was written. Hong Kong has been – though unfortunately as the mainland communist regime takes over[3] it will not remain – one of the freest, if not the freest, of countries in the world, in every respect but one. Hong Kong has had an extraordinary degree of economic freedom: no tariffs and no import or export quotas, except as we in our wisdom have forced such quotas on Hong Kong in order to protect our industries from its efficiency … Taxes have been very low … There are few regulations on business, no price controls, no wage controls.

Hong Kong's completely free economy has achieved marvels. Here is a place with no resources except a magnificent harbour, a small piece of land, an island off a peninsula, a population of 500,000, after World War II that has grown to a population close to six million – over ten times as large – and at the same time, the standard of life has multiplied more than fourfold. It has been one of the most rapidly-growing countries in the world, a remarkable example of what free markets can do if left unrestricted …

In addition to economic freedom, Hong Kong has a great deal of human freedom. I have visited many times and I have never seen any evidence of suppression of freedom of speech, freedom of the press, or any other human freedom that we regard as important.

However, in one respect Hong Kong has no freedom whatsoever. It has no political freedom. The Chinese who fled to Hong Kong were not free people. They were refugees from the communist regime and they themselves had been citizens of a regime that was very far from a free society. They did not choose freedom; it was imposed on them. It was imposed on them by outside forces. Hong Kong was governed by officials of the British Colonial Office, not by self-chosen representatives. In the past couple of years, in trying to persuade the world that Britain has not done a dastardly deed in turning Hong Kong over to the communists, the British administration has tried to institute a legislative council and to give some evidence of political representation. However, in general, over the whole of that period, there has been essentially no direct political representation.

That brings out an enormous paradox, the one that as I said caused me to rethink the relationship among different kinds of freedom. The British colonies that were given their political freedom after World War II have for the most part destroyed the other freedoms. Similarly, at the very time officials of the British Colonial Office were imposing economic freedom on Hong Kong, at home in Britain a socialist government was imposing socialism on Britain. Perhaps they sent the backward people out to Hong Kong to get rid of them. It shows how complex the relationship is between economic freedom and political freedom, and human freedom and political freedom. Indeed, it suggests that while economic freedom facilitates political freedom, political freedom, once established, has a tendency to destroy economic freedom.

[3] The UK and China had agreed in 1984 that China would resume sovereignty over Hong Kong on 1 July 1997.

Consider the example that I believe is most fascinating, India. It was given its political freedom by Britain over 40 years ago. It has continued, with rare exceptions, to be a political democracy. It has continued to be a country where people are governed by representatives chosen at the ballot box, but it has had very little economic freedom and very limited human freedom. On the economic side, it has had extensive controls over exports and imports, over foreign exchange, over prices, over wages. There have been some reforms in the past year or so, but until recently you could not establish any kind of enterprise without getting a licence from the government. The effect of such centralized control of the economy has been that the standard of life for the great bulk of the Indians is no higher today than it was 40 years ago when India was given its political freedom …

What is true for India is true much more broadly. Foreign aid has done far more harm to the countries we have given it to than it has done good. Why? Because in every case, foreign aid has strengthened governments that were already too powerful. Mozambique, Tanzania, and many another African country testify to the same effect as India.

To come back to Hong Kong, the only reason it did not get its political freedom is because the local people did not want political freedom. They knew very well that that meant the Chinese communists would take them over. In a curious way, the existence of the Chinese communist government was the major protection of the economic and human freedoms that Hong Kong enjoyed. Quite a paradoxical situation …

Another fascinating example that brings out the complexity of the situation is Chile. Chile, as you know, was first taken over by SALVADOR ALLENDE and a socialist group. Allende came into power as a result of an election in which no one of the three major parties was able to get a majority, and subsequent political manoeuvring, along with his promise to abide by the constitution. No sooner in office, however, than he reneged on his promise and proceeded to try to convert Chile into a full-fledged communist state. The important thing for my purpose is what happened after Allende's policies provoked the military to overthrow him and set up a military junta led by General Pinochet[4] to run the country.

[4] The Chilean soldier and dictator General Augusto Pinochet (1915–2006) overthrew Allende's government during a coup in September 1973, and ruled Chile as a repressive military dictatorship until 1990. In 1975, Friedman provoked controversy by visiting Chile to lecture on economics.

Almost all military juntas are adverse to economic freedom for obvious reasons. The military is organized from the top down: the general tells the colonel, the colonel tells the captain, the captain tells the lieutenant, and so on. A market economy is organized from the bottom up: the consumer tells the retailer, the retailer tells the wholesaler, the wholesaler tells the producer, and the producer delivers. The principles underlying a military organization are precisely the reverse of those underlying a market organization.

Pinochet … tried for a while to have military officers run the economy. However, inflation doubled in the first eight or nine months of their regime. When rates of inflation reached 700 to 1,000 per cent, they had to do something …

I have nothing good to say about the political regime that Pinochet imposed. It was a terrible political regime. The real miracle of Chile is not how well it has done economically; the real miracle of Chile is that a military junta was willing to go against its principles and support a free market regime designed by principled believers in a free market. The results were spectacular. Inflation came down sharply. After a transitory period of recession and low output that is unavoidable in the course of reversing a strong inflation, output started to expand, and ever since, the Chilean economy has performed better than any other South American economy.

The economic development and the recovery produced by economic freedom in turn promoted the public's desire for a greater degree of political freedom – exactly what happened (if I may jump from one continent to another) in China after 1976, when the regime introduced a greater measure of economic freedom in one sector of the economy, agriculture, with great success. That, too, generated pressure for more political freedom and was one of the major factors underlying the dissatisfaction that led to Tiananmen Square.[5]

In Chile, the drive for political freedom, generated by economic freedom and the resulting economic success, ultimately resulted in a referendum that introduced political democracy. Now, at long last, Chile has all three things: political freedom, human freedom and economic freedom. Chile will continue to be an interesting experiment to watch to see whether it can keep all three or whether, now that it has political freedom, that political freedom will tend to be used to destroy or reduce economic freedom.

In order to understand the paradox that economic freedom produces political freedom but political freedom may destroy economic freedom, it is important to recognize that free private markets have a far broader meaning than the usual restriction to narrowly economic transactions. Literally, a market is simply a place where people meet, where people get together to make deals with one another.

Every country has a market … but there are different kinds of markets. A private market is one in which the people making deals are making them either on their own behalf or as agents for identifiable individuals rather than as agents of governments. … A private market is very different from a government market. In a strictly private market, all the deals are between individuals acting in their own interest or as agents for other identifiable individuals.

Finally, you can have a private market, but it may or may not be a free market … In a free private market, all the deals are strictly voluntary. Many of the cases of private markets that I cited before were not cases of free private markets … You have a private market in India, but it is not a free private market because many voluntary deals are not permitted. An individual can deal with another to exchange a good or service only if he has the permission of the government. I may say a completely free private market exists nowhere in the world. Hong Kong is perhaps the closest approximation to it. However, almost everywhere what you have, at best, is a partly free, largely hampered, private market.

A free private market is a mechanism for achieving voluntary co-operation among people … A characteristic feature of a free private market is that all parties to a transaction believe that they are going to be better off by that transaction. It is not a zero sum game in which some can benefit only at the expense of others. It is a situation in which everybody thinks he is going to be better off … A free private market involves the absence of coercion. People deal with one another voluntarily, not because somebody tells them to or forces them to …

The essence of human freedom, as of a free private market, is freedom of people to make their own decisions so long as they do not prevent anybody else from doing the same thing. That makes clear, I think, why free private markets are so closely related to human freedom. It is the only mechanism that permits a complex, inter-related society to be organized from the bottom up rather than the top down.

[5] In April–June 1989, unprecedented student-led demonstrations at Tiananmen Square in central Beijing expressed public dissatisfaction with the Communist Chinese regime.

George Galloway
Scottish politician

George Galloway (1954–) was born in Dundee of Irish Catholic extraction, and attended the city's Harris Academy. He embraced left-wing politics as a teenager, and soon became constituency secretary for the Labour Party in Dundee. In 1974, he began to take an active interest in Palestinian affairs. In 1983, he was appointed general secretary of the charity War On Want, founded by the former Labour prime minister HAROLD WILSON. In 1987 he became Labour MP for Glasgow Hillhead (later Glasgow Kelvin) a seat he held until 2005, despite sexual and financial controversies, a vote of no confidence (1988) and expulsion from the Labour Party (2003) for public criticism of British participation in the war on Iraq. A frequent visitor to the Middle East, he has faced persistent allegations of improper dealings with the regime of Iraqi dictator SADDAM HUSSEIN. In January 2004, he formed Respect: The Unity Coalition with allies from the Socialist Alliance. Later he announced his candidature for the London seat of Bethnal Green and Bow, which he won at the general election of May 2005, overturning a Labour majority of more than 10,000. He provoked scandal in 2006 by appearing on the reality television show *Celebrity Big Brother*, further impairing an already scant parliamentary attendance record. He subsequently failed to win re-election to the House of Commons (2008) and election to the Scottish Parliament (2011). He has published several books, including the autobiography *I'm Not the Only One* (2004, updated 2005).

'You have nothing on me, Senator'
17 May 2005, Washington, DC, USA

George Galloway should have been a fish out of water when he appeared before a subcommittee of the US Senate Committee on Homeland Security and Governmental Affairs. Instead, he seemed in his element – as flamboyant, assured and provocative as ever.

Known to admirers and detractors alike as 'Gorgeous George', Galloway arrived at the Senate wearing an immaculately tailored suit and smoking a large cigar. He was accused of having profited from clandestine dealings with Saddam Hussein, deposed president of Iraq. According to a dossier of evidence prepared by the committee, Galloway had illegally received credits to buy Iraqi oil under the United Nations' oil-for-food programme, a programme which allowed Iraq to bypass UN-imposed sanctions to trade oil for food and medicine.

As Galloway concedes in this fiery speech, he has a long-standing interest in the Middle East. Following the Gulf War of 1991, he campaigned against the sanctions on Iraq. In 1998, he established the Mariam Appeal, whose focus was a four-year-old Iraqi girl who required treatment for leukemia. Once her treatment was funded, excess donations were to be directed to medical aid for other Iraqi children. Doubts were raised about whether funds were being used for charitable purposes, but a 2003 investigation by the Charity Commission found no evidence of corruption.

Galloway has often been accused of financial wrongdoing, but the charges have never stuck. In 2003, he successfully sued the *Daily Telegraph* over claims that he had profited from the 'oil-for-food' programme. He also brought a libel case over similar allegations in the *Christian Science Monitor*, which was settled out of court in 2004.

Galloway left the Senate satisfied he had cleared his name. Others were less convinced. Senator Norm Coleman, who led the committee, expressed doubt that he was a credible witness, and warned of 'consequences' if Galloway was found to have lied under oath.

Senator: I am not now, nor have I ever been, an oil trader, and neither has anyone on my behalf. I have never seen a barrel of oil, owned one, bought one, sold one – and neither has anyone on my behalf.

Now I know that standards have slipped in the last few years in Washington, but for a lawyer you are remarkably cavalier with any idea of justice. I am here today but last week you already found me guilty. You traduced my name around the world without ever having asked me a single question, without ever having contacted me, without ever having written to me or telephoned me, without any attempt to contact me whatsoever. And you call that justice.

Now I want to deal with the pages that relate to me in this dossier and I want to point out areas where there are … let's be charitable and say errors. Then I want to put this in the context where I believe it ought to be.

[1] It was at this meeting that Galloway was filmed saying to Saddam, 'Sir: I salute your courage, your strength, your indefatigability.'

[3] The Swedish diplomat Hans Blix (1928–) led the UN's Monitoring, Verification and Inspection Commission, 2000–3. The commission began searching for evidence of weapons of mass destruction in Iraq in 2002, but was withdrawn in March 2003. Blix later criticized the US and UK governments for exaggerating the case for war.

[5] The Iraqi businessman and politician Ahmed Abdel Hadi Chalabi (1944–), who fled Iraq in 1996. Despite accusations of financial impropriety and an embezzlement conviction in the 1990s, he was seen as a potential post-war leader by the US government, which flew him back into Iraq after the war ended in 2003. It transpired that much of the pre-war intelligence he had provided was false, and that he had leaked US intelligence to Iran. He was elected to the transitional National Assembly in January 2005 and became a Deputy Prime Minister.

On the very first page of your document about me you assert that I have had 'many meetings' with Saddam Hussein. This is false. I have had two meetings with Saddam Hussein, once in 1994[1] and once in August of 2002. By no stretch of the English language can that be described as 'many meetings' with Saddam Hussein.

As a matter of fact, I have met Saddam Hussein exactly the same number of times as Donald Rumsfeld[2] met him. The difference is, Donald Rumsfeld met him to sell him guns and to give him maps the better to target those guns. I met him to try and bring about an end to sanctions, suffering and war; and on the second of the two occasions, I met him to try and persuade him to let Dr Hans Blix and the United Nations weapons inspectors[3] back into the country – a rather better use of two meetings with Saddam Hussein than your own Secretary of State for Defence made of his.

I was an opponent of Saddam Hussein when British and American governments and businessmen were selling him guns and gas. I used to demonstrate outside the Iraqi embassy when British and American officials were going in and doing commerce.

You will see from the official parliamentary record, Hansard, from 15 March 1990 onwards, voluminous evidence that I have a rather better record of opposition to Saddam Hussein than you do and than any other member of the British or American governments do.

Now you say in this document, you quote a source, you have the gall to quote a source, without ever having asked me whether the allegation from the source is true, that I am 'the owner of a company which has made substantial profits from trading in Iraqi oil'.

Senator, I do not own any companies, beyond a small company whose entire purpose, whose sole purpose, is to receive the income from my journalistic earnings from my employer, Associated Newspapers in London. I do not own a company that's been trading in Iraqi oil. And you have no business to carry a quotation, utterly unsubstantiated and false, implying otherwise.

Now you have nothing on me, Senator, except my name on lists of names from Iraq, many of which have been drawn up after the installation of your puppet government in Baghdad. If you had letters against me, they would have been up there in your slideshow for the members of your committee today.

You have my name on lists provided to you by the Duelfer inquiry,[4] provided to him by the convicted bank robber and fraudster and conman Ahmed Chalabi,[5] who many people to their credit in your country now realize played a decisive role in leading your country into the disaster in Iraq.

There were 270 names on that list originally. That's somehow been filleted down to the names you chose to deal with in this committee. Some of the names on that committee included the former secretary to his Holiness Pope JOHN PAUL II, the former head of the African National Congress presidential office and many others who had one defining characteristic in common: they all stood against the policy of sanctions and war which you vociferously prosecuted and which has led us to this disaster.

You quote Mr Dahar Yassein Ramadan. Well, you have something on me, I've never met Mr Dahar Yassein Ramadan. Your sub-committee apparently has. But I do know that he's your prisoner, I believe he's in Abu Ghraib prison.[6] I believe he is facing war crimes charges, punishable by death.

[2] The US businessman and politician Donald Rumsfeld (1932–) became Secretary of Defence in January 2001.

[4] The US weapons inspector Charles A Duelfer led the investigation into Iraq's weapons of mass destruction (WMD) capability. The report, released in October 2004, showed that Iraq did not possess any WMD at the time of the US-led invasion in March 2003.

[6] A detention centre near Baghdad used for torture and executions by Saddam. Now run by US-led authorities, it was the centre of a scandal in April 2004 over US mistreatment of prisoners.

In these circumstances, knowing what the world knows about how you treat prisoners in Abu Ghraib prison, in Bagram airbase,[7] in Guantánamo Bay[8] – including, I may say, British citizens being held in those places – I'm not sure how much credibility anyone would put on anything you manage to get from a prisoner in those circumstances. But you quote 13 words from Dahar Yassein Ramadan, whom I have never met. If he said what he said, then he is wrong.

And if you had any evidence that I had ever engaged in any actual oil transaction, if you had any evidence that anybody ever gave me any money, it would be before the public and before this committee today, because I agreed with your Mr Greenblatt.[9] Your Mr Greenblatt was absolutely correct. What counts is not the names on the paper. What counts is: where's the money?

Senator: who paid me hundreds of thousands of dollars of money? The answer to that is nobody. And if you had anybody who ever paid me a penny, you would have produced them today.

Now, you refer at length to a company named in these documents as Aredio Petroleum. I say to you under oath here today: I have never heard of this company, I have never met anyone from this company. This company has never paid a penny to me. And I'll tell you something else: I can assure you that Aredio Petroleum has never paid a single penny to the Mariam Appeal Campaign. Not a thin dime. I don't know who Aredio Petroleum are, but I dare say if you were to ask them they would confirm that they have never met me or ever paid me a penny.

Whilst I'm on that subject: who is this senior former regime official that you spoke to yesterday? Don't you think I have a right to know? Don't you think the committee and the public have a right to know who this senior former regime official you were quoting against me interviewed yesterday actually is?

Now, one of the most serious of the mistakes you have made in this set of documents is, to be frank, such a schoolboy howler as to make a fool of the efforts that you have made. You assert on page 19, not once but twice, that the documents that you are referring to cover a different period in time from the documents covered by the *Daily Telegraph*, which were a subject of a libel action won by me in the High Court in England late last year.

You state that the *Daily Telegraph* article cited documents from 1992 and 1993, whilst you are dealing with documents dating from 2001. Senator, the *Daily Telegraph*'s documents date identically to the documents that you were dealing with in your report here. None of the *Daily Telegraph*'s documents dealt with a period of 1992, 1993. I had never set foot in Iraq until late in 1993 – never in my life. There could be no documents relating to Oil-for-Food matters in 1992, 1993, for the Oil-for-Food scheme did not exist at that time.[10]

And yet you've allocated a full section of this document to claiming that your documents are from a different era to the *Daily Telegraph* documents when the opposite is true. Your documents and the *Daily Telegraph* documents deal with exactly the same period.

But perhaps you were confusing the *Daily Telegraph* action with the *Christian Science Monitor*. The *Christian Science Monitor* did indeed publish on its front pages a set of allegations against me very similar to the ones that your committee have made. They did indeed rely on documents which started in 1992, 1993. These documents were unmasked by the *Christian Science Monitor* themselves as forgeries.

[7] A military base in Parvan, Afghanistan, used by US forces since 2001. US military personnel were revealed to have carried out abuse and torture on prisoners held at the site, resulting in at least two deaths.

[8] An enclave of Cuba under US control since 1903, Guantánamo Bay is the site of a US Navy base and, since 2001, of the detention centres Camp X-Ray and Camp Delta, where prisoners suspected of terrorism have been held in inhumane conditions.

[9] The US lawyer Mark Greenblatt worked as legal counsel to the US Senate subcommittee.

[10] The scheme was established in 1996.

[11] Neoconservatism is a right-of-centre political ideology characterized by aggressive interventionism in foreign affairs and relative tolerance of domestic spending on social welfare. It has influenced Republican foreign policy since the 1980s, especially the policies of President GEORGE W BUSH'S administration.

Now, the neocon[11] websites and newspapers in which you're such a hero, Senator, were all absolutely cock-a-hoop at the publication of the *Christian Science Monitor* documents, they were all absolutely convinced of their authenticity. They were all absolutely convinced that these documents showed me receiving $10 million from the Saddam regime. And they were all lies.

In the same week as the *DailyTelegraph* published their documents against me, the *Christian Science Monitor* published theirs – which turned out to be forgeries – and the British newspaper, *Mail on Sunday*, purchased a third set of documents, which also, upon forensic examination, turned out to be forgeries. So there's nothing fanciful about this. Nothing at all fanciful about it.

The existence of forged documents implicating me in commercial activities with the Iraqi regime is a proven fact. It's a proven fact that these forged documents existed and were being circulated amongst right-wing newspapers in Baghdad and around the world in the immediate aftermath of the fall of the Iraqi regime.

Now, Senator, I gave my heart and soul to oppose the policy that you promoted. I gave my political life's blood to try to stop the mass killing of Iraqis by the sanctions on Iraq which killed one million Iraqis, most of them children. Most of them died before they even knew that they were Iraqis, but they died for no other reason other than that they were Iraqis with the misfortune to be born at that time. I gave my heart and soul to stop you committing the disaster that you did commit in invading Iraq. And I told the world that your case for the war was a pack of lies.

I told the world that Iraq, contrary to your claims, did not have weapons of mass destruction. I told the world, contrary to your claims, that Iraq had no connection to al-Qaeda.[12] I told the world, contrary to your claims, that Iraq had no connection to the atrocity on 9/11 2001. I told the world, contrary to your claims, that the Iraqi people would resist a British and American invasion of their country and that the fall of Baghdad would not be the beginning of the end, but merely the end of the beginning.

[12] A loosely structured network of Islamic fundamentalist terrorists, said to be led by OSAMA BIN LADEN.

Senator, in everything I said about Iraq, I turned out to be right and you turned out to be wrong – and 100,000 people paid with their lives; 1,600 of them American soldiers sent to their deaths on a pack of lies; 15,000 of them wounded, many of them disabled forever on a pack of lies.

If the world had listened to Kofi Annan,[13] whose dismissal you demanded; if the world had listened to President Chirac,[14] who you want to paint as some kind of corrupt traitor; if the world had listened to me and the anti-war movement in Britain, we would not be in the disaster that we are in today.

[13] The Ghanaian diplomat Kofi Annan (1938–), Secretary-General of the United Nations, 1997–2006. He urged restraint when the USA and the UK were preparing to invade Iraq without UN backing; and later declared the invasion and occupation illegal.

[14] The French politician Jacques Chirac (1932–), president of France since 1995, was one of the most vocal opponents of using force against Iraq.

Senator, this is the mother of all smokescreens. You are trying to divert attention from the crimes that you supported, from the theft of billions of dollars of Iraq's wealth.

Have a look at the real Oil-for-Food scandal. Have a look at the 14 months you were in charge of Baghdad, the first 14 months when $8.8 billion of Iraq's wealth went missing on your watch. Have a look at Halliburton[15] and other American corporations that stole not only Iraq's money, but the money of the American taxpayer.

Have a look at the oil that you didn't even meter, that you were shipping out of the country and selling, the proceeds of which went who knows where? Have a look at the $800 million you gave to American military commanders to hand out around the country without even counting it or

[15] A multinational energy corporation which – sometimes via its subsidiary KBR – won many contracts in post-war Iraq. The corporation has faced persistent allegations of fraud and profiteering, partly because Vice President Dick Cheney (1941–) was its chief executive officer, 1995–2000.

weighing it.

Have a look at the real scandal — breaking in the newspapers today; revealed in the earlier testimony in this committee — that the biggest sanctions-busters were not me, or Russian politicians, or French politicians. The real sanctions-busters were your own companies, with the connivance of your own government.

Mahatma Gandhi
Indian lawyer and statesman

Mohandâs Karamchand Gandhi *known as Mahatma ('Great Soul')* (1869–1948) was born in Porbandar, the son of a politician. His mother was a devout Hindu, and Gandhi derived much of his pacifist creed from her. He studied law in London, and in 1893 left a Bombay legal practice to live frugally in South Africa, where he spent over 20 years opposing discriminatory legislation against Indians. He supported Britain in the Boer War (1899–1902). In 1914 he returned to India. While supporting the British in World War I, he took an increasing interest in home rule, acquiring control of the Congress Movement. His civil disobedience campaigns of 1919–20 led to violence, notably the massacre at Amritsar, in which around 380 people were killed and many more wounded when British troops fired into a crowd. He was imprisoned for conspiracy (1922–4). In 1930 he led a 200-mile march to the sea to collect salt in symbolic defiance of the government monopoly. He was arrested and after his release in 1931 attended a conference on Indian constitutional reform in London. Back in India, he renewed his civil disobedience campaign and was arrested again; this, along with his 'fasts unto death', formed the pattern of his activity for six years. He assisted in the adoption of the constitutional compromise of 1937, under which Congress ministers accepted office in provincial legislatures. During World War II, Gandhi urged complete independence, convinced that only a free India could give Britain effective support. In August 1942, he was arrested for encouraging civil disobedience. He was released in May 1944. He negotiated with the British Cabinet Mission (1946) which recommended the new constitutional structure, eventually realized in Partition. In May 1947 he hailed India's independence as 'the noblest act of the British nation'. This period was darkened by strife between religious factions; but his fasts to shame the instigators helped avert deeper tragedy. He was assassinated in Delhi by a Hindu fanatic on 30 January 1948. Gandhi was venerated as a moral teacher, a reformer who sought an India free from caste and materialism, and a patriot who gave the independence movement a new quality. Critics considered him a victim of self-delusion, which blinded him to the bloodshed provoked by his supposedly non-violent campaigns. However, throughout Asia he is generally regarded as a great influence for peace, whose teaching had a message not only for India but for the world.

'There is no room for anarchism in India'
4 February 1916, Benares (now Varanasi), India

Gandhi spoke in fluent English when he addressed a meeting to celebrate the opening of Benares Hindu University. He believed, however, that by using the colonial language, Indians condemned themselves to secondary status. In this speech, which marked the beginning of his campaign for Indian independence, he encourages his audience to consider an analogy, comparing the use of Indian vernacular languages in place of English with the liberation of India from British rule.

By the early 20th century, India had become a land of deep divisions. A few maharajas lived in splendour while millions endured abject poverty, ruled by English-speaking civil servants under a viceroy appointed by the British monarch. In contrast to the lavishly dressed and bejewelled participants at earlier opening ceremonies, Gandhi spoke wearing simple clothes made of hand-spun, hand-woven cloth. This symbolized the damage done to the Indian economy by exporting raw cotton to Britain, then importing finished cloth from British factories.

The English social reformer Dr Annie Besant had invited Gandhi to speak, and while supporting Indian independence, she objected strongly to parts of his speech. Indeed, her obvious disapproval led Gandhi to be more critical of anarchist actions than he had intended – he had also been disturbed by the high level of security in evidence. Dr Besant and some of the Indian princes present walked out during the speech.

> I am hoping that this university will see to it that the youths who come to it will receive their instruction through the medium of their vernaculars. Our language is the reflection of ourselves, and if you tell me that our languages are too poor to express the best thought, then I say that the sooner we are wiped out of existence the better for us. Is there a man who dreams that English can ever become the national language of India?
> [*Cries of 'Never!'*]
> Why this handicap on the nation? Just consider for one moment what an unequal race our lads have to run with every English lad. I had the privilege

of a close conversation with some Poona professors. They assured me that every Indian youth, because he reached his knowledge through the English language, lost at least six precious years of life. Multiply that by the number of students turned out by our schools and colleges, and find out for yourselves how many thousand years have been lost to the nation.

The charge against us is that we have no initiative. How can we have any if we are to devote the precious years of our life to the mastery of a foreign tongue? We fail in this attempt also. Was it possible for any speaker yesterday and today to impress his audience as [it] was possible for Mr Higginbottom?[1] It was not the fault of the previous speakers that they could not engage the audience. They had more than substance enough for us in their addresses. But their addresses could not go home to us.

I have heard it said that after all it is English-educated India which is leading and which is doing all things for the nation. It would be monstrous if it were otherwise: the only education we receive is English education. Surely we must show something for it.

But suppose that we had been receiving, during the past 50 years, education through our vernaculars, what should we have today? We should have today a free India; we should have our educated men, not as if they were foreigners in their own land, but speaking to the heart of the nation …

Let us now turn to another subject. The Congress has passed a resolution about self-government, and I have no doubt that the All-India Congress Committee and the Muslim League will do their duty and come forward with some tangible suggestions.

But I, for one, must frankly confess that I am not so much interested in what they will be able to produce as I am interested in anything that the student world is going to produce or the masses are going to produce. No paper contribution will ever give us self-government. No amount of speeches will ever make us fit for self-government. It is only our conduct that will fit us for it.

[*Applause.*]

And how are we trying to govern ourselves? I want to think audibly this evening. I do not want to make a speech and if you find me this evening speaking without reserve, pray, consider that you are only sharing the thoughts of a man who allows himself to think audibly, and if you think that I seem to transgress the limits that courtesy imposes upon me, pardon me for the liberty I may be taking.

I visited the Viswanath temple[2] last evening and as I was walking through those lanes, these were the thoughts that touched me. If a stranger dropped from above on to this great temple, and he had to consider what we as Hindus were, would he not be justified in condemning us? Is not this great temple a reflection of our own character?

I speak feelingly, as a Hindu. Is it right that the lanes of our sacred temple should be as dirty as they are? The houses round about are built anyhow. The lanes are tortuous and narrow. If even our temples are not models of roominess and cleanliness, what can our self-government be? Shall our temples be abodes of holiness, cleanliness and peace as soon as the English have retired from India, either of their own pleasure or by compulsion, bag and baggage?

… The city mostly is a stinking den. We are a people unused to city life. But if we want city life, we cannot reproduce the easy going hamlet life. It is not comforting to think that people walk about the streets of Indian

[1] The US missionary Samuel Higginbottom spent many years in India, and was Director of Agriculture in Gwalior state (1916–19).

[2] A temple in Benares, considered the home of the god Shiva.

Bombay under the perpetual fear of dwellers in the storeyed buildings spitting upon them.

I do a great deal of railway travelling. I observe the difficulty of third-class passengers. But the railway administration is by no means to blame for all their hard lot. We do not know the elementary laws of cleanliness. We spit anywhere on the carriage floor, irrespective of the thought that it is often used as sleeping space. We do not trouble ourselves as to how we use it. The result is indescribable filth in the compartment.

The so-called better-class passengers overawe their less fortunate brethren. Among them I have seen the students' world also. Sometimes they behave no better. They can speak English and they have worn Norfolk jackets[3] and therefore claim the right to force their way in and command seating accommodation. I have turned the searchlight all over, and as you have given me the privilege of speaking to you I am laying my heart bare.

[3] A loosely pleated jacket with lapels and waistband, fashionable in Britain at this time.

Surely we must set these things right in our progress towards self-government. His Highness the Maharajah who presided yesterday over our deliberations spoke about the poverty of India. Other speakers laid great stress upon it. But what did we witness in the great *pandal*,[4] in which the foundation ceremony was performed by the Viceroy? Certainly a most gorgeous show, an exhibition of jewellery which made a splendid feast for the eyes of the greatest jeweller who chose to come from Paris.

[4] A large tent made from bamboo and fabric.

I compare with the richly bedecked noblemen the millions of the poor. And I feel like saying to these noblemen, 'There is no salvation for India unless you strip yourselves of this jewellery and hold it in trust for your countrymen in India.'

[*'Hear, hear!' and applause.*]

I am sure it is not the desire of the King-Emperor or Lord Hardinge[5] that in order to show the truest loyalty to our King-Emperor, it is necessary for us to ransack our jewellery-boxes and to appear bedecked from top to toe. I would undertake, at the peril of my life, to bring to you a message from King George[6] himself that he expects nothing of the kind.

[5] The English diplomat Charles Hardinge, 1st Baron Hardinge of Penshurst (1858–1944) served as Viceroy of India, 1910–16.

[6] The British monarch GEORGE V (1865–1936), who reigned 1910–36, was also Emperor of India, a title first held (as Empress) by his grandmother, Queen Victoria, from 1876.

Sir, whenever I hear of a great palace rising in any great city of India – be it in British India or be it in India which is ruled by our great chiefs – I become jealous at once, and I say, 'Oh, it is the money that has come from the agriculturists.'

Over 75 per cent of the population are agriculturists and Mr Higginbottom told us last night, in his own felicitous language, that they are the men who grow two blades of grass in the place of one. But there cannot be much spirit of self-government about us if we take away or allow others to take away from them almost the whole of the results of their labour. Our salvation can only come through the farmer. Neither the lawyers, nor the doctors, nor the rich landlords are going to secure it.

Now, last but not the least, it is my bounden duty to refer to what agitated our minds during these two or three days. All of us have had many anxious moments while the Viceroy was going through the streets of Benares. There were detectives stationed in many places. We were horrified. We asked ourselves, 'Why this distrust? Is it not better that even Lord Hardinge should die than live a living death?'

But a representative of a mighty sovereign may not. He might find it necessary even to live a living death. But why was it necessary to impose these detectives on us? We may foam, we may fret, we may resent but let us not forget that India of today in her impatience has produced an army of anarchists.

I myself am an anarchist, but of another type. There is a class of anarchists amongst us, and if I was able to reach this class, I would say to them that their anarchism has no room in India, if India is to conquer the conqueror. It is a sign of fear. If we trust and fear God, we shall have to fear no-one, not maharajahs, not viceroys, not the detectives, not even King George.

I honour the anarchist for his love of the country. I honour him for his bravery in being willing to die for his country; but I ask him: is killing honourable? Is the dagger of an assassin a fit precursor of an honourable death? I deny it. There is no warrant for such methods in any scriptures. If I found it necessary for the salvation of India that the English should retire, that they should be driven out, I would not hesitate to declare that they would have to go, and I hope I would be prepared to die in defence of that belief. That would, in my opinion, be an honourable death.

The bomb-thrower creates secret plots, is afraid to come out into the open, and when caught pays the penalty of misdirected zeal. I have been told, 'Had we not done this, had some people not thrown bombs, we should never have gained what we have got with reference to the partition movement.'

[*Mrs Besant:*[7] *'Please stop it.'*]

... I think what I am saying is necessary. If I am told to stop I shall obey. [*Turning to the Chairman*] I await your orders. If you consider that by my speaking to my country as I am, I am not serving the country and the Empire, I shall certainly stop.

[*Cries of 'Go on!'*]

[*The Chairman: 'Please explain your object.'*]

I am explaining my object. I am simply –

[*Another interruption.*]

My friends: please do not resent this interruption. If Mrs Besant this evening suggests that I should stop, she does so because she loves India so well, and she considers that I am erring in thinking audibly before you young men.

But even so, I simply say this: that I want to purge India of this atmosphere of suspicion on either side. If we are to reach our goal, we should have an empire which is to be based upon mutual love and mutual trust. Is it not better that we talk under the shadow of this college than that we should be talking irresponsibly in our homes? I consider that it is much better that we talk of these things openly. I have done so with excellent results before now. I know that there is nothing that the students do not know. I am therefore turning the searchlight towards ourselves. I hold the country so dear to me that I exchange these thoughts with you, and submit to you that there is no room for anarchism in India.

Let us frankly and openly say whatever we want to say to our rulers, and face the consequences if what we have to say does not please them. But let us not abuse ... If we are to receive self-government, we shall have to take it. We shall never be granted self-government. Look at the history of the British Empire and the British nation; freedom-loving as it is, it will not be a party to give freedom to a people who will not take it themselves. Learn your lesson if you wish to from the Boer War. Those who were enemies of that empire only a few years ago have now become friends.

[*At this point there was an interruption and a movement on the platform to leave; the speech therefore ended here abruptly.*]

[7] The English campaigner Dr Annie Wood Besant (1847–1933) was a member of the Theosophy movement, based on Hindu principles of karma and reincarnation. After moving to India in 1893, she was a founder of the Home Rule League and the newspaper *New India*. Gandhi said that she had 'awakened India from her deep slumber'.

❧

'Why do we want to offer this non-co-operation?'
12 August 1920, Madras (now Chennai), India

Following violent campaigns for Indian independence, the Anarchical and Revolutionary Crimes Act of 1919, popularly known as the Rowlatt Act, made permanent the suspension of civil liberties enacted during World War I. These developments prompted Gandhi to organize a peaceful, principled resistance movement known as *satyagraha* ('firmness in truth'). However, this was accompanied by violence in places, leading to the imposition of martial law in the Punjab, and the Amritsar massacre of April 1919, at which British troops fired into a crowd gathered for a religious festival, killing at least 379.

The peace terms presented to Turkey by the Allies following World War I in the Treaty of Sèvres angered Indian Muslims, who launched the Khilafat movement in September 1919 to protect the Turkish Khilafa and save the Ottoman Empire from dismemberment by Britain and her allies. Gandhi supported this movement, and in June 1920 he wrote to the Viceroy announcing his intention to start a non-co-operation movement in protest against the treaty. In his letter, he referred to the right of the subject 'to refuse to assist a ruler who misrules'. Supporters of the non-co-operation movement were instructed to refuse to perform government duties, withdraw their children from schools and colleges and establish national schools and colleges. They were to boycott British courts and establish private courts. They were to advocate truth and non-violence at all times and wear Indian home-spun cloth.

Gandhi formally launched his non-co-operation movement on 1 August 1920. Soon afterwards, he spoke to a crowd of 50,000 gathered on the beach at Madras. In the speech he explains the importance of the Khilafat movement and the principles of the non-violence movement.

Mr Chairman and friends: like last year, I have to ask your forgiveness that I should have to speak being seated. Whilst my voice has become stronger than it was last year, my body is still weak; and if I were to attempt to speak to you standing, I could not hold on for very many minutes before the whole frame would shake. I hope, therefore, that you will grant me permission to speak seated. I have sat here to address you on a most important question ... I have come to ask every one of you whether you are ready and willing to give sufficiently for your country's sake, for you country's honour and religion ...

What is this non-co-operation, about which you have heard much, and why do we want to offer this non-co-operation? I wish to go for the time being into the way. There are two things before this country: the first and the foremost is the Khilafat question. On this the heart of the Mussulmans[1] of India has become lacerated. British pledges given after the greatest deliberation by the prime minister of England[2] in the name of the English nation, have been dragged into the mire. The promises given to Muslim India ... have been broken, and the great religion of Islam has been placed in danger.

The Mussulmans hold – and I venture to think they rightly hold – that, so long as British promises remain unfulfilled, so long is it impossible for them to tender whole-hearted fealty and loyalty to the British connection; and if it is to be a choice for a devout Mussulman between loyalty to the British connection and loyalty to his Code and Prophet, he will not require a second to make his choice – and he has declared his choice. The Mussulmans say frankly, openly, and honourably to the whole world that if the British ministers and the British nation do not fulfil the pledges given to them ... it will be impossible for them to retain Islamic loyalty.

It is a question, then, for the rest of the Indian population to consider whether they want to perform a neighbourly duty by their Mussulman countrymen, and if they do, they have an opportunity of a lifetime, which will not occur for another 100 years, to show their goodwill, fellowship and friendship and to prove what they have been saying for all these long years, that the Mussulman is the brother of the Hindu. If the Hindu regards that

[1] An archaic term for Muslims.

[2] DAVID LLOYD GEORGE.

before the connection with the British nation comes his natural connection with his Muslim brother, then I say to you that if you find that the Muslim claim is just … you cannot do otherwise than help the Mussulman through and through …

These are the plain conditions which the Indian Mussulmans have accepted; and it was when they saw that they could accept the proffered aid of the Hindus, that they could always justify the cause and the means before the whole world, that they decided to accept the proffered hand of fellowship. It is then for the Hindus and Mohammedans[3] to offer a united front to the whole of the Christian powers of Europe and tell them that weak as India is, India has still got the capacity for preserving her self-respect. She still knows how to die for her religion and for her self-respect.

That is the Khilafat in a nut-shell; but you have also got the Punjab. The Punjab has wounded the heart of India as no other question has for the past century. I do not exclude from my calculation the Mutiny of 1857. Whatever hardships India had to suffer during the Mutiny, the insult that was attempted to be offered to her during the passage of the Rowlatt legislation and that which was offered after its passage were unparalleled in Indian history … The House of Commons, the House of Lords, Mr Montagu,[4] the Viceroy of India,[5] every one of them knows what the feeling of India is on this Khilafat question and on that of the Punjab … [but] they are not willing to give the justice which is India's due and which she demands.

I suggest that … unless we have gained a measure of self-respect at the hands of the British rulers in India, no connection and no friendly intercourse is possible between them and ourselves. I therefore venture to suggest this beautiful and unanswerable method of non-co-operation.

I have been told that non-co-operation is unconstitutional. I venture to deny that it is unconstitutional. On the contrary, I hold that non-co-operation is a just and religious doctrine; it is the inherent right of every human being and it is perfectly constitutional … I do not claim any constitutionality for a rebellion, successful or otherwise, so long as that rebellion means in the ordinary sense of the term, what it does mean – namely wresting justice by violent means. On the contrary, I have said it repeatedly to my countrymen that violence, whatever end it may serve in Europe, will never serve us in India.

My brother and friend Shaukat Ali[6] believes in methods of violence … but because he recognizes as a true soldier that means of violence are not open to India, he sides with me, accepting my humble assistance, and pledges his word that so long as I am with him and so long as he believes in the doctrine, so long will he not harbour even the idea of violence against any single Englishman or any single man on earth. I am here to tell you that he has been as true as his word and has kept it religiously. I am here to bear witness that he has been following out this plan of non-violent non-co-operation to the very letter and I am asking India to follow …

As soon as India accepts the doctrine of the sword, my life as an Indian is finished. It is because I believe in a mission special to India and it is because I believe that the ancients of India, after centuries of experience, have found out that the true thing for any human being on earth is not justice based on violence, but justice based on sacrifice of self, justice based on Yagna and Kurbani.[7] I cling to that doctrine and I shall cling to it for ever. It is for that reason I tell you that whilst my friend believes also in the doctrine of violence and has adopted the doctrine of non-violence as a weapon of the

[3] Another term for Muslims.

[4] The English politician Edwin Montagu (1879–1924) served as Under-Secretary of State for India, 1910–14, and Secretary of State for India, 1917–22. In 1917–18, he researched and wrote a report on Indian constitutional reforms which formed the basis of the Government of India Act (1919), granting limited self-government.

[5] The English colonial administrator Frederic Thesiger, 3rd Baron Chelmsford *later 1st Viscount Chelmsford* (1868–1933) served as Viceroy of India, 1916–21.

[6] The Indian Muslim nationalist Shaukat Ali (1873–1938) founded the Khilafat movement with his brother Mohammad (1878–1931).

[7] Ceremonial rituals of sacrifice and worship.

weak, I believe in the doctrine of non-violence as a weapon of the strongest. I believe that a man is the strongest soldier for daring to die unarmed, with his breast bare before the enemy. So much for the non-violent part of non-co-operation ...

I ask further, is it unconstitutional for me to say to the British government, 'I refuse to serve you'? Is it unconstitutional for our worthy chairman to return with every respect all the titles that he has ever held from the government? Is it unconstitutional for any parent to withdraw his children from a government or aided school? Is it unconstitutional for a lawyer to say, 'I shall no longer support the arm of the law so long as that arm of law is used not to raise me but to debase me?' Is it unconstitutional for a civil servant or for a judge to say, 'I refuse to serve a government which does not wish to respect the wishes of the whole people'? I ask, is it unconstitutional for a policeman or for a soldier to tender his resignation when he knows that he is called to serve a government which traduces his own countrymen? Is it unconstitutional for me to go to the *krishan*, to the agriculturist, and say to him: 'It is not wise for you to pay any taxes, if these taxes are used by the government not to raise you but to weaken you'? I hold and I venture to submit, that there is nothing unconstitutional in it. What is more, I have done every one of these things in my life and nobody has questioned the constitutional character of it ...

I submit that in the whole plan of non-co-operation, there is nothing unconstitutional. But I do venture to suggest that it will be highly unconstitutional in the midst of this unconstitutional government – in the midst of a nation which has built up its magnificent constitution – for the people of India to become weak and to crawl on their belly. It will be highly unconstitutional for the people of India to pocket every insult that is offered to them. It is highly unconstitutional for the 70 millions of Mohammedans of India to submit to a violent wrong done to their own religion. It is highly unconstitutional for the whole of India to sit still and co-operate with an unjust government which has trodden under its feet the honour of the Punjab.

I say to my countrymen: so long as you have a sense of honour and so long as you wish to remain the descendants and defenders of the noble traditions that have been handed to you for generations after generations, it is unconstitutional for you not to non-co-operate and unconstitutional for you to co-operate with a government which has become so unjust as our government has become. I am not anti-English; I am not anti-British; I am not anti any government; but I am anti-untruth – anti-humbug and anti-injustice ...

[8] The annual session of the Indian National Congress was held at Amritsar in December 1919.

I had hoped, at the Congress at Amritsar[8] – I am speaking God's truth before you – when I pleaded on bended knees before some of you for co-operation with the government. I had full hope that the British ministers – who are wise, as a rule – would placate the Mussulman sentiment; that they would do full justice in the matter of the Punjab atrocities. And therefore I said: Let us return goodwill to the hand of fellowship that has been extended to us, which I then believed was extended to us through the Royal Proclamation. It was on that account that I pleaded for co-operation.

But today, that faith having been obliterated by the acts of the British ministers, I am here to plead not for futile obstruction in the legislative council, but for real, substantial non-co-operation, which would paralyse the mightiest government on earth.

That is what I stand for today. Until we have wrung justice, and until we have wrung our self-respect from unwilling hands and from unwilling pens there can be no co-operation … Co-operation is a duty only so long as government protects your honour, and non-co-operation is an equal duty when the government, instead of protecting, robs you of your honour. That is the doctrine of non-co-operation …

I deny being a visionary. I do not accept the claim of saintliness. I am of the earth, earthy, a common man as much as any one of you, probably much more than you are. I am prone to as many weaknesses as you are. But I have seen the world. I have lived in the world with my eyes open. I have gone through the most fiery ordeals that have fallen to the lot of man. I have gone through this discipline. I have understood the secret of my own sacred Hinduism, I have learnt the lesson that non-co-operation is the duty not merely of the saint, but it is the duty of every ordinary citizen who – not knowing much, not caring to know much – wants to perform his ordinary household functions …

I am asking my countrymen in India to follow no other gospel than the gospel of self-sacrifice which precedes every battle. Whether you belong to the school of violence or non-violence, you will still have to go through the fire of sacrifice and of discipline. May God grant you, may God grant our leaders, the wisdom, the courage and the true knowledge to lead the nation to its cherished goal. May God grant the people of India the right path, the true vision and the ability and the courage to follow this path, difficult and yet easy, of sacrifice.

❧

'Non-violence implies voluntary submission'
18 March 1922, Ahmedabad, India

❧

By now, Gandhi was fully committed to the independence movement. But where most campaigning had been violent, Gandhi advocated non-violence, and promoted good relations between Hindus and Muslims.

The success of his non-co-operation campaign, begun in 1920, had exasperated government officials. The Viceroy, Lord Chelmsford, declared it 'the most foolish of all foolish schemes', but ridicule failed to undermine Gandhi. As civil disobedience mounted, his threat to the status quo became an increasingly flagrant challenge.

In February 1922, Gandhi wrote to Lord Reading (who had become Viceroy in 1921), announcing a new campaign to withhold taxes in the state of Gujerat. Days later, 22 police were killed during a riot in United Province. Fearing escalation, Gandhi cancelled the Gujerat campaign, but to no avail. On 10 March he was arrested and charged with 'bringing or attempting to excite disaffection towards His Majesty's Government established by law in British India'. A lawyer by training, Gandhi was at home in the courtroom. He freely admitted the crime and, prior to sentencing, addressed the court.

In his speech he describes the progression from his early life as a loyal subject of the Empire to his current stance of open rebellion. Its central focus is his decision to work towards removal of the British administration, which he believed had brought many Indians close to starvation.

Sentencing Gandhi to six years' imprisonment the judge, C N Broomsfield, acknowledged his importance and noble ideals and said he would welcome political developments that might allow early parole. Gandhi was released in 1924, but by then the unrest had worsened.

❧

[1] The English lawyer Sir Thomas Strangman, then Advocate-General of Bombay, conducted the prosecution.

Before I read this statement, I would like to state that I entirely endorse the learned Advocate-General's[1] remarks in connection with my humble self. I think that he was entirely fair to me in all the statements that he has made, because it is very true and I have no desire whatsoever to conceal from this court the fact that to preach disaffection towards the existing system of government has become almost a passion with me.

And the learned Advocate-General is also entirely in the right when he says that my preaching of disaffection did not commence with my connection with *Young India*,[2] but that it commenced much earlier, and in the statement that I am about to read it will be my painful duty to admit before this court that it commenced much earlier than the period stated by the Advocate-General. It is the most painful duty with me, but I have to discharge that duty knowing the responsibility that rested upon my shoulders …

He is quite right when he says that as a man of responsibility, a man having received a fair share of education, having had a fair share of experience of this world, I should know the consequences of every one of my acts. I knew them. I knew that I was playing with fire. I ran the risk and if I was set free I would still do the same. I would be failing in my duty if I do not do so. I have felt it this morning that I would have failed in my duty if I did not say all what I said here just now. I wanted to avoid violence. Non-violence is the first article of my faith. It is the last article of my faith.

But I had to make my choice. I had either to submit to a system which I considered has done an irreparable harm to my country, or incur the risk of the mad fury of my people bursting forth when they understood the truth from my lips. I know that my people have sometimes gone mad. I am deeply sorry for it; and I am therefore here to submit not to a light penalty but to the highest penalty. I do not ask for mercy. I do not plead any extenuating act. I am here, therefore, to invite and submit to the highest penalty that can be inflicted upon me for what in law is a deliberate crime and what appears to me to be the highest duty of a citizen.

The only course open to you, Mr Judge, is, as I am just going to say in my statement, either to resign your post or inflict on me the severest penalty, if you believe that the system and law you are assisting to administer are good for the people. I do not expect that kind of conversion. But by the time I have finished with my statement you will, perhaps, have a glimpse of what is raging within my breast to run this maddest risk which a sane man can run.

[*The following is the written statement which Gandhi read to the court.*]

I owe it perhaps to the Indian public and to the public in England – to placate which this prosecution is mainly taken up – that I should explain why from a staunch loyalist and co-operator I have become an uncompromising disaffectionist and non-co-operator. To the court, too, I should say why I plead guilty to the charge of promoting disaffection towards the government established by law in India.

My public life began in 1893 in South Africa in troubled weather. My first contact with British authority in that country was not of a happy character. I discovered that as a man and an Indian I had no rights. On the contrary I discovered that I had no rights as a man because I was an Indian.

But I was not baffled. I thought that this treatment of Indians was an excrescence upon a system that was intrinsically and mainly good. I gave the government my voluntary and hearty co-operation, criticizing it fully where I felt it was faulty but never wishing its destruction.

Consequently when the existence of the Empire was threatened in 1899 by the Boer challenge, I offered my services to it, raised a volunteer ambulance corps and served at several actions that took place for the relief of Ladysmith. Similarly in 1906, at the time of the Zulu revolt, I raised a stretcher-bearer party and served till the end of the 'rebellion'. On both of these occasions I received medals and was even mentioned in dispatches. For my work in South Africa I was given by Lord Hardinge[3] a Kaiser-i-Hind[4] gold medal.

When the war broke out in 1914 between England and Germany, I raised a volunteer ambulance corps in London, consisting of the then resident Indians in London, chiefly students. Its work was acknowledged by the authorities to be valuable. Lastly in India, when a special appeal was made at the war conference in Delhi in 1917 by Lord Chelmsford[5] for recruits I struggled at the cost of my health to raise a corps in Kheda[6] and the response was being made when the hostilities ceased and orders were received that no more recruits were wanted. In all these efforts at service I was actuated by the belief that it was possible by such services to gain a status of full equality in the Empire for my countrymen.

The first shock came in the shape of the Rowlatt Act,[7] a law designed to rob the people of all real freedom. I felt called upon to lead an intensive agitation against it. Then followed the Punjab horrors, beginning with the massacre at Jallianwala Bagh[8] and culminating in crawling orders,[9] public floggings and other indescribable humiliations. I discovered too that the plighted word of the prime minister to the Mussulmans[10] of India regarding the integrity of Turkey and the holy places of Islam was not likely to be fulfilled.

But in spite of the foreboding and the grave warnings of friends, at the Amritsar Congress in 1919, I fought for co-operation and working the Montagu–Chelmsford reforms,[11] hoping that the prime minister would redeem his promise to the Indian Mussulmans, that the Punjab wound would be healed and that the reforms – inadequate and unsatisfactory though they were – marked a new era of hope in the life of India.

But all that hope was shattered. The Khilafat[12] promise was not to be redeemed. The Punjab crime was whitewashed and most culprits not only went unpunished but remained in service and some continued to draw pensions from the Indian revenue, and in some cases were even rewarded.[13] I saw too that not only did the reforms not mark a change of heart, but they were only a method of further draining India of her wealth and of prolonging her servitude.

I came reluctantly to the conclusion that the British connection had made India more helpless than she ever was before, politically and economically. A disarmed India has no power of resistance against any aggressor if she wanted to engage in an armed conflict with him.

So much is this the case that some of our best men consider that India must take generations before she can achieve the Dominion status. She has become so poor that she has little power of resisting famines. Before the British advent, India spun and wove in her millions of cottages just the supplement she needed for adding to her meagre agricultural resources. The cottage industry, so vital for India's existence, has been ruined by incredibly heartless and inhuman processes, as described by English witnesses.

Little do town-dwellers know how the semi-starved masses of Indians are slowly sinking to lifelessness. Little do they know that their miserable comfort represents the brokerage they get for the work they do for the foreign exploiter, that the profits and the brokerage are sucked from the masses. Little do they realize that the government established by law in British India is carried on for this exploitation of the masses.

No sophistry, no jugglery in figures can explain away the evidence the skeletons in many villages present to the naked eye. I have no doubt whatsoever that both England and the town-dwellers of India will have to answer, if there is a God above, for this crime against humanity which is perhaps unequalled in history.

[5] The English colonial administrator Frederic Thesiger, 3rd Baron Chelmsford *later 1st Viscount Chelmsford* (1868–1933) served as Viceroy of India, 1916–21.
[6] A district in the north-western state of Gujerat.

[7] Following an inquiry chaired by Sir Sidney Rowlatt in 1918, the Anarchy and Revolutionary Crimes Act was passed in 1919. A response to violent campaigns for independence, it permanently withdrew civil liberties which had been suspended during World War I.

[8] The village where the Amritsar Massacre occurred.
[9] In April 1919 the English missionary Marcella Sherwood was assaulted in Amritsar. The local military commander, Brigadier General R E H Dyer (1864–1927) responded by imposing a 'crawling order' requiring all Indians to traverse the street where the assault occurred 'on all fours'. The ruling was enforced on pain of flogging. Soon afterwards, Dyer was responsible for the Amritsar massacre.
[10] An archaic term for Muslims.

[11] Reforms proposed by Edwin Montagu, the Secretary of State for India, and Lord Chelmsford, the Viceroy, and subsequently enacted in the Government of India Act 1919. The measures allowed Indians to control education and public health, but recommended British control of the police, the law courts, law and order and taxation.
[12] Gandhi was a supporter of the Khilafat movement. See previous speech.
[13] On his return to Britain Dyer received an award of £18,000, collected by readers of the *Morning Post*.

The law itself in this country has been used to serve the foreign exploiter. My unbiased examination of the Punjab Martial Law cases has led me to believe that at least 95 per cent of convictions were wholly bad. My experience of political cases in India leads me to the conclusion that in nine out of every ten the condemned men were totally innocent. Their crime consisted in love of their country. In 99 cases out of 100, justice has been denied to Indians as against Europeans in the courts of India.

This is not an exaggerated picture. It is the experience of almost every Indian who has had anything to do with such cases. In my opinion the administration of the law is thus prostituted, consciously or unconsciously, for the benefit of the exploiter.

The greatest misfortune is that Englishmen and their Indian associates in the administration of the country do not know that they are engaged in the crime I have attempted to describe. I am satisfied that many English and Indian officials honestly believe that they are administering one of the best systems devised in the world and that India is making steady though slow progress. They do not know that a subtle but effective system of terrorism and an organized display of force on the one hand and the deprivation of all powers of retaliation or self-defence on the other have emasculated the people and induced in them the habit of simulation.

This awful habit has added to the ignorance and the self-deception of the administrators. Section 124–A, under which I am happily charged, is perhaps the prince among the political sections of the Indian Penal Code designed to suppress the liberty of the citizen. Affection cannot be manufactured or regulated by law. If one has no affection for a person or thing, one should be free to give the fullest expression to his disaffection, so long as he does not contemplate, promote or incite to violence.

But the section under which Mr Banker[14] and I are charged is one under which mere promotion of disaffection is a crime. I have studied some of the cases tried under it, and I know that some of the most loved of India's patriots have been convicted under it. I consider it a privilege, therefore, to be charged under it.

[14] The Indian campaigner Shankarlal Ghelabhai Banker, publisher of the *Young India* newspaper, was Gandhi's co-accused.

I have endeavoured to give in their briefest outline the reasons for my disaffection. I have no personal ill-will against any single administrator, much less can I have any disaffection towards the King's person. But I hold it to be a virtue to be disaffected towards a government which in its totality has done more harm to India than any previous system. India is less manly under the British rule than she ever was before. Holding such a belief, I consider it to be a sin to have affection for the system. And it has been a precious privilege for me to be able to write what I have in the various articles tendered in evidence against me.

In fact I believe that I have rendered a service to India and England by showing in non-co-operation the way out of the unnatural state in which both are living. In my humble opinion, non-co-operation with evil is as much a duty as is co-operation with good. But in the past, non-co-operation has been deliberately expressed in violence to the evil-doer.

I am endeavouring to show to my countrymen that violent non-co-operation only multiplies evil and that as evil can only be sustained by violence, withdrawal of support of evil requires complete abstention from violence. Non-violence implies voluntary submission to the penalty for non-co-operation with evil.

I am here, therefore, to invite and submit cheerfully to the highest penalty that can be inflicted upon me for what in law is deliberate crime and what appears to me to be the highest duty of a citizen. The only course open to you, the judge and the assessors, is either to resign your posts and thus dissociate yourselves from evil – if you feel that the law you are called upon to administer is an evil and that in reality I am innocent – or to inflict on me the severest penalty, if you believe that the system and the law you are assisting to administer are good for the people of this country and that my activity is therefore injurious to the public weal.

Giuseppe Garibaldi
Italian patriot and military leader

Giuseppe Garibaldi (1807–92) was born a sailor's son in Nice, then part of the French Empire, now in France. He went to sea at an early age. In 1833 he became involved in the Young Italy movement led by the patriot Giuseppe Mazzini. He was condemned to death for taking part in an attempt to seize Piedmont in 1834. He escaped to South America, where in the rebellion of Rio Grande against Brazil he distinguished himself as a guerrilla fighter and privateer. He was taken prisoner, later eloping with the beautiful Creole, Anita Riviera de Silva, who became the mother of his children Menotti, Ricciotti and Teresa. Returning to Italy during the 1848 revolution, he served with the Sardinian army against the Austrians and commanded the Roman Republic army in its defence of the city against the French. He lived in exile until 1854, when he returned to settle down to a life of farming, but fought the Austrians again in the war of liberation of 1859. In 1860, at the head of 1,000 volunteers ('Red Shirts'), he conquered Sicily and Naples for the new unified kingdom of Italy. In 1862 and 1867, he led two unsuccessful expeditions to liberate Rome from papal rule. He was a good commander of irregulars but his ignorance of politics sometimes harmed his cause. Nevertheless, he remains the central figure in the story of Italian independence.

'The oppressors and the mighty shall disappear like dust'
7 September 1860, Naples, Italy

Since joining the Young Italy movement in 1833, Garibaldi had been intent on freeing and uniting the nation. After interludes in South and North America, he returned to Italy in 1854, and seems to have enjoyed a peaceful life for a few years. But 1859–60 proved to be his most active years as a military leader. After defeating Austrian incursions in the Alps, he learned of uprisings in Sicily and saw the opportunity to pursue his overriding goal. From May 1860, he led the famous campaign to wrest the Kingdom of the Two Sicilies – which included Sicily itself and much of southern Italy – from King Francis II.

By September, he had taken Naples and victory seemed within reach. The final battle was yet to be fought at the River Volturno in October, but Garibaldi already scented triumph. Having declared himself Dictator of the Two Sicilies – a title he would willingly renounce in favour of Victor Emmanuel of Sardinia, who was proclaimed king of a united Italy in 1861 – he halted to rest, regroup and bolster the resolve of his volunteer army.

Garibaldi knew he lacked the political acumen of his allies Giuseppe Mazzini and Camillo Cavour, but he had a natural gift for arousing patriotic fervour among the masses. In this speech to his troops, he plays to his strengths, firing their imagination with references to invincible armies of old, inciting pride in their provincial origins and assuring them of glorious victory.

By November, he was riding into Naples alongside his new king.

We must now consider the period which is just drawing to a close as almost the last stage of our national resurrection, and prepare ourselves to finish worthily the marvellous design of the elect of 20 generations, the completion of which Providence has reserved for this fortunate age.

Yes, young men, Italy owes to you an undertaking which has merited the applause of the universe. You have conquered and you will conquer still, because you are prepared for the tactics that decide the fate of battles. You are not unworthy of the men who entered the ranks of a Macedonian phalanx, and who contended not in vain with the proud conquerors of Asia. To this wonderful page in our country's history another more glorious still will be added, and the slave shall show at last to his free brothers a sharpened sword forged from the links of his fetters.

To arms, then, all of you! All of you! And the oppressors and the mighty shall disappear like dust. You, too, women, cast away all the cowards from your embraces; they will give you only cowards for children, and you who are the daughters of the land of beauty must bear children who are noble and brave. Let timid doctrinaires depart from among us to carry their servility and their miserable fears elsewhere.

This people is its own master. It wishes to be the brother of other peoples, but to look on the insolent with a proud glance, not to grovel before them imploring its own freedom. It will no longer follow in the trail of men whose hearts are foul. No! No! No!

Providence has presented Italy with Victor Emmanuel.[1] Every Italian should rally round him. By the side of Victor Emmanuel every quarrel should be forgotten, all rancour depart. Once more I repeat my battle-cry: 'To arms, all, all of you!'

If March 1861[2] does not find one million Italians in arms, then alas for liberty, alas for the life of Italy. Ah no – far be from me a thought which I loathe like poison. March of 1861, or if need be February, will find us all at our posts – Italians of Calatafimi, Palermo, Ancona, the Volturno, Castelfidardo and Isernia; and with us every man of this land who is not a coward or a slave. Let all of us rally round the glorious hero of Palestro[3] and give the last blow to the crumbling edifice of tyranny. Receive, then, my gallant young volunteers, at the honoured conclusion of ten battles, one word of farewell from me.

I utter this word with deepest affection and from the very bottom of my heart. Today I am obliged to retire, but for a few days only. The hour of battle will find me with you again, by the side of the champions of Italian liberty. Let those only return to their homes who are called by the imperative duties which they owe to their families, and those who by their glorious wounds have deserved the credit of their country. These, indeed, will serve Italy in their homes by their counsel, by the very aspect of the scars which adorn their youthful brows.

Apart from these, let all others remain to guard our glorious banners. We shall meet again before long, to march together to the redemption of our brothers who are still slaves of the stranger. We shall meet again before long to march to new triumphs.

[1] The Italian monarch Victor Emmanuel II (1820–78) was King of Sardinia, 1849–61, which included Savoy and Piedmont. In alliance with France, he drove the Austrians out of Lombardy in 1859, and acquired most of the other northern and central areas of Italy in 1860. After the capture of Naples, Garibaldi greeted him as King of Italy.

[2] The notional date of Italian unification. In the event Victor Emmanuel took the throne on 18 February.

[3] The village in northern Italy where Victor Emmanuel's Sardinian forces, assisted by French troops, defeated the Austrian army in 1859.

Lou Gehrig
American sportsman

Henry Louis Gehrig (1903–41) was born in New York City, the son of German immigrants. He became known as the 'Iron Horse' for his remarkable endurance, playing a record number of 2,130 consecutive major-league games for the New York Yankees (1925–39). He was voted Most Valuable Player (MVP) four times (in 1927, 1931, 1934 and 1936). His career was cut short by amyotrophic lateral sclerosis, now known in the USA as 'Lou Gehrig's disease'. In 1939, he was elected to the National Baseball Hall of Fame. The story of his life was told in the film *The Pride of the Yankees* (1942), with Gary Cooper in the central role.

'The luckiest man on the face of the earth'
4 July 1939, New York City, USA

One of the most emotional speeches ever given on a sporting occasion was heard by the 62,000 fans in Yankee Stadium when Gehrig was inducted into the Baseball Hall of Fame. At the suggestion of New York sports writer Paul Gallico, a special Lou Gehrig Appreciation Day was held on Independence Day to honour this enormously popular sporting hero. During Gehrig's tenure at first base, the New York Yankees had won seven pennants and six World Series titles. Gehrig's uniform number – 4 – was the first ever to be retired from baseball.

Surrounded by his former team-mates from the 1927 and 1939 squads, he was almost overwhelmed by emotion and struggled to deliver the speech he had prepared, until he was encouraged by the team manager, Joe McCarthy. The speech is short and certainly heartfelt. Its simple and direct style is in keeping with this quiet and modest man, who played down his diagnosis with amyotrophic lateral sclerosis as 'a bad break', preferring to count his blessings. Two months previously, Gehrig had learned of his affliction, a rare condition that causes spinal paralysis.

The intense atmosphere in the stadium was heightened further when Gehrig was embraced by his rival Babe Ruth, another baseball legend, ending a five-year feud between the two.

Fans, for the past two weeks you have been reading about a bad break I got. Yet today I consider myself the luckiest man on the face of the earth. I have been in ballparks for 17 years and have never received anything but kindness and encouragement from you fans. Look at these grand men. Which of you wouldn't consider it the highlight of his career just to associate with them for even one day?

Sure, I'm lucky. Who wouldn't consider it an honour to have known Jacob Ruppert;[1] also the builder of baseball's greatest empire, Ed Barrow;[2] to have spent six years with that wonderful little fellow, Miller Huggins;[3] then to have spent the next nine years with that outstanding leader, that smart student of psychology – the best manager in baseball today, Joe McCarthy?[4] Who wouldn't feel honoured to have roomed with such a grand guy as Bill Dickey?[5]

Sure, I'm lucky. When the New York Giants, a team you would give your right arm to beat, and vice versa, sends you a gift – that's something! When everybody down to the groundskeepers and those boys in white coats remember you with trophies – that's something!

When you have a wonderful mother-in-law who takes sides with you in squabbles against her own daughter[6] – that's something! When you have a father and mother who work all their lives so that you can have an education and build your body – it's a blessing! When you have a wife who has been a tower of strength and shown more courage than you dreamed existed – that's the finest I know!

So I close in saying that I might have been given a bad break, but I have an awful lot to live for! Thank you.

[1] The US brewer Colonel Jacob Ruppert (1867–1939) was joint owner of the Yankees from 1914 until his death.
[2] The US sports manager Edward Barrow *known as Cousin Ed* (1868–1953) was general manager of the Yankees from 1921, becoming club president in 1939 and chairman in 1945.
[3] The US sportsman Miller Huggins *known as the Mighty Mite* (1879–1929) was manager of the Yankees from 1917 until his death.

[4] The US sports manager Joseph (Joe) McCarthy (1887–1978) was manager of the Yankees, 1931–46.
[5] The US sportsman William (Bill) Dickey (1907–93) played for the Yankees, 1928–43, and succeeded McCarthy as the team's manager in 1946. He also appeared in *The Pride of the Yankees*, a biographical film about Gehrig.
[6] Gehrig married Eleanor Twitchell in 1933.

George V

British monarch

George V *originally George Frederick Ernest Albert* (1865–1936) was born at Marlborough House, London. He served in the Royal Navy, travelled in many parts of the British Empire, and was created Prince of Wales in 1901. He succeeded his father, Edward VII, in 1910. His reign was marked by various important events, such as the Union of South Africa (1910), his visit to India for the Coronation Durbar (1911), World War I (1914–18), the Sinn Féin Rebellion (1916), the royal family's adoption of the surname Windsor (1917), the Irish Free State settlement (1922), the first Labour governments (1924, 1929–31), the General Strike (1926), Scottish church union (1929), economic crisis and a national government (1931), the Statute of Westminster, defining the Dominion status of the colonies (1931), and the Government of India Act (1935). He originated the monarch's Christmas Day broadcasts to the nation in 1932. Although he was suspicious of new ideas, he was responsible for the development of the monarchy as a symbol of national unity, and his silver jubilee (1935) was celebrated with genuine popular enthusiasm.

'Voices out of the air'

25 December 1932, Sandringham, England

As general manager of the recently formed British Broadcasting Company, John Reith wrote to King George's private secretary, in October 1923, proposing that the king should consider broadcasting to the British Isles. The king, however, was averse to anything 'modern', and the suggestion was unsuccessful. Reith persevered and in 1932 suggested that, since the Empire Service was to start on 19 December, the king might broadcast to the Empire at Christmas. Sir Clive Wigram, George's private secretary, asked the prime minister RAMSAY MACDONALD to encourage the king, who eventually consented.

The king was concerned that the broadcast be easily understood around the Empire, so the writer and poet RUDYARD KIPLING was invited to write it. The speech was delivered just after 3pm (the most favourable time for short-wave radio reception around the world) on Christmas Day, from a small room at the royal residence at Sandringham. The king listened to greetings broadcast from around the Empire and then spoke live, cued by a red light.

The king's short communication was a simple message to the 'family of nations'. The microphones were connected through Post Office land lines to Broadcasting House, from where the signal was sent via Home Service transmitters and short-wave transmitters at the Empire Broadcasting Service.

Following the success of this broadcast, King George made a Christmas broadcast each year for the rest of his life – a tradition upheld by British monarchs ever since.

Through one of the marvels of modern science, I am enabled, this Christmas Day, to speak to all my peoples throughout the Empire. I take it as a good omen that wireless should have reached its present perfection at a time when the Empire has been linked in closer union. For it offers us immense possibilities to make that union closer still.

It may be that our future will lay upon us more than one stern test. Our past will have taught us how to meet it unshaken. For the present, the work to which we are all equally bound is to arrive at a reasoned tranquillity within our borders; to regain prosperity without self-seeking; and to carry with us those whom the burden of past years has disheartened or overborne.

My life's aim has been to serve as I might, towards those ends. Your loyalty, your confidence in me has been my abundant reward.

I speak now from my home and from my heart to you all. To men and women so cut off by the snows, the desert, or the sea, that only voices out of the air can reach them; to those cut off from fuller life by blindness, sickness, or infirmity; and to those who are celebrating this day with their children and grandchildren. To all – to each – I wish a Happy Christmas. God bless you!

Dick Gephardt
American politician

Richard Andrew Gephardt (1941–) was born in St Louis, Missouri, the son of a milk-truck driver of German descent. He studied at Northwestern University and the University of Michigan Law School, qualifying as a lawyer in 1965. He served with the Missouri Air National Guard until 1971, meanwhile working for the Democrat Party in Missouri (1968–71). After serving as a Democrat alderman (1971–6), he was elected to Congress in 1977, and re-elected for 13 consecutive terms until he stood down in 2004. He sought the Democratic nomination in the presidential elections of 1988 and 2004, but was unsuccessful. His political career was marked by a gradual shift to the left. During the mid-1980s, he abandoned a strong anti-abortion position; having supported President RONALD REAGAN's tax cuts in 1981, he opposed similar cuts introduced by President GEORGE W BUSH. He retired from politics in January 2005 and went on to set up a Washington-based public affairs firm, Gephardt Government Affairs, and an Atlanta-based labour consultancy, the Gephardt Group. He has campaigned with his lesbian daughter Chrissy for public acceptance of homosexuality.

'A system of government of men, not of angels'
19 December 1998, Washington, DC, USA

In the autumn of 1998, Washington was beset by sex scandals. The most prominent centred on the affair between President BILL CLINTON and former White House intern Monica Lewinsky, which had first been reported in January and was finally admitted by Clinton in August.

On 19 December, four articles of impeachment were brought against Clinton, charging him with abuse of power, obstruction of justice and two counts of perjury – the last referring to his famous assertion under oath, 'I have never had sexual relations with Monica Lewinsky'.

The House of Representatives was preparing to vote on the impeachment motion when the Republican Speaker-designate Bob Livingston – whose own extramarital affairs had been exposed by Larry Flynt, publisher of *Hustler* magazine – dramatically announced his own resignation and called on Clinton to follow suit.

Dick Gephart, leader of the Democrats in the House of Representatives, responded with this speech, in which he urges a resolution of censure as a milder alternative to impeachment. He also calls for a relaxation of puritanical values in American political culture, which he felt was undermining its coherence.

It was a popular speech, repeatedly interrupted by applause, but it failed in its objective. Clinton was impeached on two of the four counts, and faced a five-week trial in the Senate, though he was ultimately acquitted in February 1999.

Mr Speaker and members of the House: I stood on this floor yesterday and implored all of us to say that the politics of slash-and-burn must end. I implored all of you that we must turn away from the politics of personal destruction and return to the politics of values.

It is with that same passion that I say to all of you today that the gentleman from Louisiana, Bob Livingston, is a worthy and good and honourable man.

[*Lengthy applause.*]

I believe his decision to retire is a terrible capitulation to the negative forces that are consuming our political system and our country. [*Applause.*] And I pray with all my heart that he will reconsider this decision.

[*Applause.*]

Our founding fathers created a system of government of men, not of angels. No-one standing in this House today can pass a puritanical test of purity that some are demanding that our elected leaders take.

[*Applause.*]

If we demand that mere mortals live up to this standard, we will see our seats of government lay empty, and we will see the best, most able people unfairly cast out of public service. We need to stop destroying imperfect people at the altar of an unobtainable morality.

[*Applause.*]

We need to start living up to the standards which the public, in its infinite wisdom, understands that imperfect people must strive towards, but too often fall short. We are now rapidly descending into a politics where life imitates farce. Fratricide dominates our public debate and America is held hostage to tactics of smear and fear.

Let all of us here today say no to resignation, no to impeachment, no to hatred, no to intolerance of each other, and no to vicious self-righteousness.

[*Lengthy applause.*]

We need to start healing. We need to start binding up our wounds. We need to end this downward spiral which will culminate in the death of representative democracy. I believe this healing can start today by changing the course we've begun. This is exactly why we need this today to be bipartisan. This is why we ask the opportunity to vote on a bipartisan censure resolution, to begin the process of healing our nation and healing our people.

We are on the brink of the abyss. The only way we stop this insanity is through the force of our own will. [*Applause.*] The only way we stop this spiral is for all of us to finally say: enough. Let us step back from the abyss and let's begin a new politics of respect and fairness and decency, which raises what has come before.

May God have mercy on this Congress and may Congress have the wisdom and the courage and the goodness to save itself today.

[*Lengthy applause.*]

William Gladstone
English statesman

William Ewart Gladstone (1809–98) was born in Liverpool, the son of a merchant and MP. He was educated at Eton and Christ Church, Oxford. In 1832 he became Conservative MP for Newark. After several junior appointments, he was appointed president of the Board of Trade (1843), then Colonial Secretary (1845). At the general election of 1847 he became MP for the University of Oxford, still as a Conservative. When Robert Peel died in 1850, Gladstone rose in prominence, and was soon recognized as a master of parliamentary debate. His first truly great speech in Parliament was made in the debate on BENJAMIN DISRAELI's budget in 1852. On the fall of the Tory administration, Lord Aberdeen formed the famous Coalition Ministry, with Lord Palmerston as Home Secretary, Lord John Russell as Foreign Secretary and Gladstone as Chancellor of the Exchequer. Gladstone's speech on the introduction of his first budget was masterly. He was again appointed Chancellor by Palmerston in 1859. In 1865, on Lord Russell's becoming prime minister, Gladstone became Leader of the House of Commons. In 1866, a minor reform bill to enlarge the franchise in boroughs and counties was defeated and the Liberals went out of office. The serious condition of Ireland, however, brought the Liberals to power with Gladstone as prime minister in 1868, the first of four periods in office. He introduced a system of national education, disestablished the Irish Church, and introduced a measure to improve university education in Ireland, but it was rejected (1873). Gladstone offered his resignation, but remained in office. The by-elections began to tell against the Liberals, and Gladstone suddenly dissolved Parliament, allowing Disraeli to return to power (1874). For some time Gladstone took the opportunity to concentrate on his literary studies. In 1880, the Liberals were returned to government with an overwhelming majority, and Gladstone (now member for Midlothian) became prime minister once more. He carried out parliamentary reforms to expand the male franchise. After a further period out of office, he attempted to introduce a home rule bill for Ireland, but it divided the Liberals and was rejected. He was defeated at the polls in 1886. In 1893, after his final return to office, the home rule bill was carried in the Commons, but was thrown out by the Lords. Gladstone resigned in 1894, aged 84. He died at Hawarden, and was buried in Westminster Abbey.

'The guilt unredeemed of causeless and unnecessary wars'
26 November 1879, Dalkeith, Scotland

After losing the general election of 1874, Gladstone had retired as Liberal Party leader, but retained his seat in Greenwich. In 1879–80, he returned to prominence, with a two-week electoral campaign in Midlothian, near Edinburgh, during which he made a series of famous speeches, largely on foreign policy. It was an unprecedented appeal to the masses which drew large audiences from all over Scotland and was widely reported in the press.

This is the final part of the second Midlothian speech, in which Gladstone appeals to the women among his audience, and more generally to 'the common nature which runs through us all'. Modern sensibilities may well rankle at Gladstone's assertion that women 'do not concern yourselves with abstract propositions', but it is impossible to resist his appeal to compassion and common sense as he exposes the cruel cost of war to civilians. His humane instincts were particularly outraged by the conflict in Afghanistan, which he describes as 'a war as frivolous as ever was waged in the history of man'.

The speech demonstrates Gladstone's capacity for passionate but well structured oratory. He won the seat easily and resumed the demanding dual post of prime minister and Chancellor of the Exchequer until 1885.

> I understand it to be your wish that I should use some words addressed to the particular share that ladies, and that women, may be thought to have in the crisis of today. I use the expression women with greater satisfaction than the former one which I uttered, the name of ladies; because it is to them – not only in virtue of a particular station, not only by reason of their possessing a greater portion of the goods of life than may have been granted to the humbler classes of society – that I appeal.
>
> I appeal to them in virtue of the common nature which runs through us all. And I am very glad, sir, that you have introduced to us with a special notice the factory girls of the place, who on this occasion have been desirous to testify their kindly feelings. I hope you will convey to them the

assurance that their particular act is not forgotten, and that the gift they offer is accepted with as lively thankfulness and as profound gratification as the most splendid offering that could be tendered by the noblest in the land.

I speak to you, ladies, as women; and I do think and feel that the present political crisis has to do not only with human interests at large, but especially with those interests which are most appropriate, and ought to be most dear, to you. The harder, and sterner, and drier lessons of politics are little to your taste. You do not concern yourselves with abstract propositions. It is that side of politics which is associated with the heart of man that I must call your side of politics. When I look at the inscription which faces me on yonder gallery, I see the words 'Peace, Retrenchment and Reform'.[1]

What some would call the desert of this world, and of the political world in particular, would be an arid desert indeed if we could not hope that our labours are addressed to the increase of human happiness; that we try to diminish the sin and the sorrow in the world, to do something to reduce its grievous and overwhelming mass, to alleviate a little the burden of life for some, to take out of the way of struggling excellence those impediments at least which the folly or the graver offence of man has offered as obstacles in his progress. These are the hopes that cheer, that ought to cheer, the human heart, amidst the labours and struggles of public life.

Of all these words – peace, retrenchment, and reform – the one word upon which I will say a few more special words on this occasion is the word 'peace'. Is this, ladies, a time of peace? Cast your eyes abroad over the world. Think what has taken place in the last three or four years. Think of the events which have deluged many a hill and many a valley with blood; and think, with regret and pain, of the share, not which you individually, but which your country collectively has had in that grievous operation.

If we cast our eyes to South Africa,[2] what do we behold? That a nation whom we term savages have, in defence of their own land, offered their naked bodies to the terribly improved artillery and arms of modern European science, and have been mowed down by hundreds and by thousands, having committed no offence, but having, with rude and ignorant courage, done what were for them – done faithfully and bravely what were for them – the duties of patriotism. You may talk of glory, you may offer rewards – and you are right to give rewards to the gallantry of your soldiers, who, I think, are entitled not only to our admiration for courage, but to our compassion for the nature of the duties they have been called to perform. But the grief and the pain nonetheless remain.

Go from South Africa to the mountains of Central Asia. Go into the lofty hills of Afghanistan,[3] as they were last winter, and what do we there see? I fear a yet sadder sight than was to be seen in the land of the Zulus. It is true that with respect to the operations of the war in Afghanistan you have seen none but official accounts, or hardly any but official accounts; and many of the facts belonging to that war have not been brought under the general notice of the British public.

I think that a great misfortune. I know that it may be necessary and wise, under certain circumstances, to restrain what might be the injudicious and exaggerated, and therefore the dangerous communications that might proceed from irresponsible persons. At the same time, I deeply regret that we were not more fully informed of the proceedings of the war in Afghanistan, especially as we must bear in mind that our army is composed

[1] The Whigs had won the election of 1830 on the platform of this slogan. In the course of the 19th century, the Liberal Party gradually replaced the Whigs.

[2] Gladstone refers to the bloody Anglo-Zulu War of 1879, in which British forces finally triumphed at the Battle of Ulundi, effectively ending the Zulu nation.

[3] Casualties were heavy on both sides during the Second Anglo-Afghan War (1878–1880). British forces occupied much of Afghanistan, and won the Battle of Kandahar in 1880, but ultimately withdrew rather than face further bloody skirmishes.

[4] Many of the troops under British command in Afghanistan were Indian or Nepali.

in great part of a soldiery not British, and not under Christian obligations and restraints.[4]

What we know is this: that our gallant troops have been called upon to ascend to an elevation of many thousand feet, and to operate in the winter months – I am going back to a period of nine or twelve months – amidst the snows of winter. We know that that was done for the most part not strictly in the territory of Afghanistan proper, but in its border lands, inhabited by hill tribes who enjoy more or less of political independence, and do not own a regular allegiance to the Afghan ruler. You have seen during last winter from time to time that from such and such a village attacks had been made upon the British forces, and that in consequence the village had been burned.

Have you ever reflected on the meaning of these words? Do not suppose that I am pronouncing a censure, for I am not, either upon the military commanders or upon those who acted subject to their orders. But I am trying to point out the responsibility of the terrible consequences that follow upon such operations. Those hill tribes had committed no real offence against us. We, in the pursuit of our political objects, chose to establish military positions in their country. If they resisted, would not you have done the same? And when, going forth from their villages they had resisted, what you find is this, that those who went forth were slain, and that the village was burned.

Again I say, have you considered the meaning of these words? The meaning of the burning of the village is that the women and the children were driven forth to perish in the snows of winter. Is not that a terrible supposition? Is not that a fact – for such, I fear, it must be reckoned to be – which does rouse in you a sentiment of horror and grief, to think that the name of England, under no political necessity, but for a war as frivolous as ever was waged in the history of man, should be associated with consequences such as these?

I have carried you from South Africa to Central Asia. I carry you from Central Asia to eastern Europe,[5] and in the history of eastern Europe in the last few years do you not again feel that this is no matter of dry political argument; that there was a wider theatre upon which for many generations a cruel and a grinding oppression, not resting upon superior civilization, not upon superior knowledge, but a domination of mere force, had crushed down to the earth races who, four or five hundred years ago, greatly excelled our own forefathers in civilization – had crushed these races to the earth, had abated in them the manhood and the nobler qualities that belong to freedom – had ground these qualities, it appeared, in some cases almost out of their composition – had succeeded in impressing upon them some of the features of slaves; and in addition to this, when from time to time the impulses of humanity would not be repressed, and an effort was made by any of these people to secure to themselves their long-lost liberties, these efforts had been put down with a cruelty incredible and unequalled, almost and perhaps entirely unequalled in the annals of mankind; and not only with that cruelty, but with a development of other horrors in the treatment of men, women and children, which even decency does not permit me to describe?

I will not dwell further on these matters than to say that I think in all these scenes, if peace be our motto, we must feel that a strong appeal is made to you as women – to you specially, and to whatever there is in men that associates itself with what is best and most peculiar in you.

[5] Since the Crimean War of 1854–6, the Ottoman Empire had been in decline, but there had been recent flashpoints, including the British occupation of Cyprus (1876) and the Russo-Turkish War (1877–8). In 1876, Gladstone had published a pamphlet on Turkish atrocities in Bulgaria.

Ladies, I am not here before you as one of those who have ever professed to believe that the state which society has reached permits us to make a vow of universal peace, and of renouncing, in all cases, the alternative of war. But I am here to say that a long experience of life leads me not towards any abstract doctrine upon the subject, but to a deeper and deeper conviction of the enormous mischiefs of war, even under the best and most favourable circumstances, and of the mischiefs indescribable and the guilt unredeemed of causeless and unnecessary wars.

Look back over the pages of history; consider the feelings with which we now regard wars that our forefathers in their time supported with the same pernicious fanaticism, of which we have had some developments in this country within the last three years. Consider, for example, that the American War,[6] now condemned by 999 out of every 1,000 persons in this country, was a war which for years was enthusiastically supported by the mass of the population. And then see how powerful and deadly are the fascinations of passion and of pride; and, if it be true that the errors of former times are recorded for our instruction, in order that we may avoid their repetition, then I beg and entreat you: be on your guard against these deadly fascinations; do not suffer appeals to national pride to blind you to the dictates of justice.

[6] Gladstone probably refers to the American War of Independence (1775–83), rather than the more recent Civil War (1861–5).

Remember the rights of the savage, as we call him. Remember that the happiness of his humble home, remember that the sanctity of life in the hill villages of Afghanistan among the winter snows, is as inviolable in the eye of Almighty God as can be your own. Remember that he who has united you together as human beings in the same flesh and blood, has bound you by the law of mutual love; that that mutual love is not limited by the shores of this island, is not limited by the boundaries of Christian civilization; that it passes over the whole surface of the earth, and embraces the meanest along with the greatest in its unmeasured scope.

And therefore, I think that in appealing to you ungrudgingly to open your own feelings, and bear your own part in a political crisis like this, we are making no inappropriate demand, but are beseeching you to fulfil a duty which belongs to you; which, so far from involving any departure from your character as women, is associated with the fulfilment of that character, and the performance of its duties; the neglect of which would in future times be to you a source of pain and just mortification, and the fulfilment of which will serve to gild your own future years with sweet remembrances, and to warrant you in hoping that, each in your own place and sphere, you have raised your voice for justice, and have striven to mitigate the sorrows and misfortunes of mankind.

❧

'I have no fear of atheism in this House'

26 April 1883, London, England

❧

In 1847, when he was Conservative MP for the University of Oxford, Gladstone had controversially voted for the admission of Jews to Parliament. Now, during his second administration as Liberal prime minister, he took up the cause célèbre of Charles Bradlaugh (1833–91) an avowed atheist who had been elected in 1880 as MP for Northampton.

Bradlaugh had initially refused to take the oath of allegiance, a requirement for new Members, since it included the phrase 'So help me God'. He later offered to take the oath 'as a matter of form' but this proposal was rejected and Bradlaugh was barred from taking up his seat. He did so anyway, and was ultimately fined £1,500 for voting in

Parliament illegally. In 1881, he was caricatured in the satirical magazine *Punch* as a demon flying on bat's wings.

Though Gladstone was a devout Christian who loathed atheism, he considered the oath an outmoded piece of legislation – worn out like an old coin, as he puts it here – and no defence against unorthodox religious views. He therefore supported the 'affirmation bill', which proposed allowing an affirmation in place of the oath. This speech was made on its second reading.

In his carefully reasoned argument, Gladstone points to the gradual extension of religious tolerance in British public life and claims that – far from safeguarding Christianity – the existing law would weaken it. The bill was narrowly defeated, but in 1886 Bradlaugh was allowed to take the oath. Two years later, the Oaths Act enshrined the right of affirmation.

I know it is said that Christianity is part of the Common Law; but am I to be told that, if it is so, every man who is not a Christian is an offender against the Common Law? If so, it is an extraordinary mode of interpreting the law. But it has been shown that no oath or religious test of any kind was ever used by this House as a condition precedent to entrance into it until the reign of Elizabeth;[1] and that, when an oath was then introduced, it was not introduced in the slightest degree as a religious test ...

[1] The Act of Supremacy of 1559 required all those in church and public office to swear allegiance to ELIZABETH I, and in effect to be adherents of the Church of England.

I venture to say, as a matter of history, that that was the principle of our law down to the year 1828.[2] If that be so, I think it will be very difficult to maintain that there is any disqualification of the unbeliever by the Common Law of England. You may tell me that it was not then merely a question of the admission of atheists to this House, but a question of permitting them to live. That was perfectly true, I think, at least down to the year 1614 – for as late as that year, the ancestors of those of us who are of English blood burnt a certain person for deficiencies in respect of belief.[3]

[2] In 1828, THE DUKE OF WELLINGTON became prime minister and repealed the Test Act, which required those holding public office to abjure transubstantiation, a key tenet of Roman Catholicism.

He was not, however, an atheist; he was an Arian – so that people had better look out if this doctrine comes again into vogue. The fact is that the state gradually adopted the principles of toleration, but where it tolerated, it did not interpose barriers against access to this House. That is the historical principle which, I think, it will be found difficult to shake ...

[3] Arianism was a sect founded in the fourth century which took an unorthodox view of Jesus as a 'created being'. Two British adherents, named Whiteman and Legate, were burned at the stake around 1612–14.

I am convinced that upon every religious, as well as upon every political ground, the true and the wise course is not to deal out religious liberty by halves, by quarters, and by fractions, but to deal it out entire, and to leave no distinction between man and man on the ground of religious differences from one end of the land to the other ...

I want to know, is your religious distinction a real distinction at all? I will, for the sake of argument, and for no other purpose whatever, go with you on this dangerous ground of splitting religion into slices, and I ask you, 'Where will you draw the line?' You draw it at the point where the abstract denial of God is severed from abstract admission of the Deity. My proposition is that your line is worthless. There is much on your side of the line which is just as objectionable as the atheism on the other side. If you call on us to draw these distinctions, let them be rational distinctions. I do not say let them be Christian distinctions; but let them be rational distinctions ...

I do not hesitate to say that the specific evil, the specific form of irreligion with which in educated society in this country you have to contend – and with respect to which you ought to be on your guard – is not blank atheism. That is a rare form of opinion and it is seldom met with. But what is frequently met with are those various forms of opinion which teach us that whatever there be beyond the visible scene, whatever there can be beyond this short span of life, you know and can know nothing of it, and that it is a visionary and a bootless undertaking to endeavour to establish relations with it.

That is the specific mischief of the age; but that mischief you do not attempt to touch. Nay, more; you glory in the state of the law that now prevails. All differences of religion you wish to tolerate. You wish to allow everybody to enter your chambers who admits the existence of Deity.

You would seek to admit Voltaire.[4] That is a specimen of your toleration. But Voltaire was not a taciturn foe of Christianity. He was the author of that painful and awful phrase that goes to the heart of every Christian – and goes, I believe, to the heart of many a man professing religion who is not a Christian – *écrasez l'infâme*.[5] Voltaire was a believer in God; he would not have had the slightest difficulty in taking the oath; and you are working up the country to something like a crusade on this question, endeavouring to strengthen in the minds of the people the false notion that you have got a real test, a real safeguard – that Christianity is still generally safe with certain unavoidable exceptions, under the protecting aegis of the oath within the walls of this chamber. And it is for that you are entering on a great religious war! I hold, then, that this contention of our opponents is disparaging to religion. It is idle; and it is also highly irrational …

My reasons, sir, for the passing of the bill may be summed up in a few words. If I were asked to put a construction on this oath as it stands, I probably should give it a higher meaning than most gentlemen opposite. It is my opinion, as far as I can presume to form one, that the oath has in it a very large flavour of Christianity.

I am well aware that … there are other forms of positive attestation, recognized by other systems of religion, which may enable the oath to be taken by the removal of the words 'So help me God', and the substitution of some other words, or some symbolical act, involving the idea of Deity, and responsibility to the Deity. But … the oath does not consist of spoken words alone. The spoken words are accompanied by the corroborative act of kissing the book. What is the meaning of that? According to the intention of the legislature, I certainly should say that that act is an import of the acceptance of the divine revelation.

There have been other forms in other countries. I believe in Scotland the form is still maintained of holding up the right hand instead of kissing the book. In Spain the form is, I believe, that of kissing the cross. In Italy, I think, at one time, the form was that of laying the hand on the Gospel.

All these different forms meant, according to the original intention, an acceptance of Christianity. But you do not yourselves venture to say that the law could be applied in that sense. A law of this kind is like a coin spick-and-span, brand-new from the mint, carrying upon it its edges in all their sharpness and freshness; but it wears down in passing from hand to hand, and, though there is a residuum, yet the distinctive features disappear. Whatever my opinion may be as to the original vitality of the oath, I think there is very little difference of opinion as to what it has now become …

It is taken as no more than a theistic test. It does, as I think, involve a reference to Christianity. But while this is my personal opinion, it is not recognized by authority, and at any rate, does not prevail in practice; for some gentlemen in the other House of Parliament, if not in this also, have written works against the Christian religion, and yet have taken the oath. But, undoubtedly, it is not good for any of us to force this test so flavoured, or even if not so flavoured, upon men who cannot take it with a full and a cordial acceptance. It is bad – it is demoralizing to do so. It is all very well to say, 'Oh, yes; but it is their responsibility'. That is not, in my view, a satisfactory answer.

[4] The French philosopher and author Voltaire (1694–1778) embraced a nonconformist religious philosophy known as deism, acknowledging a creator and a sense of divine justice, but rejecting orthodox Christianity.

[5] Voltaire's battle-cry – literally 'crush that which is infamous' – a declaration of reason over faith.

A seat in this House is to the ordinary Englishman … the highest prize of his ambition. But if you place between him and that prize not only the necessity of conforming to certain civil conditions but the adoption of certain religious words, and if these words are not justly measured to the condition of his conscience and of his convictions, you give him an inducement … to do violence to his conscience in order that he may not be stigmatized by being shut out from what is held to be the noblest privilege of the English citizen – that of representing his fellow citizens in Parliament.

And therefore I say that, besides our duty to vindicate the principle of civil and religious liberty, which totally detaches religious controversy from the enjoyment of civil rights, it is most important that the House should consider the moral effect of this test … Viewed as a theistic test, it embraces no acknowledgement of Providence, of divine government, of responsibility, or of retribution. It involves nothing but a bare and abstract admission – a form void of all practical meaning and concern.

This is not a wholesome, but an unwholesome, lesson. Yet more. I own that although I am now, perhaps, going to injure myself by bringing the name of Mr Bradlaugh into this controversy, I am strongly of opinion that the present controversy should come to a close. I have no fear of atheism in this House. Truth is the expression of the divine mind; and however little our feeble vision may be able to discern the means by which God will provide for its preservation, we may leave the matter in his hands, and we may be quite sure that a firm and courageous application of every principle of justice and of equity is the best method we can adopt for the preservation and influence of truth.

I must painfully record my opinion that grave injury has been done to religion in many minds … through the resistance offered to the man elected by the constituency of Northampton, which a portion of the community believe to be unjust. When they see the profession of religion and the interests of religion ostensibly associated with what they are deeply convinced is injustice, they are led to questions about religion itself, which they see to be associated with injustice. Unbelief attracts a sympathy which it would not otherwise enjoy; and the upshot is to impair those convictions and that religious faith, the loss of which I believe to be the most inexpressible calamity which can fall either upon a man or upon a nation.

Joseph Goebbels
German politician

Paul Joseph Goebbels (1897–1945) was born in Rheydt, the son of a Rhenish factory foreman. He was educated at a Catholic school and Heidelberg University. A club foot absolved him from military service in World War I, and he won a number of scholarships, attending eight universities. He became an enthusiastic supporter of ADOLF HITLER, and joined the Nazi Party in 1924, soon becoming editor of the Nazi sheet *Völkische Freiheit* ('People's Freedom'). With Hitler's accession to power 'Jupp' was made head of the Ministry of Public Enlightenment and Propaganda. A bitter anti-Semite, he had a gift for mob oratory which made him a powerful exponent of the more radical aspects of the Nazi philosophy. Wartime conditions greatly expanded his responsibilities and power, and by 1943, while Hitler was running the war, Goebbels was virtually running Germany. He retained Hitler's confidence to the last, and in the Berlin bunker where Hitler spent his final days, Goebbels and his wife Magda committed suicide after they had taken the lives of their six children. His diaries now represent a major historical source.

'Let the storm break loose'
18 February 1943, Berlin, Germany

The opening stages of World War II had seen Germany triumphantly overrunning much of northern Europe. By November 1942, Germany had also made significant progress on the Eastern Front, driving deep into the Soviet Union. But Soviet resistance then forced German withdrawal, isolating the German Sixth Army at Stalingrad. By the end of January 1943, the Sixth Army had surrendered to the Red Army, while German forces in North Africa had retreated from the Allies. The tide of the war had turned.

As Hitler's chief propagandist, Goebbels knew it was vital that the German people did not weaken at the news of these reverses. On 18 February 1943, in front of film cameras and radio microphones, he addressed a specially selected audience of thousands, a cross-section of German society which included veterans of the Eastern Front. In the hour-long speech, of which this an edited section, Goebbels skilfully manipulates his audience to give enthusiastic vocal support to the concept of total war – the complete mobilization of the country's material and human resources. He employed the technique of posing dramatic questions to the audience, well aware that their responses would be broadcast to the world.

Goebbels said afterwards of his listeners, 'They applauded at just the right moments: it was the politically best-trained audience you can find in Germany.' Hitler's chief architect, Albert Speer, commented that while Goebbels's delivery of the speech appeared highly emotional, it had been a calculated act. This translation is by Randall Bytwerk.

You, my hearers, at this moment represent the whole nation. I wish to ask you ten questions that you will answer for the German people throughout the world – but especially for our enemies, who are listening to us on the radio.

[*The crowd is at the peak of excitement. Each individual feels as if he is being spoken to personally. With full participation and enthusiasm, the crowd answers each question.*]

The English maintain that the German people has lost faith in victory. I ask you: Do you believe with the Führer and us in the final total victory of the German people? I ask you: Are you resolved to follow the Führer through thick and thin to victory, and are you willing to accept the heaviest personal burdens in the fight for victory?

Second: the English say that the German people are tired of fighting. I ask you: Are you ready to follow the Führer as the phalanx of the homeland, standing behind the fighting army, and to wage war with wild determination through all the turns of fate until victory is ours?

Third: the English maintain that the German people have no desire any longer to accept the government's growing demands for war work. I ask you: Are you and the German people willing to work, if the Führer orders, ten, twelve and if necessary fourteen hours a day and to give everything for victory?

Fourth: the English maintain that the German people are resisting the government's total war measures. They do not want total war, but capitulation!

[*Shouts: 'Never! Never! Never!'*]

I ask you: Do you want total war? If necessary, do you want a war more total and radical than anything that we can even imagine today?

Fifth: the English maintain that the German people have lost faith in the Führer. I ask you: is your confidence in the Führer greater, more faithful and unshakable than ever before? Are you absolutely and completely ready to follow him wherever he goes and do all that is necessary to bring the war to a victorious end?

[*Thousands of voices join in shouting: 'Führer command, we follow!' A wave of shouts of 'Heil!' flows through the hall.*]

Sixth, I ask you: are you ready from now on to give your full strength to provide the Eastern Front with the men and munitions it needs to give Bolshevism the death blow?

Seventh, I ask you: do you take a holy oath to the front that the homeland stands firm behind them, and that you will give them everything they need to win the victory?

Eighth, I ask you: do you, especially you women, want the government to do all it can to encourage German women to put their full strength at work to support the war effort, and to release men for the front whenever possible, thereby helping the men at the front?

Ninth, I ask you: do you approve, if necessary, the most radical measures against a small group of shirkers and black-marketeers who pretend there is peace in the middle of war and use the need of the nation for their own selfish purposes? Do you agree that those who harm the war effort should lose their heads?

Tenth and lastly, I ask you: do you agree that above all in war, according to the National Socialist Party platform, the same rights and duties should apply to all, that the homeland should bear the heavy burdens of the war together, and that the burdens should be shared equally between high and low and rich and poor?

I have asked: you have given me your answers. You are part of the people, and your answers are those of the German people. You have told our enemies what they needed to hear so that they will have no false illusions or ideas.

Now, just as in the first hours of our rule and through the ten years that followed, we are bound firmly in brotherhood with the German people. The most powerful ally on earth, the people themselves, stand behind us and are determined to follow the Führer, come what may. They will accept the heaviest burdens to gain victory. What power on earth can hinder us from reaching our goal? Now we must and will succeed!

I stand before you not only as the spokesman of the government, but as the spokesman of the people … We are all children of our people, forged together by this critical hour of our national history. We promise you, we promise the front, we promise the Führer, that we will mould together the homeland into a force on which the Führer and his fighting soldiers can rely on absolutely and blindly. We pledge to do all in our life and work that is necessary for victory … With burning hearts and cool heads we will overcome the major problems of this phase of the war. We are on the way to eventual victory. That victory rests on our faith in the Führer.

This evening I once again remind the whole nation of its duty. The Führer expects us to do that which will throw all we have done in the past into the shadows. We do not want to fail him. As we are proud of him, he should be proud of us.

The great crises and upsets of national life show who the true men and women are. We have no right any longer to speak of the weaker sex, for both sexes are displaying the same determination and spiritual strength. The nation is ready for anything. The Führer has commanded, and we will follow him. In this hour of national reflection and contemplation, we believe firmly and unshakably in victory. We see it before us, we need only reach for it. We must resolve to subordinate everything to it. That is the duty of the hour. Let the slogan be: 'Now, people rise up and let the storm break loose!'

[*Goebbels' final words were lost in a storm of applause.*]

Emma Goldman

American anarchist, feminist and birth-control advocate

Emma Goldman *known as Red Emma* (1869–1940) was born in Lithuania (then part of Russia) to a Jewish family who moved to Germany to escape persecution. In 1885 she emigrated to the USA, where she began active anarchist agitation against tyrannical employers and was jailed in 1893 for incitement to riot in New York City. She founded and edited the anarchist monthly *Mother Earth* (1906–17) and became internationally known for her political writing, her stirring speeches and her participation in anarchist congresses at Paris (1899) and Amsterdam (1907). In 1917 she was imprisoned for opposing government policy on registration of military recruits; she was deported to the USSR in 1919 but left in 1921, appalled by the totalitarian state. She was not allowed back into the USA until 1934, and then only for three months, on condition that she would not talk about politics. During the Spanish Civil War (1936–9), she supported the anarchists. Her publications include an autobiography, *Living My Life* (1931), *Anarchism and Other Essays* (1910) and *My Disillusionment in Russia* (1923). She lived in France, Britain and Canada until her death in 1940, after which her body was returned to the USA for burial at Waldheim Cemetery in Chicago.

'Progress is ever renewing, ever becoming, ever changing'
9 July 1917, New York City, USA

At the time of her trial, Emma Goldman was already well known to the authorities for her involvement in anarchism and the rising labour movement, and for her efforts to distribute birth-control literature. After the USA joined World War I in April 1917, she jointly founded the No-Conscription League, and she gave two major addresses against the war in New York City. One of these was on 18 May, the day when the Selective Service Act was passed, which imposed conscription and required all men aged 21–30 to register.

This was an unpopular law: refusal to comply was a criminal offence, and the law did not recognize conscientious objection except on religious grounds. On 15 June she was arrested on conspiracy charges at a meeting of the No-Conscription League, and a transcript of the speech she had just given was entered as Exhibit 33 in her subsequent trial.

Along with her co-defendant and lover Alexander Berkman (1870–1936), she was found guilty of conspiracy to obstruct conscription into the US armed services. The heavily sarcastic and ironic tone of Goldman's address did not help convince the twelve men of the jury of her innocence. They returned a guilty verdict and she was sentenced to two years in jail. Re-arrested on her release, she was deported to Russia along with other foreign-born radicals, partly through the efforts of J Edgar Hoover (1895–1972), a young director in the Justice Department's General Intelligence Division, who would later found the Federal Bureau of Investigation.

On the day after our arrest it was given out by the US Marshal and the District Attorney's office that the 'big fish' of the No-Conscription activities had been caught, and that there would be no more troublemakers and disturbers to interfere with the highly democratic effort of the government to conscript its young manhood for the European slaughter. What a pity that the faithful servants of the government … should have used such a weak and flimsy net for their big catch. The moment the anglers pulled their heavily laden net ashore, it broke, and all the labour was so much wasted energy.

The methods employed by Marshal McCarthy and his hosts of heroic warriors were sensational enough to satisfy the famous circus men, Barnum and Bailey. A dozen or more heroes dashing up two flights of stairs, prepared to stake their lives for their country, only to discover the two dangerous disturbers and troublemakers, Alexander Berkman and Emma Goldman, in their separate offices, quietly at work at their desks, wielding not a sword, nor a gun or a bomb, but merely their pens! Verily, it required courage to catch such big fish.

To be sure, two officers equipped with a warrant would have sufficed to carry out the business of arresting the defendants Alexander Berkman and Emma Goldman. Even the police know that neither of them is in the habit of running away or hiding under the bed. But the farce-comedy had to be properly staged if the Marshal and the District Attorney were to earn immortality. Hence the sensational arrest; hence, also, the raid upon the offices of *The Blast*, *Mother Earth* and the No-Conscription League.[1]

In their zeal to save the country from the troublemakers, the Marshal and his helpers did not even consider it necessary to produce a search warrant. After all, what matters a mere scrap of paper when one is called upon to raid the offices of anarchists! ... Would the gentlemen who came with Marshal McCarthy have dared to go into the offices of Morgan, or Rockefeller, or of any of those men without a search warrant? They never showed us the search warrant, although we asked them for it. Nevertheless, they turned our office into a battlefield, so that when they were through with it, it looked like invaded Belgium, with the only difference that the invaders were not Prussian barbarians but good American patriots bent on making New York safe for democracy.

The stage having been appropriately set for the three-act comedy, and the first act successfully played by carrying off the villains in a madly dashing automobile – which broke every traffic regulation and barely escaped crushing every one in its way – the second act proved even more ludicrous. Fifty thousand dollars bail was demanded, and real estate refused when offered by a man whose property is rated at $300,000 – and that after the District Attorney had considered and, in fact, promised to accept the property for one of the defendants, Alexander Berkman – thus breaking every right guaranteed even to the most heinous criminal.

Finally the third act, played by the government in this court during the last week. The pity of it is that the prosecution knows so little of dramatic construction, else it would have equipped itself with better dramatic material to sustain the continuity of the play. As it was, the third act fell flat, utterly, and presents the question, 'Why such a tempest in a teapot?'

Gentlemen of the jury: my comrade and co-defendant having carefully and thoroughly gone into the evidence presented by the prosecution, and having demonstrated its entire failure to prove the charge of conspiracy or any overt acts to carry out that conspiracy, I shall not impose upon your patience by going over the same ground, except to emphasize a few points. To charge people with having conspired to do something which they have been engaged in doing most of their lives, namely their campaign against war, militarism and conscription as contrary to the best interests of humanity, is an insult to human intelligence.

Gentlemen of the jury: the District Attorney must have learned from the reporters the gist of the numerous interviews which they had with us. Why did he not examine them as to whether or not we had counselled young men not to register? That would have been a more direct way of getting at the facts. In the case of the reporter from the *New York Times*, there can be no doubt that the man would have been only too happy to accommodate the District Attorney with the required information. A man who disregards every principle of decency and ethics of his profession as a newspaper man, by turning material given him as news over to the District Attorney, would have been glad to oblige a friend ...

Perhaps the *Times* reporter refused to go to the extent of perjuring himself. Patrolmen and detectives are not so timid in such matters. Hence Mr Randolph and Mr Cadell,[2] to rescue the situation. Imagine employing

[1] *The Blast* was edited by Berkman, *Mother Earth* by Goldman. Both were anarchist newspapers, taking an anti-war stance. Berkman and Goldman were both prominent members of the No-Conscription League.

[2] Randolph was a patrolman who claimed to have accurately recorded Goldman's remarks; Cadell was the detective assigned to the case. In Berkman's speech to the jury, he remarked: 'Mr Randolph has a very simple system. He just leaves out the words that he does not get. He leaves out the sentences he does not get, and he puts in the things he thinks should be there.'

tenth-rate stenographers to report the very important speeches of dangerous troublemakers! What lack of forethought and efficiency on the part of the District Attorney! But even these two members of the police department failed to prove by their notes that we advised people not to register. But since they had to produce something incriminating against anarchists, they conveniently resorted to the old standby, always credited to us, 'We believe in violence and we will use violence.'

Assuming, gentlemen of the jury, that this sentence was really used at the meeting of May 18, it would still fail to prove the indictment which charges conspiracy and overt acts to carry out the conspiracy. And that is all we are charged with. Not violence, not anarchism. I will go further and say that had the indictment been for the advocacy of violence, you gentlemen of the jury would still have to render a verdict of 'Not Guilty', since the mere belief in a thing or even the announcement that you would carry out that belief can not possibly constitute a crime.

However, I wish to say emphatically that no such expression as 'We believe in violence and we will use violence' was uttered at the meeting of May 18, or at any other meeting. I could not have employed such a phrase, as there was no occasion for it. If for no other reason, it is because I want my lectures and speeches to be coherent and logical. The sentence credited to me is neither.

I have read to you my position toward political violence from a lengthy essay called 'The Psychology of Political Violence'. But to make that position clearer and simpler, I wish to say that I am a social student. It is my mission in life to ascertain the cause of our social evils and of our social difficulties. As a student of social wrongs it is my aim to diagnose a wrong. To simply condemn the man who has committed an act of political violence, in order to save my skin, would be as unpardonable as it would be on the part of the physician, who is called to diagnose a case, to condemn the patient because the patient has tuberculosis, cancer, or some other disease.

The honest, earnest, sincere physician does not only prescribe medicine, he tries to find out the cause of the disease. And if the patient is at all capable as to means, the doctor will say to him, 'Get out of this putrid air, get out of the factory, get out of the place where your lungs are being infected.' He will not merely give him medicine. He will tell him the cause of the disease. And that is precisely my position in regard to acts of violence. That is what I have said on every platform. I have attempted to explain the cause and the reason for acts of political violence.

It is organized violence on top which creates individual violence at the bottom. It is the accumulated indignation against organized wrong, organized crime, organized injustice which drives the political offender to his act. To condemn him means to be blind to the causes which make him. I can no more do it, nor have I the right to, than the physician who were to condemn the patient for his disease. You and I and all of us who remain indifferent to the crimes of poverty, of war, of human degradation, are equally responsible for the act committed by the political offender. May I therefore be permitted to say, in the words of a great teacher: 'He who is without sin among you, let him cast the first stone.'

… Gentlemen of the jury: most of you, I take it, are believers in the teachings of JESUS. Bear in mind that he was put to death by those who considered his views as being against the law.

I also take it that you are proud of your Americanism. Remember that those who fought and bled for your liberties were in their time considered as being against the law, as dangerous disturbers and troublemakers. They not only preached violence, but they carried out their ideas by throwing tea into the Boston harbour … They wrote a dangerous document called the Declaration of Independence, a document which continues to be dangerous to this day, and for the circulation of which a young man was sentenced to 90 days' prison in a New York court, only the other day. They were the anarchists of *their* time – they were never within the law …

Progress is ever renewing, ever becoming, ever changing – *never is it within the law.* If that be crime, we are criminals even like Jesus, SOCRATES, Galileo,[3] Bruno,[4] JOHN BROWN and scores of others. We are in good company …

[3] The Italian astronomer and mathematician Galileo Galilei (1564–1642) was imprisoned by the Inquisition after publishing his astronomical discoveries.

[4] The Italian philosopher and scientist Giordano Bruno (1548–1600) was burned at the stake for heresy after his pantheistic doctrines attracted the attention of the Inquisition.

Gentlemen of the jury, you are not called upon to accept our views, to approve of them or to justify them. You are not even called upon to decide whether our views are within or against the law. You are called upon to decide whether the prosecution has proven that the defendants Emma Goldman and Alexander Berkman have conspired to urge people not to register, and whether their speeches and writings represent overt acts. Whatever your verdict, gentlemen, it cannot possibly affect the rising tide of discontent in this country against war which, despite all boasts, is a war for conquest and military power. Neither can it affect the ever-increasing opposition to conscription which is a military and industrial yoke placed upon the necks of the American people. Least of all will your verdict affect those to whom human life is sacred, and who will not become a party to the world slaughter …

And gentlemen: in conclusion let me tell you that my co-defendant, Mr Berkman, was right when he said the eyes of America are upon you. They are upon you not because of sympathy for us or agreement with anarchism. They are upon you because it must be decided sooner or later whether we are justified in telling people that we will give them democracy in Europe, when we have no democracy here. Shall free speech and free assemblage, shall criticism and opinion – which even the espionage bill did not include – be destroyed?

… Gentlemen of the jury, whatever our verdict will be, as far as we are concerned, nothing will be changed. I have held ideas all my life. I have publicly held my ideas for 27 years. Nothing on earth would ever make me change my ideas except one thing; and that is, if you will prove to me that our position is wrong, untenable, or lacking in historic fact. But never would I change my ideas because I am found guilty …

Please forget that we are anarchists. Forget that it is claimed that we propagated violence. Forget that something appeared in *Mother Earth* when I was thousands of miles away, three years ago. Forget all that, and merely consider the evidence. Have we been engaged in a conspiracy? Has that conspiracy been proven? … We for the defence say they have not been proven. And therefore your verdict must be not guilty.

But whatever your decision, the struggle must go on. We are but the atoms in the incessant human struggle towards the light that shines in the darkness – the ideal of economic, political and spiritual liberation of mankind!

Billy Graham
American evangelist

William Franklin Graham Jnr (1918–) was born in Charlotte, North Carolina. He began his studies at Florida Bible Institute (now Trinity College) in 1938, and was ordained a minister of the Southern Baptist Church (1940). In 1943 he graduated in anthropology from Wheaton College, Illinois, and in the same year married Ruth Bell. He made his first high-profile preaching crusade in Los Angeles in 1949 and has since conducted his crusades on all continents. During the Cold War, he preached in the USSR and other eastern European countries. It is claimed that millions have been converted to Christianity through his crusades and the subsidiary ministries of broadcasting, films and the printed word. A charismatic figure who has been the friend and counsellor of many in high office, including US president RICHARD M NIXON, Graham has consistently emerged from investigative reporting as a person of high integrity, and his Billy Graham Evangelistic Association as a model of financial accountability. He was invited to officiate at the funeral of RONALD REAGAN in June 2004, but was unable to attend, having recently undergone hip replacement surgery. Despite failing health, he launched a North American Crusade in New York in April 2005, and in August 2005 launched the building of his new library at Charlotte. His books include *Peace with God* (1952), *World Aflame* (1965), *Angels* (1975), *Storm Warning* (1992) and his autobiography, *Just as I Am* (1997).

'Billy Graham is a sinner'
18 September 1984, Novosibirsk, Siberia, Russia

At the centre of this sermon, given during one of Graham's missions to the USSR, is an anecdote that calls to mind Pascal's Wager. The French mathematician and philosopher Blaise Pascal (1623–62) famously argued for belief in God as follows: 'Let us weigh the gain against the loss in wagering that God exists ... If you gain, you gain all; if you lose, you lose nothing. Therefore do not hesitate to wager that He exists.'

But Graham is no Pascal. His enormous success as a preacher rests partly on his personal charisma, but also on an easy-going, conversational style based on direct, simple statement. By introducing stories about Helen Keller, his son, his father, a student in New Zealand and an airline passenger, he engages the imagination; by frequent reference to the Bible, he bolsters and authenticates his argument; by posing questions, he forces the audience to consider their own position.

This sermon, an edited version of which is given here, is predicated on John 3:16, a text Graham has preached more than any other. But its most dramatic moment comes when he declares himself a sinner. From this bald statement of humility, he builds a persuasive case for Christian faith, culminating in a practical, two-step programme for salvation.

Tonight I am reading from the third chapter of John, verse 16. This is perhaps the best-known verse in all the Bible. My mother taught me this verse when I was a little boy on the farm, and perhaps many of you also learned it when you were younger. For some of you it may be new – but it contains the teaching of the Bible in a nutshell.

'For God so loved the world, that he gave his only begotten Son, that whosoever believeth in him should not perish, but have everlasting life' (John 3:16).

Around the world people ask me one question: 'If there is a God of love, why does he allow all of the suffering that goes on in the world? Why doesn't God stop it?' There is so much suffering in the world – disease, poverty, war, hate, loneliness, boredom and all kinds of other problems. We are told that right now 40 small wars are going on in the world. If God loves the human race, why doesn't he stop it? In my country, at least, millions of people are getting depressed; they get discouraged with life. Many end up committing suicide. But God did not intend for the world to be this way, as we see in this verse. So let's look at this verse very closely.

The first phrase says, 'For God.' It brings us right at the start to the subject of God. Does God exist? ... Almost everybody believes there is some kind of supreme being. We are born with that belief that there is something – or someone – beyond this life, something in control of this vast universe. Down inside we are born with a yearning for God.

We had a woman in America who was born deaf, and dumb, and blind. Her name was Helen Keller.[1] She could not see; she could not hear; she could not speak. They tried for years to communicate with her. How would you communicate with a person like that? Finally, after much struggle, they communicated with her, and she became a famous and much admired scholar and writer. When they first communicated the word 'God' to her, she said, 'I knew him, but I did not know his name.' Deep in her heart she knew there is God …

There are certain things that all of us as a human race cannot escape. First, we cannot escape being born. You have been born, and you cannot be unborn. Second, we cannot escape death. You are going to die. Everybody in this room will be dead in the next 100 years. Death is total in every generation. The third thing you cannot escape is the judgement of God …

The Bible says that God has two sets of books: the book of judgement and the book of life. The moment you are born your name is written in the book of judgement, and all the sins that you commit are in that book. When you receive Christ, all of those sins are wiped out because of what Christ did for you on the cross. God cannot remember your sins any more …

Then the Bible says God is love. God says, 'I have loved [you] with an everlasting love' (Jeremiah 31:3). This is why God created man. Have you ever asked yourself, 'Who am I? Where did I come from? Why am I here? What is the purpose of my life? When I die, where am I going?' Have you ever asked yourself those questions? God created man because God loves us and wants to have a personal relationship with us, and he wants us to love him in return …

Let me tell you something. Billy Graham is a sinner. I have broken God's law. The Bible says that if we break it in one point, we are guilty of all. 'For whosoever shall keep the whole law, and yet offend in one point, he is guilty of all' (James 2:10). So what does that mean? That means I must face judgement. I am under condemnation. How can I be saved? It seems impossible. God says I have to be as holy as he is holy, and I have no way of being holy. I am a sinner, and so are you, if you measure yourself against God's goodness …

When I was still a teenager, I received Christ. The Scripture says that he clothed me in a robe of righteousness because of the cross, and when God looks at me, he does not see my sins. He sees the blood of Christ, and we celebrate that blood when we take communion. When we take the fruit of the vine, or we break the bread, we are remembering that death almost 2,000 years ago.

Why is that death so important? Because in that moment, God laid on Christ the sins of us all. He had never committed sin or broken God's moral law. He never deserved to die. But in those few moments on the cross, Christ did not die just physically; he died spiritually. Your sins and my sins were placed on him and caused him to feel the pangs of Hell. He took the Hell and the judgement I deserve on that cross. But, thank God, he didn't stay on the cross. He rose from the dead, and he is alive. And the Scripture says that someday he is coming back to establish his eternal kingdom.

I remember some years ago I was preaching in New Zealand, and I was invited to give a lecture at the University of Auckland, the capital of New Zealand.[2] During my lecture I mentioned the word 'Hell'. That night – I had

[1] The US writer and activist Helen Adams Keller (1880–1968) was not, in fact, born with her disabilities. She lost her sight, hearing and ability to speak due to illness, aged 19 months. With the help of her lifelong teacher Anne Sullivan (1866–1936), she learned to communicate, and became a prominent lecturer, author and Socialist campaigner.

[2] Aukland is the largest city in New Zealand, but the capital is Wellington.

already gone to bed – there came a loud knock at the door. I got up and rubbed the sleep from my eyes, and I went to the door and found a student.

He was very angry. He said, 'Tonight you talked to us, and you said there is a Hell. I don't believe there is a Hell or a judgement. You shouldn't talk like that to us.'

I said, 'Come in. Sit down,' and he did. We talked for a long time. I said, 'Would you admit that there is a 10 per cent chance JESUS was right and there is a Hell?' He scratched his head, and he thought a minute.

He said, 'Yes, I would say there is a 10 per cent chance, but,' he added, 'that's not much.'

I said, 'I want to ask you another question. Suppose you go out to the airport, and you are planning to take a plane to Sydney, Australia. You have the ticket, and just as you are ready to get on the plane, they make the announcement: "There is only a 10 per cent chance the plane won't make it." Would you get on the plane?'

He said, 'No.'

'And you tell me,' I replied, 'that you believe there is a 10 per cent chance there is a Hell, and you are willing to take the eternal risk?'

He said 'I suppose not.'

I said, 'Then you'll receive Christ.'

He said no. 'Because,' he said, 'I admit that my problem is not intellectual. My problem is moral. I'm not ready to surrender to Christ. His moral demands are too high.' How tragic it is to turn our backs on God and his salvation! What did God do? How could man be saved?

We live in the mountains in the southern part of America. I was walking there with my younger son one time years ago, and we stepped on an anthill. We looked down and a lot of the ants had been killed, and many of them were hurt. Their little house was destroyed. I said to my son, 'Wouldn't it be wonderful if we could go down and tell those ants we are sorry and we care about them, and then help them rebuild their house?'

And he said, 'Father, we're too big, and they're too little. There's no way we could help them. The only way we could talk with them is if we somehow could become ants and live with them.'

I wanted to teach him a little lesson, so I said, 'One time God – the mighty God of Heaven – looked down on this little speck of dust that we call the earth and saw that we were like those little ants crawling around. And God said, "I want to help them; I want to save them; I want to help them rebuild their lives." But how could the mighty God of Heaven communicate with us? You know what God did? God became a man, and that's who Jesus Christ was. Christ was the God-man who came for the purpose of showing us what God is like, and dying on the cross for our sins.'

That is what the verse I read a few minutes ago says God did for us: 'For God so loved the world, that he gave his only begotten Son, that whosoever believeth in him should not perish, but have everlasting life' (John 3:16).

Now, what does God require of you and me? He gave his Son – the most personal, costly gift he could give. But what must we do in return? What do you have to do if you are to have your name written in the book of life, have your sins forgiven and have eternal life? Listen carefully.

First, you must repent of your sins. What does repent mean? It means to change – to change your mind, to change your way of living. It means to turn away from sin, and with God's help to live the way God wants you to live. It means that you have become a man or a woman of love. It means that you are willing to live for Christ.

The first sermon Jesus ever preached was on the theme of repentance. Peter said in Acts 3:19, 'Repent ye therefore, and be converted, that your sins may be blotted out.' The apostle Paul said that God 'commandeth all men every where to repent' (Acts 17:30). Have you repented? Has your life been changed? Do people know it? Does your wife, does your husband, your father, your mother know it by the way you live?

Second, you must come by faith and trust to Christ as your Saviour and Lord. You cannot understand it all with your mind, but don't let that keep you from Christ. I don't understand light or electricity, but that doesn't keep me from turning on the light switch. The Bible says by wisdom man cannot know God. Our minds are limited, and they have been affected by sin. The Bible says, 'Without faith it is impossible to please him' (Hebrews 11:6). John 1:12, promises, 'But as many as received him, to them gave he power to become the sons of God, even to them that believe on his name.'

Some people say, 'I could never receive Christ, because I couldn't live up to what God expects of me.' That is like a person saying, 'I can never fly on an airplane, because I don't think I have the strength to keep it in the air.' Keeping the plane in the air is not the job of the passenger. It's the job of the pilot and the people that work on the plane and the people who designed and built it.

I heard about a man who had never flown in an airplane. My father, who died about 25 years ago, never flew in an airplane. I tried to get him to; but he said, 'If God had meant for man to fly, he'd have given him wings.' But anyway, this one man finally said, 'All right, I'll go up in this airplane.' When the plane landed, his son asked him, 'How did you like it?' He said, 'It was all right, but I never did put my full weight on the seat.'

That's the way many people approach faith in Christ. When you put your faith in Christ, you make a total commitment to him – you put your full weight on him – and trust him alone for your salvation. The Bible says, 'For by grace are ye saved through faith; and … not of yourselves: it is the gift of God' (Ephesians 2:8).

What are you going to do? Are you going to open your heart to Christ? The Bible says, 'Now is the accepted time; behold, now is the day of salvation' (2 Corinthians 6:2). You may be closer to God at this moment than ever before in your life. You may never be this close again. Tonight is the night to receive him, and to put your whole weight on Christ. If you have a doubt about your relationship with Christ, you can make sure tonight. Some of you belong to the church or attend church. But deep in your heart you have doubts about your relationship to Christ. Whatever your background, come to him by faith and make your commitment to him now.

Günter Grass
German writer

Günter Wilhelm Grass (1927–) was born in Danzig (now Gdansk, Poland), and educated at Danzig Volksschule and Gymnasium. Having trained as a stonemason and sculptor, he attended the Academy of Art, Düsseldorf, and the State Academy of Fine Arts, Berlin. He served in World War II and was a prisoner of war. He worked as a farm labourer, apprentice stonecutter, miner and jazz musician, and was then a speech-writer for the future Chancellor Willy Brandt (1913–92) when Brandt was Mayor of West Berlin. His novel *Die Blechtrommel* (1959, Eng trans *The Tin Drum*, 1962) was the first of numerous works that have made him Germany's greatest living novelist. Ostensibly the autobiography of Oskar Matzerath, detained in a mental hospital for a murder he did not commit, it caused a furore in Germany because of its depiction of the Nazis. Intellectual and experimental in form, theme and language, his books consistently challenge the status quo and question our reading of the past. A prolific playwright, poet and essayist, he excels in fiction. Important books are *Katz und Maus* (1961, Eng trans *Cat and Mouse*, 1963), *Hundejahre* (1963, Eng trans *Dog Years*, 1965), *Örtlich betäubt* (1969, Eng trans *Local Anaesthetic*, 1970), *Der Butt* (1977, Eng trans *The Flounder*, 1978), *Das Treffen in Telgte* (1979, Eng trans *The Meeting at Telgte*, 1981), *Die Ratten* (1987, Eng trans *The Rats*, 1987) and *Unkenrufe* (1992, Eng trans *The Call of the Toad*, 1992). He has illustrated many of his own book jackets. In 1995 he published *Ein weites Feld* ('A Broad Field'), one of the first major novels to tackle the issue of German reunification; and in 2003 *Letzte Tänze* ('Last Dances'). He has also published three volumes of memoirs (2007, 2008, 2010). He was awarded the Nobel Prize for literature in 1999.

'I'm against revolution'
October 1969, Belgrade, Yugoslavia

The late 1960s was a time of profound upheaval in central Europe. Many of those who came of age in this era embraced a rebellious 'counterculture', rejecting conformity with existing socio-political mores. Students rioted in Paris in May 1968, and unrest spread to many other European cities. Demonstrations against the Vietnam War occurred in many countries. There was also unrest in the Eastern bloc, for example in Czechoslovakia, where anti-Soviet demonstrations provoked the Russian-led invasion of August 1968.

Günter Grass was active in German politics during this era, working for the Social Democratic Party led by Willy Brandt. A few days before he gave this speech, Brandt had won a general election, ousting the Christian Democratic Party, which had been in power for 20 years.

Like many residents of the divided Germany, Grass was acutely aware of his country's position at the European front line of the Cold War. In October 1969, he crossed the Iron Curtain to attend the Belgrade Writers' Conference, where he gave this address, entitled 'Literature and Revolution, or The Rhapsodist's Snorting Hobby-horse'.

The speech, translated here by Ralph Manheim, explores the malign effects of revolution both on human society as a whole and specifically on literature. It proposes that the cost of revolution is always higher than any benefit it may bring, and contrasts the frivolity of many revolutionaries with the hard work of those striving for real change.

Ladies and gentlemen: I'll come right out with it. I'm against revolution. I detest the sacrifices that always have to be made in its name. I detest its superhuman goals, its absolute demands, its inhuman intolerance; I fear the mechanism of revolution, which had to invent permanent counter-revolution as an antidote to its efforts. From Kronstadt to Prague, Russia's October Revolution, though a military success, has been a failure, in the sense that it restored the traditional structures of political power. Revolutions replace dependence with dependence, coercion with coercion.

In other words, I am at best a tolerated guest among proponents of revolution: I am a revisionist and worse – I am a social democrat.

Since in recent years the people of western Europe, in mingled terror and fascination, have taken to consuming revolution as a topic of conversation or as material for audio-visual display, and since grandiose revolutionary (and telegenic) gestures have left nothing behind them but intensified reaction (in France, for example), a plethora of secondary revolutionary literature, and a certain influence on men's and women's outer garments, the question arises: can't the most recent revolutionary speculations, as unwarranted as they are unpromising, ultimately be attributed to the dissatisfaction of literary rhapsodists, to whom revolution seems to promise spectacular gestures?

In Germany, at all events, it was literary mediocrity that first attempted to get a free ride on the back of the student protest movement. A doctoral thesis might be devoted to the role of literary epigones[1] in proclaiming literary models of revolution. Early in the century it was said that if a revolution were ever to take place in Germany it would be in the field of music. Today, in the late sixties, the revolutionary stance has found a far better subsidized playground: even arch-conservative newspapers have been running feature articles that foam at the mouth with revolutionary fervour. Literature and revolution, or the rhapsodist's snorting hobby-horse.

You may have noticed that our topic, apparently so serious, is doing its best to make me abandon all attempts to keep a straight face. For it almost looks as if the grandiloquent heralds of the revolutionary vogue have either failed to read TROTSKY'S remarks on the subject or as if, against their better judgement – carried away, at least temporarily, by the student protest movement – they had become a demonstration *per absurdum* of the thesis that literature must be the handmaiden of revolution …

Since August of this year, Paris has been graced with an exhibition in honour of NAPOLEON, whose 200th birthday Europe is preparing, with mixed feelings, to celebrate. If we consider that, as the Paris exhibition shows, Napoleon never suffered from a lack of literary eulogists, and that Napoleon was a product of the French Revolution, and if we bear in mind that JOSEPH STALIN must be regarded as a product of the October Revolution – for neither Napoleon nor Stalin dropped from the sky – we are entitled to imagine how colourfully and with what glittering literary encomiums Stalin's 200th birthday will be celebrated when the time comes. And, come to think of it, the inevitable birthdays of the dictators MUSSOLINI and HITLER could be occasions for colossal exhibitions, featuring exquisite literary testimonials by writers ranging from Marinetti[2] to Gottfried Benn.[3]

At all times and under all systems, writers have taken advantage of revolutionary occasions to unload their anti-bourgeois exasperation. To such productive misunderstandings we owe enduringly beautiful poems by Klopstock[4] and Schiller,[5] Yesenin[6] and Mayakovsky.[7] Writers love to transfer purifying storms and showers of metaphors to white paper; but once we try to measure a line of Rimbaud[8] or an early Expressionist[9] image against reality, the puritanical zeal of the guillotine begins to weigh on us, or we get bogged down in scholastic discussions of the question: did Stalin's agrarian reform justify the murder of millions of kulaks?[10]

With blinding clarity the German writer Georg Büchner[11] exposed the deadly mechanisms of revolution: with a few changes in local colour, *Danton's Death* might apply to Cuba or China. The truism that revolution devours its children has not yet been refuted. I hear the question coming: are you implying that the French Revolution or the October Revolution was not necessary?

We have no way of finding out how and with what consequences the European Enlightenment could have developed without revolution in France, whether the victims of the Revolution might have been spared. We

---

[1] Inferior followers or imitators.

[2] The Italian author Emilio Marinetti (1876–1944) was a pioneer of Futurism in art, poetry and the novel, and published the movement's first manifesto in 1909. He was a keen supporter of Mussolini.

[3] The German poet Gottfried Benn (1886–1956) served as a military doctor during World War I, which lent his work a dark and pessimistic quality. He initially supported Hitler, but later turned against the Nazis.

[4] The German poet Friedrich Gottlieb Klopstock (1724–1803) was profoundly religious, but his later work anticipates the rebelliousness of Romanticism.

[5] The German poet and dramatist Friedrich von Schiller (1759–1805) produced works characterized by *Sturm und Drang* ('storm and urgency'), rejecting mediocrity and political restraint.

[6] The Russian poet Sergei Yesenin (1895–1925) embraced the 1917 Bolshevik Revolution as a means of utopian reform, but became deeply disillusioned, suffered a nervous breakdown and hanged himself.

[7] The Russian poet and satirical playwright Vladimir Mayakovsky (1893–1930) was jailed as a youth for his political activities. He later embraced both Futurism and the Bolshevik Revolution, becoming one of the USSR's leading writers during the 1920s.

[8] The French poet Arthur Rimbaud (1854–91) was a precursor of Symbolism in his experimental use of language and imagery.

[9] The Expressionist school of painting and literature emerged in the late 19th century as a direct expression – often through exaggeration, distortion or abstraction – of inner emotions.

[10] A pejorative Russian term for landowning peasants, who were widely regarded as class enemies after the Revolution. Later, Stalin introduced 'dekulakization' measures, under which kulaks were to be liquidated.

[11] The German playwright Georg Büchner (1813–37) is best known for two plays that set an individual against a brutalizing society: *Danton's Death* (1835) and *Woyzeck* (1837).

do not know, and we are at a loss to conjecture, how and to what degree the Kerensky government could have democratized tsarist Russia. Those who believe in the logic of revolution will not be convinced by either the English or the Swedish example. But one thing is certain: much as Eisenstein's film *Potemkin*[12] still appeals to us, the price – Stalin and his consequences – seems too high for even the most incorrigible revolutionary rhapsodist.

I come from a country with a tragi-comic revolutionary past. From 1848 through 1918 to our most recent Book Fair insurrections, most left-wing revolutions have ended by making themselves ridiculous. We are still paying dearly for what, if you'll forgive me for saying so, may be considered the one successful German revolution: the National Socialist seizure of power in 1933. It is too easy to dispose of Mussolini's march on Rome and Hitler's 30 January[13] as rightist putsches, as though only left-wing seizures of power were entitled to the name of 'revolution'.

Though far from equating the aims and motives of leftist and rightist revolutions, I believe that the mechanisms of revolution function independently, regardless of whether the revolution is animated by leftist or by rightist ideologies, of whether the aggressive drives released regard themselves as leftist or rightist. Even the relationship between right-wing literature and right-oriented revolution is not unlike the relationship between left-wing literature and left-oriented revolution. Brecht's[14] hymns to Stalin are in no way superior to Heidegger's[15] kowtowings to National Socialism ...

Hérault's[16] demand in Büchner's *Danton's Death* – 'It is time for the revolution to stop and the Republic to begin' – is still valid today. But the occupation of Czechoslovakia shows how hard it is being made for the republic to begin, precisely because the revolution can't stop. Which is all the more reason to stop thinking about 'Literature and Revolution' and give some consideration to the unspectacular, less inflammatory theme: 'Literature and the Republic'.

A few weeks ago in my country, a round in the fight for the weal and woe of the republic came to an end. A close victory for the Social Democrats seems to hold out some hope for a German parliamentary democracy whose history has been unstable, full of vicissitudes and on the whole more unhappy than continuous. It is true that the stimulus word 'revolution' was much seen and heard in the period immediately preceding the elections, but when the protest movement ended in violent action and it became clear that the essential conflict was that between the traditional power groups – on the one side the conservatives with their nationalist superstructure, and on the other side the socialist-liberal reformists – the word 'revolution' fell into disuse, except perhaps in advertisements for household appliances.

Civic common sense showed no inclination to be guided by the verbal radicalism or vulgar anti-communism of the fifties. Medium-range reformist goals, associated with plans for financing, were decisive. Reason managed to extend its base by a hand's breadth.

It was amusing and instructive to observe how this sobering process made itself felt in the political and economic sections of the press, while literature – or, rather, the branch of literature concerned with feature articles – went right on playing revolutionary sandbox games. A few publishers' readers and, responding to the trend, a few authors embittered for varying reasons, began to avenge themselves on society for its

[12] The Russian film director Sergei Eisenstein (1898–1948) is best known for his film *Battleship Potemkin* (1925), an epic dramatization of the Kronstadt revolution in 1905, which is still regarded as a landmark in cinematic history.

[13] On 30 January 1933, Hitler was sworn in as Chancellor of Germany. Exactly six years later, he spoke chillingly at the Reichstag in Berlin of a world war which would bring about 'the annihilation of the Jewish race in Europe'. The war began a few months later.

[14] The German playwright and poet Bertolt Brecht (1898–1956) was a committed Marxist and consistently opposed the Nazis, but maintained an ambiguous relationship with both the West and the Eastern bloc, settling in East Berlin after World War II. He accepted the Stalin Peace Prize in 1954.

[15] The German philosopher Martin Heidegger (1889–1976) was a member of the Nazi Party from 1933, and enforced racial cleansing laws while serving as rector of the University of Freiburg.

[16] Marie Jean Hérault de Séchelles (1759–94), was active in the French Revolution, taking part in the storming of the Bastille. He was guillotined in 1794.

coolness toward revolution by trying systematically to ruin certain reputedly left-wing publishing houses. Nothing surprising about that, for the literary variety of revolution has always been directed primarily against its own camp.

In the past three years it has never occurred to the proponents of revolutionary change to dynamite the Hanover Trade Fair; oh no, their Bastille has been the Frankfurt Book Fair.

I won't go into details and ask, for instance, whether the storming of a cold buffet is likely to call the attention of the masses to the concentration of power under late capitalism. And the depressing fact that the traditional, formerly right-oriented tendency of students to bug the bourgeoisie for a few carefree years has now slipped into leftist costume, is only one more indication of the pseudo-revolutionary character of a fashionable movement, which in the end has revealed only one thing: the internal quarrels of the radical left and its blindness to the alternative – namely, the arduous, long-range attempt to get the republic finally started.

Don't get me wrong: I'm not talking about the student protest movement, which for the most part pressed for reforms and, by radically democratic means, forced public discussion of such matters as long-overdue university reform. I'm talking about the wanton literary abuse of the stimulus word 'revolution' and about a group of fast-writing, inflammatory and immoderately ambitious writers, who never weary of celebrating the May 1968 disaster of the French left as a revolutionary achievement and collecting its outpourings in anthologies. And they continue to bask in the illusion that in France the students and intellectuals achieved solidarity with the workers.

During the last election campaign, when overextended wage contracts and failure to revaluate the mark led to spontaneous work stoppages in a number of factories, groups of the radical left – imagining no doubt that the workers were planning something revolutionary – tried to approach the strikers, who patted them good-naturedly on the back and sent them home.

Will this 'experience with the masses' teach anyone a lesson? Are the contractions of daily life in a democracy glaring and sobering enough to deter writers from engaging in do-it-yourself revolutionary activity in their leisure time?

A cynic might say that the literary market will regulate demand. At present, the need for attractively packaged revolutionary literature is more than covered. The most dim-witted high-school student is beginning to realize that the destruction of factories, even if they produce consumer goods, might encounter considerable resistance; that the industrial countries of both the East and the West have to increase their productivity if the already foreseeable catastrophes of the Third World are to be averted; and that it is not up to seminars in German literature to decide whether, when and for what reasons revolutions should take place in South America.

Let me risk a prediction: if literature wants to be taken seriously, it will have to stop trying to turn the reader on with the stimulus word 'revolution'. Already there are indications that, especially in Scandinavia (which is ahead of other European countries), more and more writers are beginning to take an interest in the potentialities and limitations of economic development as a factor in peace policy. For the first time 'peace studies' – only a few years ago identified with utopian pacifism – are beginning to figure prominently in budgetary debates; if peace, until now an exceptional condition, is to become permanent, it will be necessary to make a scientific study of the peaceful ways of solving conflicts that would normally lead to war.

Will literature be able to get away from the barricades it has been so addicted to thus far? Or will it reverse the road signs and take an interesting, esoteric and illusory course to Romanticism?

'Literature and Revolution' – a gem from Leon Trotsky's literary heritage. Marxist scholars in naïve discussion with Jesuitical left deviationists. There will always be exclusionists, and they will always applaud themselves, but literature demands realities; for there are more realities than one. I hope to become acquainted with yours, with the Yugoslavian reality; I shall be glad to tell you about mine, the German reality. I start from the assumption that your reality and mine are not mutually exclusive. Our revolutions have already taken place.

Henry Grattan
Irish politician

Henry Grattan (1746–1820) was born in Dublin and educated at Trinity College, Dublin. At the Middle Temple, he became such a fervent supporter of the pro-independence politician and orator Henry Flood (1732–91) that his father disinherited him. He deserted law for politics in 1775, when he entered the Irish parliament for Charlemont. When Flood accepted a government post Grattan immediately took his place, attempting to secure the removal of the restrictions imposed on Irish trade. When the concessions he won were revoked in 1779, he began the struggle for legislative independence. He secured the abolition of all claims by the British parliament to legislate for Ireland in 1782, but was unable to prevent the Act of Union of 1800. He sat in Parliament at Westminster until his death.

'Bad in principle, and worse in practice'
31 January 1787, Dublin, Ireland

Around 1760, bands of armed Catholic insurgents began to spring up in southern Ireland, the most notorious of which wore white uniforms and became known as White-Boys. Much feared for the barbarous cruelties they inflicted on those who resisted, they persecuted and robbed Protestants, and recruited fellow-Catholics using threats to extract oaths of secrecy and allegiance.

One chief grievance of the insurgents were the tithes – literally 'tenths' – a proportion of their income which they were obliged to pay to sustain the Church of Ireland, the established Anglican church, which had few adherents.

Further disturbances broke out in Munster in the winter of 1786–7, with assemblies of 5,000 reported, pledging to withhold their tithes. This led the Attorney-General John FitzGibbon *later 1st Earl of Clare* (1748–1802) to introduce his 'bill to prevent tumultuous risings and assemblies', modelled on the English Riot Act of 1714–15. Although he conceded that Munster peasants were in 'a more abject state of poverty than human nature could be supposed equal to bear' – placing the blame squarely on rapacious landowners – and that the protestors were unarmed and peaceful, he proposed a raft of harsh measures.

Like his colleague John Philpot Curran (1750–1817), who opposed the bill as 'written in blood', Henry Grattan regarded FitzGibbon's proposals as unnecessary and unconstitutional. In this speech, given in the Irish parliament, his acute legal mind is evident as he tackles it point by point. Despite his efforts, the bill was passed, but not before a clause calling for the destruction of Catholic chapels was removed.

Mr Speaker, sir: it is impossible to hear that bill read, or the question put on the committal of it, without animadversion. I agree that the south should be coerced. If the populace or peasantry of that district have thought proper to invade personal security, and lay the foundation of undermining their own liberties; if they have resorted to the exercise of torture as relief for poverty, I lament their savage infatuation, and I assent to their punishment. I assent to it with shame; I blush at the cast of lawlessness thrown on the country, and I lament the necessity of a strong measure, the natural result of shabby mutiny and abortive rebellion.

This is not the first time I have had occasion to express my concern at certain excesses of some part of our fellow subjects. See the fruit of those excesses; see the glorious effect of their labour: a riot act. Aggravated: a riot act, general and perpetual. Evils which it was chance to foresee, it becomes now my duty to mitigate.

I will agree to the strengthening of the civil magistrate within a certain limitation; I would enable the magistrate to disperse such meetings as are notoriously for illegal purposes; and I will agree that it is proper not to admit persons to bail who had refused to disperse, as it could only furnish them with an opportunity of repeating their transgressions. I will agree that the persons who dug graves, provided gibbets and the like, should be punished capitally; for those who made torture their amusement, and practised such inexorable barbarity, I think merit death.

I will also agree that there are several clauses in the Riot Act,[1] which it may be proper to adopt. But in the very setting out of the bill, there is an evident departure from, and contradiction of, the Riot Act. The Riot Act stated that if twelve or more persons, riotously, tumultuously *and* unlawfully assembled and refused to disperse, etc; but this act stated, if persons to the number of twelve or more, riotously, tumultuously *or* unlawfully assembled … The former was copulative; the latter disjunctive; and the difference was, that coming within any one of the descriptions, tumultuous, riotous or unlawful, felony would ensue – though in England, to constitute the crime, each must be alleged.

And when there is a deviation from the Riot Act, I am very sorry to find it is not one founded in mildness and mercy, but one founded in severity. Another difference from the Riot Act is that in England the proclamation is obliged to be read; but by this bill, nothing more was required of the magistrate than to command the rioters to disperse, in the king's name. If they did not disperse in one hour, death was the consequence; and this I consider as putting an hourglass in the hand of time, to run a race against the lives of the people; and this is certainly a great objection.

Another objection is that if a magistrate was stopped when repairing to the place of riot, the person who stopped him would be guilty of felony; that was, though the magistrate was resorting to an unlawful place, the person who obstructed him should be deemed to merit death. And if the persons did not disperse, if the magistrate was interrupted, the reckoning of time was to commence from the moment of his obstruction; and should they continue one hour they would be guilty of felony, and incur the punishment of death; that is, the interception of a magistrate, at a distance in this kingdom, was to be tantamount to the reading of a proclamation on the spot in England.

This I think one of the severest clauses that was ever brought forward, or *ever* adopted. But even though this had been premised of the English Riot Act, the measure of their severity should not be a measure for the legislation of the House: if it should, it would be bad in principle, and worse in practice.

Another clause of the bill made it felony to write, print, publish, send or carry any message, letter or notice tending to excite insurrection – that is, that a man who shall write or print any letter or notice shall be guilty – of what? – of felony! Like the Draconian laws,[2] this bill had 'blood! blood!' – 'felony! felony! felony!' in every period and in every sentence.

Now had this bill been law for some time past, what would be the situation of every man who printed a newspaper for the last nine months? What would be the situation of every man who had written upon the subject of tithes? For as the right of the clergy to tithes is acknowledged to be founded in law, and as the papers and writers have argued against them, what would be the consequence? Who could tell how their conduct might be construed in a court of law; or whether they might not be adjudged guilty of felony? But I will not ask who would be guilty under such a law; but I will ask who would *not* be guilty?

A perpetual mutiny bill had been once the law of the land, and yet gentlemen both spoke and wrote against it as dangerous, unconstitutional, and beyond the power of Parliament to sanction. Had this bill been then law, they would have all been guilty of felony, and suffer

[1] The Riot Act, introduced in England in 1714–15, was legislation 'for preventing tumults and riotous assemblies, and for the more speedy and effectual punishing of the rioters'. It required such assemblies to disperse within an hour, on pain of death.

[2] The Athenian lawgiver Draco (seventh century BC) was known for introducing an extremely harsh penal code. Recorded in 621 BC, it prescribed the death sentence for almost all offences. The word 'draconian', used to describe harsh penal systems, is derived from his name.

death.

Who could tell in what manner the words 'tending to excite disturbance' might be interpreted? The clause respecting the taking of arms, and ammunition, or money to purchase them, bears a similarity to the White-Boy Act;[3] but the White-Boy Act was more guarded.

[3] Introduced in 1765 to tackle the insurgents, the White-Boy Act criminalized oaths of secrecy, particularly those made under threat of violence.

Now, look to the clause which prostrates places of public worship.[4] I consider it as casting a stain of impiety on the whole nation, and enjoining the magistrates to commit that very act of violence which is punished with death in the peasantry. It is a revival of the Penal Laws,[5] and that in the most dangerous and exceptionable part.

[4] The bill included a clause authorizing the demolition of Catholic chapels, though this was eventually dropped.
[5] The Penal Laws of 1695–1728 prevented Catholics from voting and holding public office. They also punished participation in Catholic services with fines, imprisonment or execution.

I call upon gentlemen to consider that they had no charge against the Catholics to warrant this measure; to consider that they had not so much as cause for suspicion of them; to consider, if they were a popish peasantry, they were actuated by no popish motive; to consider that public thanks had been returned to the principal person of the Catholic religion in this country for his manly exertions to maintain the public peace, and to protect the rights of the established clergy. And I think if there be any thing sacred or binding in religion, it would operate successfully against the present measure; for it would cast a stigma on the Protestant religion.

I have heard of transgressors being dragged from the sanctuary, but I never heard of the sanctuary being demolished! It went so far as to hold out the laws as a sanction to sacrilege. If the Roman Catholics are of a different religion, yet they have one common God and one common Saviour with gentlemen themselves; and surely the God of the Protestant temple is the God of the Catholic temple.

What then does the clause enact? That the magistrate shall pull down the temple of his God – and if it be rebuilt, and as often as it is rebuilt for three years, he shall again prostrate it, and so proceed in a repetition of his abominations, and thus stab the criminal through the sides of his God. A new idea indeed!

But this was not all. The magistrate was to sell by auction the altar of the divinity to pay for the sacrilege that had been committed on his house. By preventing the chapel from being erected, I contend that we must prohibit the exercise of religion for three years; and that to remedy disturbance, we resort to irreligion, and endeavour to establish it by Act of Parliament …

Perpetuity was another principle of the bill, and another objection to it. Would any man say that the coercion which might be necessary, from the turbulence of one period, would be requisite at all future times? Was it to be handed down an inheritance to posterity? Would they tell the provinces of Ulster, Leinster, and Connaught that they would reward their tranquillity in the same manner they did the turbulence in the south? Was it to descend from the fathers to the children, as a kind of original sin, and death and felony to be spread in every quarter?

It was a fixed principle that the punishment should bear a proportion to the crime, but it was not attended to in the bill. Would any man say that a man ought to be punished with death for writing, or influencing persons, I will say, by threats or otherwise? I wish, if possible, to confine the operation of the bill to the offending counties, and contend that if the bill is to pass in its present state (but that I believe to be impossible) I will venture to pronounce that it would be absolutely ineffectual; for the crime would be overshot, and the feelings of humanity would revolt at the punishment. It would indeed be the triumph of the criminal and the stigma of the laws.

I desire to know whether it is meant to press the bill, with all its clauses;

whether it be intended to submit it to alteration. If the former, I will oppose it in the first instance; if the latter should be acceded to, I will vote for the committal.

Angelina Grimké
American abolitionist

Angelina Emily Grimké Weld *née Grimké* (1805–79) was born in Charleston, South Carolina, the daughter of a South Carolina judge and plantation owner. In 1829, she joined her sister Sarah Grimké in Philadelphia, where they vigorously appealed to the women of the USA to support their fight against slavery in their pamphlets 'Appeal to the Christian Women of the South' (1836) and 'Appeal to Women of the Nominally Free States' (1837). After Angelina had a letter published in the anti-slavery newspaper *The Liberator* (1835), they became public figures, and Angelina undertook a speaking tour. In 1838 she married the abolitionist Theodore Weld and gave up public life. With Sarah she continued, however, to be committed to reform. Their most significant work was *American Slavery as it is: Testimony of a Thousand Witnesses* (1838).

'The spirit of slavery is here'
17 May 1838, Philadelphia, Pennsylvania, USA

The Grimké sisters were among the first female abolitionists. Finding it impossible to live in the South, they moved north to Philadelphia, the 'City of Brotherly Love'. Slavery might have been a 'peculiar institution' in the South, but northern racism was both obvious and, as it proved, dangerous.

Pennsylvania Hall was purpose-built to provide a venue for abolitionist societies in Philadelphia and was opened on 14 May 1838 with speeches and letters of congratulations, including one from former president John Quincy Adams. Money for the building had been raised by public subscription, but it was immediately clear that others believed their right to property (including slave-holding) was being threatened. Violent protests grew over the next two days.

Tensions came to a head during a meeting of the Anti-Slavery Convention of American Women, at which an estimated 3,000 were present. Angry protesters disrupted the meeting; and although they were ejected from the building, they remained outside, hurling stones and abuse. Angelina Grimké's address lasted over an hour and, while a frightened audience was persuaded to remain in the hall, she was able to exploit the mob's intimidatory tactics to good effect.

When the abolitionists refused to limit their meetings to gatherings of whites only, the city's mayor cancelled all remaining meetings and locked the hall. Soon afterwards, a mob broke into the building and set fires which burned the hall to the ground, four days after it had been opened.

Men, brethren and fathers; mothers, daughters and sisters: what came ye out for to see? A reed shaken with the wind?[1] Is it curiosity merely, or a deep sympathy with the perishing slave, that has brought this large audience together?

[*A yell from the mob without the building.*]

Those voices without ought to awaken and call out our warmest sympathies. Deluded beings! 'They know not what they do.'[2] They know not that they are undermining their own rights and their own happiness, temporal and eternal. Do you ask, 'What has the North to do with slavery?' Hear it – hear it.

Those voices without tell us that the spirit of slavery is here, and has been roused to wrath by our abolition speeches and conventions: for surely liberty would not foam and tear herself with rage, because her friends are multiplied daily, and meetings are held in quick succession to set forth her virtues and extend her peaceful kingdom. This opposition shows that slavery has done its deadliest work in the hearts of our citizens.

Do you ask, then, 'What has the North to do?'. I answer, cast out first the spirit of slavery from your own hearts, and then lend your aid to convert the South. Each one present has a work to do, be his or her situation what it may, however limited their means, or insignificant their supposed influence. The great men of this country will not do this work; the church

[1] Matthew 11:7.

[2] Grimké refers to Luke 23:34, where JESUS calls upon God to forgive his persecutors.

will never do it. A desire to please the world, to keep the favour of all parties and of all conditions, makes them dumb on this and every other unpopular subject.

They have become worldly-wise, and therefore God, in his wisdom, employs them not to carry on his plans of reformation and salvation. He hath chosen the foolish things of the world to confound the wise, and the weak to overcome the mighty.

As a Southerner, I feel that it is my duty to stand up here tonight and bear testimony against slavery. I have seen it – I have seen it. I know it has horrors that can never be described. I was brought up under its wing: I witnessed for many years its demoralizing influences, and its destructiveness to human happiness.

It is admitted by some that the slave is not happy under the worst forms of slavery. But I have never seen a happy slave. I have seen him dance in his chains, it is true; but he was not happy. There is a wide difference between happiness and mirth. Man cannot enjoy the former while his manhood is destroyed, and that part of the being which is necessary to the making, and to the enjoyment of happiness, is completely blotted out. The slaves, however, may be, and sometimes are, mirthful. When hope is extinguished, they say, 'let us eat and drink, for tomorrow we die.'[3]

[3] 1 Corinthians 15:32.

[*Stones thrown at the windows, a great noise without, and commotion within.*]

What is a mob? What would the breaking of every window be? What would the levelling of this hall be? Any evidence that we are wrong, or that slavery is a good and wholesome institution? What if the mob should now burst in upon us, break up our meeting and commit violence upon our persons – would this be any thing compared with what the slaves endure? No, no: and we do not remember them 'as bound with them'[4] if we shrink in the time of peril, or feel unwilling to sacrifice ourselves, if need be, for their sake.

[4] Hebrews 13:3.

[*Great noise.*]

I thank the Lord that there is yet life left enough to feel the truth, even though it rages at it – that conscience is not so completely seared as to be unmoved by the truth of the living God.

Many persons go to the South for a season, and are hospitably entertained in the parlour and at the table of the slave-holder. They never enter the huts of the slaves; they know nothing of the dark side of the picture, and they return home with praises on their lips of the generous character of those with whom they had tarried. Or if they have witnessed the cruelties of slavery, by remaining silent spectators they have naturally become callous – an insensibility has ensued which prepares them to apologize even for barbarity. Nothing but the corrupting influence of slavery on the hearts of the Northern people can induce them to apologize for it; and much will have been done for the destruction of Southern slavery when we have so reformed the North that no-one here will be willing to risk his reputation by advocating or even excusing the holding of men as property. The South know it, and acknowledge that as fast as our principles prevail, the hold of the master must be relaxed.

[*Another outbreak of mobocratic spirit, and some confusion in the house.*]

How wonderfully constituted is the human mind! How it resists, as long as it can, all efforts made to reclaim from error! I feel that all this disturbance is but an evidence that our efforts are the best that could have been adopted, or else the friends of slavery would not care for what we say and do.

The South know what we do. I am thankful that they are reached by our efforts. Many times have I wept in the land of my birth over the system of slavery. I knew of none who sympathized in my feelings – I was unaware that any efforts were made to deliver the oppressed – no voice in the wilderness was heard calling on the people to repent and do works meet for repentance – and my heart sickened within me.

Oh, how should I have rejoiced to know that such efforts as these were being made. I only wonder that I had such feelings. I wonder when I reflect under what influence I was brought up that my heart is not harder than the nether millstone. But in the midst of temptation I was preserved, and my sympathy grew warmer, and my hatred of slavery more inveterate, until at last I have exiled myself from my native land because I could no longer endure to hear the wailing of the slave.

I fled to the land of Penn;[5] for here, thought I, sympathy for the slave will surely be found. But I found it not. The people were kind and hospitable, but the slave had no place in their thoughts. Whenever questions were put to me as to his condition, I felt that they were dictated by an idle curiosity, rather than by that deep feeling which would lead to effort for his rescue.

I therefore shut up my grief in my own heart. I remembered that I was a Carolinian, from a state which framed this iniquity by law. I knew that throughout her territory was continual suffering, on the one part, and continual brutality and sin on the other. Every southern breeze wafted to me the discordant tones of weeping and wailing, shrieks and groans, mingled with prayers and blasphemous curses. I thought there was no hope; that the wicked would go on in his wickedness, until he had destroyed both himself and his country.

My heart sank within me at the abominations in the midst of which I had been born and educated. 'What will it avail,' cried I in bitterness of spirit, 'to expose to the gaze of strangers the horrors and pollutions of slavery, when there is no ear to hear nor heart to feel and pray for the slave?'

… But how different do I feel now! Animated with hope, nay, with an assurance of the triumph of liberty and goodwill to man, I will lift up my voice like a trumpet, and show this people their transgression, their sins of omission towards the slave, and what they can do towards affecting Southern mind, and overthrowing Southern oppression.

We may talk of occupying neutral ground, but on this subject, in its present attitude, there is no such thing as neutral ground. He that is not for us is against us, and he that gathereth not with us, scattereth abroad[6] … God swept Egypt with the besom of destruction, and punished Judea also with a sore punishment, because of slavery. And have we any reason to believe that he is less just now? Or that he will be more favourable to us than to his own 'peculiar people?'.[7]

[*Shoutings, stones thrown against the windows, etc.*]

There is nothing to be feared from those who would stop our mouths, but they themselves should fear and tremble. The current is even now setting fast against them. If the arm of the North had not caused the Bastille[8] of slavery to totter to its foundation, you would not hear those cries. A few years ago, and the South felt secure, and with a contemptuous sneer asked, 'Who are the abolitionists? The abolitionists are nothing.'

…We often hear the question asked: 'What shall we do?' Here is an opportunity for doing something now. Every man and every woman

---

[5] In 1681, Charles II granted a charter to the English Quaker William Penn (1644–1718) to found a settlement in America. He established it as a Quaker colony, and named it Pennsylvania (Latin: 'Penn's woodland').

[6] See Matthew 12:30.

[7] A phrase used in the Bible to describe the Jews, God's 'chosen' people.

[8] A jail in Paris, France which was stormed on 14 July 1789, marking the start of the French Revolution. The event is regarded as a blow struck for freedom, and 14 July is a public holiday in France.

present may do something by showing that we fear not a mob, and, in the midst of threatenings and revilings, by opening our mouths for the dumb and pleading the cause of those who are ready to perish.

To work as we should in this cause, we must know what slavery is. Let me urge you then to buy the books which have been written on this subject and read them, and then lend them to your neighbours … It is said by some, our books and papers do not speak the truth. Why, then, do they not contradict what we say? They cannot. Moreover the South has entreated, nay commanded us to be silent; and what greater evidence of the truth of our publications could be desired?

Women of Philadelphia: allow me as a Southern woman, with much attachment to the land of my birth, to entreat you to come up to this work. Especially let me urge you to petition. Men may settle this and other questions at the ballot-box, but you have no such right. It is only through petitions that you can reach the legislature. It is therefore peculiarly your duty to petition.

Do you say, 'It does no good'?. The South already turns pale at the number sent. They have read the reports of the proceedings of Congress, and there have seen that among other petitions were very many from the women of the North on the subject of slavery … The fact that the South look with jealousy upon our measures shows that they are effectual. There is, therefore, no cause for doubting or despair, but rather for rejoicing.

It was remarked in England that women did much to abolish slavery in her colonies. Nor are they now idle. Numerous petitions from them have recently been presented to the Queen,[9] to abolish the apprenticeship with its cruelties nearly equal to those of the system whose place it supplies. One petition two miles and a quarter long has been presented. And do you think these labours will be in vain ?

Let the history of the past answer. When the women of these States send up to Congress such a petition, our legislators will arise as did those of England, and say, 'When all the maids and matrons of the land are knocking at our doors we must legislate.' Let the zeal and love, the faith and works of our English sisters quicken ours – that while the slaves continue to suffer, and when they shout deliverance, we may feel the satisfaction of having done what we could.

[9] The English monarch Queen Victoria (1819–1901) succeeded to the throne less than a year before this speech was given. Slavery was abolished in all British territories in 1833. Slave labour had been replaced in some places by indentured servants whose conditions were nearly as harsh.

Jo Grimond
Scottish politician

Joseph Grimond *later Baron Grimond* (1913–93) was born in St Andrews and educated at Eton and Balliol College, Oxford. He was called to the Bar in 1937, and served during World War II with the Fife and Forfar Yeomanry. In 1945 he contested the Orkney and Shetland seat, which he ultimately won in 1950. In the interim, he became Secretary of the National Trust for Scotland (1947–9). From 1956 to 1967 he was leader of the Liberal Party, during which time Liberal representation in Parliament was doubled. His aim of making the Liberal Party the real radical alternative to Conservatism was only partially realized in the creation of the Social Democratic Party, and later the (Social and) Liberal Democrats. He served again as party leader for a short period following the resignation of Jeremy Thorpe (1976). He retired from Parliament in 1983, when he was made a life peer. His publications include *The Future of Our Society* (1978), *A Personal Manifesto* (1983) and *Memoirs* (1984).

'I intend to march my troops towards the sound of gunfire'
14 September 1963, Brighton, England
❧

The once-powerful Liberal Party had been in decline since the 1920s, and in the general election of 1958, two years after Jo Grimond became their leader, the Liberals won a mere six seats, while the Conservatives had a majority of more than 100 over the Labour Party. However, the Conservative government was hit by several scandals during the early 1960s – most notably the 'Profumo affair' of 1963, in which a liaison between the Cabinet minister John Profumo (1915–2006) and the showgirl Christine Keeler was believed to have jeopardized national security. Many felt the political establishment was ripe for change.

Following the Orpington by-election of March 1962 – at which the Liberal candidate Jeremy Lubbock overturned a large Tory majority – the party's popular support was high, but it soon slumped. The party's prospects in the general election to be held in 1964 seemed poor.

When the Liberal faithful assembled in Brighton in September 1963, Grimond was determined to bolster their confidence. In this famous speech, he encourages party workers to exert themselves as if the election campaign were already under way. He inspires them with his vision of reform in British institutions and – while acknowledging that his views are controversial – encourages them to court such controversy.

The Liberals won nine seats at the election, an improvement of 50 per cent – and additionally significant because the Labour Party, having won the election by a narrow margin, was now reliant on Liberal support. However, hopes of a shift in political trends faded following the 1966 election, in which the Labour Party won an absolute majority.

❧

Fellow delegates: *we* have made this party, you and I. It has not always been easy, but we have built it up and there are a lot of people in this hall who have come into the Liberal Party and have devoted their money, their energy, their wits to building up their party. And it is your party – my party – and all of our party. We stand for partnership and we mean to practise partnership in this party.

It may be that we should run a different sort of party. Some people do. [*Laughter.*] But a Liberal Assembly comes together so that we may together fashion our policy, see each other, talk to each other as equals, take the pulse of the party, and feel the fist of the party when necessary. We like it like that, and it is our party, and we are going to have it like that.

Now, ... Mr GLADSTONE said that little is accomplished in politics without passion and it is true. The reforms we propose are not very complicated. They are widely agreed to be necessary, but this country is inert and will only be shaken by passion.

It is typical that reforms that everyone knows to be necessary, and which many other countries have carried out, should in Britain be considered to be absolutely visionary [*Laughter.*] How dare people think that when science is undergoing revolution after revolution, when the whole structure and obligations of government have changed, that it is impossible to change the political institutions by which we run our country? [*Applause.*] How can you suggest, when in the arts and sciences there is this enormous ferment, that politics alone must go on being wrapped up in a polythene bag, being more remote from the ordinary people? [*Applause.*]

… I believe we can create a society which people can admire, and to which they can respond. In every great society the citizens have been proud of proclaiming their citizenship. Men would have died rather than deny that they were Athenians or, indeed, citizens of Elizabethan Britain. Banishment from their society was a punishment less dread only than death itself. When a man claimed to be a Roman citizen, he identified himself not solely with the victories of the Roman armies or the material prosperity of the city itself. He identified himself with the public virtues of Rome, embodied in the structure of her empire and in the systems of law and administration. But who could be proud of an association with the public life of Britain in the last few years?

[*Loud applause.*]

Today too many people are backing away from Britain, backing away from their responsibilities to their country. They emigrate. They take pride, not in developing and moulding the civilization which we have inherited, but in enjoying what is ludicrous and sordid in it, and disclaiming all responsibilities for its ethics or good management. [*Applause.*]

Now I beg of you Liberals, identify yourselves with your country! Get closer to it. It is yours – and this backing away, this snide dissociation from the great past and from the beckoning future – it will be the death of this country if it continues. [*Applause.*]

… The British used to laugh at foreign bigwigs loaded with medals, posturing under meaningless titles, prating of prestige and all too often corrupt and decadent. Now no establishment in the world is so much concerned with titles and decorations as is official Britain. Nor is any governing class so concerned with its prestige and anxious about status rating. Underneath all this façade we now know what has been going on. No wonder then that there is cynicism about the conduct of our public affairs. This cynicism has led to a good deal of complacency and a great resistance to change …

We are now awaiting the report of Lord Denning[1] on, among other things, the state of public life in this country. I ask you to consider this astonishing development. Since when have the people of this country had to call in a high court judge, however eminent, to carry out a roving commission into the private lives of various individuals, so that we may be informed whether we are behaving ourselves or not?

Ladies and gentlemen: can you contemplate Mr Gladstone requiring advice on this subject? [*Laughter.*] Let us be fair. Mr DISRAELI would have laughed himself silly at the idea. Mr Asquith[2] would not have stomached it for a moment. And Mr BALFOUR would have cut it down with a phrase. As for Mr CHURCHILL, I wonder what he is thinking now?

… What should citizenship of Britain mean today? What should we create here to which people would assent, so that people will be able to say, 'I lived in the sixties and seventies and, for all my life, I shall be proud of the public life of my country'? What can we do to restore that confidence, that optimism, to draw people once again into their country's affairs and give back power to the decent, hard-working, general British citizen? I will tell you what I think British citizenship should mean.

First, that this country gets its role in the world right. To begin with, it

[1] In July 1963, prime minister HAROLD MACMILLAN appointed the law lord Alfred Thompson Denning, Baron Denning (1899–1999) to investigate the security aspects of the Profumo affair. The report, published on 26 September 1963, found there had been no breach of security.

[2] The English statesman Herbert Henry Asquith (1852–1928) served as Liberal Prime Minister, 1908–16.

should be the proud boast of everyone who is entitled to claim citizenship of our Commonwealth, that they can come to this country freely, and walk its streets, as Britons.

[*Loud applause.*]

Secondly, few things have been more inimical to the true development of Britain than the attempt to keep up as a nuclear power with the USA and Russia, while neglecting the opportunity to play a constructive part in Europe ... Europe still needs Britain, and Britain, Europe ...

Secondly, it should mean that a citizen should have a clear political choice put before him ... It is monstrous that so little information should be supplied to the public about politics. The simplest and most obvious thing is for a television edition of Parliament daily.[3] The next thing which is needed is that Parliament and the press, acting on behalf of the public, should be allowed to probe into the recesses of where decisions are taken, and to be informed how our civil service works and where it needs improvement ... As a politician I have said again and again that, however critical or indeed beastly it may be to politicians, it gives publicity to politics and without that publicity the House of Commons would die.

[*Applause.*]

... Thirdly, to be satisfactory, a society must feel some confidence in the distribution of its wealth ... We believe both that capital wealth should be more widely shared, and that the salaried workers and those in public services should be more adequately rewarded ...

Fourthly, we have made our proposals for the reform of Parliament, the executive and the civil service. But these proposals must be completed by reforms of the legal system ... I speak with some affection for the system, because I was trained as a barrister. It needs reform, under three heads. First, the reform of the penal system. When I compare some of the sentences awarded for offences against property, and sometimes on demonstrators, with the sentences which are often given to people who beat their children half dead, I wonder just whether we have our priorities in punishment quite right.

Then I draw your attention to the recruitment of the legal profession. The trades unions in this country are constantly under attack for restrictive practices. This speech requires some courage as I look around on the platform. But the restrictive practices of the most reactionary union fade into oblivion compared with the restrictive practices of the Bar. [*Applause.*]

... Most important, there is a growing divorce between the people and the law in this country. Nobody gets involved in civil action if they can avoid it. If they do, they may find themselves engaged in litigation of unknown cost, conducted in archaic and unintelligible language so that you cannot find out what is going on. And at the end of it all they may have more judges on their side than against them, and lose the case.

It is an axiom of British law that not only should justice be done, but should be seen to be done. It is also a justifiable boast of the British that the judiciary are independent of the executive. But the office of the Lord Chancellor is a standing negation of this. He is both a leading politician and head of the judicial system ... We say that the judiciary and the legal profession must be drawn from all the nation, it must be equipped to deal with cases where the individual is in conflict with the executive, and must be seen to be absolutely free from any contact with, let alone subservience to, the executive ...

As I regard this conference as focused on the future, I will finish by giving

[3] The first live radio broadcast from the House of Commons was made on 9 June 1975. The first live television broadcast from the House of Lords took place on 23 January 1985 and that from the House of Commons on 21 November 1989.

you your marching orders for the campaign which will not open when Parliament is dissolved, but which is opening now, this autumn, and will not end until polling day at the general election. We have in recent by-elections polled more votes than the Tories. We have produced before you at the conference men of higher calibre than many Tory ministers ... I make no wild or extravagant claim when I say they are men of equal ability, character, dedication and force to any you will find in public life today ...

If we return after the election with a solid block of Liberals in the House of Commons, even if we do not hold a majority, we shall be able to influence the whole thinking of the country and attitude of whatever party may be in power. We have made it clear that we intend to use that influence. As the election approaches we shall not shirk the battle, nor shall we be diverted by the great volume of criticism which we hope will pour down upon us.

[*Applause.*]

War, delegates – war has always been a confused affair. In bygone days the commanders were taught that when in doubt they should march their troops towards the sound of gunfire. I intend to march my troops towards the sound of gunfire. [*Loud applause.*] Politics are a confused affair and the fog of political controversy can obscure many issues. But we will march towards the sound of the guns.

Our government, for too long, has pretended not to see what it does not like. It has put the telescope to its blind eye in a very un-Nelsonian[4] mood, so it can say that there is no enemy in sight. But, delegates, there are enemies, there are difficulties to be faced. There are decisions to be made. There is passion to be generated. The enemy is complacency and wrong values and inertia in the face of incompetence and injustice. It is against this enemy that we march.

[4] Grimond refers to the English naval commander Horatio Nelson, 1st Viscount Nelson (1758–1805), who famously ignored an order to disengage at the Battle of Copenhagen (1801) by placing a telescope to his blind eye and remarking 'I see no ships'.

Ernesto 'Che' Guevara

Argentinian revolutionary leader

Ernesto Guevara de la Serna *nicknamed Che* (1928–67) was born in Rosario and graduated in medicine at the University of Buenos Aires (1953). He travelled widely in South America, then joined FIDEL CASTRO's revolutionary movement in Mexico (1955), and played an important part in the Cuban revolution (1956–9). He was awarded Cuban citizenship in 1959, and held several government posts under Castro. An activist of revolution elsewhere, including Africa, he left Cuba in 1965 to become a guerrilla leader in South America, and was captured and executed by government troops in Bolivia while trying to foment a revolt. He became an icon for left-wing youth in the 1960s. He wrote *Guerrilla Warfare* (1961), *Reminiscences of the Cuban Revolutionary War* (1968) and *Motorcycle Diaries* (published 1996).

'To be a revolutionary you have first to have a revolution'

19 August 1960, Havana, Cuba

The repressive policies and economic struggles that mark Castro's long regime in Cuba have diminished his folk-hero status. No such problem for his right-hand man Che Guevara, whose good looks and youthful death (aged 39) created an enduring romantic image.

But Che – whose nickname is an Argentinian greeting – was more than simply a handsome pin-up. While training as a doctor, he developed a keen understanding of politics, economics and Marxist ideology; he later became an expert guerrilla strategist. He was famously described by the French author Jean-Paul Sartre as 'the most complete human being of our time'.

During the revolution led by Castro, Guevara spent two years living in Cuba's Sierra Maestra mountains, and helped lead the peasant army to victory, overthrowing the despotic regime of General Fulgencio Batista. After Castro's installation as prime minister, Cuba underwent rapid socio-economic change, forging an alliance with the USSR in defiance of American sanctions. Guevara spearheaded revolutionary reforms, often leading by example, and won enormous affection from the Cuban people.

This speech, translated by Beth Kurti, was given to medical professionals at the Confederation of Cuban Workers. In it, Guevara harks back to his professional roots but relates all work to egalitarian principles.

He was a fiery speaker with dark, lowering eyes, who invariably wore green fatigues and black beret – even when addressing the United Nations in 1964 – and constantly smoked cigars despite severe asthma. Witnesses describe the 'charisma' and 'moral sense' of his speeches. Though his relationship with Castro ultimately soured, he is still considered a national hero in Cuba.

Almost everyone knows that years ago I began my career as a doctor. And when I began as a doctor, when I began to study medicine, the majority of the concepts I have today, as a revolutionary, were absent from my store of ideals. Like everyone, I wanted to succeed. I dreamed of becoming a famous medical research scientist; I dreamed of working indefatigably to discover something which would be used to help humanity, but which signified a personal triumph for me. I was, as we all are, a child of my environment.

After graduation … I began to travel throughout America,[1] and I became acquainted with all of it … I came into close contact with poverty, hunger, and disease; with the inability to treat a child because of lack of money; with the stupefaction provoked by continual hunger and punishment … And I began to realize at that time that there were things that were almost as important to me as becoming a famous scientist or making a significant contribution to medical science: I wanted to help those people.

But I continued to be – as we all continue to be always – a child of my environment, and I wanted to help those people with my own personal efforts … I began to investigate what was needed to be a revolutionary doctor …

[1] Guevara refers to Latin America, much of which he explored by motorbike with his friend Alberto Granado (1922–11).

Then I realized a fundamental thing. For one to be a revolutionary doctor or to be a revolutionary at all, there must first be a revolution. Isolated individual endeavour, for all its purity of ideals, is of no use, and the desire to sacrifice an entire lifetime to the noblest of ideals serves no purpose if one works alone, solitarily, in some corner of America, fighting against adverse governments and social conditions which prevent progress. To create a revolution, one must have what there is in Cuba – the mobilization of a whole people, who learn by the use of arms and the exercise of militant unity to understand the value of arms and the value of this unity.

And now we have come to the nucleus of the problem we have before us at this time. Today one finally has the right and even the duty to be, above all things, a revolutionary doctor, that is to say a man who utilizes the technical knowledge of his profession in the service of the revolution and the people. But now old questions reappear: How does one actually carry out a work of social welfare? How does one unite individual endeavour with the needs of society?

... In Cuba a new type of man is being created,[2] whom we cannot fully appreciate here in the capital, but who is found in every corner of the country. Those of you who went to the Sierra Maestra on 26 July[3] must have seen two completely unknown things. Firstly, an army with hoes and pickaxes, an army whose greatest pride is to parade in the patriotic festivals of Oriente[4] with hoes and axes raised, while their military comrades march with rifles.

But you must have seen something even more important. You must have seen children whose physical constitutions appeared to be those of eight- or nine-year-olds, yet almost all of whom are 13 or 14. They are the most authentic children of the Sierra Maestra, the most authentic offspring of hunger and misery. They are the creatures of malnutrition.

In this tiny Cuba, with its four or five television channels and hundreds of radio stations, with all the advances of modern science, when those children arrived at school for the first time at night and saw the electric light bulbs, they exclaimed that the stars were very low that night. And those children, some of whom you must have seen, are learning in collective schools skills ranging from reading to trades, and even the very difficult science of becoming revolutionaries.

Those are the new humans being born in Cuba. They are being born in isolated areas, in different parts of the Sierra Maestra, and also in the co-operatives and work centres. All this has to do with the theme of our talk today, the integration of the physician or any other medical worker, into the revolutionary movement ... The principle upon which the fight against disease should be based is the creation of a robust body; but not the creation of a robust body by the artistic work of a doctor upon a weak organism; rather, the creation of a robust body with the work of the whole collectivity, upon the entire social collectivity.

Some day, therefore, medicine will have to convert itself into a science that serves to prevent disease *and* orients the public toward carrying out its medical duties. Medicine should only intervene in cases of extreme urgency, to perform surgery or something else which lies outside the skills of the people of the new society we are creating ...

But for this task of organization, as for all the revolutionary tasks, fundamentally it is the individual who is needed. The revolution does not, as some claim, standardize the collective will and the collective initiative. On the contrary, it liberates man's individual talent. What the revolution does is

[2] Central to Guevara's political philosophy was the creation of *El Hombre Nuevo* ('The New Man'), a Cuban Communist who would be motivated by a spirit of collectivism and expect moral rather than material rewards. He strove to exemplify this ascetic doctrine with his own conduct.

[4] Until 1976, an eastern province of Cuba, the location of the Sierra Maestra.

[3] Castro's first attempt to overthrow Batista was on 26 July 1953 (see his speech of 16 October 1953, included in this book). On the same date in 1959, Castro returned to office as Prime Minister, after briefly resigning, effectively ousting President Manuel Urritia six months after his appointment. Cubans now celebrate 26 July as a national holiday.

orient that talent. And our task now is to orient the creative abilities of all medical professionals toward the tasks of social medicine.

We are at the end of an era, and not only here in Cuba. No matter what is hoped or said to the contrary, the form of capitalism we have known, in which we were raised, and under which we have suffered, is being defeated all over the world ... Such a profound social change demands equally profound changes in the mental structure of the people.

Individualism, in the form of the individual action of a person alone in a social milieu, must disappear in Cuba. In the future, individualism ought to be the efficient utilization of the whole individual for the absolute benefit of a collectivity ...

One way of getting to the heart of the medical question is not only to visit and become acquainted with the people who make up the co-operatives and work centres, but to find out what diseases they have, what their sufferings are, what have been their chronic miseries for years, and what has been the inheritance of centuries of repression and total submission. The doctor, the medical worker, must go to the core of his new work, which is the man within the mass, the man within the collectivity.

Always, no matter what happens in the world, the doctor is extremely close to his patient and knows the innermost depths of his psyche. Because he is the one who attacks pain and mitigates it, he performs an invaluable labour of much responsibility in society.

A few months ago, here in Havana, it happened that a group of newly graduated doctors did not want to go into the country's rural areas, and demanded remuneration before they would agree to go. From the point of view of the past it is the most logical thing in the world for this to occur; at least, so it seems to me, for I can understand it perfectly. The situation brings back to me the memory of what I was and what I thought a few years ago ... the gladiator who rebels, the solitary fighter who wants to assure a better future, better conditions, and to make valid the need people have of him.

But what would have happened if – instead of these boys, whose families generally were able to pay for their years of study – others of less fortunate means had just finished their schooling and were beginning the exercise of their profession? What would have occurred if two or three hundred peasants had emerged, let us say by magic, from the university halls?

What would have happened, simply, is that the peasants would have run, immediately and with unreserved enthusiasm, to help their brothers. They would have requested the most difficult and responsible jobs in order to demonstrate that the years of study they had received had not been given in vain. What would have happened is what will happen in six or seven years, when the new students, children of workers and peasant, receive professional degrees of all kinds ...

None of us – none of the first group which arrived in the *Granma*,[5] who settled in the Sierra Maestra and learned to respect the peasant and the worker living with him – had a peasant or working-class background. Naturally, there were those who had had to work, who had known certain privations in childhood; but hunger, what is called real hunger, was something none of us had experienced. But we began to know it in the two long years in the Sierra Maestra. And then many things became very clear ...

We understood perfectly that the life of a single human being is worth a

[5] The small, overloaded vessel on which Castro, Guevara and 80 others set sail from Mexico on 25 November 1956, to begin the revolution in Cuba.

million times more than all the property of the richest man on earth. And we learned it; we, who were not of the working class nor of the peasant class. And are we now going to tell the four winds, we who were the privileged ones, that the rest of the people in Cuba cannot learn it also?

Yes, they can learn it: the Revolution today demands that they learn it, demands that it be well understood that far more important than a good remuneration is the pride of serving one's neighbour; that much more definitive and much more lasting than all the gold that one can accumulate is the gratitude of a people. And each doctor, within the circle of his activities, can and must accumulate that valuable treasure, the gratitude of the people …

We shall see that diseases need not always be treated as they are in big-city hospitals. We shall see that the doctor has to be a farmer also and plant new foods and sow, by example, the desire to consume new foods, to diversify the Cuban nutritional structure, which is so limited, so poor, in one of the richest countries in the world, agriculturally and potentially. The first thing we will have to do is not to go to the people to offer them our wisdom. We must go, rather, to demonstrate that we are going to learn with the people, that together we are going to carry out that great and beautiful common experiment: the construction of a new Cuba …

I was telling you that to be a revolutionary you have first to have a revolution. We already have it. Next, you have to know the people with whom you are going to work … I ought to warn you that the doctor, in that function of soldier and revolutionary, should always be a doctor. You should not commit the same error which we committed in the Sierra … It seemed dishonourable to us to remain at the side of a wounded man or a sick one, and we looked for any way possible of grabbing a rifle and going to prove on the battlefront what we could do.

Now the conditions are different, and the new armies which are being formed to defend the country must be armies with different tactics. The doctor will have an enormous importance within the plan of the new army. He must continue being a doctor, which is one of the most beautiful tasks there is and one of the most important in war … In time of danger they should go immediately to solve the problems of the poor people of Cuba. But the militias offer also an opportunity to live together, joined and made equal by a uniform, with men of all the social classes of Cuba.

If we medical workers – and permit me to use once again a title which I had forgotten some time ago – are successful, if we use this new weapon of solidarity, if we know the goals, know the enemy, and know the direction we have to take, then all that is left for us to know is the part of the way to be covered each day. And that part no-one can show us; that part is the private journey of each individual. Now that we have all the elements for our march toward the future, let us remember the advice of Martí:[6] 'The best way of telling is doing.' Let us march, then, toward Cuba's future.

[6] The Cuban journalist and poet José Martí (1853–95) became the figurehead of the independence movement. He was one of the leaders of the Second War of Independence against Spain, but was killed during his first battle. He is still celebrated as a Cuban national hero, almost as ubiquitous as Che himself.

William Hague

English statesman and public speaker

William Jefferson Hague (1961–) was born in Wentworth, Yorkshire. Aged 16, he addressed the 1977 Conservative Party conference and received a standing ovation. He was educated at Oxford, became a political adviser to the Treasury (1983) and entered Parliament as MP for Richmond, Yorkshire, in 1989. He rose quickly to become Secretary of State for Wales (1995–7). Following Labour's landslide win in the 1997 general election, former prime minister John Major stood down as leader of the Conservative Party, and Hague succeeded him. An effective debater notable for his wit, Hague failed to win the general election of 2001, and resigned, to be succeeded by Iain Duncan Smith, Michael Howard and David Cameron. In 2005 he became Shadow Foreign Secretary and in 2010, when Cameron became Prime Minister, he was appointed Foreign Secretary. He has published critically well-received biographies of William Pitt the Younger (2004) and William Wilberforce (2007).

'What sort of world do young people want?'

12 October 1977, Blackpool, England

The 16-year-old William Hague became an overnight star with his famous speech to the Conservative Party conference. Memories abound in the British consciousness: a teenage boy, dressed in an old-fashioned tweed blazer, confidently approaches the platform and addresses the conference in a deep Yorkshire accent. The speech itself was similarly confident: Hague insisted that, contrary to voting trends, the Conservatives represented the hopes of young people. He lampooned Britain's fate under the then Labour government as 'miserable and abhorrent' and gave an accurate forecast of the changes a Conservative government – led by MARGARET THATCHER – would introduce, from ending state-run industries to increasing home ownership.

However, this speech dogged Hague as an adult: the public could never quite shake off their image of him as a precocious youth. In 2001, after losing the general election as Conservative leader, Hague again addressed his party's conference in Blackpool. This time, his humour was self-deprecating. 'I gave a speech in this hall when I said half of you won't be here in 30 years' time and, actually, I was wrong,' he said. 'Because 24 years on you're still here and I have come and gone.'

As a 16-year-old, I represent what may well seem to be the last generation for the Conservative Party. By all accounts, some ten per cent of first-time voters voted Conservative in the last general election. If that trend continues then perhaps some mathematician in the hall would care to work out just how many years it will be before it becomes impossible for the Conservative Party to win a general election.

That lack of support stems largely, in my belief, from the fact that the party is seen, rightly or wrongly, as standing for the maintenance of the existing political and economic order. The young people who voted so overwhelmingly against our party last time are people who believe in change – not change for its own sake but change because they are dissatisfied with the existing state of affairs in Great Britain. But the only form of change that has been offered to them in the past has been a change to the left – an irreversible shift of power, as the Labour Party has called it, supposedly to the people but in reality to the centralized state.

They must now be shown that it is possible to change in other directions. Indeed, not only possible to change but necessary to change. Every subsequent Labour government has encroached upon the liberty of the individual citizen. Every subsequent Conservative government has failed to do more than only marginally restore it.

What sort of world do young people want? Like the rest of the British people, they share the aspirations and hopes of the Conservative Party, but in this case it is not translated into Conservative votes. They want a society where effort and initiative are rewarded instead of stamped upon, where those who work the hardest receive the greatest reward, where those who take the greatest risk receive the largest profit.

They want to live in a world where it pays to work and, more important, where it pays to work in Britain. They do not accept the socialist argument that the government knows what is good for the people better than the people do. They do not want to go to Callaghan's[1] promised land, which must surely rank as the most miserable and abhorrent land that has ever been promised to the people of a nation. But most of all they want to be free, free from the government, the government that they think should get out of the way, not intervene, not interfere in their lives. And I trust Mrs Thatcher's government will indeed get out of the way.

There is at least one school, which I think is in London, where the pupils are allowed to win just one race each, no more, for fear that the others might feel inferior. That is a classic illustration of the socialist state, which draws nearer with every Labour government and which Conservatives have never reversed. Half of you may not be here in 30 or 40 years' time, but I will be and I want to be free.

Economic policy can guarantee that freedom. Denationalization of certain industries and forcing others to cover their costs, large and progressive cuts in public spending, the year-by-year reduction of the proportion of the GNP[2] spent by the state, in short, the creation of a free market economy.

There comes a time, as a country moves nearer towards a socialist state, when the party of the left ceases to be the dominant party, the reformer, and it is the party of the right that becomes the party of radicalism and change. If we should fail now to reverse the progress of socialism, we can write off the future of this party and of the country. But if we rise to the challenge and if we determine to roll back the frontiers of the state, we will not only capture the imagination and support of the younger people; we will save free enterprise and Great Britain, and create a capital-owning, home-owning democracy for the young people.

[1] The English politician James Callaghan (1912–2005) served as Labour Prime Minister, 1976–9. He was ousted following a vote of no confidence. The ensuing general election was won by the Conservatives.

[2] Gross National Product, a measure of productivity in goods and services.

Haile Selassie
Emperor of Ethiopia

Haile Selassie I *previously Prince Ras Tafari Makonnen* (1891–1975) was born near Harer. Son of Ras Makonnen, he led the revolution (1916) against Lij Yasu, and became regent and heir to the throne. In 1930 he became Emperor of Ethiopia, then known as Abyssinia. A Coptic Christian, he westernized the institutions of his country and took it into the League of Nations. He settled in England after the Italian conquest of Abyssinia (1935–6), but in 1941 was restored after the liberation by British forces. In the early 1960s he played a crucial part in the establishment of the Organization of African Unity (OAU). Opposition to his reign had existed since 1960, and the disastrous famine of 1973 led to economic chaos, industrial strikes and mutiny among the armed forces. In 1974 he was deposed and a Marxist military regime took power. Suspicion persists about the cause of his death. Accusations of corruption levelled against him and his family have not destroyed the unique prestige and reverence in which he is held by certain groups, notably adherents of Rastafarianism.

'If we are to survive, this organization must survive'
4 October 1963, New York City, USA

When Haile Selassie gave this legendary speech to the United Nations, he became – as he points out towards the end – the first head of state to address both the League of Nations and its successor organization. He had good reason to hope for improvement: following the Italian invasion of 1935, the League of Nations had listened sympathetically to his plea for assistance, but failed to act.

A determined and progressive leader, Haile Selassie had modernized and westernized Ethiopia, becoming the country's first leader to travel widely, and showing a flair for international diplomacy. Now, in the wake of a failed coup in 1960 – which had attempted to depose him and install his son – he was seeking stability. Five months earlier, he had convened a summit meeting of 32 African heads of state to form the Organization of African Unity, whose goals were to promote solidarity and oust colonialism.

With a view to placing his new organization in a wider international context, he spoke eloquently to the United Nations, stressing the organization's importance in maintaining global peace, and urging it to adopt more forceful policies. The famous passage on racial equality struck a chord around the world – particularly in the USA, where the civil rights movement was at its peak. It also formed the basis of the song 'War', recorded by the reggae star Bob Marley in 1976.

Today, I stand before the world organization which has succeeded to the mantle discarded by its discredited predecessor.[1] In this body is enshrined the principle of collective security which I unsuccessfully invoked at Geneva.[2] Here, in this assembly, reposes the best – perhaps the last – hope for the peaceful survival of mankind ...

The record of the United Nations, during the few short years of its life,[3] affords mankind a solid basis for encouragement and hope for the future. The United Nations has dared to act when the League dared not – in Palestine, in Korea, in Suez, in the Congo. There is not one among us today who does not conjecture upon the reaction of this body, when motives and actions are called into question. The opinion of this organization today acts as a powerful influence upon the decisions of its members. The spotlight of world opinion, focused by the United Nations upon the transgressions of the renegades of human society, has thus far proved an effective safeguard against unchecked aggression and unrestricted violation of human rights ...

For this, all men must give thanks. As I stand here today, how faint, how remote, are the memories of 1936. How different in 1963 are the attitudes of men. We then existed in an atmosphere of suffocating pessimism. Today, cautious yet buoyant optimism is the prevailing spirit.

But each one of us here knows that what has been accomplished is not

[1] The League of Nations was established in 1920 to promote international co-operation and prevent wars. It ceased to operate during World War II, and officially dissolved itself in 1946 at a meeting of the United Nations.

[2] Haile Selassie made a famous appeal to the League of Nations following the Italian invasion of 1935, during which illegal chemical weapons were used. The speech elicited sympathy but no action.

[3] The United Nations was formed by 51 nations in 1945, inheriting some of the structure and agencies of the League of Nations.

enough. The United Nations' judgements have been and continue to be subject to frustration, as individual member states have ignored its pronouncements and disregarded its recommendations. The organization's sinews have been weakened, as member states have proceeded, in violation of its commands, to pursue their own aims and ends. The troubles which continue to plague us virtually all arise among member states of this organization, but the organization remains impotent to enforce acceptable solutions …

Peace is a day-to-day problem, the product of a multitude of events and judgements. Peace is not an 'is', it is a 'becoming.' We cannot escape the dreadful possibility of catastrophe by miscalculation. But we can reach the right decisions on the myriad subordinate problems which each new day poses, and we can thereby make our contribution and perhaps the most that can be reasonably expected of us in 1963 to the preservation of peace. It is here that the United Nations has served us – not perfectly, but well. And in enhancing the possibilities that the organization may serve us better, we serve and bring closer our most cherished goals …

The goal of the equality of man which we seek is the antithesis of the exploitation of one people by another with which the pages of history – and in particular those written of the African and Asian continents – speak at such length. Exploitation, thus viewed, has many faces. But whatever guise it assumes, this evil is to be shunned where it does not exist and crushed where it does. It is the sacred duty of this organization to ensure that the dream of equality is finally realized for all men …

As a free Africa has emerged during the past decade, a fresh attack has been launched against exploitation, wherever it still exists. And in that interaction so common to history, this in turn has stimulated and encouraged the remaining dependent peoples to renewed efforts to throw off the yoke which has oppressed them and claim as their birthright the twin ideals of liberty and equality.

This very struggle is a struggle to establish peace, and until victory is assured, that brotherhood and understanding which nourish and give life to peace can be but partial and incomplete. In the United States of America, the administration of President Kennedy[4] is leading a vigorous attack to eradicate the remaining vestige of racial discrimination from this country. We know that this conflict will be won and that right will triumph. In this time of trial, these efforts should be encouraged and assisted, and we should lend our sympathy and support to the American government today.

Last May,[5] in Addis Ababa, I convened a meeting of heads of African states and governments. In three days, the 32 nations represented at that conference demonstrated to the world that when the will and the determination exist, nations and peoples of diverse backgrounds can and will work together in unity, to the achievement of common goals and the assurance of that equality and brotherhood which we desire.

On the question of racial discrimination, the Addis Ababa Conference taught, to those who will learn, this further lesson: that until the philosophy which holds one race superior and another inferior is finally and permanently discredited and abandoned; that until there are no longer first-class and second-class citizens of any nation; that until the colour of a man's skin is of no more significance than the colour of his eyes; that until the basic human rights are equally guaranteed to all without regard to race; that until that day, the dream of lasting peace and world citizenship and the rule of international morality will remain but a fleeting illusion, to be

[4] JOHN F KENNEDY had championed racial equality reforms. The Civil Rights Act, passed in 1964 after his assassination, was largely his work.

[5] Haile Selassie refers to May 1963, when the Organization of African Unity was formed.

[6] Angola, seeking independence from Portugal, was then embroiled in a guerrilla war (1961–75).

[7] Mozambique, also seeking independence from Portugal, had formed the FRELIMO liberation front, though hostilities did not break out in earnest until September 1964.

[8] South Africa was under the draconian apartheid system of racial segregation from 1948 until the 1990s.

[9] See notes 6 and 7 above.

pursued but never attained; and until the ignoble and unhappy regimes that hold our brothers in Angola,[6] in Mozambique[7] and in South Africa[8] in subhuman bondage have been toppled and destroyed; until bigotry and prejudice and malicious and inhuman self-interest have been replaced by understanding and tolerance and goodwill; until all Africans stand and speak as free beings, equal in the eyes of all men, as they are in the eyes of Heaven; until that day, the African continent will not know peace. We Africans will fight, if necessary, and we know that we shall win, as we are confident in the victory of good over evil.

The United Nations has done much, both directly and indirectly to speed the disappearance of discrimination and oppression from the earth. Without the opportunity to focus world opinion on Africa and Asia which this organization provides, the goal, for many, might still lie ahead, and the struggle would have taken far longer. For this, we are truly grateful.

But more can be done. The basis of racial discrimination and colonialism has been economic, and it is with economic weapons that these evils have been and can be overcome. In pursuance of resolutions adopted at the Addis Ababa Summit Conference, African states have undertaken certain measures in the economic field, which, if adopted by all member states of the United Nations, would soon reduce intransigence to reason.

I ask, today, for adherence to these measures by every nation represented here that is truly devoted to the principles enunciated in the [UN] Charter. I do not believe that Portugal[9] and South Africa are prepared to commit economic or physical suicide if honourable and reasonable alternatives exist. I believe that such alternatives can be found. But I also know that unless peaceful solutions are devised, counsels of moderation and temperance will avail for naught; and another blow will have been dealt to this organization …

Here, then, is the opportunity presented to us. We must act while we can, while the occasion exists to exert those legitimate pressures available to us, lest time run out and resort be had to less happy means. Does this organization today possess the authority and the will to act? And if it does not, are we prepared to clothe it with the power to create and enforce the rule of law? Or is the Charter a mere collection of words, without content and substance, because the essential spirit is lacking?

The time in which to ponder these questions is all too short. The pages of history are full of instances in which the unwanted and the shunned nonetheless occurred because men waited to act until too late. We can brook no such delay. If we are to survive, this organization must survive. To survive, it must be strengthened. Its executive must be vested with great authority. The means for the enforcement of its decisions must be fortified, and, if they do not exist, they must be devised. Procedures must be established to protect the small and the weak when threatened by the strong and the mighty. All nations that fulfil the conditions of membership must be admitted and allowed to sit in this assemblage. Equality of representation must be assured in each of its organs.

The possibilities which exist in the United Nations to provide the medium whereby the hungry may be fed, the naked clothed, the ignorant instructed, must be seized on and exploited for the flower of peace is not sustained by poverty and want. To achieve this requires courage and confidence. The courage, I believe, we possess. The confidence must be created, and to create confidence we must act courageously … Unless the smaller nations are accorded their proper voice in the settlement of the world's problems, unless the equality which Africa and Asia have struggled to attain is reflected in expanded membership in the institutions which make up the United Nations, confidence will come just that much harder.

Unless the rights of the least of men are as assiduously protected as those of the greatest, the seeds of confidence will fall on barren soil. The stake of each one of us is identical – life or death. We all wish to live. We all seek a world in which men are freed of the burdens of ignorance, poverty, hunger and disease. And we shall all be hard-pressed to escape the deadly rain of nuclear fall-out should catastrophe overtake us. When I spoke at Geneva in 1936, there was no precedent for a head of state addressing the League of Nations. I am neither the first, nor will I be the last head of state to address the United Nations, but only I have addressed both the League and this Organization in this capacity.

The problems that confront us today are unprecedented. They have no counterparts in human experience. Men search the pages of history for solutions, for precedents, but there are none. This, then, is the ultimate challenge.

Where are we to look for our survival, for the answers to the questions which have never before been posed? We must look, first, to Almighty God, who has raised man above the animals and endowed him with intelligence and reason. We must put our faith in him, that he will not desert us or permit us to destroy humanity, which he created in his image.

And we must look into ourselves, into the depth of our souls. We must become something we have never been; and for which our education and experience and environment have ill-prepared us. We must become bigger than we have been, more courageous, greater in spirit, larger in outlook. We must become members of a new race, overcoming petty prejudice, owing our ultimate allegiance not to nations but to our fellow men within the human community.

Dag Hammarskjöld
Swedish statesman

Dag Hjalmar Agne Carl Hammarskjöld (1905–61) was born in Jönköping. In 1933 he became an assistant professor at Stockholm University, and subsequently secretary (1935) and then chairman (1941–8) of the Bank of Sweden. He was Swedish Foreign Minister (1951–3), and a delegate to the Organization for European Economic Cooperation, the British–Scandinavian Economic Community (UNISCAN), the Council of Europe and the United Nations General Assembly. He became Secretary-General of the UN in 1953. Hammarskjöld, who once described himself as 'the curator of the secrets of 82 nations', played a leading part in the setting up of the UN Emergency Force in Sinai and Gaza in 1956, and worked for conciliation in the Middle East (1957–8). He died in an air crash near Ndola in Zambia, while he was engaged in negotiations over the Congo crisis, during which the country's first elected leader, PATRICE LUMUMBA, was deposed, imprisoned and ultimately assassinated. DESMOND TUTU and the Norwegian soldier Bjørn Egge (the first UN officer to examine the body) are among the many who believe Hammarskjöld was assassinated. He was awarded the Nobel Peace Prize posthumously in 1961.

'Without recognition of human rights we shall never have peace'
10 April 1957, New York City, USA

Dag Hammarskjöld's outstanding talent for diplomacy was put to the test during the final years of his life: indeed, if the conspiracy theories are true, it contributed to his early death.

As Secretary-General of the United Nations, he had relatively little power, but as a negotiator he was calm, tactful and effective. Shortly before giving this speech, he had helped defuse the Suez Crisis – in which British, French, Israeli and Egyptian forces went to war over control of the Suez Canal, and the USSR threatened to intervene. He had also created an emergency international force to maintain peace.

This address was given at the 50th anniversary celebrations of the American Jewish Committee. This had been a devastating half-century for Jews, yet had also seen the establishment of a Jewish homeland in Israel. However, Hammarskjöld refers only briefly to Jewish history, instead using his speech to explore some of the principles that informed his struggle for peace. Above all, he stresses the dependence of peace on a recognition of human rights, and the centrality of tolerance to the goals of his organization.

Four years ago today, I was inducted into my present office, to which I had been catapulted without previous soundings, indeed, without any pre-warning. I felt that it was my duty to accept it, not because of any feeling of confidence in my personal capacity to overcome the difficulties which might arise, but because, under the conditions then prevailing, the one to whom the call had come seemed to me in duty bound to respond.

The situation that faced me at the very outset has proved not to be unique. It has been repeated several times in the past few years, most recently in relation to problems of the Middle East. The other day, returning from the latest visit to that area on a UN mission, I read a book by Arthur Waley[1] – certainly well known to many of you as one of the great interpreters of Chinese thought and literature and as one of those great Jewish students of humane letters who have so splendidly enriched our cultural tradition. In his work Waley quotes what an early Chinese historian had to say about the philosopher Sung Tzu and his followers, some 350 years BC. To one who works in the United Nations, the quotation strikes a familiar note. It runs as follows:

'Constantly rebuffed but never discouraged, they went round from state to state, helping people to settle their differences, arguing against wanton attack and pleading for the suppression of arms, that the age in which they lived might be saved from its state of continual war. To this end they interviewed princes and lectured the common people,

[1] The English Orientalist Arthur Waley (1889–1966) translated numerous Chinese and Japanese texts, as well as writing extensively on the Far East.

nowhere meeting with any great success, but obstinately persisting in their task, till kings and commoners alike grew weary of listening to them. Yet undeterred they continued to force themselves on people's attention.'

Is this a description of a quixotic group, whose efforts are doomed to failure? The wording, with its tone of frustration, may lead us to think so. However, I believe that this interpretation would be wrong. The historian tells us about a group engaged in a struggle he considers very much worth while and one which will have to go on until success is achieved.

The half-ironical, half-sad note which he strikes indicates only his knowledge of the difficulties which human nature puts in the way of such work for peace. His pessimism is tempered by the mild sense of humour and the strong sense of proportion of a man seeing his own time in the long perspective of history. We can learn from his attitude, both in our efforts to move towards peace and in our work for universal recognition of human rights.

We know that the question of peace and the question of human rights are closely related. Without recognition of human rights we shall never have peace, and it is only within the framework of peace that human rights can be fully developed.

In fact, the work for peace is basically a work for the most elementary of human rights: the right of everyone to security and to freedom from fear. We, therefore, recognize it as one of the first duties of a government to take measures in order to safeguard for its citizens this very right. But we also recognize it as an obligation for the emerging world community to assist governments in safeguarding this elementary human right without having to lock themselves in behind the wall of arms.

The dilemma of our age, with its infinite possibilities of self-destruction, is how to grow out of the world of armaments into a world of international security, based on law. We are only at the very beginning of such a change. The natural distrust in the possibility of progress is nourished by unavoidable setbacks and, when distrust is thus strengthened, this in turn increases our difficulties.

The effort may seem hopeless. It will prove hopeless unless we, all of us, show the persistence of Sung Tzu and his followers, and unless peoples and governments alike are willing to take smaller immediate risks in order to have a better chance to avoid the final disaster threatening us if we do not manage to turn the course of developments in a new direction.

The United Nations finds itself in a difficult stage of its development. It is still too weak to provide the security desired by all, while being strong enough and alive enough effectively to point out the direction in which the solution must be sought. In its present phase, the organization may look to many like a preacher who cannot impose the law he states or realize the gospel he interprets. It is understandable if those who have this impression turn away in distrust or with cynical criticism, forgetting that setbacks in efforts to implement an ideal do not prove that the ideal is wrong, and overlooking also that at the beginning of great changes in human society there must always be a stage of such frailty or seeming inconsistency.

It is easy to say that it is pointless to state the law if it cannot be enforced. However, to do so is to forget that if the law is the inescapable law of the future, it would be treason to the future not to state the law simply because of the difficulties of the present. Indeed, how could it ever become a living reality if those who are responsible for its development were to succumb to the immediate difficulties arising when it is still a revolutionary element in the life of society?

The history of the Jewish people offers some of the most magnificent examples of how ideals and law may be brought to victory through courageous assertion of new universal principles, which the wise call folly when they are first introduced in a society shaped on a different pattern.

The thoughts I have tried to express apply to practically the whole field of United Nations activities, but in particular to the work of the organization for the implementation of the principles of the Charter in the fields of international security and disarmament and in the field of fundamental human rights. They apply likewise to the United Nations itself as an experiment in international organization.

But is not an experiment something tentative and passing? And should not the United Nations be regarded as something definite and lasting? I think it is important to be clear on this point. Certainly the experiences and achievements of the United Nations as it is today are helping us to build the future. The United Nations is something definite also in the sense that the concepts and ideals it represents, like the needs it tries to meet, will remain an ineluctable element of the world picture. However, that does not mean that the present embodiment of the groping efforts of mankind towards an organized world community represents a definite shape for all time. The United Nations is, and should be, a living, evolving, experimental institution. If it should ever cease to be so it should be revolutionized or swept aside for a new approach.

The growth of social institutions is always one where, step by step, the form which adequately meets the need is shaped through selection, or out of experience. Thus an effort that has not yielded all the results hoped for has not failed if it has provided positive experience on which a new approach can be based. An attempt which has proved the possibility of progress has served the cause of progress even if it has had to be renewed again and again, and in new forms or settings in order to yield full success.

When we look back over the experiences in the United Nations over the past few months, we may differ amongst ourselves as to the wisdom of this or that particular stand and we may have doubts about the end result of this or that step. But I think we all can agree on the value and historical importance of certain developments.

First of all, it proved possible in an emergency to create for the first time a truly international force. This force, although modest in size and, for constitutional reasons, also modest in aim, broke new ground which inevitably will count in future efforts to preserve peace and promote justice.

I think we can likewise agree that the fact that the United Nations could undertake and carry through a major field operation like the clearance of the Suez Canal, where no government was in a position to accomplish the task, indicated possibilities for international organization which, once proven, cannot in future be disregarded.

Finally, deeply regrettable though the conflicts of views and interests were, it should not be forgotten that those who now feel they had to sacrifice for the maintenance of a principle, in a different situation may be the first to profit from the fact that the principle was maintained. As individuals we know that the law which restrains us likewise protects us. The same holds true in international life.

Some moments ago I referred to the fact that lasting peace is not possible without recognition of fundamental human rights and that human rights cannot reach their full development unless there is peace. The United Nations cannot lay down the law for the life within any national community. Those laws have to be established in accordance with the will of the people, as expressed in the forms indicated by their chosen constitution.

But just as the United Nations can promote peace, so it can, in joint deliberations, define the goals of human rights which should be the laws of the future in each nation. Whatever the distance between these goals and the everyday reality we meet all around the world, it is not vain thus to set the targets as they present themselves to the most mature political thinking of our age …

You have put 'the pursuit of equality at home and abroad' as a motto of your anniversary. Interpreted in a broad sense these words reflect a basic human right, equal in significance to the right to security and freedom from fear …

The underlying problems now making the Middle East such a troubled area … lend special weight to the undertaking of the member nations in the Charter 'to practise tolerance'.

The words just quoted from the Charter are among those which link its text to a great ethical tradition. They are often overlooked, sometimes brushed aside as empty ornaments without political significance, sometimes honoured by lip-service. However, they represent an element without which the Charter and the system it creates would disintegrate. Both the work for peace and the work for human rights must be anchored in and inspired by a general approach which gives balance and substance to the results. Peace cannot be enforced for selfish reasons, equality cannot be imposed as an abstract concept. In fact, attempts to do so account for some of the darkest episodes in history.

The work for peace must be animated by tolerance and the work for human rights by respect for the individual. A student of the growth of human rights through the ages will recognize its close relationship to the development of tolerance inspired by intellectual liberalism or, perhaps more often, by ethical concepts of religious origin.

Attempts are made to link the development of human rights exclusively to the liberal ideas which broke through to predominance in the Age of Enlightenment. However, to do so means to me to overlook the historical background of those ideas. It means also cutting our ties to a source of strength that we need in order to carry the work for human rights to fruition and to give to those rights, when established, their fitting spiritual content.

To some, the word 'tolerance' may sound strange in a time of 'Cold War' and of negotiations 'from positions from strength'; it may have an overtone of meekness or appeasement. And yet, have we reason to believe that what was true in the past is no longer true? It is not the weak but the strong who practice tolerance, and the strong do not weaken their position in showing tolerance. On the contrary, only through tolerance can they justify their strength.

Tom Hanks
American actor and director

Thomas Jeffrey Hanks (1956–) was born in Concord, California. He made his film debut in the thriller *He Knows You're Alone* (1980) and was praised for his performance in the television sitcom *Bosom Buddies* (1980–2) before the unexpected popularity of the film *Splash* (1984) boosted his career. His relaxed manner and mischievous grin made him one of the USA's most popular young performers in comedies like *Bachelor Party* (1984) and *The Money Pit* (1985). Nominated for an Academy Award for his role as a young boy trapped in an adult world in *Big* (1988), he subsequently won best actor Oscars for his performances in *Philadelphia* (1993) and *Forrest Gump* (1994). His many popular successes include *Sleepless in Seattle* (1993), *Apollo 13* (1995), *Cast Away* (2000), *Catch Me If You Can* (2002), *The Da Vinci Code* (2006) and *Angels and Demons* (2009). He made his debut as a feature-film director with *That Thing You Do* (1995). After starring in the World War II film *Saving Private Ryan* (1998), he received the Distinguished Public Service Award, the US Navy's highest civilian honour.

'The streets of Heaven are too crowded with angels'
21 March 1994, Hollywood, California, USA

Released in 1993, *Philadelphia* was the first major Hollywood film to tackle AIDS. It was also the first to feature an openly homosexual central character, a Philadelphia lawyer who loses his job after contracting the disease and successfully sues his employer. The role is said to have been offered to Daniel Day-Lewis, Michael Keaton and Andy Garcia before Hanks accepted it.

The theme was considered daring for mainstream cinema, and Hanks later revealed that scenes exploring his character's relationship with his boyfriend – played by Antonio Banderas – had been cut. (They were later reinstated for a DVD release.) As a result, the film was criticized in some quarters as timid and anodyne. Nonetheless, it was successful at the box office and – the following year – at the Academy Awards.

When he came to accept his Oscar, Hanks observed convention by acknowledging his collaborators on the film. But most memorably, in the spirit of tolerance promoted by the film, he paid tribute to two gay men who had influenced his choice of career: his drama teacher and one of his classmates. His comments inspired the film *In and Out* (1997), about a teacher 'outed' by a former pupil during an Oscar acceptance speech.

Some critics praised *Philadelphia* for not lapsing into sentimentality; however, Hanks was barely able to contain his emotions as he conferred a blessing on people who had died from AIDS. In the rather confused final passage, he invokes both God and, unexpectedly, the city's role in the early days of the nation.

Here's what I know. I could not be standing here without that undying love that was just sung about by – not Bruce – but Neil Young.[1] And I have that in a lover that is so close to fine,[2] we should all be able to experience such heaven right here on earth.

I know also that I should not be doing this, I should not be here, but I am because of the union of such film-makers as Ed Saxon,[3] Ron Nyswaner,[4] Kristi Zea,[5] Tak Fujimoto,[6] Jonathan Demme[7] – who seems to have these [*referring to the Oscar*] attached to his limbs for every actor that works with him of late.

And a cast that includes Antonio Banderas, who, second to my lover, is the only person I would trade for. And a cast that includes many other people, but the actor who really put his film image at risk, and shone because of his integrity, Mr Denzel Washington,[8] who I really must share this with.

I would not be standing here if it weren't for two very important men in my life, so – two that I haven't spoken with in a while, but I had the pleasure of just the other evening. Mr Rawley Farnsworth, who was my high school drama teacher, who taught me to 'act well the part, there all the glory lies'. And one of my classmates under Mr Farnsworth, Mr John Gilkerson.

I mention their names because they are two of the finest gay Americans,

[1] Hanks refers to the song 'Philadelphia' by the Canadian rock star Neil Young (1945–), which was used at the end of the film. The film also featured the Oscar-winning song 'The Streets of Philadelphia' by the US rock star Bruce Springsteen (1949–), a friend of Hanks.

[2] Hanks refers to his wife, actress Rita Wilson (1956–).

[3] Producer of the film.

[4] The film's screenwriter.

[5] Associate producer.

[6] The film's director of photography, who also played a minor role in the film.

[7] The film's director. His earlier film *The Silence of the Lambs* (1991) won a string of Oscars and other awards, both for him and for actors Anthony Hopkins and Jodie Foster.

[8] The US film actor Denzel Washington (1954–) played the homophobic attorney working for the gay central character. He was praised for jeopardizing his 'virtuous' onscreen persona by taking on an unsympathetic role.

two wonderful men that I had the good fortune to be associated with, to fall under their inspiration at such a young age. I wish my babies could have the same sort of teacher, the same sort of friends.

And there lies my dilemma here tonight. I know that my work in this case is magnified by the fact that the streets of Heaven are too crowded with angels. We know their names. They number a thousand for each one of the red ribbons that we wear here tonight. They finally rest in the warm embrace of the gracious Creator of us all. A healing embrace that cools their fevers, that clears their skin and allows their eyes to see the simple, self-evident, common-sense truth that is made manifest by the benevolent Creator of us all, and was written down on paper by wise men, tolerant men, in the city of Philadelphia 200 years ago.[9]

God bless you all. God have mercy on us all. And God bless America.

[9] Hanks refers to the Declaration of Independence (1776) and perhaps the US Constitution (1787), both of which were signed in Philadelphia.

Jeremy Hanley
English politician

Sir Jeremy James Hanley (1945–) was born in London, the son of the actors Jimmy Hanley (1918–70) and Dinah Sheridan (1920–2012). He was educated at Rugby. He became a chartered accountant, contested the Lambeth Central seat in 1978 and entered Parliament in 1983 as Conservative MP for Richmond and Barnes. He served in John Major's government as a Parliamentary Under-Secretary of State for Northern Ireland (1990–2) and Minister of State for the Armed Forces (1993–4). He became a member of the Privy Council in 1994. He served as chairman of the Conservative Party (1994–5) and as Minister of State at the Foreign Office from 1995 until he lost his seat at the general election of 1997.

'The first day at Westminster'
7 November 1990, London, England

❧

Looking back at his entrance into British parliamentary life, Jeremy Hanley showed how thin the line can sometimes be between politics and stand-up comedy. He made this speech in the House of Commons at the beginning of the debate on the Queen's Speech, when he seconded the Loyal Address, the Commons' formal thanks to the Queen for her speech outlining future government legislation, given at the State Opening of Parliament each year.

In his address Hanley – the son of two actors – reflects on the fickleness of a career in politics, and on one of the House of Commons' more charismatic members, the Democratic Unionist Party (DUP) leader Rev IAN PAISLEY, of whom Hanley gives a fairly accurate impersonation. DUP and Ulster Unionist Party members sit on the same side as the Conservatives in the Commons but, as Hanley recalls Paisley telling him, seating arrangements have little relation to political support.

❧

Being elected in 1983, in somewhat surprised form, with a less-than-generous majority of 74 votes, the first day at Westminster was an occasion which – I'm sure all Members of this House will agree – you simply never forget.

With a majority that small, who is to say what quite tipped the balance? But I have to admit that, the day before the election, there was a showing on television of my father's film *The Blue Lamp*,[1] which was the old archetype bobby-on-the-beat-type movie. Now, perhaps it helped; who can tell? But when I went through the St Stephen's entrance on the day to take the oath, for the first time as the Member for Richmond and Barnes, the policeman on the door said, [*Cockney accent*] 'Mr 'Anley, I'm very sorry that your late father isn't around to see you come into this House, sir. I think he'd 'ave been very proud.'

I said, 'Well, thank you, Sergeant. That's very kind.'

He said, 'Mind you, sir, I think the shock might have killed him.'

[*Raucous laughter.*]

Absolutely true. I'm sure honourable and right honourable Members have noted those smiles which play on the face of the constabulary in this Palace of Westminster. Could it be the confidence of a job well done, or more likely the fact that whatever the result of the next election, they'll be back?

It was on that day too that I learned one of the most important lessons about the House of Commons. I sat in the chamber to take the oath and watched from a modest spot near the back of the government side as the famous and the lesser-known filed past. It was just like viewing a walking waxworks – or as one constituent said, 'It's just like Madame Tussaud's except the exhibits look slightly less lifelike.'

[*Laughter.*]

[1] *The Blue Lamp* (1950) starred Jack Warner (1896–1981) as PC George Dixon, as did the long-running television series *Dixon of Dock Green* (1955–76). Jimmy Hanley co-starred as Dixon's fresh-faced young partner PC Andy Mitchell.

And as I was sitting over there on the bench, the fourth row back, I was very conscious that somebody had sat next to me. I turned round to see who it was and I saw him and said, startled, 'How do you do? I didn't realize that you were on our side.'

The Honourable and Reverend neighbour said to me, in his unmistakable terms, [*thick Ulster accent*] 'Never confuse sitting on your side with *being* on your side.'

Hannibal
Carthaginian soldier

Hannibal *known as 'the grace of Baal'* (247–182 BC) was the son of Hamilcar Barca. At the age of nine, he swore eternal enmity to Rome. He served in Spain under Hamilcar and his brother-in-law Hasdrubal, and was elected general after Hasdrubal's death. He won control of southern Spain up to the Ebro (221–219 BC), and the fall of Saguntum in 218 BC sparked off the Second Punic War with Rome. In 218 BC he surprised the Romans by marching from Spain through southern Gaul, and crossing the Alps into Italy with an army including elephants. Thousands of his troops, accustomed to a hot climate, perished amid ice and snow; but he defeated the Taurini, forced Ligurian and Celtic tribes to serve in his army, and at the River Ticinus drove back the Romans under Publius Cornelius Scipio, the Elder (218 BC). The first great battle was fought at the River Trebia, where Roman troops were either cut to pieces or scattered in flight. In the spring, Hannibal crossed the Apennines, devastating Etruria, and marched towards Rome. At Lake Trasimene he annihilated the Roman army. Passing through Apulia and Campania, he wintered at Gerunium, and in the spring at Cannae (216 BC) utterly destroyed another Roman army under Quintus Fabius. After Cannae the tide turned. Rome's allies remained loyal, while Hannibal received inadequate support from Carthage. He was not defeated, but his veterans were lost to him and he had no means of filling their places, while the Romans could put army after army into the field. He spent the winter of 216–215 BC at Capua. The Romans wisely avoided a further pitched battle, and allowed the Carthaginians to overrun Italy, gaining minor victories. However, Capua fell in 210 BC and in 207 BC Hasdrubal, marching from Spain to his aid, was defeated and killed at the River Metaurus. For four years Hannibal remained in the hill-country of Bruttium, until in 203 BC he was recalled to Africa to meet a Roman invasion by Scipio. The following year he met Scipio at Zama. His decisive defeat there ended the war. On the conclusion of peace, Hannibal devoted himself to political reform, but he aroused such strong opposition that he fled to the court of Antiochus III at Ephesus, and then to Bithynia. When the Romans demanded his surrender, he committed suicide by taking poison.

'No middle way between victory and death'
November 218 BC at the River Ticinus (Ticino), northern Italy

In the summer of 218 BC Hannibal marched his army up the east coast of Spain, past Saguntum (a pro-Roman city which he had sacked the previous year), crossing the River Ebro and the Pyrenees into southern France. Moving with remarkable speed, he reached and crossed the Rhône before a Roman army under the consul Publius Scipio (d.183 BC) arrived there; and set off through the Alps in early winter, arriving in Italy by mid-November. In the meantime, Scipio had returned by sea, and now faced the Carthaginian army at the confluence of the Po and Ticino rivers, just west of modern Pavia. Hannibal won the battle by superior cavalry tactics.

The speech given here was not composed by Hannibal but by the Roman historian Livy (59 BC–AD17), writing 200 years later in the reign of the Emperor Augustus. In the tradition of ancient historiography, he gives a speech to each of the two generals before the battle, and both are his creations rather than the words of the speakers. After giving Scipio's speech, he tells how Hannibal put on a display of single combats between some of his own men and Gallic prisoners, previously captured in the Po valley, and uses the energy and courage of these Gauls to provide Hannibal with an exemplar for his troops. The translation is by Aubrey de Sélincourt (1965).

My soldiers: just now, as you were watching other men's fate, you were not unmoved; only think with similar feelings of what is in store for yourselves, and victory is already in our hands. What you have seen was more than a spectacle for your entertainment: it was a sort of image, or allegory, of your own condition.

It may indeed be that fate has laid upon you heavier chains and harsher necessities than upon those prisoners of ours. North and south the sea hems you in; you have not a single ship even to escape in with your lives; facing you is the Po, a greater and more turbulent river than the Rhône. Behind you is the Alpine barrier, which even in the freshness and flower of your strength you almost failed to cross.

Here then, where you have first come face to face with the enemy, you

411

must conquer or die. But have courage! Circumstances compel you to fight; but those same circumstances offer you in the event of victory nobler rewards than a man might pray for, even from the immortal gods. The prize would be great enough were we only to recover, by the strength of our hands, the islands of Sicily and Sardinia which our fathers lost;[1] but all the heaped wealth of Rome, won in her long career of conquest, will be yours; those rich possessions – yes, and the possessors too.

Forward then, and win this splendid prize! And with God's blessing draw your swords! You have chased cattle long enough in the wild mountains of Lusitania and Celtiberia,[2] with nothing to show for the long years of toil and danger. Since then you have travelled far, over mountains, across rivers, through peoples in arms, and it is time that you fought a campaign with money in it and all good things, and earned a rich reward for your efforts.

Here Fortune has granted you an end to your sweat and tears; and here she will pay you worthily for your long service in the field. You need not imagine that victory will be as hard to win as the fame of our antagonists might suggest. Fortune is fickle: often a despised enemy has fought to the death, and a feather in the scale has brought defeat to famous nations and their kings.

Take away the blinding brilliance of the name, and in what can the Romans be compared with you? To say nothing of your 20 years of brave and successful service in the field, you have come to this place from the Pillars of Hercules, from the Atlantic Ocean and the farthest limits of the world, thrusting your victorious way through all the wild and warlike nations of Spain and Gaul; and now you will be facing an army of raw recruits, beaten this very summer to its knees and penned in by the Gauls[3] – an army and a commander still strangers to one another.

And what a commander! Am I to compare myself with him – that six months' general who abandoned his own troops[4] – when I, born and bred on active service, in my illustrious father's tent,[5] subdued Spain and Gaul and vanquished not only the wild Alpine tribes but – a much harder task – the Alps themselves? Show Scipio now the soldiers of Rome and of Carthage without their standards, and I would wager he couldn't tell which were his own.

Now as for me, my men, there is not one of you who has not with his own eyes seen me strike a blow in battle; I have watched and witnessed your valour in the field, and your acts of courage I know by heart, with every detail of when and where they took place: and this, surely, is not a thing of small importance. I was your pupil before I was your commander; I shall advance into the line with soldiers I have a thousand times praised and rewarded; and the enemy we shall meet are raw troops with a raw general, neither knowing anything of the other.

Wherever I look, I see high hearts and strong arms: I see my veteran infantry, my cavalry, native and Numidian, all drawn from nations of noble blood; I see my brave and loyal allies; and, lastly, you, my fellow countrymen of Carthage, whom just resentment as well as patriotism has inspired to fight.

We are the aggressors, we the invaders of Italy – and for that reason shall fight with a courage and audacity corresponding to our hopes – with the well-known confidence of him who strikes the first blow. Anger, the sense of unmerited injury, will spur you on and give you added fire. Remember how they demanded the surrender of my person – of me, your commander – as a criminal, and later of every man amongst you who might

[1] At the end of the First Punic War in 241 BC Sicily was seized from the Carthaginians; and in 238 BC the Romans (disreputably) expelled them from Sardinia.

[2] In western and central Spain, where Hannibal had been in command for the past three years.

[3] A Roman force, under the praetor Lucius Manlius, had been ambushed by the Gauls near Mutina earlier in the year.

[4] When Scipio had left southern France to return to Italy, he had handed over the command of his army to his brother Gnaeus (d. 211 BC), in secure Roman control in Spain. His command (as was normal with Roman magistrates) had begun with his term of office as consul in March 218 BC.

[5] Hannibal's father, Hamilcar Barca (c.270–228 BC) had been the most successful Carthaginian general in the First Punic War, and had commanded in Spain thereafter.

have fought at Saguntum. Had you been given up they would certainly have put you to death with the cruellest tortures.[6]

The Romans are a proud and merciless people; they claim to make the world their own and subject to their will. They demand the right to dictate to us who our friends should be and who our enemies. They circumscribe our liberties, barring us in behind barriers of rivers or mountains beyond which we may not pass – but they do not themselves observe the limits they have set. 'Do not cross the Ebro,' they say; 'Keep your hands off Saguntum.'[7]

'But is Saguntum on the Ebro?' you say.

'Then don't go anywhere – stay where you are!'

'Is it not enough,' you say, 'that you steal our ancient possessions Sicily and Sardinia? Must you have Spain too? If I abandon Spain, you will cross into Africa.' *Will*, indeed! Why, of the two consuls elected this year they have already sent one to Africa, the other to Spain.[8]

We have nothing left in the world but what we can win with our swords. Timidity and cowardice are for men who can see safety at their backs – who can retreat without molestation along some easy road and find refuge in the familiar fields of their native land; but they are not for you. You must be brave; for you there is no middle way between victory and death. Put all hope of it from you and either conquer, or – should fortune hesitate to favour you – meet death in battle rather than in flight.

Think on these things; carry them printed on your minds and hearts. Then – I repeat – success is already yours. God has given to man no sharper spur to victory than contempt of death.

[6] Such torture is represented in Roman sources as a normal Carthaginian practice, here attributed by a Carthaginian to the Romans.

[7] In 226 BC Hasdrubal, Hannibal's predecessor and brother-in-law, had agreed to the Roman demand not to cross the River Ebro under arms. The Romans had subsequently made an alliance with Saguntum, about 100 miles south of the Ebro.

[8] In March 218 BC, in expectation of trouble with Hannibal, the Senate had sent Publius Scipio to Spain and his colleague, Tiberius Sempronius Longus, to Sicily and Africa. In the event, neither reached his designated command.

Keir Hardie
Scottish politician

James Keir Hardie (1856–1915) was born near Holytown, Lanarkshire. He worked from the age of seven and was employed in a coalmine from the age of ten. Victimized as champion of the miners (whom he organized) he moved to Cumnock and became a journalist. The first of all Labour candidates in the UK, he stood as candidate for the Scottish Labour Party in Mid-Lanark (1888), but sat for West Ham, South (1892–5), and Merthyr Tydfil (1900–15). He worked strenuously for Socialism and the unemployed both within and outside Parliament. In 1893 he founded the Independent Labour Party, then edited the *Labour Leader*, which became the party's official voice in 1903. He was chairman of the party until 1900 and again in 1913–14 (the party having been renamed the Labour Party). He strenuously opposed Liberal influence on the trade unions and strongly advocated the formation of a separate political party, as distinct from the existing Labour Representation League. A strong pacifist, he opposed the Boer War of 1899–1902, and lost his seat in 1915 after opposing Britain's involvement in World War I.

'Socialism proposes to dethrone the brute-god Mammon'
23 April 1901, London, England

This speech, made in the House of Commons around midnight, was the first full socialist address heard in that chamber. Hardie's attack on capitalism revealed a more instinctive, working-class socialism than that espoused by more intellectual contemporaries such as GEORGE BERNARD SHAW. 'The true test of progress,' he declared, 'is not the accumulation of wealth in the hands of a few, but the elevation of a people as a whole.'

One of the most powerful moments in the speech occurs in the middle of Hardie's argument that, despite the advancements brought by mechanization, most people were happier before the advent of machines and factories. In response to a Conservative MP's single interjection of 'No', Hardie boldly asserts, '"No" is not an argument.'

I make no apology for bringing the question of socialism before the House of Commons. It has long commanded the attention of the best minds in the country. It is a growing force in the thought of the world, and whether men agree or disagree with it, they have to reckon with it, and may as well begin by understanding it. In the German Empire, socialism is the one section of political thought which is making headway, and to an extent which is, I believe, alarming the powers that be.

Over 50 Socialist members occupy seats in the German Reichstag, between 40 and 50 in the Chamber of Deputies in France, and between 30 and 40 in the Belgian parliament. Socialism on the Continent therefore is an established and recognized fact, so far as its entry into politics is concerned, and if it be argued that while that may be true of the Continent it is not true of this country, I reply that the facts and conditions now existing in this country are such as to make it extremely probable that the progress of socialism in this country will be at a more rapid pace than in any other country in Europe.

Needless to say, at this hour of the evening it is impossible for me to treat this subject adequately. I will therefore summarize briefly the principal arguments that it was my intention to submit to the House, had time permitted. I begin by pointing out that the growth of our national wealth, instead of bringing comfort to the masses of the people, is imposing additional burdens on them.

We are told on high authority that some 300 years ago the total wealth of the English nation was 100 millions sterling. At the beginning of the last century it had increased to 2,000 millions, and this year it is estimated to be 13,000 millions. While our population during the last century increased three and a half times, the wealth of the community increased over six times. But one factor in our national life remained with us all through the century, and is with us still, and that is that at the bottom of the social scale there is a mass of poverty and misery, equal in magnitude to that which obtained 100 years ago.

I submit that the true test of progress is not the accumulation of wealth in the hands of a few, but the elevation of a people as a whole. I admit frankly that a considerable improvement was made in the condition of the working people during the last century. At the beginning of the 19th century, the nation industrially was sick almost unto death. It was at that time passing from the old system of handicraft – under which every man was his own employer and his own capitalist, and traded direct with his customer – to the factory system which the introduction of machinery brought into existence.

During these 100 years, the wealth of the nation accumulated, and the condition of the working classes as compared with the early years of the century improved, but I respectfully submit to the House that there was more happiness, more comfort and more independence before machinery began to accumulate wealth.

[*An honourable Member: 'No.'*]

'No' is not an argument. I ask honourable gentlemen opposite to listen, and refute my statements if they are incorrect … The high standard of comfort reached by the labouring classes at the end of the last century has not brought them that happiness which obtained in England 300 years ago, when there was no machinery, no large capitalists, no private property in land, as we know it today, and when every person had the right to use the land for the purpose of producing food for himself and his family.

I said that an improvement was made during the last century, but I would qualify that statement in this respect – that practically the whole of that improvement was made during the first 75 years. During the last quarter of the century, the condition of the working classes has been practically stationary. There have been slight increases of wages here and reductions of hours there, but the landlord with his increased rent has more than absorbed any advantage that may have been gained.

I could quote figures, if that statement is disputed, showing that in all the industrial parts of the country rents during the past 20 years have been going up by leaps and bounds. I will refer to one authority whom even honourable gentlemen opposite will not dare to call into question, Viscount Goschen,[1] when First Lord of the Admiralty, in defending the government for refusing to give increased wages to labourers at Woolwich Arsenal, said on 14 April 1899:

[1] The English politician George Goschen, 1st Viscount Goschen (1831–1907), held ministerial posts in both Liberal and Conservative governments in the late 19th century. He served as First Lord of the Admiralty, 1871–4 and 1895–1900.

'If the position of the labourers at Woolwich and Deptford was as described, it was rather due to sweating landlords than to the rate of wages. The wages had been raised 29 per cent in the last ten years, and the house rents 50 per cent. It was constantly the case in those districts that the increase of wages only led to a larger sum going into the pockets of the landlords, and he was even told that some of the men who were locally the loudest in the cry for justice to the labourers were owners of cottage property, who would benefit if the wages were raised.'

In view of a statement of that kind, made by such an authority, I submit that my assertion is not without substance.

I come now to the causes which have forced thinking people of all ranks of society to reconsider their attitude towards socialism. I refer particularly to the great and alarming growth of what are known as trusts and syndicates in connection with industry ... So long as industry is conducted by individuals competing one with another, there is a chance of the article produced being supplied at an approximation to its market value, but competition has been found to be destructive of the interests of the owners and possessors of capital in this as in every other country.

Three or four firms which formerly entered one market and competed with each other find it conducive to their interests to combine, thereby creating a monopoly which enables them to charge whatever price they like, and to treat their workpeople in any way that seems good to them.

I approach this question of trusts from two points of view: first, from that of the consumer, who is at the mercy of an uncontrolled and, it may be, perfectly unscrupulous combination which cares only for dividends; and, secondly – and this is to me of greater concern – from that of the worker. The consumer may protect himself, but the worker is helpless ...

We are rapidly approaching a point when the nation will be called upon to decide between an uncontrolled monopoly, conducted for the benefit and in the interests of its principal shareholders, and a monopoly owned, controlled, and manipulated by the state in the interests of the nation as a whole. I do not require to go far afield for arguments to support that part of my statement concerning the danger which the aggregation of wealth in a few hands is bringing upon us.

This House and the British nation know to their cost the danger which comes from allowing men to grow rich and permitting them to use their wealth to corrupt the press, to silence the pulpit, to degrade our national life, and to bring reproach and shame upon a great people, in order that a few unscrupulous scoundrels might be able to add to their ill-gotten gains.

The war in South Africa[2] is a millionaires' war. Our troubles in China[3] are due to the desire of the capitalists to exploit the people of that country as they would fain exploit the people of South Africa. Much of the jealousy and bad blood existing between this country and France is traceable to the fact that we went to war in Egypt[4] to suppress a popular uprising, seeking freedom for the people in order that the interest of our bondholders might be secured.

Socialism, by placing land and the instruments of production in the hands of the community, eliminates only the idle, useless class at both ends of the scale. Half a million of the people of this country benefit by the present system; the remaining millions of toilers and businessmen do not. The pursuit of wealth corrupts the manhood of men. We are called upon, at the beginning of the 20th century, to decide the question propounded in the Sermon on the Mount as to whether or not we will worship God or Mammon.

The present day is a Mammon-worshipping age. Socialism proposes to dethrone the brute-god Mammon and to lift humanity into its place. I beg to submit in this very imperfect fashion the resolution on the paper, merely premising that the last has not been heard of the socialist movement, either in the country or on the floor of this House, but that, just as sure as radicalism democratized the system of government politically in the last century so will socialism democratize the country industrially during the century upon which we have just entered.

[2] The South African War, or Boer War (1899–1902), waged by Britain against the South African Republic and the Orange Free State.
[3] Hardie refers to the Boxer Rebellion (1899–1901), a rejection of western influence.

[4] In 1882, Britain attacked Egypt and seized control of its government, to protect its commercial interests in the Middle East.

Václav Havel
Czech writer and statesman

Václav Havel (1936–2011) was born in Prague, where he was educated at the Academy of Dramatic Art. He began work as a stagehand at the Prague *Theater Na zábradlí* ('Theatre on the Balustrade'), becoming resident writer there (1960–9). His work includes *Zahradní slavnost* (1963, Eng trans *The Garden Party*, 1969), *Spiklenci* (1970, 'The Conspirators') and *Audience* (1976, Eng trans *Temptation*, 1976). In 1977, he was one of the founders of Charter 77, a movement which criticized violations of human and civil rights by the communist regime in Czechoslovakia. Deemed subversive, he was repeatedly arrested, and in 1979 was imprisoned for four and a half years. He was again imprisoned in February 1989, but was released three months later. In December 1989, after the overthrow of the Czechoslovak Communist Party during the so-called Velvet Revolution, he was elected president by direct popular vote. He oversaw the peaceful division of Czechoslovakia into separate Czech and Slovak states in 1992, and was elected president of the Czech Republic in 1993. He was re-elected in 1998, and left office in 2003. His later publications in English translation include *Selected Plays* (1991) and *Towards a Civil Society* (1994).

'We live in a contaminated moral environment'
1 January 1990, television and radio broadcast from Prague, Czechoslovakia

🦢

In November 1989, when the Communist Party relinquished its 41-year monopoly of power in Czechoslovakia, the dissident playwright Václav Havel remarked, 'History has begun to develop very quickly in this country.' He was proved right a month later when, as leader of the Civic Forum party, he became the country's democratically elected president. Two days later, he addressed his compatriots in a broadcast that signalled a dramatic change, not just in governance, but in the national mood.

Havel refers briefly to the environmental contamination caused in Czechoslovakia – as elsewhere in the Eastern bloc – by thoughtless industrial practices. But his central concern is the moral contamination brought about by communism: corruption, privilege and the deliberate propagation of lies.

In this he echoes the medieval Bohemian martyr Jan Hus (c.1369–1415), whose statue stands in Prague's Old Town Square. An influential church reformer, Hus is best known for his prayer: 'Seek the Truth/Listen to the Truth/Teach the Truth/Love the Truth/Abide by the Truth/And Defend the Truth /Unto Death.' Havel urges his listeners not to entertain denial, but to embrace Czechoslovakia's contamination as 'a sin we committed against ourselves'.

These concerns befit a writer concerned with ideological distortions of truth and reality. But although Havel's plays are abstract and cerebral, his inaugural address is a direct and straight-talking appeal to ordinary people tasting freedom for the first time in a generation.

🦢

My dear fellow citizens: for 40 years, you heard from my predecessors on this day different variations of the same theme: how our country flourished, how many million tons of steel we produced, how happy we all were, how we trusted our government, and what bright perspectives were unfolding in front of us.

I assume you did not propose me for this office so that I, too, would lie to you.

Our country is not flourishing. The enormous creative and spiritual potential of our nations[1] is not being used sensibly. Entire branches of industry are producing goods which are of no interest to anyone, while we are lacking the things we need. A state which calls itself a workers' state humiliates and exploits workers. Our obsolete economy is wasting the little energy we have available. A country that once could be proud of the educational level of its citizens spends so little on education that it ranks today as 72nd in the world. We have polluted our soil, our rivers and forests, bequeathed to us by our ancestors, and we have today the most contaminated environment in Europe. Adult people in our country die

[1] Havel's use of the plural here acknowledges the existence of the discrete Czech and Slovak nations, which would soon be peacefully separated.

earlier than in most other European countries.

Allow me a little personal observation: when I flew recently to Bratislava, I found time during various discussions to look out of the plane window. I saw the industrial complex of Slovnaft chemical factory and the giant Petržalka housing estate right behind it. The view was enough for me to understand that for decades our statesmen and political leaders did not look or did not want to look out of the windows of their planes. No study of statistics available to me would enable me to understand faster and better the situation in which we find ourselves.

But all this is still not the main problem. The worst thing is that we live in a contaminated moral environment. We fell morally ill because we became used to saying something different from what we thought. We learned not to believe in anything, to ignore each other, to care only about ourselves. Concepts such as love, friendship, compassion, humility, or forgiveness lost their depth and dimensions; and for many of us they represented only psychological peculiarities, or they resembled gone-astray greetings from ancient times, a little ridiculous in the era of computers and spaceships. Only a few of us were able to cry out loud that the powers that be should not be all-powerful, and that special farms, which produce ecologically pure and top-quality food just for them, should send their produce to schools, children's homes and hospitals if our agriculture was unable to offer them to all.

The previous regime – armed with its arrogant and intolerant ideology – reduced man to a force of production and nature to a tool of production. In this it attacked both their very substance and their mutual relationship. It reduced gifted and autonomous people, skilfully working in their own country, to nuts and bolts of some monstrously huge, noisy and stinking machine, whose real meaning is not clear to anyone. It cannot do more than slowly but inexorably wear down itself and all its nuts and bolts.

When I talk about contaminated moral atmosphere, I am not talking just about the gentlemen who eat organic vegetables and do not look out of the plane windows. I am talking about all of us. We had all become used to the totalitarian system and accepted it as an unchangeable fact and thus helped to perpetuate it. In other words, we are all – though naturally to differing extents – responsible for the operation of the totalitarian machinery; none of us is just its victim: we are all also its co-creators.

Why do I say this? It would be very unreasonable to understand the sad legacy of the last 40 years as something alien, which some distant relative bequeathed us. On the contrary, we have to accept this legacy as a sin we committed against ourselves. If we accept it as such, we will understand that it is up to us all, and up to us only, to do something about it. We cannot blame the previous rulers for everything, not only because it would be untrue but also because it could blunt the duty that each of us faces today – namely, the obligation to act independently, freely, reasonably and quickly.

Let us not be mistaken: the best government in the world, the best parliament and the best president, cannot achieve much on their own. And it would also be wrong to expect a general remedy from them only. Freedom and democracy include participation and therefore responsibility from us all.

If we realize this, then all the horrors that the new Czechoslovak democracy inherited will cease to appear so terrible. If we realize this, hope will return to our hearts …

We are a small country, yet at one time we were the spiritual crossroads of Europe. Is there any reason why we could not again become one? Would it not be another asset with which to repay the help of others that we are going to need?

Our home-grown Mafia – of those who do not look out of plane windows and who eat specially fed pigs – may still be around and at times may muddy the waters, but they are no longer our main enemy. Even less so is our main enemy the international Mafia. Our main enemies today are our own bad traits: indifference to the common good, vanity, personal ambition, selfishness and rivalry. The main struggle will have to be fought on this field.

There are free elections and an election campaign ahead of us. Let us not allow this struggle to dirty the so-far clean face of our gentle revolution. Let us not allow the sympathies of the world, which we have won so fast, to be equally rapidly lost through our becoming entangled in the jungle of skirmishes for power. Let us not allow the desire to serve oneself to bloom once again under the fair mask of the desire to serve the common good.

It is not really important now which party, club or group will prevail in the elections. The important thing is that the winners will be the best of us, in the moral, civic, political and professional sense, regardless of their political affiliations. The future policies and prestige of our state will depend on the personalities we select and later elect to our representative bodies …

In conclusion, I would like to say that I want to be a president who will speak less and work more. To be a president who will not only look out of the windows of his plane but who, first and foremost, will always be present among his fellow citizens and listen to them well.

You may ask what kind of a republic I dream of. Let me reply: I dream of a republic independent, free and democratic; of a republic economically prosperous and yet socially just; in short, of a humane republic which serves the individual and which therefore holds the hope that the individual will serve it in turn. Of a republic of well-rounded people – because without such it is impossible to solve any of our problems – human, economic, ecological, social or political.

The most distinguished of my predecessors[2] opened his first speech with a quotation from the great Czech educator Komenský.[3] Allow me to round off my first speech with my own paraphrase of the same statement:

People, your government has returned to you!

[2] The Moravian-born statesman Tomáš Masaryk (1850–1937) was the first president of Czechoslovakia, 1918–35.

[3] The Moravian educationalist John Komenský, or Comenius (1592–1670).

Denis Healey
English politician

Denis Winston Healey *later Baron Healey* (1917–) was born in Keighley, Yorkshire, and educated at Oxford. During World War II, he served with the Royal Engineers in North Africa and Italy (1940–5), attaining the rank of major. For seven years after the war he was secretary of the Labour Party's international department before becoming MP for Leeds in 1952. He was a member of the Shadow Cabinet for five years before becoming Secretary of State for Defence in the HAROLD WILSON government of 1964–70, a post which he held for six years. His five years as Chancellor of the Exchequer (1974–9) were a rather stormy period marked by a sterling crisis and subsequent intervention by the International Monetary Fund. Healey unsuccessfully contested the Labour Party leadership in 1976 and again in 1980 when he was somewhat unexpectedly defeated by MICHAEL FOOT. He was, however, elected deputy leader ahead of his left-wing opponent TONY BENN. He resigned from the Shadow Cabinet in 1987 and was made a life peer in 1992. His publications include the autobiography *The Time of My Life* (1989), and *My Secret Planet* (1992).

'The great she-elephant, she who must be obeyed'
27 February 1984, London, England

This was one of Denis Healey's most withering attacks on the government led by MARGARET THATCHER. It was delivered during a debate on proposals to ban union membership at the intelligence-gathering Government Communications Headquarters (GCHQ) at Cheltenham. The government, keen to reduce union power wherever possible, argued that the possibility of strike action by GCHQ workers threatened national security. On 25 January, therefore, it announced new terms for GCHQ staff: they were to be paid £1,000 as recompense for the loss of their rights; those unable to accept this would be offered transfers to other departments or would have to leave the Civil Service entirely.

Healey, then shadow Foreign Secretary, argued that the real reason for the government's action was its introduction of lie-detector tests at GCHQ, and its fear that if staff had access to industrial tribunals they would dispute any dismissals based on the tests, which were notoriously unreliable. The debate was of the utmost gravity, but Healey used his wit to devastating effect. His description of Thatcher as 'the great she-elephant' was one in a string of nicknames he concocted for her. Others included 'the dragon empress', 'Rhoda the rhino' and 'Pétain in petticoats' – a reference to Marshal Philippe Pétain (1856–1951), who led the collaborationist Vichy regime in Nazi-occupied France and was later convicted of treason.

Let me begin by agreeing on one thing with the Foreign Secretary.[1] No-one with any knowledge of the matter can underestimate the importance of this issue. GCHQ has been by far the most valuable source of intelligence for the British government ever since it began operating at Bletchley during the last war. British skills in interception and code-breaking are unique and highly valued by all of our allies. GCHQ has been a key element in our relationship with the United States for more than 40 years. I am glad that, in his final words, the Foreign Secretary recognized the skill, loyalty and dedication of the men and women who work there …

It is just over four weeks since the Foreign Secretary told the House that he had decided to rob those loyal and dedicated men and women of their right to trade union membership – a right that they have enjoyed throughout their employment there and which has been enjoyed by all employees ever since GCHQ was first set up. It is a right that is enjoyed by tens of thousands of other men and women who do work of equal secrecy and of equal national importance in other government departments and in private industry. It is a right that is enjoyed by more tens of thousands of men and women in the Post Office, the Health Service and in many other parts of the government service on whose continuity of work lives might well depend.

[1] GEOFFREY HOWE served as Foreign Secretary 1983–9.

The decision that the Foreign Secretary announced to the House just over one month ago was taken without consulting the representatives of the workers concerned and without consulting even his colleagues in the Cabinet. Since then, I must tell the Foreign Secretary, his daily contradictory statements have made him the laughing stock of the world … The Foreign Secretary has been attacked anonymously by fellow Ministers as basing his decision on emotional and not on intellectual judgement. He has been attacked publicly by Conservative backbenchers … The Conservative newspapers have been even more outspoken. The *Daily Telegraph* described the behaviour of the Foreign Secretary and the government as 'little short of shambolic'. The *Daily Express* described their decision as 'highly illiberal and authoritarian'. Moreover, they were condemned unanimously by the Select Committee of the House which has a majority of Conservative members.

More important still, the government's decision has already done immense damage to the morale, not only at GCHQ but of the Civil Service as a whole … The whole machinery of government is now seething with discontent, partly because the government's decision is seen as a precedent for attacks on union membership in other secret work – public and private – and in other areas where continuity of operation is regarded by the government as important.

The Foreign Secretary told the House that he had no intention of using this precedent elsewhere. I remember him and the prime minister telling us at election after election that they had 'no intention' of cutting Health Service provision. The fact is, however, that that phrase is used by members of the government to disguise a decision to do something by not actually denying that they will do it. For the government, the way to Hell is paved with 'no intentions'.

The government must recognize that their decision about GCHQ is a kick in the teeth for all those trade union leaders who have been prepared to develop a constructive relationship with the government. Above all, it is a kick in the teeth for Mr Lionel Murray[2] …

[2] The English trade-union leader Lionel Murray *known as Len Murray* (1922–2004) was General Secretary of the Trades Union Congress, 1973–84.

In the past month everyone has been asking why on earth the Foreign Secretary took the decision. It was not because he believed that trade unions were likely to be spies, because he knows, as we do, that most spies since the war have been public schoolboys, Masons, scientists or servicemen. I have no doubt that the government have in hand measures for dealing with that particular threat to our security. The Foreign Secretary told the House this afternoon that he took the decision because the disruption at GCHQ on certain occasions between 1979 and 1981 broke the continuity of work there and might have endangered lives. He concluded – he told us again this afternoon – that membership of the trade union produces an unacceptable conflict of loyalties.

Some honourable members may have been impressed by some of the quotations that the Foreign Secretary read out in his speech, from trade union leaders during those periods of industrial action. However, the trade unions have shown that there was no prejudice to the essential operations of GCHQ at the time, and the Foreign Secretary told the Select Committee that there was no evidence that any damage was done …

The Foreign Secretary cannot have it both ways. If the action of the unions in 1979 was as dangerous as he told us it was this afternoon, it was a gross dereliction of duty for him not to have taken then the action that he is now proposing … The proposal for a ban on union membership, which was discussed by Ministers in 1982, was brushed aside so contemptuously by Lord Carrington[3] that he could not even remember that it had been put to him when he was questioned by his friends …

Two years after Ministers rejected a ban on union membership at GCHQ, the Foreign Secretary and the prime minister took a decision to ban the unions right out of the blue. Their only excuse was that the government had not avowed the existence of GCHQ as an intelligence centre until they published the report of the Security Commission on the Prime affair.[4] I have been in the House for more than 30 years and that is the daftest excuse I have ever heard a government give for an act of policy …

The existence and function of GCHQ have been known to any interested person anywhere in the world since the end of the Second World War … For the prime minister and the Foreign Secretary to tell us in 1984 that no-one had known – the government had never admitted – until eight months ago that GCHQ was an intelligence headquarters is arrant nonsense, and they know it.

It is difficult to find any convincing reason for this sudden decision by the government – eight months after the publication of the Security Commission report on Prime – except for their fear of staff reaction to the introduction of the polygraph, or lie detector, which is due to begin on an experimental basis in a few weeks' time. The lie detector has been described by a scientist who studied it as wrong on two-thirds of the occasions on which it was used, and it was condemned by the Royal Commission on Criminal Procedure as unsuitable for use in court proceedings in Britain for that reason.

There is no doubt but that the government were terrified of how staff might react if the use of the lie detector was made a ground for dismissal … The government undoubtedly feared that staff at GCHQ might have recourse to industrial tribunals to protect themselves. However, it is interesting to note that the staff have never been interested in using industrial tribunals. In all but three cases during the past 40 years, when there has been a dispute they have taken it to the Civil Service appeals tribunal, and they are prepared to do so now …

We all agree that there is a powerful case for guaranteeing continuity of operation at GCHQ, but the unions have now offered that in terms of a contract which is legally binding on individual employees … If the government had a spark of common sense, they would have jumped at the offer made by the trade unions, and the next Labour government will do so when the opportunity arrives. But the prime minister has behaved in this affair, uncharacteristically, like General Galtieri,[5] who rejected her offer on the Falklands – a very favourable offer – preferred to fight, and lost.

She is now gambling with people's lives. Sir Brian Tovey[6] told us that if only ten per cent of the members of GCHQ in key areas refused to stay there, the operation would collapse. I put it to the Foreign Secretary that it is certain that many more than that will refuse …

The Foreign Secretary and the prime minister talk of conflicts of loyalty. They have forced on the staff in GCHQ the most damaging conflict of loyalty known to man – loyalty to principle as against loyalty to family. The staff know that in many cases, if they give up work at GCHQ, it will be impossible for them to find work anywhere else without breaking their family life …

The government's action is risking the disruption of the work of GCHQ at one of the most dangerous periods in the post-war world, when the

[3] The English politician Peter Carington, 6th Baron Carrington (1919–) served as Foreign Secretary, 1979–82.

[4] In May 1983 the government made a statement concerning Geoffrey Prime, who had been convicted of espionage at GCHQ (his identity only emerging because of police investigations into paedophilia charges against him). It was the first time the government had officially acknowledged GCHQ's existence.

[5] The soldier and dictator General Leopoldo Galtieri (1926–2003) was head of the military junta in Argentina, 1981–3. In 1982, he ordered the Argentine invasion of the Falkland Islands, precipitating a conflict in which the UK defeated Argentina. See MARGARET THATCHER'S speech of 26 May 1982, included in this book.

[6] The English civil servant Sir Brian Tovey (1926–) was the director of GCHQ, 1978–83.

[7] Between 1975 and the early 1990s, Lebanon was embroiled in a civil war which also involved Israel, Syria and the Palestinian Liberation Organization.
[8] Now usually called the Iran–Iraq War, 1980–8.

Lebanon is in chaos,[7] when the Gulf War[8] is threatening oil supplies to the western world, when the United States is warning of military intervention very close to the Soviet frontier,[9] and when there is a new leadership in the Kremlin.[10] What a wonderful moment for the government to choose to put this vital operation in jeopardy …

I have not wasted time on the Foreign Secretary this afternoon, although I am bound to say that I feel that some of his colleagues must be a bit tired by now of his hobbling around from one of the doorsteps to another, with a bleeding hole in his foot and a smoking gun in his hand, telling them that he did not know it was loaded.

The Foreign Secretary, however, is not the real villain in this case; he is the fall guy. Those of us with long memories will feel that he is rather like poor van der Lubbe in the Reichstag fire trial.[11] We are asking ourselves the question that was asked at the trial: who is the Mephistopheles behind this shabby Faust?[12] The answer to that is clear. The handling of this decision by – I quote her own backbenchers – the great she-elephant, she who must be obeyed, the Catherine the Great of Finchley,[13] the prime minister herself, has drawn sympathetic trade unionists, such as Len Murray, into open revolt. Her pigheaded bigotry has prevented her closest colleagues … from offering and accepting a compromise.

The right honourable lady, for whom I have a great personal affection, has formidable qualities, a powerful intelligence and immense courage, but those qualities can turn into horrendous vices, unless they are moderated by colleagues who have more experience, understanding and sensitivity. As she has got rid of all those colleagues, no-one is left in the Cabinet with both the courage and the ability to argue with her.

I put it to all Conservative members, but mainly to the government front bench, that to allow the right honourable lady to commit Britain to another four years of capricious autocracy would be to do fearful damage not just to the Conservative party but to the state. She has faced them with the most damaging of all conflicts of loyalty. They must choose between the interests of their country, our nation's security and our cohesion as a people and the obstinacy of an individual. I hope that they resolve this conflict in the interests of the nation. If not, they will carry a heavy responsibility for the tragedies that are bound to follow.

[9] In the early 1980s, Afghanistan became central to the Cold War after Soviet troops intervened to support a pro-Communist government. In response, the USA supplied financial assistance and armaments to resistance groups.
[10] The Russian politician Konstantin Chernenko (1911–85) became Soviet premier in February 1984. He died the following year and was succeeded by Mikhail Gorbachev (1931–).

[11] The burning of the Reichstag (parliament) building in Berlin on 27 February 1933 was believed by many to be the work of ADOLF HITLER's Nazi supporters. Hitler blamed the fire on Communists – in particular, the young Dutch activist Marinus van der Lubbe (1909–34), who was guillotined for his alleged crime.
[12] According to legend, Faust was a 16th-century scholar seduced into a demonic pact by the Devil's agent, Mephistopheles.
[13] The North London district of Finchley was Margaret Thatcher's constituency, 1959–92.

'Start by asking the right question'

15 May 1990, Cambridge, England

Regarded by many as 'the best prime minister we never had', Denis Healey drew on his long experience of international politics to give this lecture at Churchill College, Cambridge. In it he brilliantly surveyed the world following the end of the Cold War, anticipating the imminent collapse of Soviet power.

'History can be a dangerous guide,' he argues, 'but it is practically the only useful guide we have.' With this in mind, he describes how the fall of previous empires led to a rise of nationalism, and predicts with unerring accuracy the nationalistic fervour that would tear apart the Balkans as the 1990s progressed.

Just as prescient was his suggestion that allowing eastern European states to join the European Union would bring economic and security benefits beyond individual countries' borders.

The 40 years since the defeat of Hitler were dominated by a Cold War between the Soviet Union and the West; this was reflected in an arms race on which the two sides are still, in 1990, spending about $400 billion a year, deploying about 4.5 million men on active service, and have deployed about 30,000 nuclear weapons – all this in the European area alone. On top of that the two superpowers, the United States and the Soviet Union, still deploy about 25,000 strategic nuclear weapons world-wide, whose purpose is solely to threaten one another's home territory.

Now all is changed, changed utterly, and one can say with Yeats that 'a terrible beauty is born'.[1] Five years ago Mikhail Gorbachev[2] took office in the Kremlin and embarked on a course which has ended the Cold War and ended the division of Europe. As a result of his decisions, communism is now dead and gone as a factor in European affairs and … there is no chance whatever of it returning to life.

I was lucky enough to be in Berlin that weekend last November when the Wall first crumbled … It was an extraordinary moment in history: the whole population of that great city was glowing with pleasure, laughing and crying with joy.

In the six months since that weekend, things have been moving so fast that it is very difficult to keep up with them. The future is now impossible to predict; in fact you can say that if you are not confused you do not know what is going on. It is like pressing the fast rewind button on a video recorder and wondering whether it will stop in 1945,[3] 1917,[4] 1848,[5] 1789[6] or when. Certainly I think anybody with a sense of history – and this was one of WINSTON CHURCHILL's greatest gifts as a politician – must reflect on two of the lessons of the past.

The first lesson is that a revolution which destroys the institutions of the existing regime tends to produce anarchy, and anarchy in turn can produce dictatorship. This happened after 1917 with LENIN and STALIN; it happened after 1789 with NAPOLEON. On the other hand, a revolution which does not destroy the existing institutions is liable to fail; this happened in 1848, and may be happening in Romania and other parts of eastern Europe at the present time.

The other lesson of history concerns what happens when a great empire disintegrates. It looks as if the end of the Soviet Empire, like the end of the Ottoman Empire and the end of the Austro-Hungarian Empire, is releasing a suppressed nationalism of frightening force all over the region it dominated, from Kosovo in Yugoslavia, right to Mongolia in the Far East and even beyond, in some of the Muslim republics of China.

History can be a dangerous guide, but it is practically the only useful guide we have. It is a far better guide than ideology, on which people otherwise tend to rely in interpreting the present and guessing about the future. But if you use history as a guide you must examine the differences from the past as well as the similarities. The most important differences which affect what is going on in Europe and the world at the present time have been created by the development of science over the last half century. All these developments strengthen the case against nationalism or even regionalism as the basis for policy. Let us look at just four of these changes.

First, nuclear physics has produced atomic weapons, which have made large-scale war not a rational option, at least in the European area … There is no doubt that the existence of nuclear weapons and the impossibility of destroying the knowledge of how to make them is one of the major factors which led Gorbachev to abandon the doctrine of the Two Camps, on which Soviet policy had been based since the time of Lenin.

The second big scientific development is in information technology … [It has] produced an interdependent global financial system and has assisted the cross-border networking of industry, for example, through alliances,

[1] Healey quotes from WB YEATS' poem 'Easter 1916'.

[2] Mikhail Gorbachev (1931–) was leader of the USSR, 1985–91. Under his regime, the Cold War was brought to an end, as was the supremacy of the Communist Party in the USSR, which was ultimately dissolved. He received the Nobel Peace Prize in 1990.

[3] The year World War II ended, the United Nations was established and Europe was divided by what became known as the 'Iron Curtain'.
[4] The year of the Russian Revolutions.
[5] A year of revolutions in Europe, including in France, Germany, Austria, Hungary and Bohemia.
[6] The year that the French Revolution began.

mergers and acquisitions. This internationalization of finance and industry … is controlled neither by governments nor by central banks.

The third scientific development is due to chemistry. This has produced new and unforeseen dangers to the world environment, in the ozone layer and in large-scale pollution of the land, the rivers and the sea. We are feeling the effects even in the food chain; Britain is now regarded widely as the only country in the world where the sex is safer than the food.

The fourth major development in science over the last 50 years has been in the field of television and radio. Television and radio have not only increased the ability of governments to control the opinion of their peoples, they have also reduced the ability of governments to do so … These new media not only make news international, they have tended to produce the internationalization of culture. I was surprised when I was in Moscow some years ago to find young people in Gorky Park with punk haircuts carrying ghetto blasters, which were playing the latest western and Soviet pop music.

In my opinion all these scientific developments have made the creation of a world order both more necessary and more possible. Unfortunately, the international explosion of nationalism has also made it more difficult to create a world order, not only between what we call East and West but also in the Third World … Nuclear weapons, chemical weapons, biological weapons and the missiles to carry them will proliferate in the Third World where nationalism is even stronger than it is in Europe and is fuelled by religious and tribal influences which are even more virulent.

I have been trying to understand world affairs ever since I left the army in 1945. As a young man I was surprised to find that nationalism was by far the most powerful single force in world politics, far stronger than ideology, class solidarity or religion. Those who think for example, that Muslim fundamentalism is more powerful than nationalism should look at what happened in the Gulf War[7] where the Shia population of Iraq fought for the Iraqi government, for their own country, against the Shia regime in Iran.

[7] Now usually called the Iran–Iraq War, 1980–8.

Unfortunately nationalism is essentially a product of democracy. In its modern form it hardly existed before the end of the 18th century. It is in fact the most important single legacy of the French Revolution, as that great political philosopher Talmon[8] preached in his many books. Yet the nation state is a dangerous anachronism in the modern world. It is anachronistic because of the scientific developments I have described. It is dangerous because it is impossible to draw a frontier round any nationality in the world without including minorities of other nationalities which claim the same rights as the majority …

[8] The Polish historian Jacob Talmon (1916–80) was an anti-Marxist who believed that the French Revolution was the root of modern totalitarianism.

Nationalism tends to increase if an economy is failing. The economic failure of communism is total, and as a result we see xenophobia breaking out all over what used to be the Soviet Empire, including its most filthy form, anti-Semitism. Unfortunately the economic failure of communism has been made worse so far by attempts to replace it with something different. In the Soviet Union, living standards have steadily fallen since perestroika[9] began five years ago and parts of the system are breaking down altogether …

[9] A programme of political and economic restructuring introduced by Gorbachev.

At least 10,000 books have been written to tell people how to turn capitalism into Socialism. There is not yet a single book about how to turn a command economy into a market economy. The trouble is that the old structures have now gone … There are no effective communications between government and industry; there is no commercial banking system, and most worrying of all, in some of these countries the whole society seems to have lost both the desire and the capacity for working; they have lived too long in a system in which, as the old Soviet joke goes 'we pretend to work and they pretend to pay us' …

Now let us look at the implications of this for the western world. At the moment, western governments are still stunned by the disappearance of the enemy who has given their efforts meaning for the last 40 years. You will remember that poem of Cavafy[10] about the senators who are waiting for the arrival of the barbarians in Rome and are suddenly told the barbarians have turned and gone back. It ends with the immortal couplet 'What shall we do without the barbarians? They were a sort of solution.' One can't help feeling that about the western reaction to these stupendous changes in eastern Europe and the Soviet Union.

The most worrying country in the West is also the most powerful – the United States – which seems to be reclining in what was recently described as a state of 'happy apathy' … The United States is now preoccupied primarily by its internal problems, which it sees as drugs and crime, both increased by the old American dilemma of how to deal with the racial problem – which is now not only black but increasingly Hispanic and Asian. The main external enemy as seen by Americans, according to the opinion polls, is not the Soviet Union but Japan. In some areas the Americans are getting quite hysterical about what they see as the Japanese threat …

On top of that the United States has now got a very fragile financial system … Most of my American friends in financial institutions think the system would collapse if there were a recession. So far there has not been a recession because the Japanese and the Germans have been financing the enormous American fiscal and external deficits. But the German surplus is now going to be fully absorbed into paying for the digestion of eastern Germany … Meanwhile the Japanese themselves have a shrinking trade surplus …

The Americans cannot finance their deficits themselves because they do not save enough. If they consequently have to get rid of their deficits because they cannot get someone else to finance them, they will risk generating a world recession, because a collapse in America's demand for foreign goods would reduce economic growth in all other countries in the world. This is one of many reasons why big cuts in American defence spending are now absolutely inevitable. Even the administration is now saying it plans to cut American defence spending by a quarter over the next five years.

Now what is going to be the impact of all this on NATO[11] and the European Community? Unless NATO makes some very fundamental changes in its role very quickly, it will be seen as a biological monstrosity, an organ without a function … There is no risk of a major Soviet attack on western Europe. NATO will still be required to co-ordinate the strategic western response to the changes in eastern Europe, but this is essentially a political and not a military function …

The role of any security organization in Europe in the coming years will not be to deter or defeat an external attack – which has been NATO's role over the last 40 years – but to police Europe's internal frontiers and to mediate in disputes which may divide the countries of Europe … It would be fatal for NATO to try to preserve the bloc mentality that has kept it going over the last 40 years …

So far as I can see there is only one potential framework for a new

[10] The Greek poet Konstantínos Kaváfis *known as Constantine Cavafy* (1863–1933), whose work challenged religious, sexual and political orthodoxies.

[11] The North Atlantic Treaty Organization, established in 1949 to co-ordinate defence collaboration between 12 European and North American countries. There are now more than 25 member states.

security architecture ... I believe we should develop CSCE[12] into a new structure for security which would spread from Vancouver to Vladivostok, including not only the European countries of the north, as well as east and west, but also the United States and Canada and the Soviet Union itself. All are now signatories of the Helsinki Treaty.[13] NATO's main role should be to bring that about as fast as possible.

We have to see the European Community in a similar way ... I believe that the prospect of membership of the Community would be a powerful force for economic change in the east European countries ...

I cannot predict now how all this will come about. But in my political experience the important thing is to set your objective clearly. Our objective today must be to take advantage of the opportunities of uniting the whole of Europe which have been created by the end of the Cold War ... I believe this new form of European unity stretching from Brest to Bucharest, inside a new security structure stretching from Vancouver to Vladivostok, is something which could excite the imagination of both peoples and governments and particularly of the young.

When I look back on my own life – I was born in 1917 – I see governments botching the first attempt to built a world society under the League of Nations after 1918, through lack of dedication, and botching the second attempt under the United Nations after 1945, mainly because the Soviet Union and its satellites refused to join the effort. The end of the Cold War gives us a third chance. If we miss that chance I fear that anarchy in the Soviet Union and the Third World will sweep all our signposts away.

The world desperately needs at the moment the sort of vision and leadership which Winston Churchill gave us 50 years ago. The challenges we face today are physically far less formidable than those that Churchill faced in 1940. Intellectually, however, they are infinitely more formidable. However, the central problem in politics as in almost any field of effort is to start by asking the right question. The moment you have got the question rightly formulated, the possibility of a solution is imminent. Our duty now is to define that question, and to start working out the answer.

Edward Heath
English statesman

Edward Richard George Heath *also called Ted Heath; later Sir Edward Heath* (1916–2005) was born in Broadstairs, Kent, the son of a carpenter and a maid. He attended Chatham House Grammar School in Ramsgate, and won an organ scholarship to Balliol College, Oxford. After service in World War II he entered Parliament in 1950, one of R A Butler's 'One Nation' new Tory intellectuals. He became Chief Whip (1955–9), then Minister of Labour (1959–60). He was the chief negotiator for British entry into the European Common Market, and although France prevented the UK from joining, he was awarded the German Charlemagne prize (1963). In the Douglas-Home administration of 1963–4 he became Secretary of State for Industry and president of the Board of Trade (1963). Elected leader of the Conservative Party in July 1965, he led the opposition until, on winning the 1970 general election, he became prime minister. At the beginning of 1973, the UK finally became a member of the European Community, which Heath considered his crowning achievement. After a long confrontation with the miners' union in 1973, the Conservatives narrowly lost the general election of February 1974, the loss being confirmed by another election in October 1974. In 1975 he was replaced as leader by MARGARET THATCHER. From 1979 he became an increasingly outspoken critic of what he regarded as the extreme policies of Thatcherism. He resisted attempts to move him to the Lords, and retained the seat of Old Bexley and Sidcup in the 1997 general election, standing down in 2001 after more than 50 years in the House of Commons. His international credibility was evident from his meetings with SADDAM HUSSEIN before and after the 1991 Gulf War, which were instrumental in securing the release of British hostages and prisoners. He was an expert yachtsman, and, after winning the 1969 Hobart Ocean race, captained the British crew for the Admiral's Cup races of 1971 and 1979. He was also an accomplished musician.

'A Europe which is free, democratic, safe and happy'
2 January 1973, London, England

Britain's entry into the European Community on 1 January 1973 was a personal triumph for Edward Heath. When his predecessor HAROLD MACMILLAN realized the mistake Britain had made in refusing to join the EEC in 1957, Heath headed the negotiating team that applied for membership in 1961, only to be vetoed by France. He never lost sight of his ambition, however, and when the House of Commons voted by a majority of 112 to go into Europe in October 1971, he celebrated by playing Bach on the organ. Yet EC membership was and continued to be a deeply divisive issue: the Commons passed the second reading of the European Communities Bill in February 1972 by only eight votes.

Eleven months later, however, Heath was once again in jubilatory mood, as this speech – at a dinner at Hampton Court held by the British Council of the European Movement – shows. Unlike future Conservative and Labour leaders, he had no qualms over the political and social, as well as economic, aims of the European Community, 'whose scope will gradually extend until it covers virtually the whole field of collective human endeavour'. Some saw Heath as a charmless, awkward communicator, but this address demonstrates both his sense of idealism and his optimism.

Mr Chairman: I am delighted to be able to respond to a toast, moved with such eloquence by a European[1] who has brought to this cause a personal conviction, determination and compassion which we deeply admire. It is fitting that he should be with us here tonight, as we celebrate British entry into the Community. We are honoured that he should come during what are, regrettably, the last few days of his term of office as President of the European Commission. We are grateful for the remarkable achievements which have been brought about during his presidency.

Many have worked with him for this result, but we recognize with gratitude his own personal contribution which has been so considerable. For it is he who has been the permanent conductor of the Nine Muses,[2] known to us in British song as the 'Nine Bright Shiners'. Indeed Matthew Arnold[3] might have been thinking of Dr Mansholt when he wrote:

[1] The Dutch agricultural technocrat Sicco Mansholt (1908–95) served as President of the European Commission, 1972–3.

[2] Heath refers to the nine members of the EC: the six original member states were joined in 1973 by the UK, Republic of Ireland and Denmark.

[3] The English poet and critic Matthew Arnold (1822–88).

'Tis Apollo comes leading
　His choir, the Nine –
　The leader is fairest
　But all are divine.'[4]

I am happy to recognize in Dr Mansholt the Apollo of modern Europe.

Twenty-five years ago, at the first gathering of the European Movement[5] at The Hague, Sir WINSTON CHURCHILL looked forward to the day when, 'men and women of every country will think as much of being European as of belonging to their native land and wherever they go in this wide domain will truly feel, "Here I am at home".'

[5] A lobbying association established in 1948 to work towards the unification of Europe. Among its founders was Winston Churchill.

Tonight as we meet on the eve of the 'Fanfare for Europe' festival to mark British entry into the Community, we are one step nearer to making Churchill's dream a reality. It is appropriate that here to celebrate this great event there should be not only a distinguished gathering of British people but also a large number of our fellow Europeans. We welcome you all – diplomatic representatives of other Community countries, presidents of the Community's institutions and distinguished elder statesmen of the Community, the 'Fathers of Europe'.

The enlargement of the Community has finally come about in this, the 25th anniversary year of the European Movement. This movement has provided much of the impetus towards European unity, and I would like to pay tribute to its work over these years.

The European Movement has brought together people from very different political, social and professional backgrounds, who are united in their belief that Britain's future should be one of partnership with our European neighbours. In particular I would like to thank the British Council of the European Movement for their work in preparing the way for British entry into the Community.

The meaning of our accomplished membership of the Community for the British people themselves is, and is rightly, a preoccupation of many in this country. I would like to pay tribute to all those journalists and others responsible for the public media who have done so much in the last few days to ensure, by their contributions in the press, radio and elsewhere, that the real meaning of membership is understood.

[6] The English churchman and politician Cardinal Thomas Wolsey (c.1475–1530) was Henry VIII's chief minister between 1515 and 1529.

We meet tonight in a palace conceived and built by Cardinal Wolsey,[6] a statesman who wrestled with the problems of Europe at a time when nationalism was in the ascendant throughout Europe. Wolsey sought to further the interests of his church, his country and his master – but at the same time he tried to keep in check the national rivalries which threatened to destroy the medieval ideal of a Europe which was essentially one.

The forces of division proved too strong. Wolsey lost his position, he lost this palace, he was lucky not to lose his head. Europe entered on four centuries of bitter rivalry, each phase of which reached its climax in a destructive war.

Now, in 1973, we can fairly claim that since the end of the last war there has been another sea change in the history of Europe. For since 1945 the story of Europe has been essentially one of reconciliation instead of rivalry. In that story the founding of the European Community was one milestone. The enlargement yesterday of that Community from six to nine members was another milestone of equal importance. For the Community now includes within its scope all the main national traditions which over the centuries have enriched the life of our continent.

We have been accustomed during these years to hear the Community described as the Common Market. I hope that this is a habit which we can now abandon. Certainly the unified market is a fact of enormous significance. But it is only the first step in a journey which will carry us well beyond questions of tariffs and trade. For what we are building is a Community whose scope will gradually extend until it covers virtually the whole field of collective human endeavour.

I believe that the real significance of last autumn's summit meeting was precisely this. We were able to agree on the guidelines for this progress towards a wider Community. We were able to show how, in one field after another, we could come together as neighbours to achieve by co-operation the many aims which we share and which we could not hope to realize in isolation. One of our most important decisions at that meeting was that we should work urgently towards building a European foreign policy. I believe that this is not a luxury for our Community but a clear necessity.

It is a necessity if we consider our relations with the United States. I think that all of us here tonight recognize the part which the United States has played in making possible the creation of this new Community. I am not thinking mainly of the economic help given to Europe after the war, massive and timely though this was. I am thinking rather of the consistent policy of successive administrations who have held that it was a fundamental interest of the United States that Europe should unite – an interest which outweighed the increased competition and the occasional disagreements with American policy which a united Europe was bound to involve.

In this field we can see most clearly how artificial is the distinction between foreign policy and economic policy. Our aim in Europe must be to build up our own strength, and our own Community of purpose, across the whole field of policy. Our aim must be that Europe can emerge as a valid partner of the United States in strengthening the prospects for peace and prosperity across the world. That is the aim which I will have at the forefront of my mind when I discuss these matters with President NIXON at the beginning of next month.

A common policy is equally necessary in our dealings with the Soviet Union and with eastern Europe. We can see clearly enough that the whole relationship between eastern and western Europe is now once again in a state of flux. We welcome the progress which has already been made by the federal German government in working out a better relationship with its neighbours. We know that in the course of 1973 there will be further important decisions to be taken.

Our aim can be simply defined. It is to enable both western and eastern Europe to make progress without being held back by mutual suspicions or the threat of war. I am sure that we shall only succeed in this purpose if we in western Europe speak with a common voice and act with a common energy. Members of the Community, with their uniquely successful experience of the policies of reconciliation, have an important contribution to make to a better relationship with eastern Europe. For we want to build, as our ultimate objective, a Europe which is not only prosperous – but a Europe which is free, democratic, safe and happy.

This goal extends beyond the confines of our existing Community. It concerns our neighbours to the east, the Soviet Union and her allies, and the neutral nations, as well as our own member states and associates.

The political task which faces us is as ambitious as any yet undertaken by a group of nations acting together. And it embraces every aspect of our responsibilities as governments and as leaders of democratic political societies. That task requires us to fulfil the needs and ambitions of our citizens. We are, all of us throughout the Community, increasingly concerned to put right the defects and injustice of modern society.

As industry advances to the greater prosperity we expect, it has imposed new burdens on us all. Only in the last few years have we become fully aware of the effects of industrial activity on this scale: the ruin of the landscape, the pollution of the atmosphere, the poisoning of rivers and estuaries. In the densely populated lands of western Europe we can only mitigate, control and reduce the harmful effects of this activity by deliberate action on a continental scale. The atmosphere over our cities today will fall with the rain in Scandinavia tomorrow. The effluents of the Rhine in January will be washing our eastern shores in February. To stop this we must act together. I believe that we can meet this danger, and I know that the people of western Europe expect it from us.

There is another expectation, yet more difficult to fulfil. Throughout the nations of western Europe, and particularly among our young citizens, we have all noticed – and applauded – the growing demand that the richer nations should work more effectively to help the less developed countries, in their struggle to create conditions of life compatible with human dignity and self-respect.

We all know that there are many societies wrestling with this problem today. Each member of the Community has inherited special links with other countries beyond the seas, and this is specially true of Britain. As each year more of our citizens travel to distant lands, realization of this human need becomes more widely diffused within our own boundaries.

I believe that the time has come for us to formulate a collective response to this problem. Together, the nations of the Community can do more than the sum of their individual efforts, by joining our skills and resources in a concerted programme. Success in meeting this challenge will be increasingly expected of us by our citizens, and we must act speedily and effectively.

The prizes to be gained by common action are very great. There is the prize of peace. There is the prize of prosperity. There is the prize of building in Europe a society which will correspond more closely to the hopes of the peoples whom we represent. These have been the aims which have inspired the founders of the European Movement. Today we can see that they are no longer far-off dreams. They are prizes which now lie within our grasp. We must show the imagination and the strength of purpose to make them our own.

Patrick Henry
American revolutionary and politician

Patrick Henry (1736–99) was born in Hanover County, Virginia. After working as shopkeeper and farmer, he trained as a lawyer. He became a member of the colonial Virginia House of Burgesses (1765–74), where his oratory won him fame. He was an outspoken opponent of British policy towards the colonies, particularly over the Stamp Act of 1765, which levied a tax on all legal documents, publications and playing cards. He made the first speech in the Continental Congress (1774), but is best known for his 'liberty or death' speech of 1775. He became governor of independent Virginia in 1776, and was re-elected four times. He opposed the US Constitution on the grounds that the states did not need a strong central government, and when it was adopted he began to lobby for its amendment, arguing successfully for the addition of the Bill of Rights – the first ten Amendments to the Constitution, passed in 1789. He retired in 1791.

'Give me liberty or give me death!'
23 March 1775, Richmond, Virginia, America

When Patrick Henry stood in St John's Church, Richmond and told the Second Virginia Convention that war had 'already begun', he was only saying what all knew to be true. The passage of the Coercive Acts of 1774 – which removed certain rights of self-government – had led directly to the First Continental Congress in Philadelphia. The 56 delegates, representing all the colonies except Georgia, denounced these measures, refused to accept them and voted to form colonial militias. New York's assembly had already refused to accept British demands to quarter troops on civilians and had been threatened with revocation of its charter.

Virginia was the largest of the American colonies, and prided itself on having the longest-serving legislature, the House of Burgesses. Henry, now 38, was a second-generation colonist, and had already made a name for himself by writing the 'Virginia Resolutions' against the hated Stamp Act. On this occasion he spoke extemporaneously and the text was compiled by his biographer, William Wirt, from recollections of those who heard his energetic defence of liberty.

Parliament and the Crown had been at odds with the colonies for more than a decade, and their differing attitudes are clear in the language of the controversy. Parliament's voice was a paternalistic one – the colonists were like children, in need of correction and guidance. Indeed, few colonists wanted war (although Henry perhaps did); most simply wanted the same rights and privileges as other British subjects. THOMAS JEFFERSON believed Henry's famous last sentence sparked the War of Independence.

Mr President: no man thinks more highly than I do of the patriotism, as well as abilities, of the very worthy gentlemen who have just addressed the House. But different men often see the same subject in different lights; and, therefore, I hope it will not be thought disrespectful to those gentlemen if, entertaining as I do opinions of a character very opposite to theirs, I shall speak forth my sentiments freely and without reserve.

This is no time for ceremony. The question before the House is one of awful moment to this country. For my own part, I consider it as nothing less than a question of freedom or slavery; and in proportion to the magnitude of the subject ought to be the freedom of the debate. It is only in this way that we can hope to arrive at truth, and fulfil the great responsibility which we hold to God and our country. Should I keep back my opinions at such a time, through fear of giving offence, I should consider myself as guilty of treason towards my country, and of an act of disloyalty toward the Majesty of Heaven, which I revere above all earthly kings.

Mr President, it is natural to man to indulge in the illusions of hope. We are apt to shut our eyes against a painful truth, and listen to the song of that siren till she transforms us into beasts. Is this the part of wise men, engaged in a great and arduous struggle for liberty? Are we disposed to be of the number of those who, having eyes, see not and, having ears, hear not, the things which so nearly concern their temporal salvation? For my part, whatever anguish of spirit it may cost, I am willing to know the whole truth; to know the worst, and to provide for it.

I have but one lamp by which my feet are guided, and that is the lamp of experience. I know of no way of judging of the future but by the past. And judging by the past, I wish to know what there has been in the conduct of the British ministry for the last ten years to justify those hopes with which gentlemen have been pleased to solace themselves and the House. Is it that insidious smile with which our petition has been lately received? Trust it not, sir; it will prove a snare to your feet. Suffer not yourselves to be betrayed with a kiss.

Ask yourselves how this gracious reception of our petition comports with those warlike preparations which cover our waters and darken our land. Are fleets and armies necessary to a work of love and reconciliation? Have we shown ourselves so unwilling to be reconciled that force must be called in to win back our love? Let us not deceive ourselves, sir. These are the implements of war and subjugation; the last arguments to which kings resort.

I ask gentlemen, sir: what means this martial array, if its purpose be not to force us to submission? Can gentlemen assign any other possible motive for it? Has Great Britain any enemy, in this quarter of the world, to call for all this accumulation of navies and armies? No, sir, she has none. They are meant for us: they can be meant for no other. They are sent over to bind and rivet upon us those chains which the British ministry have been so long forging.

And what have we to oppose to them? Shall we try argument? Sir, we have been trying that for the last ten years. Have we anything new to offer upon the subject? Nothing. We have held the subject up in every light of which it is capable; but it has been all in vain. Shall we resort to entreaty and humble supplication? What terms shall we find which have not been already exhausted? Let us not, I beseech you, sir, deceive ourselves.

Sir, we have done everything that could be done to avert the storm which is now coming on. We have petitioned; we have remonstrated; we have supplicated; we have prostrated ourselves before the throne, and have implored its interposition to arrest the tyrannical hands of the Ministry and Parliament. Our petitions have been slighted; our remonstrances have produced additional violence and insult; our supplications have been disregarded; and we have been spurned, with contempt, from the foot of the throne! In vain, after these things, may we indulge the fond hope of peace and reconciliation.

There is no longer any room for hope. If we wish to be free; if we mean to preserve inviolate those inestimable privileges for which we have been so long contending; if we mean not basely to abandon the noble struggle in which we have been so long engaged, and which we have pledged ourselves never to abandon until the glorious object of our contest shall be obtained, we must fight! I repeat it, sir, we must fight! An appeal to arms and to the God of hosts is all that is left us!

They tell us, sir, that we are weak, unable to cope with so formidable an adversary. But when shall we be stronger? Will it be the next week, or the next year? Will it be when we are totally disarmed, and when a British guard shall be stationed in every house? Shall we gather strength by irresolution and inaction? Shall we acquire the means of effectual resistance by lying supinely on our backs and hugging the delusive phantom of hope, until our enemies shall have bound us hand and foot?

Sir, we are not weak if we make a proper use of those means which the God of nature hath placed in our power. The millions of people, armed in the holy cause of liberty, and in such a country as that which we possess, are invincible by any force which our enemy can send against us. Besides, sir, we shall not fight our battles alone. There is a just God who presides over the destinies of nations, and who will raise up friends to fight our battles for us.

The battle, sir, is not to the strong alone; it is to the vigilant, the active, the brave. Besides, sir, we have no election. If we were base enough to desire it, it is now too late to retire from the contest. There is no retreat but in submission and slavery! Our chains are forged! Their clanking may be heard on the plains of Boston! The war is inevitable – and let it come! I repeat it, sir, let it come.

It is in vain, sir, to extenuate the matter. Gentlemen may cry, 'Peace! Peace!' But there is no peace. The war is actually begun. The next gale that sweeps from the north will bring to our ears the clash of resounding arms! Our brethren are already in the field! Why stand we here idle? What is it that gentlemen wish? What would they have? Is life so dear, or peace so sweet, as to be purchased at the price of chains and slavery? Forbid it, Almighty God! I know not what course others may take; but as for me: give me liberty or give me death!

Chaim Herzog
Israeli soldier and statesman

Chaim Herzog (1918–97) was born in Belfast, Northern Ireland. He was the son of Yitzhak Halevi Herzog, who was Chief Rabbi of Ireland (1919–36) and of Palestine and the State of Israel (1936–59). He was raised and educated in Dublin. Following a period in Palestine – during which he joined the Haganah – he studied law at University College and at Cambridge, becoming a barrister. When World War II broke out, he joined the British Army and served in intelligence in Europe, reaching the rank of lieutenant colonel. He participated in the liberation of Nazi concentration camps. He returned to Palestine in 1945 and fought for the establishment of an Israeli state. After this was achieved he served as an officer in the Israel Defence Forces (IDF), fighting in the Arab–Israeli War of 1948, and becoming head of IDF military intelligence (1948–50) in the rank of colonel. He then served as Commander of the Jerusalem Brigade until 1957, and as Chief of Southern Command until 1959. This was followed by a second term as head of IDF military intelligence (1959–62) in the rank of general. In 1962, he went into private practice, founding the law firm of Herzog, Fox & Neeman, which is now the largest in Israel. He frequently appeared as a military radio commentator, earning national acclaim especially for building the morale of the people during the Six-Day War of 1967. Following the Israeli capture of the West Bank, he became its military governor. In 1975 he was appointed as Israeli Ambassador to the United Nations, a post he held until 1978, fiercely resisting Resolution 3379, which declared that Zionism should be regarded as racism. This resolution was finally repealed in 1991. In 1981 Herzog was elected as a Labour member of the Knesset. Within two years, he was elected president of Israel, serving from 1983 until his retirement in 1993. He was a popular and highly admired head of state. He advocated tolerance, supporting Arab and Druze rights, and campaigned for electoral reform. He spent much of his two terms of office engaged in diplomatic missions overseas, visiting 33 countries, including Ireland, where he opened the Irish Jewish Museum. His publications include *Who Stands Accused? Israel Answers Its Critics* (1978), *The Arab–Israeli Wars: War and Peace in the Middle East* (1982) and *Living History: A Memoir* (1996).

'This wicked resolution must sound the alarm'
10 November 1975, New York City, USA

Chaim Herzog's famous speech to the United Nations General Assembly is the most passionate defence of Zionism ever given in that chamber. Zionists had been seeking to recover Palestine since the late 19th century, but faced staunch Arab resistance. In 1947, UN Resolution 181 proposed the partition of Palestine into Arab and Israeli states. This was immediately rejected by the Arabs and war broke out. As the British mandate to govern Palestine expired in May 1948, Israel's founding prime minister DAVID BEN-GURION proclaimed a separate state, prompting another war. In the 1960s and 1970s, Israel thwarted attacks by her neighbours and made significant gains in territory.

However, the plight of Palestinian Arabs living in refugee camps attracted the world's attention, and although surrounded by enemies on all sides, Israel was widely regarded as an aggressor.

In November 1975, the UN debated Resolution 3379, which proposed to equate Zionism with racism, condemning it as a 'threat to world peace and security'. In his defiant speech, Herzog gives a historical account of his country's right to exist, vindicating Zionist principles and condemning Israel's enemies.

When he finished speaking, he tore up a copy of the resolution and stormed out, echoing a similar protest staged by his father during the British mandate. The USA and its allies backed Israel in opposing the resolution, while the USSR and other members of the Eastern bloc supported it. The resolution was passed by 72 votes to 35, with 32 abstentions.

Mr President: it is symbolic that this debate, which may well prove to be a turning point in the fortunes of the United Nations and a decisive factor in the possible continued existence of this organization, should take place on November 10.

Tonight, 37 years ago, has gone down in history as *Kristallnacht*, the 'Night of the Crystals'. This was the night in 1938 when Hitler's Nazi stormtroopers launched a co-ordinated attack on the Jewish community in Germany, burned the synagogues in all its cities and made bonfires in the streets of the Holy Books and the Scrolls of the Holy Law and Bible. It was the night when Jewish homes were attacked and heads of families taken away, many of them never to return. It was the night when the windows of all Jewish businesses and stores were smashed, covering the streets in the cities of Germany with a film of broken glass which dissolved into the millions of crystals which gave that night its name. It was the night which led eventually to the crematoria and the gas chambers, Auschwitz, Birkenau, Dachau, Buchenwald, Theresienstadt and others.[1] It was the night which led to the most terrifying holocaust in the history of man.

It is indeed befitting, Mr President, that this debate, conceived in the desire to deflect the Middle East from its moves towards peace and born of a deep pervading feeling of anti-Semitism, should take place on the anniversary of this day ... Hitler would have felt at home on a number of occasions during the past year, listening to the proceedings in this forum, and above all to the proceedings during the debate on Zionism.

It is sobering to consider to what level this body has been dragged down if we are obliged today to contemplate an attack on Zionism. For this attack constitutes not only an anti-Israeli attack of the foulest type, but also an assault in the United Nations on Judaism – one of the oldest established religions in the world, a religion which has given the world the human values of the Bible, and from which two other great religions, Christianity and Islam, sprang ...

I do not come to this rostrum to defend the moral and historical values of the Jewish people. They do not need to be defended ... I come here to denounce the two great evils which menace society in general and a society of nations in particular. These two evils are hatred and ignorance. These two evils are the motivating force behind the proponents of this resolution and their supporters ...

Zionism is one of the most dynamic and vibrant national movements in human history. Historically it is based on a unique and unbroken connection, extending some 4,000 years, between the People of the Book[2] and the Land of the Bible.

In modern times, in the late 19th century, spurred by the twin forces of anti-Semitic persecution and of nationalism, the Jewish people organized the Zionist movement in order to transform their dream into reality. Zionism as a political movement was the revolt of an oppressed nation against the depredation and wicked discrimination and oppression of the countries in which anti-Semitism flourished. It is no coincidence that the co-sponsors and supporters of this resolution include countries who are guilty of the horrible crimes of anti-Semitism and discrimination to this very day.

Support for the aim of Zionism was written into the League of Nations mandate[3] for Palestine and was again endorsed by the United Nations in 1947, when the General Assembly voted by overwhelming majority for the restoration of Jewish independence in our ancient land.

The re-establishment of Jewish independence in Israel, after centuries of struggle to overcome foreign conquest and exile, is a vindication of the fundamental concepts of the equality of nations and of self-determination. To question the Jewish people's right to national existence and freedom is not only to deny to the Jewish people the right accorded to every other people on this globe, but it is also to deny the central precepts of the United Nations ...

We in Israel have endeavoured to create a society which strives to implement the highest ideals of society – political, social and cultural – for

[1] Herzog refers to the concentration camps established by the Nazis in Germany and occupied Poland and Czechoslovakia, where Jews and other 'enemies of the state' were imprisoned and murdered.

[2] Jews use this phrase to refer to the Jewish people. (Muslims refer to both Jews and Christians as 'People of the Book'.)

[3] The UK administered Palestine under a League of Nations mandate from the Treaty of Versailles (1919) until May 1948.

all the inhabitants of Israel, irrespective of religious belief, race or sex.

Show me another pluralistic society in this world in which, despite all the difficult problems, Jew and Arab live together with such a degree of harmony, in which the dignity and rights of man are observed before the law, in which no death sentence is applied, in which freedom of speech, of movement, of thought, of expression are guaranteed, in which even movements which are opposed to our national aims are represented in our parliament.

The Arab delegates talk of racism. What has happened to the 800,000 Jews who lived for over 2,000 years in the Arab lands, who formed some of the most ancient communities, long before the advent of Islam? Where are they now?

The Jews were once one of the important communities in the countries of the Middle East, the leaders of thought, of commerce, of medical science. Where are they in Arab society today? You dare talk of racism when I can point with pride to the Arab ministers who have served in my government; to the Arab deputy speaker of my parliament; to Arab officers and men serving of their own volition in our border and police defence forces, frequently commanding Jewish troops; to the hundreds of thousands of Arabs from all over the Middle East crowding the cities of Israel every year; to the thousands of Arabs from all over the Middle East coming for medical treatment to Israel; to the peaceful co-existence which has developed; to the fact that Arabic is an official language in Israel on a par with Hebrew; to the fact that it is as natural for an Arab to serve in public office in Israel as it is incongruous to think of a Jew serving in any public office in an Arab country, indeed being admitted to many of them. Is that racism? It is not! That, Mr President, is Zionism.

Zionism is our attempt to build a society, imperfect though it may be, in which the visions of the prophets of Israel will be realized. I know that we have problems. I know that many disagree with our government's policies. Many in Israel too disagree from time to time with the government's policies … and are free to do so because Zionism has created the first and only real democratic state in a part of the world that never really knew democracy and freedom of speech …

We are seeing here today but another manifestation of the bitter anti-Semitic, anti-Jewish hatred which animates Arab society. Who would have believed that in this year, 1975, the malicious falsehoods of the 'elders of Zion'[4] would be distributed officially by Arab governments? Who would have believed that we would today contemplate an Arab society which teaches the vilest anti-Jewish hate in the kindergartens? …

We are being attacked by a society which is motivated by the most extreme form of racism known in the world today. This is the racism which was expressed so succinctly in the words of the leader of the PLO,[5] YASSER ARAFAT, in his opening address at a symposium in Tripoli, Libya: 'There will be no presence in the region other than the Arab presence …' In other words, in the Middle East, from the Atlantic Ocean to the Persian Gulf, only one presence is allowed, and that is Arab presence. No other people, regardless of how deep are its roots in the region, is to be permitted to enjoy its right to self-determination.

Look at the tragic fate of the Kurds of Iraq. Look what happened to the black population in southern Sudan. Look at the dire peril in which an entire community of Christians finds itself in Lebanon. Look at the avowed policy of the PLO, which calls in its Palestine Covenant of 1964 for the destruction

[4] The *Protocols of the Elders of Zion* was a hoax document published in 1905 by the Russian mystic Sergei Nilus (1862–1929), purporting to be a Jewish plan for world domination. Widely translated and distributed, it provided a focus for anti-Semitism, and was a key influence on Adolf Hitler. Exposed in 1921, the hoax was generally accepted as such by the late 1930s.

[5] The Palestine Liberation Organization was formed in 1964 to represent the interests of the Palestinian people. It refused to recognize Israel's right to exist until 1993.

of the state of Israel, which denies any form of compromise on the Palestine issue and which, in the words of its representative only the other day in this building, considers Tel Aviv to be occupied territory. Look at all this, and you see before you the root cause of the twin evils of this world at work, the blind hatred of the Arab proponents of this resolution, and the abysmal ignorance and wickedness of those who support them …

Over the centuries it has fallen to the lot of my people to be the testing agent of human decency, the touchstone of civilization, the crucible in which enduring human values are to be tested. A nation's level of humanity could invariably be judged by its behaviour towards its Jewish population. Persecution and oppression have often enough begun with the Jews, but it has never ended with them. The anti-Jewish pogroms[6] in Czarist Russia were but the tip of the iceberg which revealed the inherent rottenness of a regime that was soon to disappear in the storm of revolution. The anti-Semitic excesses of the Nazis merely foreshadowed the catastrophe which was to befall mankind in Europe.

[6] The organized persecution of Jews in 19th-century Russia later spread to eastern Europe and beyond.

This wicked resolution must sound the alarm for all decent people. The Jewish people as a testing agent has unfortunately never erred. The implications inherent in this shameful move are terrifying indeed.

On the issue before us, the world has divided itself into good and bad, decent and evil, human and debased. We, the Jewish people, will recall in history our gratitude to those nations who stood up and were counted and who refused to support this wicked proposition. I know that this episode will have strengthened the forces of freedom and decency in this world and will have fortified the free world in their resolve to strengthen the ideals they so cherish. I know that this episode will have strengthened Zionism as it has weakened the United Nations.

As I stand on this rostrum, the long and proud history of my people unravels itself before my inward eye. I see the oppressors of our people over the ages as they pass one another in evil procession into oblivion. I stand here before you as the representative of a strong and flourishing people which has survived them all and which will survive this shameful exhibition and the proponents of this resolution.

The great moments of Jewish history come to mind as I face you, once again outnumbered and the would-be victim of hate, ignorance and evil. I look back on those great moments. I recall the greatness of a nation which I have the honour to represent in this forum. I am mindful at this moment of the Jewish people throughout the world wherever they may be, be it in freedom or in slavery, whose prayers and thoughts are with me at this moment.

I stand here not as a supplicant. Vote as your moral conscience dictates to you. For the issue is neither Israel nor Zionism. The issue is the continued existence of this organization, which has been dragged to its lowest point of discredit by a coalition of despots and racists.

The vote of each delegation will record in history its country's stand on anti-Semitic racism and anti-Judaism. You yourselves bear the responsibility for your stand before history, for as such will you be viewed in history. We, the Jewish people, will not forget. For us, the Jewish people, this resolution based on hatred, falsehood and arrogance is devoid of any moral or legal value. For us, the Jewish people, this is no more than a piece of paper and we shall treat it as such.

Charlton Heston

American actor

Charlton Heston *originally Charles Carter* (1923–2008) was born in Evanston, Illinois. He made his film debut in an amateur adaptation of *Peer Gynt* (1941). During World War II he served in the US air force. Resuming his acting career, he made his Broadway debut in *Antony and Cleopatra* (1947). His first Hollywood film was *Dark City* (1950), but his major early successes were the Cecil B De Mille films *The Greatest Show on Earth* (1952) and *The Ten Commandments* (1956). He also played the larger-than-life heroes for which his strapping physique suited him in *Ben-Hur* (1959) – for which he won an Academy Award as best actor – and *El Cid* (1961). Other major films include *Touch of Evil* (1958), *The War Lord* (1965), *Will Penny* (1967), *Soylent Green* (1973), *Earthquake* (1974), *Tombstone* (1993) and *Genghis Khan* (2005). He frequently returned to the stage, and also directed *Antony and Cleopatra* (1972) on film and, for television, *A Man for All Seasons* (1988). He published the autobiographies *The Actor's Life* (1978) and *In the Arena* (1995).

'This rampant epidemic of new McCarthyism'

16 February 1999, Cambridge, Massachusetts, USA

🐦

Charlton Heston has never made a secret of his political beliefs. In his youth, he was active in the civil rights movement and the Democrat Party, campaigning for the presidential candidates ADLAI STEVENSON and JOHN F KENNEDY. In the 1980s, however, he came to support the Republicans, campaigning on behalf of presidents RONALD REAGAN, George H W Bush and GEORGE W BUSH.

A key area of interest was gun control. Heston is a lifelong member of the National Rifle Association (NRA) – which supports the right of American citizens to own firearms – and was its president from 1998 until 2003.

As he comments in this speech, given at the Law School of Harvard University, his NRA role made him a 'moving target' in the 'crosshairs' of those who favoured tighter control of guns. Three years later, he appeared as a harassed interviewee in *Bowling for Columbine*, the Oscar-winning documentary by MICHAEL MOORE.

Heston's speech is partly an attempt to redeem his own reputation, beginning with a humorous evocation of some of his famous acting roles – Moses, John the Baptist, THOMAS JEFFERSON, Cardinal Richelieu – and recalling his work as a civil rights campaigner.

But it also addresses the rise of 'political correctness' in American culture. Heston argues passionately and persuasively that far from liberating society, this trend is ushering in new restrictions on its freedoms, while failing to curb a growing subculture which he considers an incitement to violence and hatred. Ultimately, harking back to the rhetoric of the nation's founders, he delivers a rousing call for civil disobedience.

🐦

I remember my son, when he was five, explaining to his kindergarten class what his father did for a living. 'My Daddy,' he said, 'pretends to be people.' There have been quite a few of them. Prophets from the Old and New Testaments, a couple of Christian saints, generals of various nationalities and different centuries, several kings, three American presidents, a French cardinal and two geniuses, including Michelangelo.[1] If you want the ceiling re-painted I'll do my best …

As I pondered our visit tonight it struck me: if my creator gave me the gift to connect you with the hearts and minds of those great men, then I want to use that same gift now to re-connect you with your own sense of liberty, your own freedom of thought, your own compass for what is right.

Dedicating the memorial at Gettysburg, ABRAHAM LINCOLN said of America, 'We are now engaged in a great Civil War, testing whether that nation or any nation so conceived and so dedicated can long endure.'[2]

Those words are true again. I believe that we are again engaged in a great civil war, a cultural war that's about to hijack your birthright to think and say what lives in your heart. I'm sure you no longer trust the pulsing lifeblood of liberty inside you, the stuff that made this country rise from wilderness into the miracle that it is.

[1] Heston played the Renaissance painter and sculptor Michelangelo (1475–1564) in *The Agony and the Ecstasy* (1965).

[2] Lincoln's Gettysburg Address is included in this book.

Let me back up a little. About a year or two ago, I became president of the National Rifle Association, which protects the right to keep and bear arms of American citizens. I ran for office, I was elected, and now I serve, I serve as a moving target for the media who've called me everything from 'ridiculous' and 'duped' to a 'brain-injured, senile, crazy old man' …

As I have stood in the crosshairs of those who target Second Amendment freedoms,[3] I've realized that firearms are not the only issue. No, it's much, much bigger than that. I've come to understand that a cultural war is raging across our land, in which, with Orwellian fervour,[4] certain accepted thoughts and speech are mandated.

For example, I marched for civil rights with Dr KING in 1963 – long before Hollywood found it acceptable, I may say. But when I told an audience last year that white pride is just as valid as black pride or red pride or anyone else's pride, they called me a racist.

I've worked with brilliantly talented homosexuals all my life – throughout my whole career. But when I told an audience that gay rights should extend no further than your rights or my rights, I was called a homophobe.

I served in World War II against the Axis powers. But during a speech, when I drew an analogy between singling out the innocent Jews and singling out innocent gun-owners, I was called an anti-Semite.

Everyone I know knows I would never raise a closed fist against my country. But when I asked an audience to oppose this cultural persecution I'm talking about, I was compared to Timothy McVeigh.[5]

From *Time* magazine to friends and colleagues, they're essentially saying, 'Chuck, how dare you speak your mind like that? You are using language not authorized for public consumption.'

But I am not afraid. If Americans believed in political correctness, we'd still be King George's boys – subjects bound to the British crown.

In his book, *The End of Sanity*, Martin Gross writes that 'blatantly irrational behaviour is rapidly being established as the norm in almost every area of human endeavour …'.

Let me read a few examples. At Antioch College in Ohio, young men seeking intimacy with a co-ed must get verbal permission at each step of the process from kissing to petting to final, at last, copulation – all clearly spelled out in a printed college directive.

In New Jersey, despite the death of several patients nationwide who'd been infected by dentists who had concealed their own AIDS, the state commissioner announced that health providers who are HIV-positive need not – need not! – tell their patients that they are infected.

At William and Mary,[6] students tried to change the name of the school team 'The Tribe' because it was supposedly insulting to local Indians, only to learn that authentic Virginia chiefs really like the name 'The Tribe'.

In San Francisco, city fathers passed an ordinance protecting the rights of transvestites to cross-dress on the job, and for transsexuals to have separate toilet facilities while undergoing sex-change surgery.

In New York City, kids who don't speak a word of Spanish have been placed in bilingual classes to learn their three Rs in Spanish, solely because their own names sound Hispanic.

At the University of Pennsylvania, in a state where thousands died at Gettysburg opposing slavery, the president of that college officially set up segregated dormitory space for black students. Yeah, I know: that's out of bounds now. Dr King said 'negroes'. Jimmy Baldwin[7] and most of us on the

[3] The Second Amendment to the US Constitution, ratified on 15 December 1791, states: 'A well regulated militia being necessary to the security of a free State, the right of the People to keep and bear arms shall not be infringed.' It is a much-debated element of US legislation.

[4] Heston refers to the novel *Nineteen Eighty-Four* (1949) by the English writer George Orwell (1903–50), in which individual freedoms are brutally curtailed by a totalitarian state.

[5] The US drifter Timothy McVeigh (1968–2001) was convicted of perpetrating the Oklahoma City bombing of 1995, in which 167 people were killed and hundreds injured. He was executed in June 2001.

[6] The College of William and Mary, a university at Williamsburg, Virginia, established in 1693.

[7] The African–American novelist James Baldwin (1924–87) was active in the civil rights movement.

march said 'black'. But it's a no-no now …

Finally, just last month, David Howard, head of the Washington, DC Office of Public Advocate, used the word 'niggardly' while talking about budgetary matters with some colleagues. Of course, 'niggardly' means stingy or scanty. But within days, Howard was forced to publicly apologize and then resign.

As columnist Tony Snow[8] wrote: 'David Howard got fired because some people in public employ were morons who (a) didn't know the meaning of niggardly, (b) don't know how to use a dictionary to discover the meaning, and (c) actually demanded that he apologize for their ignorance.'

Now, what does all of this mean? It means that telling us what to think has evolved into telling us what to say, so telling us what to do can't be far behind. Before you claim to be a champion of free thought, tell me: why did political correctness originate on America's campuses? And why do you continue to tolerate it? Why do you, who're supposed to debate ideas, surrender to their suppression?

Let's be honest. Who here in this room thinks your professors can say what they really believe? (Uh-huh. There's a few …) Well, it scares me to death, and it should scare you too, that the superstition of political correctness rules the halls of reason.

You are the best and the brightest. You, here in this fertile cradle of American academia, here in the castle of learning on the Charles River, you are the cream. But I submit that you, and your counterparts across the land, are the most socially conformed and politically silenced generation since Concord Bridge.[9] And as long as you validate that and abide it, you are – by your grandfathers' standards – cowards.

Here's another example. Right now at more than one major university, Second Amendment scholars and researchers are being told to shut up about their findings or they'll lose their jobs. Why? Because their research findings would undermine big-city mayors' pending lawsuits that seek to extort hundreds of millions of dollars from firearm manufacturers.

Now, I don't care what you think about guns. But if you are not shocked at that, I am shocked at you. Who will guard the raw material of unfettered ideas, if not you? Democracy is dialogue. Who will defend the core values of academia, if you, the supposed soldiers of free thought and expression, lay down your arms and plead, 'Don't shoot me'?

If you talk about race, it does not make you a racist. If you see distinctions between the genders, it does not make you sexist. If you think critically about a denomination, it does not make you anti-religion. If you accept but don't celebrate homosexuality, it does not make you a homophobe.

Don't let America's universities continue to serve as incubators for this rampant epidemic of new McCarthyism.[10] That's what it is: new McCarthyism. But, what can you do? How can anyone prevail against such pervasive social subjugation?

Well, the answer's been here all along. I learned it 36 years ago, on the steps of the Lincoln Memorial in Washington, DC, standing with Dr Martin Luther King and 200,000 people.

You simply disobey. Peaceably, yes. Respectfully, of course. Non-violently, absolutely. But when told how to think or what to say or how to behave, we don't. We disobey social protocol that stifles and stigmatizes personal freedom.

I learned the awesome power of disobedience from Dr King, who learned it from GANDHI and Thoreau[11] and JESUS and every other great man

[8] The US journalist and broadcaster Tony Snow (1955–2008) was a nationally syndicated columnist for the *Detroit News*, 1993–2001 and *USA Today*, 1994–2000. He served as White House Press Secretary, 2006–2007.

[9] Site of the first battle of the American War of Independence, 19 April 1775.

[10] The US Senator Joseph McCarthy (1909–57) led a notorious purge of Communism in US public affairs, 1953–4. His zealous pursuit of political dissenters has often been described as a witch-hunt.

[11] The US philosopher and writer Henry David Thoreau (1817–62) was jailed for a single night in July 1846, having refused to pay poll tax for six years on the grounds that it was being used to fund the Mexican–American War of 1846–8.

[12] At the Boston Tea Party of 1773, American patriots sabotaged a British attempt to sell cheap Indian tea in America (undercutting American merchants) by dumping three shiploads of tea into Boston harbour.
[13] Until the mid-1950s, black Americans were required by law to confine themselves to the rear portion of buses. This law was declared unconstitutional in 1954, but southern states continued to enforce it.

who led those in the right against those with the might. Disobedience is in our DNA. We feel innate kinship with that disobedient spirit that tossed tea into Boston harbour,[12] that sent Thoreau to jail, that refused to sit in the back of the bus,[13] that protested a war in Vietnam.

In that same spirit, I'm asking you to disavow cultural correctness with massive disobedience of rogue authority, social directives, and onerous laws that weaken personal freedom.

But be careful. It hurts. Disobedience demands that you put yourself at risk. Dr King stood on lots of balconies. You must be willing to be humiliated – to endure the modern-day equivalent of the police dogs at Montgomery[14] and the water cannons at Selma.[15] You must be willing to experience discomfort. Now, I'm not complaining, but my own decades of social activism have left their mark on me. Let me tell you a story.

A few years ago, I heard about a rapper named Ice-T who was selling a CD called 'Cop Killer', celebrating ambushing and murdering police officers. It was being marketed by none other than Time/Warner, the biggest entertainment conglomerate in the country – in the world. Police across the country were outraged. Rightfully so – at least one of them had been murdered.

But Time/Warner was stonewalling because the CD was a cash cow for them, and the media were tiptoeing around because the rapper was black. I heard Time/Warner had a stockholders' meeting scheduled in Beverly Hills. I owned some shares at the time, so I decided to attend the meeting.

What I did was against the advice of my family and my colleagues. I asked for the floor. To a hushed room of a thousand average American stockholders, I simply read the full lyrics of 'Cop Killer' – every vicious, vulgar, instructional word:

'I got my twelve-gauge sawed-off. I got my headlights turned off. I'm about to bust some shots off. I'm about to dust some cops off.'

It got worse, a lot worse. Now, I won't read the rest of it to you. But trust me, the room was a sea of shocked, frozen, blanched faces. The Time/Warner executives squirmed in their chairs and stared at their shoes. They hated me for that. Then I delivered another volley of sick lyrics, brimming with racist filth, where Ice-T fantasizes about sodomizing the two 12-year-old nieces of Al and Tipper Gore[16]: 'She pushed her butt against my – '

No. No, I won't do to you here what I did to them. Let's just say I left the room in stunned silence. When I read the lyrics to the waiting press corps outside, one of them said, 'We can't print that, you know.'

'I know,' I replied, 'but Time/Warner is still selling it.'

Two months later, Time/Warner terminated Ice-T's contract. I'll never be offered another film by Warner Brothers, or get a good review from *Time* magazine. But disobedience means you must be willing to act, not just talk.

When a mugger sues his elderly victim for defending herself, jam the switchboard of the district attorney's office. When your university is pressured – your university – is pressured to lower standards until 80 per cent of the students graduate with honours, choke the halls of the Board of Regents. When an eight-year-old boy pecks a girl's cheek on the playground and then gets hauled into court for sexual harassment, march on that school and block its doorways. When someone you elected is seduced by political power and betrays you, petition them, oust them, banish them. When *Time* magazine's cover portrays millennium nuts[17] as deranged, crazy Christians holding a cross, as it did last month, boycott their magazine and the products it advertises.

[14] In May 1963, Martin Luther King led non-violent marches in Montgomery, Alabama. The Commissioner of Public Safety, Eugene 'Bull' Connor (1897–1973), turned fire-hoses and police dogs on black demonstrators.
[15] In March 1965, black demonstrators marched from Selma, Alabama to Montgomery to campaign for voting rights. Fifty were hospitalized after police used water-cannons, tear-gas, whips and clubs against them.

[16] The US businessman and politician Al Gore, Jr (1948–) and his wife Mary Elizabeth 'Tipper' Gore (1948–) had campaigned against 'alarming trends' in popular music. In 1985, Tipper Gore co-founded the Parents' Music Resource Center, which campaigned successfully for labelling music with 'explicit lyrics or content'.

[17] In 1999, the fear that the millennium would bring widespread computer failure, combined, in some cases, with unorthodox biblical interpretation, encouraged some fringe groups to expect an apocalyptic event.

So that this nation may long endure, I urge you to follow in the hallowed footsteps of the great disobediences of history that freed exiles, founded religions, defeated tyrants, and yes, in the hands of an aroused rabble in arms and a few great men, by God's grace, built this country.

If Dr King were here, I think he would agree.

I thank you.

Heinrich Himmler
German politician and chief of police

Heinrich Luitpold Himmler (1900–45) was born in Munich, the son of a Catholic schoolmaster, and was educated at the Landshut High School. He took a diploma in agriculture at the Munich Technical College in 1919, and became a member of several right-wing organizations, joining the Nazi Party in 1925. In 1929 ADOLF HITLER made him head of the SS (*Schutzstaffel*, 'protective force'), which he developed from Hitler's personal bodyguard into a powerful party weapon. With Reinhard Heydrich (1904–42), he used it to carry out the assassination of Ernst Röhm (1934) and other Nazis opposed to Hitler. Inside Germany and later in Nazi-occupied countries, he developed the Gestapo (*Geheime Staatspolizei*, 'secret state police'). He used this ruthless organization to unleash an unmatched political and anti-Semitic terror of espionage, wholesale detention, mass deportation, torture, execution and massacre. The systematic liquidation of whole national and racial groups, over which he presided, led to the coining of the term 'genocide'. In 1943, following defeats on the Eastern Front, Himmler was given the post of Minister of the Interior, with a remit to curb defeatism. After the attempt on Hitler's life by a group of army officers in July 1944, he was made commander-in-chief of the home forces. In April 1945, he proposed an unconditional surrender to the Allies, with whom he hoped to lead Germany against Russia. Hitler immediately stripped him of power and issued orders for his arrest. Himmler disappeared but was captured by the British near Bremen. He committed suicide at Lüneburg by swallowing a cyanide phial concealed in his mouth, and thereby escaped trial for his central role in the murder of over seven million people.

'I am talking about ... the extermination of the Jewish people'
4 October 1943, Posen (Poznan), Poland

This chilling speech illuminates the steady development of the Nazi genocide project. The official persecution of German Jews – and the establishment of concentration camps to house 'enemies of the state' – began soon after Hitler's appointment as Chancellor in 1933. The Nazi Party itself was purged in 1934, and the Nuremberg Laws of September 1935 denied German citizenship to Jews and other 'non-Aryans'. On *Kristallnacht* ('night of crystals') in November 1938, Jewish businesses were ransacked, looted and burned. Concentration camps became extermination centres following the Wannsee Conference in January 1942, at which Nazi leaders discussed the destruction of all European Jews – the 'Final Solution to the Jewish Question'.

However, the enormity of this plan was daunting, practically as well as morally. In a three-hour speech to SS officers in Nazi-occupied Poland, Himmler demanded the suppression of squeamishness and mercy. He also emphasized the need for discipline and secrecy, thus implicating his deputies in the crime of the Holocaust. Yet despite the clandestine circumstances, he had the meeting tape-recorded, even interrupting his speech to ensure the recorder was working. The tapes later fell into the hands of the US military and were preserved as evidence of Nazi war crimes. This is a short extract from the transcript.

I want to mention a very difficult subject before you, with complete candour. It should be discussed amongst us, yet nevertheless, we will never speak about it in public. Just as we did not hesitate in June[1] to carry out our duty as ordered, and stand comrades who had failed against the wall and shoot them – about which we have never spoken, and never will speak. That was, thank God, a kind of tact natural to us, a foregone conclusion of that tact, that we have never conversed about it amongst ourselves, never spoken about it. Everyone shuddered, and everyone was clear that the next time he would do the same thing again, if it were commanded and necessary.

I am talking about the evacuation of the Jews, the extermination of the Jewish people. It is one of those things that is easily said. 'The Jewish people is being exterminated,' every party member will tell you. 'Perfectly clear: it's part of our plans. We're eliminating the Jews, exterminating them, a small matter.'

And then along they all come, all the 80 million upright Germans, and

[1] In the SS purge of 30 June–1 July 1934, known as 'The Night of the Long Knives', over 70 leading Nazis were murdered.

each one has his decent Jew. They say: 'All the others are swine, but here is a first-class Jew.' [*Some laughter.*] And none of them has seen it, has endured it. Most of you will know what it means when 100 bodies lie together, when 500 are there or when there are 1,000. And to have seen this through and – with the exception of human weakness – to have remained decent, has made us hard and is a page of glory never mentioned and never to be mentioned.

Because we know how difficult things would be if today – in every city, during the bomb attacks, the burdens of war and the privations – we still had Jews as secret saboteurs, agitators and instigators. We would probably be at the same stage as in 1916/17, if the Jews still resided in the body of the German people.

We have taken away the riches that they had, and I have given a strict order, which Obergruppenführer Pohl[2] has carried out. We have delivered these riches to the Reich, to the State. We have taken nothing from them for ourselves. A few, who have offended against this, will be [judged][3] in accordance with an order that I gave at the beginning: he who takes even one mark of this is a dead man.

A number of SS men have offended against this order. They are very few, and they will be dead men *without mercy*! We have the moral right, we had the duty to our people to do it, to kill this people who would kill us. We, however, do not have the right to enrich ourselves with even one fur, with one mark, with one cigarette, with one watch, with anything that we do not have. Because we don't want, at the end of all this, to get sick and die from the same bacillus that we have exterminated. I will never see it happen that even one bit of putrefaction comes in contact with us, or takes root in us. On the contrary, where it might try to take root, we will burn it out together. But altogether we can say: we have carried out this most difficult task for the love of our people. And we have suffered no defect within us, in our soul, or in our character.

[2] The German naval officer Oswald Pohl (1892–1951) was an SS leader and a key player in the Holocaust. He survived the war and was eventually hanged for war crimes. During his trial testimony he claimed this was the first time he had been told officially that the 'Final Solution' meant the extermination of the Jews.

[3] The word was not spoken but implied.

Adolf Hitler
German dictator

Adolf Hitler (1889–1945) was born in Braunau, Upper Austria, the son of a minor customs official. He failed his school-leaving examinations, but went to Bavaria, attending art school in Munich. He moved to Vienna (1904–13), where he lived by selling sketches and doing odd jobs. During this time he developed his right-wing, anti-Semitic views. In 1913 he returned to Munich, where he volunteered for war service in 1914, rising to the rank of corporal. In 1918 he was wounded. In 1919, he worked as a spy, investigating fringe political groups. He joined one of them, and in 1920 changed its name to *Nationalsozialistische Deutsche Arbeiterpartei* ('National Socialist German Workers' Party') – later contracted to *Nazi*. In 1923, the Nazis attempted a coup in Munich; but the police machine-gunned them, and Hitler narrowly escaped serious injury. In jail, he wrote *Mein Kampf* (1925, 'My Struggle'). He failed to win the presidential election of 1932, but was appointed Chancellor in January 1933. He quickly silenced all opposition, and forced a general election. The Nazis achieved a bare majority, and Hitler assumed power. In the purge of June 1934, he ruthlessly crushed dissent within the Nazi Party. He then pursued 'Nazification' of all aspects of German life, enforced by the *Gestapo* ('secret state police') and the establishment of concentration camps. He openly rearmed, established the Rome–Berlin 'axis' with BENITO MUSSOLINI, invaded Austria (1938), and absorbed parts of Czechoslovakia (1939). Hitler then demanded from Poland the return of Danzig, and Poland's refusal, backed by Britain and France, precipitated World War II. Germany conquered much of northern and central Europe in 1939–40, but its air force was heavily defeated in the Battle of Britain (1940). Hitler attacked Romania, Yugoslavia and Greece (1940–1), then Russia. As an ally of Japan, he was soon at war with the USA (1941). In North Africa, the tide turned: BERNARD MONTGOMERY's victory at El Alamein (1942) forced Nazi withdrawal. Devastating defeat at Stalingrad (1942) was followed by the Allied invasion of Sicily, Italian capitulation (1943) and further Russian victories (1943–4), then the Allied invasion of Normandy. Using newly developed V1 and V2 missiles, Hitler attacked England, but it was too late. In July 1944 he narrowly survived an assassination attempt. The invasion of Germany followed. Hitler retreated to his Berlin bunker, where he married his mistress, Eva Braun. The evidence suggests they committed suicide.

'This art shall be of eternal value'
18 July 1937, Munich, Germany

After gaining control of Germany, Hitler set about reforming society according to Nazi principles. After years as a struggling artist, he considered himself well qualified as a judge of art, and decided to bring it under state control. He disliked current trends in international art, which rejected the past as a model for the future, producing more unsettling and experimental work. This he labelled 'degenerate art'. In 1937, his government purged German museums of 15,550 works of modern art.

He had personally commissioned the *Haus der Deutschen Kunst* ('House of German Art') in Munich, designed in Nazi neo-classical style by Paul Ludwig Troost. The gallery was completed in 1937, and inaugurated with the *Gross Deutsche Kunstausstelling* ('Great Exhibition of German Art'). The show comprised paintings and sculptures in reassuringly representational styles, celebrating the Nazi Party and the traditional German values embraced by Hitler: *Kinder, Küche, Kirche* ('children, kitchen, church').

Attending the opening ceremony, Hitler gave this speech, in which he dwells on the association between great art and great civilizations, implying that the same association would take effect under his own Third Reich. All too familiar with the bitter disappointments of artistic failure, he also expresses the hope that German artists taking part in the exhibition might come to be numbered with great artists of the past. In the speech, translated by Ilse Falk, he also launches a further attack on 'degenerate art', suggesting that those who produced it must be suffering from eye defects.

> When, four years ago, the solemn ceremony of laying the cornerstone for this building took place, we were all conscious of the fact that not only the stone for a new building must be laid, but the foundation for a new and true German art. At stake was our chance to provoke a turning-point in the development of the total German cultural output …
>
> Germany's collapse and general decline had been – as we know – not only economic or political, but probably even to a much greater extent,

cultural … [but] the cultural collapse was neither seen nor understood by the vast majority of our people …

Art, on the one hand, was defined as nothing but an international communal experience, thus killing altogether any understanding of its integral relationship with an ethnic group. On the other hand, its relationship to time was stressed, that is: there was no longer any art of peoples or even of races, but only an art of the times. According to this theory, therefore, Greek art was not formed by the Greeks, but by a certain period which formed it as their expression. The same, naturally, was true of Roman art, which, for the same reasons, coincided only by accident with the rise of the Roman Empire.

Again, in the same way, the more recent art epochs of humanity have not been created by the Arabs, Germans, Italians, French, etc, but are only appearances conditioned by time. Therefore today no German or French or Japanese or Chinese art exists, but plainly and simply only a 'modern art'. Consequently, art as such is not only completely isolated from its ethnic origins, but it is the expression of a certain vintage which is characterized today by the word 'modern' and thus, of course, will be un-modern tomorrow …

And to be sure, following the maxim: every year something new. One day Impressionism, then Futurism, Cubism, maybe even Dadaism,[1] etc. A further result is that even for the most insane and inane monstrosities, thousands of catchwords to label them will have to be found, and have indeed been found. If it weren't so sad in one sense, it would almost be a lot of fun to list all the slogans and clichés with which the so-called 'art initiates' have described and explained their wretched products in recent years …

National-Socialist Germany, however, wants again a German Art – and this art shall be of eternal value, as are all truly creative values of a people. Should this art, however, again lack this eternal value for our people, then indeed it will mean that it also has no higher value today.

When, therefore, the cornerstone of this building was laid, it was with the intention of constructing a temple, not for a so-called modern art, but for a true and everlasting German art – that is, better still, a House for the art of the German people, and not for any international art of the year 1937, '40, '50, '60. For art is not founded on time, but only on peoples …

From the history of the development of our people, we know that it is composed of a number of more or less differentiated races, which in the course of millennia, thanks to the overwhelming formative influence of one outstanding racial core, resulted in that particular mixture which we see in our people today. This power, once capable of forming a people, and thus still today an active one, is contained here again in the same Aryan[2] race which we recognize not only as the carrier of our own culture, but as that of the preceding cultures of antiquity as well …

The question has often been asked: What does it really mean to be German? Among all those definitions which through the centuries have been suggested by many men, the most valuable one for me seems to be that one which from the start does not even try to give an explanation, but which rather sets up a law. And the most beautiful law which I can envisage for my people as the task set for its life in this world, a great German has already long ago put into words: 'To be German is to be clear.' This, moreover, implies that to be German means to be logical and also, above all, to be true …

When on that fateful 6 June in 1931 the old Glaspalast[3] burnt down in

[1] Art movements of the late 19th and early 20th century.

[2] In the 19th century, some academics posited the existence of a distinct 'proto-Indo-European' master race, which had sprung from Nordic origins. The Nazi scholar Alfred Rosenberg (1893–1946) was a key proponent of the Aryan–Nordic theory, which was used to bolster Nazi anti-Semitism.

[3] The House of German Art was a replacement for the Glaspalast, built in 1853–4.

that horrible fire, an immortal treasure of such true German art went up in flames. They were called the Romantics, but in essence they were the most glorious representatives of those noble Germans in search of the true intrinsic virtue of our people and the honest and respectable expression of those only inwardly experienced laws of life …

Art can in no way be a fashion. As little as the character and the blood of our people will change, so much will art have to lose its mortal character and replace it with worthy images expressing the life-course of our people in the steadily unfolding growth of its creations. Cubism, Dadaism, Futurism, Impressionism, etc, have nothing to do with our German people.

For these concepts are neither old nor modern, but are only the artifactitious stammerings of men to whom God has denied the grace of a truly artistic talent, and in its place has awarded them the gift of jabbering or deception. I will therefore confess now, in this very hour, that I have come to the final inalterable decision to clean the house, just as I have done in the domain of political confusion, and from now on rid the German art life of its phrase-mongering.

'Works of art' which cannot be understood in themselves but, for the justification of their existence, need those bombastic instructions for their use, finally reaching that intimidated soul, who is patiently willing to accept such stupid or impertinent nonsense – these works of art from now on will no longer find their way to the German people … Whether or not anybody has a strong will or an inner experience, he will have to prove through his work, and not through gibberish …

I have observed, among the pictures submitted here, quite a few paintings which make one actually come to the conclusion that the eye shows things differently to certain human beings than the way they really are – that is, that there really are men who see the present population of our nation only as rotten cretins; who, on principle, see meadows blue, skies green, clouds sulphur yellow, and so on – or, as they say, experience them as such.

I do not want to enter into an argument here about the question of whether the persons concerned really do or do not see or feel in such a way; but, in the name of the German people, I want to forbid these pitiful misfortunates who quite obviously suffer from an eye disease, to try vehemently to foist these products of their misinterpretation upon the age we live in, or even to wish to present them as 'Art'.

No, here there are only two possibilities. Either these so-called 'artists' really see things this way and therefore believe in what they depict; then we would have to examine their eyesight-deformation to see if it is the product of a mechanical failure or of inheritance. In the first case, these unfortunates can only be pitied; in the second case, they would be the object of great interest to the Ministry of Interior of the Reich, which would then have to take up the question of whether further inheritance of such gruesome malfunctioning of the eyes cannot at least be checked.

If, on the other hand, they themselves do not believe in the reality of such impressions but try to harass the nation with this humbug for other reasons, then such an attempt falls within the jurisdiction of the penal law. This House, in any case, has neither been planned, nor was it built for the works of this kind of incompetent or art criminal …

But far more important is the fact that the labour performed here on this spot for four and a half years, the maximum achievements demanded here of thousands of workers, were not intended to serve the purpose of exhibiting the production of men who, to top it off, were lazy enough to dirty a canvas with colour droppings in the firm hope that, through the daring advertisement of their products as the lightning birth of genius, they could not fail to produce the needed impression and qualifications for their acceptance.

No, I say. The diligence of the builder of this House and the diligence of his collaborators must be equalled by the diligence of those who want to be represented in this House. Beyond this, I am not the least bit interested in whether or not these 'also-rans' of the art world will cackle among themselves about the eggs they have laid, thereby giving to each other their expert opinion.

For the artist does not create for the artist, but just like everyone else he creates for the people. And we will see to it that from now on the people will once again be called upon to be the judges of their own art …

National Socialism has made it its primary task to rid the German Reich, and thus the German people and its life, of all those influences which are fatal and ruinous to its existence. And although this purge cannot be accomplished in one day, I do not want to leave the shadow of a doubt as to the fact that sooner or later the hour of liquidation will strike for those phenomena which have participated in this corruption.

But with the opening of this exhibition, the end of German art foolishness and the end of the destruction of its culture will have begun. From now on we will wage an unrelenting war of purification against the last elements of putrefaction in our culture … From now on – I assure you – all those cliques of babblers, dilettantes and art crooks which lend support to each other and are therefore able to survive, will be eliminated and abolished. For our sake those prehistoric stone-age culture-vultures and art stammerers may just as well retreat to the caves of their ancestors to adorn them with their primitive international scribblings.

But the House for German Art in Munich has been built by the German people for their own German art. To my great pleasure, I am able to state that now already, besides the many decent older artists … a number of new youthful masters are presenting themselves. A walk through this exhibition will allow you to find quite a few things that will impress you as beautiful and, above all, as decent, and which you will sense to be good. Particularly the level of the graphic art submitted was on the average from the very beginning extremely high and thus satisfying.

Many of our young artists will now recognize in what is being offered them which road they should take … And when once again in this realm of art the holy conscientiousness will have regained its full rights, then, I have no doubt, the Almighty will elevate a few from this multitude of decent creators of art into the starry skies of the immortal, divinely inspired artists of the great past …

I can therefore express no other wish at this moment than that the new house be privileged to reveal again to the German people a large number of works by great artists in these halls during the coming centuries, and thus contribute not only to the glory of this true city of art, but also to the honour and prestige of the entire German nation.

I herewith declare the Great Exhibition of German Art 1937 in Munich opened!

'The German people in its whole character is not warlike'
20 February 1938, Berlin, Germany

❧

When Hitler gave this speech at the Reichstag, he had been Chancellor for just over five years. His political power was unassailable, but war had become virtually inevitable. He therefore set out to prepare the German people for the struggles ahead. His speech seeks to convince them of German nobility ('not warlike, but rather soldierly') and to alert them to the belligerence and moral inferiority of Russian Bolshevism ('the incarnation of the human destructive instinct') which he explicitly links to Judaism.

The speech, translated here by Norman H Baynes, is structured as an overview of Germany's foreign relations. At this time, Hitler still hoped for alliances with Britain and France, and he downplays possible causes of conflict with those countries. He is more fulsome, however, when discussing the other Axis powers, Italy and Japan – with which he had signed the Anti-Comintern Pact in November 1936 – 'those two great powers who have recognized a world danger in Bolshevism'.

The position of Austria was less secure. Not long before giving the speech, Hitler had ordered the Austrian Chancellor, Kurt Schuschnigg, to appoint a Nazi sympathizer to his government and to release imprisoned Austrian Nazis. Less than a month later, on 12 March, he launched the *Anschluss* ('connection'), effectively an invasion, which declared Austria part of 'Greater Germany'. But it would be more than a year before he annexed Poland, plunging the world into war.

Hitler's talent for demagoguery becomes ever more evident as he draws the speech to its climax, concluding with a fervently patriotic prayer.

❧

As its elected leader, I should like to assure the German people today that however much peace means to us, we are equally resolved to defend our honour and the inalienable rights of our people. Though I stand for the cause of peace, I shall always see to it that the instrument which I am convinced is the only sure and effective guarantee of peace in such troubled times is never weakened, much less taken away from the German people.

And though I can assure the world of the German people's sincere and profound love of peace, I must assert, beyond all doubt, that this love of peace has nothing to do with feeble renunciation or with cowardice and dishonour. If ever an international campaign of hatred and defamation seeks to wreck the peace of our Reich, steel and iron will protect the German people and the German homeland.

And then, as quick as lightning, the world would see to what extent this Reich, people, party and armed forces are imbued with the same fervid spirit and will ...

We are of the opinion that Germany has made many valuable contributions to co-operation with other powers. The Reich today cannot be considered isolated, either politically or economically. I have on the contrary endeavoured since taking office to establish the best possible relations with most of the other states of the world. There is only one state with which we have not sought to establish relations, nor do we wish to enter into closer relations with it: Soviet Russia. More than ever do we see in Bolshevism the incarnation of the human destructive instinct.

But we do not make the Russian people as such responsible for this ghastly ideology of annihilation. We know perfectly well that a small upper class of Jewish intellectuals plunged a great nation into a state bordering on insanity. This would not concern us so much after all, had this doctrine remained within the frontiers of Russia herself, since Germany has no intention of foisting our conceptions of life on the Russian nation. Unfortunately, however, the Bolshevism of international Jewry attempts from its central point in Soviet Russia to rot away the very core of the nations of the world, to overthrow the existing social order, and to substitute chaos for civilization …

Great Britain has repeatedly assured us, through the mouths of her responsible statesmen, of her desire to maintain the status quo in the world. This should apply here, too. Whenever a European country falls prey to Bolshevism, a shifting of positions becomes apparent. For the territories thus Bolshevized are no longer sovereign states with independent, national lives of their own, but are now mere sections of the Moscow Revolutionary Centre. I am aware that Mr EDEN[1] does not share this view. Mr STALIN does, however, and is perfectly frank about it. In my opinion Mr Stalin is still at the moment of speaking a much better judge and interpreter of Bolshevist views and aims than a British cabinet minister! Therefore we look upon every attempt to spread Bolshevism, no matter where it may be, with utter loathing, and where it menaces us, we shall oppose it.

This explains our relations with Japan. I cannot agree with those politicians who think they do Europe a service in harming Japan. I am afraid the defeat of Japan in eastern Asia would never benefit Europe or America but only Bolshevist Soviet Russia. I do not consider China strong enough, either spiritually or materially, to withstand from her own resources any attack by Bolshevism. I believe, however, that even the greatest victory gained by Japan would be infinitely less dangerous for civilization and world peace than any success achieved by Bolshevism. Germany has concluded a pact with Japan to counteract Comintern aims …

Italo-German relations are based on conceptions of life and of the state common to both nations, as well as on co-operative action in warding off the international dangers that menace us both. How greatly this fact is appreciated everywhere in Germany was most strikingly evidenced in the joyous enthusiasm with which the creator of the fascist state was welcomed in the Reich. One fact at least ought to be acknowledged by all European statesmen. If MUSSOLINI had not conquered Italy in 1922 with the help of his fascist movement, the country would in all probability have fallen a prey to Bolshevism.

The dire consequence to western culture in the event of such a collapse would be inconceivable. The very thought of such a possibility is horrifying to a man of historical vision and sense of responsibility based on a knowledge of the facts …

Italy's position resembles that of Germany in certain respects. Under the circumstances, therefore, it was but natural that – suffering as we both do from overcrowding – we should show a keen understanding of the activities of a man and his government who, refusing to allow their people to be sacrificed on the altar of the fantastic ideals of the League of Nations,[2] were rather fully determined to save their nation. And all the more so, since there is no doubt that the apparent ideals of the League of Nations coincide rather too closely with the exceedingly realistic interests of its chief powers.

Furthermore, Germany and Italy have taken a common stand with regard to the Spanish conflict. Its aim is to see a national Spain which enjoys complete independence. The Italo-German friendship, springing as it does from definite causes, has become an element of stabilization in the appeasement of Europe. The connection of both states with Japan presents the most powerful of all obstructions to the further advance of the menacing power of Russian Bolshevism.

There has been much talk and still more writing in recent years about the differences between France and England on the one hand, and Germany

[1] Anthony Eden became British Foreign Secretary in 1935. He supported non-intervention in the Spanish Civil War of 1936 and the efforts of Prime Minister NEVILLE CHAMBERLAIN to appease Hitler, but resigned around the time of this speech over Chamberlain's negotiations with Fascist Italy.

[2] The League of Nations was established in 1920 to promote international co-operation and prevent wars. It ceased to operate during World War II, and officially dissolved itself in 1946 at a meeting of its successor organization, the United Nations.

on the other. I do not quite see wherein these differences are supposed to be embodied. Germany has no further territory in Europe to claim from France, a point I have frequently stressed … Nor has Germany any quarrel with England unless perhaps it may be our wish for colonies.

There is, however, not a single reason for any kind of possible conflict. But what does poison friendly relations between the two countries, and consequently causes trouble, is an absolutely intolerable press campaign which is being conducted in France and England under the slogan of 'Liberty for expression of personal opinions'. I have little use for the reiterated sentiments of foreign statesmen and diplomats who declare that there is no law in these countries to put an end to lies and calumnies … This is a grave menace indeed, and one that endangers peace. For this very reason I refuse to tolerate any longer the unbridled and persistent scoffing and slandering to which our country and people are subjected. We shall answer these calumnies in future and with real National Socialist thoroughness …

I am happy to be able to tell you, gentlemen, that during the past few days a further understanding has been reached with a country that is particularly close to us for many reasons. The Reich and German Austria are bound together not only because they are the same people, but also because they share a long and common history, and a common culture.

The difficulties which had been experienced in carrying out the agreement of 11 July[3] compelled us to make an attempt to clear out of the way misunderstandings and hindrances to a final conciliation … I am glad to be able to assure you that these considerations corresponded with the views of the Austrian Chancellor, whom I invited to come to visit me … I want to express in this connection before the German people my sincere thanks to the Austrian Chancellor for his great understanding and the warm-hearted willingness with which he accepted my invitation and worked with me so that we might discover a way of serving the best interests of the two countries, for after all, it is the interest of the whole German people, whose sons we all are, wherever we may have been born …

I can assure you, gentlemen, that our relations with the other European powers, as well as with the states outside Europe, are either normal or else very friendly. I need only point to our especially warm friendship with Hungary, Bulgaria, Yugoslavia, and many other states. Our foreign trade balance has given you an impressive picture of our economic co-operation with the other peoples!

But above all stands our co-operation with those two great powers who have recognized a world danger in Bolshevism, just as Germany has, and are determined to unite their strength in common defence against the Comintern movement. That this work of co-operation with Italy and Japan may ever become closer is my sincere desire. In addition, we are happy for every relief of tension that can be effected in the general political situation. For however great may be the achievement of our people we are not in doubt that general prosperity would be increased if a closer international co-operation could be secured.

The German people in its whole character is not warlike, but rather soldierly – that is, while they do not want war, they are not frightened by the thoughts of it. They love peace, but they love honour and their freedom just as much. Fifteen terrible years lie behind us as a warning and a lesson, which, I believe, the German nation will always remember and never forget.

[3] The Austro-German Treaty of 11 July 1936 committed Hitler to respecting Austria's independence, and Schuschnigg to a foreign policy that treated Austria as a German state. Schuschnigg was deposed and imprisoned after the *Aschluss*.

Gentlemen: you have authorized me to act by adopting the laws giving me full power. I have laid before you an account covering five historic years in the life of the German people. I cannot close without assuring you how great is my faith in the future of our people and the Reich, that we all so warmly love. My motive as an unknown soldier in taking up the struggle for the regeneration of Germany had as its deepest ground my belief in the German people: not belief in her public institutions, her social order and social classes, her parties, her state and political power, but belief in the eternal values inherent in our people.

And above all there is my belief in the millions of individual German men and women, who, just as I was once myself, are nameless servers of our community and our people. It is for them that I endeavoured to build up this new Reich ...

This new Reich shall belong to no class, it shall belong to no group of men, for it shall belong to the whole German people. This Reich will endeavour to make it easier for the German people to find its path of life on this earth; it will seek to fashion for it a fairer existence. What I have called into life in these years cannot claim to be an end in itself – all can and will be transient.

For us the permanent element is that substance of flesh and blood which we call the German people. Party, state, army, economic organization – these are but institutions and functions which have only the value of a means to an end. They will be weighed in the balance by the judgement of history, according to the measure in which they have served that end, and that end is again and always the people.

In this hour I would ask of the Lord God only this: that, as in the past, so in the years to come he would give his blessing to our work and our action, to our judgement and our resolution, that he will safeguard us from all false pride and from all cowardly servility, that he may grant to us to find the straight path which his providence has ordained for the German people, and that he may ever give us the courage to do the right, never to falter, never to yield before any violence, before any danger.

❧

'The most memorable struggle in all German history'
4 May 1941, Berlin, Germany
❧

Following the Luftwaffe's defeat in the Battle of Britain, Hitler was forced to reconsider his strategy. During the first year of the war, much of central Europe had succumbed to the German onslaught and British forces had been driven from France. But Hitler's plan to invade the UK, Operation Sealion, had been thwarted, and he responded by launching a *Blitzkrieg* ('lightning war') of bombing raids against British cities. WINSTON CHURCHILL professed himself outraged by this development, but retaliated by sending British bombers to attack German cities.

In September 1940, US president FRANKLIN D ROOSEVELT finally responded to Churchill's pleas for help and supplied 50 destroyers. In March 1941, the USA began supplying other war materials to Britain under the Lend–Lease scheme.

Aiming to deter American involvement in Europe, Hitler decided to bring forward his invasion of Russia, originally planned for 1943. He also turned his focus to southern Europe. On 26 March 1941, Prince Pavle of Yugoslavia joined the Three-Power Pact with the Axis powers. The following day, a coup deposed Pavle and the deal was renounced. Hitler acted swiftly, invading Yugoslavia on 6 April. Britain sent 60,000 troops to Greece but Yugoslavia was swiftly defeated. Greece fell soon afterwards and British forces were forced to withdraw.

It was against this background that Hitler addressed the Reichstag in early May. His personal antipathy for Churchill (reciprocated with gusto) provides a sharp focus for a speech in which this most aggressive of leaders portrays himself as a frustrated peacemaker with no choice but to strike back.

❧

Hitler – 'The most memorable struggle in all German history'

[1] On 10 May 1940, Germany invaded neutral Holland, launched an airborne attack on Belgium and began its advance on France through the Ardennes forest. By mid-June, all three countries had fallen.

On 10 May last year,[1] perhaps the most memorable struggle in all German history commenced. The enemy front was broken up in a few days and the stage was then set for the operation that culminated in the greatest battle of annihilation in the history of the world. Thus France collapsed, Belgium and Holland were already occupied, and the battered remnants of the British Expeditionary Force were driven from the European continent, leaving their arms behind.[2]

On 19 July 1940, I then convened the German Reichstag for the third time in order to render that great account which you all still remember. The meeting provided me with the opportunity of expressing the thanks of the nation to its soldiers in a form suited to the uniqueness of the event. Once again, I seized the opportunity of urging the world to make peace.[3] And what I foresaw and prophesied at that time happened. My offer of peace was misconstrued as a symptom of fear and cowardice.

The European and American warmongers succeeded once again in befogging the sound common sense of the masses, who can never hope to profit from this war, by conjuring up false pictures of new hope. Thus, finally, under pressure of public opinion, as formed by their press, they once more managed to induce the nation to continue this struggle.

Even my warnings against night bombings of the civilian population, as advocated by Mr Churchill, were interpreted as a sign of German impotence. He, the most bloodthirsty or amateurish strategist that history has ever known, actually saw fit to believe that the reserve displayed for months by the Luftwaffe could be looked upon only as proof of their incapacity to fly by night.

So this man for months ordered his paid scribblers to deceive the British people into believing that the Royal Air Force alone – and no others – was in a position to wage war in this way, and that thus ways and means had been found to force the Reich to its knees by the ruthless onslaught of the British air force on the German civilian population, in conjunction with the starvation blockade.[4]

Again and again I uttered these warnings against this specific type of aerial warfare and I did so for over three and a half months. That these warnings failed to impress Mr Churchill does not surprise me in the least. For what does this man care for the lives of others? What does he care for culture or for architecture? When war broke out he stated clearly that he wanted to have his war, even though the cities of England might be reduced to ruins. So now he has got his war.

My assurances that from a given moment every one of his bombs would be returned if necessary a hundredfold failed to induce this man to consider even for an instant the criminal nature of his action. He professes not to be in the least depressed and he even assures us that the British people, too, after such bombing raids, greeted him with a joyous serenity, causing him to return to London refreshed by his visits to the stricken areas.

It is possible that this sight strengthened Mr Churchill in his firm determination to continue the war in this way, and we are no less determined to continue to retaliate, if necessary, a hundred bombs for every one of his and to go on doing so until the British nation at last gets rid of this criminal and his methods.

The appeal to forsake me, made to the German nation by this fool and his satellites on May Day of all days, is only to be explained either as symptomatic of a paralytic disease or of a drunkard's ravings.[5] His abnormal state of mind also gave birth to a decision to transform the Balkans into a

[2] The evacuation of Allied troops from the beaches of Dunkirk, on the north coast of France, in late May and early June 1940.

[3] On 19 July 1940, Hitler made a broadcast containing a 'final offer' of peace, proposing that he would control mainland Europe, but leave the British Empire unmolested. His offer was rejected immediately.

[4] The British naval blockade in the North Sea prompted Hitler's decision to invade Denmark and Norway.

[5] As well as being vegetarian, Hitler did not smoke and rarely drank alcohol. Churchill, by contrast, had a well-known love of cigars and whisky.

theatre of war.

For over five years, this man has been chasing around Europe like a madman in search of something that he could set on fire. Unfortunately, he again and again finds hirelings who open the gates of their country to this international incendiary. After he had succeeded, in the course of the past winter, in persuading the British people by a wave of false assertions and pretensions that the German Reich, exhausted by the campaign in the preceding months, was completely spent, he saw himself obliged, in order to prevent an awakening of the truth, to create a fresh conflagration in Europe.

In so doing he returned to the project that had been in his mind as early as the autumn of 1939 and the spring of 1940. It was thought possible at the time to mobilize about 100 divisions in Britain's interest. The sudden collapse which we witnessed in May and June of the past year forced these plans to be abandoned for the moment. But by the autumn of last year Mr Churchill began to tackle this problem once again.

The reverses suffered by the Italian army in North Africa, owing to a certain material inferiority of their tanks and anti-tank guns, finally led Mr Churchill to believe that the time was ripe to transfer the theatre of war from Libya to Greece. He ordered the transport of the remaining tanks and of the infantry division, composed mainly of Anzacs,[6] and was convinced that he could now complete his scheme, which was to set the Balkans aflame.

[6] Troops from Australia and New Zealand.

Thus did Mr Churchill commit one of the greatest strategic blunders of this war. As soon as there could be no further doubt regarding Britain's intentions of gaining a foothold in the Balkans, I took the necessary steps. Germany, by keeping pace with these moves, assembled the necessary forces for the purpose of counteracting any possible tricks of that gentleman.

Germany had no intention of starting a war in the Balkans. On the contrary, it was our honest intention as far as possible to contribute to a settlement of the conflict with Greece by means that would be tolerable to the legitimate wishes of Italy. The Duce[7] not only consented to but lent his full support to our efforts to bring Yugoslavia into a close community of interests with our peace aims. Thus it finally became possible to induce the Yugoslav government to join the Three-Power Pact, which made no demands whatever on Yugoslavia but only offered that country advantages.

[7] The Italian word for leader, commonly applied to the dictator BENITO MUSSOLINI; it corresponds to Hitler's title of Führer.

Thus on 26 March of this year a pact was signed in Vienna that offered the Yugoslav state the greatest future conceivable and could have assured peace for the Balkans. Believe me, gentlemen, on that day I left the beautiful city by the Danube[8] truly happy, not only because it seemed as though almost eight years of foreign policies had received their reward but also because I believed that perhaps at the last moment German intervention in the Balkans might not be necessary.

[8] Hitler refers to Belgrade, then capital of Yugoslavia.

We were all stunned by the news of that coup,[9] carried through by a handful of bribed conspirators who had brought about the event that caused the British prime minister to declare in joyous words that at last he had something good to report.

[9] The coup organized by Yugoslav officers led by General Dušan Simović to depose Prince Pavle, thus negating the Three-Power Pact.

You will surely understand, gentlemen, that when I heard this I at once gave orders to attack Yugoslavia. To treat the German Reich in this way is inconceivable. One cannot spend years in concluding a treaty that is in the interest of the other party merely to discover that this treaty has not only been broken overnight but also that it had been answered by insulting the representative of the German Reich, by threatening his military attaché, by injuring the aide de camp of this attaché, by maltreating numerous other Germans, by demolishing property, by laying waste the homes of German citizens and by terrorizing.

God knows that I wanted peace. But I can do nothing but protect the interests of the Reich with those means which, thank God, are at our disposal. I made my decision at that moment all the more calmly because I knew that I was in accord with Bulgaria – who had always remained unshaken in her loyalty to the German Reich – and with the equally justified indignation of Hungary.

The consequences of this campaign are extraordinary. In view of the fact that a small set of conspirators in Belgrade again were able to foment trouble in the service of extra-continental interests, the radical elimination of this danger means the removal of an element of tension for the whole of Europe.

The Danube as an important waterway is thus safeguarded against any further act of sabotage. Traffic has been resumed in full.

Apart from the modest correction of its frontiers, which were infringed as a result of the outcome of the World War, the Reich has no special territorial interests in these parts. As far as politics are concerned we are merely interested in safeguarding peace in this region, while in the realm of economics we wish to see an order that will allow the production of goods to be developed and the exchange of products to be resumed in the interests of all.

It is, however, only in accordance with supreme justice if those interests are also taken into account that are founded upon ethnographical, historical or economic conditions.

I can assure you that I look into the future with perfect tranquillity and great confidence. The German Reich and its allies represent power – military, economic and, above all, in moral respects – which is superior to any possible coalition in the world. The German armed forces will always do their part whenever it may be necessary. The confidence of the German people will always accompany their soldiers.

Ho Chi Minh
Vietnamese statesman

Ho Chi Minh *originally Nguyen That Thanh* (1890–1969) was born in the Annam region of central Vietnam, the son of a mandarin. From 1912 he worked in London and the USA. In 1918, he moved to France, where he became a founder-member of the French Communist Party. From 1922 until 1930 he frequently visited Moscow. He founded the Viet Minh Independence League in 1941, directing successful military operations against the Japanese occupiers and later against the French. After declaring independence in 1945, he led the successful military operation against the French in the Indochina War (1946–54). After the partition of the country in 1954, he became prime minister (1954–5) and president (1954–69) of communist North Vietnam. Re-elected in 1960, he enlisted Chinese support in the war between North and South Vietnam and became a leading force in the conflict in the 1960s as it widened to draw in other countries, primarily the USA. Despite massive US military intervention in support of South Vietnam (1965–73), Ho Chi Minh's Viet Cong liberation front retained the initiative, and forced a ceasefire in 1973, four years after his death. However, the war continued until 1975, when Saigon fell and was renamed Ho Chi Minh City.

'Vietnam has the right to be a free and independent country'
2 September 1945, Hanoi, Vietnam

Ho Chi Minh's opportunistic declaration of Vietnamese independence was a direct result of World War II. As part of Indochina the country had been a valued French colony since 1868, but Japan invaded in 1940 and France was forced to recognize Japanese rule, in return for nominal sovereignty.

With American support, Ho's Viet Minh Independence League waged a guerrilla war against the Japanese occupiers. In March 1945, fearing an American invasion, the Japanese ousted France's nominal colonial rulers, installing the Vietnamese emperor Bao Dai (1913–97) as their puppet ruler. Five months later, Japan surrendered, Bao Dai abdicated, and the Viet Minh gained effective control over much of Vietnam.

On 2 September 1945, Japan signed the surrender agreement ending World War II. Ho seized his opportunity to declare Vietnam's independence, which he announced in this speech, given at Ba Dinh Square in Hanoi.

He begins by quoting from the American Declaration of Independence, of which he had been given a copy by his allies in US military intelligence. Denouncing the economic enslavement of Vietnam by France, he then proclaims the formation of the Democratic Republic of Vietnam.

However, at the recently-concluded Potsdam conference (July–August 1945), the Allied leaders WINSTON CHURCHILL (replaced part-way by CLEMENT ATTLEE), HARRY S TRUMAN and JOSEPH STALIN had agreed to return to France all her pre-war colonies in Indochina. This led to the Indochina War of 1946–54, in which the Viet Minh eventually achieved North Vietnam's independence.

'All men are created equal. They are endowed by their Creator with certain unalienable rights; among these are life, liberty, and the pursuit of happiness.'

This immortal statement was made in the Declaration of Independence of the United States of America in 1776. In a broader sense, this means: all the peoples on the earth are equal from birth; all the peoples have a right to live, to be happy and free.

The declaration of the French Revolution, made in 1791, on the rights of man and the citizen also states: 'All men are born free and with equal rights, and must always remain free and have equal rights.'[1] These are undeniable truths.

Nevertheless, for more than 80 years, the French imperialists, abusing the standard of liberty, equality, and fraternity, have violated our fatherland and oppressed our fellow citizens. They have acted contrary to the ideals of humanity and justice.

In the field of politics, they have deprived our people of every democratic liberty. They have enforced inhuman laws; they have set up three distinct

[1] Ho seems to refer to the *Declaration of the Rights of Man and of the Citizen*, which was approved by France's National Assembly in August 1789.

political regimes in the north, the centre, and the south of Vietnam, in order to wreck our national unity and prevent our people from being united.

They have built more prisons than schools. They have mercilessly slain our patriots; they have drowned our uprisings in rivers of blood. They have fettered public opinion; they have practised obscurantism against our people. To weaken our race they have forced us to use opium and alcohol.

In the field of economics, they have fleeced us to the backbone, impoverished our people and devastated our land. They have robbed us of our rice fields, our mines, our forests, and our raw materials. They have monopolized the issuing of bank notes and the export trade. They have invented numerous unjustifiable taxes and reduced our people, especially our peasantry, to a state of extreme poverty. They have hampered the prospering of our national bourgeoisie; they have mercilessly exploited our workers.

In the autumn of 1940, when the Japanese fascists violated Indochina's territory to establish new bases in their fight against the Allies, the French imperialists went down on their bended knees and handed over our country to them.

Thus, from that date, our people were subjected to the double yoke of the French and the Japanese. Their sufferings and miseries increased. The result was that, from the end of last year to the beginning of this year, from Quang Tri Province to the north of Vietnam, more than two million of our fellow citizens died from starvation.

On March 9 [1945], the French troops were disarmed by the Japanese. The French colonialists either fled or surrendered, showing that not only were they incapable of 'protecting' us, but that, in the span of five years, they had twice sold our country to the Japanese.

On several occasions before March 9, the Viet Minh League urged the French to ally themselves with it against the Japanese. Instead of agreeing to this proposal, the French colonialists so intensified their terrorist activities against the Viet Minh members, that before fleeing they massacred a great number of our political prisoners detained at Yen Bay and Cao Bang.

Notwithstanding all this, our fellow citizens have always manifested toward the French a tolerant and humane attitude. Even after the Japanese putsch of March 1945, the Viet Minh League helped many Frenchmen to cross the frontier, rescued some of them from Japanese jails, and protected French lives and property.

In the autumn of 1940, our country had in fact ceased to be a French colony and had become a Japanese possession. After the Japanese had surrendered to the Allies, our whole people rose to regain our national sovereignty and to found the Democratic Republic of Vietnam. The truth is that we have wrested our independence from the Japanese and not from the French.

The French have fled, the Japanese have capitulated, Emperor Bao Dai has abdicated. Our people have broken the chains which for nearly a century have fettered them and have won independence for the fatherland. Our people at the same time have overthrown the monarchic regime that has reigned supreme for dozens of centuries. In its place has been established the present democratic republic.

For these reasons, we, members of the provisional government, representing the whole Vietnamese people, declare that from now on we break off all relations of a colonial character with France; we repeal all the international obligations that France has so far subscribed to on behalf of Vietnam, and we abolish all the special rights the French have unlawfully acquired in our fatherland.

The whole Vietnamese people, animated by a common purpose, are determined to fight to the bitter end against any attempt by the French colonialists to reconquer their country. We are convinced that the Allied nations, which at Teheran[2] and San Francisco[3] have acknowledged the principles of self-determination and equality of nations, will not refuse to acknowledge the independence of Vietnam.

A people who have courageously opposed French domination for more than 80 years, a people who have fought side by side with the Allies against the fascists during these last years, such a people must be free and independent.

For these reasons, we, members of the provisional government of the Democratic Republic of Vietnam, solemnly declare to the world that Vietnam has the right to be a free and independent country – and in fact it is so already. The entire Vietnamese people are determined to mobilize all their physical and mental strength, to sacrifice their lives and property in order to safeguard their independence and liberty.

[2] At the Teheran Conference (November–December 1943) the Allied leaders Churchill, FRANKLIN D ROOSEVELT and Stalin had discussed, inter alia, the establishment of a post-war international organization.

[3] The San Francisco Conference or United Nations Conference on International Organization (April–June 1945) was the international meeting at which the United Nations Organization was established.

Geoffrey Howe
Welsh politician

Richard Edward Geoffrey Howe *later Baron Howe of Aberavon* (1926–) was born in Port Talbot, Glamorgan, and educated at Cambridge. He was called to the Bar in 1952 and entered Parliament as a Conservative MP in 1964. Knighted in 1970, he was Solicitor-General from 1970 to 1972. During MARGARET THATCHER's first administration (1979–83), he served as Chancellor of the Exchequer, and successfully engineered a reduction in the rate of inflation. He became Foreign Secretary after the 1983 general election. In 1989, in a major cabinet reshuffle, he was moved from the Foreign Office to the leadership of the House of Commons (with the title of Deputy Prime Minister) following policy disagreements with Thatcher over European monetary union. A year later, he resigned in protest at her continuing intransigence, heightening the party split that contributed to Thatcher's downfall and replacement by John Major (1943–). In 1991, he announced his decision not to continue as an MP after the next general election. He was made a life peer in 1992 and his memoir, *Conflict of Loyalties*, was published in 1994.

'I realize now that the task has become futile'
13 November 1990, London, England

Geoffrey Howe's memorable Cabinet resignation speech in the House of Commons – delivered to gasps of disbelief from his own Conservative benches – reflected his long-standing frustration at Margaret Thatcher's mistrust of Europe. Two weeks earlier, at a European Council meeting in Rome, Thatcher had sealed Britain's isolation by announcing that she would never accept the idea of a single currency.

Howe's speech reflected personal feelings of pique, too: Thatcher had made a number of humiliating interventions during his time as Foreign Minister, and in the previous year's cabinet reshuffle he had been effectively sidelined.

Howe had often been considered too mild-mannered – the Labour frontbencher DENIS HEALEY once compared being attacked by him to 'being savaged by a dead sheep' – but this speech was devastating in its impact. It motivated Michael Heseltine, Thatcher's long-time rival, to stand against her in a leadership contest; when Thatcher failed to win outright in the first round of voting, she resigned as Conservative leader and prime minister.

I find to my astonishment that a quarter of a century has passed since I last spoke from one of the back benches.[1] Fortunately, however, it has been my privilege to serve for the past twelve months of that time as Leader of the House of Commons, so I have been reminded quite recently of the traditional generosity and tolerance of this place. I hope that I may count on that today as I offer to the House a statement about my resignation from the government.

It has been suggested … that I decided to resign solely because of questions of style and not on matters of substance at all. Indeed, if some of my former colleagues are to be believed, I must be the first minister in history who has resigned because he was in full agreement with government policy. The truth is that, in many aspects of politics, style and substance complement each other. Very often, they are two sides of the same coin.

The prime minister and I have shared something like 700 meetings of Cabinet or Shadow Cabinet during the past 18 years … The House might well feel that something more than simple matters of style would be necessary to rupture such a well-tried relationship.

It was a privilege to serve as my right honourable friend's first Chancellor of the Exchequer … Not one of our economic achievements would have been possible without the courage and leadership of my right honourable friend – and, if I may say so, they possibly derived some little benefit from the presence of a Chancellor who was not exactly a wet[2] himself.

[1] The 'front benches' at the centre of the House of Commons chamber are reserved for the Cabinet and Shadow Cabinet. Other Members of Parliament are referred to as 'backbenchers'.

[2] A usually derogatory term for moderate Conservatives.

It was a great honour to serve for six years as Foreign and Commonwealth Secretary and to share with my right honourable friend in some notable achievements in the European Community ... But it was as we moved on to consider the crucial monetary issues in the European context that I came to feel increasing concern ... I concluded at least five years ago that the conduct of our policy against inflation could no longer rest solely on attempts to measure and control the domestic money supply. We had no doubt that we should be helped in that battle – and indeed in other respects – by joining the Exchange Rate Mechanism[3] of the European monetary system.

There was, or should have been, nothing novel about joining the ERM; it has been a long-standing commitment ... However, it must be said that that practical conclusion has been achieved only at the cost of substantial damage to her administration and more serious still, to its inflation achievements ...

It is now, alas, impossible to resist the conclusion that today's higher rates of inflation could well have been avoided had the question of ERM membership been properly considered and resolved at a much earlier stage. There are, I fear, developing grounds for similar anxiety over the handling – not just at and after the Rome summit – of the wider, much more open question of economic and monetary union.

Let me first make clear certain important points on which I have no disagreement with my right honourable friend, the prime minister. I do not regard the Delors report[4] as some kind of sacred text that has to be accepted, or even rejected, on the nod. But it is an important working document. As I have often made plain, it is seriously deficient in significant respects.

I do not regard the Italian presidency's management of the Rome summit as a model of its kind – far from it. It was much the same, as my right honourable friend the prime minister will recall, in Milan some five years ago.

I do not regard it as in any sense wrong for Britain to make criticisms of that kind plainly and courteously, nor in any sense wrong for us to do so, if necessary, alone. As I have already made clear, I have, like the prime minister and other right honourable friends, fought too many European battles in a minority of one to have any illusions on that score.

But it is crucially important that we should conduct those arguments upon the basis of a clear understanding of the true relationship between this country, the Community and our Community partners. And it is here, I fear, that my right honourable friend the prime minister increasingly risks leading herself and others astray in matters of substance as well as of style ...

If we had been in from the start,[5] as almost everybody now acknowledges, we should have had more, not less, influence over the Europe in which we live today. We should never forget the lesson of that isolation, of being on the outside looking in, for the conduct of today's affairs.

We have done best when we have seen the Community not as a static entity to be resisted and contained, but as an active process which we can shape, often decisively, provided that we allow ourselves to be fully engaged in it, with confidence, with enthusiasm and in good faith.

We must at all costs avoid presenting ourselves yet again with an over-simplified choice, a false antithesis, a bogus dilemma, between one

[3] The Exchange Rate Mechanism (ERM) was a system introduced in the European Community in 1979. It was designed to stabilize exchange rates in the run-up to Economic and Monetary Union (EMU) and the introduction of a single currency.

[4] The Delors report was produced by the office of the French politician and economist Jacques Delors (1925–) in 1989, when he was serving as President of the European Commission. It set out a plan for the implementation of EMU.

[5] In 1957, Britain took the decision not to be among the founder members of the European Economic Community.

alternative, starkly labelled 'co-operation between independent sovereign states' and a second, equally crudely labelled alternative 'centralized, federal super-state', as if there were no middle way in between.

We commit a serious error if we think always in terms of 'surrendering' sovereignty and seek to stand pat for all time on a given deal – by proclaiming, as my right honourable friend the prime minister did two weeks ago, that we have 'surrendered enough'.

The European enterprise is not and should not be seen like that – as some kind of zero sum game ... What kind of vision is that for our business people, who trade there each day, for our financiers, who seek to make London the money capital of Europe or for all the young people of today?

These concerns are especially important as we approach the crucial topic of economic and monetary union. We must be positively and centrally involved in this debate and not fearfully and negatively detached. The costs of disengagement here could be very serious indeed.

There is talk, of course, of a single currency for Europe. I agree that there are many difficulties about the concept – both economic and political. Of course, as I said in my letter of resignation, none of us wants the imposition of a single currency. But that is not the real risk. The eleven others cannot impose their solution on the twelfth country against its will, but they can go ahead without us. The risk is not imposition but isolation. The real threat is that of leaving ourselves with no say in the monetary arrangements that the rest of Europe chooses for itself, with Britain once again scrambling to join the club later, after the rules have been set and after the power has been distributed by others to our disadvantage. That would be the worst possible outcome.

It is to avoid just that outcome and to find a compromise both acceptable in the government and sellable in Europe that my right honourable friend the Chancellor has put forward his hard ECU[6] proposal. This lays careful emphasis on the possibility that the hard ECU as a common currency could, given time, evolve into a single currency. I have of course supported the hard ECU plan. But after Rome, and after the comments of my right honourable friend the prime minister two weeks ago, there is grave danger that the hard ECU proposal is becoming untenable, because two things have happened.

The first is that my right honourable friend the prime minister has appeared to rule out from the start any compromise at any stage on any of the basic components that all the eleven other countries believe to be a part of EMU – a single currency or a permanently fixed exchange rate, a central bank or common monetary policy ...

The second thing that happened was, I fear, even more disturbing. Reporting to this House, my right honourable friend almost casually remarked that she did not think that many people would want to use the hard ECU anyway – even as a common currency, let alone as a single one. It was remarkable – indeed, it was tragic – to hear my right honourable friend dismissing, with such personalized incredulity, the very idea that the hard ECU proposal might find growing favour among the peoples of Europe ...

How on earth are the Chancellor and the Governor of the Bank of England,[7] commending the hard ECU as they strive to, to be taken as serious participants in the debate against that kind of background noise? I believe that both the Chancellor and the Governor are cricketing enthusiasts, so I hope that there is no monopoly of cricketing metaphors. It

[6] The 'hard ECU' (European Currency Unit), a common currency that would circulate alongside existing national currencies, was proposed in June 1990 by John Major, who was then Chancellor of the Exchequer. The ECU was replaced by the euro on 1 January 1999.

[7] The most senior executive in the Bank of England, who plays a significant role in guiding the UK's economic and monetary policy. The post was then occupied by Robin Leigh-Pemberton *later Baron Kingsdown* (1927–).

is rather like sending your opening batsmen to the crease, only for them to find, the moment the first balls are bowled, that their bats have been broken before the game by the team captain.

The point was perhaps more sharply put by a British businessman, trading in Brussels and elsewhere, who wrote to me last week, stating: 'People throughout Europe see our prime minister's finger-wagging and hear her passionate "No, No, No"[8] much more clearly than the content of the carefully worded formal texts.'

He went on: 'It is too easy for them to believe that we all share her attitudes; for why else has she been our prime minister for so long?' My correspondent concluded: 'This is a desperately serious situation for our country.'

And sadly, I have to agree.

The tragedy is – and it is for me personally, for my party, for our whole people and for my right honourable friend herself, a very real tragedy – that the prime minister's perceived attitude towards Europe is running increasingly serious risks for the future of our nation. It risks minimizing our influence and maximizing our chances of being once again shut out. We have paid heavily in the past for late starts and squandered opportunities in Europe. We dare not let that happen again …

Mr Speaker: in my letter of resignation, which I tendered with the utmost sadness and dismay, I said: 'Cabinet government is all about trying to persuade one another from within'.

That was my commitment to government by persuasion – persuading colleagues and the nation. I have tried to do that as Foreign Secretary and since, but I realize now that the task has become futile: trying to stretch the meaning of words beyond what was credible, and trying to pretend that there was a common policy when every step forward risked being subverted by some casual comment or impulsive answer.

The conflict of loyalty, of loyalty to my right honourable friend the prime minister – and, after more than two decades together that instinct of loyalty is still very real – and of loyalty to what I perceive to be the true interests of the nation, has become all too great. I no longer believe it possible to resolve that conflict from within this government. That is why I have resigned. In doing so, I have done what I believe to be right for my party and my country.

[8] The words used by Thatcher at the Rome summit to signal her rejection of a single currency.

Victor Hugo
French poet and writer

Victor Marie Hugo (1802–85) was born in Besançon, the son of one of NAPOLEON BONAPARTE's generals. He was educated in Paris at the Feuillantines, in Madrid, and at the École Polytechnique. He wrote a tragedy at the age of 14, and at 20, when he published his first set of *Odes et ballades* (1822), he had been victor three times at the Floral Games of Toulouse. In the 1820s and 1830s he produced further poetry and drama, establishing his place in the forefront of the Romantic movement, in particular with *Hernani* in 1830, the first of the five-act lyrics which are especially associated with him. In 1831 he produced one of his best-known novels, *Nôtre Dame de Paris*, an outstanding historical romance, later filmed as *The Hunchback of Nôtre Dame* (1924). During the 1840s Hugo became an adherent of republicanism, and he was elected to the Constituent Assembly in 1848. After the *coup d'état* of Louis Napoleon (Napoleon III) he was sent into exile to Guernsey in the Channel Islands (1851–70), where he issued his satirical *Napoléon le petit* (1852, 'Little Napoleon'). His greatest novel, *Les Misérables*, a panoramic piece of social history, appeared in 1862. He returned to Paris in 1870, and stayed through the Commune – the socialist government of March–May 1871 – but then departed for Brussels. He protested publicly against the action of the Belgian government in respect of the beaten Communists, in consequence of which he was again expelled. In 1872 he published *L'Année terrible* ('The Terrible Year') a series of pictures of the war, and in 1874 he published his last romance in prose, *Quatre-vingt-treize* ('Ninety-Three'). In 1876 he was made a senator. He was buried as a national hero in Paris.

'He had the tenderness of a woman and the wrath of a hero'
30 May 1878, Paris, France

In the pantheon of French literature, few names are more revered than that of the great philosopher, satirist and social critic Voltaire. On the centenary of his death, Victor Hugo – himself a writer of no small standing – gave this address in tribute to a man who had influenced him from an early age.

Hugo was by now in physical decline, and suffering from a neurological complaint known as cerebral congestion. But he was still regarded as a republican figurehead and a national hero, thanks to the popularity of *Les Misérables*, *L'Année terrible* and other works.

A long-standing opponent of the death penalty, Hugo used his speech to explore Voltaire's legacy of political protest. To do so, he describes – with unstinting vividness – two famous atrocities carried out by the Church authorities during the ostensibly genteel reign (1715–74) of Louis XV.

The cases of Jean Calas and Jean-François de la Barre became causes célèbres, largely thanks to Voltaire, who devoted himself, during the 1760s, to attacking '*l'infame*' – ie the established Church and the intolerant practices of its courts. In 1763 he published a passionate 'Treatise on Tolerance', referring to the Calas case.

But Voltaire's outrage was often cloaked in humour and the culmination of Hugo's speech is a tribute to his satirical smile, a smile captured in his famous death mask. In this translation by William F Fleming, it is impossible to miss Hugo's fast-moving and dramatic narrative style, fired by his admiration for Voltaire and the loathing they shared for cruelty and injustice.

A hundred years ago today a man died. He died immortal. He departed laden with years, laden with works, laden with the most illustrious and the most fearful of responsibilities, the responsibility of the human conscience informed and rectified. He went cursed and blessed, cursed by the past, blessed by the future; and these, gentlemen, are the two superb forms of glory. On his deathbed he had, on the one hand, the acclaim of contemporaries and of posterity; on the other, that triumph of hooting and of hate which the implacable past bestows upon those who have combated it.

He was more than a man; he was an age. He had exercised a function and fulfilled a mission. He had been evidently chosen for the work which he had done, by the Supreme Will, which manifests itself as visibly in the laws of destiny as in the laws of nature.

The 84 years that this man lived occupy the interval that separates the monarchy at its apogee from the Revolution in its dawn. When he was born, Louis XIV[1] still reigned; when he died, Louis XVI[2] reigned already; so that his cradle could see the last rays of the great throne, and his coffin the first gleams from the great abyss …

Before the Revolution,[3] gentlemen, the social structure was this: at the base, the people; above the people, religion represented by the clergy; by the side of religion, justice represented by the magistracy. And, at that period of human society, what was the people? It was ignorance. What was religion? It was intolerance. And what was justice? It was injustice. Am I going too far in my words? Judge. I will confine myself to the citation of two facts, but decisive ones.

At Toulouse, on 13 October 1761, there was found in a lower storey of a house a young man hanged. The crowd gathered, the clergy fulminated, the magistracy investigated. It was a suicide; they made of it an assassination. In what interest? In the interest of religion. And who was accused? The father. He was a Huguenot,[4] and he wished to hinder his son from becoming a Catholic.

There was here a moral monstrosity and a material impossibility; no matter! This father had killed his son; this old man had hanged this young man. Justice travailed, and this was the result. In the month of March, 1762, a man with white hair, Jean Calas, was conducted to a public place, stripped naked, stretched on a wheel, the members bound on it, the head hanging. Three men are there upon a scaffold; a magistrate, named David, charged to superintend the punishment, a priest to hold the crucifix and the executioner, with a bar of iron in his hand.

The patient, stupefied and terrible, regards not the priest, and looks at the executioner. The executioner lifts the bar of iron, and breaks one of his arms. The victim groans and swoons. The magistrate comes forward; they make the condemned inhale salts; he returns to life. Then another stroke of the bar; another groan. Calas loses consciousness; they revive him, and the executioner begins again; and, as each limb before being broken in two places receives two blows, that makes eight punishments.

After the eighth swooning the priest offers him the crucifix to kiss; Calas turns away his head, and the executioner gives him the *coup de grâce*; that is to say, crushes in his chest with the thick end of the bar of iron. So died Jean Calas.

That lasted two hours. After his death the evidence of the suicide came to light. But an assassination had been committed. By whom? By the judges.

Another fact. After the old man, the young man. Three years later, in 1765, in Abbeville, the day after a night of storm and high wind, there was found upon the pavement of a bridge an old crucifix of worm-eaten wood, which for three centuries had been fastened to the parapet. Who had thrown down this crucifix? Who committed this sacrilege? It is not known. Perhaps a passer-by. Perhaps the wind.

Who is the guilty one? The Bishop of Amiens launches a *monitoire*. Note what a *monitoire* was: it was an order to all the faithful, on pain of Hell, to declare what they knew, or believed they knew, of such or such a fact; a murderous injunction, when addressed by fanaticism to ignorance. The *monitoire* of the Bishop of Amiens does its work; the town gossip assumes the character of the crime charged.

Justice discovers, or believes it discovers, that on the night when the

[1] The French monarch Louis XIV (1638–1715) reigned for 72 years, from the age of four in 1643 until his death in 1715.
[2] The French monarch Louis XVI (1754–93) reigned 1774–92. He was tried for high treason and executed during the French Revolution.
[3] The French Revolution (1789–99), which overthrew the *ancien régime* in France.
[4] A French Protestant.

crucifix was thrown down, two men, two officers, one named La Barre, the other d'Étallonde, passed over the bridge of Abbeville, that they were drunk, and that they sang a guardroom song … Two orders for arrest were issued.

D'Étallonde escaped, La Barre was taken. Him they delivered to judicial examination. He denied having crossed the bridge; he confessed to having sung the song. The Seneschalcy[5] of Abbeville condemned him; he appealed to the parliament of Paris. He was conducted to Paris; the sentence was found good and confirmed.[6] He was conducted back to Abbeville in chains. I abridge.

The monstrous hour arrives. They begin by subjecting the Chevalier de la Barre to the torture, ordinary and extraordinary, to make him reveal his accomplices. Accomplices in what? In having crossed a bridge and sung a song. During the torture one of his knees was broken; his confessor, on hearing the bones crack, fainted away.

The next day, June 5, 1766, La Barre was drawn to the great square of Abbeville, where flamed a penitential firer, the sentence was read to La Barre; then they cut off one of his hands; then they tore out his tongue with iron pincers; then, in mercy, his head was cut off and thrown into the fire. So died the Chevalier de la Barre. He was 19 years of age.

Then, O Voltaire, thou didst utter a cry of horror, and it will be to thine eternal glory![7] Then didst thou enter upon the appalling trial of the past; thou didst plead against tyrants and monsters, the cause of the human race, and thou didst gain it. Great man, blessed be thou forever.

The frightful things that I have recalled were accomplished in the midst of a polite society. Its life was gay and light; people went and came; they looked neither above nor below themselves; their indifference had become carelessness; graceful poets, Saint-Aulaire,[8] Boufflers,[9] Gentil-Bernard,[10] composed pretty verses; the court was all festival; Versailles was brilliant; Paris ignored what was passing; and then it was that, through religious ferocity, the judges made an old man die upon the wheel and the priests tore out a child's tongue for a song.

In the presence of this society, frivolous and dismal, Voltaire alone, having before his eyes those united forces, the court, the nobility, capital; that unconscious power, the blind multitude; that terrible magistracy, so severe to subjects, so docile to the master, crushing and flattering, kneeling on the people before the king; that clergy, vile mélange of hypocrisy and fanaticism; Voltaire alone, I repeat it, declared war against that coalition of all the social iniquities, against that enormous and terrible world, and he accepted battle with it. And what was his weapon? That which has the lightness of the wind and the power of the thunderbolt. A pen.

With that weapon he fought; with that weapon he conquered. Gentlemen, let us salute that memory.

Voltaire conquered; Voltaire waged the splendid kind of warfare, the war of one alone against all; that is to say, the grand warfare. The war of thought against matter, the war of reason against prejudice, the war of the just against the unjust, the war for the oppressed against the oppressor; the war of goodness, the war of kindness. He had the tenderness of a woman and the wrath of a hero. He was a great mind, and an immense heart.

He conquered the old code and the old dogma. He conquered the feudal lord, the Gothic judge, the Roman priest. He raised the populace to the dignity of people. He taught, pacificated, and civilized. He … accepted all

[5] An administrative and judicial body of the church.

[6] A copy of Voltaire's prohibited *Philosophical Dictionary* (1764), found in La Barre's lodgings, was used in evidence against him.

[7] After Jean Calas's brutal execution, Voltaire launched a campaign to have his case retried. In March 1765 he was found not guilty and posthumously pardoned. Voltaire also campaigned to have La Barre's sentence rescinded.

[8] The French poet François-Joseph de Beaupoil de Sainte-Aulaire (1643–1742).

[9] The French poet Stanislas-Jean, Chevalier de Boufflers (1738–1815).

[10] The French poet Pierre Auguste Bernard, known as Gentil-Bernard (1708–75), whose poetry Voltaire was known to enjoy.

the menaces, all the outrages, all the persecutions, calumny, and exile.[11] He was indefatigable and immovable. He conquered violence by a smile, despotism by sarcasm, infallibility by irony, obstinacy by perseverance, ignorance by truth.

I have just pronounced the word, smile. I pause at it. Smile! It is Voltaire.

Let us say it, gentlemen, pacification is the great side of the philosopher; in Voltaire the equilibrium always re-establishes itself at last. Whatever may be his just wrath, it passes, and the irritated Voltaire always gives place to the Voltaire calmed. Then in that profound eye the smile appears.

That smile is wisdom. That smile, I repeat, is Voltaire. That smile sometimes becomes laughter, but the philosophic sadness tempers it. Toward the strong it is mockery; toward the weak it is a caress. It disquiets the oppressor, and reassures the oppressed. Against the great, it is raillery; for the little, it is pity. Ah, let us be moved by that smile! It had in it the rays of the dawn. It illuminated the true, the just, the good, and what there is of worthy in the useful. It lighted up the interior of superstitions. Those ugly things it is salutary to see; he has shown them. Luminous, that smile was fruitful also.

The new society, the desire for equality and concession, and that beginning of fraternity which called itself tolerance, reciprocal goodwill, the just accord of men and rights, reason recognized as the supreme law, the annihilation of prejudices and fixed opinions, the serenity of souls, the spirit of indulgence and of pardon, harmony, peace – behold, what has come from that great smile …

Did Voltaire always smile? No. He was often indignant. You remarked it in my first words.

Certainly, gentlemen, measure, reserve, proportion are reason's supreme law. We can say that moderation is the very breath of the philosopher. The effort of the wise man ought to be to condense into a sort of serene certainty all the approximations of which philosophy is composed …

Never, I insist upon it, will any wise man shake those two august supports of social labour, justice and hope; and all will respect the judge if he is embodied justice, and all will venerate the priest if he represents hope. But if the magistracy calls itself torture, if the church calls itself inquisition, then humanity looks them in the face and says to the judge: 'I will none of thy law!' and says to the priest: 'I will none of thy dogma! I will none of thy fire on the earth and thy Hell in the future!' Then philosophy rises in wrath, and arraigns the judge before justice, and the priest before God!

This is what Voltaire did. It was grand.

Saddam Hussein
Iraqi dictator

Saddam Hussein (1937–2006) was born into a peasant family in Tikrit, and educated in Baghdad. He joined the Ba'ath Socialist Party in 1957. In 1959 he took part in an attempt to assassinate the prime minister, General Abdul Karim Kassem. He was wounded, but escaped. He studied law in Cairo, Egypt (1962–3), returning to Iraq when the Ba'ath party came to power in 1963. The Ba'athists were soon overthrown and in 1964 Saddam was imprisoned for plotting against the new regime. After his release (1966) he took a leading part in the 1968 revolution and established a Revolutionary Command Council (RCC), of which he became vice president, then chairman and state president (1979). He waged a bitter war against Iran (1980–8) to gain control of the Strait of Hormuz, and dealt harshly with Kurdish rebels. In December 1989 an assassination attempt prompted the summary execution of 19 senior army officers. In July 1990 he ordered the invasion of Kuwait, which led to United Nations sanctions and later the Gulf War, in which he was opposed by a UN-backed force involving US, European and Arab troops. Saddam's army surrendered in February 1991. Crippling economic sanctions were imposed and Saddam was immediately confronted with civil war, but contained an uprising in the south. Under the terms of the peace treaty, a UN delegation was sent to oversee the destruction of all non-conventional weapons. Iraqi resistance to the inspections fell away when an air offensive was threatened. Saddam made further raids on Iran in 1993, defying ceasefire resolutions. In 1996 the UN 'oil-for-food' programme allowed Iraq to trade limited amounts of oil for food and medicine. However, tensions continued with the West, particularly with the USA, which claimed Saddam had resumed production of weapons of mass destruction. British and US forces launched sporadic bombing raids in 1997–8. Following the terrorist strikes in the USA in 2001, President GEORGE W BUSH identified Iraq as a member of the 'axis of evil', and renewed demands for regime change. In March 2003, amid widespread controversy over the legality of war, an invasion was launched by a US-led alliance of 35 countries. Decisive victory was accomplished within three weeks, though insurgency has persisted. Saddam went into hiding but was captured in December 2003. His trial for crimes against humanity began in July 2004. He was convicted in November 2006 and executed by hanging just under two months later.

'Iraq will be victorious'
20 March 2003, Baghdad, Iraq

Courted by the West during the Iran–Iraq War of the 1980s, Saddam Hussein was transformed into an international pariah when his forces invaded Kuwait in 1991. This prompted the Gulf War of 1991, although US president George H W Bush resisted calls to invade Iraq and topple Saddam.

Relations between Iraq and the West did not improve during the 1990s. Economic sanctions imposed by the United Nations caused severe hardship, and many Iraqi civilians were killed or wounded during US and British bombing raids. Saddam manipulated the resentment of his people towards the West – particularly towards the USA – to consolidate his power.

Following the terrorist attacks of 11 September 2001 in the USA, American fears of overseas threats were heightened and the anti-American rhetoric of Saddam reinforced a perception of his regime as a sponsor of international terrorism. His continued obstruction of the work of UN weapons inspection teams hardened international attitudes towards him and strengthened calls for President GEORGE W BUSH to complete his father's 'unfinished business'. Allied forces were assembled on Iraq's borders in the early months of 2003 and US bombers struck Baghdad on 20 March.

Saddam appeared on Iraqi television two hours after these initial 'decapitation' bombings, which announced the onset of the expected war. Wearing military uniform – and citing the date, to prove that the speech had not been pre-recorded and that he was still in control – Saddam conceded no suggestion of defeat, despite the overwhelming odds.

The fierce defiance, pious religious language and promises of humiliation for the enemy are all characteristic features of his bullish oratorical style.

> In the name of God, the merciful, the compassionate ... Those who are
> oppressed are permitted to fight and God is capable of making them
> victorious. God is greatest.
> To the great people of Iraq, to our brave strugglers, to our men in the
> heroic armed forces, to our glorious nation: at dawn prayers today on 20

March 2003, the criminal, reckless little Bush and his aides committed this crime which he was threatening to commit against Iraq and humanity. He executed his criminal act with his allies; thereby he and his followers have added to the series of shameful crimes committed against Iraq and humanity.

To the Iraqis and the good people of our nation: your country, your glorious nation and your principles are worth the sacrifices of yourself, your souls, your family and your sons.

In this context, I don't need to repeat to you what each and every one of you must and needs to do to defend our precious nation, our principles and sanctities. I say to every single member of the patient and faithful Iraqi family which is oppressed by the evil enemy to remember and not to forget everything that he has said and pledged. These days, and according to God's will, will add to the eternal history of glorious Iraq.

You brave men and women of Iraq: you deserve victory and glory and everything that elevates the stature of the faithful before their God and defeats the infidels, enemies of God and humanity at large. You, Iraqis, will be victorious along with the sons of the nation. You are already victorious, with the help of God. Your enemies will be in disgrace and shame …

To you friends, opposed to the evil in the world, peace upon you. Now that you have seen how the reckless Bush belittled your positions and views against the war and your sincere call for peace, he has committed his despicable crime today.

We pledge to you in our name and in the name of our leadership and in the name of the Iraqi people and its heroic army, in the name of Iraq's civilization and history, that we will fight the invaders and, God willing, we will take them to the limit at which they will lose their patience and any hope to achieve what they have planned and what the Zionist criminal[1] has pushed them to do …

[1] A reference to Israel, a close ally of the USA and regarded as a strong influence on US policy in the Middle East. Saddam's Iraq was one of the Arab states that did not recognize Israel's right to exist.

They will be defeated, a defeat that is wished for them by the good, faithful and lovers of peace and humanity. Iraq will be victorious, God willing, and with Iraq our nation and humanity will be victorious and the evil ones will be hit in a way that will make them unable to achieve their crime in the way that they, the American and Zionist coalition, have planned for nations and peoples, above all our glorious Arab nation.

God is greatest. Long live Iraq and Palestine. God is greatest. Long live our glorious nation; long live human brotherhood; long live lovers of peace and security and those who seek the right of people to live in freedom, based on justice. God is greatest. Long live Iraq; long live jihad[2] and long live Palestine. God is greatest. God is greatest. God is greatest.

[2] Holy war waged by Muslims in defence of their faith.

Harold Ickes

American politician

Harold LeClair Ickes (1874–1952) was born on a farm near Hollidaysburg, Pennsylvania. At 16, he moved to Chicago, where he attended the University of Chicago, then became a newspaper reporter. He returned to university to study law, graduating in 1907, but then went into politics. Initially a Republican, he supported the 'Bull Moose' candidate THEODORE ROOSEVELT in the presidential election of 1912; then campaigned for the Republicans Charles Evans Hughes and Hiram Johnson. He remained active in Chicago Republican politics until 1933, when he was recruited to the Cabinet led by Democrat president FRANKLIN D ROOSEVELT as Secretary of the Interior, a post he held until 1946. He became an important player in Roosevelt's New Deal programmes. An active campaigner for civil rights and civil liberties, he became director of the Public Works Administration, helping provide employment towards the end of the Depression. After the explosion of Germany's hydrogen-filled zeppelin *Hindenburg*, Ickes strongly resisted the sale of helium to ADOLF HITLER's Germany, fearing military use of dirigibles, and effectively halted the development of zeppelins. He later encouraged Roosevelt to enter World War II. Famous for his pugnacious debating style and his mordant wit, he continued in office following Roosevelt's death in April 1945, but resigned soon after the accession of President HARRY S TRUMAN. At the time, he wrote: 'I don't care to stay in an administration where I am expected to commit perjury for the sake of the party.' His publications include *The Autobiography of a Curmudgeon* (1943) and *Secret Diary*, published posthumously in three volumes (1953–4).

'What constitutes an American?'

18 May 1941, New York City, USA

American pressure groups such as the America First Committee were supported by prominent figures including senators, military leaders and former presidents. Their fears of foreign entanglements were exacerbated by writers such as Lawrence Dennis (1893–1977) who, in *The Coming American Fascism* (1936), declared that the liberal values of law and constitutional guarantees would in time be viewed as ridiculous in the face of the positive benefits of fascism. However, it was *The Wave of the Future* (1940) by Anne Morrow Lindbergh (1906–2001) which provided the hook upon which Ickes hung this speech.

By May 1941, most of Europe and part of North Africa were under Axis occupation, and the UK had been exhausted by the Battle of Britain and the Blitz. German submarines were threatening Atlantic shipping. President Roosevelt had promised aid to WINSTON CHURCHILL, but it was clear that he would have to counter the isolationist mood prevalent in the USA at the time. Ickes's contribution was remarkable: he declared that the war wasn't for territory but for 'men's souls'.

His reputation as Roosevelt's 'hatchet man' during elections was well-earned, and this speech is a good example of his plain-speaking style. Addressing an audience in Central Park on an 'I Am an American' Day, he spoke forcefully, without recourse to the 'gobbledegook' he so disliked. Basing his speech around questions and answers, he makes a forthright appeal to old-fashioned patriotism, with references to the Declaration of Independence. His assessment of a future after a Nazi victory is correspondingly blunt.

I want to ask a few simple questions. And then I shall answer them.

What has happened to our vaunted idealism? Why have some of us been behaving like scared chickens? Where is the million-throated, democratic voice of America?

For years it has been dinned into us that we are a weak nation; that we are an inefficient people; that we are simple-minded. For years we have been told that we are beaten, decayed, and that no part of the world belongs to us any longer. Some amongst us have fallen for this carefully pickled tripe. Some amongst us have fallen for this calculated poison. Some amongst us have begun to preach that the 'wave of the future' has passed over us and left us a wet, dead fish.

They shout – from public platforms, in printed pages, through the microphones – that it is futile to oppose the 'wave of the future.' They cry

[1] An English document, drafted in 1215 to limit the power of monarchs within the bounds of the law. The English monarch John (c.1166–1216) was forced by his barons to sign it following a string of military disasters.

that we Americans, we free Americans nourished on Magna Carta[1] and the Declaration of Independence, hold moth-eaten ideas. They exclaim that there is no room for free men in the world any more and that only the slaves will inherit the earth. America – the America of WASHINGTON and JEFFERSON and LINCOLN and Walt Whitman[2] – they say, is waiting for the undertaker and all the hopes and aspirations that have gone into the making of America are dead too.

[2] The US poet Walt Whitman (1819–92), is best-known for the twelve-volume collection of poetry *Leaves of Grass*, an attempt to define the American experience.

However, my fellow citizens, this is not the real point of the story. The real point – the shameful point – is that many of us are listening to them and some of us almost believe them.

I say that it is time for the great American people to raise its voice and cry out in mighty triumph what it is to be an American. And why it is that only Americans, with the aid of our brave allies – yes, let's call them 'allies' – the British, can and will build the only future worth having. I mean a future, not of concentration camps, not of physical torture and mental straitjackets, not of sawdust bread or of sawdust Caesars – I mean a future when free men will live free lives in dignity and in security.

This tide of the future, the democratic future, is ours. It is ours if we show ourselves worthy of our culture and of our heritage. But make no mistake about it; the tide of the democratic future is not like the ocean tide – regular, relentless, and inevitable. Nothing in human affairs is mechanical or inevitable. Nor are Americans mechanical. They are very human indeed.

What constitutes an American? Not colour nor race nor religion. Not the pedigree of his family nor the place of his birth. Not the coincidence of his citizenship. Not his social status nor his bank account. Not his trade nor his profession. An American is one who loves justice and believes in the dignity of man. An American is one who will fight for his freedom and that of his neighbour. An American is one who will sacrifice property, ease and security in order that he and his children may retain the rights of free men. An American is one in whose heart is engraved the immortal second sentence of the Declaration of Independence.[3]

[3] 'We hold these truths to be self-evident, that all men are created equal, that they are endowed by their Creator with certain unalienable Rights, that among these are Life, Liberty and the pursuit of Happiness.'

Americans have always known how to fight for their rights and their way of life. Americans are not afraid to fight. They fight joyously in a just cause. We Americans know that freedom, like peace, is indivisible. We cannot retain our liberty if three-fourths of the world is enslaved. Brutality, injustice and slavery, if practised as dictators would have them, universally and systematically, in the long run would destroy us as surely as a fire raging in our nearby neighbour's house would burn ours if we didn't help to put out his.

If we are to retain our own freedom, we must do everything within our power to aid Britain. We must also do everything to restore to the conquered peoples their freedom. This means the Germans too.

Such a programme, if you stop to think, is selfishness on our part. It is the sort of enlightened selfishness that makes the wheels of history go around. It is the sort of enlightened selfishness that wins victories.

Do you know why? Because we cannot live in the world alone, without friends and without allies. If Britain should be defeated then the totalitarian undertaker will prepare to hang crepe on the door of our own independence.

Perhaps you wonder how this could come about? Perhaps you have heard 'them' – the wavers of the future – cry, with calculated malice, that even if Britain were defeated we could live alone and defend ourselves single-handed, even against the whole world.

I tell you that this is a cold-blooded lie. We would be alone in the world, facing an unscrupulous military-economic bloc that would dominate all of Europe, all of Africa, most of Asia and perhaps even Russia and South America. Even to do that, we would have to spend most of our national income on tanks and guns and planes and ships.

Nor would this be all. We would have to live perpetually as an armed camp, maintaining a huge standing army, a gigantic air force, two vast navies. And we could not do this without endangering our freedom, our democracy, our way of life …

A perpetually militarized, isolated and impoverished America is not the America that our fathers came here to build. It is not the America that has been the dream and the hope of countless generations in all parts of the world. It is not the America that 130 million of us would care to live in.

The continued security of our country demands that we aid the enslaved millions of Europe – yes, even of Germany – to win back their liberty and independence. I am convinced that if we do not embark upon such a programme we will lose our own freedom.

We should be clear on this point. What is convulsing the world today is not merely another old-fashioned war. It is a counter-revolution against our ideas and ideals, against our sense of justice and our human values.

Three systems today compete for world domination. Communism, fascism and democracy are struggling for social–economic–political world control. As the conflict sharpens, it becomes clear that the other two, fascism and communism, are merging into one. They have one common enemy, democracy. They have one common goal, the destruction of democracy.

This is why this war is not an ordinary war. It is not a conflict for markets or territories. It is a desperate struggle for the possession of the souls of men. This is why the British are not fighting for themselves alone. They are fighting to preserve freedom for mankind. For the moment, the battleground is the British Isles. But they are fighting our war; they are the first soldiers in trenches that are also our front-line trenches …

We free, democratic Americans are in a position to help. We know that the spirit of freedom never dies. We know that men have fought and bled for freedom since time immemorial … Liberty never dies. The Genghis Khans[4] come and go. The Attilas[5] come and go. The HITLERs flash and sputter out. But freedom endures.

Destroy a whole generation of those who have known how to walk with heads erect in God's free air, and the next generation will rise against the oppressors and restore freedom. Today in Europe, the Nazi Attila may gloat that he has destroyed democracy. He is wrong. In small farmhouses all over central Europe, in the shops of Germany and Italy, on the docks of Holland and Belgium, freedom still lives in the hearts of men. It will endure like a hardy tree gone into the wintertime, awaiting the spring.

And, like spring, spreading from the south into Scandinavia, the democratic revolution will come. And men with democratic hearts will experience comradeship across artificial boundaries.

These men and women, hundreds of millions of them, now in bondage or threatened with slavery, are our comrades and our allies. They are only waiting for our leadership and our encouragement, for the spark that we can supply. These hundreds of millions of liberty-loving people, now oppressed, constitute the greatest sixth column in history. They have the will to destroy the Nazi gangsters.

[4] The warrior Genghis Khan (c.1162–1227) founded the Mongol Empire. Although a skilful administrator, he had a reputation for despotic rule and ruthless savagery.

[5] The warrior Attila the Hun (c.406–453 AD) ruled over an empire that extended from central Europe to the frontiers of China, and was also known as a remorseless tyrant.

We have always helped in struggles for human freedom. And we will help again. But our hundreds of millions of liberty-loving allies would despair if we did not provide aid and encouragement. The quicker we help them the sooner this dreadful revolution will be over. We cannot, we must not, we dare not delay much longer.

The fight for Britain is in its crucial stages. We must give the British everything we have. And by everything, I mean everything needed to beat the life out of our common enemy.

The second step must be to aid and encourage our friends and allies everywhere. And by everywhere I mean Europe and Asia and Africa and America.

And finally, the most important of all, we Americans must gird spiritually for the battle. We must dispel the fog of uncertainty and vacillation. We must greet with raucous laughter the corroding arguments of our appeasers and fascists. They doubt democracy. We affirm it triumphantly so that all the world may hear.

Here in America we have something so worth living for that it is worth dying for! The so-called 'wave of the future' is but the slimy backwash of the past. We have not heaved from our necks the tyrant's crushing heel, only to stretch our necks out again for its weight. Not only will we fight for democracy, we will make it more worth fighting for. Under our free institutions, we will work for the good of mankind, including Hitler's victims in Germany, so that all may have plenty and security …

We will help brave England drive back the hordes from Hell who besiege her and then we will join for the destruction of savage and bloodthirsty dictators everywhere. But we must be firm and decisive. We must know our will and make it felt. And we must hurry.

Edward Irving

Scottish clergyman and mystic

Edward Irving (1792–1834) was born in Annan, Dumfriesshire. He studied at the University of Edinburgh, became a schoolmaster and in 1819 was appointed assistant to the evangelical preacher Thomas Chalmers, then minister of the Tron Church in Glasgow. In 1822 he began work at the Caledonian Church, Hatton Garden, London, where he enjoyed great success as a preacher. In 1825, however, he began to announce the imminent second coming of JESUS. In 1828, he was charged with heresy for maintaining the sinfulness of Christ's nature. Convicted by the London presbytery in 1830, he was ejected from his new church in Regent's Square in 1832, and finally deposed in 1833. Much of his congregation adhered to him, and a new communion, the Catholic Apostolic Church (known as Irvingite) developed. His publications include *Homilies on the Sacraments* (1828).

'In God's name do not perish with your eyes open'

c.1823, London, England

An imposing figure with dark eyes and long black hair, Edward Irving won many admirers among the London society of the 1820s with his sermons. In 1823 the Foreign Secretary GEORGE CANNING praised Irving in the House of Commons for making the most eloquent sermon he had ever heard.

This address typifies Irving's style: God's forgiveness is not to be taken for granted, he exhorts; humanity's only salvation is to follow the Gospel, 'a chart for the great ocean of God's mercy'.

Irving's popularity began to wane, however, as he espoused increasingly apocalyptic views. These views are foreshadowed here. The sermon ends with a warning that God's 'messenger of execution is coming'; more telling still, it compares Christianity in Britain to the faith practised on the Continent, where it had been weakened by 'the most desperate throes of revolution'. Irving would later predict that the Second Coming was to occur in 1868. One sign of the imminent end of the world, he believed, was the French Revolution of 1789.

'I will sing of mercy and judgement' – Psalm 101:1

There is no man who has lived in this world who has not to accuse himself of sins against his own conscience, and the good sense of the world. Our vanity, which passeth unseen, and which often cannot be concealed; our intemperate tastes, which we often follow; our deception and false appearance, which almost in every house and in every company we are fain to assume; our licentiousness and libertine indulgences, our high crimes and misdemeanours, do all present themselves to the mind in its reflective moods.

They cannot escape the apprehension of that God who seeth not as man seeth and judgeth not as man judgeth, and knoweth all things. The recording angel of God, the angel of judgement, the book of God's remembrance – these are not images gathered from the Christian dispensation, but are congenial to the human mind in its savage state; and it is these images that have given birth to those cruel customs which have entered into the rites of all people. There is not any man that hears me, how remote soever he may be from Christian life and feeling – there is not any man that existeth under the canopy of that system which we live under, who does not forecast the consequence of his transgressions, and apprehend the responsibility which tells him in his heart he is less than nothing. No man can live under constant apprehension and anxiety; and, rather than be ever downcast, will lift a dagger to his breast, and flee from amidst the shadows of bad things to come.

Hence it comes to pass that the mind, in order to deliver herself from this fear of death, erects out of her hopes a covert, a house of refuge round about, in which she may be, to ward off her own apprehensions about that which is to come. She cannot live without a defence from her own apprehensions. God knew that, my brethren, and God sent the Gospel for the defence of the mind.

But haply she relisheth not, knoweth not, the Gospel: then, I say, she doth construct a pavilion wherein she may repose from fear. Now, of the pavilion which your mind hath constructed, independent of the Gospel which she hath chosen as a refuge from the storm, it is my intention to show, that, when the blast from the Lord will come, the soul of man, to deliver herself from those shadows of fear which look portentous from the other side of the grave, can seldom, in such a land as ours, escape into the bleak refuge of atheism, and enjoy the pleasing thoughts of annihilations (as they can and do on the Continent). But with us, in our happy realm, religion is so much better inwrought in the daily business of life, and the religious man doth above all men so philanthropically relieve the wants of his fellow men, that she hath entwined around the cords of a British heart, and cannot be ejected thence, as in other kingdoms, but by the most desperate throes of revolution in the breasts of the noblest parts of mankind …

But if the people of this country have guarded against the harbour of atheism, they have not, I am sorry to state, guarded against nourishing notions of God altogether unworthy of his character, adverse to the defence of our spiritual and moral nature, and subversive of salvation which is by Christ. The refuge … on which they rely who care little for Christ is *in the indiscriminate mercy and forgiveness of God.*

'God is merciful,' they say, 'and we have no reason to fear.' This is what they take refuge under – God's mercy and bounty; which I am not here to disparage. On the other side, I am here to uphold his mercy and forgiveness, as needful to the utmost necessity and want of human nature, and whose length, breadth, height and depth angels cannot measure: and I am to present this mercy as free and unbought as the breath we draw.

The world thinks us Christians as worshippers of a God of wrath; but they are ignorant blasphemers of our God. 'Turn ye, turn ye: why will ye die?'[1] 'Though your sins be as scarlet, they shall be as wool; though they be red like crimson, yet shall they be white as snow.'[2] O the mercy of God in Christ is a theme for poets to expend their genius upon, if they had not lost their ancient prerogative of holding commune with the skies. The forgetting of God, the disbelieving of God, the mockery of God, all that is transacted in light or in darkness – none of these can shut up the ear of our merciful God, or close the highway of pardon which Christ hath made open.

And, not content with writing mercy on himself, he has commanded to write mercy on every heart. For what is charity but mercy – the human portraiture of that mercy which came from Heaven in the person of our blessed Lord? The dimensions of divine mercy will admit being measured by nothing but by the transgressions of men – not of one man, but of all. If God were to govern the world destitute of long-suffering and mercy – if he were to deal justice on the world with the severity of a human being – then the earth would be my prison-house, and bread and water my prison allowance. By sealing up the light or heat of the sun, or by some other stroke of almighty execution, he would, if he governed by any rule but mercy, make the earth one universal grave, and restore all things into ancient chaos till another work of creation should be accomplished.

What hinders all this? 'Tis mercy. What covereth the bosom of sinful men

[1] Ezekiel 33:11.

[2] Isaiah 1:18.

with a veil and hindereth the world from seeing? 'Tis mercy. What showereth the rain and sheddeth the beams of the sun on the world? 'Tis mercy. What openeth the gates of Heaven to the penitent? 'Tis mercy. What sacrificed God's dearly beloved Son for the chief of sinners? 'Twas mercy. It is because his mercy endureth for ever that we are not in that place where it is clean gone for ever …

But, brethren, this mercy needeth to be bounded by shores and limits, else it would swallow up all the good order of human life, and allow a universal liberty to the inclinations of men, and all licentiousness, which would subvert the earth whereof God intends to be the righteous Judge … Therefore God hath constructed, for the containing of his mercy, the everlasting Gospel, by which he can be just and the justifier of every sinner.

This, though it *contains*, does not *limit* his mercy; for by it all the sins of all men can be washed away, and sanctification for Heaven fully imparted. Whoever says that the mercy of the Gospel is a finite, and not infinite, thing, understands it not at all. The Gospel is a chart for the great ocean of God's mercy, without which misery would be all-prevailing over the earth. Had the soul of man not fallen into strife with itself, had it continued entire and pure, then there would have been no display, save of the holiness and mercy of God in one harmonious union. It is because the character of man has become divisible into good and evil, therefore the character of God has become divisible into mercy and justice; and both combined together will bind again the soul of man into that condition which it hath lost …

But, as I said before, there still continues in the body of this Gospel a law of holiness as well as of pardon; the one being intended to sustain the other. This pardon in Christ is the refuge of our accusing consciences, the refuge which every man seeks after. It is the refuge from fear and apprehension in all unjoyous moods, which are the mildews of the soul's fruitfulness. Again, this pardon in Christ is the breaking down of the wall of partition between man and God. The pardon by Christ is that beginning of hope, of confidence, of joy, which are the refreshing dews to the soul's fruitfulness. This pardon is the commencement of a true knowledge of God, and a rule for the remembrance of God.

All this does the Gospel of Christ do for man, for no other intent than to disentangle him. It unfetters him; it helps, and crowns him, in the great race of holiness, into which he never attempts to enter himself while he remains locked by sin and the powers of darkness. Therefore, I say again that the Gospel is nothing but a containing vessel for the mercy of God, lest, breaking all bounds, it might overspread all the good that can arise from it. The Gospel, therefore, is your security: the Gospel is the pavilion round about you from fears for the future: it is the only place where to seek mercy: the Gospel of Jesus Christ bringing salvation to man.

But the wise of this world cannot burden themselves with any such conditions as this Gospel requires: they will take God out of the Gospel, and consecrate a God after their own fashion. Independent of that holiness wrought into the substance of the Gospel, the world look to be saved in that terrible day of the Lord. They say, 'God is merciful': they trust in his mercy. They say so, though they feel no compunction nor repentance for sin. They evince no reformation, and yet expect mercy. They make no prayer, but simply hope that, as they increase their transgressions, God will cleanse them away. They think that while they have been sinning all the day long, he will forgive all the night long; and that the next morning they will have all clear. Thus year after year is passed through; death comes, and into the arms of God's mercy they think they fall; while they sink into the bottle of his wrath and indignation.

What an attribute to bestow on a God – the tolerator of all crimes and of all wickedness, and a receptacle for all classes of transgressors! Can it be that men of understanding, of honour and honesty – men of judicial wisdom, who see and know that, while justice is tempered with mercy, mercy is regulated by justice – can it be that such men who now hear me, ministering to the government of cities and states, and knowing how needful it is to have their mercy under keeping of justice – can it be that fathers of families, and masters of households, harbour such ideas of God's all toleration, and that you can place yourselves under this canopy, more perishing than Jonah's gourd,[3] from the troubles of your conscience?

... Ye are cheated; ye are served with baits from the enemy of souls; ye are so involved in your fears, and drowned in your pleasures – so intoxicated with vanities; so vexed and driven about from care to care – that you have no notion of the true God. Solemnly I warn you that you are lost for ever – I say, if there be truth in the Word of God, you are lost for ever, while you take refuge beneath these subterfuges; while you are heedless of the Word of God, and live defiled with sin, you are lost, for ever lost.

O for the Baptist's voice which rang in the wilderness! O for the voice of the Baptist, to thrill the hearts of the various characters who now hear me, and to make them conscious of their sins, and seek to have them washed away! O for the voice of Jonah, who strolled from street to street through Nineveh, to make the tempest cease in the bosom of its people, and unmask their wickedness, that they might repent ... If every newspaper or magazine were a book of Scripture, and every contributor a prophet of the Lord, then there might be some hope.

Once more, do you for the sake of your souls repent. I call on you to look and judge for yourselves. Be at pains to consult the oracles of God with your own eyes. Sit in judgement thereon. Deal with divine wisdom as if it were your all. Be what you are, continue what you are, till you are convinced of better things; but in God's name do not perish with your eyes open ...

Hear and your souls shall live. At your peril remain ignorant of it – at your soul's everlasting peril. His messenger of execution is coming. The destroying angel is forth. He destroys not the first-born, but the last, and men of every age. He sweepeth the earth every 70 years. Wherefore look to yourselves. You are warned. Remember, you are warned. Therefore look to yourselves.

[3] Irving refers to Jonah 4:7, which tells how a worm gnawed its way into Jonah's gourd, provoking an angry response from him. His fury reflects his anger with God, who chose not to destroy the Ninevites.

Isocrates
Athenian orator and prose writer

Isocrates (436–338 BC) was born in Athens. After studying under Gorgias and SOCRATES, he worked briefly and unsuccessfully as an advocate. He then turned to speech-writing, and became an influential teacher of oratory (c.390 BC), presenting rhetoric as an essential foundation of education. Many of his writings, such as the *Symmachicus* and the *Panathenaicus*, were meant to serve as model speeches, but were widely circulated as instructional or argumentative constitutional texts, thus becoming the world's first political pamphlets. He urged the Greek city-states to unite against the Persians, but that ambition was thwarted by the victory at Chaeronea by Philip II of Macedonia in 338 BC. Isocrates starved himself to death in protest. His oratorical style employs complex sentence structure and the frequent use of antithesis.

'Our city is the oldest and the greatest in the world'
c.380 BC, Athens, Greece

Isocrates was above all a teacher of rhetoric, devoted to the idea that by instructing the young in how to speak he could provide them with a true education, through which they could discuss and determine their personal and political affairs. This speech is believed to have taken him ten years to write, and was finally released to the public about 380 BC – perhaps at a Panhellenic festival, though that is uncertain.

The speech deals with a theme common among orators of the period, that the Greek states should unite to face the threat of the Persian Empire, which had invaded Greece in the early fifth century, and remained a major force in the Greek world until its overthrow by Alexander the Great in the 320s BC. The section given here, from the beginning of the speech, sets out Isocrates' thoughts about oratory and moves on to present the reasons for Athens's claim to be the leader of the Greeks, which he elaborates in a eulogy of Athenian greatness and her service to the Greek nation.

Although of no significance as a politician, Isocrates was extremely important in the development of rhetorical style, and his influence can be seen in the works of DEMOSTHENES and CICERO. The translation is by George Norlin (1928).

Many times have I wondered at those who first convoked the national assemblies and established the athletic games, amazed that they should have thought the prowess of men's bodies to be deserving of so great bounties, while to those who had toiled in private for the public good and trained their own minds so as to be able to help also their fellow-men they apportioned no reward whatsoever, when, in all reason, they ought rather to have made provision for the latter. For if all the athletes should acquire twice the strength which they now possess, the rest of the world would be no better off; but let a single man attain to wisdom, and all men will reap the benefit who are willing to share his insight.

Yet I have not on this account lost heart, nor chosen to abate my labours; on the contrary, believing that I shall have a sufficient reward in the approbation which my discourse will itself command, I have come before you to give my counsels on the war against the barbarians and on concord among ourselves.

I am, in truth, not unaware that many of those who have claimed to be sophists[1] have rushed upon this theme, but I hope to rise so far superior to them that it will seem as if no word had ever been spoken by my rivals upon this subject; and, at the same time, I have singled out as the highest kind of oratory that which deals with the greatest affairs and, while best displaying the ability of those who speak, brings most profit to those who hear; and this oration is of that character.

In the next place, the moment for action has not yet gone by, and so

[1] Sophists were public teachers of rhetoric, politics, philosophy, etc. whom Isocrates despised. The topic had also been addressed by other more substantial rhetoricians, including Isocrates' own teacher and hero, Gorgias (c.483–375 BC).

made it now futile to bring up this question; for then, and only then, should we cease to speak, when the conditions have come to an end and there is no longer any need to deliberate about them, or when we see that the discussion of them is so complete that there is left to others no room to improve upon what has been said.

But so long as conditions go on as before, and what has been said about them is inadequate, is it not our duty to scan and study this question, the right decision of which will deliver us from our mutual warfare, our present confusion, and our greatest ills?

Furthermore, if it were possible to present the same subject matter in one form and in no other, one might have reason to think it gratuitous to weary one's hearers by speaking again in the same manner as his predecessors; but since oratory is of such a nature that it is possible to discourse on the same subject matter in many different ways – to represent the great as lowly or invest the little with grandeur, to recount the things of old in a new manner or set forth events of recent date in an old fashion – it follows that one must not shun the subjects upon which others have spoken before, but must try to speak better than they.

For the deeds of the past are, indeed, an inheritance common to us all; but the ability to make proper use of them at the appropriate time, to conceive the right sentiments about them in each instance, and to set them forth in finished phrase, is the peculiar gift of the wise. And it is my opinion that the study of oratory as well as the other arts would make the greatest advance if we should admire and honour not those who make the first beginnings in their crafts, but those who are the most finished craftsmen in each; and not those who seek to speak on subjects on which no-one has spoken before, but those who know how to speak as no-one else could.

Yet there are some who carp at discourses which are beyond the powers of ordinary men and have been elaborated with extreme care, and who have gone so far astray that they judge the most ambitious oratory by the standard of the pleas made in the petty actions of the courts; as if both kinds should be alike and should not be distinguished, the one by plainness of style, the other by display; or as if they themselves saw clearly the happy mean, while the man who knows how to speak elegantly could not speak simply and plainly if he chose.

Now these people deceive no-one; clearly they praise those who are near their own level. I, for my part, am not concerned with such men, but rather with those who will not tolerate, but will resent, any carelessness of phrase, and will seek to find in my speeches a quality which they will not discover in others. Addressing myself to these, I shall proceed with my theme, after first vaunting a little further my own powers. For I observe that the other orators in their introductions seek to conciliate their hearers and make excuses for the speeches which they are about to deliver, sometimes alleging that their preparation has been on the spur of the moment, sometimes urging that it is difficult to find words to match the greatness of their theme.

But as for myself, if I do not speak in a manner worthy of my subject and of my reputation and of the time which I have spent – not merely the hours which have been devoted to my speech but also all the years which I have lived – I bid you show me no indulgence but hold me up to ridicule and scorn; for there is nothing of the sort which I do not deserve to suffer, if indeed, being no better than the others, I make promises so great.

So much, by way of introduction, as to my personal claims.

But as to our public interests, the speakers who no sooner come before us than they inform us that we must compose our enmities against each other and turn against the barbarian, rehearsing the misfortunes which have come upon us from our mutual warfare and the advantages which will result from a campaign against our natural enemy – these men do speak the truth, but they do not start at the point from which they could best bring these things to pass.

For the Hellenes[2] are subject, some to us, others to the Lacedaemonians,[3] the polities by which they govern their states having thus divided most of them. If any man, therefore, thinks that before he brings the leading states into friendly relations, the rest will unite in doing any good thing, he is all too simple and out of touch with the actual conditions.

No, the man who does not aim merely to make an oratorical display, but desires to accomplish something as well, must seek out such arguments as will persuade these two states to share and share alike with each other, to divide the supremacy between them, and to wrest from the barbarians the advantages which at the present time they desire to seize for themselves at the expense of the Hellenes.

Now our own city could easily be induced to adopt this policy, but at present the Lacedaemonians are still hard to persuade; for they have inherited the false doctrine that leadership is theirs by ancestral right. If, however, one should prove to them that this honour belongs to us rather than to them, perhaps they might give up splitting hairs about this question and pursue their true interests.

So, then, the other speakers also should have made this their starting-point and should not have given advice on matters about which we agree before instructing us on the points about which we disagree. I, at all events, am justified by a two-fold motive in devoting most of my attention to these points: first and foremost, in order that some good may come of it, and that we may put an end to our mutual rivalries and unite in a war against the barbarian; and secondly, if this is impossible, in order that I may show who they are that stand in the way of the happiness of the Hellenes, and that all may be made to see that even as in times past Athens justly held the sovereignty of the sea, so now she not unjustly lays claim to the hegemony.

For in the first place, if it is the most experienced and the most capable who in any field of action deserve to be honoured, it is without question our right to recover the hegemony which we formerly possessed; for no-one can point to another state which so far excels in warfare on land as our city is superior in fighting battles on the sea. But, in the next place, if there are any who do not regard this as a fair basis of judgement, since the reversals of fortune are frequent (for sovereignty never remains in the same hands), and who believe that the hegemony, like any other prize, should be held by those who first won this honour, or else by those who have rendered the most service to the Hellenes, I think that these also are on our side; for the farther back into the past we go in our examination of both these titles to leadership, the farther behind shall we leave those who dispute our claims.

For it is admitted that our city is the oldest and the greatest in the world and in the eyes of all men the most renowned. But noble as is the foundation of our claims, the following grounds give us even a clearer title to distinction: for we did not become dwellers in this land by driving others out of it, nor by finding it uninhabited, nor by coming together here a

[2] The Greek nation.
[3] The Spartans, who, having defeated the Athenians in the second Peloponnesian War (431–404 BC), were the predominant Greek city-state until the 390s and 380s BC.

motley horde composed of many races; but we are of a lineage so noble and so pure that throughout our history we have continued in possession of the very land which gave us birth, since we are sprung from its very soil and are able to address our city by the very names which we apply to our nearest kin; for we alone of all the Hellenes have the right to call our city at once nurse and fatherland and mother.

And yet, if men are to have good ground for pride and make just claims to leadership and frequently recall their ancestral glories, they must show that their race boasts an origin as noble as that which I have described.

So great, then, are the gifts which were ours from the beginning and which fortune has bestowed upon us. But how many good things we have contributed to the rest of the world we could estimate to best advantage if we should recount the history of our city from the beginning and go through all her achievements in detail. For we should find that not only was she the leader in the hazards of war, but that the social order in general in which we dwell — with which we share the rights of citizenship and through which we are able to live — is almost wholly due to her.

It is, however, necessary to single out from the number of her benefactions, not those which because of their slight importance have escaped attention and been passed over in silence, but those which because of their great importance have been and still are on the lips and in the memory of all men everywhere.

Andrew Jackson
American politician

Andrew Jackson *nicknamed Old Hickory* (1767–1845) was born into an Irish immigrant family in Waxhaw, South Carolina. Aged 13, he fought in the War of Independence, losing most of his immediate family. After studying law he became public prosecutor in Nashville (1788). He helped draft the constitution of Tennessee, and became its representative in Congress in 1796, its senator in 1797 and a judge of its Supreme Court (1798–1804). When war was declared against Great Britain in 1812, he fought against the Creek Indians in Alabama, achieving a decisive victory at Horseshoe Bend (1814). Created major general, he invaded Spanish territory in Florida and successfully defended New Orleans (1815). The victory at New Orleans made Jackson a national hero, though a treaty ending the war had in fact been signed before the battle. In 1818, Jackson again invaded Florida, defeated the Seminoles and became the state's first governor. He soon resigned, and in 1823 was re-elected to the US Senate. In 1824, as a Democratic candidate for the presidency, he had the highest popular vote, but the election was decided in favour of John Quincy Adams. Strongly supported in the west and south, Jackson was elected president in 1828. Fearless and honest, he nonetheless replaced many minor officials with his partisans, relying heavily on a cadre of informal advisers (his 'Kitchen Cabinet'). He quarrelled with his vice president, JOHN C CALHOUN, on the issue of states' rights, favoured extended suffrage and sought to limit the power of the monied élite, thus promoting 'Jacksonian Democracy' – though he had little respect for the democratic system and made high-handed use of executive power. He vehemently opposed efforts to recharter the Bank of the United States, which he considered the malignant agent of centralized money power. On this issue he was re-elected by an overwhelming majority in 1832, and in his second term he pursued hard-money policies, transferring federal funds to state banks and issuing the Specie Circular of 1836, which demanded payment in gold or silver for public lands and brought about the financial panic of 1837. He pressed for the removal of American Indians to free land for settlement; and his most shameful act was refusing to enforce a decision by the Supreme Court (1832), invalidating Georgia's claim on Cherokee territory. As a plain-speaking champion of the common man, however, he won enormous popularity. In 1837 he retired to his Tennessee plantation.

'The eyes of all nations are fixed on our republic'
4 March 1833, Washington, DC, USA

Jackson's first inaugural address in 1829 had been given on the newly-completed east portico of the Capitol building. The celebrations became legendary, as his unruly friends from the west drank too much and behaved badly. By comparison, the second inauguration was a subdued affair. Due to the cold March weather the oaths were taken inside the chamber of the House of Representatives, rather than in public as before.

During his first term, Jackson had set a nationalist agenda and put in place legislation which some states found onerous. The Tariff of 1832, although moderate compared to earlier protectionist legislation, was part of an 'American System', designed to strengthen national industry by taxing imports. This was opposed in the west and the south, and South Carolina went so far as to pass an Ordinance of Nullification; the debate over this led to Vice President Calhoun's resignation.

The conflict between individual states' rights and federal power was also the subject of a famous debate between the senators Daniel Webster and Robert Hayne in January 1830. These were early skirmishes which would lead to the larger conflict of the Civil War.

Jackson recognized that the right of states to make their own laws was often in conflict with federal legislation, and in his brief second inaugural address, he speaks quite distinctly to these issues. He quotes GEORGE WASHINGTON twice, to illustrate that the tension between state and federal government was not a new challenge, but also to lend weight to his strong nationalist argument.

Fellow citizens: the will of the American people, expressed through their unsolicited suffrages, calls me before you to pass through the solemnities preparatory to taking upon myself the duties of president of the United States for another term. For their approbation of my public conduct, through a period which has not been without its difficulties, and for this renewed expression of their confidence in my good intentions, I am at a loss for terms adequate to the expression of my gratitude. It shall be displayed to the extent of my humble abilities in continued efforts so to administer the government as to preserve their liberty and promote their happiness.

So many events have occurred within the last four years which have necessarily called forth — sometimes under circumstances the most delicate and painful — my views of the principles and policy which ought to be pursued by the general government, that I need on this occasion but allude to a few leading considerations connected with some of them.

The foreign policy adopted by our government soon after the formation of our present constitution, and very generally pursued by successive administrations, has been crowned with almost complete success, and has elevated our character among the nations of the earth. To do justice to all and to submit to wrong from none has been, during my administration, its governing maxim — and so happy have been its results that we are not only at peace with all the world, but have few causes of controversy, and those of minor importance, remaining unadjusted.

In the domestic policy of this government, there are two objects which especially deserve the attention of the people and their representatives, and which have been and will continue to be the subjects of my increasing solicitude. They are the preservation of the rights of the several states and the integrity of the Union.

These great objects are necessarily connected, and can only be attained by an enlightened exercise of the powers of each, within its appropriate sphere, in conformity with the public will constitutionally expressed. To this end, it becomes the duty of all to yield a ready and patriotic submission to the laws constitutionally enacted, and thereby promote and strengthen a proper confidence in those institutions of the several states and of the United States which the people themselves have ordained for their own government.

My experience in public concerns, and the observation of a life somewhat advanced,[1] confirm the opinions long since imbibed by me, that the destruction of our state governments — or the annihilation of their control over the local concerns of the people — would lead directly to revolution and anarchy, and finally to despotism and military domination. In proportion, therefore, as the general government encroaches upon the rights of the states, in the same proportion does it impair its own power and detract from its ability to fulfil the purposes of its creation.

Solemnly impressed with these considerations, my countrymen will ever find me ready to exercise my constitutional powers in arresting measures which may directly or indirectly encroach upon the rights of the states, or tend to consolidate all political power in the general government. But of equal, and, indeed, of incalculable, importance is the union of these states, and the sacred duty of all to contribute to its preservation by a liberal support of the general government in the exercise of its just powers.

You have been wisely admonished to, 'accustom yourselves to think and speak of the Union as of the palladium of your political safety and prosperity, watching for its preservation with jealous anxiety, discountenancing whatever may suggest even a suspicion that it can in any event be abandoned, and indignantly frowning upon the first dawning of any attempt to alienate any portion of our country from the rest or to enfeeble the sacred ties which now link together the various parts.'[2]

Without union, our independence and liberty would never have been achieved; without union they never can be maintained. Divided into 24,[3] or even a smaller number, of separate communities, we shall see our internal

[1] Jackson was approaching his 67th birthday.

[2] Jackson quotes George Washington's farewell address of 1796, which is also included in this book.

[3] The number of states that then comprised the USA.

trade burdened with numberless restraints and exactions; communication between distant points and sections obstructed or cut off; our sons made soldiers to deluge with blood the fields they now till in peace; the mass of our people borne down and impoverished by taxes to support armies and navies, and military leaders at the head of their victorious legions becoming our lawgivers and judges. The loss of liberty, of all good government, of peace, plenty, and happiness, must inevitably follow a dissolution of the Union. In supporting it, therefore, we support all that is dear to the freeman and the philanthropist.

The time at which I stand before you is full of interest. The eyes of all nations are fixed on our republic. The event of the existing crisis will be decisive in the opinion of mankind of the practicability of our federal system of government. Great is the stake placed in our hands; great is the responsibility which must rest upon the people of the United States. Let us realize the importance of the attitude in which we stand before the world. Let us exercise forbearance and firmness. Let us extricate our country from the dangers which surround it and learn wisdom from the lessons they inculcate.

Deeply impressed with the truth of these observations, and under the obligation of that solemn oath which I am about to take, I shall continue to exert all my faculties to maintain the just powers of the Constitution and to transmit unimpaired to posterity the blessings of our federal Union.

At the same time, it will be my aim to inculcate, by my official acts, the necessity of exercising by the general government those powers only that are clearly delegated: to encourage simplicity and economy in the expenditures of the government; to raise no more money from the people than may be requisite for these objects, and in a manner that will best promote the interests of all classes of the community and of all portions of the Union. Constantly bearing in mind that in entering into society 'individuals ... must give up a share of liberty to preserve the rest',[4] it will be my desire so to discharge my duties as to foster with our brethren in all parts of the country a spirit of liberal concession and compromise and – by reconciling our fellow-citizens to those partial sacrifices which they must unavoidably make for the preservation of a greater good – to recommend our invaluable government and Union to the confidence and affections of the American people.

Finally, it is my most fervent prayer to that Almighty Being before whom I now stand, and who has kept us in his hands from the infancy of our republic to the present day, that he will so overrule all my intentions and actions and inspire the hearts of my fellow-citizens that we may be preserved from dangers of all kinds and continue forever a united and happy people.

[4] In a letter to the Federal Convention dated 17 September 1787, Washington wrote: 'It is obviously impractical in the federal government of these states, to secure all rights of independent sovereignty to each, and yet provide for the interest and safety of all: individuals entering into society, must give up a share of liberty to preserve the rest.'

James VI and I
King of Scotland and England

James VI and I *originally Charles James* (1566–1625) was born in Edinburgh, the son of Mary, Queen of Scots and Lord Darnley. On his mother's abdication in 1567 he was proclaimed king of Scotland as James VI. During his infancy, power was exercised through a sequence of regents; eventually some stability was achieved by James Douglas, 4th Earl of Morton. Morton was executed in 1581, largely at the instigation of James's relations, the Earl of Arran and the Duke of Lennox. An extreme Protestant reaction followed, and the King was seized by William Ruthven (1582). Although Presbyterian ministers were not involved, the General Assembly approved the action, provoking James's life-long suspicion of the Kirk. He escaped, and a counter-coup was organized by Arran. In 1584, Parliament reiterated the primacy of the Crown over all estates, including the Church. More than 20 radical ministers fled to England, along with some of Ruthven's lords. The exiles returned in 1585 and Arran was displaced from power, but the assertion of royal power continued, now under the guiding hand of the Chancellor, John Maitland of Thirlestane. The execution of Mary in 1587 drew a token protest from her son, but was not allowed to disturb his agreement with England under the Treaty of Berwick (1586). In 1589 James married Princess Anne of Denmark. During the early 1590s, he played off Catholic and Protestant factions, and by 1596 a new stability resulted. On the death of ELIZABETH I (1603), James succeeded to the throne of England as great-grandson of James IV's English wife, Margaret Tudor. He promised to visit Scotland every three years, but he did not return until 1617. However, his political skill allowed him to govern Scotland 'by his pen'. He was initially well-received by his English subjects. After the failure of the Gunpowder Plot (1605), severe laws were brought in against Catholics. Eventually, growing opposition to the joint rule of two kingdoms, Puritan resentment of his high-church stance, his use of court favourites, and his friendship with Spain embittered his fragile relations with Parliament. James's eldest son, Henry, Prince of Wales, died in 1612 and his second son, the future CHARLES I, became the heir to the throne. James's achievements as king of England are still a matter of dispute, but he is widely recognized as one of the most successful kings of Scotland, which was transformed during his long reign.

'Kings are justly called gods'
21 March 1609, London, England

James had been raised in the Protestant faith, but mistrusted Puritans, partly for their treatment of his mother. On succeeding to the English throne, he announced that he would not alter the religious settlement which had established the moderate Protestant nature of the Church of England during Elizabeth's reign, ignoring the demands of Puritans. James considered the Church of England and the monarchy interdependent, supporting the episcopal nature of the Church with the phrase 'no bishop, no king'. This angered Puritans, who wished to see the Church reformed in both doctrine and practice.

James also fell into dispute with Parliament over the extent of his sovereign powers, and was criticized for requesting what he considered an adequate income. There was also discord over John Cowell's book *The Interpreter* (1607) – whose publication James was believed to have sanctioned – which asserted that the king was an absolute ruler.

Hampered by a stutter, James was not an eloquent speaker, but in this address to Parliament, he clearly outlines his vision of the relationship between Crown, Church and state. He refers directly to the divine right of kings – which he perceived as the natural order, ordained by God. However, he does make some concessions, acknowledging that kingdoms and laws have the potential to develop; and that a just king in a settled kingdom is well advised to abide by its laws.

His conclusion leaves little room for negotiation, drawing a pointed parallel between the blasphemy of questioning the actions of God and the treason of questioning the actions of a king.

> I will reduce to three general and main grounds the principal things that have been agitated in this parliament, and whereof I will now speak.
>
> First, the errand for which you were called by me, and that was, for supporting of my state and necessities.
>
> The second is, that which the people are to move unto the king: to represent unto him such things whereby the subjects are vexed or wherein the state of the commonwealth is to be redressed, and that is the thing

which you call grievances. The third ground that hath been handled amongst you – and not only in talk amongst you in the parliament, but even in many other people's mouths as well within as without the parliament – is of a higher nature than any of the former (though it be but an incident). And the reason is, because it concerns a higher point; and this is a doubt, which hath been in the heads of some, of my intention in two things.

First: whether I was resolved in the general to continue still my government according to the ancient form of this state and the laws of this kingdom; or if I had an intention not to limit myself within those bounds, but to alter the same when I thought convenient, by the absolute power of a king.

The other branch is anent the Common Law, which some had a conceit I disliked and (in respect that I was born where another form of law was established) that I would have wished the Civil Law to have been put in place of the Common Law for government of this people. And the complaint made amongst you of a book written by Dr Cowell was a part of the occasion of this incident; but as touching my censure of that book, I made it already to be delivered unto you by the Treasurer here sitting, which he did out of my own directions and notes. And what he said in my name, that had he directly from me; but what he spake of himself therein, without my direction, I shall always make good, for you may be sure I will be loath to make so honest a man a liar or deceive your expectations: always within very few days my edict shall come forth anent that matter which shall fully discover my meaning.

The state of monarchy is the supremest thing upon earth; for kings are not only God's lieutenants upon earth and sit upon God's throne, but even by God himself they are called gods. There be three principal similarities that illustrate the state of monarchy: one taken out of the word of God and the two other out of the grounds of policy and philosophy. In the Scriptures, kings are called gods, and so their power after a certain relation compared to the divine power. Kings are also compared to the fathers of families, for a king is truly *parens patriae*, the politic father of his people. And lastly, kings are compared to the head of this microcosm of the body of man.

Kings are justly called gods, for that they exercise a manner or resemblance of divine power upon earth; for if you will consider the attributes of God, you shall see how they agree in the person of a king. God hath power to create or destroy, make or unmake at his pleasure; to give life or send death; to judge all, and to be judged nor accomptable to none; to raise low things and to make high things low at his pleasure; and to God are both soul and body due.

And the like power have kings: they make and unmake their subject; they have power of raising and casting down; of life and death; judges over all their subjects and in all causes, and yet accomptable to none but God only. They have power to exalt low things and abase high things, and make of their subjects like men at the chess, a pawn to take a bishop or a knight, and to cry up or down any of their subjects as they do their money. And to the king is due both the affection of the soul and the service of the body of his subjects …

As for the father of a family, they had of old under the law of nature *patriam potestatem*,[1] which was *potestatem vitae et necis*,[2] over their children or family (I mean such fathers of families as were the lineal heirs of those families whereof kings did originally come) for kings had their first original from them who planted and spread themselves in colonies through

---

[1] Latin: 'Fatherly power'.

[2] Latin: 'The power of life and death'.

the world.

Now a father may dispose of his inheritance to his children at his pleasure, yea, even disinherit the eldest upon just occasions and prefer the youngest, according to his liking; make them beggars or rich at his pleasure; restrain or banish out of his presence, as he finds them give cause of offence, or restore them in favour again with the penitent sinner. So may the king deal with his subjects.

And lastly, as for the head of the natural body, the head hath the power of directing all the members of the body to that use which the judgement in the head thinks most convenient. It may apply sharp cures or cut off corrupt members, let blood in what proportion it thinks fit and as the body may spare.

But yet is all this power ordained by God *ad aedificationem, non ad destructionem.*[3] For although God have power as well of destruction as of creation or maintenance, yet will it not agree with the wisdom of God to exercise his power in the destruction of nature and overturning the whole frame of things, since his creatures were made that his glory might thereby be the better expressed. So were he a foolish father that would disinherit or destroy his children without a cause, or leave off the careful education of them; and it were an idle head that would, in place of physic, so poison or phlebotomize[4] the body as might breed a dangerous distemper or destruction thereof.

But now in these our times we are to distinguish between the state of kings in their first original, and between the state of settled kings and monarchs that do at this time govern in civil kingdoms. For even as God, during the time of the Old Testament, spake by oracles and wrought by miracles, yet how soon it pleased him to settle a church which was bought and redeemed by the blood of his only son Christ, then was there a cessation of both; he ever after governing his people and church within the limits of his revealed will.

So in the first original of kings, whereof some had their beginning by conquest and some by election of the people, their wills at that time served for law; yet how soon kingdoms began to be settled in civility and policy, then did kings set down their minds by laws — which are properly made by the king only, but at the rogation of the people, the king's grant being obtained thereunto.

And so the king became to be *lex loquens*[5] after a sort, binding himself by a double oath to the observation of the fundamental laws of his kingdom: tacitly, as by being a king, and so bound to protect as well the people as the laws of his kingdom; and expressly, by his oath at his coronation, so as every just king in a settled kingdom is bound to observe that paction made to his people by his laws in framing his government agreeable thereunto — according to that paction which God made with Noah after the Deluge: 'Hereafter seed-time and harvest, cold and heat, summer and winter, and day and night shall not cease so long as the earth remains.'

And therefore a king, governing in a settled kingdom, leaves to be a king and degenerates into a tyrant as soon as he leaves off to rule according to his laws. In which case the king's conscience may speak unto him as the poor widow said to Philip of Macedon: 'Either govern according to your law, *aut ne Rex sis.*'[6]

And though no Christian man ought to allow any rebellion of people against their prince, yet doth God never leave kings unpunished when they

[3] Latin: 'To edification, not to destruction'.

[4] To make a surgical incision to a vein, for the purpose of blood-letting.

[5] Latin: 'Speaking law.'

[6] Latin 'Or you may not be a king'.

transgress these limits, for in that same Psalm[7] where God saith to kings, '*Vos Dei estis*,'[8] he immediately thereafter concludes, 'But ye shall die like men.' The higher we are placed, the greater shall our fall be. *Ut casus sic dolor*:[9] the taller the trees be, the more in danger of the wind; and the tempest bears sorest upon the highest mountains.

Therefore all kings that are not tyrants or perjured will be glad to bound themselves within the limits of their laws, and they that persuade them the contrary are vipers and pests, both against them and the commonwealth. For it is a great difference between a king's government in a settled state and what kings in their original power might do *in individuo vago*.[10]

As for my part, I thank God I have ever given good proof that I never had intention to the contrary; and I am sure to go to my grave with that reputation and comfort, that never king was in all his time more careful to have his laws duly observed, and himself to govern thereafter, than I.

I conclude, then, this point touching the power of kings with this axiom of divinity: that as to dispute what God may do is blasphemy – but *quid vult Deus*,[11] that divines may lawfully and do ordinarily dispute and discuss, for to dispute a *posse ad esse*[12] is both against logic and divinity – so is it sedition in subjects to dispute what a king may do in the height of his power; but just kings will ever be willing to declare what they will do, if they will not incur the curse of God.

I will not be content that my power be disputed upon, but I shall ever be willing to make the reason appear of all my doings, and rule my actions according to my laws.

[7] Psalm 82.
[8] Latin: 'You are gods.'

[9] Latin: 'As the fall is, so the pain will be', ie: 'The higher the tree the greater the fall'.

[10] Latin: literally, 'In an undivided wandering', but perhaps in context: 'When completely unconstrained by others'.

[11] Latin: 'What God wants.'
[12] Latin: 'From what may be to what is'.

Jean Jaurès
French Socialist leader, writer and pacifist

Auguste Marie Joseph Jean Léon Jaurès (1859–1914) was born in Castres, Tarn. He lectured on philosophy at the University of Toulouse and became deputy for the *département* of Tarn (1885–9). In the early 1890s, he wrote two theses for his doctorate; and in 1892, he supported a miners' strike in Tarn. He founded the French Socialist Party, and in 1904 co-founded the socialist newspaper *L'Humanité*, which he edited until his death. An advocate of Franco-German rapprochement in the crisis that followed the assassination of Archduke Franz Ferdinand, Jaurès was himself shot dead on 31 July 1914 by Raoul Villain, a fanatical French patriot.

'For us, Socialists, our duty is simple'
29 July 1914, Brussels, Belgium

Given just two days before his assassination, Jaurès' final speech was a doomed attempt to reverse central Europe's plunge into war. The great powers of Russia and Austria–Hungary had been vying for influence in the Balkans since the late 19th century. Two short wars in the area in 1912–13 greatly enlarged Serbian territory; and the new 'big Serbia', aligned with Russia, was viewed as a threat by Austria–Hungary and its ally Germany. A pretext to attack Serbia came on 28 June 1914 when Archduke Franz Ferdinand of Austria was assassinated by the Serbian nationalist Gavrilo Princip.

Weeks of diplomatic negotiation followed, in an effort to avert war. French leaders visited Russia offering support, while Jaurès and the French Socialists, keen to sever their country's links with tsarist Russia, continued to advocate closer ties with Germany.

On 23 July, Austria–Hungary sent an ultimatum to Serbia. Its terms (believed to be known to German leaders) were uncompromising. Unable to comply, Serbia appealed to Russia for military support. Austria–Hungary declared war on 28 July and the German Chief-of-Staff sent a telegram suggesting that if Austria–Hungary mobilized, Germany would follow.

It was still hoped that the war could be limited to Austria–Hungary and Serbia, and Jaurès visited Brussels in an attempt to persuade Socialists to strike against the war.

His efforts were in vain. Germany declared war on Russia on 1 August and on France three days later.

The diplomats negotiate. It seems that they will be satisfied to take from Serbia a little of its blood. We have, therefore, a little rest to ensure peace. But to what lessons has Europe submitted? After 20 centuries of Christianity, after 100 years of the triumph of the rights of men, how is it possible that millions of persons, without knowing why, can kill each other?

And Germany? If she knew of the Austrian note[1] it is inexcusable to have allowed such a step. And if official Germany did not know of the Austrian note, what is her governmental wisdom? You have a contract[2] which binds you and drags you into war and you don't know why you have been dragged? I ask, what people have given such an example of anarchy?

[*Applause.*]

Nevertheless, the authorities hesitate. Let us profit thereby and organize. For us, Socialists, our duty is simple. We do not need to impose upon our government a policy of peace; our government is practising it. I, who have never hesitated to bring upon my head the hatred of our patriots by my obstinate will and by my desire to bring about a Franco-German understanding, have the right to say that the French government desires peace.

[*Applause.*]

The French government is the best ally for peace of the English government, which has taken the initiative in conciliation,[3] and gives Russia advice of prudence and patience. As for us, it is our duty to insist that the

[1] Jaurès probably refers to the ultimatum of 23 July.

[2] The Dual Alliance between Germany and Austria–Hungary (1879) promised reciprocal protection should either country be attacked by Russia.

[3] The British statesman Sir Edward Grey, 3rd Baronet *later 1st Viscount Grey of Fallodon* (1862–1933) served as Foreign Secretary, 1905–16. He had proposed a four-power mediation of the Balkan crisis.

government shall speak to Russia with force so that she will refrain. If, unfortunately, Russia pays no heed, it is our duty to say, 'We know of but one treaty; the treaty which binds us to the human race.'

[*Applause.*]

This is our duty, and in expressing it we find ourselves in accord with our German comrades who demand that their government see to it that Austria moderates her acts. It is possible that the telegram of which I spoke is due partly to that desire of the German workers. One cannot go against the wish of four millions of enlightened consciences.

Do you know what the proletarians are? They are the men who have collectively an affection for peace and a horror of war. The chauvinists, the nationalists, are men who have collectively a love for war and slaughter. When, however, they feel over their heads the menace of conflicts and wars which may put an end to their capitalistic existence, then they remind themselves that they have friends who seek to reduce the storm.

But for the supreme masters, the ground is mined. In the drunkenness of the first battles they will succeed in pulling along the masses. But gradually, as disease completes the work of the shells, as death and misery strike, these men will turn to German, French, Russian, Austrian and Italian authorities and demand what reasons they can give for all the corpses. And then revolution let loose will say, 'Go and beg grace from God and man.'

Thomas Jefferson
American statesman

Thomas Jefferson (1743–1826) was born on his father's plantation in Virginia. He attended the College of William and Mary and was admitted to the Bar in 1767. Two years later he was elected to the Virginia House of Burgesses, and joined the Revolutionary Party. He played a prominent part in calling the first Continental Congress in 1774, at which he was a delegate, drafting the Declaration of Independence. He helped form the Virginia state constitution, and became governor of Virginia (1779–81). As a member of Congress in 1783, he secured the adoption of decimal coinage. In 1784, he was sent as plenipotentiary to France with BENJAMIN FRANKLIN and SAMUEL ADAMS. He succeeded Franklin as Minister in 1785. In 1789, GEORGE WASHINGTON appointed him Secretary of State. As leader of the Democratic–Republican Party, he advocated limited government, envisioning the USA as a republic of independent farmers, and he clashed repeatedly with Alexander Hamilton and the Federalist Party. In 1797, he became vice president under John Adams. Playing little part in an administration dominated by Federalists, he drafted the Kentucky Resolves of 1798 to protest the passage of the Alien and Sedition Acts. At the presidential election of 1800, he tied with Aaron Burr; the House of Representatives ultimately chose Jefferson as president, and he took office in 1801. Events of his first term included the war with Tripoli, which subdued the Barbary pirates, and the Louisiana Purchase of 1803, which Jefferson sponsored. He also planned the expedition of Captain Meriwether Lewis and Lieutenant William Clark (1804–6) to explore the lands to the west of the Mississippi, which reached the Pacific coast in 1805. Jefferson was re-elected by a large majority for a second term, which saw the Embargo Act of 1807, the trial of Aaron Burr for treason, and the prohibition of the slave import trade (1808). In 1809, Jefferson retired to his Virginian estate and devoted much time to founding the University of Virginia. A man of letters and a gifted architect, he published several books, including his *Notes on Virginia* (1785). In old age he carried on a famous correspondence with his former political rival John Adams. He and Adams both died on 4 July 1826, the 50th anniversary of the Declaration of Independence.

'Let us, then, fellow-citizens, unite with one heart and one mind'
4 March 1801, Washington, DC, USA

Jefferson's Democratic–Republican Party rejected the idea that a strong nation required a powerful central government. When he was elected president in 1800, there were many who wondered how he would fulfil his oath of office to 'preserve, protect and defend' the Constitution, which defined exactly the sort of government many thought he wished to dismantle. Foreign governments watching this experiment presumed the new country would be torn apart by civil war if the ruling Federalists did not retain power.

Jefferson's election had been decided by a special session of the House of Representatives after he and Aaron Burr received 73 votes each. The House debated for 30 hours before deciding in favour of Jefferson, establishing a precedent for peaceful handover of power between political rivals.

Jefferson gave this inaugural address in the new city of Washington, within the partially completed Capitol building, reflecting the nation-building that was underway. The speech is conciliatory and inclusive: 'We are all Republicans; we are all Federalists'. Paraphrasing widely from the Constitution – and particularly from the Bill of Rights – Jefferson delineates the gulf between the Old World and the New.

Friends and fellow-citizens: called upon to undertake the duties of the first executive office of our country, I avail myself of the presence of that portion of my fellow-citizens which is here assembled, to express my grateful thanks for the favour with which they have been pleased to look toward me, to declare a sincere consciousness that the task is above my talents, and that I approach it with those anxious and awful presentiments which the greatness of the charge and the weakness of my powers so justly inspire.

A rising nation, spread over a wide and fruitful land, traversing all the seas with the rich productions of their industry, engaged in commerce with nations who feel power and forget right, advancing rapidly to destinies beyond the reach of mortal eye: when I contemplate these transcendent objects, and see the honour, the happiness, and the hopes of this beloved country committed to the issue and the auspices of this day, I shrink from the contemplation, and humble myself before the magnitude of the undertaking. Utterly, indeed, should I despair, did not the presence of many whom I here see remind me that in the other high authorities provided by our Constitution I shall find resources of wisdom, of virtue and of zeal on which to rely under all difficulties.

To you, then, gentlemen, who are charged with the sovereign functions of legislation, and to those associated with you, I look with encouragement for that guidance and support which may enable us to steer with safety the vessel in which we are all embarked amidst the conflicting elements of a troubled world.

During the contest of opinion through which we have passed, the animation of discussions and of exertions has sometimes worn an aspect which might impose on strangers unused to think freely and to speak and to write what they think; but this being now decided by the voice of the nation, announced according to the rules of the Constitution, all will, of course, arrange themselves under the will of the law, and unite in common efforts for the common good.

All, too, will bear in mind this sacred principle, that though the will of the majority is in all cases to prevail, that will to be rightful must be reasonable; that the minority possess their equal rights, which equal law must protect, and to violate would be oppression.

Let us, then, fellow-citizens, unite with one heart and one mind. Let us restore to social intercourse that harmony and affection without which liberty and even life itself are but dreary things. And let us reflect that, having banished from our land that religious intolerance under which mankind so long bled and suffered, we have yet gained little if we countenance a political intolerance as despotic, as wicked, and capable of as bitter and bloody persecutions.

During the throes and convulsions of the ancient world, during the agonizing spasms of infuriated man, seeking through blood and slaughter his long-lost liberty, it was not wonderful that the agitation of the billows should reach even this distant and peaceful shore; that this should be more felt and feared by some and less by others, and should divide opinions as to measures of safety.

But every difference of opinion is not a difference of principle. We have called by different names brethren of the same principle. We are all Republicans; we are all Federalists. If there be any among us who would wish to dissolve this Union or to change its republican form, let them stand undisturbed as monuments of the safety with which error of opinion may be tolerated, where reason is left free to combat it. I know, indeed, that some honest men fear that a republican government cannot be strong, that this government is not strong enough; but would the honest patriot, in the full tide of successful experiment, abandon a government which has so far kept us free and firm, on the theoretic and visionary fear that this government, the world's best hope, may by possibility want energy to preserve itself? I trust not.

I believe this, on the contrary, the strongest government on earth. I believe it the only one where every man, at the call of the law, would fly to the standard of the law, and would meet invasions of the public order as his own personal concern. Sometimes it is said that man can not be trusted with the government of himself. Can he, then, be trusted with the government of others? Or have we found angels in the forms of kings to govern him? Let history answer this question.

Let us, then, with courage and confidence pursue our own Federal and Republican principles, our attachment to union and representative government. Kindly separated by nature and a wide ocean from the exterminating havoc of one quarter of the globe; too high-minded to endure the degradations of the others; possessing a chosen country, with room enough for our descendants to the thousandth and thousandth generation; entertaining a due sense of our equal right to the use of our own faculties, to the acquisitions of our own industry, to honour and confidence from our fellow-citizens, resulting not from birth, but from our actions and their sense of them; enlightened by a benign religion, professed indeed and practised in various forms, yet all of them inculcating honesty, truth, temperance, gratitude, and the love of man; acknowledging and adoring an overruling Providence, which by all its dispensations proves that it delights in the happiness of man here and his greater happiness hereafter — with all these blessings, what more is necessary to make us a happy and a prosperous people?

Still one thing more, fellow-citizens — a wise and frugal government, which shall restrain men from injuring one another, shall leave them otherwise free to regulate their own pursuits of industry and improvement, and shall not take from the mouth of labour the bread it has earned. This is the sum of good government, and this is necessary to close the circle of our felicities.

About to enter, fellow-citizens, on the exercise of duties which comprehend everything dear and valuable to you, it is proper you should understand what I deem the essential principles of our government, and consequently those which ought to shape its administration. I will compress them within the narrowest compass they will bear, stating the general principle, but not all its limitations.

Equal and exact justice to all men, of whatever state or persuasion, religious or political; peace, commerce, and honest friendship with all nations, entangling alliances with none; the support of the state governments in all their rights, as the most competent administrations for our domestic concerns and the surest bulwarks against anti-Republican tendencies; the preservation of the general government in its whole constitutional vigour, as the sheet anchor of our peace at home and safety abroad; a jealous care of the right of election by the people — a mild and safe corrective of abuses, which are lopped by the sword of revolution where peaceable remedies are unprovided; absolute acquiescence in the decisions of the majority, the vital principle of republics, from which there is no appeal but to force, the vital principle and immediate parent of despotism; a well disciplined militia, our best reliance in peace and for the first moments of war, till regulars may relieve them; the supremacy of the civil over the military authority; economy in the public expense, that labour may be lightly burdened; the honest payment of our debts and sacred preservation of the public faith; encouragement of agriculture, and of commerce as its handmaid; the diffusion of information and arraignment of all abuses at the bar of the public reason; freedom of religion; freedom of the press; and freedom of person under the protection of the habeas corpus,[1] and trial by juries impartially selected.

These principles form the bright constellation which has gone before us and guided our steps through an age of revolution and reformation. The wisdom of our sages and blood of our heroes have been devoted to their

[1] The ancient principle of English law, which requires the presence of the accused during criminal proceedings, was enshrined in the US Constitution of 1787.

attainment. They should be the creed of our political faith, the text of civic instruction, the touchstone by which to try the services of those we trust; and should we wander from them in moments of error or of alarm, let us hasten to retrace our steps and to regain the road which alone leads to peace, liberty, and safety.

I repair, then, fellow-citizens, to the post you have assigned me. With experience enough in subordinate offices to have seen the difficulties of this, the greatest of all, I have learned to expect that it will rarely fall to the lot of imperfect man to retire from this station with the reputation and the favour which bring him into it. Without pretensions to that high confidence you reposed in our first and greatest revolutionary character – whose pre-eminent services had entitled him to the first place in his country's love and destined for him the fairest page in the volume of faithful history – I ask so much confidence only as may give firmness and effect to the legal administration of your affairs.

I shall often go wrong through defect of judgement. When right, I shall often be thought wrong by those whose positions will not command a view of the whole ground. I ask your indulgence for my own errors, which will never be intentional, and your support against the errors of others, who may condemn what they would not if seen in all its parts. The approbation implied by your suffrage is a great consolation to me for the past, and my future solicitude will be to retain the good opinion of those who have bestowed it in advance, to conciliate that of others by doing them all the good in my power, and to be instrumental to the happiness and freedom of all.

Relying, then, on the patronage of your goodwill, I advance with obedience to the work, ready to retire from it whenever you become sensible how much better choice it is in your power to make. And may that Infinite Power which rules the destinies of the universe lead our councils to what is best, and give them a favourable issue for your peace and prosperity.

Jesus of Nazareth
Founder of Christianity

Jesus (c.6 BC–c.30 AD) is the central figure of the Christian faith, believed to be both human and divine, and to have been raised from the dead. Our knowledge of his life comes almost exclusively from the New Testament, although Tacitus refers to his death and he is also mentioned by Pliny, Josephus and some Hebrew sources. Of the Gospel accounts, Mark is now generally held to be the earliest, and to be a source of the other three, Matthew, Luke and John. According to the accounts in Matthew and Luke, Jesus was the first-born child of Mary, who at the time of his birth was engaged to be married to Joseph, a carpenter; through his legal father, Jesus belonged to the tribe of Judah and hence was a descendant of King David, a heritage needed by the Messiah awaited by the Jewish people. According to Matthew, he was born shortly before the death of Herod (4 BC, although the Roman census mentioned by Luke did not take place before AD 6. Jesus is believed to have become a carpenter. After three decades of obscurity, he was baptized by John the Baptist, which marked the beginning of his public life. He gathered around him twelve disciples and undertook two missionary journeys through Galilee, culminating in the miraculous feeding of the five thousand. The Gospels relate how he performed healings, exorcisms and other miracles. Jesus brought his message primarily to the Jews and only later to the Gentiles, and continued John the Baptist's message of a coming kingdom. This had dangerous political implications; and the traditionalist Pharisees were alarmed by Jesus's association with 'sinners', his flouting of orthodox religious practices and his revolutionary Sermon on the Mount. Jesus sought refuge for a while in the Gentile territories of Tyre and Sidon, where he revealed himself to the disciples as the promised Messiah. He returned to Jerusalem in triumph, a week before the Passover feast. He was betrayed by Judas Iscariot and – after a hurried trial – condemned to death by the Sanhedrin. The necessary confirmation of the sentence from Pontius Pilate, the Roman prefect, was obtained on the grounds of political expediency. Jesus was crucified, along with two criminals, on Passover or the preceding day. He was buried the same day. The following Sunday, Mary Magdalene, possibly accompanied by other women, visited the tomb and found it empty. Jesus himself appeared to her, and she told the disciples of her experiences. He also appeared to groups of his disciples after his death, according to stories that may be later insertions into the Gospel accounts. The New Testament also recounts his subsequent ascension into Heaven and the conferring of the Holy Spirit on his disciples, giving them power to preach, prophesy and heal. The cross, the instrument of his execution, became the symbol of Christianity.

'Blessed are the meek: for they shall inherit the earth'
c.30 AD, a mountainside in Galilee, Palestine

Of the four Gospels, only Matthew records this, the Sermon on the Mount (5:3–7:27), though Luke's Sermon on the Plain (6:20–49) includes some similar material. Both texts belong to a period when Jesus travelled in Palestine, preaching and performing miracles.

Given here in the King James Version, the sermon lays down the central tenets of Christianity, including the enigmatic beatitudes ('blessed are ...'), the Lord's Prayer ('Our Father, which art in Heaven ...') and the 'golden rule' ('whatsoever ye would that men should do to you, do ye even so to them').

The sermon can viewed as a commentary on the Ten Commandments handed down to Moses (Exodus 20). However, its stern mandate works as an extension of Mosaic law: for example, the prohibition of adultery is supplanted by a condemnation of any kind of lust.

Apart from the creation (Genesis 1–2), there is probably no biblical text whose interpretation has aroused more debate. Few commentators, for instance, embrace a literal reading of 'if thy right eye offend thee, pluck it out, and cast it from thee'. MARTIN LUTHER tackled the problem by dividing life into spiritual and mundane spheres, believing compromise was unavoidable in the latter. Another German theologian, Martin Dibelius (1883–1947), believed that failure to meet its demands was inevitable in a fallen world, but that the attempt to would induce repentance.

By any interpretation, the sermon offers an idealistic programme of compassion, humility and virtue, while many of its motifs (such as the 'city on a hill') have become widely used in secular contexts.

Blessed are the poor in spirit: for theirs is the kingdom of Heaven.
Blessed are they that mourn: for they shall be comforted.
Blessed are the meek: for they shall inherit the earth.
Blessed are they which do hunger and thirst after righteousness: for

they shall be filled.

Blessed are the merciful: for they shall obtain mercy.

Blessed are the pure in heart: for they shall see God.

Blessed are the peacemakers: for they shall be called the children of God.

Blessed are they which are persecuted for righteousness's sake: for theirs is the kingdom of Heaven.

Blessed are ye, when men shall revile you, and persecute you, and shall say all manner of evil against you falsely, for my sake.

Rejoice, and be exceeding glad: for great is your reward in Heaven: for so persecuted they the prophets which were before you.

Ye are the salt of the earth: but if the salt have lost his savour, wherewith shall it be salted? It is thenceforth good for nothing, but to be cast out, and to be trodden under foot of men.

Ye are the light of the world. A city that is set on an hill cannot be hid.

Neither do men light a candle, and put it under a bushel, but on a candlestick; and it giveth light unto all that are in the house.

Let your light so shine before men, that they may see your good works, and glorify your Father which is in Heaven.

Think not that I am come to destroy the law, or the prophets: I am not come to destroy, but to fulfil.

For verily I say unto you: 'till Heaven and earth pass, one jot or one tittle shall in no wise pass from the law, 'till all be fulfilled.

Whosoever therefore shall break one of these least commandments, and shall teach men so, he shall be called the least in the kingdom of Heaven: but whosoever shall do and teach them, the same shall be called great in the kingdom of Heaven.

For I say unto you that except your righteousness shall exceed the righteousness of the Scribes and Pharisees,[1] ye shall in no case enter into the kingdom of Heaven.

> [1] The legalistic custodians of Mosaic law.

Ye have heard that it was said of them of old time: 'Thou shalt not kill; and whosoever shall kill shall be in danger of the judgement.' But I say unto you that whosoever is angry with his brother without a cause shall be in danger of the judgement: and whosoever shall say to his brother, '*Raca*,'[2] shall be in danger of the council, but whosoever shall say, 'Thou fool,' shall be in danger of hell fire.

> [2] An Aramaic insult.

Therefore, if thou bring thy gift to the altar, and there rememberest that thy brother hath ought against thee; leave there thy gift before the altar, and go thy way; first be reconciled to thy brother, and then come and offer thy gift.

Agree with thine adversary quickly, whiles thou art in the way with him; lest at any time the adversary deliver thee to the judge, and the judge deliver thee to the officer, and thou be cast into prison. Verily I say unto thee: thou shalt by no means come out thence, 'till thou hast paid the uttermost farthing.

Ye have heard that it was said by them of old time: 'Thou shalt not commit adultery.' But I say unto you, That whosoever looketh on a woman to lust after her hath committed adultery with her already in his heart.

And if thy right eye offend thee, pluck it out, and cast it from thee: for it is profitable for thee that one of thy members should perish, and not that thy whole body should be cast into Hell. And if thy right hand offend thee, cut it off, and cast it from thee: for it is profitable for thee that one of thy members should perish, and not that thy whole body should be cast into

Hell.

It hath been said, 'Whosoever shall put away his wife, let him give her a writing of divorcement.' But I say unto you that whosoever shall put away his wife, saving for the cause of fornication, causeth her to commit adultery; and whosoever shall marry her that is divorced committeth adultery.

Again, ye have heard that it hath been said by them of old time, 'Thou shalt not forswear thyself, but shalt perform unto the Lord thine oaths.' But I say unto you: swear not at all; neither by Heaven; for it is God's throne, nor by the earth; for it is his footstool; neither by Jerusalem; for it is the city of the great King. Neither shalt thou swear by thy head, because thou canst not make one hair white or black. But let your communication be, 'Yea, yea'; 'Nay, nay'. For whatsoever is more than these cometh of evil.

Ye have heard that it hath been said, 'An eye for an eye, and a tooth for a tooth.' But I say unto you, that ye resist not evil, but whosoever shall smite thee on thy right cheek, turn to him the other also. And if any man will sue thee at the law, and take away thy coat, let him have thy cloak also. And whosoever shall compel thee to go a mile, go with him twain. Give to him that asketh thee, and from him that would borrow of thee turn not thou away.

Ye have heard that it hath been said, 'Thou shalt love thy neighbour, and hate thine enemy.' But I say unto you: love your enemies, bless them that curse you, do good to them that hate you, and pray for them which despitefully use you, and persecute you, that ye may be the children of your Father which is in Heaven. For he maketh his sun to rise on the evil and on the good, and sendeth rain on the just and on the unjust.

For if ye love them which love you, what reward have ye? Do not even the publicans the same? And if ye salute your brethren only, what do ye more than others? Do not even the publicans so?

Be ye therefore perfect, even as your Father which is in Heaven is perfect.

Take heed that ye do not your alms before men, to be seen of them, otherwise ye have no reward of your Father which is in Heaven. Therefore when thou doest thine alms, do not sound a trumpet before thee, as the hypocrites do in the synagogues and in the streets, that they may have glory of men. Verily I say unto you: they have their reward. But when thou doest alms, let not thy left hand know what thy right hand doeth, that thine alms may be in secret: and thy Father which seeth in secret himself shall reward thee openly.

And when thou prayest, thou shalt not be as the hypocrites are: for they love to pray standing in the synagogues and in the corners of the streets, that they may be seen of men. Verily I say unto you: they have their reward. But thou, when thou prayest, enter into thy closet, and when thou hast shut thy door, pray to thy Father which is in secret; and thy Father which seeth in secret shall reward thee openly.

But when ye pray, use not vain repetitions, as the heathen do: for they think that they shall be heard for their much speaking. Be not ye therefore like unto them: for your Father knoweth what things ye have need of, before ye ask him.

After this manner therefore pray ye: Our Father which art in Heaven, Hallowed be thy name.

Thy kingdom come, Thy will be done in earth, as it is in Heaven.

Give us this day our daily bread.

And forgive us our debts, as we forgive our debtors.

And lead us not into temptation, but deliver us from evil: For thine is the kingdom, and the power, and the glory, for ever.

Amen.

For if ye forgive men their trespasses, your heavenly Father will also forgive you; but if ye forgive not men their trespasses, neither will your Father forgive your trespasses.

Moreover when ye fast, be not, as the hypocrites, of a sad countenance, for they disfigure their faces, that they may appear unto men to fast. Verily I say unto you, they have their reward. But thou, when thou fastest, anoint thine head, and wash thy face, that thou appear not unto men to fast, but unto thy Father which is in secret; and thy Father, which seeth in secret, shall reward thee openly.

Lay not up for yourselves treasures upon earth, where moth and rust doth corrupt, and where thieves break through and steal, but lay up for yourselves treasures in Heaven, where neither moth nor rust doth corrupt, and where thieves do not break through nor steal, for where your treasure is, there will your heart be also.

The light of the body is the eye: if therefore thine eye be single, thy whole body shall be full of light. But if thine eye be evil, thy whole body shall be full of darkness. If therefore the light that is in thee be darkness, how great is that darkness!

No man can serve two masters: for either he will hate the one and love the other; or else he will hold to the one, and despise the other. Ye cannot serve God and Mammon.[3] Therefore I say unto you: take no thought for your life, what ye shall eat, or what ye shall drink; nor yet for your body, what ye shall put on. Is not the life more than meat, and the body than raiment?

Behold the fowls of the air: for they sow not, neither do they reap, nor gather into barns; yet your heavenly Father feedeth them. Are ye not much better than they?

Which of you by taking thought can add one cubit unto his stature? And why take ye thought for raiment? Consider the lilies of the field, how they grow; they toil not, neither do they spin, and yet I say unto you that even Solomon in all his glory[4] was not arrayed like one of these. Wherefore, if God so clothe the grass of the field, which today is, and tomorrow is cast into the oven, shall he not much more clothe you, O ye of little faith?

Therefore take no thought, saying, 'What shall we eat?' or, 'What shall we drink?' or, 'Wherewithal shall we be clothed?' (for after all these things do the Gentiles seek). For your heavenly Father knoweth that ye have need of all these things. But seek ye first the kingdom of God, and his righteousness; and all these things shall be added unto you.

Take therefore no thought for the morrow: for the morrow shall take thought for the things of itself. Sufficient unto the day is the evil thereof.

Judge not, that ye be not judged. For with what judgement ye judge, ye shall be judged: and with what measure ye mete, it shall be measured to you again.

And why beholdest thou the mote that is in thy brother's eye, but considerest not the beam that is in thine own eye? Or how wilt thou say to thy brother, 'Let me pull out the mote out of thine eye,' and, behold, a beam is in thine own eye? Thou hypocrite. First cast out the beam out of thine own eye; and then shalt thou see clearly to cast out the mote out of thy brother's eye.

[3] A personification of wealth and avarice as an idol. From the Aramaic *māmōnā*, meaning wealth.

[4] A great king of Israel, known for his wisdom, power and opulent lifestyle. The son and successor of David, he built the great temple in Jerusalem and three books of the Old Testament (Proverbs, Ecclesiastes and the Song of Solomon) are attributed to him.

Give not that which is holy unto the dogs, neither cast ye your pearls before swine, lest they trample them under their feet, and turn again and rend you.

Ask, and it shall be given you; seek, and ye shall find; knock, and it shall be opened unto you, for everyone that asketh receiveth; and he that seeketh findeth; and to him that knocketh it shall be opened.

Or what man is there of you, whom if his son ask bread, will he give him a stone? Or if he ask a fish, will he give him a serpent? If ye then, being evil, know how to give good gifts unto your children, how much more shall your Father which is in Heaven give good things to them that ask him? Therefore all things whatsoever ye would that men should do to you, do ye even so to them: for this is the law and the prophets.

Enter ye in at the strait gate, for wide is the gate and broad is the way that leadeth to destruction, and many there be which go in thereat; because strait is the gate and narrow is the way which leadeth unto life, and few there be that find it.

Beware of false prophets, which come to you in sheep's clothing, but inwardly they are ravening wolves. Ye shall know them by their fruits. Do men gather grapes of thorns, or figs of thistles? Even so every good tree bringeth forth good fruit; but a corrupt tree bringeth forth evil fruit. A good tree cannot bring forth evil fruit, neither can a corrupt tree bring forth good fruit. Every tree that bringeth not forth good fruit is hewn down, and cast into the fire. Wherefore by their fruits ye shall know them.

Not everyone that saith unto me, 'Lord, Lord' shall enter into the kingdom of Heaven; but he that doeth the will of my Father which is in Heaven. Many will say to me in that day, 'Lord, Lord, have we not prophesied in thy name, and in thy name have cast out devils, and in thy name done many wonderful works?' And then will I profess unto them, 'I never knew you: depart from me, ye that work iniquity.'

Therefore whosoever heareth these sayings of mine, and doeth them, I will liken him unto a wise man, which built his house upon a rock; and the rain descended, and the floods came, and the winds blew, and beat upon that house; and it fell not: for it was founded upon a rock.

And everyone that heareth these sayings of mine, and doeth them not, shall be likened unto a foolish man, which built his house upon the sand; and the rain descended, and the floods came, and the winds blew, and beat upon that house; and it fell: and great was the fall of it.

[*And it came to pass, when Jesus had ended these sayings, the people were astonished at his doctrine, for he taught them as one having authority, and not as the Scribes.*]

❧

'Behold my hands and my feet, that it is I myself'

c.33 AD, Jerusalem, Judea, Palestine

❧

It is difficult to imagine the dismay and disarray of Jesus's followers after his execution. Secular interpreters suggest, plausibly, that the abrupt end of their adventure may have left them disoriented and prone to hallucination. But to believers, the resurrection and ascension represent fulfilment of prophesies made both by Jesus himself ('They shall kill him; and after that he is killed, he shall rise the third day', Mark 9:31) and less explicitly in the Old Testament (see, for example, Isaiah 53). The apostles were destined to act as witnesses to this, and to carry Jesus's message forward.

The New Testament gives five separate accounts of Jesus's appearance to his disciples just before his ascent into Heaven. The two given here are from books attributed to the same writer, the Gospel of Luke (24:36–51) and the

Acts of the Apostles (1:2–9). Together, they reinforce the idea of Jesus as both a living man who eats to satisfy his hunger and a divine being who can manifest himself suddenly among his followers, and is ultimately carried off into the clouds. Specifically they identify him with the Messiah predicted in the Old Testament.

The prelude to Luke's account is a story about two unnamed followers. While walking to the village of Emmaus, they encounter a stranger who upbraids them for failing to understand the significance of Jesus's death. Later, over a shared meal that echoes the Last Supper, he reveals his identity to them and disappears. Hastening back to Jerusalem, they relate their story breathlessly to the eleven surviving disciples ...

And as they thus spake, Jesus himself stood in the midst of them, and saith unto them, Peace be unto you. *But they were terrified and affrighted, and supposed that they had seen a spirit.*

And he said unto them, Why are ye troubled; and why do thoughts arise in your hearts? Behold my hands and my feet, that it is I myself: handle me, and see;[1] for a spirit hath not flesh and bones, as ye see me have.

And when he had thus spoken, he shewed them his hands and his feet. And while they yet believed not for joy, and wondered, he said unto them, Have ye here any meat?

And they gave him a piece of a broiled fish, and of an honeycomb. And he took it, and did eat before them. And he said unto them, These are the words which I spake unto you, while I was yet with you, that all things must be fulfilled, which were written in the law of Moses and in the Prophets and in the Psalms, concerning me.

Then opened he their understanding, that they might understand the Scriptures, and said unto them, Thus it is written, and thus it behoved Christ to suffer, and to rise from the dead the third day: and that repentance and remission of sins should be preached in his name among all nations, beginning at Jerusalem. And ye are witnesses of these things.

And, behold, I send the promise of my Father upon you: but tarry ye in the city of Jerusalem, until ye be endued with power from on high.

And he led them out as far as to Bethany, and he lifted up his hands, and blessed them. And it came to pass, while he blessed them, he was parted from them, and carried up into Heaven.

[*The same author elaborates a little on these events in the book of Acts of the Apostles:*]

He through the Holy Ghost had given commandments unto the apostles whom he had chosen, to whom also he shewed himself alive after his passion by many infallible proofs, being seen of them 40 days, and speaking of the things pertaining to the kingdom of God: and, being assembled together with them, commanded them that they should not depart from Jerusalem, but wait for the promise of the Father, which, saith he, Ye have heard of me. For John truly baptized with water; but ye shall be baptized with the Holy Ghost not many days hence.

When they therefore were come together, they asked of him, saying, 'Lord, wilt thou at this time restore again the kingdom to Israel?' And he said unto them, It is not for you to know the times or the seasons, which the Father hath put in his own power. But ye shall receive power, after that the Holy Ghost is come upon you: and ye shall be witnesses unto me both in Jerusalem, and in all Judea, and in Samaria, and unto the uttermost part of the earth.

And when he had spoken these things, while they beheld, he was taken up; and a cloud received him out of their sight.

[1] In the account given at John 20:19–30, 'Doubting' Thomas Didymus is sceptical, until Jesus invites him to touch his death wounds, or stigmata.

Mohammed Ali Jinnah

Indo-Pakistani statesman

Mohammed Ali Jinnah (1876–1948) was born in Karachi, which was then in north-west India. He studied at Bombay and Lincoln's Inn, London, and was called to the Bar in 1897. He ran a successful legal practice in Bombay, and in 1910 was elected to the Viceroy's legislative council. Already a member of the Indian National Congress, in 1913 he joined the Indian Muslim League and as its president brought about peaceful co-existence with the Congress Party through the Lucknow Pact (1916). In 1928, the British prime minister STANLEY BALDWIN sent Sir John Simon and six other MPs to assess India's constitutional affairs. Congress regarded the Simon Commission – which included no Indians – as an insult and imposed a boycott. Although Jinnah supported this effort, he opposed MAHATMA GANDHI's civil disobedience policy and resigned from the Congress Party, which he believed to be exclusively fostering Hindu interests. He continued to try to safeguard the rights of Muslim minorities at the London Round Table Conference in 1931. By 1940, he was strongly advocating separate statehood for Muslims and he resisted all British efforts, such as the mission by Sir Stafford Cripps (1942), to retain Indian unity. On 14 August 1947, the Dominion of Pakistan came into existence and Jinnah, known as *Quaid-i-Azam* (Great Leader), became its first governor-general. Although this was a ceremonial post as representative of the British monarch (who remained head of state after independence), Jinnah was a diligent leader, working hard to contain religious violence, protect the country's many refugees and challenge Indian domination of predominantly Muslim Kashmir. He died of tuberculosis and lung cancer, 13 months after taking office.

'A united India could never have worked'

11 August 1947, Karachi, then in India

❧

As early as March 1940, the Muslim League had adopted a resolution to seek the establishment of Pakistan as an Islamic state in the north-west and north-east of India, separate from the country's Hindu-dominated regions. A key figure in the drive for Indian independence, Jinnah emerged as the leader of this movement. Though he faced opposition from Gandhi, JAWAHARLAL NEHRU and the Hindu-dominated Indian Congress Party, he pursued the project relentlessly, ultimately achieving partition with the independence of India in 1947.

Jinnah was a natural and popular choice as first governor-general of Pakistan. On his election as president of the Constituent Assembly, three days before Pakistan came into existence, he gave this address at Karachi, immediately establishing himself as an authoritative leader.

In the speech, Jinnah identifies some of the problems that faced the new country, among them bribery and corruption, black-marketing, nepotism and the mingling of rival faith communities.

He insists, however, that had partition not been achieved, the tensions in a single united state would have made it unworkable. He also firmly positions Pakistan as a secular state rather than an Islamic theocracy (he appointed a Hindu as his first law minister, and was seen as a protector of Hindus).

Though partition led to much strife and violence, Jinnah was revered as the father of the nation.

❧

I cordially thank you, with the utmost sincerity, for the honour you have conferred upon me – the greatest honour that is possible to confer – by electing me as your first president. I also thank those leaders who have spoken in appreciation of my services and their personal references to me. I sincerely hope that with your support and your co-operation we shall make this constituent assembly an example to the world …

You know really that not only we ourselves are wondering but, I think, the whole world is wondering at this unprecedented cyclonic revolution, which has brought about the plan of creating and establishing two independent sovereign dominions in this subcontinent. As it is, it has been unprecedented; there is no parallel in the history of the world. This mighty subcontinent with all kinds of inhabitants has been brought under a plan which is titanic, unknown, unparalleled. And what is very important with regards to it is that we have achieved it peacefully and by means of an evolution of the greatest possible character …

The first and the foremost thing that I would like to emphasize is this: remember that you are now a sovereign legislative body and you have got all the powers. It therefore places on you the gravest responsibility as to how you should take your decisions. The first observation that I would like to make is this: you will no doubt agree with me that the first duty of a government is to maintain law and order, so that the life, property and religious beliefs of its subjects are fully protected by the state.

The second thing that occurs to me is this: one of the biggest curses from which India is suffering – I do not say that other countries are free from it, but I think our condition is much worse – is bribery and corruption. That really is a poison. We must put that down with an iron hand and I hope that you will take adequate measures as soon as it is possible for this assembly to do so.

Black-marketing is another curse. Well, I know that black-marketeers are frequently caught and punished. Judicial sentences are passed, or sometimes fines only are imposed. Now you have to tackle this monster, which today is a colossal crime against society, in our distressed conditions, when we constantly face shortage of food and other essential commodities of life. A citizen who does black-marketing commits, I think, a greater crime than the biggest and most grievous of crimes. These black-marketeers are really knowing, intelligent and ordinarily responsible people, and when they indulge in black-marketing, I think they ought to be very severely punished, because they undermine the entire system of control and regulation of foodstuffs and essential commodities, and cause wholesale starvation and want and even death.

The next thing that strikes me is this (here again it is a legacy which has been passed on to us): along with many other things, good and bad, has arrived this great evil, the evil of nepotism and jobbery. I want to make it quite clear that I shall never tolerate any kind of jobbery, nepotism or any influence directly or indirectly brought to bear upon me. Whenever I will find that such a practice is in vogue or is continuing anywhere, low or high, I shall certainly not countenance it.

I know there are people who do not quite agree with the division of India and the partition of the Punjab and Bengal. Much has been said against it, but now that it has been accepted, it is the duty of every one of us to loyally abide by it and honourably act according to the agreement, which is now final and binding on all. But you must remember, as I have said, that this mighty revolution that has taken place is unprecedented.

One can quite understand the feeling that exists between the two communities wherever one community is in majority and the other is in minority. But the question is, whether it was possible or practicable to act otherwise than what has been done. A division had to take place. On both sides, in Hindustan[1] and Pakistan, there are sections of people who may not agree with it, who may not like it, but in my judgement there was no other solution and I am sure future history will record its verdict in favour of it. And what is more, it will be proved by actual experience as we go on that was the only solution of India's constitutional problem. Any idea of a united India could never have worked and in my judgement it would have led us to terrific disaster.

Maybe that view is correct; maybe it is not; that remains to be seen. All the same, in this division it was impossible to avoid the question of minorities being in one dominion or the other. Now that was unavoidable. There is no other solution. Now what shall we do?

[1] A term with various meanings. Jinnah here probably refers to the new Republic of India.

Now, if we want to make this great state of Pakistan happy and prosperous, we should wholly and solely concentrate on the well-being of the people, and especially of the masses and the poor. If you will work in co-operation, forgetting the past, burying the hatchet, you are bound to succeed. If you change your past and work together in a spirit that every one of you – no matter to what community he belongs, no matter what relations he had with you in the past, no matter what is his colour, caste or creed – is first, second and last a citizen of this state, with equal rights, privileges, and obligations, there will be no end to the progress you will make.

I cannot emphasize it too much. We should begin to work in that spirit and in course of time all these angularities of the majority and minority communities, the Hindu community and the Muslim community – because even as regards Muslims you have Pathans, Punjabis, Shias, Sunnis and so on; and among the Hindus you have Brahmins, Vashnavas, Khatris; also Bengalis, Madrasis and so on – will vanish. Indeed if you ask me, this has been the biggest hindrance in the way of India to attain the freedom and independence; and but for this we would have been free peoples long ago.

No power can hold another nation, and specially a nation of 400 million souls, in subjection; nobody could have conquered you, and even if it had happened, nobody could have continued its hold on you for any length of time, but for this. Therefore, we must learn a lesson from this.

You are free; you are free to go to your temples, you are free to go to your mosques or to any other place of worship in this state of Pakistan. You may belong to any religion or caste or creed – that has nothing to do with the business of the state. As you know, history shows that in England, conditions, some time ago, were much worse than those prevailing in India today. The Roman Catholics and the Protestants persecuted each other. Even now there are some states in existence where there are discriminations made and bars imposed against a particular class.

Thank God, we are not starting in those days. We are starting in the days where there is no discrimination, no distinction between one community and another, no discrimination between one caste or creed and another. We are starting with this fundamental principle that we are all citizens and equal citizens of one state.

The people of England in course of time had to face the realities of the situation and had to discharge the responsibilities and burdens placed upon them by the government of their country and they went through that fire step by step. Today, you might say with justice that Roman Catholics and Protestants do not exist; what exists now is that every man is a citizen, an equal citizen of Great Britain and they are all members of the nation.

Now, I think we should keep that in front of us as our ideal and you will find that, in course of time, Hindus would cease to be Hindus and Muslims would cease to be Muslims – not in the religious sense, because that is the personal faith of each individual, but in the political sense as citizens of the state.

Well, gentlemen, I do not wish to take up any more of your time and thank you again for the honour you have done to me. I shall always be guided by the principles of justice and fair play without any – as is put in the political language – prejudice or ill-will, in other words, partiality or favouritism. My guiding principle will be justice and complete impartiality, and I am sure that with your support and co-operation, I can look forward to Pakistan becoming one of the greatest nations of the world.

I have received a message from the United States of America, addressed to me. It reads:

'I have the honour to communicate to you, in Your Excellency's capacity as President of the Constituent Assembly of Pakistan, the following message which I have just received from the Secretary of State of the United States: [2] "On the occasion of the first meeting of the Constituent Assembly for Pakistan, I extend to you and to the members of the Assembly the best wishes of the government and the people of the United States for the successful conclusion of the great work you are about to undertake."'

[2] The post was held at this time by GEORGE C MARSHALL.

John Paul II
Polish pope

John Paul II *originally Karol Józef Wojtyła* (1920–2005) was born in Wadowice. Ordained in 1946, he became Professor of Moral Theology at Lublin and Kraków. As Archbishop and Metropolitan of Kraków (1964–78), he was created cardinal in 1967 and was elected Pope in 1978, the first non-Italian Pope in 450 years. He was noted for his energy and analytical ability, and his pontificate saw many foreign visits, in which he preached to huge audiences. He also canonized more saints than all previous Popes put together. He survived two assassination attempts. In May 1981, he was shot and wounded in St Peter's Square, Rome, by a Turkish national, Mehmet Ali Ağca; a year later the Spanish priest Juan María Fernández y Krohn attempted to stab him with a bayonet in Fatima, Portugal. John Paul later visited Ağca in jail, and formed a relationship with his family. A champion of economic justice and an outspoken defender of the Church in communist countries, he was uncompromising on moral issues. In the 1980s his visits to Poland and his meetings with the Soviet leader Mikhail Gorbachev were of great assistance to the Polish union Solidarity in promoting Polish democracy, achieved in 1989. In 1995 he participated in historic meetings to discuss relations between the Orthodox and Roman Catholic Churches and other concerns. He met Tenzin Gyatso, 14th DALAI LAMA at the Vatican in 1999. In the late 1990s, he was diagnosed with Parkinson's disease, and his final years were marked by declining health. His successor Benedict XVI (1927–) began the process to beatify him less than two months after his death in April 2005. He wrote a play and several books, including *The Freedom of Renewal* (1972) and *The Future of the Church* (1979), and his *Collected Poems* appeared in 1982.

'We wish to remember for a purpose'
23 March 2000, Jerusalem, Israel

As the first Polish pope – who lived through his country's occupation, partition and devastation during World War II – John Paul II shared more common ground with Holocaust survivors than any of his Italian predecessors. In a letter of 1998, he wrote: 'The crime which has become known as the Shoah remains an indelible stain on the history of the century that is coming to a close. Remembrance of the Holocaust is an essential component in fashioning the future.'

Two years later, when he visited the Yad Vashem Holocaust Memorial in Jerusalem, he gave a speech which – in keeping with these sentiments – was both spiritual and pragmatic. The speech does not limit itself to lamentation over human wickedness, nor to dwelling on the message of hope in adversity provided by Psalm 31 – a sacred text for both Christians and Jews. Having established common religious ground, John Paul builds on it to insist that faith can be applied practically to forestall the evils perpetrated under 'a godless ideology'.

Conspiracy theories abound about the wartime Vatican's supposed knowledge of – or even complicity in – the Nazi genocide. Perhaps mindful of this, John Paul moves on to reject firmly any suggestion of anti-Semitism in the modern Vatican. He concludes with a plea for conciliation, unity and preventative remembrance.

The words of the ancient Psalm rise from our hearts:
'I have become like a broken vessel. I hear the whispering of many – terror on every side! – as they scheme together against me, as they plot to take my life. But I trust in you, O Lord; I say, "You are my God".'[1]

In this place of memories, the mind and heart and soul feel an extreme need for silence. Silence in which to remember. Silence in which to try to make some sense of the memories which come flooding back. Silence because there are no words strong enough to deplore the terrible tragedy of the Shoah.[2] My own personal memories are of all that happened when the Nazis occupied Poland during the war. I remember my Jewish friends and neighbours, some of whom perished, while others survived.

I have come to Yad Vashem to pay homage to the millions of Jewish people who, stripped of everything, especially of their human dignity, were murdered in the Holocaust. More than half a century has passed, but the memories remain.

[1] Psalm 31:12–14. During his speech, John Paul quotes three times from this passage.

[2] The Hebrew term for the Holocaust. It translates literally as 'catastrophe'.

Here, as at Auschwitz and many other places in Europe, we are overcome by the echo of the heart-rending laments of so many. Men, women and children cry out to us from the depths of the horror that they knew. How can we fail to heed their cry? No-one can forget or ignore what happened. No-one can diminish its scale.

We wish to remember. But we wish to remember for a purpose, namely to ensure that never again will evil prevail, as it did for the millions of innocent victims of Nazism. How could man have such utter contempt for man? Because he had reached the point of contempt for God. Only a godless ideology could plan and carry out the extermination of a whole people.

The honour given to the 'just Gentiles' by the state of Israel at Yad Vashem for having acted heroically to save Jews, sometimes to the point of giving their own lives, is a recognition that not even in the darkest hour is every light extinguished. That is why the Psalms, and the entire Bible, though well aware of the human capacity for evil, also proclaim that evil will not have the last word. Out of the depths of pain and sorrow, the believer's heart cries out: 'I trust in you, O Lord; I say, "You are my God".'

Jews and Christians share an immense spiritual patrimony, flowing from God's self-revelation. Our religious teachings and our spiritual experience demand that we overcome evil with good. We remember, but not with any desire for vengeance or as an incentive to hatred. For us, to remember is to pray for peace and justice, and to commit ourselves to their cause. Only a world at peace, with justice for all, can avoid repeating the mistakes and terrible crimes of the past.

As Bishop of Rome and successor of the Apostle Peter, I assure the Jewish people that the Catholic Church, motivated by the gospel law of truth and love and by no political considerations, is deeply saddened by the hatred, acts of persecution and displays of anti-Semitism directed against the Jews by Christians at any time and in any place. The church rejects racism in any form as a denial of the image of the Creator inherent in every human being.

In this place of solemn remembrance, I fervently pray that our sorrow for the tragedy which the Jewish people suffered in the 20th century will lead to a new relationship between Christians and Jews. Let us build a new future, in which there will be no more anti-Jewish feeling among Christians or anti-Christian feeling among Jews, but rather the mutual respect required of those who adore the one creator and Lord, and look to Abraham as our common father in faith.

The world must heed the warning that comes to us from the victims of the Holocaust and from the testimony of the survivors. Here at Yad Vashem the memory lives on, and burns itself onto our souls. It makes us cry out: 'I hear the whispering of many – terror on every side! But I trust in you, O Lord; I say, "You are my God".'

Lyndon B Johnson

American statesman

Lyndon Baines Johnson *known as LBJ* (1908–73) was born near Stonewall, Texas, into a Baptist family which was involved in state politics. He worked his way through college to become a high school teacher, then a Congress-man's secretary. He was elected to Congress in 1937, and was a strong supporter of President FRANKLIN D ROOSE-VELT's 'New Deal'. He joined the US Navy immediately after the Japanese attack on Pearl Harbor in 1941, and was decorated. He was elected as senator from Texas in 1948 and became Democratic leader in the Senate in 1953. In 1960, he contested the party's presidential nomination, which was won by JOHN F KENNEDY. When Kennedy was elected, Johnson became his vice president. After Kennedy's assassination in Dallas, Texas, in 1963, he succeeded to the presidency. He was returned as president in the 1964 election with a huge majority. Under his adminis-tration the Civil Rights Act (1964) – introduced by Kennedy the previous year – and the Voting Rights Act (1965) were passed, making effective, if limited, improvements to the position of racial minorities in the USA. He also introduced, under the slogan 'Great Society', a series of important economic and social welfare reforms, inclu-ding a medical care programme for the elderly and measures to improve education. However, the ever-increasing escalation of the war in Vietnam led to active protest and growing personal unpopularity for Johnson, and in 1968 he announced his decision to retire from active politics.

'The time of justice has now come'

15 March 1965, Washington, DC, USA

In this impassioned speech to Congress, proposing the Voting Rights Bill, the key phrase is 'We shall overcome', a rallying call of African–American leaders campaigning for civil rights.

The previous year, Johnson had signed the landmark Civil Rights Act of 1964, but further legislation was required to tackle discrimination against African–American voters at state and local elections – discrimination which often took the form of literacy, knowledge or even character tests to determine a voter's eligibility. The final catalyst for the new bill came one week before Johnson's address, when an African–American voter registration march from Selma to Montgomery, Alabama, was attacked by police officers, leading to the death of one of the campaigners.

Johnson was still working on his speech less than an hour before delivering it both to a plenary session of Con-gress and to the US public via television broadcast. He was anxious as to the legislature's reaction. Later, however, he revealed that while he was giving the speech, 'a picture rose before my eyes – a picture of blacks and whites marching together, side by side, chanting and singing the anthem of the civil rights movement'.

I speak tonight for the dignity of man and the destiny of democracy. I urge every member of both parties, Americans of all religions and of all colours, from every section of this country, to join me in that cause.

At times history and fate meet at a single time in a single place to shape a turning point in man's unending search for freedom. So it was at Lexington and Concord[1]. So it was a century ago at Appomattox.[2] So it was last week in Selma, Alabama.

There, long-suffering men and women peacefully protested the denial of their rights as Americans. Many were brutally assaulted. One good man, a man of God, was killed.[3]

There is no cause for pride in what has happened in Selma. There is no cause for self-satisfaction in the long denial of equal rights of millions of Americans. But there is cause for hope and for faith in our democracy in what is happening here tonight. For the cries of pain and the hymns and protests of oppressed people have summoned into convocation all the majesty of this great government – the government of the greatest nation on earth.

Our mission is at once the oldest and the most basic of this country: to right wrong, to do justice, to serve man. In our time we have come to live with moments of great crisis. Our lives have been marked with debate

[1] Lexington and Concord were the sites of the opening battles of the War of Independence in 1775.

[2] Appomattox was the scene of the surrender that ended the American Civil War in 1865.

[3] The victim was James J Reeb (1927–65), a white clergyman from Boston.

about great issues; issues of war and peace, issues of prosperity and depression. But rarely in any time does an issue lay bare the secret heart of America itself …

The issue of equal rights for American negroes is such an issue. And should we defeat every enemy, should we double our wealth and conquer the stars, and still be unequal to this issue, then we will have failed as a people and as a nation. For with a country, as with a person, 'What is a man profited, if he shall gain the whole world, and lose his own soul?'[4]

[4] Mark 8:36.

There is no negro problem. There is no southern problem. There is no northern problem. There is only an American problem. And we are met here tonight as Americans – not as Democrats or Republicans – we are met here as Americans to solve that problem.

This was the first nation in the history of the world to be founded with a purpose. The great phrases of that purpose still sound in every American heart, north and south: 'All men are created equal'[5] – 'government by consent of the governed'[6] – 'give me liberty or give me death'.[7] Well, those are not just clever words, or those are not just empty theories. In their name Americans have fought and died for two centuries, and tonight around the world they stand there as guardians of our liberty, risking their lives.

[5] From the opening sentence of the American Declaration of Independence.
[6] An indirect quotation from the Declaration of Independence.
[7] From PATRICK HENRY'S speech of 1775, included in this book.

Those words are a promise to every citizen that he shall share in the dignity of man. This dignity cannot be found in a man's possessions; it cannot be found in his power, or in his position. It really rests on his right to be treated as a man equal in opportunity to all others. It says that he shall share in freedom, he shall choose his leaders, educate his children, and provide for his family according to his ability and his merits as a human being …

Many of the issues of civil rights are very complex and most difficult. But about this there can and should be no argument. Every American citizen must have an equal right to vote. There is no reason which can excuse the denial of that right. There is no duty which weighs more heavily on us than the duty we have to ensure that right. Yet the harsh fact is that in many places in this country men and women are kept from voting simply because they are negroes.

Every device of which human ingenuity is capable has been used to deny this right. The negro citizen may go to register only to be told that the day is wrong, or the hour is late, or the official in charge is absent. And if he persists, and if he manages to present himself to the registrar, he may be disqualified because he did not spell out his middle name or because he abbreviated a word on the application.

And if he manages to fill out an application he is given a test. The registrar is the sole judge of whether he passes this test. He may be asked to recite the entire Constitution, or explain the most complex provisions of state law. And even a college degree cannot be used to prove that he can read and write. For the fact is that the only way to pass these barriers is to show a white skin.

Experience has clearly shown that the existing process of law cannot overcome systematic and ingenious discrimination. No law that we now have on the books – and I have helped to put three of them there[8] – can ensure the right to vote when local officials are determined to deny it.

[8] Johnson refers to the Civil Rights Act of 1964, the Equal Opportunity Act of 1964 and the Elementary and Secondary Education Act of 1965.

In such a case our duty must be clear to all of us. The Constitution says that no person shall be kept from voting because of his race or his colour. We have all sworn an oath before God to support and to defend that

Constitution. We must now act in obedience to that oath.

Wednesday, I will send to Congress a law designed to eliminate illegal barriers to the right to vote. The broad principles of that bill will be in the hands of the Democratic and Republican leaders tomorrow … This bill will strike down restrictions to voting in all elections – federal, state, and local – which have been used to deny negroes the right to vote. This bill will establish a simple, uniform standard which cannot be used, however ingenious the effort, to flout our Constitution. It will provide for citizens to be registered by officials of the United States government if the state officials refuse to register them. It will eliminate tedious, unnecessary lawsuits which delay the right to vote. Finally, this legislation will ensure that properly registered individuals are not prohibited from voting …

There is no constitutional issue here. The command of the Constitution is plain. There is no moral issue. It is wrong – deadly wrong – to deny any of your fellow Americans the right to vote in this country. There is no issue of state rights or national rights. There is only the struggle for human rights. I have not the slightest doubt what will be your answer …

But even if we pass this bill, the battle will not be over. What happened in Selma is part of a far larger movement which reaches into every section and state of America. It is the effort of American negroes to secure for themselves the full blessings of American life. Their cause must be our cause too. Because it is not just negroes, but really it is all of us, who must overcome the crippling legacy of bigotry and injustice. And we shall overcome.

As a man whose roots go deeply into Southern soil, I know how agonizing racial feelings are. I know how difficult it is to reshape the attitudes and the structure of our society. But a century has passed, more than 100 years, since the negro was freed. And he is not fully free tonight.

It was more than 100 years ago that ABRAHAM LINCOLN, a great president of another party, signed the Emancipation Proclamation,[9] but emancipation is a proclamation and not a fact. A century has passed, more than 100 years, since equality was promised. And yet the negro is not equal. A century has passed since the day of promise. And the promise is unkept.

The time of justice has now come. I tell you that I believe sincerely that no force can hold it back. It is right in the eyes of man and God that it should come. And when it does, I think that day will brighten the lives of every American. For negroes are not the only victims. How many white children have gone uneducated, how many white families have lived in stark poverty, how many white lives have been scarred by fear, because we have wasted our energy and our substance to maintain the barriers of hatred and terror?

So I say to all of you here, and to all in the nation tonight, that those who appeal to you to hold on to the past do so at the cost of denying you your future. This great, rich, restless country can offer opportunity and education and hope to all: black and white, north and south, sharecropper and city dweller. These are the enemies: poverty, ignorance, disease. They are the enemies and not our fellow man, not our neighbour. And these enemies too, poverty, disease and ignorance, we shall overcome.

Now let none of us in any sections look with prideful righteousness on the troubles in another section, or on the problems of our neighbours. There is really no part of America where the promise of equality has been fully kept. In Buffalo as well as in Birmingham, in Philadelphia as well as in

[9] The Emancipation Proclamation, issued by Lincoln on 22 September 1862 and 1 January 1863, officially freed the slaves of the Confederate states.

Selma, Americans are struggling for the fruits of freedom.

This is one nation. What happens in Selma or in Cincinnati is a matter of legitimate concern to every American. But let each of us look within our own hearts and our own communities, and let each of us put our shoulder to the wheel to root out injustice wherever it exists …

The bill that I am presenting to you will be known as a civil rights bill. But in a larger sense, most of the programme I am recommending is a civil rights programme. Its object is to open the city of hope to all people of all races. Because all Americans just must have the right to vote. And we are going to give them that right …

My first job after college was as a teacher in Cotulla, Texas, in a small Mexican–American school. Few of them could speak English, and I couldn't speak much Spanish. My students were poor and they often came to class without breakfast, hungry. They knew even in their youth the pain of prejudice. They never seemed to know why people disliked them. But they knew it was so, because I saw it in their eyes. I often walked home late in the afternoon, after the classes were finished, wishing there was more that I could do. But all I knew was to teach them the little that I knew, hoping that it might help them against the hardships that lay ahead.

Somehow you never forget what poverty and hatred can do when you see its scars on the hopeful face of a young child. I never thought then, in 1928, that I would be standing here in 1965. It never even occurred to me in my fondest dreams that I might have the chance to help the sons and daughters of those students and to help people like them all over this country.

But now I do have that chance – and I'll let you in on a secret – I mean to use it. And I hope that you will use it with me … Beyond this great chamber, out yonder in 50 states, are the people that we serve. Who can tell what deep and unspoken hopes are in their hearts tonight as they sit there and listen? We all can guess, from our own lives, how difficult they often find their own pursuit of happiness, how many problems each little family has. They look most of all to themselves for their futures. But I think that they also look to each of us.

Above the pyramid on the great seal of the United States it says – in Latin – 'God has favoured our undertaking'. God will not favour everything that we do. It is rather our duty to divine His will. But I cannot help believing that He truly understands and that He really favours the undertaking that we begin here tonight.

'Force must often precede reason'
7 April 1965, Baltimore, Maryland, USA

Johnson's first major speech on Vietnam, delivered three weeks later at Johns Hopkins University, was an attempt to justify the escalating US involvement. A series of massive bombing raids, known as 'Operation Rolling Thunder', had begun the previous month in response to an attack by the Viet Cong on a US military base in Pleiku, central Vietnam.

The speech points to the difficulties Johnson faced in Vietnam. Defeat would not only make the USA look weak in the eyes of the world, but might also lead to communist expansion in Asia and beyond. On the other hand, the war threatened to overshadow Johnson's domestic agenda, running counter to the aims of civil rights and welfare reform with which he wanted to be associated. A key phrase in this speech, reflecting such aims, is the 'dream of a world' of peace, opportunity and the rule of law.

Omitted here for reasons of space is a passage in which Johnson proposed a $1 billion development programme in Vietnam, which he hoped would persuade HO CHI MINH, leader of communist North Vietnam, to end hostilities. After the speech, Johnson predicted to his press secretary that 'old Ho can't turn me down'. Ho did precisely that, however, and over the next four years the number of US soldiers in Vietnam rose from around 100,000 to 550,000.

❧

Tonight, Americans and Asians are dying for a world where each people may choose its own path to change. This is the principle for which our ancestors fought in the valleys of Pennsylvania. It is the principle for which our sons fight tonight in the jungles of Vietnam.

Vietnam is far away from this quiet campus. We have no territory there, nor do we seek any. The war is dirty and brutal and difficult. And some 400 young men, born into an America that is bursting with opportunity and promise, have ended their lives on Vietnam's steaming soil. Why must we take this painful road? Why must this nation hazard its ease and its interest and its power, for the sake of a people so far away?

We fight because we must fight if we are to live in a world where every country can shape its own destiny. And only in such a world will our own freedom be finally secure. This kind of world will never be built by bombs or bullets. Yet the infirmities of man are such that force must often precede reason, and the waste of war, the works of peace.

We wish that this were not so. But we must deal with the world as it is, if it is ever to be as we wish. The world as it is in Asia is not a serene or peaceful place. The first reality is that North Vietnam has attacked the independent nation of South Vietnam. Its object is total conquest. Of course, some of the people of South Vietnam are participating in attack on their own government. But trained men and supplies, orders and arms, flow in a constant stream from north to south. This support is the heartbeat of the war.

And it is a war of unparallelled brutality. Simple farmers are the targets of assassination and kidnapping. Women and children are strangled in the night because their men are loyal to their government. And helpless villages are ravaged by sneak attacks. Large-scale raids are conducted on towns, and terror strikes in the heart of cities.

The confused nature of this conflict cannot mask the fact that it is the new face of an old enemy. Over this war – and all Asia – is another reality: the deepening shadow of communist China. The rulers in Hanoi are urged on by Peking. This is a regime which has destroyed freedom in Tibet,[1] which has attacked India, and has been condemned by the United Nations for aggression in Korea. It is a nation which is helping the forces of violence in almost every continent. The contest in Vietnam is part of a wider pattern of aggressive purposes.

Why are these realities our concern? Why are we in South Vietnam? We are there because we have a promise to keep. Since 1954 every American president has offered support to the people of South Vietnam.[2] We have helped to build, and we have helped to defend. Thus, over many years, we have made a national pledge to help South Vietnam defend its independence. And I intend to keep that promise.

To dishonour that pledge, to abandon this small and brave nation to its enemies, and to the terror that must follow, would be an unforgivable wrong. We are also there to strengthen world order. Around the globe, from Berlin to Thailand, are people whose wellbeing rests, in part, on the belief that they can count on us if they are attacked. To leave Vietnam to its fate would shake the confidence of all these people in the value of an American commitment and in the value of America's word. The result would be increased unrest and instability and even wider war.

[1] China invaded Tibet in October 1950.

[2] This promise was made after the Viet Cong defeated the French colonial administration in 1954, and announced its intention to unify North and South Vietnam under Communist rule.

We are also there because there are great stakes in the balance. Let no-one think for a moment that retreat from Vietnam would bring an end to conflict. The battle would be renewed in one country and then another. The central lesson of our time is that the appetite of aggression is never satisfied. To withdraw from one battlefield means only to prepare for the next. We must say in south-east Asia – as we did in Europe – in the words of the Bible: 'Hitherto shalt thou come, but no further.'[3]

[3] Job 38:11.

There are those who say that all our effort there will be futile – that China's power is such that it is bound to dominate all south-east Asia. But there is no end to that argument until all of the nations of Asia are swallowed up.

There are those who wonder why we have a responsibility there. Well, we have it there for the same reason that we have a responsibility for the defence of Europe. World War II was fought in both Europe and Asia, and when it ended we found ourselves with continued responsibility for the defence of freedom.

Our objective is the independence of South Vietnam, and its freedom from attack. We want nothing for ourselves – only that the people of South Vietnam be allowed to guide their own country in their own way. We will do everything necessary to reach that objective. And we will do only what is absolutely necessary …

We hope that peace will come swiftly. But that is in the hands of others besides ourselves. And we must be prepared for a long continued conflict. It will require patience as well as bravery, the will to endure as well as the will to resist.

I wish it were possible to convince others with words of what we now find it necessary to say with guns and planes: armed hostility is futile. Our resources are equal to any challenge. Because we fight for values and we fight for principles, rather than territory or colonies, our patience and our determination are unending.

Once this is clear, then it should also be clear that the only path for reasonable men is the path of peaceful settlement …

This war, like most wars, is filled with terrible irony. For what do the people of North Vietnam want? They want what their neighbours also desire: food for their hunger; health for their bodies; a chance to learn; progress for their country; and an end to the bondage of material misery. And they would find all these things far more readily in peaceful association with others than in the endless course of battle.

These countries of south-east Asia are homes for millions of impoverished people. Each day these people rise at dawn and struggle through until the night to wrestle existence from the soil. They are often racked by disease, plagued by hunger, and death comes at the early age of 40.

Stability and peace do not come easily in such a land. Neither independence nor human dignity will ever be won, though, by arms alone. It also requires the work of peace. The American people have helped generously in times past in these works. Now there must be a much more massive effort to improve the life of man in that conflict-torn corner of our world …

This will be a disorderly planet for a long time. In Asia, as elsewhere, the forces of the modern world are shaking old ways and uprooting ancient civilizations. There will be turbulence and struggle and even violence. Great social change – as we see in our own country now – does not always come without conflict.

We must also expect that nations will on occasion be in dispute with us. It may be because we are rich, or powerful; or because we have made some mistakes; or because they honestly fear our intentions. However, no nation need ever fear that we desire their land, or to impose our will, or to dictate their institutions.

But we will always oppose the effort of one nation to conquer another nation. We will do this because our own security is at stake. But there is more to it than that. For our generation has a dream. It is a very old dream. But we have the power and now we have the opportunity to make that dream come true.

For centuries, nations have struggled among each other. But we dream of a world where disputes are settled by law and reason. And we will try to make it so.

For most of history, men have hated and killed one another in battle. But we dream of an end to war. And we will try to make it so.

For all existence most men have lived in poverty, threatened by hunger. But we dream of a world where all are fed and charged with hope. And we will help to make it so.

The ordinary men and women of North Vietnam and South Vietnam – of China and India – of Russia and America – are brave people. They are filled with the same proportions of hate and fear, of love and hope. Most of them want the same things for themselves and their families. Most of them do not want their sons to ever die in battle, or to see their homes, or the homes of others, destroyed.

Well, this can be their world yet. Man now has the knowledge – always before denied – to make this planet serve the real needs of the people who live on it. I know this will not be easy. I know how difficult it is for reason to guide passion, and love to master hate. The complexities of this world do not bow easily to pure and consistent answers. But the simple truths are there just the same. We must all try to follow them as best we can ...

Every night, before I turn out the lights to sleep, I ask myself this question: have I done everything that I can do to unite this country? Have I done everything I can to help unite the world, to try to bring peace and hope to all the peoples of the world? Have I done enough?

Ask yourselves that question in your homes – and in this hall tonight. Have we, each of us, all done all we could? Have we done enough?

We may well be living in the time foretold many years ago when it was said: 'I call Heaven and earth to record this day against you, that I have set before you life and death, blessing and cursing: therefore choose life, that both thou and thy seed may live.'[4] This generation of the world must choose: destroy or build; kill or aid; hate or understand. We can do all these things on a scale never dreamed of before.

Well, we will choose life. In so doing we will prevail over the enemies within man, and over the natural enemies of all mankind.

[4] Deuteronomy 30:19.

Samuel Johnson
English writer, critic and lexicographer

Samuel Johnson *known as Dr Johnson* (1709–84) was born in Lichfield, Staffordshire, the son of a bookseller, and he read voraciously in his father's shop. He was educated at Pembroke College, Oxford, but left without taking a degree. He moved to Birmingham, where he turned to writing. In 1735 he married Elizabeth Porter and they opened a school near Lichfield. The school failed, and in 1737, the couple moved to London, where Johnson wrote parliamentary reports for *The Gentleman's Magazine*. In it he published (anonymously) his first poem, *London: A Poem in Imitation of the Third Satire of Juvenal*. In 1744 he produced a successful *Life* of his friend Richard Savage. In 1747 he issued a prospectus for his *Dictionary of the English Language*; and in 1749 he published his long didactic poem, *The Vanity of Human Wishes*. His tragedy *Irene* was produced at Drury Lane Theatre in 1749. In 1750–2, Johnson edited a periodical, *The Rambler*, full of moral essays written (anonymously) by himself. In 1752 his wife died, plunging him into lasting depression. His great Dictionary appeared in 1755. Johnson was awarded an honorary degree at Oxford, but continued with literary hack-work, contributing to *The Literary Magazine*, *The Idler* and *The Universal Chronicle* (1758–60). When his mother died, he wrote his moral fable, *Rasselas: The Prince of Abyssinia* (1759), in a week to defray the funeral expenses. With the accession of George III in 1760, Johnson was granted a pension of £300 for life, which brought him financial security for the first time. In 1763 he met James Boswell, who would become his biographer, and with whom he would share a delightful tour of the Hebrides, recorded in *A Journey to the Western Isles of Scotland* (1775). In 1764, he founded the Literary Club with friends including EDMUND BURKE and Joshua Reynolds; later members were Boswell and CHARLES JAMES FOX. In 1765, he published a critical edition of Shakespeare's plays (8 vols), with its classic *Preface*, and began his monumental *Lives of the Most Eminent English Poets* (10 vols, 1779–81). In that year Johnson's friend Henry Thrale died; his widow, Hester, who had looked after Johnson for many years, fell in love with an Italian musician and Johnson's wounded fury at their marriage in 1784 led to estrangement. He died in dejection, and was buried in Westminster Abbey.

'All human actions terminate in vanity'
c. 1760, Ashbourne, England

Unlike most of the speeches in this book, this sermon is attributed to its writer rather than its speaker. As well as his dictionary, biographies, poetry, diaries and essays, Samuel Johnson wrote around 40 sermons, of which 28 survive. Most of these were written for his old friend Dr John Taylor, with whom he had studied both at school and university. It is likely that Taylor preached this sermon at Ashbourne in Derbyshire, where he lived in a splendid house which still stands.

Johnson's theme is the futility of all actions undertaken in anticipation of earthly reward. Drawing on the wisdom of King Solomon, the reputed author of the Old Testament book of Ecclesiastes, Johnson argues that such actions lead to frustration, never happiness. This knowledge should teach us humility, he urges, while instilling in us a zeal for the afterlife, where real happiness lies.

Johnson himself plainly struggled with this message at times. In a letter to Taylor he wrote, 'O! my friend, the approach of death is very dreadful. I am afraid to think on that which I know I cannot avoid.'

I have seen all the works that are done under the sun; and behold, all is vanity and vexation of spirit – Ecclesiastes 1:14

That all human actions terminate in vanity, and all human hopes will end in vexation, is a position from which nature withholds our credulity, and which our fondness for the present life and worldly enjoyments disposes us to doubt; however forcibly it may be urged upon us, by reason or experience.

Every man will readily enough confess that his own condition discontents him; and that he has not yet been able, with all his labour, to make happiness, or, with all his inquiries, to find it. But he still thinks it is somewhere to be found, or by some means to be procured. His envy sometimes persuades him to imagine that others possess it; and his ambition points the way by which he supposes that he shall reach, at last, the station to which it is annexed. Everyone wants something to happiness, and when he has gained what he first wanted, he wants something else; he wears out life in efforts and pursuits, and perhaps dies regretting that he must leave the world when he is about to enjoy it ...

Experience never convinces us of our impotence; and indeed our miscarriages might be reasonably enough imputed by us, to our own unskillfulness, or ignorance, if we were able to derive intelligence from no experience but our own. But surely we may be content to credit the general voice of mankind, complaining incessantly of general infelicity; and when we see the restlessness of the young, and the peevishness of the old; when we find the daring and the active combating misery, and the calm and humble lamenting it; when the vigorous are exhausting themselves, in struggles with their own condition, and the old and the wise retiring from the contest, in weariness and despondency; we may be content at last to conclude that if happiness had been to be found, some would have found it ...

But though our obstinacy should hold out against common experience and common authority, it might at least give way to the declaration of Solomon, who has left this testimony to succeeding ages: that all human pursuits and labours are vanity. From the like conclusion made by other men we may escape by considering that their experience was small and their power narrow; that they pronounced with confidence upon that which they could not know; and that many pleasures might be above their reach, and many more beyond their observation ...

But the character of Solomon leaves no room for subterfuge. He did not judge of what he did not know. He had in his possession whatever power and riches and – what is still more – whatever wisdom and knowledge could confer ... Every power of delight which others possessed he had authority to summon, or wealth to purchase; all that royal prosperity could supply was accumulated upon him; at home he had peace, and in foreign countries he had honour; what every nation could supply was poured down before him ... But after the anxiety of his inquiries, the weariness of his labours, and the loss of his innocence, he obtained only this conclusion: 'I have seen all the works that are done under the sun, and behold, all is vanity and vexation of spirit.'

That this result of Solomon's experience – thus solemnly bequeathed by him to all generations – may not be transmitted to us without its proper use, let us diligently consider:

First, in what sense we are to understand that all is vanity.

Secondly, how far the conviction that all is vanity, ought to influence the conduct of life.

Thirdly, what consequences the serious and religious mind may deduce from the position that all is vanity.

When we examine first, in what sense we are to understand that all is vanity; we must remember that the preacher is not speaking of religious practices, or of any actions immediately commanded by God, or directly referred to him; but of such employments as we pursue by choice, and such work as we perform, in hopes of a recompense in the present life ...

The event of all human endeavours is uncertain. He that plants may gather no fruit; he that sows may reap no harvest. Even the most simple operations are liable to miscarriage, from causes which we cannot foresee; and if we could foresee them, cannot prevent. What can be more vain, than the confidence of man, when the annual provision made for the support of life is not only exposed to the uncertainty of the weather and the variation of the sky, but lies at the mercy of the reptiles of the earth, or the insects of the air? The rain and the wind he cannot command; the caterpillar he cannot destroy, and the locust he cannot drive away …

The history of mankind is little else than a narrative of designs which have failed, and hopes that have been disappointed. In all matters of emulation and contest, the success of one implies the defeat of another, and at least half the transaction terminates in misery. And in designs not directly contrary to the interest of another – and therefore not opposed either by artifice or violence – it frequently happens, that by negligence or mistake, or unseasonable officiousness, a very hopeful project is brought to nothing …

Every man hopes for kindness from his friends, diligence from his servants, and obedience from his children; yet friends are often unfaithful, servants negligent, and children rebellious. Human wisdom has, indeed, exhausted its power in giving rules for the conduct of life; but those rules are themselves but vanities. They are difficult to be observed, and though observed, are uncertain in the effect.

The labours of man are not only uncertain, but imperfect … He that rises to greatness finds himself in danger; he that obtains riches, perceives that he cannot gain esteem. He that is caressed, sees interest lurking under kindness; and he that hears his own praises, suspects that he is flattered. Discontent and doubt are always pursuing us. Our endeavours end without performance, and performance ends without satisfaction.

But since this uncertainty and imperfection is the lot which our Creator has appointed for us, we are to inquire, secondly, how far the conviction that all is vanity, ought to influence the conduct of life.

Human actions may be distinguished into various classes. Some are actions of duty, which can never be vain, because God will reward them. Yet these actions, considered as terminating in this world, will often produce vexation. It is our duty to admonish the vicious, to instruct the ignorant, and relieve the poor; and our admonitions will, sometimes, produce anger, instead of amendment; our instructions will be sometimes bestowed upon the perverse, the stupid, and the inattentive; and our charity will be sometimes misapplied by those that receive it and – instead of feeding the hungry – will pamper the intemperate; but these disappointments do not make good actions vain, though they show us how much all success depends upon causes, on which we have no influence.

There are likewise actions of necessity. These are often vain and vexatious, but such is the order of the world that they cannot be omitted. He that will eat bread must plough and sow, though it is not certain that he who ploughs and sows shall eat bread. It is appointed that life should be sustained by labour and we must not sink down in sullen idleness when our industry is permitted to miscarry … We must still prosecute our business, confess our imbecility, and turn our eyes upon him whose mercy is over all his works, and who, though he humbles our pride, will succour our necessities.

Works of absolute necessity are few and simple. A very great part of human diligence is laid out in accommodations of ease or refinements of pleasure; and the further we pass beyond the boundaries of necessity, the more we lose ourselves in the regions of vanity, and the more we expose ourselves to vexation of spirit. As we extend our pleasures, we multiply our wants … When to the enjoyments of sense are superadded the delights of fancy, we form a scheme of happiness that never can be complete, for we can always imagine more than we possess …

But most certain is the disappointment of him who places his happiness in comparative good, and considers, not what he himself wants, but what others have. The delight of eminence must, by its own nature, be rare, because he that is eminent, must have many below him … He that places his delight in the extent of his renown, is, in some degree, at the mercy of every tongue; not only malevolence, but indifference, may disturb him …

What, then, is the influence which the conviction of this unwelcome truth ought to have upon our conduct? It ought to teach us humility, patience, and diffidence. When we consider how little we know of the distant consequences of our own actions, how little the greatest personal qualities can protect us from misfortune, how much all our importance depends upon the favour of others, how uncertainly that favour is bestowed, and how easily it is lost, we shall find that we have very little reason to be proud …

But however unpleasing these considerations may be, however unequal our condition is to all our wishes or conceptions, we are not to admit impatience into our bosoms, or increase the evils of life by vain throbs of discontent. To live in a world where all is vanity, has been decreed by our Creator to be the lot of man, a lot which we cannot alter by murmuring, but may soften by submission.

The consideration of the vanity of all human purposes and projects, deeply impressed upon the mind, necessarily produces that diffidence in all worldly good which is necessary to the regulation of our passions, and the security of our innocence … The full persuasion that all earthly good is uncertain in the attainment and unstable in the possession – and the frequent recollection of the slender supports on which we rest, and the dangers which are always hanging over us – will dictate inoffensive modesty and mild benevolence.

He does not rashly treat another with contempt, who doubts the duration of his own superiority. He will not refuse assistance to the distressed, who supposes that he may quickly need it himself … He will not fix his fond hopes upon things which he knows to be vanity, but will enjoy this world, as one who knows that he does not possess it.

And that this is the disposition which becomes our condition will appear when we consider, thirdly, what consequences the serious and religious mind may draw from the position that all is vanity.

When the present state of man is considered, when an estimate is made of his hopes, his pleasures, and his possessions; when his hopes appear to be deceitful, his labours ineffectual, his pleasures unsatisfactory and his possessions fugitive, it is natural to wish for an abiding city, for a state more constant and permanent, of which the objects may be more proportioned to our wishes, and the enjoyments to our capacities; and from this wish it is reasonable to infer, that such a state is designed for us by that infinite wisdom, which, as it does nothing in vain, has not created minds with comprehensions never to be filled.

[1] Johnson refers to the Book of Revelation, the final book of the Bible, which describes the conclusion of the temporal world, to be replaced with a heavenly realm.

When Revelation[1] is consulted, it appears that such a state is really promised, and that, by the contempt of worldly pleasures, it is to be obtained. We then find that, instead of lamenting the imperfection of earthly things, we have reason to pour out thanks to him who orders all for our good, that he has made the world, such as often deceives, and often afflicts us; that the charms of interest are not such, as our frailty is unable to resist, but that we have such interruptions of our pursuits, and such languor in our enjoyments, such pains of body and anxieties of mind, as repress desire, and weaken temptation.

And happy will it be, if we follow the gracious directions of Providence, and determine that no degree of earthly felicity shall be purchased with a crime. If we resolve no longer to bear the chains of sin, to employ all our endeavours upon transitory and imperfect pleasures, or to divide our thoughts between the world and Heaven; but to bid farewell to sublunary vanities, to endure no longer an unprofitable vexation of spirit, but with pure heart and steady faith to 'fear God, and to keep his commandments, and remember that this is the whole duty of man'.[2]

[2] Ecclesiastes 12:13.

Chief Joseph
Native American chief

Chief Joseph *originally Hinmatonyalatkit ('Thunder Coming up over the Land from the Water')* (c.1840–1904) was born in Wallowa Valley, Oregon, the ancestral territory of the Nez Percé, the son of a chief who had converted to Christianity. They were peaceful people occupying large ancestral lands between Idaho and northern Washington, and enjoyed good relations with incoming white settlers. In 1855 Joseph's father signed a treaty guaranteeing his people much of their territory; but in the early 1860s, gold was discovered on Nez Percé lands, and in 1863 the US government forced a new treaty on them, depriving them of their homeland. On the death of his father in 1871, Joseph became one of the leaders of a Nez Percé band that refused to accept the new treaty. He counselled peace, but his braves killed several white settlers and in 1877 US troops were sent to capture them. After a series of battles, the Nez Percé were forced to retreat. Joseph led about 750 of his people on a 1,500-mile journey across four states, fighting off pursuing US troops who greatly outnumbered them and twice crossing the Rockies. He nearly completed his plan of leading his people into safety in Canada, but when they stopped to rest 30 miles from the border, they were surrounded by fresh troops under General Nelson A Miles. Joseph's dignified speech of surrender is famous. He and his people were sent to Indian Territory (Oklahoma), and he died in the Colville Indian Reservation in Washington.

'I will fight no more forever'
5 October 1877, Chinook, Montana, USA

Since imposing the new treaty of 1863, the US government had persistently attempted to displace the Nez Percé from their ancestral land. Meanwhile Joseph had become more entrenched, convinced by his father that 'a man cannot sell what he does not own'. He gradually resigned himself to capitulation, but in the spring of 1877 General Oliver Otis Howard arrived, insisting the Nez Percé leave within one month. Joseph resisted, claiming his livestock were scattered and the rivers were high. The ensuing tension led to violence and the deaths of four white men, allowing Howard the pretext to use force.

The Nez Percé fled, pursued by US soldiers whose numbers increased to about 2,000. Joseph showed great tactical skill during the skirmishes that followed and lost few men – earning the nickname 'The Red Napoleon'. However, the journey took its toll on the Nez Percé and they failed to reach their destination.

Joseph now recognized that he and his people were condemned to live under US regulation in a reservation. His famous, poetic lament was recorded (perhaps accurately) by a journalist from *Harper's Weekly* magazine. Following their surrender, many of Joseph's people died of a combination of malaria and starvation.

[1] A Nez Percé fighter thought by many to be the group's real strategist.

[2] Ta-Hool-Hool-Shute (c. 1810–77) was a Nez Percé chief who refused to cede tribal lands. He was killed at Bear Paw, Montana less than a week before this speech was given.

Tell General Howard I know his heart. What he told me before, I have it in my heart. I am tired of fighting. Our chiefs are killed: Looking Glass[1] is dead, Ta-Hool-Hool-Shute[2] is dead. The old men are all dead. It is the young men who say yes or no. He who led on the young men is dead. It is cold, and we have no blankets; the little children are freezing to death. My people, some of them, have run away to the hills, and have no blankets, no food. No-one knows where they are – perhaps freezing to death.

I want to have time to look for my children, and see how many of them I can find. Maybe I shall find them among the dead. Hear me, my chiefs! I am tired; my heart is sick and sad. From where the sun now stands I will fight no more forever.

Leon Kass
American bioethicist

Leon R Kass (1939–) was born in Chicago to Jewish immigrant parents and studied at the University of Chicago, where he gained a degree in 1958 and qualified as a medical doctor in 1962. He took a PhD in biochemistry at Harvard (1967), then served in the US Public Health Service while conducting molecular research at the National Institutes of Health. In 1969, he was a founding fellow of the Hastings Center in New York, the first US institution to examine bioethics. He served as executive secretary of the Committee on the Life Sciences and Social Policy of the National Research Council/National Academy of Sciences (1970–2). He taught at St John's College, Annapolis, Maryland, and at the Kennedy Institute of Ethics at Georgetown University, Washington, DC; and returned in 1976 to the University of Chicago, becoming an award-winning teacher. He was chairman of the President's Council on Bioethics, 2001–5, and is now the Addie Clark Harding Professor in the Committee on Social Thought and the College at the University of Chicago and Hertog Fellow in Social Thought at the American Enterprise Institute. His publications include *Toward a More Natural Science: Biology and Human Affairs* (1984); *The Hungry Soul: Eating and the Perfecting of Our Nature* (1994); *The Ethics of Human Cloning* (1998, with James Q Wilson) and *The Beginning of Wisdom: Reading Genesis* (2003).

'Human nature itself lies on the operating table'
17 May 2001, Chicago, Illinois, USA

When the field of study known as bioethics developed in the late 20th century, Dr Leon Kass soon emerged as one of its leading – and most controversial – figures. His cautious, philosophical stance has been labelled 'bioconservative', 'romantic', even 'anti-scientific'; many saw his appointment as chair of the Council of Bioethics by the highly conservative president GEORGE W BUSH as confirmation of this. The council was later accused of politicizing bioethics by stifling dissenting views and recruiting from the religious right.

But Kass, who encourages science students to study great works of literature, is equipped to appeal to a broad spectrum of society. Like the novelist and physicist C P SNOW – whose 'Two Cultures' speech is included in this book – he advocates both scientific and philosophical thought. In this speech, given at a symposium on genetics at Chicago University, he attacks the prospect of human cloning as 'repulsive', but also as clinically bankrupt – a case he argues on four itemized grounds.

In urging an outright ban, he also demonstrates a sense of political pragmatism. If the ban cannot be imposed globally, he proposes, let it be introduced unilaterally; he also argues that this would reassure the public that scientists can be trusted to proceed responsibly without interference.

His conclusions are both legally and scientifically radical. The ban, he concedes, is unprecedented in US law; furthermore the 'technological imperative' that has traditionally driven scientific progress must be challenged. He clinches his argument with a stark statement contrasting 'free human beings' with 'slaves of unregulated innovation'.

The urgency of the great political struggles of the 20th century – successfully waged against totalitarianisms first right and then left – seems to have blinded many people to a deeper truth about the present age: all contemporary societies are travelling briskly in the same utopian direction … Leading the triumphal procession is modern medicine, becoming daily ever more powerful in its battle against disease, decay and death, thanks especially to the astonishing achievements in biomedical science and technology – achievements for which we must surely be grateful.

Yet contemplating present and projected advances in genetic and reproductive technologies, in neuroscience and psychopharmacology, and in the development of artificial organs and computer-chip implants for human brains, we now clearly recognize new uses for biotechnical power that soar beyond the traditional medical goals of healing disease and relieving suffering. Human nature itself lies on the operating table, ready for alteration, eugenic and psychic 'enhancement' and wholesale redesign.

Some transforming powers are already here. The pill. In vitro fertilization. Bottled embryos. Surrogate wombs. Cloning. Genetic screening. Genetic manipulation. Organ harvests. Mechanical spare parts. Chimeras. Brain implants. Ritalin for the young, Viagra for the old and Prozac for everyone.

Years ago Aldous Huxley saw it coming. In his charming but disturbing novel, *Brave New World*, he made its meaning strikingly visible for all to see.[1] Huxley paints human life seven centuries hence … At long last, mankind has succeeded in eliminating disease, aggression, war, anxiety, suffering, guilt, envy and grief. But this victory comes at the heavy price of homogenization, mediocrity, pacification, trivial pursuits, shallow attachments, debasement of tastes, spurious contentment and souls without loves or longings.

The Brave New World has achieved health, prosperity, community, stability, and nigh-universal contentment, only to be peopled by creatures of human shape but of stunted humanity. They consume, fornicate, take 'soma', enjoy 'centrifugal bumble-puppy' and operate the machinery that makes it all possible. They do not read, write, think, love, or govern themselves. Art and science, virtue and religion, family and friendship are all passé. What matters most is bodily health and immediate gratification. Babies and blessings both come out of bottles. Brave new man is so dehumanized that he does not even recognize what has been lost …

In Huxley's novel, everything proceeds under the direction of an omnipotent – albeit benevolent – world state. But the dehumanization he portrays does not really require despotism. To the contrary, precisely because the society of the future will deliver exactly what we most want – health, safety, comfort, plenty, pleasure, peace of mind and length of days – mankind can reach the same humanly debased condition solely on the basis of free human choice. No need for World Controllers. Just give us the technological imperative, liberal democratic society, compassionate humanitarianism, moral pluralism and free markets and we can take ourselves to Brave New World all by ourselves – and, what is most distressing, without even deliberately deciding to go. In case you hadn't noticed, the train has left the station and is gathering speed, but no-one seems to be in charge.

Not the least of our difficulties, in trying to exercise control over where biology is taking us, is the fact that we do not get to decide, once and for all, for or against the destination of a post-human world. The scientific discoveries and technical powers that will take us there come to us piecemeal, one at a time and seemingly independent from one another, each often attractively introduced as a measure that will 'help us not to be sick'. But sometimes we come to a clear fork in the road where decision is possible and where we know that the decision we make will make a world of difference, indeed, will make a permanently different world.

We stand now at the point of such a momentous decision. Events have conspired to provide us with a perfect opportunity to seize the initiative and to gain some control of the biotechnical project. I refer to the prospect of human cloning, a practice absolutely central to Huxley's fictional world. Indeed, creating and manipulating life in the laboratory is the gateway to the Brave New World, not only in fiction but also in fact.

'To clone or not to clone a human being' is no longer a fanciful question. Success in cloning first sheep,[2] then also cows, mice, pigs and goats, make it perfectly clear that a fateful decision is now at hand: whether we should welcome or even tolerate the cloning of human beings.

[1] The most famous work of the English novelist, poet and essayist Aldous Huxley (1894–1963), *Brave New World* (1932) is a pre-eminent example of dystopian fiction, which extrapolates current trends to produce alarming visions of the future.

[2] This was accomplished in 1996 at the Roslin Institute near Edinburgh, Scotland, when a ewe was cloned from an adult mammary cell. It was named Dolly, after the country singer Dolly Parton (1946–). It developed arthritis abnormally young and died of lung disease in 2003.

Human cloning, though partly continuous with previous reproductive technologies, is also something radically new, both in itself and in its easily foreseeable consequences ... We are compelled to decide nothing less than whether human procreation is going to remain human, whether children are going to be *made-to-order* rather than begotten, and whether we wish to say yes in principle to the road that leads to the dehumanized hell of *Brave New World* ...

What is cloning? Cloning, or asexual reproduction, is the production of individuals who are genetically identical to an already existing individual ... Some possible misconceptions need to be avoided. First, cloning is not Xeroxing: the clone of **BILL CLINTON**,[3] though his genetic double, would enter the world hairless, toothless, and peeing in his diapers, like any other human infant. But neither is cloning just like natural twinning: the cloned twin will be identical to an older, existing adult; it will arise not by chance but by deliberate design; and the entire genetic makeup will be pre-selected by the parents and/or scientists. Further, the success rate, at least at first, will probably not be very high. For this reason among others, it is unlikely that, at least for now, the practice would be very popular, and there is no immediate worry of mass-scale production of multicopies.

Still, for the tens of thousands of people who sustain over 300 assisted-reproduction clinics in the United States and already avail themselves of in vitro fertilization and other techniques, cloning would be an option with virtually no added fuss. Should commercial interests develop in 'nucleus banking', as they have in sperm banking and egg harvesting; should famous athletes or other celebrities decide to market their DNA the way they now market their autographs and nearly everything else; should techniques of embryo and germ-line[4] genetic testing and manipulation arrive as anticipated, increasing the use of laboratory assistance in order to obtain 'better' babies – then cloning, if permitted, could become more than a marginal practice simply on the basis of free reproductive choice.

What to think about this prospect? Nothing good. Indeed, most people are repelled by nearly all aspects of human cloning: the possibility of mass production of human beings, with large clones of look-alikes, compromised in their individuality; the idea of father-son or mother-daughter twins; the bizarre prospect of a woman bearing and rearing a genetic copy of herself, her spouse, or even her deceased father or mother; the grotesqueness of conceiving a child as an exact replacement for another who has died; the utilitarian creation of embryonic duplicates of oneself, to be frozen away or created when needed to provide homologous tissues or organs for transplantation; the narcissism of those who would clone themselves and the arrogance of others who think they know who deserves to be cloned; the Frankensteinian[5] hubris to create human life and increasingly to control its destiny; men playing at being God. Almost no-one finds any of the suggested reasons for human cloning compelling; almost everyone anticipates its possible misuses and abuses. Moreover, the belief that human cloning cannot be prevented makes the prospect all the more revolting.

Revulsion is not an argument; and some of yesterday's repugnances are today calmly accepted – though, one must add, not always for the better. In crucial cases, however, repugnance is the emotional expression of deep wisdom, beyond reason's power fully to articulate it. Can anyone really give an argument fully adequate to the horror which is father-daughter incest (even with consent), or having sex with animals, or mutilating a corpse, or

[3] Clinton was US President at this time.

[4] A sequence of cells containing genetic material that may be passed on to an offspring.

[5] Kass refers to the famous Gothic novel *Frankenstein* (1818) by Mary Shelley (1797–1851), in which the scientist Victor Frankenstein 'creates' a living creature from human body parts.

eating human flesh, or raping or murdering another human being?

Let me suggest that our repugnance at human cloning belongs in that category. We are repelled by the prospect of cloning human beings, not because of the strangeness or novelty of the undertaking, but because we intuit and feel, immediately and without argument, the violation of things that we rightfully hold dear … Shallow are the souls that have forgotten how to shudder.

Yet repugnance need not stand naked before the bar of reason. The wisdom of our horror at human cloning *can* be partially articulated. I offer four objections to human cloning: (1) it involves unethical experimentation; (2) it threatens identity and individuality; (3) it turns procreation into manufacture; and (4) it means despotism over children and perversion of parenthood.

First, any attempt to clone a human being would constitute an unethical experiment upon the resulting child-to-be. In all the animal experiments, fewer than two to three per cent of cloning attempts succeed. Not only are there foetal deaths and stillborn infants, but there is also a high incidence of late-appearing disabilities and deformities in cloned animals that attain live birth. Nearly all scientists agree that attempts to clone a human being carry grave risks of producing unhealthy and disabled children. Considered opinion (even among scientists) is virtually unanimous: attempts at human cloning are irresponsible and unethical. We cannot ethically even get to know whether or not human cloning is feasible.

Second, cloning, if successful, would create serious issues of identity and individuality. The clone may experience concerns about his distinctive identity not only because he will be in genotype and appearance identical to another human being, but, in this case, because he may also be twin to the person who is his 'father' or 'mother' – if one can still call them that. What would be the psychic burdens of being the 'child' or 'parent' of your twin? … In addition, unlike 'normal' identical twins, a cloned individual will be saddled with a genotype that has already lived. He will not be fully a surprise to the world: people are likely always to compare his performances in life with that of his alter ego, especially if he is a clone of someone gifted or famous …

Third, human cloning would represent a giant step toward turning begetting into making, procreation into manufacture (literally, something 'handmade'), a process already begun with in vitro fertilization and genetic testing of embryos. With cloning, not only is the process in hand, but the total genetic blueprint of the cloned individual is selected and determined by the human artisans. To be sure, subsequent development is still according to natural processes, and the resulting children will be recognizably human. But we here would be taking a major step into making man himself simply another one of the man-made things …

Finally, the practice of human cloning by nuclear transfer – like other anticipated forms of genetically engineering the next generation – would enshrine and aggravate a profound and mischief-making misunderstanding of the meaning of having children and of the parent-child relationship. When a couple normally chooses to procreate, the partners are saying yes to the emergence of new life in its novelty, are saying yes not only to having a child but also to having whatever child this child turns out to be. In accepting our finitude and opening ourselves to our replacement, we tacitly confess the limits of our control …

A wanted child now means a child who exists precisely to fulfil parental wants. Like all the more precise eugenic manipulations that will follow in its wake, cloning is thus inherently despotic, for it seeks to make one's children after one's own image (or an image of one's choosing) and their future according to one's will …

Whether or not they share my reasons, most people share my conclusion: Human cloning is unethical in itself and dangerous in its likely consequences, including the precedent it will establish for designing our children. For us the real questions are: what should we do about it? How best to succeed? What we should do is to work to prevent human cloning by making it illegal. We should aim for an international legal ban if possible and for a unilateral ban at a minimum – and soon, before the fact is upon us.

To be sure, renegade scientists may secretly undertake to violate such a law, but we can deter them by criminal sanctions and monetary penalties, as well as by removing any incentives to proudly claim credit for their technological bravado and success. Such a ban on clonal baby-making, moreover, will not harm the progress of basic genetic science and technology. On the contrary, it will reassure the public that scientists are happy to proceed without violating the deep ethical norms of the human community. And it will protect worthy science against a public backlash triggered by the brazen misconduct of the rogues.

I appreciate that a Federal legislative ban is without American precedent, at least in matters technological (though the British and many other European nations have banned cloning of human beings, and we ourselves ban incest, polygamy, and other forms of 'reproductive freedom'). Perhaps such a ban will prove ineffective; perhaps it will eventually be shown to have been a mistake. But – and this is maybe the most important result – it would at least place the burden of practical proof where it belongs, requiring proponents to show very clearly what great social or medical good can be had only by the cloning of human beings. Only for such a compelling case, yet to be made or even imagined, should we wish to risk this major departure in human procreation.

We Americans have lived by and prospered under a rosy optimism about scientific and technological progress. The technological imperative has, on balance, probably served us well, though we should admit that there is no accurate method for weighing benefits and harms. But there is very good reason for shifting the paradigm around, at least regarding those technological interventions into the human body and mind that will surely effect fundamental (and likely irreversible) changes in human nature, basic human relationships, and what it means to be a human being. Here we surely should not be willing to risk everything in the naïve hope that, should things go wrong, we can later set them right again.

The present danger posed by human cloning is, paradoxically, also a golden opportunity. In a truly unprecedented way, we can strike a blow for the human control of the technological project, for wisdom, prudence and human dignity. The prospect of human cloning, so repulsive to contemplate, is the occasion for deciding whether we shall be slaves of unregulated innovation, and ultimately its artifacts, or whether we shall remain free human beings who guide our technique toward the enhancement of human dignity. The humanity of the human future is in our hands.

Brian Keenan
Northern Irish teacher and writer

Brian Keenan (1950–) was born in Belfast, where he gained degrees in English and Anglo-Irish literature before working as a teacher and in community development. He worked as a teacher in the English department at the American University of Beirut, Lebanon (1985–6), where he was kidnapped and held hostage. Following his release in 1990, he became a writer and journalist. He now lives near Dublin with his wife and two children. His publications include the bestselling memoir of his captivity *An Evil Cradling* (1992) (*Irish Times* Irish Literature Prize for Non-Fiction; Christopher Ewart-Biggs Memorial Prize; *Time-Life* PEN Award), the travel books *Between Extremes* (1999, with fellow hostage John McCarthy) and *Four Quarters of Light* (2004), and the novel *Turlough* (2000). He returned to Beirut for the first time since his release from captivity in 2007.

'Hostage is a crucifying aloneness'
August 1990, Dublin, Ireland
🐦

While walking to work in Beirut on 11 April 1986, Brian Keenan was bundled into the back of an old Mercedes by four gunmen. He spent the next four and a half years as a hostage of the militant group Islamic Jihad.

For the first few months, he was kept in complete isolation and darkness in a filthy cell; but later he was confined with other western hostages, including Dr Tom Sutherland (the American dean of agriculture at the university), the American journalist Terry Anderson and the British journalist John McCarthy.

On 24 August 1990 – following negotiations credited to Iranian officials – Keenan was finally released. On arriving home in Dublin, he held a press conference, at which he made this moving speech.

Mindful of his former companions, who were still being held, he begins by urging the press to cover the story with sensitivity. Later he speaks with evident affection about his cellmates, describing the games and conversations that enabled them to survive the ordeal. But the heart of the speech is the short passage beginning 'Hostage is a crucifying aloneness', which expresses in poetic terms the spiritual agonies of captivity.

McCarthy, Sutherland and Anderson were all released, separately, towards the end of 1991.

Keenan's book *An Evil Cradling* describes his experiences as a hostage. It inspired the successful play *Someone Who'll Watch Over Me* (1992) by the Irish playwright Frank McGuinness.
🐦

I would like to begin this press conference by making a firm request and a strong appeal to all members of the press and the media. I would ask you to use all your judgement and exercise restraint in your reports, remembering [they may affect] the psychological and physical wellbeing of those who remain in captivity. In the past some members of the American press and media issued reports which … hinted and in some cases strongly suggested that the tapes that their kidnappers had given [released hostages] to bring out had been coded by the hostages. Such unfounded and irresponsible remarks came within a hair's breadth of having some of the remaining hostages summarily executed.

You must remember that hysteria with these men is not subject to reason.[1] Various other statements surrounding the release of other more recent hostages have exacerbated appalling conditions … I therefore appeal to those motives of morality and humanity which in this case must be the primary motivating urge of your profession. Remember: these are people. Hostages, wherever they are, whatever they are, regardless of nationality, religious or ethnic background, *are* human beings. All of us are but teeth on a comb — and if one is snapped off in a sudden rage it cannot, cannot be put back.

A hostage is a word that's for a long time been used in the press. May I just briefly give my own short, brief definitions for that word?

Hostage is a crucifying aloneness. There's a silent, screaming slide into the bowels of ultimate despair. [*Pause.*] Hostage is a man hanging by his

[1] Keenan later wrote that, 'the mercurial temperament and psychotic personality of some of our captors occasioned erratic but constant abuse and violence'.

fingernails over the edge of chaos, feeling his fingers slowly straightening. Hostage is the humiliating stripping away of every sense and fibre of body and mind and spirit that make us what we are. Hostage is a mutant creation, filled with fear, self-loathing, guilt and death-wishing, but he is a man, a rare, unique and beautiful creation, of which these things are no part. You now have a real opportunity to reach out and help those people, whoever and wherever they are. Seize that chance to reach out and give part of yourselves to them.

There is no victory in condemnation or retribution … I cannot now condemn a man because he is different from me. Such conceit is self-maiming. Now I have seen just a little of the world again, I know one thing at least for sure. God loves diversity. The degree to which a man is different from me is that same degree by which I am enriched and expanded through him. Our differences reconcile us to a greater whole, limitless, fathomless, in which all men can partake.

So now I want to tell you a little of those hostages, those men I knew, our differences, our oneness, these men who were as my limbs. [*Pause.*] My continuing shadow of despair and raging hope.

[*Pause and deep sigh.*] A drink. [*Drinks.*]

Dr Tom Sutherland … whose life has been spent exclusively in the service of education in England, America, Ethiopia, Beirut. A man courteous in manner and very, very great in heart who joyed tremendously in servicing young minds everywhere … For many hours we would sit with him while he delivered fascinating lectures in genetics and animal husbandry, his specific fields of study. They came to us in those awful places as a kind of light illuminating our darkness, warming that chill and that despair. His value as a patient and kind instructor fed our dreams to shield us from those long, long nights.

The Dean owns a 27-year-old Volvo which he bought brand new – 27 years ago, obviously – which he has loved, he has nourished since he bought it. We each of us know that Volvo extremely well, having talked about it at great length over many nights …

I should say that perhaps it was unfortunate that the professor's long career and service to those young people never allowed him to develop very much skill at poker, which was much to our advantage …

Perhaps, of all of us, [he was] the man least prepared by life for the horror he now endures. I watched his eyes light in dazzling enthusiasm as he took several hours a day to teach me French, with a consortium of broken matchsticks, cigarette papers and an ancient French historical novel, which I never want to read again in my life …

I'd like to talk about Terry Anderson. Old Terry's a bit of a bulky and a belligerent newspaper man – I'm sure like many of you out in front of me – who had a voracious hunger for intellectual conversation and when he could not get it would pace the floor endlessly in his patched and re-patched and much more patched but still very holy socks.

He didn't get pacing very far as the chain was only about this long [*indicates about five feet*]. Terry we affectionately and jokingly called 'Thunderbum' for his frequent bouts of Beirut belly, which everybody had regularly. It is not, not, not a pleasant illness. Though often debilitated with pain, he stoically suffered, for in truth all pain and illness was generally dismissed by our keepers, though they would eventually and always supply us with some form of antibiotic …

And so having had some ease from his Beirut belly, Terry would be back again to his forceful debates on many subjects, which kept us awake for many hours. I think Terry debated with himself a lot while we tried to plug our ears with bits of mattress and bits of pillow.

Terry would also, like us all, take his periods of despair and seek solace in his family. After many long periods of silence, Terry and perhaps myself would sit through those long nights and speak with much pain and remorse and the great longing and love for his first daughter Gabrielle. She is a much older child than when last he saw her and with many tears he would elaborate [*pause*] he would elaborate his plans to bring her to the States to have that fatherly sharing of love and affection with her to help her to shape and discover her future.

In these confessional moments which were common to us all, a deep and enduring and unbreakable bond was formed. Beyond the bluster which we each maintained, Terry's life was shaping itself towards his children with this deep burden of love, this deep burden of need …

I watched him and worked with him as he designed and evolved a project for a school for young delinquent boys in America; everything worked out in fine, meticulous and authoritative detail – indeed quite a masterpiece of thought and the depths of conviction. The doyen of hostages, as he has been called, is a man I feel so totally committed to these things that he inspired us to our own survival projects.

My soulmate [*pause*] and my cellmate. John Boy, I call him. [*Pause.*] How can I forget Johnny McCarthy – his humour, his mimicry, his abundant love of life on so many times seemed to diminish almost to extinction those grinding moments of hopelessness … When a man can find a will equal to vision and by force of the fire that is in him fuse these things, he is undiminished and can never be diminished.

In John Boy I saw a man grow; I watched a man deepen, and it was a real joy to be a witness to that. But sometimes – unfortunately for us – humour is John's forte, and it infused and infested us all. I remember how when we had no reading material for over a year we played 17-hour marathon games of dominoes. Can you imagine what it would be like to play with [*Austrian accent*] 'a Viennese doctor of ze alienation, who vos having ze most unusual but exciting sexual liaison with some amazing but very plain Hausfrau from Bavaria. Most interesting; and now I'm vinning another game, you stupid Dumkopf'?

This was usual for John and he usually beat me at these exciting stories he would tell in his huge, huge box of personalities. There is a famous quotation from John Milton: 'The mind is its own place and in itself / Can make a Heaven of Hell or a Hell of Heaven.'[2] The problem with that eloquent sentence is: how can you control the mind when the mind itself has already chosen to go its own way, independent of one's will, one's desire, one's need?

From the depths of mania or despair – that awful, howling wilderness where one felt like no more than a speck of dust in an alien cosmos – John Boy's ever-present, good-natured insanity does dissolve with light and thrust us back to the world …

In the beginning, when he was kept alone and even during the first month we were together [he] was somewhat withdrawn, fearful and initially found person-to-person communication difficult. This was repeated when we were put with the Americans after some time. It was a matter of slowly re-learning how to socialize. We all often thought: how could we relate to anyone what we had been thinking?

[2] *Paradise Lost*, Book 1, line 253.

Tiny, tiny cells; constant blindfolds; prolonged days in the dark; sometimes weeks without light create kinds of insanity that drive men deep, deep into themselves. Other people one begins to look at with strange, mistrustful apprehension – but the irrepressible wit that's the golden kernel of John [*pause*] ultimately and always emerged. He would even imitate some of the guards with a precision and a zaniness that reduced their brutality to insignificance ...

John McCarthy is a big giver. It is now time for some people to start giving to John McCarthy – and I am not referring to John McCarthy's action group. There are many stories I could tell you about John and many stories I could tell you about the Americans. Their deeply moving concern for their families and their friends, their occasional and disturbing doubts about the health of some of their families. Remember that these men have had only minimal information of their families and in that quarter-life existence with the mind's massive overload, pushing and straining for survival, these men know an awful smothering in the shadows.

But because I know them as rich, vibrant, colourful human beings I know they have also – as has been said by a better man than me – the courage to seek, to thrive, to find and not to yield.

Undoubtedly you may be asking me of my analysis, my solution. What can I say, having known nothing for four and a half years? This world has changed very greatly for me. I offer you only this solution, for it was the only solution that I had and we all had for the period of our captivity.

[*Holds up hands.*]

Look at my hands. The human body has two hands, the most complex and perhaps the most beautiful structure, and with these hands I can do many things. I can make a fist [*makes fist with left hand*] ... and I can make with it a driving force of such power. I can destroy; I can tear down; I can in my rage and in my fear and in my fury make a wasteland about me.

I can with this hand [*holds up right hand*] in its subtle and elaborate freedom, play a piece of music; I can write a book; I can paint; I can sculpt; I can make a friend. A few nights ago ... I held a new baby in these hands. I felt myself more trembling and alive than I have ever felt. But above all with this hand [*right*] I can overcome this hand [*left*]. I can contain this hand. I can conquer this hand. This power in all of us is creative, it is passionate and it is unconquerable ...

How can I thank all the people ... hundreds, thousands of people whom I have never met and may perhaps never meet, who have sent me messages, cards, flowers, gifts. To experience such love is to partake of something sublime. I thank them all; I embrace them all.

I must express my thanks to many ... Thank you, thank you to all. To all and everyone on this island, thank you. Finally [*indicating his family and friends*] I just want to say more than thanks to them – and you're not going to see it. Okay, ladies and gentlemen: thank you very much.

John F Kennedy
American statesman

John Fitzgerald Kennedy (1917–63) was born in Brookline, Massachusetts, the second son of Joseph P Kennedy. He graduated from Harvard in 1940 and the same year published *Why England Slept*, a bestselling analysis of Great Britain's unpreparedness for war. He served as a torpedo boat commander in the Pacific during World War II and was decorated for his courageous conduct when the boat was hit and sunk. Elected to the US House of Representatives as a Democrat from Massachusetts in 1946, he won a Senate seat in 1952 and the next year married Jacqueline Lee Bouvier (1929–94). While convalescing from spinal operations he wrote *Profiles in Courage* (1956), which won a Pulitzer Prize. Though he failed in his effort to gain the Democratic vice-presidential nomination in 1956, he won the presidential nomination in 1960. He defeated the Republican candidate RICHARD M NIXON by a narrow margin, to became the first Catholic and, at 43, the youngest person to be elected president. He introduced a legislative programme, the 'New Frontier', which aimed to extend civil rights and to provide funding for education, medical care for the elderly and the space programme, but much of it stalled in Congress. Through his brother ROBERT F KENNEDY he supported federal desegregation policy in schools and universities. He faced a series of foreign policy crises, including the unsuccessful invasion of FIDEL CASTRO's Cuba at the Bay of Pigs (April 1961), the building of the Berlin Wall (August 1961) and the Cuban missile crisis (October 1962). At the risk of nuclear war, he induced the Soviet Union to withdraw its missiles from Cuba, and he achieved a partial nuclear test ban treaty with the USSR in 1963. He also founded the Peace Corps and increased the US military involvement in Vietnam. On 22 November 1963, he was assassinated by rifle fire while being driven in an open car through Dallas, Texas. The alleged assassin, Lee Harvey Oswald, was himself shot and killed at point-blank range two days later. Kennedy's eloquent idealism and youthful glamour had won him much popularity in the USA and abroad, and though the legislative achievements of his brief administration were modest, his martyrdom enabled his successor and vice president, LYNDON B JOHNSON, to promote the social reforms of the 'Great Society' as his legacy.

'Ask not what your country can do for you'
20 January 1961, Washington, DC, USA

In one of the most lauded inaugural addresses of all time, John F Kennedy, who had been elected president by a narrow margin, reached out to a new generation of Americans.

Kennedy spoke from a platform erected at the east front of the Capitol. Heavy snow had fallen the night before, but any thoughts of postponing the ceremony were swiftly set aside. The new president's speech is a study in inspirational oratory: successive statements perfectly balance one another – for example the famous 'Let us never negotiate out of fear. But let us never fear to negotiate' – while a string of triumphal metaphors call on Americans to support his presidency even though its goals remain unclear.

The address was long thought to be the work of Kennedy's speechwriter, Theodore Sorensen (1928–), although recent research suggests that Kennedy himself composed the bulk of the speech, including most of its key phrases. James Reston of the *New York Times* remarked that 'the evangelical and transcendental spirit of America has not been better expressed since WOODROW WILSON and maybe not even since RALPH WALDO EMERSON.'

Vice President Johnson, Mr Speaker, Mr Chief Justice, President EISENHOWER, Vice-President NIXON, President TRUMAN, reverend clergy, fellow citizens: we observe today not a victory of party but a celebration of freedom, symbolizing an end as well as a beginning, signifying renewal as well as change. For I have sworn before you and Almighty God the same solemn oath our forebears prescribed nearly a century and three-quarters ago.

The world is very different now. For man holds in his mortal hands the power to abolish all forms of human poverty and all forms of human life. And yet the same revolutionary beliefs for which our forebears fought are still at issue around the globe – the belief that the rights of man come not from the generosity of the state but from the hand of God.

We dare not forget today that we are the heirs of that first revolution.

Let the word go forth from this time and place, to friend and foe alike, that the torch has been passed to a new generation of Americans: born in this century, tempered by war, disciplined by a hard and bitter peace, proud of our ancient heritage and unwilling to witness or permit the slow undoing of those human rights to which this nation has always been committed – and to which we are committed today, at home and around the world.

Let every nation know, whether it wishes us well or ill, that we shall pay any price, bear any burden, meet any hardship, support any friend, oppose any foe to assure the survival and the success of liberty.

This much we pledge and more. To those old allies whose cultural and spiritual origins we share, we pledge the loyalty of faithful friends. United, there is little we cannot do in a host of co-operative ventures. Divided, there is little we can do – for we dare not meet a powerful challenge at odds and split asunder.

To those new states whom we welcome to the ranks of the free,[1] we pledge our word that one form of colonial control shall not have passed away merely to be replaced by a far more iron tyranny. We shall not always expect to find them supporting our view. But we shall always hope to find them strongly supporting their own freedom – and to remember that, in the past, those who foolishly sought power by riding the back of the tiger ended up inside.

To those peoples in the huts and villages of half the globe, struggling to break the bonds of mass misery, we pledge our best efforts to help them help themselves, for whatever period is required – not because the communists may be doing it, not because we seek their votes, but because it is right. If a free society cannot help the many who are poor, it cannot save the few who are rich.

To our sister republics south of our border, we offer a special pledge: to convert our good words into good deeds, in a new Alliance for Progress;[2] to assist free men and free governments in casting off the chains of poverty.

But this peaceful revolution of hope cannot become the prey of hostile powers. Let all our neighbours know that we shall join with them to oppose aggression or subversion anywhere in the Americas. And let every other power know that this hemisphere intends to remain the master of its own house.

To that world assembly of sovereign states, the United Nations, our last best hope in an age where the instruments of war have far outpaced the instruments of peace, we renew our pledge of support, to prevent it from becoming merely a forum for invective, to strengthen its shield of the new and the weak and to enlarge the area in which its writ may run.

Finally, to those nations who would make themselves our adversary, we offer not a pledge but a request: that both sides begin anew the quest for peace, before the dark powers of destruction unleashed by science engulf all humanity in planned or accidental self-destruction.

We dare not tempt them with weakness. For only when our arms are sufficient beyond doubt can we be certain beyond doubt that they will never be employed.

But neither can two great and powerful groups of nations take comfort from our present course – both sides overburdened by the cost of modern weapons, both rightly alarmed by the steady spread of the deadly atom, yet both racing to alter that uncertain balance of terror that stays the hand of mankind's final war.

[1] Kennedy here refers to newly independent African states, most of which joined the United Nations in 1960–1.

[2] Established in August 1961, the Alliance for Progress was a programme of economic co-operation between the USA and Latin America, which offered aid as an incentive to land reform and democratization.

So let us begin anew, remembering on both sides that civility is not a sign of weakness, and sincerity is always subject to proof. Let us never negotiate out of fear. But let us never fear to negotiate.

Let both sides explore what problems unite us instead of belabouring those problems which divide us.

Let both sides, for the first time, formulate serious and precise proposals for the inspection and control of arms; and bring the absolute power to destroy other nations under the absolute control of all nations.

Let both sides seek to invoke the wonders of science instead of its terrors. Together let us explore the stars, conquer the deserts, eradicate disease, tap the ocean depths and encourage the arts and commerce.

Let both sides unite to heed in all corners of the earth the command of Isaiah – to 'undo the heavy burdens … (and) let the oppressed go free'.[3]

[3] Isaiah 58:6.

And if a beach-head of co-operation may push back the jungle of suspicion, let both sides join in creating a new endeavour, not a new balance of power, but a new world of law, where the strong are just and the weak secure and the peace preserved.

All this will not be finished in the first hundred days. Nor will it be finished in the first thousand days, nor in the life of this administration,[4] nor even perhaps in our lifetime on this planet. But let us begin.

[4] Kennedy's presidency lasted 1,037 days.

In your hands, my fellow citizens, more than mine, will rest the final success or failure of our course. Since this country was founded, each generation of Americans has been summoned to give testimony to its national loyalty. The graves of young Americans who answered the call to service surround the globe.

Now the trumpet summons us again, not as a call to bear arms, though arms we need, not as a call to battle, though embattled we are, but a call to bear the burden of a long twilight struggle, year in and year out, 'rejoicing in hope, patient in tribulation'[5] – a struggle against the common enemies of man: tyranny, poverty, disease and war itself.

[5] Romans 12:12.

Can we forge against these enemies a grand and global alliance – north and south, east and west – that can assure a more fruitful life for all mankind? Will you join in that historic effort?

In the long history of the world, only a few generations have been granted the role of defending freedom in its hour of maximum danger. I do not shrink from this responsibility: I welcome it. I do not believe that any of us would exchange places with any other people or any other generation. The energy, the faith, the devotion which we bring to this endeavour will light our country and all who serve it – and the glow from that fire can truly light the world.

And so, my fellow Americans: ask not what your country can do for you; ask what you can do for your country. My fellow citizens of the world: ask not what America will do for you, but what together we can do for the freedom of man.

Finally, whether you are citizens of America or citizens of the world, ask of us here the same high standards of strength and sacrifice which we ask of you. With a good conscience our only sure reward, with history the final judge of our deeds, let us go forth to lead the land we love, asking his blessing and his help, but knowing that here on earth, God's work must truly be our own.

'We choose to go to the Moon'

12 September 1962, Houston, Texas, USA

President Kennedy gave this speech at Rice University in Houston, during a trip to dedicate NASA's new Manned Spacecraft Center (now the Johnson Space Center). Its stirring words led Kennedy to be hailed as a space visionary; at the time, however, he faced congressional and public scepticism about America's space programme, which had begun in earnest the year before.

The speech is clear about the intellectual challenge and adventure of space exploration, and of a Moon landing in particular. It makes no mention of the USSR, whose own space programme and triumph of sending the first man into space in 1961 were the main motivations for the USA's entry into the 'space race'. Yet the political aspect of this race rings loud in Kennedy's words, vowing that space be not 'governed by a hostile flag of conquest'.

Indeed – as revealed by a tape-recording of a meeting between Kennedy and the NASA chief James Webb less than two months after this speech – rivalry with the Soviets was the sole motivating factor for the president when it came to landing a man on the Moon. If it wasn't for the pressing need to beat the Russians, he told Webb, the space programme would not go ahead because, he added, 'I'm not that interested in space.'

We meet at a college noted for knowledge, in a city noted for progress, in a state noted for strength, and we stand in need of all three, for we meet in an hour of change and challenge, in a decade of hope and fear, in an age of both knowledge and ignorance. The greater our knowledge increases, the greater our ignorance unfolds.

Despite the striking fact that most of the scientists that the world has ever known are alive and working today, despite the fact that this nation's own scientific manpower is doubling every twelve years in a rate of growth more than three times that of our population as a whole – despite that, the vast stretches of the unknown and the unanswered and the unfinished still far outstrip our collective comprehension.

No man can fully grasp how far and how fast we have come, but condense, if you will, the 50,000 years of man's recorded history in a time span of but a half-century. Stated in these terms, we know very little about the first 40 years, except at the end of them advanced men had learned to use the skins of animals to cover them. Then, about ten years ago, under this standard, man emerged from his caves to construct other kinds of shelter. Only five years ago, man learned to write and use a cart with wheels. Christianity began less than two years ago. The printing press came this year, and then less than two months ago, during this whole 50-year span of human history, the steam engine provided a new source of power.

Newton explored the meaning of gravity. Last month electric lights and telephones and automobiles and airplanes became available. Only last week did we develop penicillin and television and nuclear power, and now, if America's new spacecraft succeeds in reaching Venus, we will have literally reached the stars before midnight tonight.

This is a breathtaking pace, and such a pace cannot help but create new ills as it dispels old – new ignorance, new problems, new dangers. Surely the opening vistas of space promise high costs and hardships, as well as high reward.

So it is not surprising that some would have us stay where we are a little longer to rest, to wait. But this city of Houston, this state of Texas, this country of the United States was not built by those who waited and rested and wished to look behind them. This country was conquered by those who moved forward – and so will space.

[1] The English colonist William Bradford (1590–1657) travelled to New England on the *Mayflower* in 1620, became leader of the Pilgrims in 1621 and served as Governor of the Plymouth colony for many years.

William Bradford,[1] speaking in 1630 of the founding of the Plymouth Bay Colony, said that all great and honourable actions are accompanied with great difficulties, and both must be enterprised and overcome with answerable courage.

If this capsule history of our progress teaches us anything, it is that man, in his quest for knowledge and progress, is determined and cannot be deterred. The exploration of space will go ahead, whether we join in it or not, and it is one of the great adventures of all time, and no nation which expects to be the leader of other nations can expect to stay behind in this race for space.

Those who came before us made certain that this country rode the first waves of the industrial revolutions, the first waves of modern invention, and the first wave of nuclear power, and this generation does not intend to founder in the backwash of the coming age of space. We mean to be a part of it – we mean to lead it. For the eyes of the world now look into space, to the Moon and to the planets beyond, and we have vowed that we shall not see it governed by a hostile flag of conquest,[2] but by a banner of freedom and peace. We have vowed that we shall not see space filled with weapons of mass destruction, but with instruments of knowledge and understanding.

[2] The Soviet leader NIKITA KHRUSHCHEV had effectively thrown down the gauntlet to the USA when the USSR launched the first satellite in 1957 and conducted the first manned space flight in 1961. Khrushchev had cited these achievements as evidence of the superiority of Communism.

Yet the vows of this nation can only be fulfilled if we in this nation are first, and, therefore, we intend to be first. In short, our leadership in science and in industry, our hopes for peace and security, our obligations to ourselves as well as others, all require us to make this effort, to solve these mysteries, to solve them for the good of all men, and to become the world's leading space-faring nation.

We set sail on this new sea because there is new knowledge to be gained and new rights to be won, and they must be won and used for the progress of all people. For space science – like nuclear science and all technology – has no conscience of its own. Whether it will become a force for good or ill depends on man, and only if the United States occupies a position of pre-eminence can we help decide whether this new ocean will be a sea of peace or a new terrifying theatre of war. I do not say that we should or will go unprotected against the hostile misuse of space any more than we go unprotected against the hostile use of land or sea, but I do say that space can be explored and mastered without feeding the fires of war, without repeating the mistakes that man has made in extending his writ around this globe of ours.

There is no strife, no prejudice, no national conflict in outer space as yet. Its hazards are hostile to us all. Its conquest deserves the best of all mankind, and its opportunity for peaceful co-operation may never come again. But why, some say, the Moon? Why choose this as our goal? And they may well ask why climb the highest mountain. Why, 35 years ago, fly the Atlantic? Why does Rice play Texas?[3]

[3] Kennedy refers to sporting contests between rival Texan universities.

We choose to go to the Moon. We choose to go to the Moon in this decade and do the other things, not because they are easy, but because they are hard, because that goal will serve to organize and measure the best of our energies and skills, because that challenge is one that we are willing to accept, one we are unwilling to postpone, and one which we intend to win – and the others, too.

[4] On 25 May 1961, had Kennedy announced the Apollo space programme, committing the USA to land a man on the Moon before the end of the decade.

It is for these reasons that I regard the decision last year[4] to shift our efforts in space from low to high gear as among the most important decisions that will be made during my incumbency in the office of the presidency …

To be sure, all this costs us all a good deal of money. This year's space budget is three times what it was in January 1961, and it is greater than the space budget of the previous eight years combined. That budget now stands at $5,400 million a year – a staggering sum, though somewhat less than we pay for cigarettes and cigars every year. Space expenditures will soon rise some more, from 40 cents per person per week to more than 50 cents a week for every man, woman, and child in the United States, for we have given this programme a high national priority – even though I realize that this is in some measure an act of faith and vision, for we do not now know what benefits await us.

But if I were to say, my fellow citizens, that we shall send to the Moon, 240,000 miles away from the control station in Houston, a giant rocket more than 300 feet tall, the length of this football field, made of new metal alloys, some of which have not yet been invented, capable of standing heat and stresses several times more than have ever been experienced, fitted together with a precision better than the finest watch, carrying all the equipment needed for propulsion, guidance, control, communications, food and survival, on an untried mission, to an unknown celestial body; and then return it safely to earth, re-entering the atmosphere at speeds of over 25,000 miles per hour, causing heat about half that of the temperature of the sun – almost as hot as it is here today – and do all this, and do it right, and do it first before this decade is out, then we must be bold.

I'm the one who is doing all the work, so we just want you to stay cool for a minute.

[*Laughter.*]

However, I think we're going to do it, and I think that we must pay what needs to be paid. I don't think we ought to waste any money, but I think we ought to do the job. And this will be done in the decade of the Sixties. It may be done while some of you are still here at school at this college and university. It will be done during the terms of office of some of the people who sit here on this platform. But it will be done. And it will be done before the end of this decade.

I am delighted that this university is playing a part in putting a man on the Moon as part of a great national effort of the United States of America. Many years ago the great British explorer George Mallory, who was to die on Mount Everest,[5] was asked why did he want to climb it. He said, 'Because it is there.'

Well, space is there, and we're going to climb it, and the Moon and the planets are there, and new hopes for knowledge and peace are there. And, therefore, as we set sail we ask God's blessing on the most hazardous and dangerous and greatest adventure on which man has ever embarked.

[5] The English mountaineer George Mallory (1886–1924) and his companion Andrew Irvine (1902–1924) attempted to reach the summit of Everest in June 1924. Both died during the expedition, and it is not known whether they succeeded.

'Ich bin ein Berliner'

26 June 1963, West Berlin, West Germany

Kennedy left the USA in June 1963 for a goodwill tour of five nations in western Europe. West Germany was the first of these countries and Berlin – situated in East Germany but divided into east and west halves by the recently built wall – was his most eagerly anticipated destination.

East Germany had erected the wall in August 1961 to prevent skilled workers escaping to the more prosperous West Germany and threatening the viability of its economy. The concrete structure, replete with watchtowers, gun positions and mines, was over 15 feet high in parts and ran for 100 miles around the perimeter of West Berlin.

A crowd of 120,000 cheering Berliners gathered to hear Kennedy speak on the steps of the Schöneberger Rathaus, West Berlin's city hall, near the wall itself. His speech later caused wry smiles since, in some parts of Germany (although not Berlin), *ein Berliner* is a type of doughnut. Amusement was the last thing on the audience's mind, however: they regarded Kennedy's address as a major morale boost and a message of defiance to their communist neighbours.

❧

[1] The German statesman Willy Brandt (1913–92) served as Mayor of Berlin, 1957–66, and later Chancellor of the Federal Republic of Germany, 1969–74.
[2] The German statesman Konrad Adenauer (1876–1967) served as Chancellor of the Federal Republic of Germany, 1949–63.
[3] The US soldier General Lucius D Clay (1897–1978) was the director of civilian affairs in Germany after World War II.

I am proud to come to this city as the guest of your distinguished Mayor,[1] who has symbolized throughout the world the fighting spirit of West Berlin. And I am proud to visit the Federal Republic with your distinguished Chancellor,[2] who for so many years has committed Germany to democracy and freedom and progress, and to come here in the company of my fellow American, General Clay,[3] who has been in this city during its great moments of crisis and will come again if ever needed.

Two thousand years ago the proudest boast was *'civis Romanus sum'*.[4] Today, in the world of freedom, the proudest boast is *'Ich bin ein Berliner'*. I appreciate my interpreter translating my German!

[4] Latin: 'I am a Roman citizen.'

There are many people in the world who really don't understand, or say they don't, what is the great issue between the free world and the communist world. Let them come to Berlin. There are some who say that communism is the wave of the future. Let them come to Berlin. And there are some who say, in Europe and elsewhere, we can work with the communists. Let them come to Berlin. And there are even a few who say that it is true that communism is an evil system, but it permits us to make economic progress. *Lass' sie nach Berlin kommen.* Let them come to Berlin.

Freedom has many difficulties and democracy is not perfect, but we have never had to put a wall up to keep our people in, to prevent them from leaving us. I want to say, on behalf of my countrymen, who live many miles away on the other side of the Atlantic, who are far distant from you, that they take the greatest pride that they have been able to share with you, even from a distance, the story of the last 18 years.

I know of no town, no city, that has been besieged for 18 years that still lives with the vitality and the force, and the hope and the determination of the city of West Berlin. While the Wall is the most obvious and vivid demonstration of the failures of the communist system, for all the world to see, we take no satisfaction in it, for it is, as your Mayor has said, an offence not only against history but an offence against humanity, separating families, dividing husbands and wives and brothers and sisters, and dividing a people who wish to be joined together.

What is true of this city is true of Germany: real, lasting peace in Europe can never be assured as long as one German out of four is denied the elementary right of free men, and that is to make a free choice. In 18 years of peace and good faith, this generation of Germans has earned the right to be free, including the right to unite their families and their nation in lasting peace, with goodwill to all people. You live in a defended island of freedom, but your life is part of the main.

So let me ask you, as I close, to lift your eyes beyond the dangers of today, to the hopes of tomorrow, beyond the freedom merely of this city of Berlin, or your country of Germany, to the advance of freedom everywhere, beyond the Wall to the day of peace with justice, beyond yourselves and ourselves to all mankind.

Freedom is indivisible, and when one man is enslaved, all are not free. When all are free, then we can look forward to that day when this city will be joined as one and this country and this great continent of Europe in a peaceful and hopeful globe. When that day finally comes, as it will, the people of West Berlin can take sober satisfaction in the fact that they were in the frontlines for almost two decades.

All free men, wherever they may live, are citizens of Berlin, and, therefore, as a free man, I take pride in the words: *'Ich bin ein Berliner.'*

Robert F Kennedy
American politician

Robert Francis Kennedy (1925–68) was born in Brookline, Massachusetts, the third son of Joseph Kennedy. He was educated at Harvard and University of Virginia Law School and was admitted to the Massachusetts Bar in 1951. As chief counsel of the Senate Select Committee on Improper Activities (1957–9), he prosecuted David Bech and Jimmy Hoffa of the Teamsters union, who were charged with corruption. He was an efficient manager of his brother JOHN F KENNEDY's presidential campaign, and was an energetic Attorney-General (1961–4) in the latter's administration, notable in his efforts to promote civil rights. He resigned after President Kennedy's assassination, and was elected senator from New York in 1965. After much hesitation he declared his candidacy for the Democratic presidential nomination in 1968, quickly winning as an idealist reformer. On 5 June 1968, after winning the California primary election, he was shot by the Palestinian militant Sirhan Sirhan (1944–). He died the following day.

'Martin Luther King was shot and killed tonight'
4 April 1968, Indianapolis, Indiana, USA

This speech ranks as one of the most darkly symbolic events in 20th-century US politics, in which the brother of the murdered president, who would himself be killed two months later, announced the assassination of the country's most revered African–American leader.

The occasion was to have been a campaign rally as part of Kennedy's bid for the 1968 Democratic presidential nomination. Arriving in Indianapolis by plane, Kennedy learned of MARTIN LUTHER KING's death in Memphis, Tennessee. The police, fearful of the unrest this news would trigger, warned Kennedy against making his planned appearance in a predominantly black neighbourhood. Kennedy would not be deterred, however, and announced King's murder to a totally unprepared, stunned audience.

The civil rights activist John Lewis, who witnessed the speech, recounted how Kennedy 'spoke from his soul', and how his words 'just chilled your body'. Riots broke out in more than 100 cities across America following King's death, but in Indianapolis that night, after Kennedy's appeal for compassion and understanding of the kind King himself had shown, there was calm.

I have bad news for you, for all of our fellow citizens, and people who love peace all over the world – and that is that Martin Luther King was shot and killed tonight.

Martin Luther King dedicated his life to love and to justice for his fellow human beings, and he died because of that effort.

In this difficult day, in this difficult time for the United States, it is perhaps well to ask what kind of a nation we are and what direction we want to move in. For those of you who are black – considering the evidence there evidently is that there were white people who were responsible[1] – you can be filled with bitterness, with hatred and a desire for revenge. We can move in that direction as a country, in great polarization – black people amongst black, white people amongst white, filled with hatred toward one another.

Or we can make an effort, as Martin Luther King did, to understand and to comprehend – and to replace that violence, that stain of bloodshed that has spread across our land, with an effort to understand with compassion and love.

For those of you who are black and are tempted to be filled with hatred and distrust at the injustice of such an act, against all white people, I can only say that I feel in my own heart the same kind of feeling. I had a member of my family killed, but he was killed by a white man. But we have to make an effort in the United States, we have to make an effort to understand, to go beyond these rather difficult times.

My favourite poet was Aeschylus.[2] He wrote: 'In our sleep, pain which

[1] The US white supremacist James Earl Ray (1928–98) confessed to King's murder and was convicted on 10 March 1969. He later repudiated his confession, despite the conclusion of several federal investigations that he was indeed responsible.

[2] The Athenian dramatist Aeschylus (c.525–c.456 BC) was the first of the great Greek tragedians. Kennedy quotes here from the *Agamemnon*, written around 458 BC).

cannot forget falls drop by drop upon the heart until, in our own despair, against our will, comes wisdom through the awful grace of God.'

What we need in the United States is not division; what we need in the United States is not hatred; what we need in the United States is not violence or lawlessness, but love and wisdom and compassion toward one another; and a feeling of justice towards those who still suffer within our country, whether they be white or they be black.

So I shall ask you tonight to return home, to say a prayer; for the family of Martin Luther King, that's true; but more importantly to say a prayer for our own country, which all of us love – a prayer for understanding and that compassion of which I spoke.

We can do well in this country. We will have difficult times. We've had difficult times in the past. We will have difficult times in the future. It is not the end of violence; it is not the end of lawlessness; it is not the end of disorder.

But the vast majority of white people and the vast majority of black people in this country want to live together, want to improve the quality of our life, and want justice for all human beings who abide in our land. Let us dedicate ourselves to what the Greeks wrote so many years ago: to tame the savageness of man and to make gentle the life of this world.

Let us dedicate ourselves to that, and say a prayer for our country and for our people.

Nikita Khrushchev
Russian politician

Nikita Sergeyevich Khrushchev (1894–1971) was born in Kalinovka, near Kursk. He worked as a shepherd boy and a locksmith and is said to have been almost illiterate until the age of 25. After joining the Bolshevik Party in 1918, he fought in the civil war and rose rapidly in the party organization. In 1939 he was made a full member of the Politburo – the executive committee of the Communist Party – and of the Presidium of the Supreme Soviet. In World War II he organized guerrilla warfare in the Ukraine against the invading Germans and took charge of the reconstruction of devastated territory. In 1949 he launched a drastic reorganization of Soviet agriculture. In 1953, on the death of JOSEPH STALIN, he became First Secretary of the All Union Party. Among the events of his administration were the 1956 Poznan riots, which he quelled, the Hungarian uprising of 1956, which he crushed, and the failed attempt to install missiles in Cuba (1962). Khrushchev did much to enhance the ambitions and status of the USSR abroad, but was nevertheless deposed in 1964. Forced into retirement, he was replaced by Leonid Brezhnev (1906–82) and Alexei Kosygin (1904–80). He died in retirement in Moscow. He has been substantially rehabilitated in recent years.

'The cult of the individual and its harmful consequences'
25 February 1956, Moscow, Russia

Khrushchev's famous denouncement of Stalin was made in a closed, late-night session at the 20th Congress of the Communist Party of the Soviet Union, the first to be held since Stalin's death in 1953.

Just over a year earlier, the Shvernik Commission had been established under the leadership of Nikolai Shvernik, who had been nominal head of state during the Stalin era. Its remit was to investigate repression under Stalin, and in particular the 'Great Purge' of 1937–8, during which at least 1.5 million party members were arrested, many were tortured and some 680,000 were executed.

Though Shvernik's report was not made public, Khrushchev drew on its findings extensively while preparing this speech. In it, he focuses on several areas: Stalin's departures from the principles of Marxism–Leninism; his reliance on a terrifying police state; and his vanity: the 'cult of personality' was later used as a euphemistic umbrella term to refer to all Stalin's crimes.

The speech lasted over three hours: highlights are given here. Despite the secrecy, it soon leaked to other Eastern bloc countries, paving the way for reconciliation with Marshal Josip Tito and his Yugoslavian Communists in June.

Before long it reached the West – possibly with the tacit assent of the Soviet authorities – appearing in an American newspaper later the same year. It was not officially published in Russia until 1989. The West's relationship with Khrushchev was often troubled, but this speech is now seen as a turning point in the liberalization of eastern Europe.

Russian Comrades … a lot has been said about the cult of the individual and about its harmful consequences.

After Stalin's death, the central committee of the party began to implement a policy of explaining concisely and consistently that it is impermissible and foreign to the spirit of Marxism–Leninism[1] to elevate one person, to transform him into a superman, possessing supernatural characteristics akin to those of a god. Such a man supposedly knows everything, sees everything, thinks for everyone, can do anything, is infallible in his behaviour.

Such a belief about a man – and specifically about Stalin – was cultivated among us for many years. The objective of the present report is not a thorough evaluation of Stalin's life and activity. Concerning Stalin's merits, an entirely sufficient number of books, pamphlets and studies had already been written in his lifetime. The role of Stalin in the preparation and execution of the socialist revolution, in the civil war and in the fight for the construction of socialism in our country is universally known. Everyone knows it well.

[1] A Socialist political philosophy based on the works of MARX and LENIN.

At present, we are concerned with a question which has immense importance for the party now and for the future – with how the cult of the person of Stalin has been gradually growing, the cult which became at a certain specific stage the source of a whole series of exceedingly serious and grave perversions of party principles, of party democracy, of revolutionary legality …

Allow me first of all to remind you how severely the classics of Marxism–Leninism denounced every manifestation of the cult of the individual. In a letter to the German political worker, Wilhelm Bloss, Marx stated:

'Due to my antipathy to any cult of the individual, I never made public during the existence of the International[2] the numerous addresses from various countries which recognized my merits and which annoyed me. I did not even reply to them, except sometimes to rebuke their authors. Engels[3] and I first joined the secret society of Communists on the condition that everything making for superstitious worship of authority would be deleted from its statute …'

Some time later Engels wrote:

'Both Marx and I have always been against any public manifestation with regard to individuals, with the exception of cases when it had an important purpose. We most strongly opposed such manifestations which during our lifetime concerned us personally.'

The great modesty of the genius of the revolution, Vladimir Ilich Lenin, is known. Lenin had always stressed the role of the people as the creator of history, the directing and organizational role of the party as a living and creative organism, and also the role of the central committee …

Always unyielding in matters of principle, Lenin never imposed by force his views upon his co-workers. He tried to convince; he patiently explained his opinions to others. Lenin always diligently observed that the norms of party life were realized, that the party statute was enforced, that the party congresses and the plenary sessions of the central committee took place at the proper intervals.

In addition to the great accomplishments of V I Lenin for the victory of the working class and of the working peasants, for the victory of our party and for the application of the ideas of scientific communism to life, his acute mind expressed itself also in this: that he detected in Stalin in time those negative characteristics which resulted later in grave consequences …

Vladimir Ilich said:

'Stalin is excessively rude, and this defect, which can be freely tolerated in our midst and in contacts among us Communists, becomes a defect which cannot be tolerated in one holding the position of the Secretary General. Because of this, I propose that the comrades consider the method by which Stalin would be removed from this position and by which another man would be selected for it – a man, who above all , would differ from Stalin in only one quality, namely, greater tolerance, greater loyalty, greater kindness and more considerate attitude toward the comrades, a less capricious temper, etc.' …

As later events have proven, Lenin's anxiety was justified. In the first period after Lenin's death Stalin still paid attention to his advice, but later he began to disregard the serious admonitions of Vladimir Ilich. When we analyse the practice of Stalin in regard to the direction of the party and of the country; when we pause to consider everything which Stalin

[2] The International Working-Men's Association, formed in London in September 1864, from a loose assembly of English, French, Irish, Polish, Italian and German radicals. Marx soon emerged as its leader.

[3] The German political philosopher Friedrich Engels (1820–95) was Marx's lifelong friend and collaborator, co-author of *The Communist Manifesto*.

perpetrated, we must be convinced that Lenin's fears were justified. The negative characteristics of Stalin, which in Lenin's time were only incipient, transformed themselves during the last years into a grave abuse of power by Stalin, which caused untold harm to our party …

Stalin acted not through persuasion, explanation, and patient co-operation with people, but by imposing his concepts and demanding absolute submission to his opinion. Whoever opposed this concept or tried to prove his viewpoint, and the correctness of his position, was doomed to removal from the leading collective and to subsequent moral and physical annihilation …

Stalin originated the concept 'enemy of the people'. This term automatically rendered it unnecessary that the ideological errors of a man or men engaged in a controversy be proven; this term made possible the usage of the most cruel repression, violating all norms of revolutionary legality, against anyone who in any way disagreed with Stalin, against those who were only suspected of hostile intent, against those who had bad reputations.

This concept – 'enemy of the people' – actually eliminated the possibility of any kind of ideological fight or the making of one's views known on this or that issue, even those of a practical character. In the main, and in actuality, the only proof of guilt used, against all norms of current legal science, was the confession of the accused himself, and as subsequent probing proved, confessions were acquired through physical pressures against the accused.

This led to glaring violations of revolutionary legality, and to the fact that many entirely innocent persons, who in the past had defended the party line, became victims. We must assert that in regard to those persons who in their time had opposed the party line, there were often no sufficiently serious reasons for their physical annihilation …

Everyone knows how irreconcilable Lenin was with the ideological enemies of Marxism, with those who deviated from the correct party line. At the same time, however, Lenin … advised that such people should be patiently educated, without the application of extreme methods. Lenin's wisdom in dealing with people was evident in his work with cadres.

An entirely different relationship with people characterized Stalin. Lenin's traits – patient work with people, stubborn and painstaking education of them, the ability to induce people to follow him without using compulsion, but rather through the ideological influence on them of the whole collective – were entirely foreign to Stalin. He discarded the Leninist method of convincing and educating; he abandoned the method of ideological struggle for that of administrative violence, mass repressions and terror. He acted on an increasingly larger scale and more stubbornly through punitive organs, at the same time often violating all existing norms of morality and of Soviet laws.

Arbitrary behaviour by one person encouraged and permitted arbitrariness in others. Mass arrests and deportations of many thousands of people, execution without trial and without normal investigation created conditions of insecurity, fear and even desperation. This, of course, did not contribute toward unity of the party ranks and of all strata of working people, but, on the contrary, brought about annihilation and the expulsion from the party of workers who were loyal but inconvenient to Stalin …

Can it be said that Lenin did not decide to use even the most severe means against enemies of the Revolution when this was actually necessary? No; no-one can say this. Vladimir Ilich demanded uncompromising dealings with the enemies of the Revolution and of the working class and when necessary resorted ruthlessly to such methods.

You will recall only V I Lenin's fight with the Socialist Revolutionary organizers of the anti-Soviet uprising,[4] with the counter-revolutionary kulaks in 1918 and with others, when Lenin without hesitation used the most extreme methods against the enemies. Lenin used such methods, however, only against actual class enemies and not against those who blunder, who err, and whom it was possible to lead through ideological influence and even retain in the leadership …

Stalin, on the other hand, used extreme methods and mass repressions at a time when the Revolution was already victorious, when the Soviet state was strengthened, when the exploiting classes were already liquidated and socialist relations were rooted solidly in all phases of national economy; when our party was politically consolidated and had strengthened itself both numerically and ideologically …

Many abuses were made on Stalin's orders without reckoning with any norms of party and Soviet legality. Stalin was a very distrustful man, sickly suspicious. We know this from our work with him. He could look at a man and say: 'Why are your eyes so shifty today?' or 'Why are you turning so much today and avoiding to look me directly in the eyes?'

The sickly suspicion created in him a general distrust even toward eminent party workers whom he had known for years. Everywhere and in everything he saw 'enemies,' 'two-facers' and 'spies'. Possessing unlimited power, he indulged in great wilfulness and stifled people morally as well as physically. A situation was created where one could not express one's own volition. When Stalin said that one or another should be arrested, it was necessary to accept on faith that he was an 'enemy of the people' …

Comrades: the cult of the individual acquired such monstrous size chiefly because Stalin himself, using all conceivable methods, supported the glorification of his own person. This is supported by numerous facts. One of the most characteristic examples of Stalin's self-glorification and of his lack of even elementary modesty is the edition of his *Short Biography*, which was published in 1948.[5]

This book is an expression of the most dissolute flattery, an example of making a man into a godhead, of transforming him into an infallible sage, 'the greatest leader, sublime strategist of all times and nations'. Finally, no other words could be found with which to lift Stalin up to the heavens.

We need not give here examples of the loathsome adulation filling this book. All we need to add is that they all were approved and edited by Stalin personally. Some of them were added in his own handwriting to the draft text of the book.

What did Stalin consider essential to write into this book? Did he want to cool the ardour of the flatterers who were composing his *Short Biography*? No! He marked the very places where he thought that the praise of his services was insufficient. Here are some examples characterizing Stalin's activity, added in Stalin's own hand …

'Although he performed his tasks as leader of the party and the people with consummate skill, and enjoyed the unreserved support of the entire Soviet people, Stalin never allowed his work to be marred by the slightest hint of vanity, conceit or self-adulation.'

Where and when could a leader so praise himself? Is this worthy of a

[4] In July 1918, Socialist Revolutionaries had attempted a coup in Moscow, which was labelled the anti-Soviet uprising. Around the same time, Lenin had introduced repressive measures against peasant landowners (kulaks), who had been resisting the redistribution of their wealth and property.

[5] The first *Short Biography* was published in 1927, attributed to Stalin's secretary Ivan Tovstukha (1889–1935). A revised and expanded second edition appeared in 1948.

leader of the Marxist–Leninist type? No. Precisely against this did Marx and Engels take such a strong position. This always was sharply condemned also by Vladimir Ilich Lenin.

In the draft text of his book appeared the following sentence: 'Stalin is the Lenin of today.' This sentence appeared to Stalin to be too weak. Thus, in his own handwriting, he changed it to read: 'Stalin is the worthy continuer of Lenin's work, or, as it is said in our party, Stalin is the Lenin of today.' You see how well it is said, not by the nation but by Stalin himself ...

Further, Stalin writes:

'Stalin's military mastership was displayed both in defence and on offence. Comrade Stalin's genius enabled him to divine the enemy's plans and defeat them. The battles in which comrade Stalin directed the Soviet armies are brilliant examples of operational military skill.'

This is how Stalin was praised as a strategist. Who did this? Stalin himself, not in his role as a strategist but in the role of an author/editor, one of the main creators of his self-adulatory biography ...

Or let us take the matter of the Stalin Prizes.[6]

[*Movement in the hall.*]

Not even the Tsars created prizes which they named after themselves.

Stalin recognized as the best a text of the national anthem of the Soviet Union which contains not a word about the Communist Party; it contains, however, the following unprecedented praise of Stalin: 'Stalin brought us up in loyalty to the people. He inspired us to great toil and deeds.'[7]

In these lines of the anthem, the whole educational, directional and inspirational activity of the great Leninist Party is ascribed to Stalin. This is, of course, a clear deviation from Marxism–Leninism, a clear debasing and belittling of the role of the party. We should add for your information that the presidium of the central committee has already passed a resolution concerning the composition of a new text of the anthem, which will reflect the role of the people and the role of the party.[8]

[*Loud, prolonged applause.*]

And was it without Stalin's knowledge that many of the largest enterprises and towns were named after him? Was it without his knowledge that Stalin monuments were erected in the whole country – these 'memorials to the living'? ... Anyone who has visited the Stalingrad area must have seen the huge statue which is being built there, and that on a site which hardly any people frequent. Huge sums were spent to build it at a time when people of this area had lived since the war in huts ...

We should, in all seriousness, consider the question of the cult of the individual. We cannot let this matter get out of the party, especially not to the press. It is for this reason that we are considering it here at a closed congress session. We should know the limits; we should not give ammunition to the enemy; we should not wash our dirty linen before their eyes. I think that the delegates to the congress will understand and assess properly all these proposals.

[*Tumultuous applause.*]

Comrades: we must abolish the cult of the individual decisively, once and for all; we must draw the proper conclusions concerning both ideological–theoretical and practical work. It is necessary for this purpose: first, in a Bolshevik manner to condemn and to eradicate the cult of the individual as alien to Marxism–Leninism and not consonant with the principles of party leadership and the norms of party life, and to fight inexorably all attempts at bringing back this practice in one form or another ...

[6] Introduced in 1939, Stalin Prizes were intended as a Soviet equivalent to Nobel Prizes.
[7] The lines referred to in full: 'Through tempests the sunrays of freedom have cheered us,/Along the new path where great Lenin did lead/Be true to the people, thus Stalin has reared us,/Inspire us to labour and valorous deed!'
[8] Introduced in 1944, 'The Hymn of the Union of Soviet Socialist Republics' by Alexander V Alexandrov and Sergei V Mikhalkov was the USSR's official anthem until 1991.

Second, to continue systematically and consistently the work done by the party's central committee during the last years, a work characterized by minute observation in all party organizations, from the bottom to the top, of the Leninist principles of party leadership, characterized, above all, by the main principle of collective leadership …

Third, to restore completely the Leninist principles of Soviet Socialist democracy, expressed in the constitution of the Soviet Union, to fight wilfulness of individuals abusing their power. The evil caused by acts violating revolutionary socialist legality which have accumulated during a long time as a result of the negative influence of the cult of the individual has to be completely corrected.

Comrades: the 20th Congress of the Communist Party of the Soviet Union has manifested with a new strength the unshakeable unity of our party, its cohesiveness around the central committee, its resolute will to accomplish the great task of building Communism.

[*Tumultuous applause.*]

And the fact that we present in all their ramifications the basic problems of overcoming the cult of the individual which is alien to Marxism–Leninism, as well as the problem of liquidating its burdensome consequences, is evidence of the great moral and political strength of our party.

[*Prolonged applause.*]

We are absolutely certain that our party, armed with the historical resolutions of the 20th Congress, will lead the Soviet people along the Leninist path to new successes, to new victories.

[*Tumultuous, prolonged applause.*]

Long live the victorious banner of our party – Leninism!

[*Tumultuous, prolonged applause ending in standing ovation.*]

Martin Luther King

American clergyman and civil rights leader

Martin Luther King, Jr (1929–68) was born in Atlanta, Georgia, the son of an African–American Baptist pastor. He studied at Morehouse College in Atlanta and Crozier Theological Seminary in Chester, Pennsylvania, and earned a PhD from Boston University in 1955. Shortly after he had become pastor of the Dexter Avenue Baptist Church in Montgomery, Alabama, Rosa Parks (1913–2005) was arrested for refusing to give up her seat on a bus to a white passenger. This sparked the Montgomery bus boycott (1955–6), and King came to national prominence as its eloquent and courageous leader. In 1957 he founded the Southern Christian Leadership Conference, which organized civil rights activities throughout the country. A brilliant orator, he galvanized the movement and in 1963 led the great march on Washington, where he delivered the famous 'I have a dream' speech. Inspired by the example of MAHATMA GANDHI, he espoused a philosophy of non-violence and passive resistance which proved effective as the spectacle of unarmed black demonstrators being harassed and attacked by white segregationists and police exposed the moral weakness of the opposing side. King's efforts were instrumental in securing passage of the Civil Rights Act of 1964 and the Voting Rights Act of 1965. In 1964 he received an honorary doctorate from Yale, the Kennedy Peace Prize, and the Nobel Peace Prize. He was assassinated in Memphis, Tennessee, while on a civil rights mission. His assassin, a young white supremacist named James Earl Ray (1928–98), was apprehended in London, and in 1969 was sentenced in Memphis to 99 years' imprisonment. King's widow Coretta Scott King (1927–2006) carried on his work. The third Monday in January is celebrated as Martin Luther King Day in the USA.

'I have a dream'

28 August 1963, Washington, DC, USA

One of the most moving, inspirational and famous of all 20th-century speeches, this address was the high point of the March on Washington for Jobs and Freedom. The brainchild of the black leader Philip Randolph, it was the result of co-operation between, among others, the National Association for the Advancement of Colored People, the Congress of Racial Equality and King's own Southern Christian Leadership Conference. The organizers hoped that the march would speed the passage of President JOHN F KENNEDY's civil rights bill into law.

King gave his speech – which was broadcast on television and published in newspapers – from the steps of the Lincoln Memorial to about 250,000 people, a fifth of whom were white. The first half, on which he had been working until 4am the night before, is sprinkled with biblical and political allusions – to LINCOLN's Emancipation Proclamation and the Declaration of Independence among other texts – to build the case for African–American freedom and equality. The second part, incredibly, was improvised: King made the brilliant decision that relaying his dream of multi-racial harmony would connect with his audience at the deepest level.

I am happy to join with you today in what will go down in history as the greatest demonstration for freedom in the history of our nation.

[*Cheers and applause.*]

[1] King refers to Abraham Lincoln.

Five score years ago, a great American, in whose symbolic shadow we stand today,[1] signed the Emancipation Proclamation. This momentous decree came as a great beacon light of hope to millions of negro slaves who had been seared in the flames of withering injustice. It came as a joyous daybreak, to end the long night of their captivity.

But one hundred years later, the negro still is not free. One hundred years later, the life of the negro is still sadly crippled by the manacles of segregation and the chains of discrimination. One hundred years later, the negro lives on a lonely island of poverty in the midst of a vast ocean of material prosperity.

[*Applause.*]

One hundred years later, the negro is still languished in the corners of American society and finds himself an exile in his own land. And so we've come here today to dramatize a shameful condition.

In a sense we've come to our nation's capital to cash a cheque. When the architects of our republic wrote the magnificent words of the Constitution and the Declaration of Independence, they were signing a promissory note to which every American was to fall heir. This note was a promise that all men – yes, black men as well as white men – would be guaranteed the unalienable rights of life, liberty and the pursuit of happiness.

It is obvious today that America has defaulted on this promissory note, insofar as her citizens of colour are concerned. Instead of honouring this sacred obligation, America has given the negro people a bad cheque, a cheque which has come back marked 'insufficient funds'.

[*Cheers and applause.*]

But we refuse to believe that the bank of justice is bankrupt. We refuse to believe that there are insufficient funds in the great vaults of opportunity of this nation. And so we've come to cash this cheque, a cheque that will give us, upon demand, the riches of freedom and the security of justice.

[*Cheers and applause.*]

We have also come to this hallowed spot to remind America of the fierce urgency of now. This is no time to engage in the luxury of cooling off or to take the tranquillizing drug of gradualism. [*Cheers and applause.*] Now is the time to make real the promises of democracy. Now is the time to rise from the dark and desolate valley of segregation to the sunlit path of racial justice. Now is the time to lift our nation from the quicksands of racial injustice to the solid rock of brotherhood. Now is the time to make justice a reality for all of God's children.

It would be fatal for the nation to overlook the urgency of the moment. This sweltering summer of the negro's legitimate discontent will not pass until there is an invigorating autumn of freedom and equality. Nineteen sixty-three is not an end, but a beginning. Those who hoped that the negro needed to blow off steam and will now be content will have a rude awakening if the nation returns to business as usual.

[*Cheers and applause.*]

There will be neither rest nor tranquillity in America until the negro is granted his citizenship rights. The whirlwinds of revolt will continue to shake the foundations of our nation until the bright day of justice emerges.

But that is something that I must say to my people, who stand on the warm threshold which leads into the palace of justice. In the process of gaining our rightful place, we must not be guilty of wrongful deeds. Let us not seek to satisfy our thirst for freedom by drinking from the cup of bitterness and hatred.

[*Cheers and applause.*]

We must forever conduct our struggle on the highest plane of dignity and discipline. We must not allow our creative protest to degenerate into physical violence. Again and again, we must rise to the majestic heights of meeting physical force with soul force.

The marvellous new militancy which has engulfed the negro community must not lead us to a distrust of all white people, for many of our white brothers, as evidenced by their presence here today, have come to realize that their destiny is tied up with our destiny. [*Cheers and applause.*] And they have come to realize that their freedom is inextricably bound to our freedom. We cannot walk alone.

And as we walk, we must make the pledge that we shall always march ahead. We cannot turn back. There are those who are asking the devotees of civil rights, 'When will you be satisfied?' We can never be satisfied as long as the negro is the victim of the unspeakable horrors of police brutality. We can never be satisfied as long as our bodies, heavy with the fatigue of travel, cannot gain lodging in the motels of the highways and the hotels of the cities.

[*Cheers and applause.*]

We cannot be satisfied as long as a negro in Mississippi cannot vote and a negro in New York believes he has nothing for which to vote. No, no we are not satisfied and we will not be satisfied until justice rolls down like waters and righteousness like a mighty stream.[2]

[2] See Amos 5:24.

I am not unmindful that some of you have come here out of great trials and tribulations. Some of you have come fresh from narrow jail cells. Some of you have come from areas where your quest for freedom left you battered by the storms of persecution and staggered by the winds of police brutality. You have been the veterans of creative suffering. Continue to work with the faith that unearned suffering is redemptive.

Go back to Mississippi, go back to Alabama, go back to South Carolina, go back to Georgia, go back to Louisiana, go back to the slums and ghettos of our northern cities, knowing that somehow this situation can and will be changed. Let us not wallow in the valley of despair. I say to you today my friends – [*cheers and applause*] so even though we face the difficulties of today and tomorrow, I still have a dream. It is a dream deeply rooted in the American dream.

I have a dream that one day this nation will rise up and live out the true meaning of its creed: 'We hold these truths to be self-evident, that all men are created equal.'

[*Cheers and applause.*]

I have a dream that one day on the red hills of Georgia the sons of former slaves and the sons of former slave-owners will be able to sit down together at the table of brotherhood. I have a dream that one day even the state of Mississippi, a state sweltering with the heat of injustice, sweltering with the heat of oppression, will be transformed into an oasis of freedom and justice. I have a dream that my four little children will one day live in a nation where they will not be judged by the colour of their skin but by the content of their character. I have a dream today.

[*Cheers and applause.*]

I have a dream that one day, down in Alabama, with its vicious racists, with its Governor having his lips dripping with the words of interposition and nullification[3] – one day right there in Alabama little black boys and black girls will be able to join hands with little white boys and white girls as sisters and brothers. I have a dream today.

[3] The US politician John M Patterson served as Governor of Alabama 1958–63. His period in office was marked by opposition to the civil rights movement.

[*Cheers and applause.*]

I have a dream that one day every valley shall be exalted, and every hill and mountain shall be made low; the rough places will be made plain, and the crooked places will be made straight, and the glory of the Lord shall be revealed and all flesh shall see it together.[4]

[4] See Isaiah 40:4–5.

This is our hope. This is the faith that I go back to the South with. With this faith, we will be able to hew out of the mountain of despair a stone of hope. With this faith, we will be able to transform the jangling discords of our nation into a beautiful symphony of brotherhood. With this faith we will be able to work together, to pray together, to struggle together, to go to jail together, to stand up for freedom together, knowing that we will be free one day.

[*Applause.*]

This will be the day, this will be the day when all of God's children will be able to sing with new meaning:

'My country 'tis of thee, Sweet land of liberty, Of thee I sing: Land where my fathers died, Land of the pilgrims' pride, From every mountainside, Let freedom ring!'[5]

And if America is to be a great nation, this must become true. And so let freedom ring from the prodigious hilltops of New Hampshire. Let freedom ring from the mighty mountains of New York. Let freedom ring from the heightening Alleghenies of Pennsylvania. Let freedom ring from the snow-capped Rockies of Colorado. Let freedom ring from the curvaceous slopes of California. But not only that; let freedom ring from Stone Mountain of Georgia. Let freedom ring from Lookout Mountain of Tennessee. Let freedom ring from every hill and molehill of Mississippi. From every mountainside let freedom ring.

[*Cheers and applause.*]

And when this happens, when we allow freedom to ring, when we let it ring from every village and every hamlet, from every state and every city, we will be able to speed up that day when all of God's children – black men and white men, Jews and gentiles, Protestants and Catholics – will be able to join hands and sing in the words of the old negro spiritual: 'Free at last! Free at last! Thank God Almighty, we are free at last!'

[*Tumultuous cheers and applause.*]

[5] The hymn 'America (My Country, 'Tis of Thee)', sung to the tune of 'God Save the Queen'.

❧

'I've seen the promised land'

3 April 1968, Memphis, Tennessee, USA

❧

The context of violence and the urging of non-violence are central to this, the last speech Martin Luther King gave before his assassination on the following night. King spoke at Mason Temple, Memphis, in support of the city's predominantly black sanitation workers, who had been on strike since February. On 28 March, while leading a march for the striking workers, King had watched in distress as the peaceful protest turned angry, leading the police to shoot dead at least one of the marchers. King's return visit and this speech were attempts to restore calm.

In the five years since King's 'I have a dream' address, the Black Power movement had introduced violence into the civil rights struggle, but as King showed in this speech, his commitment to non-violence remained firm. He was clearly thinking about his own mortality, however, as demonstrated by his references to a near-fatal stabbing in 1958 and to threats made against him on the day of this speech. This focus, as well as King's biblical allusions to the promised land of freedom and equality – which he suggests he himself may not reach – and his sense of calm resignation, lend the speech a haunting prescience.

❧

Something is happening in Memphis; something is happening in our world. And you know, if I were standing at the beginning of time, with the possibility of taking a kind of general and panoramic view of the whole of human history up to now, and the Almighty said to me, 'Martin Luther King, which age would you like to live in?' I would take my mental flight by Egypt and I would watch God's children in their magnificent trek from the dark dungeons of Egypt through, or rather across the Red Sea, through the wilderness on toward the promised land. And in spite of its magnificence, I wouldn't stop there.

I would move on by Greece, and take my mind to Mount Olympus. And I would see Plato, Aristotle, SOCRATES, Euripides and Aristophanes assembled around the Parthenon.[1] [*Cheers and applause.*] And I would watch them around the Parthenon as they discussed the great and eternal issues of reality. But I wouldn't stop there.

[1] King conjures an imaginary picture of the great thinkers of ancient Athens – the philosophers Plato (c.427–c.348 BC), Aristotle (c.384–322 BC) and SOCRATES; and the dramatists Euripides (c.480–406 BC) and Aristophanes (c.448–380 BC) – gathered at the city's greatest building, the temple to Athena built around 447 BC.

I would go on, even to the great heyday of the Roman Empire. And I would see developments around there, through various emperors and leaders. But I wouldn't stop there.

I would even come up to the day of the Renaissance, and get a quick picture of all that the Renaissance did for the cultural and aesthetic life of man.

But I wouldn't stop there. I would even go by the way that the man for whom I'm named had his habitat. And I would watch MARTIN LUTHER as he tacked his 95 theses on the door at the church of Wittenberg, but I wouldn't stop there.

I would come on up even to 1863, and watch a vacillating president by the name of ABRAHAM LINCOLN finally come to the conclusion that he had to sign the Emancipation Proclamation.[2] But I wouldn't stop there.

[*Applause.*]

I would even come up to the early Thirties, and see a man grappling with the problems of the bankruptcy of his nation. And come with an eloquent cry that 'we have nothing to fear but fear itself'.[3] But I wouldn't stop there.

Strangely enough, I would turn to the Almighty, and say: 'If you allow me to live just a few years in the second half of the 20th century, I will be happy.'

[*Applause.*]

Now that's a strange statement to make, because the world is all messed up. The nation is sick. Trouble is in the land; confusion all around. That's a strange statement. But I know somehow that only when it is dark enough can you see the stars. And I see God working in this period of the 20th century in a way that men, in some strange way, are responding. Something is happening in our world.

The masses of people are rising up. And wherever they are assembled today, whether they are in Johannesburg, South Africa; Nairobi, Kenya; Accra, Ghana; New York City; Atlanta, Georgia; Jackson, Mississippi; or Memphis, Tennessee, the cry is always the same: 'We want to be free.'

[*Cheers and applause.*]

And another reason that I'm happy to live in this period is that we have been forced to a point where we're going to have to grapple with the problems that men have been trying to grapple with through history, but the demands didn't force them to do it. Survival demands that we grapple with them.

Men, for years now, have been talking about war and peace. But now, no longer can they just talk about it. It is no longer a choice between violence and non-violence in this world; it's non-violence or non-existence. That is where we are today …

We've got to give ourselves to this struggle until the end. Nothing would be more tragic than to stop at this point, in Memphis. We've got to see it through. And when we have our march, you need to be there. Be concerned about your brother. You may not be on strike. But either we go up together, or we go down together. Let us develop a kind of dangerous unselfishness …

Let us rise up tonight with a greater readiness. Let us stand with a greater determination. And let us move on in these powerful days, these days of challenge, to make America what it ought to be. We have an opportunity to make America a better nation. And I want to thank God, once more, for allowing me to be here with you.

You know, several years ago, I was in New York City autographing the first book that I had written. And while sitting there autographing books, a

[2] Lincoln's 'vacillation' over slavery was an attempt to reconcile a long-running rift in US politics. Despite conciliatory remarks in his inaugural address of March 1861, the secession of the slave-owning southern states – and the resulting Civil War – proved unavoidable. Lincoln's Emancipation Proclamation took effect on 1 January 1863, officially freeing all slaves in the rebel states.

[3] King refers to the first inaugural address of President FRANKLIN D ROOSEVELT, in March 1933, which heralded the 'New Deal', a programme of unprecedented socio-economic reforms that enabled national recovery after the Great Depression.

black woman came up.[4] The only question I heard from her was, 'Are you Martin Luther King?' And I was looking down writing, and I said, 'Yes'. And the next minute I felt something beating on my chest. Before I knew it I had been stabbed by this demented woman.

I was rushed to Harlem Hospital. It was a dark Saturday afternoon. And that blade had gone through, and the X-rays revealed that the tip of the blade was on the edge of my aorta, the main artery. And once that's punctured, you drown in your own blood – that's the end of you.

It came out in the *New York Times* the next morning, that if I had merely sneezed, I would have died. Well, about four days later, they allowed me, after the operation, after my chest had been opened and the blade had been taken out, to move around in the wheelchair in the hospital. They allowed me to read some of the mail that came in, and from all over the States and the world, kind letters came in.

I read a few, but one of them I will never forget. (I had received one from the president and the vice president. I've forgotten what those telegrams said. I'd received a visit and a letter from the governor of New York, but I've forgotten what that letter said.) But there was another letter that came from a little girl, a young girl who was a student at the White Plains High School.

And I looked at that letter and I'll never forget it. It said simply, 'Dear Dr King: I am a ninth-grade student at the White Plains High School.' And she said, 'While it should not matter, I would like to mention that I'm a white girl. I read in the paper of your misfortune, and of your suffering. And I read that if you had sneezed, you would have died. I'm simply writing you to say that I'm so happy that you didn't sneeze.'

[*Cheers and applause.*]

And I want to say tonight, I want to say tonight that I too am happy that I didn't sneeze, because if I had sneezed, I wouldn't have been around here in 1960, when students all over the South started sitting in at lunch counters. And I knew that as they were sitting in, they were really standing up for the best in the American dream, and taking the whole nation back to those great wells of democracy which were dug deep by the Founding Fathers in the Declaration of Independence and the Constitution.

If I had sneezed, I wouldn't have been around here in 1961, when we decided to take a ride for freedom and ended segregation in inter-state travel.

If I had sneezed, I wouldn't have been around here in 1962, when negroes in Albany, Georgia decided to straighten their backs up. And whenever men and women straighten their backs up, they are going somewhere, because a man can't ride your back unless it is bent. If I had sneezed –

[*Cheers and applause.*]

If I had sneezed I wouldn't have been here in 1963, when the black people of Birmingham, Alabama, aroused the conscience of this nation, and brought into being the Civil Rights Bill.

If I had sneezed, I wouldn't have had a chance later that year, in August, to try to tell America about a dream that I had had.

If I had sneezed, I wouldn't have been down in Selma, Alabama, to see the great movement there.

If I had sneezed, I wouldn't have been in Memphis to see a community rally around those brothers and sisters who are suffering. I'm so happy that I didn't sneeze.

[4] King refers to an incident in September 1958, when he was stabbed by Izola Ware Curry.

And they were telling me –

[*Cheers and applause.*]

Now it doesn't matter now. It really doesn't matter what happens now. I left Atlanta this morning and as we got started on the plane – there were six of us – the pilot said over the public address system, 'We are sorry for the delay, but we have Dr Martin Luther King on the plane. And to be sure that all of the bags were checked; and to be sure that nothing would be wrong on the plane, we had to check out everything carefully. And we've had the plane protected and guarded all night.'

And then I got into Memphis. And some began to say the threats, or talk about the threats that were out. What would happen to me from some of our sick white brothers? Well, I don't know what will happen now. We've got some difficult days ahead. But it really doesn't matter with me now. Because I've been to the mountaintop. [*Cheers and applause.*] And I don't mind.

Like anybody, I would like to live a long life: longevity has its place. But I'm not concerned about that now. I just want to do God's will. And he's allowed me to go up to the mountain. And I've looked over. And I've seen the promised land.[5] I may not get there with you. But I want you to know tonight, that we, as a people, will get to the promised land!

[*Cheers and applause.*] And so I'm happy, tonight. I'm not worried about anything. I'm not fearing any man! Mine eyes have seen the glory of the coming of the Lord![6]

[*Tumultuous cheers and applause.*]

[5] See Exodus 12:25 and Deuteronomy 9:28.

[6] The opening words of the 'Battle Hymn of the Republic', written during the American Civil War (1861–5) by Julia Ward Howe.

Neil Kinnock

Welsh politician

Neil Gordon Kinnock *later Baron Kinnock* (1942–) was born in Tredegar, Monmouthshire, and educated at University College Cardiff. He became Labour MP for Bedwellty in 1970, and leader of the British Labour Party in 1983. He was a member of the Labour Party's National Executive Committee from 1978 and chief opposition spokesman on education from 1979. He was at the centre of a controversy in 1981 when he headed a group of left-wing MPs who refused to support TONY BENN during elections for the deputy leadership of the party. A skilful orator, Kinnock was the Left's obvious choice in the Labour leadership contest of 1983, being regarded by many as the favoured candidate of the outgoing leader, MICHAEL FOOT, for whom he had worked as parliamentary private secretary. He was elected party leader by a large majority and re-elected in 1988. He succeeded in isolating the extreme elements within the party and persuaded it to adopt more moderate policies, better attuned to contemporary conditions. Nevertheless, the party was unsuccessful in the 1992 general election, after which Kinnock resigned and was replaced by John Smith. He was MP for Islwyn, 1983–95, and a member of the European Commission, 1995–2004, becoming its vice president in 1999. He became chair of the British Council in December 2004, a position he held until 2009. He was created a life peer in January 2005. His publications include *Making Our Way* (1986) and *Thorns and Roses* (1992).

'The first Kinnock in a thousand generations'

15 May 1987, Llandudno, Wales

This speech to the Welsh Labour Party conference is perhaps the most memorable of Kinnock's political career. Though he often spent all night preparing his speeches, this one is said to have been improvised from notes scribbled in the back of a car.

It was given soon after Prime Minister MARGARET THATCHER had announced a general election. Under her eight years in government, public utilities had been privatized, trade unions had been crushed, unemployment had risen (though it was now in decline), social security regulations had been tightened, the health service had been reformed, the leftist Greater London Council had been abolished and education funding had been sharply reduced.

The economy was booming, but in many sectors Thatcher was deeply unpopular. In 1985, for example, she had been refused an honorary degree by Oxford University in retaliation for education cuts.

Kinnock saw his chance to rally support against her. Unashamedly using the quasi-communist term 'comrades', his speech addresses the social concerns affecting ordinary people. Its central motif – a reference to his own and his wife's family backgrounds – vividly illustrates his argument for state-funded education.

The 'thousand generations' passage soon reappeared as part of a party political broadcast. It also resurfaced the following year in a speech by US senator Joe Biden, who was then seeking the Democratic presidential nomination. The plagiarism was identified, humiliating Biden and undermining his campaign.

Kinnock gained some ground for Labour, but most of the media supported Thatcher and she won the election with a comfortable majority of 102 seats.

I am happy to report that we are definitely in the last month of Thatcherism. We are in the last few weeks of that job-destroying, justice-trampling, oil-wasting, truth-twisting, service-smashing, nation-splitting, bunch-of-twisters-under-one-person government.[1] The last few weeks.

But apart from that they've got a great record. Well, they must have a great record! Mrs Thatcher's told them to fight on that record; to fight with pride, she said. She's been telling her party, 'Fight with pride on our record.' I hope they do. Oh, I hope they take some notice of her there. I hope they do fight on their record – I hope they do fight with pride. 'Pride goeth before destruction, and a haughty spirit before a fall.'[2] And so, surely, fall they will on 11 June.

They certainly deserve to. After eight years in government, a three million unemployment figure is not seen as the badge of shame; it's not seen as a cause of disappointment. A three million unemployment figure to

[1] This string of compound adjectives mimics a successful soft drink commercial.

[2] Proverbs 16:18.

them is a source of 'celebration' … and the prime minister has decided to mark the event by becoming immortal!

On Tuesday, I read it in the papers: 'Fourth-term target for Thatcher – on to the 21st century.' Well, I suppose that fits. She's been lecturing us about the 19th century; now she's talking about the 21st century – all she's missed out is this century, the one that we're living in! That's all she's missed out!

But I've been watching her on TV this week. Apparently that's all I'm going to be able to do, 'cause she won't debate with me face-to-face on the issues … It was Monday night's performance that I found most interesting.

She said she was full of ideas for continuing in the direction that they've been going. Full of ideas for continuing in the direction they've been going – well, we know what she means. New ideas like privatizing schools! New ideas like decontrolling rents! New ideas like paying for health care! What wonderful 'fresh,' 'new' ideas! What a great way to greet the dawn of the 21st century, with these wonderful 'new' ideas.

But anybody attracted by those 'ideas' – the privatization ideas, the decontrolling ideas; the flog-off, the sell-off ideas – had better ask themselves one question. They'd better ask themselves why every single one of those 'new' ideas was abandoned 50 and more years ago. If – if the payment for schooling was such a wonderful idea, why was it abolitioned, treated as a great leap forward for the people of this country? If uncontrolled rents did so much for housing, so much for families, why were they ever controlled? What malicious government ever decided that the landlords couldn't be left to deal with these things in their mercy?

And when it came to paying for health care, if that was such a blessing, why was the ending of that system hailed as the greatest step forward in civilization, in post-war history? Believe me, the reason is simple, very simple. The system that existed before those changes – the very system that Margaret Thatcher wants to reintroduce in this country – was wrong, and it was wretched, and it was squalid and brutal; it was rotten with injustice and with misery and with derision. That's why they got rid of it! That's why it was discarded – by popular demand! And that is why it must never be restored by prime ministerial demand.

That's why this election has come just in time! Just in time for those whose lives and skills are being wasted by unemployment. Just in time for the children in a school system that is deprived and derided by a Secretary of State for Education who won't send his own child to local schools. The election comes just in time for the old, who are being cheated out of pensions, and housing benefits and much else. It's come just in time for our health service, with its three-quarters of a million people in pain on the waiting list …

Listen, comrades. Our country has taken a beating in the last eight years, from a government with an 'on your bike' employment policy,[3] a 'stay in bed to keep warm' retirement policy, a 'flag day' health service policy, and a 'jumble sale' education system policy.[4] People all over this country know that Britain couldn't take 13 years of that. Britain can't take 13 years of Thatcherism. Britain can't serve such a life sentence without it becoming a death sentence for even more industries, and communities, and hopes – yes, and people, too! Because unemployment and poverty are not just 'ailments', not just misfortunes! They are mortal afflictions, as every experience and figure shows.

Not that it bothers the prime minister. It doesn't seem to influence her at all. She will have us think that we are in the middle of a great 'recovery'.

[3] In 1981, when he was Secretary of State for Employment, Norman Tebbit *later Baron Tebbit* (1931–) said, 'I grew up in the 1930s with an unemployed father … He got on his bike and looked for work, and he went on looking until he found it.'

[4] The 'flag day' and 'jumble sale' jibes refer to Thatcher's privatization schemes in the health and education sectors.

Difficult to see the evidence, unless of course you wait until the end of the news. *There* you can see the recovery! The stock market is up! There's the evidence for recovery! Unemployed? Don't worry, stay at home and watch the stock market going up on the television! Worried about redundancy? Don't worry, you can pass your time by looking at the Financial Times Share Index!

It strikes me very often, you know, that the reason that they put the stock market reports on the back end of the news alongside all those thrilling items about gerbils having triplets is because it's got just about as much relevance to real life as the gerbil incident. But there's the evidence for the great recovery!

'Recovery' is an awful funny word to use about eight years in which manufacturing production hasn't got back to the 1979 levels. 'Recovery' is a very strange term to describe an economy that has had an *increase* of two million unemployed since 1979. 'Recovery' is a very peculiar label for a situation in which manufacturing investment is 20 per cent *lower* than it was in 1979. 'Recovery' – it's hardly the word to describe a country that in 1979 had a £3 billion *surplus* in manufacturing goods, and in 1987 has got an £8 billion *deficit* in manufacturing goods ... Is it a recovery when one in five of 16-to-25-year-olds haven't got a job? Is it a recovery when you can hardly buy anything with a 'Made in Britain' label in any shop, in any high street in this land? Is it a recovery when scientists are leaving in droves? Does that all become a recovery? I don't think it's much of a recovery ...

When we speak of collective strength and collective freedom, collectively achieved, we are not fulfilling that nightmare that Mrs Thatcher tries to paint, and all her predecessors have tried to saddle us with. We're not talking about uniformity; we're not talking about regimentation; we're not talking about *conformity* – that's their creed. The uniformity of the dole queue; the regimentation of the unemployed young and their compulsory work schemes. The *conformity* of people who will work in conditions, and take orders, and accept pay because of mass unemployment that they would laugh at in a free society with full employment.

That kind of freedom for the individual, that kind of liberty, can't be secured by most of the people for most of the time if they're just left to themselves, isolated, stranded, with their whole life chances dependent upon luck!

Why am I the first Kinnock in a thousand generations to be able to get to university? Why is Glenys the first woman in her family in a thousand generations to be able to get to university? Was it because *all* our predecessors were thick? Did they lack talent – those people who could sing, and play, and recite and write poetry; those people who could make wonderful, beautiful things, with their hands; those people who could dream dreams, see visions; those people who had such a sense of perception as to know in times so brutal, so oppressive, that they could win their way out of that by coming together?

Were those people not university material? Couldn't they have knocked off all their A Levels in an afternoon? But why didn't they get it? Was it because they were weak – those people who could work eight hours underground and then come up and play football? Weak? Those women who could survive eleven childbearings, were they weak? Those people who could stand with their backs and their legs straight and face the great – the people who had control over their lives; the ones that owned their workplaces and tried to own them – and tell them, 'No, I won't take your orders.' Were they weak?

Does anybody really think that they didn't get what we had because they didn't have the talent, or the strength, or the endurance, or the commitment? Of course not. It was because there was no platform upon which they could stand, no arrangement for their neighbours to subscribe to their welfare, no method by which the community could translate its desires for those individuals into provision for those individuals. And now Mrs Thatcher – by dint of privatization and means test and deprivation and division – wants to nudge us back into the situation where everybody can either stand on their own feet or live on their knees …

Of course, you'll hear the Tories talking a lot about freedom. You're going to hear a lot of that over the next month; a lot of talk of freedom from people who have spent much of the last eight years crushing individual freedoms under the weight of unemployment and poverty. Squeezing individual rights with cuts, and with means tests and with charges.

I think of the youngsters I meet. Three, four, five years out of school. Never had a job. And they say to me, 'Do you think we'll ever get a job?' These are young men and women living in a free country, but they don't feel free.

I think of the 55-year-old woman I met, waiting months to go into hospital for an operation, her whole existence clouded by pain. She is a citizen of a free country, but she doesn't feel free.

I think of the young couple, two years married, living in their mam and dad's front room 'cause they can't get a home. Seeing their family relationship deteriorate from what was the greatest friendship and kinship in their family on their wedding day, to the most bitter contradictions and conflicts within that household. Those young people, they live in a free country, but they don't feel free.

I think of the old couple. We all know them. The old people, going for months through the winter afraid to turn the heat up. Staying at home, afraid to go out after dark. Old people for whom the need to buy a new pair of shoes is an economic crisis! They live in a free country – indeed they're of the generation that *fought* for a free country – but they don't feel free.

How can they, and millions like them, have their individual freedom if there is not collective provision? How can they have *strength* if they haven't that, just that little bit of support – of care? That helping hand. They can't have either. They can't have either strength or care now, because they are locked out of being able to discharge their responsibilities, just as surely as they are locked out of their ability to enjoy rights.

And they are fellow-citizens. They want to be able to use both rights and responsibilities. They don't want featherbedding. They want a foothold. They don't want cosseting, or cotton-wooling, they want a chance to *contribute*. The greatest privilege is to be able to bear responsibility, not discharge rights. Rights are great. They can be plastered on walls, written in bills; but it's responsibilities that you *can* discharge – that's when you feel strong, because you've got the means, you've got the strength, you've got the rights. They can't discharge responsibilities or rights, and they want the freedom to do so. That's the freedom we want them, as democratic socialists, to have. That's a freedom that we seek power to get and to spread in our country.

❧

'"No such thing as society," she says'
4 October 1988, Blackpool, England

❧

On 31 October 1987, an interview with Prime Minister Margaret Thatcher appeared in *Woman's Own* magazine. In it, she was quoted as saying, 'There is no such thing as society.'

It was nearly a year later when Kinnock turned her remarks to his own purposes at the Labour Party conference. Kinnock was in a strong position: the previous Sunday he had won nearly 90 per cent of his party's vote following a leadership challenge from the left-winger Tony Benn.

His confidence is apparent in his conference speech. A tendency to verbosity had led adversaries and rivals to dub him 'the Welsh windbag', but here Kinnock shows restraint and economy. His gift for a passionate, almost musical language comes to the fore as he uses Thatcher's own words to berate her for neglecting Britain's impoverished 'underclass'.

Another key issue for the Labour Party at this time was its policy of unilateral nuclear disarmament, which some critics believed had been a stumbling block at the June 1987 election. Although there had been hints of a change of policy in recent interviews, Kinnock used his speech to assert his continued commitment to disarmament.

He skilfully links the two themes by attributing both Thatcher's social policy and her defence policy to her 'narrowness of vision'. In doing so, he aligns himself with the world's most powerful leaders, the Soviet president Mikhail Gorbachev and – audaciously, given their ideological differences – the US president RONALD REAGAN.

❧

Now that everyone has had an opportunity to digest the results of Sunday night, I should like to thank you again for your support. You know that my feeling about the leadership election was that it was an unnecessary distraction from our work in the party. But the fact is, asked for or not, elections have results and results give mandates. That mandate was given democratically and it will be used democratically. It will be used very deliberately and very directly for the purpose for which I believe it was given to me by people right across the Labour movement. The purpose of unity. The purpose of change. The purpose of doing everything that can be done to secure victory for this party at the next general election. That is why I was given this mandate. I was given the mandate, too – and this is how I will serve it – in order to pursue the democratic socialist values of this movement and the social and economic vision which arises from those values.

We are socialists, we are rationalists. Our vision is insight, not a mirage. We have strong ideals, but our idealism is not naivety. We do not pretend the world is as it is not. We have a dream, but we are not dreamers. We do not simply desire ends. We understand the necessity of committing the means and it is precisely that which produces our commitment to social justice and to economic efficiency.

There are those, of course, like the present government, who consider social justice to be an impediment to economic efficiency. There are some – including, from what they say, some in our movement – who consider economic efficiency to be a threat to social justice. Both are wrong. The simple fact is that sustained social justice depends upon a foundation of economic prosperity; and economic success cannot be properly achieved without social justice. Justice and efficiency – the two go together …

If social justice and economic efficiency are not the ruling values of our society, where does our society go? Many people are asking that. They say: 'What is happening to our country and what is going to happen to our country?'

The answer is that unless we apply the policies of social justice and economic efficiency to create wealth, and unless we apply those policies to use that wealth to create a fairer society in Britain, then Britain inevitably goes further along the path that it is set upon now. It goes further along the path to a split society. It goes further towards a community divided into three unequal parts: a small, opulent superclass at the top; a larger class of people living in a reasonable but sometimes anxious affluence in the middle – especially those at the bottom end of that central class who are subject to the pressures of a credit-driven economy – and at the bottom a third class, an underclass of people living in dire need.

I am not describing some distant tomorrow, some awful decade away, I am describing Britain now. In Britain now nearly nine million men, women and children live on supplementary benefit. Another nine million on low pay. That is one in three of the population: 18 million people on poverty level, whether they earn those desperately low wages or are thrust into poverty because of unemployment, illness or disability and are confined to the dependence on what the government chooses to hand out to them in their social security system.

By 1991, that underclass will be even bigger – 22 million men, women and children – and they suffer all of the social and civil disadvantages that go with their low incomes. Our society is disfigured and endangered by such great poverty. To their credit, many who are not poor understand that. They understand, too, that a society with such great and growing differences in personal economic conditions is unlikely to be a society at peace with itself. It is an insecure society. That is what we have now.

The expressions of insecurity take many forms. They include increasing family break-up, increasing neurotic stress and breakdown, poverty and homelessness, crimes of sexual abuse and robbery, drug and alcohol abuse, a huge rise in violence for criminal ends and – incredibly and terrifyingly – a spread in violence for entertainment, whether it is in football crowds or in quiet country towns on a Saturday night. Of course, no-one could or would blame the government for all that. But it is impossible to accept that there is no connection between the fracturing of our society and the grabbing 'loadsamoney'[1] ethic encouraged by a government that treats care as 'drooling', compassion as 'wet'. A government led by a prime minister who says that: 'There is no such thing as society.'

'No such thing as society,' she says. No obligation to the community. No sense of solidarity. No principles of sharing or caring. 'No such thing as society.' No sisterhood, no brotherhood. No neighbourhood. No honouring other people's mothers and fathers. No succouring other people's little children. 'No such thing as society.' No number other than one. No person other than me. No time other than now. No such thing as society, just 'me' and 'now'. That is Margaret Thatcher's society.

I tell you, you cannot run a country on the basis of 'me' and 'now'. You cannot run domestic policy on that basis, and you certainly cannot run international policy on that basis. Nowhere is that more obvious than in defence policies. Margaret Thatcher tries to operate 'me' and 'now' policies at every level. Thankfully, other leaders do not share her narrowness or her lack of vision.

The relationship between the superpowers has been changing radically since Reykjavik.[2] But it is in the year since we last met at conference that that changed relationship has manifested itself in tangible form, with the treaty to remove intermediate nuclear weapons.[3] That relationship, whatever the outcome of the presidential elections in the United States of America,[4] will be further developed by the reduction in strategic nuclear

[1] Loadsamoney was a popular satirical character created by the English comedian Harry Enfield (1961–). A leering, self-centred tradesman who bragged about his lavish income, he represented the 'self-made man' Thatcher's policies were said to encourage.

[2] At the Reykjavik summit of October 1986, Soviet president Mikhail Gorbachev (1931–) and US president Ronald Reagan (1911–2004) discussed nuclear disarmament.

[3] On 8 December 1987, Gorbachev and Reagan signed the Intermediate-Range Nuclear Forces Treaty.
[4] On 8 November 1988, George H W Bush (1924–), who had been vice president under Reagan, was elected US president.

arms and it will be strengthened by agreements on conventional force reductions.

Those changes have taken place partly because of the fact that Mikhail Gorbachev and – I guess you never thought you would hear it from this platform – Ronald Reagan too had the courage and wisdom to take initiatives that grew, according to their own testimony, from the fact that they – as individuals and as leaders – they have accepted the moral arguments against nuclear weapons that we, and many like us across the world, have been putting for three decades and more.

When Mikhail Gorbachev and Ronald Reagan say that we have 'entered the age of nuclear disarmament', then there are opportunities for clearing countries and continents of nuclear weapons that have not existed at any time since NATO[5] and the Warsaw Pact[6] became nuclear powers. That is why we must encourage all new steps, celebrate all new achievements and seek the power to participate in that process to end dependence on nuclear weapons anywhere in the world. That is what we must do.

That power, as is obvious to everyone, can only be attained, only be exercised in government. For everyone here and throughout the Labour movement knows that if we do not get the power of government, the consequence will be that Trident[7] will definitely be completed and deployed – and in addition, other systems will be multiplied under the guise of 'modernization'. To win power is to have the means of achieving a non-nuclear defence policy ourselves and securing the reduction in the nuclear weapons systems of others. Not to win power is to make certain the increase of nuclear arms by a Tory government that wants more of such arms and not less. This party, I am certain, wants to be part of the process of nuclear disarmament. Indeed, this party wants to take a leading part in that process of nuclear disarmament. That is only possible in government. It is not possible out of government.

When we conclude our review next year and when we resolve our policy of fighting the next general election, that policy must be serious about nuclear disarmament, serious about defence. Indeed, so serious about both objectives that we are capable of earning the democratic power to achieve them.

[5] The North Atlantic Treaty Organization, an international pact for defence collaboration established 1949, which by 1988 incorporated most countries in western Europe and North America.

[7] Trident is an intercontinental ballistic missile which can be launched from a submarine. Thatcher's decision to procure Trident II from the USA prompted much debate during the mid-1980s.

[6] A similar treaty, signed in 1955, embracing the USSR and eastern European countries under Communist rule.

Rudyard Kipling
English writer

Joseph Rudyard Kipling (1865–1936) was born in Bombay, India, the son of John Lockwood Kipling (1837–1911), principal of the school of art in Lahore. He was educated at the United Services College, Westward Ho!, in Devon, England, but returned in 1880 to India, where he worked as a journalist. His reputation was established with the publication of mildly satirical verses and two short story collections. He returned in 1889 to England, where he published his first full-length novel *The Light that Failed* (1890). In London he formed a friendship with the American author and publisher Wolcott Balestier (1861–91), with whom he collaborated on *The Naulakha* (1892), and whose sister Caroline he married (1892). A spell of residence in his wife's native Vermont ended abruptly in 1899 through incompatibility with in-laws and locals, and the remainder of his career was spent in England. Meanwhile he had written brilliantly successful collections of verse, and further short stories. *The Jungle Book* (1894) and *The Second Jungle Book* (1895) have gained a place among the classic animal stories; while *Stalky and Co* (1899) presents semi-autobiographical school stories. His most successful novel *Kim* (1901) is an espionage adventure with a Buddhist theme, set in India. The children's classic *Just So Stories* appeared in 1902. The verse collection *The Five Nations* (1903) included the highly successful 'Recessional', written for Queen Victoria's diamond jubilee in 1897. Later works include *Puck of Pook's Hill* (1906), *Rewards and Fairies* (1910), *Debits and Credits* (1926). In 1932, he scripted the first Christmas radio broadcast for GEORGE V, which is included in this book. The autobiographical *Something of Myself* was published posthumously (1937). Kipling's real merit as a writer has become obscured in recent years and he has been accused of imperialism and jingoism, but this ignores not only a great body of his work far removed from this sphere, but also his own criticisms and satire on some of the less admirable aspects of colonialism. He was awarded the Nobel Prize for literature in 1907.

'The magic of the necessary word'
5 May 1906, London, England

This speech was given at an anniversary dinner for the Royal Academy, a grand affair held at its headquarters in Burlington House. Guests of honour included the Archbishop of Canterbury, the Russian Ambassador and – representing the royal family – Edward VII's brother the Duke of Connaught. Although he had arrived back only that morning from South Africa, Kipling had accepted an invitation to speak on behalf of literature.

He devoted his address to the perilous position of writers. His tone is elevated and humorous – and the speech provoked considerable laughter among his listeners. Yet a serious undercurrent can be detected as he laments the lot of those called upon to record the events and spirit of their times. Their work rarely endures, he declares, yet it is scrutinized as if it were indelible.

He weaves his argument around two pithy parables, each set in a primitive tribal community. Kipling's imperialistic instincts may perhaps be glimpsed in his depiction of these cultures, but he asserts that all societies behave according to exactly the same primal instincts. His central message is one no writer would disown: that history is made by the written word.

His opening remarks were prompted by the glowing introduction lavished upon him by Sir Edward Poynter, president of the Academy: 'You know him as the enchanter of childhood, the hero of boyhood, the grand exponent of vigorous manhood, the staunch upholder of the honour of his country ... I give you the toast of literature coupled with the name of Mr Rudyard Kipling.' Loud cheers followed.

A great and, I frankly admit, a somewhat terrifying, honour has come to me; but I think, compliments apart, that the most case-hardened worker in letters, speaking to such an assembly as this, must recognize the gulf that separates even the least of those who do things worthy to be written about from even the best of those who have written things worthy of being talked about.

There is an ancient legend which tells us that when a man first achieved a most notable deed he wished to explain to his tribe what he had done. As soon as he began to speak, however, he was smitten with dumbness; he lacked words, and sat down. Then there arose – according to the story – a masterless man, one who had taken no part in the action of his fellow, who had no special virtues, but who was afflicted – that is the phrase – with the magic of the necessary word. He saw; he told; he described the merits of the notable deed in such a fashion, we are assured, that the words 'became alive and walked up and down in the hearts of all his hearers'. Thereupon, the tribe, seeing that the words were certainly alive, and fearing lest the man with the words would hand down untrue tales about them to their children, took and killed him. But later they saw that the magic was in the words, not in the man.

We have progressed in many directions since the time of this early and destructive criticism, but, so far, we do not seem to have found a sufficient substitute for the necessary word as the final record to which all achievement must look. Even today, when all is done, those who have done it must wait until all has been said by the masterless man with the words. It is certain that the overwhelming bulk of those words will perish in the future as they have perished in the past; but it is true that a minute fraction will continue to exist, and by the light of these words, and by that light only, will our children be able to judge of the phases of our generation.

Now we desire beyond all things to stand well with our children; but when our story comes to be told we do not know who will have the telling of it. We are too close to the tellers; there are many tellers and they are all talking together; and, even if we know them, we must not kill them. But the old and terrible instinct which taught our ancestors to kill the original story-teller warns us that we shall not be far wrong if we challenge any man who shows signs of being afflicted with the magic of the necessary word.

May not this be the reason why, without any special legislation on its behalf, literature has always stood a little outside the law as the one calling that is absolutely free – free in the sense that it needs no protection? For instance, if, as occasionally happens, a judge makes a bad law, or a surgeon a bad operation, or a manufacturer makes bad food, criticism upon their actions is by law and custom confined to comparatively narrow limits.

But if a man, as occasionally happens, makes a book, there is no limit to the criticism that may be directed against it. And this is perfectly as it should be. The world recognizes that little things like bad law, bad surgery and bad food affect only the cheapest commodity that we know about – human life. Therefore, in these circumstances, men can afford to be swayed by pity for the offender, by interest in his family, by fear, or loyalty, or respect for the organization he represents, or even by a desire to do him justice.

But when the question is of words – words that may become alive and walk up and down in the hearts of the hearers – it is then that this world of ours, which is disposed to take an interest in its future, feels instinctively that it is better that a thousand innocent people should be punished rather than that one guilty word should be preserved, carrying that which is an untrue tale of the tribe.

The chances, of course, are almost astronomically remote that any given tale will survive for so long as it takes an oak to grow to timber size. But that guiding instinct warns us not to trust to chance a matter of the supremest concern. In this durable record, if anything short of indisputable and undistilled truth be seen there, we all feel, 'How shall our achievements profit us?' The record of the tribe is its enduring literature.

The magic of literature lies in the words, and not in any man. Witness: a thousand excellent, strenuous words can leave us quite cold or put us to sleep, whereas a bare half-hundred words breathed upon by some man in his agony, or in his exaltation, or in his idleness, ten generations ago, can still lead whole nations into and out of captivity, can open to us the doors of the three worlds, or stir us so intolerably that we can scarcely abide to look at our souls. It is a miracle – one that happens very seldom. But secretly, each one of the masterless men with the words has hope, or has had hope, that the miracle may be wrought again through him.

And why not? If a tinker in Bedford gaol;[1] if a pamphleteering shopkeeper, pilloried in London;[2] if a muzzy Scot;[3] if a despised German Jew;[4] or a condemned French thief;[5] or an English Admiralty official with a taste for letters[6] can be miraculously afflicted with the magic of the necessary word, why not any man at any time? Our world, which is only concerned in the perpetuation of the record, sanctions that hope just as kindly and just as cruelly as nature sanctions love.

All it suggests is that the man with the words shall wait upon the man of achievement, and step by step with him try to tell the story to the tribe. All it demands is that the magic of every word shall be tried out to the uttermost by every means, fair or foul, that the mind of man can suggest. There is no room – and the world insists that there shall be no room – for pity, for mercy, for respect, for fear, or even for loyalty between man and his fellow-man, when the record of the tribe comes to be written.

That record must satisfy, at all costs to the word and to the man behind the word. It must satisfy alike the keenest vanity and the deepest self-knowledge of the present; it must satisfy also the most shameless curiosity of the future. When it has done this, it is literature of which it will be said, in due time, that it fitly represents its age. I say in due time because ages, like individuals, do not always appreciate the merits of a record that purports to represent them. The trouble is that one always expects just a little more out of a thing than one puts into it. Whether it be an age or an individual, one is always a little pained and a little pessimistic to find that all one gets back is just one's bare deserts. This is a difficulty old as literature.

A little incident that came within my experience a while ago shows that the difficulty is always being raised by the most unexpected people all about the world. It happened in a land where the magic of words is peculiarly potent and far-reaching, that there was a tribe that wanted rain, and the rain-doctors set about getting it. To a certain extent, the rain-doctors succeeded. But the rain their magic brought was not a full driving downpour that tells of large prosperity; it was patchy, local, circumscribed, and uncertain.

There were unhealthy little squalls blowing about the country and doing damage. Whole districts were flooded out by waterspouts, and other districts annoyed by trickling showers, soon dried by the sun. And so the tribe went to the rain-doctors, being very angry, and they said, 'What is this rain that you make? You did not make rain like this in the time of our fathers. What have you been doing?'

And the rain-doctors said, 'We have been making our proper magic. Supposing you tell us what you have been doing lately?'

And the tribe said, 'Oh, our head-men have been running about hunting jackals, and our little people have been running about chasing grasshoppers! What has that to do with your rain-making?'

'It has everything to do with it,' said the rain-doctors. 'Just as long as your head-men run about hunting jackals, and just as long as your little people run about chasing grasshoppers, just so long will the rain fall in this manner.'

---

[1] Kipling refers to the English writer John Bunyan (1628–88), a tinker turned preacher, who wrote a number of devotional works during his two terms of imprisonment for his dissenting religious views; of these, the best known is *Pilgrim's Progress* (1678–84).

[2] Kipling refers to the English writer Daniel Defoe (1660–1731), a shopkeeper turned prolific journalist and pamphleteer, who was fined, pilloried and imprisoned for the satiric *The Shortest Way with Dissenters* (1702). He is best known now for his novels, including *Robinson Crusoe* (1719) and *Moll Flanders* (1722).

[3] Kipling refers to the Scottish poet and songwriter Robert Burns (1759–96), an unsuccessful farmer with a tangled love life.

[4] Kipling refers to the German social, political and economic theorist KARL MARX, a Jew whose family converted to Christianity to escape anti-Semitism. His writings included *Das Kapital* (published 1867–94), one of the most influential works of the 19th century.

[5] Kipling perhaps refers to Jeanne de St Remy de Valois, Comtesse de Lamotte (1756–91), mistress of a French cardinal, who stole a diamond necklace, was convicted, escaped from jail to England and published a memoir.

[6] Kipling refers to the English diarist Samuel Pepys (1633–1703), who worked as an Admiralty clerk from 1660 and became Secretary to the Admiralty in 1672. His diaries cover the years 1660–9, including descriptions of the Great Plague (1665–6), the Great Fire of London (1666) and the Dutch fleet sailing up the Thames (1665–7).

Vladimir Ilich Lenin
Russian revolutionary leader

Vladimir Ilich Lenin *originally Vladimir Ilich Ulyanov* (1870–1924) was born into a middle-class family in Simbirsk. He was educated at Kazan University and in 1892 began to practise law. In 1894, after five years' study of KARL MARX, he moved to St Petersburg. He organized the illegal Union for the Liberation of the Working Class, was arrested and spent several years in exile, first in Siberia and then in the West. In 1900, in Switzerland, he edited the political newspaper *Iskra* ('The Spark') and developed, with Georgi Plekhanov, an underground Social Democratic Party, to assume leadership of the working classes in a revolution against Tsarism. His evolving ideas were set out in *What is to be Done?* (1902), in which he advocated a professional core of party activists to spearhead the revolution. This suggestion was adopted by the party's Bolshevik wing at the congress in London in 1903, but was opposed by the 'bourgeois reformist' Menshevik wing. Lenin returned to Russia in 1905, and blamed the failure of the rising that year on lack of support for his programme. He determined that 'soviets' (workers' councils) should be the instruments of revolution. He left Russia in 1907 and spent a decade strengthening the Bolsheviks against the Mensheviks, studying Marx and Friedrich Engels and organizing underground work in Russia. After the February Revolution of 1917, which forced Tsar Nicholas II's abdication, Lenin travelled in a sealed train from Switzerland to Petrograd (formerly St Petersburg). He told his followers to prepare for the overthrow of the provisional government. In the October Revolution the provisional government collapsed and the Bolsheviks declared that supreme power rested in them. Lenin inaugurated the 'dictatorship of the proletariat' with the dissolution of the constituent assembly. In August 1918, he was shot by Fanya Kaplan, a member of the Socialist Revolutionary Party. He never fully recovered from his injuries. For three years he grappled with war and anarchy. In 1922 he launched his 'new economic policy' of limited free enterprise, before entering an era of giant state planning. His health declined and he died in January 1924. His body was embalmed in a mausoleum in Red Square, Moscow. A charismatic figure who lived only for the furtherance of Marxism, Lenin was shrewd, dynamic pedantic and implacable. Despite the ultimate failure of Soviet communism, his influence endures in Russia and beyond.

'To the workers, everything; to the toilers, everything!'
30 August 1918, Moscow, Russia

This speech was delivered immediately before Fanya Kaplan's dramatic assassination attempt. The occasion was a mass meeting in the hand-grenade shop of Moscow's Michelson Factory.

Much had changed in Russia after the February Revolution; and although Lenin – unwilling to compromise his careful plans to reorganize the government and economy – had not take advantage of anti-government demonstrations in July 1917, he had led the successful October Revolution. He allowed elections for a constituent assembly in November, but dissolved it in January 1918 after a majority of seats were won by the Socialist Revolutionary Party. Russia withdrew from World War I in March 1918, ceding vast areas of land and economic resources to Germany under the Treaty of Brest-Litovsk.

On 15 August, Lenin severed diplomatic relations with the USA and two weeks later he gave this speech discrediting the moderate provisional government (established after the February Revolution) and attacking the American concept of democracy. In it, he expresses his anger at the course of the war and the treatment of workers in other countries. As he was leaving the meeting, Kaplan ran towards him and fired at close range. Lenin refused to go to hospital for fear that further assassins were waiting for him there, and was treated at home.

We Bolsheviks are constantly accused of violating the slogans of equality and fraternity. Let us go into this question in detail.

What was the authority which took the place of the Tsar's authority?[1] It was the authority of Guchkov[2] and Milyukov,[3] which began to prepare for a constituent assembly in Russia. What was it that really lay behind this work in favour of a liberation of the people from its yoke of a thousand years? Simply the fact that Guchkov and the other leaders gathered around them a host of capitalists who were pursuing their own imperialist purposes.

And when the clique of Kerensky,[4] Chernov,[5] etc, gained power, this new government, hesitating and deprived of any base to stand on, fought

[1] The Romanov dynasty ruled Russia from 1613. Constitutional reforms took place in 1905 but after the February Revolution, the Tsar abdicated, ending imperial rule. The provisional government was established to rule the country until the formation of an elected constituent assembly.

[2] The Russian politician Aleksandr Guchkov (1862–1936) was Minister of War in the provisional government. He supported the war and opposed far-reaching land reform. He left office in May 1917.

[3] The Russian politician Pavel Miliukov (1859–1943) was Minister of Foreign Affairs in the provisional government until May 1917, having supported the war.

[4] The Russian socialist politician Aleksandr Kerensky (1881–1970) became Minister of War in the provisional government in May 1917, then Prime Minister in July 1917. Under Bolshevik pressure he fled Russia later that year.

[5] The Russian politician Viktor Chernov (c.1873–1952) helped to found the Socialist Revolutionary Party (SRP) in 1901. In 1917, he became Minister of Agriculture in the provisional government. He briefly chaired the constituent assembly following SRP election success, before Lenin dissolved the assembly.

only for the basic interests of the bourgeoisie, closely allied to it. The power actually passed into the hands of the *kulaks*,[6] and nothing into those of the toiling masses.

We have witnessed the same phenomenon in other countries also. Let us take America, the freest and most civilized country. America is a democratic republic. And what is the result? We have the shameless rule of a clique not of millionaires but of multi-millionaires, and the entire nation is enslaved and oppressed. If the factories and works, the banks and all the riches of the nation belong to the capitalists; if, by the side of the democratic republic we observe a perpetual enslavement of millions of toilers and a continuous poverty, we have a right to ask: where is all your lauded equality and fraternity?

Far from it! The rule of democracy is accompanied by an unadulterated savage banditry. We understand the true nature of so-called democracies.

The secret treaties of the French Republic, of England and of the other democracies,[7] have clearly convinced us of the real nature, the underlying facts of this business. Their aims and interests are just as criminally predatory as are those of Germany. The war has opened our eyes. We now know very well that the 'defender of the fatherland' conceals under his skin a vile bandit and thief. This attack of the bandit must be opposed with a revolutionary action, with revolutionary creativeness.

To be sure, it is very difficult, at an exceptional time like this, to bring about a union, particularly of the peasant revolutionary elements. But we have faith in the creative energy and the social zeal of the vanguard of the revolution – the proletariat of the factories and shops. The workers have already well grasped the fact that, as long as they permit their minds to revel in the phantasms of a democratic republic and a constituent assembly, they will have to hand out 50 million roubles a day in advance for military aims that will be destructive to themselves, and for just so long will it be impossible for them to find any outlet from the capitalist oppression.

Having grasped this, the workers created their soviets.[8] It was life itself, real, actual life, which taught the workers to understand that as long as the landholders had entrenched themselves so well in palaces and magic castles, freedom of assembly would be a mere fiction and would only perhaps be found in the other world. To promise freedom to the workers and at the same time to leave the castles, the land, the factories and all the resources in the hands of the capitalists and landowners – that this has nothing to do with liberty and equality.

We have only one slogan, one watchword: everyone who works has a right to enjoy the good things of life. Idlers, parasites, those who suck out the blood of the toiling masses, must be deprived of these blessings. And our cry is: to the workers, everything; to the toilers, everything!

We know that all this is difficult to bring about. We know what savage opposition we shall encounter on the part of the bourgeoisie; but we believe in the final victory of the proletariat; for once it has freed itself from the terrible quandary of the threats of military imperialism and once it has erected, on the ruins of the structure it has overthrown, the new structure of the socialist republic, it cannot but gain the victory.

And, as a matter of fact, we find a merging of forces in progress everywhere. Owing to our abolition of private property in land, we now find an active fraternization going on between the proletariat of the city and of the village. The clarification of the class-consciousness of the workers is also advancing apace in a far more definite manner than before.

[6] A pejorative term for landowning peasants who had acquired property following the emancipation of the serfs in 1905. The kulaks opposed Lenin's land reform.

[7] The rapid escalation of events leading to World War I was largely due to a network of treaties and pacts negotiated (often secretly) between the various European powers.

[8] Workers' and soldiers' councils, elected by popular vote.

In the West too: the workers of England, France, Italy and other countries are responding more and more to the appeals and demands which bear witness to the early victory of the cause of international revolution. And our task of the day is this: that of performing our revolutionary work, regardless of all the hypocrisy, the base shouts of rage and the sermons delivered by the murderous bourgeoisie. We must turn all our efforts on the Czecho-Slovak front,[9] in order to disperse at once this band of cut-throats which cloaks itself in the slogans of liberty and equality and shoots down hundreds and thousands of workers and peasants.

We have only one recourse: victory or death!

[9] Following the success of the October Revolution, the new regime came under attack from various anti-Bolshevik factions in a civil war between Communist 'Reds' and a coalition of conservatives, monarchists and liberals known as 'Whites'. These included the Czecho-Slovak Legion in Siberia.

Abraham Lincoln
American statesman

Abraham Lincoln (1809–65) was born in a log cabin in Kentucky, the son of a restless pioneer. The family settled in Indiana in 1816. Two years later Abraham's mother died and his father remarried shortly afterwards. In 1830 the Lincolns moved on to Illinois and Abraham went to work as a clerk in a store at New Salem. He already had political ambitions, and saw the need to study law and grammar. He won election to the legislature in 1834, and began to practise law in 1836. In 1846 he sat in Congress; but professional work was distracting him from politics when in 1854 Senator Stephen A Douglas achieved repeal of the Missouri Compromise of 1820, reopening the question of slavery in the territories. The resulting Kansas–Nebraska Act roused intense feeling throughout the North, and Lincoln delivered a powerful speech on the subject which revealed his power as a debater. He was then elected to the legislature. After the Republican Party was organized in 1854 to oppose the extension of slavery, Lincoln became its most prominent leader in Illinois, and became a candidate for the vice-presidency. In 1858 he stood against Douglas for the Illinois seat in the Senate. Lincoln lost, but his views attracted the attention of the whole country. In May 1860 the Republican convention nominated him for the presidency. The Democratic Party was then divided between Douglas and John Cabell Breckinridge. After an exciting campaign, Lincoln won with a comfortable majority. South Carolina had left the Union, and the six gulf states had formed the Confederate States of America. Not even Lincoln's oratorical skills and conciliatory efforts could prevent the impending conflict and in April 1861, the Civil War began with the Confederate attack on Fort Sumter in Charleston. Lincoln defined the issue of the war in terms of national integrity, not anti-slavery. Nonetheless, his Emancipation Proclamation (issued in two parts, September 1862 and January 1863) declared freedom for all slaves in areas of rebellion. He adhered to this theme in his re-election campaign of 1864 and was re-elected. In April 1965 at Ford's Theatre, Washington, he was shot by the actor John Wilkes Booth (1838–65) and he died the next morning. Lincoln was fair and direct in speech and action, steadfast in principle, sympathetic and charitable. He was familiar with the Bible, though not a professed member of any church.

'The central idea of secession is the essence of anarchy'
4 March 1861, Washington, DC, USA

In common with all US presidents, Lincoln took an oath to 'preserve, protect and defend' the Constitution, and there is no doubt that on the warm March day of his inauguration he believed his most important task was to uphold the Union. His first inaugural address, guiding his listeners through the legal and logical arguments for preserving the Union, was measured to strike a balance between the opposing forces that were threatening to pull the young country apart.

Dr Eugene A Goodwin from Maine, physician and diarist, attended the event and declared Lincoln to be decisive, looking well and speaking loudly and distinctly, despite rumours of assassination threats which forced him to travel to Washington in secret.

Lincoln's attempts to defend the Union without further alienating the South were doomed to failure – their hopes for success not helped by the critical time-lapse between his election in November and his inauguration four months later. By March, seven states had seceded, a convention had been called to meet in Montgomery, Alabama and the Confederate president, Jefferson Davis, had been elected and sworn in. Concurrently, the Confederate states had begun to seize military forts and arsenals. Lincoln's speech was quickly relayed via telegraph and pony express throughout the country.

Lincoln intended the address to conclude with a challenge: 'Shall it be peace or the sword?'. However, his Secretary of State, William H Seward, convinced him to soften the tone. The entire speech, with the conciliatory message contained in the final paragraph, has been immortalized within the Lincoln Memorial in Washington.

> Fellow citizens of the United States: in compliance with a custom as old as the government itself, I appear before you to address you briefly, and to take, in your presence, the oath prescribed by the Constitution of the United States, to be taken by the president 'before he enters on the execution of his office' …
>
> Apprehension seems to exist among the people of the Southern states, that by the accession of a Republican administration, their property and

their peace and personal security are to be endangered. There has never been any reasonable cause for such apprehension. Indeed, the most ample evidence to the contrary has all the while existed, and been open to their inspection. It is found in nearly all the published speeches of him who now addresses you.

I do but quote from one of those speeches when I declare that, 'I have no purpose, directly or indirectly, to interfere with the institution of slavery in the states where it exists. I believe I have no lawful right to do so, and I have no inclination to do so.' Those who nominated and elected me did so with full knowledge that I had made this and many similar declarations, and had never recanted them …

It is 72 years since the first inauguration of a president under our national Constitution.[1] During that period 15 different and greatly distinguished citizens have, in succession, administered the executive branch of the government. They have conducted it through many perils; and generally with great success. Yet, with all this scope for precedent, I now enter upon the same task for the brief constitutional term of four years, under great and peculiar difficulty. A disruption of the Federal Union heretofore only menaced, is now formidably attempted …

[1] The first US President, GEORGE WASHINGTON (1732–99), was inaugurated in New York City on 30 April 1789. His inaugural address is included in this book.

It is safe to assert that no government proper ever had a provision in its organic law for its own termination. Continue to execute all the express provisions of our national Constitution, and the Union will endure forever, it being impossible to destroy it, except by some action not provided for in the instrument itself.

Again, if the United States be not a government proper, but an association of states in the nature of contract merely, can it, as a contract, be peaceably unmade, by less than all the parties who made it? One party to a contract may violate it – break it, so to speak – but does it not require all to lawfully rescind it?

Descending from these general principles, we find the proposition that, in legal contemplation, the Union is perpetual, confirmed by the history of the Union itself. The Union is much older than the Constitution. It was formed in fact, by the Articles of Association in 1774. It was matured and continued by the Declaration of Independence in 1776. It was further matured and the faith of all the then 13 states expressly plighted and engaged that it should be perpetual, by the Articles of Confederation in 1778. And finally, in 1787, one of the declared objects for ordaining and establishing the Constitution, was '*to form a more perfect union*'.

But if destruction of the Union, by one, or by a part only, of the states, be lawfully possible, the Union is *less* perfect than before the Constitution, having lost the vital element of perpetuity. It follows from these views that no state, upon its own mere motion, can lawfully get out of the Union …

I therefore consider that, in view of the Constitution and the laws, the Union is unbroken; and, to the extent of my ability, I shall take care, as the Constitution itself expressly enjoins upon me, that the laws of the Union be faithfully executed in all the states. Doing this I deem to be only a simple duty on my part; and I shall perform it, so far as practicable, unless my rightful masters, the American people, shall withhold the requisite means, or, in some authoritative manner, direct the contrary. I trust this will not be regarded as a menace, but only as the declared purpose of the Union, that it *will* constitutionally defend and maintain itself.

In doing this, there needs to be no bloodshed or violence; and there shall be none, unless it be forced upon the national authority. The power confided to me will be used to hold, occupy, and possess the property and places belonging to the government, and to collect the duties and imposts; but beyond what may be necessary for these objects, there will be no invasion – no using of force against, or among the people anywhere. Where hostility to the United States, in any interior locality, shall be so great and so universal, as to prevent competent resident citizens from holding the federal offices, there will be no attempt to force obnoxious strangers among the people for that object. While the strict legal right may exist in the government to enforce the exercise of these offices, the attempt to do so would be so irritating, and so nearly impracticable with all, that I deem it better to forego, for the time, the uses of such offices …

In every case and exigency, my best discretion will be exercised, according to circumstances actually existing, and with a view and a hope of a peaceful solution of the national troubles, and the restoration of fraternal sympathies and affections …

Before entering upon so grave a matter as the destruction of our national fabric, with all its benefits, its memories, and its hopes, would it not be wise to ascertain precisely why we do it? Will you hazard so desperate a step, while there is any possibility that any portion of the ills you fly from have no real existence? Will you, while the certain ills you fly to are greater than all the real ones you fly from? Will you risk the commission of so fearful a mistake?

… If, by the mere force of numbers, a majority should deprive a minority of any clearly written constitutional right, it might, in a moral point of view, justify revolution – certainly would, if such right were a vital one. But such is not our case. All the vital rights of minorities, and of individuals, are so plainly assured to them, by affirmations and negations, guarantees and prohibitions, in the Constitution, that controversies never arise concerning them.

But no organic law can ever be framed with a provision specifically applicable to every question which may occur in practical administration. No foresight can anticipate, nor any document of reasonable length contain express provisions for all possible questions. Shall fugitives from labour be surrendered by national or by state authority? The Constitution does not expressly say. *May* Congress prohibit slavery in the territories? The Constitution does not expressly say. *Must* Congress *protect* slavery in the territories? The Constitution does not expressly say.

From questions of this class spring all our constitutional controversies, and we divide upon them into majorities and minorities. If the minority will not acquiesce, the majority must, or the government must cease. There is no other alternative; for continuing the government is acquiescence on one side or the other. If a minority, in such case, will secede rather than acquiesce, they make a precedent which, in turn, will divide and ruin them; for a minority of their own will secede from them, whenever a majority refuses to be controlled by such minority …

Plainly, the central idea of secession is the essence of anarchy. A majority, held in restraint by constitutional checks, and limitations, and always changing easily, with deliberate changes of popular opinions and sentiments, is the only true sovereign of a free people … Unanimity is impossible; the rule of a minority, as a permanent arrangement, is wholly inadmissable; so that, rejecting the majority principle, anarchy, or despotism in some form, is all that is left …

One section of our country believes slavery is *right*, and ought to be extended, while the other believes it is *wrong*, and ought not to be extended. This is the only substantial dispute …

Physically speaking, we cannot separate. We cannot remove our respective sections from each other, nor build an impassable wall between them. A husband and wife may be divorced, and go out of the presence and beyond the reach of each other; but the different parts of our country cannot do this. They cannot but remain face to face; and intercourse, either amicable or hostile, must continue between them.

Is it possible then to make that intercourse more advantageous, or more satisfactory, *after* separation than *before*? Can aliens make treaties easier than friends can make laws? Can treaties be more faithfully enforced between aliens, than laws can among friends? Suppose you go to war, you cannot fight always; and when, after much loss on both sides, and no gain on either, you cease fighting, the identical old questions, as to terms of intercourse, are again upon you.

This country, with its institutions, belongs to the people who inhabit it. Whenever they shall grow weary of the existing government, they can exercise their *constitutional* right of amending it, or their *revolutionary* right to dismember, or overthrow it. I cannot be ignorant of the fact that many worthy and patriotic citizens are desirous of having the national constitution amended. While I make no recommendation of amendments, I fully recognize the rightful authority of the people over the whole subject …

Why should there not be a patient confidence in the ultimate justice of the people? Is there any better or equal hope in the world? In our present differences, is either party without faith of being in the right? If the Almighty Ruler of nations, with his eternal truth and justice, be on your side of the North, or on yours of the South, that truth, and that justice, will surely prevail, by the judgement of this great tribunal, the American people.

By the frame of the government under which we live, this same people have wisely given their public servants but little power for mischief; and have, with equal wisdom, provided for the return of that little to their own hands at very short intervals. While the people retain their virtue and vigilance, no administration, by any extreme of wickedness or folly, can very seriously injure the government, in the short space of four years.

My countrymen, one and all: think calmly and *well* upon this whole subject. Nothing valuable can be lost by taking time. If there be an object to *hurry* any of you, in hot haste, to a step which you would never take *deliberately*, that object will be frustrated by taking time; but no good object can be frustrated by it.

Such of you as are now dissatisfied still have the old Constitution unimpaired − and on the sensitive point, the laws of your own framing under it − while the new administration will have no immediate power, if it would, to change either. If it were admitted that you who are dissatisfied hold the right side in the dispute, there still is no single good reason for precipitate action. Intelligence, patriotism, Christianity and a firm reliance on him who has never yet forsaken this favoured land are still competent to adjust, in the best way, all our present difficulty.

In your hands, my dissatisfied fellow countrymen, and not in mine, is the momentous issue of civil war. The government will not assail you. You can have no conflict without being yourselves the aggressors. You have no oath registered in Heaven to destroy the government, while I shall have the solemn one to 'preserve, protect and defend' it.

I am loath to close. We are not enemies, but friends. We must not be enemies. Though passion may have strained, it must not break our bonds of affection. The mystic cords of memory – stretching from every battlefield and patriot grave to every living heart and hearthstone, all over this broad land – will yet swell the chorus of the Union, when again touched, as surely they will be, by the better angels of our nature.

❧

'This nation, under God, shall have a new birth of freedom'
19 November 1863, Gettysburg, Pennsylvania, USA

❧

The Gettysburg Address is one of the world's most celebrated oratories, but it was not intended as such. The main address at the dedication of the Gettysburg war cemetery was given by Senator Edward Everett (1794–1865), the best-known orator of his time. As if acknowledging the minor part he was to play, Lincoln arrived looking faintly ridiculous, on a horse that was too small for him.

The Battle of Gettysburg had been one of the Civil War's bloodiest encounters, costing the lives of some 43,000 men. It is generally considered as the turning point in the war, at which the forces of the South under General Robert E Lee were repelled by General George Meade in their attempt to invade the North.

At the ceremony, Everett spoke for more than two hours, at the end of which much of the crowd had dispersed. Lincoln's speech lasted a mere three minutes, interrupted five times by applause. His remarks were not, as legend suggests, composed in haste; he had been working on the speech well in advance. Despite its brevity, the address artfully incorporates themes of birth and rebirth, death and resurrection, implicitly citing the USA's twin sacred texts – the Bible and the Declaration of Independence – from the biblical tone of its opening phrase.

Everett later wrote to Lincoln, admitting, 'I wish that I could flatter myself that I had come as near to the central idea of the occasion in two hours as you did in two minutes.'

❧

[1] On 4 July 1776, the Continental Congress approved the Declaration of Independence, which announced the separation from Great Britain of the 13 British colonies in North America that became the founding states of the Union.

Four-score and seven years ago,[1] our fathers brought forth on this continent a new nation, conceived in liberty and dedicated to the proposition that all men are created equal.[2] Now we are engaged in a great Civil War, testing whether that nation or any nation so conceived and so dedicated can long endure. We are met on a great battlefield of that war. We have come to dedicate a portion of that field as a final resting-place for those who here gave their lives that this nation might live. It is altogether fitting and proper that we should do this.

[2] A key phrase from the Declaration of Independence is: 'We hold these truths to be self-evident, that all men are created equal'.

But, in a larger sense, we cannot dedicate, we cannot consecrate, we cannot hallow this ground. The brave men, living and dead, who struggled here have consecrated it, far above our poor power to add or detract. The world will little note, nor long remember, what we say here, but it can never forget what they did here.

It is for us the living, rather, to be here dedicated to the unfinished work which they who fought here have thus far so nobly advanced. It is rather for us to be here dedicated to the great task remaining before us: that from these honoured dead we take increased devotion to that cause for which they gave the last full measure of devotion; that we here highly resolve that these dead shall not have died in vain; that this nation, under God, shall have a new birth of freedom, and that government of the people, by the people, for the people shall not perish from the earth.

❧

'Let us strive on to finish the work we are in'
4 March 1865, Washington, DC, USA

❧

Exactly four years and a bloody Civil War separated Lincoln's second inaugural address from his first. It had rained for days previously and Pennsylvania Avenue was awash with mud. This did not trouble the audience, which gathered at Capitol Hill to watch the president sworn in by Salmon P Chase, Chief Justice of the Supreme Court, and to hear him speak. Eyewitnesses remark upon the rapturous reception he received and the silence in which they listened to his relatively short and intensely theological speech.

Lincoln had feared that he would not be re-elected and his defeat would see the end of the Union which he had struggled hard to preserve. In the end, he received 54 per cent of the popular vote and lost only two northern states (New Jersey and Delaware). Lincoln himself was quite proud of the address, feeling it would 'wear well'. In fact, its famous statement of reconciliation – which, had he lived, would have set the tone for national reconstruction – is considered one of the most important documents shaping American history and is carved into the chamber of the Lincoln Memorial.

Among the audience outside the Capitol building and its nearly-completed dome was John Wilkes Booth, a guest of the US ambassador to Spain, John P Hale, whose daughter was his fiancée. Booth later confessed to a friend, 'What an excellent chance I had to kill the president if I had wished!'. On 14 April, in a Washington theatre, he did exactly that.

❧

Fellow-countrymen: at this second appearing to take the oath of the presidential office there is less occasion for an extended address than there was at the first. Then, a statement somewhat in detail of a course to be pursued seemed fitting and proper. Now, at the expiration of four years, during which public declarations have been constantly called forth on every point and phase of the great contest which still absorbs the attention and engrosses the energies of the nation, little that is new could be presented.

The progress of our arms, upon which all else chiefly depends, is as well known to the public as to myself, and it is, I trust, reasonably satisfactory and encouraging to all. With high hope for the future, no prediction in regard to it is ventured.

On the occasion corresponding to this four years ago, all thoughts were anxiously directed to an impending Civil War. All dreaded it, all sought to avert it. While the inaugural address was being delivered from this place, devoted altogether to *saving* the Union without war, urgent agents were in the city seeking to *destroy* it without war – seeking to dissolve the Union and divide effects by negotiation. Both parties deprecated war, but one of them would *make* war rather than let the nation survive, and the other would *accept* war rather than let it perish, and the war came.

One eighth of the whole population were coloured slaves, not distributed generally over the Union, but localized in the southern part of it. These slaves constituted a peculiar and powerful interest. All knew that this interest was somehow the cause of the war. To strengthen, perpetuate and extend this interest was the object for which the insurgents would rend the Union even by war, while the government claimed no right to do more than to restrict the territorial enlargement of it.

Neither party expected for the war the magnitude or the duration which it has already attained. Neither anticipated that the cause of the conflict might cease with or even before the conflict itself should cease. Each looked for an easier triumph, and a result less fundamental and astounding. Both read the same Bible and pray to the same God, and each invokes his aid against the other. It may seem strange that any men should dare to ask a just God's assistance in wringing their bread from the sweat of other men's faces, but let us judge not, that we be not judged.

The prayers of both could not be answered. That of neither has been answered fully. The Almighty has his own purposes. 'Woe unto the world because of offences; for it must needs be that offences come, but woe to that man by whom the offence cometh.'[1] If we shall suppose that American slavery is one of those offences which, in the providence of God, must

[1] Matthew 18:7.

needs come, but which, having continued through his appointed time, he now wills to remove; and that he gives to both North and South this terrible war as the woe due to those by whom the offence came, shall we discern therein any departure from those divine attributes which the believers in a living God always ascribe to him?

Fondly do we hope, fervently do we pray, that this mighty scourge of war may speedily pass away. Yet, if God wills that it continue until all the wealth piled by the bondsman's 250 years of unrequited toil shall be sunk, and until every drop of blood drawn with the lash shall be paid by another drawn with the sword, as was said 3,000 years ago, so still it must be said: 'the judgements of the Lord are true and righteous altogether.'

With malice toward none, with charity for all, with firmness in the right as God gives us to see the right, let us strive on to finish the work we are in, to bind up the nation's wounds, to care for him who shall have borne the battle and for his widow and his orphan, to do all which may achieve and cherish a just and lasting peace among ourselves and with all nations.

'Shall we sooner have the fowl by hatching the egg than by smashing it?'
11 April 1865, Washington, DC, USA

General Robert E Lee surrendered the Confederate Army to General Ulysses S Grant on 9 April 1865 at Appomatox Court House in Virginia. Former Confederate soldiers were allowed to return home with their horses and side-arms, but everything else – rifles, flags and banners – had to be surrendered. Almost a million men had been wounded in the Civil War; two-thirds of this number died. Grant himself commented later that, 'There were no victors. We stained America red.' Many in the North wanted retribution, but Lincoln had promised there would be no treason trials or prosecutions.

Lincoln's primary concern was that the orders of secession passed by the Southern states should be rescinded. His reconstruction plans contained three pragmatic strands: restoration of the Union, emancipation and guaranteed civil rights for the freed slaves. However, the more radical tendency refused to allow representatives from Louisiana, Arkansas and Tennessee, where 'loyal' governments had already been formed, to take their seats in Congress. The radicals eventually defeated the executive's plans, and forced through a much harsher settlement, which would divide the nation for another decade.

Lincoln appeared at a window of the Executive Mansion (as the White House was then called) in response to repeated calls by revellers who had lit bonfires and were dancing in the streets. This generous and conciliatory speech was the last important one he gave before his assassination. He read it by a candle held by his personal secretary, Noah Brooks, who later commented, 'That this was not the sort of speech which the multitude had expected is tolerably certain.'

We meet this evening, not in sorrow, but in gladness of heart. The evacuation of Petersburg and Richmond, and the surrender of the principal insurgent army, give hope of a righteous and speedy peace, whose joyous expression can not be restrained. In the midst of this, however, he from whom all blessings flow must not be forgotten. A call for a national thanksgiving is being prepared, and will be duly promulgated.

Nor must those whose harder part gives us the cause of rejoicing be overlooked. Their honours must not be parcelled out with others. I myself was near the front, and had the high pleasure of transmitting much of the good news to you; but no part of the honour, for plan or execution, is mine. To General Grant, his skilful officers and brave men, all belongs. The gallant navy stood ready, but was not in reach to take active part.

By these recent successes the re-inauguration of the national authority – reconstruction – which has had a large share of thought from the first, is pressed much more closely upon our attention. It is fraught with great difficulty. Unlike the case of a war between independent nations, there is no authorized organ for us to treat with. No one man has authority to give up the rebellion for any other man. We simply must begin with, and mould from, disorganized and discordant elements. Nor is it a small additional embarrassment that we, the loyal people, differ among ourselves as to the mode, manner and means of reconstruction.

As a general rule, I abstain from reading the reports of attacks upon myself, wishing not to be provoked by that to which I can not properly offer an answer. In spite of this precaution, however, it comes to my knowledge that I am much censured for some supposed agency in setting up, and seeking to sustain, the new state government of Louisiana. In this I have done just so much as, and no more than, the public knows.

In the Annual Message of December 1863 and accompanying Proclamation, I presented a plan of reconstruction (as the phrase goes) which, I promised, if adopted by any state, should be acceptable to and sustained by the executive government of the nation. I distinctly stated that this was not the only plan which might possibly be acceptable; and I also distinctly protested that the executive claimed no right to say when or whether members should be admitted to seats in Congress from such states.

This plan was, in advance, submitted to the then Cabinet, and distinctly approved by every member of it. One of them suggested that I should then, and in that connection, apply the Emancipation Proclamation[1] to the theretofore excepted parts of Virginia and Louisiana; that I should drop the suggestion about apprenticeship for freed-people, and that I should omit the protest against my own power, in regard to the admission of members to Congress; but even he approved every part and parcel of the plan which has since been employed or touched by the action of Louisiana.

The new constitution of Louisiana, declaring emancipation for the whole State, practically applies the Proclamation to the part previously excepted. It does not adopt apprenticeship for freed-people; and it is silent, as it could not well be otherwise, about the admission of members to Congress, so that, as it applies to Louisiana, every member of the Cabinet fully approved the plan. The message went to Congress, and I received many commendations of the plan, written and verbal; and not a single objection to it from any professed emancipationist came to my knowledge, until after the news reached Washington that the people of Louisiana had begun to move in accordance with it.

From about July 1862, I had corresponded with different persons, supposed to be interested, seeking a reconstruction of a state government for Louisiana. When the message of 1863, with the plan before mentioned, reached New Orleans, General Banks[2] wrote me that he was confident the people, with his military co-operation, would reconstruct substantially on that plan. I wrote him, and some of them, to try it; they tried it, and the result is known. Such, only, has been my agency in getting up the Louisiana government. As to sustaining it, my promise is out, as before stated. But, as bad promises are better broken than kept, I shall treat this as a bad promise and break it whenever I shall be convinced that keeping it is adverse to the public interest. But I have not yet been so convinced …

We all agree that the seceded states, so called, are out of their proper practical relation with the Union; and that the sole object of the government, civil and military, in regard to those states is to again get them into that proper practical relation. I believe it is not only possible, but in fact,

[1] Issued in two parts, September 1862 and January 1863, the Emancipation Proclamation officially freed all slaves in the rebelling Confederate states, but exempted border states and those which had not seceded from the Union.

[2] The US soldier and politician Nathaniel P Banks (1816–94) led the Union army that captured Fort Hudson in 1863, and served in Congress until 1873.

easier, to do this, without deciding, or even considering, whether these states have even been out of the Union, than with it. Finding themselves safely at home, it would be utterly immaterial whether they had ever been abroad. Let us all join in doing the acts necessary to restoring the proper practical relations between these states and the Union …

Still the question is not whether the Louisiana government, as it stands, is quite all that is desirable. The question is: 'Will it be wiser to take it as it is, and help to improve it; or to reject and disperse it? Can Louisiana be brought into proper practical relation with the Union soon by sustaining or by discarding her new state government?'

Some 12,000 voters in the heretofore slave state of Louisiana have sworn allegiance to the Union, assumed to be the rightful political power of the state, held elections, organized a state government, adopted a free-state constitution, giving the benefit of public schools equally to black and white, and empowering the legislature to confer the elective franchise upon the coloured man. Their legislature has already voted to ratify the constitutional amendment recently passed by Congress, abolishing slavery throughout the nation.

These 12,000 persons are thus fully committed to the Union, and to perpetual freedom in the state – committed to the very things, and nearly all the things the nation wants – and they ask the nation's recognition, and its assistance to make good their committal. Now, if we reject and spurn them, we do our utmost to disorganize and disperse them. We in effect say to the white men: 'You are worthless, or worse. We will neither help you, nor be helped by you.'

To the blacks we say: 'This cup of liberty which these, your old masters, hold to your lips, we will dash from you, and leave you to the chances of gathering the spilled and scattered contents in some vague and undefined when, where, and how.'

If this course, discouraging and paralysing both white and black, has any tendency to bring Louisiana into proper practical relations with the Union, I have so far been unable to perceive it. If, on the contrary, we recognize and sustain the new government of Louisiana, the converse of all this is made true. We encourage the hearts, and nerve the arms of the 12,000 to adhere to their work and argue for it and proselyte for it and fight for it and feed it and grow it and ripen it to a complete success.

The coloured man, too, in seeing all united for him, is inspired with vigilance and energy and daring, to the same end. Grant that he desires the elective franchise. Will he not attain it sooner by saving the already advanced steps toward it, than by running backward over them? Concede that the new government of Louisiana is only to what it should be as the egg is to the fowl. Shall we sooner have the fowl by hatching the egg than by smashing it?

… In the present situation, as the phrase goes, it may be my duty to make some new announcement to the people of the South. I am considering, and shall not fail to act, when satisfied that action will be proper.

David Lloyd George

Welsh statesman

David Lloyd George *later 1st Earl Lloyd-George of Dwyfor* (1863–1945) was born in Manchester of Welsh parentage. When he was two, his father died and the family moved to Llanystumdwy, Wales, the home of his uncle, Richard Lloyd, who recognized his latent brilliance and sponsored his education. Lloyd George thus acquired his religion, his industry, his vivid oratory, his radical views and his Welsh nationalism. He became a solicitor and in 1890 was elected as an advanced Liberal for Caernarvon Boroughs. He became president of the Board of Trade (1905–8) and was responsible for the Merchant Shipping Act (1906), the Census Production Act (1906), and the Patents Act (1907). As Chancellor of the Exchequer (1908–15) he achieved important social reform with the Old Age Pensions Act (1908), the National Insurance Act (1911), and the momentous 'people's budget' (1909–10). The budget's rejection by the Lords led to a constitutional crisis and the Parliament Act of 1911, which removed the Lords' power of veto. Although a pacifist, Lloyd George strongly believed in national rights and saw a parallel between the Welsh and the Boers. His condemnation of the Boer War was loud but the German threat to invade Belgium in 1914 dispelled his pacifism. He was appointed Minister of Munitions (1915), then War Secretary (1916) and became prime minister (1916–22) at the head of a Liberal–Conservative coalition government. This caused a split in the Liberal Party which never completely healed. A forceful leader through the latter half of World War I, he was also a dominant figure in the post-war peace negotiations, which he handled brilliantly although he was inclined to pay too much attention to the demands of smaller countries. In 1921 he negotiated with Sinn Féin and conceded the Irish Free State (1922). This was very unpopular with the Conservatives in the government, and led to his downfall and that of the Liberals as a party at the 1922 election. Following the general election of 1931 he resigned as Liberal leader and led a group of Independent Liberal MPs. He retained his seat until the year of his death; in the same year he was raised to the peerage. His publications include *War Memoirs* (1933–6) and *The Truth about the Peace Treaties* (1938).

'I say their day of reckoning is at hand'

20 July 1909, London, England

In this speech, Lloyd George – then Chancellor of the Exchequer – defended the controversial proposals put forward in his famous 'people's budget'. Lloyd George is generally credited with introducing old-age pensions, and one important strand of the budget was taxing the wealthy to provide revenues to fund the pensions. It also proposed taxes to fund naval rearmament, then an important contributor to national pride and security. But his most revolutionary proposal – drawing on ideas propagated by the American economist Henry George – was the introduction of new taxes for landowners.

It was this measure in particular which drew a hostile response from the House of Lords, which was dominated by Conservative landowners. In his speech, Lloyd George uses unashamedly poetic language – 'the brambles and thorns of poverty', 'the fangs of the Great Destroyer' – to pour scorn on the complacency and greed of wealthy landowners.

The Lords overthrew the budget, but the battle did not end there. Lloyd George and his prime minister, H H Asquith, rallied public opinion against the upper chamber, forcing the general election of January 1910. This resulted in a hung parliament and Asquith led a minority government with support from the Labour and Irish nationalist members. The Lords then accepted an amended people's budget, with the land tax proposal removed. But after winning a second general election in December 1910, Asquith was able to curb the power of the peerage with the Parliament Act of 1911.

A few months ago, a meeting was held not far from this hall in the heart of the City of London, demanding that the government should launch into enormous expenditure on the navy. That meeting ended up with a resolution promising that those who passed the resolution would give financial support to the government in their undertaking. There have been two or three meetings held in the City of London since, attended by the same class of people but not ending up with a resolution promising to pay. On the contrary, we are spending the money, but they won't pay.

What has happened since to alter their tone? Simply that we have sent in

[1] A class of heavily armoured, steam-turbine-powered warship, based on the revolutionary design of the HMS *Dreadnought*, launched in February 1906.

the bill. We started our four Dreadnoughts.[1] They cost eight millions of money. We promised them four more. They cost another eight millions. Somebody has got to pay; and then these gentlemen say: 'Perfectly true; somebody has got to pay but we would rather that somebody were somebody else.' We started building; we wanted money to pay for the building; so we sent the hat round. We sent it round amongst the workmen and winders of Derbyshire and Yorkshire, the weavers of High Peak and the Scotsmen of Dumfries who, like all their countrymen, know the value of money. They all dropped in their coppers. We went round Belgravia;[2] and there has been such a howl ever since that it has completely deafened us.

[2] A wealthy district of central London. Lloyd George's point is that the poor were willing to contribute but the rich were not.

But they say, 'It is not so much the Dreadnoughts we object to; it is pensions.' If they objected to pensions, why did they promise them? They won elections on the strength of their promises. It is true they never carried them out. Deception is always a pretty contemptible vice, but to deceive the poor is the meanest of all. But they say, 'When we promised pensions, we meant pensions at the expense of people for whom they were provided. We simply meant to bring in a bill to compel workmen to contribute to their own pensions.' If that is what they meant why did they not say so?

The budget, as your chairman has already so well reminded you, is introduced not merely for the purpose of raising barren taxes, but taxes that are fertile, taxes that will bring forth fruit: the security of the country, which is paramount in the minds of all. The provision for the aged and deserving poor: it was time it was done. It is rather a shame for a rich country like ours — probably the richest in the world, if not the richest the world has ever seen — that it should allow those who have toiled all their days to end in penury and possibly starvation. It is rather hard that an old workman should have to find his way to the gates of the tomb, bleeding and footsore, through the brambles and thorns of poverty. We cut a new path for him, an easier one, a pleasanter one, through fields of waving corn. We are raising money to pay for a new road, aye, and to widen it, so that 200,000 paupers shall be able to join in the march.

There are so many in the country blessed by Providence with great wealth, and if there are amongst them men who grudge out of their riches a fair contribution towards the less fortunate of their fellow-countrymen they are very shabby rich men.

We propose to do more by means of the budget. We are raising money to provide against the evils and the sufferings that follow from unemployment. We are raising money for the purpose of assisting our great friendly societies to provide for the sick and the widows and orphans. We are providing money to enable us to develop the resources of our own land. I do not believe any fair-minded man would challenge the justice and the fairness of the objects which we have in view in raising this money.

But there are some of them who say, 'The taxes themselves are unjust, unfair, unequal, oppressive — notably so the land taxes.' They are engaged, not merely in the House of Commons, but outside the House of Commons, in assailing these taxes with a concentrated and sustained ferocity which will not allow even a comma to escape with its life.

Now, are these taxes really so wicked? Let us examine them; because it is perfectly clear that the one part of the budget that attracts all the hostility and animosity is that part which deals with the taxation of land ... All we say is this: 'In future you must pay one halfpenny in the pound on the real value of your land. In addition to that, if the value goes up (not owing to your efforts – if you spend money on improving it we will give you credit for it) but if it goes up owing to the industry and the energy of the people living in that locality, one-fifth of that increment shall in future be taken as a toll by the state.'

They say: 'Why should you tax this increment on landlords and not on other classes of the community?' They say: 'You are taxing the landlord because the value of his property is going up through the growth of population, through the increased prosperity for the community. Does not the value of a doctor's business go up in the same way?'

Ah, fancy their comparing themselves for a moment! What is the landlord's increment? Who is the landlord? The landlord is a gentleman – I have not a word to say about him in his personal capacity – the landlord is a gentleman who does not earn his wealth. He does not even take the trouble to receive his wealth. He has a host of agents and clerks to receive it for him. He does not even take the trouble to spend his wealth. He has a host of people around him to do the actual spending for him. He never sees it until he comes to enjoy it. His sole function, his chief pride, is stately consumption of wealth produced by others.

What about the doctor's income? How does the doctor earn his income? The doctor is a man who visits our homes when they are darkened with the shadow of death: who, by his skill, his trained courage, his genius, wrings hope out of the grip of despair, wins life out of the fangs of the Great Destroyer. All blessings upon him and his divine art of healing that mends bruised bodies and anxious hearts. To compare the reward which he gets for that labour with the wealth which pours into the pockets of the landlord, purely owing to the possession of his monopoly is a piece – if they will forgive me for saying so – of insolence which no intelligent man would tolerate. Now that is the halfpenny tax on unearned increment.

Now I come to the reversion tax. What is the reversion tax? You have got a system in the country which is not tolerated in any other country of the world, except, I believe, Turkey: the system whereby landlords take advantage of the fact that they have got complete control over the land to let it for a term of years … You improve the building, and year by year the value passes into the pockets of the landlord, and at the end of 60, 70, 80 or 90 years, the whole of it passes away to the pockets of a man who never spent a penny upon it …

I know districts, quarry districts, in Wales, where a little bit of barren rock – where you could not feed a goat, where the landlord could not get a shilling an acre for agricultural rent – is let to quarrymen for the purpose of building houses; where 30 shillings or two pounds a house is charged for ground rent. The quarryman builds his house. He goes to a building society to borrow money. He pays out of his hard-earned weekly wage contributions to the building society for 10, 20 or 30 years. By the time he becomes an old man he has cleared off the mortgage, and more than half the value of the house has passed into the pockets of the landlord … This system – it is the system I am attacking, not individuals – is not business; it is blackmail …

Well, that is the system, and the landlords come to us in the House of Commons and they say: 'If you go on taxing reversions we will grant no more leases.' Is not that horrible? No more leases! No more kindly landlords with all their retinue of good fairies – agents, surveyors, lawyers – ready always to receive ground rents, fees, premiums, fines, reversions – no more! Never again! They will not do it. We cannot persuade them. They won't have it …

Now, unless I am wearying you, I have just one other land tax, and that is a tax on royalties. The landlords are receiving eight millions a year by way of royalties. What for? They never deposited the coal there. It was not they who planted these great granite rocks in Wales, who laid the foundations of the mountains. Was it the landlord? And yet he, by some divine right, demands as his toll – for merely the right for men to risk their lives in hewing these rocks – eight millions a year.

Take any coalfield. I went down to a coalfield the other day, and they pointed out to me many collieries there. They said: 'You see that colliery there? The first man who went there spent a quarter of a million in sinking shafts, in driving mains and levels. He never got coal, and he lost his quarter of a million. The second man who came spent £100,000 – and he failed. The third man came along, and he got the coal.' What was the landlord doing in the meantime? The first man failed; but the landlord got his royalty … The second man failed, but the landlord got his royalty. These capitalists put their money in, and I said: 'When the cash failed what did the landlord put in?' He simply put in the bailiffs. The capitalist risks, at any rate, the whole of his money; the engineer puts his brains in; the miner risks his life.

I was telling you, I went down a coal mine the other day. We sank into a pit half a mile deep. We then walked underneath the mountain, and we did about three-quarters of a mile with rock and shale above us. The earth seemed to be straining – around us and above us – to crush us in. You could see the pit-props bent and twisted and sundered until you saw their fibres split in resisting the pressure. Sometimes they give way, and then there is mutilation and death. Often a spark ignites, the whole pit is deluged in fire, and the breath of life is scorched out of hundreds of breasts by the consuming flame.

In the very next colliery to the one I descended, just a few years ago, 300 people lost their lives in that way. And yet when the prime minister[3] and I knock at the door of these great landlords, and say to them: 'Here, you know these poor fellows who have been digging up royalties at the risk of their lives? Some of them are old. They have survived the perils of their trade. They are broken; they can earn no more. Won't you give them something towards keeping them out of the workhouse?' they scowl at us. And we say: 'Only a ha'penny; just a copper.' They say: 'You thieves!' and they turn their dogs on to us, and you can hear their bark every morning. If this is an indication of the view taken by these great landlords of their responsibility to the people who at the risk of life create their wealth, then I say their day of reckoning is at hand …

I claim that the tax we impose on land is fair, is just and is moderate … The ownership of land is not merely an enjoyment, it is a stewardship. It has been reckoned as such in the past; and if they cease to discharge their functions – the security and defence of the country, looking after the broken in their villages and in their neighbourhoods – then these functions which are part of the traditional duties attached to the ownership of land, and which have given to it its title – if they cease to discharge those functions, the time will come to reconsider the conditions under which the land is held in this country. No country, however rich, can permanently afford to have quartered upon its revenue a class which declines to do the duty which it was called upon to perform since the beginning.

[3] The English statesman Herbert Henry Asquith (1852–1928) served as Liberal Prime Minister, 1908–1916.

❧

'There are no nightingales this side of the Severn'
August 1916, Aberystwyth, Wales

When Lloyd George visited ADOLF HITLER in 1936, the Führer greeted him as 'the man who won the war' – referring to World War I. A strange tribute from a German leader, perhaps – especially since Lloyd George had proposed in 1918 to 'demand the whole cost of the war from Germany'.

But Hitler had a point: Lloyd George played a central role in leading Britain through the war. Formerly a pacifist, he became Munitions Minister in 1915 and War Secretary in 1916, finally succeeding Asquith in December 1916 as prime minister of the Liberal–Conservative coalition government.

He was also one of the 'Big Three' – alongside US president WOODROW WILSON and French prime minister Georges Clemenceau – who negotiated the post-war Treaty of Versailles in 1919, urging compromise in a situation he later described as 'seated between JESUS Christ and NAPOLEON'.

Lloyd George's links with Wales had dwindled after he gained prominence in British politics, but he maintained an interest in Welsh affairs and made an annual speech at the National Eisteddfod – Wales's poetry and culture festival. This extract from his speech to the Eisteddfod at the height of World War I demonstrates his gift for poetic language; and allows him to express a romantic brand of patriotism, while bolstering wartime morale.

Why should we not sing during the war? Why especially should we not sing at this stage of the war? The blinds of Britain are not down yet, nor are they likely to be. The honour of Britain is not dead, her might is not broken, her destiny is not fulfilled. Her ideals have not been shattered by her enemies. She is more than alive, she is more potent, she is greater than she ever was. Her dominions are wider, her influence is deeper, her purpose is more exalted than ever. Why should her children not sing?

I know war means suffering; war means sorrow. Darkness has fallen on many a devoted household. But it has been ordained that the best singer among the birds of Britain should give its song in the night, and according to legend that sweet song is one of triumph over pain. There are no nightingales this side of the Severn;[1] Providence rarely wastes its gifts. We do not need this exquisite songster in Wales; we can provide better. There is a bird in our villages that can beat the best of them, he's called *y Cymro*.[2]

He sings in joy; he sings also in sorrow. He sings in prosperity; he sings also in adversity. He sings at play; he sings also at work. He sings in the sunshine; he sings in the storm. He sings in the daytime; he sings also in the night. He sings in peace; why should he not sing in war?

Hundreds of wars have swept over these hills, but the harp of Wales has never yet been silenced by one of them. And I should be proud if I had contributed something to keep it in tune during the war by urging you to hold this Eisteddfod at Aberystwyth today.

[1] The River Severn forms part of the border between England and Wales.

[2] Welsh: 'the Welshman'.

Patrice Lumumba
Congolese politician

Patrice Hemery Lumumba (1925–61) was born in Katako Kombe and educated at mission schools, both Catholic and Protestant. He became a post office clerk and later director of a brewery. As president of a trade union, he was arrested for embezzlement and served a year-long jail sentence. On his release, he helped form the Mouvement National Congolais (MNC) in 1958 to challenge Belgian rule and, when the Congo became an independent republic, he became its first prime minister (1960). A major symbolic figure in the African history of the period, he sought a unified Congo and opposed the secession of Katanga under Moise Tshombe. Less than three months after coming to power, he was arrested by his own army, handed over to the Katangese, brutalized and eventually murdered in January 1961. His name, however, remains significant as the embodiment of African nationalism and the opponent of Balkanization manipulated by ex-colonial countries and their allies. In 1966 he was declared a national hero and martyr.

'An honest, loyal, strong, popular government'
23 June 1960, Léopoldville (now Kinshasa), Congo

This speech represents a brief dawn of optimism in the stormy history of Congolese politics. In 1908, Belgium had annexed a large part of central Africa, naming it the Belgian Congo. The colonizers profited from a wealth of natural resources, but by the 1950s nationalist groups were demanding self-government.

The trade unionist and independence campaigner Patrice Lumumba had made many anti-imperialist speeches, for which he was shunned by the West but received limited support from the USSR. Lumumba's faction of the Mouvement National party won elections in December 1959 and May 1960 and – when independence was achieved in June – formed its first government.

Lumumba gave this exhilarated address to the Congolese Chamber a week before independence was officially declared. It was preceded by the announcement of the cabinet, in which Lumumba held the twin posts of prime minister and Minister of National Defence.

In his speech, translated here by H R Lane, Lumumba commends the government to the Chamber and expresses his desire to establish law and order. He also attempts to position the country as truly independent, aligned to neither the USA nor the USSR, though he does acknowledge the need for Belgian support.

He was, however, unable to stabilize the new republic, and was soon overthrown in a coup led by Colonel Joseph-Désiré Mobutu (1930–97), who handed power back to civilians in 1961 but staged a second coup in 1965 which initiated his 32-year authoritarian and corrupt regime. Lumumba's daughter Julienne later revealed that he was conscious of the threat from Mobutu and expected to die for his cause, but believed his message would survive.

Mr President, dear colleagues, ladies and gentlemen: the crisis that threatened to endanger the future of our young nation has fortunately been resolved, thanks to the Congolese wisdom that all the elected representatives have shown in the face of the danger that confronted us. You have been the first to demonstrate to everyone that is our duty to bring about union and solidarity ...

At this historic moment, I should like to recall the long and painful struggle that all the Congolese, united in their passionate desire for liberation, waged until victory was theirs.

We found we were unanimous and stood shoulder to shoulder in our opposition to a political regime that at certain times ignored the direction history was taking.

We found we were unanimous as we fought our first battles against colonialism.

We found we were unanimous as we mourned our dead brothers.

We found we were unanimous at the Round Table,[1] united in a Common Front.

Today, in victory, in triumph, we are still united and unanimous: our entire

[1] The Round Table Conference of all Congolese parties was convened by the Belgian authorities in January 1960. Lumumba's party, the MNC, had refused to participate until Lumumba was released from prison to attend the conference.

nation rejoices at this.

Gentlemen: the government that you are about to vote on is an honest, loyal, strong, popular government, which represents the entire nation, having been chosen by you to serve the interests of our homeland. All the members of my team and I formally pledge that this government will remain a government of the people, by the people and for the people.[2]

Strengthened by this popular support, the government will endeavour to keep the nation's territory and its unity intact and protect it from attack from any quarter.

The vastness of the territory and its great diversity make certain steps necessary, however. The government views this situation realistically. We must be able to modify the administrative divisions of the old regime by legal means so that each citizen may find happiness among his fellows.

This government will endeavour to establish the rule of law and order everywhere in the country, without hesitating; but as it goes about this task, it will always respect the inalienable rights of man and the citizen as a sacred good.

This government will consider its first duty to be that of leading the popular masses along the path to social justice, wellbeing and progress, carefully avoiding adventures that might lead to catastrophes that we wish to spare our people. We want nothing to do with new forms of dictatorship.

This government will endeavour to maintain friendly relations with all foreign countries, but it will not succumb to the temptations of joining one or another of the blocs that have now divided the world between them, as it might so easily do; it will also not hesitate to espouse a noble and just cause on the international plane, and in Africa in particular.

Gentlemen: in the name of the government of the Congo, in the name of the Congolese people and also in the certainty that I am speaking for all the members of this parliament, I now address our Belgian friends in particular, and have this to say to them: in the last three-quarters of a century, you have created an enormous handiwork in this country. It was not always immune to criticism, certainly, but now that the outrages perpetrated during the elections are at an end, we must recognize that it constitutes the unshakable foundation on which we are going to build our nation together.

The first missionaries, who were later joined by lay teachers, brought education to every corner of the country under difficult conditions; without this education what is happening today would not have been possible.

For three-quarters of a century the colonials, the industrialists, the various companies have endeavoured to develop the country. We are soon going to build the great Congolese nation with them.

We will need the help of Belgians and of all men of goodwill more than ever; we will do our utmost to ensure that the co-operation that will begin tomorrow will be of benefit to all. The religious missions will be assured of being able to continue their apostolate, thanks to the freedom of opinion and the religious freedom that our constitution will guarantee. The members of the former colonial administration have now turned their powers of government over to the Congolese, but their counsel and their experience will remain the surest guarantee of sound government.

Lastly, you will understand why I wish to conclude my remarks with an expression of the overwhelming emotion I feel. The members of the first government of the Congo are faced with a grave task, and they are well

[2] Lumumba quotes from ABRAHAM LINCOLN's Gettysburg Address of 19 November 1863, included in this book.

aware of how complex it is. We are face to face with an immense country, with extraordinary potentialities. We have at our side a young, resolute, intelligent people capable of being the equal of other nations.

We are privileged to be beginning our national life at the same time as other countries in Africa. This huge continent is awakening and looking toward a better future. The Congolese people will fulfil its destiny through unity and solidarity.

Gentlemen: whether or not this destiny is a happy one and one truly worthy of our people will depend on each one of us, on our work each day of our lives. I am proud to see the Congo, our homeland, take its place in the ranks of free peoples.

May I ask you, dear brothers, on this solemn day on which the Congo is achieving its total independence, on which a democratic government is taking over, on which justice is being established, on which each of us will henceforth enjoy total personal freedom, on which the sun has suddenly come out in this country to dissipate the long darkness of the colonial regime, to raise your voices with me:

Long live the independent Congo!

Long live the united Congo!

Long live freedom!

Martin Luther
German religious reformer

Martin Luther (1483–1546) was born in Eisleben, the son of a copper miner. He was educated at Magdeburg, Eisenach and the University of Erfurt, graduating in 1505. He then studied at the Augustinian monastery in Erfurt. He was ordained a priest in 1507, and in 1508 went to teach at the University of Wittenberg. On a mission to Rome in 1510–11 he was appalled by corrupt practices, in particular the sale of indulgences by Johann Tetzel and others in the lands around Saxony, and developed a strong desire for reform. As Professor of Biblical Exegesis at Wittenberg (1512–46), he began to preach the doctrine of salvation by faith rather than works. In 1517, he drew up 95 theses on indulgences, denying the Pope's right to forgive sins, and nailed them to the church door at Wittenberg. Tetzel burned them and published a set of counter-theses; and Luther's students retaliated by burning Tetzel's. In 1518 Luther was joined by Philip Melanchthon. Pope Leo X initially took little notice, but in 1518 summoned Luther to Rome. His university intervened, and ineffectual negotiations were undertaken by Cardinal Cajetan and the papal envoy Karl von Miltitz. Luther intensified his attacks on the papal system, with support from the Dutch theologian Desiderius Erasmus (1466–1536). In 1520, Luther published his address to the *Christian Nobles of Germany* and the treatise *On the Babylonian Captivity of the Church of God*, attacking the doctrines of the Church of Rome. A papal bull was issued against him, and he burned it in public at Wittenberg. Luther was summoned to appear before the Diet at Worms in 1521. On his return, he was seized, at the instigation of the Elector of Saxony, and lodged (mostly for his own protection) at Wartburg Castle. He spent a year there, translating the Bible and composing treatises. In 1522, civil unrest called him back to Wittenberg, where he made a stand against both lawlessness and tyranny. Estrangement had sprung up between Erasmus and Luther, and there was an open breach in 1525, when Erasmus published *De Libero Arbitrio*, and Luther followed with *De Servo Arbitrio*. In 1529 he attended a conference at Marburg with Huldrych Zwingli and other Swiss theologians, maintaining his views on the Eucharist. The drawing up of the Augsburg Confession (1530) – at which Melanchthon represented Luther – marked the culmination of the German Reformation. Luther died in Eisleben, and was buried at Wittenberg.

'I cannot and will not retract'
18 April 1521, Worms, Germany

The diet of Worms was one of the most important encounters in the history of the Christian church. At this assembly of the electors of the Holy Roman Empire, presided over by the Emperor Charles V, the 'poor monk' Martin Luther put forward his case that the papacy was an obstruction to true Christian practice. It was a turning point for the religious reform movement (Reformation) that had been inspired by Luther, and led to the repudiation of papal authority and the establishment of the Protestant churches.

Disgusted by the Church of Rome's corrupt practice of selling indulgences – forgiveness of sins as a marketable commodity – Luther had provoked debate with his 95 theses. A papal court had begun discussing his case in 1518, but he had burned the papal bull of 1520 which threatened him with excommunication. In January 1521 he was banned by a further bull, but by then he had enlisted broad support in Germany. Fearful of impending schism, Charles V summoned him to Worms.

His speech – translated here by the English essayist William Hazlitt (1778–1830) – was delivered on the second day of the diet. Luther's approach is notable both for its humility ('scum of the earth that I am') and for its defiance – a defiance born of unshakeable confidence. He repeatedly challenges the diet to refute his claims with scriptural evidence. Though he admits to excessive violence, he refuses to remove the 'teeth' or 'horns' of his argument, or to recant.

The diet declared Luther an outlaw, but he resumed his preaching at Wittenberg within a year. The Reformation was to prove irreversible.

Most serene Emperor, illustrious Princes, most clement Lords: I am again before you, appearing at the hour appointed, and supplicating you to listen to me with benevolence and equity. If in my statement or my replies, I should omit to give you the titles of honour due to you; if I offend against the etiquette of courts, you will, I trust, pardon me, for I have never been accustomed to palaces. I am nothing but a poor monk, the inmate of a humble cell, who have, I assure you, never preached aught, never written aught, but in singleness of heart, and for the glory of my God, and the honour of the Gospel.

Most serene Emperor and princes of the empire: to the two questions put to me yesterday, whether I acknowledged as mine the books published in my name,[1] and whether I persevered in defending them, I answer now, as before, and as I will answer to the hour of my death: yes, the books which have been published by me, or which have been published in my name, are mine. I acknowledge them, I avow them, and will always avow them, so long as they remain the same as I sent them forth, undistorted by malice, knavery, or mistaken prudence. I acknowledge, further, that whatever I have written was first matured in my mind by earnest thought and meditation.

[1] Luther refers to his works *Christian Nobles of Germany* and *On the Babylonian Captivity of the Church of God*, both published in 1520.

Before replying to the second question, I entreat Your Majesty and the states of the empire to consider that my writings do not all treat of the same matter. Some of them are preceptive, destined for the edification of the faithful, for the advancement of piety, for the amelioration of manners; yet the bull, while admitting the innocence and advantage of such treaties, condemns these equally with the rest. If I were to disavow them, what practically should I be doing? Proscribing a mode of instruction which every Christian sanctions, and thus putting myself in opposition to the universal voice of the faithful.

There is another class of writings in which I attack the papacy and the belief of the papists as monstrosities, involving the ruin of sound doctrine and of men's souls. None can deny, who will listen to the cries and the evidences of the conscience within, that the Pope's decretals[2] have thrown utter disorder into Christianity, have surprised, imprisoned, tortured the faith of the faithful, have devoured as a prey this noble Germany, for that she has protested aloud against lying tales, contrary to the Gospel and to the opinions of the fathers.

[2] Papal decrees.

If I were to retract these writings, I should lend additional strength and audacity to the Roman tyranny, I should open the floodgates to the torrent of impiety, making for it a breach by which it would rush in and overwhelm the Christian world. My recantation would only serve to extend and strengthen the reign of iniquity; more especially when it should be known that it was solely by order of Your Majesty, and your Serene Highnesses, that I had made such retraction.

Finally, there is another class of works which have been published under my name. I speak of these books of polemics, which I have written against some of my adversaries, advocates of the Roman tyranny. I have no hesitation in admitting that in these I have shown greater violence than befitted a man of my calling; I do not set up for a saint; I do not say that my conduct has been above reproach. My dispute is not about that conduct, but about the doctrine of Christ. But though I have been violent overmuch at times, I cannot consent to disavow these writings, because Rome would make use of the disavowal, to extend her kingdom and oppress men's souls.

A man and not God, I would not seek to shield my books under any other patronage than that with which Christ covered his doctrine. When interrogated before the high priest as to what he taught, and his cheek buffeted by a varlet: 'If I have spoken evil,' he said, 'bear witness of the evil.'[3] If the Lord Jesus, who knew himself incapable of sin, did not reject the testimony which the vilest mouths might give respecting his divine Word,

[3] John 18:23.

ought not I, scum of the earth that I am, and capable only of sin, to solicit the examination of my doctrines?

I therefore, in the name of the living God, entreat Your Sacred Majesty, your illustrious Highnesses, every human creature, to come and depose what they can against me, and, with the Prophets and the Gospel in their hands, to convict me, if they can, of error. I stand here ready, if anyone can prove me to have written falsely, to retract my errors, and to throw my books into the fire with my own hand. Be assured I have well weighed the dangers, the pains, the strife, and hatred that my doctrine will bring into the world; and I rejoice to see the Word of God producing, as its first fruits, discord and dissension, for such is the lot and destiny of the divine Word, as our Lord has set forth: 'I came not to send peace, but a sword, to set the son against his father'.[4]

4 Matthew 10:34–35.

Forget not that God is admirable and terrible in all his counsels; and beware, lest, if you condemn the divine Word, that Word send forth upon you a deluge of ills, and the reign of our noble young emperor, upon whom, next to God, repose all our hopes, be speedily and sorely troubled.

I might here, in examples drawn from holy writ, exhibit to you Pharaoh, king of Egypt, and the kings of Israel, ruined from seeking to reign, at first by peace and by what they termed wisdom. For God confounds the hypocrite in his hypocrisy, and overturns mountains ere they know of their fall: fear is the work of God.

I seek not herein to offer advice to your high and mighty understandings; but I owed this testimony of a loving heart to my native Germany. I conclude with recommending myself to your sacred Majesty and your Highnesses, humbly entreating you not to suffer my enemies to indulge their hatred against me under your sanction.

[*At this point the Emperor's orator posed Luther a direct question: would he retract or not?*]

Since your Imperial Majesty and your Highnesses demand a simple answer, I will give you one, brief and simple, but deprived of neither its teeth nor its horns. Unless I am convicted of error by the testimony of Scripture, or by manifest evidence (for I put no faith in the mere authority of the Pope, or of councils, which have often been mistaken, and which have often contradicted one another, recognizing, as I do, no other guide than the Bible, the Word of God), I cannot and will not retract, for we must never act contrary to our conscience.

Such is my profession of faith, and expect none other from me. I have done. God help me! Amen.

Douglas MacArthur
American soldier

Douglas MacArthur (1880–1964) was born in Little Rock, Arkansas, the son of Lieutenant General Arthur MacArthur (1845–1912). He was educated at West Point, commissioned in the Corps of Engineers in 1903, and went to Tokyo in 1905 as aide to his father. In World War I he commanded the 42nd (Rainbow) Division in France, and was decorated 13 times and cited seven additional times for bravery. In 1919 he became the youngest-ever Superintendent of the US Military Academy at West Point, and in 1930 he was made a general and Chief of Staff of the US Army. In 1935 he became head of the US military mission to the Philippines. In World War II he was appointed commanding general of the US armed forces in the Far East in 1941. In March 1942, after a skilful but unsuccessful defence of the Bataan Peninsula, he was ordered to evacuate from the Philippines to Australia, where he set up his headquarters as supreme commander of the South-West Pacific Area. As the war developed he carried out a brilliant 'leap-frogging' strategy which enabled him to recapture the Philippine Archipelago from the Japanese. He completed the liberation of the Philippines in July 1945, and in September 1945, as supreme commander of the Allied powers, formally accepted the surrender of Japan on board the USS *Missouri*. He then exercised almost unlimited authority in the occupied empire, drafting a new constitution for Japan and carrying out a programme of sweeping reform. When war broke out in Korea in June 1950, President HARRY S TRUMAN ordered MacArthur to support the South Koreans in accordance with the appeal of the United Nations Security Council. In July he became commander-in-chief of the UN forces. After initial setbacks he pressed far into North Korea, but after the Chinese entered the war in November, MacArthur demanded powers to blockade the Chinese coast, to bomb Manchurian bases and to use Chinese nationalist troops from Formosa (Taiwan) against the Communists. This led to acute differences with Truman's administration and in April 1951 he was relieved of his commands. He unsuccessfully sought nomination for the presidency in 1952. A brilliant military leader and a ruler of Japan imbued with a deep moral sense, MacArthur was a legendary figure during his lifetime. He also inspired criticism for his imperious belief in his mission and his sense of self-dramatization.

'Duty, Honour, Country'
12 May 1962, West Point, New York, USA

General MacArthur's most famous speech was his farewell address to Congress, given in 1951 after he lost his command. 'Old soldiers never die,' he intoned then, quoting a barrack-room ballad, 'they just fade away.'

It was more than a decade before MacArthur faded away altogether. In 1962, he returned to West Point military academy as recipient of its Sylvanus Thayer Award for service to the nation – and gave what he probably knew would be his final public address. His health finally failing, MacArthur addressed West Point's young cadets about 'the great moral code' of American military service.

Taking his three keywords from the motto enshrined in West Point's coat of arms, he propounds his credo: a view of the American soldier as 'the noblest development of mankind'. He illustrates his thesis with vivid examples from 20th-century combat, and even foresees future conflicts with 'the sinister forces of some other planetary galaxy'.

In the opening paragraphs, MacArthur deprecates his gifts as an orator, but the speech is astonishingly poised. His words are imbued with pride and laced with grandiose imagery; his delivery is measured, deliberate, even ponderous. The resulting speech is irresistibly stirring, and shamelessly sentimental. One eyewitness account described its impact, noting: 'there were tears in the eyes of big strapping cadets who wouldn't have shed one before a firing squad'.

[1] The US soldier General William C Westmoreland (1914–2005) was at this time Superintendent of West Point, a post previously held by MacArthur. Westmoreland went on to command military operations in Vietnam (1964–8) and became US Army Chief of Staff, 1968–72.

General Westmoreland,[1] General Groves,[2] distinguished guests and gentlemen of the Corps: as I was leaving the hotel this morning, a doorman asked me, 'Where are you bound for, General?' and when I replied, 'West Point,' he remarked, 'Beautiful place, have you ever been there before?'

[*Laughter.*]

No human being could fail to be deeply moved by such a tribute as this. Coming from a profession I have served so long, and a people I have loved so well, it fills me with an emotion I cannot express. But this award is not intended primarily to honour a personality, but to symbolize a great moral code – the code of conduct and chivalry of those who guard this beloved

[2] The US soldier General Leslie Richard Groves (1896–1970) had been the military commander behind the Manhattan Project to develop the atomic bomb, and had retired from the US Army in 1948.

land of culture and ancient descent. That is the meaning of this medallion. For all eyes and for all time, it is an expression of the ethics of the American soldier. That I should be integrated in this way with so noble an ideal arouses a sense of pride and yet of humility which will be with me always.

Duty. Honour. Country. Those three hallowed words reverently dictate what you ought to be, what you can be, what you will be. They are your rallying points: to build courage when courage seems to fail; to regain faith when there seems to be little cause for faith; to create hope when hope becomes forlorn. Unhappily, I possess neither that eloquence of diction, that poetry of imagination, nor that brilliance of metaphor to tell you all that they mean.

The unbelievers will say they are but words, but a slogan, but a flamboyant phrase. Every pedant, every demagogue, every cynic, every hypocrite, every troublemaker and – I am sorry to say – some others of an entirely different character, will try to downgrade them even to the extent of mockery and ridicule.

But these are some of the things they do. They build your basic character. They mould you for your future roles as the custodians of the nation's defence. They make you strong enough to know when you are weak, and brave enough to face yourself when you are afraid. They teach you to be proud and unbending in honest failure, but humble and gentle in success; not to substitute words for actions, nor to seek the path of comfort, but to face the stress and spur of difficulty and challenge; to learn to stand up in the storm but to have compassion on those who fall; to master yourself before you seek to master others; to have a heart that is clean, a goal that is high; to learn to laugh yet never forget how to weep; to reach into the future yet never neglect the past; to be serious yet never to take yourself too seriously; to be modest so that you will remember the simplicity of true greatness, the open mind of true wisdom, the meekness of true strength.

They give you a temper of the will, a quality of the imagination, a vigour of the emotions, a freshness of the deep springs of life, a temperamental predominance of courage over timidity, an appetite for adventure over love of ease. They create in your heart the sense of wonder, the unfailing hope of what next, and the joy and inspiration of life. They teach you in this way to be an officer and a gentleman.

And what sort of soldiers are those you are to lead? Are they reliable, are they brave, are they capable of victory? Their story is known to all of you; it is the story of the American man-at-arms. My estimate of him was formed on the battlefield many, many years ago and has never changed. I regarded him then as I regard him now – as one of the world's noblest figures, not only as one of the finest military characters but also as one of the most stainless. His name and fame are the birthright of every American citizen. In his youth and strength, his love and loyalty he gave all that mortality can give. He needs no eulogy from me or from any other man. He has written his own history and written it in red on his enemy's breast.

But when I think of his patience under adversity, of his courage under fire and of his modesty in victory, I am filled with an emotion of admiration I cannot put into words. He belongs to history as furnishing one of the greatest examples of successful patriotism. He belongs to posterity as the instructor of future generations in the principles of liberty and freedom. He belongs to the present, to us, by his virtues and by his achievements. In 20 campaigns, on a hundred battlefields, around a thousand campfires, I have witnessed that enduring fortitude, that patriotic self-abnegation and that invincible determination which have carved his statue in the hearts of his people. From one end of the world to the other, he has drained deep the chalice of courage.

As I listened to those songs, in memory's eye I could see those staggering columns of the First World War, bending under soggy packs, on many a weary march from dripping dusk to drizzling dawn, slogging ankle-deep through the mire of shell-shocked roads, to form grimly for the attack, blue-lipped, covered with sludge and mud, chilled by the wind and rain; driving home to their objective, and, for many, to the judgement seat of God.

I do not know the dignity of their birth but I do know the glory of their death. They died unquestioning, uncomplaining, with faith in their hearts, and on their lips the hope that we would go on to victory. Always for them Duty, Honour, Country. Always their blood and sweat and tears as we sought the way and the light and the truth.

And 20 years after, on the other side of the globe, again the filth of murky foxholes, the stench of ghostly trenches, the slime of dripping dugouts; those boiling suns of relentless heat; those torrential rains of devastating storms; the loneliness and utter desolation of jungle trails; the bitterness of long separation from those they loved and cherished; the deadly pestilence of tropical disease; the horror of stricken areas of war; their resolute and determined defence; their swift and sure attack; their indomitable purpose; their complete and decisive victory – always victory. Always, through the bloody haze of their last reverberating shot, the vision of gaunt, ghastly men reverently following your password of Duty, Honour, Country.

The code which those words perpetuate embraces the highest moral laws, and will stand the test of any ethics or philosophies ever promulgated for the uplift of mankind. Its requirements are for the things that are right, and its restraints are from the things that are wrong. The soldier, above all other men, is required to practise the greatest act of religious training – sacrifice. In battle and in the face of danger and death, he discloses those divine attributes which his maker gave when he created man in his own image. No physical courage and no brute instinct can take the place of the divine help which alone can sustain him. However horrible the incidents of war may be, the soldier – who is called upon to offer and to give his life for his country – is the noblest development of mankind.

You now face a new world – a world of change. The thrust into outer space of the satellite, spheres and missiles marked the beginning of another epoch in the long story of mankind – the chapter of the space age. In the five or more billions of years the scientists tell us it has taken to form the earth, in the three or more billion years of development of the human race, there has never been a greater, a more abrupt or staggering evolution. We deal now not with things of this world alone, but with the illimitable distances and as yet unfathomed mysteries of the universe. We are reaching out for a new and boundless frontier.

We speak in strange terms: of harnessing the cosmic energy; of making winds and tides work for us; of creating unheard-of synthetic materials to supplement or even replace our old standard basics; of purifying sea water for our drink; of mining ocean floors for new fields of wealth and food; of disease preventatives to expand life into the hundreds of years; of controlling the weather for a more equitable distribution of heat and cold, of rain and shine; of spaceships to the Moon; of the primary target in war, no longer limited to the armed forces of an enemy, but instead to include his civil populations; of ultimate conflict between a united human race and the sinister forces of some other planetary galaxy; of such dreams and fantasies as to make life the most exciting of all time.

And through all this welter of change and development, your mission remains fixed, determined, inviolable. It is to win our wars. Everything else in your professional career is but corollary to this vital dedication. All other public purposes, all other public projects, all other public needs, great or small, will find others for their accomplishment; but you are the ones who are trained to fight. Yours is the profession of arms – the will to win, the sure knowledge that in war there is no substitute for victory; that if you lose, the nation will be destroyed; that the very obsession of your public service must be Duty, Honour, Country.

Others will debate the controversial issues, national and international, which divide men's minds; but serene, calm, aloof, you stand as the nation's war guardian, as its lifeguard from the raging tides of international conflict, as its gladiator in the arena of battle. For a century and a half you have defended, guarded and protected its hallowed traditions of liberty and freedom, of right and justice. Let civilian voices argue the merits or demerits of our processes of government; whether our strength is being sapped by deficit financing, indulged in too long, by federal paternalism grown too mighty, by power groups grown too arrogant, by politics grown too corrupt, by crime grown too rampant, by morals grown too low, by taxes grown too high, by extremists grown too violent; whether our personal liberties are as thorough and complete as they should be. These great national problems are not for your professional participation or military solution. Your guidepost stands out like a ten-fold beacon in the night: Duty, Honour, Country.

You are the leaven which binds together the entire fabric of our national system of defence. From your ranks come the great captains who hold the nation's destiny in their hands the moment the war tocsin sounds. The Long Grey Line has never failed us. Were you to do so, a million ghosts in olive drab, in brown khaki, in blue and grey, would rise from their white crosses thundering those magic words: Duty, Honour, Country.

This does not mean that you are warmongers. On the contrary, the soldier, above all other people, prays for peace, for he must suffer and bear the deepest wounds and scars of war. But always in our ears ring the ominous words of Plato, that wisest of all philosophers: 'Only the dead have seen the end of war.'[3]

[3] Attribution of this phrase to Plato is dubious.

The shadows are lengthening for me. The twilight is here. My days of old have vanished, tone and tint; they have gone glimmering through the dreams of things that were. Their memory is one of wondrous beauty, watered by tears and coaxed and caressed by the smiles of yesterday. I listen vainly but with thirsty ear for the witching melody of faint bugles blowing reveille, of far drums beating the long roll. In my dreams I hear again the crash of guns, the rattle of musketry, the strange, mournful mutter of the battlefield.

But in the evening of my memory, always I come back to West Point. Always there echoes and re-echoes, Duty, Honour, Country.

Today marks my final roll-call with you, but I want you to know that when I cross the river my last conscious thoughts will be of the Corps, and the Corps, and the Corps.

I bid you farewell.

Thomas Macaulay
English writer and politician

Thomas Babington Macaulay *later 1st Baron Macaulay* (1800–59) was born in Rothley Temple, Leicestershire, and educated at Trinity College, Cambridge. He was called to the Bar in 1826, and then combined his legal career with writing. His article on Milton in the August 1825 issue of the *Edinburgh Review* had gained him recognition, and for nearly 20 years he was one of the most prolific and popular of the contributors to the magazine. He became MP for the borough of Calne in 1830, and took part in the Reform Bill debates. He was legal adviser to the Supreme Council of India (1834–8) and on his return in 1839 became MP for Edinburgh, and later Secretary of War under Lord Melbourne. He received a peerage in 1857. His *History of England from the Accession of James II* (5 vols, 1848–61) enjoyed unprecedented popularity for a work of its kind. His work has been found to contain historical inaccuracies, but as a picturesque narrator he has few rivals.

'England has been to the Jews less than half a country'
17 April 1833, London, England

❧

For centuries, only members of the Church of England were allowed to hold public office in Britain: this disadvantaged Nonconformists, Catholics and Jews, who also faced many other restrictions.

Although Parliament had passed the Jew Act in 1753, allowing Jews to become naturalized, public opposition had led to its repeal the following year. Some Jewish families, among them the parents of BENJAMIN DISRAELI, abandoned their faith, allowing their children to be baptized as Christians.

From 1828, Nonconformist Christians were allowed to enter Parliament and hold municipal and public office; this right was extended to Catholics the following year. These developments encouraged the Jewish community, as did a petition on their behalf, presented to Parliament in 1830 by William Huskisson, MP for Liverpool.

The Jewish situation was considered by a House of Commons committee in 1833. Afterwards, the Judge Advocate General, Robert Grant, moved: 'That it is the opinion of this committee that it is expedient to remove all civil disabilities at present existing with respect to His Majesty's subjects professing the Jewish religion, with the like exceptions as are provided with respect to His Majesty's subjects professing the Roman Catholic religion.' A warm debate followed, during which Macaulay made this speech, drawing on Christian morality to argue in favour of the Jews. The denial of rights inflicts pain, he reasons, and Christians should refrain from inflicting pain on others.

The resolution passed without a division, but was rejected in the Lords, and the Jewish Disabilities Act was not passed until 1858.

❧

[1] The English politician Sir Robert Harry Inglis (1786–1855) served as MP for the University of Oxford, 1829–54. He was vehemently opposed to Jewish relief.
[2] See Matthew 7:12.

My honourable friend[1] has appealed to us as Christians. Let me then ask him how he understands that great commandment which comprises the Law and the Prophets. Can we be said to do unto others as we would that they should do unto us[2] if we wantonly inflict on them even the smallest pain? As Christians, surely we are bound to consider, first, whether, by excluding the Jews from all public trust, we give them pain; and, secondly, whether it be necessary to give them that pain in order to avert some greater evil. That by excluding them from public trust we inflict pain on them my honourable friend will not dispute. As a Christian, therefore, he is bound to relieve them from that pain, unless he can show what I am sure he has not yet shown, that it is necessary to the general good that they should continue to suffer.

But where, he says, are you to stop, if once you admit into the House of Commons people who deny the authority of the Gospels? Will you let in a

[3] An archaic term for Muslim.

Mussulman?[3] Will you let in a Parsi? Will you let in a Hindu, who worships a lump of stone with seven heads?

I will answer my honourable friend's question by another. Where does he mean to stop? Is he ready to roast unbelievers at slow fires? If not, let him tell us why: and I will engage to prove that his reason is just as decisive against the intolerance which he thinks a duty as against the intolerance which he thinks a crime.

Once admit that we are bound to inflict pain on a man because he is not of our religion; and where are you to stop? Why stop at the point fixed by my honourable friend rather than at the point fixed by the honourable Member for Oldham,[4] who would make the Jews incapable of holding land? And why stop at the point fixed by the honourable Member for Oldham rather than at the point which would have been fixed by a Spanish Inquisitor of the 16th century? When once you enter on a course of persecution, I defy you to find any reason for making a halt till you have reached the extreme point …

In truth, those persecutors who use the rack and the stake have much to say for themselves. They are convinced that their end is good; and it must be admitted that they employ means which are not unlikely to attain the end. Religious dissent has repeatedly been put down by sanguinary persecution. In that way the Albigenses[5] were put down. In that way Protestantism was suppressed in Spain and Italy, so that it has never since reared its head. But I defy anybody to produce an instance in which disabilities such as we are now considering have produced any other effect than that of making the sufferers angry and obstinate. My honourable friend should either persecute to some purpose, or not persecute at all …

The honourable Member for Oldham tells us that the Jews are naturally a mean race, a sordid race, a money-getting race; that they are averse to all honourable callings; that they neither sow nor reap; that they have neither flocks nor herds; that usury is the only pursuit for which they are fit; that they are destitute of all elevated and amiable sentiments. Such, Sir, has in every age been the reasoning of bigots. They never fail to plead in justification of persecution the vices which persecution has engendered.

England has been to the Jews less than half a country; and we revile them because they do not feel for England more than a half patriotism. We treat them as slaves and wonder that they do not regard us as brethren. We drive them to mean occupations; and then reproach them for not embracing honourable professions. We long forbade them to possess land; and we complain that they chiefly occupy themselves in trade. We shut them out from all the paths of ambition; and then we despise them for taking refuge in avarice. During many ages we have, in all our dealings with them, abused our immense superiority of force; and then we are disgusted because they have recourse to that cunning which is the natural and universal defence of the weak against the violence of the strong.

But were they always a mere money-changing, money-getting, money-hoarding race? Nobody knows better than my honourable friend the Member for the University of Oxford that there is nothing in their national character which unfits them for the highest duties of citizens. He knows that, in the infancy of civilization, when our island was as savage as New Guinea, when letters and arts were still unknown to Athens, when scarcely a thatched hut stood on what was afterwards the site of Rome, this contemned[6] people had their fenced cities and cedar palaces, their splendid temple, their fleets of merchant ships, their schools of sacred learning, their great statesmen and soldiers, their natural philosophers, their historians and their poets.

What nation ever contended more manfully against overwhelming odds for its independence and religion? What nation ever, in its last agonies, gave such signal proofs of what may be accomplished by a brave despair? And if, in the course of many centuries, the oppressed descendants of

[4] The English agriculturalist, journalist and politician William Cobbett (1763–1835), of whom Macaulay later wrote, 'his faculties were impaired by age'. He was 70 at this time.

[5] An ascetic religious sect which sprang up in southern France during the 12th century.

[6] Despised.

warriors and sages have degenerated from the qualities of their fathers; if, while excluded from the blessings of law, and bowed down under the yoke of slavery, they have contracted some of the vices of outlaws and of slaves, shall we consider this as matter of reproach to them? Shall we not rather consider it as matter of shame and remorse to ourselves?

Let us do justice to them. Let us open to them the door of the House of Commons. Let us open to them every career in which ability and energy can be displayed. Till we have done this, let us not presume to say that there is no genius among the countrymen of Isaiah, no heroism among the descendants of the Maccabees.[7]

Sir, in supporting the motion of my honourable friend, I am, I firmly believe, supporting the honour and the interests of the Christian religion. I should think that I insulted that religion if I said that it cannot stand unaided by intolerant laws. Without such laws it was established, and without such laws it may be maintained.

It triumphed over the superstitions of the most refined and of the most savage nations, over the graceful mythology of Greece and the bloody idolatry of the northern forests. It prevailed over the power and policy of the Roman Empire. It tamed the barbarians by whom that empire was overthrown. But all these victories were gained not by the help of intolerance, but in spite of the opposition of intolerance.

The whole history of Christianity proves that she has little indeed to fear from persecution as a foe, but much to fear from persecution as an ally. May she long continue to bless our country with her benignant[8] influence, strong in her sublime philosophy, strong in her spotless morality, strong in those internal and external evidences to which the most powerful and comprehensive of human intellects have yielded assent, the last solace of those who have outlived every earthly hope, the last restraint of those who are raised above every earthly fear!

But let not us, mistaking her character and her interests, fight the battle of truth with the weapons of error, and endeavour to support by oppression that religion which first taught the human race the great lesson of universal charity.

[7] Jewish rebels who established independence in Israel, 165–63 BC.

[8] Kind, favourable.

❧

'Educate the people'
18 April 1847, London, England

❧

In England, the government had long been reluctant to intervene in the education of children. The Church of England and other religious bodies had established a system of voluntary education during the 18th century. However, not all children were able to participate; there were insufficient schools in the rapidly expanding urban areas and many could not afford the fees.

State education systems had developed in Calvinist-influenced countries such as Scotland, the Netherlands and the New England colonies of America, where the concept of education for all was valued. By the early 19th century, all states in the USA were obliged to provide schooling, and English education reformers, who admired such systems, tried to introduce a comparable scheme.

A Committee of the Privy Council on Education had been established in 1839, and in 1847 it issued a minute proposing the nationalization of education. When it was debated in Parliament, Macaulay defended this proposal. His speech links inadequate education with crime, claiming that if the state failed in its duty to educate the people, their resulting ignorance would lead them into delinquency.

Although Macaulay was at a loss to understand the 'clamour' of those opposing state provision of education, the Education Act, providing universal elementary education in England and Wales, was not passed until 1870.

❧

This then is my argument. It is the duty of government to protect our persons and property from danger. The gross ignorance of the common people is a principal cause of danger to our persons and property. Therefore, it is the duty of the government to take care that the common people shall not be grossly ignorant.

And what is the alternative? It is universally allowed that, by some means, government must protect our persons and property. If you take away education, what means do you leave? You leave means such as only necessity can justify, means which inflict a fearful amount of pain, not only on the guilty, but on the innocent who are connected with the guilty. You leave guns and bayonets, stocks and whipping-posts, treadmills, solitary cells, penal colonies, gibbets.

See then how the case stands. Here is an end which, as we all agree, governments are bound to attain. There are only two ways of attaining it. One of those ways is by making men better, and wiser, and happier. The other way is by making them infamous and miserable. Can it be doubted which way we ought to prefer? Is it not strange, is it not almost incredible, that pious and benevolent men should gravely propound the doctrine that the magistrate is bound to punish and at the same time bound not to teach?

To me it seems quite clear that whoever has a right to hang has a right to educate. Can we think without shame and remorse that more than half of those wretches who have been tied up at Newgate in our time might have been living happily, that more than half of those who are now in our gaols might have been enjoying liberty and using that liberty well, that such a hell on earth as Norfolk Island[1] need never have existed, if we had expended in training honest men but a small part of what we have expended in hunting and torturing rogues.

[1] The penal settlement on this South Pacific island during the 19th century was renowned for brutality.

I would earnestly entreat every gentleman to look at … the report made by Mr Seymour Tremenheere[2] on the state of that part of Monmouthshire which is inhabited by a population chiefly employed in mining. He found that, in this district, towards the close of 1839, out of 11,000 children who were of an age to attend school, 8,000 never went to any school at all, and that most of the remaining 3,000 might almost as well have gone to no school as to the squalid hovels in which men who ought themselves to have been learners pretended to teach.

[2] The English lawyer Hugh Seymour Tremenheere (1804–93) was a government inspector of schools.

In general, these men had only one qualification for their employment; and that was their utter unfitness for every other employment. They were disabled miners, or broken hucksters. In their schools all was stench and noise and confusion. Now and then, the clamour of the boys was silenced for two minutes by the furious menaces of the master; but it soon broke out again. The instruction given was of the lowest kind. Not one school in ten was provided with a single map. This is the way in which you suffered the minds of a great population to be formed.

And now for the effects of your negligence. The barbarian inhabitants of this region rise in an insane rebellion against the government. They come pouring down their valleys to Newport.[3] They fire on the queen's troops. They wound a magistrate. The soldiers fire in return; and too many of these wretched men pay with their lives the penalty of their crime.

But is the crime theirs alone? Is it strange that they should listen to the only teaching that they had? How can you, who took no pains to instruct them, blame them for giving ear to the demagogue who took pains to delude them? We put them down, of course. We punished them. We had no choice. Order must be maintained; property must be protected; and,

[3] Macaulay probably refers to the Newport Rising of 4 November 1839, when a Chartist protest march developed into a riot, with fighting between troops and protestors; at least 22 people were killed. Barnabas Brough's vivid account of the events, *A Night With the Chartists*, had been published in 1847.

since we had omitted to take the best way of keeping these people quiet, we were under the necessity of keeping them quiet by the dread of the sword and the halter. But could any necessity be more cruel? And which of us would run the risk of being placed under such necessity a second time?

I say, therefore, that the education of the people is not only a means, but the best means of attaining that which all allow to be a chief end of government; and, if this be so, it passes my faculties to understand how any man can gravely contend that government has nothing to do with the education of the people.

My confidence in my opinion is strengthened when I recollect that I hold that opinion in common with all the greatest law-givers, statesmen, and political philosophers of all nations and ages; with all the most illustrious champions of civil and spiritual freedom; and especially with those men whose names were once held in the highest veneration by the Protestant dissenters of England.

I might cite many of the most venerable names of the old world; but I would rather cite the example of that country which the supporters of the voluntary system here are always recommending to us as a pattern. Go back to the days when the little society which has expanded into the opulent and enlightened commonwealth of Massachusetts began to exist. Our modern dissenters will scarcely, I think, venture to speak contumeliously of those Puritans whose spirit Laud[4] and his High Commission Court could not subdue, of those Puritans who were willing to leave home and kindred, and all the comforts and refinements of civilized life, to cross the ocean, to fix their abode in forests among wild beasts and wild men, rather than commit the sin of performing, in the house of God, one gesture which they believed to be displeasing to Him.

Did those brave exiles think it inconsistent with civil or religious freedom that the state should take charge of the education of the people? No sir: one of the earliest laws enacted by the Puritan colonists was that every township, as soon as the Lord had increased it to the number of 50 houses, should appoint one to teach all children to write and read, and that every township of 100 houses should set up a grammar school. Nor have the descendants of those who made this law ever ceased to hold that the public authorities were bound to provide the means of public instruction.

Nor is this doctrine confined to New England. 'Educate the people' was the first admonition addressed by Penn[5] to the colony which he founded. 'Educate the people' was the legacy of WASHINGTON to the nation which he had saved. 'Educate the people' was the unceasing exhortation of JEFFERSON; and I quote Jefferson with peculiar pleasure, because of all the eminent men that have ever lived, Adam Smith[6] himself not excepted, Jefferson was the one who most abhorred everything like meddling on the part of governments. Yet the chief business of his later years was to establish a good system of state education in Virginia.

And, against such authority as this, what have you who take the other side to show? Can you mention a single great philosopher, a single man distinguished by his zeal for liberty, humanity, and truth, who, from the beginning of the world down to the time of this present parliament, ever held your doctrines? You can oppose to the unanimous voice of all the wise and good, of all ages, and of both hemispheres, nothing but a clamour which was first heard a few months ago, a clamour in which you cannot join without condemning, not only all whose memory you profess to hold in reverence, but even your former selves.

[4] The English clergyman William Laud (1573–1645) was appointed Archbishop of Canterbury in 1633, and was notorious for his persecution of Puritanism. A close ally of CHARLES I, he was charged with treason and beheaded.

[5] The English Quaker William Penn (1644–1718) founded the American colony of Pennsylvania.

[6] The Scottish economist and philosopher Adam Smith (1723–90) was a central figure of the Enlightenment, best known for his book *The Wealth of Nations* (1776).

Eugene McCarthy

American politician

Eugene Joseph McCarthy (1916–2005) was born in Watkins, Minnesota. A teacher of political science, he entered the House of Representatives as a Democrat (1949) and in 1958 was elected senator from Minnesota. In 1968 he challenged President LYNDON B JOHNSON for the presidential nomination, on a policy of opposition to the Vietnam War. Johnson stood down, but McCarthy did not gain the nomination and he left the Senate in 1970 to devote himself to teaching and writing, although he mounted an independent presidential campaign in 1976. During the presidential campaign of 2000, he campaigned for the inclusion of Ralph Nader (1934–), the Green candidate, in televised debates. In 2004, he joined the board of advisors of the Federation for American Immigration Reform. His publications include *Required Reading* (1988) and *Colony of the World* (1993).

'In place of near despair, let us have hope'

2 December 1967, Chicago, Illinois, USA

Eugene McCarthy's seminal anti-Vietnam War address – made two days after he declared his intention to challenge President Johnson in the 1968 Democratic primary elections – lucidly articulated the problems with the administration's Vietnam policy. The speech also laid bare divisions among Democrats, divisions that would lead ROBERT F KENNEDY to enter the presidential race and Johnson to withdraw from it.

McCarthy had supported the war in 1964, but became increasingly sceptical about its military, political and above all moral justification – a position clearly voiced in this speech, addressed to the Conference of Concerned Democrats. By 1967, disquiet about Vietnam was growing: polls carried out that summer found that fewer than 50 per cent of respondents supported Johnson's conduct of the war, while in October about 35,000 anti-war demonstrators staged a protest outside the Pentagon, the headquarters of the US Department of Defense.

In his speech, McCarthy appeals to history, both recent and classical, to make his case. He contrasts the 'joyless spirit' of the current era with the hope and confidence that followed the presidential election victory of JOHN F KENNEDY in 1963. He also cites Carthage's wars with ancient Rome; while Rome eventually defeated Carthage, the cost of doing so was so great that it led to the end of the Roman republic.

In 1952, in this city of Chicago, the Democratic Party nominated as its candidate for the presidency ADLAI STEVENSON. His promise to his party and to the people of the country then was that he would talk sense to them ... Under the presidency of John F Kennedy, his ideas were revived in new language and in a new spirit. To the clear sound of the horn was added the beat of a steady and certain drum.

John Kennedy set free the spirit of America. The honest optimism was released. Quiet courage and civility became the mark of American government, and new programmes of promise and of dedication were presented: the Peace Corps[1], the Alliance for Progress[2], the promise of equal rights for all Americans – and not just the promise but the beginning of the achievement of that promise.

All the world looked to the United States with new hope, for here was youth and confidence and an openness to the future. Here was a country not being held by the dead hand of the past, nor frightened by the violent hand of the future which was grasping at the world. This was the spirit of 1963.

What is the spirit of 1967? What is the mood of America and of the world toward America today? It is a joyless spirit – a mood of frustration, of anxiety, of uncertainty.

In place of the enthusiasm of the Peace Corps among the young people of America, we have protests and demonstrations. In place of the enthusiasm of the Alliance for Progress, we have distrust and

[1] Founded by President Kennedy in 1961, the Peace Corps is an agency of the US State Department intended to foster good relations overseas (and initially to counter the influence of Communism in developing nations). Peace Corps recruits typically serve for two years, providing practical assistance in education, agriculture and other projects.

[2] Also founded by President Kennedy in 1961, the Alliance for Progress was a programme of economic co-operation between the USA and Latin America, which offered aid as an incentive to land reform and democratization.

disappointment. Instead of the language of promise and of hope, we have in politics today a new vocabulary in which the critical word is 'war': war on poverty, war on ignorance, war on crime, war on pollution. None of these problems can be solved by war, but only by persistent, dedicated and thoughtful attention.

But we do have one war which is properly called a war – the war in Vietnam, which is central to all of the problems of America. A war of questionable legality and questionable constitutionality. A war which is diplomatically indefensible; the first war in this century in which the United States – which at its founding made an appeal to the decent opinion of mankind in the Declaration of Independence – finds itself without the support of the decent opinion of mankind. A war which cannot be defended in the context of the judgement of history.

It is being presented in the context of an historical judgement of an era which is past. Munich[3] appears to be the starting point of history for the Secretary of State[4] and for those who attempt to support his policies. What is necessary is a realization that the United States is a part of the movement of history itself; that it cannot stand apart, attempting to control the world by imposing covenants and treaties and by violent military intervention; that our role is not to police the planet, but to use military strength with restraint and within limits, while at the same time we make available to the world the great power of our economy, of our knowledge and of our goodwill.

A war which is not defensible, even in military terms, which runs contrary to the advice of our greatest generals – EISENHOWER, Ridgway,[5] Bradley,[6] and MACARTHUR – all of whom admonished us against becoming involved in a land war in Asia. Events have proved them right, as estimate after estimate as to the time of success and the military commitment necessary to success has had to be revised – always upward. More troops, more extensive bombing, a widening and intensification of the war. Extension and intensification have been the rule, and projection after projection of success have been proved wrong.

With the escalation of our military commitment has come a parallel overleaping of objectives: from protecting South Vietnam, to nation-building in South Vietnam, to protecting all of south-east Asia, and ultimately to suggesting that the safety and security of the United States itself is at stake.

Finally, it is a war which is morally wrong. The most recent statement of objectives cannot be accepted as an honest judgement as to why we are in Vietnam. It has become increasingly difficult to justify the methods we are using and the instruments of war which we are using as we have moved from limited targets and somewhat restricted weapons to greater variety and more destructive instruments of war, and also have extended the area of operations almost to the heart of North Vietnam.

Even assuming that both objectives and methods can be defended, the war cannot stand the test of proportion and of prudent judgement. It is no longer possible to prove that the good that may come with what is called victory, or projected as victory, is proportionate to the loss of life and property and to other disorders that follow from this war …

Beyond all of these considerations, two further judgements must be passed: a judgement of individual conscience, and another in the broader context of the movement of history itself.

The problem of individual conscience is, I think, set most clearly before us

[3] McCarthy probably refers to the Munich Agreement of September 1938, which permitted Nazi Germany's annexation of the Sudetenland in western Czechoslovakia.
[4] The US politician Dean Rusk (1909–94) served as Secretary of State, 1961–9, under Presidents Kennedy and Johnson.

[5] The US soldier General Matthew B Ridgway (1895–1993) was a key military commander during the Korean War (1950–3).
[6] The US soldier Omar N Bradley (1893–1981) was a leader of the campaigns in North Africa and Europe during World War II, and became a five-star general in 1950.

[7] The French poet and philosopher Charles Péguy (1873–1914).
[8] The Dreyfus Affair centred on the conviction for treason, in 1894, of the Jewish artillery officer Alfred Dreyfus (1859–1935). When evidence of Dreyfus's innocence came to light, the military authorities made a concerted effort to uphold the conviction, provoking accusations of anti-Semitism by ÉMILE ZOLA and others.

in the words of Charles Péguy[7] in writing about the Dreyfus case:[8] 'a single injustice, a single crime, a single illegality, if it is officially recorded … will bring about the loss of one's honour, the dishonour of a whole people.'

And the broader historical judgement, as suggested by Arnold Toynbee[9] in his comments on Rome's war with Carthage: 'Nemesis[10] is a potent goddess … War posthumously avenges the dead on the survivors, and the vanquished on the victors. The nemesis of war is intrinsic. It did not need the invention of the atomic weapon to make this apparent. It was illustrated more than 2,000 years before our time, by HANNIBAL's legacy to Rome.'

[9] The English historian and social campaigner Arnold Toynbee (1889–1975).
[10] In Greek mythology, Nemesis is the goddess of vengeance. The word is used to refer to any agent of retribution or harsh justice.

Hannibal gained a 'posthumous victory over Rome. Although he failed to defeat the great nation militarily, because of the magnitude of her military manpower and solidity of the structure of the Roman Commonwealth, he did succeed in inflicting grievous wounds on the Commonwealth's body social and economic. They were so grievous that they festered into the revolution that was precipitated by Tiberius Gracchus[11] and that did not cease till it was arrested by Augustus[12] 100 years later … This revolution,' Toynbee said, 'was the nemesis of Rome's superficially triumphant career of military conquest,' and ended, of course, the republic and substituted for it the spirit of the dictators and of the Caesars.

[11] The Roman tribune Tiberius Sempronius Gracchus (163–133 BC) attempted to resettle the poor on lands requisitioned by the state, provoking civil unrest and violence.
[12] The Roman Emperor Caesar Augustus (63 BC–AD 14) quelled civil wars to usher in a two-century era of peace and prosperity known as the *Pax Romana*.

Those of us who are gathered here tonight are not advocating peace at any price. We are willing to pay a high price for peace – for an honourable, rational and political solution to this war, a solution which will enhance our world position, which will permit us to give the necessary attention to our other commitments abroad, both military and non-military, and leave us with both human and physical resources and with moral energy to deal effectively with the pressing domestic problems of the United States itself.

I see little evidence that the administration has set any limits on the price which it will pay for a military victory which becomes less and less sure and more hollow and empty in promise.

The scriptural promise of the good life is one in which the old men see visions and the young men dream dreams. In the context of this war and all of its implications, the young men of America do not dream dreams, but many live in the nightmare of moral anxiety, of concern and great apprehension; and the old men, instead of visions which they can offer to the young, are projecting, in the language of the Secretary of State, a spectre of one billion Chinese threatening the peace and safety of the world – a frightening and intimidating future.

The message from the administration today is a message of apprehension, a message of fear, yes – even a message of fear of fear.[13] This is not the real spirit of America. I do not believe that it is. This is a time to test the mood and spirit.

[13] McCarthy alludes to the famous phrase used by FRANKLIN D ROOSEVELT in his inaugural address of 4 March 1933: 'the only thing we have to fear is fear itself'. The speech is included in this book.

To offer in place of doubt, trust. In place of expediency, right judgement. In place of ghettos, let us have neighbourhoods and communities. In place of incredibility, integrity. In place of murmuring, let us have clear speech; let us again hear America singing. In place of disunity, let us have dedication of purpose. In place of near despair, let us have hope.

This is the promise of greatness which was seated for us by Adlai Stevenson and which was brought to form and positive action in the words and actions of John Kennedy. Let us pick up again these lost strands and weave them again into the fabric of America. Let us sort out the music from the sounds and again respond to the trumpet and the steady drum.

Hugh MacDiarmid
Scottish poet

Hugh MacDiarmid *pseudonym of Christopher Murray Grieve* (1892–1978) was born in Langholm, Dumfriesshire. He was educated at Langholm Academy, and became a pupil-teacher at Broughton Higher Grade School, Edinburgh, before turning to journalism. He served with the Royal Army Medical Corps in Greece and France during World War I, and was a munitions worker in World War II. A founder member of the National Party of Scotland (which became the Scottish National Party) in 1928, and intermittently an active communist, he stood for election as a Communist candidate in 1964. He became the leader of the Scottish Renaissance and dedicated his life to the regeneration of Scots as a literary language, repudiated by his fellow Scottish poet, Edwin Muir, in 1936. As a journalist in Montrose, he edited anthologies of contemporary Scottish writing, such as *Northern Numbers* (1920–2) and *The Scottish Chapbook* (1922–3), in which he published his own early poetry. His early lyrical verse appeared in *Sangschaw* (1925) and *Penny Wheep* (1926), but he is best known for his long poem *A Drunk Man Looks at the Thistle* (1926). Other publications include *To Circumjack Cencrastus* (1930), the three *Hymns to Lenin* (1931, 1932, 1957), *Scots Unbound* (1932), *Stony Limits* (1934), *A Kist o' Whistles* (1947) and *In Memoriam James Joyce* (1955). He wrote numerous essays, such as 'Albyn' (1927) and 'The Islands of Scotland' (1939). He published two memoirs: *Lucky Poet* (1943) and *The Company I've Kept* (1966).

'The star of Robbie Burns is beaming more busily than ever'
25 January 1959, Edinburgh, Scotland

Despite claiming he detested Burns suppers, Hugh MacDiarmid presented many chief toasts to the poet Robert Burns, both in Scotland and abroad. Celebrating the bicentenary of Burns's birth, this speech was delivered at the Peacock Hotel in Newhaven, Edinburgh and broadcast on the BBC.

The 'Immortal Memory' speech is always a key part of traditional Burns nights and is intended to celebrate the poet's enduring importance. On this occasion, MacDiarmid expresses his well-known paradoxical opinions on Burns and the Burns culture in Scotland. Ever the elitist intellectual, MacDiarmid argues that Burns cannot be placed alongside the world's greatest poets because he is too populist. By the same token, however, MacDiarmid argues that it is precisely Burns's belief in and appeal to the masses that makes him a figure of great importance.

The speech also states, in a less aggressive tone than MacDiarmid employs elsewhere, that the celebration of Burns must be fresh and up-to-date. In *A Drunk Man Looks at the Thistle*, for example, MacDiarmid had attacked as empty and jaded the traditional celebration of Burns. Mindless and sentimental adulation of Burns prevented, in his opinion, the development of Scottish literature.

A leading campaigner for cultural reawakening in Scotland, MacDiarmid stresses that Scots, Burns's native language, must survive if Scotland is to have an independent literary tradition. It was a tradition that poets like himself, he modestly believed, should carry forward in an innovative fashion.

Mr Chairman, my lord, ladies and gentlemen: I regard it as a great honour to have been asked to propose the chief toast on this auspicious occasion.

The bicentenary of Robert Burns has shown no diminishment of homage to him, but on the contrary, an increase. Within the past few years, a vast new public has accrued to him – in the Soviet Union, China, Hungary, Bulgaria and elsewhere.[1] In all these countries, leading poets have published new translations of his poems and songs and these have circulated in hundreds of thousands of volumes.

But North America is, of course, the great stronghold of Scottish sentiment, and consequently of the Burns movement, not only because both Canada and the United States have an element in their populations of hundreds of thousands of Scots with a great array of St Andrew's societies, Edinburgh associations, clan societies and Burns clubs, most of which celebrate Burns every January, but because the preferred Scottish feeling is continually refreshed by the huge and ever-increasing number of visitors to Scotland, most of whom visit the places associated with Burns and carry

[1] The following month, MacDiarmid travelled to the Communist states of Czechoslovakia, Hungary and Bulgaria to speak at Burns celebrations.

back a renewed enthusiasm.

Nor is that merely emotional. There is a sound background to it, of practical interest in Scottish affairs and of intensive scholarship. It is for this reason that most of the best books on Burns, and on Scottish literature generally, are being written in the United States. The radio, too, has played its part in broadcasting Burns to many millions of listeners in every part of the world.

The way in which Burns continues to be celebrated annually is a phenomenon unique in literary history. Sir Alan Herbert[2] was right when he said, 'At the present time, there's a lump of metal going round the sun. I heard the other day,' he said, 'that some solemn ass described the dispatch of this lump of metal as the supreme achievement of man. How much grander is the fact that Robert Burns put a girdle round the earth with a single song – *Auld Lang Syne* – owing nothing to electricity or science, his only instrument the hearts and tongues of ordinary men.'

[*Cries of 'Hear! Hear!'*]

The secret of the whole thing is in that last phrase – 'the hearts and tongues of ordinary men'. I have said elsewhere, Burns remains the authentic and almost the only voice of Scotland in the world today. The reason for his unparallelled fame is not far to seek. It is based on his belief in the creative power of the broad masses of mankind. His glory lies in his tremendous faith in the common man and woman everywhere. No-one who does not share and live by this faith really appreciates Burns. Wordsworth[3] said of [him]: 'he showed my youth / how verse can build a princely throne on humble truth'. Longfellow[4] put the whole thing in a nutshell when he wrote, 'the burden of his song is love of right, disdain of wrong, its masterchords are manhood, freedom, brotherhood!'

[*Cries of 'Hear! Hear!'*]

Many famous poets have expressed their love of Burns, but all of them at the same time have denied him a place among the world's greatest poets. Even Walt Whitman[5] was constrained to say, 'while Burns is not at all great in the sense that Isaiah and Aeschylus[6] and the Book of Job are unquestionably great, he is not to be mentioned with Shakespeare. He has a nestling niche of his arm, all fragrant and quaint and homely; a lodge built near, but outside the mighty temple of the gods of song and art.'

Nevertheless Whitman continued to say – 'that after a full retrospect of his works and life that Burns remains almost the manliest, tenderest, and even if contradictory, almost the dearest flesh and blood figure in all the streams and cluster of bygone poets!'

[*Cries of 'Hear! Hear!'*]

How is this paradox to be resolved? If Burns is not one of the world's greatest, why has he this unprecedented worldwide acclamation? Whitman again came nearest the solution when he wrote: 'Think of the petty environage and limited area of the poets of past or present Europe. No matter how great their genius, it almost seems as if a poetry with cosmic and dynamic features, of magnitude and limitlessness suitable to the human soul were never possible before. It is certain that a poetry of absolute faith and equality for the democratic masses never was!'

Burns comes as near to that, perhaps, as any poet has yet done. Carlyle[7] was right when he said that if Burns had been a better intellectual workman he might have changed the whole cause of European literature. As it is, despite his worldwide fame, Burns has had no real successors. Most subsequent voices of any rank have appealed not to the broad masses of

[2] The English writer and politician Sir A(lan) P(atrick) Herbert (1890–1971) was known for his humorous articles in *Punch* magazine and elsewhere.

[3] The English poet William Wordsworth (1770–1850) was a prominent member of the Romantic movement.
[4] The US poet Henry Wadsworth Longfellow (1807–82) paid this tribute to the ploughman poet in 'Ultima Thule (Robert Burns)'.

[5] The US poet Walt Whitman (1819–92) is best known for the twelve-volume collection of poetry *Leaves of Grass*, an attempt to define the American experience.
[6] The Greek tragedian Aeschylus (525–456 BC) was the earliest of the great Athenian dramatists.

[7] The Scottish essayist and historian Thomas Carlyle (1795–1881) was among the most influential writers of his era.

mankind, but to a very small, specialized reading public.

To reach the common people is a glory not often achieved by the great artistic poets, but Burns has achieved it in greater measure than any other poet – so, if he is not to be counted among the world's greatest poets, he nevertheless appeals to an immensely greater public than all these other poets put together. A public that has little or no use for any other poetry, no matter how great the literature might think it.

[*Cries of 'Hear! Hear!'*]

For it is above all true of Burns that he wrote, not to extrovert his personality, nor to comply with the demands of taste, but to voice the common thought of masses of men. His poems and songs express something clamouring for utterance. 'The glory and generous shame, / The unconquerable mind and freedom's holy flame.'[8]

That is why, 200 years after his birth, the star of Robbie Burns is beaming more busily than ever all over the globe.

[*Applause.*]

The language he wrote in had a great deal to do with it, because Scots poetry is almost entirely a poetry of song, whereas English poetry is extremely deficient in song. Song is nearer to the hearts of all people; and Scottish song owes its immense effect to the open vowels of the Scots language; whereas the narrow, clipped sounds of modern English are no medium for song at all.

It would be a very sad thing if the language in which Burns wrote is allowed to die out and if the independent Scots literary tradition, to which Burns owed so much, ceases to be carried on. Burns would never have done his great work if he had not been concerned, as he said, to see subsequent bards carrying on that tradition to endless generations.

[*Cries of 'Hear! Hear!'*]

Over 3,000 books have been devoted to Burns. I think the best of them is Hans Hecht's critical and biographical study first published [in English] in 1936. Hecht summed up the whole matter splendidly when he said that into little more than 37 years of life there is compressed in Burns such a wealth of love and sorrow; of passion, success and disappointment; of errors and triumphs, as seldom fall to the lot of any individual.

He is enshrined forever in the hearts of his fellow countrymen and has become such an essential part of their spiritual possessions that it is impossible to imagine Scotland without Robert Burns. He has remained a living force in the nation. The sun that rose over the grave by the churchyard wall in Dumfries was the sun of immortality.

Nulla crux, nulla corona![9]

We toast the immortal memory of Robert Burns and the whole world agrees. But homage is not enough. We must continue his great work and carry it on in the conditions of a world that has changed out of all recognition since Burns's day. Only insofar as we inherit Burns's spirit at its very best and carry forward his work to new levels of achievement are we worthy to call ourselves Burnsians. Immortality is a word really beyond our comprehension, whereas it is within our power to ensure the future of Robert Burns and develop his influence on the world.

And now, ladies and gentlemen, I ask you to be upstanding and drink with me to the immortal memory of Robert Burns.

To Robert Burns!

[8] MacDiarmid quotes from 'The Progress of Poesy: A Pindaric Ode' by the English poet Thomas Gray (1716–71).

[9] Latin: 'Neither cross, nor garland'. The phrase is said to have been carved into the sword of Florian Geyer (1490–1525), German leader of the Black Company during the Peasants' War of 1524–6.

Ramsay MacDonald
Scottish statesman

James Ramsay MacDonald (1866–1937) was born in Lossiemouth, Morayshire, and educated at a board school. He joined the Independent Labour Party in 1894 and was secretary (1900–11), then leader (1911–14, 1922–31) of the Labour Party. A member of the London County Council (1901–4) and of Parliament from 1906, he became leader of the opposition in 1922, and from January to November 1924 was prime minister and Foreign Secretary of the first Labour government in Britain – a minority government dependent on the support of the Liberals. He was prime minister again from 1929 to 1931. He met the financial crisis of 1931 by forming a predominantly Conservative 'National' coalition government (opposed by most of his party), which he rebuilt and led (1931–5) after a general election. In 1935 STANLEY BALDWIN took over the premiership and MacDonald became Lord President of the Privy Council. He died shortly after his retirement in 1937.

'The Labour Party will face what baffled the other two parties'
11 April 1929, sound recording made in London, England

For the general election of 1929, the Columbia Gramophone Company made a series of recordings which allowed party leaders to put forward their manifestos. Ramsay MacDonald's stirring, concise address described how the Labour Party differed from the Conservatives and the Liberals, and how it would tackle the problem of unemployment in Britain – at the time running at around ten per cent of the working population.

In his slow and precise Morayshire cadence (he stumbled over the word 'adequate' in the penultimate paragraph), MacDonald put forward a melodic case for his party's policies. Although Baldwin, the incumbent prime minister, soon afterwards claimed that Labour's proposed '250 millions of fresh taxation' would fail to absorb the unemployed, MacDonald's appeal to ordinary voters won the day, and Labour narrowly defeated the Conservatives. Ironically, unemployment would become far worse under MacDonald; the Great Depression, precipitated by the Wall Street Crash in October that year, caused the numbers of jobless to reach nearly 25 per cent by 1931.

Ladies and gentlemen: I speak to you of the Labour Party, its ideas and its immediate objects. But first of all, let me welcome the goodly company of new electors, whom we have long striven to get on the register, and to whom we are now glad to appeal. May they govern their country well.

The party was born from the hearts and the needs of the people. Its programme is based on the problems of the home. Consider what it is that worries the lives of our people. First and foremost, there is the dread of an ever-overhanging poverty. The nation is rich; millions of pounds are squandered every year in deteriorating luxury, which blesses and benefits nobody. Many who have, have not earned their possessions. Multitudes who have not, have toiled all their days and at the end are no better off than when they began. This is a political and moral as well as an economic issue. It is the greatest problem of our civilization.

The Labour Party is not interested in dispossessing, but it is interested in creating a society in which the wealth-producers and service-givers may enjoy the reward of their labours. This necessitates a rural as well as a town programme. And the party's programme to build up the countryside is winning the support of farmers and labourers alike. The Labour Party does not forget that agriculture is still our greatest industry, or that the condition of the farm labourer is one of the most pressing of our national problems.

The way by which most of our dreaded poverty comes is unemployment. For nearly ten years now, this has been a menacing disgrace in our midst. The leaders of both the other parties have neglected it; have been baffled by it. When Mr LLOYD GEORGE[1] was prime minister, with a huge majority behind him and nearly two million unemployed in the

[1] Lloyd George was leader of the Liberal Party at this time. He had served as prime minister, 1916–22.

country, he promised much and did little. Since Mr Baldwin has been in office, he has neglected to face the facts and has fallen back upon charity. His great cure is to spread the unemployed over the land and knock them off insurance benefits.

The Labour Party will face what baffled the other two parties. Our claim that the unemployed should have work or maintenance still holds good. National resources, now neglected, will be used. Great highways built, transport organized as a national service, a bold policy of housing restored and slum clearances on an adequate scale begun; electrical power developed, national credit used to assist trade and recondition industrial planning, children kept at school and old workers pensioned so that they can retire.

Whilst these schemes are enlivening trade and absorbing the unemployed, those who are still out of work will be honourably maintained by adequate payments from insurance funds. They will not be driven onto the Poor Law.[2] This is accepted by the Labour Party as its first task in government: to solve it successfully and in the quickest possible time, the party will commandeer its best brains, the ripest experience of the country and what money is required. By our treatment of the unemployed problem, we shall stand or fall.

[2] Britain's Poor Laws, the first of which dated from the late 16th century, provided relief for the very young, the sick and the old. Those who were capable of it were employed in workhouses. Legislation in the 1930s and 1940s replaced the Poor Laws with a welfare system.

❧

'If we want peace we must pursue the policy of peace'
9 November 1933, London, England

❧

Established after World War I, the League of Nations was committed to the pursuit of world disarmament. To this end it organized a Disarmament Conference, which opened at Geneva, Switzerland in February 1932, attended by representatives of League of Nations countries as well as the USA and the USSR. Proceedings came to a halt, however, when Germany demanded that if other countries did not disarm to its own levels – as mandated in the Treaty of Versailles – it had the right to rearm itself. By the time MacDonald made this speech – the annual prime minister's address to the Lord Mayor's Banquet – plans to get Germany back on board had taken several major blows: ADOLF HITLER had come to power, and was already rearming. Then, on 14 October, Hitler withdrew Germany from both the Conference and the League of Nations.

MacDonald made a heartfelt, articulate case, his speech containing perfectly balanced lines such as 'Disarmament removes dangers for peace, but peace removes obstacles to disarmament.' Ultimately, it is a sense of powerlessness that comes across most; MacDonald could do nothing more than implore Germany, as tactfully as possible, to return to the fold. This weakness reflected that of the League of Nations itself, while the sympathetic attitude towards Germany foreshadowed later accusations that MacDonald had failed to stand up to Hitler.

❧

The trade of the world depends upon the peace of the world, and the peace of the world is not defined by the objective fact that nobody is fighting. When I use the expression 'the peace of the world' I mean the peace of mind of the world. I mean a world relieved of anxiety; a world composed of nations being confident of their rectitude and the honesty and the fair play of each other.

But what do we find? – that the war and the peace both left Europe unsettled. We have been walking for years on a very, very thin crust. Whilst every nation knew that coercion and repression were no cure for grievances, and no calm for minds that believed and felt that they were injured, confidence was lacking, and wise actions were in consequence postponed. The result was a formidable gathering up of forces, a fear and unhappiness which were bound, sooner or later, to be realized and dashed at the foot of heavily burdened servants, like my friend Sir John Simon,[1] who has just spoken.

[1] The English politician Sir John Simon *later 1st Viscount Simon* (1873–1954) was at this time leader of the National Liberals, as distinct from the Liberal Party, and Foreign Secretary in MacDonald's coalition cabinet.

At the League of Nations during the last 12 months we have been faced with the general problem of peace; at the disarmament conference we have been faced with the specific problems of disarmament. The policy of the British government has been to carry out its own pledges regarding disarmament, to use its good offices and its great influence, both moral and political, on the councils of the nations, so that grievances might be fairly considered and removed, and both the condition and the will to co-operate between the nations established, and thus help to provide for the nations of Europe a security of peace which is the only security that nations can ever have.

As regards our own disarmament, in the air, on the sea and land, we have reduced our armaments to a point where we can rightly claim in the face of the world that not one pound of our public money is being spent on our fighting services that is not necessary for defence in the light of present conditions. Indeed it might be argued that if we spent more than we are doing, that boundary line would still not be passed. I firmly believe, however, that by unswerving activities to get international agreement on armaments, we can still gain a much greater security against war.

We know that the point is reached when that policy cannot be pursued further, when the position of arms of offence by other nations forces the hands of the pacific nations, and they feel compelled to accumulate material for defence purposes; but let none of us imagine that by so doing we establish peace. It is, at best, a necessary makeshift. Whilst those precautions may postpone the day of war, peaceful nations must use the period of postponement to engage in even still more active endeavours to eliminate from the minds of nations those fears, those unhappinesses, that sense of injustice that in the end lead to armed conflict. Arms have never yet saved a nation from war, nor have they given security to either strong or weak nations against attack. History has placed that on the throne of unassailable truth. If we want peace we must pursue the policy of peace.

The British government, during the last 12 months, has repeatedly come to the rescue of the disarmament conference, especially last March, when we made ourselves responsible for the draft convention which was the result of a careful study of the deliberations of the conference up to date, and which has been accepted by all the powers at Geneva as a basis for a final international agreement. That, of itself, is a great achievement. It is deplorable that just at the moment when another attempt was to be made to meet German claims, Germany not only withdrew from the deliberations of the disarmament conference, but gave notice of its intention to leave the League of Nations itself. Her act almost amounted to a repudiation of the peace machinery of the world.

Some of the terms of the Peace Treaty,[2] and much which has happened since then, have undoubtedly left irritating grievances in that country, but the policy which she has just adopted to remedy those grievances has only increased the fears and suspicions which have hitherto made their removal very hard. Her motives I do not question — I have never questioned them, and I hope I shall never be rash enough to do so, but there are inevitable consequences to certain acts.

If, my Lord Mayor, out of my generosity to you I came to the conclusion that it would be a kind act of Christian and human kindness to remove your head, I might assure you before doing so that I had no intentions upon your life, but most unfortunately for me, my intentions would be of no avail, and I should be rightly held responsible for the results of my conduct. We have

[2] The Treaty of Versailles, signed in June 1919, which required Germany to pay compensation for war damages, and severely restricted the country's military strength.

always believed that the best policy in Europe was to help Germany to get out of the conditions which she resented …

Let's be perfectly clear about this: that the amount of disarmament which can be agreed to by international conference depends upon what countries think is the risk they are running by a reduction of arms. If, by the action of any country, other countries are compelled even against their wish to arm, that risk is high and the amount of disarmament is bound to be low. Convince the nations that the risk they are running is little, then the amount of disarmament will be great. Failing to understand that – if I may very respectfully and in a most friendly way make the observation – failing to understand that has been Germany's fundamental mistake.

All these delays make us heart-sore. A Job's patience[3] seems to be needed to keep the peace front unbroken and remove the obstacles to a disarmament convention. But the situation is now, subject to theory, steady in all its aspects. The British government is not going to commit itself to one way of procedure, and the British government is prepared – and I can pledge myself that it will do it – is prepared to play its full part in bringing about that confidence which alone will result in the satisfactory disarmament convention.

And in any disarmament convention that is going to be effective as a way to peace, Germany must be a signatory. What is the use of nations outside coming to agreements on the assumption that Germany may come in? What is to hinder Germany, even now, to come in to put her case before us? She will address a tribunal of men who want peace of mind, who want to be able to meet her in every way, and I know if that policy be pursued, whoever speaks where I am now speaking, next year, will tell how the success was accomplished. But it will not be accomplished until the nations who fear or suspect each other have given it their confidence that they are to pursue the way of peace, fair play and equity.

Disarmament removes dangers for peace, but peace removes obstacles to disarmament. It is not a question of putting the cart before the horse. It is a contribution first from one side, then from the other, making a further contribution from the first side, and so on, continuing until the mind of Europe is such that its reason rejects arms …

The present position of Germany is not good for Germany, it is not good for Europe. It only makes it difficult – very nearly in fact, impossible – for all of us to be both reasonable and generous. It must not be left where it is at this moment. Baron von Neurath[4] indicated two days ago, I think, that his government had some proposals to make. We should like to have them. They shall receive the most favourable and impartial consideration at our hands. It cannot be too much emphasized – and I wish it could be possible to get the German people to hear this – that the German case is so sympathetically understood that the German problem now is not to overcome hostility so much as to join with the rest of us in producing proofs which must be more than words, of goodwill, of pacific determination, of desire to be neighbourly, of being a co-operating influence, in removing from Europe the suspicions and unsettlement which prevent all of us from doing the best which we are willing to do under circumstances which will allow.

The clouds brewing over us at this moment are those vacant chairs at the European council boards. Next week the German elections will be over: I trust that the German government will then use its great authority to guide their deliberations along lines which will not only serve their own interests, but those of Europe as a whole, and of our western civilization.

[3] The story of Job, which comprises a book of the Old Testament, tells how he endured a succession of terrible misfortunes before finally complaining to God.

[4] The German politician Konstantin Baron von Neurath (1873–1956) served as Foreign Minister in Hitler's government, 1932–8.

John Maclean
Scottish Socialist politician and teacher

John Maclean (1879–1923) was born in Pollokshaws, Glasgow to parents from the Isle of Mull, and educated at Pollokshaws Academy and Queen's Park School. Sacked from his post as a schoolteacher in Govan, Glasgow in 1915, he became a full-time Marxist educator and organizer. His classes recruited many working men, and in 1916 he formed the Scottish Labour College. A member of the British Socialist Party before World War I, he became Soviet Consul on the Clyde after the Russian Revolution of 1917. When the Communist Party was formed he refused to join, instead setting up the Scottish Workers' Party, which promoted a more nationalistic message. He was arrested six times between 1916 and 1923 on various charges of sedition and incitement to strike. His health was badly broken during the ensuing prison sentences, and he died young.

'I am here as the accuser of capitalism'
9 May 1918, Edinburgh, Scotland

This speech was delivered from the dock at the High Court in Edinburgh, where Maclean, twice imprisoned already, was again facing sedition charges. He conducted his own defence, cross-examining 28 prosecution witnesses, 25 of whom were employed by the police. Instead of calling his own witnesses, he used the platform to denounce capitalism and World War I.

Maclean spoke for around 75 minutes: in this extract, he makes clear his opposition to the war and his support for the Russian Revolution the year before. His endorsement of the USSR was the main charge among the eleven brought against him.

The prospect of a third term in jail did nothing to dampen Maclean's rhetorical fire. His speech accurately predicts that economic collapse and a further world war would follow if capitalism was allowed to flourish. Unafraid of alienating or alarming the jury, he tells them their judgements of him are invalid due to their inferior, capitalist morality, as opposed to his superior 'working-class' one.

Sentenced to five years in Peterhead jail, Maclean came to believe his food was being drugged and responded by going on hunger strike. He was paroled when the war ended in November 1918, following a campaign for his release.

I wish no harm to any human being, but I, as one man, am going to exercise my freedom of speech. No human being on the face of the earth, no government is going to take from me my right to speak, my right to protest against wrong, my right to do everything that is for the benefit of mankind. I am not here, then, as the accused; I am here as the accuser of capitalism dripping with blood from head to foot ...

The country has been exploited by the capitalist in every sphere, to get the toilers to work harder to bring victory. I said at the commencement of the war that while this was being done, and while assurances were being given that at the end of the war the people would get back to normal, I said that circumstances would make such a return impossible ... because there is going to be 'the war after the war', the economic war which brought on this war ...

It was not the workers who instigated the war. The workers have no economic interest to serve as a consequence of the war – and because of that, it is my appeal to my class that makes me a patriot so far as my class is concerned. And when I stand true to my class, the working class, in which I was born, it is because my people were swept out of the Highlands,[1] and it was only because of my own ability that I remained. I have remained true to my class, the working class, and whatever I do I think I am doing in the interest of my class and my country. I am no traitor to my country. I stand loyal to my country because I stand loyal to the class which creates the wealth throughout the whole of the world.

[1] Maclean's parents were both of Highland stock, but had been forced to relocate to the industrial south of Scotland as a result of the Highland Clearances: the evictions, forced and often violent, of small-scale farmers by landowners to clear the land for large-scale sheep farming.

We are out for life and all that life can give us. I therefore took what action I did in the light of what was transpiring inside Russia, inside Austria and inside Germany. You have got to bear that in mind when you wish to understand my remarks. I therefore urged the workers of this country that if they were going to strike, mere striking was useless, because they would be starved back into work again, and that if they were going to be against the manpower bill, it meant that they were out for peace. And as there was no sign on either side of coming to an amicable constitutional conclusion, then it was the business of the workers to take the whole matter in hand themselves.

War was declared! No matter the motive, no matter the cause, all constitution and order was thrown aside, and in the prosecution of the war the British government found it necessary to throw aside every law in this country and to bring in the Defence of the Realm Act,[2] which means the negation of all law in the country. I have repeatedly pointed out that if the government wishes to get a grip of any individual, they do so under the Defence of the Realm Act. The government have power to do anything they desire. That may be right, or it may be wrong, but the position is this: that the bringing in of the Defence of the Realm Act has thrown aside all law and order as we know it during normal periods.

In the plunge into the war we have the abolition of constitutional methods, and therefore I contended, and I contend today, that if it is right and proper on the part of the government to throw aside law and order – constitutional methods – and to adopt methods that mankind has never seen before, then it is equally right that the members of the working class, if the war is not going to cease in a reasonable time, should bring about a reasonable settlement to the workers in no victory to either side.

If one side or the other wins, then the revenge will come, as France today is seeking revenge after the drubbing she got in 1871.[3] Realizing that, we, as representatives of the workers of the world, do not wish one side or the other to be the victors, we wish the status quo prior to the war to be re-established.

If the workers are going to do that, then it means that they have to adopt methods and tactics entirely different from the methods which would be adopted or could be adopted under normal circumstances. Abnormal lines of action must be taken, such as our comrades in Russia took. The very circumstances of the war forced in upon the Russian workers' committees and their national soviets the line of action which they adopted, and the only way we could do it would be to adopt methods peculiar to the working-class organization in this country in the interests of the workers themselves …

I pointed out to the workers that, in order to solve all the problems of capitalism, they would have to get the land and the means of production. I pointed out to them that if capitalism lasted after the war, with the growing size of the trusts, with the great aggregations that were taking place, with the improved machinery inside the works, with the improved methods of speeding up the workers, with the development of research and experiment, that we were going to have the workers turning out three, four and five times as much wealth as they had done in pre-war times. And a great problem would arise – a greater problem than ever before in this country – of disposing of its surplus goods on the markets of the world, not only of getting markets for these surplus goods, but of getting the raw materials …

[2] Passed in August 1914, the Defence of the Realm Act granted the government the power to requisition land and buildings, and imposed censorship. It also banned the British public from flying kites, lighting bonfires or feeding wild animals.

[3] The Franco-Prussian War of 1870–1 resulted in the German humiliation of France.

In the next five years there is going to be a great world trade depression and the respective governments, to stave off trouble, must turn more and more into the markets of the world to get rid of their produce, and in 15 years' time from the close of this war – I have pointed this out at all my meetings – we are into the next war. If capitalism lasts, we cannot escape it.

Britain has the wealth. Britain did everything she could to hold back the war. That necessarily had to be the attitude of Great Britain. But in spite of all Great Britain's skill or cunning, there has been war. I have heard it said that the western civilizations are destroying themselves as the Eastern civilizations destroyed themselves. In 15 years' time we may have the first great war bursting out in the Pacific: America versus Japan, or even Japan and China versus America. We have then the possibilities of another war, far greater and far more serious in its consequences than the present war. I have pointed that out to my audiences.

In view of the fact that the great powers are not prepared to stop the war until the one side or the other is broken down, it is our business as members of the working class to see that this war ceases today, not only to save the lives of the young men of the present, but also to stave off the next great war. That has been my attitude and justifies my conduct in recent times. I am out for an absolute reconstruction of society, on a co-operative basis, throughout all the world. When we stop the need for armies and navies, we stop the need for wars.

I have taken up unconstitutional action at this time because of the abnormal circumstances and because precedent has been given by the British government. I am a socialist, and have been fighting and will fight for an absolute reconstruction of society, for the benefit of all. I am proud of my conduct. I have squared my conduct with my intellect, and if everyone had done so this war would not have taken place.

I act square and clean for my principles. I have nothing to retract. I have nothing to be ashamed of. Your class position is against my class position. There are two classes of morality. There is the working-class morality and there is the capitalist class morality. There is this antagonism as there is the antagonism between Germany and Britain. A victory for Germany is a defeat for Britain; a victory for Britain is a defeat for Germany. And it is exactly the same so far as our classes are concerned. What is moral for the one class is absolutely immoral for the other, and vice versa.

No matter what your accusations against me may be, no matter what reservations you keep at the back of your head, my appeal is to the working class. I appeal exclusively to them because they and they only can bring about the time when the whole world will be in one brotherhood, on a sound economic foundation. That and that alone can be the means of bringing about a reorganization of society. That can only be obtained when the people of the world get the world and retain the world.

Harold Macmillan
English statesman

Maurice Harold Macmillan *later 1st Earl of Stockton* (1894–1986) was born in London. He was educated at Eton and Oxford, though his studies were interrupted by military service in World War I, during which he was seriously wounded. In 1919–20 he was in Canada as aide-de-camp to the governor-general, the 9th Duke of Devonshire, whose daughter Lady Dorothy (1900–66) he married. Returning to Britain, he partnered his brother Daniel in the family publishing firm and stood successfully as Conservative MP for Stockton-on-Tees in 1924. He was defeated in 1929, but re-elected in 1931. Not always willing to conform to the party line, he remained a backbencher until 1940, when WINSTON CHURCHILL made him Parliamentary Secretary to the Ministry of Supply. After a brief spell as Colonial Under-Secretary, in 1942 he was sent to North Africa to fill the new Cabinet post of Minister Resident at Allied Headquarters, where he proved his ability as a mediator in many clashes of factions and personalities. Defeated in the Labour landslide of 1945, he was returned later the same year for Bromley, and held this seat until he retired in 1964. He was Minister of Housing (1951–4), silencing general doubts by achieving his promised target of 300,000 houses in a year. He became Minister of Defence (1954–5), then Foreign Minister until the end of 1955, when he was appointed Chancellor of the Exchequer. On the resignation of ANTHONY EDEN in 1957 he emerged, in R A Butler's words, as 'the best prime minister we have'. As an intellectual and an aristocrat, he was regarded with suspicion by many. Nevertheless, his economic expansionism at home, his resolution in foreign affairs, his integrity and his infectious optimism inspired confidence, and his popularity soared. He embarked upon a new term as prime minister in 1959. His 'wind of change' speech in Cape Town (1960) acknowledged the inevitability of African independence. In 1962, after some electoral setbacks, he carried out a drastic 'purge' of his government, involving seven Cabinet ministers. Further setbacks followed, such as the Profumo scandal (1963), and ill health brought about his reluctant resignation in 1963. On his 90th birthday in 1984 he was ennobled as the Earl of Stockton. His publications include *Winds of Change* (1966), *Tides of Fortune* (1969), *Riding the Storm* (1971) and *At The End of the Day* (1972).

'Most of our people have never had it so good'
20 July 1957, Bedford, England

At this point in his career, Harold Macmillan's political fortunes were rising to their zenith. As Chancellor, he had been labelled 'Supermac' by the newspaper cartoonist Vicky, after presiding over a booming British economy. But his colonial policy, which facilitated independence in much of what remained of the empire, made him unpopular with the right of his party. So too did his 'One Nation Conservatism', whose economic and social philosophies more closely resembled the post-war social democratic policies of CLEMENT ATTLEE than any former Tory platform.

But whatever his issues with his party, Macmillan was popular with the country at large. Having inherited a 13-point deficit in the polls at his election to the party leadership, he would win the 1959 election with a seven-point lead.

However, this famous speech to the party faithful of Bedford was particularly taxing for Macmillan, partly because it addresses the end of Empire. What is so impressive about it is the quiet pragmatism that characterized his policy-making. He thrived by his well-known credo: 'If people want a sense of purpose they should get it from their archbishop. They should certainly not get it from their politicians.'

The dry, knowing patrician wit for which he was renowned is also in evidence here. It has been said of Macmillan that his hunting, shooting and fishing lifestyle was carefully acquired, but it played well, perhaps for the last time, with the British public.

Just over six months have passed since severe ill-health forced Sir Anthony Eden to lay down his burden. To all of us – his friends and colleagues – this was indeed a cruel blow. For he was endowed with two great qualities without which no politician, however able or however brilliant, can aspire to the name of statesman. These are courage and integrity. He had both, to a supreme degree …

It has fallen to me to be his successor; and I must tell you that I feel both encouraged and inspired by the loyalty and comradeship which have been shown to me during these six months. I know it is the fashion, especially during the last few weeks of a session, for the newspapers and political commentators to work up all kinds of stories of troubles and dangers ahead. In politics, nobody ever remembers the difficulties that have been overcome. They are old history. The commentators aren't interested in them; good news is no news.

I have on my writing table a little volume of *The Pilgrim's Progress*[1] that belonged to my grandfather. As I was coming to Bedford, I thought I would look it through again. How living the characters are: Mr Worldly Wiseman, Obstinate, Reliable; and the town of Fair Speech, with My Lord Turn About, My Lord Time Server, My Lord Fair Speech, from whose ancestors the town first took its name; also Mr Smooth Man, Mr Facing Both Ways, Mr Anything and Mr Two Tongues.

Oh, we have got them all still. But we have our Faithfuls too; and in this splendid gathering today I see thousands of them. Firm, unshaken and determined, and I am convinced that in our great Conservative and Unionist Party throughout the country – as well as among many men and women of any party affiliations – my colleagues and I can count on a great fund of sympathy and support in our pilgrimage.

This meeting, I must remind you, was originally planned to celebrate the jubilee of Bedfordshire's senior Member. Alan Lennox-Boyd[2] has served his constituency for an unbroken tenure of 25 years. Fortunately he is still quite a young man, and a man of immense vigour. He holds today one of the most arduous as well as one of the most important posts in the Cabinet. He has not spared himself. I do not suppose he has told you – but I will tell you – that since he became Colonial Secretary, only three years ago, he has travelled 80,000 miles – more than three times round the globe. He has won the admiration and respect of all the political leaders and indeed of all the people of our colonies. He has done something more – he has won their affection. Peoples of every race, religion and colour have come to look upon him as a friend.

This leads me to say something about changes and developments which have taken place in the empire during recent years. I know there are some people who feel concerned at what is happening. They even talk about the disintegration of the empire. It is changing; but it is not disintegrating. Colonial territories are taking steps everywhere towards self-government. But we should take pride in this, for it is we who have taught them; who have set them on the path. Our aim has always been to lead the colonial peoples along the road to self-government within the Commonwealth …

There is not a colony today which is not thinking of its future destiny. People are seeking new faiths and beliefs, trying to adjust themselves to the sudden impact of new thoughts, ideas and invention. But we must not be frightened by what is happening. For after all, it is of our own making.

Of all political forces, the new rise of nationalism is the most powerful, swift and elemental. It can be stubborn too. It can be led; but it cannot be driven. If we try to drive it backwards, we shall drive it to communism. Our task is to guide these forces with sympathy and understanding. To this work nobody has given greater service than the Colonial Secretary. He is supported by the splendid officers of our fine colonial service.

In the long history of the past, the world has seen the rise and fall of great empires. Let us take pride in this – that Britain is the only power which has, of its own volition, set about the task of giving full independence to all parts of its Empire as they become able to manage their own affairs. This is not a sunset; it is the coming of a new dawn …

Yet, despite all this, Great Britain is charged with 'imperialism' and

[1] A Christian allegory of mankind's struggle through life, published in 1678–84 by the English writer and preacher John Bunyan (1628–88).

[2] Alan Lennox-Boyd *later 1st Viscount Boyd of Merton* (1904–83) became MP for Mid Bedfordshire in 1931, later serving as Minister for Transport and Aviation (1952–4) and Secretary of State for the Colonies (1954–9).

'colonialism'. So constant, indeed, have these attacks become that 'colonialism' has almost come to be the signature tune of the Moscow Radio and the 'Voice of the Arabs' in Cairo.

Let us contrast our own record with that of our communist accusers. Whilst 100 million people in Europe alone have, since the war, been fully absorbed into the communist bloc, more than five times that number in Asia and Africa have been helped to nationhood by governments of this country. Turn now to the last few months – four million citizens in Ghana have been built into a new free nation, while for ten million Hungarians freedom has been crushed by the Red Army.

It is our duty to ourselves, to our friends, to the cause of freedom and to the potential victims of communist blandishments everywhere to see that these facts are known ... The pattern of the Commonwealth is changing and with it is changing Britain's position as the mother country. Our children are growing up; we can no longer treat them as we did when they were younger. Like parents with sons who are on the verge of manhood, we can achieve more by persuasion and discussion. And what does this add up to? It means that Britain's influence today is as great as ever.

The countries of the Commonwealth and of the colonial empire look to us for leadership in many fields.

First, defence. Here I am happy to tell you what a fine job the Member for Bedford, Mr Christopher Soames,[3] is doing in his new post. And by the way, your county of Bedford is really a very satisfactory county politically: all four Members support the government. Three of them are in the government – two in the Cabinet – and the fourth is an energetic and hard-working backbencher. No Mr Faint Hearts here, or among the thousands who send them to the House of Commons.

In defence I have continued the policy started by Mr Attlee and carried on by Sir Winston Churchill and Sir Anthony Eden, and now reaching its fruition. That is to say, we are making Britain an atomic and nuclear power. This is not the time for me to talk abut defence in any detail. As you know, we are engaged upon a recasting of our defence services. It will be a long job, and a difficult one. And remember, on our success depends the end of conscription and the return to volunteer or regular forces.

I would like you all to know the importance that I attribute to our efforts towards disarmament. But it must be real disarmament. It must not be a form of disarmament which leaves us at the mercy of the communist powers. Today we are defended from aggression by the power of the bomb. We are working closely with our American, French and Canadian partners to find a method by which both the tests and the manufacture of material for these terrible weapons can safely be reduced or ultimately abandoned. But I am not prepared – and I do not think you are prepared – to see Britain powerless to defend herself. Until therefore some real advance can be made, even a partial advance, on the lines that we have proposed, we must stand firm ...

For so long as I can remember, this country has been the traditional source of capital for the Commonwealth and the Empire. During the Victorian and Edwardian eras this reached immense figures. Indeed, it was to British capital that not only the Commonwealth and the colonies, but a great part of the world – including the United States – owed the foundations of their prosperity.

At the culminating point of this operation – that is, in the years immediately preceding the First War – Great Britain is believed to have

[3] Christopher Soames *later Baron Soames* (1920–87) was MP for Bedford, 1950–66, and in January 1957 had moved from a junior ministerial post at the Air Ministry to a similar post at the Admiralty.

exported some seven per cent of her national income. Now, after two World Wars – and many other calls upon our resources which are absolutely essential if we are to keep ahead in the race and maintain our investing power – we cannot hope to do as much. But we are still doing pretty well …

Our problem today is how to do all the things that we want to do. We want to invest in the Commonwealth. We want to improve conditions among the millions of people in Asia and Africa whose living standards are too low – and incidentally if we improve their conditions we shall improve the markets for our goods. We want to re-equip our factories and farms with the most up-to-date plant and machinery. We want to maintain and, if we can, improve our social services. And we must of course play our proper part in defence.

All these things together make up a heavy task, which we have succeeded in meeting over the last six years … Our general prospects are good. The balance of payments prospects are favourable – we look like earning a really worthwhile surplus this year. That is because our exports are holding up well in world markets. In the first half of this year they were six per cent higher by value – seven and a half per cent higher to North America – than a year before. Our invisible earnings too – from shipping, and oil particularly – are doing well. The gold and dollar reserves rose £88 million in the first half of this year …

These increased earnings come from the increasing production of most of our main industries – steel, coal, motor cars – a large part of the increase in output is going to exports or to investments. That is all to the good. Indeed, let's be frank about it: most of our people have never had it so good.

Go around the country, go to the industrial towns, go to the farms, and you will see a state of prosperity such as we have never had in my lifetime – nor indeed ever in the history of this country. What is beginning to worry some of us is, 'Is it too good to be true?' – or perhaps I should say, 'Is it too good to last?' For, amidst all this prosperity, there is one problem that has troubled us – in one way or another – ever since the war. It's the problem of rising prices.

Our constant concern today is – can prices be steadied while at the same time we maintain full employment in an expanding economy? Can we control inflation? This is the problem of our time.

It is true that prices have risen less since we took office. It is true that wages, and in the main salaries, have more than held their own in the race. Taking the nation as a whole, compared with six years ago, personal incomes are 40 per cent up, and though prices have risen they have only risen by 20 per cent. I read in the *Daily Mirror* this week a statement which said that the people were worried at 'too small wages chasing too big bills'. Whatever else is true, this isn't true. Wages have risen far beyond prices. But we must not, and we do not intend to allow these facts to blind us to the dangers. The great mass of the country has – for the time being, at any rate – been able to contract out of the effects of rising prices. For, if that happens, we will be back in the old nightmare of unemployment. The older ones among you will know what this meant. I hope the younger ones will never have to learn it. What folly, to risk throwing away all that we have gained.

Last year, when I was Chancellor, I described our position as brilliant but precarious. There must always be a risk, and it is surely the lesson in life not to take too much or press an advantage too far. If we do we may lose the greatest social and economic benefit that has come to us since the war – security.

The Conservative Party is not the party of any class or section. We govern in the interests of the whole nation; and we cannot forget that some sections of the people have not shared in this general prosperity.[4] These are those who live on fixed incomes, including those who have retired from active work. We cannot, as a national party, see their interests sacrificed. The government have a clear duty in this matter, and we intend to discharge it ...

In the long run, there is only one answer to the $64,000-dollar question[5] – to increase production. That's the answer. That is where the real hope lies. That is why the Chancellor of the Exchequer[6] last April gave new incentives through lower taxation. That has been our policy ever since 1951 – in six out of seven budgets, the burden of taxation has been lowered. The nation today is paying £800 million a year less in taxes than it would be paying if the Socialist rates of 1951 had been maintained.

But you know, the government cannot do this all alone. Of course, government action is needed and is being taken. But by itself it cannot solve the problem. This is a combined operation. We are all in it – government, industry, the general public. What we need is restraint and common sense – restraint in the demands we make, and common sense on how we spend our income. But the only form of restraint which can work in a free society is self-restraint ...

This then is my theme, and this my message to you. An expanding Commonwealth, changing but taking new form, shedding old methods but reaching out to great new possibilities; Britain the centre of it, trusted by all and honoured as the natural leader. A material development of the Commonwealth to which Britain is making the largest contribution of any country in the world in money, and to which she can make increasing contributions in technical skill and experience.

Our own country buoyant, determined to maintain a high rate of investment, a high rate of savings and determined too to conquer the danger of inflation by rising activity.

So, midway through this year 1957, we are masters of our own fate. It lies in our own hands; with wisdom, good sense, good feeling and comradeship, we can achieve our purpose. I have no doubt at all what the outcome will be.

[4] Macmillan's 'One Nation Conservatism' promoted connection and harmony between different social classes – particularly between the aristocracy and the working class.

[5] *The $64,000 Question* was a US television game show which screened 1955–8. The phrase entered popular parlance on both sides of the Atlantic.

[6] Peter Thorneycroft *later Baron Thorneycroft* (1909–94) had succeeded Macmillan as Chancellor of the Exchequer in January 1957. He resigned over increased government expenditure in January 1958.

'First the Georgian silver goes ...'
8 November 1985, London, England

Few people are better placed to damage a prime minister's credibility than a previous incumbent – especially one belonging to the same party. So it was when Harold Macmillan (now the Earl of Stockton) rose at the tenth anniversary dinner of the moderate Tory Reform Group to make this speech criticizing the economic policy of Prime Minister MARGARET THATCHER.

By now aged 91, Stockton was an elder statesman in the classic mould. He began by describing the roots of the economic decline which had beset Britain during the 1960s and 1970s, leading to the 'winter of discontent' (1978–9) and the overthrow of the Labour government in 1979.

He praised the efforts of former prime ministers HAROLD WILSON and James Callaghan (both Labour), attributing Britain's difficulties mainly to the rapid rise in oil prices. He also described how Thatcher had begun to effect economic recovery through 'belt-tightening' deflationary measures.

But then he turned, in the passage given here, to pass withering judgement on an 'ingenious system which the government has devised'. This was Thatcher's controversial programme to privatize national utilities by floating them on the stock market. Like many people in the country, Stockton saw this as a short-term solution which would leave Britain bereft of assets.

Stockton moves on to urge the embracing of technology (as Wilson had done in his 'white heat' speech of October 1963) and ends with a call for unity. But the most memorable part of his speech, which provoked laughter and applause, was his barbed likening of Britain to an ancestral home forced to sell off its priceless heirlooms.

❧

It is very common with individuals or estates, when they run into financial difficulties, to find that they have to sell some of their assets. First the Georgian silver goes, then all that nice furniture that used to be in the saloon, and then the Canalettos go and then the most tasty morsel, the most productive of all. Having got rid of cables and wireless,[1] and having got rid of the only part of the railways that paid and having got rid of the part of the steel industry that paid, and having sold this and that, the great thing of the monopoly of the telephone system came on the market. They were like the two Rembrandts that were still left, and they went.

Now we are promised in the Queen's Speech[2] a further sale of anything that can be scraped up. You can't sell the coal mines, I'm afraid, because nobody would buy them. In order to cover this ingenious resort, not so much to the market as to the auctioneer, we've invented a wonderful new and very ungrammatical word called 'privatization', and by giving a kind of colour of conformity with Conservative principles that seems to be run by private enterprise, it has got away with the selling of assets on a colossal scale. Assets that can never be replaced.

I'm sorry now to see that the royal dockyards are to go,[3] the dockyards where Henry VIII built our first great fleets,[4] which Pepys nurtured so long,[5] which built the ships that Nelson fought in.[6] I don't think we're going to sell the equity but we are going to get rid of all the admirals and put in a lot of private enterprise operators, which will make nice jobs for the retired civil servants and the rest. But this in itself would not have kept us afloat. What has happened, the miracle that has happened, in the decade of your lifetime as a group, has been the discovery of North Sea oil.[7]

This astonishing event has changed the whole situation of Britain. We have become accustomed to think in terms of money equal to the huge sums of the Middle Eastern powers — the Persian Gulf has flowed into the North Sea — and these huge sums, together with the sale of internal assets, has enabled the budget to be balanced: that, and that alone.

The balance of payments shows a very heavy loss. In the ordinary working of the economy we are practically bankrupt, save for oil. We are the Abu Dhabi[8] of today: a small oil island. Perhaps it will go on for ever, perhaps it won't, and surely we ought to be taking immediate steps to turn our minds from the rather narrow politics that [look] like being discussed in the next year or so, to the real issue that lies behind. It is this: that the heavy burden of a welfare state, the high costs of defence, the other needs of government expenditure in all parts of the world, cannot be sustained without an increase in the total amount of wealth produced. That is the only real test and it is in that that we have fallen behind.

Our productivity is low and shows no sign of really increasing, except with occasional spurts. Our methods are largely obsolete. We are far behind the true great nations of the East and the West, who have exploited the new industrial revolution — on which, without perhaps knowing it, we are launched.

For the third industrial revolution — which is based on the silicon chip, the

[1] Stockton probably refers to the privatization of the telecommunications utility British Telecom (BT) in 1984. Cable & Wireless was the parent company of Mercury Communications, which had been established in 1983 to challenge BT's monopoly.

[3] The privatization of London's Royal Docks in the mid-1980s was epitomized by the Canary Wharf development at the Isle of Dogs.
[4] The English monarch Henry VIII (1491–1547) sponsored the first major expansion of the Royal Navy during his reign, 1509–47.
[5] The English diarist Samuel Pepys (1633–1703) was appointed Clerk of the Acts to the Navy Board in 1660, became secretary to the Admiralty in 1672 and worked for three decades to secure the upkeep and expansion of the fleet. He also saved the Royal Navy's headquarters during the Great Fire of London in 1666.

[2] At the State Opening of Parliament, a ceremony held at the start of each parliamentary session, the reigning monarch reads a statement outlining the government's legislative programme for the session ahead.

[6] The English naval commander Horatio Nelson, 1st Viscount Nelson (1758–1805) defeated NAPOLEON BONAPARTE's fleet – but was fatally wounded – at the Battle of Trafalgar.
[7] North Sea oil and gas fields were in fact discovered in the late 1950s, but oil was first piped ashore in 1975.

[8] The largest of the highly prosperous, oil-rich United Arab Emirates.

robot and the automated plant – is taking the place of the old ones: the first which was based on coal and steam, and the second based on oil and the motor car engine. This revolution cannot be stopped. If we do not adopt it, we shall fall still further behind; if we do adopt it we shall have immense, immediate difficulties, for the more plants become capital-intensive and less labour-intensive, unemployment is likely to increase rather than decrease in the short run. But if the wealth is produced, if the productivity is increased, if we can restore the old prestige of British industry, then the wealth that follows will give employment in many secondary industries ...

There are of course many advanced and progressive and clever men leading some of the great industries, who have adopted these processes and are making a great success of them – hence the comparative high standards in the south of England. However, we have not really begun – as they have in the United States, or in Japan, or even in Taiwan – to adopt the thing that is bound to come and take the place of the old.

We cannot stop it – the tide moves on – any more than we could stop the first industrial revolution, with all its sad results: the herding of the country people into the cities, ill-built and ill-drained houses; and at the same time the destruction of the old rural industries which had kept England going for 400–500 years, that is, the cottage spinning wheel and the cottage loom. This was all abolished, swept into the factories. We know the results: the employment of children, the terrible situation against the people without trade unions and without public opinion that could defend them. They could find but very few defenders, certainly not among what is called the leaders of liberal progressive opinion, like Mr Cobden and Mr Bright.[9] This time, if we are to make the conversion to this new system which alone could save us, we must do it all together.

It is a mistake to believe that the Japanese triumphs have been produced by a system of uncontrolled private enterprise. In fact there has been a very close partnership between a highly organized government and a highly organized industry. To do this we must surely adopt a new attitude or try to reach it. It demands not the politics of confrontation but the politics of union. It demands that people should try, in achieving this great purpose, to work together and give it their best. If we do – if we can rouse our people to something like the enthusiasm and determination which has carried them in my lifetime through two devastating and terrible wars; if we can get something like the spirit that united us during that awful period – then I believe that we could approach this task, guided by the expert opinion that we can call up and supported by a strong opinion that is the only way to meet our burdens.

It is not to scrimp and save here and there, not by selling off the national assets, but by the creation of wealth on a scale much more equivalent to that which followed the creation of the steam engine in 1840 ... Let us see whether, by close co-operation among all our people in every walk of life, we can promote not merely an acceptance but a demand for the only method now available to us to meet not only the burdens of today, but the burdens of the future.

These, my friends, are even greater than appears on paper; so great that statisticians hardly dare to publish them. Pensioners are growing at an alarming rate. Old gentlemen like me insist on living to a ridiculous age! The aged grow poor all the time. Where I live, those who have to be looked after have grown enormously since I was a boy. The demands for education are

[9] The English businessmen and politicians Richard Cobden (1804–65) and JOHN BRIGHT were leading radical thinkers of their day. They formed the Anti-Corn Law League in 1838 to campaign against protective tariffs on corn imports that inflated the price of bread, a staple of the working-class diet.

very big, both for equipment and personnel, and it is on the education of very highly developed and intelligent people that our power to use the new methods will depend.

The same way, almost everything in front of us shows signs, not of natural reduction but of natural growth. Yet I say, if we can bring together the spirit which once we had – which many of us perhaps still remember, with all their horror and sorrows, with all the wounds, family tragedies – the years of war were in a sense not altogether unhappy years. And why, my friends? Because we were all on the same side.

Malcolm X
American civil rights leader

Malcolm X *originally Malcolm Little, later el-Hajj Malik el-Shabazz* (1925–65) was born in Omaha, Nebraska, the son of a radical Baptist minister. He grew up in Lansing, Michigan and Boston, Massachusetts. After an adolescence of violence, narcotics and petty crime, he evaded the draft during World War II by feigning mental illness. He was convicted of burglary in 1946 and sent to prison in Charlestown, Massachusetts, where he came under the influence of Elijah Muhammad (1897–1975), leader of the Nation of Islam movement. He embraced Islam, changed his name, and after his release in 1952 became Muhammad's chief disciple; he greatly expanded the organization's following and became the most effective spokesman for Black Power. In 1963 Malcolm was suspended from the Nation of Islam after disagreements with Muhammad and attracted the profound hatred of the leader's loyal followers. In 1964, Malcolm founded the Organization for Afro-American Unity, dedicated to the alliance of American blacks and other non-white peoples. In the last year of his life, following a pilgrimage to Mecca, Malcolm announced his conversion to orthodox Islam and put forward his belief in a possible brotherhood between blacks and whites. Malcolm's extreme stance and the inflammatory nature of his oratory, which had scared many whites, appealed to many blacks in the northern urban ghettos, but had been met with criticism by moderate civil rights leaders, who deplored his violent message. In February 1965 Malcolm died after being shot 15 times at Audubon Ballroom in Harlem, New York City. Three black men were convicted of the murder, though this verdict was controversial.

'The ballot or the bullet'
3 April 1964, Cleveland, Ohio, USA

This powerful speech is a response to the sweeping events of its time – as Malcolm X says here, 1964 'threatens to be the most explosive year America has ever witnessed'. In the run-up to the presidential elections in November, there was an urgent desire among African–Americans for President LYNDON B JOHNSON to secure passage of the civil rights legislation proposed by President JOHN F KENNEDY before he was assassinated. This was partly expressed in the increasing refusal of many black people to accept the programme of non-violent protest endorsed by MARTIN LUTHER KING.

Also in 1964 came Malcolm's own break from the Nation of Islam and a shift in his stance, in recognition that the struggle for equality was moving from the political to the economic sphere.

Malcolm urges assertion over compromise; in place of King's dream of multi-racial harmony, he describes a 'nightmare' of segregation and mistreatment – the only response to which, he urges, must be black unity and black action. Malcolm took the phrase 'the ballot or the bullet' from the 19th-century abolitionist leader FREDERICK DOUGLASS, but its roots go to the heart of American history, and the anti-colonial war of liberation from England.

[1] The US academic and writer Louis Lomax (1922–70).

[2] The US clergyman and politician Rev Adam Clayton Powell, Jr (1908–72) served in the US House of Representatives, 1945–67 and 1969–71, and chaired the Labour and Education Committee from 1961. He had succeeded his father as pastor of the Abyssinian Baptist Church, Harlem, New York in 1937.

[3] The US clergyman Rev Milton Galamison (1923–88) was pastor at the Siloam Presbyterian Church in Brooklyn, New York. He led the Committee for Integrated Schools, which imposed a city-wide student boycott on the school system.

Mr Moderator, Brother Lomax,[1] brothers and sisters, friends and enemies: I just can't believe everyone in here is a friend, and I don't want to leave anybody out. The question tonight, as I understand it, is 'The Negro Revolt, and Where Do We Go From Here?' or 'What Next?' In my little humble way of understanding it, it points toward either the ballot or the bullet.

Before we try and explain what is meant by the ballot or the bullet, I would like to clarify something concerning myself. I'm still a Muslim; my religion is still Islam. That's my personal belief. Just as Adam Clayton Powell[2] is a Christian minister who heads the Abyssinian Baptist Church in New York, but at the same time takes part in the political struggles to try and bring about rights to the black people in this country; and Dr Martin Luther King is a Christian minister down in Atlanta, Georgia, who heads another organization fighting for the civil rights of black people in this country; and Reverend Galamison[3] – I guess you've heard of him – is another Christian minister in New York who has been deeply involved in the school boycotts to eliminate segregated education; well, I myself am a minister – not a Christian minister, but a Muslim minister – and I believe in action on all fronts, by whatever means necessary.

Although I'm still a Muslim, I'm not here tonight to discuss my religion. I'm not here to try and change your religion. I'm not here to argue or discuss anything that we differ about, because it's time for us to submerge our differences and realize that it is best for us to first see that we have the same problem, a common problem, a problem that will make you catch hell whether you're a Baptist, or a Methodist, or a Muslim, or a nationalist. Whether you're educated or illiterate, whether you live on the boulevard or in the alley, you're going to catch hell just like I am. We're all in the same boat and we all are going to catch the same hell from the same man. He just happens to be a white man. All of us have suffered here, in this country, political oppression at the hands of the white man, economic exploitation at the hands of the white man, and social degradation at the hands of the white man.

Now in speaking like this, it doesn't mean that we're anti-white, but it does mean we're anti-exploitation, we're anti-degradation, we're anti-oppression. And if the white man doesn't want us to be anti-him, let him stop oppressing and exploiting and degrading us. Whether we are Christians or Muslims or nationalists or agnostics or atheists, we must first learn to forget our differences.

If we have differences, let us differ in the closet. When we come out in front, let us not have anything to argue about until we get finished arguing with the man. If the late President Kennedy could get together with **KHRUSHCHEV** and exchange some wheat,[4] we certainly have more in common with each other than Kennedy and Khrushchev had with each other.

If we don't do something real soon, I think you'll have to agree that we're going to be forced either to use the ballot or the bullet. It's one or the other in 1964. It isn't that time is running out — time has run out!

Nineteen sixty-four threatens to be the most explosive year America has ever witnessed. The most explosive year. Why? It's a political year. It's the year when all of the white politicians will be back in the so-called negro community, jiving you and me for some votes. The year when all of the white political crooks will be right back in your and my community with their false promises, building up our hopes for a letdown, with their trickery and their treachery, with their false promises which they don't intend to keep. As they nourish these dissatisfactions, it can only lead to one thing, an explosion; and now we have the type of black man on the scene in America today — I'm sorry, Brother Lomax — who just doesn't intend to turn the other cheek any longer.

Don't let anybody tell you anything about the odds are against you. If they draft you, they send you to Korea and make you face 800 million Chinese.[5] If you can be brave over there, you can be brave right here. These odds aren't as great as those odds. And if you fight here, you will at least know what you're fighting for.

I'm not a politician, not even a student of politics; in fact, I'm not a student of much of anything. I'm not a Democrat. I'm not a Republican, and I don't even consider myself an American. If you and I were Americans, there'd be no problem. Those honkies[6] that just got off the boat, they're already Americans; Polacks[7] are already Americans; the Italian refugees are already Americans. Everything that came out of Europe, every blue-eyed thing, is already an American. And as long as you and I have been over here, we aren't Americans yet.

[4] In June 1963, Kennedy arranged to sell $250 million of surplus wheat to the Soviet Union to alleviate a food shortage.

[5] Both US and Chinese troops were engaged in the Korean War. US forces lost more than 50,000 troops, many of them African–American. However this war effectively ended in 1953. Malcolm may have intended to refer to the Vietnam War, although large-scale US involvement did not begin until later in 1964.

[6] A pejorative term for white people.
[7] A pejorative term for Polish immigrants.

Well, I am one who doesn't believe in deluding myself. I'm not going to sit at your table and watch you eat, with nothing on my plate, and call myself a diner. Sitting at the table doesn't make you a diner, unless you eat some of what's on that plate. Being here in America doesn't make you an American. Being born here in America doesn't make you an American. Why, if birth made you American, you wouldn't need any legislation; you wouldn't need any amendments to the Constitution; you wouldn't be faced with civil rights filibustering in Washington, DC, right now. They don't have to pass civil rights legislation to make a Polack an American.

No, I'm not an American. I'm one of the 22 million black people who are the victims of Americanism. One of the 22 million black people who are the victims of democracy, nothing but disguised hypocrisy. So, I'm not standing here speaking to you as an American, or a patriot, or a flag-saluter, or a flag-waver – no, not I. I'm speaking as a victim of this American system. And I see America through the eyes of the victim. I don't see any American dream; I see an American nightmare.

These 22 million victims are waking up. Their eyes are coming open. They're beginning to see what they used to only look at. They're becoming politically mature. They are realizing that there are new political trends from coast to coast. As they see these new political trends, it's possible for them to see that every time there's an election, the races are so close that they have to have a recount … With Kennedy and NIXON when they ran for president, it was so close they had to count all over again.[8] Well, what does this mean? It means that when white people are evenly divided, and black people have a bloc of votes of their own: it is left up to them to determine who's going to sit in the White House and who's going to be in the dog house.

It was the black man's vote that put the present administration in Washington, DC. Your vote, your dumb vote, your ignorant vote, your wasted vote put in an administration in Washington, DC, that has seen fit to pass every kind of legislation imaginable, saving you until last, then filibustering on top of that.

And your and my leaders have the audacity to run around clapping their hands and talk about how much progress we're making. And what a good president we have. If he wasn't good in Texas, he sure can't be good in Washington, DC.[9] Because Texas is a lynch state. It is in the same breath as Mississippi, no different; only they lynch you in Texas with a Texas accent and lynch you in Mississippi with a Mississippi accent.

And these negro leaders have the audacity to go and have some coffee in the White House with a Texan, a southern cracker – that's all he is – and then come out and tell you and me that he's going to be better for us because, since he's from the South, he knows how to deal with the Southerners. What kind of logic is that? Let Eastland[10] be president, he's from the South too. He should be better able to deal with them than JOHNSON.

In this present administration, they have in the House of Representatives 257 Democrats to only 177 Republicans. They control two-thirds of the House vote. Why can't they pass something that will help you and me? In the Senate, there are 67 senators who are of the Democratic Party. Only 33 of them are Republicans. Why, the Democrats have got the government sewed up, and you're the one who sewed it up for them.

And what have they given you for it? Four years in office, and just now getting around to some civil rights legislation … They get all the negro vote,

[8] In the presidential election of 1960, Nixon received marginally more of the popular vote than Kennedy, but under the electoral college system, Kennedy won by a clear margin. Recounts were held in eleven states.

[9] Following Kennedy's assassination, he was succeeded by Vice President Johnson, a Texan, who in fact introduced reforms to tackle poverty. He also hired the first African–American White House secretary, Jerri Whittington, who became a celebrity as a result.

[10] The US politician James O Eastland (1904–86) served as a Democrat Senator from Mississippi, 1941 and 1943–1978. He was notorious for his unashamed racist and anti-Semitic views and his opposition to the civil rights movement.

and after they get it, the negro gets nothing in return. All they did when they got to Washington was give a few big negroes big jobs. Those big negroes didn't need big jobs; they already had jobs. That's camouflage, that's trickery, that's treachery, window-dressing … you put the Democrats first and the Democrats put you last … [11]

That's why, in 1964, it's time now for you and me to become more politically mature and realize what the ballot is for; what we're supposed to get when we cast a ballot; and that if we don't cast a ballot, it's going to end up in a situation where we're going to have to cast a bullet. It's either a ballot or a bullet …

What I'm trying to impress upon you, in essence, is this: you and I in America are faced not with a segregationist conspiracy, we're faced with a government conspiracy … You don't have anybody putting blocks in your path but people who are a part of the government. The same government that you go abroad to fight for and die for is the government that is in a conspiracy to deprive you of your voting rights, deprive you of your economic opportunities, deprive you of decent housing, deprive you of decent education.

You don't need to go to the employer alone, it is the government itself, the government of America, that is responsible for the oppression and exploitation and degradation of black people in this country. And you should drop it in their lap. This government has failed the negro. This so-called democracy has failed the negro. And all these white liberals have definitely failed the negro …

You take the people who are in this audience right now. They're poor. We're all poor as individuals. Our weekly salary individually amounts to hardly anything. But if you take the salary of everyone in here collectively, it'll fill up a whole lot of baskets. It's a lot of wealth. If you can collect the wages of just these people right here for a year, you'll be rich — richer than rich. When you look at it like that, think how rich Uncle Sam had to become, not with this handful, but millions of black people. Your and my mother and father, who didn't work an eight-hour shift, but worked from 'can't see' in the morning until 'can't see' at night, and worked for nothing, making the white man rich, making Uncle Sam rich. This is our investment. This is our contribution, our blood.

Not only did we give of our free labour, we gave of our blood. Every time he had a call to arms, we were the first ones in uniform. We died on every battlefield the white man had. We have made a greater sacrifice than anybody who's standing up in America today. We have made a greater contribution and have collected less. Civil rights, for those of us whose philosophy is black nationalism, means: 'Give it to us now. Don't wait for next year. Give it to us yesterday, and that's not fast enough.'

I might stop right here to point out one thing. Whenever you're going after something that belongs to you, anyone who's depriving you of the right to have it is a criminal. Understand that. Whenever you are going after something that is yours, you are within your legal rights to lay claim to it. And anyone who puts forth any effort to deprive you of that which is yours is breaking the law, is a criminal. And this was pointed out by the Supreme Court decision. It outlawed segregation.

Which means segregation is against the law. Which means a segregationist is breaking the law. A segregationist is a criminal. You can't label him as anything other than that. And when you demonstrate against segregation, the law is on your side. The Supreme Court is on your side.

Now, who is it that opposes you in carrying out the law? The police department itself. With police dogs and clubs. Whenever you demonstrate against segregation, whether it is segregated education, segregated housing, or anything else, the law is on your side, and anyone who stands in the way is not the law any longer. They are breaking the law; they are not representatives of the law.

Any time you demonstrate against segregation and a man has the audacity to put a police dog on you, kill that dog, kill him, I'm telling you, kill that dog. I say it, if they put me in jail tomorrow, kill that dog. Then you'll put a stop to it. Now, if these white people in here don't want to see that kind of action, get down and tell the mayor to tell the police department to pull the dogs in. That's all you have to do. If you don't do it, someone else will.

If you don't take this kind of stand, your little children will grow up and look at you and think 'shame'. If you don't take an uncompromising stand, I don't mean go out and get violent; but at the same time you should never be non-violent unless you run into some non-violence. I'm non-violent with those who are non-violent with me. But when you drop that violence on me, then you've made me go insane, and I'm not responsible for what I do. And that's the way every negro should get.

Any time you know you're within the law, within your legal rights, within your moral rights, in accord with justice, then die for what you believe in. But don't die alone. Let your dying be reciprocal. This is what is meant by equality. What's good for the goose is good for the gander …

Uncle Sam's hands are dripping with blood, dripping with the blood of the black man in this country. He's the earth's number-one hypocrite. He has the audacity – yes, he has – imagine him posing as the leader of the free world. The free world! And you over here singing 'We Shall Overcome'. Expand the civil rights struggle to the level of human rights. Take it into the United Nations, where our African brothers can throw their weight on our side, where our Asian brothers can throw their weight on our side, where our Latin-American brothers can throw their weight on our side, and where 800 million Chinamen are sitting there waiting to throw their weight on our side.

Let the world know how bloody his hands are. Let the world know the hypocrisy that's practised over here. Let it be the ballot or the bullet. Let him know that it must be the ballot or the bullet.

Nelson Mandela
South African lawyer and statesman

Nelson Rolihlahla Mandela (1918–2013) was born in Umtata, the son of a local chief. He practised as a lawyer in Johannesburg, establishing South Africa's first black legal practice. In 1944 he joined the African National Congress (ANC), and for the next 20 years he directed a campaign of defiance against the government and its policy of apartheid. The ANC was banned in 1960 after 69 protesters were shot dead by police at Sharpeville. In 1961, Mandela organized a three-day national strike, and in 1964 he was sentenced to life imprisonment for political offences including sabotage and treason. From his prison cell, Mandela became a symbol of resistance to apartheid, acquiring a charisma that was enhanced by his refusal to negotiate with the authorities. During the 1970s and 1980s, Mandela became an international figure and the focus of an increasingly powerful international campaign for his release, in which his second wife Winnie (1934–) played a leading part. In 1988 his 70th birthday prompted further demands for his release, and international alarm at reports of his declining health led to his being moved to a more comfortable confinement. The liberalizing measures of F W de Klerk (1936–), who served as president 1989–94, began the process of dismantling apartheid. De Klerk visited Mandela in prison within months of his election in 1989, lifted the ban on the ANC, removed restrictions on political groups, called a halt to executions and finally ordered Mandela's release in February 1990. In 1991 Mandela was elected president of the ANC and entered into talks with de Klerk about the country's future. He travelled extensively to win support for continued international pressure to abolish apartheid completely. In 1993 Mandela and de Klerk were joint winners of the Nobel Peace Prize. On 10 May 1994, following South Africa's first multi-racial elections, Mandela was inaugurated as South Africa's first black president. His marriage to Winnie came under increasing strain as a result of her controversial activities and associations. They separated in 1992 and divorced in 1996. This embarrassment, together with continued hostility between the ANC and the Zulu Inkatha movement, only slightly tarnished Mandela's triumph as the new leader of his country, and he continued to strengthen relations with South Africa's trading partners in Europe and America. His term as president ended in 1999.

'There is no easy walk to freedom anywhere'
21 September 1953, Transvaal, South Africa

Introduced by the Nationalist government from 1948, apartheid was implemented through a series of statutes. In 1950, the Group Areas Act banned black South Africans from various urban areas unless they held a 'pass'; and the Suppression of Communism Act enabled the government to restrict the movement of its political opponents. In 1953, the Bantu Education Act lowered schooling standards for black children; and the Native Labour (Settlement of Disputes) Act prohibited strike action by black workers. These developments galvanized the previously conservative ANC, which began to call for acts of public disobedience.

Mandela was elected president of the Transvaal branch of the ANC in early 1953, but had been served with a banning order. This address to the Transvaal Conference was therefore read on his behalf.

In the speech, an edited version of which is given here, he describes the dreadful conditions imposed on black South Africans by the apartheid laws. He rejects the new laws, denouncing them as measures to bolster white rule. He also reminds his hearers that white supremacy has been questioned and superseded all over the world and calls for action to challenge the unjust minority government and support the trade unions.

The living conditions of the people, already extremely difficult, are steadily worsening and becoming unbearable. The purchasing power of the masses is progressively declining and the cost of living is rocketing. Bread is now dearer than it was two months ago. The cost of milk, meat and vegetables is beyond the pockets of the average family and many of our people cannot afford them.

The people are too poor to have enough food to feed their families and children. They cannot afford sufficient clothing, housing and medical care. They are denied the right to security in the event of unemployment, sickness, disability, old age and where these exist, they are of an extremely inferior and useless nature.

Because of lack of proper medical amenities, our people are ravaged by such dreaded diseases as tuberculosis, venereal disease, leprosy, pellagra, and infantile mortality is very high. The recent state budget made provision for the increase of the cost-of-living allowances for Europeans and not a word was said about the poorest and most hard-hit section of the population – the African people.

The insane policies of the government, which have brought about an explosive situation in the country, have definitely scared away foreign capital from South Africa and the financial crisis through which the country is now passing is forcing many industrial and business concerns to close down, to retrench their staffs and unemployment is growing every day.

The farm labourers are in a particularly dire plight. You will perhaps recall the investigations and exposures of the semi-slave conditions on the Bethal farms made in 1948[1] … You will recall how human beings, wearing only sacks with holes for their heads and arms, never given enough food to eat, slept on cement floors on cold nights with only their sacks to cover their shivering bodies. You will remember how they are woken up as early as 4am and taken to work on the fields with the *indunas*[2] *sjambokking*[3] those who tried to straighten their backs, who felt weak and dropped down because of hunger and sheer exhaustion.

You will also recall the story of human beings toiling pathetically from the early hours of the morning till sunset, fed only on mealie meal served on filthy sacks spread on the ground and eating with their dirty hands. People falling ill and never once being given medical attention.

You will also recall the revolting story of a farmer who was convicted for tying a labourer by his feet from a tree and had him flogged to death, pouring boiling water into his mouth whenever he cried for water. These things which have long vanished from many parts of the world still flourish in South Africa today. None will deny that they constitute a serious challenge to Congress and we are in duty bound to find an effective remedy for these obnoxious practices.

The government has introduced in Parliament the Native Labour (Settlement of Disputes) Bill and the Bantu Education Bill. Speaking on the Labour Bill, the Minister of Labour, Ben Schoeman, openly stated that the aim of this wicked measure is to bleed African trade unions to death. By forbidding strikes and lockouts it deprives Africans of the one weapon the workers have to improve their position. The aim of the measure is to destroy the present African trade unions …

The Minister of Native Affairs, Verwoerd,[4] has also been brutally clear in explaining the objects of the Bantu Education Bill. According to him, the aim of this law is to teach our children that Africans are inferior to Europeans. African education would be taken out of the hands of people who taught equality between black and white. When this bill becomes law, it will not be the parents but the Department of Native Affairs which will decide whether an African child should receive higher or other education. It might well be that the children of those who criticize the government and who fight its policies will almost certainly be taught how to drill rocks in the mines and how to plough potatoes on the farms of Bethal. High education might well be the privilege of those children whose families have a tradition of collaboration with the ruling circles.

The attitude of the Congress on these bills is very clear and unequivocal. Congress totally rejects both bills without reservation … At a time when every genuine Congressite should fight unreservedly for the recognition of African trade unions and the realization of the principle that everyone has

[1] Bethal is a village in Mpumalanga, whose farms relied on the labour of black prisoners. This practice was exposed by investigative reporting in *Drum*, a magazine established in 1951. Produced by white British editors, it was geared to a black South African readership.

[2] A tribal headman.
[3] Hitting with a traditional long wooden stick used in war.

[4] The Dutch-born politician Hendrik Verwoerd (1901–66) became Minister of Native Affairs in 1950 and was Prime Minister from 1958 until his assassination in 1966.

the right to form and to join trade unions for the protection of his interests, we declare our firm belief in the principles enunciated in the Universal Declaration of Human Rights that everyone has the right to education; that education shall be directed to the full development of human personality and to the strengthening of respect for human rights and fundamental freedoms ... that parents have the right to choose the kind of education that shall be given to their children.

The cumulative effect of all these measures is to prop up and perpetuate the artificial and decaying policy of the supremacy of the white man. The attitude of the government to us is that: 'Let's beat them down with guns and batons and trample them under our feet. We must be ready to drown the whole country in blood if only there is the slightest chance of preserving white supremacy.'

[5] Afrikaans: 'Master race'.

But there is nothing inherently superior about the *herrenvolk*[5] idea of the supremacy of the whites. In China, India, Indonesia and Korea, American, British, Dutch and French imperialism, based on the concept of the supremacy of Europeans over Asians, has been completely and perfectly exploded. In Malaya and Indo-China, British and French imperialisms are being shaken to their foundations by powerful and revolutionary national liberation movements.

In Africa, there are approximately 190 million Africans as against four million Europeans. The entire continent is seething with discontent and already there are powerful revolutionary eruptions in the Gold Coast, Nigeria, Tunisia, Kenya, the Rhodesias and South Africa. The oppressed people and the oppressors are at loggerheads. The day of reckoning between the forces of freedom and those of reaction is not very far off. I have not the slightest doubt that when that day comes truth and justice will prevail.

The intensification of repressions and the extensive use of the bans is designed to immobilize every active worker and to check the national liberation movement. But gone forever are the days when harsh and wicked laws provided the oppressors with years of peace and quiet. The racial policies of the government have pricked the conscience of all men of goodwill and have aroused their deepest indignation. The feelings of the oppressed people have never been more bitter. If the ruling circles seek to maintain their position by such inhuman methods then a clash between the forces of freedom and those of reaction is certain. The grave plight of the people compels them to resist to the death the stinking policies of the gangsters that rule our country ...

Action has become the language of the day. The ties between the working people and the Congress have been greatly strengthened ... Our immediate task is to consolidate these victories, to preserve our organizations and to muster our forces for the resumption of the offensive. To achieve this important task the National Executive of the ANC in consultation with the National Action Committee of the ANC and the

[6] The South African Indian Congress, formed in 1924.

SAIC[6] formulated a plan of action popularly known as the 'M' Plan ... The underlying principle of this plan is the understanding that it is no longer possible to wage our struggle mainly on the old methods of public meetings and printed circulars. The aim is:

1. To consolidate the Congress machinery;
2. To enable the transmission of important decisions taken on a national level to every member of the organization without calling public

meetings, issuing press statements and printing circulars;

3. To build up in the local branches themselves local congresses which will effectively represent the strength and will of the people;

4. To extend and strengthen the ties between Congress and the people and to consolidate Congress leadership.

I appeal to all members of the Congress to redouble their efforts and play their part truly and well in its implementation. The hard, dirty and strenuous task of recruiting members and strengthening our organization through a house-to-house campaign in every locality must be done by you all. From now on, the activity of Congressites must not be confined to speeches and resolutions. Their activities must find expression in wide-scale work among the masses, work which will enable them to make the greatest possible contact with the working people.

You must protect and defend your trade unions. If you are not allowed to have your meetings publicly, then you must hold them over your machines in the factories, on the trains and buses as you travel home. You must have them in your villages and shanty-towns. You must make every home, every shack and every mud structure where our people live, a branch of the trade union movement and never surrender …

The friends of the people are distinguishable by the ready and disciplined manner in which they rally behind their organization and their readiness to sacrifice when the preservation of the organization has become a matter of life and death. Similarly, enemies and shady characters are detected by the extent to which they consistently attempt to wreck the organization by creating fratricidal strife, disseminating confusion and undermining and even opposing important plans of action to vitalize the organization … We must rid ourselves of such elements and give our organization the striking power of a real militant mass organization.

Kotane, Marks, Bopape, Tloome[7] and I have been banned from attending gatherings and we cannot join and counsel with you on the serious problems that are facing our country. We have been banned because we champion the freedom of the oppressed people of our country and because we have consistently fought against the policy of racial discrimination in favour of a policy which accords fundamental human rights to all, irrespective of race, colour, sex or language. We are exiled from our own people, for we have uncompromisingly resisted the efforts of imperialist America and her satellites to drag the world into the rule of violence and brutal force, into the rule of the napalm, hydrogen and the cobalt bombs where millions of people will be wiped out to satisfy the criminal and greedy appetites of the imperial powers.

We have been gagged because we have emphatically and openly condemned the criminal attacks by the imperialists against the people of Malaya, Vietnam, Indonesia, Tunisia and Tanganyika and called upon our people to identify themselves unreservedly with the cause of world peace and to fight against the war policies of America and her satellites.

We are being shadowed, hounded and trailed because we fearlessly voiced our horror and indignation at the slaughter of the people of Korea[8] and Kenya.[9] The massacre of the Kenyan people by Britain has aroused world-wide indignation and protest. Children are being burnt alive, women are raped, tortured, whipped and boiling water poured on their breasts to force confessions from them that Jomo Kenyatta[10] had administered the Mau Mau oath to them. Men are being castrated and shot dead. In the

[7] The South African activists Moses Kotane (1905–78), John Marks (1903–72), David Bopape (1915–2004) and Dan Tloome (1919–92) were all Communist members of the ANC.

[8] The armistice ending the Korean War had been signed on 27 July, after three years of fighting. Most of the territory between Seoul and the Chinese border had seen conflict, with civilian deaths estimated at two million.

[9] Kenya was under British rule from 1895 until independence in 1963. The violent anti-colonial Mau Mau uprising, chiefly among the Kikuyu people, caused a state of emergency in the early 1950s and was being met with great brutality by the authorities.

[10] The Kenyan nationalist Jomo Kenyatta (c.1892–1978) was jailed in April 1953 for alleged leadership of the Mau Mau uprising. After independence, he became Kenya's first Prime Minister (1963–4) and President (1964–78).

[11] A major ethnic group in Kenya. Its traditional lands, especially in the 'White Highlands', were those most affected by European settlement.

Kikuyu[11] country there are some villages in which the population has been completely wiped out. We are prisoners in our own country because we dared to raise our voices against these horrible atrocities and because we expressed our solidarity with the cause of the Kenyan people.

You can see that there is no easy walk to freedom anywhere, and many of us will have to pass through the valley of the shadow again and again before we reach the mountain tops of our desires.

Dangers and difficulties have not deterred us in the past; they will not frighten us now. But we must be prepared for them like men in business who do not waste energy in vain talk and idle action. The way of preparation lies in our rooting out all impurity and indiscipline from our organization and making it the bright and shining instrument that will cleave its way to freedom.

❧

'An ideal for which I am prepared to die'
20 April 1964, Pretoria, South Africa

❧

The government ban of 1960 drove the ANC underground. It established a military wing, *Umkhonto we Sizwe* ('The Spear of the Nation') with Mandela among its leaders. This organization undertook a sabotage campaign against military, government and civilian targets.

Mandela evaded arrest until August 1962, when he was captured and charged with organizing a strike and leaving the country illegally. He was sentenced to five years in prison.

In July 1963, South African police arrested several other prominent ANC leaders in Rivonia. They were then charged with sabotage, along with Mandela.

At the opening of the defence case in the Supreme Court, Mandela gave a long statement from the dock, of which this is an extract. This was a rare opportunity for Mandela to voice his views in public and he responded with a confident, courageous and supremely well informed speech, condemning the effects of apartheid on South Africa's black majority.

At the conclusion of the trial in June, Mandela was convicted on four charges of sabotage. He was sentenced to life imprisonment, together with seven others – Walter Sisulu, Govan Mbeki, Raymond Mhlaba, Elias Motsoaledi, Andrew Mlangeni, Ahmed Kathrada and Denis Goldberg.

❧

South Africa is the richest country in Africa, and could be one of the richest countries in the world. But it is a land of extremes and remarkable contrasts. The whites enjoy what may well be the highest standard of living in the world, whilst Africans live in poverty and misery. Forty per cent of the Africans live in hopelessly overcrowded and, in some cases, drought-stricken Reserves,[1] where soil erosion and the overworking of the soil makes it impossible for them to live properly off the land. Thirty per cent are labourers, labour tenants, and squatters on white farms and work and live under conditions similar to those of the serfs of the Middle Ages. The other 30 per cent live in towns where they have developed economic and social habits which bring them closer in many respects to white standards. Yet most Africans, even in this group, are impoverished by low incomes and high cost of living …

[1] Accommodation for black South Africans, created under the Native Land Act of 1913, and primarily intended as pools of migrant labour.

Poverty goes hand-in-hand with malnutrition and disease. The incidence of malnutrition and deficiency diseases is very high amongst Africans. Tuberculosis, pellagra, *kwashiorkor*,[2] gastroenteritis, and scurvy bring death and destruction of health. The incidence of infant mortality is one of the highest in the world. According to the Medical Officer of Health for Pretoria, tuberculosis kills 40 people a day (almost all Africans), and in 1961 there were 58,491 new cases reported. These diseases not only destroy the vital organs of the body, but they result in retarded mental conditions

[2] A disease caused by malnutrition, often developed by an infant weaned too early so that a younger sibling can be breast-fed. The name translates as 'one who is displaced'.

and lack of initiative, and reduce powers of concentration. The secondary results of such conditions affect the whole community and the standard of work performed by African labourers.

The complaint of Africans, however, is not only that they are poor and the whites are rich, but that the laws which are made by the whites are designed to preserve this situation. There are two ways to break out of poverty. The first is by formal education, and the second is by the worker acquiring a greater skill at his work and thus higher wages. As far as Africans are concerned, both these avenues of advancement are deliberately curtailed by legislation.

The present government has always sought to hamper Africans in their search for education. One of their early acts, after coming into power, was to stop subsidies for African school feeding. Many African children who attended schools depended on this supplement to their diet. This was a cruel act.

There is compulsory education for all white children at virtually no cost to their parents, be they rich or poor. Similar facilities are not provided for the African children, though there are some who receive such assistance. African children, however, generally have to pay more for their schooling than whites. According to figures quoted by the South African Institute of Race Relations in its 1963 journal, approximately 40 per cent of African children in the age group between 7 and 14 do not attend school. For those who do attend school, the standards are vastly different from those afforded to white children …

The quality of education is also different. According to the *Bantu Educational Journal*, only 5,660 African children in the whole of South Africa passed their Junior Certificate[3] in 1962, and in that year only 362 passed matric. This is presumably consistent with the policy of Bantu education, about which the present prime minister said, during the debate on the Bantu Education Bill in 1953:

> 'When I have control of native education I will reform it so that natives will be taught from childhood to realize that equality with Europeans is not for them … People who believe in equality are not desirable teachers for Natives. When my Department controls Native education it will know for what class of higher education a Native is fitted, and whether he will have a chance in life to use his knowledge.'

The other main obstacle to the economic advancement of the African is the industrial colour-bar, under which all the better jobs of industry are reserved for whites only. Moreover, Africans who do obtain employment in the unskilled and semi-skilled occupations which are open to them are not allowed to form trade unions which have recognition under the Industrial Conciliation Act. This means that strikes of African workers are illegal, and that they are denied the right of collective bargaining which is permitted to the better-paid white workers. The discrimination in the policy of successive South African governments towards African workers is demonstrated by the so-called 'civilized labour policy' under which sheltered, unskilled government jobs are found for those white workers who cannot make the grade in industry, at wages which far exceed the earnings of the average African employee in industry.

The government often answers its critics by saying that Africans in South Africa are economically better off than the inhabitants of the other

[3] An examination taken by white children at the age of 15. Very few black South Africans reached this level.

countries in Africa. I do not know whether this statement is true and doubt whether any comparison can be made without having regard to the cost-of-living index in such countries. But even if it is true, as far as the African people are concerned it is irrelevant. Our complaint is not that we are poor by comparison with people in other countries, but that we are poor by comparison with the white people in our own country, and that we are prevented by legislation from altering this imbalance.

The lack of human dignity experienced by Africans is the direct result of the policy of white supremacy. White supremacy implies black inferiority. Legislation designed to preserve white supremacy entrenches this notion. Menial tasks in South Africa are invariably performed by Africans. When anything has to be carried or cleaned the white man will look around for an African to do it for him, whether the African is employed by him or not.

Because of this sort of attitude, whites tend to regard Africans as a separate breed. They do not look upon them as people with families of their own; they do not realize that they have emotions – that they fall in love like white people do; that they want to be with their wives and children like white people want to be with theirs; that they want to earn enough money to support their families properly, to feed and clothe them and send them to school. And what 'house-boy' or 'garden-boy' or labourer can ever hope to do this?

Pass laws,[4] which to the Africans are among the most hated bits of legislation in South Africa, render any African liable to police surveillance at any time. I doubt whether there is a single African male in South Africa who has not at some stage had a brush with the police over his pass. Hundreds and thousands of Africans are thrown into jail each year under pass laws. Even worse than this is the fact that pass laws keep husband and wife apart and lead to the breakdown of family life.

Poverty and the breakdown of family life have secondary effects. Children wander about the streets of the townships[5] because they have no schools to go to, or no money to enable them to go to school, or no parents at home to see that they go to school, because both parents (if there be two) have to work to keep the family alive. This leads to a breakdown in moral standards, to an alarming rise in illegitimacy, and to growing violence which erupts not only politically, but everywhere.

Life in the townships is dangerous. There is not a day that goes by without somebody being stabbed or assaulted. And violence is carried out of the townships in the white living areas. People are afraid to walk alone in the streets after dark. Housebreakings and robberies are increasing, despite the fact that the death sentence can now be imposed for such offences. Death sentences cannot cure the festering sore.

Africans want to be paid a living wage. Africans want to perform work which they are capable of doing, and not work which the government declares them to be capable of doing. Africans want to be allowed to live where they obtain work, and not be endorsed out of an area because they were not born there. Africans want to be allowed to own land in places where they work, and not to be obliged to live in rented houses which they can never call their own. Africans want to be part of the general population, and not confined to living in their own ghettoes. African men want to have their wives and children to live with them where they work, and not be forced into an unnatural existence in men's hostels. African women want to be with their menfolk and not be left permanently widowed in the Reserves. Africans want to be allowed out after eleven o'clock at night and

[4] Originally introduced by British governors in 1923, the system which required black South Africans to carry pass books was preserved and extended under apartheid. Protests culminated in the Sharpeville massacre of 1960.
[5] Urban settlements designed for black South Africans.

not to be confined to their rooms like little children. Africans want to be allowed to travel in their own country and to seek work where they want to and not where the Labour Bureau tells them to. Africans want a just share in the whole of South Africa; they want security and a stake in society.

Above all, we want equal political rights, because without them our disabilities will be permanent. I know this sounds revolutionary to the whites in this country, because the majority of voters will be Africans. This makes the white man fear democracy.

But this fear cannot be allowed to stand in the way of the only solution which will guarantee racial harmony and freedom for all. It is not true that the enfranchisement of all will result in racial domination. Political division, based on colour, is entirely artificial and, when it disappears, so will the domination of one colour group by another. The ANC has spent half a century fighting against racialism. When it triumphs it will not change that policy.

This, then, is what the ANC is fighting. Their struggle is a truly national one. It is a struggle of the African people, inspired by their own suffering and their own experience. It is a struggle for the right to live.

During my lifetime I have dedicated myself to this struggle of the African people. I have fought against white domination, and I have fought against black domination. I have cherished the ideal of a democratic and free society in which all persons live together in harmony and with equal opportunities. It is an ideal which I hope to live for and to achieve. But if needs be, it is an ideal for which I am prepared to die.

&

'On this day of my release'
11 February 1990, Cape Town, South Africa

&

Sentenced to life imprisonment in 1964, Mandela refused to fade from the world's attention. Instead, he became the focus for a growing international anti-apartheid movement. The slogan 'Free Nelson Mandela' was heard at many demonstrations during the 1970s and 1980s – and even became, in 1984, the refrain of a hit single by the English ska band The Specials.

In the face of international disapproval, however, apartheid endured. There were outbreaks of severe violence in black townships, notably in Soweto, near Johannesburg. By the early 1980s, Prime Minister P W Botha (later President) had accepted a need for change, and announced that whites should 'adapt or die'. Some apartheid laws were repealed, but Mandela refused to renounce armed struggle in return for a conditional offer of release in 1985.

On 10 February 1990, Botha's successor F W de Klerk finally ordered Mandela's release.

The following day, the world watched Mandela walk from prison, amazed at the erect, patrician figure who had been hidden from view for so long. Later, he spoke at a rally at Cape Town's Grand Parade. In his speech, he salutes those who had supported him during his imprisonment and who had kept the struggle against apartheid alive. He then insists on the need for a democratic, non-racial South Africa.

After multi-party talks, a constitution was finally agreed in 1993. Following the ANC's election success in 1994, Mandela became president.

&

Friends, comrades and fellow South Africans: I greet you all in the name of peace, democracy and freedom for all. I stand here before you not as a prophet but as a humble servant of you, the people. Your tireless and heroic sacrifices have made it possible for me to be here today. I therefore place the remaining years of my life in your hands.

On this day of my release, I extend my sincere and warmest gratitude to the millions of my compatriots and those in every corner of the globe who have campaigned tirelessly for my release.

I send special greetings to the people of Cape Town, this city which has been my home for three decades. Your mass marches and other forms of struggle have served as a constant source of strength to all political prisoners.

I salute the African National Congress. It has fulfilled our every expectation in its role as leader of the great march to freedom.

I salute our president, Comrade Oliver Tambo,[1] for leading the ANC even under the most difficult circumstances.

I salute the rank and file members of the ANC. You have sacrificed life and limb in the pursuit of the noble cause of our struggle.

I salute combatants of *Umkhonto we Sizwe*,[2] like Solomon Mahlangu and Ashley Kriel, who have paid the ultimate price for the freedom of all South Africans.

I salute the South African Communist Party for its sterling contribution to the struggle for democracy. You have survived 40 years of unrelenting persecution. The memory of great Communists like Moses Kotane, Yusuf Dadoo, Bram Fischer and Moses Mabhida will be cherished for generations to come.

I salute General Secretary Joe Slovo,[3] one of our finest patriots. We are heartened by the fact that the alliance between ourselves and the party remains as strong as it always was.

I salute the United Democratic Front,[4] the National Education Crisis Committee,[5] the South African Youth Congress, the Transvaal and Natal Indian Congresses and COSATU[6] and the many other formations of the Mass Democratic Movement.

I also salute the Black Sash[7] and the National Union of South African Students. We note with pride that you have acted as the conscience of white South Africa. Even during the darkest days in the history of our struggle you held the flag of liberty high. The large-scale mass mobilization of the past few years is one of the key factors which led to the opening of the final chapter of our struggle.

I extend my greetings to the working class of our country. Your organized strength is the pride of our movement. You remain the most dependable force in the struggle to end exploitation and oppression.

I pay tribute to the many religious communities who carried the campaign for justice forward when the organizations for our people were silenced.

I greet the traditional leaders of our country. Many of you continue to walk in the footsteps of great heroes like Hintsa[8] and Sekhukune.[9]

I pay tribute to the endless heroism of youth, you, the young lions. You, the young lions, have energized our entire struggle.

I pay tribute to the mothers and wives and sisters of our nation. You are the rock-hard foundation of our struggle. Apartheid has inflicted more pain on you than on anyone else.

On this occasion, we thank the world community for their great contribution to the anti-apartheid struggle. Without your support our struggle would not have reached this advanced stage. The sacrifice of the front-line states will be remembered by South Africans forever.

My salutations would be incomplete without expressing my deep appreciation for the strength given to me during my long and lonely years in prison by my beloved wife and family. I am convinced that your pain and suffering was far greater than my own …

Today, the majority of South Africans, black and white, recognize that apartheid has no future. It has to be ended by our own decisive mass action

[1] The South African politician Oliver Tambo (1917–93) became acting president of the ANC in 1967, president in 1977 and national chairman in 1991.
[2] The military wing of the ANC, established in 1961.

[3] The Lithuanian-born South African politician Joe Slovo (1926–95) worked in exile after 1963 for the ANC and the South African Communist Party (SACP). He was Chief of Staff of *Umkhonto we Sizwe* from 1985, and played a leading role in negotiations with the government after 1990.

[4] A coalition of anti-apartheid groups formed in 1983, led by Allan Boesak and DESMOND TUTU.
[5] Established in 1986.
[6] The Congress of South African Trade Unions, established in 1985.
[7] An organization of white women, founded in 1955, which promoted non-violent resistance to apartheid.

[8] The African warrior Hintsa (1789–1835) was a Xhosa chief who led his people from 1804. He fought against the British army in the early 19th century and was killed and mutilated by British troops.
[9] The African warrior Sekhukune (1814–82) was King of the Marota people in the Western Transvaal from 1861. He formed the Marota Empire and tried to unite other groups to defend their lands against colonialists.

in order to build peace and security. The mass campaign of defiance and other actions of our organization and people can only culminate in the establishment of democracy.

The destruction caused by apartheid on our subcontinent is incalculable. The fabric of family life of millions of my people has been shattered. Millions are homeless and unemployed. Our economy lies in ruins and our people are embroiled in political strife. Our resort to the armed struggle in 1960, with the formation of the military wing of the ANC, *Umkhonto we Sizwe*, was a purely defensive action against the violence of apartheid. The factors which necessitated the armed struggle still exist today. We have no option but to continue. We express the hope that a climate conducive to a negotiated settlement will be created soon so that there may no longer be the need for the armed struggle.

I am a loyal and disciplined member of the African National Congress. I am therefore in full agreement with all of its objectives, strategies and tactics.

The need to unite the people of our country is as important a task now as it always has been. No individual leader is able to take on this enormous task on his own. It is our task as leaders to place our views before our organization and to allow the democratic structures to decide. On the question of democratic practice, I feel duty-bound to make the point that a leader of the movement is a person who has been democratically elected at a national conference. This is a principle which must be upheld without any exceptions.

Today, I wish to report to you that my talks with the government have been aimed at normalizing the political situation in the country. We have not as yet begun discussing the basic demands of the struggle. I wish to stress that I myself have at no time entered into negotiations about the future of our country except to insist on a meeting between the ANC and the government.

Mr de Klerk has gone further than any other Nationalist president in taking real steps to normalize the situation. However there are further steps, as outlined in the Harare Declaration,[10] that have to be met before negotiations on the basic demands of our people can begin. I reiterate our call for, inter alia, the immediate ending of the State of Emergency and the freeing of all, and not only some, political prisoners. Only such a normalized situation, which allows for free political activity, can allow us to consult our people in order to obtain a mandate.

The people need to be consulted on who will negotiate and on the content of such negotiations. Negotiations cannot take place above the heads or behind the backs of our people. It is our belief that the future of our country can only be determined by a body which is democratically elected on a non-racial basis. Negotiations on the dismantling of apartheid will have to address the overwhelming demand of our people for a democratic, non-racial and unitary South Africa. There must be an end to white monopoly on political power and a fundamental restructuring of our political and economic systems, to ensure that the inequalities of apartheid are addressed and our society thoroughly democratized.

It must be added that Mr de Klerk himself is a man of integrity, who is acutely aware of the dangers of a public figure not honouring his undertakings. But as an organization, we base our policy and strategy on the harsh reality we are faced with. And this reality is that we are still suffering under the policy of the Nationalist government.

[10] Adopted by the Organization of African Unity in August 1989, the Harare Declaration raised the possibility of negotiating an end to apartheid. It formed the basis of the 'Declaration on Apartheid and its Destructive Consequences in Southern Africa', adopted by the United Nations in December 1989.

Our struggle has reached a decisive moment. We call on our people to seize this moment, so that the process towards democracy is rapid and uninterrupted. We have waited too long for our freedom. We can no longer wait. Now is the time to intensify the struggle on all fronts. To relax our efforts now would be a mistake which generations to come will not be able to forgive. The sight of freedom looming on the horizon should encourage us to redouble our efforts.

It is only through disciplined mass action that our victory can be assured. We call on our white compatriots to join us in the shaping of a new South Africa. The freedom movement is a political home for you too. We call on the international community to continue the campaign to isolate the apartheid regime. To lift sanctions now would be to run the risk of aborting the process towards the complete eradication of apartheid.

Our march to freedom is irreversible. We must not allow fear to stand in our way. Universal suffrage on a common voters' roll in a united democratic and non-racial South Africa is the only way to peace and racial harmony.

In conclusion I wish to quote my own words during my trial in 1964. They are true today as they were then: 'I have fought against white domination and I have fought against black domination. I have cherished the ideal of a democratic and free society in which all persons live together in harmony and with equal opportunities. It is an ideal which I hope to live for and to achieve. But if needs be, it is an ideal for which I am prepared to die.'

'While poverty persists, there is no true freedom'
3 February 2005, London, England

By now in declining health, Mandela announced his partial retirement from public life in June 2004, at the age of 85. He could, however, be relied on to emerge from retirement to support causes particularly close to his heart.

The 'Make Poverty History' campaign – established by a broad coalition of UK charities, faith groups, trade unions and celebrities – was launched at the beginning of 2005 with the goal of achieving fair trading conditions, abolishing the debts crippling poor countries and organizing appropriate aid. The campaign was to be focused on the meeting of G8 leaders at Gleneagles, Scotland in July, the British presidency of the EU in the second half of the year, the 20th anniversary of the Live Aid concerts and the five-year review of the United Nations' Millennium Goals. Similar campaigns operated in other countries.

Walking with a stick and wearing a fur hat in the cold weather, a frail Mandela addressed about 20,000 supporters at the campaign's first mass rally in Trafalgar Square. He called on the G7 finance ministers and Central Bank governors, meeting in London the next day, to make a concrete commitment to overcoming poverty.

Bob Geldof, chief instigator of Live Aid, also addressed the rally, saying : 'If it isn't this year, then when? I'm tired of the politics of being nice. I'm sick of standing in squares, of linking arms, of tear gas, of records and concerts. I'm sick of this crap. Feed the world, feed the world still.' Mandela also spoke at the Live 8 concert on 3 July in Edinburgh.

I am privileged to be here today at the invitation of the Campaign to Make Poverty History. As you know, I recently formally announced my retirement from public life and should really not be here.

However, as long as poverty, injustice and gross inequality persist in our world, none of us can truly rest. Moreover, the Global Campaign for Action Against Poverty represents such a noble cause that we could not decline the invitation.

Massive poverty and obscene inequality are such terrible scourges of our times – times in which the world boasts breathtaking advances in science, technology, industry and wealth accumulation – that they have to rank alongside slavery and apartheid as social evils.

The Global Campaign for Action Against Poverty can take its place as a public movement alongside the movement to abolish slavery and the international solidarity against apartheid. And I can never thank the people of Britain enough for their support through those days of the struggle against apartheid. Many stood in solidarity with us, just a few yards from this spot.[1]

Through your will and passion, you assisted in consigning that evil system forever to history. But in this new century, millions of people in the world's poorest countries remain imprisoned, enslaved, and in chains. They are trapped in the prison of poverty. It is time to set them free.

Like slavery and apartheid, poverty is not natural. It is man-made and it can be overcome and eradicated by the actions of human beings. And overcoming poverty is not a gesture of charity. It is an act of justice. It is the protection of a fundamental human right, the right to dignity and a decent life. While poverty persists, there is no true freedom.

The steps that are needed from the developed nations are clear. The first is ensuring trade justice. I have said before that trade justice is a truly meaningful way for the developed countries to show commitment to bringing about an end to global poverty.

The second is an end to the debt crisis for the poorest countries. The third is to deliver much more aid and make sure it is of the highest quality. In 2005, there is a unique opportunity for making an impact.

In September, world leaders will gather in New York to measure progress since they made the Millennium Declaration in the year 2000.[2] That declaration promised to halve extreme poverty. But at the moment, the promise is falling tragically behind. Those leaders must now honour their promises to the world's poorest citizens.

Tomorrow, here in London, the G7 finance ministers can make a significant beginning. I am happy to have been invited to meet with them. The G8 leaders, when they meet in Scotland in July,[3] have already promised to focus on the issue of poverty, especially in Africa. I say to all those leaders: do not look the other way; do not hesitate. Recognize that the world is hungry for action, not words. Act with courage and vision.

I am proud to wear the symbol of this global call to action in 2005. This white band is from my country. In a moment, I want to give this band to you – young people of Britain – and ask you to take it forward along with millions of others to the G8 summit in July. I entrust it to you. I will be watching with anticipation.

We thank you for coming here today. Sometimes it falls upon a generation to be great. You can be that great generation. Let your greatness blossom. Of course the task will not be easy. But not to do this would be a crime against humanity, against which I ask all humanity now to rise up.

Make Poverty History in 2005. Make history in 2005. Then we can all stand with our heads held high.

Thank you.

[1] South Africa House, the South African embassy in Trafalgar Square, had been the focus of demonstrations during the apartheid years.

[2] The largest ever gathering of the world's heads of state adopted the UN Millennium Declaration in September 2000. This set out a series of Millennium Development Goals to be reached by 2015.
[3] The G8 summit meeting – between leaders of eight of the world's wealthiest countries – took place at Gleneagles Hotel in Perthshire on 6–8 July 2005.

George C Marshall
American soldier and politician

George Catlett Marshall (1880–1959) was born in Uniontown, Pennsylvania. He was commissioned in 1901, and as Chief of Staff (1939–45) he directed the US Army throughout World War II, becoming its first five-star general. After two years in China as special representative of the president he became Secretary of State (1947–9) and drafted a scheme for the post-war reconstruction of Europe, known as the European Recovery Plan or the Marshall Plan. In 1950 he was made Secretary of Defence by President HARRY S TRUMAN. Among his many admirers was WINSTON CHURCHILL, who described him as both 'a magnificent organizer and builder of armies' and 'a statesman with a penetrating and commanding view of the whole scene'. He was awarded the Nobel Peace Prize in 1953.

'The United States should do whatever it is able to do to assist'

5 June 1947, Cambridge, Massachusetts, USA

❧

General Marshall used the occasion of a Harvard commencement ceremony – at which he received an honorary doctorate – to announce his programme of aid and restructuring for post-war Europe. This scheme, which became known as the Marshall Plan, ran from 1948–51, helping to restabilize the economies of 17 countries in western and southern Europe and so discourage the encroachment of communism. Marshall and Truman recognized that insufficient US assistance during western Europe's last economic crisis (1929–31) had benefited ADOLF HITLER's rise to power.

First-hand accounts of Marshall's address, delivered from the steps of the church in Harvard Yard, describe a nervous speaker who fiddled with his glasses, barely raised his eyes from his text and was sometimes inaudible. But the power of his speech lay in its very lack of rhetoric and its modest delivery. The details of Marshall's proposals are also low-key: there is no mention of numbers, although by 1953 the USA had spent $13 billion on European recovery. All of this was deliberate: Truman's administration was concerned that the plan would not be well received by many Americans. Consequently American journalists were not alerted to Marshall's address, while European media were contacted as soon as it had been made.

❧

[1] The US chemist and public servant James Bryant Conant (1893–1978) was president of Harvard University, 1933–53. He also served as chairman of the National Defense Research Committee, 1941–6, and as an advisor to the National Science Foundation and the Atomic Energy Commission.

Mr President, Dr Conant,[1] members of the Board of Overseers, ladies and gentlemen: I am profoundly grateful, touched by the great distinction and honour and great compliment accorded me by the authorities of Harvard this morning. I am overwhelmed, as a matter of fact, and I am rather fearful of my inability to maintain such a high rating as you've been generous enough to accord to me. In these historic and lovely surroundings, this perfect day, and this very wonderful assembly, it is a tremendously impressive thing to an individual in my position.

But to speak more seriously, I need not tell you that the world situation is very serious. That must be apparent to all intelligent people. I think one difficulty is that the problem is one of such enormous complexity that the very mass of facts presented to the public by press and radio make it exceedingly difficult for the man in the street to reach a clear appraisement of the situation.

Furthermore, the people of this country are distant from the troubled areas of the earth, and it is hard for them to comprehend the plight and consequent reactions of the long-suffering peoples of Europe and the effect of those reactions on their governments in connection with our efforts to promote peace in the world.

In considering the requirements for the rehabilitation of Europe, the physical loss of life, the visible destruction of cities, factories, mines and railroads was correctly estimated, but it has become obvious during recent months that this visible destruction was probably less serious than the dislocation of the entire fabric of European economy. For the past ten years, conditions have been highly abnormal. The feverish preparation for war and the more feverish maintenance of the war effort engulfed all aspects of national economies.

Machinery has fallen into disrepair or is entirely obsolete. Under the arbitrary and destructive Nazi rule, virtually every possible enterprise was geared into the German war machine. Long-standing commercial ties, private institutions, banks, insurance companies and shipping companies disappeared through loss of capital, absorption through nationalization, or by simple destruction.

In many countries, confidence in the local currency has been severely shaken. The breakdown of the business structure of Europe during the war was complete. Recovery has been seriously retarded by the fact that two years after the close of hostilities, a peace settlement with Germany and Austria has not been agreed upon. But even given a more prompt solution of these difficult problems, the rehabilitation of the economic structure of Europe quite evidently will require a much longer time and greater effort than had been foreseen.

There is a phase of this matter which is both interesting and serious. The farmer has always produced the foodstuffs to exchange with the city-dweller for the other necessities of life. This division of labour is the basis of modern civilization. At the present time it is threatened with breakdown. The town and city industries are not producing adequate goods to exchange with the food-producing farmer. Raw materials and fuel are in short supply. Machinery, as I have said, is lacking or worn out. The farmer or the peasant cannot find the goods for sale which he desires to purchase. So the sale of his farm produce for money which he cannot use seems to him an unprofitable transaction. He, therefore, has withdrawn many fields from crop cultivation and he's using them for grazing. He feeds more grain to stock and finds for himself and his family an ample supply of food, however short he may be on clothing and the other ordinary gadgets of civilization.

Meanwhile, people in the cities are short of food and fuel,[2] and in some places approaching starvation levels. So the governments are forced to use their foreign money and credits to procure these necessities abroad. This process exhausts funds which are urgently needed for reconstruction. Thus, a very serious situation is rapidly developing which bodes no good for the world.

The modern system of the division of labour, upon which the exchange of products is based, is in danger of breaking down. The truth of the matter is that Europe's requirements for the next three or four years of foreign food and other essential products – principally from America – are so much greater than her present ability to pay that she must have substantial additional help or face economic, social and political deterioration of a very grave character.

The remedy seems to lie in breaking the vicious circle and restoring the confidence of the people of Europe in the economic future of their own countries and of Europe as a whole. The manufacturer and the farmer throughout wide areas must be able and willing to exchange their product for currencies, the continuing value of which is not open to question.

Aside from the demoralizing effect on the world at large and the possibilities of disturbances arising as a result of the desperation of the people concerned, the consequences to the economy of the United States should be apparent to all. It is logical that the United States should do

[2] The winter of 1946–7 was one of Europe's harshest on record.

[3] The offer of US aid was made to all European states, Communist and non-Communist, in order to avoid the charge that the USA was seeking to divide Europe along ideological lines. The USSR and eastern European nations rejected the plan as a threat to their sovereignty.

whatever it is able to do to assist in the return of normal economic health in the world, without which there can be no political stability and no assured peace. Our policy is directed not against any country or doctrine,[3] but against hunger, poverty, desperation and chaos. Its purpose should be the revival of a working economy in the world, so as to permit the emergence of political and social conditions in which free institutions can exist.

Such assistance, I am convinced, must not be on a piecemeal basis, as various crises develop. Any assistance that this government may render in the future should provide a cure rather than a mere palliative. Any government that is willing to assist in the task of recovery will find full co-operation, I am sure, on the part of the United States government. Any government which manoeuvres to block the recovery of other countries cannot expect help from us. Furthermore, governments, political parties or groups which seek to perpetuate human misery in order to profit therefrom, politically or otherwise, will encounter the opposition of the United States.

It is already evident that before the United States government can proceed much further in its efforts to alleviate the situation and help start the European world on its way to recovery, there must be some agreement among the countries of Europe as to the requirements of the situation and the part those countries themselves will take in order to give a proper effect to whatever actions might be undertaken by this government. It would be neither fitting nor efficacious for our government to undertake to draw up unilaterally a programme designed to place Europe on its feet economically. This is the business of the Europeans. The initiative, I think, must come from Europe.

The role of this country should consist of friendly aid in the drafting of a European programme and of later support of such a programme, so far as it may be practical for us to do so. The programme should be a joint one, agreed to by a number, if not all, European nations.

An essential part of any successful action on the part of the United States is an understanding on the part of the people of America of the character of the problem and the remedies to be applied. Political passion and prejudice should have no part. With foresight, and a willingness on the part of our people to face up to the vast responsibility which history has clearly placed upon our country, the difficulties I have outlined can and will be overcome.

I am sorry that on each occasion I have said something publicly in regard to our international situation, I have been forced by the necessities of the case to enter into rather technical discussions. But to my mind, it is of vast importance that our people reach some general understanding of what the complications really are, rather than react from a passion or a prejudice or an emotion of the moment.

As I said more formally a moment ago, we are remote from the scene of these troubles. It is virtually impossible at this distance merely by reading, or listening, or even seeing photographs and motion pictures, to grasp at all the real significance of the situation. And yet the whole world of the future hangs on a proper judgement. It hangs, I think, to a large extent on the realization of the American people of just what are the various dominant factors.

What are the reactions of the people? What are the justifications of those reactions? What are the sufferings? What is needed? What can best be done? What must be done?

Thank you very much.

Karl Marx
German social, political and economic theorist

Karl Marx (1818–83) was born in Trier to Jewish parents who converted to Protestantism to escape anti-Semitism. He studied at the universities of Bonn (1835–6) and Berlin (1836–41), where he associated with the followers of Hegel, who were concerned particularly with the critique of religion. He worked for the liberal Cologne paper *Rheinische Zeitung* ('Newspaper of the Rhine'), until it was suppressed by the government. In 1844, he emigrated to Paris, where he embraced communism and first stated his belief in the proletariat as the agent of revolution. In Paris, he wrote his first long critique of capitalism, usually called *Economic and Philosophical Manuscripts of 1844* (published 1932), which developed the important Marxist notion of the alienation of man under capitalism. He also began his lifelong friendship with Friedrich Engels (1820–95). He moved to Brussels in 1845, and in collaboration with Engels wrote *German Ideology*, a full statement of his materialist conception of history, and the famous *Communist Manifesto* (1848), a masterpiece of political propaganda. With Engels, he reorganized the Communist League, which met in London in 1847. After the 1848 Paris revolution, he returned to Cologne as editor of the radical *Neue Rheinische Zeitung* ('New Newspaper of the Rhine'), but when that folded in 1849 he took refuge in London. His family lived in some poverty, but at the British Museum he and Engels began the research which fed his major works, *Grundrisse der Kritik der politischen Ökonomie* ('Blueprint for the Critique of Political Economy', 1857–8, published in 1939–41), *Zur Kritik der politischen Ökonomie* ('On the Critique of Political Economy', 1859) and, most notably, his magnum opus *Das Kapital* ('Capital', 3 vols, 1867–94). Though it remained unfinished at his death, *Das Kapital* ranks among the most influential works of the 19th century. In it, Marx developed his mature doctrines of the theory of surplus value, class conflict and the exploitation of the working class, and predicted the victory of Socialism and the decline of the state as communism was achieved. Marx also worked as European correspondent for the *New York Daily Tribune* (1852–62). He later revived his political involvement and was a leading figure in the First International (Working-Men's Association) from 1864 until its effective demise in 1872. The last decade of his life was marked by increasing ill health. He died in 1883 and was buried in Highgate cemetery, London.

'History is the judge – its executioner, the proletarian'
14 April 1856, London, England

By the time he gave this speech, Marx was in his eighth year of residence in Britain, having been expelled from every other country he had attempted to settle in. (It is to the credit of Lord John Russell, prime minister in 1849, that he had resisted pressure from the Prussian government to deport Marx and Engels.) Although by 1856 the grinding poverty in which the Marx family lived had been alleviated by his contributions to radical newspapers in the USA, this year had also seen his wife Jenny struck down with smallpox, which she barely survived. Her health never fully recovered and the illness left her disfigured. Marx wrote to his benefactor Engels that 'such a lousy life is not worth living'.

Yet this speech, given at the Bell Hotel in London, at a banquet to celebrate the fourth anniversary of the Chartist *People's Paper*, sparks with vitality. It also serves to illustrate many of the distinctive qualities of Marx's rhetorical technique. His use of metaphor is present – he alludes both to nature and to the supernatural – as is his characteristically pointed style and brevity.

As his fellow radical Frederick Lessner said, referring to a speech of 1847: 'Marx was a born leader of the people. His speech was brief, convincing and compelling in its logic. He never said a superfluous word; every sentence contained an idea and every idea was an essential link in the chain of his argument.'

[1] A series of popular uprisings occurred throughout Europe in that year, with Russia and Britain virtually the only major nations unaffected. In most cases these were bloodily repressed within months, though social reforms occurred in many countries as a result.

The so-called revolutions of 1848[1] were but poor incidents – small fractures and fissures in the dry crust of European society. However, they denounced the abyss. Beneath the apparently solid surface, they betrayed oceans of liquid matter, only needing expansion to rend into fragments continents of hard rock. Noisily and confusedly, they proclaimed the emancipation of the proletarian – ie the secret of the 19th century, and of the revolution of that century.

That social revolution, it is true, was no novelty invented in 1848. Steam, electricity and the self-acting mule were revolutionists of a rather more dangerous character than even citizens Barbès, Raspail and Blanqui.[2] But although the atmosphere in which we live weighs upon everyone with a 20,000-pound force, do you feel it? No more than European society before 1848 felt the revolutionary atmosphere enveloping and pressing it from all sides. There is one great fact, characteristic of this, our 19th century: a fact which no party dares deny.

On the one hand, there have started into life industrial and scientific forces, which no epoch of the former human history had ever suspected. On the other hand, there exist symptoms of decay, far surpassing the horrors recorded of the latter times of the Roman Empire. In our days, everything seems pregnant with its contrary. Machinery, gifted with the wonderful power of shortening and fructifying human labour, we behold starving and overworking it. The new-fangled sources of wealth, by some strange weird spell, are turned into sources of want. The victories of art seem bought by the loss of character.

At the same pace that mankind masters nature, man seems to become enslaved to other men, or to his own infamy. Even the pure light of science seems unable to shine but on the dark background of ignorance. All our invention and progress seem to result in endowing material forces with intellectual life, and in stultifying human life into a material force.

This antagonism between modern industry and science on the one hand, modern misery and dissolution on the other hand; this antagonism between the productive powers and the social relations of our epoch is a fact – palpable, overwhelming, and not to be controverted. Some parties may wail over it; others may wish to get rid of modern arts, in order to get rid of modern conflicts. Or they may imagine that so signal a progress in industry wants to be completed by as signal a regress in politics.

On our part, we do not mistake the shape of the shrewd spirit that continues to mark all these contradictions. We know that to work well, the new-fangled forces of society, they only want to be mastered by new-fangled men – and such are the working men. They are as much the invention of modern time as machinery itself.

In the signs that bewilder the middle class, the aristocracy and the poor prophets of regression, we do recognize our brave friend, Robin Goodfellow,[3] the old mole that can work in the earth so fast, that worthy pioneer – the Revolution. The English working men are the first-born sons of modern industry. They will then, certainly, not be the last in aiding the social revolution produced by that industry, a revolution which means the emancipation of their own class all over the world, which is as universal as capital rule and wages slavery.

I know the heroic struggles the English working class have gone through since the middle of the last century – struggles less glorious because they are shrouded in obscurity, and burked by the middle-class historian. To revenge the misdeeds of the ruling class, there existed in the Middle Ages, in Germany, a secret tribunal called the *Vehmgericht*.[4] If a red cross was seen marked on a house, people knew that its owner was doomed by the *Vehm*. All the houses of Europe are now marked with the mysterious red cross.

History is the judge – its executioner, the proletarian.

[2] The French activists Armand Barbès (1809–70), François-Vincent Raspail (1794–1878) and Louis Auguste Blanqui (1805–81) were among the most prominent Socialist leaders at the time of the 1848 uprisings in Paris.

[3] An alternative name for Puck, or Pook, the English version of a mischievous forest or nature spirit common in folklore throughout Europe and depicted in Shakespeare's play *A Midsummer Night's Dream*.

[4] From *Vehme* (German: 'judgement') and *Gericht* (German: 'court'). The 'Free Judges' of the League of the Holy Court acted as a secret tribunal in Westphalia from the late 12th century to the mid-16th century. Those they condemned disappeared: their bodies were later displayed hanging from trees.

James Maxton
Scottish politician

James Maxton (1885–1946) was born in Glasgow. He attended the University of Glasgow and became a teacher in the east end of the city. The poverty he witnessed there encouraged him to become a socialist. A supporter of the Independent Labour Party, he became its chairman in 1926. He was MP for Glasgow Bridgeton from 1922 until his death. A man of strong convictions, he was a staunch pacificist, and suffered imprisonment for attempting to foment a strike of Clyde shipyard workers during World War I, in which he was a conscientious objector. One of the most turbulent 'Red Clydesiders', he was expelled from the House of Commons in 1923 for calling a minister a murderer. He remained as chairman of the Independent Labour Party until 1940, leading its secession from the Labour Party in 1932, and became increasingly isolated from mainstream Labour politics. His extreme views won few supporters, but his sincerity gained the respect of all.

'The task of the socialist movement'
August 1927, sound recording for the *New Leader* newspaper, London, England

❧

This brief recording eloquently expresses James Maxton's passion for creating a better world. It is both an optimistic celebration of humankind's technological achievements and a stinging condemnation of the failures of capitalist modernity. The revolutionary ideals that made Maxton stand out from the 'moderate' Labour crowd are evident.

At this point in his career, having initially backed the Labour prime minister RAMSAY MACDONALD, Maxton felt alienated. MacDonald had not done enough, he believed, to combat inequality through state intervention. Frustrated also by the failure of Labour leaders to prosecute the General Strike of 1926 to a revolutionary conclusion, Maxton here emphasizes the need for a more committed class struggle.

A superb orator, Maxton addressed more public audiences than most contemporary politicians and found many supporters amid the economic upheavals of the 1920s. A representative of the poor area of Bridgeton in Glasgow, he demonstrates in this speech that his politics also had a profound international dimension. Maxton's growing involvement with the anti-colonial movement is clearly evident. As chairman of the League Against Imperialism (1927–9) he repeatedly advocated self-government for British colonies in Parliament.

This speech is a poignant rallying cry for men and women across the world, labouring under the injustices of global capitalism, to unite and build a fairer future for all. In 1927 the means were there; all that was required was the will.

❧

Why should people live lives of poverty and toil? Why should people rise in the morning fearing to face life because of the evils, the cares and the sorrows the day may bring? Should life not rather be a carefree, joyous adventure that all should meet with confidence and hope?

This great world we live in is full of interest, beauty and variety, and is peopled by men and women with infinite capacity for happiness. Through the centuries, men and women have struggled to extract the secrets of nature and of Mother Earth; and today we have amassed a great store of knowledge and of skill that gives mankind a control of the earth and its forces, so that these may be pressed into the service of humanity.

From tropical zone to frigid pole, the fruits of the soil are garnered and conveyed to all parts of the globe, and men of all races work in the service of all races. Invention and discovery from day to day bring men closer together, pile up the quantities of wealth produced at ever-increasing rates and ever with increasing speed, transported thousands of miles across the earth's surface, over the sea or even through the air.

And yet, men and women starve and children cry for bread because a very few men claim the earth as their own and make the millions toil for them. The task of the socialist movement in every country in the world is to lighten the workers' toil, to increase the supply of the material things of life in every home, and to remove the horrible insecurity that kills the joy of life and to sweep the owning classes from the shoulders of the disowned.

The scientist has played his part, the writer has played his part. The traveller and explorer have played their part. And now the workers, the common people, must play their part. The wealthy and powerful, blinded by their material riches, do not see the real wealth of humanity itself. And to the workers is left the task of freeing mankind from the fetters of servitude.

The will to liberty, the will to security, the will to happiness are first necessary. Then comes the need for an organization to give expression to that will; and after that, a clear idea of the social structure which can enable mankind freely and easily to give his quota of service and receive his full reward.

The socialist movement fulfils these three functions: it strives to create the will; it builds up the organization to express it, and it has devised a social structure that can produce the world's needs and supply them in secure and certain fact. It calls aloud for the willing help of good and true men and women who are not afraid to fight for a just cause.

Golda Meir
Israeli politician

Golda Meir *née Goldie Mabovich, later Goldie Myerson* (1898–1978) was born in Kiev, Ukraine. Her family emigrated to Milwaukee, USA, when she was eight years old. She married Morris Myerson in 1917 and in 1921 emigrated to Palestine, where she took up social work and became a leading figure in the Labour movement. From 1924, she worked for the Histadrut trade union. She was an Israeli emissary to the USA (1932–4). In 1946, she became head of the Jewish Agency's Political Department, liaising with the British authorities. In 1948, DAVID BEN-GURION appointed her to his provisional government, and she undertook a diplomatic mission to Jordan. One of the signatories of the Declaration of the Establishment of the State of Israel in May 1948, she became Israeli ambassador to the Soviet Union (1948–9), Minister of Labour (1949–56), and Foreign Minister (1956–66). She retired in 1968, but after Prime Minister Levi Eshkol died in office in 1969, she returned to politics, becoming the world's third woman prime minister, aged 71. Her efforts for peace in the Middle East were halted by the fourth Arab–Israeli War (the Yom Kippur War) of 1973 and she resigned in 1974.

'Nothing unites our people more than the desire for peace'
26 May 1970, Jerusalem, Israel

When Golda Meir assumed the premiership of Israel in March 1969, she inherited a series of long-running territorial disputes. The most pressing of these was the 'war of attrition' with Egypt.

In the Six-Day War of June 1967, Israel had gained territory from Egypt, Jordan and Syria, including the Sinai peninsula. This strategically important acquisition enabled Israel to control the Suez Canal, which it closed. The Arab nations refused to recognize the new territorial boundaries, a position arguably supported by a UN resolution of November 1967, though its wording gave rise to dispute.

In June 1968, the Egyptian president Gamal Abdel Nasser launched a war to liberate the canal. Attacks and counter-attacks continued sporadically throughout 1969, and in January 1970, Nasser visited Moscow, where he was granted Soviet military assistance. This was an escalation with global implications. US president RICHARD M NIXON sent a warning letter to Soviet president Alexei Kosygin in February and pressed for peace negotiations, which resumed in April 1970.

Faced with an escalating war and American pressure to withdraw, Meir gave this speech to the Knesset, the Israeli parliament. Firm yet diplomatic, it portrays Israel as an embattled nation seeking peace; and the Arab nations as recalcitrant aggressors refusing to recognize Israel's right to exist.

A ceasefire agreement was signed in August. Neither side gained territory, and despite much heavier Egyptian casualties, both sides claimed victory. Nasser died of a heart attack the following month. His successor, Anwar Sadat, was soon planning the Yom Kippur War of 1973.

Today again, as the guns thunder, I address myself to our neighbours. Stop the killing, end the fire and bloodshed which bring tribulation and torment to all the peoples of the region! End rejection of the ceasefire; end bombardment and raids; end terror and sabotage!

Even Russian pilots will not contrive to destroy the ceasefire lines,[1] and certainly they will not bring peace. The only way to permanent peace and the establishment of secure and recognized boundaries is through negotiations between the Arab states and ourselves, as all sovereign states treat one another, as is the manner of states which recognize each other's right to existence and equality, as is the manner of free peoples, not protectorates enslaved to foreign powers or in thrall to the dark instincts of war, destruction and ruin.

To attain peace, I am ready to go at any hour to any place, to meet any authorized leader of any Arab state – to conduct negotiations with mutual respect, in parity and without preconditions, and with a clear recognition that the problems under controversy can be solved. For there is room to fulfil the national aspirations of all the Arab states and of Israel as well in the

[1] The positions reached at the end of the Six-Day War, with Israel in possession of the occupied territories.

Middle East – and progress, development and co-operation can be hastened among all its nations, in place of barren bloodshed and war without end.

If peace does not yet reign, it is from no lack of willingness on our part: it is the inevitable outcome of the refusal of the Arab leadership to make peace with us. That refusal is still a projection of reluctance to be reconciled to the living presence of Israel within secure and recognized boundaries, still a product of the hope, which flickers on in their hearts, that they will accomplish its destruction. And this has been the state of things since 1948,[2] long before the issue of the territories arose in the aftermath of the Six-Day War.

Moreover, if peace does not yet reign, it is equally not because of any lack of 'flexibility' on our part, or because of the so-called 'rigidity' of our position. That position is: ceasefire, agreement and peace. The Arab governments preach and practise no ceasefire, no negotiation, no agreement and no peace. Which of the two attitudes is stubborn and unyielding? The Arab governments' or ours?

There are some, the Arabs included, who claim that we have not accepted the United Nations resolution of 22 November 1967,[3] and that the Arabs have. In truth, the Arabs only accepted it in a distorted and mutilated interpretation of their own, as meaning an instant and absolute withdrawal of our forces, with no commitment to peace. They were ready to agree to an absolute Israeli withdrawal, but the resolution stipulates nothing of the kind.

According to its text and the exegesis of its compilers, the resolution is not self-implementing. The operative clause calls for the appointment of an envoy, acting on behalf of the Secretary-General,[4] whose task would be to 'establish and maintain contact with the states concerned in order to promote agreement and assist efforts to achieve a peaceful and accepted settlement in accordance with the provisions and principles in this resolution.' …

The Arabs and those others who assert that we are preventing progress towards peace in terms of the resolution have no factual basis for so asserting. They seek merely to throw dust in the world's eyes, to cover up their guilt and deceive the world into thinking that we are the ones who are retarding peace.

It is also argued that, by creating facts on the ground, we are laying down irrevocable conditions which render negotiations superfluous or make it more difficult to enter into them. This contention, too, is wholly mistaken and unfounded. The refusal of the Arab states to enter into negotiations with us is simply an extension of their long-drawn-out intransigence. It goes back to before the Six-Day War, before there were any settlements in the administered territories.

After that fighting, we said – and we left no room for doubt – that we were willing to enter into negotiations with our neighbours with no pre-conditions on either side. This willingness does not signify that we have no opinions, thoughts or demands, or that we shall not exercise our right to articulate them in the discussions, as our neighbours are entitled to no less …

We do not insist that, in negotiating with us, the Arab states forfeit their equal right to make any proposal that they think fit, just as they cannot annul from the outset our right to express, in the discussions, any ideas or proposals which we may form. And there assuredly is no moral or political

[2] The Declaration of the Establishment of the State of Israel was signed on 14 May 1948. The following day, Israel was attacked by Egypt, Syria, Lebanon, Transjordan and Iraq.

[3] UN Resolution 242 called for 'withdrawal of Israeli armed forces from territories occupied in the recent conflict' but this was a translation of an ambiguous text originally written in French. Israel's opponents insisted a state of war would exist until the occupied territories were restored.

[4] The Burmese diplomat U Thant (1909–74) served as UN Secretary-General, 1961–71.

ground for demanding that we refrain from any constructive act in the territories, even though the Arab governments reject the call for peace and make ready for war ...

There is no precedent of a conflict between nations being brought to finality without direct negotiations. In the conflict between the Arabs and Israel, the issue of direct negotiations goes to the very crux of the matter. For the objective is to achieve peace and co-existence, and how will our neighbours ever be able to live with us in peace if they refuse to speak with us at all?

... Only those who deny the right of another state to exist, or who want to avoid recognizing the fact of its sovereignty, can develop the refusal to talk to it into an inculcated philosophy of life, which the pupil swears to adhere to as to a political, national principle. The refusal to talk to us directly is damning evidence that the unwillingness of the Arab leaders to be reconciled with the very being of Israel is the basic reason why peace is still to seek.

I am convinced that it is unreal and utopian to think that using the word 'withdrawal' will pave the way to peace. True, those among us who do believe that the magic of that word is likely to bring us nearer to peace only mean 'withdrawal after peace is achieved' and then only to secure and agreed boundaries, demarcated in a peace treaty. On the other hand, when Arab and Soviet leaders talk of 'withdrawal', they mean complete and outright retreat from all the administered territories, and from Jerusalem, without the making of a genuine peace and without any agreement on new permanent borders, but with an addendum calling for Israel's consent to the return of all the refugees.

Israel's policy is clear, and we shall continue to clarify it at every suitable opportunity, as we have done in the United Nations and elsewhere. No person dedicated to truth could misinterpret our policy: when we speak of secure and recognized boundaries, we do not mean that, after peace is made, the Israel Defence Forces should be deployed beyond the boundaries agreed upon in negotiations with our neighbours. No-one could be misled – Israel desires secure and recognized boundaries with its neighbours.

Israel's defence forces have never crossed its borders in search of conquest, but only when the safeguarding of the existence and bounds of our state demanded it. Nasser's claim that Israel wishes to maintain the ceasefire only so as to freeze the ceasefire lines is preposterous. The ceasefire is necessary, not to perpetuate the lines, but to prevent death and destruction, to make progress easier towards a peace resting upon secure and recognized boundaries. It is necessary as a step upwards on the ladder to peace. Incessant gunfire is a step downward on the ladder to war.

The question is crystal-clear, and there is no point in clouding it with semantics or in trying to escape from reality. There is not a single article in Israel's policy which prevents the making of peace. Nothing is lacking for the making of peace but the Arab persistence in denying Israel's very right to exist. Arab refusal to acquiesce in our existence – in the Middle East, alongside the Arab states – abides. The only way to peace is through a change in that recalcitrance.

When it changes, there will no longer by any obstacle to peace negotiations. Otherwise, no formulae, sophistry or definitions will avail. Those in the world who seek peace would do well to heed this basic fact and help to bring about a change in the obdurate Arab approach, which is the real impediment to peace. Any display of 'understanding' and forgiveness, however unwitting, is bound to harden the Arabs in their obstinacy and hearten them in their gainsaying of Israel's right to exist – and will, besides, be exploited by Arab leaders to justify ideologically the continuance of the war against Israel.

Nothing unites our people more than the desire for peace. There is no stronger urge in Israel, and on joyful occasions and in hours of mourning alike it is expressed. Nothing can wrench out of our hearts or out of our policy this wish for peace, this hope of peace – not even our indignation over the killing of our loved ones, not even the enmity of the rulers of the Arab world.

The victories that we have won have never intoxicated us, or filled us with such complacency as to relinquish the wish and call for peace – a peace that means good-neighbourly relations, co-operation and an end to slaughter. Peace and co-existence with the Arab peoples have been, and are, among the fundamentals of Jewish renaissance. Generations of the Zionist movement[5] were brought up on them. The desire for peace has charted the policy of all Israel's governments, of whatever membership. No government of Israel in power, however constituted, has ever blocked the way to peace.

With all my heart, I am convinced that in Israel, in the future as in the past, there could be no government which would not bespeak the people's cardinal and steadfast aspiration to bring about a true and enduring peace.

[5] Zionism supports the existence of a Jewish homeland in Palestine. The term was coined by the Austrian Jew Nathan Birmbaum in *Self Emancipation* (1890).

John Stuart Mill
English philosopher and social reformer

John Stuart Mill (1806–73) was born in London, the son of the Scottish philosopher James Mill (1773–1836), who was wholly responsible for his son's education. He learned Greek at the age of three, Latin and arithmetic at eight, logic at twelve, and political economy at 13. He was shielded from association with other boys, his only recreation being a daily walk, during which he was tested with oral examinations. After visiting France in 1820 he studied history, law and philosophy. His forced education gave him an advantage, as he put it, of a quarter of a century over his contemporaries. In 1823 he began a career under his father at the India Office, where he became head of his department. He began enthusiastically to fulfil his father's ambition that he should become leader of the Utilitarian movement, founded on Jeremy Bentham's philosophy of universally enjoyed welfare. From 1822, he wrote for *The Traveller* newspaper, helped form the Utilitarian Society, which met in Bentham's house (1823–6), and helped found University College London (1825). He contributed to the *Westminster Review* and appeared regularly at the London Debating Society. He espoused Thomas Malthus's view that population growth would lead to food shortages, and was arrested in 1824 for distributing birth control literature. In 1826 he suffered a breakdown, usually considered a result of his precocious but emotionally restricted development. He recovered, with his sympathies broadened and his intellectual position modified. He effectively humanized Utilitarianism by recognizing differences in the quality as well as the quantity of pleasures, thereby restoring the importance of cultural and idealistic values. In 1851, after a long, intense but apparently chaste romance he married Harriet Taylor, the bluestocking widow of a wealthy London merchant. She took an active interest in his writing and contributed significantly to his major essay *On Liberty* (1859), which eloquently defines and defends the freedoms of the individual against social and political control. Elected to Parliament in 1865, he campaigned for women's suffrage and generally supported the Advanced Liberals. In 1872 he became godfather, 'in a secular sense', to BERTRAND RUSSELL. His last years were spent in France and he died in Avignon.

'The two sexes must now rise or sink together'
20 May 1867, London, England

Mill was an early and prominent supporter of women's rights: he helped found the National Union of Women's Suffrage Societies and wrote *The Subjection of Women* (published in 1869, although it was written around 1861).

This speech was made to Parliament during a debate on the reform bill, which sought to extend the franchise to every adult male householder in borough constituencies. Mill had been elected as MP for the City and Westminster at his first attempt in 1865, but his parliamentary career was short-lived. He was not re-elected in 1868, in part because of support for female suffrage. However, this speech was reprinted by women's groups in both Britain and the USA.

Mill's hesitant oratorical style belied his scholarship and sharp wit, which made him more comfortable in open debate. Though rather convoluted and complex in style, the speech employs humour and ironical common sense, deftly cutting the ground from under the feet of his opponents.

At its end, Mill moves an amendment to Clause 4, which would have changed the word 'man' to 'person' – in a stroke enabling women of similar social status to vote. He had gained supporters, but the amendment was defeated by 196 votes to 73, though the Reform Act itself was passed.

Politics, it is said, are not a women's business. Well sir, I rather think that politics are not a man's business either; unless he is one of the few who are selected and paid to devote their time to the public service, or is a member of this or of the other House. The vast majority of male electors have each his own business which absorbs nearly the whole of his time; but I have not heard that the few hours occupied, once in a few years, in attending at the polling-booth – even if we throw in the time spent in reading newspapers and political treatises – ever causes them to neglect their shops or their counting-houses.

I have never understood that those who have votes are worse merchants, or worse lawyers, or worse physicians, or even worse clergymen than other people. One would almost suppose that the British

Constitution denied a vote to everyone who could not give the greater part of his time to politics; if this were the case we should have a very limited constituency.

But allow me to ask, what is the meaning of political freedom? Is it anything but the control of those who do make their business of politics, by those who do not? Is it not the very essence of constitutional liberty, that men come from their looms and their forges to decide, and decide well, whether they are properly governed, and whom they will be governed by? And the nations which prize this privilege the most, and exercise it most fully, are invariably those who excel the most in the common concerns of life.

The ordinary occupations of most women are, and are likely to remain, principally domestic; but the notion that these occupations are incompatible with the keenest interest in national affairs, and in all the great interests of humanity, is as utterly futile as the apprehension, once sincerely entertained, that artisans would desert their workshops and their factories if they were taught to read.

I know there is an obscure feeling – a feeling which is ashamed to express itself openly – as if women had no right to care about anything, except how they may be the most useful and devoted servants of some man. But as I am convinced that there is not a single member of this House whose conscience accuses him of so mean a feeling, I may say without offence, that this claim to confiscate the whole existence of one half of the species for the supposed convenience of the other, appears to me, independently of its injustice, particularly silly. For who that has had ordinary experience of human affairs, and ordinary capacity of profiting by that experience, fancies that those do their own work best who understand nothing else?

A man has lived to little purpose who has not learnt that without general mental cultivation, no particular work that requires understanding is ever done in the best manner. It requires brains to use practical experience; and brains, even without practical experience, go further than any amount of practical experience without brains.

But perhaps it is thought that the ordinary occupations of women are more antagonistic than those of men are to the comprehension of public affairs. It is thought, perhaps, that those who are principally charged with the moral education of the future generations of men, cannot be fit to form an opinion about the moral and educational interests of a people; and that those whose chief daily business is the judicious laying-out of money, so as to produce the greatest results with the smallest means, cannot possibly give any lessons to right honourable gentlemen on the other side of the House or on this, who contrive to produce such singularly small results with such vast means.

I feel a degree of confidence, sir, on this subject, which I could not feel if the political change – in itself not great or formidable – which I advocate were not grounded, as beneficent and salutary political changes almost always are, upon a previous social change. The notion of a hard and fast line of separation between women's occupations and men's – of forbidding women to take interest in the things which interest men – belongs to a gone-by state of society which is receding further and further into the past.

We talk of political revolutions, but we do not sufficiently attend to the fact that there has taken place around us a silent domestic revolution.

Women and men are, for the first time in history, really each other's companions. Our traditions respecting the proper relations between them have descended from a time when their lives were apart – when they were separate in their thoughts, because they were separate equally in their amusements and in their serious occupations.

In former days, a man passed his life among men; all his friendships, all his real intimacies, were with men; with men alone did he consult on any serious business; the wife was either a plaything or an upper servant. All this, among the educated classes, is now changed. The man no longer gives his spare hours to violent outdoor exercise and boisterous conviviality with male associates; the two sexes now pass their lives together; the women of man's family are his habitual society; the wife is his chief associate, his most confidential friend, and often his most trusted adviser.

Now, does a man wish to have for his nearest companion so closely linked with him – and whose wishes and preferences have so strong a claim on him – one whose thoughts are alien to those which occupy his own mind; one who can neither be a help, a comfort, nor a support, to his noblest feelings and purposes? Is this close and almost exclusive companionship compatible with women's being warned off all large subjects, being taught that they ought not to care for what it is men's duty to care for, and that to have any serious interests outside the household is stepping beyond their province? Is it good for a man to live in complete communion of thoughts and feelings with one who is studiously kept inferior to himself, whose earthly interests are forcibly confined within four walls, and who cultivates, as a grace of character, ignorance and indifference about the most inspiring subjects, those among which his highest duties are cast? Does any one suppose that this can happen without detriment to the man's own character?

Sir, the time is now come when, unless women are raised to the level of men, men will be pulled down to theirs. The women of a man's family are either a stimulus and a support to this highest aspirations, or a drag upon them. You may keep them ignorant of politics, but you cannot prevent them from concerning themselves with the least respectable part of politics – its personalities. If they do not understand and cannot enter into the man's feelings of public duty, they do care about his personal interest, and that is the scale into which their weight will certainly be thrown.

They will be an influence always at hand, co-operating with the man's selfish promptings, lying in wait for his moments of moral irresolution, and doubling the strength of every temptation. Even if they maintain a modest forbearance, the mere absence of their sympathy will hang a dead-weight on his moral energies, making him unwilling to make sacrifices which they will feel, and to forego social advantages and successes in which they would share, for objects which they cannot appreciate. Supposing him fortunate enough to escape any actual sacrifice of conscience, the indirect effect on the higher parts of his own character is deplorable.

Under an idle notion that the beauties of character of the two sexes are mutually incompatible, men are afraid of manly women; but those who have considered the nature and power of social influences will know, that unless there are manly women, there will not much longer be manly men. When men and women are really companions, if women are frivolous, men will be frivolous; if women care for nothing but personal interest and idle vanities, men in general will care for little else; the two sexes must now rise or sink together.

It may be said that women may take interest in great public questions without having votes. They may, certainly; but how many of them will? Education and society have exhausted their power in inculcating on women that their proper rule of conduct is what society expects from them; and the denial of the vote is a proclamation intelligible to every one, that whatever else society may expect, it does not expect that they should concern themselves with public interests. Why, the whole of a girl's thoughts and feelings are toned down by it from her school days. She does not take the interest even in national history which her brothers do, because it is to be no business of hers when she grows up.

If there are women – and now happily there are many – who do interest themselves in these subjects, and do study them, it is because the force within is strong enough to bear up against the worst kind of discouragement, that which acts not by interposing obstacles, which may be struggled against, but by deadening the spirit which faces and conquers obstacles.

We are told, sir, that women do not wish for the suffrage. If the fact were so, it would only prove that all women are still under this deadening influence; that the opiate still benumbs their mind and conscience. But great numbers of women do desire the suffrage, and have asked for it by petitions to this House. How do we know how many more thousands there may be who have not asked for what they do not hope to get; or for fear of what may be thought of them by men, or by other women; or from the feeling, so sedulously cultivated in them by their education – aversion to make themselves conspicuous? Men must have a rare power of self-delusion if they suppose that leading questions put to the ladies of their family or of their acquaintance will elicit their real sentiments, or will be answered with complete sincerity by one women in 10,000.

No-one is so well schooled as most women are in making a virtue of necessity; it costs little to disclaim caring for what is not offered; and frankness in the expression of sentiments which may be unpleasing and may be thought uncomplimentary to their nearest connections, is not one of the virtues which a women's education tends to cultivate, and is, moreover, a virtue attended with sufficient risk, to induce prudent women usually to reserve its exercise for cases in which there is a nearer and a more personal interest at stake.

However this may be, those who do not care for the suffrage will not use it. Either they will not register, or if they do, they will vote as their male relatives advise – by which, as the advantage will probably be about equally shared among all classes, no harm will be done. Those, be they few or many, who do value the privilege, will exercise it, and will receive that stimulus to their faculties, and that widening and liberalizing influence over their feelings and sympathies, which the suffrage seldom fails to produce on those who are admitted to it.

Meanwhile, an unworthy stigma would be removed from the whole sex. The law would cease to declare them incapable of serious things; would cease to proclaim that their opinions and wishes are unworthy of regard, on things which concern them equally with men, and on many things which concern them much more than men. They would no longer be classed with children, idiots and lunatics, as incapable of taking care of either themselves or others, and needing that everything should be done for them, without asking their consent. If only one woman in 20,000 used the suffrage, to be declared capable of it would be a boon to all women.

Honoré de Mirabeau
French revolutionary politician

Count Honoré Gabriel Riqueti de Mirabeau (1749–91) was born in Bignon. He was dismissed from the cavalry for his disorderly behaviour, and wrote his *Essai sur le despotisme* in hiding in Amsterdam, having eloped with a young married woman. In May 1777 he was imprisoned for three and a half years, during which he wrote *Erotica biblion, Ma conversion,* and his famous *Essai sur les lettres de cachet* (2 vols, 1782). In 1786 he was sent on a secret mission to Berlin, and there obtained the materials for his work *Sur la monarchie prussienne sous Frédéric le Grand* (4 vols, 1787). In 1789 he was elected to the Estates-General by the Third Estate for both Marseilles and Aix. When the Third Estate constituted itself as the National Assembly, Mirabeau's political acumen made him a great force, while his audacity and volcanic eloquence endeared him to the people. He advocated a constitutional monarchy on the English model but was distrusted by both the court and the extremists. Nonetheless he was elected president of the Assembly in January 1791, but died soon afterwards.

'We look for the true safety of the French'
9 July 1789, Paris, France

On 23 June 1789, the Third Estate – those who were neither clergy nor nobility – walked out of the existing assembly, the Estates-General, and into the tennis court, declaring themselves the new National Assembly. Six days later, Louis XVI dispatched 20,000 troops to Paris to quell disturbances in the capital.

Mirabeau attempted to convince the king to withdraw the troops and work with the Assembly to draw up a new constitution, perhaps putting brakes on the slide toward revolution. His address, approved by the Assembly, is unapologetically monarchist in tone. This translation by James White, who rendered many speeches and addresses into English during the French Revolution, conveys Mirabeau's combination of servility, flattery and cunning, which sugared a bitter pill for royal consumption.

Due to spectacular arguments with his father the Marquis, Mirabeau was representing the new middle classes, rather than the nobility from Aix-en-Provence. Despite his unsavoury reputation and his dissolute youth – often blamed for his early death – he was acknowledged as a skilful and elegant orator. Hence he became the unofficial spokesman for the National Assembly.

However, at around the same time he was secretly negotiating with the king and queen, trying to convince them to accept a constitutional settlement rather than cling to a now discredited absolutist regime. Ambitious to become a minister in a new government, Mirabeau's hopes were dashed when the king rejected his advice and then proceeded to dismiss the reformist finance minister, Jacques Necker, on 11 July. The Bastille was stormed three days later.

Sire: you have invited the National Assembly to give you proofs of its confidence: this was even going beyond their most ardent wishes.

We are come to acquaint your Majesty with the cruel alarms at present existing: were we ourselves the object of them, had we the weakness to be apprehensive for ourselves, your goodness would vouchsafe to rid us of those fears, and even, while blaming us for having doubted of your intentions, would attend to our uneasinesses. You would dispel the cause of them; you would not leave the least uncertainty with respect to the situation of the National Assembly.

But, sire, we are not imploring your protection. That would be an offence against your justice. We have entertained fears, and, we are bold to say, they are connected with the purest patriotism, with the interest of our constituents, with the public tranquillity, with the happiness of the beloved sovereign, who, while smoothing for us the road to felicity, well deserves to find an unobstructed passage to it himself.

In the emotions of your own heart, sire, we look for the true safety of the French. When troops advance from every quarter, when camps are forming around us, when the capital is besieged, we ask one another with astonishment: hath the king distrusted the fidelity of his people? Had it been possible for him to have doubted of it, would he not have made our hearts the depositary of his fatherly affliction? What mean these menacing preparations? Where are the enemies of the state and of the king that are to be subdued? Where are the rebels, the leaguers, that are to be reduced?

It is unanimously answered, in the capital, and throughout the kingdom: 'We have an affection for our king; we bless Heaven for the gift which in its love it hath bestowed on us.'

Sire, the piety of Your Majesty can never be imposed upon, unless under the pretext of the public good. Had they, who have given those counsels to our sovereign, sufficient confidence in their own principles to lay them before us, this moment would confer the most glorious triumph upon truth.

The state hath nothing to dread, except from the wicked principles which daringly besiege the throne itself, and respect not the confidence of the purest, the most virtuous of princes. And upon what grounds, sire, would they induce you to doubt the attachment and affection of your subjects? Have you been prodigal of their blood? Are you cruel, are you implacable? Have you perverted the course of justice? Does the people impute its misery to you? Does it mention your name in the midst of its calamities? Can they have told you that the people is impatient of your yoke, that it is weary of the sceptre of the Bourbons?[1] No. No: they have not told you so; calumny is at least not absurd; she looks for some verisimilitude to colour her base practices.

Your Majesty hath had a recent instance of your power over your people; subordination is re-inflated in the agitated capital; the prisoners, to whom the populace had given liberty, have of themselves resumed their fetters; a single word from your mouth hath restored that public order, which perhaps, had force been used, it would have cost torrents of blood to re-establish. But that word was a word of peace; it was the expression of your heart; and your subjects glory in having never made resistance to it. How delightful to exercise such sway! It was the sway of Louis IX,[2] of Louis XII,[3] of Henry IV;[4] it is the only sway worthy of you.

We should deceive you, sire, if, forced as we are by circumstances, we neglected to add, that such a sway is the only one which, at the present day, it is possible to exercise in France. France will not endure that the best of kings should be imposed on and drawn aside, by sinister views, from the noble plan which he himself hath traced out. You have summoned us to act in concert with you in settling the constitution, in labouring at the regeneration of the kingdom: the National Assembly approaches you, in order to declare solemnly that your wishes shall be accomplished, that your promises shall not be vain; that no snares, no difficulties, no terrors shall retard its progress, nor intimidate its courage.

Where then, our enemies will affect to say, is the danger to be apprehended from the soldiery? What mean they by these complaints, if they are inaccessible to discouragement?

The danger, sire, is urgent, is universal, is beyond all the calculations of human prudence.

The danger is for the inhabitants of the provinces. Should they once be alarmed for our liberty, we should no longer have it in our power to restrain their impetuosity. Distance alone magnifies everything, exaggerates everything, doubles the disquiet, angers it, envenoms it.

The danger is for the capital. With what sensations will the people, in the

[1] The royal house to which Louis XVI and his ancestors belonged.

[2] The French monarch Louis IX (c.1214–70) reigned 1226–70. Known for his piety and compassion for the poor, he was canonized as St Louis in 1297.

[3] The French monarch Louis XII (1462–1515) reigned 1498–1515. Known for popular reforms, including tax cuts, he became known as 'the Father of the People'.

[4] The French monarch Henry IV (1553–1610) reigned 1589–1610, and was the first Bourbon king of France. He brought an end to over 40 years of religious wars in France, building a stable and efficient administration, and restoring the economy.

lap of indigence and tortured with the keenest anguish, see the relics of its subsistence disputed for by a throng of threatening soldiers? The presence of the military will cause heats and animosities, will provoke the people, will produce a universal ferment; and the first act of violence, exercised under pretence of police, may commence a train of evils truly horrible.

The danger is for the troops. French soldiers drawn close to the very centre of our discussions, partaking of the passions and the interests of the people, may forget that the ceremony of enlisting made them soldiers, and recollect that nature made them men.

The danger, sire, menaces those labours which are our primary duty, and which will only obtain their full success, and a real permanency, as long as the people looks on them to be altogether free.

There is, moreover, a contagion in commotions where the passions take the lead. We are but men: distrust of ourselves, the fear of appearing weak, may drive us beyond our object; we shall be besieged by counsels violent and immoderate; and calm reason, tranquil wisdom, utter not their oracles amidst scenes of disorder, faction and tumult.

The danger, sire, is yet more terrible, and judge of its extent by the alarms which bring us before you. Mighty revolutions have arisen from causes far less illustrious; more than one enterprise fatal to the peace of nations hath been ushered in, in a manner less inauspicious and less formidable.

Believe not those who talk to you disrespectfully of the nation and who, according to their own views, represent it to you, one while as insolent, rebellious, seditious; one while as submissive, docile for the yoke, ready to bow down the head to receive it. These two pictures are alike unfaithful.

Ever ready to obey you, sire, because you command in the name of the laws, our fidelity is unbounded, as it is untainted.

Ready to resist all the arbitrary commands of those who misuse your name, because they are hostile to the laws, our fidelity itself enjoins us such resistance; and we shall ever consider it an honour to us to merit the reproaches which our firmness brings upon us.

Sire, we conjure you, in the name of our country, in the name of your own happiness and your own glory, to send back your soldiers to the posts from which your counsellors have drawn them; send back that artillery, destined to cover your frontiers; above all, send back the foreign troops, those allies of the nation, whom we pay to defend and not to trouble our domestic peace. Your Majesty hath no need of them. Why should a monarch, adored by five-and-twenty millions of Frenchmen, assemble round the throne – in a hurry and at vast expense – some thousands of mere foreigners?

Sire, amidst your children, be guarded by their love. The deputies of the nation are summoned to consecrate, with you, the lofty rights of royalty upon the immoveable basis of the liberty of the people. But, while they are performing their duty, while they are giving way to their reason, to their sentiments, would you expose them to the suspicion of having yielded only to fear?

The authority which is delegated to you by every heart is the only pure, the only unshakeable authority. It is the just return for your benefits, and the immortal appanage[5] of the princes to whom you will be a model.

[5] A provision for maintenance, especially of a prince.

Bernard Montgomery
English soldier

Bernard Law Montgomery *later 1st Viscount Montgomery of Alamein* (1887–1976) was born in London, the son of Bishop Montgomery. He was educated at St Paul's School and the Royal Military College, Sandhurst. He served with the Royal Warwickshire Regiment in World War I. In World War II he commanded the 3rd Division, which was forced to retreat to Dunkirk in May–June 1940. In North Africa in 1941 he commanded the 8th Army, restoring their bruised confidence and the will to win. Conforming to General Harold Alexander's strategic plans, he defeated the German Field Marshal Erwin Rommel at the Battle of El Alamein (October 1942). This was followed by a series of victories that eventually drove the Axis forces back to Tunis. His subsequent activities in Sicily and Italy were solid, if somewhat pedestrian. Appointed Commander for the Ground Forces for the Normandy invasion in 1944, his strategy was characterized by wariness and unflagging tenacity. By deliberately attracting the main weight of the German counter-offensive to the British flank, he freed the US armoured formations to inaugurate the joint drive across France and Belgium. His attempt to roll up the German right flank by way of Arnhem (September 1944) lacked co-ordination and ended in disaster, but his timely intervention helped materially to frustrate Karl von Rundstedt's surprise offensive of December 1944. He accepted the German capitulation on Lüneburg Heath, and was commander of the British-occupied zone in Germany (1945–6) and Chief of the Imperial General Staff (CIGS) in 1946–8. He was Deputy Supreme Commander of NATO forces (1951–8). His publications include *Normandy to the Baltic* (1947), his *Memoirs* (1958) and *The Path to Leadership* (1961). Controversial and outspoken, he was known as a 'soldier's general' and is regarded by some military historians as the best British field commander since THE DUKE OF WELLINGTON.

'If we can't stay here alive, then let us stay here dead'
13 August 1942, Cairo, Egypt

By the end of June 1942, Rommel's Afrika Korps had driven the 8th Army out of Libya to the El Alamein Line, the last defendable position before the Nile. The British forces were dispirited, demoralized, and facing a real danger of complete destruction.

Desperate for a British victory to boost morale before the planned Allied landings in western North Africa, Prime Minister WINSTON CHURCHILL flew to Cairo in August 1942 for talks with British commander-in-chief Field Marshal Sir Claude Auchinleck. Churchill favoured a major offensive; and when Auchinleck disagreed he was summarily replaced with General Sir Harold Alexander.

Lieutenant General Bernard Montgomery, then relatively unknown, was appointed to lead the 8th Army. He irked the outgoing Auchinleck by assuming his command on 13 August, two days before he had been authorized to do so.

On arrival, Montgomery gave this bracing speech to his officers, assembled in Cairo. He acknowledged his men's low morale, but fired their confidence and determination, asserting that there would be no further retreat.

His brisk inflexibility had the desired effect. After two months of careful planning, during which Montgomery stealthily assembled a massive superiority of men and weapons, the 8th Army struck Rommel's forces at El Alamein on the night of 23 October. The battle lasted a week, with heavy losses on both sides, but eventually Rommel was defeated and the Afrika Korps began a 1,500-mile withdrawal. The stage was set for Operation Torch – the Allied invasion of Morocco and Algeria – which began on 8 November.

I want first of all to introduce myself to you. You do not know me. I do not know you. But we have got to work together; therefore we must understand each other, and we must have confidence each in the other. I have only been here a few hours. But from what I have seen and heard since I arrived I am prepared to say, here and now, that I have confidence in you. We will then work together as a team; and together we will gain the confidence of this great Army and go forward to final victory in Africa.

I believe that one of the first duties of a commander is to create what I call 'atmosphere', and in that atmosphere his staff, subordinate commanders and troops will live and work and fight.

I do not like the general atmosphere I find here. It is an atmosphere of doubt, of looking back to select the next place to which to withdraw, of loss of confidence in our ability to defeat Rommel, of desperate defence measures by reserves in preparing positions in Cairo and the Delta.[1]

[1] The Nile delta, north of Cairo.

All that must cease. Let us have a new atmosphere.

The defence of Egypt lies here at Alamein and on the Ruweisat Ridge. What is the use of digging trenches in the Delta? It is quite useless; if we lose this position we lose Egypt; all the fighting troops now in the Delta must come here at once, and will. *Here* we will stand and fight; there will be no further withdrawal. I have ordered that all plans and instructions dealing with further withdrawal are to be burnt, and at once. We will stand and fight *here*.

If we can't stay here alive, then let us stay here dead.

I want to impress on everyone that the bad times are over. Fresh Divisions from the UK are now arriving in Egypt, together with ample reinforcements for our present Divisions. We have 300 to 400 Sherman new tanks coming and these are actually being unloaded at Suez now. Our mandate from the prime minister is to destroy the Axis forces in North Africa; I have seen it, written on half a sheet of notepaper. And it will be done. If anyone here thinks it can't be done, let him go at once; I don't want any doubters in this party. It can be done, and it will be done: beyond any possibility of doubt.

Now I understand that Rommel is expected to attack at any moment. Excellent. Let him attack. I would sooner it didn't come for a week, just to give me time to sort things out. If we have two weeks to prepare we will be sitting pretty; Rommel can attack as soon as he likes after that, and I hope he does.

Meanwhile, we ourselves will start to plan a great offensive; it will be the beginning of a campaign which will hit Rommel and his army for six, right out of Africa.

But first we must create a reserve corps, mobile and strong in armour, which we will train out of the line. Rommel has always had such a force in his Afrika Korps, which is never used to hold the line but which is always in reserve, available for striking blows. Therein has been his great strength. We will create such a corps ourselves, a British Panzer Corps. It will consist of two armoured divisions and one motorized division. I gave orders yesterday for it to begin to form, back in the Delta.

I have no intention of launching our great attack until we are completely ready. There will be pressure from many quarters to attack soon. I will not attack until we are ready, and you can rest assured on that point. Meanwhile, if Rommel attacks while we are preparing, let him do so with pleasure. We will merely continue with our own preparations and we will attack when we are ready, and not before.

I want to tell you that I always work on the chief-of-staff system. I have nominated Brigadier de Guingand[2] as Chief of Staff, 8th Army. I will issue orders through him. Whatever he says will be taken as coming from me and will be acted on *at once*. I understand there has been a great deal of 'bellyaching' out here. By bellyaching I mean inventing poor reasons for not doing what one has been told to do.

[2] The British soldier Francis de Guingand *later Sir Francis de Guingand* (1900–79) served as Montgomery's Chief of Staff during the North African campaign and afterwards.

All this is to stop at once. I will tolerate no bellyaching. If anyone objects to doing what he is told, then he can get out of it: and at once. I want that made very clear right down through the 8th Army.

I have little more to say just at present. And some of you may think it is quite enough and may wonder if I am mad. I assure you I am quite sane.

I understand there are people who often think I am slightly mad; so often that I now regard it as rather a compliment. All I have to say to that is that if I am slightly mad, there are a large number of people I could name who are raving lunatics!

What I have done is to get over to you the atmosphere in which we will now work and fight; you must see that that atmosphere permeates right through the 8th Army to the most junior private soldier. All the soldiers must know what is wanted; when they see it coming to pass, there will be a surge of confidence throughout the army.

I ask you to give me your confidence and to have faith that what I have said will come to pass. There is much work to be done.

The orders I have given about no further withdrawal will mean a complete change in the layout of our dispositions; also, we must begin to prepare for our great offensive.

The first thing to do is to move our HQ to a decent place where we can live in reasonable comfort and where the army staff can all be together and side by side with the HQ of the Desert Air Force. This is a frightful place here, depressing, unhealthy and a rendezvous for every fly in Africa; we shall do no good work here. Let us get over there by the sea where it is fresh and healthy. If officers are to do good work they must have decent messes, and be comfortable. So off we go on the new line.

The Chief of Staff will be issuing orders on many points very shortly, and I am always available to be consulted by the senior officers of the staff. The great point to remember is that we are going to finish with this chap Rommel once and for all. It will be quite easy. There is no doubt about it.

He is definitely a nuisance. Therefore we will hit him a crack and finish with him.

The Marquess of Montrose
Scottish soldier

James Graham *later 5th Earl of Montrose, then 1st Marquess of Montrose* (1612–50) succeeded his father as Earl of Montrose at 14 and was educated at the University of St Andrews, later travelling in Europe. Returning to Scotland, he was one of four noblemen who drew up the National Covenant (1637) defending Presbyterianism against the imposition of Anglicanism. In 1638 he occupied Aberdeen on behalf of the Covenanters. When CHARLES I invited several Covenanting nobles to meet him, Montrose was among them, and Presbyterians later dated his 'apostasy' from that interview. At the General Assembly of the Church of Scotland in 1639 he expressed misgivings about the Covenant. It leaked out that he had been communicating with the king; he was cited before a committee of the Scottish Parliament, and imprisoned in Edinburgh Castle for five months (1641). In 1644 he was created Marquess of Montrose and advanced into Perthshire as Charles's lieutenant general. He routed the Covenanters at Tippermuir; then took Aberdeen and drove the anti-royalist Archibald Campbell, 8th Earl of Argyll, from his castle at Inveraray. An attempt to surround his forces failed when Montrose surprised Argyll at Inverlochy (1645). In June 1645, Charles was defeated at Naseby but the following month Montrose won another battle at Kilsyth; this, the most notable of his six victories, seemed to lay Scotland at his feet. With depleted forces, he was surprised on 13 September and defeated at Philiphaugh, near Selkirk. He escaped to Norway in September 1646, travelling to Paris, Germany and the Low Countries. When news of Charles's execution reached him, he swore to avenge it. He lost most of his army by shipwreck, but reached Ross-shire, where his dispirited forces were defeated at Carbisdale on 27 April 1650. He was captured and taken to Edinburgh, where he was executed. Montrose's passionately loyal poetry is little known, apart from one stanza beginning, 'He either fears his fate too much'. Its attribution to Montrose (first made in 1711) is doubtful.

'Doth not sometimes a just man perish in his righteousness?'
21 May 1650, Edinburgh, Scotland

Montrose spoke these words at the age of 38, as he faced a cruel and humiliating execution. Very nearly one of history's victors, he had ended up on the losing side in the British Civil Wars. As a principal signatory to the Covenant, he had initially sought to curtail royal authority and reduce English interference in Scottish affairs; but he had been unable to uphold the Covenanters' increasingly anti-monarchist line.

It is said that on the day of his execution bad weather gave way to sunshine at around 2pm, when he stepped onto the scaffold. In his speech, recorded by James Fraser in *The Chronicles of the Frasers*, Montrose boldly restates his loyalty to the king and his respect for the laws of nature and nations. He also challenges his executioners' authority, insisting only God can punish him for his sins.

After he was hanged, drawn and quartered, tradition states his heart was spirited away to be embalmed and placed in a steel case made from the blade of his sword. The rest of his body certainly suffered a worse fate. His rotting remains were on public display in Edinburgh for eleven years before they were buried at St Giles Cathedral.

I am sorry if this manner of my end be scandalous to any good Christian here. Doth it not often happen to the righteous according to the way of the unrighteous? Doth not sometimes a just man perish in his righteousness, and a wicked man prosper in his wickedness and malice? They who know me should not disesteem me for this. Many greater than I have been dealt with in this kind. But I must say that all God's judgements are just, and this measure, for my private sins, I acknowledge to be just with God, and wholly submit myself to Him.

But in regard of man, I may say they are but instruments. God forgive them, and I forgive them. They have oppressed the poor and violently perverted judgement and justice; but he that is higher than they will reward them.

What I did in this kingdom was in obedience to the most just commands of my sovereign, and in his defence, against those who rose up against him. I acknowledge nothing, but fear God and honour the king, according to the commandments of God and the just laws of nature and nations. I have not sinned against man, but against God; and with him there is mercy, which is the ground of my drawing near to him.

It is objected against me by many, even good people, that I am under the censure of the Church. Seeing it is only for doing my duty, by obeying my Prince's most just commands for religion, his sacred person and authority, yet I am sorry they did excommunicate me; and in that which is according to God's laws, without wronging my conscience or allegiance, I desire to be relaxed. If they will not do it, I appeal to God, who is the righteous judge of the world, and who must and will, I hope, be my judge and saviour.

It is spoken of me that I should blame the king. God forbid! For the late king, he lived a saint and died a martyr.[1] I pray God that I may end as he did. If ever I would wish my soul in another man's stead, it should be in his. For His Majesty now living,[2] never people, never any people, I believe, might be more happy in a king. His commands to me were most just, and I obeyed them. In nothing that he promiseth will he fail. He deals justly with all men. I pray God he be so dealt withal that he be not betrayed under trust, as his father was.

I desire not to be mistaken, as if my carriage at this time, in relations to your ways, were stubborn. I do but follow the light of my conscience, my rule; which is seconded by the working of the Spirit of God that is within me. I thank him I go to Heaven with joy the way he paved for me. If he enable me against the fear of death, and furnish me with courage and confidence to embrace it, even in its most ugly shape, let God be glorified in my end, though it were in my damnation. Yet I say not this out of any fear or mistrust, but out of my duty to God, and love to his people.

I have no more to say, but that I desire your charity and prayer; and I shall pray for you all. I leave my soul to God, my service to my Prince, my goodwill to my friends, my love and charity to you all. And thus, briefly, I have exonerated my conscience.

[2] Charles I's son Charles II (1630–85) was King of England, Scotland and Ireland *de jure* from the moment of his father's death, but only achieved this position *de facto* at the Restoration in 1660.

[1] Charles I was beheaded at Whitehall on 30 January 1649.

Michael Moore
American campaigner and film-maker

Michael Moore (1954–) was born in Davison, near Flint, Michigan to parents of Irish Catholic origin. At 18, he was elected to the education board of Davison. He studied at the University of Michigan–Flint, before dropping out to establish the weekly magazine *The Flint Voice* (later *The Michigan Voice*). In 1986, he became editor of the political magazine *Mother Jones*, based in San Francisco. He was fired after less then a year and sued, eventually settling out of court. He used the settlement – along with money raised by running bingo games – to fund his first film *Roger & Me* (1989). In this comic documentary, Moore hounds Roger Smith, chief executive officer of General Motors, which closed its plant in Flint at the cost of many thousands of jobs – including those of both Moore's parents – causing economic disaster in the area. The film established the tone and style of his future projects, including the film *The Big One* (1997) and the cable television series *The Awful Truth* (1999). His first big hit, *Bowling for Columbine* (2002), explored gun ownership in the USA (a lifelong shooting enthusiast, Moore is a member of the National Rifle Association). The film won an Oscar at the 2003 Academy Awards. His next documentary was *Fahrenheit 9/11* (2004), which directly attacked President GEORGE W BUSH for his 'fraudulent' election and criticized his handling of the terrorist catastrophe of 11 September 2001 and its aftermath. Moore also lambasted the Bush administration and big business in his best-selling books, *Stupid White Men* (2001) and *Dude, Where's My Country?* (2003). In his documentary *Sicko* (2007) he lambasted the American health industry while in 2009's *Capitalism: A Love Story* he examined the financial crisis of 2007–8.

'We live in fictitious times'
23 March 2003, Hollywood, California, USA

Already notorious as a thorn in the side of big business and the Republican administration, Michael Moore released his documentary *Bowling for Columbine* in 2002. An exposé of gun-control issues, the film was named after the Colorado high school where, in 1999, two teenagers shot 39 people, killing 15, including themselves. The film famously featured the actor CHARLTON HESTON, president of the National Rifle Association, who reluctantly agreed to an interview when Moore located his house on a map of stars' homes and turned up unannounced.

Bowling for Columbine became the highest-grossing documentary of all time (a record broken by Moore's next film *Fahrenheit 9/11*) and won numerous international awards. At the Cannes Film Festival, it became the first documentary in 46 years to compete in the main competition, received a 13-minute standing ovation and won an award specially created for the occasion. More surprising, perhaps, was the film's Oscar for Best Documentary at the Academy Awards, often seen as politically conservative. However, no-one was very surprised when Moore used his acceptance speech to attack President Bush.

Bush's victory at the election of November 2000 had been legally contested, and Moore was one of many who considered the outcome flawed. At the Oscar ceremony – coverage of which was interrupted twice by news of American bombing in Iraq – he also criticized Bush for pursuing a war many saw as unjustified. Joined onstage by his fellow nominees, Moore struggled to make himself heard over a cacophony of boos and cheers.

The following day, ticket sales for the film rose by 110 per cent.

[1] The Oscar was awarded jointly to Moore and his Canadian producer Michael Donovan.
[2] The US politician Tom Ridge (1946–) of the Office of Homeland Security had attracted criticism for seeming to suggest US citizens should secure their homes against chemical attack using plastic sheeting and duct tape; and for causing public panics with a colour-coded terror alert system (in

Whoa. Thank you very much. On behalf of our producers Kathleen Glynn and Michael Donovan[1] from Canada, I'd like to thank the Academy for this.

I've invited my fellow documentary nominees on the stage with us, and we would like to – they're here in solidarity with me because we like non-fiction.

We like non-fiction and we live in fictitious times. We live in the time where we have fictitious election results that elect a fictitious president. We live in a time where we have a man sending us to war for fictitious reasons – whether it's the fiction of duct tape or the fiction of orange alerts.[2]

We are against this war, Mr Bush! Shame on you, Mr Bush! Shame on you! And any time you've got the Pope[3] and the Dixie Chicks[4] against you, your time is up!

Thank you very much.

which orange was 'high').
[3] In January 2003, JOHN PAUL II had warned against the impending invasion of Iraq, describing war as 'a defeat for humanity'.
[4] The all-female country music trio the Dixie Chicks (formed in Dallas, Texas in 1989) caused a furore in March 2003 by telling a London audience they were ashamed of Bush, the Texas-born US President.

Thomas More
English politician and scholar

Sir Thomas More *later St Thomas* (1478–1535) was born in London, the son of a judge. Educated at Oxford under John Colet and Thomas Linacre, he completed his legal studies at New Inn and Lincoln's Inn, was Reader for three years in Furnival's Inn, and spent the next four years in the Charterhouse in 'devotion and prayer'. During the last years of Henry VII he became Under-Sheriff of London and a member of parliament. Introduced to Henry VIII through Thomas Wolsey, he became Master of Requests (1514), Treasurer of the Exchequer (1521) and Chancellor of the Duchy of Lancaster (1525). He was Speaker of the House of Commons, and was sent on missions to the French courts of Francis I and Charles V. On the fall of Wolsey in 1529, More, against his own strongest wish, was appointed Lord Chancellor. He executed his office with a primitive virtue and simplicity but displayed particular harshness in his sentences for religious opinions. He sympathized with John Colet and Erasmus in their desire for a more rational theology and for radical reform in the manners of the clergy, but like them he felt no promptings to break with the historic Church. He saw with displeasure the successive steps which led Henry to the final schism from Rome. In 1532 he resigned the chancellorship. In 1534 Henry was declared head of the English Church and More's steadfast refusal to recognize any head of the Church other than the Pope led to his sentence for high treason after a harsh imprisonment of over a year. Still refusing to recant, he was beheaded. With his Latin *Utopia* (1516, Eng trans 1556), More takes his place among the most eminent humanists of the Renaissance. His *History of King Richard III* (1513) is highly regarded, although it is actually a second-hand account taken from Richard's enemy, Archbishop John Morton. He was canonized in 1935. His feast day is 9 July.

'I am sorrier for your perjury than for mine own peril'
July 1535, London, England

A reluctant Lord Chancellor, Thomas More soon found himself in trouble. When King Henry broke away from Rome in 1532, More – a devout Catholic – resigned his post. In 1533, when Henry divorced Catherine of Aragon to marry Anne Boleyn, More failed to attend the new queen's coronation. In 1534, when Henry passed the Act of Succession (declaring Anne's daughter ELIZABETH I heir to the throne) and the Act of Supremacy (declaring Henry head of the English Church and denouncing papal authority), More refused to take the oath. By April 1534, Henry had jailed him and was seeking his death.

The opportunity arose in July 1535, when More's rival Lord Rich, the Solicitor-General, offered to testify that More had told him privately that 'Parliament could not make the king supreme head of the church'. Having previously refused to speak, More was forced to break his silence at the ensuing trial. His speech was recorded in a biography by his son-in-law William Roper (1496–1578).

An articulate and intelligent orator with a good grasp of the law, More tries to discredit Rich as man of ill repute, with whom he would never have traded secret thoughts. But he is ultimately obliged to declare his allegiance to the Church of Rome, sealing his fate.

In a gesture of Christian forgiveness, he responds to his death sentence by extending hope for reconciliation with his judges in the afterlife. It is said he offered his forgiveness to the executioner; and his final words are recorded as: 'The king's good servant, but God's first.'

If I were a man, my lords, that did not regard an oath, I need not, as it is well known, in this place, at this time, nor in this case to stand as an accused person. And if this oath of yours, Master Rich, be true, then pray I that I may never see God in the face, which I would not say, were it otherwise to win the whole world.

In good faith, Master Rich, I am sorrier for your perjury than for mine own peril, and you shall understand that neither I nor any man else to my knowledge ever took you to be a man of such credit in any matter of importance I or any other would at any time vouchsafe to communicate with you. And I, as you know, of no small while have been acquainted with you and your conversation, who have known you from your youth hitherto, for we long dwelled together in one parish. Whereas yourself can tell (I am sorry you compel me to say) you were esteemed very light of tongue, a great dicer and of no commendable fame. And so, in your house at the Temple, where hath been your chief bringing up, were you likewise accounted.

Can it therefore seem likely to your honourable lordships, that I would, in so weighty a cause, so unadvisedly overshoot myself as to trust Master Rich – a man of me always reputed for one of little truth, as your lordships have heard – so far above my sovereign lord the king, or any of his noble counsellors, that I would unto him utter the secrets of my conscience touching the king's supremacy, the special point and only mark at my hands so long sought for?

A thing which I never did – nor ever would after the statute thereof made – reveal unto the king's Highness himself or to any of his honourable counsellors, as it is not unknown to your honours, at sundry and several times, sent from his grace's own person unto the Tower[1] unto me for none other purpose. Can this, in your judgement, my lords, seem likely to be true? And if I had so done, indeed, my lords, as Master Rich hath sworn – seeing it was spoken but in familiar, secret talk, nothing affirming, and only in putting of cases, without other displeasant circumstances – it cannot justly be taken to be spoken maliciously; and where there is no malice there can be no offence.

And over this I can never think, my lords: that so many worthy bishops, so many noble personages, and many other worshipful, virtuous, wise and well-learned men as at the making of that law were in Parliament assembled, ever meant to have any man punished by death in whom there could be found no malice, taking *malitia pro malevolentia*.[2] For if *malitia* be generally taken for sin, no man is there that can excuse himself. *Quia si dixerimus quod peccatum no habemus, nosmetipsos seducimus, et veritas in nobis non est*.[3]

And only this word 'maliciously' is in the statute material, as this term 'forcibly' is in the statute of forcible entries, by which statute if a man enter peaceably, and put not his adversary out forcibly, it is no offence, but if he put him out forcibly, then by that statute it is an offence, and so shall be punished by this term 'forcibly'.

Besides this, the manifold goodness of the king's Highness himself, that hath been so many ways my singular good lord and gracious sovereign, and that hath so dearly loved and trusted me, even at my first coming into his noble service, with the dignity of his honourable Privy Council, vouchsafing to admit me, and to offices of great credit and worship most liberally advanced me; and finally with the weighty room of his Grace's higher Chancellor, the like whereof he never did to temporal man before, next to his own royal person the highest office in this whole realm, so far above my qualities or merits, and meet therefore of his own incomparable benignity, honoured and exalted me, by the space of 20 years or more showing his continual favours towards me, and (until, at mine own poor suit it pleased His Highness, giving me licence with His Majesty's favour to bestow the residue of my life wholly for the provision of my soul in the service of God, and of his special goodness thereof to discharge and unburden me) most benignly heaped honours continually more and more upon me; all this His Highness's goodness, I say, so long thus bountifully extended towards me, were in my mind, my lords, matter sufficient to convince this slanderous surmise by this man so wrongfully imagined against me.

[*Before judgement was given, More spoke again, breaking his silence on the issue and giving the world the statement which had been sought from*

[1] The Tower of London, where More was imprisoned from April 1534.

[2] Latin: 'sin as equivalent to malevolence'. More points to the Christian doctrine that says humanity is by nature sinful.

[3] Latin: 'If we say we have no sin, we abuse ourselves and there is no truth in us' (1 John, 1:8).

him during the months of imprisonment and interrogation.]

Forasmuch, my lord, as this indictment is grounded upon an Act of Parliament directly oppugnant[4] to the laws of God and his holy Church — the supreme government of which, or of any part thereof, may no temporal prince presume by any law to take upon him, as rightfully belonging to the See of Rome, a spiritual pre-eminence by the mouth of our Saviour himself, personally present upon the earth, to St Peter and his successors, bishops of the same see, by special prerogative granted — it is therefore in law amongst Christian men, insufficient to charge any Christian man.

[*After sentencing, More spoke for the last time.*]

More have I not to say, my lords, but that like as the blessed apostle St Paul, as we read in the Acts of the Apostles,[5] was present and consented to the death of St Stephen, and kept their clothes that stoned him to death, and yet be they now both twain holy saints in Heaven, and shall continue there friends forever; so I verily trust and shall therefore right heartily pray, that though your lordships have now in earth been judges to my condemnation, we may yet hereafter in Heaven merrily all meet together to our everlasting salvation.

[4] Hostile, opposing, warring.

[5] More refers to Acts 7:54–8:1, which describes Saul's indifference to Stephen's martyrdom. After Saul's conversion (Acts 9) he came to be known as Paul.

Toni Morrison
American novelist

Toni Morrison, *pen name of Chloe Anthony Morrison, née Wofford* (1931–) was born in Lorain, Ohio, and educated at Howard and Cornell Universities, later teaching at Texas Southern University (1955–7) and at Howard (1957–64). She moved to New York in 1965 to work in publishing as a senior editor at Random House while becoming established as a fiction writer. Labelled as a black James Joyce or WILLIAM FAULKNER, she explores in rich vocabulary and cold-blooded detail the stories of African–Americans in a white-dominated culture. *The Bluest Eye* (1970) focuses on an eleven-year-old black girl who feels a sense of inferiority at not having blue eyes, and suffers an incestuous rape; *Sula* (1974) again confronts a generation gap, but between a grandmother and the eponymous scapegoat; and *Song of Solomon* (1977) is a merciless study of genteel African–Americans. Further novels, formidable in their mastery of technique and courageous in their subject-matter, have included *Tar Baby* (1981), a story of race conflict on a Caribbean island; *Beloved* (1987), her Pulitzer Prize-winning account of a runaway slave woman who kills her baby daughter to prevent her becoming a slave; *Jazz* (1992), set in 1920s Harlem; *Paradise* (1998), an account of a black utopian experiment; and *A Mercy* (2008), which looked at the roots of slavery in early America. Her study of black literature, *Playing in the Dark: Whiteness and the Literary Imagination*, was published in 1992. Morrison taught writing at the State University of New York at Albany from 1984, and moved to Princeton University in 1989. She was awarded the Nobel Prize for literature in 1993, which confirmed her as one of the most important contemporary US novelists.

'Is the bird I am holding living or dead?'
7 December 1993, Stockholm, Sweden

The Nobel Prize includes the invitation to give a lecture, allowing laureates a prominent platform on which to discuss their work and issues relating to it. Nobel lectures are often intellectually demanding, sometimes politically charged, but rarely as philosophically beguiling as this one.

In awarding Morrison her prize, the Swedish Nobel committee spoke of a writer 'who in novels characterized by visionary force and poetic import, gives life to an essential aspect of American reality'. She spun her lecture around a dark, poetic fable about an old blind woman and a group of children, about life and death, tolerance and prejudice, violence and compassion – themes which haunt her fiction.

Morrison's tale is earthed and earthy, laced with mystical paradox ('she is both the law and its transgression') and socio-political commentary ('the city, where the intelligence of rural prophets is the source of much amusement'). She uses it to launch a meditation on language, contrasting 'the policing languages of mastery' with 'unmolested language' which 'surges toward knowledge, not its destruction'. As a writer, she positions herself, alongside the old woman, as a custodian or defender of free language.

But Morrison has a twist in store, a warning against complacency and prejudice. Returning to her story, she allows the old woman to learn from the children, in what amounts to a warning against an aloof literary culture. Her speech, ultimately, offers a bold message of hope, a celebration both of storytelling and of 'being young, when language was magic without meaning'.

Thank you all for this very warm welcome. Fiction has never been entertainment for me. It has been the work I have done for most of my adult life. I believe that one of the principal ways in which we acquire, hold and digest information is via narrative. So I hope you will understand when the remarks I make begin with what I believe to be the first sentence of our childhood that we all remember: the phrase 'once upon a time'.

'Once upon a time there was an old woman. Blind but wise.' Or was it an old man? A guru, perhaps. Or a griot[1] soothing restless children. I have heard this story, or one exactly like it, in the lore of several cultures.

'Once upon a time there was an old woman. Blind. Wise.'

In the version I know, the woman is the daughter of slaves, black, American, and lives alone in a small house outside of town. Her reputation for wisdom is without peer and without question. Among her people she is both the law and its transgression. The honour she is paid and the awe in

[1] A tribal teller of traditional stories and tribal or family history.

which she is held reach beyond her neighbourhood to places far away; to the city, where the intelligence of rural prophets is the source of much amusement.

One day the woman is visited by some young people who seem to be bent on disproving her clairvoyance and showing her up for the fraud they believe she is. Their plan is simple: they enter her house and ask the one question the answer to which rides solely on her difference from them, a difference they regard as a profound disability: her blindness. They stand before her, and one of them says, 'Old woman, I hold in my hand a bird. Tell me whether it is living or dead.'

She does not answer, and the question is repeated. 'Is the bird I am holding living or dead?'

Still she doesn't answer. She is blind and cannot see her visitors, let alone what is in their hands. She does not know their colour, gender or homeland. She only knows their motive. The old woman's silence is so long, the young people have trouble holding their laughter.

Finally she speaks and her voice is soft but stern. 'I don't know,' she says. 'I don't know whether the bird you are holding is dead or alive, but what I do know is that it is in your hands. It is in your hands.'

Her answer can be taken to mean: if it is dead, you have either found it that way or you have killed it. If it is alive, you can still kill it. Whether it is to stay alive, it is your decision. Whatever the case, it is your responsibility. For parading their power and her helplessness, the young visitors are reprimanded, told they are responsible not only for the act of mockery but also for the small bundle of life sacrificed to achieve its aims. The blind woman shifts attention away from assertions of power to the instrument through which that power is exercised.

Speculation on what (other than its own frail body) that bird-in-the-hand might signify has always been attractive to me, but especially so now – thinking, as I have been, about the work I do that has brought me to this company. So I choose to read the bird as language and the woman as a practised writer. She is worried about how the language she dreams in, given to her at birth, is handled, put into service, even withheld from her for certain nefarious purposes. Being a writer, she thinks of language partly as a system, partly as a living thing over which one has control, but mostly as agency – as an act with consequences.

So the question the children put to her – 'Is it living or dead?' – is not unreal, because she thinks of language as susceptible to death, erasure; certainly imperilled and salvageable only by an effort of the will. She believes that if the bird in the hands of her visitors is dead, the custodians are responsible for the corpse. For her, a dead language is not only one no longer spoken or written, it is unyielding language, content to admire its own paralysis. Like statist language, censored and censoring. Ruthless in its policing duties, it has no desire or purpose other than maintaining the free range of its own narcotic narcissism, its own exclusivity and dominance.

However moribund, it is not without effect, for it actively thwarts the intellect, stalls conscience, suppresses human potential. Unreceptive to interrogation, it cannot form or tolerate new ideas, shape other thoughts, tell another story, fill baffling silences. Official language, smitheried to sanction ignorance and preserve privilege, is a suit of armour polished to shocking glitter, a husk from which the knight departed long ago. Yet there it is: dumb, predatory, sentimental. Exciting reverence in schoolchildren, providing shelter for despots, summoning false memories of stability, harmony among the public.

She is convinced that when language dies, out of carelessness, disuse, indifference and absence of esteem, or killed by fiat, not only she herself, but all users and makers are accountable for its demise. In her country, children have bitten their tongues off and use bullets instead to iterate the voice of speechlessness, of disabled and disabling language, of language adults have abandoned altogether as a device for grappling with meaning, providing guidance, or expressing love. But she knows tongue-suicide is not only the choice of children. It is common among the infantile heads of state and power merchants whose evacuated language leaves them with no access to what is left of their human instincts, for they speak only to those who obey, or in order to force obedience.

The systematic looting of language can be recognized by the tendency of its users to forgo its nuanced, complex, midwifery properties for menace and subjugation. Oppressive language does more than represent violence; it is violence; does more than represent the limits of knowledge; it limits knowledge. Whether it is obscuring state language or the faux-language of mindless media; whether it is the proud but calcified language of the academy or the commodity-driven language of science; whether it is the malign language of law-without-ethics, or language designed for the estrangement of minorities, hiding its racist plunder in its literary cheek – it must be rejected, altered and exposed.

It is the language that drinks blood, laps vulnerabilities, tucks its fascist boots under crinolines of respectability and patriotism as it moves relentlessly toward the bottom line and the bottomed-out mind. Sexist language, racist language, theistic language – all are typical of the policing languages of mastery, and cannot, do not permit new knowledge or encourage the mutual exchange of ideas.

The old woman is keenly aware that no intellectual mercenary, nor insatiable dictator, no paid-for politician or demagogue; no counterfeit journalist would be persuaded by her thoughts. There is and will be rousing language to keep citizens armed and arming; slaughtered and slaughtering in the malls, courthouses, post offices, playgrounds, bedrooms and boulevards; stirring, memorializing language to mask the pity and waste of needless death.

There will be more diplomatic language to countenance rape, torture, assassination. There is and will be more seductive, mutant language designed to throttle women, to pack their throats like pâté-producing geese with their own unsayable, transgressive words; there will be more of the language of surveillance disguised as research; of politics and history calculated to render the suffering of millions mute; language glamorized to thrill the dissatisfied and bereft into assaulting their neighbours; arrogant, pseudo-empirical language crafted to lock creative people into cages of inferiority and hopelessness.

Underneath the eloquence, the glamour, the scholarly associations, however stirring or seductive, the heart of such language is languishing, or perhaps not beating at all – if the bird is already dead …

The conventional wisdom of the Tower of Babel story is that the collapse was a misfortune. That it was the distraction, or the weight of many languages that precipitated the tower's failed architecture. That one monolithic language would have expedited the building and Heaven would have been reached. Whose Heaven, she wonders? And what kind?

Perhaps the achievement of Paradise was premature, a little hasty, if no-one could take the time to understand other languages, other views, other narratives, period. Had they, the Heaven they imagined might have been found at their feet. Complicated, demanding, yes, but a view of Heaven as life; not Heaven as post-life.

She would not want to leave her young visitors with the impression that language should be forced to stay alive merely to be. The vitality of language lies in its ability to limn[2] the actual, imagined and possible lives of its speakers, readers, writers. Although its poise is sometimes in displacing experience, it is not a substitute for it. It arcs toward the place where meaning may lie.

When a president of the United States thought about the graveyard his country had become, and said, 'The world will little note nor long remember what we say here. But it will never forget what they did here,'[3] his simple words were exhilarating in their life-sustaining properties because they refused to encapsulate the reality of 600,000 dead men in a cataclysmic race war. Refusing to monumentalize, disdaining the 'final word', the precise 'summing up', acknowledging their 'poor power to add or detract', his words signal deference to the uncapturability of the life it mourns.

It is the deference that moves her, that recognition that language can never live up to life once and for all. Nor should it. Language can never 'pin down' slavery, genocide, war. Nor should it yearn for the arrogance to be able to do so. Its force, its felicity is in its reach toward the ineffable.

Be it grand or slender, burrowing, blasting or refusing to sanctify; whether it laughs out loud or is a cry without an alphabet, the choice word, the chosen silence, unmolested language surges toward knowledge, not its destruction. But who does not know of literature banned because it is interrogative; discredited because it is critical; erased because alternate? And how many are outraged by the thought of a self-ravaged tongue?

Word-work is sublime, she thinks, because it is generative; it makes meaning that secures our difference, our human difference – the way in which we are like no other life.

We die. That may be the meaning of life. But we do language. That may be the measure of our lives.

'Once upon a time ...' visitors ask an old woman a question. Who are they, these children? What did they make of that encounter? What did they hear in those final words: 'The bird is in your hands'? A sentence that gestures towards possibility or one that drops a latch? Perhaps what the children heard was, 'It's not my problem. I am old, female, black, blind. What wisdom I have now is in knowing I cannot help you. The future of language is yours.'

They stand there. Suppose nothing was in their hands? Suppose the visit was only a ruse, a trick to get to be spoken to, taken seriously as they have not been before? A chance to interrupt, to violate the adult world, its miasma of discourse about them, for them, but never to them? Urgent questions are at stake, including the one they have asked: 'Is the bird we hold living or dead?'

Perhaps the question meant: 'Could someone tell us what is life? What is death?' No trick at all; no silliness. A straightforward question worthy of the attention of a wise one. An old one. And if the old and wise who have lived life and faced death cannot describe either, who can?

But she does not; she keeps her secret; her good opinion of herself; her gnomic pronouncements; her art without commitment. She keeps her distance, enforces it and retreats into the singularity of isolation, in

[2] To depict by painting or drawing.

[3] Morrison quotes from ABRAHAM LINCOLN's Gettysburg Address of 19 November 1863, which is included in this book.

sophisticated, privileged space.

Nothing, no word follows her declaration of transfer. That silence is deep, deeper than the meaning available in the words she has spoken. It shivers, this silence, and the children, annoyed, fill it with language invented on the spot.

'Is there no speech,' they ask her, 'no words you can give us that helps us break through your dossier of failures? Through the education you have just given us that is no education at all because we are paying close attention to what you have done as well as to what you have said? To the barrier you have erected between generosity and wisdom?

'We have no bird in our hands, living or dead. We have only you and our important question. Is the nothing in our hands something you could not bear to contemplate, to even guess? Don't you remember being young, when language was magic without meaning? When what you could say, could not mean? When the invisible was what imagination strove to see? When questions and demands for answers burned so brightly you trembled with fury at not knowing?

'Do we have to begin consciousness with a battle heroines and heroes like you have already fought and lost, leaving us with nothing in our hands except what you have imagined is there? Your answer is artful, but its artfulness embarrasses us and ought to embarrass you. Your answer is indecent in its self-congratulation. A made-for-television script that makes no sense if there is nothing in our hands.

'Why didn't you reach out, touch us with your soft fingers, delay the sound bite, the lesson, until you knew who we were? Did you so despise our trick, our modus operandi you could not see that we were baffled about how to get your attention? We are young. Unripe. We have heard all our short lives that we have to be responsible. What could that possibly mean in the catastrophe this world has become; where, as a poet said, "nothing needs to be exposed since it is already barefaced"?

'Our inheritance is an affront. You want us to have your old, blank eyes and see only cruelty and mediocrity? Do you think we are stupid enough to perjure ourselves again and again with the fiction of nationhood? How dare you talk to us of duty when we stand waist-deep in the toxin of your past?

'You trivialize us and trivialize the bird that is not in our hands. Is there no context for our lives? No song, no literature, no poem full of vitamins, no history connected to experience that you can pass along to help us start strong? You are an adult. The old one, the wise one. Stop thinking about saving your face. Think of our lives and tell us your particularized world. Make up a story. Narrative is radical, creating us at the very moment it is being created. We will not blame you if your reach exceeds your grasp; if love so ignites your words they go down in flames and nothing is left but their scald. Or if, with the reticence of a surgeon's hands, your words suture only the places where blood might flow.

'We know you can never do it properly – once and for all. Passion is never enough; neither is skill. But try. For our sake and yours, forget your name in the street; tell us what the world has been to you in the dark places and in the light. Don't tell us what to believe, what to fear. Show us belief's wide skirt and the stitch that unravels fear's caul. You, old woman, blessed with blindness, can speak the language that tells us what only language can: how to see without pictures. Language alone protects us from the scariness of things with no names. Language alone is meditation. Tell us what it is to be a woman so that we may know what it is to be a man. What moves at the margin. What it is to have no home in this place. To be set adrift from the one you knew. What it is to live at the edge of towns that cannot bear your company.

'Tell us about ships turned away from shorelines at Easter, placenta in a field. Tell us about a wagonload of slaves, how they sang so softly their breath was indistinguishable from the falling snow. How they knew from the hunch of the nearest shoulder that the next stop would be their last. How, with hands prayered in their sex, they thought of heat, then sun. Lifting their faces as though it was there for the taking. Turning as though there for the taking.

'They stop at an inn. The driver and his mate go in with the lamp, leaving them humming in the dark. The horse's void steams into the snow beneath its hooves and its hiss and melt are the envy of the freezing slaves.

'The inn door opens: a girl and a boy step away from its light. They climb into the wagon bed. The boy will have a gun in three years, but now he carries a lamp and a jug of warm cider. They pass it from mouth to mouth. The girl offers bread, pieces of meat and something more: a glance into the eyes of the one she serves. One helping for each man, two for each woman. And a look. They look back. The next stop will be their last. But not this one. This one is warmed.'

It's quiet again when the children finish speaking, until the woman breaks into the silence.

'Finally', she says, 'I trust you now. I trust you with the bird that is not in your hands because you have truly caught it. Look. How lovely it is, this thing we have done – together.'

Benito Mussolini
Italian dictator

Benito Amilcare Andrea Mussolini (1883–1945) was born in Predappio, the son of a blacksmith. After working as a teacher and journalist, he travelled to Switzerland, where he developed revolutionary beliefs, returning to Italy in 1904. After a brief period of imprisonment for political activities, he became editor in 1912 of the nationalist newspaper *Avanti*. He broke with the socialists over their neutral stance in World War I, and founded his own paper, *Il Popolo d'Italia* ('The People of Italy') which argued that only by supporting the Allies could Italy retrieve the disputed Austrian territories. Mussolini fought in World War I and was wounded. In 1919 he founded the fascist movement, ostensibly to serve the interests of neglected ex-servicemen, and used it to promote the extreme nationalism to which he was now committed. He turned the fascists against the communists, and in 1921 exploited his growing popularity to win election to the Chamber of Deputies. The following year his armed Blackshirts marched on Rome in a show of might. He presented himself as the only man capable of restoring order to a country that was slipping into chaos. In October 1922 Victor Emmanuel III invited him to form a government. In 1925 he took the title *Il Duce* ('The Leader'). Through intimidation, patronage and propaganda, he turned Italy into a totalitarian state by 1929. Despite aggression over Corfu, his foreign policy was not marked by overt expansionism until the mid-1930s. However, in 1935 he launched the conquest of Abyssinia (Ethiopia), which was followed in 1936 by large-scale intervention in the Spanish Civil War on the side of General Franco. During this period he moved increasingly towards co-operation with ADOLF HITLER, which culminated in the 1939 Pact of Steel and, eventually, the invasion of France in 1940. Mussolini annexed Albania in 1939 but failed to seize Greece in 1940. German military assistance signalled the beginning of his dependence on Hitler, and thereafter his actions were dictated largely by Berlin. Dissatisfaction with this policy and the expectation of Allied victory turned many of his supporters against him. Following the Allied landings in Sicily (1943), both the king and his own Fascist Council turned on him. He was rescued by German paratroopers and taken to northern Italy, in a doomed attempt to re-establish his authority. When that failed, he tried to flee the country, but was caught and summarily executed. His corpse was displayed in a public square in Como and mutilated.

'We must win the peace'
25 June 1923, Rome, Italy

During his first year as prime minister, Mussolini was still strengthening his grasp on power. One key strand of his appeal was patriotism, and at a rally to mark the fifth anniversary of the Battle of the Piave, he gave this grandstanding speech in celebration of Italian martial success.

Italy had entered World War I in 1915 on the side of the UK and France, hoping to win territory from Austria–Hungary and Germany. A critical conflict occurred in June 1918, when Italian troops repulsed an attack by the Austro-Hungarian army across the River Piave. Four months later, the Italian army scored an even more decisive victory at the Battle of Vittorio Veneto. However, Italy received little in the peace treaties that followed the war; and it was partly out of resentment over this that Mussolini had built his popularity.

Mussolini was a charismatic and inspiring public speaker, whose oratorical techniques − like his political policies − prefigured those of Hitler. Addressing a huge crowd at the Palazzo Venezia, he feigns reluctance to speak, before unleashing a typically rousing address.

Although he insists the Blackshirts' march on Rome 'buried the past', he alludes strongly to the city's ancient heritage as an invincible military power. His purpose is to enlist popular support and discourage dissent; and he excites the crowd into a denunciation of those who would 'maim victory', before rewarding them with a vision of Italy as a great and 'imperishable' power. The translation is by Baron Bernardo Quaranta di San Severino.

Fellow soldiers: after your ranks, so well disciplined and of such fine bearing, have marched past His Majesty the King, the intangible symbol of the country; after the austere ceremony in its silent solemnity before the tomb of the Unknown Warrior − after this formidable display of sacred strength, words from me are absolutely superfluous, and I do not intend to make a speech. The march of today is a manifestation full of significance and warning. A whole people in arms has met today in spirit in the Eternal City.[1] It is a whole people who, above unavoidable party differences, finds

[1] Rome.

itself strongly united when the safety of the common motherland is at stake.

[2] A major eruption of the Sicilian volcano had started earlier that month.

On the occasion of the Etna eruption,[2] national solidarity was wonderfully manifested; from every town, every village, one might say from every hamlet, a fraternal heart-throb went out to the land stricken by calamity.

Today tens of thousands of soldiers, thousands of standards – with men coming to Rome from all parts of Italy and from the far-away colonies, from abroad – bear witness that the unity of the Italian nation is an accomplished and irrevocable fact.

After seven months of government, to talk to you, my comrades of the trenches, is the highest honour which could fall to my lot. And I do not say this in order to flatter you, nor to pay you a tribute which might seem formal on an occasion like this. I have the right to interpret the thoughts of this meeting, which gathers to listen to my words, as an expression of solidarity with the national government.

[*Cries of assent.*]

Let us not utter useless and fantastical words. Nobody attacks the sacred liberty of the Italian people. But I ask you: should there be liberty to maim victory?

[*Cries of 'No! no!'*]

Should there be liberty to strike at the nation? Should there be liberty for those who have as their programme the overthrow of our national institutions?

[*Cries of 'No! no!'*]

I repeat what I explicitly said before. I do not feel myself infallible, I feel myself a man like you. I do not repulse – I cannot – I shall not repulse any loyal and sincere collaboration.

Fellow soldiers: the task which weighs on my shoulders, but also on yours, is simply immense, and to it we shall be pledged for many years. It is, therefore, necessary not to waste, but to treasure and utilize all the energies which could be turned to the good of our country.

Five years have passed since the battle of the Piave, from that victory … It is necessary to proclaim, for you who listen to me, and also for those who read what I say, that the victory of the Piave was the deciding factor of the war. On the Piave the Austro-Hungarian Empire went to pieces, from the Piave started the flight on white wings of the victory of the people in arms.

The government means to exalt the spiritual strength which rises out of the victory of a people in arms. It does not mean to disperse them, because it represents the sacred seed of the future. The more distant we get from those days, from that memorable victory, the more they seem to us wonderful, the more the victory appears enveloped in a halo of legend. In such a victory everybody would wish to have taken part!

We must win the peace! Too late somebody perceived that when the country is in danger, the duty of all citizens, from the highest to the lowest, is only one: to fight, to suffer and – if needs be – to die!

We have won the war, we have demolished an empire which threatened our frontiers, stifled us and held us for ever under the extortion of armed menace. History has no end.

Comrades: the history of peoples is not measured by years, but by tens of years, by centuries. This manifestation of yours is an infallible sign of the vitality of the Italian people. The phrase 'we must win the peace' is not an empty one. It contains a profound truth. Peace is won by harmony, by work and by discipline. This is the new gospel which has been opened before the eyes of the new generations who have come out of the trenches; a gospel simple and straightforward, which takes into account all the elements, which utilizes all the energies, which does not lend itself to tyrannies of grotesque exclusivism, because it has one sole aim, a common aim: the greatness and the salvation of the nation!

Fellow soldiers: you have come to Rome, and it is natural – I dare to say, fated! Because Rome is always, as it will be tomorrow and in the centuries to come, the living heart of our race! It is the imperishable symbol of our vitality as a people. Who holds Rome, holds the nation.

The Blackshirts buried the past. I assure you, my fellow-soldiers, that my government, in spite of the manifest or hidden difficulties, will keep its pledges. It is the government of Vittorio Veneto.[3] You feel it and you know it, and if you did not believe it, you would not be here assembled in this square.

[3] Mussolini refers to the battle between the Italian and Austro-Hungarian armies, October–November 1918. The Austro-Hungarian army collapsed following Italy's victory.

Carry back to your towns, to your lands, to your houses, distant but near to my heart, the vigorous impression of this meeting. Keep the flame burning, because that which has not been may be, because if victory was maimed once, it does not follow that it can be maimed a second time!

[*Loud cheers, repeated cries of, 'We swear it!'*]

I keep in mind your oath. I count upon you as I count upon all good Italians, but I count, above all, upon you, because you are of my generation, because you have come out from the bloody filth of the trenches, because you have lived and struggled and suffered in the face of death, because you have fulfilled your duty and have the right to vindicate that to which you are entitled, not only from the material but from the moral point of view.

I tell you, I swear to you, that the time is past forever when fighters returning from the trenches had to be ashamed of themselves; the time when, owing to the threatening attitudes of Communists, the officers received the cowardly advice to dress in plain clothes. [*Applause.*] All that is buried. You must not forget, and nobody forgets, that seven months ago 52,000 armed Blackshirts came to Rome to bury the past!

[*Loud cheers.*]

Soldiers, fellow soldiers: let us raise before our great unknown comrade the cry which sums up our faith. Long live the King! Long live Italy, victorious, impregnable, immortal!

[*Loud cheers, with flags raised.*]

'A solemn hour is about to strike'

2 October 1935, radio broadcast from Rome, Italy

By now, Mussolini's dictatorship was well established; and his ambitions had become increasingly expansionist. His most notorious aggression overseas was in north-east Africa.

During the late 19th century, Italy had repeatedly tried to link Italian Somaliland with part of neighbouring Abyssinia (now Ethiopia) but had never succeeded. Further disappointment followed after World War I, when Italy received little in the distribution of Germany's former colonies. Mussolini was eager for overseas territories, partly to absorb Italy's surplus unemployed.

Italy had signed a 20-year treaty of friendship with Abyssinia in 1928. However, following periods of unrest (possibly provoked by Italian influence) there were border clashes between Italian and Abyssinian troops in December 1934. In June 1935, Britain offered land in British Somaliland to Mussolini if he abandoned his designs on Abyssinia, but the offer was rejected. Against the advice of the King and most of his generals, Mussolini invaded.

Keen to bolster his prestige and popular support, he made this broadcast to announce the invasion. In characteristically bullish language, he describes Italy's territorial grievances, emphasizing the strength of the fascist state and the inevitability of victory.

The League of Nations imposed sanctions but, keen to avoid escalation, restricted them to non-essential commodities – Mussolini later admitted that oil sanctions would have forced him to abandon the project within a week.

It took Italian forces several months to occupy the capital, Addis Ababa, but Abyssinia was formally annexed by Italy in May 1936. Emperor HAILE SELASSIE made a famous appeal to the League of Nations, but Italy held the country until 1941.

Blackshirts of revolution, men and women of all Italy, Italians all over the world, beyond the mountains, beyond the seas, listen. A solemn hour is about to strike in the history of the country. Twenty million Italians are at this moment gathered in the squares of all Italy. It is the greatest demonstration that human history records. Twenty millions, one heart alone, one will alone, one decision.

This manifestation signifies that the tie between Italy and fascism is perfect, absolute, unalterable. Only brains softened by puerile illusions, by sheer ignorance, can think differently, because they do not know what exactly is the fascist Italy of 1935.

For many months the wheel of destiny and the impulse of our calm determination moves toward the goal. In these last hours, the rhythm has increased and nothing can stop it now.

It is not only an army marching towards its goal, but it is 44 million Italians marching in unity behind this army. Because the blackest of injustices is being attempted against them: that of taking from them their place in the sun. When, in 1915, Italy threw in her fate with that of the Allies,[1] how many cries of admiration, how many promises were heard? But after the common victory, which cost Italy 600,000 dead, 400,000 lost, one million wounded, when peace was being discussed around the table, only the crumbs of a rich colonial booty were left for us to pick up.

[1] See introduction to previous speech.

For 13 years we have been patient while the circle tightened around us at the hands of those who wish to suffocate us. We have been patient with Ethiopia for 40 years. It is enough now.

Instead of recognizing the rights of Italy, the League of Nations dares talk of sanctions, but until there is proof to the contrary I refuse to believe that the authentic people of France will join in supporting sanctions against Italy. Six hundred thousand dead whose devotion was so heroic that the enemy commander justly admired them – those fallen would now turn in their graves.

And until there is proof to the contrary, I refuse to believe that the authentic people of Britain will want to spill blood and send Europe into a catastrophe for the sake of a barbarian country, unworthy of ranking among civilized nations. Nevertheless, we cannot afford to overlook the possible developments of tomorrow.

To economic sanctions, we shall reply with our discipline, our spirit of sacrifice, our obedience. To military sanctions, we shall reply with military measures. To acts of war, we shall reply with acts of war.

A people worthy of their past and their name cannot and never will take a different stand. Let me repeat, in the most categorical manner, that the sacred pledge which I make at this moment, before all the Italians gathered together today, is that I shall do everything in my power to prevent a colonial conflict from taking on the aspect and weight of a European war.

This conflict may be attractive to certain minds, which hope to avenge their disintegrated temples through this new catastrophe. Never, as at this historical hour, have the people of Italy revealed such force of character, and it is against this people to which mankind owes its greatest conquest, this people of heroes, of poets and saints, of navigators, of colonizers, that the world dares threaten sanctions.

Italy, Italy: entirely and universally fascist! The Italy of the Blackshirt revolution, rise to your feet, let the cry of your determination rise to the skies and reach our soldiers in East Africa. Let it be a comfort to those who are about to fight. Let it be an encouragement to our friends and a warning to our enemies. It is the cry of Italy, which goes beyond the mountains and the seas out into the great world. It is the cry of justice and of victory!

Jawaharlal Nehru

Indian statesman

Jawaharlal Nehru *known as Pandit ('Teacher')* (1889–1964) was born in Allahabad, Uttar Pradesh, the son of Motilal Nehru, a prominent politician. He was educated in England, at Harrow and Trinity College, Cambridge. He read for the Bar, then returned to India and served in the High Court of Allahabad. A persistent vision of himself as an Indian GIUSEPPE GARIBALDI drove him to join the Indian Congress Committee in 1918. It also brought him, with scientific reservations, under the spell of MAHATMA GANDHI. He was imprisoned by the British in 1921 and spent 18 of the ensuing 25 years in jail. In 1928, he was elected president of the Indian National Congress, an office he often held afterwards, as the leader of the movement's socialist wing. Although sympathetic to the Allies in World War II, he did not co-operate, in common with other Congress Party leaders, and turned down the offer of dominion status for India in 1942. When India achieved independence in 1947, Nehru became its first prime minister and Minister of External Affairs. As democratic leader of the first republic within the commonwealth, he followed a policy of neutralism and peace-making during the Cold War, often acting as a go-between between the superpowers, and originated the theory of non-alignment. He committed India to a policy of industrialization and a reorganization of its states on a linguistic basis. Although he championed his people's claim to Kashmir, he acted with restraint in his attempts to bring this long-running dispute with Pakistan to a peaceful solution. His many publications include *Soviet Russia* (1929), *India and the World* (1936), *Independence and After* (1950) and an *Autobiography* (1936). His daughter Indira Gandhi (1917–84) served as prime minister of India, 1966–77 and 1980–4.

'A tryst with destiny'

14 August 1947, New Delhi, India

At midnight on 14 August 1947, India achieved the independence it had been actively seeking for nearly a century. The same day marked Partition, when a new nation, Pakistan, was created from northern regions of the country. The significance of this event, and its effect on the people who lived through it, are explored in Salman Rushdie's prize-winning novel *Midnight's Children*.

For Jawaharlal Nehru, this was not merely the fulfilment of a political goal. He had been raised in a powerful political family and had been a vital influence in the campaign for independence, leading the Congress Party from 1930. However, his presidency of the party had been challenged by Vallabhbhai Patel during the election of 1946, by which time independence was imminent. Experienced and politically astute, Patel had received majority support, but with Gandhi's backing Nehru retained the post, which brought with it the premiership of the new republic. The sense of destiny was not lost on him.

Moments before midnight, Nehru delivered this memorable and moving address to the Indian Assembly. Highly literate and acutely aware of the momentous circumstances, he rose to the occasion with a speech notable for its lyrical, poetic tone but laced with pragmatism. Both a celebration of victory and a warning of the hard work ahead, it was greeted with ecstatic cries of '*Jai Hind!*' ('Victory to India!').

Long years ago, we made a tryst with destiny, and now the time comes when we shall redeem our pledge, not wholly or in full measure, but very substantially. At the stroke of the midnight hour, when the world sleeps, India will awake to life and freedom. A moment comes, which comes but rarely in history, when we step out from the old to the new, when an age ends, and when the soul of a nation, long suppressed, finds utterance. It is fitting that at this solemn moment we take the pledge of dedication to the service of India and her people and to the still larger cause of humanity.

At the dawn of history, India started on her unending quest; and trackless centuries are filled with her striving and the grandeur of her success and her failures. Through good and ill fortune alike, she has never lost sight of that quest, or forgotten the ideals which gave her strength. We end today a period of ill-fortune and India discovers herself again. The achievement we celebrate today is but a step, an opening of opportunity, to the greater triumphs and achievements that await us. Are we brave enough and wise enough to grasp this opportunity and accept the challenge of the future?

Freedom and power bring responsibility. The responsibility rests upon this assembly, a sovereign body representing the sovereign people of India. Before the birth of freedom we have endured all the pains of labour and our hearts are heavy with the memory of this sorrow. Some of those pains continue even now. Nevertheless, the past is over and it is the future that beckons to us now.

That future is not one of ease or resting but of incessant striving so that we may fulfil the pledges we have so often taken, and the one we shall take today. The service of India means the service of the millions who suffer. It means the ending of poverty and ignorance and disease and inequality of opportunity. The ambition of the greatest man of our generation has been to wipe every tear from every eye. That may be beyond us, but as long as there are tears and suffering, so long our work will not be over.

And so we have to labour and to work, and work hard, to give reality to our dreams. Those dreams are for India, but they are also for the world, for all the nations and peoples are too closely knit together today for any one of them to imagine that it can live apart. Peace has been said to be indivisible; so is freedom, so is prosperity now, and so also is disaster in this one world that can no longer be split into isolated fragments.

To the people of India, whose representatives we are, we make an appeal to join us with faith and confidence in this great adventure. This is no time for petty and destructive criticism, no time for ill-will or blaming others. We have to build the noble mansion of free India where all her children may dwell.

❧

'The light has gone out of our lives'
30 January 1948, radio broadcast from New Delhi, India

❧

Announcing the assassination of MAHATMA GANDHI was an early test of Nehru's mettle as leader of independent India.

Gandhi's death was perhaps the most dramatic event in the violence that erupted in India and Pakistan following Partition. He had devoted much of his life to the peaceful liberation of India from British rule and was viewed as the country's spiritual leader. A Hindu, he had promoted the unity of mankind under one God and tolerance towards followers of all religions. He had originally hoped for a united India, but Partition had proved unavoidable.

Around 500,000 people died in the ensuing turmoil; the border regions of Bengal and the Punjab were particularly badly hit. Gandhi made heroic efforts to curtail this violence, undertaking a series of fasts to shame the perpetrators. But some Hindus felt he had made too many concessions to Muslims. On 30 January 1948, he was on his way to a prayer vigil in New Delhi when he was shot dead by Nathuram Godse, a young Hindu fanatic.

Breaking the news in this radio announcement, Nehru was anxious to avoid saying anything that might prompt further bloodshed. In his speech, he pays heartfelt tribute to Gandhi's legacy, stressing the importance of peaceful conduct among those paying their respects. He urges his listeners not to react violently, invoking Gandhi's own principles of non-violence.

Godse and his co-conspirator Narayan Apte were tried and hanged the following year, but by then the worst of the violence had died away.

❧

Friends and comrades: the light has gone out of our lives and there is darkness everywhere. I do not know what to tell you and how to say it. Our beloved leader, Bapu[1] as we called him, the Father of the Nation, is no more. Perhaps I am wrong to say that. Nevertheless, we will not see him again as we have seen him for these many years. We will not run to him for advice

[1] Hindi: 'Father'.

and seek solace from him, and that is a terrible blow, not to me only, but to millions and millions in this country. And it is a little difficult to soften the blow by any other advice that I or anyone else can give you.

The light has gone out, I said, and yet I was wrong. For the light that shone in this country was no ordinary light. The light that has illumined this country for these many many years will illumine this country for many more years, and a thousand years later, that light will still be seen in this country and the world will see it and it will give solace to innumerable hearts. For that light represented something more than the immediate present; it represented the living, the eternal truths, reminding us of the right path, drawing us from error, taking this ancient country to freedom.

All this has happened when there was so much more for him to do. We could never think that he was unnecessary or that he had done his task. But now, particularly when we are faced with so many difficulties, his not being with us is a blow most terrible to bear.

A madman has put an end to his life, for I can only call him mad who did it, and yet there has been enough of poison spread in this country during the past years and months, and this poison has had an effect on people's minds. We must face this poison, we must root out this poison, and we must face all the perils that encompass us, and face them not madly or badly, but rather in the way that our beloved teacher taught us to face them.

The first thing to remember now is that none of us dare misbehave because he is angry. We have to behave like strong and determined people, determined to face all the perils that surround us, determined to carry out the mandate that our great teacher and our great leader has given us, remembering always that if, as I believe, his spirit looks upon us and sees us, nothing would displease his soul so much as to see that we have indulged in any small behaviour or any violence.

So we must not do that. But that does not mean that we should be weak, but rather that we should, in strength and in unity, face all the troubles that are in front of us. We must hold together; and all our petty troubles and difficulties and conflicts must be ended in the face of this great disaster. A great disaster is a symbol to us to remember all the big things of life and forget the small things of which we have thought too much. In his death he has reminded us of the big things of life, that living truth, and if we remember that, then it will be well with India …

It was proposed by some friends that Mahatmaji's body should be embalmed for a few days to enable millions of people to pay their last homage to him. But it was his wish, repeatedly expressed, that no such thing should happen, that this should not be done, that he was entirely opposed to any embalming of his body, and so we decided that we must follow his wishes in this matter, however much others might have wished otherwise.

And so the cremation will take place on Saturday in Delhi city by the side of the Jumna river. On Saturday forenoon, about 11.30, the bier will be taken out at Birla House[2] and it will follow a prescribed route and go to the Jumna river. The cremation will take place there at about 4 PM. The place and route will be announced by radio and the press.

[2] The large house in Delhi where Gandhi lived during his final months, and the scene of his assassination.

People in Delhi who wish to pay their last homage should gather along this route. I will not advise too many of them to come to Birla House, but rather to gather on both sides of this long route from Birla House to the Jumna river. And I trust that they will remain there in silence, without any demonstrations. That is the best way and the most fitting way to pay homage to this great soul. Also, Saturday should be a day of fasting and prayer for all of us.

Those who live elsewhere, out of Delhi and in other parts of India, will no doubt also take such part as they can in this last homage. For them also, let this be a day of fasting and prayer. And at the appointed time for cremation, that is 4pm on Saturday afternoon, people should go to the river or to the sea and offer prayers there.

And while we pray, the greatest prayer that we can offer is to take a pledge to dedicate ourselves to the truth, and to the cause for which this great countryman of ours lived and for which he had died. That is the best prayer that we can offer him and his memory. That is the best prayer that we can offer to India and ourselves.

Jai Hind.[3]

[3] Hindi: 'Hail India' or 'Victory to India'.

Ingrid Newkirk
English animal rights campaigner

Ingrid Newkirk (1949–) was born in Kingston-on-Thames and grew up in New Delhi, India, 1956–64. In 1969, she emigrated to the USA, working as a law enforcement officer in Maryland (1970–6); then for the Commission on Public Health and Washington Humane Society in the District of Columbia (1976–81). With Alex Pacheco, she founded People for the Ethical Treatment of Animals (PETA) in 1980, becoming its president in 1981. Her achievements as an animal rights·campaigner include co-ordinating the first arrest of an American scientist on animal cruelty charges, helping establish Taiwan's first anti-cruelty legislation and successfully campaigning to end General Motors' use of animals in crash tests. Her publications include *PETA's Celebrity Cookbook* (2000), *Making Kind Choices* (2001) and *The PETA Practical Guide to Animal Rights – Simple Acts of Kindness to Help Animals in Trouble* (2009).

'Animals are not inanimate objects'
April 2001, Colorado, USA

As the figurehead of PETA, Ingrid Newkirk has long experience as a public speaker. In this speech – given during a series sponsored by the USA's Public Broadcasting Service – she outlines the principles that guide her organization, using simple, coherent and well-illustrated arguments that are hard to refute.

Her central theme of 'human prejudice' proposes that we have 'miscategorized ourselves' as superior to other species. Animals, she points out, experience emotions, use forms of language, have many talents we do not possess and share much of our DNA. She moves on to describe some shocking animal rights violations, and the action taken by PETA to prevent them.

PETA continues to lobby under Newkirk's leadership, using aggressive, often controversial media campaigns to target the four areas it considers most harmful to animals: factory farming, animal testing, fur farming and animals in entertainment. It has enlisted the support of celebrities including Paul McCartney, Stella McCartney, Roger Moore and Pamela Anderson.

The animal rights movement has often been associated with violent extremist organizations, including the Animal Liberation Front and Earth Liberation Front, which the US Federal Bureau of Investigation has identified as 'a serious terrorist threat'. However, PETA has consistently refused to condemn these groups, and has at times provided funds to both organizations, causing many commentators to question its tax-exempt status.

But despite the negative publicity surrounding animal rights activism, Newkirk's common-sense appeal for compassion is hard to resist.

In 1980, a small group of friends started People for the Ethical Treatment of Animals. Back then, no-one had heard of 'animal rights'. Today, people remain confused as to what the term means, but they *do* know that how we treat animals is important. Acknowledging animals' rights can be as simple as respecting their needs. Of course, animals don't need complex rights, like the right to drive or the right to vote – although considering the mess we sometimes make of our elections, perhaps that's not such a bad idea.[1]

Animals enjoy the natural world without ruining it. All they need is to be able to take a drink of clean water, to be nourished, to have shelter from extreme weather and to be left in peace. It isn't much to ask. Yet today, few animals have those vital things. The reason they don't have them is because human beings dominate the world and, to put it bluntly, enslave animals.

That may sound harsh, but think about it. If allowed to be themselves, animals are self-sufficient, whole and vital … Animals don't despoil the waterways or woods, as humans do with our poptop bottles and plastic bags, and, far worse, with the hog and chicken waste from our intensive farming systems. The Alaskan wilderness, which is often described as 'uninhabited' and 'unspoiled' has, in fact, always been heavily inhabited by billions of animals who have kept it pristine.

[1] Newkirk refers to the US presidential election of 7 November 2000, an extremely close contest between GEORGE W BUSH and the Democrat candidate Al Gore (1948–), in which the final outcome was determined by the US Supreme Court and was not conceded until 13 December.

Although animals have wants and needs and behaviours of their own, they are often treated as nothing more than hamburgers, handbags, living test tubes, cheap burglar alarms or amusements for human beings. They are not allowed to live their lives, but instead are forced to serve us, giving us carriage rides, performing silly tricks and having their skin used for clothing. We use their flesh as food, despite knowing that we can eat far healthier food, and they are the surrogate tasters of our poisons.

I was inspired to form People for the Ethical Treatment of Animals after reading a book called *Animal Liberation*, written by the philosopher Peter Singer.[2] Dr Singer suggests that instead of just being just kind to animals, which everyone knows one should be, we might try viewing animals as individuals like ourselves, as members of other cultures or, indeed, other nations …

After all, animals are not inanimate objects; they are feeling beings who experience love and joy, loneliness and fear, in much, if not exactly, the same way we do. Although we have set ourselves up as gods who can do anything we please simply because we please, biologically we are but one animal among many. Many anthropologists believe that we have miscategorized ourselves as a separate class of animal (hominids) out of pure conceit, for now that we have unravelled the human genome, we see that we share 99 per cent of our DNA with other primates.

When we think about it, perhaps all that keeps us from treating the other animals with respect – the ultimate respect being to leave them in peace to do what they wish to do – is simple prejudice. Human beings have a sorry history of prejudice. Through the ages, our feelings of superiority have caused us to denigrate and abuse others we have felt were somehow less important or less intelligent than ourselves, instead of exercising magnanimity and protecting them. …

The questions for our generation, and for future generations, are: 'Who are animals, what are we doing to them, and should we change, no matter how comfortable we may be in our old ways?'

Some members of our own species may have been to the Moon, and some can split the atom, but there are many ways in which human talents pale in comparison to the animals' … Our own military is still learning from dolphins, who use sonar not only to navigate, but also to stun their prey, and from bats who can find their way in total darkness. We cannot decipher animals' languages, but it is indisputable that they have them.

Monkeys have separate warnings to alert the troupe to a threat from the sky, such as a hawk, and a threat from the ground, such as a poisonous snake. Prairie dogs use different calls to signal the approach of a single human being, a friend and a foe. Whales sing their histories through the great oceans, adding new bits of information every year. The tree frog drums his messages to others far away, while other frogs 'hear' with their skin …

The turtle navigates by the earth's magnetic field, and starlings read the heavens for direction. It was an albatross, not a man, who first circumnavigated the globe and knew the earth was round. As for family values, geese mate for life, and a male will risk hunters' guns to stick by his injured wife when she is shot.

When people say, 'But all that is just instinct,' I wonder how they think we human beings select our own mates, the people we love. Is it by cold logic? … I was working for a humane society[3] when I first started thinking about animals in a different way. I was already familiar with the often-terrible

[2] The Australian philosopher and teacher Peter Singer (1946–) is the author *Animal Liberation* (1975; revised 1990 and 2002), considered a seminal work in its field.

[3] The Washington Humane Society, established in 1870 to protect homeless and abused animals.

things that happen to dogs and cats and wildlife …

One afternoon, a cruelty call took me to a barn littered with broken glass. A family had moved away, leaving the animals behind. They were all dead except for one small pig. I lifted him up and held him in my arms, then gave him his first drink of water in perhaps a week. Then I bundled him off to the vet.

My job was to prosecute the people who had wilfully caused this small animal's suffering, so I made sure that I dutifully collected all the evidence. But while driving home that night, I began to wonder what I could eat for dinner. Ah, I thought, conducting a mental inventory of the contents of my refrigerator, I have some pork chops. The penny dropped! I realized how inconsistent it was of me to be preparing to charge someone with a crime for abusing one little pig while paying someone else to hurt and kill the other little pig I was going to eat for dinner.

I had never been to a slaughterhouse then, but, like most people, I knew that such places must be appalling. Today, I can tell you first-hand about the look in the eyes of the animals. As they are prodded and kicked along to their death, they can smell and hear and see what is already happening to those in front of them in the slaughter line … No animals wish to be killed and all of them – dogs and chickens and pigs – struggle fiercely to avoid the man with the knife. All are equally filled with fear.

It is perhaps awful to say, but the moment of death in the slaughterhouse may be the best part of these animals' lives. I say that because to satisfy the tastes of so many people who crave chicken wings and burgers, animals raised for meat have a truly wretched existence. They are castrated and dehorned, have their tails amputated and their beaks seared off with a hot wire, all without benefit of anaesthetics.

Calves are separated from their loving mothers soon after birth so that the milk meant for these baby animals can become cheese and ice cream and the calf can be raised for veal. After weeks in darkness, the calves stumble down the same ramp their mothers will walk when their lives are considered insufficiently profitable. Animals on factory farms are crowded together in enormous numbers. Pigs must breathe in the ammonia from their own waste, collected in troughs beneath their pens. They suffer blackened lungs and have difficulty breathing, and their limbs become infected with open sores from lying on the hard cement.

Undercover video footage shot by PETA shows pigs routinely clubbed with iron gateposts and beaten to death with claw hammers. The lame are thrown in and out of the trucks, and in bitter winter weather, the pigs' sensitive flesh freezes to the sides of the metal truck body.

'Broiler chickens' are bred to be so top-heavy that the bones in their legs splinter and they spend much of their lives in chronic pain. In the egg factories, chickens can never stretch a wing or find room to lie down. When their laying life is over, they are stuffed into crates so roughly that their wings often fracture. The dying are afforded no care. Sometimes you may pass a transport truck and see them looking out through the slats, their eyes filled with despair. What we do to them is neither 'civilized' nor humane.

In 1981, People for the Ethical Treatment of Animals embarked on its first investigation. One of us took a job in a laboratory in Silver Spring, Maryland, where a group of macaque monkeys were kept. The monkeys had been taken as babies from their homes and families in the Philippines. The nerves in their spines had been cut, and this affected their ability to control their arms. The cages in which they were kept were rarely cleaned; in fact, they were so filthy that fecal matter rose to a height of a couple of inches in some places and fungus grew on it.

The experimenter didn't bother to give the monkeys food bowls, so when their food was thrown into the cage, the pellets fell through the wire and landed in the waste collection trays below. The monkey would have to pick the food pellets out of these trays in order to eat. The animals' limbs were also injured from getting caught in the rusted and broken cage wires, and the monkeys had lost a great deal of their hair from malnutrition. The researcher had converted a small refrigerator into a shock box; inside it, the monkeys were punished if they failed to pick up objects with their damaged limbs.

We persuaded the police to do something unprecedented: to serve a search warrant on the laboratory and remove the monkeys. Seeing the faces of those monkeys turned up to the sunlight for the first time in many years as they came out of the lab encouraged people to seek alternatives to animal use.

Scientists and laypeople wondered aloud whether it was morally right to experiment on animals at all and whether, indeed, it was scientifically valid to do so. Some physicians … began clamouring for funding for human epidemiological studies, the cloning of human skin, and computer technology that can bring quick and directly applicable results.

When PETA started, most cosmetics, toiletries, and household products such as oven cleaner were still tested on animals. Today, more than 550 product companies have switched to using human skin patch tests, computer assays, and human corneas from eye banks, and from gathering guinea pig data to analysing human data. The arguments that animals must be used faded into oblivion because consumers refused to buy the products until the companies changed.

The current challenge is to shift agencies, like the US Environmental Protection Agency, away from animal use. The most common toxicity tests still in use take a substance, like weed killer or mustard gas, the effects of which we have long known from tragic human experience, and force-feed that substance to rabbits … No painkillers are given as substances like septic tank cleaner are smeared onto the animals' abraded skin to see how much flesh they corrode, the results being crudely recorded. Chemicals are also placed in animals' eyes and forced into animals' lungs. When enough people protest, this will stop …

Most people, when shown how their actions contribute to cruelty and given options, will make compassionate choices. In the US alone, while the demand for cheap flesh results in more than nine billion animals suffering for the table each year – that's one million animals eaten every hour – the number of vegetarians is growing rapidly …

PETA's message is that each one of us is a vital player in life's great orchestra. Every day, our choices perpetuate or stop needless violence … I ask that you please join us in making the world a less violent place for all living beings.

Thank you.

John Henry Newman

English clergyman, poet and religious writer

John Henry Newman *later Cardinal Newman* (1801–90) was born in London, the son of a banker of Dutch ancestry. He was educated privately in Ealing, and concluded from a youthful study of the Bible that the Pope was the Antichrist. He studied at Trinity College, Oxford from 1817, but suffered a nervous breakdown and barely graduated in 1821. He stayed in Oxford, where he was ordained an Anglican priest in 1824. From 1827, he was a central member of the Oxford Movement, which sought to link the modern Anglican church to its Catholic roots. After travel in southern Europe, 1832–3, he returned to Oxford and began writing his *Tracts for the Times* on Anglican doctrine. In 1842, he entered retreat at Littlemore, emerging the following year with a retraction of his criticisms of the Roman Catholic church, into which he was received in 1845. He visited Rome in 1846–7 and soon after his return settled in Edgbaston, Birmingham, where he founded the Oratory in 1848. His lectures on 'Anglican Difficulties' (1850) drew attention to his power of irony and delicate literary style, and were followed by lectures on 'Catholicism in England' (1851) and 'The Idea of a University' (1852). He was rector of Dublin Catholic University, 1851–9. In 1864 the novelist Charles Kingsley passed casual comment in *Macmillan's Magazine* on the indifference of the Roman Church to the virtue of truthfulness, which he asserted Newman shared. This led to a correspondence, which in turn resulted in the publication of Newman's remarkable *Apologia pro Vita Sua*. In 1865, he wrote a poem of singular beauty, 'The Dream of Gerontius', republished in *Verses on Various Occasions* (1874). In 1870, he published his *Grammar of Assent*, on the philosophy of faith. In the controversies which led to the Vatican Council of 1869–70, Newman was in vehement opposition to the Ultramontanes, who claimed papal infallibility, and the bitterness between the two parties ran high. Pope Leo XIII, anxious to show sympathy with the moderates, summoned Newman to Rome in 1879, where he was made a cardinal.

'The state of sin is a demoniacal possession'

19 March 1848, Birmingham, England

Three years after his conversion from Anglicanism to Roman Catholicism, and less than a year after his ordination as a Roman Catholic priest, Newman preached this sermon on the nature of sin in St Chad's Roman Catholic Cathedral, Birmingham.

Like his writings, Newman's sermons – which he always wrote out in longhand before he delivered them – revealed a mastery of the English language. Taking as his starting point Christ's transfiguration and exorcism of a possessed youth, Newman compares sinfulness with demoniac possession. One example of such possession, he says, aligning himself with the temperance movements of the 19th century, is drunkenness.

Newman held controversial views on matters of papal infallibility and on the relative merits of other religions. Here, however, he speaks of his gratitude in knowing 'the true religion, which has been from the beginning and has been always the same'. The relief of the convert, alienated from Anglicanism and finding refuge in Catholicism, is palpable.

In the passage of St Matthew's Gospel, part of which is read as the Gospel for this day, we have a very remarkable contrast, the contrast between this world and the unseen world. It is so distinctly drawn out and so impressive, that it may be profitable to us, with God's grace, to attempt to enlarge upon it.

Our Lord often passed the night in prayer, and as afterwards in that sad night before his Passion, he took with him three Apostles,[1] to witness his prayer in agony, so at an earlier time, he took the same favoured three with him to witness his prayer in ecstasy and glory … As he prayed, his countenance became bright and glorious, and he was lifted off the earth. So he remained communing with his father, ministered to by Moses and Elias, till a voice came from the cloud, which said, 'This is my beloved Son; hear ye him.'[2]

The sight had been so wonderful, so transporting, that St Peter could not help crying out. He knew not what he said, he did not know how to express

[1] Peter, James and John.

[2] Matthew 17:5.

³ Matthew 17:4.

his inward feelings, nor did he understand in a moment all the wonders about him. He could but say: 'Lord, it is good for us to be here.'³ Simple words, but how much they contain in them. It was good; it was the good of man; it was the great good; it was our good. He did not say that the sight was sublime and marvellous. He was not able to reflect upon it and describe it. His reason did not speak, but his affections. He did but say that it was good to be there. And he wished that great good to continue to him ever

…

Now let us see what was taking place below while they were above. When they reached the crowd, they found a dispute going on between the rest of the Apostles and the Scribes. The subject of it seems to have been the poor demoniac, who is next spoken of.

A father had brought his son to be cured by the Apostles. He was a frightful maniac, possessed by the devil. None could hold him. The spirit took away his voice and hearing. He was ordinarily deaf and dumb, but sometimes he dashed himself to the ground, threw himself into the fire or into the water, foamed at the mouth and then perhaps collapsed.

The devil was too much for the Apostles. They could not master him, they could not cast him out. They were reduced to a sort of despair, and this was the occasion, as it appears, of their dispute with the Scribes, who might be taunting them with their failure. Oh the contrast between what St Peter had come from and what he had now come to! He had left peace, stillness, contemplation, the vision of Heaven, and he had come into pain, grief, confusion, perplexity, disappointment and debate.

Now this contrast, as I have said, between the Mount of Transfiguration and the scene at its foot fitly represents to us the contrast between the world and the church, between the things seen and the things unseen. I will not dwell on the mere physical evils of this life, though they are enough to appal us – the miseries of sickness, pain, want, cold, hunger; but let us dwell upon the moral evils which it contains. The poor youth who was brought to Christ to be cured was possessed by the devil and – alas – is not a great portion, is not the greatest portion of mankind at this day possessed by the devil too?

… As the poor epileptic in the Gospel was under the mastery of the evil spirit, so that his eyes, his ears, his tongue, his limbs were not his own, so does that same miserable spirit possess the souls of sinners, ruling them, impelling them here and there, doing what he will with them, not indeed doing the same with everyone: some he moves one way, some in another, but all in some pitiable, horrible and ungodly way.

Wickedness is sometimes called madness in Scripture – so it is. As literal madness is derangement of the reason, so sin is derangement of the heart, of the spirit, of the affection. And as madness was the disorder in which possession by the devil showed itself in Scripture, so this madness of the heart and spirit is the disorder which in all ages the devil produces in the spirit. And as there are different forms of that madness which is derangement of the reason, so there are different forms of that worse madness which is sin. In an asylum there are different forms of the disorder, and so this whole world is one vast madhouse, of which the inmates, though shrewd enough in matters of this world, yet in spiritual matters are in one way or another mad.

For example, what is the drunkard but a sort of madman? Who is possessed and ruled by an evil spirit if not he? He has delivered himself over to the power of Satan, and he is his slave. He cannot do what he would.

Through his own fault he cannot do what he would. In that he differs from the real madman, whose fault it is not that he is mad, whereas it is the drunkard's own fault that he is the slave of evil.

But so it is: he has put himself under the power of evil; he puts himself away from grace; he cannot make up his mind to will to be otherwise; his will is set on what is evil – and thus he is a mere slave. The relentless spirit of evil carries him off to the haunts of intemperance. He knows that he is ruining himself, soul and body; he knows the misery he brings upon his family; he knows that he is shortening his life; he curses perhaps his own infatuation while he persists in it. He wishes he had never been born.

Perhaps he has a bad illness in consequence, and the medical man who attends him says to him that it will to a certainty be his death if he does not reform. He knows it, yet his sin is too strong for him, and in this despair and agony of mind perhaps he takes up some dreadful belief, most injurious to God's honour and glory, as if he were fated to all this and could not help it. He says: 'Every man is fated to be what he is. It can't be helped. It's not my fault. I never could have been otherwise. It did not depend on me.'

Miserable and most untrue saying. Is it not the saying of a madman? Is it not the word of one possessed with the devil? Here, then, is one instance in which the demoniac in the Gospel may be taken as a type and emblem of the state of the world.

Others are possessed by spirits of a different kind. They are not outrageous, but they are bowed down to the earth and kept in a close awful captivity. How many, for instance, are there with hard hearts! And what is hardness of heart but a sort of possession by the evil one? The drunkard has often moments of religious feeling, but there are numbers, and they perhaps are what the world calls moral, well-conditioned men, who seem to have no heart whatever for spiritual subjects.

A true Christian cannot hear the name of Christ without emotion, but in this country there are multitudes, poor and rich, who are set up on nothing else whatever but on getting money, and who have not taste whatever for religion … The demoniac in the Gospel not only cried out and tore himself, but at other times he became dry or shrivelled, which seems to mean a sort of collapse. What is this love of the world, which we see whether in rich or poor, but a sort of shrivelling up or collapse of the soul? What then is so like a possession of Satan? And can any state be more fearful than that of an immortal being, who is to live forever, attempting to live on mortal food, and having no relish for that immortal food which alone is its true nourishment?

… Accustom yourself to the idea, my brethren, and a terrible idea it is, that the state of sin is a demoniacal possession. Consider how such a possession of the body is spoken of in Scripture. Consider how the devil tormented the poor suffering body which he was allowed to get hold of. Then consider, what we may so often see now, what a fearful affliction madness is. Then, when you have considered these two things and got a clear hold of the idea, think that sin is just such a possession of the heart and spirit. It is not that the body is afflicted, as in the case of a demoniac. It is not that the reason is afflicted, as in the case of a madman. But it is that the spirit, the heart, the affections, the conscience, the will are in the power of an evil spirit, who sways them about at his please. How awful is this!

When, then, St Peter, St James and St John came down from the mount and saw the miserable youth tormented by an evil spirit, they saw in that youth a figure and emblem of that world of sinners, to whom in due time they were sent to preach. But this is not all. They found their brethren disputing with the Scribes, or at least the Scribes questioning with them. Here is another circumstance in which the scene which they saw resembled the old. The world is full of wrangling and debate – and not unreasonably, because when the heart is wrong the reason goes wrong too; and when men corrupt themselves and lead bad lives, then they do not see the truth, but have to hunt about after it, and this creates a great confusion …

When men do not see, they begin to reason. When men do not see, they begin to talk loud. When men do not see, they begin to quarrel. Look around, my brethren, is it not so? Have not you theories innumerable, arguments interminable offered to you, on all sides? One man says truth is here, another there. Alas, alas, how many religions are there in this great yet unhappy country? Here you have the Scribes wrangling with each other. There is no end of religions – there are new ones continually. Now if one is true, the other is false; if the new is true the old are false; if the old are true the new are false. All cannot be true. Can even a dozen be true, or six, or two? Can more than *one* be true? And which is that one? Thank God, we, my brethren, know which that one is – this is the true religion, which has been from the beginning and has been always the same, but on all sides there are wranglings and doubtings and disputings, uncertainty and change.

Now I will mention one other respect in which the scene before the three Apostles when they came down from the Mount resembled the world, and that is a still more miserable one. You will observe that their brethren could not cast the evil spirit out. So it is now. There is an immense weight of evil in the world. We Catholics, and especially we Catholic priests, have it in charge to resist, to overcome the evil; but we cannot do what we would, we cannot overcome the giant, we cannot bind the strong man. We do a part of the work, not all. It is a battle which goes on between good and evil, and though by God's grace we do something, we cannot do more. There is confusion of nations and perplexity. It is God's will that so it should be, to show his power. He alone can heal the soul. He alone can expel the devil. And therefore we must wait for a great deal, till he comes down, till he comes down from his seat on high, his seat in glory, to aid us and deliver us.

In that day we shall enter, if we be worthy, the fullness of that glory, of which the three Apostles had the foretaste in the moment of Transfiguration. All is darkness here, all is bright in heaven. All is disorder here, all is order there. All is noise here and there there is stillness, or if sounds are heard, they are the sweet sounds of the eternal harps on which the praises of God are sung. Here we are in a state of uncertainty; we do not know what is to happen …

But all this will be set right in the world to come, and if St Peter could say at the Transfiguration, 'It is good to be here,' much more shall we have cause to say so when we see the face of God. For then we shall be like our Lord Himself, we shall have glorified bodies, as he had then and has now. We shall have put off flesh and blood, and receive our bodies at the last day, the same indeed, but incorruptible, spiritual bodies, which will be able to see and enjoy the presence of God in a way which was beyond the three Apostles in the days of their mortality. Then the envious malignant spirit will be cast out, and we shall have nothing to fear, nothing to be perplexed at, for the Lord God shall lighten us and encompass us and we shall be in perfect security and peace.

Richard M Nixon
American politician

Richard Milhous Nixon (1913–94) was born in Yorba Linda, California, into a Quaker family of Irish descent. He was educated at Whittier College and Duke University. After practising as a lawyer, he served in the US Navy (1942–6), then ran for Congress as a Republican in California, defeating his Democratic opponent by painting him as a communist sympathizer, a strategy he would use often in his career. His fearless outspokenness and tactical brilliance boosted his political career, and he was a prominent member of the House Committee on Un-American Activities. After serving in the Senate (1951–3) he became vice president under DWIGHT D EISENHOWER in 1953 and was re-elected in 1956. In 1958 he and his wife Pat visited Peru and Venezuela, where they faced violent anti-American demonstrations. In 1959 he exchanged frank dialogue with NIKITA KHRUSHCHEV on a visit to Moscow. He became the Republican presidential candidate in 1960, losing narrowly to JOHN F KENNEDY. In 1962, he stood for the governorship of California, but was again defeated. Despite an emotional declaration that he was retiring from politics, he returned, winning the presidential election in 1968 by a small margin. In 1972, he was re-elected with a large majority. His administration (1969–74) was marked by continuing controversy over the Vietnam War, especially the invasion of Cambodia (1970) and the heavy bombing of North Vietnam, which led to a ceasefire in 1973. He initiated the Strategic Arms Limitation Talks (SALT) with the USSR (1969–72), reopened US relations with the People's Republic of China (1972), and became the first US president to visit the country. In June 1972 there was a burglary at the Democratic National Committee's headquarters in the Watergate building, Washington. Nixon's re-election team was swiftly implicated. During the official investigation which followed, Nixon lost credibility, at first claiming executive privilege for senior White House officials to prevent them being questioned; then refusing to hand over tapes of relevant conversations. On 9 August 1974, after several leading members of his government had been found guilty of involvement in the Watergate scandal, he resigned, thus averting the threat of impeachment. In his autobiographies *The Memoirs of Richard Nixon* (1978) and *In the Arena: A Memoir of Victory, Defeat, and Renewal* (1990) and other works written during his retirement, he sought to salvage his damaged reputation and rebuild his image as a statesman.

'I intend to continue the fight'
23 September 1952, radio and television broadcast from Hollywood, California, USA

At the 1952 Republican convention, Nixon won the party's nomination to run for vice president alongside the popular presidential candidate Dwight D Eisenhower. The campaign threatened to come off the rails, however, after allegations that Nixon had accepted $18,000 in illegal political contributions. Facing demands for his withdrawal from the Republican ticket, Nixon made an astute decision to appeal directly to the public through the new medium of television.

Speaking without a script from an NBC television studio in Hollywood, Nixon denied that any donations had been used improperly. He revealed every aspect of his personal finances, from his savings and loans to his debts (much of which is omitted here for reasons of space), conveying an image of prudence and austerity. He told 60 million viewers – the largest television audience ever at that time – that his wife owned a 'respectable Republican cloth coat' and not a mink coat, and famously appealed to their sentimentality by admitting he had accepted the gift of a cocker spaniel, which his six-year-old daughter had named Checkers.

Initially, Nixon feared his address had backfired. However, his blend of humility and defiance struck a chord among viewers, who bombarded Eisenhower with telegrams, urging him to keep Nixon as his running mate. The Eisenhower–Nixon ticket duly won the election in November.

Television would not always be so kind to Nixon: in a televised debate during the 1960 presidential campaign, his gaunt, perspiring appearance contrasted with the handsome, relaxed JOHN F KENNEDY. Many think this contrast lost Nixon the election.

My fellow Americans: I come before you tonight as a candidate for the vice presidency and as a man whose honesty and integrity have been questioned. The usual political thing to do when charges are made against you is to either ignore them or to deny them without giving details.

I believe we've had enough of that in the United States, particularly with the present administration in Washington, DC. To me the office of the vice presidency of the United States is a great office and I feel that the people have got to have confidence in the integrity of the men who run for that office and who might obtain it.

I have a theory, too, that the best and only answer to a smear or to an honest misunderstanding of the facts is to tell the truth. And that's why I'm here tonight. I want to tell you my side of the case.

I am sure that you have read the charge and you've heard that I, Senator Nixon, took $18,000 from a group of my supporters.

Now, was that wrong? And let me say that it was wrong – I'm saying, incidentally, that it was wrong and not just illegal. Because it isn't a question of whether it was legal or illegal, that isn't enough. The question is, was it morally wrong?

I say that it was morally wrong if any of that $18,000 went to Senator Nixon for my personal use. I say that it was morally wrong if it was secretly given and secretly handled. And I say that it was morally wrong if any of the contributors got special favours for the contributions that they made.

And now to answer those questions let me say this. Not one cent of the $18,000 or any other money of that type ever went to me for my personal use. Every penny of it was used to pay for political expenses that I did not think should be charged to the taxpayers of the United States ...

Some of you will say, and rightly, 'Well, what did you use the fund for, Senator? Why did you have to have it?' Let me tell you in just a word how a Senate office operates.

[1] Nixon meant to say $10,000.

First of all, a senator gets $15,000 a year[1] in salary. He gets enough money to pay for one trip a year, a round trip that is, for himself and his family between his home and Washington, DC. And then he gets an allowance to handle the people that work in his office, to handle his mail. And the allowance for my state of California is enough to hire 13 people ...

But there are other expenses which are not covered by the government. And I think I can best discuss those expenses by asking you some questions.

Do you think that when I or any other senator makes a political speech, has it printed, should charge the printing of that speech and the mailing of that speech to the taxpayers? Do you think, for example, when I or any other senator makes a trip to his home state to make a purely political speech, that the cost of that trip should be charged to the taxpayers? Do you think when a senator makes political broadcasts or political television broadcasts, radio or television, that the expense of those broadcasts should be charged to the taxpayers?

Well, I know what your answer is. It is the same answer that audiences give me whenever I discuss this particular problem. The answer is no. The taxpayers shouldn't be required to finance items which are not official business but which are primarily political business.

But then the question arises, you say, 'Well, how do you pay for these and how can you do it legally?' And there are several ways that it can be done ... The first way is to be a rich man. I don't happen to be a rich man so I couldn't use that one. Another way that is used is to put your wife on the payroll. Let me say, incidentally, my opponent, my opposite number for the vice presidency on the Democratic ticket,[2] does have his wife on the payroll. And has had her on his payroll for the past ten years ...

[2] The US politician John Sparkman (1899–1985), who served as the Senator from Alabama, 1946–79.

That's his business and I'm not critical of him for doing that. You will have to pass judgement on that particular point. But I have never done that for this reason. I have found that there are so many deserving stenographers and secretaries in Washington that needed the work that I just didn't feel it was right to put my wife[3] on the payroll.

My wife's sitting over here. She's a wonderful stenographer. She used to teach stenography and she used to teach shorthand in high school. That was when I met her. And I can tell you folks that she's worked many hours at night and many hours on Saturdays and Sundays in my office and she's done a fine job. And I'm proud to say tonight that in the six years I've been in the House and the Senate of the United States, Pat Nixon has never been on the government payroll ...

And so I felt that the best way to handle these necessary political expenses of getting my message to the American people and the speeches I made, the speeches that I had printed, for the most part, concerned this one message – of exposing this administration, the communism in it, the corruption in it – the only way that I could do that was to accept the aid which people in my home state of California who contributed to my campaign and who continued to make these contributions after I was elected were glad to make.

And let me say I am proud of the fact that not one of them has ever asked me for a special favour. I'm proud of the fact that not one of them has ever asked me to vote on a bill other than as my own conscience would dictate. And I am proud of the fact that the taxpayers – by subterfuge or otherwise – have never paid one dime for expenses which I thought were political and shouldn't be charged to the taxpayers.

Let me say, incidentally, that some of you may say, 'Well, that's all right, Senator; that's your explanation, but have you got any proof?'

And I'd like to tell you this evening that just about an hour ago we received an independent audit of this entire fund. I suggested to Governor Sherman Adams, who is the chief of staff of the Dwight Eisenhower campaign, that an independent audit and legal report be obtained. And I have that audit here in my hand.

It's an audit made by the Price, Waterhouse & Co firm, and the legal opinion by Gibson, Dunn & Crutcher, lawyers in Los Angeles, the biggest law firm and incidentally one of the best ones in Los Angeles.

I'm proud to be able to report to you tonight that this audit and this legal opinion is being forwarded to General Eisenhower. And I'd like to read to you the opinion that was prepared by Gibson, Dunn & Crutcher and based on all the pertinent laws and statutes, together with the audit report prepared by the certified public accountants.

> 'It is our conclusion that Senator Nixon did not obtain any financial gain from the collection and disbursement of the fund by Dana Smith;[4] that Senator Nixon did not violate any Federal or state law by reason of the operation of the fund, and that neither the portion of the fund paid by Dana Smith directly to third persons nor the portion paid to Senator Nixon to reimburse him for designated office expenses constituted income to the Senator which was either reportable or taxable as income under applicable tax laws. (Signed) Gibson, Dunn & Crutcher by Alma H Conway.'

Now that, my friends, is not Nixon speaking, but that's an independent audit which was requested because I want the American people to know all the facts ...

Pat and I have the satisfaction that every dime that we've got is honestly ours. I should say this – that Pat doesn't have a mink coat. But she does

[3] Nixon had married Thelma Catherine 'Patricia' Ryan (1912–93) in 1940. Her Irish father nicknamed her Pat as she was born on 16 May, the day before ST PATRICK's day.

[4] The US lawyer Dana Smith administered Nixon's political expenses fund.

have a respectable Republican cloth coat. And I always tell her that she'd look good in anything.

One other thing I probably should tell you – because if we don't they'll probably be saying this about me too – we did get something, a gift, after the election. A man down in Texas heard Pat on the radio mention the fact that our two youngsters would like to have a dog. And believe it or not, the day before we left on this campaign trip we got a message from Union Station in Baltimore saying they had a package for us. We went down to get it.

You know what it was? It was a little cocker spaniel dog in a crate that he'd sent all the way from Texas. Black and white spotted. And our little girl Tricia, the six-year-old, named it Checkers. And you know, the kids, like all kids, love the dog and I just want to say this right now, that regardless of what they say about it, we're gonna keep it.

It isn't easy to come before a nationwide audience and air your life as I've done. But I want to say some things before I conclude …

I know that this is not the last of the smears. In spite of my explanation tonight, other smears will be made; others have been made in the past. And the purpose of the smears, I know, is this – to silence me, to make me let up.

Well, they just don't know who they're dealing with … I intend to continue the fight. Why do I feel so deeply? Why do I feel that in spite of the smears, the misunderstandings, the necessity for a man to come up here and bare his soul as I have? Why is it necessary for me to continue this fight?

And I want to tell you why. Because, you see, I love my country. And I think my country is in danger. And I think that the only man that can save America at this time is the man that's running for president on my ticket – Dwight Eisenhower.

You say, 'Why do I think it's in danger?' and I say look at the record. Seven years of the **TRUMAN**–Acheson administration[5] and what's happened? Six hundred million people lost to the Communists, and a war in Korea in which we have lost 117,000 American casualties. And I say to all of you that a policy that results in a loss of 600 million people to the Communists and a war which costs us 117,000 American casualties isn't good enough for America.

And I say that those in the State Department that made the mistakes which caused that war and which resulted in those losses should be kicked out of the State Department just as fast as we can get 'em out of there.

And let me say that I know Mr **STEVENSON**[6] won't do that, because he defends the Truman policy; and I know that Dwight Eisenhower will do that, and that he will give America the leadership that it needs …

And, now, finally, I know that you wonder whether or not I am going to stay on the Republican ticket or resign. Let me say this: I don't believe that I ought to quit because I'm not a quitter. And, incidentally, Pat's not a quitter. After all, her name was Patricia Ryan and she was born on St Patrick's Day, and you know the Irish never quit.

But the decision, my friends, is not mine. I would do nothing that would harm the possibilities of Dwight Eisenhower to become president of the United States. And for that reason I am submitting to the Republican National Committee tonight through this television broadcast the decision which it is theirs to make.

Let them decide whether my position on the ticket will help or hurt. And

[5] Truman's vice president was Alben W Barkley (1949–53), but Nixon refers to his Secretary of State Dean Acheson (1893–71), who had advocated non-intervention in Korea and was seen by some as having a dangerously lax attitude to communism.

[6] Stevenson was the Democratic candidate for the presidency in the elections of 1952 and 1956.

I am going to ask you to help them decide. Wire and write the Republican National Committee whether you think I should stay on or whether I should get off. And whatever their decision is, I will abide by it.

But just let me say this last word. Regardless of what happens I'm going to continue this fight. I'm going to campaign up and down America until we drive the crooks and the Communists and those that defend them out of Washington.

'There can be no whitewash at the White House'
30 April 1973, broadcast from Washington, DC, USA

The Watergate scandal began on 17 June 1972, when police arrested five men who had broken into the headquarters of the Democratic Party at the Watergate building in Washington, DC. They were soon linked to the Republican Party's Committee for the Re-election of the President.

Nixon probably had no prior knowledge of the break-in – whose perpetrators had broken in three weeks earlier to install bugging devices – but quickly realized it could undermine his re-election chances. He therefore ordered the FBI to halt its investigations, paid hush money to the five burglars and instructed his special counsel, John Dean, to conceal any involvement by the administration.

By early 1973, however, the conspiracy of concealment was unravelling. *The Washington Post* had already broken news of the scandal, and in February a special Senate committee was set up to investigate the affair. In televised hearings, Dean accused Nixon of involvement in the cover-up. Nixon responded by firing Dean; three other aides swiftly resigned.

In this speech, broadcast from the Oval Office at 9pm, he announced these resignations and proclaimed his innocence. Nixon made a show of leadership, accepting responsibility for mistakes even if they were not of his making, and looking beyond the scandal to the 'great goals' of peace, opportunity, decency and civility. Later, he would be forced to make less bullish statements on the affair.

Good evening. I want to talk to you tonight from my heart on a subject of deep concern to every American.

In recent months, members of my administration and officials of the Committee for the Re-election of the President – including some of my closest friends and most trusted aides – have been charged with involvement in what has come to be known as the Watergate affair. These include charges of illegal activity during and preceding the 1972 presidential election and charges that responsible officials participated in efforts to cover up that illegal activity.

The inevitable result of these charges has been to raise serious questions about the integrity of the White House itself. Tonight I wish to address those questions.

Last June 17, while I was in Florida trying to get a few days' rest after my visit to Moscow,[1] I first learned from news reports of the Watergate break-in. I was appalled at this senseless, illegal action, and I was shocked to learn that employees of the re-election committee were apparently among those guilty. I immediately ordered an investigation by appropriate government authorities. On September 15, as you will recall, indictments were brought against seven defendants in the case.

As the investigations went forward, I repeatedly asked those conducting the investigation whether there was any reason to believe that members of my administration were in any way involved. I received repeated assurances that there were not ...

Until March of this year, I remained convinced that the denials were true and that the charges of involvement by members of the White House staff were false. The comments I made during this period, and the comments

[1] In May 1972, Nixon visited Moscow to sign arms limitation treaties with the USSR.

made by my press secretary in my behalf, were based on the information provided to us at the time we made those comments. However, new information then came to me which persuaded me that there was a real possibility that some of these charges were true, and suggesting further that there had been an effort to conceal the facts both from the public, from you, and from me.

As a result, on March 21, I personally assumed the responsibility for co-ordinating intensive new inquiries into the matter, and I personally ordered those conducting the investigations to get all the facts and to report them directly to me, right here in this office.

I again ordered that all persons in the government or at the re-election committee should co-operate fully with the FBI, the prosecutors, and the grand jury. I also ordered that anyone who refused to co-operate in telling the truth would be asked to resign from government service. And, with ground rules adopted that would preserve the basic constitutional separation of powers between the Congress and the presidency, I directed that members of the White House staff should appear and testify voluntarily under oath before the Senate committee which was investigating Watergate.

I was determined that we should get to the bottom of the matter, and that the truth should be fully brought out – no matter who was involved … Whatever may appear to have been the case before, whatever improper activities may yet be discovered in connection with this whole sordid affair, I want the American people, I want you to know beyond the shadow of a doubt that during my term as president, justice will be pursued fairly, fully, and impartially, no matter who is involved. This office is a sacred trust and I am determined to be worthy of that trust.

Looking back at the history of this case, two questions arise. How could it have happened? Who is to blame?

Political commentators have correctly observed that during my 27 years in politics I have always previously insisted on running my own campaigns for office.

But 1972 presented a very different situation. In both domestic and foreign policy, 1972 was a year of crucially important decisions, of intense negotiations, of vital new directions, particularly in working toward the goal which has been my overriding concern throughout my political career – the goal of bringing peace to America, peace to the world.

That is why I decided, as the 1972 campaign approached, that the presidency should come first and politics second. To the maximum extent possible, therefore, I sought to delegate campaign operations, to remove the day-to-day campaign decisions from the president's office and from the White House. I also, as you recall, severely limited the number of my own campaign appearances.

Who, then, is to blame for what happened in this case?

For specific criminal actions by specific individuals, those who committed those actions must, of course, bear the liability and pay the penalty.

For the fact that alleged improper actions took place within the White House or within my campaign organization, the easiest course would be for me to blame those to whom I delegated the responsibility to run the campaign. But that would be a cowardly thing to do. I will not place the blame on subordinates – on people whose zeal exceeded their judgement and who may have done wrong in a cause they deeply believed to be right.

In any organization, the man at the top must bear the responsibility. That responsibility, therefore, belongs here in this office. I accept it. And I pledge to you tonight, from this office, that I will do everything in my power to ensure that the guilty are brought to justice and that such abuses are purged from our political processes in the years to come, long after I have left this office.

Some people, quite properly appalled at the abuses that occurred, will say that Watergate demonstrates the bankruptcy of the American political system. I believe precisely the opposite is true. Watergate represented a series of illegal acts and bad judgements by a number of individuals. It was the system that has brought the facts to light and that will bring those guilty to justice – a system that in this case has included a determined grand jury, honest prosecutors, a courageous judge, John Sirica,[2] and a vigorous free press.[3]

[2] The US lawyer John Sirica (1904–92) was the Chief Judge of the District Court for the District of Columbia. He presided over the burglars' trial, and later demanded that Nixon turn over his recordings of White House conversations.

[3] Nixon alludes to the investigative reporting of the *Washington Post* journalists Bob Woodward (1943–) and Carl Bernstein (1944–), who received leaked information about the scandal from a source known then only as 'Deep Throat'. In 2005, his identity was revealed as W Mark Felt (1913–2008), a senior FBI official during the early 1970's.

It is essential now that we place our faith in that system – and especially in the judicial system. It is essential that we let the judicial process go forward, respecting those safeguards that are established to protect the innocent as well as to convict the guilty. It is essential that in reacting to the excesses of others, we not fall into excesses ourselves. It is also essential that we not be so distracted by events such as this that we neglect the vital work before us, before this nation, before America, at a time of critical importance to America and the world.

Since March, when I first learned that the Watergate affair might in fact be far more serious than I had been led to believe, it has claimed far too much of my time and my attention. Whatever may now transpire in the case, whatever the actions of the grand jury, whatever the outcome of any eventual trials, I must now turn my full attention – and I shall do so – once again to the larger duties of this office. I owe it to this great office that I hold, and I owe it to you – to my country … There is vital work to be done toward our goal of a lasting structure of peace in the world – work that cannot wait, work that I must do …

When I think of this office – of what it means – I think of all the things that I want to accomplish for this nation, of all the things I want to accomplish for you.

On Christmas Eve, during my terrible personal ordeal of the renewed bombing of North Vietnam[4] – which after twelve years of war finally helped to bring America peace with honour – I sat down just before midnight. I wrote out some of my goals for my second term as president. Let me read them to you.

[4] On 18 December 1972, Nixon ordered a new bombing campaign against North Vietnam, code-named Operation Linebacker Two. It lasted for 12 days, and resulted in the deaths of up to 1,600 North Vietnamese and 90 US airmen.

'To make it possible for our children, and for our children's children, to live in a world of peace.

'To make this country be more than ever a land of opportunity – of equal opportunity, full opportunity for every American.

'To provide jobs for all who can work, and generous help for those who cannot work.

'To establish a climate of decency and civility, in which each person respects the feelings and the dignity and the God-given rights of his neighbour.

'To make this a land in which each person can dare to dream, can live his dreams – not in fear, but in hope – proud of his community, proud of his country, proud of what America has meant to himself and to the world.'

These are great goals. I believe we can, we must work for them. We can achieve them. But we cannot achieve these goals unless we dedicate ourselves to another goal.

We must maintain the integrity of the White House, and that integrity must be real, not transparent. There can be no whitewash at the White House.

We must reform our political process, ridding it not only of the violations of the law but also of the ugly mob-violence and other inexcusable campaign tactics that have been too often practised and too readily accepted in the past, including those that may have been a response by one side to the excesses or expected excesses of the other side. Two wrongs do not make a right.

I have been in public life for more than a quarter of a century. Like any other calling, politics has good people and bad people. And let me tell you, the great majority in politics – in the Congress, in the federal government, in the state government – are good people. I know that it can be very easy, under the intensive pressures of a campaign, for even well-intentioned people to fall into shady tactics, to rationalize this on the grounds that what is at stake is of such importance to the nation that the end justifies the means. And both of our great parties have been guilty of such tactics in the past.

In recent years, however, the campaign excesses that have occurred on all sides have provided a sobering demonstration of how far this false doctrine can take us. The lesson is clear: America, in its political campaigns, must not again fall into the trap of letting the end, however great that end is, justify the means.

I urge the leaders of both political parties, I urge citizens, all of you, everywhere, to join in working toward a new set of standards, new rules and procedures to ensure that future elections will be as nearly free of such abuses as they possibly can be made. This is my goal. I ask you to join in making it America's goal.

❧

'This house has a great heart'
9 August 1974, Washington, DC, USA
❧

The beginning of the end for Nixon's presidency came when the Senate committee investigating the Watergate affair learned he had had a recording system installed in the Oval Office of the White House. The committee subpoenaed the recordings he had made of conversations that took place there, but Nixon initially refused to release them.

On 5 August 1974, however, he surrendered transcripts, in one of which he clearly discussed using the Central Intelligence Agency to block the Federal Bureau of Investigation's probe into the Watergate burglary. The House Judiciary Committee recommended that Nixon be removed from office by impeachment, but Nixon chose instead to become the first US president to resign.

On 8 August, he made a national broadcast announcing his resignation. The following morning, members of his staff gathered in the East Room of the White House for an emotional farewell. Like his Checkers speech years earlier, this one was unscripted, and demonstrates Nixon's remarkable resilience under pressure. His concluding advice, however – that his listeners should 'never get discouraged' and should remember that 'those who hate you don't win unless you hate them' – seems most readily applicable to Nixon himself.

❧

Members of the cabinet, members of the White House staff, all of our friends here: I think the record should show that this is one of those spontaneous things that we always arrange whenever the president comes in to speak, and it will be so reported in the press, and we don't mind, because they have to call it as they see it.

But on our part, believe me, it is spontaneous. You are here to say goodbye to us, and we don't have a good word for it in English – the best is *au revoir*. We will see you again.

I just met with the members of the White House staff – you know, those who serve here in the White House day in and day out – and I asked them to do what I ask all of you to do, to the extent that you can, and of course are requested to do so: to serve our next president[1] as you have served me and previous presidents – because many of you have been here for many years – with devotion and dedication, because this office, great as it is, can only be as great as the men and women who work for and with the president.

This house, for example – I was thinking of it as we walked down this hall, and I was comparing it to some of the great houses of the world that I have been in. This isn't the biggest house. Many and most, in even smaller countries, are much bigger. This isn't the finest house. Many in Europe, particularly, and in China, Asia, have paintings of great, great value, things that we just don't have here and probably will never have until we are 1,000 years old or older.

But this is the best house. It is the best house, because it has something far more important than numbers of people who serve, far more important than numbers of rooms or how big it is, far more important than numbers of magnificent pieces of art.

This house has a great heart, and that heart comes from those who serve. I was rather sorry they didn't come down. We said goodbye to them upstairs. But they are really great. And I recall after so many times I have made speeches, and some of them pretty tough, yet I always come back; or after a hard day – and my days usually have run rather long – I would always get a lift from them, because I might be a little down but they always smiled.

And so it is with you. I look around here and I see so many on this staff that, you know, I should have been by your offices and shaken hands, and I would love to have talked to you and found out how to run the world – everybody wants to tell the president what to do, and boy, he needs to be told many times – but I just haven't had the time. But I want you to know that each and every one of you, I know, is indispensable to this government.

I am proud of this cabinet. I am proud of all the members who have served in our cabinet. I am proud of our sub-cabinet. I am proud of our White House staff. As I pointed out last night, sure, we have done some things wrong in this administration, and the top man always takes the responsibility, and I have never ducked it. But I want to say one thing: we can be proud of it. Five and a half years. No man or no woman came into this administration and left it with more of this world's goods than when he came in. No man or no woman ever profited at the public expense or the public till. That tells something about you.

Mistakes, yes. But for personal gain, never. You did what you believed in. Sometimes right, sometimes wrong. And I only wish that I were a wealthy man – at the present time, I have got to find a way to pay my taxes[2] [*Laughter*] – and if I were, I would like to recompense you for the sacrifices that all of you have made to serve in government.

But you are getting something in government – and I want you to tell this to your children, and I hope the nation's children will hear it, too – something in government service that is far more important than money. It is a cause bigger than yourself. It is the cause of making this the greatest nation in the world, the leader of the world, because without our

[1] The US politician Gerald R Ford (1913–2006) served as Nixon's vice president from 1973, and succeeded him to serve as president, 1974–7. In September 1974, he granted Nixon a comprehensive pardon.

[2] In October 1973, it was revealed that Nixon had failed to pay over $400,000 in taxes. He insisted that this had been unintentional, famously asserting, 'I am not a crook'. In April 1974, he pledged to make good the underpayment, with interest.

leadership, the world will know nothing but war, possibly starvation or worse, in the years ahead. With our leadership it will know peace, it will know plenty …

[3] THEODORE ROOSEVELT.

Now, however, we look to the future. I had a little quote in the speech last night from TR.[3] As you know, I kind of like to read books. I am not educated, but I do read books – [*laughter*] – and the TR quote was a pretty good one.

Here is another one I found as I was reading, my last night in the White House, and this quote is about a young man. He was a young lawyer in New York. He had married a beautiful girl, and they had a lovely daughter, and then suddenly she died, and this is what he wrote. This was in his diary.

He said, 'She was beautiful in face and form and lovelier still in spirit. As a flower she grew and as a fair young flower she died. Her life had been always in the sunshine. There had never come to her a single great sorrow. None ever knew her who did not love and revere her for her bright and sunny temper and her saintly unselfishness. Fair, pure and joyous as a maiden, loving, tender and happy as a young wife. When she had just become a mother, when her life seemed to be just begun and when the years seemed so bright before her, then by a strange and terrible fate death came to her. And when my heart's dearest died, the light went from my life forever.'[4]

[4] Roosevelt married Alice Hathaway Lee (1861–84) in 1880, when he was 22. She died two days after giving birth to their daughter. In a cruel twist of fate, Roosevelt's mother died the same day.

That was TR in his twenties. He thought the light had gone from his life forever – but he went on. And he not only became president but, as an ex-president, he served his country, always in the arena, tempestuous, strong, sometimes wrong, sometimes right, but he was a man.

And as I leave, let me say, that is an example I think all of us should remember. We think sometimes when things happen that don't go the right way; we think that when you don't pass the bar exam the first time – I happened to, but I was just lucky; I mean, my writing was so poor the bar examiner said, 'We have just got to let the guy through.' We think that when someone dear to us dies, we think that when we lose an election, we think that when we suffer a defeat that all is ended. We think, as TR said, that the light had left his life forever.

Not true. It is only a beginning, always. The young must know it; the old must know it. It must always sustain us, because the greatness comes not when things go always good for you, but the greatness comes and you are really tested, when you take some knocks, some disappointments, when sadness comes, because only if you have been in the deepest valley can you ever know how magnificent it is to be on the highest mountain.

And so I say to you on this occasion, as we leave, we leave proud of the people who have stood by us and worked for us and served this country. We want you to be proud of what you have done. We want you to continue to serve in government, if that is your wish. Always give your best, never get discouraged, never be petty. Always remember: others may hate you, but those who hate you don't win unless you hate them, and then you destroy yourself.

And so, we leave with high hopes, in good spirit and with deep humility, and with very much gratefulness in our hearts. I can only say to each and every one of you, we come from many faiths, we pray perhaps to different gods – but really the same God in a sense – but I want to say for each and every one of you, not only will we always remember you, not only will we always be grateful to you, but always you will be in our hearts and you will be in our prayers.

Thank you very much.

Barack Obama
American politician

Barack Hussein Obama II (1961–) is the 44th President of the United States, the first African American to hold the office. The son of a white American anthropologist and a black Kenyan economist, Obama was born in Honolulu, Hawaii, where his parents met while studying at University of Hawai'i at Manoa. He studied at Columbia University and Harvard Law School, and subsequently practised as a civil rights attorney in Chicago. From 1992 to2004 he also taught at the University of Chicago Law School. In 1995 he published a memoir, *Dreams from My Father: A Story of Race and Inheritance*, a moving, lyrical account of his early life and a tribute to his father, who had been killed in a car crash in 1982.

Obama's political career began in the 1990s. From 1997 to 2004, he served three terms in the Illinois Senate, and in 2004 Obama ran a successful campaign to represent Illinois in the United States Senate. It was at this time that he first gained national media prominence, especially with his keynote address at the Democratic National Convention in the run-up to the November election. He began his presidential campaign in 2007 and in 2008 received the presidential nomination of the Democratic Party, after narrowly defeating Hillary Rodham Clinton in the primaries.

After defeating the Republican nominee, John McCain, in the general election, Obama was sworn in as president on 20 January 2009. His 2008 election was accompanied by a surge of popular optimism among liberal and left-leaning voters, especially the young, as well as globally. In the long shadow cast by the 9/11 Attacks and the wars in Afghanistan and Iraq, Obama's election seemed to herald a new age of idealism and inclusion. Obama's struggle to carry through reforms and his failure to fulfil election promises such as the closure of the detention centre at Guantanamo Bay led to a degree of disillusion. Nonetheless, he was re-elected president in November 2012 and inaugurated for a second term on 20 January 2013.

'We can be better'
12 January 2011, McKale Center, University of Arizona, Tucson

Barack Obama's power as a political orator is widely recognized and has undoubtedly played a significant role in his political career, especially during the 2008 election. A controlled but impassioned delivery, combined with the almost lyrical quality of the speeches themselves, have resulted in such masterly, crowd-pleasing master classes as the 2004 keynote speech to the Democratic National Convention and the iconic 'Yes, we can' New Hampshire primary speech of January 2008.

Obama's speech in Tucson, Arizona, was delivered as part of the memorial for the victims of the 2011 Tucson shooting. On 8 January 2011 US Representative Gabrielle Giffords and 18 others were shot by Jared Lee Loughner during a constituent meeting held in a supermarket parking lot in the Tucson suburb Casas Adobes. Six people died, including the District Court Chief Judge John Roll, Gabe Zimmerman, one of Giffords's aides, and a nine-year-old girl, Christina-Taylor Green. The primary target, Gifford, who was shot in the head at point-blank range, survived and has made a slow recovery. Loughner's motivation was unclear, although he had been recently diagnosed with schizophrenia.

The speech was written by Obama in collaboration with his speechwriter Cody Keenan and was viewed by some 30 million Americans on television. Its dignity and restraint, together with its powerful statement of the value of community and mutual responsibility, won Obama widespread praise.

Thank you. Please. Please, be seated.
To the families of those we've lost, to all who called them friends, to the students of this university, the public servants who are gathered here, the people of Tucson and the people of Arizona: I have come here tonight as an American who, like all Americans, kneels to pray with you today and will stand by you tomorrow.
There is nothing I can say that will fill the sudden hole torn in your hearts. But know this: The hopes of a nation are here tonight. We mourn with you for the fallen. We join you in your grief. And we add our faith

to yours that Representative Gabrielle Giffords[1] and the other living victims of this tragedy will pull through.

Scripture tells us, 'There is a river whose streams make glad the city of God, the holy place where the most high dwells. God is within her, she will not fall; God will help her at break of day.'[2]

On Saturday morning, Gabby, her staff, and many of her constituents gathered outside a supermarket to exercise their right to peaceful assembly and free speech.

They were fulfilling a central tenet of the democracy envisioned by our founders: representatives of the people answering questions to their constituents, so as to carry their concerns back to our nation's capital. Gabby called it 'Congress on Your Corner,' just an updated version of government of and by and for the people.

And that quintessentially American scene, that was the scene that was shattered by a gunman's bullets. And the six people who lost their lives on Saturday, they, too, represented what is best in us, what is best in America.

Judge John Roll[3] served our legal system for nearly 40 years.

A graduate of this university and a graduate of this law school, Judge Roll was recommended for the federal bench by John McCain 20 years ago, appointed by President George H W Bush, and rose to become Arizona's chief federal judge.

His colleagues described him as the hardest-working judge within the Ninth Circuit. He was on his way back from attending mass, as he did every day, when he decided to stop by and say hi to his representative.

John is survived by his loving wife, Maureen, his three sons, and his five beautiful grandchildren.

George and Dorothy Morris – 'Dot' to her friends – were high school sweethearts who got married and had two daughters. They did everything together, traveling the open road in their R.V., enjoying what their friends called a 50-year honeymoon.

Saturday morning, they went by the Safeway to hear what their congresswoman had to say. When gunfire rang out, George, a former Marine, instinctively tried to shield his wife.

Both were shot. Dot passed away.

A New Jersey native, Phyllis Schneck retired to Tucson to beat the snow. But in the summer, she would return east, where her world revolved around her three children, her seven grandchildren, and two-year-old great-granddaughter. A gifted quilter, she'd often work under her favorite tree, or sometimes she'd sew aprons with the logos of the Jets and the Giants to give out at the church where she volunteered. A Republican, she took a liking to Gabby and wanted to get to know her better.

Dorwan and Mavy Stoddard grew up in Tucson together about 70 years ago. They moved apart and started their own respective families, but after both were widowed, they found their way back here, to, as one of Mavy's daughters put it, 'be boyfriend and girlfriend again.'

When they weren't out on the road in their motor home, you could find them just up the road, helping folks in need at the Mountain Avenue Church of Christ. A retired construction worker, Dorwan spent his spare time fixing up the church along with their dog, Tux. His final act of self-lessness was to dive on top of his wife, sacrificing his life for hers.

Everything – everything Gabe Zimmerman[4] did, he did with passion, but his true passion was helping people. As Gabby's outreach director, he made the cares of thousands of her constituents his own, seeing to

[2] Psalms 46:4. Obama discussed his speech with the White House-based Pentecostal clergyman Joshua DuBois; the religious imagery, however, is restrained.

[3] John McCarthy Roll (1947–2011) served on the US District Court for the District of Arizona, from 1991 until his death, serving as chief judge from 2006.

[1] Gabrielle ('Gabby') Giffords (1970–) was Democratic member of the US House of Representative for Arizona's 8th Congressional District, 2007–12. A year after the shooting she resigned her seat, to focus on her recovery, but with the promise to return to politics.

[4] Gabriel Matthew ('Gabe') Zimmerman (1980–2011) had worked for Congresswoman Giffords for the previous five years.

[5] US national programme that guarantees access to health insurance for the over-65s and other vulnerable groups.

it that seniors got the Medicare[5] benefits that they had earned, that veterans got the medals and the care that they deserved, that government was working for ordinary folks.

He died doing what he loved: talking with people and seeing how he could help. And Gabe is survived by his parents, Ross and Emily, his brother, Ben, and his fiancee, Kelly, who he planned to marry next year.

And then there is nine-year-old Christina-Taylor Green. Christina was an A student. She was a dancer. She was a gymnast. She was a swimmer. She decided that she wanted to be the first woman to play in the Major Leagues, and as the only girl on her Little League team, no one put it past her.

She showed an appreciation for life uncommon for a girl her age. She'd remind her mother, 'We are so blessed. We have the best life.' And she'd pay those blessings back by participating in a charity that helped children who were less fortunate.

Our hearts are broken by their sudden passing. Our hearts are broken, and yet our hearts also have reason for fullness.

Our hearts are full of hope and thanks for the 13 Americans who survived the shooting, including the congresswoman many of them went to see on Saturday. I have just come from the University Medical Center, just a mile from here, where our friend Gabby courageously fights to recover even as we speak.

And I want to tell you – her husband, Mark, is here, and he allows me to share this with you. Right after we went to visit, a few minutes after we left her room and some of her colleagues from Congress were in the room, Gabby opened her eyes for the first time.

Gabby opened her eyes for the first time.

Gabby opened her eyes.

Gabby opened her eyes, so I can tell you, she knows we are here, she knows we love her, and she knows that we are rooting for her through what is undoubtedly going to be a difficult journey. We are there for her.

Our hearts are full of thanks for that good news, and our hearts are full of gratitude for those who saved others. We are grateful to Daniel Hernandez, a volunteer in Gabby's office.

And, Daniel, I'm sorry, you may deny it, but we've decided you are a hero, because you ran through the chaos to minister to your boss and tended to her wounds and help keep her alive.

We are grateful to the men who tackled the gunman as he stopped to reload.

They're right over there.

We – we are grateful for petite Patricia Maisch, who wrestled away the killer's ammunition and undoubtedly saved some lives.

[6] In the US, 'first responder' is a person qualified to give pre-hospital care in emergencies. Most US policemen and all firefighters are first responders.

And we are grateful for the doctors and nurses and first responders[6] who worked wonders to heal those who'd been hurt. We are grateful to them.

These men and women remind us that heroism is found not only on the fields of battle. They remind us that heroism does not require special training or physical strength. Heroism is here, in the hearts of so many of our fellow citizens, all around us, just waiting to be summoned, as it was on Saturday morning.

Their actions, their selflessness poses a challenge to each of us. It raises the question of what, beyond prayers and expressions of concern, is required of us going forward. How can we honor the fallen? How can we be true to their memory?

You see, when a tragedy like this strikes, it is part of our nature to demand explanations, to try to impose some order on the chaos and make sense out of that which seems senseless.

Already, we've seen a national conversation commence, not only about the motivations behind these killings, but about everything from the merits of gun safety laws[7] to the adequacy of our mental health system. And much – much of this process of debating what might be done to prevent such tragedies in the future is an essential ingredient in our exercise of self-government.

But at a time when our discourse has become so sharply polarized, at a time when we are far too eager to lay the blame for all that ails the world at the feet of those who happen to think differently than we do, it's important for us to pause for a moment and make sure that we're talking with each other in a way that – that heals, not in a way that wounds.

Scripture tells us that there is evil in the world and that terrible things happen for reasons that defy human understanding. In the words of Job, 'When I looked for light, then came darkness.'[8] Bad things happen, and we have to guard against simple explanations in the aftermath.

For the truth is, none of us can know exactly what triggered this vicious attack. None of us can know with any certainty what might have stopped these shots from being fired or what thoughts lurked in the inner recesses of a violent man's mind.

Yes, we had to examine all the facts behind this tragedy. We cannot and will not be passive in the face of such violence. We should be willing to challenge old assumptions in order to lessen the prospects of such violence in the future.

But what we cannot do is use this tragedy as one more occasion to turn on each other.

That we cannot do.

That we cannot do.

As we discuss these issues, let each of us do so with a good dose of humility. Rather than pointing fingers or assigning blame, let's use this occasion to expand our moral imaginations, to listen to each other more carefully, to sharpen our instincts for empathy, and remind ourselves of all the ways that our hopes and dreams are bound together. After all, that's what most of us do when we lose somebody in our family, especially if the loss is unexpected. We're shaken out of our routines. We're forced to look inward. We reflect on the past.

Did we spend enough time with an aging – an aging parent, we wonder? Did we express our gratitude for all the sacrifices that they made for us? Did we tell a spouse just how desperately we loved them, not just once in a while, but every single day?

So sudden loss causes us to look backward, but it also forces us to look forward, to reflect on the present and the future, on the manner in which we live our lives and nurture our relationships with those who are still with us.

We may ask ourselves if we've shown enough kindness and generosity and compassion to the people in our lives. Perhaps we question whether we're doing right by our children, or our community, whether our priorities are in order. We recognize our own mortality. And we are reminded that, in the fleeting time we have on this Earth, what matters is not wealth, or status, or power, or fame, but rather how well we have loved and what small part we have played in making the lives of other people better.

[7] Mass shootings had become a depressingly familiar feature of contemporary America society and the issue of fire arms had long been a matter of high-profile and bitter debate. The right to bear arms is enshrined in the Second Amendement to the US Constitution and is vigorously defended by such groups as the National Rifle Association. In the wake of the Sandy Hook Elementary School shooting (2012), Obama would put forward moderate proposals for improving gun control, in whch he was backed by the vast majority of the US public.

[8] Job 30:26. The biblical figure of Job has long been used as an example of human incomprehension in the face of misfortune and evildoing and of the need, nonetheless, to keep faith.

And that process – that process of reflection, of making sure we align our values with our actions, that, I believe, is what a tragedy like this requires.

For those who were harmed, those who were killed, they are part of our family, an American family, 300 million strong.

We may not have known them personally, but surely we see ourselves in them. In George and Dot, in Dorwan and Mavy, we sense the abiding love we have for our own husbands, our own wives, our own life partners.

Phyllis, she's our mom or our grandma, Gabe, our brother or son.

In Judge Roll, we recognize not only a man who prized his family and doing his job well, but also a man who embodied America's fidelity to the law.

And in Gabby – in Gabby, we see a reflection of our public-spiritedness, that desire to participate in that sometimes frustrating, sometimes contentious, but always necessary and never-ending process to form a more perfect union.

And in Christina, in Christina, we see all of our children, so curious, so trusting, so energetic, so full of magic, so deserving of our love, and so deserving of our good example.

If this tragedy prompts reflection and debate, as it should, let's make sure it's worthy of those we have lost.

Let's make sure it's not on the usual plane of politics and point-scoring and pettiness that drifts away in the next news cycle.

The loss of these wonderful people should make every one of us strive to be better, to be better in our private lives, to be better friends and neighbors and co-workers and parents.

And if, as has been discussed in recent days, their death helps usher in more civility in our public discourse, let us remember it is not because a simple lack of civility caused this tragedy – it did not – but rather because only a more civil and honest public discourse can help us face up to the challenges of our nation in a way that would make them proud.

We should be civil because we want to live up to the example of public servants like John Roll and Gabby Giffords, who knew first and foremost that we are all Americans, and that we can question each other's ideas without questioning each other's love of country, and that our task, working together, is to constantly widen the circle of our concern so that we bequeath the American dream to future generations.

They believe – they believe and I believe that we can be better. Those who died here, those who saved lives here, they help me believe. We may not be able to stop all evil in the world, but I know that how we treat one another, that's entirely up to us.

And I believe that, for all our imperfections, we are full of decency and goodness and that the forces that divide us are not as strong as those that unite us.

That's what I believe, in part because that's what a child like Christina-Taylor Green believed.

Imagine – can you imagine for a moment, here was a young girl who was just becoming aware of our democracy, just beginning to understand the obligations of citizenship, just starting to glimpse the fact that someday she, too, might play a part in shaping her nation's future.

She had been elected to her student council. She saw public service as something exciting and hopeful. She was off to meet her congress-woman, someone she was sure was good and important and might be a role model. She saw all this through the eyes of a child, undimmed by the cynicism or vitriol that we adults all too often just take for granted.

I want us to live up to her expectations.

I want our democracy to be as good as Christina imagined it. I want America to be as good as she imagined it. All of us, we should do everything we can to make sure this country lives up to our children's expectations.

As has already been mentioned, Christina was given to us on September 11th, 2001, one of 50 babies born that day to be pictured in a book called *Faces of Hope*.[9] On either side of her photo in that book were simple wishes for a child's life: 'I hope you help those in need,' read one. 'I hope you know all of the words to the National Anthem and sing it with your hand over your heart. I hope – I hope you jump in rain puddles.'

If there are rain puddles in Heaven, Christina is jumping in them today.

And here on this Earth, here on this Earth, we place our hands over our hearts and we commit ourselves as Americans to forging a country that is forever worthy of her gentle, happy spirit.

May God bless and keep those we've lost in restful and eternal peace. May he love and watch over the survivors. And may he bless the United States of America.

[9] Christine Naman, *Faces of Hope: 50 Babies Born on 9/11* (HCI, 2002).

'You are marching'
28 August 2013, Lincoln Memorial, Washington, DC

President Obama's stirring speech on the National Mall was given to mark the 50th anniversary of the March on Washington, which reached its climax with the famous 'I have a dream' speech by MARTIN LUTHER KING, JR. While it is essentially a speech commemorating another speech, it is also an impassioned call for the work of the African-American Civil Rights Movement – 'our great unfinished business' – to be revived and continued, primarily in the sphere of economic justice.

To the King family, who have sacrificed and inspired so much; to President CLINTON; President CARTER; Vice President Biden and Jill; fellow Americans.

Five decades ago today, Americans came to this honored place to lay claim to a promise made at our founding: 'We hold these truths to be self-evident, that all men are created equal, that they are endowed by their Creator with certain unalienable rights, that among these are Life, Liberty and the pursuit of Happiness.'[1]

In 1963, almost 200 years after those words were set to paper, a full century after a great war was fought and emancipation proclaimed,[2] that promise – those truths – remained unmet. And so they came by the thousands from every corner of our country, men and women, young and old, blacks who longed for freedom and whites who could no longer accept freedom for themselves while witnessing the subjugation of others.

Across the land, congregations sent them off with food and with prayer. In the middle of the night, entire blocks of Harlem[3] came out to wish them well. With the few dollars they scrimped from their labor, some bought tickets and boarded buses, even if they couldn't always sit where they wanted to sit. Those with less money hitchhiked or walked. They were seamstresses and steelworkers, students and teachers, maids and Pullman porters. They shared simple meals and bunked together on floors. And then, on a hot summer day, they assembled here, in our nation's capital, under the shadow of the Great Emancipator[4] – to offer testimony of injustice, to petition their government for redress, and to awaken America's long-slumbering conscience.

We rightly and best remember Dr. King's soaring oratory that day, how he gave mighty voice to the quiet hopes of millions; how he offered a salvation path for oppressed and oppressors alike. His words belong to the ages, possessing a power and prophecy unmatched in our time.

But we would do well to recall that day itself also belonged to those ordinary people whose names never appeared in the history books, never got on TV. Many had gone to segregated schools and sat at segregated lunch counters. They lived in towns where they couldn't vote and cities where their votes didn't matter. They were couples in love who couldn't marry, soldiers who fought for freedom abroad that they found denied to them at home. They had seen loved ones beaten, and children fire-hosed, and they had every reason to lash out in anger, or resign themselves to a bitter fate.

And yet they chose a different path. In the face of hatred, they prayed for their tormentors. In the face of violence, they stood up and sat in, with the moral force of nonviolence. Willingly, they went to jail

[1] Obama quotes the famous lines from the Preamble to the United States Declaration of Independence.

[2] The American Civil War (1861–5) was followed by the Emancipation Proclamation issued by President ABRAHAM LINCOLN on 1 January 1863.

[3] From the early 20th century, Harlem was a traditional African-American neighbourhood of the New York borough of Manhattan. It was the focus of the black cultural flourishing of the 1920s known as the 'Harlem Renaissance'.

[4] Abraham Lincoln. Lincoln's reputation as the 'emancipator' of African-Americans has been much contested; African-Americans, it is argued, freed themselves fom slavery.

to protest unjust laws, their cells swelling with the sound of freedom songs. A lifetime of indignities had taught them that no man can take away the dignity and grace that God grants us. They had learned through hard experience what FREDERICK DOUGLASS[5] once taught – that freedom is not given, it must be won, through struggle and discipline, persistence and faith.

That was the spirit they brought here that day. That was the spirit young people like John Lewis[6] brought to that day. That was the spirit that they carried with them, like a torch, back to their cities and their neighborhoods. That steady flame of conscience and courage that would sustain them through the campaigns to come – through boycotts and voter registration drives and smaller marches far from the spotlight; through the loss of four little girls in Birmingham,[7] and the carnage of the Edmund Pettus Bridge,[8] and the agony of Dallas and California and Memphis. Through setbacks and heartbreaks and gnawing doubt, that flame of justice flickered; it never died.

And because they kept marching, America changed. Because they marched, a Civil Rights law[9] was passed. Because they marched, a Voting Rights law[10] was signed. Because they marched, doors of opportunity and education swung open so their daughters and sons could finally imagine a life for themselves beyond washing somebody else's laundry or shining somebody else's shoes. [*Applause.*] Because they marched, city councils changed and state legislatures changed, and Congress changed, and, yes, eventually, the White House changed. [*Applause.*]

Because they marched, America became more free and more fair – not just for African-Americans, but for women and Latinos, Asians and Native Americans; for Catholics, Jews, and Muslims; for gays, for Americans with a disability. America changed for you and for me. And the entire world drew strength from that example, whether the young people who watched from the other side of an Iron Curtain and would eventually tear down that wall, or the young people inside South Africa who would eventually end the scourge of apartheid. [*Applause.*]

Those are the victories they won, with iron wills and hope in their hearts. That is the transformation that they wrought, with each step of their well-worn shoes. That's the debt that I and millions of Americans owe those maids, those laborers, those porters, those secretaries; folks who could have run a company maybe if they had ever had a chance; those white students who put themselves in harm's way, even though they didn't have to; those Japanese Americans who recalled their own internment; those Jewish Americans who had survived the Holocaust; people who could have given up and given in, but kept on keeping on, knowing that 'weeping may endure for a night, but joy cometh in the morning.' [*Applause.*]

On the battlefield of justice, men and women without rank or wealth or title or fame would liberate us all in ways that our children now take for granted, as people of all colors and creeds live together and learn together and walk together, and fight alongside one another, and love one another, and judge one another by the content of our character in this greatest nation on Earth. [*Applause.*]

To dismiss the magnitude of this progress – to suggest, as some sometimes do, that little has changed – that dishonors the courage and the sacrifice of those who paid the price to march in those years. [*Applause.*] Medgar Evers, James Chaney, Andrew Goodman,

[6] John Lewis (1940–), civil rights activist and the youngest speaker to address the crowds at the March on Washington; Democratic member of the House of Representatives, 1987– .

[9] Civil Rights Act 1964, banning discrimination based on 'race, color, religion, or national origin' in employment practices and public accommodations.
[10] Voting Rights Acts 1965, restoring and protecting voting rights.

[5] Frederick Douglass (1818–95), African-American abolitionist, statesman and former slave, and author of *A Narrative of the Life of Frederick Douglass, an American Slave* (1845).

[7] On 15 September 1963 four African-American girls – Addie Mae Collins, Cynthia Wesley, Carole Robertson and Denise McNair – were killed during the bombing of the 16th Street Baptist Church in Birmingham, Alabama by white racists.
[8] On 7 March 1965, 'Bloody Sunday', peaceful demonstrators taking part in a march on the Alabama state capital, Montgomery, were attacked by armed officers at the Edmund Pettus Bridge, Selma, Alabama.

Michael Schwerner, Martin Luther King, Jr. – they did not die in vain.[11] [*Applause.*] Their victory was great.

But we would dishonor those heroes as well to suggest that the work of this nation is somehow complete. The arc of the moral universe may bend towards justice, but it doesn't bend on its own. To secure the gains this country has made requires constant vigilance, not complacency. Whether by challenging those who erect new barriers to the vote, or ensuring that the scales of justice work equally for all, and the criminal justice system is not simply a pipeline from underfunded schools to overcrowded jails, it requires vigilance. [*Applause.*]

And we'll suffer the occasional setback. But we will win these fights. This country has changed too much. [*Applause.*] People of goodwill, regardless of party, are too plentiful for those with ill will to change history's currents. [*Applause.*]

In some ways, though, the securing of civil rights, voting rights, the eradication of legalized discrimination – the very significance of these victories may have obscured a second goal of the March. For the men and women who gathered 50 years ago were not there in search of some abstract ideal. They were there seeking jobs as well as justice – [*applause*] – not just the absence of oppression but the presence of economic opportunity. [*Applause.*]

For what does it profit a man, Dr. King would ask, to sit at an integrated lunch counter if he can't afford the meal? This idea – that one's liberty is linked to one's livelihood; that the pursuit of happiness requires the dignity of work, the skills to find work, decent pay, some measure of material security – this idea was not new. Lincoln himself understood the Declaration of Independence in such terms – as a promise that, in due time, 'the weights should be lifted from the shoulders of all men, and that all should have an equal chance.'[12]

And Dr. King explained that the goals of African-Americans were identical to working people of all races: 'Decent wages, fair working conditions, livable housing, old-age security, health and welfare measures, conditions in which families can grow, have education for their children, and respect in the community.'

What King was describing has been the dream of every American. It's what's lured for centuries new arrivals to our shores. And it's along this second dimension – of economic opportunity, the chance through honest toil to advance one's station in life – where the goals of 50 years ago have fallen most short.

Yes, there have been examples of success within black America that would have been unimaginable a half century ago. But as has already been noted, black unemployment has remained almost twice as high as white unemployment, Latino unemployment close behind. The gap in wealth between races has not lessened, it's grown. And as President Clinton indicated, the position of all working Americans, regardless of color, has eroded, making the dream Dr. King described even more elusive.

For over a decade, working Americans of all races have seen their wages and incomes stagnate, even as corporate profits soar, even as the pay of a fortunate few explodes. Inequality has steadily risen over the decades. Upward mobility has become harder. In too many communities across this country, in cities and suburbs and rural hamlets, the shadow of poverty casts a pall over our youth, their lives a fortress of substandard schools and diminished prospects, inadequate health care and perennial violence.

[11] The civil rights activist Medgar Wiley Evers (1925–63) was assassinated in Jackson, Mississippi; the field workers James Chaney (1943–64), Andrew Goodman (1943–1964) and Michael Schwerner (1939–64) were murdered by members of the Klu Klux Klan while engaged in a voting registration campaign among African-Americans in Philadelphia, Mississippi; King was assassinated in 1967.

[12] From a speech made by President Lincoln in Independence Hall, Philadelphia, Pennsylvania.

And so as we mark this anniversary, we must remind ourselves that the measure of progress for those who marched 50 years ago was not merely how many blacks could join the ranks of millionaires. It was whether this country would admit all people who are willing to work hard regardless of race into the ranks of a middle-class life. [*Applause.*]

The test was not, and never has been, whether the doors of opportunity are cracked a bit wider for a few. It was whether our economic system provides a fair shot for the many – for the black custodian and the white steelworker, the immigrant dishwasher and the Native American veteran. To win that battle, to answer that call – this remains our great unfinished business.

We shouldn't fool ourselves. The task will not be easy. Since 1963, the economy has changed. The twin forces of technology and global competition have subtracted those jobs that once provided a foothold into the middle class – reduced the bargaining power of American workers. And our politics has suffered. Entrenched interests, those who benefit from an unjust status quo, resisted any government efforts to give working families a fair deal – marshaling an army of lobbyists and opinion makers to argue that minimum wage increases or stronger labor laws or taxes on the wealthy who could afford it just to fund crumbling schools, that all these things violated sound economic principles. We'd be told that growing inequality was a price for a growing economy, a measure of this free market; that greed was good and compassion ineffective, and those without jobs or health care had only themselves to blame.

And then, there were those elected officials who found it useful to practice the old politics of division, doing their best to convince middle-class Americans of a great untruth – that government was somehow itself to blame for their growing economic insecurity; that distant bureaucrats were taking their hard-earned dollars to benefit the welfare cheat or the illegal immigrant.

And then, if we're honest with ourselves, we'll admit that during the course of 50 years, there were times when some of us claiming to push for change lost our way. The anguish of assassinations set off self-defeating riots. Legitimate grievances against police brutality tipped into excuse-making for criminal behavior. Racial politics could cut both ways, as the transformative message of unity and brotherhood was drowned out by the language of recrimination. And what had once been a call for equality of opportunity, the chance for all Americans to work hard and get ahead was too often framed as a mere desire for government support – as if we had no agency in our own liberation, as if poverty was an excuse for not raising your child, and the bigotry of others was reason to give up on yourself.

All of that history is how progress stalled. That's how hope was diverted. It's how our country remained divided. But the good news is, just as was true in 1963, we now have a choice. We can continue down our current path, in which the gears of this great democracy grind to a halt and our children accept a life of lower expectations; where politics is a zero-sum game where a few do very well while struggling families of every race fight over a shrinking economic pie – that's one path. Or we can have the courage to change.

The March on Washington teaches us that we are not trapped by the mistakes of history; that we are masters of our fate. But it also teaches us that the promise of this nation will only be kept when we work together. We'll have to reignite the embers of empathy and fellow feeling, the coalition of conscience that found expression in this place 50 years ago.

And I believe that spirit is there, that truth force inside each of us. I see it when a white mother recognizes her own daughter in the face of a poor black child. I see it when the black youth thinks of his own grandfather in the dignified steps of an elderly white man. It's there when the native-born recognizing that striving spirit of the new immigrant; when the interracial couple connects the pain of a gay couple who are discriminated against and understands it as their own.

That's where courage comes from – when we turn not from each other, or on each other, but towards one another, and we find that we do not walk alone. That's where courage comes from. [*Applause.*]

And with that courage, we can stand together for good jobs and just wages. With that courage, we can stand together for the right to health care in the richest nation on Earth for every person. [*Applause.*] With that courage, we can stand together for the right of every child, from the corners of Anacostia to the hills of Appalachia, to get an education that stirs the mind and captures the spirit, and prepares them for the world that awaits them. [*Applause.*]

With that courage, we can feed the hungry, and house the homeless, and transform bleak wastelands of poverty into fields of commerce and promise.

America, I know the road will be long, but I know we can get there. Yes, we will stumble, but I know we'll get back up. That's how a movement happens. That's how history bends. That's how when somebody is faint of heart, somebody else brings them along and says, come on, we're marching. [*Applause.*]

There's a reason why so many who marched that day, and in the days to come, were young – for the young are unconstrained by habits of fear, unconstrained by the conventions of what is. They dared to dream differently, to imagine something better. And I am convinced that same imagination, the same hunger of purpose stirs in this generation.

We might not face the same dangers of 1963, but the fierce urgency of now remains. We may never duplicate the swelling crowds and dazzling procession of that day so long ago – no one can match King's brilliance – but the same flame that lit the heart of all who are willing to take a first step for justice, I know that flame remains. [*Applause.*]

That tireless teacher who gets to class early and stays late and dips into her own pocket to buy supplies because she believes that every child is her charge – she's marching. [*Applause.*]

That successful businessman who doesn't have to but pays his workers a fair wage and then offers a shot to a man, maybe an ex-con who is down on his luck – he's marching. [*Applause.*]

The mother who pours her love into her daughter so that she grows up with the confidence to walk through the same door as anybody's son – she's marching. [*Applause.*]

The father who realizes the most important job he'll ever have is raising his boy right, even if he didn't have a father – especially if he didn't have a father at home – he's marching. [*Applause.*]

The battle-scarred veterans who devote themselves not only to helping their fellow warriors stand again, and walk again, and run again, but to keep serving their country when they come home – they are marching. [*Applause.*]

Everyone who realizes what those glorious patriots knew on that day – that change does not come from Washington, but to Washington; that change has always been built on our willingness, We The People, to take on the mantle of citizenship – you are marching. [*Applause.*]

And that's the lesson of our past. That's the promise of tomorrow – that in the face of impossible odds, people who love their country can change it. That when millions of Americans of every race and every region, every faith and every station, can join together in a spirit of brotherhood, then those mountains will be made low, and those rough places will be made plain, and those crooked places, they straighten out towards grace, and we will vindicate the faith of those who sacrificed so much and live up to the true meaning of our creed, as one nation, under God, indivisible, with liberty and justice for all. [*Applause.*]

Daniel O'Connell
Irish political leader

Daniel O'Connell *known as the Liberator* (1775–1847) was born near Cahirciveen, County Kerry. Called to the Irish Bar in 1798, he became a successful barrister. In 1823, he formed the Catholic Association, which successfully fought elections against the landlords. Elected MP for County Clare in 1828, he was prevented as a Catholic from taking his seat, but following the Catholic Emancipation Act (1829) he was re-elected in 1830. He denounced the ministry of THE DUKE OF WELLINGTON and Robert Peel, but in the face of a threatened prosecution he temporized, and was appointed King's Counsel. In 1832 he was elected MP for Dublin. Of the 105 Irish members, 45 were Repealers, seeking repeal of the Act of Union (1800). O'Connell was forced to bring the Repeal movement prematurely into Parliament, and a motion for inquiry was defeated by 523 to 38. For five years (1835–40) he gave steady support to the Whigs. The Earl of Mulgrave and Thomas Drummond governed Ireland so mildly that O'Connell was prepared to abandon the repeal agitation. In 1838 he founded his 'Precursor Society', and in 1840 his famous Repeal Association, but the cause languished until the appearance of the pro-repeal newspaper *The Nation* (1842). In 1841 he lost his seat at Dublin, but found another at Cork. In November he became the first Catholic Lord Mayor of Dublin. In 1843 he raised repeal in the Dublin corporation, and carried it by 41 to 15. The agitation now leaped to prominence, but the 'Young Ireland' party grew impatient, and O'Connell allowed himself to outrun his better judgement. Wellington ordered 35,000 men into Ireland and a planned meeting at Clontarf in October 1843 was abandoned. Early in 1844, with his son and five of his chief supporters, O'Connell was imprisoned and fined for conspiracy to raise sedition. The House of Lords set aside the verdict, but O'Connell spent 14 weeks in prison. He opposed Peel's provincial 'godless colleges', and abandoned the Young Ireland movement (1846) for fear it would lead to violence. The situation was exacerbated by the potato famine, which began in 1845. A broken man, he left Ireland in January 1847, planning to visit Rome, but died of heart disease in Genoa.

'England never did do justice to Ireland'
4 February 1836, London, England

After the Emancipation Act of 1829, Daniel O'Connell became the first Catholic in centuries to sit in Parliament. This privilege did not come without drawbacks, however. Unpopular in England, he faced a constant and wearying hostility, to which he tended to react angrily. In particular, he excited the rage of a young BENJAMIN DISRAELI, who called him 'an incendiary and a traitor'. O'Connell responded, 'My answer to that is he is a liar ... the most degraded of his species and kind.'

Embattled and overworked, O'Connell divided most of his time between Westminster and his Dublin constituency, but pined for his secluded home in Kerry – and his beloved wife Mary.

This speech is from a Commons debate following the King's Speech at the opening of Parliament in February 1836. Among other things, it proposed measures to tackle poverty in Ireland, but also to investigate and remedy endemic corruption in the municipal corporations 'upon the same principles as those of the Acts which have already passed for England and Scotland'.

O'Connell's old foe, the former prime minister Sir Robert Peel, took exception to this clause and proposed an amendment that would remove the necessity of applying the same principles. He was supported by Lord Stanley, another long-term enemy of O'Connell. Much of the ensuing debate focused on whether Ireland could expect to enjoy the same rights as England and Scotland. Numerous allusions were made to O'Connell, including several references to his 'tyranny'. Eventually, he was unable to resist entering the fray.

The amendment was not passed.

It appears to me impossible to suppose that the House will consider me presumptuous in wishing to be heard for a short time on this question, especially after the distinct manner in which I have been alluded to in the course of the debate. If I had no other excuse, that would be sufficient; but I do not want it. I have another and a better: the question is one in the highest degree interesting to the people of Ireland. It is, whether we mean to do justice to that country; whether we mean to continue the injustice which has been already done to it, or to hold out the hope that it will be treated in the same manner as England and Scotland. That is the question.

We know what 'lip service' is; we do not want that. There are some men who will even declare that they are willing to refuse justice to Ireland; while there are others who, though they are ashamed to say so, are ready to consummate the iniquity, and they do so.

England never did do justice to Ireland – she never did. What we have got of it we have extorted from men opposed to us on principle, against which principle they have made us such concessions as we have obtained from them. The right honourable Baronet opposite[1] says he does not distinctly understand what is meant by a principle. I believe him. He advocated religious exclusion on religious motives; he yielded that point at length, when we were strong enough to make it prudent for him to do so.

Here am I calling for justice to Ireland; but there is a coalition tonight – not a base unprincipled one, God forbid; it is an extremely natural one – I mean that between the right honourable Baronet and the noble Lord the member for North Lancashire.[2] It is a natural coalition, and it is impromptu; for the noble Lord informs us he had not even a notion of taking the part he has until the moment at which he seated himself where he now is.

I know his candour; he told us it was a sudden inspiration which induced him to take part against Ireland. I believe it with the most potent faith, because I know that he requires no preparation for voting against the interests of the Irish people.

[*Groans.*]

I thank you for that groan – it is just of a piece with the rest. I regret much that I have been thrown upon arguing this particular question, because I should have liked to have dwelt upon the speech which has been so graciously delivered from the throne today[3] – to have gone into its details, and to have pointed out the many great and beneficial alterations and amendments in our existing institutions which it hints at and recommends to the House. The speech of last year was full of reforms in words, and in words only; but this speech contains the great leading features of all the salutary reforms the country wants; and if they are worked out fairly and honestly in detail, I am convinced the country will require no further amelioration of its institutions, and that it will become the envy and admiration of the world. I, therefore, hail the speech with great satisfaction.

It has been observed that the object of a King's Speech is to say as little in as many words as possible. But this speech contains more things than words. It contains those great principles which, adopted in practice, will be most salutary not only to the British Empire, but to the world. When speaking of our foreign policy, it rejoices in the co-operation between France and this country; but it abstains from conveying any ministerial approbation of alterations in the domestic laws of that country,[4] which aim at the suppression of public liberty, and the checking of public discussion, such as call for individual reprobation, and which I reprobate as much as any one.

I should like to know whether there is a statesman in the country who will get up in this House and avow his approval of such proceedings on the part of the French government. I know it may be done out of the House amid the cheers of an assembly of friends; but the government have, in my opinion, wisely abstained from reprobating such measures in the speech, while they have properly exulted in such a union of the two countries as will contribute to the national independence and the public liberty of Europe.

[1] The English statesman Sir Robert Peel, 2nd Baronet (1788–1850) served as Prime Minister, 1834–5 and 1841–6. A staunch opponent of Catholic emancipation, he had challenged O'Connell to a duel in 1815.

[2] The English statesman Edward Smith-Stanley *known as Lord Stanley, later 14th Earl of Derby* (1799–1869) had served as Chief Secretary for Ireland, 1830–3. In 1833 he had introduced the Coercion Act for Ireland, leading to a fierce conflict with O'Connell. He resigned from government in 1834 over attempts to disestablish the Church of Ireland.

[3] The British monarch William IV (1765–1837) reigned 1830–7. On this day he had delivered the King's Speech, outlining the legislative programme proposed by the Whig government.

[4] The more liberal regime that came to power in France, after the 1830 revolution brought Louis-Philippe to the throne, became gradually more reactionary and introduced various severe measures to suppress republican agitation, including shutting down clubs and periodicals, and even outlawing the word '*républicain*'.

O'Connell – 'England never did do justice to Ireland'

[5] O'Connell was 60 when he gave this speech.

Years are coming over me,[5] but my heart is as young and as ready as ever in the service of my country, of which I glory in being the pensionary and the hired advocate. I stand in a situation in which no man ever stood yet: the faithful friend of my country, its servant, its stave, if you will. I speak its sentiments by turns to you and to itself. I require no £20 million on behalf of Ireland. I ask you only for justice: will you? Can you – I will not say dare you – refuse? Because that would make you turn the other way.

I implore you, as English gentlemen, to take this matter into consideration now, because you never had such an opportunity of conciliating. Experience makes fools wise. You are not fools, but you have yet to be convinced. I cannot forget the year 1825.[6] We begged then as we would for a beggar's boon; we asked for emancipation by all that is sacred amongst us, and I remember how my speech and person were treated on the treasury bench, when I had no opportunity of reply.

The other place turned us out and sent us back again, but we showed that justice was with us. The noble lord says the other place has declared the same sentiments with himself; but he could not use a worse argument. It is the very reason why we should acquiesce in the measure of reform, for we have no hope from that House. All our hopes are centred in this; and I am the living representative of those hopes.

I have no other reason for adhering to the ministry than because they, the chosen representatives of the people of England, are anxiously determined to give the same measure of reform to Ireland as that which England has received. I have not fatigued myself but the House, in coming forward upon this occasion. I may be laughed and sneered at by those who talk of my power; but what has created it but the injustice that has been done in Ireland?

That is the end and the means of the magic, if you please – the groundwork of my influence in Ireland. If you refuse justice to that country, it is a melancholy consideration to me to think that you are adding substantially to that power and influence, while you are wounding my country to its very heart's core; weakening that throne, the monarch who sits upon which you say you respect; severing that union which, you say, is bound together by the tightest links; and withholding that justice from Ireland which she will not cease to seek till it is obtained.

Every man must admit that the course I am taking is the legitimate and proper course. I defy any man to say it is not. Condemn me elsewhere as much as you please, but this you must admit. You may taunt the ministry with having coalesced me; you may raise the vulgar cry of 'Irishman and Papist' against me; you may send out men called ministers of God to slander and calumniate me; they may assume whatever garb they please.

But the question comes into this narrow compass: I demand, I respectfully insist on equal justice for Ireland, on the same principle by which it has been administered to Scotland and England. I will not take less. Refuse me that if you can.

[6] An emancipation bill, drafted by O'Donnell, was introduced into Parliament in 1825 by Sir Francis Burdett, 5th Baronet (1770–1844). It passed the House of Commons but was rejected by the Lords. As a Catholic, O'Donnell had been denied his elected seat and hence the opportunity to debate in Parliament.

Laurence Olivier
English actor, producer and director

Laurence Kerr Olivier *later Baron Olivier* (1907–89) was born in Dorking. His first professional appearance was as the Suliot officer in Chapman's *Byron* in 1924, and he joined the Old Vic Company in 1937. He played all the great Shakespearean roles, while his versatility was underlined by a virtuoso display as a broken-down music-hall comedian in *The Entertainer* (1957). After war service he became co-director of the Old Vic Company (1944); and he produced, directed and played in acclaimed films of *Henry V, Hamlet* and *Richard III*. He played memorable roles in several other films, including *Wuthering Heights* (1939), *Rebecca* (1940), *The Prince and the Showgirl* (which he also directed, 1957), *Sleuth* (1972) and *Marathon Man* (1976). Olivier was knighted in 1947. He was divorced from his first wife, Jill Esmond (1908–90) in 1940 and in the same year married Vivien Leigh (1913–67). They were divorced in 1960, and the following year he married Joan Plowright (1929–). In 1962 he undertook the directorship of a new venture, the Chichester Festival, where he was highly successful; later the same year he was appointed director of the National Theatre, where among many successes he directed and acted a controversial but outstanding *Othello* (1964). He was director of the National Theatre until 1973, and then associate director for a year. After 1974 he appeared chiefly in films and in television productions (notably as Lord Marchmain in *Brideshead Revisited*, 1982, and as King Lear in 1983). He was made a life peer in 1970 and was awarded the Order of Merit in 1981.

'The great firmament of your nation's generosities'
9 April 1979, Hollywood, California, USA

Although Jack Nicholson's twelve nominations mark him out as the world's most Oscar-nominated actor, Laurence Olivier can boast 13 nominations when his work as a director is taken into account. Olivier received an honorary Oscar in 1945 for his patriotic *Henry V*, made during World War II; and he was named best actor and best director for *Hamlet* (1948). Thereafter, he repeatedly left the awards ceremony empty-handed.

In 1979 he was nominated again, for his role in *The Boys from Brazil*, as a Jewish investigator seeking Nazi war criminals. This time, the best actor award went to Jon Voight for *Coming Home*, but for Olivier there was another honorary award, 'for the full body of his work, for the unique achievements of his entire career and his lifetime of contribution to the art of film'.

An honorary Oscar is often viewed as a consolation prize, but if Olivier felt slighted he was far too polite to show it. On the contrary, his acceptance speech is famous for its florid and overblown style – almost an exaggerated pastiche of British courtesy. Afterwards, Olivier is said to have remarked to Buz Kohan, scriptwriter for the awards ceremony: 'God, I mucked that up. I had no idea what I was saying but I didn't want to stop.'

O dear friends: am I supposed to speak after that?

Cary,[1] my dear old friend for many a year, from the earliest years of either of us working in this country: thank you for that beautiful citation and the trouble you have taken to make it and for all the warm generosities in it.

Mr President and governors of the Academy, committee members, fellows, my very noble and approved good masters,[2] my colleagues, my friends, my fellow-students: in the great wealth, the great firmament of your nation's generosities, this particular choice may perhaps be found by future generations as a trifle eccentric.

But the mere fact of it, the prodigal, pure, human kindness of it, must be seen as a beautiful star in that firmament which shines upon me at this moment, dazzling me a little, but filling me with the warmth of the extraordinary elation, the euphoria that happens to so many of us at the first breath of the majestic glow of a new tomorrow.

From the top of this moment, in the solace, in the kindly emotion that is charging my soul and my heart at this moment, I thank you for this great gift, which lends me such a very splendid part in this, your glorious occasion. Thank you.

[1] The English-born Hollywood star Cary Grant (1904–86) had presented the award to Olivier. They were not close friends, but Olivier regarded Grant as the exemplar of British movie stardom.

[2] A line spoken by Othello in the tragedy of the same name (c.1604) by the English playwright William Shakespeare (1564–1616). Olivier had received an Oscar nomination for his performance as Othello in Stuart Burge's 1965 film of the play.

Ian Paisley
Northern Irish clergyman and politician

Ian Richard Kyle Paisley *later Baron Bannside* (1926–) was born in Ballymena, and educated at South Wales Bible College and the Reformed Presbyterian Theological College, Belfast. He was ordained by his Baptist minister father in 1946 and founded his own denomination, the Free Presbyterian Church of Ulster, in 1951. In 1969 he entered the Northern Ireland parliament as Protestant Unionist MP for Bannside, becoming leader of the opposition in 1972. He co-founded the Democratic Unionist Party, and since 1970 has been MP for Antrim North and leader of the Democratic Unionists in the House of Commons, though he resigned briefly in protest at the Anglo-Irish Agreement, signed by the British prime minister MARGARET THATCHER and the Irish *Taoiseach* Garret FitzGerald in 1985. As a member of the European parliament since 1979, he staged a well-publicized one-man protest there against the choice of Pope JOHN PAUL II as a guest speaker in 1988. Northern Ireland's most vociferous opponent of Irish unification, he is the object of fanatical devotion from Ulster loyalists and participated in the all-party peace process of 1995–6 only with deeply held misgivings. He suffered a much-publicized spell of ill-health in 2004, but by 2005 was fit enough to fight – and win – another election. His publications include *The Massacre of Bartholo-mew* (1974), *America's Debt to Ulster Kidd* (1982) and *Those Flaming Tennents* (1983). He was made a life peer in 2010.

'The judgement of God is seen upon this nation'
17 October 1984, Belfast, Northern Ireland

On 12 October 1984, the Irish Republican Army (IRA) launched its most audacious terrorist strike: the bombing of the Grand Hotel in Brighton, where Prime Minister MARGARET THATCHER and her Cabinet were staying for the Conservative Party conference. Four people were killed, none of them Cabinet members, though Norman Tebbitt, president of the Board of Trade, and his wife Margaret were seriously injured.

Opening the conference as planned the following morning, Thatcher said: 'The attack failed. All attempts to destroy democracy by terrorism will fail'. That same day, the IRA released a statement which included the words: 'Today we were unlucky, but remember we only have to be lucky once. You will have to be lucky always.'

Four days later, Ian Paisley gave his own, outraged response in the Northern Ireland Assembly, proposing a motion to condemn the bombing. Famous for his strident debating style and staunch Unionism, Paisley tackled the issue in both religious and political terms, and with unusual eloquence.

His speech refers to divine judgement and divine mercy, and contains several biblical allusions. It also expresses compassion for the victims of terrorism, both Protestant and Catholic. But Paisley is unflinching in his support for the death penalty, his condemnation of his political foes – the Republicans and the Labour Party – and his endorsement of Unionism: 'the resolute determination of a free people'.

He concludes his speech with a prayer for peace, but the intransigent factions of Northern Ireland were not to be assuaged so easily.

We have had an outrage in the United Kingdom which is perhaps unparalleled in modern history. The Irish Republican Army has attempted to wipe out the entire government of the United Kingdom. All of us should be greatly alarmed that it is possible for such an attack to be mounted. We must spell that out very clearly: it is possible in this society for an attack on the entire government of our kingdom to be set up and almost succeed. That puts a question mark on intelligence, and on those responsible for security.

There is always a great flurry of activity after such deeds of atrocity. Doors are barred and the people are put to great inconvenience. If half the effort were put in beforehand, such atrocities would not take place. We have to spell that out in clear terms.

War is a judgement. Those acquainted with the Bible will know that there are judgements on nations. We are all concerned about moral values and about standards, and about departing from those standards and moral values. And when nations depart from standards and from moral values there is always a reaping …

The judgement of God is seen upon this nation. We saw it in the lightning that struck York Minster.[1] The scientists tell us that there was no lightning in that district, yet the lightning that struck the cathedral was more powerful than any lightning ever experienced in the United Kingdom since records began – the lightning-rod could not take the force of it. Even the *Times* editorial said that it was a reminder of the prophet Elijah and the fire of judgement from Heaven,[2] and I am forced to a similar conclusion. I am convinced that we need to wake up to the fact that there are judgements abroad in this land today. That is why in our motion we are thankful to Almighty God that in his providence and grace the government were not wiped out.

I would like to ask Members of this House[3] what would have happened if the entire government had been wiped out. Is there anyone in the House confident that a second line of leadership in the Conservative Party would have been helpful to our province? I have not got that confidence. I do not know where the party would have got the men of calibre and standing to fill the vacant posts.

We know the turmoil that exists in Britain at present, with the British Labour Party not prepared to condemn violence in the way it ought to be condemned. We know its attitude to this province as far as a united Ireland is concerned. It would have been an awful tragedy for the United Kingdom generally, but for this province in particular, if the prime minister and her Cabinet had been entirely wiped out in Brighton. It is too horrible to contemplate. Therefore, it is right that we debate this matter today.

No doubt other people will take different views on this subject, but all of us, no matter what view we take, will not in any way underestimate the seriousness of this incident and the situation that has brought it about … We need to remind ourselves of what has happened, not just here in Northern Ireland but on the British mainland: 89 people have been killed and over 1,000 injured …

When a prominent person is murdered it makes headlines in the media. However, when an ordinary citizen whose name has never reached the headlines is murdered, his family suffers every bit as much, and perhaps even more so, for sometimes that person is the breadwinner and there is nobody there to help the family carry the burden. Sometimes the mother, who cements the home, is taken and the children are left without a mother. Every one of those 89 people killed was of the utmost importance to society. I do not suppose any Member of this House can remember five, six or seven names of those killed; they are forgotten because so many have been murdered in this savage campaign.

When we turn to our own unhappy province we see that this is only a small percentage of the total killed by similar action in Northern Ireland. Why is this? Why is this trouble going on? Why is the IRA able to mount such a campaign and how, after the dastardly deeds are done, can it publicly boast about them and get headlines in the press?

… I notice that a man elected to this House – Danny Morrison[4] – exhorts us to examine what would have happened if the bomb had killed the British Cabinet. He says that there would have been a rethink within British political circles and that it would probably have led to a British withdrawal in a much shorter period; it would have been unique in British constitutional history, apart maybe from Guy Fawkes.[5] He went on to say that the moral position is irrelevant. Think of those words: 'the moral

[1] In the early hours of 9 July 1984, York Minster was set ablaze, and the roof of the south transept was destroyed. Various causes were rumoured, but most attributed the fire to a lightning strike. The damage took four years to repair.

[3] The Northern Ireland Assembly had been established in 1982, but was boycotted by Republican members since it failed to make provision for power-sharing and cross-border liaison. The assembly continued until 1986.

[4] The Irish Republican activist Danny Morrison (1953–) was director of publicity for Sinn Féin, 1979–90.

[2] See 1 Kings 18:36–39.

[5] The English Catholic Guy Fawkes (1570–1606) was a conspirator in the 'Gunpowder Plot' intended to assassinate the Protestant King JAMES VI AND I and Parliament by blowing up the Palace of Westminster in November 1605. He was caught before he could ignite the explosives, tortured until he revealed the identities of his collaborators and executed in January 1606.

position is irrelevant' – it does not matter about the sanctity of human life
…

Danny Morrison may live in Northern Ireland but he does not know what makes Loyalists tick. We are not part of the United Kingdom because there is a British presence here … It is not because there are 8,000 or 9,000 British troops here that we want to remain within the United Kingdom; it is the resolute determination of a free people who democratically, at the ballot box, have time after time, said that this is where they want to be and this is where they want to stay – and here they will be and stay here they shall. That is the position. If there were a rethink tomorrow and the Thatcher administration pulled every British soldier out of Northern Ireland, we would be as firm in our determination. Indeed, we might be a lot firmer in our determination never to bow the knee to Dublin rule or to any scheme organized and motivated by the Irish Republican Army. He needs to learn that before he says these things …

I trembled when the Secretary of State[6] started to quote statistics at the Brighton conference. I trembled because no doubt in a few days' or months' time we in Northern Ireland will reap the consequences of that. I have told successive Secretaries of State to shut their mouths and get on with the job. People did not need to be told that HITLER had been defeated. He had been defeated and everybody knew he had been defeated. When the IRA is defeated the government will not need to make announcements about statistics, because all of us will know that the defeat has taken place. I ask the Secretary of State, for the sake of the people in Northern Ireland, not to make such foolish statements but rather to get on with the real job of defeating the terrorists. The facts will speak loud enough for themselves …

The Prime Minister said something that I must emphasize today. She reiterated her personal view that the death penalty should be brought back, and she forecast another vote on the issue in the Commons before long. I am well aware that there is a division in this House on the question of the death penalty, but I want to ask those who would not go along with me on this matter why the IRA should have the right to take life. Why should the sanction for IRA crimes not be as great as the punishment it metes out to others?

When a country is being held to ransom by a group of ruthless and bloodthirsty IRA monsters, there is only one reasonable deterrent, and that is to say: 'If you go out as a terrorist and take the lives of others your own life shall be forfeited.' That is something the British government have to say as, unfortunately, whether we like it or not, it is the only language that Irish Republican terrorists understand.

I read a lot of Irish history and I have studied Republicanism, and I have discovered that perhaps the great genius of modern Republicanism was none other than DE VALERA himself. And de Valera understood the mentality of the Republican terrorist, for he himself was one. What did he do when there was an upsurge of IRA violence in his country? Did he say, 'We will treat them well. We will not have any hangings or shootings'? No. He shot them out of hand. Why? Because he knew that was the only way to stop something that would gather momentum and increase trouble in the 26 counties that he ruled.[7] How right he was …

After this bombing, the IRA had the audacity to say: 'Today we were unlucky, but remember we have only to be lucky once.'

Lucky? What is that type of luck? People's blood is what it calls luck. The IRA's statement continues: 'You will have to be lucky always. Give Ireland

[6] The English politician Douglas Hurd *later Baron Hurd of Westwell* (1930–) served as Secretary of State for Northern Ireland 1984–5. He had been appointed only five weeks earlier.

[7] The Anglo-Irish Treaty 1921 partitioned Ireland; six counties (Northern Ireland) remained British, and the other 26 formed the self-governing Irish Free State, which became an independent republic in 1937.

peace and there will be no war.'

Who has brought war to Ireland? Who is killing people in the streets of this city? Who has killed all these people in the streets of England, people who had nothing whatsoever to do with the problems of Northern Ireland? I do not suppose one of those people ever made a political speech on Northern Ireland in his life, or on the things that concern Northern Ireland. Peace? These men know nothing about peace, and if they had their united Ireland tomorrow, we would have the same situation as we had with their predecessors: we would have another civil war,[8] and how dreadful and dark that war would be …

The IRA has done a job at Brighton. It said, 'Today we were unlucky'. It has left behind broken homes and broken hearts, and when it is all forgotten there will be people with no power in their arms or legs – the forgotten people. In my pastoral duties I have to visit the victims of IRA violence. As I look at them lying in bed or sitting in a wheelchair, I say that these are truly the forgotten people. Many of them feel a great sorrow, for usually someone near and dear to them has been killed in a similar outrage to that which has happened in Brighton.

My heart bleeds for every family that has been bereaved. I care not what their religion is. I do not see any difference between the tears of a Roman Catholic mother and the tears of a Protestant mother; I do not see any difference in the heartbreak. I have been in many homes across this community and it is the same sorrow that tears at the breast and the same agony that haunts them at night when the door is closed and the darkness comes.

Surely, with resoluteness and strength, the British government can take some action to rid us of this scourge. They will not find the Loyalist people ungrateful; they will not find the Loyalist people ungenerous; they will not find the Loyalist people refusing to do what is reasonable, true and right. Ulster people are the most magnanimous people in the world. All they are asking for is their rights and when they get their rights they will be prepared to see that everyone else has the same rights.

So in passing this motion, this House is simply recalling what is recorded in one of the Psalms of David, 'Deep calleth unto deep'.[9] From the depths of our agony to the depths of the agony of those who have suffered in this outrage there is a bridge that joins us together, and upon that bridge we can seek the consolation of God Almighty and, with a bright faith, hope that these appalling clouds of darkness will eventually be dispelled and that once again this province and indeed the whole of the United Kingdom will walk in light, joy and peace. May God speed the day.

[8] A civil war was fought between rival republican factions in the Irish Free State, June 1922–April 1923.

[9] Psalm 42:7.

Emmeline Pankhurst
English suffragette

Emmeline Pankhurst *née Goulden* (1857–1928) was born in Manchester. In 1879 she married Richard Marsden Pankhurst (1834–98), a radical barrister who had been the author of the first women's suffrage bill in Britain and of the 1870 and 1882 Married Women's Property Acts. She founded the Women's Franchise League in 1889. She fought for women's suffrage with tenacity and extreme militancy, and was later joined by her daughters Christabel (1880–1958) and Sylvia (1882–1960). In 1894 she won the right for married women to vote in local elections, though not for seats at Westminster. She was frequently imprisoned and underwent hunger strikes and forcible feeding. She later joined the Conservative Party. Her 40-year campaign reached a peak of success shortly before her death, when the Representation of the People Act was finally passed (1928), establishing voting equality for men and women. She published an autobiography, *My Own Story* (1914).

'The laws that men have made'
24 March 1908, London, England

Formed in 1887 from 17 separate groups, the National Union of Women's Suffrage Societies had campaigned persistently but unsuccessfully to gain the vote for women. A growing sense of frustration drove Emmeline and Christabel Pankhurst to form breakaway groups: the Women's Social and Political Union in 1903 and the more militant Women's Freedom League in 1907.

Tactics pursued by members of these organizations included heckling political speeches and provoking the police to arrest them for disturbing the peace. Their activities attracted the desired attention, though they were also delightedly lampooned by cartoonists and mainstream newspapers. In 1907, the law was changed to allow women ratepayers to vote in local elections – but this did not satisfy Pankhurst.

In 1908, she gave a series of lectures under the umbrella title *The Importance of the Vote*. This one was given in the Portman Rooms during the Putney by-election of that year, which added urgency to its message. In her bald but patiently reasoned attack on the status quo, Pankhurst recites men's legislative shortcomings, condemning them for their failure to improve ordinary women's lives.

What I am going to say to you tonight is not new. It is what we have been saying at every street corner, at every by-election during the last 18 months. It is perfectly well known to many members of my audience, but they will not mind if I repeat, for the benefit of those who are here for the first time tonight, those arguments and illustrations with which many of us are so very familiar.

In the first place, it is important that women should have the vote in order that in the government of the country the women's point of view should be put forward. It is important for women that in any legislation that affects women equally with men, those who make the laws should be responsible to women, in order that they may be forced to consult women and learn women's views when they are contemplating the making or the altering of laws.

Very little has been done by legislation for women for many years – for obvious reasons. More and more of the time of Members of Parliament is occupied by the claims which are made on behalf of the people who are organized in various ways in order to promote the interests of their industrial organizations or their political or social organizations. So the Member of Parliament, if he does dimly realize that women have needs, has no time to attend to them, no time to give to the consideration of those needs. His time is fully taken up by attending to the needs of the people who have sent him to Parliament.

While a great deal has been done, and a great deal more has been talked about for the benefit of the workers who have votes, yet so far as women are concerned, legislation relating to them has been practically at a standstill. Yet it is not because women have no need, or because their need is not very urgent. There are many laws on the statute-book today which are admittedly out of date, and call for reformation; laws which inflict very grave injustices on women. I want to call the attention of women who are here tonight to a few acts on the statute-book which press very hardly and very injuriously on women.

Men politicians are in the habit of talking to women as if there were no laws that affect women. 'The fact is,' they say, 'the home is the place for women. Their interests are the rearing and training of children. These are the things that interest women. Politics have nothing to do with these things, and therefore politics do not concern women.' Yet the laws decide how women are to live in marriage, how their children are to be trained and educated, and what the future of their children is to be. All that is decided by act of Parliament. Let us take a few of these laws, and see what there is to say about them from the women's point of view.

First of all, let us take the marriage laws. They are made by men for women. Let us consider whether they are equal, whether they are just, whether they are wise. What security of maintenance has the married woman? Many a married woman, having given up her economic independence in order to marry, how is she compensated for that loss? What security does she get in that marriage for which she gave up economic independence? Take the case of a woman who has been earning a good income. She is told that she ought to give up her employment when she becomes a wife and a mother. What does she get in return?

All that a married man is obliged by law to do for his wife is to provide for her shelter of some kind, food of some kind and clothing of some kind. It is left to his good pleasure to decide what the shelter shall be, what the food shall be, what the clothing shall be. It is left to him to decide what money shall be spent on the home, and how it shall be spent; the wife has no voice legally in deciding any of these things. She has no legal claim upon any definite portion of his income. If he is a good man, a conscientious man, he does the right thing. If he is not, if he chooses almost to starve his wife, she has no remedy. What he thinks sufficient is what she has to be content with.

I quite agree, in all these illustrations, that the majority of men are considerably better than the law compels them to be … but since there are some bad men, some unjust men, don't you agree with me that the law ought to be altered so that those men could be dealt with?

Take what happens to the woman if her husband dies and leaves her a widow, sometimes with little children. If a man is so insensible to his duties as a husband and father when he makes his will, as to leave all his property away from his wife and children, the law allows him to do it. That will is a valid one. So you see that the married woman's position is not a secure one. It depends entirely on her getting a good ticket in the lottery. If she has a good husband, well and good: if she has a bad one, she has to suffer, and she has no remedy. That is her position as a wife, and it is far from satisfactory.

Now let us look at her position if she has been very unfortunate in marriage, so unfortunate as to get a bad husband, an immoral husband, a vicious husband, a husband unfit to be the father of little children. We turn to the divorce court. How is she to get rid of such a man? If a man has got married to a bad wife, and he wants to get rid of her, he has but to prove against her one act of infidelity. But if a woman who is married to a vicious husband wants to get rid of him, not one act nor a thousand acts of infidelity entitle her to a divorce. She must prove either bigamy, desertion or gross cruelty, in addition to immorality, before she can get rid of that man.

Let us consider her position as a mother. We have repeated this so often at our meetings that I think the echo of what we have said must have reached many. By English law, no married woman exists as the mother of the child she brings into the world. In the eyes of the law she is not the parent of her child. The child, according to our marriage laws, has only one parent who can decide the future of the child, who can decide where it shall live, how it shall live, how much shall be spent upon it, how it shall be educated and what religion it shall profess. That parent is the father.

These are examples of some of the laws that men have made, laws that concern women. I ask you, if women had had the vote, should we have had such laws? If women had had the vote, as men have the vote, we should have had equal laws. We should have had equal laws for divorce, and the law would have said that as nature has given to children two parents, so the law should recognize that they have two parents.

I have spoken to you about the position of the married woman who does not exist legally as a parent, the parent of her own child. In marriage, children have one parent. Out of marriage children have also one parent. That parent is the mother – the unfortunate mother. She alone is responsible for the future of her child; she alone is punished if her child is neglected and suffers from neglect.

But let me give you one illustration. I was in Herefordshire during the by-election. While I was there, an unmarried mother was brought before the bench of magistrates, charged with having neglected her illegitimate child. She was a domestic servant, and had put the child out to nurse. The magistrates – there were colonels and landowners on that bench – did not ask what wages the mother got; they did not ask who the father was or whether he contributed to the support of the child. They sent that woman to prison for three months for having neglected her child.

I ask you women here tonight: if women had had some share in the making of laws, don't you think they would have found a way of making all fathers of such children equally responsible with the mothers for the welfare of those children?

… The man voter and the man legislator see the man's needs first, and do not see the woman's needs. And so it will be until women get the vote. It is well to remember that, in view of what we have been told of what is the value of women's influence. Woman's influence is only effective when men want to do the thing that her influence is supporting.

Now let us look a little to the future. If it ever was important for women to have the vote, it is ten times more important today, because you cannot take up a newspaper, you cannot go to a conference, you cannot even go to church, without hearing a great deal of talk about social reform and a demand for social legislation. Of course, it is obvious that that kind of legislation – and the Liberal government tell us that if they remain in office long enough we are going to have a great deal of it – is of vital importance to women.

If we have the right kind of social legislation it will be a very good thing for women and children. If we have the wrong kind of social legislation, we may have the worst kind of tyranny that women have ever known since the world began. We are hearing about legislation to decide what kind of homes people are to live in. That surely is a question for women. Surely every woman, when she seriously thinks about it, will wonder how men by themselves can have the audacity to think that they can say what homes ought to be without consulting women.

Then take education. Since 1870 men have been trying to find out how to educate children.[1] I think they have not yet realized that if they are ever to find out how to educate children, they will have to take women into their confidence, and try to learn from women some of those lessons that the long experience of ages has taught to them. One cannot wonder that whole sessions of Parliament should be wasted on education bills ...

The more one thinks about the importance of the vote for women, the more one realizes how vital it is. We are finding out new reasons for the vote, new needs for the vote every day in carrying on our agitation.

I hope that there may be a few men and women here who will go away determined at least to give this question more consideration than they have in the past. They will see that we women, who are doing so much to get the vote, want it because we realize how much good we can do with it when we have got it. We do not want it in order to boast of how much we have got. We do not want it because we want to imitate men or to be like men. We want it because without it we cannot do that work which it is necessary and right and proper that every man and woman should be ready and willing to undertake in the interests of the community of which they form a part.

[1] The Education Act of 1870 created school districts, each with its own elected board, and allowed women both to vote and to stand as candidates. Four women were elected to school boards that year, including the English physician Dr Elizabeth Garrett Anderson (1836–1917) who received more votes than any other candidate in the country.

Charles Stewart Parnell

Irish politician

Charles Stewart Parnell (1846–91) was born in Avondale, County Wicklow, the grandson of Sir John Parnell (1744–1801), who had been Chancellor of the Irish Exchequer. His father belonged to an old Cheshire family which had purchased land in Ireland, and his mother was the daughter of an American admiral. He studied for four years at Magdalene College, Cambridge, but took no degree. He became High Sheriff of County Wicklow (1874), and in 1875 he became an MP supporting home rule. In 1877–8 he gained great popularity in Ireland through audacious and deliberate obstruction of parliamentary tactics. In 1878 he devoted himself to agrarian agitation, and was elected president of the Irish National Land League, for which he secured substantial donations from the USA. In 1880 he became chairman of the Irish Parliamentary Party. The Land League was later declared illegal, and Parnell was imprisoned 1881–2, but the organization was revived in 1884 as the National League, with Parnell as president again. In 1886, Parnell and his 85 fellow Irish MPs used their vote to help introduce WILLIAM GLADSTONE's Home Rule Bill, but failed to secure the legislation because of defections by Liberal MPs. When Salisbury took the issue to the country later the same year, he was returned with a Unionist majority of more than 100, causing Parnell to form an alliance with Gladstone. In 1889, Parnell was cleared of complicity in the murder of the Irish Under-Secretary Thomas Henry Burke (1882) and other organized outrages, following the publication of letters purportedly written by him in the *Times*. After this he received £5,000 in damages for libel. His character restored, he was given the freedom of the city of Edinburgh the same year. In 1890 Parnell was cited co-respondent in a divorce case brought by Captain William Henry O'Shea (1840–1905) against his wife Katie (1846–1921), and a decree was granted with costs against Parnell. The Irish members met to consider his position a week later, and eventually elected Justin McCarthy chairman in his place. Parnell also lost support in Ireland, and at the 1892 general election, 72 anti-Parnellites were returned, against nine of his supporters. Meanwhile, Parnell had died suddenly in Brighton, five months after his marriage to Katie O'Shea. He is buried in Glasnevin cemetery, Dublin.

'You will have to resort to coercion'

7 June 1886, London, England

As an Irish landowner and MP, Parnell was well versed in the problems of the Irish peasantry. With the devastating famine of 1845–9 within living memory, tenant farmers still faced failing crops, escalating rents and evictions. Hence the formation of the Land League to protect their welfare.

In 1880, the Mayo land agent Captain Charles Boycott received a sharp lesson in the League's power (and a permanent place in English dictionaries) when his threats of eviction resulted in ostracization by servants, labourers, shopkeepers and neighbours. More often, the League simply withheld rents.

These events prompted the Land Reform Act of 1881, which bestowed limited rights on tenants, but failed to satisfy all factions of the Land League. Parnell tried to expose the Act's weaknesses with a combination of time-consuming test cases and incendiary speeches. This led to his imprisonment, the prohibition of the League and a period of violent civil unrest, which the government tried to curb with a harsh Coercion Act (1881).

Eventually, during his brief third period as prime minister in 1886, WILLIAM GLADSTONE introduced his Government of Ireland Bill, which Parnell and his fellow Irish MPs eventually backed, after two months of debate. Here, at the end of a long, fiery speech given the day before the vote, Parnell lends cautious support to the bill, despite 'vehement objections' to a clause that would exclude members of the proposed Irish parliament from sitting in Westminster.

The bill failed, dividing the Liberals and toppling Gladstone's administration. Three further Home Rule bills were introduced before Ireland gained its own parliament in 1920.

[1] Gladstone's third period of office lasted only six months, from February to August 1886.

When the Prime Minister[1] has produced his plan, without binding myself beforehand, I shall candidly examine it, with a desire not to see in it an element that will injure the permanency of the settlement. I shall chiefly deal with it with a view of seeing whether it will diminish the permanency of the settlement, to the success of which my colleagues and I have pledged our political future.

But I confess, Sir, that if I had regard to the spirit with which the right honourable gentleman the Member for West Birmingham[2] has dealt with this question, I should have been hopelessly alienated from the plan of retaining the Irish Members. He has dealt with it in a way to attach an apparent stigma of inferiority to us, and in order that he may have the excuse for constantly meddling in our affairs, checking us, thwarting us and keeping us under his thumb. The Irish people will never submit to that. We could not agree to his scheme, for that would be fatal to the finality and durability of the scheme.

Now, Sir, what does it all come to? It comes to two alternatives, when everything has been said and everything has been done. One alternative is the coercion which Lord Salisbury[3] put before the country, and the other is the alternative offered by the Prime Minister, carrying with it the lasting settlement of a treaty of peace. If you reject this bill … I beg to say you will have to resort to coercion. That is not a threat on my part – I would do much to prevent the necessity for resorting to coercion; but I say it will be inevitable, and the best-intentioned Radical[4] who sits on those benches, and who thinks that he 'never never will be a party to coercion' will be found very soon walking into the division lobby[5] in favour of the most drastic coercion bill, or, at the very outside, pitifully abstaining.

We have gone through it all before. During the last five years I know, Sir, there have been very severe and drastic coercion bills;[6] but it will require an even severer and more drastic measure of coercion now. You will require all that you have had during the last five years, and more besides.

What, Sir, has that coercion been? You have had, Sir, during those five years – I do not say this to inflame passion or awaken bitter memories – you have had during those five years the suspension of the Habeas Corpus Act;[7] you have had a thousand of your Irish fellow-subjects held in prison without specific charge, many of them for long periods of time, some of them for 20 months, without trial and without any intention of placing them on trial. I think of all these thousand persons arrested under the Coercion Act of the late Mr Forster[8] scarcely a dozen were put on their trial; you have had the Arms Acts;[9] you have had the suspension of trial by jury – all during the last five years.

You have authorized your police to enter the domicile of a citizen, of your fellow-subject in Ireland, at any hour of the day or night, and to search every part of this domicile, even the beds of the women, without warrant. You have fined the innocent for offences committed by the guilty; you have taken power to expel aliens from this country; you have revived the Curfew Law and the blood-money of your Norman conquerors;[10] you have gagged the press and seized and suppressed newspapers; you have manufactured new crimes and offences, and applied fresh penalties unknown to your laws for these crimes and offences.

All this you have done for five years, and all this and much more you will have to do again. The provision in the bill for terminating the representation of Irish Members has been very vehemently objected to, and the right honourable gentleman, the Member for the Border Burghs,[11] has said that there is no halfway house between separation and the maintenance of law and order in Ireland by Imperial authority.

I say, with just as much sincerity of belief and just as much experience as the right honourable gentleman, that in my judgement, there is no halfway house between the concession of legislative autonomy to Ireland and the disfranchisement of the country and her government as a Crown Colony.

But, Sir, I refuse to believe that these evil days must come. I am convinced

[3] The English politician Robert Gascoyne-Cecil, 3rd Marquess of Salisbury (1830–1903) supported government of Ireland by England, saying: 'Apply that recipe … for 20 years, and at the end of that time you will find Ireland will be fit to accept any gift in the way of local government or repeal of Coercion Laws that you may wish to give.'

[7] *Habeas corpus ad subjiciendum* (Latin: 'You shall have the body to be examined') is a provision in law that requires the accused to be present in a criminal court as a safeguard against wrongful conviction. Gladstone reluctantly suspended it in 1881.
[8] The English politician William Edward Forster (1819–86) served as Chief Secretary for Ireland, 1880–2, and, having unsuccessfully prosecuted Parnell and his colleagues in 1880, he pressurized Gladstone into suspending habeas corpus. Before long, hundreds of Irish citizens had been jailed without charge.
[9] Also passed in 1881, the Arms Act removed the right of Irish citizens to bear arms.

[4] The Radicals emerged in the early 19th century as a movement favouring universal male suffrage, Catholic emancipation, free trade and other reforms. By the 1880s, parliamentary Radicals had joined with Whigs and Tory Peelites to form the Liberal Party.
[5] The division lobbies are used during voting procedures in both Houses of Parliament. Members leave the debating chamber via the Aye or No lobby, depending on how they wish to cast their vote.
[6] The Irish Coercion Act of 1881 introduced a range of severe measures.

[10] A dusk-to-dawn curfew was originally imposed by William the Conqueror in the 11th century and had been revived in 19th-century Ireland; similarly, rewards had been offered for the capture of criminals.
[11] Sir George Trevelyan, 2nd Baronet (1838–1928) served as Chief Secretary for Ireland, 1882–4.

there are a sufficient number of wise and just Members in this House to cause it to disregard appeals made to passion and to pocket, and to choose the better way of the Prime Minister – the way of founding peace and goodwill among nations; and when the numbers in the division lobby come to be told, it will also be told, for the admiration of all future generations, that England and her parliament, in this 19th century, was wise enough, brave enough and generous enough to close the strife of centuries and to give peace, prosperity, and happiness to suffering Ireland.

La Pasionaria
Spanish journalist and politician

Isidora Dolores Gómez Ibárruri *known as La Pasionaria* (1895–1989) was born in Gallarta, in Vizcaya province, the daughter of a Basque miner. She worked as a maid-servant, then joined the Socialist Party in 1917 and worked as a journalist for the workers' press, using the pseudonym La Pasionaria ('The Passion Flower'). She helped to found the Spanish Communist Party in 1920, edited several communist newspapers, and was a member of the Central Committee from 1930. She was twice imprisoned for political activities (1931–3). She was Spanish delegate to the Third International – the international Communist organization (or Comintern) founded by Lenin in 1919 – attending its conferences in 1933 and 1935. She co-founded the World Committee of Women Against War and Fascism in 1934 and was elected to the Spanish legislature, or Cortes, in 1936. During the Civil War (1936–9) she became legendary for her passionate exhortations to the Spanish people to fight against the Fascist forces, declaring: 'It is better to die on your feet than to live on your knees.' When Franco came to power in 1939 she took refuge in the USSR. After his death in 1975 she returned to Spain. She re-entered the National Assembly as Communist deputy for Asturias in 1977 at the age of 81. Her autobiography, *¡No pasarán!* ('They Shall Not Pass!'), was published in 1966.

'They shall not pass!'
19 July 1936, radio broadcast from Madrid, Spain

At dawn on 18 July 1936, Major General Francisco Franco – then occupying a command in the remote Canary Islands – released a manifesto in mainland Spain, declaring military rebellion against the leftist People's Front government. The uprising began that morning, and three years of bloody struggle followed.

La Pasionaria had her own reasons to loathe Franco: as the daughter of a miner, she had seen him put down the miner-led revolt of October 1934 in Asturias. She rightly saw the rebellion as a calamity.

Already well known as a journalist, politician and public speaker – particularly popular among women – La Pasionaria quickly emerged as the mouthpiece of the Republican cause. This call to arms, broadcast by radio the day after Franco's manifesto, was one of many rousing speeches she made around this time, and her slogan 'They shall not pass!' became a rallying cry of the Spanish Civil War.

However, her supporters were doomed to failure. By 1 October, Franco had been declared head of state, although it was April 1939 before he was able to claim total victory.

Workers, anti-fascists, and labouring people: rise as one man! Prepare to defend the republic, national freedom and the democratic liberties won by the people!

Everybody now knows from the communications of the government and of the People's Front[1] how serious the situation is. The workers, together with the troops which have remained loyal to the republic, are manfully and enthusiastically carrying on the struggle in Morocco and the Canary Islands.[2]

Under the slogan, 'Fascism shall not pass, the October butchers[3] shall not pass!' Communists, socialists, anarchists and republicans, soldiers and all the forces loyal to the will of the people are routing the traitorous rebels, who have trampled in the mud and betrayed their vaunted military honour.

The whole country is shocked by the actions of these villains. They want with fire and sword to turn democratic Spain, the Spain of the people, into a hell of terrorism and torture. But they shall not pass!

All Spain has risen to the struggle. In Madrid the people have come out into the streets, lending strength to the government by their determination and fighting spirit, so that it may utterly exterminate the reactionary fascist rebels.

Young men and women: sound the alarm! Rise and join the battle!

Women, heroic women of the people: remember the heroism of the

[1] The leftist coalition established in 1935, comprising Liberals, Socialists, Communists and anarchists under the leadership of former prime minister Manuel Azaña y Díaz (1880–1940). He was elected President in 1936.

[2] The two Spanish colonies where Franco had established bases. At the time of this speech, Franco was assembling his troops in Morocco.

[3] La Pasionaria refers to Franco's brutal crushing of the revolution of October 1934.

La Pasionaria – 'They shall not pass!'

[4] Women were active in resisting the Austrian fascist regime of 1934–8.

Austrian women![4] And you too fight side-by-side with your menfolk; together with them defend the bread and tranquillity of your children, whose lives are in danger!

Soldiers, sons of the people: stand steadfastly as one man on the side of the government, on the side of the working people, on the side of the People's Front, on the side of your fathers, brothers and comrades! March with them to victory! Fight for the Spain of 16 February![5]

[5] The election won by the People's Front was held on 16 February 1936.

Working people of all political trends! The government has placed valuable means of defence into our hands in order that we may perform our duty with honour, in order that we may save Spain from the disgrace that would be brought upon her by a victory of the bloodthirsty October butchers. Not one of you must hesitate for a single moment, and tomorrow we shall be able to celebrate our victory. Be prepared for action! Every worker, every anti-fascist, must regard himself as a mobilized soldier!

People of Catalonia, the Basque country and Galicia, and all Spaniards: rise in the defence of the democratic republic, rise to consolidate the victory won by the people on 16 February! The Communist Party calls upon all of you to join the struggle. It calls upon all working people to take their place in the struggle in order completely to smash the enemies of the republic and of the freedom of the people.

Long live the People's Front!
Long live the alliance of all anti-fascists!
Long live the people's republic!

St Patrick
Celtic Christian missionary

St Patrick *originally Succat* was born around AD 385 either in Pembrokeshire, Wales, or at Boulogne on the north coast of France, or perhaps at Kilpatrick near Dumbarton, Scotland. His father was a Romano-British deacon named Calpurnius. According to legend, he was sold by pirates to an Antrim chief called Milchu when he was 15. After six years he escaped and went to France, where he became a monk, first at Tours and afterwards at Lérins. He was consecrated a bishop at 45, and in AD 432 it is thought he was sent by Pope Celestine as a missionary to Ireland. He converted his old master Milchu and other chiefs, and after 20 years spent in missionary work, fixed his see at Armagh (AD 454). The only certainly authentic literary remains of St Patrick are his spiritual autobiography *Confession*, and a letter addressed to Coroticus, a British chieftain who had taken some Irish Christians as slaves. His feast day is 17 March.

'I cannot keep silent, nor would it be proper'
c.463 AD, Ireland

This is an extract from St Patrick's famous written work, the *Confession*, considered by many to be the transcript of a sermon which Patrick preached, in full or in part, to the Irish people. The *Confession* gives an outline of Patrick's life, including his capture and transportation to Ireland, his conversion, his escape from and – years later – return to his adopted country.

It is far from clear-cut, however. Patrick omits many details – for instance, at least two decades between his return to Ireland and the attack on him by his seniors are unaccounted for – and ascribes most of his major decisions to direct callings from God. One reason for Patrick's emphasis on these spiritual revelations is to refute British ecclesiastical opinion, which frowned on his mission to pagan Ireland and suspected him of having a financial motive.

What is clear is Patrick's deep sense of humility. This too may be seen as a response to his superiors' criticisms of the 'evidently unlearned' Patrick. However, this is unmistakably the true, self-denying voice of the zealous missionary, convinced both of God's word and his own proselytizing role.

I, Patrick, a sinner, a most simple countryman, the least of all the faithful and most contemptible to many, had for father the deacon Calpurnius, son of the late Potitus, a priest, of the settlement of Bannavem Taburniae. He had a small villa nearby where I was taken captive. I was at that time about 16 years of age. I did not, indeed, know the true God; and I was taken into captivity in Ireland with many thousands of people, according to our deserts – for quite drawn away from God, we did not keep his precepts, nor were we obedient to our priests who used to remind us of our salvation. And the Lord brought down on us the fury of his being and scattered us among many nations, even to the ends of the earth, where I, in my smallness, am now to be found among foreigners.

And there the Lord opened my mind to an awareness of my unbelief, in order that, even so late, I might remember my transgressions and turn with all my heart to the Lord my God, who had regard for my insignificance and pitied my youth and ignorance. And he watched over me before I knew him, and before I learned sense or even distinguished between good and evil, and he protected me, and consoled me as a father would his son.

Therefore, indeed, I cannot keep silent, nor would it be proper, so many favours and graces has the Lord deigned to bestow on me in the land of my captivity. For after chastisement from God, and recognizing him, our way to repay him is to exalt him and confess his wonders before every nation under Heaven ...

I am, then, first of all, countrified, an exile, evidently unlearned, one who is not able to see into the future, but I know for certain that before I was humbled I was like a stone lying in deep mire, and he that is mighty came and in his mercy raised me up and, indeed, lifted me high up and placed me on top of the wall. And from there I ought to shout out in gratitude to the Lord for his great favours in this world and for ever, that the mind of man cannot measure …

After I reached Ireland I used to pasture the flock each day and I used to pray many times a day. More and more did the love of God, and my fear of him and faith increase, and my spirit was moved so that in a day [I said] from one up to 100 prayers, and in the night a like number; besides I used to stay out in the forests and on the mountain and I would wake up before daylight to pray in the snow, in icy coldness, in rain, and I used to feel neither ill nor any slothfulness, because, as I now see, the Spirit was burning in me at that time.

And it was there of course that one night in my sleep I heard a voice saying to me: 'You do well to fast: soon you will depart for your home country.' And again, a very short time later, there was a voice prophesying: 'Behold, your ship is ready.' And it was not close by, but, as it happened, 200 miles away, where I had never been nor knew any person. And shortly thereafter I turned about and fled from the man with whom I had been for six years and I came – by the power of God, who directed my route to advantage (and I was afraid of nothing) – until I reached that ship …

And after three days we reached land, and for 28 days journeyed through uninhabited country, and the food ran out and hunger overtook them; and one day the steersman began saying: 'Why is it, Christian? You say your God is great and all-powerful; then why can you not pray for us? For we may perish of hunger; it is unlikely indeed that we shall ever see another human being.'

In fact, I said to them, confidently: 'Be converted by faith with all your heart to my Lord God, because nothing is impossible for him, so that today he will send food for you on your road, until you be sated, because everywhere he abounds.' And with God's help this came to pass; and behold, a herd of swine appeared on the road before our eyes, and they slew many of them, and remained there for two nights, and they were full of their meat and well restored, for many of them had fainted and would otherwise have been left half dead by the wayside. And after this they gave the utmost thanks to God, and I was esteemed in their eyes, and from that day they had food abundantly. They discovered wild honey besides and they offered a share to me, and one of them said: 'It is a sacrifice.' Thanks be to God, I tasted none of it …

And after a few years I was again in Britain with my kinsfolk, and they welcomed me as a son, and asked me, in faith, that after the great tribulations I had endured I should not go anywhere else away from them. And, of course, there, in a vision of the night, I saw a man whose name was Victoricus coming as if from Ireland with innumerable letters, and he gave me one of them, and I read the beginning of the letter: 'The Voice of the Irish', and as I was reading the beginning of the letter, I seemed at that moment to hear the voices of those who were beside the forest of Foclut, which is near the western sea,[1] and they were crying as if with one voice: 'We beg you, holy youth, that you shall come and shall walk again among us.' And I was stung intensely in my heart so that I could read no more, and thus I awoke …

And on a second occasion I saw him praying within me, and I was as it

[1] Historians believe the wood of Foclut is near the present-day town of Killala, County Mayo, in Ireland.

were, inside my own body, and I heard him above me — that is, above my inner self. He was praying powerfully with sighs. And in the course of this I was astonished and wondering, and I pondered who it could be who was praying within me. But at the end of the prayer it was revealed to me that it was the Spirit. And so I awoke and remembered the Apostle's words: 'Likewise the Spirit helps us in our weakness; for we know not how to pray as we ought. But the Spirit Himself intercedes for us with sighs too deep for utterance.'[2]

[2] Romans 8:26.

I did not proceed to Ireland of my own accord until I was almost giving up, but through this I was corrected by the Lord, and he prepared me so that today I should be what was once far from me, in order that I should have the care of — or rather, I should be concerned for — the salvation of others ...

When I baptized so many thousands of people, did I hope for even half a jot from any of them? Tell me, and I will give it back to you. And when the Lord ordained clergy everywhere by my humble means, and I freely conferred office on them, if I asked any of them anywhere even for the price of one shoe, say so to my face and I will give it back.

More, I spent for you so that they would receive me. And I went about among you, and everywhere for your sake, in danger, and as far as the outermost regions beyond which no-one lived, and where no-one had ever penetrated before, to baptize or to ordain clergy or to confirm people. Conscientiously and gladly I did all this work by God's gift for your salvation.

From time to time I gave rewards to the kings, as well as making payments to their sons who travel with me; notwithstanding which, they seized me with my companions, and that day most avidly desired to kill me. But my time had not yet come. They plundered everything they found on us anyway, and fettered me in irons; and on the 14th day the Lord freed me from their power, and whatever they had of ours was given back to us for the sake of God on account of the indispensable friends whom we had made before.

Also you know from experience how much I was paying to those who were administering justice in all the regions, which I visited often. I estimate truly that I distributed to them not less than the price of 15 men, in order that you should enjoy my company and I enjoy yours, always, in God. I do not regret this, nor do I regard it as enough. I am paying out still and I shall pay out more. The Lord has the power to grant me that I may soon spend my own self, for your souls.

Behold, I call on God as my witness upon my soul that I am not lying; nor would I write to you for it to be an occasion for flattery or selfishness, nor hoping for honour from any one of you. Sufficient is the honour which is not yet seen, but in which the heart has confidence. He who made the promise is faithful; he never lies ...

Behold now I commend my soul to God, who is most faithful and for whom I perform my mission in obscurity, but he is no respecter of persons and he chose me for this service that I might be one of the least of his ministers. For which reason I should make return for all that he returns me. But what should I say, or what should I promise to my Lord? For I, alone, can do nothing unless he himself vouchsafe it to me ...

And if at any time I managed anything of good for the sake of my God whom I love, I beg of him that he grant it to me to shed my blood for his name with proselytes and captives, even should I be left unburied, or even were my wretched body to be torn limb from limb by dogs or savage beasts, or were it to be devoured by the birds of the air, I think, most surely, were this to have happened to me, I had saved both my soul and my body.

For beyond any doubt on that day we shall rise again in the brightness of the sun, that is, in the glory of Christ Jesus our Redeemer, as children of the living God and co-heirs of Christ, made in his image; for we shall reign through him and for him and in him …

Behold over and over again: I would briefly set out the words of my confession. I testify in truthfulness and gladness of heart before God and his holy angels that I never had any reason, except the Gospel and his promises, ever to have returned to that nation from which I had previously escaped with difficulty.

But I entreat those who believe in and fear God, whoever deigns to examine or receive this document composed by the obviously unlearned sinner Patrick in Ireland, that nobody shall ever ascribe to my ignorance any trivial thing that I achieved or may have expounded that was pleasing to God, but accept and truly believe that it would have been the gift of God.

And this is my confession before I die.

George S Patton

American soldier

George Smith Patton *known as Old Blood and Guts* (1885–1945) was born in San Gabriel, California. He graduated from West Point in 1909 and in World War I commanded a tank brigade on the western front. A major general by 1941, he became one of the most daring US combat commanders in World War II. He trained the 1st Armoured Corps and later led the first US troops to fight in North Africa, playing a key role in the Allied invasion. In 1943 he commanded the US 7th Army in the Sicilian campaign. At the head of the 3rd Army he swept across France and Germany in 1944–5 and reached the Czech frontier. He was fatally injured in a motor accident near Mannheim in occupied Germany. His memoirs, *War as I Knew it*, were published posthumously in 1947.

'All real Americans love the sting and clash of battle'

5 June 1944, the south coast of England

General Patton was a strict disciplinarian who expected the best from his men and despised those who did not show courage under fire. Indeed, in August 1943, he assaulted a soldier hospitalized for shellshock, though the ensuing scandal was hushed up by DWIGHT D EISENHOWER, then Supreme Commander of the Allied forces in Europe. Recognizing Patton's usefulness, Eisenhower wrote to him: 'You owe us some victories. Pay up and the world will deem me a wise man.'

Patton was duly sent to Britain in early 1944 to command the 3rd Army in preparation for D-Day. It was a tense time: fierce resistance was expected from the German troops occupying Normandy; and Patton himself did not know when the order would be given to cross the Channel.

When priming his men for battle, Patton spoke spontaneously, sharing his forthright views on war and tactics. His profanity and obscenity on such occasions were legendary. Taxed on this approach, he said: 'When I want my men to remember something important, to really make it stick, I give it to them double dirty. You can't run an army without profanity, and it has to be eloquent profanity.'

In an impeccable uniform, with gleaming boots and shiny helmet, he addressed his troops on the beautiful fresh morning of 5 June 1944, shortly before they set off for the invasion of Europe. This typically down-to-earth but colourful speech was pieced together by Carlo D'Este for his biography, *Patton: Genius for War*.

Men: this stuff we hear about America wanting to stay out of the war – not wanting to fight – is a lot of bullshit. Americans love to fight – traditionally! All real Americans love the sting and clash of battle. When you were kids, you all admired the champion marble player, the fastest runner, the big league ball players, the toughest boxers. Americans love a winner and will not tolerate a loser. Americans play to win all the time. I wouldn't give a hoot in hell for a man who lost and laughs. That's why Americans have never lost and will never lose a war, for the very thought of losing is hateful to an American.

If he isn't, he's a goddam liar! Some men are cowards, yes, but they fight just the same, or get the hell shamed out of them watching men fight who are just as scared. Some of them get over their fright in a minute under fire, some take an hour, and for some it takes days. But the real man never lets fear of death overpower his honour, his sense of duty to his country, and his innate manhood.

All through your army career you men have bitched about what you call 'this chicken-shit drilling'. That is all for a purpose – *to insure instant obedience to orders and create alertness*. I don't give a damn for a man who is not always on his toes. You men are veterans, or you would not be here. You are ready! A man, to continue breathing, must be alert at all times. If not, someone, sometime, some German sonofabitch, will sneak up behind him and beat him to death with a sockful of shit.

[*A roar of approval.*]

There are 400 neatly marked graves somewhere in Sicily, all because *one man* went to sleep on his job. [*Pause.*] But they are *German* graves, for we caught the bastard asleep before they did.

We have the best food, the finest equipment, the best spirit and the best men in the world. Why, by God, I actually pity those poor sons-of-bitches we are going up against. This individual heroic stuff is a lot of crap. The bilious bastard who wrote that kind of stuff for the *Saturday Evening Post* didn't know any more about real battle than he did about fucking.

[*Howls of delight and clapping; with some men gleefully slapping their legs.*]

My men don't surrender. I don't want to hear of any soldier under my command being captured unless he is hit. Even if you are hit, you can still fight. That's not just bullshit either. The kind of a man I want under me is like the lieutenant who, with a Luger[1] against his chest, swept aside the gun with his hand, jerked his helmet off with the other and busted hell out of the Boche[2] with the helmet. Then he picked up the gun and killed another German. All the time this man had a bullet through his lung. That's a man for you!

All the real heroes are not storybook combat figures either. Every single man in the army plays a vital part. Every little job is essential to the whole scheme. What if every truck-driver suddenly decided that he didn't like the whine of those shells and turned yellow and jumped headlong into a ditch? He could say to himself, 'They won't miss me – just one guy in thousands.' What if every man said that? Where in the hell would we be now?

No, thank God, Americans don't say that. Every man does his job. Every man serves the whole. Every department, every unit, is important to the vast scheme of things. The ordnance is needed to supply the guns, the quartermaster is needed to bring up the food and clothes for us – for where we are going there isn't a hell of a lot to steal! Every last damn man in the mess hall, even the one who heats the water to keep us from getting diarrhoea, has a job to do. Even the chaplain is important, for if we get killed and he is not there to bury us we would all go to Hell.

Each man must not only think of himself, but think of his buddy fighting alongside him. We don't want yellow cowards in the army. They should be killed off like flies. If not, they will go back home after the war, goddam cowards, and breed more cowards. The brave men will breed more brave men.

One of the bravest men I saw in the African campaign was the fellow I saw on a telegraph pole in the midst of furious fire … I stopped and asked him what the hell he was doing up there at that time. He answered, 'Fixing the wire, sir.'

'Isn't it a little unhealthy up there right now?' I asked.

'Yes, sir, but this goddam wire has got to be fixed.'

There was a real soldier … [and] you should have seen those trucks on the road to Gabès.[3] The drivers were magnificent. All day they crawled along those sonofabitchin' roads, never stopping, never deviating from their course, with shells bursting all around them. We got through on good old American guts. Many of the men drove over 40 consecutive hours.

[*Dead silence.*]

Don't forget, you don't know I'm here at all. No word of that fact is to be mentioned in any letter. The world is not supposed to know what the hell they did with me. I'm not supposed to be commanding this army. I'm not even supposed to be in England. Let the first bastards to find out be the

[1] A pistol issued to German soldiers.

[2] Derogratory French slang for the Germans, originally used during World War I.

[3] A city in Tunisia which saw fierce fighting between Allied and German forces in 1943.

goddam Germans. Some day I want them to raise up on their hind legs and howl: 'Jesus Christ, it's that goddam 3rd Army and that sonofabitch Patton again!'

[*Cheers and roars of approval.*]

We want to get the hell over there. We want to get over there and clean the goddam thing up. And then we'll have to take a little jaunt against the purple-pissing Japanese and clean their nest too, before the Marines get in and claim all the goddam credit!

[*Laughter.*]

Sure we all want to go home. We want this thing over with. But you can't win a war lying down. The quickest way to get it over with is to get the bastards. The quicker they are whipped, the quicker we go home. The shortest way home is through Berlin! Why, if a man is lying down in a shell-hole, if he just stays there all the day, the Boche will get to him eventually, and probably get him first! There is no such thing as a foxhole war any more. Foxholes only slow up the offensive. Keep moving. We will win this war, but we will win it only by fighting and by showing guts.

[*Pause.*]

There is one great thing you men will be able to say when you go home. You may all thank God for it. Thank God that, at least, 30 years from now, when you are sitting around the fireside with your grandson on your knee and he asks what you did in the great World War II, you won't have to say, 'I shovelled shit in Louisiana.'

Pádraig Pearse

Irish writer and nationalist

Pádraig Henry Pearse (1879–1916) was born in Dublin, the son of an English father, a monumental sculptor, and an Irish mother. A leader of the Gaelic revival, he joined the Gaelic League in 1895, became editor of its journal *An Claidheamh Soluis* ('The Sword of Light') in 1903 and lectured in Irish at University College. In 1908 he founded a bilingual school, St Enda's, at Ranelagh, which later moved to Rath Farnham. In 1915 he joined the Irish Republican Brotherhood. In the 1916 Easter Rising he was commander-in-chief of the insurgents, and was proclaimed president of the provisional government. After the revolt had been quelled he was arrested, court-martialled and shot. He left various writings, including poems, short stories and plays in both English and Irish.

'To fight is to win'

2 May 1916, Dublin, Ireland

When Pádraig Pearse read out his declaration of an independent Irish constitution at noon on 24 April 1916, his Irish Volunteers had little support from the Irish public. Most Republican sympathy lay with the plan put forward by nationalist MP John Redmond (1856–1918) to establish home rule by peaceful means. Even Pearse's own paramilitary force – which, combined with the smaller Irish Citizen Army led by Scottish–Irish socialist James Connolly (1868–1916), amounted to somewhere between 1,000 and 1,500 men and women – was split as to the wisdom of his insurrection, and did not fully support it.

During six days' fighting against superior British forces, much of the centre of Dublin had been seriously damaged by artillery and small arms fire, with numerous civilian losses, and Pearse's capitulation at his headquarters at the Dublin General Post Office building was greeted with general relief. But British reprisals against the leaders of the rebellion – who were court-martialled in camera, without access to a legal defence, then executed on 3 May – created unprecedented sympathy for Pearse's cause. Indignation was particularly aroused by images circulated in the press of Connolly's execution while tied to a chair; wounded in the action, he was unable to stand for the firing squad. This would eventually lead to a violent independence movement, civil war and, finally, the Irish Free State.

In all, 16 leaders were executed, including Pearse's brother Willie. On being convicted, Pearse gave a rousing speech, which he later recorded in this written version.

[1] The English soldier General Sir John Maxwell (1859–1929) had been appointed in April 1916 as commander-in-chief in Dublin. With Ireland under martial law, he was effectively its governor. Instructed by Prime Minister H H Asquith (1852–1928) to crush the rebellion quickly, he is said to have remarked: 'When I am finished, there will not be a whisper of sedition in Ireland for another 100 years.'

I desire in the first place to repeat what I have already said in letters to General Sir John Maxwell[1] and to Brigadier General Lowe.[2] My object in agreeing to an unconditional surrender was to prevent the further slaughter of the civilian population of Dublin and to save the lives of our gallant fellows who, having made for six days a stand unparalleled in military history, were now surrounded and (in the case of those under the immediate command of headquarters) without food.

I fully understand now, as then, that my own life is forfeit to British law, and I shall die very cheerfully if I can think that the British government, as it has already shown itself strong, will now show itself magnanimous enough to accept my single life in forfeiture and to give a general amnesty to the brave men and boys who have fought at my bidding. In the second place I wish to be understood that any admissions I make here are to be taken as involving myself alone. They do not involve and must not be used against anyone who acted with me, not even those who may have set their names to documents with me.

[*The court assented to this.*]

I admit that I was Commandant-General commanding-in-chief of the forces of the Irish Republic, which have been acting against you for the past week, and that I was president of the provisional government. I stand over all my acts and words done or spoken, in these capacities.

When I was a child of ten, I went down on my bare knees by my bedside one night and promised God that I should devote my life to an effort to free

[2] On 29 April, the English soldier Brigadier General W H M Lowe had received Pearse's letter of surrender, which read: 'In order to prevent the further slaughter of Dublin citizens and in the hope of saving the lives of our followers now surrounded and hopelessly outnumbered, the members of the Provisional Government ... have agreed to an unconditional surrender.'

my country. I have kept my promise. For among all earthly things, as a boy and as a man I have worked for Irish freedom. I have helped to organize, to arm, to train and to discipline my fellow countrymen to the sole end that, when the time came, they might fight for Irish freedom. The time, as it seemed to me, did come and we went into the fight.

I am glad we did. We seem to have lost: we have not lost. To refuse to fight would have been to lose. To fight is to win: we have kept faith with the past and handed a tradition to the future.

I repudiate the assertion of the prosecutor that I sought to aid and abet England's enemy. Germany is no more to me than England is. I asked and accepted German aid in the shape of arms and an expeditionary force. We neither asked for nor accepted German gold, nor had any traffic with Germany but what I state.[3] My aim was to win Irish freedom. We struck the first blow ourselves but I should have been glad of an ally's aid.

I assume that I am speaking to Englishmen who value their own freedom and who profess to be fighting for the freedom of Belgium and Serbia.[4] Believe that we too love freedom and desire it. To us it is more desirable than anything in the world. If you strike us down now, we shall rise again and renew the fight. You cannot conquer Ireland; you cannot extinguish the Irish passion for freedom; if our deed has not been sufficient to win freedom then our children will win it by a better deed.

[3] On 21 April, Pearse's ally Sir ROGER CASEMENT had arrived off the coast of Kerry with a shipment of German arms, but his vessel was scuttled by its German captain when intercepted by the Royal Navy. Casement had been involved in a similar but successful shipment in July 1914.

[4] Among the stated goals of World War I, in which Britain was engaged at the time of this speech.

Pericles
Athenian statesman

Pericles (c.490–429 BC) was born into an aristocratic family in Athens. He was the son of Xanthippus, who had won the naval victory over the Persians at Mycale in 479 BC. He came rapidly to the fore as a supporter of the new democracy. With Ephialtes in 462–461 BC, he brought in measures limiting the power of the old aristocratic Areopagus. After the murder of Ephialtes, Pericles became the dominant figure in Athenian politics. He was elected 15 times to the office of *strategos* (general, but with political functions) between 451 BC (when he introduced a popular law which restricted citizenship) and his death. Athens under Pericles followed an expansionist policy, in which the Delian League, founded to keep the defeated Persians away from Greece, was turned into an Athenian empire. Tribute was exacted from the former allies, and attempts to secede were crushed by force. Colonies and other settlements were founded in the Thracian Chersonese and in southern Italy. According to some accounts, Pericles planned a grand Hellenic confederation, but the Spartans thwarted the scheme. Athens and Sparta were almost continuously at war during these years, but in 446 BC there was a peace in which Sparta recognized much of Athens's imperial ambition. Pericles undertook a major building programme which glorified Athens with the Parthenon and other buildings. He was opposed for a time by Thucydides, son of Melesias, who was ostracized in 433 BC, leaving Pericles virtually unopposed. When war broke out again with Sparta in 431 BC Pericles advocated a policy of caution on land, allowing the invading Spartans to destroy the fields while the population was concentrated behind the strong city walls and supply lines could be protected by the powerful Athenian navy. In 430 BC plague broke out in the city; the Athenians' patience broke and Pericles was removed from office. He was again elected *strategos*, but he died soon afterwards, himself a victim of the plague. Athens under Pericles was a democracy effectively ruled by its first citizen. No other Athenian statesman before or since achieved such a dominant position. He enjoyed the company of the poets and intellectuals of the day, including the dramatist Sophocles, who was a personal friend.

'Fix your eyes upon the greatness of Athens'
431 BC, Athens, Greece

Athens, a radical democracy but also mistress of a sea-born empire throughout the Aegean, was once again at war with Sparta, a land-based militaristic city, governed by an antique and oligarchic system, long regarded as the most powerful in Greece.

The Athenians had a custom, claimed as ancient, whereby those who had been killed fighting for the city were given public burial in the Ceramicus, to the north-west of the Acropolis. In the winter of 431 BC at the end of the first year of the war, Pericles – the leading man in the state and largely responsible for the policy which had led to the war – was chosen as the orator of the funeral oration.

The famous speech given here is not that given by Pericles, but the account of it written by the historian Thucydides. As always in the work of ancient historians, the author has composed a piece suitable to the occasion. However, there is reason to believe that Thucydides is closer to the gist of Pericles' actual oration than is true, for example, of the speech of Hannibal recorded by Livy, or that of Calgacus recorded by Tacitus (both of which are included in this book).

In any case, Thucydides has taken the opportunity to set out, in a terse but effective style that is particularly his own, the virtues of the Athenian democracy. It remains a classic statement of the case for the Greek democratic ideal. The translation is by Benjamin Jowett (1881).

Most of those who have spoken here before me have commended the lawgiver, who added his oration to our other funeral customs. It seemed to them a worthy thing that such an honour should be given at their burial to the dead who have fallen on the field of battle. But I should have preferred that, when men's deeds have been brave, they should be honoured in deed only, and with such an honour as this public funeral, which you are now witnessing. Then the reputation of many would not have been imperilled on the eloquence or want of eloquence of one, and their virtues believed or not as he spoke well or ill.

For it is difficult to say neither too little nor too much; and even moderation is apt not to give the impression of truthfulness. The friend of the dead who knows the facts is likely to think that the words of the speaker fall short of his knowledge and of his wishes; another who is not so well informed, when he hears of anything which surpasses his own powers, will be envious and will suspect exaggeration. Mankind are tolerant of the praises of others so long as each hearer thinks that he can do as well or nearly as well himself, but, when the speaker rises above him, jealousy is aroused and he begins to be incredulous.

However, since our ancestors have set the seal of their approval upon the practice, I must obey, and to the utmost of my power shall endeavour to satisfy the wishes and beliefs of all who hear me.

I will speak first of our ancestors, for it is right and becoming that now, when we are lamenting the dead, a tribute should be paid to their memory. There has never been a time when they did not inhabit this land, which by their valour they have handed down from generation to generation, and we have received from them a free state.

But if they were worthy of praise, still more were our fathers, who added to their inheritance, and after many a struggle transmitted to us, their sons, this great empire. And we ourselves assembled here today, who are still most of us in the vigour of life, have chiefly done the work of improvement, and have richly endowed our city with all things, so that she is sufficient for herself both in peace and war.

Of the military exploits by which our various possessions were acquired, or of the energy with which we or our fathers drove back the tide of war, Hellenic or barbarian, I will not speak; for the tale would be long and is familiar to you. But before I praise the dead, I should like to point out by what principles of action we rose to power, and under what institutions and through what manner of life our empire became great. For I conceive that such thoughts are not unsuited to the occasion, and that this numerous assembly of citizens and strangers may profitably listen to them.

Our form of government does not enter into rivalry with the institutions of others. We do not copy our neighbours, but are an example to them. It is true that we are called a democracy, for the administration is in the hands of the many and not of the few. But while the law secures equal justice to all alike in their private disputes, the claim of excellence is also recognized; and when a citizen is in any way distinguished, he is preferred to the public service, not as a matter of privilege, but as the reward of merit. Neither is poverty a bar, but a man may benefit his country whatever be the obscurity of his condition …

And we have not forgotten to provide for our weary spirits many relaxations from toil; we have regular games and sacrifices throughout the year; at home the style of our life is refined; and the delight which we daily feel in all these things helps to banish melancholy. Because of the greatness of our city the fruits of the whole earth flow in upon us; so that we enjoy the goods of other countries as freely as of our own.

Then, again, our military training is in many respects superior to that of our adversaries. Our city is thrown open to the world, and we never expel a foreigner or prevent him from seeing or learning anything of which the secret if revealed to an enemy might profit him. We rely not upon management or trickery, but upon our own hearts and hands. And in the matter of education, whereas they from early youth are always undergoing laborious exercises which are to make them brave, we live at ease, and yet are equally ready to face the perils which they face.

And here is the proof. The Lacedaemonians[1] come into Attica not by themselves, but with their whole confederacy following; we go alone into a neighbour's country; and although our opponents are fighting for their homes and we on a foreign soil, we have seldom any difficulty in overcoming them. Our enemies have never yet felt our united strength; the care of a navy divides our attention, and on land we are obliged to send our own citizens everywhere. But they, if they meet and defeat a part of our army, are as proud as if they had routed us all, and when defeated they pretend to have been vanquished by us all.[2]

If then we prefer to meet danger with a light heart but without laborious training, and with a courage which is gained by habit and not enforced by law, are we not greatly the gainers? Since we do not anticipate the pain, although, when the hour comes, we can be as brave as those who never allow themselves to rest; and thus too our city is equally admirable in peace and in war.

For we are lovers of the beautiful, yet simple in our tastes, and we cultivate the mind without loss of manliness. Wealth we employ, not for talk and ostentation, but when there is a real use for it. To avow poverty with us is no disgrace; the true disgrace is in doing nothing to avoid it. An Athenian citizen does not neglect the state because he takes care of his own household; and even those of us who are engaged in business have a very fair idea of politics.

We alone regard a man who takes no interest in public affairs, not as a harmless, but as a useless character; and if few of us are originators, we are all sound judges of a policy. The great impediment to action is, in our opinion, not discussion, but the want of that knowledge which is gained by discussion preparatory to action. For we have a peculiar power of thinking before we act and of acting too, whereas other men are courageous from ignorance but hesitate upon reflection. And they are surely to be esteemed the bravest spirits who, having the clearest sense both of the pains and pleasures of life, do not on that account shrink from danger. In doing good, again, we are unlike others; we make our friends by conferring, not by receiving favours …

I have dwelt upon the greatness of Athens because I want to show you that we are contending for a higher prize than those who enjoy none of these privileges – and to establish by manifest proof the merit of these men whom I am now commemorating. Their loftiest praise has been already spoken. For in magnifying the city I have magnified them, and men like them whose virtues made her glorious. And of how few Hellenes[3] can it be said as of them, that their deeds when weighed in the balance have been found equal to their fame?

Methinks that a death such as theirs has been gives the true measure of a man's worth; it may be the first revelation of his virtues, but is at any rate their final seal. For even those who come short in other ways may justly plead the valour with which they have fought for their country; they have blotted out the evil with the good, and have benefited the state more by their public services than they have injured her by their private actions. None of these men were enervated by wealth or hesitated to resign the pleasures of life; none of them put off the evil day in the hope, natural to poverty, that a man, though poor, may one day become rich.

But, deeming that the punishment of their enemies was sweeter than any of these things, and that they could fall in no nobler cause, they determined at the hazard of their lives to be honourably avenged, and to

[1] The Spartans. Sparta was the chief city of Lacedaemonia, and the leader of a confederacy of states based in the Peloponnese.

[2] Unlike the Spartans, Athenians made up all the soldiers in their army and the great majority of the ships and sailors in the navy.

[3] The Greek nation as a whole.

leave the rest. They resigned to hope their unknown chance of happiness; but in the face of death they resolved to rely upon themselves alone. And when the moment came they were minded to resist and suffer, rather than to fly and save their lives; they ran away from the word of dishonour, but on the battlefield their feet stood fast, and in an instant, at the height of their fortune, they passed away from the scene, not of their fear, but of their glory.

Such was the end of these men; they were worthy of Athens, and the living need not desire to have a more heroic spirit, although they may pray for a less fatal issue. The value of such a spirit is not to be expressed in words. Anyone can discourse to you forever about the advantages of a brave defence which you know already. But instead of listening to him, I would have you day by day fix your eyes upon the greatness of Athens, until you become filled with the love of her; and when you are impressed by the spectacle of her glory, reflect that this empire has been acquired by men who knew their duty and had the courage to do it, who in the hour of conflict had the fear of dishonour always present to them, and who, if ever they failed in an enterprise, would not allow their virtues to be lost to their country, but freely gave their lives to her as the fairest offering which they could present at her feast.

The sacrifice which they collectively made was individually repaid to them; for they received again each one for himself a praise which grows not old, and the noblest of all sepulchres – I speak not of that in which their remains are laid, but of that in which their glory survives, and is proclaimed always and on every fitting occasion both in word and deed.

For the whole earth is the sepulchre of famous men. Not only are they commemorated by columns and inscriptions in their own country, but in foreign lands there dwells also an unwritten memorial of them, graven not on stone but in the hearts of men. Make them your examples, and, esteeming courage to be freedom and freedom to be happiness, do not weigh too nicely the perils of war …

I do not now commiserate the parents of the dead who stand here; I would rather comfort them. You know that your life has been passed amid manifold vicissitudes; and that they may be deemed fortunate who have gained most honour – whether an honourable death like theirs, or an honourable sorrow like yours – and whose days have been so ordered that the term of their happiness is likewise the term of their life.

I know how hard it is to make you feel this, when the good fortune of others will too often remind you of the gladness which once lightened your hearts. And sorrow is felt at the want of those blessings, not which a man never knew, but which were a part of his life before they were taken from him. Some of you are of an age at which they may hope to have other children, and they ought to bear their sorrow better; not only will the children who may hereafter be born make them forget their own lost ones, but the city will be doubly a gainer. She will not be left desolate, and she will be safer. For a man's counsel cannot have equal weight or worth when he alone has no children to risk in the general danger.

To those of you who have passed their prime, I say: congratulate yourselves that you have been happy during the greater part of your days; remember that your life of sorrow will not last long, and be comforted by the glory of those who are gone. For the love of honour alone is ever young; and not riches, as some say, but honour is the delight of men when they are old and useless.

To you who are the sons and brothers of the departed, I see that the struggle to emulate them will be an arduous one. For all men praise the dead, and however pre-eminent your virtue may be, hardly will you be thought, I do not say to equal, but even to approach them. The living have their rivals and detractors, but when a man is out of the way, the honour and goodwill which he receives is unalloyed.

And if I am to speak of womanly virtues to those of you who will henceforth be widows, let me sum them up in one short admonition. To a woman not to show more weakness than is natural to her sex is a great glory, and not to be talked about for good or for evil among men.[4]

I have paid the required tribute, in obedience to the law, making use of such fitting words as I had. The tribute of deeds has been paid in part; for the dead have been honourably interred and it remains only that their children should be maintained at the public charge until they are grown up: this is the solid prize with which, as with a garland, Athens crowns her sons living and dead, after a struggle like theirs. For where the rewards of virtue are greatest, there the noblest citizens are enlisted in the service of the state. And now, when you have duly lamented, every one his own dead, you may depart.

[4] Women had no part to play in the public life of Athenian democracy, but these words are poor consolation.

Harold Pinter

English dramatist, poet and activist

Harold Pinter (1930–2008) was born in London, the son of an East End tailor of Portuguese–Jewish ancestry (da Pinta). He studied at RADA, then at the Central School of Speech and Drama in London. He became a repertory actor and wrote poetry, later turning to plays. His first London production, *The Birthday Party* (1959), was trounced by critics alarmed by its highly idiosyncratic dramatic idiom. The play uses apparently inconsequential or illogical dialogue to expose undercurrents in conversation, inducing an atmosphere of menace, claustrophobia and isolation, but also humour. This and other early works drew comparisons with the Absurdist drama of Samuel Beckett and Eugene Ionesco. His second major play, *The Caretaker* (1958, filmed 1963) was much more successful. His television play *The Lover* (1963) won the Italia Prize. Other early plays include *The Collection* (television 1961, stage 1962), *The Dwarfs* (radio 1960, stage 1963), and *The Homecoming* (1965). His early film scripts include *The Servant* (1963) and *The Pumpkin Eaters* (1964). Later plays include *No Man's Land* (1975), and *Betrayal* (1978), the story of an adulterous relationship told in reverse chronological order, which was widely believed to contain elements of autobiography. Pinter did not produce another full-length play until *Party Time* (1991) which was followed by *Moonlight* (1993). Three short pieces, under the title *Other Voices*, were staged at the National Theatre, London, in 1982, during Pinter's tenure as associate director (1973–83). *One for the Road* (1984), *Mountain Language* (1988) and *A New World Order* (1990) deal with explicitly political themes. Later film scripts include *The French Lieutenant's Woman* (1981), from the novel by John Fowles, *The Handmaid's Tale* (1987), from the novel by Margaret Atwood, and *The Comfort of Strangers* (1990), from the novel by Ian McEwan. Pinter works sporadically as an actor and theatre director. He appeared in the films *Mojo* (1997) and *The Tailor of Panama* (2000) and directed a revival of *No Man's Land* in 2001 and Simon Gray's *The Old Masters* in 2004. He underwent successful treatment for cancer in 2002. In his later years, Pinter has become increasingly outspoken about his political views, and particularly on human rights issues. In 1991 he helped launch a campaign against the celebration of Columbus's 'discovery' of America. He was made a CBE in 1992; and was awarded the Wildred Owen Award for Poetry in 2004 and the 2005 Nobel Prize for literature.

'A thing is not necessarily either true or false'
4 January 1962, Bristol, England

The mystery and suspense generated by Pinter's plays often derive from uncertainty. His characters frequently refuse to reveal what they want or who they are – indeed, they themselves often seem unsure.

Early in his career, Pinter gave this speech at the National Student Drama Festival, to explain something of the creative process behind his work. But in keeping with the enigmatic tone of his plays, he offers few hard facts. Instead, he argues that people are not subject to simple interpretation; and that therefore any drama featuring characters of easily understood motivation is fundamentally untrue.

He adds that perception and memory are highly unreliable sources of information; and even describes language – the tool of his trade – as untrustworthy, more often used to veil than to reveal. This tendency is certainly borne out in his characters' dialogue. Though clearly loath to alienate his peers, he also indicates a contempt for didactic trends in the theatre of the early 1960s – the playwright as 'prophet'.

Another key feature of Pinter's work is its humour, and the speech is laced with sly wit. For example, he puts forward a tongue-in-cheek syllogism to explain why *The Caretaker* enjoyed a warmer reception than *The Birthday Party*. Its success, he ironically proposes, resulted from the notation he used to write his famous pauses.

The speech gives few clues as to the 'meaning' of Pinter's plays, which he once described – glibly but memorably – as 'the weasel under the cocktail cabinet'. It does suggest, however, that he knows little better than anyone else what his characters are up to.

I'm not a theorist. I'm not an authoritative or reliable commentator on the dramatic scene, the social scene, any scene. I write plays, when I can manage it, and that's all. That's the sum of it. So I'm speaking with some reluctance, knowing that there are least 24 possible aspects of any single statement, depending on where you're standing at the time or on what the weather's like. A categorical statement, I find, will never stay where it is and be finite. It will immediately be subject to modification by the other 23 possibilities of it. No statement I make, therefore, should be interpreted as final and definitive. One or two of them may sound final and definitive, they may even be *almost* final and definitive, but I won't regard them as such tomorrow, and I wouldn't like you to do so today.

I've had two full-length plays produced in London. The first ran a week and the second ran a year. Of course, there are differences between the two plays. In *The Birthday Party* I employed a certain amount of dashes in the text, between phrases. In *The Caretaker* I cut out the dashes and used dots instead. So that instead of, say: 'Look, dash, who, dash, I, dash, dash, dash,' the text would read: 'Look, dot, dot, dot, who, dot, dot, dot, I, dot, dot, dot, dot.'

So it's possible to deduce from this that dots are more popular than dashes and that's why *The Caretaker* had a longer run than *The Birthday Party.* The fact that in neither case could you hear the dots and dashes in performance is beside the point. You can't fool the critics for long. They can tell a dot from a dash a mile off, even if they can hear neither.

It took me quite a while to grow used to the fact that critical and public response in the theatre follows a very erratic temperature chart. And the danger for a writer is where he becomes easy prey for the old bugs of apprehension and expectation in this connection. But I think Düsseldorf cleared the air for me. In Düsseldorf about two years ago I took, as is the Continental custom, a bow with a German cast of *The Caretaker* at the end of the play on the first night. I was at once booed violently by what must have been the finest collection of booers in the world. I thought they were using megaphones, but it was pure mouth. The cast was as dogged as the audience, however, and we took 34 curtain calls, all to boos. By the 34th there were only two people left in the house, still booing. I was strangely warmed by all this, and now, whenever I sense a tremor of the old apprehension or expectation, I remember Düsseldorf, and am cured.

The theatre is a large, energetic, public activity. Writing is, for me, a completely private activity – a poem or a play, no difference. These facts are not easy to reconcile. The professional theatre, whatever the virtues it undoubtedly possesses, is a world of false climaxes, calculated tensions, some hysteria and a good deal of inefficiency. And the alarms of this world which I suppose I work in become steadily more widespread and intrusive. But basically my position has remained the same. What I write has no obligation to anything other than to itself. My responsibility is not to audiences, critics, producers, directors, actors or to my fellow men in general, but to the play in hand, simply. I warned you about definitive statements but it looks as though I've just made one.

I have usually begun a play in quite a simple manner; found a couple of characters in a particular context, thrown them together and listened to what they said, keeping my nose to the ground. The context has always been, for me, concrete and particular, and the characters concrete also. I've never started a play from any kind of abstract idea or theory and never envisaged my own characters as messengers of death, doom, Heaven or the Milky Way – or, in other words, as allegorical representations of any particular force, whatever that may mean. When a character cannot be comfortably defined or understood in terms of the familiar, the tendency is to perch him on a symbolic shelf, out of harm's way. Once there, he can be talked about but need not be lived with. In this way, it is easy to put up a pretty efficient smokescreen, on the part of the critics or the audience, against recognition, against an active and willing participation.

We don't carry labels on our chests, and even though they are continually fixed to us by others, they convince nobody. The desire for verification on the part of all of us, with regard to our own experience and the experience of others, is understandable, but cannot always be satisfied. I suggest there can be no hard distinctions between what is real and what is unreal, nor between what is true and what is false. A thing is not necessarily either true or false; it can be both true and false. A character on the stage who can present no convincing argument or information as to his past experience, his present behaviour or his aspirations, nor give a comprehensive analysis of his motives is as legitimate and as worthy of attention as one who, alarmingly, can do all these things. The more acute the experience the less articulate its expression.

Apart from any other consideration, we are faced with the immense difficulty, if not the impossibility, of verifying the past. I don't mean merely years ago, but yesterday, this morning. What took place, what was the nature of what took place, what happened? If one can speak of the difficulty of knowing what in fact took place yesterday, one can I think treat the present in the same way. What's happening now? We won't know until tomorrow or in six months' time, and we won't know then, we'll have forgotten, or our imagination will have attributed quite false characteristics to today.

A moment is sucked away and distorted, often even at the time of its birth. We will all interpret a common experience quite differently, though we prefer to subscribe to the view that there's a shared common ground, a known ground. I think there's a shared common ground all right, but that it's more like a quicksand. Because 'reality' is quite a strong, firm word we tend to think, or to hope, that the state to which it refers is equally firm, settled and unequivocal. It doesn't seem to be, and in my opinion, it's no worse or better for that.

A play is not an essay, nor should a playwright under any exhortation damage the consistency of his characters by injecting a remedy or apology for their actions into the last act, simply because we have been brought up to expect, rain or sunshine, the last act 'resolution'. To supply an explicit moral tag to an evolving and compulsive dramatic image seem to me facile, impertinent and dishonest. Where this takes place it is not theatre but a crossword puzzle. The audience holds the paper. The play fills in the blanks. Everyone's happy.

There is a considerable body of people just now who are asking for some kind of clear and sensible engagement to be evidently disclosed in contemporary plays. They want the playwright to be a prophet. There is certainly a good deal of prophecy indulged in by playwrights these days, in their plays and out of them. Warnings, sermons, admonitions, ideological exhortations, moral judgements, defined problems with built-in solutions; all can camp under the banner of prophecy. The attitude behind this sort of thing might be summed up in one phrase: '*I'm* telling *you*!' …

If I were to state any moral precept it might be: beware of the writer who puts forward his concern for you to embrace, who leaves you in no doubt of his worthiness, his usefulness, his altruism, who declares that his heart is in the right place and ensures that it can be seen in full view, a pulsating mass where his characters ought to be. What is presented, so much of the time, as a body of active and positive thought is in fact a body lost in a prison of empty definition and cliché.

This kind of writer clearly trusts words absolutely. I have mixed feelings about words myself. Moving among them, sorting them out, watching them appear on the page: from this I derive a considerable pleasure. But at the same time I have another strong feeling about words which amounts to nothing less than nausea. Such a weight of words confronts us day in, day out, words spoken in a context such as this, words written by me and by others, the bulk of it a stale dead terminology; ideas endlessly repeated and permutated become platitudinous, trite, meaningless. Given this nausea, it's very easy to be overcome by it and step back into paralysis. But if it is possible to confront this nausea, to follow it to its hilt, to move through it and out of it, then it is possible to say that something has occurred, that something has even been achieved.

Language, under these conditions, is a highly ambiguous business. So often, below the word spoken, is the thing known and unspoken. My characters tell me so much and no more, with reference to their experience, their aspirations, their motives, their history. Between my lack of biographical data about them and the ambiguity of what they say lies a territory which is not only worthy of exploration but which it is compulsory to explore. You and I, the characters which grow on a page, most of the time we're inexpressive, giving little away, unreliable, elusive, evasive, obstructive, unwilling. But it's out of these attributes that a language arises. A language, I repeat, where under what is said, another thing is being said.

Given characters who possess a momentum of their own, my job is not to impose upon them, not to subject them to a false articulation, by which I mean forcing a character to speak where he could not speak, making him speak in a way he could not speak, or making him speak of what he could never speak. The relationship between author and characters should be a highly respectful one …

I'd like to make quite clear at the same time that I don't regard my own characters as uncontrolled, or anarchic. They're not. The function of selection and arrangement is mine. I do all the donkey-work, in fact, and I think I can say I pay meticulous attention to the shape of things, from the shape of a sentence to the overall structure of the play. This shaping, to put it mildly, is of the first importance. But I think a double thing happens. You arrange and you listen, following the clues you leave for yourself, through the characters. And sometimes a balance is found, where image can freely engender image and where at the same time you are able to keep your sights on the place where the characters are silent and in hiding. It is in the silence that they are most evident to me.

There are two silences. One when no word is spoken; the other when perhaps a torrent of language is being employed. This speech is speaking of a language locked beneath it. That is its continual reference. The speech we hear is an indication of that which we don't hear. It is a necessary avoidance, a violent, sly, anguished or mocking smokescreen, which keeps the other in its place. When true silence falls, we are still left with echo but are nearer nakedness. One way of looking at speech is to say that it is a constant stratagem to cover nakedness.

We have heard many times that tired, grimy phrase, 'failure of communication' … and this phrase has been fixed to my work quite consistently. I believe the contrary. I think that we communicate only too well, in our silence, in what is unsaid, and that what takes place is a continual evasion, desperate rearguard attempts to keep ourselves to ourselves. Communication is too alarming. To enter into someone else's life is too frightening. To disclose to others the poverty within us is too fearsome a possibility.

I am not suggesting that no character in a play can ever say what he in fact means. Not at all. I have found that there invariably does come a moment when this happens, when he says something, perhaps, which he has never said before. And where this happens, what he says is irrevocable, and can never be taken back …

I've written nine plays, for various mediums, and at the moment I haven't the slightest idea how I've managed to do it. Each play was, for me, 'a different kind of failure'.[1] And that fact, I suppose, sent me on to write the next one.

[1] A line from 'East Coker', one of the *Four Quartets* (1943) by the US poet and dramatist T S Eliot (1888–1965).

And if I find writing plays an extremely difficult task, while still understanding it as a kind of celebration, how much more difficult it is to attempt to rationalize the process, and how much more abortive, as I think I've clearly demonstrated to you this morning.

Samuel Beckett says, at the beginning of his novel *The Unnameable*,[2] 'The fact would seem to be, if in my situation one may speak of facts, not only that I shall have to speak of things of which I cannot speak, but also, which is even more interesting, but also that I, which is if possible even more interesting, that I shall have to, I forget, no matter.'

[2] Published in French as *L'Innommable* (1953) and in English translation in 1958.

❦

'What would Wilfred Owen make of the invasion of Iraq?'
18 March 2005, Shrewsbury, England
❦

Although he is still best known as a playwright, Pinter's dramatic output has dwindled since the 1980s; and he has said he will probably write no more plays. His parallel career as a poet has, however, continued; while his prominence as a political activist has risen.

A vehement critic of British support for the USA in the war against Iraq, he addressed the House of Commons in January 2003. 'One of the more nauseating images of the year 2002,' he said, 'is that of our prime minister kneeling in the church on Christmas Day praying for peace on earth and goodwill towards all men while simultaneously preparing to assist in the murder of thousands of totally innocent people in Iraq.'

In 2004, Pinter was announced as winner of the Wilfred Owen Award, given biennially to a writer seen to be upholding the tradition of Owen, the celebrated World War I poet. The award was made for a lifetime's contribution to literature, and specifically for his poetry collection *War*, published in 2003. This book included eight poems concerning the Gulf War of 1991 and the build-up to the 2003 invasion of Iraq.

When the award was presented to him at a weekend festival in Shrewsbury, where Owen grew up, Pinter used the occasion as a platform to pour scorn on President GEORGE W BUSH and Prime Minister TONY BLAIR over the war in Iraq.

❦

This is a true honour. Wilfred Owen was a great poet. He articulated the tragedy, the horror and indeed the pity of war[1] in a way no other poet has. Yet we have learnt nothing. Nearly 100 years after his death,[2] the world has become more savage, more brutal, more pitiless.

[1] 'The pity of war' is a quotation from Owen's poem 'Strange Meeting' (1917).

[2] Owen (1893–1918) was killed during the final week of World War I, aged 25.

But the 'free world' we are told (as embodied in the United States and Great Britain) is different to the rest of the world, since our actions are dictated and sanctioned by a moral authority and a moral passion condoned by someone called God. Some people may find this difficult to comprehend, but OSAMA BIN LADEN finds it easy.

What would Wilfred Owen make of the invasion of Iraq? A bandit act, an act of blatant state terrorism, demonstrating absolute contempt for the concept of international law. An arbitrary military action inspired by a series of lies upon lies and gross manipulation of the media and therefore of the public. An act intended to consolidate American military and economic control of the Middle East, masquerading – as a last resort (all other justifications having failed to justify themselves) – as liberation. A formidable assertion of military force, responsible for the death and mutilation of thousands upon thousands of innocent people.

An independent and totally objective account of the Iraqi civilian dead in the medical magazine *The Lancet* estimates that the figure approaches 100,000. But neither the US or the UK bother to count the Iraqi dead. As General Tommy Franks[3] memorably said: 'We don't do body counts.'

We have brought torture, cluster bombs, depleted uranium, innumerable acts of random murder, misery and degradation to the Iraqi people and call it 'bringing freedom and democracy to the Middle East'. But, as we all know, we have not been welcomed with the predicted flowers. What we have unleashed is a ferocious and unremitting resistance, mayhem and chaos.

You may say at this point: what about the Iraqi elections? Well, President Bush himself answered this question only the other day when he said, 'We cannot accept that there can be free democratic elections in a country under foreign military occupation.'

I had to read that statement twice before I realized that he was talking about Lebanon and Syria.

What do Bush and Blair actually see when they look at themselves in the mirror?

I believe Wilfred Owen would share our contempt, our revulsion, our nausea and our shame at both the language and the actions of the American and British governments.

[3] The US soldier General Tommy Franks (1945–) was commander-in-chief of US Central Command and oversaw the invasion of Iraq in March 2003. He retired in July 2003.

William Pitt the Elder
English statesman

William Pitt *later 1st Earl of Chatham* (1708–78) was born in Westminster. He was educated at Eton and Trinity College, Oxford. In 1735 he entered Parliament for the family borough, Old Sarum, near Salisbury. He sided with Frederick, Prince of Wales, against King George II, and as leader of the young 'Patriot' Whigs, opposed ROBERT WALPOLE. After Walpole's fall from power, the King admitted Pitt to the new administration (1746); he became Paymaster-General, but resigned in 1755. In 1756, on the outbreak of the Seven Years' War with France, Pitt became Secretary of State in a coalition government with the Duke of Newcastle. He immediately put into effect his plan of carrying on the war with France, raised the militia, and strengthened naval power. George II's hostility and German predilections led him to resign in April 1757, only to be recalled in June in response to popular demands. His vigorous war policy was widely successful against the French at sea and on land (in India, Africa, Canada and on the Rhine), but Pitt was compelled to resign (1761) when the Cabinet refused to declare war with Spain. Pitt received a pension of £3,000 a year, and his wife was created Baroness Chatham. His imposing appearance and magnificent voice greatly enhanced his oratory. His character was irreproachable, though his haughtiness irritated even his friends. He formed a new ministry (1766–8), with a seat in the House of Lords as Viscount Pitt and Earl of Chatham. However, ill health prevented him from taking any active part in politics, and he resigned in 1768. He spoke strongly against the arbitrary and harsh policy towards the American colonies; however, when a treaty was proposed, Chatham appeared at the House of Lords and in his final speech secured a majority against the motion. The effort exhausted him and he collapsed into the arms of his friends. A few weeks later, he was dead. Chatham was honoured with a public funeral and a statue in Westminster Abbey; the government voted £20,000 to pay his debts, and conferred a pension of £4,000 a year on his descendants. His second son was the future prime minister, William Pitt the Younger.

'You cannot conquer America'
18 November 1777, London, England

This speech to the House of Lords, made at the opening of Parliament, was one of the last of Chatham's career. Having retired in 1768, he spoke in the House only on matters of urgency, but his brilliance as an orator – and his legendary pomposity – are still evident as he addresses the crisis in America.

The speech's keyword is 'ruin': Britain had already suffered defeats in America, the Declaration of Independence had been signed, and Chatham, like many others, foresaw humiliating defeat. He also felt that national honour had been compromised by the deployment of German mercenaries and Native American 'savages' alongside British troops.

Conscious of the importance of America to Britain as 'the fountain of our wealth', Chatham puts forward a logical case for conciliation, arguing that it would still be possible to resurrect pro-British sympathies in America.

Although he was admired for his neutral stance, his opinions were also subject to change. At his final appearance in the House of Lords, six months later, he would successfully oppose a treaty with America which he believed granted too many concessions. He died long before the Treaty of Paris (1783) which formally ended the war.

I rise, my Lords, to declare my sentiments on this most solemn and serious subject. It has imposed a load upon my mind, which, I fear, nothing can remove; but which impels me to endeavour its alleviation, by a free and unreserved communication of my sentiments …

This, my Lords, is a perilous and tremendous moment! It is not a time for adulation. The smoothness of flattery cannot now avail; cannot save us in this rugged and awful crisis. It is now necessary to instruct the throne in the language of truth. We must dispel the delusion and the darkness which envelop it; and display, in its full danger and true colours, the ruin that is brought to our doors …

The accustomed language from the throne has been application to Parliament for advice, and a reliance on its constitutional advice and assistance. As it is the right of Parliament to give, so it is the duty of the

Crown to ask it. But on this day, and in this extreme momentous exigency, no reliance is reposed on our constitutional counsels; no advice is asked from the sober and enlightened care of Parliament; but the Crown, from itself, and by itself, declares an unalterable determination to pursue measures. And what measures, my Lords? The measures that have produced the imminent perils that threaten us; the measures that have brought ruin to our doors.

Can the minister of the day now presume to expect a continuance of support, in this ruinous infatuation? Can Parliament be so dead to its dignity and its duty, as to be thus deluded into the loss of the one and the violation of the other? … France, my Lords, has insulted you; she has encouraged and sustained America; and whether America be wrong or right, the dignity of this country ought to spurn at the officious insult of French interference. The ministers and ambassadors of those who are called rebels and enemies are in Paris; in Paris they transact the reciprocal interests of America and France.

Can there be a more mortifying insult? Can even our ministers sustain a more humiliating disgrace? Do they dare to resent it? Do they presume even to hint a vindication of their honour, and the dignity of the state, by requiring the dismission of the plenipotentiaries of America? Such is the degradation to which they have reduced the glories of England …

My Lords, this ruinous and ignominious situation, where we cannot act with success, nor suffer with honour, calls upon us to remonstrate in the strongest and loudest language of truth, to rescue the ear of Majesty from the delusions which surround it. The desperate state of our arms abroad is in part known: no man thinks more highly of them than I do. I love and honour the English troops. I know their virtues and their valour. I know they can achieve anything except impossibilities; and I know that the conquest of English America is an impossibility.

You cannot, I venture to say it, you cannot conquer America. Your army's last war[1] effected everything that could be effected; and what was it? It cost a numerous army, under the command of a most able general, now a noble Lord in this house,[2] a long and laborious campaign, to expel 5,000 Frenchmen from French America. My Lords, you cannot conquer America.

What is your present situation there? We do not know the worst; but we know that in three campaigns we have done nothing and suffered much.[3] Besides the sufferings, perhaps total loss, of the northern force; the best appointed army that ever took the field, commanded by Sir William Howe,[4] has retired from the American lines. He was obliged to relinquish his attempt, and, with great delay and danger, to adopt a new and distant plan of operations. We shall soon know, and in any event have reason to lament, what may have happened since. As to conquest, therefore, my Lords, I repeat, it is impossible.

You may swell every expense, and every effort, still more extravagantly; pile and accumulate every assistance you can buy or borrow; traffic and barter with every little pitiful German prince that sells and sends his subjects to the shambles of a foreign prince;[5] your efforts are for ever vain and impotent: doubly so from this mercenary aid on which you rely. For it irritates, to an incurable resentment, the minds of your enemies, to overrun them with the mercenary sons of rapine and plunder; devoting them and their possessions to the rapacity of hireling cruelty! If I were an American, as I am an Englishman, while a foreign troop was landed in my country, I never would lay down my arms. Never, never, never.

[1] During the Seven Years' War of 1756–63, British forces mounted land and sea assaults on French colonies in North America. By 1760, these territories were under British control.

[3] Chatham probably refers to the Siege of Boston (1775–6), the New York campaign (1776) and the Saratoga campaign (1777), all of which were costly for Britain, though New York was successfully captured and held until the end of the war.

[4] The English soldier Sir William Howe *later 5th Viscount Howe* (1729–1814) was commander-in-chief of the British Army in America, 1775–7 and led the New York campaign.

[2] The English soldier Jeffrey Amherst, 1st Baron Amherst (1717–97) commanded the British forces that captured French colonies in Canada, 1758–60.

[5] During the War of Independence, around a third of the British forces were made up of German mercenaries hired by George III. They were know as Hessians, as more than half of them came from German state of Hesse. Made up of forced conscripts and petty criminals, they were notoriously ill-disciplined.

Your own army is infected with the contagion of these illiberal allies … I know from authentic information, and the most experienced officers, that our discipline is deeply wounded. Whilst this is notoriously our sinking situation, America grows and flourishes: whilst our strength and discipline are lowered, hers are rising and improving.

But my Lords, who is the man that in addition to these disgraces and mischiefs of our army, has dared to authorize and associate to our arms the tomahawk and scalping-knife of the savage?[6] To call into civilized alliance, the wild and inhuman savage of the woods; to delegate to the merciless Indian the defence of disputed rights, and to wage the horrors of his barbarous war against our brethren? My Lords, these enormities cry aloud for redress and punishment.

Unless thoroughly done away, it will be a stain on the national character. It is a violation of the constitution. I believe it is against law. It is not the least of our national misfortunes, that the strength and character of our army are thus impaired. Infected with the mercenary spirit of robbery and rapine; familiarized to the horrid scenes of savage cruelty, it can no longer boast of the noble and generous principles which dignify a soldier; no longer sympathize with the dignity of the royal banner, nor feel the pride, pomp, and circumstance of glorious war, 'that make ambition virtue!'[7] What makes ambition virtue? – the sense of honour. But is the sense of honour consistent with a spirit of plunder, or the practice of murder? Can it flow from mercenary motives, or can it prompt to cruel deeds? Besides these murderers and plunderers, let me ask our ministers, what other allies have they acquired? Have they entered into alliance with the king of the gypsies? Nothing, my Lords, it too low or too ludicrous to be consistent with their counsels.

The independent views of America have been stated and asserted as the foundation of this address. My Lords, no man wishes for the due dependence of America on this country more than I do. To preserve it, and not confirm that state of independence into which your measures hitherto have driven them, is the object which we ought to unite in attaining.

The Americans, contending for their rights against arbitrary exactions,[8] I love and admire. It is the struggle of free and virtuous patriots; but contending for independency and total disconnection from England, as an Englishman, I cannot wish them success. For, in a due constitutional dependency, including the ancient supremacy of this country in regulating their commerce and navigation, consists the mutual happiness and prosperity both of England and America. She derived assistance and protection from us; and we reaped from her the most important advantages. She was, indeed, the fountain of our wealth, the nerve of our strength, the nursery and basis of our naval power.

It is our duty, therefore, my Lords, if we wish to save our country, most seriously to endeavour the recovery of these most beneficial subjects: and in this perilous crisis, perhaps the present moment may be the only one in which we can hope for success … Let us wisely take advantage of every possible moment of reconciliation.

Besides, the natural disposition of America herself still leans towards England; to the old habits of connection and mutual interest that united both countries. This was the established sentiment of all the continent; and still, my Lords, in the great and principal part, the sound part of America, this wise and affectionate disposition prevails; and there is a very considerable part of America yet sound – the middle and southern

[6] Native Americans fought on both sides during the war, for example at the Battle of Oriskany on 6 August 1777, a victory for the British. In the course of this debate, Lord Suffolk defended their deployment, arguing that it was 'perfectly justifiable to use all the means that God and nature put into our hands'.

[7] 'Farewell the plumed troop and the big wars/ That make ambition virtue! O, farewell!' Lines spoken by Othello in the tragedy of the same name (c.1604) by the English playwright William Shakespeare (1564–1616).

[8] During the period 1760–70, the British Crown attempted to redeem a large national debt by imposing an escalating series of taxes on America. This led to growing unrest and the notorious 'Boston Massacre' of 1770, when British troops fired into a mob of American civilians, killing five.

provinces. Some parts may be factious and blind to their true interests; but if we express a wise and benevolent disposition to communicate with them those immutable rights of nature, and those constitutional liberties, to which they are equally entitled with ourselves; by a conduct so just and humane, we shall confirm the favourable, and conciliate the adverse. I say, my Lords, the rights and liberties to which they are equally entitled with ourselves … reserving always, as the sacred right of the mother country, the due constitutional dependency of the colonies. The inherent supremacy of the state, in regulating and protecting the navigation and commerce of all her subjects, is necessary for the mutual benefit and preservation of every part, to constitute and preserve the prosperous arrangement of the whole empire.

The sound parts of America, of which I have spoken, must be sensible of these great truths, and of their real interests. America is not in that state of desperate and contemptible rebellion which this country has been deluded to believe. It is not a wild and lawless banditti, who, having nothing to lose, might hope to snatch something from public convulsions. Many of their leaders and great men have a great stake in this great contest. The gentleman who conducts their armies, I am told, has an estate of £4,000 or £5,000 a year;[9] and when I consider these things, I cannot but lament the inconsiderate violence of our penal acts, our declarations of treason and rebellion, with all the fatal effects of attainder and confiscation …

You cannot conciliate America by your present measures. You cannot subdue her by your present, or by any measures. What, then, can you do? You cannot conquer; you cannot gain; but you can address; you can lull the fears and anxieties of the moment into an ignorance of the danger that should produce them. But, my Lords, the time demands the language of truth. We must not now apply the flattering unction of servile compliance, or blind complaisance.

In a just and necessary war, to maintain the rights or honour of my country, I would strip the shirt from my back to support it. But in such a war as this, unjust in its principle, impracticable in its means, and ruinous in its consequences, I would not contribute a single effort, nor a single shilling. I do not call for vengeance on the heads of those who have been guilty: I only recommend to them to make their retreat. Let them walk off; and let them make haste, or they may be assured that speedy and condign punishment will overtake them.

My Lords, I have submitted to you, with the freedom and truth which I think my duty, my sentiments on your present awful situation. I have laid before you the ruin of your power, the disgrace of your reputation, the pollution of your discipline, the contamination of your morals, the complication of calamities, foreign and domestic, that overwhelm your sinking country. Your dearest interests, your own liberties, the constitution itself, totters to the foundation.

All this disgraceful danger, this multitude of misery, is the monstrous offspring of this unnatural war. We have been deceived and deluded too long. Let us now stop short. This is the crisis – the only crisis, of time and situation, to give us a possibility of escape from the fatal effects of our delusions. But if, in an obstinate and infatuated perseverance in folly, we slavishly echo the peremptory words this day presented to us, nothing can save this devoted country from complete and final ruin.

[9] GEORGE WASHINGTON, who commanded the colonial army, was also a landowner and planter. He enjoyed some prosperity, but was frequently in debt.

Sidney Poitier
American actor and director

Sidney Poitier (1924–) was born in Miami, Florida and raised in the Bahamas. He later studied at the American Negro Theater in New York. He appeared on stage in *Lysistrata* (1946) and *Anna Lucasta* (1946–8) before making his film debut in the documentary *From Whence Cometh My Help* (1949). His Hollywood debut followed in *No Way Out* (1950), and he gave strong performances in *Cry, the Beloved Country* (1952), *The Blackboard Jungle* (1955) and *The Defiant Ones* (1958). He won an Academy Award for *Lilies of the Field* (1963). Handsome and unassuming, he brought dignity to the portrayal of noble and intelligent characters in such films as *In the Heat of the Night* (1967) and its sequels *They Call Me Mister Tibbs* (1970) and *The Organization* (1971). He has also directed a number of comedies, including *Stir Crazy* (1980) and *Ghost Dad* (1990). He returned to acting after a ten-year absence in *Little Nikita* (1988) and *Shoot to Kill* (1988). Later television appearances include *Children of the Dust* (1995) and *To Sir With Love II* (1996). He has published three autobiographies, *This Life* (1980), *The Measure of a Man* (2000) and *Life Beyond Measure: Letters to My Great-Granddaughter* (2008). In 2009 he was awarded the Presidential Medal of Freedom by BARACK OBAMA.

'A long journey to this moment'
13 April 1964, Santa Monica, California, USA

24 March 2002, Hollywood, California, USA

In 1964, Sidney Poitier became the first black actor to win an Academy Award for a leading role (though Hattie McDaniel had been named best supporting actress in 1940 for *Gone with the Wind*). It was in keeping with his reputation as a pioneer who had fought single-mindedly for success in an industry – and a country – that tended to relegate African-Americans to minor roles.

Poitier's career began when he arrived in New York aged 18, so penniless he had to sleep in a bus station. Initially rejected by the American Negro Theater, he spent six months surviving on menial jobs while honing his skills. Gradually, his efforts paid off, and by 1949 he was playing lead roles on Broadway. His debut feature film came soon afterwards.

Throughout his early career, there was a parity between his own struggle for recognition and the travails of his characters. Time and again – *In the Heat of the Night, Guess Who's Coming to Dinner* (both 1967) – he was cast as the outsider, excluded by his race, whose nobility won out over bigotry.

He was Oscar-nominated for the prison-escape drama *The Defiant Ones* (1959), and eventually won his best actor Academy Award for the comedy-drama *Lilies of the Field* (1963) set in a remote convent. His speech was very short, referring briefly to his 'long journey' to success.

When he received an honorary Oscar in 2002, 'in recognition of his remarkable accomplishments as an artist and as a human being,' he was able to enlarge on his theme.

1964

Because it is a long journey to this moment, I am naturally indebted to countless numbers of people, principal among whom are Ralph Nelson,[1] James Poe,[2] William Barrett,[3] Martin Baum,[4] and of course the members of the Academy. For all of them, all I can say is a very special thank you.

2002

I arrived in Hollywood at the age of 22, in a time different than today's, a time in which the odds against my standing here tonight, 53 years later, would not have fallen in my favour. Back then, no route had been established for where I was hoping to go, no pathway left in evidence for me to trace, no custom for me to follow.

Yet here I am this evening, at the end of a journey that in 1949 would have been considered almost impossible and in fact might never have been set in motion, were there not an untold number of courageous, unselfish choices made by a handful of visionary American film-makers, directors, writers and producers; each with a strong sense of citizenship

[1] The US film-maker Ralph Nelson (1916–87) directed *Lilies of the Field*.
[2] The US writer James Poe (1921–80) wrote the screenplay for *Lilies of the Field*.
[3] The US writer William E Barrett (1900–86) wrote the novel *Lilies of the Field*, on which the film was based.
[4] The US actors' agent Martin Baum (1924–2010) represented Poitier.

responsibility to the times in which they lived; each unafraid to permit their art to reflect their views and values, ethical and moral, and moreover, acknowledge them as their own.

They knew the odds that stood against them and their efforts were overwhelming and likely could have proven too high to overcome. Still, those film-makers persevered, speaking through their art to the best in all of us. And I've benefited from their effort. The industry benefited from their effort. America benefited from their effort. And in ways large and small, the world has also benefited from their effort.

Therefore, with respect, I share this great honour with the late Joe Mankiewicz,[5] the late Richard Brooks,[6] the late Ralph Nelson, the late Darryl Zanuck,[7] the late Stanley Kramer,[8] the Mirisch brothers, especially Walter[9] whose friendship lies at the very heart of this moment, Guy Green,[10] Norman Jewison[11] and all others who have had a hand in altering the odds for me and for others.

Without them, this most memorable moment would not have come to pass and the many excellent young actors who have followed in admirable fashion might not have come as they have to enrich the tradition of American film-making as they have. I accept this award in memory of all the African-American actors and actresses who went before me in the difficult years, on whose shoulders I was privileged to stand, to see where I might go.

My love and my thanks to my wonderful, wonderful wife, my children, my grandchildren, my agent and friend Martin Baum. And finally, to those audience members around the world who have placed their trust in my judgement as an actor and film-maker, I thank each of you for your support through the years. Thank you.

[5] The US film-maker Joseph L Mankiewicz (1909–93) was the writer and director of *No Way Out*.
[6] The US film-maker Richard Brooks (1912–92) was the writer and director of *Blackboard Jungle*.
[7] The US film-maker Darryl Zanuck (1902–79) was the producer of *No Way Out*.
[8] The US film-maker Stanley Kramer (1913–2001) was the director and producer of *The Defiant Ones* and *Guess Who's Coming to Dinner*.
[9] The US film-maker Walter Mirisch (1921–) was the producer of *In the Heat of the Night* and its sequels. His elder brother Marvin (1918–2002) was also a producer.
[10] The British film-maker Guy Green (1913–2005) was the writer and director of *A Patch of Blue*, in which Poitier starred in 1965.
[11] The Canadian film-maker Norman Jewison (1926–) was the director of *In the Heat of the Night*.

Enoch Powell
English politician and scholar

John Enoch Powell (1912–98) was born in Stechford, Birmingham. He was educated at King Edward's School, Birmingham and Trinity College, Cambridge; then became Professor of Greek at Sydney University (1937–9). During World War II he enlisted as a private in 1939, was commissioned in 1940 and rose to the rank of brigadier. In 1946 he joined the Conservative Party, and in 1950 he entered Parliament as MP for Wolverhampton. He held offices including Parliamentary Secretary, Ministry of Housing (1955–7) and Financial Secretary to the Treasury (1957–8), from which he resigned over policy issues. He was Minister of Health from 1960, resigning again over the appointment of Sir Alec Douglas-Home as prime minister in 1963. Powell's austere brand of intellectualism, his adherence to the principles of high Toryism in economic planning, and his radical views on defence and foreign commitments made him a significant figure within his party. He created controversy with his outspoken attitude to non-white immigration and racial integration. Because of his opposition to the European Community, he did not stand for election in 1974; however, he returned to Parliament as an Ulster Unionist from October 1974 until he lost his seat in the 1987 general election. He published numerous academic and political works, including *Reflections of a Statesman* (1991). Other titles include *Collected Poems* (1990) and *The Evolution of the Gospel* (1994).

'A great administrative disaster'
27 July 1959, London, England

Hola Camp was a detention centre in Kenya, one of many set up by the British authorities to house Mau Mau rebels – Kikuyu people who, from the early 1950s, had resorted to violence in protest at Britain's colonial administration. In 1958, eleven Mau Mau detainees at Hola Camp died after being severely beaten by prison officers. A disgraceful cover-up ensued: an official statement declared the men had died not from any violence but from drinking large quantities of water in extreme heat – the 'water cart communiqué' to which Powell refers.

Powell's speech is a stinging attack on his own government for its failings in the affair. In particular this was a response to comments made by fellow Conservatives that black African lives were worth less than white British ones, and that things worked differently in Africa. Not true, Powell urged: Britain could not 'pick and choose where and in what parts of the world we shall use this or that kind of standard'.

Overshadowed as it was by his later 'rivers of blood' speech, Powell's Hola Camp address revealed a man of deep principle. As he finished speaking, he sat down in tears. In the words of the journalist W F Deedes – who was himself a Conservative backbencher at the time and witnessed Powell giving the speech – 'no racist could have made it'.

Many aspersions have been cast and many imputations made by honourable Members opposite in the course of this debate, with which I could not for an instant associate myself. And yet I cannot regret that even at this hour[1] the House is once again considering the affair of Hola Camp. For the further documents relating to the deaths, which were issued as a White Paper last week, confirm what was already pretty clear from the earlier evidence: that it could be to the credit neither of this House nor of this country that the matter should rest where it now stands.

The affair of Hola Camp was a great administrative disaster, and to that administrative disaster there were three aspects. There was the authorization of an operation which in its nature was likely to have fatal results; there was the failure to see that that operation, such as it was, was at least carried out with the minimum of risk; and finally there was the incident, which it is difficult to find a word to describe, of the water cart communiqué.

The new documents show that the responsibility for all three aspects of this administrative disaster goes higher than can be discharged by the premature retirement of the officer in charge of the camp; or by the retirement, accelerated by a few weeks, of the Commissioner of Prisons.[2]

[1] This speech was given at 1.15am.

[2] The English colonial administrator J H Lewis was Commissioner of Prisons in Kenya at this time.

The central document in the White Paper of last week, and it has often been referred to in this debate, is the minute of 17 February addressed by the Commissioner of Prisons to the Minister of Defence[3] ... It is impossible to read that document without sensing through it the state of mind of the man who wrote it or being aware of the risks which were attendant upon the situation which it reveals ...

The Minister of Defence and the Minister of African Affairs[4] took upon themselves the responsibility for authorizing an operation which they had been warned involved the risk of death, in a minute accompanied by a paper which showed to anyone who cared to read it that not even that operation, dangerous as it was, was the one which Sullivan[5] contemplated carrying out.

The right honourable lady, the Member for Blackburn[6] was a little too kind to the Minister for African Affairs. She overlooked the fact that he, as well as the Minister of Defence, had all the relevant papers in front of him. Those two men took upon themselves, with their eyes open and with full knowledge, not only the responsibility for the Cowan Plan,[7] but the responsibility for allowing the deformed version of it to go forward.

It was authorized – now we come to the second phase, the execution – with the indication that it should go forward 'subject to the proviso that' the Commissioner 'should first ensure that he has a sufficient number of warders at Hola to cope with possible eventualities'. So, warned of the danger implicit, aware from the SOS that all was not well, the ministers responsible, the ministers who had given the decision, left the matter there and just sent it down the line.

Those two men, who knew that they had authorized – without reference, as advised by the Commissioner of Prisons, to the Security Council – an operation involving the risk of death, learnt on the afternoon of 3 March that on the day on which that operation was carried out ten men had died at Hola Camp; and on 4 March, after – and these are the words of the publicity officer: 'a good deal of discussion as to whether violence was the cause of the deaths of these men' – in a meeting presided over by His Excellency the Governor, they were parties to the issue of the water cart communiqué.

Those documents, that evidence, prove to me conclusively that the responsibility here lies not only with Sullivan and Lewis, but at a level above them. It lies with those to whom they actually appealed for help, whom they warned of the danger, from whom they received indeed a decision which transferred responsibility upwards, but no other help or guidance. That responsibility, transcending Sullivan and Lewis, has not been recognized; but it cannot be ignored, it cannot be burked,[8] it will not just evaporate into thin air if we do nothing about it.

I am as certain of this as I am of anything: that my right honourable friend the Secretary of State,[9] from the beginning to the end of this affair, is without any jot or tittle of blame for what happened in Kenya; that he could not be expected to know, that it could not be within the administrative conventions that these matters should be brought to his attention before or during the execution. When I say my right honourable friend was in this matter utterly and completely blameless, that is of a piece with his administration of his high office generally, which has been the greatest exercise of the office of Colonial Secretary in modern times.

It is in the name of that record, it is in the name of his personal blamelessness, that I beg of him to ensure that the responsibility is

[3] The English politician Duncan Sandys *later Baron Duncan-Sandys* (1908–87) served as Minister of Defence, 1957–9.

[4] The English politician C M Johnston was Minister for African Affairs at this time.

[5] The English colonial administrator G M Sullivan was then commander of Hola Camp.

[6] The English politician Barbara Castle *later Baroness Castle of Blackburn* (1910–2002) served as MP for Blackburn from 1945 and was an outspoken opponent of colonialism.

[7] Devised by Prisons Superintendent John Cowan, the Cowan Plan was a programme of prison beatings designed to force Mau Mau detainees to renounce their nationalist views.

[8] Suppressed, stifled, or extinguished quietly.

[9] The English politician Alan Lennox-Boyd *later 1st Viscount Boyd of Merton* (1904–83) served as Secretary of State for the Colonies, 1954–9.

recognized and carried where it properly belongs, and is seen to belong.

I have heard it suggested that there were circumstances surrounding this affair at Hola Camp which, it is argued, might justify the passing over of this responsibility – which might justify one in saying, 'Well, of course, strictly speaking, that is quite correct; but then here there were special circumstances.'

It has been said – and it is a fact – that these eleven men were the lowest of the low; subhuman was the word which one of my honourable friends used. So be it. But that cannot be relevant to the acceptance of responsibility for their death. I know that it does not enter into my right honourable friend's mind that it could be relevant, because it would be completely inconsistent with his whole policy of rehabilitation, which is based upon the assumption that whatever the present state of these men, they can be reclaimed.

No-one who supports the policy of rehabilitation can argue from the character and condition of these men that responsibility for their death should be different from the responsibility for anyone else's death. In general, I would say that it is a fearful doctrine, which must recoil upon the heads of those who pronounce it, to stand in judgement on a fellow human being and to say, 'Because he was such-and-such, therefore the consequences which would otherwise flow from his death shall not flow'.

It is then said that the morale of the Prison Service, the morale of the whole Colonial Service, is above all important and that whatever we do, whatever we urge, whatever we say, should have regard to that morale. 'Amen,' say I. But is it for the morale of the Prison Service that those who executed a policy should suffer – whether inadequately or not is another question – and those who authorized it, those to whom they appealed, should be passed over? I cannot believe that that supports the morale of a service.

Going on beyond that, my honourable friend the Member for Leicester, South-East[10] reminded the House how proud the Colonial Service is of the integrity of its administration and its record. Nothing could be more damaging to the morale of such a service than that there should be a breath or a blemish left upon it. No, Sir; that argument from the morale of the Prison Service and the Colonial Service stands on its head if what we mean is that therefore the consequences of responsibility should not follow in this case as they would in any other similar case.

Finally it is argued that this is Africa, that things are different there. Of course they are. The question is whether the difference between things there and here is such that the taking of responsibility there and here should be upon different principles. We claim that it is our object – and this is something which unites both sides of the House – to leave representative institutions behind us wherever we give up our rule. I cannot imagine that it is a way to plant representative institutions, to be seen to shirk the acceptance and the assignment of responsibility, which is the very essence of responsible government.

Nor can we ourselves pick and choose where and in what parts of the world we shall use this or that kind of standard. We cannot say, 'We will have African standards in Africa, Asian standards in Asia and perhaps British standards here at home.' We have not that choice to make. We must be consistent with ourselves everywhere. All government, all influence of man upon man, rests upon opinion.

What we can do in Africa, where we still govern and where we no longer

[10] The English politician William John Peel *later Sir John Peel* (1912–2004) served as MP for Leicester South-East, 1957–74. He had provoked outrage in the House of Commons by describing Mau Mau detainees as 'desperate and subhuman individuals'.

govern, depends upon the opinion which is entertained of the way in which this country acts and the way in which Englishmen act. We cannot, we dare not, in Africa of all places, fall below our own highest standards in the acceptance of responsibility.

'I seem to see "the River Tiber foaming with much blood"'

20 April 1968, Birmingham, England

The background to Enoch Powell's 'rivers of blood' speech – as it was inaccurately dubbed by the press – centres on two pieces of legislation, one already in place, the other making its way through Parliament at the time.

The first, the British Nationality Act of 1948, had allowed immigrants from the Indian sub-continent, Africa and the Caribbean to claim British citizenship because their countries belonged to the Commonwealth. Powell blamed this Act for increasing the number of immigrants, whose presence, he believed, threatened to bring about a 'total transformation' of parts of Britain. The second, the Race Relations Bill, aimed to tackle discrimination on the grounds of race, colour or origin. Powell thought this 'exactly and diametrically wrong'. For him, white British people were the victims of discrimination; and he predicted racial conflict on a grand scale unless immigration was checked and foreign-born immigrants were repatriated.

Powell's speech, made at the West Midlands Area Conservative Political Centre, led to his eviction from the Shadow Cabinet led by EDWARD HEATH and earned him enduring notoriety. What is often overlooked, however, was the popular acclaim he received: in the ensuing weeks, well-wishers sent him over 100,000 messages of support.

The supreme function of statesmanship is to provide against preventable evils. In seeking to do so, it encounters obstacles which are deeply rooted in human nature. One is that by the very order of things such evils are not demonstrable until they have occurred: at each stage in their onset there is room for doubt and for dispute whether they be real or imaginary.

By the same token, they attract little attention in comparison with current troubles, which are both indisputable and pressing: whence the besetting temptation of all politics to concern itself with the immediate present at the expense of the future. Above all, people are disposed to mistake predicting troubles for causing troubles and even for desiring troubles: 'if only', they love to think, 'if only people wouldn't talk about it, it probably wouldn't happen' …

A week or two ago I fell into conversation with a constituent, a middle-aged, quite ordinary working man employed in one of our nationalized industries. After a sentence or two about the weather, he suddenly said: 'If I had the money to go, I wouldn't stay in this country.'

I made some deprecatory reply, to the effect that even this government wouldn't last for ever;[1] but he took no notice, and continued: 'I have three children, all of them been through grammar school and two of them married now, with family. I shan't be satisfied till I have seen them all settled overseas. In this country in 15 or 20 years' time, the black man will have the whip hand over the white man.'

I can already hear the chorus of execration. How dare I say such a horrible thing? How dare I stir up trouble and inflame feelings by repeating such a conversation? The answer is that I do not have the right not to do so. Here is a decent, ordinary fellow-Englishman, who in broad daylight in my own town says to me, his Member of Parliament, that this country will not be worth living in for his children. I simply do not have the right to shrug my shoulders and think about something else.

What he is saying, thousands and hundreds of thousands are saying and thinking – not throughout Great Britain, perhaps, but in the areas that are

[1] The Labour government led by HAROLD WILSON had been in power since October 1964.

already undergoing the total transformation to which there is no parallel in a thousand years of English history.

In 15 or 20 years, on present trends, there will be in this country three-and-a-half million Commonwealth immigrants and their descendants. That is not my figure. That is the official figure given to Parliament by the spokesman of the Registrar General's office. There is no comparable official figure for the year 2000; but it must be in the region of five to seven million, approximately one-tenth of the whole population, and approaching that of Great London.[2] Of course, it will not be evenly distributed from Margate to Aberystwyth and from Penzance to Aberdeen. Whole areas, towns and parts of towns across England will be occupied, largely or wholly, by different sections of the immigrant and immigrant-descended population.

As time goes on, the proportion of this total who are immigrant-descendants, those born in England, those who arrived here by exactly the same route as the rest of us, will rapidly increase. Already by 1985 the native-born would constitute the majority. It is this fact above all which creates the extreme urgency of action now, of just that kind of action which is hardest for politicians to take, action where the difficulties lie in the present but the evils to be prevented or minimized lie several parliaments ahead.

The natural and rational first question, with the nation confronted by such a prospect, is to ask: 'How can its dimensions be reduced? Granted it be not wholly preventable, can it be limited, bearing in mind that numbers are of the essence?' The significance and consequences of an alien element introduced into a country or population are profoundly different, according to whether that element is one per cent or ten per cent.

The answers to the simple and rational question are equally simple and rational: by stopping, or virtually stopping, further inflow, and by promoting the maximum outflow. Both answers are part of the official policy of the Conservative Party.

It almost passes belief that at this moment 20 or 30 additional immigrant children are arriving from overseas in Wolverhampton alone every week – and that means 15 or 20 additional families of a decade or two hence. Those whom the gods wish to destroy, they first make mad.[3] We must be mad, literally mad, as a nation to be permitting the annual inflow of some 50,000 dependants, who are for the most part the material of the future growth of the immigrant-descended population. It is like watching a nation busily engaged in heaping up its own funeral pyre …

In these circumstances nothing will suffice but that the total inflow for settlement should be reduced at once to negligible proportions, and that the necessary legislative and administrative measures be taken without delay. I stress the words 'for settlement'. This has nothing to do with the entry of Commonwealth citizens, any more than of aliens, into this country, for the purposes of study or of improving their qualifications, like (for instance) the Commonwealth doctors who, to the advantage of their own countries, have enabled our hospital service to be expanded faster than would otherwise have been possible. These are not, and never have been, immigrants.

I turn to re-emigration. If all immigration ended tomorrow, the rate of growth of the immigrant and immigrant-descended population would be substantially reduced, but the prospective size of this element in the population would still leave the basic character of the national danger unaffected. This can only be tackled while a considerable proportion of the

[2] Powell overestimates, but only slightly; according to the 2001 Census, 7.9 per cent of the population belonged to ethnic minorities.

[3] Powell, a former professor of Greek, refers to words attributed to the ancient Greek dramatist Euripides (c.480–406 BC).

total still comprises persons who entered this country during the last ten years or so.

Hence the urgency of implementing now the second element of the Conservative Party's policy: the encouragement of re-emigration. Nobody can make an estimate of the numbers which, with generous grants and assistance, would choose either to return to their countries of origin or to go to other countries anxious to receive the manpower and the skills they represent. Nobody knows, because no such policy has yet been attempted. I can only say that, even at present, immigrants in my own constituency from time to time come to me, asking if I can find them assistance to return home. If such a policy were adopted and pursued with the determination which the gravity of the alternative justifies, the resultant outflow could appreciably alter the prospects for the future …

The third element of the Conservative Party's policy is that all who are in this country as citizens shall be equal before the law and that there shall be no discrimination or difference made between them by public authority. As Mr Heath has put it, we will have no 'first-class citizens' and 'second-class citizens'. This does not mean that the immigrant and his descendants should be elevated into a privileged or special class or that any citizen should be denied his right to discriminate, in the management of his own affairs, between one fellow-citizen and another, or that he should be subjected to inquisition as to his reasons and motives for behaving in one lawful manner rather than another.

There could be no grosser misconception of the realities than is entertained by those who vociferously demand legislation (as they call it) 'against discrimination', whether they be leader-writers of the same kidney and sometimes on the same newspapers as those which year after year in the 1930s tried to blind this country to the rising peril which confronted it, or archbishops who live in palaces, faring delicately, with the bedclothes pulled right up over their heads. They have got it exactly and diametrically wrong. The discrimination and the deprivation, the sense of alarm and of resentment, lie not with the immigrant population but with those among whom they have come and are still coming. This is why to enact legislation of the kind before Parliament at this moment is to risk throwing a match onto gunpowder. The kindest thing that can be said about those who propose and support it is that they know not what they do.[4]

Nothing is more misleading than to compare the Commonwealth immigrant in Britain with the American negro. The negro population of the United States – which was already in existence before the United States became a nation – started literally as slaves and were later given the franchise and other rights of citizenship, to the exercise of which they have only gradually and still incompletely come. The Commonwealth immigrant came to Britain as a full citizen, to a country which knew no discrimination between one citizen and another, and he entered instantly into the possession of the full rights of every citizen, from the vote to free treatment under the National Health Service …

But while to the immigrant entry to this country was admission to privileges and opportunities eagerly sought, the impact upon the existing population was very different. For reasons which they could not comprehend, and in pursuance of a decision by default, on which they were never consulted, they found themselves made strangers in their own country. They found their wives unable to obtain hospital beds in childbirth, their children unable to obtain school places, their homes and

[4] Powell refers to JESUS'S forgiveness of those who crucified him. See Luke 23:34.

neighbourhoods changed beyond recognition, their plans and prospects for the future defeated. At work they found that employers hesitated to apply to the immigrant worker the standards of discipline and competence required of the native-born worker; they began to hear, as time went by, more and more voices which told them that *they* were now the unwanted …

In the hundreds upon hundreds of letters I received when I last spoke on this subject two or three months ago, there was one striking feature which was largely new and which I find ominous. All Members of Parliament are used to the typical anonymous correspondent; but what surprised and alarmed me was the high proportion of ordinary, decent, sensible people, writing a rational and often well-educated letter, who believed that they had to omit their address because it was dangerous to have committed themselves to paper to a Member of Parliament agreeing with the views I had expressed, and that they would risk either penalties or reprisals if they were known to have done so.

The sense of being a persecuted minority which is growing among ordinary English people in the areas of the country which are affected is something that those without direct experience can hardly imagine. I am going to allow just one of those hundreds of people to speak for me. She did give her name and address, which I have detached from the letter which I am about to read. She was writing from Northumberland about something which is happening at this moment in my own constituency:

'Eight years ago in a respectable street in Wolverhampton a house was sold to a negro. Now only one white (a woman old-age pensioner) lives there. This is her story. She lost her husband and both her sons in the war. So she turned her seven-roomed house, her only asset, into a boarding house. She worked hard and did well, paid off her mortgage and began to put something by for her old age. Then the immigrants moved in. With growing fear, she saw one house after another taken over. The quiet street became a place of noise and confusion. Regretfully, her white tenants moved out.

'The day after the last one left, she was awakened at 7AM by two negroes who wanted to use her phone to contact their employer. When she refused, as she would have refused any stranger at such an hour, she was abused and feared she would have been attacked but for the chain on her door. Immigrant families have tried to rent rooms in her house, but she always refused.

'Her little store of money went, and after paying her rates, she has less than two pounds per week. She went to apply for a rate reduction and was seen by a young girl, who on hearing she had a seven-roomed house, suggested she should let part of it. When she said the only people she could get were negroes, the girl said, "Racial prejudice won't get you anywhere in this country". So she went home.

'The telephone is her lifeline. Her family pay the bill and help her out as best they can. Immigrants have offered to buy her house – at a price which the prospective landlord would be able to recover from his tenants in weeks, or at most a few months. She is becoming afraid to go out. Windows are broken. She finds excreta pushed through her letterbox. When she goes to the shops, she is followed by children – charming, wide-grinning piccaninnies. They cannot speak English, but one word they know. "Racialist," they chant. When the new Race

Relations Bill is passed, this woman is convinced she will go to prison. And is she so wrong? I begin to wonder.'

… We are on the verge here of a change. Hitherto, it has been force of circumstance and of background which has rendered the very idea of integration inaccessible to the greater part of the immigrant population – that they never conceived or intended such a thing, and that their numbers and physical concentration meant that the pressures towards integration which normally bear upon any small minority did not operate. Now we are seeing the growth of positive forces acting against integration, of vested interests in the preservation and sharpening of racial and religious differences, with a view to the exercise of actual domination, first over fellow-immigrants and then over the rest of the population …

For these dangerous and divisive elements the legislation proposed in the Race Relations Bill is the very pabulum[5] they need to flourish on. Here is their means of showing that the immigrant communities can organize to consolidate their members, to agitate and campaign against their fellow citizens, and to overawe and dominate the rest with the legal weapons which the ignorant and the ill-informed have provided.

[5] Substance that gives nourishment; insipid intellectual nourishment.

As I look ahead, I am filled with foreboding. Like the Roman, I seem to see 'the River Tiber foaming with much blood'.[6] That tragic and intractable phenomenon which we watch with horror on the other side of the Atlantic, but which there is interwoven with the history and existence of the States itself, is coming upon us here by our own volition and our own neglect. Indeed, it has all but come. In numerical terms, it will be of American proportions long before the end of the century.

[6] Powell quotes from Virgil's epic poem the *Aeneid*, book VI.

Only resolute and urgent action will avert it even now. Whether there will be the public will to demand and obtain that action, I do not know. All I know is that to see, and not to speak, would be the great betrayal.

Yitzhak Rabin

Israeli soldier and statesman

Yitzhak Rabin (1922–95) was born to a Russian–Jewish family in Jerusalem and raised in Tel Aviv. After he completed his studies at Kadoorie Agricultural High School, World War II broke out. He abandoned plans to study engineering at the University of California, and embarked on an army career. During the war he took part in sabotage operations against the Vichy French in Lebanon and Syria. He fought in the Arab–Israeli War (1948–9) and represented the Israeli Defence Forces at the armistice in Rhodes. In the mid-1950s, he studied at Camberley Staff College in England. He rose to become Chief of Staff in 1964, skilfully leading the armed forces during the Six-Day War of 1967, which dramatically increased Israel's territory. After serving as ambassador to the USA (1968–73) he moved decisively into the political arena, becoming leader of the Labour Party and prime minister following the resignation of GOLDA MEIR (1974). He resigned this position in 1977 and spent several years on the opposition back benches while the Likud Party was in power. Rabin was appointed Defence Minister in the coalition government (1984–90) of Yitzhak Shamir and Shimon Peres. In 1985, he withdrew troops from Lebanon, which Israel had invaded three years earlier. His severe and sometimes brutal handling of Palestinian insurgents in the Gaza *intifada* (1987) brought him a reputation for harshness. In 1990 Shamir formed a more hardline government, which fell at the beginning of 1992, having alienated all its allies, including the USA. Rabin was re-elected leader of the Labour Party and in 1992 again became prime minister. His centre-left government favoured Palestinian self-government. In 1993, following secret talks in Oslo, he signed an accord with the Palestine Liberation Organization, granting self-rule of Gaza and Jericho to the Palestinians and stipulating a phased withdrawal of Israeli forces. In 1994 he signed a peace treaty with Jordan; the same year he was awarded the Nobel Peace Prize jointly with Shimon Peres and YASSER ARAFAT. In 1995 he signed a second accord, agreeing to further troop withdrawals from the West Bank and further expansion of Palestinian self-rule. These concessions aroused extreme opposition in Israel and he was assassinated on 4 November 1995 while attending a peace rally in Tel Aviv. He was succeeded as prime minister by his old rival, Shimon Peres.

'I wish to salute loved ones and foes'

10 December 1994, Oslo, Norway

The Nobel Peace Prize is often controversial; never more so than in 1994, when it was divided three ways for the only time in its century-long history. The recipients were Israeli prime minister Yitzhak Rabin, his Foreign Minister Shimon Peres, and Yasser Arafat, chairman of the Palestinian Liberation Organization.

'Arafat, Peres and Rabin have made substantial contributions to a historic process through which peace and co-operation can replace war and hate,' said Francis Sejersted, chairman of the Nobel committee, but many were not convinced. One committee member, Kare Kristiansen, resigned over the inclusion of Arafat, whom he described as 'too tainted by violence, terror and torture'.

Worse still, shortly before the award was announced on 14 October, the militant Palestinian group Hamas had seized a 19-year-old Israeli soldier, US-born Corporal Nachshon Wachsman. They threatened to kill him if the Israeli authorities did not release 200 Palestinian prisoners, including their leader Sheikh Ahmed Yassin. That night, during a botched rescue operation in the West Bank, Wachsman was killed, along with three of his kidnappers and another Israeli soldier.

Despite this disaster, when Rabin accepted his share of the award at a ceremony eight weeks later, he gave a speech of astonishing lyricism and optimism. Contrasting the beauty of the Middle East with the ugliness of its conflicts, he laments the crushed aspirations of people throughout the region, describes the feelings he experienced as a military officer, assumes the burden of responsibility in the search for peace and finally prays for success.

His assassination came less than a year later.

[1] The Norwegian politician Dr Gro Harlem Brundtland (1939–) served as prime minister of Norway, 1981, 1986–9 and 1990–6; and as Director-General of the World Health Organization, 1998–2003.

Your Majesty the King, Your Royal Highness, esteemed members of the Norwegian Nobel Committee, Honourable Prime Minister Madame Gro Harlem Brundtland,[1] Ministers, Members of the Parliament and Ambassadors, fellow laureates, distinguished guests, friends, ladies and gentlemen: at an age when most youngsters are struggling to unravel the secrets of mathematics and the mysteries of the Bible; at an age when first love blooms; at the tender age of 16, I was handed a rifle so that I could defend myself – and also, unfortunately, so that I could kill in an hour of danger.

That was not my dream. I wanted to be a water engineer. I studied in an agricultural school and I thought that being a water engineer was an important profession in the parched Middle East. I still think so today. However, I was compelled to resort to the gun.

I served in the military for decades. Under my command, young men and women who wanted to live, wanted to love, went to their deaths instead. Under my command, they killed the enemy's men who had been sent out to kill us.

Ladies and gentlemen: in my current position, I have ample opportunity to fly over the state of Israel, and lately over other parts of the Middle East as well. The view from the plane is breathtaking: deep-blue lakes, dark-green fields, dun-coloured deserts, stone-grey mountains, and the entire countryside peppered with whitewashed, red-roofed houses. And cemeteries. Graves as far as the eye can see.

Hundreds of cemeteries in our part of the Middle East – in our home in Israel – but also in Egypt, in Syria, Jordan, Lebanon and Iraq. From the plane's window, from thousands of feet above them, the countless tombstones are silent. But the sound of their outcry has carried from the Middle East throughout the world for decades.

Standing here today, I wish to salute loved ones and foes. I wish to salute all the fallen of all the countries in all the wars; the members of their families who bear the enduring burden of bereavement; the disabled whose scars will never heal. Tonight I wish to pay tribute to each and every one of them, for this important prize is theirs, and theirs alone.

Ladies and gentlemen: I was a young man who has now grown fully in years. And of all the memories I have stored up in my 72 years, what I shall remember most, to my last day, are the silences. The heavy silence of the moment after and the terrifying silence of the moment before.

As a military man, as a commander, I issued orders for dozens, probably hundreds of military operations. And together with the joy of victory and grief of bereavement, I shall always remember the moment just after making the decision to mount an action: the hush as senior officers or cabinet ministers slowly rise from their seats; the sight of their receding backs; the sound of the closing door; and then the silence in which I remain alone.

That is the moment you grasp that, as a result of the decision just made, people will be going to their deaths. People from my nation, people from other nations. And they still don't know it.

At that hour, they are still laughing and weeping; still weaving plans and dreaming about love; still musing about planting a garden or building a house – and they have no idea these are their last hours on earth. Which of them is fated to die? Whose picture will appear in a black border in tomorrow's newspaper? Whose mother will soon be in mourning? Whose world will crumble under the weight of the loss?

As a former military man, I will also forever remember the silence of the moment before: the hush when the hands of the clock seem to be spinning forward, when time is running out and in another hour, another minute, the inferno will erupt.

In that moment of great tension just before the finger pulls the trigger, just before the fuse begins to burn; in the terrible quiet of that moment, there's still time to wonder, alone: is it really imperative to act? Is there no other choice? No other way? And then the order is given, and the inferno begins.

'God takes pity on kindergarteners', wrote the poet Yehudah Amichai,[2] who is here with us tonight:

'God takes pity on kindergarteners, Less so on schoolchildren, And will no longer pity their elders, Leaving them to their own. And sometimes they will have to crawl on all fours, Through the burning sand, To reach the casualty station, Bleeding.'

For decades, God has not taken pity on the kindergarteners in the Middle East, or the schoolchildren, or their elders. There has been no pity in the Middle East for generations.

Ladies and gentlemen: I was a young man who has now grown fully in years. And of all the memories I have stored up in my 72 years, I now recall the hopes.

Our peoples have chosen us to give them life. Terrible as it is to say, their lives are in our hands. Tonight, their eyes are upon us and their hearts are asking: how is the authority vested in these men and women being used? What will they decide? What kind of morning will we rise to tomorrow? A day of peace? Of war? Of laughter or of tears?

A child is born into an utterly undemocratic world. He cannot choose his father and mother. He cannot pick his sex or colour, his religion, nationality, or homeland. Whether he is born in a manor or a manger, whether he lives under a despotic or democratic regime, it is not his choice. From the moment he comes, close-fisted, into the world, his fate lies in the hands of his nation's leaders. It is they who will decide whether he lives in comfort or despair, in security or in fear. His fate is given to us to resolve – to the presidents and prime ministers of countries democratic or otherwise.

Ladies and gentlemen: just as no two fingerprints are identical, so no two people are alike, and every country has its own laws and culture, traditions and leaders. But there is one universal message which can embrace the entire world, one precept which can be common to different regimes, to races which bear no resemblance, to cultures alien to each other.

It is a message which the Jewish people has borne for thousands of years, a message found in the Book of Books,[3] which my people has bequeathed to all civilized men: 'V'nishmartem me'od l'nafshoteichem', in the words in Deuteronomy: 'Therefore take good heed to yourselves'[4] – or, in contemporary terms, the message of the sanctity of life.

The leaders of nations must provide their peoples with the conditions – the 'infrastructure', if you will – which enables them to enjoy life: freedom of speech and of movement; food and shelter; and most important of all: life itself. A man cannot enjoy his rights if he is not among the living. And so every country must protect and preserve the key element in its national ethos: the lives of its citizens.

To defend those lives, we call upon our citizens to enlist in the army, and to defend the lives of our citizens serving in the army, we invest huge sums in planes and tanks, in armoured plating and concrete fortifications. Yet despite it all, we fail to protect the lives of our citizens and soldiers. Military cemeteries in every corner of the world are silent testimony to the failure of national leaders to sanctify human life.

There is only one radical means of sanctifying human lives. Not armoured plating, or tanks, or planes, or concrete fortifications. The one radical solution is peace.

[2] The Israeli poet Yehuda Amichai (1924–2000) pioneered the use of colloquial Hebrew. Born in Germany, he fled with his family to Palestine in 1936.

[3] The *Tanakh*, comprising the *Torah* (the Pentateuch), *Nevi'im* (the Prophets) and *Ketuvim* (Writings).

[4] Deuteronomy 4:15.

Ladies and gentlemen: the profession of soldiering embraces a certain paradox. We take the best and bravest of our young men into the army. We supply them with equipment which costs a virtual fortune. We rigorously train them for the day when they must do their duty – and we expect them to do it well. Yet we fervently pray that that day will never come – that the planes will never take flight, the tanks will never move forward, the soldiers will never mount the attacks for which they have been trained so well.

We pray it will never happen because of the sanctity of life.

History as a whole, and modern history in particular, has known harrowing times when national leaders turned their citizens into cannon fodder in the name of wicked doctrines: vicious fascism and fiendish Nazism. Pictures of children marching to the slaughter, photos of terrified women at the gates of crematoria must loom before the eyes of every leader in our generation, and the generations to come. They must serve as a warning to all who wield power.

Almost all the regimes which did not place man and the sanctity of life at the heart of their world-view, all those regimes have collapsed and are no more. You can see it for yourselves in our own day.

Yet this is not the whole picture. To preserve the sanctity of life, we must sometimes risk it. Sometimes there is no other way to defend our citizens than to fight for their lives, for their safety and sovereignty. This is the creed of every democratic state. …

Ladies and gentlemen: we are in the midst of building the peace. The architects and engineers of this enterprise are engaged in their work even as we gather here tonight, building the peace layer by layer, brick by brick, beam by beam. The job is difficult, complex, trying. Mistakes could topple the whole structure and bring disaster down upon us.

And so we are determined to do the job well – despite the toll of murderous terrorism, despite fanatic and scheming enemies.

We will pursue the course of peace with determination and fortitude. We will not let up. We will not give in.

Peace will triumph over all our enemies, because the alternative is grim for us all. And we will prevail.

We will prevail because we regard the building of peace as a great blessing for us, and for our children after us. We regard it as a blessing for our neighbours on all sides, and for our partners in this enterprise – the United States, Russia, Norway and all mankind.

We wake up every morning, now, as different people. Suddenly, peace. We see the hope in our children's eyes. We see the light in our soldiers' faces, in the streets, in the buses, in the fields.

We must not let them down. We will not let them down.

I do not stand here alone, today, on this small rostrum in Oslo. I am the emissary of generations of Israelis, of the shepherds of Israel, just as King David was a shepherd, of the herdsmen and dressers of sycamore trees, as the Prophet Amos was; of the rebels against the establishment, like the Prophet Jeremiah, and of men who go down to the sea, like the Prophet Jonah.

I am the emissary of the poets and of those who dreamed of an end to war, like the Prophet Isaiah.

I am also the emissary of sons of the Jewish people like **ALBERT EINSTEIN** and Baruch Spinoza;[5] like Maimonides,[6] Sigmund Freud,[7] and Franz Kafka.[8]

And I am the emissary of the millions who perished in the Holocaust,

[5] The Dutch philosopher and theologian Baruch Spinoza (1632–77) was active in optics, astronomy, theology and metaphysics.
[6] The Spanish philosopher Moshe ben Maimon *known as Maimonides* (1135–1204) was active in medicine and Aristotelian philosophy.

[7] The Austrian neurologist Sigmund Freud (1856–1939) is regarded as the founder of psychoanalysis.
[8] The writer Franz Kafka, born in Prague to German parents (1883–1924), is known for such works as *Metamorphosis* (1916), *The Trial* (1925) and *The Castle* (1926).

among whom were surely many Einsteins and Freuds who were lost to us, and to humanity, in the flames of the crematoria.

I am here as the emissary of Jerusalem, at whose gates I fought in days of siege; Jerusalem which has always been, and is today, the eternal capital of the state of Israel and the heart of the Jewish people, who pray toward it three times a day.

And I am also the emissary of the children who drew their visions of peace; and of the immigrants from Saint Petersburg and Addis Ababa.

I stand here mainly for the generations to come, so that we may all be deemed worthy of the medallion which you have bestowed on me today.

I stand here as the emissary of our neighbours who were our enemies. I stand here as the emissary of the soaring hopes of a people which has endured the worst that history has to offer and nevertheless made its mark – not just on the chronicles of the Jewish people but on all mankind.

With me here are five million citizens of Israel – Jews and Arabs, Druze and Circassians – five million hearts beating for peace – and five million pairs of eyes which look to us with such great expectations for peace.

Ladies and gentlemen: I wish to thank, first and foremost, those citizens of the state of Israel, of all generations and political persuasions, whose sacrifices and relentless struggle for peace bring us steadier closer to our goal.

I wish to thank our partners – the Egyptians, Jordanians, Palestinians and the chairman of the Palestinian Liberation Organization, Mr Yasser Arafat, with whom we share this Nobel Prize – who have chosen the path of peace and are writing a new page in the annals of the Middle East.

I wish to thank the members of the Israeli government and above all my colleague Mr Shimon Peres, whose energy and devotion to the cause of peace are an example to us all.

I wish to thank my family for their support.

And, of course, I wish to thank the members of the Nobel Committee and the courageous Norwegian people for bestowing this illustrious honour on my colleagues and myself.

Ladies and gentlemen: allow me to close by sharing with you a traditional Jewish blessing which has been recited by my people, in good times and in bad, from time immemorial, as a token of their deepest longing:

'The Lord will give strength to his people; the Lord will bless his people – all of us – with peace.'

Ronald Reagan

American actor and politician

Ronald Wilson Reagan (1911–2004) was born in Tampico, Illinois, the son of an Irish immigrant who was bankrupted during the Great Depression. He studied economics at Eureka College, Illinois, then worked as a sports broadcaster in Iowa before being signed as a film actor by Warner Brothers in 1937. He married the actress Jane Wyman (1914–) in 1940, but they divorced in 1948. He starred in 50 films, including *Bedtime for Bonzo* (1951) and *The Killers* (1964). He became interested in politics when serving as president of the Screen Actors' Guild (1947–52) and moved increasingly towards Republicanism, particularly following his marriage in 1952 to the affluent actress Nancy Davis (1921–), a devout Presbyterian. During the later 1950s he became a committed free-enterprise conservative. He joined the Republican Party in 1962 and delivering a rousing television appeal for the party's 1964 presidential election candidate, Barry M Goldwater. In 1966 Reagan was elected governor of California, and he remained in the post until 1972. He unsuccessfully contested the Republican presidential nomination in 1968 and 1976, being defeated by RICHARD M NIXON and Gerald R Ford respectively. In 1980, however, he captured the party's nomination, and convincingly defeated President Jimmy Carter (1924–). His campaign stressed the need to reduce taxes, deregulate the economy and modernize defence to enable the USA to negotiate abroad 'from a position of strength'. He survived an attempted assassination in 1981 and, despite serious economic problems between 1981 and 1983, secured re-election by a record margin in 1984. His programme of tax cuts and deficit financing brought about rapid economic upturn between 1983 and 1986. Despite advocating a space-based Strategic Defence Initiative ('Star Wars'), he became a convert to détente. He held four summit meetings with Soviet leader Mikhail Gorbachev between 1985 and 1988, and signed a treaty for the scrapping of intermediate nuclear forces. In 1986–7, however, Reagan's position was imperilled by the 'Iran-Contra Affair' concerning illegal arms-for-hostages deals with Iran and the laundering of profits intended, equally illegally, to support the anti-Marxist Contra guerrillas in Nicaragua. Despite the resignation of key aides, Reagan escaped unscathed. Dubbed 'the great communicator' for his accomplished handling of the media, Reagan had a unique, populist rapport with 'mainstream America', and left office an immensely popular figure. However, his policies towards Central America and domestic social programmes were less widely supported and his successor, George H W Bush, inherited record budget and trade deficits.

'The aggressive impulses of an evil empire'

8 March 1983, Orlando, Florida, USA

Among Reagan's priorities when he came to power was the restoration of the USA's military and moral pre-eminence; to this end, he authorized vast increases in defence spending and pursued a conservative social agenda.

This speech, made at the annual convention of the National Association of Evangelicals, is a clear reflection of Reagan's main aims: the first half (omitted here for reasons of space) dealt with the importance of Christianity in American life and discussed sexual morality and abortion; the second half dismisses calls for the USA to freeze its nuclear arsenal, and famously describes the Soviet Union as an 'evil empire'.

The speech, and this phrase in particular, divided opinion around the world. The Soviets, of course, were incensed – an official response stated that Reagan's administration could 'think only in terms of confrontation and bellicose, lunatic anti-communism'. Others, however, thought that by introducing the notion of 'evil' into the Cold War, Reagan had claimed the moral high ground and gained new confidence for the USA.

Years later, Reagan said of his speech, 'It was portrayed as some kind of know-nothing, arch-conservative statement ... [but] the Soviet system has purposely starved, murdered and brutalized its own people ... Is the system that allowed this not evil?'

During my first press conference as president, in answer to a direct question, I pointed out that, as good Marxist–Leninists, the Soviet leaders have openly and publicly declared that the only morality they recognize is that which will further their cause, which is world revolution. I think I should point out I was only quoting Lenin, their guiding spirit, who said in 1920 that they repudiate all morality that proceeds from supernatural ideas – that's their name for religion – or ideas that are outside class conceptions. Morality is entirely subordinate to the interests of class war. And everything is moral that is necessary for the annihilation of the old, exploiting social order and for uniting the proletariat.

Well, I think the refusal of many influential people to accept this elementary fact of Soviet doctrine illustrates an historical reluctance to see totalitarian powers for what they are. We saw this phenomenon in the 1930s. We see it too often today.

This doesn't mean we should isolate ourselves and refuse to seek an understanding with them. I intend to do everything I can to persuade them of our peaceful intent, to remind them that it was the West that refused to use its nuclear monopoly in the Forties and Fifties for territorial gain, and which now proposes a 50 per cent cut in strategic ballistic missiles and the elimination of an entire class of land-based, intermediate-range nuclear missiles.

At the same time, however, they must be made to understand we will never compromise our principles and standards. We will never give away our freedom. We will never abandon our belief in God. And we will never stop searching for a genuine peace. But we can assure none of these things America stands for through the so-called nuclear freeze solutions proposed by some.[1]

[1] Among those calling for a nuclear freeze was BELLA ABZUG, whose speech on that theme is included this book.

The truth is that a freeze now would be a very dangerous fraud, for that is merely the illusion of peace. The reality is that we must find peace through strength.

I would agree to a freeze if only we could freeze the Soviets' global desires. A freeze at current levels of weapons would remove any incentive for the Soviets to negotiate seriously in Geneva[2] and virtually end our chances to achieve the major arms reductions which we have proposed. Instead, they would achieve their objectives through the freeze.

[2] In 1983, negotiations between the USSR and the USA for the reduction of intermediate-range nuclear weapons were held in Geneva, Switzerland. The Soviets walked out of these discussions on 23 November of that year.

A freeze would reward the Soviet Union for its enormous and unparalleled military build-up. It would prevent the essential and long overdue modernization of United States and allied defences and would leave our aging forces increasingly vulnerable. And an honest freeze would require extensive prior negotiations on the systems and numbers to be limited and on the measures to ensure effective verification and compliance. And the kind of a freeze that has been suggested would be virtually impossible to verify. Such a major effort would divert us completely from our current negotiations on achieving substantial reductions.

A number of years ago, I heard a young father, a very prominent young man in the entertainment world, addressing a tremendous gathering in California. It was during the time of the Cold War, and communism and our own way of life were very much on people's minds. And he was speaking to that subject. And suddenly, though, I heard him saying, 'I love my little girls more than anything.'

And I said to myself, 'Oh, no, don't. You can't – don't say that.' But I had underestimated him.

He went on: 'I would rather see my little girls die now, still believing in God, than have them grow up under Communism and one day die no longer believing in God.'

There were thousands of young people in that audience. They came to their feet with shouts of joy. They had instantly recognized the profound truth in what he had said, with regard to the physical and the soul and what was truly important.

Yes, let us pray for the salvation of all of those who live in that totalitarian darkness – pray they will discover the joy of knowing God. But until they do, let us be aware that while they preach the supremacy of the state, declare its omnipotence over individual man, and predict its eventual domination of all peoples on the earth, they are the focus of evil in the modern world.

It was C S Lewis[3] who, in his unforgettable *Screwtape Letters*, wrote: 'The greatest evil is not done now in those sordid "dens of crime" that Dickens loved to paint. It is not even done in concentration camps and labour camps. In those we see its final result. But it is conceived and ordered (moved, seconded, carried and minuted) in clear, carpeted, warmed and well-lighted offices, by quiet men with white collars and cut fingernails and smooth-shaven cheeks who do not need to raise their voices.'

Well, because these 'quiet men' do not 'raise their voices,' because they sometimes speak in soothing tones of brotherhood and peace, because, like other dictators before them, they're always making 'their final territorial demand', some would have us accept them at their word and accommodate ourselves to their aggressive impulses. But if history teaches anything, it teaches that simple-minded appeasement, or wishful thinking about our adversaries, is folly. It means the betrayal of our past, the squandering of our freedom.

So I urge you to speak out against those who would place the United States in a position of military and moral inferiority. You know, I've always believed that old Screwtape reserved his best efforts for those of you in the church. So, in your discussions of the nuclear freeze proposals, I urge you to beware the temptation of pride – the temptation of blithely declaring yourselves above it all and labelling both sides equally at fault, to ignore the facts of history and the aggressive impulses of an evil empire, to simply call the arms race a giant misunderstanding and thereby remove yourself from the struggle between right and wrong and good and evil.

I ask you to resist the attempts of those who would have you withhold your support for our efforts, this administration's efforts, to keep America strong and free, while we negotiate real and verifiable reductions in the world's nuclear arsenals and one day, with God's help, their total elimination.

While America's military strength is important, let me add here that I've always maintained that the struggle now going on for the world will never be decided by bombs or rockets, by armies or military might. The real crisis we face today is a spiritual one; at root, it is a test of moral will and faith.

Whittaker Chambers, the man whose own religious conversion made him a witness to one of the terrible traumas of our time, the Hiss–Chambers case,[4] wrote that the crisis of the western world exists to the degree in which the West is indifferent to God, the degree to which it collaborates in communism's attempt to make man stand alone without God. And then he said, for Marxism–Leninism is actually the second oldest faith, first proclaimed in the Garden of Eden with the words of temptation, 'Ye shall be as gods'.[5]

The western world can answer this challenge, he wrote, 'but only provided that its faith in God and the freedom he enjoins is as great as communism's faith in man'.

I believe we shall rise to the challenge. I believe that communism is another sad, bizarre chapter in human history whose last pages even now are being written. I believe this because the source of our strength in the quest for human freedom is not material, but spiritual. And because it knows no limitation, it must terrify and ultimately triumph over those who

[3] The Anglo-Irish academic and writer C S Lewis (1898–1963) published *The Screwtape Letters* as a book in 1942. A series of fictional letters addressed by the demon Screwtape to his incompetent nephew Wormwood, this Christian cautionary tale was originally published in instalments in the *Guardian*.

[4] In 1948, the US journalist and former Communist Whittaker Chambers (1901–61) accused the former US State Department official Alger Hiss (1904–96) of being a Communist spy.

[5] Genesis 3:5.

would enslave their fellow man.

For in the words of Isaiah: 'He giveth power to the faint; and to them that have no might he increaseth strength … But they that wait upon the Lord shall renew their strength; they shall mount up with wings as eagles; they shall run, and not be weary …'[6]

Yes, change your world. One of our Founding Fathers, Thomas Paine, said, 'We have it within our power to begin the world over again.'[7] We can do it, doing together what no one church could do by itself.

God bless you, and thank you very much.

[6] Isaiah 40:29 and 31.

[7] Reagan quotes from the pamphlet 'Common Sense' by the English philosopher Thomas Paine (1737–1809) who advocated American independence and became an American citizen in 1795.

❧

'Tear down this wall!'

12 June 1987, West Berlin, West Germany

❧

On the 750th anniversary of Berlin's foundation, President Reagan spoke from the city's Brandenburg Gate. This was, as he acknowledges in the speech, an echo of the famous Berlin address given by JOHN F KENNEDY 24 years earlier.

As in 1963, East was divided from West by the Berlin Wall, but the circumstances had changed. The Soviet premier, Mikhail Gorbachev (1931–), had begun to promote a new policy of *glasnost*, or openness. Recognizing these developments, Reagan challenged Gorbachev, in possibly the most famous words of his presidency, to 'tear down this wall!'. Just over two years later, the wall did indeed come down.

Ironically, the phrase was nearly omitted from the speech. Many advisers believed it was provocative and would raise false hopes. But Reagan was determined to include it, telling an aide on the morning of his address, 'The boys at State are going to kill me, but it's the right thing to do.'

❧

[1] The German statesman Helmut Kohl (1930–) served as Chancellor of West Germany, and later of Germany, 1982–98.

Chancellor Kohl,[1] Governing Mayor Diepgen,[2] ladies and gentlemen: 24 years ago, President John F Kennedy visited Berlin, speaking to the people of this city and the world at the City Hall. Well, since then two other presidents have come, each in his turn, to Berlin. And today I myself make my second visit to your city.

[2] The German politician Eberhard Diepgen (1941–) served as Mayor of Berlin, 1984–9 and 1991–2001.

We come to Berlin, we American presidents, because it's our duty to speak, in this place, of freedom. But I must confess, we're drawn here by other things as well: by the feeling of history in this city, more than 500 years older than our own nation; by the beauty of the Grunewald and the Tiergarten; most of all, by your courage and determination. Perhaps the composer, Paul Lincke, understood something about American presidents. You see, like so many presidents before me, I come here today because wherever I go, whatever I do: *ich hab' noch einen Koffer in Berlin.*[3]

[3] German: 'I still have a suitcase in Berlin.'

Our gathering today is being broadcast throughout western Europe and North America. I understand that it is being seen and heard as well in the East. To those listening throughout eastern Europe, I extend my warmest greetings and the goodwill of the American people. To those listening in East Berlin, a special word: although I cannot be with you, I address my remarks to you just as surely as to those standing here before me. For I join you, as I join your fellow countrymen in the West, in this firm, this unalterable belief: *es gibt nur ein Berlin.*[4]

[4] German: 'There is only one Berlin.'

Behind me stands a wall that encircles the free sectors of this city, part of a vast system of barriers that divides the entire continent of Europe. From the Baltic south, those barriers cut across Germany in a gash of barbed wire, concrete, dog-runs and guard-towers. Farther south, there may be no visible, no obvious wall. But there remain armed guards and checkpoints all the same – still a restriction on the right to travel, still an instrument to impose upon ordinary men and women the will of a totalitarian state.

Yet it is here in Berlin where the wall emerges most clearly; here, cutting across your city, where the news photo and the television screen have imprinted this brutal division of a continent upon the mind of the world. Standing before the Brandenburg Gate, every man is a German, separated from his fellow men. Every man is a Berliner, forced to look upon a scar.

President von Weizsäcker[5] has said: 'The German question is open as long as the Brandenburg Gate is closed.' Today I say: as long as this gate is closed, as long as this scar of a wall is permitted to stand, it is not the German question alone that remains open, but the question of freedom for all mankind. Yet I do not come here to lament. For I find in Berlin a message of hope, even in the shadow of this wall, a message of triumph.

[5] The German politician Richard, Baron von Weizsäcker (1920–) served as president of West Germany, and later of Germany, 1984–94.

In this season of spring in 1945, the people of Berlin emerged from their air-raid shelters to find devastation. Thousands of miles away, the people of the United States reached out to help. And in 1947 Secretary of State GEORGE MARSHALL announced the creation of what would become known as the Marshall Plan. Speaking precisely 40 years ago this month, he said: 'Our policy is directed not against any country or doctrine, but against hunger, poverty, desperation, and chaos.'

In the Reichstag, a few moments ago, I saw a display commemorating this 40th anniversary of the Marshall Plan. I was struck by the sign on a burnt-out, gutted structure that was being rebuilt. I understand that Berliners of my own generation can remember seeing signs like it dotted throughout the western sectors of the city. The sign read simply: 'The Marshall Plan is helping here to strengthen the free world.' A strong, free world in the West, that dream became real. Japan rose from ruin to become an economic giant. Italy, France, Belgium – virtually every nation in western Europe saw political and economic rebirth; the European Community was founded.

In West Germany and here in Berlin, there took place an economic miracle, the *Wirtschaftswunder* … From 1950 to 1960 alone, the standard of living in West Germany and Berlin doubled. Where four decades ago there was rubble, today in West Berlin there is the greatest industrial output of any city in Germany – busy office blocks, fine homes and apartments, proud avenues, and the spreading lawns of parkland. Where a city's culture seemed to have been destroyed, today there are two great universities, orchestras and an opera, countless theatres and museums. Where there was want, today there's abundance – food, clothing, automobiles – the wonderful goods of the Ku'damm.[6] From devastation, from utter ruin, you Berliners have, in freedom, rebuilt a city that once again ranks as one of the greatest on earth …

[6] The Kurfürstendamm, an upmarket shopping district.

In the 1950s, KHRUSHCHEV[7] predicted: 'We will bury you.' But in the West today, we see a free world that has achieved a level of prosperity and well-being unprecedented in all human history. In the communist world, we see failure, technological backwardness, declining standards of health, even want of the most basic kind – too little food. Even today, the Soviet Union still cannot feed itself. After these four decades, then, there stands before the entire world one great and inescapable conclusion: freedom leads to prosperity. Freedom replaces the ancient hatreds among the nations with comity and peace. Freedom is the victor.

[7] In 1956, the Soviet leader Nikita Khrushchev told Western ambassadors at a reception in Moscow, 'Whether you like it or not, history is on our side. We will bury you!'

And now the Soviets themselves may, in a limited way, be coming to understand the importance of freedom. We hear much from Moscow about a new policy of reform and openness. Some political prisoners have been released. Certain foreign news broadcasts are no longer being jammed. Some economic enterprises have been permitted to operate with greater freedom from state control …

There is one sign the Soviets can make that would be unmistakable, that would advance dramatically the cause of freedom and peace. General Secretary Gorbachev,[8] if you seek peace, if you seek prosperity for the Soviet Union and eastern Europe, if you seek liberalization: come here to this gate! Mr Gorbachev, open this gate! Mr Gorbachev, tear down this wall!

I understand the fear of war and the pain of division that afflict this continent − and I pledge to you my country's efforts to help overcome these burdens. To be sure, we in the West must resist Soviet expansion. So we must maintain defences of unassailable strength. Yet we seek peace; so we must strive to reduce arms on both sides. Beginning 10 years ago, the Soviets challenged the Western alliance with a grave new threat, hundreds of new and more deadly SS-20 nuclear missiles, capable of striking every capital in Europe.[9] The Western alliance responded by committing itself to a counter-deployment unless the Soviets agreed to negotiate a better solution; namely, the elimination of such weapons on both sides.

For many months, the Soviets refused to bargain in earnestness. As the alliance, in turn, prepared to go forward with its counter-deployment, there were difficult days − days of protests like those during my 1982 visit to this city − and the Soviets later walked away from the table.

But through it all, the alliance held firm. And I invite those who protested then − I invite those who protest today − to mark this fact: because we remained strong, the Soviets came back to the table. And because we remained strong, today we have within reach the possibility, not merely of limiting the growth of arms, but of eliminating, for the first time, an entire class of nuclear weapons from the face of the earth. As I speak, NATO ministers are meeting in Iceland[10] to review the progress of our proposals for eliminating these weapons. At the talks in Geneva,[11] we have also proposed deep cuts in strategic offensive weapons …

While we pursue these arms reductions, I pledge to you that we will maintain the capacity to deter Soviet aggression at any level at which it might occur. And in co-operation with many of our allies, the United States is pursuing the Strategic Defence Initiative[12] − research to base deterrence not on the threat of offensive retaliation, but on defences that truly defend; on systems, in short, that will not target populations, but shield them. By these means we seek to increase the safety of Europe and all the world.

But we must remember a crucial fact: East and West do not mistrust each other because we are armed; we are armed because we mistrust each other. And our differences are not about weapons but about liberty. When President Kennedy spoke at the City Hall those 24 years ago, freedom was encircled, Berlin was under siege. And today, despite all the pressures upon this city, Berlin stands secure in its liberty. And freedom itself is transforming the globe …

In Europe, only one nation and those it controls refuse to join the community of freedom. Yet in this age of redoubled economic growth, of information and innovation, the Soviet Union faces a choice. It must make fundamental changes, or it will become obsolete. Today thus represents a moment of hope. We in the West stand ready to co-operate with the East to promote true openness, to break down barriers that separate people, to create a safer, freer world.

And surely there is no better place than Berlin, the meeting place of East

[8] Mikhail Gorbachev (1931−) served as General Secretary of the Communist Party of the Soviet Union, 1985−91; and as President of the Soviet Union, 1990−1.

[9] From the late 1970s, the Soviet Union began to replace its arsenal of nuclear warheads with SS-20 missiles, each of which carried three warheads and had the range and accuracy to hit targets anywhere in western Europe in under ten minutes.

[10] The NATO meeting in Reykjavik, Iceland was a follow-up to the summit Reagan and Gorbachev had held there in October 1986 to discuss nuclear arms control.

[12] The Strategic Defence Initiative (nicknamed 'Star Wars' by the media) was a system intended to protect the USA from nuclear attack by intercepting incoming missiles from space.

[11] Strategic arms reduction talks (START) between the USA and the USSR began in Geneva in 1982 and ultimately produced several arms treaties. The talks were also the occasion of the first meeting between Reagan and Gorbachev in November 1985.

and West, to make a start … And I invite Mr Gorbachev: let us work to bring the eastern and western parts of the city closer together, so that all the inhabitants of all Berlin can enjoy the benefits that come with life in one of the great cities of the world …

In these four decades, as I have said, you Berliners have built a great city. You've done so in spite of threats – the Soviet attempts to impose the East-mark, the blockade.[13] Today the city thrives in spite of the challenges implicit in the very presence of this wall. What keeps you here? Certainly there's a great deal to be said for your fortitude, for your defiant courage. But I believe there's something deeper, something that involves Berlin's whole look and feel and way of life – not mere sentiment … something that speaks with a powerful voice of affirmation, that says yes to this city, yes to the future, yes to freedom. In a word, I would submit that what keeps you in Berlin is love – love both profound and abiding.

Perhaps this gets to the root of the matter, to the most fundamental distinction of all between East and West. The totalitarian world produces backwardness because it does such violence to the spirit, thwarting the human impulse to create, to enjoy, to worship. The totalitarian world finds even symbols of love and of worship an affront.

Years ago, before the East Germans began rebuilding their churches, they erected a secular structure: the television tower at Alexanderplatz. Virtually ever since, the authorities have been working to correct what they view as the tower's one major flaw, treating the glass sphere at the top with paints and chemicals of every kind. Yet even today when the sun strikes that sphere – that sphere that towers over all Berlin – the light makes the sign of the cross. There in Berlin, like the city itself, symbols of love, symbols of worship, cannot be suppressed.

As I looked out a moment ago from the Reichstag, that embodiment of German unity, I noticed words crudely spray-painted upon the wall, perhaps by a young Berliner, 'This wall will fall. Beliefs become reality.' Yes, across Europe, this wall will fall. For it cannot withstand faith; it cannot withstand truth. The wall cannot withstand freedom.

And I would like, before I close, to say one word. I have read, and I have been questioned since I've been here, about certain demonstrations against my coming. And I would like to say just one thing to those who demonstrate so. I wonder if they have ever asked themselves that if they should have the kind of government they apparently seek, no-one would ever be able to do what they're doing again.

Thank you and God bless you all.

[13] Reagan refers to the crisis of 1948–9, when the Soviet Union attempted to force the western Allies out of Berlin by imposing an East German currency and blockading communication and transport links between Berlin and the West.

Red Jacket
Native American chief

Chief Red Jacket *originally Otetiani, also called Sagoyewat-ha* (c.1758–1830), was born near Canoga, New York. His Indian name, Sagoyewat-ha, is translated as 'He Keeps Them Awake' or 'He Makes Them Look for It in Vain'. He became a chief of the Seneca tribe during the American War of Independence, and developed good relationships with both American officials and British troops (from whom he obtained the red coats that gave him his English name). He negotiated property agreements with white settlers against the interests of his own people, leading to accusations of cowardice, duplicity and even witchcraft. However, his skill as an orator served to sustain his reputation, and he later made genuine efforts to protect Seneca culture and traditions from corruption by settlers, expelling all Christian missionaries from Seneca reservations in 1824. His later life was troubled by alcoholism. A tribal council eventually deposed him (1827) but intervention from the US Office of Indian Affairs led to his reinstatement as a chief.

'We never quarrel about religion'
Summer 1805, Buffalo Grove, New York, USA

Chief Red Jacket's Seneca tribe was the largest of the Six Nations of the Iroquois, who mostly fought alongside the British in the War of Independence. His great skill was diplomacy, and he worked hard to broker agreements between the British, the Americans and other Native American tribes. He was involved in every major treaty council concerning the Seneca from 1780 until his death in 1830. Above all, he was determined to retain Seneca lands within the newly-formed state of New York.

He preferred not to deal with Christian missionaries, but this was sometimes unavoidable. In 1805, a Mr Cram arrived from the Evangelical Missionary Society of Massachusetts with a proposal to preach in the region. He addressed his request to a council meeting of the Six Nations, at which Red Jacket was a spokesman.

Cram told the meeting: 'There is only one religion, and only one way to serve God ... You have never worshipped the Great Spirit in a manner acceptable to him, but have all your lives been in great error and darkness.'

In the reply given here, Red Jacket implies that the Six Nations were united, but this was misleading. His rival, Joseph Brant of the Mohawks, had led almost half the Iroquois to British-controlled Canada in 1785. Others, seeking accommodation with the new US government, denounced Red Jacket in 1801 and he narrowly escaped execution.

After hearing Red Jacket's response, Cram is said to have refused to shake hands, saying, 'There is no fellowship between the religion of God and the Devil.'

Friend and brother: it was the will of the Great Spirit that we should meet together this day. He orders all things and has given us a fine day for our council. He has taken his garment from before the sun, and caused it to shine with brightness upon us. Our eyes are opened, that we see clearly; our ears are unstopped, that we have been able to hear distinctly the words you have spoken. For all these favours we thank the Great Spirit; and him only.

Brother: this council fire was kindled by you. It was at your request that we came together at this time. We have listened with attention to what you have said. You requested us to speak our minds freely. This gives us great joy; for we now consider that we stand upright before you, and can speak what we think. All have heard your voice, and all speak to you now as one man. Our minds are agreed.

Brother: you say you want an answer to your talk before you leave this place. It is right you should have one, as you are a great distance from home, and we do not wish to detain you. But we will first look back a little and tell you what our fathers have told us, and what we have heard from the white people.

Brother: listen to what we say. There was a time when our forefathers owned this great island. Their seats extended from the rising to the setting of the sun. The Great Spirit had made it for the use of the Indians. He had created the buffalo, the deer and other animals for food. He had made the bear and the beaver, and their skins served us for clothing. He had scattered them over the country, and had taught us how to take them. He had caused the earth to produce corn for bread. All this he had done for his red children, because he loved them. If we had any disputes about our hunting grounds, they were generally settled without the shedding of much blood.

But an evil day came upon us. Your forefathers crossed the great waters and landed on this island. Their numbers were small. They found friends and not enemies. They told us they had fled from their own country for fear of wicked men, and had come here to enjoy their religion. They asked for a small seat. We took pity on them, granted their request and they sat down amongst us. We gave them corn and meat; they gave us poison in return.

The white people, brother, had now found our country. Tidings were carried back, and more came amongst us. Yet we did not fear them. We took them to be friends. They called us brothers. We believed them and gave them a large seat. At length their numbers had greatly increased. They wanted more land; they wanted our country. Our eyes were opened and our minds became uneasy. Wars took place. Indians were hired to fight against Indians, and many of our people were destroyed. They also brought strong liquors among us. It was strong and powerful and has slain thousands.

Brother: our seats were once large, and yours very small. You have now become a great people, and we have scarcely a place left to spread our blankets. You have got our country, but you are not satisfied; you want to force your religion upon us.

Brother: continue to listen. You say that you are sent to instruct us how to worship the Great Spirit agreeably to his mind. And if we do not take hold of the religion which you white people teach, we shall be unhappy hereafter. You say that you are right, and we are lost. How do you know this to be true?

We understand that your religion is written in a book. If it was intended for us as well as for you, why has not the Great Spirit given it to us? And not only to us: why did he not give to our forefathers knowledge of that book, with the means of understanding it rightly? We only know what you tell us about it. How shall we know when to believe, being so often deceived by the white man?

Brother: you say there is but one way to worship and serve the Great Spirit. If there is but one religion, why do you white people differ so much about it? Why not all agreed, as you can all read the book?

Brother: we do not understand these things. We are told that your religion was given to your forefathers and has been handed down from father to son. We also have a religion which was given to our forefathers and has been handed down to us, their children. We worship that way. It teaches us to be thankful for all the favours we receive; to love each other, and to be united. We never quarrel about religion.

Brother: the Great Spirit has made us all, but he has made a great difference between his white and red children. He has given us a different complexion and different customs. To you he has given the arts. To these he has not opened our eyes. We know these things to be true. Since he has made so great a difference between us in other things, why may we not conclude that he has given us a different religion according to our understanding? The Great Spirit does right. He knows what is best for his children; we are satisfied.

Brother: we do not wish to destroy your religion, or to take it from you. We only want to enjoy our own.

Brother: you say you have not come to get our land or our money, but to enlighten our minds. I will now tell you that I have been at your meetings, and saw you collecting money from the meeting. I cannot tell what this money was intended for, but suppose it was for your minister – and if we should conform to your way of thinking, perhaps you may want some from us.

Brother: we are told that you have been preaching to the white people in this place. These people are our neighbours. We are acquainted with them. We will wait a little while and see what effect your preaching has upon them. If we find it does them good and makes them honest and less disposed to cheat Indians, we will then consider again what you have said.

Brother: you have now heard our answer to your talk, and this is all we have to say at present. As we are going to part, we will come and take you by the hand, and hope the Great Spirit will protect you on your journey, and return you safe to your friends.

Paul Reynaud

French statesman

> Paul Reynaud (1878–1966) was born in Barcelonnette, the son of a wealthy businessman. He studied law at the Sorbonne and became a barrister, then fought in World War I. In 1919, he was elected to the Chamber of Deputies and he went on to hold several senior government posts. He was ejected from the Cabinet in 1932 after pursuing hardline defence and foreign policies, but returned in 1938 as Minister of Justice. In March 1940, he was elected prime minister by a narrow margin. He attempted to instigate a more rigorous war effort but the German onslaught led to his resignation. He was replaced by Marshal Philippe Pétain, who signed an armistice with the Germans and had Reynaud arrested and imprisoned. After the war, Reynaud re-entered politics and became, at 71, a delegate to the Council of Europe (1949). However, he failed to regain his former influence, and lost his seat in 1962, aged 84.

'The soul of France is not broken'

13 June 1940, radio broadcast from Tours, France

Under the influence of CHARLES DE GAULLE, Paul Reynaud believed France should have a modern, mechanized army, but had been unable to convince his Cabinet colleagues. He became prime minister during the *'drôle de guerre'* or 'phoney war', the six-month period of military inactivity that followed France's declaration of war on Germany in September 1939. By this time it was too late to rearm, and the country was left to rely on the static defences favoured by Pétain – the Maginot Line, constructed in 1930–5.

In May 1940, German troops swiftly overran Luxembourg, Belgium and the Netherlands, and 330,000 British and French troops were forced to retreat to Dunkirk. By early June, German forces had conquered northern and south-western France. The French government abandoned Paris on 10 June; on the same day Italy declared war on the Allies.

On 13 June, WINSTON CHURCHILL visited Reynaud at Tours, urging further French resistance to the German advance. Reynaud had already requested help from US President FRANKLIN D ROOSEVELT, but with Churchill's encouragement he renewed his appeal.

He then broadcast this defiant, morale-boosting address to the French people. In it, he praises French forces for their heroism, stresses the government's determination to resist German superiority and places his faith in US and British intervention.

However, German troops entered Paris on 14 June and Reynaud's plea to Roosevelt was rejected on 15 June. He resigned the following day and was succeeded by Pétain, who signed the armistice on 22 June and formed the Vichy government.

In the misery that has descended upon the motherland, one thing above all must be said. Now, as fortune overwhelms them, I wish to declare to the world the heroism of France's armies, the heroism of our soldiers, the heroism of our leaders. I have witnessed, returning from the battle, men who have not slept in five days, harassed by aeroplanes, exhausted by long marches and heavy combat.

These men, whose nerves the enemy thought broken, were in no doubt about the final outcome of the war. They were in no doubt about the future of the motherland. The heroism of the armies of Dunkirk[1] has been exceeded in the fighting from the sea to the Argonne. The spirit of France is not broken.

Our race does not allow itself to be trampled by invasion. The soil on which we live has endured so many over the centuries; yet our race has always thrown back or dominated the invaders. The world must know of the sufferings of France. Everyone must know what they owe her. The hour has come for them to pay their debt.

The French army has been the vanguard of the army of the democracies. It has sacrificed itself, but in losing this battle it has dealt severe blows to

[1] The Allied troops were evacuated from the beaches at Dunkirk between 26 May and 2 June 1940.

our mutual enemy. The hundreds of tanks destroyed, aeroplanes shot down, losses in men, the petroleum factories and planes – it all accounts for the current morale of the German people, despite their victories.

Wounded France is now entitled to turn to other democracies and say: 'We have claims on you.' No-one who believes in justice can deny this.

But it is one thing to consent; and another to act. We know how highly ideals are held in the life of the great American people. Will they hesitate still to declare themselves against Nazi Germany?

As you know, I have demanded it from President Roosevelt. Tonight, I have sent him a new and final appeal. Every time I have asked the president of the United States to step up in every way the help permitted by American law, he has generously agreed, and his people have approved.

But things have advanced further. Today, the life of France is at stake – or at least France's essence of life. Our struggle, which grows more painful each day, becomes futile if in persevering we can perceive no hope, however distant, of a shared victory.

The superiority and quality of British aviation is improving. Clouds of warplanes from across the Atlantic must come to crush the evil power that is dominating Europe.

Despite our losses, the democracies still possess enormous power. We are entitled to hope that the day will arrive when all that power will be mustered. That is why our hearts must remain hopeful. That, too, is why we have wished France to keep a free government and have left Paris.

It was essential to prevent HITLER from suppressing the legal government and announcing to the world that France had only a puppet government, in his pay, similar to those he has been trying to establish elsewhere.

During the struggles of our history, the French people have known times when we were beleaguered by the advice of defeatists. But our greatness lies in never abdicating.

Whatever happens in the days ahead, the French people are going to suffer. May they be worthy of the nation's history. May they unite as brothers. May they hold fast around their wounded motherland.

The day of resurrection will arrive.

Maximilien Robespierre
French revolutionary politician

Maximilien Marie Isidore de Robespierre (1758–94) was born at Arras, of Irish parentage. He became a successful advocate, and entered the Estates-General (National Assembly) in 1789. Aligning himself with the far left, he spoke at virtually every sitting. He soon became immensely popular within the Paris Commune, the revolutionary government of Paris (1789–95). He also found favour with the extreme republican members of the Jacobin Club, the powerful left-wing group of deputies from Breton. His impartiality and support of democratic principles won him the nickname 'L'incorruptible'. In 1792, he resigned his office as public accuser and petitioned for a revolutionary tribunal and a new convention. Elected for Paris to the National Convention – the constitutional and legislative assembly (1792–5) – he emerged as leader of the diverse political faction La Montagne, which was strenuously opposed to the Girondins, whom, with the support of Georges Danton and Jean-Paul Marat, he helped destroy; the Girondins were proscribed following Marat's murder in July 1793. With support from the Jacobins, he brought about Louis XVI's execution on 21 January 1793. The same year, Robespierre was elected to the Committee of Public Safety, created to defend France from both internal and external enemies. With real power at his disposal for the first time, he purged the National Assembly of ultra-revolutionaries in the bloody Reign of Terror of 1793–4. He also introduced strict economic control, and began to establish a form of welfare state. However, his growing autocracy coincided with a new era of ascendancy for the army, resulting from successes such as the Battle of Fleurus in 1794, and the prospect of Robespierre heading a dictatorship finally spurred his enemies into action. On 27 July 1794, he was denounced in the Convention, and a deputy called for his arrest. He was apprehended by the National Guard, after being shot in the jaw, and the following day he and 21 of his supporters were guillotined without trial.

'The day has finally come'
8 June 1794, Paris, France

The Roman Catholic Church had held enormous influence under the *ancien regime* of pre-Revolutionary France, owning a fifth of the country's land. Following the Revolution, the clergy lost their power and the Church's property was confiscated by the state. An atheistic Cult of Reason was established in its place, celebrating the glories of human intelligence.

Influenced by the deist theories of Jean-Jacques Rousseau, Robespierre rejected the Cult of Reason. In March 1794, one of its founders, Jacques Hébert, was executed. The following month, Robespierre, perhaps seeking to unify the masses against the Revolution's enemies, conceived a new state religion based on deism.

The Cult of the Supreme Being embraced the worship of a creator God and rejected atheism. On 7 May, Robespierre proposed the new religion to the Convention, which made a decree recognizing the Supreme Being. Robespierre, as president, inaugurated the religion during a special public ceremony on 8 June, at which he made two short speeches, effigies were burned and a new statue was unveiled.

A careful thinker and a persuasive political speaker, he had been an important voice in the Assembly and Convention. Now, as he saw his ambitions fulfilled, he expressed his excitement in a florid oratorical style, translated here by the editor. But Robespierre's popularity had waned as his power grew, and he himself faced the guillotine some weeks later.

French republicans: the day has finally come – that day of eternal good fortune which the French people consecrate to the Supreme Being! Never before has this world which he created offered up to him a spectacle so worthy of his attention. He has seen tyranny, crime and fraud reign over the earth. Now, at this moment, he sees a whole nation – which has in its clutches all the oppressors of the human race – rest for a moment from its heroic efforts to raise its thoughts and vows towards the Supreme Being, who entrusted it with the mission to undertake them, and the power to execute them!

Is this not he whose immortal hand, in engraving the code of justice and equality on the heart of man, has inscribed there the death sentence of tyrants? Is this not he who, from the beginning of time, decreed the

Republic, and commanded – for every century and for every people – liberty, good faith and justice?

He did not create kings so that they might devour the human race; he did not create priests to tether us like base animals to the chariots of kings, and to offer the world an example of depravity, of pride, of betrayal, of greed, of debauchery, of falsehood. He created the universe to demonstrate his power; he created men to help one another, to love one another and to arrive at happiness through virtue.

He it was who filled the breast of the triumphant oppressor with remorse and dread; the heart of the oppressed innocent with serenity and pride; he it was who compelled the just man to hate the wicked and the wicked man to respect the just; he it was who decorated the face of beauty with modesty, to enhance its loveliness; he it was who caused mothers' bellies to quiver with tenderness and joy; he it was who bathed the son's eyes with fragrant tears as his mother pressed him to her breast; he it was who subdued the most urgent and tender of passions to the sublime love of the motherland; he it was who decked the natural world in grace, richness and majesty. Everything that is good is his work, or else it is he himself: evil belongs to the corrupted man who oppresses or permits the oppression of his own people.

The author of nature has linked all mortals by an immense chain of love and joy; perish those tyrants who have dared to break it!

French republicans: it is for you to purify the earth which they have soiled, and restore to it the justice they have banished! Freedom and justice have issued together from the breast of divinity: among men, one cannot survive without the other. Generous people: do you aspire to victory over all your enemies? Practise justice; and render unto God only the veneration of which he is worthy. People: under his auspices, let us deliver ourselves today to the transports of pure elation! Tomorrow we shall resume our struggle against vice and tyranny; we shall offer the world an example of republican virtue, and that will be to honour him still more!

[*Between the two speeches, an effigy representing atheism was burned, to be replaced with a statue representing wisdom.*]

This monster, vomited onto France by the spirit of kings, has been returned to nothing! May all the crimes and all the miseries of the world be destroyed with it! Armed, one after another, with the daggers of fanaticism and the poisons of atheism, the kings conspired perpetually to assassinate humanity. If they could no longer disfigure divinity with superstition and thus associate it with their infamy, then they made every effort to banish it from the earth, to rule here alone by criminal means.

People: you must no longer fear their sacrilegious plots; they can no more sever the world from the breast of its author than the remorse from their own hearts! Unfortunates: raise your lowered heads; you can once again lift your eyes to Heaven without fear! Heroes of the motherland: your unstinting devotion is not by any means an inspired lunacy; the agents of tyranny may assassinate you, but they lack the power to destroy you altogether. You can now turn again to higher thoughts; you can bind your brief life to God himself and to immortality. May nature reclaim its brilliance; and wisdom its empire! The Supreme Being is in no way destroyed. Above all, our unvindicated enemies strove to drive wisdom out of the Republic: it is for wisdom alone to strengthen empires, for wisdom alone to vouchsafe the fruits of our enterprise! Let us therefore bring wisdom to bear on all our undertakings! Let us be grave and discreet in our deliberations, like men representing the interests of the world; let us be ardent and unyielding in our wrath towards these tyrannical conspirators; unperturbable in danger, patient in labour, fearsome in retaliation, modest and vigilant in success; let us be generous towards the virtuous, compassionate towards the unfortunate, relentless towards the wicked, just towards everyone; let us never rely on prosperity without complication, or triumph without obstacle, nor on anything which depends upon fortune or on the perversity of others: let us depend upon nothing but our loyalty and our virtue, the sole but certain guarantees of our independence; let us crush the impious union of kings by the greatness of our character, even more than by the strength of our arms.

Frenchmen: you are waging war on kings; you are therefore worthy of honouring Divinity! Being of Beings, Author of Nature: the brutish slave, the filthy instrument of despotism, the cruel, treacherous aristocrat outrages you by invoking your name, but we, the defenders of liberty, can abandon ourselves with confidence to your paternal breast!

Being of Beings: we have no need to address you with unjust prayers. You know well those creatures which sprang from your hands; their needs do not escape your attention, any more than do their most secret thoughts. Hatred for bad faith and tyranny burns in our hearts, alongside love of justice and of the motherland: our blood is flowing for the cause of humanity: behold our prayer, behold our sacrifices, behold the praise we offer unto you!

John D Rockefeller, Jr
American tycoon and philanthropist

John Davison Rockefeller, Jr (1874–1960) was born in Cleveland, Ohio, the only son of the oil magnate John D Rockefeller. He was educated at the Browning School in New York City and Brown University in Providence, Rhode Island. He joined his father's business, then became chairman of the Rockefeller Institute of Medical Research, and built the Rockefeller Center in New York (completed 1939). He also established the Rockefeller Foundation and Rockefeller University in New York City. In 1945, he donated the land in Manhattan on which the headquarters of the United Nations were built; and in 1958 he donated $5 million to establish New York City's Lincoln Center for the Performing Arts. He funded numerous conservation projects, buying and donating land for several National Parks, and restoring colonial Williamsburg in Virginia. His six children included John Davison Rockefeller III (1906–78) who became chairman of the Rockefeller Foundation in 1952, and Nelson Aldrich Rockefeller (1908–79), who served as governor of New York, 1959–73 and US vice president, 1974–7.

'The brotherhood of man and the fatherhood of God'
8 July 1941, radio broadcast from New York City, USA

This radio address was originally intended to help raise funds for the newly-created United Service Organizations (USO), but soon became famous for its evocation of true-blue American values.

The USO was established in February 1941 to provide off-duty recreation for US armed forces. FRANKLIN D ROOSEVELT, who served – like subsequent US presidents – as its honorary chairman, resisted attempts by the Department of Defence to bring it under military control. Instead it was formed as a charitable corporation, pooling resources from the Salvation Army, the YMCA and YWCA, the National Jewish Welfare Board, the National Catholic Community Service and the Travelers Aid Association.

Originally proposed by General GEORGE C MARSHALL, the USO offered 'wholesome' recreational services, food and entertainment. Staffed mainly by volunteers, it soon succeeded in booking well-known entertainers such as Bob Hope, Bing Crosby and the Marx Brothers – a practice which it has maintained to the present day.

John D Rockefeller, Jr – two of whose sons served in World War II – was a founding member of USO. He helped raise funds for the organization, partly through radio broadcasts like this one, which explains and promotes its goals. The best remembered section, however, comes at the end, where Rockefeller details his personal and political philosophy in a famous series of 'I believe' statements. This simple, democratic creed was subsequently displayed on a commemorative plaque at the Rockefeller Center. It was also quoted in part by Michael Howard, then leader of the UK Conservative Party, on campaign posters in 2003.

Fellow parents and neighbours: we stand together tonight on a common basis and with a common purpose. The common basis is that we are each of us the parent of a son who is in the defence forces of our country. I am proud, as you are, that my son, like yours, is serving his country in this important field. Like you I would to God that none of our boys should have to go into war training, for I hate war. At the same time, you could never have forgiven yourself, nor could I, with my son, had I put a straw in the way of his going, or done anything other than back him to the limit as he volunteered for service.

The common purpose which unites us is to see to it that there are made available to these sons of ours in the time they spend outside of the training areas, opportunities that will satisfy their normal desire for wholesome companionship and recreation, and will protect them from those forces that seek their undoing, and influences that will develop that splendid something called morale, without which the finest military training can not make a good soldier.

In the service, these sons of ours are only 'Private Jones' or 'Seaman Smith'. To us they are our pride and joy. They have often meant heartache and sleepless nights. But what worthwhile boy does not have his problems, his temptations and his defeats as well as his victories? For a quarter of a century we have watched them grow and develop as we have dreamed of their future.

And now they have gone out from our homes into a new and strange life to become the proud defenders of their country, but they have not gone out from our hearts; they are more than ever in our thoughts. We do not propose to see what we have been doing for them all these years go for naught. We do not propose to have them cut off after training hours, from activities that are normal and wholesome. It is to provide these activities that we so gladly turn to the United Service Organizations, which are fitted, each one of them, not only by long years of successful experience in their respective fields, but also by similar work in the last war, to do for our sons what we covet for them and they eagerly seek, after the day's work is done …

Some people say, 'But too much is being done for the trainees; what they need is to be made hard and tough and not to be babied and pampered. We are not sympathetic with the work of the USO.'

Those who say that the man who is tough makes the best soldier know little of human nature. He who carries on when physical forces are exhausted is the man who is buoyed up by the spiritual force called morale, who is fighting, not for the lust of killing, but for a principle, a great cause, dearer than life itself. I certainly do not want my son made tough by his military training; nor do you. I do not want my son, just because he is a soldier, to be abandoned by those influences that make for character.

I want him to come back home, whatever his military experiences may be, still a man with ideals, holding duty and honour above life. That you share fully with me these views I am confident. It is for that reason that we, the parents and neighbours of these boys, want to see provided for them – when outside of the training areas – a wholesome atmosphere, the companionship of fine women and girls, recreations that are normal and influences that will keep them clean, and worthy.

But unfortunately, there are far too few such places available as yet for soldiers and sailors when off duty. Many of the boys, as they flock into the nearby towns and cities, are today having that enervating and wholly discouraging feeling forced upon them that nobody cares. There is nothing that more quickly leads to demoralization. That is why the campaign for the USO must be pressed, not only to success, but to an overwhelming success. Nothing could prove more conclusively to our defence forces that the people of this country are solidly behind them and that everybody cares about their well being, than to have the fund largely oversubscribed. Moreover, every dollar, every penny that can be secured is needed, and more too, to provide the facilities which we as parents have promised our sons, and we as citizens have promised our defence forces.

Not long since, I sought to formulate in my own mind the things that make life most worth living, without which it would have little meaning. Some of these things have been relegated to bygone days; some are regarded as long since outgrown. Nevertheless I believe they are, every one of them, fundamental and eternal. They are the principles on which my wife and I have tried to bring up our family; they are the principles in which my father believed and by which he governed his life. They are the principles, many of them, which I learned at my mother's knee. They point the way to usefulness and happiness in life, to courage and peace in death. If they mean to you what they mean to me, they may perhaps be helpful also to our sons for their guidance and inspiration. Let me state them:

I believe in the supreme worth of the individual and in his right to life, liberty and the pursuit of happiness.[1]

[1] Rockefeller quotes from the US Declaration of Independence.

I believe that every right implies a responsibility; every opportunity, an obligation; every possession, a duty.

I believe that the law was made for man and not man for the law; that government is the servant of the people and not their master.

I believe in the dignity of labour, whether with head or hand; that the world owes no man a living but that it owes every man an opportunity to make a living.

I believe that thrift is essential to well-ordered living and that economy is a prime requisite of a sound financial structure, whether in government, business or personal affairs.

I believe that truth and justice are fundamental to an enduring social order.

I believe in the sacredness of a promise, that a man's word should be as good as his bond; that character – not wealth or power or position – is of supreme worth.

I believe that the rendering of useful service is the common duty of mankind and that only in the purifying fire of sacrifice is the dross of selfishness consumed and the greatness of the human soul set free.

I believe in an all-wise and all-loving God, named by whatever name; and that the individual's highest fulfilment, greatest happiness and widest usefulness are to be found in living in harmony with his will.

I believe that love is the greatest thing in the world; that it alone can overcome hate; that right can and will triumph over might.

These are the principles, however formulated, for which all good men and women throughout the world, irrespective of race or creed, education, social position or occupation are standing; and for which many of them are suffering and dying. These are the principles upon which alone a new world, recognizing the brotherhood of man and the fatherhood of God, can be established.

It is to help usher in this new day that our sons have dedicated themselves to the service of their country. And it is that they may be kept worthy of this high service that we call upon all parents and neighbours in this city and throughout the length and breadth of this fair land to stand with us in supporting the United Service Organizations and their campaign.

Franklin D Roosevelt
American statesman

Franklin Delano Roosevelt (1882–1945) was born into a wealthy family in Hyde Park, New York, a distant cousin of THEODORE ROOSEVELT. He was educated in Europe and at Harvard and Columbia law schools. He was admitted to the New York Bar in 1907 and later served as a New York state senator (1910–13) and as Assistant Secretary of the Navy (1913–20), before becoming the Democratic nominee for the vice presidency in 1920. Stricken by polio and paralysed (1921–3), he was nonetheless elected governor of New York (1928–32). He defeated Herbert Hoover in the presidential election of 1932, in which the repeal of alcohol prohibition was a decisive issue. He came to power during the Great Depression of 1929–39; he met this by launching his innovative New Deal programme, which involved abandonment of the gold standard, devaluation of the dollar, state intervention in the credit market, agricultural price support and the passage of a Social Security Act (1935) which provided for unemployment and old-age insurance. On the strength of his success in these reforms, Roosevelt was re-elected by a landslide in 1936, and he secured a third term in 1940 and a fourth in 1944. Roosevelt inculcated a new spirit of hope through his skilful and optimistic radio 'fireside chats', and constructed a new rural-urban 'majority coalition' for the Democratic Party. During the late 1930s he endeavoured to avoid involvement in the coming European conflict, but on the outbreak of World War II he modified the USA's neutrality in favour of the Allies (for example, by providing armaments and equipment through the Lend–Lease Programme). Eventually the USA was brought fully into the conflict by Japan's attack on Pearl Harbor (December 1941). A conference with WINSTON CHURCHILL at sea produced the 'Atlantic Charter', a statement of peace aims; and there were other notable meetings with Churchill and JOSEPH STALIN at Teheran (1943) and Yalta (1945). He died three weeks before the Nazi surrender.

'The only thing we have to fear is fear itself'
4 March 1933, Washington, DC, USA

Franklin D Roosevelt's first inaugural address, delivered in the depths of the Great Depression, brought a much-needed message of hope. With over half the American workforce unemployed, farm prices at rock bottom and industry in disarray, the country was in despair. On accepting the nomination as Democratic candidate for the 1932 election, Roosevelt had promised a 'new deal for the American people'. Now he was able to begin implementing policies that were little short of revolutionary in a country deeply mistrustful of socialism.

Roosevelt had been remarkably vague during the election campaign about how he planned to tackle the huge economic problems facing the nation. Now he set out his vision clearly and confidently, speaking both to the crowd gathered at the White House and to the country at large via radio broadcast, which was to become his favourite medium.

His tone is solemn, but displays the forthright style that was his trademark. All the major tenets of the New Deal are here, presented almost as a covenant between the government and the people. The speech is one of extraordinary optimism, portraying a bright future and evoking the still-potent national mythology of the pioneer spirit without ever underestimating the impact of the Depression on ordinary citizens.

The immediate result was the so-called 'Hundred Days', in which an emergency session of Congress pushed through most of the necessary reforming legislation.

I am certain that my fellow Americans expect that, on my induction into the presidency, I will address them with a candour and a decision which the present situation of our nation impels. This is pre-eminently the time to speak the truth, the whole truth, frankly and boldly. Nor need we shrink from honestly facing conditions in our country today. This great nation will endure as it has endured, will revive and will prosper.

So, first of all, let me assert my firm belief that the only thing we have to fear is fear itself – nameless, unreasoning, unjustified terror which paralyses needed efforts to convert retreat into advance. In every dark hour of our national life, a leadership of frankness and vigour has met with that understanding and support of the people themselves which is essential to victory. I am convinced that you will again give that support to leadership in these critical days.

In such a spirit, on my part and on yours, we face our common difficulties. They concern, thank God, only material things. Values have shrunken to fantastic levels; taxes have risen; our ability to pay has fallen; government of all kinds is faced by serious curtailment of income; the means of exchange are frozen in the currents of trade; the withered leaves of industrial enterprise lie on every side; farmers find no markets for their produce; the savings of many years in thousands of families are gone.

More important, a host of unemployed citizens face the grim problem of existence and an equally great number toil with little return. Only a foolish optimist can deny the dark realities of the moment.

Yet our distress comes from no failure of substance. We are stricken by no plague of locusts. Compared with the perils which our forefathers conquered because they believed and were not afraid, we have still much to be thankful for. Nature still offers her bounty and human efforts have multiplied it. Plenty is at our doorstep, but a generous use of it languishes in the very sight of the supply. Primarily, this is because rulers of the exchange of mankind's goods have failed through their own stubbornness and their own incompetence, have admitted their failure and have abdicated. Practices of the unscrupulous money-changers stand indicted in the court of public opinion, rejected by the hearts and minds of men.

True they have tried, but their efforts have been cast in the pattern of an outworn tradition. Faced by failure of credit, they have proposed only the lending of more money. Stripped of the lure of profit by which to induce our people to follow their false leadership, they have resorted to exhortations, pleading tearfully for restored confidence. They know only the rules of a generation of self-seekers. They have no vision, and when there is no vision the people perish.

The money-changers have fled from their high seats in the temple of our civilization. We may now restore that temple to the ancient truths. The measure of the restoration lies in the extent to which we apply social values more noble than mere monetary profit.

Happiness lies not in the mere possession of money; it lies in the joy of achievement, in the thrill of creative effort. The joy and moral stimulation of work no longer must be forgotten in the mad chase of evanescent profits. These dark days will be worth all they cost us if they teach us that our true destiny is not to be ministered unto but to minister to ourselves and to our fellow men.

Recognition of the falsity of material wealth as the standard of success goes hand in hand with the abandonment of the false belief that public office and high political position are to be valued only by the standards of pride of place and personal profit; and there must be an end to a conduct in banking and in business which too often has given to a sacred trust the likeness of callous and selfish wrongdoing. Small wonder that confidence languishes, for it thrives only on honesty, on honour, on the sacredness of obligations, on faithful protection, on unselfish performance; without them it cannot live. Restoration calls, however, not for changes in ethics alone. This nation asks for action, and action now.

Our greatest primary task is to put people to work. This is no unsolvable problem if we face it wisely and courageously. It can be accomplished in part by direct recruiting by the government itself, treating the task as we would treat the emergency of a war, but at the same time, through this employment, accomplishing greatly needed projects to stimulate and reorganize the use of our natural resources.

Hand in hand with this, we must frankly recognize the overbalance of population in our industrial centres and – by engaging on a national scale in a redistribution – endeavour to provide a better use of the land for those best fitted for the land. The task can be helped by definite efforts to raise the values of agricultural products and with this the power to purchase the output of our cities. It can be helped by preventing realistically the tragedy of the growing loss, through foreclosure, of our small homes and our farms. It can be helped by insistence that the federal, state, and local governments act forthwith on the demand that their cost be drastically reduced. It can be helped by the unifying of relief activities which today are often scattered, uneconomical and unequal. It can be helped by national planning for and supervision of all forms of transportation and of communications and other utilities which have a definitely public character. There are many ways in which it can be helped, but it can never be helped merely by talking about it. We must act and act quickly.

Finally, in our progress toward a resumption of work we require two safeguards against a return of the evils of the old order: there must be a strict supervision of all banking and credits and investments, so that there will be an end to speculation with other people's money; and there must be provision for an adequate but sound currency.

These are the lines of attack. I shall presently urge upon a new Congress, in special session, detailed measures for their fulfilment, and I shall seek the immediate assistance of the several states.

Through this programme of action, we address ourselves to putting our own national house in order and making income balance outgo. Our international trade relations, though vastly important, are in point of time and necessity secondary to the establishment of a sound national economy. I favour as a practical policy the putting of first things first. I shall spare no effort to restore world trade by international economic readjustment, but the emergency at home cannot wait on that accomplishment.

The basic thought that guides these specific means of national recovery is not narrowly nationalistic. It is the insistence, as a first consideration, upon the interdependence of the various elements in and parts of the United States – a recognition of the old and permanently important manifestation of the American spirit of the pioneer. It is the way to recovery. It is the immediate way. It is the strongest assurance that the recovery will endure.

In the field of world policy I would dedicate this nation to the policy of the good neighbour – the neighbour who resolutely respects himself and, because he does so, respects the rights of others; the neighbour who respects his obligations and respects the sanctity of his agreements in and with a world of neighbours.

If I read the temper of our people correctly, we now realize as we have never realized before our interdependence on each other; that we cannot merely take but we must give as well; that if we are to go forward, we must move as a trained and loyal army, willing to sacrifice for the good of a common discipline, because without such discipline no progress is made, no leadership becomes effective. We are, I know, ready and willing to submit our lives and property to such discipline, because it makes possible a leadership which aims at a larger good. This I propose to offer, pledging that the larger purposes will bind upon us all as a sacred obligation with a unity of duty hitherto evoked only in time of armed strife.

With this pledge taken, I assume unhesitatingly the leadership of this great army of our people, dedicated to a disciplined attack upon our common problems.

Action in this image and to this end is feasible under the form of government which we have inherited from our ancestors. Our constitution is so simple and practical that it is possible always to meet extraordinary needs by changes in emphasis and arrangement without loss of essential form. That is why our constitutional system has proved itself the most superbly enduring political mechanism the modern world has produced. It has met every stress of vast expansion of territory, of foreign wars, of bitter internal strife, of world relations.

It is to be hoped that the normal balance of executive and legislative authority may be wholly adequate to meet the unprecedented task before us. But it may be that an unprecedented demand and need for undelayed action may call for temporary departure from that normal balance of public procedure.

I am prepared under my constitutional duty to recommend the measures that a stricken nation in the midst of a stricken world may require. These measures, or such other measures as the Congress may build out of its experience and wisdom, I shall seek, within my constitutional authority, to bring to speedy adoption.

But in the event that the Congress shall fail to take one of these two courses, and in the event that the national emergency is still critical, I shall not evade the clear course of duty that will then confront me. I shall ask the Congress for the one remaining instrument to meet the crisis — broad executive power to wage a war against the emergency, as great as the power that would be given to me if we were in fact invaded by a foreign foe.

For the trust reposed in me, I will return the courage and the devotion that befit the time. I can do no less.

We face the arduous days that lie before us in the warm courage of national unity; with the clear consciousness of seeking old and precious moral values; with the clean satisfaction that comes from the stern performance of duty by old and young alike. We aim at the assurance of a rounded and permanent national life.

We do not distrust the future of essential democracy. The people of the United States have not failed. In their need they have registered a mandate that they want direct, vigorous action. They have asked for discipline and direction under leadership. They have made me the present instrument of their wishes. In the spirit of the gift I take it.

In this dedication of a nation we humbly ask the blessing of God. May he protect each and every one of us. May he guide me in the days to come.

❧

'A world founded upon four essential human freedoms'
6 January 1941, Washington, DC, USA

❧

Article II, section 3, clause 1 of the US Constitution requires the president to provide Congress 'from time to time' with 'information of the state of the Union'. Since 1790, the State of the Union Address has been given once a year, usually in January. Every president, including GEORGE WASHINGTON, has either spoken directly to the legislature or given written submissions, intimating executive policy for the coming term. This is a showcase event, and as the president makes his way to the podium he is usually greeted by a standing ovation.

The Japanese attack on Pearl Harbor was still eleven months off when Roosevelt gave his 'Four Freedoms' speech, but his conviction that American entry into World War II was inevitable runs through his address to Congress. Bold and straightforward in tone, it is characteristic of Roosevelt's style. Fully aware that Americans feared becoming entangled in another European war, FDR proposed to raise taxes to cover defence spending and broaden assistance to the Allies' war effort – though he carefully neglected to mention the proposed Lend–Lease Act by name. (It was passed in March.)

This discourse on the meaning and responsibilities of freedom in a democracy has had many imitators. It is among the best-known of presidential speeches, and is widely considered one of the most influential speeches of the 20th century.

❧

I address you, the members of the 77th Congress, at a moment unprecedented in the history of the Union. I use the word 'unprecedented', because at no previous time has American security been as seriously threatened from without as it is today.

Since the permanent formation of our government under the Constitution, in 1789, most of the periods of crisis in our history have related to our domestic affairs. Fortunately, only one of these – the four-year war between the states[1] – ever threatened our national unity. Today, thank God, 130 million Americans, in 48 States, have forgotten points of the compass in our national unity.

[1] The American Civil War of 1861–5.

It is true that prior to 1914 the United States often had been disturbed by events in other continents. We had even engaged in two wars with European nations and in a number of undeclared wars in the West Indies, in the Mediterranean and in the Pacific for the maintenance of American rights and for the principles of peaceful commerce. But in no case had a serious threat been raised against our national safety or our continued independence.

What I seek to convey is the historic truth that the United States as a nation has at all times maintained clear, definite opposition to any attempt to lock us in behind an ancient Chinese wall while the procession of civilization went past. Today, thinking of our children and of their children, we oppose enforced isolation for ourselves or for any other part of the Americas …

Every realist knows that the democratic way of life is at this moment being directly assailed in every part of the world – assailed either by arms, or by secret spreading of poisonous propaganda by those who seek to destroy unity and promote discord in nations that are still at peace. During 16 long months, this assault has blotted out the whole pattern of democratic life in an appalling number of independent nations, great and small. The assailants are still on the march, threatening other nations, great and small.

Therefore, as your president, performing my constitutional duty to 'give to the Congress information of the state of the Union', I find it, unhappily, necessary to report that the future and the safety of our country and of our democracy are overwhelmingly involved in events far beyond our borders.

Armed defence of democratic existence is now being gallantly waged in four continents. If that defence fails, all the population and all the resources of Europe, Asia, Africa and Australasia will be dominated by the conquerors. Let us remember that the total of those populations and their resources in those four continents greatly exceeds the sum total of the population and the resources of the whole of the Western hemisphere – many times over.

In times like these it is immature – and incidentally, untrue – for anybody to brag that an unprepared America, single-handed and with one hand tied behind its back, can hold off the whole world. No realistic American can expect from a dictator's peace international generosity, or return of true independence, or world disarmament, or freedom of expression, or freedom of religion – or even good business. Such a peace would bring no security for us or for our neighbours. 'Those, who would give up essential liberty to purchase a little temporary safety, deserve neither liberty nor safety.'[2]

[2] Roosevelt quotes from *Pennsylvania Assembly: Reply to the Governor*, published by BENJAMIN FRANKLIN on 11 November 1755. An amended version is engraved on a plaque at the Statue of Liberty in New York City.

As a nation, we may take pride in the fact that we are soft-hearted; but we cannot afford to be soft-headed … We must especially beware of that small group of selfish men who would clip the wings of the American eagle in order to feather their own nests.

I have recently pointed out how quickly the tempo of modern warfare could bring into our very midst the physical attack which we must eventually expect if the dictator nations win this war …

As long as the aggressor nations maintain the offensive, they – not we – will choose the time and the place and the method of their attack. That is why the future of all the American republics is today in serious danger. That is why this Annual Message to the Congress is unique in our history. That is why every member of the executive branch of the government and every member of the Congress faces great responsibility and great accountability. The need of the moment is that our actions and our policy should be devoted primarily – almost exclusively – to meeting this foreign peril. For all our domestic problems are now a part of the great emergency.

Just as our national policy in internal affairs has been based upon a decent respect for the rights and the dignity of all our fellow men within our gates, so our national policy in foreign affairs has been based on a decent respect for the rights and dignity of all nations, large and small. And the justice of morality must and will win in the end …

Today it is abundantly evident that American citizens everywhere are demanding and supporting speedy and complete action in recognition of obvious danger.

Therefore, the immediate need is a swift and driving increase in our armament production. Leaders of industry and labour have responded to our summons. Goals of speed have been set. In some cases these goals are being reached ahead of time; in some cases we are on schedule; in other cases there are slight but not serious delays; and in some cases – and I am sorry to say very important cases – we are all concerned by the slowness of the accomplishment of our plans … None of us will be satisfied until the job is done …

New circumstances are constantly begetting new needs for our safety. I shall ask this Congress for greatly increased new appropriations and authorizations to carry on what we have begun. I also ask this Congress for authority and for funds sufficient to manufacture additional munitions and war supplies of many kinds, to be turned over to those nations which are now in actual war with aggressor nations. Our most useful and immediate role is to act as an arsenal for them as well as for ourselves. They do not need manpower, but they do need billions of dollars' worth of the weapons of defence.

The time is near when they will not be able to pay for them all in ready cash. We cannot, and we will not, tell them that they must surrender, merely because of present inability to pay for the weapons which we know they must have … For what we send abroad, we shall be repaid within a reasonable time following the close of hostilities, in similar materials, or, at our option, in other goods of many kinds, which they can produce and which we need.

Let us say to the democracies: 'We Americans are vitally concerned in your defence of freedom. We are putting forth our energies, our resources and our organizing powers to give you the strength to regain and maintain a free world. We shall send you, in ever-increasing numbers, ships, planes, tanks, guns. This is our purpose and our pledge.'

In fulfilment of this purpose we will not be intimidated by the threats of dictators that they will regard as a breach of international law or as an act of war our aid to the democracies which dare to resist their aggression. Such aid is not an act of war, even if a dictator should unilaterally proclaim it so to be.

When the dictators, if the dictators, are ready to make war upon us, they will not wait for an act of war on our part. They did not wait for Norway or Belgium or the Netherlands to commit an act of war. Their only interest is in a new one-way international law, which lacks mutuality in its observance and therefore becomes an instrument of oppression.

The happiness of future generations of Americans may well depend upon how effective and how immediate we can make our aid felt. No-one can tell the exact character of the emergency situations that we may be called upon to meet. The nation's hands must not be tied when the nation's life is in danger …

As men do not live by bread alone,[3] they do not fight by armaments alone. Those who man our defences, and those behind them who build our defences, must have the stamina and the courage which come from unshakable belief in the manner of life which they are defending. The mighty action that we are calling for cannot be based on a disregard of all things worth fighting for.

The nation takes great satisfaction and much strength from the things which have been done to make its people conscious of their individual stake in the preservation of democratic life in America. Those things have toughened the fibre of our people, have renewed their faith and strengthened their devotion to the institutions we make ready to protect.

Certainly this is no time for any of us to stop thinking about the social and economic problems which are the root cause of the social revolution which is today a supreme factor in the world.

For there is nothing mysterious about the foundations of a healthy and strong democracy. The basic things expected by our people of their political and economic systems are simple. They are: equality of opportunity for youth and for others; jobs for those who can work; security for those who need it; the ending of special privilege for the few; the preservation of civil liberties for all; the enjoyment of the fruits of scientific progress in a wider and constantly rising standard of living …

I have called for personal sacrifice. I am assured of the willingness of almost all Americans to respond to that call. A part of the sacrifice means the payment of more money in taxes. In my budget message I shall recommend that a greater portion of this great defence programme be paid for from taxation than we are paying today. No person should try, or be allowed, to get rich out of this programme; and the principle of tax payments in accordance with ability to pay should be constantly before our eyes to guide our legislation. If the Congress maintains these principles, the voters, putting patriotism ahead of pocketbooks, will give you their applause.

In the future days, which we seek to make secure, we look forward to a

[3] 'Man doth not live by bread only, but by every word that proceedeth out of the mouth of the Lord doth man live' – originally Deuteronomy 8:3; also quoted by JESUS at Matthew 4:4 and Luke 4:4.

world founded upon four essential human freedoms.

The first is freedom of speech and expression – everywhere in the world.

The second is freedom of every person to worship God in his own way – everywhere in the world.

The third is freedom from want – which, translated into world terms, means economic understandings which will secure to every nation a healthy peacetime life for its inhabitants – everywhere in the world.

The fourth is freedom from fear – which, translated into world terms, means a worldwide reduction of armaments, to such a point and in such a thorough fashion, that no nation will be in a position to commit an act of physical aggression against any neighbour – anywhere in the world.

That is no vision of a distant millennium. It is a definite basis for a kind of world attainable in our own time and generation. That kind of world is the very antithesis of the so-called new order of tyranny which the dictators seek to create with the crash of a bomb …

This nation has placed its destiny in the hands and heads and hearts of its millions of free men and women; and its faith in freedom under the guidance of God. Freedom means the supremacy of human rights everywhere. Our support goes to those who struggle to gain those rights or keep them. Our strength is our unity of purpose. To that high concept there can be no end save victory.

&

'Our Christmas celebrations have been darkened'
24 December 1943, radio broadcast from Hyde Park, New York, USA

&

Straightforward in tone and full of reassurance, this was the 27th of Roosevelt's 30 radio 'fireside chats', and the only one not broadcast from the White House. Christmas Eve 1943 found the president in his private home along the Hudson River, 'Springwood' in Hyde Park, New York, which he visited some 200 times during his presidency.

Roosevelt understood well the power of an informal radio broadcast to communicate with such a large and disparate nation – though the phrase 'fireside chat' is thought to have been coined by Harry Butcher, Washington manager of the Columbia Broadcasting System. The speech-writers were instructed to make each speech short, simple and effective, and the broadcasts continued from 1933 until 1944. 'I never saw him – but I knew him,' wrote the academic and poet Carl Carmer in 1945. 'He came into our house, the president of these United States, calling us friends.'

The USA had now been at war for two years, and American servicemen were fighting in all parts of the world. Roosevelt used this Christmas broadcast to pay tribute to them, offer comfort to their loved ones at home and explain some of his diplomatic efforts with other Allied leaders. By describing conferences he had held during the past few weeks with WINSTON CHURCHILL and the Chinese leader Chiang Kai-shek in Cairo; and with Churchill and JOSEPH STALIN in Teheran, he was able to present a reassuring picture of unity and military strength.

&

My friends: I have recently returned from extensive journeyings in the region of the Mediterranean and as far as the borders of Russia. I have conferred with the leaders of Britain and Russia and China on military matters of the present – especially on plans for stepping up our successful attack on our enemies as quickly as possible and from many different points of the compass …

That this is truly a world war was demonstrated to me when arrangements were being made with our overseas broadcasting agencies for the time to speak today to our soldiers, sailors, marines and merchant seamen in every part of the world.

In fixing the time for this broadcast, we took into consideration that at this moment here in the United States, and in the Caribbean and on the north-east coast of South America, it is afternoon. In Alaska and in Hawaii and the mid-Pacific, it is still morning. In Iceland, in Great Britain, in North Africa, in Italy and the Middle East, it is now evening. In the south-west Pacific, in Australia, in China and Burma and India, it is already Christmas Day. So we can correctly say that at this moment, in those Far Eastern parts where Americans are fighting, today is tomorrow.

But everywhere throughout the world – throughout this war that covers the world – there is a special spirit that has warmed our hearts since our earliest childhood, a spirit that brings us close to our homes, our families, our friends and neighbours – the Christmas spirit of 'peace on earth, goodwill toward men.' It is an unquenchable spirit.

During the past years of international gangsterism and brutal aggression in Europe and in Asia, our Christmas celebrations have been darkened with apprehension for the future. We have said, 'Merry Christmas – a Happy New Year', but we have known in our hearts that the clouds which have hung over our world have prevented us from saying it with full sincerity and conviction …

But on Christmas Eve this year, I can say to you that at last we may look forward into the future with real, substantial confidence that, however great the cost, 'peace on earth, goodwill toward men' can be and will be realized and ensured. This year I can say that. Last year I could not do more than express a hope. Today I express a certainty – though the cost may be high and the time may be long.

Within the past year – within the past few weeks – history has been made, and it is far better history for the whole human race than any that we have known, or even dared to hope for, in these tragic times through which we pass.

A great beginning was made in the Moscow conference last October by Mr Molotov, Mr EDEN, and our own Mr Hull.[1] There and then the way was paved for the later meetings. At Cairo and Teheran we devoted ourselves not only to military matters; we devoted ourselves also to consideration of the future – to plans for the kind of world which alone can justify all the sacrifices of this war.

Of course, as you all know, Mr Churchill and I have happily met many times before, and we know and understand each other very well. Indeed, Mr Churchill has become known and beloved by many millions of Americans, and the heartfelt prayers of all of us have been with this great citizen of the world in his recent serious illness.[2]

The Cairo and Teheran conferences, however, gave me my first opportunity to meet the Generalissimo, Chiang Kai-shek, and Marshal Stalin – and to sit down at the table with these unconquerable men and talk with them face to face. We had planned to talk to each other across the table at Cairo and Teheran; but we soon found that we were all on the same side of the table. We came to the conferences with faith in each other. But we needed the personal contact. And now we have supplemented faith with definite knowledge.

It was well worth travelling thousands of miles over land and sea to bring about this personal meeting, and to gain the heartening assurance that we are absolutely agreed with one another on all the major objectives – and on the military means of attaining them.

At Cairo, Prime Minister Churchill and I spent four days with the Generalissimo, Chiang Kai-shek. It was the first time that we had an opportunity to go over the complex situation in the Far East with him

[1] A conference was held at Moscow in October 1943 between the Soviet Foreign Minister Vyacheslav Molotov (1890–1986), the British Foreign Secretary Anthony Eden and the US Secretary of State Cordell Hull (1871–1955). All parties signed the Moscow Declaration, which declared Hitler's annexation of Austria in 1938 illegal.

[2] Churchill left the Cairo conference suffering from pneumonia, which he himself feared might become fatal.

personally. We were able not only to settle upon definite military strategy, but also to discuss certain long-range principles which we believe can assure peace in the Far East for many generations to come …

Increasingly powerful forces are now hammering at the Japanese at many points over an enormous arc which curves down through the Pacific from the Aleutians to the jungles of Burma. Our own army and navy, our air forces, the Australians and New Zealanders, the Dutch, and the British land, air and sea forces are all forming a band of steel which is slowly but surely closing in on Japan …

I met in the Generalissimo a man of great vision, great courage and a remarkably keen understanding of the problems of today and tomorrow. We discussed all the manifold military plans for striking at Japan with decisive force from many directions, and I believe I can say that he returned to Chungking[3] with the positive assurance of total victory over our common enemy. Today we and the Republic of China are closer together than ever before in deep friendship and in unity of purpose.

After the Cairo conference, Mr Churchill and I went by airplane to Teheran. There we met with Marshal Stalin. We talked with complete frankness on every conceivable subject connected with the winning of the war and the establishment of a durable peace after the war.

Within three days of intense and consistently amicable discussions, we agreed on every point concerned with the launching of a gigantic attack upon Germany. The Russian army will continue its stern offensives on Germany's eastern front, the Allied armies in Italy and Africa will bring relentless pressure on Germany from the south, and now the encirclement will be complete as great American and British forces attack from other points of the compass …

During the last two days at Teheran, Marshal Stalin, Mr Churchill and I looked ahead to the days and months and years that will follow Germany's defeat. We were united in determination that Germany must be stripped of her military might and be given no opportunity within the foreseeable future to regain that might.

The United Nations have no intention to enslave the German people. We wish them to have a normal chance to develop, in peace, as useful and respectable members of the European family. But we most certainly emphasize that word 'respectable' for we intend to rid them once and for all of Nazism and Prussian militarism and the fantastic and disastrous notion that they constitute the 'master race'.

We did discuss international relationships from the point of view of big, broad objectives, rather than details. But on the basis of what we did discuss, I can say even today that I do not think any insoluble differences will arise among Russia, Great Britain, and the United States.

In these conferences we were concerned with basic principles – principles which involve the security and the welfare and the standard of living of human beings in countries large and small.

To use an American and somewhat ungrammatical colloquialism, I may say that I 'got along fine' with Marshal Stalin. He is a man who combines a tremendous, relentless determination with a stalwart good humour. I believe he is truly representative of the heart and soul of Russia; and I believe that we are going to get along very well with him and the Russian people – very well indeed.

Britain, Russia, China and the United States and their allies represent more than three-quarters of the total population of the earth. As long as

[3] The Chinese leader Chiang Kai-shek (1887–1975) established a provisional seat of government at Chungking (or Chongqing) during the Second Sino-Japanese War (1937–45). The city was heavily bombed by Japanese forces.

these four nations with great military power stick together in determination to keep the peace there will be no possibility of an aggressor nation arising to start another world war …

For too many years we lived on pious hopes that aggressor and warlike nations would learn and understand and carry out the doctrine of purely voluntary peace … There have always been cheerful idiots in this country who believed that there would be no more war for us if everybody in America would only return into their homes and lock their front doors behind them. Assuming that their motives were of the highest, events have shown how unwilling they were to face the facts.

The overwhelming majority of all the people in the world want peace. Most of them are fighting for the attainment of peace – not just a truce, not just an armistice – but peace that is as strongly enforced and as durable as mortal man can make it. If we are willing to fight for peace now, is it not good logic that we should use force if necessary, in the future, to keep the peace?

… In all my travels, at home and abroad, it is the sight of our soldiers and sailors and their magnificent achievements which have given me the greatest inspiration and the greatest encouragement for the future … Some of our men overseas are now spending their third Christmas far from home. To them and to all others overseas or soon to go overseas, I can give assurance that it is the purpose of their government to win this war and to bring them home at the earliest possible time …

The American people have had every reason to know that this is a tough and destructive war. On my trip abroad, I talked with many military men who had faced our enemies in the field. These hardheaded realists testify to the strength and skill and resourcefulness of the enemy generals and men whom we must beat before final victory is won. The war is now reaching the stage where we shall all have to look forward to large casualty lists – dead, wounded and missing. War entails just that. There is no easy road to victory. And the end is not yet in sight …

Less than a month ago I flew in a big army transport plane over the little town of Bethlehem, in Palestine. Tonight, on Christmas Eve, all men and women everywhere who love Christmas are thinking of that ancient town and of the star of faith that shone there more than 19 centuries ago.

American boys are fighting today in snow-covered mountains, in malarial jungles, on blazing deserts; they are fighting on the far stretches of the sea and above the clouds, and fighting for the thing for which they struggle. I think it is best symbolized by the message that came out of Bethlehem.

On behalf of the American people – your own people – I send this Christmas message to you who are in our armed forces: in our hearts are prayers for you and for all your comrades in arms who fight to rid the world of evil.

We ask God's blessing upon you – upon your fathers, mothers, wives and children – all your loved ones at home. We ask that the comfort of God's grace shall be granted to those who are sick and wounded, and to those who are prisoners of war in the hands of the enemy, waiting for the day when they will again be free.

And we ask that God receive and cherish those who have given their lives, and that He keep them in honour and in the grateful memory of their countrymen forever.

God bless all of you who fight our battles on this Christmas Eve.

God bless us all. Keep us strong in our faith that we fight for a better day for humankind – here and everywhere.

Theodore Roosevelt
American statesman

Theodore Roosevelt *known as Teddy Roosevelt or TR* (1858–1919) was born in New York City of Dutch and Scottish descent. After studying at Harvard, he became leader of the New York legislature (1884) and president of the New York Police Board (1895–7). As Assistant Secretary of the Navy (1898) he raised and commanded the volunteer cavalry known as the 'Rough Riders', active in Cuba during the Spanish–American War (1898). He returned to serve as governor of New York State (1898–1900). Elected vice president in 1900, he became president on the assassination of William McKinley (1901), and was re-elected in 1904. During his presidency (1901–9), he strengthened the US Navy and introduced a 'Square Deal' policy between labour and business, enforcing anti-trust laws. A firm believer in sports and bracing outdoor pursuits, he boxed regularly, undertook a knife-fight with a cougar (1901) and in 1902 became the first US president to ride in a motor car. His administration acquired the Panama Canal Zone (1903) and began the construction of the canal. In 1906, he visited the site, becoming the first US president to make an official trip overseas. He received the Nobel Peace Prize in 1906 for his part in the negotiations which ended the Russo-Japanese War. Having made way for his protégé William H Taft in the presidential election of 1908, he travelled in Europe and made a hunting tour in central Africa. He returned in time to take an active part in the congressional elections of 1910, and created a split in the Republican Party, forming a 'Progressive' faction with his supporters. As Progressive candidate for the presidency in 1912 he survived an assassination attempt but was defeated by the Democratic candidate, WOODROW WILSON. After exploring the Rio Duvida in Teodoro, Brazil (1914), he campaigned vigorously for US intervention in World War I. An immensely popular president, he was also a prolific correspondent and author. As well as the eight-volume *Letters of Theodore Roosevelt* (published posthumously, 1951–4), he wrote books on American ideals, ranching, hunting and zoology, including *Hunting Trips of a Ranchman: Sketches of Sport on the Northern Cattle Plains* (1885) and *The Strenuous Life* (1910). The Teddy bear is named after him, and he is one of the four former presidents represented in the monumental sculpture at Mount Rushmore, South Dakota (completed 1941).

'The Man with the Muck-rake'
14 April 1906, Washington, DC, USA

This address was given at a cornerstone-laying ceremony for the Cannon House Office Building, which was to provide office space for the expanding US government. Minority representatives, usually Democrats, had previously been forced to work in their lodgings, for lack of suitable accommodation.

Roosevelt's real subject, however, is the media. By the turn of the 19th century, the 'yellow journalism' of sensationalized stories in cheap popular magazines had given way to a more considered and thoroughly researched approach. The press now provided detailed coverage of the issues of the day, including political corruption, exploitative business practices and fraudulent claims by manufacturers. Exposés were published in magazines such as *McClure's* and supported in the mainstream press. Fiction writers also contributed to this new approach. Upton Sinclair's novel *The Jungle* (1906) – which deals with malpractice in the meat-packing industry – is an example of crusading literature which brought about changes in the law.

Roosevelt abhorred corruption, and acknowledged the need for investigative journalism; but he was also alert to the dangers of indiscriminate attacks on the reputations of public figures. These, he believed, would deplete citizens' trust in all elected officials.

In this speech, he refers to a character from John Bunyan's Christian allegory *The Pilgrim's Progress* (1678–84), who is so steeped in the filth of the world that he fails to perceive the glory of God. Characteristically folksy and paternalistic, it clearly sets out Roosevelt's reformist credentials. Legislation he introduced during this year included the Pure Food and Drug Act and the Meat Inspection Acts.

Over a century ago, WASHINGTON laid the cornerstone of the Capitol in what was then little more than a tract of wooded wilderness here beside the Potomac. We now find it necessary to provide great additional buildings for the business of the government. This growth in the need for the housing of the government is but a proof and example of the way in which the nation has grown and the sphere of action of the national government has grown. We now administer the affairs of a nation in which the extraordinary growth of population has been outstripped by the growth of wealth and the growth in complex interests.

The material problems that face us today are not such as they were in Washington's time, but the underlying facts of human nature are the same now as they were then. Under altered external form we war with the same tendencies toward evil that were evident in Washington's time, and are helped by the same tendencies for good.

It is about some of these that I wish to say a word today. In Bunyan's *Pilgrim's Progress* you may recall the description of the Man with the Muck-rake, the man who could look no way but downward, with the muck-rake in his hand; who was offered a celestial crown for his muck-rake, but who would neither look up nor regard the crown he was offered, but continued to rake to himself the filth of the floor.

In *Pilgrim's Progress*, the Man with the Muck-rake is set forth as the example of him whose vision is fixed on carnal instead of on spiritual things. Yet he also typifies the man who in this life consistently refuses to see aught that is lofty, and fixes his eyes, with solemn intentness, only on that which is vile and debasing. Now, it is very necessary that we should not flinch from seeing what is vile and debasing. There is filth on the floor and it must be scraped up with the muck-rake; and there are times and places where this service is the most needed of all the services that can be performed. But the man who never does anything else, who never thinks or speaks or writes, save of his feats with the muck-rake, speedily becomes, not a help to society, not an incitement to good, but one of the most potent forces for evil.

There are, in the body politic, economic and social, many and grave evils, and there is urgent necessity for the sternest war upon them. There should be relentless exposure of and attack upon every evil man, whether politician or businessman, every evil practice, whether in politics, in business or in social life. I hail as a benefactor every writer or speaker, every man who – on the platform, or in book, magazine or newspaper – with merciless severity makes such attack, provided always that he in his turn remembers that the attack is of use only if it is absolutely truthful.

The liar is no whit better than the thief, and if his mendacity takes the form of slander, he may be worse than most thieves. It puts a premium upon knavery untruthfully to attack an honest man; or even with hysterical exaggeration to assail a bad man with untruth. An epidemic of indiscriminate assault upon character does not good, but very great harm. The soul of every scoundrel is gladdened whenever an honest man is assailed, or even when a scoundrel is untruthfully assailed.

Now, it is easy to twist out of shape what I have just said, easy to affect to misunderstand it, and, if it is slurred over in repetition, not difficult really to misunderstand it. Some persons are sincerely incapable of understanding that to denounce mud-slinging does not mean the endorsement of whitewashing; and both the interested individuals who need whitewashing, and those others who practise mud-slinging, like to encourage such confusion of ideas.

One of the chief counts against those who make indiscriminate assault upon men in business or men in public life is that they invite a reaction which is sure to tell powerfully in favour of the unscrupulous scoundrel who really ought to be attacked, who ought to be exposed; who ought, if possible, to be put in the penitentiary ...

Any excess is almost sure to invite a reaction; and, unfortunately, the reaction, instead of taking the form of punishment of those guilty of the excess, is very apt to take the form either of punishment of the unoffending or of giving immunity, and even strength, to offenders. The effort to make financial or political profit out of the destruction of character can only result in public calamity. Gross and reckless assaults on character, whether on the stump or in newspaper, magazine, or book, create a morbid and vicious public sentiment, and at the same time act as a profound deterrent to able men of normal sensitiveness and tend to prevent them from entering the public service at any price.

As an instance in point, I may mention that one serious difficulty encountered in getting the right type of men to dig the Panama Canal is the certainty that they will be exposed, both without, and, I am sorry to say, sometimes within, Congress, to utterly reckless assaults on their character and capacity.

At the risk of repetition let me say again that my plea is not for immunity to, but for the most unsparing exposure of, the politician who betrays his trust, of the big businessman who makes or spends his fortune in illegitimate or corrupt ways. There should be a resolute effort to hunt every such man out of the position he has disgraced. Expose the crime, and hunt down the criminal; but remember that even in the case of crime, if it is attacked in sensational, lurid and untruthful fashion, the attack may do more damage to the public mind than the crime itself.

It is because I feel that there should be no rest in the endless war against the forces of evil that I ask that the war be conducted with sanity as well as with resolution. The men with the muck-rakes are often indispensable to the well-being of society; but only if they know when to stop raking the muck, and to look upward to the celestial crown above them, to the crown of worthy endeavour.

There are beautiful things above and round about them; and if they gradually grow to feel that the whole world is nothing but muck, their power of usefulness is gone. If the whole picture is painted black there remains no hue whereby to single out the rascals for distinction from their fellows. Such painting finally induces a kind of moral colour-blindness; and people affected by it come to the conclusion that no man is really black, and no man is really white, but they are all grey.

In other words, they neither believe in the truth of the attack, nor in the honesty of the man who is attacked; they grow as suspicious of the accusation as of the offence; it becomes well-nigh hopeless to stir them either to wrath against wrong-doing or to enthusiasm for what is right; and such a mental attitude in the public gives hope to every knave, and is the despair of honest men.

To assail the great and admitted evils of our political and industrial life with such crude and sweeping generalizations as to include decent men in the general condemnation means the searing of the public conscience. There results a general attitude either of cynical belief in and indifference to public corruption, or else of a distrustful inability to discriminate between the good and the bad. Either attitude is fraught with untold damage to the country as a whole. The fool who has not sense to discriminate between what is good and what is bad is well-nigh as dangerous as the man who does discriminate and yet chooses the bad.

There is nothing more distressing to every good patriot, to every good American, than the hard, scoffing spirit which treats the allegation of dishonesty in a public man as a cause for laughter. Such laughter is worse than the crackling of thorns under a pot, for it denotes not merely the vacant mind, but the heart in which high emotions have been choked before they could grow to fruition.

There is any amount of good in the world, and there never was a time when loftier and more disinterested work for the betterment of mankind was being done than now. The forces that tend for evil are great and terrible, but the forces of truth and love and courage and honesty and generosity and sympathy are also stronger than ever before. It is a foolish and timid, no less than a wicked, thing to blink the fact that the forces of evil are strong, but it is even worse to fail to take into account the strength of the forces that tell for good.

Hysterical sensationalism is the very poorest weapon wherewith to fight for lasting righteousness. The men who with stern sobriety and truth assail the many evils of our time, whether in the public press or in magazines, or in books, are the leaders and allies of all engaged in the work for social and political betterment. But if they give good reason for distrust of what they say, if they chill the ardour of those who demand truth as a primary virtue, they thereby betray the good cause, and play into the hands of the very men against whom they are nominally at war.

❧

'It takes more than that to kill a bull moose'
14 October 1912, Milwaukee, Wisconsin, USA

❧

This is probably the only political speech ever delivered by a man bleeding from a bullet wound. Roosevelt gave it while campaigning for re-election as president. On arriving in Milwaukee, he was shot in the chest by John Schrank, who had followed him around the country waiting for an opportunity. The bullet lodged in his ribs, having been deflected both by the manuscript of his speech and the steel case in which he kept his spectacles.

In keeping with his reputation for robust virility, Roosevelt staggered to his feet, spat into his hand to ensure his lungs had not been pierced, and brushed aside assistance to address the crowd.

By this time, Roosevelt was representing the Progressive Party – nicknamed the 'Bull Moose Party' under his leadership – established as a reaction to rapid industrialization and urbanization. The rise of 'big business' – often aligned with dishonest politicians – had led to a breakdown in the democratic process, which in turn allowed poverty and slum living conditions to spread.

During his two terms as president (1901–9), Roosevelt had attempted to rectify exploitative practices, reforming health and safety regulations and implementing existing anti-trust laws. He had stood down at the height of his popularity in 1908, although he was expected to win the subsequent election. In 1910, frustrated by the pace of reform, he returned to politics, hiving off the Progressive wing of the Republican Party.

He failed to win the election, but the speech bears testimony to his remarkable hardiness and vigour.

❧

Friends: I shall ask you to be as quiet as possible. I don't know whether you fully understand that I have just been shot; but it takes more than that to kill a bull moose. But fortunately I had my manuscript, so you see I was going to make a long speech, and there is a bullet – there is where the bullet went through [*indicating blood-stained papers, pierced by the bullet*] and it probably saved me from it going into my heart. The bullet is in me now, so that I cannot make a very long speech, but I will try my best.

And now, friends: I want to take advantage of this incident to say a word of solemn warning to my fellow countrymen. First of all, I want to say this about myself: I have altogether too important things to think of to feel any concern over my own death; and now I cannot speak to you insincerely within five minutes of being shot. I am telling you the literal truth when I say that my concern is for many other things. It is not in the least for my own life.

I want you to understand that I am ahead of the game, anyway. No man has had a happier life than I have led; a happier life in every way. I have been able to do certain things that I greatly wished to do, and I am interested in doing other things.

I can tell you with absolute truthfulness that I am very much uninterested in whether I am shot or not. It was just as when I was colonel of my regiment. I always felt that a private was to be excused for feeling at times some pangs of anxiety about his personal safety, but I cannot understand a man fit to be a colonel who can pay any heed to his personal safety when he is occupied, as he ought to be, with the absorbing desire to do his duty.

I am in this cause with my whole heart and soul. I believe that the Progressive movement is making life a little easier for all our people; a movement to try to take the burdens off the men and especially the women and children of this country. I am absorbed in the success of that movement.

Friends: I ask you now this evening to accept what I am saying as absolutely true, when I tell you I am not thinking of my own success. I am not thinking of my life or of anything connected with me personally. I am thinking of the movement. I say this by way of introduction, because I want to say something very serious to our people and especially to the newspapers.

I don't know anything about who the man was who shot me tonight.[1] He was seized at once by one of the stenographers in my party, Mr Martin, and I suppose is now in the hands of the police. He shot to kill. He shot – the shot, the bullet went in here – I will show you …

Now, I do not know who he was or what he represented. He was a coward. He stood in the darkness in the crowd around the automobile and when they cheered me, and I got up to bow, he stepped forward and shot me in the darkness.

Now, friends: of course, I do not know, as I say, anything about him; but it is a very natural thing that weak and vicious minds should be inflamed to acts of violence by the kind of awful mendacity and abuse that have been heaped upon me for the last three months by the papers, in the interest of not only Mr DEBS but of Mr WILSON[2] and Mr Taft.[3]

Friends: I will disown and repudiate any man of my party who attacks with such foul slander and abuse any opponent of any other party; and now I wish to say seriously to all the daily newspapers, to the Republicans, the Democrat and Socialist parties, that they cannot, month in month out and year in and year out, make the kind of untruthful, of bitter assault that they have made and not expect that brutal, violent natures, or brutal and violent characters, especially when the brutality is accompanied by a not very strong mind; they cannot expect that such natures will be unaffected by it.

Now, friends: I am not speaking for myself at all, I give you my word, I do not care a rap about being shot; not a rap.

I have had a good many experiences in my time and this is one of them. What I care for is my country. I wish I were able to impress upon my people, our people, the duty to feel strongly but to speak the truth of their opponents. I say now, I have never said one word on the stump against any opponent that I cannot defend. I have said nothing that I could not substantiate and nothing that I ought not to have said; nothing that, looking back at, I would not say again.

Now, friends: it ought not to be too much to ask that our opponents [*speaking to someone on the stage*] I am not sick at all; I am all right; I

[1] John F Schrank (d.1943) was born in Bavaria, southern Germany, and emigrated to New York City, where he ran a tavern and later became an evangelical preacher. After shooting Roosevelt, he was ruled insane. He spent the rest of his life in a Wisconsin mental hospital.

[2] Woodrow Wilson, the Democratic candidate, who won the presidential election.
[3] William H Taft (1857–1930) had succeeded Roosevelt as President in 1909. Although Roosevelt had endorsed him on standing down in 1908, he became dissatisfied with Taft's performance in office.

cannot tell you of what infinitesimal importance I regard this incident as compared with the great issues at stake in this campaign, and I ask it not for my sake, not the least in the world, but for the sake of common country, that they make up their minds to speak only the truth, and not use that kind of slander and mendacity which, if taken seriously, must incite weak and violent natures to crimes of violence. Don't you make any mistake. Don't you pity me. I am all right. I am all right – and you cannot escape listening to the speech either.

And now, friends: this incident that has just occurred – this effort to assassinate me – emphasizes to a peculiar degree the need of the Progressive movement. Friends, every good citizen ought to do everything in his or her power to prevent the coming of the day when we shall see in this country two recognized creeds fighting one another, when we shall see the creed of the 'Have-nots' arraigned against the creed of the 'Haves'. When that day comes, then such incidents as this tonight will be commonplace in our history. When you make poor men, when you permit the conditions to grow, such that the poor man as such will be swayed by his sense of injury against the men who try to hold what they improperly have won; when that day comes, the most awful passions will be let loose and it will be an ill day for our country.

Now, friends: what we who are in this movement are endeavouring to do is forestall any such movement for justice now – a movement in which we ask all just men of generous hearts to join with the men who feel in their souls that lift upward which bids them refuse to be satisfied themselves while their countrymen and countrywomen suffer from avoidable misery. Now, friends: what we Progressives are trying to do is to enrol rich or poor – whatever their social or industrial position – to stand together for the most elementary rights of good citizenship, those elementary rights which are the foundation of good citizenship in this great republic of ours.

[*At this point a renewed effort was made to persuade Roosevelt to conclude his speech.*]

My friends are a little more nervous than I am. Don't you waste any sympathy on me. I have had an A1 time in life and I am having it now. I never in my life was in any movement in which I was able to serve with such whole-hearted devotion as in this; in which I was able to feel as I do in this that common weal. I have fought for the good of our common country.

And now, friends: I shall have to cut short much of that speech that I meant to give you, but I want to touch on just two or three points.

In the first place, speaking to you here in Milwaukee, I wish to say that the Progressive Party is making its appeals to all our fellow citizens without any regard to their creed or to their birthplace. We do not regard as essential the way in which a man worships his God or as being affected by where he was born. We regard it as a matter of spirit and purpose …

At one time I promoted five men for gallantry on the field of battle. Afterward in making some inquiries about them I found that two of them were Protestants, two Catholic, and one a Jew … I did not promote them because of their religion. It just happened that way … If he was a good fighting man, then I saw that Uncle Sam got the benefit of it. That is all.

I make the same appeal to our citizenship. I ask in our civic life that we in the same way pay heed only to the man's quality of citizenship, to repudiate as the worst enemy that we can have whoever tries to get us to discriminate for or against any man because of his creed or birthplace.

Now, friends: in the same way I want our people to stand by one another without regard to differences or class or occupation … It is essential that here should be organizations of labour. This is an era of organization. Capital organizes and therefore labour must organize. My appeal for organized labour is two-fold; to the outsider and the capitalist I make my appeal to treat the labourer fairly, to recognize the fact that he must organize that there must be such organization, that the labouring man must organize, for his own protection, and that it is the duty of the rest of us to help him and not hinder him in organizing. That is one-half appeal that I make.

Now, the other half is to the labour man himself. My appeal to him is to remember that as he wants justice, so he must do justice. I want every labour man, every labour leader, every organized union man, to take the lead in denouncing disorder and in denouncing the inciting of riot; that in this country we shall proceed under the protection of our laws and with all respect to the laws, I want the labour men to feel in their turn that exactly as justice must be done them so they must do justice. They must bear their duty as citizens, their duty to this great country of ours, and that they must not rest content unless they do that duty to the fullest degree.

I know these doctors, when they get hold of me, will never let me go back and there are just a few more things that I want to say to you …

I ask you to look at our declaration and hear and read our platform about social and industrial justice and then, friends, vote for the Progressive ticket without regard to me, without regard to my personality, for only by voting for that platform can you be true to the cause of progress throughout this Union.

[*After speaking for around an hour, Roosevelt was eventually ushered from the stage and taken to hospital. He survived the shooting, and received more votes than either Taft or Debs, but was defeated by Wilson.*]

Bertrand Russell

English philosopher, mathematician and writer

Bertrand Arthur William Russell *later 3rd Earl Russell* (1872–1970) was born in Trelleck, Gwent; his parents died when he was very young and he was raised by his grandmother, the widow of Lord John Russell (the former prime minister and 1st Earl). He was educated privately and at Trinity College, Cambridge, where he took first-class honours in mathematics and philosophy. He became a Fellow of Trinity in 1895. His most original contributions to mathematical logic were expounded in *The Principles of Mathematics* (1903) and the monumental *Principia Mathematica* (1910–13, with Alfred North Whitehead). In 1912, he wrote his first genuinely popular work, the brilliantly stimulating *Problems of Philosophy*. During World War I, his active pacifism led to his imprisonment (1918), which allowed him to write his *Introduction to Mathematical Philosophy* (1919). He made a living by lecturing and journalism, and became a celebrated controversialist. He visited the USSR, where he met LENIN, LEON TROTSKY and the writer Maxim Gorky, which led to his critical *Theory and Practice of Bolshevism* (1919). He also taught in China (1920–1). In 1927, with his second wife Dora Black, he founded a progressive school near Petersfield, setting out his views in *On Education* (1926) and *Education and the Social Order* (1932). In 1931 he succeeded his elder brother as Earl Russell. His second divorce (1934) and marriage to Patricia Spence (1936) endowed his earlier book *Marriage and Morals* (1929) with controversy. The rise of fascism led him to renounce his pacifism in 1939; his fellowship at Trinity was restored in 1944, and after World War II he was awarded an Order of Merit. He received the Nobel Prize for literature in 1950. He had meanwhile continued publishing important philosophical works including *An Enquiry into Meaning and Truth* (1940), *The History of Western Philosophy* (1945) and *Human Knowledge: Its Scope and Limits* (1948). Some of his popular and provocative essays were later collected in *Why I am Not a Christian* (1957). After 1949 he became preoccupied with nuclear disarmament, taking a leading role in the Campaign for Nuclear Disarmament, and engaging in a remarkable correspondence with various world leaders. In 1961 he was again imprisoned for his part in a sit-down demonstration in Whitehall. His last years were spent in North Wales, and he retained his lucidity, independence of mind and humour to the end. His last major publication was a three-volume *Autobiography* (1967–9).

'I cannot believe that this is to be the end'

30 December 1954, broadcast from London, England

❧

Bertrand Russell leaned towards pacifism throughout his life, famously during World War I, though during World War II he recognized the need for armed resistance to ADOLF HITLER, 'as a necessary prelude to anything good'.

Although he seemed, briefly, to favour a pre-emptive nuclear strike against the USSR (which he posited during a speech of November 1948), he soon joined the anti-nuclear lobby.

He used this BBC broadcast to condemn hydrogen-bomb testing, urging his listeners to 'learn to think in a new way' to reverse the trend towards catastrophe. Russell was a well-known and revered public figure at this time, despite his often unorthodox views. (In 1964, for example, he published his *16 Questions on the Assassination*, disputing the official account of JOHN F KENNEDY's murder.) This speech is an appeal to the common man – and the commonality of mankind – soberly tackling a terrifying scenario which he was convinced required a radical response. His words attracted the attention of ALBERT EINSTEIN (whose 1950 broadcast on the follies of nuclear proliferation is included in this book). In 1955, they jointly compiled and published the Russell–Einstein Manifesto, in which they and nine other prominent scientists called for arms limitations.

This in turn led the philanthropist Cyrus Eaton to sponsor a Conference on Science and World Affairs at Pugwash, Nova Scotia in 1957. Russell was elected president, though ill-health prevented him from attending. In 1958 he became founding president of the Campaign for Nuclear Disarmament. The Pugwash Conferences still continue, and were awarded the Nobel Peace Prize in 1995.

❧

I am speaking not as a Briton, not as a European, not as a member of a western democracy, but as a human being, a member of the species Man, whose continued existence is in doubt. The world is full of conflicts: Jews and Arabs; Indians and Pakistanis; white men and negroes in Africa; and, overshadowing all minor conflicts, the titanic struggle between communism and anti-communism.

Almost everybody who is politically conscious has strong feelings about one or more of these issues; but I want you, if you can, to set aside such feelings for the moment and consider yourself only as a member of a biological species which has had a remarkable history and whose disappearance none of us can desire. I shall try to say no single word which should appeal to one group rather than to another. All, equally, are in peril, and if the peril is understood, there is hope that they may collectively avert it.

We have to learn to think in a new way. We have to learn to ask ourselves not what steps can be taken to give military victory to whatever group we prefer, for there no longer are such steps. The question we have to ask ourselves is: what steps can be taken to prevent a military contest of which the issue must be disastrous to all sides?

The general public, and even many men in positions of authority, have not realized what would be involved in a war with hydrogen bombs. The general public still thinks in terms of the obliteration of cities. It is understood that the new bombs are more powerful than the old and that, while one atomic bomb could obliterate Hiroshima,[1] one hydrogen bomb could obliterate the largest cities, such as London, New York and Moscow. No doubt in a hydrogen-bomb war, great cities would be obliterated.

But this is one of the minor disasters that would have to be faced. If everybody in London, New York and Moscow were exterminated, the world might, in the course of a few centuries, recover from the blow. But we now know, especially since the Bikini test,[2] that hydrogen bombs can gradually spread destruction over a much wider area than had been supposed.

It is stated on very good authority that a bomb can now be manufactured which will be 25,000 times as powerful as that which destroyed Hiroshima. Such a bomb, if exploded near the ground or under water, sends radioactive particles into the upper air. They sink gradually and reach the surface of the earth in the form of a deadly dust or rain. It was this dust which infected the Japanese fishermen and their catch of fish although they were outside what American experts believed to be the danger zone.

No-one knows how widely such lethal radioactive particles might be diffused, but the best authorities are unanimous in saying that a war with hydrogen bombs is quite likely to put an end to the human race. It is feared that if many hydrogen bombs are used there will be universal death – sudden only for a fortunate minority, but for the majority a slow torture of disease and disintegration …

Here, then, is the problem which I present to you, stark and dreadful and inescapable: shall we put an end to the human race or shall mankind renounce war?

People will not face this alternative because it is so difficult to abolish war. The abolition of war will demand distasteful limitations of national sovereignty. But what perhaps impedes understanding of the situation more than anything else is that the term 'mankind' feels vague and abstract. People scarcely realize in imagination that the danger is to themselves and their children and their grandchildren, and not only to a dimly apprehended 'humanity'. And so they hope that perhaps war may be allowed to continue, provided modern weapons are prohibited.

I am afraid this hope is illusory. Whatever agreements not to use hydrogen bombs had been reached in time of peace, they would no longer be considered binding in time of war, and both sides would set to work to

[1] The Japanese city which was devastated by the first atomic bomb strike on 6 August 1945, which killed an estimated 80,000 civilians. Radiation poisoning caused many thousands of subsequent deaths.

[2] More than 20 atomic and hydrogen bomb tests took place at Bikini Atoll in the Marshall Islands between 1946 and 1958. The first hydrogen-bomb test was at neighbouring Eniewetok Atoll in 1952. In a test codenamed 'Castle Bravo', on 1 March 1954, the USA detonated a 15-megaton hydrogen bomb. The secret test attracted world-wide publicity and concern about the effects of testing after the fallout poisoned the crew of a nearby fishing boat.

manufacture hydrogen bombs as soon as war broke out, for if one side manufactured the bombs and the other did not, the side that manufactured them would inevitably be victorious …

As geological time is reckoned, Man has so far existed only for a very short period – one million years at the most. What he has achieved, especially during the last 6,000 years, is something utterly new in the history of the cosmos, so far at least as we are acquainted with it. For countless ages the Sun rose and set, the Moon waxed and waned, the stars shone in the night, but it was only with the coming of Man that these things were understood. In the great world of astronomy and in the little world of the atom, Man has unveiled secrets which might have been thought undiscoverable.

In art and literature and religion, some men have shown a sublimity of feeling which makes the species worth preserving. Is all this to end in trivial horror, because so few are able to think of Man rather than of this or that group of men? Is our race so destitute of wisdom, so incapable of impartial love, so blind even to the simplest dictates of self-preservation, that the last proof of its silly cleverness is to be the extermination of all life on our planet? For it will be not only men who will perish, but also the animals, whom no-one can accuse of communism or anti-communism.

I cannot believe that this is to be the end. I would have men forget their quarrels for a moment and reflect that, if they will allow themselves to survive, there is every reason to expect the triumphs of the future to exceed immeasurably the triumphs of the past. There lies before us, if we choose, continual progress in happiness, knowledge, and wisdom.

Shall we, instead, choose death, because we cannot forget our quarrels? I appeal, as a human being to human beings: remember your humanity, and forget the rest. If you can do so, the way lies open to a new Paradise; if you cannot, nothing lies before you but universal death.

Gerhard Schröder
German politician

Gerhard Schröder (1944–) was born in Mosenburg, Lippe, and never knew his father, who was killed in action in Romania. Raised in poverty by his mother, a cleaner, he studied at night school, won a place at the University of Göttingen and began a career in law. He joined the Social Democratic Party (1963) and became national chairman of the Young Socialists (1976–80) and a member of the Bundestag (1980–86). He was leader of the opposition (1986) and Minister President (1990–8) in the State Parliament of Lower Saxony before becoming Chancellor of Germany on leading the Social Democrats to electoral victory in 1998. As Chancellor, he distanced himself from the extreme left within his party and built a reputation as a reformer and modernizer with a somewhat less enthusiastic approach towards the European Union than his Christian Democrat predecessor, Helmut Kohl. He won a second term in 2002, but in October 2005 he conceded a much-contested election, and controversially declined a cabinet position in the coalition government formed by Christian Democrat leader Angela Merkel. He is currently chairman of the board of the construction consortium Nord Stream AG.

'I express my shame'
25 January 2005, Berlin, Germany
❧

Known for his broad smile, smart suits and fat cigars, Schröder is a popular and charismatic politician – though his administrations were dogged by economic decline, rising unemployment and controversial social security reform. He also risked ridicule and accusations of attacking freedom of speech in 2002, when he launched a lawsuit against a newspaper that claimed he dyed his hair.

Born during World War II to a father killed in combat, he was the first post-war Chancellor young enough to reposition Germany as a military power, sending troops on peacekeeping missions in the Balkans and combat operations in Afghanistan. Conversely, he was a key dissenter, alongside President Jacques Chirac of France, when the USA and UK sought support for war against Iraq – a stance which helped secure his narrow election victory in 2002.

He was invited to speak at a remembrance ceremony on the 60th anniversary of the liberation of Auschwitz–Birkenau, the most notorious of the death camps used by the Nazis to imprison and exterminate Jews and other 'undesirables' during the Holocaust. It was a historic opportunity to apologize on behalf of a country long dogged by the sins of its fathers.

From a lectern overshadowed by large projected photographs of the grim, fence-lined road to the camp and its inmates, he made this bold, moving statement. It is both an acknowledgement Germany's collective guilt for 'the greatest crime in the history of mankind' and a stiff call for vigilance against anti-Semitism, neo-Nazi activity and Holocaust denial.

❧

Survivors of Auschwitz–Birkenau; ladies and gentlemen: I would like to thank the International Auschwitz Committee for the invitation to speak to you here today.

In my estimation, an invitation of this kind is still not something that can be taken for granted. It would be fitting for us Germans to remain silent in the face of what was the greatest crime in the history of mankind. Words by government leaders are inadequate when confronted with the absolute immorality and senselessness of the murder of millions.

We look for rational understanding of something that is beyond human comprehension. We seek definitive answers, but in vain.

What is left is the testimony of those few who survived and their descendants. What is left are the remains of the sites of these murders and the historical record. What is left, also, is the certainty that these extermination camps were a manifestation of absolute evil.

Evil is not a political or scientific category. But after Auschwitz, who could doubt that it exists, and that it manifested itself in the hate-driven genocide carried out by the Nazi regime?

However, noting this fact does not permit us to circumvent our responsibility by blaming everything on a demonic Hitler. The evil manifested in the Nazi ideology was not without its precursors. There was a tradition behind the rise of this brutal ideology and the accompanying loss of moral inhibition. Above all, it needs to be said that the Nazi ideology was something that people supported at the time and that they took part in putting into effect.

Now, 60 years after the liberation of Auschwitz by the Red Army, I stand before you as the representative of a democratic Germany. I express my shame for the deaths of those who were murdered and for the fact that you, the survivors, were forced to go through the hell of a concentration camp.

Chelmno, Belzec, Sobibor, Treblinka, Maidanek and Auschwitz–Birkenau[1] are names that will forever be associated with the history of the victims as well as with German and European history. We know that. We bear this burden with sadness, but also with a serious sense of responsibility.

[1] Schröder lists the sites of Nazi concentration camps in Poland.

Millions of men, women, and children were gassed, starved, or shot by German SS troops and their helpers. Jews, gypsies, homosexuals, political prisoners, prisoners of war, and resistance fighters from across Europe were exterminated with cold industrial perfection; or were enslaved and worked to death.

Never before had there been a worse breakdown of thousands of years of European culture and civilization. After the war it took some time before the full extent of this breakdown was realized. We are aware of it, but I doubt that we will ever be able to understand it.

The past cannot be 'overcome'. It is the past. But its traces and, above all, the lessons to be learned from it extend to the present.

There will never be anything that can make up for the horror, the torment, and the agony that took place in the concentration camps. It is only possible to provide the families of those who died and the survivors a certain amount of compensation.

Germany has faced this responsibility for a long period of time now with its government policies and court decisions, supported by a sense of justice on the part of the people. The young men and women in the photo we see here were freed in the summer of 1945. Most survivors went in different directions after their liberation: to Israel, to North and South America, to neighbouring European countries, or back to their countries of origin.

However, some of them stayed in or returned to Germany, the country where the so-called 'final solution'[2] originated. It was an extraordinarily difficult decision for them, and often enough it was not a voluntary decision, but rather the result of total desperation. However, hope did return to their disrupted lives, and many did remain in Germany, and we are grateful for that.

[2] The *Endlösung der Judenfrage* ('Final Solution to the Jewish Question') was a term coined by Adolf Eichmann (1906–62), one of the architects of the Holocaust, for the decision to exterminate the Jews, rather than merely dispossessing and imprisoning them.

Today the Jewish community in Germany is the third-largest in Europe. It is full of vitality and growing rapidly. New synagogues are being built. The Jewish community is and will remain an irreplaceable part of our society and culture. Its brilliant as well as painful history will continue to be both an obligation and a promise for the future.

We will use the powers of government to protect it against the anti-Semitism of those who refuse to learn the lessons of the past. There is no denying that anti-Semitism continues to exist. It is the task of society as a whole to fight it. It must never again become possible for anti-Semites to attack and cause injury to Jewish citizens in our country or any other country and in doing so bring disgrace upon our nation.

Right-wing extremists, with their spray-painted slogans, have the special attention of our law-enforcement and justice authorities. But the process of dealing politically with neo-Nazis and former Nazis is something we all need to do together.

It is the duty of all democrats to provide a strong response to neo-Nazi incitement and recurrent attempts on their part to play down the importance of the crimes perpetrated by the Nazi regime. For the enemies of democracy and tolerance there can be no tolerance.

The survivors of Auschwitz have called upon us to be vigilant, not to look away, and not to pretend we don't hear things. They have called upon us to acknowledge human rights violations and to do something about them. They are being heard, particularly by young people – for instance by those who are looking at the Auschwitz memorial today with their own eyes. They are speaking with former prisoners. They are helping to maintain and preserve the memorial. They will also help to inform future generations of the crimes committed by the Nazi regime.

The vast majority of the Germans living today bear no guilt for the Holocaust. But they do bear a special responsibility. Remembrance of the war and the genocide perpetrated by the Nazi regime has become part of our living constitution. For some this is a difficult burden to bear.

Nonetheless this remembrance is part of our national identity. Remembrance of the Nazi era and its crimes is a moral obligation. We owe it to the victims, we owe it to the survivors and their families, and we owe it to ourselves.

It is true, the temptation to forget is very great. But we will not succumb to this temptation. The Holocaust memorial in the centre of Berlin cannot restore the lives or the dignity of the victims. It can perhaps serve survivors and their descendants as a symbol of their suffering. It serves us all as a reminder of the past.

We know one thing for sure. There would be no freedom, no human dignity, and no justice if we were to forget what happened when freedom, justice, and human dignity were desecrated by government power. Exemplary efforts are being undertaken in many German schools, in companies, in labour unions, and in the churches. Germany is facing up to its past.

From the Shoah[3] and Nazi terror a certainty has arisen for us all that can best be expressed by the words 'never again'. We want to preserve this certainty. All Germans, but also all Europeans, and the entire international community need to continue to learn to live together with respect, humanity, and in peace.

The Convention on the Prevention and Punishment of the Crime of Genocide[4] was a direct effect of the Holocaust on international law. It requires people of different cultural, religious, and racial origins to respect and protect life and human dignity throughout the world. You in the International Auschwitz Committee support this with the exemplary work you are doing in the interest of all people.

Together with you, I bow my head before the victims of the death camps. Even if one day the names of the victims should fade in the memory of mankind, their fate will not be forgotten. They will remain in the heart of history.

[3] The Hebrew term for the Holocaust. It translates literally as 'catastrophe'.

[4] The convention was framed by the United Nations in Geneva, Switzerland in December 1948, and came into force in January 1951.

Chief Seattle
Native American leader

Chief Seattle *also called Noah Sealth* (c.1786–1866), was born on Blake Island in central Puget Sound, now in Washington State, where he witnessed the arrival of white settlers. Descended from noble Suquamish and Duwamish families, he became known among his people as a formidable leader, and participated in numerous raids on other Native American groups. After the death of one of his sons in the 1830s, he was converted to Christianity by French Roman Catholic missionaries and turned away from fighting, seeking instead to forge harmonious relationships between native groups and white settlers in the area. The newly established settlement of Seattle was named in his honour. Chief Seattle's willingness to negotiate with Americans attracted some criticism from his people, particularly after he signed the Fort Elliot Treaty of 1855, ceding land rights to settlers. Despite this, he maintained his friendships with Americans, holding meetings with presidents William McKinley and THEODORE ROOSEVELT, while continuing to work diligently on behalf of native groups. Barred by an ordinance of 1865 from making his home within the city that bore his name, he spent his last years on the Suquamish reservation at Port Madison, Washington.

'Day and night cannot dwell together'
January 1855, near Seattle, Washington, USA

At least four versions of this speech exist, and the most familiar is the least accurate: a modern apology traced to a screenplay and rewritten (without the writer's permission) in 1972; then adopted as authentic by the US environmental movement. The original version given here is almost as mysterious.

Chief Seattle was an elderly man – and had pointedly refused to learn English – when he addressed the governor of Washington Territory, Issac Stevens, at a reception in 1855. Stevens had been closely involved in buying – and sometimes seizing – Salish lands along Puget Sound; and the native peoples had been moved to reservations. Seattle reputedly had tremendous presence: he stood six feet tall and spoke in a deep voice. Governor Stevens was rather shorter, and Seattle is said to have given his half-hour speech holding one hand on Stevens's head and the other with index finger pointing skyward.

Dr Henry J Smith, a surgeon and part-time poet with a Victorian taste for the flowery phrase, is credited with taking notes at the time, and reproduced the speech much later in an article for the *Seattle Sunday Star* of 29 October 1887. Neither his original transcription nor his diaries have been found. Smith had only been in the territory for a year, and it is unlikely he fully understood Seattle's Lushootseed oration. It is more plausible that he heard a translation, possibly through the medium of another tribal language such as Chinook, before recasting it in English, in his own style.

Yonder sky, that has wept tears of compassion upon my people for centuries untold, and which to us appears changeless and eternal, may change. Today is fair. Tomorrow it may be overcast with clouds.

My words are like the stars that never change. Whatever Seattle says, the great chief at Washington can rely upon with as much certainty as he can upon the return of the sun or the seasons. The white chief says that big chief at Washington sends us greetings of friendship and goodwill. This is kind of him, for we know he has little need of our friendship in return.

His people are many. They are like the grass that covers vast prairies. My people are few. They resemble the scattering trees of a storm-swept plain. The great and – I presume – good white chief sends us word that he wishes to buy our land, but is willing to allow us enough to live comfortably. This indeed appears just, even generous, for the red man no longer has rights that he need respect, and the offer may be wise, also, as we are no longer in need of an extensive country.

There was a time when our people covered the land as the waves of a wind-ruffled sea cover its shell-paved floor, but that time long since passed away with the greatness of tribes that are now but a mournful memory. I will not dwell on, nor mourn over, our untimely decay, nor reproach my paleface brothers with hastening it, as we too may have been somewhat to blame.

Youth is impulsive. When our young men grow angry at some real or imaginary wrong, and disfigure their faces with black paint, it denotes that their hearts are black, and that they are often cruel and relentless, and our old men and old women are unable to restrain them. Thus it has ever been. Thus it was when the white man began to push our forefathers ever westward.

But let us hope that the hostilities between us may never return. We would have everything to lose and nothing to gain. Revenge by young men is considered gain, even at the cost of their own lives, but old men who stay at home in times of war, and mothers who have sons to lose, know better.

Our good father in Washington — for I presume he is now our father as well as yours, since King George[1] has moved his boundaries further north — our great and good father, I say, sends us word that if we do as he desires he will protect us. His brave warriors will be to us a bristling wall of strength, and his wonderful ships of war will fill our harbours, so that our ancient enemies far to the northward — the Haidas and Tsimshians — will cease to frighten our women, children and old men. Then in reality he will be our father and we his children.

But can that ever be? Your god is not our god! Your god loves your people and hates mine! He folds his strong protecting arms lovingly about the paleface and leads him by the hand as a father leads an infant son. But he has forsaken his red children, if they really are his.

Our god, the Great Spirit, seems also to have forsaken us. Your god makes your people wax stronger every day. Soon they will fill all the land. Our people are ebbing away like a rapidly receding tide that will never return. The white man's god cannot love our people or he would protect them. They seem to be orphans who can look nowhere for help. How then can we be brothers? How can your god become our god and renew our prosperity and awaken in us dreams of returning greatness?

If we have a common heavenly Father he must be partial, for he came to His paleface children. We never saw Him. He gave you laws but had no word for his red children, whose teeming multitudes once filled this vast continent as stars fill the firmament. No; we are two distinct races with separate origins and separate destinies. There is little in common between us.

To us the ashes of our ancestors are sacred and their resting place is hallowed ground. You wander far from the graves of your ancestors and seemingly without regret. Your religion was written upon tablets of stone by the iron finger of your god so that you could not forget. The red man could never comprehend or remember it.

Our religion is the traditions of our ancestors — the dreams of our old men, given them in solemn hours of the night by the Great Spirit; and the visions of our *sachems*,[2] and is written in the hearts of our people.

Your dead cease to love you and the land of their nativity as soon as they pass the portals of the tomb and wander away beyond the stars. They are soon forgotten and never return. Our dead never forget this beautiful world that gave them being. They still love its verdant valleys, its murmuring rivers, its magnificent mountains, sequestered vales and verdant lakes and bays, and ever yearn in tender fond affection over the lonely-hearted living, and often return from the happy hunting ground to visit, guide,

[1] The traders in Hudson's Bay still called themselves 'King George's Men' because it was felt the native population would not respect them if they knew their ruler, Queen Victoria, was a woman.

[2] Native American chiefs.

console and comfort them.

Day and night cannot dwell together. The red man has ever fled the approach of the white man, as the morning mist flees before the morning sun. However, your proposition seems fair and I think that my people will accept it and will retire to the reservation you offer them. Then we will dwell apart in peace, for the words of the great white chief seem to be the words of nature speaking to my people out of dense darkness.

It matters little where we pass the remnant of our days. They will not be many. The Indian's night promises to be dark. Not a single star of hope hovers above his horizon. Sad-voiced winds moan in the distance. Grim fate seems to be on the red man's trail, and wherever he goes he will hear the approaching footsteps of his fell destroyer and prepare stolidly to meet his doom, as does the wounded doe that hears the approaching footsteps of the hunter.

A few more moons, a few more winters, and not one of the descendants of the mighty hosts that once moved over this broad land or lived in happy homes, protected by the Great Spirit, will remain to mourn over the graves of a people once more powerful and hopeful than yours. But why should I mourn at the untimely fate of my people? Tribe follows tribe, and nation follows nation, like the waves of the sea. It is the order of nature, and regret is useless.

Your time of decay may be distant, but it will surely come, for even the white man – whose god walked and talked with him as friend to friend – cannot be exempt from the common destiny.

We may be brothers after all. We will see. We will ponder your proposition and when we decide we will let you know. But should we accept it, I here and now make this condition: that we will not be denied the privilege, without molestation, of visiting at any time the tombs of our ancestors, friends and children.

Every part of this soil is sacred in the estimation of my people. Every hillside, every valley, every plain and grove, has been hallowed by some sad or happy event in days long vanished. Even the rocks, which seem to be dumb and dead as they swelter in the sun along the silent shore, thrill with memories of stirring events connected with the lives of my people, and the very dust upon which you now stand responds more lovingly to their footsteps than yours, because it is rich with the blood of our ancestors and our bare feet are conscious of the sympathetic touch. Our departed braves, fond mothers, glad, happy-hearted maidens and even the little children who lived here and rejoiced here for a brief season, will love these sombre solitudes and at eventide they greet shadowy returning spirits.

And when the last red man shall have perished and the memory of my tribe shall have become a myth among the white men, these shores will swarm with the invisible dead of my tribe. And when your children's children think themselves alone in the field, the store, the shop, upon the highway, or in the silence of the pathless woods, they will not be alone.

In all the earth there is no place dedicated to solitude. At night, when the streets of your cities and villages are silent and you think them deserted, they will throng with the returning hosts that once filled them and still love this beautiful land. The white man will never be alone.

Let him be just and deal kindly with my people, for the dead are not powerless. Dead, did I say? There is no death; only a change of worlds.

George Bernard Shaw
Irish dramatist and critic

George Bernard Shaw (1856–1950) was born in Dublin of Protestant parents. After unhappy years at school and work for a firm of land agents, he moved to London. There he entered a period of struggle and poverty, writing five unpublished novels. Under the influence of KARL MARX, he developed a belief in socialism which underlay all his future work. He joined the Fabian Society (1884–1911), edited *Fabian Essays* (1889) and wrote many socialist tracts. He became a music critic for the *Star* (1888–90), and a drama critic for *Saturday Review* (1895–8). In 1898, he published *The Perfect Wagnerite* – which represents Wagner's *Ring* cycle as a social allegory – and married the Irish heiress Charlotte Payne-Townshend (1857–1943). His first play was *Widowers' Houses* (1892). This was followed by *Mrs Warren's Profession* (1898), *Arms and the Man* (1898), *Candida* (1897), *The Devil's Disciple* (1897), *Captain Brassbound's Conversion* (1900) and *Caesar and Cleopatra* (1901). Shaw's long correspondence with the actresses Ellen Terry (1847–1928) and Mrs Patrick Campbell (1865–1940) also developed during these years. His growing reputation was reinforced by *Man and Superman* (1902), one of his greatest philosophical comedies. Other notable plays from this period are *Major Barbara* (1905), *The Doctor's Dilemma* (1906) and *Misalliance* (1910). These embrace a wide range of subject matter, from politics to family life, prostitution and vaccination, and he sometimes fell foul of the censors. In the years before World War I came *Androcles and the Lion* (1912), a 'religious pantomime', and *Pygmalion* (1913), an anti-romantic comedy which was later adapted as a musical play, *My Fair Lady* (1956). He provoked controversy with *Common Sense About the War* (1914). Three of his greatest dramas followed the war: *Heartbreak House* (1919), an attempt to analyse moral and political discontents, *Back to Methuselah* (1921), five plays in one, and *Saint Joan* (1923), which displays Shaw's religious nature and genius for characterization. In 1931 he visited Russia, and in 1932 travelled widely with his wife. Greater perhaps than any of the late plays are two prose works: *The Intelligent Woman's Guide to Socialism and Capitalism* (1928) and *The Black Girl in Search of God* (1932). Of the later drama, only *The Apple Cart* (1929) has been regularly staged. Shaw was a passionate advocate of spelling reform and bequeathed money to fund a new phonetic writing system. He received the Nobel Prize for literature in 1925.

'A woman is really only a man in petticoats'
20 May 1927, London, England

Shaw's feminism may date from his earliest years. Certainly, his estrangement from his alcoholic father, George Carr Shaw, has been widely noted. The family did not attend his funeral in 1885, such was their profound disaffection.

By 1927, Shaw's views on the equality of the sexes had been widely disseminated for over three decades. His most notable early contribution was the play *Mrs Warren's Profession*, in which his economic rationalism on the subject of women and prostitution caused such controversy that it was not performed for many years. Meanwhile, his comment, in 1896, on 'the naïve impertinences of St Peter, who, on the subject of Woman, was neither Catholic nor Christian, but a boorish Syrian fisherman', was more feminist than theological.

But Shaw was interestingly cold in his personal relations with women. The Irish writer and editor Frank Harris, who knew him well, called him 'the first man to have cut a swathe through the theatre and left it strewn with virgins', and this description seems to be borne out by other members of his social circle.

In this speech – given on behalf of the Cecil Houses Fund at the King's Theatre, Hammersmith – Shaw's plea for refuges for homeless women seems to balance his two greatest political passions, socialism and feminism. Describing himself as hard-hearted became a favourite rhetorical device for Shaw, whose lack of sentiment was used to advantage in both theatre and public speaking. The speech also shows his ironical sense of humour.

I am addressing you in the character of a curious old relic of the Victorian age[1] ... I have something to tell you which the younger members of my audience have probably no adequate conception of – something which has a great deal to do with the extraordinary neglect on the part of organized society to provide for women the accommodations and conveniences that are provided as a matter of course for men.

The Victorian age attempted and, to an extraordinary extent, did actually succeed in one of the most amazing and grotesque enterprises ever

[1] Shaw was 71 when he made this speech.

undertaken by mankind. The Victorians were romantic people. Confronted as they were with the real human animal, male and female, they said, 'This is unendurable'. The men looked at one another, and did not like each other very much; and that sort of feeling that you must have something to adore, something to worship, something to lift you up, gave them the curious notion that if they took the women and denied that they were human beings; if they dressed them up in an extraordinary manner which entirely concealed the fact that they were human beings; if they set up a morality and a convention that women were angels; then they would succeed in making women angels, and have a society in which men found happiness in adoring a large congregation of angels.

This was very nice for the men. Also it was rather flattering to the women. But there were limits. It is all very well to be regarded as an angel up to a certain point; but there come moments at which you are seriously inconvenienced by the fact that you are not an angel; that you very seriously require certain accommodations and conveniences which angels can do without; and that when these are denied to you on the ground that you are an angel, you suffer for it. However, in the Victorian age they did not mind that. They went on dressing up the women as angels and pretending accordingly.

I well remember, when I was a small boy, receiving perhaps a greater shock than I have ever received since. I had been brought up in a world in which woman, the angel, presented to me the appearance of a spreading mountain, a sort of Primrose Hill. On the peak there was perched a small, pinched, upper part, and on top of that a human head. That, to me, at the period of life when one is young and receiving indelible impressions, was a woman.

One day, when I was perhaps five years of age, a lady paid us a visit, a very handsome lady who was always in advance of the fashion. Crinolines were going out; and she had discarded hers. I, an innocent unprepared child, walked bang into the room and suddenly saw, for the first time, a woman not shaped like Primrose Hill, but with a narrow skirt which evidently wrapped a pair of human legs. I have never recovered from the shock, and never shall.

After that, there was a certain reaction. Primrose Hill began to be reproduced again in various shapes, with bustles at the back and things of that sort. You see them in the old numbers of *Punch*, in pictures by Leech[2] and others. But, generally speaking, the reduction of women to vulgar flesh and blood continued to be prevented by a system of dressing not at all like what we now know as dressing a woman. In fact, woman was not dressed in the sense we are familiar with. She was upholstered. She was dressed in upholstering fabrics called reps; and if she was not studded with buttons all over her tempting contours like a sort of super-sofa, she was pinched in and padded out so as to produce as much of that effect as possible. You do not remember that. I do. The last woman who bravely kept up the upholstered appearance to the end was my late friend Marie Corelli.[3] She being gone, I look round the world, and I do not see any woman now who is upholstered.

I lived on to an advanced age and received another shock. I received a visit at Adelphi Terrace from a foreign princess, a very charming woman bearing the name of one of Napoleon's marshals. She sat down on the sofa, and I talked to her; and as she had a very pretty face I was principally occupied by that. But after we had been conversing – though I do not

[2] The cartoonist John Leech (1817–64), who was known for his work in the satirical magazine *Punch*.

[3] The romantic novelist Marie Corelli *real name Mary Mackay* (1855–1924) was critically abhorred but extremely popular with readers.

know that she had much chance in the conversation; so let us say when I had been shewing off for a quarter of an hour – I paused for breath, and in the course of my pausing I happened to look down. To my utter amazement I discovered that her skirt came only to her knees. I had never before seen such a spectacle, except on the stage. I thought, 'Great Heavens! The princess has forgotten her skirt!'; and I almost lost my presence of mind. Well, now all that is gone; I can stand any amount of ladies with their skirts to their knees without turning a hair.

I am telling you all this with a serious purpose. The dress has changed, but the morality has not. People are still full of the old idea that woman is a special creation. I am bound to say that of late years she has been working extremely hard to eradicate that impression, and make one understand that a woman is really only a man in petticoats. People sometimes wonder what is the secret of the extraordinary knowledge of women which I shew in my plays. They very often accuse me of having acquired it by living a most abandoned life. But I never acquired it. I have always assumed that a woman is a person exactly like myself, and that is how the trick is done.

But the world has not come to that frame of mind yet. In spite of Mr Kipling's attempt to make you understand that the woman is only the female of the species,[4] there is still an idea that men and women are different creatures, the man having many needs and the woman being only one of them.

[4] Shaw refers to the poem 'The Female of the Species' (1911) by the English writer RUDYARD KIPLING.

When I went into active municipal life, and became a member of the Health Committee of a London Borough Council,[5] the question of providing accommodation for women, which was part of our business, was one which I conceived to be pressingly important. And you can have no idea of the difficulty I had in getting that notion, to a limited extent, into the heads of the gentlemen who were working with me on the Committee …

[5] Shaw had served on the St Pancras Borough Council, 1897–1904.

A doctor rose to call attention to a case in which a woman was concerned. He happened to mention that she had been in his hands because she was expecting her confinement. Now, I notice that you all receive that in perfectly decorous silence; there does not seem to you anything funny about it. But I assure you that on that Health Committee – and it is not much more than twenty years ago – no sooner had the doctor uttered this revelation than the whole Committee burst into a roar of laughter. You see, there was not only the angel conception: there was also the inevitable reaction against it. If anyone betrayed the secret or gave it away, half the world was shocked, and the other half roared with laughter.

There was a noteworthy feature in the pantomimes of my early days. No part of the harlequinade was complete unless one of the scenes shewed an old woman dropping from a top window or climbing over a wall, the joke being that in the course of these gymnastics she thrust her leg from under her skirt, in a white stocking, and allowed the audience to see almost up to her knee, eliciting a shriek of laughter. Propriety was saved by the fact that the old woman was obviously a man dressed up as a woman. You can tell from the old comic pictures of those days that to see even a woman's ankle was considered half a shocking thing and half an obscene joke!

I have taken up the time of the meeting with all this because really, unless you grasp it, unless you understand that this thing remains still with us as a superstition even now, when we think we have completely freed ourselves of it, you will be bewildered when, in dealing with this question of lodging-houses for women, you come right up against it. It is the real reason why, when on that public body I talked and talked to get proper, common, sanitary accommodation for women, I found it impossible for a long time to get over the opposition to it as an indecency. A lavatory for women was described as an abomination. Exactly the same feeling stands in the way of providing for women what is popularly called a 'doss house'.

Now, this work ought not to be left to Mrs Chesterton.[6] Not that she is not doing it remarkably well; but it is not her job. It is the job of all of us. It ought to be done by the London County Council. But this is not a reason for saying: 'Oh, well, we may leave it to the London County Council.' If you do, it will not be done.

Before a public body takes up something of this kind, its practicability and the public need for it generally has to be demonstrated by private initiative. If you will help Mrs Chesterton to set up, say, a dozen of these doss houses in London, to do for women what Lord Rowton[7] did for men – and why he never thought of the women I am sure I do not know; but he did not: he left it to you – if you set up a dozen of these houses, and prove that they work well, and that they are wanted, then there will be a very fair chance of inducing the London County Council to take them over and to make more of them, until there is a really adequate supply.

But it is we who must begin; and when the Council takes up the work it will make all the other people who are not here today contribute their share. That is why we are beginning as we are today. You must build another house, and another house; and then in the course of another 100 years or so the London County Council will wake up and do its duty.

Let me end with one or two general moral observations. To qualify herself for this work, Mrs Chesterton had to become a waif and an outcast;[8] but it was impossible for her to go on with that long enough: I can quite understand why. If you cast a glance at the people sleeping out on the Thames Embankment and in the Adelphi Arches (I live in the Adelphi, but not in the Arches) or huddling on the Waterloo Bridge steps or the other places where you can get out of the wind, your feeling always is, 'This thing is a social shame.'

It is an individual shame to you. It is outrageous that these things should be. You do not lack sympathy. You think it is cruel. Your imagination assumes despair, misery and so on. Ladies and gentlemen: that is not altogether the case. If you will steel yourselves to investigate; if you will, with a perfectly unbiased mind, look at the homeless people, the people who have got into the way of having no place to live in, and nothing material to think of; if you make a careful study of their faces, and estimate their happiness by their expression; and if you will then turn from them and study, say, an ordinary congregation in a respectable church, or even a number of well-dressed people taken at random in the rich parts of the town, you will suddenly begin to doubt very much which are the happier people.

The truth of the matter is that one of the things that we have to do is to prevent people finding out what a jolly thing it is to be a destitute and therefore irresponsible person. That is the real danger. That is the reason why you must not only do your best to provide lodging-houses for the women, but also do your best to provide them with the shilling to go to the house. That is also important; because if a woman has not got a shilling she cannot go to Mrs Chesterton's house.

If I were to pretend to be deeply moved by the lot of all these homeless women, I should be a mere hypocrite. I am more than 70 years of age; and so much human suffering has been crowded into those 70 years that I am in

[6] The English philanthropist and writer Ada Chesterton (1886–1962) provided accommodation for destitute women via the charity Cecil Houses, on behalf of which this speech was given. It was named after her late husband, the campaigning journalist Cecil Chesterton (1879–1918).

[7] The English philanthropist Montagu William Lowry-Corry, 1st Baron Rowton (1838–1903) was private secretary to BENJAMIN DISRAELI. He built six houses in London to provide cheap and clean accommodation for workmen otherwise forced to live in filthy lodging houses. JOSEPH STALIN stayed in a Rowton house in 1907.

[8] Ada Chesterton had spent time living among destitute women, and wrote of her experiences in the books *In Darkest London* (1926) and *I Lived in a Slum* (1936).

the condition of Macbeth in his last Act: 'I have supped full with horrors: direness, familiar to my slaughterous thoughts, cannot once start me.'[9]

Another million of starving children has become as nothing to me. I am acquiring the curious callousness of old age. At first, when I was beginning to get on in years, I used to feel sad when my old friends and even enemies began dropping round me. Nowadays I have got over that: I exult every time another goes down. I am a man of the most extraordinary hardness of heart; and I suggest to you that this is an undesirable condition for an old man to be in. I suggest to you that it is a frightful thought that if you are not careful, if you are not more thoughtful and humane than my generation was, there may be, 70 years hence, another old man looking on at horrible preventable evils with a heart as hard as mine. That is clearly an undesirable thing; and so I will sit down and leave the appeal to younger people who have still some sensibilities left.

❧

'They enforce your slavery and call it freedom'
18 June 1935, radio broadcast from London, England

❧

By now well advanced in years, Shaw retained a sense of the zealous socialism that had informed his work and thinking since the 1880s. His opinions had always been controversial, but public disapproval had grown since 1931, when he had visited JOSEPH STALIN's Soviet Union and returned with some enthusiasm for the project. He had also, by then, provided BENITO MUSSOLINI's new regime in Italy with an endorsement – albeit a qualified and ambivalent one. Although in both cases Shaw's admiration was rich in caveats, he was now treated with suspicion even by some fellow Fabians.

However, thanks to the historical context, much of what he said in this BBC radio address was accessible to a surprisingly wide audience. Particularly pertinent are his comments about the electoral process. In 1931, the national government had been formed – an uneasy coalition between RAMSAY MACDONALD's Labour Party and the Conservatives led by STANLEY BALDWIN. To many, it seemed there were few ideological differences between the main political parties. Shaw's flirtations with Oswald Mosley – the former Labour minister and British Fascist leader – should be seen in the context of the Great Depression of the early 1930s, a time when extremism flourished in Britain as well as elsewhere in Europe.

❧

What is a perfectly free person? Evidently a person who can do what he likes, when he likes and where he likes, or do nothing at all if he prefers it. Well, there is no such person, and there never can be any such person. Whether we like it or not, we must all sleep for one third of our lifetime, wash and dress and undress. We must spend a couple of hours eating and drinking. We must spend nearly as much in getting about from place to place. For half the day we are slaves to necessities which we cannot shirk, whether we are monarchs with a thousand slaves or humble labourers with no servants but their wives. And the wives must undertake the additional heavy slavery of childbearing, if the world is still to be peopled.

These natural jobs cannot be shirked. But they involve other jobs which can. As we must eat we must first provide food; as we must sleep, we must have beds, and bedding in houses with fireplaces and coals; as we must walk through the streets, we must have clothes to cover our nakedness. Now, food and houses and clothes can be produced by human labour. But when they are produced they can be stolen. If you like honey you can let the bees produce it by their labour, and then steal it from them. If you are too lazy to get about from place to place on your own legs you can make a slave of a horse. And what you do to a horse or a bee, you can also do to a man or a woman or a child, if you can get the upper hand of them by force or fraud or trickery of any sort, or even by teaching them that it is their religious duty

[9] Towards the end of the tragedy *Macbeth* (c.1606) by the English playwright William Shakespeare (1564–1616), the central character is psychologically overwhelmed by the consequences of his actions. Shaw quotes from Act V, scene i.

to sacrifice their freedom to yours.

So beware! If you allow any person, or class of persons, to get the upper hand of you, he will shift all that part of his slavery to nature that can be shifted on to your shoulders; and you will find yourself working from eight to fourteen hours a day when, if you had only yourself and your family to provide for, you could do it quite comfortably in half the time or less. The object of all honest governments should be to prevent your being imposed on in this way.

But the object of most actual governments, I regret to say, is exactly the opposite. They enforce your slavery and call it freedom. But they also regulate your slavery, keeping the greed of your masters within certain bounds. When chattel slavery of the negro sort costs more than wage slavery, they abolish chattel slavery and make you free to choose between one employment or one master and another, and this they call a glorious triumph for freedom, though for you it is merely the key of the street. When you complain, they promise that in future you shall govern the country for yourself. They redeem this promise by giving you a vote, and having a general election every five years or so.

At the election two of their rich friends ask for your vote, and you are free to choose which of them you will vote for to spite the other – a choice which leaves you no freer than you were before, as it does not reduce your hours of labour by a single minute. But the newspapers assure you that your vote has decided the election, and that this constitutes you a free citizen in a democratic country. The amazing thing about it is that you are fool enough to believe them.

Now mark another big difference between the natural slavery of man to nature and the unnatural slavery of man to man. Nature is kind to her slaves. If she forces you to eat and drink, she makes eating and drinking so pleasant that when we can afford it we eat and drink too much. We must sleep or go mad: but then sleep is so pleasant that we have great difficulty in getting up in the morning. And firesides and families seem so pleasant to the young that they get married and join building societies to realize their dreams. Thus, instead of resenting our natural wants as slavery, we take the greatest pleasure in their satisfaction. We write sentimental songs in praise of them. A tramp can earn his supper by singing 'Home, Sweet Home'.

The slavery of man to man is the very opposite of this. It is hateful to the body and to the spirit. Our poets do not praise it: they proclaim that no man is good enough to be another man's master. The latest of the great Jewish prophets, a gentleman named MARX, spent his life in proving that there is no extremity of selfish cruelty at which the slavery of man to man will stop if it be not stopped by law …

When we grumble, we are told that all our miseries are our own doing because we have the vote. When we say 'What good is the vote?' we are told that we have the Factory Acts,[1] and the Wages Boards,[2] and free education, and the New Deal,[3] and the dole;[4] and what more could any reasonable man ask for? We are reminded that the rich are taxed a quarter, a third, or even a half and more of their incomes; but the poor are never reminded that they have to pay that much of their wages as rent in addition to having to work twice as long every day as they would need if they were free.

Whenever famous writers protest against this imposture – say Voltaire[5] and Rousseau[6] and Tom Paine[7] in the 18th century, or Cobbett[8] and Shelley,[9] Karl Marx and Lassalle[10] in the 19th, or LENIN and TROTSKY in the

[1] The Factory Acts of 1833–1901 introduced a series of limitations on the minimum age of child workers and the hours that women and children could work.
[2] Independent National Wages Boards were established during the 1920s to help resolve industrial disputes.
[3] A general term for the programme of legislation introduced from 1933 in the USA by President FRANKLIN D ROOSEVELT, designed to bring about economic and social recovery after the Great Depression.
[4] An informal term for the benefits paid to unemployed workers.
[5] The French writer, philosopher and satirist François-Marie Arouet *known as Voltaire* (1694–1778) was a fierce social campaigner and a central figure of the Enlightenment.
[6] The French philosopher and writer Jean-Jacques Rousseau (1712–78) is best known for his book *The Social Contract* (1762), advocating a collectivist society. He was a key influence on French revolutionary thinking.
[7] The English philosopher Thomas Paine (1737–1809) advocated American independence in his pamphlet 'Common Sense' (1776). His book *The Rights of Man* supported the French Revolution and proposed abolition of the British monarchy. He became an American citizen in 1795.
[8] The English journalist and agriculturist William Cobbett (1763–1835) was known for his radical views and distaste for authority, which led to his imprisonment for treasonous libel (1810–12).
[9] The English poet Percy Bysshe Shelley (1792–1822) was a key figure of the Romantic movement and after his death was embraced by Socialists for his radical opinions.
[10] The German Socialist politician Ferdinand Lassalle (1825–64) formed the General German Workers' Association in 1863, but was ostracized by Marx's followers for negotiating with the Prussian leader Otto von Bismarck (1815–98) over universal suffrage.

20th – you are taught that they are atheists and libertines, murderers and scoundrels; and often it is made a criminal offence to buy or sell their books. If their disciples make a revolution, England immediately makes war on them and lends money to the other powers to join her in forcing the revolutionists to restore the slave order ...

So far I have mentioned nothing but plain natural and historical facts. I draw no conclusions, for that would lead me into controversy, and controversy would not be fair when you cannot answer me back. I am never controversial over the wireless. I do not even ask you to draw your own conclusions, for you might draw some very dangerous ones, unless you have the right sort of head for it.

Always remember that though nobody likes to be called a slave, it does not follow that slavery is a bad thing. Great men, like Aristotle,[11] have held that law and order and government would be impossible unless the persons the people have to obey are beautifully dressed and decorated, robed and uniformed, speaking with a special accent, travelling in first-class carriages or the most expensive cars, or on the best-groomed and best-bred horses, and never cleaning their own boots, nor doing anything for themselves that can possibly be done by ringing a bell and ordering some common person to do it. And this means, of course, that they must be made very rich without any obligation other than to produce an impression of almost godlike superiority on the minds of common people. In short, it is contended, you must make men ignorant idolaters before they will become obedient workers and law-abiding citizens.

To prove this, we are reminded that, although nine out of ten voters are common workers, it is with the greatest difficulty that a few of them can be persuaded to vote for the members of their own class. When women were enfranchised and given the right to sit in Parliament, the first use they made of their votes was to defeat all the women candidates who stood for the freedom of the workers and had given them years of devoted and distinguished service. They elected only one woman – a titled lady of great wealth and exceptionally fascinating personality ...[12]

The practical question at the bottom of it all is how the income of the whole country can best be distributed from day to day. If the earth is cultivated agriculturally in vast farms with motor ploughs and chemical fertilizers, and industrially in huge electrified factories full of machinery that a girl can handle, the product may be so great that an equal distribution of it would provide enough to give the unskilled labourers as much as the managers and the men of the scientific staff. But do not forget, when you hear tales of modern machinery enabling one girl to produce as much as a thousand men could produce in the reign of good Queen Anne,[13] that this marvellous increase includes things like needles and steel pins and matches, which we can neither eat nor drink nor wear. Very young children will eat needles and matches eagerly – but the diet is not a nourishing one. And though we can now cultivate the sky as well as the earth, by drawing nitrogen from it to increase and improve the quality of our grass and, consequently, of our cattle and milk and butter and eggs, Nature may have tricks up her sleeve to check us if the chemists exploit her too greedily.

And now to sum up. Wipe out from your dreams of freedom the hope of being able to do as you please all the time. For at least twelve hours of your day Nature orders you to do certain things, and will kill you if you don't do them. This leaves twelve hours for working; and here again Nature will kill you unless you either earn your living or get somebody else to earn it for

[11] The Greek philosopher Aristotle (384–322 BC) is one of the greatest influences on European thought. His central idea was empiricism: the reliance of knowledge on experience.

[12] Lady NANCY ASTOR.

[13] The British monarch Queen Anne (1665–1714) reigned in England, Scotland and Ireland from 1702 until her death, and in 1707 became the first monarch of Great Britain. Her reign was politically turbulent, but is regarded as a time when culture flourished.

you. If you live in a civilized country your freedom is restricted by the laws of the land enforced by the police, who oblige you to do this, and not to do that, and to pay rates and taxes …

But as society is constituted at present, there is another far more intimate compulsion on you: that of your landlord and that of your employer. Your landlord may refuse to let you live on his estate if you go to chapel instead of to church, or if you vote for anyone but his nominee, or if you practise osteopathy, or if you open a shop. Your employer may dictate the cut, colour, and condition of your clothes, as well as your hours of work. He can turn you into the street at any moment to join the melancholy band of lost spirits called the Unemployed. In short, his power over you is far greater than that of any political dictator could possibly be.

Your only remedy at present is the Trade Union weapon of the strike, which is only the old Oriental device of starving on your enemy's doorstep until he does you justice. Now, as the police in this country will not allow you to starve on your employer's doorstep, you must starve on your own – if you have one. The extreme form of the strike – the general strike of all workers at the same moment – is also the extreme form of human folly, as, if completely carried out, it would extinguish the human race in a week. And the workers would be the first to perish. The general strike is Trade Unionism gone mad. Sane Trade Unionism would never sanction more than one big strike at a time, with all the other trades working overtime to support it …

We must change our politics before we can get what we want; and meanwhile we must stop gassing about freedom, because the people of England in the lump don't know what freedom is, never having had any. Always call freedom by its old English name of leisure, and keep clamouring for more leisure and more money to enjoy it in return for an honest share of work …

And now suppose we at last win a lot more leisure and a lot more money than we are accustomed to. What are we going to do with them? I was taught in my childhood that Satan will find mischief still for idle hands to do. I have seen men come into a fortune and lose their happiness, their health, and finally their lives by it as certainly as if they had taken daily doses of rat poison instead of champagne and cigars. It is not at all easy to know what to do with leisure unless we have been brought up to it.

I will therefore leave you with a conundrum to think over. If you had your choice, would you work for eight hours a day and retire with a full pension at 45, or would you rather work four hours a day and keep on working until you are 70? Now, don't send the answer to me, please. Talk it over with your wife.

Margaret Chase Smith
American politician

Margaret Chase Smith *née Chase* (1897–1995) was born in Skowhegan, Maine, the daughter of a barber. She worked as a teacher, then on a newspaper, marrying its publisher, Clyde Smith, in 1930. He became US Representative in Washington and when he died in 1940 she took over his position, becoming Maine's first Congresswoman. Eight years later, she became the first woman elected as a US senator in her own right and the first woman to be elected to both houses of the US Congress. She was also the first woman to read the address to the Senate. Re-elected three times, she served until 1973. In 1950 she became one of the first Republican senators to speak out against the anti-communist activities of Senator JOSEPH MCCARTHY, and in 1964 she campaigned for the office of US president, the first woman to do so since Victoria Woodhull in 1872. She wrote the books *Gallant Women* (1968) and *Declaration of Conscience* (1972). In 1989 she was awarded the Presidential Medal of Freedom.

'A forum of hate and character assassination'
1 June 1950, Washington, DC, USA

When the softly-spoken junior Republican senator from Maine concluded this 15-minute address to the Chamber, her listeners might have reflected that her reputation for courage and independence was well founded. She never named Senator McCarthy, but received widespread recognition for denouncing hearings that were virtually charging people with treason on the flimsiest of evidence and without due process of law. Her picture appeared on the cover of *Newsweek* magazine, and she was personally congratulated by President HARRY S TRUMAN.

By 1950, the Cold War had reached a critical phase. The 'Red Scare' had grown out of tensions following World War II, including specific diplomatic disputes, and had been exaggerated by political polarization, broadly between communism and Western capitalism. Fear of internal subversion by communists or 'fellow travellers' intensified after the revolution in China in 1949 and the test detonation of the first Soviet nuclear device the same year. By the end of June 1950, the Cold War would turn hot in Korea.

McCarthy's anti-communist 'witch hunt' was sanctioned by the Senate and publicized throughout the USA. In many respects it was not unlike the Soviet show-trials taking place at the behest of JOSEPH STALIN around the same time. Reputations were destroyed, and the ripples from the McCarthy hearings reached all walks of life, particularly education and the media. It was only in 1954, when McCarthy began investigating the army and the administration of former president DWIGHT D EISENHOWER that he was himself investigated, and officially censured by the Senate.

Mr President: I would like to speak briefly and simply about a serious national condition. It is a national feeling of fear and frustration that could result in national suicide and the end of everything that we Americans hold dear. It is a condition that comes from the lack of effective leadership, either in the legislative branch or the executive branch of our government.

That leadership is so lacking that serious and responsible proposals are being made that national advisory commissions be appointed to provide such critically needed leadership.

I speak as briefly as possible, because too much harm has already been done with irresponsible words of bitterness and selfish political opportunism. I speak as simply as possible because the issue is too great to be obscured by eloquence. I speak simply and briefly in the hope that my words will be taken to heart.

Mr President: I speak as a Republican. I speak as a woman. I speak as a United States senator. I speak as an American.

The United States Senate has long enjoyed worldwide respect as the greatest deliberative body in the world. But recently that deliberative character has too often been debased to the level of a forum of hate and character assassination, sheltered by the shield of congressional immunity.

It is ironical that we senators can, in debate in the Senate, directly or indirectly, by any form of words, impute to any American who is not a senator any conduct or motive unworthy or unbecoming an American – and without that non-senator American having any legal redress against us – yet if we say the same thing in the Senate about our colleagues we can be stopped on the grounds of being out of order.

It is strange that we can verbally attack anyone else without restraint and with full protection, and yet we hold ourselves above the same type of criticism here on the Senate floor. Surely the United States Senate is big enough to take self-criticism and self-appraisal. Surely we should be able to take the same kind of character attacks that we 'dish out' to outsiders.

I think that it is high time for the United States Senate and its members to do some real soul-searching and to weigh our consciences as to the manner in which we are performing our duty to the people of America and the manner in which we are using or abusing our individual powers and privileges.

I think that it is high time that we remembered that we have sworn to uphold and defend the Constitution. I think that it is high time that we remembered that the Constitution, as amended, speaks not only of the freedom of speech but also of trial by jury instead of trial by accusation. Whether it be a criminal prosecution in court or a character prosecution in the Senate, there is little practical distinction when the life of a person has been ruined.

Those of us who shout the loudest about Americanism in making character assassinations are all too frequently those who, by our own words and acts, ignore some of the basic principles of Americanism: the right to criticize. The right to hold unpopular beliefs. The right to protest. The right of independent thought.

The exercise of these rights should not cost one single American citizen his reputation or his right to a livelihood; nor should he be in danger of losing his reputation or livelihood merely because he happens to know someone who holds unpopular beliefs. Who of us does not? Otherwise none of us could call our souls our own. Otherwise thought control would have set in.

The American people are sick and tired of being afraid to speak their minds lest they be politically smeared as 'communists' or 'fascists' by their opponents. Freedom of speech is not what it used to be in America. It has been so abused by some that it is not exercised by others.

The American people are sick and tired of seeing innocent people smeared and guilty people whitewashed. But there have been enough proved cases – such as the *Amerasia* case,[1] the Hiss case,[2] the Coplon case,[3] the Gold case[4] – to cause nationwide distrust and strong suspicion that there my be something to the unproved, sensational accusations.

As a Republican, I say to my colleagues on this side of the aisle that the Republican Party faces a challenge today that is not unlike the challenge which it faced back in LINCOLN's day. The Republican Party so successfully met that challenge that it emerged from the Civil War as the champion of a united nation – in addition to being a party which unrelentingly fought loose spending and loose programmes.

Today, our country is being psychologically divided by the confusion and the suspicions that are bred in the United States Senate to spread like cancerous tentacles of 'know nothing; suspect everything' attitudes. Today we have a Democratic administration which has developed a mania for loose spending and loose programmes. History is repeating itself – and the Republican Party again has the opportunity to emerge as the champion

[1] *Amerasia* was a US magazine concerned with Asian affairs. In June 1945, six people associated with it were arrested, including three government employees, following the theft of classified documents. The charges were dropped because government agents had acquired evidence during a burglary on *Amerasia*'s offices.

[2] The US government official Alger Hiss (1904–96) was arrested in 1948 on charges of spying for the USSR. He was ultimately convicted of perjury and jailed in January 1950. However, it was later revealed that the FBI had given perjurious evidence, and the government had illegally withheld relevant information.

[3] The US Justice Department employee Judith Coplon (1922–2011) became a Soviet spy in 1944. She was convicted of espionage and conspiracy (1949–50), but her convictions were overturned due to legal blunders by the FBI, which had arrested her without a warrant.

[4] The Russian–American chemist Harry Gold (1910–74) worked as a Soviet spy from 1934 until his arrest in 1950. During his FBI interrogation and trial, he provided evidence that was later found to be unreliable. He was convicted in 1951, and after serving half of a 30-year sentence was released in 1966.

of unity and prudence.

The record of the present Democratic administration has provided us with sufficient campaign issues, without the necessity of resorting to political smears. America is rapidly losing its position as leader of the world, simply because the Democratic administration has pitifully failed to provide effective leadership.

The Democratic administration has completely confused the American people by its daily, contradictory, grave warnings and optimistic assurances, which show the people that our Democratic administration has no idea of where it is going.

The Democratic administration has greatly lost the confidence of the American people by its complacency to the threat of communism here at home, and the leak of vital secrets to Russia through key officials of the Democratic administration. There are enough proved cases to make this point without diluting our criticism with unproved charges.

Surely these are sufficient reasons to make it clear to the American people that it is time for a change and that a Republican victory is necessary to the security of the country. Surely it is clear that this nation will continue to suffer so long as it is governed by the present ineffective Democratic administration.

Yet to displace it with a Republican regime embracing a philosophy that lacks political integrity or intellectual honesty would prove equally disastrous to the nation. The nation sorely needs a Republican victory. But I do no want to see the Republican Party ride to political victory on the Four Horsemen of Calumny — Fear, Ignorance, Bigotry and Smear.

I doubt if the Republican Party could do so, simply because I do not believe the American people will uphold any political party that puts political exploitation above national interest. Surely we Republicans are not that desperate for victory.

I do not want to see the Republican Party win that way. While it might be a fleeting victory for the Republican Party, it would be a more lasting defeat for the American people. Surely it would ultimately be suicide for the Republican Party and the two-party system that has protected our American liberties from the dictatorship of a one-party system.

As members of the minority party, we do not have the primary authority to formulate the policy of our government. But we do have the responsibility of rendering constructive criticism, of clarifying issues, of allaying fears by acting as responsible citizens.

As a woman, I wonder how the mothers, wives, sisters, and daughters feel about the way in which members of their families have been politically mangled in Senate debate — and I use the word 'debate' advisedly.

As a United States senator, I am not proud of the way in which the Senate has been made a publicity platform for irresponsible sensationalism. I am not proud of the reckless abandon in which unproved charges have been hurled from this side of the aisle. I am not proud of the obviously staged, undignified counter-charges which have been attempted in retaliation from the other side of the aisle.

I do not like the way the Senate has been made a rendezvous for vilification, for selfish political gain at the sacrifice of individual reputations and national unity. I am not proud of the way we smear outsiders from the floor of the Senate and hide behind the cloak of congressional immunity and still place ourselves beyond criticism on the floor of the Senate.

As an American, I am shocked at the way Republicans and Democrats alike are playing directly into the communist design of 'confuse, divide, and conquer'. As an American, I do not want a Democratic administration 'whitewash' or 'cover-up' any more than I want a Republican smear or witch-hunt.

As an American, I condemn a Republican fascist just as much as I condemn a Democrat communist. I condemn a Democrat fascist just as much as I condemn a Republican communist. They are equally dangerous to you and me and to our country.

As an American, I want to see our nation recapture the strength and unity it once had when we fought the enemy instead of ourselves.

It is with these thoughts that I have drafted what I call a Declaration of Conscience. I am gratified that the Senator from New Hampshire,[5] the Senator from Vermont,[6] the Senator from Oregon,[7] the Senator from New York,[8] the Senator from Minnesota,[9] and the Senator from New Jersey[10] have concurred in that declaration and have authorized me to announce their concurrence.

The declaration reads as follows:

1. We are Republicans. But we are Americans first. It is as Americans that we express our concern with the growing confusion that threatens the security and stability of our country. Democrats and Republicans alike have contributed to that confusion.

2. The Democratic administration has initially created the confusion by its lack of effective leadership, by its contradictory grave warnings and optimistic assurances, by its complacency to the threat of communism here at home, by its oversensitiveness to rightful criticism, by its petty bitterness against its critics.

3. Certain elements of the Republican Party have materially added to this confusion in the hopes of riding the Republican Party to victory through the selfish political exploitation of fear, bigotry, ignorance, and intolerance. There are enough mistakes of the Democrats for Republicans to criticize constructively without resorting to political smears.

4. To this extent, Democrats and Republicans alike have unwittingly, but undeniably, played directly into the communist design of 'confuse, divide, and conquer'.

5. It is high time that we stopped thinking politically as Republicans and Democrats about elections and started thinking patriotically as Americans about national security based on individual freedom. It is high time that we all stopped being tools and victims of totalitarian techniques – techniques that, if continued here unchecked, will surely end what we have come to cherish as the American way of life.

[5] The US politician Charles W Tobey (1880–1953) served as Republican senator from New Hampshire, 1933–53.

[6] The US politician George D Aiken (1892–1984) served as Republican senator from Vermont, 1941–74.

[7] The US politician Wayne L Morse (1900–74) served as Republican senator from Oregon, 1945–68.

[8] The US politician Irving M Ives (1896–1962) served as Republican senator from New York, 1947–58.

[9] The US politician Edward J Thye (1896–1969) served as Republican senator from Minnesota, 1947–58.

[10] The US politician Robert C Hendrickson (1898–1964) served as Republican senator from New Jersey, 1949–54.

C P Snow

English novelist and physicist

Charles Percy Snow *later Baron Snow* (1905–80) was born in Leicester and was educated at Alderman Newton's School. He studied science at Leicester University College, and Christ's College, Cambridge, and became a Fellow of Christ's College (1930–50) and a tutor there (1935–45). He was chief of scientific personnel for the Ministry of Labour during World War II, and a Civil Service commissioner from 1945 to 1960. His major sequence of novels began with *Strangers and Brothers* (1940), which gave its name to the series, and features the character Lewis Eliot, through whose eyes the dilemmas of the age are focused. It was followed after the war by *The Light and the Dark* (1947) and *Time of Hope* (1949). *The Masters* (1951) stages the conflict aroused by the election of a new master in a Cambridge college. *The New Men* (1954) poses the dilemma faced by scientists in the development of nuclear fission. Other books include *Corridors of Power* (1964) and *The Sleep of Reason* (1968). Several have been adapted for theatre and television. Though the chief characters of his cycle are rather supine, being manipulated to exhibit the expressed problems, mostly of power and prestige, his work shows a keen appreciation of moral issues in a science-dominated age. His controversial Rede lecture 'The Two Cultures' discussed the dichotomy between science and literature and his belief in closer contact between them. Created a life peer in 1964, he was made Parliamentary Secretary at the Ministry of Technology (1964–6) and was Rector of St Andrews University (1961–4). In 1950 he married the novelist Pamela Hansford Johnson.

'The misunderstandings between the two cultures'

7 May 1959, Cambridge, England

As both a successful novelist and a scientist of distinction, C P Snow was almost uniquely placed to observe a fundamental schism in the intellectual life of his culture. He is probably best known for having addressed this problem in his essay 'The Two Cultures', on which he later expanded in his Rede lecture at Cambridge University.

There is insufficient space here to give the whole lecture: this is an abridged version of the first section, in which Snow laid out the basis of the problem. Later in the lecture, he tried to warn both factions of the difficulties they would face in addressing the world's problems if they failed to communicate.

Despite his academic credentials, Snow is careful to phrase his argument in terms easily understood by anyone. He also occupies an even-handed position, though he is critical of arrogance on both sides. He applauds scientists for their altruism, but defends artists from the charges of cynical indifference or worse attracted by a few individuals.

Later published as a book, the lecture was widely discussed on both sides of the Atlantic, leading Snow to publish *The Two Cultures: A Second Look* in 1964. His ideas were not, however, universally admired. In an essay of 1962, the distinguished literary critic F R Leavis dismissed Snow as a 'public relations man' for the scientific fraternity.

Nor has Snow been much heeded. Although, as he concedes, a few members of each school are conversant with the other, the two cultures are no closer to uniting half a century later.

It is about three years since I made a sketch in print of a problem which had been on my mind for some time.[1] It was a problem I could not avoid just because of the circumstances of my life. The only credentials I had to ruminate on the subject at all came through those circumstances, through nothing more than a set of chances. Anyone with similar experience would have seen much the same things and I think made very much the same comments about them. It just happened to be an unusual experience. By training I was a scientist; by vocation I was a writer. That was all. It was a piece of luck, if you like, that arose through coming from a poor home.[2]

But my personal history isn't the point now. All that I need say is that I came to Cambridge and did a bit of research here at a time of major scientific activity … So for 30 years I have had to be in touch with scientists, not only out of curiosity, but as part of a working existence. During the same 30 years I was trying to shape the books I wanted to write, which in due course took me among writers.

[1] This lecture was a development of ideas first put forward in an essay 'The Two Cultures', published in the *New Statesman*, 6 October 1956.

[2] Raised in a poor family, Snow undertook a scientific training in the belief that this would provide him with better employment opportunities.

There have been plenty of days when I have spent the working hours with scientists and then gone off at night with some literary colleagues. I mean that literally. I have had, of course, intimate friends among both scientists and writers. It was through living among these groups and much more, I think, through moving regularly from one to the other and back again that I got occupied with the problem of what, long before I put it on paper, I christened to myself as the 'two cultures'. For constantly I felt I was moving among two groups – comparable in intelligence, identical in race, not grossly different in social origin, earning about the same incomes – who had almost ceased to communicate at all; who in intellectual, moral and psychological climate had so little in common that instead of going from Burlington House or South Kensington to Chelsea,[3] one might have crossed an ocean.

[3] Burlington House in Piccadilly, London, houses the secretariats of several learned scientific societies. South Kensington is the location of several national museums, including the National Science Museum and the Natural History Museum. Chelsea attracted many literary and artistic residents in the 19th and 20th centuries.

In fact, one had travelled much further than across an ocean – because after a few thousand Atlantic miles, one found Greenwich Village[4] talking precisely the same language as Chelsea, and both having about as much communication with MIT[5] as though the scientists spoke nothing but Tibetan. For this is not just our problem … By and large this is a problem of the entire West.

[4] Greenwich Village is a district of Manhattan, New York City particularly known for its artistic residents and bohemian culture.
[5] The Massachusetts Institute of Technology, opened in 1865, is one of the world's leading scientific and technology research institutions.

By this I intend something serious. I believe the intellectual life of the whole of western society is increasingly being split into two polar groups. When I say the intellectual life, I mean to include also a large part of our practical life, because I should be the last person to suggest the two can at the deepest level be distinguished. I shall come back to the practical life a little later. Two polar groups: at one pole we have the literary intellectuals, who incidentally while no-one was looking took to referring to themselves as 'intellectuals' as though there were no others …

Literary intellectuals at one pole; at the other scientists, and as the most representative, the physical scientists. Between the two a gulf of mutual incomprehension; sometimes (particularly among the young) hostility and dislike, but most of all lack of understanding. They have a curious, distorted image of each other. Their attitudes are so different that, even on the level of emotion, they can't find much common ground.

Non-scientists tend to think of scientists as brash and boastful. They hear Mr T S Eliot,[6] who just for these illustrations we can take as an archetypal figure, saying about his attempts to revive verse-drama, that we can hope for very little, but that he would feel content if he and his co-workers could prepare the ground for a new Kyd or a new Greene.[7] That is the tone, restricted and constrained, with which literary intellectuals are at home: it is the subdued voice of their culture.

[6] The US poet and playwright T S Eliot (1888–1965) wrote verse dramas including *Murder in the Cathedral* (1935) and *The Cocktail Party* (1950).
[7] The English playwrights Thomas Kyd (c.1557–1595) and Robert Greene (c.1558–92) are considered minor dramatists of the Elizabethan era. Their work has been overshadowed by that of their contemporary, William Shakespeare (1564–1616).

Then they hear a much louder voice, that of another archetypal figure, Rutherford,[8] trumpeting: 'This is the heroic age of science! This is the Elizabethan age!'. Many of us heard that – and a good many other statements beside which that was mild – and we weren't left in any doubt whom Rutherford was casting for the role of Shakespeare. What is hard for the literary intellectuals to understand, imaginatively or intellectually, is that he was absolutely right …

[8] The New Zealand-born British physicist Ernest Rutherford, 1st Baron Rutherford (1871–1937) is considered the father of nuclear physics. He was known for his ebullient public persona.

The non-scientists have a rooted impression that the scientists are shallowly optimistic, unaware of man's condition. On the other hand, the scientists believe that the literary intellectuals are totally lacking in foresight, peculiarly unconcerned with their brother men, in a deep sense anti-intellectual, anxious to restrict both art and thought to the existential moment. And so on.

Anyone with a mild talent for invective could produce plenty of this kind of subterranean back-chat. On each side there is some of it which is not entirely baseless. It is all destructive. Much of it rests on misinterpretations which are dangerous. I should like to deal with two of the most profound of these now, one on each side.

First, about the scientists' optimism. This is an accusation which has been made so often that it has become a platitude. It has been made by some of the acutest non-scientific minds of the day. But it depends upon a confusion between the individual experience and the social experience, between the individual condition of man and his social condition. Most of the scientists I have known well have felt – just as deeply as the non-scientists I have known well – that the individual condition of each of us is tragic. Each of us is alone: sometimes we escape from solitariness, through love or affection or perhaps creative moments, but those triumphs of life are pools of light we make for ourselves while the edge of the road is black: each of us dies alone.

Some scientists I have known have had faith in revealed religion. Perhaps with them the sense of the tragic condition is not so strong. I don't know. With most people of deep feeling, however high-spirited and happy they are, sometimes most with those who are happiest and most high-spirited, it seems to be right in the fibres, part of the weight of life. That is as true of the scientists I have known best as of anyone at all.

But nearly all of them – and this is where the colour of hope genuinely comes in – would see no reason why, just because the individual condition is tragic, so must the social condition be. Each of us is solitary; each of us dies alone: all right, that's a fate against which we can't struggle. But there is plenty in our condition which is not fate, and against which we are less than human unless we do struggle.

Most of our fellow human beings, for instance, are underfed and die before their time. In the crudest terms, that is the social condition. There is a moral trap which comes through the insight into man's loneliness: it tempts one to sit back, complacent in one's unique tragedy, and let the others go without a meal. As a group, the scientists fall into that trap less than others. They are inclined to be impatient to see if something can be done: and inclined to think that it can be done, until it's proved otherwise. That is their real optimism, and it's an optimism that the rest of us badly need.

In reverse, the same spirit, tough and good and determined to fight it out at the side of their brother men, has made scientists regard the other culture's social attitudes as contemptible. That is too facile: some of them are, but they are a temporary phase and not to be taken as representative.

I remember being cross-examined by a scientist of distinction. 'Why do most writers take on social opinions which would have been thought distinctly uncivilized and démodé at the time of the Plantagenets?[9] Wasn't that true of most of the famous 20th-century writers? YEATS,[10] Pound,[11] Wyndham Lewis[12] – nine out of ten of those who have dominated literary sensibility in our time – weren't they not only politically silly, but politically wicked? Didn't the influence of all they represent bring Auschwitz[13] that much nearer?'

I thought at the time, and I still think, that the correct answer was not to defend the indefensible … It was no use denying the facts, which are broadly true. The honest answer was that there is, in fact, a connection, which literary persons were culpably slow to see, between some kinds of early 20th-century art and the most imbecile expressions of anti-social

[9] The Plantagenets were a royal dynasty originating in Anjou, France, who ruled in England, 1154–1485.
[10] Yeats expressed admiration for the Italian fascist leader BENITO MUSSOLINI, and was a supporter of Eoin O'Duffy's right-wing 'Blueshirts' movement in Ireland. He later rejected fascism, but was involved in the eugenics movement, which helped inspire the racial policies of Nazi Germany.
[11] The US poet Ezra Pound (1885–1972) moved to Rapello, Italy in the mid-1920s, and expressed ardent support for Mussolini and anti-Semitism. He opposed US involvement in World War II and was arrested and tried for treason. He also supported racial segregation in the US South.

[12] The Anglo-American artist and painter Wyndham Lewis (1882–1957) was shunned for his even-handed biography *Hitler* (1931). Although he distanced himself from Nazism with *The Hitler Cult* (1939), he was widely considered an apologist for fascism.
[13] One of the most notorious concentration camps established in Nazi-occupied Poland for the imprisonment and later the extermination of Jews and political prisoners.

feeling. That was one reason, among many, why some of us turned our backs on the art and tried to hack out a new or different way for ourselves.

But though many of those writers dominated literary sensibility for a generation, that is no longer so, or at least to nothing like the same extent. Literature changes more slowly than science. It hasn't the same automatic corrective, and so its misguided periods are longer. But it is ill-considered of scientists to judge writers on the evidence of the period 1914–50 …

The degree of incomprehension on both sides is the kind of joke which has gone sour. There are about 50,000 working scientists in the country and about 80,000 professional engineers or applied scientists. During the war and in the years since, my colleagues and I have had to interview somewhere between thirty to forty thousand of these – that is, about 25 per cent. The number is large enough to give us a fair sample, though of the men we talked to most would still be under 40. We were able to find out a certain amount of what they read and thought about. I confess that even I, who am fond of them and respect them, was a bit shaken. We hadn't quite expected that the links with the traditional culture should be so tenuous, nothing more than a formal touch of the cap.

As one would expect, some of the very best scientists had and have plenty of energy and interest to spare, and we came across several who had read everything that literary people talk about. But that's very rare. Most of the rest, when one tried to probe for what books they had read, would modestly confess, 'Well, I've tried a bit of DICKENS,'[14] rather as though Dickens were an extraordinarily esoteric, tangled and dubiously rewarding writer, something like Rainer Maria Rilke.[15] In fact that is exactly how they do regard him: we thought that discovery, that Dickens had been transformed into the type- specimen of literary incomprehensibility, was one of the oddest results of the whole exercise …

Remember, these are very intelligent men. Their culture is in many ways an exacting and admirable one. It doesn't contain much art, with the exception, an important exception, of music …

But what about the other side? They are impoverished too – perhaps more seriously, because they are vainer about it. They still like to pretend that the traditional culture is the whole of 'culture', as though the natural order didn't exist. As though the exploration of the natural order was of no interest either in its own value or its consequences. As though the scientific edifice of the physical world was not, in its intellectual depth, complexity and articulation, the most beautiful and wonderful collective work of the mind of man. Yet most non-scientists have no conception of that edifice at all. Even if they want to have it, they can't. It is rather as though, over an immense range of intellectual experience, a whole group was tone-deaf. Except that this tone-deafness doesn't come by nature, but by training, or rather the absence of training.

As with the tone-deaf, they don't know what they miss. They give a pitying chuckle at the news of scientists who have never read a major work of English literature. They dismiss them as ignorant specialists. Yet their own ignorance and their own specialization is just as startling. A good many times I have been present at gatherings of people who, by the standards of the traditional culture, are thought highly educated and who have with considerable gusto been expressing their incredulity at the illiteracy of scientists. Once or twice I have been provoked and have asked the company how many of them could describe the Second Law of Thermodynamics.[16] The response was cold: it was also negative. Yet I was

[14] Dickens's novels are notable for their gripping plots, humour and accessibility.

[15] The Austrian poet Rainer Maria Rilke (1875–1926) is known for abstruse work steeped in mysticism.

[16] The Second Law of Thermodynamics states, broadly, that energy density dissipates over time. It is often cited as the reason why a perpetual motion machine is not possible.

asking something which is about the scientific equivalent of: 'Have you read a work of Shakespeare's?'

I now believe that if I had asked an even simpler question, such as, 'What do you mean by mass, or acceleration?' – which is the scientific equivalent of saying, 'Can you read?' – not more than one in ten of the highly educated would have felt that I was speaking the same language. So the great edifice of modern physics goes up, and the majority of the cleverest people in the western world have about as much insight into it as their neolithic ancestors would have had …

There seems then to be no place where the cultures meet. I am not going to waste time saying that this is a pity. It is much worse than that … at the heart of thought and creation we are letting some of our best chances go by default. The clashing point of two subjects, two disciplines, two cultures – of two galaxies, so far as that goes – ought to produce creative chances. In the history of mental activity that has been where some of the breakthroughs came. The chances are there now. But they are there, as it were, in a vacuum, because those in the two cultures can't talk to each other.

Socrates

Greek philosopher

Socrates (469–399 BC) was born in Athens, and became, like his father, a stonemason. In middle age he married Xanthippe, by whom he had three sons. He fought bravely as a hoplite in the Peloponnesian War (431–404 BC), opposed the collective sentence on the generals convicted after Arginusae (406 BC) and refused to co-operate with the Thirty Tyrants – the Spartans who ruled Athens after its defeat in 404 BC. He is represented as ugly, with a snub-nose and a paunch. He wrote nothing, founded no school and had no formal disciples, but along with Plato and Aristotle, he is one of the three great figures in ancient philosophy. His pivotal influence was such that all earlier Greek philosophy is classified as 'pre-Socratic', and he was responsible for the shift of philosophical interest from speculations about the natural world and cosmology to ethics and conceptual analysis. He was caricatured by the comic dramatist Aristophanes in *The Clouds* – in which he is associated with the Sophists, whom in fact he opposed – and was adulated by Xenophon. The principal sources for his life are the dialogues of Plato, especially the *Apology*, *Crito* and *Phaedo*, which describe Socrates' trial, last days and death. In later dialogues, Plato makes Socrates the mouthpiece for what were undoubtedly his own opinions. He held aloof from politics, guided by his 'voice', which impelled him to philosophy and to the examination of conventional morality. The 'Socratic method' was to ask for definitions of familiar concepts such as justice, courage and piety, to elicit contradictions in the responses of his interlocutors, and thus to demonstrate their ignorance, which he claimed to share. This unpopular activity no doubt contributed to the demands for his indictment, and he was tried at the age of 70. He rejected the option of merely paying a fine, declined a later opportunity to escape from prison, and was sentenced to die.

'I shall go away condemned by you to death'

399 BC, Athens, Greece

Socrates was prosecuted by three Athenians, Meletus, Anytus and Lycon, on charges of impiety, having allegedly corrupted the young and neglected the gods of the city. It is clear that he very unpopular among a considerable part of the population of Athens, perhaps because several of his former pupils had been associated with the oligarchic regime which briefly overthrew the democracy in Athens after it was conquered by Sparta at the end of the Peloponnesian War.

The trial took place before a jury of 501 Athenian citizens, and resulted in the death sentence. A month later, Socrates was executed by a self-administered dose of the poison hemlock. Socrates' speeches during his trial do not survive, but several versions of it were written subsequently by other followers, of which two – one by Plato and a much shorter sketch by Xenophon – have survived.

In both, Socrates argues that he is not guilty of corrupting the young or denying the gods, and in both he is sanguine about the prospect of death. Plato's Socrates, however, presents a philosophical defence of his life as a search for truth and the way one should live, which is largely absent from Xenophon. The passage from Plato's version given here – in a translation by Hugh Tredennick and Harold Tarrant (1993) – is Socrates' last speech to the jury, after the death sentence has been delivered.

Well, gentlemen: for the sake of a very small gain in time you are going to earn the reputation – and the blame from those who wish to disparage our city – of having put Socrates to death: 'that wise man' – because they will say I am wise even if I am not, these people who want to find fault with you. If you had waited just a little while, you would have had your way in the course of nature. You can see that I am well on in life and near to death. I am saying this not to all of you but to those who voted for my execution, and I have something else to say to them as well.

No doubt you think, gentlemen, that I have been condemned for lack of the arguments which I could have used, if I had thought it right to leave nothing unsaid or undone to secure my acquittal. But that is very far from the truth. It is not a lack of arguments that has caused my condemnation, but a lack of effrontery and impudence, and the fact that I have refused to address you in the way which would give you most pleasure. You would have liked to hear me weep and wail, doing and saying all sorts of things which I declare to be unworthy of myself, but which you are used to hearing from other people.

But I did not think then that I ought to stoop to servility because I was in danger, and I do not regret now the way in which I pleaded my case; I would much rather die as the result of this defence than live as the result of the other sort. In a court of law, just as in warfare, neither I nor any other ought to use his wits to escape death by any means.

In battle it is often obvious that you could escape being killed by giving up your arms and throwing yourself upon the mercy of your pursuers; and in every kind of danger there are plenty of devices for avoiding death if you are unscrupulous enough to stop at nothing. But I suggest, gentlemen, that the difficulty is not so much to escape death; the real difficulty is to escape from wickedness, which is far more fleet of foot.

In this present instance I, the slow old man, have been overtaken by the slower of the two; but my accusers, who are clever and quick, have been overtaken by the faster: by iniquity. When I leave this court I shall go away condemned by you to death, but they will go away convicted by Truth herself of depravity and injustice. And they accept their sentence even as I accept mine. No doubt it was bound to be so, and I think that the result is fair enough.

Having said so much, I feel moved to prophesy to you who have given your vote against me; for I am now at that point where the gift of prophecy comes most readily to men: at the point of death. I tell you, my executioners, that as soon as I am dead, vengeance shall fall upon you with a punishment far more painful than your killing of me. You have brought about my death in the belief that through it you will be delivered from submitting the conduct of your lives to criticism; but I say that the result will be just the opposite. You will have more critics, whom up till now I have restrained without your knowing it; and being younger they will be harsher to you and will cause you more annoyance.

If you expect to stop denunciation of your wrong way of life by putting people to death, there is something amiss with your reasoning. This way of escape is neither possible nor creditable; the best and easiest way is not to stop the mouths of others, but to make yourselves as well behaved as possible. This is my last message to you who voted for my condemnation.

As for you who voted for my acquittal, I should very much like to say a few words to reconcile you to this result, while the officials are busy and I am not yet on my way to the place where I must die. I ask you, gentlemen, to spare me these few moments; there is no reason why we should not exchange a few words while the law permits. I look upon you as my friends, and I want to show you the meaning of what has now happened to me.

Gentlemen of the jury — for you deserve to be so called — I have had a remarkable experience. In the past the prophetic voice to which I have become accustomed has always been my constant companion, opposing me even in quite trivial things if I was going to take the wrong course.[1] Now something has happened to me, as you can see, which might be thought and is commonly considered to be a supreme calamity; yet neither when I left home this morning, nor when I was taking my place here in the court, nor at any point in any part of my speech, did the divine sign oppose me.

In other discussions it has often checked me in the middle of a sentence; but this time it has never opposed me in any part of this business in

[1] Socrates at several points in Plato's dialogues refers to a 'divine being' (*daimon*) which advised him. This may have been one of the reasons for the charge of impiety.

anything that I have said or done. What do I suppose to be the explanation? I will tell you. I suspect that this thing that has happened to me is a blessing, and we are quite mistaken in supposing death to be an evil. I have good grounds for thinking this, because my accustomed sign could not have failed to oppose me if what I was doing had not been sure to bring some good result.

We should reflect that there is much reason to hope for a good result on other grounds as well. Death is one of two things. Either it is annihilation, and the dead have no consciousness of anything; or, as we are told, it is really a change: a migration of the soul from this place to another.

Now, if there is no consciousness but only a dreamless sleep, death must be a marvellous gain. I suppose that if anyone were told to pick out the night on which he slept so soundly as not even to dream, and then to compare it with all the other nights and days of his life, and then were told to say, after due consideration, how many better and happier days and nights than this he had spent in the course of his life – well, I think that the Great King himself, to say nothing of any private person, would find these days and nights easy to count in comparison with the rest. If death is like this, then, I call it gain; because the whole of time, if you look at it in this way, can be regarded as no more than one single night.

If, on the other hand, death is a removal from here to some other place, and if what we are told is true, that all the dead are there, what greater blessing could there be than this, gentlemen of the jury? If on arrival in the other world, beyond the reach of these so-called jurors here, one will find there the true jurors who are said to preside in those courts, Minos and Rhadamanthys and Aeacus[2] and Triptolemus[3] and all those other demi-gods who were upright in their earthly life, would that be an unrewarding place to settle?

Put it in this way: how much would one of you give to meet Orpheus and Musaeus, Hesiod and Homer?[4] I am willing to die ten times over if this account is true. For me at least it would be a wonderful personal experience to join them there, to meet Palamedes[5] and Ajax the son of Telamon[6] and any other heroes of the old days who met their death through an unjust trial, and to compare my fortunes with theirs – it would be rather amusing, I think – and above all I should like to spend my time there, as here, in examining and searching people's minds, to find out who is really wise among them, and who only thinks that he is.

What would one not give, gentlemen, to be able to scrutinize the leader of that great host against Troy,[7] or Odysseus,[8] or Sisyphus,[9] or the thousands of other men and women whom one could mention? Their company and conversation – like the chance to examine them – would be unimaginable happiness. At any rate I presume that they do not put one to death there for such conduct; because apart from the other happiness in which their world surpasses ours, they are now immortal for the rest of time, if what we are told is true.

You too, gentlemen of the jury, must look forward to death with confidence, and fix your minds on this one belief, which is certain: that nothing can harm a good man either in life or after death, and his fortunes are not a matter of indifference to the gods. This present experience of mine does not result from mere earthly causes; I am quite clear that the time had come when it was better for me to die and be released from my distractions. That is why my sign never turned me back.

For my own part I bear no grudge at all against those who condemned

[2] According to Greek myths, these were the judges of the underworld.
[3] Triptolemus was associated with hope for the afterlife in Greek legend.
[4] In Greek legend, Orpheus was the chief representative of the art of song, and Musaeus was the founder of poetry. Hesiod and Homer were early Greek poets and professional reciters of poetry believed to have lived in the eighth century BC.
[5] In Greek mythology, Palamedes was responsible for sending Odysseus to the Trojan War against his wishes. Odysseus subsequently had him tried for treason and executed on false evidence.
[6] A legendary hero who survives the Trojan War but after committing a shameful act, kills himself rather than live with the shame.

[7] Agamemnon, who led the Greek armies against Troy.
[8] Also known as Ulysses, Odysseus was a Greek hero of the Trojan War, who features in the *Iliad* and is the protagonist of the *Odyssey*.
[9] Another mythical figure, a sinner punished in the underworld by being set to pushing a boulder up a hill repeatedly for eternity.

me and accused me, although it was not with this kind intention that they did so, but because they thought that they were hurting me; and that is culpable of them. However, I ask them to grant me one favour. When my sons grow up, gentlemen, if you think that they are putting money or anything else before goodness, take your revenge by plaguing them as I plagued you; and if they fancy themselves for no reason, you must scold them just as I scolded you, for neglecting the important things and thinking that they are good for something when they are good for nothing. If you do this, I shall have had justice at your hands — I and my children.

Well, now it is time to be off, I to die and you to live; but which of us has the happier prospect is unknown to anyone but God.

Aleksandr Solzhenitsyn
Russian writer and dissident

Aleksandr Isayevich Solzhenitsyn (1918–2008) was born in Kislovodsk into an intellectual Cossack family, though his father died before his birth. His mother raised him in Rostov-on-Don, where he graduated in mathematics and physics in 1941. After distinguished service with the Red Army in World War II, he was imprisoned (1945–53) for commenting unfavourably on JOSEPH STALIN's conduct of the war. He was rehabilitated in 1956, and his first novel, *Odin den' Ivana Denisovicha*, (1962, Eng trans *One Day in the Life of Ivan Denisovich*, 1963), set in a prison camp, was acclaimed both in the USSR, now led by NIKITA KHRUSHCHEV, and in the West, but his denunciation in 1967 of the strict censorship in Russia led to the banning of his later novels, *Rakovy Korpus* (1968, Eng trans, *The Cancer Ward*, 2 vols, 1968–9) and *V Kruge pervom* (1968, Eng trans *The First Circle*, 1968). He was expelled from the Soviet Writers' Union in 1969, but was awarded the Nobel Prize for literature in 1970. *Arkhipelag Gulag* (3 vols, 1973–76, Eng trans *The Gulag Archipelago 1918–56*, 1974–78), a factual account of the Stalinist terror, was first published in the West between 1973 and 1975. In 1974 he was deported to West Germany; he later settled in the USA, and in 1994 returned to Russia. His memoirs, *Bodalsya telyonok s dubom* (1975), were published in translation in 1980 as *The Oak and the Calf*, and *Kak Nam Obustroit' Rossiyu?* (Eng trans *Rebuilding Russia*, 1991) in 1990. In the same year his citizenship was restored and he won the Russian State Literature prize. In 1997, he was elected a member of the Russian Academy of Science and established his own literary award. A well-received ten-part dramatization of *V Kruge pervom* began screening on Russian television in January 2006.

'I have been in the dragon's belly'
9 July 1975, New York City, USA

On 12 February 1974, Alexandr Solzhenitsyn was arrested and charged with treason, following the publication of the first volume of *The Gulag Archipelago*. This critical survey of the USSR's harsh Gulag correctional system drew on his own experience, which began in 1945 when he was imprisoned for criticizing Stalin.

By 1974, treatment of dissidents had relaxed somewhat, but Solzhenitsyn's reputation in the West probably contributed to his relatively lenient treatment: he was stripped of citizenship and exiled to West Germany, along with his wife and sons. In December 1974, he was able to attend a banquet in Stockholm, where he formally accepted the Nobel Prize he had been awarded in 1970.

Settling in the USA, Solzhenitsyn used his liberty to alert the West to the threat he believed the USSR posed to its security and freedom. In 1975, he embarked on a lecture tour in which he described and criticized the communist regime under which he and millions of others had suffered.

With the Cold War barely beginning to thaw, Solzhenitsyn's rejection of communism and endorsement of Christianity were of course warmly received in the USA – though his warnings against complacency must have induced shivers. In this speech – given at a lunch held in his honour by the American Federation of Labour and Congress of Industrial Organizations – he attacks not the 'disguises' assumed by communism and the betrayals of Soviet foreign policy, but the 'essence' laid out in the *Communist Manifesto*.

Is it possible or impossible to transmit the experience of those who have suffered to those who have yet to suffer? Can one part of humanity learn from the bitter experience of another or can it not? Is it possible or impossible to warn someone of danger?

How many witnesses have been sent to the West in the last 60 years? How many waves of immigrants? How many millions of persons? They are all here. You meet them every day. You know who they are: if not by their spiritual disorientation, their grief, their melancholy, then you can distinguish them by their accents or their external appearance. Coming from different countries, without consulting with one another, they have brought out exactly the same experience. They tell you exactly the same thing: they warn you of what is now taking place and of what has taken place in the past. But the proud skyscrapers stand on, just into the sky, and say: 'It will never happen here. This will never come to us. It is not possible here.'

It can happen. It is possible. As a Russian proverb says: 'When it happens to you, you'll know it's true.'

But do we really have to wait for the moment when the knife is at our throat? Couldn't it be possible, ahead of time, to assess soberly the world-wide menace that threatens to swallow the whole world? I was swallowed myself. I have been in the dragon's belly, in its red-hot innards. It was unable to digest me and threw me up. I have come to you as a witness to what it is like there, in the dragon's belly.

It is astonishing that communism has been writing about itself in the most open way, in black and white, for 125 years, and even more openly, more candidly in the beginning. The *Communist Manifesto*,[1] for instance, which everyone knows by name, and which almost no-one ever takes the trouble to read, contains ever more terrible things than what has actually been done. It is perfectly amazing. The whole world can read, everyone is literate, yet somehow no-one wants to understand. Humanity acts as if it does not understand what communism is, as if it does not want to understand, is not capable of understanding.

I think it is not only a question of the disguises that communism has assumed in the last decades. It is rather that the essence of communism is quite beyond the limits of human understanding. It is hard to believe that people could actually plan such things and carry them out. And it is precisely because its essence is beyond comprehension, perhaps, that Communism is so difficult to understand.

In my last address in Washington I spoke a great deal about the Soviet state system, how it was created and what it is today. But it is perhaps more important to discuss with you the ideology that inspired the system, created it and still governs it. It is much more important to understand the essence and above all the legacy of this ideology, which has not changed at all in 125 years. It has not changed since the day it was created.

That Marxism is not a science is entirely clear to intelligent people in the Soviet Union. One would even feel awkward to refer to it as a science. Leaving aside the exact sciences, such as physics, mathematics and the natural sciences, even the social sciences can predict an event – when, in what way and how an event might occur. Communism has never made any such forecasts. It has never said where, when and precisely what is going to happen. Nothing but declamations. Rhetoric to the effect that the world proletariat will overthrow the world bourgeoisie and the most happy and radiant society will then arise. The fantasies of Marx, Engels and LENIN break off at this point. Not one of them goes any further to describe what this society would be like. They simply say: the most radiant, most happy society. Everything for the sake of man.

I wouldn't want to enumerate for you all the unsuccessful predictions of Marxism, but I can give you a few. For example, it was claimed that the conditions of the working class in the West would deteriorate steadily, get more and more unbearable, until the workers would be reduced to total poverty. (If only in our country we could feed and clothe our working class, provide it with everything and give it as much leisure as you do!)

Or the famous prediction that communist revolutions would begin in such advanced industrial countries as England, France, America, Germany. (But it worked out exactly the other way, as you know.) Or the prediction that socialist states would not even exist. As soon as capitalism was overthrown, the state would at once wither away. (Look about you: where

[1] Co-written by the German political philosophers KARL MARX (1818–83) and Friedrich Engels (1820–95). *The Manifesto of the Communist Party* was published as a pamphlet in 1848. It became the basis of all socialist and communist doctrines.

can you see states as powerful as in the so-called socialist or communist countries?) Or the prediction that wars are inherent only to capitalism; as soon as communism is introduced, all wars will come to an end. (We have also seen enough of this: in Budapest,[2] in Prague,[3] on the Soviet–Chinese border,[4] in the occupation of the Baltic countries[5] and when Poland was stabbed in the back.[6] We have seen enough of this already and we will surely see more yet.)

Communism is as crude an attempt to explain society and the individual as if a surgeon were to perform his delicate operations with a meat axe. All that is subtle in human psychology and in the structure of society (which is even more complex), all of this is reduced to crude economic processes. This whole created being – man – is reduced to matter. It is characteristic that communism is so devoid of arguments that it has none to advance against its opponents in our communist countries. It lacks arguments and hence there is the club, the prison, the concentration camp and insane asylums with forced confinement.

Marxism has always opposed freedom. I will quote just a few words from the founding fathers of communism, Marx and Engels (I quote from the first Soviet edition of 1929): 'Reforms are a sign of weakness';[7] 'Democracy is more to be feared than monarchy and aristocracy';[8] 'Political liberty is a false liberty, worse than the most abject slavery'.[9]

In their correspondence, Marx and Engels frequently stated that terror would be indispensable after achieving power, that, 'it will be necessary to repeat the year 1793.[10] After achieving power, we'll be considered monsters, but we couldn't care less.'[11]

Communism has never concealed the fact that it rejects all absolute concepts of morality. It scoffs at any consideration of 'good' and 'evil' as indisputable categories. Communism considers morality to be relative, to be a class matter. Depending upon circumstances and the political situation, any act, including murder, even the killing of hundreds of thousands, could be good or could be bad. It all depends upon class ideology. And who defines this ideology? The whole class cannot get together to pass judgement. A handful of people determine what is good and what is bad.

But I must say that in this very respect communism has been most successful. It has infected the whole world with the belief in the relativity of good and evil. Today, many people apart from the communists are carried away by this idea. Among progressive people, it is considered rather awkward to use seriously such words as 'good' and 'evil'. Communism has managed to persuade all of us that these concepts are old-fashioned and laughable. But if we are to be deprived of the concepts of good and evil, what will be left? Nothing but the manipulation of one another. We will sink to the status of animals.

Both the theory and the practice of communism are completely inhuman for that reason. There is a word very commonly used these days: 'anti-communism'. That is a poor, tasteless locution. It makes it appear as though communism were something original, fundamental. Therefore, it is taken as the point of departure, and anti-communism is defined in relation to communism. I say that this word was poorly selected, that it was put together by people who do not understand etymology.

The primary, the eternal concept is humanity, and communism is anti-humanity. Whoever says 'anti-communism' is saying, in effect, 'anti-anti-humanity'. A poor construction. So we should say: that which is against

[2] The pro-reform Hungarian Uprising of October–November 1956 was suppressed by the forces of the Soviet-controlled Warsaw Pact, at a cost of 30,000–50,000 lives.
[3] In August 1968, Warsaw Pact forces invaded Czechoslovakia to end the Prague Spring, a period of political liberalization. Around 100 were killed.

[7] Volume 23, page 339.
[8] Volume 2, page 369.
[9] Volume 2, page 394.

[10] Marx and Engels refer here to the Terror, a purge carried out by the leaders of the French Revolution.

[4] Tension between the USSR and communist China, 1960–89, flared up into a border war in 1969.
[5] The Baltic republics Estonia, Latvia and Lithuania were annexed by the USSR in 1940, then again in 1944 after liberation from the Germans.
[6] Poland was invaded by both Germany and Russia in 1939. During the Warsaw Uprising of 1944, the Polish resistance, denied assistance promised by Stalin, was crushed by the Germans, allowing the Russians to install a puppet regime in 1945.

[11] Volume 25, page 187.

communism is for humanity. Not to accept, but to reject this inhuman communist ideology is simply to be a human being. Such a rejection is more than a political act. It is a protest of our souls against those who would have us forget the concepts of good and evil.

Charles, Earl Spencer

English landowner and writer

Charles Edward Maurice Spencer *later 9th Earl Spencer* (1964–) was born in Sandringham, Norfolk, and became known as Viscount Althorp when his father succeeded as 8th Earl Spencer in 1975. Educated at Eton and Magdalen College, Oxford, he worked as a broadcast journalist for the American network NBC before succeeding to the earldom in 1992, when he moved to the ancestral home, Althorp House in Northamptonshire. After restoring and refurbishing the house he relocated his family to Cape Town, South Africa in 1996. He returned to England after the death of his sister Diana, Princess of Wales the following year, and subsequently oversaw the construction of a permanent memorial at the site of her burial in the grounds at Althorp. He is the author of *Althorp: The Story of an English House* (1998) and *The Spencer Family* (1999).

'She remained intact, true to herself'

6 September 1997, London, England

❧

Millions around the world were shocked by the death of Diana, Princess of Wales, killed in a high-speed car crash in Paris while fleeing from paparazzi. The six days between her death and her funeral saw a tremendous outpouring of public grief, both within the UK and around the world.

However, the reaction of the Royal Family was widely perceived as cold and unfeeling. Ironically, given the role played by the media in the Princess's death, some newspapers railed at Queen ELIZABETH II for her muted response, although she paid tribute to her former daughter-in-law in a live television broadcast on the eve of the funeral.

The ceremony was held at Westminster Abbey in central London; and the surrounding streets were thronged with crowds eager to pay their respects. The abbey was filled with a wide range of guests, including celebrities such as Sir Elton John, who performed his song 'Candle in the Wind'. The eulogy was given by Earl Spencer, Diana's brother.

His speech is a dignified and moving expression of grief from a man not known for public speaking. He alternates between eulogising his sister in a detached way, and addressing her directly; describing both his love for her and his rage at the media, which he felt had hounded her to her death. He also obliquely criticizes the Royal Family for its dealings with Diana, and expresses the hope that her sons, Prince William and Prince Harry, will be allowed to enjoy a healthy upbringing, free from the stifling formality she had endured when she was married to CHARLES, PRINCE OF WALES.

❧

I stand before you today the representative of a family in grief, in a country in mourning, before a world in shock. We are all united not only in our desire to pay our respects to Diana but rather in our need to do so. For such was her extraordinary appeal that the tens of millions of people taking part in this service all over the world via television and radio who never actually met her, feel that they too lost someone close to them in the early hours of Sunday morning. It is a more remarkable tribute to Diana than I can ever hope to offer her today.

Diana was the very essence of compassion, of duty, of style, of beauty. All over the world she was a symbol of selfless humanity. All over the world, a standard-bearer for the rights of the truly downtrodden, a very British girl who transcended nationality. Someone with a natural nobility who was classless and who proved in the last year that she needed no royal title[1] to continue to generate her particular brand of magic.

Today is our chance to say thank you for the way you brightened our lives, even though God granted you but half a life. We will all feel cheated, always, that you were taken from us so young and yet we must learn to be grateful that you came along at all. Only now that you are gone do we truly appreciate what we are now without and we want you to know that life without you is very, very difficult.

We have all despaired at our loss over the past week and only the

[1] Following her divorce from the Prince of Wales in 1996, the Princess was no longer styled 'Her Royal Highness'.

strength of the message you gave us through your years of giving has afforded us the strength to move forward.

There is a temptation to rush to canonize your memory; there is no need to do so. You stand tall enough as a human being of unique qualities not to need to be seen as a saint. Indeed to sanctify your memory would be to miss out on the very core of your being, your wonderfully mischievous sense of humour with a laugh that bent you double.

Your joy for life transmitted wherever you took your smile and the sparkle in those unforgettable eyes, your boundless energy, which you could barely contain.

But your greatest gift was your intuition and it was a gift you used wisely. This is what underpinned all your other wonderful attributes; and if we look to analyse what it was about you that had such a wide appeal, we find it in your instinctive feel for what was really important in all our lives.

Without your God-given sensitivity we would be immersed in greater ignorance at the anguish of AIDS and HIV sufferers, the plight of the homeless, the isolation of lepers, the random destruction of landmines.

Diana explained to me once that it was her innermost feelings of suffering that made it possible for her to connect with her constituency of the rejected.

And here we come to another truth about her. For all the status, the glamour, the applause, Diana remained throughout a very insecure person at heart, almost childlike in her desire to do good for others so she could release herself from deep feelings of unworthiness, of which her eating disorders were merely a symptom.

The world sensed this part of her character and cherished her for her vulnerability whilst admiring her for her honesty.

The last time I saw Diana was on July 1, her birthday, in London, when typically she was not taking time to celebrate her special day with friends but was guest of honour at a special charity fundraising evening. She sparkled of course, but I would rather cherish the days I spent with her in March when she came to visit me and my children in our home in South Africa. I am proud of the fact that, apart from when she was on display meeting President MANDELA,[2] we managed to contrive to stop the ever-present paparazzi from getting a single picture of her – that meant a lot to her.

These were days I will always treasure. It was as if we had been transported back to our childhood when we spent such an enormous amount of time together – the two youngest in the family.

Fundamentally she had not changed at all from the big sister who mothered me as a baby, fought with me at school and endured those long train journeys between our parents' homes with me at weekends.

It is a tribute to her level-headedness and strength that despite the most bizarre-like life imaginable after her childhood, she remained intact, true to herself.

There is no doubt that she was looking for a new direction in her life at this time. She talked endlessly of getting away from England, mainly because of the treatment that she received at the hands of the newspapers.[3] I don't think she ever understood why her genuinely good intentions were sneered at by the media, why there appeared to be a permanent quest on their behalf to bring her down. It is baffling.

My own and only explanation is that genuine goodness is threatening to those at the opposite end of the moral spectrum. It is a point to remember

[2] The South African statesman Nelson Mandela (1918–) was president of South Africa, 1994–9.

[3] From the moment in 1981 when her engagement to Prince Charles was announced, Diana had been the target of intrusive press interest. Although some commentators believed she had courted it, the constant pressure became unbearable and is thought to have contributed to her well-publicized eating disorders.

that of all the ironies about Diana, perhaps the greatest was this: a girl given the name of the ancient goddess of hunting was, in the end, the most hunted person of the modern age.

She would want us today to pledge ourselves to protecting her beloved boys William and Harry from a similar fate and I do this here, Diana, on your behalf. We will not allow them to suffer the anguish that used regularly to drive you to tearful despair.

And beyond that, on behalf of your mother and sisters, I pledge that we, your blood family, will do all we can to continue the imaginative way in which you were steering these two exceptional young men so that their souls are not simply immersed by duty and tradition but can sing openly as you planned.

We fully respect the heritage into which they have both been born and will always respect and encourage them in their royal role; but we, like you, recognize the need for them to experience as many different aspects of life as possible to arm them spiritually and emotionally for the years ahead. I know you would have expected nothing less from us.

William and Harry, we all cared desperately for you today. We are all chewed up with the sadness at the loss of a woman who was not even our mother. How great your suffering is, we cannot even imagine.

I would like to end by thanking God for the small mercies he has shown us at this dreadful time. For taking Diana at her most beautiful and radiant and when she had joy in her private life. Above all we give thanks for the life of a woman I am so proud to be able to call my sister, the unique, the complex, the extraordinary and irreplaceable Diana whose beauty, both internal and external, will never be extinguished from our minds.

Joseph Stalin
Russian revolutionary and leader

Joseph Stalin *originally Iosif Vissarionovich Dzhugashvili* (1879–1953) was born near Tiflis, Georgia, the son of a shoemaker. He trained for the priesthood at the Theological Seminary, but was expelled, probably for propagating Marxism. He joined the Bolshevik underground, was arrested and transported to Siberia, but escaped in 1904. During the ensuing years he identified closely with revolutionary Marxism, escaped repeatedly from captivity, grew intimate with LENIN and Nikolai Bukharin, and joined the illicit Bolshevik Central Committee (1912). After the October Revolution (1917), Stalin was appointed Commissar for Nationalities and a member of the Politburo. With his appointment as General Secretary to the Central Committee in 1922, Stalin stealthily began to build up the power that would ultimately ensure his leadership. After Lenin's death (1924) he assumed control, successfully testing his authority by engineering the downfall of LEON TROTSKY (1928). Stalin's reorganization of the USSR's resources with successive five-year plans suffered many setbacks and encountered stubborn resistance in rural regions, where the *kulaks*, or peasant proprietors, refused to accept the principle of collectivization. Stalin moved to 'discipline' those who opposed his will, bringing death by execution or famine to some 10 million peasants (1932–3). This mass slaughter – which eliminated the Old Bolsheviks and the allegedly right-wing intelligentsia – was followed by a purge of thousands of army officers, who were accused of pro-German sympathies. Stalin provided military support to the Spanish communist government overthrown by Franco in 1936, but was careful not to commit too deeply. After his exclusion from the Munich Conference (1938), he signed a non-aggression pact with Nazi Germany, which allowed him to prepare for the invasion of 1941. Eventually, the Germans were defeated in a war of attrition: the harsh Russian winter contributed to an enormous toll of casualties. Quick to exploit the Anglo-American fear that the USSR might withdraw from the alliance, Stalin outwitted WINSTON CHURCHILL and FRANKLIN D ROOSEVELT at the conferences at Teheran (1943) and Yalta (1945), and gained control of eastern Europe. He inaugurated the 'Cold War' against all non-communist countries, which included the blockade of Berlin (1948–9). At home, his ruthless purge of all opposition continued, and his fierce anti-Semitism resulted in the execution of a number of Jewish doctors for alleged conspiracy (1953). Stalin died in mysterious circumstances; the official cause was a brain haemorrhage. His body was embalmed and placed in the Mausoleum of Lenin but was later moved to an ordinary grave.

'The issue is one of life and death for the Soviet state'
3 July 1941, radio broadcast from Moscow, Russia

The USSR was ill-prepared for the German invasion of June 1941, code-named Operation Barbarossa after a twelfth-century Holy Roman Emperor. Despite the non-aggression pact of 1939 – which included plans to divide up the countries of eastern Europe – Stalin had foreseen the possibility of German aggression, but did not expect it as soon as this.

The Red Army was well-armed and plentiful in numbers – giving rise to some complacency – but its troops lacked training and communications equipment. Moreover, many of its most experienced officers and strategists had been killed or imprisoned during the purges of 1936–8, and those who remained tended to tell Stalin what he wanted to hear. Their German adversaries, meanwhile, were supremely well-drilled and confident, having conquered much of Europe. The Luftwaffe – far better equipped than the Soviet air force – and Panzer tank divisions swiftly decimated Soviet positions.

This radio address, given less than two weeks after the invasion, was an effective morale-booster, employing familiar martial slogans such as 'Forward to victory!'. Its fiery rhetoric fuels faith in the Soviet forces, encourages civilians to participate in the fray and incites hatred for the invaders.

But it was not enough to forestall the rapid advance of German forces. By August 1941 they had reached the outskirts of Leningrad, which was under siege for 90 days. The Germans were eventually halted in November, after failing to take Moscow. A long and bitter struggle ensued, with heavy losses both to the combatants and to civilians.

Comrades, citizens, brothers and sisters, men of our Army and Navy: my words are addressed to you, dear friends!

The perfidious attack by Hitlerite Germany on our fatherland, begun on 22 June, is continuing. In spite of the heroic resistance of the Red Army, and although the enemy's finest divisions and finest air force units have already been smashed and have met their doom on the field of battle, the enemy continues to push forward, hurling fresh forces to the front. Hitler's troops have succeeded in capturing Lithuania, a considerable part of Latvia, the western part of Byelorussia and part of western Ukraine. The fascist aircraft are extending the range of their operations, bombing Murmansk, Orsha, Moghilev, Smolensk, Kiev, Odessa, Sevastopol. Grave danger overhangs our country.

How could it have happened that our glorious Red Army surrendered a number of our cities and districts to the fascist armies? Is it really true that the German-fascist troops are invincible, as the braggart fascist propagandists are ceaselessly blaring forth?

Of course not! History shows that there are no invincible armies and never have been. NAPOLEON's army was considered invincible, but it was beaten successively by the armies of Russia, England and Germany. Kaiser Wilhelm's German army in the period of the First Imperialist War was also considered invincible, but it was beaten several times by Russian and Anglo-French troops, and was finally smashed by the Anglo-French forces. The same must be said of Hitler's German-fascist army of today.

This army had not yet met with serious resistance on the continent of Europe. Only on our territory has it met with serious resistance. And if, as a result of this resistance, the finest divisions of Hitler's German-fascist army have been defeated by our Red Army, this means that it too can be smashed and will be smashed, as were the armies of Napoleon and Wilhelm …

It may be asked, how could the Soviet government have consented to conclude a non-aggression pact with such perfidious people, such fiends as Hitler and Ribbentrop?[1] Was this not an error on the part of the Soviet government? Of course not! Non-aggression pacts are pacts of peace between two states. It was such a pact that Germany proposed to us in 1939. Could the Soviet government have declined such a proposal? I think that not a single peace-loving state could decline a peace treaty with a neighbouring state, even though the latter were headed by such monsters and cannibals as Hitler and Ribbentrop. But that, of course, only on the one indispensable condition − that this peace treaty did not jeopardize, either directly or indirectly, the territorial integrity, independence and honour of the peace-loving state. As is well known, the non-aggression pact between Germany and the USSR was precisely such a pact.

What did we gain by concluding the non-aggression pact with Germany? We secured our country peace for a year and a half and the opportunity of preparing our forces to repulse fascist Germany should she risk an attack on our country despite the pact. This was a definite advantage for us and a disadvantage for fascist Germany.

What has fascist Germany gained and what has she lost by perfidiously tearing up the pact and attacking the USSR? She has gained a certain advantageous position for her troops for a short period of time, but she has lost politically by exposing herself in the eyes of the entire world as a bloodthirsty aggressor. There can be no doubt that this short-lived military gain for Germany is only an episode, while the tremendous political gain of the USSR is a weighty and lasting factor that is bound to form the basis for the development of outstanding military successes of the Red Army in the war with fascist Germany.

That is why the whole of our valiant Red Army, the whole of our valiant Navy, all the falcons of our Air Force, all the peoples of our country, all the

[1] The Nazi politician Joachim von Ribbentrop (1893−1946) served as German Foreign Minister, 1938−45. On 23 August 1939, he signed a non-aggression pact in Moscow with the Soviet Foreign Minister Vyacheslav Molotov (1890−1986). This held until 22 June 1941, when Hitler launched Operation Barbarossa.

finest men and women of Europe, America and Asia, and, finally, all the finest men and women of Germany – denounce the treacherous acts of the German-fascists, sympathize with the Soviet government, approve of its conduct, and see that ours is a just cause, that the enemy will be defeated, and that we are bound to win …

What is required to put an end to the danger imperilling our country and what measures must be taken to smash the enemy?

Above all, it is essential that our people, the Soviet people, should appreciate the full immensity of the danger that threatens our country and give up all complacency, casualness and the mentality of peaceful constructive work that was so natural before the war, but which is fatal today, when war has radically changed the whole situation.

The enemy is cruel and implacable. He is out to seize our lands, watered by the sweat of our brows, to seize our grain and oil secured by the labour of our hands. He is out to restore the rule of the landlords, to restore Tsarism, to destroy the national culture and the existence as states of the Russians, Ukrainians, Byelorussians, Lithuanians, Latvians, Estonians, Uzbeks, Tatars, Moldavians, Georgians, Armenians, Azerbaijanians and the other free peoples of the Soviet Union, to Germanize them, to turn them into the slaves of German princes and barons.

Thus the issue is one of life and death for the Soviet state, of life and death for the peoples of the USSR; the issue is whether the peoples of the Soviet Union shall be free or fall into slavery. The Soviet people must realize this and abandon all complacency; they must mobilize themselves and reorganize all their work on a new, war-time footing, where there can be no mercy to the enemy.

Further, there must be no room in our ranks for whimperers and cowards, for panic-mongers and deserters. Our people must know no fear in the fight and must selflessly join our patriotic war of liberation against the fascist enslavers. Lenin, the great founder of our state, used to say that the chief virtues of Soviet men and women must be courage, valour, fearlessness in struggle, readiness to fight together with the people against the enemies of our country. These splendid virtues of the Bolshevik must become the virtues of millions and millions of the Red Army, of the Red Navy, of all the peoples of the Soviet Union.

All our work must be immediately reorganized on a war footing; everything must be subordinated to the interests of the front and the task of organizing the destruction of the enemy. The peoples of the Soviet Union now see that German fascism is untameable in its savage fury and hatred of our native country, which has ensured all its working people labour in freedom and prosperity. The peoples of the Soviet Union must risk against the enemy and defend their rights and their land.

The Red Army, Red Navy and all citizens of the Soviet Union must defend every inch of Soviet soil, must fight to the last drop of blood for our towns and villages, must display the daring, initiative and mental alertness that are inherent in our people …

We must exterminate spies, sabotage agents and enemy parachutists, rendering rapid aid in all this to our extermination battalions. We must bear in mind that the enemy is crafty, unscrupulous, experienced in deception and the dissemination of false rumours. We must reckon with all this and not fall victims to stratagem. All who by their panic-mongering and cowardice hinder the work of defence, no matter who they may be, must be immediately hauled before a military tribunal …

In areas occupied by the enemy, guerrilla units, mounted and on foot, must be formed; sabotage groups must be organized to combat enemy units, to foment guerrilla warfare everywhere, blow up bridges and roads, damage telephone and telegraph lines, set fire to forests, stores and transports. In occupied regions conditions must be made unbearable for the enemy and all his accomplices. They must be hounded and annihilated at every step, and all their measures frustrated.

The war with fascist Germany cannot be considered an ordinary war. It is not only a war between two armies, it is also a great war of the entire Soviet people against the German-fascist armies. The aim of this national patriotic war in defence of our country against the fascist oppressors is not only to eliminate the danger hanging over our country, but also to aid all the European peoples groaning under the yoke of German fascism.

In this war of liberation we shall not be alone. In this great war we shall have true allies in the peoples of Europe and America, including the German people which is enslaved by the Hitlerite misrulers. Our war for the freedom of our country will merge with the struggle of the peoples of Europe and America for their independence, for democratic liberties. It will be a united front of the peoples standing for freedom and against enslavement and threats of enslavement by Hitler's fascist armies …

Comrades, our forces are numberless. The overweening enemy will soon learn this to his cost. Side by side with the Red Army, many thousands of workers, collective farmers and intellectuals are rising to fight the enemy aggressor. The masses of our people will rise up in their millions. The working people of Moscow and Leningrad have already begun to form huge People's Guards in support of the Red Army. Such People's Guards must be raised in every city which is in danger of enemy invasion; all the working people must be roused to defend with their lives their freedom, their honour and their country in this patriotic war against German fascism.

In order to ensure the rapid mobilization of all the forces of the peoples of the USSR and to repulse the enemy who has treacherously attacked our country, a State Committee of Defence has been formed and the entire state authority has now been vested in it. The State Committee of Defence has entered on the performance of its functions and calls upon all our people to rally around the party of Lenin and Stalin and around the Soviet government, so as to render self-sacrificing support to the Red Army and Red Navy, to exterminate the enemy and secure victory.

All our forces for the support of our heroic Red Army and our glorious Red Navy! All the forces of the people for the destruction of the enemy! Forward to victory!

Elizabeth Cady Stanton
American social reformer and suffragist

Elizabeth Cady Stanton *née Cady* (1815–1902) was born in Johnstown, New York. While studying law under her Congressman father Daniel Cady (1773–1859), she determined to address the inequality that she discovered in women's legal, political and industrial rights and in divorce law. In 1840 she married the lawyer and abolitionist Henry Brewster Stanton (1805–87), but insisted on dropping the word 'obey' from the marriage vows. Later that year, she accompanied him to the World's Anti-Slavery Convention in London, where she encountered, with much indignation, a ruling that women delegates were excluded from the floor. In 1848, with Lucretia Mott (1793–1880), she organized the first Women's Rights Convention at Seneca Falls, New York, which accepted a set of resolutions which Stanton had drawn up, including suffrage for women. From 1851, she worked in partnership with Susan B Anthony (1820–1906). Together they produced the feminist magazine *Revolution* (1868–70) and founded the National Woman Suffrage Association in 1869. From then until 1892, Stanton was president of the organization (renamed the National American Woman Suffrage Association in 1890). With Mott and Matilda Joslyn Gage (1826–98) she compiled three of the six volumes of *The History of Woman Suffrage* (1881–6). She also wrote an autobiography, *Eighty Years and More, 1815–1897* (1898). Her daughter was the suffragette Harriot Stanton Blatch (1856–1940).

'The male element is a destructive force'
January 1869, Washington, DC, USA

In this vigorous speech, given to a women's suffrage convention, Elizabeth Cady Stanton calls for an amendment to the US Constitution that would grant women the right to vote. In ferocious terms, she describes the ruinous effects of a 'high carnival' of male dominance; and calls for a radical reinvention of society with much greater feminine influence, which she likens to the harmonizing power of nature.

Many commentators considered Stanton's speech the only oration of note at the conference. Yet it ran counter to the prevailing mood which, in the main, was hostile to campaigning for suffrage. This had never been a straightforward issue, and had proved divisive even at the groundbreaking meeting at Seneca Falls in 1848. Many delegates feared the idea would be considered ridiculous, not only by their political opponents and the general public, but by potential allies such as the Quakers, whose male adherents often refused on principle to vote.

Nevertheless, momentum toward female suffrage was building. The success of this convention led to the foundation, later the same year, of the National Woman Suffrage Association (NWSA), which supported Stanton's call for a 16th Amendment to the US Constitution. This policy proved too revolutionary for some members, many of whom broke away to form the American Woman Suffrage Association. However, the NWSA remained a powerful force, and the two groups were eventually reunited in 1890.

I urge a 16th Amendment, because 'manhood suffrage', or a man's government, is civil, religious and social disorganization. The male element is a destructive force: stern, selfish, aggrandizing; loving war, violence, conquest, acquisition; breeding in the material and moral world alike discord, disorder, disease and death. See what a record of blood and cruelty the pages of history reveal! Through what slavery, slaughter and sacrifice, through what inquisitions and imprisonments, pains and persecutions, black codes and gloomy creeds, the soul of humanity has struggled for the centuries, while mercy has veiled her face and all hearts have been dead alike to love and hope!

The male element has held high carnival thus far. It has fairly run riot from the beginning, overpowering the feminine element everywhere, crushing out all the diviner qualities in human nature, until we know but little of true manhood and womanhood – of the latter comparatively nothing, for it has scarce been recognized as a power until within the last century. Society is but the reflection of man himself, untempered by woman's thought; the hard iron rule we feel alike in the church, the state, and the home. No-one need wonder at the disorganization, at the fragmentary condition of everything, when we remember that man, who represents but half a complete being, with but half an idea on every subject, has undertaken the absolute control of all sublunary matters.

People object to the demands of those whom they choose to call the strong-minded, because they say 'the right of suffrage will make the women masculine'. That is just the difficulty in which we are involved today. Though disfranchised, we have few women in the best sense; we have simply so many reflections, varieties and dilutions of the masculine gender. The strong, natural characteristics of womanhood are repressed and ignored in dependence, for so long as man feeds woman, she will try to please the giver and adapt herself to his condition. To keep a foothold in society, woman must be as near like man as possible, reflect his ideas, opinions, virtues, motives, prejudices, and vices. She must respect his statutes, though they strip her of every inalienable right and conflict with that higher law written by the finger of God on her own soul.

She must look at everything from its dollar-and-cent point of view or she is a mere romancer. She must accept things as they are and make the best of them. To mourn over the miseries of others, the poverty of the poor, their hardships in jails, prisons, asylums, the horrors of war, cruelty and brutality in every form – all this would be mere sentimentalizing. To protest against the intrigue, bribery, and corruption of public life, to desire that her sons might follow some business that did not involve lying, cheating and a hard, grinding selfishness, would be arrant nonsense.

In this way, man has been moulding woman to his ideas by direct and positive influences; while she, if not a negation, has used indirect means to control him and in most cases developed the very characteristics, both in him and herself, that needed repression.

And now, man himself stands appalled at the results of his own excesses, and mourns in bitterness that falsehood, selfishness and violence are the law of life. The need of this hour is not territory, gold-mines, railroads, or specie payments[1] but a new evangel of womanhood, to exalt purity, virtue, morality, true religion, to lift man up into the higher realms of thought and action.

We ask woman's enfranchisement, as the first step toward the recognition of that essential element in government that can only secure the health, strength, and prosperity of the nation. Whatever is done to lift woman to her true position will help to usher in a new day of peace and perfection for the race.

In speaking of the masculine element, I do not wish to be understood to say that all men are hard, selfish, and brutal – for many of the most beautiful spirits the world has known have been clothed with manhood – but I refer to those characteristics, though often marked in woman, that distinguish what is called the stronger sex. For example: the love of acquisition and conquest – the very pioneers of civilization when expended on the earth, the sea, the elements, the riches and forces of nature – are powers of destruction when used to subjugate one man to another or to sacrifice nations to ambition.

Here that great conservator of woman's love, if permitted to assert itself – as it naturally would in freedom against oppression, violence and war – would hold all these destructive forces in check, for woman knows the cost of life better than man does, and not with her consent would one drop of blood ever be shed, one life sacrificed in vain.

[1] Stanton refers to the 'male' political issues of the day, including the long-running debate over the gold standard, which linked currency to the value of gold. Certain payments had to be made 'in specie' – in the form of actual gold – rather than in paper currency.

With violence and disturbance in the natural world, we see a constant effort to maintain an equilibrium of forces. Nature, like a loving mother, is ever trying to keep land and sea, mountain and valley, each in its place, to hush the angry winds and waves, balance the extremes of heat and cold, of rain and drought, that peace, harmony and beauty may reign supreme.

There is a striking analogy between matter and mind; and the present disorganization of society warns us that in the dethronement of woman we have let loose the elements of violence and ruin that she only has the power to curb. If the civilization of the age calls for an extension of the suffrage, surely a government of the most virtuous educated men and women would better represent the whole and protect the interests of all than could the representation of either sex alone.

David Steel
Scottish politician

David Martin Scott Steel *later Baron Steel of Aikwood* (1938–) was born in Kirkcaldy, Fife. He became a journalist and broadcaster, and was the youngest MP when first elected in 1965. His constituency was first Roxburgh, Selkirk and Peebles (1965–83), then Ettrick and Lauderdale (1983–97). He sponsored a controversial bill to reform the laws on abortion (1966–7) and was active in the Anti-Apartheid Movement before succeeding Jeremy Thorpe as leader of the Liberal Party in 1976. He led his party into an electoral pact with Labour (1977–8) and subsequently an alliance with the Social Democratic Party (SDP) (1981–8), but despite Steel's undoubted popularity, they won only 23 seats at the 1983 general election. After a similar result at the election of 1987, Steel called for a merger of the Liberals and SDP; this took place in 1988 and Paddy Ashdown became leader as Steel declined to seek the leadership. He published his autobiography, *Against Goliath: David Steel's Story*, in 1989, and was awarded a knighthood in 1990 and a life peerage in 1997. In 1999, he became first Presiding Officer of the new Scottish Parliament. He stepped down in 2003. In 2004 he was created a Knight of the Order of the Thistle – the highest honour in Scotland.

'Prepare for government'
18 September 1981, Llandudno, Wales

When David Steel took on the leadership of the Liberal Party in 1976, it had not been in power since 1922, nor even the main opposition party since 1924. The pact with James Callaghan's Labour Party in 1977–8 had failed to yield the desired results. But in 1981, Steel saw his chance in a new alliance.

Britain's political landscape was perhaps as polarized as it had ever been, with the Conservatives under Prime Minister MARGARET THATCHER tending towards the far right and the Labour Party under MICHAEL FOOT moving further to the left. In 1981, four former Labour ministers formed the new, centrist Social Democatic Party (SDP), officially launched in March 1981. Within three months, the natural affinity between the Liberals and SDP was confirmed in an electoral pact.

This was a time of great optimism for the Liberals, and the SDP historians Ivor Crewe and Anthony King described Steel's performance at the Liberal Assembly in Llandudno as 'more confident and commanding than ever before'. But with the benefit of hindsight Steel's famous final words are cruelly ironic. At the 1983 election, the alliance received just over a quarter of the votes, but won only 23 seats: fewer than four per cent.

Steel himself managed to see the funny side when a comedian lampooned his speech at the Edinburgh Fringe. In his memoir *Against Goliath*, he quotes the punchline: 'Go back to your constituencies and bloody well stay there!'

It is five years since we were last here in Llandudno, when I made my first speech to you as the party's new leader. What an extraordinary five years it has been for all of us. I've been looking back at what I said then:

> 'We are in being as a political party to form a government so as to introduce the policies for which we stand … I do not expect to lead just a nice debating society … We shall probably have – at least temporarily – to share power with somebody else to bring about the changes we seek … I want Liberals to be an altogether tougher and more determined force. I want us to be a crusading and campaigning movement, not an academic think-tank, nor occasional safety-valve in the political system … The road I intend to travel may be a bumpy one, and I recognize the risk that in the course of it we may lose some of the passengers, but I don't mind so long as we arrive at the end of it reasonably intact and ready to achieve our goals.'

The road over the last few years has certainly been a bumpy one. Life for the passengers has at times been very uncomfortable and worrying, but we've lost surprisingly few. Actually, life in the driving seat hasn't been all that smooth either. But you may have noticed we've picked up some hitchhikers.

Here again in Llandudno in 1981, we can see our party more tested, more organized, more mature and more prepared for the final electoral breakthrough.

It is as well for our country that the Liberal Party is so ready. For just look at the state of the nation in 1981. We have the highest unemployment figures since the 1930s. We have an annual inflation rate which – in spite of two years' so-called priority fight against it – is nearly twelve per cent and now rising again. We have a house-building rate which has sunk to its lowest level since 1948. In fact there are now more homeless people than when the Shelter campaign started.

We have a commitment to the escalating costs of Trident[1] which will make our expenditure on Concorde look like pocket money for Dinky toys. We have riots in our city streets, with many young people, both black and white, feeling angry and shut out. The nation's tax burden has increased in the last two years, and yet our educational system is falling apart from the cuts in government expenditure. This government is so penny-pinching that it has even been prepared to cut back the overseas service of the BBC – in which we have justly taken worldwide pride for decades.

[1] 'Trident' is a submarine-launched ballistic nuclear weapons system which entered service in 1984; the government had announced its intention to acquire the system in 1980.

It is a grim picture which Britain presents to the rest of the world in this last quarter of the 20th century – tired, shoddy and mean-spirited – a picture made all the uglier because neither the government nor the official opposition hold out any prospect that we can solve our problems.

Cabinet reshuffles cannot disguise the fact that this Tory government has prove a total failure. Our prime minister is a woman who has first turned her back on those who elected her and then had the nerve to claim that the people are behind her. Well, she had seven per cent of them behind her at Warrington.[2]

[2] At the Warrington by-election in July 1981, Labour retained the seat, but the Conservative share of the vote was 7 per cent, compared to 28 per cent at the 1979 general election.

Margaret Thatcher has portrayed herself as the nation's nurse, administering nasty but necessary medicine in the belief that whatever short-term pain we may suffer, in the long run it will do us good. I am surprised that, as a qualified chemist, she seems to have forgotten the warning on every bottle: 'Caution. It is dangerous to exceed the stated dose.'

When I listen to her I am reminded of Somerset Maugham's description of her predecessor NEVILLE CHAMBERLAIN as, 'sincere, no doubt, and honest, but muddled with self-conceit, who put his party before his country, and by his ineptitude and stubbornness brought it to the verge of ruin.'

As for the Labour opposition, who should be riding high in the effort to turn out this government, they claim to be the party of brotherhood, but they seem to have taken their interpretation of it from the earliest biblical example – Cain and Abel. It doesn't really matter whether DENIS HEALEY or TONY BENN is the bloodstained victor.[3] Neither the bankrupt right nor the hard left of the Labour Party have anything to offer this country any more. The party's over.

[3] At this time, Healey and Benn were vying for deputy leadership of the Labour Party. Healey won narrowly.

Michael Foot said the other day that if his party didn't come to its senses they would generate a decade of Thatcher government. But he's wrong, because at the next election, we intend to provide the British electorate with a wider choice than that between the frying pan and the fire …

The task of putting together our Alliance on the ground is not going to be an easy one. We must secure a reasonable balance in our deployment of forces in every area. It will be immeasurably complicated. It will call for a high degree of vision, of trust and of forbearance, both by our party and by the SDP.

It will require trust between our two parties. The members of the SDP who have been here this week have been greatly impressed in their first close contact with the Liberal Party. They have also enjoyed the warmth of their welcome, and we were right to treat them kindly since they've come from a broken home – the Labour Party. I hope they won't mind if I give them one piece of advice: as the ship of the Labour Party sinks, be careful and be discriminating about who you let clamber on board ours. Ours is a ship on a voyage of adventure. Don't let it become a lifeboat for those whose only real interest is saving their parliamentary or council skins.

It will also require trust *within* our party. I want to thank you for the very considerable trust you have shown me in what I realize must at times have been a tortuous and anxious period. Now it is my turn to trust you, as you proceed to give effect to our Alliance throughout the country. And I do trust you to make a success of it.

Our political situation is unique. Political parties normally seek to persuade the public to follow them. For the last few months, the voice of the public, as registered in the polls, has been desperately pleading with our two political parties. Their message has been: 'get together for our sakes'. They know our country is at a low ebb. The years of mismanagement have destroyed confidence. Broken promises have bred cynicism. The taste of failure is sour and bitter. We don't simply face an economic slump in Britain. What we have to deal with is more complex, a crisis of a whole society which has lost its way and turned in upon itself.

The challenge is daunting. It is a challenge to new leadership and new imagination. Four great tasks await the next government: *industrial reconstruction* – to get factories, offices and workshops humming with activity again; *social reconciliation* – to bring together a people divided against each other and restore a sense of the common weal amongst all our peoples; *a new constitutional settlement* – which makes democratic and open self-government its guiding principle; *an international role* – which restores our influence abroad and makes us a force for peace and prosperity in the world. These are the four cornerstones of the great reforming government I expect us to form with our Social Democratic allies.

Yes, government … This Assembly has seen the Liberal Party discard its role of eternal opposition and face up to the realities of power. It is an awesome responsibility. Instead of criticizing, we must contribute. Instead of shouting on the sidelines, we must take over the game. For I tell you this. When our Alliance government takes office, it will represent the last, best hope for the British people. Our fellow-citizens don't want another set of broken promises, followed by the usual search for scapegoats. They have seen enough of that from the Tory and Labour Parties. They want honesty, commitment and imagination. Our Alliance can only succeed if it calls upon the greatest under-used resource of all, the people themselves. Our plan for recovery must depend upon creating a common purpose in which everyone has a part to play …

Liberalism is not just the creed of a political party. It is the expression of a profoundly moral view of human nature and its possibilities. For too long, the Liberal values of tolerance, mutual respect and co-operation have been on the defensive against the zealots of right and left. Liberals themselves have sometimes been defensive, with the attitudes and concerns of a persecuted minority. There has even been a tendency to say: keep Liberalism out of politics.

But that time is over. The relevance of Liberalism, which has sometimes been drowned out by the clamour of the extremists, is sharp and clear today. It is time to assert our Liberalism proudly – and nowhere more so than in this new Alliance. We must provide the heart and soul of the Alliance, proud of being Liberals and glad to work with those who have come to agree with us.

The great debate we have had this week about our future has not just been of importance to the party, it has been of supreme importance to the country. There are those who say the Liberals and Social Democrats are like two teams of people who find themselves on the summit of the same mountain, having got there from different starting places and by different routes. I am not sure that that analogy is entirely correct. Of course we have come by different routes, but I am not certain that the starting place wasn't in fact the same.

Remember that the Social Democrats, who worked within the Labour Party for years, based their creation of the welfare state and the planned economy on the work of great Liberals like Beveridge and Keynes.[4] Somewhere after we left our common starting point they lost their way. The Labour Party took the wrong path, to state socialism, bureaucracy, centralized controls and mandate by caucus – that perversion of democracy. But the Social Democrats have now found their way to rejoin us …

[4] Steel refers to William Beveridge, 1st Baron Beveridge (1879–1963) and the English economist John Maynard Keynes (1883–1946), both of whom developed influential theories on unemployment and welfare.

Our Alliance has caught people's imaginations. You can see it in opinion polls and in local by-election victories … The voters are responding to the sight of politicians of different tradition but similar persuasion getting together and sinking differences for the common good. They respect an alliance of principle because they can see that an alliance is the way forward: the alliance for Britain, where people can be brought together.

An alliance between management and labour, a real partnership to restore pride in our work and confidence in our industry. An alliance between young and old, in which the young are given the chance they need and the old the respect they deserve. An alliance in the economy, between a private sector dedicated to productivity and a public sector committed to service and efficiency. An alliance between black people and white people, so that all the communities of Britain can make a contribution to the solution of our problems. In short, an alliance which pulls our country together – instead of the old parties, which have torn it apart.

An alliance which discards the envy and pettiness of the past, which stands for all the people and our hope for the future. This has been the dream that has sustained the Liberal Party for so many long, weary years. Now, at last, we have the reality in our grasp. We must have the nerve and courage not to let it slip. I have the good fortune to be the first Liberal leader for over half a century who is able to say to you, at the end of our annual assembly: go back to your constituencies and prepare for government.

Adlai Stevenson
American politician and lawyer

Adlai Ewing Stevenson II (1900–65) was born in Los Angeles, the grandson of Adlai Ewing Stevenson (1835–1914) who had been US vice president, 1893–7, under Grover Cleveland. He studied at Princeton, spent two years editing a family newspaper and then took up law practice in Chicago. From 1943 he took part in several European missions for the State Department and from 1945 served on US delegations to the foundation conferences of the United Nations Organization. In 1948 he was elected governor of Illinois, where his administration was exceptional for efficiency and lack of corruption. He stood against General DWIGHT D EISENHOWER as Democratic presidential candidate in 1952 and 1956, but each time his urbane and intellectual campaign speeches, published under the titles *Call to Greatness* (1954) and *What I Think* (1956), had more appeal abroad than at home. He was US ambassador to the United Nations (1962–5).

'I have not sought the honour you have done me'
26 July 1952 Chicago, Illinois, USA

In 1951, after the 12-year presidency of FRANKLIN D ROOSEVELT, 1933–45, the 22nd Amendment to the US Constitution was passed, which limits US presidents to two terms in office, apart from in exceptional circumstances. By this time, President HARRY S TRUMAN had served almost two terms, although as a former vice president who succeeded Roosevelt on his death, he had been elected only once (in 1948). He was therefore entitled to run for re-election in 1952, but with his popularity dwindling, he made it known that he would stand down and began seeking a successor.

As they had in 1948, both main parties courted Eisenhower, regarded as a war hero and therefore a well-favoured candidate. In 1948 he had declined to stand, but this time he accepted the Republican nomination. The Democrats turned instead to the popular and intelligent governor of Illinois, Adlai Stevenson, grandson of a former vice president.

Initially reluctant, Stevenson eventually accepted the nomination with this characteristically humble and fluent speech. His intellect and oratorical skills are evident here, but proved alienating to the American public. 'Ike' Eisenhower's running mate RICHARD M NIXON characterized Stevenson as an 'egghead', a reference to both his 'elitist' professorial image and his distinctive bald crown.

Stevenson stood little chance against the populist appeal of the 'We Like Ike' campaign, and although he won 44 per cent of the popular vote, the election result was a landslide for the Republicans. Stevenson ran against Eisenhower again in 1956, losing again by a slightly wider margin.

Mr President, ladies and gentlemen of the Convention, my fellow citizens: I accept your nomination and your programme. I should have preferred to hear those words uttered by a stronger, a wiser, a better man than myself. But after listening to the President's speech, I even feel better about myself. None of you, my friends, can wholly appreciate what is in my heart. I can only hope that you understand my words. They will be few.

I have not sought the honour you have done me. I could not seek it, because I aspired to another office,[1] which was the full measure of my ambition, and one does not treat the highest office within the gift of the people of Illinois as an alternative or as a consolation prize.

I would not seek your nomination for the presidency, because the burdens of that office stagger the imagination. Its potential for good or evil, now and in the years of our lives, smothers exultation and converts vanity to prayer.

I have asked the Merciful Father – the father of us all – to let this cup pass from me, but from such dreaded responsibility one does not shrink in fear, in self-interest, or in false humility. So, 'If this cup may not pass from me, except I drink it, Thy will be done.'[2]

That my heart has been troubled, that I have not sought this nomination, that I could not seek it in good conscience, that I would not seek it in honest

[1] Stevenson had planned to run for a second term as Governor of Illinois.

[2] Stevenson refers to JESUS's prayer in the garden of Gethsemane on the night before his arrest, when he resigned himself to his sacrifice. (See Matthew 26:39; Luke 22:42; Mark 14:36.)

self-appraisal, is not to say that I value it the less. Rather, it is that I revere the office of the presidency of the United States. And now, my friends, that you have made your decision, I will fight to win that office with – with all my heart and my soul. And, with your help, I have no doubt that we will win.

You have summoned me to the highest mission within the gift of any people. I could not be more proud. Better men than I were at hand for this mighty task, and I owe to you and to them every resource of mind and of strength that I possess, to make your deed today a good one for our country and for our party. I am confident too, that your selection for – of a candidate for vice president[3] will strengthen me and our party immeasurably in the hard, the implacable work that lies ahead of all of us.

I know you join me in gratitude and respect for the great Democrats and the leaders of our generation, whose names you have considered here in this convention, whose vigour, whose character, whose devotion to the republic we love so well have won the respect of countless Americans and have enriched our party. I shall need them; we shall need them, because I have not changed in any respect since yesterday.

Your nomination, awesome as I find it, has not enlarged my capacities, so I am profoundly grateful and emboldened by their comradeship and their fealty; and I have been deeply moved by their expressions of goodwill and of support. And I cannot, my friends, resist the urge to take the one opportunity that has been afforded me to pay my humble respects to a very great and good American, whom I am proud to call my kinsman, Alben Barkley of Kentucky.[4]

Let me say, too, that I have been heartened by the conduct of this convention. You have argued and disagreed, because as Democrats you care and you care deeply. But you have disagreed and argued without calling each other liars and thieves, without despoiling our best traditions – you have not spoiled our best traditions in any naked struggles for power.

And you have written a platform that neither equivocates, contradicts, nor evades. You have restated our party's record, its principles and its purposes, in language that none can mistake, and with a firm confidence in justice, freedom and peace on earth that will raise the hearts and the hopes of mankind for that distant day when no-one rattles a sabre and no-one drags a chain.

For all things I am grateful to you. But I feel no exultation, no sense of triumph. Our troubles are all ahead of us. Some will call us appeasers; others will say that we are the war party. Some will say we are reactionary; others will say that we stand for socialism. There will be inevitable – the inevitable cries of 'throw the rascals out', 'it's time for a change' and so on and so on.

We'll hear all those things and many more besides. But we will hear nothing that we have not heard before. I'm not too much concerned with partisan denunciation, with epithets and abuse, because the working man, the farmer, the thoughtful businessman – all know that they are better off than ever before, and they all know that the greatest danger to free enterprise in this country died with the Great Depression, under the hammer blows of the Democratic Party.

Nor am I afraid that the precious two-party system is in danger. Certainly the Republican Party looked brutally alive a couple of weeks ago – and I mean both Republican Parties.[5] Nor am I afraid the Democratic Party is old and fat and indolent. After 150 years, it has been old for a long time, and it will never be indolent as long as it looks forward and not back, as long as it

[3] The US politician John J Sparkman (1899–1985) was the Senator from Alabama who stood as Stevenson's running mate. The inclusion of a southerner on the ticket was significant: the Democrats feared their choice of a northern liberal as presidential candidate would alienate the South. In the event, the nine states won by the Democrats were all in the South.

[4] The US politician Alben W Barkley (1877–1956) had served as Vice President in the Truman administration of 1949–53 and had campaigned for nomination as the Democratic presidential candidate in 1952.

[5] The Republican Party at this time comprised two main factions: east-coast moderates represented by Eisenhower and the more conservative Midwest who supported Robert A Taft. The primaries had divided the vote fairly evenly.

commands the allegiance of the young and the hopeful who dream the dreams and see the visions of a better America and a better world.

You will hear many sincere and thoughtful people express concern about the continuation of one party in power for 20 years. I don't belittle this attitude. But change for the sake of change has no absolute merit in itself. If our greatest hazard is preservation of the values of Western civilization, in our self-interest alone, if you please, it is the part – is it the part of wisdom to change for the sake of change to a party with a split personality, to a leader whom we all respect, but who has been called upon to minister to a hopeless case of political schizophrenia?

If the fear is corruption in official position, do you believe, with Charles Evans Hughes,[6] that guilt is personal and knows no party? Do you doubt the power of any political leader, if he has the will to do so, to set his own house in order without his neighbours having to burn it down?

What does concern me – in common with thinking partisans of both parties – is not just winning this election, but how it is won; how well we can take advantage of this great quadrennial opportunity to debate issues sensibly and soberly. I hope and pray that we Democrats, win or lose, can campaign not as a crusade to exterminate the opposing party, as our opponents seem to prefer, but as a great opportunity to educate and elevate a people whose destiny is leadership, not alone of a rich and prosperous, contented country, as in the past, but of a world in ferment.

And my friends: even more important than winning the election is governing the nation. That is the test of a political party, the acid, final test. When the tumult and the shouting die, when the bands are gone and the lights are dimmed, there is the stark reality of responsibility in an hour of history haunted with those gaunt, grim spectres of strife, dissension and materialism at home and ruthless, inscrutable and hostile power abroad.

The ordeal of the 20th century, the bloodiest, most turbulent era of the whole Christian age, is far from over. Sacrifice, patience, understanding and implacable purpose may be our lot of years to come. Let's face it. Let's talk sense to the American people. Let's tell them the truth: that there are no gains without pains, that there – that we are now on the eve of great decisions, not easy decisions, like resistance when you're attacked, but a long, patient, costly struggle which alone can assure triumph over the great enemies of man – war, poverty and tyranny – and the assaults upon human dignity which are the most grievous consequences of each.

Let's tell them that the victory to be won in the 20th century, this portal to the Golden Age, mocks the pretensions of individual acumen and ingenuity. For it is a citadel guarded by thick walls of ignorance and of mistrust which do not fall before the trumpets' blast or the politicians' imprecations or even a general's baton. They are, they are, my friends, walls that must be directly stormed by the hosts of courage, of morality and of vision, standing shoulder to shoulder, unafraid of ugly truth, contemptuous of lies, half-truths, circuses and demagoguery.

The people are wise, wiser than the Republicans think. And the Democratic Party is the people's party – not the labour party, not the farmers' party, not the employers' party – it is the party of no-one because it is the party of everyone.

That, I think, is our ancient mission. Where we have deserted it, we have failed. With your help, there will be no desertion now. Better we lose the election than mislead the people; and better we lose than misgovern the people. Help me to do the job in these years of darkness, of doubt and of

[6] The US jurist and politician Charles Evans Hughes (1862–1948) had exposed huge frauds in the insurance industry and established a reputation as a reformer before becoming Governor of New York (1907–10). He was also Secretary of State (1921–5) and Chief Justice of the Supreme Court (1930–41).

crisis which stretch beyond the horizon of tonight's happy vision, and we will justify our glorious past and the loyalty of silent millions who look to us for compassion, for understanding, and for honest purpose, Thus we will serve our great tradition greatly.

I ask of you all you have. I will give you all I have, even as he who came here tonight and honoured me, as he has honoured you, the Democratic Party, by a lifetime of service and bravery that will find him an imperishable page in the history of the republic and of the Democratic Party – President Harry S Truman.

And finally, my friends, in this staggering task you have assigned me, I shall always try 'to do justly, to love mercy, and to walk humbly with my God'.[7]

[7] See Micah 6:8.

Charles Sumner
American politician and lawyer

Charles Sumner (1811–74) was born in Boston, where he attended the Latin School. He then studied at Harvard and Harvard Law School, graduating in 1834. He became a crusading lawyer, campaigning for prison and education reform, as well as world peace. He travelled in Europe (1837–40), becoming fluent in several languages and meeting prominent political figures, including JOHN BRIGHT and WILLIAM GLADSTONE. He then returned to the USA and legal practice, also lecturing and contributing to journals. In 1845, he made his name as an orator with an Independence Day address on peace, 'The True Grandeur of Nations'. He became a widely admired public speaker with a strong, clear voice and elaborate gestures. His speeches were filled with literary and biblical references, but humourless: as he himself put it, 'You might as well look for a joke in the Book of Revelations'. He became vigorously opposed to slavery, and joined the abolitionist Free Soil Party. He stood unsuccessfully for the House of Representatives in 1848, but in 1852 he was elected as Free Soil senator from Massachusetts, a post he held until his death (though he represented the Republican Party from 1857). In 1856, following his speech opposing the extension of slavery into Kansas and Nebraska, he was savagely beaten by a Congressman, and incapacitated for over three years. The secession of the southern states which led to the Civil War left the Republican Party in full control of both Houses of Congress, and in 1861 Sumner was elected chairman of the Senate Foreign Relations Committee. After the war, he opposed the reconstruction policies of President ABRAHAM LINCOLN, preferring to regard the South as a conquered territory which was not protected by the provisions of the US Constitution. He supported the impeachment of President Andrew Johnson over his treatment of the South and his veto of civil rights bills (1868), and opposed President Ulysses S Grant's project for the acquisition of San Domingo. Grant responded by having Sumner removed from his post on the Foreign Relations Committee. His continuous and acrimonious censures on Grant's administration brought about a rupture with the leading Republican politicians, which worsened when he supported Horace Greeley as presidential candidate in 1872. He died of a heart attack.

'With finite power he wrestles with the infinite'
19 May 1856, Washington, DC, USA

In a precursor to the impending Civil War, this speech brought the passions – and the violence – of the slavery debate into the US Senate chamber.

The westward expansion of the USA during the first half of the 19th century and the consequent creation of new states brought the question of slavery to the top of the political agenda. The pro-slavery and anti-slavery factions in the Congress were each afraid of the other achieving a superiority in numbers and either extending or abolishing slavery. The Missouri Compromise of 1820 was an agreement under which a territory with slavery and one without it were admitted to statehood simultaneously, to maintain parity. But it was only a temporary solution, and the situation came to a head when the Kansas–Nebraska Act was passed in 1854, allowing each state – including newly-established Kansas – to decide its own position on slavery.

As Kansas flooded with both pro-slavers and abolitionists, leading to violent confrontations, the debate raged on in the Senate. Its highlight was Charles Sumner's speech, known as 'The Crime against Kansas', which was delivered over two days. Breathtaking in both eloquence and ferocity, it is filled with literary, historical and mythological references.

In this extract, Sumner pours scorn on the two men principally responsible for the attempt to establish Kansas as a slave state. Senator Stephen A Douglas, the Democrat leader who had framed the Kansas–Nebraska Act, heard himself characterized as a Sancho Panza; but his colleague Andrew P Butler was not in the chamber to receive the full force of Sumner's vituperative attack.

Retribution came two days later, when Butler's nephew, Congressman Preston S Brooks, attacked Sumner in the Senate, beating him with a cane as if he were 'an unruly dog'. Sumner suffered severe injuries; Brook left the chamber unhindered. Both were heroes to their respective parties.

[1] The Presiding Officer of the Senate is normally the US vice president. At this time, however, there was no vice president. The post

Mr President:[1] you are now called to redress a great transgression ... Take down your map, sir, and you will find that the territory of Kansas, more than any other region, occupies the middle spot of North America, equally distant from the Atlantic on the east, and the Pacific on the west; from the

of president *pro tempore* of the United States Senate was held by Jesse D Bright (1812–75).

frozen waters of Hudson's Bay on the north, and the tepid Gulf Stream on the south, constituting the precise territorial centre of the whole vast continent.

To such advantages of situation, on the very highway between two oceans, are added a soil of unsurpassed richness and a fascinating, undulating beauty of surface, with a health-giving climate, calculated to nurture a powerful and generous people, worthy to be a central pivot of American institutions ... Against this territory, thus fortunate in position and population, a crime has been committed which is without example in the records of the past ...

The wickedness which I now begin to expose is immeasurably aggravated by the motive which prompted it. Not in any common lust for power did this uncommon tragedy have its origin. It is the rape of a virgin territory, compelling it to the hateful embrace of slavery; and it may be clearly traced to a depraved longing for a new slave state, the hideous offspring of such a crime, in the hope of adding to the power of slavery in the national government.

Yes, sir, when the whole world, alike Christian and Turk, is rising up to condemn this wrong, and to make it a hissing to the nations, here in our republic, force, aye, sir, *force* has been openly employed in compelling Kansas to this pollution, and all for the sake of political power. There is the simple fact, which you will in vain attempt to deny, but which in itself presents an essential wickedness that makes other public crimes seem like public virtues.

But this enormity, vast beyond comparison, swells to dimensions of wickedness which the imagination toils in vain to grasp, when it is understood that for this purpose are hazarded the horrors of intestine feud not only in this distant territory, but everywhere throughout the country.

Already the muster has begun. The strife is no longer local, but national. Even now, while I speak, portents hang on all the arches of the horizon threatening to darken the broad land, which already yawns with the mutterings of civil war. The fury of the propagandists of slavery, and the calm determination of their opponents, are now diffused from the distant territory over widespread communities and the whole country, in all its extent marshalling hostile divisions; and foreshadowing a strife which – unless happily averted by the triumph of freedom – will become war fratricidal, parricidal war with an accumulated wickedness beyond the wickedness of any war in human annals ...

Such is the crime which you are to judge. But the criminal also must be dragged into day, that you may see and measure the power by which all this wrong is sustained. From no common source could it proceed. In its perpetration was needed a spirit of vaulting ambition which would hesitate at nothing; a hardhood of purpose which was insensible to the judgement of mankind; a madness for slavery which would disregard the Constitution, the laws, and all the great examples of our history; also a consciousness of power such as comes from the habit of power; a combination of energies found only in a hundred arms directed by a hundred eyes; a control of public opinion through venal pens and a prostituted press; an ability to subsidize crowds in every vocation of life – the politician with his local importance, the lawyer with his subtle tongue, and even the authority of the judge on the bench; and a familiar use of men in places high and low, so that none, from the president to the lowest border postmaster, should decline to be its tool. All these things and more were needed, and they were found in the slave power of our republic.

There, sir, stands the criminal, all unmasked before you – heartless, grasping, and tyrannical – with an audacity beyond that of Verres,[2] a subtlety beyond that of Machiavel,[3] a meanness beyond that of Bacon,[4] and an ability beyond that of Hastings.[5] Justice to Kansas can be secured only by the prostration of this influence …

It is related in Northern mythology that the god of force, visiting an enchanted region, was challenged by his royal entertainer to what seemed an humble feat of strength: merely, sir, to lift a cat from the ground. The god smiled at the challenge and, calmly placing his hand under the belly of the animal, with superhuman strength strove, while the back of the feline monster arched far upward, even beyond reach and one paw actually forsook the earth, until at last the discomfited divinity desisted; but he was little surprised at his defeat when he learned that this creature, which seemed to be a cat and nothing more, was not merely a cat, but that it belonged to and was a part of the great Terrestrial Serpent which, in its innumerable folds, encircled the whole globe.

Even so the creature, whose paws are now fastened upon Kansas, whatever it may seem to be, constitutes in reality a part of the slave power which, in its loathsome folds, is now coiled about the whole land. Thus do I expose the extent of the present contest, where we encounter not merely local resistance, but also the unconquered sustaining arm behind. But out of the vastness of the crime attempted, with all its woe and shame, I derive a well-founded assurance of a commensurate vastness of effort against it by the aroused masses of the country, determined not only to vindicate right against wrong, but to redeem the republic from the thraldom of that oligarchy which prompts, directs and concentrates the distant wrong.

Such is the crime, and such the criminal which it is my duty in this debate to expose – and by the blessing of God, this duty shall be done completely to the end. But before entering upon the argument, I must say something of a general character, particularly in response to what has fallen from senators who have raised themselves to eminence on this floor in championship of human wrongs.

I mean the senator from South Carolina,[6] and the Senator from Illinois,[7] who, though unlike as Don Quixote and Sancho Panza,[8] yet, like this couple, sally forth together in the same adventure. I regret much to miss the elder Senator from his seat; but the cause against which he has run a tilt, with such activity of animosity, demands that the opportunity of exposing him should not be lost; and it is for the cause that I speak.

The Senator from South Carolina has read many books of chivalry, and believes himself a chivalrous knight, with sentiments of honour and courage. Of course he has chosen a mistress to whom he has made his vows and who, though ugly to others, is always lovely to him; though polluted in the sight of the world, is chaste in his sight. I mean the harlot, Slavery. For her, his tongue is always profuse in words. Let her be impeached in character, or any proposition made to shut her out from the extension of her wantonness, and no extravagance of manner or hardihood of assertion is then too great for this senator.

The frenzy of Don Quixote on behalf of his wench, Dulcinea del Toboso, is all surpassed. The asserted rights of slavery, which shock equality of all kinds, are cloaked by a fantastic claim of equality. If the slave states cannot enjoy what, in mockery of the great fathers of the republic, he misnames

[2] The Roman politician Gaius Verres (c.115–43 BC) was notorious for abusing his authority for personal gain, through bribery, looting and arbitrary executions. He was prosecuted by CICERO in a famous speech of 70 BC.
[3] The Florentine politician and philosopher Niccolò Machiavelli (1469–1527) is best known for *The Prince* (published 1532), a handbook of political philosophy whose main theme is that rulers must be prepared to do evil if good will come of it. His name is associated with cunning and connivance.

[4] The Virginian colonist and plantation owner Nathaniel Bacon (c.1643–76) attempted to defraud a neighbour of his inheritance, and in 'Bacon's Rebellion' (1675–6) led an attack on peaceful Native Americans.
[5] The English colonial administrator Warren Hastings (1732–1818) served as governor-general of the East India Company, 1773–86, transforming it from a trading society to an arm of the British state. His impeachment (1787) and six-year trial for corruption, led by EDMUND BURKE, ended in acquittal.

[6] The US politician Andrew P Butler (1796–1857), Democrat senator from South Carolina, 1846–1857.
[7] The US politician Stephen A Douglas (1813–61), Democrat senator from Illinois, 1847–61.

[8] A fictional nobleman and his squire, created by the Spanish novelist Miguel de Cervantes (1547–1616) in his novel *Don Quixote* (1605–15). Quixote is notable for acting impetuously on misplaced ideals of chivalry.

'equality under the Constitution' – in other words, the full power in the National Territories to compel fellow men to unpaid toil, to separate husband and wife and to sell little children at the auction block – then, sir, the chivalric senator will conduct the state of South Carolina out of the Union! Heroic knight! Exalted senator! A second Moses come for a second exodus!

But not content with this poor menace, which we have been twice told was 'measured', the senator, in the unrestrained chivalry of his nature, has undertaken to apply opprobrious words to those who differ from him on this floor … The men who strive to bring back the government to its original policy – when freedom and not slavery was sectional – he arraigns as 'sectional'. This will not do. It involves too great a perversion of terms. I tell that senator that it is to himself, and to the 'organization' of which he is the 'committed advocate' that this epithet belongs. I now fasten it upon them.

For myself, I care little for names; but since the question has been raised here, I affirm that the Republican Party of the Union is in no just sense sectional, but, more than any other party, national; and that it now goes forth to dislodge from the high places of the government the tyrannical sectionalism of which the Senator from South Carolina is one of the maddest zealots.

As the Senator from South Carolina is the Don Quixote, the Senator from Illinois is the squire of slavery, its very Sancho Panza, ready to do all its humiliating offices … The senator dreams that he can subdue the North. He disclaims the open threat, but his conduct still implies it. How little that senator knows himself or the strength of the cause which he persecutes! He is but a mortal man; against him is an immortal principle. With finite power he wrestles with the infinite, and he must fall. Against him are stronger battalions than any marshalled by mortal arm – the inborn, ineradicable, invincible sentiments of the human heart against him is nature in all her subtle forces; against him is God. Let him try to subdue these …

Senators such as these are the natural enemies of Kansas, and I introduce them with reluctance, simply that the country may understand the character of the hostility which must be overcome. Arrayed with them, of course, are all who unite, under any pretext or apology, in the propagandism of human slavery. To such, indeed, the time-honoured safeguards of popular rights can be a name only, and nothing more. What are trial by jury, habeas corpus, the ballot-box, the right of petition, the liberty of Kansas, your liberty, sir, or mine, to one who lends himself not merely to the support at home, but to the propagandism abroad, of that preposterous wrong which denies even the right of a man to himself? Such a cause can be maintained only by a practical subversion of all rights. It is, therefore, merely according to reason that its partisans should uphold the usurpation in Kansas.

To overthrow this usurpation is now the special, importunate duty of Congress, admitting of no hesitation or postponement. To this end it must lift itself from the cabals of candidates, the machinations of party, and the low level of vulgar strife. It must turn from that slave oligarchy which now controls the republic, and refuse to be its tool. Let its power be stretched forth toward this distant territory, not to bind, but to unbind; not for the oppression of the weak, but for the subversion of the tyrannical; not for the prop and maintenance of a revolting usurpation, but for the confirmation of liberty.

Sun Yat-sen
Chinese revolutionary politician

Sun Yat-sen (Sun Yixian) *also known as Sun Zhongshan (Sun Chung-shan)* (1866–1925) was born in Zuiheng near Guangzhou (Canton), the son of a Christian farmer. He was brought up by his elder brother in Hawaii, and graduated in medicine at Hong Kong (1892), practising at Macao and Guangzhou. He visited Honolulu (1894) and founded his first political organization there, the Xing Zhong Hui (Cantonese: 'Revive China Society'). After his first abortive uprising against the imperial regime in Guangzhou in 1895, he lived in Japan, the USA and the UK, studying western politics and canvassing support among expatriate Chinese communities. While in London in 1896, he was kidnapped and imprisoned in the Chinese legation. He was saved from certain death by the intervention of his former tutor, the surgeon Sir James Cantlie, and the British Foreign Office. After engineering ten unsuccessful uprisings from abroad, he was victorious in the revolution of 1911. In February 1912 China was proclaimed a republic, with Sun as its provisional president, but he ceded to the northern military leader General Yuan Shikai, who had forced the Emperor's abdication. Yuan sought to establish himself as a dictator and Sun, opposing him from the south, was defeated and found himself again in exile. In 1916, he married his former secretary Song Qingling. He returned to China in 1917 and, with help from the Russians, reorganized the Guomindang – the Chinese Nationalist Party, influenced by LENIN. He was elected president of the Southern Republic in 1921, and later established the Whampoa Military Academy in Guangzhou. Part of his speech at its inauguration in June 1924 was set to music as the Chinese National Anthem. The academy's first principal was Chiang Kai-shek (1887–1975) who – three years after Sun's death – achieved the unification of China, inspired by Sun's *San Min Zhuyi* ('Three Principles of the People'): nationalism, democracy and social reform. Sun was essentially empirical in his political teachings and rejected the communist dogma of the class war. During a conciliatory conference with other Chinese political leaders in Beijing, Sun died of cancer. Acknowledged by all political factions as the father of the Chinese Republic, he was re-interred in a mausoleum built in his honour in Nanjing in 1928.

'How can we restore the standing of our nation?'
2 March 1924, Guangzhou, Southern Republic of China

❦

Sun Yat-sen began to develop his doctrine of 'Three Principles of the People' during the early 20th century. He planned to publicize it in a book written in Shanghai around 1919, but his manuscript was destroyed in 1922 when the presidential palace burned down during an uprising led by his rival Chen Jiongming. Hence his ideas were mostly disseminated via lectures. Partly inspired by ABRAHAM LINCOLN's Gettysburg Address, the Three Principles were the basis of his plan to reconstruct China as a free, prosperous and powerful modern democracy. They had a lasting influence on Chinese political thought.

Within five years of the revolution, the government of the Chinese republic had broken down. Although the first president's move towards dictatorship had been thwarted and an increasingly nominal Beijing government maintained relations with the West, central authority no longer existed. Much of the country was in a state of chaos, disputed by shifting alliances of regional warlords and subject to encroachments by Japan in the north-east. In 1919, Sun re-established the Guomindang to oppose the Beijing government, and set up a military government in Guangzhou (Canton) in 1921 of which he was elected president. He then began to expound his political philosophy.

This address – lecture number six on 'The Principle of Nationalism' – was given at the first party congress of the Guomindang. Here, Sun describes China's long decline as a world power to its current anarchic condition. He calls for the people to restore Chinese ascendancy by embracing ancient morality, which had been rejected in the desire to absorb foreign ideas. He also criticizes the Japanese for shifting their allegiance from weak to strong countries. The translation is by Frank W Price (1927).

❦

Gentlemen: my subject today is, how can we restore the standing of our nation? ... What kind of position in the world did China occupy in ancient times? China was once an exceedingly powerful and civilized nation, the dominant state of the world, with a standing higher than that of the modern great powers – Great Britain, the United States, France, and Japan. Because China was once the sole great power of the world and because our forefathers once reached a position of such eminence, therefore I say that we are now not even a colony … If we want to restore our national standing, we must first revive our national spirit. If we want to revive our national spirit, we must fulfil two conditions.

First, we must utilize China's ancient social groups, as the family and the clan, and consolidate them to form a great national body. When this is accomplished and we have the strength of 400 millions united to fight, no matter how low our present position we should be able to lift it up. So, to know and to unite are the two essentials for reviving our nationalism. When all of you have come to understand these essentials, you must proclaim them among the 400 millions of the whole country, until everybody understands them. Then we can begin to revive our lost national spirit. Our old national spirit is asleep; we must awaken it and then our nationalism will begin to revive. When our nationalism is revived, we can go a step farther and study how to restore our national standing.

China did not reach her former position of greatness by one road only. Usually a nation becomes strong at first by the expansion of its military power, then by the development of various forms of culture; but if the nation and the state are to maintain a permanent standing, moral character is essential. Only by attaining a high standard of morality can the state hope to govern long and exist at peace.

In former times, Asia had no stronger people than the Mongols. In the east they overthrew China; in the west they subjugated Europe … Yet the Mongol dynasty did not last long, while the other dynasties, although not so strong as the Mongol, lasted very long. We find the reason in the moral standards of the former, which were below those of other dynasties …

Because of the high moral standards of our race, we have not only been able to survive in spite of the downfall of the state, but we have had power to assimilate these outside races. So, coming to the root of the matter, if we want to restore our race's standing, besides uniting all into a great national body, we must first recover our ancient morality – then, and only then, can we plan how to attain again to the national position we once held.

As for China's old moral standards, they are not yet lost sight of by the people of China. First come loyalty and filial devotion, then kindness and love, then faithfulness and justice, then harmony and peace. The Chinese still speak of these ancient qualities of character. But since our domination by alien races and since the invasion of foreign culture, which has spread its influence all over China, a group intoxicated with the new culture have begun to reject the old morality, saying that the former makes the latter unnecessary. They do not understand that we ought to preserve what is good in our past and throw away only the bad. China now is in a period of conflict between old and new currents and a large number of our people have nothing to follow after.

A few days ago I was in the country and entered an ancestral temple. On going to the innermost court to rest, I saw on the right-hand side the character for 'filial devotion', but on the left side a blank where there must have been previously, I think, the character for 'loyalty'. This I have seen more than once; many ancestral or family temples are in the same condition. But the character for 'filial devotion,' which I observed the other day, was extra large, while the marks on the left wall where the character had been scratched off looked very recent. It may have been the work of the country folk themselves or of soldiers living in the temple, yet I have seen many ancestral temples which had not been billets for soldiers with the character for 'loyalty' rubbed off the walls.

This shows the thinking of a certain type of people today: because we have a republic, we need not talk about loyalty. They say that in former days loyalty was shown to princes, and that as there are no princes in a democracy, so loyalty is not needed and can be cast aside.

Such an argument is certainly due to misunderstanding: we do not want princes in the country, but we cannot do without loyalty. If we say that loyalty is outworn today, what about the nation? Can we not direct our loyalty towards the nation? Of course we cannot now speak of loyalty to princes, but how about loyalty to the people and loyalty to our tasks?

When we undertake a task we should not falter from first to last until the task is done; if we do not succeed, we should not begrudge our very lives as a sacrifice — this is loyalty. The ancient teaching of loyalty pushed to its limit meant death. To say that ancient loyalty was due to kings and, since now we have no kings, we do not need loyalty and can do as we please, is absolutely wrong … It stands to reason that we should still show loyalty, not to princes but to the nation and to the people. Loyalty to 400 millions must naturally be on a much higher level than loyalty to one individual; so I say that the fine moral quality of loyalty must still be cherished.

Filial devotion is even more a characteristic of China, and we have gone far beyond other nations in the practice of it. Filial duty as revealed in the *Classic of Filial Piety*[1] covers almost the whole field of human activity, touching every point; there is no treatise on filial piety in any civilized country today that is so complete. Filial devotion is still indispensable. If the people of the democracy can carry out loyalty and filial devotion to the limit, our state will naturally flourish.

Kindness and love are also part of China's high morality. In the past, no-one discussed love better than Motze.[2] His 'love without discrimination' is the same thing as JESUS's 'universal love'.[3] The ancients applied the principle of love to government, saying, 'Love the people as your children', and, 'Be kind to all the people and love all creatures'. Love was used to embrace all duties, from which we can see how well they put kindness and love into effect.

Since our foreign intercourse began, some people have thought that the Chinese ideal of kindness and love was inferior to the foreigners' because foreigners in China, by establishing schools and carrying on hospitals to teach and relieve the Chinese, have been practising kindness and love. In the practical expression of the fine qualities of kindness and love, it does seem as though China were far behind other countries, and the reason is that the Chinese have been less active in performance. Yet kindness and love are old qualities of Chinese character, and as we study other countries let us learn their practical methods, revive our own kindness and love, the spirit of ancient China, and make them shine with greater glory.

Faithfulness and justice. Ancient China always spoke of faithfulness in dealing with neighbouring countries and in intercourse with friends. In my estimation, the quality of faithfulness is practised better by Chinese than by foreigners. This can be seen in business intercourse: Chinese in their business relations do not use written contracts; all that is necessary is a verbal promise which is implicitly trusted. Thus, when a foreigner places an order for goods with a Chinese, no contract is necessary; there is simply an entry on the books and the bargain is closed. But when a Chinese places an order with a foreigner, there must be a detailed contract; if there is no attorney or diplomatic officer at the place, the foreigner may follow the Chinese custom and simply enter the transaction in his books. But such

[1] One of the Five Classics attributed to the ancient Chinese philosopher Confucius (551–479 BC).

[2] The Chinese philosopher Motze (c.470–390 BC) propounded a doctrine of universal love, on which the school of Mohism was based.

[3] Sun was familiar with the teachings of Jesus as a result of his conversion to Christianity in the 1880s.

cases are rare; a contract is nearly always required …

Justice. China in her mightiest days never utterly destroyed another state … One day, about the time that the European war was raging most fiercely, I was talking with a Japanese friend about world problems, when Japan had just joined the Entente in their fight against Germany. My Japanese friend said that he himself did not approve of Japan's going to war against Germany, that he favoured Japan's remaining neutral or joining Germany against the Entente. But he went on to say that since Japan and England were allies and had signed an international treaty, Japan had to be 'faithful and just' and keep the agreement, sacrifice her own rights and take the side of the Entente.

I immediately asked that Japanese gentleman: 'Did not China and Japan sign the Treaty of Shimonoseki,[4] the most important provision of which was a guarantee of absolute independence to Korea? Why is Japan willing to sacrifice her national rights to keep a treaty with England while with China she is faithless and breaks the Treaty of Shimonoseki? The independence of Korea was proposed and demanded by Japan herself and effected by threats of force; now Japan is fat from eating her own words. What kind of faithfulness and justice do you call that?'.

Indeed, Japan advocates keeping her treaty with England but not with China, because England is strong and China is weak. Japan's entry into the European war is because of feat of compulsion, not because of any 'faithfulness' or 'justice'. China was a strong state for thousands of years and Korea lived on; Japan has been a strong state for not over twenty years and Korea is already destroyed. From this one can see that Japan's sense of 'faithfulness and justice' is inferior to China's and that China's standards have advanced beyond those of other nations.

China has one more splendid virtue – the love of harmony and peace. Among the states and the peoples of the world today China alone preaches peace; other countries all talk in terms of war and advocate the overthrow of states by imperialism. Only in recent years, since the experience of many great wars and the huge, tragic death losses, have they begun to propose the abolition of war …

The intense love of peace which the Chinese have had these thousands of years has been a natural disposition. In individual relationships great stress has been laid upon 'humility and deference'. In government the old saying was, 'He who delights not in killing a man can unify all men'. All of this is very different from the ideals of foreigners. China's ancient virtues of loyalty, filial devotion, kindness, love, faithfulness and such are in their very nature superior to foreign virtues – but in the moral quality of peace we will further surpass the people of other lands. This special characteristic is the spirit of our nation and we must not only cherish it, but cause it to shine with greater lustre; then our national standing will be restored.

[4] A peace accord between China and Japan, signed on 17 April 1895.

Jonathan Swift

Anglo-Irish satirist and clergyman

Jonathan Swift (1667–1745) was born in Dublin, of English parents. He was educated at Kilkenny Grammar School and Trinity College, Dublin, where he obtained his degree only by 'special grace' in 1685. He became secretary to the diplomat Sir William Temple, and supported him on the side of the Ancients in the 'Querelle des Anciens et des Modernes', a literary dispute on the relative merits of classical and contemporary sensibilities. His contribution was the mock-epic *Battle of the Books*, which was published along with his satire on religious dissension, *A Tale of a Tub* (1704). His visits to London were largely political, but he also participated in literary and aristocratic circles. Initially, he supported the Whigs, but his interest in the church steered him towards the Tory party. His *History of the Four Last Years of the Queen* [Anne] (published posthumously in 1758) describes the intrigue and pamphleteering that were rife during that period. The death of Queen Anne (1714) disappointed all the hopes of Swift and his Tory friends. He accepted his 'exile' to the Deanery of St Patrick's Cathedral, Dublin, and from then on, except for two visits in 1726 and 1727, stayed away from London. He threw himself into a strenuous campaign for Irish liberties, denied by the Whig government. The *Drapier's Letters* (1724), concerning England's restrictions on Irish trade, is the most famous outcome of this activity. Swift's charitable efforts for the poor of Dublin greatly enhanced his reputation. In 1726 he published his world-famous satire *Gulliver's Travels*. This was followed in 1729 by *A Modest Proposal*, which sarcastically suggested the poor of Ireland should satisfy their hunger by feeding their children to the rich. His light verse now ranged from *The Grand Question Debated* (1729) to the satirical *Verses on His Own Death* (1731). Swift considered *On Poetry; a Rhapsody* (1733) his best verse satire. The ironical *Directions to Servants* and *A Complete Collection of Genteel and Ingenious Conversation* appeared in 1731. Politics apart, Swift's influence was directed powerfully against the vogue of deistic science and modern invention and in favour of orthodoxy and good manners.

'The great evil of this neglect and scorn of preaching'

c.1720–30, Dublin, Eire

The south wall of St Patrick's Cathedral in Dublin is adorned with a plaque on which is inscribed the epitaph of Jonathan Swift, who became its dean in 1713. Written in Latin by Swift himself, the motto's key phrase translates as 'fierce indignation', a spirit which informed much of his work.

He had been disappointed in English politics, and as a Tory pamphleteer received a frosty reception on arriving in predominantly Whig Dublin. Nonetheless, this was a productive period in his creative life, during which he produced *Gulliver's Travels* and *A Modest Proposal* – the latter inspired, at least partly, by the poverty he witnessed in the weavers' district adjacent to the cathedral.

From this period too date many of his sermons. The precise dates are uncertain, but nine of them were published posthumously in 1763. In a short preface, Swift's friend and biographer John Boyle, the 5th Earl of Orrery, notes: 'These sermons are curious; and curious for such reasons as would make other works despicable. They were written in a careless hurrying manner; and were the offspring of necessity, not of choice: so that one will see the original force of the Dean's genius more in these compositions, that were the legitimate sons of duty, than in other pieces that were the natural sons of love.'

In this, perhaps the best known, Swift's 'fierce indignation' is very much in evidence, as he regales his congregation on the importance of attending church – and paying heed to the preacher.

'And there sat in a window a certain young man named Eutychus, being fallen into a deep sleep; and while Paul was long preaching, he sunk down with sleep, and fell down from the third loft, and was taken up dead.'[1]

[1] Acts of the Apostles 20:9.

I have chosen these words with design, if possible, to disturb some part in this audience of half an hour's sleep, for the convenience and exercise whereof this place, at this season of the day, is very much celebrated.

There is indeed one mortal disadvantage to which all preaching is subject; that those who, by the wickedness of their lives, stand in greatest need, have usually the smallest share; for, either they are absent upon the account of idleness, or spleen, or hatred to religion, or in order to doze away the intemperance of the week; or, if they do come, they are sure to employ their minds rather any other way than regarding or attending to the business of the place.

The accident which happened to this young man in the text hath not been sufficient to discourage his successors, but because the preachers now in the world, however they may exceed Saint Paul in the art of setting men to sleep, do extremely fall short of him in the working of miracles,[2] therefore men are become so cautious as to choose more safe and convenient stations and postures for taking their repose, without hazard of their persons … However, this being not the only way by which the lukewarm Christians and scorners of the age discover their neglect and contempt of preaching, I shall enter expressly into consideration of this matter …

First, I shall produce certain instances to show the great neglect of preaching now among us.

These may be reduced under two heads. First, men's absence from the service of the church; and, secondly, their misbehaviour when they are here. The first instance of men's neglect is in their frequent absence from the church.

There is no excuse so trivial, that will not pass upon some men's consciences to excuse their attendance at the public worship of God. Some are so unfortunate as to be always indisposed on the Lord's Day, and think nothing so unwholesome as the air of a church. Others have their affairs so oddly contrived as to be always unluckily prevented by business. With some it is a great mark of wit, and deep understanding, to stay at home on Sundays.

Others again discover strange fits of laziness, that seize them, particularly on that day, and confine them to their beds. Others are absent out of mere contempt of religion. And, lastly, there are not a few who look upon it as a day of rest, and therefore claim the privilege of their castle, to keep the Sabbath by eating, drinking and sleeping, after the toil and labour of the week. Now, in all this the worst circumstance is that these persons are such whose companies are most required, and who stand most in need of a physician.

Secondly, men's great neglect and contempt of preaching appear by their misbehaviour when at church.

If the audience were to be ranked under several heads, according to their behaviour, when the Word of God is delivered, how small a number would appear of those who receive it as they ought? How much of the seed then sown would be found to fall by the wayside, upon stony ground, or among thorns? And how little good ground would there be to take it?[3] A preacher cannot look around from the pulpit without observing that some are in a perpetual whisper, and, by their air and gesture, give occasion to suspect that they are in those very minutes defaming their neighbour.

Others have their eyes and imagination constantly engaged in such a circle of objects, perhaps to gratify the most unwarrantable desires, that they never once attend to the business of the place; the sound of the preacher's words doth not so much as once interrupt them …

But of all misbehaviour, none is comparable to that of those who come here to sleep; opium is not so stupefying to many persons as an afternoon sermon. Perpetual custom hath so brought it about that the words of whatever preacher become only a sort of uniform sound at a distance, than which nothing is more effectual to lull the senses …

[2] In the story chosen by Swift as his text, St Paul proceeds to restore Eutyclus to life. (See Acts of the Apostles 20:10–12.)

[3] Swift refers to the Parable of the Sower. See Matthew 13:3–23; Mark 4:3–9, 13–20; Luke 8:4–15.

I proceed, *secondly*, to reckon up some of the usual quarrels men have against preaching, and to show the unreasonableness of them …

First, they object against the particular preacher; his manner, his delivery, his voice are disagreeable; his style and expression are flat and low, sometimes improper and absurd; the matter is heavy, trivial and insipid; sometimes despicable and perfectly ridiculous, or else, on the other side, he runs up into unintelligible speculation, empty notions and abstracted flights, all clad in words above usual understandings.

Secondly, they object against preaching in general; it is a perfect road of talk; they know already whatever can be said; they have heard the same an hundred times over. They quarrel that preachers do not relieve an old beaten subject with wit and invention; and that now the art is lost of moving men's passions, so common among the orators of Greece and Rome …

But let us examine the reasonableness of them. The doctrine delivered by all preachers is the same: so we preach and so ye believe. But the manner of delivering is suited to the skill and abilities of each, which differ in preachers just as in the rest of mankind. However, in personal dislikes of a particular preacher, are these men sure they are always in the right? Do they consider how mixed a thing is every audience, whose taste and judgement differ, perhaps every day, not only from each other, but themselves?

… These men, whose ears are so delicate as not to endure a plain discourse of religion, who expect a constant supply of wit and eloquence on a subject handled so many thousand times; what will they say when we turn the objection upon themselves, who with all the lewd and profane liberty of discourse they take, upon so many thousand subjects, are so dull as to furnish nothing but tedious repetitions and little paltry, nauseous commonplaces, so vulgar, so worn, or so obvious as upon any other occasion but that of advancing vice, would be hooted off the stage.

Nor, lastly, are preachers justly blamed for neglecting human oratory to move the passions, which is not the business of a Christian orator, whose office it is only to work upon faith and reason. All other eloquence hath been a perfect cheat, to stir up men's passions against truth and justice, for the service of a faction, to put false colours upon things and by an amusement of agreeable words, make the worse reason appear to be the better. This is certainly not to be allowed in Christian eloquence …

I go on *thirdly*, to set forth the great evil of this neglect and scorn of preaching, and to discover the real causes from whence it proceedeth.

I think it is obvious to believe that this neglect of preaching hath very much occasioned the great decay of religion among us. To this may be imputed no small part of that contempt some men bestow on the clergy; for whoever talketh without being regarded is sure to be despised. To this we owe, in a great measure, the spreading of atheism and infidelity among us; for religion, like all other things, is soonest put out of countenance by being ridiculed … Thus are the last efforts of reforming mankind rendered wholly useless. 'How shall they hear,' saith the apostle, 'without a preacher?'[4]

[4] Romans 10:14.

But, among all neglects of preaching, none is so fatal as that of sleeping in the house of God. A scorner may listen to truth and reason, and in time grow serious; an unbeliever may feel the pangs of a guilty conscience; one whose thoughts or eyes wander among other objects, may, by a lucky word, be called back to attention: but the sleeper shuts up all avenues to his soul …

The great evil of this neglect will further yet appear from considering the real causes whence it proceedeth, whereof the first I take to be an evil conscience. Many men come to church to save or gain a reputation; or because they will not be singular, but comply with an established custom; yet all the while, they are loaded with the guilt of old rooted sins. These men can expect to hear of nothing but terrors and threatenings, their sins laid open in true colours, and eternal misery the reward of them; therefore no wonder they stop their ears and divert their thoughts and seek any amusement, rather than stir the hell within them.

Another cause of this neglect is a heart set upon worldly things. Men whose minds are much enslaved to earthly affairs all the week cannot disengage or break the chain of their thoughts so suddenly as to apply to a discourse that is wholly foreign to what they have most at heart. Tell a usurer of charity and mercy and restitution: you talk to the deaf. His heart and soul, with all his senses, are got among his bags, or he is gravely asleep and dreaming of a mortgage …

A third cause of the great neglect and scorn of preaching ariseth from the practice of men who set up to decry and disparage religion. These, being zealous to promote infidelity and vice, learn a rote of buffoonery that serveth all occasions and refutes the strongest arguments for piety and good manners. These have a set of ridicule, calculated for all sermons and all preachers, and can be extreme witty as often as they please upon the same fund.

Let me now, *in the last place*, offer some remedies against this great evil.

It will be one remedy against the contempt of preaching, rightly to consider the end for which it was designed … It is become an impertinent vein among people of all sorts, to hunt after what they call a good sermon, as if it were a matter of pastime and diversion. Our business, alas, is quite another thing, either to learn or at least be reminded of our duty, to apply the doctrines delivered, compare the rules we hear with our lives and actions and find wherein we have transgressed. These are the dispositions men should bring into the house of God; and then they will be a little concerned about the preacher's wit or eloquence, nor be curious to enquire out his faults of infirmities, but consider how to correct their own.

Another remedy against the contempt of preaching is, that men would consider, whether it be not reasonable to give more allowances for the different abilities of preachers than they usually do? Refinements of style and flights of wit, as they are not properly the business of any preacher, so they cannot possibly be the talents of all … Why should they be so over-nice in expectation of eloquence, where it is neither necessary nor convenient, is hard to imagine.

Lastly, the scorners of preaching would do well to consider that this talent of ridicule they value so much is a perfection very easily acquired … It is in any man's power to suppose a fool's cap on the wisest head, and then laugh at his own supposition …

To conclude, these considerations may, perhaps, have some effects while men are awake; but what argument shall we use to the sleeper? What methods shall we take to hold open his eyes? Will he be moved by considerations of common civility? We know it is reckoned a point of very bad manners to sleep in private company, when, perhaps, the tedious impertinence of many talkers would render it at least as excusable as at the dullest sermon. Do they think it is a small thing to watch four hours at a play, where all virtue and religion are openly reviled; and can they not watch one half hour to hear them defended? Is this to deal like a judge (I mean like a good judge) to listen on one side of the cause, and sleep on the other?

I shall add but one word more: that this indecent sloth is very much owing to that luxury and excess men usually practise upon this day, by which half the service thereof is turned into sin; men dividing the time between God and their bellies, when after a gluttonous meal, their senses dozed and stupefied, they retire to God's house to sleep out the afternoon. Surely, brethren, these things ought not so to be.

Rabindranath Tagore
Indian writer and philosopher

Rabindranath Tagore (1861–1941) was born in Calcutta. He studied law in England (1878–80) and for 17 years managed his family estates at Shileida, where he collected the legends and tales he later used in his work. In 1901 he founded, at Santiniketan near Bolpur in West Bengal, a communal school aiming to blend Eastern and Western systems of philosophy and education, which became Visva–Bharati University. He was openly critical of the non-co-operation campaign led by MAHATMA GANDHI, but also of the British government's treatment of Bengal. His first book was a volume of poetry, *A Poet's Tale* (1878). This was followed by a novel, *Karuna*, and a drama, *The Tragedy of Rudachandra*. His major works include *Binodini* (1902, Eng trans 1964), the first modern novel by an Indian writer; *The Crescent Moon* (1913), poems about childhood; *Gitanjali* (1912, Eng trans *Song Offerings*, 1912), a volume of spiritual verse; and his best-known play, *Chitra* (1914). He also wrote *My Reminiscences* (1917) and *My Boyhood Days* (1940). He received the Nobel Prize for literature in 1913, the first Asian to do so, and was knighted in 1915 – an honour which he resigned in 1919 as a protest against British policy in the Punjab.

'Money has established its universal sovereignty'
April/May 1923, Peking (Beijing), China

After receiving his Nobel Prize, Tagore was invited to speak at institutions around the world, and spent some time lecturing in Japan and the USA. Meanwhile, at home, he founded the Visva–Bharati University, a development of the school he had established in 1901 at Santiniketan. This became a centre for Indian culture and a meeting place of East and West.

In 1923, Liang Chi-chao, president of the Universities Lecture Association of Peking, invited him and a number of his Visva–Bharati colleagues to China. They left in March 1924, arriving in Shanghai after visiting south-east Asia, and toured in China for six weeks. Tagore spoke in many cities, without reference to notes, and his speeches were recorded in Chinese newspapers and the journals of Visva–Bharati.

This is the final part of a lecture entitled 'Civilization and Progress', which contrasts Western imperialism with the Eastern idea of *dharma*. This was an important theme on the Chinese tour. In an earlier lecture, 'To My Hosts', Tagore told his fellow Asians, 'The West is becoming demoralized through being the exploiter, through tasting the fruits of exploitation.'

Here, he laments increasing materialism in Western societies, which he describes as 'a huge degradation, like a slimy reptile' whose influence is spreading around the world. With reference to Indian and Chinese sacred texts, he argues that civilization can only thrive when connected to an inner ideal. Tagore's lectures provoked some hostile responses among young Chinese Communists, who regarded his arguments as reactionary and ideologically dangerous.

[1] The source of this quotation is uncertain.

It is said in our scriptures: 'In greed is sin, in sin death.'[1] Your philosopher has said: 'No greater calamity than greed.'[2] These sentences carry the wisdom of ages. When greed becomes the dominant character of a people it forebodes destruction for them and no mere organization like the League of Nations can ever save them.

To let the flood of self-seeking flow unchecked from the heart of the nation and at the same time try to build an outer dam across its path can never succeed. The deluge will burst forth with a greater force because of the resistance. Lao-tze says: 'Not self-seeking, he gaineth life.'[3] Life's principle is in this and therefore, in a society, all the trainings and teachings that make for life are those that help us in our control of selfish greed.

When civilization was living – that is to say, when most of its movements were related to an inner ideal and not to an external compulsion – then money had not the same value as it has now. Do you not realize what an immense difference that fact has made in our life, and how barbarously it has cheapened those things which are invaluable in our inheritance? We have grown so used to this calamitous change that we do not fully realize

[2] Verse 46:2 of the *Tao te-Ching*, the assembled ideas of the Chinese philosopher Lao-tze (sixth century BC), which form the basis of the Taoist religion.

[3] *Tao te-Ching* 22:2.

the indignity it imposes upon us.

I ask you to imagine a day, if it does ever come, when in a meeting everybody will leave his chair and stand up in awe if a man enters there who has a greater number of human skulls strung in his necklace than have his fellow beings. We can have no hesitation today in admitting that this would be pure barbarism. Are there no other tokens of a similar degradation for man? Are there no other forms of human skulls than those which the savages so proudly wear?

In olden times, the mere hoarding of millions was never considered as wealth unless it had some crown of glory with which to proclaim its ideal greatness. In the East as well as in the West, man, in order to save his inherent dignity, positively despised money that represented merely a right to possession and no moral responsibility. Money-making as a profession was everywhere contemptuously treated, and men who made big profits the sole end of their life were looked down upon.

There was a time in India when our Brahmins were held in reverence, not only for their learning and purity of life, but for their utter indifference to material wealth. This only shows that our society was fully conscious that its very life depended upon its ideals, which were never to be insulted by anything that belonged to a passion for self-seeking. But because today progress is considered to be characteristic of civilization – and because this progress goes on gathering an unending material extension – money has established its universal sovereignty. For in this world of ambition, money is the central power-house, sending impulsions in all directions.

In former days, the monarchs of men were not ashamed humbly to pay their respect to men of intellect or those who had spiritual or creative gifts. For the qualities of the higher life were the motive force of the civilization of those times. But today, men, whatever their position, never think that they are humiliating themselves when they offer their homage to men of corpulent cash, not always because they expect any benefit therefrom, but because of the bare fact of its possession. This denotes a defeat of the complete man by the material man.

This huge degradation, like a slimy reptile, has spread its coils round the whole human world. Before we can rescue humanity from the bondage of its interminable tail, we must free our mind from the sacrilege of worship offered to this unholy power, this evil dragon which can never be the presiding deity of the civilization of man.

I am sure you know that this soulless progeny of greed has already opened its elastic jaws wide over the fair limbs of your country, wider perhaps than in any other part of the world. I earnestly hope that you will develop some means to rescue her from her destination towards the hollow of its interior.

But the danger is not so much from the enemy who attacks, but from defender who may betray. It fills my heart with a great feeling of dismay when, among your present generation of young men, I see signs of their succumbing to the depravity of fascination for an evil power which allures with its enormity. They go about seeking for civilization amongst the wilderness of skyscrapers, in the shrieking headlines of news journals, and the shouting vociferation of demagogues. They leave their own great prophets, who had a far-seeking vision of truth, and roam in the dusk, begging for the loan of light from some glow-worm which can only hold its niggardly lantern for the purpose of crawling towards its nearest dust.

They will learn the meaning of the word civilization when they come back home and truly understand what their great master, Lao-tze, wanted to teach when he said: 'Those who have virtue attend to their obligations; those who have no virtue attend to their claims.'[4] In this saying he has expressed in a few words what I have tried to explain in this paper. Progress which is not related to an inner ideal, but to an attraction which is external, seeks to satisfy our endless claims. But civilization, which is an ideal, gives us power and joy to fulfil our obligations.

About the stiffening of life and hardening of heart caused by the organization of power and production, he says with profound truth:

'The grass as well as the trees, while they live, are tender and supple; when they die they are rigid and dry. Thus the hard and the strong are the companions of death. The tender and the delicate are the companions of life. Therefore he who in arms is strong will not conquer. The strong and the great stay below. The tender and the delicate stay above.'[5]

Our sage in India says, as I have quoted before: 'by the help of anti-*dharma* men prosper, they find what they desire, they conquer enemies, but they perish at the root'.[6] The wealth which is not welfare grows with a rapid vigour, but it carries within itself the seed of death. This wealth has been nourished in the West by the blood of men and the harvest is ripening. The same warning was also given centuries ago by your sage when he said: 'Things thrive and then grow old. This is called Un-Reason. Un-Reason soon ceases.'[7]

Your teacher has said: 'To increase life is called a blessing.'[8] For the increase of life, unlike the increase of things, never transcends the limits of life's unity. The mountain pine grows tall and great, its every inch maintains the rhythm of an inner balance, and therefore even in its seeming extravagance it has the reticent grace of self-control. The tree and its productions belong to the same vital system of cadence; the timber, leaves, flowers and fruits are one with the tree; their exuberance is not a malady of exaggeration, but a blessing. But systems which mainly are for making profits and not for supplying life's needs encourage an obesity of ugliness in our society, obliterating the fine modulations of personality from its features. Not being one with our life, they do not conform to its rhythm.

Our living society, which should have dance in its steps, music in its voice, beauty in its limbs; which should have its metaphor in stars and flowers, maintaining its harmony with God's creation, becomes, under the tyranny of a prolific greed, like an over-laden market-cart jolting and creaking on the road that leads from things to the Nothing, tearing ugly ruts across the green life till it breaks down under the burden of its vulgarity on the wayside reaching nowhere. For 'This is called Un-Reason,' as your teacher has said, 'and Un-Reason soon ceases.'[9]

---

[4] *Tao te-Ching* 79:2.

[5] *Tao te-Ching* 76:2–5.

[6] The source of this quotation is uncertain.

[7] *Tao te-Ching* 30:4 and 55:4–5.

[8] *Tao te-Ching* 55:4.

[9] *Tao te-Ching* 30:4

Mother Teresa of Calcutta
Albanian-born nun and missionary

Mother Teresa *originally Agnes Gonxha Bojaxhiu* (1910–97) was born of Albanian parents at Skopje in present-day Macedonia, where she spent her childhood. When she was eight, her father died, leaving the family in financial difficulties, and she was raised in poverty by her mother. In 1928, she went to Ireland to join the Order of the Sisters of Loreto, taking her name from St Thérèse of Lisieux. She left for India at the end of the year. From 1931, she taught at St Mary's School for girls in Calcutta, taking her final vows in 1937. She became principal of the school in 1944, but later felt called to help the poor. In 1948, she left the convent. Following a brief training in basic nursing at Patna she returned to Calcutta and lived temporarily with the Little Sisters of the Poor. From here, she began working in the slums, visiting and treating the sick and needy. She was gradually joined by other nuns, and in 1950 established the Missionaries of Charity, which became a pontifical congregation (answering directly to the Pope) in 1965. She opened her House for the Dying in 1952; and began working with lepers in 1957. Her leper colony, Shanti Nagar ('Town of Peace') was inaugurated in West Bengal in 1970. She founded the Missionaries of Charity Brothers in 1963. She also collaborated with multi-faith groups, including the Co-Workers of Mother Teresa, and established missions in communist countries, including the USSR, Cuba and Albania. By the end of her life, there were 4,000 sisters in her order, running over 610 charity houses in 123 countries. She was awarded the Pope John XXIII Peace Prize in 1971 and the Nobel Peace Prize in 1979. She was beatified in 2003.

'For love to be true it has to hurt'
10 June 1977, Cambridge, England

Mother Teresa gave this address at the parish church of St Mary the Great with St Michael, which is also the university church of the University of Cambridge. The occasion was the conferment on her of an honorary doctorate by the University, presented by Prince Philip, Duke of Edinburgh, the newly installed chancellor of the university.

In her address, Mother Teresa describes the work of her order, the Missionaries of Charity, pointing to love as the motivating factor for her and her fellow nuns. Poverty is not limited to the material dimension, she argues; there is great spiritual poverty too, especially in the West. Love, she urges, must begin at home, in our daily contact with partners, children and the elderly. It should also inform our views on abortion. 'Where is the unborn child?' she asks. 'Dead! Why? Because we do not want him.'

In later life Mother Teresa's views on contraception and abortion became more outspoken, leading critics to argue that she ignored the consequences of overpopulation in developing nations such as India. Yet many also praised her devotion and humility, qualities which this sermon reflects. As Cardinal Basil Hume declared on her death, 'The utter sincerity with which she lived out her faith gave her an energy and radiance which is unforgettable.'

A Hindu gentleman was asked, 'What is Christian religion?', and he answered, 'It's a giving'. For God loved the world so much that he gave his Son. He gave him to Mary to be his mother, and he became a person, just like you and me in all things except sin. He, too, proved his love to us by giving his own life, his own being …

That is the giving of Christ. And today God keeps on loving the world. He keeps on sending you and me to prove that he loves the world, that he still has that compassion for the world. It is we who have to be his love, his compassion in the world of today. But to be able to love we must have faith, for faith in action is love, and love in action is service. That is why JESUS made himself the Bread of Life,[1] that we may be able to eat and live and be able to see him in the distressing disguise of the poor. For us to be able to love we need to see, we need to touch, and that is why, as we read in the Gospel, Jesus made the poor the hope of salvation for you and for me. He said that 'whatever you did to the least of my brethren you did it to me'.[2]

That is why the work of the Missionaries of Charity is so beautiful. I think that we are not really social workers, but that we are really contemplatives

[1] Jesus describes himself as the 'bread of life' at John 6:35. The phrase is also associated with God's provision of manna to the Israelites in exile (Exodus 16:4–35), with the Last Supper (Mark 14:22), and hence with the Eucharist.

[2] Matthew 25:40.

right in the heart of the world today, if we take Jesus at his word when he said, 'I was hungry, I was naked, I was homeless, and you did it to me'.[3] So we are really touching him 24 hours a day, and that is why that contemplation, that touching of Christ in the poor, is so beautiful, so real, so loving. Our poor people do not need sympathy; they do not need pity from us; they really need love and compassion. But we must know that they are lovable people, that they are great people, and that knowledge will lead us to love them and love, to serve them.

[3] See Matthew 25:35–40.

Do we really know our poor? Right here! Maybe the poor are in our own family, for love begins at home. Do we know them? Do we know the lonely ones? Do we know the unwanted ones? Do we know the forgotten ones? I picked up a woman from a dustbin and she was burning with fever. She was in her last days and she kept on saying, 'My son did this to me'. I picked her out and I took her home, then I brought her to the convent.

On the way, I tried to make her accept to forgive her son. It took me a long time to make her say, 'I forgive my son'. Just before she died she was able to say that with a real forgiveness. But she was not concerned that she was dying, she was not concerned that she was burning with fever, she was not concerned that she was suffering so much. The breaking of the heart was that her son did not want her. I think this is something that you and I must understand.

[4] See 1 John 4:20.

St John has said, 'How can you say that you love God whom you do not see when you do not love your neighbour whom you do see'. He uses a very strong word; he says, 'You are a liar if you say you love God and you don't love your neighbour'.[4] I think this is something that we must all understand, that love begins at home. Today we see more and more that all the suffering in the world has started from the home. Today we have no time even to look at each other, to talk to each other, to enjoy each other, and still less to be what our children expect from us, what the husband expects from the wife, what the wife expects from the husband. And so more and more we are out of our homes and less and less we are in touch with each other ...

Where are our old people today? They are in institutions. Where is the unborn child? Where? Dead. Gone. Why? Because we do not want him. I find it great, great poverty that in the West, here in this country, a child must die because we are afraid to feed one more child, to educate one more child. The child must die before it is born. Is that not great poverty? The fear of having to feed one more child marks that child for death ... God has put all his love into creating that human life and that is why we have no right to destroy it, especially we who understand that Christ has died for that life, to save that life. Christ has died and given everything for the child and if we really are Christians, then for us, too, as the Hindu man put it, 'It's a giving'.

We must give until it hurts. For love to be true it has to hurt. It hurt Jesus to love us; it hurt God to love us because he had to give. He gave his Son. Today here we are together. I can give you nothing; I have nothing to give. But what I want from you is that when we look together and we see the poor in our own family, that we begin at home to love until it hurts, that we have a ready smile, that we have time for our people. If we know our people, then we will know who is our next-door neighbour. We will know them ...

Our Sisters are very much engaged with the poorest of the poor, with the crippled, with the blind, with the mental. We have homes for the sick and dying. This year we are celebrating the silver jubilee of our first home for the dying in Calcutta. In these 25 years, we have picked up over 36,000 people from the streets and over 16,000 have died with us …

I am very sure that all those people who have died with us are in Heaven; they are really saints, they are in the presence of God. It may be that they were not wanted on this earth, but they are very beloved children of God. And so, I would like you to pray and to thank God for all the beautiful things our Sisters have done in the Home for the Dying. Though it is a part of the Kali Temple, the Goddess of Fear,[5] yet there beside it is to be found the joy of helping people to die in peace with God. You would be surprised how beautifully they die. They brought a man from the street, half-eaten with maggots, and he said, 'I've lived like an animal in the street but I'm going to die like an angel, loved and cared for.' And he did die like an angel, he died a beautiful death …

In Calcutta some time ago, we were very hard-up for sugar. I do not know how the word went round that Mother Teresa had no sugar for her children, but a little child told his parents, 'I will not eat sugar for three days. I want to give my sugar to Mother Teresa.' So the parents, who had never been to our house, brought him and he brought a little bottle of sugar and said, 'I will not have sugar for three days, have this for your children.' He could hardly speak because he was only four years old, but that little child loved with great love. He loved until it hurt.

We who know Jesus, who love Jesus, who belong to Jesus, we must love as he has loved us. This is why he instituted the Bread of Life, that we may love as he loved us. And he continues saying the same thing, 'As My Father has loved me …' – How did his Father love him? By giving him to us – '… I have loved you.'[6] And how did he love us? By giving himself to us. That is the way that we have to love one another: by giving ourselves to each other. And the giving must be until it hurts …

We deal with thousands of people and yet there has not been one occasion when we have had to say to somebody, 'Very sorry, we don't have …'. In Calcutta we cope with 7,000 people every day and the day we don't cook, they don't eat.

I can remember a Sister came and told me, 'Mother, there is no more rice for Friday and Saturday; we will have to tell people that we don't have it.' I was a little surprised because in all 25 years I had never heard that before. On Friday morning, at about nine o'clock, a truck full of bread, thousands of loaves of bread, arrived. Nobody in Calcutta knew why the government closed the schools, but the schools were closed and all the bread was brought to us, and for two days our people ate bread, and bread, and bread!

I knew why God closed the schools! For there it was: he closed the schools because he wanted our people to know that they are more important than the grass, and the birds, and the flowers of the fields; that they are special to him.[7] Those thousands of people had to know that he loved them, that He cared for them. And this is a repeated evidence of tender love, of the tender thoughtfulness of God himself for his people.

To be able to do this work each Sister's life is woven with the Eucharist and with prayer. You will be very surprised to know that we are getting hundreds of wonderful young vocations, and the young people in their application write something very beautiful: 'I want a life of poverty, prayer and sacrifice that will lead me to the service of the poor'. This is our young people – so full of love, so full of generosity. In a moment, they can be sent anywhere at any time to do any humble work. The whole of our Society is

---

[5] In Hinduism, the goddess Kali is usually associated with violence and destruction, though some sects of the religion accord her benevolent, life-giving attributes.

[6] John 15:9.

[7] Mother Teresa alludes to Matthew 6:25–32, where Jesus describes the provision made by God for humankind.

just engaged in doing that – feeding the hungry Christ, clothing the naked Christ, taking care of the sick Christ and giving a home to the homeless Christ.

It is very beautiful to see our young people so fully devoted, so full of love for God's poor. In our Society, we take the three vows of loving Christ with undivided love in chastity, through the freedom of poverty, in total surrender to obedience. We also take a fourth vow of giving wholehearted free service to the poorest of the poor, that is to Christ in the distressing disguise of the poor.

We need your prayers that we do not spoil God's work. Pray for us that the work remains his work and that we remain completely at his disposal. We have Brothers also who do the same work in the same total surrender to God. The aim of the Society is to satiate the thirst of Jesus on the Cross for love, for souls. The spirit of the congregation is total surrender to God, loving trust in our superiors, and cheerfulness, because without joy there is no love, and love without joy is not true love …

Make us worthy, Lord, to serve our fellow men throughout the world who live and die in poverty and hunger.

Give them, through our hands, this day their daily bread;[8] and by our understanding love, give peace and joy.

Amen.

[8] See the Lord's Prayer, Matthew 6:11.

Margaret Thatcher
English politician

Margaret Hilda Thatcher *née Roberts, later Baroness Thatcher* (1925–2013) was born in Grantham. She read chemistry at Somerville College, Oxford (1943–7) and stood unsuccessfully as a Conservative candidate for Dartford in 1950 and 1951. She qualified as a barrister in 1953 and specialized in tax law. She was elected MP for Finchley in 1959 and joined the Shadow Cabinet in 1967. In EDWARD HEATH's government (1970–4) she served as Secretary of State for Education and Science. She was elected leader of the Conservative Party in 1975 and became prime minister in May 1979. In her first administration, she reduced inflation, but unemployment rose. Her popularity was boosted by the recapture of the Falkland Islands following the Argentinian invasion of 1982 and she was reelected in June 1983. During her second term, she placed greater emphasis on the market economy. The sale of shares to small investors became known as 'popular capitalism'. A miners' strike that began in March 1984 lasted a year without success. During the party conference in October 1984, the Irish Republican Army detonated a bomb in Brighton in an attempt to assassinate the Cabinet: Thatcher escaped injury but there were four deaths. She went on to negotiate the Anglo-Irish Agreement in 1985. The economy continued to grow during her second administration, with unemployment declining from January 1986, but her tough stance was unpopular in several quarters. Her reputation for intransigence was strengthened by the resignation of Defence Secretary Michael Heseltine (1986). She was returned for a third term in 1987. On the international stage, she established a close friendship with US president RONALD REAGAN, won the admiration of Soviet president Mikhail Gorbachev, and was credited with helping end the Cold War. At home, the introduction of the community charge (popularly called the poll tax) was highly unpopular. In October 1989 her Chancellor of the Exchequer Nigel Lawson resigned, followed a year later by her Foreign Secretary GEOFFREY HOWE. Her leadership of the party was challenged, and in November 1990, after narrowly failing to win re-election on the first ballot, she resigned. She declined to stand for Parliament in 1992, and was created a life peer. Much of her economic legacy became common ground between the British political parties after TONY BLAIR became Labour leader in 1994. She largely withdrew from public life following health problems in 2002.

'The lady's not for turning'
10 October 1980, Brighton, England

Margaret Thatcher's keynote speech to the 1980 Conservative Party conference, the middle section of which is reproduced here, was a rousing statement of defiance against critics outside and within the party who had attacked her government's counter-inflationary policies, blaming them for the growth in unemployment. While the Prime Minister acknowledged the 'human tragedy' of Britain's two million unemployed, she insisted that low inflation offered the only real hope of long-term prosperity. Additional measures, she hinted, were curbing the wastefulness of local authorities and nationalized utilities – curbs which Thatcher would increasingly effect during her eleven years in office, limiting the powers of local authorities and privatizing the utility companies.

    The most famous line of the speech – and one of the most memorable of her career – was a direct riposte to those commentators who were predicting that Thatcher would be forced to make a 'U-turn' on her economic policy, just as Edward Heath's government had been in 1972. However, an equally telling moment – in terms of the national mood and the Prime Minister's mettle – occurred earlier in the speech, when protesters burst into the conference hall, shouting 'Tories out! We want jobs!'. Thatcher replied, to thunderous applause, 'Never mind, it's wet outside. I expect they wanted to come in. You can't blame them; it's always better where the Tories are.'

> The level of unemployment in our country today is a human tragedy. Let me make it clear beyond doubt: I am profoundly concerned about unemployment. Human dignity and self-respect are undermined when men and women are condemned to idleness. The waste of a country's most precious assets – the talent and energy of its people – makes it the bounden duty of government to seek a real and lasting cure.
>
>   If I could press a button and genuinely solve the unemployment problem, do you think that I would not press that button this instant? Does anyone imagine that there is the smallest political gain in letting this unemployment continue, or that there is some obscure economic religion which demands

[1] Earlier in the speech, Thatcher had asserted that 'control of the money supply was ... an essential condition for the recovery of much of continental Europe'.

this unemployment as part of its ritual? This government are pursuing the only policy which gives any hope of bringing our people back to real and lasting employment. It is no coincidence that those countries of which I spoke earlier,[1] which have had lower rates of inflation have also had lower levels of unemployment.

I know that there is another real worry affecting many of our people. Although they accept that our policies are right, they feel deeply that the burden of carrying them out is falling much more heavily on the private than on the public sector. They say that the public sector is enjoying advantages but the private sector is taking the knocks and at the same time maintaining those in the public sector with better pay and pensions than they enjoy.

I must tell you that I share this concern and understand the resentment. That is why I and my colleagues say that to add to public spending takes away the very money and resources that industry needs to stay in business let alone to expand. Higher public spending, far from curing unemployment, can be the very vehicle that loses jobs and causes bankruptcies in trade and commerce. That is why we warned local authorities that since rates are frequently the biggest tax that industry now faces, increases in them can cripple local businesses. Councils must, therefore, learn to cut costs in the same way that companies have to.[2]

[2] 'Rate-capping', which limited local councils' entitlement to levy property tax – or 'rates' – became a contentious issue during Thatcher's first administration.

That is why I stress that if those who work in public authorities take for themselves large pay increases they leave less to be spent on equipment and new buildings. That in turn deprives the private sector of the orders it needs, especially some of those industries in the hard-pressed regions. Those in the public sector have a duty to those in the private sector not to take out so much in pay that they cause others unemployment. That is why we point out that every time high wage settlements in nationalized monopolies lead to higher charges for telephones, electricity, coal and water, they can drive companies out of business and cost other people their jobs.

If spending money like water was the answer to our country's problems, we would have no problems now. If ever a nation has spent, spent, spent and spent again, ours has. Today that dream is over. All of that money has got us nowhere but it still has to come from somewhere.

Those who urge us to relax the squeeze, to spend yet more money indiscriminately in the belief that it will help the unemployed and the small businessman, are not being kind or compassionate or caring. They are not the friends of the unemployed or the small business. They are asking us to do again the very thing that caused the problems in the first place. We have made this point repeatedly.

I am accused of lecturing or preaching about this. I suppose it is a critic's way of saying, 'Well, we know it is true, but we have to carp at something'. I do not care about that. But I do care about the future of free enterprise, the jobs and exports it provides and the independence it brings to our people. Independence? Yes, but let us be clear what we mean by that. Independence does not mean contracting out of all relationships with others. A nation can be free but it will not stay free for long if it has no friends and no alliances. Above all, it will not stay free if it cannot pay its own way in the world. By the same token, an individual needs to be part of a community and to feel that he is part of it. There is more to this than the chance to earn a living for himself and his family, essential though that is.

Of course, our vision and our aims go far beyond the complex arguments of economics, but unless we get the economy right we shall deny our people the opportunity to share that vision and to see beyond the narrow horizons of economic necessity. Without a healthy economy we cannot have a healthy society. Without a healthy society the economy will not stay healthy for long.

But it is not the state that creates a healthy society. When the state grows too powerful, people feel that they count for less and less. The state drains society, not only of its wealth but of initiative, of energy, the will to improve and innovate as well as to preserve what is best. Our aim is to let people feel that they count for more and more. If we cannot trust the deepest instincts of our people we should not be in politics at all. Some aspects of our present society really do offend those instincts.

Decent people do want to do a proper job at work, not to be restrained or intimidated from giving value for money. They believe that honesty should be respected, not derided. They see crime and violence as a threat, not just to society but to their own orderly way of life. They want to be allowed to bring up their children in these beliefs, without the fear that their efforts will be daily frustrated in the name of progress or free expression. Indeed, that is what family life is all about.

There is not a generation gap in a happy and united family. People yearn to be able to rely on some generally accepted standards. Without them you have not got a society at all, you have purposeless anarchy. A healthy society is not created by its institutions, either. Great schools and universities do not make a great nation, any more than great armies do. Only a great nation can create and involve great institutions – of learning, of healing, of scientific advance. And a great nation is the voluntary creation of its people – a people composed of men and women whose pride in themselves is founded on the knowledge of what they can give to a community of which they in turn can be proud.

If our people feel that they are part of a great nation and they are prepared to will the means to keep it great, a great nation we shall be, and shall remain. So, what can stop us from achieving this? What then stands in our way? The prospect of another winter of discontent?[3] I suppose it might.

But I prefer to believe that certain lessons have been learnt from experience, that we are coming, slowly, painfully, to an autumn of understanding. And I hope that it will be followed by a winter of common sense. If it is not, we shall not be diverted from our course.

To those waiting with bated breath for that favourite media catchphrase, the 'U-turn', I have only one thing to say. 'You turn if you want to. The lady's not for turning.'[4]

[3] In the winter of 1978–9, James Callaghan's Labour government faced a series of public sector strikes, leaving the country at various times without postal, firefighting or rubbish collection services. This period, which led to Labour's defeat in the 1979 general election, became known as the 'winter of discontent', a phrase drawn from the opening line of *Richard III* (c.1592) by the English dramatist William Shakespeare (1564–1616).

[4] This line plays on the title of the verse play *The Lady's Not for Burning* (1949) by the English dramatist Christopher Fry (1907–2005).

❧

'To appease an aggressor is to invite aggression'
26 May 1982, London, England

❧

This speech to the Conservative women's conference at the Royal Festival Hall came at a crucial moment in the Falklands War, both militarily and politically. Argentine troops had invaded the Falkland Islands on 2 April, but it was not until 21 May – five days before this address – that British soldiers landed at Port San Carlos, on the north coast of East Falkland. From there they advanced to capture Darwin, Goose Green and the capital, Port Stanley, forcing the Argentines to surrender on 14 June. At the time of this speech, however, victory was far from assured; as Thatcher acknowledges, Argentine Exocet missiles had damaged (in fact, they had sunk) the British destroyer HMS *Coventry* and the container ship *Atlantic Conveyor* only the day before.

Speaking at a sensitive moment in terms of public support for the conflict, Thatcher responds to the 'questioning voices' raised about its necessity and potential consequences, and draws an implicit parallel with Britain's role in World War II. Like that war, she argues, this was a similarly just cause, protecting British values at home as well as on the Falkland Islands, 8,000 miles away. The Churchillian overtones hit exactly the right note. Repeated in Parliament and elsewhere, they boosted Thatcher's previously dwindling popularity, while the retaking of the Falklands helped the Conservatives to a landslide victory in the general election of 1983.

❧

Madam Chairman: our conference takes place at a time when great and grave issues face our country. Our hearts and minds are focused on the South Atlantic. You have been debating defence policy at a time when our fighting men are engaged in one of the most remarkable military operations in modern times.

We have sent an immensely powerful task force – more than 100 ships and 27,000 sailors, marines, soldiers and airmen – some 8,000 miles away in the South Atlantic.

In a series of measured and progressive steps, over the past weeks, our forces have tightened their grip of the Falkland Islands. They have retaken South Georgia.[1] Gradually they have denied fresh supplies to the Argentine garrison.

Finally, by the successful landing at San Carlos Bay in the early hours of Friday morning, they have placed themselves in a position to retake the islands and reverse the illegal invasion by Argentina.[2]

By the skill of our pilots, our sailors and those manning the Rapier missile on shore they have inflicted heavy losses on the Argentine Air Force – over 50 aircraft have been destroyed.

There have, of course, been tragic losses and you will have heard of the further attacks on our task force. HMS *Coventry* came under repeated air attack yesterday evening and later sank. One of our merchant ships supporting the task force, the *Atlantic Conveyor*, was also damaged and had to be abandoned. We do not yet know the number of casualties, but our hearts go out to all those families who had men in these ships.

Despite these grievous losses, neither our resolve nor our confidence is weakened.

We in Britain know the reality of war. We know its hazards and its dangers. We know the task that faces our fighting men. They are now established on the Falkland Islands with all the necessary supplies. Although they still face formidable problems, in difficult terrain with a hostile climate, their morale is high.

We must expect fresh attacks upon them, and there can be no question of pressing the Force Commander[3] to move forward prematurely – the judgement about timing must be his and his alone, and we have confidence in his judgement.

Madam Chairman: the theme of this conference is 'Living with our Neighbours' and it may seem inappropriate to be debating such a thing when there was open conflict between Britain and Argentina, and the lives of young men on both sides are being lost.[4] But the whole basis of our foreign and defence policy, and indeed of the international political order, depends on the friendship of neighbours, co-operating with them and abiding by the rule of law.

These are the very things which the illegal invasion of the Falkland Islands, had it gone unchallenged, would have subverted and destroyed. The Falkland Islands are British. The Falkland Islanders are British. They don't want to be ruled by Argentina, as those pictures of the welcome given to British marines and soldiers showed more clearly than a thousand words.

[1] British troops retook South Georgia, an island 1,000 miles south-east of the Falklands, on 25 April 1982.

[2] Since 1833, Britain had governed the Falklands, rejecting Argentina's claims of sovereignty over the islands. The 1982 invasion, launched by Argentina's military junta largely to boost popular support for the government, was condemned by the United Nations Security Council by ten votes to one (with four abstentions).

[3] The English soldier Major General Sir Jeremy Moore (1928–2007) was commander of British land forces during the Falklands War.

[4] About 750 Argentines are believed to have died in the Falklands conflict, while Britain lost 255 members of its armed forces. Three Falkland islanders were also killed.

The phlegmatic, matter-of-fact welcome to our troops by the Falkland Islanders – 'We were expecting you. We only wondered why you didn't get here sooner' – that is entirely characteristic of British people wherever they may be.

There is another wider aspect of neighbourliness which has been revealed by this crisis. It is the strength of our links with our friends and allies in the commonwealth and NATO, and we are most grateful for their support. No nation these days can stand completely alone.

It was eight weeks ago today, Wednesday, that information reached us that the Argentine fleet was sailing towards the Falklands, 8,000 miles away from home. At that stage there were only two ways of trying to stop it: through President Reagan – whose appeal to Argentina was rebuffed – and the United Nations, whose plea was also rejected.

Now there were those who said we should have accepted the Argentine invasion as a fait accompli. But Madam Chairman: whenever the rule of force rather than the rule of law is seen to succeed, the world moves a step closer to anarchy.

The older generation in our country, and generations before them, have made sacrifices so that we could be a free society and belong to a community of nations which seeks to resolve disputes by civilized means.

Today it falls to us to bear the same responsibility. We shall not shirk it. What has happened since that day, eight weeks ago, is a matter of history – the history of a nation which rose instinctively to the needs of the occasion.

For decades, the peoples of the Falkland Islands had enjoyed peace with freedom; peace with justice; peace with democracy. They are our people and let no-one doubt our profound longing for peace. But that peace was shattered by a wanton act of armed aggression by Argentina in blatant violation of international law. And everything that has happened since has stemmed from the invasion by the military dictatorship of Argentina. And sometimes I feel people need reminding of that fact more often. We want peace restored. But we want it with the same freedom, justice and democracy that the islanders previously enjoyed.

For seven weeks we sought peace by diplomatic means; through the good offices of our close friend and ally, the United States; through the unremitting efforts of the Secretary-General of the United Nations.[5]

[5] The Peruvian diplomat Javier Pérez de Cuéllar de la Guerra (1920–), who was Secretary-General of the United Nations, 1982–91.

We studied seven sets of proposals and finally we drew up our own. Without compromising fundamental principles, we made a variety of reasonable and practical suggestions in a supreme effort to avoid conflict and loss of life. We worked tirelessly for a peaceful solution. But when there is no response of substance from the other side, there comes a point when it is no longer possible to trust the good faith of those with whom one is negotiating.

Playing for time is not working for a peaceful solution. Wasting time is not willing a peaceful solution. It is simply leaving the aggressor with the fruits of his aggression. It would be a betrayal of our fighting men and of the islanders if we had continued merely to talk, when talk alone was getting nowhere.

And so, seven weeks to the day after the invasion, we moved to recover by force what was taken from us by force. It cannot be said too often: We are the victims; they are the aggressors. We came to military action reluctantly.

But when territory which has been British for almost 150 years is seized and occupied; when not only British land, but British citizens, are in the power of an aggressor; then we have to restore our rights and the rights of the Falkland Islanders.

There have been a handful of questioning voices raised here at home. I would like to answer them. It has been suggested that the size of the Falkland Islands and the comparatively small number of its inhabitants – some 1,800 men, women and children – should somehow affect our reaction to what has happened to them.

To those – not many – who speak lightly of a few islanders beyond the seas and who ask the question, 'Are the few worth fighting for?' let me say this: right and wrong are not measured by a head-count of those to whom that wrong has been done. That would not be principle but expediency.

And the Falklanders, remember, are not strangers. They are our own people. The prime minister of New Zealand, Rob Muldoon – and what a marvellous friend he is – went to the heart of the matter in his usual straightforward way. 'With the Falkland Islanders,' he said, 'it is family.'

When their land was invaded and their homes were overrun, they naturally turned to us for help – and we, their fellow citizens, 8,000 miles away in our own much larger island, could not and did not beg to be excused. We sent our men and our ships with all speed, hoping against hope that we would not have to use them in battle; but prepared to do so if all attempts at a peaceful solution failed. When those attempts did fail, we could not sail by on the other side.

And let me add this. If we, the British, were to shrug our shoulders at what had happened in the South Atlantic and to acquiesce in the illegal seizure of those faraway islands, it would be a clear signal to those with similar designs on the territory of others to follow in the footsteps of aggression. Surely we, of all people, have learned the lesson of history: that to appease an aggressor is to invite aggression elsewhere, and on an ever-increasing scale?[6]

Other voices – again only a few – have accused us of clinging to colonialism or even imperialism. Let us remind those who advance that argument that we British have a record second to none of leading colony after colony to freedom and independence. We cling not to colonialism but to self-determination of peoples everywhere.

Still others – again only a few – say we must not put at risk our investments and interests in Latin America; that trade and commerce are too important to us to put in jeopardy some of the valuable markets of the world. What would the islanders, under the heel of the invader, say to that?

What kind of people would we be if, enjoying the birthright of freedom ourselves, we were to abandon British citizens for the sake of commercial gain? We would never do it.

Now we are present in strength on the Falkland Islands. Our purpose is to repossess them and we shall persevere until that purpose is accomplished. When the invader has left, there will be much to do rebuilding, restoring homes and farms and above all renewing the confidence of the people in their future.

Their wishes will need time to crystalize and of course they will depend in some measure on what we and others are prepared to do, to develop untapped resources and to safeguard the islands' future.

Madam Chairman: our cause is just. It is the cause of freedom and the rule of law. It is the cause of support for the weak against aggression by the strong. Let us then draw together in the name, not of jingoism, but of justice.

[6] Thatcher alludes to the appeasement of Hitler in the 1930s by British governments, and especially the Munich Agreement negotiated by NEVILLE CHAMBERLAIN, which postponed but did not prevent the outbreak of World War II.

[7] Thatcher quotes the final lines from the play *King John* (c.1596) by William Shakespeare (1564–1616).

Finally, let our nation, as it has so often in the past, remind itself – and the world: 'Nought shall make us rue / If England to herself do rest but true'.[7]

'What are the distinctive marks of Christianity?'
21 May 1988, Edinburgh, Scotland

Margaret Thatcher's speech to the General Assembly of the Church of Scotland, given at the Assembly Hall on the Mound in Edinburgh, was swiftly dubbed 'the Sermon on the Mound' by the media. It revealed a more reflective, private side to the 'Iron Lady', as well as the support she found for her political views in the Bible. The address touched on many of the broad themes of Thatcherism: personal choice, individual responsibility, the centrality of the family and the creation of wealth. She quotes St Paul's injunction that 'If a man will not work he shall not eat', and points out that he is cautioning against the love of money for its own sake, rather than the generation of wealth.

Thatcher's words were met with warm applause from the Assembly, but many present were unhappy with the decision to let the prime minister speak – the Church of Scotland opposed the Conservative government on a range of issues, including its plans to replace local council rates with a poll tax. But the Church hierarchy had its own point to make: after her address, the Rev James Whyte – then Moderator (the head of the Church of Scotland) – presented the prime minister with a report entitled 'Just Sharing: A Christian Approach to the Distribution of Wealth, Income and Benefits'.

Moderator: I am greatly honoured to have been invited to attend the opening of this 1988 General Assembly of the Church of Scotland; and I am deeply grateful that you have now asked me to address you.

I am very much aware of the historical continuity extending over four centuries, during which the position of the Church of Scotland has been recognized in constitutional law and confirmed by successive sovereigns. It sprang from the independence of mind and rigour of thought that have always been such powerful characteristics of the Scottish people, as I have occasion to know. [*Muted laughter.*] It has remained close to its roots and has inspired a commitment to service from all people.

I am therefore very sensible of the important influence which the Church of Scotland exercises in the life of the whole nation, both at the spiritual level and through the extensive caring services which are provided by your church's department of social responsibility. And I am conscious also of the value of the continuing links which the Church of Scotland maintains with other churches.

Perhaps it would be best, Moderator, if I began by speaking personally as a Christian, as well as a politician, about the way I see things. Reading recently, I came across the starkly simple phrase: 'Christianity is about spiritual redemption, not social reform'.

Sometimes the debate on these matters has become too polarized and given the impression that the two are quite separate. But most Christians would regard it as their personal Christian duty to help their fellow men and women. They would regard the lives of children as a precious trust. These duties come not from any secular legislation passed by Parliament, but from being a Christian.

But there are a number of people who are not Christians who would also accept those responsibilities. What then are the distinctive marks of Christianity?

They stem not from the social but from the spiritual side of our lives, and personally, I would identify three beliefs in particular. First, that from the beginning man has been endowed by God with the fundamental right to choose between good and evil. And second, that we were made in God's own image and, therefore, we are expected to use all our own power of thought and judgement in exercising that choice; and further, that if we open our hearts to God, he has promised to work within us. And third, that Our Lord Jesus Christ, the Son of God, when faced with his terrible choice and lonely vigil, chose to lay down his life that our sins may be forgiven.

I remember very well a sermon on an Armistice Sunday when our preacher said, 'No-one took away the life of Jesus; he chose to lay it down.'

I think back to many discussions in my early life when we all agreed that if you try to take the fruits of Christianity without its roots, the fruits will wither. And they will not come again unless you nurture the roots.

But we must not profess the Christian faith and go to church simply because we want social reforms and benefits or a better standard of behaviour; but because we accept the sanctity of life, the responsibility that comes with freedom and the supreme sacrifice of Christ expressed so well in the hymn:

'When I survey the wondrous Cross / On which the Prince of glory died, / My richest gain I count but loss / And pour contempt on all my pride.'

May I also say a few words about my personal belief in the relevance of Christianity to public policy – to the things that are Caesar's?

The Old Testament lays down in Exodus the Ten Commandments as given to Moses, the injunction in Leviticus to love our neighbour as ourselves and generally the importance of observing a strict code of law. The New Testament is a record of the Incarnation, the teachings of Christ and the establishment of the Kingdom of God. Again we have the emphasis on loving our neighbour as ourselves and to 'Do-as-you-would-be-done-by'.

I believe that by taking together these key elements from the Old and New Testaments, we gain a view of the universe, a proper attitude to work, and principles to shape economic and social life.

We are told we must work and use our talents to create wealth. 'If a man will not work he shall not eat,' wrote St Paul to the Thessalonians.[1] Indeed, abundance rather than poverty has a legitimacy which derives from the very nature of Creation.

[1] 2 Thessalonians 3:10.

Nevertheless, the Tenth Commandment – 'Thou shalt not covet' – recognizes that making money and owning things could become selfish activities. But it is not the creation of wealth that is wrong, but love of money for its own sake. The spiritual dimension comes in deciding what one does with the wealth. How could we respond to the many calls for help, or invest for the future, or support the wonderful artists and craftsmen whose work also glorifies God, unless we had first worked hard and used our talents to create the necessary wealth? And remember the woman with the alabaster jar of ointment.[2]

[2] In an incident described in Matthew 26:6–13, a woman pours costly perfumed oil over JESUS's head. Accused of waste by his disciples, she is absolved by Jesus for symbolically preparing him for burial.

I confess that I always had difficulty with interpreting the biblical precept to love our neighbours 'as ourselves' until I read some of the words of C S Lewis.[3] He pointed out that we don't exactly love ourselves when we fall below the standards and beliefs we have accepted. Indeed we might even hate ourselves for some unworthy deed.

None of this, of course, tells us exactly what kind of political and social institutions we should have. On this point, Christians will very often genuinely disagree, though it is a mark of Christian manners that they will do so with courtesy and mutual respect.

[*Applause.*]

[3] The Anglo-Irish academic and writer C S Lewis (1898–1963) was a late convert to Christianity and wrote several books on faith and religious practice. He is best known for his 'Narnia' series, a Christian allegory for children in seven books (1950–7).

What is certain, however, is that any set of social and economic arrangements which is not founded on the acceptance of individual responsibility will do nothing but harm.

We are all responsible for our own actions. We can't blame society if we disobey the law. We simply can't delegate the exercise of mercy and generosity to others. The politicians and other secular powers should strive by their measures to bring out the good in people and to fight down the bad: but they can't create the one or abolish the other. They can only see that the laws encourage the best instincts and convictions of the people, instincts and convictions which I'm convinced are far more deeply rooted than is often supposed.

Nowhere is this more evident than the basic ties of the family which are at the heart of our society and are the very nursery of civic virtue. And it is on the family that we in government build our own policies for welfare, education and care.

You recall that Timothy was warned by St Paul that anyone who neglects to provide for his own house (meaning his own family) has disowned the faith and is 'worse than an infidel'.[4]

[4] 1 Timothy 5:8.

We must recognize that modern society is infinitely more complex than that of biblical times and of course new occasions teach new duties. In our generation, the only way we can ensure that no-one is left without sustenance, help or opportunity is to have laws to provide for health and education, pensions for the elderly, succour for the sick and disabled.

But intervention by the state must never become so great that it effectively removes personal responsibility. The same applies to taxation; for while you and I would work extremely hard whatever the circumstances, there are undoubtedly some who would not unless the incentive was there. And we need their efforts too.

Moderator: recently there have been great debates about religious education. I believe strongly that politicians must see that religious education has a proper place in the school curriculum.

[*Applause.*]

In Scotland, as in England, there is an historic connection expressed in our laws between church and state. The two connections are of a somewhat different kind, but the arrangements in both countries are designed to give symbolic expression to the same crucial truth: that the Christian religion – which, of course, embodies many of the great spiritual and moral truths of Judaism – is a fundamental part of our national heritage. And I believe it is the wish of the overwhelming majority of people that this heritage should be preserved and fostered.

[*Applause.*]

For centuries it has been our very lifeblood. And indeed we are a nation whose ideals are founded on the Bible.

Also, it is quite impossible to understand our history or literature without grasping this fact, and that's the strong practical case for ensuring that children at school are given adequate instruction in the part which the Judaic–Christian tradition has played in moulding our laws, manners and institutions. How can you make sense of Shakespeare and Sir Walter Scott, or of the constitutional conflicts of the 17th century in both Scotland and England, without some such fundamental knowledge?

But I go further than this. The truths of the Judaic–Christian tradition are infinitely precious, not only, as I believe, because they are true, but also because they provide the moral impulse which alone can lead to that peace, in the true meaning of the word, for which we all long.

To assert absolute moral values is not to claim perfection for ourselves. No true Christian could do that. What is more, one of the great principles of our Judaic–Christian inheritance is tolerance. People with other faiths and cultures have always been welcomed in our land, assured of equality under the law, of proper respect and of open friendship. There's absolutely nothing incompatible between this and our desire to maintain the essence of our own identity. There is no place for racial or religious intolerance in our creed.

When ABRAHAM LINCOLN spoke in his famous Gettysburg speech of 1863 of 'government of the people, by the people, and for the people', he gave the world a neat definition of democracy which has since been widely and enthusiastically adopted. But what he enunciated as a form of government was not in itself especially Christian, for nowhere in the Bible is the word 'democracy' mentioned. Ideally, when Christians meet, as Christians, to take counsel together, their purpose is not (or should not be) to ascertain what is the mind of the majority but what is the mind of the Holy Spirit – something which may be quite different.

[*Applause.*]

Nevertheless I am an enthusiast for democracy. And I take that position, not because I believe majority opinion is inevitably right or true – indeed no majority can take away God-given human rights – but because I believe it most effectively safeguards the value of the individual and, more than any other system, restrains the abuse of power by the few. And that is a Christian concept.

But there is little hope for democracy if the hearts of men and women in democratic societies cannot be touched by a call to something greater than themselves. Political structures, state institutions, collective ideals – these are not enough. We parliamentarians can legislate for the rule of law. You, the church, can teach the life of faith.

But when all is said and done, the politician's role is a humble one. I always think that the whole debate about the church and the state has never yielded anything comparable in insight to that beautiful hymn 'I Vow to Thee My Country'.[5] It begins with a triumphant assertion of what might be described as secular patriotism, a noble thing indeed in a country like ours: 'I vow to thee my country all earthly things above; / Entire, whole and perfect the service of my love'.

It goes on to speak of 'another country I heard of long ago' whose king can't be seen and whose armies can't be counted, but 'soul by soul and silently her shining bounds increase'. Not group by group, or party by party, or even church by church, but soul by soul – and each one counts.

That, members of the Assembly, is the country which you chiefly serve. You fight your cause under the banner of an historic church. Your success matters greatly – as much to the temporal as to the spiritual welfare of the nation. I leave you with that earnest hope that may we all come nearer to that other country whose 'ways are ways of gentleness and all her paths are peace'.

[*Applause.*]

[5] A patriotic song and Anglican hymn with lyrics by the English diplomat Cecil Spring-Rice (1859–1918). Written weeks before his death, it was later set to the music of 'Jupiter', from the *Planets Suite* (1916) by the English composer Gustav Holst (1874–1934).

Dylan Thomas
Welsh writer

Dylan Marlais Thomas (1914–53) was born in Swansea, the son of a schoolmaster. He worked for a time as a reporter on the *South Wales Evening Post* and established himself as a poet with the publication of *Eighteen Poems* in 1934. The same year, he moved to London, later settling permanently back in Wales at Laugharne (1949). In 1937 he married Caitlin Macnamara and published *Twenty-Five Poems*. His other works include *The Map of Love* (1939), *Portrait of the Artist as a Young Dog* (1940), *The World I Breathe* (1940), *Deaths and Entrances* (1946) and a scenario, *The Doctor and the Devils* (1953). His *Collected Poems, 1934–52*, were published in 1952. From 1944 he worked intermittently on a radio 'play for voices' about a Welsh seaside village and in its first form it was called *Quite Early One Morning*. Thomas expanded it into *Under Milk Wood*, taking part in a reading of it in New York just before his death, from chronic alcohol abuse, while on a lecture tour of the USA. It was published posthumously in 1954. Until then his work had been praised by critics, among them Edith Sitwell, for its striking rhythms, original imagery and technical ingenuity, but he could in no sense be called a popular writer. However, *Under Milk Wood* was immediately comprehensible, funny and fresh, with moments of lyric tenderness. It had a second success as a stage play and inspired a jazz suite by the English jazz composer Stan Tracey (1965). In 1955 an unfinished novel, *Adventures in the Skin Trade*, was published; also *A Prospect of the Sea*, a collection of stories and essays.

'Windbags and bigwigs and humbugs'
11 May 1953, Cambridge, Massachusetts, USA

Dylan Thomas had long dreamed of visiting the USA, but had been prevented from doing so by World War II. In 1945, he wrote to his friend, the American poet Oscar Williams, proposing a tour. 'I can read aloud, through sonorous asthma, with pomp,' his letter declared. 'I can lecture on "The Trend of Y", or "X at the Crossroads", or "Z: Whither?" with lower case an assurance whose shiftiness can be seen only from the front row.'

It was February 1950 before he finally arrived in New York for his first American reading tour, which he regarded primarily as an opportunity to make money. This three-month visit proved less inspirational than expected, but provided ample opportunity for heavy drinking and bad behaviour, which dissipated most of his earnings.

However, he had been well-received, and returned in 1952, accompanied by his long-suffering wife Caitlin, who had identified the attractions of touring as 'flattery, idleness and infidelity'. In April 1953 he was back, this time on his own. By now, the routine had become familiar, and he satirized it – and himself – magnificently in this speech written for the third American tour, which he first performed at the Massachusetts Institute of Technology.

In June 1953, he returned to Wales, recording this speech for the BBC's Welsh Home Service in October. The following week, he set off on his fourth and final jaunt to the USA, which culminated in his death, aged 39, following a drinking binge in New York.

Across the United States of America, from New York to California and back, glazed, again, for many months of the year there streams and sings for its heady supper a dazed and prejudiced procession of European lecturers, scholars, sociologists, economists, writers, authorities on this and that and even, in theory, on the United States of America. And, breathlessly between addresses and receptions, in planes and trains and boiling hotel bedroom ovens, many of them attempt to keep journals and diaries. At first, confused and shocked by shameless profusion and almost shamed by generosity, unaccustomed to such importance as they are assumed, by their hosts, to possess, and up against the barrier of a common language, they write in their notebooks like demons, generalizing away, on character and culture and the American political scene.

But, towards the middle of their middle-aged whisk through Middle-Western clubs and universities, the fury of the writing flags; their spirits are lowered by the spirit with which they are everywhere strongly greeted and which, in ever-increasing doses they themselves lower; and they begin to mistrust themselves, and their apparent popularity – for they have found, too often, that an audience will receive a lantern-lecture on, say, ceramics, with the same uninhibited enthusiasm that it accorded the very week before to a paper on the Modern Turkish Novel.

And, in their diaries, more and more do such entries appear as, 'No way of escape!' or 'Buffalo!' or 'I am beaten', until at last they cannot write a word. And, twittering all over, old before their time, with eyes like rissoles in the sand, they are helped up the gangway of the home-bound liner by kind bosom friends (of all kinds and bosoms) who boister them on the back, pick them up again, thrust bottles, sonnets, cigars, addresses into their pockets, have a farewell party in the cabin, pick them up again, and, snickering and yelping, are gone: to wait at the dockside for another boat from Europe and another batch of fresh, crisp green lecturers.

There they go, every spring, from New York to Los Angeles: exhibitionists, polemicists, histrionic publicists, theological rhetoricians, historical hoddy-doddies, balletomanes, ulterior decorators, max-factored actors,[1] windbags and bigwigs and humbugs, men in love with stamps, men in love with steaks, men after millionaires' widows, men with elephantiasis of the reputation (huge trunks and teeny minds), authorities on gas, bishops, bestsellers, new spellers, editors looking for writers, writers looking for publishers, publishers looking for dollars, existentialists, serious physicists with nuclear missions, men from the BBC who speak as though they had the Elgin Marbles in their mouths,[2] potboiling philosophers, professional Irishmen (very lepri-corny), and, I am afraid, fat poets with slim volumes.

And see, too, in that linguaceous stream, the tall monocled men, smelling of saddle soap and club armchairs, their breath a nice blending of whisky and fox's blood, with big protruding upper-class tusks and county moustaches, presumably invented in England and sent abroad to advertise *Punch*,[3] who to one's surprise one finds are here to lecture to women's clubs on some such unlikely subject as 'The History of Etching in the Shetland Islands'.

And the brassy-bossy men-women, with corrugated-iron perms and hippo hides, who come, self-announced, as 'ordinary British housewives', to talk to rich minked chunks of American matronhood about the iniquity of the English Health Service, the criminal sloth of the miners, the *visible* tail and horns of Mr ANEURIN BEVAN[4] and the fear of everyone in England to go out alone at night because of the organized legions of cosh boys against whom the police are powerless, owing to the refusal of those in power to equip them with revolvers and to flog to ribbons every adolescent offender on any charge at all.

And there shiver and teeter also, meek and driven, their little eyes lost and rabbit-scared behind big glasses steamed over by the smoke of countless cocktail parties, those British authors unfortunate enough to have written, after years of unadventurous forgotten work, one bad novel which became enormously popular on both sides of the Atlantic. At home, when success first hit them, they were mildly delighted; a couple of literary luncheons went sugar-tipsy to their heads, like the washing sherry served before those luncheons; and perhaps, as the lovely money rolled lushly in, they began to dream, in their moony writers' way, of being able to retire to the country, keep wasps (or was it bees?), and never write another lousy word.

But in come the literary agent's triggermen and the publisher's armed

[1] The Polish-born US make-up manufacturer Max Factor (1877–1938) created a make-up suitable for film actors in 1914 and supplied his 'flexible greasepaint' and wigs to the Hollywood film industry. He introduced cosmetics for general use in the 1920s.

[3] A satirical British magazine, published 1841–1992 and 1996–2002.

[2] The Elgin Marbles are marble statues from the Parthenon in Athens brought to Britain in 1801–5 by Thomas Bruce, 7th Earl of Elgin (1766–1841). Thomas deliberately confuses them with the small glass spheres also called marbles; the expression 'marbles in one's mouth' is used to characterize an excessively elevated form of English pronunciation.

[4] The former Labour minister had resigned from the cabinet in 1951 and espoused more Socialist views than the government. These views, and even the more moderate policies of the government had aroused deep suspicion among conservative elements in the British public.

narks: 'You must go to the States and make a Personal Appearance. Your novel is *killing* them over there, and we're not surprised either. You must go round the States lecturing to women.' And the inoffensive writers, who've never dared lecture anyone, let alone women – they are frightened of women, they do not understand women, they write about women as creatures that never existed, and the women lap it up – these novelists cry out: 'But what shall we lecture about?'

'The English Novel.'

'I don't read novels.'

'Great Women in Fiction.'

'I don't like fiction *or* women.'

But off they're wafted, first class, in the plush bowels of the *Queen Victoria* with a list of engagements long as a New York menu or a half-hour with a book by Charles Morgan,[5] and soon they are losing their little cold-as-goldfish paws in the great general glutinous handshake of a clutch of enveloping hostesses.

It was Ernest Raymond, the author of *Tell England*, who once made a journey round the American women's clubs, being housed and entertained at each small town he stopped at by the richest and largest and furriest lady available. On one occasion he stopped at some little station, and was met, as usual, by an enormous motor-car full of a large, horn-rimmed businessman, looking *exactly* like a large horn-rimmed businessman on the films – and his roly-poly pearly wife.

Mr Raymond sat with her in the back of the car, and off they went, the husband driving. At once, she began to say how utterly delighted she and her husband and the committee were to have him at their Women's Literary and Social Guild, and to compliment him on his books. 'I don't think I've ever, in all my life, enjoyed a book so much as *Sorrel and Son*,' she said. 'What you don't know about human nature! I think Sorrel is one of the most beautiful characters ever portrayed.'

Ernest Raymond let her talk on, while he stared, embarrassed, in front of him. All he could see were the three double chins that her husband wore at the back of his neck. On and on she gushed in praise of *Sorrel and Son* until he could stand it no longer. 'I quite agree with you,' he said. 'A beautiful book indeed. But I'm afraid I didn't write *Sorrel and Son*. It was written by an old friend of mine, Mr Warwick Deeping.'

And the large horn-rimmed double-chinned husband at the wheel said without turning: 'Caught again, Emily.'

See the garrulous others, also, gabbing and garlanded from one nest of culture-vultures to another: people selling the English way of life and condemning the American way as they swig and guzzle through it; people resurrecting the theories of surrealism for the benefit of remote parochial female audiences who did not know it was dead, not having ever known it had ever been alive; people talking about Etruscan pots and pans to a bunch of dead pans and wealthy pots near Boston. And there, too, in the sticky thick of lecturers moving across the continent, go the foreign poets, catarrhal troubadours, lyrical one-night-standers, dollar-mad nightingales, remittance-bards from at home, myself among them, booming with the worst.

Did we pass one another, en route, all unknowing, I wonder, one of us, spry-eyed, with clean, white lectures and a soul he could call his own, going buoyantly west to his remunerative doom in the great State University factories, another returning dog-eared as his clutch of poems and his

[5] The English critic, novelist and dramatist Charles Morgan (1894–1958) wrote a number of technically competent but colourless novels.

carefully typed impromptu asides? I ache for us both. There one goes, unsullied as yet, in his Pullman[6] pride, toying, oh boy, with a blunderbuss bourbon, being smoked by a large cigar, riding out to the wide open spaces of the faces of his waiting audience.

He carries, besides his literary baggage, a new, dynamic razor, just on the market, bought in New York, which operates at the flick of a thumb, but cuts the thumb to the bone; a tin of new shaving-lather which is worked with the other, unbleeding, thumb and covers not only the face but the whole bathroom and, instantly freezing, makes an arctic, icicled cave, from which it takes two sneering bell-boys to extract him; and, of course, a nylon shirt. This, he dearly believed from the advertisements, he could himself wash in his hotel, hang to dry overnight, and put on, without ironing, in the morning. (In my case, no ironing *was* needed, for, as someone cruelly pointed out in print, I looked, anyway, like an unmade bed.)

He is vigorously welcomed at the station by an earnest crew-cut platoon of giant collegiates – all chasing the butterfly culture with net, note-book, poison-bottle, pin and label, each with at least 36 terribly white teeth – and nursed away, as heavily gently as though he were an imbecile rich aunt with a short prospect of life, into a motorcar in which, for a mere 50 miles or so, travelled at poet-breaking speed, he assures them of the correctness of their assumption that he is half-witted, by stammering inconsequential answers in an over-British accent to their genial questions about what international conference Stephen Spender[7] might be attending at the moment or the reactions of British poets to the work of a famous American whose name he did not know or catch.

He is then taken to a small party of only a few hundred people, all of whom hold the belief that what a visiting lecturer needs before he trips onto the platform is just enough Martinis so that he can trip *off* the platform as well. And, clutching his explosive glass, he is soon contemptuously dismissing, in a flush of ignorance and fluency, the poetry of those androgynous literary ladies with three names who produce a kind of verbal ectoplasm to order as a waiter dishes up spaghetti – only to find that the fiercest of these, a wealthy huntress of small, seedy lions (such as himself), who stalks the Middle-Western bush with ears and rifle cocked, is his hostess for the evening. Of the lecture he remembers little but the applause and maybe two questions: 'Is it true that the young English intellectuals are *really* psychological?' or, 'I always carry Kierkegaard[8] in my pocket. What do you carry?'

Late at night, in his room, he fills a page of his journal with a confused but scathing account of his first engagement; summarizes American advanced education in a paragraph that will be meaningless tomorrow, and falls to sleep, where he is immediately chased through long, dark thickets by a Mrs Mabel Frankincense Mehaffey, with a tray of Martinis and lyrics.

And there goes the other happy poet bedraggledly back to New York which struck him all of a sheepish never-sleeping heap at first, but which seems to him now, after the ulcerous rigours of a lecturer's spring, a haven cosy as toast, cool as an icebox and safe as skyscrapers.

[6] Thomas refers to the railroad cars produced by the Pullman Palace Car Co., notable for their luxurious comfort.

[7] The English poet and critic Stephen Spender (1909–95).

[8] The Danish philosopher and theologian Søren Kierkegaard (1813–55) is regarded as one of the founders of Existentialism.

Leon Trotsky
Russian revolutionary

Leon Trotsky *originally Lev Davidovich Bronstein* (1879–1940) was born in Yanovka, Ukraine, and educated in Odessa. At the age of 19, he was arrested as a Marxist and sent to Siberia. He escaped in 1902, joined LENIN in London, and in the abortive revolution of 1905 became president of the St Petersburg Soviet, or workers' council. After escaping from a further period of exile in Siberia, he became a revolutionary journalist among Russian émigrés in the West. He returned to Russia in 1917, joined the Bolshevik Party and with Lenin played a major role in the October Revolution. As Commissar for Foreign Affairs, he conducted negotiations with the Germans for the peace treaty of Brest–Litovsk (1918). In the Russian Civil War, as Commissar for War, he created the Red Army of five million men from a nucleus of 7,000. On Lenin's death in 1924 Trotsky's influence began to decline. JOSEPH STALIN, who opposed his theory of 'permanent revolution', ousted him from the Politburo, and he was exiled to Central Asia (1927), and later expelled from the USSR (1929). He continued to agitate and intrigue as an exile in several countries. In 1937, having been sentenced to death in his absence by a Soviet court, he found asylum in Mexico City. There he was assassinated with an ice-pick by Ramón del Río Mercader *alias Jacques Mornard* (1914–78). Ruthless, energetic, a superb orator and a messianic visionary, Trotsky became the focus of those Communists, Soviet and otherwise, who opposed the endless opportunism of Stalin. He was a writer of power, wit and venom, an advocate of permanent revolution and – in contrast to Stalin's 'socialism in one country' – world revolution. His publications include *History of the Russian Revolution* (1932), *The Revolution Betrayed* (1937), *Stalin* (1948) and *Diary in Exile* (Eng trans 1959). They remain influential in western Marxist circles. In January 1989, as part of the policy of *glasnost* under Mikhail Gorbachev, it was revealed that Trotsky's murder was arranged by the Soviet secret police.

'Our party will in the fire of repression become the true leader'
August 1917, Petrograd (now St Petersburg), Russia

❦

The February Revolution of 1917 was a series of demonstrations, strikes and military mutinies which led to the abdication of Tsar Nicholas II. A series of provisional governments, formed largely of Liberal and socialist ministers, briefly ruled the country while the formalities of electing a constituent assembly were agreed.

Lenin arrived back from exile in April, Trotsky in early May. Dissatisfied with the outcome of this 'bourgeois–democratic' revolution, Lenin called for a Bolshevik 'proletarian-socialist' revolt, under the slogan 'all power to the Soviets'. Soviets (workers' councils) emerged throughout the country, creating a confused power structure and preventing decisive government.

In the summer, dissatisfaction with the government led to the 'July Days' demonstrations, though these were not endorsed by Lenin, who was not yet ready to take power. Several factions were engaged in the power struggle, but Trotsky emerged as a fiery and persuasive spokesmen for the Bolsheviks.

In this speech, he pours scorn on Prime Minister Alexander Kerensky's proposal to crush the anarchists on the Left and counter-revolutionaries on the Right 'with blood and iron'. Identifying Kerensky's 'anarchic elements' as trade unions, he calls on these 'unadulterated organizations of the proletariat' to unite with the Bolsheviks, overthrow the bourgeois provisional government, and seize control of Russia.

The Bolshevik uprising in Petrograd failed, and Trotsky spent several weeks in jail, but he was released in September. In the October Revolution, the Bolsheviks overthrew the provisional government, and a Soviet state was established under Lenin.

❦

Any intelligent person (or any fool) knows that to save Russia a merciless struggle with anarchy on the left and counter-revolution on the right is essential. This constitutes the essence of the entire programme of *Izvestia*,[1] *Delo Naroda*,[2] *Rabochaya Gazeta*[3] … Kerensky's[4] historic speech at the 'historic' state conference amounted to variations on just this theme. With blood and iron against anarchy on the left; counter-revolution on the right.

This sounds very good; in any event symmetrical. But does it make sense? When they speak of counter-revolution, they have in mind not certain attitudes or random disorderly actions, but particular class interests, incompatible with the securing and development of the

[1] 'News', a revolutionary newspaper.
[2] 'People's Cause', a revolutionary newspaper.
[3] 'Workers' Gazette', a revolutionary newspaper.

[4] The Russian revolutionary leader Alexander Kerensky (1881–1970) was a minister in the provisional government established after the February Revolution and became prime minister in July 1917.

revolution. It is the landowners and imperialist capital who support the counter-revolution. Which classes are supporting anarchy?

The mayor of Moscow, the SR[5] Rudnyev answered this very clearly. He welcomed the state conference on behalf of the 'entire' population of Moscow – minus those anarchic elements who had arranged a general protest strike in Moscow. But who arranged the strike? The Moscow trades unions … The trades unions decreed and brought about a general strike against the government's foisting of a counter-revolutionary parliament on Moscow.

The trades unions are the purest, most unadulterated organizations of the proletariat, of that class which by its unstinting toil creates Moscow's power and wealth. And it is these trades unions who unite the flower of the working class – the fundamental driving force of the present-day economy. It is these trades unions that the SR mayor of Moscow has called anarchic elements. And it is against these conscientious, disciplined workers that the iron of the government's violence will have to be directed.

It would be unforgiveable, however, to believe the leaders of the petty bourgeoisie when they promise to fight the right and left with equal strength. That is not happening and cannot happen. In spite of its numerical strength, the petty bourgeoisie as a class is economically and politically weak. It is extremely unco-ordinated, economically dependent, politically unstable. The petty bourgeois democracy is in no position to engage in a simultaneous struggle with two such powerful forces as the revolutionary proletariat and the counter-revolutionary bourgeoisie. All the experience of history proves this.

For serious political struggle, the present-day petty bourgeoisie in the towns and the country needs not only an ally but also a leader. As it enters the struggle with 'anarchy', in the person of the organized proletariat, the 'democracy' of Kerensky and Tsereteli[6] – whatever they may have said – inescapably falls under the leadership of the imperialist bourgeoisie. That is why attacks on the right remain only at the planning stage, and come to be replaced by bows of humility to the right.

The provisional government has closed *Pravda*[7] and about ten other Bolshevik newspapers, which were the guiding organs of the advanced proletariat. Avksentyev's[8] attack on the right was the closure of *Narodnaya Gazeta*.[9] But was *Narodnaya Gazeta* the guiding organ of the counter-revolutionary bourgeoisie? No, it was solely the clandestine organ of those swine the Black Hundred.[10] The role played by *Pravda* for the revolutionary working class was played among the imperialist bourgeoisie by the newspaper *Rech*;[11] but is it not clear that at the mere thought of closing *Rech* those most gallant power-bearers are quaking with fear?

But let us return for a minute to the Moscow strike. *Rabochaya Gazeta*, that most pitiful organ … emits the usual stock abuse aimed at the strikers, who are destroying the power of 'revolutionary democracy'. Here we find 'betrayal', 'the stab in the back' and 'anarchy' … *Rabochaya Gazeta* regards the workers as criminals for refusing to subordinate their own class struggle in all its manifestations to the will of the non-proletarian section of the Moscow Soviet.

The supremacy of the petty bourgeoisie over the proletariat is elevated to the supreme principle of social-democratic principles. For a coalition with the imperialist bourgeoisie, Tsereteli and his party are prepared to make monstrous concessions and humiliations … The leaders of the lower middle class demand from the workers the very attitude towards the petty

[5] Abbreviation for a member of the Socialist Revolutionary Party, a Russian Socialist party formed in 1902, in opposition to the Russian Social Democrats.

[6] The Georgian revolutionary leader Irakli Tsereteli (1881–1960) was the leader of the Mensheviks, the Social-Democratic Labour Party.

[9] 'People's Gazette', a secret newspaper circulated by the Black Hundred (see note 10).
[10] A pro-tsarist movement, which upheld the Tsar's guiding motto: 'autocracy, orthodoxy and national character'.
[11] 'Speech', a right-wing newspaper.

[7] 'Truth', a revolutionary newspaper.
[8] The Russian revolutionary leader Nikolai Avksentyev (1878–1943) served as Minister for the Interior in Kerensky's government.

bourgeoisie that they themselves display towards the representatives of capital …

Retribution is not slow in coming. Hunted, persecuted, slandered, our party has never grown as quickly as of late. And this process will not be slow to spill over from the capital to the provinces, from the cities into the country and army. The peasants can see and hear that it is those very authorities, for the very same reasons, that are crushing the land committees and are persecuting the Bolsheviks. The soldiers can observe the wild hallooing directed at the Bolsheviks and at the same time sense the counter-revolutionary noose growing ever tighter round their neck.

All the working masses of the country will learn from their new experiences to tie their fate to the fate of our party. Without for one minute ceasing to be the class organization of the proletariat – but, on the contrary, completely fulfilling this role only now – our party will in the fire of repression become the true leader, the support and hope of all oppressed, crushed, deceived and persecuted masses.

❧

'Universal and compulsory military training'
22 March 1918, Moscow, Russia

❧

As Commissar of War in LENIN's new government, Trotsky immediately had to prepare the country for a possible civil war. The Russian army, perceived as a tool of the former government, had been demobilized following the Revolution; Trotsky therefore had to assemble a new army. Unsuccessful in securing military assistance from Western allies, he was obliged to employ officers from the former Russian army, for which he faced criticism.

By 22 March, however, he had raised his Red Army. Celebrations were held all over Moscow under the slogan 'Organize Socialist Defence', and Trotsky addressed a meeting at Alexeyevskaya People's House.

Russia had been committed to World War I by Tsar Nicholas II's backing for Serbia when it was threatened by Austria–Hungary in 1914. Soon after the Revolution, the country's new Soviet leaders had agreed an armistice with Germany and Austria. However, in the ensuing treaty, signed at Brest–Litovsk on 6 March, Lenin had been forced to accept very damaging terms, which obliged Russia to surrender substantial territory and economic resources to Germany.

In his speech, translated here by Brian Pearce, Trotsky refers to the injustices of the treaty, the shattered and vulnerable condition of Russia and the need for a powerful army. He also defends the introduction of conscription and the deployment of former Russian army officers.

'Red Army Day' became an annual holiday, which moved to 23 February after Russia switched to the Gregorian calendar in 1918. The Soviet government annulled the Brest–Litovsk Treaty in November 1918, but gained very little at the Treaty of Versailles the following year.

❧

[1] The series of uprisings which engineered the collapse of Tsarist rule and the abdication of Nicholas II in February 1917.
[2] The Bolshevik coup, which ousted the weak provisional government that took office after the February Revolution, and established Russia as a Soviet state.

The February Revolution[1] and then the October Revolution[2] took place largely under the sign of struggle for a peace, on honest democratic principles. The bourgeoisie, which obtained power in the first period of the revolution, very gravely hindered the cause of peace through its imperialistic policy.

Only with the October Revolution, when state power passed directly into the hands of the Soviets, did Russia enter a phase of real, active struggle for peace.

We put forth all possible efforts, made every sacrifice toward this end, going so far as complete demobilization of the old army and declaration that Russia was no longer at war with the central powers: but German imperialism, feeling no serious revolutionary pressure from within, brought down all its weight upon almost-disarmed Russia and – dealing a series of treacherous blows at her – obliged our country to sign an impossibly burdensome treaty of peace.[3]

[3] The Brest–Litovsk Treaty was agreed by Russia, Germany and Austria–Hungary on 3 March 1918. It was approved by the Congress of the Bolshevik Party of 6–8 March. At the same meeting, delegates agreed to change the party's name to the Russian Communist Party.

Such a peace – with the ever-present threat to Soviet Russia's very existence from Germany, Japan and other imperialist powers – cannot last long, and for this reason the urgent, essential task that the present moment sets before us is that of organizing the country's defence, mobilizing all its forces to give an armed rebuff to the enemy, both external and internal.

What are the concrete measures which must be taken immediately and fully, right now?

Universal and compulsory military training of the entire population of Russia. Every worker and peasant must devote a certain number of hours every day to military study. We must invite experienced old soldiers, non-commissioned officers and members of the old commanding apparatus to serve as instructors.

All the officers, all the doctors and engineers, all the educated specialists who have hitherto been zealously engaged in sabotage, will be dragged out into the open. It is said that the attitude of the former officers is counter-revolutionary, that it will be dangerous to entrust them with military work in a socialist army. But in the first place, they will be allotted only the technical and operational-strategic aspects of the work, while the entire apparatus of the army as a whole, its organization and internal structure will be entirely and completely a matter for the Soviets of Workers' and Soldiers' Deputies. And in the second place, the officers and generals were objects of fear to us only when they controlled the entire mechanism of state power. Now, they are helpless to shake and undermine the foundations of Soviet power.

But let every one of them realize, and firmly keep in mind, that if they make the slightest attempt to use their position for counter-revolutionary purposes, they will suffer severe punishment; they will be dealt with in accordance with the full strictness of revolutionary order; they will be shown no mercy.

As regards discipline in the army, this must be the discipline of people who are bound together by one and the same firm revolutionary consciousness – consciousness of their socialist duty. This will not be a discipline based on orders from above – a discipline enforced by the officer's stick – but fraternal, conscious, revolutionary discipline.

In view of the approach of spring and of the work in the fields that this brings with it, we cannot carry out universal mobilization at this moment. For the time being we shall confine ourselves to introducing universal compulsory military training and the formation of volunteer fighting units which will serve as the skeleton of the new mass army.

The country is in a shattered state, the economy has been disorganized, there is no strict accounting, and without that it is difficult to organize defence. Besides ruthless and resolute struggle against the speculators and capitalists – who even now have not tired of profiteering from the people's misfortunes, intensifying the already chaotic state of the country – we shall wage an equally stern and resolute struggle against those hooligan elements from among the working people themselves who are plundering and destroying the people's property to the value of tens and hundreds of thousands of roubles. The revolutionary people will authorize struggle against these hooligan elements in the name of defence and preservation of the people's property.

We have enemies everywhere, but we also have friends in Europe, namely, the working class. It is incomparably harder for them than it was for us to fight against their own well organized and still-strong bourgeoisie, but the four years' war is inevitably preparing the objective basis for an all-Europe revolution.

Sooner or later, the conflagration of revolutionary civil war will burst forth in Europe. In this war, too, we must not be the last to come forward. We must be fully armed and ready for battle. We must conquer – and we shall conquer in this war because the working class of all countries, risen in revolt, cannot but be victorious in the final decisive conflict with its age-old enemies, those who started and who are prolonging this plundering butchery, the bloodiest ever known!

Harry S Truman
American statesman

Harry S Truman (1884–1972) was born in Lamar, Missouri, and educated in Independence, Missouri. He served during World War I as an artillery captain on the Western Front. After the war he returned to his farm and later went into partnership in a men's clothing store which failed. In 1922 he became judge for the Eastern District of Jackson County in Missouri, and in 1926 presiding judge, a post he held until 1934 when he was elected as the Democrat senator from Missouri. He was elected vice president in 1944 and became president in April 1945 on the death of FRANKLIN D ROOSEVELT. He was re-elected in 1948, in a surprise victory over Thomas E Dewey. During his presidency he took many historically important decisions. These included dropping the atom bombs on Hiroshima and Nagasaki (1945); pushing through Congress a huge post-war loan to Great Britain (the MARSHALL Plan, 1946); making a major change in US policy towards the USSR, the Truman Doctrine of Communist containment and support for free peoples resisting subjugation (1947); organizing airlifts of supplies into West Berlin during the Soviet blockade of roads and railways (1948–9); helping establish NATO (1949); and sending US troops on behalf of the United Nations to resist the Communist invasion of South Korea (1950), a commitment which ultimately helped erode his popularity. In the USA he established the Criminal Investigation Agency (CIA) in 1947; and introduced the 'Fair Deal', a liberal programme of economic reform. He did not stand for re-election in 1952 and retired to Missouri. Later he became a strong critic of DWIGHT D EISENHOWER's Republican administration.

'It must be the policy of the United States to support free peoples'
12 March 1947, Washington, DC, USA

❧

This speech was Truman's response to an early crisis of the Cold War. During the Nazi occupation of Greece (1941–4), hostilities had sprung up between politically polarized factions of the Greek resistance. After the Nazi withdrawal in 1944, this power struggle worsened as the government returned from exile and the Greek Communist Party attempted to gain control. Elections in 1946 failed to unite the country and by early 1947, Greece was embroiled in an escalating civil war.

Turkey, meanwhile, was facing internal economic crisis and territorial claims from the USSR, notably over control of the Dardanelle Straits. Then, in February, the British government announced that it would be obliged to halt aid payments to Greece and Turkey within six weeks. The result, some experts feared, would be the establishment of two communist states in the south-east Mediterranean, with a possible 'domino effect' as Soviet influence spread through the region.

This set a pressing deadline for Truman. A confident and effective leader, he called a joint session of Congress to emphasize the gravity of the situation and propose urgent aid for Greece and Turkey. The policy of containment he outlined was a significant departure from the USA's traditionally isolationist stance, and became known as the Truman Doctrine.

Truman's plea was successful; the Republican-dominated Congress agreed to bankroll a $400 million aid package, which was signed into law on 22 May. The Truman Doctrine formed the basis of US policy towards communism until the REAGAN era.

❧

Mr President, Mr Speaker, members of the Congress of the United States: the gravity of the situation which confronts the world today necessitates my appearance before a joint session of the Congress. The foreign policy and the national security of this country are involved.

One aspect of the present situation, which I present to you at this time for your consideration and decision, concerns Greece and Turkey. The United States has received from the Greek government an urgent appeal for financial and economic assistance. Preliminary reports from the American economic mission now in Greece and reports from the American Ambassador in Greece corroborate the statement of the Greek government that assistance is imperative if Greece is to survive as a free nation. I do not believe that the American people and the Congress wish to turn a deaf ear to the appeal of the Greek government.

Greece is not a rich country. Lack of sufficient natural resources has always forced the Greek people to work hard to make both ends meet. Since 1940, this industrious, peace-loving country has suffered invasion, four years of cruel enemy occupation and bitter internal strife.

When forces of liberation entered Greece they found that the retreating Germans had destroyed virtually all the railways, roads, port facilities, communications and merchant marine. More than 1,000 villages had been burned. Eighty-five per cent of the children were tubercular. Livestock, poultry and draft animals had almost disappeared. Inflation had wiped out practically all savings.

As a result of these tragic conditions, a militant minority, exploiting human want and misery, was able to create political chaos which, until now, has made economic recovery impossible. Greece is today without funds to finance the importation of those goods which are essential to bare subsistence ...

The very existence of the Greek state is today threatened by the terrorist activities of several thousand armed men, led by Communists, who defy the government's authority at a number of points, particularly along the northern boundaries. A commission appointed by the United Nations Security Council[1] is at present investigating disturbed conditions in northern Greece and alleged border violations along the frontier between Greece on the one hand and Albania, Bulgaria and Yugoslavia on the other.

[1] Established in October 1945, the United Nations was a relatively untried organization at this stage.

Meanwhile, the Greek government is unable to cope with the situation. The Greek army is small and poorly equipped. It needs supplies and equipment if it is to restore authority to the government throughout Greek territory. Greece must have assistance if it is to become a self-supporting and self-respecting democracy.

The United States must supply this assistance. We have already extended to Greece certain types of relief and economic aid but these are inadequate. There is no other country to which democratic Greece can turn. No other nation is willing and able to provide the necessary support for a democratic Greek government.

The British government, which has been helping Greece, can give no further financial or economic aid after March 31. Great Britain finds itself under the necessity of reducing or liquidating its commitments in several parts of the world, including Greece.

We have considered how the United Nations might assist in this crisis. But the situation is an urgent one requiring immediate action, and the United Nations and its related organizations are not in a position to extend help of the kind that is required ...

No government is perfect. One of the chief virtues of a democracy, however, is that its defects are always visible and under democratic processes can be pointed out and corrected. The government of Greece is not perfect. Nevertheless it represents 85 per cent of the members of the Greek parliament who were chosen in an election last year. Foreign observers, including 692 Americans, considered this election to be a fair expression of the views of the Greek people.

The Greek government has been operating in an atmosphere of chaos and extremism. It has made mistakes. The extension of aid by this country does not mean that the United States condones everything that the Greek government has done or will do. We have condemned in the past, and we condemn now, extremist measures of the right or the left. We have in the past advised tolerance, and we advise tolerance now.

Greece's neighbour, Turkey, also deserves our attention. The future of Turkey as an independent and economically sound state is clearly no less important to the freedom-loving peoples of the world than the future of Greece. The circumstances in which Turkey finds itself today are considerably different from those of Greece. Turkey has been spared the disasters that have beset Greece. And during the war, the United States and Great Britain furnished Turkey with material aid.

Nevertheless, Turkey now needs our support. Since the war, Turkey has sought additional financial assistance from Great Britain and the United States for the purpose of effecting that modernization necessary for the maintenance of its national integrity. That integrity is essential to the preservation of order in the Middle East.

The British government has informed us that, owing to its own difficulties, it can no longer extend financial or economic aid to Turkey. As in the case of Greece, if Turkey is to have the assistance it needs, the United States must supply it. We are the only country able to provide that help.

I am fully aware of the broad implications involved if the United States extends assistance to Greece and Turkey, and I shall discuss these implications with you at this time.

One of the primary objectives of the foreign policy of the United States is the creation of conditions in which we and other nations will be able to work out a way of life free from coercion. This was a fundamental issue in the war with Germany and Japan. Our victory was won over countries which sought to impose their will, and their way of life, upon other nations.

To ensure the peaceful development of nations, free from coercion, the United States has taken a leading part in establishing the United Nations. The United Nations is designed to make possible lasting freedom and independence for all its members. We shall not realize our objectives, however, unless we are willing to help free peoples to maintain their free institutions and their national integrity against aggressive movements that seek to impose upon them totalitarian regimes. This is no more than a frank recognition that totalitarian regimes imposed upon free peoples, by direct or indirect aggression, undermine the foundations of international peace and hence the security of the United States.

The peoples of a number of countries of the world have recently had totalitarian regimes forced upon them against their will. The government of the United States has made frequent protests against coercion and intimidation, in violation of the Yalta agreement,[2] in Poland, Romania and Bulgaria. I must also state that in a number of other countries there have been similar developments.

At the present moment in world history, nearly every nation must choose between alternative ways of life. The choice is too often not a free one. One way of life is based upon the will of the majority, and is distinguished by free institutions, representative government, free elections, guarantees of individual liberty, freedom of speech and religion, and freedom from political oppression.

The second way of life is based upon the will of a minority, forcibly imposed upon the majority. It relies upon terror and oppression, a controlled press and radio, fixed elections and the suppression of personal freedoms.

I believe that it must be the policy of the United States to support free peoples who are resisting attempted subjugation by armed minorities or by outside pressures. I believe that we must assist free peoples to work out

[2] At the Yalta conference of February 1945, FRANKLIN D ROOSEVELT, WINSTON CHURCHILL and JOSEPH STALIN agreed plans for the defeat of Germany, including how far across Europe their respective armies should advance. The meeting point of the Allied forces and the Red Army hardened into the post-war division between Communist and non-Communist Europe, as the USSR did not withdraw from the territories it had liberated and allow democratic governments to be set up. Instead it subverted democratic elections to ensure that Communist regimes gained power and then created one-party states.

their own destinies in their own way. I believe that our help should be primarily through economic and financial aid, which is essential to economic stability and orderly political processes.

The world is not static; and the status quo is not sacred. But we cannot allow changes in the status quo in violation of the charter of the United Nations by such methods as coercion, or by such subterfuges as political infiltration. In helping free and independent nations to maintain their freedom, the United States will be giving effect to the principles of the Charter of the United Nations.

It is necessary only to glance at a map to realize that the survival and integrity of the Greek nation are of grave importance in a much wider situation. If Greece should fall under the control of an armed minority, the effect upon its neighbour, Turkey, would be immediate and serious. Confusion and disorder might well spread throughout the entire Middle East.

Moreover, the disappearance of Greece as an independent state would have a profound effect upon those countries in Europe whose peoples are struggling against great difficulties to maintain their freedoms and their independence while they repair the damages of war.

It would be an unspeakable tragedy if these countries, which have struggled so long against overwhelming odds, should lose that victory for which they sacrificed so much. Collapse of free institutions and loss of independence would be disastrous, not only for them but for the world. Discouragement and possibly failure would quickly be the lot of neighbouring peoples striving to maintain their freedom and independence.

Should we fail to aid Greece and Turkey in this fateful hour, the effect will be far-reaching to the West as well as to the East. We must take immediate and resolute action ...

The seeds of totalitarian regimes are nurtured by misery and want. They spread and grow in the evil soil of poverty and strife. They reach their full growth when the hope of a people for a better life has died. We must keep that hope alive.

The free peoples of the world look to us for support in maintaining their freedoms. If we falter in our leadership, we may endanger the peace of the world – and we shall surely endanger the welfare of this nation.

Great responsibilities have been placed upon us by the swift movement of events. I am confident that the Congress will face these responsibilities squarely.

Sojourner Truth

American abolitionist and suffragist

Sojourner Truth *originally Isabella Van Wagener* (c.1797–1883) was born a slave in Ulster County, New York. She worked for a variety of owners, but was freed in 1827 by Isaac Van Wagener and settled in New York City, where she became an ardent evangelist. In 1843 she felt called to change her name, and to fight against slavery and for women's suffrage. Preaching widely across the USA, she drew large crowds with her infectious style of speaking. In 1850 she produced an autobiography, *The Narrative of Sojourner Truth*, which she had dictated to her neighbour Olive Gilbert. She was appointed counsellor to the freedmen of Washington by President ABRAHAM LINCOLN, and continued to promote black rights, including educational opportunities, until her retirement in 1875.

'I want women to have their rights'
9 May 1867, New York City, USA

❧

The American Equal Rights Association had a short but colourful life. Formed after the Civil War in 1866, its aim was to 'secure Equal Rights to all American citizens, especially the Right of Suffrage, irrespective of race, colour or sex' and its membership included most of the important campaigners of the day, such as Susan B Anthony and Lucretia Mott.

The first annual meeting included speeches on suffrage and civil rights by, among others, ELIZABETH CADY STANTON, FREDERICK DOUGLASS, Frances D Gage, and Sojourner Truth. The organization was to split after 1870 over the issue of another amendment to guarantee women the vote (see Stanton's speech in this book) but the factions merged in 1890 as the National American Woman Suffrage Association.

This speech, one of several 'talks' Truth planned to give during the conference, illustrates her style very well. She refers to her own life with grim humour to illustrate the indefensible differences between men and women in law, and the often ridiculous excuses given to maintain them. Although she was illiterate, her unadorned speaking style was persuasive, and she made a great impact by breaking into song. She was nicknamed the 'Libyan Sibyl' in an essay of 1863 by Harriet Beecher Stowe (1811–96), author of *Uncle Tom's Cabin*.

The 15th Amendment (1870) had freed slaves and guaranteed black men the vote. As her speech makes clear, Truth considered slavery only 'partly destroyed'.

❧

My friends: I am rejoiced that you are glad, but I don't know how you will feel when I get through.

I come from another field – the country of the slave. They have got their liberty – so much good luck to have slavery partly destroyed; not entirely. I want it root and branch destroyed. Then we will all be free indeed.

I feel that if I have to answer for the deeds done in my body just as much as man, I have a right to have as much as a man. There is a great stir about coloured men getting their rights, but not a word about the coloured women; and if coloured men get their rights, and not coloured women theirs, you see the coloured men will be masters over the women, and it will be just as bad as it was before.

So I am for keeping the thing going while things are stirring; because if we wait till it is still, it will take a great while to get it going again. White women are a great deal smarter, and know more than coloured women, while coloured women do not know scarcely anything. They go out washing, which is about as high as a coloured woman gets, and their men go about idle, strutting up and down; and when the women come home, they ask for their money and take it all, and then scold you because there is no food.

I want you to consider on that, chil'n. I call you chil'n; you are somebody's chil'n, and I am old enough to be mother of all that is here. I want women to have their rights. In the courts women have no right, no voice; nobody speaks for them. I wish woman to have her voice there among the

[1] Truth's date of birth is uncertain, but this seems to be an exaggeration.

[2] An agricultural worker employed in harvesting grain.

pettifoggers. If it is not a fit place for women, it is unfit for men to be there.

I am above 80 years old;[1] it is about time for me to be going. I have been 40 years a slave and 40 years free, and would be here 40 years more to have equal rights for all. I suppose I am kept here because something remains for me to do; I suppose I am yet to help to break the chain.

I have done a great deal of work; as much as a man, but did not get so much pay. I used to work in the field and bind grain, keeping up with the cradler,[2] but men doing no more got twice as much pay; so with the German women. They work in the field and do as much work but do not get the pay. We do as much, eat as much, we want as much.

I suppose I am about the only coloured woman who goes about to speak for the rights of the coloured women. I want to keep the thing stirring, now that the ice is cracked. What we want is a little money. You men know that you get as much again as women when you write, or for what you do. When we get our rights we shall not have to come to you for money, for then we shall have money enough in our pockets; and maybe you will ask us for money. But help us now until we get it. It is a good consolation to know that when we have got this battle once fought we shall not be coming to you any more.

You have been having our rights so long that you think, like a slaveholder, that you own us. I know that it is hard for one who has held the reins for so long to give up; it cuts like a knife. It will feel all the better when it closes up again.

I have been in Washington about three years, seeing about these coloured people. Now coloured men have the right to vote. There ought to be equal rights now more than ever, since coloured people have got their freedom. I am going to talk several times while I am here; so now I will do a little singing. I have not heard any singing since I came here.

[*She sings.*]

Desmond Tutu
South African clergyman

Desmond Mpilo Tutu (1931–) was born in Klerksdorp in the Transvaal, the son of a primary school headmaster. He studied theology at the University of South Africa and King's College London. After working as a schoolteacher for about four years he attended theological college and became an Anglican parish priest (1961). He rose rapidly to become Bishop of Lesotho (1976–8), Secretary-General of the South African Council of Churches (1978–85), the first black Bishop of Johannesburg (1985–6) and Archbishop of Cape Town (1986–96). A fierce opponent of apartheid, he repeatedly risked imprisonment for his advocacy of punitive international sanctions against South Africa, although he deplored the use of violence. He was awarded the Nobel Peace Prize in 1984, was appointed Chancellor of the University of the Western Cape in Cape Town in 1988, and chaired the post-apartheid Truth and Reconciliation Commission, 1995–9. He was awarded the Sydney Peace Prize in 1999, the Delta Prize for Global Understanding in 2000 and the Presidential Medal of Freedom in 2009.

'Apartheid's final solution'
11 December 1984, Oslo, Norway

Well-known as an outspoken critic of South African apartheid, Archbishop Tutu was awarded the Nobel Peace Prize in 1984. He used his acceptance speech to condemn South Africa's 'racist dream', and to scorn the limited concessions of the country's new constitution, introduced the previous year.

NELSON MANDELA (who would receive the Nobel Peace Prize in 1993) once remarked of his ally: 'Sometimes strident, often tender, never afraid and seldom without humour, Desmond Tutu's voice will always be the voice of the voiceless.'

Presenting the award, Egil Aarvik, chairman of the Norwegian Nobel Committee, spoke of Tutu's determination that peace should triumph over violence. He recalled seeing an example of Tutu's ministry during television coverage of a massacre in Johannesburg: 'After the police vehicles had driven away with their prisoners, Desmond Tutu stood and spoke to a frightened and bitter congregation: "Do not hate," he said. "Let us choose the peaceful way to freedom."'

He is, nonetheless, a forceful speaker. Having described individual cases and their tragic consequences for both black and white South Africans, Tutu turns briefly lyrical, before dissecting the iniquities of apartheid.

Since the dismantling of apartheid in the early 1990s, Tutu has continued to campaign, drawing attention to its economic and social after-effects for black South Africans. He has also campaigns on other issues. He has criticized Israel for its treatment of the Palestinians, Indonesia for its takeover of the western part of New Guinea (Irian Jaya), and Robert Mugabe's dictatorial regime in neighbouring Zimbabwe. Unlike many other African churchmen, he has declared the sexual orientation of clergymen unimportant.

I come from a beautiful land, richly endowed by God with wonderful natural resources, wide expanses, rolling mountains, singing birds, bright shining stars out of blue skies; with radiant sunshine, golden sunshine. There is enough of the good things that come from God's bounty, there is enough for everyone, but apartheid has confirmed some in their selfishness, causing them to grasp greedily a disproportionate share, the lion's share, because of their power.

They have taken 87 per cent of the land, though being only about 20 per cent of our population. The rest have had to make do with the remaining 13 per cent. Apartheid[1] has decreed the politics of exclusion. Seventy-three per cent of the population is excluded from any meaningful participation in the political decision-making processes of the land of their birth.

The new constitution[2] ... perpetuates by law and entrenches white minority rule. Blacks are expected to exercise their political ambitions in unviable, poverty-stricken, arid, bantustan[3] homelands, ghettoes of misery, inexhaustible reservoirs of cheap black labour, bantustans into which South Africa is being balkanized.

[1] Apartheid was first introduced in 1948, enshrining racial segregation in South African law, greatly restricting the freedom of movement and residence, and access to education and jobs of the non-white population (including Asians and mixed race people as well as native Africans), as well as denying them political, civil and legal rights.

[2] The South African constitution was revised in 1983, allowing Asian and 'coloured' (mixed race) citizens limited participation in subordinate houses of a tricameral parliament. It decreed that the black majority were to be regarded as citizens of 'independent' 'homelands'.

[3] Bantu is a generic term for over 400 native ethnic groups in the southern part of the African continent. Bantustan refers to the 'homelands' of which black South Africans were designated 'citizens' during the apartheid regime.

Blacks are systematically being stripped of their South African citizenship and being turned into aliens in the land of their birth. This is apartheid's final solution, just as Nazism had its final solution for the Jews in Hitler's Aryan madness. The South African government is smart. Aliens can claim but very few rights, least of all political rights.

In pursuance of apartheid's ideological racist dream, over three million of God's children have been uprooted from their homes, which have been demolished, whilst they have then been dumped in the bantustan homeland resettlement camps. I say dumped advisedly: only things or rubbish is dumped, not human beings. Apartheid has, however, ensured that God's children, just because they are black, should be treated as if they were things, and not as of infinite value as being created in the image of God.

These dumping grounds are far from where work and food can be procured easily. Children starve, suffer from the often irreversible consequences of malnutrition – this happens to them not accidentally, but by deliberate government policy. They starve in a land that could be the bread basket of Africa, a land that normally is a net exporter of food.

The father leaves his family in the bantustan homeland, there eking out a miserable existence, whilst he, if he is lucky, goes to the so-called white man's town as a migrant, to live an unnatural life in a single-sex hostel for 11 months of the year, being prey there to prostitution, drunkenness and worse. This migratory labour policy is declared government policy, and has been condemned, even by the white Dutch Reformed Church,[4] not noted for being quick to criticize the government, as a cancer in our society. This cancer, eating away at the vitals of black family life, is deliberate government policy. It is part of the cost of apartheid, exorbitant in terms of human suffering.

[4] The principal church of the Afrikaner ruling minority.

Apartheid has spawned discriminatory education, such as Bantu Education, education for serfdom, ensuring that the government spends only about one-tenth on one black child per annum for education what it spends on a white child. It is education that is decidedly separate and unequal. It is wantonly wasteful of human resources, because so many of God's children are prevented, by deliberate government policy, from attaining to their fullest potential. South Africa is paying a heavy price already for this iniquitous policy, because there is a desperate shortage of skilled manpower, a direct result of the short-sighted schemes of the racist regime …

Apartheid is upheld by a phalanx of iniquitous laws, such as the Population Registration Act, which decrees that all South Africans must be classified ethnically and duly registered according to these race categories. Many times, in the same family one child has been classified white whilst another, with a slightly darker hue, has been classified coloured, with all the horrible consequences for the latter of being shut out from membership of a greatly privileged caste. There have, as a result, been several child suicides.

This is too high a price to pay for racial purity, for it is doubtful whether any end, however desirable, can justify such a means. There are laws such as the Prohibition of Mixed Marriages Act, which regard marriages between a white and a person of another race as illegal. Race becomes an impediment to a valid marriage. Two persons who have fallen in love are prevented by race from consummating their love in the marriage bond. Something beautiful is made to be sordid and ugly.

The Immorality Act decrees that fornication and adultery are illegal if they happen between a white and one of another race. The police are reduced to the level of Peeping Toms to catch couples red-handed. Many whites have committed suicide rather than face the disastrous consequences that follow in the train of even just being charged under this law …

There are the laws which permit the indefinite detention of persons whom the Minister of Law and Order has decided are a threat to the security of the state. They are detained at his pleasure, in solitary confinement, without access to their family, their own doctor or a lawyer. That is severe punishment when the evidence apparently available to the minister has not been tested in an open court – perhaps it could stand up to such rigorous scrutiny, perhaps not; we are never to know.

It is a far too convenient device for a repressive regime, and the minister would have to be extra-special not to succumb to the temptation to circumvent the awkward process of testing his evidence in an open court, and thus he lets his power under the law to be open to the abuse where he is both judge and prosecutor. Many – too many – have died mysteriously in detention. All this is too costly in terms of human lives.

The minister is able, too, to place people under banning orders without being subjected to the annoyance of the checks and balances of due process. A banned person for three or five years becomes a non-person, who cannot be quoted during the period of her banning order. She cannot attend a gathering, which means more than one other person. Two persons together talking to a banned person are a gathering! She cannot attend the wedding or funeral of even her own child without special permission. She must be at home from 6pm of one day to 6am of the next and on all public holidays, and from 6pm on Fridays until 6am on Mondays for three years. She cannot go on holiday outside the magisterial area to which she has been confined. She cannot go to the cinema, nor to a picnic.

That is severe punishment, inflicted without the evidence allegedly justifying it being made available to the banned person, nor having it scrutinized in a court of law. It is a serious erosion and violation of basic human rights, of which blacks have precious few in the land of their birth. They do not enjoy the rights of freedom of movement and association. They do not enjoy freedom of security of tenure, the right to participate in the making of decisions that affect their lives. In short, this land, richly endowed in so many ways, is sadly lacking in justice.

Once a Zambian and a South African, it is said, were talking. The Zambian then boasted about their Minister of Naval Affairs. The South African asked, 'But you have no navy, no access to the sea. How then can you have a Minister of Naval Affairs?' The Zambian retorted, 'Well, in South Africa you have a Minister of Justice, don't you?'

It is against this system that our people have sought to protest peacefully since 1912 at least, with the founding of the African National Congress.[5] They have used the conventional methods of peaceful protest – petitions, demonstrations, deputations, and even a passive resistance campaign. A tribute to our people's commitment to peaceful change is the fact that the only South Africans to win the Nobel Peace Prize are both black.[6]

Our people are peace-loving to a fault. The response of the authorities has been an escalating intransigence and violence, the violence of police dogs, tear gas, detention without trial, exile and even death. Our people

[5] The African National Congress (ANC) was formed as the South African Native National Congress in 1912 to defend the rights of South Africa's black majority.

[6] The previous South African to win the Nobel Peace Prize was Albert Lutuli (c.1898–1967), President-General of the African National Congress, who received the award in 1960.

[7] The Pass Laws required black citizens to carry identity documents at all times.

protested peacefully against the Pass Laws[7] in 1960, and 69 of them were killed on March 21, 1960, at Sharpeville, many shot in the back running away.[8]

Our children protested against inferior education, singing songs and displaying placards and marching peacefully. Many in 1976, on June 16 and subsequent times, were killed or imprisoned.[9] Over 500 people died in that uprising. Many children went into exile. The whereabouts of many are unknown to their parents …

[9] In April 1976, schoolchildren in Soweto (an abbreviation of 'South-Western Townships') on the outskirts of Johannesburg) went on strike, refusing to attend classes. At a mass rally on 16 June, children threw stones at police, who responded with bullets, and 566 children were killed.

There has been little revulsion or outrage at this wanton destruction of human life in the West. In parenthesis, can somebody please explain to me something that has puzzled me? When a priest goes missing and is subsequently found dead, the media in the West carry his story in very extensive coverage.[10] I am glad that the death of one person can cause so much concern. But in the self-same week when this priest is found dead, the South African Police kill 24 blacks who had been participating in the protest, and 6,000 blacks are sacked for being similarly involved, and you are lucky to get that much coverage.

Are we being told something I do not want to believe – that we blacks are expendable and that blood is thicker than water; that when it comes to the crunch, you cannot trust whites, that they will club together against us? I don't want to believe that is the message being conveyed to us.

Be that as it may, we see before us a land bereft of much justice, and therefore without peace and security. Unrest is endemic, and will remain an unchanging feature of the South African scene until apartheid, the root cause of it all, is finally dismantled.

At this time, the army is being quartered on the civilian population. There is a civil war being waged. South Africans are on either side. When the African National Congress and the Pan-Africanist Congress[11] were banned in 1960, they declared that they had no option but to carry out the armed struggle. We in the South African Council of Churches have said we are opposed to all forms of violence – that of a repressive and unjust system, and that of those who seek to overthrow that system. However, we have added that we understand those who say they have had to adopt what is a last resort for them.

[11] A splinter group of the ANC, which sought government 'of the African, by the African, for the African'. The two organizations were banned in the wake of the Sharpeville massacre.

Violence is not being introduced into the South African situation *de novo* from outside by those who are called terrorists or freedom fighters, depending on whether you are oppressed or an oppressor. The South African situation is violent already, and the primary violence is that of apartheid, the violence of forced population removals, of inferior education, of detention without trial, of the migratory labour system, etc …

I have spoken extensively about South Africa, first because it is the land I know best; but because it is also a microcosm of the world and an example of what is to be found in other lands in differing degree … Because there is global insecurity, nations are engaged in a mad arms race, spending billions of dollars wastefully on instruments of destruction, when millions are starving. And yet, just a fraction of what is expended so obscenely on defence budgets would make the difference in enabling God's children to fill their stomachs, be educated, and given the chance to lead fulfilled and happy lives. We have the capacity to feed ourselves several times over, but we are daily haunted by the spectacle of the gaunt dregs of humanity shuffling along in endless queues, with bowls to collect what the charity of the world has provided, too little too late.

[8] On 21 March 1960, a crowd gathered in the Sharpeville township to demonstrate against the Pass Laws. Estimated numbers vary widely, from 300 to 20,000. As the singing protesters congregated around the police station, the police opened fire, killing 69 and injuring 186. The officer in charge, Colonel J Pienaar, was quoted as saying, 'If they do these things they must learn their lesson the hard way.'

[10] In October 1984, the Polish priest Father Jerzy Popieluszko (1947–84) was abducted and murdered by police. The incident sparked an international outcry.

When will we learn? When will the people of the world get up and say, 'Enough is enough'? God created us for fellowship. God created us so that we should form the human family, existing together because we were made for one another. We are not made for an exclusive self-sufficiency but for interdependence, and we break the law of our being at our peril …

Unless we work assiduously so that all of God's children, our brothers and sisters, members of our one human family, all will enjoy basic human rights, the right to a fulfilled life, the right of movement, of work, the freedom to be fully human, with a humanity measured by nothing less than the humanity of JESUS Christ Himself, then we are on the road inexorably to self-destruction; we are not far from global suicide – and yet it could be so different.

When will we learn that human beings are of infinite value because they have been created in the image of God, and that it is a blasphemy to treat them as if they were less than this, and to do so ultimately recoils on those who do this? In dehumanizing others, they are themselves dehumanized. Perhaps oppression dehumanizes the oppressor as much as, if not more than, the oppressed. They need each other to become truly free, to become human. We can be human only in fellowship, in community, in *koinonia*,[12] in peace.

Let us work to be peacemakers, those given a wonderful share in Our Lord's ministry of reconciliation. If we want peace, so we have been told, let us work for justice. Let us beat our swords into ploughshares.[13]

God calls us to be fellow workers with Him, so that we can extend his kingdom of *shalom*,[14] of justice, of goodness, of compassion, of caring, of sharing, of laughter, joy and reconciliation, so that the kingdoms of this world will become the Kingdom of our God and of his Christ, and he shall reign forever and ever. Amen.

[12] Greek: 'fellowship'.

[13] Isaiah 2:4.

[14] Hebrew: 'peace'.

Mark Twain
American writer and journalist

Mark Twain *pen name of Samuel Langhorne Clemens* (1835–1910) was born in Florida, Missouri. He was first a printer (1847–55) and later a Mississippi river-boat pilot (1857–61). He took his pen name from piloting parlance. In 1861 he went to Carson City, Nevada, as secretary to his brother, who was in the service of the governor, and made an unsuccessful attempt at goldmining. He then edited the Virginia City *Territorial Enterprise* for two years and in 1864 moved to San Francisco as a reporter. His first success was *The Celebrated Jumping Frog of Calaveras County* (1865), which was published as a book with other sketches in 1867. Also in 1867 he visited France, Italy and Palestine, gathering material for *Innocents Abroad* (1869), which established his reputation as a humorist. After his return he was for a time editor of a newspaper in Buffalo, New York, where he married the wealthy Olivia Landon. Later he moved to Hartford, Connecticut, and joined a publishing firm which failed, recouping his losses by lecturing and writing. *Roughing It* (1872) is a humorous account of his Nevada experiences, while *The Gilded Age* (1873), written with Charles Dudley Warner (1829–1900), describes the readjustment period after the Civil War. He visited England for a lecture tour in 1872, and afterwards wrote *The Prince and the Pauper* (1882) and *A Connecticut Yankee in King Arthur's Court* (1889). His two greatest masterpieces, *The Adventures of Tom Sawyer* (1876) and *The Adventures of Huckleberry Finn* (1884), are drawn from his own boyhood experiences, and give vivid accounts of life on the Mississippi frontier. In 1883 he published *Life on the Mississippi*, an autobiographical account of his days as a river-boat pilot. From the 1890s to the end of his life, Twain was afflicted by financial problems, aggravated by unsuccessful business ventures. He tried to recover his fortunes on lecture tours in New Zealand, Australia, India and South Africa, but his difficulties intensified with the death of his wife and two of his three daughters. His writing from these years has a more sombre tone, notably in *The Man that Corrupted Hadleyburg* (1900) and *The Mysterious Stranger* (published posthumously in 1916). In these last years he dictated his autobiography to his secretary A B Paine, and it was published in different versions.

'There is a sumptuous variety about the New England weather'
22 December 1876, New York City, USA

The tone of this speech might appropriately be described as breezy. Given relatively early in Twain's literary career, in the year when *Tom Sawyer* was published, it illustrates not only his fanciful imagination and playful sense of humour but also, in its final passage, his capacity for dazzling verbal fireworks.

Twain was one of several guest speakers at the New England Society's annual dinner in New York. The event was held at Delmonico's restaurant, decorated, in this centennial year of the USA, with an array of banners, shields and flowers. The following day's *New York Times* reported it as 'one of the most brilliant celebrations of the kind that has ever been held in this city'.

Having lived since 1871 in Hartford, Connecticut, Twain had plentiful experience of New England's fickle climate, and chose it as his theme, perhaps intending to counterbalance a more earnest speech on 'New England Culture' by the clergyman and writer Edward Everett Hale (1822–1909). Though later described as 'rambling', Twain's speech was said to have 'provoked a storm of laughter', and was greeted with thunderous applause.

> I reverently believe that the Maker who made us all makes everything in New England but the weather. I don't know who makes that, but I think it must be raw apprentices in the weather-clerk's factory who experiment and learn how, in New England, for board and clothes, and then are promoted to make weather for countries that require a good article, and will take their custom elsewhere if they don't get it.
>
> There is a sumptuous variety about the New England weather that compels the stranger's admiration — and regret. The weather is always doing something there; always attending strictly to business; always getting up new designs and trying them on the people to see how they will go. But it gets through more business in spring than in any other season. In the spring I have counted 136 different kinds of weather inside of four-and-twenty hours.

It was I that made the fame and fortune of that man that had that marvellous collection of weather on exhibition at the Centennial,[1] that so astounded the foreigners. He was going to travel all over the world and get specimens from all the climes. I said, 'Don't you do it; you come to New England on a favourable spring day.' I told him what we could do in the way of style, variety, and quantity.

Well, he came and he made his collection in four days. As to variety, why, he confessed that he got hundreds of kinds of weather that he had never heard of before. And as to quantity – well, after he had picked out and discarded all that was blemished in any way, he not only had weather enough, but weather to spare; weather to hire out; weather to sell; to deposit; weather to invest; weather to give to the poor.

The people of New England are by nature patient and forbearing, but there are some things which they will not stand. Every year they kill a lot of poets for writing about 'Beautiful Spring'. These are generally casual visitors, who bring their notions of spring from somewhere else, and cannot, of course, know how the natives feel about spring. And so the first thing they know, the opportunity to inquire how they feel has permanently gone by.

Old Probabilities[2] has a mighty reputation for accurate prophecy, and thoroughly well deserves it. You take up the paper and observe how crisply and confidently he checks off what today's weather is going to be on the Pacific, down south, in the middle states, in the Wisconsin region. See him sail along in the joy and pride of his power till he gets to New England, and then see his tail drop.

He doesn't know what the weather is going to be in New England. Well, he mulls over it, and by-and-by he gets out something about like this: 'Probably north-east to south-west winds, varying to the southward and westward and eastward, and points between, high and low barometer swapping around from place to place; probably areas of rain, snow, hail and drought, succeeded or preceded by earthquakes, with thunder and lightning.'

Then he jots down his postscript from his wandering mind, to cover accidents. 'But it is possible that the programme may be wholly changed in the meantime.'

[*Loud laughter.*]

Yes, one of the brightest gems in the New England weather is the dazzling uncertainty of it. There is only one thing certain about it: you are certain there is going to be plenty of it – a perfect grand review; but you never can tell which end of the procession is going to move first. You fix up for the drought; you leave your umbrella in the house and sally out, and two to one you get drowned. You make up your mind that the earthquake is due; you stand from under and take hold of something to steady yourself, and the first thing you know you get struck by lightning.

These are great disappointments; but they can't be helped. The lightning there is peculiar; it is so convincing, that when it strikes a thing it doesn't leave enough of that thing behind for you to tell whether – Well, you'd think it was something valuable, and a Congressman had been there.

[*Loud laughter and applause.*]

And the thunder. When the thunder begins to merely tune up and scrape and saw, and key up the instruments for the performance, strangers say, 'Why, what awful thunder you have here!' But when the baton is raised and

[1] In 1876, the USA celebrated its centenary with the huge *International Exhibition of Arts, Manufactures and Products of the Soil and Mine*, which opened on 10 May at Fairmount Park, Philadelphia. Almost nine million people attended this display of technological wonders.

[2] Professor Cleveland Abbe (1838–1916), a civilian meteorologist who was employed by the US Army Signal Service, founded the Weather Bureau and advocated the use of time zones. Weather forecasts were then described as 'probabilities' of the weather, from which his nickname of 'Old Probabilities' or 'Old Probs' was derived.

the real concert begins, you'll find that stranger down in the cellar with his head in the ash-barrel.

Now as to the *size* of the weather in New England – lengthways, I mean. It is utterly disproportioned to the size of that little country. Half the time, when it is packed as full as it can stick, you will see that New England weather sticking out beyond the edges and projecting around hundreds and hundreds of miles over the neighbouring states. You can see cracks all about where she has strained herself trying to do it.

I could speak volumes about the inhuman perversity of the New England weather, but I will give but a single specimen. I like to hear rain on a tin roof. So I covered part of my roof with tin, with an eye to that luxury. Well, sir, do you think it ever rains on that tin? No, sir; skips it every time.

Mind, in this speech I have been trying merely to do honour to the New England weather – no language could do it justice. But, after all, there is at least one or two things about that weather (or, if you please, effects produced by it) which we residents would not like to part with. If we hadn't our bewitching autumn foliage, we should still have to credit the weather with one feature which compensates for all its bullying vagaries: the ice-storm.

When a leafless tree is clothed with ice from the bottom to the top, ice that is as bright and clear as crystal; when every bough and twig is strung with ice-beads, frozen dew-drops, and the whole tree sparkles cold and white, like the Shah of Persia's diamond plume. Then the wind waves the branches and the sun comes out and turns all those myriads of beads and drops to prisms that glow and burn and flash with all manner of coloured fires, which change and change again with inconceivable rapidity from blue to red, from red to green, and green to gold – the tree becomes a spraying fountain, a very explosion of dazzling jewels; and it stands there the acme, the climax, the supremest possibility in art or nature, of bewildering, intoxicating, intolerable magnificence. One cannot make the words too strong.

[*Prolonged applause.*]

Month after month I lay up my hate and grudge against the New England weather; but when the ice storm comes at last, I say: 'There, I forgive you, now; the books are square between us; you don't owe me a cent; go, and sin no more;[3] your little faults and foibles count for nothing; you are the most enchanting weather in the world!'

[3] The instruction given by JESUS to the woman caught in adultery. See John 8:11.

'If there is an awful, horrible malady in the world, it is stage-fright'
5 October 1906, Norfolk, Connecticut, USA

Much later in life, as an established man of letters, Twain gave one of his most personal speeches. The occasion was the debut recital given by his daughter Clara Clemens, a contralto. Mindful of the emotional pressures attending on such an occasion, Twain rose at the end to thank the audience, and rewarded them with a characteristically humorous anecdote about his own debut performance.

In fact, the father-daughter relationship was not altogether harmonious. Neither parent had wholly approved of Clara's musical career, and her father had openly favoured her elder sister Susie, who died in 1896. When her mother Olivia died in 1904, Clara found herself acting as a surrogate for the two women Twain had most adored. In 1909, she married a Russian-born concert pianist, Ossip Gabrilowitsch, and moved to Europe, leaving her father with her epileptic younger sister, Jean, who died later that year.

Yet Twain and Clara held each other in much affection. In June 1908, during a tour of the UK, she wrote a newspaper article that bears some of the hallmarks of her father's prose style. In it she recalls how, on the afternoon before a demanding recital, she persuaded him to stand in for her at a social function. 'At first he objected strongly, but finally, in a burst of impetuosity, he said: "Yes, Clara, I'll go to that reception. I'd go to Hell for you."

'To which I thoughtfully replied: "If ever, father, you should be called upon to go there, please go labelled, *I'm for Clara*."'

❧

My heart goes out in sympathy to any one who is making his first appearance before an audience of human beings. By a direct process of memory I go back 40 years, less one month – for I'm older than I look.

I recall the occasion of my first appearance. San Francisco knew me then only as a reporter, and I was to make my bow to San Francisco as a lecturer. I knew that nothing short of compulsion would get me to the theatre. So I bound myself by a hard-and-fast contract so that I could not escape. I got to the theatre 45 minutes before the hour set for the lecture. My knees were shaking so that I didn't know whether I could stand up.

If there is an awful, horrible malady in the world, it is stage-fright – and sea-sickness. They are a pair. I had stage-fright then for the first and last time. I was only sea-sick once, too. It was on a little ship on which there were 200 other passengers. I – was – sick. I was so sick that there wasn't any left for those other 200 passengers.

It was dark and lonely behind the scenes in that theatre, and I peeked through the little peek-holes they have in theatre curtains and looked into the big auditorium. That was dark and empty, too. By-and-by it lighted up, and the audience began to arrive.

I had got a number of friends of mine, stalwart men, to sprinkle themselves through the audience armed with big clubs. Every time I said anything they could possibly guess I intended to be funny they were to pound those clubs on the floor. Then there was a kind lady in a box up there, also a good friend of mine, the wife of the Governor. She was to watch me intently and whenever I glanced toward her she was going to deliver a gubernatorial laugh that would lead the whole audience into applause.

At last I began. I had the manuscript tucked under a United States flag in front of me, where I could get at it in case of need. But I managed to get started without it. I walked up and down – I was young in those days and needed the exercise – and talked and talked.

Right in the middle of the speech I had placed a gem. I had put in a moving, pathetic part which was to get at the hearts and souls of my hearers. When I delivered it they did just what I hoped and expected. They sat silent and awed. I had touched them. Then I happened to glance up at the box where the Governor's wife was. You know what happened.

Well, after the first agonizing five minutes, my stage-fright left me, never to return. I know if I was going to be hanged I could get up and make a good showing, and I intend to. But I shall never forget my feelings before the agony left me, and I got up here to thank you for helping my daughter, by your kindness, to live through her first appearance.

And I want to thank you for your appreciation of her singing – which is, by the way, hereditary.

Bartolomeo Vanzetti

Italian–American political activist

Bartolomeo Vanzetti (1888–1927) was born in Villafalletto, Italy. He emigrated to the USA at the age of 20 and settled in Massachusetts, where he had a succession of casual jobs. Through his developing interest in socialism and radical political activities, he met fellow immigrant Nicola Sacco (1891–1927), who worked in a shoe factory. The two men became friends and, as both were opposed to World War I for political reasons, they crossed the border to Mexico to avoid conscription into the US Army. They returned to the USA after the end of the war and continued their involvement with radical left-wing groups, Vanzetti now peddling fish for a living. Arrested and brought to trial for murdering two men while robbing a shoe-factory at South Braintree, Massachusetts (1920), Sacco and Vanzetti were found guilty, although the evidence was conflicting and circumstantial. Worldwide protests and appeals for clemency – on the grounds that Sacco and Vanzetti were widely believed to be victims of prejudice – led to an investigation. However, the verdict of the trial was upheld, and the men were executed in the electric chair (1927). The case remained controversial for many years.

'I never committed a crime in my life'

9 April 1927, Dedham, Massachusetts, USA

Sacco and Vanzetti were arrested at the height of the 'Red Scare', and their trial in 1921 was conducted in the midst of hysteria over communism and trade unionism. The Department of Justice, under Attorney-General Mitchell Palmer, was particularly active in Massachusetts, and bankers were taking out newspaper advertisements denouncing 'reds'. Both defendants had previously been under surveillance; they had evaded war service; and they were known radicals and atheists.

In 1920, in a raid on the South Braintree shoe factory, paymaster Frederick Parmenter and security guard Alessandro Berardelli were murdered and $15,800 was stolen. Sacco and Vanzetti were not arrested until several weeks later, and were initially questioned only about their political beliefs. They were able to explain why they carried guns (Sacco was a night watchman and Vanzetti needed protection against robbers). But alibis offered by other Italian immigrants were dismissed. In 1925, a Portuguese immigrant, Celestino Madeiros, confessed to the murders, but his claim was never fully investigated.

As the trial and appeals progressed, doubts over the men's guilt grew, but a combination of prejudice, fear and gullibility led to the guilty verdict being upheld. Both men knew they had been condemned for their political beliefs. Vanzetti's address to the court, spoken in simple English at his final appeal, is a moving response to this gross miscarriage of justice.

Leading public figures of the day – including GEORGE BERNARD SHAW, BERTRAND RUSSELL and the poet Dorothy Parker – called for a retrial, but in vain. On 23 August 1927, the day of the execution, 250,000 people demonstrated silently in Boston. In 1977, Sacco and Vanzetti were posthumously pardoned.

[*Clerk Worthington: 'Bartolomeo Vanzetti, have you anything to say why sentence of death should not be passed upon you?'*]

Yes. What I say is that I am innocent, not only of the Braintree crime, but also of the Bridgewater crime.[1] That I am not only innocent of these two crimes, but in all my life I have never stolen and I have never killed and I have never spilled blood. That is what I want to say. And it is not all. Not only am I innocent of these two crimes, not only in all my life I have never stolen, never killed, never spilled blood, but I have struggled all my life, since I began to reason, to eliminate crime from the earth …

Not only have I struggled hard against crimes, but I have refused myself of what are considered the commodity and glories of life, the prides of a life of a good position, because in my consideration it is not right to exploit man. I have refused to go in business because I understand that business is a speculation on profit upon certain people that must depend upon the businessman, and I do not consider that that is right and therefore I refuse to do that.

[1] In 1920 Vanzetti had been tried and found guilty of an attempted robbery at Bridgewater, Massachusetts, in December 1919.

Now, I should say that I am not only innocent of all these things, not only have I never committed a real crime in my life — though some sins but not crimes — not only have I struggled all my life to eliminate crimes, the crimes that the official law and the moral law condemns, but also the crime that the moral law and the official law sanction and sanctify — the exploitation and the oppression of the man by the man, and if there is a reason why I am here as a guilty man, if there is a reason why you in a few minutes can doom me, it is this reason and none else.

There is the best man I ever cast my eyes upon since I lived, a man that will last and will grow always more near to and more dear to the heart of the people, so long as admiration for goodness, for virtues, and for sacrifice will last. I mean EUGENE VICTOR DEBS.

He has said that not even a dog that kills chickens would have found an American jury disposed to convict it with the proof that the commonwealth has produced against us …

He knew, and not only he knew, but every man of understanding in the world, not only in this country but also in other countries — men to whom we have provided a certain amount of the records of the case at times — they all know and still stick with us, the flower of mankind of Europe, the better writers, the greatest thinkers of Europe, have pleaded in our favour. The scientists, the greatest scientists, the greatest statesmen of Europe, have pleaded in our favour.

Is it possible that only a few — a handful of men of the jury, only two or three other men, who would shame their mother for worldly honour and for earthly fortune — is it possible that they are right against what the world, for the whole world has said that it is wrong and I know that it is wrong? If there is one that should know it, if it is right or if it is wrong, it is I and this man.

You see it is seven years that we are in jail. What we have suffered during these seven years no human tongue can say; and yet you see me before you, not trembling, you see me looking you in your eyes straight, not blushing, not changing colour, not ashamed or in fear …

They have given a new trial to Madeiros for the reason that the judge had either forgot or omitted to tell the jury that they should consider the man innocent until found guilty in the court, or something of that sort. That man has confessed. The man was tried on his confession and was found guilty, and the Supreme Court gave him another trial. We have proved that there could not have been another judge on the face of the earth more prejudiced, more cruel and more hostile than you have been against us. We have proven that.

Still they refuse the new trial. We know — and you know in your heart — that you have been against us from the very beginning, before you see us. Before you see us you already know that we were radicals, that we were underdogs, that we were the enemy of the institutions that you can believe in good faith in their goodness — I don't want to discuss that — and that it was easy at the time of the first trial to get a verdict of guiltiness …

The first lawyer of the defence, Mr Vahey,[2] has not defended me, has sold me for 30 golden money like Judas sold JESUS Christ. If that man has not told to you or to Mr Katzmann[3] that he knew that I was guilty, it is because he cannot; it is because he knew that I was not guilty.

That man has done everything indirectly to hurt us. He has made a long speech to the jury about things that do matter nothing, and on the point of essence to the trial he has passed over with few words or with complete

[2] The US lawyer John P Vahey, practising locally, had advised Vanzetti against testifying on his own behalf, to avoid revealing his radical politics to the jury.

[3] The US lawyer Frederick Katzmann was the prosecution attorney. Vahey and Katzmann had been partners in a legal firm since 1924.

silence. This was a premeditation, in order to give to the jury the impression that my own defender has nothing good to urge in defence of myself, and therefore is compelled to go around the bush on little things that amount to nothing and let pass the essential points, either in silence or with a very weakly resistance.

We were tried during a time whose character has now passed into history. I mean by that, a time when there was a hysteria of resentment and hate against the people of our principles, against the foreigner, against slackers and it seems to me – rather, I am positive of it, that both you and Mr Katzmann have done all what it were in your power in order to work out, in order to agitate still more the passion of the juror, the prejudice of the juror, against us …

In the best of my recollection and of my good faith, during the trial Katzmann has told to the jury that a certain Coacci[4] has brought in Italy the money that, according to the state theory, I and Sacco have stolen in Braintree. We never stole that money. But Katzmann, when he told that to the jury, he knew already that that was not true. He knew already that that man was deported in Italy by the federal police, soon after our arrest. I remember well that I was told that the federal policemen had him in their possession – that the federal policemen had taken away the trunks from the very ship where he was, and brought the trunks back over here and look them over and found not a single money.

Now, I call that murder, to tell to the jury that a friend or comrade or a relative or acquaintance of the charged man, of the indicted man, has carried the money to Italy, when he knows it was not true. I can call that nothing else but murder, a plain murder …

What I want to say is this: everybody ought to understand that the first beginning of our defence has been terrible. My first lawyer did not try to defend us. He has made no attempt to collect witnesses and evidence in our favour … I have already say that I not only am not guilty of these two crimes, but I never committed a crime in my life. I have never stolen and I have never killed and I have never spilled blood and I have fought against crime and I have fought and I have sacrificed myself even to eliminate the crimes that the law and the church legitimate and sanctify.

This is what I say: I would not wish to a dog or to a snake, to the most low and misfortunate creature of the earth – I would not wish to any of them what I have had to suffer for things that I am not guilty of. I am suffering because I am a radical and indeed I am a radical. I have suffered because I was an Italian, and indeed I am an Italian. I have suffered more for my family and for my beloved than for myself. But I am so convinced to be right that you can only kill me once, but if you could execute me two times, and if I could be reborn two other times, I would live again to do what I have done already.

I have finished. Thank you.

[4] The Italian anarchist Feruccio Coacci had been employed in a Bridgewater shoe factory. He was due to be deported on 15 April 1920, the day when the Braintree crime took place, but failed to turn himself in. He was deported on 18 April.

George G Vest

American lawyer and politician

George Graham Vest (1830–1904) was born in Frankfort, Kentucky. He was admitted to the bar in 1853 and began practising law in Georgetown, Missouri. He served as a Missouri state representative (1860–1) and Confederate Congressman (1862–5) before resuming his legal practice, but later returned to politics, enjoying a long career as a Democrat senator from Missouri (1879–1903).

'A man's dog stands by him in prosperity and in poverty'

23 September 1870, Warrensburg, Missouri, USA

This speech is Vest's summation to the jury in the matter of *Burden* v *Hornsby*. This bizarre case involved two brothers-in-law, three trials, some fine legal minds and the 'murder' of a hunting dog. The speech's sentimentality played directly to the jury in the case before the Court of Common Pleas and had very little to do with the facts of the case. Vest was considered one of the most accomplished extemporaneous speakers of his day, and his 'eulogy to the dog' became such a classic that he repeated it many times throughout his life.

The case, which spanned two years, was brought by Charles Burden, whose dog, Old Drum, had been shot by a farmhand on the orders of Burden's neighbour and brother-in-law Leonidas Hornsby. Some of Hornsby's sheep had been savaged by a dog, and he vowed to kill the next one to appear on his land. Burden, astonishingly, eventually won – thanks more to Vest's eloquence than to the facts – and furthermore was awarded $50 compensation for the death of his favourite hunting dog. Although Hornsby pursued the case to the Missouri Supreme Court, the verdict was upheld.

In the long run no harm was done. The neighbours remained friends, although both families took some time to recover financially from the expense of going to law.

Gentlemen of the jury: the best friend a man has in the world may turn against him and become his enemy. His son or daughter that he has reared with loving care may prove ungrateful. Those who are nearest and dearest to us; those whom we trust with our happiness and our good name may become traitors to their faith. The money that a man has, he may lose. It flies away from him, perhaps when he needs it most. A man's reputation may be sacrificed in a moment of ill-considered action. The people who are prone to fall on their knees to do us honour when success is with us, may be the first to throw the stone of malice when failure settles its cloud upon our heads.

The one absolutely unselfish friend that man can have in this selfish world, the one that never deserts him, the one that never proves ungrateful or treacherous is his dog. A man's dog stands by him in prosperity and in poverty, in health and in sickness.

He will sleep on the cold ground, where the wintry winds blow and the snow drives fiercely, if only he may be near his master's side. He will kiss the hand that has no food to offer. He will lick the wounds and sores that come in encounters with the roughness of the world. He guards the sleep of his pauper master as if he were a prince. When all other friends desert, he remains. When riches take wings and reputation falls to pieces, he is as constant in his love as the sun in its journey through the heavens.

If fortune drives the master forth, an outcast in the world, friendless and homeless, the faithful dog asks no higher privilege than that of accompanying him, to guard him against danger, to fight against his enemies. And when the last scene of all comes, and death takes his master in its embrace and his body is laid away in the cold ground, no matter if all other friends pursue their way, there by the graveside will the noble dog be found, his head between his paws, his eyes sad, but open in alert watchfulness, faithful and true, even in death.

William Wallace
Scottish rebel leader

> William Wallace *also known as Walays or Wallensis ('Welshman'), later Sir William* (c.1274–1305) was reputedly the second son of Sir Malcolm Wallace of Elderslie, near Paisley. Wallace's biographer, the minstrel Blind Harry (c.1440–1492), refers to his early years in Dundee and Ayrshire. However, it is uncertain whether he took part in the raid on the English garrison at Ayr (1292) which is treated in some accounts as the start of the War of Scottish Independence (1292–1328). In 1297, leading a small band of men, Wallace sacked Lanark and killed the English sheriff William de Hazelrig. Later that year, he met Edward I's army and won a decisive victory at Stirling Bridge, after which he was knighted by King Robert I (1274–1329). Following this, the English were expelled from Scotland and a devastating raid was inflicted on the north of England. In retaliation, Edward invaded Scotland in 1298, meeting Wallace at Falkirk, where the Scots were crushed. For a short time, Wallace continued to wage a guerrilla war, but in 1299 he escaped to France, where he tried to enlist support for the Scottish cause. He returned in 1303, but in 1305 he was arrested near Glasgow by Sir John Monteith, Sheriff of Dumbarton. Taken to London, he was convicted of treason, then executed.

'Do with me what you will. Scotland shall yet be free!'
23 August 1305, London, England

This passionate gallows speech is a defiant call to arms by the former Guardian of Scotland, who spent two decades resisting the occupation of his country by Edward I of England. After his capture on 3 August, Wallace was taken to the Great Hall at Westminster, where he stood trial for treason against the king of England. Wallace was also accused of slaughter, arson, atrocities against the English Church and the murder of William de Hazelrig.

It was a show trial, whose outcome was decided beforehand. Wallace was then dragged at the tails of horses from London to Smithfield, the place of his execution, where he gave a short but powerful speech. In the words attributed to him, he refuses to be branded a traitor since he had never been a subject of the English Crown, and states that, though they may kill him, the English will never conquer Scotland.

He was hanged but cut down while still alive to be disembowelled and mutilated. His head was displayed on a pike at London Bridge, while his quarters were taken to Newcastle (sacked by Wallace's army in 1297) and the Scottish towns of Berwick, Perth and Stirling.

Wallace's grisly death was a warning to the Scots, but one that would ultimately be ignored. Even before chronicles of his life began appearing, Wallace was a martyr to Scottish independence.

Written many centuries later in support of the Scottish Home Rule movement, this notional speech evokes the spirit, if not the letter, of a condemned patriot's final words.

I cannot be a traitor to Edward, as I never was his subject. I was born and bred a Scotsman, and as such owe no allegiance to a foreign monarch … For what am I in chains? For defending my country. For raising my arm in defence of the land dearer to me than life itself.

Was this a crime? Are we calmly to sit down and bow our necks to the yoke of the oppressor? Is this the manner of England? No, nor of Scotland either. My country shall yet be free. Not Edward's armies nor his tyranny shall subdue her, or enslave her children. Her mountains and her valleys shall again re-echo with the cry of liberty; her brave sons shall again expel the invader from the land. It avails not that ye have me in your power.

Do with me what you will. Scotland shall yet be free! Other patriots shall arise to assert her independence and maintain her rights though I perish in the attempt.

Robert Walpole
English statesman

Robert Walpole *later 1st Earl of Orford* (1676–1745) was born in Houghton in Norfolk, and educated at Eton and King's College, Cambridge. He was destined for the Church, and entered politics largely by accident when his two elder brothers died, leaving him the family estate and sufficient wealth to follow a political career. He entered the House of Commons in 1701 as the Whig member for Castle Rising, Norfolk, and in 1702 for King's Lynn. He was a formidable speaker and quickly rose in the ranks of his party. During Queen Anne's reign (1702–14) he was appointed Secretary for War in 1708 and Treasurer of the Navy in 1710. During the Tory administration that followed the Whig collapse in 1710, he was sent to the Tower for alleged corruption (1712), but he was recalled when George I succeeded to the throne in 1714 and became a Privy Councillor and Chancellor of the Exchequer (1715). George I could not speak English and gave up attending the proceedings of Parliament, thereby leaving Walpole considerable freedom and discretion as leader of the government. Gradually Walpole established his supremacy, chairing, on the king's behalf, a small group of ministers which was the forerunner of the present-day Cabinet. As a result, he came to be seen as Britain's first prime minister, although he himself rejected the title. He was knighted in 1725 and created Earl of Orford in 1742. Walpole's foreign policy was based on a determination to maintain peace. He did not fully recover from the outbreak of the so-called 'War of Jenkins' Ear' with Spain (1739–48) which he had opposed, and he resigned in 1742. He enjoyed good relations with the Prince of Wales, who became George II, and with his wife, Queen Caroline. In addition to his earldom, Walpole was presented with No. 10 Downing Street, which was to become the London home of all future prime ministers.

'Is it no imputation to be arraigned before this House?'
13 February 1741, London, England

Sir Robert Walpole had presided over meetings of ministers for many years, becoming the most prominent figure in the British government. He had initially been popular, establishing economic stability following the South Sea Company's collapse (1720), keeping taxes low and avoiding war. During the 1730s, however, his taxation plans had become unpopular, as had his extensive use of patronage. He had failed to prevent war with Spain in 1739; and Britain, like most European powers, had become involved in the War of the Austrian Succession (1740–8).

By February 1741, Parliament had grown weary of Walpole's powerful position and protracted period in office; and his opponents demanded his removal. Their description of him as 'sole and prime minister' highlighted his unorthodox position, which allowed him to meddle with other ministers' roles. They also complained about the conduct of foreign affairs and in particular the progress of the Austrian war.

In this bullish reply, Walpole answers his accusers. He accepts responsibility for foreign policy, but refuses to accept blame for the war; and argues that domestic taxation had been jointly agreed by all ministers. He also hotly denies any impropriety in his granting of patronage, and the suggestion of any personal benefit.

The motion was defeated by 106 votes to 290, but Walpole's position was weakened. A year later, following a motion of no confidence, he resigned.

It has been observed by several gentlemen, in vindication of this motion, that if it should be carried, neither my life, liberty, nor estate will be affected. But do the honourable gentlemen consider my character and reputation as of no moment? Is it no imputation to be arraigned before this House, in which I have sat 40 years, and to have my name transmitted to posterity with disgrace and infamy? I will not conceal my sentiments that to be *named* in Parliament as a subject of inquiry is to me a matter of great concern …

Had the charge been reduced to specific allegations, I should have felt myself called upon for a specific defence. Had I served a weak or wicked master, and implicitly obeyed his dictates, obedience to his commands must have been my only justification. But as it has been my good fortune to serve a master who wants no bad ministers, and would have harkened to none, my defence must rest on my own conduct.

The consciousness of innocence is also a sufficient support against my present prosecutors. A further justification is derived from a consideration of the views and abilities of the prosecutors. Had I been guilty of great enormities, they want neither zeal and inclination to bring them forward, nor ability to place them in the most prominent point of view. But as I am conscious of no crime, my own experience convinces me that none can be justly imputed …

My great and principal crime is my long continuance in office; or, in other words, the long exclusion of those who now complain against me. This is the heinous offence which exceeds all others. I keep from them the possession of that power, those honours and those emoluments to which they so ardently and pertinaciously aspire …

But whence this cry of corruption, and exclusive claim of honourable distinction? Compare the estates, characters and fortunes of the Commons on one side with those on the other. Let the matter be fairly investigated. Survey and examine the individuals who usually support the measures of government, and those who are in opposition. Let us see to whose side the balance preponderates. Look round both Houses, and see to which side the balance of virtue and talents preponderates! Are all these on one side, and not on the other? Or are all these to be counterbalanced by an affected claim to the exclusive title of patriotism!

Gentlemen have talked a great deal of 'patriotism'. A venerable word, when duly practised. But I am sorry to say that of late it has been so much hackneyed about that it is in danger of falling into disgrace. The very idea of true patriotism is lost, and the term has been prostituted to the very worst of purposes.

A patriot, sir! Why, patriots spring up like mushrooms! I could raise 50 of them within the four-and-twenty hours. I have raised many of them in one night. It is but refusing to gratify an unreasonable or an insolent demand, and up starts a patriot. I have never been afraid of making patriots; but I disdain and despise all their efforts …

I shall now consider the articles of accusation which they have brought against me, and which they have not thought fit to reduce to specific charges; and I shall consider these in the same order as that in which they were placed by the honourable member who made the motion: first, in regard to foreign affairs; secondly, to domestic affairs; and, thirdly, to the conduct of the war.[1]

As to foreign affairs, I must take notice of the uncandid manner in which the gentlemen on the other side have managed the question by blending numerous treaties and complicated negotiations into one general mass.

To form a fair and candid judgement of the subject it becomes necessary not to consider the treaties merely insulated, but to advert to the time in which they were made, to the circumstances and situation of Europe when they were made, to the peculiar situation in which I stand, and to the power which I possessed. I am called, repeatedly and insidiously, 'prime and sole minister'. Admitting, however, for the sake of argument, that I am prime and sole minister in this country, am I, therefore, prime and sole minister of all Europe? Am I answerable for the conduct of other countries as well as for that of my own?

Many words are not wanting to show that the particular view of each court occasioned the dangers which affected the public tranquillity; yet the whole is charged to my account. Nor is this sufficient. Whatever was the conduct of England, I am equally arraigned. If we maintained ourselves in

[1] Walpole refers to the War of the Austrian Succession (1740–8), in which Frederick II of Prussia challenged Maria Theresa of Austria's succession to the Habsburg empire. Britain supported Austria in a war that embroiled much of Europe.

peace, and took no share in foreign transactions, we are reproached for tameness and pusillanimity. If, on the contrary, we interfered in these disputes, we are called Don Quixotes,[2] and dupes to all the world ...

I now come, sir, to the second head: the conduct of domestic affairs. And here a most heinous charge is made, that the nation has been burdened with unnecessary expenses for the sole purpose of preventing the discharge of our debts and the abolition of taxes. But this attack is more to the dishonour of the whole Cabinet council than to me. If there is any ground for this imputation, it is a charge upon king, Lords and Commons, as corrupted or imposed upon. And they have no proof of these allegations, but affect to substantiate them by common fame and public notoriety!

No expense has been incurred but what has been approved of and provided for by Parliament ... In all such cases there will be a variety of opinions. I happened to be one of those who thought all these expenses necessary, and I had the good fortune to have the majority of both houses of Parliament on my side.

But this, it seems, proceeded from bribery and corruption. Sir, if any one instance had been mentioned, if it had been shown that I ever offered a reward to any member of either House, or ever threatened to deprive any member of his office or employment, in order to influence his vote in Parliament, there might have been some ground for this charge. But when it is so generally laid I do not know what I can say to it unless it be to deny it as generally and as positively as it has been asserted. And – thank God – till some proof be offered, I have the laws of the land as well as the laws of charity in my favour ...

I shall now advert to the third topic of accusation – the conduct of the war. I have already stated in what manner and under what circumstances hostilities commenced; and as I am neither general nor admiral – as I have nothing to do either with our navy or army – I am sure that I am not answerable for the prosecution of it. But were I to answer for everything no fault could, I think, be found with my conduct in the prosecution of the war ...

If my whole administration is to be scrutinized and arraigned, why are the most favourable parts to be omitted? If facts are to be accumulated on one side, why not on the other? And why may not I be permitted to speak in my own favour? Was I not called by the voice of the king and the nation to remedy the fatal effects of the South Sea project[3] and to support declining credit? Was I not placed at the head of the treasury when the revenues were in the greatest confusion? Is credit revived, and does it now flourish? Is it not at an incredible height, and if so, to whom must that circumstance be attributed? Has not tranquillity been preserved both at home and abroad, notwithstanding a most unreasonable and violent opposition? Has the true interest of the nation been pursued, or has trade flourished?

Have gentlemen produced one instance of this exorbitant power; of the influence which I extend to all parts of the nation; of the tyranny with which I oppress those who oppose, and the liberality with which I reward those who support me? But having first invested me with a kind of mock dignity, and styled me a prime minister, they impute to me an unpardonable abuse of that chimerical authority which they only have created and conferred ...

Let me expose to their view the real condition of the public weal. Let me

[2] Don Quixote was a fictional nobleman created by the Spanish novelist Miguel de Cervantes (1547–1616) in his novel of the same name (1605–15). Quixote is notable for acting impetuously on misplaced ideals of chivalry.

[3] The South Sea Company, formed in 1711 to manage English trade with Spanish South America, in 1719 proposed to manage part of the National Debt. The exaggerated claims at the launch of this scheme encouraged excessive speculation and it collapsed in 1720, leaving thousands of British investors destitute.

show them that the Crown has made no encroachments, that all supplies have been granted by Parliament, that all questions have been debated with the same freedom as before the fatal period in which my counsels are said to have gained the ascendancy – an ascendancy from which they deduce the loss of trade, the approach of slavery, the preponderance of prerogative and the extension of influence. But I am far from believing that they feel those apprehensions which they so earnestly labour to communicate to others; and I have too high an opinion of their sagacity not to conclude that, even in their own judgement, they are complaining of grievances that they do not suffer, and promoting rather their private interest than that of the public.

What is this unbounded sole power which is imputed to me? How has it discovered itself, or how has it been proved? What have been the effects of the corruption, ambition and avarice with which I am so abundantly charged?

Have I ever been suspected of being corrupted? A strange phenomenon, a corrupter himself not corrupt! Is ambition imputed to me? Why then do I still continue a commoner? I, who refused a white staff[4] and a peerage?

... Have I given any symptoms of an avaricious disposition? Have I obtained any grants from the Crown since I have been placed at the head of the treasury? Has my conduct been different from that which others in the same station would have followed? Have I acted wrong in giving the place of auditor to my son and in providing for my own family? I trust that their advancement will not be imputed to me as a crime unless it shall be proved that I placed them in offices of trust and responsibility for which they were unfit.

But while I unequivocally deny that I am sole and prime minister, and that to my influence and direction all the measures of the government must be attributed, yet I will not shrink from the responsibility which attaches to the post I have the honour to hold; and should – during the long period in which I have sat upon this bench – any one step taken by government be proved to be either disgraceful or disadvantageous to the nation, I am ready to hold myself accountable.

To conclude, sir, though I shall always be proud of the honour of any trust or confidence from His Majesty, yet I shall always be ready to remove from his councils and presence when he thinks fit ... But I must think that an address to His Majesty to remove one of his servants, without so much as alleging any particular crime against him, is one of the greatest encroachments that was ever made upon the prerogatives of the Crown.

And therefore, for the sake of my master, without any regard for my own, I hope all those that have a due regard for our constitution and for the rights and prerogatives of the Crown – without which our constitution can not be preserved – will be against this motion.

[4] The symbol of the Lord High Treasurer, historically the head of the King's Treasury and administrator of its functions. Since 1714 the 'office' has been held by a board of members of the government, the Lords Commissioners of the Treasury. The First Lord of the Treasury is now, by convention, the prime minister. From 1721 until 1741, Walpole held the title First Lord of the Treasury; the title of prime minister was not in use at that date.

Booker T Washington

American educationist

Booker Taliaferro Washington (1856–1915) was born a slave in Franklin Country, Virginia. After emancipation, he was educated at Hampton Institute, and became a teacher, writer and speaker on black issues. In 1881, he was appointed principal of the newly opened Tuskegee Institute, Alabama, which he built into a major centre of education for black Americans. The foremost black leader in the late 19th century, he encouraged black citizens to focus on economic equality rather than fight for social or political equality. He was strongly criticized by the civil rights activist William Du Bois, and his policies were repudiated by the 20th-century civil rights movement. He is the author of *Up from Slavery* (1901). This – with its less well-known predecessor *The Story of My Life and Work* (1900) – is one of the classic American life-stories, recalling in vivid detail the hardships and racial hatreds of the South.

'Cast down your bucket'

18 September 1895, Atlanta, Georgia, USA

The 1895 Cotton States and International Exposition was part of a long-term plan to boost the economy of the southern states following the devastating Civil War. A public showcase for technological innovations, it was held at what is now Piedmont Park in Atlanta.

Booker T Washington was enlisted as one of the keynote speakers. This was a bold move, since the audience was predominantly white, but the organizers believed visitors would welcome evidence of progress on racial issues. His address, delivered on the Exposition's opening day, was received more enthusiastically by whites than blacks, and became known as the 'Atlanta Compromise'.

Building his speech on a parable about travellers cast adrift at sea and desperate for water, Washington urges black Americans not to ignore the opportunities presented to them. He encourages them to accept labouring work in agriculture and industry rather than seeking more exalted positions in society. Conversely, he urges white employers to hire black workers, rather than promoting the immigration of whites from other countries.

His speech calls for consideration and co-operation from white people, but dismisses the notion of social equality between the races as extremist folly. This was significantly at odds with the rebellious cry of 'Agitate, agitate, agitate!' delivered by FREDERICK DOUGLASS seven months earlier, on the last day of his life.

Under the patronage of the millionaire industrialist Henry Huttleston Rogers, Washington became a popular public figure, campaigning widely for co-operation between black and white Americans. But many black activists labelled him an 'accommodator' and never forgave him.

> Mr President and gentlemen of the Board of Directors and citizens: one-third of the population of the South is of the negro race. No enterprise seeking the material, civil or moral welfare of this section can disregard this element of our population and reach the highest success. I but convey to you, Mr President and Directors, the sentiment of the masses of my race when I say that in no way have the value and manhood of the American negro been more fittingly and generously recognized than by the managers of this magnificent exposition, at every stage of its progress. It is a recognition that will do more to cement the friendship of the two races than any occurrence since the dawn of our freedom.
>
> Not only this, but the opportunity here afforded will awaken among us a new era of industrial progress. Ignorant and inexperienced, it is not strange that in the first years of our new life we began at the top instead of at the bottom; that a seat in Congress or the state legislature was more sought than real estate or industrial skill; that the political convention or stump speaking had more attractions than starting a dairy farm or truck garden.
>
> A ship lost at sea for many days suddenly sighted a friendly vessel. From the mast of the unfortunate vessel was seen a signal, 'Water, water; we die of thirst!' The answer from the friendly vessel at once came back, 'Cast

down your bucket where you are.'

A second time the signal, 'Water, water; send us water!' ran up from the distressed vessel, and was answered, 'Cast down your bucket where you are.' And a third and fourth signal for water was answered, 'Cast down your bucket where you are.' The captain of the distressed vessel, at last heeding the injunction, cast down his bucket, and it came up full of fresh, sparkling water from the mouth of the Amazon River.

To those of my race who depend on bettering their condition in a foreign land or who underestimate the importance of cultivating friendly relations with the southern white man, who is their next-door neighbour, I would say: 'Cast down your bucket where you are' – cast it down in making friends in every manly way of the people of all races by whom we are surrounded.

Cast it down in agriculture, mechanics, in commerce, in domestic service and in the professions. And in this connection, it is well to bear in mind that whatever other sins the South may be called to bear, when it comes to business, pure and simple, it is in the South that the negro is given a man's chance in the commercial world, and in nothing is this exposition more eloquent than in emphasizing this chance.

Our greatest danger is that in the great leap from slavery to freedom we may overlook the fact that the masses of us are to live by the productions of our hands, and fail to keep in mind that we shall prosper in proportion as we learn to dignify and glorify common labour, and put brains and skill into the common occupations of life; shall prosper in proportion as we learn to draw the line between the superficial and the substantial, the ornamental gewgaws of life and the useful. No race can prosper till it learns that there is as much dignity in tilling a field as in writing a poem. It is at the bottom of life we must begin, and not at the top. Nor should we permit our grievances to overshadow our opportunities.

To those of the white race – who look to the incoming of those of foreign birth and strange tongue and habits for the prosperity of the South – were I permitted I would repeat what I say to my own race, 'Cast down your bucket where you are.' Cast it down among the eight millions of negroes whose habits you know, whose fidelity and love you have tested in days when to have proved treacherous meant the ruin of your firesides. Cast down your bucket among these people who have, without strikes and labour wars, tilled your fields, cleared your forests, builded your railroads and cities, and brought forth treasures from the bowels of the earth, and helped make possible this magnificent representation of the progress of the South.[1]

Casting down your bucket among my people, helping and encouraging them – as you are doing on these grounds, with education of head, hand and heart – and you will find that they will buy your surplus land, make blossom the waste places in your fields and run your factories. While doing this, you can be sure in the future, as in the past, that you and your families will be surrounded by the most patient, faithful, law-abiding and unresentful people that the world has seen.

As we have proved our loyalty to you in the past, in nursing your children, watching by the sick-bed of your mothers and fathers, and often following them with tear-dimmed eyes to their graves, so in the future, in our humble way, we shall stand by you with a devotion that no foreigner can approach, ready to lay down our lives, if need be, in defence of yours, interlacing our industrial, commercial, civil and religious life with yours in a way that shall

[1] Washington refers to the technological innovations in agriculture, manufacturing, mining and transport displayed at the Exposition.

make the interests of both races one. In all things that are purely social, we can be as separate as the fingers, yet one as the hand in all things essential to mutual progress.

There is no defence or security for any of us except in the highest intelligence and development of all. If anywhere there are efforts tending to curtail the fullest growth of the negro, let these efforts be turned into stimulating, encouraging and making him the most useful and intelligent citizen. Effort or means so invested will pay 1,000 per cent interest. These efforts will be twice blessed – blessing him that gives and him that takes.

There is no escape through law of man or God from the inevitable:

[2] Washington quotes from a poem by the Quaker poet and abolitionist John Greenleaf Whittier (1807–92).

'The laws of changeless justice bind / Oppressor with oppressed; / And close as sin and suffering joined / We march to fate abreast.'[2]

Nearly 16 millions of hands will aid you in pulling the load upward, or they will pull against you the load downward. We shall constitute one-third and more of the ignorance and crime of the South, or one-third its intelligence and progress; we shall contribute one-third to the business and industrial prosperity of the South, or we shall prove a veritable body of death, stagnating, depressing, retarding every effort to advance the body politic.

Gentlemen of the exposition, as we present to you our humble effort at an exhibition of our progress, you must not expect overmuch. Starting 30 years ago[3] with ownership here and there in a few quilts and pumpkins and chickens (gathered from miscellaneous sources), remember the path that has led from these to the inventions and production of agricultural implements, buggies, steam-engines, newspapers, books, statuary, carving, paintings, the management of drug stores and banks, has not been trodden without contact with thorns and thistles.

[3] The Emancipation Proclamation, declared by President ABRAHAM LINCOLN, took effect on 1 January 1863. It emancipated slaves in the southern states of the Confederacy, but could only be applied in those states after the Civil War ended in April 1865.

While we take pride in what we exhibit as a result of our independent efforts, we do not for a moment forget that our part in this exhibition would fall far short of your expectations but for the constant help that has come to our educational life, not only from the southern states, but especially from northern philanthropists, who have made their gifts a constant stream of blessing and encouragement.

The wisest among my race understand that the agitation of questions of social equality is the extremist folly; and that progress in the enjoyment of all the privileges that will come to us must be the result of severe and constant struggle rather than of artificial forcing. No race that has anything to contribute to the markets of the world is long in any degree ostracized. It is important and right that all privileges of the law be ours, but it is vastly more important that we be prepared for the exercise of these privileges. The opportunity to earn a dollar in a factory just now is worth infinitely more than the opportunity to spend a dollar in an opera-house.

In conclusion, may I repeat that nothing in 30 years has given us more hope and encouragement, and drawn us so near to you of the white race, as this opportunity offered by the exposition; and here – bending, as it were, over the altar that represents the results of the struggles of your race and mine, both starting practically empty-handed three decades ago – I pledge that in your effort to work out the great and intricate problem which God has laid at the doors of the South, you shall have at all times the patient, sympathetic help of my race.

Only let this be constantly in mind: that while from representations in these buildings of the product of field, of forest, of mine, of factory, letters, and art, much good will come, yet far above and beyond material benefits will be that higher good that – let us pray God – will come in a blotting-out of sectional differences and racial animosities and suspicions; in a determination to administer absolute justice; in a willing obedience among all classes to the mandates of law. This, coupled with our material prosperity, will bring into our beloved South a new heaven and a new earth.

George Washington
American soldier and statesman

George Washington (1732–99) was born in Bridges Creek, Virginia, to a wealthy family. However, his father died while George was still a boy, leaving a large family and inadequate means. The story of his confession to cutting down a tree is probably the invention of his biographer, Mason Weems. In 1747 George went to Mount Vernon to live with his half-brother, Lawrence, who had received most of the Washington property. He worked as a surveyor, learned to hunt and studied military strategy. After the death of Lawrence (1752) and then his family, George inherited the estate and joined the local militia. In 1754, he became a lieutenant colonel and drove the French out of Fort Duquesne, though he was later besieged and forced to surrender. In 1755, the British general Edward Braddock was killed at Fort Duquesne. Washington saved the British remnant and became commander of the Virginia forces (1756). In 1759 he married a rich widow, Martha Custis (1732–1802), becoming one of the wealthiest men in the country. He entertained liberally, hunted, farmed successfully and entered politics, representing his county in the House of Burgesses. He became interested in the dispute of the colonies with the British Crown, and represented Virginia in the Continental Congresses of 1774 and 1775. He became commander-in-chief of the Continental Army (1775) and launched an ambitious programme of recruitment and training. During the War of Independence, his poorly-armed men trapped a well-equipped British army in Boston and forced their evacuation (1776). Following reverses in the New York area, Washington retreated through New Jersey, winning victories at Trenton and Princeton (1777). He suffered further reverses at Brandywine and Germantown, but sustained his army through the winter of 1777–8. The French entered the war in 1778, and with their assistance, Washington won victory at Yorktown in 1781, virtually ending the war. In 1783, he retired to Mount Vernon, seeking to secure a government by constitutional means. In 1787, he presided over the convention at Philadelphia which formulated the US Constitution; and the government was established in 1789 with Washington as president. He appointed THOMAS JEFFERSON and Alexander Hamilton as Secretary of State and Treasury Secretary respectively. In 1793, he was elected to a second term, but by now differences had developed between Jefferson's Democratic Republicans and Hamilton's Federalists. Washington favoured the Federalists; in the face of fierce personal attacks from the Republicans he retired in 1797. He died at Mount Vernon.

'This transcendent proof of the confidence of my fellow-citizens'
30 April 1789, New York City, USA

Washington had hoped for a peaceful retirement on his plantation at Mount Vernon, but once the new Constitution had been ratified in 1788, he was unanimously elected to serve as the first president of the USA. He was a popular figure, and all along the route from his home to New York City, he found himself fêted and cheered. After he had reached New Jersey and boarded the launch which would row him to Manhattan island, a Spanish royal packet-boat, which happened to be in harbour, fired a 13-gun salute (one for each of the newly united states). The battery on the island replied, repeating the salute with a 13-gun volley of its own.

Congress spent a week deciding how to conduct the inauguration, which was eventually held in a private session of the Senate. There were no precedents, either for the ceremony or for the duties of the office. Eyewitness accounts describe Washington as a very nervous speaker who would prefer to face a cannon than a room full of expectant representatives. In the event, his address was brief and practical, though he refers in it to his 'conflict of emotions'.

The natural diffidence exhibited here would occasionally be mistaken for self-aggrandizement; and Washington himself recognized the importance of separating the man from the office. He entertained all his congressional colleagues on a rota basis (and was respected for his excellent table) but greeted official guests dressed in black velvet, standing on a dais and wearing a sword. He did not shake hands.

Fellow-citizens of the Senate and of the House of Representatives: among the vicissitudes incident to life, no event could have filled me with greater anxieties than that of which the notification was transmitted by your order, and received on the 14th day of the present month.

On the one hand, I was summoned by my country, whose voice I can never hear but with veneration and love, from a retreat which I had chosen with the fondest predilection, and, in my flattering hopes, with an immutable decision, as the asylum of my declining years[1] – a retreat which

[1] Washington was 57 at this time.

917

was rendered every day more necessary as well as more dear to me by the addition of habit to inclination, and of frequent interruptions in my health to the gradual waste committed on it by time.

On the other hand, the magnitude and difficulty of the trust to which the voice of my country called me, being sufficient to awaken in the wisest and most experienced of her citizens a distrustful scrutiny into his qualifications, could not but overwhelm with despondence one who (inheriting inferior endowments from nature and unpractised in the duties of civil administration) ought to be peculiarly conscious of his own deficiencies.

In this conflict of emotions, all I dare aver is that it has been my faithful study to collect my duty from a just appreciation of every circumstance by which it might be affected. All I dare hope is that if, in executing this task, I have been too much swayed by a grateful remembrance of former instances, or by an affectionate sensibility to this transcendent proof of the confidence of my fellow-citizens, and have thence too little consulted my incapacity as well as disinclination for the weighty and untried cares before me, my error will be palliated by the motives which mislead me, and its consequences be judged by my country with some share of the partiality in which they originated.

Such being the impressions under which I have, in obedience to the public summons, repaired to the present station, it would be peculiarly improper to omit in this first official act my fervent supplications to that Almighty Being who rules over the universe, who presides in the councils of nations, and whose providential aids can supply every human defect, that his benediction may consecrate to the liberties and happiness of the people of the United States a government instituted by themselves for these essential purposes, and may enable every instrument employed in its administration to execute with success the functions allotted to his charge. In tendering this homage to the Great Author of every public and private good, I assure myself that it expresses your sentiments not less than my own, nor those of my fellow-citizens at large less than either.

No people can be bound to acknowledge and adore the Invisible Hand which conducts the affairs of men more than those of the United States. Every step by which they have advanced to the character of an independent nation seems to have been distinguished by some token of providential agency; and in the important revolution just accomplished in the system of their united government, the tranquil deliberations and voluntary consent of so many distinct communities from which the event has resulted cannot be compared with the means by which most governments have been established without some return of pious gratitude, along with an humble anticipation of the future blessings which the past seems to presage. These reflections, arising out of the present crisis, have forced themselves too strongly on my mind to be suppressed. You will join with me, I trust, in thinking that there are none under the influence of which the proceedings of a new and free government can more auspiciously commence.

By the article establishing the executive department it is made the duty of the president 'to recommend to your consideration such measures as he shall judge necessary and expedient'. The circumstances under which I now meet you will acquit me from entering into that subject further than to refer to the great constitutional charter under which you are assembled, and which, in defining your powers, designates the objects to which your attention is to be given. It will be more consistent with those circumstances – and far more congenial with the feelings which actuate me – to substitute, in place of a recommendation of particular measures, the tribute that is due to the talents, the rectitude and the patriotism which adorn the characters selected to devise and adopt them.

In these honourable qualifications, I behold the surest pledges that, as on one side no local prejudices or attachments, no separate views nor party animosities, will misdirect the comprehensive and equal eye which ought to watch over this great assemblage of communities and interests, so, on another, that the foundation of our national policy will be laid in the pure and immutable principles of private morality, and the pre-eminence of free government be exemplified by all the attributes which can win the affections of its citizens and command the respect of the world.

I dwell on this prospect with every satisfaction which an ardent love for my country can inspire, since there is no truth more thoroughly established than that there exists in the economy and course of nature an indissoluble union between virtue and happiness; between duty and advantage; between the genuine maxims of an honest and magnanimous policy and the solid rewards of public prosperity and felicity; since we ought to be no less persuaded that the propitious smiles of Heaven can never be expected on a nation that disregards the eternal rules of order and right which Heaven itself has ordained; and since the preservation of the sacred fire of liberty and the destiny of the republican model of government are justly considered, perhaps, as deeply, as finally, staked on the experiment entrusted to the hands of the American people.

Besides the ordinary objects submitted to your care, it will remain with your judgement to decide how far an exercise of the occasional power delegated by the fifth article of the Constitution[2] is rendered expedient at the present juncture by the nature of objections which have been urged against the system, or by the degree of inquietude which has given birth to them. Instead of undertaking particular recommendations on this subject, in which I could be guided by no lights derived from official opportunities, I shall again give way to my entire confidence in your discernment and pursuit of the public good; for I assure myself that – whilst you carefully avoid every alteration which might endanger the benefits of an united and effective government, or which ought to await the future lessons of experience – a reverence for the characteristic rights of freemen and a regard for the public harmony will sufficiently influence your deliberations on the question how far the former can be impregnably fortified or the latter be safely and advantageously promoted.

To the foregoing observations I have one to add, which will be most properly addressed to the House of Representatives. It concerns myself and will therefore be as brief as possible. When I was first honoured with a call into the service of my country, then on the eve of an arduous struggle for its liberties, the light in which I contemplated my duty required that I should renounce every pecuniary compensation. From this resolution I have in no instance departed; and being still under the impressions which produced it, I must decline as inapplicable to myself any share in the personal emoluments which may be indispensably included in a permanent provision for the executive department, and must accordingly pray that the pecuniary estimates for the station in which I am placed may, during my continuance in it, be limited to such actual expenditures as the public good may be thought to require.[3]

[2] The fifth article allows for amendments to the Constitution, 'whenever two-thirds of both houses shall deem it necessary'.

[3] Congress had offered a salary of $25,000, which Washington, a wealthy man, declined to accept.

> Having thus imparted to you my sentiments as they have been awakened by the occasion which brings us together, I shall take my present leave; but not without resorting once more to the benign Parent of the Human Race in humble supplication that, since he has been pleased to favour the American people with opportunities for deliberating in perfect tranquillity, and dispositions for deciding with unparalleled unanimity on a form of government for the security of their union and the advancement of their happiness, so his divine blessing may be equally conspicuous in the enlarged views, the temperate consultations and the wise measures on which the success of this government must depend.

'I am again called upon by the voice of my country'
4 March 1793, Philadelphia, Pennsylvania, USA

Washington's period in office set the tone for the US presidency for many years to come. His pioneering first term demanded a plethora of decisions, both major and minor. The agenda included the appointment of executive posts and the Supreme Court; legislation over coinage, slavery and treatment of the native population; the establishment of the US Navy; and decisions concerning the establishment of a new capital city on the Potomac river, which would later bear his name.

He was very reluctant to stand in the second presidential election of 1792, and only agreed after much persuasion from both main factions in Congress. Although not without ambition, he was a modest man. Furthermore, his wife Martha resented his appointment to the presidency, and had refused to attend his first inauguration. He was, however, elected unanimously.

The appointment of a vice president was less easily determined. The post was awarded to the man receiving the next highest number of votes, which proved to be John Adams, a Federalist. This placed the party in a very strong position: although Washington tried to stay above political wrangling, he favoured the strong central government promoted by the Federalists.

The second inaugural ceremony took place in Philadelphia, the temporary capital, before a small group of Congressmen, judges and townspeople. A reluctant public speaker, Washington made the shortest inaugural speech ever given.

> Fellow-citizens: I am again called upon by the voice of my country to execute the functions of its Chief Magistrate.[1] When the occasion proper for it shall arrive, I shall endeavour to express the high sense I entertain of this distinguished honour, and of the confidence which has been reposed in me by the people of united America.
>
> Previous to the execution of any official act of the president, the Constitution requires an oath of office. This oath I am now about to take, and in your presence: that if it shall be found during my administration of the government I have in any instance violated willingly or knowingly the injunctions thereof, I may (besides incurring constitutional punishment) be subject to the upbraidings of all who are now witnesses of the present solemn ceremony.

[1] An early title given to the US president.

'The disinterested warnings of a parting friend'
19 September 1796, Philadelphia, Pennsylvania, USA

Washington's decision not to stand for a third term set a precedent that stood until FRANKLIN D ROOSEVELT was re-elected for third and fourth terms in 1940 and 1944. The limitation of a presidency to two terms was enshrined in law by the 22nd Amendment to the Constitution (1951).

When Washington came to announce his retirement, he sought help in drafting his speech from two other 'Founding Fathers', James Madison and Alexander Hamilton, the latter the quintessential Federalist. Together, they attempted for the first time to define what it meant to be an American. The speech they composed serves as a caution against internal factionalism and entanglements in foreign wars – an attitude which would in time harden into a more isolationist stance not intended by the speaker.

The presidential election that followed was the first to be truly contested, and the peaceful handing of power from Washington to his former vice president John Adams marked an important coming-of-age for the new republic. As in so much else, Washington set the tone for the behaviour of a president. He refused to retire from the room when Adams was sworn in, emphasizing that, as a former president, he was now merely a citizen.

The farewell address was published around the country. Extracts found their way into embroidery patterns and children's textbooks, and were even engraved on watches. For decades afterwards, it was read out annually in Congress.

❧

Friends and fellow-citizens: the period for a new election of a citizen to administer the executive government of the United States being not far distant, and the time actually arrived when our thoughts must be employed in designating the person who is to be clothed with that important trust, it appears to me proper, especially as it may conduce to a more distinct expression of the public voice, that I should now apprise you of the resolution I have formed to decline being considered among the number of those out of whom a choice is to be made.

I beg you, at the same time, to do me the justice to be assured that this resolution has not been taken without regard to all the considerations appertaining to the relation which binds a dutiful citizen to his country; and that, in withdrawing the tender of service which silence in my situation might imply, I am influenced by no diminution of zeal for your future interest, no deficiency of grateful respect for your past kindness; but am supported by a full conviction that the step is compatible with both …

In looking forward to the moment which is intended to terminate the career of my public life, my feelings do not permit me to suspend the deep acknowledgement of that debt of gratitude which I owe to my beloved country for the many honours it has conferred upon me; still more for the steadfast confidence with which it has supported me, and for the opportunities I have thence enjoyed of manifesting my inviolable attachment by services, faithful and persevering, though in usefulness unequal to my zeal.

If benefits have resulted to our country from these services, let it always be remembered to your praise, and as an instructive example in our annals, that under circumstances in which the passions, agitated in every direction, were liable to mislead; amidst appearances sometimes dubious, vicissitudes of fortune often discouraging; in situations in which not unfrequently want of success has countenanced the spirit of criticism, the constancy of your support was the essential prop of the efforts and a guarantee of the plans by which they were effected.

Profoundly penetrated with this idea, I shall carry it with me to my grave, as a strong incitement to unceasing wishes that Heaven may continue to you the choicest tokens of its beneficence; that your union and brotherly affection may be perpetual; that the free Constitution which is the work of your hands may be sacredly maintained; that its administration in every department may be stamped with wisdom and virtue; that, in fine, the happiness of the people of these states, under the auspices of liberty, may be made complete by so careful a preservation and so prudent a use of this blessing as will acquire to them the glory of recommending it to the applause, the affection and adoption of every nation which is yet a stranger to it.

Here, perhaps, I ought to stop. But a solicitude for your welfare, which cannot end but with my life, and the apprehension of danger, natural to that solicitude, urge me, on an occasion like the present, to offer to your solemn contemplation and to recommend to your frequent review, some sentiments, which are the result of much reflection, of no inconsiderable observation, and which appear to me all-important to the permanency of your felicity as a people. These will be offered to you with the more freedom, as you can only see in them the disinterested warnings of a parting friend, who can possibly have no personal motives to bias his counsel …

Interwoven as is the love of liberty with every ligament of your hearts, no recommendation of mine is necessary to fortify or confirm the attachment. The unity of government which constitutes you one people is also now dear to you. It is justly so; for it is a main pillar in the edifice of your real independence, the support of your tranquillity at home, your peace abroad, of your safety, of your prosperity, of that very liberty which you so highly prize.

But as it is easy to foresee that from different causes and from different quarters much pains will be taken, many artifices employed, to weaken in your minds the conviction of this truth; as this is the point of your political fortress against which the batteries of internal and external enemies will be most constantly and actively – though often covertly and insidiously – directed, it is of infinite moment that you should properly estimate the immense value of your national union to your collective and individual happiness; that you should cherish a cordial, habitual and immovable attachment to it; accustoming yourselves to think and speak of it as of the palladium of your political safety and prosperity,[1] watching for its preservation with jealous anxiety; discountenancing whatever may suggest even a suspicion that it can in any event be abandoned; and indignantly frowning upon the first dawning of every attempt to alienate any portion of our country from the rest, or to enfeeble the sacred ties which now link together the various parts …

To the efficacy and permanency of your Union, a government for the whole is indispensable. No alliances, however strict, between the parts can be an adequate substitute; they must inevitably experience the infractions and interruptions which alliances in all times have experienced. Sensible of this momentous truth, you have improved upon your first essay by the adoption of a Constitution of government better calculated than your former for an intimate union and for the efficacious management of your common concerns.

This government, the offspring of our own choice, uninfluenced and unawed, adopted upon full investigation and mature deliberation, completely free in its principles, in the distribution of its powers, uniting security with energy, and containing within itself a provision for its own amendment, has a just claim to your confidence and your support. Respect for its authority, compliance with its laws, acquiescence in its measures, are duties enjoined by the fundamental maxims of true liberty …

Remember especially that for the efficient management of your common interests, in a country so extensive as ours, a government of as much vigour as is consistent with the perfect security of liberty is indispensable. Liberty itself will find in such a government, with powers properly distributed and adjusted, its surest guardian. It is, indeed, little else than a name where the government is too feeble to withstand the enterprises of faction, to confine each member of society within the limits

[1] In Greek mythology, the Palladium was a Trojan shrine to the goddess Athena, which had the power to safeguard the city where it was kept. When laying siege to Troy, the Greek warriors Odysseus and Diomed stole the statue, rendering the city vulnerable.

prescribed by the laws, and to maintain all in the secure and tranquil enjoyment of the rights of person and property …

Let me now take a more comprehensive view, and warn you, in the most solemn manner, against the baneful effects of the spirit of party generally. This spirit, unfortunately, is inseparable from our nature, having its root in the strongest passions of the human mind. It exists under different shapes in all governments, more or less stifled, controlled, or repressed. But in those of the popular form it is seen in its greatest rankness, and is truly their worst enemy.

The alternate domination of one faction over another, sharpened by the spirit of revenge, natural to party dissensions, which, in different ages and countries, has perpetrated the most horrid enormities, is itself a frightful despotism. But this leads at length to a more formal and permanent despotism. The disorders and miseries which result gradually incline the minds of men to seek security and repose in the absolute power of an individual; and, sooner or later, the chief of some prevailing faction, more able or more fortunate than his competitors, turns this disposition to the purposes of his own elevation on the ruins of public liberty.

Without looking forward to an extremity of this kind (which, nevertheless, ought not to be entirely out of sight) the common and continual mischiefs of the spirit of party are sufficient to make it the interest and duty of a wise people to discourage and restrain it.

It serves always to distract the public councils and enfeeble the public administration. It agitates the community with ill-founded jealousies and false alarms; kindles the animosity of one part against another; foments occasionally riot and insurrection. It opens the door to foreign influence and corruption, which finds a facilitated access to the government itself through the channel of party passion. Thus the policy and the will of one country are subjected to the policy and will of another.

There is an opinion that parties, in free countries, are useful checks upon the administration of the government, and serve to keep alive the spirit of liberty. This, within certain limits, is probably true; and in governments of a monarchical cast, patriotism may look with indulgence, if not with favour, upon the spirit of party. But in those of popular character, in governments purely elective, it is a spirit not to be encouraged. From their natural tendency, it is certain there will always be enough of that spirit for every salutary purpose. And, there being constant danger of excess, the effort ought to be, by force of public opinion, to mitigate and assuage it. A fire not to be quenched, it demands a uniform vigilance to prevent its bursting into a flame, lest, instead of warming, it should consume …

Of all the dispositions and habits which lead to political prosperity, religion and morality are indispensable supports. In vain would that man claim the tribute of patriotism who should labour to subvert these great pillars of human happiness, these firmest props of the destinies of men and citizens … Let us with caution indulge the supposition that morality can be maintained without religion. Whatever may be conceded to the influence of refined education on minds of peculiar structure, reason and experience both forbid us to expect that natural morality can prevail in exclusion of religious principles …

Observe good faith and justice towards all nations; cultivate peace and harmony with all: religion and morality enjoin this conduct; and can it be that good policy does not equally enjoin it? It will be worthy of a free, enlightened, and, at no distant period, a great nation to give to mankind the magnanimous and too novel example of a people always guided by an exalted justice and benevolence …

In the execution of such a plan, nothing is more essential than that permanent, inveterate antipathies against particular nations, and passionate attachments for others, should be excluded; and that, in place of them, just and amicable feelings towards all should be cultivated. The nation which indulges towards another an habitual hatred, or an habitual fondness, is in some degree a slave. It is a slave to its animosity or to its affection, either of which is sufficient to lead it astray from its duty and its interest. Antipathy in one nation against another disposes each more readily to offer insult and injury, to lay hold of slight causes of umbrage, and to be haughty and intractable when accidental or trifling occasions of dispute occur. Hence frequent collisions, obstinate, envenomed and bloody contests …

Harmony and a liberal intercourse with all nations are recommended by policy, humanity and interest. But even our commercial policy should hold an equal and impartial hand; neither seeking nor granting exclusive favours or preferences; consulting the natural course of things; diffusing and diversifying, by gentle means, the streams of commerce, but forcing nothing; establishing, with powers so disposed, in order to give trade a stable course, to define the rights of our merchants, and to enable the government to support them, conventional rules of intercourse, the best that present circumstances and mutual opinion will permit, but temporary, and liable to be, from time to time, abandoned or varied, as experience and circumstances shall dictate …

In offering to you, my countrymen, these counsels of an old and affectionate friend, I dare not hope they will make the strong and lasting impression I could wish – that they will control the usual current of the passions, or prevent our nation from running the course which has hitherto marked the destiny of nations. But if I may even flatter myself that they may be productive of some partial benefit, some occasional good – that they may now and then recur to moderate the fury of party spirit; to warn against the mischief of foreign intrigues; to guard against the impostures of pretended patriotism – this hope will be a full recompense for the solicitude for your welfare by which they have been dictated.

How far, in the discharge of my official duties, I have been guided by the principles which have been delineated, the public records and other evidences of my conduct must witness to you and to the world. To myself, the assurance of my own conscience is that I have at least believed myself to be guided by them.

The Duke of Wellington
Anglo-Irish soldier and statesman

Arthur Wellesley *originally Arthur Wesley, later 1st Duke of Wellington* (1769–1852) was born in Dublin, the son of an Irish peer. He studied at Eton and Brussels, and at a military school at Angers, changing his name to Wellesley in 1798. After joining the army, he served as aide-de-camp to two Lord Lieutenants of Ireland. He was also Member for Trim in the Irish parliament (1790–5). His brother bought him command of the 33rd Foot, and he campaigned with it in Holland in 1794. In 1797 he was sent to India, where he participated in the Seringapatam expedition, becoming administrator of the conquered territory. His campaigns resulted in the capture of Poona (1803), the breaking of Maratha power and final victory at Argaum (1803). On returning home he was knighted (1805). He became MP for Rye (1806–9), and was appointed Irish Secretary in 1807. He was released from his parliamentary duties to accompany the Copenhagen expedition the same year, and defeated the Danes at Sjaelland. In 1808 he was sent to help the Portuguese against the French in the Peninsular War. After victory at Talavera (1809), he was elevated to the peerage as Viscount Wellington. Salamanca (1812) was a decisive victory and ultimately the French were driven out of Spain and defeated at Toulouse (1814). Created Duke of Wellington in 1814, he became ambassador to Louis XVIII, the restored king of France. After NAPOLEON's escape from Elba, Wellington took command of the force mustered to oppose him. Two days after Napoleon defeated Blücher at Ligny, Wellington routed the French at Waterloo (June 1815). He became commander-in-chief during the occupation of France (1815–18). In 1818 he returned to politics, becoming Master-General of the Ordnance. In 1826 he was made Constable of the Tower, and in 1827 commander-in-chief. In 1827 he resigned over GEORGE CANNING's foreign policy, but with Canning's death in 1827 and the collapse of the Goderich administration, Wellington became prime minister (1828–30). In 1829 he assisted in Robert Peel's reorganization of the Metropolitan Police. His opposition to the enlargement of the franchise brought widespread unpopularity. In 1834 Wellington again formed a government, and in Peel's temporary absence abroad he acted for all the secretaries of state. With Peel's return to power in 1841 Wellington joined his Cabinet. He retired from public life in 1846. He was appointed Lord High Constable of England, and in 1848 organized the military in London against the Chartists.

'If this democratic assembly should once be established in England'
4 October 1831, London, England

The broadening of the parliamentary franchise was an issue that dominated mid-19th century politics in Britain, but Wellington might be said to have had a particular personal interest in opposing it on this occasion. A few months earlier, his outspoken antipathy to extending the vote had led to protests at his London home, Apsley House, during which windows were broken by an angry mob. His nickname, the Iron Duke, came not from his final victory over Napoleon, but from the iron shutters he installed to protect his home after this event. By this time, Wellington's universal acclaim following the victory over France had long since dissipated, to be replaced by quiet resentment of what were judged to be narrow-minded policies, even among some fellow Tories.

In this speech to the House of Lords – and elsewhere – Wellington insisted on conserving what had been established by precedent in the parliamentary system. This led to the label Conservative Party being applied to his faction, a name that would stick.

For all his efforts, the bill was passed. Of the waverers who had eventually voted for it, Wellington wrote, 'They have ruined themselves and us'.

[1] The English politician George Finch-Hatton, 10th Earl of Winchelsea (1791–1858), who in March 1829 had fought a duel with Wellington over the latter's support for Catholic emancipation. Neither man was harmed.

A noble Earl who has spoken on this side of the House[1] has made an observation to your Lordships, which well deserves your attention. The noble Earl has told you that if you increase but a little the democratic power in the state, the step can never be withdrawn. Your Lordships must continue in the same course till you have passed through the miseries of a revolution, and thence to a military despotism and the evils which attend that system of government. It is not denied that this bill must increase beyond measure the democratic power of the state; that it must constitute in the House of Commons a fierce democracy: what must be the consequences, your Lordships will judge.

I will not detain your Lordships by adverting to the merits of the system of government which has existed up to the present moment, upon which my opinion is by no means altered. No man denies that we have enjoyed great advantages; that we have enjoyed a larger share of happiness, comfort and prosperity, for a long course of years, than were ever enjoyed by any nation; that we have more riches, the largest fortunes, personal as well as real, more manufactures and commerce, than all the nations of Europe taken together; the richest, most extensive, most peopled, and most prosperous foreign colonies and possessions, that any nation ever possessed. There is not an important position in the world, whether for the purpose of navigation, commerce, or military defence, that does not belong to us.

If this democratic assembly should once be established in England, does anyone believe that we should continue to enjoy these vast advantages? But a democracy has never been established in any part of the world that it has not immediately declared war against property, against the payment of the public debt and against all the principles of conservation, which are secured by and are, in fact, the principal objects of the British constitution, as it now exists.

Property and its possessors will become the common enemy. I do not urge this argument as one in which your Lordships are peculiarly interested: it is not you alone, nor even other proprietors, who are interested in the protection of property; the whole people, middling classes as well as the lower orders, are interested in this subject. Look at the anxiety prevailing in every part of London, in respect to the great revolution to be made by this bill.

My noble friend the noble Baron[2] has been ridiculed for adverting to the opinions of tradesmen in Bond Street and St James's Street. Those in Bond Street consist of more than 200 respectable persons, who are well able to form an opinion of the effect of this bill upon the resources of themselves, the middling classes and the poor, as they supply the luxuries of persons in easier circumstances, residing in that quarter of the town. Anything which can affect the resources of their customers must be interesting to them, and they do feel that this bill must affect property, private expenditure and the resources of themselves and of those whom they employ.

A noble Lord on the other side, who adverted to this topic, greatly under-rated the wealth of these tradesmen. I know of one, residing in Bond Street, who employs at all times from 2,000 to 4,000 workmen, whose trade depends, as well as the employment of this body of people, upon the expenditure of his customers: is he not interested in upholding the public faith and the system of property now established in England? Are not the people, of all classes and descriptions, down to the lowest, interested in the maintenance of our extensive manufactures and commerce, in the conservation of our enormous dominions abroad, and the continued respect of all nations?

If I am right in thinking that this fierce democracy will be established in the House of Commons, does any man believe that that harmony can continue between the King and his government and the House of Commons — so necessary to insure to both general respect, and to the King's government the strength which is necessary to enable His Majesty to protect and keep in order his foreign dominions and to insure the obedience of their inhabitants? We shall lose these colonies and foreign possessions; and with them our authority and influence abroad.

There is no instance of any country having maintained its strength or its

[2] The English politician James Archibald Stuart-Wortley-Mackenzie, 1st Baron Wharncliffe (1776–1845), also a former soldier.

influence in its foreign possessions, or the respect of foreign nations, during the existence of internal troubles and disturbance; and there is no case of the existence, without such troubles, of a government consisting of king, Lords and Commons, independently of each other, and the members of the latter depending solely upon the popular choice and being delegates of the people.

We have had an example in England of a House of Commons which was independent of the influence of the Crown; and of this House, turning the spiritual Lords out of it, murdering their sovereign, and voting the House of Lords useless. I will read your Lordships the account given by a man, who was knowing in his time of what this House became.

'The parliament, which had so vigorously withstood the encroachments of the royal power, became themselves too desirous of absolute authority; and not only engrossed the legislative, but usurped the executive power.

'All causes, civil and criminal, all questions of property, were determined by committees, who, being themselves the legislature, were accountable to no law, and for that reason their decrees were arbitrary, and their proceedings violent. Oppression was without redress, unjust sentence without appeal; there was no prospect of ease or intermission. The parliament had determined never to dissolve themselves.

'At length the army interfered. They soon perceived that, unless they made one regulation more, and crushed this many-headed monster, they had hitherto ventured their lives to little purpose and had, instead of assuring their own and their country's liberty, only changed one kind of slavery for another.'

This is the account of the state of a House of Commons acting independently of all influence; and of the state to which it brought the country.

Charles Wesley
English clergyman and hymnwriter

Charles Wesley (1707–88) was born in Epworth, Lincolnshire, the younger brother of JOHN WESLEY. He studied at Christ Church College, Oxford, where in 1729 he formed a small group of fellow students, nicknamed 'The Oxford Methodists' or 'The Holy Club', later joined by his brother. Ordained in 1735, he accompanied John to the colony of Georgia in America, as secretary to Governor James Oglethorpe (1696–1785). He returned to England in 1736. He was the indefatigable lieutenant of his more famous brother. After an evangelical conversion in 1738, he wrote over 5,500 hymns, including 'Hark, the Herald Angels Sing', 'Love Divine, All Loves Excelling' and 'Jesu, Lover of my Soul'.

'In the tears of the righteous there is joy'
18 April 1736, Frederica, Georgia, America

In 1735, the Wesley brothers set sail for Georgia, where they were to act as pastors to the colonists and missionaries to the native population. However, the expedition was a failure, particularly from Charles's point of view. He had only recently been ordained – in all likelihood at his brother's insistence – and found his American experience physically and emotionally draining. This sermon on the spiritual rewards that result from temporal adversity must have seemed particularly relevant to his circumstances.

Some historians see Charles as little more than a prodigious hymn-writer, and a drag on his brother's efforts to establish Methodism. This eloquent and uplifting sermon suggests otherwise, however. Charles gave it at least twice in America and repeated it in England; like countless other sermons he gave, it moved congregations with its poetic language and clear message.

John succinctly captured the difference in preaching style – and character – between him and his brother when he said, 'In connexion [ie reasoned argument] I beat you; but in strong pointed sentences you beat me.'

Psalm 126:7 'He that now goeth on his way weeping, and bearing forth good seed, shall doubtless come again with joy, and bring his sheaves with him.'

Experience shows us that even they who are Christians indeed, who serve God with all their strength, may go on their way weeping, perhaps for many years, perhaps to the end of their lives. They are followers of him who was a man of sorrows and acquainted with grief. And if any man will come after him, he must deny himself and take up his cross. He must suffer with his master more or less; being, like him, to be made perfect through sufferings.

Indeed for this very cause are those sufferings sent to lead them to higher perfection. They go on their way weeping, that the good seed they bear forth may yield them the more fruit. And that good seed, even all those Christian virtues which are perfected by affliction shall in due time grow up into a plentiful harvest of rest and joy and life eternal.

The certainty of this great truth is pointed out to us by the very manner wherein it is revealed. Heaven and earth may, nay they must pass away; but not one tittle of this shall pass. As sure as God is, and as he is a rewarder of them that diligently seek him, so sure no one virtue of any follower of Christ shall in any wise lose its reward. Only let him bear forth this good seed unto the end and though he may now go on his way weeping, he shall doubtless come again with joy and bring his sheaves with him.

What I intend at present is briefly to explain how every virtue is the seed of joy eternal: a great truth, such as deserves your frequent thoughts and deepest consideration. The time indeed will not suffer me to consider now every particular Christian virtue, but only those general graces which we can never consider enough: humility and faith and hope and love. Yet this is almost the same thing; since these are the common root of all the particular virtues: none of which has any worth, nor in truth any being, unless it spring from these. It will therefore suffice to show, in few words, that each of these is the seed of joy; that every one of these graces, although when first sown it may be small as a grain of mustard seed, yet as it groweth up shooteth out great branches full of delight and blessedness.

This joy I therefore called eternal, because the holy scriptures assure us that it is the same in kind, though not in degree, with that we shall enjoy to eternity. For it should be well observed and always remembered, that Heaven is begun upon earth. And accordingly our saviour often means by 'the kingdom of Heaven' that temper of mind which a Christian now enjoys. He begins to enjoy it when he begins to be a Christian, when Christ begins to reign in his soul. And the more absolutely he reigns there, the more happiness he enjoys. For as all the poor in spirit, all that believe in God, all that trust in him, all that love him, are blessed; so the greater their humility, faith, hope and love, the greater is their blessedness. And thus as they go on from strength to strength, they go on from one measure of joy to another, till what was sown on earth be removed into a better soil, and grow up to perfection in Heaven …

Yet 'tis most true, as was before observed, that till that happy hour when God shall wipe away all tears from their eyes, even they who bear forth this seed of joy may go on their way weeping. They may, nay they must, endure affliction, for so did the captain of their salvation. But 'tis true that a Christian knows to rejoice not only after but even in tribulation. As in the laughter of the wicked, the heart is sorrowful, so in the tears of the righteous there is joy. He does not stay till his afflictions are overpassed, but in everything giveth thanks. Though he cannot but feel when he is in pain, yet in the midst of it, he can 'rejoice in the Lord'.

Let us now consider this great truth a little more particularly. The first of all Christian graces and the foundation of all is humility: a deep sense of our spiritual poverty, a feeling knowledge that we are nothing but sin and deserve nothing but shame. And a clear sight that we have nothing and can do nothing – no, not so much as think a good thought. And is such a virtue as this the seed of joy? Yea, as surely as it is the seed of all other virtues. As surely as it is contrary to pride, which is the seed of all torment.

No sooner does humility enter a soul, which before was all storm and tempest, but it says to that sea, 'Peace, be still', and there is a great calm. There is indeed in every branch of humility a sweetness which cannot be uttered. There is pain, 'tis true, in the entrance into it, but that very pain is full of pleasure. There is mourning joined with it; but even that mourning is blessedness; it is health to the soul, and marrow to the bones. It heals even while it wounds; it delights at the same time and in the same degree wherein it softens the heart. Humility not only removes all that pain and anguish with which pride drinks up the blood and spirits; it not only plants peace wherever it comes, and brings rest to the weary soul; but joy too and such joy as together with it increases more and more unto the perfect day.

Humility cannot but lead to faith: a sight of our disease makes us soon fly to the cure of it. Who can feel himself sick and not long to be made whole? What contrite sinner is not glad of a saviour? And he is the more glad, the more firmly he believes that he is able and willing to save to the uttermost; able to save all that believe, for he is God! And willing, for he is man! Here is joy! Joy which none can divide from faith! Joy unspeakable and full of glory!

God, the Lord God, Jehovah, God over all, the God to whom all things are possible, hath undertaken the cause of lost man! He hath promised, he hath sworn to save them! Nay, he hath done more than this: he hath bowed the heavens and come down: he hath been made man! He hath lived, suffered, died to save them! Yea, tell it out in all lands! God hath died! He hath died to save man! Let the heavens rejoice, and let the earth be glad. Publish ye, praise ye and say, this is the victory which overcometh the world, even our faith. If we can believe, all things are possible to him that believeth: to him it is easy, 'to rejoice evermore'! Yea, he cannot but rejoice in thy strength, O Lord Christ, and be exceeding glad of thy salvation!

Now if it be so joyful a thing to believe that Christ died to save sinners, what must it be to add to our faith hope? To be assured that he died to save us? If the knowing that a ransom is paid for lost man, and a new covenant of mercy given him, be the source of a peace which passeth all understanding, yea, of joy unspeakable, and full of glory, how does he rejoice, who feels within his own soul, that this ransom is paid for him? Whose heart assures him that he is within that covenant and shall find mercy even in the day of vengeance?

If the belief that all who are faithful servants of their great master have an house eternal in the heavens be a continual spring of gladness of heart; how shall not his heart sing for joy, with whom the spirit of God bears witness that he is faithful? Who can lay hold of those great and precious promises, and lay them close to his own soul! Whose eye God hath opened to look into eternity, and to take a view of those mansions of glory, into which he knows his blessed Lord is gone before, to prepare a place for him.

Such joy have all they that hope in God, and the stronger their hope, the greater their joy. But this is not all: for hope leads to love; and in the love of God joy is perfected. Very excellent things are spoken of the happiness that flows from loving God.

But whosoever has this love shed abroad in his heart feels more than can ever be spoken, yea though he spake with the tongue of men and angels, he could not utter the joy of charity. It is the hidden manna, the inexpressible sweetness, whereof none can know but he that tastes it … How is his soul satisfied, as it were, with marrow and fatness, when his mouth praiseth him with joyful lips! How does his joy still increase when he joins with the congregation of the faithful in prayer and praise and thanksgiving.

He needeth not the exhortations of man, no, nor even the *command* of God to drag him to the house of prayer. He needeth not to be assured that if he does forbear assembling himself with the people of God, as the manner of *most* is, he thereby breaks the communion of saints, he renounces the privileges of his baptism, he casts himself out of the congregation of faithful people; he excommunicates, or cuts himself off from the body of Christ, and that consequently Christ shall profit him nothing. No – on the contrary he is glad when they say unto him, 'Let us go unto the house of the Lord,'[1] but his joy overflows all bounds when in memory of him whom his soul loveth, he eateth the living bread which came down from Heaven, and drinketh the cup of salvation.

Lo: thus is the man blessed that feareth the Lord; that beareth forth good seed! These sheaves shall he bring home in this life, however he may now go on his way weeping! These are the first fruits which he shall receive, even here: but the harvest is not yet. He as yet knows and loves God only in part, therefore he as yet enjoys him in part only.

[1] Psalm 122:1.

But the hour is at hand when that which is perfect shall come and that which is in part be done away. Yet a little while and he shall come again with fullness of joy, to reap his entire harvest. Behold, one standeth at the door who will complete what he hath begun, who shall ripen the seeds of grace into glory; and instead of that dew of Heaven which now refreshes his soul, shall give him rivers of pleasures evermore!

John Wesley
English clergyman

John Wesley (1703–91) was born in Epworth, Lincolnshire, where his father was rector. He studied at Christ Church, Oxford, was ordained deacon in 1725 and priest in 1728, and in 1726 was appointed a Fellow of Lincoln College. He became the leader of a small, dedicated group which had gathered round his younger brother CHARLES WESLEY, nicknamed 'The Holy Club' or 'The Oxford Methodists'. John later adopted the word 'Methodism' for the great evangelical movement which developed from it. After their father's death in 1735, John and Charles went on a missionary voyage to Georgia, but they aroused the hostility of the colonists and returned to England. During a religious meeting, John heard a reading of MARTIN LUTHER's preface to the Epistle to the Romans, and experienced an assurance of salvation which he felt must be shared with others. His unwonted zeal alarmed most of the parish clergy, who closed their pulpits to him. He began preaching in the open air at Bristol (1739), where he also founded the first Methodist chapel. In London, he bought the ruined Foundry in Moorfields, which became his headquarters: Methodist anniversaries have sometimes been reckoned from this event. He spoke often to crowds of 10,000–30,000, giving strength to working-class neighbourhoods: most of his converts were colliers, miners, foundrymen, weavers and day-labourers. He travelled 250,000 miles and preached 40,000 sermons. He also founded the *Methodist Magazine* (1778) and achieved an enormous amount of literary work, including grammars, extracts from the classics, histories, abridged biographies, collections of psalms, hymns and tunes, his own sermons and journals. These proved popular, earning him £30,000, which he distributed in charity during his life. He founded charitable institutions at Newcastle and London, and Kingswood School in Bristol. Determined to remain loyal to the Church of England, he urged his followers to do the same. He always regarded Methodism as a movement within the Church and it remained so during his lifetime. In 1751 he married the widow Mary Vazeille, who deserted him in 1776.

'One thing is needful'
20 August 1764, Canterbury, England

In a speech given in November 1928, when he was prime minister, STANLEY BALDWIN had this to say about John Wesley: 'He was a true son of the 18th century: he disliked extravagance and fanaticism, he loathed sentimentality ... he was calm and cool, and preached without rhetorical exaggeration. Broadly speaking, the emotional appeal was conspicuous by its absence.'

In this characteristically level-headed sermon, John Wesley takes his text from Luke 10:42, warning his listeners to 're-exchange the image of Satan for the image of God' or face eternal darkness. The sermon, which he used on numerous occasions throughout his long preaching career, has a sombre, repetitive tone – designed to press home its message as firmly as possible. The image of men walking a 'narrow, weak, tottering bridge' between this world and the next echoes John Milton's epic poem *Paradise Lost*, written more than 100 years earlier.

Early Methodists met to worship out of doors or in each other's homes, but as their numbers grew they began to build meeting houses. One such building was the Round House or Pepper-Box Chapel in Canterbury, Kent, where Wesley's diary records that he gave this sermon.

In the tenth chapter of the Gospel according to St Luke, at the 42nd verse, it is thus written: 'One thing is needful'.

Could we suppose an intelligent being, entirely a stranger to the state of this world and its inhabitants, to take a view of their various enterprises and employments, and thence conjecture the end of their existence, he would surely conclude that these creatures were designed to be busied about many things. While he observed not only the infinite difference of the ends which different men were pursuing, but how vast a multitude of objects were successively pursued by almost every different person, he might fairly infer that for all these things were the sons of men placed upon the earth, even to gratify their several desires with sensual pleasure, or riches, or honour, or power.

How surprised then would he be to hear their Creator declare to all, without distinction, 'One thing is needful!'. But how much more when he knew that this one thing needful for men, their one business, the one end of their existence, was none of all those things which men were troubled about, none of all those ends they were pursuing, none of all those businesses wherein they were so deeply engaged, which filled their hearts and employed their hands. Nay, that it was an end not only distinct from but contrary to them all – as contrary as light and darkness, Heaven and Hell, the kingdom of God and that of Satan.

The only thought he could form in their favour must be, that they had a surplusage of time at their command; that they therefore trifled a few hours, because they were assured of thousands of years wherein to work. But how beyond measure would he be amazed when he heard farther that these were creatures of a day; that as they yesterday arose out of the dust, so tomorrow they were to sink into it again …

When he saw that all men were placed on a narrow, weak, tottering bridge, whereof either end was swallowed up in eternity; that the waves and storms which went over it were continually bearing away one after another, in an hour when they looked not for it; and that they who yet stood, knew not but they should plunge into the great gulf the very next instant, but well knew that if they fell before they had finished their work they were lost, destroyed, undone – forever: how would all utterance, nay, all thought, be lost! How would he express, how would he conceive the senselessness, the madness, of those creatures who, being in such a situation, could think of anything else, could talk of anything else, could do anything besides, could find time for any other design or care, but that of ensuring the one thing needful …

Now this great work, this one thing needful, is the renewal of our fallen nature. In the image of God was man made, but a little lower than the angels. His nature was perfect, angelical, divine. He was an incorruptible picture of the God of glory. He bore his stamp on every part of his soul; the brightness of his Creator shone mightily upon him. But sin hath now effaced the image of God. He is no longer nearly allied to angels. He is sunk lower than the very beasts of the field. His soul is not only earthly and sensual, but devilish. Thus is the mighty fallen! The glory is departed from him! His brightness is swallowed up in utter darkness!

From the glorious liberty wherein he was made, he is fallen into the basest bondage. The devil, whose slave he now is, to work his will, hath him so fast in prison that he cannot get forth. He hath bound him with a thousand chains, the heavy chains of his own vile affections. For every inordinate appetite, every unholy passion, as it is the express image of the god of this world, so it is the most galling yoke, the most grievous chain, that can bind a free-born spirit. And with these is every child of Adam, everyone that is born into this world, so loaded that he cannot lift up an eye, a thought to Heaven; that his whole soul cleaveth unto the dust!

But these chains of darkness under which we groan do not only hold us in on every side, but they are within us too … We are all over, within and without, in the eye of God, full of diseases, and wounds, and putrefying sores. Every one of our brutal passions and diabolical tempers, every kind of sensuality, pride, selfishness, is one of those deadly wounds, of those loathsome sores, full of corruption, and of all uncleanness.

To recover our first estate, from which we are thus fallen, is the one thing now needful – to re-exchange the image of Satan for the image of God, bondage for freedom, sickness for health. Our one business is to rase out of our souls the likeness of our destroyer, and to be born again, to be formed anew after the likeness of our Creator. It is our one concern to shake off this servile yoke and to regain our native freedom; to throw off every chain, every passion and desire that does not suit an angelical nature. The one work we have to do is to return from the gates of death to perfect soundness; to have our diseases cured, our wounds healed and our uncleanness done away.

Let us in the second place consider a few of the numberless reasons which prove that this is the one thing needful; so needful that this alone is to be had in view, and pursued at all times and in all places; not indeed by neglecting our temporal affairs, but by making them all minister unto it; by so conducting them all, that every step therein may be a step to this higher end.

Now that the recovery of the image of God, of this glorious liberty, of this perfect soundness, is the one thing needful upon earth, appears first from hence, that the enjoyment of them was the one end of our creation. For to this end was man created, to love God; and to this end alone, even to love the Lord his God with all his heart, and soul, and mind, and strength.

But love is the very image of God: it is the brightness of his glory. By love man is not only made like God, but in some sense one with him … Love is the health of the soul, the full exertion of all its powers, the perfection of all its faculties. Therefore, since the enjoyment of these was the one end of our creation, the recovering of them is the one thing now needful.

May not the same truth appear, secondly, from hence, that this was the one end of our redemption; of all our blessed Lord did and suffered for us; of his incarnation, his life, his death? All these miracles of love were wrought with no other view than to restore us to health and freedom … For this only he lived, that he might heal every disease, every spiritual sickness of our nature. For this only he died, that he might deliver those who were all their lifetime subject to bondage. And it was in pursuance of the very same design that he gave us his merciful law.

The end of his commandment, too, was only our health, liberty, perfection, or, to say all in one word, charity. All the parts of it centre in this one point, our renewal in the love of God; either enjoining what is necessary for our recovery thereof, or forbidding what is obstructive of it. Therefore this, being the one end of our redemption as well as creation, is the one thing needful for us upon earth.

This is the one thing needful, thirdly, because it is the one end of all God's providential dispensations. Pleasure and pain, health and sickness, riches and poverty, honour and dishonour, friends and enemies, are all bestowed by his unerring wisdom and goodness with a view to this one thing. The will of God, in allotting us our several portions of all these, is solely our sanctification; our recovery from that vile bondage, the love of his creatures, to the free love of our Creator. All his providences, be they mild or severe, point at no other end than this …

To the same end are all the internal dispensations of God, all the influences of his Holy Spirit. Whether he gives us joy or sorrow of heart, whether he inspires us with vigour and cheerfulness, or permits us to sink into numbness of soul, into dryness and heaviness, 'tis all with the same view, viz: to restore us to health, to liberty, to holiness.

These are all designed to heal those inbred diseases of our nature, self-love, and the love of the world. They are all given together with the daily bread of his external dispensations, to enable us to turn that into proper nourishment, and so recover his love, the health of our souls. Therefore the renewal of our nature in this love being not only the one end of our creation and our redemption, but likewise of all the providences of God over us, and all the operations of his Spirit in us, must be, as the eternal wisdom of God hath declared, the one thing needful.

How great reason is there, then, even in the Christian world, to resume the Apostle's exhortation, 'Awake, thou that sleepest, and arise from the dead!'[1] Hath not Christ given thee light? Why then sittest thou still in the shadow of death? What slumber is this which hangs on thy temples? Knowest thou not that only one thing is needful? What then are all these? Why hath any but that the least place in thy thoughts, the least share in thy affections? Is the entertainment of the senses the one thing needful? Or the gratifying the imagination with uncommon, or great, or beautiful objects? Our Lord saith not so. Saith he then that the one thing is to acquire a fortune, or to increase that thou hast already? I tell you, nay: these may be the thoughts of those that dream, but they cannot [be those] of waking men. Is it to obtain honour, power, reputation, or (as the phrase is) to get preferment? Is the one thing to gain a large share in that fairest of the fruits of earth, learning? No.

Though any of these may sometimes be conducive to, none of them is, the one thing needful. That is simply to escape out of the snare of the devil, to regain an angelical nature; to recover the image wherein we were formed; to be like the Most High …

Let us well observe that our Lord doth not call this our main concern, our great business, the chief thing needful, but the *one* thing – all others being either part of this or quite foreign to the end of life. On this then let us fix our single view, our pure unmixed intention; regarding nothing at all, small or great, but as it stands referred to this. We must use many means; but let us ever remember we have but one end. For as while our eye is single our whole body will be full of light, so, should it ever cease to be single, in that moment our whole body would be full of darkness.

Be we then continually jealous over our souls, that there be no mixture in our intention. Be it our one view in all our thoughts and words and works, to be partakers of the divine nature, to regain the highest measure we can of that faith which works by love, and makes us become one spirit with God. I say, the highest measure we can; for who will plead for any abatement of health, liberty, life and glory?

Let us then labour to be made perfectly whole, to burst every bond in sunder; to attain the fullest conquest over this body of death, the most entire renovation of our nature, knowing this: that when the Son of Man shall send forth his angels to cast the double-minded into outer darkness, then shall the single of heart receive the one thing they sought, and shine forth as the sun in the kingdom of their Father.

[1] Ephesians 5:14.

William Allen White
American journalist and writer

William Allen White *known as the Sage of Emporia* (1868–1944) was born in Emporia, Kansas. In 1895, he became proprietor and editor of the *Emporia Gazette*, a post he held until his death. He gained national fame during the presidential election of 1896 as a result of his ferocious anti-Populist editorial 'What's the Matter with Kansas?', much used by the successful presidential campaign on behalf of the Republican William McKinley. White later lent support to the growing Progressive movement, backing New York Governor and then President THEODORE ROOSEVELT. He published short stories of mordant social criticism, *Stratagems and Spoils* (1901), and a novel in the same vein, *A Certain Rich Man* (1909). His daughter Mary died in a horse-riding accident in 1921, aged 17, and he wrote a famous eulogy to her in the *Gazette*. He later wrote about national politicians of his time in *Masks in a Pageant* (1928), and an ironic life of President Calvin Coolidge, *A Puritan in Babylon* (1933). He won a Pulitzer Prize in 1923 for his editorials.

'We are all children of John Q Public'
20 September 1938, Washington, DC, USA

William Allen White was very well known for his pithy editorials in the *Gazette*. A liberal Republican, he considered himself an archetypal resident of small-town America. He was a quintessential civic-minded journalist, and made plain speaking his trademark.

This address to the Seventh International Management Congress in Washington, DC, was an unusual departure for White, who rarely spoke in public. The congress was attended by 2,000 delegates from 21 nations, united in the belief that world peace could be maintained by forging ever-closer world trading links, a precursor to globalization. If their messages of international co-operation were muted it was hardly surprising. ADOLF HITLER – who had annexed Austria six months earlier – was to meet the British prime minister NEVILLE CHAMBERLAIN in Munich two days later over the crisis in Czechoslovakia. Before the Congress adjourned, that country would be plundered of territory by Germany and neighbouring east European countries.

White's remarks about the failings of both management and labour in corporate America would have given neither side much comfort, but still resonate today. The solutions he suggests epitomize his personal optimism that the Great Depression was lifting, even if he blames greedy 'Mr Capitalist' for the election of FRANKLIN D ROOSEVELT, whose 'New Deal' policies were badly needed in the early 1930s. His speech also underscores how divorced American opinion was from crucial events which would lead Europe into war within a year and the USA two years after that.

In this discussion I am supposed to represent the public – the American consumer. He is a mythical character who never lived on land or sea, but for that matter, the capitalist is a myth and the worker's status is an economic hypothesis. It is trite to say that in America we are all more or less owners, all workers of high or low degrees, and certainly we are all consumers. We are all the children of John Q Public, and our interests as members of the consuming public are, after all, our chief end and objective as citizens of our democracy.

Let me begin by telling you both, labourer and capitalist, that you have got us citizen consumers in a pretty sad mess. Every time we consumers think of what one of you has done we are dead sore at each of you until we begin to think of what the other has done.

Let me start on capital, the employer. Not that he is more to blame than labour. But he is more responsible. He enjoys more freedom. He could have done better. You employers have wasted 20 years since the end of the World War. In those 20 years, a little intelligent self-interest, a little foresight – not much – would have solved equitably the problems that are now pressing upon us, problems that have been adjusted in haste and in the emergency of calamity.

Take the eight-hour day. You knew that it was coming. Why didn't you men willingly, sensibly, grant it? But no. You had to fight it, every inch, and make the consuming public think you were greedy – when you were not. You were just dumb – dumb to give labour a sense of deep antagonism.

Take the old-age pension and job insurance to cover seasonal and technological unemployment. A thousand voices rose across the land, telling you of the trouble ahead. What did you do? You put cotton in your ears, and if you could hear through the cotton you began yelling 'Communism!' at the academician and the liberal politician and spokesmen of the consuming public.

Everyone realized, 20 years ago and more, that sooner or later, with the pensions of the Civil War gone which took care of the aged until the World War, we should have old-age pensions as a federal problem. Yet you employers let a generation of old people, unprovided for, begin to clamour for old-age pensions and begin to listen to demagogues with silly panaceas.

Then, having squandered your substance, you turned your men on the street in the days of the locust, and put into the hands of the most adroit politician America has ever seen[1] the votes of ten million men whom your slipshod social viewpoint rendered jobless.

[1] White refers to President Franklin D Roosevelt.

If a dozen or 20 years ago you, Mr Capitalist, had used the social sense of the average man in the street, this problem of unemployment and old-age pensions would not be handing to your arch-enemies an organized, subsidized, class-conscious proletariat which can be voted to your destruction. By your sloth you created the particular head devil who is mocking you. He is your baby. You begot him two decades ago in the days of your youth when you were going to handle your business in your own way and no man could come into your shop and tell you how to run it!

[2] The biblical King Solomon was celebrated for his wisdom.

But labour has been no Solomon.[2] The proper business of a labour union is to get higher wages, better hours and good shop conditions for the workmen. But when labour *en masse* plunks its vote for its own party, then the spirit of party loyalty begins to obscure labour's objectives – high wages, short hours, decent shop conditions. Thus class-conscious labour leaders become more interested in their party welfare than in the fundamental objectives of labour unions.

So we shall have the class-conscious political worker trading his vote not for the immediate objective of wages, hours and shop conditions, but for power for his political labour boss. The political labour boss will ask the workers to swallow a whole ticket in order to dominate a whole government. He would turn a democracy into a contest between two class-conscious parties, a class-conscious proletariat and a class-conscious plutocracy.

In that set-up where is the consumer? Where indeed is the compromise between labour and capital, under the supervision of a middle class? In short, with only two class-conscious political parties, what becomes of democracy? The labour union, militant and undefiled? Yes. The vertical union and the closed shop? Yes. But a class-conscious Labour Party in a democracy? No! If labour insists upon maintaining its class lines of bitter, intransigent hostility to all capital, the American middle class – old John Q Public and his heirs and assigns – will not support labour.

This is a middle-class country and the middle class will have its will and way. For the middle class is the real owner of American industry. The middle class is also 80 per cent worker and the consumer of 80 per cent of American industrial production in the home market. The middle class thinks and feels chiefly as The Consumer. And before the middle class demands an increase in either interest for inventors or higher wages for the worker, the middle class will demand fair prices and a stable industry.

That means industrial peace. No peace is lasting until it is founded upon that essential equitable compromise between the contending forces – capital and labour – known as justice.

Gough Whitlam

Australian statesman

Edward Gough Whitlam (1916–) was educated at the University of Sydney. After war service in the Royal Australian Air Force he became a barrister. He entered politics in 1952 and led the Australian Labor Party (1967–77), forming the first Labor government since 1949. His administration (1972–5) was notable for its radicalism, ending conscription and withdrawing Australian troops from the Vietnam War, recognizing communist China, relaxing the restrictions on non-white immigrants, abolishing university fees and creating Medibank (the state-funded health care system). He was controversially dismissed by the governor-general John Kerr in 1975, after the Senate had blocked his money bills; Labor lost the subsequent election. Whitlam retired from politics in 1977, but went on to become Australian ambassador to UNESCO in Paris (1983–6) and a member of its executive board (1985–9). His publications include *The Whitlam Government* (1985).

'It's time'

13 November 1972, Blacktown, New South Wales, Australia

In the late 1960s the Australian electorate had become restive, and the election of the first Australian Labor Party (ALP) government since the 1940s seemed a real possibility. A progressive agenda – championed jointly by the party's traditional working-class support and young middle-class professionals – became a new electoral force across the country. Their demands for the withdrawal of Australia's forces from Vietnam, the revocation of conscription and extension of rights for Aboriginals and women became increasingly vocal and persuasive.

After a narrow defeat in the 1969 federal election, Whitlam's ALP looked sure to win in 1972. The decline of the Democratic Labor Party – a conservative Roman Catholic party that had eroded the traditional labour vote – seemed to augur well for the ALP.

So too did the performance of Sir William McMahon's coalition government, which attempted a belated liberalization of policy but to little effect. Having dispensed with former prime minister John Gorton – a populist who was much loved by the public, but resented within his own party for his high-handed attitude to both his Cabinet and the rights of state legislatures – the coalition was left with a leader who had been much admired as a federal treasurer, but made a desperately uncharismatic prime minister.

Whitlam mocked McMahon as 'Tiberius on the telephone' – likening him to a notoriously reclusive Roman emperor – and seized the advantage with this speech (of which the long middle section, giving details of proposed legislation, has been omitted).

Coming at the end of a clever campaign, accompanied by the half-gospel, half pop-song jingle, 'It's time', it assured Whitlam's electoral triumph on 2 December 1972.

Men and women of Australia: the decision we will make for our country on 2 December is a choice between the past and the future; between the habits and fears of the past, and the demands and opportunities of the future. There are moments in history when the whole fate and future of nations can be decided by a single decision. For Australia, this is such a time. It's time for a new team, a new programme, a new drive for equality of opportunities. It's time to create new opportunities for Australians, time for a new vision of what we can achieve in this generation for our nation and the region in which we live. It's time for a new government – a Labor government.

My fellow citizens: I put these questions to you. Do you believe that Australia can afford another three years like the last 20 months? Are you prepared to maintain at the head of your affairs a coalition which has lurched into crisis after crisis, embarrassment piled on embarrassment, week after week? Will you accept another three years of waiting for next week's crisis, next week's blunder? Will you again entrust the nation's economy to the men who deliberately, but needlessly, created Australia's worst unemployment for ten years? Or to the same men who have presided over the worst inflation for 20 years? Can you trust the last-minute promises of men who stood against these very same proposals for 23 years? Would you trust your international affairs again to the men who gave you Vietnam? Will you trust your defences to the men who haven't even yet given you the F-111?[1]

We have a new chance for our nation. We can recreate this nation. We have a new chance for our region. We can help recreate this region.

The war of intervention in Vietnam is ending. The great powers are rethinking and remoulding their relationships and their obligations. Australia cannot stand still at such a time. We cannot afford to limp along with men whose attitudes are rooted in the slogans of the 1950s – the slogans of fear and hate. If we made such a mistake, we would make Australia a backwater in our region and a back number in history. The Australian Labor Party – vindicated as we have been on all the great issues of the past – stands ready to take Australia forward to her rightful, proud, secure and independent place in the future of our region.

And we are determined that the Australian people shall be restored to their rightful place in their own country – as participants and partners in government, as the owners and keepers of the national estate and the nation's resources, as fair and equal sharers in the wealth and opportunities that this nation should offer in abundance to all its people. We will put Australians back into the business of running Australia and owning Australia. We will revive in this nation the spirit of national co-operation and national self-respect, mutual respect between government and people.

In 24 hours Mr McMahon[2] will present to you a series of proposals purporting to be the Liberal Party programme. But it is not what he will say in 24 hours that counts; it is what could have been done in the past 23 years, what has happened in the last 20 months, on which the Liberals must be judged. It is the Liberal Party which asks you to take a leap in the dark – the Liberal Party which dispossessed the elected prime minister[3] in mid-term, the Liberal Party which has produced half-baked, uncosted proposals in its death-bed repentance. It is the Liberal Party whose election proposals are those which it has denounced and derided for 23 years.

By contrast, the Australian Labor Party offers the Australian people the most carefully developed and consistent programme ever placed before them. I am proud of our programme. I am proud of our team. I am proud to be the leader of this team.

Our programme has three great aims. They are: to promote quality; to involve the people of Australia in the decision-making processes of our land; and to liberate the talents and uplift the horizons of the Australian people.

We want to give a new life and a new meaning in this new nation to the touchstone of modern democracy – to liberty, equality, fraternity.

We propose a new charter for the children of Australia. The real answer to the modern malaise of juvenile crime, drugs and vandalism is not repression and moralizing. The answer is to involve the creative energies of our children and our youth in a creative, concerned community.

We will make pre-school education available to every Australian child. We do this not just because we believe that all Australian children should have the opportunities now available only to children in Canberra, but because pre-school education is the most important single weapon in promoting equality and in overcoming social, economic and language inequalities.

[1] In a decision that was controversial from the start, the General Dynamics F-111A, a US-built fighter-bomber, had been purchased 'off the drawing board' in 1963. Due for completion in 1967, the project was beset with technical difficulties and escalating costs.

[2] The Australian politician William McMahon (1908–88) was leader of the Liberal Party, 1971–3, and Prime Minister of the coalition government, 1971–2.

[3] The Australian politician John Gorton (1911–2002) served as Liberal Prime Minister, 1968–71. He resigned the leadership following a premiership and party vote of confidence, and was replaced by McMahon.

Under a Labor government, commonwealth spending on schools and teacher-training will be the fastest expanding sector of budget expenditure. This must be done, not just because the basic resource of this nation is the skills of its people, but because education is the key to equality of opportunity. Sure – we can have education on the cheap ... but our children will be paying for it for the rest of their lives.

We will abolish fees at universities and colleges of advanced education. We believe that a student's merit rather than a parent's wealth should decide who should benefit from the community's vast financial commitment to tertiary education. And more, it's time to strike a blow for the ideal that education should be free. Under the Liberals, this basic principle has been massively eroded. We will re-assert that principle at the commanding heights of education, at the level of the university itself.

We intend to raise the basic pension rate to 25 per cent of average weekly earnings. Australia did that in the late Forties. Does anyone say we cannot afford it now? The important thing is this: the present method of irregular, uneven and politically inspired pension increases has been a source of needless anxiety, insecurity and indignity to those who depend on pensions for their sole income.

We will establish a universal health insurance system – not just because the Liberal system is grossly inadequate and inefficient, but because we reject a system by which the more one earns the less one pays, a system by which a person on $20,000 a year pays only half as much as a person on $5,000 a year.

We will establish a National Compensation Scheme to reduce the hardships imposed by one of the great factors for inequality in society – inequality of luck.

We will make a massive attack on the problem of land and housing costs. The land is the basic property of the Australian people. It is the people's land, and we will fight for the right of all Australian people to have access to it at fair prices ...

We will exert our powers against prices. We will establish a Prices Justification Tribunal, not only because inflation will be the major economic problem facing Australia over the next three years, but because industrial co-operation and goodwill is being undermined by the conviction among employees that the price for labour alone is subject to regulation and restraint.

Under Labor, the national government – itself the largest customer – will move directly and solidly into the field of consumer protection.

We will change the emphasis in immigration from government recruiting to family reunion and to retaining the migrants already here. The important thing is to stop the drift away from Australia. We believe that the Australian people rather than governments should have the real say in the composition of the population.

We will issue national development bonds through an expanded Australian Industry Development Corporation – not just because we are determined to reverse the trend towards foreign control of Australian resources, but because we want ordinary Australians to play their part in buying Australia back.

We will abolish conscription forthwith.[4] It must be done not just because a volunteer army means a better army, but because we profoundly believe that it is intolerable that a free nation at peace and under no threat should cull by lottery the best of its youth to provide defence on the cheap.

[4] Although there had been periods of compulsory military service for duty within Australia at various times since the country's independence in 1901, in 1965 the Liberal government introduced new powers enabling conscripts to be sent overseas. Over 19,000 national servicemen served in the Vietnam War. National Service was abolished by the ALP government in December 1972.

[5] By the early 1970s there was a strengthening civil rights movement among Aborigines, especially for land rights to property forcibly taken by British settlers. Although courts had rejected claims by tribes in the Northern Territory in the 1960s, the Aboriginal Land Rights Act 1976 covered territories with tribal associations.

We will legislate to give Aborigines land rights[5] – not just because their case is beyond argument, but because all of us as Australians are diminished while the Aborigines are denied their rightful place in this nation.

We will co-operate whole-heartedly with the New Guinea House of Assembly in reaching successfully its timetable for self-government and independence – not just because it is Australia's obligation to the United Nations, but because we believe it wrong and unnatural that a nation like Australia should continue to run a colony.[6]

All of us, as Australians, have to insist that we can do so much better as a nation. We ought to be angry, with a deep determined anger, that a country as rich and skilled as ours should be producing so much inequality, so much poverty, so much that is shoddy and sub-standard. We ought to be angry – with an unrelenting anger – that our Aborigines have the world's highest infant mortality rate. We ought to be angry at the way our so-called leaders have kept us in the dark – Parliament itself as much as the people – to hide their own incapacity and ignorance ...

For 13 years now I have had the honour to fill the second highest and then the highest place my party can bestow. Throughout that time I have striven to make the policies of the Australian Labor Party, its machinery, its membership, more and more representative of the whole Australian people and more and more responsive to the needs and hopes of the whole Australian people.[7] This at least I have tried to do, and will continue to do; and, supporting me, I have the best of colleagues and the best of friends.

We of the Labor Party have used these crucial last years in opposition to prepare ourselves for the great business of moving our nation ahead, to uniting our people in a common co-operative endeavour and to making the democratic system work once more. The determination of a few and the dedication of thousands have reconstructed and welded the Australian Labor Party into the most representative political party Australia has yet known.

We come to government with malice toward none; we will co-operate wholeheartedly with all sections of this nation in a national endeavour to expand and equalize for all our people.

We shall need the help and seek the help of the best Australians. We shall rely, of course, on Australia's great public service; but we shall welcome advice and co-operation from beyond the confines of Canberra.

But the best team, the best policies, the best advisers are not enough. I need your help. I need the help of the Australian people; and given that, I do not for a moment believe that we should set limits on what we can achieve, together, for our country, our people, our future.

[6] Papua New Guinea was a merger of German New Guinea, annexed on the outbreak of World War I, and British territory transferred to Australia in 1906. Australia administered the territory under a League of Nations mandate, 1920–42, and a UN mandate, 1947–75. A home rule campaign had begun in the late 1960s and independence was achieved peacefully in 1975.

[7] After his election to the party leadership in 1967, Whitlam had been instrumental in curbing the influence of the party's all-powerful federal executive, made up of trade unionists and largely unelected party officials, which decided party policy.

William Wilberforce
English philanthropist, politician and abolitionist

William Wilberforce (1759–1833) was born in Hull, the son of a wealthy merchant, and educated at St John's College, Cambridge. In 1780 he was elected MP for Hull, and in 1784 for Yorkshire. He became a close friend of William Pitt, the Younger, while remaining independent of any party. In 1784–5, during a tour of Europe, he was converted to evangelical Christianity, and in 1787 he founded an association for the reformation of manners. In 1788, supported by Thomas Clarkson and the Quakers, he began a 19-year campaign for the abolition of the slave trade in the British West Indies, which he finally achieved in 1807. He next sought to secure the abolition of the slave trade abroad and the total abolition of slavery itself; but declining health compelled him to retire from Parliament in 1825. He died one month before the Slavery Abolition Act was passed in 1833. He published *A Practical View of Christianity* in 1797, helped to found the *Christian Observer* (1801), and promoted many schemes for the welfare of the community. He was buried in Westminster Abbey.

'Let us put an end at once to this inhuman traffic'
12 May 1789, London, England

This parliamentary tour de force was Wilberforce's first attempt to convince the House of Commons of the need to abolish slavery. It was supported by his friends and allies, William Pitt, the Younger, CHARLES FOX and EDMUND BURKE. Wilberforce was considered something of a radical, and had spoken previously in favour of Catholic emancipation and parliamentary reform.

The abolition movement drew its strength from a combination of Enlightenment thinking on freedom and the rise of evangelical Christianity. Wilberforce's adherence to the evangelical faith put him in touch with others of a like mind; he was a leading member of the 'Clapham Sect', named after the area in London where the group met, at Holy Trinity Church. He also helped establish the Society for Effecting the Abolition of the Slave Trade (1787) which is often credited with being the first truly political movement.

Wilberforce draws on a report recently produced by the legislature of Jamaica, a British colony since 1655, whose prodigious sugar trade relied on slaves from Africa. In his speech's most vivid passage, he dwells unsparingly on the disgraceful treatment of slaves as they were transported around the world, and scorns the attempts of slavers to justify the appalling conditions aboard slave ships.

At the time of this speech, no official record of parliamentary debates was kept. Wilberforce's speech comes down through newspapers (such as the *Morning Star*) and other edited versions, the most famous being included in William Cobbett's *Parliamentary History of England* (1803), produced by a printer named Thomas Curson Hansard.

In opening, concerning the nature of the slave trade, I need only observe that it is found by experience to be just such as every man who uses his reason would infallibly conclude it to be. For my own part, so clearly am I convinced of the mischiefs inseparable from it, that I should hardly want any further evidence than my own mind would furnish, by the most simple deductions.

Facts, however, are now laid before the House. A report has been made by His Majesty's Privy Council, which, I trust, every gentleman has read, and which ascertains the slave trade to be just as we know. What should we suppose must naturally be the consequence of our carrying on a slave trade with Africa? With a country vast in its extent, not utterly barbarous, but civilized in a very small degree?

Does any one suppose a slave trade would help their civilization? Is it not plain that she must suffer from it; that civilization must be checked; that her barbarous manners must be made more barbarous; and that the happiness of her millions of inhabitants must be prejudiced with her intercourse with Britain? Does not everyone see that a slave trade carried on around her coasts must carry violence and desolation to her very centre? That in a continent just emerging from barbarism, if a trade in men is established, if her men are all converted into goods and become commodities that can be bartered, it follows they must be subject to ravage just as goods are; and this, too, at a period of civilization when there is no protecting legislature to defend this, their only sort of property, in the same manner as the rights of property are maintained by the legislature of every civilized country.

We see then, in the nature of things, how easily the practices of Africa are to be accounted for. Her kings are never compelled to war, that we can hear of, by public principles, by national glory, still less by the love of their people. In Europe it is the extension of commerce, the maintenance of national honour, or some great public object, that is ever the motive to war with every monarch; but, in Africa, it is the personal avarice and sensuality of their kings …

The slave trade, in its very nature, is the source of such kind of tragedies; nor has there been a single person, almost, before the Privy Council, who does not add something by his testimony to the mass of evidence upon this point. Some, indeed, of these gentlemen, and particularly the delegates from Liverpool,[1] have endeavoured to reason down this plain principle; some have palliated it; but there is not one, I believe, who does not more or less admit it. Some, nay most, I believe, have admitted the slave trade to be the chief cause of wars in Africa.

Having now disposed of the first part of this subject, I must speak of the transit of the slaves to the West Indies. This, I confess, in my own opinion, is the most wretched part of the whole subject. So much misery condensed in so little room is more than the human imagination had ever before conceived. I will not accuse the Liverpool merchants. I will allow them, nay, I will believe them, to be men of humanity; and I will therefore believe, if it were not for the multitude of these wretched objects, if it were not for the enormous magnitude and extent of the evil which distracts their attention from individual cases, and makes them think generally, and therefore less feelingly on the subject, they never would have persisted in the trade.

I verily believe, therefore, if the wretchedness of any one of the many hundred negroes stowed in each ship could be brought before their view, and remain within the sight of the African merchant, that there is no-one among them whose heart would bear it.

Let any one imagine to himself 600 or 700 of these wretches chained two and two, surrounded with every object that is nauseous and disgusting, diseased, and struggling under every kind of wretchedness! How can we bear to think of such a scene as this? One would think it had been determined to heap on them all the varieties of bodily pain, for the purpose of blunting the feelings of the mind; and yet, in this very point (to show the power of human prejudice), the situation of the slaves has been described by Mr Norris, one of the Liverpool delegates, in a manner which I am sure will convince the House how interest can draw a film over the eyes, so thick that total blindness could do no more; and how it is our duty therefore to trust not to the reasonings of interested men, nor to their way of colouring a transaction.

'Their apartments,' says Mr Norris, 'are fitted up as much for their advantage as circumstances will admit. The right ankle of one, indeed, is connected with the left ankle of another by a small iron fetter, and if they are turbulent, by another on their wrists. They have several meals a day, some of their own country provisions, with the best sauces of African cookery; and by the way of variety, another meal of pulse, etc, according to

[1] From around 1740 until abolition in 1807, Liverpool was the centre of the British slave trade. It is believed that at least a third of the city's workers were involved in the trade in some way during this period.

European taste.

'After breakfast they have water to wash themselves, while their apartments are perfumed with frankincense and lime juice. Before dinner they are amused after the manner of their country. The song and the dance are promoted,' and, as if the whole were really a scene of pleasure and dissipation, it is added that games of chance are furnished.

'The men play and sing, while the women and girls make fanciful ornaments with beads, with which they are plentifully supplied.'

Such is the sort of strain in which the Liverpool delegates, and particularly Mr Norris, gave evidence before the Privy Council. What will the House think when, by the concurring testimony of other witnesses, the true history is laid open?

The slaves, who are sometimes described as rejoicing at their captivity, are so wrung with misery at leaving their country, that it is the constant practice to set sail in the night, lest they should be sensible of their departure. The pulse which Mr Norris talks of are horse beans; and the scantiness of both water and provision was suggested by the very legislature of Jamaica, in the report of their committee, to be a subject that called for the interference of Parliament.

Mr Norris talks of frankincense and lime juice: when the surgeons tell you the slaves are stored so close that there is not room to tread among them; and when you have it in evidence from Sir George Young,[2] that even in a ship which wanted 200 of her complement, the stench was intolerable.

The song and the dance are promoted, says Mr Norris. It had been more fair, perhaps, if he had explained that word 'promoted'. The truth is, that for the sake of exercise, these miserable wretches, loaded with chains, oppressed with disease and wretchedness, are forced to dance by the terror of the lash, and sometimes by the actual use of it.

'I,' says one of the other evidences, 'was employed to dance the men, while another person danced the women.' Such, then, is the meaning of the word 'promoted'; and it may be observed, too, with respect to food, that an instrument is sometimes carried out in order to force them to eat, which is the same sort of proof how much they enjoy themselves in that instance also.

As to their singing: what shall we say when we are told that their songs are songs of lamentation upon their departure which, while they sing, are always in tears, insomuch that one captain (more humane as I should conceive him, therefore, than the rest) threatened one of the women with a flogging, because the mournfulness of her song was too painful for his feelings.

In order, however, not to trust too much to any sort of description, I will call the attention of the House to one species of evidence, which is absolutely infallible. Death, at least, is a sure ground of evidence, and the proportion of deaths will not only confirm, but, if possible, will even aggravate our suspicion of their misery in the transit. It will be found, upon an average of all ships of which evidence has been given at the Privy Council, that exclusive of those who perish before they sail, not less than twelve-and-one-half per cent perish in the passage.

Besides these, the Jamaica report tells you that not less than four-and-one-half per cent die on shore before the day of sale, which is only a week or two from the time of landing. One-third more die in the seasoning, and this in a country exactly like their own, where they are healthy and happy, as some of the evidences would pretend. The diseases, however, which they

[2] The English naval officer Admiral Sir George Young (1732–1810). The Dolben Act of 1788 limited the number of enslaved people that a ship was allowed to carry between Africa and the Americas. The Royal Navy was responsible for ensuring that regulatory and, subsequently, abolition legislation was observed.

contract on shipboard, the astringent washes which are to hide their wounds, and the mischievous tricks used to make them up for sale, are, as the Jamaica report says − a most precious and valuable report, which I shall often have to advert to − one principal cause of this mortality.

Upon the whole, however, here is a mortality of about 50 per cent, and this among negroes who are not bought unless quite healthy at first, and unless (as the phrase is with cattle) they are sound in wind and limb.

When we consider the vastness of the continent of Africa; when we reflect how all other countries have for some centuries past been advancing in happiness and civilization; when we think how in this same period all improvement in Africa has been defeated by her intercourse with Britain; when we reflect that it is we ourselves that have degraded them to that wretched brutishness and barbarity which we now plead as the justification of our guilt; how the slave trade has enslaved their minds, blackened their character, and sunk them so low in the scale of animal beings that some think the apes are of a higher class, and fancy the orang-utan has given them the go-by, what a mortification must we feel at having so long neglected to think of our guilt, or attempt any reparation!

It seems, indeed, as if we had determined to forbear from all interference until the measure of our folly and wickedness was so full and complete; until the impolicy which eventually belongs to vice was become so plain and glaring that not an individual in the country should refuse to join in the abolition; it seems as if we had waited until the persons most interested should be tired out with the folly and nefariousness of the trade, and should unite in petitioning against it.

Let us then make such amends as we can for the mischiefs we have done to the unhappy continent; let us recollect what Europe itself was no longer ago than three or four centuries. What if I should be able to show this House that in a civilized part of Europe, in the time of our Henry VII,[3] there were people who actually sold their own children? What if I should tell them that England itself was that country? What if I should point out to them that the very place where this inhuman traffic was carried on was the city of Bristol?[4]

Ireland at that time used to drive a considerable trade in slaves with these neighbouring barbarians; but a great plague having infested the country, the Irish were struck with a panic, suspected (I am sure very properly) that the plague was a punishment sent from Heaven for the sin of the slave trade, and therefore abolished it. All I ask, therefore, of the people of Bristol is, that they would become as civilized now as Irishmen were 400 years ago. Let us put an end at once to this inhuman traffic − let us stop this effusion of human blood.

[3] The English monarch Henry VII (1457−1509) reigned in England and Ireland, 1485−1509.

[4] From the late 17th century until the mid-18th century, Bristol was Britain's leading centre for the slave trade. It was overtaken by Liverpool around 1740 but remained active in slavery.

Oscar Wilde

Irish writer and wit

Oscar Fingal O'Flahertie Wills Wilde (1854–1900) was born in Dublin. He was educated at Portora Royal School in Enniskillen, Trinity College, Dublin (1871–4), and Magdalen College, Oxford (1874–8), where he was dandified, sexually ambiguous, sympathetic towards the Pre-Raphaelites, and contemptuous of conventional morality. He was also an accomplished Classicist, and won the Newdigate Prize at Oxford in 1878 for his poem 'Ravenna'. His first collection of poetry was published in 1881. In the same year he was ridiculed in Gilbert and Sullivan's *Patience* as an adherent of the cult of 'art for art's sake'. The next year he embarked on a lecture tour of the USA. He married Constance Lloyd, the daughter of an Irish barrister, in 1884 and had two sons for whom he wrote the classic children's fairy stories *The Happy Prince and Other Tales* (1888). His only novel, *The Picture of Dorian Gray* (1891), was inspired by his presumed lover, the poet John Gray, and was originally published in *Lippincott's Magazine* (1890), to a scandalized reception. In 1891, he published more fairy stories in *A House of Pomegranates*, as well as *Lord Arthur Savile's Crime and Other Stories*, and his second play, the uninspired verse tragedy *The Duchess of Padua*. Over the next five years he built his reputation as a dramatist, with *Lady Windermere's Fan* (1892), *A Woman of No Importance* (1893), *An Ideal Husband* (1895) and his masterpiece, *The Importance of Being Earnest* (1895). *Salomé*, originally written in French (1893), was refused a production licence in England as it featured biblical characters, but was published in 1894 in a translation by his lover Lord Alfred Douglas (1870–1945). By now Wilde's homosexuality was commonly known in the circles in which he moved, and Lord Alfred's father, the 9th Marquess of Queensberry, left a card at Wilde's club addressed 'To Oscar Wilde posing as a Somdomite' (*sic*). Wilde sued for libel. He lost the case, and was prosecuted and imprisoned for indecency (1895). His bitter reproach to Lord Alfred was published as *De Profundis* (1905). Released in 1897, he went to France under the alias Sebastian Melmoth. *The Ballad of Reading Gaol* was published in 1898. He also wrote literary essays, and *The Soul of Man Under Socialism* (1891), a riposte to GEORGE BERNARD SHAW. His last years were spent wandering on the Continent, and he died in Paris.

'Bad art is a great deal worse than no art at all'

11 May 1882, New York City, USA

Properly entitled 'The Practical Application of the Principles of Aesthetic Theory to Exterior and Interior House Decoration, with Observations upon Dress and Personal Ornaments', this speech was given during Wilde's American lecture tour of 1882.

Though it would be a decade before he established himself as a major literary figure, Wilde was already known as a prominent member of the Aesthetic movement, which rejected Victorian morality, paid homage to the Romantics and embraced the cult of beauty.

The Aesthetes had been lampooned in the Gilbert and Sullivan operetta *Patience*, whose central character, Reginald Bunthorne, was modelled on Wilde. Following the operetta's success in the USA, its producer Richard D'Oyly Carte conceived the idea of a lecture tour.

Written for the tour, Wilde's haughty survey of American décor illustrates his witty, epigrammatic style and lofty artistic ideals. The following day, the *New York Times* reported on his performance: 'He has a cultivated habit of leaning back in a sort of Ajax-defying-the-lightning attitude, with his left hand poked far into his left side and the elbow bent. When he leans back in this position, throws his hair gracefully back from his massive forehead ... and lets loose one of his massive jokes, he is simply irresistible.'

Though Wilde alludes fairly openly to his homosexual leanings at the end of the first paragraph, his flamboyant appearance and effeminate mannerisms belonged to the heterosexual tradition of the dandy. Consequently, his sexual proclivities were little suspected outside his circle until publicized by his libel case against the Marquess of Queensberry the following decade.

In my last lecture I gave you something of the history of art in England. I sought to trace the influence of the French Revolution upon its development. I said something of the song of Keats[1] and the school of the Pre-Raphaelites.[2] But I do not want to shelter the movement, which I have called the English Renaissance, under any palladium[3] however noble, or any name however revered. The roots of it have, indeed, to be sought for in

[1] The English poet John Keats (1795–1821) was a prominent figure of the Romantic movement.

[2] A British art movement of the mid-19th century, led by the Pre-Raphaelite Brotherhood of English painters, principally Dante Gabriel Rossetti, (1828–82) John Everett Millais (1829–96) and Holman Hunt (1827–1910). Their work was characterized by close study of nature, biblical and literary subject matter, and obsessive naturalism.
[3] In Greek mythology, the Palladium was a Trojan shrine to the goddess Athena, which had the power to safeguard the city where it was kept

things that have long passed away, and not, as some suppose, in the fancy of a few young men – although I am not altogether sure that there is anything much better than the fancy of a few young men.

When I appeared before you on a previous occasion, I had seen nothing of American art, save the Doric columns and Corinthian chimney-pots visible on your Broadway and Fifth Avenue. Since then, I have been through your country to some 50 or 60 different cities, I think. I find that what your people need is not so much high imaginative art, but that which hallows the vessels of everyday use.

I suppose that the poet will sing and the artist will paint regardless whether the world praises or blames. He has his own world and is independent of his fellow men. But the handicraftsman is dependent on your pleasure and opinion. He needs your encouragement and he must have beautiful surroundings. Your people love art but do not sufficiently honour the handicraftsman.

Of course, those millionaires who can pillage Europe for their pleasure need have no care to encourage such; but I speak for those whose desire for beautiful things is larger than their means. I find that one great trouble all over is that your workmen are not given to noble designs. You cannot be indifferent to this, because art is not something which you can take or leave. It is a necessity of human life.

And what is the meaning of this beautiful decoration which we call art? In the first place, it means value to the workman and it means the pleasure which he must necessarily take in making a beautiful thing. The mark of all good art is not that the thing done is done exactly or finely, for machinery may do as much, but that it is worked out with the head and the workman's heart. I cannot impress the point too frequently that beautiful and rational designs are necessary in all work.

I did not imagine, until I went into some of your simpler cities, that there was so much bad work done. I found, where I went, bad wallpapers horribly designed, and coloured carpets, and that old offender the horsehair sofa, whose stolid look of indifference is always so depressing. I found meaningless chandeliers and machine-made furniture, generally of rosewood, which creaked dismally under the weight of the ubiquitous interviewer. I came across the small iron stove which they always persist in decorating with machine-made ornaments, and which is as great a bore as a wet day or any other particularly dreadful institution. When unusual extravagance was indulged in, it was garnished with two funeral urns.

It must always be remembered that what is well and carefully made by an honest workman, after a rational design, increases in beauty and value as the years go on. The old furniture brought over by the Pilgrims, 200 years ago, which I saw in New England, is just as good and as beautiful today as it was when it first came here. Now, what you must do is to bring artists and handicraftsmen together. Handicraftsmen cannot live, certainly cannot thrive, without such companionship. Separate these two and you rob art of all spiritual motive.

Having done this, you must place your workman in the midst of beautiful surroundings. The artist is not dependent on the visible and the tangible. He has his visions and his dreams to feed on. But the workman must see lovely forms as he goes to his work in the morning and returns at eventide. And, in connection with this, I want to assure you that noble and beautiful designs are never the result of idle fancy or purposeless daydreaming. They come only as the accumulation of habits of long and delightful observation. And yet such things may not be taught. Right ideas concerning them can certainly be obtained only by those who have been accustomed to rooms that are beautiful and colours that are satisfying …

Now, what America wants today is a school of rational art. Bad art is a great deal worse than no art at all. You must show your workmen specimens of good work so that they come to know what is simple and true and beautiful. To that end I would have you have a museum attached to these schools – not one of those dreadful modern institutions where there is a stuffed and very dusty giraffe, and a case or two of fossils, but a place where there are gathered examples of art decoration from various periods and countries …

You have too many white walls. More colour is wanted. You should have such men as Whistler[4] among you to teach you the beauty and joy of colour. Take Mr Whistler's 'Symphony in White', which you no doubt have imagined to be something quite bizarre. It is nothing of the sort. Think of a cool grey sky flecked here and there with white clouds, a grey ocean and three wonderfully beautiful figures robed in white, leaning over the water and dropping white flowers from their fingers. Here is no extensive intellectual scheme to trouble you and no metaphysics, of which we have had quite enough in art. But if the simple and unaided colour strike the right keynote, the whole conception is made clear.

I regard Mr Whistler's famous Peacock Room[5] as the finest thing in colour and art decoration which the world has known since Correggio painted that wonderful room in Italy where the little children are dancing on the walls.[6]

Mr Whistler finished another room just before I came away – a breakfast room in blue and yellow. The ceiling was a light blue, the cabinet-work and the furniture were of a yellow wood, the curtains at the windows were white and worked in yellow, and when the table was set for breakfast with dainty blue china nothing can be conceived at once so simple and so joyous.

The fault which I have observed in most of your rooms is that there is apparent no definite scheme of colour. Everything is not attuned to a keynote as it should be. The apartments are crowded with pretty things which have no relation to one another. Again, your artists must decorate what is more simply useful. In your art schools I found no attempt to decorate such things as the vessels for water. I know of nothing uglier than the ordinary jug or pitcher. A museum could be filled with the different kinds of water vessels which are used in hot countries. Yet we continue to submit to the depressing jug with the handle all on one side. I do not see the wisdom of decorating dinner-plates with sunsets and soup-plates with moonlight scenes. I do not think it adds anything to the pleasure of the canvas-back duck to take it out of such glories. Besides, we do not want a soup-plate whose bottom seems to vanish in the distance. One feels neither safe nor comfortable under such conditions. In fact, I did not find in the art schools of the country that the difference was explained between decorative and imaginative art.

The conditions of art should be simple. A great deal more depends upon the heart than upon the head. Appreciation of art is not secured by any elaborate scheme of learning. Art requires a good healthy atmosphere. The motives for art are still around about us as they were round about the ancients. And the subjects are also easily found by the earnest sculptor and the painter. Nothing is more picturesque and graceful than a man at work. The artist who goes to the children's playground, watches them at their

[4] The US painter and etcher James McNeill Whistler (1834–1903) was based in London. He and Wilde were friends and rival wits. He is best known for 'An Arrangement in Grey and Black', (1871), a portrait of his mother, but his Pre-Raphaelite-influenced 'Symphony in White' series of 1862–4 is also well known.

[6] The Italian Renaissance painter Antonio Allegri da Correggio (c.1494–1534) is known for religious and mythological scenes. He painted many frescoes – including those at Parma cathedral – featuring *putti*, or frolicking children.

[5] In 1876, Whistler was commissioned to decorate a dining room in the London home of shipping magnate Frederick Leyland. The elaborate result, featuring golden peacocks, was bought by the US art collector Charles Lang Freer in 1904 and is on permanent display at the Freer Gallery in Washington, DC.

sport and sees the boy stop to tie his shoe will find the same themes that engaged the attention of the ancient Greeks and such observation and the illustrations which follow will do much to correct that foolish impression that mental and physical beauty are always divorced.

To you, more than perhaps to any other country, has nature been generous in furnishing material for art workers to work in. You have marble quarries where the stone is more beautiful in colour than any the Greeks ever had for their beautiful work, and yet day after day I am confronted with the great building of some stupid man who has used the beautiful material as if it were not precious almost beyond speech. Marble should not be used save by noble workmen. There is nothing which gave me a greater sense of barrenness in travelling through the country than the entire absence of wood carving on your houses. Wood carving is the simplest of the decorative arts. In Switzerland the little barefooted boy beautifies the porch of his father's house with examples of skill in this direction. Why should not American boys do a great deal more and better than Swiss boys?

There is nothing to my mind more coarse in conception and more vulgar in execution than modern jewellery. This is something that can easily be corrected. Something better should be made out of the beautiful gold which is stored up in your mountain hollows and strewn along your river beds. When I was at Leadville[7] and reflected that all the shining silver that I saw coming from the mines would be made into ugly dollars, it made me sad. It should be made into something more permanent. The golden gates at Florence[8] are as beautiful today as when Michelangelo[9] saw them ...

I said in my last lecture that art would create a new brotherhood among men by furnishing a universal language. I said that under its beneficent influences war might pass away. Thinking this, what place can I ascribe to art in our education? If children grow up among all fair and lovely things, they will grow to love beauty and detest ugliness before they know the reason why. If you go into a house where everything is coarse, you find things chipped and broken and unsightly. Nobody exercises any care. If everything is dainty and delicate, gentleness and refinement of manner are unconsciously acquired.

When I was in San Francisco I used to visit the Chinese Quarter frequently. There I used to watch a great hulking Chinese workman at his task of digging, and used to see him every day drink his tea from a little cup as delicate in texture as the petal of a flower, whereas in all the grand hotels of the land, where thousands of dollars have been lavished on great gilt mirrors and gaudy columns, I have been given my coffee or my chocolate in cups an inch and a quarter thick. I think I have deserved something nicer ...

No better way is there to learn to love Nature than to understand art. It dignifies every flower of the field. And the boy who sees the thing of beauty which a bird on the wing becomes when transferred to wood or canvas will probably not throw the customary stone. What we want is something spiritual added to life. Nothing is so ignoble that art cannot sanctify it.

[7] A town in Colorado which flourished through silver mining during the 1880s.

[8] Created by the goldsmith Lorenzo Ghiberti (1378–1455), the 'Gates of Paradise' at Florence's Baptistry (completed 1452) are among the masterpieces of the early Renaissance.

[9] The Florentine sculptor, painter and poet Michelangelo Buonarroti (1475–1564) is regarded as one of the great artists of the Renaissance.

❧

'The love that dare not speak its name'
30 April 1895, London, England

❧

This noble defence of homosexual love was given during the second of three court cases which were Wilde's undoing. Though his marriage to Constance Lloyd seemed happy and had produced two children, Wilde had made little secret of his sexual proclivities.

Since 1891 he had been conducting an affair with Lord Alfred Douglas, 16 years his junior. Lord Alfred's father, the Marquess of Queensberry, became increasingly outraged. Four days after the opening of Wilde's play *The Importance of Being Earnest* in February 1895, he left an offensive note for Wilde at the Albemarle Club in London (see biography, above). Wilde, feeling invulnerable, chose to bring a libel action against his accuser.

Ignoring the advice of friends including GEORGE BERNARD SHAW, but encouraged by his mother Lady Jane Francesca Wilde, he went ahead with the case, initially treating the court as a platform for his witty aphorisms. But when Queensberry announced he intended to produce as witnesses several men with whom Wilde had consorted, he was forced to withdraw his case.

Neglecting his chance to escape, Wilde was arrested the following day, and prosecuted under the recently-introduced Criminal Law Amendment Act, which criminalized acts of 'gross indecency'.

At his first criminal trial (26 April–1 May) the jury found it impossible to reach a verdict and Wilde was released on bail. But at a retrial (20–26 May) he and his procurer Alfred Taylor were convicted and sentenced to two years' hard labour. Wilde wrote of this in his long poem *The Ballad of Reading Gaol*.

❧

[1] The line is from 'Two Loves', a poem by Lord Alfred Douglas, which had been produced as evidence.
[2] Some biblical commentators believe a homosexual liaison is suggested by 1 Samuel 18:21.

The 'love that dare not speak its name'[1] in this century is such a great affection of an elder for a younger man as there was between David and Jonathan,[2] such as Plato made the very basis of his philosophy,[3] and such as you find in the sonnets of Michelangelo and Shakespeare.[4] It is that deep, spiritual affection that is as pure as it is perfect. It dictates and pervades great works of art like those of Shakespeare and Michelangelo, and those two letters of mind, such as they are.

It is in this century misunderstood, so much misunderstood that it may be described as the 'love that dare not speak its name', and on account of it I am placed where I am now.

It is beautiful, it is fine, it is the noblest form of affection. There is nothing unnatural about it. It is intellectual, and it repeatedly exists between an elder and a younger man, when the elder man has intellect and the younger man has all the joy, hope and glamour of life before him.

That it should be so the world does not understand. The world mocks at it and sometimes puts one on the pillory for it.

[3] In Plato's *Symposium*, the purest form of love is said to exist between a man and a younger boy.
[4] Both the Florentine sculptor, painter and poet Michelangelo Buonarroti (1475–1564) and the English playwright and poet William Shakespeare (1564–1616) expressed homosexual passions in their sonnets.

Harold Wilson
English politician

James Harold Wilson *later Baron Wilson of Rievaulx* (1916–95) was born in Huddersfield. He was educated there, in Cheshire and at Oxford, where he became a lecturer in economics in 1937, contributing to William Beveridge's report on social welfare (1942). In 1943–4 he was director of economics and statistics at the Ministry of Fuel and Power. He became MP for Ormskirk in 1945, and was then appointed Parliamentary Secretary to the Ministry of Works. In 1947 he became Secretary for Overseas Trade, then president of the Board of Trade, but he resigned with ANEURIN BEVAN in April 1951 over the introduction of National Health Service charges to fund the Korean War. In 1951 and 1955 he was re-elected MP for Huyton, the division he had represented since 1950. In 1956 he became the principal opposition spokesman on economic affairs. An able and hard-hitting debater, he succeeded Hugh Gaitskell as leader of the Labour Party in 1963, becoming prime minister the following year with a precariously small majority. His government's economic plans were badly affected at home by a crisis in the balance of payments, leading to severe restrictive measures. Abroad he was faced with the Rhodesian problem – when a white minority illegally declared independence – continued intransigence from the French president CHARLES DE GAULLE over Britain's proposed entry into the Common Market, and the important question of Britain's new status in world politics as a lesser power. In 1965, he ended capital punishment and established the Open University. He was re-elected in 1966 with comfortably large support. However, he was forced to devalue the pound in 1967, and his popularity declined in the late 1960s. The Labour Party lost power in the 1970 general election, but after four years in opposition, Wilson led Labour back into government in 1974, resigning as party leader two years later. He was knighted in 1976 and created a life peer in 1983. Although he cultivated a homely, man-of-the-people public image he was noted for his skill as a debater, and is considered one of the shrewdest political operators of the 20th century. His *Memoirs* were published in 1986.

'The white heat of this revolution'
1 October 1963, Scarborough, England

This speech, which opened a debate on science at the Labour Party conference of 1963, contains one of the most famous phrases from 1960s Britain. It was made eight months after Harold Wilson became party leader, following the unexpected death of Hugh Gaitskell.

Wilson set out to present Labour as the forward-thinking, modern party, in contrast to the Conservative government, racked by the scandal of the Profumo Affair and led by the aristocratic Sir Alec Douglas-Home. As this speech clearly demonstrates, Wilson wanted the public to see him as a man of the people, in touch with changing times – a desire shared by President JOHN F KENNEDY, who had conveyed similar ideas to broad acclaim.

Wilson's professed knowledge of 'modern computers' and 'machine-tools' may have been shaky, and from today's perspective appears quaint, but at the time it had an enormous effect on the public, helping Labour to its narrow victory in the general election of 1964.

This morning, we present this document to the nation, *Labour and the Scientific Revolution*, because the strength, the solvency, the influence of Britain, which some still think depends upon nostalgic illusions or upon nuclear posturings – these things are going to depend, in the remainder of this century, to a unique extent on the speed with which we come to terms with the world of change ...

It is, of course, a cliché that we are living at a time of such rapid scientific change that our children are accepting as part of their everyday life things which would have been dismissed as science fiction a few years ago ... It is only a few years since we first in this conference debated automation, when almost every word uttered in that debate is already as out of date today as if we had been talking about the advent of the spinning jenny[1] ...

Let us be frank about one thing. It is no good trying to comfort ourselves with the thought that automation need not happen here; that it is going to create so many problems that we should perhaps put our heads in the sand

[1] A machine for spinning yarn, invented around 1746 by the weaver and carpenter James Hargreaves (1720–78), which dramatically increased productivity in the textile industry.

[2] Named after their (possibly mythical) leader Ned Ludd, the Luddites were textile workers who tried to protect their jobs by sabotaging the new machines as the textile industry mechanized in the early 19th century. The term came to signify reluctance to embrace technological progress.

and let it pass by. Because there is no room for Luddites[2] in the Socialist Party. If we try to abstract from the automative age, the only result will be that Britain will become a stagnant backwater, pitied and held in contempt by the rest of the world.

The danger, as things are, is that an unregulated private enterprise economy in this country will promote just enough automation to create serious unemployment, but not enough to create a breakthrough in the production barrier. Let us look at what is happening in automation all over the world – and what I may say is elementary compared with the knowledge that some of our trade union delegates could present to you this morning.

Already in the engineering and automobile industries in the United States they have reached a point where a programme-controlled machine-tool line can produce an entire motor car – and I mean an American motor car, with all the gimmicks on it – without the application of human skill or effort. They can do this without a single worker touching it. It is not commercially worthwhile yet, but it is technically possible.

Because we have to recognize that automation is not just one more process in the history of mechanization, if by mechanization we mean the application of technology to eliminate the need for human muscle. The essence of modern automation is that it replaces the hitherto unique human functions of memory and of judgement. And now the computers have reached the point where they command facilities of memory and of judgement far beyond the capacity of any human being or group of human beings who have ever lived.

A modern computer, in a fraction of a second, can make calculations and can make decisions of judgement which all the mathematicians in Britain and America combined could not make by ordinary methods in the space of a year. You have computers at work now controlling a planned productive system of machine-tools which have an impulse-cycle of three millionths of a second. They do their calculations and take their decisions in a period of three millionths of a second. Yet already those machines are out of date. New mass controllers are in production now with a speed 1,000 times as fast.

It was not easy, for me at any rate, to be able to appreciate what three billionths of a second – one 300-millionth of a second – really means – perhaps some of you find it easier to visualize it – until it was explained to me that if you were to set out to walk right round the earth at the Equator, assuming there was no water there, taking a step every 300-millionth of a second – that is, taking one step every time these machines actually do their thinking process – then you would circle the entire earth in one second. Now perhaps we have got it …

We can now set a programme-controlled machine-tool line so that, without the intervention of any human agency, it can produce a new set of machine-tools in its own image. And when machine-tools have acquired, as they now have, the faculty of unassisted reproduction, you have reached a point of no return where if man is not going to assert his control over machines, the machines are going to assert their control over man …

The problem is this. Since technological progress left to the mechanism of private industry and private property can lead only to high profits for a few, a high rate of employment for a few, and to mass redundancies for the many, if there had never been a case for socialism before, automation would have created it. Because only if technological progress becomes part of our national planning can that progress be directed to national ends.

So the choice is not between technological progress and the kind of easy-going world we are living in today. It is the choice between the blind imposition of technological advance – with all that means in terms of unemployment – and the conscious, planned, purposive use of scientific progress to provide undreamed of living standards and the possibility of leisure, ultimately on an unbelievable scale.

That is why we must, in the Labour Party, devote a lot more thought to providing facilities for the use of leisure; and this is why, again, as this document suggests, we shall have to be a lot more imaginative about the provision for retraining the workers made redundant by the development of new skills and new techniques …

In all our plans for the future, we are redefining and we are restating our socialism in terms of the scientific revolution. But that revolution cannot become a reality unless we are prepared to make far-reaching changes in economic and social attitudes which permeate our whole system of society.

The Britain that is going to be forged in the white heat of this revolution will be no place for restrictive practices or for outdated methods on either side of industry. We shall need a totally new attitude to the problems of apprenticeship, of training and retraining for skill. If there is one thing where the traditional philosophy of capitalism breaks down it is in training for apprenticeship, because quite frankly it does not pay any individual firm – unless it is very altruistic or quixotic or far-sighted – to train apprentices, if it knows at the end of the period of training they will be snapped up by some unscrupulous firm that makes no contribution to apprenticeship training. That is what economists mean when they talk about the difference between marginal private cost and net social cost.

So we are going to need a new attitude … For the commanding heights of British industry to be controlled today by men whose only claim is their aristocratic connections, or the power of inherited wealth, or speculative finance is as irrelevant to the 20th century as would be the continued purchase of commissions in the armed forces by lordly amateurs. At the very time that even the MCC[3] has abolished the distinction between amateurs and professionals, in science and industry we are content to remain a nation of gentlemen in a world of players.

For those of us who have studied the formidable Soviet challenge in the education of scientists and technologists – and above all, in the ruthless application of scientific techniques in Soviet industry – know that our future lies not in military strength alone, but in the efforts, the sacrifices, and above all the energies which a free people can mobilize for the future greatness of our country.

Because we are democrats, we reject the methods which communist countries are deploying in applying the results of scientific research to industrial life. But because we care deeply about the future of Britain, we must use all the resources of democratic planning, all the latent and underdeveloped energies and skills of our people, to ensure Britain's standing in the world. That is the message which I believe will go out from this conference to the people of Britain and to the people of the world.

[3] The Marylebone Cricket Club, established in London in 1787, hosted annual matches between amateur 'gentlemen' (from schools and universities) and semi-professional 'players' from 1806 to 1963.

❧

'The pound here in Britain, in your pocket or purse'

19 November 1967, radio and television broadcast from London, England

❧

This national address was a valiant effort to accentuate the positive in what was a disaster for the Labour government: the devaluation of sterling by 14 per cent against the US dollar. The decision was the result of economic difficulties that had been simmering during the Conservatives' long spell in government (1951–64) and which came to the boil under Labour: trade union agitation, low productivity levels and, above all, an unstable pound.

As ever, Wilson spoke in optimistic, no-nonsense terms about attacking the 'root cause' of Britain's economic problems, claiming that devaluation would boost exports, thereby increasing productivity and jobs. Most famously of all, he said that while sterling was worth less in terms of other currencies, the 'pound in your pocket' was not devalued. Few were convinced, however, and the phrase was to haunt Wilson, becoming the punchline of jokes everywhere.

Public scepticism was not unfounded; spending cuts caused by devaluation led to the reintroduction of prescription charges for the National Health Service. As the Conservative leader EDWARD HEATH said at the time, Labour had devalued 'against all their own arguments'.

❧

Since the Cabinet last Thursday took its unanimous decision to devalue sterling, it's been impossible for me to speak to you, because of the need for secrecy while this tremendous international monetary operation was being carried through. Now I can tell you why we have taken this action, and more important what it means.

Because we had to maintain silence, there have inevitably been rumours, some of them very strong, that we were taking a different course. It would have been possible to ride out this present tide of foreign speculation against the pound by borrowing from central banks and governments abroad, banks and governments to whom I pay tribute for their help and co-operation over these past years. In our view it would have been irresponsible to go on dealing with these successive waves of speculation by borrowing for three months, six months at a time, without attacking the root cause of the speculation. Failure to attack the root cause would have meant trying to borrow, this time in conditions in which our creditors abroad might well insist on guarantees about this or that aspect of our national policies.

Last weekend, the government decided that we were not prepared to accept any solution which placed rigid limitations on the ability of our people and government to solve our problems by our own exertions; that we could not accept restrictions on our national growth, on industrial expansion, on our determination to achieve and maintain full employment. We are determined to break out from the straitjacket which has constricted us under successive governments now for 15 years, a straitjacket which meant that every time we tried to solve our problems by expanding production, by mobilizing the efforts and skill of our people, on the basis of full employment, the immediate result was a desperate trade and payments deficit.

The deficit we inherited three years ago – over £800 million – was itself the result of an attempt by our predecessors to fight their way out of this dilemma by an unrestrained boom. And for three years we have fought – and it was our duty to fight – to overcome that deficit, to maintain the external value of sterling. And no-one could doubt, at home or abroad, our determination to win through. No-one will underrate what we've had to do in that fight, nor the heavy price we've paid and have had to ask the country to pay.

But by our policies, by the efforts of our people, we'd reduced that deficit last year to less than a quarter, our exports had risen at about double the rate of the past few years, and we were all set to get into balance, indeed into surplus this year. But there was never enough margin to meet the chance and change of world events, nor to guarantee the repayment of the vast borrowing we'd incurred to pay for the deficit that we found on taking office.

I'm not going to go into all the details of the events which this year have once again put us in the red: the heavy cost to our trade and payments of the war in the Middle East;[1] the temporary disruption to our exports by the dock strike.[2] And tonight is not the time to attribute blame to the policies of the last government or this government, or to unofficial strikers, or to the manoeuvring of speculators at home and abroad.

But all along we've had to face this: exports – even our increasing exports – could not earn enough to meet the successive waves of speculation against sterling. Time was needed to restructure and modernize our industries; to build up our trade – and we've been doing this at a rate about double what was previously achieved. Time was needed to cut down our overseas defence commitments; but that time was denied us. Whenever Britain ran into short-term difficulties, there were some who sold sterling in a panic and there were others who gambled against us in the hope of a quick gain. And all this, even though our basic position was showing a steady improvement ...

And the problem is this: we, Britain, are a major trading country. And like any business firm, our financial position depends on how much we sell to others. But because we're also an international bank; because sterling is an international currency, it's subject to speculative attacks for short-run reasons which have nothing to do with Britain's trading position.

Now our decision to devalue attacks our problems at the root. And that is why the international monetary community have rallied round with a display of formidable strength to back the operation. This backing is, of course, to deter the speculators, not for us to live on. And that's why it doesn't involve unacceptable conditions.

Tonight, we must face the new situation. First, what this means. From now on, the pound abroad is worth 14 per cent or so less in terms of other currencies. That doesn't mean, of course, that the pound here in Britain, in your pocket or purse or in your bank, has been devalued. What it does mean is that we shall now be able to sell more goods abroad on a competitive basis. This is a tremendous opportunity for all our exporters, and for many who have not yet started to sell their goods overseas.

But it will also mean that the goods we buy from abroad will be dearer. And so for many of these goods it will be cheaper to buy British. Because one of the great problems we in Britain have had over these past five or six years has been the great increase year by year in imports of goods manufactured abroad. And then farm production will be stimulated. We'll be able to do more to replace food imported from abroad.

Saving imports, and still more the export drive, will mean that industrial production will go up. Many industries and firms, which are now working below capacity, will have a chance to get into full production. This means more work, more jobs in the development areas, because we intend to be ruthless in diverting new enterprise to those areas.

But all this will be at a cost, at any rate for a time. The needs of the export

[1] Wilson refers to the Six-Day War (June 1967) between Israel and its Arab neighbours Egypt, Syria and Jordan.

[2] In May 1966 a strike over working hours, organized by the National Union of Seamen, brought British ports and docks to a standstill.

drive will mean that we've got to shift £500 million of our national output into exports and into import saving. That is why we're tightening the control on bank lending, except for priority borrowers such as exporters. The bank rate is being raised to eight per cent, for as long as is necessary. Hire purchase is being tightened on cars, an industry which can now go out and get an immediate boost in its exports.

We're cutting back public expenditure. We're making further sharp cuts in defence spending, effective in this coming year. There'll be cuts in the capital expenditure programmes of some of the publicly owned industries and the other cuts in public expenditure the Chancellor announced last month. But the priority programmes of housing, school building and hospital building will be safeguarded in all these measures, and the job of bringing work to development areas will be given a still higher priority than it's had.

I've said that imports will cost more, and this means higher prices, over a period, for some of our imports, including some of our basic foods. And it's vital that price rises are limited to those cases where increased import costs make this unavoidable. Our people will not tolerate traders who are not affected by import costs trying to cash in by unjustifiable price increases. We shall keep a very tight watch on prices, and we shall use the powers we have under the Prices and Incomes Act.[3]

And it's just as vital that any prices that do go up are not used as an excuse for excessive wage demands, because that would simply increase our export costs and this would cut into the benefit our export industries have now got, with all that would mean for trade, and at the end of the day, for employment.

The government, for our part, in addition to our policy for prices, will keep a strict watch on dividends. The corporation tax on profits is to be increased. We will do everything in our power to create the climate in which an effective prices and incomes policy can be pursued by those whose job it is. And this must mean rent. The government have decided to refer to the National Board for Prices and Incomes certain council rent increases, and we're particularly after those cases where the increases seem exceptionally steep and provocative.

It's the duty of the government to ensure by special measures that when burdens have to be borne, those who are liable to be hardest hit are protected – and your government will fulfil that duty.

This has been – devaluation has been – a hard decision, and some of its consequences will themselves be hard for a time. But now the decision has been taken, all of us together must now make a success of it. We must take with both hands the opportunity that's now been presented to us. Our exporters; our industrial managers; our salesmen – what a chance they've got now. Our workers in every industry; our scientists and engineers; our designers; the professionals responsible for our invisible earnings are now on their mettle – and any who fail, through laziness or self-seeking; any who frustrate the work of others by unofficial strikes, will imperil the right to work not only of themselves, but of the nation.

I have told you tonight what led to this decision. I told you the alternative which we could have sought and why we rejected that alternative. This is a proud nation. As I've said, we have the chance now to break out from the straitjacket of these past years. We're on our own now. It means: Britain first.

[3] The 1966 Act required that wage claims be reported to the government within a week, and introduced various measures to control pay rises. It was highly unpopular with the trade unions.

Woodrow Wilson
American statesman

Thomas Woodrow Wilson (1856–1924) was born in Staunton, Virginia, the son of a Presbyterian minister of Scottish–Irish ancestry. He studied at Princeton and Johns Hopkins University, then practised law at Atlanta, and lectured at Bryn Mawr and Princeton, becoming president of Princeton in 1902. In 1910 he became president of the American Political Science Association and in 1911, governor of New Jersey. In 1912, as candidate for the Democratic Party, he was elected president of the USA, a post he held for two terms. Despite his efforts to keep the USA out of World War I, he declared war on Germany in 1917. His 'Fourteen Points', a peace programme outlined to Congress in 1918, was instrumental in bringing about the armistice with Germany and the peace talks that produced the post-war treaties (1919) and the establishment of the League of Nations (1920); he was a leading player in the peace talks at Versailles and received the Nobel Peace Prize in 1919. However, the US Senate rejected the Treaty of Versailles and, in 1920, membership of the League of Nations. Wilson's administration also saw the 18th and 19th Amendments to the US Constitution (1917–20) which introduced, respectively, prohibition of alcohol and women's suffrage. In October 1919, he suffered a stroke which severely incapacitated him and forced his retirement from politics. His publications include a *History of the American People* (1902).

'The world must be made safe for democracy'
2 April 1917, Washington, DC, USA

This momentous speech was given during an extraordinary joint session of Congress, at which Wilson recommended declaring war on Germany.

His decision was prompted in part by indiscriminate submarine warfare conducted against shipping in the Atlantic. After the British passenger cruiser RMS *Lusitania* was sunk in 1915, torpedo strikes had been briefly checked by international outcry. But by 1917, German U-boats had resumed attacks on all shipping entering and leaving Allied ports.

Although he had previously resisted involvement in World War I, Wilson was an internationalist, who believed the USA should play a larger part on the world stage. He argued that the values of 'western civilization' were in peril. The rise of the Bolsheviks in Russia at this time intensified his belief that democracy was under threat. He had been narrowly re-elected on a neutralist platform, but now, less than a month after beginning his second term as president, he pressed for war.

The USA had only a small standing army at this time and Wilson was forced to introduce conscription for men aged 21 to 30, suppressing dissent with the Espionage Act of 1917 and the Sedition Act of 1918.

Wilson signed no treaty with France or Britain, but news that the 'Yankees' were entering the war boosted morale among the Allies. Few American troops were deployed in Europe before summer 1918, but their expected arrival undermined what might have been a decisive German spring offensive.

We have no quarrel with the German people. We have no feeling toward them but one of sympathy and friendship. It was not upon their impulse that their government acted in entering this war. It was not with their previous knowledge or approval. It was a war determined upon as wars used to be determined upon in the old, unhappy days, when peoples were nowhere consulted by their rulers and wars were provoked and waged in the interest of dynasties, or of little groups of ambitious men who were accustomed to use their fellow men as pawns and tools. ...

We are accepting this challenge of hostile purpose because we know that in such a government, following such methods, we can never have a friend; and that in the presence of its organized power, always lying in wait to accomplish we know not what purpose, there can be no assured security for the democratic governments of the world. We are now about to accept gage of battle with this natural foe to liberty and shall, if necessary, spend the whole force of the nation to check and nullify its pretensions and its power. We are glad, now that we see the facts with no veil of false pretence about them, to fight thus for the ultimate peace of the world and for the liberation of its peoples, the German peoples included: for the rights of nations great and small and the privilege of men everywhere to choose their way of life and of obedience.

The world must be made safe for democracy. Its peace must be planted upon the tested foundations of political liberty. We have no selfish ends to serve. We desire no conquest, no dominion. We seek no indemnities for ourselves, no material compensation for the sacrifices we shall freely make. We are but one of the champions of the rights of mankind. We shall be satisfied when those rights have been made as secure as the faith and the freedom of nations can make them.

Just because we fight without rancour and without selfish object, seeking nothing for ourselves but what we shall wish to share with all free peoples, we shall, I feel confident, conduct our operations as belligerents without passion and ourselves observe with proud punctilio[1] the principles of right and of fair play we profess to be fighting for.

I have said nothing of the governments allied with the imperial government of Germany because they have not made war upon us or challenged us to defend our right and our honour. The Austro-Hungarian government has, indeed, avowed its unqualified endorsement and acceptance of the reckless and lawless submarine warfare adopted now without disguise by the imperial German government, and it has therefore not been possible for this government to receive Count Tarnowski, the ambassador recently accredited to this government by the imperial and royal government of Austria–Hungary; but that government has not actually engaged in warfare against citizens of the United States on the seas, and I take the liberty, for the present at least, of postponing a discussion of our relations with the authorities at Vienna. We enter this war only where we are clearly forced into it, because there are no other means of defending our rights.

It will be all the easier for us to conduct ourselves as belligerents in a high spirit of right and fairness because we act without animus, not in enmity toward a people or with the desire to bring any injury or disadvantage upon them, but only in armed opposition to an irresponsible government which has thrown aside all considerations of humanity and of right and is running amok. We are, let me say again, the sincere friends of the German people, and shall desire nothing so much as the early re-establishment of intimate relations of mutual advantage between us – however hard it may be for them, for the time being, to believe that this is spoken from our hearts.

We have borne with their present government through all these bitter months because of that friendship – exercising a patience and forbearance which would otherwise have been impossible. We shall, happily, still have an opportunity to prove that friendship in our daily attitude and actions toward the millions of men and women of German birth and native sympathy who live among us and share our life, and we shall be proud to prove it toward all who are in fact loyal to their neighbours and to the government in the hour of test. They are, most of them, as true and loyal Americans as if they had never known any other fealty or allegiance. They will be prompt to stand with us in rebuking and restraining the few who may be of a different mind and purpose. If there should be disloyalty, it will be dealt with with a firm hand of stern repression; but, if it lifts its head at all, it will lift it only here and there and without countenance except from a lawless and malignant few.

[1] Punctiliousness.

It is a distressing and oppressive duty, gentlemen of the Congress, which I have performed in thus addressing you. There are, it may be, many months of fiery trial and sacrifice ahead of us. It is a fearful thing to lead this great peaceful people into war, into the most terrible and disastrous of all wars, civilization itself seeming to be in the balance.

But the right is more precious than peace, and we shall fight for the things which we have always carried nearest our hearts – for democracy, for the right of those who submit to authority to have a voice in their own governments, for the rights and liberties of small nations, for a universal dominion of right by such a concert of free peoples as shall bring peace and safety to all nations and make the world itself at last free.

To such a task we can dedicate our lives and our fortunes, everything that we are and everything that we have, with the pride of those who know that the day has come when America is privileged to spend her blood and her might for the principles that gave her birth and happiness and the peace which she has treasured. God helping her, she can do no other.

'Unless justice be done to others it will not be done to us'
8 January 1918, Washington, DC, USA

Wilson himself undertook diplomatic duties in his War Cabinet. In this speech – again to a joint session of Congress – he outlined his proposals for brokering a liberal and fair peace in Europe.

This abridged version includes his famous 'Fourteen Points': a detailed programme intended to settle territorial questions at the end of the war. Though he describes his terms as 'too concrete to admit of any further doubt or question', Wilson includes both specific provisions (the restoration of territory to Russia, Belgium, France and other nations) and broader principles, such as 'absolute freedom of navigation upon the seas'.

He concludes with a proposal for an international body with the authority to adjudicate in future disputes: the basis of the League of Nations and its successor, the United Nations Organization.

Parts of the Fourteen Points would later be enshrined in the Treaty of Versailles of 1919. However, US ratification of both this and membership of the League of Nations was overruled by Republicans in the Senate. Against his doctors' advice, Wilson undertook a frantic public campaign to reverse this outcome. He gave 39 speeches in just three weeks, which may well have contributed to his stroke.

His successor as president, Warren G Harding, officially ended hostilities with Germany.

Not once, but again and again, we have laid our whole thought and purpose before the world, not in general terms only, but each time with sufficient definition to make it clear what sort of definite terms of settlement must necessarily spring out of them. Within the last week Mr LLOYD GEORGE has spoken with admirable candour and in admirable spirit for the people and government of Great Britain. There is no confusion of counsel among the adversaries of the Central Powers, no uncertainty of principle, no vagueness of detail.

The only secrecy of counsel, the only lack of fearless frankness, the only failure to make definite statement of the objects of the war, lies with Germany and her allies. The issues of life and death hang upon these definitions. No statesman who has the least conception of his responsibility ought for a moment to permit himself to continue this tragical and appalling outpouring of blood and treasure unless he is sure beyond a peradventure that the objects of the vital sacrifice are part and parcel of the very life of society and that people for whom he speaks think them right and imperative as he does.

There is, moreover, a voice calling for these definitions of principle and of purpose which is, it seems to me, more thrilling and more compelling than any of the many moving voices with which the troubled air of the world is filled. It is the voice of the Russian people. They are prostrate and all but helpless, it would seem, before the grim power of Germany, which has hitherto known no relenting and no pity.

Their power, apparently, is shattered. And yet their soul is not subservient. They will not yield, either in principle or in action. Their conception of what is right, of what it is humane and honourable for them to accept, has been stated with a frankness, a largeness of view, a generosity of spirit, and a universal human sympathy which must challenge the admiration of every friend of mankind; and they have refused to compound their ideals or desert others that they themselves may be safe.

They call to us to say what it is that we desire; in what, if in anything, our purpose and our spirit differ from theirs; and I believe that the people of the United States would wish me to respond, with utter simplicity and frankness. Whether their present leaders believe it or not, it is our heartfelt desire and hope that some way be opened whereby we may be privileged to assist the people of Russia to attain their utmost hope of liberty and ordered peace.

It will be our wish and purpose that the processes of peace, when they are begun, shall be absolutely open and that they shall involve and permit henceforth no secret understandings of any kind. The day of conquest and aggrandizement is gone by; so is also the day of secret covenants entered into in the interest of particular governments and likely at some unlooked-for moment to upset the peace of the world. It is this happy fact – now clear to the view of every public man whose thoughts do not still linger in an age that is dead and gone – which makes it possible for every nation whose purposes are consistent with justice and the peace of the world to avow, now or at any other time, the objects it has in view.

We entered this war because violations of right had occurred which touched us to the quick and made the life of our own people impossible, unless they were corrected and the world secured once for all against their recurrence. What we demand in this war, therefore, is nothing peculiar to ourselves. It is that the world be made fit and safe to live in; and particularly that it be made safe for every peace-loving nation which, like our own, wishes to live its own life, determine its own institutions, be assured of justice and fair dealing by other peoples of the world as against force and selfish aggression. All the peoples of the world are in effect partners in this interest, and for our own part we see very clearly that unless justice be done to others it will not be done to us. The programme of the world's peace, therefore, is our programme; and that programme, the only possible programme as we see it, is this:

One: open covenants of peace, openly arrived at, after which there shall be no private international understandings of any kind, but diplomacy shall proceed always frankly and in the public view.

Two: absolute freedom of navigation upon the seas, outside territorial waters, alike in peace and in war, except as the seas may be closed in whole or in part by international action for the enforcement of international covenants.

Three: the removal, so far as possible, of all economic barriers and the establishment of an equality of trade conditions among all the nations consenting to the peace and associating themselves for its maintenance.

Four: adequate guarantees given and taken that national armaments will be reduced to the lowest point consistent with domestic safety.

Five: a free, open-minded, and absolutely impartial adjustment of all colonial claims, based upon a strict observance of the principle that in determining all such questions of sovereignty, the interests of the populations concerned must have equal weight with the equitable claims of the government whose title is to be determined.

Six: the evacuation of all Russian territory and such a settlement of all questions affecting Russia as will secure the best and freest co-operation of the other nations of the world, in obtaining for her an unhampered and unembarrassed opportunity for the independent determination of her own political development and national policy, and assure her of a sincere welcome into the society of free nations, under institutions of her own choosing; and, more than a welcome, assistance also of every kind that she may need and may herself desire. The treatment accorded Russia by her sister nations in the months to come will be the acid test of their goodwill, of their comprehension of her needs as distinguished from their own interests, and of their intelligent and unselfish sympathy.

Seven: Belgium, the whole world will agree, must be evacuated and restored, without any attempt to limit the sovereignty which she enjoys in common with all other free nations. No other single act will serve as this will serve to restore confidence among the nations in the laws which they have themselves set and determined for the government of their relations with one another. Without this healing act, the whole structure and validity of international law is forever impaired.

Eight: all French territory should be freed and the invaded portions restored, and the wrong done to France by Prussia in 1871 in the matter of Alsace-Lorraine, which has unsettled the peace of the world for nearly 50 years,[1] should be righted, in order that peace may once more be made secure in the interest of all.

[1] Under the Treaty of Frankfurt, which ended the Franco-Prussian War of 1870–1, France was obliged to cede much of Alsace-Lorraine to the newly unified Germany.

Nine: a readjustment of the frontiers of Italy should be effected along clearly recognizable lines of nationality.

Ten: the peoples of Austria-Hungary, whose place among the nations we wish to see safeguarded and assured, should be accorded the freest opportunity of autonomous development.

Eleven: Romania, Serbia and Montenegro should be evacuated; occupied territories restored; Serbia accorded free and secure access to the sea; and the relations of the several Balkan states to one another determined by friendly counsel along historically established lines of allegiance and nationality; and international guarantees of the political and economic independence and territorial integrity of the several Balkan states should be entered into.

Twelve: the Turkish portions of the present Ottoman Empire should be assured a secure sovereignty, but the other nationalities which are now under the Turkish rule should be assured an undoubted security of life and an absolutely unmolested opportunity of autonomous development, and the Dardanelles should be permanently opened as a free passage to the ships and commerce of all nations under international guarantees.

Thirteen: an independent Polish state should be erected, which should include the territories inhabited by indisputably Polish populations, which should be assured a free and secure access to the sea, and whose political and economic independence and territorial integrity should be guaranteed by international covenant.

Fourteen: a general association of nations must be formed under specific covenants for the purpose of affording mutual guarantees of political independence and territorial integrity to great and small states alike.

In regard to these essential rectifications of wrong and assertions of right, we feel ourselves to be intimate partners of all the governments and peoples associated together against the imperialists. We cannot be separated in interest or divided in purpose. We stand together until the end.

For such arrangements and covenants, we are willing to fight and to continue to fight until they are achieved; but only because we wish the right to prevail and desire a just and stable peace such as can be secured only by removing the chief provocations to war, which this programme does remove. We have no jealousy of German greatness, and there is nothing in this programme that impairs it.

We grudge her no achievement or distinction of learning or of pacific enterprise, such as have made her record very bright and very enviable. We do not wish to injure her or to block in any way her legitimate influence or power. We do not wish to fight her, either with arms or with hostile arrangements of trade, if she is willing to associate herself with us and the other peace-loving nations of the world in covenants of justice and law and fair dealing. We wish her only to accept a place of equality among the peoples of the world – the new world in which we now live – instead of a place of mastery.

Neither do we presume to suggest to her any alteration or modification of her institutions. But it is necessary, we must frankly say, and necessary as a preliminary to any intelligent dealings with her on our part, that we should know whom her spokesmen speak for when they speak to us, whether for the Reichstag majority or for the military party and the men whose creed is imperial domination.

We have spoken now, surely, in terms too concrete to admit of any further doubt or question. An evident principle runs through the whole programme I have outlined. It is the principle of justice to all peoples and nationalities, and their right to live on equal terms of liberty and safety with one another, whether they be strong or weak. Unless this principle be made its foundation no part of the structure of international justice can stand. The people of the United States could act upon no other principle; and to the vindication of this principle they are ready to devote their lives, their honour and everything that they possess. The moral climax of this, the culminating and final war for human liberty has come, and they are ready to put their own strength, their own highest purpose, their own integrity and devotion to the test.

John Winthrop
English colonialist

John Winthrop (c.1587–1649) was born in Groton, Suffolk. He studied at Trinity College, Cambridge and Gray's Inn, London, becoming a lawyer at the Court of Wards. He was elected governor of Massachusetts Bay colony in 1629, and the following year he led pilgrims on a transatlantic voyage to settle in the New World. He was periodically re-elected, and probably had more influence than anyone else in forming the political institutions of the northern states of America. His *Journal* was published long after his death, the first part in 1790 and the remainder in 1825–6.

'We shall be as a city upon a hill'
March/April 1630, on board the *Arbella* on the Atlantic Ocean

John Winthrop has been viewed variously as a social reformer, a utopian visionary, or a misguided reactionary. But his conception of the new colony to be founded in wilderness of Massachusetts was a commanding one.

In this on-board sermon, which became known as 'A Model of Christian Charity', he uses biblical imagery to great effect. Establishing a tension between the real world the pilgrims had left behind and the ideal world they hoped to inhabit, Winthrop instructs his listeners to show discipline and individual responsibility, presenting their society as an example of faith and good practice.

In 17th-century England, Puritans were regarded with suspicion, often facing persecution. The 700 exiles who came to the New World viewed themselves in a quite different way; they were 'the godly', who held a special covenant with God. They had emerged during the Reformation as a radical Protestant group, broadly seeking to purify church practice.

However, Winthrop's followers were not impoverished. Their expedition was well-planned and financed, and a royal charter had been bestowed on the Massachusetts Bay Company.

Although Winthrop's speech is not simple to read – and presumes a thorough familiarity with the Bible – it has had a great influence on the American sense of identity. The phrase 'city on a hill', drawn originally from the Sermon on the Mount, is felt to reinforce a sense of America's unique destiny in the world. It has been quoted in speeches by US presidents as disparate as JOHN F KENNEDY and RONALD REAGAN.

Herein are four things to be propounded: first the persons, secondly the work, thirdly the end, fourthly the means.

For the persons: we are a company professing ourselves fellow members of Christ, in which respect only, though we were absent from each other many miles, and had our employments as far distant, yet we ought to account ourselves knit together by this bond of love, and live in the exercise of it, if we would have comfort of our being in Christ. This was notorious in the practice of the Christians in former times …

Secondly, for the work we have in hand, it is by a mutual consent through a special overruling providence – and a more than an ordinary approbation of the churches of Christ – to seek out a place of cohabitation and consortship under a due form of government both civil and ecclesiastical. In such cases as this, the care of the public must oversway all private respects, by which not only conscience, but mere civil policy doth bind us; for it is a true rule that particular estates cannot subsist in the ruin of the public.

Thirdly, the end is to improve our lives to do more service to the Lord and increase of the body of Christ whereof we are members, that ourselves and posterity may be the better preserved from the common corruptions of this evil world …

Fourthly, for the means whereby this must be effected, they are twofold: a conformity with the work and end we aim at. These we see are extraordinary, therefore we must not content ourselves with usual, ordinary means. Whatsoever we did, or ought to have done, when we lived in England, the same must we do and more also where we go. That which the most in their churches maintain as a truth in profession only, we must bring into familiar and constant practice, as in this duty of love: we must love brotherly without dissimulation,[1] we must love one another with a pure heart fervently,[2] we must bear one another's burdens,[3] we must not look only on our own things, but also on the things of our brethren.

Neither must we think that the Lord will bear with such failings at our hands as he doth from those among whom we have lived, and that for three reasons.

Firstly, in regard of the more near bond of marriage between him and us, wherein he hath taken us to be his, after a most strict and peculiar manner which will make him the more jealous of our love and obedience. So he tells the people of Israel: 'You only have I known, of all the families of the earth; therefore will I punish you for your Transgressions.'[4]

Secondly, because the Lord will be sanctified in them that come near him. We know that there were many that corrupted the service of the Lord, some setting up altars before his own, others offering both strange fire and strange sacrifices also; yet there came no fire from Heaven, or other sudden judgement upon them, as did upon Nadab and Abihu,[5] who yet we may think did not sin presumptuously.

Thirdly, when God gives a special commission, he looks to have it strictly observed in every article. When he gave Saul a commission to destroy Amalek[6] he indented with him upon certain articles; and because he failed in one of the least, and that upon a fair pretence, it lost him the kingdom, which should have been his reward, if he had observed his commission.[7]

Thus stands the cause between God and us: we are entered into covenant with him for this work; we have taken out a commission. The Lord hath given us leave to draw our own articles. We have professed to enterprise these actions upon these and these ends. We have hereupon besought him of favour and blessing.

Now, if the Lord shall please to hear us and bring us in peace to the place we desire, then hath he ratified this covenant and sealed our commission [and] will expect a strict performance of the articles contained in it. But if we shall neglect the observation of these articles, which are the ends we have propounded and – dissembling with our God – shall fall to embrace this present world and prosecute our carnal intentions, seeking great things for ourselves and our posterity, the Lord will surely break out in wrath against us, be revenged of such a perjured people and make us know the price of the breach of such a covenant.

Now the only way to avoid this shipwreck and to provide for our posterity is to follow the counsel of Micah: 'to do justly, to love mercy, to walk humbly with our God'.[8] For this end, we must be knit together in this work as one man. We must entertain each other in brotherly affection. We must be willing to abridge ourselves of our superfluities, for the supply of others' necessities. We must uphold a familiar commerce together in all meekness, gentleness, patience and liberality. We must delight in each other, make others' conditions our own, rejoice together, mourn together, labour and suffer together, always having before our eyes our commission and community in the work, our community as members of the same body.

So shall we keep 'the unity of the spirit in the bond of peace',[9] the Lord will be our God and delight to dwell among us as his own people and will command a blessing upon us in all our ways, so that we shall see much more of his wisdom, power, goodness and truth than formerly we have been

[1] See Romans 12:9–10.

[2] See 1 Peter 1:22.

[3] See Galatians 6:2.

[4] Amos 3:2.

[5] See Leviticus 10:1–2.

[6] See 1 Samuel 15.

[7] See 1 Samuel 28:16–18.

[8] Micah 6:8.

[9] Ephesians 4:3.

acquainted with. We shall find that the God of Israel is among us when ten of us shall be able to resist a thousand of our enemies, when he shall make us a praise and glory, that men shall say of succeeding plantations: the Lord make it like that of New England.

For we must consider that we shall be as a city upon a hill.[10] The eyes of all people are upon us, so that if we shall deal falsely with our God in this work we have undertaken, and so cause him to withdraw his present help from us, we shall be made a story and a byword through the world; we shall open the mouths of enemies to speak evil of the ways of God and all professors for God's sake; we shall shame the faces of many of God's worthy servants, and cause their prayers to be turned into curses upon us, till we be consumed out of the good land whether we are going.

And to shut up this discourse with that exhortation of Moses, that faithful servant of the Lord, in his last farewell to Israel beloved,[11] there is now set before us life and good, death and evil: in that we are commanded this day to love the Lord our God, and to love one another, to walk in his ways and to keep his commandments and his ordinance, and his laws, and the articles of our covenant with him that we may live and be multiplied, and that the Lord our God may bless us the land whither we go to possess it. But if our hearts shall turn away so that we will not obey, but shall be seduced and worship other gods – our pleasures and profits – and serve them; it is propounded unto us this day, we shall surely perish out of the good land whither we pass over this vast sea to possess it.

Therefore let us choose life, that we and our seed may live by obeying his voice and cleaving to him, for he is our life, and our prosperity.

[10] Matthew 5:14; part of JESUS's Sermon on the Mount, which is included in this book.

[11] See Deuteronomy 30:15–18.

Frances Wright
Scottish – American reformer and abolitionist

Frances Wright *also known as Fanny, later Frances Darusmont* (1795–1852) was born in Dundee, Scotland, the heiress to a large fortune. She emigrated to the USA in 1818 and toured widely, publishing *Views of Society and Manners in America* in 1821. In 1826 she founded a short-lived community for freed slaves at Nashoba in Western Tennessee. Following its collapse in 1829, she settled in New York City, where she published with the Welsh reformer Robert Dale Owen a socialist journal, *Free Enquirer*. In 1831, she married a French physician, Guillaume Darusmont. One of the early suffragettes, she campaigned vigorously against religion and for the emancipation of women.

'To be free we have but to see our chains'
4 July 1828, Nashoba, Tennessee, USA

The early 19th century was a time of expanding boundaries – not only mass migration but also social experimentation. One pioneer was the utopian visionary Frances Wright, who put her philosophy into action at Nashoba.

The commune she founded there was intended as an implementation of the ideas in her book *A Plan for the Gradual Abolition of Slavery* (1825). She bought 30 slaves in order to establish the community, teaching them skills so they could earn the money to buy their freedom. They would then be sent either to Africa or to Haiti to begin a new life.

Meetings at Nashoba were held in New Harmony Hall. The building was named in honour of New Harmony, Robert Owen's utopian commune in Indiana, a model for Wright's own experiment. It was here that she gave this Independence Day speech which, unusually, was addressed to both men and women.

She was a gifted speaker and her audience was sympathetic to her message. Here, she describes with almost evangelical fervour and optimism her view of human progress through rational thinking, co-operation and education, principles she sees enshrined in the US Constitution.

However, Nashoba did not enjoy the success of similar communities such as Owen's New Lanark in Scotland, which was profitable as well as socially responsible. Nashoba began poorly and when Wright had to leave for medical reasons it was at the centre of a scandal in which reports of mistreatment were overshadowed by rumours of 'free love' and interracial partnerships. The experiment was abandoned in 1829.

The custom which commemorates in rejoicing the anniversary of the national independence of these states has its origin in a human feeling, amiable in its nature and beneficial, under proper direction, in its indulgence.

From the era from which dates the national existence of the American people, dates also a mighty step in the march of human knowledge … Dating, as we justly may, a new era in the history of man from 4 July 1776,[1] it would be well – that is, it would be useful – if on each anniversary we examined the progress made by our species in just knowledge and just practice. Each 4 July would then stand as a tidemark in the flood of time, by which to note the rise and fall of each successive error, the discovery of each important truth, the gradual melioration in our public institutions, social arrangements, and, above all, in our moral feelings and mental views. Let such a review as this engage annually our attention, and sacred, doubly sacred, shall be this day: and that not to one nation only, but to all nations capable of reflection.

The political dismemberment of these once-British colonies from the parent island – though involving a valuable principle and many possible results – would scarcely merit a yearly commemoration, even in this country, had it not been accompanied by other occurrences more novel, and far more important. I allude to the seal then set to the system of representative government, till then imperfectly known in Europe, and

[1] The date on which the US Declaration of Independence was signed.

insecurely practised in America; and to the crown then placed on this system by the novel experiment of political federation. The frame of federative government that sprang out of the articles signed in '76 is one of the most beautiful inventions of the human intellect. It has been in government what the steam engine has been in mechanics, and the printing press in the dissemination of knowledge.

But it needs not that we should now pause to analyse what all must have considered. It is to one particular feature in our political institutions that I would call attention, and this because it is at once the most deserving of notice, and the least noticed … There is, in the institutions of this country, one principle, which, had they no other excellence, would secure to them the preference over those of all other countries. I mean – and some devout patriots will start – I mean the principle of change.

I have used a word to which is attached an obnoxious meaning. Speak of change and the world is in alarm. And yet where do we not see change? What is there in the physical world but change? And what would there be in the moral world without change? The flower blossoms, the fruit ripens, the seed is received and germinates in the earth, and we behold the tree. The aliment we eat to satisfy our hunger incorporates with our frame, and the atoms composing our existence today are exhaled tomorrow. In like manner, our feelings and opinions are moulded by circumstance and matured by observation and experience. All is change. Within and about us, no one thing is as it was, or will be as it is.

Strange, then, that we should start at a word used to signify a thing so familiar. Stranger yet that we should fail to appreciate a principle which, inherent in all matter, is no less inherent in ourselves; and which, as it has tracked our mental progress heretofore, so will it track our progress through time to come.

But will it be said change has a bad, as well as a good sense? It may be for the better, and it may be for the worse? In the physical world it can be neither the one nor the other. It can be simply such as it is. But in the moral world – that is, in the thoughts and feelings and inventions of men – change may certainly be either for the better or for the worse, or it may be for neither.

Changes that are neither bad nor good can have regard only to trivial matters, and can be as little worthy of observation as of censure. Changes that are from better to worse can originate only in ignorance, and are ever amended so soon as experience has substantiated their mischief. Where men then are free to consult experience they will correct their practice, and make changes for the better.

It follows, therefore, that the more free men are, the more changes they will make. In the beginning, possibly, for the worse; but most certainly in time for the better, until – their knowledge enlarging by observation, and their judgement strengthening by exercise – they will find themselves in the straight, broad, fair road of improvement. Out of change, therefore, springs improvement; and the people who shall have imagined a peaceable mode of changing their institutions, hold a surety for their melioration. This surety is worth all other excellences.

Better were the prospects of a people under the influence of the worst government who should hold the power of changing it, that those of a people under the best who should hold no such power. Here, then, is the great beauty of American government. The simple machinery of representation carried through all its parts, gives facility for its being moulded at will to fit with the knowledge of the age. If imperfect in any or all of its parts, it bears within it a perfect principle – the principle of improvement.

And let us observe that this principle is all that we can ever know of perfection. Knowledge, and all the blessings which spring out of knowledge, can never be more than progressive; and whatsoever sets open the door does all for us; does every thing. The clear-sighted provision in the national Constitution – as in the constitutions of the different states – by which the frame of government can be moulded at will by the public voice and so made to keep pace in progress with the public mind, is the master-stroke in constitutional law. Were our institutions far less enlightened and well digested than they are, were every other regulation erroneous, every other ordinance defective – nay, even tyrannous – this single provision would counterbalance all. Let but the door be opened, and be fixed open, for improvement to hold on her unimpeded course, and vices, however flagrant, are but the evils of an hour.

Once launch the animal man in the road of iniquity, and he shall – he must – hold a forward career. He may be sometimes checked; he may seem occasionally to retrograde; but his retreat is only that of the receding wave in the inning tide. His master movement is always in advance … To hold him still, he must be chained. Snap the chain, and he springs forward …

Supposing that our laws – constitutional, civil or penal – should in any thing cripple us at the present, the power will be with us to amend or annul them so soon (and how might it be sooner?) as our enlarged knowledge shall enable us to see in what they err. All the liberty, therefore, that we yet lack will gradually spring up – there, where our bondage is – in our minds. To be free we have but to see our chains.

Are we disappointed? Are we sometimes angry because the crowd or any part of the crowd around us bows submissively to mischievous usages or unjust laws? Let us remember that they do so in ignorance of their mischief and injustice, and that when they see these, as in the course of man's progressive state they must see them, these and other evils will be corrected. Inappreciable is this advantage that we hold (unfortunately) above other nations.

The great national and political revolution of '76 set the seal to the liberties of North America. And but for one evil, and that of immense magnitude, which the constitutional provision we have been considering does not fairly reach – I allude to negro slavery and the degradation of our coloured citizens – we could foresee for the whole of this magnificent country a certain future of uniform and peaceful improvement.

While other nations have still to win reform at the sword's point, we have only to will it. While in Europe men have still to fight, we have only to learn. While there they have to cope with ignorance – armed cap-à-pie, encircled with armies and powerful with gold – we have only peacefully to collect knowledge, and to frame our institutions and actions in accordance with it.

It is true that we have much knowledge to collect and consequently much to amend in our opinions and our practice. It is also true that we are often ignorant of what has been done, and quite unaware that there is yet any thing to do. The very nature of the national institutions is frequently mistaken, and the devotion exhibited for them as frequently based on a wrong principle.

Here, as in other countries, we hear of patriotism; that is, of love of country in an exclusive sense; of love of our countrymen in contradistinction to the love of our fellow-creatures; of love of the Constitution, instead of love or appreciation of those principles upon which the Constitution is, or ought to be, based – and upon which, if it should be found not to be based, it would merit no attachment at all …

The only rational purpose for which we can suppose men congregated into what are called nations, is the increase of happiness – the ensuring of some advantage, real or imagined. The only rational purpose for which we can suppose governments organized, the same. If, upon examination, we should find the object not gained, the experiment, so far as it went, would have failed, and we should then act rationally to break up such national congregations, and to change or annul such governments. Our character as citizens, therefore, must ever depend upon our finding it for our interest as human beings to stand in that relation …

In continental Europe, of late years, the words 'patriotism' and 'patriot' have been used in a more enlarged sense than it is usual here to attribute to them, or than is attached to them in Great Britain. Since the political struggles of France, Italy, Spain, and Greece, the word patriotism has been employed, throughout continental Europe, to express a love of the public good; a preference for the interests of the many to those of the few; a desire for the emancipation of the human race from the thrall of despotism, religious and civil. In short, patriotism there is used rather to express the interest felt in the human race in general, than that felt for any country, or inhabitants of a country, in particular …

Used in this sense, patriotism is a virtue, and a patriot a virtuous man. With such an interpretation, a patriot is a useful member of society, capable of enlarging all minds, and bettering all hearts with which he comes in contact; a useful member of the human family, capable of establishing fundamental principles, and of merging his own interests, those of his associates, and those of his nation, in the interests of the human race …

If such a patriotism as we have last considered should seem likely to obtain in any country, it should be certainly in this – in this, which is truly the home of all nations, and in the veins of whose citizens flows the blood of every people on the globe. Patriotism, in the exclusive meaning, is surely not made for Americans. Mischievous everywhere, it were here both mischievous and absurd. The very origin of the people is opposed to it. The institutions, in their principle, militate against it. The day we are celebrating protests against it.

It is for Americans more especially to nourish a nobler sentiment; one more consistent with their origin, and more conducive to their future improvement. It is for them more especially to know why they love their country, but because it is the palladium[2] of human liberty – the favoured scene of human improvement.

It is for them more especially to know why they honour their institutions, and feel that they honour them because they are based on just principles. It is for them more especially to examine their institutions, because they have the means of improving them; to examine their laws, because at will they can alter them. It is for them to lay aside luxury, whose wealth is in industry; idle parade, whose strength is in knowledge; ambitious distinction, whose principle is equality.

It is for them not to rest satisfied with words, who can seize upon things; and to remember that equality means not the mere equality of political rights, however valuable, but equality of instruction, and equality in virtue; and that liberty means not the mere voting at elections, but the

[2] In Greek mythology, the Palladium was a Trojan shrine to the goddess Athena, which had the power to safeguard the city where it was kept. When laying siege to Troy, the Greek warriors Odysseus and Diomed stole the statue, rendering the city vulnerable.

free and fearless exercise of the mental faculties, and that self-possession which springs out of well-reasoned opinions and consistent practice.

It is for them to honour principles rather than men – to commemorate events rather than days; when they rejoice, to know for what they rejoice, and to rejoice only for what has brought, and what brings, peace and happiness to men. The event we commemorate this day has procured much of both, and shall procure, in the onward course of human improvement, more than we can now conceive of. For this – for the good obtained, and yet in store for our race – let us rejoice! But let us rejoice as men, not as children; as human beings, rather than as Americans; as reasoning beings, not as ignorants. So shall we rejoice to good purpose and in good feeling; so shall we improve the victory once on this day achieved, until all mankind hold with us the jubilee of independence.

W B Yeats
Irish writer and politician

William Butler Yeats (1865–1939) was born in Sandymount, Dublin, but grew up in London. In 1881, the family returned to Dublin. In 1884 he enrolled in the Metropolitan School of Art and his first lyrics appeared in *Dublin University Review* (1885). He became preoccupied with Irish mythology and mysticism, and helped found the Dublin Hermetic Society in 1885. His literary debut, *Mosada: A Dramatic Poem*, was published in 1886. He returned to London and edited *Fairy and Folk Tales of the Irish Peasantry* (1888). His circle of friends widened to include GEORGE BERNARD SHAW and OSCAR WILDE. In 1889 he published *The Wanderings of Oisin and Other Poems*, which was well reviewed. He returned to Ireland in 1891. In 1892, he published the drama *The Countess Kathleen* (1892) and helped found the Irish Literary Society. In 1893 he published *The Celtic Twilight*, a collection of stories and legends. His drama *The Land of Heart's Desire* (1894) was produced in London. His collected *Poems* (1895) established him as a major poet. He helped found the Irish Literary Theatre in 1899 and in 1902 contributed *Cathleen ni Houlihan*, a nationalist propaganda play. This theatre became the Irish National Theatre, which opened the Abbey Theatre in Dublin (1904). Yeats's *Collected Works in Prose and Verse* (8 volumes) appeared in 1906. In 1914 he published *Responsibilities*. His play *The Player Queen* premiered at the Abbey in 1919. He developed an interest in psychic research which influenced later work, including *The Wild Swans at Coole* (1919) and *A Vision* (1925). *Michael Robartes and the Dancer* (1921) pre-empted outbreak of the Irish civil war. With the foundation of the Irish Free State (1922) he became a member of the Irish Senate. In 1923 he was awarded the Nobel Prize for literature. In 1928 he moved to Rapallo, Italy and published *The Tower*, a dark vision of the future. This, with the collection *The Winding Stair* (1933), is considered his best poetic work. His idiosyncratic anthology, *The Oxford Book of Modern Verse 1892–1935*, appeared in 1936. In 1938, he moved to Cap Martin, where he died. Yeats was a titan of 20th-century literature, although his reputation was tainted by flirtations with fascism and eugenics. His various memoirs are collected in *Autobiographies* (1955).

'There is no use quarrelling with icebergs in warm water'
11 June 1925, Dublin, Ireland

In this speech to the Irish Senate, Yeats argues forcefully that legislation should be determined on secular rather than religious principles. It was given during a heated debate on divorce. The issue was a divisive one: according to the rulings of their respective churches, Protestants were allowed to divorce while Catholics were not. In theory, therefore, the Catholic majority would not be affected by any relaxation of divorce laws.

Yeats, whose background was Protestant, rejected in principle any legal restriction on divorce, but his speech also pursues a pragmatic argument: that such a restriction would hinder Irish reunification. When the Anglo-Irish Treaty was signed in 1921, granting qualified independence to Ireland, the six largely Protestant northern counties chose to remain under British rule. The other 26 counties became the Catholic-dominated Irish Free State.

Reunification was the goal of many Irish politicians, but as Yeats points out, northern Protestants would be unwilling to surrender personal freedoms, such as the right to divorce. Laws dictated by Catholic doctrine, he insists, would 'put a wedge in the midst of this nation'. He reminds the Senate that the Irish constitution had been carefully framed to exclude a clause banning divorce, and urges senators to resist pressure from the Roman Catholic Church.

Though he anticipated defeat in the short term, Yeats foresaw a time when the 'iceberg' would melt in the 'warm water' of youthful public opinion. He cannot have guessed that it would be 70 years before divorce was legalized in Ireland.

> I speak on this question after long hesitation and with a good deal of anxiety, but it is sometimes one's duty to come down to absolute fundamentals for the sake of the education of the people …
>
> I have no doubt whatever, if circumstances were a little different, a very easy solution would be found for this whole difficulty. I judge from conversations that I have had with various persons that many would welcome a very simple solution, namely, that the Catholic members should remain absent when a bill of divorce was brought before the House that concerned Protestants and non-Catholics only … It is obvious, I think, that that would be a wise policy.

It is perhaps the deepest political passion with this nation that North and South be united into one nation. If it ever comes that North and South unite, the North will not give up any liberty which she already possesses under her constitution. You will then have to grant to another people what you refuse to grant to those within your borders. If you show that this country, Southern Ireland, is going to be governed by Catholic ideas and by Catholic ideas alone, you will never get the North. You will create an impassable barrier between South and North, and you will pass more and more Catholic laws, while the North will, gradually, assimilate its divorce and other laws to those of England. You will put a wedge into the midst of this nation.

I do not think this House has ever made a more serious decision than the decision which, I believe, it is about to make on this question. You will not get the North if you impose on the minority what the minority consider to be oppressive legislation. The minority will make it plain that it does consider it exceedingly oppressive to deprive it of rights which it has held since the 17th century. These rights were won by the labours of John Milton[1] and other great men, and won after strife, which is a famous part of the history of the Protestant people …

When the committee was set up to draw up the constitution of the Free State, it was urged to incorporate in the constitution the indissolubility of marriage and refused to do so. That was the expression of the political mind of Ireland. You are now urged to act on the advice of men who do not express the political mind, but who express the religious mind. I admit it must be exceedingly difficult for members of this House to resist the pressure that has been brought upon them. In the long warfare of this country with England the Catholic clergy took the side of the people, and owing to that they possess here an influence that they do not possess anywhere else in Europe …

I am sure it is difficult for members of this House to resist the advice of Archbishop O'Donnell … Addressing the Catholic Truth Society in October last he used these words:

> 'No power on earth can break the marriage bond until death … that is true of all baptized persons no matter what the denomination may be. To be sure we hear that a section of our fellow-countrymen favour divorces. Well, with nothing but respect and sympathy for all our neighbours, we have to say that we place the marriages of such people higher than they do themselves. Their marriages are unbreakable before God and we cannot disobey God by helping break them.'

That is to say that you are to legislate on purely theological grounds and you are to force your theology upon persons who are not of your religion. It is not a question of finding it legally difficult or impossible to grant to a minority what the majority does not wish for itself. You are to insist upon members of the Church of Ireland[2] or members of no church taking a certain view of biblical criticism, or of the authority of the text upon which that criticism is exercised, a view that they notoriously do not take. If you legislate upon such grounds there is no reason why you should stop there. There is no reason why you should not forbid civil marriages altogether seeing that civil marriage is not marriage in the eyes of the Church … It is just as much adultery, according to that view, as the remarriage of divorced persons is.

[1] The English writer John Milton (1608–74) argues for divorce on the grounds of incompatibility in his *Doctrine and Discipline of Divorce* (1643).

[2] The Protestant church.

Nor do I see why you should stop at that, for we teach in our schools and universities and print in our books many things which the Catholic Church does not approve of. Once you attempt legislation on religious grounds, you open the way for every kind of intolerance and for every kind of religious persecution. I am not certain that there are not people in country who would not urge you on to that course. I have nothing but respect for Most Reverend Dr O'Donnell. I am told that he is a vigorous and able man, and I can say this for the speech from which I quoted, that if unwise in substance it was courteous in form. But what have I to say of the following extract from an article by Father Peter Finlay:

'The refusal to legalize divorce is no denial of justice to any section of our people; it is no infringement of the fullest civil and religious liberty which our Constitution guarantees to all. As well say that prohibition of suttee is a denial of justice to the Hindu widow. The Hindu widow had a far clearer right to do herself to death on her husband's funeral pyre – her religion imposed it upon her as a duty – than any member of a Christian community can have to put away his wife and enter into a state of public legalized adultery. England acted justly, and in fulfilment of a plain and grave moral obligation, when she forbade suttee in India. The Irish Free State will act justly, and in fulfilment of a plain and grave moral obligation, in refusing to legalize absolute divorce and re-marriage among ourselves.'

In a previous part of the essay he compares divorce with polygamy, robbery and murder. I know little or nothing about Father Finlay's career. It may have been eminent and distinguished, but I am sure that very few members of this House will think with pleasure of following the guidance of a man who speaks with such monstrous discourtesy of a practice which has been adopted by the most civilized nations of the modern world – by Germany, England, America, France and Scandinavian countries.

He must know that by every kind of statistics, by every standard except the narrowest, that those nations, because they so greatly exceed us in works, exceed us in virtue.

Father Peter Finlay has been supported by an ecclesiastic of the Church of Ireland, the Bishop of Meath, who has even excelled him in invective. Perceiving, no doubt, that indissoluble marriage – which for the guilty party at least, he passionately desires – has in other countries made men and women exceedingly tolerant of certain forms of sexual immorality, he declares that every erring husband or erring wife should be treated as a robber, a forger or a murderer.

Now, there is one great difference between Father Finlay in his relation to this House and the Bishop of Meath. I think that Father Finlay may influence votes in this House, but I am sure that the Bishop of Meath has not influenced one. What is more, if the entire Protestant episcopacy in Ireland came out with a declaration on this subject, it would not influence a vote in this House. It is one of the glories of the church in which I was born that we have put our bishops in their places in discussions requiring legislation. Even in those discussions involving legislation on matters of religion they count only according to their individual intelligence and knowledge.

The rights of divorce, and many other rights, were won by the Protestant communities in the teeth of the most bitter opposition from their clergy. The living, changing, advancing human mind sooner or later refuses to accept this legislation from men who base their ideas on the interpretation of doubtful texts in the Gospels. It is necessary to say – and I say it without fear of contradiction – that there is not a scholar of eminence in Europe today who considers that the Gospels are, in the strict sense of the words, historical documents. Their importance is devotional, not historical. For any ecclesiastic to advise statesmen to base legislation on a passage that may lack historical validity is to appeal to the ignorance of the people.

I am sure that the majority of those who favour the indissolubility of marriage are under the impression that it preserves sexual morality in the country that adopts it. I think that before they are entirely certain on that point, they should study the morality of countries where marriage is indissoluble – Spain, Italy, and the South American nations. We are not proposing to take from those nations our economics, our agricultural or technical instruction, but we are proposing to take from them our marriage laws. Before doing so, I think it would be well to make some study of the effect of the marriage laws on those nations.

I have gone to the authorities available, and I find that, on the whole, they have successfully suppressed much evidence of immorality. There are no reports in the newspapers of divorce proceedings. The usual number of children are born in wedlock, but I do find there is a great uncertainty as to the parentage of these children – but then, public opinion discourages curiosity on that subject, and it is a habit to discourage any inquiry into the emotional relations of men and women.

Among modern communities there is a demand for happiness, which increases with education, and men and women who are held together against their will and reason soon cease to recognize any duty to one another.

You are going to have indissoluble marriage, but you are going to permit separation. You are going to permit young people who cannot live together, because of some intolerable wrong, to separate. You are going to invite men and women in the prime of life to accept for the rest of their existence the law of the cloisters. Do you think you are going to succeed in what the entire of Europe has failed to do for the last 2,000 years? Are you going to impose the law of the cloister on those young people? If not, you are not going to raise the morality of this country by indissoluble marriage. A great English judge, speaking out of the immensity of his experience, said that there is no cause of irregular sexual relations so potent as separation without the possibility of remarriage.

This is a question which I know to be exciting a good deal of interest. I know something of the opinions of those who will make the next generation in this country. I know it, perhaps, better than most of the members of this House, and I am going to give those young people a piece of advice. I urge them not to be unduly excited. There is no use quarrelling with icebergs in warm water. These questions will solve themselves. Father Peter Finlay and the Bishop of Meath will have their brief victory, but we can leave them to it …

This is a matter of very great seriousness. I think it is tragic that within three years of this country gaining its independence we should be discussing a measure which a minority of this nation considers to be grossly oppressive. I am proud to consider myself a typical man of that minority. We against whom you have done this thing are no petty people. We are one of the great stocks of Europe. We are the people of BURKE; we are the people of GRATTAN; we are the people of SWIFT, the people of EMMET, the people of PARNELL. We have created most of the modern literature of this country. We have created the best of its political intelligence.

Yet I do not altogether regret what has happened. I shall be able to find out – if not I, my children will be able to find out – whether we have lost our stamina or not. You have defined our position and given us a popular following. If we have not lost our stamina then your victory will be brief and your defeat final, and when it comes, this nation may be transformed.

'Feed the immature imagination upon that old folk life'
30 November 1925, London, England

As one of Ireland's pre-eminent literary figures, Yeats took a keen interest in reforming the education system following the establishment of the Irish Free State. At the time of this speech to the Irish Literary Society, Parliament was considering a compulsory education bill, and Yeats was anxious to provide advice and enlist support.

Having inspected many of the school buildings in the country, he believed the bill should not be passed until the facilities had been improved. However, most of his speech is devoted to discussion of the school syllabus. Steeped in the Irish literary tradition, he proposes that Irish children should be introduced at an early age to their country's folk stories, later progressing to the works of great – and distinctively Irish – philosophers such as George Berkeley and EDMUND BURKE. He also endorses religious education, prohibited under British rule.

The developments in Italy under BENITO MUSSOLINI had also attracted Yeats, and here he praises the changes introduced to Italian education by the Gentile Act, passed in 1923.

At this time, following the recent unrest in Ireland, many children were unruly, and some teachers believed their lessons should centre on the new Irish nation and their duty to it. Yeats argues that by interweaving the country's rich cultural tradition with other aspects of the curriculum, Ireland's schools could feed the both the immature imagination and the mature intellect, creating an education system that would be truly inspiring.

Ireland has been put into our hands that we may shape it, and I find all about me in Ireland today a new overflowing life. To this overflowing life I attribute that our audiences at the Abbey Theatre have doubled, that the interest in music is so great that the Royal Dublin Society,[1] which a few years ago was content with a hall that held 700 people, finds its new hall that holds some 1,500 so much too small, that every afternoon concert has to be repeated in the evening …

[1] The Society was founded in 1731 to encourage the development of Ireland's agriculture, arts, science and industry.

I know no case where the best teaching has been brought to Ireland in vain, and today there is a greater desire than ever before for expression – I think I may also say for discipline. The whole nation is plastic and receptive, but it is held back – and will be held back for some time to come – by its lack of education, education in the most common and necessary subjects.

For that reason I put so much reliance in your patriotism and your patience that I am going to talk to you about education in the primary schools. Perhaps, indeed, I but speak of it because it is so running in my head that I would speak badly of anything else. I have been going round schools listening at a school attendance committee, talking to schoolmasters and inspectors.

Many of you have influence in Ireland, influence through the press, or through your friends, and I want to impress upon you that the schools in Ireland are not fit places for children. They are insanitary, they are out of repair, they are badly heated, and in Dublin and Cork they are far too small.

The government inherited this state of things, this old scandal. They want to put it right, but they will not be able to do so unless public opinion is with them, above all, perhaps, unless just the kind of people who are here tonight are prepared to defend them and support them. The government is introducing a compulsory education bill, but we have all our individual responsibility, and we must see to it that compulsory education does not come into force – I do not say does not pass – until those schools are fitted for their work. And if the children are going to be forced to school you must not only see that those schools are warm and clean and sanitary, but you must do as other countries are doing more and more, and see that children during school hours are neither half-naked nor starved ...

Only when the schools have been made habitable will the question arise that most interests us – what are you going to teach there? Whether Gaelic be compulsory or voluntary, a great deal of it will be taught. At present Gaelic scholars assure me that there is nothing to read in modern Irish except for very young children who love fairy tales. You must translate, you must modernize.

A Committee of the Senate, of which I was chairman, has made a recommendation to the government, asking it to endow research into Old, Middle and Modern Irish. Nothing is decided, but I think the government will make this grant. Probably most of the books so produced will be in Middle or Ancient Irish, and in any case unsuitable for young children. They will, however, supply the material from which in some degree a vivid modern literature may be created. I think the government should appoint some committee of publication and so make possible a modern Gaelic literature ... Up to, say, ten years old, a child is content with a wild old tale, but from ten years on you must give it something with more of the problems of life in it. I would like to see the great classics, especially of the Catholic Latin nations, translated into Gaelic.

The tendency of the most modern education – that in Italy, let us say – is to begin geography with your native fields, arithmetic by counting the school chairs and measuring the walls, history with local monuments, religion with the local saints, and then to pass on from that to the nation itself ...

If your education, therefore, is efficient in the modern sense, it will be more national than the dreams of politicians. If your education is to be effective, you must see to it that your English teaching also begins with what is near and familiar. I suggest therefore [a] commission or committee to find writers who can create English reading books and history books, which speak of Ireland in simple vivid language ... Yet I do not think that I would exclude from the children's books any simple masterpiece of English literature.

Let them begin with their own, and then pass to the world and the classics of the world ... The Italian Minister of Education[2] has advised his teachers continually to study the great classics, and he adds that those great classics will be as difficult to them as is the lesson to the child, and will therefore help them to understand the mind of a child.

In Gaelic literature we have something that the English-speaking countries have never possessed – a great folk literature. We have in Berkeley[3] and in Burke a philosophy on which it is possible to base the whole life of a nation. That, too, is something which England, great as she is in modern scientific thought and every kind of literature, has not, I think. The modern Irish intellect was born more than 200 years ago when Berkeley defined in three or four sentences the mechanical philosophy of Newton,[4] Locke[5] and Hobbes,[6] the philosophy of England in his day, and I think of England up to our day, and wrote after each 'We Irish do not hold with this,' or some like sentence.

Feed the immature imagination upon that old folk life, and the mature

[2] The Italian philosopher and politician Giovanni Gentile (1875–1944) served in Mussolini's Fascist regime as Education Minister, 1922–4, and as president of the Supreme Council of Public Education, 1926–8.

[4] The English physicist, mathematician and astronomer Isaac Newton (1642–1727).
[5] The English political philosopher John Locke (1632–1704).

[3] The Irish philosopher and clergyman George Berkeley (1685–1753).

[6] The English political philosopher Thomas Hobbes (1588–1679).

intellect upon Berkeley and the great modern idealist philosophy created by his influence, upon Burke, who restored to political thought its sense of history, and Ireland is reborn, potent, armed and wise. Berkeley proved that the world was a vision, and Burke that the state was a tree, no mechanism to be pulled in pieces and put up again, but an oak tree that had grown through centuries.

Teacher after teacher in Ireland has said to me that the young people are anarchic and violent, and that we have to show them what the State is and what they owe to it. All over the world during the Great War, the young people became anarchic and violent, but in Ireland it is worse than elsewhere, for we have in a sense been at war for generations, and of late that war has taken the form of burning and destruction under the eyes of the children.

They respect nothing, one teacher said to me. 'I cannot take them through Stephen's Green[7] because they would pull up the plants.' Go anywhere in Ireland and you will hear the same complaint. The children, everybody will tell you, are individually intelligent and friendly, yet have so little sense of their duty to community and neighbour that if they meet an empty house in a lonely place they will smash all the windows. Some of the teachers want lessons on civic duty, but there is much experience to show that such lessons, being of necessity dry and abstract, are turned to mockery.

[7] A park in Dublin.

The proper remedy is to teach religion, civic duty and history as all but inseparable. Indeed, the whole curriculum of a school should be as it were one lesson and not a mass of unrelated topics. I recommend Irish teachers to study the attempt now being made in Italy, under the influence of their Minister of Education, the philosopher Gentile, the most profound disciple of our own Berkeley, to so correlate all subjects of study.

I would have each religion, Catholic or Protestant, so taught that it permeate the whole school life, and that it may do so, that it may be good education as well as good religion, I would have it taught upon a plan signed, as it is in Italy, by the representative of the government as well as by the religious authority. For instance, the Italian teachers are directed by the minister to teach 'no servile fear'.

Up to three years ago in Ireland, religion could not be taught in school hours, and even now, though that regulation is no longer binding, it is often nothing but a daily lesson in the Catechism. In Italy it takes four forms, that it may not be abstract, and that it may be a part of history and of life itself, a part, as it were, of the foliage of Burke's tree. First, praying, the learning and saying of simple prayers; second, singing, the learning and singing of famous religious songs; third, narration, the reading, or perhaps among the younger children the hearing and writing out in the child's own words of stories out of the Bible, and stories of the great religious personages of their own country; fourth, contemplation, by which I mean that dogmatic teaching which stirs the mind to religious thought.

The prayers and songs for an Irish school exist in abundance. There are, for instance, many religious songs in Gaelic with their traditional music, and they are already published in little books.

Every child, in growing from infancy to maturity, should pass in imagination through the history of its own race and through something of the history of the world, and the most powerful part in that history is played by religion. Let the child go its own way when maturity comes, but it is our business that it has something of that whole inheritance, and not as a mere thought … but as part of its emotional life.

One never knows where one's words carry, and I, in speaking, though I speak to you all, am thinking perhaps of some one young man or some one young girl who may hear my words and bear them in mind years hence. Even he and she may do nothing with my thought, but they may carry it, or some other amongst you may carry it, as a bird will carry a seed clinging to its claws. I am thinking of an Egyptian poem, where there are birds flying from Arabia with spice in their claws.

I do not think any of you are millionaires, and yet permit me to dream that my words may reach one that is. If the government were to do all that I suggest, if after the schools are put in good repair it were to get together the right editors and they find the right authors, if all the textbooks necessary to create a religious and secular culture in Irish and English were published, there would still be much that no government, certainly no government of a poor country, can accomplish.

England has had great educational endowments for centuries. Everyone knows with what lavish generosity the rich men of America have endowed education. Large sums of money have been sent to Ireland for political ends, and rich Irish—Americans have largely contributed, and we all hope, I think, that there is no further need for that money.

If societies like this interest themselves in Irish education and spread that interest among the Irish educated classes everywhere, money may be sent to us to cheapen the price of school books for the poor, or to clothe the poorer children, or to make the school buildings pleasanter to a child's eyes, or in some other way to prepare for an Ireland that will be healthy, vigorous, orderly and above all, happy.

Émile Zola
French writer

Émile Zola (1840–1902) was born in Paris, the son of an Italian engineer. He entered the publishing house of Hachette as a clerk, and soon became an active journalist. His first short stories were published as *Contes à Ninon* (1864, 'Stories for Ninon'), and other collections followed. In the later years of the Empire he formed a sort of informal society along with the French writers Gustave Flaubert, Alphonse Daudet, Edmond and Jules de Goncourt, and the Russian writer Ivan Turgenev, out of which grew the Naturalist school of novel. His first major novel, *Thérèse Raquin* (1867), a powerful picture of remorse, belongs to this school. Later he began the series of novels called *Les Rougon-Macquart*, a collection of some 20 volumes, all connected by the appearance of members of the same family. These include *Nana* (1880), *Germinal* (1885), *L'Oeuvre* (1886, 'The Work'), *La Terre* (1887, 'The Earth'), *Le Rêve* (1888, 'The Dream') and *La Bête humaine* (1890, 'The Human Beast'). In his research of the human condition, Zola mastered the technical details of most professions, trades and crafts, as well as the history of recent events in France: this is seen for example in *Germinal* (mining), *L'Oeuvre* (art and literature), *Le Rêve* (church ritual) and *La Bête humaine* (railways). In 1898 Zola was sentenced to a jail term following his involvement in the 'Dreyfus Affair', but he escaped to England and on his return a year later was welcomed back a hero. He died in Paris, accidentally suffocated by charcoal fumes.

'The salvation of this country is at stake'
23 February 1898, Paris, France

The 'Dreyfus Affair' centred on Alfred Dreyfus, a Jewish officer in the French army. In 1894, after military secrets were leaked to Germany, he was court-martialled for treason, convicted and imprisoned. The conviction depended on flawed evidence and a more likely culprit emerged in Major Ferdinand Walsin-Esterhazy; but anti-Semitism in the army and the press encouraged high-ranking officers to suppress fresh evidence.

Dreyfus became a *cause célèbre*, dividing French society into 'Dreyfusards' – who wanted the case reopened – and 'anti-Dreyfusards'. A famous cartoon by the satirical artist Caran d'Ache shows a whole family brawling over the issue.

In January 1898, Zola published an open letter 'J'Accuse ...!' in the newspaper *L'Aurore*. Addressed to the President, it denounced a miscarriage of justice and singled out members of the military hierarchy for blame.

Zola knew he risked prosecution for libel, and the following month he stood trial. His speech to the jury – translated here by Eleanor Levieux – is an appeal to common decency and national pride. Zola insists that the underlying principles of democracy, truth and patriotism are of greater importance than either Dreyfus or himself.

Zola was convicted and sentenced to a year in jail and a heavy fine. He launched an appeal, then fled to England. In August 1898, Major Hubert Henry – who had forged the original evidence – confessed and committed suicide. Dreyfus was retried by court martial and found guilty again, but pardoned. He was finally exonerated by a retrial in a civil court in 1906.

Zola returned to France in June 1899. He never went to jail, but died before Dreyfus was vindicated.

[1] The French politician Felix Jules Méline (1838–1925) served as Prime Minister of France, 1896–8.

Gentlemen of the jury: in the Chamber of Deputies, at its session of 22 January, M Méline, the prime minister,[1] declared – to frantic applause from his indulgent majority – that he had faith in the twelve citizens in whose hands he was placing the defence of the French army. Gentlemen, it was you he was talking about.

And just as General Billot[2] had dictated his order to the court martial – which had been instructed to acquit Major Esterhazy – by directing his military subordinates, from on high, to observe the most absolute respect for the previous verdict, so M Méline tried to order you to convict me in the name of respect for the army, which he accuses me of having offended.

[2] The French soldier and politician General Jean-Baptiste Billot (1828–1907) served as French Minister of War, 1882–3 and 1897–8.

I declare before the consciences of all decent people that I denounce this attempt by the government to put pressure on the system of justice in this country. Such conduct in politics is abominable. It is a dishonour to a free nation.

Gentlemen: will you obey him? We shall see. But it is not true that it was M Méline's wish that I stand here before you. Only with the utmost reluctance did he bow to the necessity of taking legal action against me, for it meant the truth would be on the march, taking a new stride, and he was terrified. Everyone knows this. I stand here before you because I wanted it that way …

I personally am of no importance. I have sacrificed all personal considerations. It is enough for me to know that I have placed in your hands not only the honour of the French army but the endangered honour of the entire nation …

I hoped to lay all the evidence before you, because I believed you were the only people worthy to have it and competent to deal with it. The first thing they did was to take away from you, with their left hand, what they had seemed to give you with their right. They pretended to accept your jurisdiction, but whereas they trusted you to avenge the members of a court martial, some of the other officers remained beyond your reach, above any justice you might dispense. Understand who may. It is as absurd as it is hypocritical, and what is dazzlingly clear is this: they were afraid of your common sense; they did not dare run the risk of allowing us to say everything and allowing you to judge everything.

They claim that they wanted to keep the scandal from spreading. Well, what do you think of *my* scandal? Of the action I took because I wanted to lay this affair before you? Because I wanted the people, as embodied in you, to judge it? … There is only one thing that terrifies them: the idea of your being in complete control. The law – the law of the sovereign people – is fully represented by you, and it is this law that I, as a good citizen, have insisted on and profoundly respect …

Now, the debate you have heard here proves to you that every step of the way, we have had to combat the most extraordinary tenacious determination to keep things dark. We have had to struggle to reveal every scrap of truth. They have argued over everything, refused us everything and terrified our witnesses, hoping to prevent us from establishing the evidence. It was for you and you alone that we have been fighting, so that the evidence would be submitted to you in full and you could then reach your decision with no remorse, as your consciences dictate. I am confident that you will take account of our efforts, and moreover, I am confident that matters have been clarified sufficiently.

I categorically deny what M Méline asserts: I have never offended the army; quite the contrary. I have expressed my affection and respect for a nation in arms, for France's beloved soldiers who would rise up at the very first hint of a threat and defend French soil. And it is also false that I have attacked their leaders, the generals who would lead those soldiers to victory. If a few individuals at the War Office have compromised the army itself by their skulduggery, the mere fact of saying so does not insult the entire army, does it? Indeed, saying so is the duty of a good citizen; saying so spares the army from being compromised …

I maintain that our valiant army is insulted every single day by scoundrels who claim to defend it, yet actually besmirch it with their sneaking plots and drag in the mud every good and noble attribute France still has. I maintain that it is they who dishonour our nation's great army when they mingle cries of 'Long live the army!' with shouts of 'Down with the Jews!' …

A legend has been built up; no doubt it is familiar to you. Dreyfus was sentenced fairly and legally by seven infallible officers, and if we so much as suspect them of having made a mistake we offend the entire army. Amid vengeful torments he is expiating his appalling deed. And since he is Jewish, a Jewish syndicate has been formed – has it not? – an international syndicate of individuals who are not loyal to any state, who are manipulating vast sums, hundreds of millions, for the purpose of saving this traitor through the most shameless manoeuvres.

Indeed, this syndicate has piled crime upon crime, buying people's silence, stirring up France into a state of murderous agitation. It is determined to sell France to the enemy and plunge all of Europe into the inferno of war rather than renounce its terrifying purpose … That is the poisonous diet that the foul press has been feeding to this poor nation for months. And if a disastrous crisis ensues, we mustn't be surprised, for when one sows stupidity and lies on such a scale, what else can one harvest but madness?

Certainly, gentlemen, I would not insult you by supposing that until now you have been content to believe such an old wives' tale. I know you, I know who you are. You are the heart and mind of Paris, my great Paris, the Paris I was born in, the Paris I love with infinite tenderness, the Paris I have been exploring and whose praises I have been singing for nearly 40 years. And I also know what you are thinking this very minute, because before I came here as a defendant I sat where you are sitting now. You are there to represent the opinion of the average citizen; together you are striving to embody wisdom and justice … You may make a mistake; but if you do, it will be with the intention of protecting the welfare of all while protecting your own.

I can picture you, at home with your families, in the evening, in the lamplight; I can hear you talking with your friends; I go with you as you enter your workshops and your places of business. All of you work; some of you are tradesmen, others are in industry, and still others are in the professions. And your very legitimate concern is with the deplorable condition that business has fallen into. Everywhere, the current depression threatens to turn into a disaster: receipts are declining, transactions becoming more and more difficult. And as a result the idea you have brought with you here (I can see it in your faces) is, 'Enough is enough! It's time to put an end to all this!' … And if you convict me, gentlemen, at bottom your verdict will be based on just that one consideration: the wish to reassure your families, the need to see business improve and the belief that in striking me down you will put a halt to a campaign whose demands are undermining the interests of France.

Well, gentlemen, you would be totally, totally wrong. Do me the honour of believing that I have not come here to defend my own freedom. If you strike me down, you will only be raising me up. He who suffers for the sake of truth and justice becomes august and sacred.

Gentlemen, look at me. Do I look like a man who has sold out? Am I a liar? Am I a traitor? Then why on earth would I be going to such trouble? I have no political ambitions, no sectarian axe to grind. I am a writer and a free man; I have devoted my life to work; tomorrow I will melt back into the crowd and resume my task where I left off …

A miscarriage of justice occurred; and every single day since then, the attempt to cover it up has engendered a new insult to common sense and fairness. Because an innocent man was convicted, a guilty man had to be acquitted; and now they are telling you it is my turn to be convicted because I have voiced my terrible anguish at seeing the country so lost in this dreadful maze. Go ahead and convict me – but you will just be making one more mistake and piling it on top of all the others, and history will judge you harshly for it.

If you find me guilty, your verdict will not restore the peace and quiet that you yearn for – that we all yearn for; it will merely sow the seeds of passion and disorder once again. The cup is full, I warn you. Do not make it overflow …

By now, gentlemen, the Dreyfus Affair is a very minor matter, very remote and very blurred, compared to the terrifying questions it has raised. There is no Dreyfus Affair any longer. There is only one issue: is France still the France of the Revolution and the Declaration of the Rights of Man? The France which gave the world liberty, and was supposed to give it justice? Are we still the noblest, most fraternal, most generous of peoples? Are we going to keep our reputation in Europe as a humane and fair-minded nation? Every single conquest we have made is in danger of being compromised.

Open your eyes! Realize that if the soul of France is in such disarray, it must have been stirred to its inmost depths because the danger is truly awful. No nation can be wrought up to this extent without the very core of its moral sense being endangered. The hour is one of exceptional gravity; the salvation of this country is at stake.

Once you have realized that, gentlemen, you will understand that speaking the truth and acting with justice are the only possible remedies. Anything which delays the revelation and makes the darkness more murky still will only aggravate and prolong the crisis. Good citizens feel how crucial it is to end all this; their duty is to demand a complete revelation. Already, a good many of us hold that conviction. Men of letters, philosophers and scientists are rising up on all sides, pleading on behalf of intelligence and reason …

Alas, gentlemen, like so many other people you may be waiting for a thunderbolt, for proof of Dreyfus's innocence to flash out of the sky like lightning. But as a general rule that is not how the truth proceeds; it calls for a certain amount of diligence and intelligence.

Proof? We know very well where we could find it, but only in the depth of our souls do we think of that. As patriots, we tremble, for we have made the honour of our army hang on a lie, and one day the proof may hit us like a slap in the face … The truth is making the rounds of the embassies; it will soon be known to everyone, but at this time we cannot drag out the truth ourselves from where it is concealed, shielded by relentless formalities. The government is not unaware of anything; the government is convinced, as we are, that Dreyfus is innocent; and the day the government is ready, it will be able, at no risk whatsoever, to find the witnesses who will reveal the truth at last.

Dreyfus is innocent, I swear he is. I stake my life on that. I stake my honour on it. The hour is a solemn one. Before this court, which represents human justice, before you, gentlemen of the jury – who are the very embodiment of the entire nation – before all of France, before all the world, I swear that Dreyfus is innocent. With all the authority that my 40 years of labour confer on me, I swear that Dreyfus is innocent.

By everything that I have achieved, by the name I have carved out for myself, by my works which have expanded the influence of French literature, I swear that Dreyfus is innocent. May all of this turn to dust, may my works perish if Dreyfus is not innocent! He is innocent.

Zola – 'The salvation of this country is at stake'

> Everything seems to be arrayed against me ... All I have on my side is an idea, the ideal of truth and justice. I am confident. I shall carry the day. I did not wish my country to remain mired in lies and injustice. My opponents may strike me down now; but one day, France will thank me for having helped to salvage its honour.

Index